THE NEW
KOBBÉ'S
OPERA BOOK

THE NEW
KOBBÉ'S
OPERA BOOK

EDITED BY

THE EARL OF HAREWOOD

AND

ANTONY PEATTIE

G.P. PUTNAM'S SONS
NEW YORK

First published in Great Britain 1922
Ninth edition 1976
Tenth edition 1987
Eleventh edition 1997

G.P. Putnam's Sons
Publishers Since 1838
a member of
Penguin Putnam Inc.
200 Madison Avenue
New York, New York 10016

Project manager: Elisabeth Ingles
Design and typesetting: Penny and Tony Mills
Music setting: Wessex Music Services
Index: Ingrid Lock
Additional research: Janet Jempson
Typist: Kim Griffiths

Printed and bound in the United States of America by
RR Donnellys & Sons Company.

1 3 5 7 9 10 8 6 4 2

This book is printed on acid-free paper.

CONTENTS

LIST OF ILLUSTRATIONS

PREFACE

Gustav Kobbé (1857–1918) was a New Yorker by birth and his musical education took place there and at Wiesbaden in Germany. He was co-editor of the *Musical Review* when in 1882 he was sent by the *New York World* as correspondent to Bayreuth for the première of *Parsifal*. For eighteen years he was music critic of the *New York Herald*, and he was a regular contributor of articles on music to prominent American magazines. His death was unusual and occurred while he was sailing in the Great South Bay, Long Island, when a seaplane struck his boat and killed him instantly.

When *Kobbé's Complete Opera Book* was first published (posthumously), it was a pioneering work, replicated to some extent maybe on the continent of Europe but not otherwise in the English language. The scale was large, so was the view taken of the operas he tackled, and it was easy to see where his sympathies lay. He took, as was natural around the end of the Great War, what would have been considered a progressive view: Opera, he believed, like for instance Medicine, developed, and, as it did so, older discoveries were superseded. That for him as a man of his time meant that Gluck's *Orfeo* (the earliest opera then still playing) provided a parameter for his work. With *Orfeo*, he believed modern opera began.

Revising and enlarging the book just before the end of the twentieth century – the fourth time I have done it – I realise our parameters have necessarily changed and now stretch from the time of Monteverdi up to the present day. Immediately, an element of personal judgement comes into play – choice, if you prefer the word. If the contents now include your own preference among modern works – say, *Klinghoffer*, *Greek*, *Harvey Milk* or Goehr's *Arianna* – the *New Kobbé* meets with your approval; if they do not, it's not so sound! It's as simple as that. Or is it?

Our tendency now has been to include virtually anything Wagner, Mozart, Verdi, Puccini or Richard Strauss ever wrote; to treat everything by Handel or Rossini as a strong candidate for inclusion; and then to worry about space – the book is now in larger format

than before but it should not require a lectern to make it readable. Kobbé expatiated on his favourite works – Mozart or Wagner – and went into much less detail about others he thought less important; similar criteria inevitably govern his successors. We have thought whoever uses the book would want only the bones of Verdi's *Oberto* or Heise's *Drot og Marsk*, but would expect something nearer a dissertation on *Don Carlos* or *War and Peace* or *Die Soldaten* as works of greater importance and profounder complexity. All choice such as we have had to make tends to the controversial: the field consists of thousands of operas; Kobbé includes only 500. Not everyone can be expected to agree with precisely what we have chosen.

Apart from choice, space is a consideration we have had to take into account. Is there likely to be renewed interest in Kienzl's *Der Evangelimann* or Mascagni's *Le maschere*, fringe operas at best in recent times, or should we leave them out in favour of something statistics suggest as more likely to be encountered by the operatic traveller? Will one-time favourites like *L'amico Fritz* and *Die Königin von Saba* disappear completely, as current lists imply, or will they regain a bit of favour? Is there any chance of revival of something once considered basic repertory like *The Bohemian Girl* – a big success (and hugely enjoyable) under Beecham in 1951, virtually unheard (though recorded) since? Will current interest in the lesser works of Verdi, to say nothing of Massenet (in either case to be applauded), blot out the chances of valuable but essentially non-repertory operas like *Padmâvatî* or *Cardillac* finding regular favour with operatic planners? Kobbé himself might have speculated in such a fashion, but in his time it would have been *Così* and *Don Carlos* that he would have cited as top priorities for production at the Met or Covent Garden and therefore for listing in anything purporting to be 'complete'.

The inclusion or omission of operetta has posed a problem. There are now admirable books devoted exclusively to operetta and the musical and embracing almost anything in the category. On the other hand, certain works, not only *Die Fledermaus* and *The Merry Widow* but *Mikado* and *Sweeney Todd*, are likely to find themselves in the repertory of opera companies and therefore to be encountered by subscribers or ordinarily enterprising opera-goers. Compromise here, as for instance in the area of 'national' operas – works to be found regularly in one country but virtually never exported – has to be the order of the day, and inevitably some compromise turns out to be controversial.

Kobbé's original scheme divided the book into centuries and subdivided by 'Schools' – German, Italian, French initially; Russian, Czech and so on did not get much of a look-in at the time he was writing. There were some odd choices, Flotow for instance being classified under 'French Opera' because Kobbé, with some but not total justification, decided that this was his style, as if he were Meyerbeer. We have decided, not without misgiving, to list composers alphabetically, thus making it easier for those unwilling to use an index to locate them but separating for instance *Cavalleria rusticana* from *Pagliacci*. On the other hand, such a listing obviates the soul-searching attendant on deciding whether Spontini and Cherubini were Italian composers (which they were) or Italians who wrote French operas (which is also true); and Stravinsky becomes an alphabetical entry without the need to classify *Mavra* as a Russian opera and *The Rake's Progress* as American – or might chauvinism stretch a couple of points and claim that the subject and one of the librettists qualify it as English?

By tradition operatic commentators have predicted woe – the repertory is ossified; no new works of any merit are being written; performance standards have never been lower; there are no good singers left; you can't cast Wagner/Verdi/Mozart any more; audiences are falling/getting older every day; and so on. At least the last complaint seems no longer true: audiences *aren't* falling off in most countries – maybe in Italy, but not in the U.S.A. or Britain. Nor is the repertory as narrow as it used to be, even if the widening is due more to revival than to new creations: we have the chance today of seeing works which a generation or more ago were hardly dictionary entries, let alone to be found in Kobbé.

A shadow of sadness hangs over this new edition. When in 1995 the *New Kobbé* was mooted, we rapidly settled on Nicholas John as co-editor – I had after all on my own filled that capacity for more than forty years and the book needed a new point of view to supplement the old. Nick John trained as a lawyer but worked at English National Opera for over twenty years, finishing up in the influential job of Dramaturge, which embraced everything from editing the daily programmes to research for directors, often advising them as well. At E.N.O. I had known him as a good colleague, over the years he had become a friend, and – even more important in the context – was steeped in opera and knew his way about the repertory and well beyond it as few others. Tragically, in June 1996 he was killed in an accident in Switzerland. Kobbé planning was well advanced; Nick's notes were voluminous, though he had written only a couple of new entries (*Turandot* appears under Puccini), but at short notice we looked for a new collaborator with more or less immediate availability and, as London taxi-drivers say, the Knowledge as well. We are lucky to have persuaded Antony Peattie, who had at Welsh National Opera filled a comparable job to Nick's at E.N.O., to take over and be associated with Kobbé in the future.

The Complete Opera Book was published after Kobbé's death, with a certain number of operas added to what he had written. In 1954, 1976 and 1985 I added more operas, and then as before the entry for each work was signed with an initial, 'K.' standing for what Kobbé wrote; 'K.W.' for the operas added after his death by Katherine Wright, who put together his material; 'F.B.' for Ferruccio Bonavia, who added a few more; and 'H.' for those I contributed. The same holds good for the *New Kobbé*, except that the earlier initials are supplemented by 'P.' for Antony Peattie, and, in one instance only, by Nicholas John's 'N.J.' Running times of operas (without intervals of course) have been included as a useful feature; needless to say they can only be approximate, lengths varying widely from conductor to conductor and edition to edition.

Many musicians and operatic friends have helped in one way or another to prepare the book, and I am particularly grateful to Charles Mackerras, David Lloyd-Jones, Winton Dean, Edmund Tracey and John Warrack for their suggestions, as well as, it goes without saying, to Antony Peattie and Nicholas John for their contributions. Elisabeth Ingles, as an indefatigable and constructive editor, helped vastly to see the new edition through the press.

HAREWOOD
July 1997

THE OPERAS

A

ADOLPHE ADAM

(born 24 July 1803, died 3 May 1856)

Adam assisted his teacher Boïeldieu in 1825 with the preparation of *La Dame Blanche* for the Opéra-Comique but it was his early collaboration with Eugène Scribe which set him off on the road to success. From 1826 until his death in 1856 he produced a stream of mainly light operas, and it is ironical that only one, *Le Postillon de Longjumeau*, is remembered today, and it mainly because of the brilliance of its one hit number. On the other hand, the music of his ballet *Giselle* is known wherever a ballet company points its toes.

LE POSTILLON DE LONGJUMEAU

The Coachman of Longjumeau

Opera in three acts, text by A. de Leuven and L.L. Brunswick. Première at Opéra-Comique, Paris, 13 October 1836, with Roy, Chollet, Henri. First performed St James's Theatre, London, 1837 (in English); Drury Lane, 1845 (in French); New York, 1840 (in English). Revived Berlin, 1930, with de Garmo, Roswaenge, Helgers, conducted by Blech; Vienna Volksoper, 1964, with Murray Dickie. Still performed in German opera houses. The most famous of all Chappelous was Theodor Wachtel, who himself began life as a stableman.

Madeleine, *Chappelou's wife*	Soprano
Rose	Soprano
Chappelou, *a coachman*	Tenor
Le Marquis de Corcy, *head of the Paris Opéra*	Tenor
Bijou, *Chappelou's friend*	Baritone
Bourdon	Bass

Place: Longjumeau; Paris
Time: Early Nineteenth Century
Running Time: 2 hours 5 minutes

Act I. Chappelou, the coach-driver of Longjumeau, is about to be married to the young mistress of the post-house, Madeleine. The wedding over, his friends make him stay behind – as is the custom – to sing. He says he has no heart for it, but in response to their urging chooses a favourite song, on the subject of the Coachman of Longjumeau, who wins the love of a beautiful princess, mainly, one gathers from the music, because of his exquisitely beautiful post-horn playing. This is the song which has made the opera famous, and the tenor who can imitate the post-horn when it comes to the top Ds is sure of a success.

The effect of the song is further-reaching than either singer or those who asked for it could have guessed. Chappelou is heard by the Marquis de Corcy, who is head of the Opéra in Paris, and who urges Chappelou to come with him to augment the sadly depleted ranks of the tenors of his company. Chappelou tries to postpone his departure, but the Marquis is adamant; if he wants to come to Paris, he must leave straight away. Chappelou charges his friend Bijou, who also has a voice, to tell Madeleine he will be back tomorrow, or next week, but that he has had to leave hurriedly, to meet the King in Paris and to make his fortune. Madeleine is broken-hearted and furious with her inconstant husband, but Bijou makes up his mind to follow Chappelou, so that his voice may be given to the world as well.

Act II. Madeleine is now in Paris under the assumed name of Madame Latour. Having inherited a fortune from an old aunt who has died, she passes as a rich and noble lady, but the whole object of her expedition is to find her errant husband and punish him for what he has done to her. These sentiments she puts forward in an aria at the beginning of the act; but it is clear that in spite of the ten years of absence she still loves her husband.

A rehearsal is in progress at the Opéra, where

Chappelou, under the name of St Phar, has become principal tenor, and where his friend Bijou (called Alcindor) is leader of the chorus. St Phar protests that they are all asked to sing too much, and he at any rate has a sore throat. The Marquis is in despair; the performance they are rehearsing is to be given in honour of Madame Latour, and the Marquis is in love with her. Immediately, St Phar seems better – he too is violently in love with the lady – and he is able to sing his song, top C, top D, and all.

There is an interview between St Phar and Madame Latour in which the tenor lays bare his heart and Madame eventually agrees to marry him. He is congratulated by his comrades and invites them all to the wedding. St Phar, it should be mentioned, unwilling to commit bigamy, has persuaded his friend Bijou to dress up as a priest and take the wedding ceremony, but Madame has somehow got to know about this and has locked Bijou up, together with the second leader of the chorus, so that the ceremony is performed by a real priest.

Act III. The Marquis remembers that St Phar has a wife at home and so is fully conscious that bigamy is being committed; however, since he is himself in love with the beautiful Madame Latour, he does nothing to prevent the marriage going through, but he rejoices to himself that tomorrow he will be able to bring the police to arrest his rival. St Phar is full of happiness in his marriage, but it is short-lived. Bijou escapes, and reveals the horrid truth to him; it was not he but a priest who officiated at the wedding, which is thus not mock, but real.

Madeleine has not yet finished with her husband, but comes to him in her original country clothes, and with Madeleine's voice. Then, blowing out the candle, she proceeds to hold a conversation with herself, altering her voice from that of Madeleine to that of Madame Latour and back again. Chappelou does not know what to say, and his despair is complete when the police are heard knocking at the door. Headed by the Marquis, they prepare to take him away – to be hanged, says the Marquis. Madeleine demands to be allowed to go with him – and then suddenly puts on her 'grand' voice, saying that there are two witnesses to the crime. She reveals the truth, and all is forgiven.   H.

JOHN ADAMS
(born 15 February 1947)

NIXON IN CHINA

Opera in three acts, libretto by Alice Goodman. Première Houston, 22 October 1987, with James Maddalena and Carolann Page as the Nixons, John Duykers as Mao Tse-Tung and Sanford Sylvan as Chou En-Lai; conductor John DeMain. Seen in New York, Amsterdam and at the Edinburgh Festival with largely the same cast. First performed Adelaide Festival, 1992, with Maddalena and Eilene Hannan, conductor David Porcelijn.

Chou En-Lai, *Chinese Prime Minister* ....Baritone

Richard Nixon, *President of the U.S.A.* ....Baritone

Henry Kissinger, *American
    Secretary of State* ....Bass-Baritone

Nancy T'ang, *First Secretary to
    Mao Tse-Tung* ....Soprano

Second Secretary to Mao ....Soprano

Third Secretary to Mao ....Contralto

Mao Tse-Tung, *President of China* ....Tenor

Pat Nixon ....Soprano

Chiang Ch'ing *(Madam Mao)*................High Soprano

Chinese Servicemen, Newsmen, Workers, Citizens

Place: Beijing, China
Time: 21–25 February 1972
Running Time: 2 hours 25 minutes

Born ten years after Philip Glass and described by Alice Goodman as 'a minimalist bored with minimalism', John Adams is nonetheless regularly grouped with Steve Reich and Philip Glass. It was Peter Sellars, because he prefers to work on a new opera rather than an existing one, who came up

Nixon in China *(Houston Grand Opera at Edinburgh Festival, 1988, director Peter Sellars, designer Adrianne Lobel). John Duykers (Mao), James Maddalena (Nixon), Thomas Hammons (Kissinger).*

with *Nixon in China* as an operatic subject. The three collaborators agreed from the start that this was to be a heroic opera and in no sense a satire. Its strength they believed would come from the extreme familiarity all over the world of characters such as the Nixons and Kissinger.

Adams has said: 'Something tremendously powerful was lost when composers moved away from tonal harmony and regular pulses ... Among other things the audience was lost.' He sees his score as 'ultra-American' and goes on, 'it is very important that people going to see this opera understand that what may seem on the surface like a *divertissement* or a comic strip, is actually a multilayered and extremely complex work.'

Act I. As prelude, the violins, violas and keyboards of the orchestra play rising scales, joined after a bit by woodwinds which add slower scales, the bass constantly changing. The scales continue as Chinese soldiers, waiting for the arrival of the American President, engage in slow, repetitive patriotic singing. Tension grows as the tempo gradually quickens and a *crescendo*

develops to the moment when the Presidential 'plane (*The Spirit of '76*) comes to a stop, at which point banality takes over: 'Your flight was smooth, I hope? Oh yes, smoother than usual, I guess.' Nixon's aria, 'News has a kind of mystery' (the word 'news' reiterated twelve times), is neo-classical in style, with a nod to Stravinsky, and during its course Chou attempts to introduce various civic worthies while Nixon goes into ecstasy over the idea that the 'eyes and ears of Hissstory' are taking note of their actions. Clichés are resoundingly exchanged but the extensive aria suggests idealism ('The Eastern Hemisphere beckons to us, and we have flown east of the sun, west of the moon, across an ocean of distrust') as well as platitudes ('It's prime time in the U.S.A. ... they watch us now').

Scene ii. Chairman Mao's study. Mao receives President Nixon. His three secretaries echo Mao's words almost throughout and the ensemble bubbles along, with Mao dispensing (as Alice Goodman has written) 'philosophical apophthegms, unexpected political observations, and gnomic jokes'. Nixon falls back on diplomatic fencing, and Kissinger, cast throughout as a kind of villain,[1] is constantly, as he himself admits, out of his depth.

Mao continues to wax philosophical, the secretaries to echo, and Nixon and Kissinger only occasionally to get half an idea in edgeways. Suddenly Mao has a brainwave: 'Founders come first, then profiteers', and this will return to him every now and then until the end of the scene.

As Mao appears to doze off in his chair, Nixon attempts to seize the initiative:

> ... I think this leap
> Forward to light is the first step
> Of all our youth, all nations' youth;
> History is our mother, we
> Best do her honour in this way.

But Mao is not to be out-smarted:

> History is a dirty sow:
> If we by chance escape her maw
> She overlies us.

The scene draws to a close and Mao is left to his books and his dictation: 'Founders come first ...'

Scene iii. A banquet is being held in the Great Hall of the People. President and First Lady sit on either side of Premier Chou. The atmosphere is more relaxed and Nixon and Pat exchange a few words at the start. Gentle verbal fencing between the principals precedes a toast – 'Gambei' – before Premier Chou's speech, which is assured and yet subtle, gaining in poise until Chou reaches his peroration:

> All patriots were brothers once:
> Let us drink to the time when they
> Shall be brothers again. Gambei!

Nixon seems at first nervous but confidence grows as he speaks, not without a glance at the watching media, until he reaches a purple climax and Enthusiasm takes over. Nixon plays a trump card:

> ... Everyone
> Listen, just let me say one thing.
> I opposed China. I was wrong.

The act ends in an orgy of toasts.

Act II, scene i. It is the morning of the second day. Snow has fallen in the night and it is Mrs Nixon's turn to meet China – or at least that part of it she is officially to be shown. She is taken to a glass factory, a clinic and a pig farm, she meets crowds of children and finishes with a visit to the Ming Tombs. The action occurs in the interludes of an extended *scena* and aria: 'I don't day-dream and don't look back.' The aria is personal in tone, full of home-spun wisdom and patriotic utterance.

Scene ii. Together with Madam Mao and Premier Chou, the Nixons are to see a ballet performance, 'The Red Detachment of Women', a revolutionary farrago (devised in real life for the cultural revolution in 1966) by Chiang Ch'ing. Her aim was to remove Western cultural influences and to replace them with scenarios of political significance. The trouble is that the music written specially for them (as John Adams once suggested, probably by a committee) had distinct overtones of the nineteenth-century Russian ballets they so despised.

From the outset the atmosphere for the ballet is one of expectancy. It is a bizarre affair. Young women are chained to posts on an estate and Lao Szu, the landlord's factotum (played by the singer of Kissinger), has one of them, Ching Hua, beaten into insensibility. Pat Nixon cannot bear the stage action and intervenes in spite of all the President's attempts to stop her. The stage rain (as is consistent with the surrealist action) appears to soak them both and Ching Hua is raised to her feet. The People's Army takes over and Ching Hua is presented with a rifle. In the courtyard of the tyrant's mansion, the girls dance and Ching Hua attempts rebellion. This is the cue for Chiang Ch'ing to start an aria and somehow bring the action to an end.

The music is ostinato-based and builds a considerable head of rhythmic steam. At one point the composer quotes Richard Strauss (Jokanaan from *Salome*) and at another Wagner (*Götterdämmerung*) and the dance grows again in rhythmic intensity, not without a debt to Carl Orff. Chiang Ch'ing's aria 'I am the wife of Mao Tse-Tung' is an extended solo, studded with top B flats, Cs and the occasional D, and the music's relentless nature mirrors that of the character.

Act III. It is the last night in Beijing and the elegiac music suggests we are in another world, contemplative and almost devoid of action. Too much action over the six days of the opera's duration has drained all energy from the protagonists, so that they are reduced to

---

[1] A Harvard in-joke apparently on the part of the three alumni, Goodman, Adams and Sellars, on their former professor.

musing on present, past and future. Only Mao appears to retain a semblance of vitality, and he dances with his wife and remembers their first meeting. Chiang Ch'ing is as irrepressible as always but Dr Kissinger excuses himself and leaves. Conversations cross and duets momentarily blend to ensembles.

The atmosphere intensifies, the tempo quickens but the drama stays on a contemplative plane. Chou is the most cogently philosophical, Mao content to babble more or less purposelessly, Chiang Ch'ing mostly to reiterate Marxist slogans, Nixon to talk aimlessly of the war and risks perceived but not quite confronted, Pat to react to what her husband says. Often the composer, while writing lyrical music of considerable beauty, seems unconcerned to make the words audible. Nonetheless, we hear Chou's summing up of his own outlook and of the memorable five days:

'I'm old and I cannot sleep
For ever, like the young ...
How much of what we did was good?'

Nixon in China is not concerned with the dramatic situations and confrontations dear to the hearts of Verdi or Mozart, rather with the clashes of will and point of view and the meeting of opposites which inform Wagner's *Ring*. Of course John Adams's method differs from that of operatic masters of the past. But the acute observation of character set out and implied in the libretto – Mao's babbling nonetheless enshrining moments of truth, the Nixons' small talk revealing significant patterns of behaviour, Chou ready with a phrase to bridge gaps or encapsulate a philosophy – these verbal leads stimulate Adams's music so that it captivates listeners with its accessibility, holds their attention as he skilfully avoids patterns coagulating with repetition, and finally steers the opera not only through its use of a modern and historically important event but ensures that it adds up to a true dramatic experience.   H.

THE DEATH OF KLINGHOFFER

Opera in a prologue and two acts, commissioned by Brooklyn Academy of Music, La Monnaie, Opéra de Lyon, Glyndebourne, Los Angeles Festival and San Francisco Opera, libretto by Alice Goodman. First performance at the Théâtre Royal de la Monnaie, Brussels, 19 March 1991, with James Maddalena as the Captain, Sanford Sylvan as Klinghoffer, Thomas

Hammons as the First Officer and 'Rambo', Stephanie Friedman as Omar. U.S. première at the Brooklyn Academy of Music, New York, 1991. Performed in all the opera houses that commissioned it (except for Glyndebourne), as well as in Vienna.

The Captain *of the* Achille Lauro ....Baritone
The First Officer (Giordano Bruno) ....Bass-Baritone
'Rambo', *a terrorist* ....Bass-Baritone
Swiss Grandmother ....Mezzo-Soprano
Austrian Woman ....Mezzo-Soprano
British Dancing Girl...........................Mezzo-Soprano
Molqi, *a terrorist* ....Tenor
Mamoud, *a terrorist*......................................Baritone
Leon Klinghoffer...Baritone
Omar, *a terrorist* ....Mezzo-Soprano
Marilyn Klinghoffer ....Contralto

Running Time: 2 hours 30 minutes

*T*he Death of Klinghoffer is based on the hijacking of the Italian cruise liner *Achille Lauro* by Palestinian terrorists between 7 and 9 October 1985. As in *Nixon in China*, the subject was proposed by Peter Sellars, who directed both operas. The events were just as real, yet the same team of composer, librettist, director and choreographer (Mark Morris) treated them in very different ways. John Adams has suggested that his model in his second opera was Bach's Passions. This is helpful, in that it 'explains' why there is so little interaction between the opera's characters: most of the time they sing by themselves, looking back on the events on board. The opera's prologue comprises two symmetrical choruses; the first act has two scenes, each of which is made up of five separate monologues. The second act repeats this format in its first scene, and precedes it with a choral prologue devoted to the story of Hagar. Four other choruses interrupt the sequence of individuals expressing themselves. They are distinguished as Ocean, Night, Desert and Day Chorus. In the first production the same baritone sang The First Officer and 'Rambo'; the same mezzo-soprano sang the Swiss Grandmother, Austrian Woman and British Dancing Girl, and dancers shadowed several singers as their *alter egos*.

Prologue. Exiled Palestinians remember how Israel destroyed their houses. Exiled Jews left with nothing but 'empty hands' long for the promised land, Zion.

Act I. The Captain of the *Achille Lauro* remembers how the hijacking began. Most of the tourists were ashore, leaving the old and infirm. When he was told of the terrorists, he went to the restaurant where he saw two boys with guns. A Swiss Grandmother had stayed on board with her two-year-old grandson. The First Officer remembers how he supervised taking a wounded man to the sick bay and so had to imagine the Captain's speech exhorting calm. Molqi relives the hijacking: 'Give these orders. Nobody stirs.' The portentously slow Ocean Chorus asks 'Is not the ocean itself their past?'

Scene ii. As the ship moves towards Syria, Mamoud remembers firing his first gun and how his mother 'could not remember' expulsion or interment. He remembers closing his brother's eyes, after he had been decapitated. When the Captain suggests that if only Mamoud could talk like that with his enemies, peace would result, Mamoud replies that, then 'our hope dies and I shall die too'. For the Captain, the ship should be like a hotel, but is inevitably more like a prison. He sings this simultaneously with the Austrian Woman's reminiscence in mannered *Sprechgesang* of how she kept her distance, stayed in her locked cabin and sustained herself on fruit and chocolate, unafraid. The Night Chorus brings the first act to a dramatic close with a reflection on persecution, ending, 'I am afraid for myself, for myself, for myself'.

Act II, scene i. The Chorus tell the story of Hagar and her son Ishmael, whom Islam reveres as the prophet Mohammed's ancestor. Hagar was expelled by the barren Sarah, jealous that her handmaiden had given birth to her husband Abraham's son. Hagar had no milk for her son, who grew weak. Determined that 'My son will die as a free man on his own land' she turned from him (in despair, presumably), 'Then the angel struck open the abandoned well'. After the grim cross-rhythms of the accompaniment and the grinding vocal line, the last line lacks any epiphanic charge. Ominously introduced by stuttering keyboard figures and tense, high violin wails, Molqi comments on the impasse and dreads what he may have to do. The Captain reports that they have received no answer to the terrorists' demands. Mamoud announces 'Now we will kill you all.' Leon Klinghoffer tells the hijackers, 'There's so much anger in you. And hate.' He refuses to take their political aims seriously. 'You just want to see

people die', he tells them, 'You're crazy.' Omar's monologue harps on the exile's feeling of exclusion and the desperation it engenders. The role is sung by a mezzo-soprano, following the eighteenth-century convention for stage adolescents, an apt comment on his passion for a martyr's 'Holy Death'. The Desert Chorus asks mysteriously: 'Is not their desert the garden of the Lord?' In silence, 'Omar and Molqi fight. Molqi wheels Klinghoffer away.'

Scene ii. Marilyn Klinghoffer imagines her husband has been taken to the ship's hospital. During a lengthy, loud orchestral passage he is killed off-stage. Unaware, she resolves to shut her eyes and pretend the hijacking never happened. Molqi hands over her husband's passport with the laconic (spoken) phrase, 'American kaput'. Mamoud announces that every fifteen minutes one more will be shot. The Captain remembers rebuking them; now he asks them to kill him and redeem his honour. Molqi asks, if they kill again, what will 'their answer' be?

During the 'Aria of the Falling Body (*Gymnopédies*)', Klinghoffer's double dances with the singer's body. Mamoud reports that it is 'over. It's done.' The Day Chorus ends the act, asking, 'Is not the day made to disperse their grief?'

Scene iii. The Captain tells Marilyn that her husband has been killed ('I am told his body was thrown overboard in the wheelchair') and attempts to comfort her. A saxophone adds its mournful comment, then she turns on him in fury, in some of the most convincing music of the opera: 'You embraced them!' For once, the music made of fragments speaks for feelings that cannot be articulated. She looks back on their close, loving marriage and ends the opera bitterly but with great dignity, 'They should have killed me. I wanted to die.'

While Bach's Passions supply an analogy for *The Death of Klinghoffer*'s formality, the analogy unhelpfully raises high expectations of its emotional charge: perhaps because it deals with such an explosive topic as the relations between Jews and Arabs (or between the West and Islam) and was completed while the United States was bombing Baghdad, the opera distances itself from emotion. For all its instrumental inventiveness (particularly for woodwind, but also featuring three electronic synthesizers/samplers), the music deals in monotony occasionally inflected with orientalist melismas. Introductory ostinatos set a cracking pace, as they do in Handel (or Verdi, for that matter), but when the solo voices enter they add disappointingly little: in trying to avoid rhetoric, they take no risks. Alice Goodman's libretto veers from poetry to 'Poetry' – a vivid, colloquial idiom that has room for compact eloquence occasionally sinks into obscurantist bathos (particularly in the opera's choruses), which repels comprehension.   P.

THOMAS ADÈS
(born 1 March 1971)

POWDER HER FACE

Opera in two acts, libretto by Philip Hensher. First performance by Almeida Opera, Cheltenham, 1 July 1995, with Jill Gomez as Duchess, Roger Bryson as Hotel Manager, Niall Morris as Electrician and Valdine Anderson as Maid, conducted by Brad Cohen. German première, Magdeburg, 21 September 1996, conducted by Mathias Husmann; U.S. première at University of California, Berkeley, 25 April 1997, conducted by Kent Nagano.

Duchess ....Dramatic Soprano

Hotel Manager, *also* Duke, Laundryman,
    Other Guest ....Bass

Electrician, *also* Lounge Lizard, Waiter, Priest,
    Rubbernecker, Delivery Boy ....Tenor

Maid, *also* Confidante, Waitress, Mistress,
    Rubbernecker, Society Journalist ....High Soprano

Time: 1934–90
Running Time: 1 hour 55 minutes

*P*owder Her Face owes as much to myth as to history. The Duchess has an archetypal quality not unrelated to Lulu, the subject of the librettist's first novel (*Other Lulus*, 1994). As in Berg's *Lulu*, multiple roles suggest that the action may take place in the heroine's mind. The opera alludes to Margaret, Duchess of Argyll (1912–93), but as an exemplar of a life devoted to what would not last. It helps to know that a photograph produced at her divorce trial showed her engaged in fellatio with 'a headless man' (his face was out of shot). To understand the opera she should be thought of as someone who 'died, as we all do, with nothing, and like all of us, left nothing behind except her memory'.[1]

Act I follows a Laughter-Prologue. 1990. The Electrician mimics the Duchess to amuse the Maid: 'I was betrayed, girl'. As he quotes a popular song celebrating her infamy, he fails to notice that the Duchess herself has come in behind him. A door opens as the Duchess reminisces, anticipating the arrival of the Duke, 'my better angel'. During the interlude it shuts slowly and the Maid and Electrician dress up as Confidante and as Lounge Lizard respectively.

1934. A country house. The Confidante and Lounge Lizard discuss Mrs Freeling's divorce from her husband and look forward to the arrival of the Duke. Mrs Freeling's aria, 'I could never grow bored of dukedoms. But now I'm so bored', is sung simultaneously with the others' duet. The Lounge Lizard starts the gramophone and sings the song written about Mrs Freeling, 'Respectability stretch'. The door opens to reveal the Hotel Manager as Duke.

1936. A series of tableaux, lit only by flash bulbs, traces the course of the Duke's and Mrs Freeling's wedding before the Electrician as Priest. Frozen moments from the ceremony alternate with scenes from a troilistic orgy, illustrating the Maid as Waitress's Fancy Aria.

1953. Another hotel bedroom. The Duchess in a dressing gown rings room service and orders beef sandwiches and wine. The Electrician as Waiter brings her order, and walks over to the bed where she is sitting. In the words of the Radio 3 announcer, 'Room service takes a rather unusual form': her words stop and she 'goes off into humming'. A flashbulb goes off as the Waiter has an orgasm. The Duchess succumbs to a fit of coughing.

---

[1] Philip Hensher, note in the programme for the première.

1953. The Duke's bedroom. The Maid as Mistress hints to the Hotel Manager as Duke that the Duchess is promiscuously unfaithful and suggests he look in her case. He finds the camera.

Act II. 1955. A courtroom. The Maid and the Electrician as Rubberneckers agree that the Duke knew what his wife was up to. The Duchess enters, followed by the Hotel Manager, who puts on a robe and a wig to act as Judge and give his verdict. He condemns the Duchess as a pervert, a beast, 'insatiable, unnatural and altogether fairly appalling'. The Duchess unveils herself and bravely faces the consequences, believing 'I am still loved.'

1970. The hotel bedroom. Interviewed by the Maid as Journalist for a women's magazine, the Duchess gives the secrets of her beauty regime, 'Go to bed early and often', but then goes on to rant against blacks, Jews, concrete. Meanwhile the Electrician as Delivery Boy delivers various hat boxes. The scene ends as the Duchess rips up the bill.

1990. The hotel bedroom. The Hotel Manager tells the Duchess that because her bill hasn't been paid for eight months, 'Everything is used up. And now you must go.' The Duchess looks back on a life surrounded by servants: 'The only people who were good to me were paid for it.'

Ghost Epilogue. The Electrician and Maid emerge from under the bed and then strip it in a 'sheet-folding Tango'. They flirt before she leaves.

Words and music are closely allied in *Powder her Face*. The librettist said that in choosing the subject itself, he was thinking of Thomas Adès's music, since the composer's 'tottering, extravagant inventions on the ruins of tonality' suggested 'the wrecked beauty of an old woman'. Philip Hensher also explained in a programme note that the title can be read as 'an instruction to a maquilleuse' and as a reflection on the Duchess's fate, our common fate as 'food for worms'. The music in Adès's first opera is not afraid to acknowledge its debts, to Astor Piazzola, in the tangos that frame *Powder Her Face* and connote a dance with death, for example, or to *The Rake's Progress*, so as to parallel the divorce trial with the auction scene. The wit and the spectacle, the music's occasional bursts of pastiche and its jokes accentuate a disturbing seriousness, which emerges ungloved in the interludes (as so often in twentieth-century operas). The première was marked by the unique

Powder her Face (*Cheltenham Festival, 1995, director David Farr, sets by Angela Davies). Jill Gomez as the Duchess.*

performance of Jill Gomez, who invested the role of the Duchess with both glamour and pathos. She brought out the intensity of the Duchess's needs – Adès sets 'Come in' over thirty-two bars of music – and, as a result, ensured that the opera that began as a joke ended in something like tragedy.   P.

EUGEN D'ALBERT

(born 10 April 1864, died 3 March 1932)

TIEFLAND

The Lowlands

Opera in a prologue and two acts, text by Rudolph Lothar after a Catalonian play *Tierra Baixa*, by Angel Guimerà. Première, Neues Deutsches Theater, Prague, 15 November 1903. First performed in Berlin, 1907, with Labia as Marta; Vienna, 1908; Metropolitan, 1908, with Destinn, Schmedes, Feinhals, conductor Hertz; Covent Garden, 1910, with Terry, Teyte, John Coates, Frederick Austin, conductor Beecham. Revived Berlin, 1939, with Rünger, Völker, Bockelmann; Vienna, 1947, with Helena Braun, Friedrich, Kamann, conductor Loibner. Kirsten Flagstad made her operatic debut as Nuri.

Sebastiano, *a rich landowner* ....Baritone

Tommaso, *the village elder (aged ninety)* ....Bass

Moruccio, *a miller* ....Baritone

Marta ....Soprano

Pepa ....Soprano

Antonia ....Soprano

Rosalia ....Contralto

Nuri, *a little girl* ....Soprano

Pedro, *a shepherd* ....Tenor

Nando, *a shepherd* ....Tenor

The Priest ....Mute

Place: The Pyrenees and the Lowlands of Catalonia
Time: Early Twentieth Century
Running Time: 2 hours 25 minutes

D'Albert, who was born in Glasgow, was not only a pianist of very high attainments, but also a successful composer, whose operas range from comedy to a German form of *verismo*; *Tiefland* is an example of the latter aspect of his style. D'Albert was married no fewer than six times, his second wife being the great pianist Teresa Carreño.

Prologue. A rocky slope high up in the Pyrenees. A shepherd's hut can be seen. Pedro and Nando greet each other, Pedro observing that he has not seen anyone for three months, and has not spoken to a soul for six. He protests that he finds the shepherd's life perfect, but that he has in his prayers asked God to send him a wife ('Zwei Vaterunser bet' ich').

Sebastiano appears at the top, accompanied by Marta and Tommaso; he sends Tommaso off to look for Pedro. He explains the object of their errand to Marta, who has been his mistress for some time. He has brought her up here to show her to Pedro, whom he has picked out as a suitable husband!

Pedro tells Nando of his good fortune, but the latter warns him about conditions down there in the valley. Pedro sings a last greeting to the mountains ('Ich grüss' noch einmal meine Berge').

Act I. The interior of the mill. Moruccio is working, but is interrupted by the arrival and importunate questioning of Pepa, Antonia, and Rosalia; is it true that Marta is getting married?

Marta comes in for a moment, but, seeing all the people there, hurries out again. The three women begin to laugh at the curious situation which her marriage will create, not least for the duffer who is to become her husband. Marta comes back and drives them out. She seems pleased to see Nuri, and it looks as though she will confide in the child.

Marta reflects on her misery. She is Sebastiano's property, and had not the courage to free herself by drowning herself in the stream. Now she is to marry a mountain lout... She hurries out when she hears what she thinks may be the noise of the escort bringing her bridegroom-to-be. Moruccio asks Tommaso how he came to be a party to the arrangement of such a wicked marriage. Pedro arrives, closely followed by Sebastiano, who orders that Marta be brought from her room.

While Pedro is getting dressed outside, Marta and Sebastiano are alone. There is an extensive duet in which Sebastiano claims that Marta's love will be his even after she is married to Pedro. That very night, if she sees a light, it will be the signal that he is there.

Pedro comes with other villagers for Marta, and they leave for the church. Tommaso, however, asks to speak to Sebastiano. He hints at the accusation which Moruccio has made against Marta, but Sebastiano says it is false; moreover, he who made it shall no longer remain in his service.

The moon rises, the wedding procession can be heard returning, and Marta comes in, followed by Pedro. She will have none of him, and even refuses to accept the wedding present he offers her, a silver Taler. It was hard-earned, he says, and proceeds to tell Marta the story of his fight with a wolf which preyed on the sheep, and which he eventually managed to kill with his knife, receiving as a reward the Taler from Sebastiano's own hands ('Wolfserzählung').

Marta seems impressed by his narrative and touched that he wants to give the piece of silver to her. But she bids him goodnight, and points to a room which she describes as his in exactly the opposite direction from hers. When he protests, she presumes that he has been told what a shameful bargain he made when he married her. But Pedro knows nothing of her past, and speaks of nothing but his love for her. Suddenly, Pedro sees a light in her room. He feels in his pocket for his knife and is about to approach the curtain which covers the door when the light disappears and Marta says that she saw nothing. She resigns herself to spending the night in the main room, and Pedro lies down on the floor, determined to see her vigil through with her.

Act II. The curtain rises to show Marta and Pedro as at the end of Act I. Nuri is heard singing behind the scenes, and Marta goes out to her room. Nuri wakes Pedro, who thinks for a moment it is Marta. He says he will not stay any longer; he is sure there was a man in her room last night.

His suspicions are confirmed when Nuri says she is sorry everyone is laughing at him on account of the marriage he has made. He now knows that his dishonour is public property – but at whose hands is he dishonoured?

Marta sees him with Nuri, and has a spasm of jealousy. He goes out with Nuri, and Marta is about to follow them when she meets Tommaso coming to see her. He curses her for what she has let him all unwittingly do to Pedro. In a moving passage ('Ich weiss nicht, wer mein Vater war') she tells him her story, how she was left alone with her mother and they earned their living by begging in the streets. One day an old man, a cripple, joined them, and after that he lived with them. Her mother died, and she stayed with the cripple, who would not let her go as her dancing brought them money. Eventually their wanderings led them to this valley, where she was seen by Sebastiano, who spoke the first kind words she had ever heard. The cripple was installed as miller, and she became mistress of Sebastiano, the lord of the manor. She was fourteen years old when she arrived. Now she has been forced into marriage with Pedro; but a wonderful thing happened to her in the chapel when she fancied she heard a voice proclaiming him as her destined mate. Tommaso tells her she must, if she loves Pedro, tell him her secret.

As Tommaso is leaving, the women start to question him; what does he know? Nothing, he answers. Pedro is the next to be cross-questioned. He loses his temper and tries to force them to tell him why they laugh at him. Ask Marta, they tell him. Marta brings him his food, but he tells her that he should kill her, not forgive her, as she asks. She tells him she was another man's before she was married to him; everyone was laughing at the wedding for that reason. Pedro stabs her in the arm, and Marta weeps for joy. At last he has punished her for her fault; will he not strike her dead? Pedro is in despair; will she not come with him to the mountains where they will live together in peace? Marta joins her voice with his.

They are about to leave arm-in-arm when Sebastiano appears at the gate. Pedro tells him that he must take back his gift of the mill; he and his bride are returning to the mountains – but Sebastiano does not even notice Pedro. He commands Marta to dance for him, as she used to ('Hüll in die Mantille'). Pedro orders Marta to follow him. When Marta tells him whose light it was in her room the previous night, Pedro is with difficulty restrained from attacking Sebastiano. Men seize Pedro and drag him away, while Marta falls unconscious.

Tommaso appears and tells Sebastiano that the father of his bride-to-be will not be seeing him that day, as Sebastiano was expecting. He, Tommaso, has made it his business to inform him of the background to the projected marriage, and he will have nothing further to do with Sebastiano. There is a violent duet between Marta and Sebastiano, the latter proclaiming that she is all that is left to him now, Marta objecting that she loves Pedro. Pedro comes in, ready to fight Sebastiano for Marta.

Sebastiano makes for the gate, but Pedro heads him off. He draws his knife, but throws it away, saying that they will fight with bare hands. Sebastiano makes an effort to reach the knife but Pedro seizes him by the throat in a grip of iron, not releasing him until all signs of life are extinct. Pedro goes to the entrance of the mill calling for the villagers. They see the corpse on the floor. Now is the time to laugh, orders Pedro. As for him, he will away into the hills, taking Marta his wife with him.   H.

DOMINICK ARGENTO
(born 27 October 1927)

Born of Sicilian immigrant parents, Argento studied with Nicolas Nabokov and Hugo Weisgall, and later with Dallapiccola. His first opera (1954) started a line of successful works, large and small, some with a dodecaphonic basis. *Postcard from Morocco* has proved the most successful, though *The Aspern Papers* has been described as a score 'having both twelve-note and bel canto implications'.

POSTCARD FROM MOROCCO

Opera in one act, libretto by John Donahue. Première, Minneapolis, by Center Opera Company, 14 October 1971, conductor Philip Brunelle. First performed King's College, London, 1976.

Lady with a Cake Box	Soprano
Man with a Shoe Sample Kit/ Second Puppet	Baritone
Man with a Cornet Case/Puppet Maker	Bass
Lady with a Hat Box/Foreign Singer	Mezzo-Soprano
Man with Old Luggage/First Puppet/Operetta Singer	Tenor
Lady with a Hand Mirror/Operetta Singer	Coloratura Soprano
Mr Owen, *the man with a paintbox*	Tenor

Place: A Railway Station in Morocco
Time: 1914
Running Time: 1 hour 35 minutes

The opera is scored for seven singers with eight instrumentalists in the orchestra. The abstract libretto has only one named character, Mr Owen, and the opera is built up of a series of surrealistically connected episodes, to which composer and librettist have attached a collage of nonsense sentences, ideas, disparate, often attractive, even lyrical, in themselves but little related apparently to what went before or comes later. Any number of dramatic interpretations are obviously possible, and the absurdist overtones are apparent. The scenery is described as wacky or exotic; there are entertainments present, says the librettist, and some of the people visible are real, some not. 'The decor is false but charming ... Accompanying this little comedy is an Algerian orchestra ... in costume and fez ... The live characters play more than one role ... We see each one trying hard to protect whatever small part of himself he has in his suitcase.'

Seven people are stranded at a station. Each character has a solo in which he or she seems as prepared to reveal some element of personality as they are unprepared to reveal the contents of the item of luggage they carry.

The Lady with a travelling mirror sings in high, coloratura style; two puppets plan to build a boat; the mezzo-soprano rather expressively sings nonsense. In lyrical phrases, one tenor declares he only travels with old luggage, not wanting to risk anything important. The Man with a cornet admits his uncle was a pro, which he is not; but he won't show the instrument. The Lady with the hat box is equally enigmatic. The band tunes, and there follows a version of the Spinning Chorus from *The Flying Dutchman*, some percussion and brass jokes, a snatch of the *Ring*, all lumped together as 'Souvenirs de Bayreuth'.

The Man with a shoe sample kit admits his case is specially made, but will show them his wares only by appointment. It is the turn of Mr Owen with his paintbox. What kind of pictures does he paint? Shoes, for example? Lovers sing in Viennese fashion before the lady with the cake box is quizzed in her turn. She keeps her beloved in a box, she says. You're joking, of course? In a duet of some charm, she and Mr Owen converse at cross purposes. Mr Owen kisses her, then confesses a dream to a cardboard priest.

The puppeteer declares he gets ideas by looking at people – their luggage, shoes, hats and so on. A passacaglia begins, the coloratura soprano ascending climactically to a high E (or even G, if she has one), and Mr Owen's paintbox is revealed as empty. Isolated, he becomes the Captain of a ship, issues orders, and his grandiose tenor statements lead to an ensemble and the opera's end.   H.

EMILIO ARRIETA
(born 21 October 1823, died 11 February 1894)

Opera in Spain was always much concerned with Italian influence and Italian works. In the nineteenth century, sporadic attempts at Spanish opera began to bear fruit. The rapid rise from about 1850 of a grand, four-act form of *zarzuela*, with composers like Barbieri, Chapi and Serrano leading the way, established something approaching a school. In Catalonia, Pedrell was followed by Vives and later by Albéniz and Granados, Falla and Turina, but the flag was kept flying mainly by derivatives of *zarzuela*, whether direct (as for instance Arrieta's *Marina*) or simply *zarzuelas* on a bigger scale. The latter often had a less popular-style plot so that elsewhere they would have been styled as operas, or at least operettas, and would have been played in opera houses and sung by opera singers.

Arrieta, orphaned early on, contrived to reach Milan where he studied and even achieved the writing of an Italian opera, *Ildegonda*, with libretto by one of Verdi's collaborators, Solera. In Madrid, he was encouraged by Barbieri's success to take up *zarzuela*, and in 1853 was highly successful with *El Dominó azul*, every one of whose numbers is said to have been encored at the première. *Marina* followed in 1855, and he wrote over fifty *zarzuelas*, deciding in 1871 with a little doctoring to turn the successful *Marina* into an opera (he replaced spoken dialogue with recitative and restructured the two-act *zarzuela* into a three-act opera with a quantity of added music). He was professor of composition in Madrid from 1857, numbering Chapi and Bretón among his pupils, and director from 1868 to his death. Arrieta was regarded as a technically adroit composer, though Lionel Salter tells us some contemporaries regarded him as unromantic and 'the most academic and circumspect Spanish musician of his time'. Fortunately, that does not show in the very attractive score he wrote for *Marina*, where, in spite of the ups and downs of the story, the musical atmosphere is predominantly lively and full of the cheerfulness which so distinguishes the *zarzuela* genre.   H.

MARINA

Opera in three acts, libretto by Francisco Camprodon. Première (as *zarzuela*), Teatro del Circo, Madrid, 21 September 1855; (as opera) Madrid, 16 March 1871, with Angioliana Ortolani and Enrico Tamberlik.

Marina, *an orphan*	Soprano
Jorge, *a sea captain*	Tenor
Roque, *Jorge's boatswain*	Baritone
Pascual, *a boat-builder*	Bass
Teresa	Soprano
Alberto, *a sea-captain*	Baritone

Place: Lloret, a Fishing Village
Time: The Recent Past
Running Time: 1 hour 30 minutes

Act I. Marina is waiting for Jorge's return from sea. She is an orphan, adopted by Jorge's parents, and she and Jorge have fallen in love without ever declaring their feelings. Alberto, like Jorge a sea captain, tells her that he has a letter from her father, written to her mother just before his death in Trinidad. On her death, it was found among her papers, and he promises to send it to Marina. The boat-builder Pascual woos her ardently but vainly, until Marina hits on the device of accepting Pascual as a means to spur Jorge's interest.

A crowd welcomes Jorge back from his voyage, and he is confident enough of Marina's love to announce that he is shortly getting married. Pascual however steals a march on him and reveals that his fiancée is Marina. Jorge is thunderstruck but tries to disguise his feelings, nonetheless admitting his misery to Roque.

Act II. In the shipyard, Pascual with Marina at his side invites the workmen to his wedding, and Alberto promises to let her have the letter before long, which somehow rouses Pascual's jealousy. Jorge assures everyone that while he lives Marina will never want, Pascual asks Marina to visit his mother, who cannot leave the house, and Jorge is left downcast; even Roque is unable to suggest comfort.

Act III. With a group of seafarers, Jorge drinks to drown his sorrows, a Brindisi which skilfully alternates high spirits with Jorge's melancholy. Marina tries to provide some solace, believing another woman is the root of the problem, but she gets nowhere and leaves in tears. Pascual meanwhile prepares for the wedding festivities. A sailor comes in with the letter Alberto promised Marina, but Pascual, who is suspicious of Alberto and jealous of Marina, contrives to intercept it. He thinks it is a love letter to Marina and his accusation that she loves another brings from her an immediate admission of the charge, whereupon he breaks off the engagement. Jorge discovers that the letter from Marina's father was a wholly innocent affair and not, as he had suspected, a love letter from Alberto. He also finds out that it is he whom she loves, and he and Marina fall into each other's arms. H.

DANIEL-FRANÇOIS AUBER

(born 29 January 1782, died 12 May 1871)

Auber lived to be nearly ninety and played a prominent part in the history of French opera. After some early work of little lasting significance, he began a collaboration with the librettist Eugène Scribe which, with *La Muette de Portici* in 1828, created effectively a new genre, Grand Opera. Even Wagner was impressed with the novelty of the opera's revolutionary ideas and the scale of its stage production, and Auber followed it a couple of years later with the tuneful but much lighter *Fra Diavolo*, whose success was hardly less great. He wrote regularly for both the Opéra and the Opéra-Comique until the century was well past the half-way mark, and at least the names of many of these works are still half-familiar – *Gustave III* (on the story known from Verdi's *Ballo*, and itself an enjoyable precursor of a later masterpiece), *Le Cheval de Bronze*, *Les diamants de la couronne*, and *Manon Lescaut* (with its famous laughing song). Auber's work was enormously popular during his lifetime though later composers esteemed him less than had Wagner. He was sufficiently renowned to be appointed to succeed his old teacher Cherubini as Director of the Paris Conservatoire.

LA MUETTE DE PORTICI

The Dumb Girl of Portici

Opera in five acts, text by Scribe and Delavigne. Première at the Opéra, Paris, 29 February 1828, with Noblet, Cinti-Damoreau, Nourrit, Dabadie. First performed at Drury Lane, London (in English), 1829; New York, 1829 (in English); Covent Garden, 1845 (in French); 1849 (in Italian), with Grisi and Mario; Metropolitan, 1884, with Bely, Schott, Kögel, conductor Damrosch. Braham was a noted Masaniello. Revived with explicit revolutionary overtones, Berlin, Staatsoper, 1953, with Stolze.

Alphonse (Alfonso) d'Arcos, *son of the Spanish Viceroy of Naples*	Tenor
Lorenzo, *his confidant*	Tenor
Selva, *an officer of the Viceroy's guard*	Bass
Masaniello, *a fisherman of Naples*	Tenor
Pietro, *his friend*	Baritone
Fenella, *Masaniello's sister*	Dancer
Borella, *a fisherman*	Bass
Moreno, *a fisherman*	Bass
Elvire (Elvira), *a Spanish Princess*	Soprano
A Maid of Honour to the Princess	Mezzo-Soprano

Place: Naples
Time: 1647
Running Time: 2 hours 30 minutes

The story of *La Muette de Portici* is based on the historical happenings of the year 1647, when the people of Naples rose against their Spanish oppressors. The opera is perhaps the most successful Auber ever wrote; within twelve years of the first performance, there had been 100 representations at the Paris Opéra, and the 500th occurred in 1880. 'It is well known', says Loewenberg, 'that a performance (not the first performance though as sometimes stated) at Brussels, 25 August 1830, gave the signal to the outbreak of the Belgian revolution, which led to the independence of the country.'

Act I. After an overture of almost Rossinian animation, the setting is the garden next to the palace of the Duke of Arcos, Spanish Viceroy of Naples. Against a chorus of rejoicing, the Viceroy's son, Alphonse, laments his conduct in seducing an innocent and poor Neapolitan maid, Fenella, who loved him but whom he has had to cast off in view of his approaching marriage with Elvire, the Spanish Princess whom he loves. Fenella, who is dumb, has disappeared, and for a month there has been no sign of her. In a large-scale aria, Elvire proclaims her happiness to the girls who are attending her to the altar. Dances are performed for her entertainment, but Elvire hears that a fishermaid, pursued by soldiers, is asking for her protection. She questions Fenella, who tells her story in dumb show.

The Princess with her attendants goes into the chapel. When she emerges with her bridegroom, Alphonse recognises Fenella, whom Elvire beckons towards them. Fenella indicates that it is Alphonse who has betrayed her. Elvire is horrified, and the act ends in general consternation.

Act II. Portici, on the seashore between Naples and Mount Vesuvius. Fishermen are assembling, and greet their leader, Masaniello. He sings a barcarolle ('Amis, la matinée est belle'), which is fuller of foreboding than of the joy of living. As yet only Pietro, Masaniello's friend, knows of the sad fate of Fenella, but he now reports that he has been unable to find her anywhere. The two friends swear vengeance on the tyrants who have oppressed their people for so long and who have now done so grievous an injury to the most defenceless of their subjects; 'Amour sacré de la patrie' runs the refrain of the famous patriotic duet, which once provided the signal for the start of the Belgian revolution.

Fenella comes to seek Masaniello, and tells him her story. She will not admit her lover's name, but signifies that he is married and so cannot redeem her shame. Masaniello swears to be revenged, and calls the fishermen to arms. They swear perdition to the enemies of the country.

Act III. A public square in Naples. Alphonse tries to persuade Elvire that he loves her, and that his penitence for the wrong he did the fishergirl is sincere. She yields to his entreaty, and he commands the guards to find Fenella and bring her before Elvire. The market is in full swing, and people buy and sell;

a tarantella is danced. The guards think they see Fenella and attempt to arrest her. Masaniello intervenes and, when the guards would arrest him too, calls on the people to rise. The soldiers are driven off, but before leading his improvised army off to further conquests, Masaniello calls on them to pray for God's guidance in their just enterprise. The act comes to an end as they prepare to subdue the city.

Act IV. Portici; the hut of Masaniello. Masaniello laments that the battle for liberty should have bred licence and destructiveness among the conquering rabble he led to victory. Fenella appears, pale and with faltering steps, and her brother gently sings her to sleep. Pietro and his companions come to incite Masaniello once more to place himself at their head and lead them to victory and revenge. He pleads for moderation, and for a cessation of bloodshed.

They go to the back of the house, and shortly afterwards a knock is heard. Alphonse and Elvire come to seek shelter from the bloodthirsty mob, little knowing from whom they are asking it. At first Fenella does not want to save Elvire, whom she thinks of as her rival, but Elvire's pleading wins her pity, and she vows to save them or die with them in the attempt. Much to Fenella's joy, Masaniello agrees to shelter the two fugitives.

Pietro appears with representatives of the people to ask Masaniello to take the keys of government and rule over them. Pietro recognises Alphonse, and an ensemble ensues between the two Spanish fugitives, Masaniello, Pietro, and the chorus. Pietro wishes to put them straight away to death, Masaniello urges that his oath of hospitality is binding. In the end Masaniello gives the Spaniards safe-conduct and threatens to slay anyone who makes a move against them. Pietro and his followers swear that Masaniello shall be the next to fall.

Act V. In front of the Viceroy's palace at Naples. Pietro sings a barcarole with the chorus; in between the two verses he confides to a friend that he has already administered poison to Masaniello, who seemed likely to become a greater tyrant than those they deposed in his favour. Even as he sings, the 'king of the day' is dying, and nothing can save him.

News comes that Alphonse is marching against them at the head of troops, and, almost as bad, that Vesuvius is in eruption; the credulous peasants think that the wrath of heaven is being visited on the rebels. Only Masaniello can save them, cry the people, but Pietro and his friends reveal that the poison has made the hero the victim of hallucinations. Masaniello himself comes out of the palace, and is obviously not in his right mind. All appeal to him as their only hope; but he takes no notice and sings the barcarole we heard in the second act. Not until Fenella appears can he grasp the import of the situation, but then he places himself at the head of the rebels and marches off with them.

Fenella prays for his safe return. Elvire appears, explaining that Masaniello has saved her life from the murderous stroke of one of his followers; Alphonse, who follows her, continues the story – Masaniello himself was struck down in revenge for his saving of Elvire. Fenella is overcome by the news and commits suicide.   H.

FRA DIAVOLO

Opera in three acts, text by Scribe. Première at Opéra-Comique, Paris, 28 January 1830, with Prévost, Boulanger, Chollet. First performed Drury Lane, 1831; New York, 1831; Lyceum, 1857 (in Italian), with Borsio, Gardoni, Ronconi, Tagliafico. Last performance at Covent Garden, 1896, with Engle, de Lucia, Pini-Corsi, Arimondi, Bispham. Revived Metropolitan, 1910, with Alten and Clément, conductor Hertz; Berlin, 1934, with Eisinger, Pattiera, Schützendorf, Hüsch, conductor Blech; la Scala, Milan, 1934, with Carosio, Pertile, Autori, Bettoni, Nessi, conductor Santini; Sadler's Wells, 1935 (in English), with Naylor, Arthur Cox (Carron); Berlin, 1936, with Berger, Völker; Stockholm, 1948; Naples, 1962, with Vicenzi, Lazzari; Wexford Festival, 1966, with Valentini, Benelli; Marseilles, 1966, with Mady Mesplé and Michel Sénéchal; San Francisco, 1968, with Mary Costa, Nicolai Gedda. Fra Diavolo was a favourite role of many famous tenors, among them Bonci and Schipa.

Fra Diavolo, *a bandit chief*....................................Tenor

Lord Cockburn, *an English tourist*......................Tenor

Lady Pamela, *his wife*..........................Mezzo-Soprano

Lorenzo, *an officer of carabiniers* ....Tenor

Matteo, *an innkeeper* ....Bass

Zerlina, *his daughter*..Soprano

Giacomo, *a bandit*...Bass

Beppo, *a bandit*...Tenor

Place: Near Naples
Time: Eighteenth Century
Running Time: 2 hours 10 minutes

*F*ra Diavolo, one of the most popular of all *opéras-comiques*, is now remembered chiefly through recordings of its virtuoso arias. All the same, its admirable music and excellent story seem to entitle it to more frequent revival than in fact, outside Germany, it seems to receive.

The story is concerned with Fra Diavolo, a famous bandit leader in the district round Naples. His reputation is to some extent that of a Robin Hood, his chivalry being above question and his habit to give generously to the poor out of what he has taken from the rich. At the time of the story, he is travelling under the name of the Marquis of San Marco.

Act I. Matteo's tavern. A reward of 10,000 *piastres* has been offered for the apprehension of the bandit Fra Diavolo. Lorenzo and his troop of carabiniers are drinking at the inn, but the brigadier seems unusually preoccupied. It soon turns out that he is full of sadness at the prospect of losing his sweetheart, Zerlina, the innkeeper's daughter, whom her father has destined for a wealthier suitor. The party is interrupted by the precipitate arrival of Lord Cockburn, a wealthy English traveller, and his wife, Lady Pamela, complaining loudly that they have been set upon and robbed. Lorenzo starts off to look for the brigand, after hearing that Lord Cockburn means to offer a reward of 6,000 *scudi* for the return of his wife's jewels.

The English couple have only just finished an altercation on the subject of the attentions of a certain Marquis of San Marco to her ladyship when a carriage draws up at the door, and the Marquis himself is announced. He seems delighted to see Pamela, and says that he is going to stay the night. Matteo hastens to see that he is suitably provided with food, and then bids his daughter look after the Marquis well while he himself is away for the night making arrangements for her wedding.

The Marquis asks why the English lord seems in such a bad temper and is told that he has just been robbed by the notorious Fra Diavolo. The Marquis expresses incredulity at the idea that there should be bandits in such a civilised part of the country, but Zerlina is told to sing him the local ballad of Fra Diavolo. He joins in the last verse. A couple of beggars come in, and the Marquis says he will pay for their board and lodging. When the innkeeper and his daughter have gone out, these turn out to be

Giacomo and Beppo, two members of Fra Diavolo's band, and they discuss the affair of the English nobleman, admitting that they were unable to find the gold he was reputed to have with him. Fra Diavolo says he will try to find out its whereabouts from Lady Pamela. He dismisses his retainers, and starts to pay compliments to the lady, turning their emotional duet into a barcarole when he catches sight of her husband. The Marquis flatters Milord into giving away the secret hiding-place of his money; he boasts that it is in bills, sewn into his cloak and his wife's gown.

There is a noise outside; it is the troop of carabiniers returning after a most successful sortie against the bandits. They report that they have killed at least twenty and recaptured the stolen property. Lady Pamela insists that Lorenzo be given his reward straight away, so that he can convince Matteo that he is wealthy enough to marry Zerlina. The act ends with Lorenzo and the soldiers announcing their intention to capture the bandit chief himself, Fra Diavolo swearing to be revenged for the loss of his followers.

Act II. The curtain rises to show Zerlina's bedroom. Lord Cockburn and his wife are sleeping next door, and the only way into their room is through hers. Zerlina prepares the room, singing a brilliant aria the while. Its occupants come up to bed, quarrelling as they do so sufficiently for Zerlina to remark that she and her husband will not be like that a year after their wedding day. Zerlina goes with them to their room to help Lady Pamela undress and to see if there is anything they need.

Enter Fra Diavolo, who has discovered that Zerlina's room is next to that of the English travellers, and who means to hide there himself, with his two followers, so as to relieve them for the second time of their valuables. He sings a barcarole to attract the attention of Giacomo and Beppo, and lets them in through the window. They hear Zerlina's voice and all hide, Beppo and Giacomo going through some glass doors from which the bedroom is in full view. Zerlina undresses and pauses for a moment to admire her face and figure in the looking-glass; this is too much for the watchers who cannot restrain their laughter. Zerlina says her prayers and goes to bed. Diavolo and his followers make their way towards Milord's rooms. Giacomo is about to stab Zerlina – might she not give them away if there were to be any noise? – but she murmurs a prayer in

her sleep and he cannot bring himself to do the deed.

Suddenly, there is a sound downstairs; Zerlina wakes up to hear Lorenzo calling for her. He and his men have not found Fra Diavolo and would like food and shelter for the rest of the night. She admits them; Lord Cockburn makes an appearance to complain about the noise but that is forgotten when Beppo knocks something over in the cupboard in which he is hidden. All is not lost however, Fra Diavolo taking it upon himself to step out and confront the brigadier and the Englishman. He had, he confesses to each of them separately, a rendezvous; he whispers the names of Zerlina and Lady Pamela into the appropriate ear. He is challenged by Lorenzo, and accepts. When Zerlina and Lady Pamela appear, they are met with nothing but coldness by respectively the lover and the husband on whom they were counting for comfort.

Act III. The mountains, not far from Matteo's inn. Fra Diavolo has laid his plans carefully. He means to be revenged on Lorenzo for what he and his soldiers have done to the rest of his band. Meanwhile, he sings of the charms of a bandit's life. The Easter procession is about to start out from the inn, watched by Beppo and Giacomo, who have orders to wait until Lorenzo and his soldiers have moved off, then ring the church bell to indicate to Fra Diavolo that the way is clear. Lorenzo, in a romance, sings sadly of the love he had thought faithful but has found to be false. Suddenly, he remembers that he has a debt of honour to pay at exactly this hour. He reproaches Zerlina for her unfaithfulness, which she indignantly denies. Just then Beppo and Giacomo catch sight of her and recognise her as the girl they watched going to bed the previous night. They laugh at the memory and repeat some of her phrases, just a little too loudly it appears, for she hears them and demands that someone find out the truth about how they overheard her when she was alone in her own bedroom. A paper giving Fra Diavolo's plan is found on one of them and the plot is revealed.

Lorenzo orders that Giacomo be taken to ring the bell, and that when Fra Diavolo appears Beppo tell him the way is clear. He will then fall into their hands. All goes as he has hoped. Diavolo descends to the square, where he is ambushed and shot. (In a later version, the ending has Fra Diavolo surrounded by carabiniers and made prisoner.)   H.

LE DOMINO NOIR

The Black Domino

Opera in three acts, text by A.E. Scribe. Première at Opéra-Comique, Paris, 2 December 1837, with Cinti-Damoreau as Angèle. Enormously successful all over Europe and in France, where it had reached 1000 performances at the Opéra-Comique by 1882.

Angèle d'Olivarès, *a novice*............................Soprano

Brigitte de San Lucar, *a novice* ....Soprano

Horace de Massarena, *a young nobleman* ....Tenor

Count Juliano, *his friend* ....Tenor

Jacinthe, *Juliano's housekeeper* ....Mezzo-Soprano

Gil Perez, *porter at the convent* ....Bass

Ursule, *a nun at the convent* ....Soprano

An Extern Sister...Contralto

Lord Elfort, *Attaché at the British Embassy* .....Baritone

Place: Madrid
Running Time: 1 hour 35 minutes

*L*e *Domino Noir* is one of the most successful of Auber's many light operettas, moreover one with his regular collaborator, the indefatigable Scribe. The music is lively, graceful and stylish, the plot would seem not inappropriate to one of the fancies of Offenbach himself, of whose comedies it seems a perfectly logical precursor.

A year before the story begins, Horace de Massarena, a young man about town, met at a masked ball given by the Queen a young woman with whom he fell in love but whose face he never saw. She is in fact a cousin of the Queen's, and she is not only about to take her vows but at the Queen's wish immediately to become abbess of the convent.

At the ball once again, Juliano thinks he will help his friend Horace's pursuit of the unknown lady by advancing the clock so that her friend Brigitte speeds off to the convent alone, leaving Angèle fearful that her late return will ruin her reputation. Meanwhile, Juliano's housekeeper, Jacinthe, expecting her master back with friends for supper, takes in a stranded Angèle, whom she passes off as the niece she is expecting from the country. Angèle waits at table and captivates the company with her charm but is recognised by Horace, who, mystified by the development and trying to save Angèle from the attentions of his friends, contrives to lock her in Jacinthe's room. There she is discovered by Jacinthe's admirer Gil Perez, the convent porter, who receives such a shock at the sight of Angèle in her mask and domino that he surrenders the keys which he is conveniently carrying, thus providing Angèle with the means of re-entering the convent.

Brigitte is overjoyed to see her, but Ursule, wildly jealous of Angèle's imminent preferment, nearly blows the situation until the arrival of a letter from the Queen at the same time gives the abbess's job to Ursule and instructs Angèle to find a husband forthwith. The coincidental appearance of Horace solves the problem and the opera ends with a chorus of rejoicing, Angèle and Horace engaged, likewise Brigitte and Juliano, the cross-grained Ursule about to be enthroned, and happiness and fulfilment in sight for all. (The English attaché plays a peripheral, if comical, role as he searches for a wife he suspects of two-timing him.)

The music skips along in as carefree a manner as the story, whether in the jaunty ensembles which abound or in arias on a grand scale like the *Aragonaise* ('La belle Inès fait florès') Angèle sings to convince Juliano's guests of her country origins. With her grand patter song in the third act ('Ah! quelle nuit!') as well as the *Aragonaise*, Angèle's is a virtuoso role, but Auber allots admirable solos to Jacinthe at the start of Act II ('S'il est sur la terre'), to Gil Perez when he sings the praises of left-overs from a feast ('Nous allons avoir grâce à Dieu'), and even to Brigitte in a sad little number in Act III ('Au réfectoire, à la prière').   H.

B

MICHAEL WILLIAM BALFE

(born 15 May 1803, died 20 October 1870)

THE BOHEMIAN GIRL

Opera in three acts, text by Alfred Bunn founded on the ballet-pantomime *The Gipsy*, by St Georges. Première, Drury Lane, London, 27 November 1843. First performed New York, 1844; Her Majesty's Theatre (in Italian), 1858. Revived Sadler's Wells, 1932, with Kemp, Coates, Tudor Davies, Kelsey, Austin; Covent Garden Company at Liverpool, 1951, and subsequently at the Royal Opera House, in a new version by Sir Thomas Beecham and Dennis Arundell with Roberta Peters, Coates, Marlowe and Lanigan, Dickie, Walters, Glynne, conductor Beecham. Like *Maritana*, continuously in the repertories of British touring companies until the 1930s.

Arline, *daughter of the Count* ....Soprano
Thaddeus, *a proscribed Pole*...............................Tenor
Queen of the Gipsies ....Alto
Devilshoof, *chief of the gipsies*...............................Bass
Count Arnheim, *Governor of Pressburg* ....Bass
Florestein, *his nephew* ....Tenor
Captain of the Guard...Bass
Officer ....Tenor
Buda, *Arline's attendant* ....Soprano

Place: Pressburg, Poland
Running Time: 3 hours

The *Bohemian Girl*, now rarely given, owed its initial popularity to the easy melodies which abound in its score. There are no subtleties in the libretto, but the action is vigorous and as remote from everyday life as one could well imagine. The chief characters are either noblemen or gipsies – noblemen who have the power of life and death over the people, and gipsies who may rob and cheat but also number among their companions beings as innocent and pure as the hero and heroine of the story.

Act I. Thaddeus, a Polish noble exiled after a rebellion, has sought the company of Devilshoof and his gipsies in order to escape the punishment to which he has been condemned. As a gipsy he saves the life of Arline, the daughter of Count Arnheim, the Austrian governor of the province. The delighted father invites both Thaddeus and Devilshoof to his castle. They go, but refuse to drink the health of the Emperor as loyal subjects should. Devilshoof is cast into prison; Thaddeus, who saved the child, is allowed to go free. Devilshoof, however, is a master locksmith; he escapes from prison and, in revenge, steals Arline and hides her among the gipsies.

The chief numbers in Act I are Thaddeus's entrance aria, ''Tis sad to leave our fatherland', and 'In the gipsy's life you read', the gipsy chorus, which recurs often during the course of the action.

Act II. Twelve years have gone by and Arline, grown to womanhood, has fallen in love with her rescuer, Thaddeus, who returns her love and wishes to marry her. There is, however, an obstacle. The Queen of the Gipsies is herself in love with Thaddeus, and the Queen is not a woman to be slighted with impunity.

Devilshoof and his friends have robbed Florestein, nephew of Count Arnheim, of all he possessed while he was returning from a feast. The Queen, fearing the Count's power, orders the booty to be returned. The trinkets are returned accordingly, all but a medallion which Devilshoof has taken as his share, but which the Queen retains with a view to its later use. When she is forced by gipsy custom to unite Thaddeus and Arline, she begins to plot the girl's downfall, and the opportunity is not long in coming.

The gipsies have mingled with the crowds at the fair and there the Queen presents Arline with the medallion stolen from Florestein. This young nobleman, who was at first attracted to Arline and then piqued by her lack of response, on seeing the trinket accuses her of theft. In spite of the gipsies' resistance, Arline is taken to the castle to be tried. Count Arnheim would be merciful since the accused woman is just the age of his lost daughter, but the evidence is against her and he is forced to find her guilty. Arline does not know the secret of her birth although she has dreamt, as she confided to Thaddeus earlier on, that she 'dwelt in marble halls with vassals and serfs at my side'. Blood, however, will tell; feeling herself disgraced, she is about to stab herself to the heart when the Count himself stops her and, in grasping her hand, notices a scar, similar to that his lost daughter bore, on her arm. Recognition follows, to the great joy of all but Thaddeus, who fears that Arline is lost to him.

This act contains the best-known aria in the score, Arline's 'I dreamt that I dwelt in marble halls', a simple tune which, when well sung as it was by, for instance, Roberta Peters in the Covent Garden revival in 1951, is of truly appealing character. There are also the Count's 'The heart bowed down', a duet for Arline and Thaddeus, and the repetition of the gipsies' chorus.

Act III. Arline is faithful to her lover, in spite of her high station and its advantages. The Count sternly objects to the marriage of his daughter with a gipsy, whereupon Thaddeus, stung to the quick, reveals his real identity. The fact that he rebelled against the Austrians is forgotten and forgiven, and a wedding-feast arranged. The Queen alone is angry and disappointed. She aims a shot at Arline, but the bullet ricochets and kills her. Thaddeus's aria, 'When other lips and other hearts', occurs early in Act III.

The Bohemian Girl, Maritana and *The Lily of Killarney* were collectively known for many years as 'The English Ring'. F.B.

SAMUEL BARBER
(born 9 March 1910, died 23 January 1981)

A nephew of the celebrated American mezzo-soprano Louise Homer (Toscanini's Orfeo at the Metropolitan), Barber studied at the Curtis Institute of Music and was a sufficiently good singer to record his own *Dover Beach*. Fame came when Toscanini conducted a broadcast of his *Adagio for strings* but, although he regularly wrote for the voice, his first mature opera, *Vanessa*, was not written until 1958 when it had its première at the Metropolitan; the same company commissioned *Antony and Cleopatra* for the opening of its new theatre in 1966. In the meanwhile, *Vanessa* had been performed at the Salzburg Festival in 1958, and the following year at Spoleto (Menotti's Festival north of Rome) was heard a nine-minute chamber opera for four soloists, *A Hand of Bridge*, written before *Vanessa*. Barber's style is basically lyrical and traditional.

VANESSA

Opera in four acts, libretto by the composer, based on a story in *Seven Gothic Tales* by Isak Dinesen. Première at Metropolitan Opera, New York, 15 January 1958, with Steber, Elias, Resnik, Gedda, Tozzi, conductor Mitropoulos. First performed Salzburg, 1958, with the Metropolitan cast but Malaniuk instead of Resnik. In 1964 Barber revised the score, and the three-act version was heard for the first time at the Metropolitan in 1965, with Costa, Elias, Thebom, Alexander, Tozzi, conductor Steinberg.

Vanessa, *an ageing beauty*	Soprano
Erika, *her niece*	Mezzo-Soprano
The Old Baroness, *Vanessa's mother*	Mezzo-Soprano
Anatol, *a handsome young man*	Tenor
The Old Doctor	Bass
Nicholas, *the Major-Domo*	Baritone
A Footman	Tenor

Servants, Guests, Peasants

Place: Vanessa's House in a Northern Country
Time: c. 1905
Running Time: 2 hours

For twenty years, Vanessa has waited for the return of Anatol, the only man she has ever loved. The mirrors and a large painting are covered over.

Act I. Winter. Vanessa, her mother and her niece are awaiting the arrival of a guest. The Baroness, who won't speak to Vanessa, leaves; Erika sings a ballad: 'Must the winter come so soon?' Vanessa has her back to the door but her intense excitement is expressed lyrically: 'Do not utter a word, Anatol.' She does not want him to see her unless he still loves her, but excitement turns to something closer to revulsion as she realises the man she sees is not the man she loved. It is Anatol's son, searching for the woman whose very name so excited his father. Vanessa goes, and he asks Erika at least to share supper with him.

Act II. A month later. Erika confesses to her grandmother that she slept with Anatol the night he arrived – the Anatol 'who entered our house like a thief', comments the Baroness. Erika does not know if she loves him – perhaps he is incapable of love – but she knows that Vanessa does. Vanessa and Anatol come in from skating, followed soon by the Doctor; they dream of the past to the strains of a *Ländler*, 'Under the willow tree' (trio). Vanessa tells Erika she is in love, that this after all *is* the man she was waiting for (a coloratura passage cut in the 1964 version). When she goes to talk to the Pastor, the Baroness insists Erika speak up if she is not to lose her love. 'It is his love I want and not his capture.' He will choose the easier option, says the Baroness. Erika taxes Anatol with the position but when he proposes (Aria: 'Outside this house the world has changed'), she seems to turn him down. The others go off to the chapel, and an orchestral interlude precedes the act's end, with Erika sobbing on the sofa.

Act III. New Year's Eve, a ball in progress. The Doctor indulges in nostalgia, then practises his speech announcing the engagement. Vanessa is upset that her mother and niece seem to be boycotting the evening. Anatol attempts comfort, but reminds her that 'love has a bitter core'. Erika appears in time to hear the Doctor's voice, then faints at the crucial moment. Dances go on in the ballroom next door. Erika revives, clutches her stomach – she is carrying Anatol's child – then goes out. The Baroness suspects what is happening.

Act IV. Vanessa, the Baroness and the Doctor wait anxiously for news of Erika. Vanessa is close to despair, but Erika is found, Anatol carries her in, then assures Vanessa that Erika does *not* love him. Erika tells the Baroness the child will not be born.

Vanessa and Anatol are married and about to set off for Paris. More nostalgia for the Doctor before Vanessa unavailingly tries to get Erika to talk.

Anatol and Erika say goodbye, apparently without rancour, and the music reaches a climax with a quintet: 'To leave, to break, to find, to keep'. All say goodbye, leaving Erika with the Baroness, who except in the quintet does not utter. Erika orders the Major-Domo to cover the mirrors as they had been when it was Vanessa who was waiting. The gatekeeper is to admit no one; it is her turn now to wait. The quintet dominates the end of the opera.   H.

ANTONY AND CLEOPATRA

Opera in three acts; libretto from Shakespeare's *Antony and Cleopatra*. Première at Metropolitan Opera, New York, 16 September 1966, with Leontyne Price, Rosalind Elias, Jess Thomas, Justino Diaz, Ezio Flagello, conductor Thomas Schippers. Revised version, 1976, Juilliard School, New York; 1983, Spoleto, with Esther Hines, Jeffrey Walls, conductor Christian Badea.

Antony, *Roman general* ....Bass-Baritone
Enobarbus, *Antony's comrade*................Bass-Baritone
Iras, *Cleopatra's attendant*....................Mezzo-Soprano
Charmian, *Cleopatra's attendant*..................Contralto
Cleopatra, *Queen of Egypt*..............................Soprano
Caesar, *ruler of Rome* ....Tenor
Maecenas, *a senator*...Bass
Agrippa, *a senator*..Bass
A Messenger ....Tenor
Eros, *Antony's shieldbearer* ....Tenor
Dolabella, *Caesar's emissary* ....Baritone
Thidias, *Caesar's ambassador*.............................Tenor
Alexas, *Cleopatra's attendant*..........................Baritone
A Soothsayer ....Bass
Four Guards............................Tenor, Baritone, Bass
A Rustic ....Bass

Soldiers, Senators, Egyptians

Place: Egypt and Rome
Time: 42–31 B.C.
Running Time: 2 hours 5 minutes

*A*ntony and Cleopatra was written for the opening in 1966 of the new building of the Metropolitan Opera at Lincoln Center in New York, a glittering occasion which tended to put the new work in second place. Franco Zeffirelli, who directed the opera, had collaborated with the composer on the reduction of one of Shakespeare's richest plays to manageable length, but a fine cast failed to shrug off a lavish production which overwhelmed singers, audience and particularly critics. The Met went through with the scheduled performances in the 1966–67 season but cancelled the revival and Barber was apparently devastated by the negative critical reaction to his work. He nonetheless worked with the aid of Gian Carlo Menotti on revising the score, removing characters, reducing spectacle, even adding a love duet for the protagonists and amending the *tessitura* of some of the vocal line. The revision, extensive as it was, did not carry complete conviction, and Andrew Porter wrote in *The New Yorker*: 'If the opera is revived a century or so hence, directors ... will want to combine both scores ... reinstating valued passages which the composer himself cut but retaining passages he strengthened by recomposition.' This synopsis concentrates on the revised version of the opera.

Act I. The Chorus angrily asserts that Antony in Alexandria neglects his duties for Cleopatra. Antony for his part tells Enobarbus he is resolved to leave, but Cleopatra will never accept it and the two lovers bid each other what can be no more than a temporary farewell. An orchestral interlude takes us to the Senate in Rome, where Antony and Caesar quarrel. To cement an alliance, Agrippa proposes a marriage between Antony and Caesar's sister, Octavia.

Cleopatra in the midst of her court whiles away Antony's absence, watches slaves dance, then chastises a messenger who brings news that Antony and Octavia are married. No amount of denigratory references to Octavia's physical disabilities can undo the initial damage.

At a banquet in Rome, Antony bids Octavia goodnight and she leaves with her brother. The soldiers doze and Enobarbus assures Dolabella that Antony will never give up Cleopatra. He recalls the entrancing sight of her in her barge, and she appears as if in a vision. Antony resolves to return to Egypt.

Act II. In the Senate, Caesar denounces Antony for his actions in Egypt. He will meet him on the battlefield.

In Alexandria, a Soothsayer enigmatically foretells Charmian's future, before Antony and Cleopatra make an entrance to hear Enobarbus bring the bad news that Caesar has captured part of the empire. Antony will lead the army against him but Cleopatra inveighs against Enobarbus for preventing her following him into battle. Soldiers outside Antony's tent are inclined to believe the defection of the god Hercules, who has hitherto protected him. To the words of 'Take, o take those lips away', Antony and Cleopatra sing ecstatically of love.

The Egyptian army is ready for battle at Actium. Enobarbus brings news that Cleopatra led her fleet away from the action, and Antony followed. Enobarbus will find a way to desert. To Eros Antony admits that he is defeated and must beg for clemency. Cleopatra prepares to surrender to Caesar, but Antony orders the ambassador whipped, then flings Cleopatra to the ground and leaves. Her women advise her to repair to the monument and give out that she is dead.

Enobarbus is overwhelmed with remorse when he hears that Antony has so far forgiven him as to send his possessions after him. Orchestral interlude.

Antony hears from Eros the false news that Cleopatra is dead and resolves to the accompaniment mainly of flute and timpani to emulate her. Eros refuses to kill him but stabs himself, and Antony has no option but to fall on his own sword. Alexas follows him as he is borne away dying to the Queen.

Act III. Cleopatra's monument. With Charmian and Iras she resolves never to leave her stronghold, then hears that Antony is being carried to her. He is drawn up into the monument and dies in her arms, to be mourned by the Queen and her women. Caesar comes to make formal peace both with the Egyptian Queen and his dead adversary.

Cleopatra hears from Dolabella what she most dreads: that Caesar plans to display her in Rome as part of his triumph. Cleopatra's reaction is instantaneous and violent. A rustic brings her an asp in a basket of figs and she dies, nobly, her robe on her shoulders, her crown on her head. The chorus, in Greek style, mourns the lovers.   H.

BÉLA BARTÓK

(born 25 March 1881, died 26 September 1945)

DUKE BLUEBEARD'S CASTLE

A kékszakállú Herceg Vára

Opera in one act, text by B. Balázs. Première, Budapest, 24 May 1918, with Olga Haselbeck, Oszkar Kalman. First performed Frankfurt, 1922; Berlin, 1929. Revived Budapest, 1937; Florence Festival, 1938 (by Budapest company), with Ella di Nemethy, Szekely, conductor Failoni; New York, City Center, 1952, with Ayars, Pease, conductor Rosenstock; B.B.C., London, 1953, with Cross, Matters; Sadler's Wells, 1954, with Elliott, Ward; Edinburgh Festival, 1963,[1] by Budapest Opera with Olga Szönyi, Andras Farago.

Duke Bluebeard ....Bass

Judith, *his wife* ....Mezzo-Soprano

Bard...Spoken

Three Wives..Silent

Running Time: 55 minutes

Bartók's short opera is one of the most impressive of his early works. Whatever it may owe in conception to Debussy and to Maeterlinck, the music is characteristic of its composer. Wrote Desmond Shawe-Taylor in 1972 in *The Sunday Times*: 'The fable can be understood on many levels: as a foreshortened process of mutual discovery between two persons such as in real life would take many years; as a conflict between rational, creative Man and emotional, inspiring, never fully comprehending Woman; more deeply still, as an allegory of the loneliness and solitude of all human creatures. Bartók, whose own need for inner solitude was imperious, and whose remoteness could be frightening, threw himself into the subject with an intensity which grips the listener.' The piece has almost no action, and yet the music is essentially dramatic, just as the orchestral colour retains life and vigour even in its most sombre moments.

A bard appears before the curtain to establish in spoken word that the action of the opera is legendary. When the curtain rises, it reveals a large round room, gothic in style.[2] On the left, a staircase leads up to a little iron door. To the right of this staircase can be seen seven larger doors. There are no windows or ornaments of any kind. The room is like a great, empty cavern.

Bluebeard enters, leading Judith by the hand. She has left her parents and her home to follow him, and is only just regaining her courage. She sees the doors and wants to open them to let light and air into the castle. She knocks at the first door, and hears a long sigh like that of the wind. With the key that Bluebeard gives her, she opens the door, from which immediately streams red light (violins *tremolo*, flutes *arpeggio*). It is the Torture Chamber, and Judith exclaims that the walls are wet with blood; but she is not afraid.

In succession, she opens four more doors. A shaft of bronze-coloured light (solo trumpet, woodwind trills) comes from the Armoury; golden light (violin solo, three trumpets) pours from the Treasury, from which she takes a jewelled cloak and a crown; bluish light (harp *glissando*, strings *tremolo*, solo horn) comes from behind the door which conceals the Garden; and a dazzling white light (full orchestra, organ) blinds her as she opens the door which gives on to Bluebeard's Kingdom. Not even perhaps in *Fidelio* or *Die Meistersinger* has C major been more grandly confident than in the magnificent outburst which accompanies the opening of the fifth door. At each door Judith sees signs of blood: on the weapons in the Armoury, on the jewels and robes in the Treasury, on the flowers in the Garden, even in the colour of the cloud over the Kingdom itself.

Judith will not heed Bluebeard's warning, but opens the sixth door (harp, clarinet *arpeggios*). When she asks Bluebeard what is the significance of the water behind it, he answers 'Tears'. He tries to turn her from completing her purpose and takes her lovingly in his arms. She asks him if he has loved other women, and, when he tries to evade the question, demands that he give her the seventh key so that she may find out what the door conceals. As he gives it her, he tells her that it will show her all his former wives.

---

[1] The three Bartók stage works, this opera and the ballets *The Wooden Prince* and *The Miraculous Mandarin*, conducted by János Ferencsik, played together in one theatrical evening as the composer (retrospectively) wanted.

[2] Such are the stage directions now more honoured in the breach than the observance.

She opens the seventh door and immediately the sixth and fifth doors close; at the same time the light in the hall begins to grow dimmer. Three beautiful women emerge. Bluebeard kneels before them and assures them that they are not forgotten; even Judith is filled with awe at their beauty. In his first wife Bluebeard sees the embodiment of the morning of his existence, in the second of his noonday, in the third of evening. One by one they disappear through the door, and the fourth door closes. Then he addresses Judith. She is the most beautiful of all, and her he met in the night; after her is eternal darkness. He goes slowly to fetch the crown and robe from the third door, which closes after him, and adorns Judith with them. For a moment she pleads with him, then turns and goes through the seventh door which shuts after her. Bluebeard is alone once more.   H.

LUDWIG VAN BEETHOVEN
(born c. 17 December 1770, died 26 March 1827)

FIDELIO

Opera in two acts, text by Joseph Sonnleitner and Georg Friedrich Sonnleithner after a drama by Jean Nicolas Bouilly. Première at the Theater an der Wieden, Vienna, 20 November 1805 (in three acts), with Anna Milder, Louise Müller, Demmer, Meier, Rother, Weinkopf and Cache, conducted by Beethoven.

Florestan, *a nobleman*..Tenor
Leonore, *his wife, in male attire as Fidelio*........Soprano
Don Fernando, *the King's Minister* ....Bass
Don Pizarro, *Governor of the fortress* ....Baritone
Rocco, *chief jailer*...Bass
Marzelline, *Rocco's daughter*...........................Soprano
Jaquino, *assistant to Rocco* ....Tenor
Soldiers, Prisoners, People

Place: A Fortress near Seville
Time: Eighteenth Century
Running Time: 2 hours 20 minutes

Bouilly's original libretto was written for the French composer Pierre Gaveaux in 1798 and was set by two other composers. The French Revolution subject for Beethoven and his audiences was as contemporary as Menotti's *The Consul*, Poulenc's *La Voix humaine* and Adams's *Nixon in China* in the late twentieth century.

The opera is in *Singspiel* form, with spoken dialogue between the musical numbers, and Beethoven cannot have found it easy to reconcile his predilection for high-minded, heroic themes with his chosen form's more domestic tendencies. The original version (1805), with an audience mostly made up of French troops occupying Vienna, was not a success. The 1806 revision reduced three acts to two, and the final re-working (1814) substantially revised music and text – alterations to every musical number except the March. The versions of 1805 and 1806 are very far from either incompetent or negligible, as revivals in 1970, the Beethoven bicentenary year, or on record testify, demonstrating too that dramatic improvement came with a maturer view – it is hard to agree with Ernest Newman who believed that the resigned *andante* second section of Florestan's *scena* in the original was preferable to the hallucinated and feverish ending Beethoven supplied in 1814. One is dramatically apt, the other a stroke of nothing less than genius.

Confusion reigns over the four overtures. *Leonora No. 2* was played at the première in 1805, *Leonora No. 3* at the 1806 revision, and a new, less 'symphonic' prelude (the *Fidelio* overture) was composed for 1814, though, modern scholarship says, not ready until the second performance. *Leonora No. 1* (published as Op. 138 and first performed eleven months after Beethoven's death) may have been meant for the 1805 production and discarded before the first night, or for one planned for Prague in 1807 and never realised.

Before the opera begins, Florestan, who worked for the progressive Minister of State Don Fernando, has disappeared in mysterious circumstances. Only his wife Leonore refuses to believe he is dead and has narrowed her search for him to a prison whose reac-

Fidelio (Salzburg Festival, 1931). Lotte Lehmann as Leonore and Franz Völker as Florestan.

tionary governor was an enemy of Florestan's; there she works disguised as a young man.

Act I. A prison courtyard. A brisk duet between Jaquino and Marzelline suggests that he is in love with her but that she prefers Fidelio, her father's new assistant, as her subsequent aria confirms. She is joined by her father, but the appearance of Fidelio brings, in a remarkable canon quartet, a change of mood to something almost mystic. The theme enunciated by each character is the same but their sentiments differ, and the quartet ('Mir ist so wunderbar') establishes, in contrast to the two earlier numbers, the lofty aspirations of much of the rest of the opera. With Rocco's jocular, almost vulgar, aria in praise of money and young people's need for it, the *Singspiel* convention reappears (the aria was dropped for 1806, reinstated in 1814), but it wavers again with the subsequent trio. Fidelio in effect volunteers for the more taxing side of a prison jailer's job, and Rocco praises him for his resolution; Marzelline continues her generalised adoration, and the trio is dominated by a heroic phrase

for Fidelio, 'Ich habe Muth' (I have the strength).

A short, rhythmically striking March bridges the scenes and proclaims the arrival of Pizarro, the governor. One of the dispatches he peruses warns him that Don Fernando is on his way to inspect the fortress, and he weighs in with a hefty aria ('Ha! welch' ein Augenblick') presaging immediate action against Florestan. He posts a trumpeter to warn of the Minister's approach, then tosses a purse to Rocco with instructions to do away with the most dangerous of the prisoners. Rocco's reluctance grows in the course of a repetitious but effective duet, during which Pizarro determines to do the job himself. Fidelio overhears and reacts in the highly dramatic 'Abscheulicher! wo eilst du hin?' (Abominable man! Where are you hurrying?) The grandiose aria, with its moving middle section expressing continuing hope for the success of her rescue mission, is quite outside the *Singspiel* convention.

On Fidelio's intercession and because it is the King's birthday, the prisoners are allowed into the open air. Fidelio scans their faces to see if Florestan is among them. Act II's lofty aspirations are perhaps most fully anticipated in Fidelio's aria and the music of the prisoners as they grope their way towards light and hope (Prisoners' Chorus). With a great cry of 'Noch heute!' Fidelio learns that as Rocco's assistant she will that very day help him dig the grave in what may be her husband's cell. If she cannot save him, she can die with him! On Pizarro's reappearance, the prisoners are hustled back to their cells, but Rocco staves off retribution by an astute reference to the plot Pizarro wants him to be part of.

Act II. A dungeon. An orchestral introduction of extraordinary dramatic import, all heavily weighted chords, grinding turns on the strings and an apparently endless descent into the depths, prepares us for a first sight of Florestan in chains. His arioso-recitative is a triumph of word-setting, and, if the *adagio cantabile* aria relies on recollection of things past, the quick section that follows parts company with normality as Florestan's vision of Leonore leads to hysteria. A whispered scene between Fidelio and Rocco

ends as Florestan recovers from his swoon and she recognises her husband. She is permitted to offer him a drink and a morsel of food and his thanks for an unexpected kindness lead to a trio of remarkable beauty and in the circumstances amazing serenity.

Pizarro enters and initiates the highly dramatic ensemble by making himself known to Florestan but, as he draws his dagger, Fidelio stands between him and Florestan, then reveals herself as Leonore: 'Tödt erst sein Weib!' (First, kill his wife!). A trumpet call rings out, Jaquino announces the Minister, and Pizarro's moment has gone. There ensues a rapturous duet ('O namenlose Freude!') and a happy ending to an opera, much of whose music has presaged tragedy, is in sight.

The chorus rejoices at the freeing of the prisoners (in C major, the brilliance of which is upstaged if the *Leonora No. 3* is played to cover the scene change), Don Fernando recognises Florestan and sets Leonore to free him from his fetters, Pizarro is arrested, and the opera, with an anticipation of the Ninth Symphony, comes to a triumphant end.   H.

VINCENZO BELLINI
(born 3 November 1801, died 23 September 1835)

Bellini came of a musical family in Sicily, and his early experience was in church music. Six years in Naples ended in 1826 with a successful operatic première (his second work for the stage), *Bianca e Gernando* (*sic* in earlier version), and a resulting commission for la Scala. *Il Pirata* was the first libretto written for him by Felice Romani, henceforth (apart from *I Puritani*) his invariable collaborator, and with it he emerged as a major operatic force.

IL PIRATA
The Pirate

Opera in two acts, libretto (from the French translation of a five-act tragedy by the Irish writer, the Rev. R.C. Maturin, *Bertram, or The Castle of St Aldobrando*) by Felice Romani. Première, la Scala, Milan, 27 October 1827, with Henriette Méric-Lalande, Giovanni Rubini and Antonio Tamburini; scenery by Alessandro Sanquirico (fifteen performances that season, twelve

in 1830 and twelve in 1840). First performed King's Theatre, London, 1830, with la Scala cast; Paris, 1832, with Schroeder-Devrient, Rubini, Santini; New York, 1832. Revived Rome, 1935, with Iva Pacetti, Gigli, Mario Basiola, conductor Serafin; la Scala, 1958, with Callas, Corelli, Bastianini; New York (both times in concert), 1959 with Callas, 1966 with Montserrat Caballé; Philadelphia, 1968, with Caballé; London (in concert), 1969, with Caballé; Wexford, 1972, and York Festival, 1973, with Christiane Eda-Pierre.

Ernesto, *Duke of Caldora*	Baritone
Imogene, *his wife*	Soprano
Gualtiero, *former Count of Montalto*	Tenor
Itulbo, *Gualtiero's lieutenant*	Tenor
Goffredo, *a hermit, once tutor to Gualtiero*	Bass
Adele, *Imogene's companion*	Soprano
A Little Boy, *son to Imogene and Ernesto*	Silent

Fishermen and Women, Pirates, Knights, Ladies

Place: The Castle of Caldora and Nearby, in Sicily
Time: Thirteenth Century
Running Time: 2 hours 55 minutes

The background of the Sicilian story has Ernesto, Duke of Caldora, and Gualtiero, Count of Montalto, as rivals in politics as well as for the hand of the fair Imogene. Gualtiero and Imogene's father followed the cause of King Manfred, Ernesto that of Charles of Anjou. Imogene loves Gualtiero, who is however banished following the death of King Manfred and the defeat of his followers by the Anjou party. In exile, he leads a band of pirates from Aragon to ravage the shores of Sicily, in the hope of revenge and recovering Imogene. She, however, has been forced through threats to her father's life to marry the Duke of Caldora. He has recently commanded the fleet which defeated the Aragonese pirates, their leader escaping only to be shipwrecked on the coast not far from Caldora.

Act I. After a conventional overture, the curtain rises to agitated music to show the anguished populace watching the shipwreck. The storm over, survivors come on shore, and the hermit Goffredo recognises Gualtiero, who proclaims that nothing but his continuing love for Imogene has supported him through his trials ('Nel furor delle tempeste').

Honouring old custom, the Duchess herself comes to offer hospitality to the strangers, for whom Itulbo acts as spokesman. Horrified at the idea that their leader may be dead, Imogene in a beautiful aria ('Lo sognai ferito') confides her fears to Adele. At sight of Imogene, Gualtiero can barely restrain himself and the sound of his involuntary cry awakes poignant memories for her.

At night, the pirates, drinking rousingly on the castle terrace, are warned by Itulbo not to give away their identity. Imogene is still troubled by thoughts of the stranger who has taken refuge with Goffredo, and it does not take long before he reveals to her who he is. The story of Imogene's coercion by Ernesto comes out, and Gualtiero's stupefaction, expressed in one of Bellini's most melting cantilenas ('Pietosa al padre'), turns, when he sees Imogene's small son, to thoughts of revenge.

Imogene, left alone in her grief, hears the sounds of carousal within, and the scene changes to the great hall of the castle, where the Duke's men celebrate. Ernesto himself rejoices in an aria (to the accompaniment of strings and three trombones, *piano*) and reproaches Imogene that she alone remains outside the general festivities. For himself, the sole shadow on his joy is doubt about the fate of the hated Gualtiero. He will question the fugitives and their leader. Itulbo poses as the pirate chief, Ernesto threatens imprisonment, Imogene pleads the general cause, the hermit restrains the frantic Gualtiero, who emulates Ernesto in his willingness to breathe fire and slaughter at every opportunity. A quintet (and soon a sextet) develops with comments from the chorus, and the act ends in a *stretta* but without public disclosure of Gualtiero's identity.

Act II. In the ante-chamber to Imogene's apartments, Adele tries to reassure her entourage as to Imogene's health. She tells her mistress that Gualtiero will not leave without seeing her, but it is the Duke who now confronts her squarely with accusations of infidelity. She defends herself by saying that it is true she still loves Gualtiero but as someone she knew in the past; Ernesto must be content that she is his wife and the mother of his son. The slow music of their fine duet suggests a degree of acceptance of the situation, but Ernesto's fury is unleashed when he gets a message to the effect that Gualtiero is even now sheltering in the castle.

On the terrace, Itulbo unsuccessfully tries to persuade Gualtiero to forgo his meeting with Imogene. The tone of the lovers' scene is one of passion as well as resignation, and towards its end they are watched by Ernesto, who remains in hiding to add his voice to a trio of finest inspiration. Ernesto is discovered, and he and Gualtiero go off to end their rivalry in mortal combat.

To the great hall of the castle come the Duke's retainers to mourn his death and to swear vengeance on his killer. To their amazement, Gualtiero surrenders voluntarily and is handed over to the Council of Knights, bidding farewell in an aria ('Tu vedrai la sventurata') to the absent Imogene and asking her forgiveness.

In Bellini's operas, it is the woman who is customarily protagonist and *Il Pirata* is no exception, in spite of its title and the unusual robustness of much of the music. Imogene's reason and strength of will have collapsed under the strain of events, and her last scene is introduced by a plaintive and beautiful cor anglais solo, which movingly expresses her anguished state. She thinks she sees Ernesto, and later their son, who pleads with his father for the life of Gualtiero who once spared Ernesto's. Musically, Bellini already inhabits the world of 'Casta diva' of four years later, and the slow 'Col sorriso d'inno-cenza' is a beautiful inspiration, with a worthy pendant in the cabaletta 'Oh sole, ti vela di tenebre oscure'; together, and after Imogene hears that the Council has condemned Gualtiero to death, they bring the opera to an impressive conclusion. H.

LA STRANIERA

The Stranger

Opera in two acts, text by Felice Romani based on Vicomte d'Arlincourt's novel *L'Etrangère*. Première, la Scala, Milan, 14 February 1829, with Henriette Méric-Lalande, Caroline Unger, Domenico Reina, Antonio Tamburini. First produced London, King's Theatre, 1832, with Giuditta Grisi, Rubini, Tamburini; New York, Park Theatre, 1834. Revived Catania, 1954, with Adriana Guerrini; Palermo, 1968, with Renata Scotto; New York (concert performance), 1969, with Montserrat Caballé; Edinburgh Festival, 1972, by Palermo company with Scotto, conductor Sanzogno.

Alaide *(la Straniera)* ....Soprano

Il Signore di Montolino ....Bass

Isoletta, *his daughter* ....Mezzo-Soprano

Arturo, *Count of Ravenstal* ....Tenor

Baron Valdeburgo ....Baritone

The Prior of the Templars ....Bass

Osburgo, *confidante of Arturo* ....Tenor

Place: Brittany
Time: Middle Ages
Running Time: 3 hours 5 minutes

*L*a Straniera was written in 1829 for la Scala, Bellini's second opera with Felice Romani. Like *Il Pirata, La Straniera* shows a more vigorous approach to drama than the later Bellini operas, where elegiac melody is as much in evidence as romantic passion. Leslie Orrey in his book about Bellini lays great stress on the fine quality of the choral writing in *La Straniera*.

All these operas were written like Handel's to display the skill and dexterity of the great prima donnas of the day. More recently, Callas for a few short unforgettable years at la Scala made works of this period her own, recreating perhaps three operas every two years. Newer claimants with technique but less imagination have attempted to emulate her, but one of these revivals is hardly to be distinguished from the other. Instant Bellini or Donizetti is not at all what Callas made.

Act I, scene i. Near the castle of Montolino, peasants and members of Lord Montolino's entourage celebrate in a barcarolle chorus the forthcoming marriage of Isoletta, his daughter, to Arturo, Count of Ravenstal. Only Isoletta cannot share in the rejoicing because, as she confides to her friend Baron Valdeburgo, she has detected a change in her fiancé. She fears he is in love with an unknown woman who lives across the lake – *la Straniera*. Valdeburgo, and later Isoletta's father and Arturo's friend Osburgo, do their best to comfort her, and in the distance they hear the voices of the crowd who are inveighing against *la Straniera* as a witch.

Scene ii. *La Straniera*'s hut in the woods. Arturo has come to seek her out. Alaide, the Stranger, enters (introduced by harp) and muses on the sadness which can result from a love which trusts too much ('Ah! Sventurato il cor che fida'). She reproaches Arturo for having sought her out, and, in answer to a passionate declaration of love, assures him that Heaven has put an insurmountable barrier between them.

Scene iii. Osburgo is near the dwelling of the dreaded *Straniera* with a hunting party. Valdeburgo tries to persuade Arturo to return to his proper place at the heart of the wedding festivities. When he refers to the Stranger as unworthy of Arturo, the latter begs him at least to see her and to judge whether he can then still condemn her. As soon as he sees Alaide, Valdeburgo gives a cry of recognition. Alaide is equally delighted, and Arturo's suspicions are first aroused and then, when Valdeburgo tells him that for reasons he cannot reveal Arturo must renounce his love, as he thinks, confirmed. Only the intervention of Alaide prevents him falling upon his erstwhile friend with his sword. Arturo leaves only when Alaide reluctantly agrees to see him again.

Scene iv. A gloomy prelude brings us to the shore of the lake near the castle. Arturo learns from Osburgo and his friends that they have heard Alaide and Valdeburgo planning to elope. He himself believes he knows the worst when he overhears Alaide address Valdeburgo as Leopoldo, whereupon he attacks and wounds him so that he falls into the lake. Alaide in her horror reveals that he is her brother. Arturo jumps in after him and a group of countrymen, led by Osburgo, surprise her alone with a bloodstained sword and accuse her of murder.

Act II, scene i. In a room in the castle, the Prior of

the Order of the Hospitallers is hearing the evidence of Osburgo against *la Straniera*. When she appears, he seems for a moment to recognise her voice. Arturo rushes in to say that it is he who is guilty of murder, but the problem is resolved with the re-appearance of Valdeburgo to announce that neither Arturo nor Alaide is guilty. Valdeburgo offers to protect Alaide and, when the members of the court demand that she shall unveil, she consents to do so only to the Prior himself. He is astonished at what he sees and announces that she is free to depart.

Scene ii. Arturo makes for Alaide's hut, but in a vigorous duet Valdeburgo heads him off. Arturo is persuaded to go back to Isoletta, after Valdeburgo has conceded that he will bring Alaide to the wedding.

Scene iii. The church. Isoletta is full of foreboding and in an aria, 'Ah! se non m'ami più' (flute obbligato) reveals her sorrow.[1] A wedding hymn starts the proceedings, but Arturo is obviously distraught and Isoletta threatens to abandon the ceremony. Suddenly Alaide intervenes, and insists that Isoletta and Arturo shall go towards the altar, Alaide herself rushing outside to pray movingly for God's forgiveness ('Pago, o ciel tremendo'). Arturo, with drawn sword, tries to order her to follow him, but the Prior announces that she must take her rightful place as Queen of France.[2] Arturo reacts by throwing himself on his sword, Isoletta falls on his dead body and *la Straniera* fulfils the prophecy contained in her opening words, to dwell on the sadness of a love which trusted too well.

It has been suggested – reasonably I think – that the impossibly violent loves of the romantics were less erotic in origin than manifestations of rebellion against the norms of society. By these canons, both Arturo and *la Straniera* are romantic figures sacrificed on the altar of self-fulfilment.   H.

I CAPULETI E I MONTECCHI

The Capulets and the Montagues

Opera in four parts (two acts), libretto by Felice Romani, a reworking of his libretto for Nicola Vaccai's *Giulietta e Romeo* (1825), derived very remotely from Shakespeare's *Romeo and Juliet*. Première, Venice, 11 March 1830 (in a double bill with the ballet *Chiara di Rosenberg*), with Giuditta Grisi as Romeo,

Rosalbina Caradori-Allan as Giulietta. First produced London, King's Theatre, 1833, with Giuditta Pasta, Joséphine de Méric; New Orleans, 1847; Dresden, 1831. Revived Catania, 1935, for Bellini Centenary, with Ines Alfani-Tellini, Aurora Buades and Franco Lo Giudice, conductor Marinuzzi; Palermo, 1954, with Rosanna Carteri, Giulietta Simionato, conductor Vittorio Gui. A 'new' version of the score by Claudio Abbado with Romeo sung by a tenor was first given at la Scala, Milan, in 1966, with Renata Scotto, Giacomo Aragall, Luciano Pavarotti (Tebaldo); this production was seen at the 1966 Holland Festival, the 1967 Edinburgh Festival, and the same year in Montreal. The opera was staged in Philadelphia in 1968, with Scotto, Aragall (Romeo), Giuseppe Campora; Boston, 1975, with Beverly Sills, Tatiana Troyanos; Vienna, 1977, with Sona Ghazarian, Agnes Baltsa; London, Covent Garden, 1984, with Edita Gruberova, Agnes Baltsa, conductor Riccardo Muti.

Giulietta (Juliet), *a Capulet* ....Soprano

Romeo, *head of the Montagues*.............Mezzo-Soprano

Tebaldo (Tybalt), *a Capulet partisan* ....Tenor

Capellio (Capulet), *head of the Capulets,*
    Juliet's father .... Bass

Lorenzo, *physician in the employ*
    of the Capulets..Baritone

Capulets, Montagues, Ladies, Soldiers

Place: Verona
Time: Thirteenth Century
Running Time: 2 hours 10 minutes

B ellini was at work on the score of *I Capuleti e I Montecchi* for a period of no more than six weeks, not signing the contract for the new opera for la Fenice until 20 January 1830, with rehearsals beginning at the end of February and the first night on 11 March! Bellini's opera was replacing one due from Giovanni Pacini, who could not deliver in time, and for it he plundered his recent and unsuccessful opera *Zaira*, and even pressed into service music from his earlier *Adelson e Salvini*. Romani also drew extensively on his own book for an opera he had written for Vaccai, and it is an irony of fate that the great Maria Malibran should herself have jettisoned Bellini's last act in favour of Vaccai's when it came to her turn to star in the opera – all this while both Vaccai and Bellini were still alive and flourishing!

Act I. A short, urgent prelude takes us to the Capulet palace, where Capulet's followers are gathered. Are they as Guelphs threatened again by Ghibellines?

---

[1] In the Palermo revival of 1968 transferred quite appropriately to the first scene of Act I.

[2] The historical King of France fled on his wedding night from his bride

Isamberga of Denmark, and later married Agnes of Pomerania, the opera's heroine. The Pope ordered the King to return to his first wife, Agnes going into exile. With the death of Isamberga, Agnes may now return to the King.

Tybalt tells them that Romeo, the most hated of the Montagues, is leading an army against them, the same man who earlier slew Capulet's son, and who now sends an envoy to offer peace terms. Lorenzo urges that the terms be considered, but Capulet says his son's death was never avenged and Tybalt in his cavatina swears in the name of Juliet, whom he loves, to carry out the act which will purge the offence against Capulet. During the course of his cabaletta, could the audience but catch his words through the ensemble, they would hear Lorenzo refer to Capulet's implacable outlook, which will not soften when he learns the secret his daughter Juliet conceals.

Preparations for Juliet's wedding to Tybalt are in hand as Romeo makes his entrance incognito, announced only as the Ghibelline envoy offering peace to the Guelphs. His soft words propose equal status in Verona for Montagues and Capulets, the peace to be signalled by the marriage of Juliet with Romeo. Capulet rejects the possibility but Romeo, still unrecognised, in a beautiful passage ('Se Romeo t'uccise un figlio') urges that Capulet's son was slain in the heat of battle, that his death has been mourned ever since by Romeo, and that Romeo will replace the son Capulet has lost. His pleading is dignified and persuasive but Capulet and his followers remain obdurate and the scene ends with Romeo in his cabaletta vowing to continue the feud; but let there be no mistake, the blood which will flow will be on the heads of those who rejected the peace offer.

In her own room, Juliet sadly contrasts her joyful wedding garment with her unhappy situation, and longs in a beautiful romanza ('O quante volte') for Romeo, whom she loves. Lorenzo brings her beloved Romeo to her and there ensues one of Bellini's most ardent love duets, ending with a sublime passage mainly in thirds which foreshadows Norma and Adalgisa. Romeo begs Juliet to leave with him, Juliet urges her duty to her father. In the end, he makes his escape through the secret passage by which he entered.

The scene changes to a courtyard of the palace, where the wedding festivities have started. Romeo, disguised as a Guelph, is urged by Lorenzo to save himself, but Romeo tells him that a force of Ghibellines is loose in Verona disguised as Guelphs and planning to descend on the palace to halt the wedding. Lorenzo's sympathy is with the young lovers but he cannot betray his allegiance to Capulet. Fighting can be heard as Romeo rushes off. Juliet is torn between fear for her lover's life and despair at the bloodshed. When Romeo reappears once again to urge her to flee with him, he is quickly discovered, and, when he announces himself as Tybalt's rival for Juliet's hand, his true identity is revealed. A grand finale starts with a slow, soft unaccompanied passage of much delicacy, but the intervention of armed Montagues brings the act to a spirited if more conventional end.

Act II. Juliet has no idea who was victorious in the fighting, and whether she should now mourn the death of kinsmen or lover. Lorenzo tells her Romeo is safe, but that, if she is not to be taken to Tybalt's abode, she must take a sleeping draught which he will deliver to her. This way she will appear dead, be buried in the family tomb and then later rejoin Romeo. In an aria, she denies fear of death, but takes the potion only when her father can be heard approaching. He is deaf to her pleas, but orders watch to be kept on Lorenzo, whom he now suspects of double-dealing.

In the grounds of the palace, preluded by clarinet, Romeo gloomily suspects that Lorenzo has deserted him. He and Tybalt confront one another and prepare to fight – the martial duet for mezzo-soprano and tenor is a rarity – until the sound of a funeral dirge for Juliet diverts them from their purpose. Both are horror-stricken and long for death.

The tomb of the Capulets. Romeo and the Montagues come to the vault to mourn Juliet, and, even though he knows she cannot hear him, Romeo begs Juliet to allow him to join her in death ('Deh! tu bell'anima').[1] Lorenzo has been prevented from informing Romeo of the plan and he takes poison, only for Juliet to wake to hear from her lover the dread truth. After a short but heartfelt duet, he dies in her arms and she expires from grief, leaving her father to contemplate the dead lovers. 'Killed! By whom?' Even his own followers join in the cry: 'By you, pitiless man!'   H.

---

[1] It was Malibran (in 1832 in Bologna) who first started the practice of substituting for Bellini's last scene, with its aria and duet, Vaccai's setting of the same scene, containing the aria 'Ah! Se tu dormi'. Many mezzos follow her.

LA SONNAMBULA
The Sleepwalker

Opera in two acts, text by Felice Romani. Première at the Teatro Carcano, Milan, 6 March 1831, with Pasta, Rubini. First performed in London, Haymarket, 1831, with Pasta, Rubini; Drury Lane, 1833 (in English), with Malibran (her début); Covent Garden, 1835, with same cast; New York, 1835 (in English); 1844 (in Italian). Performed at Covent Garden, 1910, with Tetrazzini, McCormack, Edmund Burke; revived Metropolitan, New York, 1932, with Pons, Gigli, Pinza, conductor Serafin; la Scala, Milan, 1935, with dal Monte, Schipa, Pasero, conductor Guarnieri; 1939, with Carosio, Malipiero, Pasero, conductor Marinuzzi; la Scala, 1955, with Callas, Monti, Zaccaria in Visconti's production (also Edinburgh, 1957, with Callas and later Scotto); Covent Garden, 1960, with Sutherland, conductor Serafin; Metropolitan, New York, 1963, with Sutherland, Gedda.

Count Rodolfo, *lord of the castle* .... Bass

Teresa, *proprietress of the mill* .... Mezzo-Soprano

Amina, *her foster-daughter* .... Soprano

Lisa, *proprietress of the village inn* .... Soprano

Elvino, *a young farmer* .... Tenor

Alessio, *a villager* .... Bass

Place: A Village in Switzerland
Time: Early Nineteenth Century
Running Time: 3 hours 10 minutes

Bellini wrote *La Sonnambula* for two of his finest collaborators, the great Giuditta Pasta and the hardly less magnificent tenor, Rubini. The pastoral opera which resulted is stylistically in strong contrast to Bellini's next work *Norma*, but it has never been long out of the repertory when a coloratura soprano of quality has been available.

Act I. The village green. The villagers are making merry, for they are about to celebrate a nuptial contract between Amina, an orphan brought up as the foster-child of Teresa, the mistress of the village mill, and Elvino, a young landowner of the neighbourhood. These preparations, however, arouse the jealousy of Lisa, the proprietress of the inn, for she is in love with Elvino. Nor do Alessio's ill-timed attentions please her. Amina enters with Teresa, and thanks her neighbours for their good wishes. She has two attractive solos, 'Come per me sereno' and the cabaletta 'Sovra il sen la man mi posa'.

When the village notary and Elvino appear, the contract is signed, and Elvino places a ring on Amina's finger, in a duet: 'Prendi, l'anel ti dono', a composition in long-flowing expressive measures.

A handsome stranger appears. Night is approaching, and, and urged by Lisa, he decides to spend the night at the inn. The villagers do not know it, but he is Rodolfo, the lord of the castle. He recalls the scenes of his youth ('Vi ravviso'), then gallantly addresses himself to Amina in a charming cabaletta.

Elvino is piqued at the stranger's attentions to his bride, but Teresa warns all present to go home, for the village is said to be haunted by a phantom. The stranger treats the superstition lightly, and, ushered in by Lisa, retires to the village inn. Elvino upbraids Amina for seemingly having found much pleasure in the stranger's gallant speeches, but before they part there are mutual concessions and forgiveness ('Son geloso del Zefiro errante').

Rodolfo's room at the inn. He enters, conducted by Lisa. She is coquettish, he quite willing to meet her halfway. He learns from her that his identity has now been discovered by the villagers, and that they will come to the inn to offer their congratulations.

He is annoyed, but quite willing that Lisa's attractions shall atone for the discovery. At that moment, however, there is a noise outside, and Lisa hurries out, in her haste dropping her handkerchief, which Rodolfo picks up and hangs over the bedpost. A few moments later he is amazed to see Amina, all in white, raise his window and enter his room. He realises almost immediately that she is walking in her sleep, and that it is her somnambulism which has given rise to the superstition of the village phantom. In her sleep Amina speaks of her approaching marriage, of Elvino's jealousy, of their quarrel and reconciliation. Rodolfo, not wishing to embarrass her by his presence should she suddenly awaken, extinguishes the candles, steps out of the window and closes it lightly after him. Still asleep, Amina sinks down upon the bed.

The villagers enter to greet Rodolfo. As the room is dark, and, to their amusement, they see the figure of a woman on the bed, they are about to withdraw discreetly, when Lisa, who knows what has happened, enters with a light, brings in Elvino, and points out Amina to him. The light, the sounds, awaken her. Her natural confusion at the situation in which she finds herself is mistaken by Elvino for evidence of guilt. He rejects her. The others, except for Teresa, share his suspicions. Teresa takes the handkerchief hanging over the bedpost and places it around Amina's neck, and when the poor, grief-stricken girl faints as Elvino turns away from her, her foster-mother catches her in her arms.

In this scene, indeed in this act, the most striking musical number is the duet near the end. It begins with Amina's protestations of innocence: 'D'un pensiero, e d'un accento'. When Elvino's voice joins hers there is no comfort for her in his words. An unusual and beautiful effect is the closing of the duet with an expressive phrase for tenor alone: 'Questo pianto del mio cor'.

Act II, scene i. A shady valley between the village and the castle. The villagers are going to the castle to beg Rodolfo to intercede with Elvino for Amina. Elvino meets Amina. Still enraged at what he considers her perfidy, he snatches from her finger the ring he gave her. Amina still loves him. He expresses his mixed feelings in the aria 'Ah! perchè non posso odiarti'.

Scene ii. The village, near Teresa's mill. A slender wooden bridge gives access from a window in the mill roof to a flight of steps.

Lisa has induced Elvino to promise to marry her, and preparations for the wedding are afoot. Rodolfo endeavours to dissuade Elvino from the step he is about to take, explaining that Amina is a somnambulist. But Elvino has never heard of somnambulism, and remains incredulous.

Teresa begs the villagers to make less disturbance as poor Amina is asleep in the mill. The girl's foster-mother learns of Elvino's intention of marrying Lisa. Straight away she takes from her bosom Lisa's handkerchief, which she found hanging over Rodolfo's bedpost. Lisa is confused. Elvino feels that she, too, has betrayed him. Rodolfo again urges Elvino to believe that Amina was never false to him – that she is the innocent victim of sleepwalking. Elvino demands proof, and at that moment Rodolfo points to the mill roof, where Amina, in her nightdress, lamp in hand, emerges from a window. Still asleep, she walks to the bridge spanning the mill wheel. She sets foot on the narrow, insecure bridge. The villagers fall on their knees in prayer that she may cross safely. As Amina crosses a rotting plank breaks under her footsteps, and the lamp falls from her hand into the torrent beneath. Still walking in her sleep, she advances to the villagers and Rodolfo. She kneels and prays for Elvino. Then she speaks of the ring he has taken from her, and draws from her bosom the flowers given to her by him on the previous day.

Gently Elvino replaces the ring upon her finger, and kneels before her. 'Viva Amina!' cry the villagers. She awakens and sees Elvino, with arms outstretched, waiting to beg her forgiveness and lead her to the altar. Amina's 'Ah! non giunge' is one of the show-pieces of Italian opera. Nor is its brilliance hard and glittering; it is the brightness of a tender soul rejoicing at casting off sorrow. Indeed, there is about the entire opera a sweetness and a gentle charm that account for its having endured so long in the repertory.   K.

NORMA

Opera in two acts, text by Felice Romani, founded on L.A. Soumet's tragedy. Première at la Scala, Milan, 26 December 1831, with Pasta, Grisi, Donzelli, Negrini; London, Haymarket, 1833, with Pasta, de Meric, Donzelli, Galli; Drury Lane, 1837; Covent Garden, 1841, with Adelaide Kemble; New Orleans, 1836; New York, 1841 (in English); 1843 (in Italian); Metropolitan, New York, 1891, with Lilli Lehmann; 1927, with Ponselle, Telva, Lauri-Volpi, Pinza, conductor Serafin; Covent Garden, 1929, with Ponselle; Metropolitan, New York, 1936, with Cigna, Castagna, Martinelli, Pinza, conductor Panizza; 1943, with Milanov; la Scala, 1952, with Callas, Stignani, Penno, Rossi-Lemeni; Covent Garden, 1952, with Callas, Stignani, conductor Gui; 1967, with Sutherland, Marilyn Horne, conductor Bonynge.

Pollione, *Roman pro-consul in Gaul* ....Tenor

Oroveso, *Archdruid, father of Norma* ....Bass

Norma, *high priestess of the druidical temple*....Soprano

Adalgisa, *a virgin of the temple*........................Soprano

Clotilda, *Norma's confidante* ....Soprano

Flavio, *a centurion* ....Tenor

Priests, Officers of the Temple, Gallic Warriors, Priestesses and Virgins of the Temple

Place: Gaul
Time: Roman Occupation, about 50 B.C.
Running Time: 3 hours

Act I. The sacred grove of the Druids. The high priest Oroveso comes with the Druids to the sacred grove to beg the gods to rouse the people to war and accomplish the destruction of the Romans. Scarcely have they gone than the Roman pro-consul Pollione appears and confides to his centurion, Flavio, that he no longer loves Norma, although she has broken her vows of chastity for him and has borne him two sons. He now loves Adalgisa.

At the sound of the sacred instrument of bronze that calls the Druids to the temple, the Romans disappear. The priests and priestesses approach the altar, and Norma, the high priestess, ascends the steps. No one suspects her intimacy with the Roman enemy. But she loves Pollione and seeks to avert the danger that would threaten him, should Gaul rise against the Romans, by prophesying that Rome will fall through its own weakness, and declaring that it is not yet the will of the gods that Gaul shall go to war. She also prays to the goddess for the return of the Roman leader, who has left her.

In the sacred grove, Adalgisa is waiting for Pollione, who joins her and begs her to fly with him to Rome, where their happiness would be secure. After some hesitation, she agrees to go with him.

Norma's dwelling. The priestess is steeped in deep sadness, for she knows that Pollione plans to desert her and their offspring, although she is not yet aware of her rival's identity. Adalgisa comes to unburden her heart to her superior. She confesses that she has become untrue to her faith through love – and, moreover, love for a Roman. Norma, thinking of her own unfaithfulness to her vows, is about to free Adalgisa from hers, when Pollione appears. For the first time Norma learns the identity of the Roman Adalgisa loves. When she learns the truth the latter turns from Pollione; she loves Norma too well to go away with the betrayer of the high priestess.

Act II. Norma, filled with despair, is beside the cradle of her children. An impulse to kill them comes over her, but motherhood triumphs over unrequited love. She will relinquish her lover to Adalgisa, who must promise to take the place of mother to her children. Adalgisa, however, will not hear of treachery to Norma. She will go to Pollione, but only to remind him of his duty.

Scene ii. The temple. Norma awaits the result of Adalgisa's plea to Pollione; then learns that she has failed and has come back to the grove to pass her life as a priestess. Norma's wrath is now beyond control. She strikes the brazen shield, and, when the warriors have gathered, proclaims her message: war against the Romans! But with the war song now mingles the sound of tumult from the temple. A Roman has broken into the sacred edifice and has been captured. It is Pollione, who Norma knows has attempted to carry off Adalgisa. The penalty for his intrusion is death. But Norma, moved by love to pity and still hoping to save

her errant lover, submits a new victim to the enraged Gauls – a perjured virgin of the priesthood. They ask her to name the wrong-doer, and to their amazement she utters her own name, then confesses all to her father, Oroveso, and confides her children to his care.

A pyre has been erected. She mounts it, but not alone. Pollione, his love rekindled at the spectacle of her greatness of soul, joins her. In the flames he, too, will atone for their offences before God.   K.

Norma is a work of great lyrical beauty and considerable dramatic tension. The music unfolds in long scenes, but the listener never loses the feeling that the threads are drawing gradually and inevitably together towards the final tragic dénouement.

The overture is in the nature of a dramatic prelude. The Druids are shown first in a solemn introduction (in which occurs a haunting woodwind phrase), followed by an inflammatory pronouncement by Oroveso, which leads to a typical early nineteenth-century Italian march. Next we are introduced to the Romans, in the persons of Pollione and his friend Flavio; Pollione has a cavatina, 'Meco all'altar di Venere', whose ending is interrupted by the sounds of the Druids gathering for their ceremony, but he has time for a cabaletta before he disappears from view. The introduction to the great scene of Druidical rites is in the form of a march which is later used for the quick section of Norma's great and justly famous 'Casta diva', which forms the centrepiece of this scene and indeed of the whole opera. This prayer to the 'chaste goddess' is one of the most celebrated of soprano arias, and its form and melodic contour are said (with other pieces of the same kind in Bellini's works) to have had the strongest influence on the character and mood of Chopin's Nocturnes. Even transposed, the *fioriture* ornaments are taxing to the average soprano – but the truth is that the average soprano cannot (and never could) tackle the title role.

Adalgisa is the fourth character to be presented musically; her impressive recitative, 'Sgombra è la sacra selva', is her only solo opportunity, but it leads to a big-scale duet with Pollione, 'Va crudele, al dio spietato', and is followed by an extensive scene with Norma herself as she confesses her guilt, and a trio which ends the act. Better known and even more beautiful is the great scene for the two sopranos in Act II, 'Mira, o Norma', after Norma has begged Adalgisa

Norma *(Metropolitan Opera House, New York, c. 1927). Rosa Ponselle as Norma and Marian Telva as Adalgisa.*

to marry Pollione and to look after the two children Norma has had by him. Adalgisa's devotion is touchingly and beautifully shown in this duet, which contains one of Bellini's finest melodies. Norma and Adalgisa sing in thirds together in the slow section and again in the decorated quick section with which it ends.

The last part of the opera begins with Oroveso's solo, 'Ah, del Tebro' (marked 'con ferocia' in the score), gathers momentum when Norma summons the Druids and with them sings a determined chorus, 'Guerra!', and reaches its climax when Pollione is left alone with Norma. Their two great duets, of which 'In mia man alfin tu sei' takes place in private, 'Qual cor tradisti' in public and with choral support, form the climax of the opera. Bellini's vocal writing is at its most expressive, and the drama is no less intense than in, for instance, the duet between Radames and Amneris in the last act of *Aida*. The opera ends fittingly with a beautiful trio, 'Deh, non volerli vittime', for Norma, Pollione, Oroveso and the chorus.

'Bellini's and Romani's *Norma*', wrote Andrew Porter in *The New Yorker* in 1973, 'remains one of the most demanding parts in opera, both vocally and dramatically. It calls for power; grace in slow cantilena; pure, fluent coloratura; stamina; tones both tender and violent; force and intensity of verbal declamation; and a commanding stage presence. Only a soprano who has all these things can sustain the role. There have not been many such sopranos. The critics of the nineteenth century delighted to describe and compare the fine points of the performances by Giulia Grisi, Malibran, Adelaide Kemble, and, later, Lilli Lehmann.'

In the two periods before and after the 1939–45 war, *Norma* acquired two great protagonists: Rosa Ponselle and Maria Callas. With such exponents, *Norma*, above all Bellini's operas, flowers, gains in expressiveness and dramatic impact and the music grows to full stature. Partly, this gain is general and the result of technical attainments, of superior, more penetrating imagination; partly it is particular and the product of an ability to colour and weight every phrase individually and leave nothing open to the risks of the automatic or the routine. But, whatever the reason, let no one imagine he has genuinely heard *Norma* without a truly great singer in the title

role. Not to have one is as dire in its consequences as a performance of *Götterdämmerung* with an inadequate Brünnhilde. The trouble as far as Bellini is concerned is that, in the twentieth century, there have been fewer great Normas than fine Brünnhildes.   H.

BEATRICE DI TENDA

Opera in two acts, text by Felice Romani. Première at la Fenice, Venice, 16 March 1833, with Giuditta Pasta, Anna dal Serre, Alberico Curioni, Orazio Cartagenova. First performed Palermo, 1833; Naples, 1834, with Persiani; London, 1836; Vienna, 1837; Paris, 1841; New Orleans, 1842; New York, 1844. Revived Palermo, 1959, with Rubio, conductor Gui; New York (American Opera Society), 1961, with Sutherland, Horne, conductor Rescigno; la Scala, 1961, with Sutherland, Kabaivanska, conductor Gavazzeni; Naples, 1962, with Sutherland; Venice, 1964, with Gencer, conductor Gui.

Filippo Maria Visconti, *Duke of Milan* ....Baritone

Beatrice di Tenda, *his wife*.............................Soprano

Agnese del Maino, *beloved of Filippo*....Mezzo-Soprano

Orombello, *lord of Ventimiglia* ....Tenor

Anichino, *friend of Orombello and formerly minister to Facino, Duke of Milan*....................Tenor

Rizzardo del Maino, *Agnese's brother* ....Tenor

Courtiers, Judges, Officials, Soldiers, Women-in-Waiting

Place: The Castle of Binasco
Time: 1418
Running Time: 2 hours 50 minutes

*B*eatrice di Tenda is the composer's penultimate opera, first performed just over a year after *Norma* and nearly two before *I Puritani*. It was commissioned for the Carnival of 1833, and, by November 1832, Bellini and Romani, in agreement with the great singer Pasta, had settled on *Beatrice di Tenda*. By mid-December, Bellini, in Venice to produce *Norma*, had received nothing from Romani and by the end of the month police action had been invoked to persuade Romani to leave Milan to fulfil his contract. Between the beginning of January and 16 March 1833, the normally slow-working Bellini received his verses, set them, rehearsed the performers and produced the opera – to finish up with something of a failure with the audience[1] and to have Romani apologising to the public for the haste with which he had been con-

---

[1] '*Beatrice* is musically speaking one of Bellini's richest operas,' wrote that considerable authority, Vittorio Gui.

strained to work! The similarity of the story to that of *Anna Bolena* (Romani's libretto was set by Donizetti in 1830) is too marked to be disregarded.

The story is based on an event in Italian history. Filippo Visconti, after the death of his brother and of their father Gian Galeazzo, joined with the general Facino Cane to restore order, and in due course married his widow Beatrice di Tenda, through whom he inherited army and possessions. When the opera begins, Filippo is bored with Beatrice and has fallen in love with Agnese del Maino.

Act I. The overture, which features Beatrice's fourth scene 'Deh! se mi amasti', brings us to the courtyard of the castle of Binasco. The courtiers are amazed that Duke Filippo has left the festivities early and hear from him that it is because of his lack of sympathy with his wife, who presides over them. The voice of Agnese can be heard singing from the castle ('Ah, non pensar che pieno sia'), and Filippo, encouraged by his sycophantic entourage, mellifluously admits his love for her ('Come t'adoro').

In her own apartments, Agnese awaits the result of an anonymous letter of assignation she has sent Orombello, lord of Ventimiglia, with whom she is secretly in love. In the course of their duet, Agnese comes to understand that Orombello is in love with Beatrice, and her furious reaction presages danger for the Duchess.

Beatrice, strolling in the grounds of the ducal palace with her maids of honour, laments in a beautiful cavatina ('Ma la sola, ohimé, son' io') and cabaletta ('Ah! la pena in lor piombò') her husband's oppressive treatment of her subjects as well as his spurning of her love, which had raised him to his present position as Duke. As she leaves, Agnese's brother, Rizzardo, brings Filippo to the scene. He longs for an excuse to rid himself of Beatrice but, now that he suspects her (falsely, as it turns out) of an amorous intrigue, finds himself furious at the discovery. Their confrontation, mildness itself at first on her side, is composed of insults and accusations on his, culminating in his claim to possess proof that she is plotting with their subjects to remove him.

The fourth scene takes place in a remote part of the castle. Armed soldiers discuss the Duke's behaviour – love or anger, they say, will soon force him to show his hand. Beatrice enters and kneels in front of a statue of Facino, her first husband, from whom she

begs forgiveness ('Deh! se mi amasti un giorno') that she so soon forgot his memory in marriage with another. She is, she says, by all forsaken – by all, cries Orombello, but not by him! He knows her plight, knows too that her subjects venerate her still and will with him at their head come to her aid. But Beatrice knows she can accept no aid from Orombello, wishing to avoid all danger of compromising herself. As Orombello kneels at her feet, Filippo with his entourage appears on the scene to accuse her of furnishing him with proof of all his suspicions. A great ensemble, Verdian in its thrust and directness, builds up as each character protests his or her emotions, and the act comes to an end with Filippo, enraged at Orombello's protestations of Beatrice's innocence, ordering them both to prison.

Act II. A tribunal court inside the castle. A vigorous orchestral prelude leads to the revelation by the gentlemen of the court that Orombello has succumbed to the pressure of torture and confessed. Filippo is deaf to the pleas of Anichino, and at the appearance of the judges he demands an exemplary sentence for the guilty woman. When confronted with Orombello and the news that he has confessed, Beatrice berates him for what she can only think is a futile effort to buy his life, until, in a burst of revulsion, he proclaims that his confession was made under duress and is false. An ensemble develops, with Beatrice voicing her thanks to Orombello and to heaven, Orombello his newfound steadfastness, Agnese her doubts and remorse, Anichino his certainty of their joint innocence, Filippo his increased determination to make the charge stick, if necessary through further torture. There is a moment of pathos as Beatrice warns her husband that heaven is watching his actions, then Filippo baldly states his conviction that the law must run its course with maximum severity.

Filippo is face to face with his conscience. At first he cannot understand how others can feel remorse where he cannot, then, as he fancies he hears Beatrice's voice under torture, wonders whether he himself is as obdurate as he tries to make out, finally discovering the truth about his feelings as he learns from Anichino that, in spite of Beatrice's refusal to confess under torture, the judges have agreed on her death warrant, which now lacks only his signature. He cannot sign and so send to the block the woman who saved him from the life of a wandering fugitive ('Qui m'accolse oppresso, errante') – it is the one moment of humanity in a character otherwise drawn too black for credibility. But Filippo's clemency is short-lived, and the news that the people and elements of Facino's army are massing against him causes him to sign the decree, insisting that it is not he but Beatrice's own villainy which condemns her ('Non son io che la condanno').

A hall leading to the castle dungeons. Her maids of honour have left Beatrice at prayer in her cell, but soon she emerges to tell them that heaven has helped her triumph over the pain of her ordeal, that she will die wrapped in virtue's mantle, while Filippo and her enemies await God's punishment for their crimes against truth and justice. The appearance of Agnese to confess her part in Beatrice's torment – it was she who stole her letters, and with her own honour bought the death of Beatrice – leads to a change of heart in Beatrice as, in a beautiful trio initiated by Orombello from his nearby cell ('Angiol di pace'), she grants Agnese her pardon.

A funeral dirge announces the guards who are to escort Beatrice to the scaffold, and, as Agnese faints in anguish, Beatrice poignantly asks for prayers for Filippo and Agnese and not for herself ('Ah! se un'urna'), then in a brilliant cabaletta ('Ah! la morte a cui m'appresso') appears to welcome the prospect of death as amounting to victory over the sorrows of earth.   H.

I PURITANI

The Puritans

Opera in three acts, words by Count Pepoli. Produced Paris, Théâtre des Italiens, 25 January 1835, with Grisi as Elvira, Rubini as Arturo, Tamburini as Riccardo, and Lablache as Giorgio. London, King's Theatre, 21 May 1835 (in Italian); la Scala, Milan, 1835; Philadelphia, 1843; New York, 1844; Academy of Music, 1883, with Gerster. Revived, Manhattan Opera House, 1906, with Bonci as Arturo and Pinkert as Elvira; and in 1909 with Tetrazzini; Metropolitan, 1918, with Barrientos, Lazaro, de Luca, Mardones; Florence, 1933, with Capsir, Lauri-Volpi, Basiola, Pinza, conductor Serafin; la Scala, Milan, 1942, with Carosio; Rome Opera, 1948, with Pagliughi; la Scala, 1949, with Carosio, conductor Capuana; Fenice, Venice, 1949, with Callas, conductor Serafin; Glyndebourne, 1960, with Sutherland, conductor Gui; Covent Garden, 1964, with Sutherland; 1992 with June Anderson, Sabbatini.

Lord Walton, *of the Puritans*..............................Bass

Giorgio (Sir George Walton), *his brother,*
    of the Puritans .... Bass

Arturo (Lord Arthur Talbot), *of the Cavaliers*.....Tenor

Riccardo (Sir Richard Forth),
    of the Puritans...Baritone

Sir Benno Robertson, *of the Puritans*..................Tenor

Queen Enrichetta (Henrietta),
    widow of Charles I ....Soprano

Elvira, *daughter of Lord Walton*......................Soprano

Puritans, Soldiers of the Commonwealth, Men-at-Arms, Women, Pages

Place: Near Plymouth, England
Time: English Civil War
Running Time: 2 hours 45 minutes

Though the quartet of leading singers was the same in each case, nothing could be in stronger contrast to Bellini's opera than Donizetti's *Don Pasquale* of eight years later. In spite of a happy ending, Bellini's *I Puritani* demonstrates the melancholy side of his genius as few of his operas; a seriously prepared performance is as convincing an advocate for the lyrical tragedies of the first part of the nineteenth century as is Donizetti's *Lucia*.

Act I. A fortress, near Plymouth, held by Lord Walton for Cromwell. Lord Walton's daughter, Elvira, is in love with Lord Arthur Talbot, a cavalier and adherent of the Stuarts, but her father has promised her hand to Sir Richard Forth, like himself a follower of Cromwell. He relents, however, and Elvira is bidden by her uncle, Sir George Walton, to prepare for her nuptials with Arthur, for whom a safe conduct to the fortress has been provided.

Queen Henrietta, widow of Charles I, is a prisoner in the fortress. On discovering that she is under sentence of death, Arthur, loyal to the Stuarts, enables her to escape by draping her in Elvira's bridal veil and conducting her past the guards, as if she were the bride. There is one critical moment. They are met by Sir Richard, who had hoped to marry Elvira. The men draw their swords, but a disarrangement of the veil shows Sir Richard that the woman he supposes to be Lord Arthur's bride is not Elvira. He permits them to pass. When the escape is discovered, Elvira, believing herself deserted, loses her reason. Those who had gathered for the nuptials now, in a stirring chorus, invoke maledictions upon Arthur's head.

Act II. Another part of the fortress. The action is mainly to do with the exhibition of Elvira's madness. There is also the famous martial duet, 'Suoni la tromba' (Sound the trumpet), in which Sir George and Sir Richard announce their readiness to meet Arthur in battle and avenge Elvira's sad plight.

Act III. A grove near the fortress. Arthur, although proscribed, seeks out Elvira. Her joy at seeing him again temporarily lifts the clouds from her mind, but renewed evidence of her disturbed mental state alarms her lover. He hears men, whom he knows to be in pursuit of him, approaching, and is aware that capture means death, but he will not leave Elvira. He is apprehended and is about to be executed when a messenger arrives with the news of the defeat of the Stuarts and a pardon for all prisoners. Arthur is freed. The sudden shock of joy restores Elvira's reason. The lovers are united.

As an opera *I Puritani* lacks the naïveté of *La Sonnambula*, nor has it any one number of the celebrity of 'Casta diva' in *Norma*. However, it is sometimes revived for a tenor whose elegance of phrasing finds exceptional opportunity in the role of Arthur; or for some renowned prima donna of the brilliant coloratura type, for whom Elvira is a grateful part.

The principal musical numbers are, in Act I, Sir Richard Forth's cavatina, 'Ah! per sempre io ti perdei'; Arthur's romance, 'A te o cara'; and Elvira's sparkling polacca, 'Son vergin vezzosa'. In Act II we have Sir George's romance, 'Cinta di fiori', and Elvira's mad scene, 'Qui la voce sua soave'. This is a *legato* melody of infinite pathos and beauty – one of Bellini's finest inspirations and perhaps the loveliest and most purely musical of all nineteenth-century mad scenes. It is followed by a beautiful cabaletta, 'Vien, diletto'.

The act closes with the duet for baritone and bass, between Sir Richard and Sir George, 'Suoni la tromba', a fine sonorous proclamation of martial ardour. It was in this duet, on the occasion of the opera's revival for Gerster, that I heard break and go to pieces the voice of Antonio Galassi, the great baritone of the heyday of Italian opera at the Academy of Music. 'Suoni la tromba!' – he could sound it no more. The career of a great artist was at an end.

'A una fonte afflitto e solo', a beautiful number for Elvira, occurs at the beginning of the third act. There is also in this act the impassioned 'Vieni fra queste braccia' for Arthur and Elvira, with its two top Ds for the tenor. It is followed by a big ensemble, 'Credeasi, misera', dominated by the tenor's part, in which occurs a rare example of a top F written for the tenor.

K., H.

JULIUS BENEDICT
(born 27 November 1804, died 5 June 1885)

THE LILY OF KILLARNEY

Opera in three acts, text by J. Oxenford and D. Boucicault, after the latter's play *Colleen Bawn*. Première, Covent Garden, 8 February 1862, with Louise Pyne, Henry Haigh, Charles Santley, William Harrison. First produced New York, 1868; Brunswick, Hamburg and other German cities, 1863, as *Die Rose von Erin*. Revived Covent Garden, 1902, with Fanny Moody, Joseph O'Mara; Sadler's Wells, 1931, with Jean Kemp, Arthur Cox, Henry Wendon, Harry Brindle.

Eily O'Connor (The Colleen Bawn)................Soprano

Hardress Cregan, *secretly married to Eily*...........Tenor

Mrs Cregan, *his mother* ....Contralto

Mr Corrigan ....Bass

Myles na Coppaleen, *in love with Eily* ....Tenor

Danny Mann, *a boatman, devoted to Hardress* ....Baritone

Miss Ann Chute, *an heiress* ....Soprano

Sheelah ....Contralto

Father Tom ....Bass

O'Moore ....Bass

Place: Ireland
Time: Nineteenth Century
Running Time: 1 hour 30 minutes

Act I, scene i. The hall at Tore Cregan. Hardress Cregan, whose secret marriage to the beautiful peasant girl Eily O'Connor is unknown even to his mother, is entertaining his friends. Two guests squabble about the merits of their horses, and Hardress decides that only a steeplechase can satisfactorily settle the argument. Mrs Cregan is left alone, to be visited by Mr Corrigan, a vulgarian who holds a mortgage on the Cregan property and threatens that, if Hardress does not marry the heiress Ann Chute and so obtain the money, he will demand her own hand in marriage. She is outraged at the suggestion.

At this point Danny Mann is heard singing in the distance, and Corrigan tells Mrs Cregan that Mann is waiting to take Hardress to visit the Colleen Bawn. He forces her to watch the lantern signals as proof of her son's infatuation. They listen as Hardress and Danny sing 'The Moon has raised her lamp above', a duet that is probably the best-known piece in the score. In a quartet ('Ah, never was seen') Mrs Cregan and Corrigan sing of their anger and suspicion, while Danny and Hardress are heard singing on their way to Eily.

Scene ii. Eily's cottage. Corrigan tries to extract information about Hardress from Myles na Coppaleen, a peasant hopelessly in love with Eily, who sings of his unrequited love ('From Inchigela' and 'It is a charming girl'). Eily, with Myles, Sheelah and Father Tom (a good priest who watches over her), is waiting for her husband. She tells the story of her secret marriage in a romance ('In my wild mountain valley'), and the four sing a lively quartet which is interrupted, to the chagrin of Myles, by the sound of Hardress approaching. Father Tom begs Eily to make her marriage public, but when Hardress arrives he tries to induce her to surrender her marriage certificate to him and so conceal the matter altogether. Myles and Father Tom succeed in making Eily promise never to part with the precious document, and Hardress leaves in a passion.

Act II. There is a hunting chorus as Hardress begins to pay court to Ann Chute. She sings a florid air ('The eye of love is keen') which is followed by a duet ('Ah, never may that faithful heart'), in which Hardress is nagged by conscience as he thinks of Eily. Hardress is horrified when Danny Mann suggests that he should murder Eily so as to clear the way for him; if he decides on her death, he has only to send Danny his glove as a signal.

Scene ii. There follows a tempestuous scene with Hardress flying into a rage at Corrigan's attentions to his mother; Mrs Cregan crying that her son could save her from him if he wished, and Corrigan taunting Hardress with his love for Eily. All this is overheard by Danny Mann, who darkly hints to Mrs Cregan that if she can persuade Hardress to send him his glove, her troubles will be over. Mrs Cregan is puzzled but goes off to do as he suggests. She returns with the glove and gives it to Danny, whose momentary pangs at the prospect of his self-imposed task eventually yield to his feelings of loyalty to his master.

Scene iii. At her cottage, Eily sings of her loneliness and longing for her husband. Danny Mann, much the worse for drink, comes to tell her that he will row her across the lake to Hardress. Myles begs her not to go, but Eily mocks his fears and goes off in Danny's boat.

Scene iv. To a lonely cave comes Myles, still singing of his hopeless love for Eily. Seeing an otter slither off a rock, he goes to get his gun. Danny rows Eily into the cave, sets her ashore on a rock and demands her marriage lines or her life. She refuses to give them up and Danny pushes her into the water. A shot is heard and Danny too falls into the sea. Myles comes to look for the otter he thinks he has shot and finds Eily under the water. He plunges in and drags her out, as the song of the boatmen can be heard in the distance.

Act III. Myles sings a lullaby to Eily and he, Eily and Father Tom together thank heaven for her rescue. The scene changes to the town, where Hardress is about to marry Ann Chute. Suddenly, Corrigan arrives with soldiers who arrest Hardress for his part in the murder of Eily, Danny Mann having made a dying confession. Villainy is only kept from triumph by the timely arrival of Myles and Eily to refute the allegation. The truth about the marriage is revealed, Mrs Cregan allays suspicion about her son by admitting that he knew nothing about Danny Mann and the glove; and all ends in a bright Rondo Finale.   H.

ALBAN BERG

(born 9 February 1885, died 24 December 1935)

WOZZECK

Opera in three acts and fifteen scenes, text adapted by the composer from Büchner's drama *Woyzeck*. Première, Berlin Staatsoper, 14 December 1925, with Sigrid Johanson, von Scheele-Müller, Leo Schützendorf, Waldemar Henke, Martin Abendroth, conductor Erich Kleiber. First performed Vienna, 1930, with Pauly, Manowarda, conductor Krauss; Philadelphia, 1931, with Roselle, Ivantzoff, conductor Stokowski; New York, 1931, same cast; London (Queen's Hall, in concert form), 1934 with Blyth, Bitterauf, conductor Boult; Rome, 1942, with Gatti, Gobbi, conductor Serafin. Revived Düsseldorf, 1948, with Mödl, Nillius, conductor Hollreiser; Naples, 1949, with Danco, Gobbi, conductor Böhm; Covent Garden, 1952, with Goltz, Rothmüller, Parry Jones, Dalberg, conductor Erich Kleiber; la Scala, Milan, 1952, with Dow, Gobbi, conductor Mitropoulos; New York, Metropolitan, 1959, with Steber, Uhde, conductor Böhm; Paris, 1963 and 1966, conductor Boulez.

Wozzeck, *a soldier* ....Baritone
The Drum-Major ....Tenor
Andres, *a soldier*...Tenor
The Captain...Tenor
The Doctor ....Bass
First and Second Workmen...........Baritone and Bass
An Idiot ....Tenor
Marie ....Soprano
Margret..Contralto
Marie's Child...Treble

Soldiers, Maids, Servants, Children

Place: Germany
Time: c. 1830
Running Time: 1 hour 25 minutes

Conceived in 1914, when Berg saw a performance of *Woyzeck*, the stylistically prophetic play by Georg Büchner (1813–37), *Wozzeck*'s composition was interrupted by the First World War, in which Berg served. The music was completed in 1921, and in 1923 Universal Edition undertook to publish the opera. In the meanwhile, Berg tried to persuade some opera house or other to mount the work (he was helped by the noted pianist Eduard Steuermann, who played the score to one uninterested General-

musikdirektor after another). It was eventually accepted by Erich Kleiber for production at the Staatsoper, Berlin, but, eighteen months before the Berlin première, the public had the opportunity of hearing the so-called Fragments from *Wozzeck* (the first half of Act I, scene iii; Act III, scene i; and Act III, scene v and the interlude which precedes it), sung by Sutter-Kottlar and conducted by Scherchen. From that moment *Wozzeck* became a centre of controversy, and musicians and opera-goers divided into those who loved and those who loathed the work – in either case, the reaction was often stronger than the reasons which could be found to support the impression.

Wozzeck is in three acts, each of five scenes. The music is continuous and often Berg provides no more than a few seconds of interlude music during which the scene change must be made.

Berg himself has related music and drama in the most succinct way in the following key:

ACT I

STAGE	MUSIC	
Wozzeck in his relationship to his surroundings	*Five Character-Pieces*	
Wozzeck and the Captain	Scene i	Suite
Wozzeck and Andres	Scene ii	Rhapsody
Marie and Wozzeck	Scene iii	Military March and Lullaby
Wozzeck and the Doctor	Scene iv	Passacaglia
Marie and the Drum-Major	Scene v	*Andante affettuoso (quasi Rondo)*

ACT II

Dramatic development	*Symphony in Five Movements*	
Marie and the Child, later Wozzeck	Scene i	Sonata Movement
Captain and Doctor, later Wozzeck	Scene ii	Fantasy and Fugue
Marie and Wozzeck	Scene iii	*Largo*
Beer-Garden	Scene iv	Scherzo
Sleeping Quarters in the Barracks	Scene v	*Rondo con introduzione*

ACT III

However, the composer (in an article published in the *Neue Musik-Zeitung* 1928, and reprinted in Willi Reich's book on Berg) has given a warning to anyone who may be tempted to perform a mental analysis of *Wozzeck* during performance: 'However thorough one's knowledge of the musical forms which are to be found within the opera ... from the moment when the curtain rises until it falls for the last time, nobody in the audience ought to notice anything of these various Fugues and Inventions, Suite and Sonata movements, Variations and Passacaglias – everyone should be filled only by the idea of the opera, an idea which far transcends the individual fate of Wozzeck.'

Berg was a pupil of Schoenberg's, and his musical style is influenced by many of his teacher's theoretical and practical ideas. *Wozzeck* is not, however, composed according to Schoenberg's so-called dodecaphonic method, although the theme of the Passacaglia in Act II has twelve notes. Key signatures, except in the Act III Interlude, are discarded, and the composer makes considerable and subtle use of *Sprechstimme*, known from Schoenberg's employment of it in *Pierrot Lunaire*. *Sprechstimme* is best described as 'musically defined speech'. Rhythm and intonation are exactly prescribed, but 'in the execution each note is only defined in the moment when it is articulated, immediately afterwards the voice drops or rises as in natural speech'.[1] All authorities are agreed that an over-vocal and *cantabile* style in *Sprechstimme* is unfortunate, and that the finished result should sound something like the poetic declamation of a good actor.

Act I. The curtain rises in the third bar of the opera on Scene i, which takes place in the Captain's room. The Captain is being shaved by Wozzeck, his soldier-servant. The Captain is a garrulous, digressive individual, and he moralises to the bewildered Wozzeck: if he hurries so much, what will he do with the ten minutes he saves? He puts aside the subject of Eternity, and asks Wozzeck if the wind is not blowing south-north, chortling at the automatic 'Jawohl, Herr Hauptmann' which he gets as answer. The observation that Wozzeck is a good fellow, but without moral sense – witness the fact that he is unmarried but has a child – finally breaks through Wozzeck's preoccupation. Did not the Lord God say 'Suffer little children to come unto me', asks Wozzeck. The Captain's voice rises to a top C in his astonishment at this, and Wozzeck explains that only the rich can afford conventional morality (Ex. 1).

Wir ar - me Leut!

Wozzeck thinks too much, muses the Captain, and he dismisses him with the admonition that he is not to hurry so dreadfully.

Scene ii. Wozzeck and Andres are cutting sticks at sundown in a field from which can be seen the town. Andres sings to himself, but Wozzeck cannot rid his mind of an impression that the place they are in is haunted. He imagines every sort of thing, babbles of the intrigues of the Freemasons, thinks the ground is going to open under his feet, and is convinced the whole world is on fire when the setting sun colours the horizon red. This short scene contains some of Berg's most dazzling orchestral invention.

Scene iii. Marie's room; evening. The sound of a military march played behind the scenes makes it quite plain that what Marie is looking at out of the window is the band going back to barracks. The Drum-Major waves to her, and she sings happily to the band's tune, so happily in fact that her neighbour Margret cannot resist a malicious comment about her lively interest in soldiers. After an exchange of abuse Marie slams the window and shuts out the sound of the band. She sings a lyrical cradle song to her child, before there is a knock at the window, and Wozzeck himself is seen standing there. He cannot come in as it is too late, he has not even time to look at his child whom Marie holds up to

---

[1] Erwin Stein's article on *Wozzeck*, in *Opera*, January 1952.

him. His confused talk worries her and, after he is gone, she rushes out of the door.

Scene iv (the Passacaglia). The Doctor's study, next day. Wozzeck, in return for a small pittance, is prepared to act as a guinea-pig for the Doctor's dietetic experiments. The Doctor complains that Wozzeck does not follow out all his instructions, and his scientific talk further confuses the unhappy man, whose outburst causes the Doctor to suggest that he may well end up in a lunatic asylum. The Doctor is ecstatic about the fame which will result when his new theories are published, and the curtain goes down as he re-examines Wozzeck's tongue.

Scene v. The street in front of Marie's house, where the Drum-Major is posturing to her evident admiration. He assures her that his present finery is as nothing to what he wears on Sundays. Marie repulses him once when he tries to embrace her, but the second time does not resist him, and, with the exclamation 'What does it matter? It's all the same', takes him into her house.

Act II. In her room, Marie is admiring herself and her new earrings in a bit of broken mirror. She tries to get the child to go to sleep, then falls to admiring herself again. Wozzeck comes in, and asks what it is that she is trying to hide. She says she found the earrings, and he observes that he has never had the luck to find things like that in pairs. He looks at the sleeping child, then, with a reference to No. 1, reflects that life is nothing but work, and that even in sleep man sweats. He gives Marie the money he has earned from the Captain and the Doctor (to the accompaniment of a string chord of C major) and goes out, leaving her to reflect sadly on her infidelity to him.

Scene ii. The street. The Doctor is hurrying along when he is stopped, in spite of his protests, by his friend the Captain, on whom he revenges himself by giving him details of various fatal cases he has recently seen, ending with a warning that the Captain's own flushed condition may easily be a symptom of an impending apoplectic fit, from which death, or at least paralysis, is likely to result. The Captain becomes lyrical at the thought of his own demise, but consoles himself with thoughts of what nice things people will say of him after he has gone.

His reverie is interrupted when Wozzeck comes rapidly down the street – he cuts through the world like one of his own razor blades, says the Captain in a depressed way. The mention of shaving reminds him of the scandal about Marie and the bearded Drum-Major, and he and the Doctor proceed to torment Wozzeck with innuendo (has he not lately found a hair of a beard in his soup?) and even the imitation of a military march. The seriousness with which Wozzeck takes their insinuations quite shocks his tormentors, and he bursts out with a *fortissimo* imprecation at the impossibility of finding satisfaction in life. The Doctor feels his pulse to see if emotion is affecting it, and both he and the Captain exclaim in surprise as their victim rushes off down the street.

Scene iii. The street in front of Marie's house. It is the slow movement of the symphony (*largo*) and is scored for a chamber orchestra of fourteen players, composed according to the distribution of Schoenberg's *Kammer-symphonie*. Marie is standing in front of her house when Wozzeck comes up to her. She is as beautiful as sin, he says – but how can sin be beautiful? Did *he* stand there? Marie replies that she cannot control who walks in the street, and, when Wozzeck looks as though he will strike her: 'Better a knife blade in my heart than lay a hand on me ... My father would never dare when I was little.' Wozzeck repeats her words in a dazed sort of way as she goes into the house.

Scene iv. A beer-garden, where dancing is in progress to a slow *Ländler* played on the stage by a Heurige orchestra: two to four fiddles tuned a tone high, clarinet in C, accordion, several guitars, a bombardon in F (bass tuba). There is general dancing, and a couple of exceedingly drunk workmen sing in a maudlin way of the effect of brandy on the soul. Wozzeck comes in and sees Marie dancing with the Drum-Major; his jealousy grows until he is about to rush on to the dance floor and separate them, when the dance stops. The soldiers, with Andres as soloist, begin a lusty hunting song, ending on a sustained C for the soloist. The first workman climbs on to a table and starts a most effective example of one of those wholly logical, wholly nonsensical discourses traditionally associated with the very drunk. It is entirely conducted in *Sprechstimme*, and shows how effective and expressive a medium that can be.

A snatch of the male chorus succeeds the sermon, after which an Idiot appears on the scene, wanders over to where Wozzeck is sitting, and observes 'Lustig, lustig ... aber es riecht ... ich riech blut' (Joyful, joyful ... and yet it reeks ... I smell blood). The whole role contains only thirteen notes, and yet the tiny scene in which the Idiot appears, to a mainly accordion accompaniment, has an extraordinary fascination and significance. The dancing begins again and Wozzeck's imagination is obsessed with the idea of blood.

Scene v. Wozzeck's barrack room at night. Before the curtain goes up, the sound of snoring can be heard from the sleeping occupants of the room (the chorus in five parts hum wordlessly with half-open mouths), and as soon as the stage can be seen, Wozzeck is heard complaining to Andres that he cannot sleep for memories of the dance hall. The Drum-Major staggers into the room, proclaiming his conquest at the top of his voice and demanding that Wozzeck drink with him. The latter turns away and whistles to himself, whereupon the Drum-Major yanks him from where he stands; they fight for a moment, Wozzeck is knocked to the ground, and the Drum-Major shakes him and threatens to knock all the breath out of his body. He goes out, leaving Wozzeck staring in front of him. 'He bleeds', exclaims Andres. The suggestion of blood seems to Wozzeck like fate's prompting: 'One time after another.'

Act III. Musically, this act is particularly concentrated and consists of six Inventions (that is Berg's name for them).

Scene i. Marie's room at night. The solo viola gives out the theme. Marie is reading the story of Mary Magdalen in the Bible, and cannot help comparing what she reads with her own life. She ends with a cry for mercy: 'Saviour ... as You had mercy on her, have mercy now on me, Lord!' The scene, which is of haunting beauty, has *Sprechstimme* when Marie reads from the Bible, singing when she comments on what she has read.

Scene ii. A pond in the wood, later that night. Wozzeck appears with Marie, whom he prevents from going home as she wishes. He reflects on how long they have known each other, and, when Marie sees the moon rise, draws a knife and cuts her throat, then bends over her: 'Dead!' The interlude consists of two long *crescendi* on B natural, beginning with a *ppp* solo horn, and continuing through the whole orchestra until, after a percussive rhythm, the second *crescendo* takes in the percussion as well. Straight away the curtain rises on Scene iii, with the hammering of a quick polka on an out-of-tune piano. The scene represents an inn. Wozzeck is among the dancers. He takes

Margret for partner, and leads her to a table, where he starts to flirt with her. She sings a short song, but stops when she sees blood on Wozzeck's hand. He makes some attempt to explain it away by saying he cut his arm, then pushes through the dancers who have by now crowded round him, and rushes from the room.

Scene iv. The pond, once again. Wozzeck searches for the knife, which he dropped after the murder and which would incriminate him if found. He finds it, pauses for a moment to look at the body of Marie, then throws the knife into the water, into which he watches it sink. The whole world seems to him bathed in blood; he sees spots on his hands and his clothes, and walks hopelessly into the water to wash it off. He walks further, until he has disappeared from sight. As the Doctor and the Captain come into view and comment on the sound they hear – the sound of a man drowning, hazards the Doctor – the orchestra suggests the waters closing over Wozzeck's head in rising chromatic scales.

The great D minor interlude forms the climax of the opera, and at the same time a lament for Wozzeck himself, the opera's hero. Reference is made to music from earlier scenes, and the themes most closely connected with Wozzeck himself are heard in ennobled form.

Scene v. The street outside Marie's house. Children are playing. Apart and playing by himself is Marie's child. Other children come running in, and one of them says that Marie has been found dead. The child cannot take in what he is being told, and goes on playing his game: 'Hopp-hopp, hopp-hopp, hopp-hopp.' The curtain drops slowly.   H.

LULU

Opera in three acts, text adapted by the composer from Wedekind's *Erdgeist* and *Die Büchse der Pandora*. Première in the unfinished (two-act) form in which it was left by the composer at the time of his death in Zürich, 2 June 1937, with Nuri Hadzic as Lulu, Aster Stig (Dr Schön), Emmerich (Athlete), Peter Baxevanos (Alwa), Maria Bernhard (Geschwitz), Feichtinger (Gymnasiast), Paul Feher (Painter), Honisch (Schigolch), conductor Denzler. First performed Venice, 1949, with Styx, Rehfuss, Demetz, Zareska, conductor Sanzogno; Essen, 1953, with Spletter, conductor König; Hamburg, 1957, with Pilarczyk, conductor Ludwig, producer Rennert; Sadler's Wells, 1962, by Hamburg Company; Santa Fe, 1963, with Joan Carroll, conductor Craft; Stuttgart, 1966, in Wieland Wagner's production, with Silja, conductor Leitner, and Edinburgh Festival, 1967. The three-act version, completed by Friedrich Cerha, first performed Opéra, Paris, 1979, with Teresa Stratas, Yvonne Minton, Kenneth Riegel, Franz Mazura, produced by Patrice Chéreau, conducted by Pierre Boulez; Covent Garden, 1981, with Karan Armstrong, conductor Colin Davis; Glyndebourne, 1996, with Christine Schäfer, conductor Andrew Davis.

Lulu ....High Soprano
Gräfin Geschwitz ....Mezzo-Soprano
A Wardrobe-Mistress..................................Contralto
A Schoolboy ('Der Gymnasiast')..................Contralto
The Doctor, *Lulu's husband* ....Speaking Part
The Painter, *Lulu's second husband* ....Lyric Tenor
Dr Schön, *a newspaper editor* ....Heroic Baritone
Alwa, *Dr Schön's son, a composer*............Heroic Tenor
An Animal-Tamer ....Bass
Rodrigo, *an athlete*...Bass
Schigolch, *an old man* ....High Character Bass
The Prince, *a traveller in Africa* ....Tenor
The Theatre Director ....Buffo Bass
Clown..Baritone
Manservant...Tenor
The Banker ....Bass
The Journalist...Tenor
The Marquis ....Tenor
Lady Artist...Mezzo-Soprano
Young Girl ....Soprano
Her Mother ....Contralto
Page...Mezzo-Soprano
Servant ....Bass
Police Commissioner...Bass
The Professor...Tenor
The Negro...Lyric Tenor
Jack the Ripper..................................Heroic Baritone

Pianist, Stage Manager, Attendants of the Prince, Policemen, Nurses, Wardresses, Dancers, Party Guests, Servants, Workers

Place: A German City
Time: Last Quarter of the Nineteenth Century
Running Time: 2 hours 40 minutes

*L*ulu, Berg's second and last opera, is written throughout in the dodecaphonic system. When the composer died, he had finished Acts I and II, and part of Act III. In addition, he had sketched, in more or less elaborate form, the whole of the rest of the work, which is to say that, except for some lines in the ensemble, all the words had been set. Some of the music of this act was included among the five Symphonic Pieces from the opera, which he completed first. The Symphonic Suite (which requires a singer for performance) consists of (1) *Rondo* (duet Lulu-Alwa, II, i, and end of II, ii), (2) *Ostinato* (Interlude II, i-ii), (3) *Song of Lulu* (II, i), (4) *Variations* (Interlude III, i-ii), (5) *Adagio* (Interlude I, ii-iii, and end of opera, including arietta of Geschwitz).

Efforts were made after Berg's death to have the opera finished by one of his contemporaries sympathetic to his music. Schoenberg turned it down, on the grounds that the libretto contained unnecessary anti-Semitic references (there are two of them) and, when initial attempts failed, the composer's widow gradually imposed an embargo on any work on her late husband's opera. The two acts were performed and most commentators accepted *Lulu* as one of the great operatic masterpieces of the twentieth century, even without its third act. Frau Berg's reasons for refusing access to the manuscript, it was advanced by apologists, were artistic – also because she hated the decadent tone of the libretto, particularly of the last act. Others found them more personal and connected with an affair Berg is said to have had during the composition of *Lulu*. Backed by pressure from Pierre Boulez, Universal Edition eventually allowed Friedrich Cerha, the Viennese composer, to complete the work, which emerged in 1979 under the baton of Boulez as a masterpiece, even if rather a lengthy one, with its third act restored to full length.

Prologue. An animal-tamer, accompanied by the clown from his circus, steps in front of the curtain and introduces his troupe, among whom is Lulu, dressed in Pierrot's costume.

Act I. The curtain goes up on scene i to reveal a painter's studio, where Lulu, as Pierrot, is being painted. Dr Schön, a newspaper editor, watches the proceedings. Schön's son, Alwa, enters and is surprised to find Lulu there without her husband. She explains that she expects him at any moment, and Alwa, who works in the theatre, takes his father off to his dress rehearsal, leaving Lulu and the Painter alone. The latter admits he cannot give his mind to his work, and tries to embrace Lulu. He chases her vigorously round the room – the two voices are in canon and begin with Lulu's motif (heard first in the

Prologue) – and kisses her hands just before the sound of her husband's knocking is heard.

He succeeds in forcing the door, only to collapse at their feet with the shock of finding them in a compromising position. They gradually come to realise he is dead and Lulu comments, with more interest than regret, on his death (*Canzonetta* introduced by saxophone solo). There is a duet for Lulu and the Painter, in which his questions about her beliefs receive the unvaried answer 'I don't know', and the Painter sings an *arioso* when Lulu leaves him alone while she goes to change her clothes.

An interlude leads to scene ii, which takes place in an elegant room in which hangs Lulu's portrait as Pierrot. The Painter, who is now her husband, comes in with the mail, and Lulu reads with amazement a notice of the engagement of Dr Schön. There follows a light-hearted *Duettino* between her and the Painter, at the end of which the studio bell rings. The Painter looks out and says it is a beggar. He goes off to his studio to work, and Lulu lets in the 'beggar', who turns out to be Schigolch, who is supposed to be her father, but in reality may be a former lover. He expresses admiration for her present surroundings; she has come a long way since he last saw her.

As he leaves, Schön enters (Sonata movement begins), recognises Schigolch with some surprise, and then tells Lulu that she must stop coming to see him now that he is engaged. She retorts that she belongs to him (the slow beginning of the coda of the sonata's exposition has something of the significance of a love theme); he rescued her from the streets as a child, and anyhow her husband is blind to anything she does, and does not think of her as a person but as his 'little darling'.

The Painter enters, Lulu leaves, and Schön urges him to watch Lulu carefully, then, as the music gains in urgency, gradually reveals something of her past. He himself introduced her to Dr Goll, her previous husband; it was just after the death of his (Schön's) own wife, and Lulu was doing her utmost to take her place. She has been known by a different name to each of her lovers; Schön calls her Mignon, Dr Goll called her Nelly, and the Painter refers to her as Eva. The Painter makes as if to go out and talk to Lulu,

but presently groans are heard and Lulu and Dr Schön force open a locked door (rhythmical canon of percussion) to find the Painter lying dead.

The bell rings and Alwa comes in full of excitement at the news that revolution has broken out in Paris. Schön fears that the scandal which will inevitably follow discovery of the Painter's suicide will endanger his own engagement, but, editor-wise, hopes the sensation of the news from France may serve to cover it up. The curtain falls to Lulu's words, sung to her motif: 'You will marry me after all.'

An extended Interlude, in which the love theme is developed, leads to a third scene, which takes place in Lulu's dressing-room at a theatre. Alwa waits for Lulu to come off the stage, and reminds her how, as a young man, he wanted to induce his father to marry her after his mother's death. Lulu replies that she knows perfectly well that Dr Schön put her on the stage so that somebody rich should take her off his hands.

She goes out for the next part of her act, and Alwa observes that her life history would make a splendid story for an opera. A Prince, who intends to marry her, enters and launches into extravagant praise of Lulu. There is a noise off-stage, and Lulu is carried in after fainting during her act – an accident caused, Lulu explicitly says, because she had to dance in front of Schön's prospective bride.

Lulu and Schön are left alone (development section of the Sonata) and a scene ensues between them, Lulu taunting him for not having already married his innocent bride and for his unavailing attempts to free himself from her own domination. In despair, he tries to tear himself away, but she shows herself the stronger (recapitulation of the Sonata) and forces him to write, to her dictation, a letter to his fiancée, breaking off the engagement. The curtain falls as Schön exclaims 'Now comes my execution' (love music). Lulu prepares to continue the act interrupted by her fainting fit.

Act II, scene i. A palatial hall decorated in the German Renaissance style. Gräfin (Countess) Geschwitz, a lesbian and dressed in clothes of distinctly masculine cut, is paying a call on Lulu, to whom she is obviously very much attracted. Schön, who is now Lulu's husband, is present, and when Lulu has left with Geschwitz, he shows that jealousy has brought him to the verge of madness. He looks behind the curtains, a loaded revolver in his hand, as if he expected to find some lover there. Lulu returns and she and Schön leave the stage together.

No sooner have they gone than Geschwitz sneaks back into the room and conceals herself, just before Schigolch, an Athlete and a Schoolboy come in (the last-named a 'Hosenrolle', or travesty part). The boy is in love with Lulu and Schigolch has acted as go-between in arranging a meeting. They are drinking and smoking when Lulu comes in, but all hide when Alwa is announced. Alwa with rising excitement declares his love for Lulu. She counters that it was she who was responsible years ago for poisoning his mother. Dr Schön watches the scene from a hiding-place, and catches sight of the Athlete, who is also hiding. Schön leads Alwa, who is no longer in control of himself, from the room, and returns to launch a tirade against Lulu, offering her the revolver, with which he has been pursuing the Athlete, and telling her to use it against herself.

Next he finds Geschwitz and drags her from the room, all the time continuing to urge Lulu to commit suicide. Here follows Lulu's song (it is dedicated by the composer to Anton von Webern); in it, she justifies herself and says she has never tried to seem other than she is. Schön again attempts to force the revolver against Lulu, there is a cry from the boy, and Lulu fires five shots into Schön's body. The entire scene between Schön and Lulu is built up on an aria of five verses for Schön, the different episodes coming as interruption between the verses.

Lulu is horrified by what she has done; Schön was her only love. Alwa returns, and Schön's last words to him are in the nature of a demand for vengeance. Lulu in an arietta pleads to Alwa for mercy, but the curtain falls as the police appear.

The exciting Interlude between the scenes is designed to accompany a silent film, showing what happens to Lulu in the time which intervenes. It involves a court scene, during whose course Lulu is condemned for the murder of Schön; her entry into hospital after she has contracted cholera; and the means of escape (about which more later) through the intervention of Geschwitz.

Scene ii takes place in the same set as scene i, the room however looking dirty and ill-kept. Geschwitz, Alwa and the Athlete (dressed as a footman) are together, and from the conversation we gather that Lulu has had cholera, from which Geschwitz has also only just recovered, that Lulu is to be rescued from the prison hospital where Geschwitz will take her place, and that Lulu is going to marry the Athlete. Schigolch takes Geschwitz off to put the plan into execution – we hear that Geschwitz in her passion for Lulu purposely contracted cholera to make the plan of escape possible.

No sooner are Alwa and the Athlete alone than the Schoolboy appears with a plan for Lulu's escape. They try to convince him that she is dead, and hustle him out of the room just before she comes in, supported by Schigolch. The Athlete is so put out when he sees her looking pale and emaciated that he shouts abuse at her, and leaves the room. Schigolch goes off to collect the tickets for Paris, and Alwa and Lulu are alone. After a passionate love duet, they leave together for Paris.

Act III, scene i. A salon in a casino in Paris, obviously frequented by characters of the demi-monde. The Athlete proposes a toast to Lulu, and the company, as it moves into the gaming room, talks about the rise in the value of some railway shares in which they have all invested. The Marquis, an elegant white-slave trafficker who knows of Lulu's past, suggests that she should enter a brothel in Cairo; if she declines his suggestion, he threatens to expose her to the police. Lulu offers to pay, and the company returns in great heart from their gambling, everyone having won. The Athlete now threatens Lulu if she doesn't pay him too, and at this juncture the page brings the banker a telegram with news of the collapse of the railway shares. Even Schigolch asks Lulu for money and when she tells him of the Athlete's threats, Schigolch proposes to lure him to his hotel room and dispose of him. The Marquis leaves to inform the police and Lulu persuades Countess Geschwitz to go with the Athlete to Schigolch's hotel. The banker's announcement and insistence on payment in cash means that almost everyone present is bankrupt. Lulu dresses up the page in her clothes and herself puts on the boy's. The police find only the page.

Scene ii. An attic in a London slum. Lulu is now on the streets and with her earnings keeps Alwa and Schigolch. Her first client is a professor, whose overcoat pockets Schigolch searches while Lulu is in her room with him. It doesn't take long, and Geschwitz appears from Paris having saved Lulu's Pierrot portrait which she shows them. Lulu is back on the beat and Schigolch hides as a second client, the negro, argues with Lulu about money and Alwa, who tries to help, is struck dead before the negro leaves.

Lulu's last pick-up is Jack the Ripper. Geschwitz makes up her mind to return to Germany as a fighter for women's rights. Jack murders Lulu and, when Geschwitz tries to come to her aid, kills her as well. He washes his hands and leaves as Geschwitz dies.

After the first public hearing of the work, Erwin Stein wrote as follows: 'The music itself shows Berg at the height of his musical achievement. It enriches the picture we had already gained of the composer through his original and important achievements and is another confirmation of the fact that twelve-tone compositions are capable of the greatest variety of expression.

'The lyrical passages ... are some of the most beautiful things Berg ever wrote. They belong for the most part to the character of Alwa, the contemplative artist who represents the opposite pole to the impulsive Lulu. No less effective is the drawing of the other characters. The music surrounds every figure with a special atmosphere, showing up the features and giving weight to their miming and gestures. The comic element, represented by Schigolch and the Athlete, is also depicted with incisive humour. Yet the whole is enveloped in sound of a unique character. And in spite of occasional powerful *crescendos*, the orchestration of *Lulu* shows a preference for the delicate, gracious colours befitting the heroine.'   H.

LUCIANO BERIO
(born 24 October 1925)

LA VERA STORIA
The True Story

Opera in two acts, libretto by Italo Calvino. First performance, la Scala, Milan, 9 March 1982, with Alexandrina Milcheva as Ada, Mariana Nicolesco as Leonora, Oslavio di Credico as Ugo, Roeloff Oostwoud as Luca, Alberto Noli as Ivo, conducted by Luciano Berio. French première, Théâtre National de l'Opéra de Paris, 1985, conducted by Sylvain Cambreling. U.K., Royal Festival Hall, 1989 (concert), staged performance, 1994 (with Felicity Palmer as Ada), both conducted by the composer.

Leonora ....Soprano

Luca..Tenor

Ada..Mezzo-Soprano

Ivo, Comandante...Baritone

Condemned Man...Bass

Ugo, Priest ....Tenor

Ballad-Singers

Three Passers-By ....Actors

Passer-By..Soprano

Vocal Group .... Two Sopranos, Two Contraltos, Two Tenors, Two Basses

Three Voices in the Street, Mimes, Dancers, Acrobats

Running Time: 2 hours

The 'true story' of the title has affinities with that quintessentially operatic work, *Il trovatore*, in terms of the distribution of the voices and the story. A Condemned Man is shot. In revenge, his daughter Ada steals one of Ugo the Commander's young sons. The boy, Luca, becomes the political opponent of Ugo's other son, Ivo. Ugo dies of grief, Ivo takes over as Commander. In a duel Luca wounds Ivo and is shot by an execution squad headed by his brother. This skeletal story constitutes part of the action of the first act, which celebrates the nature of the crowd and is punctuated by four *feste*. A *festa* is an important part of Italian culture, reflecting the role of street life in Italian history.

Act I explores the nature of crowds: one crowd 'contains in itself all crowds'.

First Festa. An empty square in the blazing light of midday. The score direction reads 'anxious and dreamy'. The music recreates the swirling movement of a group that forms a crowd. A Condemned Man in handcuffs is led in by soldiers. The fragmentary phrases that the crowd have been chanting complete themselves: 'at a festa everything is spent, enjoyed and burnt, a festa was and is a ferocious sacrifice'.

The Condemned Man reflects that while he is now a victim, 'you may be one tomorrow, if the city continues to suffer the nightmare of the man who wants us to be slaves.'

Second Festa. The crowd explodes and the palace goes up in flames.

The Abduction. Ada, the Condemned Man's daughter, steals the little son of Ugo, the city's commander. Calling Ugo 'the beast', she tells him that she stole his son because he has 'reduced us to beasts who tear one another apart. You killed pity.'

'If you Know what a Son is' (First Ballad). A Ballad-Singer recites the same text, accompanied by two electric guitar players. Berio makes haunting use of folksong-like intonations here, melismas that sound Islamic, to bring out the archetypal nature of the process: the mother who has lost her son has been treated like a beast and she will inflict the same on the man responsible.

Revenge. In a dark duet with his elder son Ivo, Ugo swears revenge: though even a thousand dead will not satisfy him, his son must exact bloody reprisals. At the end, he dies and the police disperse the onlookers.

Time. Leonora's aria, marked 'always very intense and tense', consists of almost incoherent impressions reminiscent of Lucky's monologue in *Waiting for Godot.* Fragments of meaning relating to public and to private time, to anxiety, to a vortex, a volcano and meteors occasion vivid illustrative details in the music.

'When We Remember' (Second Ballad). A Ballad-Singer accompanied by an accordion player surveys the panorama of history: it teaches us not to expect anything to improve in the future. The police remove them both brutally.

The Night. Berio opposes two disparate sound worlds for this scene, with woodwind (some sumptuous clarinet arabesques) for Leonora and Luca, hard-edged brass for Ivo. Leonora stands between tenor and baritone, as she does in *Il trovatore.* Separate lines for each soloist converge in a major concerted section as the two men confront each other, enmity bringing them as close as brothers.

The Duel. The antagonism between Ivo and Luca results in a fight, mimed by dancer-acrobats, with Ivo backed by the guards and Luca by the rebels. Luca wounds Ivo. The guards arrest him and the rebels retreat.

The Prayer. The crowd forms into a military parade, led by Ivo, surrounded by dignitaries of the church, the army and the police. A Priest sings Latin 'in a head voice'. The chorus produce noise with their hands and with maracas, claves, wood blocks, wood chimes, glass chimes, tamburelli. The scene has a grotesque liveliness.

'Nobody Knows' (Third Ballad). As the Priest reaches a hysterical pitch, the Ballad-Singer points out that 'Nobody knows who the other one is; nobody wants to know, but everybody knows why they do not want to see. This is how crime leads to crime.' Ada tries to get near Ivo to plead for Luca, but is always pushed back.

'Enemy Brothers' (Fourth Ballad). The pianola accompaniment gives it the feel of a blues song, while the text enumerates typical operatic stuff, such as enemy brothers and tyrannical fathers, instruments of revenge and jealousy, contrary sighs and tender griefs, ending, 'in every catalogue, however, there is always a hidden story'. The procession disappears. Leonora and Ada enter in a close embrace.

The Cry. Leonora and Ada share their grief, which is like 'a cry in the night'.

'Let the Song Make' (Fifth Ballad). Someone passes by, singing in the dusk, accompanied by a violinist and an accordion player. Her haunting song relates closely to the previous scene.

The Prison. Luca moves through despair, the feeling that living is no different from dying, to an awareness that outside there is change: hearing 'the roar of a crowd which will not disperse' and a song, he recovers his sense of meaning.

Third Festa. The crowd which was a passive participant in others' schemes now intervenes. It protests violently but, assaulted by the police, it disperses, leaving many dead on the ground. The singing takes on the character of wailing.

'Evening Comes Down' (Sixth Ballad). The battle-field seems to have become a vast cemetery. A woman passes through the bodies.

The Sacrifice. Luca is brought out in handcuffs; Ivo heads the execution squad. Ada and Leonora are among the crowd who watch the shooting. The ensemble is one of the highpoints of the opera.

Fourth Festa. In the crowd's last outburst the chorus accept that 'We advance, we fall, even one feast day we'll know defeat; waiting begins again; the festa was and will be at the end of ills.'

Memory. Ada looks forward to the possibility, after centuries, that evil may cancel itself out.

Act II. Berio himself said that while Act I was horizontal in structure, Act II is vertical. Act II's radical reworking of Act I's words and music is reminiscent of Berg's *Lulu*, but there are differences, too. In a sense, Berio here redresses the fundamental balance between words and music. There is literal meaning (more exploration of what the *festa* means) and narrative action, but the overall emphasis has shifted, from the stage to the pit. While the chorus is kept offstage, Berio uses a virtuoso Vocal Group who fragment single lines and even words from Act I and create extraordinary and memorable sound patterns.

Scene i. Two Passers-By try to get into a building, while they stress that everything is contained in a *festa*. One of them gets in, the other is surrounded by the police. He is dragged inside.

Scene ii. Passer-By III, a soprano, recycles Luca's scene in prison, dislocating words to an elaborate effect. Passerby I is seen to be interrogated, beaten up and eventually thrown out of the window.

Scene iii (*Encore*). Gendarmes carry away the lifeless body of Passer-By I. There are cries (one evoking Tosca's words to Scarpia): 'I want to see him! Let's run away! Everyone's killing everyone!'

Scene iv (*Pas de quoi*). Picturesque movement on the street. An accordion player at her side, a reciter of poetry (Passer-By IV) addresses the crowd, recycling the words of Ada's scene and the First Ballad. She duets with her own, recorded voice. A man abducts a child, recreating the primal scene of Act I.

Tango. During the playfully sinister tango, which owes something to Weill, but rather more in its acerbic flavour to Berg's dances in *Wozzeck*, the man disappears briefly into the crowd and reappears without the baby.

Scene v (*Rondo*). The crowd experiences terror; the street gradually becomes the arena for guerrilla warfare. Fragments of text from Act I are treated to more intricate reworkings. The words at one point refer to Luca's experience of dislocation in prison, as though the music can resolve his dilemma.

Scene vi opens with a piano duet. Phrases from Act I's duel are recited mechanically by three voices from the crowd. The Priest returns, in a blowsy jazz-inflected passage. The building at the back explodes with lights and violence.

Scene vii. A magnificent concerto or duel for alto saxophone and wind (predominantly clarinet) is heard as the Vocal Group intone fragments from the prison scene, moving from despair to Luca's vision of hope outside the walls.

Scene viii. All the soloists join a huge ensemble, sparsely accompanied by harp and bells. They call for resistance and allow for defeat.

Scene ix. Ada ends the opera, as she ended Act I, contemplating a future in which, perhaps, evil may have ended.

La vera storia uses the Brechtian device of ballad-singers to comment on the action, and to relay the meaning of selected moments in directly accessible form. Another level of meaning is opera itself: the 'story' of the title is fiction as well as fact. The references to *Il trovatore* are symptomatic of a more general operatic content. Most of the scenes have titles, as they do in early nineteenth-century opera.

Calvino's poetry can be explicit in protestation but more often prefers the oblique. For all the score's complexity Berio aims at full-blooded theatrical impact: his favourite score marking is 'intensely'; the crucial endings to both acts could not be more powerful. Ada exhorts us to remember. If there is compensation for so much suffering, it may come in the distant future. Perhaps, 'forsè', is the keyword, as the poet and musician construct something on which to rejoice. *La vera storia* culminates in Ada's moving recapitulation of her Act I lament and what could be more operatic than that?   P.

UN RE IN ASCOLTO
A King Listens

Azione musicale in two parts, texts by Italo Calvino, including material by Friedrich Wilhelm Gotter and W.H. Auden. Première, in German, Salzburg, 7 August 1984, with Theo Adam as Prospero, Heinz Zednik as the Director and Patricia Wise as the Protagonist, conducted by Lorin Maazel. Same production performed at Vienna State Opera, 1984, and at la Scala, Milan, 1986, with Victor Braun as Prospero. Revived Düsseldorf, 25 May 1988. U.K. première, Covent Garden, London, 1989, with Donald McIntyre as Prospero, Robert Tear as the Director, Graham Valentine as Venerdì, Kathryn Harries as the Protagonist, conducted by the composer. U.S. première, Chicago, 1996, conducted by Dennis Russell Davies.

Prospero..Bass-Baritone

Director ....Tenor

Venerdi (Friday).................................Actor
Protagonist......................................Soprano
Soprano I (with her Pianist)
Soprano II
Mezzo-Soprano
Three Singers...........................Tenor, Baritone, Bass
Nurse...Soprano
Wife.......................................Mezzo-Soprano
Doctor...Tenor
Lawyer..Bass
Pianist, *who sings*

Accordion-Player, Mime, Messenger, Designer,
    Assistants, Tailor, Circus Performers etc.

Running Time: 1 hour 30 minutes

In calling *Un re in ascolto* an *azione musicale* Berio
alludes to *Tristan und Isolde*, which Wagner calls a
Handlung or 'action'. Like Wagner, Berio explores
music's capacity for action independent of the drama,
so that it is 'the musical processes that are primarily
responsible for the narration'. According to Berio
himself, Italo Calvino 'wrote some very beautiful fragments describing the inner thoughts of a grand old
man of the theatre as he lies dying'. Berio then fragmented them further: the political strand has been
diminished while the thread of artistic endeavour
emerges strongly – Berio highlights the action of *listening*, in terms of its import for music, rather than as an
element in the plot (which it was for Calvino). Trying to
track any one strand too closely misses the point,
which is to accept the continuum of 'acoustic material'
(the composer's phrase for music) and the accidental,
incidental meanings it throws up. Berio warns us that
'when your "theatrical consumer" hears opera he feels
a Pavlovian need for linear, finalised stories that will
provoke tension in relation to the outcome rather than,
as Brecht said, to the way things are.'

Part I, *Aria I*. In his room at the side of the stage,
Prospero remembers his dream of 'another theatre ...
where an "I" whom I do not know, sings ... the music
that I do not remember and that I now would like to
sing'. Berio highlights the word 'sing' ('canta'), which
is so important for the opera as a whole, asking it to be
sung as though 'from extremely far away and flexibly,
with a different voice'. The rest of the stage reveals a
rehearsal in progress.

Duet I. The Director takes Venerdi (i.e. Man
Friday, a version of Caliban) through his 'aria',

preparing the audience for a circus act. Meanwhile,
the stage exhibits 'a kaleidoscope of actions'.

Concertato I. A Pianist and Venerdi rehearse and
rework the same text; Three Singers envisage an
idyll 'protected from the tempest'. While the Director
shows the Chorus their moves, they sing of an
ominous storm to come.

Audition I. A Soprano auditions with an aria that
is a farewell to Prospero. It ends with the first of the
many 'addio's that punctuate the work. They epitomise one sort of opera and highlight a valedictory
note in this *azione*.

Duet II. The Director discusses the plot with
Prospero. Their conversation hints at a plot, a king
frightened of conspiracy, who confides only in his
ugly servant, and experiences rebellion or a tempest.

Concertato II with performers. Prospero watches as
the rehearsal continues to recycle fragments of text
that has been heard already. The Director, Three
Singers and Chorus intone Prospero's farewell speech
from *The Tempest* in a magnificent threnody. One
phrase, 'Ecco la vera storia: è finita la festa' (This is the
true story, the festa is over), refers to Berio's previous
opera and points to the important but elusive autobiographical level in this work.

Serenata. Venerdi repeats fragments from his duet
scene. Prospero returns to his room.

Aria II. Prospero listens to the sounds that reach
him from the harbour and the theatre, where
another audition takes place.

Audition II. The Mezzo-Soprano sings of evening at
sea and insists that her compass ('bussola') is hers,
the first of the auditioning singers to claim some
property or quality as her own.

Duet III. The Mime and Venerdi parody the scene
between Prospero and the Director. Venerdi ends,
'You imagined.'

Aria III. Prospero hears 'a voice hidden among
voices' that intimates his death. The act ends on a
theatrical high note: he admits, 'I am afraid', then
attempts to destroy the set and collapses.

Part II, *Duet IV*. As the cast gather round him,
Prospero contemplates death. In a highly charged
ensemble, Prospero's wife and the cast comment on
his changed appearance, and singers and orchestra
go into spasm, as though enacting a heart attack.
The Chorus sing his farewell to theatre.

Air for orchestra alone, an emotive, highly con-

Un re in ascolto *(Covent Garden, 1989, director Graham Vick, designer Chris Dyer)*. *Donald McIntyre as Prospero, Robert Tear as the Director.*

densed passage of some twenty-seven bars, as Prospero sits enthroned in the middle of the stage. Another Soprano comes for an audition.

Audition III. The Soprano sings of evening at sea. She is taken away by armed men, 'as though she were a guilty queen'.

Aria IV. Prospero contemplates his kingdom of music. The Protagonist arrives.

Aria V. The Protagonist asserts her independence (from any composer, from Prospero), claiming that her person, her will, her compass, her voice and her theatre are all her own. In some ways she represents the performer as heroine, rather in the mould of Cathy Berberian, the extraordinary singer whom Berio married and for whom he wrote some of his greatest works. The marriage was dissolved in 1964 and she died in 1983. Perhaps the Protagonist can

be read as his tribute to her memory.

Concertato IV. The people surrounding Prospero react as a crowd (that vital element in *La vera storia*), first exploding with excitement, then calming down. They take off their costumes, bid farewell to Prospero and leave the stage.

Aria VI. Accompanied by the Chorus Prospero sings of a voice hidden among voices, hidden in silence, chasing memory and imagining the future, before he dies.

Un re in ascolto invites interpretation but it also supplies, almost against its will, a highly charged evening in the theatre. One fruitful way to approach it is to see it as a reflection on the complex nature of opera itself, the encounter (conflict or collaboration) between words, music, singers, production, chorus, stage, theatre and drama.   P.

HECTOR BERLIOZ
(born 11 December 1803, died 8 March 1869)

BENVENUTO CELLINI

Opera in three acts, words by de Wailly and Barbier. Première Opéra, Paris,[1] 10 September 1838, with Dorus-Gras, Stolz, Duprez, Derivis; there were twenty-nine rehearsals, four complete performances. First performed London, Covent Garden, 1853, under Berlioz's own direction, with Julienne, Tamberlik, Tagliafico (in Italian); by Liszt, at Weimar, 1852; by von Bülow, Hanover, 1879. Revived Vienna, 1911; Théâtre des Champs-Elysées, Paris, 1912, conducted by Weingartner; Glasgow, 1939 (in English); Carl Rosa in London, 1957, with Charles Craig, conductor Arthur Hammond; Amsterdam, 1961, with Gedda, conductor Prêtre; London, Covent Garden, 1966, with Elizabeth Vaughan, Minton, Gedda, conductor Pritchard; San Carlo, Naples (Italian première), 1967; la Scala, Milan, 1976, by Covent Garden company with Nicolai Gedda, conductor Colin Davis.

Cardinal Salviati[2]	Bass
Balducci, *Papal treasurer*	Bass
Teresa, *his daughter*	Soprano
Benvenuto Cellini, *a goldsmith*	Tenor
Ascanio, *his apprentice*	Mezzo-Soprano
Francesco ⎫ *artisans in Cellini's workshop*	...Tenor
Bernardino ⎭	.....Bass
Fieramosca, *sculptor to the Pope*	Baritone
Pompeo, *a bravo*	Baritone

Place: Rome
Time: 1532
Running Time: 2 hours 40 minutes

Berlioz's pull towards opera, foreshadowed, it is easy to see, in earlier concert works, did not reach fruition until in his mid-thirties *Benvenuto Cellini*, which had been conceived as an *opéra-comique*, and turned down at the eponymous theatre, was staged with little success at the Opéra. It was too difficult for audience and performers alike. Liszt admired it and chose it, after *Lohengrin*, as the second opera in his term as Kapellmeister in Weimar, but this was in a reduced version. In the later twentieth century, a return to the full version, with spoken dia-

logue and Pope rather than Cardinal, has tended to be the norm.

The overture, which makes use of material from the opera, is one of Berlioz's best-known.

Act I. The carnival of 1532. Shrove Monday. We are in the house of the Papal treasurer, Balducci, who scolds his daughter Teresa for having looked out of the window. The old man is vexed, because the Pope has summoned the Florentine goldsmith Cellini to Rome.

Teresa, however, is delighted. For she has found a note from Cellini in a bouquet that was thrown to her from the street by a mask – Cellini, of course. She sings of her delight in an attractive *cavatina*, followed by an *allegro con fuoco*. A few moments later Cellini appears at her side. There is a broad, *andante* tune for them both to sing (it is later used for the *Carnaval Romain* overture). Cellini proposes a plan of elopement. In the morning, during the carnival mask, he will wear a white monk's hood, his apprentice Ascanio a brown one. She will join them and they will flee together. But a listener has sneaked in – Fieramosca, the Pope's sculptor and no less Cellini's rival in love than in art. He overhears the plot and also the slighting remarks made about him by Teresa and Cellini. Unexpectedly, too, Balducci comes back. His daughter still up? In her anxiety to find an excuse, she says she heard a man sneak in. During the search Cellini disappears, and Fieramosca is apprehended. Before he can explain, women neighbours, who have hurried in, drag him off to the public bath house and treat him to a ducking.

Act II. In the courtyard of a tavern Cellini is seated with his assistants. In a romance, he sings that he is happy in his love, for he places it even higher than fame, which alone hitherto he has courted. He must pledge his love in wine. Unfortunately the host will no longer give him credit. Ascanio brings some money from the Papal treasurer, but in return Cellini must promise to complete

---

[1] The importance of a Paris production dominated French operatic history until late in the nineteenth century, and Berlioz, much as he despised the standards of the Opéra, moved heaven though not invariably earth in his efforts to get his work performed there.

[2] The part of Cardinal Salviati was originally allotted by Berlioz to Pope Clement VII. The Paris censorship forbade the representation of a Pope on the stage; but the ascription was restored in the Covent Garden production of 1966.

his *Perseus* by morning. He promises, although the avaricious Balducci has profited by his necessity and has sent too little money. Ascanio is informed by Cellini of the disguises they are to wear at the carnival, and of his plan that Teresa shall flee with him. Again Fieramosca has been spying and overhears the plot. Accordingly he hires the bravo Pompeo to assist him in carrying off Teresa.

A change of scene shows the crowd of maskers on the Piazza di Colonna. It is carnival time and the music is a brilliant representation of the gaiety and spirit of the scene. Balducci walks by with Teresa and together they see the play in which, in revenge for his niggardly payment to them, Cellini and his friends have arranged that the snoring Midas shall look like Balducci. Cellini takes advantage of the confusion caused by Balducci's protests to approach Teresa with Ascanio. At the same time, from the other side come two more monks, also in the disguise she and her lover agreed upon. Which is the right couple? Soon the two couples fall upon each other. A scream, and one of the brown-hooded monks (Pompeo) falls mortally wounded to the ground. A white-hooded monk (Cellini) has stabbed him. The crowd hurls itself upon Cellini. At that moment the boom of a cannon gives notice that the carnival celebration is over. Cellini escapes, and in his place the other white-hooded monk, Fieramosca, is seized.

Act III. Before Cellini's house, in the background of which, through a curtain, is seen the foundry, the anxious Teresa is assured by Ascanio that her lover is safe. Soon he arrives in person to describe his escape. With his white habit he was able to join a procession of monks similarly garbed and so make his way home. While Ascanio prepares for their flight, the beautiful line of the duet Cellini and Teresa sing together makes this one of the most attractive episodes of the score.

Balducci and Fieramosca enter precipitately. Balducci wants to force his daughter to become Fieramosca's bride. The scene is interrupted by the arrival of Cardinal Salviati (or the Pope) to see the completed *Perseus*. Cellini's predicament seems dire. Accused of murder and the attempted kidnapping of a girl, the *Perseus* unfinished, the money received for it spent! Heavy punishment waits, and another will receive the commission to finish the *Perseus*.

The artist flies into a passion. Another finish his masterpiece! Never! The casting shall be done on the spot! He is left alone and sings a beautiful 6/8 *andante* aria. Then the casting begins. Not metal enough? He seizes his completed works and throws them into the molten mass. Eventually, the master shatters the mould. The *Perseus* in all its glory appears before the eyes of the astonished onlookers – a potent plea for the inspired master. Once more have Art and her faithful servant triumphed over all rivals.   K., H.

LA DAMNATION DE FAUST
The Damnation of Faust

In its original form a 'dramatic legend' in four parts for the concert stage, words, after Gérard de Nerval's version of Goethe's play, by Berlioz, Gérard and Gandonnière. Produced as a concert piece at the Opéra-Comique, Paris, 6 December 1846; London, two parts of the work, under Berlioz's direction, Drury Lane, 7 February 1848; first complete performance in England, Free Trade Hall, Manchester, 5 February 1880; New York, 12 February 1880, by Dr Leopold Damrosch. Adapted for the operatic stage by Raoul Gunsbourg, and produced by him at Monte Carlo, 18 February 1893, with Jean de Reszke as Faust; Liverpool, 1894. Revived Monte Carlo, March 1902, with Melba, Jean de Reszke, and Maurice Renaud. Given in Paris with Calvé, Alvarez and Renaud, to celebrate the centenary of Berlioz's birth, 11 December 1903. New York, Metropolitan, 1906, with Farrar, Rousselière, Plançon. Revived la Scala, Milan, 1929, with Cobelli, Merli, Galeffi, conductor de Sabata; Paris Opéra (in Béjart's production), 1964; Sadler's Wells, 1969, with Curphey (later Janet Baker), Alberto Remedios, Herincx, conductor Charles Mackerras.

Marguerite..Soprano

Faust...Tenor

Méphistophélès...Bass

Brander...Bass

Students, Soldiers, Citizens, Men and Women, Fairies
Running Time: 2 hours 15 minutes

Part I. In the first part of Berlioz's dramatic legend Faust is supposed to be on the plains of Hungary. Introspectively he sings of nature and solitude. There are a chorus and dance of peasants and a recitative. Soldiers march past to the stirring measures of the *Rákóczi March*. This splendid march Berlioz orchestrated in Vienna, during his tour of 1845, and conducted at a concert in Pest, when it created the greatest enthusiasm. It was in order to justify the interpolation of this march that he laid the first scene of his dramatic legend on the plains of Hungary.

The next part only required a stage setting to make it operatic. Faust is in his study, lamenting his joyless existence. He is about to quaff poison, when the walls part and disclose a church interior. The congregation, kneeling, sings the Easter canticle, 'Christ is Risen', and Faust is comforted by their singing. Méphistophélès appears and offers to show Faust all that his soul can desire. The two start off together to sample what joy and pleasure can be had on earth.

Auerbach's cellar, Leipzig. Revel of students and soldiers. Brander sings the 'Song of the Rat', whose death is mockingly grieved over in a 'Requiescat in pace' and a fugue on the word 'Amen', sung by the roistering crowd. Méphistophélès follows this up with the 'Song of the Flea'.

Part II. Faust is supposed to be asleep on the banks of the Elbe. Méphistophélès sings the beautiful 'Voici des roses', after which comes the most exquisite effect of the score, the 'Dance of the Sylphs', a masterpiece of delicate and airy illustration. Violoncellos, *con sordini*, hold a single note as a pedal point, over which is woven a gossamer fabric of melody and harmony, ending with the faintest *pianissimo* from drum and harps. Gunsbourg employed here, with admirable results, the aerial ballet, and gave a rich and beautiful setting to the scene, including a vision of Marguerite. The ballet is followed by a chorus of soldiers and a students' song.

Part III. The scenic directions of Gounod's *Faust* call Marguerite's house – so much of it as is projected into the garden scene – a pavilion. Gunsbourg made it more like an arbour, into which the audience could see through the elimination of a supposedly existing wall, the same as in Sparafucile's house in the last act of *Rigoletto*. Soldiers and students are strolling and singing in the street. Faust sings 'Merci doux crépuscule', and rejoices to be in Marguerite's room. He hides, Marguerite comes in and sings the ballad of the King of Thule. Berlioz's setting of the song is primitive, and he aptly characterises the number as a *Chanson Gothique*. It is a marvellously effective re-creation of the medieval spirit. The Invocation of Méphistophélès is followed by the 'Minuet of Will-o'-the-Wisps'; then comes Méphistophélès's serenade, 'Devant la maison', a brilliant, elusive piece of mockery (*Allegro* in *tempo di valse*).

Faust enters Marguerite's house. There is a love duet, 'Ange adorable', which becomes a trio when Méphistophélès joins the lovers and urges Faust's departure.

Part IV. Marguerite is alone. Berlioz, instead of using Goethe's song, 'Meine Ruh ist hin' (My peace is gone), substitutes a poem of his own. Introduced by the sad strains of the cor anglais, the unhappy Marguerite sings 'D'Amour, l'ardente flamme', an aria of extraordinary beauty. The singing of the students and the soldiers grows fainter. The 'retreat' – the call to which the flag is lowered at sunset – is sounded by the drums and trumpets. Marguerite, overcome by remorse, swoons at the window.

A mountain gorge. The scene begins with Faust's soliloquy, 'Nature, immense, impénétrable et fière', an invocation to nature that is enormously impressive. There follows the *Ride to the Abyss*; moving panorama; pandemonium; redemption of Marguerite, whom angels are seen welcoming in the softly illumined heavens, far above the town in which the action is supposed to have transpired.

The production by Damrosch in its original concert form in New York was one of the sensational events in the concert history of America. As an opera, however, the work has failed outside France to make the impression that might have been expected from its effects on concert audiences. K.

LES TROYENS
The Trojans

Opera in five acts, text by the composer after Vergil. The work was not produced in its entirety until twenty-one years after the composer's death. Part II was first performed at the Théâtre-Lyrique, Paris, 4 November 1863, with Charton-Demeur as Dido and Monjauze as Aeneas. Between that date and 20 December 1863, there were twenty-one performances of the opera, which was then dropped. The entire work was given at Karlsruhe on 5 and 6 December 1890 in a German version conducted by Mottl (Part I thus had its world première on 5 December 1890). Concert performances in U.S.: Part I, New York, 1877; Part II, 1887. Part I was first performed in French at Nice, 1891; in Paris, Opéra, 1899, with Delna, Lucas, Renaud, conducted by Taffanel. Part II was revived Opéra, Paris, 1892, with Delna, Laffarge; first performed Liverpool (in concert), 1897; first performed in Italy, Naples, 1951, with Cavelti, Tygesen, conductor Cluytens. Both parts on the same evening (i.e. *Les Troyens* as Berlioz conceived it) were performed in Cologne, 1898 (in German); Stuttgart, 1913 (arr. Schillings); Opéra, Paris, 1921 (in a reduced version); revived there 1939, with Anduran, Ferrer, de Trévi,[1] Singher; 1961, with Crespin, Chauvet, Massard. First performed Berlin, 1930 (in four acts), with Leider, Roswaenge, conductor Blech; Glasgow, 1935 (English translation by E.J. Dent), conductor Erik Chisholm; Oxford (reduced version), 1950, with Arda Mandikian and John Kentish, conductor Westrup; Covent Garden (virtually complete, in English), 1957, with Thebom, Shuard, Vickers, conductor Kubelík; la Scala (extensively cut), 1960, with Simionato, del Monaco, conductor Kubelík; Buenos Aires, 1964, with Crespin (as Cassandra and Dido), Chauvet; Scottish Opera, 1969, with Janet Baker, Ronald Dowd, conductor Gibson (uncut, in English); 1983, Metropolitan, New York, with Jessye Norman, Troyanos, Domingo, conductor Levine.

PART I: *La Prise de Troie* (The Fall of Troy)

Cassandre (Cassandra), *a Trojan prophetess* ...Soprano

Ascagne (Ascanius), *son of Enée* ....Soprano

Hécube (Hecuba), *wife of Priam* ....Mezzo-Soprano

Polyxène (Polyxenes), *daughter of Priam* ....Soprano

Enée (Aeneas), *a Trojan hero* ....Tenor

Chorèbe (Choroebus), *fiancé of Cassandre* ......Baritone

Panthée (Pantheus), *a Trojan priest*......................Bass

Ghost of Hector ....Bass

Priam, *King of Troy*..Bass

A Trojan Soldier ....Baritone

A Greek Captain..Bass

Helenus, *son of Priam*...Tenor

Andromaque (Andromache), *widow of Hector*...Mime

Astyanax, *her son*...Mime

Soldiers of Greece and Troy, Citizens, Women, Children

PART II: *Les Troyens à Carthage* (The Trojans at Carthage)

Didon (Dido), *Queen of Carthage* ....Mezzo-Soprano

Anna, *her sister*..Contralto

Ascagne...Soprano

Enée...Tenor

Iopas, *a Carthaginian poet*...................................Tenor

Hylas, *a young Phrygian sailor*............................Tenor

Narbal, *Didon's minister* ....Bass

Panthée..Bass

Two Soldiers...Baritone, Bass

Two Trojan Captains............................Baritone, Bass

The Ghost of Cassandre ....Mezzo-Soprano

The Ghost of Chorèbe ....Baritone

The Ghost of Hector ....Bass

The Ghost of Priam ....Bass

The God Mercure (Mercury) ....Bass

Trojan Captains, Courtiers, Hunters, Carthaginians, Invisible Ghosts, Workmen, Sailors, Labourers, Naiads, Fauns, Satyrs, Wood Nymphs

Place: Troy; Carthage
Time: Twelfth (or Thirteenth) Century B.C.
Running Time: 4 hours; see below

*L*es Troyens is Berlioz's greatest opera, and in many respects his greatest achievement. In it he unites his yearning for the classicism of Gluck, for design and form, with his own passion for what is expressive and vivid. The work is on the grandest scale, and Berlioz himself noted the timings which the five acts would require: Act I, 52 minutes; Act II, 22 minutes; Act III, 40 minutes; Act IV, 47 minutes; Act V, 45 minutes – a total of 206 minutes.[2] With four intervals, each lasting a quarter of an hour (*if* the elaborate sets did not require more), the performance would thus take four hours and twenty-six minutes, he calculated. But he was fated never to hear his opera in the form in which he conceived it; when it was performed at the Théâtre-Lyrique, the first two acts were removed, and only the second part – known in vocal scores, and in most performances for that matter, as *Les Troyens à Carthage* – was given.

Les Troyens was until the mid-twentieth century one of the neglected masterpieces of opera from the past waiting to be discovered. On this subject, Donald Grout, in his *A Short History of Opera* (O.U.P.), wrote: '... *Les Troyens* is the most important French opera of the nineteenth century, the masterpiece of one of France's greatest composers, the Latin counterpart of Wagner's Teutonic *Ring*; its strange fate is paralleled by nothing in the history of music unless it be the century-long neglect of Bach's *Passion according to St Matthew* ... in a country properly appreciative of its cultural monuments it would seem that *Les Troyens* ought to be produced regularly at state expense until singers, conductors and public are brought to realise

---

[1] Georges Thill, the maker of a famous record of the great tenor *scena*, sang Aeneas in a revival in 1930 at the Paris Opéra of Part II.

[2] But these timings are usually exceeded in performance. Scottish Opera's

had just over four hours of music, and the performance, with a dinner interval of one hour, lasted five hours 48 minutes. The acts were timed as 60 minutes; 25 minutes; 60 minutes; 45 minutes; 53 minutes.

its greatness. Of all the works of the French grand-opera school in the nineteenth century, this is the one most worthy of being so preserved.'

Berlioz's life-long enthusiasm for Vergil was second only to his love for Shakespeare; both contribute to the libretto of *Les Troyens*, the former to the narrative of the love of Dido for Aeneas as told in the first, second and fourth books of the *Aeneid*, the latter to the interpolation of the scene for Jessica and Lorenzo from *The Merchant of Venice*, which provides words for the great love duet between Didon and Enée in Act IV.

Les Troyens begins at the point in the Trojan war when the Trojans have lost Hector, the Greeks Achilles and Patroclus, and the Trojans have reason to believe that their enemies have had enough. The war has gone on for over nine years already, and the Greeks have retired, leaving behind them the wooden horse.

Part I, Act I. The scene is the abandoned camp of the Greeks on the wooded plain in front of Troy. On one side stands a throne, on the other an altar, at the back the tomb of Achilles, on which sit three shepherds playing the double-flute. The Trojans rejoice that their ten years of confinement are over. There is talk of the wooden horse, and all rush off to see this curiosity, everyone except Cassandre, who remains behind prophesying the doom of Troy ('Malheureux roi!'). Even Chorèbe, her lover, believes that her mind is deranged. He tries to console her, but she continues to predict the fall of the city and his death. She can't persuade him to leave Troy, and resigns herself to death on the morrow.

The character of Cassandre is splendidly depicted in the opening scene, Cassandre of whom Berlioz exclaimed when he finally gave up hope of hearing the first part of his opera: 'Ah, my noble Cassandre, my heroic virgin, I must needs resign myself to never hearing thee'. The classical feeling of the opening aria shows Berlioz's affinity with his beloved Gluck.

The second scene is set in front of the Citadel, again with an altar on one side, a throne on the other. The Trojans celebrate their deliverance from the Greeks with a procession and public games. The music is a great hymn of thanksgiving. Hector's widow and her son Astyanax, dressed in white clothes of mourning, place flowers at the foot of the altar, while Cassandre foretells for them an even greater sorrow than they have yet known.

The scene is broken in upon by the precipitate arrival of Enée who distractedly describes the terrible scene he has just witnessed on the seashore. The priest, Laocoön, suspecting some hidden design of the Greeks, threw a javelin into the side of the wooden horse, whereupon two serpents came up out of the sea and devoured him before the eyes of the Trojans. All assembled express their horror and fear at this phenomenon in a magnificent octet with chorus ('Châtiment effroyable'). Enée suggests that the disaster may have been brought upon them by Pallas, outraged at the insult to the horse, which has been dedicated to her. They should placate her by bringing the image within the walls and taking it to her temple. Cassandre alone remains behind as they leave to give effect to Enée's suggestion. The step they are taking will, she predicts, lead to disaster.

To the sound of a march, the horse is dragged inside the city walls (this is the 'Trojan March' sometimes heard in concerts).

In spite of the rumour that the sound of arms has been heard coming from inside the horse, the people persist in greeting its arrival with joy, and the sound of their song grows gradually in volume until it fills the whole city. Only Cassandre dissents from the rejoicing, but her suggestion that the horse should be destroyed forthwith meets with no favourable response from the crowd.

Act II. The first scene plays in Enée's palace. Enée's son, Ascagne, comes in, but seeing his father asleep, dare not wake him, and leaves the room. The ghost of Hector appears and marches slowly across

Les Troyens *(Welsh National Opera, 1987, director Tim Albery, designers Tom Cairns, Antony McDonald). The Trojans celebrate the Greeks' departure from the city.*

the room.[1] Enée wakes, greets the hero, and hears from him that Troy has fallen. He is instructed to take his son and the images of the gods and to take ship across the seas, there – in Italy – to found a new empire. Hector's speech is impressively set to a descending chromatic octave, each sentence delivered on one note, a semitone below the previous one. At its end, Panthée comes to Enée bringing the images of the Trojan gods. He tells Enée of the happenings in the centre of the town; in the middle of the night, the horse opened to disgorge a troop of well-armed Greek soldiers. Priam is dead, and the town sacked and on fire. Enée rushes off to lead his men into battle.

The second scene takes place in the Temple of Vesta, where the Trojan women are gathered together, lamenting the fall of Troy. To them comes Cassandre, announcing the escape of Enée. For herself nothing remains, she says, since Chorèbe is dead. She urges the women to take their own lives rather than fall as slaves into the hands of the Greeks, and drives out the few who are unwilling to choose death rather than dishonour, herself staying as leader of those who are resolved to die. The tension mounts, some Greeks come in and demand to know where the treasure is hidden. Cassandre answers by stabbing herself. Some of the women throw themselves from the gallery of the temple, and as they die all cry 'Italie!'

Part II. The rest of the opera takes place in Carthage. When it was decided to give the second part alone, Berlioz composed a prelude to it, which is now printed in the vocal scores (although not in the one Berlioz prepared). At the first performance he made up his mind that it was crucial for the audience to know the events that should have taken place in the first half; he therefore had the story recited by a speaker in Greek costume, and followed this with a performance of the Trojan march together with the chorus which accompanies the entrance of the wooden horse within the walls of Troy.

Act III. An amphitheatre in the garden of Didon's palace at Carthage. A festival is taking place to cele-

---

[1] Patrick J. Smith in *The Tenth Muse* points out that this strikingly dramatic scene is a descendant of the *ombra* scene of seventeenth-century operas, itself often allied to the slumber scene (*cf.* the play in *Hamlet*).

brate the progress which has been made in building the city. Didon herself is greeted with a rapturous chorus, 'Gloire à Didon', when she takes her place on the throne. In a majestic aria ('Chers Tyriens'), she speaks of the work required to raise the city from nothing, and of what still remains to be done. The people for their part swear to protect her and her kingdom against Iarbas, who has demanded her hand in marriage and is invading their territory.

A harvest festival of a kind now takes place. Each section of national life files past the Queen, and is rewarded for its industry. Singing 'Gloire à Didon', the people march out, leaving Didon alone with her sister, Anna. In the conversation which ensues, it is made clear that Anna thinks Didon is badly in need of a husband (she is a widow), and that Carthage needs a king just as much. Didon thinks sadly of her dead husband, and Anna does not press the point, which she feels is already gained.

Iopas comes in to tell the Queen that a foreign fleet has anchored in their harbour, driven apparently by the recent storm, and the leaders are asking to see the Queen. She gives orders that she will receive them. The Trojan march is heard (this time in the minor), and the survivors are led in by Ascagne, Enée having assumed a disguise and allowing his son to speak for the whole company. Didon welcomes them, and says that Enée, the noble warrior and friend of the great Hector, cannot be anything but an honoured guest at her court. At that moment, Narbal enters in great perturbation; Iarbas at the head of a horde of Numidian troops is even now threatening Carthage itself. Instantly Enée proclaims himself leader of the Trojans and offers his services and theirs to help repel the Queen's enemies. His offer is accepted, and at the head of the army he marches out to fight the invader, leaving his son in Didon's hands.

In Berlioz's original plan, the third act ended with the great symphonic intermezzo, the *Chasse royale et orage* (Royal Hunt and Storm). In modern scores this appears at the end of the following act, where it is perhaps less happily placed.

The scene is a virgin forest near Carthage. The sound of the hunt can be heard in the distance; naiads listen anxiously, then disappear. There are signs that a storm is approaching. Ascagne is seen, and after him

come Didon and Enée, the former dressed as Diana, the latter as a warrior, and both take shelter. Fauns and satyrs dance, and cries of 'Italie!' are heard. The storm dies down, and gradually peace returns. Ernest Newman[1] has described this scene as 'the finest and most sustained piece of nature painting in all music; it is like some noble landscape of Claude come to life in sound'. Later on he adds: 'The reader who knows his Vergil will not make the mistake, however, of seeing in the *Royal Hunt and Storm* only a piece of nature painting in music. He will listen imaginatively to it, as Berlioz certainly intended him to do, as the passionate climax to the realisation by Dido and Aeneas of their love for each other.'

Act IV. Didon's gardens, by the sea. Everything is decorated to celebrate Enée's victorious return. Narbal confides to Anna his fear that Enée's coming will not be for Carthage's or for Didon's good. Already she neglects affairs of state. Anna asks him if he cannot see that Didon is in love with her guest; where else could Carthage find a better king?

To an orchestral reminiscence of the crowd's greeting early in the previous act, Didon comes in with her royal guest. A ballet is danced for their entertainment. At its end, Didon asks Iopas to sing; he does so, charmingly, to the accompaniment of a harp and various instruments ('O blonde Cerès'). But Didon can find no pleasure in anything that diverts her attention from Enée. She asks him to continue his recital of the fate of Troy. What happened to Andromaque, she asks. Though at first determined to die, in the end she submitted to love's urgings and married her captor Pyrrhus. 'O pudeur', sings Didon, 'Tout conspire à vaincre mes remords' (All conspires to vanquish my remorse).[2]

Ascagne removes her ring, and Anna comments on his likeness to Cupid. Enée's voice has already been heard, but now Iopas and Narbal add theirs to make up the quintet. It is one of the loveliest moments in the score, and the ensemble is built up like one of Verdi's on the individual reactions to the now apparent love of Didon for Enée. It is followed by a septet (Didon, Enée, Anna, Ascagne, Iopas, Narbal, Panthée, and the chorus) which is no less beautiful.

Everyone leaves the scene except Didon and Enée, who are alone in the garden ('Nuit d'ivresse et d'ex-

[1] In *Opera Nights*: Putnam.

[2] Translations by Edward Dent.

tase infinie'). It is the beginning of the incomparable Shakespearean love duet, one of the finest in all opera: 'Par une telle nuit' (In such a night as this). Idea succeeds idea, and a reference to their own names brings the duet to an idyllic close. They go off with Didon leaning on Enée's shoulder, just as a shaft of moonlight reveals a statue of the god Mercure which comes to life and reiterates the knell of their hopes: 'Italie!'

Act V. The harbour at night. The Trojan ships are lying at anchor, and a young sailor, Hylas, sings sadly of his homeland ('Vallon sonore'). Panthée and the Trojan chiefs direct that preparations be made for the fleet's departure, which is only delayed because of Enée's love for Didon; every moment wasted is likely to bring down the anger of the gods – even now the disembodied cry of 'Italie' can be heard again. Two soldiers on sentry duty have little use for what they undoubtedly think of as the high-falutin' talk about 'Italie'. They are perfectly content in Carthage, where the food and the women are entirely to their liking. This new voyage is likely to lead to nothing but inconvenience for them – but they break off as they see Enée coming towards them.

Enée is torn between his overwhelming love for Didon, to whom he has broken the news that he must leave, and his sense of duty and of destiny: 'Inutiles regrets. Je dois quitter Carthage' (There is no turning back; this land I must relinquish). But he thinks longingly of Didon, and cannot bear the thought of their farewell: 'Ah, quand viendra l'instant des suprêmes adieux?' His initial agitation returns: 'En un dernier naufrage'. Once again he hears the voices, and now sees the spectre of King Priam, followed by those of Chorèbe, Cassandre and Hector, each in turn ordering him to follow his destiny. His mind is made up and he orders the Trojans to their boats: 'Debout, Troyens' (Awake, awake, Trojans awake), ending with a sad, slow farewell to the absent Didon. The *scena* is one of the most magnificent in the tenor repertory.

Didon has followed Enée, and a short scene takes place between them, Didon reproaching, weeping, begging him to stay, Enée almost prepared to give way until the sound of the Trojan march is heard in the distance. Then, with a cry of 'Italie', Enée rushes on to one of his vessels.

The second scene takes place in Didon's palace.

Didon tries to persuade her sister Anna to go to the harbour to intercede for her. Anna says Enée's departure had become inevitable, if the gods were to be obeyed; but she maintains that, in spite of the gods, he still loves her. Didon says this is impossible; *her* love would compel her to disobey Jupiter himself. When Iopas describes the ships putting out to sea, Didon bursts out in fury, ordering the Carthaginians to pursue and destroy the traitorous Trojans. She herself has done wrong by not from the start treating the Trojans as they have finished by treating her. Why did she not serve up the body of Ascagne to Enée at a feast? One thing only is left her: to raise an awful pyre to the god of the underworld, and on it burn everything that was ever connected with the traitorous Enée.

Anna and Narbal leave her, and Didon's grief overflows; she tears her hair and beats her breast in her anguish: 'Ah, je vais mourir'. Perhaps from his ship Enée will catch sight of the flames which will signal her terrible end. She bids farewell to the great city.

The last scene takes place on a terrace overlooking the sea. A funeral pyre is presided over by priests of Pluto. Didon, preceded by Anna and Narbal, comes slowly in. Anna and Narbal solemnly curse the Trojans, after which Didon prepares to mount the steps of the pyre. She looks sadly at Enée's accoutrements on it; then, taking his sword, stands with it while she prophesies that her people will one day produce a warrior to avenge on his descendants the shame now brought by Enée. Then she plunges the sword into her breast, reviving only long enough to communicate her further vision, in which she sees Rome triumphant. She dies as the Carthaginians hurl further curses at the Trojans. But the Trojan March contradicts them, and a vision of the eternal Rome rises behind Didon's pyre.   H.

BÉATRICE ET BÉNÉDICT

Opera in two acts, words by the composer, after Shakespeare's *Much Ado about Nothing*. Produced at Baden-Baden, 9 August 1862, with Charton-Demeur, Monrose, Montaubry. First performed Weimar, 1863; Karlsruhe, 1888, conducted by Mottl; Vienna, 1890; Opéra-Comique, Paris, 1890; Glasgow (in English), 1936; Opéra-Comique, Paris, 1966; Cambridge, 1967, with Anne Howells, Kenneth Bowen, conductor David Atherton; Buxton Festival, 1981, with Ann Murray, Philip Langridge; Opera North, Leeds, 1983, with Claire Powell, John Brecknock.

Don Pedro, *a general* ....Bass
Léonato, *governor of Messina* ....Actor
Héro, *his daughter* ....Soprano
Béatrice, *his niece* ....Mezzo-Soprano
Claudio, *an officer* ....Baritone
Bénédict, *an officer* ....Tenor
Ursula, *Hero's companion* ....Contralto
Somarone, *orchestral conductor* ....Bass

Place: Messina, Sicily
Running Time: 1 hour 25 minutes

Berlioz envisaged an opera on the subject of *Much Ado about Nothing* nearly thirty years before *Béatrice et Bénédict* in 1862 became the last major work from his pen. He had given regular concerts at Baden-Baden when he was commissioned to write an opera, and after the première he added the female trio and a chorus to the original score. He himself famously described the score as 'a caprice written with the point of a needle'.

The story is an adaptation of a shortened version of Shakespeare's play, which preserves the spirit of the comedy, but omits the saturnine intrigue of Don John against Claudio and Hero. The gist of the comedy is the gradual metamorphosis of the brilliant but captious Béatrice from pique and partially feigned indifference towards the witty and gallant Bénédict, to love. Both have tempers. In fact they reach an agreement to marry as a result of a spirited quarrel.

The overture, like that for *Benvenuto Cellini*, is made up of tunes used elsewhere in the opera. Thus the opening *allegretto scherzando* later accompanies the duet at the end of the opera, and the *andante* tune is Béatrice's 'Il m'en souvient'. The overture is a brilliant, lively piece of music, and it has become popular in the concert hall, where, probably, many of its admirers are entirely ignorant of the fact that it belongs to an opera.

Allegretto scherzando

Act I. The garden of Léonato, the governor of Messina. There is general rejoicing that the town is no longer in danger from the besieging army of Moors, which has finally been driven off. After some dialogue – this is an *opéra-comique*, with much of the action carried on in ordinary speech – the chorus starts to repeat its praises of the victorious general and his troops, much to Béatrice's dissatisfaction. There is a dance, a *Sicilienne* in 6/8 time, of charming individuality, and the stage empties.

Héro has a splendid aria in which she looks forward to seeing Claudio again. The lovely, calm tune of the opening *larghetto* section, 'Je vais le voir', is a fine example of that stylistic refinement and purity which is a feature of Berlioz's music, and the quick section, 'Il me revient fidèle', makes an exhilarating finish. Bénédict and Claudio arrive, and the skirmishing of the protagonists begins. 'Comment le dédain pourrait-il mourir?' (Is it possible disdain should die?), begins their duet, a true inspiration. It is followed by a trio for the three men, Bénédict, Claudio, and Don Pedro: 'Me marier? Dieu me pardonne' (Get married? God forgive me), a 3/8 *allegretto*, in which Bénédict makes furious answer when he is twitted on the subject of marriage. The trio is dominated by long musical sentences for Bénédict, upon which the others comment.

Berlioz introduces a non-Shakespearean character, Somarone, a *maître de chapelle*, who rehearses his chorus and orchestra in an *Epithalame grotesque*, a choral fugue on the subject of love. Gradually Bénédict is brought to realise that all is not well with his plans for perpetual bachelorhood. He sings a spirited *rondo*, 'Ah, je vais l'aimer'.

It is evening, and Héro and Ursula close the act with a slow duet – a Nocturne, 'Nuit paisible et sereine', 'a marvel of indescribable lyrical beauty in which Berlioz's feeling for nature is wonderfully expressed' (so says W.J. Turner). One has to turn to *Così fan tutte* to find idyllic writing for combined female voices of comparable beauty.

Act II opens with a version of the *Sicilienne* already heard. There is a dialogue between the servants, and Somarone starts up a drinking song, whose accompaniment is provided by guitars, trumpets, and tambourines (the guitar was the instrument on which Berlioz most enjoyed performing). The stage empties, and Béatrice comes in. Bénédict loves her; how to overcome her own increasing feeling for him? She has an aria on the grand scale, 'Il m'en souvient', whose tune has already been heard in the overture. The impressive *scena* finishes with an *allegro agitato*, 'Je l'aime donc?' (Do I love him, then?)

There is a flowing, 6/8 trio of outstanding lyricism

Béatrice et Bénédict (Welsh National Opera, 1994, director Elijah Moshinsky, set designer Michael Yeargan, costume designer Dona Granata). Seated, Donald Kaasch (Bénédict), Sara Fulgoni (Béatrice), Karl Morgan Daymond (Claudio).

for Héro, Béatrice and Ursula, in which Béatrice reveals that her feelings have undergone a considerable change since we first met her. She positively welcomes the tenderness which she earlier despised: 'Et ton époux restera ton amant'. This and the succeeding number, an off-stage chorus with guitar accompaniment, Berlioz added to the score after returning from Baden-Baden, where the opera was first produced.

Both Béatrice and Bénédict try to conceal their mutual love, but it is in vain. After a general *Marche nuptiale*, the two marriage contracts are signed between Béatrice and Bénédict, Héro and Claudio – and the opera finishes with a brilliant duet for Béatrice and Bénédict: 'L'amour est un flambeau'. This, called a *scherzo-duettino* by the composer, is accompanied by the opening figure of the overture, and its sparkle and gaiety make the perfect comedy ending.

Béatrice et Bénédict not only reflects Berlioz's love of Shakespeare but also a mid-nineteenth-century view of the playwright. The 'serious' side of the story has gone, but in its place is a rich warmth of invention such as virtually no other composer has brought to Shakespeare. To try to re-interpret Berlioz's interpretation of his favourite poet – by for instance introducing Shakespearean elements Berlioz omitted – has no other effect than to distort (particularly since *Much Ado* can still be performed without Berlioz) an operatic masterpiece.   H.

LEONARD BERNSTEIN
(born 25 August 1918, died 14 October 1990)

A QUIET PLACE

Opera in three acts, libretto by Stephen Wadsworth, incorporating *Trouble in Tahiti* (opera in seven scenes, libretto and music by Leonard Bernstein, Brandeis University, 12 June 1952). Commissioned by Houston Grand Opera, the Kennedy Center, Washington D.C., and la Scala, Milan. First performance in Houston (as a one-act opera in four scenes to follow *Trouble in Tahiti*), on 17 June 1983, with Chester Ludgin as Sam, Sheri Greenawald as Dede, Timothy Nolen as Junior and Peter Kazaras as François, conducted by John DeMain. Rewritten, as Stephen Wadsworth put it, with *Trouble in Tahiti* 'folded ... into' scene ii, it was first performed at la Scala on 19 June 1984, with Julian Robbins as Junior, Chester Ludgin as Old Sam, Diane Kesling as Dinah and Beverly Morgan as Dede, conducted by John Mauceri. Same production, Kennedy Center, 1984. Vienna State Opera, 1986, with John Brandstetter as Junior, Wendy White as Dinah and Chester Ludgin as Old Sam, conducted by Bernstein.

Old Sam	Baritone
Dede	Soprano
Junior	Baritone
François	Tenor
Susie	Mezzo-Soprano
Bill	Baritone
Mrs Doc	Mezzo-Soprano
Doc	Bass
Funeral Director	Tenor
Analyst	Tenor
Dinah	Mezzo-Soprano
Young Sam	Baritone
Jazz Trio	Soprano, Tenor, Baritone
Vocal Ensemble	

Running Time: 2 hours 30 minutes

Prologue. 'Dark night'. A chorale establishes the ideal that reality will never reach. Voices evoke the car crash in which Dinah died.

Act I, scene i is set in the funeral parlour and comprises eleven dialogues. Dinah's brother Bill deals with the Funeral Director, her Analyst is evasive, Doc finds Dinah had been drinking, Mrs Doc exposes the Funeral Director's hypocrisy, and they wait for Dinah and Sam's two children – Junior, who is gay and mentally disturbed, Dede, who married François, previously a lover of Junior. Sam has seen neither for years. The dialogue is edgy, fragmented, while the music mixes disparate idioms, including jazz for the drunk, sarcastic Mrs Doc. Dede and François arrive first. Dede's nervousness leads her to a manic description of the drive ('Have you got an hour or two?') that ends enthusiastically, 'It's just to die', before she realises what she has said. She admits that she dreams about her mother, though they were never close. Bill tries to welcome François, Sam greets Dede. 'Words mean so little at a time like this', says the Chorus, adding 'So I made a pie'.

They start the ceremony before Junior has arrived. Private reminiscences occur simultaneously with the public readings and hint at unresolved tensions: 'What a fucked-up family'. Junior enters, dishevelled, rambling nervously, while the orchestra passes a sad, fragmentary motif from the lower strings to higher instruments to powerful effect. Amidst different reactions to Dinah, Bill's contribution emerges clearly: 'Dinah fought for her own private place. Her garden.' The guests file by the coffin, leaving Sam, his children and François behind. Sam's anger erupts in an aggressive aria, in which he attacks his son. Sam weeps alone. In a lyrical, nostalgic trio with prominent solo violin, Junior, Dede and François reflect on their troubled relationships with their fathers. Junior insults his father and stages a menacing strip show, but, in the moving postlude, he 'approaches the coffin tenderly'.

Act II, scene i. Sam reads Dinah's diary which records how much they had grown apart. He remembers how the idyll of married life became a nightmare, which is how we encounter the first extract from Bernstein's *Trouble in Tahiti*, written more than thirty years before *A Quiet Place*.

Scene ii. A Jazz Trio celebrates the suburban idyll ('Mornin' sun kisses the windows') and a Girl sings a delightful, apparently improvised nonsense song ('Ratty boo'). In the kitchen Dinah and Young Sam consume breakfast 'in grim silence'. Junior expects them to see him in his school show, Sam insists on taking part in a tournament at the gym, and they quarrel, although they both long for a reconciliation. Sam goes to the office and Dinah sees her analyst, recounting her dream of love leading them to 'a quiet place'. They meet by chance in the street and lie that they already have lunch appointments. 'Can't we find the way back to the garden where we began?'

Scene iii. Sam can't bring himself to read Dinah's diary entry 'To Whom It May Concern'. Dede helps Sam go through Dinah's things and their conversation leads to a partial reconciliation. Junior's mind is disturbed. François criticises Junior's behaviour to his father and rejects his embrace. Junior sings a song suggesting that as a child he had a sexual relationship with his sister. Dede puts on one of her mother's dresses (the one she wears in the *Trouble in Tahiti* flashback). In an elaborately constructed quartet Sam and Dede begin to understand one another, while Junior fantasises that Sam shot him. As Dede, Sam and François sing 'We all can help us all', Dede helps Junior to recover a memory of a happy family Christmas, and to accept that he loves his father. A chorale ends the scene: 'Give all for love. For love is strong as death.'

Scene iv. *Trouble in Tahiti* returns: the Jazz Trio evokes an idyllic suburbia. Sam celebrates winning the tournament in a show-stopping aria with butch brass fanfares, and exults in his fitness and his youth. Dinah has an equivalent bravura aria: having been to the cinema to see *Trouble in Tahiti*, 'escapist Technicolor twaddle', she performs its beguine or rhumba rhythm ballad. She rushes home, but after dinner they cannot bring themselves to talk truthfully about their problems. Sam suggests they go out to a film, then goes into Junior's room and kisses his sleeping son.

Act III. After an intensely serious, tormented, but not unrhetorical prelude the scene is Dinah's garden. Dede has done some therapeutic weeding. Junior brings coffee and they remember quarrels at meals.

Tag 1. They play an elaborate game of tag and François parodies a line from *Candide*, 'What a day, what a day for a *café au lait*!' In an elegant trio they re-enact Dede's twenty-first birthday, when she first met François, then Junior's boyfriend.

Tag 2. Back in the present, Sam joins in the game and eventually embraces François, with the words, 'Welcome to the family'. Sam reads out some of Dinah's diary, and her voice is heard off-stage. The family's reconciliation splinters on the question of changing bedrooms. A full-blown quarrel develops. Junior hurls the diary in the air. They collect the pages

in silence, the chorus hums the opening chorale, and gradually the family make peace: Sam embraces his son, Dede takes François' hand and tentatively reaches for Sam's hand. The Chorus add the last word, 'Amen'.

It is hard to do justice to such a combustible work: the original one-act *Trouble in Tahiti* satirises the 'bright falsehood' of cheap sentimentality, whether evoked in suburban idylls of the conventional family unit or in escapist musicals. *A Quiet Place* adds several other levels, some of which work well: when Sam quotes from Dinah's diary the 'cheap slogan ... "Pretty as a picture"', Dinah's own voice can be heard singing 'Lie, lie, lie, lie Island Magic I'. But the conjunction of two separate works makes for an explosive combination. Elements such as the perfunctory pastoral and the psychobabble of François 'helping' Junior have already dated badly. The obvious parallel with Tippett's work can help, if it encourages us to look beyond *A Quiet Place*'s disconcerting rubs and stylistic inconsistencies to appreciate its musical brilliance, its willingness to confront several different kinds of truth. It is meant to be, as the characters would say, 'conflicted'; it is never going to be an easy experience.   P.

CANDIDE

Comic operetta in two acts, libretto based on Voltaire's story *Candide* (1756). Original orchestrations by Leonard Bernstein and Hershy Kay; book by Lillian Hellman, lyrics by Richard Wilbur, additional lyrics by John Latouche, Dorothy Parker, Lillian Hellman and Leonard Bernstein. Première at the Colonial Theatre, Boston, 29 October 1956 (and on 1 December at the Martin Beck Theatre, New York), with Max Adrian as Doctor Pangloss/Martin, Barbara Cook as Cunegonde/Scrub Lady, Robert Rounseville as Candide, Robert Mesrobian as Baron/Prince Ivan and Irra Petina as Old Lady/Sofronia. This version is not available for performance. U.K. première at the New Theatre, Oxford, 30 March 1959, and in London at the Savile Theatre, 30 April 1959, in a version where the book was credited to Hellman assisted by Michael Stewart and for which Bernstein wrote a new number, 'We are women'. The cast included Laurence Naismith, Mary Costa, Denis Quilley, Edith Coates (as The Old Lady), Ron Moody (Governor of Buenos Aires) and Dennis Stephenson (Maximilian). Harold Prince directed a new one-act version, Chelsea Theatre Center of Brooklyn, 20 December 1973. The book was credited to Hugh Wheeler adapted from Voltaire; additional lyrics by Stephen Sondheim; orchestrations by Hershy Kay; music re-scored for thirteen players. Produced in a version revised for an opera house by the New York City Opera on 13 October 1982. John Wells and John

Mauceri produced a new version for Scottish Opera, Theatre Royal, Glasgow, 19 May 1988, directed by Jonathan Miller and John Wells, with Nickolas Grace, Bonaventura Bottone, Mark Beudert, Marilyn Hill Smith and Ann Howard. Bernstein himself gave his blessing to a final version, based on Scottish Opera's edition, which he conducted in 1989 at the Barbican, London, and recorded.

Voltaire/Pangloss/ Martin/Cacambo	Baritone or Tenor
Candide	Tenor
Cunegonde	High Soprano
Maximilian	Baritone
The Old Lady	Mezzo-Soprano
Captain	Baritone
Paquette	Soprano
Governor	Tenor
Vanderdendur	Tenor
Bear-Keeper	Bass
Cosmetic Merchant	Tenor
Doctor	Baritone
Junkman	Baritone
Alchemist	Tenor
Inquisitor I/Judge	Tenor
Inquisitor II/Judge	Baritone
Inquisitor III/Judge	Bass
Señor I	Tenor
Señor II	Tenor
Prince Charles Edward	Tenor
King Hermann Augustus	Baritone
Sultan Achmet	Tenor
Tsar Ivan	Bass
Croupier	Baritone
Ragotski	Tenor or Baritone
Crook	Tenor or Baritone

19 Non-Singing Roles; Chorus

Place: Westphalia, Lisbon, Paris, Cadiz, Buenos Aires, Eldorado, Surinam, Venice
Time: Eighteenth Century
Running Time: 1 hour 50 minutes (1989 version)

Even in his metropolitan musicals, *On the Town* (1944) and *Wonderful Town* (1953), Bernstein was aiming beyond the obvious limitations of the genre. With *Candide*, he set out to write 'a big, three-act opera with chorus and ballet'.[1] Composition was a long-drawn-out affair. During this period, he wrote a dialogue between himself and his demonic Id, who complained that *Candide* was 'beginning to look like a real fine old-fashioned operetta. Or a comic opera, or opéra comique ... but not a musical comedy, surely?' Bernstein answers himself and settles the matter: 'The particular mixture of styles and elements that go into this work makes it perhaps a new kind of show ...'[2] It is certainly operatic in its difficulties: Cunegonde calls for expert coloratura, for example, which was insouciantly tossed off by Barbara Cook, as the original cast album records. Voltaire satirised self-satisfied celebrations of the status quo. Bernstein and Hellman set out to fight against the prevailing climate of ideological intolerance, as America rode a wave of anti-communist sentiment. 'Puritanical snobbery, phony moralism, inquisitorial attacks on the individual, brave-new-world optimism, essential superiority – aren't all these charges leveled against American society by our best thinkers? And they are also charges made by Voltaire against his own society.'[3]

Act I. Candide is a bastard in the noble Westphalian family who inhabit the castle of Thunder-ten-Tronck. Though illegitimate, Candide is satisfied with his lot ('Life is happiness indeed'). The Baron and Baroness's two children, Maximilian and Cunegonde, are equally at ease ('Life is absolute perfection'). Candide falls in love with Cunegonde and she with him. For the moment, everything works out for the best in this, 'the best of all possible worlds', as the resident philosopher Dr Pangloss teaches. Inspired by watching Pangloss give 'private coaching' to Paquette, the maid, Cunegonde and Candide decide to marry. He looks forward to 'a rustic and a shy life' and she to the high life. Maximilian alerts the Baron who expels Candide. Candide is abducted and forced to join the army.

In the course of the war, Thunder-ten-Tronck is liberated, the inhabitants slaughtered. Candide finds Cunegonde's corpse and bids farewell to his love. After many months of wandering, he is given some money by an Anabaptist, which he gives away at once to a beggar. This turns out to be Pangloss, who has lost his nose from venereal disease, which he caught from Paquette. Pangloss and Candide travel

---

[1] Quoted Humphrey Burton, *Leonard Bernstein*, London, 1994.
[2] *New York Times*, 18 November 1956.
[3] Quoted Meryle Secrest, *Leonard Bernstein*, London, 1995.

to Lisbon, but they are wrecked in a storm. Lisbon is destroyed in an earthquake. On shore, they are arrested for heresy and sentenced to hang ('What a day, what a day/ For an auto-da-fé!'). Pangloss argues in vain that he is too sick to die ('Oh, my darling Paquette'). Candide, left alive, blames himself for his misfortunes.

Meanwhile in Paris, having escaped death, Cunegonde shares her favours between a rich Jew, Don Issachar, and the Cardinal Archbishop of Paris ('Glitter and be gay'). She meets Candide again, who kills both her protectors. Advised by an Old Lady, who accompanies them, they flee to Cadiz, where she tells them her story. Born the daughter of (the imaginary) Pope Urban the Tenth, she lost her fiancé to poisoned chocolate and her virginity to a Pirate Captain, repeatedly. As a slave in northern Turkey, she was deprived of one of her buttocks during the Russians' siege. Now she resolves to restore their fortunes ('I was not born in sunny Hispania ... I am easily assimilated', a show-stopping number to words by Bernstein). A South American half-caste called Cacambo arranges for Candide to travel to South America to join the war to save the Jesuits from being slaughtered by Protestants. The act ends with a quartet finale ('Once again we must be gone'), as they all set off for the New World.

Act II. The Governor of Buenos Aires inspects the new slaves. Among them are Paquette and Maximilian in drag. He rejects the former and chooses the latter, but when Candide, his servant Cacambo and Cunegonde arrive, the Governor falls in love with Cunegonde ('Poets have said'). She insists on marriage but substitutes her brother for herself at the wedding ceremony. When Maximilian's gender is discovered, Father Bernard buys him from the Governor for his seminary. Cacambo warns Candide that he has been denounced: he must escape. Cunegonde and the Old Lady wait impatiently until the Governor agrees to marriage ('No doubt you'll think I'm giving in').

Meanwhile, Candide and Cacambo encounter the Jesuits, who turn out to be Paquette and Maximilian. Candide and Maximilian quarrel over Cunegonde. Candide stabs Maximilian and escapes in his Jesuit robes, but abandons them just in time to avoid being killed by the Mump Indians. Candide and Cacambo arrive by chance in the land of Eldorado, where food

is free and precious stones litter the ground. Candide grows sad without his love, however ('Up a seashell mountain') and they leave, loaded with gold and jewels. They reach the Dutch colony of Surinam. Candide charges Cacambo to ransom Cunegonde and bring her to Venice.

Candide's new companion, Martin, laughs at the absurdity of the world ('Words, words, words, words', words by Bernstein). Vanderdendur cheats Candide out of the rest of his wealth when he sells him a perfect wreck of a boat ('Bon voyage, dear fellow'). Martin drowns, but Candide is rescued. He finds that Pangloss is now a wretched galley slave. When four crowned heads appear in the water and are rescued, they resolve to pursue the simple life. In Venice, a croupier welcomes them to his casino. Candide is cheated out of his money by a Sailor who pretends that Paquette is his long-lost Cunegonde. He is briefly arrested by Maximilian, now Prefect of Police. Cacambo tells Candide that Cunegonde is kept as a slave by Prince Ragotski, who runs the most notorious casino in Venice.

Cunegonde and the Old Lady reflect on their privileged, captive state ('We are women'). In turn, the Old Lady, Ragotski, Maximilian and a Crook resent the way they have to work ('What's the use', in Venetian waltz time). Candide is cornered by two beggars, the Old Lady and Cunegonde, neither of whom recognises him. Ladies surround Pangloss when he wins at roulette. Suddenly, everyone recognises everyone else. Candide has enough money left to buy a small farm outside Venice. Having learned, in the words of the chorus, that 'Life is neither good nor bad', he proposes to Cunegonde and she accepts him ('You've been a fool and so have I'). He suggests that they 'try before we die/ To make some sense of life'. In the finale, everyone resolves to 'make our garden grow'.

Candide was reworked almost continuously as soon as it was written. Inevitably it takes lots of liberties with the original story, yet its spirit remains close to that of Voltaire in its exhilarating, picaresque pace: like the story, it never remains long in any one place or mood. This hectic sequence also means that as a work it has had room for any number of new ideas. Operetta? Musical? Comic opera? *Candide* succeeds on its own terms, with a homey sentimentality that is always undercut by biting New York or Voltairean cynicism.   P.

HARRISON BIRTWISTLE
(born 15 July 1934)

Harrison Birtwistle was born at Accrington, Lancashire, and was associated with the Manchester New Music Group at an important period of his musical development (the composers Alexander Goehr and Peter Maxwell Davies, the trumpet player and conductor Elgar Howarth, the composer and pianist John Ogdon were other members). He was an active clarinettist in his early days, but an admiration for Stravinsky's music and theory as well as preoccupation with the emotional release of Greek drama are perhaps the most important influences on the early and middle periods of his creativity.

PUNCH AND JUDY

A tragical comedy, or a comical tragedy, in one act, libretto by Stephen Pruslin. Première, Aldeburgh Festival, 8 June 1968, with Jenny Hill, Maureen Morelle, John Winfield, John Cameron, Geoffrey Chard, Wyndham Parfitt, conducted by David Atherton (repeated that year at Edinburgh Festival and Sadler's Wells). First performed Minneapolis, 1970; London (concert), 1979, with Phyllis Bryn-Julson, Jan DeGaetani, Philip Langridge, Stephen Roberts, David Wilson-Johnson, John Tomlinson, London Sinfonietta, conductor David Atherton; Copenhagen, 1981; Gelsenkirchen, 1985. Opera Factory London performed the opera with great success in 1982 in a production by David Freeman.

Pretty Polly, *later Witch* ....High Soprano
Judy, *later Fortune-Teller* ....Mezzo-Soprano
Lawyer...High Tenor
Punch...Higher Baritone
Choregos, *later Jack Ketch* ....Lower Baritone
Doctor...Basso Profondo

Running Time: 1 hour 40 minutes

Birtwistle has said, 'When I embarked on *Punch and Judy* ... I knew the kind of world I wanted to create long before I'd chosen the subject ... I wanted a theatrical event that ... was very formal, a myth and English. The subject ... had the advantage of having a story everyone knew so that it wouldn't distract people from understanding what I was really trying to say.'[1] He worked with the pianist Stephen Pruslin to produce what the librettist has described as 'a stylised and ritualistic drama for adults that used all of the imagery, the trappings and paraphernalia of the original as a departure-point'.

Punch and Judy was commissioned on the basis of its scenario for the Aldeburgh Festival, written between January 1966 and January 1967 (partly while the composer was a visiting fellow at Princeton University), and performed in 1968. Critical acclaim was considerable but so was a certain public dismay, not least perhaps because the harsh, abrasive instrumental writing sounded harsher still in the confined space of the Jubilee Hall – 'his brass roars and brays, voices are pushed to their extremities and the woodwind squeals and screams so implacably in its uppermost register that it is not long before the ear is begging for mercy,' wrote Peter Heyworth in 1979, eleven years after the première (but he did not neglect to single the opera out for special praise then and at the première itself). With *Punch and Judy* the Theatre of Cruelty had set its mark on opera.

The scoring is for fifteen instrumentalists, including five wind players on a platform on stage, according to the composer's direction. It is to be played without interval, an instruction not invariably followed. In organisation it is highly stylised, full of set-pieces – over a hundred separate items altogether, some lasting only a few seconds. Bach's *St Matthew Passion* was the model for composer and librettist, and *Punch and Judy* is a baroque opera in shape, a morality rather than a tragedy in content, but also in certain aspects a 'quest' opera – the quest of Punch for his ideal.

This last claim requires some justification. The librettist invented the idea of Quest for Pretty Polly as a 'positive analogue' (as he calls it) to Punch's 'apparently motiveless acts of violence'. It is, to my mind, a very successful device and Pruslin emphasises that there is 'no *necessary* connection between the two sides of Punch's schizoid nature' – though

---

[1] From *Harrison Birtwistle* by Michael Hall (Robson Books, 1984).

Punch and Judy *(première, Aldeburgh, 1968, director Anthony Besch, designer Peter Rice). John Cameron as Punch and Maureen Morelle as Judy.*

there may be. In other words, that Punch murders in order to win Pretty Polly is plausible rather than an essential aspect of the plan. Both composer and librettist, says Pruslin, 'saw the work ultimately as an opera *about* opera. It is an opera in quotation marks. The characters are stock-characters raised to a principle. The set-pieces (quartet, love duet, etc.) are likewise formulas that recur with different meanings in many operas. Our aim was the collective generalisation of known operas into a "source-opera" which, though written after them, would give the illusion of having been written before them.'

Michael Nyman, who collaborated with the composer in his next operatic essay, *Under the Greenwood Tree*, sees the opera's shaping, with its dozens of short musical forms, in terms of cinema, 'for, as with a film scenario, each action is broken down into a series of shots, each shot being a short self-contained musical entity. These units – word games, chorales, ensembles – gradually increase in number during the opera, as the plot progresses, and are repeated throughout the recurrent action-cycles.'[1]

Choregos sings the prologue.

Melodrama I. Punch titters, sings to the baby a lullaby, described in the libretto as a serenade, emits his so-called war-cry, then throws the baby into the fire. Judy too has a lullaby, discovers baby burned to death, confronts Punch as a murderer and plays with him a word-game in which Choregos joins in comment. Murder is in the air and Choregos proclaims 'Punch ... consecrates the altar of arrogance ... for the holy sacrament of murder'. Doctor and Lawyer sing the first Passion Aria, Judy prepares for death and, after again venting his war-cry, Punch stabs her, celebrating in a catchy little gavotte of self-satisfaction (called Resolve, it will recur in connection with the other murders).

A very short toccata precedes and succeeds Passion Chorale I, for mezzo-soprano, tenor, baritone and bass, one of three very impressive ensembles described by this title.

The Quest for Pretty Polly I. In six short numbers – Travel Music, Weather Report, Prayer, Serenade, Pretty Polly's Rhapsody, Moral – Punch searches for Pretty Polly, woos her only to lose her, and leaves Choregos to mourn his failure and attempt consolation. There are four such Quests in the opera, and in each Punch travels on a hobby-horse, a Prayer is made for clement weather, and Pretty Polly is unsuccessfully wooed, in the first instance being offered a vast flower which she rejects with an oblique reference to the murder of the baby.

A short sinfonia introduces Melodrama II, leading up to the second Murder Ensemble, Punch's war-cry, and Punch's murder of Doctor and Lawyer. There

follow Passion Chorale II, a condemnation of Punch's murderous propensities, and the second Quest for Pretty Polly. Melodrama III is a battle of wits between Choregos and Punch and includes a fine tune for Punch to the words 'Let the Winds be gentle' (Preyer it is called, consistent with the libretto's delight in puns). Punch contrives to shove Choregos into a bass viol case, bows vigorously on the viol, and opens the case to reveal Choregos dead.

A splendid aria for Judy is followed by a muted version of Punch's war-cry, before we embark on a shortened version of the Quest cycle, ending in Nightmare. Choregos, musically essential and therefore miraculously indestructible, introduces Tarot Games with Judy as Fortune-Teller. Pretty Polly's Black Rhapsody culminates in the rather surprising stage direction 'Punch faints and the Nightmare dissolves'.

The third Quest for Pretty Polly goes through the hoops but Passion Chorale III which follows foresees the possibility of redemption through love. Melodrama IV finds Punch in prison, visited by Choregos disguised as Jack Ketch, the Public Hangman, whom Punch by a trick contrives to hang. The last movement is called Punch Triumphant. Pretty Polly sings exultantly of spring, the love duet for her and Punch signals release – Punch has turned the tables with his one good deed, the murder of the Hangman! – and Choregos is left with the Epilogue.

Punch and Judy is an extraordinary work, inimitable in its construction, which is devised to suit Birtwistle's needs, as full of music as an egg is of meat. Michael Nyman in *The Listener* (10 October 1968) summed it up when he said that it is 'at once simple, obscure, direct and puzzling'.   H.

THE MASK OF ORPHEUS

Opera in three acts, libretto by Peter Zinovieff. Première, 21 May 1986, by English National Opera, with Philip Langridge and Nigel Robson, Jean Rigby and Ethna Robinson, Tom McDonnell and Rodney Macann, Marie Angel, Richard Angas, conductors Elgar Howarth and Paul Daniel, producer David Freeman.

Orpheus:	The Man	Tenor
	The Hero	Mime
	The Myth/Hades	Tenor

[1] *Spectator*, 30 August 1968.

Euridice:	The Woman	Mezzo-Soprano
	The Hero	Mime
	The Myth/Persephone	Mezzo-Soprano

Aristaeus:	The Man	Bass-Baritone
	The Hero	Mime
	The Myth/Charon	Bass-Baritone

The Oracle of the Dead/Hecate.....................Soprano

The Troupe of Ceremony/Judges of the Dead

The Caller...Bass

First Priest ....Tenor

Second Priest...Baritone

Third Priest ....Baritone

The Three Women/Furies

First Woman...Soprano

Second Woman ....Mezzo-Soprano

Third Woman....................................Mezzo-Soprano

Mimes; The Troupe of Passing Clouds; Small Snakes;
    Large Snake

Running Time: 3 hours 15 minutes

When in the late 1960s Covent Garden's appointed but not yet resident joint artistic directors, Colin Davis and Peter Hall, were looking for a new opera with which to give point and 'signature' to their aspirations for the company, the obvious composer – after *Punch and Judy* – to write it was Harrison Birtwistle. Later, Peter Hall decided against taking up the position at Covent Garden, preferring to run the National Theatre and to put his operatic energies into regular summer work at Glyndebourne, and it was natural enough for Birtwistle to emigrate with him and to plan the new work for Glyndebourne. Its theme was originally Faust but by now had become Orpheus.

Two acts were sketched out before in 1973 it became apparent that neither scale nor box office potential suited Glyndebourne and the composer offered it accordingly to English National Opera, who grabbed it with both hands. The writing of the third act, after an interval and the composition of several other successful works, proved harder for the composer than had the last act of *Siegfried* for Wagner 100 years before in slightly comparable circumstances. 'It was a piece of archaeology,' said Birtwistle in an interview, 'months and months and months of unravelling

what I'd done and where I'd got to and why I had made certain decisions. It was like piecing together a civilisation.' A period of a year free of other work had to be found for composition and work on the electronics, but the opera was finally declared in a fit state to be scheduled for performance. At this point E.N.O. could not see where the production money was coming from, but the cost of extra instruments and the substantial electronic set-up (not only the technical apparatus but the highly skilled technicians) was eventually covered and the work reached the stage in May 1986.

It is a work of infinite complication. 'Essentially I'm concerned with repetition, with going over and over the same event from different angles so that a multi-dimensional musical object is created, an object which contains a number of contradictions as well as a number of perspectives. I don't create linear music, I move in circles; more precisely, I move in concentric circles ... To find a narrative to match this way of proceeding, I had to turn to myth, for only in myth do you find narratives which are not linear. Myths are multi-dimensional narratives containing contradictions and ambiguities. In telling a myth, you have to tell the whole myth, not just a part of it.'[1] In the first act, Orpheus is instructed by Apollo, and we then see him falling in love with Euridice, married to her, her seduction by Aristaeus, her death, and finally the Oracle of the Dead telling Orpheus how to rescue her from the Underworld. For each major figure in the drama – Orpheus, Euridice, Aristaeus – there are three performers, two singers and a mime, and the story is constantly re-told and the music re-worked. The second act describes how Orpheus journeys to the Underworld, meets Euridice, attempts to lead her back to the world, until he looks back and she dies. He hangs himself. Orpheus' life after his return from the Underworld is the subject of the third act, and the various versions of his death are all woven into the musico-dramatic structure. Says the composer: 'I don't think it's an opera anyway. It doesn't necessarily use song to carry the narrative forward. It uses dance, dumb action, other things.'

Electronic music is important in *The Mask of Orpheus*, and Birtwistle worked on and off for two years with Barry Anderson at I.R.C.A.M. in Paris.

---

[1] Harrison Birtwistle interviewed by Michael Hall in the programme for the opera's première.

According to Elgar Howarth, who has conducted most of Birtwistle's music and who prepared the E.N.O. performance, it 'functions in different ways: periodically to provide background auras (of summer, of winter, of bees, etc.); as signals representing the voice of Apollo; and, most adventurously, to halt the flow of the normal music, abruptly "freezing" the action to present "panels" of extra drama outside the Orpheus–Euridice story, panels depicting other Greek myths ... stories told by Orpheus as examples of his magic gift of song, and here acted, mimed and danced without words or singing. These episodes – Three Passing Clouds and Three Allegorical Flowers – wrench our attention from the main drama quite deliberately, and contain some of the most remarkable music of the whole score.'

In all the circumstances, the carefully worked out synopsis[1] of the opera, prepared for English National Opera, seems the most succinct way of presenting a précis.

Parodos. *The voice of Apollo, composed of purely electronic sound, dominates the action, uttering commands in his own language.* Apollo presides at the birth of Orpheus. His first memory is of his heroic voyage on the *Argos* with Jason and his men.

Act I, scene i. Orpheus falls in love with Euridice. She agrees to marry him.

The myth of Dionysus. The Titans captured Dionysus, who tried in vain to escape by assuming the form of a bull, a snake and a lion. Although they killed him, Rhea, his grandmother, reconstituted him and brought him up as a woman. He discovered wine and its effects.

In the wedding ceremony, Hymen (god of marriage) is invoked and the priests ask ritual questions; but there are bad omens: Hymen arrives late and Euridice stumbles repeatedly in the ritual. Not even Orpheus can dispel this atmosphere with his love-song for Euridice.

Scene ii. Two versions of the death of Euridice. Euridice wanders by the river.

The myth of Lycurgus. Lycurgus and his men fought Dionysus and captured his followers. Rhea released them and made Lycurgus so mad that he killed his own son thinking he was pruning a vine. The earth turned barren at the crime. Dionysus returned and Lycurgus, taken by his people to a mountain, was torn apart by wild horses.

Aristaeus, Man and Hero, make love at the same time to Euridice. In one case she resists and in the other she does not. In both versions she dies from the bite of a water-snake.

The myth of the anemone. Venus loved the beautiful Adonis. Despite her warnings, he hunted wild boar and was fatally wounded in the genitals. She decreed that every year his death should be commemorated. From his blood sprang the anemone.

Aristaeus tells Orpheus of Euridice's death.

Scene iii. *The first time distortion:* Orpheus imagines it was he, not Aristaeus, who saw Euridice die.

There are echoes of the love duet during Euridice's funeral ceremony, and the priests invoke Hermes, who, it is hoped, will guide her to the Underworld. They enact a ritual of the Tree of Life. Orpheus leaves the ceremony to consult the Oracle of the Dead.

The Oracle envies his magic and gives him three clues to the Underworld in exchange for his magical power of music: 'Always face the way of the sun'; 'Choose without choosing'; 'Never address anyone directly'. But when the Oracle tries to copy his song, all she can manage is hysterical screeching.

Orpheus now imagines he can find the way to the Underworld. While he describes seventeen arches which connect the mountain of the living to that of the dead, Euridice is metamorphosed into myth.

Act II. *The second time distortion:* another version of Euridice's death, in which she is killed by a giant snake.

Orpheus Man, exhausted, has a deep and terrible sleep, in which he dreams that he, as Orpheus the Hero, descends through the arches into the Underworld. All the figures he confronts are grotesque versions of the characters he has encountered in Act I. As the Oracle instructed, he walks backwards, always facing the sun he is leaving behind.

The Descent. 1st Arch. 'Countryside'. Orpheus sings to Charon and crosses the River Styx.

2nd Arch. 'Crowds'. Orpheus' music brings tears to the eyes of the Furies.

3rd Arch. 'Evening'. The judges of the dead foretell his death. Orpheus sees a vision of Euridice.

---

[1] Which is reproduced here with permission, and which at some points refers to action specifically devised by David Freeman for the Coliseum staging. It was written by Nicholas John.

4th Arch. 'Contrasts'. Orpheus drinks from the pool of memory but refuses to drink from the pool of forgetfulness. He has a second vision of Euridice.

5th Arch. 'Dying'. Orpheus notices those in torment as he passes.

6th Arch. 'Wings'. His magic overcomes even the fiercest of the characters of the Underworld.

7th Arch. 'Colour'. At last Orpheus reaches the centre of the Underworld and stands before its rulers: Hades, his wife Persephone, and the Goddess of Witches, Hecate. He fails to see their resemblance to himself, Euridice or the Oracle.

8th Arch. 'Secrecy'. Orpheus is surrounded by the awesome trio but continues to sing.

9th Arch. 'Glass'. Orpheus escapes from them.

The Return. 10th Arch. 'Buildings'. He finds himself among myriads of wispy shadows resembling Euridice.

11th Arch. 'Weather'. Although the Euridice phantoms dance around him, he makes no choice.

12th Arch. 'Eyes'. Orpheus begins his return, imagining that the real Euridice is following, but in fact it is Persephone who follows.

13th Arch. 'Knives'. Persephone stumbles and another Euridice takes her place. Orpheus overcomes the same obstacles as on his descent. Euridice tries to follow but the dead cannot leave the Underworld. One form of Euridice takes the place of another. As Orpheus journeys, he hears Apollo's voice in his head.

14th Arch. 'Animals'. Orpheus crosses the River Styx. Charon refuses to take Euridice and she falls back. As Orpheus emerges into the sunlight, he awakes. Too late. Euridice is already fading from his memory.

15th Arch. 'Ropes'. Orpheus has lost Euridice for ever.

16th Arch. 'Order'. Orpheus realises he has dreamt his entire journey, and, as Orpheus Hero, he re-enacts it.

17th Arch. 'Fear'. Orpheus mourns Euridice and rejects the three women who offer to marry him.

The myth of the hyacinth. Apollo and the youth Hyacinth competed at the discus. Apollo's returning discus killed Hyacinth. He changed him into a flower, with the mournful Greek characters 'Ai-Ai' upon its petals. Orpheus hangs himself.

Act III. *The structure of the act is based on the movement of tides on an imaginary beach. Nine episodes of the myth are played in an artificial time-sequence, which starts by receding into the past, then comes forward into the future and finally begins to return to the past.*

The third time distortion: Orpheus Hero is rejected by the Underworld and is re-born as a myth.

Episode 1. Orpheus Hero re-enacts his journey out of the Underworld with Euridice. She dies and he hangs himself.

Episode 2. Orpheus Man sings of his imaginary descent to the Underworld.

Episode 3. The death of Euridice is seen again but this time observed by Orpheus Man and Hero, instead of Aristaeus.

The myth of the lotus. Beautiful Dryope was suckling her child by a pool. When she plucked a lotus flower, to her horror she found drops of blood upon her hand.

Orpheus sings a second verse and remembers his imaginary ascent from the Underworld.

Episode 4. Orpheus Hero re-enacts his journey out of the Underworld with Euridice. She dies and he hangs himself.

Even the animals gather and listen as Orpheus sings a third verse in a secret language which he has invented.

Episode 5. Aristaeus is punished by his bees. Orpheus consoles him. But Zeus is angered by Orpheus' presumption in revealing divine mysteries in his arcane poetry and music, and strikes him dead with a thunderbolt.

Orpheus sings a fourth verse of his magic song.

Episode 6. Orpheus Myth is sacrificed and dismembered by the Dionysiac women. His head is thrown into the River Hebrus.

Orpheus sings a fifth verse of his song.

Episode 7. The head of Orpheus floats down the river. He still murmurs. Orpheus challenges the sun-god with his song.

Episode 8. Orpheus Myth has become an oracle, and is consulted by Aristaeus. A snake, which tries to silence the oracle, is killed by Apollo. But the god himself finally silences Orpheus for rivalling his own oracle at Delphi.

The myth of Pentheus. Dionysus dressed Pentheus as a woman so that he could penetrate secretly into the Dionysiac women's revels. He tried to stop them tearing a bull apart with their bare hands, and instead, in their frenzy, they tore him apart. His own mother ripped off his head.

Episode 9. The sacrifice of Orpheus Myth is continued as if the two previous episodes had not happened. The Dionysiac women eat his flesh.

Exodos. The myth of Orpheus decays.   H.

YAN TAN TETHERA

'Mechanical pastoral' in one act, libretto by Tony Harrison, based on K.M. Briggs's *A Dictionary of British Folktales* (1970–71). Première, Queen Elizabeth Hall, London, 7 August 1986, with Omar Ebrahim as Alan, Helen Charnock as Hannah, Richard Suart as Caleb Raven, Philip Doghan as the Bad 'Un and Piper, and Tom McDonnell as Ram, conducted by Elgar Howarth; broadcast on Channel 4/Radio 3, 19 April 1987. Revived by Opera Factory at Queen Elizabeth Hall, 1992, with Geoffrey Dolton, Patrick Donnelly and Marie Angel, conductor Mark Wigglesworth.

Shepherd Alan......................................Bass/Baritone

Hannah, *his wife*...Soprano

Davie and Rab, *their twin sons*.........................Trebles

Caleb Raven...Bass/Baritone

The Piper/The Bad 'Un.....................................Tenor

Jack and Dick, *the dark-haired twins*.................Trebles

Black-Faced Cheviot Sheep, Horned Wiltshire Sheep, Twins

Place: Wiltshire
Running Time: 1 hour 30 minutes

Commissioned for television by the B.B.C., this work takes its title from a numbering system for counting sheep in the North of England, i.e. 'One, Two, Three'.

The work begins with 'the "music" of the hill, which is composed of voices.' The hill is an ancient burial mound. As the sun rises, the music 'becomes less audible, goes "underground" ... There should be one or two sarsen stones on the scene.' Shepherd Alan sits at the foot of the hill with a Cheviot Ram and Ewe. On another hill in the distance stands Caleb Raven with his herd of horned Wiltshire sheep. The two hills revolve, rather like figures in an intricate clock mechanism. Alan has recently arrived from the North. Though he waves at Caleb Raven on the other mound, Raven never waves back. Alan longs to go back to the North, but his ewe is likely to lamb any day.

The hills revolve, bringing Caleb Raven to the foreground; he complains that Alan's sheep have black faces and don't have bells, unlike his. The Wiltshire sheep sing 'This is the sound of the bells folk hear in the valley', whenever the sheep move. Birtwistle sets the first line for overlapping entries of high-lying voices, sounding slightly like bells, but this is no idyll. Caleb Raven tells the audience that he stole the village bell and melted it down to make bells for his sheep. He is looking for the gold left in the graves under the mounds.

The hills revolve. Alan has two more sheep now. He explains that while his sheep have no bells, he hears music, a Northern air, which reminds him 'of how I'm not very happy and how my heart's not very content in these foreign parts'. It is played by the Piper behind Alan, but every time he turns round, the Piper vanishes. Alan counts his sheep up to ten: 'Yan, Tan, Tethera, Methera, Pimp, Sethera, Lethera, Hovera, Dovera, Dik', and recites the charm 'Yan, Tan, Tethera, One–Two–Three, Sweet Trinity, keep me and my sheep', hoping it will stop him hearing the Piper play. His wife is about to give birth, so he is determined to stay where he is. Since it lost its bell, the church has fallen into decay, so all they have to keep the 'Bad 'Un' (the devil) away is this charm. Hannah learns the charm in a duet that becomes an ensemble when Alan's sheep join in.

Caleb Raven watches as Alan counts his sheep, furious that he has so many more. Their powerful duet takes the form of competitive systems of counting. Alan counts in tens, Caleb Raven in sinister units of thirteen. The phantom Piper lures Alan away with his music. When the Piper reappears, Caleb wonders whether the Piper taught him his spell. He recites 'Yan, Tan, Tethera', causing the Piper to spin round and round; his hat falls off, revealing a pair of horns – the Piper is the Bad 'Un. Caleb wants the 'Northman' dead, so he can have Hannah for himself. The Bad 'Un promises to lure away both Alan and the twins his wife will bear. Caleb also asks for gold. In an eery ritual sequence, the Bad 'Un encourages Caleb to poke the mound with his crook. He finds a bracelet, brooch and ring.

Alan attempts to ward off the Piper by repeating his shepherd's charm, but he succumbs to the lure of his tune and disappears. Hannah's labour begins; her high-lying music becomes intensely anguished, she recites the shepherd's charm and appeals to the sarsen stones to lessen her pains. We see the Bad 'Un carrying two small bundles away.

Caleb leaves the gold at the foot of the mound, but Hannah is not impressed. As she tends the Cheviot sheep she counts the seven years that have passed since Alan and her twins disappeared. She and her sheep recite the charm, which sends Caleb off into a spin. He returns with two dark-haired twin boys, Jack and Dick; Hannah knows they are not her children, but agrees to look after them. The use of treble voices inevitably makes a powerful impact. Jack and Dick promise Hannah that the twins will return tomorrow at dawn.

Just before dawn, we see them kneeling in front of the mound. Birtwistle's music is at its most atmospheric here, with horn calls over the orchestra's collective sighing, yielding to upwardly spiralling woodwind. The hill opens. Hannah's twins Davie and Rab emerge, along with the ram and the ewe that Alan had brought with him. They promise that Alan himself will return the next day.

Caleb returns with his sheep, determined to steal more of the gold, so he can escape from the Bad 'Un. Caleb watches Jack and Dick go round the mound three times, clockwise. The hill opens and Alan emerges, carrying the church bell, now covered in gold. Caleb tries to imitate their ritual, but he goes round the mound thirteen times, anti-clockwise. The hill opens, Caleb rushes inside 'and the hill closes on him with a snap'. As the restored church bell chimes, Alan explains that 'when you're out on the downs alone', you can hear an agonised voice for ever stuck at 'Tethera Dik' (thirteen).   P.

GAWAIN

Opera in two acts, libretto by David Harsent, based on the medieval legend of *Sir Gawain and the Green Knight*. Première, Covent Garden, 30 May 1991, with Marie Angel as Morgan le Fay, Elizabeth Laurence as Lady de Hautdesert, Richard Greager as Arthur, Penelope Walmsley-Clark as Guinevere, François Le Roux as Gawain, John Tomlinson as the Green Knight/Bertilak de Hautdesert, conducted by Elgar Howarth. When Covent Garden revived it on 14 April 1994, Anne Howells sang Lady de Hautdesert and the composer shortened the 'turning of the seasons'.

Morgan le Fay, *Arthur's half-sister* ....Soprano
Lady de Hautdesert, *wife of Bertilak* ....Mezzo-Soprano
Arthur, *King of Logres* ....Tenor
Guinevere, *Arthur's wife* ....Soprano
A Fool ....Baritone
Agravain, *a knight, Gawain's brother* ....Bass
Ywain, a knight, *Arthur's nephew* ....Tenor
Gawain, a knight, *Arthur's nephew* ....Baritone
Bishop Baldwin, *Arthur's confessor* ......Counter-Tenor
Bedevere, *a knight* ....Actor
The Green Knight/
    Bertilak de Hautdesert ....Bass-Baritone
Clerics, Off-Stage Chorus

Place: King Arthur's Court; Hautdesert; The Green Chapel
Time: Medieval
Running Time (revised version): 2 hours 30 minutes

As he came off-stage from the première of *The Mask of Orpheus* in 1986, Birtwistle told the conductor Elgar Howarth that he had been asked to write an opera for Covent Garden. Howarth himself commented that 'Orpheus is a piece which a young man knew he had to write. *Gawain* is the work of a mature master. All of [his] theatrical virtuosity has gone into it.'

Act I. Camelot at Christmas. King Arthur and his court are attended by two invisible people, the witch Morgan le Fay and Lady de Hautdesert. Morgan hates King Arthur and his wife Guinevere, and hopes to destroy them. Lady de Hautdesert is chilled and excited by Morgan's purpose. Arthur feels that the 'rituals of the season [have been] tamed by habit'. His wife invites him to join the feast but he asks to hear or see some demonstration of courage.

The Green Knight rides in holding a branch of holly in one hand and an axe in the other. He insults Arthur (as Siegfried does Gunther in the Gibichungs' hall) by asking which is the King, and points out that 'There's a smell of timidity in the place, like rot.' He then issues a challenge: he will let anyone strike at his neck with the axe, as long as he is then allowed to do the same in return, a year and a day later. Arthur is intrigued: 'How can you kill a man if you are dead?' Gawain accepts the challenge and strikes off the Green Knight's head with his axe. In a moment of rare theatrical magic, the Green Knight picks up his own head, which continues to sing. He tells Gawain, 'Ride north ... the bargain's struck.'

In a long and elaborate ritual sequence, Gawain is stripped, washed and armed during the 'Turning of the Seasons', beginning and ending in winter. The Fool tells Gawain to look out of his window, out of

Gawain (Covent Garden, 1991, director Di Trevis, designer Alison Chitty). John Tomlinson as the Green Knight holds up his severed head.

the door, over the moor, in his mirror, where he might see someone: 'Who is it?'

Act II. Morgan describes and controls Gawain's journey. Bertilak and Lady de Hautdesert wait for Gawain to arrive. Morgan prompts them to ask him to teach them something of courtly love, which Lady de Hautdesert compares to hunting. Bertilak offers him their house and everything within it. Gawain explains that he has a debt to pay and cannot rest until he has found the Green Chapel. Learning that it is not more than two miles away, he agrees to stay until he has rested. Bertilak is going hunting from dawn to dusk. He offers Gawain a pact: each evening they will give one another whatever they have gained during the day. Lady de Hautdesert leads Gawain to his bed and Morgan sings him a lullaby. Next day, the hunt and the attempted seduction of Gawain by Lady de Hautdesert are interwoven. She flatters Gawain and offers him her body. He ignores this and she kisses him. Bertilak kills a stag, throws the offal outside and the head at Gawain's feet. Gawain responds by kissing Bertilak. The sequence of lullaby,

hunt and seduction is repeated, when Bertilak throws a boar's head at Gawain's feet and Gawain kisses him, and, when Bertilak hunts a fox and Lady de Hautdesert kisses Gawain again. However, she then offers him her sash as well: while he wears it, nothing can hurt him. At the exchange, Bertilak throws the carcass of the fox at Gawain's feet, but Gawain merely kisses him three times and does not mention the sash.

He sets off for the Green Chapel where he confronts the Green Knight and bows to receive the axe-blow. The Green Knight merely grazes his neck with the axe and explains that the first two blows were feints, because Gawain was honest on two occasions in the exchange of gifts with Bertilak. He cut him with the third blow, because Gawain lied to keep the sash, not out of greed or love, but fear of death, 'not sin enough to die for'. The Green Knight refuses to accept the sash that Gawain tries to give him and loops it round his chest. Morgan reveals that the Green Knight was Bertilak: the man has become the hero and is now a man again. She tells Gawain 'I've done the same to you. Become yourself; your purpose has just begun.'

Back at Arthur's court, the King is still longing to whet his appetite with courage. Someone knocks at the door three times. The Fool opens it and Morgan enters, though she is invisible to the court. Gawain returns and receives a warm welcome. They ask for news of brave feats, but he protests that he is 'not that hero'. As they disarm him, his responses disappoint them and he feels out of place. Morgan ends the opera by telling him and us, 'Think only of dreams and promises. Then with a single step your journey starts.'

Birtwistle's librettist David Harsent shared the composer's interest in the English folk tradition. A ritual element was already present in the medieval poem, with its two mirror scenes in Arthur's court, its journeys and mythical confrontation. According to Rhian Samuel (in a programme note for the première) Birtwistle 'chose the poem mainly for its wealth of formal patternings and its capacity for the inclusion of more (he claims the seasons sequence and the hunt/seduction intercutting in particular as his own creation)'. For some of the audience, the masque of the 'Turning of the Seasons' was a highpoint of the evening; for others, the year seemed to last forever. As Paul Griffiths pointed out in *The Times*, the libretto contains 'a certain amount of poetic phrase-making which looks wonderful on the page but sounds regrettably portentous in the theatre'. It is the mock-medievalisms that seem egregious: 'Now celebrate the hearth, the boar's head and the wine'. The text's facility, pomposity and sentimentality consort oddly with the grittiness, the intellectual complexity and emotional impact of Birtwistle's music.   P.

THE SECOND MRS KONG

Opera in two acts, libretto by Russell Hoban. First performance by Glyndebourne Touring Opera at Glyndebourne, 24 October 1994, with Philip Langridge as Kong, Helen Field as Pearl, Michael Chance, Steven Page, Omar Ebrahim, conducted by Elgar Howarth. In German, Operntheater im Jugendstiltheater, Vienna, 1996, conducted by Andreas Mitisek; Theater der Stadt Heidelberg, 1996, conducted by Thomas Kalb.

Kong, *the idea of him* ....Tenor
Pearl, *Vermeer's 'Girl with a Pearl Earring'* .....Soprano
Orpheus, *for ever singing his loss* ....Counter-Tenor
Anubis, *a jackal-headed boatman* ....Bass-Baritone
Death of Kong, *a wrong assumption* ....Bass-Baritone
Vermeer, *left behind by Pearl* ....Baritone
Inanna, *Mrs Dollarama, dead former
    beauty queen* .... Mezzo-Soprano
Mr Dollarama, *dead film producer* ....Baritone
Swami Zumzum, *Inanna's dead
    spiritual adviser* .... Character Tenor
Mirror ....Lyric Soprano
Mirror Echo ....Soprano
Madame Lena, *the customary sphinx* ....Contralto
Eurydice...Soprano
Woman Model ....Soprano
Model 1 and Terror ....High Soprano
Model 2 and Despair ....Soprano
Model 3 and Fear ....Mezzo-Soprano
Model 4 and Doubt ....Mezzo-Soprano
Joe Shady ....Bass
Monstrous Messenger ....Bass

Chorus of the Dead

Running Time: 1 hour 55 minutes

Act I. An island in the world of shadows, inhabited by the dead. Anubis the jackal-headed boatman brings the souls of the dead to the world of shadows. At his command the dead relive their memories. Mr Dollarama finds his wife Inanna in bed with her guru Swami Zumzum. Orpheus looks back and loses Eurydice. Vermeer the painter sees Pearl in his mind and falls in love with her.

Vermeer's memory. Vermeer relives the moment when he first met Pearl in Delft, 1664.

As the dead watch the scene unfold, a monstrous messenger delivers a print of the film *King Kong*. Kong was taken to the World of Shadows by mistake in 1933, when the puppet ape died in the film. Kong himself knows he is an idea that will not die. But he is not sure what he is an idea of.

Meanwhile in Delft, 1664, Vermeer cannot find the model he needs to inspire him. Pearl comes collecting for the church. Vermeer invites her to sit for him. Kong cries out from the World of Shadows, a lost and lonely call. Vermeer finishes the painting, irritated at Pearl's lack of interest in him.

Kong's room, the world of shadows. Kong watches *King Kong* and realises that he is more than 'the giant head, the giant hand, the little puppet moving on the screen'. Inanna comes to him, hoping for love. Now that Kong has heard Pearl's voice, however, he can think of no one else.

Pearl, Pearl, the Vermeer Girl. Now in the twentieth century, the painting has become a popular icon, widely available.

Penthouse flat, Mammon House. Pearl has become part of the furnishings of a stockbroker's flat. She puts on the television and catches a re-run of *King Kong*. But this Kong is a puppet. The Mirror enlightens her, and she uses the computer to search for Kong. They fall in love. Kong vows to find her.

The dead have been watching from the World of Shadows. A quarrel between Mr Dollarama, Inanna and Swami Zumzum turns into a fight. In the confusion, Kong escapes and sets off to find Pearl among the living. He brings Orpheus to act as his pilot.

Act II. At sea. Kong and Orpheus are lost. Kong asks Orpheus the way to the world of the living. They are attacked by Doubt, Fear, Despair and Terror. Orpheus loses his head; Kong remains resolute: 'Beyond the soul's dark sea ... there waits my Pearl.' Kong rescues the head of Orpheus.

Anubis and some of the dead have followed. Inanna disparages Pearl to Dollarama, 'all she's ever done is hang on walls ... she's two-dimensional'. Vermeer defends her.

Customs barrier, a tunnel. The sphinx, Madame Lena, controls the customs barrier between the two worlds. She tries to seduce Kong and is disappointed when he runs off to find Pearl. Her riddle, 'What has two hearts and one desire?' remains unanswered.

On the road to the city. Kong and the head of Orpheus lose confidence in their quest for Pearl and Eurydice. The song of Orpheus charms a telephone and Kong calls Pearl to get directions. They remember falling in love.

A menacing figure challenges Kong. As an idea, however, Kong refuses to die. They fight and the dead bet on the outcome. Kong wins. He now knows who he is: 'I am the wild and wordless, lost and lonely child of all the world'.

Penthouse flat, Mammon House. Pearl cannot find her own reflection. Kong arrives. This is the moment they have waited for: 'there is nothing ... more real than our love'. Kong and Pearl try to touch each other. The Mirror intervenes: 'Look at me, see in my silver-shadowed waters yourselves together and apart forever. You cannot have each other.' Inanna, Dollarama, the head of Orpheus and Eurydice try to intercede but are helpless.

The Mirror tells them that 'it is not love that moves the world from night to morning ... it is the longing for what cannot be.' The love of Pearl and Kong cannot be fulfilled. They remember how they first fell in love.

The Second Mrs Kong represents an exciting development in Birtwistle's oeuvre. For the first time, the libretto stretches the composer: instead of merely supplying the ritual elements he needs, it takes him into new areas of humour and of human emotions. There is still a mythical quality to the story, and the music is as cerebrally rich as ever, yet it can also sound simple, and have a direct impact. Among the work's highlights are Madame Lena the Sphinx's formidable aria; the shimmering duet for two sopranos, the Mirror and Pearl; Inanna's longing for Kong; Kong's pathos; Orpheus mourning Eurydice. The work's open ending, its refusal to settle for a neat formula, also represents an advance on previous works. At the opera's core is the recognition that all lovers return to the moment when they fell in love, a phenomenon that seems ideally suited to Birtwistle's mind (his love of repetitive patterns) and heart.   P.

GEORGES BIZET
(born 25 October 1838, died 3 June 1875)

Bizet was a prolific composer, pre-eminent in the theatre, where paradoxically his operas never achieved instant success. His delightful Symphony in C was written when he was only seventeen, *Le Docteur Miracle* a year later, and in 1857 he won the Prix de Rome, spending three years in that city. On his return, *Les Pêcheurs de Perles* was commissioned for the Opéra-Comique, where however it had little success. In 1871 he married the daughter of the composer Halévy, who had been his teacher. His career is littered with operas started and then abandoned, but *Djamileh* (1872) impressed du Locle, the co-director of the Opéra-Comique, sufficiently for him to commission Bizet and the librettists Henri Meilhac and Ludovic Halévy (his wife's cousin) to write *Carmen*.

LE DOCTEUR MIRACLE
Doctor Miracle

Operetta in one act, text by Léon Battu and Ludovic Halévy. Première at the Bouffes Parisiens, 9 April 1857. Not revived until 1951.

The Magistrate ....Baritone
Laurette, *his daughter*....................................Soprano
Véronique, *his wife*..Soprano
Captain Silvio/Pasquin/Dr Miracle ....Tenor

Running Time: 1 hour

At eighteen, with the composition of the Symphony in C already behind him (though unperformed), and just before winning the Prix de Rome which entitled him to a sojourn in the eternal city, Bizet entered a competition organised by Offenbach. This was for an operetta in connection with the Théâtre des Bouffes Parisiens which Offenbach was about to open. All composers had to set the same libretto; there were over seventy entries, and Bizet shared first prize with Charles Lecocq. The premières of the two operettas occurred on 8 and 9 April 1857 and Bizet's effort was sufficiently successful with the public to clock up eleven successive performances.

A young soldier is in love with the daughter of an anti-militarist magistrate and contrives to get a job as the magistrate's cook. The omelette he serves up is so horrible that his beloved's father is convinced he has been poisoned and sends for the doctor. That worthy when he arrives – the soldier in disguise, of course – promises a cure in return for the hand of the daughter of the house. Happy ending!

All buzzes along as light-heartedly as if it were by Offenbach himself, sometimes tongue-in-cheek in parody of operatic practice, occasionally straight and lyrical. The music's climax comes with the 'Quatuor de l'omelette', an ensemble worthy of Rossini, an excellent example of the ensemble of misunderstanding in which the Italian master was so expert.   H.

DON PROCOPIO

Opera in two acts, text (in Italian) by Carlo Cambiaggio after Luigi Prividali's libretto *I pretendenti delusi*. Première Monte Carlo (in French) 10 March 1906, with Angèle Pornot, Rousselière, Jean Périer, Max Bouvet, conductor Léon Jehin (the opera was twinned with *Pagliacci* in which Rousselière and Bouvet played the leads opposite Geraldine Farrar). First performed University College, London, 1955.

Don Andronico ....Bass
Bettina, *his niece*...Soprano
Ernesto, *her brother*.......................................Baritone
Don Procopio, *an old miser* ....Bass
Odoardo, *Bettina's lover* ....Tenor
Eufemia ....Mezzo-Soprano

Running Time: 1 hour

Having won the Prix de Rome, Bizet found a libretto in a bookshop and set it as the first composition he would send back to Paris. It was finished in 1859 but never performed in his lifetime, coming to light nearly twenty years after his death, when Charles Malherbe arranged the score and (quite superfluously) added recitatives.

Act I. Bettina loves Don Odoardo but her uncle, much to her chagrin, has arranged for her to marry the well-off Don Procopio. She plans with her brother Ernesto and Odoardo to pretend that she is delighted with the match, which will enable her to live in some style. Don Procopio has misgivings about the prospect even before he and Bettina are introduced.

Act II. Bettina is evidently planning to live it up, much to the horror of the thrifty Don Procopio, who wants to get out of the whole affair. He is pressed to keep to his side of the bargain, until Don Andronico decides to make the best of a bad job and allow the young lovers to marry.

The music is thoroughly Italianate in style, with Donizetti as Bizet's avowed model, and charming in effect – inventive, swift-moving, full of wit and patter, replete with the idiomatic twists and turns which make *Don Pasquale* such a masterpiece. The score includes a march borrowed from Bizet's earlier Symphony in C, and some music was later used in *Les Pêcheurs de Perles* and *La Jolie Fille de Perth*, the very attractive serenade in the last-named opera appearing first in *Don Procopio*.   H.

LES PÊCHEURS DE PERLES
The Pearl Fishers

Opera in three acts, text by Carré and Cormon. Première at the Théâtre-Lyrique, Paris, 30 September 1863, with de Maesen, Morini, Ismaël. First performed Covent Garden, 1887, as *Leïla*, with Fohström, Garulli, Lhérie; Philadelphia, 1893; Opéra-Comique, Paris, 21 April 1893, with Calvé, Delmas, Soulacroix, conductor Danbé; Metropolitan, 1896 (two acts only, in combination with *La Navarraise*), with Calvé, Cremonini, Ancona. Revived Metropolitan, 1916, with Hempel, Caruso, de Luca; Covent Garden, 1920, with Pareto, Tom Burke, Badini, conductor Beecham; Berlin, 1934, with Berger, Wittrisch, Schlusnus, conductor Blech; la Scala, Milan, 1938, with Carosio, Lugo, Biasini, conductor Capuana.

Leïla, *priestess of Brahma*..............................Soprano

Nadir, *a fisherman*...Tenor

Zurga, *king of the fishermen*...........................Baritone

Nourabad, *high priest of Brahma* ....Bass

Place: Ceylon
Time: Antiquity
Running Time: 1 hour 40 minutes

Act I. The scene is the seashore, where the fishermen are holding fête preparatory to choosing a chief. They sing and dance, and eventually select Zurga to rule them; he accepts their confidence. Nadir appears, is greeted after his long absence, and describes his adventures in the jungle. There is a fond reunion between Zurga and Nadir. They were formerly friends, but recall their rivalry for the hand of the beautiful priestess, Leïla, whom they had seen together in the Brahmin temple of Candy. Their love for her had brought enmity between them, but they recall that the oath of friendship which they swore has never since been broken. Their duet, 'Au fond du temple saint', is an example of Bizet's melodic inspiration at its finest. Its theme is used throughout the opera as a friendship motto.

News is brought that a boat has arrived, bringing with it the unknown virgin whose duty is to pray during the time the fishermen are at sea, so as to ward off evil spirits. Zurga tells Nadir that she is veiled and must not be approached or seen by anyone during the time of her vigil. She is brought in by the old priest Nourabad, and welcomed by the fisherfolk. Zurga swears her in as the inviolate virgin protectress of the fishermen, and threatens her with death if she prove false to her oath.

Leïla and Nadir recognise each other, and he stands watching as if in a dream as she ascends the cliff. In an aria of great beauty he reflects on his love, which has never been dimmed by the passing of time: 'Je crois entendre encore'. This is the best-known section of the score, not least in its Italian translation, 'Mi par d'udir ancora', and it is concerned, like the duet for tenor and baritone, like the love duet, with a kind of erotic hypnosis, gentle and seductive, musically elusive and yet compelling, with which Bizet ensnares his young lovers and impregnates his score – hence one of the secrets of its attraction. Leïla reappears, and sings an invocation to Brahma, echoed by the chorus, before she is left alone on her rock for her vigil. Before the end of the act, Nadir, gazing up at Leïla, sings ardently of his love for her and swears to protect her.

Act II. In a ruined temple, the high priest, Nourabad, warns Leïla on pain of death to be faithful to her religious vows. She will be alone but well guarded. Leïla tells him he need have no fear; she never breaks her promise. The necklace she wears was given her by a fugitive, whose hiding-place she refused to reveal although the daggers of his pursuers were pointed at her heart.

Nourabad leaves her, and she sings of the love which fills her heart ('Comme autrefois dans la nuit sombre'). Suddenly, she hears the voice of Nadir singing a serenade: 'De mon amie fleur endormie'. A moment later he is with her, and a passionate duet of almost Verdian character develops: 'Ton cœur n'a pas compris le mien'. Leïla begs Nadir to leave her, and they agree to meet again the next day; but Nourabad has seen Nadir, and he calls down anathema on both their heads, while the chorus mutter that they can see a storm arising. Nadir is captured by the guards, Nourabad accuses the lovers of sacrilege, the crowd take up his cry for vengeance. Zurga claims the right, as chief and therefore judge, to settle the case himself, and he inclines to be merciful for the sake of his friend. But Nourabad tears the veil from Leïla's head, and Zurga, recognising Leïla, swears to be revenged on Nadir for his treachery. The crowd call on him to avenge the sacrilege.

Act III. Zurga's tent. The chief contrasts his own restless state of mind with the abated storm, which for a time threatened destruction of the fishing fleet ('L'orage s'est calmé'). He laments the breaking of his friendship with Nadir: 'O Nadir, tendre ami de mon

Les pêcheurs de perles *(Metropolitan Opera House, New York, c. 1916). Giuseppe De Luca (1876–1950) as Zurga, Frieda Hempel (1885–1955) as Leïla, Enrico Caruso (1873–1921) as Nadir.*

cœur'. It is a fine lyrical *scena* of considerable power. Leïla appears before him, and expresses her willingness to die, but in a melting tune pleads for Nadir. Zurga eventually gives in to jealousy at the idea of losing Leïla to Nadir, and is cursed by Leïla for his jealous cruelty. Just before leaving him, she asks that a last favour may be granted her; she has a necklace which she would like to have sent to her mother far away. This she puts into Zurga's hands.

The second scene of Act III is set at the place of execution, where a funeral pyre has been erected. There are savage dances and choruses before Nourabad leads Leïla out into the middle of the populace. Just as the guilty lovers are to meet death, a distant glow is seen. Zurga dashes in crying that the camp is on fire, and the people rush out to fight the flames. Zurga tells Leïla and Nadir that it was he who set fire to the camp; the necklace she gave him was once his, and he the fugitive she saved from death long ago. He unfastens their chains and bids them flee.[1] Zurga impedes their pursuers, but is denounced by Nourabad, who had stayed behind in hiding when the others left. The music of 'Au fond du temple saint' is heard in the orchestra, and the top line is sung by Leïla and Nadir in octaves as they appear safe on the top of the rock.

It is easy to mock the paste-board, over-romantic story – the kind of thing you would make up to show opera's fustian side – but not the lyricism of the music, which keeps it a best-seller some 150 years after the première.   K., H.

---

[1] Godard, in a misguided attempt to strengthen Bizet's ending, composed a trio, 'O lumière sainte', for insertion at this point, where for many years it was performed. Later editing of Bizet's score has been extensive and the duet for tenor and baritone usually closes with a reprise of the refrain, more effective one may think than the quick section Bizet intended.

LA JOLIE FILLE DE PERTH

The Fair Maid of Perth

Opera in four acts, text by J.H. Vernoy de Saint-Georges and J. Adenis, founded on Scott's novel *The Fair Maid of Perth*. Première Théâtre-Lyrique, Paris, 26 December 1867, with Devriès, Ducasse, Massy, Barré, Lutz. First produced Manchester, 1917, by the Beecham Opera Company with Sylvia Nelis, Walter Hyde, Webster Millar, and in London at Drury Lane, 1917, by the same cast; Covent Garden, 1919. Revived Oxford, 1955; B.B.C. (in concert, English), 1956, with Mattiwilda Dobbs, Alexander Young, conductor Beecham; B.B.C. again, 1973, with Eda-Pierre, Delia Wallis, Young, conductor David Lloyd-Jones.

Simon Glover, *glove-maker* ....Bass

Catherine Glover, *his daughter* ....Soprano

Mab, *Queen of the gipsies* ....Soprano

Henri (Henry) Smith, *the armourer* ....Tenor

The Duke of Rothsay ....Baritone or Tenor

Ralph, *Glover's apprentice* ....Bass or Baritone

A Lord in the service of Rothsay ....Tenor

The Duke's Major-Domo ....Bass

Place: Scotland
Running Time: 2 hours

Bizet signed a contract with Carvalho for *La Jolie Fille de Perth* in July 1866 when he was twenty-seven and finished it in December of the same year; Winton Dean in his book about the composer describes the libretto as the worst Bizet ever had to set. Certainly it is far from Walter Scott, and the libretto's naive treatment of the novel's characters has probably led to the music's under-valuation. The part of Catherine was intended for Christine Nilsson, but that great prima donna preferred to create Ophelia in Ambroise Thomas's *Hamlet*. *La Jolie Fille de Perth* was well received at its first performance, better than any other opera of Bizet's during his lifetime, but it had a mere eighteen performances and was not heard again in Paris until 1890.

Act I. After a bout of communal singing in his workshop, Smith laments the absence of his beloved Catherine Glover, but his thoughts are interrupted by sounds from outside. He opens the door to give shelter to the gipsy Mab, who is being mobbed by a group of young men. She hides as Catherine comes in with her father and the apprentice Ralph, Ralph

making little attempt throughout the scene to hide his jealousy of the sympathy between Smith and Catherine. Glover has brought provisions for a wedding feast, venison, pâté, pudding and whisky among them – his gourmand tendencies are recognised throughout the opera, not least in the first-act finale – and Catherine celebrates the holiday in a brilliant and rapid Polonaise.[1] Glover prefers Smith to Ralph as a suitor for Catherine's hand, and Smith and Catherine are left to sing sweetly in duet together. Will she be his Valentine? As token of his devotion, he gives her a gold-enamelled flower.

Enter the Duke of Rothsay, arrogant and at first unrecognised. He asks for Smith's professional services, but his interest is in Catherine and, in the course of a trio, he invites her to his castle at night, much to the rage of Smith, who seems at one point to be out-hammering Sachs in his effort to drown the words of a rival far more dangerous than any Beckmesser – all this to the most mellifluous music imaginable. The quarrel is about to blaze into a fight when Mab emerges from her hiding-place, to Catherine's considerable dismay and everybody else's embarrassment. The lively trio becomes a livelier quartet, and in the course of the finale, after her father's entry and recognition of the Duke, Catherine quarrels with Smith, throws down the flower which he had earlier given her – Mab picks it up – and flounces out.

Act II is introduced by a nocturnal march. But it is not a night for sleep, and carnival is in full swing, the Duke dispensing hospitality and all watching the gipsies dance to a musical number of real fame, which was encored at the first performance. The Duke enlists the help of Mab in his scheme to abduct Catherine, Mab (who was once his mistress) seeming in a charming song to fall in with the scheme but in fact determined to substitute herself for Catherine.

Smith sings a most attractive serenade in 6/8 outside Catherine's window ('A la voix d'un amant fidèle'),[2] one of the four numbers known outside performance, and it is followed immediately by the splendid, if lugubrious, drinking song of the bibulous Ralph, 'Quand la flamme de l'amour', hardly less well-known and perhaps even better.

---

[1] A more lyrical aria (by Bizet but unauthorised here) appears in an appendix to the vocal score as an alternative for the singer of Catherine.

[2] Its popularity in Britain is due to Heddle Nash's celebrated recording and it

is comparatively far less known in France. Bizet originally wrote it for *Don Procopio* (1859).

Ralph collapses out of breath, and it is unfortunate that the Duke's major-domo chooses to ask him the way to Catherine's house, even more so that he watches a masked female figure, to a reminiscence of the Duke's love song, accompany the major-domo towards the castle. Ralph is indignant at the turn of events and rouses both Glover and Smith, who rush off, leaving Ralph in his befuddled state to observe the real Catherine lean out of her window in an attempt to answer Smith's serenade.

Act III. Introduced by a graceful minuet entr'acte,[1] familiar from its introduction into the second *L'Arlésienne* suite, the Duke of Rothsay in his castle is gaming with the gentlemen of his house and describes in a *cavatina* the effect his new love has had on him before starting to woo her (it is of course Mab unrecognisably masked). Mab is suitably cynical about the Duke's sincerity as he uses much the same words to his supposed Catherine as he had once upon a time used to her (and Bizet the tune of his entr'acte minuet). The Duke takes Catherine's rose, which Mab is wearing, and eventually Mab makes her escape pursued by the Duke, to be succeeded by Smith, who, albeit rather gently, voices his despair and determination to be revenged. Smith hides and is indignant when Glover accompanied by Catherine asks the Duke to give his permission for her to marry Smith. In the course of the extended finale – the score's most ambitious section – the unfortunate Catherine finds herself at first forgiven for her supposed infidelity, then apparently sharing a guilty secret with a lord of the manor whom she hardly knows, finally rejected by a lover whose fury knows no bounds when he sees the golden flower pinned to the Duke's tunic.

Act IV. It is the morning of St Valentine's Day, and Smith and Ralph quarrel when the latter defends Catherine's honour. They arrange to fight a duel. Catherine appears, and she and Smith sadly recall past love. Smith is aware that Ralph is likely to kill him in the duel, and Catherine collapses. The chorus greets St Valentine's Day, Mab enters to relate that the Duke at her insistence has stopped the duel, and all now turn their attention to Catherine, whose wits have conveniently, at least from the nineteenth-century operatic point of view (though in defiance of Sir Walter Scott), deserted her. Her Ballade is a graceful example of the mad scene – for all that Winton Dean in his splendid book on Bizet says it 'raises a critical blush' – but the situation is apparently resolved when Smith serenades under Catherine's window, and Mab acts her part. Smith greets her as his Valentine, and all ends happily.

'The development shown in *La Jolie Fille de Perth* is in some ways negative rather than positive: Bizet has eliminated many of the weaknesses of the two previous operas, but not pursued his advances, particularly in the harmonic sphere. It is a less arresting and a less uneven opera, and consequently has been underrated. For much of its apparent tameness the libretto is responsible'.[2] That it is a step on Bizet's road from graceful melody to major achievement (in *Carmen*) of the perfect *opéra-comique* is undeniable, as witness the serenade, Ralph's drinking song, the skilful, even ironic, use of the music associated with the Duke's wooing of Catherine, notably in the finale of Act II and in Act III. The opera, like *Pêcheurs de Perles*, is more than just a signpost on a road to a great capital city, and one hopes revivals – they will be no more than that – will continue while the tradition of *opéra-comique* (to which it belongs in spirit if not in literal fact) continues.   H.

DJAMILEH

Opera in one act, text by Louis Gallet, based on a poem by Alfred de Musset. Première Opéra-Comique, Paris, 22 May 1872, with Aline Prelly (a notorious beauty but a bad singer), Duchesne, Potel. Poorly cast, it received only eleven performances and was not revived at the Opéra-Comique until 1938, with Jennie Tourel, Louis Arnoult and Roger Bourdin, conductor Cloëz. The first English performance was in 1919, with Gladys Ancrum, Webster Millar, Walter Hyde, conductor Beecham. It had been given in Vienna under Mahler in 1898, was well thought of by Richard Strauss who recommended it in his 'artistic testament' to Karl Böhm, and was revived in Munich in 1965.

Djamileh, *a slave girl* ....Mezzo-Soprano
Haroun, *a rich playboy* ....Tenor
Splendiano, *Haroun's servant* ....Baritone (or Tenor)
A Slave Merchant................................Speaking Role

Slaves and Friends of Haroun's

Running Time: 1 hour 5 minutes

---

[1] Arranged by Guiraud.

[2] Winton Dean: *Bizet, His Life and Works* (Dent).

Haroun, a Cairo playboy, is in the habit of changing his mistress every month, Splendiano, his servant and once his tutor, buying him new ones at the slave market. His heart is ice-cold, he claims, and he loves only love. The snag to this scenario is that his latest, Djamileh, is in love with him and contrives to change places with Splendiano's newest candidate for his master's favours, with the expected result. Splendiano is left mourning his dream of himself enjoying Djamileh.

The story is too flimsy and too short of drama to carry the weight that the music with its instrumental subtleties, its nuances, twists and turns of colour, deserves. Haroun is an unattractive if melodious cypher, Splendiano a bawd in search of musical comedy, and only Djamileh engages sympathy. Nonetheless, the failure of his short opera did not cause Bizet to lose his conviction that, with this score, he had at last found his way in the theatre. Within three years, *Carmen* was in front of the public and within four Bizet was dead. Even so, Richard Strauss's advocacy says more for his sense of musical quality than for his theatrical instincts.   H.

CARMEN

Opéra-comique in four acts, words by Henri Meilhac and Ludovic Halévy, founded on the novel by Prosper Mérimée. Première at Opéra-Comique, Paris, 3 March 1875, the title role being created by Galli-Marié with Chapuy, Lhérie, Bouhy. Her Majesty's Theatre, London (in Italian), 22 June 1878, with Minnie Hauck; same theatre, 5 February 1879 (in English); same theatre, 8 November 1886 (in French), with Galli-Marié. Covent Garden, 1882, with Pauline Lucca, Valleria, Lestellier, Bouhy. Minnie Hauck also created the role in America, 23 October 1879, at the Academy of Music, New York, with Campanini, del Puente. Calvé made her New York début as Carmen at the Metropolitan, 20 December 1893, with Jean de Reszke and Eames.

Don José, *a corporal of dragoons*	Tenor
Escamillo, *a matador*	Baritone
El Dancairo ⎱ *smugglers*	Tenor
El Remendado ⎰	Tenor
Zuniga, *a captain*	Bass
Moralès, *an officer*	Baritone
Micaela, *a peasant girl*	Soprano
Frasquita ⎱ *gipsies*	Soprano
Mercédès ⎰	Soprano
Carmen, *a cigarette girl*	Mezzo-Soprano

Innkeeper, Guide, Officers, Dragoons, Boys, Cigarette Girls, Gipsies, Smugglers, etc.

Place: Seville, Spain
Time: c. 1830
Running Time: 2 hours 40 minutes

Carmen is an *opéra-comique* with a tragic story and a tragic ending, and a substantial portion of the action is carried on in dialogue. For Vienna in 1875, it was thought helpful to have portions (but not all) of the dialogue set as recitative, and Bizet's pupil/colleague, Ernest Guiraud, later responsible for 'doctoring' Offenbach's *Les Contes d'Hoffmann* before its première, undertook the task with sufficient success for his 'version' to be adopted for some eighty years in most of the large non-French opera houses (in a few, it is still used). But *Carmen* is a better work with the dialogue Bizet intended, so that his brilliantly inventive, subtly scored genre music recreates the world he aimed at so precisely, a world of sophisticated gestures on a small scale rather than grand arias, large ensembles or rumbustious finales. Even so, in any version and in theatres large or small, the opera has for well over a century been probably the most popular in the repertory, and is almost invariably revealed as a masterpiece of virtual perfection and unerring design.

In 1964 was published Oeser's so-called complete edition, which prints much material cut during and before rehearsal, but falsifies the text by re-writing stage directions and excising Bizet's own modifications and improvements. To follow it slavishly is to fall into new and by no means shallow pits.

The opera was not initially a success (nor yet quite the failure legend would have it – forty-five performances in its first year), mainly due to its low-life theme and violent conclusion offending against the traditionally family atmosphere of the Opéra-Comique. By 1883, after success abroad, *Carmen* returned in triumph to Paris and by the end of the year had clocked up its hundredth performance.

Act I. A square in Seville, containing cigarette factory and guard-house. The prelude introduces the music of the *Corrida*, then Escamillo, the bullfighter, finally the brooding, apprehensive motif of fate and Carmen's obsession with it.

The atmosphere is heat-laden as townsfolk idly watch the world go by. Corporal Moralès tries to pick up Micaela, who is looking for Don José and will return later, but the action proper starts with a march heralding the relief guard; children parody the soldiers' drill. Corporal José tells Lieutenant Zuniga that the girls from the cigarette factory tend to be pretty but that he has eyes for no one but Micaela, his foster-sister. A bell rings; the male crowd voyeuristically anticipates the arrival of the girls, who emerge to sing melodiously of the factory's produce. Electricity is in the music as the gipsy Carmen darts out of the factory to become the cynosure of all eyes but proof against any advances. She sings a sultry *Habanera* ('L'amour est un oiseau rebelle'). A musical reference to the fate motif brings Carmen face to face with José, who seems not to notice her. She chucks a flower at him and runs into the factory, leaving him to pick it up as Micaela returns. Micaela brings José money and news of his mother ('Parle-moi de ma mère') and they sing an extended duet full of charm but devoid of passion.

Shouts from the factory suggest that someone has been stabbed – by Carmen, cries one faction. Zuniga tries to get sense from the hubbub, then sends José to sort it out inside. He escorts Carmen out, but she answers Zuniga's questioning only with humming and singing and José is instructed to tie her hands. Zuniga makes out a warrant while Carmen urges José to let her go – because, she says, he is in love with her ('Près des remparts de Séville'). She is right, as is immediately clear when he joins his voice to hers, loosens the knots and lets her give him a shove and run off to freedom, the crowd frustrating the soldiers' pursuit.

Act II. Lillas Pastia's tavern. The prelude (or Entr'acte as it is called) anticipates Don José's entrance song of a little later. A crowd is drinking and smoking, soldiers as well as gipsies like Carmen, Frasquita and Mercédès, who form a trio to sing a *Chanson Bohémienne* ('Les tringles des sistres tintaient'). The soldiers including Zuniga want to flirt and Carmen elicits from him the information that José has finished his prison sentence. There follows the entry of Escamillo, the matador, attended by an admiring crowd (Toreador's Song). He is plainly attracted to Carmen, but she brushes him off, at least for the moment, and, when he has gone, she does the same to Zuniga, all for love of José, whom she expects at any moment in the inn.

Lillas Pastia shuts the inn, and smugglers in the persons of Dancairo and Remendado emerge as it were from the woodwork, and in a quintet of outstanding brilliance plan with the three gipsies the immediate future. Frasquita and Mercédès will of course join that night's foray, but Carmen says she has unfinished business: she is in love and they must go without her. They can't believe it and protest, but to no avail.

The sound of José's voice is heard outside (singing the melody of the Entr'acte), and Carmen sets about seducing him with a dance, interrupted to her fury when José hears the bugle sound 'retreat'. He must obey what amounts to an order and Carmen rounds on him, silenced only when he pours out his feelings in the so-called Flower Song ('La fleur que tu m'avais jetée'), a declaration of love wrung from the very heart. Carmen returns to the attack ('Non! tu ne m'aimes pas!') and embarks on an attempt to get him to join the outlaws ('Là-bas, là-bas, dans la montagne'). Don José is already almost in the net when Zuniga barges his way in, to be defied by José and disarmed by smugglers attracted by the noise of the fight. Don José has drawn his sword against a superior officer and has no option but to join the smugglers' band.

Act III. A rocky spot on the frontier. An Entr'acte of ethereal beauty, all solo wind and strings, has little relevance to the action, which involves the smugglers preparing to reconnoitre their route and starts with a big-scale ensemble with chorus. José cannot easily accept that he is a deserter; Carmen hints that their affair is winding down. Frasquita and Mercédès spread the cards and Carmen joins them to read her fortune. She foresees death and her fatalistic creed means she cannot evade it: 'En vain pour éviter'. The smugglers prepare to move off, the three girls, in a passage of high swagger and to José's jealous indignation, promising to take care of the guards.

José is left on watch and is out of sight when Micaela, led by a guide, comes to look for him. Her aria ('Je dis que rien ne m'épouvante') is a beautiful lyrical invention, but Micaela hides when José takes an unsuccessful shot at a stranger. Escamillo has come looking for a girl he admits he fancies, but it is not long before he squares up to José, the dragoon Carmen (he has heard) once loved. As Escamillo slips and looks likely to lose, their fight is interrupted by the returning smugglers. Escamillo and Carmen exchange glances, and he invites the whole band to the *Corrida* in Seville.

Carmen *(Metropolitan Opera House, New York, c. 1900). Emma Calvé (1858–1942) as Carmen.*

Micaela is discovered and Carmen advises José to comply with her plea to go to his dying mother. José is frantic ('Dût-il m'en coûter la vie') in one of the score's most dramatic incidents, but the act ends with the reiteration of Escamillo's song.

Act IV. Outside the bullring in Seville. The Entr'acte is a Spanish dance. Crowd animation precedes the entry of the various elements of the quadrilla (the music of the prelude to Act I), and eventually the crowd hails Escamillo himself. He embraces Carmen ('Si tu m'aimes, Carmen') and she is warned by Frasquita and Mercédès that José is lurking in the crowd. She confronts him alone but will not listen as his pleas turn to threats. To the sound of applause for the victorious Escamillo, she hurls at José the ring he once gave her. He stabs her and surrenders as the crowd starts to leave .   H.

DAVID BLAKE
(born 2 September 1936)

A pupil of Hanns Eisler's in East Berlin, David Blake was Professor of Music at York University before being commissioned to write for English National Opera following the success in 1972 of his cantata *Lumina*. *Toussaint* was composed between 1973 and 1976 and is a historical epic on a scale inspired perhaps by Prokofiev's *War and Peace*, which was in E.N.O.'s repertory at the time. Its success was mitigated by what was thought of as limited pace and excessive length and the 1983 revival was considerably shortened. His second opera, the conversation piece *The Plumber's Gift*, was in sharp contrast and, in spite of admiration for its musical quality, gained rather less success.

TOUSSAINT,
OR THE ARISTOCRACY OF THE SKIN

Opera in three acts and twenty-two scenes, text by Anthony Ward. Première, English National Opera, London, 28 September 1977, with Sarah Walker, Neil Howlett, conductor Mark Elder, producer David Pountney.

Toussaint Bréda, *a black slave* ....Baritone
Suzanne, *his wife* ....Mezzo-Soprano
Boukman, *a Voudoun priest* ....Bass
Moïse, *Toussaint's nephew*.....................................Bass
Jean François...Tenor
Dessalines, *a black general* .... Baritone
Mars Plaisir, *a mulatto, Toussaint's valet* ....Tenor
Bayon de Libertat, *a fussy old French* colon,
      Toussaint's master..Tenor
Madame de Libertat, *his wife* ....Soprano
Christine, *a rich mulatto, passing as white*.......Soprano
Boucannier, *a French* colon ....Baritone
Laveaux, *French general* ....Bass
Darban, *a French* colon ....Bass
Bricard, *a French* colon ....Tenor
Millet, *delegate of the Colonial Assembly* ....Tenor
Sonthonax, *French Chief Commissioner* ....Tenor
Napoleon Bonaparte, *First Consul*.................Baritone
Pauline Leclerc, *Napoleon's sister*..................Soprano

Leclerc, *French General* ....Tenor

French *Colons*, Commissioners, Generals, Members of the National Convention; Spanish Generals; Black Soldiers, Servants

Place: Saint Domingue (later Haiti)
Time: 1791–1803
Running Time: 2 hours 45 minutes

The story is concerned with Toussaint's successful revolt against the French on the island of Saint Domingue, and his gradual decline, due partly to his own arrogance, partly to the alienating as well as corrupting effect of power. After his early triumph, the story develops into a struggle between Toussaint and Napoleon, and ends with the betrayal of Toussaint. Composer and librettist use a Brechtian device in the person of Mars Plaisir as dispassionate (often spoken) commentator on events.

Act I, scene i. 1791. Toussaint does the accounts. Elsewhere, a Voudoun Priest chants and three self-appointed leaders proclaim revolt.

Scene ii. Toussaint deplores violence, advises his master and mistress to escape, then himself joins the revolutionaries.

Scene iii. Life in a society based on slavery: a rich mulatto woman is accused of illegally dressing like a white woman; in spite of her spirited defence, the 'poor whites' kill her.

Scene iv. Jean François and Toussaint discuss the possibility of coming to terms with the French. Jean François's willingness to compromise is noted.

Scene v. French commissioners demand unconditional surrender, which Toussaint refuses, and for good measure has Jean François shot.

Scene vi. General Laveaux, a soldier of integrity and Republican principles, opts not to fight the black insurgents.

Scene vii. In the National Assembly in Paris, Millet's speech in favour of slavery and its benefits is fiercely interrupted.

Scene viii. Toussaint and his wife Suzanne movingly discuss the realities of his new position, unable to trust even his friends, uncertain whether to ally himself to Spanish or English, King or Republic.

Scene ix. Sonthonax proclaims the emancipation of slaves.

Scene x. Toussaint, once in league with the Spanish, repudiates the alliance.

Scene xi. In April 1796, Laveaux announces Toussaint's appointment as French Lieutenant Governor; Dessalines and Moïse mistrust the latest turn of events. Toussaint's sons will be educated under French protection in Paris. Suzanne protests it is a trick; Toussaint agrees but can see no way out of a trap. Suzanne laments.

Act II, scene i. July 1801. At a reception, Toussaint vigorously proclaims the need for economic discipline. Mars is now his valet. Moïse is unconvinced: 'The voice of the politician takes the place of the voice of the people.' Over Quadrilles, Toussaint questions a Frenchman as to Napoleon's attitude to Saint Domingue. Toussaint, Moïse and Suzanne mull over the situation.

Scene ii. Paris. Napoleon decides to invade Saint Domingue. Leclerc will lead, Toussaint's sons and Napoleon's sister will sail with the fleet. Leclerc will publicly confirm Toussaint's status but must clandestinely restore slavery and capture Toussaint.

Scene iii. Moïse revolts against Toussaint, who orders his execution. Moïse cogently argues that the revolution has lost the very people for whom it was intended. Dessalines announces the arrival of a well-armed French fleet.

Scene iv. In her apartment at Port-au-Prince, Pauline (scantily dressed, says the libretto, 'as in Canova's sculpture') bitches about the boredom of a military wife. She and her maids sing a so-called 'Chant du Sens interdit'.

Scene v. The battle of Crête à Pierrot. Toussaint leaves Dessalines in charge while he goes to fight in the south. Dessalines's rabble-raising speech does the trick and battle is prepared. Suzanne volunteers to tend the wounded. Battle continues, the noise abates and Suzanne is left with the wounded.

Scene vi. Toussaint makes his sons choose between the French and the Black causes.

Scene vii. A fresh attack is expected. Women lament but all again take up battle positions.

Act III, scene i. April 1802. An uneasy truce; the people are miserable, Toussaint is growing old, Dessalines has defected and is bargaining for what he can get out of it.

Scene ii. Toussaint and Suzanne have retired to his estate, where he laments the way things have gone, the people theoretically free but the land uncultivated. He allows the French to arrest him. He and Suzanne in canon take a last desolate farewell of each other.

Scene iii. April 1803. Toussaint, in prison in the Jura Mountains, is looked after by Mars but dies of cold, alone and betrayed.

Scene iv. December 1803. The French have withdrawn; Dessalines, decked out in French finery, proclaims the first Black Republic – with himself as Emperor!   H.

MARC BLITZSTEIN

(born 2 March 1905, died 22 January 1964)

REGINA

Opera in three acts, libretto by the composer from Lillian Hellman's play *The Little Foxes*. Première Shubert Theater, New Haven, Connecticut, 6 October 1949; New York, 46th Street Theater, 1949. Première in 'operatic' scoring, New York City Center, 1953, with Brenda Lewis as Regina, Ellen Faull, Lucretia West, William Wilderman, conductor Julius Rudel. First performed Houston, 1980, with Maralin Niska, Elizabeth Carron, Jennifer Jones, Giorgio Tozzi (Ben), Don Garrard (Horace), conductor John DeMain; Chicago, 1982; Wolf Trap, Virginia, 1982; Scottish Opera, 1991, with Katherine Terrell, Nan Christie, McCue, conductor Mauceri.

Regina Giddens	Soprano
Alexandra Giddens (Zan), *her daughter*	Soprano
Birdie Hubbard, *Oscar's wife*	Soprano
Addie, *Regina's housekeeper*	Contralto
Horace Giddens, *Regina's husband*	Bass
Benjamin Hubbard, *Regina's elder brother*	Baritone
Oscar Hubbard, *Regina's younger brother*	Baritone
Leo Hubbard, *Birdie and Oscar's son*	Tenor
Cal, *Regina's house man*	Baritone

William Marshall, *a businessman
      from the North* ....Tenor

Jabez, *trumpeter in the Angel Band*..................Baritone

John Bagtry, *an old flame of Regina's*...................Silent

Belle..Silent

The Angel Band; a Chamber Trio; Townspeople

Place: The Town of Bowden, Alabama
Time: 1900
Running Time: 2 hours 40 minutes

Though his training was cosmopolitan and included study with Nadia Boulanger in Paris and Arnold Schoenberg in Berlin, Blitzstein's apprenticeship was served in the American theatre. He believed that all art is inevitably propaganda, and that conviction is the foundation of his operas as of his plays with music. *The Cradle Will Rock* (1936) was once banned for political reasons but on its first appearance became a Broadway hit, produced by Orson Welles and John Houseman, and, to beat the ban, with the composer playing the instrumental parts on the piano (it was not heard with orchestra until 1947). Popular music was the opera's foundation, as it was too for the play with music, *No for an Answer*, which followed it in 1941.

Regina was conceived on a much grander scale, and its orchestration eventually enlarged for operatic as opposed to theatrical performance. For all its sidelong glances at Broadway and the 'hit' tune, it is one of the most successful operas to come out of America. Revivals have been more rather than less successful than the original performances and *Regina* has found favour with critics as well as audiences. Its subject is American but that should no more inhibit performance outside the United States than the same quality has inhibited foreign production of Arthur Miller's plays.

Bowden, Alabama, is in the Deep South of America, and the action takes place on the veranda of the Giddens' house as well as in its living-room and ballroom.

Prologue. The Prokofiev-like violence of the prelude contrasts at curtain-rise with the gentle mood of an Alabama spring morning, adumbrated by Addie's leading of spiritual singing (black life and music stand in *Regina* for the ideals of the Good Life, the Hubbard men represent corruption, and the Deep South in general the decay of capitalism). Cal and Alexandra add their voices to the music, which turns to relaxed ragtime before Regina is heard demanding to know what the racket is, and peace retreats before her.

Act I. An orchestral introduction takes us to the dinner party Regina is giving for a visitor from the North, William Marshall, with whom she and her brothers intend to make a business deal which will safeguard the fortunes of the Hubbard clan. Birdie in an arietta (complete with cadenza) considers the pleasures of listening to music, something to which her father and mother were addicted. Mr Marshall seemed to appreciate hearing about it, she thinks, but her husband nonetheless berates her for taking up too much of their visitor's time.

The others come out, and their small talk is carried on partly through stylised and unaccompanied singing, partly in pregnant *arioso*, and partly in straight speech (Blitzstein throughout *Regina* achieves a successful solution to the perennial operatic problem of conveying information). Regina in an arietta hymns the virtues of old-fashioned gallantry, reference is made to the Hubbards having taken over the land (and the daughter) of the previous owners, and all drink to the new firm of Hubbard Sons and Marshall, Birdie touching a top D flat in her by now slightly sozzled enthusiasm. Goodbyes are said to an *allegro grazioso*, and after a moment of contented vocalising, Regina and her brothers celebrate *con fuoco* what they are all convinced is a 'big, rich' future. Regina dreams of shopping, but her enthusiasm tails off as Ben, acknowledged leader of the family, calls them to order: 'I am waiting'.

Regina must put up her share of the capital, the brothers insist, but Regina knows they can't raise enough without her and wants more than the straight one-third she is entitled to. Ben offers forty per cent for her share and Horace's, and says it will come out of Oscar's portion. To keep it all in the family, they start to plan a marriage between Regina's innocent daughter, Zan, and Leo, the feckless, not to say brutish, son of Oscar and Birdie. Zan shall set off to Baltimore now, says Regina, to fetch her father from hospital, where he is having treatment for a severe heart condition. Zan must tell him it is she who misses him and wants him back. Regina's aria is jazzy in tone to begin with, moving to 6/8 later, and in it she professes to admire her daughter's spirit in not giving in to her mother's wishes without at least some show of independence, a quality no one could think missing in Regina herself.

Birdie spills the beans to Zan about the marriage plans, and Zan speculates in an arietta about love and marriage (Zan is adolescent and there is perhaps less sense of character here than in ensembles, dialogue or the opera's satirical sections). Birdie much prefers Zan to her own son and the idea of their marriage is abhorrent to her, but her unbuttoned tongue earns her as the curtain falls a resounding and far from metaphorical slap from her husband.

Act II. Regina in a state of over-excitement waits for the start of the party she is giving to welcome Marshall back to Alabama. Above everything, when will Zan bring her father home to Bowden?

Leo's pleasure-conscious outlook and disinclination to take life seriously come over well in an attractive *scherzando*[1] scene with his father Oscar, who reads him a lecture about working harder. Leo lets drop the information that he has opened his Uncle Horace's safe deposit box and seen the bonds it contains – $88,000 worth, no less. Uncle Horace himself never looks inside it. Might he perhaps *lend* them the bonds, wonders Oscar; he wouldn't in any case miss them. From the knowing nature of Leo's music, in Blitzstein's best showbiz manner, it's hard to believe that the penny won't drop with him, but Oscar seems to think it hasn't.

Addie helps Horace into the room. He doesn't look at all well. Horace stops them announcing his return; now that he *is* home, he wants to savour it for a moment, but all that goes out of the window the moment he hears about the plot to marry off Zan. The others offer hypocritical greetings, and it is time for the confrontation between Horace and Regina. They both seem disposed to try to avoid quarrelling, Horace describing himself as an old dry-bones, and Regina in her rather soft-grained arietta attempting to maintain the mood. Horace admits he can't last very long, but this starts them quarrelling – about his infidelities, about her ten-year-long refusal of her bed which caused them. Regina wants him to talk business with Ben, but Horace would like to wait until tomorrow. Ben is beginning to explain the deal with Marshall when Horace feels an attack coming on and starts upstairs, just as the possibilities of the safe deposit dawn on Leo. Zan assumes that, with her father in a

bad way, the party will be postponed, but that is the last thing in Regina's mind.

The scene changes to the ballroom, and the turning point of the opera, as Wilfrid Mellers says when 'the tension explodes in music that is also dramatic action. The piano on stage, playing ("in the style of Louis Moreau Gottschalk") prettied arpeggios in the fancy key of B major, is the tawdrily elegant façade behind which lurks the fury. This breaks out first in the chorus of merrymakers ... in E flat (which has become the stock key of Tin Pan Alley) ... the tune is both brutal and banal, its pulsing rhythm crude.' The guests relish the Hubbards' hospitality but detest the hosts, who have cheated and double-crossed each and every one of them. So the toast is 'Sing. Eat. Gobble. Guzzle. Swill. Perish. Rot. For what? For Hubbard!'

Horace instructs his lawyer to bring his safe-deposit in the morning so that he can make a new will; there is talk between the Hubbard menfolk about the chances of Leo pulling off the coup with Horace's bonds, after which polite salon music gives way to a jazz band.

Oscar attempts, on orders from Ben, to be nice to Birdie but only succeeds in putting her down once again, and it is left to the gentle, compassionate Addie to comfort her in a slow, low-lying lullaby of real beauty. Regina flirts with an old beau, more to hurt Horace than out of genuine interest. In her bravura aria, Regina makes no bones about being the most important person in her own life and valuing Things above People – and when she hears Leo and Ben reassure Marshall that the money is to hand and the deal on, her astonishment and expostulations are drowned in the brilliance of the choral Gallop. Through its whirling vulgarity Horace can be heard: 'It's a great day when you and Ben cross swords', but Regina gets the last word, on a top C: 'I hope you die soon. I'll be waiting.'

Act III. Next afternoon. The act begins with a gentle orchestral *adagietto*, followed by the Rain Quartet. The four people in the opera on the side of the angels – Birdie, Zan, Addie and Horace – luxuriate in spring and listen contentedly to the sound of the rain peacefully falling. Theirs is gentle, sophisticated music of great potency, quick and light in tempo but

---

[1] In *Music in a New Found Land*, Wilfrid Mellers has observed that 'the nastiest characters in *Regina* have a bastardised musical idiom hovering between jazz and the nineteenth-century salon'.

unemphatic in manner except in its frank enjoyment of company, agreeable weather and an absence of immediate worries. Horace for once feels well (his solo in the middle of the quartet: 'Consider the rain') and just before the quartet ends, there is interruption from gospel singing at the back of the house. Nonetheless, the quartet finishes on a note of confidence, the opera's highpoint, and 'musically Blitzstein's most mature affirmation, and the most beautiful and original music he (had) so far created'.[1]

The Rain Quartet gives way to Birdie's confession aria. People say she gets headaches, but she knows she drinks – in order to remember her mother, her home at Lionnet, and singing, and in order to forget the horrors of the Hubbards, her beastly son and the husband who married her for her inheritance, for Lionnet. It is a moment not only of nostalgia but of lyrical self-revelation, a twentieth-century high coloratura soliloquy of power and truth. Zan takes her arm and guides her home – not, sadly, to Lionnet.

It is a time for revelation. Horace asks Addie to take Zan away after he is dead; he will make this possible by means of the legacy he had always planned for Addie. When Regina comes in, Horace tells her that he has discovered Leo has taken the bonds, and that without knowing it, they have already invested in Hubbard Sons and Marshall. Regina is instantly convinced they have Ben and Oscar in their hands, but Horace counters by saying he will tell the world the bonds are a loan from her – what's more, they are all she's getting in his will. His arietta is passionate but muted; by contrast Regina's aria ('You hate me very much') is a lot more vehement. She says she has always been confident he would die first. 'Horace,' she says, 'I've always been lucky.'

Horace can take no more, has an attack, and Regina sends for the doctor. But with her brothers, the upper hand is once more hers. Her terms are simple: while Horace lives, she tells the others they are safe. But when he dies, as she expects him to, she wants seventy-five per cent in exchange for the bonds – without which the deal with Marshall cannot be completed. If they refuse, it is jail.

Ben is trying to joss her out of it when they hear Addie keening on the stairs. Zan erupts in passionate grief – what was her father doing on the stairs? Regina in an aria appears to regain the initiative: either she gets the money or she will prosecute. Ben acts the good loser and all seems settled.

But the last word is Zan's. She will be going away and nothing her mother can do will stop her. That is what her father would have wanted her to do, and, to the sound of 'Certainly, Lord', she and Addie stare out of the window as Regina in defeat goes upstairs.   H.

---

[2] Mellers: *Op. cit.*

FRANÇOIS ADRIEN BOÏELDIEU
(born 16 December 1775, died 8 October 1834)

LA DAME BLANCHE
The White Lady

Opera in three acts, text by Scribe, founded on Scott's *Guy Mannering* and *The Monastery*. Première at the Opéra-Comique, Paris, 10 December 1825, with Rigaud, Boulanger, Ponchard, Henry. First performed Drury Lane, London, 1826 (in English); Haymarket, 1834 (in German); New York, 1827 (in French). Revived Metropolitan, 1904, with Gadski, Naval, conductor Mottl; Paris, 1925, with Féraldy, Villabella; Brussels, 1936; London, Philopera Circle, 1955; Toulouse, 1961; Ghent and Bordeaux, 1963, the latter with Michel Sénéchal; Opéra-Comique, 1997, with Raphanel, Kunde, conductor Minkowski.

Gaveston, *steward to the late Comte d'Avenel*.........Bass
Anna, *his ward*..Soprano
George Brown, *a young English officer*...............Tenor
Dickson, *tenant on the estate*.............................Tenor
Jenny, *his wife*..Soprano
Marguerite, *old servant of the Comte d'Avenel* ....Soprano

Gabriel, *employed by Dickson* ....Bass

MacIrton, *Justice of the Peace* ....Bass

Place: Scotland
Time: 1759
Running Time: 1 hour 50 minutes

*L*a Dame Blanche had one of the most successful pre-mières in all operatic history, and still stands as one of the notable hits in the history of *opéra-comique*. The 1,000th performance at the Opéra-Comique in Paris was in 1862, the 1,675th in 1914. It was revived at the Opéra-Comique for the centenary in 1925 with Féraldy and Villabella and, notwithstanding a lack of sparkle in the libretto, remains a distinguished example of *opéra-comique* for the period.

Act I. In front of Dickson's house. Dancing and singing are in progress in honour of the christening of Dickson's small child. George Brown arrives, makes himself known as an officer in the King's service, and accepts to take the place of the child's missing godfather. He enquires about the history of the castle of Avenel, which dominates the countryside, and is told that, among other things, it boasts a ghost, not a malicious one, but a female, known as 'the White Lady', whose special office is to protect her sex from false-hearted suitors. Everyone believes in her, and most are firmly convinced that one time or another they have seen her. Dickson is summoned to meet her that very night, and, in spite of his very definite fears, he dare not disobey. George offers to go in his stead, and the offer is gratefully accepted. They wish him godspeed.

Act II. A Gothic room in the Castle. It is only half-lit and Marguerite is sitting there spinning. Anna comes in to tell Marguerite something of the story of the old Count's missing heir, whom Gaveston is thought to have spirited away so as to obtain the castle for himself. Gaveston tries unsuccessfully to discover from Anna where the Countess hid the treasure before she died. There is a ring at the door-bell and Gaveston says he will not allow anyone to enter; but Anna pleads with him – has he not enemies enough without making any more? She believes that it is Dickson, come at the order of the 'white lady' (for it is Anna who appears as the ghost, and who has summoned Dickson, hoping through him to prevent the castle falling into Gaveston's hands). Anna tells Gaveston that she will the next day reveal the Countess's secret if he will allow the traveller in. Marguerite opens the doors.

George Brown, who has come in Dickson's place, says that he has heard that the castle has a ghost, and he would like to have the opportunity of seeing it. He is left alone in the great room, stokes up the fire, and sings a serenade, hoping to entice the ghost to appear. She does, in the person of Anna, who to her amazement discovers that it is George Brown and recognises him as a wounded officer she had once nursed and grown fond of. He is astonished that the ghost should know such details of his past – he has been trying ever since to find his benefactress, with whom he fell in love – and promises that he will perform whatever she orders on the morrow.

She disappears and Gaveston invites George to stay for the auction which is about to take place. Jenny and Dickson ply George with questions, but he reveals nothing of what he has seen.

Dickson has been charged by his fellow farmers to bid as high as he dare in order to prevent the castle falling into Gaveston's hands. The bidding rises, Dickson is obliged to drop out, but George Brown comes into the reckoning. He is about to give up when the sight of Anna spurs him to greater efforts, and eventually the castle is knocked down to George. He must pay, says the justice, by midday. Gaveston is beside himself with fury.

Act III. The same room. Anna and Marguerite discuss the whereabouts of a certain statue of the 'white lady' in which, says Anna, all the family money was once hidden. Marguerite remembers a secret passage, and they go off to explore it. The crowd meanwhile assembles to do honour to the new owner, and sings a version of the old Scottish tune 'Robin Adair', which he recognises and is able to finish.

Gaveston asks George for some explanation of his extraordinary behaviour of that morning; has he the money to pay for the castle? No, says George, but the 'white lady' will provide it. George leaves and his place is taken by MacIrton, a friend of Gaveston's who warns him that the lost son of the house has turned up in England and now goes under the name of George Brown. Anna, in hiding, overhears.

Just before midday, MacIrton comes with representatives of the law to collect the money; George asks for time to communicate with the white lady, who is financing the whole transaction. Anna appears in the guise of the white lady, bringing the treasure chest with her – she has found it after all.

Moreover she declares that George Brown is the missing heir to the estates of Avenel.

The freshness of the tunes, the effervescent personalities at work in it – these qualities seem to survive the passing of years as far as *La Dame Blanche* is concerned. Such passages as George's invigorating 'Ah, quel plaisir d'être soldat', the agreeable ballad of 'la dame blanche' sung by Jenny and Dickson, and the charming *allegretto* section of the duet in Act II for Anna and George – these have the lightness of touch and distinction that even now personify the

expression 'Opéra-comique'. Anna's aria at the beginning of Act III has an almost Weber-like feeling about it. The figure of George Brown himself is particularly attractive, his part in the action romantic, debonair and devil-may-care and yet never for a moment going against the logic of the drama. Highly successful are his two romantic solos, the one in Act II when he is waiting for the ghost to appear ('Viens gentille dame'), the other equally charming when he tries to catch the tune of 'Robin Adair' as the chorus starts to sing it in Act III.   H.

ARRIGO BOITO

(born 24 February 1842, died 10 June 1918)

MEFISTOFELE

Mephistopheles

Opera in a prologue, four acts, and an epilogue, words by the composer. Première at la Scala, Milan, 5 March 1868, with Reboux, Flory, Spallazzi Junca. Revised version produced at Bologna, 1875, with Borghi-Mamo, Campanini, Nannetti, with great success. First performed at Her Majesty's Theatre, London, 1880, with Christine Nilsson, Campanini, Nannetti, conductor Arditi; New York, 1880, with Valleria, Campanini, Novara; Metropolitan, New York, 1883, with Nilsson, Campanini, Mirabella; revived there 1889, with Lilli Lehmann, 1896, with Calvé, 1907, with Farrar, Martin, Chaliapin; Covent Garden, 1914, with Muzio, Raisa, McCormack, Didur; 1926, with Scacciati, Merli, Chaliapin; la Scala, 1918, with Cannetti, Gigli, de Angelis, conductor Toscanini; 1934, with Caniglia, Bruna Rasa, Masini, Pinza; 1952, with Tebaldi, Martinis, Tagliavini, Rossi-Lemeni, conductor de Sabata; Metropolitan, 1920, with Alda, Easton, Gigli, Didur; San Francisco, 1952, with Sayao, Fenn, Tagliavini, Rossi-Lemeni; Chicago, 1961, with Ligabue, Christa Ludwig, Bergonzi, Christoff; Sadler's Wells (Welsh National Opera), 1957, with Herincx; 1987, Genoa, with Burchaladze in a Ken Russell production which caused a scandal; 1989, San Francisco, with Beňačková, O'Neill, Ramey; 1991, Chicago, with Millo, Kristiansson, Ramey.

Mefistofele (Mephistopheles)...............................Bass
Faust...Tenor
Margherita ....Soprano
Martha...Contralto
Wagner ....Tenor
Elena (Helen of Troy)...................................Soprano
Pantalis ....Mezzo-Soprano

Nereo ....Tenor
Mystic Choir, Cherubs, Penitents, Wayfarers, Men-at-Arms, Huntsmen, Students, Citizens, Witches, Greek Chorus, Sirens, Naiads, Dancers, Warriors

Place: Frankfurt; Vale of Tempe; Ancient Greece
Time: Middle Ages
Running Time: 2 hours 20 minutes

The history of Arrigo Boito's two operas (as opposed to his several, mostly successful, libretti for other composers) is full of surprises, even contradictions. He seems to have settled on two subjects, Goethe's *Faust* and the Roman Emperor Nero, while still a student and to have worked on them throughout his life. *Mefistofele* was a disastrous failure at la Scala in 1868, only two years after he had returned from service as a volunteer with Garibaldi's forces in 1866, partly perhaps because the composer's refusal to sanction the cuts insisted upon by the conductor, who had also been his teacher at the Milan Conservatory, led not only to the latter's withdrawal but his replacement by the inexperienced Boito himself. Revision not only shortened the opera but restored the title role from baritone to tenor, and the result was a considerable success, in Bologna this time rather than Milan. Further revision initiated a process of constant tinkering with work in hand that was to dominate the composer's other great preoccupation, his opera *Nerone*, which had still not reached a final version at the composer's death over forty years after the rehabilitation of *Mefistofele*.

Toscanini championed both operas, conducting the première of *Nerone* at la Scala in 1924, including the Prologue of *Mefistofele* in many concert programmes, and choosing it, together with Act III of the same opera and an act of *Nerone*, for his solitary postwar operatic appearance in a mixed bill at la Scala in June 1948.

Boito was anything but a dilettante composer, and his two operas were worked and re-worked with diligence and skill. But the fact remains that these two operas, together with half a dozen early works of little significance, comprise his entire *oeuvre*. At least ten libretti written for other composers suggest that the written word came more easily than music to this nevertheless highly gifted man.

Prologue. Announced in a slow prelude with frequent trumpet calls, it opens in space, populated by invisible legions of angels, cherubs and seraphs, who raise their voices in a hymn of praise to the Creator. Mefistofele, heralded by *scherzo* music, addresses God ('Ave Signor!') and sardonically offers to wager that he can win the soul of Faust. God through the chorus assents, and cherubim (a boys' chorus) and finally a group of penitents return to their chorus of praise, bringing to an end a movement which contains little action but plenty of drama through music – the very stuff of opera.

Act I. Frankfurt. Easter is being celebrated, a Cavalcade with the Elector at its head passes by, and the aged Dr Faust and his pupil Wagner shadowed by a mysterious grey friar make their entrance. Wagner thinks nothing of him but Faust senses something supernatural. The scene changes to Faust's study where his thoughts turn to eternal peace ('Dai campi, dai prati'), only to be interrupted by a shriek from the friar, who throws off his disguise and impressively declares himself as the spirit of negation ('Son lo spirito che nega sempre'). He offers in exchange for Faust's soul to serve him on earth, and Faust agrees to the bargain ('Se tu mi doni un' ora di riposo'), whereupon Mefistofele spreads his cloak and both disappear through the air.

Act II. A garden. Faust (rejuvenated and under the name of Henry) is strolling with Margherita, her friend Martha, and Mefistofele. Margherita agrees to meet him and he provides her with a sleeping draught for her mother. It is a scene of some charm and contains Faust's solo, 'Colma il tuo cor d'un palpito', and a quartet of farewell.

Scene ii. The heights of the Brocken mountain. Faust watches the orgies of the Witches' Sabbath. The Witches present a glass globe, reflected in which Mefistofele sees the earth which in a grand soliloquy he despises: 'Ecco il mondo' (Behold the earth). The Witches dance and Faust sees a vision of Margherita, her throat encircled by a blood-red necklace. The act ends in a witches' orgy.

Act III. In prison. Margherita lies on a heap of straw. She has drowned her baby, her mind is wandering and her lament is heart-felt: 'L'altra notte in fondo al mare'. Mefistofele and Faust appear outside her cell and Faust begs for Margherita's life. Mefistofele opens the prison door.

Margherita thinks her jailers have come to release her, but recognises her lover. She begs him to let her die beside her baby and her mother, whom she is accused of poisoning, but finally consents to flee with Faust; in some distant place they might yet be happy: 'Lontano, sui flutti d'un ampio oceano'. Mefistofele's voice recalls her to reality. She prays to Heaven for mercy ('Spunta l'aurora pallida') and dies. Voices of the celestial choir (as in the Prologue) sing softly, 'She's saved!' Faust and Mefistofele escape as the executioner appears in the background.

Act IV. Mefistofele takes Faust to the shores of the Vale of Tempe, where Helen and Pantalis hymn the rising moon. Faust is ravished with the beauty of the scene, while Mefistofele remarks that the orgies of the Brocken were more to his taste.

It is the night of the Classical Sabbath. A band of young maidens appears, singing and dancing, much to the annoyance of Mefistofele, who retires. Helen enters and rehearses the story of Troy's destruction. Kneeling before Helen, Faust addresses her as his ideal of beauty and purity ('Forma ideal purissima') and in a rapturous duet they pledge love and devotion ('Ah! Amore! misterio celeste').

Epilogue. Faust's study. Once more an old man, Faust feels death approaching, his last dream filling his mind ('Giunto sul passo estremo'). It is his farewell to life but Mefistofele fears Faust may yet escape him and urges him to new adventures. He hesitates, then seizing the Bible, cries, 'Here at last I find salvation', and dies to the sound of a celestial choir. H.

NERONE
Nero

Opera in four acts, text by the composer. Première at la Scala, Milan, 1 May 1924, with Raisa, Bertana, Pertile, Galeffi, Journet, Pinza, conductor Toscanini. First performed Rome, 1928, with Scacciati, Bertana, Lauri-Volpi, Franci, Maugeri, conductor Marinuzzi; Buenos Aires, 1926, with Arangi-Lombardi, Bertana, Pertile, Franci, Formichi, Pinza, conductor Marinuzzi. Revived la Scala, 1939, with Cigna, Stignani, Voyer, Sved, conductor Marinuzzi; Rome, 1950, with Annaloro; RAI, Turin, 1975, conductor Gavazzeni; Carnegie Hall, New York (in concert), 1982, conductor Eve Queler.

Nerone (Nero), *Emperor of Rome*	Tenor
Simon Mago, *a sorcerer*	Baritone
Fanuèl, *a Christian leader*	Baritone
Asteria	Soprano
Rubria, *a Vestal Virgin*	Mezzo-Soprano
Tigellino, *follower of Nero*	Bass
Gobrias, *follower of Simon Mago*	Tenor
Dositèo, *a Roman*	Baritone
Pèrside, *a Christian*	Soprano
Cerinto	Contralto

Place: Rome and Nearby
Time: c. 60 A.D.
Running Time: 2 hours 40 minutes

Act I. The Appian Way. Simon Mago and Tigellino are waiting for Nero on his way to bury the ashes of his mother, Agrippina, whom he has murdered. He arrives almost penitent but for the fact that in the *Oresteia* he finds a precedent for matricide. He has heard an unearthly voice saying 'I am Orestes', and he finds comfort in the thought that he is the reincarnation of Orestes. He apostrophises the grave where the ashes of Agrippina must be buried: 'Queste ad un lido fatal'. Simon Mago gives him absolution. Just as the rite is ending the figure of a woman, whose neck is encircled by snakes, seems to rise from the ground. Nero flees, but Simon stays and boldly challenges her.

The newcomer is Asteria, who loves Nero and follows him everywhere. Simon believes she may be of use to him and promises to bring her to Nero if she will do his bidding. Simon descends to the crypt where the Christians gather, while two Christians, Rubria and Fanuèl, meet above. Rubria loves Fanuèl, but Fanuèl has no other thought than his mission. Rubria recites the Lord's Prayer, watched by Asteria. When the two Christians see their arch-enemy, Simon, issuing from the crypt, Rubria is sent to warn the others, while Fanuèl remains to face whatever danger there is. But Simon has no hostile intentions. He sees the old world going to ruin and now offers power and wealth to Fanuèl if Fanuèl will but teach him how to work miracles. The music at this point works in the traditional 'intonation' of the Credo. Fanuèl, dreaming of a world in which neither power nor wealth has a share, indignantly refuses. The two must henceforth be enemies.

The news of Nero's return has reached Rome and a great procession comes to meet him. A scene of triumph closes the act.

Act II. The temple of Simon Mago. The stage is divided into two by the altar where Simon pretends to work a miracle. The faithful worship and pray; Simon's adepts laugh and count their gains. The mock ceremony over, Simon prepares the temple for the expected visit of Nero. To persuade the Emperor that Simon can work miracles, Asteria will pretend to be a goddess; echoes must be arranged, mirrors placed so as to make it appear that phantoms visit the temple. Nero addresses the supposed goddess: 'Oh, come viene a errar'. Everything follows the appointed course until Nero touches Asteria and the goddess reveals herself as a woman. In vain the metallic voice of the oracle is heard warning Nero. The Emperor no longer fears these gods. He calls to his guards, who arrest Simon and set about destroying the temple. Standing over the ruins, Nero takes a cithara and sings.

Act III. In an orchard away from the noise of Rome the Christians meet and their leader, Fanuèl, expounds the Beatitudes; Rubria tells the parable of the foolish virgins in music of utmost suavity. Asteria has escaped from her prison house to warn them that Simon has tried to purchase freedom by betraying the Christians to Nero. Rubria urges Fanuèl to fly but he refuses. Two beggars come to them in the darkness; they are Simon and one of his assistants who have come to spy. Discovering Fanuèl, Simon sends to warn the guards; there is a short scene of considerable power between Fanuèl and Simon Mago. When the guards arrive, Fanuèl orders the Christians to submit. He tells them his journey is ended. As he goes the women make a path of flowers before him. Rubria is left alone while the Christians' hymn dies away in the distance. The whole passage, with its mixture of Christian serenity and dramatic power, is most impressive.

Act IV. The first scene takes place in the 'Oppidum', where the mob has gathered to applaud the victors and abuse the vanquished. Here Simon and Gobrias plot to burn Rome and escape the punishment which awaits Simon. The conspiracy is made known by Tigellino to Nero, who refuses to interfere. He has planned the games; he is determined to succeed and to please the mob; if the mob demands victims it shall have them. Fanuèl is brought in together with other Christians, who go to their martyrdom in the circus.

A vestal demands their pardon. Nero angrily orders the veil to be torn from her. It is Rubria, who has come to help Fanuèl. She too is condemned. The Christians go to their deaths; Simon follows, and then the light of the flames which are consuming the city is seen in the distance.

The second scene takes us to the 'spoliarium', where those who died in the circus are thrown. Asteria and Fanuèl, who, thanks to the fire, have escaped, find Rubria wounded to death. Before dying, she confesses her sin. She was a vestal; she worshipped with the Christians and then returned every day to Vesta. There is time for another confession; she loves Fanuèl. He too loves and now calls her his bride. She asks Fanuèl to tell her once more of Galilee and of the sea on whose shore Christ prayed. Fanuèl obeys, and with that image in her eyes and in her mind, Rubria dies.

Nerone was originally planned in five acts. Boito worked at the opera all his life, adding and cancelling and improving till he wrote on the last page: 'The End: Arrigo Boito and Kronos'.   F. B.

ALEKSANDR PORFIRYEVICH BORODIN
(born 12 November 1834, died 27 February 1887)

PRINCE IGOR
Knyaz Igor

Opera in a prologue and four acts, text by the composer after a play by V.V. Stassov; completed by Rimsky-Korsakov and Glazunov. Première at St Petersburg, 4 November 1890. First performed London, Drury Lane, 1914, with Kousnetzova, Petrenko, Andreev, Chaliapin; Metropolitan, New York, 1915, with Alda, Amato, Didur; Covent Garden, 1919 (in English), with Licette, Thornton, Millar, Edmund Burke, Allin, conductor Coates. Revivals include Berlin, 1930, with Branzell, Roswaenge, Schorr, Scheidl, conductor Blech; Covent Garden, 1935, with Rethberg, Branzell, Kullman, Janssen, Kipnis, conductor Beecham; la Scala, 1940; Vienna, 1947, with Hilde Konetzni, Nikolaidi, Rothmüller, Alsen, conductor Krips; Montreal (EXPO 1967), by Bolshoi Company; New York City Opera, 1969; Opera North, 1982.

Igor Sviatoslavich, *Prince of Seversk*		Baritone
Yaroslavna, *his wife*		Soprano
Vladimir Igorevich, *Igor's son*		Tenor
Vladimir Yaroslavich, *Prince Galitzky, brother of Yaroslavna*		Bass
Khan Kontchak	*Polovtsian leaders*	Bass
Khan Gzak		Bass
Kontchakovna, *Kontchak's daughter*		Mezzo-Soprano
Ovlour, *a Polovtsian*		Tenor
Skoula	*Gudok players*	Bass
Eroshka		Tenor
Yaroslavna's Nurse		Soprano
A Young Polovtsian Maiden		Soprano

Russian Princes and Princesses, Boyars and their Wives, Russian Warriors, People; Polovtsian Chiefs, Kontchakovna's Women, Slaves of Khan Kontchak, Russian Prisoners of War, Polovtsian Troops

Place: The Town of Poutivl; the Polovtsian Camp
Time: 1185
Running Time: 3 hours 20 minutes

Borodin, who divided his life between science and music, wrote his opera piece by piece. Rimsky-Korsakov often found him working in his laboratory. 'When he was seated before his retorts, which were filled with colourless gases of some kind, forcing them by means of tubes from one vessel to another, I used to tell him that he was spending his time in pouring water into a sieve. As soon as he was free he would take me to his living-rooms and there we occupied ourselves with music and conversation, in the midst of which Borodin would rush off to the laboratory to make sure that nothing was burning or boiling over, making the corridor ring as he went with some extraordinary passage of ninths or seconds. Then back again for more music and talk.'

Borodin himself wrote: 'In winter I can only compose when I am too unwell to give my lectures. So my friends, reversing the usual custom, never say to me, "I hope you are well" but "I do hope you are ill". At Christmas I had influenza, so I stayed at home and wrote the Thanksgiving Chorus in the last act of *Igor*.'

He never finished his opera. It was completed by Rimsky-Korsakov and his pupil Glazunov, and three years after his death received its first performance. Borodin never wrote down the overture, but Glazunov heard him play it so frequently that it was easy for him to orchestrate it according to Borodin's wishes. The composer left this note about his opera: 'It is curious to see how all the members of our set agree in praise of my work. While controversy rages amongst us on every other subject, all, so far, are pleased with *Igor* – Mussorgsky, the ultra-realist, the innovating lyrico-dramatist, Cui, our master, Balakirev, so severe as regards form and tradition, Vladimir Stassov himself, our valiant champion of everything that bears the stamp of novelty or greatness.'

The overture is composed entirely of music heard later. It opens with the music which precedes Igor's great aria in the second act, continues with themes later associated with Kontchak and Kontchakovna, before reaching the impassioned Ex. 1:

and Ex. 2:

Prologue. The market-place of Poutivl, where rules Igor, Prince of Seversk. Although implored to postpone his departure because of an eclipse of the sun, which his people regard as an evil omen, Igor with his son Vladimir departs to pursue the Polovtsi, a Tartar tribe, formerly driven to the plains of the Don by Igor's father, Prince Sviatoslav of Kiev.

Act I. The house of Prince Vladimir Galitzky, brother of Igor's wife, Yaroslavna. Galitzky in Igor's absence has been appointed to govern Poutivl and watch over the Princess Yaroslavna. He is popular with the crowd, on account of his easy-going, profligate ways. In an incisive, vigorous aria, which perfectly sets off his irresponsible character, he makes it clear that he is a man of mettle, and one to be reckoned with.

Some young girls venture into Galitzky's presence to appeal for his help and protection against his hangers-on, who have abducted one of them. He refuses to take any steps in the matter. Skoula and Eroshka, a pair of drunken *Gudok* players who have deserted from Igor's army, try to stir up the mob against their absent chief. They sing the praises of their patron, Galitzky, and demand rhetorically why he should not become their prince and rule over them.

The scene changes to Yaroslavna's room, where the same party of girls as had failed to enlist Galitzky's sympathy comes to ask for aid. This is preceded by a beautiful, warm *arioso* passage for Yaroslavna alone. That she is a match for her brother she proves a moment later when he enters her room. She compels him to agree to give up the girl who was abducted.

In the finale, an account is given of the disasters which have befallen Igor – he has been defeated, he and the young prince are prisoners, and the enemy is marching on Poutivl. The alarm bell is sounded, but the act ends on a note of defiance, the loyal boyars swearing to defend Yaroslavna, their Princess.

Act II. The camp of the Polovtsi. In this and the next act, Borodin has been highly successful in giving his music (to our western ears at any rate) something of an oriental colour. Khan Kontchak sings music that is totally different from Galitzky's (although the two roles are often, valuably, sung by the same singer), and Kontchakovna obviously inhabits a different world from Yaroslavna. This difference is immediately apparent when the young Polovtsian maidens sing their languorous song to their mistress. They dance for her, but the day is drawing to a close, and she puts an end to their activities, and herself sings a beautiful nocturne whose languishing, chromatic melody speaks longingly of love.

Kontchakovna sees a group of Russian prisoners coming into the camp, and bids her women give them water to drink. The prisoners sing their thanks, and move on towards captivity, followed by the Polovtsian guards. Prince Vladimir, Igor's son, has already fallen in love with the Khan's daughter, and he expresses his feelings in an aria of exquisite beauty, 'Daylight is fading away'. Kontchakovna tells Vladimir that she is confident her father will not oppose their marriage, but Vladimir is sure Igor will not even consider giving his approval to a match with the daughter of his enemy. They leave as Igor approaches, filled with longing for his homeland, and walks through the camp where he is held prisoner. We hear the music which began the overture. He sings desperately of his past happiness and present misery (Ex. 1), and longs for freedom to re-establish his glory and to ensure the safety of his people. There is tenderness in his reference to Yaroslavna (Ex. 2), but his *scena* dies away in a mood of despair.

To him comes the Tartar traitor Ovlour, and, in music of insinuating character, offers to help him escape. He refuses – honour prevents him taking such a course, however strong the temptation.

Hardly has Ovlour gone than Khan Kontchak himself appears. In a great bass *scena*, the Khan offers the Prince anything he may desire to make his captivity less irksome. He looks upon him as an honoured guest, not as a prisoner; will he choose hawks, horses, a finer tent, slaves? Igor answers that nothing in his captivity irks him – only his loss of liberty. Even liberty the Khan will restore him, if he will pledge his word not to make war on him again. Why should they not unite? Together the world would be at their feet. But Igor admits that if he were given his freedom, his first action would be to raise an army and march against the Tartars who threaten the peace of his land. The Khan appears to like his guest's frankness, and gives orders that the dancing slaves should be brought in to perform for their joint entertainment.

Now begin the famous Polovtsian dances, known from frequent performance with or without the chorus (which is in reality an integral part of them), in concert hall, and as a separate ballet. In scope they range from soft enticing melody to harsh vigour, with more than a touch of the barbaric in it. In context, they make a thrilling finale to an act whose varied musical splendours constitute perhaps Borodin's most enduring memorial.

Act III. The prelude is a savage Polovtsian march, augmented by the chorus, accompanying the entrance of Khan Gzak and his warriors, who, like Kontchak, have been victorious over their Russian foes, and who bring in their train a crowd of prisoners. We see the primitive side of Kontchak's character in the vigorous and triumphant aria in which he welcomes his brothers-in-arms and rejoices in the slaughter and devastation they have left behind them. The sound of trumpets announces the division of the spoils, as the two Khans go off to make new plans for their campaigns against the Russians. The Tartars keep up the mood of urgency, but the Russians, when they are left alone by their captors, lament the state into which their country has fallen. Is it not incumbent on Igor, they ask, to escape from captivity and lead his countrymen to revenge and freedom? Igor is persuaded that he must sacrifice honour to duty.

In celebration of their victory, the Polovtsi guards make merry, and it is not long before they are drunk. It is Ovlour's chance. He settles the details of the escape with Igor and Vladimir and arranges to meet them with the horses he has in waiting on the other side of the river. But Kontchakovna has had word that an escape is plotted, and she is full of reproaches, not at the treachery which is planned but that Vladimir should be prepared to leave her without so much as an attempt to take her with him. She pleads that the voice of love should be heard as well as that of duty. Vladimir is undecided, but his father hears what Kontchakovna is suggesting, and a fine trio ensues, in which Igor (to the tune of Ex. 1) opposes his will to Kontchakovna's. The Khan's daughter finally has recourse to a desperate expedient, and rouses the camp. Igor escapes, but Vladimir is left behind in the hands of the Polovtsi.

The Polovtsi pursue Igor, and at first cry for the death of Vladimir, in spite of the pleas of Kontchakovna. However, Kontchak appears on the scene, and admits his admiration for Igor; in his position, he would have followed the same course. In a couple of phrases, he shows both sides of his simple yet complex nature; let them hang the guards who should have prevented Igor's flight, but may Vladimir be spared to live among them as Kontchakovna's husband, and their ally. A chorus of praise to Kontchak brings the act to an end.

Act IV. The city walls and public square of Poutivl. Yaroslavna laments her lost happiness. Her plaintive phrases eventually give way to the passionate theme associated with Igor's love for her (Ex. 2). After the extensive *scena* for Yaroslavna, who sits absorbed in her gloomy thoughts, some peasants pass by, also full of woe.

But the tide is due to turn for the Russians. Yaroslavna sees in the distance two horsemen riding furiously towards the city; one of them seems arrayed like a prince, the other is evidently from his dress a Polovtsian. She recognises Igor, and in a moment they are in each other's arms. Their duet is rapturous with delight, and they go off towards the citadel, pausing in front of the gate just as Eroshka and Skoula come into sight, slightly drunk as is their habit, and giving vent to disloyal sentiments on the subject of their rightful prince. Igor is the cause of all their woes, they sing – but they are filled with consternation when they recognise the subject of their conversation standing only a few yards from them. Shall they go into voluntary exile to escape the penalty that must surely be theirs? No! The thought of enforced wandering is hardly less repugnant than the possibility of death; let them brave it out.

Borodin was much too fond of his drunken rascals to let them finish the opera with anything but a flourish (cf. Mussorgsky with Varlaam and Missail), and Eroshka and Skoula duly emerge on top when they announce the return of Igor to his as yet unsuspecting subjects. They are hailed as at any rate partially responsible for the joy which has come to the city and are allowed to participate in the finale (marked *allegro marziale*), in which the return of Igor and the imminent fall of Galitzky are jointly celebrated.

Borodin did not 'finish' *Prince Igor* (although he wrote all the music) and the kind of revision to which a composer of an epic of this sort might be expected to subject his work was not available to him. The organisers of modern performances are faced with a dilemma when confronted with an opera which sprawls (as to my mind does *Prince Igor*) and which yet contains music of such evident value. Some have revised it entirely as did Eugene Goossens for Covent Garden in 1937, others have simply omitted Act III, thus bringing the opera within manageable length while omitting little of the drama though much that is of musical value (some was included at the New York City Opera in 1969 and by Opera North in Leeds in 1982). A final – even an interim – editorial solution has not yet been reached, hardly even attempted.   K.W., H.

RUTLAND BOUGHTON

(born 23 January 1878, died 25 January 1960)

THE IMMORTAL HOUR

Opera in two acts, the libretto being adapted from the play and poems of Fiona Macleod. Performed at Glastonbury on 26 August 1914. It was an immediate success, and Elgar pronounced it a work of genius. The chief interpreters on that occasion were Irene Lemon (Etain), Frederic Austin (Eochaidh), Muriel Boughton (Spirit Voice), Neville Strutt (Manus), Agnes Thomas (Maive), Arthur Trowbridge (Old Bard), Arthur Jordan (Midir), and the composer himself sang the part of Dalua. The war delayed its production in London, and it was only in 1920 that it was given there at the Old Vic Theatre. In 1922 the Birmingham Players brought it to London, where it played at the Regent Theatre for 216 performances, with Gwen Ffrangcon Davies as Etain; Kingsway Theatre, London, 1926; New York, 1926; Royal Academy of Music, 1939; Sadler's Wells, 1953, with Patricia Howard, Lanigan, Hargreaves, Clarkson, conductor James Robertson.

Dalua	Baritone
Etain	Soprano
Eochaidh	Baritone
Spirit Voice	Mezzo-Soprano
Manus	Bass
Maive	Contralto
Old Bard	Bass
Midir	Tenor

Chorus of Druids and Warriors

Running Time: 2 hours

Act I, scene i. A forest. A pool in the background. Dalua, the Lord of Shadow, a creature of the fairy world, passes wearily through the forest. The trees dance around him while a ghostly chorus mocks him. He tells them to be still for he hears the voice of another wanderer. The spirits disappear. Dalua hides while Etain comes haltingly forward. Dalua recognises her and salutes her, 'daughter of Kings and Star among the dreams that are lives and souls'. She has forgotten the fairy world to which she belongs and which Dalua seeks to recall to her. She does not know why she is in the wood. But Dalua knows. A King of men has wooed the 'Immortal Hour'. He has called upon the gods to send him one fairer than any mortal maid, and the gods sent Etain. Who is this King? asks Etain. He is coming hither now, answers Dalua. Etain goes out slowly while the sound of the horn heralds the coming of Eochaidh, the King. Dalua salutes him and the King recognises in him one whom he has known in dreams – why is he in this lonely wood?

Scene ii. The hut of Manus and Maive. Manus sits before the pine-log fire. His wife stands at the back, plucking feathers from a dead cockerel. In a sheltered recess sits Etain.

Manus and Maive are discussing the stranger who has given them three pieces of gold – one for Etain, one for any stranger who might come, and one for keeping silence. Etain laments the beauty of her world, lost to her, and asks the peasants if they know of it. But Manus is afraid to answer. Just then the horn is heard outside. It is Eochaidh calling to the people in the hut. He is told to enter and, exchanging a greeting with his humble host, the King sees Etain. Manus and Maive retire in the shadow.

The King makes himself known to Etain who can only tell him her name because she is still bewildered by a strange darkness on her mind. The course of true love runs smooth enough until voices are heard singing the praise of the lordly ones 'who dwell in the hills'. The curtain descends, with Eochaidh kneeling by the side of Etain, who listens spellbound as the voices outside slowly melt away in the distance.

Act II. Druids are celebrating the anniversary of the meeting of King Eochaidh and his bride. Etain would like to thank them for their welcome when she is suddenly assailed by strange thoughts and longings. Wearily she bids them farewell and would retire, when Eochaidh begs her to remain and not leave him alone this night. He is full of forebodings. Surely Dalua has bewitched his eyes. Etain too has heard the magic music; she must go. Slowly she descends from her throne and goes out. The King sends away the bards and the warriors. As they move to go they are confronted by a stranger, Midir, who comes to claim a boon. He is himself a king's son. He wishes the King well; may he obtain his heart's desire. Eochaidh grants the boon and requests the bards and Druids to leave him alone with the stranger.

As soon as they are gone the King turns eagerly to Midir whose power he feels to be more than mortal, and asks: 'Give me my heart's desire. Tell me there is to be no twilight upon my joy.' Midir answers him by throwing off his cloak and, clad in pure gold, tells the story of Aedh the shining god and of Dana; how they loved and how Oengus was born of their union. Murmuring 'dreams, dreams', Eochaidh turns to the subject of Midir's request for a boon. Midir asks to be allowed to kiss the Queen's hand. Eochaidh has promised, and he sends for her. An old bard sings of dreams that have passed silent and swift like shadows.

Etain appears in the doorway dressed as she was when Eochaidh first saw her, in green with the mystic mistletoe in her hair. She does not recognise Midir but readily allows him, at the King's request, to kiss her hand and to sing a song he has made. The song is the one that has been heard at the close of the first act, exalting the 'lordly ones in the hollow hills'. Its effect on Etain is that of a spell, and when Eochaidh would come near her she seems unaware of his presence. Midir sings another more joyous song of the land of youth where there is no death, of the land of heart's desire, and Etain feels drawn irresistibly to him. Eochaidh implores Etain to stay, but Etain no longer hears him.

An unseen chorus takes up the haunting melody and Etain slowly follows Midir as in a trance. The stage grows dark; only a light shines where Midir stands. As he passes out of sight complete darkness falls on the stage. Dalua enters, and rapidly touches Eochaidh, who falls inert to the ground. F.B.

BENJAMIN BRITTEN
(born 22 November 1913, died 4 December 1976)

The story of Benjamin Britten's sixteen operas can be told in terms of a search for twentieth-century operatic form. Essentially, he cut for himself four different paths. First, a traditional-force line, involving a big apparatus, designed by implication for nineteenth-century-style buildings and comprising *Peter Grimes*, *Billy Budd* and *Gloriana*. Next, he invented a new form of chamber opera, with initially an orchestra of thirteen, no chorus, a small number of soloists, and intended for smaller theatres (*The Rape of Lucretia*, *Albert Herring*, *The Beggar's Opera* and *The Turn of the Screw*). Even more out of the ordinary, and also made for smaller forces and buildings, were the children's operas – *The Little Sweep*, *The Golden Vanity* and *Noye's Fludde*, the last designed for performance in church. A fourth and wholly original category was the church parable, of which there were three examples: *Curlew River*, *The Burning Fiery Furnace* and *The Prodigal Son*. There is contrast between the forms he evolved but flexibility within them, and *A Midsummer Night's Dream*, *Owen Wingrave*, and *Death in Venice* (which are neither traditional nor chamber in form, nor in the forces they require) have proved almost as viable in theatres as large as the San Francisco Opera, Covent Garden and the Metropolitan as in Aldeburgh's Jubilee Hall, on television, or at the Snape Maltings, for which they were first designed.

Formal diversity then distinguishes the sixteen operas, from the Coronation Gala work, *Gloriana*, with its big solo statements, its pageantry and its ballet, to the loosely-knit *Noye's Fludde*, with its tuned mugs and children's bugle band; from the farcical comedy of *Albert Herring* to the almost ritualistic shaping of *The Turn of the Screw*; from the often deliberate and monodic church parables to the lightning changes and prestidigital compression of *Owen Wingrave*; from the relatively traditional *Peter Grimes* to the convention-defying *Death in Venice*.

When the last of the operas – as one had come to accept *Death in Venice* would be – had been heard the whole perspective was suddenly altered by the re-appearance of a precursor, the hitherto suppressed *Paul Bunyan*. This was written a couple of years before *Peter Grimes*, and made no attempt either to keep or to defy operatic rules, but invented its own as it went along: improvising brilliant and effective stage stuff out of Auden's often mock-sophisticated, bookish libretto; paying no attention to the conventions of stage realism and characterisation, but instead scattering operatic seeds on ground which in the event proved stony – the work was a failure – but which might, had it been fertile, have immediately grown an operatic forest. Had that initial experiment met with acceptance, the elaborately-tested experiments of subsequent years might never have had to be made, and Minerva could have sprung fully-armed from the (invisible) head of Paul Bunyan!

PAUL BUNYAN

Operetta in two acts and a prologue, libretto by W.H. Auden and Chester Kallman. Première by Columbia University, New York, 5 May 1941, with Helen Marshall (Tiny), William Hess (Inkslinger), Mordecai Bauman (Narrator). First performed B.B.C. Radio, 1976, with Norma Burrowes, Peter Pears (Inkslinger), George Hamilton IV (Narrator), conductor Steuart Bedford; Aldeburgh Festival, 1976, with Iris Saunders, Neil Jenkins, Russell Smythe (and at Florence Festival, 1978); Cassel (in German), 1978, conductor James Lockhart; Albany Opera, London, 1981; St Louis, 1984.

Narrator	Baritone or Tenor
The Voice of Paul Bunyan	Spoken
Johnny Inkslinger, *bookkeeper*	Tenor
Tiny, *Paul Bunyan's daughter*	Soprano
Hot Biscuit Slim, *a good cook*	Tenor
Sam Sharkey ⎱ *two bad cooks*	Tenor
Ben Benny ⎰	Bass
Hel Helson, *foreman*	Baritone
Four Swedes	Tenors, Basses
John Shears, *a farmer*	Baritone
Western Union Boy	Tenor
Fido, *a dog*	High Soprano
Moppet ⎱ *two cats*	Mezzo-Soprano
Poppet ⎰	Mezzo-Soprano

Lumberjacks, Farmers, Frontier Women; Herons, Moon, Wind, Beetle, Squirrel

Place: United States of America
Time: Early Times
Running Time: 2 hours

Thirty-five years separate the first performance of Benjamin Britten's so-called operetta and its second, and there is a vast difference between the circumstances of the première in New York by the Music Department of Columbia University and the grandly cast B.B.C. broadcast of February 1976. In New York, it was a failure, and the composer withdrew the work, for years treating it as a youthful indiscretion, although he would occasionally play a snatch or two from it to friends.

Its origins are uncomplicated. Britten and Auden were living in New York and the composer's publishers, Boosey and Hawkes, wanted them to write something suitable for performance in high schools. Paul Bunyan, the giant lumberman hero, was conceived as ' ... a projection of the collective state of mind of a people whose tasks were primarily the physical mastery of nature ... Paul Bunyan says goodbye because he is no longer needed' (from the original programme note).

Britten began revising the operetta (or as he preferred to say, adjusting it) in 1974 with a view to performance by the about-to-be-formed English Music Theatre, deciding in the process to omit the original overture and composing a brief introduction in its place; revising Slim's and Tiny's songs in Act I and the mocking of Hel Helson in Act II. As well as the original overture, he dropped a song for Inkslinger and the lumberjacks in Act I, and composed a new finale to the first act.

Prologue. A slow solemn introduction suggesting the awakening of giant forces leads to a scene in the forest. The chorus quietly celebrates rivers, rain, trees. We hear the name of Paul Bunyan, who will only be born 'at the next Blue Moon'. Immediately the moon turns blue.

The operetta is interspersed with ballads in a folk-style sung by a Narrator. The first one, leading to Act I, describes the birth and raising of Paul Bunyan.

Act I. A clearing in the forest. The voice of Paul Bunyan (who is too big ever to be seen) can be heard: 'It is a spring morning without benefit of young persons ... It is America, but not yet'. Lumberjacks from Sweden, France, Germany and even England sing in full flood, and Bunyan welcomes them. Who shall be foreman? Four Swedes volunteer but can't

agree which is the best, but the problem is solved when the Western Union boy brings 'A telegram from overseas'. The King of Sweden is sending his finest logger, Hel Helson, and he will be foreman.

Two cooks sing seductively together, *larghetto*, and the mention of food brings in Johnny Inkslinger, bookkeeper, poet, ultimately the camp's intellectual. He can join – and eat – only if he works. He says he won't. The cooks need dogs to clean up and chase away salesmen, and cats to catch mice and rats. A trio of animals, two of the former, one of the latter (singing always together), solve that problem, and Bunyan says goodnight, for the first of several times.

The next number is a highly effective Blues for alto, tenor, baritone and bass solos, after which Inkslinger enters to accept a job – on Bunyan's conditions: no work, no supper! Bunyan's second goodnight.

A second ballad interlude, during which the growing up of the lumberjacks is described and also Paul Bunyan's search for a wife of appropriate dimensions for someone of his vast size. He finds one and they marry, have a daughter called Tiny, are unhappy together, part, and later she dies.

Food is one of the camp's main preoccupations, and it is apparently not good enough. Inkslinger is most articulate in complaint, and after he has gently told Sam and Ben they are looking for more variety, the two cooks walk out. The others rat on Inkslinger and blame it all on him, but there is an interruption as Slim comes in. In his attractively lyrical song, he makes clear that he is looking for the self he knows he hasn't yet found. Is he perhaps the cook they need?

Bunyan returns with his daughter Tiny, a pretty girl, as the lumberjacks are not slow to notice.

Inkslinger tells the story of his life in a large-scale song which articulates the style of the new American writers, born and bred in the sticks. The others are more interested in Bunyan's daughter and each hopes he can supply what she lacks. Her song is more one of sadness for her mother's death than of confidence in the future.

Inkslinger regrets that life's timing seems constantly awry, but when Bunyan comes back, he warns him that Hel Helson seems a bit restive, like some of the others. Bunyan's third goodnight.

Act II. Bunyan's good-morning starts the act, and he reads the men a lecture about their conduct. Hel Helson is left in charge while Bunyan is away.

Helson and four cronies are alone together and though off-stage the chorus sings 'No! I'm afraid it's too late, Helson never will be great', he makes plain in his song that he is not without ambition.

It is the turn of the animals, and first Fido then the two cats parade their not-so-simple philosophies.

Bunyan is back and the cronies egg Helson on to challenge him. As Helson runs out, the chorus rushes in and their graphic description of what is going on off-stage is intercut with a love duet for Tiny and Slim on stage, an early example of Britten's ability to invent an operatic situation where none truly exists. To a mock funeral march, Helson is carried in unconscious. Bunyan suggests they let bygones be bygones. There is a choral hymn 'O great day of Discovery'.

The third ballad interlude celebrates peace between Helson and Bunyan and their future partnership which will be part of the founding of America.

It is Christmas Eve and the party is musically a very lively affair, with sung interjected solos from the animals and a speech from Inkslinger, who announces the engagement of Tiny and Slim and the latter's promotion to run a hotel in Manhattan. The chorus is delighted, the animals join in, and Hel's contribution to their life – he converts Paul's ambitious dreams into practical schemes – is not forgotten. Even the Western Union boy has a job as he brings Inkslinger a telegram from Hollywood; he will be famous! Paul is leaving and his Farewell bids them remember their freedom.

The operetta ends with a so-called litany, in which they ask to be saved from (for instance) 'a tolerance that is really inertia and disillusion'. But Paul reminds them that 'America is what you do, America is what you choose to make it', which may make a less than rumbustious ending to an operetta, but then this, with its soft, downbeat finish (marked *solenne*), is unlike other specimens, if in no other way than that its vocal score proclaims it an operetta on the title page, an opera under its last bar!   H.

PETER GRIMES

Opera in a prologue, an epilogue, and three acts, text by Montagu Slater, after the poem by George Crabbe. Première, Sadler's Wells, London, 7 June 1945, with Joan Cross, Coates, Iacopi, Blanche Turner, Bower, Pears, Roderick Jones, Donlevy, Brannigan, Morgan Jones, Culbert, conductor Goodall. First performed Stockholm, 1945, with Sundström,

Svanholm, Sigurd Björling, conductor Sandberg; Berkshire Festival, U.S.A., 1946, with Manning, William Horne, Pease, conductor Bernstein; Zürich, 1946, with Cross, Cordy, von Sieben, della Casa, Moor, Pears, Andreas Boehm, Rehfuss, Vichegonov, Libero de Luca, conductor Denzler; Hamburg, 1947, with Schlüter, Markwort, conductor Hollreiser; Berlin, 1947, with Grümmer, Witte, conductor Heger; Covent Garden, 1947, with Cross, Pears, conductor Rankl, later Goodall; la Scala, Milan, 1947, with Danco, Ticozzi, Prandelli, Colombo, Borriello, conductor Serafin; Metropolitan, New York, 1948, with Resnik (later Stoska), Jagel (later Sullivan), Brownlee, Hines, Garris, conductor Emil Cooper; 1967, with Amara, Vickers, Geraint Evans, conductor Colin Davis. After Peter Pears, Jon Vickers had a marked success in the title role, playing it all over English-speaking countries.

Peter Grimes, *a fisherman*	Tenor
John, *his apprentice*	Silent
Ellen Orford, *a widow, schoolmistress of the Borough*	Soprano
Captain Balstrode, *retired merchant skipper*	Baritone
Auntie, *landlady of 'The Boar'*	Contralto
Her Two 'Nieces', *main attractions of 'The Boar'*	Sopranos
Bob Boles, *fisherman and Methodist*	Tenor
Swallow, *a lawyer*	Bass
Mrs (Nabob) Sedley, *a rentier widow of an East India Company's factor*	Mezzo-Soprano
Rev. Horace Adams, *the rector*	Tenor
Ned Keene, *apothecary and quack*	Baritone
Dr Thorp	Silent
Hobson, *the carrier*	Bass

Chorus of Townspeople and Fisherfolk

Place: The Borough, a Fishing Village, East Coast of England
Time: Towards 1830
Running Time: 2 hours 35 minutes

The idea of *Peter Grimes* came to Britten in America in 1941 after reading an article by E.M. Forster on the subject of George Crabbe, the poet of England and more particularly of East Anglia. Shortly afterwards, Koussevitzky, the conductor, offered to commission him to write an opera, and, immediately on his return to England (in the spring of 1942), he set to work with Montagu Slater to hammer out the libretto.

This is freely adapted from Crabbe's story, which forms a part of his long poem, *The Borough*. The venue remains Aldeburgh, where Crabbe was born and where Britten, shortly after the première of *Peter Grimes*, made his home, but the character of Peter Grimes is softened; he is no longer the uncomplicated

Peter Grimes *(Sadler's Wells, London, 1947). Peter Pears as Grimes and Joan Cross as Ellen Orford.*

sadist of Crabbe's poem, but a proud, self-willed out-sider, whose uncompromising independence and un-willingness to accept help bring him in the end to disaster.

The immediate success of Britten's opera is a matter of history. Its first performance came a month after the end of the war in Europe and coincided with the return of the Sadler's Wells Company to its London home; the music has unflagging vitality and inven-tion; the subject was susceptible enough to traditional big-scale operatic treatment to please old opera-goers, and the anti-hero (an early example of the type) suffi-ciently 'different' to please the more sophisticated.

Prologue. The Moot Hall of the Borough, where the inquest is being held on Grimes's apprentice who died at sea. As the curtain goes up, we hear in the woodwind a theme which is associated with Swallow, the Borough lawyer and Coroner. The people of the Borough suspect Grimes of having caused the boy's death, and feeling runs high. When asked to give evidence, Grimes repeats the oath after Swallow in notes an octave higher and of double the time value. He tells a story of distress at sea, how he and the boy, when out fishing, were driven off course, how they were three days without water, and how the boy died of exposure.

When it comes to confirming what occurred when Grimes landed his boat, Swallow and Grimes refer in turn to Ned Keene, the Rector, Bob Boles, Auntie, Mrs Sedley, and Ellen Orford, who corroborate the evi-dence. There is some interruption from the onlookers, and at the end the Coroner gives his verdict: '... your apprentice died in accidental circumstances. But that's the kind of thing people are apt to remember', and advises Grimes to get a grown-up, not a boy, to help him in future. Grimes tries to make himself heard above the growing uproar, but it is impossible, and Hobson clears the court.

Grimes and Ellen Orford are left alone, and Ellen tries to give comfort. Their duet begins with Ellen singing in E major, Peter in F minor, but as Peter warms to her quiet confidence in his future, he takes up her key and they finish together: 'here is a friend'.

Britten begins each of his three acts with a so-called Interlude, and also connects the two scenes of each of them with a similar orchestral piece. Prologue and Act I are joined by a calm piece which seems to express the typical movement of waves and water so often heralding a new day for the fishermen of the Borough.

Act I. The beach, showing the Moot Hall, Boar Inn, and the church. The first part of the scene is in the form of an extended chorus, 'Oh, hang at open doors the net, the cork', with interruptions from Auntie, who opens up for the day; Boles, who protests at anything which comes into the category of fun; Balstrode, who is concerned with the weather; the Rector and Mrs Sedley, who wish each other 'Good morning'; and Ned Keene, who says he is anxious for an assignation with one of Auntie's 'Nieces' that night.

Meanwhile, the fishermen and their womenfolk go about their daily business, mending nets and preparing for the day's work. Grimes's voice is heard off, calling for help with his boat, which is refused him until Balstrode and Keene give him a hand.

Keene tells Grimes that he has found him another apprentice whom he has only to fetch from the workhouse. Carter Hobson refuses to have anything to do with the transaction: the cart's full. 'I have to go from pub to pub,' sings Hobson, in what Britten describes as a 'half number'. The chorus supports Hobson's refusal, but Ellen Orford takes up his tune and offers to help him mind the boy if he will agree to bring him back. The chorus's protest rises in vigour until Ellen takes her stand firmly against them: 'Let her among you without fault cast the first stone.' Hobson yields to her pleading, and Mrs Sedley asks Keene if he yet has her laudanum. He says she must meet him in the pub to collect it.

Balstrode sees the storm cone has been hoisted, and leads a great fugal ensemble. Bob Boles calls on the Borough to repent, and the passage ends with the fervent prayer: 'O tide that waits for no man, spare our coasts.' The storm music dominates the rest of the act.

Balstrode comments on Grimes's apparently convinced isolation – even now, he stays out in the storm, instead of coming into the pub – and suggests that he would be better off working on a merchantman. He is 'native, rooted here', replies Grimes: 'By familiar fields, marsh and sand.' Touched however by the old captain's kindliness, he tells him in an *arioso* passage

the story of his horrifying experience with only the corpse of the dead boy to keep him company. He plans to stop the gossips with the one thing they listen to – money (a rapid *scherzando* passage). The duet grows in intensity as he refuses to listen to Balstrode's advice. Left alone, he reflects passionately on the peace which could be his were Ellen to become his wife.

The interval of the ninth has been thought to characterise Grimes's maladjustment, and we hear it in its minor form at the beginning of the scene with Balstrode (Ex. 1a)

and resolved into the major when he thinks of Ellen and his possible salvation (Ex. 1b).

With the fall of the curtain, we hear for the first time the full force of the storm in the orchestral interlude which follows, and which is developed from the storm themes already heard, with a reference in the middle to Ex. 1b.

Scene ii. The interior of The Boar; the storm enters each time one of the characters opens the door. Mrs Sedley is an unexpected visitor, but she explains that she is waiting for Ned Keene.

Two episodes characterise the music: Balstrode complains about the noise the frightened 'Nieces' make, and is rebuked by Auntie in a half-humorous piece; Bob Boles makes drunken advances to one of the Nieces, tries to hit Balstrode, who overpowers him and leads the company in 'We live and let live, and look we keep our hands to ourselves.'

Grimes come in, and Mrs Sedley promptly faints. Grimes takes little notice of what has been or is going on inside The Boar but sings introspectively of the mystery of the skies and human destiny: 'Now the Great Bear and Pleiades'. The melody is in the orchestra and in canon, but the effective words, the contrasting *molto animato* in the middle, and the suggestive and reiterated 'Who, who, who, who can turn skies back and begin again' make this a *scena* of haunting beauty.

The reaction to Grimes's mood is, not unnaturally, one of consternation, and Ned Keene saves the situation by starting off a round: 'Old Joe has gone fishing', in which three distinct tunes are used and combined in the metre of 7/4. The storm is heard again, and Hobson the carter comes in with Ellen and Grimes's new apprentice. The bridge is down, they almost had to swim, and everyone is chilled to the bone. Auntie offers refreshment, but Grimes wants to be off. Ellen tells the boy gently: 'Peter will take you home', upon which the chorus comments derisively, 'Home! do you call that home!'

Act II. The opening prelude is in complete contrast to what has gone before. It is Sunday morning, and the sunlight is reflected off the waves as everyone goes to church. The interlude is made up of a brilliant *toccata* which contrasts with a broad, appealing lyrical tune, heard first on the violas and cellos and again, immediately on the rise of the curtain, sung by Ellen who comes in with John, the new apprentice ('Glitter of waves and glitter of sunlight').

The scene which follows takes place within a frame provided by the music of the church service which is heard from time to time off-stage. During the hymn (*maestoso*) Ellen talks to the boy about the workhouse, and her determination that the new apprentice's life shall be different from that of the old. The beginning of the Confession and Responses (*Recitativo agitato*) coincides with Ellen's discovery that the boy has a torn coat and – worse – a bruise on his neck. With the Gloria (*Andante con moto*) she tries, in music of aria-like stature, to provide comfort for herself almost as much as for the boy. Peter Grimes comes in quickly as the chorus begins the Benedicite (*Allegro agitato*), and tells the boy they are off to work, answering Ellen roughly when she reminds him that it is Sunday, a day of rest. The chorus starts the Creed (*Adagio*) as Ellen pleads with Peter to adjust his ways to the boy's tender years. 'Were we mistaken when we schemed to solve your life by lonely toil?' she asks him in music of the utmost tenderness, and concludes: 'Peter! we've failed.' At this he cries out in agony and strikes her, matching the chorus's 'Amen' with his own *fortissimo* 'So be it, and God have mercy upon me!' Grimes drives the boy off, and leaves Ellen to make her way weepingly home.

Auntie, Bob Boles, and Ned Keene sing a brisk trio based on Grimes's phrase: 'Grimes is at his exercise', and the service comes to an end, spilling its congregation on to the beach. Some of them, Mrs Sedley naturally among them, have heard the noise of the quarrel during the service, and the chorus murmurs in indignation at what it only half understands. Balstrode tries to exert a calming influence, Swallow chips in with a sitting-on-the-fence platitude, but Bob Boles inflames popular sentiment and calls on Ellen Orford, who has come back to collect her things, to tell them what was going on.

She attempts to explain in terms of what they tried to do, but the weight of opinion is too solidly against her and though her voice rises higher and higher in her effort to make herself understood, the ensemble and the chorus cap her efforts with a cry of 'Murder!' In spite of Balstrode's protest that they are wasting their time, the Rector and Swallow organise a party to investigate what is going on at Grimes's hut, Carter Hobson beats his drum, and they march off together to the tune of a vindictive chorus.

As their voices die away in the distance, two flutes in seconds introduce a 6/8 'trio' for the two Nieces, Auntie, and Ellen (except in the first and last phrases the Nieces sing in unison), whose calm beauty provides a contemplative ending to a scene which has otherwise been dramatic and even violent.

The interlude joining the first scene of Act II to the second is a *Passacaglia*, which is the centrepiece of the whole opera. It is built up on the 'God have mercy upon me' theme, and through it runs a desolate viola solo, which represents the fate of the apprentice caught up in Grimes's destiny.

Scene ii. Grimes's hut, an upturned boat full of ropes and fisherman's tackle. Until the sound of the chorus off-stage just before its end, the scene consists of an extended monologue for Grimes, the boy's part being confined to a single scream.

The music settles down to an aria, in which Grimes seeks to contrast what he is in reality with what he has always dreamed and planned, with Ellen's help, to be. The florid cast of the music and the idyllic nature of the words eventually give place to a feverish description of that awful vigil with the dying apprentice in the boat. The aria comes to an end, and in the next bar the sound of the investigatory procession from the village can be heard. Grimes

So be it   And God have mer- cy upon me

reacts violently to it, thinks the boy is the cause of its coming to his hut, and shouts his defiance of what it can do to him. With an admonition to be careful, Grimes hustles the boy down the cliff steps, turns as he senses the unwelcome visitors nearing his door, and hears the boy scream as he falls down the cliff to his death. Grimes climbs quickly after him. With the scream, the orchestral sound cuts off suddenly and leaves only an eerie echo on the celesta.

The Rector puts his head round the door, and is followed by Swallow, Keene, and Balstrode. They find nothing, but comment on the open door with the precipice almost directly beyond it, and the neatness of the hut, and Swallow sums up the feelings of all when he says that the whole episode seems to have ended by quieting village gossip once and for all.

Act III opens with a Moonlight prelude of great simplicity and beauty, whose rising theme is punctuated now and then by a little figure for flute and harp.

The same scene as the first of Act I (the Borough street and beach), this time at night. A dance is in progress in the Moot Hall, and there is a steady procession between there and The Boar. The off-stage band plays a rustic jig, and Swallow appears, all dignity discarded, chasing one of the Nieces and singing a raffish tune. The first Niece is presently joined by the second – they find safety in numbers – and together they elude Swallow, who angrily goes into The Boar, leaving the orchestra to enjoy his tune. Ned Keene's intentions are in no way dissimilar from Swallow's, but he is waylaid by Mrs Sedley, who, to the accompaniment of a *Ländler* from the off-stage orchestra, tries to enlist his interest in proving Peter Grimes a murderer.

While the orchestra starts up a hornpipe, the older members of the community bid each other goodnight, the Rector outdoing everyone in affability, a section of extraordinary musical refinement and inspiration. Mrs Sedley broods in the darkness and watches Ellen and Balstrode as they walk up from the beach, the latter revealing that Grimes's boat is in but he is nowhere to be found, the former overcome by recognising the boy's jersey, which Balstrode has found washed up by the tide.

Ellen's aria, 'Embroidery in childhood was a luxury of idleness', is, like the quartet at the end of the first scene of the previous act, a moment of stillness in the drama, which is here commented upon in music that is florid and exacting, but whose effect is one of tranquillity and resignation. It is the most extended aria of the opera.

Balstrode says there may yet be something they can do for Peter. Mrs Sedley now has the clue she needs, and she goes officiously towards the door of The Boar, and calls for Mr Swallow. When he hears that Grimes's boat is back he orders, as mayor of the Borough, that Hobson take a posse of men and find Grimes. In an atmosphere of hysteria and brutality, which is horrifyingly reflected in the big ensemble, 'him who despises us we'll destroy', the inhabitants set out to hunt down the fellow-citizen they cannot understand. The scene ends with *fortissimo* cries of 'Peter Grimes' before the curtain comes down.

The sixth interlude, a short one, has been described by Edward Sackville-West as 'one of the strangest and most imaginative passages in the opera … The music, which transfers us from the one-track hysteria of the crowd to the echoing limbo of Grimes's mind, is … bound together by a single chord, a dominant seventh on D – held, *ppp*, throughout the interlude by three muted horns. Figures of nightmare sea-birds fly through the fog uttering fragments of themes which Grimes has sung earlier …'.

As the curtain rises, the search-party can be heard crying 'Peter Grimes', and at the same time a fog-horn (tuba off-stage) makes itself heard. Grimes drags himself in and has a long mad scene to himself, accompanied only by the off-stage chorus and the fog-horn against the background of the horn chord. He babbles of home, and sings snatches that remind him of the various stages of his tragic story. Ellen comes in with Balstrode and tells him they have come to take him home, but he appears not to recognise her until he sings a reminiscence of Ex. 1b, which represents his aspirations and is now associated with what he has failed to obtain. Balstrode drops into ordinary speech to tell Peter to take his boat out to sea and sink her there.

Very quietly, three violins begin to play the music of the prelude to Act I, as the stragglers return from the unsuccessful chase. It is morning, and the chorus sings the same tune as at the beginning of Act I. Swallow looks through his glasses to confirm that a boat has been seen sinking out at sea, but no one is interested. The Borough has forgotten its manhunt and prepares to get on with another day.   H.

THE RAPE OF LUCRETIA

Opera in two acts, text by Ronald Duncan, based on André Obey's play, *Le Viol de Lucrèce*. Première at Glyndebourne, 12 July 1946; the work was later toured throughout England with a double cast, the first-named singer in each case having sung at the première: Cross (Nielsen), Ferrier (Nancy Evans), Ritchie (Duff), Pollak (Lawson), Pears (Schiøtz), Kraus (Rogier), Donlevy (Sharp), Brannigan (Norman Walker), conductor Ansermet (Goodall). First performed Basle, 1947, with Lorand, von Sieben, Wosniak, Gschwend, conductor Krannhals; Chicago, 1947, with Resnik, Kibler, Kane, Rogier, conductor Breisach; New York, 1949, with Kitty Carlisle, conductor Breisach; Rome, 1949, with Vitali-Marini, Gardino, Manuritta, Franci, conductor Santini; Salzburg Festival, 1950, with Kupper, Höngen, Gueden, Dagmar Hermann, Patzak, Uhde, Poell, Böhme, conductor Krips; English National Opera, 1983, with Kathryn Harries, Jean Rigby, Anthony Rolfe Johnson, Russell Smythe, conductor Steuart Bedford.

Male Chorus ....Tenor

Female Chorus...Soprano

Lucretia..Contralto

Collatinus, *her husband*..Bass

Lucia, *her attendant* ....Soprano

Bianca, *her nurse*...Contralto

Tarquinius, *Prince of Rome* ....Baritone

Junius, *a Roman general* ....Baritone

Place: In or Near Rome
Time: 500 B.C.
Running Time: 1 hour 40 minutes

In early 1946, the team which had successfully pioneered *Peter Grimes* at Sadler's Wells resigned from the company. Britten decided to accept an invitation from Glyndebourne to re-open the theatre, which had been closed during the war, and, for practical as much as aesthetic reasons (although he strongly developed the latter), set out the new opera for a relatively small but varied cast, no chorus, and an orchestra of thirteen instruments including piano.[1] The basis of the new venture was the Sadler's Wells team, and the opera was well enough received to encourage a tour of leading British cities (which lost money heavily), and of Holland, which has since always been receptive to Britten's works.

Although *The Rape of Lucretia* is the most lyrical of Britten's operas, its actual organisation is more formal than for instance that of *Peter Grimes*. The two acts, which are divided into two scenes each, take place within a musical and dramatic frame provided by a Male and a Female Chorus. These two commentators assume, together with the orchestra, the duties of preparation, comment, heightening of the tension, and summing-up which, in *Grimes*, were allotted to the orchestra alone, and in fact the interludes in the middle of each act are vocal as opposed to the purely instrumental equivalents in the earlier opera.

Act I. The Male and Female Choruses are discovered sitting on either side of the stage.

We are *in medias res* straight away as the Male Chorus announces *con forza* in the third bar: 'Rome is now ruled by the Etruscan upstart, Tarquinius Superbus.' In a nervous half *arioso*, half recitative style, he introduces the story by sketching in the historical background against which it is set. The particular situation – war against Greece – is specified by the Female Chorus before the two voices join in a lyric statement, 'Whilst we as two observers stand between this present audience and that scene'. The orchestra (muted strings and harp) suggests an atmosphere of oppressive heat, a night alive with the noise of crickets and bull-frogs. The scene is a camp outside Rome. The Male Chorus and the orchestra are interrupted in their description of the lights of distant Rome by an explosive drinking song for the officers.

The officers discuss the outcome of their bet the night before, when they rode home unannounced to see what their wives were doing in their absence. Only Lucretia, Collatinus' wife, was at home, and the others were all found in compromising situations. 'And Collatinus has won the bet', shouts Tarquinius, 'And Junius is a cuckold, a cuckold's a cock without a crow ... ' Tarquinius' motif is heard for the first time at the words 'You forget I am the *Prince of Rome*' (the four descending notes C, B, A, and G sharp).

Tarquinius and Junius quarrel but are separated by Collatinus, who suggests they drink a toast together. Tarquinius immediately proposes it 'To the chaste Lucretia!' in a phrase which forms her motif.

To the chaste Lu - cre - - tia!

Junius rushes angrily from the tent. He is furi-

---

[1] Flute (doubling piccolo and bass flute), oboe (doubling English horn), clarinet (doubling bass clarinet), bassoon, horn, percussion, harp, piano (doubling celesta), string quartet, double bass.

ously jealous of Lucretia's chastity, and repeats her name again and again, easing his agony by abusing her. His aria is developed to a point at which the idea of revenge fills his mind, when for the second time the Male Chorus takes over from him. What Junius might not have said aloud, but what he would have admitted to feeling, is sung by him; the jealousy which causes his anger and the thoughts it suggests to him – things he would *not* have admitted to feeling – are described by the Male Chorus in music of insinuating character (Ex. 2).

Junius ends his aria with a final explosive 'Lucretia!', and Collatinus walks out to reason with him and persuade him to take a less directly personal view of the situation. Collatinus' aria, 'Those who love create', replaces one written for the first version of the opera, which had the dramatic disadvantage of showing Collatinus not understanding that Junius' driving motive is jealousy. Collatinus goes off to bed, leaving Tarquinius and Junius to resolve their differences in a striking duet, which finishes with a canon at the half bar; as they put it,

It seems we agree,
But are not of the same opinion!

Junius leaves Tarquinius alone, after suggesting that to prove Lucretia chaste is something even the Prince will not dare to attempt. The Male Chorus comments on Tarquinius' indecision, until his cry of 'My horse! My horse!' reveals that his mind is now all too firmly made up.

The curtain falls rapidly and immediately the Male Chorus begins a graphic description of Tarquinius' Ride to Rome. The music's energy mounts until the Ride is brought to a temporary halt by the River Tiber. Tarquinius and his horse take to the water, and the Chorus describes their crossing (Ex. 2). The slow *crescendo* from the solo flute's *ppp* to the full orchestra's *ff* is extraordinarily evocative, and the Ride culminates in

the Chorus's *ff* 'Lucretia' as the curtain goes up to reveal the hall of Lucretia's house.

All is apparently at peace. She and her two female companions are spinning, and the Female Chorus's beautiful spinning song, with its flute and harp accompaniment, not only sets the mood but also frames the three solo verses, each with its 'nostalgic ninth', which Lucretia, Bianca, and Lucia sing in turn. Lucretia thinks she hears a knock, but finding it is not Collatinus or his messenger, as she had hoped, sings an *arioso*, 'How cruel men are to teach us love'. The women prepare for bed, and a trio develops between Lucia and Bianca, who vocalise on 'Ah' while folding linen, and the Female Chorus who comments on this regular and calming feminine action.

'How quiet it is tonight', reflects Lucretia; '... it must be men who make the noise', retorts Bianca, and immediately we hear a suggestion of Tarquinius' Ride in the orchestra. A loud knocking announces that Tarquinius has arrived. The rest of the scene is carried on in pantomime, to the expressive comment of the two Choruses, until Lucretia's two companions remark on the strangeness of a visit so late from the Prince whose palace lies only just across the city, but who is asking for Lucretia's hospitality. She cannot refuse it, and there starts a chain of 'Goodnights', each one based on Tarquinius' motif but subtly different from the next, and each introduced by one or other of the Choruses.

Act II. The two Choruses introduce the act. Lucretia sleeps as the bass flute, muted horn, and bass clarinet introduce the Female Chorus's Lullaby 'She sleeps as a rose upon the night', a tune of exquisite sensitivity. The hushed atmosphere is continued in the next section, in which the Male Chorus, accompanied only by percussion, describes Tarquinius' approach to Lucretia's room. As Tarquinius reaches the head of the bed, the first phrase of the Female Chorus's Lullaby is heard again. In an extended and impressive aria, Tarquinius sings of his feelings for Lucretia; the middle section is heard against the Female Chorus's Lullaby, and at the end of the aria Tarquinius bends over Lucretia to wake her, as he has planned, with a kiss.

Lucretia wakes (to the sound of the 'whip' – a little-used orchestral instrument) and is confronted with the sight of Tarquinius. Lucretia pleads for mercy in music of rapidly rising tension, and Tarquinius does his best to establish that her resistance is diminishing:

'Can you deny your blood's dumb pleading?' The Choruses take Lucretia's part in the quartet which ensues, but it is too late, and Tarquinius pulls the cover from the bed and threatens Lucretia with his sword. The scene ends with a statement by the quartet *a cappella* of the music heard originally in Junius' soliloquy (Ex. 2), and Tarquinius beats out the candle with his sword as the curtain falls rapidly.

The Interlude takes the form of a figured chorale sung by the two commentators, in which they interpret in Christian terms the scene they have just witnessed, while the orchestra depicts the physical events of the rape. The Interlude dies away and the front-drop goes up to show the hall of Lucretia's house as in the second scene of Act I. Lucia and Bianca exult in the beauty of the day. Their *aubade* gives them plenty of opportunity for coloratura display before they discuss whether it was Tarquinius they heard gallop out of the courtyard earlier in the morning. Lucia sings a little arietta, 'I often wonder whether Lucretia's love is the flower of her beauty', before Lucretia is seen coming into the hall.

She is obviously full of foreboding, and her initially quiet behaviour gives way to hysteria when she is offered the orchids to arrange: 'How hideous! Take them away!' She bursts into wild activity and orders Lucia to send a messenger to Collatinus, telling him to come home. She calms sufficiently to arrange the rest of the flowers, which she does while she sings an aria, a miniature of beauty and pathos, and one of the major inspirations of the score. Bianca's aria is in complete contrast; she remembers when life was still sweet and fresh for all of them before the fatal yesterday.

There is a short interchange between Bianca and Lucia (Lucretia has left the stage) in which the former bids the latter prevent the messenger reaching Collatinus; but it is too late, and in a moment Collatinus and Junius are with them, demanding to know where Lucretia is.

Lucretia herself comes in, dressed in purple mourning, and in eleven bars of orchestral music (cor anglais and strings) the essence of her tragedy is conveyed. Collatinus addresses his wife in words and music that are calculated to comfort and sustain her, affirming that they must never again be parted. Their voices blend before Lucretia makes her confession to Collatinus, the orchestra punctuating what she has to say with *sotto voce* memories of the music which went

with what she is describing. Finally she sings a modified version of Ex. 2, ending, 'For me this shame, for you this sorrow'. Collatinus attempts to forgive her, but she is overcome by what has happened, and stabs herself, dying in Collatinus' arms.

Her funeral march (marked *alla marcia grave*) takes the form of an extended *chaconne*. It is sung by all the characters in tableau, Collatinus and Junius first, then Bianca and Lucia, and finally the two commentators joining their voices in the magnificent ensemble. The Female Chorus cannot accept the finality with which the story has closed, and ends incredulously 'Is this it all?' to which she receives conclusive answer from her male companion: 'It is not all ... For now He bears our sin, and does not fall ... In His passion is our hope, Jesus Christ, Saviour, He is all, He is all.' The Christian ethic has been allowed – some commentators have said 'forced' – to draw a moral from the pagan story. The opera ends with a final statement of the lyrical passage heard at the end of the prologue.   H.

ALBERT HERRING

Opera in three acts, text by Eric Crozier, adapted from Maupassant's story *Le Rosier de Madame Husson*. Première, Glyndebourne, 20 June 1947, with Joan Cross, Ritchie, Nancy Evans, Pears, Sharp, Parsons, Lumsden, conductor Britten. First performed Tanglewood, U.S.A., 1949; Hanover, 1950; Berlin, 1950; New York, 1952, by Opera Futures Workshop; Berlin, Komische Oper, 1958, producer Herz; New York City Opera, 1971, conductor Bernardi; Glyndebourne, 1985, with Patricia Johnson, John Graham-Hall, conductor Bernard Haitink, producer Peter Hall.

Lady Billows, *an elderly autocrat*.....................Soprano

Florence Pike, *her housekeeper*......................Contralto

Miss Wordsworth, *head teacher*.....................Soprano

Mr Gedge, *the Vicar* ....Baritone

Mr Upfold, *the Mayor*.....................................Tenor

Superintendent Budd...Bass

Sid, *a butcher's assistant* ....Baritone

Albert Herring, *from the greengrocer's*...............Tenor

Nancy, *from the bakery*........................Mezzo-Soprano

Mrs Herring, *Albert's mother*...............Mezzo-Soprano

Village children
    Emmie...Soprano
    Cis ....Soprano
    Harry...Treble

Place: Loxford, a Small Market-Town in East Suffolk, England
Time: April and May of 1900
Running Time: 2 hours 25 minutes

During a tour of English cities with *Lucretia* in 1946, Britten decided for the future to form his own chamber opera company, the English Opera Group, with the result that, though *Albert Herring* like *Lucretia* was first given at Glyndebourne, it was presented under the management of the English Opera Group. *Albert Herring* kept the chamber opera form of *Lucretia* but, as a comedy, represented a new departure for Britten, a fact given additional emphasis by his original choice, subsequently discarded, of *Mansfield Park* as the subject of his next opera. Kathleen Ferrier was to have had a leading part in it, but in 1947 at Glyndebourne she sang instead Gluck's *Orfeo* for the first time.

Act I. The curtain rises after two bars of the busy prelude to show the breakfast room of Lady Billows's house, where Florence, her housekeeper, is tidying up. Lady Billows is heard calling instructions from her room, and Florence checks off in her notebook what she has to see to that morning; sample: 'Advert in chemist's window ... indecent ... tear it up!' Florence seems about to favour us with some revelation of her private aspirations, when a knock is heard at the door, which Florence opens to admit Miss Wordsworth, the Vicar, the Mayor, and Mr Budd, the committee which is to decide between the rival candidates for the position of Queen of the May.

An *alla marcia* introduces her Ladyship, who seems at one point in danger of not noticing her visitors, except to complain that the room stinks of tobacco. But the situation is saved, and, while she greets the committee, the orchestra begins the fugal tune which develops after a bit into a full-blooded quintet: 'We've made our own investigations.'

Lady Billows rhapsodises on the subject of the position of May Queen, her first four notes constituting a 'Festival motif', and grows eloquent as she considers the 'state of complete moral chaos' from which it is expected to rescue the town. Names are put forward and vetoed with uncommon gusto by Florence. A short quartet, beginning with the Vicar's 'Oh, bitter, bitter is the fruit' and ending with Budd's pregnant 'and darkness has its uses', leads to a furious aria for Lady Billows.

It is the moment for a brainwave, and Super-intendent Budd has it: why not a *King* of the May? He launches headlong into an aria: 'Albert Herring's clean as new-mown hay', but the other committee members hint delicately that he is perhaps an unusually backward boy. Lady Billows calls helplessly on the Vicar for some comfort in an awkward situation; there *are* apparently no virgins in Loxford. The Vicar rises to the occasion with a string of persuasive platitudes and a big *cantabile* tune which is taken up by the others.

'Right! We'll have him! May King! That'll teach the girls a lesson!' she says, and leads off the fugal finale. She leaves the room for a moment and returns to transform the finale into a florid, Purcell-like choral ode, with which the scene ends.

The interlude prepares us for the village children, and the curtain goes up to show the interior of Mrs Herring's grocer's shop, outside which can be seen playing Emmie, Cis, and Harry. The ball bounces, and Harry goes in after it, taking the opportunity to pinch some apples. They are interrupted by Sid, who empties Harry's pockets, and, pausing to take an apple for himself, shouts for Albert.

The hero makes his entrance backwards through the door, and carrying a hundredweight of turnips (or so he tells us). Sid gives his order and offers to toss Albert for it. But gambling is not in Albert's line. Sid tempts him to break the apron strings with a recital of the pleasures of independence. Albert tries not to listen, and Sid is just off, when Nancy, his girlfriend, comes in, obviously in the middle of her shopping.

Sid buys Nancy a couple of peaches, and tells her to bring them that night and meet him at quarter past eight for a walk in the moonlight. Albert comments on their duet, which thus becomes a trio. Sid and Nancy go off together, Sid of course forgetting to pay, and Albert is left alone. His monologue begins as he wonders if his mother's strictness really leads to anything valuable, and continues as he reflects on what he misses. It is interrupted by another customer – Emmie come to buy herbs for a stew – but ends with a half-defiant 'Golly, it's about time!'

Florence sends for Mrs Herring to tell her that the Festival Committee is about to pay her a visit. There is no time for further explanation before Lady Billows is upon them, announcing, 'We bring great news to you upon this happy day'. Once the visiting party has departed, the winner is left alone with the jubilant Mrs Herring, who is only momentarily put out when Albert says firmly that he intends to refuse the prize. Mum's firmness is very much to the fore as she sends him upstairs, to delighted cries of 'Albert's Mum took a stick, Whacked him on the thingmijig' from the children.

Act II. Horn calls on the Festival motif run through a short prelude, before the curtain goes up on the inside of a marquee set up in the vicarage garden. 'There is a long trestle-table loaded with cakes, jellies, and other good things.'

Sid tells Nancy what has been going on down at the church, in an aria that is richly ironical. What of Albert? 'The poor kid looks on tenterhooks. He's in the mood to escape if he could.' 'You've got some scheme,' says Nancy, and Sid takes her outside to tell her what it is.

With the flute twittering away *presto* above the strings, Miss Wordsworth brings in the children to run through the anthem in celebration of Albert's coronation as King of the May.

They are excited at the prospect of the feast, but at last, in spite of difficulties of pitch and enunciation, the rehearsal comes to an end, and teacher and children leave the tent just as Nancy and Sid return to it, the plot having been revealed. Sid pours rum into the lemonade glass in Albert's place (to the accompaniment of the *Tristan* chord) and all is ready for the reception of the official procession.

Miss Wordsworth hurries the children back, and Superintendent Budd, Mrs Herring, the Mayor, Florence, the Vicar, and Lady Billows come in successively, each singing characteristic music. The anthem goes off quite well, flowers are presented, and the children are thanked for their contribution to the feast before the Vicar rises to introduce the first speaker.

This, of course, is Lady Billows, who begins with phrases of an ambitious range that rivals even Fiordiligi's. She loses her notes, but general applause covers the gap and she presents Albert with his prize of twenty-five sovereigns. In turn come speeches from the Mayor, Miss Wordsworth and Mr Budd, and finally Albert is called on to make some sort of reply. He can get no further than 'Er ... er ... thank you ... very much', but rejoicing is general, and the Vicar leads off a congratulatory ensemble, 'Albert the Good! Long may he reign!'

Albert drinks to the toast, enormously likes what he tastes, and comes round to Nancy for more,

reaching her with a resounding hiccup (on a top C flat). He is cured, by drinking from the wrong side of a glass, and the curtain goes down as a fugue starts on the melody of 'Albert the Good'.

The interlude continues with the noise of the feast, then changes character as May Day turns into May Night and becomes a nocturne. Scene ii takes place inside Mrs Herring's shop. Albert comes back from the feast and sings exuberant reminiscences of his triumph, punctuating his song by banging the shop door and ringing the bell. In his *scena*, he runs through a variety of subjects, starting with the necessity of finding some matches to the charms of Nancy – and at mention of her, Sid's whistle can be heard outside in the street. Nancy comments sympathetically on Albert's plight, they sing a short but forceful duet, kiss, and are off, leaving behind a much shaken, even an excited Albert. He remembers the money in his pocket and decides to toss for it, whether he shall go off on the bust ... or not. It comes down 'heads for yes', and he starts off to find out what he has been missing.

Act III. The *prestissimo* prelude immediately suggests the atmosphere of man-hunt which follows the discovery of Albert's disappearance. Nancy sings three verses of an aria which has been aptly described as Mahlerian in feeling, before Sid comes wearily into the shop, complaining that one can hear nothing but Albert's name everywhere.

Superintendent Budd asks for Mrs Herring, who comes down, a picture of inconsolable grief. She has only one photograph of Albert, but the Superintendent is welcome to that for identification purposes. Mrs Herring begins the quartet (*come un lamento*) which ensues.

Harry complicates matters with his shouted: 'There's a Big White Something in Mrs Williams' well', and Mrs Herring collapses, just as Lady Billows comes to join in the practical side of the hunt. A procession appears escorting the Mayor, who carries a tray on which is Albert's orange-blossom wreath – 'Found on the road to Campsey Ash, crushed by a cart'. There ensues the Threnody, 'In the midst of life is death, Death awaits us one and all', a great ensemble for nine voices, on an *ostinato*. Each individual has a characteristic verse to himself, the others meanwhile continuing the lament, marked *grave*.

The shop bell rings, and Albert peers round the door. Immediately a storm of recrimination breaks around his head. Only Sid and Nancy take his part as Albert starts to tell them a story in which more is hinted at than actually described. Albert blames it all on the life of repression and mollycoddling he has been forced to lead. At the end of his recital of his doings, Albert sings a tune which is at the same time ridiculously mild and inoffensive, and also warm and curiously full of understanding, even wisdom. Its effect on everyone is electrical; they have met their match and can no longer patronise their innocent May King. 'I didn't lay it on *too* thick, did I?' Albert asks Sid and Nancy; then, seeing the children mocking him from the window, he invites them inside to sample what the shop can offer in the way of fruit. The opera concludes as they all sing Lady Billows' 'Great news' theme, and Albert throws his orange-blossom wreath into the audience.   H.

LET'S MAKE AN OPERA!

An entertainment for young people, in two parts (and three acts), text by Eric Crozier. Première at the Aldeburgh Festival, June 1949, with Gladys Parr, Anne Sharp, Elizabeth Parry, Max Worthley, Norman Lumsden, John Moules, conducted by Norman Del Mar. First performed St Louis, 1951, and subsequently all over the world.

The Opera	*The Play*	
Miss Baggott, *the housekeeper*	Gladys Parworthy	...Contralto
Black Bob, *the sweep-master, and* Tom, *the coachman*	Norman Chaffinch, *a composer*	Bass
Clem, *Black Bob's assistant, and* Alfred, *the gardener*	Max Westleton	Tenor
Rowan, *the nursery-maid*	Pamela Wilton	Soprano
Juliet Brook *(aged fourteen)*	Anne Dougall	Soprano
The Conductor of the Opera	Mr Harper	Spoken
Sam, *the new sweepboy (eight)*	John	Treble
Gay Brook *(thirteen)*	Bruce	Treble
Sophie Brook *(ten)*	Monica	Soprano
John Crome *(fifteen)*	Peter	Treble
Tina Crome *(eight)*	Mavis	Soprano
Hugh Crome *(eight)*	Ralph	Treble

Place: Children's Nursery of Iken Hall, Suffolk
Time: 1810
Running Time: 45 minutes (opera only)

It is suggested that the names of the actual performers be used for the characters of the play. The accompaniment is for solo string quartet, piano duet (four hands on one piano), and percussion (one player is enough). For the grown-ups, professionals or gifted amateurs are needed, but the children (apart from Juliet) should be played by children. The composer characteristically adds a note to the effect that the boys should not be scared of using their chest voices.

Britten had written more than once for boys' voices (notably in *A Ceremony of Carols* and the *Spring Symphony*) before his first children's opera, which started a productive line taking in *The Turn of the Screw*, *Noye's Fludde* and *A Midsummer Night's Dream*.

The first two acts of *Let's Make an Opera!* are in the form of a play and illustrate the preparation and rehearsal of *The Little Sweep*, a children's opera which is performed in Act III.

Act I. The drawing-room of Mrs Parworthy's house. Mrs Parworthy tells a story handed down to her by her own grandmother, the Juliet Brook of the opera. There is a discussion as to whether it would be better to do it as an opera or as a play, but the decision is never really in doubt.

The second scene is concerned with some early stages of rehearsal and the successful auditioning of Max Westleton, of the local building office.

Act II represents the stage of the hall or theatre just before the dress rehearsal of *The Little Sweep*. The conductor takes the opportunity of rehearsing the audience in the four songs it is required to sing.

Act III. *The Little Sweep* has no overture but opens with the first of the four audience songs, the 'Sweep Song'. When the curtain rises, the nursery can be seen in all its prettiness, and Clem and Black Bob in their turn are heard singing the 'Sweep Song' as they drag in little Sammy, their apprentice. One of the things attempted earlier in the play is an explanation of 'ensemble' – each person has his or her own musical line. An ensemble of exactly this type is the second number of the opera, and the definition is made doubly clear, since each character sings his own line as a solo before joining in with it in the ensemble.

Miss Baggott takes Rowan next door to cover everything up with dust-sheets, leaving the two sweeps to get on with the job. With horrid relish, they pull Sammy's clothes off, tie a rope round his waist and send him up the chimney, with the unambiguous instruction: 'Scrape that flue clean, or I'll roast you alive.'

The children can be heard off-stage organising a game of hide-and-seek. Juliet runs in, hides under a dust-sheet and is discovered by Jonny who promptly hides with her. Before the others arrive, they hear sounds from the chimney: 'Help! I'm stuck.' They call the others, who take hold of the rope and start to pull, at first gently, then more vigorously.

Sammy comes tumbling out of the chimney, there is a moment of gasped astonishment, and then 'Is he wounded?' is the question to which all want an answer. The best Sammy can do is repeat pathetically 'Please don't send me up again.' The children quickly decide that they must hide Sammy and lead him across the dust-sheets towards the window as they lay the false trail. Footsteps can be heard, and the children bundle Sammy into their toy-cupboard, and themselves disappear under the dust-sheets. When Miss Baggott and the sweeps come into the room it is apparently empty. Straight away they notice the tell-tale footsteps, and Clem and Black Bob yell for Sam; there is no answer, and, with Miss Baggott, they launch into a ferocious vengeance trio.

Rowan is left in the room, which is still apparently empty, and she gives fervent expression to her hope that Sammy will evade his masters. The children enlist her help, and decide that the first thing to do is to give Sammy a bath. Sammy's ablutions are described in the second audience song, 'Sammy's Bath', a syncopated tune in triple time and of vigorous character.

Rowan and the children, still to the tune of 'Sammy's Bath' and (our eyes tell us) with complete justification, sing: 'O Sammy is whiter than swans as they fly.' Sammy thanks them, and they ask him how he came to be mixed up with his blackguardly employers. Sammy explains that his father broke his hip and had to sell him to find money to support the family. There is a slow, sad ensemble in which Rowan and the children try to offer Sammy comfort ('O why do you weep through the working day?'). Jonny suggests that they should take Sammy away with them, and, after some persuasion, Rowan agrees to leave a space in the top of a trunk.

Suddenly, Miss Baggott is heard coming along the passage. To the accompaniment of music marked *presto furioso* Sammy is hidden in the toy-cupboard, and the toys produced as if by magic. Miss Baggott

punctuates her imprecations against the sweeps with frequent references to her poor feet. The children smother her with compassion, but it is not long before Miss Baggott is at her old games again, criticising the way Rowan has done the room ('Curtains crooked') and expecting to find that the toys have not been properly tidied in the cupboard. She goes towards it to make certain, but Juliet saves the situation by collapsing dramatically.

There is another interlude, and the audience sings 'The Night Song', whose haunting tune well lives up to its description of *andante tenebroso*. The last scene takes place the following morning. Juliet brings Sammy his breakfast and after kisses all round he is packed into the trunk.

Tom, red-faced and permanently short of breath, with the assistance of Alfred, laid low by chronic lumbago, comes to take the trunk downstairs. It won't shift. Miss Baggott makes a great deal of fuss, but Tom and Alfred are adamant: 'Either that there box is unpacked or we leave her where she lies.' Finally a solution is found when Rowan and the children offer to lend a hand, and the trunk is triumphantly transported from the room, Miss Baggott following it with her habitual grumble: 'Don't drop it!'

There remains only the finale – the *envoi* it might be called. Jonny, the Twins and Rowan rush in to say good-bye, Juliet, Gay, and Sophie wave from the window and describe the progress of the carriage down the drive. The percussion imitates the horse's hooves, and the entire cast returns to the stage and sings the verses, with the audience supplying the refrain:

BILLY BUDD

Opera in four acts, words by E.M. Forster and Eric Crozier, based on the story by Herman Melville. Première, Covent Garden, 1 December 1951, with Pears, Uppman, Dalberg, conductor Britten. First performed Wiesbaden, 1952, with Liebl, Gschwend, Stern, conductor Elmendorff; Paris, 1952, with London cast; N.B.C. Television, New York, 1952; Bloomington, U.S.A., 1952.

Revised version,[1] B.B.C. broadcast, 1961, with Pears, Joseph Ward, Langdon, conductor Britten; Covent Garden, 1964, with Richard Lewis, Kerns, Forbes Robinson, conductor Solti; Florence Festival, 1965, with Picchi, Alberto Rinaldi, Rossi-Lemeni; New York, concert performance, 1966, with Richard Lewis, Kerns, Forbes Robinson, conductor Solti; Hamburg, 1972, with Harald Ek, Richard Stilwell, Louis Hendrikx.

Captain Vere, *in command of H.M.S. 'Indomitable'*	Tenor
Billy Budd	Baritone
Claggart, *Master-at-Arms*	Bass
Mr Redburn, *First Lieutenant*	Baritone
Mr Flint, *Sailing Master*	Baritone
Lieutenant Ratcliffe	Bass
Red Whiskers, *an impressed man*	Tenor
Donald, *a member of the crew*	Baritone
Dansker, *an old seaman*	Bass
A Novice	Tenor
Squeak, *ship's corporal*	Tenor
Bosun	Baritone
First and Second Mates	Baritones
Maintop	Tenor
The Novice's Friend	Baritone
Arthur Jones, *an impressed man*	Baritone
Four Midshipmen	Boy's Voices

Officers, Sailors, Powder Monkeys, Drummers, Marines

Place: On board H.M.S. *Indomitable*, a 'Seventy-Four'
Time: During the French Wars of 1797
Running Time: 2 hours 35 minutes

Britten had already discussed the possibility of collaboration with the novelist E.M. Forster before deciding on a subject, and the story goes that writer and musician simultaneously and independently suggested Herman Melville's last story, *Billy Budd*, to each other. The co-operation of Eric Crozier was enlisted when Forster insisted that his own knowledge of stage procedure was inadequate. The libretto, apart from the shanties and a direct quotation from Melville's own ballad, 'Billy in the Darbies', is in prose, and there are no women in the cast.

The background to the story is to be found in the ideas aroused by the philosophical implications of the French Revolution, and in conditions in the British Navy at that time. The action is set in 1797, just after the mutinies at Spithead and the Nore,

when memories of 'the floating Republic' were still very much in people's minds. Fear of mutiny, and of anything which might be a prelude to mutiny, dominated the reactions of the officers, and conditions on board ship in 1797 were such as to be conducive to unrest and disaffection.

Act I. In the Prologue, Captain Vere is shown as an old man. Years after his retirement, he meditates on his career and what it has taught him, on the mystery of good and evil, and on the unfathomable ways of Providence which allows a flaw in every attempt at good. Doubt, expressed musically by an ambiguity between the keys of B flat major and B minor, provides the emotional key to the scene. We hear the music later associated with Billy's stammer when Vere refers to 'some imperfection in the divine image'. The Prologue comes to an end as Vere's mind goes back to the year 1797.

The lights go up on the main deck and quarter-deck of H.M.S. *Indomitable*. An area of the main deck is being 'holy-stoned' by some sailors, who sing while they work. Their music has a double significance: it suggests the half-contented, half-dangerous swell of a calm sea in its motion, and derivations from it are used throughout the opera in connection with the idea of mutiny. In the last scene of the opera, it returns with increased emotional effect (Ex. 1):

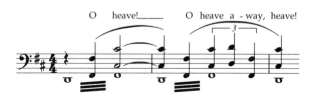

Mr Flint watches the work, pulls a man up for not taking his full share in it, and gives orders to the Bosun; a party of young Midshipmen (trebles) try to show their authority by giving orders in their turn; and all the while the working song continues. One of the men, the Novice, collides accidentally with the Bosun and is threatened with the cat; the Bosun organises a working party to hoist a sail. The Novice slips and the Bosun turns savagely on him and has Squeak, the police corporal, list him for twenty strokes.

The stage empties, leaving Mr Flint alone on the quarter-deck. The look-out spots the guard-boat returning from a press-ganging expedition, Mr

---

[1] See footnote page 113.

Redburn comes up on deck, Claggart is sent for, and preparations are made for the reception of the recruits, while Mr Flint grumbles away. Mr Ratcliffe, who has led the party which boarded the merchantman, *Rights o' Man*, reports that he has returned with three recruits. As Claggart steps forward to question them, he is announced by the tuba and timpani, and his first utterance constitutes his motif: 'Your honour, I am at your disposal'.

Red Whiskers does his best to protest, Arthur Jones replies meekly enough, and finally Billy Budd answers confidently and enthusiastically that the sea is his life and his trade is 'Able Seaman'. When asked about his parents, he is undismayed: 'Haven't any. They say I was a ... was a ...' – and the stammer music is heard as he tries to get out the word 'foundling'. The officers are delighted with their new recruit and place him in the foretop watch. In an exhilarating passage Billy rejoices in his new life: 'Billy Budd, king of the birds!' He ends with a farewell to the ship on which he served: 'Farewell to you, old comrades, farewell to you for ever ... Farewell, *Rights o' Man*' (Ex. 1). This brings an immediate reaction from the officers, who jump to the conclusion that it has political significance.

The decks are cleared, and Mr Redburn instructs Claggart to keep a watch on the new recruit. Claggart waits until the First Lieutenant has gone below, then vents his spleen: 'Do they think I am deaf? ... These officers! They are naught but dust in the wind.' He summons Squeak, who thinks at first it is Red Whiskers he is to watch but is told to keep an eye on Billy Budd, and to provoke him by petty thefts from his kit-bag. Claggart continues to express his hatred of the life in which he finds himself, but is interrupted by the arrival of the Novice's friend to report that the flogging has taken place and that the offender has collapsed as a result of it; he cannot walk. 'Let him crawl' is Claggart's cynical reaction as a sad little procession comes in to a pathetic tune on the saxophone (the particular colour of this instrument is associated with the Novice). In the subdued ensemble which follows (a trio, as the semi-chorus sings in unison), the Novice expresses utter despair and the others try to comfort him, in spite of their conviction 'We're all of us lost for ever on the endless sea' (Ex. 3):

As they go out, Billy and Dansker, followed by Donald and Red Whiskers, emerge from the shadows. Their *scherzando* quartet is in complete contrast to what has gone before. The old hands make fun of Red Whiskers and assure him and Billy that it will be their turn next. The horse-play comes to a sudden end as Claggart appears on deck, and a moment later Captain's Muster is heard (on the flutes). Donald has just time to refer to the captain as 'Starry Vere' (it is Vere's motif, the inversion of Ex. 3, the lament) before

the ship's company comes quickly on deck, and is ordered by Claggart to fall in without delay.[1]

The officers make their way on to the quarter-deck, and as the music reaches a climax, Vere himself appears. In language and music that are quite free from bombast, he addresses the ship's company: they are nearing action. He will do everything he can for

---

[1] In 1961 Britten condensed the opera to two acts, a version which has found slightly less than universal favour. Act I's finale disappeared completely, with the consequence that Captain Vere is seen first in private, and not until Act IV face to face with the ship's company; and that direct contact with Billy Budd is postponed to the second scene of that act. The music at the opening of Act IV being similar to that at the end of Act III, the running of those two acts together has the effect of eliding no more than a few bars of music. The original version has been followed in this synopsis.

Billy Budd (Covent Garden, 1951). Claggart (Frederick Dalberg) interrupts the fight in Act II (now Act I scene iii); Theodor Uppman as Billy.

them when it comes to battle, and victory must come from their combined efforts. There is enthusiasm for what he has to say, and Billy leads a chorus of praise for Vere as the act comes to an end.

Act II. Evening, a week later. Vere, alone in his cabin, is reading, but looks up from his book, and in a few beautiful *arioso* phrases prays that he and his company may be allowed grace to emulate the virtues and the courage of the people of ancient times: 'O God, grant me light'. Mr Redburn and Mr Flint are announced, and together they and Vere drink the King's health, then fall to discussing the prospect of action. Flint takes a bluff seaman's view of the war, and starts a *scherzando* duet, 'Don't like the French', in which Redburn joins. Vere admits he shares their sentiments; another toast – 'The French, down with them!'

The word 'mutiny' creeps into the conversation, and in a short aria Redburn takes up Flint's reference to 'Spithead, the Nore, the floating republic' (Ex. 1). He was there, and he knows what mutiny of that sort can mean. Vere denounces the ideas, French in their origin, which gave rise to the scandal of the Nore. 'We must be on our guard' is his conclusion. The others remember 'that young chap who shouted out "Rights o' Man"', but Vere is of the opinion that there is nothing to fear from that quarter. The sound of singing can be heard from below, and Vere makes a kindly reference to the loyalty of their crew, before Mr Redburn knocks briskly on the door and announces, 'Land on the port bow ... Enemy waters.' The two officers leave Vere to go to their stations and the Captain is left alone, first reading, then listening more and more intently to the sound of the shanty which wells up from the berth-deck.

Scene ii. The berth-deck. It is preceded by an orchestral interlude, making use of the shanty which has already been hinted at in the cabin scene ('Blow her to Hilo'), going on to a second ('Over the water'), and then returning to the first to land with overwhelming effect on a great golden chord of E flat major (chorus and orchestra) as the curtain rises. The scene is animated and yet contented. The first shanty drifts slowly to an end and Donald starts another in a brisker tempo: 'We're off to Samoa, by way of Genoa.'

Billy and Red Whiskers try to persuade Dansker to join in the fun, but he pleads age and indifference. Billy offers to lend him the tobacco he wants and goes off to get it from his kit-bag. The sound of his stammer is heard, and a moment later he drags Squeak out, the corporal protesting that he has not been at Billy's kit-bag as Billy seems to think. A fight begins, Billy floors him, and next thing Claggart is among them, demanding to know how the whole thing started. He turns to Dansker for an explanation. Squeak is arrested, and, when he threatens to blow the gaff on

Claggart, gagged as well. 'As for you ...', says Claggart, turning to Billy, 'Handsomely done, my lad. And handsome is as handsome did it, too' (the words are Melville's).

Claggart remains motionless, muttering 'Handsomely done, my lad' to himself. When the lights have receded from the hammocks, he permits expression of the thoughts which govern his heart: 'O beauty, O handsomeness, goodness, would that I never encountered you!' Claggart recognises in Billy what Iago found in Cassio, or, as Claggart himself puts it, 'The light shines in the darkness, and the darkness comprehends it and suffers'. His musical denunciation of the power of good with which he finds his own evil face to face is accompanied by a trombone solo, and the sinister power of the aria reaches a climax with its ending: 'I, John Claggart, Master-at-Arms upon the *Indomitable*, have you in my power, and I will destroy you.'

Claggart's revelation of his evil purpose is immediately followed by the entrance of the Novice (Ex. 3). Two curious scenes ensue, both nocturnal in character and marked *pianissimo*. The first is between Claggart and the Novice, whom he has summoned with a view to forcing him, through his fear of future punishment, to obtain evidence against Billy. The Novice, after a moment of revulsion against the scheme, accepts the guineas which Claggart gives him to pass on to Billy.

The second nocturne-like scene is between Billy and the Novice, and it is introduced by a tune of uncanny peace, on a solo cello over two bass clarinets (Ex. 5; the tune is heard again in a far more extended form at the beginning of Act IV):

Billy takes time to wake up, and even longer before he understands the import of what the Novice is driving at, with his talk of pressing and gangs and whether Billy won't lead them. When he tumbles to it, the Novice scampers off as Billy is seized with another fit of stammering, which resolves itself when Dansker appears on the scene. Billy's nervousness betrays itself in some agitated phrases as he tries to tell Dansker what the fuss is about. But Dansker understands all too well when he hears what Billy has to say about guineas and mutiny. The act ends with a big-scale duet for Billy and Dansker, which is cast in the form of a *passacaglia*. Dansker enunciates its theme with a variation of Claggart's motif:

Billy is convinced that Claggart likes him, that he himself likes the life on board where his ship-mates are his friends, that he is rumoured as a candidate for promotion. Dansker's rejoinder is unvarying: 'Jemmy-legs is down on you'.

Act III[1] brings the action with the French to an unachieved climax, and sees the conclusion of Claggart's efforts to pull down the power for good which he has detected in the ship's company.

The first scene is as for Act I, some days later. The music is already dominated by the *ostinato* rhythm which is used for the battle. Vere and Redburn are worried by the look of the rapidly increasing mist, but further conversation is prevented by the appearance of the Master-at-Arms, who removes his cap as a sign that he wishes to speak to the Captain. Vere's thoughts are still concerned with the effect the weather is likely to have on the prospect of action, but he consents to see Claggart. The latter, with frequent reference to his own long and faithful service, starts to formulate a charge against some sailor as yet unnamed, who, he says, is likely to endanger the safety of the ship. Vere grows impatient at Claggart's circumlocution, but the interview is cut short by a yell from the main-top: 'Enemy sail on starboard bow!'

The mist lifts and instantly the ship (like the music) hums with activity. Sail is crowded on, Vere orders action stations, and the heartfelt relief of the crew at the prospect of a reward for the weeks of waiting is expressed in an exhilarating, rising theme, 'This is our moment, the moment we've been waiting for'. Gunners run to their guns and start loading, seamen go to the nettings with lashed hammocks and stow them as a rough screen against shot, sand is scattered

on deck, water-tubs and matches are made ready, powder monkeys with a high-pitched and continuous yell scramble to their stations, and finally the marines march into position. A call for volunteers for a boarding party is answered by Donald, Red Whiskers, Dansker, and (from high up in the rigging) Billy. All is ready and excitement reaches fever-pitch, but the enemy is still out of range. There is a general prayer for wind to fill the sails, a moment when it looks as though anticipation will be realised, the climax when a shot is fired, and then frustration which amounts almost to despair when the mist returns. Orders are given to dismiss.

Claggart is again seen standing cap in hand waiting to be noticed by the Captain. This time Vere makes no attempt to hide his impatience at the evasive way in which Claggart starts out to tell his story. When the Master-at-Arms shows the Captain the gold, Vere is sceptical; how would a sailor have gold in his possession? At Claggart's naming of Billy Budd, Vere is frankly incredulous. The Master-at-Arms persists, and Vere flares up at him: 'Claggart! Take heed what you say. There's a yard-arm for a false witness.' He sends a boy for Billy and tells Claggart to follow the accused into his room.

As the officers come forward Vere exclaims vehemently: 'O this cursed mist.' There is a short quartet, one of those moments of tenderness in which the score abounds and which seems to express a sympathy with the aspirations of the crew, as well as (from Vere's point of view) a determination to clear up a mystery which is rapidly becoming inextricably connected with the physical phenomenon of the mist. In the interlude which follows, the music of the mist surrounds chorale-like statements of Vere's prayer for light, and the conflict is clearly that going on in the mind of Vere.

Fanfares associated with Billy bring the interlude to an end, and the curtain goes up to reveal Vere with the mists cleared and his mind made up. Billy is confident he has been summoned to hear that he has been promoted, and Vere encourages him to talk, which he does enthusiastically, while, to a lyrical tune, Vere reflects 'this is the man I'm told is dangerous'.

Claggart is admitted, and, after Vere has cautioned both men to speak only the truth, proceeds

---

[1] Act II in the revised version.

immediately to charge Billy with mutiny. Billy is seized with stammering and suddenly hits out at Claggart, striking him a blow in the middle of the forehead. Claggart falls, and lies motionless. Vere quickly realises he is dead, sends Billy into his state-room, then orders his cabin boy to fetch the officers.

Vere is in no doubt as to his predicament. Claggart's evil purpose is clear enough, and yet his innocent victim by his own action has doomed himself. Vere's agony is made very apparent in a monologue. The officers enter the cabin and are immediately told the facts.

Vere summons a drumhead court, which he will attend as witness. Billy is brought in, and Vere states the bare facts. Billy agrees that they are true, and can plead nothing but his innocence of what Claggart charged him with. Vere declines to add supposition to the facts. The three officers appeal for guidance to Vere, but he refuses to intervene. The verdict is 'Guilty'. Vere accepts the verdict, and orders that sentence be carried out next morning.

In *Billy Budd*, the tragedy is seen as it were through the eyes of Vere, and poignant expression of it comes at the end of this act, first in an *arioso* for Vere himself, and then in the extraordinary ending when, after Vere has gone to inform Billy of the verdict and the stage is left empty, Britten writes a succession of thirty-five common chords, whose different dynamics and scoring convey the changes of emotion with which the message is given and received. It is in effect a great cadence in F major, and in the last half-a-dozen bars recurs a suggestion of the 6/8 tune heard when Billy was woken up by the Novice in Act II (Ex. 5).

Act IV. The first scene shows a bay of the gun deck. Billy is in irons. The music continues where Act III left off, and above the gently swaying accompaniment Billy sings a slow, pathetic tune of resignation (Ex. 5). The words are Melville's, taken from the poem which he describes as composed by a shipmate after the execution and put posthumously into the mouth of Billy himself ('Billy in the Darbies').

Billy's introspection comes to an end when Dansker steals in. 'All's trouble,' he says, 'Some reckon to rescue you ... they swear you shan't swing.' The notion that his death may precipitate the mutiny which he abhors fills Billy with new courage. What has happened and is going to happen to him he ascribes to the workings of fate: he had to 'strike down that Jemmy-legs', and 'Captain Vere has had to strike me down, fate'. His new courage finds expression in an ecstatic ballad tune, which is as simple as it is moving ('And farewell to ye old "Rights o' Man!"'). The chords from the previous act recur in the accompaniment.

The interlude is made up from the calls associated with the ship's routine and the music of the verdict. Daylight is just beginning to show, and the ship's crew assembles to the sound of a funeral march, which can be described as a fugue on a rhythm of timpani and drums, on which is imposed music characteristic of each group as it enters to watch the grim pageantry of the execution. Vere takes his place and straight away Billy is led in between a guard of marines. Mr Redburn reads the sentence, Billy turns to Vere and shouts to him 'Starry Vere, God bless you', and his cry is taken up by the crew. He marches smartly out. Vere removes his hat and all eyes turn to follow Billy as he ascends the mast.

The men on the main deck suffer an immediate revulsion of feeling, and turn in revolt to the quarter-deck. This is the moment described in Melville: 'Whoever has heard the freshet-wave of a torrent suddenly swelled by pouring showers in tropical mountains, showers not shared by the plain; whoever has heard the first muffled murmur of its sloping advance through precipitous woods, may form some conception of the sound now heard.'

Britten writes a *presto* fugue on a variation of the mutiny theme (to the sound of 'ur' in 'purple'), but this savage incoherence gradually changes to a passionate echo of the swelling music associated with the routine work in the first act (Ex. 1). Such ending to the drama seems to indicate that this is no theme of disillusionment but rather carries a message of confidence, if not in Good itself, at least in Man's capacity to understand.

The light fades and presently Vere is seen standing alone, an old man as in the Prologue. For a moment it looks as though he finds the memory of what he might have prevented too much for him ('I could have saved him ... O what have I done?'), but he takes strength from Billy's ballad and this is combined with the 'cadence of comfort' from the end of Act III. The Epilogue comes quietly to an end as the orchestra stops playing, the lights fade, and only Vere's voice is heard rounding out the story.   H.

GLORIANA

Opera in three acts, words by William Plomer. First performed Covent Garden at a Gala in connection with the Coronation of Queen Elizabeth II, 8 June 1953, with Cross (later Shacklock), Vyvyan (later Sutherland), Sinclair, Leigh, Pears (later Lanigan), Geraint Evans, Matters, Dalberg, Te Wiata, conductor Pritchard; Cincinnati, 1955, with Borkh, Conley, conductor Krips; London, Royal Festival Hall, 1963, with Fisher, Pears; Sadler's Wells, 1966, with Fisher, Vyvyan, Wakefield, John Cameron, Garrard, conductor Bernardi (by Sadler's Wells Company in Brussels and Lisbon, 1967); Münster, 1968, with Martha Mödl; English National Opera, Munich, 1972, Vienna, 1975, conductor Mackerras; 1984, San Antonio, New Orleans and Metropolitan, New York, in U.S. stage première, with Sarah Walker, Arthur Davies, conductor Mark Elder; Opera North, 1994, with Barstow, Thomas Randle, conductor Paul Daniel, producer Phyllida Lloyd.

Queen Elizabeth the First	Soprano
Robert Devereux, Earl of Essex	Tenor
Frances, Countess of Essex	Mezzo-Soprano
Charles Blount, Lord Mountjoy	Baritone
Penelope (Lady Rich), *sister to Essex*	Soprano
Sir Robert Cecil, *Secretary of the Council*	Baritone
Sir Walter Raleigh, *Captain of the Guard*	Bass
Henry Cuffe, *a satellite of Essex*	Baritone
A Lady-in-Waiting	Soprano
A Blind Ballad-Singer	Bass
The Recorder of Norwich	Bass
A Housewife	Mezzo-Soprano
The Spirit of the Masque	Tenor
The Master of Ceremonies	Tenor
The City Crier	Baritone

Chorus, Dancers, Actors, Musicians

Place: England
Time: The Later Years of the Reign (1558–1603) of
    Queen Elizabeth I
Running Time: 2 hours 30 minutes

Britten in 1952 became intrigued at the idea of writing a 'national' opera in connection with the coronation the following year of Queen Elizabeth II. He decided on a subject from an earlier, golden Elizabethan age, taking as his theme not the supposed romance between Elizabeth I and the Earl of Essex, rather the contrast between the public and private life of the Queen, the conflict between instinct and duty.

Act I, scene i. The prelude is marked 'very lively', and the rhythm of the brass calls anticipates the chorus's commentary on the events of scene i, which take place outside a tilting ground. A tournament is in progress inside. Cuffe watches and reports to Essex that Mountjoy has accepted a challenge and that the crowd acclaims its favourite. Essex is furiously jealous, when, to the evident delight of the crowd, Mountjoy is victorious and receives his prize – a golden chessman – from the Queen herself.

At this point the bustle and excitement of the tournament give way to a hymn-like tune sung by the crowd in praise of the Queen (Ex. 1):

> Green leaves are we, Red rose our golden Queen,
> O crowned rose among the leaves so green.

The music symbolises the affectionate relationship between the Queen and her subjects, and is one of the opera's dominant themes.

Mountjoy appears and bids his page bind his prize upon his arm. Essex accuses him of arrogance and provokes him to fight. A trumpet fanfare off-stage causes Essex to drop his guard, and he is slightly wounded in the arm. The trumpets draw nearer, and the Queen emerges from the tilting ground, surrounded by her court. She wastes no time in summing up the situation and upbraids both lords for offending against the rule that no duel may be fought at court. It is to Raleigh for his view that she turns, and he gives it – as one 'of riper age'. In an aside, both Essex and Mountjoy make quite clear that they bitterly resent what they regard as Raleigh's insolence – he is older and more experienced than they are but of far less exalted rank, and they object the more for that.

The Queen summons the two late combatants and tells them she has need of them both; let them come to court as friends, and they can count on her support and protection. After an ensemble, a trumpet march brings the scene to an end (Ex. 1).

Scene ii. The Queen's ante-room in Nonesuch Palace. The Queen is closeted alone with Cecil. She refers to the recent duel between the two young lords, and asks Cecil whether he has had news of the reaction of Lady Rich to the fight – 'the dark Penelope' who is sister to Essex, mistress to

Mountjoy.[1] When she admits her liking for Essex, 'the lordly boy', Cecil (whom she calls by his historical nickname of 'pigmy elf') warns her to be on her guard. In a short lyrical passage the Queen reminds Cecil that she has wedded herself to the realm; she seeks no husband and is content if her people are happy (Ex. 1). Cecil reminds her of his father's ancient counsel to the sovereign whom he loved and served so long:

> There comes a moment when to rule
> Is to be swift and bold:
> Know at last the time to strike:
> It may be when the iron is cold!

As the Queen and her counsellor turn to affairs of state, a theme is heard which is associated throughout the opera with the cares of government, and often, because his presence betokens preoccupation with them, with Cecil as well. Its optimistic rise in the major and measured fall in the minor are characteristic. At mention of the possibility of a new Armada from Spain, the Queen laments the certain waste of life and money:

Essex is announced and Cecil withdraws. Essex's greeting to his sovereign and his cousin[2] is exuberant ('Queen of my life'), and the Queen asks her

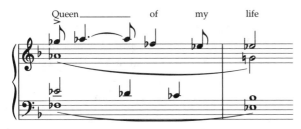

Robin – as she calls him – to soothe her worries by singing and playing to her. Suiting the tune to the words and accompanying himself on the lute, Essex sings 'Quick music's best when the heart is

oppressed', a little lyric whose enchanting, quicksilver grace is too remote from the Queen's mood to afford her the comfort she seeks. Essex sings again, this time quietly, slowly, and with a depth of feeling and sensitivity that affords a musical recreation of that quality which one may suppose caused the Queen to pin her faith for the future to her brilliant but unpredictable cousin (Ex. 4):

The music has a far-reaching significance in the opera and epitomises their relationship. For Essex it stands for the trust and affection which he can give as well as receive in his most intimate moments with his sovereign; for Queen Elizabeth it symbolises the one link with youth and brilliance which is left her in her old age – a link that is as much practical as sentimental, since Essex's prowess is in her mind as intimately linked with the fortunes of England as with those of England's Queen. The words of the poem Britten has set in one of his finest inspirations are by Essex himself.[3]

There is an affectionate duet between the two, which is interrupted when Elizabeth points to the silhouette of Raleigh, which can be seen at the entrance. Essex refers to Raleigh as 'the jackal', and denounces him as his enemy who is, with Cecil, determined to prevent him going to Ireland, there to overthrow the Queen's enemy, Tyrone. At this point occurs a phrase associated with Essex's fatal ambitions, which plays a prominent part in the opera (Ex. 5):

---

[1] Whom she married after the death of her husband, Lord Rich.
[2] His mother, Leicester's widow, was niece to Anne Boleyn, Queen Elizabeth's mother.

[3] Its first phrase is based on the opening of a madrigal by Wilbye, 'Happy were he'.

The Queen dismisses Essex and is alone.

Her thoughts run to duty and to love – the claims of one, the solace of the other, and their mutual incompatibility. Her soliloquy begins with a *forte* statement on the trombones of Ex. 1, which dominates it. After a triumphant resolution,

> I live and reign a virgin,
> Will die in honour,
> Leave a refulgent crown,

the Queen prays to God for strength and grace to fulfil the high office to which she has been called.

Act II, scene i. The Guildhall at Norwich. It was Queen Elizabeth's custom to make periodic tours of England – during which time she was said to be 'On Progress' – and, when the curtain rises (in crushed-note chords, the town bells peal in the orchestra), she is attended by her court, Essex, Cecil, Raleigh, and Mountjoy among them, and the Recorder of the City of Norwich is coming to the end of his address of welcome. The Queen thanks him and the citizens for their greetings, and, when the Recorder comes to kneel in homage and stumbles, helps him solicitously to his feet. The Recorder asks her if she will see the Masque they have prepared in her honour, an invitation to which the Queen signifies her assent but which provokes an impatient aside from Essex, chafing at the enforced inactivity (Ex. 5). Ireland is again uppermost in his mind.

The Masque begins. The music is a set of six contrasted dances, introduced by the Spirit of the Masque and set for unaccompanied voices. The Queen graciously returns thanks to the citizens of Norwich, and the finale makes great use of Ex. 1.

Scene ii. The garden of Essex's house. It is evening. The fresh, lyrical atmosphere of the early part of the scene is immediately established. Mountjoy sings of his love for Penelope Rich, who presently appears and greets him rapturously. Their duet has not run its course before it is interrupted by the voices of Essex and Lady Essex, who do not see them and are dis-

cussing the Queen's continued refusal to advance Essex to the position of Lord Deputy in Ireland. Essex's anger mounts – 'In time, I'll break her will, I'll have my way' – and a quartet develops, in which Essex's impatience overflows, Lady Essex urges caution, and first Penelope, later even Mountjoy, encourage him to hope for preferment as time reduces the Queen's grasp on power.

Scene iii. The palace of Whitehall, at a ball given by the Queen. The whole scene is built up on a series of dances in the Elizabethan style, which are played on the stage and used to frame a considerable development of the dramatic situation. A majestic Pavane is taken up by the stage band as soon as the curtain rises; the court is dancing. The Queen's lady-in-waiting comments admiringly on the splendour of Lady Essex's dress. 'Will the Queen approve?' is Frances's less confident reply as the Master of Ceremonies announces a Galliard, a quick dance to slow music (it is marked *gently flowing*).

The Queen enters (Ex. 1), catches sight of Lady Essex and looks her up and down, then orders that 'La Volta' be played. This is a brilliant piece in 6/4 time; its salient feature was the tossing of the ladies in the air by their partners (a famous picture of Queen Elizabeth dancing 'La Volta' exists at Penshurst). The vigorous nature of the dance exhausts even the apparently inexhaustible Queen, and she commands that the ladies go to change their linen, while a Morris dancer performs for the entertainment of those who remain. At the end of the dance, Lady Essex hurries in, breathlessly complaining that her new dress has disappeared while she was changing. The reason is not far to seek, for the Queen suddenly returns, wearing the missing dress. It is much too short for her, and she looks grotesque. She stalks around, while the court looks on in amazement, then turns to Lady Essex:

> If being too short it becometh not me
> I have it in mind it can ne'er become thee.[1]

The Queen leaves, and in an ensemble Essex, Mountjoy, and Penelope attempt to comfort the stricken Frances Essex, who for her part is more concerned with the inflammatory effect the episode may

---

[1] The episode may at first strike a modern audience as too grotesque to be credible, but it is based on an authenticated incident, when the Queen humiliated a lady of the court suspected of being Essex's mistress.

have on her husband than with the insult offered to herself. Her anxiety is not without foundation; to her own conciliatory 'And as the Queen hath her conditions, Robert, take care!' Essex retorts 'Conditions! Her conditions are as crooked as her carcase!' So unguarded and extreme an utterance dismays even Penelope, but as usual the Queen turns out to be unpredictable. She caps her insult to Essex's wife by returning to the stage with her Councillors to proclaim formally that Essex is appointed Lord Deputy in Ireland and charged to subdue the rebellious Tyrone (Ex. 5). The chorus salutes the 'Victor of Cadiz' and implores him to overcome the foreign threat, while the Queen and the other principal characters react to the appointment in their different ways. Essex himself sings of the charge entrusted to him (Ex. 5), and the scene comes to an end when the Queen commands a 'Coranto' which is danced by the entire court as the curtain comes down, the full orchestra, with its intimations of Essex's star in the ascendant, gradually swamping the stage band with its dance music.

Act III. The tragedy of *Gloriana* is first of all that which almost inevitably, in some way or other, attends a ruling prince, and only secondly that of Essex, the individual in whose fate the sovereign's hopes for the future of the country are epitomised. The catastrophe which is to bring about the fall of Essex – the failure in Ireland – has already taken place when Act III begins; and it is the Queen we see take the 'tragic' decision, not Essex. The working out of his destiny involves the tragedy of the Queen whose trust he held.

Scene i. The prelude is marked *quick and agitated*. When the curtain goes up we are in the Queen's anteroom at Nonesuch. It is early morning and the maids of honour are in conversation. The subject is Ireland. The news is of delay, and instead of the defeat of Tyrone, it looks as though they will soon be talking of the fall of Essex. Suddenly another lady-in-waiting enters in great perturbation to ask if the Queen is yet dressed. There is a great stir below ... She need go no further, for Essex himself bursts into the room, demanding to see the Queen. When told she is not yet ready, he sweeps back the curtain behind which she can be seen at her dressing-table without her wig.

She dismisses her attendants, and turns to him. At first the interview is quiet. There is a moment of sadness ('You see me as I am'), which leads to a tender duet, and it is not until Essex mentions the foes who 'beset me now here in England, at home' (Ex. 5) that the Queen rounds on him and puts her as yet unspoken accusations into words. He has failed in his trust; he is not only unfit but untrue. Essex pleads his devotion, and the scene grows in intensity as the music gets slower and softer, anger replaced by the agony of the might-have-been, until Essex and the Queen together recall the song which has symbolised their relationship (Ex. 4). 'Go, Robin, go! Go!'

The Queen is joined by the ladies-in-waiting, who sing gently and comfortingly to their mistress. When Cecil arrives, the Queen is majestically arrayed (Ex. 1). He tells her that Tyrone is still unsubdued, and that Essex has not only failed in his mission but has brought with him a horde of his unruly followers. The Queen makes up her mind without delay and gives orders that Essex be kept under supervision. The music is dominated by Ex. 5.

Scene ii. A street in the City of London. The short orchestral prelude is based on a theme that is taken up by a blind Ballad-Singer[1] who sits outside a tavern and relays what he hears to his listeners. He is the medium through which we hear of the progress of Essex's rebellion, from the moment when it is first discovered that the Earl is free until Essex is publicly proclaimed a traitor by the City Crier. The scene is built up on the Ballad-Singer's tune ('To bind by force, to bolt with bars the wonder of this age').

Scene iii. A room in the Palace of Whitehall. The orchestra preludes on a theme later sung by the Queen ('Essex is guilty and condemned to die'). The curtain goes up to show Cecil, Raleigh, and other members of the Council waiting to acquaint the Queen with their decision in the case of the Earl of Essex. They are unanimously agreed that he is guilty, but Cecil warns them that the Queen may yet hesitate to make up her mind, may even pardon him. They inform her of the verdict and, when Cecil tries to press her to make a quick decision, she forbids him to prate to her of her duty.

She is alone and in a crucial scene her dilemma is

---

[1] In Elizabethan times, ballad-singers were accustomed to convey the news of the day in their impromptu ballads, which they sang accompanying themselves on the gittern, a stringed instrument; they were thus a cross between newspaper-seller, news commentator and calypso singer.

forcefully portrayed until Raleigh steps in and announces that Lady Essex, Penelope Rich, and Mountjoy have come to intercede for the fallen Essex. After an ensemble, Lady Essex is promised (Ex. 1) that, whatever happens to her husband, her children will not suffer. It is the turn of Penelope to make her plea, which she does in terms which can only be described as feudal: it is not only Essex's service to his Queen but his rank which entitles him to a pardon. The Queen is roused to fury by her words, and sends for the warrant to sign it in the presence of the woman who opened her eyes to danger. Penelope shrieks with anguish as the orchestra has a *fff* statement of Ex. 4, which is to dominate the rest of the opera.

From the departure of Essex's three supporters, the stage darkens and the action becomes unrealistic – as if to emphasise this, the dialogue is mostly spoken against an orchestral background of Ex. 4. Various episodes of the end of Queen Elizabeth's life are recalled – Cecil pleads to be allowed to approach James VI of Scotland about his succession, the Queen makes her so-called Golden Speech to the House of Commons ('I have ever used to set the last Judgement Day before mine eyes'), Cecil appears again in an effort to get the Queen to go to bed. As the Queen's life draws to its close, from behind the scenes can be heard the chorus singing softly to the tune of Ex. 1.

Gloriana together with its composer was under strident attack at the time of its Coronation première, some critics, amateur rather than professional, deciding that it was an insult to the young Queen Elizabeth to show her ageing predecessor partly in a human rather than an exclusively regal light. Yet the work is a product of the composer's early maturity, full of operatic insight, arguably the most relaxed he had yet written, and a complete vindication, one might think, of his attempt to write at the same time a 'national' opera and for a specifically 'grand' occasion. That it was misunderstood and disliked by a 1953 assemblage of grandees and courtiers provides a rather acid comment on the different standards prevailing in the mid-twentieth and the late sixteenth centuries, when a luminary of the aristocracy could be the author of the words of 'Happy were he'.   H.

THE TURN OF THE SCREW

Opera in a prologue and two acts, libretto by Myfanwy Piper, after the story by Henry James. Première by the English Opera Group at the Venice Festival, 14 September 1954, with Jennifer Vyvyan, Joan Cross, Arda Mandikian, Olive Dyer, David Hemmings, Peter Pears, conductor Britten. First performed Sadler's Wells (by English Opera Group), 6 October 1954, by the same cast; Florence Festival, 1955; Stratford, Ontario, 1957; Berlin, 1957, all by the English Opera Group. First independent production, Darmstadt, 1958, with Ursula Lippmann, Martha Geister, Dorothea von Stein, George Maran, conductor Hans Zanotelli; Stockholm, 1959, with Elisabeth Söderström; Boston, U.S.A. (first professional American performance), 1961, with Patricia Neway, Richard Cassilly, conductor Julius Rudel; Scottish Opera, 1970, with Catherine Wilson, Gregory Dempsey; English National Opera, 1979, with Eilene Hannan, Ava June, Rosalind Plowright, Graham Clark, conductor Lionel Friend, producer Jonathan Miller.

The Prologue ....Tenor
The Governess ....Soprano
Miles   ⎫   ....Treble
        ⎬ *children in her charge*
Flora   ⎭   ....Soprano
Mrs Grose, *the housekeeper* ....Soprano
Miss Jessel, *the former governess* ....Soprano
Peter Quint, *the former manservant* ....Tenor

Place: Bly, an English Country House
Time: The Middle of the Nineteenth Century
Running Time: 1 hour 50 minutes

*T*he Turn of the Screw is an operatic adaptation of Henry James's story, preserving almost every detail intact; certain episodes have been run together, but almost nothing has been omitted. The composition of the orchestra is the same as in Britten's other chamber operas, except that a thirteenth player has been added to take care of piano and celesta, which figure largely in the orchestration.

With a view to musical unity in an opera which is continuous and has a prologue and sixteen scenes (with each of which is associated a dominant instrument), the work is based on a single Theme. Each scene is connected to its successor by a musical variation on this Theme, which itself involves the twelve notes of the scale and is built up on alternatively rising fourths and falling minor thirds. It first occurs after the Prologue and before the first scene of Act I. The Theme employs the twelve semitones of the scale, but the music is so far from being dodecaphonic that each variation and its succeeding scene

The Turn of the Screw *(English Opera Group, Venice, 1954, director Basil Coleman, designer John Piper).*
Jennifer Vyvyan (the Governess), David Hemmings (Miles), Peter Pears (Quint).

has in fact a definite tonal centre, an exact calculation of key sequence being a principal means of preserving musical unity. One of the features of James's story is a series of reflections on its implications, particularly on the exact states of tension and emotion in his central character, and the variations turn the screw and form musical counterparts to these literary soliloquies, increasing the tension little by little until the final catastrophe is reached.

Prologue, for tenor accompanied by piano alone: 'It is a curious story. I have it written in faded ink ... '. The visit to the children's handsome guardian, the conditions which should govern the engagement (that she must assume complete responsibility and make all decisions, referring nothing to him), her doubts, and her final acceptance influenced by the trust her charming employer was prepared to put in

her – these are set out in the explanatory prologue.

Act I. The Theme is presented on the piano above tremolo strings before the first scene, Ex. 1:

The presentation of the Theme is followed by music illustrating the Governess's journey to Bly. In the first bar is heard the music associated with the main emotional influences on Miles's life, that is to say, Quint and the new Governess; it occurs a few moments later in more characteristic vocal form, Ex. 2:

The Governess voices her misgivings and wonders what her charges will be like. The variation, beginning with Ex. 1 in a higher position, takes us straight into the busy, everyday world of Bly.

The children are agog to know what their future governess will be like, Mrs Grose is more interested in getting them to practise their bows and curtseys, and before either enquiries or rehearsals are completed, the Governess is there to greet them (immediately, Ex. 2 is heard on solo violin). The children bow and curtsey and then, while Mrs Grose chatters unconcernedly on, the Governess rhapsodises on the beauty of the children and the grandeur of Bly.

The second variation (theme in the bass, otherwise music associated with the children's everyday life) takes us to the porch at Bly (scene 3). Mrs Grose brings the Governess a letter: 'Mrs Grose! He's dismissed his school.' (Here, for the first time, occurs the sound of the celesta, later associated with Quint; Ex. 3.)

The reason? 'An injury to his friends.' Has Mrs Grose ever known Miles bad? Wild, she says, but not bad, and as if to reinforce her conviction the children are heard singing the nursery rhyme 'Lavender's blue'; the duet becomes a quartet, and the scene ends with the Governess's determined answer to Mrs Grose's anxious question: 'I shall do nothing.'

Variation III, an idyllic synthesis of bird-calls on the woodwind. The Governess's lyrical aria (scene iv) shows that the peaceful environment has quieted her initial fears, but it is just at the moment when she admits herself 'alone, tranquil, serene' that a chill comes over the evening (Ex. 3) and she turns to see an unknown male figure high up on one of the towers of the house. The guardian? No! Is it a stranger or some madman locked away?

Variation IV (Ex. 1 again in the bass) marked 'very quick and heavy', anticipates the children's vigorous singing of 'Tom, Tom, the piper's son' (scene v), which in spite of its apparent gaiety takes on the character of a sinister march. The Governess comes in, and, as the children's tune dies away, Ex. 3 is heard again and the enigmatic figure of the tower is visible outside the window. She runs to see who is there, finds nobody, and returns to describe to Mrs Grose what she has seen: 'His hair was red, close-curling, a long pale face, small eyes ... He was tall, clean-shaven, yes, even handsome, but a horror!' Mrs Grose's reaction is instantaneous: 'Quint! Peter Quint!' (Ex. 3), and her grief and terror are made very evident as she tells the story of his domination of the household and of his death, Ex. 4:

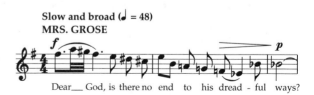

Gradually Mrs Grose explains her hatred and fear of Quint, and a new figure emerges on her words 'It was not for me to say, Miss, no indeed', indicative of her diffidence. At first mention of Miss Jessel the characteristic sound of a low gong is heard, but the music is pervaded by Ex. 4.

The way the colour drains from the orchestra, like blood from the face, as the Governess understands she saw a ghost, is one of Britten's most potent strokes. The Governess thinks she understands. Her peace at Bly is at an end. Quint, in death as in life, returns to dominate the children, and her main charge must henceforth be their protection against influences which, if she cannot withstand their power, will ruin them.

A brisk double fugue introduces and rhythmically prepares the lesson scene. Miles recites the Gender Rhymes once to be found in every English schoolboy's Latin Grammar ('Many nouns in -is we find ...') and Flora's enthusiasm for history is not allowed to divert him from repeating his lesson. What other tags does he know, asks the Governess; he answers in a curious, haunting melody, Ex. 5:

that seems to summarise everything mysterious that may lie behind his natural childlike gaiety. It disconcerts the Governess in its strangeness, and there is no reassurance in Miles's explanation 'I found it, I like it, do you?'

The seventh scene shows Flora in a not dissimilar light. She and the Governess are by the lake at Bly, and Flora asks if it figures in her geography book. She announces dramatically that the lake they are standing beside is called the Dead Sea. She turns from geography to the task of singing her doll to sleep while the Governess reads nearby. She arranges the covers for the doll, and deliberately turns to face the audience as the ghost of Miss Jessel appears at the other side of the lake. The Governess looks up from her reading, sees Miss Jessel (to the sound of her characteristic gong and chords), Ex. 6:

who disappears, and immediately deduces from Flora's unnatural silence that she has seen her too. She hurries Flora away, and then faces a situation (Ex. 2) rendered doubly desperate by the certainty that each of the children under her charge is haunted by a presence from the dead.

Celesta and harp (Ex. 3) usher in the last scene of the first act, while the horn reminds us of Ex. 1 (Variation VII). It is night, and the sound of Quint's voice quietly breaks the silence with a long reiterated coloratura flourish (derived from Ex. 3), Ex. 7:

It is a moment of chilling beauty, made more effective because it is the first time a man's voice has been heard since the Prologue, and it might never have been put in quite these musical terms if the composer had not heard Peter Pears, the original Quint, singing unaccompanied Pérotin ('Beata viscera') in Aldeburgh Church a year or so earlier. Quint is eventually made out, high in the tower, as when the Governess first saw him, and Miles can be seen in the garden below him. 'I'm all things strange and bold ...', he sings to Miles who answers him. Miss Jessel's voice can be heard calling Flora, who responds. A *pianissimo* duet in 3/8 time, marked 'quick and lightly', develops for Quint and Miss Jessel. At its end the voices of the Governess and Mrs Grose can be heard calling for the children (Ex. 1 in the horn). As soon as they appear, the ghosts vanish, Mrs Grose hustles Flora indoors, and the Governess is left to hear Miles's enigmatic answers to her question – one of Henry James's unforgettable strokes: 'You see, I am bad, aren't I?'

Act II. Variation VIII begins with the clarinet imitating Quint's opening flourish, Ex. 7. It introduces a colloquy between Miss Jessel and Quint which mounts in urgency as each participant asserts (Ex. 2) that, with his or her peace of mind established, 'the ceremony of innocence is drowned' (the line is a quotation from Yeats, the theme derived from Ex. 2). As the ghosts fade from sight, the Governess can be heard in an agony of meditation, her aria 'Lost in my labyrinth, I see no truth', sung over a complicated ostinato bass.

The churchyard scene is heralded with an orchestral invocation of church bells (Variation IX) and the lights fade in on the children as they sing a *Benedicite* which is half straight, half parody ('O amnis, axis, caulis, collis ... bless ye the Lord'). Mrs Grose does not realise the implications until her attempts at comfort elicit from the Governess 'Dear, good Mrs Grose, they are not playing, they are talking horrors'. Mrs Grose bustles Flora into church, but Miles hangs back and asks when he is going back to school. His final remark before going inside – 'You trust me, my dear, but you think and think ... of us, and of the others. Does my uncle think what you think?' – elicits from the Governess a horrified 'It was a challenge!' She must leave Bly, now, straight away, while they are at church. She runs out, and Variation X (the theme in the bass) is a postlude to her flight.

The moment she is inside her room the Governess can feel Miss Jessel's presence and sees her sitting at the desk. In their duet, Miss Jessel exudes calm and inexorability: 'Here my tragedy began! Here my revenge begins!', but the Governess's nerves are screwed almost to breaking pitch (it is her nearest approach to the madness which in the story is a conceivable alternative to the haunting the Governess senses) and she now knows that she cannot after all abandon the children. When Miss Jessel has gone, she cries 'I must write to him now', then, in one of the most beautiful passages of the whole opera, sits at her desk and writes to ask the children's guardian if he will see her, as there are things she must tell him (Ex. 8).

At Variation XI's start, bass clarinet and bass flute have a canon on the Theme, interrupted by Ex. 3, and, as the curtain rises, the cor anglais adds Ex. 5 which the boy is heard humming (tragically?) when the lights go up, and on which the following scene is based, a scene where taut nerves threaten at any moment to crack into the relief of tears. The Governess tries to get him to tell her what happened at school. Quint's voice is heard, Miles shrieks and the candle goes out leaving the question still unanswered, the tears unshed. The short Variation XII has Quint's voice singing and the theme in *pizzicato* strings. Quint tempts Miles to take the Governess's letter: 'Take it! Take it!' He does so.

With the thirteenth Variation the mood changes sharply and the solo piano imitates a late eighteenth-century sonata and nerves are seemingly under control again. Miles is seen playing to an audience of the Governess and Mrs Grose. Mrs Grose nods – Flora's peremptory 'Go to sleep!', from scene vii of Act I, has a sinister ring to it – and Flora steals out. Miles's triumphant attack on the piano (it reaches into Variation XIV) leaves no room for doubt that he was acting as a decoy to distract the grown-ups' attention.

Variation XIV is built up on Quint's 'on the paths'. Mrs Grose and the Governess find Flora by the lake. The Governess is aware of Miss Jessel's presence (Ex. 6) and tries to force Flora to acknowledge it, but her efforts are successful only in making Flora take refuge with Mrs Grose. Flora's furious 'I can't see anybody, can't see anything' is sung to the theme of the drowning of innocence and she leads a quartet of female voices in which Miss Jessel rallies Flora to her side and Mrs Grose affirms that she can see nothing. With the departure of Mrs Grose and Flora comes again the theme of Mrs Grose perplexed, and the Governess's cadence, dramatically transposed from Ex. 2, accompanies her acknowledgement of failure.

Variation XV begins with a twelve-note chord, and is concerned mostly with the music of 'I can't see anybody' (piccolo and timpani). The last scene takes place out of doors. Mrs Grose takes Flora away (Ex. 4) and, as if to atone for her own lack of support in the previous scene, reveals to the Governess that her letter to the children's guardian must have been stolen. Miles's entrance coincides with the beginning of a loose *passacaglia* on the first six notes of the theme. The melody in the upper parts, on strings when Miles is concerned, on clarinet when it is the Governess singing, is highly expressive and the whole scene one of great tension. It remains for the Governess, almost as in a ritual, to ask Miles to place his confidence in her and to tell her whether he stole her letter. His attempts at being straightforward are complicated by the admonitions of Quint, but, when the Governess presses him to tell her who it is that he can see (Ex. 1), the struggle for his soul reaches a climax and he dies with a scream of 'Peter Quint! You devil!', aimed, equivocal to the last, at one – or other – of his tormentors. Quint's voice joins with the Governess's, and in the end is heard at a distance with Ex. 3. The Governess is left with the body of the little boy, and it is with pathetic repetitions of his 'Malo' song that the opera comes to an end.   H.

NOYE'S FLUDDE

The Chester Miracle Play[1] set to music. Première, Orford Church, during Aldeburgh Festival, 18 June 1958, with Gladys Parr, Owen Brannigan, Trevor Anthony, conductor Charles Mackerras.

The Voice of God	Speaking Part
Noye	Bass-Baritone
Mrs Noye	Contralto
Sem, Ham and Jaffett	Boy Trebles
Mrs Sem, Mrs Ham, Mrs Jaffett	Girl Sopranos
Mrs Noye's Gossips	Girl Sopranos
Chorus of Animals and Birds	Children

The Congregation

Running Time: 1 hour

Britten's skilful writing for immature performers, in a way that is within their scope and still mean-ingful for audiences, is virtually unrivalled, as witness numerous examples in *The Turn of the Screw*, *Albert Herring*, *Let's Make an Opera*, the cantata *St Nicholas*, *A Midsummer Night's Dream* and the Church Parables. *Noye's Fludde* may contain nothing so disturbingly apt as Miles's 'Malo' song, but it carries the principle of adolescent participation further than in the other operas. Noye and his wife are adult, as is the Voice of God, and probably conductor and a few key musicians of the orchestra, but the bulk of the cast consists of children: there is a sizeable children's chorus, and children provide a full string orchestra, groups of recorders and bugles, and a number of percussion players, the last-named contributing notably to the brilliant colouring of the score.

As Overture, Britten uses the hymn 'Lord Jesus, think on me',[2] sung by the congregation – the work is intended for church performance. God's voice commands Noye to build the Ark, and Sem, Ham, Jaffett and their wives enter to lively music. Mrs Noye and her chorus of gossips mock the preparations. Noye in solemn music leads his family in the building of the Ark, which is accomplished in a few minutes of music, but Mrs Noye remains vociferously sceptical and she and Noye quarrel.

God's voice commands Noye to take the animals into the Ark and, heralded by bugles, a march leads them in two by two and singing 'Kyrie eleison'. Only Mrs Noye resists, but in the end her children pick her up, more than a little drunk, and carry her inside.

The great centrepiece of the opera is an extended *passacaglia* in C, a favourite device of the composer's and here used to depict the various phases of the flood's progress: rain, wind, lightning, thunder and the rising waves. Various instrumental colours are used to point up each aspect of the disaster, Noye and his family sing a prayer before committing themselves to the Ark, and the climax of the episode comes with the singing of the hymn 'Eternal Father, strong to save'.[3]

The flood music ends and there is a kind of postscript, an inversion of the raindrop figuration which has appeared earlier on, played now on tuned mugs and piano; during it I once experienced a torrential downpour in normally dry Mexico when the opera was given in the open air with local forces in

---

[1] The text is from *English Miracle Plays, Moralities and Interludes*, edited by Alfred W. Pollard and published by the Clarendon Press, Oxford.

[2] Damon's Psalter, words by Bishop Synesius, translated by Chatfield.
[3] J.B. Dykes, words by W. Whiting.

Guadalajara at the time of the 1970 World Cup (soccer) – a singularly inappropriate interruption of an otherwise enchanting performance.

Raven and dove are despatched, Noye rejoices at dry land, God's Voice commands disembarkation, and bugles cue the animals into an 'Alleluia' as they leave. The finale is built up on Tallis's *Canon*, 'The spacious firmament on high', the six verses differently treated and with the congregation joining in the last two to make the opera's climax.   H.

A MIDSUMMER NIGHT'S DREAM

Opera in three acts, text after Shakespeare by the composer and Peter Pears. Première, Aldeburgh Festival, 11 June 1960, with Jennifer Vyvyan, April Cantelo, Marjorie Thomas, Alfred Deller, George Maran, Thomas Hemsley, Owen Brannigan, Peter Pears, conductor Britten. First produced Holland Festival with Joan Carlyle replacing April Cantelo as Helena, and Forbes Robinson singing Bottom, conductor George Malcolm; Covent Garden, 1961, with Joan Carlyle, Irene Salemka, Marjorie Thomas, Margreta Elkins, Russell Oberlin, André Turp, Louis Quilico, Geraint Evans, John Lanigan, conductor Georg Solti; Hamburg State Opera, 1961, produced by Rennert; Berlin, Komische Oper, 1961, produced by Felsenstein; la Scala, Milan, 1961; San Francisco, 1961; New York, City Center, 1963; Glyndebourne, 1981, with Ileana Cotrubas, Felicity Lott, Claire Powell, James Bowman, Ryland Davies, Dale Duesing, Curt Appelgren, Patrick Power, produced by Peter Hall, conductor Bernard Haitink.

Oberon, *King of the Fairies* ....Counter-Tenor (or Contralto)

Tytania, *Queen of the Fairies* ....Coloratura Soprano

Puck ....Speaking Role (Acrobat)

Theseus, *Duke of Athens* ....Bass

Hippolyta, *Queen of the Amazons, betrothed to Theseus* ....Contralto

Lysander ....Tenor

Demetrius ....Baritone

Hermia, *in love with Lysander* ....Mezzo-Soprano

Helena, *in love with Demetrius* ....Soprano

Bottom, *a weaver* ....Bass-Baritone

Quince, *a carpenter* ....Bass

Flute, *a bellows-maker* ....Tenor

Snug, *a joiner* ....Bass

Snout, *a tinker* ....Tenor

Starveling, *a tailor* ....Baritone

Fairies
Cobweb
Peaseblossom
Mustardseed   } ....Trebles
Moth

Chorus of Fairies ....Trebles or Sopranos

Running Time: 2 hours 30 minutes

To turn a masterpiece in one medium into a work of similar calibre in another is a mighty undertaking and yet this is what Benjamin Britten has succeeded in doing. His adaptation, with the perspicacious aid of Peter Pears, caused David Drew[1] to write *à propos* the première in 1960 of *A Midsummer Night's Dream*, 'A corner of Shakespeare's Empire has undergone a subtle change. It has not been ruthlessly invaded, it has not even been quietly exploited. But for those who were at Aldeburgh on 11 June, and for those who will follow them to Britten's new opera in the months and years to come, Shakespeare's *A Midsummer Night's Dream* will never be quite the same again.'

The opera elevates the fairies, and particularly Oberon, to a position of prime influence and also, to become the framework of the whole opera, places all except the final scene in the wood, and relegates the question of anachronistic Athenian ambience to the background. Britten's music moves on three sharply differentiated planes: fairies, mortals (lovers) and rustics. The snakes which infest Shakespeare's imagery are never far from the drama's surface, the fairies dispense a magic which is sure and purposeful but not inevitably benign, the equivocal figure of Oberon[2] flaunts the power to chill if he does not choose to warm, and only the wood is omnipresent, all-consoling.

Act I. The wood is represented by a slow-breathing string texture which rises and falls as the curtain goes up, and is heard again frequently throughout the opera (Ex. 1). The fairies make their entrance with 'Over hill, over dale, thorough bush, thorough briar'. They are Tytania's instruments, interrupted by Puck (trumpet and drum accompaniment throughout), of whom they are afraid. Puck announces Oberon and Tytania (slow march) who have quarrelled over an Indian page boy. Tytania departs and Oberon alone plots vengeance, summons Puck and sends him to

[1] *New Statesman*, 18 June 1960.
[2] 'Whether intended or not', wrote David Drew in the *New Statesman*,

'Britten's Oberon is a more grimly effective horror than the Peter Quint who called from the Tower and had no Puck to help him.'

(Ex. 1) **Slow and mysterious**
portamento
Str. *pp*
less p

fetch that herb whose juice 'will make or man or woman madly dote Upon the next live creature that it sees'. Celesta lends colour in its *ostinato* accompaniment to the spell motif, Ex. 2:

20 (Slow and gentle)

OBERON

Be it on Lion, Bear or Wolf or Bull,

Or med-dling Mon-key or bu - sy Ape.

Oberon, his plot in motion, disappears and the wood is left empty (Ex. 1).

It is the turn of the lovers, whose themes throughout the opera are derived from Lysander's 'The course of true love never did run smooth'. We meet first Lysander and Hermia, eloping to avoid the forced betrothal of Hermia and Demetrius. If one senses at the start of the duet that they may not emerge from their predicament by their own efforts, the fire that has earlier been lacking in them starts to appear in the passage beginning 'I swear to thee'. They leave, the wood is empty again (Ex. 1), Oberon returns with schemes in his heart and music (Ex. 2), and the lovers, Lysander and Hermia, are succeeded by the quarrelling Demetrius and Helena, the latter breathlessly pursuing the former, who for his part wants nothing more than to be re-united with his betrothed Hermia. Helena has a short, character-revealing solo, 'I am your spaniel', and when they

depart Oberon decides to put right the destinies of these star-crossed lovers. He sends for Puck who gives him the flower he demanded and lies at his feet. 'I know a bank where the wild thyme blows' is, for all its sinister undertones, an aria of exquisite sensibility, introduced by Ex. 2 with cellos supplying the vocal line and horns adding colour, and it marvellously rounds off the first half of the act.

Into the silent wood (Ex. 1) cautiously come six rustics, heralded by trombone *pp*. Peter Quince calls the roll and, not without frequent interruption from Bottom, assigns to each a part in the play. Each is neatly characterised, from the swaggering Bottom through the shy but tenacious Francis Flute to Snug the joiner, who is 'slow of study' and tends therefore to come in on the weak beat of the bar. Bottom at one point offers to play Lion as well as Pyramus, but Flute and the others think that the ladies would take fright, 'and that were enough to hang us all'. With promises to con their parts, they whisper 'Adieu' and once more leave the wood empty (Ex. 1).

Hermia and Lysander are exhausted with their wanderings and lie down together, only for Puck mistakenly to squeeze the juice of the magic flower on Lysander's eyes (celesta). Helena and Demetrius, still quarrelling, enter in their turn to look for a resting place. Helena perceives Lysander, he wakes and declares love for her and hatred for Demetrius, in either instance to her considerable discomfiture. She runs out, followed by Lysander; Hermia wakes and distractedly follows where Lysander led.

Tytania soon enters with her retinue whom she bids sing her to sleep. They oblige with an astonishingly fresh setting of 'You spotted snakes with double tongue', but Oberon moves invisibly past the single sentinel they have posted and (Ex. 2) squeezes the magic juice on to Tytania's eyes, bidding her 'Wake when some vile thing is near'.

Act II is concerned with sleep, and the prelude is based on four chords, very differently scored, covering the twelve notes of the scale (there is little twelve-notish about the score but its gradual influence on Britten, even more than in *The Turn of the Screw*, is here apparent). The curtain discloses Tytania asleep. The six rustics enter for rehearsal. Bottom is full of suggestions: ladies will like neither a killing on the stage nor the roaring of Lion – let there be a prologue to explain them. Quince himself has a couple of conundrums: how 'to bring the moonlight into the chamber' (the word 'moonshine' has a particular resonance for the rustics), and how to represent the wall. Rehearsal starts, watched now by Puck who follows Bottom at his exit and, when Flute has voiced his entire role without a pause, brings Bottom back with an ass's head on his shoulders, to the disgruntlement of the cast which runs off at top speed.

Bottom sings – or bellows – to keep his spirits up and Tytania wakes to love him. Her attendants are introduced to him, detailed to attend his every want, and in their turn greet him ceremoniously. A languorous tune on A flat clarinet and flute expresses Tytania's infatuation and eventually she sets the fairies to play and sing to him.[1] Bottom announces 'I have an exposition of sleep come upon me', Tytania sings ecstatically and then in her turn falls asleep.

A short interlude brings Puck on the scene and after him Oberon, who soon expresses his delight at Tytania's predicament. But Puck has been mistaken over the Athenians, and Demetrius and Hermia are clearly at cross-purposes. Puck is dispatched to find Helena, and Oberon squeezes more juice (Ex. 2) on to Demetrius' eyes, before Puck returns with Helena and Lysander. Helena upbraids Lysander for his faithlessness to Hermia, but Demetrius wakes up, sees Helena, and provides her with a second adoring swain. Hermia's re-entry adds a further complication, as Helena decides she is at the bottom of a plot against her. Helena's short aria ('O is all forgot?') describing her schooldays' friendship for Hermia starts off an ensemble of misunderstanding at the end of which the two girls quarrel bitterly (Hermia: 'She hath urg'd her height' ... Helena: 'Get you gone, you dwarf') and all leave, the girls at odds, the men to fight.

Oberon comes forward dragging Puck by the ear and complaining at what must either be incompetence or knavishness. He instructs him so to order the comings and goings of Demetrius and Lysander that their efforts to confront each other in mortal combat shall end in exhaustion before they contrive to come to blows. Puck carries out his instructions, until curtain-fall finds the four lovers correctly lined up. The fairies steal in to sing a benediction, and Puck squeezes the antidote to the juice on Lysander's eyes (Ex. 2).

Act III. From the strings at the outset we sense re-conciliation and resolution in the morning air. In the wood can be seen lying asleep Tytania with Bottom, and the four lovers slightly apart. Oberon likes what he sees and having acquired the Indian boy who was the cause of the trouble, is prepared to undo 'This hateful imperfection of her eyes'. To the sound of the celesta, he undoes the spell: 'Be as thou wast wont to be; See as thou wast wont to see' (Ex. 2). Tytania awakes, is released from the spell and reconciled (very slow; *quasi saraband*) with Oberon, who himself proposes to unite the pairs of lovers to coincide with the marriage of Duke Theseus with Hippolyta.

Oberon, Tytania and the fairies disappear as the lovers, to the sound of horns (Theseus' rather than the horns of Elfland), awake and are in their turn reconciled: 'And I have found Demetrius like a jewel. Mine own, and not mine own', in a fine flowing ensemble.

Bottom, alone on the stage, starts to wake. Snatches of what has passed before go through his mind and he is indignant that his fellow mummers have abandoned him. He has dreamt – mysteries. But a ballad shall be made of his dream, 'And I will sing it in the latter end of the play before the Duke'. It is a key statement, not only musically and dramatically but because in it we have proof of the opera's mainspring, the omnipotent fairy power of Oberon; Bottom could not have *imagined* what he describes without its influence. As he walks away the others come in. Had it been possible to perform the play in front of the Duke and had Bottom been with them, he would surely have been granted sixpence a day for life for his playing of Pyramus! Bottom's voice is heard. All questioning is halted at the news that 'The Duke hath dined and our play is preferred'. In a flurry of ensemble, they prepare to leave, and horns and woodwind carry the burden of a quick march as the scene changes to:

Theseus' palace. Theseus and Hippolyta enter with their court and in a few phrases voice their impatience that the day's wedding events have not yet given way to the night's consummation. The four lovers enter to beg for the Duke's blessing, before Peter Quince comes in confidently with a playbill which he hands to Hippolyta: 'A tedious brief scene of young Pyramus, And his love Thisby.'

What follows is nothing less than a condensed

---

[1] To the tune of 'Boys and girls come out to play'.

comic opera, occupying thirty-six pages of vocal and forty of full score. Its introduction has all six rustics singing together in block harmony and marked *pomposo*: 'If we offend, it is with our good will' – but straight away there is a sting in the tail when they attempt a canon on 'All for your delight' and the climactic top D proves too high for Flute. Prologue, in the person of Quince, introduces the characters, predictably failing to fit action to word as he pushes them out while reiterating the word 'Remain'.

Wall, played by Snout, introduces himself in *Sprechstimme*, before Bottom launches himself, in the character of Pyramus, into a short if full-blooded apostrophe to Night and to the obstacle between him and his love, in the manner of a big Italianate aria – indeed the whole thing is a satire on nineteenth-century romantic opera, as is plain from the rather timid flute tune introducing Flute in the character of Thisby and the overwrought if insubstantial duet for Thisby and Pyramus which follows it. Wall prepares to leave, still in *Sprechstimme*, and is succeeded by Snug as Lion and eventually Starveling as Moon. Thisby continues her *allegretto* flute-beset mood of before, but the music is quickly superseded by the roaring of Lion, who chases Thisby out. Pyramus enters, finds Thisby's mantle, assumes the worst and plunges a sword into his bosom. Thisby finds the body of Pyramus and, at the end of her wits, enters upon a mad scene to which the flute does full justice, before embarking on an *adagio lamentoso* with full orchestral postlude. Bottom offers the assembled worthies an epilogue or a Bergomask dance and it is the dance which is chosen. It involves a maximum of misunderstanding between the players and is in two parts, the first hesitating between 6/8 and 9/8, and the second a very fast 2/4. Midnight sounds, the rustics stop dancing and Theseus and Hippolyta, followed by the four lovers, adjure them and us 'Sweet friends, to bed'.

There is no change of scene but enter Cobweb, Mustardseed, Peaseblossom and Moth to sing 'Now the hungry lion roars, And the wolf behowls the Moon'. Puck comes in with his broom, but the major musical statement is left to Oberon and the fairies with some help from Tytania. 'Now until the break of day' with its mesmeric Scotch snap is uncannily cathartic in its effect. Not even Captain Vere with his consolatory chords, not the return of the Borough's working chorus, not the reiteration of 'Malo' makes

a greater effect, and for anything comparable in Britten one has to go back to *Gloriana*'s final orchestral Lute Song and 'Green leaves'. After this, who could gainsay Puck's valedictory 'Gentles, do not reprehend'?   H.

PARABLES FOR CHURCH PERFORMANCE

The period following *A Midsummer Night's Dream* seems to have involved the composer in considerable reappraisal of his position, and his stage output for the decade is confined significantly to three Church Parables, *Curlew River*, *The Burning Fiery Furnace* and *The Prodigal Son*. That these parables derive to some degree from the successful church opera *Noye's Fludde* is obvious, but it should not be missed that their ancestry includes so dramatic (though non-stage) a church work as *Saint Nicholas* (1948). Formally they demonstrate a new conciseness, economy of means (rather under twenty singers each and an accompanying chamber orchestra of either seven or eight players), and stylistically a particularly successful synthesis of East and West as well as remarkable freedom for the performers.

Their genesis is interesting and must be seen against the background of something near crisis in the composer's approach to his art, a crisis growing perhaps out of seven or eight years of public and critical acclamation – as hard to digest for so serious and private an artist as Britten as had been a longer period of critical misunderstanding – culminating in the adulation which greeted the *War Requiem* (1961), a work the composer had felt embodied a very personal point of view.

During a journey to the Far East in February 1956, Britten underwent two new and fruitful musical experiences: in Bali, he heard gamelan music extensively for the first time (the influence comes out in his ballet *The Prince of the Pagodas* later the same year); and in Tokyo he encountered the Japanese Noh play. The Noh play seems to have haunted his imagination: 'The whole occasion made a tremendous impression upon me: the simple, touching story, the economy of the style, the intense slowness of the action, the marvellous skill and control of the performers, the beautiful costumes, the mixture of chanting, speech, singing which, with the three instruments, made up the strange music – it all offered a totally new "operatic" experience.'[1]

Seven years later, it was the Noh play *Sumidagawa* which he asked William Plomer to transform into what became the first of his three 'Parables for church performance', and it was *Curlew River* which provided the formal terms of reference for the complete set. The story and its overtones were retained but the Japanese setting gave way to a modern version of the English medieval liturgical drama with the music based on a plainsong hymn. So successful did the formula prove in *Curlew River* that composer and librettist retained it throughout the set, each parable introduced by a different plainsong tune and based upon it, each deemed to be taking place inside a monastic community, which processes in at the start of the action, and which provides from its male ranks all the characters of the drama, whether masculine or feminine.

Unlike say *Lucretia*, *Albert Herring* or *Les Mamelles de Tirésias*, which are miniature 'Grand' operas and where the small orchestra skilfully substitutes a big one, these Parables are chamber operas of potentially seminal nature. Whether the seed is finally proved fertile or sterile is a matter only time can resolve. These works will remain.

CURLEW RIVER

Parable for Church Performance, libretto by William Plomer. Première, Aldeburgh Festival, 12 June 1964, at Orford Church, with Peter Pears, John Shirley-Quirk, Bryan Drake, Don Garrard. First performed Holland Festival, 1964, and Tours, 1965, by English Opera Group with substantially the above cast. First performed Denmark, Copenhagen, 1966; U.S.A., Caramoor, New York, 1966, with Andrea Velis; Mulhouse, 1968, with Michel Sénéchal; Australia at Adelaide Festival, 1970, with Peter Pears, where it was repeated in 1988 (in parallel with Noh performances of *Sumidagawa* by a Japanese company) with Gerald English.

The Abbot, Eleven Monks, Four Acolytes, Seven Lay Brothers who make up the cast of the Parable:

The Madwoman ....Tenor

The Ferryman ....Baritone

The Traveller..Baritone

The Spirit of the Boy *(an acolyte)*......................Treble

Leader of the Pilgrims *(the Abbot)* ....Bass

Chorus of Pilgrims

Instrumentalists: Flute (doubling Piccolo), Horn, Viola, Double Bass, Harp, Percussion, Chamber Organ

Running Time: 1 hour 10 minutes

The story outline of *Curlew River* remains close to that of *Sumidagawa*, as evidenced when the Prince of Hesse and the Rhine, who went with Britten to Tokyo, described the Noh play in his diary[2]: 'The ferryman is waiting in his boat, a traveller turns up and tells him about a woman who will soon be coming to the river. The woman is mad, she is looking for her lost child. Then she appears and the ferryman does not wish to take a mad person, but in the end he lets her into his boat. On the way across the river the two passengers sit behind each other on the floor as if in a narrow boat, while the ferryman stands behind them, symbolically punting with a light stick. The ferryman tells the story of a little boy who came this way a year ago this very day. The child was very tired for he had escaped from robbers who had held him. He crossed the river in his boat, but he died from exhaustion on the other side. The woman starts crying. It was her son. The ferryman is sorry for her and takes her to the child's grave. The mother is acted by a tall man in woman's clothing with a small woman's mask on his face. Accessories help you to understand what is going on ... The play ends in the chanting of the chorus.'

It is precisely the 'plot' of *Curlew River*. To the three main characters Britten and Plomer add the Abbot of the monastery where the performance is taking place, the voice of the dead child, and nine pilgrims who act as chorus. In addition – and crucially – the action and motivation are changed from medieval Japanese and Buddhist to medieval English and Christian, and music and action start with ritual, the procession of monks up the nave of the church singing the Compline (i.e. evening) Office hymn, 'Te lucis ante terminum, Rerum Creator, poscimus', a prayer for protection at the ending of the day. The drama proper begins with the Ferryman's vigorous announcement of his role in the action.

Much has been written about *Curlew River* and the

---

[1] From the composer's sleeve-note to the recording of *Curlew River*.

[2] Printed in *Tribute to Benjamin Britten* (Faber, 1963).

other Church Parables, each of which embodies the paradox of very highly organised musical material (derived from the simple basis of plainchant) and a style of performance much freer than in Britten's other dramatic works. To take characterisation of performance first, the composer dispenses with a conductor, and treats the singers as being as much a part of a chamber ensemble as the instrumental musicians.

Eric White[1] has drawn attention to 'an element of rhapsody' in the vocal parts which is a consequence of the freedom allotted the performers, and the score specifies the leading voice at each moment as well as making liberal use of dotted (as opposed to solid) barlines, in order to diminish the emphasis on regular pattern.

Much of the writing is monophonic (confined to a single part) or heterophonic (the simultaneous sounding of simple and decorated versions of the same theme) rather than polyphonic (individual voices moving in apparent independence though fitting together harmonically).

In *Curlew River*, each character is represented by certain motifs and has associated with him his own instrument. The Ferryman has an agitated version of the Compline hymn and his instruments are horn and to a lesser extent viola. The Traveller has harp and double bass, playing arpeggios to his 'heavy, trudging step'.[2] The Madwoman has flute, additionally flutter-tongued before her entry ('Whither I, Whither I go').

The Madwoman's original motif, all fourths and sevenths, leads to an entrance scene modelled on the traditional operatic mad scene, the difference here being that *Curlew River*'s central figure starts insane and moves towards sanity rather than the more customary reverse. In her narrative aria, expression from an otherwise monotone line is achieved by means of the rising or falling of the final note by a tone or occasionally a semitone, upwards when she recalls her life or the child's loss, down when she refers to her grief. This simple, unemphatic yet in context highly expressive variation of the line is a precise echo of the simple, unemphatic gesture (the back of his hand slowly to his forehead) which the Noh player of the Madwoman in Adelaide (and in Japan) made to denote weeping.

The Parable moves through various stages of tension – notably the chorus's repeated enunciation of the Curlew River's Song of Separation, and an ensemble for Ferryman, Traveller, Chorus and flutes before the Madwoman is allowed to board the ferry – towards a climax as the Madwoman, now convinced that the grave on shore is that of her lost child whom the river people think of as a saint, prays with the travellers at the grave. Abbot and Chorus sing the hymn 'Custodes hominum' while Ferryman and Traveller pray in their turn, before, in a few phrases high in the treble (and followed by piccolo), the spirit of the boy releases his mother from her torment. At the final 'Amen' she has shed her madness, and the little drama of compassion can end as it began with the disrobing of the monks, an exhortation from the Abbot and the singing of the initial plainchant. It is a work of extraordinary tension and emotive power, which was hailed in the headline to Wilfrid Mellers's notice in the *New Statesman*,[3] punningly and appropriately, 'Britten's Yea-Play'. H.

THE BURNING FIERY FURNACE

Parable for Church Performance, libretto by William Plomer. Première, Aldeburgh Festival, 9 June 1966, at Orford Church, with Peter Pears, Bryan Drake, Robert Tear, Victor Godfrey, John Shirley-Quirk, Peter Leeming. First performed U.S.A., Caramoor, New York, 1967, with Andrea Velis; in Australia, at Adelaide Festival, 1970, with John Fryatt.

The Abbot, Twelve Monks, Five Acolytes and Eight
    Lay Brothers who make up the cast of the Parable:
Nebuchadnezzar...Tenor
The Astrologer *(The Abbot)* ....Baritone
Ananias..Baritone
Misael ....Tenor
Azarias...Bass
The Herald and Leader of the Courtiers ....Baritone

Chorus of Courtiers; Five Attendants (treble)

Instrumentalists: Flute (doubling Piccolo), Horn,
    Alto Trombone, Viola, Double Bass (doubling
    Babylonian Drum), Harp, Percussion, Chamber
    Organ (doubling Small Cymbals).

Running Time: 1 hour 5 minutes

---

[1] In his invaluable *Benjamin Britten, his Life and his Operas* (Faber, 1983).
[2] Patricia Howard: *The Operas of Benjamin Britten* (Barrie and Rockliff, 1969).
[3] 3 July 1964.

The story, much less esoteric than that of *Curlew River*, is drawn from the Old Testament and is concerned with the theme of steadfastness in the face of tyranny.

In sixth-century B.C. Babylon, three young Israelites have been brought to the city as captives. On the advice of Daniel, they are appointed by King Nebuchadnezzar to rule over three provinces, their names changed to the Babylonian forms of Shadrach, Meshach and Abednego. When at a feast they refuse to betray the faith of their forefathers by eating and drinking with the courtiers, the Astrologer persuades the King that this is an insult to nation and faith. The Herald announces that all must bow down to a great golden image of the Babylonian god Merodak when the royal music sounds, but Shadrach, Meshach and Abednego refuse to worship. At Nebuchadnezzar's command, a furnace is prepared for their execution and they are thrown in, only for an angel to join them in the furnace, whose heat their faith successfully defies. When they reappear untouched by the fire, Nebuchadnezzar repudiates the Astrologer and is converted to their faith.

Instrumentation remains the same as in *Curlew River* except that alto trombone is added to the eight players of the first Church Parable. Once again, plainchant – the Advent sequence 'Salus aeterna, indeficiens mundi vita' (Eternal Saviour of the world) – provides the musical basis of the work, this time with a wider intervalic range than before, and is followed as in *Curlew River* by instrumental heterophony (more Eastern-sounding than in *Curlew River*), as the processing monks robe for the drama. This is in two parts, each introduced by an important announcement by the Herald. In the first part, the main episode is the King's Feast; and in part II come the Processional March and Hymn to Merodak, and the Furnace and Conversion of the King.

Instrumental characteristics are associated with the Herald, alto trombone; and with Nebuchadnezzar (and his *alter ego*, the Astrologer – a role taken by the Abbot), flutter-tongued flute over harp and horn with chords on double bass and viola. Ananias, Misael and Azarias are more directly identified with the plainchant theme than the Babylonians, who are characterised at the Abbot's first pronouncement. The Feast itself is distinguished by an Entertainment given by three boys, two singers and a tumbler, the music deliberately in that simpler style regularly adopted by Britten in his writing, dramatic or otherwise, for children's voices, the words in the form of riddles, or at least question and answer. By the end of the Feast, Shadrach, Meshach and Abednego are isolated and in a touching scene reiterate their position of, as it were, passive resistance.

After the Herald's proclamation at the start of part II, we hear the sound of 'cornet, flute, harp, sackbut, psaltery, dulcimer and all kinds of music', at the first sound of which every subject of the King must fall down and worship the image of gold he has set up. In the Processional Music, the eight instruments have eight key phrases which they combine in ten different 'verses' of the march to astonishingly varied effect, after which comes the Hymn to Merodak, god of the Babylonians, whose slurs were suggested by the Herald when he first mentions the Feast, and later by Nebuchadnezzar and the Astrologer before the isolation of the three in part I.

The final episode is that of the Furnace, with the solvent of the Benedicite,[1] sung by the three with the addition of a solo treble voice to symbolise the Angel of the Lord and recalling the treble sound of the Spirit of the Boy in *Curlew River*. Nebuchadnezzar's conversion comes during a pause in the psalm, to which he later joins his voice.   H.

THE PRODIGAL SON

Parable for Church Performance, libretto by William Plomer. Première, Aldeburgh Festival, 10 June 1968, at Orford Church, with Peter Pears, John Shirley-Quirk, Bryan Drake, Robert Tear. First performed in U.S.A., Caramoor, New York, 1969, with Andrea Velis; Australia, Adelaide Festival, 1970, with Peter Pears.

The Abbot, Eleven Monks, Five Acolytes, Eight Lay
    Brothers who make up the cast of the Parable:

Tempter *(the Abbot)*	Tenor
Father	Bass-Baritone
Elder Son	Baritone
Younger Son	Tenor

Chorus of Servants, Parasites and Beggars; Young
    Servants and Distant Voices (trebles)

---

[1] Also set in the first scene of *Peter Grimes*'s Act II and parodied in *The Turn of the Screw*.

Instrumentalists: Alto Flute (doubling Piccolo), Trumpet (in D), Horn, Viola, Double Bass, Harp, Chamber Organ, Percussion

Running Time: 1 hour 10 minutes

The story of the Prodigal Son, with its emphasis on repentance and forgiveness, is one of the best known and most beautiful of all New Testament stories, and it appropriately furnishes out the trio of Noh play, Old Testament legend and Christian parable which make up Britten's Triptych.

A family consisting of Father, Elder Son, Younger Son and their Servants lives by the fruit of its toil on the land. When the Elder Son and the men go off to work in the fields, the Younger Son hears a voice tempting him to unknown delights, his 'most secret longings'. He asks for and obtains his inheritance, but in the city, Parasites remove it from him and he is left penniless and alone. He joins some Beggars, shares the food of swine, and determines to return home to ask his father's forgiveness. He is received with rejoicing, orders are given that the fatted calf be killed, and even the envious Elder Son is finally reconciled to the restored situation.

The ground plan of *The Prodigal Son* is on lines made familiar by the other Church Parables, starting with a plainchant theme, the Prime (i.e. morning) Office hymn, 'Iam lucis orto sidere', the morning prayer for protection. As the characteristic tone colour of *Curlew River* comes from solo flute, so does that of *The Burning Fiery Furnace* from alto trombone, and of *The Prodigal Son* from trumpet and viola (alto flute, doubling piccolo, and trumpet replace *The Burning Fiery Furnace*'s flute and alto trombone). Alto flute is associated with the Father, viola with the Younger Son, double bass with the Elder Son, horn with pastoral toil and its workers. The trumpet embodies the idea of Temptation.

Dramatic excitement is kindled from the moment the initial plainchant ends with the monks' 'Amen' echoed a third higher and then mocked a sixth higher as the Tempter introduces himself from the end of the nave in the garb of the as yet unseen Abbot, who in previous Church Parables has decorously introduced the burden of the drama before robing to take part in it himself. Here we plunge *in medias res* from the start, and it is not until the Tempter has put forward himself and his motives that we hear with heightened effect the plainchant theme in heterophonic statement to accompany, as in the previous Parables, the robing of the principal characters.

'See how I break it up,' breathes Quint-like the Tempter over the idyllic family scene with which we are introduced to the drama, and this is musically speaking the liveliest character, working his wiles on the Younger Son as they walk, gourd-accompanied, towards the City of Sin in splendid duet. With its two tenor voices, it recalls Monteverdi and Purcell in its outline just as it states Britten (and anticipates Tippett's Mel and Dov) in its melodic contours.

Choral writing is more prominent in *The Prodigal Son* than in its predecessors, and the quarter-hour sequence of the City and its temptations contains nine different choral sections as the Younger Son progresses from welcome by the Parasites to disintegration in face of the Beggars.

Apart from perhaps the opening *arioso* statement of the Father to his Sons and Servants, the duet for Tempter and Younger Son, and the City sequence, there are no set pieces in *The Prodigal Son* to compare with those of *The Burning Fiery Furnace*, nor has this Church Parable the musical or dramatic intensity of *Curlew River*, but the fact remains that there have been commentators to find it the best of the three. H.

OWEN WINGRAVE

Opera in two acts, libretto by Myfanwy Piper, based on the short story by Henry James. Commissioned for B.B.C. Television and first shown 16 May 1971, with Heather Harper, Jennifer Vyvyan, Sylvia Fisher, Janet Baker, Peter Pears, Nigel Douglas, Benjamin Luxon, John Shirley-Quirk, conductor Britten. Stage première, Covent Garden, 10 May 1973; Glyndebourne Touring Opera, 1995.

Owen Wingrave, *the last of the Wingraves* .....Baritone

Spencer Coyle, *head of a military cramming establishment* ....Bass-Baritone

Lechmere, *a young student of Coyle's* ....Tenor

Miss Wingrave, *Owen's aunt* ....Soprano

Mrs Coyle...Soprano

Mrs Julian, *a widow and dependant at Paramore* ....Soprano

Kate, *her daughter* ....Mezzo-Soprano

General Sir Philip Wingrave, *Owen's grandfather* ....Tenor

Narrator, *the ballad singer* ....Tenor

Distant Chorus ....Trebles

Place: London; Paramore
Time: Late Nineteenth Century
Running Time: 1 hour 55 minutes

*O*wen *Wingrave* was written for television, a fact which may have spurred the composer's creative dexterity, not least in transitional techniques already adumbrated in his earlier operas, but which should be taken to imply neither that it is unsuitable for stage nor that it makes very specific use of television techniques. Britten and Myfanwy Piper have together returned to Henry James for their subject (as with *The Turn of the Screw*), and the theme is the effort of the young scion of the military house of Wingrave to escape from the tyranny of the past and his family's military tradition and, more specifically, to make it possible for his pacifist conscience to prevail over the conventional instincts of his family. In a sense he wins, but at a cost.

The prelude to the opera consists of a dozen bars marked *marziale*, and ten instrumental 'portraits' of ten military forebears of Owen. In these few minutes Britten has set out the musical material of the opera. In the *marziale* section we are introduced to a rhythmic idea, which later gives rise to very many others in the course of the opera, and is always associated with the percussion. Owen's theme eventually provides the eleventh of the portraits. The other ten, each intended to go with a visual realisation of some member of the family, constitute a great orchestral cadenza, and are associated successively with bassoon; oboe; horn; clarinet; trombone and piccolo (Colonel and Boy); trumpet; woodwind; trombone; woodwind; all wind (Owen's father).

Act I, scene i. The study of Mr Coyle's military establishment. Discussion between Mr Coyle and his pupils, Owen Wingrave and Lechmere, is initially accompanied by consolatory and flowing triplets, but mention of casualties brings a bitter reaction from Owen. Coyle refers to the conduct of war as a science while Owen is inclined to condemn everyone who takes part in it. He confesses that he cannot go through with his military studies; he despises a soldier's life. This is too much for Coyle who finishes the scene wondering how he is either to set Owen's mind to rights or else contrive to intercede with Miss Wingrave on his behalf.

The interlude is based on the *marziale* as regimental banners wave brilliantly to instrumental cadenzas, notably a dialogue for two trumpets.

The second scene has Owen in Hyde Park, Miss Wingrave and Coyle in her London lodgings. There is cross-cutting between the two scenes as Owen reiterates his determination not to follow in his forefathers' footsteps, Miss Wingrave hers that tradition shall be upheld. To one of the most positive of the percussion rhythms of the opera, Owen is impressed by the beauty of the Horse Guards trotting by, Miss Wingrave by the military glory they represent. Coyle tries to persuade her that Owen's is not a childish fancy, but she decides that he shall be straightened out at Paramore.

The second interlude is subtitled 'A Sequence of Old, Faded, Tattered Flags', and Owen recites from Shelley's 'Queen Mab'.

The third scene finds Mr and Mrs Coyle at home with Lechmere. The three discuss the predicament Owen's decision seems to face them all with. Lechmere's offer to 'tell him it's a shame' – or more particularly the last word he uses – provokes a miniature ensemble, one of many in the course of this opera which contrive to define the attitudes of more than one character, bring the scene to a musical climax and lead into the next episode within the space of a few seconds; this one lasts forty-four seconds. The moment it is over Owen joins them and reiterates his determination not to change his mind. He plainly dreads facing his family.

The third interlude is concerned with Paramore, where the remainder of the act plays.

Scene iv introduces us to Kate and Mrs Julian, friends and dependants of the Wingraves who live at Paramore (Kate's uncle was Miss Wingrave's lover in the long distant past). They bemoan the latest turn of events, but both believe Owen will 'listen to the house'.

Owen returns to the very reverse of a hero's welcome, Mrs Julian resistant, Kate positively hostile, and the scene ends as Miss Wingrave ushers him peremptorily towards his grandfather's room, from which comes a cry of 'Sirrah! how dare you'.

Scene v. In four bars of music and to reiterated cries from the family of 'How dare you!' a week passes. They accuse him of rejecting the family's tradition and insulting not only the memory of his ancestors but everyone present as well. It is the most extended ensemble of the opera and ends as it begins with cries of 'How dare you!'

Scene vi. Mr and Mrs Coyle have arrived at Paramore and find the atmosphere eerie, the family gruesome. At mention of the possibility of the house being haunted, we hear the first adumbration of the Ballad theme. Owen tries to welcome them nonchalantly, but Coyle admits he has come down to make a last attempt at persuading Owen to conform.

Scene vii is preceded by an interlude and consists of the family dinner party. Small talk continually threatens to grow and is at best uncomfortable. As the dishes are cleared, each character in turn betrays his or her thoughts, in close-up as it were and in characteristic music (the nearest to a use of specifically television technique in the opera). After a particularly barbed comment from Sir Philip, Mrs Coyle is left pleading 'Ah! Sir Philip, Owen has his scruples'. A brilliant *scherzando* ensemble on this final word ensues for the family, and it goads Owen to the final insult: 'I'd make it a crime to draw your sword for your country, and a crime for governments to command it.' Sir Philip hobbles out in a fury and the Ballad theme is again heard in the orchestra (on the horn), a symbol no doubt of the inevitable clash between the head of the family and its rebellious son.

Act II. The stage directions of the Prologue: 'A ballad-singer is heard alternating with the distant chorus and trumpet. The verses of the ballad are illustrated by the actions in slow motion.' The haunting melody, to the words 'There was a boy, a Wingrave born', lies literally and figuratively at the heart of the work and the narrator tells the story of the young Wingrave from the past who, challenged by his friend at school to fight, refused, and was accused of cowardice by his father, only later to be struck down to his death in an upstairs room at Paramore. (The narrator, a tenor like Sir Philip, was in the original production[1] sung by the same singer.) A chorus of trebles sings a variation of Owen's motif ('Trumpet blow, Paramore shall welcome woe'), and accompaniment is confined to solo trumpet until just before Owen's voice joins that of the narrator. Lechmere is walking with the ladies and Owen contrives again to offend Kate; Mrs Coyle pleads with her for patience.

Suddenly Sir Philip shuffles out of his room and demands to see his grandson, whom he refers to as the traitor. Owen follows him in and the door is shut, but the drift of the interview can be heard outside and it is no surprise when Owen re-appears to say that he has been disinherited.

Mrs Julian breaks down sobbing at this shattering blow to her hopes. Lechmere instinctively starts to make up to Kate, who plays up to him, to the indignation of the Coyles. He would do anything to prove his worth to Kate, even sleep in the haunted room! Miss Wingrave ushers them all to bed and refers to Owen in his presence as if he did not exist.

Owen is left alone. He turns away from the portraits and in what is in many ways the climax of the opera sings, 'In peace I have found my image, I have found myself.' Suddenly he sees the ghosts of the old man and the boy slowly walk up the stairs and for a moment he thinks his rejection by the family has in some way expiated all sins of the past.

Kate appears thinking she is alone and sings sadly of what might have been. It is the first sign of her affection for Owen and their encounter quickens into a duet as they remember innumerable shared impressions of the past. But Kate will not change to please Owen, and their quarrel culminates in Owen's rating her for flirting with Lechmere. Kate accuses him of being a coward, and demands he prove his courage by sleeping in the haunted room. There is a moment of stridency from the orchestra as, at Owen's insistence, she turns the key behind him in the lock, before the scene changes to the Coyles' bedroom.

Coyle tries to reassure his wife, who is full of indignation about Kate, but an hour later (only a few bars of music) she is still not asleep, and later still Lechmere knocks at the door saying he knows of Kate's 'dare' and is worried at its possible consequences for Owen. As they are about to go off to investigate, they hear Kate's agonised cry from the distance, 'Ah, Owen, Owen, you've gone!' It might be the Governess with the dead Miles, but with her assumption of full responsibility she reaches towards tragic stature, as Sir Philip himself pushes open the door to disclose Owen lying dead on the floor. With a last *piano* reference to the ballad (narrator and chorus) the opera comes to an end.   H.

---

[1] And as in *The Turn of the Screw*.

DEATH IN VENICE

Opera in two acts, libretto by Myfanwy Piper after the story by
Thomas Mann. Première at the Maltings during Aldeburgh
Festival, 16 June 1973, with Peter Pears, John Shirley-Quirk,
James Bowman, conductor Steuart Bedford, producer Colin
Graham. First performed Covent Garden, 1973, and
Metropolitan, New York, 1974, with same cast; Adelaide
Festival, 1980, with Robert Gard; Geneva, 1983, with Anthony
Rolfe Johnson; Glyndebourne Touring Opera, 1989, and 1992
at the Festival, with Robert Tear, Alan Opie, Michael Chance.

Gustav von Aschenbach, *a novelist* ....Tenor

The Traveller...Baritone
    who also sings
    The Elderly Fop
    The Old Gondolier
    The Hotel Manager
    The Hotel Barber
    The Leader of the Players
    Dionysus

Voice of Apollo ....Counter-Tenor

The Polish Mother ....Dancer

Tadzio, *her son* ....Dancer

Her Two Daughters.......................................Dancers

Their Governess...Dancer

Jaschiu, *Tadzio's friend* ....Dancer

Hotel Porter ....Tenor

Lido Boatman...Baritone

Hotel Waiter...Baritone

Strawberry-Seller ....Soprano

Guide..Baritone

Glass-Maker..Tenor

Lace-Seller ....Soprano

Beggar-Woman.................................Mezzo-Soprano

Newspaper-Seller..Soprano

Strolling Players............................Soprano, Tenor

English Clerk at the Travel Bureau ....Baritone

Two Acrobats...Dancers

Russian Mother and Father.................Soprano, Bass

Russian Nanny...Soprano

German Mother................................Mezzo-Soprano

Gondoliers..Tenor, Baritone

Place: Munich; Venice, and the Lido
Time: 1911
Running Time: 2 hours 45 minutes

After Shakespeare, Melville and two stories by
Henry James, Britten turned his attention to
Thomas Mann, tackling in *Death in Venice* what is in
most ways a more intractable problem precisely
because Mann's story concerns itself so unremittingly
with the thoughts, aspirations and worries of a single
man. Britten and Myfanwy Piper have solved the
problem by making Aschenbach himself, the successful writer at the centre of the story, serve additionally
as narrator, so that his monologues provide something of the detached, ironic comment which is a
feature of Mann's story. In place of the nuances and
cumulative impact of Mann's writing – inevitably
(and rightly) omitted from the libretto – Britten, wrote
Peter Evans in *Opera*[1] before the Aldeburgh première,
'offers ... characteristic refinements of musical detail
and a motivic chain, more complex yet less obtrusive
than in his previous operas, that makes of the whole
work his most sustained study of festering obsession'.

Aschenbach is a solitary, and opposite him are
ranged two groups of characters. The main function of
one group is to propel Aschenbach towards his predes-
tined end: Traveller, Elderly Fop, Old Gondolier, Hotel
Manager, Hotel Barber, Leader of the Players, off-stage
voice of Dionysus. They are all played by the same
baritone singer and they share the same musical
material, much of it related to Ex. 2. The function of
the other group is to lure him towards self-destruction,
towards the Dionysian upsetting of his Apollonian
(and therefore classical) balance. This group, headed
by Tadzio and his mother but including also the other
children who play on the beach, are represented by
dancers. This emphasises the inability of Aschenbach
to speak to Tadzio, the impossibility he, the most articulate of men, finds in formulating words for his
thoughts, his basic failure in fact to communicate.

As Tadzio, his family and his companions are distinguished from the other dramatic characters by being
danced and mimed rather than sung, so is the music
associated with them generically different in that it is
given to percussion. Tadzio's theme in fact is derived
from the sounds of the gamelan orchestra, a sound
Britten used extensively years previously in his ballet
The Prince of the Pagodas (1956), and is played on the
vibraphone. Its haunting, liquid A major (the key associated with Tadzio) suggests that it stands for the effect
Tadzio has on Aschenbach[2] rather than for the
healthy, vigorous youth himself, and it remains static
throughout the opera, as does the beauty of Tadzio.

---

[1] *Opera*, June 1973.

[2] There is some kinship with Quint's celesta theme in *The Turn of the Screw*.

Aschenbach in contrast develops and changes musically just as he does morally and physically, and a number of themes are associated with him and his vision of his surroundings – the whole story in fact is seen through his eyes, as a psychoanalyst sees events through the mind of his patient. Exx. 2 and 4 (and to a lesser extent Ex. 3) are prominent exponents of Aschenbach's state of mind, changing as they do in the course of the action to show the changes within his mind. Ex. 2, for example, starts as the purest of diatonic scales, but by the end of Act I, distorted and dissonantly thickened, accompanies that moment of self-knowledge when his cry of 'I love you' brings him to his own particular key of E major.

Act I, scene i. Munich. Aschenbach muses on his inability to work. He is confronted by a Traveller, whose presence as much as his words conjures up an image (Ex. 1) so that Aschenbach obeys his injunc-

tion 'Go, travel to the South'. Varied and played usually on tuba, this theme later symbolises the physical plague which itself parallels the canker eating into Aschenbach's mind.

For the first time are heard the urgent yet un-worried scales of Ex. 2:

and it is not long before Aschenbach embarks on the first of several monologues in which he comments on the course of events and the motives which have led him to his current position. These piano-accom-

panied, prose monologues are a major feature of the score, with the singer's pitch indicated for him, but the duration of the notes and the 'shaping' of the phrases left to his imagination and discretion.

Scene ii. On the boat to Venice, youths shout to their girlfriends on shore (quiet chorus of 'Serenissima' underneath the banter), joined by an Elderly Fop, who has frequent recourse to a mincing falsetto and leads a vigorous song about the possibilities of life in Venice. Aschenbach finds him repulsive and starts to wonder why he ever decided to come ('Serenissima' theme in chorus and Ex. 2 in orchestra below his voice line).

Scene iii is preceded by an instrumental overture (Venice), marked *Lazily*, derived from the 'Serenissima' theme and consisting of barcarolle-like gondola music of some tenderness (Ex. 3):

(it even partly recalls the Lullaby in Act II of *Lucretia*), depicting the journey to the Lido. Aschenbach, by now looking forward to his stay, is rowed against his will (Ex. 3) by the Old Gondolier to his hotel on the Lido. There he is greeted by a Boatman and the Hotel Porter, but he finds when he turns to pay that the Old Gondolier has disappeared. He recognises the black gondola as a harbinger of death.

Scene iv. The first evening at the hotel. Aschenbach is welcomed by the Hotel Manager to a typically expansive Britten phrase, Ex. 4:

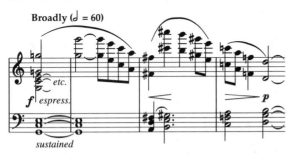

Aschenbach soliloquises on the prospect before him in Venice (with Ex. 4 and its variants very much in evidence), then watches the hotel guests assemble for dinner. Aschenbach sees the Polish family enter (Tadzio's theme heard for the first time) – Governess, two girls and Tadzio – and comments on Tadzio: 'Surely the soul of Greece lies in that bright perfection, a golden look ... mortal child with more than mortal grace.' When the Polish family goes in to dinner, Aschenbach in a further monologue reflects on the relationship of form and content, on the discipline of the family and its beauty, and concludes, 'There is indeed in every artist's nature a wanton and treacherous proneness to side with beauty.'

Scene v. On the beach (Ex. 4). Aschenbach is not at his ease, but watches the children playing (rhythmical percussion). He buys fruit from a strawberry-seller, watches Tadzio coming along the beach, approves as Tadzio mimes dislike of the Russian family, listens as voices apparently call 'Adziù' from the distance (Ex. 4 varied), but finally catches the boy's true name.

Scene vi. The foiled departure. On a visit to the city (Ex. 3), importunate guides, street-vendors and beggars together with the discomfort he feels from the sirocco prompt Aschenbach to leave Venice. He returns to the hotel where the Manager remains

courteous and understanding, but the sight of Tadzio crossing the lobby impels second thoughts, which are confirmed when he discovers his luggage has been put on the train to Como. He will return to the Lido (Ex. 3) and his luggage must be sent to him there! He is greeted by the Hotel Manager with the news that the wind is now from a healthier quarter, and when he looks out of his window (Ex. 4) he sees Tadzio and the others playing on the beach. He begins to understand his relief at the foiled departure.

Scene vii. The games of Apollo. Aschenbach from his chair allows his fancy to play with thoughts of ancient Greece. He seems to hear the voice of Apollo, in imagination turns the children's beach games into some sort of Olympiad with Tadzio crowned victor of the pentathlon. The music is a series of choral dances, percussion-accompanied, linked by the off-stage counter-tenor Voice of Apollo. Competitive running, long jump, discus, javelin-throwing and wrestling leave Tadzio the winner, and Aschenbach, after his impressive Hymn to Apollo (founded on Tadzio's theme), comes to the realisation that through Tadzio he may find inspiration to write again. He tries vainly to congratulate the winner of the games, Tadzio smiles at him on his way to the hotel and Aschenbach falls helplessly back on what he thinks of later as the supreme cliché: 'I love you' (preceded by a distorted version of Ex. 2).

Act II sees an end of joy and the start of the process of destruction through corruption to which Aschenbach is inevitably committed. A slow orchestral introduction leads us to Aschenbach, who has been writing but is hardly less scornful of his inability to communicate with Tadzio than he is of his guilty feelings for the boy.

Scene viii. The Hotel Barber's shop. From the professional patter of the Barber, Aschenbach picks up a reference to 'the sickness'.

Scene ix. The pursuit. On his way to Venice (Ex. 3), Aschenbach starts to worry and subsequent events confirm his fears: the city is too quiet, people are reading notices advising against eating shellfish, the German newspapers talk of 'rumours of cholera in Venice officially denied'; and yet, when he sees the Polish family, his one thought is to keep the rumours from them in case they decide to leave Venice. Here the Tadzio theme is conflated on the top line, while beneath it can be seen and heard the yearning theme (in crotchets) and at the bottom on the tuba (Ex. 1), in the form in which it is connected with the plague, Ex. 5:

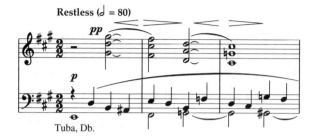

Aschenbach follows the Poles, sits near them in a café, watches them pray in St Mark's and realises that Tadzio is conscious of his nearness. He follows them back to the hotel, then tries in soliloquy to justify his infatuation by reference to Greek examples.

Scene x. The strolling players. Outside the hotel, a group of performers sing and dance, and their Leader sings a ditty before going round with his hat. Aschenbach tries to pump him about the plague but he starts a laughing song.

Scene xi. The travel bureau. A young English clerk is attempting to cope with a crowd of hotel guests frantically seeking reservations to leave the city. To Aschenbach, when they have left, he admits that Asiatic cholera has spread from India and was diagnosed in Venice earlier that year. The authorities deny it – but his advice is that Aschenbach should leave.

Scene xii. The Lady of the Pearls. Aschenbach decides he must warn Tadzio's mother, the Lady of the Pearls, but, when she appears, he goes towards her, then turns into his room.

Scene xiii. The dream. He hears (Ex. 2) the Voices of Dionysus and Apollo and tries to reject the former's advice to 'stumble in the reeling dance', but finally in dream participates in a Dionysian orgy (the Tadzio theme distorted and Ex. 1 in the orchestra). Awake, he is resigned to his fall.

Scene xiv. The empty beach. Tadzio and a few friends are playing, watched by Aschenbach.

Scene xv. The Hotel Barber's shop. Aschenbach in a frenzied search for youth allows his grey hair to be tinted, his cheeks rouged, not without ironical recall of the Elderly Fop of Scene ii.

Scene xvi. The last visit to Venice. Aschenbach, in what the libretto describes as 'his new appearance', goes by gondola to Venice, follows the Polish family, sees Tadzio detach himself from his family and look full at him, then turn away. He buys some fruit from a strawberry-seller, finds it musty and over-ripe, and starts to take stock of his situation. In the most sustained lyrical section of the opera, he recalls the Socratic dilemma of the poet who perceives beauty only through the senses: 'Does beauty lead to wisdom, Phaedrus?', an inspired passage drawing on the reserves of the Donne Sonnets and *Abraham and Isaac* from more than twenty years before. One may doubt if Britten set out to prove that the strands of a drama can be drawn together and the work so revealed in a cantilena melody with only a characteristic rhythmical snap at the end of key lines, but in the event he did so.

Scene xvii. The departure (preceded by Ex. 4 as postlude to the previous scene). Hotel Manager and Porter discuss the weather and the departing guests, and it appears that the Lady of the Pearls and her party are leaving. Aschenbach comes in wearily and goes to the beach (Ex. 4 diminished so that no exuberance or expansion is left in it). He watches Tadzio and his friends playing at first listlessly, then more roughly, until Tadzio's face is pressed into the sand. Aschenbach starts to protest, but hears distant cries of 'Adziù' and is only able to answer them gently with 'Tadzio' before slumping dead in his chair as Tadzio walks slowly away. The final twenty-bar orchestral comment provides Aschenbach's threnody, with Tadzio's theme in percussion still plaintively, seductively, above the orchestra.   H.

FERRUCCIO BUSONI
(born 1 April 1866, died 27 July 1924)

Busoni, whose father was Italian, his mother Austrian, grew up in a mainly Germanic atmosphere and before he was thirty had married a Swede. His career as a virtuoso pianist – those who heard him thought he was the greatest since Liszt – eclipsed during his lifetime his fame as a composer. He was drawn early to opera but produced only four during his maturity. He came to regard Berlin as home, in spite of an appointment in 1913 as director of the Liceo Musicale in Bologna and living in Zürich during the Great War.

He was theorist as well as practical musician and composer, and as far as opera was concerned believed that the proper subjects involved 'the incredible, the untrue or the unlikely', and that music was particularly apt for portraying the supernatural and the unnatural.

ARLECCHINO
Harlequin

Opera in one act, text by the composer. Première Zürich, 11 May 1917, with Alexander Moissi as Arlecchino. First performed Frankfurt, 1918; Berlin, 1921, conducted by Blech; Vienna, 1926; London (B.B.C.), 1939; Venice Festival, 1940, with Tellini, Mazziotti, Gelli, conductor Gui; New York, Carnegie Hall (semi-staged), 1951; Glyndebourne, 1954, with Malbin, Dickie, conductor Pritchard. Revived Berlin Staatsoper, 1946, with Beilke, Witte, conductor Schüler; Berlin, German Opera, 1966, with Johnson, Grobe, McDaniel, Lagger, conductor Patanè; Bologna, 1967.

Ser Matteo del Sarto, *a tailor*...........................Baritone

Abbate Cospicuo ....Baritone

Dottor Bombasto..Bass

Arlecchino (Harlequin).....................................Actor

Leandro ....Tenor

Annunziata, *Matteo's wife* ....Silent

Colombina (Columbine),
      Arlecchino's wife.............................Mezzo-Soprano

Place: Bergamo
Time: Nineteenth Century
Running Time: 1 hour 5 minutes

Busoni called *Arlecchino* 'ein theatralisches Capriccio' (a theatrical caprice), and Edward Dent in his biography of the composer has suggested that it is in the nature of a play for puppets. As if to emphasise this, Arlecchino speaks a prologue in which he warns the audience not to take the play too literally; it is all in the spirit of a proverb.

The work is in four parts, each corresponding to an aspect of Arlecchino; we see him as rogue, soldier, husband, and conqueror. A lively introduction leads to the first scene. Matteo is sitting in front of his house sewing and reading Dante to himself. In a window upstairs, Arlecchino can be seen ardently wooing Matteo's wife. Matteo comments on his reading, which reminds him, he says, of opera (the orchestra plays a bit of 'Fin ch'han dal vino' from *Don Giovanni*). Arlecchino wonders how he is to get away. In the end he jumps blatantly out of the window, and, when Matteo seems surprised to see him, says to him in an agitated way, 'Don't you know barbarians are surrounding the town?', which so upsets the good man that he forgets where Arlecchino came from. In his confusion, Matteo drops the key to his front door, and Arlecchino picks it up and locks the door from outside, putting the key into his pocket when he has finished. Arlecchino can be heard singing briskly from behind the scenes.

The doctor and the abbé come into sight, arguing together rather in the manner of the doctor and the captain in *Wozzeck*. The abbé sings a song in praise of Tuscany and wine. Their slanging match abates, and they shout to Matteo, who is not, they notice, in his usual place in front of his house. In a trio in which a march theme is prominent, he explains about the barbarians who are surrounding the town and asks why they have not taken refuge themselves. They say they will go and consult the Burgomaster.

Arlecchino reappears dressed as a recruiting sergeant. The music is a parodistic reference to the march from *La Fille du Régiment.* He tells Matteo he is wanted immediately for the army. Matteo asks for permission to take his Dante with him, and then, to the sound of a funeral march, is marched away.

A minuet starts in the orchestra as Arlecchino

tries the key he has copied from Matteo's; it fits, but at that moment he is spoken to from behind. He turns to find it is no other than his own wife, Colombina. Why, she demands in an aria, is he so cruel and unfaithful to her? She starts to flatter him but it is no use and Arlecchino disappears.

Colombina is determined to find out what Arlecchino was after in this particular house, but at that moment she hears the tenor voice of Leandro singing a romance, and she is quite unable to resist it. Leandro hears her version of her story, and immediately offers to revenge her honour. His first song is a parody of romantic German song, his second of a classical Italian equivalent. There is a flowery love scene for the two, which is almost too much for Colombina. At any rate, she enquires whether Leandro is not being just the least little bit sloppy in the aria he is singing; let her wait for the *stretta*, is his answer. Arlecchino comes on the scene, announces that Colombina is his wife and draws his wooden sword to fight Leandro. He knocks him out and, shouting 'murder' at the top of his voice, disappears into Matteo's house.

Colombina emerges from the tavern, together with the abbé and the doctor, who are both by now very drunk. They remember that they have to see the Burgomaster about the barbarian invaders, but the subject does not appear to be entirely clear in their minds. Suddenly, the doctor stumbles over the body of Leandro. With a shriek, Colombina recognises it. The other two start to wonder what they are to do at this hour of the night with the body of a dead man. On further investigation, Colombina decides he is not dead after all, which suggestion at first causes consternation in the minds of the other two. However, they eventually come round to her way of thinking, and try to enlist the help of the neighbours; heads appear at the windows, but are immediately withdrawn when it becomes known what is wanted of them. Suddenly a donkey appears, hitched to a cart. It is the work of providence, is the comment. In a quartet, the abbé prays, Leandro returns to consciousness, the doctor comments on the medico-philosophical aspects of the affair, and Colombina pours scorn on all men impartially. In the end, all get into the donkey cart and drive off.

Arlecchino looks down from the window of Matteo's house and waves to them as they go. He and Matteo's wife go off together. Matteo is seen coming towards his house. His companions have gone, he presumes peace has been concluded, and is returning home. He finds his wife has left the house, and so philosophically gets out his Dante and his sewing as before, and starts to read where he left off. The passage has to do with infidelity ...

A drop-curtain falls. In pairs, the various characters, including the donkey and his driver, come to make their bows to the audience. Last come Arlecchino and Annunziata, Matteo's wife. Arlecchino speaks an epilogue: he introduces Annunziata to them – they have not been lucky enough to see much of her during the evening – and then asks what the moral of the story is to be. Everything is new, everything goes on as before, is his conclusion; but his advice to the audience is that they should make up their own minds.

The stage directions suggest that if a second curtain call is needed, the drop should be raised to reveal Matteo still sitting and sewing and reading and waiting.

'Few of Busoni's compositions gave him so much satisfaction as *Arlecchino*,' says Edward Dent in his biography (O.U.P., 1933). 'Both from a literary and musical point of view he regarded it as his most individual and personal work. One reason for its lack of popularity up to the present is that it demands an unusual alertness of mind on the part of the spectator. The libretto is extremely terse in style, and was considerably reduced in the process of setting it to music, for Busoni was always determined to make the musical form the deciding factor in his works for the stage. With the older composers this principle led to the expansion of the libretto by frequent repetition of the words; with Busoni it led to compression.'   H.

TURANDOT

A Chinese fable in two acts, after Gozzi, text by the composer. Première Zürich, 11 May 1917. First performed Frankfurt, 1918; Berlin, 1921, with Lola Artôt de Padilla, Ober, conductor Blech. Revived Venice Festival, 1940, with Carbone, Limberti, Ziliani, Colella, conductor Previtali; Hamburg, 1948, with Werth, Melchert, conductor Grüber; la Scala, 1962, with Kabaivanska, Cioni, conductor Sanzogno; Berlin, German Opera, 1966, with Annabelle Bernard, Haefliger, conductor Patanè. New York, Little Orchestra Society, 1967, with Hannelore Kuhse.

The Emperor Altoum ....Bass
Turandot, *his daughter* ....Soprano
Adelma, *her confidante* ....Mezzo-Soprano
Calaf, *a young unknown prince* ....Tenor
Barak, *his faithful servant* ....Baritone
The Queen Mother of Samarkand ....Soprano
Truffaldino, *chief eunuch* ....High Tenor
Tartaglia ⎱
          } *Altoum's ministers* ....Bass
Pantalone ⎰ ....Bass
Eight Doctors ....Tenor, Bass
A Singer..Mezzo-Soprano

Slaves, Weeping Women, Eunuchs, Soldiers, Dancers

Place: The Far East
Time: Antiquity
Running Time: 1 hour 25 minutes

In 1905, Busoni composed incidental music for Carlo Gozzi's *Turandot*, not used for the stage until Reinhardt's production of 1911, and the opera was composed rapidly as a companion piece to *Arlecchino* in 1917. The action follows in the main the course which has become familiar to opera-goers through Puccini's later opera of the same name.

Act I. An introduction in march rhythm leads to the first scene. Calaf dashes through the city gates and rapturously greets Peking. His old servant Barak recognises him; not having seen him for so long, he had thought he was dead. Calaf tells him that his father, Timur, is also alive, and that he himself is looking for fortune in Peking. Barak tells him the story of Turandot and the riddles, whereupon Calaf laughs and seems unable to take the riddles too seriously, even though he catches sight of some heads impaled on spears at Turandot's order. Barak points to the procession which is at that moment going by, mourning the Prince of Samarkand, who has been put to death that very day. The lament is led by the Prince's mother, an aged negress. At its end, she curses Turandot, and throws the portrait of the Princess from her. Barak comments that even the portrait of Turandot is said to enslave those who gaze upon it. Calaf looks at it, and in an *arioso* proclaims his love for its subject. He will try his luck.

Scene ii. Truffaldino comes in front of the curtain and, in a high piping tenor, summons some slaves.

Slow, solemn music heralds the appearance of the Emperor Altoum, Turandot's father, preceded by wise doctors and attendants. The Emperor complains about his daughter's cruel behaviour, while his two comic advisers, Pantalone and the stuttering Tartaglia, gather round to flatter him. In a short aria, the Emperor prays to Confucius that he may at long last win a son in the coming trial between the stranger and Turandot. He commands that the unknown suitor be brought before him. Trumpets sound, and Calaf throws himself at the Emperor's feet. The old man is immediately impressed by the stranger's looks; who is he? Calaf answers that he is a prince, but his name must remain unknown for the present. The Emperor bids him retire now, but Calaf's reply is that he desires only Turandot or death: for him there can be no third option. Altoum offers him honours and riches if he will renounce the trial. Pantalone and Tartaglia add their voices in an effort to dissuade Calaf, but he is adamant. The brilliant quartet ends as Calaf reaffirms his determination on a series of high As.

Turandot enters, veiled. She demands to know who dares match his wisdom with hers, but, when she catches sight of the stranger, admits to herself that she is moved by the sight of him. Adelma, Turandot's confidante, in an aside recognises the Prince as the young man she fell in love with when she was a girl.[1] Calaf again denies that there is any possibility for him but Turandot or death; Turandot's rejoinder is that his death will be her death.

The Emperor suggests that Turandot ask three easy riddles so that the form of the trial may be honoured; after that the wedding can take place. Turandot refuses – the riddles are laid down by law. Truffaldino rings a bell and announces each riddle in turn. They are on a more metaphysical plane than those in Puccini's opera, and the answers are respectively Human Understanding, Morals, Art. After Calaf has guessed the second, Turandot offers to let her suitor go free and to forgo the last question. He refuses, but when Turandot unveils herself as she asks the third question, it looks as though he is lost. However, he pulls himself together and answers the third as he has the first two.

The Emperor and his entourage are delighted with Calaf's success; he calls for music, and the rejoicing is

---

[1] From this figure, Puccini and his librettist fabricated the tragic Liù.

general. Turandot admits she has lost, but says the shame is more than she can bear; at the altar she will kill herself. Calaf admits that his victory is hollow if she still hates him. He offers her a fourth chance; he will ask her a riddle. What is his name?

Act II. The chorus and its leader sing before the curtain goes up showing Turandot's room. Slaves dance and sing, but Turandot stops them abruptly and sends them away. She cannot make out her own feelings: does she love the victorious stranger after all? She knows that if she were to give way she would soon regret it. Turandot shall die untouched, is her decision. Her aria is highly dramatic and, in spite of its greater economy, almost as taxing for the singer as the music Puccini wrote for his heroine.

Truffaldino has headed the search for the stranger's name. His aria is exactly calculated for the high, thin voice which has characterised him throughout the opera. When he interrogated the stranger, he got the answer, 'Death or Turandot'.

The Emperor comes to say he knows the stranger's name, but nothing will make him tell Turandot. She faces him bitterly – he will be sorry for his unjust words. She turns in her misery to Adelma. Adelma says the Emperor is not alone in knowing the Prince's name. In a pathetic, proud tune, Adelma says that the Princess has just addressed her as 'friend', and yet keeps her a slave; if she will give her her freedom she will in return reveal the stranger's name. The Prince once laughed at her when she was a girl, and she wants revenge more than anything in the world. Turandot greets her as sister, and Adelma whispers into her ear.

An intermezzo leads to the last scene, which takes place in the throne-room. Drums beat the rhythm of a funeral march, during which Tartaglia and Pantalone lament, asking themselves the while what the sound of mourning can be about. They are answered by the Emperor; it is for Turandot, no one else. Turandot at first agrees that it is for her, and Calaf admits that he is deeply grieved at the misery which his success induces in her. The Emperor thereupon orders bright music, but suddenly Turandot rounds on them and admits that the funeral music was part of her scheme to make her revenge the sweeter. She knows the stranger's name: Calaf! She dismisses Calaf, to the Emperor's obvious sorrow, and he turns to go, saying that he will easily find

death in the wars. As he leaves, however, Turandot welcomes him as her husband, and lamentation is instantly turned to rejoicing, not least for the Emperor, for whom this means an end of sorrow.   H.

DOKTOR FAUST

Opera in six tableaux (two prologues, one scenic interlude, and three scenes), text by the composer. Première, Dresden, 21 May 1925, with Meta Seinemeyer, Theo Strack, Robert Burg, conductor Fritz Busch. First performed Berlin, 1927, with Leider, Soot, Schorr; London, Queen's Hall (concert), in English translation by E.J. Dent, 1937, conducted by Boult, with Blyth, Parry Jones, Noble; Florence Festival, 1942, with Oltrabella, Renato Gigli, Manacchini, conductor Previtali; Berlin, 1954, with Fischer-Dieskau; London, 1959 (concert), with Harper, Richard Lewis, Fischer-Dieskau, conductor Boult; la Scala, 1960, with Roberti, Bertocci, Dondi; Holland Festival, 1962, by Wupperthal Opera; New York, Carnegie Hall, 1964 (concert), with Bjoner, Shirley, Fischer-Dieskau; Florence Festival, 1964; Stockholm, 1969, with Söderström, Erik Saeden; Bologna, 1985, in Anthony Beaumont's new edition; English National Opera, 1986, with Eilene Hannan, Graham Clark, Thomas Allen, conductor Mark Elder, producer David Pountney (Beaumont edition).

Doctor Faust......................................Baritone
Wagner, *his famulus* .... Baritone

Mephistopheles in his various disguises ....Tenor
　　A Man Dressed in Black
　　A Monk
　　A Herald
　　A Chaplain
　　A Courier
　　A Nightwatchman

The Duke of Parma..Tenor
The Duchess of Parma...................................Soprano
The Master of Ceremonies....................................Bass
The Girl's Brother, *a soldier* ....Baritone
A Lieutenant ....Tenor
Three Students from Cracow ....Tenor, Two Basses
A Theologian ....Bass
A Jurist..Bass
A Doctor of Natural History ....Baritone
Four Students from Wittenberg ....Four Tenors

Spirit voices
　　Gravis ....Bass
　　Levis ....Bass
　　Asmodeus..Baritone
　　Beelzebub..Tenor
　　Megärus...Tenor
　　Sixth Voice (Mephistopheles)........................Tenor

Church-Goers, Soldiers, Courtiers, Students

Place: Wittenberg; Parma
Time: Sixteenth Century
Running Time: 2 hours 35 minutes

Busoni drew his text from the old puppet-play of *Faust*, and he is indebted to Goethe only for the richness and nobility of the language in which he expressed his conception – he was a life-long student and devotee of Goethe. *Doktor Faust* represents the summing-up of his life's work.

Prologue I. The orchestral prelude is in the nature of an 'impressionistic study of distant bells'.[1] Towards the end of the prelude the chorus behind the scenes can be heard singing the single word 'Pax' (Edward Dent has aptly pointed out that this part of the work was written at Zürich in 1917). The curtain goes up and an actor steps out in front of a drop-curtain to recite the verse prologue, in which Busoni explains how the subject came to be chosen.

He disappears and the first scene is revealed: Faust's study in Wittenberg, where he is superintending some alchemical process. Wagner tells him that three students are asking to see him, and, when Faust seems reluctant to receive them, explains that they have with them a remarkable book, called 'Clavis Astartis Magica'. Faust is excited; this is perhaps the book which will give him the magic power he has so long sought. The three announce themselves as students from Cracow. Faust is reminded of his youth, with its hopes and its dreams and its plans. The students give him the book, a key with which to unlock it, and a letter which makes it his property. They take their leave. Will he see them again? 'Perhaps' is their only answer. Wagner returns, and Faust wonders why he does not show the visitors out. He saw no one, says Wagner. The pots on the hearth begin to hiss and crackle.

Prologue II. The scene is unchanged. It is night. With the key in hand which the students have given him, Faust loosens his girdle and with it draws a magic circle. Standing inside it, he calls upon Lucifer to send down his servant. Six tongues of flame appear hovering in the air. Each of them represents one of Lucifer's intimates. Faust questions the first five – how fast is each? – and dismisses each with

contempt at the answer he gets. He steps out of the circle and seems reluctant to question the last spirit in case it too should disappoint him. A voice addresses him by name, and proclaims that it is as fast as human thought. 'The scene with six flames', says Edward Dent, ' is conceived musically as a set of variations on a theme; the first spirit is a deep bass, and the voices rise progressively, so that the last – Mephistopheles – is a high tenor'. Mephistopheles's musical entrance is cruelly exacting, as he is asked to sustain successively a high A natural, a B flat, and a B natural, and the phrase in which he boasts of his speed ends on a sustained C natural.

Faust appears satisfied by the answer of the sixth voice, and he summons him to appear in physical shape. Of Mephistopheles, Faust makes an unusual demand: 'Give me for the rest of my life the unconditional fulfilment of every wish ... let me understand the actions of mankind and extend them; give me Genius! give me its pain too, that I may be happy like no other – make me *free*.'[2] But Faust has stepped outside the magic circle, and Mephistopheles will only agree to serve him at a price: after he has done Faust's bidding, Faust must agree to serve him for ever. Faust says he will serve no one, and is about to dismiss him like the others, when Mephistopheles reminds him that his creditors are at the door, that the brother of the girl he has seduced is searching for him to kill him, and that no help but the devil's will suffice to extricate him from his predicament.

Faust reluctantly agrees to Mephistopheles's bargain, and the scene ends as he signs the agreement. During the later part of the scene, an unseen chorus sings the 'Credo' and the 'Gloria' and the curtain falls as an 'Alleluiah' is heard.

Intermezzo. This takes place in the Romanesque side-chapel of a great cathedral. The whole scene is dominated by the sound of the cathedral organ – Dent says that Busoni 'wanted the organ to be no mere background; it was to fill the whole theatre with its reverberation. Unfortunately there are few theatres which possess organs of sufficient power to carry out the composer's design.' A soldier, described as 'the girl's brother', is praying that he may be enabled to avenge her seduction. Mephistopheles points him out to Faust and then sets about the task

---

[1] E.J. Dent, *Ferruccio Busoni* (O.U.P.).

[2] E.J. Dent, *op. cit.*

of removing him. He takes on the aspect of a monk and kneels beside the soldier, who does his best to get rid of him. Suddenly, soldiers appear in the doorway and point out the soldier as the man who killed their captain. They fall upon him and kill him, leaving Mephistopheles triumphant; sacrilege and murder – and both laid to Faust's account – seems pretty good going for one day.

Scene i. The main part of the action now begins. The scene is the court of the Duke of Parma who has just married a beautiful wife. The celebrations are suggested by the orchestral Cortège with which the scene starts (this in an extended form constitutes the second part of the 'Sarabande and Cortège from *Doktor Faust*', which Busoni arranged for the concert hall). Having regard to the end of this scene, when Faust elopes with the Duchess, it is hardly surprising that the music for all its brilliance has a sinister tang to it and Busoni's diabolism seems to owe something to Berlioz's crackling essays in the same vein. The pageant and ballet which introduce the rejoicing also make use of Busoni's *Tanzwalzer*, a work dating from 1920 and dedicated to the memory of Johann Strauss; this is a separate composition, unlike the Sarabande and Cortège which date from the same year but were always intended as sketches for *Doktor Faust*.

The master of ceremonies proposes that the Duke and his newly-wed Duchess shall receive Faust, by now famous throughout the world for his learning. Mephistopheles is on hand as Faust's herald, and he announces his master, who makes a distinguished appearance, with (according to the stage directions) either black boys or monkeys carrying his train. The chorus welcomes him and expresses open admiration; the Duchess wholeheartedly concurs but the Duke has misgivings.

Faust proceeds to show his powers by turning light into darkness. He asks the Duchess what he shall do for her delectation; ask for something impossible, suggests the Duke. She would like to see Solomon, she declares; in a moment he appears before them, with the Queen of Sheba at his side. The Duke is quick to notice that the Queen has a look of the Duchess about her, and that Solomon closely resembles Faust. For her next wish, the Duchess insists that Faust shall not only perform it but divine what it is. Samson and Delilah appear; under Delilah's bed hides a black slave holding the fatal shears. Once again the visions wear the features of the Duchess and Faust. The third apparition is conjured up by Faust of his own accord; Salome and John the Baptist stand before the court, and near them the executioner. Again, the protagonists seem to have borrowed the masks of Faust and his noble hostess, and this time the executioner resembles the Duke. 'At a word from Salome, his head falls,' comments Faust. 'He must not die,' answers the Duchess eagerly. Faust is confident that the Duchess loves him.

The Duke makes an end of the performance by inviting Faust to the ducal table, but Mephistopheles dissuades his master, warning him that the food is poisoned, and together they leave the stage. For a moment, no one is visible, but presently the Duchess comes into sight once more, convinced that Faust is calling her. She sings rapturously of her love for him, then goes slowly out.

It is suddenly daylight. The Duke of Parma is in excited conversation with his Chaplain, who tells him that the Duchess has eloped with Faust; he saw them disappear together on winged horses. It would be best to hush everything up and marry the sister of the Duke of Ferrara, who otherwise threatens war. The Duke accepts his Chaplain's counsel, and as the curtain falls, we see the hand raised in blessing turn to a claw.

Scene ii. The Sarabande, an extended and solemn orchestral piece described as a symphonic intermezzo, ushers in the next scene, an inn at Wittenberg, where Faust sits drinking and discussing philosophy with his students. The discussion soon approaches a quarrel, and Faust does his best to calm things down: nothing can be proved, he says; let them follow Luther's example ... He has not even time to get out Luther's name when the company divides into Catholics and Protestants, and a Latin *Te Deum* is heard in violent opposition to 'Ein' feste Burg'.

Faust sits pensively aside until one of the students asks him to tell them of his amorous adventures with women. The orchestra *sotto voce* remembers the Cortège, and Faust starts to tell them of the most beautiful woman he ever loved, a Duchess, on her wedding day, only a year ago. Does she ever think of him now, he wonders. At that moment, in comes Mephistopheles in the guise of a messenger. The Duchess of Parma, who has just died, sends something to Faust for a remembrance. At Faust's feet he places the corpse of a new-born baby, to the general horror of the company. He proceeds to tell Faust's story in unromantic terms, and caps it by setting fire to the bundle, which was only straw. From the smoke he summons Helen of Troy.

At this point Mephistopheles leaves Faust alone. Faust raves of his dream of beauty but, just as he seems about to grasp the vision, it disappears into nothing, and he is alone once more. He turns to see three figures standing in the shadow, demanding the return of the book, the key and the letter which went with them. Faust motions them away: he has destroyed what they are demanding. They tell him his hour has come, but he has nothing but contempt for them and welcomes the end of his life.

Scene iii. A street in Wittenberg. It is winter, snow is on the ground, the Nightwatchman's voice informs the citizens that ten has struck (it is Mephistopheles in his last disguise). Students congratulate Wagner on his opening speech as Rector of the University, where he has succeeded Faust.

Faust comes in, recognises Wagner's house as once his, listens as the *Dies Irae* is sung in the church, and sees a beggar woman opposite, a child in her arms. He gives her some money, but as soon as he sees her, knows her as the Duchess. She gives him the child saying that she has already tried twice to do so. It is dead. She disappears. Faust tries to get into the church to pray, but his way is barred by the soldier who was killed in the Romanesque chapel. Faust removes him – his power still extends to spirits – and tries to pray before a crucifix at the door. But he cannot find words, and, when the light from the Nightwatchman's lantern shines on the crucifix, he sees the form of Helen of Troy upon it.

With a cry of horror he turns away, then masters himself for a supreme trial of strength. (At this point Busoni's score ends; the ending was supplied by Jarnach,[1] working from Busoni's papers. Research some fifty years later by the English conductor Anthony Beaumont suggested that the composer had music in mind other than that selected by Jarnach and he re-worked the ending of the opera with results that were first heard in Bologna in 1985 and which have been deemed an improvement on what Jarnach provided.) Faust lays the dead body of the child on the ground and covers it with his cloak. He throws his girdle on the ground, and steps within the circle. He exerts his will in a final effort to project his personality into the body of the child. May his faults be rectified in this child, and may it accomplish what he has failed to do. He dies, and as the Watchman announces midnight, a naked youth with arms uplifted and bearing a green twig in his hand rises from Faust's body and walks unconcernedly through the snow. The Nightwatchman lifts his lamp and looks down at the dead body. Has this man had an accident, he asks?   H.

---

[1] Philipp Jarnach was Busoni's pupil. At one time, there was talk of asking Schoenberg to undertake the completion.

C

JOHN CASKEN
(born 15 July 1949)

THE GOLEM

Chamber opera, prelude and legend, libretto created in collaboration with Pierre Audi. First performed at the Almeida Theatre, London, 28 June 1989, with Adrian Clarke, Christopher Robson, Patricia Rozario and John Hall, conducted by Richard Bernas and directed by Pierre Audi. U.S. première at Orpheum Theater, Omaha, 1990, conducted by Richard Pittman. Revived for a tour by the Contemporary Music Network, beginning at the Playhouse, Newcastle, 1991. In German, Dortmund, 1994, conducted by Peter Kuhn.

The Maharal, a Rabbi;
      leader of his community ....Baritone
Golem, a large figure made from clay.......Bass-Baritone
Miriam, Maharal's wife ....Soprano
Ometh, a wounded, chained person........Counter-Tenor
Stoikus, a senior figure..Tenor
Gerty, a middle-aged woman.................Mezzo-Soprano
Stump, a cripple...Tenor
Jadek, an old man ....Baritone

These voices also sing chorus parts (ghostly madrigalists in the Prelude and Celestial Voices in the Legend)

*T*he Golem won the first Britten Award for Composition in 1990.

Prelude. The Maharal looks back on his youth, when he made a golem from clay. He is criticised by four ghostly madrigalists, as he remembers how his experiment failed: though not a man, the golem longed to live as one. The Maharal relives the golem's death. This touching scene is beautifully written. Its effect comes not just from the discreet, effective use of five clay plant-pots, suspended and struck like bells (with their reminder of how clay returns to clay); but also from the rigorously unsentimental use of solo wind, violin and cello to make the most of the simple text. Ometh's voice pleading not to be forgotten reminds the Maharal of how that wounded man supplanted the Maharal in the golem's eyes. The prelude ends with a lyrically nostalgic 'aria' for the Maharal, who longs for summer, for love, for solitude. A girl detaches herself from the chorus and becomes Miriam, his wife. She hands the Maharal a rose.

Legend, scene i. The Maharal creates the golem from clay, idealistically intending him to be 'A saint to do God's work in secret'. The voices of unborn spirits warn the Maharal and Ometh's voice is heard in pain.

Scene ii. The golem's coming to life occasions some extraordinary, apt orchestral effects: he stands with the bass clarinet and then the cello; staggers to glissandos from the double bass; hears to the sound of a bowed sizzle cymbal and speaks to the cor anglais. The Maharal names him Olem and harnesses his agitation to useful activity, chopping wood. His wild movements frighten the people from the village, Jadek, Stump and Gerty. He hears Miriam singing. She brings bread. The Maharal sees the attraction between them and sends Olem away.

Scene iii. The golem meets Stoikus, who is mourning the death of his son. Stoikus's angular, distorted vocal lines, accompanied by bitter alto saxophone runs, are followed by Miriam's sensuous, legato singing, offset by spare harp notes, as she washes sheets in the river. Olem helps her and their voices blend in a frenzied climax. The Maharal intervenes.

Scene iv. The Maharal also stops Miriam from helping Ometh, who is following the golem.

Scene v. An encampment. The four townspeople are plotting rebellion. Stoikus, their elder, tells them to wait for 'the saviour'. The golem arrives but Stoikus rejects him and leaves. When he returns, wild and uncontrolled, he tries to grab Olem's axe and the golem kills him.

Ometh and Olem recognise that they need one another. In a memorable duet, wreathed with arabesques from individual instruments, punctuated by rigorously controlled percussion and including a central lullaby section, initiated by oscillating clarinet and cello, Casken creates a powerful mood of reconciliation and intimacy. The Maharal prevents their union, however: he turns the golem into a rock which collapses, destroying Ometh. The Maharal insists that the golem, 'fearless, invincible', will defeat 'those who plot to destroy us'. A sinister, relentless rhythm on the bass drum alerts us to the funereal nature of this destiny. When the Maharal notices Stoikus's dead body, he realises the golem is not, after all, 'Our Saviour'. His pride turns to despair, as Jadek, Stump and Gerty drag away Stoikus's body. Their wordless lament ends the opera.

According to the composer, the legend of the golem 'warns of the dangers of creating the artificial in order to make our feelings of outrage more tolerable. It also warns against assuming that the solution to man's problems rests not within man himself, but can be found in spite of man.' If there is a hidden allegory about retaliation, it may point to the issue of Jewish revenge on an enemy identified by Maharal as 'Those who desecrate our graves, abduct our children'. Ometh, in chains, wounded and in desperate, but somehow unsympathetic need, could represent the Palestinians. Surely there is even, occasionally, a distinctively Islamic flavour to his melismatic vocal line. The implications of the story extend rather further, however. Ometh declares he will 'stand unbound'; the Maharal reminds him that 'The ancient Gods, whose purpose you opposed to save mankind with gifts of fire and hope, they saw your tricks.' Ometh, like his name, is at least in part Prometheus: his name incarnates his nature and his role. One of the rare strengths of *The Golem* is its openness: it will always mean different things to different people, at different times.   P.

ALFREDO CATALANI

(born 18 June 1854, died 7 August 1893)

LA WALLY

Opera in four acts, text by Luigi Illica. Première at la Scala, Milan, 20 January 1892, with Darclée, conductor Mascheroni. First performed Metropolitan, 1909, with Emmy Destinn, Riccardo Martin, Amato, Campanari, conductor Toscanini; Manchester, 1919. Revived la Scala, 1922, with Sheridan, conductor Panizza; 1936, with Cigna; Rome, 1944, with Caniglia; 1946, with Caniglia; la Scala, 1953, with Tebaldi, Scotto, del Monaco, Giangiacomo Guelfi, conductor Giulini.

Wally ....Soprano
Stromminger, *her father* ....Bass
Afra, *a landlady*..Contralto
Walter, *a strolling minstrel* ....Soprano
Giuseppe Hagenbach, *of Sölden* ....Tenor
Vincenzo Gellner, *of Hochstoff* ....Baritone
The Messenger of Schnals ....Tenor

Place: Tyrol
Time: 1800
Running Time: 2 hours

Catalani died at the age of thirty-nine with effectively only four operas to his credit. *La Wally* was championed by Toscanini, who named his daughter after it; it is still occasionally revived.

Act I. Stromminger is celebrating his seventieth birthday. There is shooting, and Gellner hits the target. Hagenbach of Sölden would not have thought much of that, says Stromminger, adding that he cares little for the boasts of this individual, who is anyhow the son of his greatest enemy. While Stromminger and Gellner drink, Walter sings a song, which, he says, has been written by Wally. Hagenbach enters, flushed with triumph and holding the skin of a bear he has shot. Stromminger mocks his skill, then insults his father, so that Hagenbach throws Stromminger to the ground.

Wally recognises Hagenbach, who does not know her, as the youth she has been secretly in love with for some time. Gellner, who himself is in love with

Wally, warns Stromminger that his daughter has fallen for his enemy, and Stromminger tells Wally that she must marry Gellner within the month. Wally tries to persuade Gellner to give her up, but Stromminger threatens to throw her out of his house if she does not agree to his demand. Wally retorts that if he does she will go off alone into the snow, and in a famous aria, 'Ebben, ne andrò lontana', confirms her resolve.

Act II. The Eagle Tavern at Sölden. The landlady Afra is engaged to Hagenbach. Stromminger is now dead, and Wally has inherited a fortune. Gellner is no longer carefree, but taciturn and even sinister. A festival is in progress, to which Wally is sure to come, they say, particularly since she will there meet her adored Hagenbach. He comes in, and seems to have little regard for Wally. He is bet that he will not succeed in snatching a kiss from Wally, and, in spite of the warnings of Afra that you cannot play with love, he accepts the challenge.

Someone suggests the kissing game, but Wally says that this is not the sort of thing that amuses her. Wally, who has not seen Gellner since she left home on his account, offers him money if he will go away. He protests that he still loves her madly, and that in any case there is no use her setting her cap at Hagenbach as he is engaged to Afra. Wally is furious, and insults Afra; Hagenbach tells her that he will avenge her.

The dance starts. Hagenbach has turned the eagle's wing in his hat upside down, which means that any promise made has no value. Only Gellner notices, but Wally dances all the same with Hagenbach. In the end, he finds her passionate fascination is too much for him, and what has started as a game has gone rather further. He kisses her, but is then dragged away amid shouts of 'Hagenbach has won his bet and Afra is revenged'. Wally turns to Gellner, asks if he still wants her, and then says that Hagenbach, for what he has done to her, must die.

Act III. Hochstoff. Wally's bedroom can be seen on one side, on the other is the bridge over the Ache. Wally returns from the dance, laments her broken dream of love, but finds enough forgiveness in her heart to wonder whether she should tell Gellner that he must not do her bidding and rid the world of Hagenbach. Suddenly there is a knock at the door; Gellner tells her he has taken advantage of the dark and has just pushed Hagenbach into the abyss.

Wally is horror-stricken, and drags Gellner out, promising Afra that Hagenbach shall be hers if he survives. She herself goes down with a rope to rescue him. He is brought up unconscious. Wally tells Afra that he has been restored to her by the grace of God. She kisses him, and says that Afra should tell him she has returned the kiss he gave her at the dance.

Act IV. Tired and hopeless, Wally contemplates the glacier near her house. Walter comes by and tells her that she is in danger from the avalanches which are prevalent at that time of the year – it is Christmas; why does she not come down to celebrate with them? She says goodbye to Walter, asking him only that he will pause on his way down and sing for her the song of the Edelweiss which was heard earlier in the opera.

He leaves her, and she prepares to die like the girl in the song. Suddenly, she hears another voice, not Walter's. She thinks at first that it is the elves of the glacier who are coming to fetch her, but soon understands that it is Hagenbach, recovered from his injuries and come to confess his love for her. Wally does not like to believe him, even when he tells her that his accident occurred when he was on his way to tell her he loved her. She admits her share in his 'accident', and he embraces her and tells her that it makes no difference to his love. Hagenbach goes to look for the path down. He shouts up to Wally, but the sound of an avalanche is heard. Wally calls anxiously to him, but all is silent. Opening her arms wide, she throws herself after the avalanche.   H.

FRANCESCO CAVALLI
(born 14 February 1602, died 14 January 1676)

Having sung as a boy in the choir of St Mark's, Venice, under Monteverdi, whom he eventually succeeded as *maestro di cappella*, Cavalli worked as an organist, as a tenor soloist, as a composer of sacred music and of over thirty operas. His music is characterised by its breadth of feeling – it has room for witty, even salacious ditties and for many heartfelt laments. From the beginning, Cavalli worked with good writers: their lively invention continues to surprise. Among his greatest works are *Didone* to a text by Busenello that contrives a happy ending (1641); *L'Egisto* (1643), *L'Ormindo* (1644) and *La Calisto* (1651), to texts by Giovanni Faustini; *Giasone* (1649) to a text by C.A. Cicognini, and *Ercole Amante*, commissioned by Mazarin to celebrate the marriage of Louis XIV and the Infanta of Spain (1662).

L'ORMINDO

Opera in three acts, libretto by Giovanni Faustini. Première at the Teatro San Cassiano, Venice, 1644. Revived in 1967, in a radically re-worked, two-act edition by Raymond Leppard (which he also conducted) at Glyndebourne Festival, with John Wakefield as Ormindo, Peter-Christoph Runge as a baritone Amida, Irmgard Stadler as Sicle, Hugues Cuénod as Erice, Anne Howells as Erisbe, Jane Berbié as Mirinda and Federico Davia as Hariadeno.

Ormindo, *Prince of Tunis* ....Tenor
Amida, *Prince of Tremisene* ....Alto
Nerillo, *his page*...Soprano
Sicle, *Princess of Susio, in Egyptian*
    (i.e.gipsy) dress ....Soprano
Melide, *her lady-in-waiting,*
    dressed likewise ....Soprano
Erice, *her old nurse, dressed likewise*...................Tenor
Erisbe, *Queen of Morocco and Fez* ....Soprano
Mirinda, *her waiting-woman*...........................Soprano
Hariadeno, *King of Morocco and Fez* ....Bass
Harmony ....Soprano
Destiny ....Tenor

Love ....Soprano
Fortune...Mezzo-Soprano
Osmano, *Captain of Hariadeno's forces*...............Tenor
Guard in Ansa's Arsenal ....Tenor
Messo...Mezzo-Soprano

Soldiers of Ormindo and Amida, Mauretanian (i.e. Moorish) Soldiers, Erisbe's Waiting-Women, the Winds

Place: Ansa, City in the Kingdom of Fez
Running Time: 2 hours 20 minutes (1967 version)

As Harmony points out in the prologue, opera was then new in Venice: it moved from private spaces to public theatres only seven years before the first night of *L'Ormindo*. Cavalli balances opera's noble, inherited ambition to revive the ancient synthesis of drama and music, whose primary medium was recitative, with the more popular entertainment of arias. *L'Ormindo* was the first of Cavalli's operas to be rediscovered this century, by Raymond Leppard. His edition of *L'Ormindo*, however, 'a response to unique circumstances', in Jeremy Noble's words, has since been discredited.[1] Any revival now would have to go back to the manuscript score.

Ormindo was born from the love between Hariadeno and Nearbe, who died in giving birth to him. He was brought up in ignorance of his parenthood by Nearbe's sister Cedige, Queen of Tunis. Now an adult, he has come to Fez to help Hariadeno in his fight against Spain. With him is his friend Prince Amida, who has abandoned Sicle, the woman he was betrothed to marry. The two princes have fallen in love with Hariadeno's young wife Erisbe.

Prologue. Harmony appears before a curtain representing the Piazza San Marco. Since she came to tread the boards in Venice, she has gained in glory. The ancient Athenian and Roman stages, which she saw, never equalled the splendour of theatres in Venice, that immortal and most serene virgin.

Act I. Ormindo reflects that love has brought him to Fez and inspired him in battle. He overhears Amida's

---

[1] 'Cavalli's "Ormindo"', *Musical Times*, cx, 1969.

lovesick lament ('Cari globi di fiamme'). Gradually, they realise they both love the same woman, Erisbe, and agree to make her choose between them. Amida's young page Nerillo blames women's beauty for dividing such friends. Sicle, her nurse and her lady-in-waiting offer to tell Nerillo's fortune. Inadvertently, he reveals that Amida's love has been stolen by Erisbe. Lamenting that she has been betrayed, Sicle longs for death ('Chi, chi mi toglie al die'). Her nurse Erice advises women to love as she herself did, without getting involved.

The Royal Garden. Erisbe longs for admirers, since her husband, King Hariadeno, is so old. Happily, she now has two suitors. When they approach, she sings a song about roses that wither on the stalk, unplucked, neglected. She boldly encourages first Ormindo and then Amida and explains that she loves them both. They withdraw, discomfited, when Hariadeno comes. The King asks his wife to give his allies a warm welcome. Mirinda reflects that she would never marry an old man. Destiny orders Love to ensure that Sicle's sufferings will now cease.

Act II. Erisbe and Mirinda celebrate beauty's power to reconcile discord ('Auree trecce'). The 'gipsies' appear. Sicle reads Amida's hand in Erisbe's presence and tells him that he once abandoned a princess whom he loved. She therefore warns Erisbe to love only Ormindo. Erice offers to help Amida win Erisbe. Melide reflects that now she's seen what servitude love brings, she will not get involved. Nerillo is outraged by his experience of impudent people in the city ('Che citta, che citta'), and longs to go home. Erisbe has decided to love only Ormindo ('No, no, non vo' piu amare'). He comes to take leave of her. She decides to run away with him. Mirinda comments that if she had an old husband she would do the same.

Act III. Erice reflects that in vulgar hearts, gold stimulates love. Telling Amida that Sicle committed suicide when she was betrayed she pretends to summon her spirit. Struck by Sicle's beauty, Amida begs for forgiveness. Once she has convinced him that she is alive, they are happily reunited. Fortune intervenes at the command of Destiny, and orders the Winds to send the ship carrying Ormindo and Erisbe back to Ansa. When Hariadeno hears that the fugitives have been recaptured, he orders Osmano to kill them with poison. Osmano is Ormindo's friend, however. Mirinda imagines Osmano's sighs are those of a frustrated lover and rejects his advances. When she hears that he is determined to save Ormindo's life, or die with him, she relents. Osmano meets the lovers and Ormindo tries to save Erisbe's life. She accepts her guilt, seizes and swallows some of the poison. Ormindo drinks it too; they look forward to death together and collapse. Seeing their bodies, Hariadeno repents of his fury. Osmano reveals his trick: he substituted a sleeping draught. The lovers awaken, Ormindo begs for forgiveness and blames Cupid for his treachery. Hariadeno acknowledges love's power ('Io son humano al fine'). When he learns from Cedige's letter that Ormindo is his long-lost son, he offers him his wife and his throne. They all celebrate love: it torments its followers only to reward them the more sweetly.

Francesco Bussi called *L'Ormindo* 'almost a *Tristan und Isolde* with a happy ending'.[1] While there are parallels in the plot, that makes no allowance for the work's false bottom: the way it interleaves comedy and serious opera in alternate scenes. This is not only so as to appeal to the new market: the servants' low-life solos generally comment satirically or ironically on their masters' predicaments. The opera boasts a remarkable range of characters, with a central pair of highly contrasted women. The characters also develop: Erisbe begins as a trivial flirt and ends as a passionate lover. Amida's return to his first love is a fully motivated response to the trauma of seeing her 'ghost'. Faustini's libretto for Cavalli is formulaic, however: typically, the dénouement is made the neater, rather than more interesting, when the hero's father gracefully allows him to marry his step-mother.   P.

LA CALISTO

Opera in a prologue and three acts, words by Giovanni Faustini, after Ovid. Première at Teatro Sant'Apollinari, Venice, 28 November 1651.

Nature	Mezzo-Soprano
Eternity	Mezzo-Soprano
Destiny	Soprano
Giove (Jupiter), *King of the Gods*	Bass

[1] *Storia dell'opera*, Turin, 1977, vol.I.

Mercurio (Mercury) ....Baritone

Calisto, *one of Diana's nymphs* ....Soprano

Endimione (Endymion), *in love
      with Diana*....................................Counter-Tenor

Diana, *Jupiter's daughter and goddess
      of hunting*...................................... Mezzo-Soprano

Linfea, *an aged nymph* ....Tenor

A Little Satyr ....Mezzo-Soprano

Pan, *ruler of the sylvan world* ....Bass

Silvano, *Pan's henchman* ....Bass

Giunone (Juno), *Jupiter's consort* ....Soprano

Chorus of Wood Creatures, Furies

Running Time: 2 hours 25 minutes

Cavalli (who took the name of his patron, Venetian governor of Crema, where he was born) wrote some forty operas, and was, after Monteverdi, seventeenth-century Venice's leading composer. He sang in the choir of St Mark's when Monteverdi was director, and his first opera was performed in 1639, a mere two years after the first Venetian operatic performance to a paying audience, for which all Cavalli's operas were to be written. His style mixes Monteverdi's strikingly expressive recitative with the lyrical songs and arias which were becoming the vogue as audiences developed a taste for the medium. A curiosity is that it was the custom at the time, often to suit vagaries of staging, to add short instrumental *ritornelli* or *sinfonie*, frequently imported from outside and not by the composer of the opera itself. Reconstruction of his operas by Raymond Leppard, starting at Glyndebourne in 1967, played a considerable role, particularly in England, in re-establishing his work, of which *La Calisto* is a late and particularly brilliant example.

Prologue. Destiny persuades Nature and Eternity to agree, somewhat reluctantly, to add Calisto to the stars in heaven; instrumental *ritornelli* punctuate their formalised utterances.

Act I. A parched forest. Jupiter laments the state of the earth, waterless and laid waste by fire. Mercury reminds him that he has the power to restore nature but Jupiter's eye has already lit on Calisto, who is gentleness personified as she laments the lost beauties of a shattered world. Jupiter immediately replenishes a spring which gushes out for the delectation of Calisto, who nonetheless and in spite of the blandishments of Jupiter and Mercury rejects Jupiter as an old

lecher and proclaims she will die a virgin. The King of the gods appeals to Mercury and is advised to take on the form of Diana, in whose retinue Calisto belongs and to whose charms she will surely succumb. Calisto, no longer bothered by importunate strangers, celebrates in song her enjoyment of the fountain's renewed freshness, seems all too easily to forget her recent proclamation, and accepts the affectionate greetings of Jupiter-Diana. They go to explore neighbouring groves and, their duet suggests, other pleasures as well, Mercury commenting cynically on the crucial role in courtship of deceit.

Endymion despairs at what he feels is his hopeless pursuit of Diana, but the goddess appears, attended by an ill-natured old harridan, Linfea, and proceeds to lament the barren state of the forest ('Ardò, sospiro e piango'). Diana is plainly far from immune to the attractions of Endymion, but Linfea's mocking tongue drives him away, and Diana finds herself face to face with Calisto, ecstatic at the pleasure she has experienced with, as she thinks, her patroness, and anxious to renew it. Diana's indignation knows no bounds and she threatens, to Calisto's amazed incomprehension, to banish her from her entourage.

Linfea is plainly intrigued at passion breaking out all around her and wonders whether there could not after all be something in it for her. With an eye to the main chance, a little Satyr, who has been listening, offers himself as a solution to Linfea's problems, but this produces a barrage of insults from the aged nymph, and the way is left clear for Pan in his turn to declare his passion for Diana. But his love is in vain and he is left with only the support of Silvano, the Satyr, to fall back on. A *ciaccona* ends the act.

Act II. The summit of Mount Latmos. Endymion sings gloriously to the moon on the subject of his love for Diana, who comes in as he falls asleep and seems as smitten by what she sees before her as he was by what he only recalled in imagination. He dreams that he holds Diana in his arms and wakes to find the reality as attractive as the dream and as conducive to an impassioned love scene. Duty and her vow of chastity nevertheless call Diana away. The little Satyr, roused as always to thoughts of emulation by amorous behaviour, comments acidly on what he has witnessed and allows his imagination full play.

The plain of the Erymanthus. Juno in jealous majesty inveighs against her husband's amorous pro-

La Calisto *(Glyndebourne, 1971, director Peter Hall, designer John Bury). Ileana Cotrubas as Calisto,*
Ugo Trama as Giove.

clivities. When Calisto innocently tells of her delicious experiences with 'Diana', the description convinces Juno that Jupiter has again been at his favourite exercise. Jupiter-Diana and Mercury come into view, the former assuring the latter of the pleasurable nature of his encounter with Calisto. Juno watches as her husband and Calisto prepare for a more private assignation but Jupiter-Diana remains behind to face out the confrontation with Juno, which ends with a little duet of triumph (premature, as we may think) between Jupiter and Mercury.

Endymion returns, sees what he supposes is Diana (but is in reality Jupiter) and causes the aroused god more than a little embarrassment with his lovesick blandishments. The situation is saved and at the same time complicated by the arrival of Pan and his followers, led on by the little Satyr. In revenge for his love of Diana, who is also loved by Pan, they take Endymion prisoner, a situation he mourns with less vigour than he does the rapidity with which Diana has abandoned him to his plight. Endymion's captors rejoice with some vigour in their triumph. Linfea makes matters worse by appearing in urgent search of a lover, a situation the little Satyr interprets as an opportunity to gratify vengeance and lust at one and the same time. He and his cohorts lose no time in putting theory into practice. The act ends with a dance.

Act III. The source of the Ladon. Calisto waits expectantly for her lover but things take a totally unexpected turn as an implacable Juno accompanied by the Furies appears to wreak jealous revenge. Calisto is metamorphosed into a little bear and Juno finishes the scene with a celebration of her triumph, ending with a sigh of regret at the propensity of presumably erring husbands to fall asleep the moment they get into bed.

Jupiter attended by Mercury attempts to turn the clock back and for a moment Calisto recaptures human form, but not for long. After Jupiter's reassurance that her place in the firmament is secure, Calisto seems reconciled to her now semi-divine status as a star, which after a nostalgic farewell she assumes.

Another part of the forest. Endymion is at the mercy of Pan and his followers who propose to teach Diana a lesson by beating him, but Diana routs them and leaves them only the satisfaction of spreading rumours about her lustful behaviour. Diana indulges in a tender love scene with Endymion during whose course, with more conviction than kindness, she reiterates her pledge of chastity.

It is time for Calisto to be received into the firmament as a star with Celestial Spirits preparing the way. Jupiter in his true form welcomes her lovingly and she takes her place as Ursa Minor, thus providing an ending seemingly full of propriety to an operatic libretto singularly – and entertainingly – devoid of that quality.   H.

ALEXIS EMMANUEL CHABRIER
(born 18 January 1841, died 13 September 1894)

Chabrier was the French composer with strongest connections with fellow artists, collaborating when he was in his twenties with the poet Paul Verlaine and numbering Manet among his friends (he owned the *Bar aux Folies-Bergère* soon after it was painted). At his family's insistence he trained for the law and joined the Civil Service, with the result that only in his thirties did his two comic operas *L'Etoile* and *Une Education manquée* mark him out as a composer to be watched. In the event *L'Etoile* had less than complete success, and two of his three remaining operas (*Briséis* unfinished) are profoundly serious. He was a keen Wagnerian and was regularly accused, even, amazingly, in *L'Etoile*, of Wagnerian tendencies. A visit to Munich brought him under the spell of *Tristan* and another soon after to Spain produced *España* and enrolled him in the list of French composers who excelled at Spanish music. There is a painting by Fantin-Latour of French Wagnerians, with Chabrier at the piano and d'Indy standing nearby.

L'ÉTOILE

The Star

Opéra bouffe in three acts, libretto by E. Leterrier and A. Vanloo. Première at Bouffes Parisiennes, Paris, 28 November 1877. First produced in New York (as *The Merry Monarch*), 1890, adapted by J.C. Goodwin and W. Morse, with the music arranged by J.P. Sousa. This version was given at the Savoy Theatre, London, in 1899, with new dialogue and lyrics and additional music by I. Caryll, the whole retaining little of Chabrier's original. Revived Paris, 1925; 1941, first given at Opéra-Comique, with Fanély Revoil, Lilie Grandval, Madeleine Grandval, Madeleine Mathieu, René Hérent, Balbon, Derroja, conductor Roger Desormière; revived 1985 in a production first seen in Lyons, with Michel Sénéchal, Colette Alliot-Lugaz; Opera North, 1991.

King Ouf I ....Tenor

Siroco, *Court Astronomer*......................................Bass

Hérisson de Porc Épic ....Tenor

Tapioca, *his private secretary* ....Baritone

The Chief of Police ....Speaking

The Mayor..Speaking

Lazuli, *a pedlar* ....Mezzo-Soprano

Princess Laoula ....Soprano

Aloès, *wife of Hérisson*....................................Soprano

Ladies and Gentlemen of the Court, People, Guards

Running Time: 1 hour 40 minutes

Act I. After a bracing, unpretentious overture, the curtain rises on a public square; on the right is some form of observatory, on the left a small hotel. Rumour has it that King Ouf in disguise is prowling round the town, and the citizens warn each other to be on the watch. Why? The appearance of a cloaked figure, which proceeds to ask leading questions of individuals about King and Government, soon provides the answer. The King must provoke one of his too law-abiding subjects into subversive talk if the rest of them are not to be cheated of their main pleasure at his birthday celebrations – a public execution. Nobody obliges with an anti-Ouf remark, so he vents his disappointment on Siroco, the Astronomer Royal, who descends opportunely from his observatory. The King explains a clause in his will under which Siroco must die a quarter of an hour after his employer, then orders Siroco to look into the omens which surround Ouf's projected marriage with Princess Laoula, the daughter of his neighbour, King Mataquin, by which he proposes to bring peace between the two countries and provide his own with an heir to the throne.

On to the empty stage come four cloaked figures, respectively Hérisson de Porc Épic, King Mataquin's ambassador, Tapioca, his confidential secretary, Princess Laoula, and Aloès, wife of Hérisson. In chorus they announce their intention of remaining incognito under the guise of shopkeepers. For reasons that he says are diplomatic, like those for their incognito, Hérisson has been passing Laoula off as his wife – a complicated manoeuvre, but where would diplomacy be without complications?

They all go into the hotel as Lazuli, a pedlar, comes on singing gracefully of the power of cosmetics in the female world ('Je suis Lazuli') – an undoubted 'hit' number. Lazuli admits to himself that he has fallen in love with one of four travellers, and he gives his last golden piece to Siroco in return for a promise to consult the stars about his future. While his horoscope is being cast, Lazuli prepares to sleep and sings a touching romance to the star on which so much appears to depend.

No sooner have Hérisson and Tapioca left the inn, than Aloès and Laoula come out too, resolved on adventure. They catch sight of the recumbent Lazuli and decide to wake him up. The obvious way is to tickle him, and this method is graphically illustrated in the music ('Il faut le chatouiller pour le mieux réveiller'). Lazuli pretends to be asleep until he has the chance of seizing hold of his tormentors. He declares his love for Laoula and gives practical proof of it in the form of a kiss, but the return of Hérisson and Tapioca spoils a promising scene. Lazuli is desolate to hear that Laoula is the wife of Hérisson, and when King Ouf, still on the lookout for a victim for the public holiday, approaches him, he is understandably out of humour, speaks ill of the government and finishes by boxing the ears of his interrogator. Beside himself with joy, Ouf summons his guards and reveals to Lazuli that the ears he has just boxed are the King's. For his offence he must die – and the King sends for the instruments of torture whose praises he sings in the 'Couplets du Pal'. As Lazuli is about to be ceremonially impaled, Siroco interrupts to say that the stars reveal that the King's death will closely follow Lazuli's. There is a quick change of plan, Lazuli is pardoned, and the King announces that he will install him in the royal palace.

Act II. The Throne Room in the King's palace; at the back, windows giving a view on to a lake. Lazuli, now richly caparisoned and waited on by maids of honour whom he thanks in a *brindisi*, is visited by the King and Siroco, who have come to satisfy themselves about his health, on which so much depends for each of them. Their solicitude leaves him a prey to considerable misgivings, and he escapes with the aid of a tablecloth through the window. Ouf and Siroco return, are seized with consternation at what they see, promise to grant Lazuli his liberty and so persuade him to climb back again. He tells them he is in love with a married woman but, in a lively song, rejoices that husbands have never bothered him much – at worst he challenges them to a duel. When Hérisson the new ambassador is announced and recognised by Lazuli as the husband of his *innamorata*, King Ouf, much to Hérisson's fury, cannot give him his full attention. He is very little concerned with the details of Hérisson's mission as an ambassador, very much with his skill as a duellist, so much so that he unwittingly almost provokes Hérisson to deliver the ultimatum he always carries in his pocket against emergencies. The crisis however is averted when Hérisson goes off to fetch Princess Laoula.

So that Lazuli may be assisted to win Hérisson's wife, Hérisson when he reappears is arrested and removed by Siroco, leaving the way clear for the lovers. At this point there is a charming quartet for Lazuli and Laoula, Tapioca and Aloès, which becomes a sort of double love duet as it is clear that Tapioca means to practise on Aloès all the attentions which Lazuli lavishes on Laoula. Ouf not unnaturally takes Aloès for the Princess he is betrothed to. Nobody disillusions him. Ouf offers Lazuli freedom and money, Laoula expresses gratitude in a charming song ('Moi, je n'ai pas une âme ingrate') and, in a trio, Ouf speeds them on their way – none too soon as Hérisson, who has escaped, at this moment charges into the room. Ouf calms him and everything is prepared for a ceremonial welcome to the Princess, when Hérisson returns, leading in Aloès and Tapioca, furious not only that Princess Laoula has disappeared but that he has found his wife and Tapioca in a highly compromising situation. The embroilment soon becomes plain even to Ouf, his dismay mounting as Hérisson reveals that he has sent the guards off in pursuit of the eloping lovers; the King's consternation explodes at the sound of a shot. Laoula is led in alone, and sadly starts to tell her story. When she describes how Lazuli suddenly disappeared to the bottom of the lake, her tune becomes

brilliant and merry ('Et puis crac! Tout changea dans une minute').

Act III. An entr'acte based on the tickling trio brings up the curtain on another room in the palace. Even surreptitiously putting the clock back cannot disguise from Ouf and Siroco the unhappy fact that they are waiting for death. It is plain to them that only a glass of cordial can restore their spirits.

Lazuli now emerges from hiding. Confident of his own prowess as a swimmer, he had dived from the boat and so evaded his pursuers. The trouble is, as we learn in a song ('Enfin je me sens mieux'), that his ducking has given him a horrible cold and he sneezes throughout his number. He hides as Ouf and Siroco reappear. Even a glass of yellow chartreuse has not completely restored the King's morale and wits, and Lazuli from his hiding place sees him inadvertently insult Hérisson, receive the ever-ready ultimatum, but successfully evade the consequences by pleading that it is Hérisson's fault that Lazuli is dead and that the King must therefore shortly die.

The scene, with its references to his impending end, has tired Ouf, and Siroco timidly suggests that the remedy is another glass of cordial – this time perhaps some green chartreuse, at double the strength. There ensues the *Duetto de la chartreuse verte*, a hilarious parody of an early nineteenth-century Italian piece. Ouf and Siroco leave together, and Lazuli comes out of hiding a good deal clearer in his understanding of the situation than before. He listens while Aloès tries to console Laoula, who is clearly very unhappy at his (Lazuli's) death, then he himself joins in to make the duet a trio. There is a grand reunion, and Lazuli tries to explain to Laoula that he will eventually marry her.

Re-enter Ouf, clear in his mind about only one thing, that on the whole he prefers green to yellow chartreuse, because green is stronger. He has another look at Laoula then decides on a quick wedding, urging the joys of widowhood on the disconsolate Princess, who in a sweetly pretty song in 6/8 compares herself with a rose that once picked starts to wither and die. Just in time for Laoula, Ouf is reminded by the observatory clock that he has been tampering with the one in the palace, and seeing that the hour is at hand, renounces the proposed wedding. When the clock strikes and he remains alive, he finds time amidst his relief to assure Siroco of impending punishment, but regains his good humour in time to pardon Lazuli, who has been arrested by the diligent Chief of Police, and, to the tune of 'Le Pal', to bless Laoula and Lazuli and provide the necessary happy ending.   H.

GWENDOLINE

Opera in three acts, text by Catulle Mendès. Première Brussels, 10 April 1886 (there were only two performances as the Director of la Monnaie was declared bankrupt). First performed Karlsruhe, 1889, conductor Mottl; Munich, 1890, with Ternina, conductor Hermann Levi; Lyons, 1893, conductor Luigini; Opéra, Paris, 1893, with Berthet and Renaud, conductor Mangin, by which time the composer was mortally ill. The opera was revived in Paris in 1911 with Kousnetsova and conducted by Messager, and there had been thirty-eight performances by 1941. It was revived at San Diego in 1982 with Rosalind Plowright.

Harald, *a Dane, king of the sea* ....Baritone

Old Armel, *a Saxon chief*....................................Tenor

Gwendoline, *his daughter*..............................Soprano

Aella, *Armel's retainer*....................................Baritone

Erik, *Armel's retainer*...Tenor

Danes; Saxon Men and Women

Place: Coast of Britain
Time: Eighth Century
Running Time: 2 hours 45 minutes

Chabrier after his visit to Munich in 1879 became an ardent Wagnerian, but the music of *Gwendoline* is that of a French composer and there is little Wagnerian about his third opera except maybe the bones of the slightly absurd plot. It was turned down by the Opéra and only heard there after performance in Germany under conductors such as Mottl and Hermann Levi. There had been a private performance at the Princesse de Polignac's in 1888, when Fauré and Chabrier himself on harmonium and piano, d'Indy and Messager playing percussion, twenty-four chorus members plus harp and string quartet, accompanied Mme Lureau-Escalaïs and the baritone Melchissédec. But there was no follow-up.

The action is uncomplicated. A peaceful Saxon fishing village is overrun by Danish invaders, whose leader, Harald, is prevented from killing Armel, their chief, by Armel's daughter Gwendoline. Harald is overcome by Gwendoline's beauty, is persuaded by her to bend his rough manners to her more civilised ways – he even sits at her spinning wheel – and he ends by asking her father to be allowed to marry her. The idyllic second act is dominated by an Epithalamium and a duet for the lovers, but Armel presses a knife into Gwendoline's hand instructing her to kill Harald while he sleeps. Harald will not listen to Gwendoline's warning, and in spite of his valiant defence with only the knife as weapon, he is mortally wounded. Gwendoline stabs herself and they die together upright against a tree.

Francis Poulenc, in his book on the composer, singles out for particular praise the brilliant overture, and in the first act Gwendoline's Légende as well as Harald's aria; also Harald's request to Armel for his daughter's hand. In the second, he particularly praises the tender prelude, the Epithalamium – which he calls the jewel of the score – and the duet for the protagonists.   H.

LE ROI MALGRÉ LUI
King in Spite of Himself

Opéra-comique in three acts, libretto by Emile de Najac and Paul Burani. Première 18 May 1887, Opéra-Comique, Paris, with Adèle Isaac, Cécile Mézéray, Max Bouvet, Delaguerrière, Lucien Fugère, conductor Danbé. Revived in a new dramatic version by Albert Carré, at Opéra-Comique, 1929, with Brothier, Guyla, Bourdin, Musy; 1946, with Turba-Rabier, Vina Bovy, Bourdin, Musy; 1959, with Micheau, Castelli, Clément, Musy; Toulouse, 1978, conductor Plasson; Opera North, 1994.

Henri de Valois, *King of Poland* ....Baritone

Comte de Nangis, *a member of his suite* ....Tenor

Duc de Fritelli ....Buffo Baritone

Count Laski, *a Polish patriot* ....Bass

Basile, *an innkeeper*...Tenor

French noblemen
    Villequier..Bass
    Liancourt ....Tenor
    Elbeuf ....Tenor
    Maugiron..Baritone
    Quélus ....Baritone

A Soldier ....Bass

Minka, *one of Count Laski's serfs*....................Soprano

Alexina, *Duchess of Fritelli* ....Soprano

Six Serfs, Pages, French Noblemen, Polish
    Noblemen, Soldiers, Polish Ladies, People

Place: Poland
Running Time: 2 hours 40 minutes

Written in only nine months following the successful première in Brussels of Chabrier's ambitious serious opera *Gwendoline*, *Le Roi malgré lui*, in spite of a clumsy libretto (re-cast by Albert Carré for the revival in 1929 at the Opéra-Comique), is often considered Chabrier's masterpiece. Of it, Maurice Ravel, with as much use of hyperbole as Sir Thomas Beecham in his famous comparison of *Manon* and the Brandenburg Concertos, wrote, 'I would rather have written *Le Roi malgré lui* than the *Ring of the Nibelung*'! In truth, it is a score full of wit and erudition, of tender lyricism and comedy, perhaps amongst French *opéras-comiques* as much underrated in world estimation as was once Berlioz's more heroic *Les Troyens*.

Henri de Valois is King of Poland but he is bored with position and surroundings alike and nothing would please him better than to be rid of both.

Act I. The French nobles of Henri's court are gathered together in the castle near Cracow, playing cards and chess, fencing and generally whiling away the tedium of life in a court far from home. Nangis sings of the penance of existence in a barbarous capital, relieved only by the possibilities of a diverting love affair, then takes credit for the new soldiers he has succeeded in recruiting. The King enters, is acclaimed, reviews disinterestedly the soldiers drawn up for him, and receives in reply to an enquiry the answer that a bodyguard is necessary for him as many Poles opposed his election as their King – Villequier suspects a plot against his life. The post from France is brought ceremonially to the King, who in a beautiful romance hymns the praises of his longed-for native land. He is depressed at the unreality of his position: his senior French advisers fear he will rush off to France, his Polish subjects, led by Count Laski, dread his staying in Poland.

Enter Duke Fritelli, an Italian attached to the court but married to a Polish wife, niece moreover to the suspect Count Laski. With his conceit and cowardice and his lack of physical attraction, he is a recognised figure of fun, but the King asks him for his interpretation of the Polish character – this he gives in a remarkable and brilliantly characterised Mazurka ('Le Polonais est triste et grave'). The King insists on the attractions of Italian women, instancing an adventure he recently had with a masked Venetian in her native city. The Duke goes to fetch his wife, whom the King wishes presented, and the King discovers from Nangis that he is in love with Minka, a serf in the household of Count Laski. She regularly passes on information of her master's plots against the King. The King tells Nangis that they will go together in disguise to Cracow to spy out the land.

No sooner have the King and his attendants gone than sounds of a scuffle are heard, and Nangis has to rescue Minka from a soldier. In tender music they celebrate the love they feel for one another. Minka reveals that there is to be a ball that night at Count Laski's, then protests her love for Nangis in a graceful romance ('L'amour, ce divin maître'). She hides at the approach of the Duke and Duchess of Fritelli, intent on making obeisance to the King.

Thinking themselves alone, Alexina, the Duchess, reveals to her husband, who is also in the plot, that the Polish opponents of Henri de Valois meet that night at her uncle's house. When Fritelli suggests that he, her husband, should be the object of her passion, she bursts out laughing, and in a rapid interchange advises her husband to concentrate on ambition, while he urges on her the claims of love. She starts to tell him of an adventure she had in Venice when Fritelli realises that, for all the innocent slant she gives it, it is complementary to the one the King has just told; *she* was the Italian under whose spell he fell! When news comes that the King is too busy to receive the Duchess, Fritelli is overjoyed and announces to her his convinced adherence to the plot to drive out the foreign ruler.

Minka is about to tell Nangis of the plot against the King's life, when the King himself comes from his room. Minka, believing him like Nangis a member of the King's entourage, in a charmingly lyrical duet tells him about the plot, then points out Fritelli as one of the conspirators. The King immediately confronts Fritelli with the accusation, then pardons him on condition that Fritelli take him (the King) to the ball at Laski's that very night. The King looks for a pretext for a Frenchman to present himself as a prospective conspirator, then pretends to lose his temper with Nangis and sentences him to immediate imprisonment. The finale works up to a fine ensemble of perplexity à la Rossini ('Qu'a-t-il fait? En effet qu'a-t-il pu commettre?': What's he done? My goodness, what could he have done?) and the King departs as Nangis is led off.

Fritelli starts to explain to his wife that the King cannot now receive her, when he appears unannounced. It is immediately clear that each recognises the other as the nameless lover from Venice, but that neither has an inkling of the identity of the other. Fritelli is made to introduce the King as Nangis, who as a result of his unjust treatment is anxious to join the conspirators. The trio ('Quelle surprise, ma beauté de Venise') makes a brilliant effect but is interrupted by the voice of Minka, singing in the park as she waits for her rendezvous with Nangis. Henri brings the act to a close: 'Conspirons tous trois contre Henri de Valois'.

Act II. The great hall of Count Laski's palace at the start of the ball. The music – the well-known *Fête Polonaise* – is a choral dance, brilliantly orchestrated and altogether in the tradition of Berlioz (*cf.* the scene of the Roman Carnival in *Benvenuto Cellini*). Suggestions of Mazurka lead to an intoxicating and glitteringly orchestrated waltz sequence. The ball is an excuse for Count Laski to gather together the conspirators. Alexina presents as a sympathiser the Comte de Nangis (the King in disguise) but a complication is introduced when the ubiquitous Minka overhears the introduction and knows that some deception is afoot. During the course of a choral ensemble of conspirators, which rivals Meyerbeer for massive effect and far outdoes him for musical excitement, the *soi-disant* Nangis swears with the others to do all possible to remove the King from Poland, and Fritelli, in spite of efforts at evasion, is charged with abducting his master. However, when most have gone, the disguised King takes pity on Fritelli and says he has a more subtle plan to effect the removal of the King – who was once, Alexina points out, his greatest friend. 'Rien n'est aussi près de la haine que l'amitié' (Nothing is closer to hatred than friendship) is the burden of a witty and exquisite quartet, in which Alexina and the King are joined by Fritelli and Laski.

There follows an interlude, the Sextuor des Serves and the Chanson tzigane, dramatically superfluous but musically very much to the point, with its sensuous writing for concerted female voices and its exceptionally brilliant solo for Minka, who relates the story of her happy love to her fellow serfs.

The King enters, followed by Alexina, who is still ignorant of his identity but knows him as the man who swore eternal faith in Venice and then disappeared. 'Oui, je vous hais' (Oh yes, I hate you), she sings, but the duet turns to a barcarolle reminiscence of their rapturous experience – it is patently a delectable precursor of Reynaldo Hahn's operetta style. Alexina is clearly in love, and when she leaves, the King asks Fritelli whose wife she may be, is put off with vague hints of six children, false teeth and a wooden leg, but has the last word when he says he will ask Laski to release him from his promise. The reason: he is in love with a Pole!

Minka alone sings to attract her lover who appears just long enough to be told about the King's supposed presence at the ball before hiding. The news passes round until Laski has the doors shut and guarded. When Nangis does not remove his mask, Laski assumes that he is the King and an ensemble begins, Offenbachian in spirit and culminating in Nangis's spritely song (prompted by the real King), 'Je suis le roi'. The Poles demand his signature to an act of abdication, but prompted by Minka he refuses, and is immediately put gently but firmly under lock and key. When his death is voted as alternative to abdication, the real King proposes himself as the true victim.

Consternation is general, led by Alexina, who vouches for his *bona fides* as a mere member of the court. When the conspirators draw lots for the man to deal the fatal blow, each puts the name of Nangis on a paper, but when the King makes as if to enter and deal a death blow to himself, Minka appears and admits she has helped Nangis escape. The conspirators realise that vengeance may at any moment overtake them, and, the King promising to keep his oath, they agree to leave the house, to a thundering reprise of the *ensemble de la conjuration*.

Act III. The complications must be resolved, which they are, though not before some fairly extensive and choice red-herrings have been found, chased, pickled and discarded. The scene is the hall of an inn on the Polish frontier; numbered doors give off on either side and the hall is full of decorations, most of them bearing the letter H. A crowd sings of its joy at the prospect of a new King for Poland, but Fritelli has to explain that the new King is Archduke Ernest, not Henri de Valois! The music is a vivid *allegro tempo mazurka*, chorus and ensemble in the style of the opening of the last act of *Carmen*, spiced with ingredients peculiar to the composer of *España* and the *Joyeuse Marche*. In the course of a not too satisfactory conversation with Basile, the innkeeper, Fritelli learns that a distinguished-looking traveller arrived at the inn the night before and is now lodged in room eight. Obviously, thinks Fritelli, Archduke Ernest. Immediately bouquets are handed out, and Fritelli steps forward with a smile – only to see Henri de Valois step with a grin through the door.

The explanation is simple: horses were prepared to take him to the frontier but no further, and the coachman deposited him here – will the Duke please order a carriage to take him a stage further? More than that, will he convey his infinite regrets to the charming niece of Count Laski that he had to leave without saying goodbye? The Duke does not know whether to be angry or relieved, but goes off to do the King's bidding, leaving the field clear for the entrance of Alexina and Minka, who has been allowed to accompany her in her carriage. Together they lament the precipitate departure of the men they love (the sentiments are genuine enough, even if by now the names have got thoroughly mixed up).

At this moment Fritelli comes in carrying the hot water the King has demanded, delivers it, intimates to the despair of Alexina and Minka that the King and Nangis have both left for France, and then explodes at Alexina's complaint at his cavalier dismissal of her: 'Nous ne sommes plus à Venise, Madame!' He rates her for her indiscretions in a comic song: 'Je suis du pays des gondoles' (what is the reference to Berlioz's *Marche Hongroise* as refrain at the end of each verse?), explains that he is on an errand for the Archduke, and enters room number eight. Alexina for her part goes through the performance of collecting the peasants and preparing to salute the new King, only to see her lover come out.

All is explained, his identity as King and hers as the Duke's wife, but there is an interruption as Minka runs in, crying that Count Laski is at hand; she will be taken back to Cracow, the King will be slain. Henri consents to leave, saying that he has kept his word and the King is no more; Minka believes he has killed her lover and runs after him, vowing revenge; and Laski is told 'Le roi n'est plus' (The King is dead!). But an important change has taken place that morning, when news was received that the Archduke had renounced the throne, and the Polish nobles, impressed by Henri's chivalrous conduct the night before, had decided to renounce their opposition. He must be stopped before it is too late!

It remains to resolve Minka's dilemma, expressed in a despairing aria. Nangis appears to explain the deception and claim her in a love duet, before Henri returns in something like triumph. He extends grace to everyone, and the opera ends with the shields bearing the royal H once more to the front, and a general acclamation for 'Le Roi malgré lui'.   H.

GUSTAVE CHARPENTIER
(born 25 June 1860, died 18 February 1956)

LOUISE

Opera in four acts, text by the composer. Première Opéra-Comique, Paris, 2 February 1900, with Marthe Rioton, Deschamps-Jéhin, Maréchal, Fugère, conductor Messager. First performed Berlin, 1903, with Destinn, Goetze, Philipp, Baptist Hoffmann; Vienna, 1903, with Gutheil-Schoder, Slezak, Demuth, conductor Mahler; New York, Manhattan Opera House, 1908, with Garden, Bressler-Gianoli, Dalmorès, Gilibert, conductor Campanini: Covent Garden, 1909, with Edvina, Bérat, Dalmorès, Gilibert, conductor Frigara; Metropolitan, 1921, with Farrar, Harrold, Whitehill. Revivals include Covent Garden, 1919, with Edvina, Ansseau, Cotreuil, conductor Coates; 1928, with Heldy, Kaisin, Journet; 1936, with Delprat, Verdière (later Maison), Bouilliez, conductor Sargent; Metropolitan, 1930, with Bori; 1939, with Moore, Maison, Pinza; 1947, with Dorothy Kirsten, Jobin, Brownlee, conductor Fourestier; la Scala, Milan, 1923, with Heldy, Casazza, Pertile, Journet, conductor Toscanini; 1929, with dalla Rizza; 1934, with Favero, Casazza, Ziliani, Stabile; New York, City Opera, 1962, with Arlene Saunders; English National Opera, 1981, with Valerie Masterson, John Treleaven, Richard Van Allan, conductor Cambreling.

Louise ....Soprano

Her Mother ....Contralto

Irma...Soprano

Camille..Soprano

Gertrude	Contralto
Elise	Soprano
Blanche	Soprano
Suzanne	Contralto
Marguerite	Soprano
Madeleine	Contralto
An Errand Girl	Soprano
A Street-Sweeper	Mezzo-Soprano
A Young Rag-Picker	Mezzo-Soprano
A Forewoman	Mezzo-Soprano
A Milk Woman	Soprano
A Newspaper-Girl	Soprano
A Coal-Gatherer	Mezzo-Soprano
A Dancer	
Julien, *a young artist*	Tenor
Louise's Father	Bass
A Night-Prowler ('Noctambule')	Tenor
A Ragman	Bass
An Old Bohemian	Baritone
A Song Writer	Baritone
A Junkman	Bass
A Painter	Bass
Two Philosophers	Tenor, Bass
A Young Poet	Baritone
A Student	Tenor
Two Policemen	Baritone
A Street Arab	Soprano
A Sculptor	Baritone
An Old Clothes Man	Tenor
An Apprentice	Baritone
The King of Fools	Tenor

Street Pedlars, Workmen, etc.

Place: Paris
Time: 'The Present'
Running Time: 2 hours 20 minutes

*L*ouise is not so much the best of Charpentier as, a few early works apart, virtually his only musical legacy. He re-worked *La vie du poète*, a product of his sojourn in Rome after winning the Prix, for *Julien*, a sequel to *Louise* which, even with the benefit of Farrar and Caruso in the leads, failed at the Metropolitan. The large-scale *Fête du couronnement de la Muse*, written for an open-air ceremony in Montmartre, had already been cannibalised for *Louise*.

Charpentier was socially aware and nothing if not a believer in his own preaching, and in 1902 he founded the *Conservatoire populaire Mimi Pinson* in order to provide a free artistic education for the working girls of Paris. About the poverty of the working classes and women's emancipation he felt passionately, and in *Louise* he mixed realism and symbolism with the skill of a master, realism dominating the outer acts and the scene in the atelier, symbolism taking over with the intertwined figures of the Night Prowler, who stands for the evils of Paris (which Charpentier deplored) and free love (which he endorsed), and the King of the Fools, who presides over the city's glamour. When street criers and workers crawl like insects from the woodwork, the two ingredients mingle easily, and the mixture they make emerges half actual, half allegorical.

Paris is in the end Charpentier's theme – his own love story – and he has succeeded in suggesting a sense of freedom and pleasure against a background of struggle and even misery. The emancipated story as much as the music worked initially for *Louise*, but even today when you hear the swirl of the waltz which suggests the intoxification of Paris, you can see how the theme caught hold of a whole generation. Here was the pull of the forbidden at its most seductive. After its first night, Paul Dukas, a composer five years younger than Charpentier, pronounced an elegant verdict: 'The first and last acts are those of a master; the other two are those of an artist; the whole is the work of a man.'

There is a short prelude, which reiterates a figure used extensively in the course of the opera:

It is associated rather with the call of freedom, which, to Louise, is inextricably bound up with Julien, than with Julien himself. Three bars before the end of the prelude is heard a motif which refers to Louise's father.

Act I. A room in a working man's tenement. Opposite, a terrace belonging to an artist's studio. As the curtain goes up, Julien can be heard and seen serenading Louise to Ex. 1. Louise comes into the room in answer to his cries, and a conversation ensues between them. Louise has suggested Julien should write formally to her parents asking for her hand in marriage; if they refuse permission, she will run away with him. This, she insists, must be a last resort, as she loves her parents and hates the thought of parting with them on bad terms.

Louise asks Julien to tell her again how he first fell in love with her. He goes over it in detail – not for the first time we may imagine – from a description of his dreams (he is a poet) to the meeting of their realisation – herself – on the staircase: 'Depuis longtemps j'habitais cette chambre'. At the climax of his story, in comes Louise's Mother. She does not immediately make her presence known (except in the orchestra), but hides to listen to what is being said. The tender conversation continues and is not without its disparaging reference to the Mother, who finally puts an end to it by dragging Louise away. She sneaks back for just long enough to see the letter to her parents that Julien holds up to her.

The Mother reappears and shuts the window. Louise makes an effort to keep up appearances and arranges the supper, but her Mother imitates the tone of the conversation she has overheard, and mocks Louise's love for Julien. Only the sound of the Father coming up the stairs from work stops her laying hands on her unfortunate daughter. The Father comes in, asks whether supper is nearly ready, and proceeds to open the letter which Julien has left for him. Louise and her Father embrace – they are obviously very fond of one another – and the family sits down to table.

Louise takes the letter to her Father, who re-reads it, and appears to want to give the whole matter his consideration. But the Mother is furious, and, when Louise contradicts a particularly vicious insinuation about Julien, she slaps her face, to the Father's obvious displeasure. Her Father asks Louise to read the paper to him. She starts, but mention of spring in Paris is too much for her, and she dissolves in tears.

Act II. The prelude is called 'Paris s'éveille' (Paris awakes). A street at the foot of the hill of Montmartre, five o'clock on an April morning. The house where Louise works as a dressmaker is seen on one side of the stage. Various derelict citizens of Paris go about their business, whether it be the setting up of a stall from which to sell milk, or the search for something worthwhile among the rags and refuse of the city. One of the figures in this scene is the Night-Prowler. He is represented as a late reveller returning home, but he is also intended to symbolise the

'Plaisirs de Paris' for which Louise and those like her long so ardently. In his symbolism, Charpentier has made use of a pun on the word 'plaisir', which is also a kind of wafer, and whose street-seller's cry is associated musically with the Night-Prowler.

Julien and some Bohemian friends come to wait for Louise, in order to find out the answer to his letter. The girls who work at the dressmaker's begin to arrive, and they are soon followed by Louise and her Mother. The Mother leaves, Louise goes inside but is soon dragged out by Julien, who questions her about the letter. He is furious at her lack of rebellion; will she go back on her promise to come away with him?

The work room of the dressmaker's establishment. The girls sit round the tables, sewing and chattering. They notice that Louise has been crying, and suggest that she is in love. She denies it furiously, but Irma launches into a song on the subject of love, and soon the sound of a polka is heard from down below, immediately followed by the voice of Julien serenading: 'Dans la cité lointaine'. The girls are at first pleased, but seeing that his song is addressed apparently to none of them they begin to find it a bore. Louise can bear it no longer, asks them to explain that she has had to go home, and is later seen arm in arm with Julien in the street. Peals of laughter from the girls.

Act III. A little garden on the side of Montmartre. The prelude sets the scene with adumbrations of 'Tout être a le droit d'être libre'. Panorama of Paris; almost twilight. As the curtain rises, Louise sings her celebrated romance, 'Depuis le jour où je me suis donnée' (Oh day of joy when you became my lover). Life has changed for her since she came to live with Julien. 'Depuis le jour' has become a favourite aria, and its soaring lyricism has sufficient fervour to enable it to make a considerable impression even when heard out of context.

Louise explains that in her workshop no one took trouble about her or appeared to like her; even her father, who loves her, always treated her as a little girl, and her mother beat and scolded her ('Qui aime bien, châtie bien'). Together she and Julien rejoice at the sight of the lights of Paris coming up one after another, together they sing rapturously of their freedom: 'Tout être a le droit d'être libre' (All men have a right to be free), as much the egalitarian Charpentier's philosophy as theirs.

There follows the curious episode of the 'Couronnement de la Muse'.[1] Into the garden come Bohemians, who proceed to decorate the front of the house with paper lanterns and streamers. They are followed by a procession whose centrepiece turns out to be none other than the Night-Prowler of Act II, now dressed up as the King of the Fools. Louise is crowned Muse of Montmartre. But the jollity is suddenly interrupted when a sad figure is seen standing apart. It is Louise's Mother, who seems very different from the fire-eater of Act I. She comes to say that Louise's Father is very ill and desperately anxious to see her again. For a time, they had kept up the pretence that she was dead, but she had found him creeping along to Louise's room at night, and crying out her name. Julien is at first suspicious, but he eventually agrees that Louise may go home, the Mother promising that she shall return to him as soon as she wishes.

Act IV. The scene is the same as that of the first act. Julien's terrace is no longer visible. Louise is still with her parents, who have broken the promise to allow her to return to Julien. Her Father is just recovering from the illness which has kept him from work, but he has changed a good deal since we last saw him, and the contented and resourceful man of the first act has become a grumbler: 'Les pauvres gens peuvent-ils être heureux?' Everything is against him now, and he complains of the ingratitude of children, who would throw off the authority of those who love them and are prepared to die for them.

The significance of what he says is not lost on Louise. But she looks longingly through the window at Paris, and when her Mother says that they cannot think of letting her go back to Julien, in spite of their promise, she says wanly that he who laughs last laughs best. She goes to say goodnight to her Father, who kisses her lovingly and long and takes her in his arms. She draws away unresponsively, but he calls her to him, puts her on his knee as if she were still a child, and sings a *berceuse* to her: 'Reste ... repose-toi ... comme jadis toute petite' (Stay here ... stay here and rest ... as once you did when you were little). There is real feeling in this music, and for a moment the Father's self-pity can be forgotten.

But Louise's distress is too poignant to be ignored for long – and that is just what her parents seem to be trying to do. Louise reminds them of their promise, and then quietly but feelingly asserts her right to be free: 'Tout être a le droit d'être libre'. The sound of a waltz she heard during her brief period of freedom – the voice of Paris itself – calls to Louise. She responds passionately and invokes the name of the city to set her free. All the efforts of her Father are not enough to stifle the feeling growing within her. At last her Father loses his temper completely, orders her from the house, and even chases her round the room, until she runs out of the door. His anger spent, the father calls pitiably for Louise. Then he shakes his fist at the city, and the curtain falls on his cry: 'O Paris'.   H.

---

[1] The music is drawn from a composition of Charpentier's specially written for just such a ceremony in 1897. The Muse of Montmartre, chosen by popular vote, was to be publicly crowned, but owing to the appalling weather the function had to be put off until two years later.

ERNEST CHAUSSON
(born 20 January 1855, died 10 June 1899)

LE ROI ARTHUS
King Arthur

Opera in three acts, text by the composer. Première Brussels, 30 November 1903, with Paquot-d'Assy, Dalmorès, Albers, conductor Sylvain Dupuis. First performed Paris, 1916 (Act III only), conducted by Vincent d'Indy.

Guinevere, *Arthur's queen*..............Soprano
Arthur, *King of the Britons*............Baritone
Lancelot, *a knight*................................Tenor
Mordred, *Arthur's nephew* ....Baritone
Lyonnel, *Lancelot's retainer*................................Tenor
Allan, *an old squire* ....Bass
Merlin, *the wizard* ....Baritone
A Labourer ....Tenor
A Knight ....Bass
A Squire ....Bass
Four Soldiers ....Two Tenors, Two Basses

Knights, Squires, Pages, Bards, Women of Guinevere's Court

Running Time: 2 hours 50 minutes

Chausson, a man of wide culture, was captivated first by the music of Wagner, second by Celtic literature in general and by Arthurian legend in particular. His only opera was begun as early as 1885 and took most of the rest of his short working life (he was killed in a bicycling accident). The influence of *Tristan* is undeniable, both story and theme having much in common, but the music is very much that of a French composer, some commentators claiming it as the best of the group of works written under Wagnerian influence.

Act I. In his castle, Arthur welcomes his victorious knights, praising particularly Lancelot, to the disgust of his nephew Mordred. The latter is not only jealous of Lancelot's fame but of his clandestine love for Queen Guinevere, who has spurned the advances of Mordred.

The second scene consists of an extended love duet for Guinevere and Lancelot, over whose tryst watches a reluctant Lyonnel. Mordred surprises the lovers and is wounded by Lancelot, who leaves at Guinevere's behest. Mordred survives.

Act II. The atmosphere is peaceful as a peasant sings folk-like of the deeds of heroes. Lancelot is racked with guilt but Guinevere arrives to tell him that in spite of Mordred's accusations Arthur believes in him. She begs him to return to court, where she has publicly lied but where his testimony can still save her. He recoils from the lie, but she insists: only that will save her. Lancelot makes up his mind; he will go before the King ... and lie. Then, he will go into battle, and die. Guinevere having won one battle now urges their love, but Lancelot changes his tack and will tell no lie but escape with her.

At Arthur's court, the King is a prey to doubt. Merlin finally answers his call and prophesies nothing but doom. Their joint work is finished, the Round Table will perish, let the King ask him no more! He gets no answer to his questions about Guinevere and Lancelot, and the act ends in confusion as the old King sets off after his betrayer.

Act III. Lancelot has fled in horror at the prospect of battle with Arthur, whose right he acknowledges, and in spite of Guinevere's entreaties, he entrusts her to esquires who will take her to his ship. In despair she strangles herself with her own hair.

Lancelot has rushed unarmed into battle but is not dead as the King gazes on his body. He revives and begs Arthur to take revenge, then falls dead. Arthur mourns the loss of Guinevere and Lancelot, the two beings he held most dear, and the opera ends as he is apparently borne away to a better world.

Each act contains an extended duet for Guinevere and Lancelot, in some contrast to each other: a love duet; a duet of seduction as she persuades him to lie to the King; a duet where their power to control each other has evaporated. In spite of the apparent centrality of the love of Lancelot for Guinevere, it is Arthur who is the opera's most powerful figure, from his dignified address to his court at the outset, through the agonised consultation with Merlin to the final transfiguration.   H.

LUIGI CHERUBINI

(born early September 1760, died 15 March 1842)

MÉDÉE

Medea

Opera in three acts, text (in French) by François Benoit Hoffmann, after Euripides. Première at Théâtre Feydeau, Paris, 13 March 1797, with Scio, Gaveaux, Dessaules. First performed in Berlin, 1800; Vienna, 1814, with Milder-Hauptmann; London, 1865, at Her Majesty's, with Tietjens, Günz, Santley; 1870, at Covent Garden, with Tietjens. The spoken dialogue of the original was set to music by Franz Lachner in 1854 and by Arditi for the London production of 1865 (Lachner's recitatives have been used for most modern presentations). The opera was heard at la Scala in 1909 with Mazzoleni, conductor Vitale, but not subsequently revived until in 1953 at the Florence Festival Callas sang it for the first time with Tucci, Barbieri, Picchi, Petri, conductor Gui (subsequently Callas was responsible for revivals at la Scala, Venice, Rome, and in 1958 at Dallas and at Covent Garden). Revived 1958, Cassel, with Gerda Lammers; 1959, Covent Garden, with Callas, Carlyle, Cossotto, Vickers, Zaccaria; 1962, Paris Opéra with Rita Gorr; 1968, Venice, with Gencer; 1969, Buenos Aires, with Gwyneth Jones; 1971, Frankfurt, with Silja; 1971, Mantua, with Olivero; 1972, Vienna, with Rysanek. First performance in England of original Cherubini score, Durham, by the Palatine Group, 1967; 1984, Buxton Festival, with Rosalind Plowright, and 1996 by Opera North with Josephine Barstow.

Médée (Medea), *former wife of Jason* ....Soprano
Jason, *leader of the Argonauts* ....Tenor
Dircé (Glauce), *daughter of Créon* ....Soprano
Créon, *King of Corinth* ....Bass
Néris, *servant of Médée* ....Mezzo-Soprano
First Maidservant ....Soprano
Second Maidservant ....Soprano

Two Children of Médée, Servants of Dircé,
  Argonauts, Priests, Soldiers, People of Corinth

Place: Corinth
Time: Antiquity
Running Time: 2 hours 10 minutes

Cherubini, after study in Italy and performance there and even in England, found success in France in 1788 and remained there for effectively the rest of his life, writing operas for Paris well into the Napoleonic period. In spite of the intensely serious nature of the subject and indeed Cherubini's treatment of it, *Médée* with its spoken dialogue is technically an *opéra-comique*, and it was thus produced with great success in both Berlin and Vienna, the German-speaking stage providing the composer with some of his most lasting success.

In 1855, in response to contemporary taste, the German composer Franz Lachner turned *Médée* into a through-composed opera, adding extensive recitative in place of the spoken dialogue, and in this guise it continued intermittently in the repertory for more than a century. Recordings, starting with Callas in the 1950s, were by and large of the Lachner version and only relatively late in the twentieth century did the original version replace Lachner's successful but unidiomatic (because highly romanticised) edition.

Jason, rightful heir to the throne of Thessaly, at his coming of age was set the task of recovering the Golden Fleece by his uncle, the usurper, Pelias. In the *Argo* he sailed to Colchis, where with the help of the King's daughter Médée he accomplished his mission and ended by eloping with her. King Aeetes followed the *Argo*, but Médée, to delay the pursuit, had her young brother Absyrtus cut up and thrown into the sea, knowing that Aeetes would collect the pieces in order that they might be decently buried. Arrived safely in Thessaly, Médée caused the death of Pelias, but Jason eventually abandoned her, and with his two sons fled to Corinth.

Act I. The overture's format, content and style perhaps explain why Beethoven held Cherubini in such esteem – it is a piece of high seriousness and a fitting precursor of an operatic version of Greek tragedy by one of the composers who most benefited from Gluck's theories. The curtain rises on the royal court of Créon at Corinth. Dircé, Créon's daughter, is surrounded by her women, two of whom lead the others in a graceful serenade to their mistress, whose marriage to Jason is planned for the next day. Eventually their pleas seem to allay some of her forebodings and she sings an aria, praying the God of Love to help her against Médée: 'Hymen, viens dissiper' ('O Amore, vieni a me!') – a rewarding solo of considerable technical difficulty and built on an ample scale.

Créon enters with Jason and assures him of his support, even when the people, incensed against Médée, demand the lives of her children in default of her own. Jason announces that his sailors wish to offer the Golden Fleece in homage to Dircé. Dircé still fears that Médée will disrupt her happiness, but Jason in an aria does his best to reassure her: 'Eloigné pour jamais d'une épouse cruelle' ('Or che più non vedrò quella sposa crudele'). In a beautiful solo, to which Dircé, Jason and the Chorus later add their voices, Créon invokes the blessings of the Gods on the forthcoming marriage: 'Dieux et Déesses tutélaires' ('Pronube Dive, Dei custodi').

This trio is the end of tranquillity throughout the opera. An unknown woman enters and unveils herself to reveal Médée. The citizens and Argonauts retire, fearful of what may result from Médée's presence. Créon threatens her with imprisonment if the next day dawns to find her still in Corinth, and then all depart, leaving her face to face with Jason.

Médée is confident that the new and the old love struggle in his breast for supremacy: he can never forget his love for her nor what she has done for him. In a great aria, 'Vous voyez de vos fils la mère infortunée' ('Dei tuoi figli la madre tu vedi'), she pleads her love for him – she, who has never before abased herself in front of anyone, begs for his pity and his love. Her repeated cries of 'Ingrat!' ('Crudel!') would melt the heart of a stronger man than Jason, and it is quite clear from the succeeding duet that his resistance will not stand up unaided against Médée's wiles. Together they curse the fatal Golden Fleece, and he bids her go. She rounds on him: 'Si tel est son malheur ton épouse en fuyant te percera le coeur! Ingrat!' ('Medea col suo fuggir il cor strapperà! Crudel!')' The whole scene between Médée and Jason – her aria and the extended duet – is a splendid example of Gluckian music drama.

Act II. The scene represents Créon's palace on one side of the stage, the Temple of Hera on the other, and the drama begins straight away in the orchestra. Médée inveighs against an injustice that would teach her children to hate their mother. Néris, her confidante, tells her that the mob is gathering and demands her blood, but Médée does not hesitate. She will stay. At that moment, Créon comes out, urging her to fly the country – if she remain, even he will not be able to save her. In a scene of some power Médée pleads her cause with Créon, but he is adamant, supported by his warriors. Suddenly Médée seems to realise that her case is hopeless; she begs for one more day and Créon has not the heart to refuse her. As Créon and his retinue retire to the palace, Médée collapses on the steps. Néris dare not interrupt her brooding silence; she will weep with her mistress and be faithful until death. It is a beautiful, mournful aria ('Ah, nos peines': 'Solo un pianto') that Néris sings with bassoon obbligato, the only moment of repose that the drama allows between the entrance of Médée and the final catastrophe.

Médée is implacable – Créon has granted her a day's grace, she will know how to use it! Her rival must die. More – is Jason not a father? As her thoughts begin to appal even her, Jason enters. Médée asks to see her children and rejoices at his evident love for them. In the course of their duet, Médée pretends that her heart will break if she never sees them again and Jason agrees to let them stay with her until her departure from Corinth.

Médée orders Néris to bring her children to her, moreover to fetch as a wedding-present for Dircé the diadem and mantle once blessed by Phoebus Apollo. Néris is astonished at such generosity but leaves to fulfil her mistress's command as the wedding music

is heard. Créon, Jason, Dircé, priests, warriors and citizens go in procession to the Temple of Hera, while Médée curses the wedding hymns to which she is listening. As the procession emerges from the temple, Médée hurls herself at the altar, seizes a burning brand and runs with it out of sight.

Act III. A hill, surmounted by a temple, on one side of which can be seen Créon's palace. It is night and there is thunder. A short orchestral prelude of considerable power leads to the appearance of Médée before the temple. For the first time we see the sorceress in her true colours as she invokes the Infernal Gods to aid her purpose, the more so as she feels her resolve weaken at the sight of the children brought to her by Néris. She cannot bring herself to plunge a dagger into their defenceless breasts, and laments the power they still have over her: 'Du trouble affreux' ('Del fiero duol'), but ends the aria with a renewed threat of vengeance on Jason.

Néris tells of Dircé's grateful reception of Médée's gift, and Médée gloats over the fate that will be hers once she places the poisoned jewels on her forehead. Néris begs her to be content with this revenge and spare her children. At her mistress's command she takes them into the temple, and Médée is a prey to indecision; she must have a full revenge, but they are her children as well as Jason's. At last all pity is purged from her heart. The cry can be heard from those in the temple who are witnesses to Dircé's horrible death, and Médée sets off like a wild beast to complete her vengeance. Jason appears with the crowd, Néris reveals Médée's purpose, but before he can reach the entrance of the temple, Médée emerges, flanked by the three Furies and brandishing in her hand the knife with which she has killed the children. As Jason, Néris and the crowd scatter, the temple bursts into flames. It is Médée's ultimate revenge.

Médée is a serious work of art and contains a splendid title role. Teresa Tietjens made it her most famous impersonation in the 1870s and '80s, and it is one of the several operas of the classical epoch revived in the middle of the twentieth century for Maria Callas. Her dramatic intensity and magnificently constructive musical gifts were peculiarly well suited to this role, and she, a Greek, was assisted in the London revival of 1959 by a Greek producer, Alexis Minotis, a Greek designer, John Tsarouchis, and a Greek bass, Nicola Zaccaria.   H.

FRANCESCO CILEA
(born 26 July 1866, died 20 November 1950)

ADRIANA LECOUVREUR

Opera in four acts, text by Colautti, from the play by Scribe and Legouvé. Première at Teatro Lirico, Milan, 26 November 1902, with Pandolfini, Ghibaudo, Caruso, de Luca, conductor Campanini. First performed Covent Garden, 1904, with Giachetti, Anselmi, Sammarco, conductor Campanini; Metropolitan, New York, 1907, with Cavalieri, Caruso, Scotti, conductor Ferrari. Revived la Scala, Milan, 1932, with Cobelli, Pederzini, Pertile, Ghirardini, conductor Ghione; 1942, with Cobelli; Metropolitan, New York, 1963, with Tebaldi, Corelli; Edinburgh Festival, 1963 (by San Carlo Opera, Naples), with Magda Olivero, Oncina, Bruscantini. Magda Olivero has been one of the most famous of recent exponents of the title role.

Maurizio, *Count of Saxony*..................................Tenor

Prince de Bouillon..Bass

The Abbé de Chazeuil.......................................Tenor

Michonnet, *stage director of the*
    Comédie-Française .... Baritone

Members of the company
    Quinault.. Bass
    Poisson .... Tenor
    Mlle Jouvenot... Soprano
    Mlle Dangeville ....Mezzo-Soprano

Major-Domo ....Tenor

Adriana Lecouvreur.......................................Soprano

Princesse de Bouillon ....Mezzo-Soprano

Ladies, Gentlemen, Servants

Place: Paris
Time: 1730
Running Time: 2 hours 15 minutes

Cilea wrote two successful operas, *L'Arlesiana* and *Adriana Lecouvreur*, before he was forty, but for the remainder of his long life his success was limited, apart from his appointment as Director of the Naples Conservatory where he had been a student.

Act I. The foyer of the Comédie-Française. Actors and actresses going on to the stage demand their swords, hats, coats from Michonnet, who complains that everyone expects him to do everything at once. The Prince de Bouillon comes in with his crony the Abbé and greets the company. The Prince is the 'protector' of the actress Duclos, Adriana's rival, but he flatters Adriana as she tries over her speech. She says she is only the handmaid of the arts: 'Io son l'umile

ancella'. It is Cilea's finest inspiration, and the tune is heard frequently throughout the opera as a 'motto'.

Michonnet is her best friend, she tells them all, and the faithful Michonnet bursts into tears of emotion; when all have left he admits the reason – he has been in love with Adriana since she joined the company. Dare he tell her now? He starts to, but she tells him she is in love with an unknown officer, Maurizio, attached to the Count of Saxony. Michonnet leaves her alone, and in a moment her as yet unknown lover is at her side. He addresses her in a passionate arioso: 'La dolcissima effigie'. Adriana says she will play only for him tonight, giving him before she leaves violets for his buttonhole.

Now begins the comedy of the letters. The Abbé has found a *billet-doux* which he and the Prince decide is from Duclos making an assignation for that very night with the Count of Saxony at the Prince's villa outside Paris. He will invite the company to surprise them! Meanwhile, Michonnet has mislaid a property letter which, when found, is used by the Count to warn Adriana that he cannot sup with her that night as he had intended – Maurizio is of course the Count himself.

Act II. The Prince and the Abbé were mistaken; the letter they found was not from Duclos to the Count but from the Prince's wife, who now reflects agitatedly on the torments of love: 'Acerba voluttà'. Maurizio arrives and the Princess says she has interceded for him with the Queen. She notices the violets and asks whether they had nothing to do with his lateness; he says it was for her he brought them ('L'anima ho stanca').

A carriage is heard outside; it is her husband, exclaims the Princess – she must hide. The Prince de Bouillon, accompanied by the Abbé, comes in to find Maurizio alone. They taunt him with being caught and are astonished when he threatens a duel. Why make so much fuss? The Prince is tired of Duclos; why should not the Count of Saxony take her on? Maurizio begins to understand when, a moment later, Adriana is let in and introduced to him. This time, the astonishment is hers: the man she had thought a retainer turns out to be the Count of Saxony himself. The Prince and the Abbé don't like being kept waiting for supper and Adriana and Maurizio are alone.

In a short duet they renew their passionate vows. Michonnet comes in asking that he may speak to Duclos, as an important decision has to be made over a new role before morning. She is here, says the Abbé; Maurizio tries to silence him, but Michonnet takes the decision into his own hands and goes firmly into the room which Maurizio has tried to bar. Maurizio swears to Adriana that Duclos is not there; his appointment had to do with his political position, not with love. She believes him, and Michonnet comes out saying it was not Duclos. The Abbé wants to discover the lady's identity and this time Adriana tells Michonnet she means to keep her word to Maurizio and help the unknown lady.

Adriana knocks at the door and tells whoever is inside that, with the aid of the key of the garden, she can save her. The Princess plies her with questions and eventually admits that she loves Maurizio. Adriana proudly, to the tune of her recent duet with him, claims his love as her own. The act ends as the Princess escapes before the Prince and his followers can catch her.

Act III. A party is in preparation at the house of the Prince de Bouillon. The Princess wonders to herself where she has heard the voice of her rival. The guests come in, amongst them Adriana, whom the Princess naturally recognises immediately, and who sings the tune originally heard to the words of 'Io son l'umile ancella'. The Princess mutters something about Maurizio being wounded in a duel, and Adriana shows obvious signs of emotion. Maurizio comes in and is persuaded to talk about his battle experiences. A ballet entertainment has been arranged, and during its course the conversation continues, developing in the end into a battle of wits between the Princess and Adriana, which the latter wins as she recites the confession of adultery from Racine's *Phèdre* and aims the speech at the Princess.

Act IV. The scene is as in Act I. Michonnet waits for Adriana who seems in a mood bordering on suicide. Various actors and actresses congratulate her on her birthday and presently a casket is brought in. Adriana opens it and sees in it the violets she had given Maurizio the previous evening, by now old and mouldy. She sings sadly to the violets, in whose shrivelled appearance she sees the dying of Maurizio's love for her: 'Poveri fiori'. Michonnet comforts her and smiles when he hears Maurizio outside. Adriana cannot resist Maurizio's protestation of innocence, least of all when he proposes marriage to her and tells her in the same breath that all his claims have been met and he is once more in possession of his rightful titles. She tries to impress him by saying that the stage is the only throne she can ever mount, but his love is too much for her and she and Maurizio rest happily in each other's arms.

Suddenly, she seems about to faint and thinks it had something to do with the flowers that she gave Maurizio and which he sent back to her, but he denies ever having done such a thing. Adriana is convulsed with pain, and for a moment does not recognise him. Maurizio sends for help; Michonnet thinks the flowers were poisoned and suggests a rival has done it. After a further convulsion, Adriana dies. The Princess's revenge is complete.

Some of the figures in the opera were real people, Adrienne Lecouvreur a star at the Comédie-Française. But the plot is fiction and cuts made during rehearsal often make it hard to follow.   H.

DOMENICO CIMAROSA
(born 17 December 1749, died 11 January 1801)

IL MATRIMONIO SEGRETO
The Secret Marriage

Opera buffa in two acts, text by Giovanni Bertati after Colman's *The Clandestine Marriage*. First performed at the Burgtheater, Vienna, 7 February 1792; la Scala, Milan, 1793; London, 1794; New York, 1834; Her Majesty's, 1842. Revivals include Metropolitan, 1937; Rome, 1948, with Alda Noni and Cesare Valletti; la Scala, Milan, 1949, with Alda Noni, Hilde Gueden, Fedora Barbieri, Tito Schipa, Boris Christoff, and Sesto Bruscantini; Fortune Theatre, London,

1949; Edinburgh Festival, by Piccola Scala, 1957, with Sciutti, Ratti, Alva, conductor Sanzogno; Glyndebourne, 1965; Buxton Festival, 1994, and Opera North, 1995, in Jonathan Miller's production.

Geronimo...Buffo Bass

Elisetta, *his daughter*.......................................Soprano

Carolina, *another daughter* ....Soprano

Fidalma, *Geronimo's sister* ....Mezzo-Soprano

Count Robinson, *an English milord*.......................Bass

Paolino ....Tenor

Place: Bologna
Time: Eighteenth Century
Running Time: 2 hours 50 minutes

Cimarosa's most famous opera has the distinction of being reputedly the only work ever encored *in toto* on the occasion of its first performance. History has it that the Emperor Leopold II, for whom Mozart wrote *La Clemenza di Tito* a few months earlier, so enjoyed the work that he invited all the participants to supper, after which the performance was repeated!

The story is concerned with events at the house of one Geronimo, a wealthy citizen of Bologna, whose sister Fidalma is installed as mistress of his house, and who has two daughters, Elisetta and Carolina.

Act I. We meet Carolina and Paolino, the latter a junior business associate of Geronimo's and secretly married to Carolina. In their first duet she urges him to hide the secret of their marriage no longer but to reveal it to everyone. There is another duet in lighter vein as Carolina says goodbye to her husband. Geronimo appears, inclined to deafness and definitely afflicted by the golden malady of the *nouveau riche*. He learns from Paolino that the latter's friend, the English Count Robinson, is on his way to Bologna with the firm intention of arranging a match with Elisetta, Geronimo's other daughter. Nothing will please him but to recount the news with all its import to his family, which he does in a *buffo* aria. The sisters immediately find cause to quarrel, much to Fidalma's annoyance; a trio brings the quarrel to a musical climax.

Fidalma admits to Elisetta that she herself is in love – she underlines it in a song – but she will not admit with whom, though she whispers in an aside to the audience that it is Paolino.

Geronimo cannot wait for the Count's arrival. The English nobleman duly appears and proceeds to address everyone with a maximum of words and a minimum of content – he hates a man who cannot

be brief, he says. The situation develops until it becomes, musically speaking, a sextet, and the Count mistakes both the other ladies in turn for the Elisetta who is his bride-to-be. In conversation with Paolino shortly afterwards he reveals that the prospect of marriage with Elisetta fills him with consternation, while he looks with nothing but favour on union with Carolina – a fact which causes Paolino not a little concern. The Count proposes to Carolina, but is told as politely as possible that she is not disposed to welcome his proposal; she even lists in her aria the faults which she says she possesses.

Preparations are being made for the banquet which is to be given in the Count's honour when that worthy himself enters, protesting his love to Carolina. Elisetta interrupts and upbraids them for their conduct, but Fidalma manages to silence the quarrel which ensues by warning them that Geronimo approaches. He does his best to discover what is the cause of all the fuss, but his deafness, Paolino's unwillingness to let him find out that the Count wishes to marry Carolina, Fidalma's preoccupation with avoiding a family quarrel, and the fact that everyone talks at once, prevent him from carrying out his intention.

Act II. Geronimo is still trying to find out what it is all about, and he is found alone with the Count. After some misunderstanding, he gathers that his prospective son-in-law has not taken kindly to his bride-to-be. After voicing their mutual dissatisfaction, the two parties come to an agreement when the Count suggests that he relinquish half the dowry he has been promised if Geronimo will allow him to marry the younger of his two daughters. This arrangement suits Geronimo admirably, and their duet ends in complete accord.

Paolino is told of the new arrangement, and in his desperation is just going to throw himself on Fidalma's mercy, when she, encouraged by what she takes to be glances and sighs directed at her, says that she will accept his proposal and marry him! Paolino can stand the strain no longer and faints away. It is while Fidalma is trying to revive him that Carolina comes on the scene. Fidalma goes to fetch some smelling salts, and the wretched Paolino tries to explain the situation to Carolina, but it is not until the trio is over and he is able to embark on an aria that he manages to convince her that his protestations of love are not mere deceit.

The Count now tries, by depicting himself as an ogre and a monster of iniquity, to persuade Elisetta to break off the marriage. He fails in his object, and Elisetta and Fidalma (who has revealed that Carolina, though the object of the Count's affections, is herself in love with Paolino) plot to rid themselves of their rival and send her to a convent. Geronimo agrees, and tells her himself of his decision. Poor Carolina is broken-hearted, and her music takes on a moving character as she thinks of the future without her husband. The Count offers his help in her distress, and she is just about to tell him the whole truth when her sister, her aunt, and her father jump out on them declaring that there can be no further doubt since they have caught them in the act. Geronimo sends Paolino off at once with a letter to the Mother Superior of the convent.

The finale begins. The Count is out of his room, although it is night, and muses on the possibility of helping Carolina, when he is surprised by the watchful Elisetta; they say goodnight to each other and depart, to be succeeded by Paolino and Carolina planning an elopement. Disturbed by a noise, they quickly hide in Carolina's room, and in a moment the suspicious Elisetta is on the scene. She listens at the door, hears whispers, and rouses the house to come and catch the Count in her sister's room. Everyone rushes to the spot and together they demand that the Count shall come forth and reveal her perfidy. He does – but from his own room, where he has been asleep until woken up by the din. A moment later, Carolina and Paolino come out of their room and admit that they were married two months ago. Eventually, all is forgiven, the Count agrees to marry Elisetta, and happiness reigns supreme.

Cimarosa's main disadvantage *vis-à-vis* a modern audience is that his music reminds them, now of Mozart, now of Rossini, and that in each case they are inclined to compare him unfavourably with the greater and more familiar master. But there is a quantity of excellent music in this opera; the two finales are models of their kind, as are the arias for Carolina and Paolino, and the comedy duet between Geronimo and the Count.   H.

PETER CORNELIUS

(born 24 December 1824, died 26 October 1874)

DER BARBIER VON BAGDAD

The Barber of Baghdad

Opera in two acts, text, based on a story from the *Arabian Nights*, by the composer. First performed at Weimar, conducted by Liszt, on 15 December 1858. As a result of the feud between Liszt, Weimar's head of music, and Dingelstedt, the manager of the theatre, the first night was made the occasion of a showdown on the part of their rival adherents, and the opera was a fiasco; Liszt resigned his position, and the opera was not given again during the composer's lifetime. Revived Hanover, 1877, and again a failure. Revised and re-orchestrated by Felix Mottl, produced at Karlsruhe, 1885, and in many other German theatres. Metropolitan, New York, 1890, conducted by Damrosch; Savoy Theatre, London, 1891, by students of the Royal College of Music; Covent Garden, 1906, conducted by Richter. Revived Metropolitan, 1925, with Rethberg, Laubenthal, and Bender; London Opera Club, 1949; Vienna Volksoper, 1949, with Jurinac, Dermota and Edelmann; Edinburgh Festival, 1956, by Hamburg Opera.

The Caliph ....Baritone
Baba Mustapha, *a Cadi* ....Tenor
Margiana, *his daughter* ....Soprano
Bostana, *a servant of the Cadi* ....Mezzo-Soprano
Nureddin ....Tenor
Abul Hassan Ali Ebn Bekar, *a barber*....................Bass

Nureddin's Servants, Friends of the Cadi, the Caliph's Entourage

Place: Baghdad
Running Time: 2 hours 5 minutes

When he was twenty-five, Cornelius wrote that he was clear in his mind that his natural bent was towards operatic comedy. Considering the success which he achieved in his one attempt at this genre (a posthumous success unfortunately), it seems a pity that his two other operas should have been on serious subjects; neither has had anything like the number of performances *Der Barbier* has collected since the composer's death.

Originally Cornelius planned *Der Barbier* in one act, with an extended final scene occupying something like a third of the whole work. Later, he decided on two acts of equal length. After the unsuccessful première, Liszt persuaded the composer to re-write his overture, and instead of the comedy prelude to substitute something based on the themes of the opera itself. Cornelius died before he could orchestrate the new overture, and this was done after his death by Liszt. For the revivals they conducted, both Mottl and Levi made a number of changes in the orchestration, and it was not until 1904 that the opera was given in the form (and orchestral dress) Cornelius had intended.

The D major overture – that is to say the one written at Liszt's suggestion – is based on references to the Barber's theme, his patter song, Nureddin's appeal to the absent Margiana, the assignation duet between Nureddin and Bostana, and the chorus of Nureddin's servants.

Act I. Nureddin is lying on a couch at his house, nursing his apparently hopeless love for Margiana. He and his servants, scorning the more scientific forms of diagnosis, fear that his life is in danger. The servants' chorus and Nureddin's love song are delightfully sentimental, and he repeats the name Margiana in the apparent hope that it will ameliorate his sufferings. Left alone, Nureddin again conjures up a vision of his beloved, 'Vor deinem Fenster die Blumen versengte der Sonne Strahl', a song of charmingly romantic character.

To assuage his sufferings comes Bostana, an aged relation of Margiana's father, the Cadi. She tells him that Margiana will receive him that very day when her father goes to the mosque at noon. Before she goes, she prescribes a bath and a shave for him. With a last 'Don't forget the barber' (she has recommended her own favourite to him), she leaves the lover to contemplate his prospective bliss in an ecstatic *allegro*, 'Ach, das Leid hab' ich getragen, wie ertrag' ich nun mein Glück?'

He is too occupied to notice the entrance of the barber, Abul Hassan Ali Ebn Bekar, carrying with him his towel, his basin, a looking-glass and other apparatus of his calling, and, in addition, an astrolabe, with which he is accustomed to foretell his clients' futures. Nureddin is anxious to be shaved straight away, but he has to do with the most garrulous man in Baghdad, and the barber tells him at length and in a series of ingenious multiple rhymes exactly how fortunate it is that Nureddin should have chosen him.

Nureddin tries to make him get on with the shaving, but Abul must first cast his horoscope. This he does to the accompaniment of Nureddin's rapidly rising impatience, and having finished, once again puts forward his own qualifications in a brilliant patter song. Nureddin, not without justification by now, tells him he is nothing but a chatterbox. This fills the barber with righteous indignation; his brothers it is true were talkative, but he, the youngest of the family, has always been known for his virtue and his taciturnity. Things seem to be out of hand, and Nureddin yells for his servants to come and deliver him from this plague of a barber. Their attempts are successful up to a point, but, just as they get him to the door, the barber flourishes his razor and succeeds in turning them out.

Nureddin resorts to tact, and the barber is soon ready to begin operations, ready that is to say until his client lets fall the word 'Margiana' from his lips. This starts a flood of reminiscence; the barber himself was once in love with a Margiana – and this is the song he used to sing to her. He is delighted that Nureddin is in love, but horrified to hear that his Margiana is the daughter of Cadi Baba Mustapha, a villain, he says, who shaves himself.

Nureddin advises him to go back to his doubtless innumerable other customers, but the barber soliloquises in his absence on the disastrous effect women can have on a man's life: 'So schwärmet Jugend'. What was the ruin of all his six brothers? Love – and the catalogue of their respective misfortunes is punctuated by references to the world 'Lieben'. Cornelius's ingenuity in varying this repetition is no less to be admired than the old man's ability to find a topic to suit every occasion and, having found it, to dilate upon it endlessly.

Nureddin returns, and is horrified to find the barber still there and fully intending to accompany him to Margiana's house. He calls his servants again, and instructs them to minister to the barber, who, he tells them, is very ill; let them put him to bed and keep him there, sparing no remedy whatsoever. The servants are delighted at the prospect of getting their own back. The last we hear of them is their recital of the barber's names in five-part harmony.

Act II. The Intermezzo is based on the figure associated with the Muezzin's call to prayer. The melody is varied throughout and the effect is a delightful anticipation of the moment when Nureddin meets his Margiana for the first time. We are in the Cadi's house. Margiana expresses her delight at the prospect of Nureddin's arrival: 'Er kommt, er kommt, o Wonne meiner Brust!' Bostana rushes in and expresses the same sentiment in an identical melody, only to be joined some moments later by the Cadi, whose sentiments are made known in exactly similar terms, but of course for very different reasons. The women rejoice that Nureddin is coming, the Cadi is excited at the thought of his rich friend Selim's arrival from Damascus, bringing with him splendid presents and a request for the hand of Margiana in marriage. The trio is one of the most beautiful numbers in the score. A chest arrives from Damascus full of the expected treasures, and Margiana is dutifully pleased that her father is happy. Into the general rejoicings comes the sound of the Muezzin, sung off-stage by a bass and two tenors; the chant is taken up by the three characters on-stage, and the Cadi goes off to the mosque.

In a moment Nureddin is in the room, and he launches into a declaration of his love, which is taken up by Margiana: 'O holdes Bild in Engelschöne'. The duet has a cool, almost innocent feel about it, as is suitable for a first, almost formal declaration of love. The idyllic scene is interrupted by the sound of the Barber's voice from down below. He assures Nureddin that he is safe with so faithful a watchdog, and starts to sing his own love song. To it are added the howls of a slave who has broken the Cadi's favourite vase and is being punished out of hand by his master on his return from the mosque.

The situation takes a turn for the worse when Abul, hearing the screams of the slave, construes them as meaning the Cadi is murdering Nureddin, and yells for help. The sound of a crowd shouting hostile remarks about the Cadi can be heard below, as Nureddin is bundled into the treasure chest, which is quickly emptied. When Abul bursts into the room, bringing with him some of Nureddin's servants, Bostana tries to tell him that the unlucky lover has been hidden in the chest, but he takes it into his head

that the box contains nothing but his friend's corpse. The servants are on the point of carrying out the chest when the Cadi returns and thinks they are stealing his treasure. The ensuing alliterative abuse was thought by Ernest Newman to have been intended as a parody of Wagner's alliterative methods in *The Ring*: Cornelius was Liszt's secretary and must certainly have seen the printed copy of the libretto which Liszt had as early as 1853.

The Cadi, the barber, the Cadi's friends and retainers, Nureddin's servants, women already in mourning for him, and a mixed crowd of inhabitants of Baghdad join in an ensemble of accusation and counter-accusation, during which the chest is turned upside down. It is only brought to an end by the arrival of the Caliph, suitably attended by magnificently uniformed soldiers. The Cadi explains that Abul is a thief who is stealing his daughter's treasure. Abul denies that he is a thief but accuses the Cadi of having murdered his friend and hidden the body in the chest. Margiana and Bostana return, and the Caliph tells Margiana to open the chest and show him what her father persists in describing as her treasure.

Nobody's consternation could be more genuine than the Cadi's when the senseless body of Nureddin is disclosed in the chest. 'He! Mustapha!' he exclaims, and the cry is taken up by the Caliph and Abul in an ensemble, which is later joined by Margiana and Bostana, who lament the untimely death of the young man. Abul has been bending over the 'dead' body and he brings the lamentation to an end by announcing that Nureddin is not dead after all, but only unconscious. The Caliph suggests that this is the moment when the barber's miraculous healing powers can suitably be brought into use. Abul starts off with a line from his love song to Margiana but with no result; he tweaks Nureddin's nose and ears and tries smelling salts on him. But the simultaneous application to his nose of the rose Margiana has given him, and to his ears of the second line of the love song, works the trick: Nureddin opens his eyes and gets up.

The Cadi joins the lovers' hands but the Caliph tells his soldiers to arrest the barber – merely, he assures him, in order that he may benefit from his advice and his story-telling which have been denied him so long. Abul leads the assembly in a song of praise to the Caliph, 'Heil diesem Hause', and everyone repeats the refrain, 'Salamaleikum'. H.

D

LUIGI DALLAPICCOLA

(born 3 February 1904, died 19 February 1975)

IL PRIGIONIERO

The Prisoner

Opera in a prologue and one act, text by the composer from *La Torture par l'espérance* by Villiers de l'Isle-Adam and *La Légende d'Ulenspiegel et de Lamme Goedzak* by Charles de Coster. Première, 1949, by Radio Italiana, Turin, in concert with Magda Laszlo, Emilio Renzi, Scipione Colombo, conductor Hermann Scherchen. First staged at Teatro Comunale, Florence, 20 May 1950, with Mario Binci replacing Renzi. First performed Essen, 1954; London (in concert), 1954, with Laszlo, Krebs, Willy Heyer, conductor Scherchen, and on stage in English, Sadler's Wells (by New Opera Company), 1959, with Rosina Raisbeck, Alexander Young, John Cameron, conductor Leon Lovett; Teatro Colon, Buenos Aires, 1954; City Center, New York, 1960, with Anne McKnight, Richard Cassilly, Norman Treigle, conductor Stokowski; la Scala, Milan, 1962, with Laszlo, Aldo Bertocci, Eberhard Wächter, conductor Sanzogno, producer Rennert. The publisher records that in the first dozen years after its première, there were no fewer than 186 performances of this modern opera on radio, concert platform and stage.

The Mother ....Dramatic Soprano
The Prisoner..Baritone
The Jailer ....Tenor
The Grand Inquisitor.......................................Tenor
Two Priests ....Tenor and Baritone
A 'Fra Redemptor' (or Torturer) ....Silent

Place: Saragossa
Time: Second Half of the Sixteenth Century
Running Time: 50 minutes

In 1955, Roman Vlad, in one[1] of an illuminating series of commentaries on Dallapiccola's music, described the composer's activity to date as having been in three periods: the first, 1930–36, predominantly diatonic; the second, lasting in to the war years, 'characterised ... by the constantly increasing number of chromatic threads which Dallapiccola wove into the diatonic fabric of his works. They tended to resemble actual twelve-note rows and ultimately absorbed the diatonic elements.' In the third phase, 'he began to adopt a systematic row-technique', and Vlad describes this as a period 'in which the composer achieves mastery of his own language', an arrival in effect at artistic maturity. *Il Prigioniero* belongs to this period of Dallapiccola's activity, and is the composer's second stage work, its predecessor the successful one-act opera *Volo di Notte* (1937–39, based on Saint-Exupéry's novel of night-flying, *Vol de Nuit*), its successors the 'sacra rappresentazione', *Job* (1950), and the ambitious *Ulisse*.

The opera was written between 1944 and 1947 and orchestrated in spring 1948. At the Maggio Musicale in 1950, the composer, at the last of many solo curtain calls, bowed ironically to a solitary detractor in the gallery (so enthusiastic as to have brought a whistle with him), as if in sympathy with Shaw's famous curtain speech in a comparable situation: 'You and I may know there's nothing in it, but who are we against so many?'

Dallapiccola substituted the anonymous Prisoner for the named hero of Villiers de l'Isle-Adam's story and added the figure of the Mother.

Prologue. The Mother is waiting to visit her son in prison, and sings in a *Ballata*[2] of the recurring dreams which haunt her sleep and in which she sees at the end of a dark cavern a figure, which terrifies her as it approaches and can be recognised as King Philip II until it changes imperceptibly into the image of Death. 'The Prologue is based', says Vlad, 'on the dodecaphonic combination set out in the impetuous dramatic statement with which the opera opens', Ex. 1:

---

[1] This and other quotations by Roman Vlad are from *The Score*.

[2] This and similar descriptions are quoted from *The Score*.

As the Mother's voice rises to a hysterical B flat, the off-stage chorus cuts her short with 'Fiat misericordia tua, Domine, super nos' (Let thy mercy prevail, O Lord) in the first *Intermezzo Corale*.

Act I. The curtain rises on a dark cell within the Inquisitor's Prison in Saragossa, where the Prisoner is in process of telling his Mother of the torture he has suffered and of how the Jailer, addressing him finally as 'Fratello' (Brother), Ex. 2, has led him back to faith

(Ex. 2)

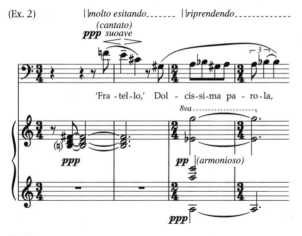

(Ex.3)

and hope and even to want to pray as in childhood (Ex.3). This is one of the three fundamental rows on which the whole opera is based.

Scene ii. The conversation is interrupted by the Jailer who gently encourages the Prisoner to new hope with the news that Flanders is in revolt and the great

bell Roelandt, symbol of liberty, about to ring out again. In this section of the opera appear first the two other fundamental rows which Dallapiccola has described as 'rows of hope and liberty'. The Jailer's description of events takes place in an *Aria in tre strofe*, and he leaves the Prisoner with the words 'There is one who watches over you ... Have faith, brother. Sleep now ... and hope.' The prisoner repeats the words as if he cannot believe them, then notices that the Jailer has left the cell door slightly ajar and rushes out.

Scene iii, following a short orchestral interlude, shows the successive stages of the Prisoner's slow and agonised attempt to make his way through the underground passages of the prison to freedom. The path of the Prisoner's 'escape' is complicated by the sight of a torturer, who does not see him, the passage of a couple of monks too engrossed in theological discussion to notice him, and finally by his perception of a draught of fresh air which encourages him to think he is nearing safety. He prays 'Signore, aiutami a salire!', and a moment later opens the door to hear as he thinks the great bell Roelandt.

A second *Intermezzo Corale*, sung as before by off-stage chorus, provides a climax, and indeed in the score the composer instructs that its 'sonority ... must be formidable; every spectator must feel literally swept away and drowned in the immensity of the sound. Mechanical means (loudspeakers etc.) should unhesitatingly be used if necessary to obtain this effect.'

Scene iv. The Prisoner is in a spring garden, under a starry sky. 'Alleluiah!' he sings at the prospect of freedom and moves towards a great cedar which dominates the foreground. In a kind of ecstasy, he spreads his arms towards the tree in a gesture of love towards all humanity – only for the choral background to his exuberant cries to shut off abruptly and to be succeeded by a soft 'Fratello' this time from the lips of the Grand Inquisitor, whose arms open as if part of the tree to embrace his captive: 'Why do you want to leave us now, on the very eve of your salvation?' As if to underline the thoughts of both protagonists, a brighter light is seen in the background, and the Prisoner comes to see that his ultimate fate is to gain salvation at the stake, just as certainly as he knows that the ultimate torture was hope. A small chorus intones a quotation from the *Canti di Prigionia*, almost muffling the last whispered 'La libertà?' (Freedom?) of the Prisoner.   H.

ULISSE

Opera in two acts, text by the composer. Première (in German) in Berlin, 29 September 1968, by Deutsche Oper, with Erik Saeden, conductor Lorin Maazel. First performed at la Scala, 1971.

Ulisse (Ulysses), *King of Ithaca*........................Baritone
Calypso ....Soprano
Penelope, *Ulisse's wife*..................................Soprano
Nausicaa, *daughter of King Alcinoo*.................Soprano
Two Maids ....Contralto, Soprano
King Alcinoo (Alcinous) ....Bass
Demodoco, *a bard at Alcinoo's court* ....Tenor
Tiresia (Tiresias), *a seer*....................................Tenor
Circe, *a siren*.......................................Mezzo-Soprano
Melanto, *a girl in Penelope's
    entourage* ....Mezzo-Soprano
Anticlea, *Ulisse's mother*...............................Soprano
Penelope's suitors
    Antinoo (Antinous)................................Baritone
    Pisandro (Pisander) ....Baritone
    Eurimaco (Eurymachus)............................Tenor
Eumeo (Eumaeus), *a shepherd*...........................Tenor
Telemaco (Telemachus), *son of
    Ulisse and Penelope* ....Counter-Tenor

Sailors, Lotus-Eaters, Courtiers

Place: The Mediterranean
Time: Thirteenth Century B.C.
Running Time: 2 hours 30 minutes

If Dallapiccola stands in the mid-twentieth century in relation to Italian music as Busoni did in the first quarter of the century, then *Ulisse* is his *Doktor Faust*, the culmination of a life's work, even though it was finished some seven years before he died. At the time of the première in 1968, he declared that he had been caught by the story of the *Iliad* since boyhood, that interest had been reawakened in 1938 by the prospect (unfulfilled) of a ballet on the subject, by work on Monteverdi's *Il Ritorno d'Ulisse* in 1941, and by a life-long admiration for Dante's interpretation of the legend. As with all his dramatic works, he said, he was intrigued by the theme of man's struggle against a superior force.

Prologue, scene i. Calypso laments Ulisse's abandonment of her. Poseidon, an invisible but potent influence, is evoked in the orchestral interlude.

Scene ii. Nausicaa. Girls play. Nausicaa in high-lying, lyrical music dreams of a man from afar who will become her husband. She joins in the game and flushes out Ulisse who is struck by her beauty.

Act I, scene iii. In King Alcinoo's palace, Demodoco recites the deeds of the Greek heroes of the Trojan War. The reference to himself prompts Ulisse to take up the narrative in flashback.

Scene iv. Ulisse starts his story as his ship reaches the Island of the Lotus-Eaters; some of his companions succumb to temptation and stay.

Scene v. After a year in her thrall, Ulisse finds strength to leave Circe, who takes revenge by assuring him his adventures are reflections of his own inner turmoil.

Scene vi. In search of clues to his destiny, Ulisse visits Hades, where he meets his mother, Anticlea, who tells him she died of despair at his absence; and Tiresia, who prophesies that he will return home but will later continue his wanderings.

Scene vii. At Alcinoo's court, the King promises to take Ulisse to Ithaca. Nausicaa is left disconsolate.

Act II, scene viii. Penelope's suitors plan to kill Telemaco, her son, returned to Ithaca after a fruitless search for his father. Melanto, a frivolous girl attracted to Antinoo, will report on events. Ulisse disguised as a beggar is welcomed by Eumeo, who has warned Telemaco. When Telemaco appears, Ulisse demands the names of the plotters, amazing Telemaco and Eumeo with his vehemence.

Scene ix. Ulisse arrives home and is sad his son failed to recognise him. The sound of Penelope singing indoors reminds him of Calypso, Nausicaa and his mother. Melanto remembers the look in the beggar's eyes, but is comforted by Antinoo. Ulisse decides it is time to act.

Scene x. In the banqueting hall, Antinoo gives Melanto Ulisse's bow, and asks her to dance. Telemaco enters to general consternation. Ulisse reveals his identity, takes the bow, orders the hanging of Melanto, shoots the suitors one by one, and is reunited with Penelope.

Scene xi. Tiresia was right; Ulisse finds no peace at home and is left on the open sea, a prey to doubts. H.

ALEKSANDR DARGOMIZHSKY

(born 14 February 1813, died 17 January 1869)

THE STONE GUEST

Kamennyi Gost'

Opera in three acts, text by Aleksandr Pushkin. Première at Mariinsky Theatre, St Petersburg, 20 February 1872, with F.P. Kommissarzhevsky as Don Juan. U.S. première, 1986; U.K. by English National Opera, 1987, with Graham Clark as Don Juan.

Don Juan ....Tenor
Leporello...Baritone
Donna Anna...Soprano
Laura ....Mezzo-Soprano
Don Carlos..Baritone
Monk..Bass
The Statue..Baritone
Guests ....Tenor, Baritone, Bass

Running Time: 1 hour 20 minutes

Dargomizhsky was encouraged in his studies by Glinka, but early failure in Russia as a composer induced him, like Glinka before him, to go abroad, in his case to Paris. His opera *Rusalka* (1856) is still current in Russia, but after it Dargomizhsky set to work on a radical scheme, the word-for-word setting of Pushkin's 'Little Tragedy' *The Stone Guest*, allowing as he said the words to dictate music and form. The work consists of continuous recitative, apart from two songs called for in the text, and is better known in discussion than in performance.

Act I. Don Juan with Leporello has returned from exile to Madrid, spurred by the boredom of provincial life, drawn by longing for the actress Laura, and defying both the royal order of banishment and the potential vengeance of the murdered Commendatore's relations. He is told that Donna Anna, the Commendatore's widow (Pushkin is the only writer to make Donna Anna widow rather than daughter), will come to pray at her husband's tomb and he waits for her, vowing to add her to his list of conquests.

Laura's latest flame Don Carlos is jealous when he learns her song was written by Don Juan, who once killed her brother in a duel. When Don Juan interrupts their scene, a duel quickly results in the death of Don Carlos. Laura resents the strife in her house, but cannot resist Don Juan.

Act II. At the Commendatore's tomb, Don Juan disguised as a monk waits for Donna Anna, who is impressed by his ardour and invites him, under the name of Don Diego di Calvido, to her home. He tells Leporello of the progress of his latest affair, then demands Leporello invite the statue to supper to witness in silence the seduction of his widow. The statue seems to move in response.

Act III. Donna Anna finds her guest irresistible and, even when she learns his true identity, cannot bring herself to send him away. There is a knocking at the door, and Don Juan when he goes to answer it finds the statue standing on the threshold. He accepts the hand the statue offers, but its grip is lethal.　　　　H.

PETER MAXWELL DAVIES

(born 8 September 1934)

The music of Sir Peter Maxwell Davies represents a rare and welcome fusion between native British tradition and a wider, European musical dimension. He has written some sixteen operas, whose formats have ranged from tradition-ally operatic, such as *Taverner* (1972) and *The Doctor of Myddfai* (1996), to masques, *Blind Man's Buff* (1972), *Le jongleur de Notre Dame* (1978), *Songs of Hoy* (1982) and *The No.11 Bus* (1984); chamber opera, *The Martyrdom of St Magnus* (1977) and *The*

Lighthouse (1980); children's opera, *The Two Fiddlers* (1978), *Cinderella* (1980) and *The Rainbow* (1981); and music theatre, *Eight Songs for a Mad King* (1969) and *The Medium* (1981). With the possible exception of *Resurrection* (1988), he has demonstrated an acute sense of theatre and a marked sensitivity to words (he has written many of his own librettos).

TAVERNER

Opera in two acts, libretto by the composer, inspired by 'John Taverner' in *Tudor Church Music*, ed. P.C. Buck, E.H. Fellowes, A. Ramsbotham and S. Townsend Warner, and based on sixteenth-century documents. First performed Covent Garden, 12 July 1972, with Ragnar Ulfung as Taverner, John Lanigan, Benjamin Luxon, Raimund Herincx, James Bowman and Gillian Knight, conducted by Edward Downes. First U.S. performance Boston, 1986, conducted by Sarah Caldwell.

John Taverner ....Tenor
Richard Taverner, *later* St John.....................Baritone
Cardinal, *later* Archbishop ....Tenor
King ....Bass
Jester, *later* Death *and* Joking Jesus................Baritone
White Abbot..Baritone
Priest-Confessor, *later*
    God the Father...............................Counter-Tenor
Boy..Treble
Captain ....Bass
Antichrist ....Tenor (Spoken)
Archangel Gabriel ....High Tenor
Archangel Michael......................................Deep Bass
Two Monks ....Tenors
Rose Parrowe, *later* Virgin Mary ....Mezzo-Soprano

Council, Monks, Demons, Townspeople, Choirboys

Place: London and Boston, Lincolnshire
Time: c. 1538
Running Time: 1 hour 55 minutes[1]

Peter Maxwell Davies began sketching music for an opera based on the life of John Taverner (1495–1545) while he was studying at Manchester University in the mid-1950s. In 1962 he wrote the First Fantasia on an 'In Nomine' by the earlier composer. He worked on the text while he was at Princeton (1962–64), and finished the music in 1970. Davies incorporates several elements of Taverner's own music, from his mass *Gloria Tibi Trinitas*, his 'In Nomine' and his Five Motets, into *Taverner*. Like *Lulu*, the opera balances around a central pivot: Act I's scenes are repeated in Act II in altered, parodied form.

Act I. A courtroom. John Taverner is on trial for heresy before the White Abbot. His father Richard blames Taverner's temper, but insists, 'His music is witness that he believes'. Taverner's mistress and muse, Rose Parrowe, defends him. His grotesque priest-confessor accepts a bribe and testifies against him, as does a boy from Taverner's choir-school. The Council expounds dogma and justifies capital punishment for heretics. Taverner is condemned to death by slow burning but reprieved by the Cardinal, because he is useful as a musician.

The chapel. Taverner has his doubts.

The throne room. A consort of viols and lute accompanies the Cardinal's consultation with the King, who is irritated by the Pope's delay in allowing him to get rid of his first wife. The Jester comments ironically. At the end of the scene he removes his mask to reveal the skull-face of Death.

Darkness, identified at the 1972 première as 'Taverner's skull'. The scene dramatises the conflict in Taverner's soul, which appears as a white dove, strangled by two Monks. Death challenges Taverner to be saved, to reject the paraphernalia of the Church of Rome, and also to reject his own art, his music and his mistress. Rose warns him that if he denies his art, he will betray what is divine in him. Death orders demons to perform a gaudy mystery play of the passion. Taverner is persuaded to repent.

Act II. The courtroom. In a scene 'conceived as a parody of Act I, Scene i', Taverner prosecutes the White Abbot for idolatry, but there is no reprieve: Death controls the Wheel of Fortune.

The throne room. A pantomime-ballet (Dance of Death) is performed aside. When the King learns the Pope has prohibited his second marriage he replaces the Church of Rome with the Church of England and is licensed by the Cardinal, recostumed by the Jester as the Archbishop of Canterbury. The King announces the dissolution of the monasteries.

The chapel. While the White Abbot celebrates mass

---

[1] Composer's own timing from the score.

and the monks chant, Taverner confesses that he took part in the corruption of the old order. Soldiers take over the monastery. Monks sing Taverner's setting of the *Benedictus*.

The market-place in Boston. From the scaffold the White Abbot speaks out: 'I am fell into the hands of those who, preaching free thought, do burn me for opposing it'. As the fire burns, Taverner appeals to God, 'Forsake not thy faithful servant'.

As it happens, the facts on which Maxwell Davies based the story have now been discredited. In the opera longueurs occur, partly because of the obscurity of the ideas themselves. On the other hand, *Taverner*'s scoring boasts an almost Puccinian variety and intensity: the opera is bell-haunted, using extraordinary means to simulate tintinnabulation; it delights in juxtaposing such extremes as monks chanting in Latin, over brass and wind, with an orchestral interlude featuring mournfully eloquent solo cello, violin and viola. It is perhaps characteristic of the opera's priorities that, when Taverner is corrupted by the Devil, the strings are asked to play with 'a maximum of nauseatingly sentimental vibrato'. The emotional weight of the opera is borne by the orchestra: none of the fiercely demanding vocal lines is as touching as the deeply felt, even romantic, *pianissimo* elegy for lower strings in the last scene's silent confrontation between Taverner and the Abbot.   P.

THE LIGHTHOUSE

'A chamber opera in a prologue and one act', libretto by the composer, based, in his words, on an incident described in 'Craig Mair's book on the Stevenson family in Edinburgh',[1] commissioned for the 1980 Edinburgh Festival. First performed there, 2 September 1980, with Neil Mackie (tenor), Michael Rippon (baritone) and David Wilson Johnson (bass), conductor Richard Dufallo. First U.S. performance Boston, 1983, directed by Peter Sellars and conducted by David Hoose. Toured widely by the Fires of London; Bremen, 1982; Salzburg and Copenhagen, 1983; Sydney and Gothenburg, 1984; Barcelona, 1986.

Sandy/Officer 1 ....Tenor

Blazes/Officer 2 ....Baritone

Arthur, Voice of the Cards/Officer 3 ....Bass

Place: Edinburgh and the Flannan Isles
Time: 1900
Running Time: 1 hour 25 minutes

*T*he Lighthouse is probably Maxwell Davies's most successful opera so far. Written for a small ensemble, the Fires of London which he founded in 1971, its theatricality exploits minimal means to considerable effect.

Prologue (Part I). The scene begins in the Courtroom, Edinburgh, where the officers who discovered the deserted lighthouse answer 'questions' posed by a solo horn, sometimes played from the back of the auditorium ('From the records of a court of enquiry into the unnatural disappearance of three lighthouse-keepers'). The officers relive their strange journey to the lighthouse, meeting first a sudden eddy 'where none had been' and then emerging into a calm that was 'more nerve-wracking than the storm'. The first officer sees a triangle of lights, which he calls 'the Angel of Death', but neither of the other officers sees it. They all hear foghorns from different directions, where there are no foghorns. As they step ashore they are watched by birds, but no lighthouse-keepers meet them. A chair and a cup have been broken. The court of enquiry records an open verdict. No one wants to replace the dead men, so an automatic lantern has been installed.

Part II. 'The Cry of the Beast'. Arthur's blessing on their meal is rejected by Sandy: storms have forced them to stay together longer than the normal three months, so their nerves are frayed. Arthur goes up to light the lantern. As Sandy and Blazes play cribbage together, the Voice of the Cards is heard from above. The two men quarrel. Arthur returns and rebukes them. Sandy tries to keep the peace and Blazes agrees to sing a song if the others do too. Blazes' jaunty song about a dysfunctional family involves alcoholism, child abuse and murder. Its moral is, 'If you're both clever and lucky, you can do just what you please.' The others join in Sandy's sad, sentimental love-song. Arthur's religious song is, as Blazes says, 'a bit of old blood and thunder'. Sandy hopes they will be preserved from Arthur's imagination and from his God.

The mists come down, so Arthur goes up to start the foghorn, 'The cry of the beast across the sleeping world'. Blazes sees a vision of the old woman he mur-

---

[1] 'The Composer's Notes on his Works', Paul Griffiths, *Peter Maxwell Davies*, London, 1982.

dered in his song. Sandy sees faces from his past, his sister and a boy who now invites him to go away into the night. Arthur returns, singing a crazed 'Hymn', 'The Beast is called out from his grave'. Gradually, he himself assumes what the stage directions call 'characteristics of the Beast'. As Blazes and Sandy follow Arthur towards the door, they plead with God to turn his wrath against the Fiend and to spare them. Suddenly, the three lighthouse-keepers become the three officers from the Lighthouse Commission boat, while the eyes of the Beast are revealed as the lights of their ship. The officers' comments seem to indicate that when they found the keepers had become 'unnatural, demonic beasts' and run amok, they killed them to protect themselves and then decided to report that the men had simply disappeared. In a final brief episode, we relive the scene's opening blessing 'to keep the Beast from the door', but in an eery, *pianissimo* version. Are they the relief keepers or, perhaps, ghosts of those who disappeared? The opera ends with the lighthouse lantern flashing in automatic mode.

The ghost that haunts *The Lighthouse* is obviously Britten, but it is a case of influence digested. The open-ended ghost story format may be reminiscent of *The Turn of the Screw*; its structure of official enquiry followed by re-enactment and its seascape may suggest *Peter Grimes*, while Arthur whistles the same marine hymn that runs through *Noye's Fludde*; yet the opera's integrity is never in doubt. The way the composer handles the central theme of the Beast also recalls Britten: Maxwell Davies leaves its exact nature open to interpretation but its 'daemonic' quality obviously includes an element of homoeroticism ('No. I didn't, we didn't'). According to the composer, the musical structure is based on number symbolism taken from the Tarot. The orchestration is dazzlingly inventive, not just because it asks for new instrumental colours (a 'plastic soap-dish [is] scraped around inside of tam-tams to produce a "howl" resembling electronic "feedback"') but in the fascinating way he combines conventional instruments, such as a high-lying, muted violin eerily paired with the bass clarinet as 'fingers of mist, clammy, unnatural, reached down from the tower towards us'.   P.

CLAUDE DEBUSSY

(born 22 August 1862, died 25 March 1918)

PELLÉAS ET MÉLISANDE

Opera in five acts, text from Maeterlinck's play of the same name. Première at Opéra-Comique, Paris, 30 April 1902, with Garden, Gerville-Réache, Périer, Dufranne, Vieuille, conductor Messager. First performed New York, Manhattan Opera House, 1908, with Garden, Gerville-Réache, Périer, Dufranne, Arimondi, Crabbé, conductor Campanini; Covent Garden, 1909, with Féart, Bourgeois, Warnéry, Vanni Marcoux, conductor Campanini; Metropolitan, New York, 1925, with Bori, Johnson, Whitehill, Rothier. Revivals include Covent Garden, 1920, with Edvina, Maguénat, conductor Pitt; 1930, with Teyte, Bourdin, Brownlee; 1937, with Perli, Gaudin, Vanni Marcoux; 1949, with Joachim, Jansen, Etcheverry, conductor Désormière; 1969, with Söderström, George Shirley, conductor Pierre Boulez; la Scala, 1925, with Heldy, Bertana, Legrand, Journet, conductor Toscanini; 1949, with Géori Boué, Bourdin, Etcheverry, conductor de Sabata; Glynde-bourne, 1962, with Duval, Henry Gui, Roux, conductor Gui; English National Opera, 1981, with Eilene Hannan, Robert Dean, Neil Howlett, conductor Mark Elder (in English).

Arkel, *King of Allemonde*		Bass
Geneviève, *mother of Pelléas and Golaud*		Alto
Pelléas }	*King Arkel's grandsons*	Tenor[1]
Golaud }		Baritone
Mélisande		Soprano
Yniold, *Golaud's son by his first marriage*		Soprano
A Physician		Bass

Some works of art sum up the past, some presage the future – amongst operas, one thinks of Mozart's in the first category, of *Tristan* or *Falstaff* or

---

[1] Or high baritone. Jean Périer, the original Pelléas, also sang Scarpia, Colline. Sharpless; Warnéry was Gonzalve in *L'Heure Espagnole*, Mime in *Siegfried*; Bourdin an Onegin, Shirley a celebrated Don Ottavio.

Wozzeck in the second. *Pelléas* seems to do neither. It belongs to no line and (unlike Debussy's piano and orchestral works) has few imitators. However, if the work is something of a dead end, it is anything but sterile; in fact, every time one hears it, one is more convinced than ever that it is a work of outstanding, uncanny beauty, of incredibly perceptive imagination, and its very lack of followers is some indication that what it has to say has been said once and for all.

So much has been written about the tenuous nature of *Pelléas* that it is perhaps worth while emphasising that such a description applies only to the dramatic side of the work. The characters do not reveal the full extent of their feelings in their every utterance – to that limited extent *Pelléas* is a 'realistic' opera – and they prefer to deal in indefinite, non-committal phrases rather than in a grandiose flaunting of feelings. But there is no musical under-emphasis in the ordinary sense of that term; what Debussy was after was surely the exact opposite – a precise, unexaggerated musical statement of the sentiments which are expressed, and an equally precise indication of what the characters concerned clearly feel to lie behind those sentiments.

Each scene is connected to its predecessor by an orchestral interlude, and the acts are thus musically continuous.

Act I, scene i. In a forest, Golaud, grandson of King Arkel, while hunting has lost his way following a wild boar and come to a place he does not know. There he sees a girl sitting by a spring. She behaves like a person isolated from the world but Golaud succeeds in inducing Mélisande – she at last tells him her name – to follow him out of the woods.

Scene ii. A room in the castle. Geneviève, mother of Golaud and Pelléas, is reading to the aged, almost blind King a letter which Golaud has written to his half-brother: 'Voici ce qu'il écrit à son frère Pelléas'. From this letter we learn that Golaud has already been married for six months to the mysterious Mélisande. He loves her, but knows no more today than he did at first in the woods. He is worried that his grandfather may not accept that he has married Mélisande and asks Pelléas to give him a sign that the King is ready 'to honour the stranger as his daughter'. Otherwise, he will steer his ship to a remote land and never return home. King Arkel has arrived at that time of life when the wisdom of experience makes one forgive whatever happens. He pardons Golaud

and commissions his grandson Pelléas to give his brother the sign agreed upon. Pelléas has asked him if he may leave to say farewell to a dying friend; but Arkel reminds him that his duty is to await his brother's return, and look after his father who lies sick in a room above them.

Scene iii. Before the castle. Geneviève seeks to calm Mélisande's distress at the gloominess of the world into which she has wandered. Pelléas is there. Together they watch a ship sail away out to sea.

Act II, scene i. A fountain in the park. Pelléas and Mélisande go together to this thickly shaded spot in the heat of the day. Is Mélisande a Melusine-like creature? Water attracts wonderfully. Pelléas bids her take care: 'Prenez garde de glisser'. She is tempted to play with the ring that Golaud gave her. It slips from her hand to the sound of a harp *glissando*, and sinks.

Scene ii. There must have been some peculiar condition attached to the ring. At the precise time that it fell into the fountain, Golaud's horse shied so that he fell and now lies injured in bed. Mélisande is looking after him. She tells Golaud that she does not feel well and is oppressed by foreboding. Golaud tries to comfort her; he takes her hands and sees that the ring is missing. She must go immediately to look for it. Pelléas will help her find it.

Scene iii. Mélisande has lied to Golaud by telling him that the ring slipped from her hand into the sea. Pelléas must therefore show her the place she has suggested so that she may at least know where she claimed to have lost the ring – a horrible place in which the shadow of death stalks. They see three mysterious bearded beggars asleep.

Act III, scene i. A tower in the castle. At the window of the tower Mélisande is combing her hair: 'Mes longs cheveux'. Pelléas comes to say goodbye; early next morning he is going away. Mélisande will at least once more reach out her hand to him so that he may press it to his lips. Their hands do not touch but as Mélisande leans forward, her hair falls over Pelléas's head and fills him with passion. Their words become warmer – then Golaud comes by and reproves their 'childishness'. He goes off with Pelléas.

The whole scene, from the ravishing harp sound of the opening until the appearance of Golaud, is no more no less than a passionate love scene (although no word of love is spoken) – but with what sensitivity has Debussy set it!

Scene ii. In the vault under the castle. Golaud leads Pelléas into these underground rooms where the breeze of death blows. Seized with shuddering they leave.

Scene iii. At the entrance to the vault, Golaud warns Pelléas to keep away from Mélisande.

Scene iv. Before the castle. Jealousy fills Golaud's heart and he lifts up his little son, Yniold, offspring of his first marriage, to spy through a window on Pelléas and Mélisande inside. The child cannot describe anything remotely improper, yet Golaud senses that there is something between the couple. He himself is much older than Pelléas or Mélisande. Dramatically, this is one of the tensest scenes of the whole score, and Golaud's agony and impotence are made more apparent by the innocence and fright of Yniold as he reports what he sees.

Act IV, scene i. In a room in the castle, Pelléas tells Mélisande that he must see her that evening. She promises to go to the old fountain in the park where she lost the ring. It will be their last meeting. She still has no idea what is driving Pelléas away.

Scene ii. Old King Arkel enters the room. He has taken Mélisande to his heart and feels she is deeply unhappy. Golaud also comes in. The sight of his wife, apparently the picture of innocence, irritates him so much ('Une grande innocence') that in a fit of madness he throws her down and drags her across the room by her hair. Only Arkel understands and pities.

Scene iii. By the spring in the park. There is a feeling of disaster in the air. Yniold has dropped something behind a stone and is looking for it. He catches sight of some sheep being driven past and listens to them as they go. (This scene is often omitted in performance.)

Scene iv. It is dark when Mélisande goes to her rendezvous with Pelléas. As they say goodbye, perhaps because of Golaud's outburst of anger, they clearly see what has caused the situation and are overcome with something like an affirmation of death and the joy of dying. Fate shuts the gates of the castle upon them; like fate they see Golaud coming. Pelléas falls from a thrust of Golaud's sword, while Mélisande flees from her husband into the night.

Act V. A room in the castle. Mélisande lies in bed, Arkel, Golaud and the Physician talking softly in the room. Mélisande is not dying from the insignificant wound Golaud gave her and perhaps her life can be saved. Golaud's bitter remorse at what he has done cannot be calmed: 'J'ai tué sans raison! ... Ils s'étaient embrassés comme des petits enfants ... Je l'ai fait malgré moi' (I have killed without cause! ... They were kissing like children, just playing games ... An uncontrollable impulse).[1] Mélisande wakes up. Everything that has happened seems to her like a dream. Desperately Golaud begs her pardon but still asks her for the truth. He is willing to die too, but before his death he must know whether she has betrayed him with Pelléas. She denies it. Golaud presses her so forcibly that she seems near death. Earthly things fall away as if her soul were already free. Arkel brings her the child she has borne and offers the last services for the dying girl, to make her free of earthly pain and the pressure of persons left behind.   H.

---

[1] Translation by Hugh Macdonald.

LÉO DELIBES
(born 21 February 1836, died 16 January 1891)

LAKMÉ

Opera in three acts, text by Edmond Gondinet and Philippe Gille, after Pierre Loti's *Le Mariage de Loti*. Première at the Opéra-Comique, Paris, 14 April 1883, with van Zandt, Talazac, conductor Danbé. First performed London, Gaiety Theatre, 1885, with van Zandt; New York, 1886, with Pauline L'Allemand; Metropolitan, 1892, with van Zandt, Montariol, Edouard de Reszke; Covent Garden, 1910, with Tetrazzini, McCormack. Revived Metropolitan, 1916, with Barrientos, Martinelli, Rothier; 1931, with Pons, Thill; 1938, with Pons, Jagel, Pinza; Wexford, 1970, with Christiane Eda-Pierre. New productions of *Lakmé* were mounted for Joan Sutherland in Philadelphia, 1964, Seattle, 1967, Sydney, 1976; and for Luciana Serra in Trieste, 1979, Bologna, 1981, Chicago, 1983.

Lakmé..Soprano

Mallika, *her slave* ....Mezzo-Soprano

Ellen ⎫ ....Soprano
Rose ⎭ *English ladies* ....Soprano

Mistress Bentson, *their governess* ....Mezzo-Soprano

Gérald, *an English officer* ....Tenor

Frédéric, *an English officer*.............................Baritone

Nilakantha, *a Brahmin priest* ....Bass-Baritone

Hadji, *servant of Nilakantha*................................Tenor

Place: India
Time: Nineteenth Century
Running Time: 2 hours 10 minutes

Delibes's reputation after his death relies on four theatrical successes, the operas *Lakmé* and *Le roi l'a dit* and the ballets *Coppélia* and *Sylvia*, yet his career as a leading French musician took him from the organ loft through the theatre to the heights of a professorship at the Paris Conservatoire.

Lakmé was written after the two successful ballets and had achieved at the Opéra-Comique over 1500 performances within 100 years of its première. As drama through music its rating on the Kerman scale cannot be high, but the composer had a great melodic gift and knew moreover precisely how to flatter the French voice. For Lakmé herself, Delibes wrote expressive lyrical music of a high order, only the Bell Song demanding an extravagant coloratura technique.

Act I. Lakmé is the daughter of Nilakantha, a fanatical Brahmin priest. While he nurses his hatred of the British invaders who have forbidden him to practise his religion, his daughter and other devotees of his cult sing an invocation to the gods: 'Blanche Dourga, Pâle Siva, Puissant Ganea'. Lakmé's vocal embroidery over the top of the chorus is full of coloratura work. Nilakantha leaves for another gathering of the faithful, and Lakmé is alone with her companions in the idyllic garden which surrounds the temple. Lakmé and Mallika sing together a most attractive barcarolle as they prepare to bathe in the stream: 'Dôme épais, le jasmin'. The rippling theme of the music and the oriental beauty of the surroundings perfectly set the atmosphere in which Lakmé moves.

We are next introduced to the English figures of the opera, two army officers, a couple of young girls, and their ineffably comic governess, Mistress Bentson. They are all in varying degrees suspicious of the Orient and its mystery, which they profess to find very peculiar indeed. They break through the bamboo fence which surrounds the temple, and exclaim with delight at what they can see inside. Frédéric warns them that several of the flowers are poisonous; he also says that the hut belongs to a dangerous and implacable Brahmin, whose one delight is in his beautiful daughter. In a quintet they speculate on the feelings of such a girl, who is shut off by her priestly vocation from contact with the outside world.

The women want a sketch done of Lakmé's jewels, and Gérald, who is something of an artist, says he will stay behind and do one, if they will go back to the town. Left alone, he is fascinated by the jewels, and he speculates on the beauty and youth of their owner. Gérald's aria, 'Fantaisie aux divins mensonges', is one of the gems of the score, in aptness, melodic freshness and unpretentious charm.

He sees Lakmé and Mallika returning, and hides. Lakmé dismisses Mallika and wonders to herself why she should feel so oddly sad and happy at the same time ('Pourquoi dans les grands bois'). She sees Gérald, and, filled with alarm, cries for help. But, when Mallika and Hadji come to her aid, she sends them off to look for her father. Alone with Gérald, she tells him that a word from her could have brought about his death; he must leave and forget he ever saw her. But Gérald is infatuated, and he sings passionately of love: 'C'est le dieu de la jeunesse, c'est le dieu du printemps'. Lakmé's voice joins his, until the sound of her father returning brings her back to reality. As Gérald disappears through the gap in the bamboo Nilakantha cries for vengeance on whoever has dared profane his temple precincts.

Act II. The scene is a bazaar, with a temple in the background. The stage is crowded with soldiers, sailors, and tourists, who mingle with the street-sellers and people. Mistress Bentson is surrounded by beggars and sellers, who, in the course of conversation, relieve her of her watch and handkerchief, before she is rescued by Frédéric. A bell rings to signal the closing of the market, and the festival begins. Girls perform various exotic dances, and Nilakantha appears, disguised as an old Hindu penitent and accompanied by his daughter. By now Gérald and his fiancée Ellen have appeared on the scene, and Gérald, out of earshot of the girls, has been told by Frédéric that their regiment leaves before dawn. Lakmé hints to her father that Brahma might not be averse to pardoning an offence by a stranger, but her father indignantly denies any such possibility. He sings tenderly of his love for Lakmé: 'Lakmé, ton doux regard se voile'.

Nilakantha demands that his daughter sing to attract the man who has dared to venture on to sacred ground – drawn, Nilakantha is sure, by the beauty of Lakmé herself. A brilliant passage of roulades is designed to attract the attention of the crowd, to whom Nilakantha introduces his daughter as a traditional Hindu singer. She tells the story of the Indian maiden, a pariah, who one day sees a handsome stranger lost in the forest and asleep, defenceless against the wild beasts, who wait to devour him. She plays on her bells and charms the animals, thus keeping the stranger safe from them. When he awakens, she discovers that it is Vishnu, the son of Brahma. He transports her with him to the skies, and ever since that day the traveller has heard the sound of bells in that particular part of the forest. This is the famous Bell Song ('Où va la jeune Hindoue?'), to which more than to anything else the opera owes its continued renown. Its bell effects and seductive melody have made it a favourite of sopranos with pretensions to vocal agility; in the hands of a coloratura soprano who is also musically inclined its effect is considerable.

To Nilakantha's fury, nobody appears in answer to Lakmé's singing, and he bids his daughter continue, which she reluctantly does, until, seeing Gérald, she utters a cry of anguish and faints in his arms. Nilakantha is convinced that he knows his enemy, and plots to isolate and destroy him during the course of the procession of the goddess which takes place later that night.

Lakmé is left alone with the faithful Hadji, who tries to console her, and promises to do whatever she asks him, whether to help a friend or dispose of an enemy. Hardly has he finished speaking when Gérald returns and rushes to Lakmé's side. There is a love duet for them ('Dans la vague d'un rêve'), during whose course Lakmé admits her love for the young officer whose religion is not her own. Lakmé plans a new life for them far away: 'Dans la forêt près de nous'.

The procession comes into sight, the priests chanting their hymn to Durga. Frédéric comments ironically on Gérald's infatuation for the Hindu 'goddess', and says that he would be really worried were it not that they have to leave that very night. As the procession passes, Nilakantha's plan is put into operation, and Gérald falls stabbed. Lakmé rushes despairingly to him, but finds that he is only slightly injured. Hadji will help her to remove him to her secret hiding-place, and he will be hers.

Act III. The entr'acte suggests a lullaby, and when the curtain goes up, we are in the hut in the forest, where Gérald is lying on a couch, while Lakmé sings to him ('Sous le ciel tout étoilé'). When he wakes up, he is at first not sure what has happened to him, but Lakmé reminds him that it was Hadji who carried him to the forest. In one of the happiest pieces of the score, 'Ah, viens dans la forêt profonde', Gérald gives lyrical expression to his happiness far from the world with Lakmé as his only companion.

From afar off can be heard the sound of singing, and Lakmé tells Gérald that it is a band of lovers come to drink of the sacred spring. She herself will fetch water from the spring in which they may pledge their love. As she goes, Frédéric, who has been watching, appears at Gérald's side. He reminds Gérald that he is due to go with his regiment that very night, but Gérald is intoxicated with his love for Lakmé. He can forget Ellen, to whom he was engaged, but can he, asks Frédéric, forget his honour as a soldier? As he leaves, Frédéric knows he has triumphed over Gérald's infatuation, and Gérald himself knows it too when he hears in the distance the sound of soldiers marching.

Lakmé notices the change which has come over her lover during her short absence, and, while his attention is concentrated on the sound of the march, she tears off a leaf of the fatal *datura* tree, and bites it. 'Tu m'as donné le plus doux rêve', she tells Gérald when he again becomes conscious of her existence. Together they drink the water from the cup, and swear to love each other through all eternity. Lakmé admits to Gérald that she thinks he is in no danger of breaking his oath, since she is dying. Their voices join again in a duet, but Lakmé dies a moment later, though not before she has had time to tell Nilakantha, who discovers them, that she and her lover have together drunk of the sacred spring. As Gérald cries out in despair, Nilakantha thinks of Lakmé transported to eternal life, and is content.   H.

FREDERICK DELIUS
(born 29 January 1862, died 10 June 1934)

KOANGA

Opera in three acts, original libretto by C.F. Keary from an episode from George Cable's *The Grandissimes*. Première, Elberfeld, Germany, 30 March 1904, with Rose Kaiser and Clarence Whitehill, conducted by Fritz Cassirer. Revived Covent Garden, 1935, with Oda Slobodskaya and John Brownlee, conducted by Sir Thomas Beecham; Washington, 1970, and Camden Festival, London, 1972, with Claudia Lindsey and Eugene Holmes, conductor Sir Charles Groves.

Uncle Joe, *an old slave* ....Bass

Planters' daughters
    Renée ....Soprano
    Hélène ....Soprano
    Jeanne ....Soprano
    Marie..Soprano
    Aurore ....Contralto
    Hortense...Contralto
    Olive ....Contralto
    Paulette..Contralto

Don José Martinez, *a planter* ....Bass

Simon Perez, *Don José's overseer* ....Tenor

Koanga, *an African prince and Voodoo priest* ...Baritone

Rangwan, *a Voodoo priest*.....................................Bass

Palmyra, *a quadroon, half-sister to Clotilda* .....Soprano

Clotilda, *wife to Don José Martinez* ....Contralto

Black Slaves, Creole Dancers, Servants

Place: A Plantation on the Mississippi in Louisiana
Time: Second Half of the Eighteenth Century
Running Time: 1 hour 50 minutes

*K*oanga is based on an episode from George Cable's book *The Grandissimes* (1880). Charles Keary wrote a libretto for Delius in 1895 and the score was finished in Paris in 1897. Two years later, some of the music was heard in a concert of Delius's works in London and in 1904 the opera was staged at Elberfeld in a German translation by Jelka Rosen, Delius's wife. Many changes seem to have been made from the original libretto, which itself may not have been the finished work of Keary, with whom Delius had quarrelled, and in 1933 – to complicate matters – Jelka translated it back into English for the London

première, adding an element of Christianity versus Voodoo to the existing mixture. A further and more coherent revision was made by Douglas Craig and Andrew Page in connection with the 1972 London revival and this has been published.

Prologue. The verandah of a southern plantation house. Uncle Joe agrees, after a graceful ensemble for female voices, to tell the young plantation ladies one of their favourite stories, that of Koanga and Palmyra.

Clouds descend during the beautiful interlude, which is redolent of spirituals,[1] and lift to disclose the garden of a sugar-cane plantation on the Mississippi in Louisiana, with slave huts to the right and the forest at the back.

Act I. Palmyra, a mulatto slave-girl, sings sadly of the turmoil in her mind: 'How far removed my spirit seems from that of master or of slave'. Simon Perez, foreman of the plantation, rouses the slaves and then starts to pester Palmyra, who, not for the first time it would appear, rejects his advances.

Don José Martinez, the owner of the plantation, appears and demonstrates his authority. His instructions must if necessary be reinforced by use of the whip, and, as for the new batch of slaves due that day, it includes a Dahomey prince, and 'we must find a way to render him of service'. Black workers sing a variety of spirituals and working songs throughout the scene but the entrance of Koanga, prince and Voodoo priest, gives rise to a grandiose solo utterance which has its effect on all, not least Palmyra. Martinez insists he must work like the others, but Perez feels even the whip will be of little avail. Don José notices the mutual attraction of Koanga and Palmyra and offers Palmyra to Koanga if he will work. The act ends in an ensemble which grows in intensity and in volume as the slaves add their disinterested singing to the voices of the principal characters who voice their feelings, Koanga and Palmyra of mutual attraction, Martinez of satisfaction at the working of his stratagem, Perez alternating between

---

[1] Beecham, in his book on the composer (Hutchinson, 1959), tells of Delius's playing black tunes on the fiddle to his future wife Jelka and his poet Keary one day in summer 1896 at Bourron, near Grez-sur-Loing, some forty miles from Paris.

pleasure at the prospect of getting Koanga to work and fury at the likelihood of losing Palmyra for himself. There is a lull in the music's flow as Clotilda enters to protest at the prospective loss of Palmyra as her maid ('She was placed in my care by my father when she was a little girl'), but her voice joins the ensemble as the act's finale runs its course with gathering momentum.

Act II. The main entrance to Don José's house, where the slaves are celebrating their master's birthday and the wedding-day of Koanga and Palmyra. Clotilda enjoins Perez to prevent the forthcoming marriage, revealing to him that Palmyra is the daughter of Clotilda's father and so her half-sister. She promises to give Palmyra to Perez if he is successful. Palmyra, at first behind the scenes, sings an aria full of confidence for the future, 'How time flows on!' When Clotilda tries to head her off from her marriage to Koanga as likely to bring everlasting shame – 'Would you renounce your faith and creed?' – Palmyra rounds on her with '*Your* faith! *Your* creed!' The wedding music starts, and even though Simon Perez tells Palmyra the secret of her birth, she continues to reject him. Palmyra sings a beautiful aria, 'The hour is near when I to him my soul surrender' (composed apparently during rehearsals for the 1904 Elberfeld première), and in response to her pledging of her soul to him, Koanga expressively renounces his inheritance in order to be a slave for love of her. Palmyra gives him wine, and the slaves sing to the seductive rhythm of the Creole dance, *la Calinda*, which, shorn of chorus and ensemble, has become one of Delius's most attractive and best-known concert pieces.[1]

During the dance, Palmyra and Koanga pledge their troth but before its end Palmyra is swept to the back of the stage and abducted by a group of servants under the direction of Simon Perez.

Koanga at first cannot understand what is happening but then demands the return of his bride until, threatened by Martinez, he is driven to strike his master down. There is a clap of thunder and Koanga, alone on the stage, kneels to bring a Voodoo curse down on the white men who have seduced him from his ancient allegiance. Lit by flashes of lightning, he can be seen making his way through the forest and, just before the fall of the curtain, his voice is heard again in the distance, threatening doom.

Act III. A swamp at nightfall. The attractive and atmospheric prelude replaced the original piece during rehearsals at Elberfeld. It is taken from Delius's first opera, then unperformed, *The Magic Fountain*,[2] and its charm is undoubted even if its suitability to open an act of sinister import may be in question.

Off-stage voices establish the eerie overtones of the scene as it is prepared for the arrival of Koanga, who proceeds to cast a magic spell with Rangwan, another Voodoo priest. Koanga and Rangwan gash their arms with knives, blood from a gourd is poured on a fire, the chant continues impressively and there is a wild dance before the fire dies down and a mist covers the scene, to change to a vision of Martinez's stricken plantation, where slaves lie prostrate on the ground. The men bemoan their fate and Koanga imagines he hears Palmyra's voice raised in lamentation, which rouses him to a splendid outburst in which he calls on the morning star to lead him to her.

The scene returns to the plantation where Christian slaves pray for deliverance and Don José curses their feebleness of spirit and promises vengeance on Koanga. Palmyra appears in a state of collapse but Perez still pursues her with protestations of love, until Koanga emerges from hiding, and, urged on by Palmyra, follows Perez into the forest and kills him. Palmyra's moment of triumph is short-lived as a band of horsemen set on Koanga behind the scenes and beat him. He is carried in and set down beside Palmyra, dying, torn between his love for her and his repentance at having even momentarily forsaken Voodoo. Palmyra sings in lyrical ecstasy over his body, then stabs herself. After a long, sinuous and beautiful postlude to this latter-day *Liebestod*, the scene changes for the epilogue to the girls sitting on the verandah and listening to Uncle Joe's story. The gentle charm of the ending, as they watch the day dawn, is in considerable contrast to the heroic qualities of the act it follows.   H.

---

[1] In reality, *la Calinda* was a frenzied dance and appears to have been banned in Louisiana on the grounds of obscenity. It is thus hard to stage in anything like its original form to the graceful music Delius wrote for it!

[2] *The Magic Fountain* was first publicly heard in a B.B.C. studio performance recorded during 1977.

A VILLAGE ROMEO AND JULIET

Opera in six scenes, text by the composer, based on a story by
Gottfried Keller. Première, Berlin, 21 February 1907. First performed Covent Garden, 1910, with Ruth Vincent, Walter
Hyde, Dearth, Maitland, conductor Beecham. Revived 1920
with Miriam Licette, Hyde, Heming, Michael, conductor
Beecham; Royal College of Music, 1934, conductor Beecham;
Bradford, 1962, by Sadler's Wells with Morison, Wakefield,
conductor Meredith Davies. American première, Washington,
1972, with Patricia Wells, John Stewart, John Reardon.

Manz, *a rich farmer* ....Baritone

Marti, *another farmer* ....Baritone

Sali, *son of Manz, as a child* ....Soprano

Sali, *son of Manz, as a man*.................................Tenor

Vreli, *daughter of Marti*....................................Soprano

The Dark Fiddler, *rightful heir to the wood*......Baritone

Two Peasants ....Baritone

Three Women ....Soprano, Mezzo-Soprano

Gingerbread Woman......................................Soprano

Wheel-of-Fortune Woman ....Soprano

Cheap Jewellery Woman....................Mezzo-Soprano

Showman ....Tenor

Merry-go-Round Man ....Baritone

The Slim Girl..Soprano

The Wild Girl ....Mezzo-Soprano

The Poor Horn-Player ....Tenor

The Hunchbacked Bass Fiddler...........................Bass

Place: Seldwyla, Switzerland
Time: Mid-Nineteenth Century
Running Time: 1 hour 45 minutes

Professor Arthur Hutchings, author of an authoritative book on Delius, admonishes the listener:
'Opera-goers who require the stage properties and
dramatic interruptions of Italian opera, the pageantry
and ballet of Russian opera, the discrimination of
character and emotional versatility of Mozartian
opera, cannot fail to be disappointed in *A Village
Romeo and Juliet*. No opera is more musical, because in
no opera has the composer been more certain that by
music he would tell the tale; Cecil Gray has called it "a
symphonic poem with the implicit programme made
explicit upon the stage." ... In this work the opera-
goer must expect only music, and music chiefly of the
same kind – sustained, dreamy beauty, slightly off-set
by the sinister strains of the Dark Fiddler or the liti-
gious quarrels of the farmers.'

Scene i. September. A piece of land luxuriously
overgrown on a hill. The broad fields of Manz and
Marti lie on either side, only a small piece of either
field being visible. Manz and Marti are rivals for the
strip of wild land which lies between their fields.
They are both ploughing when the action begins,
and each, when the other is not looking, takes an
extra furrow out of the waste land.

Sali and Vreli brings their parents' midday meals,
then go off to play together in the woods. Manz and
Marti reappear to eat together. The children come
out of the wood as the Dark Fiddler can be heard in
the distance. Marti recognises him, and knows that
the land should be his, but that, being a bastard, he
has no legal right to it. The Fiddler disappears,
watched by the children. Their parents start to
discuss the prospective sale of the land, each criticising the way the other has stolen a furrow here and
there. They quarrel furiously, and forbid their respective children ever again to play with each other.

Scene ii. Six years later. Outside Marti's house,
which has a neglected air about it. The children are
now grown up, and ever more closely drawn
towards one another. Sali comes towards the house,
from which Vreli presently looks out longingly. They
patch up a quarrel, caused one imagines by the
lawsuit in which their parents have been frittering
away their heritages. They are pessimistic about the
situation, but Sali hopes all may yet come right if
they stick together. They make an appointment for
the evening, in the fields.

Scene iii. The wild land, overgrown with poppies.
Sali waits for Vreli, who comes in and calls him, then
hides until he finds her. Their delight in each other's
company is obvious. The sound of the Dark Fiddler's
playing is heard, and he reminds them that they
played on his land. Now that they are all beggars, he
feels they are equal. Why do they not come with him
and share his vagabond's existence? He does not
seem to expect an answer, but is confident they will
meet again. Vreli remembers that the last time they
saw him was on the dread day when their fathers
quarrelled. Sali reassures her, and they talk happily
of their childhood days. They embrace.

Marti can be seen looking for Vreli. He spies them,
and is dragging Vreli away when Sali fells him with a
blow.

Scene iv. A slow introduction leads to a new
scene, the interior of Marti's house, now quite bare,

apart from a bed and a bench. Vreli is sitting in front of the fire, reminding herself sadly that this is her last night in her old home. Sali comes in, and after an ecstatic greeting, they sing of their love, and pledge never to leave each other again. Vreli tells Sali that she has just taken her father away, as he has lost his mind as a result of Sali's blow. She will have to leave as the house has been sold. They sit down together in front of the fire, and fall asleep in each other's arms. The stage grows dark as they dream they are being married in the old church of Seldwyla. Church bells ring, the organ plays, a hymn is sung, and finally the bells ring out again merrily.

Dawn breaks, and the lovers awake to understand that it was all a dream. Can they not have a whole day together, asks Vreli, in which to wander through the woods and dance? 'To Berghald,' exclaims Sali. The sound of yodelling can be heard in the distance as they leave.

Scene v. The fair. The various sellers cry their wares, and the showman leads some of the crowd into a tent. Sali and Vreli arrive, looking happy, and join in the gaiety until they are recognised by a woman from Seldwyla, with her companions. They buy everything that attracts them, but suddenly notice that they are being watched curiously by the crowd. Self-consciously they leave the fair, and make for the Paradise Garden, another dancing place.

The interlude during the change of scene is the famous Walk to the Paradise Garden (composed five years later than the rest of the opera to themes from it). During it, Sali and Vreli rest on their journey.

Scene vi. The vagabonds are heard in the distance before the curtain rises to reveal a dilapidated country house, now used as an inn. The river flows nearby, and a barge full of hay is moored on it. The Dark Fiddler and his vagabond companions sit round a table. It is evening. The Dark Fiddler is evidently telling his friends the story of the strife between Manz and Marti and its origin.

Sali and Vreli come into the garden. The Dark Fiddler strongly advises them to take to the road and join him and his friends. He plays while they dance. All join him in trying to persuade the two young lovers to join them, but they fear they are too respectable for a vagabond's life. Bargemen are heard singing in the distance, and gradually it dawns on Sali and Vreli that the only way out for them is to 'drift down the river' like the bargemen, but with a difference; they can never return.

Watched by the Dark Fiddler and the vagabonds, they get into the barge. Vreli throws her nosegay into the river, and Sali draws the plug from the bottom of the boat and throws it in too. As the boat moves out into the middle of the stream, Sali and Vreli fall into each other's arms on the bed of hay. Boatmen can be heard in the distance singing 'Ho, travellers we a-passing by'. Of the end, Professor Hutchings has written: 'The orchestra alone then concludes the work with a perfection unattainable by words; the music can suggest the deep and enfolding waters. However much the pathetic emotions have been stirred, we are satisfied and comforted almost as by the "happy ending" of comedy.'   H.

GAETANO DONIZETTI
(born 29 November 1797, died 8 April 1848)

Donizetti, like Rossini and Verdi, unlike Beethoven and Wagner, was a practitioner not a questioner. He could invent music that was original, but he accepted the aesthetic conventions of his day and sought inspiration within them, seldom attempting to break new ground. By his time, Beethoven and romantic striving had burst the moulds of symphonic form but Italian opera in the first half of the nineteenth century was nonetheless a period of certainty. Viable forms (different for tragedy and comedy) had been forged by Rossini and his contemporaries and were being exploited by Bellini, Donizetti, and even (for his first dozen creative years) Verdi. This process satisfied audiences, who knew what to expect; singers, whose status it enshrined and whose prowess it displayed; and composers, whose formal problems were largely solved and who had merely – merely! – to find the notes to express the situations which were to hand.

In Donizetti's tragedies, you will find the expected introductory chorus, the heroine's opening cavatina, the meetings and partings of lovers and would-be lovers, the confrontations of rivals, the mistakes of identity, and of course the mad scenes (sometimes masquerading as death scenes, but mad scenes nonetheless, with their jumps through time and space so that a quotation of earlier music may poignantly recall earlier bliss). A Donizetti subject, whether from Schiller or Scott, whether concerned with a Scottish queen or an Amazonian heroine, will follow the same well-trodden path. Occasionally a great scene will emerge – the sextet in *Lucia*, or the pathetic end of *Anna Bolena* – but the form will be predictable throughout, which need be no more than to say that some Haydn symphonies are better than others, that a choice is permissible even among the many examples of Madonna and Child by Giovanni Bellini.   H.

LE CONVENIENZE ED INCONVENIENZE TEATRALI

Conventions and Inconveniences of the Stage

Dramma-giocoso in two acts, libretto by Domenico Gilardoni, based on Antonio Simone Sografi's plays *Le convenienze teatrali* (1794) and *Le inconvenienze teatrali* (1800). Original one-act *farsa* with dialogue *Le convenienze teatrali* first performed at Teatro Nuovo, Naples, 21 November 1827. Revised, with recitatives, incorporating part of *Le inconvenienze teatrali*, first performed at Teatro Cannobiana, Milan, 20 April 1831. First U.S. performance Terre Haute, Indiana, 1966, as *An Unconventional Rehearsal*. Revived in Munich, 1969, as *Viva la Mamma*. First U.K. performance broadcast by B.B.C. Radio 3, 1969, as *Upstage and Downstage*; 1827 version by Opera Rara, Collegiate Theatre, London, 1972, as *The Prima Donna's Mother is a Drag*, with Lissa Gray, Peter Lyon. 1831 version, Teatro Donizetti, Bergamo, 1995, with Maria Costanza

Nocentini and Bruno De Simone, conducted by Fabrizio Maria Carminati; Teatro Regio, Turin, 1996, with Luciana Serra, José Fardilha, conducted by Fabrizio Carminati.

Daria Garbinati[1], *prima donna*........................Soprano
Procolo[2], *her husband* ....Bass
Biscroma Strappaviscere[3], *conductor*.............Baritone
Donna Agata Scanagalli, *Luigia's mother,*
    a Neapolitan..Baritone
Luigia Castragatti[4], *seconda donna* ....Soprano
Guglielmo Antolstoinoff, *primo tenore,*
    German..Tenor
Pippetto[5], *primo musico*......................Soprano/Tenor
Cesare Salzapariglia[6], *druggist and poet* ....Baritone
Impresario...Bass
Director of the Theatre.......................................Bass

Soldiers, Servants, Workmen

Place: A Hotel next to the Theatre in Lodi
Running Time: 1 hour 40 minutes

Donizetti wrote *Le convenienze ed inconvenienze teatrali* for his benefit evening. While it pokes fun at contemporary operatic clichés, and can prove genuinely funny, it also serves to display his skills at *opera seria* exhibitionism and at *opera buffa*. The target is provincial mediocrity.

Act I. After a short prelude the chorus are rehearsing a new opera based on Metastasio.[7] The conductor takes the Prima Donna through her aria, explaining that she will move the audience to feel 'pietà'. She and her husband Procolo look forward to the furore her trill will produce. The rest of the cast resent being asked to supply the *pertichini*, the small vocal entries that support the main feature. In her aria the Prima Donna rebukes a tyrant and warns him that heaven will avenge her suffering. The tyrant (played by the Musico, i.e. the castrato) yields to compassion, which occasions the equally conventional cabaletta expressing relief.

The rest of the cast plead with the conductor for larger roles. The Maestro passes their requests to the Poet, who is so evasive that they suspect the Prima Donna's influence. Publicly, everyone looks forward

---

[1] 'Garbato' would mean polite, so her surname may suggest she is not quite that. Piero Molli gives her name as Corilla Scortichini (from *scorticare*, to flay or scratch), *Donizetti: 70 Melodrammi*, 1988.

[2] Piero Molli (*idem*) gives his surname as Cornacchia, which must be derived from *corno*, horn.

[3] His name means, literally, Demisemiquaver Bowel-Ripper.

[4] Her surname means, literally, Cat-Castrator.

[5] This is bound to be rude. Piero Molli gives his name as Neocle Frescopane, literally, 'Fresh bread'.

[6] This is, probably, obscurely funny.

[7] In his one-act *farsa* Donizetti used a scene from his own 'inane heroic opera *Elvida*, which would have been readily identifiable to the original audience because [it] had been heard at the San Carlo sixteen months earlier', William Ashbrook, *Donizetti and his Operas*, 1982.

to the important stage rehearsal; privately, several of the cast plan to be elsewhere. Donizetti builds up a magnificent ensemble: the cast's lyrical effusions soar above the librettist and conductor's pattering (and unrealistic) anticipation of bravos for their contribution. Their squabbling is interrupted by Mamm'Agata, played by a baritone *en travesti*. Threatening to beat them up if they don't show respect for her and for her daughter, the Seconda Donna, she dictates the musical effects she wants Luigia's rondo to contain ('Mascalzoni, sfaccendati'[1]). Her cavatina is as funny as it is illuminating: the instrumental effects she prescribes are reproduced in the pit, more or less faithfully, such as muted violins going 'zinghete, zinghete', accompanied by an oboe going 'piripi', while the double bass's 'frunchete' go in thirds with the horn's 'tuturutu'.

When the Librettist reads out the playbill for the new opera, the singers insist on enlarging their credit lines. Mamm'Agata reminds the Prima Donna that she knew her when she sold cakes on the street. Her husband leaves in a huff. Mamm'Agata reminds the Librettist that he promised to write a duet for the Prima and the Seconda Donna. Daria refuses adamantly: she never sinks to the level of her inferiors. Her duet with Mamm'Agata, in which each insults the other, verges on slapstick: while the soprano navigates some delicious, aerial vocal lines, Mamm'Agata promises a pomegranate will be thrown from the auditorium ('Ch'io canti un duetto').

The Impresario returns with bad news: the Musico has fled. Mamm'Agata volunteers to replace him in the travesti role of Romolo, as long as her daughter can sing the duet with the Prima Donna. The Tenor returns and finds to his horror that he must sing a duet with Mamm'Agata. Faced with the score, she asks about the 'forest of houses and little boats' (i.e., quavers and semiquavers). In the trio Mamm'Agata sings out of tune. The Tenor refuses to sing with her. She flies into a rage, and threatens to have a fainting fit, but recovers in time to launch the *stretta*, attack the Tenor physically and tear up her score. Procolo happens to have learnt the Tenor's part and offers to sing the role, as long as his wife

does not have to sing a duet with Luigia and he is given a box, eleven free tickets, portraits and sonnets in honour of his wife. Mamm'Agata returns, the singers' incompatible demands lead to an impasse, but this time it's the Impresario who walks out.

Luigia reads out a letter from the agent in Livorno and so launches the remarkable sextet: three separate lines reflect ironically on one another and occasion more quarrelling. The Impresario in Livorno offers Luigia a contract, as long as she tells her mother to go to hell; meanwhile, the Librettist reads the Conductor the new dialogue he has written (inevitably, it involves 'Vendetta') and Procolo reads out the devastating review of a new opera in Cremona. This becomes a larger and more animated ensemble when the Stage Director summons the cast to rehearse in the theatre. They refuse to leave, so soldiers intervene and carry them away in sedan chairs.

Act II. The stage, in chaos. The crowds outside have forced the management to make the rehearsal an open one. The Prima Donna feels tired and insists that the Seconda Donna sing first. In the event Mamm'Agata begins, with a Romanza that parodies Desdemona's 'Willow Song' from Rossini's *Otello*, featuring sardines, turnips and limpid broccoli. A very long ritornello with prominent bassoons is the only overt sign of humour, for the aria succeeds on its own terms (*larghetto*: 'Assisa a pie d'un sacco'). Describing herself as a timid débutante, Mamm'Agata rejects any criticism and goes to dress. The rehearsal moves on to the triumphal march for Procolo's entry. In a neat detail, the Poet teaches the Chorus their moves during its introduction. They salute Procolo as the 'Trionfator' of his 'Vendette'. Appalled by his performance, the Maestro hurries on to the Funeral March. Mamm'Agata overacts her role as sacrificial victim. The Impresario interrupts with the news that the Director has cancelled the performance, which launches the finale ('Ch'è successo?'). They all wonder how they can repay their creditors. At Procolo's suggestion, the entire cast agree to run away. This brings events to an exhilarating, aptly absurd climax. The opera ends on their unison 'Scappiamo!' (Let's clear off!). P.

---

[1] The role was originally written (and is still occasionally sung) in the Neapolitan dialect, when Agata sang 'Lazzarune, scauzacane'.

ANNA BOLENA

Anne Boleyn

Opera in two acts, libretto by Felice Romani. Première, Teatro Carcano, Milan, 2O December 1830, with Giuditta Pasta, Rubini, Galli. First performed at la Scala, 1832, with Pasta (later Grisi), Deval and Negrini. London, King's Theatre, 1831, with Pasta, Rubini, Lablache; New York, 1843 (in French). Revived Covent Garden, 1847, with Giulia Grisi, Alboni, Mario, Tamburini; Drury Lane, London, 1871, with Tietjens; Bergamo, 1956 (after 113 years' absence from Italy) with Marina Cucchio; la Scala, 1957, with Callas, Simionato, Raimondi, Rossi-Lemeni, producer Luchino Visconti, conductor Gavazzeni; New York (in concert), 1957, with Gloria Davy, Simionato; Glyndebourne, 1965, with Gencer, Patricia Johnston, Oncina, Cava, conductor Gavazzeni; New York (in concert), 1967, with Suliotis, Horne and Domingo.

Enrico (Henry) VIII, *King of England* ....Bass

Anna Bolena (Anne Boleyn), *his second wife*..Soprano

Giovanna (Jane) Seymour, *her lady-in-waiting*..Soprano

Lord Rochefort, *Anne's brother*............................Bass

Lord Richard Percy..Tenor

Smeaton, *the Queen's page*............................Contralto

Hervey, *official at the court* ....Tenor

Courtiers, Officials, Lords, Huntsmen, Soldiers, etc.

Place: Windsor and London
Time: 1536
Running Time: 3 hours 10 minutes

Operatic legend once had it that in the autumn of 1830 – a year which saw the première in Paris of that source of the romantic movement, Victor Hugo's *Hernani* – both Bellini and Donizetti were working on operatic commissions from the impresario of the Teatro Carcano, Milan. Each composer had a libretto from the celebrated Felice Romani and each was determined to outdo the other. Like most legends, the facts are a little different; Donizetti's libretto for *Anna Bolena* was in his hands on 10 November (the composition was finished by 10 December), Bellini's for *La Sonnambula* only in December.

At the time of Donizetti's death, the critic of the *Revue des Deux Mondes* pointed to five of his operas as most likely to survive: *Lucia, La Favorite, L'Elisir, Don Pasquale* and *Anna Bolena*, and certainly the opera was in as high favour with the public as with prima donnas, who found a perfect vehicle for their gifts in Anne's 'Piangete voi?' and 'Al dolce guidami', a mad scene to vie with those from *Sonnambula* and *Puritani*,

Lucia and *Linda*. In the 1950s, *Anna Bolena* was one of the most successful of the operas benefiting from the sovereign interpretative powers of Maria Callas.

It was with Callas in the title role and in a magnificent production by Visconti that the opera triumphed at la Scala in 1957, and it was in this role a year later that Callas returned to the Italian stage after the most resounding scandal of her career. She had inaugurated the 1957–58 season in Rome in *Norma* and, with the President of the Republic in the house, withdrew after the first act, at which point the performance came to an unscheduled end. The storm which broke about her head next day accused her among other things of insulting the Head of State, and quite ignored the fact that she was ill and had asked for a substitute but had mistakenly yielded to the pleas of the management to sing. She did not appear in Italy again until nearly four months later, at which time la Scala's Gala for the President was rather ostentatiously changed from the originally scheduled *Anna Bolena* with Callas to something less controversial. I was present when a few days later *Anna Bolena* had its seasonal première. The atmosphere in the house was full of nervous expectancy and not until the finale of Act I did the hostility abruptly change, but then it would have taken an even more partisan audience than la Scala's to ignore Callas's 'Giudici, ad Anna! Ad Anna! Giudici!', a less than Italianate reaction to operatic drama to resist her impassioned attack in the *stretta* and her ability at the repeat to cap the intensity of the first section. That hundreds of enthusiastic Milanese waited two hours at the stage door to escort the exhausted prima donna to supper at three in the morning seemed no more than a fitting ending to an evening that had begun with assassins lurking round every corner and had ended in triumph.

Act I. The great staircase at Windsor Castle. A crowd of courtiers discuss the King's growing love for Jane Seymour, who presently appears, troubled that the Queen should show such solicitude to one whom she does not recognise as her rival. To solemn music, the Queen enters, full of forebodings which are only increased by the sad little song with which her page Smeaton tries to beguile her mood. The Queen's slow cavatina ('Come, innocente giovane') is followed by a cabaletta, after which she and the Court withdraw. Jane Seymour gives voice to her anxiety, but the appearance of the King and his ardent wooing soon remove her doubts and the scene ends with a duet, in whose course the King reveals that he intends to expose the unfaithfulness of his wife and marry Jane.

Scene ii. A courtyard in the castle. The Queen's brother Rochefort is astonished to see Percy, whom the King has recalled from exile in the hope that he will provide the evidence against the Queen. Percy admits that the love he felt for Anne Boleyn as a girl is not dead (cavatina, 'Da quel dì che lei perduta'). When the King and Queen appear, Percy's hopes are encouraged by the Queen's obvious confusion. The scene ends with an impressive quintet ('Io sentii sulla mia mano'), during whose course the King instructs Hervey to watch Percy's behaviour with the Queen, Rochefort laments Percy's lack of discretion, and the courtiers are filled with apprehension at the new turn of events.

Scene iii.[1] In a corridor leading to the Queen's private apartments, Smeaton is gazing enraptured at a miniature of the Queen, which he kisses as he sings of his love for her ('Ah, parea che per incanto'). He hides when the Queen comes into view with her brother, who is trying to persuade her to grant an audience to Percy. When Percy appears, the Queen remains adamant: she is a wife and a Queen and will not listen to his protestations. At the end of their duet, the Queen refuses to see him again and Percy draws his sword to kill himself, only for Smeaton to rush from his hiding place. The Queen faints as Rochefort runs to warn her that the King is on his way, and Henry arrives to catch her in what he purports to find a compromising situation: 'Tace ognuno è ognun tremante!' Smeaton's protestation of her innocence is rendered less credible by the discovery of the portrait he wears round his neck. The King condemns the conspirators to separate cells and orders the Queen to make her defence before the judges, not to him. 'Giudici, ad Anna' comes her despairing cry; 'Ah, segnata è la mia sorte' (My fate is sealed), she leads the *stretta* to what with a Callas can be extraordinary effect.

Act II. The Queen is in custody. In the first scene, her ladies-in-waiting try to comfort her as she waits for trial, but Hervey announces that the King has decided to deprive her of even their support. Jane Seymour comes to advise her to try to save her life with a plea of guilty, then confesses that she is the one the King has designated to take the Queen's place. In the course of a grandiose duet, Anne generously forgives her.

Scene ii. A vestibule before the Council Chamber. Hervey tells the assembled courtiers that Smeaton has confessed and implicated the Queen. The King passes through and the Queen proudly refutes the accusations which are about to be levelled at her, at the same time admitting that before becoming Queen she had loved Percy. The King's rage and determination to be revenged ('Ambo morrete'), Percy's ecstatic proclamation of his love, the Queen's regret that no hope now is left her, are combined in a noble trio, after whose *stretta*, as the Queen and Percy are led off by guards, Jane Seymour herself comes to intercede for the unfortunate Queen ('Per questa fiamma indomita'). Her plea avails nothing since Hervey comes to announce the Council's unanimous sentence of death on the Queen and her accomplices.

In the Tower of London lie the conspirators. When Hervey comes to convey the King's clemency to Percy and Rochefort, each indignantly refuses to live while the guiltless Queen must die. (This scene, which contains a beautiful lyrical aria for Percy, 'Vivi tu, te ne scongiuro', was omitted in la Scala's revival.)

The last scene is one of Donizetti's great masterpieces of melodic and dramatic inspiration. In the Tower of London the Queen waits for death. She has lost her senses and chides her ladies for weeping (in a fine preludial chorus) on her wedding day when the King awaits her. Her mood shifts from terror to joy and, when she thinks she sees Percy smile at her, she sings ecstatically 'Al dolce guidami', movingly preluded by cor anglais solo. Hervey comes to order the Queen and the three condemned with her to proceed to the scaffold, and Smeaton admits that the false confession he made, hoping to save his own life, has contributed to her downfall. Anne again loses her reason, orders Smeaton to tune his harp and sing to her, then intones a prayer ('Cielo, a miei lunghi spasimi')[2] while Smeaton, Percy and Rochefort join their voices to hers. The firing of a cannon and ringing of bells are heard acclaiming the new Queen, and the opera ends with an impassioned outburst of denunciation from Anne ('Coppia iniqua'). H.

---

[1] Now, often Act II.

[2] The tune is a decorated version of 'Home Sweet Home' (from Bishop's opera *Clari*, 1823), which enjoyed enormous popularity at the time.

L'ELISIR D'AMORE
The Elixir of Love

Opera in two acts, text by Felice Romani after Scribe's libretto for Auber's *Le Philtre*. Première at the Teatro della Canobbiana, Milan, 12 May 1832, with Sabina Heinefetter, Genero, Dabadie (who sang the equivalent role in Auber's opera the previous year), Frezzolini. First performed in London, Lyceum Theatre, 1836; New York, 1838; Metropolitan, New York, 1904, with Sembrich, Caruso, Scotti, Rossi, conductor Vigna; revived 1941, with Sayao, Landi, Valentino, Baccaloni, conductor Panizza. Covent Garden, 1950, with Carosio, Tagliavini, Gobbi, Tajo, conductor Capuana (during la Scala's visit); Glyndebourne, 1961, with Ratti, Alva, Sordello, Badioli, conductor Cillario. Famous Nemorinos of this century have also included Schipa, Gigli, di Stefano, and Pavarotti.

Nemorino, *a young peasant* ....Tenor

Adina, *wealthy owner of a farm*.......................Soprano

Belcore, *a sergeant*..Baritone

Dulcamara, *a quack doctor*..................................Bass

Giannetta, *a peasant girl*................................Soprano

Place: A Small Italian Village
Time: Nineteenth Century
Running Time: 2 hours 10 minutes

Romani derived his text – rather closely – from Scribe's for *Le Philtre*, but Donizetti's music was sufficiently beguiling to keep the opera in the repertory from the time of composition to the present day. Auber's opera appeared only a year before Donizetti's. The opera has always been liked – thirty-three performances in its first season in Milan – and the role of Nemorino one of the most popular with Italian tenors.

Act I. The entrance to Adina's farm. It is midday, the sun is hot and Giannetta and the harvesters are sheltering under a tree. Adina reads, watched by Nemorino, who loves her but laments, in a cavatina (the famous 'Quanto è bella'), the impossibility of someone so beautiful and so clever as Adina ever falling in love with a goose like himself. Suddenly, Adina bursts out laughing. It is the bizarre love story she is reading which has provoked her mirth: Tristan won Isolde, she explains, by means of a magic love potion that made him irresistible! 'If only I had such a recipe', sings Adina, as the others (including Nemorino, who is listening from the sidelines) urge her to continue the tale.

To the sound of a drum, in marches a detachment of soldiers, headed by Sergeant Belcore, who presents Adina with a posy of flowers and loses no time in proposing marriage. In a quartet, Belcore urges her rapid acceptance, Adina seems in no particular hurry, Nemorino pleads for courage from above, and Giannetta predicts that Adina is too shrewd to be so easily caught out.

Nemorino begs for a word and tries to tell Adina how desperately he loves her. She for her part says his efforts are in vain as she is as fickle as the wind ('Chiedi all'aura lusinghiera'), but Nemorino's response is to the effect that his feelings for her are as inevitable as the course of a river.

The village square. A trumpeter announces the arrival in a splendid carriage of a travelling quack doctor, Dulcamara, who, in a *buffo* cavatina, 'Udite, udite, o rustici', offers the crowd startlingly effective cures for anything from wrinkles to toothache. Nemorino plucks up courage to ask Dulcamara for Queen Isolde's love potion – an elixir of love, in effect, like the one he has heard Adina reading about from her book. He engages in attractive duet with Dulcamara ('Voglio dire') and manages to buy from him what he thinks is just the job, in point of fact a bottle of cheap Bordeaux. It should take effect within twenty-four hours, says Dulcamara, allowing himself plenty of time to leave town. Nemorino drains the flask at a draught, and becomes happily inebriated.

Adina, attracted by her shy swain's raucous singing and dancing, is astounded at his unaccustomed indifference to her. Belcore in contrast comes back to renew his offer of marriage which Adina promptly accepts, saying she will marry him within the week. Unfortunately, no sooner is this agreed than Belcore receives an order for him and his party to leave the village the next morning. Adina, stung to fury by Nemorino's apparently detached reaction, agrees to Belcore's request to bring the marriage forward to that very day. The news has a temporarily sobering effect on Nemorino, who begs Adina to wait just twenty-four hours. Adina reassures Belcore that this village lad is nothing more than an infatuated boy. Belcore threatens Nemorino and in a lively finale, Adina invites everyone to her wedding banquet and she and Belcore head off to the notary to make the arrangements, allowing time for a serious, lyrical intervention in Nemorino's 'Adina credimi'. Nemorino finds his store of Dutch courage running out and calls urgently for Dulcamara's help.

Act II. Inside Adina's farm. The wedding breakfast is in progress, even though Adina has not as yet signed the marriage contract. Rejoicing is general and Dulcamara produces a piece of music which he says is the latest thing from Venice. He and Adina sing the barcarolle, 'Io son ricco, e tu sei bella', a catchy number which tells how a girl rejects a senator's wealth in order to marry instead the young gondolier whom she truly loves.

The notary arrives, the opening chorus is repeated, and now Nemorino becomes desperate to secure Dulcamara's aid. Another dose of the elixir should help, advises Dulcamara, adding *sotto voce* that he'll be gone in half an hour. The only way Nemorino can find the money for another bottle, as he learns from Belcore in a lively duet, is to enlist in the Sergeant's regiment, which will earn him twenty *scudi*. Nemorino signs the paper, takes the money and rushes off to find Dulcamara.

The story takes another twist with Giannetta's news that Nemorino's uncle has died, leaving him a fortune. He knows nothing of all this but will become quite a catch as a husband. An ensemble develops as Nemorino comes back, Dutch courage bolstered by another draught of Bordeaux, and is immediately pounced on by Giannetta and the girls, which makes him believe that the potion is at last working. Adina comes in with Dulcamara, and both are astonished at Nemorino's new-found way with the girls. Adina makes an attempt to tell him that he has made a mistake in enlisting in Belcore's regiment but he is dragged away to dance.

In a duet, 'Quanto amore!', Dulcamara explains Nemorino's behaviour to Adina, and tells her about the elixir. He quickly twigs that she is herself in love with Nemorino and offers her a bottle, which she has the gumption to refuse, saying she needs nothing further by way of elixir than her eyes.

When they leave, Nemorino returns. He sings one of the great tenor arias of all opera, 'Una furtiva lagrima', whose tranquil introduction, dominated by a plaintive bassoon, suggests Nemorino's discovery: as she gazes enviously at the flirting village girls, there is a furtive tear in Adina's eye. She loves him after all!

In a most attractive aria ('Prendi, per me sei libero'), Adina tells Nemorino that she has bought him out of his contract with Belcore and then admits she loves him and will do so forever. The finale begins with the phlegmatic Belcore accepting that he

is losing Adina. Dulcamara for his part tells the world that, thanks to his uncle, Nemorino is now a wealthy man, and that the elixir not only cures the lovesick but also makes them rich! He sells his remaining stock of cheap red wine to the eager villagers, hops into his carriage and rides away to a chorus of admiration and farewell.   H.

LUCREZIA BORGIA

Opera in a prologue and two acts, text by Felice Romani (after Victor Hugo's fictional account of the doings of this legendary heroine, who has been acquitted by modern research of much of what she was once accused). Première at la Scala, Milan, on 26 December 1833, with Méric-Lalande, M. Brambilla, Pedrazzi, Mariani; Her Majesty's Theatre, London, 1839, with Grisi, Ernesta Grisi, Mario, Tamburini; New York, 1844; Covent Garden, 1847, with Grisi, Alboni, Mario, Tamburini; Metropolitan, 1904, with de Macchi, Edyth Walker, Caruso, Scotti, conductor Vigna. Revived Colón, Buenos Aires, 1919, with Mazzoleni, Gigli; Florence, 1933, with Arangi-Lombardi, Pederzini, Gigli, Pasero, conductor Marinuzzi; la Scala, 1951, with Mancini, Pirazzini, Picchi, Rossi-Lemeni, conductor Capuana. Teresa Tietjens in the last century, Montserrat Caballé and Leyla Gencer in the 1960s and Beverly Sills and Joan Sutherland in the 1970s have been five of the most famous exponents of the title role.

Alfonso d'Este, *Duke of Ferrara* ....Baritone
Lucrezia Borgia...Soprano
Maffio Orsini ....Contralto
Young noblemen
    Gennaro...Tenor
    Liverotto ....Tenor
    Vitellozzo ....Bass
Gazella ....Bass
Rustighello, *in the service of Don Alfonso* ....Tenor
Gubetta, *in the service of Lucrezia* ....Bass
Astolfo, *in the service of Lucrezia* ....Bass

Gentlemen-at-Arms, Officers, Nobles and Ladies of the Venetian Republic and the Este Court

Place: Venice and Ferrara
Time: Early Sixteenth Century
Running Time: 2 hours 20 minutes

After the opera was first given in Paris in 1840, Victor Hugo, on the grounds that the French translation (not the whole work) infringed his copyright, successfully sued for plagiarism, and the opera was not quite so quick as some others by Donizetti to make its way in Italy. Nonetheless, it is one of the more successful of his serious works and the title role remains a magnet for a soprano of an appropriate type.

Prologue. Gennaro, unbeknown to him, is the son of the infamous Lucrezia Borgia. When the opera opens, he is in Venice celebrating carnival with his friends, who include Maffio Orsini. Gennaro falls asleep and is discovered by Lucrezia, who sings of her love for the young man ('Com'è bello! quale incanto'). The aria is in Donizetti's grandest vein, and Gennaro wakes and appears to return her love. 'Di pescatore ignobile' he sings, describing (quite untruthfully) his humble origin as the supposed son of a fisherman. Gennaro's companions return, recognise Lucrezia and one by one denounce her as the murderer of their relations. Gennaro, who had no idea of the identity of the woman with whom he was falling in love, is horror-stricken.

Act I. A public place in Ferrara. Duke Alfonso, Lucrezia's fourth husband, has identified Gennaro as Lucrezia's lover and vents his fury in a full-scale aria ('Vieni, la mia vendetta'). Gennaro and his friends arrive in the square, see the letters BORGIA under the escutcheon of the palace, and Gennaro, to show his detestation of Lucrezia's crimes, with his sword hacks away the first letter of the name, leaving only ORGIA. On command of the Duke, he is arrested. Not knowing who has committed the outrage, Lucrezia demands that its perpetrator be put to death. Alfonso consents, but when Gennaro is led in, Lucrezia recognises him and pleads for his life. Alfonso remains firm, even when Lucrezia reminds him that he is her fourth husband and may yet share the fate of the other three. His rejoinder is to insist that Gennaro meet death by drinking a goblet of poisoned wine handed to him by Lucrezia herself. In the course of an ensemble, the Duke pours poison into Gennaro's cup unaware that Lucrezia has an antidote which, when he has left, she gives to Gennaro with the injunction to flee from Ferrara.

Act II. At a ball in Princess Negroni's palace in Ferrara, Maffio, who has sworn eternal faith with Gennaro, sings the most famous number of the opera, 'Il segreto per esser felici', a ballata which has proved to the taste of mezzo-sopranos since the opera's first performance. Sinister voices are heard from next door and Lucrezia appears to announce that, in revenge for their insults, she has poisoned all the guests at the banquet. She is horrified to find Gennaro of the company but he

refuses the antidote she offers him, even though she tells him she is his mother and pleads with him ('M'odi, ah m'odi') in an aria which is one of the most impressive passages of the score. He dies in her arms.   H.

MARIA STUARDA
Mary Stuart

Opera in three acts, text by Giuseppe Bardari. First performed under the name of *Buondelmonte* at the Teatro San Carlo, Naples, 18 October 1834, with Ronzi de Begnis. Produced under its original title but with alterations at la Scala, Milan, 30 December 1835, with Maria Malibran. Revived Bergamo, 1958, with Renata Heredia Capnist; Stuttgart, 1958, with Maria Kouba, Grace Hoffman; London, St Pancras Festival, 1966; Florence Festival, 1967, with Leyla Gencer, Shirley Verrett, Franco Tagliavini, conductor Francesco Molinari-Pradelli (Edinburgh Festival, 1969, with the same cast); Barcelona, 1968, with Montserrat Caballé. Rome, 1970, with Caballé; la Scala, 1971, with Caballé, Verrett; London (concert), 1971, with Caballé, Verrett; San Francisco, 1971, with Sutherland; New York, City Opera, 1972, with Sills, Tinsley, conductor Rudel; London Coliseum, 1973, with Janet Baker, Tinsley, Erwen, Garrard, conductor Mackerras.

Elisabetta (Elizabeth), Queen of England ......Soprano

Maria Stuarda (Mary, Queen of Scots) ....Soprano

Anna (Hannah Kennedy)...................Mezzo-Soprano

Robert Dudley, Earl of Leicester.........................Tenor

Talbot (Earl of Shrewsbury) ....Baritone

Cecil (Lord Burleigh) ....Bass

A Herald..Bass

Place: The Palace of Westminster, London; Fotheringay Castle, Northamptonshire
Time: 1567
Running Time: 2 hours 25 minutes

*M*aria Stuarda's early history is stormy, involving censorship troubles in Naples and a first night with a new libretto under the title of *Buondelmonte*; rivalry between prima donnas ending in fisticuffs on the stage; and a rehabilitation in Milan for which Malibran (in the title role) was wretchedly out of voice but refused to give up the part because of the fees involved.

At the start of the opera Mary, Queen of Scots, has fled from Scotland and been imprisoned in Fotheringay Castle by her cousin, Elizabeth, Queen of England. We do not meet her until Act II of Donizetti's opera, which is modelled on Schiller's play and includes the famous scene of the encounter between the two Queens, a dramatically effective falsification of history on Schiller's part.

Act I. In the Palace of Westminster, courtiers await with some excitement the arrival of Queen Elizabeth, rumoured to be about to unite by marriage the thrones of England and France. The Queen, however, has inclinations towards another and less exalted man, as she reveals in her graceful cavatina 'Ah, quando all'ara scorgemi'. The court and Talbot urge clemency in her dealings with her cousin Mary Stuart, Cecil reminds her of the untrustworthiness of her rival, while the Queen remains firm in her path of indecisiveness. When Leicester enters, she appoints him her ambassador to France, notices his reluctance to accept, raises suspicions in the minds of the bystanders that this may be the man whom she secretly loves, and leaves the stage.

Talbot reveals to Leicester that he has been to Fotheringay and that Mary Stuart (referred to throughout the opera indiscriminately as 'Maria' and 'Stuarda') has asked by letter for Leicester's help in her predicament. Leicester, impressed again by the beauty of her portrait ('Ah, rimiro il bel sembiante') and the poignancy of her situation, longs to free her but promises Talbot not further to jeopardise her safety by any impetuous action. When the Queen returns and demands to see the letter he is holding, she realises from it that Mary has at one time or another had designs both on the throne which she herself occupies and the man whom she at present favours. In the course of their duet, Leicester pleads successfully that the Queen agree to visit Mary in prison at Fotheringay ('Era d'amor l'immagine', and 'Sul crin la rivale').

Act II. In the Park at Fotheringay, Mary recalls with her companion Hannah the soft, far-off days of her happy life at the French court ('Oh nube! che lieve per l'aria ti aggiri'). Her reminiscences turn to agitation at the approach of the Queen's hunting party and the prospect of the meeting which she has yearned for and now dreads. Leicester is first on the scene, to counsel her to adopt a submissive attitude towards Elizabeth, to swear himself to exact vengeance if the Queen remain obdurate, and, at the end of their duet, to ask for Mary's hand in marriage.

When Elizabeth appears, she brings with her an atmosphere of suspicion (egged on by Cecil), mistrust (because of her doubts of Leicester's motives), and

apprehension (because she and her imprisoned cousin are to meet face to face for the first time). The confrontation is preceded by one of those moments of frozen drama that are peculiar to opera, a sextet in the composer's best vein, which opens with Elizabeth's reaction to her first sight of Mary: 'E sempre la stessa, superba, orgogliosa' (Unchanged she remains, proud and haughty). Mary forces herself to kneel before her cousin and beg for forgiveness, only to hear herself accused of treachery and in effect of murdering her husband, Darnley. In furious reaction, she insults the Queen, addressing her as 'Figlia impura di Bolena' and 'bastarda'. Her cause is all too evidently lost as the Queen summons the guards, and the act ends with Elizabeth in impassioned tones condemning her rival and cousin to death.

Act III. The first scene plays at the Palace of Westminster, where Queen Elizabeth waits to sign the death warrant ('Quella vita a me funesta'). The appearance of Leicester, whom she suspects of an amorous involvement with her cousin, and the persistent promptings of Cecil combine to resolve her doubts and she signs, to start a fine trio of mutual recrimination, during whose course she orders Leicester to witness the execution.

At Fotheringay, Mary hears of the sentence from Cecil and is offered and refuses the services of an Anglican priest. There follows the great scene of the confession by the loyal Talbot, which, with its linked chain of expressive melodic sections, seems to look forward to Verdi and the series of similarly constructed scenes, such as Gilda's with Rigoletto in the first act of *Rigoletto* and Leonora's with Padre Guardiano in the second of *Forza*. Mary at one moment seems to see, and we and Talbot through Donizetti's trombones to perceive, the ghost of her second husband, Henry Darnley, whom the librettist makes her refer to as Arrigo ('Delle mie colpe lo squallido fantasma'). She poignantly remembers the murdered Rizzio, but, as she clears her conscience ('Quando di luce rosea'), denies all complicity in her husband's death, which she claims was the direct result of Elizabeth's jealousy of their mutual love. Schiller's play leaves this issue unresolved, but there is no doubt that Donizetti's music demands that, though she admits to complicity in the Babington plot, Mary be judged innocent of murder.

In a room next to the scene of the impending execution, Mary's supporters protest what they think of as a crime against an innocent woman. Hannah tries to stop them disturbing the last hours of her mistress, who enters, sees them for the first time since her condemnation and prays calmly and movingly to God ('Deh! tu di un umile preghiera'). We hear the first of the three cannon shots which are to announce the moment of the execution, and Cecil brings the Queen's offer of a last wish. Mary asks that Hannah may go with her to the steps of the scaffold. She continues in a mood approaching resignation ('Di un cor che more') until the appearance of the distraught Leicester and the sound of the second cannon shot precipitate a last protest of innocence ('Ah, se un giorno da queste ritorte'). The third cannon shot sounds and Mary walks upright and dignified to her death.   H.

LUCIA DI LAMMERMOOR

Lucy of Lammermoor

Opera in three acts, text by Salvatore Cammarano after Sir Walter Scott's novel. Première at Teatro San Carlo, Naples, 26 September 1835, with Persiani, Duprez, Coselli. Her Majesty's, 1838; New Orleans, 1841; New York, 1843; Metropolitan, New York, 1883, with Sembrich, Campanini, Kaschmann. Revived Covent Garden, 1925, with Toti dal Monte, Dino Borgioli; 1959, with Sutherland, conductor Serafin; la Scala, Milan, 1923, with dal Monte, Pertile, Stracciari, Pinza, conductor Toscanini; 1936, with dal Monte, Schipa; 1938, with Pagliughi, Gigli, conductor Marinuzzi; 1947, with Pagliughi, Gigli, conductor Panizza; 1954, with Callas, di Stefano, Panerai, under Karajan. Other celebrated Lucias have been Lucca, Patti, Gerster, Melba, Tetrazzini, Galli-Curci, Barrientos, Pacini, Pareto, Scotto.

Enrico (Lord Henry Ashton) *of Lammermoor* ...Baritone
Lucia (Lucy), *his sister* ....Soprano
Edgardo (Edgar), *Master of Ravenswood*.............Tenor
Arturo (Lord Arthur Bucklaw)........................Tenor
Raimondo (Raymond), *chaplain at Lammermoor*..Bass
Alisa (Alice), *companion to Lucia* ....Mezzo-Soprano
Normanno (Norman), *follower of Ashton*...........Tenor

Relatives, Retainers, Friends of the House of
    Lammermoor

Place: Scotland
Time: c. 1700
Running Time: 2 hours 25 minutes

Lord Enrico Ashton, in order to retrieve his fallen fortunes and extricate himself from a political position endangered by his former opposition to the King, has unbeknown to her arranged a marriage between his sister Lucia and Lord Arturo Bucklaw. He for his part has only just become aware of an attachment which has grown up between Lucia and their neighbour Edgardo of Ravenswood, whose family and the Ashtons are sworn enemies.

Act I. A wood near Lammermoor. On suspicion that Edgardo has been seen lurking near the castle, retainers beat the bounds but to Ashton's fury find nothing. He inveighs against Edgardo (aria: 'Cruda, funesta smania').

A fountain in the park. Atmospherically introduced by the harp, Lucia, who has an assignation with Edgardo, in the first of two graceful solos tells Alisa the legend of the fountain: 'Regnava nel silenzio'. Here an ancestress of hers was stabbed to death by her lover and has reappeared as a ghost, which the impressionable Lucia believes she has seen. Alisa begs Lucia to give up Edgardo, but she affirms he is the light of her life: 'Quando, rapita in estasi'. Edgardo comes to tell Lucia he leaves in the morning for a mission abroad but wants to make peace with his traditional enemies – the Ashtons have apparently in the past usurped his family's inheritance. Lucia warns him that her brother still breathes fire and slaughter at mention of his name and the duet proper ('Sulla tomba') starts with his fiery reiteration of his hatred for her family. Lucia is melting and conciliatory and eventually, as he puts a ring on her finger, Edgardo sings of his feelings of ardent love. Their voices join in an expression of tenderness ('Verranno a te sull' aure'), the only time in this opera of deception and madness when there is room for such sentiments.

Act II. Ashton's apartment. Ashton has decided that nothing but a politically correct marriage on Lucia's part will save his fortunes and he tells her Lord Arturo Bucklaw will shortly arrive for their betrothal ceremony. He has not only intercepted and destroyed letters from Edgardo but now shows her a forgery purporting to prove Edgardo's unfaithfulness. Already the music suggests Lucia's mental instability and during the long scene with her brother, he rages at her daring to oppose his wishes and she dissolves into another, less real world ('Soffriva nel pianto, languia nel dolore'). Ashton remains adamant.

Though she now believes herself betrayed by Edgardo and is moved that only she can save her brother from a traitor's death, Lucia will not take the

Lucia di Lammermoor *(Covent Garden, 1959, director/designer Franco Zeffirelli). Lucia (Joan Sutherland) descends the stairs, having murdered her husband. Sutherland became famous almost overnight for her performance, particularly her singing of the celebrated mad scene.*

fatal step without the family chaplain's advice. He advises her unequivocally to accept her brother's plans (this scene is sometimes omitted).

A hall in the castle of Lammermoor. Guests rejoice, Arturo makes his entrance, Lucia is led in like a sacrificial lamb, and the wedding contract is signed. It is the moment for Edgardo's grand gesture, as he returns from his foreign duties to find what he thought was his prospective bride about to be affianced to another. The great sextet begins ('Chi mi frena in tal momento?') and builds as Lucia's and the other voices are added to create an edifice of sound from the tensions of the antagonists. Before the act ends with a *stretta* the chaplain adjures all to return swords to scabbards. Edgardo curses the day he fell in love with Lucia.

Act III. Edgardo's castle. Edgardo is alone when Ashton comes to challenge him in an extended and impressive duet (the scene is often – wrongly – omitted to bring the opera more swiftly to its climax, and indeed the heroine to hers).

The great hall of Lammermoor Castle. The chaplain interrupts the wedding celebrations with news of disaster. Lucia, her mind unhinged by the sequence of events, has, on her wedding night, killed her husband. She appears, pale and with a dagger in hand, and there follows the Mad Scene. In her hallucination Lucia, heralded by the flute, believes she and Edgardo are to be married. She is now reminded of past happiness – the love duet; now spurred to fear by memory of the ghost at the fountain; now involved in the marriage itself ('Ardon gli incensi'). The aria traditionally finishes with a huge cadenza with the voice vying for brilliant effect with a flute; though Donizetti originally allowed for a cadenza, this was elaborated starting in the mid-nineteenth century until it grew to its present proportions, indeed in many ways to dominate the opera. On the other hand, it must be said that the effect of the duet for soprano and flute is so full of virtuosity and so well known that to abandon it would demand a conductor of strong conviction and a soprano of monumental complacency. The expressive lyricism of the aria proper is set off by the grand scale of the cabaletta ('Spargi d'amaro pianto').

Finale. The Ravenswood cemetery. Edgardo still believes Lucia has betrayed him and longs for death. His recitative ('Tombe degli avi miei'), and aria ('Fra poco a me ricovero'), as if to balance Lucia's great scene, are on the grandest scale, and the finale of the opera, as a procession leaves Lammermoor and approaches Ravenswood, is no less impressive. The chaplain announces Lucia's death, Edgardo sings despairingly of his lost love ('Tu che a dio spiegasti l'ali') and stabs himself.

Once regarded as the epitome of early nineteenth-century romantic opera, *Lucia* deteriorated into little more than a vehicle for a brilliant high soprano until the advent of Maria Callas in mid-twentieth century freed the opera from the light sopranos whose exclusive property it seemed to have become. No longer was attention focused almost exclusively on the Mad Scene and *Lucia* was once again seen as a work of real musical subtlety and genuine dramatic skill, indeed a highlight of pre-Verdian Italian opera. It requires a tenor on as high a level as the soprano and its wealth of dramatic music makes it just as likely to appeal to audiences used to modern music theatre as to canary-fanciers anxious to compare the newest soprano sensation with their recordings.   H.

IL CAMPANELLO
The Doorbell

Opera in one act, text by the composer. Première 1 June 1836, with Amalia Schütz, Giorgio Ronconi, Raffaele Casacci.

Serafina, *a young bride* ....Soprano
Don Annibale di Pistacchio, *an apothecary, her husband* ....Bass
Spiridione, *Don Annibale's servant*......................Tenor
Madama Rosa, *Serafina's aunt* ....Mezzo-Soprano
Enrico, *Serafina's cousin*.................................Baritone

Place: Naples
Time: The 1830s
Running Time: 55 minutes

After the traumatic events of late 1835 – the death of his father coincided with the difficult rehearsals in Milan of *Maria Stuarda*, with Malibran in the title role – Donizetti was delighted to be offered a French *vaudeville*, which he proceeded himself to translate and adapt as *Il Campanello*, one of the not so common one-act comedies with which he punctuated the full-length melodramas in which he specialised. It was successful from the start.

The story (it amounts to little more than a sketch) revolves round the marriage of a young wife to an older man which, unlike the much more substantial *Don Pasquale*, is neither a fake nor, it would appear, does the bride's younger suitor win her in the end.

Don Annibale di Pistacchio, a village apothecary who is a stickler for the rules, has just been married to Serafina and the chorus celebrates in style. Annibale himself, not without smugness, rejoices in his new condition until Spiridione announces the arrival of none other than Enrico, Serafina's cousin, whom he greatly dislikes. It is not long before Serafina herself puts in an appearance, dancing a galop with Don Annibale's *bête noire*. In an extended duet, Enrico remonstrates with her for having married and left him desolate. There is some tenderness in her insistence that he is himself nothing but a ladies' man, but Donizetti skilfully avoids eliciting sympathy for Enrico by giving him no romantic music.

Don Annibale interrupts, but Enrico tries to gain a point by describing a ludicrous scenario of which he is the hero, until midnight sounds and, even though Enrico encourages a dispensation of wine all round, he is sent packing.

Enrico will see to it that Don Annibale's wedding night does not go uninterrupted. Spiridione's offer to dispense drugs for him elicits from the chemist an insistence on keeping to the rules which lay down that he must do so himself. First comes a Frenchman, cross-eyed with hangover and requiring from the apothecary a bottle of champagne. As he leaves, he manages to blow the candle out and rearrange crucial bits of furniture, so that Annibale knocks over his best china. Next, an opera singer rings the bell to say that his début is at hand and he has lost his voice serenading a girl. The cure is either to marry her or forget her, says the chemist. But what about my début, asks the singer? He gets some pills and tries out his voice in a virtuoso display.

When he has gone, Don Annibale finds in his keyhole a hostile note – probably from Enrico, helpfully suggests Spiridione. Next, the bell is rung by an old man with a prescription to be made up. He reels off his friend's symptoms, then suggests a list of nonsense ingredients he maintains the prescription contains. As he leaves, Spiridione returns and by mistake in the dark grabs Don Annibale.

Enrico bounces in to announce the imminent departure of the stage coach Don Annibale must catch the morning after his wedding night, and Serafina leads a grandly romantic start to the Finale. For all the mockery and horseplay, Annibale's marriage, as he departs with his baggage, seems intact and Enrico has not won the girl.   H.

L'ASSEDIO DI CALAIS
The Siege of Calais

Opera in three acts, libretto by Salvatore Cammarano. Première at San Carlo, Naples, 19 November 1836, with Paul Barroilhet, Almareinda Manzocchi, Caterina Barilli-Patti. Barilli was the mother of Adelina Patti.

Eustachio de Saint-Pierre, *Mayor of Calais* ....Baritone
Aurelio, *his son* ....Mezzo-Soprano
Eleonora, *Aurelio's wife*.................................Soprano
Burghers of Calais
    Giovanni d'Aire ....Tenor
    Jacomo de Wisants ....Tenor
    Pietro de Wisants....................................Baritone
    Armando...Bass
Eduardo (Edward) III, *King of England*...........Baritone
Isabella, *Queen of England*[1] ....Soprano
Edmundo, *English general* ....Tenor
An English Spy..Bass

Place: Inside and Outside Besieged Calais
Time: 1347
Running Time: 1 hour 50 minutes

The opera starts with a scene in which Aurelio lets himself down from the battlements in order to steal some loaves for his starving family. He ties them to the rope, is discovered but escapes.

Inside the besieged city, Eustachio rapidly establishes himself as a powerful figure, as he sings nobly and with resignation of the city's plight – commentators have compared him as a figure to Simon Boccanegra. In a duet with Eleonora, his daughter-in-law, he mourns the loss of his son then celebrates the news of Aurelio's safety. Aurelio is a *virtuoso musico* (trouser role) typical of the period and his aria expresses his joy at seeing his family again.

There is little optimism within Calais but a bold face is put on the situation, starting when a stranger makes his appearance to stir popular feeling against Eustachio, who is the sole impediment, he maintains,

---

[1] Historically incorrect: Isabella was Edward III's mother, his wife was Philippa of Hainault.

between them and a reasonable peace with the English. The finale is dominated by the resolute figure of Eustachio who loses no time in unmasking the stranger as an English spy, and the act comes to an energetic conclusion.

Act II. Eleonora and Aurelio pray for Calais and Aurelio reveals a sinister dream he has had in which his son is murdered. The duet is on a grand scale and full of attractive invention.

The citizens are in despair as Edmundo, an English general, comes to lay down the conditions under which the English King will accept the city's surrender. Failing this his army, reinforced by the English army which has conquered the Scots, will renew its attack on Calais and destroy the city. Six nobly born citizens must present themselves ready for death in expiation of the crime, as King Edward sees it, of the city having resisted him. Reaction to the demand is one of devastation but Aurelio leads a moment of spirited defiance. Eustachio reluctantly agrees to the harsh conditions. Before the sun sets, he says, six burghers will be brought to the English camp.

Edmundo leaves and Eustachio explains that death may to a soldier seem preferable; for the women and children to fall into enemy hands would be little short of disaster. He himself is the first volunteer and five others follow suit including, to Eustachio's great distress, his son Aurelio. The act ends with a great ensemble of lamentation.

Act III. The English encampment. King Edward receives news that his demands will be met and rejoices in an aria less warlike in character than one might have expected from the ferocity of his earlier sentiments. He greets his Queen at the head of her victorious army and assures her Calais will soon be his. A military show and dance in her honour precede the arrival of hostages (Donizetti appears to have provided only two out of the four ballet movements, and his letters after the première suggest he was dissatisfied with the undramatic effect made by Act III, particularly its opening scene).

With the appearance of the hostages, the mood changes to one of universal gloom. Edward appears adamant, Eustachio is dignity personified as he leads an ensemble of resignation, Aurelio bids farewell to his wife and child, but finally Edward's Queen pleads successfully with her husband, who relents amid general rejoicing and pardons the hostages.   H.

ROBERTO DEVEREUX
Robert Devereux

Opera in three acts, libretto by Salvatore Cammarano after Ancelot's *Elisabeth d'Angleterre*. Première, Naples, 29 October 1837, with Giuseppina Ronzi de Begnis. First performed in Venice in 1838 with Carolina Ungher and Moriani; Paris, 1838, with Grisi, Rubini, Tamburini; la Scala, 1839; London, 1841, with Grisi and Rubini; New York, 1849. After 1882, when it was given in Pavia, there is no record of performance until it was revived in 1964 at the San Carlo, Naples, with Leyla Gencer. Revived in concert form, 1965, Carnegie Hall, New York, with Montserrat Caballé; Barcelona, 1968, with Caballé; Bonn, 1969; London (in concert), 1970, with Caballé; New York City Opera, 1970, with Sills, Domingo.

Elisabetta (Elizabeth), *Queen of England* ....Soprano

Duke of Nottingham.....................................Baritone

Sarah, *Duchess of Nottingham* ....Mezzo-Soprano

Roberto (Robert Devereux), *Earl of Essex* ....Tenor

Lord Cecil..Tenor

Sir Walter Raleigh ....Bass

A Page...Bass

Nottingham's Servant ....Bass

Ladies of the Court, Courtiers, Pages, Guards, Nottingham's Attendants

Place: England
Time: 1598
Running Time: 2 hours 10 minutes

*R*oberto Devereux is the fifty-seventh of Donizetti's seventy operas, and it was written only nineteen years after his first, under circumstances about as unpropitious as can be imagined. In 1836, he lost his father and his mother within a few weeks of each other and his wife died in July 1837. *Roberto Devereux* was commissioned for Naples, which city, while he was struggling to complete the opera, was in the grip of a disastrous cholera epidemic. The opera was nonetheless a success at its première, though it was not long before Donizetti was speaking of a jinx on the work, both the baritone and the prima donna falling ill during the first run of performances and the opera being performed elsewhere in a pirated edition, a disaster more from the point of view of his pocket than his pride.

The overture, written for the Paris première, includes anachronistically a woodwind variant of *God Save the Queen*.

The opera has only a slender basis in historical fact, but it is convenient to place it in 1598, the year of

Essex's rebellion and execution. As a background to the story it is important to know only that Essex is back from his unsuccessful military mission to Ireland and is about to stand trial. Sarah, Duchess of Nottingham, pines with love for Robert Devereux, Earl of Essex, and cannot hide her tears from the other ladies of the court as she reads the story of fair Rosamond (the heroine incidentally of Donizetti's opera *Rosamunda d'Inghilterra*): 'All'afflitto è dolce il pianto'. The Queen enters and reveals to Sarah that she has consented to see Essex, without whom her life has no meaning, and whom she suspects not of the treason of which he is accused but of infidelity to her: 'L'amor suo mi fe' beata'. Cecil comes to demand the Queen's approval of his Peers' judgement on Essex, but she asks for further proof of treason and says she will see him, her cabaletta revealing her unabated feelings for her subject.

Essex proclaims his fidelity to his Sovereign but, in the course of a grandiose *scena* during which she refers to the ring she once gave him and which he has only to produce for her to guarantee his safety, so far forgets himself as to fancy for a moment that the Queen knows of his secret passion for Sarah. No amount of protestation can allay the suspicion he has created and the unhappy Essex is left alone to lament the turn fate has taken against him. His friend Nottingham, come to assure him of his support in the Council, reveals in a cavatina ('Forse in quel cor sensibile') that his wife Sarah, a prey to grief and weeping, has even aroused his own jealous suspicions. Cecil summons Nottingham to the Council and he goes reiterating his devotion to Essex.

Scene ii. To Sarah's apartments in Nottingham House, Essex comes to upbraid her that she married another. She pleads that her father's sudden death while Essex was abroad precipitated her into a loveless marriage and urges him to turn towards the Queen. Protesting that his heart is dead to love, he tears the Queen's ring from his finger and throws it on the table. In the course of their duet, Sarah gives him a blue scarf she has embroidered and he swears to wear it near his heart.

Act II. The Hall at the Palace of Westminster (as Act I, scene i). Lords and Ladies of the court brood on Essex's likely fate; without the Queen's aid, he is lost – and her present mood suggests this will not be forthcoming. Cecil enters to tell the Queen that the Council, in spite of Nottingham's defence of his friend,

has brought in a sentence of death, which now awaits only her approval. Cecil leaves and Raleigh comes to tell Elizabeth that when Essex was arrested and searched a silk scarf was found next to his heart. No sooner has the Queen recognised it as the Duchess of Nottingham's than Nottingham himself comes in to plead in a duet for Essex's life. Essex himself is brought in under guard, and the Queen confronts him with the scarf, proof that he lied to her once when he denied being in love. Nottingham, too, recognises his wife's scarf and calls down the vengeance of Heaven on his faithless friend. The trio ('Un perfido, un vile, un mentitore tu sei') runs the gamut of emotions of the betrayed friend, the discovered and anxious lover, and above all the scorned woman before, with the summoning of the courtiers, it becomes a finale in which all voices join for their different reasons in condemning Essex's treachery.

Act III. Sarah Nottingham's apartments. She receives news of Essex's condemnation, plans immediately to take the ring Essex has left with her to the Queen in token of his plea for mercy, only to look up into the unforgiving eyes of her husband. In the course of their duet, he denounces Essex and, when sounds of a procession taking the condemned man to prison are heard in the distance, makes clear his intention of preventing her conveying the ring to the Queen.

The scene changes to the Tower of London, where Essex waits for news of the pardon which he believes will certainly follow delivery of the ring to the Queen. He pictures offering himself to the sword of Nottingham and with his dying breath assuring his friend that Sarah has remained chaste in spite of all temptation ('Come uno spirito angelico'). But the anticipated pardon does not arrive, rather are heard the sounds of the guard approaching to take him to his death. In spite of the urgency of the situation, it is not hard to see in Donizetti's reaction to it, both in march and cabaletta, the sort of operatic cliché on which Sullivan in his comic operas seized with such relish.

The last scene shows the Queen in the Great Hall surrounded by her ladies and anxiously awaiting the arrival of the trusted Sarah to comfort her, as well as a sight of the ring which she believes Essex will send her (she does not of course connect the two events). Her beautiful aria ('Vivi ingrato') shows a forgiving side to her nature not before revealed in the opera, but the sight of the distraught Sarah bringing the ring, and her immediate recognition of a hated rival, does not sway her from her purpose. She orders a stay of execution at the very moment when a cannon shot is heard giving the signal to the headsman. The Queen turns in misery to blame Sarah until Nottingham himself reveals his guilt in preventing the ring reaching the Queen. The opera ends as Elizabeth, beside herself with grief, sees visions of the Crown bathed in blood, of a man running through the palace corridors carrying his own head, of a tomb opening for her where once stood her throne. It is rare among cabalettas in being marked *maestoso* for most of its course, and only in the last few seconds is it superseded by the more conventional *allegro*.   H.

POLIUTO

Tragedia lirica in three acts, libretto by Salvatore Cammarano, based on Pierre Corneille's *Polyeucte* (1641–42). Banned in rehearsal in 1838 by the King of Naples because of its Christian subject (St Polyeuctus d. A.D. 259). First performed in a four-act French version by Scribe as *Les martyrs*, Opéra, Paris, 1840. Teatro San Carlo, Naples, 1848. First U.S. performance New Orleans, 1846. First U.K. performance Covent Garden, London, 1852. Often staged for great tenors, such as Tamberlik, Tamagno, Gigli, Corelli (opposite Callas at la Scala in 1960). Revived Vienna, 1986, for Carreras; Rome, 1989, with Nicola Martinucci, Elizabeth Connell, Renato Bruson, conducted by Jan Latham-Koenig.

Poliuto, *Roman convert to Christianity* ....Tenor

Paolina, *his wife* ....Soprano

Severo, *Roman proconsul* ....Baritone

Felice, *Paolina's father, governor of Armenia* ....Tenor

Callistene, *high priest of Jupiter* ....Bass

Nearco, *a Christian, Poliuto's friend* ....Tenor

A Christian ....Tenor

Place: Armenia
Time: c. A.D. 259
Running Time: 1 hour 55 minutes

Donizetti wrote *Poliuto* for Naples, but he always intended it for export. Its religious, spectacular element was directly inspired by Halévy's *La Juive*, which he had admired in an awesome staging at the Opéra in 1835, while he was directing *Marino Faliero* at the rather less prestigious Théâtre des Italiens. From the very beginning, when timpani rolls introduce an extraordinary passage for four bassoons, *Poliuto* was intended to make its mark. Donizetti

wrote the title role for Adolphe Nourrit, the most important French tenor of the day, who had created leading roles for Rossini and Meyerbeer, but felt threatened by the arrival of Gilbert Duprez. Nourrit came to Italy to study with Donizetti and make his Neapolitan début as Poliuto. Discouraged by the opera's cancellation and by continuing vocal problems, he committed suicide on 8 March 1839.

Act I. 'The Baptism'. A gloomy cave. Christians have assembled in secret to witness the baptism of Poliuto. Urging discretion on one another, they also anticipate martyrdom for their faith. Poliuto confesses to his friend Nearco that he suspects his beloved Paolina is unfaithful to him with Callistene, the high priest of Jupiter. She knows nothing of his conversion to Christianity. Poliuto prays that God will make him worthy of his new faith ('D'un'alma troppo fervida'). Paolina appears, to an elaborate clarinet solo over pizzicato strings. She has followed her husband, suspecting that he has joined the prohibited sect. Nearco confirms her suspicions but begs her to keep the secret since, as he reminds her, a recent law condemns neophytes to death. She hears the Christians praying for their enemies, and is deeply moved and impressed. Poliuto confirms his wife's fears. In the distance military music announces the arrival of the new Roman proconsul, Severo, whose death in battle had been prematurely reported. Paolina had previously been in love with Severo. She is delighted at the news of his return, but represses her feelings – her F major music seems unrestrainedly jolly, however (cabaletta, 'Perchè di stolto giubilo').

In a magnificent piazza the people salute Severo. The proconsul declares that he has been sent to Armenia by the Emperor to root out the Christians' rebellious cult. Privately, he looks forward with joy and trepidation to seeing Paolina, whom he adores, in a cavatina that is a gift to a sensitive baritone ('Di tua beltade immagine'). Felice, Paolina's father, tells him that she has been married to Poliuto. Severo now wishes he had died in battle ('No, l'acciar non fu spietato').

Act II. 'The Neophyte'. A hall in Felice's house. Callistene tells Severo that Paolina's father forced her to become engaged to Poliuto. Severo declares his love for Paolina, while she tries in vain to conceal her feelings (duet, 'Il più lieto dei viventi'). She begs him to leave and allow her to keep her honour. Poliuto overhears their encounter; convinced that Paolina has betrayed him, he swears revenge. A Christian tells him that Nearco has been dragged in chains to the temple of Jupiter. Poliuto bows to the will of God and resolves to forgive, not punish ('Sfolgoro divino raggio').

The temple of Jupiter. The people's prayers mingle with the priests' invectives against the Christians.[1] Callistene accuses Nearco of having recruited a new convert last night. Nearco refuses to name the neophyte. Severo prescribes imprisonment and torture. Poliuto steps forward and reveals that he was the neophyte. All the observers are amazed and furious, except for Paolina, who offers the Christian God a deal: if the 'Nazarene' saves Poliuto's life, she will accept Him as her only god. Paolina then begs her father to pardon Poliuto, but he remains adamant. She throws herself at Severo's feet. Poliuto is so outraged by the sight that he repudiates his wife and upsets the altar to Jupiter, the 'lying, worthless' god who presided at his marriage. The priests curse him, while Callistene drags Paolina away and Poliuto and Nearco are taken back to prison.

Act III. 'Martyrdom'. The sacred wood. The people look forward to the bloody spectacle of martyrdom in the circus. Callistene worries that Paolina may convince Severo to pardon the Christians. He therefore commands the priests to mingle with the crowds and insist that punishment is exacted.

In prison, Poliuto has a celestial vision, in which his wife's virtue is exalted. Paolina confesses to him that she did indeed once love Severo, but insists that she has since followed the path of virtue. As for Callistene, his calumnies are caused by his infatuation with her. Convinced that she is innocent, Poliuto declares that he is now ready to die. Paolina begs him to abjure his faith and to have pity on her, but Poliuto remains firm (duet 'Ah! fuggi da morte'). Poliuto's courageous example inspires Paolina to embrace the Christian faith and share his martyrdom. Poliuto is momentarily abashed but then he seals Paolina's conversion by baptising her. United in the face of death, they are rapt with divine ecstasy ('Il suon dell'arpe angeliche').

Forced by Severo to choose between life and death, Poliuto confirms his decision. Paolina reveals that she has become a Christian and asks to share her husband's fate. Severo tries to make her change her mind, on the grounds that her father will suffer. As the priests curse and the people cry out, Paolina and Poliuto anticipate the joys of paradise, while Severo admits that he loves the guilty, blasphemous woman more than he loves Jupiter, but is prevented from committing suicide.

Poliuto is what matters, not the artificially inflated frenchified version that Donizetti made for Paris, *Les martyrs*, even though that omits the jealousy motif, which was only included to distract from the story's (potentially offensive) religious elements. *Les martyrs* does include a magnificent new trio in Act I, as well as excrescences such as a 'gladiatorial combat'. The tenor role was rewritten to suit Gilbert Duprez, and went as high as the F above high C; the soprano role was made even more demanding.   P.

LA FILLE DU RÉGIMENT
The Daughter of the Regiment

Opera in two acts, text by J.H. Vernoy de Saint-Georges and F. Bayard. Première at the Opéra-Comique, Paris, 11 February 1840. First performed in Milan, 1840; New York, 1843 (in French); London, Her Majesty's, 1847; Metropolitan, New York, 1902, with Sembrich, Salignac, Gilibert; revived 1917, with Hempel, Carpi, Scotti, and 1940, with Pons, Jobin, Baccaloni. Heard at la Scala, Milan, 1928, with dal Monte, Lomanto, di Lelio; Covent Garden, 1966, with Sutherland, Pavarotti, Malas; la Scala, Milan, 1968, with Freni, Pavarotti, Ganzarolli. Famous Maries have also included Lind, Sontag, Lucca, Patti, Tetrazzini.

Marie, *the 'Daughter of the Regiment'*..............Soprano
Sulpice, *sergeant of French Grenadiers*..................Bass
Tonio, *a Tyrolese peasant in love with Marie*........Tenor
Marquise de Birkenfeld................................Soprano
Hortensio, *steward to the Marquise*......................Bass
Corporal...Bass
A Peasant ....Tenor
Duchesse de Krakenthorp ....Soprano

Soldiers, Peasants, Friends of the Marquise

Place: Mountains of the Swiss Tyrol
Time: 1815
Running Time: 1 hour 25 minutes

---

[1] Marked to be sung 'with fanatic zeal', this scene is, as William Ashbrook says, 'one of Donizetti's major accomplishments' and clearly set a precedent that Verdi followed in *Aida*.

Act I. A valley in the Tyrolese mountains, the outskirts of a village. Tyrolese peasants are grouped on rising ground, as if on the lookout. Their wives and daughters kneel before a shrine to the Virgin. The Marquise de Birkenfeld is seated on a rustic bench; beside her stands Hortensio, her steward. They have been caught in the eddy of the war. A battle is in progress not far away. The Tyrolese chorus sings valiantly, the women pray: the French are victorious – no surprise, since the unbeaten Twenty-First Regiment of Grenadiers are among them.

One of them comes in, Sergeant Sulpice, an old grumbler. After him comes a pretty girl in uniform, a vivandière – Marie, the daughter of the regiment, found on the field of battle when she was a mere child, and brought up by a whole regiment of fathers, the spoiled darling of the grenadiers. She sings 'Au bruit de la guerre j'ai reçu le jour' ('Apparvi alla luce, sul campo guerrier'), which ends in a brilliant cadenza.

The Sergeant puts her through a drill. Then they have a 'Rataplan' duet, a repetition of Marie's solo with an accompaniment of drum-rolls. The drum is the music that is sweetest to her; and, indeed, Marie's manipulation of the drumsticks is a feature of the role.

But for a few days Marie has not been as cheerful as usual. She has been seen with a young man, and Sulpice asks her about him. She tells the Sergeant that this young man saved her life by preventing her from falling over a precipice. That, however, establishes no claims upon her. The regiment has decreed that only a grenadier shall have her for wife.

There is a commotion. Some soldiers drag in Tonio, whom they charge as a spy. They have discovered him sneaking about the camp. He would receive short shrift, but Marie pleads for him, for he is none other than her rescuer. As he wants to remain near Marie, he decides to become a soldier. The grenadiers celebrate his decision by drinking his health and calling upon Marie to sing the 'Song of the Regiment', a dapper tune, which is one of the best-known numbers of the score: 'Chacun le sait, chacun le dit' ('Ciascun lo dice, ciascun lo sà!'). There is then a love scene for Marie and Tonio, followed by a duet for them, 'De cet aveu si tendre' ('A voti cosi ardente').

Afterwards the grenadiers sing a 'Rataplan' chorus. But the Sergeant has been informed that the Marquise de Birkenfeld desires safe conduct. Birkenfeld is the name to which were addressed certain papers found on Marie when she was discovered as a baby on the battlefield. The Marquise examines the papers, declares that Marie is her niece and henceforth must live with her in the castle. Poor Tonio has become a grenadier in vain. The regiment cannot help him; it can only lament with him that their daughter is lost to them. She herself is none too happy. She sings a sad farewell, 'Il faut partir, mes bons compagnons d'armes' ('Convien partir! o miei compagni d'arme').

Act II. In the castle of the Marquise. Marie is learning to dance the minuet and to sing classical airs. But in the midst of her singing she and Sulpice, whom the Marquise also has brought to the castle, break out into the 'Song of the Regiment' and stirring 'Rataplans'. The liveliness, however, is only temporary, for poor Marie is to wed, at her aunt's command, a scion of the ducal house of Krakenthorp. The march of the grenadiers is heard. They come in, led by Tonio who has been made a captain for valour. Sulpice can now see no reason why Marie should not marry him instead of the nobleman selected by her aunt. And, indeed, Marie and Tonio decide to elope. But the Marquise confesses to the Sergeant, in order to win his aid in influencing Marie, that the girl is really her daughter, born out of wedlock. Sulpice informs Marie, who now feels that she cannot go against her mother's wishes.

In the end, however, it is Marie herself who saves the situation. The guests have assembled for the signing of the wedding contract, when Marie, before them all, sings fondly of her childhood with the regiment, and of her life as a vivandière. The society people are scandalised. But the Marquise is so touched that she leads Tonio to Marie and places the girl's hand in that of her lover. The opera ends with an ensemble, 'Salute to France!'   K.

LA FAVORITE

The Favourite

Opera in four acts, text in French by Alphonse Royer and Gustav Vaez after a drama *Le Comte de Comminges* by Baculard d'Arnaud. Première at the Paris Opéra, 2 December 1840. First performed in London, Drury Lane, 1843 (in English); New Orleans, 1843 (in French); Covent Garden, 1845 (in French); Her Majesty's, 1847 (in Italian); Metropolitan, New York, 1895, with Mantelli, Cremonini, Ancona, Plançon; 1905, with Edyth Walker, Caruso, Scotti, Plançon; 1912, at

London Opera House, with Augusta Doria, Orville Harrold. Revived la Scala, 1934, with Stignani, Pertile; Rome, 1935, with Cobelli, Gigli; la Scala, 1939; Rome, 1946; la Scala, 1949, with Stignani, Poggi, Silveri, Siepi; Rome, 1951, with Barbieri, Lauri-Volpi; la Scala, 1962, with Simionato, Raimondi; Chicago, 1964, with Cossotto, Alfredo Kraus, Bruscantini, and Florence, 1966, with same cast.

Alphonse (Alfonso) XI, *King of Castile* ....Baritone

Fernand (Ferdinand), *a young novice of the*
    Monastery of St James of Compostella ....Tenor

Don Gaspard (Gaspare), *the King's Minister* ......Tenor

Balthazar (Baldassare), *Superior of the*
    Monastery of St James.......................................Bass

Léonor (Leonora) di Gusman ....Mezzo-Soprano

Inès (Inez), *her confidante* ....Soprano

Courtiers, Guards, Monks, Ladies of the Court,
    Attendants

Place: Castile, Spain
Time: c. 1340
Running Time: 2 hours 50 minutes

Fernand, a novice in the Monastery of St James of Compostella, has chanced to see and has fallen in love with Léonor, the mistress of Alphonse, King of Castile. He neither knows her name, nor is he aware of her equivocal position.

Act I. The interior of the monastery. Fernand tells Balthazar, the Superior, that he desires to renounce his novitiate, because he has fallen in love and cannot banish his beloved from his thoughts. He describes her to the priest as 'Un ange, une femme'.

Balthazar's questions elicit from Fernand that his only knowledge of the woman is of her youth and beauty. Name and station are unknown to him, although he believes her to be of high rank. Balthazar, who had hoped that in time Fernand would become his successor as superior of the monastery, releases him reluctantly from his obligations, and prophesies that he will retrace his steps to seek refuge once more within the monastery's walls.

The scene changes to an idyllic prospect on the island of St Leon, where Léonor lives in splendour. She is deeply enamoured of Fernand, yet is convinced that, because of her relations with King Alphonse, he will despise her once he discovers who she is. But, without letting him learn her name or station, she has arranged for him to be brought blindfolded to the island.

'Rayons dorés', a graceful solo and chorus for Inès, Léonor's confidante, and her woman companions, opens the scene. The boat conveying Fernand touches the island; he has the bandage withdrawn from his eyes, and looks in amazement upon the charming surroundings amid which he stands. He questions Inès regarding the name and station of her who holds gentle sway over the island, but in vain. Inès and her companions retire, as Léonor enters. She interrupts Fernand's delight at seeing her by telling him – but without giving her reasons – that their love can lead only to sorrow; they must part. He protests vehemently. She, however, cannot be moved from her determination, and hands him a parchment, which she tells him will lead him to a career of honour.

Inès, entering hurriedly, announces the approach of the King. Léonor bids Fernand farewell and goes hastily to meet Alphonse. Fernand now believes that the woman with whom he has fallen in love is of so high a rank that she cannot stoop to wed him, yet expresses her love for him by seeking to advance him. This is confirmed when, on reading the scroll she has given him, he discovers that it gratifies his highest ambition and confers upon him a commission in the army. The act closes with his martial air, 'Oui, ta voix m'inspire'. He sees the path to glory open up before him, and with it the hope that some great deed may yet make him worthy to claim the hand of the woman he loves.

Act II. Gardens of the palace of the Alcazar. Fernand's dream of glory has come true. We learn, through a brief colloquy between Alphonse and Don Gaspard, his minister, that the young officer has led the Spanish army to victory against the Moors. The King, who has no knowledge of the love between Fernand and Léonor, sings of his own passion for her in the expressive air, 'Léonore, viens, j'abandonne'.

The object of his love enters, accompanied by her confidante. The King has prepared a fête in celebration of Fernand's victory, but Léonor, while rejoicing in the honours destined to be his, is filled with foreboding. Moreover, these fears find justification in the return of Gaspard with a letter in Fernand's handwriting, and intended for Léonor, but which the minister has intercepted in the hand of Inès. The King's angry questions regarding the identity of the writer are interrupted by Balthazar, preceded by a priest bearing a scroll with the Papal seal. He faces the King and Léonor while the lords and ladies, who have gathered for the fête, look on in apprehension, though not wholly without knowledge of what is impending.

There is at the court a strong party that condemns

the King's illicit passion for Léonor, so openly shown; this party has appealed to the Papal throne against the King. The Pope has sent a Bull to Balthazar, in which the Superior of the Monastery of St James is authorised to pronounce the interdict on the King if the latter refuses to dismiss his favourite and restore his legitimate wife to her rights. It is with this commission that Balthazar has now appeared before the King, who at first is inclined to refuse obedience. He wavers. Balthazar gives him until the next day, and until then withholds his anathema. His vigorous yet dignified denunciation of the King, 'Redoutez la fureur d'un Dieu terrible' (Do not call down the wrath of God, the avenger), forms a broadly sonorous foundation for the finale of the act.

Act III. A salon in the palace of the Alcazar. In a brief scene the King informs his minister that he has decided to heed the behest of the Church and refrain from braving the Papal malediction. He bids Gaspard send Léonor to him, but, at the first opportunity, to arrest Inès, her accomplice.

It is at this juncture, as Gaspard departs, that Fernand returns from the war, in which he has not only distinguished himself by his valour but actually has saved the kingdom. Alphonse asks him to name the prize he desires as recompense for his services. Léonor enters. Fernand at once asks for the bestowal of her hand upon him in marriage. The King, who loves her deeply, and has nearly risked the wrath of the Pope for her sake, nevertheless gives his assent, but with reluctance, as appears from the irony that pervades his impressive solo, 'Pour tant d'amour'.

Léonor, touched by the King's magnanimity, inspired by her love for Fernand, yet shaken by doubts and fears, because aware that he knows nothing of her past, now expresses these conflicting feelings in her principal air, 'O mon Fernand'. She considers that their future happiness depends upon Fernand's being truthfully informed of her relations with the King. Accordingly she despatches Inès with a letter to him. Inès is intercepted by Gaspard, who orders her arrest. She is therefore unable to place in Fernand's hands the letter from Léonor.

Into the presence of the assembled nobles the King now brings Fernand, and announces that he has created him Count of Zamora. The jealous lords whisper among themselves about the scandal of Fernand's coming marriage with the mistress of the King; but Léonor, who enters in bridal attire, finds Fernand eagerly waiting to wed her, notwithstanding, as she believes, his receipt of her communication and complete knowledge of her past.

While the ceremony is being performed in another apartment, the nobles discuss further the disgrace to Fernand in this marriage. That Léonor was the mistress of the King is, of course, a familiar fact at court, and the nobles regard Fernand's elevation to the rank of nobility as a reward not only for his defeat of the Moors, but also for accommodatingly taking Léonor off the hands of the King to save him from the malediction of Rome. They cannot imagine that the young officer is ignorant of the relations that existed between his bride and the King.

Fernand re-enters. In high spirits he approaches the courtiers, offers them his hand, which they refuse. Balthazar now comes to learn the decision of the King. Fernand, confused by the taunting words and actions of the courtiers, hastens to greet Balthazar, who, not having seen him since he has returned victorious and loaded with honours, embraces him, until he hears Gaspard's ironical exclamation, 'Léonor's bridegroom!' Balthazar starts back, and it is then Fernand learns that he has just been wedded to the mistress of the King.

At this moment, when Fernand has just been informed of what he can only interpret as his betrayal by the King and the royal favourite, Alphonse enters, leading Léonor, followed by her attendants. In a stirring scene, the dramatic climax of the opera, Fernand tears from his neck the chain Alphonse has bestowed upon him, breaks his sword and casts it at the King's feet, then departs with Balthazar, the nobles now making a passage for them.

Act IV. The cloisters of the Monastery of St James. The ceremony of Fernand's entry into the order takes place: 'Les Cieux s'emplissent d'étincelles', a distinguished solo and chorus for Balthazar and the monks. Left alone, Fernand gives vent to his sorrow in the romance, 'Ange si pure' (Spirit of Light), one of the most exquisite solos in the Italian repertory.

Balthazar and the monks return, with them Fernand. Léonor, disguised as a novice, comes in and hears the chanting of the monks, Fernand's voice enunciating his vows. He comes out from the chapel, recognises Léonor, bids her be gone: 'Va-t-en d'ici de cet asile'. She tells him of her unsuccessful effort to let him know of her past, and craves his forgiveness for the seeming wrong she has done him: 'Fernand, imite la clémence'.

All of Fernand's former love for her returns: 'Viens, viens, je cède éperdu'. He wants to bear her away to other climes and there happily pass his days with her. But it is too late. Léonor dies in his arms. 'By tomorrow my soul, too, will want your prayers', are Fernand's words to Balthazar, who calls upon the monks to pray for a departed soul.   K.

LINDA DI CHAMOUNIX

Opera in three acts, text by Gaetano Rossi. Première at the Kärnthnertortheater, Vienna, 19 May 1842. First performed in London, Her Majesty's Theatre, 1843; New York, 1847; London, 1888, with Fursch-Madi, Trebelli, Navarini. Revived Metropolitan, New York, 1934, with Pons, Swarthout, Crooks, de Luca, Pinza, conductor Serafin; San Carlo, Naples, 1934, with dal Monte; la Scala, Milan, 1939, with dal Monte, Elmo, Malipiero, Basiola, Pasero, conductor Marinuzzi; Trieste, 1949, with Carosio.

Marquis de Boisfleury....................................Baritone
Carlo, *Vicomte de Sirval*......................................Tenor
Prefect..Bass
Pierotto ....Contralto
Linda...Soprano
Antonio, *Linda's father*..................................Baritone
Maddalena, *Linda's mother* ....Soprano
Intendant ....Tenor

Peasant Men and Women, Savoyards

Place: Chamounix and Paris
Time: 1760, During the Reign of Louis XV
Running Time: 2 hours 35 minutes

Claiming pride of place among Donizetti's pastoral operas, and belonging to a line that includes such works as Bellini's *La Sonnambula* and Meyerbeer's *Dinorah* and of which Mascagni's *L'Amico Fritz* is a late representative, *Linda* is still the subject of occasional revival, as a repository of several admirable singing roles and much highly agreeable music, including one of Donizetti's most famous soprano arias.

Act I. An overture typical of its period and excellent of its kind leads to a chorus of villagers on their way to church. The scene is Chamounix, a village of Savoy, at dawn. Maddalena awaits with some trepidation the return of her husband Antonio from a visit

to the Marchesa, who owns their farm and the mortgage which has been raised on it. Antonio returns, says they have the Marchesa's brother, the Marquis de Boisfleury, speaking for them, and then sings melodiously of the valley they have both known all their lives as their home: 'Ambo nati in questa valle'.

The shout of the villagers outside heralds the arrival of the Marquis de Boisfleury himself, a man by no means averse to self-congratulation and unquestionably on the prowl for Linda, Antonio's daughter, of whose charms he has received excellent reports – hence his supposed support in the matter of the mortgage. He is disappointed not to see her, but promises for them his protection in the future and for Linda a position at the castle.

All leave, and Linda comes out of the house. She has been to an assignation with her lover, a young and penniless painter named Carlo, but has arrived late and found only the flowers he left for her. There is no doubt she is in love and hopes to see him again in the very near future – 'O luce di quest' anima' she sings in the best-known aria of the score, a delightful *allegretto* piece in the repertory of all coloratura sopranos.

A group of young men and women from the village are on their way to France, among them Pierotto, the village poet and a childhood friend of Linda's. All beg him to sing his latest song and he obliges with a sentimental ditty ('Per sua madre andò una figlia'), about a young girl who leaves her native village to earn money for her mother, loves, is betrayed, and dies. When they have gone Carlo comes in to find Linda plunged by the ballad into sombre thoughts, from which his ardent protestations lead her into an impassioned love duet.

They leave and the Prefect comes to see Antonio, warning him that the Marquis has sinister designs on Linda. In an extended and beautiful duet, Antonio protests to heaven against such a fate for her, the Prefect goes on to suggest more practically that she be sent away with the band of Savoyards. Antonio agrees. Linda accepts to go and for the finale the Prefect bestows a blessing on the departing group.

Act II. Linda is in Paris. Her beloved Carlo has caught up with her, made known his real identity as the Vicomte de Sirval, son of the Marchesa, and installed her in style preparatory to their marriage. She hears Pierotto's tune outside and has him brought in to her. He is astonished to find her in these circumstances, but she explains her forthcoming marriage to Carlo. In a florid duet Linda and Pierotto declare their devotion to one another and Pierotto leaves.

No sooner has Pierotto gone than the old Marquis bursts into the room, to Linda's surprise and dismay. In a *buffo* duet, the old man offers to better in every respect the comparative splendour in which she now lives. Linda protests and in a charming *andante mosso* tune, the Marquis wonders if he has got himself in too deep, and Linda (in the accents of *Don Pasquale*'s Norina) worries in case Carlo were to come in unexpectedly. Finally, amidst much ado, Linda sends him packing.

Carlo, alone, laments in a beautiful aria his inability either to combat his mother's decision that he shall make a rich marriage or to communicate this thoroughly unwelcome news to Linda ('Se tanto in ira'). Linda returns and their duet ('Ah! dimmi, dimmi io t'amo') is full of passion, but Linda refuses a kiss when she hears the sound of Pierotto's hurdy-gurdy which reminds her of childhood and innocence.

Carlo leaves, and this time her own father appears at Linda's apartment. He has come to plead with the son of the owner of his farm and he urges his suit with what he takes to be the Vicomte's mistress ('Un buon servo del Visconte di Sirval'). Linda hides her identity from him at first, but inevitably he discovers who she is. Pierotto bursts in: he has seen a wedding feast in progress at Carlo's house! The news and her father's repeated curses carry Linda over the borderline of sanity, a state of mind so ardently coveted by the nineteenth-century soprano. In the beautiful and expressive duet which ends the act, she takes Pierotto for Carlo, demands to be taken by him to the altar, and ends singing with Pierotto for all the world as heartrendingly mad as Lucia.

Act III. The village square at Chamounix: a scene of rejoicing as the Savoyards return home, considerably richer than when they set out. Only Antonio, says the Prefect, is denied the pleasure of welcoming home his child. At that moment, there rushes in the young Vicomte de Sirval. His mother has relented and he may now marry the girl of his choice. She is dead, replies the Prefect. In a duet of considerable warmth, the Prefect begs Carlo to trust in the mercy of heaven.

The square fills again as the Marquis is heard returning from his Parisian jaunts. The teasing of the Savoyards – some of them saw his flirtations in Paris – disconcerts him not at all, and he expatiates in a *buffo* aria on the forthcoming marriage between his nephew and a beautiful and virtuous girl.

But a happy ending is in store. Pierotto leads Linda into the village, playing his hurdy-gurdy to remind her of home and so bring her step by step nearer Chamounix, her family and friends. Carlo, bringing the deed of Antonio's farm, is appalled to see Linda in so parlous a condition. Suddenly she recognises her mother and seems to know Carlo's voice. His aria ('E la voce che primiera') half convinces her that it is he, and after a repetition of their first-act duet, her reason returns and she recognises everyone gathered compassionately round her. Only the Marquis has to create some diversion until Linda addresses him as 'Uncle'. The opera ends with a short and joyful duet for Linda and Carlo.   K.

DON PASQUALE

Opera in three acts, text by Giovanni Ruffini and the composer. Première at the Théâtre-Italien, Paris, 3 January 1843, with Grisi, Mario, Tamburini, Lablache. First performed la Scala, Milan, 1843; Her Majesty's, London, 1843; New Orleans, 1845; New York, 1846. Revived Metropolitan, 1899, with Sembrich, Salignac, Scotti, Pini-Corsi, conductor Mancinelli; 1935, with Bori, Schipa, de Luca, Pinza, conductor Panizza; 1940, with Sayao, Martini, Valentino, Baccaloni, conductor Papi (1945, conductor Busch); Covent Garden, 1920, with Pareto; 1937, with Favero, Dino Borgioli, Biasini, di Lelio; Glyndebourne, 1938, with Mildmay, Dino Borgioli, Stabile, Baccaloni, conductor Busch; Cambridge Theatre, London, 1946, with Noni, MacPherson, Stabile, Lawrence, conductor Erede. Revived la Scala, Milan, 1930, with dal Monte, Lomanto, Stabile, Autori; 1936, with Carosio, Schipa, de Luca, Badini, conductor Marinuzzi; 1950, with Noni, Prandelli, Taddei, Pasero, conductor Capuana. Revived Vienna, 1944, with Noni, Dermota, Kunz, Vogel, conductor Paulik; Piccola Scala, Milan, 1959, with Sciutti, Alva, Panerai, Bruscantini, conductor Sanzogno; Edinburgh Festival, 1963 (by San Carlo Opera, Naples), with D'Angelo, Alfredo Kraus, Capecchi, Corena, conductor Erede; Covent Garden, 1973, with Elizabeth Harwood, Ryland Davies, Gabriel Bacquier, Geraint Evans, conductor Pritchard.

Don Pasquale, *an old bachelor*	Bass
Dr Malatesta, *his friend*	Baritone
Ernesto, *Don Pasquale's nephew*	Tenor
Norina, *a young widow*	Soprano
A Notary	Baritone

Place: Rome
Time: Early Nineteenth Century
Running Time: 2 hours 15 minutes

Written for Paris and performed with the four most celebrated singers of the day, *Don Pasquale* is Donizetti's most masterly comic opera. It combines the product of his lyrical gift at its most mellifluous – the soprano and tenor arias of the first act, the tenor's of the second and third, and his duet with Norina – and of his comical genius – Malatesta and Don Pasquale in the last scene. By the end of the year of its première, the first signs of Donizetti's mental illness were apparent.

The overture is mainly concerned with Ernesto's serenade from the last act, and Norina's aria from the first. It admirably suggests the lively tone of the opera.

Act I. Don Pasquale's room. The wealthy Don Pasquale is about to marry. Though determined himself to have a wife, he is very angry with his nephew Ernesto for wishing to do likewise, and threatens to disinherit him on that account. Ernesto is greatly disturbed by these threats, and so is his lady-love, the sprightly young widow Norina, when he reports them to her.

When the curtain rises, Don Pasquale is impatiently waiting for Malatesta, who, unable to dissuade his friend from marriage and still less able to influence him to allow his nephew to follow the dictates of his heart, pretends to acquiesce in the madcap scheme. He proposes that his 'sister' shall be the bride (Don Pasquale has no one in particular in mind), and describes her in a graceful aria, 'Bella siccome un'angelo', as a timid, ingenuous girl, brought up, he says, in a convent. She is, however, none other than Norina, who is in no way related to Malatesta. At this description, Don Pasquale is quite unable to contain his delight and when he is alone, he breaks into a cavatina, 'Ah, un foco insolito'.

Don Pasquale lectures his nephew on the subject of his future conduct, and tells him that he is proposing to take a wife himself. This arouses Ernesto's incredulity, and his uncle is obliged to repeat it several times before he can take it in. When he does, it is to realise that it finally cuts him off from the marriage he himself proposed to enter into: 'Sogno soave e casto', he sings, in one of Donizetti's soaring inspirations, while the old uncle grumbles away in the bass. When Don Pasquale says he has already consulted Malatesta, Ernesto's last remaining hope vanishes; there is no one now to dissuade the old fool.

The scene changes to Norina's room, where she is reading. Her aria, 'So anch'io la virtù magica', shows her sprightly nature in an enchanting tune. A letter is brought to her, and when Malatesta comes to tell her that Ernesto's old uncle has fallen for the scheme which shall finally make him agree to his nephew's marriage, she is anything but pleased with the way things have gone; they have not had time to tell Ernesto about their scheme and he has written that he is furious. However, Malatesta is convinced all is going well, and he and Norina rehearse how they shall behave with Don Pasquale when finally he meets his convent-bred bride. The music is pure effervescence, with its sparkling coloratura and its brightly changing tunes.

Act II. Ernesto's lodgings. The owner is in despair at the prospect of losing his bride and his home (Don Pasquale has told him to clear out of the house). A long horn prelude ushers in the recitative and aria, 'Cercherò lontana terra', one of the best known of the opera.

At home, Don Pasquale receives his prospective bride and her sponsor, his friend, Malatesta. She is shy, he urges her on, and the husband-to-be watches every manoeuvre enraptured. Norina is eventually persuaded to speak to Pasquale, and assures him that she is only interested in the things of the household – sewing, making clothes, and looking after the kitchen. A notary has been sent for, and Malatesta dictates the terms of the marriage, the others, including the notary, repeating his words after him. A witness is needed, but none seems forthcoming until Ernesto rushes in proclaiming his betrayal to anyone who chooses to listen. Malatesta has his work cut out to explain the situation to him, without letting Don Pasquale know the way the wind is blowing.

The moment the contract is signed, Norina's temper seems to change, and she spits fire at every one of Don Pasquale's attempts at either conciliation or authority. He is confounded at the contrast, and dumb with horror when she says that Ernesto is just the person to take her out walking, something that is plainly beyond the capacity of a man of his years – or girth, for that matter. The quartet redoubles in vigour, and Norina and Ernesto have a charming lyrical aside which leaves no one in any doubt as to their mutual feelings. When Norina calls together the servants, and, finding there are only three in all, laughingly directs that more be engaged and that the wages of those at present in service be doubled, Don

Pasquale can bear it no more. 'Son tradito, son tradito' he shouts in his rage, and the *stretta* of the quartet brings the act to a spirited conclusion.

Act III. Don Pasquale's house. Servants are rushing hither and thither executing Norina's commands. Don Pasquale sees her dressed up to the nines and about to go out of the house; may he ask where? To the theatre, she says – without him. Their duet works the quarrel up until Norina finds occasion to box her 'husband's' ears. As far as Don Pasquale is concerned, it is the end of his hopes and pretensions as well as his hateful marriage, and even Norina is sorry that she has had to go so far. She rushes from the room, but takes care to drop a note as she goes. It purports to be from Ernesto, and makes an assignation for that very evening in the garden. Don Pasquale reads it, and sees in it his chance of getting quit of the whole affair; he will send for Malatesta.

When he has left the room, the servants flock back into it, and in a charming chorus comment on the happenings in the house. Malatesta arrives and proceeds to give Don Pasquale the benefit of his advice. The two men confer in a famous comic duet, whose every performance has reduced an audience somewhere to helpless laughter. Its *buffo* 6/8 finish is one of the funniest pieces of music in the post-Rossinian repertory.

The scene changes to the garden, where Ernesto sings to Norina the beautiful serenade, 'Com'è gentil'. The story is that after one of the rehearsals Donizetti asked the music publisher, Dormoy, to go with him to his lodgings. There he rummaged among a lot of manuscripts until, finding what he was looking for, he handed it to Dormoy. 'There,' he said, 'give this to Mario and tell him to sing it in the last scene in the garden as a serenade to Norina.' When the opera was performed, Mario sang it, while Lablache, behind the scenes, played an accompaniment on the lute. Most of the great lyric tenors of history, from Mario to Schipa, have tried at one time or another to prove that never before has it been so stylishly sung.

It is immediately followed by a duet that is no less charming and hardly less well known, 'Tornami a dir'. This is all thirds and sixths for the two voices, but the effect is entrancing. Don Pasquale and Malatesta surprise the lovers, Ernesto escapes, but Norina stays as if to brave it out. Malatesta twists everything round to everyone's satisfaction, and

soon Ernesto and Norina are waiting to be married, and moreover with the full approval of Don Pasquale. Suitably, Malatesta leads off the *Rondo finale* with which the work ends.   K., H.

DOM SÉBASTIEN, ROI DE PORTUGAL
Don Sebastian, King of Portugal

Opera in five acts, libretto by Eugène Scribe, after Paul-Henri Foucher's play *Dom Sébastien de Portugal* (1838), dedicated to the Queen of Portugal. First performed Paris Opéra, 13 November 1843, with Gilbert Duprez as Dom Sébastien, Paul Barroilhet as Camoëns and Rosine Stoltz as Zayda. Shortened version (in German), Kärthnertortheater, Vienna, 6 February 1845, conducted by the composer. First U.S. performance, New York, 1864; New Orleans, 1875. Revived Maggio Musicale, Florence, 1955, conducted by Carlo Maria Giulini.

Dom Sébastien, *King of Portugal* ....Tenor

Dom Antonio, *his uncle*......................................Tenor

Dom Juam de Sylva,
    Grand Inquisitor..............................Basso Profundo

Dom Louis, *Spanish ambassador* ....Tenor

Camoëns, *soldier and poet*....................................Tenor

Ben-Selim, *governor of Fez* ....Bass

Abayaldos, *leader of the Arab tribe*..................Baritone

Zayda, *his betrothed,*
    daughter of Ben Selim ....Mezzo-Soprano

Dom Henrique Sandoval,
    Dom Sébastien's lieutenant ....Bass

Ladies and Gentlemen of the Court; Portuguese Soldiers and Sailors; Arab Soldiers and Women; Members of the Inquisition

Place: Lisbon and the Moroccan desert
Time: 1577

*D*om Sébastien was intended to trump the success Donizetti had enjoyed in Paris with *Don Pasquale* earlier in 1843. Its original *raison d'être* was as a vehicle for Donizetti's friend, the tenor Gilbert Duprez, then thirty-two, who had created Edgardo in *Lucia* and Arnold in the Italian version of *Guillaume Tell*. But Donizetti was the victim of his own success: French composers resented the way his works had enjoyed a monopoly on stages and in popular acclaim for so long. It is grand opera on the grandest scale, with a number of set pieces that tend to dwarf individual characters. It also has an overwhelmingly tragic impact: Donizetti himself called it 'arcitrista'.

Of all his unknown works, *Dom Sébastien* is the one most neglected, neither commercially recorded nor performed in recent times.

Act I. The King of Portugal, Dom Sébastien, is about to lead a crusade to Africa. His uncle, Dom Antonio, who will act as regent in the King's absence, intends to share power with the Grand Inquisitor, Juam de Sylva. Meanwhile the Inquisitor is secretly determined to help Philip II, King of Spain, usurp the Portuguese throne. Dom Antonio tries to stop a soldier importuning the King, but the King insists on knowing his identity. The poet Camoëns introduces himself in a splendid cavatina: he followed Vasco da Gama and was inspired to write his *Lusiads*, which will bring lustre to his ungrateful country. He himself has gained only grief from his travels and his writing. The King declares himself Camoëns's protector. Camoëns asks for the honour of following the King.

A procession passes, as the Inquisition leads heretics to the stake. The beautiful African girl Zayda is among them. Juam de Sylva explains that she was captured in Africa and baptised in front of Dom Sébastien, who remembers he was touched by her grief. Some months later, however, her heart broken by secret pain (presumably her love for the King), she took refuge in a convent and swore to remain there for ever. Later she broke her sacred oath. Zayda explains that she only wanted to see her country and her aged father again. Even though Juam de Sylva insists the King should not interfere with the Inquisition's death sentence on this apostate, Dom Sébastien commutes her sentence to eternal exile in Africa, near her father. The people, led by Camoëns, applaud this verdict, while Juam and the Inquisitors rage. Zayda herself, in the *cantabile* romance 'O mon Dieu sur la terre', swears to consecrate her life to her tutelary god, the King. There is a chorus with trumpet fanfares as the Portuguese look forward to conquering a new world. They request a song of departure and ask Camoëns what fate awaits them. In his dramatic, pianissimo accompanied *prophétie*, he predicts disaster: the desert wind will bring the cries of triumphant warriors. How many? What does it matter? He concludes: 'En avant soldats!' The soldiers swear to die for their King. When the sun comes out, Camoëns gives a more positive forecast of their bravery. In a major ensemble the King asks heaven's blessing, while the Grand Inquisitor swears aside that monarch and soldiers will never leave Africa. Donizetti ensures that the Inquisitors' cries of 'Anathème' are heard in isolation.

Act II. A ballet and chorus of Arab women celebrate Zayda's return: she had been captured on the eve of her marriage to the warrior Abayaldos. In a touching *larghetto* romance, Zayda admits that her soul is still Dom Sébastien's ('Sol adoré de la patrie'). Her father, Beni Salem, governor of Fez, knows that she no longer favours Abayaldos, but insists she receive her friends' homage. This occasions much ballet.

Abayaldos points out that the Christians are in their deserts, and calls them to arms (in a phrase that must have resonated strangely in Paris), 'Aux armes, Africains'. Holy war is declared and, for once, the Moors beat the Christians. Dom Sébastien is more concerned to save Camoëns than himself. To save the King's life, his friend Sandoval pretends to be Dom Sébastien as he dies. Zayda finds the King and determines to save him in a harp-inflected *larghetto*, 'Grand Dieu sa misère est si grande'. They declare their love; he promises to make her his Queen.

The Moors are still bent on killing the survivors. Zayda bargains with Abayaldos: she will marry him, if he lets the prisoners return home. He agrees to her terms and in another powerful ensemble Zayda and the King implore heaven to watch over one another.

Back in Portugal, Dom Sébastien sings an affecting and very difficult aria in a half voice ('Seul sur la terre'): it includes an octave leap up to a high D flat on 'l'amour', which Donizetti optimistically asks to be sung sweetly.

Act III. Abayaldos comes as an ambassador to Portugal offering a peace treaty. Zayda has accompanied him. He knows he has not won her heart. She asks him to kill her. Camoëns appears and sings a beautiful romance in 6/8, as his broken soul revives on seeing Lisbon ('O Lisbonne, o ma patrie'). Camoëns and Dom Sébastien meet and recognise each another. Dom Sébastien explains that a greedy uncle has usurped the throne, believing him dead. A Funeral March is heard: with consummate hypocrisy, Dom Antonio mourns the 'death' of his nephew. When Camoëns disrupts the occasion, Dom Juam has him arrested. Dom Sébastien intervenes and reveals his identity. He is acclaimed by the crowd, but Abayaldos swears he buried the real king. Dom Juan summons Dom Sébastien to appear before the Inquisition. Abayaldos warns Zayda that he will watch her every move.

Act IV. Members of the Inquisition swear to keep its secrets. Dom Juam pretends not to recognise the King. Zayda comes to witness in his defence, though Dom Sébastien tells her to keep quiet. When she reveals she saved the King's life, Dom Juan greets this as blasphemy and a remarkable septet is launched.[1] Zayda gives in to despair and terror; Dom Juam calls her an apostate and condemns her to be burnt to death. Abayaldos rejects her as an impious perjurer and curses her. She defies them all, *fortissimo* ('Que le bûcher').

Act V. Dom Juam hears that the Spanish will be under Lisbon's walls by evening. He is promised power in return for giving the crown to Philip II – as long as he can make this look legitimate. With breathtaking cynicism, Dom Juam offers to pardon Zayda and save the King's life if Dom Sébastien agrees to abdicate in Philip II's favour.

Zayda is ready, even happy, to die for the King ('Mourir pour ce qu'on aime'[2]). Dom Sébastien realises he can live only at the expense of his honour. He and Zayda agree it would be better to die and Donizetti shares the line 'l'avvilir jamais' (life must never be vilified) between the two lovers to express their unanimity. However, when Dom Sébastien realises that Zayda will die if he refuses to sign the abdication, he does sign it.

Camoëns has recruited sailors to save them and in a memorable off-stage barcarolle, which Donizetti was forced to cut by one verse because the original Zayda refused to stay on stage and listen to it all, he addresses his song of hope to the tower prison ('O matelots, o matelots').

Abayaldos and Dom Antonio, however, know of the conspiracy. The prisoners are allowed to escape, so they can be executed. Their bodies fall into the sea. Dom Antonio assumes he is therefore now King but the Inquisitor brandishes the act of abdication and disillusions him: 'Glory to Philip II'. Camoëns has the last word: 'Glory to Dom Sébastien'.

Donizetti himself realised that *Dom Sébastien*'s dénouement was problematic: in a letter of 9 November 1843 he commented that 'the music can do nothing... my opera finishes with a rat's tail, as they say, or like wax in the sun'.[3] He added a new 'largo concertato' for the Vienna revival, which will be included in Mary Ann Smart's impatiently awaited new critical edition from Ricordi. *Dom Sébastien* has enjoyed the status of rough diamond for a long time now: it will be interesting to see whether the work itself can deliver all that is expected of it.   P.

---

[1] During one performance of *Dom Sébastien* in Vienna in 1845 this septet was repeated three times.
[2] Donizetti had to fight for this phrase, when his librettist Scribe preferred 'saving someone you love' to 'dying for someone you love'.
[3] Quoted by William Ashbrook, *Donizetti*, 1965.

PAUL DUKAS

(born 1 October 1865, died 17 May 1935)

ARIANE ET BARBE-BLEUE

Ariadne and Bluebeard

Opera in three acts, text after Maeterlinck's play of the same name. Première, Opéra-Comique, Paris, 10 May 1907, with Georgette Leblanc (Maeterlinck's wife), Brohly, Vieuille. First performed Metropolitan, New York, 1911, with Farrar, Rothier, conductor Toscanini; la Scala, Milan, 1911, with Pierich, Ludikar, conductor Serafin; Covent Garden, 1937, with Lubin, Etcheverry; Paris, 1975, with Grace Bumbry, Irina Arkhipova, Jacques Mars; Amsterdam, 1989, with Kathryn Harries; Opera North, 1990, with Anne Marie Owens, conductor Paul Daniel; Paris, 1991, with Françoise Pollet, conductor Inbal, producer Berghaus.

Barbe-Bleue (Bluebeard)	Bass
Ariane	Mezzo-Soprano
The Nurse	Contralto
Sélysette	Mezzo-Soprano
Ygraine	Soprano
Mélisande	Soprano
Bellangère	Soprano
Alladine	Mime
Three Peasants	Tenor, Basses

Peasants, Crowd

Place: Barbe-Bleue's Castle
Running Time: 2 hours

Two works for the stage – *Ariane et Barbe-Bleue* and the ballet *La Péri* – and the orchestral *L'apprenti sorcier* comprise the work for which Dukas is known. Other operas were contemplated, may even have been started and then destroyed, but Dukas was a slow worker and lacked confidence; late in life he destroyed the unpublished residue of his work. *Ariane* was from the start intended by Maeterlinck as an operatic libretto.

Act I. A vast and sumptuous hall of semicircular form in Barbe-Bleue's castle. Through the open window can be heard the sound of an angry crowd. They believe that Barbe-Bleue has murdered his wives one by one, and that the beautiful Ariane is to be the next victim. They comment on the arrival of the carriage. Is it true that the previous five wives are *not* dead, but still alive in a dungeon?

The windows of the hall shut, the roar of the crowd recedes to a murmur, and Ariane and her nurse come in by a side door. The nurse starts to lament their fate; he is mad and has already killed five wives. Ariane is calmer; she is convinced that Barbe-Bleue loves her. He has given her seven keys, six of silver, and one of gold; those of silver she may use to open any door she likes, that of gold she must not touch. It must be that one, then, that guards his secret; she will have nothing to do with the silver keys, only the gold will answer her purpose.

Taking the silver keys, the nurse unlocks the six doors. From them in succession pour cascades of amethysts, sapphires, pearls, emeralds, rubies and diamonds. Ariane is not looking for treasures, but she cannot resist the sight of the diamonds: 'O mes clairs diamants!' she sings, in a great lyrical outburst, whose high *tessitura* makes one wonder whether any true mezzo-soprano ever negotiated the title role successfully.

Ariane is intent on discovering what is behind the seventh, forbidden door. Nothing can be seen when the door opens, but a sad, subdued sound is heard; it is the sound of the other five wives, says Ariane. Barbe-Bleue himself comes into the hall. He reproaches Ariane for her faithlessness, but she demands to know the truth. He takes her by the arm, she struggles to free herself, the nurse joins in and the sounds of the quarrel penetrate to the crowd

waiting outside. A stone is thrown through the windows, and the nurse runs to unbolt the door, through which streams a crowd of peasants. Barbe-Bleue prepares to defend himself, but Ariane goes gently but firmly to the people and assures them that she has not been hurt. She closes the door.

Act II. A vast subterranean hall. It is nearly dark. Ariane and the nurse appear, the former holding a lamp. Ariane stumbles on the other wives, lying huddled in the middle of the vaulted hall. In her joy that they are alive, she rushes to them and embraces them: 'Ah! Je vous ai trouvées!' They look dazed and frightened at the unaccustomed light. One by one Ariane calls them to her[1] and reassures them; she has not come to join them as a captive but to free them, has in fact obeyed a higher law than Barbe-Bleue's. A drop of water extinguishes Ariane's light, but she shows no signs of fear. The others, who are used to the dark, lead her to the light – they say there is some light in the corner of the dungeon. When she gets there, Ariane finds that there are bars and bolts, which, say the other wives, they have never tried to open. The sea is behind the wall, and to open it would let in the waves. Ariane throws herself against it, and opens it, like a door, to admit light through what appears to be a great window: 'Ah, ce n'est pas encore la clarté véritable.' She takes a stone and smashes this, and immediately the whole chamber is bathed in brilliant, blinding light. Ariane encourages the others to look out at the world from which they have been cut off, and she leads them off to freedom, singing joyfully as they go.

Act III. The scene is the same as that of Act I. All the wives are adorning themselves with the jewels which were revealed with the aid of the six silver keys. They were unable to escape from the castle, since the drawbridges rose when they approached them, the moats filled magically with water. They speculate as to where Barbe-Bleue has gone, but Ariane bids them concentrate on adorning themselves for the freedom which will surely be theirs.

The nurse comes in hurriedly to say that Barbe-Bleue has returned. He is attacked by the villagers, who are determined to end what they consider his tyranny. His bodyguard deserts and Barbe-Bleue himself is wounded. The peasants bind him and offer

---

[1] When Mélisande's name is mentioned, the theme from Debussy's Act I, scene iii is heard.

him to the wives; let them take what revenge they like – he is securely fastened. Ariane thanks them and bids them go to their homes to tend their wounds.

When they have left the castle, the women all crowd round Barbe-Bleue to see what can be done for his wounds. They are found not to be serious, but the bonds with which he is secured are so tight as to

risk strangling him. Ariane cuts them with a dagger, and he is able to get up. She herself departs, although Barbe-Bleue makes a movement as if he wished her to remain. But when she in turn asks the five wives to go with her, they decline and she leaves them with Barbe-Bleue in the castle. In the composer's own words, 'no one wants to be liberated'.   H.

ANTONÍN DVOŘÁK
(born 8 September 1841, died 1 May 1904)

As an operatic composer, Dvořák is less widely known outside Czechoslovakia than he should be. His symphonic, choral and chamber music has been successful from relatively early times, initially perhaps because of the advocacy of Brahms, who introduced him to his publisher, Simrock, but the operas with their subjects embedded in Czech history and folklore have had a rougher ride. It would be foolish to deny that there may have been a grain of truth behind his remark to a friend that he regretted the amount of time he had spent writing operas; his natural bent lay elsewhere. Nonetheless, he wrote one opera of quite sovereign merit – *Rusalka* – and not only Czechs would mourn if the others did not exist.

Dvořák played the viola in the orchestra of the Prague Provisional Theatre from 1862 to 1871 (in that respect learning his trade, like Nielsen in Copenhagen), and his operatic output falls quite neatly into two halves: works written early in his career (between 1870 and 1888) and comprising seven operas, from *Alfred* to *The Jacobin*; and the three belonging to the final period, 1898–1903, comprising *The Devil and Kate*, *Rusalka* and *Armida*, as well as revisions of *Dimitrij* and *The Jacobin*. Rivalry between Dvořák and Smetana seems to have been a matter more for their adherents than for the composers themselves, who were on respectful terms, but the writer Zdeněk Nejedly, in his enthusiasm for Smetana, stirred up feeling against Dvořák which Czech commentators maintain affected Czech musical life up to and including the scheduling by Supraphon of long-playing gramophone records in the second half of the twentieth century.   H.

DIMITRIJ

Opera in four acts, libretto by Marie Červinková-Riegrová. Première, Prague, 8 October 1881; revision, Prague, 1894.

Dimitrij Ivanovic, *assumed son of*
    Ivan the Terrible.. Tenor

Marfa Ivanovna, *widow of Ivan the Terrible* ... Soprano

Marina Mnishkova *of the Sandomirs* .... Soprano

Xenia Borisovna, *daughter of the late Tsar,*
    Boris Godunov... Soprano

Pyotr Fyodorovich Basmanov, *commander of the*
    Tsar's armies.. Bass

Prince Vasili Ivanovich Shuisky ....Baritone

Yov, *the Patriarch of Moscow* ....Bass

Neborsky, *member of the Polish Contingent*.........Tenor

Buchinsky, *member of the Polish Contingent*...Baritone

Place: Moscow
Time: 1605–06
Running Time: 3 hours 10 minutes

Dvořák's longing for international repute as an opera composer was a natural follow-up to his success in the symphonic and chamber fields. Wagner's enemy, the critic Eduard Hanslick, influenced him to re-write the episode of Xenia's murder in Act IV of *Dimitrij*, his sixth opera, in order to make it more acceptable for Vienna. Various other changes followed but, disappointingly, no performances abroad materialised and in 1894 the composer revised the entire score. This was not his last word on the subject and for the last production of the work in his lifetime (in 1904) he allowed a certain mixing of the two versions. Students of Janáček will not be surprised that Karel Kovařovic when he was Director of the National Opera in Prague subjected the score to further revision before he produced it in 1906, with considerable reversion to the original of 1886. Modern opinion inclines towards the first version, with some admixture of the later revision.

The subject matter of the libretto concerns the struggles for the Russian throne in the early seventeenth century, following the period of Tsar Boris Godunov's death. The pretender, Dimitrij, is here convinced (in contradistinction to the drama of Pushkin and Mussorgsky) of the legitimacy of his claim to the throne. That he owes his victory to Polish intervention in Russian politics is a considerable contributory factor to the tragedy which unfolds and ends with his death.

Act I. Boris is dead and factions quarrel about the succession. An invading army of Poles led by Dimitrij is nearing the city but the crowd hears from Patriarch Yov that the Boyars have taken an oath of allegiance to the late Tsar's children. Prince Shuisky adds his voice and warns of the consequences of victory for the Poles and the ruler they bring with them, but when Basmanov, the Commander of the Army, tells them that the Russian army has gone over to Dimitrij's side, the people swear loyalty to the new ruler. The mob has murdered Boris's son Feodor, and his daughter Xenia takes refuge with Shuisky, who sides with the old regime.

Dimitrij enters Moscow in a spirit more conciliatory than triumphant and immediately encounters Czarina Marfa, widow of Ivan the Terrible. She soon realises that Dimitrij is not her son but his charismatic behaviour she finds sympathetic and, partly driven by an instinct for revenge, she makes up her mind to acknowledge him publicly.

Act II. The wedding of Dimitrij and Marina Mnishkova is solemnised in the Kremlin. They are alone after the ceremony but their happiness is threatened by Marina's refusal to accede to Dimitrij's request that she become a Russian. At the celebratory court ball, Russians and Poles quarrel – the latter incited by the ambitious Marina – and only the intervention of Dimitrij prevents a serious clash.

Dimitrij goes to pray for peace in the cathedral of Uspensk. To this sanctuary comes Xenia in flight from marauding Poles and when Dimitrij successfully intervenes to protect her, it becomes evident in their extended duet that there is powerful mutual attraction between him and Xenia, who as yet has no idea who it was who saved her.

Prince Shuisky leads a group of Boyars met to form a patriotic alliance against the invading Dimitrij and the Poles, but their cause undergoes a severe setback when no sooner has Shuisky sworn that it was long ago that he himself saw the corpse of the true Dimitrij, than Dimitrij himself stands in front of the conspirators, and persuades the majority of them to join his faction.

Act III. Moscow. In a beautiful soliloquy, Dimitrij yearns for Xenia. He is saluted as Tsar by the assembled company and the Patriarch asks him publicly to intervene against the increasingly overweening Poles, in particular to forbid the Latin Mass being celebrated in the Kremlin. If it persists, the Orthodox Church will withhold recognition of his marriage to Marina. This causes consternation and fury among the Poles, but in Dimitrij's mind suggests the possibility of union with Xenia.

Xenia interrupts the altercation to intercede movingly for mercy for Prince Shuisky who is under sentence of death. She is taken aback when she recognises as Tsar the man who protected her earlier from molestation.

Dimitrij's luck is running out and when he pardons Shuisky, the Russians rejoice but the Poles are brought to the edge of rebellion. Marina, alone with Dimitrij and jealous of Xenia, tells him that she knows his true origin: his name is Grishko Optrepjev. Ever since he was a child, he was passed off as the murdered son of Tsar Ivan. Partly to save his position and partly to forestall the chaos which would follow his abdication, Dimitrij resolves to stay on the throne and, if he can, to reject Marina. The confrontation is on a grand scale and Marina for her part is sufficiently impressed by Dimitrij's determination to long to win him back.

Act IV. Shuisky's house in Moscow. Xenia is convinced she has been betrayed but Dimitrij pleads with her that his emotions have always been sincere.

Marina has overheard everything and attacks Xenia with a dagger (successfully, in the original version). Xenia convinces her that her love for Dimitrij originated long before she had any idea he was Tsar, and Marina takes her part against the Poles, who would have her killed. When the Patriarch makes his appearance, Xenia takes a vow to spend the rest of her days in a nunnery, which

Dimitrij, even with the authority of the Tsar, cannot reverse. Marina in a spirit of revenge denounces him as a Pretender, Shuisky does his best to persuade Marfa to stand by her supposed son, Marfa agonises between expediency and the truth, but Dimitrij in the highly effective ensemble emerges at last as a true hero and prevents Marfa from committing the perjury demanded of her. The opera ends with the people praying over the dead body of the false Tsar whom Shuisky has shot.   H.

THE JACOBIN
Jakobín

Opera in three acts, text by Marie Červinková-Riegrová. Première, Prague, 12 February 1889; revised version, Prague, 1898.

Count Vilém of Harasov, *a retired general*.............Bass
Bohuš of Harasov, *his son*...............................Baritone
Adolf, *his nephew* ....Baritone
Julie, *wife of Bohuš* ....Soprano
Filip, *the Count's steward (burgrave)* ....Bass
Jiří, *a young forester*...Tenor
Benda, *teacher and village choirmaster* ....Tenor
Terinka, *his daughter*.....................................Soprano
Lotinka, *housekeeper at the castle* ....Contralto

Townspeople, Schoolchildren, Musicians, Country Folk

Place: A Country Town in Bohemia
Time: During the French Revolution, 1793
Running Time: 2 hours 40 minutes

*T*he Jacobin was very much a product of Dvořák's maturity, in his canon coming after *Dimitrij* and before *The Devil and Kate*, another opera firmly rooted in the Czech nationalist tradition. It is odd to reflect that Dvořák was apparently in 1884, at the time he received Marie Červinková-Riegrová's libretto, looking for something a little less emphatically Czech, which would travel easily to the foreign capital cities where his symphonic work was now being performed. After some initial misgivings he had started to compose by November 1887 and a year later had completed the full score.

Act I. Bohuš and his wife Julie are returning from France to his native town, where he longs to be reconciled with his father. The machinations of his cousin Adolf have caused an estrangement, the old Count falsely believing Bohuš's liberal inclinations to have turned to positive support for the revolutionaries in France.

Townspeople come from church, among them Filip the Count's pompous steward, who flatters Benda, the schoolmaster, as a prelude to paying court to his daughter, Terinka. This infuriates Jiří, who is himself in love with Terinka and, egged on by his friends, makes elaborate mockery of the steward. Filip for his part threatens them all with conscription, but, in spite of his sarcastic interruptions, Jiří and Terinka sing ecstatically of their love for one another. The mood changes with the return of Bohuš and Julie, who describe themselves as itinerant performers and ask to see the Count. Filip is suspicious of this unexpected turn of events but matters are taken out of his hands by the appearance of the Count, who peremptorily announces that Bohuš is disinherited, Adolf now his heir.

Act II. A schoolroom, where Benda is rehearsing a serenade for performance up at the castle, a rehearsal with more affection in the way it is depicted than parody. Terinka is worried in case her father prefers Filip to Jiří as a suitor, and when, after a long and attractive duet, he catches her and Jiří together, she finds that he does. The young people threaten to ruin the serenade in which they have solo parts, but the contretemps is interrupted if not resolved by the exciting news that soldiers are searching the town for revolutionaries.

Bohuš and Julie come to ask for lodging. They are plainly speaking from the heart when (in a fine duet with nationalist overtones) they insist that only music sustained them in their wanderings abroad, and Benda finds it easy to agree to their request and let them stay. But things are not destined to go smoothly and the arrival of Filip to pursue his wooing of Terinka leads to his discovery of Jiří and immediate decision to list him for conscription. Even Benda's pleas on behalf of the serenade do no good and things go from bad to worse when Adolf puts a spoke in Jiří's wheel by backing Filip. Disaster looms nearer when Bohuš speaks up for Jiří and at the same time denounces Adolf, with the result that he is arrested as a revolutionary.

Act III. Up at the castle, Jiří attempts to tell the Count his son has come back, but Adolf has him ejected. With the help of Lotinka, the housekeeper,

Julie and Benda manage to get near enough to the Count to make a plea for Bohuš, but the Count won't hear a word on behalf of his son whom he persists in thinking of as a Jacobin and a revolutionary. The Count reflects sadly on how hard he has made it to believe in his son's innocence, but he has reckoned without Julie who has concealed herself next door and, to the accompaniment of his dead wife's harp, sings what was once her favourite lullaby. Resistance crumbles and disappears altogether when she shows him a document which proves that, so far from having joined the Jacobins, Bohuš was once condemned to death by them.

The Count learns that his son is imprisoned in the castle, and as he listens to the serenade makes up his mind to see him after all. Reconciliation is in the air, and in an arioso added in the later revision, Bohuš sings with the utmost conviction of his dream of remaining at the home he has only just rediscovered. Bohuš and the Count are reunited, Adolf and Filip thwarted, and the way is clear for the marriage of Jiří and Terinka. Choral dancing brings this most Czech of operas to an end.

Apart from the period setting, the opera's subject matter is for Dvořák full of autobiographical overtones. He was born in a village a few miles north of Prague, near a castle; his mother's uncle and grandfather had served as stewards to a certain Count Kinsky; and his German teacher was a local schoolmaster-organist, an obvious model for Benda even to the coincidence that he had a daughter called Terinka. His sister-in-law, whom he at one time wanted to marry, eventually became the wife of a nobleman on whose estate Dvořák himself built his family home.

Much of the music of *The Jacobin* is in the vein of Smetana's *Bartered Bride*, rhythmically very lively, full of dance overtones, peasant choruses and so on; but the story, based like Smetana's masterpiece on the idea of reconciliation, is far from full-blown comedy. Darker themes, music of considerable seriousness, characters whose very existence is threatened – these sombre shadows colour the score almost as insistently as its folkloric basis. The comedy figures of the affectionately drawn Benda and the only just less-than-sinister Filip bulk large in the opera but its character derives hardly less from the lyricism of Jiří and Terinka, and the darker, near-tragic predicament of Bohuš and his wife.   H.

THE DEVIL AND KATE
Čert a Káča

Opera in three acts, text by Adolf Wenig on a Czech folk tale. Première, Narodni Divadlo, Prague, 23 November 1899, with well-known Czech singers – Ružena Maturová as the Princess, Bohumil Pták as Jirka – in the leading roles, Adolf Čech conducting.

Jirka, *a shepherd* ....Tenor
Kate, *a middle-aged spinster* ....Mezzo-Soprano
Her Mother ....Contralto
Marbuel, *a devil* ....Baritone
Lucifer...Bass
The Door-Keeper Devil ....Bass
The Princess ....Soprano
The Chambermaid...Soprano
The Marshal ....Baritone
A Musician ....Tenor

Courtiers, Villagers, Devils

Place: A Country Inn in Summer; Hell; the Princess's Castle

Running Time: 2 hours 45 minutes

More than ten years elapsed between *The Jacobin* (1888) and *The Devil and Kate*, a period Dvořák filled, operatically speaking, with revisions to *Dimitrij* and *The Jacobin* under his newly acquired interest in Wagnerian aesthetic. The latest opera, though a product of Dvořák's 'late' period, returns to the 'village comedy' atmosphere of the composer's earlier work, but the new emphasis on orchestral music gives it a fresh dimension, and, in spite of the oddity of its subject – no love interest! – it remains one of the most often played of Dvořák's operas.

Act I follows a substantial overture. A country inn. The villagers have some fun at Jirka's expense over the obviously amorous intentions of Kate towards him, a situation only underlined when the village lads so pointedly ignore Kate during a waltz that she announces she would willingly dance with the devil. Marbuel, dressed as a hunter, answers her call with exemplary alacrity, and starts to ask questions about the Princess and her overbearing steward – perhaps they are candidates for Hell? – but Kate is more interested in a drink, a spot of flirtation and a dance, the last to a whirlwind tune. Marbuel suggests she go with him, Jirka reappears to say he has been given the sack and has told the steward to go to Hell, whereupon Marbuel stamps his foot so that he and Kate disappear through a hole in the floor. The villagers have a fair idea where they have gone; Jirka says he will follow them.

Act II. Hell, where the gate-keeper snoozes, devils play cards and kettles are kept constantly on the boil. The prelude is atmospheric; Lucifer (tagged with a very attractive tune) asks for news of Marbuel's whereabouts. He appears with Kate, who scolds him about everything that comes into her mind. Lucifer wants the steward at least temporarily reprieved but the Princess brought down to Hell; he insists meanwhile they get rid of Kate. Jirka appears and suggests they pay her to go back to earth. What about some gold for him too? If Marbuel were to threaten the steward, Jirka could chase him away and claim a reward, suggests Marbuel. A great dance begins and during its course Jirka dances Kate out of the door, to general relief.

Act III. The Princess's castle. The Princess begins to see the error of her ways and to lament the prospect of Hell. Jirka persuades her to abolish serfdom, then suggests Kate should hide behind the palace door and so surprise the devil, who will have to pay ransom to get away from her. When Marbuel comes to take the Princess to Hell, Kate's appearance puts him to instant flight – Czech devils, it would appear (see Smetana's *The Devil's Wall*, page 739), are a bumbling crew, attempting much but achieving little; but that's how they like them. Kate gets her reward – a new house – and is confident she will soon get a bridegroom; the peasants get their freedom; and the Princess gets in Jirka a new Prime Minister.   H.

RUSALKA
The Water Nymph

Opera in three acts, libretto by S.J. Kvapil. Première, National Theatre, Prague, 31 March 1901, with Maturová, Kabátová, Pták, Kliment, conductor Kovařovič (by 1950, the opera had been performed over six hundred times at the National Theatre). First performed in London by John Lewis Musical Society in 1950 in an English version by Christopher Hassall; Sadler's Wells, 1959, with Joan Hammond, Charles Craig, Howell Glynne, conductor Vilem Tausky; English National Opera, 1983, with Eilene Hannan, Lois McDonall, Sarah Walker, John Treleaven, Richard Van Allan, conductor Mark Elder.

Wood Nymphs ....Soprano, Contralto
The Spirit of the Lake ....Bass
Rusalka, *his daughter* ....Soprano
Ježibaba, *the Witch*..............................Mezzo-Soprano
Voice of a Huntsman....................................Baritone
The Prince ....Tenor
The Forester...................................Baritone or Tenor
The Kitchen Boy ....Mezzo-Soprano
The Foreign Princess ....Soprano

Water Nymphs, Courtiers and Wedding Guests

Running Time: 3 hours 15 minutes

In 1899, six months after finishing his comedy *Čert a Kača* (The Devil and Kate), Dvořák let it be known that he was looking for a new libretto. The thirty-one-year-old poet and dramatist, Jaroslav Kvapil, responded with one already written and Dvořák set *Rusalka* without asking for changes. The origins of the story lie in the French *Mélusine*, Hans Christian Andersen's *Little Mermaid*, Friedrich de la Motte Fouqué's *Undine*, and Gerhart Hauptmann's *The Sunken Bell*, and the resulting story and score are far from the kind of subject which was popular in Prague in the 1890s, when the tendency was for younger composers to turn to *verismo* rather than fairy story and folklore. But *Rusalka* is a triumph of lyricism at the service of a major symphonist, in the annals of Czech opera next in popularity to Smetana's *Bartered Bride*, and it is peculiar that for his last opera, *Armida* (1902/3), Dvořák should have chosen an almost baroque libretto.

Act I. The short and beautiful prelude admirably suggests the poetical, twilit atmosphere of the opera, its tenderness and yearning. In the fourth bar occurs an important melodic phrase associated with Rusalka and her native watery element (Ex. 1). A clearing on the shore of the lake; in the background, a cottage. The good-natured old Spirit of the Lake is tempted out of the lake depths, where he has his abode, by the spirited singing of the Wood Nymphs. When they have gone, Rusalka, heralded by the harp, rises from the water and sadly asks her father for advice. The music has a warmth and tenderness that is Dvořák at his finest as she tells him in an aria that she has fallen in love with a handsome young prince and wants to become human in order to know the bliss of union with him. Her confession fills her father with sadness, but he advises her to visit the old Witch who lives nearby. When she is alone Rusalka confides to the moon the secret of her longing – this passage is justly famous as one of the most touching and yet chaste of operatic love songs.

(Ex. 1)

Rusalka calls to Ježibaba, the Witch, and in a passionate *scena* (Ex. 1 prominent in the orchestra) begs for her help. Ježibaba will grant her human attributes, but she will not be able to speak and, if he prove false to her, both she and her lover will be damned for ever. Together Rusalka and Ježibaba cast the spell. The voice of the Spirit of the Lake is raised in anguish from the depths, but Rusalka's decision is irrevocably taken.

The sound of horns and of a huntsman's song in the distance – rapt, intense, lyrical music – sets the scene for the Prince's entrance. He is in pursuit of a white doe, but feels a mysterious attraction when he is by the shores of the lake. He suspects magic but sends his companions back to the palace saying he wants to stay alone with whatever power rules the place. To the strains of Ex. 1, Rusalka comes into sight. The Prince is immediately enchanted at her appearance and sings her praises in music of the utmost tenderness (derived from the huntsman's distant song). Her sisters and the Spirit of the Lake are filled with alarm but without a word – in the Prince's presence she is dumb – Rusalka clings to

him. He is enraptured – the music becomes a kind of one-handed love duet – and flinging his cloak round her, takes Rusalka off towards his palace.

Act II. The palace grounds. The palace is full of guests invited to the wedding of the Prince and the mysterious Rusalka. In a charming scene, a forester and a boy from the palace kitchen exchange the latest news – the kitchen boy is frankly scared by Rusalka, who gives him the creeps; the forester suspects witchcraft. There is more gossip: the Prince is said already to have begun to tire of his silent beauty and his eyes have turned towards a foreign Princess. They hurry out as the Prince and Rusalka are seen approaching. That she has given him so little sign of her love has begun to baffle him, and he fears for his happiness once they are married. When the foreign Princess comes by, the Prince sends Rusalka into the palace to dress for the ball and he himself goes off with the Princess, who clearly takes it as a personal slight that he is to marry Rusalka. Rusalka goes sadly into the palace as Ex. 1 is heard.

The dance music strikes up and a brilliant scene follows as the ball begins. It is temporarily interrupted by the melodious lament of the Spirit of the Lake, who emerges from the fountain to express his despair at the downfall of his favourite daughter. He continues to mourn while the chorus sings the beautiful 'White flowers are blooming by the way'. Rusalka runs to him and is now able to give passionate voice to her misery that the Prince has all evening paid court to the foreign Princess and not to her. Before long the Prince leads his new lady-love away from the dancing and their fiery duet contains all the warmth that the Prince had missed in Rusalka. They embrace, but Rusalka throws herself into her bridegroom's arms, and the Spirit of the Lake proclaims that the Prince will now never be free of her. The Prince implores the foreign Princess's help, but she turns proudly away from him.

Act III. A glade by the side of the lake, as in Act I. Evening. Rusalka is now the victim of her lover's infidelity and condemned to wander for ever as a will-o'-the-wisp. In a grandiose aria, with insidiously beautiful orchestral accompaniment, she longs for death, but Ježibaba comes out of her hut to say that only the shedding of human blood can now redeem her from the curse which hangs over her. Rusalka sings touchingly and resignedly of her fate and, as the Wood Nymphs comment on her short sojourn in the world, she sinks alone into the waters.

The forester and the kitchen boy come to ask the Witch to help the Prince, who is, they fear, under supernatural influence. The forester pushes the boy forward, but neither dares knock at the door. When Ježibaba answers to the cries of her name, she makes short work of their plea to help restore the confidence of the Prince, and between them she and the Spirit of the Lake put the timid pair to flight.

The Wood Nymphs gather at the side of the lake and sing and dance to music of graceful character – the first Nymph has a particularly appealing solo 'Golden is my Hair' – until stopped by the Spirit of the Lake, who reminds them of Rusalka's melancholy fate.

The Prince staggers out of the wood, muttering about the snow-white doe, which first led him here to Rusalka. He recognises the place and to the music in which he addressed her at their first meeting, calls on Rusalka to come back. It is a magically tender setting of Ex. 1 which returns Rusalka to him. The Prince begs her if she is a ghost to take his life too, and he asks her forgiveness for his cruelty towards her. Tenderly she reproaches him for having lied to her; she was not able to give him the passion he craved, and now, if she were to embrace him, he would die at her caress. In ecstatic phrases he begs for the kiss which will end his life, and he dies in her arms. Even the Spirit of the Lake's pronouncement that Rusalka's fate will not be mitigated by her lover's sacrifice cannot mar the apotheosis of Rusalka and the Prince through the love that finally they share.

In 1983 for English National Opera, David Pountney staged the opera as a young girl's dream of adolescence and awakening. The Spirit of the Lake was Rusalka's grandfather, the Wood Nymphs her sisters, the Prince an older man in whose presence the young girl is tongue-tied, and the foreign Princess a sophisticated threat to first love. The Witch became that Victorian source of comfort and enlightenment as well as of alarm, a black-bombazined and beetle-browed governess. The psychoanalysts Freud and Jung, the painters Magritte and Delvaux, the writer Apollinaire, bulk larger in this production than Hans Christian Andersen or de la Motte Fouqué, and there was protest at the lack of romantic trappings. Nonetheless, without the distancing almost inevitable with Prince and Witch, Water Spirit and trailing Nymphs, the tendency was for critics and most audiences to fall under the opera's spell as too seldom outside Czechoslovakia – too seldom at least for those of us who always found in *Rusalka* a rare and in my view complete vindication of the power of inspired lyricism to express drama and human emotion.   H.

E

GOTTFRIED VON EINEM

(born 24 January 1918, died 12 July 1996)

DANTONS TOD

The Death of Danton

Opera in two parts, text by the composer and Boris Blacher after Büchner's drama of the same name (1835). First produced at the Salzburg Festival, 6 August 1947, with Maria Cebotari, Julius Patzak, Paul Schoeffler, conductor Ferenc Fricsay. Subsequently produced in Vienna, Hamburg, Berlin and Brussels. Revived Munich, 1956, conductor Lovro von Matacic; New York, City Opera, 1966 (in English), with John Reardon, conductor Ernst Märzendorfer; Berlin, 1967, with Dietrich Fischer-Dieskau; Vienna, 1967, with Lisa Della Casa, Eberhard Wächter, conductor Josef Krips; Rome, 1970, with Maria Chiara, Mario Basiola (jr.), conductor Bruno Bartoletti; Brighton Festival, 1997.

Georges Danton	Baritone
Camille Desmoulins	Tenor
Hérault de Séchelles	Tenor
Robespierre	Tenor
Saint-Just	Bass
Herrmann, *President of the Revolutionary Tribunal*	Baritone
Simon, *a prompter*	Buffo Bass
A Young Man	Tenor
First Executioner	Tenor
Second Executioner	Tenor
Julie, *Danton's wife*	Mezzo-Soprano
Lucile, *Desmoulins's wife*	Soprano
A Woman	Soprano
Madame Simon	Contralto

Men and Women of the People

Place: Paris
Time: 1794
Running Time: 2 hours 20 minutes

Einem's first opera was written towards the end of the Second World War at the suggestion of his teacher, Boris Blacher, with whom he collaborated in adapting Büchner's play for the operatic stage. Few operas of this vintage and of German or Austrian background have stayed so persistently in the repertory, a survival due as much to musical strength as to dramatic excellence.

Act I, scene i. Danton and his friends are in the Gaming Rooms. The scene is lively and conversational and there are spirited and pointed exchanges – it is the year 1794 and the power of Robespierre is absolute. Most of those who fought in the struggle for freedom have by now been liquidated. Camille Desmoulins, a younger revolutionary leader and a friend of Danton's, states his view that the moment has now come to call a halt. He is revolted by the ever-increasing number of executions and urges Danton himself to oppose Robespierre's reign of terror. Danton however seems to have grown tired and sceptical and events have caused him to lose his faith in human virtue. 'The statue of freedom is not yet cast; the furnace is glowing and we can all burn our fingers on it.'

Scene ii. An urgently lyrical interlude takes us from the leaders of the revolution to the people who are led. The theatrical prompter, Simon, is furious with his wife because, as he thinks, she has put their daughter on the streets, and the choruses have a savage note as the crowd masses to listen to Simon inveigh against the rich who can buy the love of the poor. They seize a young aristocrat and are about to hang him from the nearest lamp-post when he catches their fancy with a cool witticism and to his surprise finds his death sentence commuted to a round of applause. Robespierre himself appears before the excited crowd and announces new death sentences, to popular acclaim. The lonely figure is chillingly characterised in music and, when the crowd leaves the square and Danton enters it, the contrast between the two is very marked. Danton challenges his opponent with 'You are disgustingly upright', but Robespierre's reaction is completely without heat, though the short scene is one of considerable power. No sooner has Danton departed, to Robespierre's comment that he must clearly be done away with, than St-Just enters with documentary evidence to support Danton's indictment before the tribunal. Camille Desmoulins must also die – Robespierre hesitates for a moment since Camille was his friend, then, as near to passion as his nature can contrive, makes his decision: 'Away with them. Quickly. Only the dead do not return.' The orchestra's *larghetto* coda underlines the dictator's final words, 'They all desert me. All is bare and empty. I am alone.'

Scene iii. The Desmoulins' house. Camille, who is an enthusiastic patriot and humanist, is in conversation with Lucile his wife and Danton his friend. Danton is called out of the room, and immediately the tone of the music becomes lyrical as Camille and Lucile sing of their involvement, only a moment later to be interrupted by Danton's re-entry to tell them that he has been denounced and that the committee has decided on his arrest. His friends beg him to escape but he refuses: 'I shall know how to die courageously. It is easier than living.' Camille, who has no suspicion that his own arrest is impending, wants to talk to Robespierre, but his departure leaves Lucile full of foreboding. In an effective aria she reflects on the horror of the times in which they live, then rushes out into the street to look for Camille, their thoughts underlined by a funeral march in the orchestra.

Act II, scene iv. Arrests have continued and Danton and Camille and many of their friends now lie in prison. The dark scene shows at the same time the interior of the prison and its exterior, where the mob rages. At first their enthusiasm is for the newly arrested leaders, but soldiers are in front of the jail, and Simon stirs them to hatred with his allegations that Danton has lived in luxury, for all the world like any aristocrat, while Robespierre has trodden the path of virtue and righteousness: 'Long live Robespierre, down with the traitors.'

The interior of the prison now lights up, showing a group of prisoners, among them Danton and Camille, who are awaiting trial. Camille is full of thoughts of Lucile and cannot accept that his life hangs in the balance. Danton, in contrast, awaits death with sad composure, and his beautiful monologue perfectly expresses his resignation. Lucile appears at the barred window of the prison, driven mad by sorrow but still able to recognise Camille and speak to him. The voices of Danton, Camille and Lucile blend in a beautiful trio which is supported and then interrupted by the shouting of the other prisoners as they rattle the bars of their windows.

Scene v. The Revolutionary Tribunal. Herrmann presides and the scene begins with the hearing of Danton's case, to constant interruptions from the mob. Danton passionately denies the charge that he has conspired with the royalists and the aristocrats, and when he reminds the court of his own revolutionary achievements, the power of his oratory starts to win over the crowd. Herrmann announces a recession, and Saint-Just brings in new evidence. When the court reassembles, Danton speaks even more boldly than before and in a great prophetic speech the accused becomes the accuser of a bloody regime. The mob starts to turn against Robespierre, and the scene ends in tumult as the prisoners are hustled out by soldiers.

The last scene takes place in the public square, where a mob surrounds the guillotine, dancing and singing the Carmagnole in celebration of the impending executions. Danton's passion may have carried the mob at his trial, but the verdict has already been decided and nothing now will prevent the mob's enjoyment of its favourite form of entertainment. A tumbril brings in Danton, Camille and Hérault who sing bravely: 'Our enemy is the stupidity of the masses which can be pierced only by the sword of the spirit.' The crowd continues to roar the Carmagnole as Danton and his two friends mount the scaffold and, after a few words from each to the crowd, the executions proceed.

The heads are in the basket, the show is over, the crowd can leave and night has fallen. Two executioners are tidying up after the day's work, singing a sentimental song as they clean. When they leave, Lucile appears and stands on the steps of the guillotine, singing forlornly of what she and France have lost. Whatever her state of mind, she cannot forget Camille and the last word will inevitably be with the guillotine.   H.

DER BESUCH DER ALTEN DAME
The Visit of the Old Lady

Opera in three acts, libretto by Friedrich Dürrenmatt, adapted from his tragi-comedy of the same name (1956). First performed at the Staatsoper, Vienna, 23 May 1971, with Christa Ludwig as Claire Zachanassian, conducted by Horst Stein. First U.S. performance, War Memorial Opera House, San Francisco, 1972, with Regina Resnik, conducted by Maurice Peress, directed by Francis Ford Coppola. First U.K. performance, Glyndebourne (in English, at the composer's insistence), 1973, with Kerstin Meyer, conducted by John Pritchard. Revived Zurich, 1971, with Astrid Varnay; Berlin, 1972, with Patricia Johnson.

The Visitors
Claire Zachanassian,
    multi-millionairess.....................Mezzo-Soprano
Her Husband VII ....Actor
Husband IX..Tenor
The Butler ....Character Tenor
Toby, Roby, *chewing chewing-gum* ....Actors
Koby, Loby, *blind* ....Tenors

The Visited
Alfred Ill..High Baritone
His Wife...Lyrical Soprano
His Daughter................................Mezzo-Soprano
His Son...Tenor
The Mayor..Heldentenor
The Preacher................................Bass-Baritone
The Teacher....................................Baritone
The Doctor......................................Baritone
The Policeman ....Bass-Baritone
First Woman ....Soprano
Second Woman.............................Soprano
Hofbauer   } *citizens* ....Tenor
Helmesberger }   ....Baritone

The rest
Station Master.............................Bass-Baritone
Train Driver..Bass
Conductor...Tenor
Reporter.......................................Spoken Role
Cameraman ....Bass
A Voice ....Tenor

Citizens of Güllen

Place: Güllen, a Small Town in Central Europe
Time: The Present
Running Time: 2 hours 15 minutes

Act I, scene i. Station I. Güllen's male citizens wait for the return of Claire Zachanassian: she left the town forty-five years ago. Now Güllen is bankrupt and she is a billionairess. Her close friend, when they were young, was Alfred Ill, now the most popular man in town, scheduled to be mayor next year. Can he persuade her to save Güllen? He remembers her as 'devilishly beautiful' and claims that it was only life itself that separated them. The express train stops unexpectedly: Zachanassian pulled the emergency cord. Her entry is to an elegant adagio: von Einem's music highlights an unexpected aspect to her character, her grace and her unlikely charm. Ill assures her she hasn't changed, but she laughs and reveals that her left leg is an ivory prosthesis. She presents her seventh husband, an actor with a black moustache, whom she calls Moby. Before leaving in a litter to visit the sites of her affair with Alfred, the barn and the wood, she mentions that she brought a coffin along with her luggage. The last members of her entourage appear, Koby and Loby, two smiling, blind eunuchs.

Scene ii. The Konradsweil wood. An atmospheric chorus representing the 'authentic German, rooted wilderness' sets the Romantic scene. Zachanassian remembers how she and Alfred met and kissed here, when she was seventeen and he was twenty. Then he married a grocer's daughter and she an Armenian millionaire, who found her in a Hamburg brothel. Alfred tells her that since she left, he has been living in hell. 'And I have become hell', she replies. She promises that she won't leave Güllen in the lurch.

Scene iii. The Golden Apostle. Zachanassian asks the Doctor if he fills out death certificates and tells him in future to put 'heart attack'. In his speech the Mayor praises her sense of justice and her philanthropy. She offers 500 million to the town and 500 million to be distributed among the citizens – on one condition. Her butler Boby, formerly Güllen's judge, explains that forty-five years ago he presided over the case brought by Claire Zachanassian, then Klara Wäscher, who accused Alfred Ill of being the father of her child. Ill denied the charge and bribed two false witnesses to swear that they slept with Klara. Now called Koby and Loby, they recount how Zachanassian later had them tracked down, blinded and castrated. Claire's child died after a year; the verdict forced her to become a prostitute. Now she wants justice: she offers a billion to Güllen, if someone kills Alfred Ill. The Mayor rejects her offer – 'better poor than spotted with blood' – to tremendous applause. The act ends with Claire's words, 'I'm waiting'.

Act II, scene iv. The grocer's shop I. A series of customers buy expensive goods from Alfred Ill, all on credit, in exquisite, lilting 3/4 time. They insist that they support him and are 'dead sure' he will be mayor next year. Ill loses his temper, shouts 'What are you going to pay with?' and throws goods at them.

Scene v. The sacristy. Ill comes for comfort, but the Priest is more concerned about Ill's immortal soul than his life, and suggests he should repent. This scene is one of the best: the confrontation between high baritone and bass-baritone manages to refer to the scene in *Don Carlos* between Philip II and the Grand Inquisitor without merely imitating it. When the church bell rings (to magnificent effect), Ill realises it is new. The Priest cannot keep up the hypocrisy: embracing Ill he tells him to run away: to stay is 'to lead [them] into temptation'.

Scene vi. Station II. The station has been smartened up. A poster advertises the Passion Plays in Oberammergau, a parallel made in the music by the choral writing, which briefly borrows from Bach's Passions.[1] Ill appears with his suitcase, but is soon surrounded, 'as though by chance', by all the inhabitants of Güllen. They assure him no one wants to kill him. When the train arrives, they even tell him to go on board. He hides his face in his hands and admits, 'I am lost!'

Act III, scene vii. The barn. Claire Zachanassian is wearing a wedding dress, veil etc., having married her ninth husband in Güllen's church.[2] The Teacher and Doctor ask her to spend less and invest in the town, but it turns out that she already owns everything and has deliberately let it rot. The Teacher appeals to her humanity. 'The world turned me into a whore', she answers, 'now I turn it into a brothel.' The brass intervene between the sung phrases to highlight the menace that is not apparent on the surface.

Scene viii. The grocer's shop II. The shop has been redecorated. Ill's children now have expensive tastes; his wife has a fur coat ('on approval'). The Mayor calls in, and leaves a gun, even though Ill says he does not need it. The community are to meet that evening. Ill agrees to abide by their decision. The Mayor goes on to suggest that Ill *does* need the gun, as a man of honour ... With great dignity, Ill agrees

to accept the verdict, but not to execute it himself. The scene ends in a gruesomely lightfooted dance, as Ill's family assemble in their best clothes for a drive to the wood in his son's new Mercedes.

Scene ix. The Konradsweil wood II. Claire introduces Ill to her ninth husband, a Nobel prizewinner. Ill tells her that when the town meets tonight, he expects to be sentenced to death. She promises to bury his body in the mausoleum she has built in Capri.

Scene x. The theatre auditorium. The media are present. The Teacher asks the citizens to consider the injustice they had tolerated, for 'This is not a question of money (*tremendous applause*)'. Apart from Ill, they vote unanimously 'with a pure heart to see justice realised'. The proceedings take on a solemn, ritual aspect, though the sequence has to be repeated when the cameraman reports a technical hitch. Once the media and the women have left, the Mayor orders the doors to be shut and the lights extinguished. In the moonlight the men form a tunnel. Ill is surrounded and disappears from view. The percussion erupt and die down, but drumbeats continue to the end. The Doctor kneels at the corpse's side and diagnoses 'heart attack', which the Mayor interprets 'dead from joy'. Claire gazes at Ill's face and orders his body to be brought to the coffin. On her way out she hands the Mayor a cheque. The tempo changes to *molto allegro*, the Mayor begins to dance and everybody joins in. The infectious jollity makes for a memorable, gruesomely repellent end.

There are several moments, particularly in the opening scenes, when von Einem seems to have been daunted by the demanding, witty density of Dürrenmatt's text. For the sake of audibility, he reins the music in so sharply that it seems unduly reticent. He makes up for it in the interludes, miniconcertos for percussion and timpani that keep the issue of violence at the forefront of our awareness. When it was first performed in Britain *Der Besuch der Alten Dame* made a mixed impression: Desmond Shawe-Taylor in *The Sunday Times* playfully quoted his companion, who insisted it was '*Albert Herring* refurbished'. He then explained that the 'action,

---

[1] In case we still have not got the point, the Teacher mentions in the next scene that his 'mixed choir' performed extracts from Bach's *St Matthew Passion* at Zachanassian's wedding.

[2] The score specifies ninth, but productions generally amend this to eighth husband.

superficially amusing, fundamentally appalling, is an obvious allegory of the corruption of capitalism and liberal democracy, but it stirs no indignation or pity, or satiric rage in the spectator, it just keeps him comfortably entertained – which might, I suppose, be regarded as the final turn of the screw'. For William Mann in *The Times* it was 'musically forgettable'.

P.

GEORGES ENESCO
(born 19 August 1881, died 3 May 1955)

OEDIPE
Oedipus

Opera in four acts, libretto by Edmond Fleg (after Sophocles and earlier sources). Première, Opéra, Paris, 13 March 1936, with André Pernet, conductor Philippe Gaubert (revived there 1937 but not thereafter). First performed Brussels, 1956, with Germain Ghislain; Bucharest in Romanian, 1958 (in 1963 in Paris in this version, which was also recorded); Berlin and Vienna, 1996–7, conductor Lawrence Foster.

Oedipe (Oedipus) ....Bass-Baritone
Tirésias (Tiresias), *a seer*........................Bass-Baritone
Créon (Creon), *a Prince of Thebes* ....Bass
A Shepherd..Tenor
Theban High Priest ....Bass
Phorbas, *Queen Mérope's counsellor* ....Baritone
A Watchman ....Bass
Thésée (Theseus), *King of Attica* ....Baritone
Laïos (Laius), *King of Thebes*..............................Tenor
Jocaste (Jocasta), *Queen of Thebes*........Mezzo-Soprano
The Sphinx ....Contralto
Antigone, *Oedipe's daughter* ....Soprano
Mérope (Merope), *Queen of Corinth* ....Contralto
A Theban Woman.............................Mezzo-Soprano

Men and Women of Thebes, Corinth and Athens

Place: Thebes, Corinth, Attica
Time: Antiquity
Running Time: 3 hours

Enesco was a musical polymath: composer, violinist, pianist, conductor, teacher, mentor. As a composer, he worked slowly and painstakingly, leaving only thirty-three works to which he attached opus numbers.

The genesis of *Oedipe* itself was slow. Enesco had for several years wanted to write an opera when in 1909 at the Comédie-Française he saw a performance of Sophocles' *King Oedipus* with Mounet-Sully in the title role. Wartime commitments prevented him starting the music until the beginning of 1921. Excerpts were performed in the 1920s but the orchestration was not completed until mid-1931 and Enesco continued to work on it up to the première in 1936.

Act III corresponds roughly with Sophocles' *King Oedipus* (Stravinsky's source) and Act IV with *Oedipus at Colona*, but the first two acts are taken from Greek legends not previously staged. *Oedipe* amounts to a vast work, and its greatest admirers make vast claims for it – 'one of the peaks of twentieth-century music, it is among a handful of works that are to be reckoned on a par with *Pelléas*, *Wozzeck*, *Lulu* or *Die Soldaten*', says Harry Halpreich in notes to the complete French recording – and there is no doubt that it is a work of high seriousness and noble aspiration, though not yet one which has caught the imagination of opera planners.

Act I. A gloomy prelude in G minor introduces the Royal Palace of Thebes, where the people hymn the child newly born to Queen Jocasta and King Laius. As Jocasta and Laius discuss how to name the baby they are warned by Tiresias that the child is doomed to kill his father and marry his mother. As the horror of the prophecy sinks in, Laius gives the baby to the Shepherd; he is to abandon him in the mountains.

Act II, scene i. Twenty years later. King Polybus' and Queen Merope's palace in Corinth. Oedipus, who has consulted the Oracle and knows what is foretold, refuses to reveal to Phorbas, the Queen's counsellor, the cause of his gloom. But to Merope, whom he believes his mother, he confesses. Her protests are genuine enough; she has no idea that her own child died at birth and was replaced by Oedipus. He tells Merope of the prophecy and leaves Corinth.

Scene ii. A vigorous orchestral interlude leads to the insidious flute playing of the Shepherd. We are at the crossroads.

A chariot appears, and the impetuous King Laius strikes out at Oedipus, who in a scene of uncommon violence kills him, his guard and the charioteer. Sombre music of less vigorous cast takes us towards Thebes (scene iii) where crouches the sleeping Sphinx. A watchman attempts to warn off Oedipus. Whoever can answer the Sphinx's riddles will save the town, be offered the crown and win Jocasta as wife. The Sphinx wakes to mock Oedipus. Then comes the question: name something or someone greater than Destiny. 'Man is stronger than Destiny', answers Oedipus – correctly – and the Sphinx, cackling with manic laughter – ironical? triumphant? – expires. The watchman is transformed from harbinger of doom to herald of victory and peace. Jocasta comes out to welcome Oedipus and the music of rejoicing changes to the sound of the Shepherd's flute; destiny has caught up with Oedipus.

Act III. Thebes; twenty years later. Funeral processions pass in the background. Oedipus has sent an envoy, the Queen's brother Creon, to Delphi to consult the Oracle. Creon returns to say that the murderer of Laius is within the city; if he can be found and punished, the plague will pass. A shep-

herd witnessed the murder all those years ago and Creon has summoned him, together with the seer Tiresias. Oedipus endorses the action taken: the murderer shall be exiled. Tiresias prevaricates, then points to Oedipus as the killer of Laius. Oedipus rails at Tiresias, and turns on Creon and banishes him.

Jocasta is unconvinced by Tiresias' pronouncement; did he not once foretell that her son would kill his father, whereas Laius was in point of fact killed by brigands? Oedipus feels the trap closing. The Shepherd confirms his worst fears as Phorbas comes in to reveal that Merope and Polybus were not his parents but he was their adopted son. With a great cry Oedipus acknowledges the truth and rushes into the palace, to re-appear blind. A woman announces that Jocasta has killed herself. Oedipus' daughter Antigone prepares to help him on his way into exile.

Act IV. A sacred wood near Attica. Theseus, King of Athens, sings of justice and peace. Oedipus and Antigone come into sight, but the peaceful atmosphere is shattered by the arrival of Creon, hypocritically trying to bolster his own shaky position by persuading Oedipus to resume the throne of Thebes. Theseus intervenes and Oedipus is allowed a grand *apologia*: 'I have done nothing! Did I have any part in the crimes ordained by Destiny before I was born?'[1]

The opera ends in an atmosphere of serenity as Oedipus, followed by Theseus and leading Antigone, goes peacefully towards his last resting place, his sight restored.   H.

---

[1] Translation by John Rushby-Smith.

F

MANUEL DE FALLA

(born 23 November 1876, died 14 November 1946)

LA VIDA BREVE

The Short Life

Opera in two acts, text by C. Fernandez Shaw; French version by P. Milliet. Première, Nice, 1 April 1913, with Lillian Grenville, David Devriès, Cotreuil, conductor Miranne. First performed Opéra-Comique, Paris, 1914, with Carré, Brohly, Francell, Vieuille, conductor Ruhlmann; Madrid, 1914; Buenos Aires, 1923, with Hina Spani; Metropolitan, 1926, with Bori, Tokatyan, d'Angelo, conductor Serafin. Revived la Scala, Milan, 1952, with Araujo, Francesco Albanese, Beuf, conductor Giulini; Holland Festival, 1953, with de los Angeles, Vroons; Edinburgh Festival, 1958, with de los Angeles.

Salud, *a gipsy*	Soprano
Her Grandmother	Mezzo-Soprano
Carmela, *a young girl*	Mezzo-Soprano
Paco	Tenor
Uncle Sarvaor	Bass
A Singer	Baritone
Manuel, *Carmela's brother*	Baritone
A Voice in the Forge	Tenor
Voice of a Street-Seller	Tenor
A Distant Voice	Tenor

Place: Granada
Time: 'The Present'
Running Time: 1 hour 10 minutes

*L*a Vida Breve is the earliest of Falla's works which is still generally performed. It was written in 1904–05 and won a prize in Madrid, but was not immediately mounted on the stage. When Falla went to Paris, he took the score with him, and the work was finally performed in 1913.

Act I. The curtain rises after a dozen bars of introduction. Courtyard of a gipsy habitation. On one side of the stage, the house where the gipsies live, on the other the entrance to a smithy, from which can be heard a mysterious sound of singing. Salud's old grandmother is feeding some birds in a cage. One is going to die, she thinks – perhaps of love, like Salud. The voices of street-sellers (off-stage, like that of the soloist in the smithy) can be heard.

Salud comes in from the street, looking unhappy. Her grandmother tries to reassure her; of course Paco will come. Salud is fearful that she may lose one of the two things she most values: the love of Paco and of her grandmother. Alone Salud listens to the voices from the forge, and then sings a song with a sad philosophy – long live those who laugh, short life to those who cry: 'Vivan los que rien!' The poignant beauty of the music is like that of a folk-song, and indeed it is founded on the Andalusian style.

Her grandmother comes to tell Salud that Paco is on his way. Her joy is complete, and in their duet her sincerity and innocence contrast with his more conventional utterances. Salud's grandmother and her uncle observe the scene, and he mutters that he would gladly take revenge on Paco, whom he knows to be going to marry another girl the very next day. He is only playing with Salud.

The second scene is in the form of an intermezzo. A view of Granada from Sacro Monte can be seen.

Act II. A small street in Granada. Through the open railings can be seen the courtyard in which is being celebrated the betrothal of Paco and Carmela with song and dance. A professional singer performs an Andalusian song, which is followed by a dance, made famous all over the world by generations of fiddlers who have appropriated it as an encore piece.

Just before the dance finishes, Salud appears and rushes to see what is going on. She is in despair when she finds her worst fears realised, and Paco laughing and talking with the girl who is separating them for ever. Her grief spills over in a terrible lament, and she longs for death. Her grandmother and uncle arrive, and the latter tries to relieve the situation by cursing Paco and everything to do with him. Salud hears Paco's voice and makes up her mind to speak to him once again. She repeats the sad song of the forge.

During an interlude the scene changes to the court-yard of the house. Immediately the curtain rises there is a dance, hardly less well known than the previous one. Paco has heard the voice of Salud and is uneasy. Manuel makes a speech to congratulate the happy pair, but Paco becomes more and more uncomfortable as Uncle Sarvaor comes into the patio, followed by Salud. Sarvaor offers their services to entertain the company, but Salud denounces Paco's treachery towards her in tones that would almost appear calm did they not so obviously conceal deep feeling. She falls dead of shock at Paco's feet, and her grandmother and Uncle Sarvaor curse Paco as the curtain falls.   H.

EL RETABLO DE MAESE PEDRO

Master Peter's Puppet Show

Opera in one act, libretto by the composer from an episode in the twenty-sixth chapter of the second part of Cervantes's *Don Quixote de la Mancha*. Written for Princesse Edmond de Polignac, the première was in her drawing room, 25 June 1923, with Amparito Peris, Thomas Salignac, Hector Dufranne, conductor Golschmann (publicly in Paris later the same year). First performed Seville in concert, 23 March 1923, with Redondo, Segura, Lledo, conductor Falla; Bristol, 1924 (in English). Revived Ingestre Festival, England, 1957, with Adèle Leigh, conductor Pritchard.

Don Quixote ....Bass or Baritone

Master Peter ....Tenor

The Boy (El Trujamán)
.....................Boy Soprano or High Mezzo-Soprano

Sancho Panza ....Silent

The Innkeeper...Silent

The Scholar..Silent

The Page ....Silent

The Man with the Lances and Halberds ....Silent

Figures in the puppet show
   Charlemagne
   Don Gayferos
   Don Roland

Melisendra
King Marsilius
The Enamoured Moor

Heralds, Knights, etc., at Court of Charlemagne; Moors

Running Time: 30 minutes

The little opera was originally intended to be performed entirely with puppets, double-sized when doing duty for human beings, ordinary-sized when representing puppets. The action takes place in the stable of an inn at la Mancha on the borders of Aragon. At the back of the stable is the puppet-show itself, standing on legs covered by curtains, behind which Master Peter works the puppets. The work introduces Master Peter and the stage audience, and then tells the story of the Deliverance of Melisendra, each episode being first introduced by the boy narrator in an extraordinary recitative style and afterwards mimed by the puppets. At the end Don Quixote interrupts the action. The grave beauty of much of the music, the irresistible liveliness of the boy's narration (when it is properly performed[1]), and Falla's fastidious orchestration (note the subtle use of muted trumpet throughout) and vivid sense of contrast as evidenced in the different sections, combine to make a work of peculiar distinction.

The wind section over a side drum plays a southern, *cornemuse* type of tune, a bell rings and Master Peter invites the guests at the inn to come to the show. While the orchestra plays Master Peter's Symphony, a combination of dignity and impudence in 6/8, the audience assembles, the last to appear being Don Quixote and Sancho Panza. The boy announces that they will see the story of the Deliverance of the fair Melisendra by her husband Don Gayferos from her captivity by the Moors. In the first scene, Don Gayferos is discovered playing chess with Don Roland. The Emperor Charlemagne, Melisendra's father, is furious that Don Gayferos prefers gaming to rescuing his imprisoned wife. Gayferos overturns the chess board, tries unsuccessfully to borrow Roland's sword, then prepares to set out alone to rescue his wife.

The second scene shows the Moorish Tower of Saragossa, where Melisendra appears on a balcony. A Moor creeps up behind her and steals a kiss,

---

[1] The boy's voice must be 'nasal and rather forced – the voice of a boy shouting in the street ... devoid of all lyrical feeling. It should be sung by a boy soprano, but when this is not possible, a woman's voice (high mezzo-soprano) may be used.'

whereupon Marsilius, King of the Moors, orders that he be whipped. In the third scene, he is to receive 200 strokes, a sentence carried out summarily, says the boy, and without legal proceedings. At this Don Quixote interrupts to complain about the boy's embroidery of the story: there must always be a legal weighing of the evidence – Master Peter agrees with him: 'Sing your proper plainsong and do not meddle with other voices, for much counterpoint ruins the lute strings.' The fourth scene shows Don Gayferos crossing the Pyrenees on horseback – a perfect piece of musical stylisation – from time to time sounding his hunting horn. In the fifth scene, Melisendra, who at first does not recognise her husband, is rescued and carried away to safety.

The sixth scene shows the pursuit by the Moors. The boy starts by wishing the couple happiness and long life in the most flowery terms, and is again pulled up by Master Peter for departing from the text. The alarm is given and the bells ring out from the mosques and minarets – Don Quixote objects: 'among Moors is no ringing of bells, but beating of drums and squealing hautboys'. Master Peter pleads stage licence, and the boy describes the Moorish horsemen setting out to overtake the fugitives. Don Quixote can bear the tension no longer, but sword in hand leaps into the puppet show and proceeds to attack the Moorish puppets, beheading some, knocking others over and dealing destruction all round, in spite of the protests of Master Peter. In some beautiful phrases Don Quixote invokes Dulcinea, praises the deeds of the knights errant, and the opera ends with him triumphant, and Master Peter sadly contemplating the ruin of his puppets.   H.

GABRIEL FAURÉ

(born 12 May 1845, died 4 November 1924)

PÉNÉLOPE

Opera in three acts, libretto by René Fauchois. Première Monte Carlo, 4 March 1913, with Lucienne Bréval, Charles Rousselière, conductor Léon Jéhin. First performed in Paris at Théâtre des Champs-Elysées, 1913, with Bréval, Muratore, conductor Hasselmans; Brussels, 1913, with Croiza, Darmel; Opéra-Comique, 1919, with Germaine Lubin, Rousselière. Revived Opéra, 1943, with Lubin, Jouatte; Bordeaux, 1957, with Régine Crespin, Raoul Jobin; Buenos Aires, 1962, with Crespin, Guy Chauvet; Nantes, 1996, with Isabelle Vernet.

Ulysse (Ulysses), *King of Ithaca*...........................Tenor

Eumée (Eumaeus), *an old shepherd* ....Baritone

Pénélope's suitors
    Antinoös...Tenor
    Eurymaque (Eurymachus) ....Baritone
    Léodès (Laertes) ....Tenor
    Ctésippe (Ctesippos) ....Baritone
    Pisandre (Pisander) ....Baritone

A Shepherd...Tenor

Pénélope, *Queen of Ithaca* ....Soprano

Euryclée (Eurycleia), *Ulysse's nurse*....Mezzo-Soprano

Servants
    Cléone ....Mezzo-Soprano
    Melantho ....Soprano
    Alkandre ....Mezzo-Soprano
    Phylo..Soprano
    Lydie ....Soprano

Eurynome, *the housekeeper*............................Soprano

Shepherds, Servants, Dancers and Flute Players

Place: Ithaca
Time: Twelfth (or Thirteenth) Century B.C.
Running Time: 2 hours 15 minutes

*P*énélope is Gabriel Fauré's first true opera, composed when he was fifty, thirteen years after *Prométhée*, a big-scale drama, which used many operatic ingredients. Its success has been spasmodic, Fauré's admirers, such as the composer Koechlin, insisting on it not only as a major work of one of France's leading composers but also as something of a landmark in the history of French lyric drama, its detractors finding it undramatic. It has been the subject of occasional revival but has never truly established itself, even in the French capital.

Act I. Pénélope waits for her husband Ulysse, plagued not only by the pretenders to his throne and his marriage bed, but also by her own efforts to retain faith in his ultimate return. The first three scenes, playing in an ante-room to Pénélope's chamber, serve as exposition. After a prelude, which aptly sets out the opera's seriousness of purpose, we meet Pénélope's serving maids, who admit that in Pénélope's place they would long since have succumbed to the suitors' blandishments. The suitors suddenly push their way in, demanding to see the Queen, and opposed by the aged Euryclée; when Pénélope herself appears, it is with incomparable dignity of posture, music and phrase, and the music is fired to splendour as she protests that Ulysse, her husband, has bidden her wait for him; every day she expects him to return, in all the glory in which he left. The suitors are cynical but worried that the shroud she has been weaving for old Léodès, the father of Ulysse, is still far from finished, and the Queen thus protected from their wooing by their promise to respect her privacy until she has finished the shroud. She must work under their supervision.

Eurymaque signs for flute players and dancers to enter, which they do to a most attractive tune in triple time. Deaf to the suitors' blandishments, Pénélope, in another moment of musical inspiration, launches a last appeal: 'Ulysse, proud husband ... gentle warrior ... come, help me in my distress', and outside a voice answers her appeal. It is Ulysse, disguised as an old beggar. In spite of the opposition of the suitors, Pénélope receives him and promises him hospitality. As every other night, she refuses an invitation to the feast, and the suitors go off with the more amenable of the palace girls.

Pénélope confides the old man to the care of Euryclée, who is not long in recognising him. When she is alone, Pénélope starts, as is her wont every night, to unravel the work she has done during the day, but this time the suitors surprise her and insist that the very next day she choose between them.

The old beggar returns, and his words are of such comfort that Pénélope agrees to take him with them when she and Euryclée mount their nightly vigil on the hill which commands a view of the sea and any approaching ship. Left alone for a moment, Ulysse voices his excitement in exuberant phrases.

Act II. A shepherd is singing mournfully of his occupation. Pénélope comes to the promontory, followed by Euryclée and Ulysse. Memories of her husband crowd in on her, and in a duet with the old man she is told that the warrior king has lived under his roof in Crete for twelve days. His description of Ulysse convinces Pénélope, and before long he is assuring her of Ulysse's innermost feelings. Suddenly the old man proposes a stratagem: let Pénélope yield only to the suitor who can bend the great bow Ulysse left behind him! She agrees and goes sadly home, while Ulysse, galvanised to life, calls together the shepherds, makes himself known to them, and enlists their help.

Act III. The act opens with great urgency as Ulysse reveals that he has chosen the great sword of Hercules with which to wreak his vengeance. Euryclée is overcome by the Queen's distress, but Ulysse reassures her: the stratagem will work and by nightfall she will have seen her mistress smile again. Eumée arrives to tell the King that fate has played into their hands in that the shepherds have been ordered by the pretenders to bring beasts to the court for a sacrifice.

The suitors enter and summon Pénélope to make her choice. She tells them that the man among them who can bend the bow of Ulysse shall remain in the palace; then, struck by a sudden revulsion of feeling, begs them to leave before her presentiment of death is fulfilled. Each in turn tries his hand and each fails, until Ulysse, still in disguise, asks to be allowed his turn, to the undisguised contempt of the suitors. He bends the bow, shoots an arrow through the twelve rings of axes, then aims the bow in turn at each of the suitors, and with the aid of Eumée and the shepherds, slays the pretenders and their followers. Justice is done and the opera ends in triumph as the court rejoices in the happiness of the reunited couple.　　　H.

FRIEDRICH von FLOTOW
(born 27 April 1812, died 24 January 1883)

MARTHA

Opera in five acts, text by W. Friedrich after a ballet-pantomime, *Lady Henriette, ou La Servante de Greenwich*, by St-Georges, for which Flotow wrote part of the music. Première at the Kärnthnertortheater, Vienna, on 25 November 1847. First performed New York, 1852, with Anna Bishop; London, Drury Lane, 1849 (in German), 1858 (in English); Covent Garden, 1858, in Italian with Bosiol, Didiée, Mario, Graziani; Paris, Théâtre-Lyrique, 16 December 1865, when was interpolated the famous air 'M'Appari', from Flotow's two-act opera *L'Ame en Peine*. Metropolitan, New York, 1884, with Sembrich, Trebelli, Stagno, Novara; 1905, with Sembrich, Walker, Caruso, Plançon; 1923, with Alda, Howard, Gigli, de Luca; 1961, with de los Angeles, Tucker. Revived Covent Garden, 1930, with Edith Mason, Gigli; la Scala, 1931, with Favero, Pederzini, Pertile, Stabile; 1938, with Favero, Gigli.

Lady Harriet Durham, *Maid of Honour
    to Queen Anne* ....Soprano

Sir Tristram Mickleford, *her cousin*.......................Bass

Plunkett, *a young farmer* ....Bass

Lionel, *his foster-brother*....................................Tenor

Nancy, *waiting-maid to Lady Harriet* ....Contralto

Sheriff..Bass

Three Manservants ....Tenor, Basses

Three Maidservants...........Soprano, Mezzo-Sopranos

Courtiers, Pages, Ladies, Farmers

Place: In and Near Richmond
Time: c. 1710
Running Time: 2 hours 10 minutes

In his original article, Gustav Kobbé went so far as to group *Martha* with the French repertory on stylistic grounds. Its rightful place is among German works – oddly enough, it was as an Italian (rather than French or German) opera that it made its way in the international repertory, but in the latter half of the twentieth century, it has held its position mainly in Germany. Although I cannot agree with Kobbé's view of *Martha* as a French opera, his reasoning is interesting and this is what he wrote:

'It is not without considerable hesitation that I have classed *Martha* as a French opera. For Flotow was born in Teutendorf, and died in Darmstadt. Moreover, *Martha* was produced in Vienna, and his next best known work, *Alessandro Stradella*, in Hamburg (1844).

'The music of *Martha*, however, has an elegance that not only is quite unlike any music that has come out of Germany, but is typically French. Flotow, in fact, was French in his musical training, and both the plot and score of *Martha* were French in origin. The composer studied composition in Paris under Reicha, 1827–30, leaving Paris solely on account of the July revolution, and returning in 1835, to remain until the revolution in March 1848 once more drove him away. After living in Paris again, 1863–8, he settled near Vienna, making, however, frequent visits to that city, the French capital, and Italy.

'During his second stay in Paris he composed for the Grand Opéra the first act of a ballet, *Henriette, ou La Servante de Greenwich*. This ballet, the text by Vernoy de St-Georges, was for Adèle Dumilâtre. The reason Flotow was entrusted with only one of the three acts was the short time in which it was necessary to complete the score. The other acts were assigned, one each, to Robert Bergmüller and Edouard Deldevez. Of this ballet, written and composed for a French dancer and a French audience, *Martha* is an adaptation. This accounts for its being so typically French and not in the slightest degree German.'
                                              H.

Act I, scene i. Lady Harriet's boudoir. It is dull at the court of Queen Anne. Even the resourceful Nancy is at last driven to exclaim: 'If your ladyship would only fall in love!'

But Lady Harriet has bewitched every man at court only to remain unmoved by their protestations of passion. Just as Nancy has spoken, a footman announces the most persistent of her suitors, Sir Tristram Mickleford, an elderly cousin who presumes upon his relationship to ignore her rebuffs. When Sir Tristram opens the window, in come the strains of a merry chorus. Who are these women? Nancy knows all about them. They are servants on the way to Richmond Fair to hire themselves out to the farmers, according to time-honoured custom.

The Richmond Fair! 'Nancy,' cries Harriet, 'let us go to the fair dressed as peasant girls. Who knows, someone might want to hire us! I will call myself Martha, you can be Julia, and you, cousin, can go along with us as plain Bob!'

Scene ii. Richmond Fair is at its height. The Sheriff

reads the law by which all contracts for service made at the fair are binding for at least one year as soon as money has passed. Among those who have come to bid are a young farmer, Plunkett, and his foster-brother Lionel. The latter's parentage is shrouded in mystery. As a child he was left with Plunkett's mother by a fugitive, who confided the boy to her care, first, however, handing her a ring with the injunction, if misfortune ever threatened the boy, to show the ring to the Queen.

One after another the girls proclaim their deftness at cooking, sewing, gardening, poultry-tending. Lionel and Plunkett see two attractive girls arguing with a testy old man, and when they hear one of them call out 'No, we won't go with you!' they hurry over. 'Can't you hear her say she won't go with you?' asks Lionel. Martha and Julia are in high spirits. After a few reassuring glances, Plunkett speaks up: 'You're our choice, girls!' 'Done!' cry the girls, who think it all a great lark. The escapade seems to have gone far enough and the two girls look about for Sir Tristram to take them away, even though money has passed to bind the bargain. 'None of that', say the two farmers, and they hurry the girls off and drive away.

Act II. Plunkett's farmhouse. The adventure has carried Lady Harriet and Nancy further than they had expected. To prepare supper is more than they had bargained for and Lionel suggests that they be allowed to try their hands at the spinning-wheels. Nancy brings the lesson to an abrupt close by overturning Plunkett's wheel and dashing away with the young farmer in pursuit, leaving Lionel and Martha alone.

It is an awkward moment; to relieve the situation Martha begins to sing a favourite air, 'The Last Rose of Summer'. But it has the very opposite effect to what she had planned. Lionel completely carried away exclaims: 'Ah, Martha, if you were to marry me, you would no longer be a servant, for I would raise you to my own station!' A distant tower clock striking midnight, the young farmers allow their servants to retire to their room.

Act III. When morning comes, the birds have flown. There is neither a Martha nor a Julia in the little farmhouse, but at the court of Queen Anne a certain Lady Harriet and her maid Nancy are congratulating themselves that Sir Tristram has had sense enough to be in waiting with a carriage near

the farmhouse at midnight and help them escape through the window. Lady Harriet is no longer bored; even Nancy has lost her sprightliness. The simple fact is that they are in love.

It chances that Lionel, in much the same state of mind, comes upon a young rider in whom, in spite of her different costume, he recognises the Martha over whose disappearance he has been grieving. However her heart might go out towards Lionel, her pride of birth rebels against allowing a farmer to address words of love to her. 'You are mistaken. I do not know you!' she exclaims. Her cries for help bring not only Sir Tristram but a host of other riders to her side, and Lionel now perceives the trick that has been played upon himself and Plunkett at the fair.

Act IV. The farmhouse. Before very long there is a material change in the situation. Lionel remembers his ring and asks Plunkett to show it to the Queen and plead his cause. The ring proves to have been the property of the Earl of Derby. He it was who, after the failure of a plot to recall James II from France, had died a fugitive and confided his son to the care of Plunkett's mother, and that son was none other than Lionel, now seen as the rightful heir to the title and estates. Lionel is nonetheless miserably unhappy. He is deeply in love with Lady Harriet, yet he can hardly bring himself to speak to her, let alone notice the advances which she, in her contrition, so plainly makes towards him.

Nancy's nimble wit comes to the rescue. She and Plunkett have been quick to come to an understanding, and they plan to bring Lionel and Lady Harriet together. One afternoon, Plunkett joins Lionel in his lonely walk and guides him into Lady Harriet's garden. There Lionel hears a sweet, familiar voice singing ''Tis the last rose of summer'. A moment later, he holds his Martha in his arms.

Martha teems with melody. The best known airs are 'Letzte Rose' (The Last Rose of Summer) and Lionel's 'Ach, so fromm' ('M'appari')[1]; the finest ensemble, a quintet with chorus, occurs near the close of Act III – 'Mag der Himmel euch vergeben' ('Ah! che a voi perdoni Iddio'). But, as indicated, there is a steady flow of light and graceful melody in this opera. Almost at the very opening of Act I, Lady Harriet and Nancy have a duet, 'Von den edlen Kavalieren' ('Questo duol che si v'affana'). Bright, clever music abounds in the

---

[1] Internationally, the Italian words are better known than the original German and are here kept in brackets throughout.

Richmond Fair scene, and Lionel and Plunkett express their devotion to each other in 'Ja, seit früher Kindheit Tagen' ('Solo, profugo, reietto'). Then there is the lively quartet when the two girls leave the fair with their masters, while the crowd surrounds Sir Tristram and prevents him from interfering. It was in this scene that the bass singer Castelmary, the Sir Tristram of a performance of *Martha* at the Metropolitan Opera House, 10 February 1897, was stricken with heart failure and dropped dead upon the stage.

A capital quartet opens Act II, in the farmhouse, and leads to the spinning-wheel quartet 'Was soll ich dazu sagen?' ('Che vuol dir ciò?'). There is a duet between Lady Harriet and Lionel, in which their growing attraction for each other finds expression; there follows 'Letzte Rose' ('Qui sola, vergin rosa'),

the music an old Irish air, 'The Groves of Blarney', to which Tom Moore adapted 'The Last Rose of Summer'. The scene ends with another quartet, one of the most beautiful numbers of the score, known as the 'Good Night Quartet', 'Schlafe wohl! Und mag Dich reuen' ('Dormi pur, ma il mio riposo').

Act III opens with a song in praise of beer, the 'Porterlied' by Plunkett, 'Lass mich euch fragen' ('Chi mi dirà'). The *pièces-de-résistance* of this act are 'Ach, so fromm' ('M'appari'); a solo for Nancy, 'Jägerin, schlau im sinn' ('Il tuo stral nel lanciar'); Martha's song written for Nantier Didiée, 'Hier in stillen Schattengründen' ('Qui tranquilla almen possio') and the stirring quintet with chorus. In Act IV there is a solo for Plunkett, 'Il mio Lionel perira', and a repetition of the sprightly music of the fair scene.   K.

CARLISLE FLOYD
(born 11 June 1926)

Brought up in South Carolina, Floyd has tended to give his operas a Southern background. He taught the piano at Florida State University in Tallahassee and eventually became professor of composition. Two one-act operas preceded *Susannah*, which by the composer's own account took him six and a half months – ten days for the libretto, three months to compose, three months to orchestrate – and turned out an enormous success, first in Tallahassee and eighteen months later in New York. *Susannah* started a successful line, his eight subsequent operatic ventures maintaining the essentially veristic style of plot, based (as one might claim for Virgil Thomson) on traditional American folk genres.

SUSANNAH

Opera in two acts, words by the composer. Première at Florida State University, Tallahassee, 2 May 1949, with Phyllis Curtin, who also sang in the first performance in New York, at the City Opera in 1956, with Erich Leinsdorf conducting. First performed in Europe, by New York City Opera at Brussels, with Curtin, Norman Treigle, conductor Julius Rudel; Chicago, 1993, with Renée Fleming, Samuel Ramey.

Recorded 1994, Lyon Opéra, with Cheryl Studer, Ramey, conductor Nagano.

Susannah Polk ....Soprano
Sam Polk, *her brother*...Tenor
Olin Blitch, *an itinerant preacher*............Bass-Baritone
Little Bat McLean, *a fifteen-year-old* ....Tenor
Elder McLean, *his father* ....Bass
Elder Gleaton ....Tenor
Elder Hayes...Tenor
Elder Ott ....Bass
Mrs McLean.......................................Mezzo-Soprano
Mrs Gleaton ....Mezzo-Soprano
Mrs Hayes...Soprano
Mrs Ott...Soprano

Citizens of New Hope Valley, Tennessee

Place: The Mountains of Tennessee
Time: The Recent Past
Running Time: 1 hour 30 minutes

Act I. The mountains of Tennessee; New Hope Valley. A menacing prelude leads to a square dance which is in progress in front of the church; the wives of the Elders are gossiping maliciously about

Susannah Polk, the belle of the ball. Her mother is dead and her brother drinks. Olin Blitch arrives with a reputation for bringing sinners to repentance, and it is not long before Mrs McLean is bad-mouthing Susannah to him, which does not prevent him joining the dance and making for her square.

The same evening outside the Polk farm. Susannah has been walked home by Little Bat, a fifteen-year-old. She is affected by the beauty of the night sky (Aria: 'Ain't it a pretty night?') and wonders what it's like away from the valley. Sam comes in and asks about the dance, then sings the Jay-bird song she's liked since childhood before dancing her round the yard.

The Elders are out looking for a baptism creek; their search brings them near the Polks' farm and they catch sight of Susannah bathing. Seeing her naked sets them all off and they blame her for their own randy thoughts. She must be reported to the Church and made to confess her sin.

There is a picnic supper set up outside the church. The Elders and their wives mutter about Susannah when she arrives carrying a dish. Elder McLean tells her she is not welcome there and she runs off in distress. Little Bat steals up to the Polk place and tells her that his father and the other Elders saw her bathing naked that morning and mean to punish her. She protests that it was they who were in the wrong spying, not her. Little Bat says it's worse than he said; his father and mother forced him to say publicly 'you'd let me love you up'. Sam tries to comfort her; when she sees he has nothing more to say, she sobs as she asks him to sing the Jay-bird song again.

Act II. Outside their house, Sam and Susannah discuss the hostile atmosphere. Sam is afraid it won't improve until she confesses – but she says she has nothing to confess. She tells him the preacher talked pleasantly to her in the store and wants her to go to the meeting that evening, but she feels she can't face it. Sam has to go away that night to empty his traps, which fills Susannah with foreboding. But he persuades her against her will to agree to go.

Inside the church the same evening, the Rev Blitch starts to preach. He tells them of a dying man in Texas who failed to confess and was damned to eternal fire. Are any of them in the same state? During the hymn, some boys and girls come forward and he lays his hands on them until they all turn towards Susannah. He urges her to leave her seat and she walks towards him, then turns with a cry and runs into the night.

Susannah is alone singing a folk-like aria ('The trees on the mountains are cold and bare'). The preacher steals up and tells her to pray with him. She refuses, then tells him Little Bat confessed to her he lied. She is at the end of her tether and Blitch starts to leave, then turns back: 'I'm a lonely man, Susannah, An' every now an' then it seems I gotta have somebody, Somebody I can love'. He leads her into the house.

Next day, Blitch in church castigates himself for his sin before the Elders and their wives gather. In mounting disbelief they hear his attempt to exonerate Susannah – 'I ask y' to beseech her fergiveness An' humbly ask her pardon fer your misjudgement' – then leave. Blitch asks Susannah to forgive him but to no avail.

Susannah at home watches Sam come back from his expedition, as ever slightly drunk but as ever affectionate. Susannah tells her terrible story, Sam starts to threaten revenge, then, as she goes into the house, takes down his gun. Susannah waits in anguish, a shot rings out, and Little Bat comes running to tell Susannah what has happened, then makes his escape as the mob comes to get Sam. She bursts into uncontrollable laughter, pulls a gun on them when they threaten to find Sam and string him up, and they leave muttering curses. Little Bat emerges from the bushes, Susannah cajoles him into embracing her, then slaps him hard across the face, and is left standing defiantly in the doorway – as the libretto says, 'an inviolably strong and inexorably lonely figure in self-imposed exile'.   H.

G

JOHN GAY and J. C. PEPUSCH

(born September 1685, died 4 December 1732; born 1667, died 20 July 1752)

THE BEGGAR'S OPERA

Ballad opera in three acts; words by John Gay, music collected and arranged by John Christopher Pepusch. Première, Lincoln's Inn Fields, 9 February 1728, with Mr Walker as Macheath and Lavinia Fenton (later Duchess of Bolton) as Polly. First performed Covent Garden, 1732; New York, 1750. Revived at Covent Garden in an abridged, two-act version in 1813 with Miss Stephens, Mrs Davenport, Incledon; 1878, with Sims Reeves as Macheath. In a new version by Frederic Austin, revived Lyric, Hammersmith, 1920, where it ran for 1,463 consecutive nights, with Frederick Ranalow as Macheath, Sylvia Nelis, and Frederic Austin; revived there 1925, 1926, 1928, 1929, 1930; at Brighton, 1940 (under Glyndebourne auspices), with Audrey Mildmay, Michael Redgrave, Roy Henderson. New version by Benjamin Britten produced Cambridge, 1948, and subsequently at Sadler's Wells, with Nancy Evans, Rose Hill, Peter Pears, Otakar Kraus, conductor Britten; Vienna, 1949, with Rohs, Funk, Liewehr, conductor Zallinger; Hamburg, 1950, conductor Schmidt-Isserstedt. The English Opera Group mounted a new production at Aldeburgh in 1963 with Janet Baker, Harper, Pears, which was subsequently heard (with various cast changes) in Edinburgh, London, Montreal and other centres.

Beggar ....Speaking Role

Mrs Peachum ....Mezzo-Soprano

Mr Peachum, *a 'fence'* ....Bass

Polly, their daughter ....Soprano

Captain Macheath, *a highwayman*.....................Tenor

Filch, *in Peachum's employment* ....Tenor

Lockit, *the jailer* ....Baritone

Lucy Lockit, *his daughter*................................Soprano

Ladies of the town ....Sopranos,
    Mrs Vixen   Mezzo-Sopranos,
    Suky Tawdry   Contraltos
    Mrs Coaxer
    Dolly Trull
    Mrs Slammekin
    Molly Brazen
    Jenny Diver
    Betty Doxy

Gentlemen of the road ....Tenors,
    Harry Paddington   Baritones,
    Ben Budge   Basses
    Wat Dreary
    Matt of the Mint
    Jemmy Twitcher
    Nimming Ned

Mrs Trapes, *the 'tally woman'*..............Mezzo-Soprano

Place: London
Time: Early Eighteenth Century
Running Time: 3 hours

Opera in the early part of the eighteenth century, for England as for the rest of Europe, meant Italian opera. Such works as Clayton's *Rosamond* were freaks and, more important, failures. But in 1728, *The Beggar's Opera* was a success. It is a ballad opera, the music a compilation of tunes drawn from every imaginable source – contemporary opera, traditional ballads, folk songs – and arranged to form a whole connected by dialogue.

Swift remarked to Gay: 'A Newgate Pastoral might make an odd, pretty sort of thing', and Gay's libretto aims partly at satire, partly at parody. Fun is poked at the fashionable – for instance Handelian – opera of the day ('I have observed such a nice impartiality to our two Ladies that it is impossible for either of them to take offence ... I hope I may be forgiven that I have not made my Opera throughout unnatural, like those in vogue; for I have no recitative'). There is political and social satire, aimed at the Prime Minister, Sir Robert Walpole, and everyone in a position of authority and able to give and receive bribes. Corruption is the stuff of the drama, and the objects of its political satire were seriously worried at the effect it had.

In its own time, *The Beggar's Opera* had its imitators, none so successful as the original, and in the twentieth century composers have attempted forms of modernisation. Frederic Austin, who also sang the role of Peachum, arranged the tunes in 1920 and his version ran in London for several years. Kurt Weill and Bertholt Brecht adapted the theme two hundred years after the première, Weill using few of the old tunes and Brecht modernising the setting to conform to his rather than Gay's political ideas. Benjamin Britten made a new version in 1948, keeping more of the original melodies than had Austin and re-setting them with the aim of producing 220 years later some of the sharpness of 1728.

So strong is Britten's reaction to the drama and the old tunes, so vigorous his new setting, harmonically and orchestrally, so sharp his sense of operatic 'shape', that this amounts to a Britten opera in its own right and is so listed in his catalogue, as Op. 43.

There is a Prologue, spoken by a Beggar and a Player and explaining that the piece is written 'for the celebrating the marriage of James Chaunter and Moll Lay, two most excellent Ballad-Singers'.

Act I. The curtain goes up to reveal a room in Peachum's house where the owner is sitting at a table, before a book of accounts. He sings 'Through all the employments of life, Each Neighbour abuses his brother'. Filch reports on the fates of various members of Peachum's gang who are up before the courts, and sings the smoothly-flowing ''Tis Woman that seduces all mankind' before being sent off to deliver Peachum's messages to the various prisoners.

Peachum goes through a register of his gang, commenting on the earning (i.e. pick-pocket) capacities of each. Some, he thinks, he will give up at the next sessions and take the money offered for their apprehension. He reaches the name of Bob Booty, when his wife interrupts to enquire why he should mention that name; women, she admits, are notoriously bad judges of a man whom they love primarily for his courage: 'If any wench Venus' girdle wear'. They exchange words on the subject of murder, a crime Mrs Peachum seems to fancy less than her husband, and fall to talking about Captain Macheath. It appears that Polly, their daughter, 'thinks him a very pretty man'. 'If love the virgin's heart invade', sings Mrs Peachum; if she does not marry, 'she's – what I dare not name'. But Peachum is still worried: ' ... I would indulge the girl as far as prudently we can. In anything but marriage.' Leaving his wife to take the

coronets out of some handkerchiefs, he goes off to 'terrify her from it, by the example of our neighbours'.

Mrs Peachum is philosophical – 'Why must Polly's marriage, contrary to all observations, make her the less followed by other men?' – and she sings 'A maid is like the golden ore'. Filch comes in and Mrs Peachum questions him on the relationship between Captain Macheath and Polly. He seems embarrassed, and she takes him off to tell her more in private.

Enter Polly and her father. She urges her ability to look after herself, 'Virgins are like the fair flower in its lustre'. Peachum utters a stern warning against her marrying, when 'enter Mrs Peachum, in a very great passion'. 'Our Polly is a sad slut' she sings in her fury, and proclaims for all to hear that Polly has got herself married. 'Can Love be control'd by advice?' asks Polly, but Mrs Peachum in a delectable tune objects, 'O Polly, you might have toy'd and kiss'd'. Polly tries to keep her end up ('I, like a ship in storms, was tossed'), but is sent off to deal with customers in the front room. Peachum and his wife plot to turn the whole affair to their advantage, not forgetting that a lawyer may get his hands into the business and take all profit out of it: 'A fox may steal your hens, sir'. Polly returns and is told she must straightaway make plans to become a widow; in a word, Macheath must be delivered up to the law in time for the next session! 'O ponder well! be not severe', objects Polly; as a widow, she would cry her heart out: 'The turtle thus with plaintive crying'.

Polly goes, but hides to hear her parents continue their plot, which even gets to the stage when the Old Bailey is mentioned. She is in despair, but the scene changes and she is shown with Macheath. Their duet goes through half-a-dozen emotions and as many glorious melodies, starting

Pretty Polly, say,
When I was away,
Did your fancy never stray
To some newer lover?

Macheath protests his own constancy: 'My heart was so free, It rov'd like the Bee, 'Till Polly my passion requited', and they swear mutual adoration in 'Were I laid on Greenland's coast', with its refrain of 'Over the hills and far away'. But Polly remembers that Macheath's life is not now safe; her father is plotting against him. 'Oh what pain it is to part', she sings.

Their love scene reaches its climax with 'The miser thus a shilling sees', a superb and entirely appropriate ending which is unaccountably omitted from Austin's published score.

Act II. A tavern near Newgate. Macheath's gang discuss their profession and its hazards, but drown their sorrows: 'Fill every glass'. Macheath comes to tell them that he cannot go with them that night, owing to his 'difference' with Peachum. He wishes them luck and they go off singing 'Let us take the road', to the tune of the march from Handel's *Rinaldo*.

Macheath, alone, muses on the delights to be had from women – he is emphatic about the plural. His romance, 'If the heart of a man', is set to one of the most delightful tunes of the whole score. He does not have to wait long; the women of the town begin to arrive in answer to his invitations previously sent out. He welcomes them and leads them in a dance, 'Youth's the season made for joys'. After some dalliance, Jenny Diver sings suggestively 'Before the Barn-door crowing', and, while the ladies sing 'The gamesters and lawyers are jugglers alike', manages to secure one of his pistols, Suky Tawdry getting hold of the other. They signal to Peachum, who is waiting outside, and he comes in with constables and arrests the Captain. Macheath turns furiously on the women ('At the tree I shall suffer with pleasure'), and is led away, leaving them to dispute the division of the reward for their work.

The scene changes to Newgate Jail. Macheath is received by the sinister Lockit, who reminds him that nothing can be had in prison free of charge; 'garnish' is the custom. Macheath, alone, reflects that it is Woman that has brought him to his present condition: 'Man may escape from rope and gun'. The tune marvellously combines the lyrical with the dramatic.

Enter Lucy, daughter of Lockit. She loses no time in referring to the 'load of infamy' which she carries, and does not hesitate to blame her pregnancy on Macheath. Revenge is what she is after, she tells him, 'Thus when a good housewife sees a rat'. Macheath pleads with her, and refers to himself as her husband. Lucy is not so easily taken in ('How cruel are the traitors'), but Macheath works on her to good purpose, and explains away Polly's report of their marriage as mere vanity on her part: 'The first time at the looking-glass'. Lucy takes Macheath off in search of the priest attached to the prison.

Enter Peachum and Lockit, intent on the record of their mutual transactions. Working for the law and at the same time helping to organise crime, they are in a position to make the best of both worlds. Peachum refers openly to the betrayal of friends, and Lockit cautions him to be more careful in his use of words: 'When you censure the age'. Peachum goes further, and questions the probity of Lockit's dealing. There is a row and the two men are at each other's throats until more moderate counsels prevail, and Peachum eventually leaves, with the two reprobates in seeming accord.

It is Lucy's turn to have a disagreement with her father; she begs for mercy for Macheath: 'Is then his fate decreed, sir?' Lockit rejoins with rough comfort – be grateful for release, like other widows: 'You'll think ere many days ensue' (Britten combines the two tunes in an effective duet). Macheath rejoins Lucy, and speculates on his chance of bribing his way out of prison: 'If you at an office solicit your due'. Lucy promises to do what she can to help him – but at that moment Polly herself appears and throws herself about Macheath's neck – 'my dear husband'. Seeing him thus languishing she feels an ornithological comparison appropriate: 'Thus when the swallow seeking prey'.

Macheath's situation seems desperate: 'How happy could I be with either, Were t'other dear charmer away!' he sings in one of the best-known airs of the opera. The two 'wives' come back at him with a duet, 'I'm bubbled. I'm bubbled. O how I am troubled'. (Britten follows the air with the duet and combines the two to make a trio.) Things look black, but at last the two women begin to notice one another. Polly addresses Lucy, 'Cease your funning', and presently they have at one another, 'Why how now, Madam Flirt'. Peachum enters in search of Polly, but she resists his efforts to take her away: 'No power on earth can e'er divide', set to the 'Irish Howl'. Peachum eventually prises her away from Macheath, and it is left to Lucy, after comparing herself to a fox's mate ('I like the fox shall grieve'), to release him from his chains.

Both Austin and Britten have omitted the short final scene for Lucy and Macheath, and have taken the eminently suitable tune of 'No power on earth', set it as an ensemble, and used it as a finale.

Act III. Newgate. Lockit is admonishing Lucy for her part in Macheath's escape. She explains that it was not through bribes but from love that she was impelled to help him, and blames Lockit for teaching her to be promiscuous with her kisses – Macheath's naturally tasted so sweet after what she had been through that she lost her heart to him: 'When young at the bar' (the tune is Purcell's). Her mood changes from one of regret for her lost lover to one of recrimination, 'My love is all madness and folly', and Lockit sends her out to repent where he cannot hear her caterwauling. He sums up the whole matter; Peachum is evidently trying to outwit him in the affair of the Captain, and he must at all costs get even with him. 'Of all animals of prey', he reflects, 'Man is the only sociable one.' The aria, 'Thus gamesters united in friendship are found', is bitingly satirical.

The scene changes to a gaming-house, where are assembled ladies and gentlemen, together with Macheath, who there meets Ben Budge and Matt of the Mint, and gives them money. They discuss their affairs, but the scene is dominated by the singing of 'The modes of the court so common are grown' to the magnificent tune of 'Lillibulero'.

Peachum's house. Peachum and Lockit are again making an attempt to arrive at a settlement of their intricate accounts. They give it up and fall to drinking, agreeing at the same time that it will not be long before Macheath is in their hands again, if they keep a careful watch on Polly: 'What gudgeons are we men'. Mrs Diana Trapes calls on them, and, before getting down to the business of her visit, toasts them in a fascinating tune, 'In the days of my youth I could bill like a dove'. They join in the refrain. She has come, she says, to see what they have got for her in the way of 'Blacks of any kind ... Mantoes – velvet scarfs – petticoats ...' In the course of conversation she lets on that she has seen Captain Macheath that very day. Immediately they are all over her, and bid her name her own price for the goods, provided she lead them to the Captain forthwith.

The scene returns to Newgate. Lucy, although still bemoaning her fate ('I'm like a skiff on the ocean tossed'), is planning to even her account with Miss Polly Peachum, whom she is expecting and against whose coming she has the rat's-bane handy. Polly is announced and Lucy receives her graciously: 'When a wife's in her pout'. She tries to get her to drink the gin she pours out, but nothing will induce Polly to let a drop pass her lips. They are outwardly all affection; 'A curse attends that woman's love' is not the quarrel the

words might suggest, and Polly could not be more affable ('Among the men, coquets we find') nor Lucy more pressing ('Come sweet lass') as she presses her guest to accept her offer of a drink. The scene is brought to an abrupt conclusion by the precipitate entrance of Macheath, again in chains.

The quarrel is almost forgotten in the duet of commiseration which Lucy and Polly sing together, 'Hither dear husband, turn your eyes', but Macheath seems to take a rather different view of events: 'Which way shall I turn me'. Both Polly and Lucy plead with their respective fathers ('When my hero in court appears', and 'When he holds up his head arraign'd for his life'). Peachum and Lockit remain adamant ('Ourselves like the great'), and order Macheath to prepare himself to be conducted to the Old Bailey. He sings 'The charge is prepared', which, in Britten's version, leads to an extensive ensemble.

The condemned hold. Macheath laments his fate, and fortifies himself with copious draughts of liquor for the ordeal of hanging. He sings snatches of tune, culminating in an outburst against the injustice of the times, set to the tune of 'Greensleeves'. Austin uses only four of the ten tunes specified for this scene, and omits 'Greensleeves'. Britten makes it into a *scena* on the lines of Purcell's Mad Scenes – it is the climax of the opera – and binds it together on a bass derived from 'Greensleeves' itself. The result is impressive, and lends real dignity, not only to the figure of Macheath, but to the ideals for which the satire was battling – and satire is mere bitterness unless reared on an ideal and a truth.

Ben Budge and Matt of the Mint come to say farewell to Macheath; his last request is that they should revenge him upon Peachum and Lockit before they themselves come to the sorry pass in which he finds himself. Lucy and Polly appear, protesting that they would gladly take his place: 'Would I might be hanged'. Macheath joins in and the piece takes on the character of a dirge, more particularly when the sound of the passing-bell is heard (Britten uses this to good effect). Four more wives appear claiming Macheath as husband, until he protests that he is ready to go with the Sheriff's officers to execution. At this point, the Player protests to the Beggar that, if Macheath is hanged, the piece will be downright tragedy. The Beggar is persuaded to allow a reprieve, and Macheath returns to lead the finale, 'Thus I stand like the Turk, with his doxies around'.   H.

ROBERTO GERHARD
(born 25 September 1896, died 5 January 1970)

Gerhard, the son of Austrian and Swiss parents, a pupil at one time in Barcelona of Felipe Pedrell, at another in Vienna and Berlin of Arnold Schoenberg, was born and brought up in Spain, lived in England from the fall of the Republican Government in 1939, and was the most Spanish – the most Catalan – of composers. His music was never completely sidelined, as happened with other refugees, but heard intermittently throughout the war and afterwards, in the concert hall, on radio, in the theatre, as a basis for ballet, but it was only in the last decade of his life that he began to acquire an international reputation.

THE DUENNA

Opera in three acts, text by the composer from the play by Richard Brinsley Sheridan. First performance, B.B.C. broadcast, 1949, with Victoria Sladen, Gambell, Joan Cross, Pears, Dowling, Martin Lawrence, conductor Stanford Robinson; Wiesbaden (in concert; the planned stage performance was cancelled because of illness), 1951, conductor Franz-Paul Decker; 1972, B.B.C. broadcast with Jill Gomez, Delia Wallis, Coster, Keith Erwen, Thomas Allen, conductor Atherton. Stage première Madrid, 21 January 1992, with Sheila Cooper, Anne Mason, Felicity Palmer, Rendall, Anthony Michaels Moore, Richard Van Allan, conductor Antoni Ros Marbá; Opera North, Leeds, 1992, conductor Ros Marbá.

Don Jerome, *a nobleman of Seville* ....Bass

Don Ferdinand, *his son* ....Baritone

Donna Luisa, *his daughter* ....Soprano

The Duenna, *her chaperone* ....Mezzo-Soprano

Don Antonio, *Luisa's suitor* ....Tenor

Donna Clara d'Almanza ....Mezzo-Soprano

Don Isaac, *a Portuguese Jew* ....Baritone

Father Paul...Tenor

A Gipsy ....Soprano

Brethren of Deadly Sin ....Tenor, Baritone

López, *servant in Don Jerome's house* ....Spoken

Don Antonio's servant ....Spoken

Maid to Donna Luisa ....Spoken

Ladies and Gentlemen of Fashion, Townspeople, Beggars, Strumpets etc.

Place: Seville
Time: Eighteenth Century
Running Time: 2 hours 25 minutes

The chance find in 1945 on a Cambridge bookstall of a copy of Sheridan's *The Duenna* (itself originally a play with music by the Linleys, father and son) started Gerhard writing an opera that was almost immediately accepted by the B.B.C. for broadcast. In his music Gerhard's youthful enthusiasm for the Spanish *zarzuela* was tempered by the 'learned' outlook he naturally acquired from Pedrell and Schoenberg, but the combination found favour neither initially in England, where it was thought too 'modern' for contemporary taste, nor at the I.S.C.M. Festival in Germany, where it was too romantically 'tuneful' to please the *avant garde*. Gerhard's own, written, claim[1] – 'students of Spanish Art and Literature know that the opposition between the "popular" and the "high-brow" has never been allowed in Spain to lead to a real divorce' – has until recently been tacitly ignored. Yet it is important. Only twenty-two years after his death did the opera find a natural outlet in Spain, where it was acclaimed as 'a Catalan masterpiece', and in the English production which immediately followed.

Gerhard set great store by *The Duenna*, which has been described as a summation of the first thirty years of his creative life, and refused to contemplate another opera until it had been produced. He revised the score immediately after its first broadcast, and continued to alter and improve it until in 1967 he contemplated a major re-think, which was prevented by urgent work on new music and by the onset of his final illness. David Drew was responsible for the edition which finally reached the stage, the composer Dmitri Smirnov for reconciling the orchestral score of the broadcasts with the composer's revisions, which had been confined to the vocal score.

Act I. In front of Don Jerome's house, Antonio's serenading of his beloved Donna Luisa is interrupted

---

[1] In *Opera* magazine, 1952.

by the gloomy Brethren of Deadly Sin chanting a *memento mori* and by a strumpet and her bawd, but Luisa joins her voice to his before Don Jerome pokes a blunderbuss through the window and Antonio makes his escape. The Brethren reappear.

Antonio's friend Ferdinand feels less than secure in his love for Donna Clara (aria), and he confides to Antonio, in flight from Don Jerome, that he had contrived access to Clara's bedroom at dead of night, with the intention of foiling the scheme by her father and stepmother to consign her to a convent. His intentions were of the purest but she chased him from the room, and he is wondering if she is at that very moment in the process of eloping with another lover – Clara with whom Antonio himself was once in love! Antonio jauntily (and to a tune Lalo used in the *Symphonie espagnole*) admits that used to be the case, but 'I ne'er could any lustre see in eyes that would not look on me'. Ferdinand must have confidence in Antonio's love for his sister, Luisa, he says – and is he not in just as bad a case as Ferdinand, with Don Jerome planning the very next day to marry Luisa to Don Isaac, the Jew? All the same, Antonio seems more buoyant than he perhaps should.

At home, Donna Luisa and her Duenna plot. She will thwart her father's plan to marry her to Don Isaac by leaving the house disguised as the Duenna and agrees that, if their plan works, she will resign to the Duenna all right to Don Isaac. To Don Jerome and Ferdinand Luisa reaffirms her refusal to contemplate marriage to Don Isaac and her father declares he will neither see nor speak to her until she falls in with his wishes. Ferdinand is in despair for Antonio, but Jerome returns dragging the Duenna after him, not suspecting that the note from Antonio he has intercepted was a plant. He fires her on the spot, the plot is afoot, and a few minutes later he ejects Luisa dressed as the Duenna, who is left in a solo to enjoy their joint triumph.

Nearby, Luisa meets her friend Clara, in her turn escaped from home. Clara in a striking aria which turns into a duet tells Luisa the story of Ferdinand's arrival in her room. If she had not summarily dismissed him, she could not vouch for what her feelings might have led her to. Clara will now find refuge in a convent where the Abbess is her cousin, and Luisa will use Don Isaac, who has no inkling what she looks like, to help her find Antonio!

By Seville's riverside, Don Isaac, in conversation with Father Paul, is waylaid by Luisa, who claims to be Clara and says she is in love with Antonio. Don Isaac thinks to remove his rival for Luisa's hand and falls for the ruse, deputing Father Paul to help find Antonio. The crowd, recognising the runaway Clara and scenting scandal, seems at one point likely to impede Luisa's getaway, particularly as her brother Ferdinand, in love with the real Clara, puts in an appearance and, distraught as ever, takes the disguised Luisa for his beloved. Don Jerome complicates things, but not enough to stop everyone making an escape, leaving a Gipsy, in the absence of Donna Luisa, to top the ensemble's soprano line for the rest of the act.

Act II alternates between Don Jerome's house and Don Isaac's lodgings. At home, Don Jerome and Don Isaac make Clara's disappearance an occasion to mock her father. Jerome waxes lyrical on the subject of Luisa's beauty, which Isaac is convinced will overpower him completely. Don Isaac's wooing of the Duenna, or in many respects the other way round as she makes most of the running, is a scene of high comedy; the music a Habanera. He is horror-stricken as she unveils, then falls totally for her flattery until in the end she proposes they elope together. After all, she is the daughter of a rich man and Don Isaac sees a way of dodging an expensive marriage settlement, the Duenna of avoiding an uncomfortable meeting with her erstwhile employer. In a duet, the bargain is struck.

Isaac nearly ruins everything with some snide remarks to Don Jerome about his daughter's age and looks but, with the unexpected but opportune arrival of Ferdinand, contrives to wriggle out of a nasty situation. A rousing drinking trio ensues (another number in triple time), at whose end Ferdinand still does not know Clara's whereabouts and Isaac is carried out dead drunk. Ferdinand's attempt to plead Antonio's cause with his father has the sole effect of bringing him a lecture on the conflicting demands of love and money.

At Don Isaac's lodgings, where Luisa is in temporary hiding, the poor girl alone muses on her odd situation – the man she does not want to marry looking on her behalf for the man she does! The aria has nocturnal overtones.

Antonio arrives protesting to the insistent Don Isaac and Father Paul that Clara loves another and not him. Nonetheless, they push him through the door and watch his rapturous reunion – with Luisa. Father Paul disappears and the act ends in a spirited trio.

Act III. The priory where Antonio and Isaac plan to marry, the one the true and the other the false Luisa. Offstage voices of the Brethren of Deadly Sin cast no more than a momentary pall over proceedings, and it takes but a sniff of a purse of money to overcome Father Paul's scruples about the two clandestine marriages he is to perform. The appearance of Ferdinand is another matter; only the arrival of Clara prevents a duel and provides the occasion for a double marriage of young couples, celebrated with a wedding march for five voices (Don Isaac presumably has left to make an honest woman of the Duenna elsewhere).

The last scene is in Don Jerome's house, where guests are expected. The host is plainly disconcerted by a letter announcing his daughter's elopement with Don Isaac, the very man she refused that morning to contemplate, but he shrugs his shoulders and prepares for the party. Ferdinand introducing his bride Clara disguised as a nun hardly disconcerts him; she is an heiress after all. He waits impatiently to forgive Luisa, who is led in by Don Isaac; fulminates at recognition of the Duenna; melts and admits defeat when Antonio arrives married to the real Luisa; and joins in the laughter as the Duenna routs Don Isaac, who leaves in dudgeon, but returns for a scene of reconciliation with his bride. Don Jerome throws his doors open to everyone and the opera ends in rejoicing and conviviality.   H.

GEORGE GERSHWIN
(born 26 September 1898, died 11 July 1937)

Gershwin was not only the leading writer of American musicals for fifteen years from the early 1920s to his death but a fairly frequent composer of instrumental music, most notably *Rhapsody in Blue* (1924). In addition, he dabbled in opera from as early as 1922, when his twenty-minute jazz opera *Blue Monday* was a feature of George White's *Scandals of 1922*. *Porgy and Bess* was the climax of his career, the first American opera to score a world-wide success, also the only opera founded on the jazz of the 1920s to survive the Second World War, perhaps because European composers tended to use the medium satirically (e.g. Křenek in *Jonny spielt auf*), Gershwin as the folk basis of a story whose participants use jazz as a natural means of expression.

Fifty years after *Porgy*'s première, the opera received the not wholly relevant accolade of a production at the Metropolitan in New York. By the terms of Gershwin's will and the inflexible rule of the Gershwin Estate, English-speaking countries may only produce Gershwin's masterpiece with black casts, which limits its possibilities in for instance England, whereas paradoxically productions in translation may employ non-black singers in appropriate or even highly stylised make-up. The decision is admittedly not without point but a Swiss production had its singers coloured blue-black and included in the cast a Peter Grimes, Wotan and Baron Ochs; this may not be folk opera at its truest but the potential is close to mind-boggling!

PORGY AND BESS

Opera in three acts, text by du Bose Heyward and Ira Gershwin. Première, Boston, 30 September 1935, with Todd Duncan (Porgy), Anne Brown (Bess), Warren Coleman (Crown), Eddie Matthews (Jake), Abbie Mitchell (Clara), Bubbles (Sporting Life), Eva Jessye Choir, produced by Rouben Mamoulian, conductor Alexander Smallens. First performed Copenhagen, 1943; Zürich, 1945, with Cordy, Boehm, conductor Reinshagen; Copenhagen, 1946, with Anne Brown and Einar Nørby. In 1952, an all-black company set out from the States and toured with the opera through the capitals of Europe (notably Berlin and Vienna), ending up in London in the autumn at the Stoll Theatre, where they stayed until 10 February 1953, playing to packed houses. The cast included Leontyne Price, Thigpen, Warfield, Cab Calloway, conductor Smallens. Produced Vienna Volksoper, 1965, with Olive Moorefield, William Warfield; Metropolitan, New York, 1985, with Grace Bumbry, Simon Estes, conductor Levine; Glyndebourne, 1986, with Cynthia Haymon, Willard White, conductor Simon Rattle.

Porgy, *a cripple* ....Bass-Baritone

Bess, *Crown's girl* ....Soprano

Crown, *a tough stevedore*...............................Baritone

Serena, *Robbins's wife* ....Soprano

Clara, *Jake's wife*...Soprano

Maria, *keeper of the cook-shop* ....Contralto

Jake, *a fisherman*...Baritone

Sportin' Life, *a dope pedlar* ....Tenor

Mingo ....Tenor

Robbins, *an inhabitant of Catfish Row*................Tenor

Peter, *the honeyman*...Tenor

Frazier, *a black 'lawyer'* ....Baritone

Annie..Mezzo-Soprano

Lily, *Peter's wife, strawberry woman*....Mezzo-Soprano

Jim, *a cotton picker* ....Baritone

Undertaker ....Baritone

Nelson ....Tenor

Crab Man...Tenor

Speaking parts
   Mr Archdale, *a white man*
   Detective
   Policeman
   Coroner
   Scipio, *a small boy*

Place: Charleston, South Carolina, U.S.A.
Time: 'Recent Past'
Running Time: 3 hours 15 minutes

The scene is laid in Catfish Row – 'a former mansion of the aristocracy, but now a negro tenement on the waterfront of Charleston, South Carolina'.

Act I, scene i. The inside of the tenement. After a short *allegro con brio* introduction, we are introduced to the variegated night life of the building. There is singing and dancing and presently a lazy lullaby can be heard, sung by Clara, who nurses her baby. It is 'Summer time', and the song's lyric beauty has made it the most famous in the opera, and one of the best known in the entire song literature. A crap game is going on. The episodic music reflects the varied nature of the stage action, and the Lullaby is heard again as background to the game. Jake says he will take it on himself to send his and Clara's baby to sleep, and he sings 'A woman is a sometime thing'.

The honeyman's call is heard before Porgy is spied coming towards the tenement. He is a cripple who gets about in a little goat-cart. Everybody seems pleased to see him, and they twit him about his love life – 'I think

he's soft on Crown's Bess,' says Jake. Porgy defends Bess's reputation and blames her present low ebb on 'the Gawd fearin' ladies an' the Gawd damnin' men'. Crown comes in with Bess, calling loudly for drink and going unsteadily to join the crap school. He finds difficulty in reading the dice and objects to losing his money when Robbins beats him. He throws Robbins to the ground, attacking him with a cotton hook and killing him, to the horror of the inhabitants of Catfish Row. Bess gives Crown money and urges him to be off out of the way of the police; he says firmly that he will be back; any arrangement she may care to make in the meanwhile with another man will be with his permission – but strictly temporary.

Sportin' Life approaches Bess and offers to take her to New York with him, but she spurns his offer, and tries to find shelter from someone in the tenement – unsuccessfully, until Porgy opens his door and lets her in, just as police whistles can be heard outside.

Scene ii. Serena's room; Robbins's body lies on the bed, a saucer on its chest to receive contributions against the expense of his burial. Porgy and Bess enter and put money in the saucer, and Porgy leads a rhythmic spiritual before a detective puts his head round the door. By accusing Peter of the murder he gets the others to say that Crown did it – but he hauls off the protesting Peter as a 'material witness'.

Porgy reflects on the injustice of taking off an old man who never did anyone any harm, while a criminal like Crown wanders about scot-free. The wake goes on, and Serena begins a grandiose lament, 'My man's gone now'. The undertaker agrees to bury Robbins for the $15 which is all that is in the saucer. Bess leads the last of the spirituals, 'Oh, we're leavin' for the Promise' Land'.

Act II. A month later. Jake and the fishermen are repairing their nets, singing as they do so, 'It take a long pull to get there'. In spite of the warning that the time of year is coming round for the September storms, Jake and his friends are determined to go. Porgy appears at his window singing his Banjo song, 'Oh, I got plenty o' nuttin'', a brilliant piece with an infectious lilt which causes comment on the improvement since Bess has been living with him.

Sportin' Life is sauntering around the tenement when Maria the cook sees that he has dope on him, catches him by the throat and treats him to a lecture on what he has got coming to him. Lawyer Frazier

Porgy and Bess *(Glyndebourne, 1986, director Trevor Nunn, sets John Gunter, costumes Sue Blane).*
Willard White as Porgy and Cynthia Haymon as Bess.

comes in, looking for Porgy, to whom he sells a 'divorce' for Bess, clinching the bargain when he points out that it is naturally more difficult (and expensive) to divorce somebody who has never even been married.

There is another visitor, when Mr Archdale appears, also asking for Porgy. At first everybody is too suspicious to tell him, but he wins them over, and informs Porgy that he will go bond for his friend Peter now in jail. Porgy exclaims in horror at the sight of a buzzard flying over the tenement. If it alights, it brings bad luck. Porgy's Buzzard song, with the chorus, is sometimes omitted,[1] seemingly at the suggestion of Gershwin himself, who thought the role of Porgy needed shortening if the singer were going to stand the strain of eight performances a week for a

long run (one may be forgiven, too, if one thinks of it as a long way from the best number in the opera).

Sportin' Life sidles up to Bess and again suggests they should team up and go off to New York, but she tells him she hates the sight of him and his 'happy dust'. Porgy twigs what is going on and reaches round his door to catch hold of Sportin' Life's wrist, making him cry out with the strength of his grip.

It is the day of the organised picnic, and everybody disappears to get ready, leaving Porgy alone with Bess, who tells him she does not want to go since he cannot. There is an extended love duet for the two of them, 'Bess, you is my woman now', at whose end the stage fills with life, a military band strikes up a *tempo di marcia giocoso*, and with a maximum of noise the picnickers are on their way.

1 In the 1952 London production it was transferred to the last act.

Maria persuades Bess that she must come along after all, and she takes a fond farewell of Porgy, who is left singing happily 'I got plenty o' nuttin''.

Scene ii. Kittiwah Island, the evening of the same day. The picnickers dance riotously and Sportin' Life treats them to a sermon in praise of the virtues of scepticism, whose jaunty tune and brilliant lyrics have made it one of the most popular numbers of the score. Two samples of its outrageous rhymes:

It ain't necessarily so,
De t'ings dat yo' li'ble
To read in de Bible,
It ain't necessarily so;

and

Oh, Jonah, he lived in de whale,
Fo' he made his home in
Dat fish's abdomen
Oh, Jonah, he lived in de whale.

Serena denounces the whole pack of them for sinners, reminding them, more prosaically, that the boat is leaving soon.

Bess waits behind a moment, and Crown appears in front of her. He tells her that he will be back for her soon, but she pleads to be allowed to stay in peace with Porgy, who has taught her to live decently. Crown laughs, and says he regards her living with Porgy as a temporary arrangement. Bess suggests he find some other woman ('Oh, what you want wid Bess?'), but she cannot resist Crown's old fascination, and when he takes her in his arms, she is too weak to deny him anything. She stays behind with him as the boat leaves.

Scene iii. Jake and the fishermen prepare to go to sea, singing a snatch of 'It take a long pull to get there'. Peter is back from prison, and the sound of Bess's voice coming in a delirium from Porgy's room indicates that she too has returned from Kittiwah Island. She was lost for two days and was incoherent when she got home. Serena prays for her, and at the end tells Porgy: 'Alright now, Porgy. Doctor Jesus done take de case.' The cries of respectively the strawberry woman, the honeyman, and the crab man are heard, before Bess calls from off-stage, evidently on the way to recovery. Porgy says that he knows she has been with Crown, but that it makes no difference to his love for her. She pleads with Porgy to keep her for himself; she wants to stay but is

afraid of the effect Crown's presence may have on her: 'I loves you, Porgy.' Porgy tells her he will take good care of Crown if he returns.

Clara is anxiously watching the sea, and presently her apprehension is confirmed, and the sound of the hurricane bell can be heard.

Scene iv. Serena's room. Outside there is a terrific storm; inside all pray that the danger may be averted. 'I hear death knockin' at de do'', sings Peter – and almost immediately a real knock comes, and is answered with a hysterical rush to hold the door. It turns out to be Crown. He orders Bess to him, throwing down Porgy who makes a move to come between them. Serena warns him against violent behaviour; at any moment the storm may get him. 'If God want to kill me,' he sings, 'He had plenty of chance 'tween here an' Kittiwah Island.'

The keening seems likely to go on indefinitely, but Crown strikes up a cheerful jazz number, 'A redheaded woman makes a chow-chow jump its track'. Suddenly, Clara sees Jake's boat floating upside down in the river. She goes off to learn the worst. Bess urges some man to follow her, but only Crown will venture out. The act ends with a renewal of the prayer for mercy.

Act III, scene i. Inside the courtyard. The inhabitants are mourning Clara, Jake, and Crown, all of whom they think lost in the storm. When they reach the point of praying for Crown, they are interrupted by laughter from Sportin' Life who hints that he knows Crown is not dead. He slyly wonders what will be the upshot of the rivalry between Crown and Porgy. Bess is heard singing Clara's Lullaby to the baby she left behind her, and the inhabitants of the tenement drift off to bed.

Suddenly, Crown can be seen at the gate. He picks his way stealthily across the courtyard, then crawls towards Porgy's door. As he passes the window, the shutter opens silently and an arm is extended, grasping a long knife, which it plunges into Crown's back. Crown staggers into an upright position, and is seized round the neck in Porgy's iron grip and slowly throttled. Porgy exclaims: 'Bess, you got a man now, you got Porgy.'

Scene ii. Next afternoon. The police come to clear up the mystery of Crown's death. They question Serena, who it appears has been ill and knows nothing of the death of the man who – every inhabitant of Catfish Row is prepared to swear – was responsible for killing her husband, Robbins. Porgy is roped in to identify Crown's body, and is dragged away protesting that he won't have anything to do with Crown, his reluctance increased by Sportin' Life's helpful suggestion that Crown's wound will begin to bleed the moment the man that killed him comes into the presence of his body.

Bess is left alone, and Sportin' Life offers her some 'happy dust' to tide over her nerves at the prospect of losing Porgy. She cannot resist it, and Sportin' Life sings a persuasive *Blues*, 'There's a boat dat's leavin' soon for New York'. He leaves a second packet of dope, and Bess sneaks out of her room and takes it inside.

Scene iii. Catfish Row, a week later. Normal life is going on, children dance and sing, and Porgy is welcomed home after his week away – he would not look

at Crown and was jailed for contempt of court. Everyone is disconcerted by Porgy's arrival, but he distributes the presents he has brought them (as a result of some successful crap-shooting in prison), and does not notice anything wrong until he looks for Bess, whose present is the last and best. She is nowhere to be found, and he sees Serena looking after Clara's baby, which had been left in Bess's charge. 'Oh, Bess, oh where's my Bess?' he sings; Serena and Maria join in his song with explanations, the one excusing, the other condemning Bess. Porgy's longing is admirably expressed in this trio, and in the final 'Oh, Lord, I'm on my way', a spiritual with chorus, which Porgy sings as he starts off to follow Bess to New York. He drives out of Catfish Row in his goat-cart with his mind made up that, wherever she is, he will find her and bring her back.   H.

ALBERTO GINASTERA
(born 11 April 1916, died 25 June 1983)

BOMARZO

Opera in two acts (fifteen scenes), libretto by Manuel Mujica Lainez. Première, 19 May 1967, Washington, D.C., with Salvador Novoa, Isabel Penagos, Joanna Simon, Claramae Turner, Richard Torigi, conductor Julius Rudel. First performed City Opera, New York, 1968, with substantially the same cast. European première, Kiel, 1970 (in German), with Charles O'Neill; performed Buenos Aires, 1972, with Novoa; English National Opera, 1976, with Graham Clark, Barbara Walker, Katherine Pring, Sarah Walker, Geoffrey Chard.

Pier Francesco Orsini, *Duke of Bomarzo* ....Tenor
Silvio de Narni, *astrologer* ....Baritone
Gian Corrado Orsini, *father of Pier Francesco* ....Bass
Girolamo ⎫ ....Baritone
Maerbale ⎭ *brothers of Pier Francesco* ....Baritone
Nicolas Orsini, *nephew of Pier Francesco* ....Tenor
Julia Farnese, *wife of Pier Francesco* ....Soprano
Pantasilea, *a Florentine courtesan* ....Mezzo-Soprano
Diana Orsini, *grandmother of*
    Pier Francesco ....Contralto
Messenger ....Baritone
Shepherd Boy..Treble
Pier Francesco, Girolamo, Maerbale as Children

Place: Bomarzo, Florence and Rome
Time: Sixteenth Century
Running Time: 2 hours 15 minutes

The rather prolific output of Alberto Ginastera, who was born in Buenos Aires, had included music in every form, including a successful ballet (*Panambi*, 1939–40) and an even more successful opera, *Don Rodrigo* (1964), when he was commissioned to write a new opera for the Opera Society of Washington. Over the years, his style changed from something with a basically Argentinian flavour to an international professionalism that allowed him in the new work to range (in the words of Norman Fraser) 'from neo-organum in some of the chorales to serial variations and free-for-all pandemonium when they are required'.

His librettist was the Argentinian writer Manuel Mujica Lainez (born Buenos Aires, 1910), who had published in 1962 a novel on the subject of the strange monsters in the gardens of Bomarzo, near Viterbo, north of Rome, and their creator in the sixteenth century, Pier Francesco Orsini. Lainez's programme notes (somewhat shortened) are reproduced in italics at the beginning of each scene. Ginastera's comment on his hero: 'I see Bomarzo not as a man of the Renaissance, but as a man of our time. We live nowadays in an age of anxiety, an age of sex, an age of violence. Bomarzo struggles with violence, and is tormented by anxiety, the metaphysical anxiety of death.'

Slow, deep, preludial mutterings in the orchestra lead to the intervention of the chorus (confined, unamplified, to the pit throughout), sometimes precisely notated, sometimes aleatoric[1] – a portent of things to come.

Act I, scene i. The potion. *I, Pier Francesco Orsini, on the last day of my life went through the park until I reached a figure carved into the rock known as The Mouth of Hell. My astrologer, Silvio de Narni, and Nicolas, my nephew, came with me. We heard a shepherd boy sing that he would not change places with the Duke because I went through life dragging in my hump the burden of my sins. I heard the voice of my beloved grandmother saying they had betrayed me and I was going to die. I saw pass before my eyes all the events of my secret life which, like the hump on my back, encumbered my soul.*

The music is concerned mainly with the innocent security of the boy's 'folk song', with its medieval overtones, and with Pier Francesco's two short solos, one bewailing the lack of peace and certainty in his life and the other a monologue when he confronts his fate. The first interlude, which uses the chorus, derives from the prelude and leads to:

Scene ii. Pier Francesco's childhood. *I saw my brothers Girolamo and Maerbale, when they were children, playing in one of the rooms of the castle. Girolamo decided that, since he was to be the Duke, I would be the Duchess of Bomarzo, and that Maerbale would marry us. They dressed me in an absurd female costume, but when my eldest brother tried to kiss me, I escaped. Suddenly, Girolamo fell upon me in a fury, pierced the lobe of my ear with an earring, saying that it was a present for the Duchess. My father heard my agonised cries and calling me an effeminate hunchback pushed me into the inner cell. Inside, I saw a skeleton crowned with rose-like rags.*

The Orsini children speak their roles, and the music supplies background to their sinister pantomime, until it assumes more importance at the entry of the warrior Duke himself, characterised by the decisive tapping of his stick on the floor. The dance of the skeleton is suggestively depicted by string *glissandi* and assorted percussion.

Scene iii. The horoscope. *I next found myself as a young man in my study with the astrologer, who told me that I should be immortal, and consequently the most glorious of the Orsinis. A messenger announced that my father, the condottiere, was returning to Bomarzo badly wounded. I realised that the astrologer's forecast was coming true.*

Silvio's incantation is rendered the more impressive by a whispered choral background, and the screams of peacocks are heard from the orchestra. An extended interlude, depicting perhaps the mixed nature of Pier Francesco's reaction to the news of his father's serious wounds, leads to:

Scene iv. Pantasilea. *The Duke sent me to Florence to a famous courtesan, Pantasilea, who was naturally disappointed when she saw a hunchback enter her chamber. I was attended by Abul, my slave, whom I loved dearly. I remember the terror I felt when I was left alone with Pantasilea in a room of mirrors peopled by my shameful image. I gave the voluptuous creature my sapphire necklace, and I asked her to let me go. I ran away, as the peacocks echoed the ominous cry I had heard in the castle.*

The scene opens with Pantasilea's song of praise to Florence. Pier Francesco's horror of mirrors and their revelation to him of his crooked body is exposed for the first time, as also his homosexual security with the faithful, dumb Abul.

Scene v. By the Tiber. *Memory then took me to a place in Bomarzo, where my grandmother told me the story of the marvellous Orsinis. Suddenly I saw Girolamo on top of the rocks about to bathe in the river. He jeered at me and, as he stepped back, lost his footing and fell into the river. My grandmother wouldn't let me go to his assistance, though I realised he had hit his head on a rock and was dying.*

Musically, the scene is dominated by the powerful figure of Diana Orsini. The interlude consists mainly of bells – on the whole festive for the proclamation of the new Duke rather than mournful for the death of the old.

Scene vi. Duke of Bomarzo. *Soon after Girolamo's death, my father died, and I succeeded to the Dukedom. We held the traditional ceremony in the castle, where my*

---

[1] Allowing a strong element of choice for the performer.

grandmother introduced me to one of the guests, the beautiful Julia Farnese. Julia left the hall with my brother, Maerbale. I remained alone with Abul, and a hooded man approached; I recognised the ghost of my father.

The scene opens with a brilliant chorus, 'O Rex Gloriae', contains the disconcerting reappearance of Pier Francesco's father (accompanied by his stick-tapping), and ends with Diana Orsini's affirmation 'You are the Duke'.

Scene vii. Fiesta at Bomarzo. *The courtiers were dancing and I passed from one dream to another, and had the impression Abul, the slave, Julia Farnese and Pantasilea were dancing with me.*

A march and a musette precede Pier Francesco's soliloquy, in which he declares his identification with Bomarzo. This in turn is followed by two galliards and a masquerade, the latter in a maniacal *tempo di Saltarello* and the occasion for one of the scenes which has been most praised by critics as a successful fusion of dance and opera.

Scene viii. The portrait by Lorenzo Lotto. *I was back from the Picardy campaign, and I went to my study, my eyes eager for my portrait painted by Messer Lorenzo Lotto. I told Abul that the artist had reflected in it the best of myself. In a large mirror, I saw a version of my painful body in contrast with that in the lordly portrait. From the depth of the mirror, there emerged the countenance of the Devil. I shattered the mirror with my helmet.*

While looking at the portrait with Abul, Pier Francesco speaks over orchestral background, regretting incidentally that Julia Farnese does not love him as does Abul. He breaks into song for an aria of longing for Julia, and, in a faster tempo, expression of his fear and loathing for the mirror and the demon which appears to him in it. The chorus at the end of the scene echoes his cries of horror.

Act II, scene ix. Julia Farnese. *Julia Farnese was a constant obsession with me. I saw her in her father's palace in Rome. Maerbale was singing with her and when he and Julia were about to drink a glass of red wine, I could bear it no longer and involuntarily spilt the contents of the goblet on Julia's dress.*

In one of the main lyrical passages of the score, Julia's madrigal becomes a duet as Maerbale takes up the tune, and a trio when Pier Francesco, Otello-like, overhears it and in his jealousy interrupts the scene.

Scene x. The bridal chamber. *Julia and I were married in Bomarzo. After the ceremony, we retired to*

the bridal chamber. *I pointed out to Julia the mosaics that in heraldic design combined the roses of the Orsinis and the lilies of the Farneses. Suddenly I saw, among the designs, one that represented the face of the Devil.*

A slow nuptial hymn precedes Julia's *Canto triste de amor*, in which Pier Francesco, almost reluctantly it seems, finally joins. As the ladies-in-waiting finish undressing the Duchess, she hums to herself the song of the previous scene, until Pier Francesco screams in anguish at the apparition of the Devil, visible only to him. He orders the courtiers to leave him, and, clutching his bride by the wrist, seems to be trying to outstare the demon of the mosaics.

Scene xi. The dream. *I couldn't possess Julia that night and sank into despair, made worse by a dream. The painted figures of the men and women that people the Etruscan graves of Bomarzo came to life capturing Julia and myself in their dances.*

Pier Francesco's fruitless attempts to consummate his marriage are symbolised by the momentary substitution of the figure of Pantasilea for that of Julia, and, in between his soliloquy of frustration and a short, violent lament that it is only in dream that he can possess his wife, there takes place an erotic ballet to aleatoric music. The G sharp of Pier Francesco's concluding cry of 'Dios mío' becomes the basis of an aleatoric choral interlude, intended to 'produce the sensation that Pier Francesco's shout is extended to the chorus and orchestra'.

Scene xii. The Minotaur. *Like a madman, I left the chamber and made my way along the corridor, until I came to the central sculpture, the Minotaur. I felt the proud Orsinis around me, and on recognising my fated brother in the dreadful image, the Minotaur, I kissed its marble lips. Bomarzo trembled with passion, yet I found solace only in that sweet brother.*

As Pier Francesco enters, he repeats the sustained G sharp of his lament, then sings to the Minotaur, subsequently in a final stanza embracing the marble body as the only refuge of his lips, his passion, his doubts. The interlude is a beautiful, unaccompanied choral Villanella.

Scene xiii. Maerbale. *I couldn't erase from my feverish mind a suspicion that Julia and Maerbale were deceiving me. To ascertain whether it was true, Silvio de Narni convinced Maerbale that Julia was awaiting him on the loggia. Nicolas Orsini, my brother's son, was also watching. They kissed, and Nicolas, sensing the danger, warned his father to escape. Urged on by me, Abul pursued him with his naked dagger. Thus Maerbale met his end.*

There is a short duet for Maerbale and Julia, and the scene ends with Maerbale's murder and cries from Julia and Maerbale as Pier Francesco violently embraces his wife. The interlude provides savage comment on Pier Francesco's crime.

Scene xiv. The alchemy. *Silvio de Narni devoted all those years to search for the formula that would win eternity for me and at last he found it. I didn't realise that Nicolas was watching us. He had sworn to avenge his father.*

As the scene of the invocation mounts in intensity the chorus joins its mouthings to the exhortations of Silvio. The last interlude is in the nature of a threnody for the dying Duke.

Scene xv. The park of the monsters. *And now, for Nicolas Orsini mixed the potion of immortality with poison, I know I am going to die. The monsters of Bomarzo keep watch by the Duke whose life is dying away.*

The music recalls that of the first scene, as the chorus echoes the dying ravings of Pier Francesco. The little shepherd boy, who thinks the Duke may be asleep, finishes the opera as he had begun it.

'*Bomarzo*', wrote the critic Robert Jacobson in the *Saturday Review*, 'is governed by a strict structure, beginning with the division of its fifteen scenes (separated by fourteen interludes), each of which is subdivided into three microstructures reproducing the classical Greek form of exposition, crisis and conclusion.' His partial employment of a post-Webern serialism avoids, says the same critic, the greyness which is often found in a twelve-tone opera, and the result, wrote Irving Lowens in the Washington *Evening Star* at the time of the première, 'is the masterwork which *Don Rodrigo* foretold'. Such a laudatory press did not prevent a ban on its production in the composer's native Argentina, where it had been accepted for the Teatro Colón only to be thrown out by decree of the Mayor, who had apparently read the American notices! The whole episode seems not wholly unconnected with the official visit shortly before of President Ongario to a performance in the same theatre of the ballet *Sacre du Printemps*: 'If you show me anything dirty like that again, I'll close this place' was his reported reaction.   H.

UMBERTO GIORDANO
(born 28 August 1867, died 12 November 1948)

Giordano's first full-length opera, an essay in Neapolitan low-life, *Mala Vita*, enjoyed some success in German-speaking countries but was thought inappropriately shocking for the Italian stage. He was not without influential connections (his parents-in-law owned the hotel in Milan where Verdi customarily stayed), and the composer Alberto Franchetti, for whom Luigi Illica had written *Andrea Chénier*, allowed him to take over the libretto. Its success at la Scala established his position and *Fedora* (an opera of much lesser calibre) two years later seemed to confirm his standing but was in fact to prove the first step in a long decline. His operas continued to be performed by leading artists – the names of Geraldine Farrar, Martinelli, Amato, Zenatello, de Luca, Toti dal Monte, Lina Pagliughi and Arturo Toscanini figure in the casts of his operatic premières and revivals – but only *Chénier* and to a lesser extent (and only with a leading singing-actress) *Fedora* have continued in the repertory since his death.

ANDREA CHÉNIER

Opera in four acts, text by Luigi Illica. Première at la Scala, Milan, 28 March 1896, with Carrera, Borgatti, Sammarco. First performed New York, 1896; Manchester, 1903 (in English); Camden Town Theatre, London, 1903 (in English); Covent Garden, 1905, with Strakosch, Zenatello, Sammarco, conductor Mugnone; Metropolitan, New York, 1921, with Muzio, Gigli, Danise. Revived Covent Garden, 1925, with Sheridan, Lauri-Volpi, Franci; 1930, with Sheridan, Gigli, Inghilleri; la Scala, fiftieth anniversary performance in 1946, with Caniglia, Beval, Piero Guelfi, conductor Giordano; 1949,

Giordano Commemoration performance, with Tebaldi, del Monaco, Silveri, conductor de Sabata; Metropolitan, New York, 1954, with Milanov, del Monaco, Warren; 1962, with Eileen Farrell, Corelli, Merrill; London, Drury Lane, 1958; London, Sadler's Wells, 1959, with Victoria Elliott, Craig, Glossop.

A Major-Domo ....Baritone

Charles Gérard ....Baritone

Maddalena (Madeleine) Coigny....................Soprano

Countess de Coigny, *her mother*..........Mezzo-Soprano

Bersi, *Maddalena's mulatto maid*..........Mezzo-Soprano

Fléville, *a cavalier ('Romanziere')* ....Baritone

The Abbé ....Tenor

Andrea Chénier, *a poet* ....Tenor

Mathieu, *a waiter*...Baritone

Incredibile,[1] *a spy*...Tenor

Roucher, *a friend of Chénier's*..............................Bass

Madelon, *an old woman*.......................Mezzo-Soprano

Dumas, *president of the tribunal*.....................Baritone

Fouquier-Tinville, *attorney-general*................Baritone

Schmidt, *jailer at St Lazare prison*....................Baritone

Courtiers and Ladies, Citizens of France, Soldiers, Servants, Peasants, Prisoners, Members of Revolutionary Tribunal

Place: Paris
Time: Before and After the French Revolution
Running Time: 2 hours 20 minutes

Historical as a character though André Chénier was, Giordano's librettist, Luigi Illica, has turned his life into fiction. Chénier was a poet, dreamer, and patriot; he was born in Constantinople, but returned to Paris for his education, and there became a participant in the Revolution, and later a victim of it.

Act I. Ballroom in a château. Preparations are in train for a party, and Gérard is among the servants setting the room to rights. He mocks at the falsities and conventions of aristocratic life, but his words take on a more menacing character when, provoked by the sight of his old father carrying in some furniture, he launches into a denunciation of the masters he works for and the system which keeps them in their unearned luxury: 'Son sessant'anni'. The Countess, her daughter Maddalena, and Bersi come to see that the last-minute preparations for the party are going well. Gérard comments on the beauty of the daughter of the house, with whom he is secretly in love.

The guests arrive, notable among them the Abbé and Fléville, the latter of whom introduces an Italian musician and the poet Chénier. The Abbé wants to talk politics, but with some graceful phrases Fléville bids the guests turn their minds to the serious business of the Pastoral they are about to see and hear. There is a pastoral chorus, and then Chénier agrees to recite at Maddalena's invitation.

He sings the well-known *Improvviso di Chénier*, 'Un dì, all'azzurro spazio', in which he contrasts the beauty of nature with the misery man makes around him; he denounces the selfishness of those in authority – priests, politicians, aristocrats – and his extremist sentiments find little favour with the guests (though the aria itself has become enormously popular since first sung).

Maddalena apologises to him for the situation her request has brought about, but the Countess quickly gets the band to strike up a gavotte. Even that is interrupted when Gérard bursts in at the head of a band of beggars, announcing, butler-like, 'His Lordship, Misery!' The major-domo gets them to leave, but not before Gérard has torn his coat from his back, and denounced it as a sign of slavery. The gaiety goes on as if nothing has happened.

Act II. The Café Hottot in Paris. The first phase of the Revolution is over, and at one side of the stage stands a bust of Marat. Chénier sits alone at a table, and at another are Bersi and Incredibile, the spy. Bersi asks whether it is true that there are spies about and remarks that she herself has nothing to fear; is she not a true daughter of the Revolution, who thoroughly enjoys the new freedom, the drinking, and even watching a tumbril go by? Incredibile reads aloud from the note he is making about Bersi and about Chénier, each of whom he thinks a suspicious character.

Roucher appears and goes up to Chénier with a passport which he has been influential in getting for him. It is important he should flee at once, as he has powerful enemies. Chénier rejects such counsel of despair, and sings of his confidence in his own destiny ('Credo a una possanza arcana'). Chénier moreover has received several anonymous letters from a woman, whose image has been built up in his mind until she is the most beautiful creature he has ever imagined. Chénier is about to leave,

---

[1] 'Incroyable' = a beau, of the French Directoire period. This one is an informer, or spy.

when Robespierre and several other leading Revolutionaries appear, followed by a cheering crowd. Gérard is one of the leaders, and Incredibile stops him to enquire more details about the woman he is trying to find. Gérard gives him a lyrical description of the beauty of Maddalena. Roucher is approached by Bersi, who tells him that someone wishes to see Chénier, someone who is in danger.

Maddalena arrives at the meeting-place and is soon joined by Chénier. It is some moments before he recognises her and discovers that it was she who wrote the letters; at the same time, Incredibile looks from his hiding-place, makes up his mind that this is the woman Gérard is looking for, and goes off to tell him where she is. Maddalena asks Chénier for help in her loneliness, and he declares his love in a passionate duet. They are about to rush away together, when Gérard appears in their path, closely followed by the spy and by Roucher. Chénier shouts to his friend Roucher to take Maddalena into his charge, and he and Gérard draw their swords. They fight, Gérard falls wounded, and recognises his opponent; he murmurs to him to be on his guard – he is on Fouquier-Tinville's list as a counter-revolutionary.

Incredibile returns with police, the crowd demands vengeance on the assailant of a leader of the people; but Gérard says he did not recognise his attacker.

Act III. The Revolutionary Tribunal. Mathieu tries to get the crowd to contribute money and valuables to the common fund. The response is listless, until Gérard makes an impassioned speech. Immediately, all are ready to give, among them an old woman (Madelon), who says that she has already lost two sons fighting for France, but now offers the youngest, a boy of about fifteen. The crowd disperses singing the revolutionary song, *La Carmagnole*.

Gérard asks Incredibile whether there is news of either Chénier or Maddalena – as to the former, a newsboy can be heard crying that he is arrested, and the latter, says the spy, will not be long in coming to look for her lover. Gérard is shocked by the spy's cynicism, still more so when Incredibile urges him to write out the indictment against Chénier; it will be needed for the forthcoming session of the Tribunal.

Gérard is haunted by conscience and memory of his former patriotic enthusiasm. Can he in all honesty denounce Chénier as 'an enemy of his country' ('Nemico della patria')? His revolutionary zeal, which formerly fed on such ideals as brotherly love, is now kept alive by jealousy and lust. It is an effective outburst. Swayed by his desire for Maddalena, he impulsively signs the indictment.

Maddalena is brought in by Mathieu, and Gérard explains that Chénier has been arrested by his orders and because of his own passion for her. She turns from him, but then offers her love in exchange for Chénier's freedom. She tells Gérard the story of her mother's horrible death, in the flames of her house as it was burned by the mob: 'La mamma morta'. The Tribunal is ready to sit and Gérard tells her he will do what he can for Chénier.

The Tribunal is in session. Several prisoners are summarily condemned, to applause from the crowd, and when Chénier's turn comes, he is refused permission by the court to answer the charge. On Gérard's insistence, he is finally allowed to defend himself. He has fought for his country and his ideals with sword and with pen; let them now take his life, but leave his honour unstained: 'Sì, fui soldato' (Yes, I was a soldier). Gérard raises his voice in Chénier's defence; the indictment was false, he says. But all is in vain, and the death sentence is duly passed.

Act IV. In the courtyard of the Prison of St Lazare, Chénier waits for the tumbril. Roucher is with him, and when he finishes writing, his friend asks him to read the poem he has written. 'Come un bel dì di Maggio' (Just as a fine day in May time) he sings in a beautiful aria which describes his feelings as a poet in the face of death. Roucher bids him farewell and leaves him to return to his cell.

Gérard appears at the outer gate, with Maddalena. The jailer agrees to allow Maddalena to take the place of a female prisoner condemned to death, and so to die with Chénier. Gérard leaves, determined to make a last effort in their defence, and Chénier is brought in. Their duet is on a grand scale; they exult in their love and rejoice that death will unite them for ever ('Vicino a te'). In an opera in which Giordano has indulged to the full his gift for passionate, lyrical melody, it is fitting that the most lyrical and the most passionate moments should come in the short last act, in the shape of Chénier's aria and the great duet.   H.

FEDORA

Opera in three acts, text by A. Colautti from the play by Sardou. Première at the Teatro Lirico, Milan, 17 November 1898, with Bellincioni, Caruso, conductor Giordano. First performed Covent Garden, 1906, with Giachetti, Zenatello, Sammarco, conductor Mugnone; New York, Metropolitan, 1906, with Cavalieri, Caruso, Scotti, conductor Vigna. Revived Metropolitan, 1923, with Jeritza, Martinelli, Scotti, conductor Papi; Covent Garden, 1925, with Jeritza, Lappas; la Scala, Milan, 1932, with Cobelli, Pertile, Stabile, conductor de Sabata; 1939, with Pacetti, Gigli, conductor Marinuzzi; 1941, with Pederzini; 1948, with Caniglia, conductor de Sabata; 1956, with Callas, Corelli, Colzani, conductor Gavazzeni; Covent Garden, 1994, with Freni, Carreras.

Princess Fedora Romanov ....Soprano
Count Loris Ipanov ....Tenor
De Siriex, *a French diplomat* ....Baritone
Countess Olga Sukarev...................................Soprano
Grech, *a police officer*...Bass
Cirillo, *a coachman* ....Baritone
Dmitri, *a groom* ....Contralto
A Little Savoyard.............................Mezzo-Soprano
Désiré, *a valet* ....Tenor
Baron Rouvel ....Tenor
Lorek, *a surgeon* ....Baritone
Borov, *a doctor*..Baritone
Nicola, *footman*..Tenor
Sergio, *footman*..Baritone
Boleslao Lazinski, *a pianist* ....Mime

Place: St Petersburg, Paris, Switzerland
Time: Late Nineteenth Century
Running Time: 1 hour 50 minutes

Act I. St Petersburg, at the house of Count Vladimir Andreyevich. The Count's servants are waiting for his return home, playing dominoes and gossiping about his way of life – gambling, drinking, and women are his diversions, which, they say, will have to stop now that he is marrying the rich widow, Princess Fedora. A bell rings; it is the Princess herself, asking where her fiancé is.

The sound of a sledge is heard, and Grech enters quickly, asking where the Count's room is. The Count is carried to it, gravely wounded. No one knows who has wounded him, and Grech, the police officer in charge of the case, questions everyone present. The coachman gives his evidence dramatically and with emotion. He drove his master to the shooting gallery, he said, and, a quarter of an hour

after arriving, he heard two shots. Someone rushed out and disappeared into the darkness. He (Cirillo) hailed a passing cab (in which was de Siriex) and together they went into the house, to find the Count upstairs covered in blood. It comes to light that the Count received a letter that very morning, brought by an old woman – and the building in which he was found wounded was let to an old woman. Was anyone else seen in the house during the morning? Yes, a young man who eventually rushed out.

Suddenly, one of the servants remembers that it was Count Loris Ipanov who was there that morning – and Fedora jumps at the idea that it must have been he who carried out the attack. Grech goes to his rooms – he lives just opposite – but returns to say that their quarry has escaped them. In the meanwhile the doctor summons Fedora, whose shriek of consternation tells us that Vladimir is dead.

Act II. Fedora has determined to devote herself to the capture of the man she presumes is her fiancé's murderer, Count Loris Ipanov, and to extract a confession of guilt from him. A reception is in progress at her house in Paris, and Countess Olga introduces her friend, the pianist Boleslao Lazinski, to the guests. Fedora comes up to de Siriex, now French Foreign Secretary, and says to him with peculiar emphasis: 'I may need your help. You are an old friend, this is a newer one – Count Loris Ipanov.' De Siriex is astonished at the speed with which Fedora has caught up with Loris.

Fedora is alone with Loris, and he declares his love in the passionate *arioso*, 'Amor ti vieta', whose flowing *cantilena* is one of the best-known songs in the repertory of the Italian tenor.

Fedora tells Borov, who asks her if she would like to give him a message for any Russian friend, that she too is going back to Russia almost immediately. She has been pardoned and her possessions restored to her. Loris is disconsolate, and admits that he cannot go. Fedora says she will intercede for him, but he tells her that this in itself is unlikely to prove sufficient to have his sentence revoked. While Lazinski, with much comic pantomime, starts to play for the guests, Loris confesses to Fedora that he was in fact responsible for the death of Count Vladimir, but that he is innocent of his murder. Fedora can hardly contain her triumph. Loris says he can bring proof of his innocence, and she bids him return that very night with his documents.

Fedora, alone, sits down at her writing table. She calls to Grech and confirms that he and his men are to kidnap Loris once he has given her proof of his guilt and convey him on board a Russian ship. She has written to General Yarichkin in St Petersburg to inform him of the way events have been moving, and has added the names of Loris's brother and of his friend Sokolev as accomplices in his crime.

Loris arrives, and Fedora immediately accuses him of being a Nihilist and implicated in the plot against the Tsar's life, as well as guilty of the murder of Count Vladimir. He denies that this act was murder, and tells her the story of the Count's duplicity in carrying on a clandestine affair with Loris's wife, Wanda. He discovered the liaison by chance, and found proof in the shape of a letter from Wanda to Vladimir. He shows Fedora letters from Vladimir to Wanda, and she knows that he is speaking the truth. Loris's confession, 'Mia madre, la mia vecchia madre', is one of the best-known passages in the score. He continues his story: he went to the place of assignation and caught the guilty pair together, was shot at by Vladimir and wounded, and, when he fired in his turn, inflicted a mortal wound on his enemy.

Fedora is overcome at the story, but Loris tells her he is still pursued by an unknown adversary, who sets spies on him and will not let him live out his exile in peace. 'Vedi, io piango' (See, I am weeping), he sings, thinking of the mother and the native land he cannot see again. The signal is heard, and Fedora with difficulty prevents Loris from rushing out to meet his accusers. Only when she admits she loves him and will keep him with her does he succumb to her persuasion.

Act III. Fedora's villa in Switzerland. Mountaineers sing a Swiss song as a prelude to a short but passionate interchange between Fedora and Loris, who are living happily together. Olga interrupts the idyllic scene, and is prepared to be enthusiastic about everything – even the bicycle she sees propped up against the wall. Loris recommends a tandem as better suited to Olga's amatory purposes. Loris goes to collect his mail as de Siriex enters. He cannot resist telling Olga that her Polish pianist was in reality a spy, set on her trail to pump information from her.

When they are alone, de Siriex tells Fedora that Yarichkin had pursued his vengeful career until his dismissal by the new Tsar. Two young men, accomplices so it was said in the murder of Count Vladimir, were arrested; one disappeared, the other was shut up in a prison on the banks of the Neva, where, the tide rising suddenly, he was slowly drowned in his dungeon. It was Valerian, Loris's brother. The news of his death proved such a shock to his aged mother that she fell ill and died.

Fedora is left alone, and prays that Loris may be saved from the net she has unwittingly drawn around him ('Dio di giustizia'). Loris enters and finds a telegram telling him he has been pardoned and is free to return to Russia. His joy knows no bounds. But he has a letter from his friend Borov, who also sent the telegram, in which he indicates that a woman's accusation has been the means of prolonging his exile, and has even caused the deaths of his supposed 'accomplices', Valerian and Sokolev, which in their turn have broken the heart of his mother.

Loris will not listen to Fedora's attempt to suggest that the woman in question may have done what she did believing him to have been guilty of a monstrous crime, but a renewal of her pleading shows him that his enemy has been none other than Fedora herself. He rushes at her in fury, but she drinks poison, and Borov arrives to find her dying. Loris's grief knows no bounds, and to the tune of 'Amor ti vieta', he forgives the woman who has brought such hate and such love into his life.   H.

PHILIP GLASS
(born 31 January 1937)

EINSTEIN ON THE BEACH

Opera in four acts by Robert Wilson–Philip Glass, spoken texts by Christopher Knowles, Samuel M. Johnson and Lucinda Childs, lyrics by the composer. First performance Avignon Festival, 25 July 1976. First U.S. performance, Metropolitan Opera, New York, November 1976, conducted by the composer. Revived Brooklyn Academy of Music, New York, 1984; Stuttgart, 1989, in a production designed by Achim Fryer, which did not meet with the composer's approval.

Soprano, Tenor, Actors, Dancers, Violinist, Chorus

Running Time: 4 hours 40 minutes

*E*instein on the Beach was inspired by Robert Wilson's drawings (which often resemble architectural plans and sketches) and by his performance art (which aims to change audiences' perception of time, usually by doing very little, very slowly, very often). Robert Wilson had more influence on the opera than the libretto itself. There are literary threads running through the work, but it would be misleading to suggest that their role is much more than anecdotal. While the title refers to the historical figure, his relation to this opera is playfully relative: a violinist on-stage is dressed as Albert Einstein – but so are the other performers. The composer himself has highlighted a series of recurring images, Train, Trial and Field with Spaceship. He has added, with disarming caution, 'one might say that, in a general way, the opera begins with a 19th-century train and ends with a 20th-century spaceship. Events occur en route – trials, prison, dances – and throughout, the continuity of the Knee Plays.' The Knee Plays connect one joint of the opera to another, incidentally. The lyrics by Philip Glass himself are in a sense more straightforwardly abstract and consist of numbers (which represent the music's rhythmic structure) and solfège ('do, re, mi') which does the same for the pitch. Like a Jasper Johns painting of numbers (and the relationship may not be entirely coincidental), this is art that focuses on minimal subjects, in order to celebrate the means of expression themselves (paint/sound, colour, texture and surface pattern/rhythm, etc.). While the

music is undoubtedly complex in its creation, as the composer has eloquently described, its most obvious feature is its apparent simplicity. The effect is still controversial. Minimally varied phrases are repeated so often that they can generate a mesmerised, trance-like state of bliss or numbing boredom.

Knee Play 1 (chorus and electronic organ).

Act I, scene i. Train. The 'scene' is headed 'These are the days', a quotation from a Beatles song that recurs in the spoken text,[1] and Chapter 1.

Scene ii. Trial. The words,[1] ignoring repetition and lineation, are 'Mr Bojangles if you see any of those Baggy pants It was huge Chuck the hills If you know it was a violin to be Answer the telephone And if anybody asks you please It was trees It...It... It... is like that Mr Bojangles, Mr Bojangles, Mr Bojangles, Mr Bojangles I reach you'.

Paris. A speaker intones a mostly banal (very probably a deliberately banal) text[2] about Paris. Another speaker repeats a section of the previous text[1] longing for 'some wind for the sailboat'.

Knee Play 2 (violin solo). Taking off from Bach, it does not get far before two voices intervene, echo and overlap with one another, reciting a text[1] involving gasoline and the Beatles line.

Act II, scene i. Dance 1 – Field with Spaceship. Two notes are repeated fast and then slowly and then fast again in unpredictable groupings. Time slows: while tiring to listen to, this sequence inhibits sleep; it is indeed evocative of a journey, 'not so much in a spaceship, as on a Night Train'.

Scene ii. Night Train. Language fragmented under the impact of a very simple musical figure is briefly audible as 'One, two, three, four, five, six', before relapsing into what may be Japanese, and later consists of 'Baa, baa, baa', proving the ultimate secondariness of literary material in opera of this nature.

Knee Play 3 (chorus *a cappella*). A virtuoso choral recitation of 'One, two, three, four' at a very fast tempo sandwiches an arresting, multiple-layered exercise in solfège, repeated twice.

---

[1] Text by Christopher Knowles.

[2] Text by Samuel M. Johnson.

Act III, scene i. Trial/Prison. Electronic organ patterns introduce and then underlie choral recitations of numbers and a spoken text, repeated reminiscences of shopping in a supermarket.[1] This is followed by the text from Trial 1, by 'Bank robbery is punishable by twenty years in Federal prison', increasingly fragmented, and by 'I feel the Earth move',[2] a haunting recitation 'about' court and jail, ending with the night schedule of a New York radio station. As before, moments of coherence are disconcertingly (though inevitably) undercut by incoherence.

Scene ii. Dance 2 – 'Field with Spaceship'. Choral patterns adhere to organ patterns, at first rhythmically and melodically nearly monotonous, then taking off into looser structures. The syllables are indistinguishable, the effect by turns irritating and bewildering. In the last few bars the choral sequence is revealed as identical to a phrase Bach wrote for the solo violin.

Knee Play 4 (chorus and violin). The chorus articulate solfège patterns of a simple, blockish kind, while a violinist works away tirelessly. Is there something monkish about this dedicated chanting and scraping? If so, whose glory is it for?

Act IV, scene i. Building/Train (chorus and ensemble). Slow, choral crescendos and diminuendos build and decay over a constant bass, giving the effect of another train journey, complete with sirens.

Scene ii. Bed (solo electric organ and voice). The organ's right-hand doodling after Bach yields after a trill to a repetitive sequence that nevertheless refuses to settle down to predictable formulae. A soprano voice then soars over a simple, even simple-minded organ accompaniment in a long, wordless *vocalise*, faintly reminiscent of Mendelssohn.

Scene iii. Spaceship (chorus and ensemble). More organ doodling is abruptly overlaid by choral muttering which in turn yields to some fast scales.

Knee Play 5 (women's chorus, violin and electric organ). The chorus continue to count again, before a speaking voice joins in, reciting the text from Knee Play 1. Two female voices alternate, counting and reciting. A third, male voice recites 'Lovers on a Park Bench',[2] over a solo violin. The impact of the passion that emerges ('I love you more than tongue can tell') has a curiously stronger effect for all the aural impediments. The opera ends with his voice: 'How much do I love you? Count the stars in the sky... Number the grains of sand on the sea shore. Impossible, you say.' Its eloquence disarms all criticism and renders further analysis otiose.

In 1976 *Einstein on the Beach* was designed and directed by Robert Wilson. It lasted four hours and forty minutes without an interval, but by all accounts it worked well. Since then, following a well established historical pattern, the margin has appropriated the centre: what was once radically different, exotic, unique to Robert Wilson, has become a widely available manner: it is not just that his vision has become an overworked stylistic device in the hands of epigones, but rather that Mr Wilson's own work is now widely available all over the world, even in conservative contexts, like the Opéra de la Bastille. It is no longer quite so refreshing to see arbitrary, chic, unemotive but exquisitely lit stage pictures. On the poster for the 1976 performances at the Met *Einstein on the Beach* was described as 'by Robert Wilson–Philip Glass'. Having chained the work so definitively to one man's vision it remains to be seen whether it can survive it. The recording can give a misleading impression, because some of its musical events 'take place at a somewhat quicker pace than would occur in a live performance'. Perhaps it will always need the participation of a visual artist whose authority is at least the equal of the composer's.   P.

AKHNATEN

Opera in three acts, libretto by the composer in association with Shalom Goldman, Robert Israel and Richard Riddell (vocal text derived from original sources by Shalom Goldman). Première, Stuttgart, 24 March 1984, with Paul Esswood in the title role, conductor Dennis Russell Davies, producer Achim Freyer. First performed in Houston, 1984, with Marie Angel (Queen Tye), Christopher Robson; English National Opera, 1985, with Angel, Robson, Sally Burgess (Nefertiti), conductor Paul Daniel, producer David Freeman.

Akhnaten, *King of Egypt*......................Counter-Tenor
Nefertiti, *Akhnaten's wife* ....Alto
Queen Tye, *Akhnaten's mother*......................Soprano
Horemhab, *General and future Pharaoh*..........Baritone
Aye, *Nefertiti's father and Pharaoh's adviser* ....Bass
The High Priest of Amon ....Tenor

---

[1] Text by Lucinda Childs.   [2] Text by Christopher Knowles,

Akhnaten's Six Daughters ....Female Voices

Funeral Party ....Eight Men's Voices

Tourist Guide ....Actor (voice-over)

Place: Egypt
Time: 1370 B.C. to Present Day
Running Time: 2 hours 15 minutes

Philip Glass's third opera follows the tradition of the previous two, about Einstein and Gandhi, in taking a central figure in world thinking and mythology and portraying him on the operatic stage. Narrative is at a discount – the introduction to *Satyagraha* (1980) describes it as 'not a "story" opera but an episodic-symbolic portrait of an historical personality' – and the libretto of *Akhnaten* draws on ancient texts mostly sung in the original languages. If there is a similarity here with Stravinsky's use of sung Latin in *Oedipus Rex*, it might be argued that Glass's music has something in common with the neo-classical outlook of its great predecessor. Infinite repetitions of cell-like musical statements – often triads, arpeggios, patterns derived perhaps from Monteverdi's procedures, ostinati, bounding rhythms – this is the stuff of the 'minimalist' school, as it has been called. The sophistication and fastidious sense of instrumental colouring in Glass's music (no violins in the orchestra of *Akhnaten*) belong however to the techniques of the 'learned' composer (as have been most other members of the school), and words like 'serene', 'incantatory', expressions such as 'elegantly mechanised simplicities', 'gently atmospheric', 'trance-like' were used to describe the music at the first English performances of *Akhnaten* in 1985. More important, Glass has certainly demonstrated an ability with his operas to touch the public's sensibility as have few of his contemporaries.

Amenhotep IV changed his name to Akhnaten and after five or six years on the throne of Egypt abandoned its capital Thebes for a site to the north. There he took up a position of hostility to Amon, the God of Thebes, and not only built a new capital but developed a monotheistic and exclusive worship of the sun under the name of the Aten (or solar disc). Twenty-five years later, he was dead and his capital abandoned. His mummy was never found, but his capital, Akhetaten, has been excavated to reveal a ground plan which suggests a city of great splendour. He and his wife, Queen Nefertiti, were constantly depicted by artists, and the effigy of Nefertiti,

now in Berlin, suggests a classical beauty of the Middle East.

Act I. Thebes, 1370 B.C. Prelude. The funeral of King Amenhotep III is being prepared by the priests of Amon. Amenhotep's son, together with his widow, Queen Tye (who ruled as Regent until her son came of age) and other members of the royal entourage join the procession – Aye, Queen Tye's brother and the late King's counsellor; Horemhab, commander of the army; and Nefertiti, Aye's daughter and wife to the new Pharaoh.

The funeral of Amenhotep III. With beating of drums and chanting, eight Priests of Amon, together with Aye, celebrate the rites of Isis, Osiris and Horus, and the King's body is carried in procession through the temple.

The Coronation. A gentler mood prevails as the new King undergoes a purification ceremony before he is crowned. Then the double crown of Egypt is placed on his head and he is greeted by the High Priest of Amon, Horemhab and Aye in trio as the incarnation of Horus, son of Isis and Osiris. The chorus solemnly follows their lead in the chant.

The Window of Appearances. The new Pharaoh, who has the other-worldly voice of a counter-tenor, is a reformer with religious ideas quite different from those of his predecessor. He draws the symbol of the Aten, with the rays of the sun containing each an Ankh, the symbol of life. The High Priest of Amon, who does not yet know that the King will change his name to Akhnaten, is bewildered and affronted by the rejection of the old God and he departs, leaving the voices of Akhnaten, Nefertiti and Queen Tye – that powerful figure, the Queen Mother – to combine almost ritualistically before they dance blasphemously through the Temple of Amon. The scene, with its infinite repetitions and its incantatory quality, has a power that is little short of hypnotic.

Act II. The Temple. Amon's Priests, led by the High Priest, chant ritually, surrounded by the images and totems of the many gods among whom Amon was supreme. It is not long before, almost gently, they are overthrown by the King, his mother and their followers. Everything – temple, the images of the gods, even the priests – is destroyed, and Queen Tye's reiterated top As, Bs, and A flats provide a trumpet-like top line to the implacable chant before the music dies away.

Akhnaten and Nefertiti. Queen Tye is the leader of

the new thinking and she teaches Akhnaten a poem to the Aten, which he in duet (slow, as has been all the vocal music, even when at its most urgent) teaches to Nefertiti. The Queen Mother gives over to Akhnaten the maiden Bekhetaten, whom many believe to have been their daughter.

The City. The plan for the city is ready and celebrated in a solemn dance.

Hymn. Akhetaten is built and Akhnaten sings a hymn to the Sun, one of the score's most appreciable and extended vocal movements. The words are by Akhnaten himself. Psalm 104 is intoned by the chorus and Aye is rewarded for the part he has played in bringing the new city to reality. Akhnaten in his delight and ecstasy attempts to touch the sun.

Act III. Akhetaten, 1358 B.C.

Portrayals of Akhnaten and his family are well known, he slouching, with spindly legs and slanting eyes, pot-bellied and full-hipped, Nefertiti beautiful and long-necked, and the pair surrounded by their nude daughters with shaven heads. The opening of the act shows them living inside the city which the King has built.

The Family. The six daughters sing in block harmony, Nefertiti and Akhnaten join them (Nefertiti now, unlike in their duet in Act II, taking the higher line) and the gentle, almost idyllic mood of togetherness is inescapable. But in this case, contentment goes before a fall. Letters to the King from princes in outlying provinces are read to him by Aye and Horemhab, all calling for help against the hostile powers which threaten to invade Egypt. The King will not listen and finally even the faithful Aye in despair deserts him. In the unkindest cut, he takes with him his daughter Nefertiti and her eldest daughter, and Akhnaten is left with only two of his daughters beside him.

Attack and Fall. The High Priest of Amon is now in a position to ally with Aye and Horemhab to overthrow the King. The new triumvirate in music of energy and resolve, soon joined by the chorus, destroys the city. Akhnaten disappears – perhaps, if theories connecting him with Oedipus are to be believed, he blinds himself.

The Ruins. A prologue celebrates the eclipse of Akhnaten and reinstatement of Amon as Egypt's God.

Akhetaten; the present. Tourists are being guided round the ruins of Akhnaten's city (the disembodied voice of the guide provided the present writer with his only operatic role – spoken, some will be relieved to hear – in the last new production of his time as Managing Director of English National Opera).

Epilogue. The spirits of its founder, his mother and his wife still hover ghost-like over the ruins of the city, and theirs is, vocally speaking, the last word, though dramatically in David Freeman's production for Houston, New York and English National Opera it belonged to the constants of life by the Nile – the threshing of wheat, the making of bricks, and the slow-motion fighting continue in the precise form they have taken over the centuries.   H.

MIKHAIL IVANOVICH GLINKA

(born 1 June 1804, died 15 February 1857)

Glinka, a landowner by birth and upbringing but far from the amateur composer such a background might suggest, received his early training in Russia but was heavily influenced by Italian composers of the day, notably Rossini, a round dozen of whose operas he heard in Moscow from a touring Italian company. A period in Milan and Berlin preceded his return to Russia and with his first opera the establishment of a Russian operatic school. *A Life for the Tsar* not only treats a nationalist subject but was the first opera to use a Russian text.

In *Russlan* the composer mixes style and idiom even more than in his first opera, the Italianate cut of Lyudmila's music (like Antonida's in the earlier opera) alternating with music of oriental and fantastic colouring to make an early 'Russian' masterpiece, if such a word can be applied to an opera whose pacing is so relentlessly undramatic. Glinka's use of whole-tone scales (particularly in connection with the villainous Tchernomor) is innovative, as is his employment of strikingly new rhythmic patterns.

A LIFE FOR THE TSAR[1]

Ivan Susanin

Opera in four acts and an epilogue, text by G.F. Rozen. Première 9 December 1836, St Petersburg. This work opened every new season at St Petersburg and Moscow until 1917. First performed la Scala, Milan, 1874; Covent Garden, 1887, with Albani, Scalchi, Gayerre, Devoyod; Manchester, 1888 (in Russian); San Francisco, 1936 (in Russian); Stuttgart, 1937; Berlin, Staatsoper, 1940, with Cebotari, Roswaenge, Prohaska; la Scala, 1959, with Scotto, Raimondi, Christoff; San Carlo, Naples, 1967, with Christoff.

Antonida, *Susanin's daughter* ....Soprano

Ivan Susanin, *a peasant* ....Bass

Sobinin, *Antonida's bridegroom* ....Tenor

Vanya, *an orphan boy adopted by Susanin*......Contralto

A Polish Commander ....Baritone

Place: Domnin, Moscow, and a Polish Camp
Time: 1613
Running Time: 3 hours 15 minutes

Act I. A village street at Domnin. The peasants sing a patriotic song to celebrate the imminent return of Sobinin from the wars. Antonida, his fiancée, is no less glad, and in a *cavatina* she pours out her happiness at the prospect of seeing him again. Susanin enters with news that is less to the taste of the company; a Polish army is advancing on Moscow. The bystanders are alarmed, but their fears lessen when Sobinin himself appears and tells them that the Poles have been repulsed. He is anxious that his marriage with Antonida should immediately be celebrated, but Susanin is full of forebodings at the state of the country and will not bless their union until a Tsar has been elected. Sobinin finds this objection easy to overcome; a Tsar has in fact just been chosen, and it is none other than their own landlord, Romanov. Susanin withdraws his objections, and agrees to the wedding.

Act II. The Polish headquarters. A magnificent ball is in progress, and the Poles are full of confidence that their forthcoming campaign against the Russians will be crowned with success. A series of dances follows, including a Cracoviak and two Mazurkas. A messenger tells the Polish commander of the Polish defeat and of the election of Romanov as Tsar of Russia. The Poles plan to capture the young Tsar at the monastery where he lives.

Act III. Susanin's house. Vanya sings a song, and Susanin comments on Russia's present happy state. He goes on to say that he hears rumours that the Poles are planning to capture the young Tsar. Vanya and Susanin look forward to the day when the boy will be old enough to take his place among Russia's soldiers. Peasants enter to congratulate Antonida and Sobinin on their wedding, and a quartet follows for Antonida, Vanya, Sobinin, and Susanin.

In the middle of the rejoicing Polish troops enter and try to force Susanin to tell them the way to the monastery where the Tsar lives. Susanin at first refuses, but then manages to convey to Vanya that he must ride ahead to warn the Tsar while Susanin himself leads the Poles out of their way. He pretends to accept their bribe, and goes off with them much to the despair of Antonida, who comes in just in time to see her father taken away.

She tells Sobinin of the disaster which has come upon them; he does his best to console her, and gathers together a band of peasants whom he leads in an attempt to rescue Susanin.

Act IV. A forest, at night. Sobinin's men are disheartened by the intense cold, but in a vigorous aria he restores their confidence. Glinka composed an alternative version for this scene, and set it in the forest near the monastery. Vanya, who has ridden his horse to death, rushes in, knocks at the monastery doors and convinces the servants of the danger which threatens the Tsar's life.

The scene changes to another part of the forest. Everything is covered in snow, and the Poles accuse Susanin of having lost the way. He denies it, and they light a fire before settling down to rest for the night. Susanin is left alone, and in a famous scene he makes up his mind that it is his duty to give his life for his country. A storm blows up, the Poles awake, and Susanin tells them that he has led them astray into the

---

[1] Glinka originally called his opera *Ivan Susanin* and changed it only after prompting from the Imperial Court to *A Life for the Tsar*. In Soviet Russia (though not invariably outside) the original title was used.

wildest part of the forest; the Tsar is safe and beyond their reach. They kill him.

Epilogue. A street in Moscow. Everyone is festively dressed and they sing the praises of the Tsar. Antonida, Vanya and Sobinin join the crowd. The news of Susanin's death has reached the capital, and the crowd shares the grief of his dependants.

The scene changes to a square in front of the Kremlin. The Tsar's procession enters the capital.   H.

RUSSLAN AND LYUDMILA

Opera in five acts, text after Pushkin. Première at St Petersburg, 9 December 1842.

Svietosar, *Prince of Kiev*	Bass
Lyudmila, *his daughter*	Soprano
Russlan	Baritone
Ratmir, *an oriental prince*	Contralto
Farlaf, *a warrior*	Bass
Gorislava, *Ratmir's slave*	Soprano
Finn, *a good fairy*	Tenor
Naina, *a bad fairy*	Mezzo-Soprano
Bayan, *a Bard*	Tenor
Tchernomor, *an evil dwarf*	Silent

Place: Russia
Time: Antiquity
Running Time: 3 hours 15 minutes

Glinka's second opera is based on one of Pushkin's early dramatic poems. The poet had already agreed to prepare a dramatic version of his fairy tale when he was killed in a duel. As a result, no fewer than five different librettists worked on the opera and Glinka wrote much of the music before having any words to set. The opera was a considerable success at first but it was soon superseded by the Italian operas enjoyed by the Tsar, and Glinka left Russia totally disillusioned.

The overture is a brilliant piece, based partly on the music of the last act's finale and partly on the theme of Russlan's aria in the third scene of the second act.

Act I. Svietosar is entertaining the suitors of his daughter Lyudmila – Russlan, whom he and she prefer; Ratmir, an oriental prince; and Farlaf, a cowardly warrior. The bard Bayan prophesies wonders in the future in connection with Lyudmila and Russlan, and Lyudmila herself welcomes her suitors and sings of her reluctance to leave her own home where she has been so happy. Russlan is quite obviously the favoured suitor but a loud clap of thunder interrupts music and drama alike, and when darkness gives way to light, Lyudmila has disappeared. After a canon for Lyudmila's father and her three suitors, Svietosar promises her hand in marriage to whoever succeeds in rescuing her.

Act II. The first scene takes place in the cave of Finn, the wizard, to whom Russlan has come for advice. Finn tells him the abduction is the work of Tchernomor, the dwarf, and warns him against the interference of Naina, a wicked fairy.

The next scene shows Farlaf in consultation with Naina, who encourages him to overcome his natural cowardice. He sings his famous Rondo, a brilliant patter song whose indebtedness to Italian models is as obvious as is its own ancestry of Varlaam's song in *Boris Godunov*.

Russlan is found on a battlefield, strewn with spears, helmets, shields and swords. He muses on the silent field, where perhaps he will die, then sings exultantly of his beloved Lyudmila. The mist clears and he sees a gigantic head, which by its superhuman breathing creates a storm. The head is represented musically by a chorus, but Russlan subdues it with a single stroke of his lance. He finds the magic sword which will make him victorious over Tchernomor and the head explains that it belonged to the brother of that evil dwarf, whom Russlan with the aid of the sword will now be able to behead.

Act III. The enchanted palace of Naina. Here the oriental atmosphere and the magic dances provide Glinka with his most dramatically compact and therefore musically cogent section in an opera which can easily appear disjointed.

Naina's Persian girls sing enticingly before Gorislava, languishing for love of Ratmir, sings a cavatina. Ratmir himself, exhausted after his long journey, with cor anglais demonstrates in a beautiful aria that his erotic inclinations, given that Lyudmila is no longer likely to be his, are easily aroused by the harem in Naina's palace. The girls dance – a well contrasted series of several movements – and even the reappearance of Gorislava does not at first distract his attention.

The arrival of Russlan, still intent on finding Tchernomor and rescuing Lyudmila, provides a distraction and at first it is quite evident that he is far from immune to Gorislava's charms. Ratmir continues to hesitate, Gorislava to pine, but the appearance of Finn causes the Persian girls to disappear, the castle to turn into a forest, and the act ends with a fine quartet in which all, even Gorislava, assert their determination to deliver Lyudmila from her captivity.

Act IV. Tchernomor's magic garden on the borders of a lake. Lyudmila in an aria refuses to be consoled by any distraction but she is soothed to sleep before a band of musicians and Tchernomor's serfs enter in procession, with the old dwarf finally carried in on cushions by black slaves. Dances (described as Turkish, Arabian, and Caucasian) are performed for his delectation before a trumpet announces the imminent arrival of Russlan. He is victorious over Tchernomor but fails, even with the assistance of Gorislava and Ratmir, to rouse Lyudmila.

Act V. Ratmir's romance testifies to his love for Gorislava and when slaves bring the news that Lyudmila has again been abducted and Russlan has disappeared in pursuit, only the intervention of Finn with the offer of a magic ring breaks the impasse.

Back in Svietosar's castle, Lyudmila lies asleep, having apparently been brought there by Farlaf who is quite unable to wake her. This however Russlan, with the aid of the magic ring, succeeds in doing and he joins with Gorislava, Ratmir, Svietosar and the courtiers in the music which began the overture and now provides a brilliant finale. H.

CHRISTOPH WILLIBALD GLUCK
(born 2 July 1714, died 15 November 1787)

Gluck was an Austrian composer of Bohemian parentage, who studied in Prague and Italy and wrote his first operas for Milan, Venice and London ('Gluck knows no more counterpoint than my cook, Waltz' famously, but maybe apocryphally, opined Handel, neglecting to say that his cook was a trained musician) before settling in Vienna, where he wrote for the court. Encouraged by the Viennese impresario Count Durazzo, after 1761 he became identified as the leader of a move to reform opera, producing in succession for the Court Opera *Orfeo ed Euridice* (1762), *Alceste* (1767) and *Paride ed Elena* (1770).

When he became active in Paris, the Italian composer Nicola Piccinni was set up in opposition (1772), but Gluck held an important court card in the person of Queen Marie Antoinette, the Austrian princess who had been his pupil in Vienna. Piccinni's work was no match for that of the Viennese, whose achievement with hindsight can be seen as both more and less than the claims made for it in Gluck's manifesto – his 1769 preface to the published edition of *Alceste* sets out his precepts. *Orfeo* is a model of classical integrity, put forward with a marmoreal correctness which in no way precludes dramatic fervour; *Alceste* and *Iphigénie en Aulide* carry the movement forward in not dissimilar vein; *Paride ed Elena* and, even more, *Armide*, add passion and fantasy to the earlier classicism; and *Iphigénie en Tauride* rounds out the picture – a work of classical proportions imbued with sufficient romantic fervour to cause many to claim it as his masterpiece. That *Echo et Narcisse* was a failure in Paris in 1779 sent him back disillusioned to Vienna, where in 1781 his last operatic venture, a German reworking of *Iphigénie en Tauride*, ended his theatrical career with a resounding success.

ORFEO ED EURIDICE
Orpheus and Eurydice

Opera in three acts, libretto by Ranieri da Calzabigi. Productions and revivals: Vienna, 5 October 1762, in Italian, with Guadagni as Orfeo; Paris, as *Orphée et Eurydice*, with Legros, the tenor, as Orphée, 1774, in French; London, 1770, with Guadagni. Berlioz's revision of the opera was first heard in 1859 in Paris, with Pauline Viardot-Garcia in the title role; New York, 1863 (in English).

Famous revivals: Covent Garden, 1890, with Giulia and Sofia Ravogli; Metropolitan, New York, 1909, with Homer (later Delna) and Gadski under Toscanini; Covent Garden, 1920, with Clara Butt and Miriam Licette under Beecham; Metropolitan, 1938 and 1941, with Thorborg and Jessner (later Novotna) under Bodanzky (later Walter); Glyndebourne, 1947, with Kathleen Ferrier; Salzburg Festival, 1948, with Höngen, 1959, with Simionato, both conducted by Karajan; Covent Garden, 1953, with Kathleen Ferrier.

A summary of the different versions of *Orfeo* may be useful. In effect, Gluck composed the opera twice: for Vienna in 1762, and for Paris in 1774. Each version was written for a male hero, in Vienna for the contralto castrato Guadagni, in Paris for the tenor Legros. The 1762 version is short (about 90 minutes) and dates from *before* Gluck's conscious attempt at reforming opera (the famous manifesto forms the preface to the 1769 printing of *Alceste*,[1] whose première in 1767 provided the first hearing of a reform opera). The 1774 recomposition retains the old material while adding much that is new, and gives Orfeo himself bravura music ranging up to a D. The 1762 version was produced at Drottningholm and brought by that company with Kerstin Meyer in the title role to the 1972 Brighton Festival, but most modern revivals which claim to be of the original version in fact retain the 1762 score, recitatives and all, but slyly incorporate the most famous of the 1774 additions. The 1774 Paris version has been frequently revived, usually with some discreet transposition, notably at Sadler's Wells in 1967, and at the Paris Opéra in 1973 to inaugurate the Liebermann regime. The first attempt at a compromise between the two versions was made by Berlioz (with the help of Saint-Saëns) in 1859 for Pauline Viardot. Then, the 1774 version was used, but the tenor role of Orfeo was transposed to fit a female alto voice. (One example of the transmogrification of key and therefore *tessitura*: 'Che farò' in 1762 was in C major, in 1774 in F, in 1859 in C, and at Sadler's Wells in 1967 in E flat!)   H.

Orfeo (Orpheus) ....Contralto

Euridice (Eurydice) ....Soprano

Amor, *God of Love* ....Soprano

A Happy Shade...Soprano

Shepherds and Shepherdesses, Furies and Demons, Heroes and Heroines in Hades

Running Time: 1 hour 55 minutes

Act I. Following a brief and solemn prelude, the curtain rises to show a grotto with the tomb of Euridice. The beautiful bride of Orfeo has died. Her husband and friends mourn at her tomb. During an affecting aria and chorus ('Chiamo il mio ben così'[2]) funeral honours are paid to the dead bride. A second orchestra, behind the scenes, echoes, with moving effect, the distracted husband's cries to his bride, until, in answer to the piercing cries, Amor appears. He tells the bereaved husband that Zeus has taken pity on him. He shall have permission to go down into Hades and endeavour to propitiate Pluto and his minions solely through the power of his music. But, should he rescue Euridice, he must on no account look back at her until he has crossed the Styx.

Upon that condition, so difficult to fulfil because of the love of Orfeo for his bride, turns the whole story. For should he, in answer to her pleading, look back, or explain to her why he cannot do so, she will immediately die. But Orfeo, confident in his power of song and in his ability to stand the test imposed by Zeus and bring his beloved Euridice back to earth, receives the message with great joy.

'Fulfil with joy the will of the gods', sings Amor, and Orfeo, having implored the aid of the deities, departs for the Nether World.

Act II. Entrance to Hades. When Orfeo appears, he is greeted with threats by the Furies. The scene, beginning with the Chorus, 'Chi mai dell'Erebo?' is a masterpiece of dramatic music. The Furies call upon Cerberus, the triple-headed dog monster that guards the entrance to the Nether World, to tear in pieces the mortal who so daringly approaches, and the bark of the monster is reproduced in the score. What lifts the scene to its thrilling climax is the infuriated 'No!' which is hurled at Orfeo by the dwellers at the entrance to Hades, when, having recourse to song, he tells of his love for Euridice and his grief over her death and begs to be allowed to seek her. The sweetness of his music wins the sympathy of the Furies. They allow him to enter the Valley of the Blest, a beautiful spot where the good spirits in Hades find rest, a state that is uniquely expressed in their slow dance with its famous flute solo. Euridice (or a Happy Spirit)[3] and her companions sing of their bliss in the Elysian Fields: 'E quest'asilo ameno e grato'. Orfeo comes seeking Euridice. His peaceful aria (with its oboe obbligato) 'Che puro ciel' is answered by a chorus of Happy Shades. To him they bring the lovely Euridice. Orfeo, beside himself with joy but remem-

---

[1] See page 264.
[2] The original Italian words are here used, although it is the French version, moreover in Berlioz's edition, which is described. The only logic behind such a decision involves the fact that the opera was originally in Italian, and that something like Berlioz's edition is most likely to be heard.

[3] As to whether Euridice or another singer should be entrusted with this aria, Edward Dent wrote: 'Managers never realise that Euridice in Act III is a highly sexed person, and wants conjugal rights at once, whereas the Happy Spirit is clearly quite devoid of all human instincts. It is almost impossible to find one singer who can express both these things.'

bering the warning of Amor, takes his bride by the hand and, with averted gaze, leads her from the vale.

Act III. She cannot understand his action. He seeks to soothe her injured feelings (duet: 'Sù, e con me vieni, o cara'). But his efforts are in vain; nor can he offer her any explanation, for he has also been forbidden to make known to her the reason for his apparent indifference. She cannot comprehend why he does not even cast a glance upon her and protests in a passionate aria and duet, 'Che fiero momento', that without his love she prefers to die.

Orfeo, no longer able to resist the appeal of his beloved bride, forgets the warning of Amor. He turns and passionately clasps Euridice in his arms. Immediately she dies. It is then that Orfeo intones the lament, 'Che farò senza Euridice', that air in the score which has truly become immortal. In fact it is so beautiful that Amor, affected by the grief of Orfeo, appears to him, touches Euridice and restores her to life and to her husband's arms.

The role of Orfeo was written for the celebrated male contralto Gaetano Guadagni. For the Paris production the composer transposed the part of Orfeo for the tenor Legros, for whom he introduced a vocal number entirely out of keeping with the role[1] – a bravura aria which for a long while was erroneously ascribed to the obscure Italian composer Ferdinando Bertoni. It is believed that the tenor importuned Gluck for something that would show off his voice, whereupon the composer handed him the air. Legros introduced it at the end of the first act, where to this day it remains in the printed score. When the tenor Nourrit sang the role many years later, he substituted the far more appropriate aria 'O transport, ô désordre extrême', from Gluck's own *Echo et Narcisse*. It may be of interest to note that, for the revival which he conducted at the Metropolitan in 1910, Toscanini introduced the aria 'Divinités du Styx' (from Gluck's *Alceste*) into the scene in Hades.

Einstein sums up: '*Orfeo ed Euridice* marked an epoch not only in Gluck's work, but in the whole of operatic history. Here for the first time is an opera without *recitativo secco* ... here for the first time was a work so closely grown together with its text that it was unique and could not be composed again. ... An opera at last whose manner of performance required the composer's supervision, the first opera that culminated in the musician's labour!'   K., H.

ALCESTE
Alcestis

Opera in three acts, text by Ranieri da Calzabigi. Première at the Burgtheater, Vienna, 26 December 1767, with Antonia Bernasconi (Alceste), Giuseppe Tibaldi (Admète), Laschi (High Priest and Voice of Apollo), in Italian. Produced in Paris in a revised version, 23 April 1776, with Mlle Levasseur, and sung in French. First performance in London, King's Theatre, 1795 (in Italian). Important revivals include Florence Festival, 1935 (in Italian) under Gui, with Gina Cigna, Nicola Rakowski and Benvenuto Franci; at Covent Garden, 1937, in French, under Gaubert, with Lubin, Jouatte and Martial Singher; at the Metropolitan, New York, 1941 (in French), under Panizza, with Marjorie Lawrence, René Maison and Leonard Warren, and in 1952 (in English) with Flagstad; at Glyndebourne, 1953, with Laszlo; at la Scala, Milan, 1954, with Callas, conductor Giulini; 1974, Edinburgh Festival, with Julia Varady, conductor Alexander Gibson; 1983, Covent Garden, with Janet Baker, conductor Mackerras.

Admète (Admetus)	Tenor
Alceste (Alcestis)	Soprano
High Priest	Baritone
Hercule (Hercules)	Baritone
Evandre (Evander)	Tenor
Thanatos	Baritone
Voice of Apollo	Baritone
Herald	Baritone
Leaders of the People	Soprano, Mezzo-Soprano, Baritone
A Woman	Soprano

Place: Ancient Thebes
Running Time: 2 hours 10 minutes

Gluck goes down to history as a reformer, who turned from a capable practitioner of the art of opera as currently practised to a zealot for unadorned dramatic truth. Einstein has suggested that the normal eighteenth-century method of reform being by means of satire and parody, and Gluck being constitutionally unfitted to this medium or to that of *opera buffa*, he was obliged to become the first

---

[1] So it may once have been thought, but tastes change and Kathleen Ferrier, with John Barbirolli conducting, did not scorn to include it and indeed made a great hit with it in what turned out to be her last operatic appearance; Janet Baker at Glyndebourne did no less in hers.

critical creator in opera's history if he was to express his thoughts on the subject; he had no other 'safety valve'. His preface to *Alceste* (1769) is one of the most famous documents in the annals of opera, and it is reproduced here in the translation of Eric Blom (which occurs in his translation of Einstein's biography of Gluck in Dent's 'Master Musicians' Series):

'When I undertook to write the music for *Alceste*, I resolved to divest it entirely of all those abuses, introduced into it either by the mistaken vanity of singers or by the too great complaisance of composers, which have so long disfigured Italian opera and made of the most splendid and most beautiful of spectacles the most ridiculous and wearisome. I have striven to restrict music to its true office of serving poetry by means of expression and by following the situations of the story, without interrupting the action or stifling it with a useless superfluity of ornaments; and I believed that it should do this in the same way as telling colours affect a correct and well-ordered drawing, by a well-assorted contrast of light and shade, which serves to animate the figures without altering their contours. Thus I did not wish to arrest an actor in the greatest heat of dialogue in order to wait for a tiresome *ritornello*, nor to hold him up in the middle of a word on a vowel favourable to his voice, nor to make display of the agility of his fine voice in some long-drawn passage, nor to wait while the orchestra gives him time to recover his breath for a cadenza. I did not think it my duty to pass quickly over the second section of an aria of which the words are perhaps the most impassioned and important, in order to repeat regularly four times over those of the first part, and to finish the aria where its sense may perhaps not end for the convenience of the singer who wishes to show that he can capriciously vary a passage in a number of guises; in short, I have sought to abolish all the abuses against which good sense and reason have long cried out in vain.

'I have felt that the overture ought to apprise the spectators of the nature of the action that is to be represented and to form, so to speak, its argument; that the concerted instruments should be introduced in proportion to the interest and intensity of the words, and not leave that sharp contrast between the aria and the recitative in the dialogue, so as not to break a period unreasonably nor wantonly disturb the force and heat of the action.

'Furthermore, I believed that my greatest labour should be devoted to seeking a beautiful simplicity, and I have avoided making displays of difficulty at the expense of clearness; nor did I judge it desirable to discover novelties if it was not naturally suggested by the situation and the expression; and there is no rule which I have not thought it right to set aside willingly for the sake of an intended effect.

'Such are my principles. By good fortune my designs were wonderfully furthered by the libretto, in which the celebrated author, devising a new dramatic scheme, had substituted for florid descriptions, unnatural paragons and sententious, cold morality, heartfelt language, strong passions, interesting situations and an endlessly varied spectacle. The success of the work justified my maxims, and the universal approbation of so enlightened a city has made it clearly evident that simplicity, truth and naturalness are the great principles of beauty in all artistic manifestations. For all that, in spite of repeated urgings, on the part of some most eminent persons to decide upon the publication of this opera of mine in print, I was well aware of all the risk run in combating such firmly and profoundly rooted prejudices, and I thus felt the necessity of fortifying myself with the most powerful patronage of Your Royal Highness[1] whose August Name I beg you may have the grace to prefix to this my opera, a name which with so much justice enjoys the suffrages of an enlightened Europe. The great protector of the fine arts, who reigns over a nation that had the glory of making them rise again from universal oppression and which itself has produced the greatest models, in a city that was always the first to shake off the yoke of vulgar prejudices in order to clear a path for perfection, may alone undertake the reform of that noble spectacle in which all the fine arts take so great a share. If this should succeed, the glory of having moved the first stone will remain for me, and in this public testimonial of Your Highness's furtherance of the same, I have the honour to subscribe myself, with the most humble respect,

'Your Royal Highness's most humble, most devoted and most obliged servant,

      'CHRISTOFORO GLUCK.'

This summary and the cast list refer to the Paris

---

[1] Leopold, Duke of Tuscany, who, on the death of Joseph II, was to become Emperor Leopold II.

version of *Alceste*, almost as much a recomposition of the opera as was the Paris version of *Orfeo*.

Calzabigi has not followed the lines of Euripides' tragedy, where the role of Admetus is an inglorious one, and the intervention of Hercules due to his desire to abide by the laws of hospitality, not to any motive of pity for the sorry plight of Alcestis and Admetus.

Act I. A magnificently sombre overture fully vindicates Gluck's avowed intention as set forth in the preface; here indeed is the argument of the action. The scene represents a great court in front of the palace of Admetus; at the back can be seen the temple of Apollo. The people crowd into the courtyard and mourn the illness of their King, which, the herald tells them, is likely to prove fatal. Evander announces the entrance of Alcestis, and the Queen appears flanked by her two children. She laments the prospect in front of her children, soon to be fatherless, and bids the crowd come with her to the temple, there to offer sacrifice to the gods.

In the temple of Apollo, we hear first a simple tune, designated 'Pantomime' in the score, which may serve as background for a dance as well as for the entrance of Alcestis. The High Priest and the chorus call upon the god to avert the fate which is about to overtake Admetus, and, through him, his wife and his people. Alcestis adds her prayer, and a sacrifice is prepared, to the music of another 'Pantomime'. The High Priest, in music that grows more and more awe-inspiring, invokes the god and commands the people to be silent to hear the Oracle's judgement. When it comes, it is more terrible than they had expected: Admetus must die, unless a friend can be found to die in his stead. The people lament the harsh pronouncement and rush from the temple in fear, leaving Alcestis and the High Priest alone. Alcestis comes to understand the reality of the situation and resolves to die for her husband, without whom she cannot live. 'Non, ce n'est point un sacrifice', she sings in an aria of noble simplicity. The High Priest tells her that her prayer is granted and she has the rest of the day to prepare herself for the advent of death.

In an aria which has become the most famous of the opera, Alcestis invokes the gods of the underworld and defies them to do their worst. 'Divinités du Styx' is Gluck at his most intense, justifying his own maxims as regards the situation, but with a result that is no less impressive as music than as drama.

Act II. In a great hall of his palace, Admetus stands to receive the congratulations of his people, headed by Evander, on his apparently miraculous recovery. Dances are performed in his honour. The King enquires what brought about his recovery, and Evander tells him the condition imposed by the Oracle but does not name the victim. The King is horror-stricken and refuses to accept such a sacrifice. Alcestis joins him and shares his joy that they are reunited. The chorus of praise and rejoicing continues, but Alcestis is quite unable to hide the grief she feels as the moment draws near when she must leave her husband and her children for ever. Admetus tries to comfort her in a *da capo* aria of great beauty, 'Bannis la crainte et les alarmes', but to no avail. The Queen avows her love, but finally admits that it is she the gods are taking in place of Admetus. Dramatically, he refuses to accept the sacrifice: 'Non, sans toi, je ne puis vivre'. Alcestis is left alone with the people, and, as they mourn for her grief, sings 'Ah, malgré moi, mon faible coeur partage vos tendres pleurs'.

Act III. The courtyard of the palace. The people are mourning the deaths of both Alcestis and of Admetus, who has followed her. Hercules arrives, rejoicing that his labours are over, but Evander informs him of the death of his friend Admetus, and of the circumstances surrounding it, and he swears to restore their King and Queen to the people of Greece.

The scene changes to the gates of Hell. Alcestis pleads with the gods of Hell (who remain invisible) that her torment be not prolonged, that she be received at once. Admetus joins her, asking only to be reunited with her in death. He reminds her of her duty to their children, but their duet is interrupted by the voice of Thanatos announcing that the time has come for one of them to offer themselves to Death; the choice is left to Alcestis as to which of the two it shall be. Alcestis will not renounce her right to die for her husband, and the choice appears to have been made, much to the grief of Admetus, when Hercules appears on the scene, determined to deprive the underworld of its prey. He and Admetus defy Hell and its rulers and fight to rescue Alcestis. At the moment of their success, Apollo appears, and announces to Hercules that his action has won him the right to a place among the gods themselves, while Admetus and Alcestis are to be restored to earth, there to serve as a universal example of the power of conjugal love.

The scene changes to the palace court, and Apollo bids the people rejoice that their King and Queen are restored to them. Alcestis, Admetus, and Hercules join in a trio, and the opera ends with rejoicing.

More perhaps than any other of the operas of his maturity, *Alceste* illustrates the ideal of 'beautiful simplicity' which Gluck's preface tells us is his aim. Berlioz's admiration for the temple scene is well known, but Ernest Newman quotes this composer's detailed objection to the changes made in what we now know as 'Divinités du Styx' when the opera was translated from Italian, changes which ruined the beginning of the aria, according to Berlioz. Ironically, when an Italian soprano now sings this aria, she will use an Italian translation of the French translation of the original Italian, and of course employ the musical form of the French version! It should be noted that the original score included a scene in a gloomy forest near Pherae at the beginning of the second act, omitted in the French version, which begins with the festivities attending the recovery of Admetus. The third act, while employing much of the music of the original, is entirely altered dramatically, and, says Ernest Newman, distinctly for the worse. Du Roullet's[1] introduction of Hercules has, according to Newman, a vulgarising effect, and only the new scene at the gates of Hell (the entire act originally took place in the courtyard of the palace, where Alcestis died, Admetus tried to commit suicide, and a happy ending was provided by the appearance of Apollo) constitutes a worthwhile addition to the score as it stood.   H.

PARIDE ED ELENA

Paris and Helen

Opera in five acts, libretto by Raniero di Calzabigi. Première in Vienna, 3 November 1779, with Katherina Schindler as Helen and Giuseppe Millico as Paris. Success was limited, with only twenty-five performances reported in Vienna before 1800. First performed in Naples 1777, then forgotten until 1901 when it was revived in Prague. Modern performances have been uncommon.

Paride (Paris), *son of King*
   Priam of Troy...............................Soprano Castrato
Elena (Helen), *Queen of Sparta*........................Soprano
Cupid, *under the name of Erasto,*
   Helen's confidant ....Soprano
Pallas Athene, *the goddess*.............................Soprano
A Trojan ....Soprano

Place: Sparta
Time: Just before the Start of the Trojan War
Running Time: 1 hour 40 minutes

*P*aride ed Elena is the last of Gluck's Italian works, written for Vienna in the line of his so-called 'reform' operas. That it is a curious work, concentrating throughout its five acts on Helen's wooing by Paris and without a hint of drama, let alone tragedy, accounts for its relative lack of success through more than two hundred years. On the other hand, with its contrast between Spartan rigour on the one hand and Asiatic hedonism on the other, it is one of the composer's more notable musical achievements, of which he was justly proud. Moreover, there is great passion in the final two acts.

Act I. The seashore near Sparta. Paris has heard that Helen is the most beautiful woman in the world, as he makes clear in two exceptionally graceful arias, separated by dances: 'O del mio dolce ardor' and 'Spiagge amate', the first regularly recorded by sopranos, mezzos, tenors, even baritones throughout the twentieth century. Erasto comes to spy out the lie of the land and in soliloquy avows he will help Paris win Helen. The act ends with an extended dance.

Act II. The royal palace. Helen admires Paris as much as he does her and Erasto encourages their mutual admiration. Paris pins his hopes on Venus ('Le belle imagini').

Act III. Paris is invited to judge the winners in a Spartan version of the Olympic games, but confesses in a fervent scene (*Orfeo*-like, with its harp accompaniment) that he has eyes only for Helen. When she urges her virtue and loyalty, he thinks the gods have betrayed him, and seems to fall in a faint. The festivities nonetheless continue.

Act IV. Helen asserts that she remains loyal, but Erasto acts as intermediary between her and Paris, who pleads his love. In the trio, full of urgency, Erasto echoes Amor in *Orfeo* (even to the earlier opera's hint of 'John Peel'). Paris reacts to Helen's suggestion he should forget her in an aria of real

---

[1] Lebland du Roullet was responsible for the French translation and some adjustments in 1776.

feeling ('Di te scordami e vivere!'); this is no philandering prince but a youth overcome by love. Helen alone follows with a splendid aria – her first of the opera – full of indecision as well as passion, but the situation, minutely examined in the course of the act, remains unresolved at its end.

Act V. The palace gardens. Paris is about to leave but Erasto tells Helen his own misgivings on the subject of the imminent departure, and announces when Paris appears that Helen truly loves him. He is revealed as Cupid, Venus' son, but the situation moves beyond his control when Pallas Athene with theocratic authority proclaims that the love of Paris and Helen will lead to much suffering. They bow to their destiny and the opera's only love duet, slightly formal in expression and joined by Erasto, leads to the finale.   H.

IPHIGÉNIE EN AULIDE

Iphigenia in Aulis

Opera in three acts, text by Lebland du Roullet. First performed at the Académie de Musique, Paris, 19 April 1774, with Sophie Arnould (Iphigénie), du Plant (Clitemnestre), Legros (Achille), Larrivée (Agamemnon).

In 1846 Wagner revised the opera, changing the orchestration, re-writing some of the recitatives. This version, produced at Dresden in 1847, was given on many German stages. There was a famous revival under Mahler in Vienna in 1904 with Gutheil-Schoder, Mildenburg, Schmedes and Demuth. The opera was heard in England for the first time as late as 1933 (at Oxford) and in 1937 (Glasgow). First American performance 1935, in Philadelphia, conducted by Alexander Smallens, and sung by Rosa Tentoni, Cyrena van Gordon, Joseph Bentonelli, and George Baklanoff. Revived at Florence Festival of 1950 (in the Boboli Gardens), with Guerrini, Nicolai, Penno, and Christoff; and at la Scala, Milan, in 1959, with Simionato, Lazzarini, Pier Miranda Ferraro, Christoff; New York (concert performance), 1962, with Gorr, Marilyn Horne, Simoneau, Bacquier; Salzburg, 1962, with Christa Ludwig, Borkh, King, Berry, conductor Böhm; Drottningholm (Sweden), 1965, with Elisabeth Söderström in the title role; 1996, Opera North, in Leeds.

Agamemnon, *King of Mycenae* .... Bass-Baritone

Clitemnestre (Clytemnestra), *his wife* .... Soprano

Iphigénie (Iphigenia), *their daughter* .... Soprano

Achille (Achilles), *a Greek hero* .... Tenor

Patrocle (Patroclus) .... Bass

Calchas, *the High Priest* .... Bass

Arcas .... Bass

Diane (Diana) .... Soprano

Chorus of Priests, People

Place: The Island of Aulis
Time: The Beginning of the Trojan War
Running Time: 2 hours 30 minutes

*I*phigénie en Aulide was Gluck's first opera written originally to a French text, and its success was immediate. He insisted, contemporaries record, on the distinguished French cast throwing themselves into the drama of their roles, and the opera has kept a hold however precarious on the repertory ever since. Wagner's 1847 revision amounted in certain passages to no less than a recomposition; it was this version Mahler mounted in 1904.

Act I. Agamemnon, after consulting the oracle, has vowed to sacrifice his daughter, Iphigenia, to Diana in return for a favourable wind to take him and his army safely to Troy. He is persuaded to send for his daughter, on the pretext that her marriage to Achilles shall be solemnised in Aulis. He secretly sends word to his wife, Clytemnestra, telling her to delay the voyage as the marriage has been postponed. When the opera opens, Agamemnon is seen a prey to agonising remorse, and torn by the conflicting claims of duty and love. The Greeks demand to know the reason for the gods' continued displeasure, and Calchas, the high priest, is filled with sorrow at the thought of the sacrifice that is demanded. He prays to the goddess to find another victim, Agamemnon joins him in prayer, and the Greeks demand the name of the victim that they may immediately make the sacrifice the goddess demands. Calchas assures them that the victim shall be found that very day.

Calchas reasons with Agamemnon in an effort to persuade him to agree to the sacrifice, but the Greek King breaks out into an agonised expression of his overwhelming sorrow. Is it possible that the gods wish him to commit so dreadful a crime? Calchas asks him if his intention is to go against his oath, but Agamemnon replies that he has sworn to sacrifice Iphigenia only if she sets foot on the soil of Aulis. At that very moment, and in the midst of Calchas' denunciation of the King's duplicity, they hear the cries of the Greeks as they welcome Clytemnestra and Iphigenia, newly arrived on the island. As the King and the High Priest comment on the possible consequences of the arrival, the Greeks sing the praises of the Queen and her daughter. Agamemnon secretly informs his wife that Achilles has proved unworthy of Iphigenia and that she and her daughter are therefore to return immediately on their journey. She denounces Achilles to Iphigenia, who is ready to believe her until Achilles himself appears on the scene, overjoyed at her unexpected arrival. Iphigenia is at first cold and unwelcoming, but explanations follow and the act ends with a duet of reconciliation.

Act II. In spite of the chorus's attempts at reassurance and congratulation on her forthcoming marriage, Iphigenia is filled with foreboding at the prospect of a meeting between Agamemnon and Achilles who by now knows that his prospective father-in-law was responsible for the rumour of his infidelity to Iphigenia. Clytemnestra bids her daughter rejoice, Achilles, after introducing the warrior Patroclus to her, leads a chorus in her praise, and songs and dances are offered in honour of the happy couple. As Achilles is about to lead his bride to the altar, Arcas, Agamemnon's messenger, intervenes and protests that Agamemnon waits at the altar to sacrifice her in fulfilment of his sacred vow. Clytemnestra begs Achilles to protect his young bride from the consequences of her father's rash action. Achilles impulsively swears to defend her, but Iphigenia reminds him that Agamemnon is her father, and that she loves him in spite of the terrible situation in which fate has placed him.

Agamemnon and Achilles meet, and, in answer to Achilles' reproaches, Agamemnon reminds him that he is supreme commander of the Greek forces and that all owe allegiance to him and obedience to his decisions. Achilles defies him and says that whoever means to lay hands on Iphigenia will have to overcome him first. Agamemnon is left alone with his conscience and the necessity to decide between his duty to the gods and his love for his daughter. In the end he decides to send Clytemnestra and Iphigenia straight away to Mycenae, and by this means he hopes to avoid the consequences of his oath.

Act III. The Greeks demand that the vow shall be fulfilled as the only means by which the present wrath of the gods may be averted. Achilles begs Iphigenia to fly with him, but she protests her willingness to die, he his determination to save her. Clytemnestra is left alone with her daughter, and tries every means to save her, but the Greeks are implacable in their demand that the sacrifice shall

take place. Clytemnestra calls down the fury of Jove on the cruel hosts of the Greeks.

All is ready for the sacrifice and the Greeks beg for an answer to their prayer. The ceremony is interrupted by the arrival of Achilles at the head of the Thessalians, who fall on the assembled Greek troops. A pitched battle is averted by Calchas, who announces that the gods are appeased and prepared to grant fair weather even though Agamemnon's oath is not fulfilled. Husband and wife, parent and child, lover and beloved are reconciled and the opera ends with rejoicings as the Greeks prepare to set sail for Troy.

Although *Iphigénie en Aulide* has not quite the unity of style and construction that is so marked a feature of the later *Iphigénie en Tauride*, it is full of remarkable music. The leading figures are strongly characterised. Agamemnon is never less than a heroic figure, and the conflict which is the result of his vow makes him the most interesting character in the drama. His arias are magnificently expressive, that of the first act ('Diane impitoyable') immediately establishing his commanding stature and essential nobility as well as the appalling dilemma he sees before him, the great *scena* at the end of the second act (after the scene with Achilles) even more impressively dramatic ('O toi, l'objet le plus aimable'). Clytemnestra is less positively involved in the drama, but her intense reaction to its events is expressed in wonderfully dramatic music. In her solo scenes, she passes from straightforward fury when she hears from Agamemnon of Achilles' supposed unfaithfulness to Iphigenia, through the extremes of grief when she pleads with Achilles to save her daughter, until in the third act she collapses altogether when her pleas to the Greeks go unheeded. The intensity of her emotions is immediately apparent, and one can imagine that such musical expressiveness must have made an extraordinary effect in Gluck's time.

Like Ilia in *Idomeneo*, Iphigenia is the victim rather than the agent of the tragedy, but her resignation and acceptance of her cruel fate gives rise to music of remarkable beauty. Achilles is the ancestor of Radames and a whole line of heroic tenors, uncomplicated as a person and accustomed to express himself vigorously and uncompromisingly. His aria in Act III when he resolves to save Iphigenia by force of arms apparently made an effect at the first performance comparable to that felt by Italian audiences hearing

Verdi's music at the time of the Risorgimento. We are told that the gentlemen in the theatre could hardly refrain from drawing their swords and joining him on stage in his attempt to rescue his Princess.   H.

ARMIDE

Opera in five acts, libretto by Philippe Quinault (originally written in 1686 for Lully). Quinault based his libretto on Tasso's *La Gerusalemme liberata*. Première, Paris, 23 September 1777, with Rosalie Levasseur, Joseph Legros (Gluck's tenor Orphée). Performed in Germany, notably in 1843 when it was heard in Berlin and Wagner conducted it in Dresden with Wilhelmine Schröder-Devrient in the title role. Revived in Paris in 1905 for Lucienne Bréval (Litvinne in 1907); it opened the season in 1911 at the Metropolitan, New York, with Toscanini conducting and Fremstad, Caruso, Homer and Amato in leading roles; and at la Scala the following year Serafin conducted it with Burzio in the title role. Heard at Covent Garden, 1928, with Frida Leider, Olszewszka, Walter Widdop, conductor Heger (in German); at Spitalfields, London, 1982, with Felicity Palmer and Anthony Rolfe Johnson. Only in Paris was it regularly in the repertory, with 399 performances between 1777 and 1913.

Armide, *a sorceress; Princess of Damascus*.......Soprano
Renaud, *a Crusader*..Tenor
Phénice ⎱ *confidantes of Armide* ....Soprano
Sidonie ⎰ ....Soprano
Hidraot, *a magician, King of Damascus*........... Baritone
Hate ....Contralto
The Danish Knight ⎱ *Crusaders* ....Tenor
Ubalde ⎰ ....Baritone
Aronte, *in charge of Armide's prisoners*...........Baritone
Artémidore, *a Crusader*.....................................Tenor
A Naiad...Soprano

Spirits, Demons, Soldiers, Citizens of Damascus, Nymphs, Shepherds

Place: Damascus
Time: The First Crusade
Running Time: 3 hours 10 minutes

For his fifth French opera Gluck boldly took over the text Lully had set some ninety years before, and set it to music almost unaltered. There is some truth in the contention that it is musically the richest of all his works, just as there is rationale behind its neglect at a time when its convention was as far from contemporary experience as was once Handel's. Though its première occurred at the height of the war of the Gluckists and the Piccinnists – roughly speaking, supporters of French and Italian music, but a war just as much literary and political as musical – its merits have little to do with that controversy, and it is interesting that Gluck in retirement (quoted by Max Loppert in a revealing sleeve note for the Spitalfields recording) wrote of *Armide* as 'perhaps the best of all my works'.

Act I. Sidonie and Phénice congratulate Armide on her triumph against the Crusaders but she is dissatisfied that the bravest of them, Renaud, is still free. When Hidraot, her uncle, urges her to marry, she says that she would consider only the man who vanquishes Renaud. Aronte announces that Renaud has freed all the prisoners she was holding. She calls for revenge.

Act II. Renaud and Artémidore (one of the prisoners Renaud freed) have been lured by magic into deserted country. Renaud is determined to resist the wiles of Armide, but Hidraot and Armide pursue him. He falls asleep under her spell – a beautiful aria precedes this episode ('Plus j'observe ces lieux'). Demons disguised as nymphs beguile him. As Armide raises a dagger to kill him, she understands that nothing but the power of love holds her back. To make him love her is the revenge she determines to take (aria: 'Ah! Quelle cruauté de lui ravir le jour!').

Act III. Although she is now secure in Renaud's love, Armide has failed to control her own feelings, as she admits in a magnificent monologue: 'Ah! si la liberté me doit être ravie'. Her destiny is to choose between love for Renaud and hatred and revenge, and she summons Hate to save her from her love. The impressive incantations of Hate and her entourage and their dances have the effect of confirming Armide's love. Hate curses her; let her never seek her help again.

Act IV. Ubalde and the Danish Knight have been commissioned to free Renaud. A magic shield and sceptre first protect them against Armide's demons and then keep them proof against visions conjured up to seduce them.

Act V. Armide's palace. In the only approach to a love scene in the opera, Armide tells Renaud he taught her to know love; now she feels he may be seduced by the pull of glory. When Armide leaves him in order to secure the aid of dark powers, the elaborate attempts of her retinue (chaconne and dance) fail to entertain Renaud, and Ubalde and the Danish Knight have no difficulty with the help of their talismanic shield and sceptre in breaking the spell which binds him. He resolves to return to his comrades and Armide comes back to find her worst fears realised. Renaud is torn between love and duty but, with some reluctance, embraces duty, and Armide, unable to decide whether to give way to despair or pursue revenge – a Dido before her time – eventually destroys her own palace and is carried off in a chariot.   H.

IPHIGÉNIE EN TAURIDE
Iphigenia in Tauris

Opera in four acts, words by François Guillard. Produced in the Académie de Musique, Paris, 18 May 1779, with Levasseur, Legros, Larrivée; London (in da Ponte's Italian translation), 1796; Metropolitan Opera House, New York, 25 November 1916, with Kurt, Sembach, Weil, Braun, and Rappold (in German, arranged Richard Strauss). Revived la Scala, 1937, with Caniglia, Parmeggiani, Armando Borgioli, Maugeri, conducted by de Sabata; Berlin, 1941, with Müller, Svanholm, Domgraf-Fassbänder, Ahlersmeyer; Aix, 1952, with Neway, Simoneau, Mollet, Massard, conductor Giulini; la Scala, 1957, with Callas; Edinburgh Festival and Covent Garden, 1961, with Gorr, conductor Solti; Holland Festival, 1964, with Brouwenstijn, Ilosfalvy, Přibyl,[1] conductor Erede; Opéra, Paris, 1965, with Crespin, Chauvet, Massard.

Iphigénie (Iphigenia), *Priestess of Diana* ....Soprano
Oreste (Orestes), *her brother*...........................Baritone
Pylade (Pylades), *his friend* ....Tenor
Thoas, *King of Scythia* ....Bass
Diane (Diana) ....Soprano

Scythians, Priestesses of Diana, Greeks

Place: Tauris
Time: After the Trojan War
Running Time: 2 hours

There is much to support the argument that this is Gluck's greatest opera. Here he comes nearest to a complete reconciliation of his dramatic style with his lyrical, and the extremes represented by *Alceste* and *Armide* are to some extent amalgamated. The dramatic and the sensuous meet in *Iphigénie en Tauride* to form a whole that is more consistent and more expressive than anything Gluck had previously written. Nowhere else did he achieve such homogeneity of style, with whole scenes dominated by a single idea expressed in music of the greatest power, and seldom before had

he displayed such invention in the individual arias.

Gluck's last work for Paris has retained its hold on the repertory since its initial success. Richard Strauss's re-working in 1900 was less radical than Wagner's for *Aulide*.

Iphigenia is the daughter of Agamemnon, King of Mycenae. Agamemnon was slain by his wife, Clytemnestra, who, in turn, was killed by her son, Orestes. Iphigenia is ignorant of these happenings. She has become a priestess of Diana on the island of Tauris and has not seen Orestes for many years.

Act I. Before the atrium of the temple of Diana. To priestesses and Greek maidens, Iphigenia tells of her dream that misfortune has come to her family in the distant country of her birth. Thoas, entering, calls for a human sacrifice to ward off danger that has been foretold to him. Some of his people, hastily coming upon the scene, bring with them as captives Orestes and Pylades, Greek youths who have landed on the coast. They report that Orestes constantly speaks of having committed a crime and of being pursued by Furies.

Act II. Temple of Diana. Orestes bewails his fate. Pylades sings of his undying friendship for him. Pylades is separated from Orestes, who temporarily loses his mind. Iphigenia questions him. Orestes, under her influence, becomes calmer, but refrains from disclosing his identity. He tells her, however, that he is from Mycenae, that Agamemnon (their father) has been slain by his wife, that Clytemnestra's son, Orestes, has slain her in revenge, and is himself dead. Of the once great family only a daughter, Electra, remains.

Act III. Iphigenia is struck with the resemblance of the stranger to her brother and, in order to save him from the sacrifice demanded by Thoas, charges him to deliver a letter to Electra. He declines to leave Pylades, nor, until Orestes affirms that he will commit suicide rather than accept freedom at the price of his friend's life, does Pylades agree to take the letter, and then only because he hopes to bring succour to Orestes.

Act IV. All is ready for the sacrifice. Iphigenia has the knife poised for the fatal thrust, when, through an exclamation uttered by Orestes, she recognises him as her brother. The priestesses offer him obeisance as king. Thoas, however, enters and demands the sacrifice. Iphigenia declares that she will die with

[1] In 1780–1, Gluck revised his opera for its performance in German in Vienna, giving the role of Orestes to Josef Valentin Adamberger (like Vilem Přibyl in Holland in 1964, a tenor). Antonia Bernasconi, Josef Souter and Ludwig Fischer made up the remainder of the cast. Fischer, like Adamberger, was to sing the first performance of Mozart's *Entführung* the following year.

Iphigénie en Tauride *(Welsh National Opera, 1992, directors Patrice Caurier and Moshe Leiser,*
sets Christian Rätz, costumes Etienne Couleon). Diana Montague as Iphigénie, Simon Keenlyside as Oreste.

her brother. At that moment Pylades at the head of a rescue party enters the temple. A combat ensues in which Thoas is killed. Diana herself appears, pardons Orestes and returns to the Greeks her likeness which the Scythians had stolen and over which they had built the temple.

The mad scene for Orestes, in the second act, has been called Gluck's greatest single achievement. Mention should also be made of Iphigenia's 'O toi, qui prolongeas nos jours', the dances of the Scythians, the air of Thoas, 'De noirs pressentiments mon âme intimidée'; the airs of Pylades, 'Unis dès la plus tendre enfance' and 'O mon ami'; Iphigenia's 'O malheureuse Iphigénie', and 'Je t'implore et je tremble';

and the hymn to Diana, 'Chaste fille de Latone'.

Here may be related an incident at the rehearsal of the work which indicates the dramatic significance Gluck sought to impart to his music. In the second act, while Orestes is singing 'Le calme rentre dans mon coeur', the orchestral accompaniment continues to express the agitation of his thoughts. During the rehearsal the members of the orchestra came to a stop. 'Go on all the same,' cried Gluck. 'He lies. He has killed his mother!'

The version used at the Metropolitan was that made by Richard Strauss, which involves changes in the finales of the first and last acts. Ballet music from *Orfeo* and *Armide* was also introduced.   K., H.

HERMANN GOETZ

(born 7 December 1840, died 3 December 1876)

DER WIDERSPÄNSTIGEN ZÄHMUNG

The Taming of the Shrew

Comic opera in four acts, libretto from Shakespeare's comedy by Joseph Viktor Widmann. Première, Mannheim, 11 October 1874, with Ottilie Ottiker and Eduard Schlosser. First performed Vienna, 1875; London, Drury Lane, 1879; New York, 1886. Revived Metropolitan, New York, 1916, with Ober and Goritz, conductor Bodanzky; Berlin, 1952; London, City Opera Club, 1959.

Baptista, *a rich gentleman of Padua*........................Bass
Bianca ⎫ *his daughters* ....Soprano
Katharina ⎬ ....Soprano
Hortensio ⎫ *Bianca's suitors* ....Bass
Lucentio ⎬ ....Tenor
Petruchio, *a gentleman of Verona* ....Baritone
Grumio, *Petruchio's servant*................................Bass
A Tailor ....Tenor
Hortensio's Wife ....Mezzo-Soprano

Baptista's and Petruchio's Servants, Wedding Guests, Neighbours, etc.

Place: Acts I, II, III in Padua; Act IV in Petruchio's House in the Country
Running Time: 2 hours 15 minutes

Goetz, a pupil in Berlin of Ulrich and Hans von Bülow, spent much of his life in Switzerland as organist in Winterthur and Zürich. Apart from *The*

Taming of the Shrew, he wrote one other opera, *Francesca da Rimini*, which was much less successful than the first, some songs, piano and chamber music, a symphony, concertos for piano and for violin, and some works for chorus and orchestra. *The Taming of the Shrew* is his masterpiece.

The overture, for the most part vigorous and forthright, suggests the changes of mood of the opera itself and its underlying lyricism.

Act I. Outside Baptista's house in Padua, at night. Introduced by the clarinet, Lucentio sings an ardent and beautiful serenade to Bianca ('Klinget, klinget, liebe Töne'), until he is interrupted by the noise of Baptista's servants, about to leave his employment because of the scolding ways of his daughter, Kate, whose fury at her father's attempts to pacify them seems warrant enough for their decision. Bianca appears and there follows a charming love duet for her and Lucentio ('O wende dich nicht ab'). The arrival of Bianca's grey-beard suitor, Hortensio, with a band of musicians, puts a stop to the tender scene, and the quarrel of Hortensio and Lucentio eventually wakes up Baptista, to whom Lucentio reveals his love for Bianca. None shall pay suit to Bianca, declares Baptista, until her elder sister is married; meanwhile, Bianca shall study with the best masters in Italy.

In their *allegretto* duet, Lucentio and Hortensio offer Katharina to one another, until each is struck by the bright idea of disguising himself as a teacher and so gaining admittance to Bianca's presence. Petruchio arrives with his servant, Grumio; he would like nothing better than to share his wealth with a woman worthy of his metal. Hortensio immediately suggests Kate, Petruchio falls for the idea and proclaims his determination to marry her ('Sie ist ein Weib, für solchen Mann geschaffen').

Act II. A room in Baptista's house. Kate mocks Bianca about the previous night's serenades; her sister's supine behaviour, she says, shows why men call women the weaker sex. She makes Bianca accompany her on the lute while she sings 'Ich will mich Keinem geben' (I'll give myself to no one). Petruchio comes in and asks Baptista for Kate's hand in marriage; he will listen to no warning about her character, and resolves that nothing will stop him winning her as his wife. Their first exchange leaves Kate wondering whether she has not at last met her match, in both senses of the word. At the end of the duet, Kate sings of her dawning tenderness for Petruchio.

Baptista comes in to be told by Petruchio that he and Kate are to be married, by Kate that nothing could be further from the truth. Petruchio dominates the quintet which follows (Hortensio and Lucentio have come in as well), and at its end Kate agrees to marry him, more apparently to pay him out than for any other reason.

Act III. Baptista, with Katharina and Bianca, Lucentio and Hortensio (still disguised as teachers), are waiting to welcome the wedding guests, to whom shortly Baptista has to make excuses for the absence of Petruchio. Bianca resumes her lessons, and, under guise of translating the *Aeneid*, Lucentio makes himself known. Hortensio joins them to turn the duet into a trio, one moreover in the best traditions of German comic opera. Baptista bursts in to say that Petruchio has arrived. Deaf to remonstrance about his lateness or the untidiness of his dress, he leads the procession to church, while the servants prepare the wedding breakfast. It is not long before they are back, Hortensio describing Petruchio's disgraceful behaviour during the ceremony, and Petruchio himself announcing that he and Kate have no time to stay for the party but must be off at once.

Act IV. Petruchio's house. When the newly married couple come in, Kate is pale, Petruchio flourishing a riding whip and complaining about everything in sight. The food is whisked away untouched, and Kate is left to soliloquise on her troubles and admit that her spirit is broken: 'Die Kraft versagt'.

Grumio announces a tailor, who urges the qualities of his wares. Kate likes them, but Petruchio finds fault as usual. Next he plays tricks with the times of day; at first, according to Petruchio it is moonlight, then, when Kate agrees with him, midday. She owns she is beaten; she is now his loving wife. Immediately, Petruchio consoles her, and reconciled, they hear Grumio announce the arrival of Baptista with the newly married Bianca and Lucentio, and also Hortensio and his wife. They rejoice to hear of the taming of the shrew (in the last century, when Minnie Hauck sang Kate, this excellent septet was omitted and a waltz for Kate substituted), and the opera ends with a chorus of wedding guests congratulating Petruchio and Kate.   H.

KARL GOLDMARK

(born 18 May 1830, died 2 January 1915)

DIE KÖNIGIN VON SABA

The Queen of Sheba

Opera in four acts, text by Hermann von Mosenthal. Première at the Hofoper, Vienna, 10 March 1875, with Materna, Wild, and Beck. First performance Metropolitan, New York, 1885, with Lilli Lehmann (Sulamith; in 1889 at the same house, she sang the Queen of Sheba), Krämer-Wiedl, Marianne Brandt, Albert Stritt, Adolf Robinson, Emil Fischer, conducted by Anton Seidl; Metropolitan, 1905, with Rappold (Sulamith), Walker, Alten, Knote, van Rooy, Blass, and conducted by Hertz; Manchester, 1910; London, Kennington Theatre, 1910. The opera was in the repertory of the Vienna Staatsoper continuously from 1875 to 1938. Revived New York in concert, 1970, with Kubiak, Alpha Floyd, Arley Reece.

King Solomon...Baritone

Baal Hanan, *the Palace overseer* ....Baritone

Assad...Tenor

The High Priest ....Bass

Sulamith, *his daughter* ....Soprano

The Queen of Sheba............................Mezzo-Soprano

Astaroth, *her slave* ....Soprano

Voice of the Temple-Watchman ....Bass

Place: Jerusalem
Time: Tenth Century B.C.
Running Time: 3 hours 35 minutes

Goldmark was a Viennese composer of Hungarian and Jewish origin, whose *Königin von Saba* made a big enough success in 1875 to establish him as a leading composer. Only his comedy *Das Heimchen am Herd* (1896: from Dickens' *The Cricket on the Hearth*) made a remotely comparable effect. Of his later operas, *Wintermärchen* (1908: on Shakespeare's *Winter's Tale*) won a certain réclame with a strong cast in Vienna.

Act I. In Solomon's magnificent palace everybody is preparing for the reception of the Queen of Sheba. Nobody is more delighted than Sulamith, the daughter of the High Priest, for Assad, whom she is to marry and who had gone to meet the foreign queen, will return with her. But when he comes in, Assad confesses to King Solomon that he has not yet seen the Queen of Sheba, but at a cedar grove in Lebanon a wonderful woman favoured him with her love and since then his mind has been confused. The King tells the young man that God will restore his peace of mind through marriage to Sulamith. The Queen's train approaches, she greets Solomon, and unveils herself. Assad rushes towards her; this was the woman of the cedar grove! What does the young man want of her? She does not know him.

Act II. The Queen declined to recognise Assad but the woman in her is consumed with longing for him. Happy love unites them. The scene changes and shows the interior of the Temple, where the wedding of Assad and Sulamith is about to be solemnised. At a decisive moment the Queen appears; Assad, throwing the ring on the floor, hurries to the Queen, who, for her part, declares a second time that she has never seen him; she came only to bring a wedding gift for Sulamith. Assad has offended the Almighty and has incurred the penalty of death.

Act III. Solomon is alone with the Queen. She has one request to make of him, that he shall release Assad. Why? He is nothing to her but she wants to test whether the King has regard for his guest. Solomon sees through his guest's scheme and refuses her request. The Queen, breathing vengeance, strides out of the palace. Sulamith is in the depths of despair but Solomon consoles her; Assad will shake off the unworthy chains. Far away on the borders of the desert, she will find peace with him.

Act IV. On the border of the desert stands the asylum of the young woman consecrated to God in which Sulamith has found rest from a deceitful world. Assad staggers thither, a weary, banished man. Again the Queen of Sheba appears before him offering him her love, but he flees from the false woman for whom he had sacrificed the noble Sulamith. A desert storm arises, burying Assad in the sand. When the sky becomes clear again Sulamith, taking a walk with her maidens, finds her lover. She pardons the dying man and sings of the eternal joys which they will taste together.

Die Königin von Saba belongs in the category of operas whose music is basically conventional and which require a lavish scenic display if they are to be seen at their best. Much of the music in its day must have sounded agreeably exotic; on the other hand, such a section as Assad's narration to Solomon (Act I) reaches an almost Wagnerian length without displaying quite Wagnerian expressiveness. The beginning of the second act, however, with the *scena* for the Queen followed by Astaroth's luring song (marvellously effective in the hands of a great artist), Assad's well-known 'Magische Töne' and the extended love duet for him and the Queen are, musically speaking, of considerable appeal. Sulamith's two great scenes with the chorus ('Der Freund ist dein' in the opening scene, and the wailing lament in Act III) have a passionate, exotic colouring and demand considerable powers of execution on the part of the singer. The Queen has a striking duet with Solomon at the beginning of Act III, when she attempts to seduce him from the path of duty and to obtain Assad for herself.   K.W., H.

BERTHOLD GOLDSCHMIDT
(born 18 January 1903, died 17 October 1996)

Berthold Goldschmidt studied at the Berlin Hochschule with Franz Schreker, worked as co-répétiteur at the Berlin State Opera under Erich Kleiber, and had his first success as a composer in 1925, around the time he helped coach *Wozzeck*. In 1932 his first opera, *Der gewaltige Hahnrei*, was successfully staged. Carl Ebert scheduled it for the Städtische Oper, Berlin, but the advent of the Nazis brought cancellation and Goldschmidt's flight as a refugee to England, where he subsisted as a composer for ballet and with the B.B.C.'s Overseas Service.

After 1945 he worked for Glyndebourne, of which Ebert was artistic director, conducting a famous revival of Verdi's *Macbeth* at the 1947 Edinburgh Festival. In 1951 his second opera, *Beatrice Cenci*, won an Arts Council prize, but no performance followed and, in spite of sporadic success as a conductor – notably, the first performance in 1964 of Deryck Cooke's reconstruction of Mahler's Tenth Symphony – his music found little favour in a period dominated by reverence for the *avant garde*. In his eighties, Goldschmidt's career came back on the rails when conductors, particularly Simon Rattle, rediscovered his music and a concert performance in 1988 of *Beatrice Cenci* put him once again, in the last few years of his life, on the musical map.

DER GEWALTIGE HAHNREI
The Magnificent Cuckold

Opera in three acts, after *Le Cocu magnifique* (1920) by the Flemish playwright Fernand Crommelynck, which had success in Paris, Russia, Berlin and London. Première in Mannheim, 14 February 1932, with Else Schulz, Heinrich Kuppinger, conductor Joseph Rosenstock. First performed Berlin (concert), 1992, with Roberta Alexander, Robert Wörle, conductor Zagrosek; Komische Oper, Berlin, 1994, with Yvonne Weidstruck, Günter Neumann, conductor Yakov Kreizberg, director Harry Kupfer.

Stella..Soprano
Bruno, *her husband* ....Tenor
Petrus, *Stella's cousin*....................................Baritone
An Oxherd..Baritone
Mémé, *Stella's old nurse*.......................Mezzo-Soprano
Estrugo, *Bruno's secretary*..................................Tenor
A Young Man ....Tenor
Cornelie, *a neighbour*.......................................Soprano
Florence, *a neighbour* ....Mezzo-Soprano
A Policeman...Baritone

Neighbours

Running Time: 2 hours 5 minutes

Act I. After a brisk overture, domestic small talk establishes Stella's devotion to her husband Bruno. An Oxherd asking for help with a letter makes play for Stella so roughly as to amount to attempted rape, but Mémé sends him packing with a whack over the head. A burst of lyricism accompanies the ecstatic greeting of Bruno and Stella, before, for her seafaring cousin Petrus, Bruno bids Stella show her paces, capping it all by baring her breast. In a fit of jealousy, Bruno knocks Petrus to the ground, then questions his secretary Estrugo as to Stella's faithfulness. He tries to get Stella to admit to some misdemeanour while he was away, then chucks Petrus out of the house.

Act II. Stella wears a black coat and mask as Bruno demands the name of her lover. For a moment the interrogation gives way to Bruno's old affection, but a knock at the door rouses new suspicions. A young man asks Bruno to write a letter for him, which Bruno affects to believe is addressed to Stella – who else could be 'the most beautiful girl in the district'? Estrugo has the sense to warn him to get away while the going is good.

Bruno announces the only cure for his insane suspicions is certainty: Stella must be unfaithful beyond any doubt. He comes quickly to the point: Petrus must put him out of his misery by providing proof. Goaded by insults, Petrus takes Stella upstairs and a furious interlude brings back Estrugo to spy through the keyhole and report what he sees. Bruno reacts by fetching a gun. Villagers gather and with a touch of solemnity mock Bruno as a cuckold.

Act III. Bruno regulates traffic as young men queue up outside, assuring one another anyone can have Stella. The policeman is scandalised. Estrugo and Bruno put a ladder up to Stella's window and Bruno sings extravagant love music. Stella seems to recognise his voice and eventually, after an extensive duet, lets him in. Village women armed with pitchforks attack the masked figure of Bruno, quickly turning their fury against Stella herself. They plan to throw her in the canal but the Oxherd rescues her and demands she come with him. After a struggle of conscience – she still loves Bruno – and a moment of fastidious revulsion – her saviour is a filthy fellow – she starts to give in, and when Bruno takes aim at the Oxherd, instinctively protects him. Nonetheless, it is Bruno, her husband and tormentor, she begs to force her to swear an oath of eternal fidelity. Bruno agrees but as he watches them leave, 'the magnificent cuckold' allows an expression of satisfaction to cross his face as he says: 'Ah no, I'm not so stupid! Another of her tricks! I won't be taken in again!'   H.

BEATRICE CENCI

Opera in three acts, libretto by Martin Esslin after *The Cenci* by Percy Bysshe Shelley. Excerpts 1952, B.B.C.; Queen Elizabeth Hall, London, 1988, with Helen Lawrence, Henry Herford, conductor Odaline de la Martinez. Première, Berlin (concert and recording), 1994, with Roberta Alexander, Simon Estes, conductor Zagrosek; Magdeburg, 1994, with Heather Thomson, David Cumberland, conductor Matthias Husmann.

Count Francesco Cenci ....Bass-Baritone

Lucrezia, *his second wife* ....Mezzo-Soprano

Beatrice, *his daughter from a first marriage* .....Soprano

Bernardo, *her brother* ....Mezzo-Soprano

Cardinal Camillo ....Bass

Orsino, *a Prelate* ....Tenor

Marzio, *a hired murderer* ....Baritone

Olimpio, *a hired murderer* ....Baritone

A Judge ....Tenor

A Singer *at Count Cenci's feast* ....Tenor

Prince Colonna ....Baritone

Andrea, *a servant* ....Baritone

An Officer ....Tenor

Carpenter I ....Tenor

Carpenter II ....Baritone

Servants, Dancers, Jailers, People

Place: In and Near Rome
Time: 1599
Running Time: 2 hours

In spite of the Arts Council prize won by the composer at the 1951 Festival of Britain for *Beatrice Cenci*, it remained unstaged, apart from a couple of widely spaced concert performances of excerpts, until Goldschmidt was in his nineties.

Shelley's verse drama (1819) was printed but not seen in his lifetime because of the shocking subject – Count Francesco Cenci, a rich nobleman born in 1549, was known for a life of debauchery: he hated his sons and was guilty of incest with his daughter Beatrice. He was three times imprisoned for his vile behaviour but always able to buy freedom through hefty donations to the Papal Treasury. Beatrice and her mother were found guilty of employing murderers to kill him and the death sentence was upheld by the Pope, incensed, it is said, in the knowledge that the Count could no longer pay the heavy ransoms which after each crime procured his release.

Act I. The garden of the Cenci palace. Heavy chords and music of some solemnity usher in the drama. Lucrezia and Beatrice join with Bernardo, who has just been struck by his father out of pure malice, to lament their sufferings.

Orsino is announced and they go in, leaving Count Cenci to hear Cardinal Camillo deliver the Pope's judgment: the murder the Count has recently committed will be hushed up provided he cedes a certain property, which he describes as a third of his possessions. No doubt, says Cenci, the Pope will pray that he long enjoy the strength to sin.

Beatrice remembers the love she and Orsino once felt for each other, to which the prelate replies that he remains hopeful the Pope will not only sympathetically consider her petition against her father's cruelty but may even grant Orsino a dispensation to marry – something, the moment Beatrice's back is turned, he denies he has any intention of pursuing.

At a grand reception in Count Cenci's palace, the host greets his guests. They dance and listen to an arietta before the Count with relish announces the death of his two elder sons, long the object of his hatred. Cardinal Camillo hopes it was a jest but Cenci in a little song gloats triumphantly before defying the guests' revulsion and even Beatrice's eloquent plea for help. They fear Cenci's revenge.

Act II. A tumultuous prelude precedes Beatrice's impassioned denunciation to Lucrezia of her father's as yet unspecified crime. Orsino's arrival sets in motion the terrible chain of events which will lead to the deaths of each of them. He will procure a trustworthy pair of assassins – and when the Count calls for Beatrice, she pours an opiate in his wine. As she and Beatrice wait for deliverance, Lucrezia sings impressively of their hopes.

The deed is quickly done but no sooner have the murderers left than Cardinal Camillo thunders at the door, demanding to see the Count, who must answer new and grave charges. Tension mounts, the murder is discovered, and the Cardinal is obliged to arrest Lucrezia and Beatrice as suspects.

Act III. Bernardo is brought to Lucrezia and Beatrice as they lie in prison and he hears Beatrice describe how she dreamed of Paradise. Camillo, the Judge and their attendants tell them one of the murderers has confessed under torture, but neither woman will admit guilt. The incriminating letter found on the murderer is in Orsino's writing, but he is not to be found and the Judge decrees Lucrezia be put to the torture. Beatrice tries to comfort Bernardo but Lucrezia confesses and in despair Beatrice follows suit. The Judge sentences them to death but the Cardinal attempts a word of comfort with a promise to plead for mercy from the Pope.

They sleep and an eloquent orchestral nocturne precedes Camillo's return with the news that the Pope has confirmed the Judge's sentence. Beatrice sings a gentle lullaby in an effort to comfort Lucrezia and an interlude takes us to the square, where carpenters prepare the scaffold and the mob waits for victims. Beatrice bids a brief farewell to Bernardo, and they are led away to a short reprise of the lullaby, the Cardinal after a moment confirming their deaths. The Pope himself is heard passing in procession 'to pray for forgiveness for the souls of these poor sinners' and the sound of a Requiem brings the opera to an end. H.

ANTÔNIO CARLOS GOMES
(born 11 July 1836, died 16 September 1896)

For the Brazilian composer Gomes, opera meant Italian opera. Geographical remoteness from the musical mainstream produced not originality, but old-fashioned *bel canto* within a spectacular, if conventional theatrical framework borrowed from Meyerbeer. *Il Guarany* brought him success at la Scala, Milan, and is the only one of his works to have lasted.

IL GUARANY

Opera-ballo in four acts, libretto by Antonio Enrico Scalvini and Carlo D'Ormeville, based on the novel *O Guarany* by Jose Martiniano de Alencar (1857). Première at la Scala, Milan, 19 March 1870, with Teodoro Coloni as Antonio, Maria Sass as Cecilia, Giuseppe Villani as Pery, Enrico Storti as Gonzales, Victor Maurel as Il Cacico, conducted by Eugenio Terziani. British première Covent Garden, 1872, with M. Sessi, Ernesto Nicolini, Antonio Cotogni and Jean Baptiste Faure. First U.S. performance in San Francisco, 1884. Recent production at the Oper der Stadt, Bonn, 5 June 1994, with Veronica Villaroel, Placido Domingo, Carlos Alvarez and Boris Martinovic, conducted by John Neschling.

Don Antonio de Mariz, *elderly*
   Portuguese nobleman ....Bass

Cecilia, *his daughter*.......................................Soprano

Pery, *chief of the Guaraní tribe* ....Tenor

Don Alvaro, *Portuguese adventurer* ....Tenor

Gonzales, *Spanish adventurer* ....Baritone

Ruy-Bento, *Spanish adventurer* ....Tenor

Alonso, *Spanish adventurer* ....Bass

Il Cacico, *chief of the Aimoré tribe* ....Bass

Pedro, *Don Antonio's man-at-arms* ....Mute

Adventurers, Men and Women of the Portuguese
   Colony, Savages of the Aimoré Tribe

Place: Rio de Janeiro
Time: c.1560
Running Time: 3 hours 25 minutes

The opera's strong suit is melodies of a popular slant that are hard to resist. His characters remain conventional types, beneath a thin veneer of exoticism, but they can prove grateful roles. Cecilia calls for exquisite vocalism from the trilling start (typically off-stage, like Bellini's Elvira and many others). Victor Maurel (Verdi's Iago and Falstaff) created the role of Il Cacico, while Pery, the noble savage, represents a quintessential tenor role, popular with Tamagno and Mario del Monaco; Placido Domingo has since championed its cause outside South America.

The Portuguese nobleman Don Antonio de Mariz governs a part of Brazil that is home to two indigenous tribes, the bellicose Aimoré, led by Il Cacico, the Cacique, and the peaceable Guaraní, whose chief, Pery, loves Antonio's daughter, Cecilia.

Act I. In front of Don Antonio's castle. The Spaniard Gonzales resolves to deprive the Portuguese Don Alvaro of Cecilia, whom they both love. Her father Antonio brings news that one of his men accidentally killed a girl from the Aimoré tribe: now the Indians insist on revenge. His daughter Cecilia was recently saved from the Aimoré; Antonio introduces the Guaraní, Pery, and embraces him as his brother and friend. All are struck by Pery's nobility. Pery swears to protect the Europeans from the Aimoré. Cecilia is heard singing a love song off-stage (polacca). Antonio introduces her to the husband he chose for her, Don Alvaro. She goes white, but before Antonio can find out why, bells ring for the Ave Maria. They all kneel in prayer for peace ('Salve, possente Vergine'). Pery notices how furtively Gonzales arranges to meet Ruy and Alonso later, in secret, at the Savage's Grotto. He determines to prevent any treachery. The act ends with a duet for Pery and Cecilia ('Sento una forza indomita', recorded by Caruso and Destinn), in which they explore their burgeoning feelings for one another.

Act II. The Savage's Grotto. In a *scena* and aria ('Vanto io pur') Pery reflects that although he is in thrall to his 'signora', Cecilia, he himself is of high birth. He watches as Gonzales tempts Ruy and Alonso with a story of a rich silver mine, but when they agree to let Gonzales abduct Cecilia, Pery calls out 'Traditori!' (Traitors). Ruy and Alonso go to investigate. Pery fights Gonzales, but spares his life when the Spaniard swears to leave ('Giurar debbo').

The adventurers' barracks. Alonso and Ruy bribe the adventurers with the promise of gold ('L'oro è un ente sì giocondo'). Gonzales himself sings a lilting song celebrating the adventurer's life ('Senza tetto, senza cuna'). They all swear to follow wherever he leads.

Cecilia's bedroom. She takes up her guitar and sings a *ballata* about the power of love ('C'era una volta un principe'), before retiring to rest and dream of Pery. Gonzales climbs through the window. When Cecilia refuses to yield ('Donna, tu forsè l'unica'), he tries to seize her. From outside Pery fires an arrow that wounds Gonzales in the hand. Don Alvaro rushes in, but so do the adventurers. Pery accuses Gonzales of treachery. Discordant music for 'savage instruments' signifies that the Aimoré have surrounded the castle. They all rush off to defend it.

Act III. The camp of the Aimoré. Cecilia has been taken prisoner in the recent battle. The Indians swear to exterminate the Portuguese. The Aimoré chief, the Cacique, protects Cecilia: he wants her to be the queen of his tribe ('Giovinetta, nello sguardo'). The Indians have captured Pery, who defiantly admits that he intended to kill the Cacique. The Cacique insists that sacred rites must be accomplished before Pery can be killed and eaten. Cecilia will first be given to him as his 'bride of death'. She urges Pery to escape. He refuses ('Perchè di meste lagrime'), and secretly swallows poison, intended to kill the Aimoré when they eat him. The Cacique offers Pery in prayer to their god; Cecilia prays for deliverance. Don Antonio leads the Portuguese in an attack which rescues his daughter. He gives the credit to God.

Act IV. The cellars of the castle, lit by a flaming torch. Gonzales tells the adventurers that he is going to let the Aimoré into the castle, though he will save Cecilia for himself ('In quest'ora suprema'). Antonio has overheard them and swears to forestall their treachery. Pery also appears: he used his knowledge of forest herbs to concoct an antidote to the poison he took. He asks Antonio to allow him to save Cecilia. When Antonio points out that he worships idols, Pery asks to be initiated into Christianity. Antonio baptises him. Cecilia runs in: the Aimoré are coming, bent on destruction. Antonio entrusts her to Pery's care, but she refuses to leave her father. When she faints, Pery carries her away to safety. The adventurers burst in. Antonio seizes the torch and ignites the barrels of gunpowder. An explosion destroys the castle. In the distance, on a hill, Cecilia can be seen, supported by Pery, who points to heaven.

Il Guarany is the national opera of Brazil. For audiences elsewhere, its subject matter is little more than harmless hokum. As a drama, it moves jerkily towards static tableaux. On the other hand, its music, like its hero, throbs with a full-blooded naïveté: the various set pieces, Christian and heathen prayers, curses and lovesongs, disarm criticism with their full-frontal *Italianità* – by 1870 Verdi's operas sounded less Italian than this. And when Verdi himself heard *Il Guarany* he saluted Gomes's 'true musical genius'.   P.

CHARLES FRANÇOIS GOUNOD
(born 17 June 1818, died 18 October 1893)

Gounod divided his life between writing music for Church and for stage. His earliest opera was written for Pauline Viardot when he was over thirty, but *Sapho* heralded a list of regular if not unremitting successes, starting with *Faust* (1859) and running through the brilliantly written *Le Médecin malgré lui*, the mythological comedy *Philémon et Baucis*, the grandiose *La Reine de Saba*, the Provençal *Mireille*, culminating in the lyrical and tragic *Roméo et Juliette*. What transpired after the Franco-Prussian War is another matter. A sojourn in England produced a mass of songs, which on his return to France he turned into French and sold as new work, and unsuccessful operas like *Cinq-Mars*, *Polyeucte* and *Le tribut de Zamora*. That his last operatic effort was a re-hash of *Sapho*, his first, has been taken as a sign of the short distance he had travelled in the more than thirty years involved. Nonetheless, the composer of at least four operas of very high quality, wholly representative of the era of their composition, is entitled to forget a rather large number of near-misses.

LE MÉDECIN MALGRÉ LUI
Doctor in Spite of Himself

Opera in three acts, text by Barbier and Carré after Molière's *Le Médecin malgré lui*. Première Théâtre Lyrique, Paris, 15 January 1858. Revived at the Opéra-Comique in 1902 with Lucien Fugère as Sganarelle, and later with Louis Musy, conductor Désormière; 1978 with Jean-Philippe Lafont, conductor Cambreling, during which run it achieved its 100th performance in the house.

Sganarelle, *a woodcutter*	Baritone
Léandre, *Lucinde's lover*	Tenor
Martine, *Sganarelle's wife*	Mezzo-Soprano
Jacqueline, *Lucas's wife*	Mezzo-Soprano
Lucinde, *Géronte's daughter*	Soprano
Géronte, *a wealthy bourgeois*	Bass
Valère, *Géronte's valet*	Baritone
Lucas, *Géronte's servant*	Tenor

Running Time: 2 hours 15 minutes

When *Faust*, already scheduled, was in 1857 postponed, Gounod was lucky that the impresario Léon Carvalho, to make up for the disappointment, asked him to write this opera to a Molière text. Berlioz praised the score but the short work was not often performed during the composer's lifetime. Nonetheless its charms are considerable and demonstrate that Gounod was accomplished in comedy as well as lyric tragedy – Queen Mab and *Faust*'s Dame Marthe come into their own! Revivals reveal attractive solo numbers like Sganarelle's 'Qu'ils sont doux' and Léandre's second-act serenade 'Est-on sage dans le bel âge', and overall lively, elegant, rewarding invention of a sort which will agreeably surprise opera-goers familiar only with the composer's more sentimental effusions.

The text of the opera closely follows Molière's play, to such an extent that the Comédie-Française tried initially to block performance. Sganarelle the woodcutter is inclined to get drunk and beat his wife. She vows to get her own back. Valère and Lucas, who work for Géronte, are looking for a doctor to

Le médecin malgré lui *(Paris, Opéra-Comique at Salle Favart, 1978, director Jean-Louis Martin-Barbaz, designer Pierre-Yves Leprince). Jean-Philippe Lafont as Sganarelle, Joscelyne Taillon as Jacqueline.*

cure Lucinde, Géronte's daughter, of a mysterious loss of speech, in reality a pretext to extricate her from an undesirable engagement.

Martine points Sganarelle out as a learned but eccentric doctor, who acknowledges his profession only to those who beat him. Léandre, Lucinde's impoverished but otherwise eligible lover, explains to Sganarelle the precise nature of Lucinde's malady and they become accomplices when Sganarelle takes him on as his assistant. Sganarelle pays court to Lucas's wife Jacqueline, and enables Léandre to get into Géronte's house. Denounced by Lucas, Sganarelle seems to have run out of luck but Léandre informs Géronte that an uncle has just died leaving him a fortune, information which diverts that worthy's fury and sets a happy ending in train.   H.

FAUST

Opera in five acts, words by Barbier and Carré. Première at Théâtre Lyrique, Paris, 19 March 1859, with Miolan-Carvalho, Barbot, Reynald, Balanqué. Gounod composed 'Even bravest heart may swell' for the great English baritone Charles Santley in 1864 when the opera was first performed in English; for many years French performances omitted this splendid aria.

Faust, *a learned doctor* ....Tenor

Méphistophélès (Mephistopheles).......................Bass

Marguerite...Soprano

Valentin, *a soldier, Marguerite's brother*.........Baritone

Siébel, *a village youth in love
    with Marguerite* .... Mezzo-Soprano

Wagner, *a student*...Baritone

Martha Schwerlein, *Marguerite's
    neighbour*.......................................Mezzo-Soprano

Students, Soldiers, Villagers, Angels, Demons

Place: Germany
Time: Sixteenth Century
Running Time: 3 hours 30 minutes

Originally composed with sections of spoken dialogue, *Faust* was re-worked more than once, sung recitatives being added in 1860, Valentin's aria in 1864, and an extensive ballet at the time the work reached the Opéra (1869).

A brief prelude is mostly concerned with the aria Gounod wrote for Santley, which was indeed derived from the prelude's melody.

Act I. Faust's study. The philosopher is alone reading, before dawn. In despair he is about to drink poison when he hears cheerful singing outside. He curses life and advancing age and calls for Satan's help. Méphistophélès appears and offers him wealth and power but Faust wants neither unless accompanied by the gift of youth. A vision of Marguerite at her spinning wheel produces a rapturous response: 'A moi les plaisirs!'

Act II. A fair outside a city. Students, among them Wagner, soldiers, burghers of every age are drinking and making the most of carnival. Siébel and Valentin make their entrance, the latter examining a medal given him by his sister Marguerite as a talisman against harm in battle. He sings the aria written for Santley. Méphistophélès sings the song of the Calf of Gold, an ironic celebration of man's worship of Mammon, before telling Siébel that every flower he touches will henceforth wither. He picks a quarrel with Valentin by toasting Marguerite, swords are drawn but Valentin finds his powerless until he and the other soldiers extend their swords' cruciform hilts and counter the might of Méphistophélès.

Méphistophélès and Faust watch as develops the famous waltz, whose grace undulates exquisitely throughout the action. Siébel is in love with Marguerite but Méphistophélès manoeuvres him away from her and Faust is at last allowed to meet his vision. In a short but telling episode he offers her his arm, only, with matching elegance, to be rejected (notoriously, the only time the soprano voice is heard during two and a half acts of operatic action!). The waltz scintillates to the end.

Act III. Marguerite's garden. Siébel in a charming song attempts to leave flowers in front of his beloved's house but they wither as he touches them, and only when he has dipped his fingers in holy water do they remain fresh. Faust sings rapturously ('Salut! demeure chaste et pure'); the graceful aria with its floated top C is a touchstone of the French romantic tenor repertory. Méphistophélès substitutes a casket of jewels for Siébel's flowers and Marguerite, with the handsome stranger in mind, at first daydreams at her spinning wheel ('Il était un roi de Thulé') then bursts into the brilliant Jewel Song.

There is a short interlude in the form of a quartet for Faust and Marguerite, Méphistophélès and Martha, before Méphistophélès invokes night and the scent of flowers to render lovers impervious to all but their own mounting passion. Faust declares his love in an extended and justly famous duet, at whose end he and Marguerite agree to meet next day. He listens to her soliloquising into the night ('Il m'aime'), then folds her in his arms as Méphistophélès shakes with laughter outside.

Act IV. Marguerite's room. Though she has been betrayed and deserted, Marguerite cannot find it in her heart to respond to Siébel's callow protestations of love ('Versez vos chagrins'); she still loves Faust.

A church. Marguerite kneels to pray but the voice of the invisible Méphistophélès reminds her of her sin and demons call her name. The 'Dies irae' resounds, Marguerite joins in, but Méphistophélès condemns her to eternal damnation.

The street in front of Marguerite's house. Soldiers return from war and sing a rousing chorus (the attempts of modern producers to suggest in general the horrors of war and in particular wounded men returning from the front involve so great a solecism as to be doomed to failure). Valentin enters the house, alerted to trouble by the obvious distress of Siébel. Méphistophélès sings a ribald serenade which provokes Valentin to an attempt to avenge what he rightly takes to be an insult. A spirited trio leads to a duel, in which Faust mortally wounds his lover's brother. Marguerite throws herself on his body but with his dying breath Valentin curses her.

Act V. The ballet which was obligatory for the Paris Opéra produced one of Gounod's most mellifluous scores, and the action involves the courtesans of antiquity who pass before Faust. A vision of Marguerite causes Faust to demand of Méphistophélès that he see her again. She is in prison, condemned to death for killing her child, and Faust tries by recalling past happiness to persuade her to escape with him. The reappearance of Méphistophélès banishes any idea of flight and Marguerite thinks only of the salvation she prayed for and which he interrupted in church. 'Anges purs, anges radieux' she sings in a soaring melody which brings a final cry from an angelic chorus: 'Sauvée!' (Saved!)

Faust's fame is built on its principal numbers – the tenor-bass duet in Act I; the waltz, Valentin's solo, and the scene between Faust and Marguerite in Act II; in Act III, the tenor aria, Marguerite's two solos, the love duet; the ballet and the trio in the last act.

Gounod's gift was for lyricism of a high order, but also for a theatrical effectiveness which has over the years brought audiences to opera. The popularity of *Faust* in the nineteenth century and the frequency with which it was given there were so great that the Metropolitan Opera in New York came for a time to be known as the Faustspielhaus!   H.

MIREILLE

Opera in five acts, text by Michel Carré after Frédéric Mistral's poem *Mireio*. Première at the Théâtre-Lyrique, Paris, 19 March 1864, with Miolan-Carvalho and Michot. First performed at Her Majesty's, London, 1864, with Tietjens, Giuglini, Santley; Philadelphia, Covent Garden, 1864; 1891, with Eames. Revived at Metropolitan, 1919, with Barrientos, Hackett, Whitehill, conductor Monteux. In the open air at the Val d'Enfer, Les Baux, 1954, with Vivalda, Gedda, Dens, conductor Cluytens. English National Opera, 1983, with Valerie Masterson, Adrian Martin.

Mireille	Soprano
Vincent, *her lover*	Tenor
Ourrias, *a bull-tender*	Baritone
Maître Ramon, *father of Mireille*	Bass
Taven, *an old woman*	Mezzo-Soprano
Vincenette, *Vincent's sister*	Soprano
Andreloun, *a shepherd*	Mezzo-Soprano
Maître Ambroise, *father of Vincent*	Bass
Clémence	Soprano

Place: In and Near Arles
Time: Mid-Nineteenth Century
Running Time: 2 hours 50 minutes

Even before the first performance, the compliant Gounod allowed his pastoral tragedy to be savaged, mostly at the behest of the director of the Théâtre-Lyrique and his wife, who created the title role. There were cuts and additions, characters were amalgamated, the tragic dénouement was even changed into an operetta-style marriage. No wonder the opera failed to achieve the success which it deserved. Only seventy-five years later, under the determined leadership of Reynaldo Hahn, Henri Busser and Guy Ferrant, the producer, was the work in 1939 performed as Gounod had composed it, and a worthy element in the French repertory revealed.

Act I. The overture sets the Provençal atmosphere, with its *cornemuse* tunes. The scene is a mulberry plantation. After a pastoral chorus, Mireille

Faust. *The great bass-baritone Vanni-Marcoux (1877–1962) as Méphistophélès, a role which he first sang at the Paris Opéra in 1908.*

confesses that she is in love with Vincent, who returns her affection. Her song, 'O légère hirondelle', in the waltz rhythm in which Gounod liked to introduce his heroines, is attractively ingenuous, and was written at the express request of Miolan-Carvalho, wife of the all-powerful manager of the Théâtre-Lyrique.[1] In spite of the warning of Taven that a girl should not give her heart away so openly, least of all when there is little possibility of parental approval for the proposed match, Mireille makes no pretence of hiding her feelings when Vincent comes towards her. In duet they repeat their vows, and pledge each other to meet in a particular sanctuary if ever trouble should threaten their lives.

Act II. A festival is in progress at Arles. A *farandole* chorus makes a vigorous introduction to the act. Mireille and Vincent are there together and, when asked by the company to sing, they perform the graceful *Chanson de Magali*: 'La brise est douce'. Taven warns Mireille that Vincent has a rival, Ourrias, who has admitted his love for her. Mireille is indignant at the idea that she might prove unfaithful to Vincent: 'Trahir Vincent!' She will be true to him all her days: 'Non, jamais, jamais! A toi mon âme'.

Mireille's fervent avowal of her love is followed by the entrance of Ourrias, 'Si les filles d'Arles', a typically bucolic song. Before the act ends, Ourrias has asked for Mireille's hand and been refused, Vincent's father, Ambroise, has likewise pleaded for his son and been told that his reasons were nothing short of mercenary, and Mireille has emphasised the firmness of her attachment for Vincent, in spite of her father's preference for Ourrias.

Act III. Near Taven's cave, late at night. Ourrias is furiously jealous, strikes Vincent and leaves him for dead. Taven revives him and hurls a curse after Ourrias. Ourrias tries to escape across the Val d'Enfer, only to be confronted by the reproaching voices of conscience in the shape of the spirits of deceived lovers which haunt the place. Even the ferryman who comes to his aid seems to know of his crime, and he drowns attempting to escape.

Act IV. Late the same evening, at Ramon's farm. Midsummer night celebrations are in progress, and Ramon is full of regret that his opposition to Mireille's marriage seems to have broken her heart

and may blight his own old age. Mireille recalls the song of Magali and thinks enviously of the carefree life of the shepherds. She hears from Vincenette what has happened to Vincent and decides that this is just such a situation of crisis as made them in happier times vow to meet at the Church of Les Saintes Maries by the sea. There she will go.

The scene is the plain of La Crau, where little has a chance to grow before being burnt up by the heat of the sun. Mireille, on her way to the sanctuary, hears a charming shepherd's song: 'Le jour se lève', sung by Andreloun. His life in contrast with hers seems wonderfully free of care: 'Heureux petit berger'. With a supreme effort, she goes on her way.

Act V. The scene changes to the sanctuary itself, the Church of Les Saintes Maries. There is a march and chorus for the pilgrims, after which Vincent appears, vainly searching for Mireille. In an effective aria, 'Anges du Paradis', he prays that she may win her way to their meeting place, in spite of the torrid heat of the Provençal sun. Mireille arrives in a state of collapse, and, by the time Ramon arrives to forgive her, she is already dying. A heavenly voice welcomes her soul into the realm of God.   H.

ROMÉO ET JULIETTE
Romeo and Juliet

Opera in five acts, words by Barbier and Carré, after the tragedy by Shakespeare. Produced Paris, Théâtre-Lyrique, 27 April 1867, with Miolan-Carvalho, Michot, Barre, Cazaux; January 1873, taken over by the Opéra-Comique; Opéra, 28 November 1888, with Patti, Jean and Edouard de Reszke, Delmas.

The Duke of Verona	Bass
Count Paris	Baritone
Count Capulet	Baritone
Juliette (Juliet), *his daughter*	Soprano
Gertrude, *her nurse*	Mezzo-Soprano
Tybalt, *Capulet's nephew*	Tenor
Roméo (Romeo), *a Montague*	Tenor
Mercutio	Baritone
Stéphano, *Roméo's page*	Soprano
Grégorio, *a Capulet retainer*	Baritone
Benvolio, *retainer to the Montagues*	Tenor

---

[1] It is now sometimes omitted in performance as being a display piece and out of character for the introvertly lyrical Mireille.

Frère Laurent (Friar Lawrence) ....Bass

Frère Jean (Friar John) ....Bass

Nobles and Ladies of Verona, Citizens, Soldiers,
    Monks and Pages

Place: Verona
Time: Fourteenth Century
Running Time: 3 hours 20 minutes

Having pillaged Goethe for *Faust*, Gounod's librettists went to Shakespeare for *Roméo et Juliette*, which, like *Faust*, reached the Paris Opéra by way of the Théâtre-Lyrique. This is not Shakespeare distilled in music (like Verdi's *Otello*); it is, on the contrary and like Ambroise Thomas's *Hamlet*, a French romantic opera of high calibre, containing moreover some of Gounod's finest lyrical music.

The libretto is in five acts and follows closely, often even to the text, Shakespeare's tragedy. There is a prologue in which the characters and chorus briefly rehearse the story that is to unfold.

Act I. The grand hall in the palace of the Capulets. A masked ball is in progress. Tybalt speaks to Paris of Juliet, to whom Paris is engaged and who at that moment appears with her father. Capulet greets his guests – 'Allons! jeunes gens! Allons! belles dames!'

Romeo, Mercutio, Benvolio and half a dozen followers arrive in masks. Despite the deadly feud between the two houses, the Montagues have decided to come to the Capulets' ball in disguise. Mercutio sings the ballad of Queen Mab, a number as gossamer-like in the opera as the monologue is in the play (or indeed in Berlioz's dramatic symphony).

The Montagues head off to another part of the palace as Juliet returns with her nurse, Gertrude. Full of high spirits, she sings the graceful and animated waltz, 'Je veux vivre dans ce rêve, qui m'enivre'. Gertrude is called away and Romeo encounters Juliet. Their attraction, as in the play, is instantaneous. Romeo, with great passion, addresses his new-found love: 'Ange adorable'.

Tybalt comes in and Romeo quickly replaces his mask. But Tybalt's suspicions are aroused, and Juliet learns that the youth she finds so attractive is a Montague. Tybalt is all for revenge, but old Capulet, respecting the laws of hospitality, orders that the ball proceed.

Act II. The garden of the Capulets. Romeo is with his page, Stéphano, below Juliet's apartment. He sings one of Gounod's finest tenor arias, 'Ah! lève-toi soleil'. Juliet comes out on to the balcony and Romeo hides. From her soliloquy he learns that, although he is a Montague, Juliet loves him. Their exchange of pledges is interrupted briefly, as Grégorio and servants unsuccessfully search the gardens for a suspected intruder.

Gertrude calls and Juliet goes into her apartment. Romeo sings meaningfully 'O nuit divine', and Juliet steals out on to the balcony. The act ends with a ravishing duet, 'Ah! ne fuis pas encore!', and a brief farewell.

Act III, part i. Friar Lawrence's cell. The Friar, hoping that Romeo and Juliet's union may lead to peace between the two houses, is to marry the couple. Lawrence's hopes are summed up in his prayer, 'Dieu, qui fis l'homme à ton image'. There is an effective trio, in which Romeo and Juliet respond passionately to the marriage vows the Friar intones, and a final quartet for Juliet, Romeo, Friar Lawrence and Gertrude, 'O pure bonheur'.

Part ii. A street near Capulet's house. Stéphano, thinking Romeo may still be hiding in Capulet's garden, sings an attractive song ('Que fais-tu, blanche tourterelle') calculated to bring the Capulets into the street and allow Romeo to escape. Grégorio rushes out and he and Stéphano fight. This brings out various Montagues and Capulets, including Mercutio, who fights Tybalt and is killed. Romeo in revenge kills Tybalt. At the height of the fighting, the Duke appears and banishes Romeo from Verona.

Act IV. Juliet's room. Romeo has come to bid her farewell before he goes into exile. Their feelings, their despair, find utterance in the music. There follows the duet, 'Nuit d'hyménée, O douce nuit d'amour', during whose course Romeo hears the lark, a sign of dawn. Juliet protests, 'Non, ce n'est pas le jour', Romeo follows with 'Ah! reste! encore dans mes bras enlacés'; and the composer rises to new heights of eloquence.

Hardly has Romeo gone than Gertrude appears to warn Juliet that her father is approaching with Friar Lawrence. Tybalt's dying wish, says Capulet, was that Juliet marry Count Paris at once. Capulet orders her to prepare and no one dares tell him of Juliet's secret marriage to Romeo. Capulet leaves and Friar Lawrence gives Juliet a potion which, when taken, will make her appear dead ('Buvez donc ce breuvage').

In a scene often omitted, in the grand hall of the palace, there occurs a ballet (essential for a production at the Opéra), after which Juliet drinks the potion and falls senseless.

Act V. The tomb of the Capulets. After an exchange between Friar Lawrence and Friar John, there occurs a short interlude, an exquisite miniature, which Gounod called 'Le Sommeil de Juliette' (Juliet's sleep). Romeo, having in exile heard that Juliet is dead, has broken into the vault ('Salut, tombeau sombre et silencieux').

He sings to what he takes to be the corpse of Juliet, 'O ma femme! o ma bien aimée!', then takes poison. Juliet, who is beginning to recover from the effects of the potion and is unaware that Romeo is dying, awakens. They sing 'Viens, fuyons au bout du monde', but it is too late: Romeo, feeling the poison working, tells Juliet what he has done, 'Console-toi, pauvre âme'. Juliet will not live without Romeo and stabs herself.   H.

ENRIQUE GRANADOS
(born 27 July 1867, died 24 March 1916)

GOYESCAS

Opera in three scenes (one act), text by Fernando Periquet. Première, Metropolitan, New York, 28 January 1916, with Fitziu, Perini, Martinelli, de Luca, conductor Bavagnoli (in Spanish). First performed Opéra, Paris, 1919; Buenos Aires, 1929; la Scala, Milan, 1937, with Carbone, Elmo, Civil, Poli, conductor Capuana; Royal College of Music, London, 1951; Florence, 1963; London, Morley College, 1965.

Rosario, *a highborn young lady* ....Soprano

Fernando, *a young officer, her lover* ....Tenor

Paquiro, *a toreador*...Baritone

Pepa, *a young girl of the people,*
      Paquiro's sweetheart........................ Mezzo-Soprano

Majas and Majos

Place: Madrid
Time: About 1800
Running Time: 1 hour 5 minutes

Granados is mainly famous as an inspired composer of piano music and songs, though his early stage works for Barcelona achieved some local success and are thought of as contributions to the establishment of opera in Spain. *Goyescas* was developed from existing piano music, and once the composer had organised the musical form, the librettist wrote round what had been composed. The work was intended for Paris but the war caused cancellation and it was given in New York; the composer was drowned when his ship was torpedoed by a German submarine as he was returning to Europe.

The characters and setting of the opera are sug-gested by the work of the great Spanish painter Goya. The opera opens with a crowd of majas and majos enjoying a holiday on the outskirts of Madrid. Some of the majas are engaged in the popular pastime of tossing the *pelele* (a man of straw) in a blanket. Paquiro the toreador is paying compliments to the women. Pepa, his sweetheart of the day, arrives in her dogcart. Soon Rosario, a lady of rank, arrives in her sedan-chair to keep a tryst with her lover, Fernando, a captain in the Royal Spanish Guards. Paquiro reminds her of a *baile de candil* (a ball given in a room lit by candlelight) which she once attended. He invites her to go again. Fernando overhears his remarks, and his jealousy is aroused. He informs Paquiro that Rosario will go to the ball, but that he, Fernando, will escort her. He extracts Rosario's promise to go with him, while Pepa, enraged by Paquiro's neglect, vows vengeance upon her.

The second tableau shows the scene at the ball. Fernando appears with Rosario. His haughty bearing and disdainful speech anger all present. The two men arrange for a duel that evening, and when Rosario recovers from a swoon, Fernando takes her away.

The third tableau reveals Rosario's garden. She is sitting on a bench listening in pensive mood to the song of the nightingale. This is the famous aria called 'The Lover and the Nightingale' (La Maja y el Ruiseñor), one of the most beautiful and luxuriant nocturnes ever written for voice and orchestra.

Fernando visits Rosario before keeping his appoint-ment with Paquiro. When a bell strikes the fatal hour,

Fernando tears himself away. He is followed hesitatingly by Rosario. Soon the silence is broken by a cry from Fernando, followed by a shriek from Rosario. They reappear. Rosario supports Fernando to a stone bench where he dies in her arms.

Granados adapted the music of his opera from a set of piano pieces (1911) inspired by the paintings of Goya:

1. Los Requiebos (Endearments)
2. Coloquio en la Reja (Conversation at the Window)

3. El Fandango del Candil (The Fandango by Moonlight)
4. Quejas o la Maja y el Ruiseñor (Complaints, or the Maiden and the Nightingale)
5. El Amor y la Muerte (Love and Death)
6. La Serenada del Espectro (The Spectre's Serenade)
7. El Pelele (The Straw-Man)

The first tableau begins and ends with No. 7; No. 3 starts the second; and the third is almost entirely based on the music of Nos. 4, 2 and 5.   H.

ANDRÉ-ERNEST-MODESTE GRÉTRY
(born 8 February 1741, died 24 September 1813)

Grétry began his career with *Les Mariages samnites*, privately performed for the Prince de Conti in 1768. Given in a public theatre, it brought him widespread recognition. The day after *Le Huron* was first performed at the Comédie-Italienne (i.e. the Opéra-Comique) in 1769, Grétry was offered five librettos to set; his career was made and his popularity endured for the next thirty years and over fifty operas. He set out to write French operas in the Italian style and mostly succeeded, particularly when he collaborated with the *encyclopédiste* Jean-François Marmontel (1723–99), who managed to treat serious themes lightly. Together, between 1768 and 1775, they created a string of distinguished works that defined and extended the *opéra-comique* tradition, among them *Zémire et Azor*, a version of *Beauty and the Beast* which has proved Grétry's most lasting opera. Marie-Antoinette loved *Zémire et Azor*, but Grétry was also pleased that one of the guards in the palace was such a fan that he presented arms when the composer passed.[1] Grétry received a pension from Louis XVI and from Napoleon.

ZÉMIRE ET AZOR

Comédie-ballet mêlée de chants et de danses in four acts, dedicated to the Comtesse du Barry, libretto by Jean-François Marmontel, based on Mme J.M. Le Prince de Beaumont's story *La belle et la bête* (1756). First performed at Fontainebleau, 9 November 1771, and later at the Comédie-Italienne, 16 December 1771. It reached Moscow in 1775; first U.K. performance, King's Theatre, London, 1779 (in Italian); American première, Philadelphia, 1787. Leipzig, 1993, conducted by Volker Robde.

Sander, *a Persian merchant* ....Baritone

Ali, *his servant/slave*...Tenor

Azor, *a Persian prince, King of Kamir* ....Tenor

Sander's daughters
    Zémire..Soprano
    Fatmé...Soprano
    Lisbé..Soprano

A Fairy ....Spoken

Troupes of Genies and Fairies (mute)

Place: Ormuz, Persia
Time: Legendary
Running Time: 2 hours

Act I. Inside a fairy palace at night. The overture portrays the storm that forces Sander and Ali to shelter in a deserted palace. Terrified, Ali tells himself that the storm has stopped, but, as the score points out, 'the accompaniment contradicts his words' (ariette, 'L'orage a cessé'). Sander is not frightened: since he lost all his worldly goods in a shipwreck, he does not care. Ali stays, for the sake of the food and wine that appear magically. He just wants to sleep (duet, 'Le temps est beau'), but before they leave, Sander remembers that

---

[1] Grétry *neveu*, *Grétry en famille*, Paris, 1814.

his youngest daughter Zémire asked him to bring back a rose. He cuts one, which causes their host to appear. Azor is a prince who has been transformed into a monster. He demands Sander's life in exchange for the rose. Sander pleads to be allowed to see his daughter for the last time, promising that one of his daughters or he himself will return.

Act II. Sander's house. Zémire and her sisters wait for their father to return. He tells them that they face poverty. The prospect does not daunt Zémire, who loves the rose he brings her (ariette, 'Rose chérie'). She realises something else is worrying her father. Ali swears he'll never travel again, certainly not by air ('Plus de voyage qui me tente'). Foreseeing his death, Sander writes a farewell letter to his daughters. Zémire forces Ali to tell her the truth and then to lead her to Azor (duet, 'Je veux le voir, je veux lui dire').

Act III. Inside Azor's palace. The spell that turned Azor into a monster forces him to love in vain, until he can find someone to love him as he is ('Ah! quel tourment d'être sensible'). Zémire sees that an apartment has been prepared for her and tells Ali to reassure her father. Genies dance for her. Zémire faints when she sees Azor, but soon realises how noble he is. Azor commands Ali to leave and promises Zémire he will not devour her. At his invitation, she sings a song ('La fauvette avec ses petits'). When he realises how much Zémire misses her family, he shows them to her in a magic vision. Azor tells Zémire he loves her, but allows her to return to her family for an hour, giving her a magic ring which frees her from his power, as long as she wears it. She promises to come back before sunset.

Act IV. Sander's house. Zémire arrives by flying chariot. Her family will not believe what she says about Azor (quartet, 'Ah! Je tremble. Quelles alarmes'). She throws the ring away and vanishes.

In a grotto of his palace, Azor sees the sun set and despairs ('Le soleil s'est caché dans l'onde'). Zémire searches for him, her voice echoed by distant horn-calls ('Azor, Azor! en vain ma voix t'appelle'), and when she declares that she loves him, the scene changes to another palace. The Fairy restores Azor's beauty and presides over the couple's wedding.

Given the opera's date and courtly provenance, it would be unwise to expect Grétry and Marmontel to plumb the mythic depths of the story of Beauty and the Beast. Indeed, the librettist intervened in the first production to reject the original designs for Azor's costume, and as a result, Marmontel congratulated himself that Azor's mask looked 'frightening, but not at all deformed, nor anything like a snout'. Marmontel's enlightened, eighteenth-century framework enabled him to tell the story with a striking degree of truth. If it is no longer about monstrosity, it is still about fathers, daughters and growing up. Music and words are marked by the cult of sensibility, yet the result is far from a *grisaille* or a Greuze.   P.

RICHARD COEUR-DE-LION
Richard the Lionheart

Comédie mise en musique in three acts, libretto by Michel-Jean Sedaine, based on a story in the *Bibliothèque universelle des romans* (1776). First performance, Salle Favart, Comédie Italienne, Paris, 21 October 1784, with Philippe as Richard, Clairval as Blondel, Madame Dugazon as Laurette and Mademoiselle Rosalie as Antonio. First U.K. performance, Covent Garden, London, 1786, adapted by Shield in an English translation by Thomas Linley, with Kemble as Richard and Mrs Jordan as Matilda. Revived Opéra Comique, 1841, when Adolphe Adam revised the orchestration.

Richard Coeur-de-Lion,
  King Richard I of England ....Tenor
Blondel, *his squire, a troubadour*.....................Baritone
Antonio ....Soprano
Sir Williams, *a Welsh knight*..............................Bass
Laurette, *his daughter*...................................Soprano
Colette...Soprano
Florestan, *Governor of the castle* ....Baritone
Countess Marguerite d'Artois......................Soprano

Peasants, Soldiers, Marguerite's Retinue

Place: Austria
Time: Twelfth Century
Running Time: 2 hours

Act I. The opera opens with a lilting, rustic chorus, as peasants look forward to the party to celebrate the fiftieth anniversary of old Mathurin's marriage to Mathurine. It sets up a vision of harmony, to which the opera eventually returns, in the last scene.

Seeking his master King Richard, who may have been incarcerated in the nearby castle, Blondel pretends to be blind. He is guided by the young peasant, Antonio. When Blondel asks if he likes to dance, Antonio replies there are other activities he prefers, such as embracing his fifteen-year-old girlfriend.

Unlikely as it may sound, his song has much charm ('La danse n'est pas ce que j'aime'). In a rather grander vein, Blondel reflects that, though the universe abandons Richard, he remains faithful, as does Marguerite, the woman who loves him. As a troubadour, Blondel is bound by love, faithfulness and constancy ('O Richard, o mon roi'). Sir Williams rebukes Guillot for having brought love letters from the Governor of the castle to Sir Williams's daughter, Laurette. Realising that this may provide him with access to the castle, Blondel tries to pacify him. Laurette arrives and denies that she sees or talks to the Governor. Antonio reads out the letter: the Governor explains that he cannot leave 'the prisoner', but if she appoints a time to see him at night, he will come.

We learn that Sir Williams is a Welshman who followed King Richard to the crusades, but when he returned home, he lost his property and was obliged to flee. When Sir Williams leaves, Blondel has a chance to question his daughter. Unfortunately, Laurette has no idea of the prisoner's identity, but she is not unhappy to learn that the Governor, or Chevalier Florestan, as he signed himself, longs to throw himself at her feet. Blondel tells her that Florestan hopes to see her tonight, which occasions her haunting *ariette*, 'Je crains de lui parler, la nuit'. This is the song that the old Countess sings in Tchaikovsky's *Queen of Spades*. In that context, Laurette's tremulous heartbeat (occasioned by Florestan's declaration of love) takes on a new, rather sinister sound, which is not appropriate in its original setting. Laurette confides in Blondel, who encourages her to see Florestan this evening. He sings her a little song, about love's blindness. She determines to learn it, so as to sing it to Florestan, and repeats it one beat after him ('Un bandeau couvre les yeux').

Blondel asks whether he can stay the night in her father's house. She explains that Sir Williams has agreed to let a 'grand lady' take over his entire house for one night, so the decision is up to her. When the lady arrives, Blondel recognises her as Marguerite, whom Richard loves. To make sure, he plays a fragment of a tune that Richard himself once composed. She recognises the tune at once and willingly allows Blondel to stay. The orchestra takes over the melody and elaborates it beautifully. The Countess's men offer him a drink. In return, Blondel sings his 'Chanson du Sultan Saladin'.

Act II. An entr'acte portrays the 'Ronde de Nuit', or night watch, in which Florestan allows Richard to enjoy the fresh air: when day dawns he must return to his cell. The Governor refuses to listen to his prisoner's attempts to enlist his support, rather as Rocco in *Fidelio* refuses to listen to another, rather different, Florestan. The parallel has even more point in the prisoner's aria, the highlight of the opera as its grand introduction suggests. Richard's vocal line is full of heroic leaps, as he reflects that his glory and his worth are of no use if the world is to forget his existence. He consoles himself by summoning the image of Marguerite to comfort him, but ends by longing for death to break his chains. His air is as moving as it is spectacular ('Si l'univers entier m'oublie').

Antonio leads Blondel to the edge of the parapet and then leaves. Blondel sings the romance that Richard himself once composed, and it becomes a duet as Richard recognises Blondel's voice. Curiously, the orchestral playout is the most effective section of all ('Une fièvre brulante'). Soldiers arrive (their music has a markedly Turkish flavour) and interrogate Blondel. They threaten to incarcerate him, but relent when he pleads blindness. When the Governor arrives, Blondel relays Laurette's reply to his letter: she will see him, if he comes to the party given by the noble lady that evening.

Act III. Blondel promises to give his friends Urbain and Guillot gold if they enable him to talk to the Countess. Their trio has a rather heartless vivacity ('Mon cher Urbain, mon ami Charle [*sic*]'). Blondel's singing can be heard from off-stage. He reveals that he recognised the Countess, tells her who he is and that Richard is nearby. She summons her knights and Sir Williams. Blondel tells Sir Williams to hold a party, ostensibly to celebrate Mathurin's anniversary. The Governor will attend, hoping to see Laurette. They will take advantage of his absence to storm the castle. Laurette is delighted to hear that the Governor will come. Peasants dance, led by Guillot, who sings a comic song in praise of marriage: when cattle couple, ploughing improves; everything goes better *à deux*.

The castle is successfully attacked to stirring, brass-inflected music. The finale proves disappointingly undistinguished: perhaps its very faint anticipation of *Fidelio*'s final scene makes it seem even worse than it is. They all salute King Richard, celebrate their happiness and the faithful friendship that ended their sadness. P.

H

JACQUES FRANÇOIS FROMENTAL HALÉVY
(born 27 May 1799, died 17 March 1862)

LA JUIVE
The Jewess

Opera in five acts, text by Scribe. Première at the Opéra, Paris, 23 February 1835, with Falcon, Dorus-Gras, Nourrit, Levasseur. First performed New Orleans, 1844; Drury Lane, London, 1846; Covent Garden, 1850 (in Italian), with Pauline Viardot, Tamberlik; Metropolitan, 1885, with Materna, conductor Damrosch. Revived Metropolitan, 1887, with Lilli Lehmann, Niemann, Fischer; 1919, with Ponselle, Caruso, Rothier, conductor Bodanzky; 1936, with Rethberg, Martinelli, Pinza; Paris, 1933, with Hoerner, Franz, Huberty; New York, 1944, with Dorée, Carron; Karlsruhe, 1952; Ghent, 1964, with Tony Poncet; London (in concert), 1973, with Richard Tucker. Rosa Raisa was famous in the role of Rachel, and Duprez one of Nourrit's most famous successors in the role of Eléazar. Both Caruso and Martinelli enjoyed great success as Eléazar.

Princess Eudoxie, *niece of the Emperor* ....Soprano

Rachel, *daughter of Eléazar*............................Soprano

Eléazar, *Jewish goldsmith*...................................Tenor

Léopold, *prince of the Empire* ....Tenor

Ruggiero, *provost of the city of Constance* ....Baritone

Albert, *sergeant in the army of the Emperor* ....Bass

Cardinal de Brogni, *president of the Council* ....Bass

Place: Constance, in Switzerland
Time: 1414
Running Time: 3 hours

Halévy was thirty-five at the time of the first performance of *La Juive*; later he wrote a number of other operas, many of them successful, but *La Juive* remains the work by which his name goes down to posterity. Wagner had more than a little admiration for his work, and he was, apart from Rossini, Verdi and Berlioz, perhaps the most talented of the composers who tackled the specifically French form of 'grand opera' – more so on the evidence of *La Juive* than Meyerbeer, but unfortunately without quite Meyerbeer's drive and energy.

The original plan was to give the role of Eléazar, one of the greatest in the nineteenth-century tenor repertory, to a high bass, and to place the scene of the opera in Spain at the time of the Inquisition's greatest power, but in the end the chief role was written for the great tenor Nourrit, who himself, if tradition is to be believed, had a hand in the writing of certain portions of the opera, notably the famous aria 'Rachel, quand du Seigneur'.

Before the opera opens, various relevant events have taken place. De Brogni was once chief magistrate of Rome. During one of his periodical absences from the city, it was captured by the besieging Neapolitans and considerable portions burnt. Among the houses pillaged and destroyed was Brogni's own; he returned to find his wife dead and his child vanished. In his agony, Brogni gave up his civic dignities and joined the Church, later rising to become the Cardinal who is one of the principal figures of the story.

Act I. The overture is concerned with contrasting the themes representing the Jewish and the Christian elements of the story, and the curtain rises to reveal a square in the city of Constance. On one side, the great door of a church; on the other, the house and workroom of Eléazar. Inside the church, the choir is chanting a *Te Deum*, outside a bystander resents the fact that some Jew seems to be working on a Christian feast-day. Léopold, the young general who has just triumphantly led his armies to victory over the Hussites, is in Constance in disguise – on a previous visit he had met and fallen in love with Eléazar's daughter, Rachel, and he wishes to resume the acquaintance. He is recognised by one of his own soldiers but enjoins the fellow to silence, at the same time enquiring the cause of the festivity he seems to have stumbled upon. Albert tells him that it is in honour of the state visit of the

La Juive *(Metropolitan Opera House, New York, c. 1919). Enrico Caruso (1873–1921) and Rosa Ponselle (1897–1981) as Eléazar and his daughter Rachel.*

Emperor, who has called a great council with a view to uniting all the Christians of the world into one solid faith, an undertaking only envisaged since Léopold's own victories over the dissident Hussites.

A great choral 'Hosanna' resounds from the church, and the congregation pours out, to listen to the proclamation in the Emperor's name of a public holiday by Ruggiero, the provost of the town. Nothing could better suit the temper of the people, but no sooner have they voiced their enthusiastic reaction than Ruggiero hears the sound of work going on in Eléazar's shop and orders the occupants to be brought before him. Eléazar answers Ruggiero's questions with defiance; did he not watch his own sons burned by Christians? Why should he bow to their laws? Ruggiero threatens him with a similar death, but Cardinal Brogni is passing with his retinue, and asks what is the cause of the noise. He recognises Eléazar, and the jeweller reminds him that it was in Rome that they formerly knew each other (there is no mention of it in the opera, but in Scribe's original story it is made clear that Brogni had banished Eléazar from Rome, thus saving his life after he had been condemned to death as an usurer). Brogni sings a smoothly flowing *cavatina*, 'Si la rigueur et la vengeance', in which he prays that enlightenment may come to the Jewish unbelievers.

Only Léopold is left behind. He takes up a position outside Eléazar's house (he has been taken on there as a workman under the name of Samuel, and they believe him to be Jewish), and proceeds to serenade Rachel. It is a charming, high-lying melody, and it is not long before Rachel answers it from inside. She bids him come that very evening, when her father and his fellow-believers will be celebrating the feast of the Passover. Léopold is about to object when a crowd rushes into the square, intent on making the most of the Emperor's largesse. The choruses pile up on one another, there is a brisk dance, and drinking is general. Eléazar and Rachel, trying to cross the square, are recognised as Jews by Ruggiero and set upon by the mob. Eléazar confronts them with dignity, but they are for throwing him in the lake, when salvation comes in the person of Léopold who, though still disguised, is immediately recognised by Albert, who causes the crowd to leave the Jewish pair alone. Rachel is astonished at the effect Samuel has on the Christians and at first tries to restrain him from intervening. Eléazar continues to pour scorn on the hated Christians.

Act II. A room in Eléazar's house, where the feast of the Passover is being celebrated. Eléazar leads the chant ('O Dieu, Dieu de nos pères'), which the others, together with Rachel, repeat after him. Eléazar pronounces a curse upon anyone who dares profane the holy feast ('Si trahison ou perfidie') and then distributes the unleavened bread, Samuel being the last to receive it. He thinks he has escaped notice when he drops it without tasting it, but Rachel has seen his gesture, and is worried by what it may mean. The scene is immensely impressive, and the measured incantation of the opening is one of the most remarkable moments in the opera.

Eléazar's supplication to God ('Dieu, que ma voix tremblante') is barely finished when there is a knock at the door. He commands the Jews to put away the ritual vessels and candles, and the table is removed, the Jews themselves going out through a back door. Léopold is about to depart, when Eléazar commands him to stay with him. The door is opened, and in comes the Princess Eudoxie. She makes herself known, and Eléazar kneels before her. Her object is to buy from him a fine chain for her husband Léopold, whom that day she expects back from the wars. Léopold overhears the conversation, and is filled with remorse at his deceit.

While Eléazar sees Eudoxie to the door, Rachel returns and asks Samuel to explain his conduct when saving them from the mob, and also, that evening, at the Passover service. He protests that he must see her in great privacy.

Rachel comes back to keep her rendezvous with Léopold. Her heart is full of foreboding, even fear ('Il va venir! et d'effroi je me sens frémir'). The aria admirably expresses the mixture of feelings of which she is conscious, and is full of the apprehension with which she awaits their meeting. Léopold admits that he has deceived her, and is in fact a Christian. Rachel bitterly reproaches him for his deception; he can but defend himself by saying that there was no thought in his mind but love of her. His pleading is so passionate that Rachel is on the point of yielding, when her father confronts them.

Eléazar declares that their offence is such that they shall not escape punishment. In a trio they admit their guilt and express terror at the wrath of Eléazar, who tells them that only the fact that Samuel is a Jew prevents him from striking him dead on the spot for his falsity. Léopold bids him strike; he is a Christian. Rachel intercepts the blow, and pleads distractedly for her lover; she also is guilty. Eléazar declares himself willing to agree to the marriage, but his wrath knows no bounds when Léopold says that he is unable to marry Rachel.

Act III in some versions begins with a scene for Eudoxie and Rachel, who asks to be allowed to serve as a slave in her palace for one day only; she has trailed Léopold to the palace, and does not yet know his real identity. Eudoxie agrees to her request.

When this scene is omitted, the act begins in the gardens of the Emperor's palace, where a festival in honour of Léopold is in progress. The Emperor himself is seated at the high table, together with Brogni, Léopold and Eudoxie. A ballet is performed for their entertainment, and at its end, Eléazar and Rachel come to bring Eudoxie the chain she has bought for Léopold. When she is about to place it round her husband's neck, Rachel snatches it from her and announces that Léopold has committed the heinous crime of consorting with a Jewess, and that she herself is the Jewess in question.

There is a moment of stupefied horror. When Eléazar asks if the Christian laws are directed only against Jews or apply equally to themselves – Léopold has silently admitted the charge – Cardinal Brogni rises to his feet and pronounces a terrible anathema on all three, who have dared to break the laws of heaven ('Vous, qui du Dieu vivant': You, who defy the living God).

Act IV. All have been condemned to death, but Eudoxie resolves to risk humiliation in order to save Léopold, whom she still loves. She begs Rachel to retract her charge. Rachel at first proudly refuses, then says she will do as she has been asked, saying to herself that a Jewess can outdo a Christian in magnanimity. The scene is highly dramatic and is succeeded by one hardly less compelling when the Cardinal confronts Rachel and begs her to abjure her faith and to save herself from death. She refuses.

Brogni resolves to send for Eléazar in a last effort to save Rachel. He pleads with him to renounce his faith, and in so doing to save her life; but the old man is resolute in the face of temptation, and refuses to deny his forefathers' creed. He reminds Brogni of the time when his house and family perished in the conflagration; his daughter was saved by a Jew who came to fight the flames, and she is alive now. But though her whereabouts are known to him, he will take his revenge by carrying the secret with him to death. Brogni implores him to reveal what he knows, but he will say no more.

Eléazar is torn with doubts; can he bear, by his orthodoxy and his own uncompromising hatred of Christians, to send his daughter to her death? The thought tortures him, and resolves itself into a great expression of emotion ('Rachel, quand du Seigneur'). This is the climax of the opera, and Eléazar is at one and the same time at his noblest and his most human. He hears the savage cries: 'Au bûcher, les Juifs' (The Jews to the scaffold!) from outside, and is strengthened in his decision; Rachel shall die a victim of their hate. The end of the act is hardly less moving than the great aria a little earlier.

Act V. From a tent a view is to be had of the ground on which the scaffold is erected for the martyrdom of the two Jews – Léopold's sentence has been commuted to one of banishment. The people howl for the death of the Jews, and presently Eléazar and Rachel are seen coming slowly into view. Just as he is about to mount the scaffold Eléazar asks Rachel if she would like at the last moment to abjure her faith and adopt Christianity, but she proudly disdains any such idea. She is thrown into the cauldron at the very moment when Brogni is told by Eléazar, 'Your daughter perished in those flames'.   H.

IAIN HAMILTON

(born 6 June 1922)

Iain Hamilton's success as a composer included no staged opera before *The Catiline Conspiracy*, after Ben Jonson's play, was mounted in 1974 by Scottish Opera. The earlier *The Royal Hunt of the Sun*, based on Peter Shaffer's highly successful play and described by the composer as 'much more a music-theatre work than an opera', followed in a performance by English National Opera in 1977. *Tamburlaine*, written for radio, was his third opera concerned, as has been written, with the use and misuse of power. With *Anna Karenina*, commissioned for English National Opera, both his music and the drama inspiring it moved from a largely atonal basis to something much more lyrical and tonal. *Raleigh's Dream* was performed at Duke University, Durham, in the U.S.A. (1984), *Lancelot* in the open air at Arundel Castle in 1985, and the large-scale *Dick Whittington* has so far remained unperformed.

ANNA KARENINA

Opera in three acts, libretto by the composer after Tolstoy's novel. Première by English National Opera, London, 7 May 1981, with Lois McDonall and Geoffrey Pogson, conductor Howard Williams. First performed Los Angeles, 1983, conductor Chris Nance, who also conducted E.N.O.'s revival in 1985.

Alexei Karenin, *Minister in Imperial
    Government* ....Baritone
Anna, *his wife* ....Soprano
Count Alexei Vronsky ....Tenor
Prince Stiva Oblonsky, *Anna's brother*...........Baritone
Dolly, *his wife*.....................................Mezzo-Soprano
Kitty, *her sister*..Soprano
Colonel Yashvin, *friend of Vronsky's*.....................Bass
Countess Betsy, *Anna's friend*..............Mezzo-Soprano
Countess Vronskaya, *Vronsky's mother*.........Soprano
Countess Lydia, *friend of Karenin's* ....Contralto
Seriosha, *Anna's son*..Treble
Landau, *a mystic*...Tenor

Servants, Guests, Travellers

Place: In or Near St Petersburg and Moscow
Time: 1870s
Running Time: 2 hours 15 minutes

Act I. Vronsky is at Moscow's railway station to meet his mother, who arrives from St Petersburg with Anna, whom Vronsky meets for the first time. Anna is deeply affected when a railwayman is crushed to death.

Dolly is distraught at Stiva's unfaithfulness, and Anna tries to comfort her. There is talk that Vronsky will propose to Kitty, Dolly's sister. A visitor is announced. Stiva goes to meet him and says it was Vronsky but he wouldn't come up. Anna seems a little nervous.

Waltz music introduces the ball and a sequence of five dances. Vronsky and Anna are obviously drawn to each other, to the dismay of Dolly and Stiva and the consternation of Kitty, who runs from the room.

Countess Betsy's, St Petersburg. There is gossip about Anna and Vronsky, who arrive and are soon in close conversation. Vronsky says they will either be the most happy or the most miserable of people. When Karenin arrives he warns Anna people are talking. He is left alone with his jealousy.

At the racecourse and watched by the fashionable crowd, Vronsky has a bad fall. Karenin observes Anna's horror and tries to take her home, but she rounds on him and declares her love for Vronsky.

In a garden house at Karenin's, Anna hears that Vronsky is safe. She regrets telling him before the race that she is carrying his child, but when he comes in, their love consoles them and they dream of travelling to Italy.

Act II. Karenin decides not to give Anna a divorce. Vronsky drinks with Yashvin, then tries to dispel Anna's forebodings. Anna sings a lullaby for Seriosha, her son, then has a bitter exchange with Karenin.

Dolly is coldly received when she asks Karenin not to divorce Anna because of the scandal. Anna's telegram begging Karenin to come to Moscow where she is dying produces a dilemma: he fears a trick but worries what people would say if he did not go.

In St Petersburg, Anna is delirious after giving birth to a daughter. Karenin arrives, Vronsky on his own expresses his love for Anna, who demands he and Karenin forgive each other. If he does not divorce Anna, says Stiva, she will die. Karenin agrees and the three men reflect on what she means to each of them. Vronsky and Anna again dream of Italy.

Act III. Vronsky's estate outside Moscow. Stiva is optimistic about Anna's acceptance in society, but Dolly and Vronsky discuss a recent snub at the opera. Vronsky fears that without a divorce, even their children will be legally Karenin's. Anna feels she cannot ask Karenin for anything: even Seriosha is now with Countess Lydia.

Stiva finds Karenin changed, declining, since Anna once refused it, to countenance divorce. Karenin is totally under the influence of Countess Lydia and the mystic Landau.

In Moscow, Dolly and Yashvin visit Anna and Vronsky who, once they have gone, quarrel over something as trivial as the day they should leave for the country. Vronsky leaves, is about to turn back, then goes. Time becomes vague, Anna tries to contact him by message and note, then is found at the railway station where, half out of her mind, she staggers on to the track in front of a train. Vronsky, overcome with remorse that he never turned back when instinct suggested it, falls by her body.

It is interesting that the composer decided that the important figure of Levin was peripheral to the drama he was looking for. In structure, the opera is traditional, with ensembles like the trio between Vronsky, Stiva and Karenin in Act II; and large-scale scenes such as the opening at the station, the ballroom dances, and the racecourse. The music, in comparison with what he had written before, might be described as romantic, and as the composer has written, 'one thing matters above all else – love. It is born, rejoiced in, suffered through, betrayed, and finally lost.'   H.

GEORGE FRIDERIC HANDEL
(born 23 February 1685, died 14 April 1759)

The music of Handel's operas represents a high point of the first half of the eighteenth century, and such obstacle as there is between us and them lies in conventions which they respect and from which we were until recently remote. This was a period of consolidation in operatic history, and in Handel's day convention had become entrenched, with the aria, and more particularly the 'aria da capo' with its obligatory repeat, reigning supreme; with an exit following virtually every aria, itself a purely individual expression; with virtually no ensembles and no chorus, so that even a final number tended to be sung by the principals together; with libretti geared to provide opportunities for 'typical' arias (expressing pity, sorrow, amorous intention, regret, despair, determination, martial ardour, etc.) rather than for character development and surprise. Castrati ruled the roost, and the music for such heroes as Julius Caesar and Tamburlaine was written for vocal virtuosi whose breath control and volume were apparently sufficient to compensate for a physique which was often obese.

The revival of interest in Handel's operas which came in the early 1920s brought with it much revision, sometimes of musical detail in the interest of musico-dramatic continuity, almost always in the *tessitura* of the voices, so as to preserve an attempt at physical verisimilitude. In a word, castrato heroes became baritones or basses. In the mid-twentieth century, during the consolidation period of the Handel revival, an opposite and more scholarly attitude began to prevail, so that more or less strapping mezzos tackled the great heroes of antiquity, with results which were occasionally surprising to look at and not always heroic vocally, but which allowed Handel's orchestration to be retained and such anomalies avoided as for instance the changing of an obbligato for flute to one for oboe, in order to cut out the solecism of matching the higher instrument to a baritone when Handel had intended it to be in double harness with a mezzo. Each solution has its snags, as has the more obviously reprehensible (but, in view of length, tempting) practice of truncating 'da capo' arias, which when cut often sound either pointless or too long, sometimes paradoxically both. All the same, performance of Handel's operas, more or less complete, with the pitch of the original voices maintained (even in an age with no castrati), is by the late twentieth century the accepted norm.

Handel himself often made changes to suit the exigencies of a new situation, altering a soprano part for tenor, importing a number from another work (and another situation) for a new prima donna, adding or subtracting as seemed to him best in each new set of circumstances. But his changes often involved recomposition, and there is an overwhelming case to be made for his dramatic awareness within the convention, for his sheer stagecraft; most modern revivals which are sung to anything like the composer's requirements, and respect his intentions, serve to demonstrate that Handel's operas are the product of one of the medium's sovereign composers of genius.   H.

AGRIPPINA

Opera in three acts, libretto by Cardinal Vincenzo Grimani. Première Venice, January 1710, with Durastanti, Diamante Maria Scarabelli, Valeriano Pellegrini (castrato), Francesca Vanini-Broschi, Antonio Carli. First performed Naples, 1713; Hamburg, 1718; Vienna, 1719. Revived Halle, 1943; first English performance, Abingdon, 1963; Buxton Festival, 1992.

Agrippina, *the Emperor's wife*	Soprano
Poppea (Poppaea)	Soprano
Nerone (Nero), *Agrippina's son*	Soprano
Claudio (Claudius), *the Emperor*	Bass
Ottone (Otho)	Contralto
Pallante (Pallas), *a freedman*	Bass
Narciso, *a freedman*	Alto
Lesbo, *Claudio's servant*	Bass
Giunone (Juno)	Contralto

Place: Rome
Time: First Century A.D.
Running Time: 2 hours 55 minutes

*A*grippina was the second of the two operas Handel wrote during his sojourn in Italy (1706–10), one of the few texts written specially for him and not set by other composers. The serious issues and conflicts which arise in the course of the action are far from flippantly treated, but there is no doubt that composer and librettist have a satirical intent in mind, in this respect following, according to Winton Dean,[1] Italian taste of an earlier generation – nearer to Busenello and Monteverdi in their treatment of a classical subject in *L'Incoronazione di Poppea* than to Metastasio.

The plot is involved but not unnecessarily complicated. Agrippina, the Empress, schemes untiringly to secure the throne after Claudius' death for her son Nero by her first marriage. Claudius is weak and self-indulgent, Poppea self-seeking, Nero youthful and far from the monster of later life. Ottone, the loyal lieutenant, is in love with Poppea whom he subsequently marries, though later losing her to Nero once he becomes emperor.

Act I. The overture suggests the brilliant, fast-moving character of the opera. Agrippina has no difficulty in rousing Nero's ambitions by convincing him that the recently received news of Claudius' death suggests he should set about wooing the plaudits of the mob. She will use both Pallante and Narciso, each of whom is in love with her, to further her ambitions, but these receive a setback when to the sound of trumpets the safe arrival of the Emperor is announced. Ottone has saved Claudius' life and won a promise of the succession; he is however in love with Poppea, as, we quickly discover, are both Claudius and Nero, and would if need be sacrifice the throne for her. Poppea learns Claudius will visit her that very night but would much prefer Ottone, whom she fancies, as in an unguarded moment she admits to Agrippina. The Empress sees her chance and persuades Poppea to arouse Claudius' jealousy by convincing him Ottone has bargained to give her up in return for the succession. Poppea, furious at Ottone's apparent duplicity, successfully works on Claudius, who little knows that Poppea and Agrippina are in deadly league.

Act II. Pallante and Narciso now believe Agrippina has hoodwinked both of them. Agrippina effusively greets Claudius and turns him against Ottone, who is soon proclaimed a traitor, Agrippina,

---

[1] *Handel's Operas* (O.U.P. 1987), a definitive study.

Poppea and Nero all joining in denunciation of his conduct. Poppea still yearns for Ottone and, when he protests his innocence of the charge that he bartered her love, returns the sword he has handed her rather than plunging it into his heart. In pursuit of her goal, Poppea strings Nero along as well as Claudius, while Agrippina to strengthen her position promises her favours in succession to Pallante and Narciso, provided each will dispose of the other as well as Ottone. She persuades Claudius in his own interest and for his own safety to announce Nero as his successor, then crows over her manipulative success.

Act III. Poppea in succession hides Ottone and Nero behind curtains in her apartment, then manoeuvres Claudius when he too comes for an assignation into denouncing Nero, who to his fury is caught apparently *in flagrante delicto*. Only if Claudius protects her against Agrippina's rage, insists Poppea, will he enjoy her love. It is Ottone's turn; he must promise Poppea he loves her more than the throne itself. Nero asks for Agrippina's help and is told the throne is more important than Poppea. Narciso and Pallante meanwhile decide a full confession to Claudius is their one chance of preferment, but Claudius is baffled as to who is telling the truth and who not. Agrippina, in a masterstroke, when accused of plotting against the Emperor, admits the charge but insists it was all done to protect him. Pallante and Narciso shamefacedly feel forced to confirm her claim.

Claudius in an effort to sort things out sends for Poppea, Nero and Ottone, gets Nero to admit he was hiding in Poppea's room and orders him to marry her, confirming Ottone as his successor. Ottone chooses Poppea rather than the throne, Claudius reverses his previous decision, seems glad to be rid of Poppea, and has Juno solemnly bless the new arrangement.

The figures of the opera, apart from Lesbo, are real enough though historical facts are rearranged, and opinion is agreed that this is one of the most satisfactory texts Handel ever set – compact, logical, freely flowing. Apart from Ottone who behaves with decency throughout, the characters are by and large immoral though not wholly without redeeming features: Agrippina is ferociously ambitious, but for her son, not herself; the scheming Poppea is courageous and seems genuinely in love with Ottone; even the bumbling

Claudius ends by being magnanimous. Handel's music splendidly mirrors their faults and foibles, the arias full of feeling however ambivalent the situations in which they find themselves and however much Handel was indebted to earlier works of his own, to say nothing of his borrowings from composer-colleagues like Keiser and Mattheson. Of more than forty numbers, only five arias are completely new – but when was borrowing to greater effect?

Agrippina is a formidable figure, richly endowed with arias of power and character, rising to a climax in the *scena* late in Act 2 ('Pensieri, voi mi tormenta') when, her ambitions apparently working out, she is overcome with foreboding. Later, triumphant now that Nero's star is in the ascendant and in G major now after G minor, she ends the act in exuberant mood. Poppea, however manipulative, is a superficially more attractive figure – a 'sex kitten' like Cleopatra, Winton Dean calls her – with arias which depict her essential frivolity, from the light-hearted mirror-gazing when we first meet her ('Vaghe perle') to the most attractive of all ('Bel piacere'), a kind of love song to Ottone, with which she closes her solo account. Ottone, written for a contralto, is in strong contrast, full of passion, preferring to demand justice rather than pity.

Altogether and in spite of borrowings, an extraordinary opera for a composer not yet twenty-five.   H.

RINALDO

Opera in three acts, libretto by Giacomo Rossi after Aaron Hill. Première Haymarket, London, 24 February 1711 (7 March new style), with Francesca Boschi as Goffredo, Isabella Girardeau as Almirena, Nicolini as Rinaldo, Elisabetta Pilotti Schiavonetti as Armida and Boschi as Argante. First performed in Dublin, 1711, by Nicolini's company; Hamburg, 1715, in German; Naples, 1718 (with additional music by Leonardo Leo). *Rinaldo* was very successful in London, given fifteen times in the first season, twenty-two times between then and 1715 and revived with extensive alterations in 1717 and 1731. First performed in America at Houston in Martin Katz's musical edition, in March 1975, with Marilyn Horne, Noëlle Rogers, Evelyn Mandac, Samuel Ramey, conductor Lawrence Foster. Revived Halle, 1954, in German; London, Sadler's Wells, by Handel Opera Society, 1961 and 1965, with Helen Watts/Yvonne Minton, Jennifer Vyvyan; New York, Metropolitan, 1984, with Horne, Benita Valente, Edda Moser, Ramey, conductor Mario Bernardi.

Goffredo, *Captain General of the*
    Christian Army ....Contralto[1]

---

[1] See note opposite.

Almirena, *his daughter, affianced to Rinaldo*.... Soprano
Rinaldo, *a Christian hero*................... Mezzo-Soprano[1]
Eustazio, *Goffredo's brother* ....Contralto[1]
Argante, *King of Jerusalem and Armida's lover* .... Bass[1]
Armida, *a sorceress, Queen of Damascus*..........Soprano
A Christian Magician ....Bass[1]
A Herald...Bass
A Siren...Soprano
Two Mermaids...Soprano

Time: The Crusades
Place: Palestine
Running Time: 2 hours 55 minutes

*R*inaldo was the foundation of Handel's success in England. At the instigation of the impresario John James Heidegger, manager of the Queen's Theatre, London, he met Aaron Hill, an extraordinary character, learned in many arts and sciences, not least those of the theatre, and Hill very rapidly wrote a libretto on the legend of Rinaldo and Armida, drawing on Tasso and Ariosto. Giacomo Rossi translated it into Italian for Handel, who composed the opera in what seems an incredibly short space of time, some say as little as fourteen days. Since he re-used, for as much as two-thirds of the opera, music he had already written, the feat is partly one of skill in re-organising existing material.

One of the features of *Rinaldo* is extravagant use of stage spectacle, one of Aaron Hill's specialities, and a modern production has to provide magic and transformation scenes if justice is to be done to the original concept. Handel altered the opera a number of times, re-allocating the roles according to the voices available to sing them (Goffredo moving from soprano to castrato, Rinaldo from castrato to mezzo-soprano, Eustazio starting as contralto and being eventually eliminated altogether). In 1731, he substantially remodelled the whole work, rewriting most of the role of Almirena, toning down some extravagances, omitting subsidiary characters and fashioning a more convincing ending, with Armida and Argante no longer converted to Christianity but rather descending to hell in a chariot.

Act I. The Crusaders are besieging Jerusalem and, in expectation of victory, their general, Goffredo, promises the hand of his daughter Almirena to the hero, Rinaldo, who is in love with her, a passion she indicates she returns.

A Saracen herald announces that Argante, King of Jerusalem, is asking that Goffredo will treat with him. Spectacularly preceded by his troops and announced by trumpets and drums, Argante arrives to ask for a three-day truce. His aria ('Sibillar gli angui d'Aletto') is a mighty and magnificent challenge to a bass and in it Samuel Ramey won the Metropolitan audience in a night. Goffredo unhesitatingly accepts and Argante, who is more confident in the wiles of Armida (for whose charms he admits he languishes) than in the force of arms of his troops, is delighted with the result of his action.

Armida makes her appearance, drawn by dragons and, in a fine aria marked *furioso*, invoking the Furies. She leaves Argante in no doubt that only with the disappearance of Rinaldo can the Crusaders be defeated, and indicates that she herself will undertake his elimination.

In charming surroundings, Rinaldo and Almirena exchange pledges of love. Almirena's aria, 'Augelletti, che cantate', is with its twirling recorders not only charming in its own right but was accompanied in 1711, says Winton Dean in *Handel and the Opera Seria*, 'by the release of a flock of live birds, which left their mark not only on the opera and the press, in the persons of Addison and Steele, but on the heads of the audience'. She and Rinaldo sing a delightful duet but Armida suddenly appears and with the help of her supernatural powers abducts Almirena. Rinaldo movingly laments ('Cara sposa') that he is powerless to intervene. When Goffredo and Eustazio arrive, they mourn together the misfortune which has overtaken them. Goffredo and Eustazio believe that they may get help from a Christian magician – the aria demonstrates optimism that is nothing short of jaunty – and Rinaldo recovers his fortitude and in a rapid virtuoso aria ('Venti, turbini, prestate') swears vengeance.

Act II. A boat, at its helm a spirit in the guise of a lovely woman, lies at anchor in the bay. Seductive songs in 6/8 fill the night and when Rinaldo, Goffredo and Eustazio arrive, Rinaldo is invited on board to be conducted to Almirena. Goffredo, horror-struck to see Rinaldo apparently forgetting his warlike duties in favour of the charms of a siren, has not understood that Rinaldo's departure has as objective the rescue of his beloved, and tries vainly to restrain him.

---

[1] These five parts were sung in one or other of the groups of performances in Handel's own day by castrati, and four of them in the same period by female singers.

Rinaldo (Houston Grand Opera, 1975; first U.S. performance). Marilyn Horne in the title role.

In Argante's palace, Almirena is held prisoner and continues to mourn her captive state, deaf to declarations of love from the King, whose attachment to Armida has faded. Her aria ('Lascia chi'io pianga') is one of Handel's most celebrated, and is derived from a sarabande in his *Almira* (1705).

When Rinaldo arrives, he is immediately intercepted by Armida, who herself has fallen in love with the Christian knight, and, in order to seduce him, takes on the outward appearance of Almirena. Rinaldo is on the point of succumbing to temptation, but something holds him back. His bravura aria ('Abbruggio, avampo, e fremo') is followed by an outburst from Armida, who is furious that Rinaldo is proof against her blandishments and yet cannot bring herself to invoke the Furies against someone she loves. The *largo* section is all tenderness and warmth, but in a short *presto* middle section she rivals Rinaldo's virtuosity.

Argante comes on the scene and, believing in his turn that he is talking to Almirena, continues to protest his love, promising to deliver her from the spells of Armida. When the sorceress Queen resumes her own personality, there is a violent quarrel between her and her former lover, and in a splendid aria ('Vo' far guerra') she swears to remove from him the support she has so far supplied.

Act III. Goffredo finds himself near a mountain on whose summit is Armida's magic castle, guarded by monsters. The monsters repel the first assault but the Christian Magician eventually promises to help deliver Goffredo's daughter and the knight Rinaldo, and he gives him magic wands which will help overcome Armida's spells.

In the garden of the palace, Armida plans to kill Almirena. Rinaldo however arrives in time to prevent the crime and himself is about to strike Armida with his sword when the Furies intervene and save the sorceress.

With Goffredo's arrival and with the help of the magic wands, the castle disappears to be replaced by a desert in which can be seen the city of Jerusalem. For the Christians, it is victory, which Rinaldo celebrates with much conviction. Armida and Argante are reconciled and their troops pass before them (March). Their duet celebrates the forthcoming battle and their own reconciliation.

Goffredo, Almirena and Rinaldo rejoice in deliverance from Armida's thrall – Almirena's aria ('Bel piacere'), the singing in unison with violin, is a charmingly airy inspiration – before Eustazio recalls them all to the task in hand. It is the turn of the Christian army to march in review before its commander; the catchy tune of the March, with its drum and trumpets, is known from the *Beggar's Opera* (see page 239). Rinaldo retains trumpets and drum for his bravura proclamation of his resolve ('Or la tromba'), which is shortly followed by the battle itself, and marching and counter-marching by both sides, until the outcome is settled by Rinaldo's intervention. Argante and Armida are taken prisoner, but are pardoned and converted to Christianity (in his 1731 version, Handel changed this dénouement). Rinaldo is free to marry Almirena and a final chorus glorifies virtue.   H.

TESEO

Dramma tragico per musica in five acts, libretto by Nicola Haym, based on Philippe Quinault's *tragédie lyrique Thésée* for Lully (1675).[1] First performance, Queen's Theatre, Haymarket, London, 10 January 1713, with Valeriano Pellegrini, Margherita L'Epine and Elisabetta Pilotti-Schiavonetti. Not revived until 1947 at Göttingen. U.S. première, Boston College Theater Arts Center, 1985.

Teseo, *Egeo's son, unknown to his father* ....Soprano

Agilea, *engaged to Egeo, in love with Teseo*.......Soprano

Medea, *enchantress, in love with Egeo* ....Soprano

Egeo, *King of Athens, in love with Agilea* ....Alto

Clizia, *Agilea's confidante, in love
     with Arcane*...Soprano

Arcane, *Egeo's general, in love with Clizia*..............Alto

Fedra, *Medea's confidante* ....Mute

Minerva, *goddess*...Mute

Priest of Minerva...Bass

Running Time: 3 hours

Handel was at the beginning of his career when he wrote *Teseo*. The title-page to the libretto published in 1713 describes him as *Maestro di Cappella di S.A.E. di*

Hannover. Having found that his pastorale *Il Pastor Fido* was in advance of contemporary London taste, with *Teseo* the composer returned to safer ground and imitated the spectacular magic and machinery of *Rinaldo*.

Act I. Overture. The temple of Minerva. Agilea is engaged to marry Egeo, the aged King of Athens. As battle rages, she tells her confidante Clizia that Egeo's heroic general, Teseo, led her to safety here and confesses that she has fallen in love with him. When Arcane brings news of Teseo's bravery, Agilea prays to the gods to protect him. Arcane loves Clizia, who feels, however, that she cannot trust him completely. When she sends him to report on Teseo, he assumes Clizia is in love and is tormented by jealousy ('Ah! cruda gelosia!'). They say goodbye to one another (duetto, 'Addio! mio caro bene').

King Egeo tells Agilea to rejoice, now that the rebels have been defeated: soon she will share his throne ('Serenatevi, o luci belle'). He discounts her suggestion that she should honour him as a father, rather than as a lover, and when she further reminds him that he was supposed to marry Medea, he explains that he plans to marry the sorceress to the son he has had brought up in Troezen. Egeo reminds Agilea that he loves only her. Agilea comforts herself with the thought that she and Teseo love one another ('M'adora l'idol mio').

Act II. Egeo's palace. Medea envies the happiness of anyone who enjoys rest and innocent peace. Having already been driven by passion to murder her brother and children, she recognises that love that is forced can never last. Egeo arrives and thanks Medea for her contribution to his victory. She sees through his scheme to marry her off to his son, so that he himself can marry Agilea, but agrees, as long as she can marry Teseo. Arcane warns the King that the troops want their hero Teseo to succeed him.

A square in Athens. Teseo enters in triumph; he tells Medea that he loves Agilea. She promises to intercede for him. Alone, Medea resolves either to secure Teseo for herself or to destroy her rival.

Act III. Clizia asks the friendly stars to use their influence on her behalf. Arcane promises her he will ask the King to let them marry. Agilea longs for Teseo to return ('Vieni, torna, idolo mio'). He comes to tell her that he will either appease the King's

---

[1] For further details of how a French opera became Italian, Handel's only five-act opera, see David Kimbell, 'The Libretto of Handel's *Teseo*', *Music & Letters*, vol. xliv, Oxford, 1963.

jealousy or leave with her for some other country.

When her threats have no effect on her rival Agilea, Medea changes the scene into 'a horrid Desert full of frightful Monsters'[1] ('Numi, chi ci soccorre!'). Medea then summons spirits that 'bring Eternal Night'. On her instructions, they torment Agilea before carrying her off.

Act IV. Hearing that Medea has attacked Agilea, Egeo determines on revenge. When Agilea refuses to obey Medea, the enchantress brings on Teseo, sleeping; Agilea cannot wake him. Medea threatens his life and so forces Agilea to yield and agree to the royal marriage. Medea changes the scene into an 'Inchanted Island' and wakes Teseo, who wonders who restored him to consciousness. Faithful to her word to Medea, Agilea refuses to speak to Teseo. He cannot understand what has changed her affections so drastically. She weeps and eventually admits that she had to seem pitiless to save him. He reveals that he is in fact Egeo's son, brought up in Troezen, so she can indeed make a 'royal marriage'. Having overheard their conversation Medea appears to them out of a cloud and seems to bless their union, since their virtues withstand her fury. The lovers in duet affirm their fidelity to one another.

Act V. Medea's enchanted palace. Medea determines that Teseo and Agilea must die to satisfy her longing for revenge ('Morirò, ma vendicata'). Knowing Egeo is ignorant that Teseo is his son, she persuades the King that Teseo threatens the throne's stability. At first, Egeo stands firm, but Medea persuades him that Teseo must die for the sake of his son in Troezen. She hands him a poisoned cup to give Teseo, who arrives leading Agilea and followed by a crowd of admirers. Teseo takes the cup and swears fidelity to the King on his sword. At once the King recognises the sword as the one he left with his son as a token. 'Medea flies away, having heard [Teseo] own'd by his Father.' United by his father with Agilea, Teseo 'expresses his Joy in the Approach of his Happiness'. Egeo also gives his blessing to Arcane's marriage to Clizia and the happy couple declare their love for one another, now free from any jealous suspicions (duo, 'Unito a un puro affetto'). Medea appears, 'in a Chariot drawn by flying Dragons', but her threats to destroy the palace are answered by the Priest of Minerva who relays the goddess's blessing. Everyone (except Medea) joins in celebrating the peace that is love's sweet reward.

The eponymous hero Teseo seems to interest Handel rather less than the contrast and conflict between the two principal women, Agilea and Medea. Handel writes beautifully for Agilea in her first aria, 'E pur bello', the disarming simplicity of whose vocal line takes us inside her heart, and even more so in her second aria, 'Deh' serbate, o giusti Dei', where string figures portray her agitation, going first one way then the other, while the bass beats out her agitated pulse. Medea is one of Handel's great character studies, a sorceress in the line of Armida (*Rinaldo*, 1711) and Melissa (*Amadigi*, 1715), all of whom were written for the same remarkable soprano, Elisabetta Pilotti-Schiavonetti, whom Handel already knew in Hanover before he came to London. Medea is capable of spectacular fire and fury, but also of considerable tenderness: by a master-stroke, the aria which introduces her explores her soft, pitiful side. When she invokes the spirits of Hell, Handel invests her intensity with an extraordinary, unmelodramatic charge. This means that the *Deus ex machina*, Minerva's descent, the Priest's intervention with her blessing and the final *coro* all carry unusual weight: after such chaos, there is a real need for order to be re-established. In particular, Handel turns the *coro* into something like an anthem for deliverance from peril. P.

ACIS AND GALATEA

A masque in two acts to English words, ascribed at a 1739 revival to John Gay. Première 1718, probably at Cannons, the country house of the Earl of Carnarvon (later Duke of Chandos), for whom Handel wrote it. First performed in London, 1731; 1732 by Thomas Arne's English company, with the future Mrs Cibber as Galatea; 1732 by Handel's company, in a conflation of the mature work together with music from his earlier Neapolitan serenade and other works, and in a mixture of English and Italian (the performance was an attempt on Handel's part to establish his copyright to the music). The masque became the most popular of all his works during his lifetime.

Galatea ....Soprano

Acis, *a shepherd*..Tenor

Damon, *their friend*...Tenor

Polyphemus, *a giant*...Bass

Chorus

---

[1] Quotations here and later are from the 1713 translation of the libretto.

Place: Near Mount Etna
Time: Antiquity
Running Time: 50 minutes

Act I. The action takes place in what the score calls 'a rural prospect'; Acis and Galatea are seated by a fountain, the chorus round about, and Polyphemus on a mountain.

The overture, *presto* followed by a very short *adagio*, sets the undemanding pastoral scene for the chorus to hymn the pleasures of being alive in idyllic surroundings. Galatea languishes away from Acis ('Hush, ye pretty warbling quire'), who returns her sentiment no less melodiously ('Where shall I seek the charming fair?'). Damon gently urges Acis to bask in present pleasures rather than pursuing elusive love, but sight of Galatea leaves no doubt of Acis' devotion and spurs him to one of Handel's most glorious love songs, 'Love in her eyes sits playing'. Galatea for her part won't be outdone ('As when the dove'), and together they briskly celebrate the joys that are so evidently theirs ('Happy we!').

Act II. The chorus predicts an end to lovers' bliss ('Wretched lovers') with the intervention of the monster Polyphemus, who strides through the forest to proclaim his infatuation with Galatea. Polyphemus is half comic, half serious, his recitative ('I rage, I melt, I burn') in the style of a true bass villain, the aria ('O ruddier than the cherry') decked out with obbligato for *flauto piccolo* or flageolet to provide a note of mockery for the giant's gawky love song.

Galatea protests her antipathy but Polyphemus renews his protestations ('Cease to beauty to be suing'). Damon attempts advice but Acis valiantly protests he will defy the monster ('Love sounds th' alarm'). More advice from Damon ('Consider, fond shepherd') leads to the dénouement, a trio in which the lovers protest eternal fidelity ('The flocks shall leave the mountains'), while Polyphemus blusters at his frustration. He hurls a stone down the mountain, Acis is crushed beneath it and the chorus is left to mourn: 'The gentle Acis is no more'. In two exceptionally beautiful arias, one with chorus, Galatea mourns her loss, then is left to accept the chorus's assurance: 'Acis now a god appears!'

Acis and Galatea, Handel's first dramatic essay with English words, is generally pointed to as a precursor of his oratorio style. Its gentle pastoral atmosphere, little preoccupied with drama, puts it into quite another category from the operas. But it was intended to be staged and the music is of too high a quality for it to be divorced entirely from Handel's other stage work.   H.

RADAMISTO

Opera in three acts, text by Nicola Francesco Haym from Domenico Lalli. Première at Haymarket Theatre, London, 2 April 1720, with Margherita Durastanti (Radamisto), Anastasia Robinson (Zenobia), Ann Turner Robinson (Polissena) and Alexander Gordon (Tiridate). In December 1720, the opera was substantially revised and presented with a new cast: Senesino as Radamisto, Durastanti as Zenobia, the bass Giuseppe Boschi as Tiridate. Revised again in 1728.

Radamisto, *son of Farasmane* ....Soprano
Zenobia, *Radamisto's wife*.............................Contralto
Farasmane, *King of Thrace*....................................Bass
Tiridate, *King of Armenia* ....Tenor
Polissena, *Tiridate's wife and
    Farasmane's daughter*............................... Soprano
Tigrane, *Prince of Pontus*...............................Soprano
Fraarte, *Tiridate's brother*..............................Soprano

Place: Near Mount Ararat, West of the Caspian Sea
Time: About A.D. 51
Running Time: 2 hour 55 minutes

Though Handel regularly revised his operas, mostly to suit singers new to their roles, not many are so substantially re-written as *Radamisto*. That the title role moved from soprano to castrato in the mezzo range accounts for some of the changes, the assumption by Durastanti (a soprano and the original Radamisto) of the role of Zenobia (at first a contralto) for others, while Farasmane turned from tenor to bass. But that was far from all. There were ten new arias in all, a duet and, most significantly, a fine quartet to be inserted in the penultimate scene to its great advantage.

The plot has seemingly a minor historical basis and deals in the quarrels of the lesser kings of Asia Minor, their dynastic marriages and their efforts to ally military victory to amorous conquest. Farasmane, King of Thrace, has a son, Radamisto, living in married bliss with Zenobia, and a daughter, Polissena, less happily matched with Tiridate, king of neighbouring Armenia. Tiridate, visiting his father-in-law when Radamisto was absent, fell in love with Zenobia and, seeing no other way of satisfying his amorous longings, attacked and conquered Thrace, taking Farasmane prisoner. Tigrane, Prince of Pontus, is his ally as is his brother, Fraarte, but as the opera begins, they have as yet failed to capture Thrace's capital.

Act I. The overture, *allegro* after a solemn introduction, takes us straight to Tiridate's camp in front of the city. In noble accents ('Sommi dei') his wife Polissena prays for divine help as she learns from Tigrane that her husband's motive for attacking Thrace was his passion for Zenobia. She nevertheless repulses Tigrane who loves her.

Tiridate now shows his muscle. Radamisto must die, the city and its inhabitants be wiped out! Polissena pleads in vain, but Farasmane asks to be allowed to speak to his son. Tiridate agrees – but if the city does not surrender, not only will its inhabitants be slaughtered but Farasmane himself will die. Tiridate celebrates in a triumphant aria with trumpet obbligato.

Radamisto and Zenobia emerge from the city, and when she refuses to leave him, he comforts her in music of surpassing beauty ('Cara sposa'). Farasmane and Fraarte deliver Tiridate's terms, the former urging his son to place his own honour above his father's life. Both Zenobia and Radamisto have arias of defiance, and Tigrane prevents the wholly unjustifiable killing of Farasmane. The old man leaves on a note of resolution: 'Son lievi le catene'.

During a *sinfonia*, the city is taken. Tiridate rejoices but is furious Farasmane still lives, acceding nonetheless to Tigrane's pleas provided Radamisto and Zenobia are brought captive before him. Polissena pleads unsuccessfully for Radamisto, then begs Tigrane, grateful as she is that he saved her father, to save Radamisto too. Her expansive resolve in the face of adversity brings the act to an end.

Act II. Radamisto and Zenobia have escaped and, on the banks of the river Araxes, she slowly and movingly laments their plight, then begs him to kill her rather than let her fall into enemy hands. He succeeds only in lightly wounding her and she flings herself into the river. A prisoner, Radamisto laments what he erroneously believes to be the loss of Zenobia in one of Handel's most affecting arias ('Ombra cara'). Zenobia, however, saved by Fraarte from drowning, calls down the vengeance of the Furies on the tyrant Tiridate.

When Zenobia is brought before him, Tiridate tells her that far from losing a kingdom, she has gained an empire, then exuberantly celebrates the zenith of his

success. Fraarte urges his own love, but Zenobia asserts her loyalty to her husband in an impressive slow aria.

Tigrane is by now disillusioned with Tiridate's implacability and brings Radamisto in disguise to his sister Polissena, while he laments his predicament, caught between love of Polissena and loyalty to the King. Polissena refuses to side with her brother, however great her affection for him, against the husband she still loves, but Radamisto is unreservedly indignant that she remains loyal to a man who keeps her father imprisoned and would kill her brother ('Vanne, sorella ingrata').

Tiridate renews his assault on Zenobia's defences and hears from Tigrane the (false) news of Radamisto's death. Radamisto, disguised as one of his own servants, Ismeno, is immediately recognised by Zenobia (Tiridate has never seen his brother-in-law), but delivers what purports to be Radamisto's dying message of love for Zenobia and hatred for Tiridate. In a remarkable passage, Zenobia alternately denounces Tiridate's pretensions and reiterates her love for Radamisto. Tiridate offers Ismeno a reward if he can shake Zenobia's loyalty, and Radamisto and Zenobia end the act by pledging in duet their undying love.

Act III. Tigrane and Fraarte, disgusted by Tiridate's excesses, plot revolt, with reform rather than his death their objective. Zenobia warns Radamisto not to risk discovery by sticking too close to her, and in a spacious aria ('Dolce bene di quest'alma') he assures her of his constancy. When Tiridate attempts to embrace Zenobia, Radamisto rushes forward to protect her. Polissena saves his life and the King orders Radamisto's execution. This is too much for Polissena who warns him her love will turn to hate in the face of such intransigence, to which Tiridate replies that Radamisto shall be pardoned if he will hand over Zenobia ('Alzo al volo di mia fama'). Zenobia and Radamisto bid solemn farewell to each other and to life.

Tiridate reiterates his threats, but Polissena brings news that the army is in revolt. He fails to rally his supporters, is arrested, and the throne offered to Farasmane. Radamisto, invited by his father to avenge his wrongs, asks Polissena to forgive her husband. That worthy in the twinkling of an eye manages total repentance, with the result that he and Polissena are confirmed on the throne of Armenia. Only Fraarte seems out on a limb, and he takes it on himself publicly to repent of his unhallowed love for Polissena. Zenobia rejoices in the new situation and the opera comes to an end with a grand chorus for all seven voices.   H.

OTTONE, RE DI GERMANIA
Otho, King of Germany

Opera in three acts, libretto by Nicola Haym, adapted from Stefano Benedetto Pallavicino's libretto for *Teofano* (1719). First performance, King's Theatre, London, 12 January 1723, with Senesino as Ottone, Francesca Cuzzoni as Teofane, Giuseppe Broschi as Emireno, Margherita Durastanti as Gismonda, Berenstadt as Adalberto, Anastasia Robinson as Matilda. Handel introduced three more arias for Teofane for the twelfth performance, a benefit for Cuzzoni, and he strengthened Ottone's part in a revival in 1726. It was the first of Handel's operas to be revived in the twentieth century, at Göttingen, 1921, though Oskar Hagen's corrupt edition initiated an unfortunate tradition of altering the characters' vocal pitches. Handel Opera Society at Sadler's Wells, London, 1971; Göttingen, 1992.

Ottone (Otho II), *King of Germany*..........Alto Castrato

Teofane (Theofano), *daughter of Romano,*
    emperor of the East.................................... Soprano

Emireno, *a pirate, actually Teofane's brother*
    Basilio...Bass

Gismonda, *widow of Berengario,*
    Italian tyrant...Soprano

Adalberto, *her son*...........................Soprano Castrato

Matilda, *Ottone's cousin,*
    Adalberto's fiancée......................... Mezzo-Soprano

Place: Rome
Time: 972 A.D.
Running Time: 2 hours 55 minutes

Handel wrote *Ottone* for his Royal Academy venture, and changed the part of Teofane at the last minute to suit the great Italian soprano, Francesca Cuzzoni, who was making her London début. When she objected that the touching but vocally unspectacular 'Falsa imagine' was unsuitable for her entrance aria, Handel threatened to throw her out of the window. She agreed to sing it and it soon proved a popular hit. Anastasia Robinson, who sang Matilda, wrote to an intermediary to try to persuade Handel to rewrite the role to suit her. Her indirect approach paid off, since Handel did indeed change the role for her.

On his way to be acclaimed king of Italy, Ottone has been delayed by an encounter with the pirate Emireno. In Rome, Ottone is due to marry the Princess Teofane, who is already there. Neither has seen the other, though Teofane has a small portrait of Ottone.

Act I. A courtyard. Gismonda is ambitious for her son Adalberto to reign. When he agrees to impersonate Ottone so as to marry Teofane, his mother is delighted ('La speranza è giunta in porto'). Teofane meets Adalberto and is disappointed to discover that the portrait she carries is nothing like the man. He proposes marriage, as if he were Ottone, and looks forward to marital delights ('Bel labbro, formato'). Teofane, confused and upset, blames the portrait for cheating her ('Falsa imagine'). A Concerto is heard as Ottone arrives, bringing Emireno as his prisoner. Emireno hints that he is more than a pirate but boasts that his pride will remain inviolate, even in defeat. Unmoved, Ottone consigns him to prison. When Matilda tells Ottone about Adalberto, he swears to help her have revenge. Meanwhile, he longs to embrace Teofane ('Ritorna, o dolce amore'). Matilda is torn between her affection for Adalberto and her longing to punish him for his treachery.

A square within the palace. Gismonda pretends that she is Ottone's mother, Adelaide, and tells Teofane that she must love Adalberto and not merely do her duty. Gismonda's haughty manner offends Teofane. She is about to mount the throne at Adalberto's side, when Gismonda returns with the news that the real Ottone has arrived in Rome. Gismonda commands her son to fight him at once. Realising that someone has been impersonating Ottone, Teofane feels overwhelmed by mental anguish. Ottone's troops fight Adalberto's supporters. Adalberto remains defiant in defeat and refuses to reveal where Teofane is. Ottone remains optimistic, declares an amnesty in the city and looks ahead to his marriage ('Dell'onda ai fieri moti').

Act II. Adalberto is on his way to prison, when he is rebuked by Matilda for his infidelity and by Gismonda for failure. When Matilda suggests that the two women should beg Ottone for mercy, Gismonda rejects the idea as beneath her. Matilda's priority remains Adalberto's freedom ('Ah! tu non sai'). Alone, Gismonda reveals that she too feels compassion for her son.

Before Ottone and Teofane can actually meet and talk, Matilda begs Ottone to be merciful. Teofane hides and misunderstands as Ottone embraces Matilda in pity, when he refuses her request to save Adalberto's life. Outraged, Matilda calls on heaven to punish

Ottone for his inflexibility. Teofane accuses Ottone of betraying her with Matilda. When he in turn rebukes her for agreeing to marry Adalberto, she asks Ottone to tell her truthfully whether he does not love her, now that he sees her ('Alla fama, dimmi il vero'). Wondering who has turned her against him, Ottone compares the suffering heart to a stormy sky that is calm once more ('Dopo l'orrore').

A garden. Abandoned and alone, Teofane appeals to nature to comfort her ('O grati orrori, o solitarie piante!'). She knows, however, that if she could admit to Ottone how unhappy she is, he would have pity on her ('S'io dir potessi').

Matilda has helped Emireno and Adalberto to escape. Emireno intends to become a pirate again and swears to exact revenge. Adalberto hides when he hears people coming. Matilda realises that Ottone is looking for Teofane and offers to help him. Teofane recognises her voice, hides and hears Ottone ask Matilda not to tell everyone how ridiculous love makes him. Naturally, she misunderstands again. When Emireno invites Adalberto to sail away with him, Adalberto seizes the fainting Teofane and abducts her in the boat. Matilda returns, having shaken off Ottone. She and Gismonda rejoice that Adalberto escaped with Emireno, under cover of the kind night, a welcome accomplice in love's enterprises ('Notte cara, a te si deve').

Act III. A royal apartment. Ottone grieves at Teofane's disappearance ('Dove sei? dolce mia vita!'). Though Gismonda realises it will cost her her life, she warns him that he can never rest in peace again, now her son is free. Ottone is convinced that everyone has betrayed him ('Io son tradito'). If he cannot even find Teofane, he will lose all hope ('Tanti affanni').

A wood beside a stormy sea, where the fugitives have been forced to disembark. Adalberto hopes that the storm will be over soon, if only so that Teofane calms down and eventually feels sorry for him ('D'innalzar i flutti al ciel'). He leaves to find a refuge. When Teofane assures Emireno that either Ottone, her father Romano, or her brother Basilio will punish her abductors, Emireno realises she is his sister and tries to embrace her. Adalberto comes to her defence, but Emireno disarms him and promises Teofane that she will soon be happy. Teofane anticipates death

but determines to remain true to Ottone, even if he is unfaithful to her ('Benchè mi sia crudele').

A courtyard in the palace. Gismonda tells Ottone that Matilda helped the prisoners to escape. Matilda repents and swears to kill Adalberto. Emireno brings Adalberto back as his prisoner. When Ottone orders his death, Matilda asks to execute him herself. Adalberto confesses all and arouses her pity. Teofane stops Gismonda killing herself and rejoices with Ottone that they are reunited ('A' teneri affetti'). She also explains that Emireno is her brother Basilio. Gismonda swears loyalty to Ottone, while Matilda admits that she still loves Adalberto and frees him. They all invoke peace to take the place of pride and call on love to purge treachery.

Haym's libretto compresses the original story crudely, so that the motivation is often perfunctory. Another problem seems to be that the title role, written to suit the castrato Senesino's expressive brilliance in tender pathos, lacks heroic dynamism. Perhaps we need to adjust our expectations of heroic behaviour? The irony would not be beyond Handel's sense of humour. The other castrato role, Adalberto, is notable for its equivocal manner: weak-minded toy in the hands of his dominant mother (the three-dimensional virago-with-a-heart Gismonda), he rises to a peak of sensuality in the aria 'Bel labbro, formato', but remains wordless when the Amazon Matilda proposes marriage in the final scene. Of course, both men cannot help looking and sounding limp next to the blustery rodomontade of the pirate Emireno (the historical Emperor Basil II, known as 'the Slayer of the Bulgarians'[1]).   P.

FLAVIO

Opera in three acts, libretto by Nicola Haym after Matteo Novis's *Flavio Cuniberto* (1682). Première at the King's Theatre, Haymarket, London, 14 May 1723, with Cuzzoni as Emilia, Durastanti as Vitige, Mrs Robinson as Teodata, Senesino as Guido, Berenstadt as Flavio, Alexander Gordon as Ugone and Giuseppe Boschi as Lotario. After Handel revived it in 1732 it was not staged again until 1967 in Göttingen. Innsbruck, 1989.

Flavio, *King of the Lombards* .... Alto

Guido, *Ugone's son* .... Contralto

Emilia, *Lotario's daughter* .... Soprano

---

[1] Winton Dean and John Merrill Knapp, *Handel's Operas, 1704–1726*, rev. ed., Oxford, 1995.

Teodata, *daughter to Ugone* ....Alto
Vitige, *Teodata's lover* ....Soprano
Ugone, *counsellor* ....Tenor
Lotario, *counsellor* ....Bass

Place: Lombardy
Time: Early Middle Ages
Running Time: 2 hours 30 minutes

Handel originally called this work *Emilia* but changed the name to avoid confusion with another opera then on in London. It is in the serio-comic style with which he initiated his operatic career in Venice (*Agrippina*) and ended it in London (*Deidamia*). This may have militated against *Flavio's* popularity, yet it is a remarkable opera, covering an unusually broad range of human feeling. Guido and Emilia inhabit the world of *opera seria*, more or less, with some varied, but spectacular and serious arias. The other characters are presented in ways that involve elements of comedy, irony and parody. Flavio himself has three love-songs, including a gavotte and a gigue. There is a lot of truth in the unpredictable way they all react to one another.

Ugone, father of Teodata and Guido, and Lotario, father of Emilia, attend the court of King Flavio, who rules over Italy and Britain. Guido and Emilia have fallen in love and will marry; Teodata's affair with Vitige, a courtier, remains a secret.

Act I. Vitige leaves Ugone's house, having secretly spent the night with Teodata. The two fathers, Lotario and Ugone, approve of the marriage between Guido and Emilia and agree to seek the King's blessing on the union. When Ugone presents his daughter Teodata to King Flavio, the King falls in love with her. She feels respect rather than love.

Flavio learns that his deputy in Britain wishes to resign and at first favours Lotario to replace him, but then appoints Ugone. Lotario determines on revenge. When Flavio asks Vitige what he thinks of Teodata, Vitige pretends to find her unattractive. Alone, Vitige admits that he is tormented by jealousy. Ugone tells his son Guido that Lotario insulted him: he must now restore the family's honour. Guido presumes that honour lasts, unlike beauty or love, so he determines on revenge: family loyalty has triumphed over his feelings for Emilia. When the lovers meet, Guido tests her and she remains resolute: for her, love takes precedence over all other claims.

Act II. Ugone tells his daughter that he has been dishonoured. Misunderstanding him, Teodata confesses that she has been sleeping with Vitige, but adds that he has promised to marry her. Ugone rages against fate, which has made him look ridiculous. Lotario orders Emilia to forget Guido. She assures Guido, however, that she remains constant to him. Flavio asks Vitige to procure Teodata for him. Vitige urges Teodata to hide their love: she agrees to pretend to be attracted to the King, as long as Vitige won't torment her with his jealousy. Guido fights a duel with Lotario to avenge the insult to his father and wounds him severely. Lotario dies in the arms of his daughter Emilia, leaving her longing for death.

Act III. Emilia and Ugone both appeal to the King for justice. When Vitige brings Teodata, Flavio asks him to court her on his behalf. Covertly, Vitige urges her to dissimulate but when Flavio's offer to make Teodata his Queen seems to appeal to her, he suffers bitterly. Emilia attacks Guido for killing her father, yet when Guido invites her to kill him, she draws back. Flavio overhears Teodata and Vitige and realises they lied to him. She confesses that they love one another. Guido offers to die for his crime, if that is what Emilia wishes. To test her, Flavio tells her that Guido has already been executed. She immediately asks for death and when she finds Guido is alive, she forgives him, since it was for his honour's sake. Flavio 'punishes' Vitige by marrying him to Teodata and reconciles Guido with Ugone. Everyone rejoices.

Handel gives Emilia one of his most beautiful and saddest laments, moving gracefully to his favourite *siciliano* rhythm. Her arias are also distinguished by their orchestration. Apart from this, for its refreshing variety of moods and characters alone, *Flavio* deserves to be better known.   P.

GIULIO CESARE

Julius Caesar

Opera in three acts, libretto by Nicola Haym. Première Haymarket Theatre, London, 20 February 1724, with Cuzzoni as Cleopatra, Durastanti as Sesto,[1] Mrs Robinson as Cornelia,

---

[1] Margherita Durastanti was a soprano, but when the opera was revived in 1725, the role of Sesto, rewritten, was sung by the tenor Borosini.

Senesino as Caesar, Berenstadt as Ptolemy.[1] First performed in Germany, Brunswick, 1725; Hamburg, 1725; Vienna, 1731. First performed in Oskar Hagen's revision, 1922, Göttingen, with Wilhelm Guttmann as Caesar, Hagen-Leisner as Cleopatra, G.A. Walter as Sesto, Eleanor Reynolds as Cornelia. First performed Northampton, Mass., U.S.A., 1927; London, Scala Theatre, 1930. In the post-war period, heard at Leipzig, 1950; Düsseldorf, 1953; Vienna, 1954, with Seefried, Höngen, Schoeffler, Berry; Munich, 1955, with della Casa, Malaniuk, Metternich, conductor Jochum; Rome, 1956, with Fineschi, Barbieri, Christoff, Petri; la Scala, 1956, with Zeani, Simionato, Rossi-Lemeni; New York, 1956 (concert version), with Leontyne Price and the counter-tenor Russell Oberlin; and on several German stages during the Handel bicentenary celebrations in 1959. By Handel Opera Society at Sadler's Wells, 1963, with Joan Sutherland and Margreta Elkins; at Barber Institute, Birmingham, in 1977 with the 1724 score complete and uncut; London, English National Opera, 1979, with Valerie Masterson, Janet Baker, Sarah Walker, Della Jones, John Angelo Messana (Ptolemy), conductor Charles Mackerras (this production in San Francisco, 1982).

Giulio Cesare (Julius Caesar)......................Contralto

Curio, *a Roman tribune* ....Bass

Cornelia, *widow of Pompeo (Pompey)* ....Contralto

Sesto, *son to Cornelia and Pompeo* ......Soprano (Tenor)

Cleopatra, *Queen of Egypt*............................. Soprano

Tolomeo (Ptolemy), *King of Egypt* .... Contralto

Achilla, *General and counsellor to Tolomeo* ....Bass

Nireno, *Cleopatra's confidant* ....Contralto

Place: Egypt
Time: 48 B.C.
Running Time: 3 hours 25 minutes

Undoubtedly, the historical overtones and associations of *Julius Caesar* had something to do with the positive reaction of audiences in the early days of the Handel revival in Germany in the 1920s. But that accounts for only part of its success. Few other scores contain so many numbers which have made their way with the public out of context – and it is generally admitted that Handel's arias are far more effective in the dramatic circumstances which provide for the situation and the emotion they are intended to express than without them. It is in fact one of his most completely satisfactory works for the stage.

Act I. Egypt, after Caesar's victory over his rival Pompey at Pharsalus. During a short overture the curtain rises to show a broad plain by the Nile with a bridge over the river. The Egyptians in chorus greet the victorious Romans, who fill the scene until Julius Caesar himself enters to celebrate his triumph ('Presti omai l'Egizia terra'). To him come Cornelia and her son Sesto to beg him to show clemency in his hour of victory, only for Achilla in the same moment to offer Caesar the hospitality of Ptolemy (whose military help Pompey had invoked) and to show him the severed head of Pompey as proof of Ptolemy's change of heart. Caesar condemns the senseless cruelty ('Empio, dirò, tu sei, togliti') and leaves Cornelia to attempt suicide, to dismiss the proffered love of Curio, the Roman tribune, and to lament her wretched loneliness in a beautiful slow aria ('Priva son d'ogni conforto'). Her son Sesto in his turn excitedly vows vengeance on the criminals ('Svegliatevi nel core').

The scene changes to the palace of Ptolemy, where Cleopatra resolves to pit her celebrated beauty against her brother's gift of Pompey's head in a bid for Caesar's favour ('Non disperar'). Now Achilla tells Ptolemy of Caesar's fury at the murder of Pompey and himself offers to kill Caesar and so stabilise Ptolemy's throne if the King will grant him in reward the hand of the beautiful Cornelia. Ptolemy agrees and inveighs against Caesar ('L'empio, sleale, indegno').

In his camp, Caesar in an expressive recitative contemplates the monument he has raised to Pompey's memory and reflects on the transience of fame. To him comes Cleopatra, describing herself as Lidia, one of the Queen's women. Caesar is completely captivated by her beauty ('Non è si vago e bello') and Cleopatra celebrates her success ('Tutto può donna vezzosa') and then with Nireno hides to watch Cornelia dressed in mourning kneel before the monument of her dead husband and movingly apostrophise the urn which contains all that she adored ('Nel tuo seno, amico sasso'). When she vows vengeance on her husband's murderer, her son takes the burden upon himself. Cleopatra, still calling herself Lidia, offers her help. Sesto rejoices because his dream of justice may now come true ('Cara speme'), and the scene ends as Cleopatra exults at the prospect of victory over Ptolemy, then sings an aria ('Tu la mia stella sei'), whose melodious and lovelorn accents to some degree contradict the uncompromising nature of the recitative.

---

[1] Deutsch's *Handel, a Documentary Biography* refers to Berenstadt as a bass, presumably, suggests Winton Dean, because a German castrato (which he *was*) seemed like a contradiction in terms.

Giulio Cesare *(English National Opera, 1979, director John Copley). Janet Baker in the title role.*

The scene changes to the palace of Ptolemy. The King greets Caesar effusively, offering him entertainment but in no way deceiving the Roman, who in a fine aria with (uniquely in Handel's operas) a horn obbligato, invokes a hunting simile ('Va tacito e nascosto') to describe the relationship of Egyptian king and Roman general. Caesar and the Romans leave Ptolemy and his Egyptian courtiers, and Achilla points out Cornelia to Ptolemy, who is no less struck by her beauty than is his general. When the Roman lady and Sesto advance and challenge Ptolemy to mortal combat, guards are ordered to take the youth to prison and Cornelia to the King's harem. When the King has gone, Cornelia scorns Achilla's offer of freedom in return for marriage, and the act ends with a fine duet of farewell for mother and son.

Act II. Cleopatra has planned to have Caesar brought to her palace, where she can ravish his senses with the sight of Virtue enthroned on Mount Parnassus. The orchestral *sinfonia* which accompanies his entrance and the revelation of the goddess starts a process of seduction which is fully accomplished when Cleopatra herself, in the guise of the goddess, sings the delectable 'V'adoro pupille', an aria of a tender, sensual beauty that puts it among Handel's greatest melodic inspirations. Though the vision of his beloved is removed from him when the mountain closes, Caesar's growing passion is evident in his aria 'Se in fiorito ameno prato'.

The scene changes to the garden of the harem where Cornelia sings sadly of her departed happiness ('Deh piangete, oh mesti lumi'), and resists the blandishments successively of Achilla and Ptolemy, who, unbeknown to Achilla, is his rival for her favours. Ptolemy's determination is well portrayed in his aria 'Si spietata, il tuo rigore sveglia'. Cornelia is now joined by Sesto, bent on avenging his father's death, to which end Nireno contributes by offering to take him secretly to the King's presence. Cornelia urges him onward ('Cessa omai di sospirare') and Sesto proclaims his resolve in a splendid martial aria.

The scene returns to Cleopatra, who waits in the guise of Lidia for Caesar. As they are about to declare their love, Curio announces an imminent attempt by Ptolemy's soldiers on Caesar's life, whereupon Cleopatra declares herself in her true identity and, announcing she will quell the conspirators herself, leaves the scene. In a moment she is back urging Caesar to flee the danger, a solution he scorns ('Al lampo dell'armi'). He rushes out and the conspirators can be heard shouting for his death. In a splendidly realised scene of accompanied recitative and aria ('Se pietà di me non senti'), the music depicts the Queen's conflicting emotions – her desire for revenge on her enemies and her self-pity, set against her fears for the safety of the man whose love she now craves more than the political favour she once sought.

The scene changes again to Ptolemy's harem where the King sits surrounded by his favourites, among them Cornelia, and sings of his amorous feelings. Sesto rushes in and attempts to stab him, but is prevented by Achilla, who brings news that Caesar defended himself against the attacking soldiers and succeeded in jumping from the palace window into the harbour, where he was presumably drowned. Cleopatra is now bringing her troops against Ptolemy to avenge Caesar's death. As Ptolemy leaves, Achilla asks for the promised reward of Cornelia's hand in marriage, is sharply turned down by Ptolemy, and, as the King departs for battle, goes off muttering of the revenge that will be his. Sesto in despair tries to kill himself, but Cornelia again nerves him to the task in hand.

Act III. In a wood near Alexandria. Achilla, with a band of soldiers, prepares to defect to Cleopatra's side, in revenge for Ptolemy's treachery towards him in the matter of his love for Cornelia ('Dal fulgor di questa spada').

A Battle Symphony describes the conflict, from which Ptolemy's supporters emerge victorious. The King orders his sister to prison ('Domerò la tua fierezza') and the scene ends with her great lament at the turn her fortunes have taken ('Piangerò la sorte mia'), a beautiful *largo* aria with a vocal line of the greatest possible simplicity and containing, as contrasting middle section, a vision of herself returning as a ghost to haunt her wicked brother.

By the side of the harbour, and to *andante* music that breathes the very spirit of consolation, Caesar reappears to describe his escape from death by drowning ('Dall'ondoso periglio') and to pray for comfort in his loneliness ('Aure, deh, per pietà') in music that is as touchingly simple and as memorable as the famous 'Ombra mai fu'. Also to the harbour side come Sesto and Achilla, the latter mortally wounded in the battle which, he explains, he joined to revenge himself on the treacherous Ptolemy. Caesar sees him give Sesto the signet ring which will gain them the instant obedience of his troops, who know a subterranean approach to the palace where they may overthrow Ptolemy. Caesar takes charge of the situation and his determination is displayed in his comparison of his progress to that of a waterfall ('Quel torrente che cade dal monte'). With Achilla's death and Caesar's departure to organise the final assault, Sesto feels that the processes of justice are nearing completion ('La giustizia ha già sull'arco').

The scene changes to Cleopatra's apartments where her sad farewell to her attendant women is interrupted by the precipitate and victorious arrival of Caesar to free her. Immediately, Cleopatra's mood changes to one of jubilation and she celebrates the prospect of victory ('Da tempeste il legno infranto').

Ptolemy meanwhile makes a last attempt to persuade Cornelia of his love for her, is threatened by her with a dagger, and eventually falls dead after a duel with Sesto, whose entry prevents his mother from herself avenging her murdered husband, a deed she nevertheless greets with proper enthusiasm.

The harbour at Alexandria is the scene of the final triumph of Caesar and Cleopatra, celebrated with a march, a duet for the happy couple and a chorus of rejoicing.   H.

TAMERLANO
Tamburlaine

Opera in three acts, text by Nicola Haym from Agostino Piovene's original text after Jacques Pradon's tragedy *Tamberlan ou La Mort de Bajazet*. Première King's Theatre, Haymarket, London, 31 October 1724, with the castrati Senesino and Andrea Pacini as Andronicus and Tamburlaine, the tenor Francesco Borosini as Bajazet, Francesca Cuzzoni as Asteria, and Anna Dotti (Irene) and Giuseppe Boschi (Leone). First performed in Germany, Hamburg, 1725, in German, with the music adapted by Telemann (the arias were sung in Italian and between the acts *intermezzi*, probably Telemann's *Die ungleiche Heyrath*, were performed). Revived London, 1731 (abridged by Handel). Modern revivals: Karlsruhe, 1924; Leipzig, 1925; Halle, 1940 and 1952; Birmingham, 1962 (first performance in England since 1731) in English translation by Nigel Fortune and Brian Trowell with Catherine Wilson, Patricia Clark, Janet Baker, Alexander Young, conductor Anthony Lewis; Batignano, 1976; Edinburgh Festival, 1982, by Welsh National Opera with Eiddwen Harrhy, Anthony Rolfe Johnson; Bloomington, U.S.A., 1985 (first American performance) in English; Opera North, Leeds, 1985, with Eiddwen Harrhy, Felicity Palmer, Sally Burgess; Lyons, 1985, conductor John Eliot Gardiner.

Tamerlano (Tamburlaine), *Emperor
    of the Tartars*.. Alto

Bajazete (Bajazet), *Emperor of the Turks,
    Tamerlano's prisoner* ....Tenor

Asteria, *Bajazete's daughter,
    in love with Andronico* .... Soprano

Andronico (Andronicus), *a Grecian Prince,
    Tamerlano's ally* ....Contralto

Irene, *Princess of Trabisond,
    Tamerlano's fiancée* .... Contralto

Leone, *friend to Andronico and Tamerlano*............. Bass

Zaida, *Asteria's confidante* .... Silent

Place: Prusa, Capital of Bithinia
Time: 1402
Running Time: 3 hours

Tamerlano seems to have been written in the astonishingly short time of twenty days, between 3 and 23 July 1724. The Tartar ruler, Tamerlano, has conquered the Ottoman Emperor, Bajazete the First, and holds him prisoner. Tamerlano, who has yet to see his betrothed, Irene, the Princess of Trabisond, falls in love with Bajazete's daughter, Asteria, and renounces Irene. But Andronico, Tamerlano's Grecian ally, himself has come to love Asteria.

Act I. The overture, with its solemn introduction, contrapuntal *allegro* (rather severe in tone) and minuet, leads not without foreboding to Tamerlano's palace, where Bajazete has been brought captive. At Tamerlano's behest, Andronico frees Bajazete from his chains but Bajazete rejects what he feels is Tamerlano's false-hearted clemency. Only his love for his daughter Asteria, as he insists in an aria characteristically firm in tone ('Forte e lieto a morte andrei'), prevents his suicide. Tamerlano now enters to order Andronico to plead his cause with Bajazete and Asteria, offering (in recitative and aria) as reward for success the throne of Greece, the hand of Irene in marriage, and freedom for Bajazete.

Andronico's predicament is harsh. He it was who brought Asteria to Tamerlano, thinking to soften the tyrant's heart, but the result has been to cause Tamerlano instantly to fall in love with her. Andronico himself loves her deeply, as we learn from an aria full of the tenderest feeling ('Bella Asteria'). Nonetheless, Tamerlano approaches Asteria and makes clear at the same time his intentions towards her and the bargain he thinks he has struck with Andronico. Asteria is both saddened and angered by what seems to her Andronico's betrayal of her love.

Bajazete scorns the freedom his enemy offers and in an aria reacts vigorously to the apparently ambivalent attitude of Asteria. Alone Asteria reveals ('Deh! lasciatemi il nemico') that, however wounded she might be by Andronico's apparent treachery, the tenderness of her feelings is unchanged.

The arrival of Irene adds further complication, since she learns from Andronico that Tamerlano has resolved on a change of plan: she is now to marry Andronico rather than the Tartar monarch. The situation may yet be saved, he suggests, if she, still unknown to Tamerlano, will represent herself as

Irene's confidante in order to remonstrate with him. She agrees in music of rather placid cast, in contrast to the heartfelt and grandiose recitative and aria in which Andronico laments the cruel twists of fortune which have brought him to his present plight.

Act II. Tamerlano tells Andronico that Asteria has accepted to be his Empress and their wedding, together with that of Andronico and Irene, will shortly be celebrated. There is a note of triumph in his aria ('Bella gara'), mockery in Asteria's 'Non è più tempo' as she dissembles. Andronico is left alone to his grief ('Cerco in vano').

The disguised Irene is conducted by Leone into Tamerlano's presence, where her pleading of the real Irene's cause is received with surprising equanimity by the tyrant, and then, when they are alone together, with sympathy by Asteria, who unburdens her own true feelings to Irene. That unfortunate if imperturbable lady discerns a ray of hope in what she has heard – her 'Par che mi nasca' is described by Winton Dean[1] as 'a miracle of beauty and psychological insight'.

Bajazete learns with horror that Asteria is to join Tamerlano on his throne and resolves in an aria of tragic gloom to prevent her ('A suoi piedi'). Andronico is stung at last to fury as he threatens vengeance on Tamerlano and an end to his own life ('Più d'una tigre').

Asteria, secretly resolved to slay the tyrant who holds her and her father in his power, is about to ascend Tamerlano's throne but Bajazete vigorously intervenes. Tamerlano attempts to force him to the ground in homage only for Bajazete to kneel and forestall the attempted humiliation. Asteria, with meaningful looks at Bajazete and Andronico, prepares to mount the dais but Bajazete interposes his body in protest. Asteria draws a dagger and announces that this would have been her wedding present to Tamerlano. A trio for Asteria, Tamerlano and Bajazete ensues, at the end of which Tamerlano orders their execution. This is followed by a great scene in which Asteria in a bar or two of recitative demands in succession of her father, her lover and her rival for Tamerlano's throne whether she was unworthy or untrue. Each, in short arias with no *da capo* and starting with the word 'No!', admits the

---

[1] *Handel and the Opera Seria* (O.U.P. 1970).

purity of Asteria's actions. Alone Asteria rejoices in her vindication, regretting only that she failed in her assassination attempt.

Act III. Asteria and Bajazete determine to commit suicide by the poison Bajazete has concealed, and Asteria, who grows in stature as her plight worsens, is left alone to lament that she will soon bid farewell to father and lover alike ('Cor di padre'). Tamerlano now reveals another side of his nature in his renewed attempt to enlist Andronico's aid in persuading Asteria of his love, even of his resolve to pardon Bajazete. Andronico screws up his courage to defy Tamerlano and he and Asteria declare their mutual love. Tamerlano's mood changes and in a splendid though technically very difficult aria of rapid semi-quavered fury he vows revenge. Bajazete tries to raise the courage of the lovers who mellifluously in duet lament the prospect before them.

How fares Irene? In a lively *allegro* aria she announces that her love, provided it is requited, is pledged to Tamerlano.

Tamerlano is set to indulge his rage by humbling his victims, and first Bajazete, later Asteria, are summoned to his presence. Andronico protests that this is the unjust action of a tyrant and pleads for clemency. Tamerlano is obdurate and orders Asteria to act as his cup-bearer. She pours the poison Bajazete had given her into Tamerlano's cup, but Irene observes her action and gives her away, at the same time revealing to Tamerlano her own true identity. On Tamerlano's orders Asteria must choose whether to offer the cup first to her father or her lover, after which she may bring it to him. She is about to drink it herself when Andronico knocks it from her hand. Tamerlano rages at Asteria and orders her arrest; he will hand her over to the common seraglio – and Bajazete shall witness her shame! Bajazete is outraged and in his virtuoso aria ('Empio, per farti guerra') vows that his ghost will return to haunt the tyrant. Tamerlano and Irene, dramatically as if they were Monteverdi's and Busenello's Nero and Poppea, musically more like Handel's own Caesar and Cleopatra, celebrate in duet the prospect of future pleasure.

Asteria enters Tamerlano's presence followed by Bajazete. Bajazete astonishes them by his apparent serenity but it is not long before he reveals that he has taken poison and will soon be free of his tormentor. In a *scena* of great power he takes an agonised farewell of his beloved daughter, then turns to scarify Tamerlano. As his words become more incoherent, he staggers out to die.

Asteria comes back to beg for death in an aria of great beauty ('Padre amato'), as her submission is something Tamerlano can never win. Irene and Andronico send after Asteria to prevent her suicide, but Tamerlano himself, now moved to pity by the horror of events and the dignity and pleas of Irene, pardons his erstwhile foes. The opera ends with Tamerlano and Irene pledging love, and the chorus announcing that love's bright torches have dispelled the dark of night, albeit in accents more appropriate to the opera's gloomy events than the statutory happy ending of *opera seria*.   H.

RODELINDA

Opera in three acts, libretto by A. Salvi (originally written for Perti's opera of 1710), revised by Nicola Haym. Completed in January 1725, première at King's Theatre, Haymarket, 13 (or 24) February 1725, with Cuzzoni, Senesino, Dotti, Paccini, Boschi, Borosini. First performed in Germany in Hamburg, 1734. Revived Göttingen, 1920 (the beginning of the German Handel revival) in a new German version by Oskar Hagen; Smith College, Northampton, Mass., 1931; Old Vic, London, 1939. More recently Göttingen, 1953; Leipzig, 1955; Sadler's Wells, London, by Handel Opera Society, 1959, with Sutherland, Elkins, Janet Baker, Hallett, Herincx, conductor Farncombe.

Rodelinda, *Queen of Lombardy*...................... Soprano
Bertarido, *King of Lombardy* ....Contralto
Grimoaldo, *usurper of Bertarido's throne* .... Tenor
Eduige, *sister of Bertarido* .... Contralto
Unulfo, *adviser to Grimoaldo*
   but secretly loyal to Bertarido................... Contralto
Garibaldo, *Duke of Turin, friend to Grimoaldo* .... Bass
Flavio, *Rodelinda's son* ....Silent

Place: The Royal Palace, Milan
Running Time: 3 hours 15 minutes

Rodelinda has always been one of Handel's most successful operas,[1] revived many times during his lifetime and frequently in the twentieth century. It casts a tenor in the villain's role – there are few important tenor parts in Handel's operas, the heroic

---

[1] Not only was its initial success quite out of the ordinary, but Cuzzoni's brown and silver dress became the rage for the rest of the London season!

roles which the nineteenth century might have assigned to tenors being customarily taken by castrati. The opera's one really famous air, 'Dove sei', was once well known in England as 'Art thou troubled', but has also been given biblical words and sung as 'Holy, Holy, Holy, Lord God Almighty' – a curious example of the English nineteenth century's tendency to turn all music to oratorio.

After a *maestoso* opening, the overture is brilliant and florid.

Act I. A room in Rodelinda's apartments. Rodelinda, alone, mourns the death of her husband, Bertarido ('Ho perduto il caro sposo'), little knowing that he is alive and awaiting his opportunity for revenge on the treacherous Grimoaldo, who has deposed him. Grimoaldo proposes marriage to Rodelinda, but she furiously rejects him.

Grimoaldo consults his friend Garibaldo as to the best method of ridding himself of Bertarido's sister, Eduige, to whom he is betrothed, and of winning Rodelinda. Garibaldo promises to help him, and, when Eduige enters and reproaches Grimoaldo with his fickleness, Grimoaldo vigorously tells her that he is going to find a more worthy consort than she. When he has gone, the despised Eduige castigates him, leaving Garibaldo to sing of his aspiration to her hand and so to the throne itself.

The second scene is set in a cypress wood, where the kings of Lombardy are traditionally buried. Bertarido in disguise contemplates his own tomb which has lately been erected by Grimoaldo, and gives vent to his longing for his beloved Rodelinda in the chaste and very famous 'Dove sei'. When Rodelinda and her son Flavio approach to lay a wreath, Bertarido is prevented from speaking to them by his friend Unulfo, and the two men conceal themselves behind the tomb as Rodelinda mourns her husband in a *largo* aria, hardly less beautiful than its predecessor.

Garibaldo appears and, to the fury and despair of the hidden Bertarido, tells Rodelinda that unless she marries Grimoaldo her son will be killed. She agrees, but in a tempestuous *allegro* ('Morrai sì, l'empia tua testa') swears to have Garibaldo's head as forfeit. Garibaldo tells Grimoaldo the outcome of his efforts, not forgetting his fear of Rodelinda's revenge once she is queen. Grimoaldo will protect him. Unulfo tries to comfort the distraught Bertarido who is forced to admit that Rodelinda does believe him dead.

Act II. A room in Grimoaldo's palace. Eduige swears to be revenged on Grimoaldo. Rodelinda refuses to marry him until he has killed her son – in this way he will appear in the sight of the world as a monster ('Spietati, io vi giurai'). Grimoaldo hesitates, but Garibaldo urges him to agree to what Rodelinda exacts. Garibaldo expounds his Machiavellian theories to Unulfo and leaves the grief-stricken young man to reflect on the horror of the situation ('Frà tempeste funeste a quest'alma').

The scene changes to 'a delightful place' where Bertarido calls upon the brooks and fountains to share his sorrow. Eduige enters and after recovering from her amazement at finding her brother alive, assures him that Rodelinda is faithfulness itself. Unulfo supports her, and Bertarido rejoices at this sign of a change in his fortunes.

Rodelinda in her apartment is told by Unulfo that her husband lives and sings of her happiness. Husband and wife are united, but Grimoaldo bursts in and tells Bertarido to say farewell to Rodelinda as prison and death await him. He sings to Rodelinda of his hatred for her husband. Bertarido comforts Rodelinda and the act ends with a duet of great tenderness.

Act III. Eduige gives Unulfo a key to Bertarido's dungeon and they plan to rescue him. Garibaldo and Grimoaldo are agitated at the possible effect of the death of Bertarido on their respective ambitions and Grimoaldo expresses his fears.

The scene changes to a dark dungeon where Bertarido sings of the cruelty of love: 'Chi di voi fù più infedele, cieco Amor'. He is interrupted as a sword thrown through the window by Unulfo crashes to the ground. In the darkness and confusion, Bertarido slightly wounds his friend as he enters but the two escape by way of a secret passage.

Rodelinda and Eduige, also bent on rescue, find Bertarido's bloodstained cloak and jump to the conclusion that he has been murdered – Rodelinda demands movingly, with the force of a cry from the heart, why such pain must be endured.

In the palace garden Bertarido binds Unulfo's wound and sings of freedom. Grimoaldo meanwhile in a fine *scena* is troubled by conscience and finds consolation only in the idea of changing places with a simple shepherd (a charming Siciliana: 'Pastorello d'un povero armento'). He falls asleep after his reverie, and Garibaldo attempts to kill him with his own sword but is himself slain by Bertarido. Grimoaldo in gratitude renounces the throne and returns Rodelinda to her husband. The happy Queen sings joyfully 'Mio caro bene', and the opera ends with a triumphant chorus, sung originally of course by the principals. H.

PARTENOPE

Opera in three acts, libretto after Silvio Stampiglia's *La Partenope* (published 1699; previously set by Manzo and Caldara). Première King's Theatre, Haymarket, London, 24 February 1730, with Strada in the title role, Bernacchi as Arsace. Senesino sang Arsace the following year. Performed in Brunswick and Hamburg during Handel's lifetime, revived at Covent Garden, 1737. Revived 1935, Göttingen; Abingdon, 1961.

Partenope, *Queen of Naples* ....Soprano
Arsace, *Prince of Corinth* ....Contralto
Rosmira, *Princess of Cyprus* ....Alto
Armindo, *Prince of Rhodes*[1]..................................Alto
Emilio, *Prince of Cuma*..Tenor
Ormonte, *captain of Partenope's Guard*[1]................Bass

Guards, Soldiers, People of Naples

Place: Naples
Time: Antiquity
Running Time: 3 hours 10 minutes

Anyone familiar with Stampiglia's libretto for *Serse* and Handel's treatment of it will not be surprised to find that *Partenope* partakes of some of the mocking spirit of *Agrippina* and *Serse* rather than of the solemnity of *opera seria*. It is one of Handel's most attractive operas, though not as yet the most frequently revived.

Act I. In a scene of great ceremony, Partenope invokes the blessing of Apollo on her newly founded city of Naples, but soon finds herself the centre of a multi-faceted intrigue such as could serve as the plot of a Feydeau farce. Arsace and Partenope renew vows of eternal fidelity, but Arsace has already tacitly admitted he loves Rosmira, who has arrived in Naples disguised as an Armenian prince. Armindo also loves Partenope, but will not say so publicly as he knows of her involvement with Arsace. To complicate matters, Rosmira in her male disguise as

Prince Eurimene claims also to love Partenope, whose hand as his queen is solicited by the invading Prince Emilio. When she refuses Emilio, he declares war. Even the appointment of a prince to command her army causes confusion, and she eventually decides to do the job herself.

Act II. The troops face up to each other, Partenope is saved from death by Armindo, Arsace rescues Rosmira and captures Emilio, and Partenope's triumph is apparently complete. But not for long. Rosmira/Eurimene reminds her that it was Armindo who saved her life, Emilio claims to be Arsace's prisoner rather than Eurimene/Rosmira's, and Rosmira prepares to fight Arsace, who cannot accept the challenge since he, and he alone, knows her true identity as a woman but has sworn not to reveal it. Though Partenope sticks by him, Arsace loses face with the others, who think him a coward, all except Rosmira/Eurimene, who defends him. Partenope orders the release of Eurimene, then starts to make up her mind whether she prefers Arsace or Armindo, the latter of whom has just declared his love. Rosmira complicates matters by asking (as Eurimene) to impart a secret to Partenope which will help the cause of Armindo.

Act III. Eurimene's secret comes into the open: 'his' quarrel with Arsace is on account of Arsace's abandonment of a certain Rosmira, Princess of Cyprus, a charge Arsace admits. In the forthcoming duel, Emilio will be Arsace's second, Armindo Eurimene's. Arsace is in a trap and, to the surprise of Partenope, addresses Rosmira, who wakens him from sleep, by her true name. Rejected by both women, he inveighs against love's cruelty, then prepares for the duel. He is mocked for his half-hearted efforts by Rosmira, but turns the tables by demanding they should fight bare-chested. Rosmira is outwitted, admits who she is, and claims Arsace has proved his love by maintaining silence in the face of provocation. Partenope renounces Arsace to Rosmira, takes Armindo for her husband, and finishes the opera by proclaiming Emilio her ally.

Partenope consistently parodies *opera seria* and the heroic style which have been mainstays of Handel's output so far. Handel comments on various aspects of love, alluding off and on to military matters but, the battle at the start of Act II apart, not taking them

---

[1] For the 1737 revival, Armindo became a soprano and Ormonte an alto, and Handel made various alterations to the score, in particular to the conclusions of the second and third acts.

too seriously. Partenope herself starts as a buoyant if many-sided personality, but her music takes on a serious tone after her victory. Arsace, written for virtuoso castrato (Bernacchi originally, Senesino at revival) initially shows unaccustomed restraint, later revealing more than one side of his personality and finishing Act II with considerable bravura ('Mà quai note'). Rosmira is lively and lyrical by turns; with horns in attendance, she has brought Act I to a resounding conclusion, and the love between her and Arsace is tantalisingly but touchingly portrayed in the extended music of Act III.   H.

PORO, RE DELL'INDIE
Porus, King of India

Opera in three acts, libretto based on Pietro Metastasio's libretto *Alessandro* for Leonardo Vinci (1729). First performance, King's Theatre, London, 2 February 1731, with Senesino, Anna Maria Strada del Po, Margherita Antonia Merighi, Francesca Bertolli, Annibale Pio Fabri, and Giovanni Giuseppe Commano. Revived December 1731, when Antonio Montagnana sang Timagene and Handel gave him three arias from earlier operas. At Covent Garden in 1736 Strada sang Cleofide and the mezzo-soprano castrato Domenico Annibali sang Poro. Handel himself conducted *Poro* at Covent Garden on 5 May 1737. Revived 1928 in Brunswick and staged in Britain at Bangor, 11 September 1966. U.S. première (in concert) Washington, 1978.

Poro, *King of one part of India,*
    in love with Cleofide ....Soprano
Cleofide, *Queen of another part of India,*
    in love with Poro.. Soprano
Erissena, *Poro's sister,*
    engaged to Gandarte........................Mezzo-Soprano
Gandarte, *a general in Poro's army,*
    in love with Erissena .... Contralto
Alessandro (Alexander the Great)....................Tenor
Timagene, *Alessandro's confidant*
    and secret enemy..Bass

Time: Antiquity
Place: The River Hydaspes; Alessandro's Camp,
    Cleofide's Palace
Running Time: 3 hours 10 minutes

*P*oro was one of Handel's last settings of a text by Metastasio. As Jonathan Keates points out, Handel's treatment is cavalier and his revisions 'grew more radical as the drama progressed'.[1]

Handel adapted Metastasio for his own ends: where Metastasio stresses public, political intrigues, Handel is interested more in the private world of emotions. Crucially, the duet at the end stresses not Alessandro as role model, but the private love of two individuals.

Act I. A battlefield on the banks of the river Hydaspes. Having been defeated by Alessandro, Poro prepares to commit suicide. Gandarte encourages him to fight and not yield his beloved Cleofide to the conqueror. He exchanges helmets with him. When Poro is brought before Alessandro and Timagene he tells them he is Asbite, a chieftain loyal to Poro. Impressed by his boldness, Alessandro asks him to obtain Poro's avowal of defeat and gives him Darius's sword to protect him. Poro takes it, meaning to use it against him ('Vedrai con tuo periglio'). Alessandro also frees Poro's sister Erissena from her chains, telling her that her tears shame him. Seeing that she is impressed, Timagene asks whether she has fallen for Alessandro. Erissena points out that she displays none of the symptoms of love.

In Cleofide's palace. Cleofide assures Poro that she pretends to like Alessandro only for her lover's sake. Poro swears he will not feel jealousy. Cleofide also swears fidelity to Poro ('Se mai turbo il tuo riposo'). Yet when she leaves to see Alessandro, Poro ignores Gandarte's arguments and gives way to jealousy ('Se possono tanto due luci vezzose'). Erissena tells Gandarte that she admires Alessandro and when he complains, she warns him that he asks too much in the way of exclusive fidelity.

Alessandro's tent. Cleofide arrives in state and makes a great impression on Alessandro. Still in disguise as Asbite, Poro returns from his mission and reports to Alessandro that the King refuses to admit defeat. Poro's jealousy so annoys Cleofide that she flirts with Alessandro, who remains impervious. Poro and Cleofide rebuke one another for failing to keep their word: she seems unfaithful, while he is jealous (duet, 'Se mai turbo').

Act II. Cleofide welcomes Alessandro, but suddenly Poro's men attack. Alessandro's troops drive them away, however. Gandarte destroys the bridge and escapes. Cleofide convinces Poro that she is faithful to him when she threatens to commit suicide (duet, 'Caro amico amplesso!'). He prepares to kill her

[1] Jonathan Keates, *Handel: the Man and his Music*, London, 1985.

to save her from being taken prisoner, but is prevented by Alessandro. Cleofide protects Poro's identity. Alessandro leaves to calm his troops, who blame Cleofide for the Indians' revolt and demand her death. He tells Cleofide not to heed the barbarians' discourtesy and leaves Timagene to guard Asbite. Cleofide asks Asbite to assure Poro that she remains faithful ('Digli ch'io son fedele'). Timagene then lets Asbite go and gives him a letter promising to help Poro; meanwhile, he will report that Asbite died. Poro reflects that it is easy to fool a man who trusts too easily: like a sleeping helmsman, he is liable to wake and find himself in the midst of a storm ('Senza procelle').

In Cleofide's palace Alessandro is so concerned to protect her from his troops' fury that he offers to marry her. Gandarte tries to save Poro by claiming that he himself is Poro and was responsible for the revolt. Alessandro refuses to lose face, confronted by such magnanimity: he frees Cleofide and gives her to the man he believes to be Poro. Erissena brings news that Poro drowned in the river. Cleofide mourns him ('Se il ciel mi divide'). Gandarte resolves that if he cannot live with Erissena, he will die with her. Erissena will no longer trust in hope that cannot be trusted ('Di rendermi la calma').

Act III. The gates to the royal gardens. Poro asks Erissena not to tell anyone that he is still alive, even Cleofide, and to ensure that Timagene brings Alessandro to this garden, where Poro will kill him. He tries to rouse her anger, since he depends on his sister completely. Cleofide now agrees to marry Alessandro, apparently to protect herself from the Greeks' anger. She warns Erissena against judging on appearances. Erissena reveals Timagene's treachery to Alessandro but warns him not to let doubt of her fidelity poison their relationship. When Timagene begs for forgiveness Alessandro pardons him: as long as he now behaves nobly, Alessandro will be satisfied. Poro overhears this and realises his hopes are lost. He asks Gandarte to kill him.

Erissena reveals that Cleofide is preparing to marry Alessandro. Torn apart by jealousy, love and fury, Poro longs for death. Before he follows Poro to the temple, and possibly to death, Gandarte asks Erissena to remember how much he loved her ('Mio

ben, ricordati'). Terrified, like a shepherdess lost in a dark wood, Erissena has lost all hope of seeing day ('Son confusa pastorella').

The temple of Bacchus. Poro prepares to kill both Alessandro and Cleofide. The pyre is lit. Suddenly, she announces that she will be united with Poro in death. Poro is recaptured but his courage so impresses Alessandro that he restores to him his crown, his wife and his freedom. Gandarte is allowed to marry Erissena and is granted the lands beyond the Ganges that Alessandro conquered. Poro and Cleofide embrace and after so much suffering, everyone looks forward to the compensations of joy.

The highlights of *Poro* include the eponym's intense aria 'Se possono tanto due luci vezzose', the quarrel duet, whose melting discords are from voices superimposed on one another, the lovely duet of reconciliation, what Winton Dean and John Merrill Knapp call the 'haunting poetry'[1] of 'Senza procelle', scored for two horns, two recorders and four-part strings, the aria of mourning, 'Se il ciel mi divide', the regal grandeur of 'Serbati a grandi imprese', and Poro's remarkable 'Dov'è', which Burney described as 'in a grand style of theatrical pathetic'.   P.

EZIO

Opera in three acts, libretto by Pietro Metastasio for Nicola Porpora (1725), adapted and abridged by Handel. First performance, King's Theatre, London, 15 January 1732, with Senesino, Anna Strada del Po, Anna Bagnolesi, Francesca Bertolli, Giovanni Battista Pinacci, and Antonio Montagnana. After five performances it was not given again until Göttingen, 1926; revived in Britain by the Handel Opera Society at Sadler's Wells, 1977. Performed at the Théâtre des Champs-Elysées, Paris, 1995, with James Bowman, in his last operatic appearance, as Ezio, Dominique Visse and Susan Gritton. [2]

Valentiniano III, *Emperor of Rome,*
  in love with Fulvia..Alto

Fulvia, *Massimo's daughter,*
  promised to Ezio ....Soprano

Ezio, *general, in love with Fulvia*....................Contralto

Onoria, *Valentiniano's sister,*
  secretly in love with Ezio.................................. Alto

Massimo, *Roman patrician,*
  secret enemy of Valentiniano ....Tenor

---

[1] Quoted in Winton Dean and John Merrill Knapp, *Handel's Operas 1704–1726*, Oxford, 1995.

[2] 'Probably not one of Handel's masterpieces', Hugh Canning, *Opera*, September 1995.

Varo, *prefect of the Praetorian Guard,*
    Ezio's friend..Bass

Place: Rome
Time: c. A.D. 451
Running Time: 3 hours

There is nothing perfunctory about *Ezio*: Handel makes the most of his third Metastasio text, which he also cut skilfully, and writes gratefully for his excellent cast. The bass, Antonio Montagnana, was new and needed to be shown off, which is why the minor role was so well endowed with arias. The title role, in the safe hands of the star castrato Senesino, allows for much tenderness, as well as the heroic vocalism you would expect in an operatic general. His first aria could not be more different from that of the other (travesti) alto, Valentiniano: where the latter displays a hard-edged, grand public manner, Ezio's unsupported vocal entry creates the impression of great intimacy. And the roles of the ruthlessly duplicitous Massimo and ambivalent Onoria assume the singers can act as well as they can sing.

Act I. Ezio returns from defeating Rome's enemy, Attila the Hun, and is acclaimed by Valentiniano, who descends from his throne to congratulate him, confident that with Ezio's help, Rome will always triumph. Ezio loves Fulvia and is expecting to marry her, so he is shocked when her father Massimo, the Emperor's confidant, reveals that the Emperor wants her for himself. Undaunted, Ezio reassures Fulvia: he can resolve everything.

Massimo explains to Fulvia that he wants her to marry the Emperor, who once insulted Massimo's wife, because then she can help her father murder him. She is appalled. Alone, Massimo swears that the Emperor will be dead by dawn: if his accomplice Emilio does not succeed, Massimo will pretend that Ezio was behind the attempt.

Onoria, Valentiniano's sister, rebukes Varo, who adores her, for being part of Ezio's victories, instead of achieving sole glory. She is in fact in love with Ezio, but scheming to exploit Varo's love for her. Meanwhile Massimo feeds Valentiniano's incipient resentment of Ezio's glory. Valentiniano decides to marry Ezio to his own sister Onoria, but Ezio explains that this honour is to him a punishment, since he loves Fulvia. Horrified, Valentiniano warns Ezio to be wiser and curb the daring needed in battle but inappropriate elsewhere. His peremptory aria bristles with emphatic, but brief,

rising and falling phrases, expressive of someone on a short fuse ('So chi t'accese').

Onoria takes pleasure in announcing to Fulvia that the Emperor intends to marry Fulvia tomorrow and is surprised when Ezio makes a covert threat. More in sorrow than in anger, Ezio explains that if the Emperor wishes him faithful, then he should not wound him in his heart ('Se fedele brama il regnante'). Onoria and Fulvia quarrel, since each knows that the other loves Ezio. Fulvia reflects that Fortune is testing her constancy.

Act II opens with a darkly atmospheric Sinfonia. Massimo waits to hear whether Emilio has succeeded in his attempt on the Emperor's life. Fulvia is horrified. Valentiniano himself appears, intact, having foiled Emilio. He assumes that Ezio was behind this scheme. When Fulvia defends him, the Emperor turns on her but is reassured when Massimo insists that she was motivated by pity, not by love. The Emperor entrusts Massimo with his life ('Vi fida lo sposo').

Fulvia rebukes her father for his hypocrisy. He responds by accusing her of treachery, since she would sacrifice her father to save her lover, in an F minor aria charged with a jagged, bullying rhythm ('Va! va, dal furor portata'). Fulvia's dilemma is expressed in a brief but highly emotional passage of orchestrally accompanied recitative, before Ezio arrives and she warns him to flee. He is fearless. When Varo asks for his sword, on behalf of the Emperor, Ezio hands it over, asking him to remind Valentiniano who he is. The voice enters without a ritornello and is shadowed by unison strings ('Recagli quell'acciaro'). Varo advises Fulvia that if she wants to save Ezio, she needs to marry the Emperor and, as a woman, she won't find it hard to pretend; she disagrees. Varo reflects that fortune can take a man born a shepherd and make him rule the empire, while someone royally born can end up grazing sheep. The aria makes spectacular demands on the extremes of the bass voice and on the singer's flexibility, suggesting, perhaps, how suitable he is for promotion ('Nasce al bosco in rozza cuna').

Onoria longs to save Ezio. When the Emperor asks her, for political reasons, to marry someone she may dislike, she assumes he means Ezio and is horrified when he names Attila. She suggests he still needs to hear from Ezio and explains that while she still worries about her brother's safety, she cannot feel love. Fulvia asks Valentiniano to pardon Ezio. The Emperor summons Ezio and asks Fulvia to sit in judgement at his side. Ezio himself points out that the Emperor is at once prosecutor, judge and witness. He antagonises him further by reminding the ungrateful Emperor that he is in his debt. Fulvia tries to leave, but the Emperor forces her to confirm she once loved Ezio. When Ezio accuses her of breaking her word, she confesses that she loves only him, adding in a remarkable allegro aria that her feelings will never change. Handel expresses her constancy and her bravery in a heroic vocal line, holding one note for over six bars ('costanza') and with splendidly showy coloratura on the word 'speranza' (hope), and octave leaps. Consumed with jealousy, the Emperor consigns Ezio to his worst prison. Ezio's relief at finding that Fulvia still loves him is expressed in a memorably poignant F sharp minor siciliano: relief that 'Caesar yields to me' is complicated by regret for having doubted Fulvia.

Act III. Inside the prison. Onoria sends for Ezio: she loves him the more for the danger he faces, while his smiling calm proves his innocence. She declares her love for him. He promises her that, as his innocence is evident, his fate will arouse envy, not pity ('Guarda pria se in questa fronte'). Onoria tells the Emperor that she cannot believe in Ezio's guilt and urges her brother to let them marry. She has just as much to lose by their union; love is enemy to them both, a symmetry Handel echoes in the phrasing of her sympathetic aria ('Peni tu per un ingrata'). Valentiniano orders Varo to stand by for a test: if Ezio is not at his side, he must be made to commit suicide. Valentiniano offers to let Ezio marry Fulvia, if only he will betray the conspiracy against the Emperor's life. Ezio prepares to return to prison. Surprisingly, the Emperor seems convinced of Ezio's innocence; he frees him and unites him with Fulvia. Ezio responds in an *Andante larghetto* festively coloured by horns, recorders and bassoons, swearing that he'll make 'the Snow-clad *Scythia* give, With the scorch'd *Aethiop*'s torrid Land Their Realms to Caesar's great Command'. He leaves.

Almost immediately, Varo reports to the Emperor that 'Following your orders, Ezio has died'. Meanwhile, Onoria blithely announces good news: before Emilio died, he swore Ezio was innocent and identified the malefactor as 'the person Caesar loved best and who was injured by him in love'. Onoria identifies this as Massimo. The Emperor asks him to clear himself. To save her father, Fulvia takes the blame on herself. Valentiniano feels he may as well die now, since in one day fate has deprived him of hope, peace, his love and his friend ('Per tutto il timore periglia m'addita'). With its busy accompaniment, jaunty allegro tempo and vocal line of marked limited compass, its cumulative effect is of monstrous petulance, which may be what Handel intended. When Massimo is left alone with Fulvia, she rejects his comforting embraces and asks him to kill her. With typical lack of tact, Massimo tries to cheer her up by reminding her that she can still become the Emperor's wife. Fulvia reflects that she cannot be living, she must be in hell. In her remarkable aria (aptly distinguished by its eloquence) grief has taken over her identity and speaks for her ('Ah! non son io che parlo').

The Capitol, full of people. Massimo inflames the crowd with news of Ezio's death and invites them to avenge their hero. Varo is outraged by his behaviour. Trumpets are heard in the opening of his aria ('Già risonar d'intorno'). Guards descend and fight with the mutineers. When the Emperor asks for help, Massimo tries to kill him. His daughter prevents him and suddenly Ezio saves his life: Varo had pretended that he had died. Ezio is rewarded with Fulvia. He further intercedes for Massimo and the disobedient Varo. In the finale happy, short solos for Ezio, Fulvia, Onoria and Varo are followed by the *coro* in which everyone agrees 'That Constancy the brightest shines Which Anguish with its Flame refines; So to the Fire that fiercely glows, The Gold its purest Lustre owes'.   P.

ORLANDO

Opera in three acts, text after Carlo Sigismondo Capece's *L'Orlando, overo La Gelosia pazzia*, based on Ariosto's *Orlando Furioso*. Première King's Theatre, London, 27 January 1733, with Senesino (Orlando), Strada (Angelica), Francesca Bertolli (Medoro), and Montagnana (Zoroastro). Revived Cambridge, Massachusetts, 1981.

Orlando, *a warrior* .... Contralto
Angelica, *Queen of Cathay, beloved of*
    Medoro .... Soprano
Medoro, *African prince, beloved of Angelica* .... Contralto
Dorinda, *a shepherdess* .... Soprano
Zoroastro, *a magician* .... Bass

Running Time: 2 hours 55 minutes

Orlando is an opera in some contrast with the works that preceded it, and involves not only magic and the supernatural but also considerable musical innovation – short songs as well as the customary *da capo* arias; instrumental novelty; a famous, flexibly shaped mad scene. It has been conjectured that this scene in Act II may have as antecedents English mad scenes such as Purcell's and that the whole work was influenced by the spectacular aspects of the English masque – the stage directions are highly ambitious.

The opera ran for ten performances in 1733 and was not revived in Handel's lifetime. It was produced in the penultimate season for which the composer was responsible, in partnership with the impresario J.J. Heidegger; after these performances, Senesino resigned and went over to Handel's rivals, a new company later known as the Opera of the Nobility.

Act I. Zoroastro surveys the firmament and reads the stars to the effect that the knight Orlando will in the future return to deeds of valour, a prediction Orlando finds hard in prospect, preferring to laud the feats of valour Hercules performed while pursuing his affair with Omphale.

In a wood, Dorinda laments her love-lorn situation. Angelica, despite the recent attentions of Orlando, is now in love with Medoro, who once paid court himself to Dorinda but now returns Angelica's affections. He gives out that Angelica is a relation of his in order to comfort Dorinda, who enjoys the pretence but sees through it. Zoroastro warns Angelica that Orlando is likely to seek revenge, and when her erstwhile suitor appears, Angelica has not the heart to confront him with the new situation but instead pretends to jealousy of the Princess Isabella he has just rescued. Zoroastro conceals the approaching Medoro behind a fountain and Angelica demands Orlando prove his love by renouncing the Princess.

Medoro and Angelica continue a demonstration of their love, to the discomfiture of Dorinda, who finds a jewel given her by Angelica a poor substitute for the lover she has lost. Medoro's efforts to comfort her are less than successful – he will never know the pangs she feels, she says, and the act ends with a rare trio, Dorinda having the last word.

Act II. The love-lorn Dorinda now confuses matters; berated by Orlando for spreading the rumour that he loves Isabella, she says she was misunderstood and was referring to the new-found love

of Angelica for Medoro. Orlando is beside himself with jealousy and fury.

Urged to escape by Zoroastro, Medoro and Angelica leave a memento behind when he carves her name on a tree. She feels gratitude to Orlando for having saved her life but affects to think he will understand that her new love cannot be bound by mere gratitude or reason.

Orlando pursues Angelica but is prevented from catching her by the magic of Zoroastro, who hides her behind a cloud. Rage and jealousy now destroy the balance of Orlando's mind. In his madness, he believes Angelica has been transported to the underworld, crosses the Styx with Charon, hears Cerberus bark and is attacked by the Furies. He thinks Medoro is among his foes, but, as he sees Proserpina weep for him, Orlando's torment momentarily abates, then returns with redoubled fury, until Zoroastro comes with his chariot and bears off the stricken hero.

Act III. Dorinda gives refuge to Medoro, but before long Orlando comes to declare his love for her, seeming to believe she is Venus. He is plainly still unhinged, as evidenced by his subsequent conviction that Dorinda is Angelica's murdered brother, whose death he must avenge. Dorinda tells Angelica of Orlando's pitiable condition, news she accompanies with the not too surprising opinion that love is liable to set the brain a-whirling.

Zoroastro attempts to mend matters and transforms the scene to a 'horrid cavern'. Dorinda brings news that Orlando in his insanity has destroyed her cottage (which is true) and buried Medoro in the ruins (which is not). Orlando now mistakes Angelica for a sorceress and hurls her into the cavern, which changes instantly into a temple of Mars. Orlando boasts he has slain the monsters there and falls asleep (Handel showed a propensity to treat sleep as an aspect of the supernatural, says Winton Dean).

Zoroastro determines to restore Orlando's senses, and the eagle of Jupiter brings a golden vessel containing healing liquid which Zoroastro sprinkles on the sleeping hero. He is no sooner back to normal than Dorinda tells him he has in his frenzy killed Medoro, news which causes him to contemplate suicide, from which he is deterred only when Angelica assures him Zoroastro intervened to save Medoro. Orlando finally accepts the betrothal of Angelica and Medoro and invites all to join him in celebrating love and glory.

The role of Orlando is one for a singer of the utmost

virtuosity, and the mad scene at the end of Act II with its many sections is one of the peaks of Handel's operatic creation. Though he has no more than three of the majestic *da capo* arias a singer like Senesino would have expected (and none in the last act), Orlando offers to fight monsters to prove his love for Angelica in brilliant coloratura, reacts to the news of Angelica's love for Medoro with a vigour which is nothing less than martial and already presages madness, and, purged of his frenzy, falls asleep to music of haunting beauty. The music the composer has allotted to Angelica is only a little less original, spirited and serene by turns; Dorinda is a soubrette role full of charm; Zoroastro's function is to act as *deus ex machina* but he does so four times in music that is as full of determination as it is of coloratura writing.   H.

ARIODANTE

Opera in three acts, libretto by Antonio Salvi, after Ariosto's poem *Orlando furioso* (1516), originally called *Ginevra, Principessa di Scozia*, and first set to music by Perti in 1708. Première Covent Garden, London, 8 January 1735 (19 January new style), with Carestini in the title role and Anna Strada[1] as Ginevra, and Maria Negri, Cecilia Young, John Beard, Gustavus Waltz, and Michael Stoppelaer. Revived Covent Garden, May 1736. First produced Stuttgart in German, September 1926; New York, Carnegie Hall, March 1971, with Sophia Steffan, Judith Raskin, Patricia Wise. Revived Berlin State Opera, 1959, with new German text and Gerhard Unger in title role, Jutta Vulpius, Martin Ritzman, Theo Adam, Kurt Rehm (production later given in Prague, 1959, and Halle); Birmingham, Barber Institute, 1964, with Janet Baker, Jacqueline Delman, Patricia Clark, conductor Anthony Lewis; Drottningholm, 1965; London by Handel Opera Society, 1974, in English version by Brian Trowell with Maureen Lehane, Janet Price, Patricia O'Neill, James Bowman, Philip Langridge, conductor Charles Farncombe; Nancy, 1983 (first performance in France) with Zehava Gal; English National Opera, 1993, with Amanda Roocroft, Lesley Garrett, Ann Murray, Christopher Robson, conductor Nicholas McGegan.

Ariodante, *a prince*............................Mezzo-Soprano

Ginevra, *daughter of the King of Scotland* ....Soprano

Dalinda, *a lady of the court*.............................Soprano

Polinesso, *Duke of Albany* ....Contralto

Lurcanio, *Ariodante's brother* ....Tenor

King of Scotland..Bass

Odoardo, *a courtier*..Tenor

Place: Scotland
Running Time: 3 hours 10 minutes

Handel's operatic career was full of ups and downs, depending less on the ebb and flow of inspiration than on the vagaries of fashion and the strength or weakness of rivalries, whether artistic or political – the King's support of Handel's Royal Academy of Music against the Whigs' Opera of the Nobility by no means guaranteed Handel a winning hand. 1735 saw one of the high points of his career, with a move to Covent Garden and the production in succession of *Ariodante* and *Alcina*, two of his most inspired operas, moreover works in which the forces to hand suggested greater emphasis than before on chorus and on dance.

Act I. A formal overture introduces us to the palace of the King of Scotland, where Ginevra, his daughter, sings buoyantly of her love for her affianced Ariodante, an engagement which has the full blessing of her father. Polinesso bursts in declaring his love but Ginevra, in an aria of some determination, rebuffs him. Dalinda, Ginevra's attendant lady, has quite different feelings for Polinesso and reveals them in a charmingly artless aria, leaving Polinesso scheming an intrigue whereby Dalinda's infatuation may be made to serve his purposes.

In the idyllic surroundings of the royal gardens, Ariodante dreams of his love for Ginevra, who soon appears to join her voice with his in duet. The King interrupts to confirm his blessing on their anticipated union and Ginevra celebrates her happiness. The King once more assures Ariodante of his affection and of the pleasure he takes in the prospect of his daughter's marriage. Ariodante in his own happiness reckons without Polinesso's plotting, which moves forward as he persuades Dalinda, dressed against her better judgment in Ginevra's clothes, to admit Polinesso himself to her chambers. When she succumbs to his blandishments, Polinesso compliments her with the aplomb of a successful predator. Lurcanio pays court to Dalinda, who advises him to look elsewhere, then declares the lasting nature of her own love for Polinesso. There ensues a pastoral scene redolent of requited love for Ariodante and Ginevra, opening with a duet and finishing with chorus and dance as all celebrate the royal love.

---

[1] One of the most celebrated sopranos of the day, Strada is quoted by Čapek and Janáček in *The Makropulos Affair* (see page 393) at the same time as an example of renowned vocalism and proof of the heroine's longevity.

Ariodante *(Welsh National Opera, 1994, director David Alden, designer Ian MacNeil). Ariodante (Della Jones) comes to free Ginevra (Alwyn Mellor), watched by Lurcanio (Gregory Cross).*

Act II. Moonlight is gracefully painted in ten bars in the orchestra before Polinesso ensnares Ariodante by pretending to know nothing of his engagement to Ginevra but declaring that she rather favours him with every token of love. Ariodante challenges him in an aria of some grandeur to prove the calumny, which he proceeds to do. Dalinda, dressed as Ginevra, opens the door of the private apartments, observed by Lurcanio as well as by Ariodante. Ariodante is beside himself and would commit suicide if not restrained by Lurcanio, who urges him not to throw away his life on a worthless woman. Ariodante magnificently laments his despair ('Scherza infida'), and Polinesso gloats in triumph.

The King, who has as yet heard nothing of the untoward events, is about to declare Ariodante his heir when news comes by the hand of Odoardo that the prince has thrown himself into the sea and is dead. When the King tells Ginevra, she collapses. It is Lurcanio who comes now to accuse Ginevra of having by her unchaste behaviour been the cause of his brother's death. Lurcanio asks for justice and promises to fight in the lists anyone who will champion Ginevra's cause. The King is not prepared to acknowledge a wanton as his daughter and Ginevra, totally bewildered, in music of tragic cast goes out of her mind ('Il mio crudel martoro'). The act ends with a series of dances as Ginevra lies dreaming.

Act III. Ariodante in disguise laments a fate which has both destroyed him and left him alive. By chance he is at hand to save Dalinda from the two assassins whom Polinesso has hired to murder her and so conceal the only evidence against him. From her Ariodante learns the truth and impressively inveighs against night, disguise, suspicion, which have contributed to rob him of all he held most dear.

The King insists a champion for Ginevra's cause be found, and when Polinesso offers himself, in spite of her refusal, orders that she accept him, at the same time offering her pardon from his heart whatever his public position may be ('Al sen ti stringo'). Trumpets announce the setting of the scene for single combat, Polinesso fights Lurcanio, who fells him with a mighty blow and then, not content with that, in order that he may avenge the slight to his brother's honour, offers to fight anyone else who comes forward. An unknown knight with lowered visor appears but it is not long before he is revealed as Ariodante, come to explain all on condition the King will pardon Dalinda for her unwitting part in the shameful masquerade. News comes that Polinesso as he lay dying has confessed his guilt, and the King hastens to find his daughter and tell her the welcome news, Ariodante meanwhile ('Dopo notte') rejoicing at the happy turn of events. Dalinda, at Lurcanio's special urging, consents to become his wife (one of Handel's most beautiful duets: 'Dite spera, e son contento').

Ginevra, confined in her apartment, awaits death. The King brings her the news of her vindication, embraces her, and she is reunited with Ariodante. The opera ends in general rejoicing, not excluding the balm of dancing.   H.

ALCINA

Opera in three acts, text by A. Marchi from Ariosto's *Orlando Furioso* (originally set by Albinoni, 1725). Première Covent Garden, London, 27 April 1735, with Anna Strada, Signora Negri, Carestini, Beard, Waltz. First performed in Germany, Brunswick, 1738. Revived Leipzig, 1928; Halle, 1952; London, St Pancras Town Hall, 1957, by Handel Opera Society with Sutherland, Monica Sinclair, conductor Farncombe; Venice, 1960, with Sutherland, Dominguez, Monica Sinclair, in Zeffirelli's production, later seen in Dallas, Texas, with Sutherland; Covent Garden, 1960, by Stockholm Opera, with Hallin, Söderström, Meyer, Wixell, and in 1962, in Zeffirelli's production, with Sutherland.

Alcina, *a sorceress* ....Soprano

Ruggiero, *a knight*...............................Mezzo-Soprano

Morgana, *sister of Alcina*...............................Soprano

Bradamante, *betrothed to Ruggiero*...............Contralto

Oronte, *commander of Alcina's troops* ....Tenor

Melisso, *Bradamante's guardian* ....Bass

Oberto, *a young nobleman*................................Soprano

Place: An Enchanted Island
Running Time: 3 hours 35 minutes

*A*lcina was among the most popular of Handel's later works and was much performed from 1735 to 1737, after which it was unaccountably neglected, the next performance in England not taking place until 1957. Then the revival was associated with the as yet uncelebrated Joan Sutherland, who for the next few years chose Handel operas and Handel arias as vehicles for her skill as often as she selected Bellini or Donizetti.

Alcina's original performances were not without set-back and incident. It is related that the famous castrato Carestini refused at first to have anything to do with what became his most celebrated aria 'Verdi prati', on the grounds that it did not suit his voice, and it took a severe dose of spleen from the irascible composer to convince him of his mistake.

Act I. The enchantress Alcina lives with her sister Morgana and her General Oronte on a magic island, which she rules. Many a brave knight has come to woo her but at her hands has suffered transformation into alien form, animal, vegetable or even mineral. Her latest captive is Ruggiero, who still retains human form but in his infatuation has entirely forgotten Bradamante, to whom he is betrothed. Bradamante, disguised as her own brother Ricciardo, sets off in search of her lover with her guardian, Melisso, and the two are shipwrecked on the very island ruled over by Alcina.

When the action begins, Bradamante and Melisso are discovered by Morgana, who is distinctly attracted by 'Ricciardo' and after a short *andante* aria leads them off to Alcina's court, where they meet the still bedazzled Ruggiero and Oberto, a young nobleman searching for his father. Ruggiero, really believing that he speaks to Ricciardo, announces that he is now in love with Alcina. Morgana rejects Oronte, and announces that she will protect Bradamante, who sings a florid aria on the perils of jealousy. The infuriated Oronte tries to revenge himself by telling Ruggiero that Alcina has fallen in love with Ricciardo, and sings a spirited 12/8 aria in which he mocks Ruggiero for having believed in Alcina.

Bradamante and Melisso vainly attempt to convince Ruggiero that his supposed rival is really his betrothed, but he rushes off to plead with Alcina to do away with Ricciardo. Morgana begs Bradamante to leave the island, and the act ends with a brilliant aria 'Tornami a vagheggiar', which, appropriated to Alcina, became one of the most spectacular vehicles of Joan Sutherland's talents.[1]

Act II. Melisso, in the form of Ruggiero's old tutor Atlante, rebukes him for his behaviour and gives him a magic ring which has the power to remove the spell Alcina has cast over him. Ruggiero at once recovers from his infatuation, and thoughts of his beloved Bradamante come flooding back to him. The plot takes another twist when Bradamante reveals her true identity to Ruggiero, only to have him conclude that this is another of Alcina's spells and rebuff her angrily. Bradamante renews her efforts to convince him and eventually he believes her. In order to escape from Alcina he asks her to allow him to go hunting.

Oberto comes to beg Alcina to help him discover his father's whereabouts; she promises, not intending to keep her word, and he sings of his anxiety.

Oronte tells Alcina that Ruggiero has fled, taking with him the sword and shield which she had hidden because of their magic powers, and in a glorious and extended aria Alcina calls on the gods to witness her distress ('Ah! mio cor!'). Oronte taunts Morgana with the loss of her new lover, but she refuses to believe him. However, she comes upon the lovers and confronts them with accusations of treachery. At this point, Ruggiero sings the justly famous 'Verdi prati', whose apparently simple melody carries with it Ruggiero's subconscious reluctance to leave the scene of the happiness on which he is turning his back. The act ends with a scene in the subterranean cave, where Alcina weaves her spells; in a dramatic accompanied recitative she bewails her betrayal, then in an aria ('Ombre pallide') invokes the spirits from whom proceed her powers. This is Handel's operatic genius working at the top of its bent – richly melodious writing, grateful to the singer and expressive of the dramatic situation.

Act III. Morgana with some difficulty persuades Oronte to forgive her fickleness. Alcina makes a last desperate attempt to hold Ruggiero, but without success, and he sings a triumphant aria ('Stà nell' Ircana pietrosa tana'). Bradamante rejoices at the happy outcome of her efforts. Alcina for her part

realises the futility of her love for Ruggiero and in downcast mood sings 'Mi restano le lagrime', whose tender cast of melody seems to suggest unexpected depths in the sorceress.

An invisible chorus foretells that the marriage of Ruggiero and Bradamante will found a great family. The unfortunate Oberto, still pleading with Alcina for the release of his father, is ordered by her to kill a lion, but he realises just in time that it is in fact his father, transformed by Alcina.

Alcina tries once more to part Ruggiero and Bradamante (a beautiful and expressive trio: 'Non è amor, nè gelosia') and once more fails. Ruggiero now smashes the urn in which rest all Alcina's magical gifts, and immediately all the knights, including Oberto's father, are restored to human shape. All ends happily in a lively chorus and dance, once familiar to British ears by its inclusion in the ballet 'The Gods go a-begging'. H.

GIUSTINO

Opera in three acts, libretto based on a three-act version of Nicolò Beregan's libretto for Giovanni Legrenzi (1683), originally made for Antonio Vivaldi (1724). First performance Covent Garden Theatre, 16 February 1737, with Domenico Annibali, Anna Maria Strada del Po, Gioacchino Conti, William Savage. Revived Brunswick, 1741, in a version by G.C. Schurmann. Not performed again until 1963 at Abingdon. U.S. première San Francisco, 1989. Göttingen Handel Festival, 1994, in an edition by Nicholas McGegan, who also conducted, with Michael Chance, Dorothea Roschmann and Dawn Kotoski.

Giustino, *a ploughboy*	Alto
Arianna, *betrothed to Anastasio*	Soprano
Anastasio, *emperor of Byzantium*	Soprano
Fortune, *goddess*	Soprano
Polidarte, *confederate of Vitaliano*	Bass
Leocasta, *Anastasio's sister*	Soprano
Vitaliano, *a tyrant of Asia Minor*	Tenor
Amanzio, *Anastasio's general*	Contralto
Voice from Within	Bass

Knights, Ladies, Guards, People, Spirits of Fortune

Time: Sixth Century A.D.
Place: Byzantine Empire
Running Time: 3 hours 10 minutes

---

[1] Handel gave the aria to Alcina in the brief revival of November 1736, when his Morgana, Rosa Negri, was a mezzo of limited voice and capacity.

Giustino's spectacular series of plot reversals and elaborate changes of scene reflect Handel's need to compete with his commercial and artistic rivals, the Opera of the Nobility. The composer ensures, however, that they are organic to the work by giving a central, emblematic role to Fortune. Her influence and the motion of her wheel are mirrored in the music's impetuous flow at several points, from the overture onwards. The political lesson *Giustino* teaches – that merit is found outside the inner circle of the court – would have had a particular contemporary resonance for the Hanoverian kings. They would particularly have liked the allusions to the age of gold that both begin and end *Giustino*. That may explain why no less than three numbers in Act I recall Arne's setting of 'Rule Britannia'.

Act I. A majestic hall decorated for the coronation of Anastasio as Emperor of Byzantium. Arianna, widow of the previous emperor, crowns him with the imperial laurel wreath, as the congregation salute him. Amanzio warns the emperor that Vitaliano advances on Byzantium. The enemy's emissary Polidarte brings his master's terms: Anastasio can enjoy peace, as long as he surrenders and allows Vitaliano to have Arianna. Anastasio rejects the offer and goes to lead the attack, strengthened, as he tells Arianna, by her love. She decides to follow her beloved, using the charms that she has learnt from him ('Da tuoi begl'ochi impara').

In the countryside, leaning on his plough, Giustino considers the role Fortune plays in men's affairs, how nobility and courage are her gifts. Sleep overpowers him. The goddess of Fortune appears and invites Giustino to find success on the battlefield ('Corri, vola, a' tuoi Trofei'). He saves Leocasta, the emperor's sister, from a bear and she is so impressed that she invites him to accompany her to court.

Arianna commands Amanzio to lead her to her husband. Amanzio has his own agenda, however, and will employ deceit as a means to power.

Arianna has been taken hostage by Vitaliano. Anastasio appoints Giustino to rescue her. Giustino swears fidelity in a spectacular aria with trumpet obbligato ('Allor ch'io forte avro').

A vast plain below Byzantium. Vitaliano urges his troops to take the city. When his prisoner Arianna dares to reject him, he threatens to punish her. He orders Polidarte to expose Arianna to a monster's murderous appetite. Undaunted in her constancy, she regrets only that her beloved will not hear her last farewell ('Mio dolce amato Sposo').

Act II. Having been shipwrecked, Anastasio is inspired by Giustino's courage and they take shelter nearby. While Arianna is chained to a rock to await the monster, Polidarte tells her that beauty so disdainful deserves to be condemned, not admired or pitied. A terrible monster makes for the rock. Arianna cries for help and the echoes reach Giustino, who kills the monster. Arianna and Anastasio celebrate their happy reunion (duet, 'Mio bel tesoro!'). Amanzio brings a boat in which they embark, welcomed by sailors who wish them a calm sea.

Leocasta has fallen in love with Giustino. Vitaliano has been defeated. Anastasio celebrates his victory, as his brows are crowned with laurels ('Verdi Lauri, cingetemi il crine'). He also congratulates Giustino, who looks forward to still greater triumphs in the Emperor's service. When Vitaliano is brought before Arianna in chains he declares that he loves her. She consigns him to the tower, confident that his love has been vanquished by her contempt, as a torrent is swallowed by the sea ('Quel Torrente che s'inalza').

Act III. Vitaliano escapes and looks forward to revenge. Amanzio disturbs Anastasio by suggesting that he has lavished too much honour on that ploughboy Giustino. Anastasio accepts Amanzio's present of a jewelled sash (taken from Vitaliano) and asks him to keep an eye on Giustino. Against his will, the Emperor begins to doubt his wife's fidelity.

As Arianna rewards Giustino with the same jewelled sash that Anastasio gave her, Amanzio watches suspiciously. Giustino reflects that, like a breeze playing over a field, suspicion can reach the heart's recess ('Zeffiretto, che scorre nel prato').

Hearing that Arianna gave Giustino the jewelled sash, Anastasio assumes they have betrayed him and condemns Giustino to death. He refuses to listen to his wife and tries to frighten her with an outburst of anger. Arianna is overwhelmed with grief but refuses to display her feelings ('Il mio cor già più non sa'). Leocasta resolves to save Giustino. Amanzio congratulates himself on the success of his ambitious plans: soon the whole world will applaud him.

Thanks to Leocasta, Giustino has escaped. Exhausted, he falls asleep. Vitaliano is about to kill him, when the mountain opens to reveal the tomb of his father. A voice from within warns Vitaliano not to kill Giustino, his brother, who will both save his life and bring him power. Vitaliano wakes Giustino and tells him they are brothers. They agree to avenge Anastasio and punish Amanzio.

A delicious landscape with a structure representing the Temple of Fame and a throne. While Anastasio, Arianna and Leocasta are in chains Amanzio enjoys wearing the victor's laurels ('Or che cinto ho il crin d'alloro'). They hear the crowd saluting Giustino who orders Amanzio's execution. He then reunites Anastasio with Arianna, who declares her unchanging love for her husband ('Ti rendo questo cor'). At Giustino's behest the emperor forgives Vitaliano, who swears allegiance to him. Anastasio appoints Giustino his successor as Caesar and joins him in marriage to Leocasta. Everyone celebrates the new reign of peace.

'Few of his operas display such a remarkable catholicity of style, and the various troughs of doodling and banality typical of an overburdened invention such as Handel's during this period are counterbalanced by the untiring range of his resources.'[1] The constellation of characters in *Giustino* sets up some unexpected juxtapositions: in comparison with the dogged, *Boy's Own* heroics of Giustino himself, Anastasio's waverings look pointedly erratic, and his easily aroused jealousy is of a piece with his inconsistency. Handel refuses to set the straightforwardly heroic words of his aria 'Non si vanti un'alma audace' heroically: instead, the melting music breathes vulnerability and sensibility. On the other hand, Anastasio's character gains a third dimension when he gives in to an access of jealousy, because Handel ensures that the emotion is made real, even tragic, in the music for his aria 'O fiero e rio sospetto'. The opera pivots on a central contrast between pastoral innocence and courtly intrigue (Giustino and Leocasta's straightforwardness as against Amanzio's and Vitaliano's deviousness), followed through into the orchestration, with its rich writing for a consort of 'rural' recorders set against splendid parts for the brass section. *Giustino*'s instrumentation is one of its glories and shows how Handel relished having a good, even virtuoso oboist in his orchestra.   P.

BERENICE, REGINA D'EGITTO
Berenice, Queen of Egypt

Opera in three acts, libretto adapted from Antonio Salvi's libretto (1709). Alternative title: *Le gare di politica e d'amor* (The Quarrels between Love and Politics). First performance at Covent Garden, 18 May 1737, with Anna Strada del Po as Berenice, Francesca Bertolli as Selene, Gioachino Conti as Alessandro, Domenico Annibali, Maria Caterina Negri, John Beard and Thomas Reinhold. It was probably revived in Brunswick in 1743 and then not heard until Keele University staged it in April 1985 (Handel's tercentenary), conducted by George Pratt. Cambridge Handel Opera Group, 1993.

Berenice, *Queen of Egypt* ....Soprano
Selene, *her sister, Demetrio's lover*........................Alto
Alessandro, *a Roman prince* ....Soprano
Demetrio, *a Macedonian, Selene's lover*.................Alto
Arsace, *an Egyptian, in love with Selene*................Alto
Fabio, *envoy from Rome*.....................................Tenor
Aristobolo, *court councillor*..................................Bass

Place: Egypt
Time: c.81 B.C.
Running Time: 3 hours 15 minutes

Act I. Berenice loves Demetrio, who is allied with Egypt's enemy, King Mitridate, but she is ready to allow politics to govern her heart: for the sake of an alliance with Rome, she will marry a Roman. Fabio, the Roman envoy, introduces the man Rome has chosen as her husband, Alessandro. He falls in love with Berenice as soon as he sees her. She, however, now refuses to have her choice made for her. Fabio reminds the love-struck Alessandro that if Berenice refuses him, he must marry her sister Selene. He suggests that Alessandro follow the example of the bee, which never stops long at one blossom.

In Princess Selene's royal chambers. Demetrio and Selene are secretly in love. Selene knows that her sister the Queen would be furious if she found out, and urges him to leave. He suggests that his friend Mitridate would help Selene depose her sister. He leaves and Selene learns from Aristobolo that Rome now insists on Berenice's marrying Alessandro; Demetrio is to be executed. The news shocks Selene. Berenice comes to tell Selene that she must marry 'a royal prince'. When she hears this means Arsace Selene is bitterly disappointed. Berenice deliberately misinterprets her burning cheeks as evidence of love. Arsace imagines

[1] Jonathan Keates, *Handel: the Man and his Music*, London, 1985.

that his love for Selene now has some hope of success.

A hall in the palace. Alessandro saves Demetrio's life, which makes Berenice look at him with new eyes. But he rejects her gratitude: he seeks only the merit of honour. Berenice promises Demetrio that she will stand by him: his enemies shall be her enemies (duet 'Se il mio amor').

Act II. In the Queen's chambers. Without his beloved Selene Demetrio pines and has lost his taste for power. He is appalled when he hears Fabio announce that Rome now wishes Alessandro to marry Selene. Berenice refuses the request, saying that Selene is already engaged to marry Arsace. Fabio presents her with a simple alternative, war or peace. Demetrio remains undaunted by the prospect of war, which pleases Berenice, who loves to see him angry. Alone, Demetrio presumes that Selene has betrayed him by agreeing to marry Arsace. In revenge, he'll conspire with Mitridate, and even with the furies from Hell, against Egypt ('Su, Megera, Tisifone, Aletto!').

Alessandro dreams of worshipping his goddess Berenice. He hears Aristobolo instructing Arsace to give up Selene to Alessandro, to keep peace with Rome. Alessandro refuses to marry without love and is therefore happy to yield Selene to Arsace. Aristobolo persuades Arsace that he must give up Selene. Arsace weighs up the conflicting demands of love and glory and agrees doubtfully. As Aristobolo points out, without politics the world would be a more honest place.

In Selene's apartments. Jealousy drives Demetrio to accuse Selene of infidelity, threaten to kill his rival Arsace and admit he pretended to love Berenice. Berenice overhears this and erupts in fury against Demetrio's treachery. Vindictively, the Queen forces Selene to give her hand to Arsace. Arsace, however, insists on sacrificing his own happiness for Egypt's sake, and therefore offers Selene to Alessandro. He in turn refuses Selene, because she does not love him. Infuriated, Berenice sends Demetrio to the tower. At last, he declares himself: he will always love Selene, even in prison ('Si, tra i ceppi'). Selene rejects Arsace, on the grounds that he has proved himself unworthy of her.

Act III. Berenice hears Demetrio confirm that he is ready to die for Selene. Rome is losing patience with Egypt. Berenice entrusts Fabio with her royal signet ring: he shall decide whom she is to marry; that man will bring the ring back to her. Alone, she reflects that the caprices of that blind deity, love, are incomprehensible ('Chi t'intende?').

The royal garden. When Arsace pays court to Selene again, she promises to marry him, as long as he frees Demetrio. Alessandro brings Arsace the royal ring: since it came from Fabio, and not from Berenice herself, Alessandro naturally refuses to take advantage of it. Arsace accepts it and promises to let the Queen know this is how Alessandro feels. When Fabio returns to lead Alessandro to his wedding he is horrified to discover that the Roman still insists on letting Berenice choose her husband for herself. Alessandro explains that Cupid has placed his fate in the Queen's hands.

Berenice determines to punish Demetrio for his double treachery and commands Aristobolo to bring his head to her in the temple. She orders herself not to weep ('Avvertite, mie pupille').

Berenice consigns Demetrio to the goddess Isis and to her ministers. Selene begs for his life and then asks to join him in death. Arsace intervenes to offer his own life and return Berenice her ring. Alessandro explains that he gave it to Arsace, as he wishes Berenice, rather than Rome, to choose him as her husband. Moved by Alessandro's noble gesture, she finds that she now loves him. In duet, they celebrate their mutual love. When Berenice lets Alessandro decide Demetrio's fate, he spares his life. Arsace then allows Demetrio to marry Selene and they all join in celebrating an end to the quarrels between love and politics.

Handel's distinctively thin orchestration for *Berenice* may reflect the economic pressure on a composer who persisted in presenting Italian opera to a London public that, by 1737, had largely lost its taste for the genre. Handel's use of his resources is as inventive as ever, while the opera itself shows no sign of fatigue. It explores a world dominated by *Realpolitik* with playful objectivity. This is the real world, it seems to say, pompously coloured by splendid Sinfonias, but seething with vicious, internecine intrigue, occasionally illuminated by altruism. Perhaps this is why the distinguished Handelian Curtis Price recently called it 'a rather seedy opera', when it is one of Handel's most graceful.[1]

---

[1] *Opera*, July 1985.

One of the strengths of *Berenice* is its richness of characterisation. Not all are complex: Alessandro never wavers in his sentimental, even Romantic, high-principled devotion to his goddess Berenice; Selene the survivor seems to waver fecklessly but merely displays an engaging resourcefulness. Handel's wide sympathies even embrace a Polonius-like courtier, Aristobolo, whose repellent precepts buzz appropriately as they meander, in 'Vedi l'ape'. The soprano-alto duet that ends Act I, 'Se il mio amor', presents a public statement of solidarity, built on an exuberant march rhythm that breathes the determined optimism of those over-long, flash-lit public handshakes that end summits. The harmony between Berenice and Demetrio lasts as long as the act-break. Yet Handel also gives Demetrio an aria whose seriousness reminds one how near are Handel's late oratorios: 'No, che soffrir non può' is matched only by Selene's aria 'Tortorella che rimira', which suggests how well suited they are. Demetrio's later arioso 'Se non ho l'idol mio', his accompagnato 'Selene, infedele' and magnificent aria 'Su, Megera, Tisifone, Aletto!' show a consistent depth of feeling. Handel draws a three-dimensional portrait of the eponymous Queen, wayward as the violin line in her first aria, surrounded by yes-men, longing for someone to stand up to her, but desperately hurt and almost inarticulate with rage when her lover betrays her. In her ruminative address to the god of love 'Chi t'intende', a virtuoso oboe obbligato, the frequent changes of tempo and four-part string harmony speak for the complexity of her feelings. All in all, *Berenice* deserves to be heard more often.   P.

SERSE

Xerxes

Opera in three acts, libretto by Nicola Minato and Silvio Stampiglia. Première 26 April 1738, with Caffarelli as Serse, La Francesina (Elisabeth Duparc) as Romilda, Maria Antonia Merighi (Amastre), Maria Antonia Marchesini (Arsamene), Margherita Chimenti (Atalanta), Antonio Montagnana (Ariodate). There were only five performances and the opera waited until 1924 before it was revived at Göttingen, the fifth in the series of Handel resuscitations by Oskar Hagen; a tenor, Gunnar Graarud, sang Serse (he was later a Bayreuth Tristan), another tenor, Georg S. Walter, was Arsamene, Thyra Hagen-Leisner sang Romilda, Marie Schultz-Dornburg Amastris and Emmy von Hettin Atalanta. The opera has been frequently revived since, notably by the Barber Institute, Birmingham, with

Alexander Young, Heather Harper, Helen Watts, conductor Anthony Lewis, 1959; 1985 for the Handel Tercentenary by English National Opera, London, with Valerie Masterson, Lesley Garrett, Jean Rigby, Ann Murray, Christopher Robson, conductor Mackerras, producer Nicholas Hytner.

Serse (Xerxes), *the King*......................Mezzo-Soprano
Arsamene (Arsamenes), *his brother*....Mezzo-Soprano
Amastre (Amastris), *a foreign
   princess* .... Mezzo-Soprano
Ariodate, *Commander of the Army* ....Bass
Romilda, *his daughter*....................................Soprano
Atalanta, *her sister*...Soprano
Elviro, *servant to Arsamene* ....Baritone

Place: Persia, King Serse's Court
Running Time: 2 hours 50 minutes

In 1737 Handel's London opera company, the Royal Academy of Music, collapsed, as did its rival, the Opera of the Nobility, even though the latter had the great castrato Farinelli under contract. Handel fell ill but his powers of recovery were great and, engaged in autumn 1737 by the impresario Heidegger, he had finished *Faramondo* by Christmas Eve and started *Serse* on Boxing Day! The libretto of *Serse* is an adaptation made by Stampiglia for Bononcini (whose opera of the same name had its première in 1694) from an original by Minato set by Cavalli for Venice in 1654. Anyone acquainted with Monteverdi's masterpiece *L'Incoronazione di Poppea* (or indeed one of Cavalli's operas) will know that in them serious, even tragic, scenes alternate with comedy and farce. *Serse* belongs in this category.

Handel's reaction, conscious or unconscious, to the success of such a ballad opera as *The Beggar's Opera* (1728) led him to write three comedies in his last four operas, moreover in a less formal style than hitherto, and it is strange that nonetheless the public should have rejected him as a composer of Italian opera to such a degree that *Serse* had only five performances in 1738 and was not revived in the composer's lifetime; indeed it remained unperformed for 190 years. Not so strange perhaps that, following the success of an oratorio season in 1735 and the triumph in 1738 of *Saul*, the composer abandoned Italian opera and embarked on a new line of dramatic works, sung in English, based on the chorus, employing solid but not flamboyant singers, and with it found something much more to the English taste than the 'exotic and irrational entertainment' as Dr

Johnson had, not wholly without reason, described the Italian opera, with its strict conventions, foreign language, singers of often bizarre appearance, and an audience understanding hardly a word.

Serse (Xerxes) is the ancestor of the Persian King Darius III, whom Alexander the Great spectacularly defeated in 331 B.C., but his invasion of Greece figures hardly at all in the opera, apart from a mention of the destruction of the bridge of boats across the Hellespont. Instead, it is his misfortunes in love with which Minato is concerned, that and the absolute authority wielded by a tyrant. Serse and his brother Arsamene are in love with the same girl, Romilda. Romilda loves Arsamene, and Serse in retaliation banishes him from his kingdom. Serse is already betrothed to Amastre, who is distressed by his infidelity but disguises herself in military uniform in order to be near him and regain his love. Atalanta, Romilda's sister, is also in love with Arsamene and tries to make certain that Romilda marries Serse in order that she may have Arsamene. Two other less than serious figures play their part in the story: the comic servant Elviro, ancestor of those to be found in later Italian opera; and the sisters' father, Ariodate, the bumbling commander of Serse's army, whose crass misunderstanding of the King's instructions leads to the opera's dénouement.

Act I. The overture, slow, then quick, and ending with a gigue, leads straight to one of the most famous tunes ever written. Once known as 'Handel's celebrated Largo', this Victorian sanctification does less than justice to a glorious tune (itself apparently developed from Bononcini's setting of 1694) in which Serse whimsically apostrophises the beauties of a tree in his garden in a tune of chaste simplicity and total memorability. It has been noted that Handel marks it *larghetto* and not *largo* at all.

Arsamene and the always grumbling Elviro arrive in time to hear the sinfonia which heralds the off-stage singing of Arsamene's beloved Romilda, who sings charmingly of love's victims, and not least of Serse, who now appears to listen to and be enraptured by her singing. Romilda's second aria ('Va godendo vezzoso e bello') has two flutes in the accompaniment.

Arsamene shall be the ambassador to declare his brother's new love, orders Serse, in a charming song, whose melody is taken up in a second verse with precisely opposite sentiments by Arsamene, declaring his confidence in Romilda's love for him. Arsamene alerts Romilda to Serse's intentions, a turn of events which intrigues Atalanta (arietta). Serse's advances to Romilda are rejected, whereupon, finding Arsamene false to his charge, Serse banishes him from his kingdom. Arsamene laments the new situation in a beautiful aria, and the lovelorn Serse addresses Romilda in music only slightly less serious in tone, but to no avail. In an aria of touching simplicity, Romilda asserts that she is proof against temptation.

It is the turn of Serse's spurned betrothed, the foreign Princess Amastre, to take the stage in an aria of resolute character as befits the military disguise she has adopted, and she observes Serse congratulate his victorious general Ariodate whose daughter Romilda he promises shall marry a member of the Royal Family. Ariodate's simplistic philosophy is never to question, and he puts it forward in an aria of some complacency. Serse celebrates the strength of his new love in an extended *da capo* aria.

Elviro is entrusted by Arsamene with a letter for Romilda, an assignment he accepts with an easy show of confidence, leaving his master to lament his fate in a touching *larghetto* aria. Amastre for her part takes a more robust view of her situation, vowing vengeance on her false betrothed.

Confronting Romilda, Atalanta refers to the King as 'your Serse', but Romilda refuses to listen to insinuations that Arsamene may be false to her. Atalanta alone has temporarily the last word as she brings the act to a close with an extended and convincing exposition of her soubrette philosophy which amounts to a belief that all's fair in love as in war.

Act II. Elviro, disguised as a flower-seller and singing snatches of street cries, is on his way to deliver Arsamene's letter to Romilda, but pauses to tell Amastre about Serse's passion for Romilda. Amastre inveighs against her false lover, and Elviro is easily persuaded to deliver Arsamene's letter to Atalanta who promises to give it to Romilda. The plot thickens when, encountering the lovesick Serse, Atalanta gives him the letter, pretending it was written to her and that Arsamene is only feigning to love Romilda, which, she assures the King in a charming aria, Arsamene will persist in denying.

Serse seizes his chance and shows the letter to Romilda, who seems to believe it was written to Atalanta but persists in rejecting the advances of the monarch. He reacts with considerable passion in a grand *da capo* aria ('Se bramate d'amar'), which is as full of pain as of spleen. Romilda alone gives way melodiously to jealousy, but Amastre takes her case even harder and only Elviro's intervention prevents her suicide. Elviro tells the unfortunate Arsamene what he has heard from Atalanta, namely that Romilda has yielded to the importunity of Serse.

Serse comes with Ariodate to inspect the famous bridge but Arsamene, still suffering the shock of love betrayed, continues his lamentations, until discovered by Serse, who proclaims his intention not only to pardon his brother but to unite him with the woman he now knows he loves: none other than Atalanta! Arsamene, in spite of disappointment, seems to take heart from the new situation, and continues to express confidence not only in his love for Romilda but in the belief that it is requited. Atalanta will have none of the advice offered by Serse on hearing this, that she should forget Arsamene, but Serse half convinces himself to take comfort from the precarious position of the lover who does not know whether to hope or despair.

Elviro witnesses the storm which causes the bridge of boats to collapse. Serse, overheard by Amastre, in duet bemoans the sting of jealousy, Serse sighing for Romilda, Amastre for Serse, a dramatic situation both complex and full of irony. Amastre unobserved watches Serse attempt yet again to seduce Romilda but Romilda stands firm and when Amastre in soldierly guise takes her side, the guard on Serse's orders intervenes. Only Romilda's standing with the King induces them to withdraw, and Amastre leaves Romilda to finish the act with a splendid celebration of the steadfast quality of her love for Arsamene.

Act III. Romilda and Arsamene finally force Atalanta to admit her devious scheming, but she buoyantly looks to the future and a new lover. Serse takes advantage of Romilda's presumption in freeing what he thinks of as the young soldier and Romilda goes so far as to agree to marry him if her father consents. Serse rejoices in a *da capo* aria of confident elegance, but Arsamene turns angrily on Romilda. She goes off, as she says, to death, leaving Arsamene to bemoan his solitary fate in music of true poignancy .

Serse, in terms which turn out to be too oblique by half, tells Ariodate that his daughter shall soon be affianced to one equal in rank to the King himself. Ariodate assumes Serse must mean his brother

Arsamene, and rejoices at the honour. Serse for his part attempts to press his advantage with Romilda, but she confesses that Arsamene once loved her and contrives to make him doubt her virtue. His immediate reaction is to order the guards to kill Arsamene and Romilda in despair seeks help from her supposed champion, Amastre, who gives her a letter for the King.

Arsamene and Romilda return to indulge in lovers' quarrelling, their duet a charming expression of misunderstanding, and they go off in opposite directions, only to return, still arguing to the same tune, to interrupt the ceremony which Ariodate is preparing and which promises, when once they grasp its full import, to become their wedding. Serse arrives in time to hear that Ariodate's bungling misunderstanding of his instructions has resulted in his beloved Romilda marrying Arsamene. Only the disconcerting arrival of Amastre's letter turns his fury away from Ariodate and towards his own frustration, which he vents in a magnificent virtuoso aria ('Crude furie'). It remains for Amastre to reappear, offer Serse her love and prepare for an ending apparently happy for all except Atalanta. H.

SEMELE

Opera in three acts, libretto by William Congreve. The music was written between 3 June and 4 July 1743, but the work was not performed (and then in oratorio form) until 10 February 1744, when it was put on at Covent Garden with the French soprano Elisabeth Duparc (better known as La Francesina) as Semele and John Beard as Jupiter. Six performances in this and the following season, always in oratorio form, preceded a century and a half of neglect, until in 1925 the work was first performed on the stage, at Cambridge, in a version prepared by Dennis Arundell. First stage performance in U.S.A. at Northwestern University, Evanston, 1959. First London stage performance, Sadler's Wells by Handel Opera Society, 1959, with Heather Harper, Monica Sinclair, John Mitchinson, Owen Brannigan, conductor Charles Farncombe; Caramoor Festival, New York, 1969, with Beverly Sills, Elaine Bonazzi, Leopold Simoneau, conductor Julius Rudel; Sadler's Wells, 1970, with Lois McDonall, Alexander Young, conductor Charles Mackerras; Covent Garden, 1982, with Valerie Masterson, Robert Tear, Gwynne Howell, conductor Charles Mackerras.

Jupiter, *King of the Gods* ....Tenor
Juno, *his wife*..Contralto
Iris, *her messenger* ....Soprano
Cadmus, *King of Thebes* ....Bass
Semele, *his daughter*.......................................Soprano
Ino, *his other daughter* ....Contralto

Athamas, *a Prince of Boeotia*..................................Alto

Somnus, *God of sleep*..Bass

Apollo..Tenor

Cupid ....Soprano

Chief priest of Juno..Bass

Priests and Augurs, Zephyrs, Nymphs and Swains,
   Attendants

Running Time: 3 hours

The Novello vocal score (about 1878) of Handel's *Semele* carries the following introduction: 'The libretto was originally written as an opera-book by Congreve *but, being found unsuitable for the stage,* was converted by some slight alteration into an Oratorio.' What the unsuitability was and why stage performances in England had exclusively been given by amateurs until the summer of 1959 – the bicentenary year of Handel's death – remain a matter of very considerable mystery. To decide which is the best of Handel's mature operatic works involves recourse to individual preference, but the music of *Semele* is so full of variety, the recitative so expressive, the orchestration so inventive, the characterisation so apt, the general level of invention so high, the action so full of credible situation and incident – in a word, the piece as a whole is so suited to the operatic stage – that one can only suppose its neglect to have been due to an act of abnegation on the part of opera companies, unless of course it is caused by sheer ignorance.

Act I. There is an Overture, *maestoso* followed by an *allegro* of no less consequence. A stately gavotte sets the scene – the Temple of Juno at Thebes, where religious ceremonies are in progress. Semele, the daughter of King Cadmus, is betrothed to Athamas, Prince of neighbouring Boeotia, but is secretly in love with Jupiter, who has appeared to her in disguise. The priest proclaims the acceptance by Juno of a sacrifice, and the assembled people rejoice. Her father and her fiancé ask Semele to delay the wedding ceremony no longer, and she begs the deity to help her in her predicament.

In a scene, which could in performance be omitted, Semele describes her mournful state and Athamas urges his love for her. Ino is afraid Semele will yield to Athamas' pleas, and seems about to admit her own passion for Athamas; Semele urges her to tell all her thoughts. Cadmus admonishes Ino ('Why dost thou grieve?'), and her comments on the situation, together with those of Semele and Athamas, turn what seems to begin as a bass aria into a magnificent quartet. The fire on the altar dies down and this sign of godly displeasure is received with dismay by the populace. Once more the flames rise, but when they die down again, it is clear that it is Jupiter's displeasure they have incurred. The people are alarmed and rush out of the temple. There is a scene for Ino and Athamas, by the end of which the latter has understood Ino's love for him. Cadmus returns with his followers, and tells of having seen Semele snatched aloft by an eagle. The priests hail Cadmus and tell him that Jove's favour has lit on his family, an explanation of events which brooks no contradiction, as Semele from a cloud appears to reassure them in a beautiful aria: 'Endless pleasure, endless love Semele enjoys above'.

Act II. A purposeful *sinfonia* leads to a scene where Juno inveighs against Semele and vows vengeance. Iris tells her of the protective obstacles with which Jupiter has surrounded his new favourite; they include two fierce dragons. In a vigorous aria full of resolution ('Hence, hence, Iris hence away') Juno tells her attendant they will together persuade Somnus, the God of sleep, to 'seal with sleep the wakeful dragons' eyes'.

Semele is asleep in her palace, surrounded by Loves and Zephyrs. Cupid sings an aria ('Come, Zephyrs, come while Cupid sings') which is omitted from older vocal scores, as in the arrangement of Congreve's libretto the character of Cupid was cut out altogether – in fact Handel used the first half of the aria in *Hercules* as 'How blest the maid!'

Semele wakes and sings one of the most famous of Handel's inspirations, 'Oh sleep, why dost thou leave me?', an air of chaste and immaculate beauty, much admired away from the opera but doubly effective in context. Jupiter comes to her side and lyrically reassures her of his love. Pressed to say whether she has any wish Jupiter may gratify, Semele refers to the fact that she is mortal and he a god, and Jupiter, alarmed at the way her thoughts are inclining, hastens to provide distraction: 'I must with speed amuse her'. He announces his intention of bringing Ino to provide company for Semele, in an Arcadian setting to which he will transport them. If his serene aria ('Where'er you walk'[1]) is any indication of the

---

[1] Words by Alexander Pope.

bliss that should obtain there, the sisters' lot will indeed be a fortunate one.

Ino understands that she has come at Jove's express command to a hallowed spot, and together she and Semele sing 'Prepare, then, ye immortal choir', leaving the final comment to the chorus: 'Bless the glad earth with heavenly lays'.

Act III. Rocking quavers introduce the Cave of Sleep where Somnus lies in slumber. Music that is suddenly energetic accompanies the entrance of Juno and Iris, intent on enlisting Somnus' help to remove the barricade Jupiter has set up around Semele. Somnus' slow aria, 'Leave me, loathsome light' – perfect characterisation and a wonderfully beautiful piece of music – ends with the evocative line 'Oh murmur me again to peace'. Juno knows how to rouse him – at the mention of Pasithea's name he springs to life: 'More sweet is that name than a soft purling stream'. Juno gives her orders: Jupiter is to be distracted by dreams of Semele, the dragons are to be soothed by Somnus' leaden rod, and Ino must sleep so that Juno may appear to Semele in her guise. In a duet ('Obey my will') the amorous Somnus, in return for the promise of Pasithea, agrees to all her demands.

Juno disguised as Ino appears to Semele, comments on her beauty and asks if this is a sign that Jupiter has already made her immortal. She holds up a magic mirror and Semele is overcome with admiration of herself. Her bravura aria ('Myself I shall adore'), with its echo effects, shows how miracu-

lously Handel could transform a frivolous idea into music of surpassing grace and loveliness. Juno, still in Ino's shape, urges her to refuse her favours to Jupiter until he promises her immortality and himself appears, not as mortal, but in his own godly shape – Juno knows that at sight of the god, Semele will be destroyed. Juno retires as Jupiter approaches.

Jupiter tells Semele that he has had a dream in which she repulsed him, but in spite of the ardour of his aria ('Come to my arms, my lovely fair') she keeps to her resolve: 'I ever am granting, you always complain'. Jupiter solemnly swears to grant her desire, whatever it may be, and immediately Semele asks him to appear in all his godly splendour. Jupiter cannot conceal his consternation, which shows in agitated ornamentation, but Semele, in coloratura which is no less emphatic, insists: 'No, no, I'll take no less'. In a moving recitative, Jupiter, alone, laments his oath and its inevitable consequence. Juno celebrates her forthcoming triumph ('Above measure is the pleasure'). What the libretto describes as 'a mournful symphony' accompanies Jupiter as he appears to Semele, who realises too late that the vision will scorch her to death. She dies.

At Cadmus' court, the people comment on the story they have heard Ino tell of Semele's love and death. Ino reveals that it has been prophesied she shall marry Athamas. A *sinfonia* heralds the appearance on a cloud of Apollo, who announces that a phoenix will arise from Semele's ashes, and the people rejoice.   H.

JOSEPH HAYDN

(born 31 March 1732, died 31 May 1809)

As Kapellmeister at the court of Prince Nicholas Esterházy, Haydn conducted (and rearranged ad lib) roughly a different opera every week, including Italian operas by the leading composers of the day. Not content with repeating a formula, when he composed opera himself he made several important innovations. In particular, he wrote more interestingly for the orchestra than was normal. Nearly all his works are comic; his *opera seria L'isola disabitata* was

given few performances after its première in 1779. After pioneering work by Glyndebourne, Garsington Festival near Oxford has led the way in stimulating interest in Haydn's operas, staging them in a setting that usefully recalls the court ambience for which he composed them. As soon as they are heard (and, of course, preferably seen) they tend to convert their audiences into admirers. Perhaps the only thing that stands in the way of their wider appreciation is their long stretches of dry recitative. The most prominent feature of Haydn's operas may seem the weakest: their charm which, in a sympathetic performance, is as difficult to resist as it is to analyse.

L'INFEDELTÀ DELUSA

Infidelity Prevented

Burletta per musica in two acts, libretto adapted (probably by Carl Friberth, the first Filippo) from a libretto by Marco Coltellini (1773). First performed at Eszterháza, 26 July 1773, to celebrate the name-day of Prince Nicholas Eszterházy's sister, the Dowager Princess Maria Anna Louise. Revived 1773 to celebrate the Empress Maria Theresa's visit. First British performance by the Haydn Opera Society, in concert, Royal Festival Hall, 1960; revived at St Pancras Town Hall, 1964, and at Garsington in 1993 with Philip Doghan, Paul Harrhy, David Mattinson, Claire Daniels and Patricia Rozario, conducted by Wasfi Kani.

Vespina, *Nanni's sister, in love with Nencio*.....Soprano

Sandrina, *in love with Nanni* ....Soprano

Filippo, *her father, a farmer*.................................Tenor

Nencio, *a rich farmer, in love with Sandrina* ....Tenor

Nanni, *a young farmer, in love with Sandrina*.........Bass

Place: The Italian Countryside
Time: 1700
Running Time: 2 hours

Act I. Filippo, Vespina, Nencio and Nanni enjoy the evening breeze that relieves the day's heat, hoping it will grant them their wishes ('Bella sera'). Like the overture, this ensemble is on a large scale (over ten minutes) and was the most important addition Haydn made to the original libretto. H.C. Robbins Landon suggests it is there because Haydn 'considered that the traditional sequence of aria after aria was dull; [it] establishes right from the outset that this is not a conventional Italian opera.'[1] It has an emblematic function, initiating various patterns of behaviour (obedience and rebellion; order and disorder; hope and reality) that will be enacted in the rest of the work. Sandrina seems prepared to do what her father decides, which is that Nencio shall be her husband rather than Sandrina's choice, Nanni, who is poor. She offers to marry Nencio if she can still love Nanni, but such behaviour is unacceptable in the country,

though common in town. In an aria combining elegance and authority, Filippo insists, but Sandrina cannot quite forget Nanni. After courting her for three years, Nanni for his part feels cheated and swears that either he or Filippo must die. His aria covers a surprising amount of emotional and vocal ground, but ends in reassuringly farcical patter and horn fanfares.

As she washes the salad in Nanni's kitchen, Vespina muses on her experience of love: so far, she has felt its sting but not tasted any honey. Nanni tells her that he has lost Sandrina to Nencio and they swear revenge.

Nencio serenades Sandrina, a lilting rhythm and pizzicato strings standing in for the guitar he holds. Vespina and Sandrina overhear Nencio threaten, if necessary, to abduct Sandrina. Vespina emerges and slaps him, thus occasioning the lively finale, which opposes Vespina and Nanni against everyone else.

Act II. Disguised as an old woman, Vespina pretends to Filippo that Nencio seduced and married her daughter in secret and had three children by her. She also claims to be suffering from several illnesses, and her aria limps and coughs in sympathy. Sandrina sees it is better to stay poor, and Filippo tells Nencio that he clearly cannot marry Sandrina. Vespina, now disguised as a drunken German servant, forces wine on Nencio and lets him know Sandrina is going to marry his master, a Marquis. Vespina returns, dressed as the Marquis in question and explaining that he means to trick Filippo: Sandrina will in fact marry his servant. Nencio agrees to witness the marriage and looks forward to seeing Filippo foam at the mouth in fury. Meanwhile Vespina has no time to tell Nanni what is going on. Haydn enriches the hunting metaphor in this splendid aria with bird-like melismas for the soprano imitating her prey, tiptoeing strings and horn flourishes.

Filippo is delighted Sandrina will marry a Marquis. All Sandrina herself wants is bread, onions and her Nanni; peace, rather than luxurious pomp, as she explains in a surprising (but aptly) grand, expansive aria, distinguished by its richly decorated vocal line. Vespina has now dressed up as a notary public (anticipating Despina in *Così*), while Nanni pretends to be the Marquis's servant, there to act as proxy bridegroom. The notary's dry, pedantic deliv-

---

[1] '*L'Infedelta Delusa* in context', Garsington Festival programme, 1993.

ery of the date (1700) launches the ceremony and a particularly delicious finale, which is undercut by chuckling string figures and includes an unexpected solo for timpani ('Nel mille settecento'). Its relentless rhythm makes the explosive revelations still more funny: once the ceremony is complete, Vespina and Nanni reveal themselves. Filippo and Nenci are furious, but reconciliation is not long delayed. They agree that what's done cannot be undone (kettle-drums emphasise the point). A double wedding follows for Sandrina and Nenni, Vespina and Nencio.

The way Haydn's *Infedeltà delusa* pre-echoes Mozart's operas is intriguing. It is known that Mozart copied out sections of Haydn's *Armida* and he may well have known other works. Mozart frequently referred to Haydn as his teacher and dedicated six quartets to him. In particular, he praised him for his ability to move people and make them laugh – the aptest criticism of this opera.   P.

L'INCONTRO IMPROVVISO

The Unexpected Encounter

Dramma giocoso per musica in three acts, libretto by Carl Friberth after L.H. Dancourt's libretto for Gluck, *La Rencontre imprévue* (1764), first performed in Eszterháza on 29 August 1775. Revived, broadcast in Russian, on Leningrad radio, 1956; performed Moscow, 1962. First U.K. performance, St Pancras Town Hall, 23 March 1966, in a translation by Andrew Porter; revived Garsington, 1994, with Thomas Randle, Eirian Davies, Paul Nilon, Roger Bryson, conducted by Wasfi Kani.

Ali, *Prince of Balsóra, in love with Rezia* ....Tenor

Rezia, *Princess of Persia,*
  the Sultan's favourite ....Soprano

Balkis ⎫
Dardane ⎭ *Rezia's slaves and confidantes* ....Sopranos

Osmin, *Ali's slave* ....Tenor

A Calender, *supervisor of the caravan*
  storehouse ....Bass

Three Calenders..Basses

Sultan of Egypt..Bass

An Officer ....Tenor

Slaves, Janissaries

Place: Cairo
Running Time: 2 hours 55 minutes

Haydn wrote *L'incontro improvviso* for the celebrations attendant on the visit of the Archduke and Archduchess to Eszterháza. The first performance was followed by a masked ball for 1,380 guests in the Chinese ballroom. Accounts for the lavish production survive and were reprinted in the Garsington programme, showing that most of the soloists' costumes incorporated tufts of heron's feathers.

Prince Ali of Balsóra has come to Cairo in pursuit of his beloved Rezia. She had eloped with Ali to avoid marriage to a man her father had chosen for her. Since the lovers were separated by pirates, she has become the Sultan's favourite in his harem.

Act I. In the storehouse. The Calender and his dervishes celebrate their secret hoard of gold, food and wine. As professional beggars, they accumulate money by pretending to be starving.

Ali's servant Osmin encounters the Calender, whose begging routine consists of a nonsense song. Osmin explains he has no money and the Calender invites him to join them as a fake Dervish.

Rezia learns that Ali has been seen in Cairo. Surprised by the intensity of her feelings, she prays that they will soon be reunited for ever. She tells her confidantes Balkis and Dardane, who are as delighted as she is. Their large-scale terzetto is, as Robbins Landon says, ravishing ('Mi sembra un sogno').

In despair, Ali prays that heaven will either give him his beloved back or let him die. He watches as Osmin and the Calenders arrive and rehearse a Turkish-sounding begging-song. Ali refuses to join this 'crowd of madmen', but Osmin explains that their astute 'madness' has practical benefits, as their kitchen and cellars prove. Balkis pretends to Ali that the Sultan's favourite (who, incidentally, resists his advances) has seen him from her window and fallen in love with him. Ali politely explains that he has sworn fidelity to another.

Osmin is enjoying a feast but he remembers to pack some food away for his master. The sound of trumpets and drums punctuates their toasts. Ali is offended when Osmin urges him to respond to such generosity, but he distracts himself by reading aloud from a book. Dardane pretends that she has fallen in love with Ali. When he rejects her politely, she explains that she was only pretending: it is her mistress who loves him. Rezia reveals that it was she who was testing his fidelity. She also reassures Ali that the Sultan is, in effect, her slave and promises to escape from the harem. Balkis determines to leave the harem as well and longs for freedom.

Osmin tells the Calender that he is going to escape with his master and Rezia, using the Sultan's money that she has accumulated. They celebrate with wine, while the Calender rebukes the Prophet, who forbade it. Osmin mentions they will escape at night.

At Rezia's request, Ali sings the song in praise of her eyes that he used to sing to her (duet, 'Son quest'occhi un stral d'Amore'). Suddenly Balkis and Dardane report that the Sultan has returned to the harem. They turn to Osmin for help and on his advice leave by the secret staircase.

Act III. Night. They have taken refuge in the Calender's storehouse. Osmin brings back a notice offering a large reward for Rezia's recapture. The Calender leaves and Rezia prays that her guiding star will be propitious. Guards surround the store. Osmin thinks up a solution: Ali must dress in a smock as a French painter, the ladies must dress as dervishes and he will pretend to be a camel-driver. The Calender brings in the guards and Ali sings a splendid song about some paintings of a banquet, musicians, a stream and a battle. The Officer lifts Ali's smock, however, and shows him the Sultan's warrant. They abandon their disguises and prepare to die, but the Officer has another surprise. The Sultan only feigned severity: he knows that Rezia is really a princess and Ali a prince. He reveals that the Calender's punishment for treachery is to be flayed alive and impaled. They promise to plead for him.

The Sultan unites the two lovers and Rezia salutes him as their beloved father. Everyone celebrates the end of sorrow and fear. When Rezia and Ali plead for the Calender, the Sultan commutes his sentence to banishment. He promises to cultivate integrity and the opera ends amid renewed rejoicing.

When Garsington revived *L'incontro improvviso*, Leonard Ingrams noted in the programme that 'Haydn ... lavished a prodigious quantity of inspired music on this alternately witty and feeble text.' Even H.C. Robbins Landon, who has done so much to awaken interest in Haydn's operas, has his doubts about the work, calling it 'not really a first-rate opera: it is too long, too diffuse and lacks the driving pace of its 1773 predecessor [*L'infedeltà delusa*]'.   P.

IL MONDO DELLA LUNA
The World of the Moon

Dramma giocoso in three acts, libretto by Carlo Goldoni. First performance at Eszterháza on 3 August 1777. First U.K. performance, Scala Theatre, London, 1951; first U.S. performance, Greenwich Mews Playhouse, 1949; revived Holland Festival and Aix-en-Provence, 1959, Camden Festival, 1960; Schleswig, 1984; Garsington, 1991, with Philip Doghan, Martin Nelson, Carol Smith and Riikka Hakola, conducted by Peter Ash.

Ecclitico, *a false astrologer*	Tenor
Ernesto, *a cavalier*	Alto
Buonafede, *a protective father*	Baritone
Clarice ⎫ *his daughters*	Soprano
Flaminia ⎭	Soprano
Lisetta, *his maidservant*	Contralto
Cecco, *Ernesto's servant*	Tenor

Pupils of Ecclitico, Gentlemen, Dancers, Pages, Servants, Soldiers

Place: Italy
Time: Eighteenth Century
Running Time: 2 hours 55 minutes

The *dramma giocoso Il Mondo della luna* was commissioned to celebrate the marriage of Count Nicholas Esterházy to Countess Maria Anna Weissenwolf.

Act I. A terrace before Ecclitico's house, night. For all its jokiness, the opera begins on a serious note: Ecclitico and his four students sing a hymn to the moon, distinguished by its genuine graciousness. Ecclitico boasts of his capacity to fool stupid people. Buonafede comes to consult him: as a dilettante in astrology, he has never understood what the moon is. Ecclitico explains that his new telescope is so powerful he can see through the moon's transparent surface and into the houses inside it to spy on women as they undress before bed. Buonafede looks through the telescope, while Ecclitico's servants move puppet figures about in front of it. This fools Buonafede who says that he has seen a beautiful girl with an old man, a husband punishing his wife for infidelity and a man leading his beloved by the nose. He rewards Ecclitico with some money. When he is alone, Ecclitico reveals that he is in fact in pursuit of Buonafede's lovely daughter Clarice. He is joined by Ernesto, who loves her sister, Flaminia, and Cecco, his valet, who loves Lisetta, Buonafede's servant. Unfortunately, Buonafede is bent on marrying his daughters off to more important husbands. Ecclitico promises to get them all they want, as long as they can supply a little money. In another, more serious aria Ernesto dreams of Flaminia's eyes and looks forward to their life together. Cecco, on the other hand, assumes that everyone pretends and insists on seeing the funny side.

Inside Buonafede's house. Clarice and Flaminia long to escape from their tyrannical father. In a major aria of *opera seria* weight, Flaminia accepts that while reason should rule in the soul, when love intervenes, it takes control. Buonafede rebukes Clarice, who responds by asserting she will find herself a husband, if he will not. As in *Così*, the sisters are clearly differentiated: Clarice has her feet on the ground and her aria bristles with determined practicality. Buonafede attempts to make up to Lisetta and offers to let her look through the telescope. Bent on getting his money, she assures him of her love, her fidelity and her virtue, none of which is for real.

Ecclitico comes to take his leave of Buonafede, as the emperor of the moon has invited him to attend his court. He is to travel there by drinking 'a certain liquid'. Buonafede asks to have some and to travel with him. Ecclitico agrees. Buonafede drinks it and, as he falls asleep, he imagines he is flying to the moon. Once again, the idea of the moon inspires some delightful, airy music. Clarice and Flaminia assume their father has died, but when Ecclitico reads out the will the thought of their dowries consoles them.

Act II. Ecclitico's garden, transformed into the moon. An orchestral prelude sets the scene. Buonafede wakes to see dances performed by the moon's inhabitants. He is dressed in appropriate costume and congratulated on his good fortune. Ecclitico promises Buonafede that his daughters and his maid will arrive soon and will be humble and obedient. A march announces the entry of the emperor (Cecco in disguise), who welcomes Clarice and Flaminia but demands Lisetta for his wife. Buonafede is delighted by everything he has seen in this friendly world. His aria is one of the opera's highpoints, and not just because he is required to whistle along with the woodwind at one point ('Che mondo amabile'). He is presented to Lisetta, who wears a blindfold and resists his wooing. The emperor (Cecco) insists, however, on marrying her. She agrees delightedly. The emperor unites Ernesto with Flaminia, who welcomes the news ecstatically,

and Ecclitico with Clarice, who is just as pleased. During the finale the wedding ceremonies are completed. Buonafede suddenly realises that his daughters have achieved what they wanted.

Act III. Inside Ecclitico's house. Before they agree to release Buonafede, Ecclitico and Ernesto force him to free his daughters' dowries. Ecclitico and Clarice celebrate their union and everyone joins in the final chorus of rejoicing at the 'world of the moon'.   P.

LA FEDELTÀ PREMIATA
Fidelity Rewarded

Dramma pastorale giocoso in three acts, libretto adapted from Giambattista Lorenzi's text for Cimarosa's *L'infedeltà fedele* (1779). First performed at Eszterháza, 25 February 1781. Revised version 1782. First modern revival, Holland Festival, 1970, with Romana Righetti, Pietro Bottazzo and Eugenia Ratti, conducted by Alberto Erede. First U.K. performance, Collegiate Theatre, London, 1971; Zürich, 1975; Glyndebourne, 1979; Garsington, 1995, with Sara Fulgoni, Neill Archer, Janis Kelly, Mary Hegarty, conducted by Wasfi Kani.

Fillide/Celia, *lover of Fileno*	Mezzo-Soprano
Fileno, *lover of Fillide*	Tenor
Amaranta, *a vain and arrogant woman*	Mezzo-Soprano
Count Perrucchetto	Baritone
Nerina, *a nymph, inconstant in love*	Soprano
Lindoro, *brother of Amaranta*	Tenor
Melibeo, *high priest*	Bass
The Goddess Diana	Soprano

Nymphs, Shepherds, Hunters, Followers of Diana

Place: Near Cumae, Italy
Running Time (revised version): 2 hours 45 minutes

Haydn wrote *La fedeltà premiata* for the opening of Eszterháza's new opera house, some two years and three months after the old one had gone up in flames. The overture, which is more familiar as the last movement of his Symphony No. 73 in D, 'La Chasse', declares the festive nature of the work with its horn calls and timpani part.

Act I. Nymphs and shepherds assembled in front of Diana's temple beg the goddess to show mercy and restore peace. Melibeo the priest welcomes the flirtatious Amaranta, who reads out the oracle's text: each year two faithful lovers must be sacrificed to the monster, until some brave man offers his life voluntarily. This has been going on for ten years; the latest sacrifice is due today. Melibeo loves Amaranta and assumes she loves him – as a priest, he is exempt from this cruel law. Meanwhile Nerina rebukes Lindoro, Amaranta's brother, who has been neglecting her for Celia. Nerina annoys Amaranta, who encourages Lindoro to marry Celia. Amaranta reassures Melibeo that she loves him and will marry him one day. With its intricately worked introduction, slow pace and touching tone, this aria portrays a rather more serious capacity for love, even though we know she is faking it ('Per te m'accese amore'). Count Perrucchetto enters, faint, having been attacked by robbers. He asks for help and some wine and is horrified when Melibeo offers him water, but comforted when he sees and falls in love with Amaranta. She is thrilled to meet a count. Melibeo warns him off, in an aria about the conflict between two jealous bulls, featuring an apt role for the horns.

Fileno cannot forget his beloved Fillide. Haydn's memorable adagio setting makes this one of his most beautiful and affecting tenor arias ('Dove, oh dio, rivolgo il piede'). Nerina is immediately attracted to him. He explains that on the eve of his marriage to Fillide, she was bitten by a snake and died. She tells him that on the eve of her marriage to Lindoro, he left her for a nymph who calls herself Celia.

As she tends her sheep, Fillide (who now calls herself Celia) asks the streams whether they ever saw a more unhappy heart than hers. Once again, Haydn transforms a conventional text into an intensely individual cavatina, only faintly reminiscent of the great aria Gluck wrote for Orfeo in the Elysian Fields. She falls asleep. Nerina points out Celia to Fileno and leaves him to present her case. Celia awakes to see her beloved Fileno. She sees they are being watched by Lindoro and Melibeo. She realises that they risk being sacrificed as faithful lovers, and therefore avoids Fileno's questioning. He presumes she no longer loves him. When Melibeo questions her, Celia denies that she ever saw Fileno before. Understandably, Fileno feels betrayed. His sense of shock is brilliantly evoked in a spasmodic vocal line and staccato accompaniment, later punctuated by passionate cello accents ('Miseri affetti miei'). Celia follows him; Lindoro and Perrucchetto follow her. The count's fickleness appals Amaranta, who threat-

ens to pursue him as an avenging fury in a long, spectacular aria ('Vanne ... fugge ... traditore!').

Melibeo threatens Celia: either she marries Lindoro, or he will send her and her lover Fileno to the monster. Celia asks Nerina to find Fileno and tell him to flee. In 1781, this major aria ('Deh soccorri un'infelice') included parts for three horns, with an elaborate solo part for one of them, muted, played by the virtuoso Anton Eckhardt, whose wife created the role of Amaranta. In the revival, the role of Celia was rewritten for a soprano, and the solo was reallocated to the bassoon. Perrucchetto tries to court Nerina, but when she runs away, in mid-aria, and he realises Amaranta has been listening, he tells her her doubts of his fidelity are insufferable ('Coll'amoroso foco'). She launches the first finale in a towering fury that prevents her from saying what caused it. Celia enters, worried about Fileno's fate. When Lindoro tries to court her, she slaps his face and leaves. Nerina rejects Perrucchetto almost as brutally. Amaranta drags Celia in and Melibeo tries blackmail: if she does not agree to marry Lindoro, Fileno will die. Fileno's entry is given intensely serious, beautiful music, as he looks forward to death. Nerina enters, pursued by satyrs, one of whom carries Celia off.

Act II. Melibeo swears to destroy the count, his rival for Amaranta's love. He encourages Nerina to pursue Fileno, reminding her that heartless beauty is of no avail. When Fileno sees Celia he punishes her supposed cruelty by declaring his love for Nerina.

The hunt in honour of Diana is taking place. Perrucchetto is pursued by a bear. Amaranta runs on, fleeing from a boar, and faints. Fileno kills it, but Perrucchetto tries to take the credit. When this version of events is disputed, he appeals to the boar for confirmation. As the boar stirs, he begs for mercy and runs away.

The scale of the orchestral introduction reaffirms the seriousness with which Haydn treats Fileno. He resolves to commit suicide, but first he carves the reason on a tree: 'For Fillide ... unfaithful ... died ... Fileno'. Celia reads the inscription. She seems to hear her lover's reproaches and determines to join him on the banks of Lethe ('Ombra del caro bene').[1]

Melibeo tells Nerina to send the count into the cave and orders shepherds to prevent anyone leaving it.

[1] The best and longest analysis of this aria was first published in 1783 and is reprinted in H.C. Robbins Landon, *Haydn at Eszterháza*, London, 1978.

When Amaranta asks after the count, Lindoro tells her that, according to some shepherds, he was seen making love to Celia 'in a desperate manner'. Melibeo declares that the goddess has chosen her victims. He sends Lindoro and shepherds to enter the cave and dress the sacrificial couple in white. Lindoro returns, appalled, to report that Celia and Perrucchetto are inside. Amaranta flies into another rage, asking whether this is the reward for her faithful love, but this time there is nothing comic about her plight. Fileno arrives and asks where Celia is. When nobody answers, he presumes the worst and so launches the second, grief-stricken finale. The victims emerge from the cave to some haunting, exquisitely mournful music. Melibeo presents them to Diana, refusing to listen to Perrucchetto's plea that he is an innocent little lamb. We are no longer in the realm of unmitigated tragedy.

Act III. The sacrifice has not happened yet. Celia and Fileno meet but, instead of sorting out their misunderstanding, neither listens to the other. Perrucchetto pleads that he is ineligible because he has never been faithful, and Amaranta tries to discredit the priest but Melibeo remains adamant.

The monster appears but suddenly Fileno steps forward and offers himself as a victim. The monster turns into a grotto with Diana enthroned. She promises that peace will now return to Cumae; announces that Melibeo has been killed, as punishment for his fraud; prescribes Amaranta's marriage to the count and reunites Celia and Fileno. In a straightforward, four-square allegro chorus, nymphs and shepherds point out that we enjoy peace all the more when it is preceded by trouble and grief. Everyone concurs ('Quanto più diletta e piace').   P.

ORFEO ED EURIDICE ossia L'ANIMA DEL FILOSOFO[1]
Orpheus and Eurydice or The Philosopher's Soul

Dramma per musica in four acts, libretto by Carlo Francesco Badini, based on Ovid's *Metamorphoses* IX and X. Commissioned by Salomon for the newly rebuilt King's Theatre and written in London, 1791 – the title role was conceived for the virtuoso tenor Giacomo Davide – it was rehearsed but never staged. Recorded by the Haydn Opera

Society, 1950, and staged at the Maggio Musicale in Florence, 9 June 1951, with Maria Callas as Euridice, Tygge Tyggesen as Orfeo and Boris Christoff as Creonte, conducted by Erich Kleiber. Revived Theater an der Wien, Vienna, 1967, with Joan Sutherland as Euridice (and, for 'Al tuo seno fortunato', as the Genio) and Nicolai Gedda as Orfeo; 1987, for Cecilia Bartoli. Performed in concert at Queen Elizabeth Hall, London, 1997, with Christiane Oelze, Kurt Streit, Claron McFadden, conducted by Frieder Bernius.

Euridice, *King Creonte's daughter*...................Soprano
Orfeo, *a singer* ....Tenor
A Sibyl ('Genio', *spirit guide*) ....Soprano
Creonte, *King of Athens*................................Baritone

Servants, Cupids, Virgins, Men, Furies, Unburied Bodies, Bacchantes

Running Time: 2 hours 15 minutes

After some twenty-four years in service at the court at Eszterháza, Haydn was at last free to travel and work elsewhere when his employer Prince Nicholas Esterházy died. Haydn relished the new possibilities that London represented, particularly the chorus, which plays a major role in *Orfeo*, but also the enlarged orchestra (now including clarinets, trombones and a harp). Some mysterious features of this opera, such as its 'real' title, or the oratorio-style role of the chorus, reflect the fact that Haydn never saw it performed and may not even have completed it. There is more than enough in *Orfeo* as we now know it, however, to astonish and delight.

The tragic overture immediately sets the scene for a tale of grief and drama, in the solemn tones of *opera seria*.

Act I. A wood with a pyre visible in the middle. Euridice is in despair; the Chorus warn her not to enter the wood, whose inhabitants are more savage than the beasts. They run away as savage shepherds surround her. She guesses that they mean to sacrifice her to their god, but she is ready to die. Her aria begins modestly and the voice enters demurely, but by the time she reaches the word 'crudeltà' she has taken flight into spectacular melismas. Two members of the Chorus call for Euridice's beloved Orfeo to help her. He uses his lyre (represented by the orchestra's harp) to appeal to the savages to show mercy. They release her and the lovers embrace, while the Chorus pay tribute to the power of music.

---

[1] This was its real, though rarely used title.

Creonte had arranged for his daughter to be married to Arideo, though she loves Orfeo. She fled to the forest and a servant reports that Orfeo rescued her from the savages. Creonte is now convinced that she should be allowed to marry Orfeo. He gives his blessing to the lovers' marriage.

Act II. In the countryside. Orfeo and Euridice are surrounded by cupids who tell them to 'drink love's nectar from the cup of pleasure' while they are young. When Orfeo goes to investigate a noise, Arideo and his followers burst in to abduct Euridice. As she attempts to escape she steps on a snake which bites her. She can feel death coming. Her magnificent, moving recitative and aria comprise a miniature tribute to Gluck: Haydn evokes with diagnostic skill the way Euridice feels the poison slow her blood, but in a markedly more simple, affecting style than any of her earlier, bravura showpieces ('Del mio core'). Orfeo discovers her body and is overwhelmed with grief, which finds expression in some spectacular coloratura, coloured by clarinets.

A messenger tells Creonte that Arideo now threatens his court, his throne and his life. Creonte swears to avenge Arideo's insults and declares war on him.

Act III. Groups of Virgins and Men offer sympathy to Orfeo. He says goodbye to Euridice and asks nature to echo back his laments. Creonte hears that Orfeo is near to losing his mind. He reflects how love lets a man live more intensely, but leaves him vulnerable. He tries to console Orfeo.

Orfeo consults the Sibyl in her cave. She offers to lead him into the underworld and promises, in an exceptionally florid, beautiful aria, that if he can be brave and constant, he will recover his beloved ('Al tuo seno fortunato'). The Chorus twice admonish him to let justice reign in his heart and adore only one god. The words have only a forced relevance to Orfeo at this moment; in 1791 they may have had a Masonic meaning, such as has been posited for Creonte's Act I aria.

Act IV. In the underworld, Orfeo passes through limbo and is greeted by the Furies, who suffer from 'horrible, desperate howls' that torment the soul, in a chorus distinguished by the trombones that Haydn uses here for the first time.

When Orfeo arrives at the gates of the King of the Underworld he begs him to feel pity. Pluto is impressed by Orfeo's devotion and allows him to pass.

Orfeo is delighted with the Elysian Fields. A chorus of the blessed explain that Orfeo can have Euridice back, as long as he does not look at her when he leads her to the world of the living. Euridice approaches, limping from the wound to her foot, but Orfeo cannot help himself: he looks at her and she dies. Orfeo's grief is expressed in his aria, 'Mi sento languire', charged with urgency, built on short, impetuous vocal phrases as he repeatedly asks 'Perchè?' (Why?) and rages against fate's cruelty.

The opera's last scene, which may have been its fifth act, is set on the seashore, where Orfeo weeps. A group of Bacchantes try to seduce him into joining their life of pleasure. Their chorus, with overlapping entries, moves to an unemphatic, lilting dance rhythm. He refuses but they force him to drink something they call the 'nectar of love', which is a lethal poison. Once again the orchestra describes its course through his body. Orfeo accepts that his suffering will end with his death.

The Bacchantes feel a strange fury possess them. The music suggests this is less a Bacchic frenzy, more a stimulating itch. They aim for the 'island of pleasure', but before they can take refuge, they feel 'a hundred furies' in their hearts, a violent storm arises and destroys them.

Haydn was aware of previous operas on the Orpheus myth. Marc Viglan has suggested that the overture's graceful *presto* refers in the oboe's theme to the aria 'Ho perduto il caro bene' from Gluck's *Orfeo ed Euridice* of 1762, which Haydn had conducted at Eszterháza. Haydn avoided dramatising the central scene of Orpheus pacifying the Furies, perhaps because he wished to avoid competing on Gluck's territory, and surprises us by placing his demonstration of music's power to soothe savage hearts in the opera's very first scene. The ending is a remarkable, if temptingly loose treatment of another aspect of the Orpheus myth, his involvement in the Dionysiac cult and his death at the hands of the maenads.   P.

PETER HEISE

(born 11 February 1830, died 12 September 1879)

DROT OG MARSK

King and Marshal

Opera in four acts, text by Christian Richardt. Première, Copenhagen, 25 September 1878. A recording was made in 1981, with Inga Nielsen.

King Erik Glipping ....Tenor

Marshal Stig Andersen................................Baritone

Ingeborg, *his wife*..Soprano

Rane Johnsen, *a courtier*...................................Tenor

Count Jakob af Halland.....................................Bass

Archdeacon Jens Gand ....Bass

Arved Bengtsen, *a conspirator*...........................Tenor

Aase, *a charcoal-burner's daughter*.................Soprano

A Herald...Bass

Knights, Ladies, Courtiers, Servants, Soldiers

Place: Jutland
Time: 1286
Running Time: 3 hours 5 minutes

Heise, one of the most successful and prolific of Denmark's song-writers, though he had written incidental music for stage and ballet, was not experienced as a writer of music drama when, at the age of forty-five, he began work on his only opera, although nearly twenty years earlier he had composed an overture on the same subject. *Drot og Marsk* is something of a landmark in nineteenth-century Danish musical history and has been fairly often revived.

The characters are historical and the story has been the subject of literary treatment in Denmark, but historians are divided as to whether Marshal Stig Andersen was in fact guilty of the King's murder.

The King in the opera is represented as a compulsive womaniser and we meet him first chasing Rane away from Aase, whom he loses no time in seducing; then, after a moment of dalliance with Aase at court, he is all too plainly captivated by the charms of Ingeborg, the Marshal's wife, whose virtue he has just promised her husband to protect while he is away at war. Rane cynically watches as he prepares to break his promise. On his return, the Marshal discovers his wife has been seduced, and she demands revenge. At the People's Council at Viborg, the Marshal denounces the King, and it is apparent churchmen as well as senior courtiers have been waiting for a chance to rebel against him.

Rane has his own grievances and agrees to betray his master; other conspirators join Marshal Stig and Ingeborg in swearing revenge. Preparing to go hunting, the King has a crisis of conscience as he remembers his wanton burning of the heath long ago and equates its current desolation with the destruction of his own soul, but he leaves with a cry of defiance. In the hut where he takes refuge, he finds Aase. She rejects him, but her instinct to save him is to no purpose when Rane betrays him to the conspirators. The Marshal stabs him to death but recognises that he will be looked on as an outcast, and the people end the opera with a cry of 'Now the land is plunged in sorrow'.

Heise studied in Germany in the 1850s but *Drot og Marsk* suggests no evidence of exposure to Wagner's operas. Nonetheless, right from the purposeful-sounding overture, the music is well contrasted, with charm in the opening scene in Aase's hut, and animation in the dance rhythms of the court. There is grandeur in the Council scene and an atmosphere of menace and gloom surrounds the conspirators as they plot, led by the implacable Ingeborg. Aase is in many ways the opera's most attractive figure, and her folk-like song in the first scene contrasts well with the large-scale lyrical utterance in the last act which ends with a prayer.   H.

HANS WERNER HENZE

(born 1 July 1926)

Henze was the first to come to international attention of the musicians associated with Darmstadt, where after 1945 a centre grew up for German composers whose interests lay in the currents of contemporary music banned as decadent by the Nazi regime. He was a pupil of Wolfgang Fortner and rapidly became the leading composer of his generation and rose 'to be inspiration, and interpreter and prophet for those whose musical understanding was formed after the war. Then, Schoenberg and Stravinsky were the old gods, still speaking; but Henze speaks for, and with, us.'[1]

Henze has contributed to the continuing vitality of the operatic form as much perhaps as anyone of his generation, and his versatility comes partly from the wealth of practical experience he gained as a conductor for ballet and opera in provincial theatres. The long list of his compositions comprises a number of symphonies and other music with orchestra, chamber music on a considerable scale, a full-length ballet for Covent Garden (*Ondine*) as well as, by 1990, no fewer than nine full-length operas, all richly and variously wrought. All the more disconcerting was it to read in the summer of 1970 an interview with the composer which suggested he was disposed to reject the medium altogether. He was quoted (accurately, I am quite sure) as saying: 'My crisis was not so much about opera as about music, music-making and people, and in this context I could see that I would contribute no more new operas, masquerades, charades ... I feel opera is finished. Of course, the basic idea of putting drama to music is not finished.' He went on to give a more or less Marxist explanation of his current position, but believers in the cause of opera took comfort from the reference to 'putting drama to music', which had an encouraging ring to it. And indeed, 'drama through music' has continued to flow from his pen.   H.

BOULEVARD SOLITUDE

Opera in seven scenes, text by Grete Weil, after the play by Walter Jockisch, in its turn a modern version of *Manon Lescaut*. Première, Hanover, 17 February 1952, with Sigrid Klaus, Walter Buckow, conductor Johannes Schüler. First produced Düsseldorf, 1953, with Anna Tassopoulos; San Carlo, Naples, 1954, with Lydia Styx, conductor Jonel Perlea; Rome, 1954, with Magda László, conductor Nino Sanzogno; London, at Sadler's Wells by New Opera Company, 1962, with April Cantelo, John Carolan, Peter Glossop.

Manon Lescaut ....High Soprano
Armand des Grieux, *a student*...................Lyric Tenor
Lescaut, *Manon's brother* ....Baritone
Francis, *Armand's friend* ....Baritone
Lilaque *père, a rich old gentleman*......High Tenor Buffo
Lilaque *fils* ....Baritone
A Prostitute ....Dancer
Servant to Lilaque *fils*...Mime
Two Drug Addicts ....Dancers
A Cigarette Boy ....Dancer

Newspaper-Sellers, Beggars, Whores, Police, Students, Travellers

Place: Paris
Time: After the End of the 1939–45 War
Running Time: 1 hour 15 minutes

Henze's first opera (1950–51) is a modern version of the Manon story and with it he secured an immediate success with the critics and before long with the public as well. Henze's style is eclectic, and this thoroughly attractive little work – small in pretensions and length, considerably greater in achievement – invokes some jazz and popular elements as well as Stravinsky and Berg.

Scene i. The crowded waiting room of a large French railway station; the music at first entirely timpani and percussion. When a train is announced, Francis claps his friend Armand on the shoulder and leaves. Manon comes in with her brother who steers her in the direction of Armand's table. Manon takes out a cigarette which Armand lights, asking her if

---

[1] Andrew Porter writing in 1962.

she too is going to Paris. No, says Manon, to a finishing school in Lausanne. Armand launches into a sad account of the loneliness of student life in Paris. Manon joins in and the two get up and leave together; the pick-up is complete.

Scene ii. A small attic room in Paris. Armand and Manon lie in bed in the morning and sing a wistful song. Manon announces her intention of buying a hat which has caught her fancy. No, protests Armand; his father has cut off his allowance and they have no money. He goes off in search of his friend Francis. Lescaut comes in. What does he need – more money? No, says Lescaut coarsely, just her two ravishing breasts. He has found her a new admirer, old and fat and rich. Armand comes back and Manon embraces him tenderly. Lescaut in a wild song sardonically compliments his sister on her cruelty to Armand – the more brutally she treats her lovers, the higher will she rise – then gives her five minutes to make up her mind. Manon reproaches the absent Armand for leaving her a prey to the old temptations; but as she sings, she is preparing to leave him.

Scene iii. An elegant boudoir in the house of Lilaque père. Manon sings an aria as she writes to Armand, reassuring him that she is treated with every consideration by the generous Monsieur Lilaque. The only flaw in her existence is that Armand cannot visit her, and that could easily be remedied as every day at five in her own little carriage she drives in the Bois de Boulogne. Lescaut is furious that she prefers to write to her lover instead of looking after Lilaque and tears the letter up. When Manon protests, he retorts that she is his source of income and he needs more money at once. He notices a strongbox, forces it and in spite of Manon's protests steals from it. Lilaque enters, greets Manon tenderly and Lescaut with courtesy, at once offering to leave brother and sister alone. However, as he is about to leave the room he notices the broken safe and his good humour turns to rage as he throws the two out. The grotesque (but not by any means despicable) figure of Lilaque is characterised by very high tenor writing notably in the lyrical trio which constitutes the musical form of the scene.

Scene iv. A university library. Armand and Francis, with other students (who provide a choral background), are studying Catullus. Francis is enthralled, but Armand can think only of Manon, and when Francis tells him that she and Lescaut have been

chucked out of Lilaque's house, Armand protests that he would believe anything of Lescaut but that Manon could commit no crime. Francis goes off in a huff as Manon enters and sits by Armand. They join in reading a love poem which gradually becomes an impassioned love duet. The parallel with Massenet's St Sulpice scene is apt and only the protests of des Grieux are absent.

Scene v. A dive. The reconciliation has not lasted long, Armand has taken to drugs, and while he sings of the forgetfulness he buys, everyone else dances to music that recalls *Wozzeck* with overtones of Gershwin. Lescaut comes in with Lilaque's son – Manon's latest 'suitor' – and they sit at the bar. Lescaut asks Armand where Manon is, but Armand's only interest is in more cocaine, which he gets from Lescaut.

Manon enters and joins her brother and Lilaque *fils*. Stimulated by the drug, Armand starts to rave and tries to stop Lilaque touching Manon. Lescaut orders him off but Lilaque finally loses patience and goes off with Manon and her brother. A beautiful girl comes in and gives Armand a letter. As he reads it, Manon's voice is heard telling him to come and see her the following night as Lilaque will be away; as consolation she sends him one of the prettiest girls in Paris. But Armand is too far gone to notice her and the girl shrugs apathetically and leaves him asleep.

Scene vi. After a striking interlude, we find ourselves in a room in the apartment of Lilaque *fils*. Manon and Armand are together. Manon gaily remarks on the change in her fortunes but Armand reminds her that once they were alone together, a point of view Manon cannot understand. Lescaut, who has been keeping watch, hurries in and tells Armand he must be off. As he is about to take Armand out, he notices an abstract painting on the wall. Is it a Picasso? No, but all the same beautiful, says Armand. Manon and Lescaut ridicule the picture, but Lescaut, with an eye to the main chance, rips it from its frame and hides it under his coat. They hear the voice of Lilaque père who has been called by a suspicious servant and Manon quickly hides the two men behind a curtain. The old man protests that his delight at seeing her quite erases his memories of her past misdeeds, but to her horror he insists they return to the room she has just left, especially because it contains a modern painting which, although he personally finds it incomprehensible, is said by psychiatrists to be most beneficial to the subconscious. All Manon's efforts are in vain and he steers her back the way she has come. The moment he sees the picture has gone he starts to raise the roof with his accusations. Lilaque shouts to the servant to call the police and himself bars the door. Lescaut draws a revolver and shoots him dead, pressing the gun into Manon's hand as he escapes. Lilaque *fils* enters and sees Manon and Armand standing over his father's body.

Scene vii. An intermezzo introduces the last scene, outside a prison on a grey winter's day. Armand waits to catch a last glimpse of Manon as she is taken off to prison and sings an aria of hopelessness. The police herd Manon and other prisoners away before she and Armand can exchange a word and from this point the action becomes a symbolical pantomime, involving people from the railway station, police, singing children, Lilaque *fils* following the corpse of his father, even (in the London production) Lescaut and a bikini-ed girlfriend holidaying by the sea on the proceeds of what we have been watching. 'Et c'est là l'histoire de Manon, de Manon Lescaut.'   H.

KÖNIG HIRSCH

Il Re Cervo/King Stag

Opera in three acts, text by Heinz von Cramer after the story by Carlo Gozzi. Première (as *König Hirsch*), Berlin, Städtische Oper, 23 September 1956, with Helga Pilarczyk, Nora Jungwirth, Sandor Konya, Martin Vantin, Helmut Krebs, Tomislav Neralic, conductor Hermann Scherchen. First performed Darmstadt, 1959. Revised (as *Il Re Cervo*) 1962, Cassel, conductor Henze; Munich, 1964, with Felicia Weathers, Claude Heater, Hans-Günter Nöcker, conductor Christoph von Dohnanyi; Santa Fe, 1965; Helsinki, 1971; B.B.C., 1973 (in English), with Philip Langridge; Stuttgart, 1985, with cuts restored and Toni Krämer as the King, conductor Dennis Russell Davies.

Leandro, *the King*	Tenor
Costanza, *his beloved*	Soprano
Tartaglia, *the Chancellor*	Bass-Baritone
Scollatella I	Coloratura Soprano
Scollatella II	Soubrette
Scollatella III	Mezzo-Soprano
Scollatella IV	Alto
Checco, *a melancholy musician*	Tenor Buffo
Coltellino, *an unsuccessful murderer*	Tenor Buffo
Six Alchemists	Silent
Two Statues	Contraltos
Cigolotti, *a magician*	Speaking Role
The Stag	Speaking Role

Voices of the Wood, Voices of the People, Voices of the Wind, Courtiers, Pages, Wild Animals, People from the City, Soldiers, Huntsmen

Place: Near Venice, between Sea and Forest
Time: Antiquity
Running Time: 4 hours 20 minutes

Henze's second opera, *Il Re Cervo*, is an adaptation of one of the fables of Carlo Gozzi, the Venetian contemporary and rival of Goldoni and source of such twentieth-century operas as Busoni's and Puccini's *Turandot*, Casella's *La Donna Serpente* and Prokofiev's *The Love for Three Oranges*. Much of it was written on the island of Ischia, where Henze went to live in 1953, so that the music is perhaps the most influenced by the composer's chosen Italian environment of any opera he has yet written. The first version of the opera was heavily cut for the Berlin première in 1956, according to those who already knew it, to its considerable detriment. By 1962, the composer had decided on a revised version, about half as long. The full-length version was restored in Stuttgart in 1985.

King Leandro (Deramo in Gozzi's play) has grown up in the forest among animals. He succeeds to the throne, returns as an innocent to the complicated world of men, is crowned, chooses a bride, only to abdicate when his Chancellor, Tartaglia, has her arrested. Through a magic spell the King takes possession of the body of a dead stag, with the result that the Chancellor is able to use the same spell to assume the lifeless form of the King and take control. He reduces the country to ruins until the Stag King reappears to the joy of the populace. The false king is killed and the true one re-enters his body to general acclamation.

Act I. The King's castle, where preparations are in hand for his coronation. A fearful storm rages (depicted in the *Vivace* orchestral opening) and an early candidate for the role of Queen – Scollatella – emerges to complain of the appalling effect the weather has had on her clothes. She feels she will win the King's hand, but is frightened at being alone while the thunder rages; she looks into a mirror and summons up a double. Scollatella II comes out of the mirror, and it is not long before Scollatella III and IV are also involved in thinking up schemes to win the

King's favour. Scollatella I insists that, if their plans go right, she alone will be called Queen.

The coronation procession. Scollatella I hides as Tartaglia, the King's Chancellor, comes in and, obviously up to no good, conceals himself, storming about the futility of it all – a boy King being led like a lamb to the slaughter, fawning courtiers all over the place, while he is not accorded his just deserts. From the attitudes he strikes Scollatella thinks Tartaglia must be King and makes herself known before disappearing into the background.

At this point, Costanza is brought in by two guards. Tartaglia questions her and assures her that the King is a monster. He gives her a dagger with which he instructs her to murder him.

The animals, who have been the King's friends in the forest, form a semi-circle round him as in movingly direct vocal terms he bids them goodbye. Two statues warn him of the dangers he faces among men. Their music goes some way towards evoking the purity of the world of the boys in *The Magic Flute*, and they assure the King that they will help him by laughing the moment anyone tells him an untruth.

Tartaglia makes his entrance and announces that the moment to choose the royal bride is at hand. To more fanfares, Scollatella I comes in and makes her obeisance, followed by II, III and IV. They compete for the King's interest, and he asks which of them, if married to him, would be saddest if he died; the answer eludes them. The King assures Scollatella I that no one has given him more pleasure than she. The statues laugh and the King knows that none so far is worthy to be his bride.

Tartaglia introduces Costanza. She admits she is no longer afraid of the King and he is reassured by the silence of the statues. They sing together in an *adagio* section, the first love duet in the opera, and at its end, Leandro, unable to bear the idea that he may lose Costanza, attacks the statues and breaks them. Immediately Tartaglia shows the King Costanza's concealed weapon. She is arrested and when the King says he will exercise clemency, Tartaglia insists on death for a potential regicide. The King decides he will abdicate and Cigolotti (disguised as a parrot) leads him away.

The stage is Tartaglia's; he rejoices that he has set his net and the fishing has been good. Spirits of the Wind dash across the stage, and Coltellino, Tartaglia's hired assassin, and Checco, a musician who follows Cigolotti and carries a guitar on his back, enter after them. Coltellino, who has lost his pistol and dagger to the Spirits of the Wind, hastens to Tartaglia's summons. Doesn't he want to be an honest murderer like his father? Let him then follow the King and murder him! Even the loss of dagger and pistol is not accepted as excuse, and Tartaglia hands Coltellino replacements. The act ends with a curious postscript as alchemists come in announcing that they have come to give a party for King Leandro. They are too late, says Tartaglia.

Act II takes place in the wood – a great breathing organism – and we hear the forest sounds. There is a stranger present, a voice announces, and soon others proclaim that the wood is full of men. Leandro appears and it is not long before Scollatella's voice joins with his. Scollatella is obsessed with the idea that she is in reality a Queen, and Leandro turns from her. Animals flee from humans; the alchemists reappear disguised as animals and are themselves terrified of the huntsmen, who will try to kill them, and of the other animals, who may find them even easier prey. Tartaglia attempts to murder Leandro, and both Checco and Coltellino complicate the action with their fears and failures.

Cigolotti plans that Checco alone shall know the secret of the transformation spell, which he shall give only to the King and thus save the King's life. Checco has a beautiful, enigmatic song, nearer perhaps to Britten or Tippett than to most other Italian or German music, and lightly accompanied on guitar. A stag appears and Tartaglia wounds it so that it escapes. Tartaglia's designs are murderous. He tries to get news of the King's whereabouts from Checco. By magical means, they see the stag die and Tartaglia hears the transformation spell from Checco, who intends only to give it to the King. Leandro by its aid changes into the stag and goes off, but Tartaglia in his own turn repeats the spell and assumes the King's body. Tartaglia's *credo* follows: he will impose his will on the country, stamp on it if he choose. Meanwhile, he sets in motion a stag hunt which will eliminate Leandro for ever.

Act III plays in the deserted city, where Tartaglia has been exercising absolute rule. The people are oppressed and their only hope comes from the legend that when a stag appears in the streets, the rule of peace will return. This is in effect what happens. Quite quietly, Leandro as the Stag King walks through the streets, finding that no one answers his calls, although Coltellino melodiously laments his lack of prowess as a murderer.

Even the alchemists are persecuted under Tartaglia's rule, but gradually news of the King's return reaches the city, and Costanza comes to look for the man she was allowed to love for so short a time. The Stag King approaches her, and their second duet confirms their mutual love until her touch makes the stag flee the scene, just in time too, as Tartaglia appears, in the guise of the King and armed to the teeth. He greets Costanza as if he were the King she loves, but she detects the fraud and disappears.

People start to become conscious of the presence in their midst of the stag, against whom Tartaglia continues to rail, demanding that it be shot. Finally, Coltellino, taking straight aim with the assistance of Cigolotti but mistakenly thinking the King he sees is the King whom Tartaglia has retained him to murder, shoots his target – but it is of course Tartaglia who falls dead just as he is about to kill the stag.

Leandro works the transformation spell and the opera ends with choral rejoicing, enclosing a short, simple duet for Leandro and Costanza, in which he claims her as his bride.

The plot is said to have been one which Brahms contemplated for an opera and it has obvious affinities with Bartók's *Cantata Profana*. For Henze at the age of twenty-nine it was a fairy story with overtones of the Nazi Germany of his boyhood, and the opera has excited ardent admiration so that William Mann in *The Times*, at the time of the B.B.C.'s English performance in 1973, was able to write: 'in 1955 ... Henze's head was full of marvellous vocal and orchestral music, longing to be released'.   H.

DER PRINZ VON HOMBURG
The Prince of Homburg

Opera in three acts, text by Ingeborg Bachmann after the drama by Heinrich von Kleist. Première, Hamburg State Opera, 22 May 1960, with Liselotte Fölser, Mimi Aarden, Helmut Melchert, Vladimir Ruzdak, Toni Blankenheim, Herbert Fliether, conductor Leopold Ludwig. First performed London, Sadler's Wells Theatre, 1962, by Hamburg Company; Paris, Frankfurt Opera, 1962; Düsseldorf, 1964, with the title role rewritten for tenor and sung by Andor Kaposy; English National Opera, 1996, with Peter Coleman-Wright (in the baritone version).

Friedrich Wilhelm, *Elector of
    Brandenburg* ....Dramatic Tenor
The Electress, *his wife*....................................Contralto
Princess Natalie von Oranien, *her niece,
    Colonel-in-Chief of a Dragoon Regiment* ....Soprano
Field Marshal Dörfling....................................Baritone
Prince Friedrich Artur von Homburg,
    General of Cavalry ....High Baritone
Colonel Kottwitz, *of the Princess's Regiment* ....Bass
Count Hohenzollern, *attached to the
    Elector* ....Lyric Tenor
Three Officers...........................Tenor, Baritone, Bass
Three Ladies of the Court
    ....Soprano, Mezzo-Soprano, Contralto
Sergeant ....Baritone
First and Second Orderly ....Tenor, Baritone
Other Officers...............................Tenors and Basses

People of the Court (Pages, Servants, etc.), Military
    Personnel (Guards, Cadets, Soldiers)

Place: Fehrbellin, Germany
Time: 1675
Running Time: 2 hours 10 minutes

The libretto by Ingeborg Bachmann, a regular collaborator of Henze's, is based on Kleist's last play, *Prinz Friedrich von Homburg* (1811). The background is the successful world of Prussian militarism in the seventeenth century, and the hero of the play is a poet and dreamer who nonetheless accepts the values of his environment. It was at a performance by Jean Vilar's Théâtre National Populaire, with Gérard Philippe as the hero, that Ingeborg Bachmann discovered, far from Prussia and outside Germany, that she loved the play. To some degree, composer and librettist have consciously de-Germanised what Kleist wrote, and Kleist's lines for the Elector, 'He will teach you, be assured, what military discipline and obedience are', have been changed in the libretto to ' ... what freedom and honour are'.

Act I, scene i. Garden of a castle in Fehrbellin. The Prince of Homburg is sitting as if in a trance, twining a wreath in his hand. The remainder of the Elector's entourage is killing time before the battle, and they have noticed that their General of Cavalry is missing. They find him alone and some wonder whether he is ill. The Elector takes the wreath from his hand, places a silver chain round his neck and gives him the hand of Princess Natalie. They depart and the Prince is left stroking the glove of the Princess. Count Hohenzollern wakes his friend from his dream ... but the glove remains for him as an unexplained link between dream and reality, with fantasy still to him, in his state of half-trance, the more believable condition.

The whole scene has the softness of a dream but the interlude takes us to a different world, a military conference in a hall in the castle. Field Marshal Dörfling dictates the plan of battle, instructing the Prince to hold the attack with his cavalry force until he receives specific orders. The Prince listens dreamily, has to be continually reminded where he is, and is obsessed with the idea that Princess Natalie is looking for the glove she has lost.

Scene iii. The battlefield of Fehrbellin. Officers wait for the battle to begin and Homburg tries to check with his friend Hohenzollern as to the orders he received yesterday. He is dreaming of Natalie when the first cannon shot is heard. Officers watch its progress, the Swedes are seen to be giving way and suddenly Prince Friedrich, without waiting for his orders, orders a fanfare to be sounded, and rushes into battle.

During the interlude with its plaintive saxophone solo, it becomes dark and then gradually lightens to show the scene the following morning. Dead and wounded are being carried away and rumour has it that the Elector has been killed. The Electress and Princess Natalie are overcome with grief and the Prince of Homburg joins them in their mourning. Friedrich and Natalie avow their love for one another. But rumour was false, and the Elector stands before them safe and sound. The Elector declares that victory was endangered because the cavalry attack was started too early and that he will have whoever was responsible court-martialled and condemned to death. When the Prince comes to bring him trophies of victory, he orders his sword taken from him and the act ends, after an ensemble, with the Prince escorted towards Fehrbellin and prison.

Act II, scene iv. Prison. Prince Friedrich has been condemned to death, and he realises the gravity of the situation when he hears that the Elector has sent for the death warrant in order to sign it.

Scene v. On his way to appeal, he sees with horror the grave which has been dug for him in the courtyard of the castle.

Scene vi. The Electress's room. Homburg begs the Electress to intervene on his behalf but she feels, however great her love for him, that she is powerless in the present situation. Natalie tells him she loves him and will make an attempt to persuade the Elector to change his mind.

Scene vii. The Elector's room. Natalie begs her uncle to pardon Homburg; he is taken aback to find that the young man has so far forgotten his training as to think exclusively of his freedom. Finally, the Elector gives Natalie a letter in which he offers to let Homburg go free if he can find it in his heart and mind to consider the judgement made against him unjust.

Scene viii. Prison. Natalie brings the Prince the Elector's letter and tells him that he will immediately be free. But Friedrich hesitates, then decides the judgement was just and that he cannot write the Elector the letter which would set him free. Natalie kisses him and says that if he feels it right to follow the dictates of his own heart, she will follow hers – she decides to order her Regiment of Dragoons to free the Prince by force.

Act III, scene ix. The Elector's room. The Field Marshal brings the news that Princess von Oranien's Regiment is in the town intending to free the Prince of Homburg from prison. At the same time, the Elector receives a letter conveying the Prince's decision. Officers come to the Elector to request that the Prince be pardoned and the Elector decides to bring him from prison, saying that he will teach them what freedom and what honour are. The Prince comes in, but will not change his decision. The Elector is overjoyed, believes Friedrich has re-established his honour and gives orders that he be conducted back to prison. As he prepares to go, he makes it plain that he will not change his mind. But the Elector believes he has established a crucial point of principle and can now tear up the death warrant.

Scene x. To the sound of a funeral march, Prince Friedrich is brought blindfold by Count Hohenzollern into the garden. The Prince, who believes he is about to be executed, feels himself already withdrawn from life. Suddenly, the Elector leads in his court, the Prince's blindfold is removed as he stands before the Elector, just as in his dream before the battle. What had been a dream of victory wreath, princely chain and bride becomes reality. H.

ELEGY FOR YOUNG LOVERS

Opera in five acts, libretto by W.H. Auden and Chester Kallman. Première (in German), 20 May 1961, at Schwetzingen Festival (Munich Opera), with Dietrich Fischer-Dieskau, producer Henze, conductor Heinrich Bender. First performed in England, Glyndebourne, 1963 (in English), with Dorow, Söderström, Kerstin Meyer, Turp, Carlos Alexander, Hemsley, conductor John Pritchard; Zürich, 1961, by Munich Opera; Berlin, 1962, with Catherine Gayer, Martha Mödl, Fischer-Dieskau.

Gregor Mittenhofer, *a poet* .... Baritone

Dr Wilhelm Reischmann, *a physician* .... Bass

Toni Reischmann, *his son* .... Lyric Tenor

Elisabeth Zimmer .... Soprano

Carolina, *Gräfin von Kirchstetten* .... Contralto

Frau Hilda Mack, *a widow* .... High Soprano

Josef Mauer, *an alpine guide* .... Speaker

Servants at the 'Black Eagle' .... Silent

Place: Austrian Alps
Time: 1910
Running Time: 2 hours 35 minutes

*E*legy for Young Lovers, like *The Bassarids*, was first performed in German translation. The librettists have told us that Henze asked them late in autumn of 1958 for a libretto with 'a subject and situation which would call for tender, beautiful noises' and the composer planned a 'small, subtle orchestra' as the basis for his chamber opera, in which certain instruments could be associated with various leading characters, a flute for instance with Hilda Mack, the brass with Mittenhofer, violin and viola with the young lovers, cor anglais with Carolina, bassoon or saxophone with Dr Reischmann.

The story is packed with incident, psychological nuance and wit. It is concerned basically with (wrote the composer in 1970) 'the Birth of a Poem that is in process throughout the three acts, from the moment of the first idea to the final public reading. What happens around this process of birth, the hilarious, the wicked, the vulgar, the banal, the murderous, serves mainly to put into question the figure of the *Artist as Hero* as the nineteenth century created it, as the twentieth century has not yet completely liquidated it.'

'The artist as hero' is the great poet Gregor Mittenhofer, who goes every year to a mountain inn, the Schwarze Adler, in the Austrian Alps. This particular spring he arrives with Carolina von Kirchstetten, his patroness and unpaid secretary, Elisabeth Zimmer,

his young mistress, Dr Reischmann, his doctor. He hopes that as in former years he will get inspiration from the crazy 'visions' of the widow Mack, who has lived at the inn for the past forty years, ever since her bridegroom was killed climbing the Hammerhorn on the first day of their honeymoon. Not all the poet's hopes are realised. The body of the long dead Herr Mack is found preserved in a glacier and the widow's lunacy is replaced by pungent insight into the motives of her neighbours. Elisabeth falls in love with Toni, Dr Reischmann's son; and Mittenhofer, deprived of one of his sources of inspiration, finds another in the predicament of the two young lovers who have, with his knowledge, ventured up the mountainside, a fact he neglects to mention to a guide who could save them. The opera ends as he reads his new *Elegy for Young Lovers* to a fashionable audience.

Act I: *The Emergence of the Bridegroom* (each act and each scene have been given a title by the librettists).

I. *Forty years past.* Hilda Mack, still dressed and made up in the style of a young woman of the 1870s, sings in eloquent music of wide range (well over two octaves) of the day her husband went to climb the Hammerhorn.

II. *The order of the day.* The inside of the inn shows Carolina at her desk. Dr Reischmann watches her sort press cuttings. Each is summoned in turn, the one to take the Master his second egg, the other to give him his morning injection, and the doctor feels Carolina's pulse to diagnose a bout of flu. That Carolina must finance the poet by hiding coins where he may expect to find them, elicits from Dr Reischmann a 'What would poets do without their nannies?'

III. *A scheduled arrival.* The doctor is waiting for the arrival of his son Toni, who is going through a 'phase' and seems likely to prove poor company.

IV. *Appearances and visions.* Carolina entices Frau Mack inside just as Mittenhofer, his arm round Elisabeth Zimmer, makes his entrance. 'His high forehead and Beethoven-like mane of snow-white hair are impressive, and he is apt to accentuate both by shaking his head back.' Frau Mack starts on one of her coloratura visions, to the intense satisfaction of the poet, who begins to take notes. It is a big-scale aria in typically wide-ranging style that Frau Mack sings, and in it she seems to foretell what hindsight tells us is the death of the two young lovers.

V. *Worldly business.* Mittenhofer is delighted at what he has got, then starts to read yesterday's typing, interrupting it to yell at Carolina about a mistake she has made until she falls in a faint.

VI. *Help.* Mittenhofer disappears to his study, but reappears a moment later to search the room for his money, like a child looking for sweets.

VII. *Unworldly weakness.* Poor Carolina is in a state – 'death in fact looks dazzlingly attractive' is her comment.

VIII. *Beauty in death.* Josef Mauer, an Alpine guide, comes in to tell them that a body has been found on the Hammerhorn – fresh and young-looking, his skull cracked at the back. It must be Frau Mack's husband!

IX. *Who is to tell her?* Carolina says she is feeling too ill; it must be Elisabeth.

X. *Today's weather.* Gently and kindly, Elisabeth breaks the news to Frau Mack, who is full of foreboding for Elisabeth's own future. In the end she succeeds (in a beautiful canonic duet) in telling her the news, which Frau Mack appears to understand. Toni watches the end of the scene.

XI. *A visionary interlude.* Toni sings a song in tender remembrance of his mother.

XII. *Tomorrow: two follies cross.* Hilda, who has remained still throughout Toni's song, suddenly rises in a state bordering on ecstasy. To end the act, she joins in climactic duet with Toni, she because 'the crystal is broken', he because he realises he is falling in love with Elisabeth.

Act II: *The Emergence of the Bride.*

I. *A passion.* Elisabeth and Toni are now plainly in love, and Toni urges her to break with Mittenhofer. Carolina catches them in each other's arms and calls for the doctor to help her settle what she thinks of as nonsense.

II. *Sensible talk.* Dr Reischmann tries to reason with Toni inside, Carolina with Elisabeth outside.

III. *Each in his place.* In a duet which is composed of two separate monologues, the two young people express their outrage.

IV. *The Master's time.* Elisabeth in one room asks Toni to take her away, Mittenhofer in another is told by Carolina that there is a situation between Elisabeth and Toni, and asks Carolina to have Elisabeth join him at tea.

V. *Personal questions.* Mittenhofer's tack is to criti-

cise himself and play on Elisabeth's guilt feelings. The gist of the scene is an *apologia pro vita sua*. Elisabeth leaves, without having told him anything.

VI. *The troubles of others.* Elisabeth (and later the orchestra) is sad.

VII. *What must be told.* Elisabeth admits to Toni that she has said nothing, partly because they know nothing about each other, partly because she did not dare. Toni says he will do the job.

VIII. *The wrong time.* As Toni goes towards Mittenhofer's door, the poet himself emerges, to listen to Toni's protestations of love for Elisabeth. An ensemble of considerable dimensions builds up, involving Mittenhofer, Elisabeth (Carolina taking her place at its end), Toni, the doctor.

IX. *The bride.* Elisabeth bursts into tears, and Frau Mack comes into sight, singing tipsily (and higher than ever) and rejoicing in the new situation, which she relishes to the full. Top Cs abound, Frau Mack demands ten per cent of Mittenhofer's future royalties, and after a ringing top E natural, turns to Elisabeth and starts to comfort her. Mittenhofer resolves the situation by asking Dr Reischmann to bless the lovers.

X. *The young lovers.* In a grandiose ensemble, Mittenhofer explains his new poem, 'The Young Lovers'. The characters seem to breathe life from his words, which perfectly express their different situations for them.

XI. *The flower.* The doctor blesses the match and Mittenhofer, taking advantage of the moment and the fact that in a day or two's time he will be sixty, begs the young couple to pick him on the slopes of the Hammerhorn an Edelweiss, which he needs to finish his poem. They agree; Frau Mack plans her departure.

XII. *The vision of tomorrow.* The young lovers will stay, Mittenhofer refuses his tonic – to watch young love is enough – and, after a moment of six voices together, the rest leave and Mauer comes in to tell Mittenhofer that tomorrow will be warm and the weather on the slopes of the Hammerhorn propitious enough for them to find the Edelweiss he craves.

XIII. *The end of the day.* The atmosphere changes from one of acquiescence to another of unbridled fury. Mittenhofer inveighs against all around him, from Frau Mack to the doctor, from Carolina to Elisabeth. 'Why don't they die?' He is about to hurl an inkwell across the room when Frau Mack comes back to confront him, so that he departs with a bellow of rage leaving her in peals of uncontrollable laughter.

Act III: *Man and Wife.*

I. *Echoes.* Hilda is ready to travel; Toni and Elisabeth ascend the mountain. An ensemble mounts, during whose course Mittenhofer can be heard trying out rhymes and prepositions.

II. *Farewells.* It remains for Frau Mack to bow tenderly out of the opera, giving Carolina the colossal scarf she has been knitting for the past forty years. Mittenhofer comes out to persuade Carolina to laugh, and Frau Mack has a good word even for him.

III. *Scheduled departures.* 'The young in pairs, the old in two proceed'; the music is a quartet.

IV. *Two to go.* Carolina makes some attempt to damp down the fires which still burn within Mittenhofer, but to little avail. Mauer hurries in to say that a threatening blizzard is blowing up. Is anyone still up there? Mittenhofer, without looking at Carolina, denies knowledge of anyone, and Mauer hurries off to ask the question elsewhere.

V. *Mad happenings.* As the sky darkens, Mittenhofer and Carolina confront each other and the Master slyly suggests that she go away 'for a change of scene'. If she was ever quite sane, she is no longer.

VI. *A change of scene.* For the first time we are outside the inn, and the Hammerhorn is visible, in a blizzard. An extended orchestral interlude leads us to Toni and Elisabeth in the last stages of exhaustion on the mountain.

VII. *Man and wife.* Their duet takes the form of reminiscences of a long-married husband and wife.

VIII. *Toni and Elisabeth.* They have discovered something beyond love: Truth. This will help them to die.

IX. *Elegy for young lovers.* Mittenhofer is tying his white tie before going on stage to read poetry in Vienna. He goes through a cheer sequence – 'One. Two. Three. Four. Whom do we adore?' – then dedicates the poem he is about to read to 'the memory of a brave and beautiful young couple, Toni Reischmann and Elisabeth Zimmer'. He mouths beneath an invisible ensemble of Hilda Mack, Elisabeth, Carolina, Toni and the doctor; the poem is, with the help of others, finished, and the opera therefore at an end.   H.

DER JUNGE LORD
The Young Lord

Comic opera in two acts, libretto by Ingeborg Bachmann, after a fable from *Der Scheik von Alexandria und seine Sklaven* by Wilhelm Hauff. Première, Deutsche Oper, Berlin, 7 April 1965, with Edith Mathis, Patricia Johnson, Loren Driscoll, Donald Grobe, Barry McDaniel, conductor Christoph von Dohnanyi. First performed Stuttgart, 1965; Rome, 1965, with Maria Chiara, Fedora Barbieri, Giuseppe Campora, Aldo Bottion, conductor Henze; London, 1969 (by Cologne company), with Wendy Fine, Cvetka Ahlin, Hubert Mohler, James Harper, Claudio Nicolai, conductor Marek Janowski.

Sir Edgar	Silent
His Secretary	Baritone
Lord Barrat, *Sir Edgar's nephew*	Tenor
Begonia, *his Jamaican cook*	Mezzo-Soprano
The Mayor	Bass-Baritone
Councillor Hasentreffer	Baritone
Councillor Scharf	Baritone
Professor von Mucker	Buffo Tenor
Baroness Grünwiesel	Mezzo-Soprano
Frau von Hufnagel	Mezzo-Soprano
Frau Hasentreffer	Soprano
Luise, *the Baroness's ward*	Soprano
Ida, *her friend*	Soprano
A Maid	Soprano
Wilhelm, *a student*	Tenor
Amintore La Rocca, *a circus director*	Dramatic Tenor
A Lamplighter	Baritone
Monsieur La Truiare, *dancing master*	Silent
Meadows, *the butler*	Silent
Jeremy, *a Moor*	Silent

Circus Performers, a Teacher, a Military Band, a Dance Band, Ladies and Gentlemen of Society, Men and Women of the People, Children

Place: Hülsdorf-Gotha, Germany
Time: 1830
Running Time: 2 hours 30 minutes

Henze's fifth opera written for the stage (as opposed to radio) is a black comedy, based on Wilhelm Hauff's parable *Der Affe als Mensch*, written after he had been living for some time in Italy and drawing on his enthusiasm for early nineteenth-century opera composers – Rossini and Bellini for instance. There is lyrical writing in plenty – *Der junge Lord* is a thoroughly 'vocal' opera – but the main expression is through the ensemble as developed by Rossini and the Verdi of *Falstaff*. It all bustles along at a capital pace, easy to listen to, witty, but in no sense a classical comedy with a happy ending. The monkey screams because he is learning the hard way, the rose he gives to Luise has a sharp enough thorn to draw blood.

Act I. The small but pretty square of the town. It is autumn and the leaves are turning yellow. Rumour has it that a rich Englishman – a man of learning – is about to arrive in the town, where he has rented a house and where he proposes to spend some time (and doubtless money too). The senior citizens speculate on the possibilities and rehearse their speeches of greeting. Luise, the most eligible girl in the town, is obviously attracted to Wilhelm, a student, and they sing lyrically standing a few yards apart. Schoolchildren are rehearsed in a cantata of greeting for the visitor, when the arrival of the first carriage is signalled. The Mayor and the other worthies form up as a welcome committee and watch, with some stupefaction, as emerge one after another, not the grandee they had expected, but his retinue, starting with a collection of animals, continuing with a black page and some other servants, and finishing with Begonia, his black cook from Jamaica, who succeeds in dominating the scene. She takes a swig of rum, lapses occasionally into English, and then joins with the others in expectation of a third, even more splendidly decorated carriage.

From it with much ceremony (including a snatch of Turkish music from *Die Entführung*) emerges Sir Edgar,[1] a little tired from his journey but prepared through his secretary to make a relatively gracious answer to the blandishments of the reception committee. Nonetheless he refuses all invitations; he only wants to put the town to no inconvenience whatsoever. The skies grow dark, Begonia puts up her umbrella, and embarrassment if anything increases at the way the weather has added to the general farce and confusion. Only Luise and Wilhelm welcome the distraction.

Scene ii. Baroness Grünwiesel's salon. Even though Sir Edgar has so far turned down all invitations, Baroness Grünwiesel, as Hülsdorf-Gotha's leader of society, has gathered together its ladies to meet him,

hoping that an appropriate exception will be made in her case. Her plans for him and Luise are all too obvious, but everything changes when a message is brought by Jeremy, the black page, to the effect that Sir Edgar cannot accept her invitation. Such an insult is not to be borne and nothing will calm the Baroness's mounting fury. From now on she has only one aim, to make life in the town impossible for their odious visitor! Will she prove a worthy successor to Rossini's Don Basilio? The interlude suggests she may.

Scene iii. The town square. An unpretentious country circus has established itself and its performance is coming to an end. Its Neapolitan director, Amintore La Rocca, thanks the public just as Sir Edgar emerges to watch the circus. The only gesture of recognition he makes towards the townspeople is at their children, and comments – for instance that he goes to the circus but not to church – are fairly free. The town council attempts to flatter Sir Edgar, his secretary tries to put them off, Wilhelm and Luise indulge in the mildest of flirtations, La Rocca continues to salute the public, until a crisis develops when the councillors decide to deny the circus a licence to perform. Sir Edgar offers to pay their dues and ends by inviting director, dancing girl, fire-eater and 'human monkey' into his house, leaving the citizens outside, the humblest admiring his generosity, the more puffed up complaining at the slight he seems to offer them. Two men creep in to percussive accompaniment and write the word SHAME on the front of Sir Edgar's house.

Act II, scene iv. The front of Sir Edgar's house with snow on the ground. The sympathy of the townspeople has turned against the Englishman, and children pelt the unfortunate Jeremy with snowballs as he returns from a shopping expedition. A lamplighter is making his rounds and hears from the house bloodcurdling cries and shrieks suggestive of something appalling going on inside. He rushes off, and the scene is clear for Luise and Wilhelm to confess their love to each other in a lyrical duet.

Their idyll is interrupted by more shrieks from the house and then by the arrival of the Mayor and town council, led by the lamplighter to the scene of the supposed crime. The Mayor demands to be admitted to investigate. Sir Edgar's secretary tells them that

---

[1] An operatic curiosity was the appearance of Sir Rudolf Bing, long-time General Manager of New York's Metropolitan Opera, in this silent role at New York's City Opera in 1973. Bing, who had retired from the Metropolitan in 1972, had always maintained a lofty hostility towards rival companies, particularly those close to home.

the door is open and indeed Sir Edgar appears at it, but leaves the secretary to explain that what they have heard are the sighs and complaints of Sir Edgar's nephew, recently arrived from London and now hard at work learning German, a process he finds thoroughly disagreeable and against which they have heard his protests. As soon as he is proficient, they will all be invited to meet him! They depart in a much better mood.

Scene v. A reception in the library of Sir Edgar's house. Final preparations for a party are in hand, and Begonia waltzes across the stage with a vast dish of goodies in either hand. She is on top of the world and breaks into English to inform us (as so often before) of Napoleon's attitude towards these edibles, in this case favourable. All is ready for the entrance of the guests, headed by the Baroness herself, with Luise and Ida and the other worthies of the town, not forgetting Wilhelm. The secretary greets them, tea or punch or champagne is served and there are expressions of general gratification.

The secretary says that Sir Edgar still has reservations about his nephew's ability to speak German, but everyone makes light of the problem and in a moment Sir Edgar becomes visible on a staircase, with the young Lord. Sir Edgar kisses the Baroness's hand, and so after a moment's hesitation does Lord Barrat. He is wearing gloves and spectacles and is very smartly dressed. His conversation is a bit limited but everyone is impressed, not least Luise, whose handbag he seizes, and, after a quick look round, chucks behind him. The Baroness appears by no means nonplussed and tells Luise to offer him a cup of tea. After a moment's hesitation and conversation with Ida, she brings him the cup, which he takes in both hands, empties and then throws behind him. When he starts to kiss in rapid succession the hands of the Baroness and Luise, everyone, after a moment's stupefaction, breathes again.

Nothing goes absolutely right, in spite of the Mayor's interest in Begonia, and when Lord Barrat puts first one leg and then the other on the table, there is nothing to do for the ladies but comment on the elegance with which he pursues his eccentricities, a point of view with which Wilhelm is not in accord. The Mayor continues to pay court to Begonia, and the ladies cluster round Lord Barrat. This worthy distinguishes himself by pulling a ribbon off Luise's dress and then starts to dance. He plays with Luise's shawl,

and Begonia comments 'Jamaica girls call this *hanky-panky*. Napoleon hated it.' Wilhelm can stand it no longer and faces up to Lord Barrat, to whom Sir Edgar and the Secretary make signs to depart. Luise faints, and Wilhelm feels everyone against him.

Scene vi. The great ballroom in the Casino. Luise leaves the scene of activity and comes in by one of the doors to sing of her happiness in an aria. Her love for Lord Barrat has transformed her from the naïve girl who fell for Wilhelm to somebody much more knowing. Lord Barrat comes in giving her a rose so that the thorn scratches her hand until the blood flows. Barrat and Luise sing together and after a moment Wilhelm comes in. Soon everyone is a party to the secret of the betrothal.

The room fills up and all start to dance (Débutantes' waltz), Lord Barrat in so exaggerated a manner as to cause everybody else to try at first to copy him (as they have earlier his clothes and manners) until, after a bit, he takes Luise alone on to the floor and the others draw back. Watched all the time by Sir Edgar's secretary, he seizes an instrument from one of the band and blows it savagely to the mild astonishment of the councillors, who continue to contrive some form of admiration. When he starts to swing from the chandeliers, astonishment gives way to alarm, and even the appearance of Sir Edgar, who greets Wilhelm, does not prevent an element of panic creeping in. Lord Barrat dances Luise into exhaustion, then proceeds to tear his gloves, tie and clothes off, throwing them in every direction. Before long the monkey is revealed and led from the room at a sign from Sir Edgar. Luise and Wilhelm clutch one another, but the comedy comes to an end in general consternation.   H.

THE BASSARIDS

Opera seria with intermezzo (cut in 1992 revision of the score) in one act, libretto, based on *The Bacchae* of Euripides, by W.H. Auden and Chester Kallman. Première, Salzburg, 6 August 1966, with Ingeborg Hallstein, Kerstin Meyer, Vera Little, Loren Driscoll, Helmut Melchert, Kostas Paskalis, conductor Christoph von Dohnanyi. First produced Deutsche Oper, Berlin, 1966, with the same cast and conductor; la Scala, Milan, 1967, in Italian, conductor Sanzogno; Santa Fe, 1967, in English, with Regina Safarty, Driscoll, John Reardon, conductor Henze; English National Opera, 1974, with Barstow, Katherine Pring, Dempsey, Woollam, Welsby, producer and conductor Henze.

Dionysus (also Voice and Stranger) ....Tenor

Pentheus, *King of Thebes*................................Baritone

Cadmus, *his grandfather, founder of Thebes*............Bass

Tiresias, *an old blind prophet*..............................Tenor

Captain of the Royal Guard.........................Baritone

Agave, *Cadmus' daughter and mother
   of Pentheus*......................................Mezzo-Soprano

Autonoe, *her sister*...Soprano

Beroe, *an old slave, once nurse to Semele and later to
   Pentheus*...Mezzo-Soprano

Young Woman, *slave in Agave's household*..........Mute

Child, *her daughter* ....Mute

Bassarids (Maenads and Bacchants), Citizens of
   Thebes, Guards, Servants

Place: The Royal Palace, Thebes, and Mount
   Cythaeron
Time: Antiquity
Running Time: 2 hours 40 minutes

*T*he Bassarids,[1] Henze's second collaboration with
W.H. Auden and Chester Kallman, is a free adaptation of *The Bacchae* of Euripides. The composer asked his librettists to mould the opera in the form of a symphony, and the result is a continuous work, about as long as *Das Rheingold*, cast in four movements – composer and librettists use this title to designate the changes of mood. It was freely said at the time of the opera's première that the writers agreed to provide the tragic libretto of *The Bassarids* provided Henze 'made his peace with Wagner'. Peter Heyworth[2] suggested that this stipulation was very much in the composer's interests. 'In a period when the orchestra has evolved into such a uniquely supple and expressive instrument and the springs of melody have run so low ... there has seemed something almost perverse in Henze's devotion to the closed and essentially melodic forms of the old Italian opera ... in his manner of manipulating material, Henze is deeply indebted to the Schoenbergian dodecaphonic technique, and the most natural means of applying this to opera lies in the quasi-symphonic Wagnerian music drama, if only because both are rooted in the art of variation.'

The story symbolises 'the terrible revenge taken by the sensual Dionysian side of human nature if its existence is denied and its demands repressed',[3] and the achievement of the librettists is to have not only reflected the brutality of the century in which they write (and during which we watch and listen) but also to have filled the book with a web of psychological motivation. In the process, they have inspired the composer to one of his most important operatic scores.

Thebes was founded by Cadmus, son of Agenor, King of Tyre, and brother of Europa, who had been loved by Zeus in the guise of a bull. Five warriors, known as the Sown Men because they sprang from the dragon's teeth Cadmus sowed, helped him to build the citadel of Thebes and themselves founded the city's noble families, one of their number Echion marrying Cadmus' youngest daughter Agave. Another of Cadmus' daughters was Semele, whom Zeus courted as a mortal. Zeus' wife, Hera, disguised herself as Semele's servant, Beroe, and persuaded her to demand that Zeus should reveal himself in all his divine splendour, a piece of mortal folly whose gratification reduced her to ashes.[4] Zeus, legend goes, succeeded in rescuing her unborn child, Dionysus, and sewing him into his thigh from which eventually the boy was born.

Before the opera starts, Semele's tomb is already a shrine of pilgrimage for devotees of the cult of Dionysus, but some people, including Semele's own sisters, believe that Semele's lover was a mortal and not Zeus at all and consequently view the cult with contempt. Cadmus has abdicated in favour of his grandson Pentheus, who now reigns as King of Thebes. On his shoulders rather than on those of his grandfather lies the momentous responsibility of deciding whether to risk offending the other gods by recognising Dionysus' divinity, or run the consequences of Dionysus' wrath by opting for the theory that Semele's lover was mortal. Pentheus' invidious position is complicated by his absolute belief in reason and conviction that the source of all human blindness and wrongdoing lies in the passions of the flesh.

First movement. The courtyard of the royal palace in Thebes, with the palace on one side and the tomb of Semele on the other; in front of the tomb is an altar on which a flame burns. The citizens of Thebes are gathered in tribute to their new King. Their theme is the founding of Thebes and its present – they hope auspicious – rule by a Sown Man's son, Pentheus.

---

[1] The title *Bassarids* is an alternative name for *Bacchae*, or worshippers of Dionysus.

[2] Writing in *The Observer* after the Salzburg première.

[3] *The Times* after the première in Salzburg.

[4] See pp. 327–29.

Suddenly a voice is heard from a distance: 'Ayayalya! the God Dionysus has entered Bœotia!' The musical atmosphere dramatically changes from the matter-of-fact to one of mystery, and the reaction of the people is instantaneous: they take up the chant and go off in the direction from which the singing seems to have come – the populace has turned in the course of a few bars of music into Bassarids.

When Cadmus, Beroe, Agave and Tiresias make their entry, it is to find the space in front of the palace empty. Tiresias, the old blind prophet whose weakness is that he cannot bear to be excluded from the latest movement, longs to join the worshippers of Dionysus and go to Mount Cythaeron. Cadmus urges caution, on the grounds that no one yet knows for sure that Dionysus is a god, and moreover the mere mention of his name seems to infuriate Pentheus the King. When Agave asks Beroe if Semele was loved by Zeus, she can elicit from her no more than 'I know nothing', which only increases her contempt for Tiresias' enthusiasm.

During the following scene, the Bassarids' hymn continues as background. Cadmus is concerned with the crucial matter of whether Dionysus is divine or not, but Agave's attention is quickly diverted by the sight of the Captain of the Guard, a handsome man no longer in his first youth but sufficiently attractive to appeal to her deprived, widow's eyes. Autonoe comes in behind Agave, and it is plain that she too is attracted by the Captain of the Guard. Beroe tells them that the King wants his most prominent relations to hear the first proclamation of his reign, which the Captain of the Guard now reads; the royal message denounces the idea that Semele was the object of the affections of one of the immortals and therefore that her offspring could himself be a god, and forbids Thebans to subscribe to any such belief.

Before his grandfather, mother, aunt and nurse have had time to do more than begin their comment on his proclamation, Pentheus himself appears. He is a young man, spare, athletic, even ascetic in appearance, and immediately starts to dilate on the ignorance which has permitted women to light a flame on Semele's tomb. After a moment's hesitation, he flings his cloak over the flame on the altar and extinguishes it. Only then does the King notice that the people, who had been summoned to listen to his proclamation, are not in the square and, when Agave reveals to him that they danced off to Cythaeron, he departs in a fury, leaving his relations to comment on the course of events. Suddenly the off-stage voice of Dionysus is heard singing mysteriously and beautifully the praises of Cythaeron (usually referred to as his Serenade). Agave and Autonoe are hypnotised by what they hear and dance away so that they are out of sight by the time Pentheus reappears.

Second movement. Cadmus in his despair reasserts his authority – Pentheus after all rules by his consent. But Pentheus refuses to listen to him, proclaims that in future Thebes will know a harder rule, and, to Cadmus' evident dismay, orders the guards out, instructing them to proceed to Cythaeron and return with what prisoners they can take. The sound of the Bassarids' chant is heard again, and during Pentheus' aria (its burden: Thebes must once again know Truth and spurn what is false) his old nurse Beroe mutters a prayer to herself. When he has finished, Pentheus turns to Beroe, and swears in her presence to 'abstain from wine, from meats, and from woman's bed, live sober and chaste till the day I die'.

The guards return with their prisoners, among them Agave, Autonoe, Tiresias, a youthful stranger who is in fact Dionysus, a few male Bacchants, and a young woman with her child. All are in a state of trance and the Bassarids' chant continues as Pentheus, unable to get any sensible answer from his prisoners, orders the Captain to take them away and question them with torture, leaving behind only Tiresias, the unknown young man, and his own relations to be examined by the King himself.

Agave is the first to be questioned and in an aria she attempts to describe what she saw on Mount Cythaeron – 'a kind of Wordsworthian mystical vision of nature', the librettists have called it. Beroe tries to warn Pentheus, but the scene is soon out of his control as each one present pursues his or her own line of thinking. To the King's fury, not only can he himself get nothing out of the prisoners, but the Captain tells him that even under torture the others seemed to feel no pain and gave no information. The King orders Agave and Autonoe to their palace, bids the Captain of the Guard demolish Tiresias' house, and himself starts to question the stranger (whom he imagines a priest of Dionysus), at first casually, but gradually, as he reacts to the answers he gets, with barely suppressed fury. In the course of an aria, the stranger tells him of the curious adventure which befell him in the Aegean, when he hired a ship and crew to take him to the island of Naxos. The sailors turned out to be pirates and altered course, meaning to sell him as a slave. But Dionysus caused a vine to grow from the deck and wild animals to appear on board, so that the seamen leapt overboard in terror and were turned into dolphins.

Third movement. The Bassarids continue to sing, the Captain returns and waits for orders, and Pentheus' calm finally breaks with the result that he orders the Captain to take the stranger away and 'break that smiling mouth of its lie. Lay whips to his pampered flesh ... '.

Influences beyond Pentheus' control take over. There is the sound of an earthquake, Pentheus' cloak is plucked from Semele's tomb so that the flame shoots up again, and the prisoners can be heard shouting as they escape towards Cythaeron. The King orders the Captain to take the guard on to the hill and wipe out all the worshippers of Dionysus he can find, but the stranger urges a more cautious course, his words having a curious effect on Pentheus, who seems to agree with the advice he is being given and who welcomes, repelled and fascinated at the same time, the offer which is made to him, that he may by magic see the rites in which his mother and his aunt are engaged. The audible laughter of the Bassarids serves as a link as the scenery disappears to be replaced by what is described in the score as 'a realistically painted representation of a Boucher-like garden, with statues of mythological groups'.

Intermezzo.[1] In a period, up-dated setting – 'Marie Antoinette' is the style – Agave and Autonoe are breathless with laughter in their reaction to the behaviour of Pentheus. With the Captain of the Guard, whom each thinks of as a kind of sexual plaything, they enact the story of the Judgement of Calliope – as will be seen at the end, in reality Pentheus' repressed fantasies, where sex is far from the robust thing known to Thebes but, in a decadent world, the subject of giggles.

Cinryas, King of Cyprus, has boasted that his daughter Smyrna is more beautiful than the goddess Aphrodite. In revenge, Aphrodite has had Smyrna fall in love with her own father by whom, while he is drunk, she becomes pregnant. When Cinryas discov-

ers what has happened, sword in hand he chases his daughter, whom Aphrodite turns into a myrrh tree at the moment Cinryas' sword splits her in two. Out falls the infant Adonis. With an eye to the future, Aphrodite hides him in a chest and entrusts it to Persephone, Queen of the Dead, who herself falls a prey to feminine curiosity and opens the chest, immediately to fall in love with Adonis, whom she takes off to her own palace. Aphrodite appeals to Zeus and he appoints the Muse Calliope to make judgement. The verdict of Calliope is that each of the goddesses has rendered Adonis signal service and therefore has an equal claim on him; his year should therefore be divided into three parts, one for Aphrodite, one for Persephone and one to be spent as he himself chooses. Aphrodite cheats and by her magic contrives that Adonis spends all the year with her, with the result that Persephone, with more than a little justification, goes to Ares (Mars) and tells him that Aphrodite has a mortal lover whom she prefers to him. The god in his jealous rage disguises himself as a boar and gores Adonis to death on Mount Lebanon.[1] As part of the up-dating process (for the modern audience in the theatre rather than the voyeur king) the names of the characters in the story are changed from their Greek versions to Mars, Pluto, Jove, Venus, Proserpine.

The story is worked out in semi-formal musical terms and played as a charade by Agave, Autonoe and the Captain, while Tiresias enters dressed as a kind of Bacchant to act as Calliope. A pair of mandolins and a guitar on the stage give the accompaniment an element of period flavour, and recitatives, arias (usually with a specified *cabaletta*), duets, a round for four voices, a formal trio and a final quartet follow each other in sequence, to music which owes something to the Stravinsky of the 1920s, until all four dissolve in laughter and the Captain starts to make good his escape, averring 'my prospects here are gross and grim: those two will have me limb from limb'. The laughter of the Bassarids ends the Intermezzo as it had begun it.

A courtyard of the palace once again. Pentheus is beside himself with righteous horror and indignation and determines to go off to Mount Cythaeron to learn the worst. The stranger seems to warn him of the

---

[1] In 1992 the composer revised the score to exclude the Intermezzo, which was henceforth to be known as 'Das Urteil der Kalliope' and to be available to be performed separately.

[1] See page 355 for Henze's later approach to this legend.

perils he will run but insists that he must dress as a woman if he is to have any chance of escaping detection. Beroe begs the stranger to spare him, addressing him as Dionysus. He refuses, and Pentheus emerges tricked out incongruously in one of Agave's dresses. The voices of Dionysus and Pentheus join and by the end of their scene together sound – literally, as they sing together – as one. Dionysus takes Pentheus by the hand and leads him towards Cythaeron. Beroe is left alone lamenting the loss of the King and Cadmus adds his own lament, this time for the prospective fall of Thebes.

With the sound of the Bassarids becoming insidiously audible again, the scene changes, a procession of torches can be seen, the world of the senses has again taken over and through the foliage Pentheus can be observed crouching on a branch of a tree. The Bacchic orgy proceeds, Pentheus temporarily disappears and the voice of Dionysus himself is heard greeting the Maenads and inviting them to hunt down a trespasser who must, he says, be in their midst. The movements of the Bassarids have started as ritual but, as the music mounts in tension, they acquire purpose and the manhunt is on. Suddenly, a shaft of light falls on Pentheus and he is seen to be surrounded. In a moving final statement, half dignified, half imploring, he begs his mother to recognise him, but in vain, and as the lights go out, nothing but his scream is left of what had once been King of Thebes.

Fourth movement. The Maenads are heard in a chorus of triumph, and, back in the courtyard of the palace, Cadmus and Beroe are still keeping watch. When they appear, Agave is seen to be carrying the head of Pentheus torn from his body, and, shuddering, Cadmus attempts to introduce an element of the rational into a situation which, he sees clearly, poses the end of the Thebes he himself had created. When Agave demands to see the King, he starts slowly to question her, as to what she can see, what she can remember and finally, what she can recognise in the gory object she carries. She tries to maintain her belief that it is the head of a young lion, but in the end – agonisingly – recognises her own son. As the Captain and the guards carry in the mangled corpse of King Pentheus on a litter, Autonoe and the Chorus

disclaim all part in the murder, but Agave understands and asks her father to take Pentheus' sword and slay her with it. An ensemble of lamentation covers the efforts of Agave to move from a state of shock to one where the deepest grief is possible, and she mourns the death of her son in a slow aria.

Suddenly, Dionysus is on the scene, proclaiming, with so little preamble that the effect is one of insensitivity, his godly condition, and banishing Cadmus, Autonoe and Agave from Thebes, ordering the Captain to set fire to the palace. In a sudden burst of defiance, Agave turns to Dionysus and tells him to remember the fate of Uranus and Chronos.[1] Tartarus waits for them all in the end.

As the stage is bathed in flame, Dionysus sings of his purpose in coming to Thebes – vengeance for what the city and its inhabitants have done to his mother; it only remains now for him to restore Semele to the position from which her enemies tried to remove her. As the opera ends in a soft chorus of the Bassarids, two statues are seen standing on Semele's tomb, representing Dionysus and Thyone (the new name of the translated Semele) and appearing to the eyes of the twentieth-century audience as 'two enormous primitive fertility idols of an African or South Seas type'.   H.

THE ENGLISH CAT

Opera in two acts, libretto by Edward Bond (from a short story by Honoré de Balzac). Première Schwetzingen, 2 June 1983, by Württemberg State Theatre, Stuttgart. First performed Edinburgh Festival, 1987.

Lord Puff, *a cat, President of the Royal*
    Society for Protection of Rats ....Tenor

Arnold, *his nephew* ....Bass

Jones, *a cat, money-lender,*
    member of R.S.P.R. ....Baritone

Judge, *a dog*..Baritone

Tom, *a cat* ....Baritone

Peter, *Tom's friend, a cat* ....Tenor

Mr Keen, *member of R.S.P.R.* ....Tenor

Defence, *a dog* ....Tenor

---

[1] Uranus in Greek mythology was the personification of Heaven. He hated his children, the Titans, and confined them in Tartarus. But they broke out and his son Chronos dethroned him, only later in his turn to be dethroned by his own son Zeus.

Parson, *a sheep*...Tenor
Lucian, *a fox* ....Tenor
Minette, *a cat* ....Soprano
Babette, *Minette's sister* ....Mezzo-Soprano
Louise, *a mouse* ....Soprano
Miss Crisp, *a cat, member of R.S.P.R.* ....Soprano
Miss Gomfit, *a cat, member of R.S.P.R.* ....Soprano
Lady Toodle, *a cat* ....Mezzo-Soprano
Mr Plunkett, *a cat, member of R.S.P.R.* ..Bass-Baritone
Prosecutor, *a dog*..................................Bass-Baritone

Ensemble of Moon and Stars

Place: London
Time: 1900
Running Time: 2 hours 40 minutes

Written between 1978 and 1982, *The English Cat* is a satirical black comedy, in form a sophisticated ballad opera with separate songs, in the manner as it were of John Gay or Brecht. It is Henze's fourth opera written to an original English text, his second with Edward Bond. It is scored for big chamber orchestra, with a large percussion section. Different instrumental colours are associated with the leading characters, Lord Puff with chamber organ, Minette with zither, Arnold with heckelphone.

Act I. Mrs Halifax's drawing room. Lord Puff announces his plan to marry; his impecunious, prospectively bankrupt nephew Arnold schemes to frustrate the match. Enter Babette, Minette's sister, to spy out the land. Minette follows and is plainly unused to city ways (cavatina). Enter Louise, a mouse, collecting for the R.S.P.R. (*Ländler*). Arnold contends that Minette, from a rough, unsophisticated country background, is an unfit mate for his uncle; Lord Puff demurs (ensemble).

The roof of Mrs Halifax's house. Lovers are heard mellifluously serenading, and Minette warns Tom and Peter they are trespassing. She sings wistfully (aria) until Tom returns and almost immediately tells her he is in love with her (cavatina). Minette wants him to join the R.S.P.R. – to please her husband! Moon and Stars provide the scene's extended nocturnal finale.

The instrumental interlude is labelled 'Collages'. Mrs Halifax's chapel. Arnold's money-lender, Jones, pretends to be a doctor and on medical grounds warns Lord Puff against his marriage. Lord Puff's friends frustrate an attempt to poison him, but, when Minette comes in dressed as a bride (waltz), Arnold demands

she publicly declare what she and Tom were doing on the roof the previous night. Lord Puff still wants to go through with the marriage, on which depends his forthcoming election as President of the R.S.P.R., and as it is celebrated the act ends with an ensemble.

Act II. Mrs Halifax's drawing room. Babette and Minette bemoan the former's country poverty (duet). Tom appears outside the window, and Minette lets him in (tango). He is a deserter from the army but throws himself at her feet and is caught in this compromising position by Lord Puff and his friends (waltz). Minette explains she and Tom plan to marry when Lord Puff dies and devote themselves to serving the R.S.P.R. Lord Puff would forgive (trio) but his friends urge divorce. Minette thinks of Tom and ends the scene with a lament.

Divorce Court. The Judge and Jury are assembled and Arnold gives his evidence. Tom, pretending to act for the defence, cross-examines Lord Puff and when the court is empty seems about to throw himself at Minette's feet until she remembers the disastrous effect the last time he did it and tries to stop him. Nonetheless he completes the manoeuvre and is again caught in the act. Defence counsel has been discovered bound and gagged and now reveals that Tom is far from being counsel but is himself the co-respondent in the case. Minette is found guilty and heavily fined; Tom is made ready for prison (canzonetta), until suddenly the prosecutor recognises him as the heir of Lord Fairport who has just died. He is now the possessor of a large fortune. The Judge recognises him too.

Mrs Halifax's drawing room. Babette discovers Minette bundled up in a sack and ready on Mrs Halifax's orders to be thrown from London Bridge. Tom would gladly die with her if that would help but since it won't, he plans to console Babette, and at the same time himself (terzetto). Tom again throws himself at Minette's feet, just in time to reject Lord Puff's request that he hand over his new fortune to the R.S.P.R. (moresco). He leaves, Lord Puff and the others rack their brains for a way to get hold of the money, and the odd-job man carries the sack out and dumps it in the river (arietta and rondo).

Lincoln's Inn Fields: Lawyer's chambers. Tom is stabbed to death by Lucian, a lawyer's clerk. As he died intestate, his money passes, as Lord Puff and friends had hoped, to the R.S.P.R. Tom and Minette sing a duet of death, and it remains for Louise, the mouse, to steal a coin from her collecting box, put it in Tom's pocket and sing a requiem which celebrates her return to a life of thieving and frightening ladies into standing on chairs (villanella). H.

DAS VERRATENE MEER
The Betrayed Sea

Musikdrama in two acts, libretto by Hans-Ulrich Treichel, after Yukio Mishima's *Gogo no eiko* (1963). First performed Berlin by Deutsche Oper, 5 May 1990, conducted by Markus Stenz, with Beverly Morgan singing, Stephanie Sundine miming Fusako, Clemens Bieber as Noboru, Andreas Schmidt as Ryuji. Revived Wiesbaden, 1990, conducted by Ulf Schirmer. Italian première, Teatro Lirico, Milan, 1991, with Morgan, Sacca and Lenus Carlson, conductor Stenz; first U.S. performance, San Francisco, 1991, with Ashley Putnam, Craig Estep and Tom Fox.

Fusako Kuroda,
    a thirty-three-year-old widow.............High Soprano

Noboru, *her thirteen-year-old son,*
    known as No. Three ....Tenor

Ryuji Tsukazaki, *a merchant navy officer*........Baritone

The Gang, friends of Noboru
    No. One, *the leader*....................................Baritone
    No. Two ....Tenor
    No. Four...Baritone
    No. Five ....Bass-Baritone

Ship's Mate ....Bass-Baritone

Ship's Officer, Sailors, Harbour Master, Boutique
    Manager, Three Shop Assistants

Place: Yokohama
Time: 1950s
Running Time: 1 hour 55 minutes

Henze's *Das verratene Meer* surprised a lot of people: why would a left-wing European composer want to adapt a story by the right-wing Japanese author Yukio Mishima? The story has been read as an allegory on Japan's willing surrender to Western, industrial culture. Fusako runs a boutique selling Western clothes, called 'Rex', while the gang occupy an ex-U.S. army installation. To some extent, Henze colours the conflict with his instrumentation: saxophone on one side; exotic percussion instruments (Chinese gongs, *o-daiko* and *guiro*) on the other. He certainly does not present the conflict as between sickness and health, however: divided violas and cellos invite our sympathy with the love affair between Fusako and Ryuji, whereas the gangleader's psychopathic ravings sound

particularly lurid because they mostly lack string support and are backed by lower woodwind. Yet Henze refuses to conclude: the opera ends not with the murder and the chord marked quadruple forte, but in the silence before it.

Part I: Summer. Scene i. Fusako Kuroda puts her son Noboru to bed, promising that they will visit the ship tomorrow. She locks him into his bedroom, to prevent him meeting his gang of friends during the night. She goes into her room and undresses. Noboru gets up and looks through a hole in the wall between their rooms. In the moonlight she rubs oil into her skin, looks at a photo of her dead husband and compares herself to a garden buried under snow. Noboru gazes in rapture, his thoughts ranging from his gang of friends ('When they call I must follow; they order I obey') to his longing to have 'no heart' and, instead, the pounding engine of a ship. The interlude evokes 'Noboru's dream'.

Scene ii. In Yokohama harbour, Fusako and Noboru are welcomed on board the freight-ship *Rakuyo-Maru* by the Second Officer, Ryuji Tsukazaki. Fusako and Ryuji are drawn together as Noboru investigates the machinery. Fusako invites the officer to dinner in a French restaurant. Ryuji's dream emerges as 'perhaps a kind of bourrée'.

Scene iii. Two days later, in a park near Fusako's house, Ryuji tells Fusako about his life at sea: at first he dreamed of travelling further than his eyes could see. But now, all ports seem the same. They kiss.

Scene iv. An hour later, in Fusako's bedroom. She is fascinated by Ryuji; he reflects that until now he has always paid for sex. Meanwhile, Noboru watches them through the spyhole. Their feelings are superimposed in a trio. Having looked into the sailor's eyes, Noboru is convinced that 'He belongs to me, the night belongs to me.'

Scene v. Next morning, at the gang's meeting place, Noboru excitedly describes the sailor in idealised terms, as 'an animal from the depths, with iron muscles and shoulders of stone'. But the gangleader ridicules his hero-worship, and suggests that Ryuji is just after Fusako's money.

Scene vi. Later that afternoon in a park high above the sea, Ryuji cools himself off with some water from the fountain and inadvertently soaks himself. He encounters Noboru and the gang, who look critically at his wet shirt.

Scene vii. A few days later, at the port, Ryuji leaves, but promises that he will be back for the new year. The ship's siren drowns out Noboru's farewell cries.

Scene viii. The gangleader has brought a sack to their meeting point and pulls out a kitten. The others are chilled, uneasy. The leader puts on rubber gloves and lays out instruments such as scissors and knives on a work bench. They all hand the kitten around and, on the leader's instructions, Noboru kills it.[1]

Part II: Winter. Scene ix. New Year's Day, before dawn. Fusako and Ryuji look forward to the new day and the new year in a duet inflected by the rhythm of a tango. Ryuji asks Fusako to marry him and offers her all his savings. Fusako cries but reminds him his ship is waiting. Ryuji tells her that it must wait for him, 'perhaps... for ever'.

Scene x. The gang agree all fathers are cowards. They laugh at Noboru's hero Ryuji and are appalled to hear that the sailor now helps Fusako in her boutique. The scene ends as the leader pulls on his leather glove and turns back the cuff to reveal its red lining.

Scene xi. While Fusako lays the table for dinner, Ryuji reads out of a textbook on 'Selling Textile Wares'. Noboru is appalled to hear that his mother plans to marry him. She asks her son to call Ryuji 'Papa'. Noboru retreats to his bedroom and uncovers his spyhole but falls asleep with his light on. In their bedroom Fusako and Ryuji see light coming from the hole in the wall and realise what this implies. Fusako is furious, but Ryuji refuses to beat Noboru; instead, to Noboru's disgust, he forgives him.

Scene xii. In the warehouse where the gang assemble, Noboru summarises Ryuji's 'crimes' while the leader awards him penalty points. Worse than Ryuji's flattery of Noboru, or his exaggerated laughter (glissando on solo soprano saxophone), is the fact that he forgave Noboru (total: 150 penalty points). The leader insists that they cannot do anything more for the sailor and orders Noboru to bring Ryuji to them, using the excuse that they would like to hear about the sea and his adventures. The violent interlude raises the tension further.

Scene xiii. Fusako prepares to leave the shop. In a rhapsodic, melismatic arioso she looks forward to Noboru's further education and assumes he will learn to love Ryuji. Meanwhile the boys are seen climbing up to their 'dry dock', the remains of a U.S. Forces installation.

Scene xiv. A tape of *musique concrète* colours in the frantic industrialisation around Yokohama. Ryuji starts to tell the boys about the reality of life at sea, beginning with seasickness (vividly evoked in a mass outbreak of instrumental trills). Sensing their evident lack of interest, instead, he sings them his favourite song 'Ich setzte grosse Segel auf'. This just makes them snigger. Ryuji explains that he became a sailor not because he loved the sea, but because he hated the land. The leader takes off his leather gloves and puts on long rubber ones, while the other boys assemble their weapons. Ryuji does not notice. He drinks a cup of drugged tea. His voice becomes weaker, almost delirious, as he reminisces about tropical birds, the sun and the longing that gripped his heart in the evening, 'darker than the darkest night'. In the ensemble that ends the opera the boys' reflections all end with the same resonant phrase, 'darker than the darkest night'. The sailor falls asleep and the boys raise their weapons.

Das verratene Meer is a work of astonishingly powerful theatricality, owing more to the tradition of Puccini, say, than Verdi. The score registers every nervous tremor in the relationships between the characters, both their surface reactions (the heat in the ship's engine-room; the chill before dawn on New Year's Day) and their emotional implications. The masterly orchestration is an object lesson in inventiveness – the oboe d'amore used to sound hard and cold, for example. Only close inspection of the score convinced me the seagull cries were indeed taped seagull cries and not some exquisitely witty writing for woodwind.   P.

VENUS UND ADONIS

Opera in one act, text by Hans-Ulrich Treichel. Première, Bavarian State Opera, Munich, 11 January 1997, with Nadine Secunde, Chris Merritt, Ekkehard Wlaschiha, conductor Marcus Stenz.

The Prima Donna ....Soprano

Clemente, *a young opera singer*...........................Tenor

The Leading Actor..Baritone

---

[1] Never has an interval drink seemed more necessary: listening to a tape of B.B.C. Radio 3's broadcast of the première, which I attended, reminded me how shocked the audience was at this point.

Six Madrigalists (Shepherds)
.................Soprano, Mezzo-Soprano, Tenor, Bass

Venus ⎫
Adonis ⎬ ....Dancers
Mars ⎭

Running Time: 1 hour 15 minutes

The action is simple. Preparation is in hand for an opera involving Venus, Adonis and Mars. Love develops between Venus and Adonis, Mars is overcome with jealousy and a wild boar kills Adonis.

Dancers mirror the singers, reflecting the action in between episodes where the solo singers dominate. Additionally, there are six madrigal singers, described as shepherds, but in Munich, in the production super-vised by the composer, remaining hidden throughout the opera in a tree which dominated the set. They comment obliquely on what takes place.

As they rehearse, Clemente is attracted to the prima donna, with whom the leading actor is himself besotted. His jealousy grows as he watches the amorous couple and, when the boar kills Adonis, the actor stabs Clemente. As the opera ends, Adonis flies up to the planet Venus, the singer in Munich finishing the opera symbolically in the Royal Box at the front of the Grand Circle.

Features of the score are the division of the sizeable orchestra into three to accompany the three singers, and the comments on the action in music of ravishing quality by the invisible madrigalists.

PAUL HINDEMITH
(born 16 November 1895, died 28 December 1963)

Hindemith's career in opera follows a sad trajectory. Success came to him at an early age: when he was twenty-six, Fritz Busch conducted the premières of his two one-act operas, *Morder, Hoffnung der Frauen* and *Das Nusch-Nuschi*, in Stuttgart. They demonstrated how at home Hindemith was in radically chic, contemporary culture, where Expressionism and its parody could co-exist happily on the same playbill. He added a third one-act piece in 1922, the scandalous *Sancta Susanna*. His first full-length opera followed in 1926, with a prestigious première at the Staatsoper, Dresden: *Cardillac*, the first of three works in which Hindemith considered the role of the artist in society. They were never conceived as a trilogy (and individual revivals of any of them are rare enough), but they add up to a coherent treatment of the theme. They reveal that the composer thought of himself in progressively grander and more remote terms: as a murderous goldsmith, as the painter Mathias Grünewald, as the astronomer who discovers the 'harmony of the world', Johannes Kepler. The middle opera, *Mathis der Mahler* (1938), has long enjoyed the reputation of Hindemith's greatest work, in terms of sustained musical argument. It is another, comparatively neglected work, however, *Neues vom Tage* (1929), that proves to be his most enjoyable opera. Hindemith had worked with the poet Marcellus Schiffer on the sketch *Hin und zurück* (1927), which featured a married couple quarrelling. *Neues vom Tage* is a *Zeitoper*, part of the wave of operas that surfaced in the late Twenties, concerned to reflect contemporary reality, such as Křenek's *Jonny spielt auf* (1927) and Weill's *Die Burgschaft* (1932). Its theme of the media's corrupting influence on private life has not dated. The musical richness that Hindemith lavishes on Schiffer's spare frame provides repeated delights: bureaucratic ineptitude, stenographical rhapsody, tourism, hot baths, escorts and media intrusions generate wonderful melodies and brilliant comedy. Ironically, the magnum opus with which Hindemith hoped to secure his reputation, *Die Harmonie der Welt* (1957), never lived up to the composer's expectations. He once began a lecture by reflecting on what 'A composition of everlasting value' means.[1] When he eschewed actuality in

---

[1] The Charles Eliot Norton Lectures, 1949–50, reprinted as *A Composer's World, Horizons and Limitations*, 1952.

pursuit of what were meant to be eternal verities, however, Hindemith created a work that died as soon as it was born.   P.

CARDILLAC

Opera in three acts, libretto by Ferdinand Lion, from E.T.A. Hoffmann's story *Das Fräulein von Scuderi*. Première in Dresden, 9 November 1926, with Robert Burg, Claire Born, Grete Merrem, Max Hirzel, Ludwig Eybisch, Adolph Schoepfin, Paul Schöffler, conductor Fritz Busch. First performed in Vienna, 1927, with Jerger, Stünzner, Achsel, Hofer, Maikl, conductor Heger; Prague, 1927; Berlin, 1928, with Krenn, Hüni-Mihacsek, de Strozzi, Fidesser, conductor Klemperer; London, 1936, Broadcasting House (concert in English) with Arthur Fear, Noel Eadie, Miriam Licette, Frank Mullings, John McKenna, conductor Clarence Raybould; Venice, 1948, conductor Sanzogno. New version: Zürich, 1952, with Herbert Brauer, conductor Reinshagen. Revived (in original version), Wuppertal, 1960, producer Reinhardt, conductor Ratjen (and at Holland Festival); Vienna, 1964, with Wiener, Lipp, Seefried, Nocker, Stolze, conductor Ludwig; Munich, 1965, with Fischer-Dieskau; Santa Fe, 1967, with Reardon, conductor Craft (the outdoor opera house was burned out following the first night); London, New Opera Company, 1970.

The Goldsmith Cardillac	Baritone
His Daughter	Soprano
The Lady	Soprano
The Officer	Tenor
The Cavalier	Tenor
The Gold Merchant	Bass
The Officer of Police	High Bass

The King; Knights and Ladies of the Court; the Police; the Crowd

Place: Paris
Time: Seventeenth Century
Running Time: 1 hour 30 minutes

*C*ardillac was Hindemith's fifth opera, his first of full length, and written after the one-acters *Mörder, Hoffnung der Frauen* (to libretto by the painter Kokoschka), *Das Nusch-Nuschi* (in 1921), *Sancta Susanna* (rejected as obscene by Stuttgart but given in Frankfurt in 1922) and the Christmas fairytale, *Tuttifäntchen*. It concerns itself with the relationship between the artist and society, a theme stated here in more extreme form than in the composer's

later operas *Mathis der Maler* and *Die Harmonie der Welt*.

As befits a period of Hindemith's creative life which was combative and progressivist, the original score of *Cardillac*, if cool, is muscular and purposeful, and its energy suits a story which shows the artist insisting on his prerogatives rather than the philosophical Mathis setting the world more patiently to rights. The music is scored for inflated chamber orchestra (eighteen strings are specified) and is in style contrapuntal and linear, in form baroque – Hindemith uses Aria, Duet, Fugato, Passacaglia, etc., and the tension of the opera comes less from the drama and inherent moments of pathos than from the musical impetus of taut, closed forms.

Cardillac expresses a reaction against the German tradition of through-composed dramatic music, as epitomised by Wagner and carried on during Hindemith's youth by Strauss. The more astonishing is it that the composer saw fit in 1952, nearly a generation after the opera's first performance, to revise it extensively.[1] An act is added (consisting musically of Lully's opera *Phaeton*, with the Lady of Act I transformed into a leading singer), a new and milder text by the composer himself is substituted for Ferdinand Lion's original adaptation of E.T.A. Hoffmann, there are some cuts and some new music, but basically the orchestral part is retained with a new vocal line above it setting new words.

Hindemith's revised version of the opera had its première in Zürich and was generally looked upon as watered-down, even sentimentalised, in comparison with the original. The composer's embargo on the 1926 version was not generally lifted until his death in 1963.

Act I. An energy-laden prelude takes us into the first scene, a street in the city on to which lead streets from all sides. The Paris mob is in the grip of panic, as we hear when the curtain goes up. A series of murders has been committed and their mysterious perpetrator cannot be found. The mob is looking for a victim to assuage its fear and seizes on one suspect after another, threatening to come to blows within itself, until interrupted by a posse of the King's Guard. Its officer, in an extended declamatory passage (sung at the first performance by the young

---

[1] One must not forget that Hindemith had already produced, many years apart, two quite different versions of *Das Marienleben*, a song cycle to words by Rainer Maria Rilke.

Paul Schöffler), announces the King's edict: that the murderer shall be slowly burnt alive. The crowd seems satisfied, even appeased at this announcement and starts to disperse, making way with some reverence for a lone figure, who salutes them and leaves the square.

A Lady asks the Cavalier who it is that is treated with such unusual respect. He explains that it is the goldsmith Cardillac, an artist of unsurpassed skill, whose creations moreover are intimately connected with the recent series of murders; each of the victims is known to have bought an example of Cardillac's work shortly before death. As the Cavalier grows more pressing, the Lady has an idea: she will be his that very night if he bring her the finest piece to be found in Cardillac's workshop! She leaves and the Cavalier's ardent reaction finds expression in an aria, contrasting the possibility of a night of love with a night of death, one of which he feels must within hours be his reward.

The curtain falls quickly and we are taken into the second scene by an interlude, during whose course the atmosphere of action is exchanged for the languor of the bedchamber. The mood is sustained as the Lady sings a nocturne of considerable lyrical appeal, surrendering sensuously to sleep at the prospect of the arrival of her lover and the great gift he will bring her. There follows a scene which quickly became notorious, a pantomime to the accompaniment of a duet started by two solo flutes. The Cavalier arrives, bringing with him a golden belt of the greatest splendour. The Lady wakes, seems at first about to express surprise at the intrusion but then succumbs to the beauty of Cardillac's creation and the proximity of her lover. Before they can consummate their desire, at the duet's climax (if the word can be used in connection with so cool a structure) a dark figure appears cloaked and masked in the room. The intruder stabs the Knight to death and disappears, taking the belt with him – the action takes place in a moment of complete silence before the curtain music dashes to a conclusion.

Act II. Cardillac's workshop, with the master in full activity. To the cool, impersonal sound of a tenor saxophone, Cardillac sings an *arioso*, with gold as his subject ('Mag Sonne leuchten!'). A gold merchant, plainly nervous at the prospect of the interview, brings him gold, which he rejects as impure. The gold merchant already suspects that it is more than

coincidence that the murder victims have all been customers of Cardillac's. He believes that the great artist's creations possess a beauty beyond the deserts of men, and must be thought of as causes of the crimes rather than their innocent accompaniment. Cardillac's firm 'Was ich erschuf, ist mein' ('What I created is mine') causes the gold merchant to leave the shop, muttering that he will keep a watch on the goldsmith. Cardillac leaves his daughter in charge and goes off with the merchant.

In an aria, cast in the form of a *concerto grosso* movement with violin, oboe and horn *concertante*, the daughter waits in a mood of some trepidation for her lover. He is a young officer (in Hindemith's 1952 revision, as in Hoffmann's original story, Cardillac's apprentice), and their duet together reveals her as divided between her love for him and their plan to elope, and her duty towards her father.

Cardillac returns, this time with gold that he has passed as unalloyed. His daughter chides him for caressing the metal with an affection he never shows her, then tells him she is in love – but that she will nevertheless not leave him! To the first part of her announcement, Cardillac blandly asserts that he noticed a change in her weeks ago, but to the second he retorts that he is no old man but able to renew his hold on life with each new creation. He will give her to her lover. Their scene ends with a slow *fugato* duet, after which the girl goes inside.

In a curious episode, Cardillac observes the King and his court outside, shows the monarch (who remains silent throughout) his finest works, and ends by contriving to rebuff the King when he wishes to buy, and admitting when he is alone, 'I should have had to murder him! He would have had to die!' The golden belt, which the Cavalier bought, is now restored to its place in the collection, to its creator's unconcealed glee. He notices a spot of blood on the belt and cleans it with loving care.

Into the shop comes the Officer, announcing that he must have the most beautiful of all Cardillac's creations. He asks for his daughter's hand in marriage, much to Cardillac's relief; shows surprise at the ease with which his request is granted; then in Cardillac's rejoinder receives a clue to the latter's obsession: 'Could I ever love what is not entirely mine?' The Officer tries to buy the golden chain, Cardillac attempts to dissuade him, but the purchase is completed. The curtain falls after an aria (saxophone *obbligato* again) in which Cardillac appears at first to be contemplating the replacement of the chain he has just sold, only, by its end, to have donned the black coat and mask in pursuit of his obsession.

Act III. A street in front of a tavern. The gaiety of roisterers at night is expressed in the orchestra (including instruments behind the scenes), and the Officer strolls by, singing an arietta as he goes and wearing the chain round his neck. Observed by the gold merchant, Cardillac is following him. He attacks and slightly wounds the Officer, is recognised and bidden make good his escape, while the gold merchant raises the alarm at the top of his voice. Guards and members of the crowd drag in Cardillac, but the Officer says this was not his assailant and points to the gold merchant as possibly the criminal. All express various shades of amazement in an extended and full-blooded quartet in which the original three voices are joined by that of Cardillac's daughter. There is a duet between the daughter and her lover in which the former calls down damnation on the assailant's head only to be rebuked by the Officer, and the crowd celebrates Cardillac's vindication.

In the last section of the opera (a *Passacaglia*), Cardillac has a final confrontation with the mob and ultimately with his conscience. The gold merchant is at most an accomplice, he asserts; he himself understands the workings of the mind of such a criminal, has even been watching him, but he will never give him away. The crowd turns against Cardillac, threatening to destroy his workshop and all it contains if he will not reveal the murderer's identity. To save his works, he cries out that he himself is the murderer, and the mob beats him to death as the Officer fights his way through to put a stop to the riot. He it was against whom Cardillac raised his dagger that very evening; why does the mob set itself up as Cardillac's judge? He is no murderer but the victim of a sacred madness. As his daughter and her lover raise Cardillac's body, a flicker of life runs through him and, catching sight of the chain – *his* chain – with a last despairing effort he raises his head to kiss it, then falls back dead.

The opera finishes with a beautiful threnody over the dead Cardillac, with the high voices of the daughter and the Officer raised above those of the crowd ('Nacht des Todes ... Ein Held starb': 'Night of death ... a hero died').   H.

NEUES VOM TAGE
News of the Day

Opera in three acts, text by Marcellus Schiffer. Première, Kroll Oper, Berlin, 8 June 1929, with Grete Stückgold, Fritz Krenn, Erik Wirl, Artur Cavara, Sabine Kalter, Deszö Ernster, conductor Otto Klemperer. Revised version San Carlo, Naples, 1954, with Fortunati, Valdengo, Pirazzini, Modesti and Sinimberghi, conducted by the composer; Santa Fé, 1961, again conducted by Hindemith.

Laura	Soprano
Eduard	Baritone
The Handsome Herr Hermann	Tenor
Herr M.	Tenor
Frau M.	Mezzo-Soprano
Hotel Director	Baritone
Marriage Clerk	Bass
Six Business Types	Tenor, Baritone, Bass
Museum Guide	Baritone
Chamber Maid	Soprano

Secretaries, Museum Visitors, Tourists, Show Girls, Theatre-Goers

Place: Germany
Time: The 1920s
Running Time: 1 hour 50 minutes

Hindemith had already collaborated with Marcellus Schiffer on the short, palindromic *Hin und Zurück* (Round Trip) in 1927 before he worked with him on the full-scale *Neues vom Tage*, a product of the later Weimar Republic, when such topical operas had become the vogue. *Von heute auf morgen* was written at almost exactly the same time, but Schoenberg's music, and indeed his attitude to the little story of marital crisis, is wholly serious, in strict contrast to Hindemith's, which is satirical and obviously written with the intention of tweaking the ears of the establishment. This it succeeded in doing – some of the hostility of the Nazis towards the composer, and indeed part of the row between officialdom and Furtwängler over Hindemith's planned *Mathis der Maler*, can be traced not so much to the theme of *Mathis* as to what the Nazi authorities thought of as the frivolity of the soprano's aria in the bath in praise of hot water!

Part I. Preludial music bustles mellifluously along before we find Laura and Eduard arguing over breakfast. By the end of their duet they have agreed on a divorce and Herr and Frau M., back from honeymoon, are drawn into the contretemps and, in less time than it takes to tell, find themselves in the same situation as Laura and Eduard.

At the Marriage Licence Bureau, Herr and Frau M. are delighted with their newly awarded divorce, and recommend Eduard and Laura to find grounds for their own separation by applying to another office, advice that couple, after an argument with the Marriage Clerk, seem inclined to follow.

The Office of Family Affairs (third scene) revolves round the handsome Herr Hermann (thus described in the cast list), who is much admired by the secretaries but whose main function it seems is to provide couples with grounds for divorce. He has however apparently committed a professional solecism and fallen in love with a client, none other than Frau M.

The fourth scene takes place in a museum, where a guide fatuously describes a famous statue of Venus. Laura is there waiting to meet the potential co-respondent but surprised he is so good-looking. She and Herr Hermann (for it is he) sing together what Hindemith calls the Duett-Kitsch, a hilarious parody of an operatic love scene, but not sufficiently hilarious for it to do other than enrage Eduard. He attacks Herr Hermann and ends up by breaking the famous Venus, to the consternation of the other museum visitors. He is arrested. Soon after the première, the whole scene was the subject of considerable approval by none other than the musical sage Wiesengrund Adorno, who disliked most of the rest of the opera but was full of praise for this episode, which he felt might with advantage be performed on its own!

Part II. A hotel bathroom. Laura sits naked in the bath singing the praises of the hot water supply – parody of opera, however easy on the ear, had not hitherto gone further, and scandal at early performances was inevitable and presumably anticipated. The bathroom is between two hotel rooms and Herr Hermann comes in from next door and, in spite of Laura's protestations, starts to undress. The appearance of Frau M., by now Herr Hermann's lover, provides an unexpected complication but only when the two women start to argue over who has prior rights to the bathroom do things start to go wrong. The row rouses the entire hotel and ends with cries of 'Oh, how embarrassing!'

The sixth scene shows simultaneously Laura in her hotel room and Eduard languishing in jail. The tentacles of the media hold them fast and each reads aloud headlines about scandals involving the other.

In the seventh scene, Eduard, out on probation, adds up what he owes in fines and discovers he's broke. Herr Hermann, who now loves Laura as well as Frau M., offers him money but in the finale six business types take him over, the scene culminating in a march which Hindemith called 'The Wreath of Fame crowns your Head', a sentiment unlikely to endear him overmuch to the German establishment.

Part III. In the Office of Family Affairs, a chorus of secretaries sings happily, and Herr Hermann seems not dissatisfied with the way business is going.

In the foyer of a theatre, Herr and Frau M., back from a second honeymoon, are about to witness a stage representation of the matrimonial upheavals of Laura and Eduard.

On the stage, after a couple of contrasting dance scenes, we find Laura and Eduard re-enacting their marital rows, even to the fight in the museum at the end of Part I.

In the final scene, Eduard and Laura have saved enough for their divorce, though they confess they would much rather retire to married life. But their existences no longer belong to them so much as to the media, and they finish by finding the evening paper as full of their doings as they are of the activities in Rome of *il Duce*.

In the last decade of his life, Hindemith turned to revision of early works in order to remove what he felt were youthful excesses. *Neues vom Tage* was not immune (Laura and Eduard for instance early on repent their decision to divorce), but its attraction some three generations after its creation lies in the way its relentless parody and the music which goes with it represent a period of history.   H.

MATHIS DER MALER
Mathias the Painter

Opera in seven scenes, text by the composer. Première, 28 May 1938, Zürich Stadttheater, with Hellwig, Funk, Stig, Baxevanos, Mossbacher, Honisch, Rothmüller, Emmerich, conductor Denzler. First performed London, Queen's Hall (concert version), 1939, with Stiles-Allen, Eadie, Noble, conductor Raybould; Stuttgart (first performance in Germany), 1946; Edinburgh Festival, 1952, by Hamburg ensemble; 1967 in Montreal and at Metropolitan, New York; 1995, Covent Garden.

Cardinal Albrecht von Brandenburg .... Tenor

Mathis, *painter in his employ* ....Baritone

Lorenz von Pommersfelden, *Dean of Mainz* ....Bass

Wolfgang Capito, *the Cardinal's counsellor* ....Tenor

Riedinger, *a rich citizen of Mainz; a Lutheran* ....Bass

Hans Schwalb, *leader of the peasants' army* ....Tenor

Truchsess von Waldburg, *leader of the*
    Confederate army ....Bass

Sylvester von Schaumberg, *one of his officers* .....Tenor

Graf von Helfenstein ....Silent

Gräfin von Helfenstein, *his wife* ....Contralto

Ursula, *Riedinger's daughter* ....Soprano

Regina, *Schwalb's daughter* ....Soprano

Place: In and Near Mainz
Time: The Peasants' War, c. 1525
Running Time: 3 hours 15 minutes

Hindemith was a native of Mainz, and for his eighth opera he took as his central figure the early sixteenth-century painter Mathias Grünewald, who spent much of his life in the service of the Archbishop of Mainz, and who is famous for the great altarpiece of Isenheim. Hindemith worked on the opera during the early period of the Nazi regime in Germany, and it is not hard to trace a direct relationship between the political circumstances of Germany at that time and the happenings of the opera, whose philosophical argument had to Hindemith, as to Mathis, a significance that was practical as well as theoretical.

The story takes place against a background of the Reformation and of the Peasants' War in Germany. It is divided into seven scenes, which are not continuous, and it is customary to have an interval after the fourth scene, by which time the opera has already lasted nearer two hours than one.

The prelude to the opera bears the subtitle of 'Engelkonzert' (Concert of Angels) and is inspired by part of the Isenheim polyptych. It is well known in the concert hall from its position as the first movement of the symphony Hindemith arranged from the music of his opera, and its contrapuntal character is typical of the composer's method in this opera as in many of his other works.

Scene i. The courtyard of St Anthony's monastery at Mainz, where Mathis is painting a fresco. The seriousness of purpose which distinguishes the opera is immediately shown in Mathis's introspective monologue, in which his rejoicing at the coming of spring

cannot be separated from his doubts as to whether he is worthily fulfilling his mission as a painter. His thoughts are interrupted by the breathless arrival of Schwalb and his daughter Regina, who are seeking sanctuary from the pursuing troops of the Fürstenbund. Mathis extends his help to them, and takes pity on Regina, who, in the midst of her misery, sings a sad little folk-song. Mathis gives her a ribbon with which she binds her hair, and their conversation is interrupted by the return of Schwalb, refreshed and with his wounds bound up. He expresses astonishment that Mathis is content to occupy himself with painting instead of taking part in the struggle for freedom. The painter appears convinced by his argument, and their voices join in an expression of conviction in the importance of the peasants' cause.

Regina rushes in to warn her father that their pursuers are in sight, and Mathis gives them his horse, telling Schwalb that he can in future count on his help. The scene ends after Mathis has admitted to Sylvester that he has helped the rebel leader to escape, and has claimed his right to answer for his actions to no one but the Cardinal.

Scene ii. The hall in the Martinsburg, the Archbishop's palace in Mainz. The rival factions of Papists and Lutherans dispute while waiting for the arrival of the Archbishop. Pommersfelden stands with the Papists, Capito with the Lutherans, amongst whom can be seen Riedinger and his daughter, Ursula. Peace comes momentarily with the Archbishop's entrance, and all leave except Pommersfelden, Capito, Riedinger and his daughter. Mathis comes in after his year of absence to be greeted with an expansive phrase from Ursula, who is in love with him. A quartet ensues in which Mathis and Ursula talk of their pleasure in seeing each other again, while the Cardinal promises Riedinger that the order to burn Lutheran books shall not be executed in Mainz. Pommersfelden objects that the order is from Rome and the Cardinal reluctantly agrees that it must be carried out.

There is some dispute about the suitability or otherwise of Mathis's representation of the saints in his pictures, which turns before long to a discussion of the empty state of the Cardinal's treasury. Sylvester enters and accuses Mathis before the Cardinal of having helped Schwalb's escape. Mathis admits the accusation but pleads strongly for the peasants' cause, and begs the Cardinal not to furnish the Fürstenbund with the money they have just asked for, but instead to support the juster cause of the rebels; in return, he will serve his patron without payment for the rest of his life. The Cardinal replies that his official conduct is bound by treaties; only where art is concerned has he a free hand. Let Mathis not interfere with what he does not understand. Mathis defies his patron and his prince, and the differing points of view of the Cardinal, Mathis, Pommersfelden, Capito, and the warlike Sylvester are combined in a noble quintet. The scene ends with Mathis receiving permission to withdraw from the Cardinal's service.

Scene iii. A room in Riedinger's house; in the background can be seen the preparations for the public burning of the Lutheran books. Riedinger and his friends attempt to hide their treasured possessions, but Capito reveals the hiding place. He appeases the wrath of the Lutherans by showing them a letter purporting to have come from Luther to the Cardinal in which he urges him strongly to give a lead to the clergy by renouncing his celibacy. Capito's scheme is to persuade the Cardinal, who is in urgent need of money, to make a rich marriage – and with whom more suitable than Riedinger's daughter, Ursula, who at that moment comes into the room. Riedinger himself hints at what is planned for her before he leaves Ursula, to join his fellow-Lutherans as their books are burnt in the market-place, a scene that is suggested by the chorus in the background. Ursula inveighs against her role as a mere chattel in a man's world.

Mathis appears to bid Ursula farewell. She welcomes him exultantly, and tells him how much she has missed him during his year of leave from the Cardinal's service. He answers that his spirit is sick within him and he must leave her and his work to join in the struggle for freedom; only through contact with misery can he recover his own soul. They protest their undying love for each other, but their duet ends with the cry: 'The love, the unity in which we have lived, gives way to suffering.' Mathis embraces Ursula and leaves.

When Riedinger asks her how she can preserve her calm through the calamity which has befallen those who share her religious beliefs, Ursula says she has made up her mind to accept the sacrifice demanded of her by her faith. Riedinger rejoices and proclaims that the fire lit by their enemies has sig-

nalled the beginning of a new period of determination which shall end in victory.

Scene iv. The rebellious peasants have seized a war-ravaged village and are terrorising the local nobility. They drag in Count Helfenstein and his wife, and kill the Count almost before her eyes. Mathis protests against this betrayal of the principles for which they are fighting, and tries to defend the Countess from their molestations, but he is knocked down. Only the advent of Schwalb saves him from further injury. The peasants' leader calls them all to arms to fight the Fürstenbund army, which is even now entering the village. But they are already downhearted at the prospect of meeting trained troops, and soon come back in disorder. Schwalb himself is trapped and falls before the lances of his enemies, who come through the village to the sound of a march. Mathis only escapes with his life through the Countess's intervention, and he comes to understand his own complete failure as a man of action; his lofty ambitions, his efforts to better the lot of the peasants, have ended in this. He sees Regina, overcome with horror at her father's death, and takes her away with him to look for shelter.

[Act II] Scene v. The Cardinal's study in the Martinsburg in Mainz. Capito has been trying to persuade the Cardinal to renounce his oath of celibacy and to adopt the course Luther advocates, and marry. His most cogent argument is that a rich wife would solve the Cardinal's very considerable financial difficulties; but Albrecht resents Capito's attempt to interfere with his conscience, and to treat him as if he were not capable of making up his own mind. Capito tries flattery, and then introduces Ursula as the prospective bride. The Cardinal is astonished to see her. In music of ever-increasing fervour she explains to him that only her abiding faith in Lutheranism would have driven her to the position in which she now finds herself. Love has grown cold within her, but she is willing to submit to marriage for the sake of the cause she loves.

The Cardinal calls Capito and Riedinger into the room and tells them that he is convinced by Ursula's show of faith: her example has shown him that he too must stand by what he has been taught. He dismisses Capito from his post as adviser, saying he will lead a simpler life in the future; and he gives permission to the Lutherans to declare themselves openly.

Mathis der Maler *(Covent Garden, 1995, director Peter Sellars, sets George Tsypin, costumes Dunya Ramicova). Alan Tytus (Mathis), Inga Nielsen (Ursula), Stig Andersen (Cardinal Albrecht), Christiane Oelze (Regina, on floor).*

There is an impressive quartet between the Cardinal, Ursula, Capito, and Riedinger, and at its end Ursula asks the Cardinal to bless her before she goes out again into the world. He consents to do this, and Ursula departs, leaving behind her a man whom she has ennobled by teaching him at one and the same time the meaning of Faith and of Tolerance.

Scene vi. In the Odenwald, Mathis and Regina pause during their flight. Regina says she still dreams she is pursued by the image of her dead father. Mathis tries to calm her by describing to her his vision of the Concert of Angels, accompanied in the orchestra by the music we heard in the prelude. Together they sing the chorale ('Es sungen drei Engel'), also heard in the prelude, until Regina falls asleep and Mathis despairingly contrasts his present spiritual misery with the comparative state of grace in which he painted the picture he has just described.

In the manner of the Temptation of St Anthony, Mathis is tempted by Luxury, wearing the face of the Countess; by wealth (Pommersfelden); a beggar, a courtesan, and a martyr (Ursula); scholarship (Capito); and a knight in shining armour (Schwalb). They enter successively, Mathis answers each in turn, and the music works up to a climax when the demons appear to torment the Saint. There is a great ensemble, at whose end the Cardinal, in the guise of St Paul, comes to comfort and advise St Anthony (part of the Isenheim altar depicts the Conversation between St Paul and St Anthony). St Anthony asks what he has done that he should have reached his present state of uncertainty. St Paul tells him that he has been untrue to himself. In throwing in his lot with the people, he has denied the gifts he had from God, and has in fact withdrawn from the people he tried to help. Let him return to his art, denying himself but dedicating his work to God. In so doing he will become part of the people. The tree knows nothing of its fruits. At the end of the vision, in which the composer speaks his mind on the subject of the artist, the two voices join together in a paean of praise, ending with a magnificent 'Alleluiah'.

It is the crucial scene of the opera (Hindemith has used the themes from it as a basis for the last movement of his symphony), and it was presumably from the Temptation section of the Isenheim altar and the Conversation of St Anthony and St Paul that the composer initially drew inspiration for his theme and his central figure.

Scene vii. Mathis's studio in Mainz. Mathis is lying asleep, exhausted with his work, and Ursula watches alone by the side of the dying Regina. Ursula reflects on the meaning of their lives, and on Mathis's unprecedented inspiration since his return to Mainz and to art. Regina wakes and raves about the memory of her dead father, whose face she can see in Mathis's painting of the Crucifixion. She asks Ursula to give Mathis the ribbon which she originally received from him at their first meeting, and Ursula recognises it as one she herself had given Mathis. Regina sings a couple of sentences of the chorale, before dying with Mathis by her side.

The interlude, marked 'Very slowly', is entitled 'Entombment' (it serves as the slow movement of the symphony). At its end, the curtain rises to show the studio empty except for a table, on which lie several objects. The Cardinal comes to say farewell to Mathis, embracing him for the last time. Mathis himself takes a case and puts away materially and symbolically the things which have represented the main efforts of his life. It is in this spirit of utter humility that the opera ends.

Hindemith's concentration on the issues at stake never blinded him to the need for putting them forward dramatically within the framework he chose; he made no concessions, but he worked in terms of opera as a medium. No listener who is seriously interested in opera can come away from a performance of the work without having been impressed by Hindemith's lofty conception of the artist's responsibility, and his equally lofty view of what opera can and must accomplish. Integrity shines through *Mathis*, and the opera is perhaps strongest in the composer's conviction in his theme and its expression. And there is no denying that the theme is an elevated one.   H.

DIE HARMONIE DER WELT
The Harmony of the World

Opera in five acts, libretto by the composer. First performed Prinzregententheater, Munich, 11 August 1957, conducted by the composer. Revived, with cuts, Bremen, 1957, conducted by Heinz Wallberg; Linz, 1967, conducted by Kurt Wöss; Wuppertal, 1980, conducted by Hanns-Martin Schneidt.

Emperor Rudolf II/Ferdinand II, *Sol*.....................Bass
Kepler, *the Imperial mathematician, Earth* ......Baritone
Wallenstein, *the General, Jupiter* ....Tenor
Ulrich Grusser, *Kepler's assistant, Mars* ....Tenor
Daniel Hitzler, *a priest, Mercury* ....Bass
Tansur, *Saturn* ....Bass
Baron Starhemberg.....................................Baritone
Christoph, *Kepler's brother*................................Tenor
Susanna, *Kepler's second wife, Venus*..............Soprano
Katharina, *Kepler's mother, Luna* ....Contralto
Susanna, *Kepler's daughter by his first wife*.....Soprano

Bailiff and Lawyer, People, Soldiers, Sternbilder

Place: Prague and Linz
Time: 1607–30
Running Time: 3 hours

Hindemith started thinking about an opera centred on the historical figure of Johannes Kepler as early as 1939, when he wrote sonatas for several different instruments in preparation for what was always intended to be his *magnum opus*. Hindemith wrote the text himself, as he had with *Mathis der Maler*.

Act I. A street in Prague, 1607. The Town Crier, Tansur, warns that the comet will bring disaster. Ulrich, who assists the imperial astronomer Johannes Kepler, contradicts Tansur and spoils his business. General Wallenstein orders his horoscope from Kepler. He then enlists Tansur, because of his capacity for lying, to act as recruiter for his army.

A cemetery in Württemberg. Three scenes are juxtaposed simultaneously on stage. Katharina, Kepler's mother, disinters her father's skull to make a drinking bowl out of it. She means to warn Kepler against the spiritual self-aggrandisement which leads him to attempt to uncover nature's secrets. Christoph, her younger son, is disgusted by his mother's recourse to magic.

Four women appear briefly: in susurrations reminiscent of the love-sick secretaries of *Neues vom Tage* they decide Katharina is a witch and must be tried.

In another part of the stage, Kepler tells the old Emperor Rudolf about the order that determines the movements of the stars. The Emperor looks through a telescope but sees only a reflection of the chaos on earth.

Kepler returns to his home, having lost his wife and his son. He sings his daughter Susanna a song of mourning, using words by the historical Kepler written in 1611, and music by Johann Hermann Schein from 1627. When Kepler hears that Rudolf has been forced to abdicate in favour of his brother Matthias, he decides to go to Linz.

Act II, 1613. Wallenstein decides to raise an army to be put at the disposal of Ferdinand, the pretender to the throne. Tansur acts as his recruiting officer.

In Linz Kepler has become an object of scorn: having had a difference of opinion with the pastor Hitzler, he is excluded from communion. Susanna, the foster-daughter of Baron Starhemberg, supports Kepler. Her behaviour arouses the jealousy of Kepler's assistant Ulrich Grusser, who had his eye on her for himself.

Kepler and Susanna recognise that they love one another. The tempo changes, four muted horns enter quietly and 'with elegiac expression', as Kepler resolves to teach the world to recognise the harmony that he has found.

As Tansur recruits an army, Ulrich, embittered by his failure to secure Susanna's love, is the first to sign up to become a soldier. Meanwhile Susanna describes, in an exquisite wedding hymn, how she became a bride.

Act III, 1616–21. Kepler's little daughter Susanna sings a child's song to the moon, while Kepler's second wife Susanna quietly reads the bible. Suddenly her stepmother Katharina bursts in, seeking refuge from persecution. After another burst of the child's song, the two older women are seen reading from bibles in separate rooms. A quartet builds up, made up of Kepler's and the child's musings on the moon and the older women's bible readings. Kepler asks his mother to return to Württemberg.

Katharina is tried for witchcraft. She is about to undergo torture when Kepler intervenes and saves her. She asks him to help her in her search for ways of healing, but he refuses.

Act IV, 1628. The act opens with a 'Ballet, Polonaise', as Wallenstein, now at the height of his power, gives a party in his palace in Prague. Ulrich is so fascinated by the spectacle that he leaves his guard-post. When Wallenstein discovers Ulrich's derogation of duty he flies into a rage. He tries to enlist Kepler as his 'house astrologer', in his campaign for world domination. Having been more moved by Kepler's *Harmonie der Welt* than by any other book, he now plans to harness the world's harmony and create heaven on earth. 'What does an ocean of blood matter', Wallenstein asks Kepler, 'if at the end it gives birth to an Eden?' Despite his doubts, Kepler agrees and joins in a trio along with Wallenstein and his major-domo, Tansur. Ulrich swears revenge for the humiliation he suffered: he will 'exchange roles' with Wallenstein. Tansur comments that often the smallest insect can, with its poison, bring down the greatest beast of prey.

Act V, 1630. Now lonely and desperate, Susanna feels that Kepler avoids her and their children, driven by his pursuit of knowledge. Ulrich appears, at first bent on punishing Kepler, who 'stole' Susanna and witnessed his humiliation at Wallenstein's hands. Ulrich despises Kepler's obstinate search for the key to the world's harmony: for him, chance rules everything. When he leaves, Susanna contemplates her lonely life, concluding that she never achieved harmony.

Regensburg. After an 'Old Warsong' and variations, the princes warn Emperor Ferdinand that Wallenstein aims to depose him.

Kepler, lying ill nearby, addresses the assembly in his mind, but cannot prevent the fall of his master. He reflects that he left his home and wife in order to see, for once, harmony on earth. Now he accepts that harmony can only be achieved in death itself, and his last words suggest disillusionment, despair. He dies, but a chorus advocates optimism.

The Emperor appears, now in his planetary form as Sol, and urges Kepler to join him 'above, in order to understand the greater picture'. The stage directions call for a Baroque painting of heaven to fill the stage gradually, as a passacaglia begins. Sol is joined by Hitzler as Mercury, Susanna as Venus. Wallenstein is rebuked for his bloodthirsty hubris ('a false tone in the world's chord') and murdered by Ulrich, among others. But soon after Kepler is taken up into the harmony of the world (as Earth), Wallenstein joins him as Jupiter, Ulrich as Mars and Tansur as Saturn, all of whom have their part to play in the 'Harmony of the World'.

With exemplary tact, Hindemith's biographer Geoffrey Skelton comments on *Harmonie der Welt*:

'That it was overlong he himself acknowledged by making cuts. Whether much of the music is uninteresting, as even some of Hindemith's supporters claim, is of course a matter of opinion, but the circumstances under which a good deal of it was written, in hotels and dressing-rooms, suggest that it would not be surprising if this were so.'

The mystical aspects of the opera should not obscure its more immediate pathos: towards the end of his life, Hindemith felt out of step with most trends in contemporary music. He identified with Kepler's lonely pursuit of the truth. In composing *Harmonie der Welt* he aimed to redress in music the imbalance he found in the world. He was much struck by the comparatively invidious celebrity that posterity has (rightly) visited on his earlier, so-called 'occasional' works.   P.

DAS LANGE WEIHNACHTSMAHL
The Long Christmas Dinner

Opera in one act, libretto by Thornton Wilder after his own play *The Long Christmas Dinner* (1931), in a German version by the composer. First performance Nationaltheater, Mannheim, 17 December 1961, with Hindemith conducting. First U.K. performance, International Students' House, London, 1967, conducted by Michael Graubart. First U.S. performance, Juilliard School of Music, New York, in a double bill with Hindemith's ballet *Der Dämon*, 1963, with the composer conducting.

Lucia[1]	Soprano
Mother Bayard[2]	Contralto
Roderick[3]	Baritone
Brandon	Bass
Charles	Tenor
Genevieve	Mezzo-Soprano
Leonora	High Soprano
Ermengarde[2]	Alto
Sam[3]	High Baritone
Lucia II[1]	Soprano
Roderick II	Tenor

Place: The Dining Room of the Bayard House
Running Time: 1 hour

The 'dining table is handsomely spread for Christmas dinner'. The note in the score goes on to identify three doors in the set: the middle one leads to

---

the hall; the left-hand one signifies birth and the right-hand one death. 'Ninety years are to be traversed in this play which represents in accelerated motion ninety Christmas dinners in the Bayard household.' It begins with 'God rest you merry, gentlemen' in the orchestra.

Lucia announces, 'We're ready'. The family assemble for their first Christmas dinner in the new house. Roderick pushes Mother Bayard in in her wheelchair. He also carves, offering her 'The light, or the dark?', alternatives which, alas, turn out to have symbolic resonance. Mother Bayard remembers their first Christmas Day in the West, as a child, when there was no city there. Cousin Brandon takes his place; Roderick proposes a toast to the firm of Bayard and Brandon. A Nursemaid pushes a baby carriage through the Door of Birth, left. They call the child Charles. Mother Bayard rises and 'starts walking uncertainly to the Door of Death, right'. She has scarcely left when the Nursemaid appears, left, with the baby carriage, this time containing Genevieve. Twenty-seven bars after Mother Bayard has exited, Lucia says, 'I was thinking this morning of Mother Bayard, – two years ago!' There are a few more incidents: Cousin Ermengarde comes to stay; Roderick yields his place at table to Charles; Roderick dies; Charles marries Leonora, who takes Lucia's place; they have a child that dies, then twins; there is a war overseas...

The longest ensemble ('We talk of the weather') occurs when Sam, one of the twins, 'stands with his back to the dark door', saying, 'I shall remember you so'. We are not surprised when he is referred to in the past tense in the bar subsequent to his exit. Genevieve leaves to go 'to a town where something happens'; shortly afterwards, Roderick II does the same thing. Leonora follows to visit them and Ermengarde reads in a letter from her of 'a little new Roderick. And a little new Lucia, too'. But it's what doesn't change that matters: the ritual comments about the weather, the toasts to the family and the firm, the continuity 'from father to son, from cousin to cousin, from husband to wife' and so on.

Das lange Weihnachtsmahl suffers like so many good one-act operas from its format. Hindemith hoped Thornton Wilder would write him a libretto for a companion piece (a comic opera, incidentally), based on Wilder's play *Pullman Car Hiawatha*, about a journey on a night train. According to Hindemith's wife Gertrud, the composer 'dreams of the travelling virtuoso who practises at night on his violin'. Geoffrey Skelton points out that *Das lange Weihnachtsmahl*'s lack of a companion piece has contributed to its failure to establish itself firmly on the stage.[1]   P.

GUSTAV HOLST

(born 21 September 1874, died 25 May 1934)

Holst's interests included the whole range of Indian culture, not least music, and he taught himself Sanskrit and set Hindu texts. Several early operas precede *Sita*, on a Hindu story, finished in 1906 but still unperformed, and *Sāvitri*, also Hindu-based. In the years before the Great War of 1914–18, Holst set a number of other Hindu texts, but his future operatic essays comprised *The Perfect Fool* (1923), which involved spoofing Wagner, Italian opera and Debussy, and was performed at Covent Garden in 1923; *At the Boar's Head* (1925); and *The Wandering Scholar* (1934). None of them has made much mark on the repertory.

SĀVITRI

An episode from the Mahā Bhārata in one act. Words by the composer. Première Wellington Hall, London, 5 November 1916. First performed Lyric Theatre, 1921; Covent Garden, 1923, with Dorothy Silk, William Heseltine, Farrington, conductor Pitt; Chicago, 1934; Sadler's Wells, 1935; Oxford, 1937; Cincinnati, 1939; St Pancras Town Hall, London, 1952, with Cantelo, Young, Hemsley, conductor Colin Davis; Aldeburgh, 1956, with Mandikian, Pears, Hemsley, conductor Mackerras.

Satyavān, *a woodman* ....Tenor
Sāvitri, *his wife*..Soprano
Death ....Bass
Female Chorus

---

[1] *Paul Hindemith: the Man behind the Music*, 1975.

Place: A Wood at Evening in India
Running Time: 30 minutes

The following note has been added to the score by the composer: 'The piece is intended for performance in the open air or in a small building. When performed out of doors there should be a long avenue or path through a wood in the centre of the scene. When a curtain is used, it should be raised before the voice of Death is heard. No curtain, however, is necessary. The orchestra consists of two string quartets, a contra-bass, two flutes and an English horn. There is also a hidden chorus of female voices.'

The stage is empty. A voice is heard calling to Sāvitri. Death, the Summoner, whose path may not be turned, draws near to carry Satyavān, Sāvitri's husband, through the dark gates that sooner or later open for all. Sāvitri enters, distracted by the awful cry she has heard, unable to realise how or why Satyavān, young, strong, and fearless, should be taken from her. His voice is heard as he approaches on the homeward way after the day's labour, singing of Sāvitri's loveliness. He finds her sick with fear and trembling. The distant voices of the chorus give an eerie colour to the scene while Sāvitri laments the vanity of all things. The only reality is Death. Hearing her cry out wildly, 'He comes', Satyavān picks up his axe and boldly challenges the stranger. The brave words die on his lips, the axe falls from his hand, and after an appeal to Sāvitri he sinks to the ground while Death slowly approaches to claim him. Sāvitri gathers the body in her arms and sings softly to weave a spell so that no evil thing may come near.

When Death is quite close she is herself overcome for a moment, but conquering her fears, she finds the strength to welcome the 'Just One'. She asks Death to take her together with Satyavān. That may not be, answers Death, but, since Sāvitri, far from shrinking, gave him welcome, he will grant her a boon which, however, must not be Satyavān's life. 'Well then,' says Sāvitri after a while, 'grant me life.' 'But thou hast life now,' objects Death. 'If thou art not a blind spirit,' retorts Sāvitri, 'thou must understand that, for a woman, Life means stalwart sons and bright-eyed daughters: Life is a communion and eternal.' Her passionate pleading succeeds. Death grants her the boon – Satyavān's life, because if Satyavān dies Sāvitri's voice must become mute and she herself but 'an image floating on the waters of memory'. True to his word, Death

goes away and Satyavān comes to life again. The opera ends with Sāvitri singing gently to Satyavān as she sang when she held him lifeless in her embrace.   F. B.

AT THE BOAR'S HEAD

Musical interlude (the composer's description) in one act. Première Manchester, 3 April 1925, by British National Opera Company, with Norman Allin as Falstaff, Tudor Davies as Prince Hal (a hurried replacement for a sick Walter Hyde; Steuart Wilson sang it later); conductor Malcolm Sargent.

Prince Hal	Tenor
Falstaff	Bass
Hostess (Dame Quickly)	Soprano
Doll Tearsheet	Mezzo-Soprano
Pistol	Baritone
Peto	Tenor
Bardolph	Baritone
Poins	Bass
Gadshill	Baritone
Pistol's Companions	Baritones

Running Time: 1 hour

As a result of a fall, Holst was ordered to spend much of 1924 resting in the country, and he took the opportunity to compose *At the Boar's Head*. Looking through an album of folk music, he was struck by the way certain tunes fitted sentences from Shakespeare's *Henry IV*; following up his discovery, he found it 'an opera that wrote itself'. His daughter, Imogen Holst, nonetheless describes it as something at the time 'condemned by nearly everyone who heard it ... a brilliant failure'. At the same time she praises the skill with which he accomplished the self-imposed task, the dexterity with which he joined one tune to another, the touches of characterisation wrought with a harmonic twist here or a pizzicato discord there. Yet 'there are far too many excitements happening all the time', concludes the composer's daughter. The opera's early audiences were bewildered by its pace and unfamiliarity, and success in the composer's lifetime was very limited. Subsequent appraisal has been considerably more generous.

Holst has taken the Falstaff scenes of *Henry IV* and added two of the Sonnets for the Prince to sing. The tunes are from Playford's *English Dancing Master* of

1651 and other collections, particularly those by Cecil Sharp. Only three are Holst's own.

Falstaff accuses Prince Hal and Poins of deserting him when that morning he was set on and robbed. His own story of the encounter is embroidered to such a degree that Hal can hardly contain himself before admitting that it was he and Poins who robbed Falstaff of the money he had just taken – from unarmed travellers at that! When a messenger from the court is announced, the Prince is left alone and in a soliloquy likens himself in his present condition to the sun who permits clouds to obscure his glory.

Falstaff comes to tell him civil war has broken out. If he is to return to court, he had better practise what to say to the King his father. In a scene of some length, Falstaff at first plays the King, then roles are reversed.

Hal and Poins get themselves up as servants to watch Falstaff woo Doll Tearsheet. When Falstaff calls for a song, Hal obliges with one of Shakespeare's sonnets, 'Devouring Time, blunt thou the lion's claws', which with its references to old age is not at all to Falstaff's taste. Bardolph runs in calling on Prince Hal to return at once to Westminster, and the Prince and Poins remove their disguises and to a march go off to court.

Pistol comes looking for his crony Falstaff. He is let in against better judgement but quarrels with Doll and is thrown out. A dozen captains are below looking for Falstaff, announces Bardolph, and he and Falstaff march off to the war, leaving the women weeping. But it is not long before the situation improves as Bardolph pokes his head round the door and whispers 'Bid Mistress Tearsheet come to my master.' H.

ENGELBERT HUMPERDINCK
(born 1 September 1854, died 27 September 1921)

HÄNSEL UND GRETEL

Opera in three acts, text by Adelheid Wette (the composer's sister). First performed at the Hoftheater, Weimar, 23 December 1893; Daly's Theatre, London, 1894 (in English), conductor Arditi; Drury Lane, 1895 (in German), by the Ducal Court Company of Saxe-Coburg and Gotha; Covent Garden, 1896, conductor Mancinelli; New York, Daly's Theatre, 1895 (in English); Metropolitan, 1905 (in German), with Lina Abarbanell, Bella Alten, Louise Homer, Marion Weed, Otto Goritz, conductor Alfred Hertz; Covent Garden, by B.N.O.C., January 1923 (first broadcast of a complete opera from an opera house in Europe).

Hänsel ....Mezzo-Soprano

Gretel, *his sister*..Soprano

The Witch ....Mezzo-Soprano[1]

Gertrude, *mother of Hänsel and Gretel*.............Soprano

Peter, *their father, a broom-maker*...................Baritone

Sandman ....Soprano

Dew Fairy ....Soprano

Running Time: 2 hours

Act I follows the well-known overture, which is based on themes from the opera. In the broommaker's hut, Hänsel is binding brooms and Gretel is knitting. The children romp, quarrel, and make up – they have a long duet, culminating in a dance. When their mother, Gertrude, enters she is angry to see them idle, and trying to smack them she upsets a pitcher of milk instead. With all hope of supper vanished she sends the children out into the woods to look for strawberries, while she herself, bemoaning their poverty, sinks down exhausted upon a chair and falls asleep. A riotous 'Tra-la-la-la' song announces the approach of her husband, drunk as usual. She is about to reproach him when she notices that he has brought sausages, bread and butter, coffee – enough for a feast. He tells her that he has had good luck at the fair and bids her prepare supper. When he asks for the children he is horrified to hear that they have been sent into the woods, for a wicked witch lives near the Ilsenstein who entices

---

[1] Occasionally sung by a character tenor.

children in order to bake them in her oven and devour them. Both parents rush off in search of Hänsel and Gretel.

Act II. Near the Ilsenstein. The act opens with the Witch's Ride. Hänsel has filled his basket with berries and Gretel has made a wreath with which her brother crowns her. Before they realise what they are doing the children have eaten all the berries; then they see that it is too dark to look for more or to find their way home. Gretel weeps with fear and Hänsel comforts her. They grow sleepy. The Sandman in a delightful song sprinkles sand into their eyes, but before going to sleep the children are careful not to forget their evening prayer. Fourteen guardian angels are seen descending the heavenly ladder to protect them, in a long orchestral passage which reminds us that Humperdinck was devoted to Wagner.

Act III. Morning. The Dew Fairy sprinkles dew on the children. Suddenly they notice a little house made of cake and sugar. Hungry, they start to break off small pieces when a voice cries out from within and the Witch opens the door. She throws a rope around Hänsel's throat, and tells them both to come in. Frightened, they try to escape, but after binding them with a magic spell she imprisons Hänsel in a kennel, and forces Gretel to go into the house.

When she believes Hänsel to be asleep she turns her attention to lighting the oven, then rides around the house on her broomstick. When she alights she orders Hänsel to show her his finger. But he pokes a stick through the bars and, finding the 'finger' still thin, the Witch orders more food for him. While she turns her back, Gretel seizes the juniper bough with which the old woman makes her spells, speaks the magic words and breaks her brother's enchantment. Then the Witch tells Gretel to get into the oven and see if the honey cakes are done. But Gretel pretends to be stupid and asks her to show her how to get in. Together the children push the old Witch into the oven and slam the door, and the oven soon falls apart. The children then see a fence of gingerbread figures standing stiffly against the house. Gretel breaks the spell for them as she had done for Hänsel, and they turn into a row of boys and girls. There is general rejoicing, Gertrude and Peter appear, the old Witch is pulled out of the ruined oven as a gigantic honey cake and everyone on the stage joins in a hymn of thanksgiving.   K.W.

KÖNIGSKINDER
King's Children

Opera in three acts, libretto by Ernst Rosmer. Rosmer's play was produced in 1897 with incidental music by Humperdinck and the opera's première was on 28 December 1910, at the Metropolitan, with Geraldine Farrar, Louise Homer, Hermann Jadlower, Otto Goritz, conductor Alfred Hertz. First performed Berlin, 1911; Covent Garden, 1911, with Gura-Hummel, Otto Wolff, Hofbauer, conductor Schalk; Milan, 1911, with Lucrezia Bori, Giuseppe Armanini, Taurino Parvis; English National Opera, 1992, conductor Mark Elder, producer David Pountney.

A King's Son..Tenor
A Goose-Girl ....Soprano
A Fiddler...Baritone
The Witch...Mezzo-Soprano
A Woodcutter ....Bass
A Broom-Maker...Tenor
Children ....Sopranos
A Senior Councillor ....Bass
The Innkeeper ....Baritone
The Innkeeper's Daughter.................Mezzo-Soprano
A Tailor ....Tenor
A Stable Maid ....Mezzo-Soprano
Gate-Keepers......................................Tenor, Baritone

Place: Germany
Time: Medieval
Running Time: 2 hours 40 minutes

Act I is preceded by a lively and colourful orchestral introduction, which will surprise no one who knows *Hänsel und Gretel*. An old witch has cast a spell upon a King's daughter and forces her to act as a goose-girl in the forest. The witch wants to teach her all the magic arts and compels her to bake a magic loaf, to eat which will bring death. 'Ach, bin ich allein' begins the girl's attractive solo as she admires her reflection in the water and calls to her geese. At this point appears a Prince, who has come into the forest in search of adventure. The goose-girl has never seen a human being apart from the witch, and is greatly impressed by him. The Prince tells her of the world beyond the wood and they fall in love. The wind blows off her garland of flowers but he gives her his crown and wants her to go away with him. She however cannot break the spell which holds her prisoner.

A broom-maker and a woodcutter are guided by a wandering fiddler to the witch's hut. They have come on behalf of the townspeople to ask her who will be their King. The answer is simple: the first person to enter the gates of the city after the bells have rung the hour of noon on the following day, which is the festival day of Hella. The woodcutter and the broom-maker refuse to share with the minstrel their reward from the townspeople and go off, but the fiddler has been impressed by the beauty of the goose-girl and recognises her to be of royal blood. She tells him about the Prince, invokes her father and mother to help free her and, with the aid of the fiddler, breaks the witch's spell. They leave together.

Act II. A lively dance introduces the scene, a square outside the town gates of Hellabrunn. The news has reached the people, who await the arrival of their new King in a state of considerable excitement. Meanwhile, the Prince has entered the town at midnight and is lodged in the innkeeper's pigsty. That worthy's daughter is greatly impressed by the handsome young man, but he dreams of the goose-girl and remains indifferent. Even a slap from the infuriated innkeeper's daughter cannot deflect his thoughts, and the sight of the goose-girl's garland, with the flowers revived and fresh, confirms his love. He will wait for her in Hellabrunn. He ends by accepting the innkeeper's offer of a job as swineherd.

Woodcutter and broom-maker are among the crowd, the latter with a brood of children. His youngest daughter offers to sell the Prince a broom. He cannot pay and instead offers her a dance, which she happily accepts.

The Prince suggests that the King when he comes may be wearing simple garments and not splendid robes, but he is laughed at as a fool – moreover the innkeeper's daughter accuses him of not paying for food and drink.

At that moment, bells announce midday, and the gates are thrown open. Through them comes the goose-girl wearing her golden crown, followed by her geese, with the fiddler at her side. The lovers embrace, the Prince greeting her as his Queen. At first there is laughter but that is succeeded by fury at what the townspeople think of as a trick, and they make as if to attack the girl, whom the Prince defends. They are run out of town and the fiddler, who takes their side, is beaten. An old town councillor asks why the broom-maker's little daughter is crying and she says: 'They were the King and Queen.'

Act III. Before the curtain comes a long prelude, quite devoid of the dance undertones of the earlier orchestral music. A woodland clearing as in Act I. It is midwinter, and the fiddler is living in what was the witch's hut, by now much dilapidated and damaged. He sings eloquently of his sadness. The broom-maker has been charged with the job of getting the fiddler to return to Hellabrunn and he comes to the hut with his children. The fiddler accepts, saying that for the sake of the children and because of the Prince and Princess he is ready to go. But first, he must look for them and, taking the townspeople's children with him, he sets out on his mission. Woodcutter and broom-maker return to the hut to get warm. The fiddler's song can be heard in the distance.

On the hillside can be seen the Prince and the goose-girl coming down towards the hut, starving and half-frozen. At first the woodcutter refuses to let them in, but the Prince forgets his indignation, so shocked is he at the state of misery to which the goose-girl has come. She tries to dance and sing to show him that all is still well, but she collapses. To obtain a little food, the Prince gives his crown to the woodcutter, but it is the witch's deadly magic loaf that they are given. They eat it and in a last embrace fall happily into a final sleep. The children of Hellabrunn and the fiddler find them dead, the fiddler mourns them movingly – his last song, he says – and on a litter they carry the two bodies back towards the town. K., H.

J

LEOŠ JANÁČEK
(born 3 July 1854, died 12 August 1928)

In the canon of Janáček's operas, *Jenůfa* (1904) is preceded by *Šárka* and the one-act *The Beginning of a Romance*, two early and unsuccessful works, *Šárka* not even reaching the stage until 1926. Between *Jenůfa* and the four great works of his maturity are two operas which have not achieved universal fame: *Osud* (Fate), 1903/4, a highly unconventional conversational piece, and the fantastic burlesque *The Adventures of Mr Brouček* (written between 1908 and 1917). *Osud* is usually thought of as representing a transition between Janáček's early style, which reached its height in *Jenůfa*, and his later and more mature work. Though it does not exclude folk derivations, it is not based on folk music like the earlier works. Its production in Brno during the International Janáček Congress in 1958 (in a doctored version) was by no means a failure, but in spite of its quality the work has not made an impact on the international repertory. *Mr Brouček* has however gradually gained ground and has even been produced successfully outside Czechoslovakia.

The final flowering of Janáček's operatic genius, generated, it would not be fanciful to say, by his meeting with Kamila Stösslová in 1917 in Luhačovice, demonstrates four quite different styles of operatic creation, the one thing they have in common being their extraordinary conciseness of musical utterance. *Kátya*, for all the intensity of its drama, is a lyrical piece. *The Cunning Little Vixen* is something quite unique in opera, a pantheistic work in which animals and humans can apparently move on the same plane and with equal facility. *The Makropulos Affair* allows for little lyrical flowering in an extraordinary drama, and in *From the House of the Dead* the composer attempts and achieves the impossible, the encapsulating of a major and lengthy novel in a comparably major and extremely short opera.

Janáček admired Dvořák rather than Smetana (compare *Kátya*'s prelude with that of *Rusalka*), was a close student of folk music (though in his mature operas he composes rather than quotes it), and he recommended the operatic composer to study the natural rhythms (particularly those of speech) around him. He was an operatic master, slow to be appreciated outside his native Moravia, but now established as one of the form's pre-eminent practitioners in the twentieth century.   H.

JEJÍ PASTORKYŇA
(JENŮFA)
Her Stepdaughter

Opera in three acts, text by the composer founded on a story by Gabriella Preissová. Première, Brno, 21 January 1904, with Marie Kabeláčová, Leopolda Svobodová, Staněk-Doubravsky, Procházka; it was Janáček's first performed opera and scored a considerable local success. First performed Prague, 1916, with Ungrová, Horvátová, Schütz, Lebeda, when it immediately became a popular favourite. Translated into German by Max Brod (from whose version most other translations have been taken), and performed Vienna, 1918; Cologne, 1918; Berlin, 1924, with Jurjewskaya, Ober, Soot, Jöken, conductor Erich Kleiber; Metropolitan, New York, 1924, in German, with Jeritza, Matzenauer, Oehmann, Laubenthal, conductor Bodanzky; Venice, 1941, with Cigna; Stockholm, 1941, with Herzberg, Wettergren, Beyron, Svanholm; Berlin, 1942, with Müller, Marta Fuchs, Argyris, Anders; Vienna, 1948, with Welitsch, Helena Braun, Patzak, Treptow; Holland Festival, 1951, with Brouwenstijn, Vroons; Buenos Aires, 1951, with Lemnitz, Fischer; London, Covent Garden, 1956, with Shuard, Fisher, conductor Kubelík; Chicago, 1959, with Brouwenstijn, Fisher, conductor von Matacic; Vienna, 1964, with Jurinac, Höngen, conductor Krombholc; Edinburgh Festival, 1974, in Swedish Opera production by Götz Friedrich, with Söderström, Kerstin Meyer, Höiseth, Johnny Blanc; Metropolitan, 1974, with Teresa Kubiak, Astrid Varnay, Jon Vickers.

Grandmother Buryjovká, *owner of the mill* ..Contralto
Laca Klemeň...Tenor
Števa Buryja, *Laca's half-brother*.......................Tenor
Kostelnička Buryjovká ....Soprano
Jenůfa, *her stepdaughter* ....Soprano
Foreman at the Mill......................................Baritone
Mayor of the Village...Bass
His Wife ....Mezzo-Soprano
Karolka, *his daughter* ....Mezzo-Soprano
A Maid..Mezzo-Soprano
Barena, *servant at the mill* ....Soprano
Jano, *shepherd boy*..Soprano
Old Woman ....Contralto

Musicians, Village People

Place: A Village in Moravia
Time: Nineteenth Century
Running Time: 2 hours 10 minutes

Jenůfa, to give the opera the name by which it is known abroad, was the composer's first success, earned at the age of fifty, and in the natural course of events it should have been given immediately in Prague. Unfortunately, some years earlier, Janáček had written woundingly about a composition of Karel Kovařovic, and Kovařovic was now head of the opera in Prague. He put off hearing the new work, and it was only after extraordinary efforts by the composer's friends and admirers that twelve years later he accepted *Jenůfa* for Prague, and then only with the stipulation that he should 'edit' the work. The editing consisted of some re-orchestration and a large number of small cuts, often only of a bar or two, but for this edition Kovařovic received a royalty and his widow after him. The opera triumphed nonetheless in Prague and eighteen months later in Vienna, the latter a rather extraordinary success considering that Czechoslovakia had just declared its independence of the Austrian Empire.

Long before the opera begins, Grandmother Buryjovká has had two sons, each of them dead before the action starts. The elder, who owned the family mill, married the widow Klemeň, who already had a son Laca. Together she and the Miller had another son Števa, who is of course heir to his father and grandmother. The second son, Tomas, had by his first wife a daughter named Jenůfa; after the death of Jenůfa's mother, he married Kostelnička (as she was later known because of her work as sacristan of the village chapel).

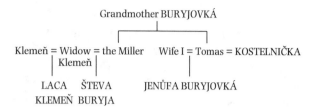

Grandmother BURYJOVKÁ

Klemeň = Widow = the Miller   Wife I = Tomas = KOSTELNIČKA
    | Klemeň |
    LACA   ŠTEVA   JENŮFA BURYJOVKÁ
   KLEMEŇ BURYJA

Act I. A lonely mill in the mountains. Jenůfa, a pot of rosemary in her arms, stands by the stream looking into the distance. The Old Grandmother sits in front of the mill peeling potatoes. Laca is near her, shaping a whip-handle with his knife. It is late afternoon. The prelude (in 6/4 time) has running through it the tinkling sound of the mill at work (xylophone). Jenůfa laments that Števa has not yet returned, and wonders despairingly whether he has been taken as a soldier by the recruiting officer. She is in love with him – in fact, carries his child within her – and her heart will break if he leaves her.

Laca makes sarcastic reference to his place in the household; he is only worth his food and lodging in return for the work he can do, and Števa has always been the idol of old Grandmother Buryjovká. At this point the orchestra shows the pity for the foibles and misfortunes of his characters which is one of Janáček's strongest qualities and which pervades his operas, but Laca's vocal line remains uncompromisingly bitter, and Jenůfa reproaches him for the way in which he speaks to the old woman. Laca wonders aloud what would be Jenůfa's reaction if Števa were taken for the army.

Jano, the shepherd boy, is heard calling happily from the mill. A new sense of joy comes into the music as he announces that he really can read now. Grandmother Buryjovká observes that Jenůfa is as much the teacher at heart as her stepmother.

The foreman of the mill comes on to the scene, and asks Laca what he is working at. A whip-handle – but his knife is blunt, says Laca, and gives it to be sharpened. Laca and Jenůfa quarrel for a moment, and Laca remarks bitterly to the foreman that she will make a splendid sister-in-law with those sweet ways of hers. The foreman, however, is not deceived and pays a compliment to Jenůfa's beauty, commenting that this is anyhow not news to Laca. What if Števa be taken for a soldier, says Laca; but the foreman has heard that he has been passed over. Jenůfa and Grandmother Buryjovká are delighted at his words, but Laca cannot conceal his jealousy. Kostelnička appears and goes into the mill, and Grandmother Buryjovká suggests they follow her.

The jaunty song of the approaching recruits can be heard in the distance, and they are followed by Števa, who is extremely drunk. With an almost hysterical cry, Jenůfa tries to bring Števa to his senses, but he answers crossly, boasting of his prowess with the girls and throwing money to his companions. They start up a song, in which Števa joins, and the orchestra plays for the dance, into which Števa drags the unwilling Jenůfa.

Kostelnička interrupts imperiously. She is a formidable and authoritative – almost authoritarian – character, and when she reads the company a lecture there is no gainsaying her. Until Števa can prove that he has stopped drinking by a year of sobriety, there is to be no more talk of a wedding with Jenůfa. Nobody tries to contradict her, although the chorus comments that she is a bit too severe.

Grandmother Buryjovká sends the musicians packing, and tells Števa to go and sleep off his drunken condition. It is partly the fault of his companions that he is so drunk, she says – this causes an ironic comment from the said companions. The scene comes to an end with a short *fugato* in which her Grandmother warns Jenůfa that life is full of sorrow, which must be borne. In turn, she is joined by the foreman, Laca, the chorus and finally Jenůfa herself, whose line soars up to C flat.

Jenůfa and Števa are left alone, and Jenůfa pleads her love for him and her fear that her secret should be found out. Her music at this point is dominated by a recurrent figure (Ex.1). Jenůfa's confession of love and anxiety is dragged out of her, almost in spite of herself, with long pauses between phrases, yet the music never fails to convey the warmth of her nature. Števa answers crossly, and practically accuses Jenůfa and her stepmother of nagging at him, so that Jenůfa loses her patience. Even when he partially pulls himself together, his answers have a conventional gallantry. When Laca returns Jenůfa is alone in her misery; he makes derisive reference to Števa's hang-dog look when he felt the rough side of Kostelnička's tongue, but this only provokes Jenůfa

to take Števa's side even more firmly than before. Laca picks up the flowers which Števa has dropped and which were given him by some female admirer; let her pin *them* on her dress! Even this attempted insult Jenůfa accepts defiantly, for Števa's sake. Laca's comment is that Števa only looks at her because of her rosy-apple cheeks. He makes as if to embrace Jenůfa and slashes her across the cheek with the knife.

She runs into the house screaming, while Laca laments the horrible thing he has done. The servant Barena suggests that it happened accidentally, but the foreman accuses Laca of having, for all his present remorse, committed the crime on purpose.

Act II. The living-room of Kostelnička's house. A tense atmosphere is established in the music straight away, and the curtain goes up to show Kostelnička and Jenůfa sewing, the latter's wound still visible. They are talking about Jenůfa's secret; the baby has been born, but Jenůfa has not seen his father for weeks now. Kostelnička cannot find it in her heart to forgive Števa. Every utterance of Jenůfa's shows her joy in her child, every one of Kostelnička's the pride which has been so cruelly hurt by the shame which has come to her beloved stepchild and which has become an obsession. Kostelnička gives Jenůfa a drink with a narcotic in it to make her sleep, and Jenůfa goes into the bedroom.

Kostelnička has sent for Števa. She admits to herself that she has prayed that the child might die, but now she must steel herself to the thought of a marriage between Jenůfa and Števa. When Števa comes, she reproaches him for not having been to see them before; he admits he did not even know that the child had been born. He seems half remorseful for what he has done to Jenůfa, half resentful that her beauty has been spoilt – for that at least he cannot be blamed, although it means the end of his love for her. He will not grudge the child money – but no one must know that it is his.

Kostelnička pleads with him; at least he must see his child. As Števa says, her pleas would melt the heart of a stone:

They grow in intensity when Števa breaks down, but he eventually admits that he is contracted to marry Karolka, the mayor's daughter. Števa runs out and, as Kostelnička screams in horror, Jenůfa's voice is heard calling in her sleep. For a moment Kostelnička is afraid she has woken up, but there is no further sound and she continues to brood on the problem which seems now to be left to her to solve.

Laca comes in, angry that Števa was there but still anxious above all things to win the love of Jenůfa. He asks Kostelnička if Jenůfa is yet back from Vienna – it was given out that she went away – and is delighted to hear that she has returned. But Kostelnička has not the heart to hide the truth from him any longer, and she tells him about the child. He is horrified at the idea that marriage with Jenůfa involves taking Števa's baby, and Kostelnička makes her decision and tells him that the baby is dead. She sends him out to make enquiries about the wedding of Števa and Karolka, and is left alone, face to face with the facts as they are and the facts as she has represented them. For a moment she wonders whether she can hide the baby. No, he would always bring bad luck on Jenůfa; he is a true child of Števa. There is no other way but to kill him. The music represents her agony and indecision, and the scene is one of terrible power, particularly towards its end, when Kostelnička yells her own name in horrible reproach at her

shadow. She goes into the bedroom and brings the child out, wrapped in her shawl.

Jenůfa wakes, and calls for Kostelnička, tenderly at first, then more urgently as she begins to realise, half-drugged by the sleeping draught as she is, that Kostelnička is not there. She suddenly sees that her baby has gone too; Kostelnička must have taken him to the mill to show to Števa. She prays for his future, and the music is suffused with sadness and tenderness, which is dispelled for a moment when Kostelnička comes back in a state of extreme agitation, but returns after Jenůfa has been told that her child is dead and buried (Kostelnička explains this by saying that Jenůfa has been unconscious and delirious for two days, during which time his death and burial occurred).

Kostelnička tells Jenůfa that Števa has been there, and has offered to give the child money, but steadfastly refused to marry her. When Laca comes in, his joy at seeing Jenůfa again is touching in its sincerity. He asks Jenůfa if they cannot finish their lives together. Jenůfa is at first dignified and reserved, but she cannot hide her tender feelings for Laca, and Kostelnička exclaims to herself that her action has put everything right. Just then, the window blows open, and the icy blast brings a horrible sense of foreboding and disaster to Kostelnička who cries out in alarm, and clings desperately to Jenůfa and Laca.

Act III. The scene is the same as in Act II. Jenůfa, now looking much better, is preparing for the wedding, and Laca sits by her side. Near them is old Grandmother Buryjovká. Kostelnička, looking haggard and worn, paces up and down the room. The maid prattles away, but Kostelnička is obviously in a state of nervous exhaustion, and, when there is a knock at the door, she startles them all with her agitated reaction. It turns out to be only the mayor come to offer his congratulations, but even his equanimity cannot restore Kostelnička's calm. Eventually, she takes them all in to see the trousseau she has made for Jenůfa, and bride and bridegroom are left alone. Jenůfa is unhappy that her decision not to wear the customary wedding garland should have occasioned comment from the mayor's wife, but Laca gives her flowers and she pins them to her dress. He cannot stop reproaching himself for what he has done to her; all his life must be spent making her amends, if that is ever possible. It transpires that it is at Jenůfa's insistence that Laca has been reconciled to Števa, even to the extent of asking him to the wedding, with his bride-to-be.

Karolka comes in with Števa to congratulate the happy couple. The visit looks likely to be completed without a word from Števa, but Laca asks him whether his own wedding-day is yet fixed. In two weeks' time, says Števa; but Karolka is determined to play the minx, and says she may yet change her mind. Števa is indignant at the idea, but relapses into silence when Jenůfa expresses the hope that true love will never hurt him. The others return, and outside gathers a group of girls, headed by Barena. They sing a little wedding song, and then bride and bridegroom are blessed by Grandmother Buryjovká.

Suddenly, cries are heard outside. The body of the murdered baby has been discovered in the mill-stream now that the ice has melted. All rush out except Števa, Kostelnička and Grandmother Buryjovká. Kostelnička becomes hysterical, but attention shifts from her when the voice of Jenůfa can be heard from outside crying that she recognises the baby as hers. In spite of Laca's efforts, she continues to ask why the baby was not properly buried, and feeling against her rises until the mob is ready to stone her. Laca prepares to defend her, but silence falls on them all when Kostelnička raises her arms and tells them quite quietly that the guilt is hers. She tells the story, and for a moment Jenůfa turns from her in revulsion. But it is only too clear that her crime has been committed in an effort to do good, and Jenůfa's great act of forgiveness towards Kostelnička somehow redeems her action from its criminal implications. For a moment it looks as though Kostelnička will kill herself, then she remembers she will be needed as a witness if Jenůfa is not to suffer for something of which she is guiltless, and she goes quietly away with the mayor.

The others leave, but Jenůfa and Laca remain behind. Sadly Jenůfa tells him to follow them. She must live out her life alone, though she is grateful to him for his greatness of spirit, and readily forgives him for the injury he did her. Laca begs to be allowed to remain at her side, and his reward is Jenůfa's great cry of exultation as she understands that their sufferings have brought them a greater love than she has ever known. This is not just a conventional happy ending. The music has a freshness of its own, and the quality of Laca's devotion is pointed up by situation and music alike.   H.

OSUD

Fate

Opera in three acts, libretto by the composer and Fedora Bartošová. Première on Brno radio, September 1934; stage première, Brno, October 1958, with Jindra Pokorná, Jaroslav Ulrych, conductor František Jílek; Stuttgart, 1958, with Lore Wissmann, Josef Traxel; B.B.C. (radio), 1972, with Marie Collier, Gregory Dempsey, conductor Vilem Tausky (in English); 1978, Česke Budějovice, in original form; London (in Czech, in concert), 1983, with Eilene Hannan, Philip Langridge, conductor Simon Rattle; English National Opera, 1984, with Hannan, Langridge, conductor Mark Elder (in English).

Míla Valková	Soprano
Živny, *a composer*	Tenor
Míla's Mother	Soprano
Dr Suda	Tenor
Two Ladies	Sopranos
Old Slovak Woman	Soprano
Major's Wife	Soprano
Councillor's Wife	Soprano
Lhotsky, *a painter*	Baritone
Konečny	Baritone
Miss Stuhlá, *a teacher*	Mezzo-Soprano
Miss Pacovská, *a student*	Soprano
Two Guests	Baritone, Bass
Waiter	Tenor
An Engineer	Tenor
A Young Widow	Soprano
A Student	Tenor
Fanča	Soprano
Doubek, *Míla and Živny's son*	(Act II) Treble, (Act III) Tenor
Hrázda	Tenor
Verva	Baritone
Součková	Soprano
Košinká	Soprano

Schoolmistresses, Students, Schoolgirls, Guests at the Spa, Students at the Conservatory

Place: A Spa Town
Time: About 1900
Running Time: 1 hour 20 minutes

The genesis of *Osud* is one of the most curious in operatic history, just as curious as its almost total rejection for more than seventy-five years of its existence. In 1903, with *Jenůfa* completed but unperformed, his beloved daughter Olga dead, and his marriage more or less at an end, Janáček went on his own to the spa town of Luhačovice (a holiday in Luhačovice became a habit in later life). In 1903, he met Kamila Urválková, a pretty young woman who told him that the composer Vítězslav Čelansky had written an opera called *Kamila* and in it depicted her as a heartless flirt who jilted her sincere admirer (the composer disguised as poet). Would Janáček right this wrong by composing another opera whose theme would clear her name? The astonishing thing is that Janáček agreed, attracted presumably by the idea of the wronged composer who writes an opera which he cannot finish because he cannot predict the future. He himself drafted a scenario, calling the principal female character Míla Valková, and asked a young female friend of Olga's to put the whole thing into verse.

Real life continued to play a part in the drafting and, when Mrs Urválková's husband discovered her relationship with Janáček, the correspondence was brought to an abrupt end. Janáček showed remarkable consistency and Míla Valková, who is prominent in the first act of *Osud*, plays a lesser part in Act II and is killed off at its end. What had started as some kind of justification of Kamila Urválková finishes as an exposition of Janáček's own creed and particularly his feelings about the interplay of an artist's private life and his creative function.

The opera seems to have been accepted in principle for production at Brno but not performed, and it was even accepted by a small theatre on the outskirts of Prague where none other than Čelansky was music director. Later on, even his friend and translator Max Brod, whom Janáček trusted, felt that because of its weak libretto there was little future for *Osud*, and it was not until a broadcast in 1934 that the work was first heard at all. When it was staged in 1958, its shape was altered and the first two acts were inserted into Act III as a huge flashback. In 1978 it was at last heard and seen as Janáček planned it.

Perhaps 'flashback' is an important word, as it was after a hugely successful concert performance under Simon Rattle at the Queen Elizabeth Hall in London that David Pountney was inspired to present the opera at the Coliseum, not using the technique of flashback, but making use of the quick cutting between scenes which is a cinematic commonplace. In this way the work's unusual shaping – it was Janáček's work after all, and he was by then an experienced composer – and the close juxtaposition of one disparate event with another emerged as perfectly natural and the opera could be seen as a mature work. In Pountney's view, Fedora Bartošová was inexperienced but far from incompetent and acted as the composer's faithful collaborator, turning into verse the unusual scenario of a man whose ideas were ahead of their times.

Before the opera begins, we are to know that Míla has had an affair with the composer Živny. He was neither rich nor respectable enough to please Míla's mother, who contrived to drive a wedge between them and even introduced Míla to someone more appropriate as her future husband. But Míla was pregnant by Živny and her mother's marriage plans came to nothing. Nevertheless, Živny was convinced that he had been jilted for someone richer, and he put his bitter personal feelings into the opera he was writing.

Act I. It is a beautiful day in a spa town and everyone – Dr Suda, his female companions, students, schoolgirls – to a seductive waltz worship the sun and the pleasures that come with it. Míla, fashionably dressed, is greeted by Lhotsky and Dr Suda, before she notices Živny, whom she has not seen since their affair was abruptly ended. Živny's identity is a matter for speculation among the other bystanders, but Konečny knows him. Živny cannot keep away from Míla and seems to make rather acid reference to the subject of his opera.

Míla asks Živny if he has come to see their son. It is obvious that for him the affair is not at an end and that her interest has quickly returned, but their conversation is interrupted by Miss Stuhlá, a schoolteacher, as she exhorts her group of ladies at their choral rehearsal. Students mock them and it is pretty obvious that the rehearsal is not going to go uninterrupted. Organised for a picnic, Dr Suda and Lhotsky bring in a bagpiper and that doesn't help the rehearsal either. Schoolgirls join in and decorate Dr Suda's umbrella with ribbons, and the fun includes a song from Dr Suda and chorus. Guests sit down for a meal, Miss Stuhlá can be seen and heard having another go at rehearsal, but even respectable people like Dr Suda don't seem to take her seriously and the hubbub increases until Míla's mother can be made out pushing through the throng looking for her daughter, and very put out when someone suggests that she was seen with Živny. To a jaunty tune, Dr Suda and the bagpiper set off followed by the schoolgirls. Miss Stuhlá's rehearsal is all too plainly in ruins.

Živny and Míla have not found it difficult to get together again and they sit ostensibly ordering something in the restaurant but in reality falling in love all over again. Živny is romantic, even passionate, and after she has heard his account of how his love survived the grief of separation, Míla in a beautiful passage more calmly describes the false position her mother forced her into, confessing that she was always in love with Živny, even once willing him to look at her while he was conducting in the opera house, but in vain. She used to fantasise about a rapprochement, and believed somebody must have spoken badly about her to Živny. They are interrupted by the return of the excursion, and Konečny starts to read a poem. Janáček's 'poetic' timescale, as at the end of *Kátya*, is very much his own, and a quarter of an hour after they have hymned the rising sun, the picnickers are returning home in pairs at night! Míla and Živny plan to go away together but she still worries about the effect that might have on her mother. The mother comes in, and explodes when it is suggested that Míla is with Živny. Students flirt, Míla's mother metaphorically wrings her hands, the other guests at the spa call it all 'just a summer romance'.

The first act adds up to an extraordinary mosaic of crowd activity depicted in music of brilliance and variety and contrasted well with the joyful intensity of the revived relationship between Míla and Živny.

Act II. Four years later. Míla and Živny are married, but the atmosphere is uneasy and somehow dominated by the instability of her mother's personality. It is evening in winter, we are in Živny's study, the piano in the background, their son Doubek at play. Živny and Míla look through his opera and they seem unable to resist reliving the pain its story recalls. Whether they now like it or not, he wrote the early part of the opera when he was in a state of shock and indignation after what he felt was her infidelity; can Míla now hear it without recrimination? Míla's mother continues to fulminate like a background dragon, and Míla sends her little boy off to his nanny. Živny plays, and takes the initiative in asking Míla to put her trust in him; in a sinister way Míla's mother continues to echo his sentiments. He tries to excuse the way he wrote the opera; he wanted to strike at her, but in one sense it was always a lie.

At this point Doubek intervenes. His nanny and her boyfriend have impressed the child with their love and he wants his mother to explain what love is. Míla's mother is distraught, nothing can restrain her, and she rushes at Živny. In her mad struggles, both mother and daughter fall over the balcony. Míla is dead and the little boy can't understand what has happened. To Živny it all appears 'a bolt from the blue', with no warning thunder.

Act III. It is eleven years later – the present. The orchestral introduction is stormy. At the conservatory where Živny works, students are singing a chorus from his opera. They will be at the première; Živny has told them that it is finished apart from the finale, which is in God's hands. The hero is Živny himself, Verva says, and starts to explain it, quoting bits from the opera including the scene of Doubek and his nanny. When Živny comes in, they ask him to tell them about it and this he does in a long *scena* in which he talks of Míla's beauty and sweetness, and moves on to a grandiose apology for his own life and creed, rising to moments of almost hysterical intensity. It is one of Janáček's great scenes and Živny explains his sense of failure, which painfully matches what must have been Janáček's own feelings: years of teaching students, years of trying to get his music performed in Prague, years convinced of failure. He is roused to an impassioned climax and when his son brings him a glass of water, lightning seems to strike the room and Živny collapses. He continues to murmur snatches of the opera but insists that the last act is 'in God's hands'. Janáček's biographer, Jaroslav Vogel, astutely says that his last remark somehow implies to the listener that *Osud* as well as Živny's opera-within-an-opera lacks a last act.

It is on record that Janáček himself attempted more than once to have the libretto re-written but it is doubtful if that would have solved the opera's problems, which in terms of balance between acts (or 'scenes', as we may think of them), to say nothing of the lack of overt drama in the last act (in spite of its magnificent inner tensions), are very real. Curiously enough, the solution seems uncomplicated: play the opera for what it is worth and on its own terms and, with a powerfully musical singer as Živny, it will justify the dislocated but poetic scenario, which was after all Janáček's own. To be in advance of one's times may seem unrealistic at the moment, but with hindsight, not unjustified.   H.

THE ADVENTURES OF MR BROUČEK

Vylety Páně Broučkovy

Opera in two parts, libretto by V. Dyk and F.S. Procházka, after Svatopluk Čech. Première, Prague, 23 April 1920, with M. Stork, M. Jenik, E. Miriovská, V. Pivonková, V. Zitek, B. Novak, conductor Otakar Ostrčil.[1] Revived Brno, January 1939. First performed Munich, 1959, with Lorenz Fehenberger, Wilma Lipp, Antonie Fahberg, Fritz Wunderlich, Kurt Böhme, Keith Engen, conductor Joseph Keilberth. Revived Prague, 1968, with Beno Blachut and Helena Tattermuschová, conductor Jaroslav Krombholc (this production seen at Holland and Edinburgh Festivals, 1970); Berlin, German Opera, 1969, with Martin Vantin; B.B.C. broadcast, 1970, with John Winfield, conductor Mackerras; English National Opera, 1978, with Gregory Dempsey, conductor Mackerras; 1992, with Graham Clark, conductor Mark Elder, producer David Pountney.

Prague 1888	The Moon	Prague 1420	
Mathias Brouček,[2] a landlord		....	Tenor
Mazal, *a painter*	Blankytny[3]	Petřik	Tenor
Sacristan	Lunobor	Domšík	Bass-Baritone
Málinka	Etherea	Kunka	Soprano
Würfl	President[3]	A Magistrate	Bass
Pot-Boy at the Inn	An Infant Prodigy	Student...................	Soprano
Mrs Fanny Novak	——	Kedruta	Contralto
A Guest at the Inn	Oblačny[3]	Vacek	Baritone
A Professor	Duhoslav, *the painter*	Vojta of the Peacocks	Tenor
A Composer	Professor Harfoboj[3]	Miroslav *the goldsmith*	Tenor
Apparition of the Poet[4]	——	——	Baritone[4]

Place: Prague, 1888; the Moon; Prague, 1420
Time: The Night of 12/13 July, 1888
Running Time: 2 hours 15 minutes

For many years *Mr Brouček* was criticised, partly because the book is peculiar and some commentators have felt that the composer made an unhappy choice, and partly because it neither continues the 'folk' line of *Jenůfa* nor employs the concise and fully evolved style of the last four operas.

The story is taken from two novels by the poet Svatopluk Čech chosen from several works in which he satirises a worldly but typical citizen of Prague – *The Excursion of Mr Brouček to the Moon* (1887) and *New, Sensational Excursion of Mr Brouček, this time into the 15th Century* (1888). No fewer than nine different literary figures contributed something to the first part of the libretto, which was on the stocks between 1908 and 1917 and was finally edited and put into its present shape by Viktor Dyk. The second part was written by F.S. Procházka, and Janáček set it in a matter of seven months in 1917, spurred on no doubt by the war situation, the prospect of a better future for the Czech nation, and the parallel with events of five hundred years earlier. In the figure of Mr Brouček, Janáček satirises the philistinism of Bohemia's middle class, just as ridiculous on the unattainable Moon as in the equally remote past, and identifies his unimaginative hero firmly with the *petit bourgeois* of his own times.

Part I. The Adventures of Mr Brouček on the Moon. The prelude, in typically Janáček vein, alternates a matter-of-fact rapid staccato quaver figure associated with Brouček (first heard early on in bassoon), Ex. 1:

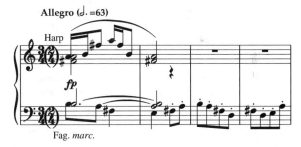

and a glorious and expansive lyrical phrase, Ex. 2:

associated with the love of Málinka and Mazal initially but perhaps also with the idealism which a compassionate spirit can find within us all. The two conflicting themes and their variants permeate the music.

It is a moonlight night outside the Vikárka Inn

---

[1] Ostrčil was second conductor in Prague at the time, newly engaged, and Janáček's old enemy Kovařovic was still music director.

[2] Brouček in Czech is a small beetle.

[3] For the London Coliseum in 1978 translated respectively as Starry-Eyes,

Wonderglitter, Dreamy Cloud and the Harper.

[4] Written in the bass clef and sung by a high baritone, or even (as in the Prague recording) by a tenor.

below Hradčany Castle in Prague. To the right is the Cathedral and near it the home of the Sacristan. Málinka, the Sacristan's daughter, is quarrelling with her lover, Mazal, whose quasi-ecstatic phrases contrast throughout with the more fragmentary sounds of the argument. Yesterday he was out dancing with Fanny, Mr Brouček's housekeeper – and she for her part might as well marry Mr Brouček! Their quarrel is interrupted first by the Sacristan, then by carousing in the inn, and a moment later by Mr Brouček, each of whom contributes to further misunderstanding, the Sacristan by supposing that he must defend his daughter's honour, Mr Brouček by his quarrelsome tipsiness and unfortunate references to Fanny and by his insistence on the possibility of life on the Moon. Mazal tries to divert his landlord's attentions by references to the Moon and then goes back inside the inn. Brouček makes an absent-minded attempt to comfort the distraught Málinka by telling her she is not bad-looking and will certainly find a man.

Artists are drinking in the inn and everyone shouts something after the departing Mr Brouček, some about the sausages he has forgotten, Málinka about marriage, and Würfl the innkeeper merely with his mechanical invitation to come again soon. Initiated by Ex. 2, there is a short duet of considerable tenderness for Mazal and Málinka at the end of which Mr Brouček comes unsteadily back into sight, staring at the Moon. At least up there he would have no worries about tenants like Mazal who don't pay their rent. Gradually, to the sound of hidden voices, Brouček seems to rise towards this desirable dwelling place, everything is covered in a white mist and we are conducted by an ecstatic violin solo to the Moon itself.

In the background is a castle and in the foreground Brouček lies asleep. A moonbeam, Blankytny by name but wearing the aspect and voice of Mazal, arrives on a horse and ties it to the stem of a flower. He is a poet and reacts with astonishment and horror when Brouček addresses him as Mazal and tries to shake him by the hand. Brouček is equally angry that his tenant fails to recognise him and misunderstanding grows as Blankytny speaks with mounting lyrical enthusiasm of beauty and the exalted nature of his lady love (whom to touch would be to dissolve), only for Brouček's answers to be as matter-of-fact as the sausages which fall out of his pocket. Lunobor, a sort of Moon wizard-monster to look at, an aesthete by outlook, announces the arrival of the object of Blankytny's exaggerated affections, his daughter Etherea, who sounds like Málinka and sings a pretty waltz. The sight of Brouček has the strangest effect on them all, and the trio of Etherea, Blankytny and Brouček ends with Etherea embracing Brouček and flying off with him on the back of the horse on which Blankytny arrived, just as Lunobor returns to read them some chapters of Moon wisdom.

We move (with Ex. 2 to the fore in the orchestral preamble) to the Temple of Arts. The scene seems to be presided over by the President (Würfl), who says he himself lacks all talent and might have decided to become a critic had he not been kind-hearted by nature. He corrects and praises the musicians, and describes himself as a patron, regularly painted and sculpted by the artists and the subject of their songs. The horse alights at the foot of the staircase with Etherea and Brouček on board. She proclaims them lovers and asks for the protection of the President, who reacts with some mildness to the highly matter-of-fact answers Brouček returns to his questioning. Blankytny laments his lost love, but Lunobor, Etherea's father, catches her and starts to take her away, while Brouček remains an object of admiration and wonder to all the lunar dwellers.

Oblačny leads the artists in their attempts to welcome Brouček, dancers perform in his honour, a child-prodigy (with an ever-playing piccolo at its lips) joins the chorus of admiration, until the President suggests a meal. The prodigy sings the National Anthem,[1] whose gist is that Moon creatures smell their food instead of eating it, Etherea returns to the scene and makes up to Brouček again, but he finds her little more than a cobweb, will never kneel down when he is asked to, and finally shocks them by falling asleep and in a half-voice muttering, 'Waiter! Roast and two veg., please!'

The flowers which the child prodigy waves under his nose succeed in waking him up and he tells them that he has had sufficient delectation for his nose. The coarse word shocks them again and they start to withdraw from him. Duhoslav the painter insists that he admire the picture which he is painting –

---

[1] A verbal parody of the (in 1917) newly established Czech National Anthem.

such glorious colours! Brouček surreptitiously covers his face and eats a sausage, deceiving the artists at first into thinking that he is weeping, only, a moment later, for the horrible truth to emerge. They are sorry for him and are astonished that he cannot feed on flowers like them. He tells them in a matter-of-fact way that only vegetarians behave like that on earth, sensible people preferring meat. Etherea makes a last attempt on his virtue, dancing round him until Brouček blows furiously at her and she subsides on the ground in a tangled cobwebby mess. Brouček mounts Pegasus and flies away, leaving Harfoboj and the child-prodigy to lead the musicians in praising the President.

Fog starts to invade the scene and an ecstatic interlude (Ex. 2 important again) takes us back to the Vikárka Inn, with the artists about to leave and Mr Würfl standing at the door. They thank him and say goodnight, the pot-boy announcing that Mr Brouček is being carried helplessly home (Ex. 1). The scene is left to Málinka and Mazal, the former returning home after a night of love with the latter; the music touchingly foreshadows the great double love duet of *Kátya Kabanová*'s second act.

Part II. The Excursion of Mr Brouček into the Fifteenth Century.

Act I. In the foreground, the Vikárka Inn; in the background, the Treasure Chamber of King Wenceslas IV. The period will shortly be that of the Hussite Wars,[1] 1420; jewels, helmets and armour in gold and silver, swords, shields, dishes, crowns and so on stand all around. The music at first is much less lyrical than that of Part I. Voices can be heard in the distance talking of subterranean passages and underground hideouts, and Brouček in an aside proclaims his belief in such a passage. Würfl is unkind enough to mention Brouček's excursion to the Moon and there is laughter, but when Würfl bids them all goodnight, Brouček is left calling for help and light and, in an extended monologue, wondering what on earth has happened.

The portrait of King Wenceslas suddenly turns round and Brouček falls into the treasure chamber.

Suddenly he is confronted with the apparition of the poet Svatopluk Čech,[2] from whose works the opera derives, in an unearthly light and explaining in a passage of measured solemnity,[3] Ex. 3:

that the idealistic actions of the past necessarily, in view of present circumstances, inspire him to celebrate freedom with a certain irony. It is not just an old man longing for the past, but the statement of a disappointed patriot,[4] and the chorale-like music (*not* derived from subsequent chorale quotations) colours the whole of the medieval section of the opera.

Brouček now stands outside, wondering if he has found a short-cut to remember in future. There is no proper light – he must write to the press and complain – but he is very taken aback when a moment later he is stopped by a citizen who at first does not understand what he says and then takes him for a German, moreover a spy for King Zikmund. The Magistrate (who sings with the voice of Würfl) is astonished at Brouček's reference to 'the late Žižka' and at his insistence that Žižka beat King Zikmund in 1420 but that this is now history as he speaks in 1888. In spite of his cries for help they take him before the judge.

In front of his house, and as the voices of the armed populace can be heard singing from the distance, the judge Domšík (Sacristan) asks Brouček who he is. Brouček at last grasps the situation and, remembering the Moon, says that he has come from the land of the Turks, which explains why his Czech sounds strange. They agree to enroll him, as the Hussites, the warriors of God, enter the square singing a chorale and going into church – a concise but splendid musical climax to the scene.

Act II. A room in Domšík's house. Through the window can be seen the Town Hall and the Square. Brouček sits on the bed and wonders what on earth has happened to him that he should find himself a Hussite –

[1] Jan Hus, burnt at the stake in 1415 for heresy, was influenced by the Englishman Wycliffe and like him advocated the printing of the Scriptures in the vernacular. His followers split into two, one group based on Prague, the other – the Taborites – adopting an extremist position and opposing much of the Church's ritual. In 1420, King Zikmund led an army against the Hussites, who, under Jan Žižka, defeated their opponents at the battle of Vitkov Hill.
[2] In Brno's production of 1967 transferred to form a prologue to Part II.

[3] Heard first at the rise of the curtain in the orchestra.
[4] In Edinburgh in 1970, at the opera's first British performance, the role of Svatopluk Čech was sung by the baritone Zdeněk Otava, who had been the original Baron Prus at the première of *The Makropulos Affair* in 1926 – an opera many in the audience had been listening to the night before. The poised intensity of his singing made an extraordinary effect, as if the veteran baritone were embodying all that is best in the Czech soul.

the music suggests his nervous state. He is interrupted by the sight of Kedruta, whom he takes for his house-keeper Fanny (referred to but not visible in the first scene). Domšík comes in and tells him to put on some proper – medieval – clothes, which Brouček does with neither enthusiasm nor competence. The people can be heard coming from church, again singing, this time the Hussite chorale 'Hear ye, the warriors of God'.[1]

Kunka (the daughter of Domšík and bearing as much resemblance to Málinka as her father does to the Sacristan) leads in her father's guests. In succession, Brouček is introduced to Vacek, Miroslav and Vojta. Kunka reports a militant sermon and all drink to the future, not least Brouček, who is congratulated on his prowess as a potman. When he says that abroad the Czechs are not much liked, all agree that this is a calumny which must be repudiated as soon as possible by victory over the oppressors. A student blames it all on the Taborite priests, to the anger of Vacek, but Brouček diverts attention by proclaiming that he is not interested in fighting Zikmund, who means nothing to him. Domšík is in process of rescuing him from an embarrassing situation when the voice of Petřík can be heard calling them to arms. Brouček cannot elude the distribution of arms and finishes by finding a pike in his hands. The music momentarily takes a lyrical turn as Kunka bids her father a tender farewell, kneeling at his departure and praying for victory for him and for the patriots (Ex. 3 in orchestra). As soon as they have gone she seizes a weapon and runs out in spite of the efforts of Kedruta to restrain her. Kedruta is left behind singing the Lord's Prayer while the Hussite chorale is heard outside. Suddenly Brouček appears, tears off his costume to put back his own clothes, lights a cigar and rushes out.

The next scene is in the old Town Square. The sun is setting and the square is full of people. The return-ing armies of Praguers and Taborites, Jan Žižka at their head, enter after their victory over King Zikmund, to the acclamation of children and popu-lace alike in a scene of considerable musical splen-dour. Brouček is noticed trying to escape from Domšík's house, and he spins an obviously false story to the questioning Taborites. Before Petřík can finish explaining what really happened, Kunka appears lamenting the death of her father and trying to take comfort from Petřík's presence among them. She goes into the house as Petřík recounts the story of Brouček's cowardice: he ran straight up to one of the German knights, knelt before him crying, 'My lord, I am yours! No Praguer, no Hussite! *Gnade!*' The Councillor, Vojta and the people demand his death. Brouček's excuses – that he is a child of the future and not yet born – seem of little avail.

As the barrel, Brouček inside it, catches fire, the stage grows cloudy again, tension relaxes (music from the Moon) and the light of the fire turns into a candle in Würfl's hand outside the Vikárka Inn, where Mr Brouček can be seen in a barrel (into which he fell drunk before going to sleep). His cries seem nearer to lamentation in his predicament than to rejoicing at his salvation, but he accepts Würfl's help up the stairs, assuring him that his adventures have indeed been strange – but let nobody be told about them! The opera ends, fast and brilliant without even a glance at the idealistic Ex. 2, but with a sly reference in the harps to Ex. 3.

In the past, commentators in and out of Czechoslovakia used to describe the music as feeble and stress the savage nature of Janáček's attack on the shortcomings of his fellow-countrymen through the central figure of Brouček, preferring his musical mockery of Prague-1420 as compared with the Moon-1888. Granted the sheer peculiarity of the stories Janáček has chosen, the music remains engaging, moving, and above all original. With its kaleidoscopic mixture of satire and sentiment, of genuine patriotic fervour and relentless spoofing of aesthetic and chauvinistic pretension, it will yet win acclaim due to the power of its musical invention, which creates a sound world of its own, enveloping, invigorating and wholly delightful.   H.

KÁTYA KABANOVÁ

Opera in three acts, text by Cervinka, founded on Ostrovsky's *The Storm*. Première, Brno, 23 October 1921, with Marie Veselá, Karel Zavřel, conductor Neumann. First performed in Prague, 1922, conductor Ostrčil; in German, translated by Max Brod, at Cologne, 1922, with Rose Pauly, Schröder, con-ductor Klemperer; Berlin, 1926. First performed in England, Sadler's Wells, 1951, with Shuard, Rowland Jones, conductor

---

[1] Used by Smetana in the finale of *Libuše*.

Mackerras (later Kubelík); in America, New York, 1960, with Shuard, Doree, Gari, Petrak, conductor Halasz; Edinburgh Festival, 1964, by Prague Opera with Domaninská; Florence (Italian première), 1957, by Belgrade Opera; Glyndebourne, 1988 (in Czech), with Nancy Gustafson, Felicity Palmer, Louise Winter, Barry McCauley, conductor Andrew Davis, producer Nikolaus Lehnhoff.

Vanya Kudrjash, *clerk to Dikoy*..........................Tenor

Glasha, *a servant*.................................Mezzo-Soprano

Dikoy, *a rich merchant* ....Bass

Boris Grigoryevich, *his nephew* ....Tenor

Feklusha, *a servant*............................Mezzo-Soprano

Marfa Kabanová, *a rich merchant's widow*
(Kabanicha) ....Contralto

Tikhon Ivanich Kabanov, *her son*......................Tenor

Varvara, *foster-child in the Kabanov*
household......................................Mezzo-Soprano

Katerina Kabanová (Kátya), *Tikhon's wife*.....Soprano

Kuligin, *friend of Vanya*................................Baritone

Place: The Little Town of Kalinov on the Banks of the Volga, in Russia
Time: About 1860
Running Time: 1 hour 55 minutes

Janáček's marriage in 1880 to a German-speaking girl from Brno seems to have been a stormy affair from the start – within a year, Zdenka had returned to her parents and the young composer was attempting to woo her back by escorting her to the door of the German-speaking theatre, which he would himself on principle not enter. In 1917, on holiday in Luhačovice, he met Kamila Stösslová, and at the age of sixty-three fell in love with this twenty-five-year-old married woman in such a way as to revolutionise the remainder of his life. Two-thirds of his greatest music was written in his last dozen years, much of it explicitly inspired by Kamila, and nowhere else in musical history is there an instance of such late flowering on so prolific a scale, and for so romantic a reason. Czech musical historians are not charitable about Kamila, but the rest of the world has reason for gratitude for what she meant to the composer. Their association lasted to the end of Janáček's life, and its first musical fruit is *Kátya*.

In *Kátya Kabanová*, written between 1918 and 1921, Janáček contrasts the old and the new, the ancient Slavonic matriarchy (symbolised in Kabanicha) and the independent, enlightened modern generation (symbolised by Varvara and Vanya Kudrjash). In between these two conflicting forces are

found the unemancipated Kátya and Boris; Kátya is oppressed by Kabanicha and Boris by his uncle, Dikoy.

The prelude, with its *pp* B flat chords and its fateful drum figure against muted trombones, is concerned with setting the atmosphere which is to prevail throughout the opera, but at the same time it serves as an exposition of leading motifs. We are made acquainted soon after the opening with an agonised figure of three (later four) adjacent chromatic notes which, it has been suggested, symbolises the painful friction of people living too closely together; the first *allegro* passage has an important theme in the oboe (much used later in the opera) against a background of flute and sleigh-bells (Tikhon's departure); but most important of all is the tender

which dominates the prelude, and, with its derivations, is heard frequently in the course of the opera.

Act I. The curtain rises to show the outside of the Kabanovs' house, which stands on the banks of the Volga. Kudrjash exclaims at the beauty of the river – a point of view with which Glasha, who works for Kabanicha, cannot sympathise. In the distance can be seen Dikoy, waving his arms about angrily as is his custom; Vanya and Glasha retire out of sight in case he takes it into his head to give them a piece of his mind. Dikoy comes in, complaining at his nephew Boris's laziness – though what he is expected to work at on a Sunday morning Boris himself is unable to guess. Dikoy makes no secret of his impatience with Boris, but he goes away when he learns from Glasha that Kabanicha is still in church.

Kudrjash listens sympathetically while Boris explains that he only stays with his tyrannical relation because of the terms of his grandmother's will; the money is to go to him and his sister when they come of age, provided they do what their uncle tells them. His sister has so far been kept away from Dikoy by their mother's family in Moscow, and if it were not for her, Boris himself would long ago have left Dikoy and given up his inheritance.

At that moment, church-goers are seen coming back from the service, and Kudrjash has to be

Kátya Kabanová *(Welsh National Opera, 1982, director David Pountney, designer Maria Bjørnson).*
Rita Gorr as Kabanicha, Elisabeth Söderström as Kátya.

restrained from leaving by the overwrought Boris. As Boris laments his rapidly-departing youth, Kátya's theme is stated *dolce* and for the first time by the oboe.

At the same time, Glasha tells Feklusha that her employer, Kabanicha, is a hypocritical old tyrant. Boris gazes into the distance and his rapturous phrases tell the listener as plainly as his words that he is in love. To the accompaniment of repeated statements of Kátya's theme, he admits to Kudrjash that Kátya is the object of his adoration – a married woman! The theme is heard in its most characteristic form as Kátya comes into sight:

Kabanicha leads her little family party back from church. She pauses in front of the house to urge Tikhon, if he wants to please his mother, to go that very day to the market at Kazan. He immediately agrees, but Kabanicha makes a sneering reference to his wife Kátya, and suggests that since his marriage he has paid his mother less than the respect and deference due to her. Tikhon hotly protests that he loves both, but when Kátya also gently claims to love her mother-in-law, Kabanicha turns and insults her. Varvara is sarcastic: 'Oh, what a place to choose for a sermon!'[1] Kátya goes into the house, and Kabanicha continues her abuse; Tikhon is too soft with Kátya, and would make no protest even if she were to take a lover. Kabanicha goes, and Varvara abuses Tikhon for not taking Kátya's part more firmly; she knows exactly what he will do now – drink to forget the scene. Varvara is alone as the curtain falls; 'Oh, how could anyone *not* love her?' is her comment on Kátya's unhappiness.

The second scene is set inside the Kabanovs' house. Kátya and Varvara are in conversation, and the former pours out her heart to Varvara. She is unhappy in her present surroundings – a fact Varvara knows well. When she was young and unmarried, she was as free as the birds, and like them she wandered unhindered wherever she wished. She describes her girlhood. Even then, her mother knew nothing of her fancies and longings. The music grows

in intensity as she describes going to church alone: 'I felt as if I was entering Paradise', she says. She saw visions of angels, lofty golden cathedrals high in the sky; she felt as if she were flying over the mountains and forests, surrounded by invisible choirs.

Varvara encourages her to describe her dreams. She says she feels that a voice is whispering in her ear, someone is embracing her and urging her to go with him – and she yields to his persuasion. Kátya breaks off; how can Varvara, a child, understand what she means? But Varvara protests that she is not as innocent as Kátya thinks; she has sins on her own conscience. Kátya says that no sin can be worse than that of loving some other man than one's own husband, but Varvara asks why that should seem so dreadful; perhaps when Tikhon has gone, Kátya will see this other man.

Kátya protests vehemently, and at this moment Tikhon appears, saying that he must leave immediately for Kazan, as his mother wishes him to. In spite of Kátya's protests, he can neither remain nor take her with him. Kátya asks him to make her swear a dreadful oath not to see or speak to a stranger while he is away, but he flatly refuses to ask her to do any such thing. Kátya starts to formulate an oath, but Kabanicha comes in and bids her son prepare for the journey. Before he leaves, he must give his orders to his wife – and in the presence of his mother, so that she may hear exactly what he says. He repeats in a milder form the injunctions of Kabanicha, and, in spite of his protests, they include a prohibition against seeing other men. It looks as though Kátya will break down as she kisses her husband goodbye – Kabanicha's grim comment is 'Shameless girl! Is he your lover?'

Act II. Living-room of the Kabanovs' house, later the same day. When the curtain rises, Kabanicha is obviously in the middle of a spate of nagging at Kátya. Why can't she be like other wives – those that love their husbands, that's to say – and stay weeping in her room for the rest of the day when he goes away? She might at least pretend to weep; that would show people her word is to be trusted! Having vented her spleen, Kabanicha leaves the room.

Varvara says the room is stuffy; she will go into the garden, using the key which Kabanicha *thinks* she has hidden, but for which Varvara has substituted

---

[1] Translation by Norman Tucker.

another. If she should see 'him', says Varvara cryptically, she will tell him that Kátya is waiting by the gate
of the garden. Varvara goes out leaving the key. For a
while Kátya wrestles with temptation; she has the key
to hand, should she use it? Suddenly, she can hear the
voice of Kabanicha, but the danger passes, and the
flood of relief which succeeds it tells her more certainly
than could anything else that her love for Boris is too
strong for her. Nothing could be more psychologically
right than the musical portrayal of this sudden and
involuntary crumbling away of resistance.

Kátya goes out, to be succeeded by Kabanicha, followed by Dikoy. Straight away he admits that he is a
bit drunk but protests that he does not want to go
home. 'Speak to me harshly' is the request he has
come to make of Kabanicha – she alone dares do such
a thing. Money is the thing that causes him to sin.
The other day a peasant asked him to repay some
money; he cursed him, all but thrashed him, and then
went down on his knees to beg forgiveness. 'You
should learn better manners' is Kabanicha's retort.
The whole episode has a coarse and overblown erotic
base, the very converse of what is to follow.

The scene changes to the garden below the house.
The summer night is hot. Vanya arrives first and
sings a carefree peasant song to balalaika accompaniment. He is waiting for Varvara, and is surprised to
see Boris, who explains that someone he passed in the
dark told him to come there, and he felt that he
should not ignore the suggestion. Vanya tries to warn
him, but Boris is plainly too much in love to benefit
from warnings. Varvara signals her arrival by singing
another snatch of folk-like melody, to which Vanya
makes appropriate answer. As she passes Boris, she
tells him that Kátya will not be long. He waits impatiently and with growing excitement as Kátya comes
into sight. In spite of herself, Kátya admits her love for
him and falls into his arms. There is apprehension as
well as poignancy and yearning in their duet. The
whole scene is saturated with the magic of the
summer night, and a unique effect is produced by the
blend and contrast of the characteristics of the two
pairs of lovers, the one passionate and carefree, the
other rapturous but guilty. The singing ends with a
little folk-like duet for Varvara and Vanya, but the
shattering emotional climax comes in the orchestra,
when Kátya and Boris return to the stage and their
pent-up feelings are expressed in three highly charged

orchestral phrases, which are more revealing than
might be a vocal section of ten times the length.

Act III. Ten days later. A tumbledown summerhouse on a terrace by the Volga. Kudrjash and
Kuligin, his friend, take shelter from the storm which
threatens, and which bursts upon them with considerable violence. They look at the pictures on the
walls; there is one of Ivan the Terrible, which elicits
the sarcastic comment that Russia has never wanted
for tyrants – there is one in every family. As if to
match the words, Dikoy comes in, pushing everyone
out of his way, and complaining that he sees far too
much of Kudrjash every day to want to see him
again. Kudrjash suggests that the frequent storms
indicate the village should have lightning-conductors; he tries to explain what they are, but meets
short shrift from the superstitious Dikoy, who takes
each storm to be a warning from God.

The rain stops and all leave the shelter, except Boris
and Kudrjash. Varvara appears, and whispers to Boris
that Tikhon is back, and his return has driven Kátya
quite out of her senses, so that she seems ill with
worry. Boris hides as Kátya comes in, supported by her
husband and preceded by Kabanicha. Thunder can be
heard in the distance and the storm starts all over
again at just the moment when Kátya catches sight of
Boris. In spite of the efforts of Varvara, who tries to
restrain her, she calls to Tikhon and Kabanicha at the
top of her voice, and confesses not only her adultery
but names the man with whom she has sinned. The
scene has an added horror in that it builds up with
incredible rapidity from comparative calm to climax
and catastrophe. Tikhon at first does not want to listen
to Kátya's confession, and is beside himself with
unhappiness, but Kabanicha's comment is one of self-
justification: 'Son, your mother warned you!'

The second scene re-introduces the great unifying
influence of the story, taking place as it does on the
banks of the Volga. Kátya has fled from her family
after her confession, and they are looking for her. It
is night, and Tikhon's remarks to Glasha reveal that
his mind is a turmoil of doubt; women like that
should not just be killed, he says, but buried alive –
and yet he still loves Kátya, and how could he harm
her? Varvara and Vanya run in, the former explaining the behaviour of Kabanicha. They agree that
there is nothing for it but to run away together, and
their careless decision accords well with what the

music has told us about them earlier in the opera.

The voices of Tikhon and Glasha can be heard calling in the distance. Kátya comes slowly on to the empty stage, hoping sadly to see Boris once again. The thought of the night overwhelms her with horror, but she reflects that she will never see another night. Suddenly, remembrance of her love fills her heart with longing; she calls for Boris, and, as if in answer to her cry, he appears. Perhaps nothing in the opera is more poignant than the quiet way in which the two lovers accept one another and each finds consolation in the presence of the other. Boris tries to comfort her, but her mind wanders and she cannot remember what she wants to say to him. At first she wants to go away with him, then changes her mind. Sadly she asks him to give alms to all the beggars he meets, with the request that they pray for her. They say goodbye.

Kátya is alone. She thinks of the birds and the flowers which have comforted her in life and will be with her in death, 'so peaceful, so lovely ... and I must die'. She throws herself into the river. Voices are heard of one or two men who have seen her fall; Tikhon and Kabanicha rush to the spot, Tikhon protesting that it is Kabanicha who has killed Kátya. Her body is carried up on to the bank by Dikoy, and the last words of the opera are sardonically given to Kabanicha: 'Let me thank you, friends and neighbours, for your kindness.'

Kátya is the logical development of *Jenůfa*. The extraordinarily tense atmosphere of the story is matched by the music, which has an economical, compressed quality rare in other composers' operas. It is from the very close juxtaposition of the broadest of lyrical themes with the most insistent of dramatic that Janáček derives his unusual power.   H.

THE CUNNING LITTLE VIXEN

Příhody Lišky Bystroušky

Opera in three acts, text by the composer from R. Tešnohlídek's stories. Première, Brno, 6 November 1924, with H. Hrdlicková, Flögl, conductor František Neumann. First performed Mainz, 1927, conductor Paul Breisach; Zagreb, 1939, conductor Milan Sachs; Leipzig, 1951; Komische Oper, Berlin, 1956, in Felsenstein's production (in German), with Irmgard Arnold,

Rudolf Asmus, conductor Václav Neumann (this production was subsequently seen at Wiesbaden and Paris); la Scala, Milan, 1958 (in Italian), with Mariella Adani, Dino Dondi, conductor Sanzogno; London, Sadler's Wells, 1961 (in English), with June Bronhill, Neil Easton, conductor Colin Davis; U.S. première, Mannes College of Music at Hunter College, 1964; Edinburgh Festival, 1970, by Prague Opera with Tattermuschová, conductor Gregor; Glyndebourne, 1975, with Norma Burrowes, Benjamin Luxon, producer Jonathan Miller.

Animals

Bystrouška, *the Vixen*	Soprano
The Fox	Soprano[1]
Lapák, *the Dachshund*	Mezzo-Soprano[1]
The Cock	Soprano
Chocholka, *the Hen*	Soprano
The Badger	Bass[2]
The Screech-Owl	Contralto[3]
The Woodpecker	Soprano

Humans

The Forester	Bass-Baritone
The Forester's Wife	Contralto[3]
The Schoolmaster	Tenor
The Parson	Bass[2]
Pásek, *the innkeeper*	Tenor
The Innkeeper's Wife	Soprano
Harašta, *the pedlar*	Bass

Birds, Flies, Insects, Cricket, Grasshopper, etc.

Running Time: 1 hour 40 minutes

F‌ew operas, even by Slavs, have an odder genesis than Janáček's *The Cunning Little Vixen*. The composer had read with growing pleasure a series of newspaper articles by the journalist Tešnohlídek, based on a Czech rural community and featuring a half-tame vixen. He was particularly enthusiastic about the way the writer could jump naturally from the human to the animal worlds and, to the astonishment of Tešnohlídek himself, he asked if he might make an operatic text from the newspaper strips.

The opera, with its juxtaposition of humans and animals, was once thought unstageable, but in 1956 at the Komische Oper, Berlin, came complete vindication of Janáček's ideas in the wonderful production of Walter Felsenstein. The work was performed over 120 times in the four years following 1956.

---

[1] In some productions, the Fox and the Dachshund have been sung by tenors.

[2,3] The score *instructs* that the following parts are to be doubled: Badger and Parson; Forester's Wife and Owl.

Just as Vaclav Talich in his shortened orchestral arrangement of Act I of *The Cunning Little Vixen* (brilliantly preserved in a Supraphon disc) has pointed up the orchestration for the purposes of the suite, so Janáček's friend Max Brod in his German translation occasionally went further than the original libretto allows, underlining points Janáček no more than hinted at and stressing the implied symbolism. The glosses of this translation were once substantially accepted in German performances, even in Felsenstein's, but by no means in Czechoslovakia, though Brod was a close friend of the composer's. When the Forester in the first scene lies down for a nap, Brod introduces a first reference to the gipsy girl Terinka, of whose beauty and love of freedom all humans in the opera are reminded when they meet the little Vixen. It doesn't contradict what one may think of as the sub-text, but it isn't what Janáček wrote.

Act I, scene i. The curtain rises in the first bar, to show a shady spot in the woods; the early afternoon sunlight plays through the leaves of the trees. Animals and insects dance in the heat, a badger smoking a pipe pokes his head out of his earth, a blue dragonfly hovers in a dance. The Forester comes looking for a place for an afternoon nap – he feels as tired as after his wedding night!

He goes to sleep, the insect noises begin again, there is an enchanting waltz as the flies dance round the Forester, and the tempo (now in duple time) quickens as a frog chases a mosquito. A vixen cub looks in amazement at the frog; can one eat it, she wonders. She pounces, the frog jumps quickly and lands cold and slippery on the Forester's nose, much to his disgust. His eyes meet the vixen's, and after a couple of feints he catches her and goes away with her under his arm. The dragonfly darts towards the place where the vixen cub was playing, looks for her, and dances a touching little lament for his lost friend.

The interweaving forest motifs, the contrasting dance rhythms, the varying and unfailingly apt orchestral invention, above all the homogeneity of the themes and Janáček's skill and lightness of touch in putting the whole thing together contribute to a musical scene in its way unparalleled in operatic literature. The mixture of peaceful contemplation and feverish animal and insect activity which goes to make up the atmosphere of a hot summer afternoon

is a familiar enough country phenomenon but not one often attempted in music.

The second scene is set outside the Forester's house. From the outset the music is pregnant with heartache and longing, Ex. 1:

The Forester's wife pours some milk for dachshund and fox cub, which she and her husband are bringing up as a pet. The little vixen is miserable and the dog tries to preach resignation as a desirable state of mind; he has learnt to make the best of a bad job. When the Forester's son teases the cub, he is rewarded with a sharp nip. The Forester quickly ties her up, and she is left in a state of dejection as the others go in.

As it gets dark, there begins an extraordinary musical episode, built up on Ex. 1. The vixen seems almost to change into a girl – perhaps the gipsy Terinka? – and provokes passionate orchestral love music starting in B flat, Ex. 2:

In Felsenstein's production in Berlin, the already highly charged situation was pointed up by having the Forester stare at the little vixen on her chain until what he saw merged with his memory of his free gipsy love. It is music of great intensity and one could think of Ex. 2, with its exhilarating leaps, as contrasting with the pathetic Ex. 1, with its close intervals and repeated notes, in the same way as does an extraordinary experience with everyday life.

With the dawn, the Forester's wife throws out food for the chickens, who cluck to a parody of Ex. 2 and strut around the yard until the vixen starts a revolutionary harangue. It is a brave new feminist world that she preaches, but the hens are unresponsive and in disgust the vixen digs herself a grave, and shams dead. There is a headlong orchestral *stretta* as

The Cunning Little Vixen (Komische Oper, Berlin, 1956, director Walter Felsenstein, designer Rudolf Heinrich). The Vixen (Irmgard Arnold) is taunted by children, Act I.

the vixen suddenly springs up and bites off the heads of one chicken after another. The Forester's wife runs out in alarm, and the vixen snaps her leash, trips up the Forester and escapes.

Act II. For the first scene, we are back again in the sanctuary of the wood. The vixen teases the badger, enlists the sympathy of the other animals, and when the badger goes off in a huff, moves as she always intended into his vacated sett.

We arrive at the village inn by means of an interlude, which suggests the bustling atmosphere inside. There we find Forester and Schoolmaster playing cards, watched by the village priest. The Forester mocks the Schoolmaster for his backwardness in courting his sweetheart, but the ribaldry is general, and it is not long before they tease the Forester about the exploits of his pet fox. The Innkeeper is worried at the amount of noise coming from the back room, the Parson takes comfort in his Latin tag, 'Non des mulieri corpus tuum' (Give not thy body to a woman) and the Forester wonders if one can describe a bag of bones like the Schoolmaster as a body. The

Innkeeper warns the Parson to leave if his drinking is not to become a scandal with his new parishioners, and the Forester is left to wonder whether the Schoolmaster may not get married after all. He orders another beer, the Innkeeper says he will one of these days get him to tell the details of his adventures with the vixen, but the Forester reacts crossly and leaves the pub in a bad temper.

The wood at night. Moonlight shows a bridge; there are sunflowers behind the fence. The Schoolmaster comes a little shakily down the road, lamenting his propensity to waste his time drinking. The vixen peeps out from behind a sunflower, to the joy of the Schoolmaster, who takes her for the gipsy Terinka, a past love, and in his ardour topples over the fence and lies supine. Next it is the turn of the Parson, who comes down the road trying to remember the source of a classical tag. He catches sight of the vixen, confuses her in his mind with Terinka, whom he also loved in student days and for whose pregnancy he was unjustly blamed. The appearance of the Forester puts an end to his moralising, and he and the Schoolmaster fall into each other's arms in their fear of where the Forester may shoot at this time of night. The Forester mutters that he is shooting at the vixen whom he has seen slinking through the woods – but the explanation seems scarcely sufficient to the frightened Parson and Schoolmaster.

The scene changes back to the vixen's earth. Moonlight. Behind the scene the voices of the forest sing a wordless chant, which will play a great part at the end of the scene. The vixen meets a fox and tells him a romanticised story of her life. When the fox refers to her as beautiful, she starts to wonder about the significance of his remark. He brings her a rabbit he has killed, kisses her, and a full-scale duet ensues, at the end of which they go off together into the vixen's earth, leaving the dragonfly – her guardian angel, surely – to rejoice. The owl positively bubbles with joy with such a juicy bit of gossip. When the foxes emerge, the vixen whispers to the fox that she is now an expectant mother, and his reaction is to send for a priest, the woodpecker, who marries them as the wood voices celebrate the wedding in a paean of wordless joy.

Act III. It is midday under a clear autumn sky. The quiet is disturbed by the singing of Harašta, out on a poaching foray. He comes on a dead hare lying where it has been killed by a fox, is about to pick it up when he catches sight of the Forester, who greets him sarcastically. Does he enjoy his lonely life? 'Lonely? I'm going to marry Terinka', is Harašta's answer. To cover his chagrin, the Forester sets a trap for the foxes near the hare they have killed and goes off, leaving Harašta to laugh at his discomfiture.

The vixen's family of cubs rush out and dance round the clumsily set trap. Harašta's song is heard in the distance and all hide except for the cunning little vixen herself. She attracts Harašta's attention as she limps away from him, and leads him a dance which finishes with him flat on the ground. He gets up to see the fox cubs pulling the poultry out of his basket, shoots into the middle of them and by pure chance kills the vixen, who lies dead on the ground as the curtain falls.

The garden of the inn. The Innkeeper's wife brings the Forester his beer. He is out of humour and tells the Schoolmaster that every time recently he has been to the fox's earth he has found it deserted; he will never get the muff he has promised his wife. Terinka gets married today, says the Schoolmaster; *and* gets a new muff, sniffs the Innkeeper's wife. The Forester is even more put out than before but he tries to console himself by telling the Schoolmaster that Terinka was wrong for either of them. They miss the Parson with his ready Latin tag: he writes sometimes, says the Innkeeper's wife, and sounds homesick – Janáček's few bars of orchestral comment exactly hit off their regret at this news of someone they liked, who through nothing but goodness of heart has been hurt. The Forester pays and goes, as he tells them, off to the wood.

The last scene takes us back to the clearing where the Forester caught the little vixen. He is looking for peace, but the scene's introduction is much more turbulent, more full of longing, than the music at the start of the opera. Again the Forester muses in music of movingly human character on the forest, where life provides never an ending, only a new beginning, and where men if they know how to look may find the happiness of eternal things. As he starts to fall asleep, he sees a fox cub playing on the edge of the clearing. 'I'll catch you like I did your mother, only this time I'll bring you up better, so that people don't talk about you and me in the newspapers.' He makes a move towards the cub, and finds a frog in his hand!

The wheel has come full cycle, and with it the end of an opera that is the product of a wise (and passionate) old age, a unique example of pantheism in music drama – one of the great masterpieces of opera.   H.

THE MAKROPULOS AFFAIR
Věc Makropulos[1]

Opera in three acts, libretto by the composer, founded on Karel Čapek's play of the same name. Première, Brno, 18 December 1926, with Čvanová, Zdeněk Otava, E. Olsovsky, conductor František Neumann. First performed Prague, 1928; Frankfurt, 1929, with Gentner-Fischer, Jean Stern, conductor Josef Krips. Revived Düsseldorf, 1957 (and the following year at the Holland Festival), with Hildegard Hillebrecht, Patzak, Wiener. First performed Sadler's Wells, 1964, in English, with Collier, Dempsey, Herincx, conductor Mackerras; revived 1972 and 1984, with Josephine Barstow; Edinburgh Festival, 1970 (by Prague Opera), with Kniplová, conductor Bohumil Gregor; New York City Opera, 1970, with Maralin Niska; San Francisco, 1976, with Anja Silja; Glyndebourne, 1995, with Anja Silja.

Emilia Marty, *a singer*	Dramatic Soprano
Albert Gregor	Tenor
Vítek, *a solicitor's clerk*	Tenor
Kristina, *his daughter*	Mezzo-Soprano
Jaroslav Prus, *a Hungarian nobleman*	Baritone
Janek, *his son*	Tenor
Dr Kolenaty, *a barrister*	Bass-Baritone
A Stage Hand	Bass
A Stage 'Dresser'	Contralto
Count Hauk-Šendorf, *an old man-about-town*	Operetta Tenor
Chamber-Maid	Contralto

Place: Prague
Time: The 1920s
Running Time: 1 hour 40 minutes

For his penultimate opera (November 1923– December 1925), Janáček himself adapted Karel Čapek's *The Makropulos Secret*, using the play in spite of Čapek's offer to write him something round the figure of the 300-year-old woman, but more suitable for opera. The background to the story emerges gradually during the opera's action, but might be conveniently summarised beforehand. In 1565, Hieronymus Makropulos, court physician to the Habsburg Emperor

---

[1] The Czech word 'Věc' means 'thing', so that the title literally translated should be *The Makropulos Thing*, the object in question being the paper on which is written in Greek the secret of eternal life. Charles Mackerras, whose splendid conducting of the opera has been one of the glories of Sadler's Wells, suggests that *The Makropulos Secret* is both a more accurate and a more suggestive translation than the commoner *The Makropulos Case* or *The Makropulos Affair*.

Rudolph II, succeeded in finding an elixir of life. The Emperor refused to believe him and compelled his daughter Elina, a girl of sixteen, to drink it first. Makropulos died years later in prison, but Elina's life was prolonged through the potion. Every sixty or seventy years, she changes her identity to avoid suspicion, but throughout her 300 years and more of existence she has retained the initials 'E.M.'

As the Scottish singer Ellen MacGregor (in the opera, *Ellian*), early in the nineteenth century, she had a love affair in Prague with Baron 'Peppi' Prus, by whom she had a son, Ferdinand MacGregor, whom she entered under the name Makropulos in the parish register of the village in which he was born. In 1827,[1] Baron Prus died intestate, and the estate went to a cousin. It was not long before a new claimant appeared, one Ferdinand MacGregor, whose case was circumstantially plausible in spite of there being no written proof. All the same, Baron Prus conceded that there was reasonable evidence to suggest that a certain Gregor Mack should be a major beneficiary. Since no one could claim this identity, the case between the families of Prus and Gregor has continued for nearly a century.

Action in the opera revolves around Emilia Marty, sated with life so that her reaction to virtually everything is cold and negative; only two things rouse her interest: memories of the past and her fear of death.

The prelude contrasts, as is Janáček's habit (in for instance *Kátya Kabanová*), lyrical themes like Ex. 1:

from which much later material derives, with orchestral ejaculations, and includes brilliant fanfares for brass and kettle drums, Ex. 2:

symbolising the Rudolphian period of Elina Makropulos's birth.

The curtain rises on the office of the lawyer Dr Kolenaty, where the chief clerk Vítek is tidying away papers for the night. He is concerned with the case of Gregor v. Prus, which has been going on for as long as anyone can remember, and which Albert Gregor now comes in to discuss. They are interrupted by the arrival of Vítek's daughter Kristina, who is studying singing and is full of enthusiasm for the famous prima donna Emilia Marty, whose reputation greatly intrigues Gregor. Kolenaty's voice is heard and he introduces none other than Marty herself, with viola d'amore to play her rather old-fashioned theme.

She explains that she is interested in the Gregor-Prus case, and proceeds to show extraordinary knowledge of its details. Kolenaty, with frequent comments from Emilia Marty, goes through the case from its origins in 1827, when Baron Prus died apparently childless and intestate. Marty states categorically that the son of the Baron Prus in question was Ferdinand MacGregor, his mother a singer at the Hofoper, Ellian MacGregor. Her motif is Ex. 3:

Questioned further, she reveals the probable hiding place of the paper which could furnish proof, and Gregor excitedly insists that Kolenaty examine this crucial evidence, even though it appears to be among some love letters (derivation of Ex. 1 on clarinet) in the archives of his adversary in the case, the present Baron Prus. (Ellian MacGregor had left the paper containing the elixir's secret in Prus's hands, perhaps as a kind of pledge that she would return, and Emilia badly wants it back.)

Kolenaty goes off protestingly on what he is sure will prove a wild-goose chase, and Gregor is left alone with Emilia Marty, enthusiastically convinced that at one and the same time she can furnish the proof to win him his case, the evidence he has so long sought about his ancestry (particularly the mysterious Ellian MacGregor), and the love of his life

---

[1] Norman Tucker in his translation for Sadler's Wells changed this date to 1817, having worked out that Čapek had miscalculated by ten years!

The Makropulos Affair *(Glyndebourne, 1995, director Nikolaus Lehnhoff, designer Tobias Hoheisel).*
Anja Silja as Emilia Marty, Nigel Douglas as Hauk-Šendorf.

(Ex. 3 in various manifestations). But Emilia will have none of him, and he is shocked to see her take on the look of an old woman. As she insists, apparently on the spur of the moment, that he give her some old Greek papers he will on inheriting find among his great-great-grandfather's effects, the scene is interrupted by the return of Kolenaty, who has found all exactly as Emilia Marty had described. Prus follows him and congratulates Gregor on having collected almost – but not quite – all the evidence he needs. Emilia offers to furnish written proof that the Ferdinand of the will and Ferdinand Gregor (Ex. 3) are the same person, but the curtain comes down with Kolenaty refusing to be persuaded to accept her assistance again.

Act II. On to the empty stage of the opera house, where a stage-hand and a dresser are gossiping, comes Prus, looking for Emilia Marty. He is followed by his son, Janek, and Kristina, who is mesmerised by Marty and tells Janek that their romance must take second place to her career. La Marty makes an entrance and Prus introduces to her Janek, who makes a poor showing. She is irritable and not in the mood for compliments, reimbursing Gregor for the jewellery hidden in a bunch of flowers which he brings her, commenting when Vítek essays a comparison between her and the prima donna of the past that Strada[1] used to sing out of tune, and asking Kristina if she has yet slept with Janek.

There follows a curious episode as a stammering old roué, Count Hauk-Šendorf, brings flowers for the diva in whom he finds an uncanny resemblance to his one-time Spanish mistress, Eugenia Montez. In the course of a short but sharply-etched scene, it transpires to Hauk's amazement that Marty is in fact the Andalusian singer of fifty years ago.

An autograph for Vítek, a wave of dismissal for Janek and Kristina, an evasion of Gregor's attempt to stay with her, and Emilia Marty is alone with Prus. Immediately he questions her about her special interest in Gregor, and goes on to ask about the mysterious Ellian MacGregor,[2] from whose illegitimate child by the Baron Prus of more than a hundred years ago stems the present litigation. Prus is fascinated by the mystery surrounding her; what was her real name? In her letters to his ancestor, she signs only 'E.M.' (Ex. 3 dominates the discussion), and this could equally stand for Ellian MacGregor, Eugenia Montez, Emilia Marty – or even Elina Makropulos.[3] He has discovered that it was in the last name that the birth of a child, Ferdinand, was registered on the appropriate day, which seems to disprove Gregor's claim to the estate. His archives contain one further packet, still unopened; with the announcement of this new mystery, Prus withdraws, refusing even to respond to Emilia Marty's offer to buy the document.

Marty is sitting exhausted when Gregor returns and, in spite of his presentiment that there is something unnatural about her, renews his protestations of love. When she asks him to get back from Dr Kolenaty the document he found in the Prus archives, he threatens to kill her, at which she shows him a scar on her neck where such an attempt has been made in the past. When he renews his pleas, he is astonished to find her fast asleep in her chair. He kisses her hand and leaves, and, when she wakes, it is to find the tongue-tied Janek gazing at her. Will *he* help her? His father has an old letter addressed 'To my son Ferdinand' in a sealed packet; will he steal it for her? He is about to agree when he is shamed and put to flight by the appearance of his father. Prus and Emilia Marty now face each other as adversaries but, like the others, he succumbs to her beauty and agrees in return for her favours to give her the unopened packet.

Act III. Behind a curtain in Marty's hotel bedroom, two people can be seen dressing. Emilia emerges and demands the promised letter, which Prus silently gives her – due to her coldness, it seems that the night together amounted to fraud. She breaks the seal and agrees it is what she wanted. To Prus, already depressed and disillusioned, is brought a message – his only son Janek has committed suicide for love of Emilia. Emilia for her part continues to arrange her hair and refuses to accept any responsibility for his death. Hauk reappears to invite Emilia to come to Spain with him, and in a short while Gregor,

---

[1] See Handel's *Ariodante*, page 318.

[2] Emilia has sent Dr Kolenaty a paper signed by Ellian MacGregor acknowledging Baron Prus as the father of her son Ferdinand.

[3] Janáček took immense pains to base his musical conversation on the rhythms and stresses of spoken Czech, but when it came to setting foreign languages (in this opera, Spanish for Hauk, some German for Kolenaty and Greek for the heroine), he behaved as if the stresses were Czech. Thus the word 'Makropulos', where the Greek stress would be on the second syllable, is accented in the opera on the first, so that it tends to emerge as **Mak**ropulos!

Dr Kolenaty, Vítek, Kristina, Prus and a doctor are announced. The doctor removes the senile old man and Kolenaty says he has some questions he must ask Emilia Marty. To begin with, the autograph she gave Kristina and the writing on the sealed packet found in Prus's house are the same, indicating presumably that the old letter was forged by her. She answers wearily that it was nobody but Ellian MacGregor who wrote the letter and goes off into the bedroom, while Kolenaty and the others start to search her luggage. Finally, reeling from the effects of drinking half a bottle of whisky but with her toilet complete, she starts to answer Kolenaty's questions.

Her name is Elina Makropulos, and she was born in Crete in 1549. Her father was Hieronymus Makropulos, physician and alchemist to Emperor Rudolph II (Ex. 2), and she it was who, to convince the Emperor that it was not poisoned, was made to drink the elixir of life her father had brewed. She was the Elina Makropulos who registered her son by Baron Prus a hundred years ago as Ferdinand Makropulos. Ellian MacGregor was her theatrical name, but she had at various times used the names Ekaterina Myshkin and Elsa Müller. To her son she left the most precious thing she owned, the prescription for the elixir of life which has caused her for 300 years to vindicate his alchemical skill. Now the 300 years is up and she must renew life with the elixir, or shrivel into old age and die.

In the course of the scene, Emilia Marty ages until at its end she can hardly stand up. Her sceptical listeners begin to suspect she may have been speaking the truth after all, and carry her to bed. When she reappears, preceded by the orchestra's insistence on a beautiful variant of Ex. 1, played initially on solo violin and perhaps denoting finally Marty's resignation to death and therefore her salvation, she looks like a ghost. The former hardness of manner has disappeared and she has come to understand how desperately she has wanted to die. She gives the Makropulos 'secret' (Ex. 2) to Kristina, who throws it into the fire as Marty sinks gratefully into death. With the understanding that Elina Makropulos can – must – die, comes the end of a splendid final scene, in which the music transcends the details and carries the burden of Čapek's drama – that length of life is far less important than man's fulfilment within it, that mankind's fear of death must be replaced by an awareness of what life would be without death.   H.

FROM THE HOUSE OF THE DEAD
Z Mrtvé ho Domu

Opera in three acts, text by the composer from Dostoevsky's novel. Première, Brno, 12 April 1930, with F. Olšovsky (Filka Morosov), A. Pelc (Skuratov), G. Fischer (Shishkov), V. Sima (Goryanshikov), conductor Břetislav Bakala. First produced Mannheim, 1930, conductor Rosenstock; Berlin, Kroll Opera, 1931, with Soot, Cavara, Domgraf-Fassbänder, conductor Fritz Zweig (last première at Kroll before its closure); Düsseldorf, 1931, conductor Horenstein; Wiesbaden, 1954, conductor Elmendorff; Holland Festival, 1954; Edinburgh Festival, 1964, by Prague Opera with Blachut, Zidek, Přemysl Koci, conductor Gregor; London, Sadler's Wells, 1965, with Dowd, Dempsey, D. Bowman, conductor Mackerras; Milan, la Scala, 1967; New York (television), conductor Adler; Hamburg, 1972, with Cassilly, W. Caron, Mittelman, conductor Kubelík; Welsh National Opera, 1982, with John Mitchinson, Graham Clark, Donald Maxwell, conductor Richard Armstrong, producer David Pountney.

Alexander Petrovich Goryanshikov, *a political prisoner* ....Bass

Alyeya, *a young Tartar* ....Soprano (or Tenor)

Filka Morosov, *in prison under the name of Luka Kuzmich* ....Tenor

The Big Convict ....Tenor

The Small Convict ....Baritone

The Commandant ....Baritone

The Very Old Convict ....Tenor

Skuratov..Tenor

Chekunov...Baritone

The Drunken Convict ....Tenor

The Cook ....Baritone

The Smith ....Bass

The Priest ....Baritone

The Young Convict ....Tenor

A Whore...Mezzo-Soprano

A Convict (*playing the roles of Don Juan and the Priest*) ....Baritone

Kedril...Tenor

Shapkin ....Tenor

Shishkov..Baritone

Cherevin ....Tenor

A Guard..Tenor

Chorus of Convicts and Guards; Silent Persons in the Play: a Knight, Elvira, the Cobbler's Wife, the Priest's Wife, the Miller, the Miller's Wife, a Scribe, the Devil

Place: Siberia
Time: Nineteenth Century
Running Time: 1 hour 25 minutes

From February 1927 until the end of the year Janáček was engaged on *From the House of the Dead*, finishing the score, according to his letter to Kamila Stösslová, on 4 January, having it copied out, and then, at the end of January 1928, starting to compose his second String Quartet. But later dates (7.v.1928 at the end of Act II, 24.iv.1928 at the end of Act III) appear on the score, and in point of fact the opera was not truly finished at the time of the composer's death, some of it existing only in short score. Orchestration and the filling of whatever gaps remained was undertaken by the composer's disciples, Břetislav Bakala, the conductor, and Osvald Chlubna, the composer. The juxtaposition of the Glagolitic Mass with the new opera contrasts the extremes of the Slav mind, from the gentle but convinced exultation of the Mass to the despair of some of the characters in the opera.

Janáček's art developed as time went on (one can hardly write 'as he grew older' about a composer whose first *local* success came when he was fifty and who was not known in the capital of his native land until he was well over sixty). Roman Vlad's comment about *Brouček* – that melodic motifs flower throughout the drama and are not employed in Wagnerian fashion – becomes less true over the years. In *The Cunning Little Vixen* he already weaves a motivic tapestry in order to create his forest, *The Makropulos Affair* carries the process a stage further, and by the time of *From the House of the Dead*, it is possible for Erik Chisholm to write with justice 'From even a casual study (of the music of Shishkov's story) it should be clear that Janáček employs as highly complex a system of leitmotif as any composer has attempted since the death of Wagner.'

Act I. There is an extended prelude, moving and evocative and derived from material originally intended for a Violin Concerto to be called 'Wanderings of the Soul'. The curtain rises on a penal settlement on the river Irtysh in Siberia; it is winter and early morning. The prisoners waiting about aimlessly outside their huts hear that a new prisoner is to arrive, a city man, perhaps an aristocrat. They argue and quarrel until Alexander Petrovich Goryanshikov is brought in by the guard. The Camp Commandant

reacts sarcastically to the prisoner's smart clothes, then orders him to behave while in prison. Questioned about the nature of his crime, Goryanshikov says he is a political prisoner, which answer produces a spasm of rage in the Commandant, who yells for him to be taken away and flogged. Nobody but Alyeya, a young Tartar prisoner, takes much notice when cries of pain are heard coming from behind the huts, but the music reacts in sympathy. The other prisoners occupy themselves with an eagle with a broken wing, which they keep in a cage. The eagle in his present condition clearly has symbolic significance to them, and an old man contrasts the eagle's pride with man's smallness of mind. The episode is interrupted by the Commandant, and the prisoners are forced to resume work by the guards, singing a lament for the homes they suspect they will never see again. Skuratov, the camp's self-appointed entertainer, joins the group and sings a folk song. There is clearly some tension between him and Luka Kuzmich, and Skuratov suddenly pours out his homesickness for Moscow, where he was happy in his work as a cobbler. He dances and collapses exhausted.

The remainder of the act is dominated by Luka's story of how he came to be in the camp. Baited by a brutal Commanding Officer, he first lulled him into a sense of security and then stabbed him to death. During the beating and torture which followed, he thought all the time that he would die. When he finishes his story, full of hideous detail, the old prisoner looks up and asks him, 'And did you die?' The characteristic speech of the prisoners is ejaculatory, as if they were forced to relieve nervous tension by their confessions.

Alexander Petrovich is brought back after his flogging; all watch the gates close after him and eventually stop working. In the revisions which were made to the score after Janáček's death and before the première at Brno, a dramatic episode was here superimposed on the music, in which Goryanshikov makes a futile attempt to kill the Commandant, an addition which is wholly questionable, since the music at this point is dominated by Skuratov's motif.

Act II. The banks of the River Irtysh.[1] The sun is shining and the steppes stretch away to the horizon

---

[1] Janáček clearly wants contrast as a relief between the gloom of Act I and the grim horror of the hospital in Act III and in order to obtain it has not scrupled to put Dostoevsky's account of the play into the open air. To play this act inside is wrong, and Max Brod, in his German translation, has underlined this by additionally placing it in summer.

(empty fifths on the flutes and then plaintive singing in the distance characterise the barren loneliness of the plain). Before the curtain rises, the working sound of hammers can be heard as the convicts break up an old boat. Goryanshikov asks Alyeya about his sister, but Alyeya is convinced she has died of grief at his disgrace. Goryanshikov tries to distract his attention and, much to Alyeya's delight, offers to teach him to read and write.

It is a holiday and the other prisoners have no patience with anything that distracts them from one of their few opportunities for rest and pleasure. They are going to have a theatrical performance of sorts, and a satirical march ushers into the camp the Commandant, the guards and the priest. The prisoners are given food, and Skuratov starts to describe the circumstances of his crime. It is a simple case of murder for jealousy, described with much of the conviction and agony which must have accompanied its commission. He was head over heels in love with a German girl, Luisa, who lived with her aunt. Unfortunately, though she had agreed to marry him, a richer compatriot asked for her hand in marriage and her aunt insisted that she make the better match. Skuratov shot him, was captured after escaping and condemned to prison for life. It is a touching narrative, and in its course Skuratov attacks and knocks to the ground a drunken man who has been continually interrupting with cries of 'It's lies!' Someone at the end asks what happened to Luisa, and Skuratov's cry of 'Oh, Luisa' remains to haunt the imagination.

It is time for the play to start and one may at first think it contradictory that, apart from dance tunes, Janáček employs similar musical language here as for the main action, his point being presumably that the fantasies of the prisoners are at least as real as their everyday thoughts and actions, in fact hardly to be distinguished from them. Don Juan and his servant Kedril are beset by devils, but Don Juan has three adventures before he finally succumbs to them. He makes love to Elvira and, when a knight appears to defend her, kills him. He spurns a cobbler's wife introduced by Kedril, but shows interest in the wife of a priest before the reappearance of the devils heralds his end. After a good deal of general laughter stylised in the music, Kedril announces that the next piece will be the Tale of the Beautiful Miller's Wife.

The Miller says goodbye to his wife, who is satirised in a tune with the bite of early Prokofiev in it and proceeds to take advantage of his absence to receive a succession of lovers, each one hiding when the next is about to appear. The last is Don Juan, dressed as a priest; when the Miller returns, Don Juan kills him and dances with the woman to the music of a slow waltz of considerable intensity.

The play is over and the prisoners start to disperse, leaving Alexander Petrovich and Alyeya sitting together and drinking tea. They watch a young prisoner make off with a particularly unprepossessing whore and shortly afterwards one of the other prisoners takes it into his head that they are privileged in having tea and attacks Alyeya, leaving a gaping wound in his head. The guards advance on the prisoners as the curtain falls.

Act III. It is again winter, and the scene shows the inside of the prison hospital. The Muslim, Alyeya, lying in bed, tells Alexander Petrovich that what has most impressed him in the Bible – he can now read a bit – is the idea that men should love their enemies. Luka mumbles away from the bed in which he lies dying, Shapkin's story of how he was caught poaching and had his ears pulled by the Chief of Police is told against an accompaniment more than usually consolatory, and Skuratov's feverish but heartrending cries of 'Oh, Luisa' eventually exasperate the other prisoners who drag him back to his own bed.

Shishkov now embarks on what is to prove the longest of the three major narratives of the opera. With a bitter irony, his story is punctuated by the death agony of Luka, who eventually turns out to have been the villain of Shishkov's narrative. A young girl called Akulka is generally believed on his evidence to have lost her honour to a certain Filka Morosov. Her parents beat her but eventually Shishkov is persuaded to marry her, and on his wedding night he discovers that she is a virgin and has been grossly slandered. When Filka is called up to the army, Akulka admits that she has been in love with him all along and that after her marriage she has in fact been guilty of the sin of which she was once falsely accused. Shishkov in his shame and agony takes her out into the woods and cuts her throat. The story is punctuated by the vain efforts of his listeners to hurry Shishkov on to the point, by the heavy breathing of the sick prisoners, and by the groans and sobs of Luka, who dies and is carried out as the story comes to an end. As it passes, Shishkov recognises the body as Filka Morosov's masquerading under another name, and in spite of the forgiving comment of an old prisoner, Shishkov curses the corpse all the way out of the door. The scene ends as the guards call Alexander Petrovich Goryanshikov, Alyeya clutching despairingly at him as he is taken out.

The camp as in the first scene. The sun is shining, the prisoners are at their work as the Commandant addresses himself drunkenly to Goryanshikov and asks his forgiveness for having had him flogged on his arrival. He is to go free straight away and his fetters are taken off him. As Alexander Petrovich tries to comfort the despairing Alyeya, the music takes on a character almost of optimism that lies somewhere at the heart of Dostoevsky's masterpiece, the optimism that believes, in spite of the evidence, that there is goodness in life, honesty and integrity in man, a purpose behind it all. Goryanshikov leaves the camp and the prisoners free the eagle, whose wings have now recovered their strength, and the music is momentarily in the nature of a hymn to freedom.

The end is controversial. In Janáček's original, after Goryanshikov has left, the guard shouts at the remaining prisoners 'March!', and with their chains clanking they are herded back to their huts – after a glimpse of freedom, life in the House of the Dead returns to stark normality. Only Alyeya, in his hospital nightgown and forgetful of everything else now that he has lost Goryanshikov, remains behind, 'as a symbol of God's spark in man'. At the suggestion of the producer, Ota Zítek, Bakala the conductor and Janáček's pupil, the composer Chlubna, omitted the intervention of the guard and chose to maintain the optimism of the final chorus, carrying it through to the end. Conductors responsible for a revival of the opera must decide which of the two versions to adopt; the vocal score contains only the revision, but the original is reproduced in Jaroslav Vogel's *Leoš Janáček: His Life and Works*.

Perhaps no other composer than Janáček would have attempted to turn Dostoevsky's vast book into an opera. Certainly no one else could have compressed it into three acts of less than thirty minutes each, and still have preserved so magnificently the spirit of the original. H.

K

WILHELM KIENZL
(born 17 January 1857, died 3 October 1941)

DER EVANGELIMANN
The Travelling Preacher

Opera in two acts, text by the composer. Première Berlin, 4 May 1895. First performed 1897, Covent Garden, with Ernest van Dyck; New York, 1924.

Friedrich Engel, *magistrate in St Othmar* ....Bass
Martha, *his niece* ....Soprano
Magdalena, *her friend*..................................Contralto
Johannes Freudhofer, *teacher in St Othmar* ...Baritone
Mathias Freudhofer, *his younger brother*............Tenor

Tradesmen, Monks, Peasants, Children

Place: St Othmar in Lower Austria; Vienna
Time: 1820; 1850
Running Time: 1 hour 30 minutes

Kienzl was an Austrian composer whose experience in 1876 of the first *Ring* at Bayreuth left him a convinced Wagnerian. In spite of a reactionary style, his operas enjoyed success in his native country until after his death. The story of *Der Evangelimann* is said to be founded on fact.

Act I. Johannes is jealous of his brother Mathias's love for Martha, and warns her uncle who forbids them to see each other. Johannes proposes to Martha and is rejected. That evening, after the villagers' regular session of ninepins, Johannes overhears Mathias and Martha pledge eternal fidelity and in a mad fit of jealousy sets fire to the barn. Mathias is discovered near the scene of the crime and arrested.

Act II. Thirty years later, Magdalena, Martha's friend, is nursing Johannes who is dying. Nothing has been heard of Mathias. Children dance, and an 'Evangelimann' – a travelling reciter of biblical verses such as once existed in Austria – teaches them Christ's Sermon on the Mount. Magdalena recognises him as Mathias, and hears he has been twenty years in prison for a crime he did not commit. Martha drowned herself soon after he was condemned and as an ex-convict he found himself unemployable. Next day, Johannes recognises Mathias's singing and confesses his crime to him, begging for forgiveness, which Mathias after a struggle concedes. Johannes dies as Magdalena prays and the children are heard singing outside: 'Blessed are they that are persecuted for righteousness' sake; for theirs is the Kingdom of Heaven'.

The music is mainly memorable for the popular, much-recorded episode of the Sermon on the Mount, the genuine pathos of whose tone dominates the score and which remains a scene of affecting power. Beside it the liveliness of the ninepins, Martha and Mathias's love-making, Magdalena's over-ripe if shapely memories of youth ('O schöne Jugendtage'), even Johannes's confession and forgiveness amount to not much more than the building blocks of a well-made opera – valuable in their own way but unlikely to alter significantly one's view of *Der Evangelimann*'s place in operatic history.   H.

OLIVER KNUSSEN

(born 12 June 1952)

WHERE THE WILD THINGS ARE

A fantasy opera in one act (nine scenes), with libretto by Maurice Sendak from his children's book of the same name. Première, Brussels, 28 November 1980, with Jane Manning, conductor Ronald Zollman (as *Max et les Maximonstres*). First performed London in concert, 1982; by Glyndebourne Opera at National Theatre, London, 1984, and at Glyndebourne, 1985, all with Rosemary Hardy or Karen Beardsley as Max, and the London Sinfonietta conducted by the composer or Jane Glover. First heard in U.S.A. in concert in 1984 and on stage in 1985 by Minnesota Opera.

Max, *a small boy*	Soprano
Mama	Mezzo-Soprano
Tzippy, *the female Wild Thing*	Mezzo-Soprano
Wild Thing with Beard	Tenor
Goat Wild Thing	Tenor
Wild Thing with Horns	Baritone
Rooster Wild Thing	Bass-Baritone
Bull Wild Thing	Bass

Running Time: 40 minutes

Let the very articulate composer speak for himself:[1] 'Conceived for the resources of an opera house – six singers, dancers, an orchestra of forty-seven players, and extensive scenic requirements – *Where the Wild Things Are* is an attempt to revive and develop the too long neglected genre of fantasy opera, in the traditions of, among others, *Hänsel und Gretel*, *Le Rossignol*, and *L'Enfant et les Sortilèges* (whose final 'Maman' was in a sense the sound from which our ideas grew) ... What resulted, to me at least, is a very big work articulated in miniature.'

The composer goes on: 'The score is headed by quotations from Mussorgsky (*Boris Godunov*) and Debussy (*La boîte à joujoux*). These references are symbolic: Mussorgsky is the supreme composer of music *about* children (*The Nursery* and Act 2 of *Boris*), and Debussy's music for his daughter Chouchou is the perfect example of how a composer can make children's music not by "writing down" to them, but by illuminating his harmonic language in particularly gentle and subtle ways. Both quotations can be heard in the music of *Wild Things*, overtly and covertly – which is a polite way of saying that virtually every note of the opera grows from one or the other.'

It is nonetheless Knussen's music and his response to the book (one can't say 'response to the text' when most of Sendak's story is told in his marvellous pictures) which made the opera (perhaps because of, rather than in spite of, its short duration) something of an instant classic for children, one of the few operas which seems aimed at them rather than at the grown-ups who go to the opera with them.

Its gestation was not easy. Maurice Huisman, the perspicacious director of the Opéra National, Brussels, wanted an opera from Oliver Knussen on the occasion of the International Year of the Child, and Sendak wrote the scenario and libretto in 1978–79. Knussen composed the first version of the opera in 1979–80 and this was heard in Brussels in late 1980, still not yet quite finished and with elements of the score repeated to cover the areas not yet composed. Substantial revision brought a further version to the concert platform in 1982, still without the sixth scene (The Wild Rumpus), but the complete opera hit London in a Glyndebourne production by January 1984, and proved well worth waiting for.

The story is simple. Max, like the child in Ravel's *L'Enfant et les Sortilèges*, is wilful, and after being cheeky to his mother, is sent to bed without any supper. His confrontation with the Wild Things parallels that of the child in *L'Enfant* with his toys and characters from his books, but once he has learned to dominate the Wild Things, he puts his room in order and is ready for the food – *hot* food! – he can smell cooking.

The overture is short, quiet, even menacing. During its course, in less time than it takes to tell, a curtain with the face of a Wild Thing on it becomes visible, and soon, through it, the hall of the house where Max lives. A *scherzino* develops as Max cavorts into view, threatening his toy soldiers, and hanging a bear melodramatically from a coat-hanger. He turns confidently to humming – there is no need to ask

---

[1] In the sleeve note for the first recording of the opera (by Unicorn Records), which he conducted himself.

who is king of the castle. But his mother's shadow comes into view, and to her, particularly when he jumps out from ambush, he is a naughty rascal, and fit to be sent to bed without any supper. There is the noise of the vacuum cleaner as she comes into sight, an angry mother–son dialogue (Max: 'And I'll tell Papa *you* were bad'), and, as Max jumps down at her, a reprise of the *scherzo* music to which she made her entrance, and during whose course she shouts 'Wild Thing' at him.

They freeze, his mother leaves and the vacuum cleaner pursues Max round the hall and into his own room. He is alone and out of humour and sings Arietta 1, whose angular vocal writing does not conceal its innate lyricism. The atmosphere is that of *L'Enfant*, most of all when Max's room is transformed into a forest, round which he dances ecstatically (Arietta 2 to a quicker 'Rag' music). Water invades the scene and Max gets into a boat, which moves off.

Interlude 1, with its horn solo and jabbering flutes, is mysteriously atmospheric. It is black night, but the sun rises and proceeds to play Box and Cox with the moon. At dawn, the sea becomes turbulent and a great Sea Monster – the first of the Wild Things – appears, only to subside at a gesture from Max. He moors the boat to an island – we are by now far from the world of Ravel – and quite soon the sound of the Wild Things, still off-stage, begins to make itself heard. They are pretty threatening, even though sleep sounds mingle with something more startling, and their noise rises to a great *crescendo* before they hurtle on to the stage, baiting Max and doing their best to scare the pants off him. It is a simple musical moment of inspired complication.

The row continues for a bit, the monsters using what Sendak has called 'a childish, naughty, upside-down pidgin Yiddish', sometimes yelled, sometimes whispered, until Max loses patience, stamps his foot and quells the din. He stares into the eyes of the Wild Things and they cower before him, and in turn sing quietly and gently, taking the opportunity to creep up on him threateningly when his back is turned, only to freeze when they think he can see them.

It is the beginning of the Coronation scene, which starts with the Goat-Dance. One by one, they prepare the accoutrements of the Coronation – velvet cushion, sceptre, casket, crown – and form a procession. The throne lights up and, after a chant of something like adoration on the part of the Wild Things, Max reaches it, sits and is crowned, at which point the opera's climax starts to build: a brilliantly direct, if highly compact, paraphrase of the Coronation scene from *Boris Godunov*, with the Goat as Shuisky and the other Wild Things, *andantino alla marcia*, standing in for the Russian crowd.

Max announces *fortissimo* 'And now let the WILD RUMPUS start!!' The music begins *molto vivace*, moves into a *Valse-Mazurka* and, with Max on the Bull's back and the other Wild Things stamping round him, there is general jubilation, the music perhaps remotely indebted to Ravel, but to the Ravel of *La Valse*, not of *L'Enfant*. This is the opera's centre-piece, and it was the last section to be completed to the composer's satisfaction.

Abruptly, Max stops the riot, dominating and controlling the Wild Things just as surely as his mother had him, and orders them too off to bed without supper. Max is alone and sings a tender aria about his dream of flying so high he was scared, his music for the first time a slow cantilena, marked at one point 'like an incantation, *calmissimo*'. He gets into his boat and suddenly there is a recrudescence of suppressed violence as the monsters whisper furiously, nightmarishly ('like an unbelievable rage when heard through ear-plugs'). Max turns round and the music changes instantly, first into a sanctimonious Barbershop quintet and then into nothing less than passionate fury again. The island recedes until, with the voices of the Wild Things still audible, the music becomes gently consolatory and in the Second Interlude a point of reconciliation seems achieved. After the Rumpus, we rejoin the world of *L'Enfant*, Max's vocal line takes on a note of ecstasy, and it is not long before Mama is heard singing reassuringly off-stage, a palpable rather than a visible comfort. We are back in Max's room – and he can smell hot soup.   H.

ZOLTÁN KODÁLY

(born 16 December 1882, died 6 March 1967)

HÁRY JÁNOS

Fable in three acts, text by Béla Paulini and Zsolt Harsányi. Première, Budapest, 16 October 1926, with Isabella Nagy and Imre Palló, conductor Nador Rékai. First performed Cologne, 1931; Zürich, 1950, with Malaniuk, Boehm, conductor Reinshagen. New production Budapest, 1952, with Maria Matyas, Imre Palló. New York, Juilliard School, 1960, in English; London, Camden Town Hall, 1967, with Frank Olegario; Vienna Volksoper, 1967, with Mirjana Irosch, Harald Serafin, conductor Carl Melles; Buxton Festival, 1982. Very successful in Hungary.

Háry János ....Baritone

Ilka (Orzse), *his fiancée* ....Soprano

Empress of Austria..Soprano

Emperor Napoleon ....Baritone

Marie-Louise, *his Austrian wife* ....Mezzo-Soprano

Old Marczi, *Marie-Louise's coachman* ....Baritone

Ritter von Ebelasztin,
    Chamberlain to Empress Marie-Louise ....Tenor

Speaking roles
Kaiser Franz of Austria
Countess Melusine } *ladies-in-waiting*
Countess Estrella   } *to Marie-Louise*
Hungarian Sentry
Russian Sentry
General Blood-and-Thunder
General Dufla
First and Second Hussars
First and Second Artillerymen
Village Elder
A Student
Abraham, *an innkeeper*
First and Second Peasants

Generals, Hungarian and French Soldiers, Peasant
    Women, Court Servants, People

Place: Hungary
Time: Beginning of the Nineteenth Century
Running Time: 1 hour 20 minutes

*H*áry János is less a true opera than a play with a quantity of incidental music. Nevertheless its home in Hungary is in the opera house, and it has been successfully played abroad. Only a few of the large number of characters actually sing, but there are no fewer than thirty musical numbers in the score, varying from a full-dress operatic finale to a few bars of incidental, atmospheric music. The play is conceived as a fantastic adventure told to his cronies by an uneducated but imaginative Hungarian peasant, and nothing that happens in it bears any relation to reality, being based exclusively on what Háry would expect it to be like. Kodály has clothed the story in music of great charm and individuality, as will be readily acknowledged by anyone who knows the attractive orchestral suite drawn from the opera.

Prologue. The prelude (called *The story begins* in the suite) aptly sets the 'once upon a time' atmosphere. The scene is in an inn, on one of whose walls hangs a crude picture of Napoleon. What sort of story is Háry János likely to tell today, asks the village elder. When Háry appears, a student points to the picture of Napoleon: that was a great hero. I once took him prisoner with my own hands, is Háry's rejoinder!

First adventure. The scene is the border of Galicia and Russia. On the Russian side, it is deep winter; the sentry is muffled in furs and stamps about, blowing on his hands. On the Hungarian side, the sun is shining, the flowers are out, and the Hussar drips with sweat. They comment on the weather. One's drink is too hot, the other's is frozen; they exchange. As the curtain goes up and during the early part of the conversation, a flute solo gives out the tune of the duet, which occurs later in the scene.

Ilka appears, singing a little unaccompanied song. When the sentry makes eyes at her, she warns him that she will set Háry János on him if he does not stop. Háry appears, asks for Ilka, is told which way she went, and goes off to find her.

Herr von Ebelasztin, Chamberlain at the French court, puts his head out of the Russian side of the guardroom and complains that his Empress has not been allowed to pass the frontier. The Hungarian coachman employed at the French court tells Háry that the Empress is being kept in the Russian guardroom. Háry demands of the guard that she be let through. 'No one in, no one out' is the Russian's answer. There seems no solution until Háry takes hold of the guardroom and pulls it bodily into Hungarian territory, whereupon the ice and snow immediately begin to melt.

Háry and Ilka sing a beautiful duet: 'Tiszán innen, Dunán túl'. The tune, of haunting, nostalgic beauty, occurs as the third item in the orchestral suite.

Marczi, the coachman, returns and toasts the lovers in a drinking song, but Ebelasztin complains of the noise and they are all ashamed at the thought that they may have disturbed the Empress's rest. She, however, emerges and asks who it was who sang so attractively. When told it was Háry, she asks him to come to Vienna with her.

The Russian re-appears, full of apprehension that he will be hanged if the guardroom's altered position is found. Ebelasztin tries to push it back but cannot, and it is not until Háry consents to do it that any progress is made. It immediately starts to freeze again.

Second adventure. This section is introduced by the famous Intermezzo with its intoxicating rhythms. The scene is the park of the Imperial Palace in Vienna, viewed strictly through the eyes of Háry's imagination, i.e. the bushes have blossoms in the shape of an Imperial crown, the trees are of gold, the dovecot is inhabited by a two-headed eagle. It appears that all are conscious of the animosity with which Ebelasztin regards Háry, although they are somewhat reassured when, a moment later, Ebelasztin sends Háry off to the riding-school. There he is put on to the fiercest horse in the stable, which immediately dashes on to the roof. Háry returns quite unconcerned, having put Lucifer quietly away in his stall. Marie-Louise gives Háry a violet she has picked, much to the fury of Ebelasztin, who has asked for it for himself.

The Austrian Empress joins the group, and Marie-Louise blushingly points out the mighty Háry to her. Ilka appears from the kitchen with a dish of sweet-corn, whose seeds she proceeds to feed to the two-headed eagle. Ebelasztin joins her, and says he carries in his bag Napoleon's declaration of war on Austria, to use when he thinks fit. Marie-Louise's gift of the violet to a peasant bumpkin is quite sufficient provocation, and he will use it forthwith. Military noises are heard from the palace, and everyone rushes in saying that war has been declared by France. Háry, by now promoted Captain by the Emperor, kisses Ilka goodbye, and the curtain falls as General Dufla wheels on an enormous cannon.

Following the Intermezzo, the music of the Second Adventure consists of three songs and an extended orchestral incident depicting the palace clocks striking midday, much to the delight of the astonished Háry (this is included in the suite). Marie-Louise sings a little song about a cuckoo as she picks the violet which is to cause the ructions between Ebelasztin and Háry. Ilka has two songs, one almost pathetic in character as she reflects on the danger Háry ran when he rode the wild Lucifer, the other brisk and lively as she feeds the Imperial fowls.

Third adventure. The battlefield; in the background is the fortress of Milan, and behind that the mountains. Cannon are in evidence, and Hussars stand about, among them Háry, by now promoted Colonel. Hussars discuss the military situation with General Blood-and-Thunder; shots are heard, and the General's immediate reaction is to give the order: 'Withdraw according to plan.' French soldiers appear, Háry draws his sabre and, by the mere act of doing so, creates a draught which fells his opponents. The music of the battle (included in the suite) is in three stages. First of all, the French band can be heard off; when it comes on, Háry is laying low the army with the wind of his sword, with the result that the playing of the band becomes more and more confused. Very soft percussion heralds the entry of Napoleon but soon the brass enters *fortissimo*, with a hint of the 'Marseillaise' somewhere in the music. Napoleon falls on his knees and is taken prisoner by Háry, who declares the war over. There is a funeral march, dominated by a moaning little tune on the saxophone.

Marie-Louise comes on the scene and is contemptuous of the beaten Napoleon, who has a little song to the tune of the funeral march. Everyone congratulates Háry and to the accompaniment of gipsy music a feast is prepared. Ebelasztin and Ilka come in, the latter admitting that the former's warnings seem to have had something behind them when she sees how Háry is behaving – 'Is this war's hardship?' she asks bitterly.

There is an acrimonious exchange between Ilka and Marie-Louise, when the former dances with Háry. Marie-Louise announces she is going to marry Háry, and when the latter demurs, she rushes off threatening to commit suicide. Háry naturally manages to save the situation, and he leads a marching ensemble as the episode comes to an end.

Fourth adventure. Háry's room in Vienna. The Empress and Marie-Louise sing a duet, Marie-Louise wondering which of her ten suitors to marry, her mother plumping for Háry.

To the accompaniment of outrageously noisy music, the Emperor leads in a procession in honour of Háry, who will in future, he announces, be endowed with half the Empire and half the Imperial Palace. At the feast Háry is not himself and will eat nothing; he is even cross when told that double-headed chickens are normal fare for the Imperial table. The Emperor toasts Háry in a speech, and then, to a march, in come the little archdukes to shake hands with the hero of the day.

Háry admits that he cannot marry Marie-Louise, not least because he has a sweetheart of his own – Ilka. If he is to have a reward, says Háry, may he be let off half his military service, so that he can go home and get married. Ilka comes in, knowing nothing of what has happened, and sings a melancholy and very beautiful song. Háry, now dressed as an infantryman, returns (for a Hussar, infantry uniform is practically the same as civilian clothes, he observes), and swears allegiance to the Emperor. There is only one more complication to clear up. Ebelasztin is sent in chains to Háry by the Emperor Napoleon, but Háry magnanimously pardons him and leads him over to his beloved Marie-Louise. The finale, for Háry, Ilka, and the chorus, makes use of material already used in the opera, notably the love duet and the intermezzo.

Epilogue, set in the same inn as the prologue. Háry János finishes his story: he and Ilka walked home and were married. Now, Ilka having died, there is no one to witness his story but he.   H.

JOONAS KOKKONEN
(born 13 November 1921, died 2 October 1996)

THE LAST TEMPTATIONS
Viimeiset kiusaukset

Opera in two acts, libretto adapted from Lauri Kokkonen's play of the same name (1959). First performed in Helsinki, Finnish National Opera, 2 September 1975, with Martti Talvela, Ritva Auvinen and Seppo Ruohonen, conducted by Ulf Söderblom. After an unprecedented 166 performances it toured to seven foreign opera houses, including the Metropolitan Opera, New York. Yet to be staged in Britain.

Paavo Ruotsalainen, *Finnish farmer, leader of a religious revival*..................................Bass
Riita, *his first wife*..Soprano
Juhana, *their son*..Tenor
Jaako Högman, *the smith who converted Paavo* ....Baritone
Anna Lovisa, *Paavo's second wife*.............Spoken Role
Albertiina Nenonen, *servant* ....Spoken Role
First Man ....Tenor
Second Man..Baritone
Third Man...Bass
First Woman..Soprano
Second Woman ....Mezzo-Soprano
Third Woman ....Alto

Place: Finland
Time: 1852, and Flashback
Running Time: 2 hours 15 minutes

Paavo Ruotsalainen (1777–1852) was a revivalist preacher who led a movement that briefly galvanised Christianity in Finland. He was inspired by the writings of Thomas Wilcox, gathered in *A Choice Drop of Honey from the Rock Christ*, 1739, which the smith Hogman gives Paavo in the opera. Kokkonen follows his brother Lauri Kokkonen's play in portraying the inner, rather than the outer man: we scarcely hear Paavo preach but we do see what a disastrous impact his mission has on his family; his cruelty, vanity and selfishness, which are part of his journey towards redemption. The ambivalence of this portrait, the storm music and the community's hostility to a visionary probably witness to the influence of Britten's *Peter Grimes*.

Act I, scene i. Paavo's deathbed. As Paavo Ruotsalainen lies dying, he calls out for Riita, his first wife who died twenty years ago. He refuses to recognise either the servant, Albertiina, or his second wife Anna Lovisa. The two women's roles are spoken (except when they sing a hymn 'with untrained voices') and their speech is independent of the orchestra, while all Paavo's singing is shadowed and enriched by complex layers of orchestration. At Albertiina's suggestion, the two women sing a hymn: hymns form one of the keystones of the work's construction. After one verse, he joins in so passionately that the others fall silent. He sends them away, convinced, as he says, that Heaven's gate must be approached alone, that 'there's no need for women past or present'. This leads to the first of the interludes that link all the scenes.

Scene ii. Riita at the dance. Like the others, this scene is experienced by Paavo at the end of his life: he is young here, but also on the edge of death. When he asks Riita to come with him, three men and three women mock him and warn her that she faces thirty-three years of suffering. She agrees to go, to retrace his steps in life. She suggests they start with a visit to the smith who inspired Paavo with a sense of his Christian mission. The trudging interlude seems to take up Paavo's last line, that he will 'plod on'.

Scene iii. The smith. Riita blames the smith for making Paavo so religious that he neglected his family. He rejects her criticisms firmly but does not answer them, contemptuously dismissing women's contribution to doctrinal discussion. Paavo himself confesses that he now has no strength, that the gate is shut. The smith reassures him that Christ will open it.

Scene iv. The frost. Paavo and Riita with their first child are in their first home in summer, playfully contemplating the future. Paavo plans to build a proper house but is daunted when a farm gate reminds him of Heaven's gate that he cannot open. A crowd appears, led by the same men and women as in Scene ii, who menace Paavo and describe how the frost is rising to threaten his crops. Paavo's frantic efforts to dispel it lead to disaster when the baby is trampled underfoot.

Scene v. Juhana and Riita. While Juhana mends Paavo's knapsack he tells his mother that he longs to get away and experience the world. She despairs at being left alone and Juhana abandons the idea for the moment. Riita hides the knapsack.

Scene vi. The last loaf. Riita begs Paavo to stay at home and not go off to meetings. He is more concerned to do God's business than look after his family and takes the last loaf in the house, as he is going on a long journey. In desperation, unable to feed their children, Riita throws an axe at Paavo. It misses.

Scene vii. Paavo's monologue. Paavo describes how he cannot open the door and remembers how he was drawn to the outside world, how people flocked to see and hear him. The orchestra vividly portrays their rowing across the water to him. He could not help them: 'I was talking to the air'. The interlude for strings that follows is particularly poignant.

Scene viii. Juhana's death revealed. The village women visit Riita, and reveal brutally that her son Juhana has died. She comments that the frost is destroying the corn, but she can no longer weep. Paavo himself sees this as God's just punishment on him.

Scene ix. Riita's death. It is late winter and she longs for spring. Despite everything, she looks back on a good life and thanks God for it. In her mind, she sees that the gate is open and asks Paavo to recite the psalm of thanksgiving ('Bless the Lord O my soul', psalm 103). He realises that, unlike her, he has wavered in his faith. He begins the psalm, but Juhana appears in a bright light and continues it. The act ends as Riita moves towards Juhana, saying, 'Now the gate is open'.

Act II, scene i (x). The Klajoki assizes. Even if we did not recognise Paavo's tormentors in the men sitting on the flagstones, the music would remind us of their taunts at the dance. It is the site of Paavo's famous victory against the authorities who once accused him and others of heresy. The men determine to hang him with his own words. His enemies distort what happened and what he said, and bring on beautiful women to tempt him. Paavo appeals to Christ to have mercy and falls down. The chorus sing a hymn.

Scene ii (xi). The fisherman (Paavo's second monologue). Riita appears (to shimmering strings and xylophone) and asks him 'Where are you?' 'In hell' he answers (to a clarinet descending into the lowest depths). In a memorably lyrical, soaring phrase she invites him 'to the island' ('Tul saareen'). In his second long monologue he reaffirms his mission. Riita begs him again to come to the island and give thanks, but he is determined to attack academic Christianity 'in its lair', at the graduation ceremony of the University of Helsinki.

Scene iii (xii). The graduation. The First, Second and Third Men wait in front of Helsinki Cathedral, still determined to destroy Paavo. Pretending not to recognise him, they laugh at him for being dressed as a farmer and imagining that he belongs with guests of honour. The works of devotion he has read do not count or even exist, according to them. He hears his hymn being played as the procession approaches and they stop him joining it.

Scene iv (xiii). The call to the island. Riita again invites Paavo to come to the island. She reassures him that he will be accepted.

Scene v (xiv). The dead. '*Only Paavo's face is visible... Suspended, "timeless" atmosphere*'. The smith explains that 'All temptations are caused by self-righteousness'. The smith, Riita and Juhana remind Paavo of important elements in his life, such as the book (his mission), the scythe (his duties at home) and the axe. He leaves the resolution to God.

Scene vi (xv). Paavo's prayer. On his deathbed once again, Paavo imagines he is going to join the procession (we hear fragments of his hymn in the orchestra). When the First, Second and Third Men and Women enter they are revealed as Paavo's family and household, all speaking, rather than singing. Paavo gradually returns to consciousness, and the orchestra stops playing as he speaks. Recognising that his death is near, he tells his girls not to cry and orders them to plant a tree on his grave – an extremely prickly one, to reflect his own nature. He asks Albertiina to read from the book the smith gave him. She does so, in speech that verges touchingly on song, or chant. Paavo begins his hymn. Soon the others take over and the chorus enter the room to join in as well. Until now we have only heard the minor-key version; Kokkonen reserves for this moment the major-key version, accompanied by the full orchestra. Finally, we hear Riita's lyrical invitation from off-stage. Paavo asks Christ to intercede for him. The orchestra has the last, eloquent word: a prolonged discord followed by timpani beats, silence, then resolution.

The Last Temptations has no formal numbers and only two extended solo passages (Paavo's monologues). Kokkonen orders his prose material with ensembles based on the interaction of the six anonymous soloists. He also uses recurrent rhythmic patterns: in the first and last scenes the timpani tap out a fairly constant rhythm that is at once Paavo's heartbeat and an anticipatory funeral march. Kokkonen delights in dances; the score's other principal structural motif is generated by the hymns' sacred, as opposed to the dances' secular patterns. It is characteristic of the opera's complex portrayal of its hero that Paavo loves dancing.

The opera proved an immense success in Finland, where it has become the national opera, and has been enthusiastically received wherever it has played abroad, thanks to its musical accessibility, occasional grim humour and the intensity of its near-*verismo* domestic scenes. It also helps that it stresses the human rather than the theological aspects of the story. The sustained string phrases under the biblical quotations go back to Bach passions, but are also not so far removed from Strauss's presentation of Jokanaan. When the dying Riita sees a vision of her dead son Juhana reciting a psalm 'in a bright light' and then moves towards him, sentimentality is only very nearly avoided – the situation is all too reminiscent of the dying nun's vision in *Suor Angelica*.

The role of Paavo Ruotsalainen was created and to a large extent defined by Martti Talvela, who managed superbly to incarnate the character's strengths and, of equal importance to this opera, his weaknesses, all the more touching for being portrayed by a magnificent bass voice: Kokkonen does not shirk from showing the inhumanity of the visionary, as well as his heroism.   P.

ERICH KORNGOLD
(born 29 May 1897, died 29 November 1957)

DIE TOTE STADT
The Dead City

Opera in three acts, libretto by Paul Schott (pseudonym for the composer and his father Julius), based on Georges Rodenbach's novel *Bruges-la-morte* (1892). First performances Hamburg, conducted by Egon Pollak; Cologne, conducted by Klemperer, both 4 December 1920. First U.S. performance, Metropolitan Opera, New York, 1921, with Maria Jeritza making her New York début as Marietta, Orville Harrold as Paul, conducted by Artur Bodanzky. Not yet apparently staged in the U.K.

Paul ....Tenor
Marietta, *dancer*/The Ghost of Marie,
    Paul's late wife ....Soprano
Frank, *Paul's friend* ....Baritone
Brigitta, *Paul's housekeeper* ....Mezzo-Soprano
Fritz, *Pierrot in Marietta's troupe* ....Baritone
Juliette, *dancer* ....Soprano
Lucienne, *dancer* ....Soprano
Gaston, *dancer* ....Tenor
Victorin, *stage director* ....Tenor
Count Albert..Tenor

Dancers, Beguine Sisters, Children, People

Place: Brussels
Time: Late Nineteenth Century
Running Time: 2 hours 15 minutes

Act I. Brigitta lets Paul's friend Frank in to the room where Paul keeps mementoes of his dead wife Marie. Brigitta warns him about Paul's unhealthy obsession with the past. Yesterday, however, Paul changed and wanted light to come inside his 'temple', saying, 'The dead rise again!' Brigitta uncovers a portrait of Marie wearing a shawl and holding a lute and shows Frank the braid of her golden hair that Paul keeps under glass. Paul explains to Frank that Marie is *not* dead: he has seen her in Bruges; she will visit him today. Korngold lavishes all his seductive art on Paul's narration, his 'fairytale, a miracle'. Somehow the shadowy, oneiric dankness of Bruges wells up, as Paul evokes his strolls by the canal, the vision of Marie... Frank warns him that he should not fantasise, but let the dead sleep. The score is haunted by Strauss, by

Salome at this point, with Paul as obsessed as the Princess of Judaea was. When Frank has gone, Paul tells the painting of Marie that he is waiting for her.

Somewhat reluctantly, for she is afraid of scandal, Brigitta lets Marietta in. The dancer is full of life, uninhibited. Paul wraps Marie's shawl around her shoulders and hands her the lute. She sings an intensely romantic, sad *Lied*, which she calls 'the song of true love that must die'. They sing the second verse together ('Glück, das mir verblieb'). She sees to her amused surprise that he is moved by 'the stupid song'. When she hears her lover Gaston singing outside, Marietta comments on how she likes his voice. She explains she is a dancer on tour and begins to dance, accompanying herself on the lute. The dance is supposedly an ecstatic celebration of Dionysiac life, which rouses Paul to try and embrace her. In avoiding him, she inadvertently draws back the curtain over Marie's portrait and recognises the lute and shawl. She refuses to take anything seriously, however, and reminds him that she can be found at the theatre, where she is dancing Hélène in Meyerbeer's *Robert le Diable*. Paul yields to desire. In the darkness, Marie steps out of the portrait and asks whether Paul has remained true to her. Assuring him that their love 'was, is and will be', she urges him to go into life, to see and understand. The act ends as Marietta appears to Paul in a fantastic costume.

Act II. The stage directions tells us that we briefly see Paul in his armchair, 'as at the end of Act I', to indicate that this scene is still part of his dream. We are on a deserted quay in Bruges, outside Marietta's house, near a convent with a bell-tower. In the exceptionally beautiful prelude, the bells ring out repeatedly. We need to know that in Bruges they are known as 'Iron Confessors'. They remind Paul of Marie's funeral and rouse his conscience: his longing to see Marietta is mixed with fear. Nuns cross the bridge and remind him that he, too, was once pure in heart. Suddenly he recognises Brigitta among them. She left Paul because he betrayed Marie's memory. Paul sees Frank approach Marietta's door and realises that his friend is his rival.

Marietta's troupe arrive in a boat without her. They pretend to be in Venice. Victorin, one of the dancers, and the Count, their rich patron, sing in honour of Marietta. The others suggest that as Gaston missed the show, he is probably in bed with Marietta. We are haunted by Strauss again, by *Ariadne auf Naxos*, with the troupe serenading their soprano. Marietta turns up on Gaston's arm and flirts with the Count. They drink a toast, 'Down with Bruges', and Marietta calls for a song. Franz obliges, accompanied by a piano and, at one point, by eight off-stage sopranos. The song is a display piece for the baritone voice, as Harlequin's was in *Ariadne*. Its aptly haunting refrain says it all: 'My yearning, my imagining, my dreams return to the past.' At its end Franz sinks to Marietta's feet. She decides to dance her solo from Meyerbeer's opera in the open air and lies down on the bench as though in a coffin, saying: 'As soon as I am a resurrected corpse, I'll seduce Robert.' Victorin whistles the resurrection theme, bells toll, an organ heaves and the music builds to a nightmarish climax – to Paul's disgust. She welcomes him as a 'true Robert', but he accuses her of lying and corruption. She refuses to let him judge her. He reveals that he only ever loved his dead wife in her; now he despises her. She pities him, however, and justifies her ecstatic life as necessary for her art. She offers him life, the sun, herself. He lets himself be seduced, agrees that he loves her for herself and even agrees that they should spend the night together in his house, in *her* (i.e. Marie's) room.

Act III. The entr'acte's blaring horns, repeatedly rising strings, and busy percussion make it quite clear how Marietta and Paul spent the night. The next morning, Marietta tells the portrait of Marie that she has now died again: since Paul loves Marietta, he is free from Marie ('Dich such'ich Bild!'). Bells chime once more: a religious procession goes by outside, to the sound of a potently mysterious march, garlanded with solo violin, cello and children's voices to ensure it resonates with innocence. Paul watches and describes the procession: monks carry statues and banners; citizens portray historical figures from the past. The procession seems to come through the room, glowing with radiant light (the scene is clearly intended to trump *Tosca*). Everyone

kneels, including Paul. Marietta is piqued by Paul's piety, a part of him that remains inaccessible to her. As the procession invades the room, Marietta resolves to confront the ghosts and superstition that fill Paul's mind. In a major passage, almost an aria, she looks back on her hard struggle to succeed: she made her own faith, when she made her own way in life. She insists that Paul kiss her. He rejects her. She declares the fight is between her and Marie, between life and death. Seizing the braid of Marie's hair she drapes it around her neck and begins to dance, expressing, as she does so, 'the conquering power of life'. He strangles her with it and then sees, to his horror, that she is, at last, exactly like Marie.

Paul wakes up and realises it was all a dream. Brigitta announces that Marietta has returned for her umbrella. She hints that perhaps she should stay. Paul remains silent, so she leaves. Frank sees Marietta and comments ironically, 'So that was the miracle?' The short scene between Paul and Frank carries a surprisingly high emotional charge, managing to be both realistic and nostalgic: some sort of resolution has been achieved. Paul will not see Marietta again. He has learnt his lesson: Bruges is the dead city; he agrees to try and leave with Frank. Alone, he sings another verse of the *Lied* he sang with Marietta. This time, he concludes that life and death must remain separate: 'Here on earth', as the composer himself wrote on the occasion of the opera's first performance in Vienna in 1921, 'there can be no reunion with those who have left us, there can be no resurrection.'

Die tote Stadt's dream-device enables Korngold to have it both ways: his music invites us to revel in obsession, to mix Dionysiac, sensuous abandonment with proto-blasphemous indulgence in religiosity, while also offering to make it all right by presenting this combination as the past which we have now superseded: so it was only a phase, after all... This makes for a heady combination even now: far from being a period piece, its power to disturb has brought it a new popularity on the continent and in New York as a thriller, an 'opéra noir'. When he directed it in Düsseldorf, Günter Krämer used apt references to Hitchcock's films (*Psycho*, *Vertigo*) to reveal it as 'a first-rate stage work' (*Opera*, May 1987).   P.

L

ÉDOUARD LALO

(born 27 January 1823, died 22 April 1892)

LE ROI D'YS
The King of Ys

Opera in three acts, text by Edouard Blau. Première at the Opéra-Comique, Paris, 7 May 1888, with Deschamps-Jéhin, Simonnet, Talazac, conductor Danbé. First performed New Orleans, 1890; Covent Garden, 1901, with Paquot, Adams, Jerome, Plançon; Metropolitan, 1922, with Ponselle, Alda, Gigli, Danise, Rothier, conductor Wolff.

Le Roi d'Ys	....	Bass
Margared ⎫ *His daughters*	....	Soprano
Rozenn ⎭	....	Soprano
Mylio	....	Tenor
Karnac	....	Baritone
Saint Corentin	....	Bass
Jahel	....	Baritone

Nobles, Warriors, Soldiers, People

Running Time: 1 hour 40 minutes

Lalo's career lay in orchestral and chamber music but there is evidence that his aspirations were operatic, for all that he composed only one substantial example. Even *Le Roi d'Ys*, successful the moment it was publicly heard and never long out of the repertory since, had to wait a dozen years from the time it was written until it was staged.

The story is founded upon a Breton legend. The impressive overture uses themes from the opera, prominent among them the duet 'En silence pourquoi souffrir?', which occurs as a cello solo, and Margared's aria in the second act.

Act I. Outside the palace of Ys. The people rejoice that the war in which they have recently been engaged is at an end, and that peace has been brought to them through the betrothal of the King's daughter Margared to the enemy leader, Karnac. As the crowd leaves the stage, the two sisters appear. Rozenn asks Margared why her looks are sad on the day on which her engagement is announced: 'En silence pourquoi souffrir?' At first Margared will not share her grief with anyone else, but eventually she admits that her heart was secretly given to a man, and that man was in the ship on which sailed the soldier Mylio, whom nobody has seen since the cessation of hostilities. She hates Karnac with a double loathing; he takes her away from the man she loves, and he is the enemy of her country. Rozenn tries to comfort her; she must lose no time in admitting her repugnance for Karnac, before it is too late and the marriage contract signed and sealed.

Alone, Rozenn in an aria avows her own love for Mylio himself. He appears suddenly at her side, and they pledge eternal faith to each other. Mylio disappears, and the King leads out Margared to meet Karnac, who appears with his followers. The people rejoice at the marriage which will put an end to their sufferings. During the course of the ceremony, Rozenn whispers to Margared that not only has Mylio returned – she has seen him – but his companions too, and among them must be the man for whom Margared languishes. Margared turns impulsively to her father, and repudiates Karnac; she cannot marry, she says, a man she does not love. The general consternation grows when Karnac pledges himself in revenge to carry the war through until Ys is totally destroyed. But at this moment, Mylio pushes his way through the crowd and swears to fight for Ys until the war is brought to a victorious conclusion. The people acclaim their champion.

Act II. The great hall of the palace. Margared looks from the window at Karnac's troops assembling on the plain below. Mylio will lead the armies of Ys, and Margared is filled with turbulent feelings on his account, which she expresses in a fine aria: 'Lorsque je t'ai vu soudain'. She suspects that Mylio loves Rozenn; if it is so, her love for her sister and Mylio would turn to implacable hate.

No sooner are the words out of her mouth than Rozenn and the King enter with Mylio. Margared hides, and hears Mylio reassure Rozenn – Saint Corentin has blessed the battle on which he is embarking – and, a moment later, her sister proclaims her love for the valiant general. The King gives his blessing to them, and then leaves with Mylio. Margared confronts Rozenn as her rival for the love of Mylio. May he die rather than be united with Rozenn! Rozenn is horror-stricken at her sister's words and tries to defend herself; were she in Margared's place, her heart might break, but she would not give way to hate: 'Tais-toi, Margared!' (Be silent, Margared!) But Margared is not to be appeased; she curses her sister and vows vengeance on her for having stolen Mylio.

The scene changes to the great plain in front of the castle of Ys. Mylio is proclaimed victorious, but ascribes the enemy's defeat to the intervention of Saint Corentin, the patron saint of Ys. The stage empties, and Karnac appears, dishevelled and worn after his unsuccessful fight. Margared stands before him, and offers him revenge for his defeat; she will, with his help, open the flood-gates and let in the sea to drown the town. As they go off together past the chapel of Saint Corentin, Margared challenges the saint to avert the disaster she will bring on Ys. The sky darkens, the statue of the Saint comes to life and calls on her to repent.

Act III. Gallery in the palace. On one side is the door to Rozenn's apartments. In accordance with Breton marriage custom, it is protected by young girls against the efforts of the friends of the bride-groom to force an entrance. Mylio himself joins his retainers and pleads his own cause. He sings the famous *Aubade*, 'Vainement, ma bien-aimée', a tune of delicious fragrance, accompanied by the female chorus. It accomplishes its purpose, and Rozenn to a Breton tune says she will grant his request. The procession forms up, and makes its way into the chapel opposite. As the sound of the *Te Deum* can be heard from the chapel, Margared and Karnac make their way into the castle. Karnac demands that Margared fulfil her promise, and when she seems reluctant to bring disaster on her relations and her countrymen, he taunts her until she is mad with jealousy.

Karnac and Margared leave together, and Mylio and Rozenn emerge from the ceremony, and sing of their love ('A l'autel j'allais rayonnant'). Margared reappears and overhears Rozenn and her father pray for her return. She is overcome with remorse and, when cries of alarm are heard outside, hastens forward to warn them of their impending fate. She tells them that Karnac has thrown open the gates which keep the sea from drowning the city, but that she herself has killed him for his deed.

The scene changes to the highest point of the city, where the people have taken refuge to escape the fate which threatens them all. The noise of the angry sea can be heard, and the crowd prays for deliverance from death. The water still mounts, and the King laments that half the city has already disappeared, carrying away most of his subjects. Suddenly Margared, as if in a trance, reflects that the waters will not recede until they have claimed the required victim. She herself is that victim, she opened the gates; she will die in expiation of her crime. She throws herself into the sea, which immediately grows calmer, and the people thank Saint Corentin for their deliverance.   H.

FRANZ LEHÁR

(born 30 April 1870, died 24 October 1948)

Franz Lehár was of Czech and Hungarian parentage, studied in Prague and later led military bands. With the dawn of a new century, he forsook bands and took exclusively to the theatre, where he had one success after another, hitting the bull's eye in 1905 with *The Merry Widow*, an operetta of something approaching perfection. In the 1920s his association with the tenor Richard Tauber brought fortune to each, and after a series of new or re-written operettas with Tauber in the lead (*Das Land des Lächelns – The Land of Smiles* – is perhaps the most famous), his last new work was an opera, *Giuditta*, written for the Vienna Opera with Jarmila Novotná and Tauber in the leads.   H.

DIE LUSTIGE WITWE

The Merry Widow

Operetta in three acts, text by Victor Léon and Leo Stein after Henri Meilhac's *L'attaché d'ambassade*. Première Theater an der Wien, Vienna, 30 December 1905, with Mizzi Günther and Louis Treumann (who made one or two early recordings). The operetta almost immediately became a hit and has been seen and heard all over the world ever since.

Baron Mirko Zeta, *Pontevedrian*
   Ambassador in Paris ....Bass
Valencienne, *his wife* ....Soprano
Count Danilo Danilovitsch, *First Secretary*........Tenor
Hanna Glawari, *a rich widow*.........................Soprano
Camille de Rosillon, *a Parisian*...........................Tenor
Raoul de St Brioche, *a Parisian* ....Tenor
Vicomte Cascada, *a Parisian*..........................Baritone
Bogdanowitsch, *Pontevedrian Consul*.............Baritone
Sylviane, *his wife*...Soprano
Kromow, *Pontevedrian Councillor* ....Baritone
Olga, *his wife*..Mezzo-Soprano
Pritschitsch, *Pontevedrian Military Attaché* ....Bass
Praskowia, *his wife* ....Mezzo-Soprano
Njegus, *an Embassy secretary*............................Tenor

Grisettes, Dancers, Guests

Place: Pontevedrian Embassy, Paris; Hanna
   Glawari's House in Paris

Time: Early Twentieth Century
Running Time: 2 hours 40 minutes

*T*he *Merry Widow*'s première turned out to be the opening of an era for the 'musical', but, sadly, the start of the obituary of the operetta, as from 1905 the genre began to decline and, with the death of Lehár after World War II, to die.

Count Danilo back in Pontevedro fell in love with Hanna, but his family disapproved of marriage to an impecunious girl, and she married a rich, elderly banker, by name Glawari, who promptly died leaving a very rich widow. She has now taken a house in Paris, to whose Pontevedrian embassy Count Danilo is posted.

In 1940 Lehár wrote a quite unnecessary but occasionally revived overture, but the operetta customarily begins with only a few bars of quick music.

Act I. The Prince's birthday is being celebrated in the Pontevedrian Embassy by Parisian guests and the Embassy staff led by the Ambassador, Baron Mirko Zeta. His present preoccupation, toasts and greetings out of the way, is to find the wealthy widow Hanna Glawari and make quite sure she doesn't marry a Frenchman, her millions being vital to the future of the shaky Pontevedrian economy. The Baron's young French wife Valencienne flirts with Camille de Rosillon, and, in spite of her protestation 'Ich bin eine anständ'ge Frau' (I'm a highly respectable wife[1]), their duet contains bittersweet seeds which may well – who knows? – bear fruit in the future. Hanna Glawari is expected and the Baron has sent Njegus, a trusty Embassy secretary, to make sure Count Danilo is around when she arrives. He seems like a good match for her, thinks the Ambassador, who has been assured that the only Frenchman of comparable standing is out of the reckoning as he is known to be in love with a married woman.

La Glawari is announced and, to general acclaim, makes her entrance, the cynosure of all male eyes, singing a mazurka over the murmured admiration of the male throng. She invites everyone to a party next day at her house. Valencienne, to keep her own nose clean, orders Camille to marry Hanna, then countermands her order immediately. It is time for Danilo to put in an appearance after a night on the town, and his song, 'Da geh' ich zu Maxim' (I'm off to chez Maxim), is justly famous as one of the great throwaway entrances of all time. He is a patriotic man all right, he says, but his first duty is to the girls at Maxim's restaurant. He subsides onto a sofa where Hanna finds him, and their sparring, which is to continue for most of the rest of the action, gets under way. At the outset, because he refuses to be branded a

---

[1] Translation throughout by Christopher Hassall.

Die lustige Witwe *(The Merry Widow). Maurice Chevalier as Count Danilo in the 1934 MGM film, directed by Ernst Lubitsch.*

fortune-hunter, he swears never to say to Hanna 'I love you'.

Camille and Valencienne daydream prettily of an unattainable future, but the Ambassador, thinking he sees a chance, instructs Danilo that it is his duty to marry the widow and so secure the Pontevedrian financial future. The finale is 'Ladies' Choice', with Danilo working hard to outmanoeuvre all the men who want to dance with Hanna until she chooses him, whereupon he offers to auction the prize he has seemingly won. Finally, partly out of instinct to beat the opposition, partly out of re-kindling of the old flame which pride insists no longer burns, he dances a waltz with her with all the genuine warmth which lies at the heart of this operetta.

Act II. The garden of Hanna Glawari's Parisian palace. Pontevedrian dancing precedes Hanna's singing of the score's best-known solo, the Vilja-Lied, 'Es lebt' eine Vilja' (There once lived a Vilja), the legend of a mountain sprite, with its haunting refrain and floated final top B. When Danilo arrives, Hanna continues her not-so-subtle advances, Danilo his impressive but constantly less believable evasions until they confront each other in a wooing duet disguised as a piece of fooling but so full of charm as to fool nobody: 'Dummer, dummer Reitersmann' (Silly, silly cavalryman).

The mood changes and Pontevedrians and Frenchmen, led of course by Danilo but including the unsuspecting Baron, nudge each other on the subject of women and fidelity, a rollicking septet which concludes that the whole subject is shrouded for most of them in mystery ('Ach, die Weiber, diese Weiber!': Oh these women, dreadful women). The Baron for his part believes the fool of a husband of the married woman Camille loves should be persuaded to give her up. To the rhythms of *kolo* and then waltz – *the* waltz – Hanna and Danilo remain determinedly, at least on his part, at cross-purposes but move nonetheless ever closer together. As far as Hanna is concerned, the hunt is on!

The rest of the act's action revolves round a pavilion in the garden. Valencienne is still determined to keep her flirtation with Camille at that level and nothing more, but he pursues her not only with ardour but, for an operetta, with quite exceptional gallantry. His aria, 'Wie eine Rosenknospe' (Red as the rose of Maytime), with its elegant balance, stands out in Lehár's output as a solo of quite extraordinary quality.

They go into the pavilion, and are observed by the all-seeing, nil-revealing Njegus, who knows that the Baron and Danilo are due to meet there. The Baron's curiosity is aroused and he looks through the keyhole to see to his horror Valencienne with an anonymous man. The situation requires all Njegus's skill if it is to be resolved happily and he contrives somehow to get Valencienne out of the pavilion and Hanna into it before the Baron comes back to open the door. When he does, it is Hanna who emerges with Camille, who repeats the declaration of love he has just made to Valencienne, to the Baron's relief but to the consternation of the by now thoroughly jealous Danilo.

The cat is truly among the pigeons, and Hanna keeps the pot boiling by announcing her engagement to Camille, somewhat to that worthy's surprise. Danilo reacts with sarcasm about marriage and its durability, but celebration seems general until Danilo embarks on a sad little parable, beginning 'There once were two royal children', outlining the unwilling silence of one and the ultimate betrayal by the other, and ending in such obvious distress that Hanna is left in no doubt of his love.

Act III. The ballroom of Hanna's house is now decorated like Maxim's. Valencienne and grisettes – real ones – dance and sing to general delight, but a telegram from Pontevedro announces imminent bankruptcy unless Hanna's millions are retrieved for the national treasury. Hanna tells Danilo that not everything that took place in the pavilion was quite as it seemed, and she and Danilo plight their troth – after so much ado, what other expression will serve? – to the strains of the *Merry Widow* waltz – lazy, over-familiar perhaps, but still packing a romantic punch.

Explanations pour out. The Baron's rejoicing turns to ashes as Valencienne's fan is found in the pavilion; he declares himself divorced and free to marry Hanna, but all is saved when Hanna tells him her late husband's will declares her fortune forfeit if she re-marries, and the fan turns out to have 'I am a respectable wife' written on it in Valencienne's unmistakable hand. 'I never knew that', says the Baron, shaken but not stirred. Danilo without risk of appearing a fortune-hunter can openly declare his love for Hanna, and even revelation of another clause in the will giving the fortune to Hanna's new husband causes no new twist to the tale. The last chorus hymns, as it had halfway through Act II, the eternal mystery of women as seen through men's eyes, only this time the women are allowed to shed some light on proceedings by joining in.

Casting of the operetta is not quite straightforward. Hanna is no soubrette, closer, a Viennese soprano once said to me, to a young Tosca than to a Susanna; Danilo on the other hand is a personality, preferably (to avoid transposition) belonging to a tenor, or at least a baritone with an easy top G. Camille is a straightforward tenor, essentially one with a top C, and Valencienne is the kind of singer Viennese operetta throws up, a soubrette with an ability to sing the low *tessitura* Lehár often writes. But the whole is much more than the sum of its parts: an operetta not only of apparently unquenchable popularity but with a splendid, witty book, and a variegated, brilliant score, each with uniquely erotic overtones. A quite unusual masterpiece!   H.

RUGGIERO LEONCAVALLO

(born 23 April 1858, died 9 August 1919)

PAGLIACCI

Strolling Players

Opera in two acts, words by the composer. Première, Teatro dal Verme, Milan, 21 May 1892, with Stehle, Giraud, Maurel, Ancona, Daddi, conductor Toscanini.

Canio *(in the play, 'Pagliaccio'),*
   head of a troupe of strolling players..................Tenor

Nedda *(in the play, 'Colombina', Columbine),*
   wife of Canio .... Soprano

Tonio *(in the play, 'Taddeo'), a clown*..............Baritone

Beppe *(in the play, 'Arlecchino', Harlequin)*.........Tenor

Silvio, *a villager*...Baritone

Villagers

Place: Montalto, in Calabria
Time: The Feast of the Assumption in about 1865–70
Running Time: 1 hour 5 minutes

It would not be accurate to suggest that *Pagliacci* was Leoncavallo's only successful opera, *La Bohème* and *Zazà* figuring at least spasmodically in the repertory for much of the twentieth century. But *Pagliacci* far outstrips the others in number of performances.

Pagliacci opens with a prologue as Tonio pokes his head through the curtains – 'Si può? Signore, Signori' (By your leave, ladies and gentlemen). The prologue, successful even as a concert piece, rehearses the story of the opera in musical phrases which recur later.

Act I. The outskirts of the village. People are celebrating the Feast of the Assumption and waiting for the arrival of a group of peripatetic players. Beppe in his Harlequin costume leads in a donkey cart in which reclines Nedda, followed by Canio in his Pagliaccio costume and Tonio, dressed as Taddeo.

Canio addresses the crowd. At eleven o'clock their play will begin; the troubles and vengeance of Pagliaccio is the theme. Tonio starts to help Nedda out of the cart but Canio shoves him aside and Tonio goes off muttering. A villager suggests Tonio might in real life be after Nedda, and Canio grimly replies that in the play he would risk a beating, but in life much more.

Nedda is alone. Canio's manner worries her but the birds are singing and she thinks of her childhood (*ballatella*: 'Oh! che volo d'augelli'). Tonio sneaks back to protest his love. The more he pleads, the more she mocks him and the angrier he gets. He attempts a kiss, but she strikes him across the face and he goes off, muttering revenge.

Nedda's lover Silvio comes in, telling her their meeting is perfectly safe as Canio is drinking at the inn. Nedda must leave with him that very night after the performance. She is not confident but eventually agrees. After an impassioned love duet, 'E allor perchè, di', tu m'hai stregato', the lovers agree not to see each other again until after the play.

Tonio has been listening and goes to fetch Canio, who arrives in time to hear Nedda call after Silvio. Canio, knife in hand, rushes forward but Nedda obstructs him and Silvio escapes. The enraged Canio demands his name, but Nedda refuses to give it. Tonio and Beppe restrain him: Nedda's lover will be at the play.

Left alone to prepare for the performance, Canio laments his predicament. His soliloquy, 'Vesti la giubba' (On with the motley), is one of opera's famous moments. 'Ridi Pagliaccio' (Laugh then, Pagliaccio), he sobs; the clown must make others laugh even though his heart is breaking.

Act II. The audience is waiting and the play begins. Colombina's husband, Pagliaccio, is away until morning, Taddeo is at the market and she is waiting for her lover, Arlecchino. A minuet provides the musical background. Arlecchino/Beppe sings a serenade, 'O Colombina, il tenero fido Arlecchin'.

Taddeo enters and makes advances to Colombina, who summons Arlecchino to throw him out. As well as his bottle of wine, Arlecchino has brought a sleeping potion for Pagliaccio. Taddeo bursts in – Pagliaccio is on his way, full of suspicions and hopping mad at her. Arlecchino nips out of the window, instructing Colombina to pour the philtre into her husband's wine. She calls after him 'Tonight, love, and forever I am yours!' – the very words Canio heard his wife use to her lover a few hours before.

Colombina tells Pagliaccio that she is alone, apart from Taddeo who is hiding in the cupboard. The audience laughs, but Canio loses control and demands Nedda tell him her real lover's name. The more Nedda tries to stay in character, the more desperate Canio becomes, insisting that he is not Pagliaccio but a man with real feelings. The audience sees his intensity as great acting. Still trying to keep up appearances, Nedda begins a gavotte, 'Suvvia, così terribile'. She stops, Canio grabs a knife and demands the name. Nedda tries to leave but Canio catches and stabs her. Silvio rushes to help and Canio stabs him in his turn, then stands stupefied: 'La commedia è finita' (The comedy is ended).

Confidence behind the première of *Pagliacci* is suggested by the engagement of a brilliant cast of leading singers (no less than two top baritones) as well as the up-and-coming Toscanini. That confidence has been justified and tenors and baritones of the top rank have queued for the leading roles, de Lucia and Caruso making an early mark as Canio, Battistini and Ruffo as Tonio. Nedda, less showy, was sufficiently well thought of early on to have Melba as her first exponent both at Covent Garden and the Metropolitan. The opera, which Leoncavallo maintained was based on a true story witnessed by his father, a magistrate, is admirably shaped, highly effective, and has been paired with a number of other one-acters, though never so compatibly it would seem as with *Cavalleria Rusticana*.   H.

LA BOHÈME

Commedia lirica in four acts, libretto by the composer, based on Henry Murger's novel *Scènes de la vie de Bohème* (1847–49) and his play (with Barrière) *La vie de Bohème* (1849). First performance at La Fenice, Venice, 6 May 1897. Leoncavallo's revision (with Rodolfo as a tenor) as *Mimì Pinson, scene della vita di Bohème* given at the Teatro Massimo, Palermo, 1913, revived Teatro San Carlo, Naples, 1957, La Fenice, Venice, 1990. First U.K. performance, Camden Town Hall, London, 1970.

Marcello, *a painter*	Tenor
Rodolfo, *a poet*	Baritone
Schaunard, *a musician*	Baritone
Barbemuche	Bass
Visconte Paolo	Baritone
Gustavo Colline	Baritone
Gaudenzio	Tenor
Durand	Tenor
The Gentleman from the First Floor	Tenor
Musette	Mezzo-Soprano
Mimì	Soprano
Eufemia, *a laundress*	Mezzo-Soprano

Students, Neighbours, Café Customers, Waiters, Salesmen

Place: Paris, Latin Quarter
Time: 1837–38
Running Time: 2 hours 15 minutes

Leoncavallo began to construct a libretto from Murger's *Scènes de la vie de Bohème* in 1892 and only thought of setting it himself when Puccini refused it. Puccini, however, was always keener on a project for an opera if someone else had already shown interest in it. In 1893 he denied that Leoncavallo had told him he was writing an opera on the subject and welcomed the competition. Puccini finished first (in 1895) and his opera was given in Turin the following year. Leoncavallo followed with his *La Bohème* in 1897 and for a time both operas co-existed in the repertory.

Act I. 24 December 1837. In a room on the first floor of the Café Momus, Gaudenzio, its proprietor, rebukes Schaunard and his Bohemian friends for eating little and paying less. Marcello imported his easel and models; Schaunard taught singing there. A potential student arrives in answer to the advertisement and is chased away by Gaudenzio. Schaunard promises they will reform. His friends the poet Rodolfo and the painter Marcello arrive, both almost penniless. The philosopher Colline turns out to have no money, either, when he arrives with Eufemia, Schaunard's girlfriend. Mimì, Rodolfo's girlfriend, a flower-girl, introduces her friend Musette, a seamstress who has left her wealthy banker friend in order

to meet the Bohemians. Marcello falls instantly in love with her (parodying Raoul's recitative from Meyerbeer's *Les Huguenots*). Schaunard introduces them all to her. In return, Mimì presents Musette to them as a delicious flirt, in love with love.

They sit down and consume a hearty meal. Musette sings for them, this time about Mimì ('Mimì Pinson la biondinetta'). Marcello makes love to Musette, who warns him that she is vain and capricious, while the others complain about the service. When the bill comes they realise they have no money to pay for it. One of the other guests, Barbemuche, a teacher and writer who longs to join the Bohemians, offers to pay but his offer is refused. Instead, Schaunard challenges him to a game of billiards. The Bohemians' comments on the match counterpoint Musette's scene with Marcello. He offers to paint her portrait and declares his love; she agrees to mend his waistcoat, but warns him to be her friend, rather than her lover ('Signorina Musette'). Schaunard wins, Gaudenzio is paid and the bells ring out for Christmas Day.

Act II. 15 April 1838. Musette lost the apartment her rich banker rented for her when he discovered she had installed her lover, Marcello. Her furniture has been piled up in the courtyard. Marcello offers to share his attic with her, if she will sometimes sing for him and the swallows that haunt it ('Io non ho che una povera stanzetta'). She remembers she has invited guests for a party that evening, and decides to hold it in the courtyard itself. Rodolfo bribes the concierge, Durand, and explains that he has sold his tragedy *Vendicator* (The Avenger). The Bohemians arrange the furniture and look forward to the party in a hectic ensemble obviously inspired by Verdi's *Falstaff*.

Durand announces the guests. Barbemuche brings his pupil, the rich Viscount Paolo. Schaunard rebukes Eufemia: for the second time he has found evidence she has another lover. Schaunard goes to the piano and directs a performance of the Bohemians' Hymn, celebrating youth and love. Schaunard threatens to perform his cantata 'On the Influence of Blue on the Arts'. The Viscount tempts Mimì by offering her riches. She knows she would regret it forever... At Marcello's suggestion Musette sings her song in praise of the voluptuous waltz. An ensemble builds up as the Viscount tempts Mimì to leave poverty and accept his 'protection'. Schaunard imitates Rossinian opera in his cantata on the theme of blue. Mimì leaves in the Viscount's carriage. Other lodgers complain at the Bohemians' riotous party and, in a noisy finale, chase them away.

Act III. October 1838. Marcello's attic. Schaunard and Marcello are hungry and sick of poverty. They comment on Rodolfo's unhappiness, since Mimì left him for the Viscount. Musette is still there, but very hungry, which Marcello takes as a reproach. He sees their rose has died. When Musette came to him, she promised to stay till it died. The two men go off to find some money. Musette decides to leave Marcello and writes him a letter: hunger is driving her out to wander the boulevards. She asks the porter to hand the letter to him. She meets Mimì, who has come back to Rodolfo, and they compare notes in a duet. Mimì hides behind a screen when Marcello arrives in fury, having read Musette's letter. She tells him how much pain the letter cost her and he realises she does love him. When she asks for a farewell kiss, he repulses her violently. The screen is overturned, revealing Mimì. Marcello blames her for finding Musette a new protector. Rodolfo arrives and refuses to listen to her. She leaves. Once Musette has also left, Marcello gives in to his grief at losing his beloved.

Act IV. 24 December 1838. Rodolfo's attic. In a sumptuous showpiece for the baritone voice, Rodolfo welcomes the bitter wind that suits his new poem: rejecting glory, riches and poetry, since he cannot have love, he welcomes death ('Scuoti, o vento'). Schaunard brings lunch (bread, potatoes and herrings) and all three remember their last Christmas. Mimì arrives, near to death. Abandoned by the Viscount, she could not afford to stay in hospital and has nowhere to go. Musette arrives, singing her song from Act II, and immediately sends Schaunard to pawn her jewels for money. It is too late, however: Mimì dies, remembering the last Christmas Eve they spent together, with 'Natale!' (Christmas!) on her lips.

Inevitably, Puccini's masterpiece has pushed Leoncavallo's version of *La Bohème* out of the limelight. Where they try to do the same things, such as manipulating bitter-sweet emotions, Puccini's opera is funnier, sadder, more intense, more real – better. Instead of interleaving them, Leoncavallo devotes the first two acts to comedy, the last two to tragedy. The superiority of Puccini's opera is most evident in its ending, whose overwhelming theatrical power makes the sentimentality of Leoncavallo's ending sound even cheaper than it is. It would be easy to say they are very different works; they are not. And yet, on its own merits, Leoncavallo's *La Bohème* undoubtedly deserves to be more widely performed. It is full of meaty, grateful roles. It is refreshingly unmealy-mouthed about money and sex: when Marcello asks, 'What is your new lover's name?' Musette answers, 'I don't know yet'. It also moves fluently, with frequent brief excursions into lyricism, while many of the arias are incorporated into the drama as performances of songs, a hymn, a cantata and a letter. The tension doesn't slacken, as it does with Puccini occasionally – when the tenor sits, you know it's time for the soprano's aria.   P.

ZAZÀ

Opera in four acts, text by the composer. Première at the Teatro Lirico, Milan, 10 November 1900, with Storchio, Garbin, Sammarco, conductor Toscanini. First performed in London at Coronet Theatre, 1909; Metropolitan, New York, 1920, with Farrar, Crimi, Amato. Revived la Scala, 1940, with Favero, Gigli, Bechi; Naples, 1950, with Favero, Prandelli, Tagliabue.

Zazà, *a music-hall singer* ....Soprano
Anaide, *her mother*..............................Mezzo-Soprano
Floriana, *a music-hall singer*..........................Soprano
Natalia, *Zazà's maid* ....Mezzo-Soprano
Mme Dufresne ....Mezzo-Soprano
Milio Dufresne, *a young man-about-town* ....Tenor
Cascart, *a music-hall performer* ....Baritone
Bussy, *a journalist*...Baritone
Marlardot, *proprietor of a music-hall*..................Tenor
Lartigon, *monologist*...Bass
Duclou, *stage manager*..Bass
Michelin, *journalist*..Tenor
Courtois ....Bass
Marco, *Dufresne's butler*...............................Baritone
Toto, *Dufresne's child*..................................Soprano
Auguste..Tenor
Claretta ....Soprano
Simona ....Soprano

Place: Paris
Time: The Present
Running Time: 1 hour 50 minutes

Leoncavallo is supposed to have preferred *Zazà* to *Pagliacci*, but the public has been reluctant to accept the later opera at the composer's own valuation. All the same, it has enjoyed a certain success whenever a singing actress of sufficient personal appeal has been available for the title role.

Act I. The scene is backstage at the music-hall where Zazà is the star attraction. On one side of the stage can be seen her dressing-room, on the other the back of a stage set. Zazà and her stage partner Cascart are lovers, but Zazà has taken a fancy to Milio Dufresne, and she boasts to the journalist Bussy that it will not be long before Dufresne in his turn succumbs to her charms. Zazà and her rival Floriana argue furiously and we meet her drunken mother before Zazà and Cascart sing a charming 'kiss' duet, a parody of the sentimental music-hall ditties of the period. Dufresne waits for Zazà to come off-stage, and gossips with Bussy, revealing as he does so that he is considerably attracted to Zazà. He describes her smile with more rapture than caution: 'È un riso gentil'. It is obvious to Bussy that Zazà's conquest is already made.

Act II. The love affair between Dufresne and Zazà is quickly under way, and the two of them go off to Zazà's house in the suburbs of Paris. Dufresne says that he must go away on business, and Zazà accepts this philosophically enough, until Cascart comes to see her. He hints that the trip may have other reasons than business behind it, and says that Dufresne has been seen with another woman in Paris. The scene includes a well-known aria for Cascart, 'Buona Zazà'. Zazà resolves to see for herself whether these suspicions are justified or not; she will follow Dufresne.

Act III. Dufresne's Paris residence. Dufresne sings unhappily of his prospective separation from Zazà ('Mai più, Zazà'), then leaves the house with his wife. Zazà, accompanied by Natalia, goes to the address she has been given. She sees a letter addressed to Madame Dufresne and realises with a shock that the 'other woman' in Dufresne's life is his wife. Dufresne's little child tells Zazà that her mother is out, and, when she is alone, Zazà gives way to her grief: 'Mamma usciva di casa'. She makes an excuse that she has come to the wrong address and leaves.

Act IV. Zazà's house. Cascart tries to persuade Zazà to give up Dufresne, who is likely to bring nothing but sorrow and suffering into her life. The stage is her career, and his old affection for her is just as strong as ever: 'Zazà, piccola zingara'. But she cannot go against the dictates of her heart, for all her affection for Cascart, and she sends him away. When Dufresne returns to the house, Zazà taxes him with what she has discovered. She says that his being married makes no difference to her love for him, but, in an effort to punish him for his deception, pretends that she revealed their liaison to Madame Dufresne. Dufresne furiously curses her for what she has done and throws her to the floor in his anger. Zazà's love is cured, and she sends Dufresne away, after telling him that she revealed nothing to his wife, who does not even know of her existence.   H.

GYÖRGI LIGETI
(born 28 May 1923)

LE GRAND MACABRE

Opera in two acts (four scenes), libretto by Michael Meschke and the composer after Michel de Ghelderode's 'La Ballade du Grand Macabre'. Première, Stockholm, 12 April 1978, with Britt-Marie Aruhn, Elisabeth Söderström, Kerstin Meyer, Barbro Ericson, Sven-Erik Vikström, Erik Saeden, Arne Tyren, conductor Elgar Howarth. First performed Hamburg, 15 October 1978; Bologna, 1979 (in Italian); Paris, 1981;

English National Opera, 1982, with Marilyn Hill Smith, Penelope Mackay, Jean Rigby, Ann Howard, Roderick Keating, Geoffrey Chard, Dennis Wicks, conductor Howarth.

Chief of the Secret Police
  (Gepopo)[1] ....Coloratura Soprano
Venus[1] ....High Soprano
Clitoria..Soprano
Spermando[2] ....Mezzo-Soprano

---

[1] May be sung by the same singer.

[2] Trouser role.

Prince Go-Go[1] ....Soprano

Mescalina, *Astradamors's wife* ....Mezzo-Soprano

Piet the Pot ....High Buffo Tenor

Nekrotzar ....Baritone

Astradamors, *an astrologer*................................Bass

Three ruffians
    Ruffiak ....Baritone
    Schobiak ....Baritone
    Schabernak ....Baritone

White Minister ....Speaking Role

Black Minister ....Speaking Role

Secret Police, Prince Go-Go's Servants

Place: Breughelland
Time: Nebulous
Running Time: 2 hours 15 minutes

It was more than a dozen years before its eventual première that the then director of the Stockholm Opera, Göran Gentele, asked Ligeti to write an opera. Initially the composer envisaged a music drama without narrative but, when Gentele was killed in a motor accident, he abandoned the work and only after several false starts settled on a play by the Flemish dramatist Michel de Ghelderode (1893–1962).

After the première, Ligeti's music was described as 'a brilliant, exotic music-box of medleys, set pieces, recurrent motifs, quotations and references proposed with the greatest delicacy, bound together with a quick, taut thread'.[2] It is an individual work, bizarre for much of the time, often jocular, always imaginative, and so far from narrative-opera that no one of its several productions in the first years of its life closely resembled any other. If the composer appeared to prefer the one in Bologna, because its jocularly pornographic nature most resembled his imaginings, he seems not to have favoured its original staging (with which he was closely associated), but to be an opera composer constantly in search of the perfect realisation.

The prelude is written for twelve tuned motor-horns, precisely notated, less precise in intonation, but producing an effect that combines rhythmical, even melodic, interest with the sheer quirkiness that somehow typifies one aspect of Ligeti's vision.

Act I, scene i. Breughelland. It is a mixture of the *Dies Irae* and the praises of his own country which Piet the Pot sings while an epicene pair of lovers,

Clitoria and Spermando, search for a place where they can make eternal love. Piet is sometimes tipsy, sometimes drunk (say the stage directions). Clitoria and Spermando duet in a land of unending 'O altitudo!' and have found, if the gentle strains of their love duetting are to be believed, the secret of suspended, but continually erotic, animation (Clitoria climaxes on a top D). As Piet watches them in amazement and delight, Nekrotzar can be heard prophesying death, and indeed grandiloquently claiming to be no less a person than Death himself. It is, he says, his task to bring the world to an end. The music of Piet and Nekrotzar cavorts until it almost gets out of hand, and in the end Piet, in spite of his efforts at evasion, is conscripted to help Nekrotzar in what he conceives to be his mission. Piet collects scythe, hat, cloak, from the tomb which Clitoria and Spermando have appropriated for love-making, and Nekrotzar makes a proclamation of doom as he rides off on Piet's back.

The last word, amorous needless to say, goes to Clitoria and Spermando before motor-horns take us in a short interlude to scene ii. Astradamors, the astrologer, is fortunate, as a masochist, in that his nymphomaniac wife Mescalina is a sadist. She is seen whip in hand at curtain rise and their love play is extensive and explicit, she in leather, he at first in female clothing. But Astradamors after all concerns himself primarily with the heavens and he goes to his telescope only to discover elements of the skyscape just as alarming, it would appear, as what has been going on on earth. Mescalina falls asleep totally drunk, and implores Venus to send her down a lover a bit more active than her husband.

It is not long before her prayer is answered as Nekrotzar comes in with Piet, and he turns out to be not at all backward in responding to her appeal. His love-making is so vigorous that she expires.

Astradamors, who does not conceal his delight to be quit of her, joins Nekrotzar and Piet in their journey to the Prince's palace.

Act II, scene iii. In contrast to Act I, Act II starts with tuned and tinkling electric bells, which bring us to Prince Go-Go's palace. The Prince at first seems scared of anything, but in the course of the action turns out to be not without his effective moments. Two politicians are trading insults and the Prince does not seem dis-

---

[1] Trouser role; may be sung by countertenor.

[2] Dominic Gill in the *Financial Times*.

posed to intervene. At one point he is lifted against his will on to a rocking horse for his riding lesson, and later he is required to memorise a speech. Eventually, the Ministers in dudgeon resign and the Prince, to their astonishment, accepts their resignations.

The Chief of the Secret Police, disguised as a brightly coloured bird (so say the stage directions), comes in, all brilliant coloratura, staccatos, high notes, two-octave jumps, to bring news of serious public disturbances and the approach of a procession. This galvanises the Prince to action and he makes a speech to produce quiet among the people.

The peace turns out to be short-lived, as the imminent arrival of Nekrotzar, with his retinue of Piet and Astradamors, will produce little short of panic. The Chief of Police starts to expostulate in even greater flights of coloratura, and, after reading a dispatch, he warns of some terrible coming. When Astradamors appears, he is jovial, it must be admitted, rather than terrible.

Here in the published score (but in Stockholm at the première it preceded Act II) comes a large-scale instrumental number based on the theme from the finale of Beethoven's *Eroica* (on timpani and lower strings) with four solo instruments (violin, piccolo, E flat clarinet, bassoon; in Stockholm, on stage) playing variations above it. During its very attractive course, Nekrotzar, still riding on Piet's back, enters in procession. Nothing apparently can stop his prophecies of doom, but Piet and Astradamors unwittingly cause a diversion by filling him up with drink, which he takes at first absent-mindedly from them. Eventually, after a lengthy and in the end almost ritualistic carousal, Nekrotzar starts to wax almost lyrical, so that, with Prince Go-Go joining in, when it comes to it, he has just enough control of speech to utter the words that should, as midnight strikes, bring the world to an end.

Scene iv. The music at first is as dimly lit as the scene, but briefly accelerates before the trombones apparently run out of steam and we are in calmer waters, back in Breughelland, with Piet and Astradamors hovering just above the ground, dreaming that they are in heaven. They leave the scene but Prince Go-Go seems to have survived as well, nervous when he finds himself apparently alone, and, it would seem, with some reason when three cut-throats set about him. He is rescued by Nekrotzar, thoroughly hung-over from the night before and amazed to find any survivors of the apocalypse. When Nekrotzar tries to get back into the tomb from which he emerged in the first place, Mescalina jumps out of it and starts chasing him. Prince Go-Go tries to assert his authority, and it is not long before the two Ministers, as well as Piet and Astradamors, come on to the scene. Piet, Astradamors and Prince Go-Go drink, and there ensues a quiet and very beautiful musical section marked *andante calmo* during which Nekrotzar starts to shrivel up and collapse, until by the end of this mirror canon, he has entirely disappeared.

At this point, the two lovers emerge from the tomb, quite ignorant of what has been going on. Their mood, post-coital and serene, starts to affect everyone and in a final *passacaglia* they decide that there is nothing to fear in death.

Le Grand Macabre (how translate the title? *The Great Horseman of the Apocalypse?*) is, it has been said, an opera for a time without answers, an opera whose subject is sex and death, and in which the only victim of the holocaust is the bringer of death himself. The composer called it an 'anti-anti-opera' (in 1965, he had planned to write no more than an anti-opera, in the vein of the attractive *Aventures* and *Nouvelles Aventures*), and yet the publisher of *Le Grand Macabre* was able at the end of a brochure devoted to it to quote from an English newspaper: 'If anyone can resurrect the art of opera, Ligeti looks the man.'   H.

ALBERT LORTZING

(born 23 October 1801, died 21 January 1851)

ZAR UND ZIMMERMANN

Tsar and Carpenter

Comic opera in three acts, text by the composer, founded on a French play by J.T. Merle. First produced Leipzig, 22 December 1837; New York, 1851; London, Gaiety Theatre, 1871 (in English, as *Peter the Shipwright*), with Santley and Blanche Cole.

Peter I, *Tsar of Russia*.....................................Baritone

Peter Ivanov, *a runaway soldier* ....Tenor

van Bett, *Burgomaster of Saardam* ....Bass

Marie, *his niece*..Soprano

Admiral Lefort, *Russian Ambassador* ....Bass

Lord Syndham, *English Ambassador*....................Bass

Marquis de Châteauneuf, *French Ambassador* ...Tenor

Witwe Browe ....Contralto

Place: Saardam, Holland
Time: 1698
Running Time: 2 hours 30 minutes

The composer's popularity in German-speaking theatres was demonstrated during 1958–59 when 565 operas by 290 composers were performed. Lortzing, with 1,044 performances in sixty-two theatres, came fourth in the list of composers, after Verdi, Mozart and Puccini. His *Der Wildschütz* was the second most popular individual opera! This popularity waned in late twentieth century.

Act I. Peter the Great of Russia, under the name of Peter Michaelov, is working in the shipbuilding yards at Saardam, in Holland, with a view to gaining experience and knowledge such as he could never find in Russia itself. He has become friends with Peter Ivanov, another Russian and a deserter from the armed forces. Peter Ivanov has fallen in love with Marie, the Burgomaster's niece, a coquette who cannot resist showing him that he is not the only attractive man about the place. Van Bett, the comically self-opinionated Burgomaster, has been approached by the Ambassadors of England and France to find out if the Tsar is secretly working in Saardam. He calls together the shipworkers, and finding many are called Peter, determines on a subtle and, he thinks, foolproof stratagem: which of them, he asks, is a foreigner? To his con-

sternation, two step forward – Peter Ivanov and Peter Michaelov. He needs time to fathom it all out; let everyone go back to work – he has all the information he requires. He decides that Peter Ivanov is the man he is looking for, and accordingly offers him whatever he chooses, even the hand of his niece in marriage, if he will admit his identity to the foreign gentleman to whom he will presently introduce him. At the end of the act, the French Ambassador has recognised the Tsar and even made contact with him, while Syndham and van Bett, thinking Ivanov is their man, start to pay court to him.

Act II. A local festivity is in progress. All watch the dancing and listen to the singing, and the French Ambassador even sings a song in praise of Flemish beauty, much to the chagrin of Peter Ivanov, who takes it to be aimed at Marie. The principal characters divide into two groups: Peter Michaelov, the French and Russian Ambassadors on one side, Peter Ivanov, van Bett, and Lord Syndham on the other, and negotiations proceed. Van Bett has had a good deal to drink, and he thinks the time has come for him to solve his problem in his own way. He demands, with more forthrightness than manners, the names and identification of the three Ambassadors present in the inn. Somewhat taken aback by their answers, he announces he will arrest the two Peters, and is only prevented from carrying out his design when the Tsar draws his sword and announces he will not be taken alive.

Act III. Van Bett prepares to send 'the Tsar' on his way with full musical honours. He rehearses his choir and tells them that he himself will sing the solo part; nothing is too much trouble if it will honour their noble visitor. The Tsar himself has in the meanwhile found the means to provide himself with a ship in which to sail home, promising before he leaves a safe conduct for Peter Ivanov. Van Bett starts off his anthem (which he directs at Ivanov, still thinking him the Tsar), but is interrupted by the sound of a cannon shot; the real Tsar is about to leave the harbour. He pauses for a moment to take leave of his friends, and is gone, to the acclamation of the crowd.

The best role is for van Bett, whose entrance aria in Act I, with its catch-phrase, 'Oh, ich bin klug und weise', is a favourite with German comic basses. Perhaps the most enjoyable moment in the opera is his rehearsal in the last act; this is capital fun, with van Bett's 'diddle-dum, diddle-dum, diddle-dum' to show when the orchestra plays alone, and his relish of the excellence of his own words. In Act II, the French Ambassador has a charming solo, 'Lebewohl mein flandrisch' Mädchen', and in the last act occur the Tsar's song, 'Sonst spielt' ich mit Szepter und Kron', and the Clog dance, the latter a direct fore-runner of Wagner's apprentices.   H.

DER WILDSCHÜTZ

The Poacher

Opera in three acts, text by the composer based on a play by A. von Kotzebue. First produced at Leipzig, 31 December 1842. First performance in England, Drury Lane, 1895 (in German); New York, 1856. Edinburgh Festival, 1958, by Stuttgart Opera, with Lore Wissmann, Plümacher, Wunderlich, Schmitt-Walter, Fritz Linke, conductor Leitner.

The Count of Eberbach .... Baritone

The Countess, *his wife* .... Contralto

Baron Kronthal, *her brother* .... Tenor

Baroness Freimann, *the Count's sister* .... Soprano

Nanette, *her maid* .... Soprano

Baculus, *a schoolmaster on the
    Count's estate* .... Buffo-Bass

Gretchen, *his fiancée* .... Soprano

Pancratius, *major-domo to the Count* ..... Speaking Part

Servants, Huntsmen, Peasants, Schoolboys

Running Time: 2 hours 50 minutes

*D*er Wildschütz is, with *Zar und Zimmermann*, Lortzing's most popular opera; the story is enter-taining, and the excellent comic role of Baculus has the additional merit of being unique – there can be no other poaching schoolmaster in operatic annals. His 'Fünftausend Thaler' aria is one of the most cele-brated solos in the repertory of the German bass. In addition, the score contains another unique feature, a fine comedy quintet – at the billiard table!

Act I. Baculus has accidentally shot a buck in a wood belonging to Count Eberbach, on whose estate he is employed as schoolmaster. He is filled with con-sternation when he receives a summons to the castle to account for his poaching. Gretchen, his bride-to-be, says she will intercede for him, but Baculus mistrusts this offer and will not allow her to go. A young student offers to help them in their dilemma and go dressed as Gretchen to ask for the Count's pardon (the student is in reality the Baroness Freimann in disguise; accom-panied by her maid Nanette – also dressed as a boy – she wishes, unknown to him, to observe her betrothed, Baron Kronthal). Count Eberbach and the Baron arrive at the school and the Count, taking an instant liking to the supposed Gretchen, invites her and her friends to his birthday celebrations next day.

Act II. Baculus accompanies the disguised Baron-ess to the castle. Here everybody is enchanted by her country airs, the Count tries to make love to her on the sly, Baron Kronthal even goes so far as to con-template matrimony. To save the situation, the Countess takes the 'village girl' into her own room for the night. Meanwhile the Baron offers Baculus no less than 5,000 thalers if he will give up his bride. It is more than the schoolmaster can resist.

Act III. Baculus sets about persuading Gretchen to fall in with the new situation, only to find to his consternation that the Baron is interested in the Gretchen he first met, not in the real bearer of that name. Baculus's admission that this was a student in disguise has unforeseen consequences: Baron Kronthal is furious that a man should have passed the night in his sister's room – for the Countess, it appears, is his sister. The discovery that the supposed Gretchen is really a student who is really Baroness Freimann solves all problems: the Count, who has been caught kissing her, is able to pass it off as only natural that he should kiss his sister, and the Countess is cleared of all blame.

As for the unhappy Baculus, he receives a full pardon from the Count, and he is even reconciled to Gretchen.   H.

M

HEINRICH AUGUST MARSCHNER
(born 16 August 1795, died 14 December 1861)

Thought of historically as the link between Weber and Wagner, Marschner was far from negligible as a composer in his own right. *Der Vampyr* was his first notable success, but with *Der Templer und die Jüdin* (an adaptation of Scott's *Ivanhoe*) and *Hans Heiling* he showed that his way with high romanticism, the supernatural and horror was no flash in the pan. If his style is firmly rooted in *Singspiel*, he experimented sufficiently boldly to make his widely touted influence on his much greater successor a matter of more than conjecture. Wagner knew his music well and even wrote additional music for his operas.

DER VAMPYR
The Vampire

Opera in two acts, text by Wilhelm August Wohlbrück after Ritter's play *Der Vampyr* (an adaptation of John Polidori's story *The Vampyre*, itself derived from an idea of Byron's). Première in Leipzig, 29 March 1828. Performed all over Germany, as well as in Moscow, St Petersburg and London, it was taken up and revised in 1924 by the composer Hans Pfitzner, a version which had considerable success. In 1987 it was revived at the Gärtnerplatztheater, Munich.

Lord Ruthven,[1] *the vampire* ....Baritone
Sir John Berkley ....Bass
Janthe, *his daughter*..Soprano
Sir Humphrey Davenaut.....................................Bass
Malwina, *his daughter* ....Soprano
Edgar Aubry, *employee of Davenaut's* ....Tenor
The Vampire Master..Spoken
John Perth, *Lord Ruthven's steward* ....Spoken

Emmy, *his daughter and Dibdin's fiancée*..........Soprano
George Dibdin, *servant of Davenaut's*..................Tenor
Berkley's Manservant ....Bass

Peasants on Davenaut estate
   James Gadshill ....Tenor
   Richard Scrop ....Tenor
   Robert Green ....Bass
   Toms Blunt...Bass
Suse Blunt, *Toms's wife*......................Mezzo-Soprano

Demons and Creatures of the Underworld; Peasants and Retainers; Ladies and Gentlemen

Place: Sir Humphrey Davenaut's Estate in Scotland
Time: Eighteenth Century
Running Time: 2 hours 40 minutes

Act I. Ruthven, a vampire, is about to be dragged to hell but is granted by the Vampire Master another year on earth provided he can sacrifice three brides by midnight. Janthe is the first victim; Berkley stabs Ruthven and leaves him for dead. He is rescued by Aubry, who realises to his horror that Ruthven is a vampire but, because Ruthven once saved his life, swears to keep his secret.

From a window in the castle, Malwina watches the approach of her beloved Aubry, who is appalled to find that her father, Sir Humphrey, has plans for her to marry none other than the Earl of Marsden – Ruthven in person!

Act II. Guests are arriving for the wedding of George Dibdin and Emmy, whom Ruthven contrives to lead off as his next victim. Gadshill, Scrop, Green and Blunt provide comic relief in a drunken scene (encored at early performances), Suse remonstrates, and they are interrupted by a shot. George has found Emmy murdered but has, he says, shot the vampire.

---

[1] Pronounced 'Rivven', even in German.

Malwina, who has no idea he is a vampire, is resigned to marrying Ruthven. With the ceremony about to begin, Aubry denounces Ruthven, who is dragged off to hell, leaving Malwina and Aubry to be united with Davenaut's blessing.

The world of Carl Maria von Weber is not far away and Marschner in *Der Vampyr* plainly thinks of his opera as in line of succession to *Der Freischütz*. It presents singers and audiences with lyrical music for each of the three sopranos, with dramatic opportunities such as Ruthven's first-act aria and Emmy's Romance in Act II, and with a highly effective male-voice drinking ensemble. The composer knows how to advance the action by musical means as in Act I's trio for Malwina, Aubry and Davenaut or the same act's finale, when Aubry, watched by the eager Davenaut and the apprehensive Malwina, tries, without breaking his sworn oath, to warn Ruthven off Malwina who is plainly marked out as the next victim. Act II's extended finale is a brilliant affair, its action developing rapidly, as preparations for Malwina's wedding to Ruthven are advanced and then dramatically interrupted by Aubry's denunciation of the bridegroom as a vampire.

H.

BOHUSLAV MARTINŮ
(born 8 December 1890, died 28 August 1959)

Bohuslav Martinů was born in Polička in the Bohemian-Moravian highlands. For a time he was a pupil of Josef Suk but when he was thirty-three he started to study in Paris with Albert Roussel, a significant influence on his development. He wrote no fewer than fourteen operas including two for radio and two for television. Most of his life was spent outside Czechoslovakia and it was while he was living in Paris in the 1930s that he embarked upon the first of three collaborative ventures with the poet Georges Neveux, French surrealist and self-styled anarchist.

COMEDY ON THE BRIDGE
Veselohra na mostě

Radio opera in one act and six scenes, libretto by the composer, based on Václav Kliment Klicpera's play of the same name (1826). First broadcast by Czech Radio on 18 March 1937, conducted by Otakar Jeremiáš, first staged on 9 January 1948 at the State Theatre, Ostrava, conducted by Frantisek Jílek. First U.K. production 1965, Lamda Theatre, London. First U.S. production, staged on 28 May 1951, at the Mannes School, New York.

Popelka, *the village beauty* ....Soprano

Sykos, *a fisherman, her fiancé* ....Baritone

Bedroň, *a hops-grower* ....Bass

Eva, *his wife*...Contralto

The Schoolmaster...Tenor

Friendly Sentry...Spoken

Enemy Sentry...Spoken

Friendly Officer..Spoken

Place: A Bridge over a River
Running Time: 40 minutes

Having already written some six operas, Martinů was commissioned by Prague Radio which had started shortly before. The success of his first radio opera, *The Voice of the Forest* (*Hlas lesa*), led to the second commission, which has since established itself independently as a stage work.

A war is on. The river separating friendly from enemy forces is crossed by a bridge that is manned at its left by the Enemy sentry and at the right by the Friendly sentry. Coming from the Enemy camp and on her way home, Popelka presents her safe-conduct and is allowed on to the bridge. At the other end, however, the Friendly sentry refuses to recognise its validity. Popelka turns back, only to discover that the Enemy sentry will not let her through again: she is trapped on the bridge. She is joined by Bedroň, the hops-grower, who comes from the right, but is equally trapped on the bridge. Each refuses to tell the other why they had been on the opposite side. He insinuates that she may have been unfaithful to her fiancé, Sykos, and then himself kisses her. Sykos sees this and rebukes Popelka bitterly, when he joins them on the bridge. When he discovers he can't get off it, he threatens to jump into the river, but instead tells Bedroň's wife Eva that he saw her husband embracing Popelka. She determines to sue him and turns to the newly arrived School-master for help. The Schoolmaster has no time for their worries or for such matters as victory or peace. He cannot solve a riddle that Officer Ladinsky told him: a stag is trapped inside a high-walled game pre-serve; how can it escape, when there is no gate, hole or ditch? They cannot help him.

As the battle resumes around them, Popelka puts Sykos's mind at ease: she went across the bridge because she heard that her brother had been killed. She found his headless corpse and buried it. Bedroň confesses to Eva that he went across (in the other direction) to tell the soldiers how to get the better of the 'enemy'. Eva confesses that although she pre-tends to be innocent, she once kissed another man. Sykos admits to Popelka that he once kissed another girl. Voices are heard, crying 'Victory!' The Friendly Officer thanks Bedroň for the information he gave them, reassures Popelka that her brother is still alive and answers the Schoolmaster's riddle: how can the stag escape? It can't. They all laugh and the opera ends with their cries of 'Victory!'

The overture begins with a trumpet fanfare, echoed in a jarringly different key by a violin: it illus-trates the gulf between the military principle and humanity, a dislocation which is emblematic for the whole opera. None of the anonymous soldiers sings:[1] dialogue between them and the named characters is across an unbridged gulf. The two Kafkaesque sen-tries repeat the Czech injunction 'Zpatky!' (Go back!) no less than twenty-nine times. When war resumes and cannons boom, the civilians are reduced to shouting, rather than singing.

With the smallest details, Martinů and Klicpera achieve the most resonant effects. *Comedy on a Bridge* certainly has farcical elements, patter sequences started off by Bedroň's verbal twitch of 'Aj!', for example, and a Rossinian frozen ensemble, but it also has elements in common with Beckett's work. The way it mixes the trivial and the serious is reminiscent of Smetana's *Bartered Bride*. Martinů refers to this, the first Czech opera, in occasional polka rhythms and in the moment when all the characters repeat 'A millstone weighs the secret down'. Character-istically, the Schoolmaster's riddle, which Martinů's music associates with childhood, nursery rhyme and fairytale, turns out to have a bleak non-solution: the stag cannot escape. No wonder that the civilians' laughter should sound so well drilled and that the final victory march seems nicely ambiguous, even, perhaps, hollow. It is symptomatic of the opera's live-liness, of its unmistakeable contemporaneity, that *Comedy on the Bridge* was awarded the New York Critics' Award for opera of the year in 1951, four-teen years after its first performance.   P.

JULIETTA

Opera in three acts, based on the play *Juliette ou La Clé des Songes* by Georges Neveux. Première at National Theatre, Prague, 16 March 1938, with Horáková, Jaroslav Gleich, con-ductor Václav Talich. First performed in Germany, 1959, Wiesbaden; London, 1978, by English National Opera, with Stuart Kale and Joy Roberts, conductor Charles Mackerras. Revived Prague, 1963, with Maria Tauberová, Ivo Zidek, con-ductor Krombholc.

Michel	Tenor
Julietta	Soprano
An Old Arab	Bass
A Man at a Window	Bass
A Man in a Helmet	Baritone

Act I

A Small Arab	Mezzo-Soprano
A Woman Selling Poultry	Mezzo-Soprano
A Woman Selling Fish	Soprano
A Policeman/Postman	Tenor
Six Townsfolk	Soprano, Mezzo-Soprano

Act II

Three Gentlemen	Soprano, Mezzo-Soprano
Grandfather 'Youth'	Bass
An Old Man	Bass
An Old Woman	Mezzo-Soprano
A Fortune-Teller	Mezzo-Soprano
A Seller of Memories	Baritone

---

[1] The Schoolmaster names the Friendly Officer as Ladinsky, but he remains anonymous in the cast list and the score.

An Old Sailor..Bass
A Young Sailor ....Tenor
A Gamekeeper ....Tenor
An Old Lady...Soprano

Act III
An Official...Tenor
A Bell Boy ....Mezzo-Soprano
A Beggar ....Baritone
A Convict ....Bass
An Engine Driver...Tenor
A Nightwatchman...Bass
Men in Grey ....Silent
A Small Arab ....Mezzo-Soprano

Place: A Small Coastal Town in France
Time: The 1930s
Running Time: 2 hours 15 minutes

Georges Neveux's play *Juliette ou La Clé des Songes* was written in 1927 and first performed in 1930, and it immediately became a subject of controversy in Paris. Martinů seems not to have seen it but to have read it and then to have been seized with the idea of setting it. Before the opera's first English performance, Neveux himself told me that the first enquiry about setting the play came from Kurt Weill. Neveux was soon after invited by Martinů to hear his first act, which was already written. Neveux went, not without misgivings, only to find that Martinů had exactly caught the mood he had sought, so that he gave him the rights to the play and withdrew them from Weill. He himself went by sleeper from Paris in March 1938 to attend the first performance in Prague, and travelled entirely alone in an otherwise unoccupied train, arriving in Prague as Hitler advanced his threats to occupy the Sudetenland. In the circumstances, it was not surprising that the poet was on his own in the train, but somehow suitable as a prelude to the première of a work which puts forward so ambivalent a view of the nature of reality.

The spectator must make of *Julietta* what he chooses. It is a philosophical poem on the nature of man and experience; it is a dream, in which inevitably all situations, all persons, however sharply defined, are projections of the dreamer's subconscious; it shows the lurching of a mind between sanity and madness; it is pure schizophrenia.

Act I. Michel, the travelling bookseller from Paris – the only 'real' man in the story, through whose eyes we view it all – once paid a visit to a village with a harbour, and ever since, back in Paris, he has been haunted by the memory of a song he heard a beautiful girl singing through an open window. He wants to find her again and returns to the town. It seems to be more or less the same, but something crucial has changed: none of the people he meets has any memory of the past and all are aware only of the present. A little Arab boy has never heard of the Sailors' Inn and can't carry Michel's bag because he has no legs. Michel starts to give him some money but the boy demands more, and then jumps up and calls his father, who threatens and jostles Michel. Two shopkeepers wonder what the row was about and the argument becomes general and heated until the little Arab calls for someone to play the accordion, which has the effect of calming people down. A man in a window has been playing it and he says it helps jog his memory; a moment of lyrical nostalgia in the music. But the sound is too much for the man in a helmet, who has more authority than the others and is captain of a ship.

Michel seems to be fighting his way out of the inn and the Policeman is quickly on the scene. The bystanders are less than helpful and when Michel complains about the Sailors' Inn, no one seems to know of it or indeed any other hotel. Michel maintains that the old Arab threatened him with a knife until he told the story of his life. The trouble, explains the Policeman, is that all in the town have lost their memories. Only a few can remember anything at all from the past and when a stranger arrives people try to persuade him to tell stories, adopting them afterwards as their own memories. Michel gets more and more embroiled. Suddenly the man at the window asks if he has ever been to Warsaw, which seems to provide a note of reassurance, and the Policeman is happy that someone will vouch for Michel. The Policeman asks him about his earliest memories and Michel dredges something up.

The Policeman remembers that the village statutes lay down that anyone who can precisely recall any subject from his childhood by sunset will be chosen Mayor. Michel is therefore now Mayor! He is invested with chain and top hat and a parakeet to remind him of his office. Also a pistol, which he must not use.

Michel starts to talk about going home and of having reached the village by train, but this proves a new bone of contention as nobody remembers either train or station. Matters take a turn for the worse when, having reassured the man with a helmet he does not propose to steal his ship, he starts to recall his election as Mayor, only to have everyone tell him he is dreaming. At last he gets a chance of telling the man with a helmet about his shop in Paris, his earlier visit to the village and the sight (and sound) of the beautiful girl he saw there. He tries to remember the song which has haunted him ever since, and then to get corroboration from the shopkeepers, but they are shutting for the night. He returns to the man with a helmet, who has forgotten about listening to a story but maintains they were interrupted in the middle of a game of dominoes; Michel says he does not even know how to play!

Just then, the sound of Julietta's voice can be heard and with it lyricism returns to the music, as for a moment she and Michel seem to recognise each other. She is perhaps an idealised fantasy and represents for him security, and she leaves him promising to come back.

Michel sees the Policeman coming by but he claims he is the village postman and they play cards for a moment until Julietta returns. Michel and Julietta come very close to declaring their mutual love and she makes a date to meet him at the crossroads in the forest.

Act II. The Forest. Michel goes off to keep his assignation with Julietta as three gentlemen who have lost their way appear (their singing and in some ways their behaviour derive from the Water Sprites in Dvořák's *Rusalka*). They call for Julietta and are confident they will find her. Michel is offered a glass of wine by Grandfather 'Youth', who keeps a roadside stall and makes no more sense than anyone else. He gossips with an old couple and then a Fortune-Teller offers to read his hand – foretelling the past, naturally, not the future. The music has a new intensity and seems to foreshadow the next scene.

When Julietta appears, she seems to exhibit true affection and Michel is overwhelmed, even though she obviously does not know his name. They embark on a love scene, of deep seriousness on Michel's side but mostly of fantasy on Julietta's. They are interrupted for a moment by the Seller of Memories and Julietta collects all sorts of things from him which she says were once theirs or at least connected with shared past experiences. Michel tries to tell her what really hap-

pened when he saw her first three years ago, but she will have none of it and in the end she starts to tease him and they quarrel. As Julietta leaves, Michel draws the pistol and shoots in her direction. A scream comes from the woods. He cannot believe that he really fired, but the inhabitants of the village descend on him and seem more likely to lynch him than give him proper trial. The Fortune-Teller intervenes and suggests he tell them some story of his past – that way they will forget why he is there. He embarks on some nonsense derived from Julietta's bogus memories of their times together, and gradually all leave.

Michel starts to make himself scarce but a Gamekeeper turns up and agrees he heard a shot; he himself fired it. Michel meets some sailors and begs them to go back and see if Julietta is in the wood. They do as he asks and can find nothing but her scarf. The man with a helmet asks Michel if he is not the passenger who booked on his ship and Michel confesses that he is so muddled he can't make head or tail of anything. In desperation, Michel bangs on a door but an old woman complains that he has just woken her up to tell her a pack of silly stories and it is quite lucky that the young sailor comes along at that moment to ask if he can keep the veil they've found. The man with a helmet shouts 'all aboard!', as Julietta's melody can be heard from the distance. There seems no escape for Michel.

Act III. The Central Office of Dreams, where everyone, on payment of a small fee, may choose his dream. Tension mounts as the official in charge says that Michel, a regular, has already been to visit him a few hours ago, before his journey. Now it is time to wake up and go home. 'I am the only one not dreaming. I have no time to dream!' says the official. In succession come a bell-boy, to dream about Westerns; a beggar to dream of a stay at the seaside; a convict to dream about rooms whose vastness will contrast with his tiny cell; and an engine driver to look at photographs of his dead daughter in the blank pages of an album – deeply-etched musical portraits, all of them.

Michel meets them all and tries, as each leaves the inside room – a cinema, as it might be – to get in to look for Julietta, whose image somehow seems to dominate every customer's conversation.

The official warns Michel that his dream is ending and, if he stays there when it is finished, he will become like the men in grey, who are wandering about and who failed to wake from their dream and had to stay for ever. All of them are lost in dreams – or is it insanity? But his obsession remains too strong.

Michel is near breaking point when suddenly Julietta's voice can be heard; but he cannot open the door. The Nightwatchman announces closing time and when Michel demands to go in, flashes his torch round the empty space and shows that there is no one there. Michel's obsession is now total and, in the words of the composer (written in New York in April 1947), 'rejecting sanity and reality, he settles for the half life of dreams'.

The Arab boy reappears and the action ends, or starts again.

Martinů weaves his dream-web with considerable musical subtlety from the basic material of a kind of post-Debussyism associated with Michel; the often motoric music of the various situations in which he finds himself; and the string-supported lyricism of Julietta herself. Echoes in music and words, sometimes chorally behind the scenes, sometimes in the orchestra, help to depict the unreality of the scene, which is set by music, illustrative for the most part, always apt and attention-catching, if seldom with the compelling power of Martinů's greater Czech predecessor, Janáček. The opera has though the great merit that musical and dramatic interest increase throughout and Act III has usually been found the best.   H.

THE GREEK PASSION
Řecke Pasije

Opera in four acts, text after the novel *Christ Recrucified* by Nikos Kazantzakis. Première, Zürich, 9 June 1961, with Sandra Warfield as Katerina, Glade Peterson as Manolios, James Pease as Grigoris, conductor Paul Sacher. First performed Brno, 1964, with Vilem Přibyl as Manolios; Antwerp, 1969; Prague, 1969, with Kniplová, Zidek, Haken, Kroupa; Welsh National Opera, 1981, with Helen Field, Mitchinson, Richard Van Allan, Geoffrey Moses, conductor Mackerras.

Village elders
    The Priest Grigoris ....Bass-Baritone
    Patriarcheas ....Baritone
    Ladas ....Speaking
Michelis, *Patriarcheas's son*................................Tenor
Kostandis, *proprietor of the café* ....Baritone

Yannakos, *a merchant*..Tenor
Manolios, *a shepherd*..Tenor
Nikolio, *a shepherd boy*..................................Soprano[1]
Andonis, *the village barber*.................................Tenor
Katerina, *a widow* ....Soprano
Lenio, *Manolios's fiancée* ....Soprano
The Priest Fotis ....Bass-Baritone
Despinio, *a refugee*...Soprano
An Old Refugee ....Bass
Panait..Tenor
An Old Woman...Contralto

Villagers, Refugees

Place: In and Near the Village of Lycovrissi in Greece
Time: Early Twentieth Century
Running Time: 2 hours 10 minutes

It was as far back as 1953 that Martinů first started to look for a tragic subject on a grand scale, and, after rejecting Dostoevsky's *The Devils* as too large for operatic treatment, he suggested to Nikos Kazantzakis that he might turn *Zorba the Greek* into a two-hour opera. Kazantzakis convinced him that *Christ Recrucified* would make better operatic material, and the composer himself between August 1954 and January 1956 compressed the 400-page novel to forty pages of libretto, losing some important aspects of the original and involving a too ruthless compression of, for instance, the figure of Manolios. Rafael Kubelík for Covent Garden and Herbert von Karajan for the Vienna Opera successively showed interest in the work but various delays caused interest to cool, so that in the event, the première took place nearly two years after its composer's death.

Act I. On Easter morning in the village of Lycovrissi, Mass is over and the villagers are leaving church, among them the priest Grigoris, and the other village elders, the rich Patriarcheas and the miserly Ladas. Grigoris appoints individual villagers (as at the more famous Oberammergau) to the roles they will fill at the Passion Play in a year's time. Kostandis, the café proprietor, will be the Apostle James – and henceforth mix no barley with the coffee he serves, come to church more often, and stop beating his wife! Yannakos, the merchant, will play Peter – and cease from the practice of giving short measure. Yannakos

---

[1] Sometimes, for reasons of verisimilitude, taken by a baritone.

The Greek Passion *(Welsh National Opera, 1981, director Michael Geliot, sets John Gunter, costumes Sally Gardner). The Priest Fotis (Geoffrey Moses) leads the refugees into exile.*

offers his donkey for Christ's ride into Jerusalem. Michelis, Patriarcheas's son, will be John, the disciple Jesus loved. Mary Magdalene by popular acclaim will be incarnated by the widow Katerina, and Judas Iscariot, in spite of his protests, by Panait. Manolios, the shepherd, though he proclaims his unworthiness, will be Jesus. They receive the priest's blessing and, as the crowd disperses, are left to wonder how they may live up to their new responsibility.

Lenio, Manolios's fiancée, now comes to beg Manolios to name their wedding day. She cannot understand his reluctance even to look at her, a protest given some substance when he appears less interested in her than in the sounds of a crowd singing the Greek chant 'Lord save thy people', which can be heard from the direction of Mount Sarakina. A band of refugees reaches the village square and Fotis, the priest who leads them, asks in the name of all for land on which to settle and from which to scratch a new living.

Grigoris seems disposed to turn them away and seizes on the collapse and death from starvation of Despinio, one of the band, to proclaim that she is a victim of cholera. During the impressive confrontation of Fotis and Grigoris, the two priests, Katerina has tried to attract the attention of Manolios, a move jealously observed by Panait. Manolios suggests the refugees go to Mount Sarakina where there is at least brushwood to burn, and Fotis leads his flock sadly away.

Act II. The musical atmosphere brightens and the houses of Yannakos and Katerina can be seen. Yannakos whispers to his donkey of the honour which will be his the following Easter, and Katerina compliments Yannakos on his cheerfulness and tells him about the dream she has had in which Manolios plays a leading part. Yannakos is approached by old Ladas with a proposition. Let Yannakos offer the refugees the necessities of life in return for their rings and bracelets; Ladas will get rich and Yannakos be in a position to buy the respect of the village. Yannakos agrees.

By the spring of St Basil, Katerina approaches Manolios, who is drawing water. She talks of her dreams – to her he is like an archangel – and their mutual attraction is obvious, but he manages to turn away from her.

An extensive interlude takes us to a desolate spot on Mount Sarakina, where the refugees have settled. There Fotis and his flock dedicate the foundations and the gates of the village community they mean to establish, in a scene which, with the chanting priest and answering chorus, makes a considerable effect. To them comes Yannakos, intent on the profitable mission he and old Ladas have cooked up between them, but he watches the preparations for the 'gate' and the 'city' with a mixture of incredulity and awe. An old man bids the refugees dig and himself jumps into the pit proclaiming that a village can only flourish if a human being is entombed in its foundations. Fotis welcomes Yannakos, who breaks down and is starting to confess his sinful mission when the people call out that the old man has died. Fotis again proclaims his faith in the future of the village as the act comes to an end.

Act III. Manolios's hut on Mount Parragia, near Sarakina. As they warm themselves in their blankets beside the fire, Manolios tells Nikolio to play on his pipe (cor anglais solo). In his dream Manolios starts to identify himself with Christ and hears the voices first of the pleading Lenio, then of the admonitory Grigoris, and finally of the temptress Katerina. He wakes up for a moment, then sleeps again, and this time Yannakos in the dream accuses him of making no more than a pretence of his role as Christ in the Passion Play, the reality being that he is thinking all the time of his impending marriage. The dream continues until a woman dressed in black, possibly the Holy Virgin, appears, only as Manolios stretches towards her to reveal herself as Katerina. He wakes again, and Nikolio wonders if someone is putting the evil eye on him. Next Lenio appears in person and asks Manolios, if they are not to marry, to free her from her betrothal vows. Manolios does not dissent but goes down to the village and Nikolio is left alone playing his pipe. Lenio comes back and Nikolio seizes her passionately as the stage darkens.

There is an interlude, after which the sound of a waltz played on an accordion brings us to Katerina's room. Manolios comes in and their encounter turns into a love scene in reverse, he asking her to think of

him no more, she telling him ecstatically that he is her saviour, without him she is damned.

The accordion waltz introduces an interlude. The road leading to Sarakina. Yannakos is sitting eating olives as Katerina comes in carrying a bundle of provisions and leading a couple of goats. She is plainly taking what she can to the refugees on the mountain, and he offers her an onion. It is obvious too that her interest in Manolios is increasing rather than diminishing, and she speaks of washing, in her role of Mary Magdalene, the feet of her Lord. Yannakos since his visit to Mount Sarakina appears nearer to understanding the mysterious events which seem to be overtaking them all.

The village Elders, together with Panait and others, are infuriated with the increasing tendency of Manolios to live out his Passion Play role and preach to the people. He is the sort of man, says Panait, to prepare the way for a revolution (a theme much developed in the novel, little emphasised in the opera) and in a moment the voice of Manolios can be heard speaking with an eloquence which causes an old woman, the mother of Andonis, to wonder whether these aren't the words of Christ himself. Andonis says he will give one tenth of his harvest to the poor, but Grigoris now denounces Manolios in public: he will hound him from the village.

The cor anglais introduces Michelis's news that Lenio has asked her father to give her in marriage to Nikolio rather than to Manolios, and at that moment Nikolio appears, assuming that Manolios will want to fight him because of the new turn of events and surprised when he does not. The act ends with the Passion Players, now joined by Katerina, somehow more united than ever.

Act IV. Lenio's wedding to Nikolio is celebrated with suitable musical jollity until the figure of Grigoris appears at the church door, fulminating about the canker which eats into the peaceful life of the village. Manolios must be driven from the community, just as a sheep with mange is separated from the flock and destroyed. No one may henceforth speak to him. But Grigoris does not have everything his own way, and successively Michelis, son of the rich Patriarcheas, Yannakos and Kostandis – the Passion Players – proclaim that Manolios does not stand alone: they are with him. Grigoris extends his interdiction to them, but, as the village people echo his words, Manolios himself comes from the church. In a big-scale utterance of great lyrical beauty he proclaims that his first attempts to live his Passion Play role were inadequate. He continued to think of his impending marriage to Lenio, and he was sorely tempted by the rosy lips of Katerina as she sat by the well. It is his confession, and his faith is now confirmed – but he is interrupted by the distant sound of the refugees from Mount Sarakina approaching Lycovrissi. He starts to plead their cause – they and their children are starving and Christian charity demands that Lycovrissi help them. The reaction of the villagers, egged on by Grigoris, is violent, and Panait-Judas strikes Manolios dead.

The procession of fugitives, led by Fotis, fills the square, there is an impressive choral threnody with the voices of Lenio and Katerina over all, Katerina sings a valediction and then Fotis to a 'Kyrie' leads the fugitives sorrowfully away.   H.

PIETRO MASCAGNI

(born 7 December 1863, died 2 August 1945)

Mascagni's career in retrospect can be seen as the story of a composer seeking more and more desperately to cap initial and worldwide success, and on the whole failing. He was twenty-six when *Cavalleria Rusticana* in 1890 won the Sonzogno competition and catapulted him to fame. The rustic comedy *L'Amico Fritz* (1891) was in strong contrast and suggested more versatility than the composer was later able to demonstrate successfully, and even his well-received conducting in Italy and abroad did not make up for several years of relative failure before *Iris* in 1898 to some extent restored public faith. *Le Maschere* in 1901 had simultaneous premières in six different Italian theatres; *Isabeau* (1911), a romantic derivation from the story of Lady Godiva, started well but failed to maintain its initial success; *Il piccolo Marat* (1921) saw a return to *verismo* set in the French Revolution; and his career shone again briefly at the height of the Fascist régime with *Nerone*, whose première at la Scala achieved at least a *succès d'estime* with Pertile in the title role and the composer conducting. H.

CAVALLERIA RUSTICANA

Rustic Chivalry

Opera in one act, text by G. Menasci and G. Targioni-Tozzetti, based on a story of G. Verga. Première at Teatro Costanzi, Rome, 17 May 1890, with Bellincioni, Stagno, Salasso, conductor Mugnone.

Turiddu, *a young soldier*	Tenor
Alfio, *the village carter*	Baritone
Lola, *his wife*	Mezzo-Soprano
Mamma Lucia, *Turiddu's mother*	Contralto
Santuzza, *a village girl*	Soprano

Villagers, Peasants, Boys

Place: A Village in Sicily
Time: The 1890s, Easter Day
Running Time: 1 hour 10 minutes

Cavalleria Rusticana is based on a compact short story by Giovanni Verga, which also inspired a stage play. It is a drama of swift action and high emotion; of passion, betrayal, and retribution. In this opera, Mascagni, at the age of twenty-six, 'found himself', and ever after through fourteen operas was trying, less successfully, to find himself again.

The prelude contains three significant passages in the development of the story: the phrase of the despairing Santuzza; the melody of the duet between Santuzza and Turiddu; and the *Siciliana*, which, as part of the prelude, is sung by Turiddu behind the curtain in the manner of a serenade to Lola: 'O Lola, ch'ai di latti'.

The scene is a public square in a Sicilian village. It is Easter morning. Church bells ring, followed by a chorus which combines delight in the beauty of the day with the lilt of religious feeling.

Santuzza approaches Mamma Lucia's house, as she comes out. She asks for Turiddu, but his mother says he has gone to Francofonte to fetch wine for the trattoria. Santuzza tells her that he was seen during the night in the village. Mamma Lucia, touched by the girl's distress, asks her in to her house, an offer Santuzza refuses – she is pregnant and feels excommunicated and unclean. Mamma Lucia's questions about her son's whereabouts are interrupted by the sounds of a whip cracking and bells jingling. Alfio, the carter, makes an entrance (in the libretto, with horse and cart), accompanied by the villagers. He sings his cheerful song, praising a carter's life and the beauty of his wife, Lola, and the villagers join in the chorus, 'Il cavallo scalpita'. Alfio asks Mamma Lucia if she still has some of her fine old wine, but she tells him that Turiddu has gone to buy fresh supplies. Alfio says he has seen her son that very morning, not far from his own cottage. Santuzza signals to Mamma Lucia to keep silent.

Alfio leaves. Singing can be heard from the church – the 'Regina Coeli'; the people in the square join in with the 'Alleluiahs', and all kneel and led by Santuzza sing the Easter Hymn, 'Inneggiamo, il Signor non è morto'.

Mamma Lucia asks Santuzza to explain Turiddu's presence in the village. 'Voi lo sapete, o mamma', she sings, and in one of the most impassioned numbers of the score tells the story of her betrayal. Turiddu was in love with Lola but left to go into the army, whereupon the fickle Lola married Alfio. On his return, Turiddu took up with Santuzza, has made her pregnant, but meanwhile has gone back to Lola, whom he sees when Alfio is on one of his frequent absences. Mamma Lucia pities Santuzza, who asks her to pray for her in church.

We see and hear Turiddu for the first time since his Siciliana. Santuzza reproaches him for pretending to have gone away when he is really visiting Lola, but when Turiddu admits his life would be in danger if he were rumbled by Alfio, Santuzza is terrified: 'Battimi, insultami, t'amo e perdono'. The mood is interrupted by Lola with a happy-go-lucky song, 'Fior di giaggiolo'. She mocks Santuzza and goes into church. As Turiddu follows her, Santuzza begs him to stay: 'No, no, Turiddu'. Turiddu shoves her aside and, as he goes into church, she curses him.

Alfio comes on the scene, looking for Lola. Santuzza, in the fewest possible words and in the white heat of suppressed passion, tells him of his wife's infidelity ('Turiddu mi tolse l'onore'). Alfio's

reaction has brute strength and the outcome can no longer be in doubt. Santuzza and Alfio leave.

The famous *intermezzo* recapitulates in its forty-eight bars what has gone before, foreshadows the impending tragedy, and so justifies a century of worldwide popularity.

The congregation emerges into the sunshine. Turiddu, in high spirits because he is with Lola and because Santuzza is no longer hanging round to reproach him, invites his friends over to his mother's wineshop. Their glasses are filled and Turiddu dashes off a drinking song, 'Viva il vino spumeggiante'. Alfio appears and Turiddu offers him wine which he refuses. The women sense trouble and take Lola off with them. In a quick exchange Alfio challenges Turiddu and in Sicilian fashion the two men embrace, Turiddu, in token of acceptance, biting Alfio's ear. Alfio goes off to get ready for the fight.

Turiddu calls for his mother. He tells her he is going away. 'Mamma, quel vino è generoso', he sings, and his aria mounts in tension as in great melodic phrases and a flood of remorse he begs his mother to look after Santuzza.

He goes, as Santuzza comes in to comfort the weeping Mamma Lucia. People crowd in and all is suppressed excitement. There is a murmur of distant voices. A woman's voice can be heard and shrieks: 'Hanno ammazzato compare Turiddu!' (They have murdered neighbour Turiddu!). The women support Mamma Lucia but Santuzza falls in a swoon.

Verismo in *Grove's Dictionary* (1954) is 'a term used to classify Italian Opera of a sensational, supposedly "realistic" kind, including the works of Mascagni, Leoncavallo, Puccini, Giordano, etc.' Other works of reference (including the *New Grove*, 1980), less tendentiously, allow that the essential difference between *verismo* operas and their predecessors lies in the libretti, which deal with everyday situations as opposed to costume plays, historical episodes or poetic legends. By that definition, *Stiffelio* and *Traviata* are *verismo* operas as opposed to *Aida* and *Simon Boccanegra*.

Whatever definition may be preferred, the average opera-goer has throughout the twentieth century understood from the word a distinct comment *on the music* and expects something demanding first and foremost power and attack from the singer and only secondarily a smooth legato or any relevance to the art of *bel canto*. This is not the whole truth, and it is the more unfortunate that the *verismo* school is often (in dictionary or history) held to have started with *Cavalleria Rusticana* in that it deals with a violent story contemporary to the 1880s but whose composer at that time wrote more as an instinctive successor to Bellini. Only occasionally in *Cavalleria* (notably in the duet for Alfio and Santuzza) is the score touched by the violence audiences have come in an over-simplified way to think of as *verismo*, and to interpret the composer otherwise is to do him an injustice.

The opera's motivation moreover is tragic and steeped in the ritual of a primitive, believing people. Turiddu knows that, if Alfio challenges him, he cannot refuse to fight and he knows too that in justice he will be killed. In comparison, *Pagliacci*, with which *Cavalleria* is usually teamed, is highly effective, but as a lurid, newspaper anecdote of a *crime passionel* rather than tragedy.   K., H.

L'AMICO FRITZ

Friend Fritz

Opera in three acts, text by P. Suardon (N. Daspuro), founded on Erckmann-Chatrian's novel. Première at Teatro Costanzi, Rome, 1 November 1891, with Calvé, de Lucia. First performed Covent Garden, 1892, with Calvé, Ravogli, de Lucia; Philadelphia, 1892; Metropolitan, New York, 1893, with Calvé, Scalchi, de Lucia, Ancona. Revived Metropolitan, 1923, with Bori, Fleta, Danise; la Scala, Milan, 1930, with Marengo, Dino Borgioli, conductor Mascagni; 1937, with Favero, Schipa, Danise; London, Drury Lane, 1958, with Panni, Misciano; la Scala, Milan, 1963, with Freni, Raimondi, Panerai, conductor Gavazzeni; Chicago, 1986; Trieste, 1987; Zürich, 1994, with Dessi, La Scola.

Fritz Kobus, *a rich bachelor landowner* ....Tenor

Suzel, *a farmer's daughter* ....Soprano

Beppe, *a gipsy*.....................................Mezzo-Soprano

David, *a Rabbi*...Baritone

Hanezò, *friend of Fritz*..Bass

Federico, *friend of Fritz*......................................Tenor

Caterina, *Fritz's housekeeper* ....Soprano

Place: Alsace
Time: 'The Present'
Running Time: 1 hour 30 minutes

After the success of *Cavalleria Rusticana*, Mascagni settled on a simple, pastoral successor, *L'Amico Fritz*, which had its première in Rome only eighteen months later. Though its reception in no way duplicated that of *Cavalleria*, it was well liked and its melodic charm has overcome a low-key dramatic scheme to ensure regular revival.

Act I. The dining-room of Fritz's house. He complains to his friend David that he has once again been asked to provide the dowry for two neighbours who want to get married. He himself cannot understand this business of falling in love and sighing for a woman. Two friends, Hanezò and Federico, come in with Caterina his housekeeper to wish him luck on his fortieth birthday. They are coming to sup with him, but David must leave to give the good news to the young lovers; he prophesies that within a year Fritz himself will be married.

Caterina brings in Suzel, the daughter of one of Fritz's tenants, who gives him flowers as a present: 'Son pochi fiori' she sings, a pretty little song. Fritz makes her sit beside him; before long they hear the sound of Beppe's fiddle outside and he is asked to sing for the company. This he does, and at the same time contrives to pay Fritz a graceful compliment on his charitable disposition: 'Laceri, miseri'.

Suzel leaves to rejoin her family, and her attractiveness now that she is nearly grown-up is generally remarked on. David comments that he is likely soon to be marrying her off to someone or other, and Fritz protests that she is only a girl. David says he is prepared to bet Fritz that he will soon be married himself, and they agree that Fritz's vineyard shall be the subject of their wager. A party of orphans who have been befriended by Fritz come in to the sound of a march, and the act ends in general rejoicing.

Act II. An orchard near a farm. Suzel is picking cherries; she sings a little ditty to express her happiness and the whole scene is full of pastoral charm. Fritz comes in ('Suzel, buon dì'), compliments Suzel on her singing, and thanks her for the flowers she has picked; she tells him the cherries are already ripe. She mounts a ladder, picks the cherries and throws them down to Fritz, who is charmed and captivated by her youth and freshness. Where else can he find such peace and innocence ('Tutto tace'); when but in spring ('Tu sei bella, O stagion primaverile')? Did Mascagni ever elsewhere write music of such delicacy and inspiration?

The sound of bells and cracking whips heralds the arrival of David, Beppe, Hanezò, and Federico. They suggest a drive round the countryside, but David pleads fatigue and stays behind. When Suzel offers him some water to drink, he tells her the scene reminds him of the story of Isaac and Rebecca, and makes her read the appropriate passage from the Bible. This she does, David thinks, with evident understanding of its relevance to her situation. When Fritz and the others return, David determines to test Fritz's reaction and tells him that he has found a suitable husband for Suzel and that her father approves. Fritz is horrified at the idea, and when David has left him, he admits to himself that he must be in love, but immediately determines to return with his friends to town. David does his best to comfort the unhappy Suzel, who watches him go – he has not even said goodbye – with a heavy heart.

Act III. The *intermezzo* which begins the act attained considerable popularity with Italian audiences, and was at one time more likely to be encored than the famous vocal numbers of the score. The scene is the same as that of the first act. Fritz is distracted with the worry that the discovery of love has brought him. Beppe comes in and tries to comfort him, even going so far as to sing him a song he wrote while himself under the influence of unhappy love.

Left alone, Fritz laments that even Beppe should have been troubled with love; what hope, he implies, is there for him? He launches into a full-scale aria on the subject of the fatal passion: 'O amore, o bella luce del core'. David comes to him and tells him that all is arranged for Suzel's wedding; only his consent is now needed. Fritz distractedly refuses it, and rushes from the room. David calls in Suzel, who has brought fruit for Fritz. Why does she look so sad? he asks. She sings plaintively of her love for Fritz: 'Non mi resta che il pianto'.

Fritz himself comes in and asks her if it is true that she is going to be married. She begs him to save her from a match she does not want. He finally admits that he loves her himself, and they sing happily of their future bliss. David wins his bet, and all congratulate Fritz on his new-found happiness.   H.

IRIS

Opera in three acts, text by Luigi Illica. Première at the Teatro Costanzi, Rome, 27 November 1898, with Darclée, de Lucia, conductor Mascagni; revised version performed at la Scala, Milan, 1899, with the same singers. First performed Philadelphia, 1902, conductor Mascagni; New York, 1902,

with Farneti; Metropolitan, 1907, with Eames, Caruso, Scotti, Journet; Covent Garden, 1919, with Sheridan, conductor Mugnone. Revived Metropolitan, 1915, with Bori; Chicago, 1929, with Mason, Cortis; Metropolitan, 1931, with Rethberg, Gigli, de Luca, Pinza; la Scala, 1924, with Vigano, Pertile, conductor Toscanini; 1936, with Pampanini; 1944, with Carbone, conductor Guarnieri. Revived London, Opera Viva, 1967, with Victoria Elliott and Robert Thomas; Wexford, 1995.

Il Cieco, *the blind man* ....Bass

Iris, *his daughter* ....Soprano

Osaka, *a rich young man* ....Tenor

Kyoto, *a takiomati* ....Baritone

Ragpickers, Shopkeepers, Geishas, *Mousmés* (laundry girls), Samurai, Citizens, Strolling Players, Three Women representing Beauty, Death, and the Vampire; a Young Girl

Place: Japan
Time: Nineteenth Century
Running Time: 2 hours 35 minutes

Six years after the success of *Cavalleria Rusticana*, Mascagni went to the successful librettist Luigi Illica for a new subject and was much taken with the idea of an opera set in Japan, with the possibilities for local colour and novelty that it suggested (only Sullivan with *Mikado* seems to have preceded him; *Madama Butterfly* was still eight years away). The opera's story is not strong and with its paucity of action presents the composer with problems.

Act I. The home of Iris near the city; before dawn. The music depicts the passage from night into day. It rises to a crashing climax – the instrumentation including tamtams, cymbals, drums, and bells – while voices reiterate, 'Calore! Luce! Amor!' (Warmth! Light! Love!). In warmth and light there are love and life; a naturalistic philosophy, to which this opening 'Hymn to the Sun' gives the key, runs through *Iris*.

Iris, who loves only her blind father, comes to the door of her cottage. She has dreamed that monsters sought to injure her doll, asleep under a rosebush. With the coming of the sun the monsters have fled.

Iris is young and beautiful. She is desired by Osaka, a wealthy rake, and Kyoto, keeper of a questionable resort, plots to obtain her for him. While her father prays and *mousmés* sing on the bank of the stream, Iris tends her flowers: 'In pure stille'. Osaka and Kyoto come to her cottage with a marionette show. The play starts, and after a while Osaka, in the person of Jor, son of the sun god, sings a serenade: 'Apri la tua finestra'. While Iris is intent upon the performance, three geisha girls, representing Beauty, Death, and the Vampire, dance about her. They conceal her from view by spreading their skirts. She is seized and carried off. Osaka, by leaving money for the blind old father, makes the abduction legal. When Il Cieco returns, he is led to believe that his daughter has gone voluntarily to the Yoshiwara. In a rage he starts out to find her.

Act II. Interior of the 'Green House' in the Yoshiwara. Kyoto and Osaka regard the sleeping Iris, who awakens. At first she thinks it is an awakening after death. But death brings paradise, while she is unhappy. Osaka, who has placed jewels beside her, comes to woo, but vainly seeks to arouse her passions. In her purity she remains unconscious of the significance of his words and caresses. His brilliant attire leads her to mistake him for Jor, the sun god, but he tells her he is Pleasure. That frightens her. For, as she narrates to him, one day, in the temple, a priest told her that pleasure and death were one: 'Un dì (ero piccina) al tempio'.

Osaka embraces her in a last effort to win her love ('Or dammi il braccio tuo'), then wearies of her innocence and leaves her. But Kyoto, wishing to lure him back, attires her in transparent garments and places her upon a balcony. The crowd in the street cries out in amazement over her beauty. Again Osaka wishes to buy her. She hears her father's voice, and joyously makes her presence known to him. He, ignorant of her abduction and believing her a voluntary inmate of the 'Green House', takes a handful of mud from the street, flings it at her, and curses her. In terror, she leaps from a window into the sewer below.

Act III. Ragpickers and scavengers are dragging the sewer before daylight. In song they mock the moon. A flash of light from the mystic mountain awakens what is like an answering gleam in the muck. They discover and drag out the body of Iris. They begin to strip her of her jewels. She shows signs of life. The sordid men and women flee. The rosy light from Fujiyama spreads over the sky. Warmth and light come once more. Iris regains consciousness. Spirit voices whisper of earthly existence and its selfish aspirations typified symbolically by the knavery of Kyoto, the lust of Osaka, the desire of Iris's father, Il Cieco, for the comforts of life through her ministrations.

Enough strength comes back for her to acclaim the sanctity of the sun. In its warmth and light – the expression of Nature's love – she sinks, as if to be absorbed by nature into the blossoming field about her. Again, as in the beginning, there is the choral tribute to warmth, light, love – the sun!   K., H.

LE MASCHERE
The Maskers

Opera in three acts, text by Luigi Illica. Première 17 January 1901, simultaneously at la Scala, Milan (conductor Toscanini), and in Rome (conductor Mascagni), Genoa, Turin, Venice and Verona; and, two days later, in Naples (conductor Mugnone), where the première was delayed by the illness of the tenor. Revived at la Scala, 1931, with Caniglia, Favero, Minghetti, conductor Mascagni; 1941 with Magnoni, Adami Corradetti, Ferrauto, Luise, Maugeri, Bettoni, conductor Marinuzzi; Bologna, 1988 (successfully), with Maria José Gallego, La Scola, Romero, Dara, conductor Gelmetti.

Giocadio, *impresario*	Speaking Part
Pantalone de' Bisognosi	Soprano
Rosaura, *his daughter*	Soprano
Florindo, *her lover*	Tenor
Doctor Graziano, *a lawyer*	Baritone
Colombina, *his maid*	Soprano
Brighella, *a pedlar, confidant of Florindo*	Tenor
Captain Spavento, *a fraud*	Baritone
Arlecchino Battocchio, *his servant*	Tenor
Tartaglia, *Pantalone's servant*	Baritone

Citizens, Peasants, Musicians, Scribes, Maskers

Place: Venice
Time: The Present
Running Time: 2 hours 50 minutes

The extraordinary matter of the opera's six coincidental premières is famous. All but the one in Rome, where the composer conducted, were failures, and at la Scala Toscanini led a cast which included Emma Carelli as Colombina and the twenty-eight-year-old Caruso as Florindo. Cuts were the order of the day and when the Naples première followed the other six, the Furlana had to be cut after the first night. Revision in 1905 did not improve the opera's fortunes.

The overture is interrupted by the impresario and the characters introduce themselves, but when it arrives it is as lively as the Opera's *commedia dell'arte* action. We are in Venice, in Wolf-Ferrari territory – or could Mascagni legitimately, as the older man, have claimed to have started it all? The story, for all its complications, is basically simple. Rosaura and her lover Florindo combine with Colombina, the maid for all circumstances who works for Doctor Graziano, and Brighella the pedlar who is also Florindo's confidant and Colombina's lover, to outwit the rest of the world and its untoward schemes. Specifically, Pantalone, Rosaura's father, plans to marry her off to a certain Captain Spavento and this must be prevented. Brighella has a scheme involving a magic powder which has the power of spreading untold confusion. Also involved are Tartaglia, Pantalone's stuttering servant, and Arlecchino, Captain Spavento's not so faithful follower. Captain Spavento turns out to be nothing but a swaggering braggart and eventually Pantalone renounces Rosaura to Florindo, and there is general praise of the Italian maskers.

The first act takes place in a piazza, the second in Pantalone's house. There is a party with dances – the slow, elegant Pavan, the hot and hectic Furlana. The third act is in a piazza behind Pantalone's house with the powder still having its effect and much nonsense talked all round.

Le Maschere appeared eleven years after *Cavalleria rusticana*, and Mascagni later complained that people thought of him as a one-opera composer without knowing most of his operas – did they for instance know *Le Maschere*? At the time of the première he went on record to say 'When I wrote *Le Maschere* I went recklessly against the current of public opinion.' Nearly a hundred years later, the opera appears to be full of graceful music – lively ensembles, Florindo's attractive serenade, the love duet, and the hardly less romantic scene for Colombina and Arlecchino. Yet its initial fiasco is a matter of history.   H.

JULES MASSENET
(born 12 May 1842, died 13 August 1912)

Massenet was a prolific and highly gifted composer of French opera, who for over thirty years dominated the French operatic stage, not so much because of the weight of his contribution as by its variety of subject, his dramatic and musical skill, fluency, lyrical invention, and that underestimated virtue, charm. From a few years before his death and particularly after World War II, his operas went into partial eclipse, though *Manon* and *Werther* never disappeared from the repertory, but revivals in the last quarter of the twentieth century suggest that even his lesser-known works – *Chérubin*, *Cendrillon*, *Grisélidis* for instance – contain much to attract later audiences, longing paradoxically for an antidote to the newer styles which had once elbowed Massenet's work out of favour.

He composed in all forms, but it is a truism that he was most at home writing music for intimate scenes, for conversations, where his inspired ordering of the small as opposed to the large gesture paid high dividends. Here, in a performance of proper sensibility, Massenet can still catch the operatic listener by the throat and bend him to the human situation he encapsulated with such skill.   H.

HÉRODIADE

Opera in four acts, libretto by Paul Milliet and Henri Grémont. Première Théâtre de la Monnaie, Brussels, 19 December 1881, with Duvivier, Blanche Deschamps, Vergnet, Manoury, Gresse. Forty-five performances in Brussels in its first season did not qualify the opera for Paris until 1884, when it was staged (in Italian, as it had been at la Scala in 1882) at the Théâtre Italien, with Jean and Edouard de Reszke and Maurel. Covent Garden saw it in 1904 with Emma Calvé, Dalmorès, Renaud and Kirkby Lunn, but with numerous modifications in order to mollify the censor. It was first heard in New York in 1908, with Lina Cavalieri, Gerville-Réache, Dalmorès and Renaud.

Phanuel, *a Chaldean astrologer* ....Bass
Salomé (Salome), *daughter of Hérodiade* ....Soprano
Hérode (Herod), *King of Galilee* ....Baritone
Hérodiade (Herodias), *wife of Hérode* ..Mezzo-Soprano
Jean (John the Baptist) ....Tenor
A Young Babylonian ....Soprano

Vitellius, *Roman Proconsul*............................Baritone

The High Priest ....Baritone

A Voice from the Temple ....Tenor

Merchants, Romans, Slaves, Priests, Soldiers, Temple
  Guards, People

Place: Jerusalem
Time: The Reign of King Herod Antipas
Running Time: 3 hours 10 minutes

Massenet's characteristic musical gesture belonged to the world of feeling, conversation and human interaction rather than to the pomp and circumstance of Grand Opera, but it is generally felt that *Hérodiade* is the best of his three attempts at the less sympathetic form, *Le Roi de Lahore* and *Le Cid* being the others. Massenet subjected the score to some revision between the performances at Brussels and la Scala and those in 1884 in Paris, but it would be a fervent admirer who could put his hand on his heart and maintain that total dramatic coherence had thus at a stroke been achieved. What *is* certain is that, in spite of some success here in the world of the large gesture, the memorability of Massenet's score comes precisely in the areas of his greatest expertise – the music connected with Salomé's vulnerability and love for the prophet, Hérode's erotic fascination with what turns out to be his stepdaughter, Jean's highly charged scenes with the infatuated Salomé.

Crucial to the development of Flaubert's *conte*, on which the opera is rather surprisingly based, is the fact that Salomé is in Jerusalem searching for the mother who abandoned her in childhood, and that neither Hérode nor Hérodiade has any idea who she is until just before the opera's end.

Act I. In the courtyard of Hérode's palace, merchants and slaves prepare for the day's trading. Quarrels are quelled by the appearance of Phanuel, who insists Rome is the common enemy, not each other. When Salomé makes her appearance, she voices her determination to find her mother, somewhat to the surprise of Phanuel who knows her identity. In a large-scale aria ('Il est doux, il est bon') she insists that only the prophet Jean, known as the Baptist, shows her understanding. They depart and are succeeded by the King and Queen, the former searching for Salomé, with whom he is infatuated, the latter vowing vengeance on the so-called prophet, who this very morning anathematised her (aria, 'Hérode! ne me refuse pas'). She has abandoned

family and child for Hérode and demands retribution. For political reasons, Hérode turns her down, but Jean comes to assail her ears with shattering cries of 'Jezebel!', until Hérode and his queen retreat into the palace.

Salomé returns and the mood changes from public recrimination to private involvement. A lyrical theme emerges as Salomé movingly declares her love, only for Jean to turn her gently away. The music grows in passion but the Baptist commands her to 'love as one loves in dreams'. This is a scene of the greatest lyrical fervour – thus three years later might Manon have proffered her love and thus, had he been so minded, might des Grieux have resisted it.

Act II. Hérode's apartments. Slaves dance but Hérode in one of the great baritone solos of French opera sings obsessively of his love for Salomé ('Vision fugitive et toujours poursuivie'). Phanuel comes to accuse him of hiding behind private preoccupation in order to avoid a confrontation with the Romans, but Hérode says he relies on the pull of Jean with the mob to defeat the Romans, after which he will deal with what he thinks of as religious agitators.

A public square in Jerusalem. In a scene of some grandeur, Hérode incites the mob to revolutionary frenzy until the appearance of Vitellius, the Roman Proconsul, quells their ardour. Vitellius promises religious freedom, and the act ends as Canaanites, led by Salomé and the Baptist, urge the greater effectiveness of spiritual power over temporal force.

Act III. At home at night, Phanuel (in a scene inserted for Edouard de Reszke in 1884) muses ('Astres étincelants') on the significance of the Baptist: prophet or revolutionary? Hérodiade asks him the name of the girl who has stolen her husband's love and he, hinting at the child she left when she married Hérode, indicates that she and Hérode's *inamorata* are one. Hérodiade refuses to believe him.

The temple, where Jean lies in prison. Salomé's musings are interrupted by Hérode, gloomy and downcast at the turn of events which seems to leave him at the Romans' mercy. He drags her from hiding to indulge in a desperate outpouring of love ('Salomé! Demande au prisonnier'). Salomé repulses him and he threatens her and the man she loves with death as the High Priest summons the people to prayer. The ritual over, the Jews demand of Vitellius that he sentence the Baptist to death as a false Messiah. Vitellius hands justice over to Hérode, who presides over a trial which, once Salomé has made it plain that it is Jean she loves and whose fate she would share, condemns him to death.

Act IV. In prison, the Baptist in an eloquent aria prepares for death ('Adieu donc, vains objets') and, when she appears, admits to Salomé his love for her.

In the banqueting hall of the Proconsul's palace, celebrations in the manner of Meyerbeer and including a ballet are in full swing. Salomé begs for the Baptist's life so that even Hérodiade is moved, but it is too late. The executioner appears with a blood-stained sword. Salomé's attempt to stab Hérodiade is prevented by a despairing cry of 'Grâce! je suis ta mère!' (Mercy! I am your mother). Salomé turns her dagger on herself.   H.

MANON

Opera in five acts, text by Meilhac and Gille, based on the story by the Abbé Prévost. Première, Opéra-Comique, Paris, 19 January 1884, with Marie Heilbronn, Talazac, Taskin, Cobalet, conductor Danbé. First performed in England, Liverpool, 1885, with Marie Roze; Drury Lane (in English), with Roze, Maas, conductor Eugene Goossens (Snr.); Covent Garden, 1891, with Sybil Sanderson, van Dyck; New York, Academy of Music, 1885, with Minnie Hauck, Giannini, del Puente; 1895 (in Italian), with Sybil Sanderson, Jean de Reszke, Ancona, Plançon. Covent Garden revivals include 1919, with Edvina and Ansseau, conductor Beecham; 1926, with Heldy and Ansseau; since 1947, McWatters, Schwarzkopf, de los Angeles, Leigh, Scotto, Valerie Masterson, Elizabeth Harwood, Leontina Vaduva have sung the title role in London.

Chevalier des Grieux ....Tenor

Comte des Grieux, *his father*................................Bass

Lescaut, *Manon's cousin*[1] ....Baritone

Guillot de Morfontaine, *an old roué*....................Tenor

De Brétigny, *a nobleman*.................................Baritone

Manon Lescaut..Soprano

Poussette, Javotte, Rosette, *actresses*............Sopranos

Students, Innkeeper, a Sergeant, a Soldier, Gamblers, Merchants and their Wives, Croupiers, Guards, etc.

Place: Amiens, Paris, Le Havre
Time: 1721
Running Time: 2 hours 40 minutes

Manon, the fifth of Massenet's twenty-five operas, was partly written in 1882 in The Hague in the very house where the Abbé Prévost had once lived. It is dedicated to Madame Miolan-Carvalho, wife of the Opéra-Comique's Director, Léon Carvalho – she is supposed after the composer had played it to her and her husband to have exclaimed 'If I were only twenty years younger!' – and was a success in its initial run at the Opéra-Comique, withdrawn after twenty-four performances only on the death of the leading soprano, Marie Heilbronn. The Opéra-Comique was burned down in 1887 but *Manon* was revived in the new House with the American Sybil Sanderson, who was still singing there at its 200th performance. At the time of Massenet's death in 1912 it had passed its 740th performance at the Opéra-Comique, where it marked its 1000th performance in 1919 with Marguerite Carré and Charles Fontaine, and by the 1950s its 2000th.

Act I. All glitter and bustle at the start (the music foreshadows the crowd in the big public scene of the Cours la Reine, III, i), the prelude moves, after a brief hint at Le Havre (V), to a statement on the clarinet of des Grieux's impassioned confession of total if occasionally disillusioned love which illuminates Act IV:

After a further reference to Le Havre, we are involved in the bustle of the inn at Amiens, where the first scene takes place. Guillot and de Brétigny are waiting impatiently to dine with three lively ladies of the town, and supper is served and in advance celebrated by the five diners. Townspeople come to ogle the passengers as they descend from a stagecoach, watched also by Lescaut, who takes time off from gambling to meet his cousin on her way to a convent. Manon duly makes her appearance, heralded by a naive tune on the clarinet which becomes her first song: 'Je suis encore tout étourdie', in which, partly self-possessed, partly chattering with over-excitement, she celebrates the joys and surprises of her first

---

[1] In the novel, he is her brother.

experience of travel. The coach once again on its way, Guillot comes out to be dazzled by the sight of Manon, elegantly mocked by the three ladies, and to suggest to Manon that, when his postilion appears, his carriage is at her disposal. Lescaut reappears, puts Guillot to flight, then reads Manon a lecture as to her future conduct: 'Ne bronchez pas' (Don't move!).

Manon is alone and a little sad that the brilliance of the outside world, which she perceives for the first time, seems to be forbidden her: 'Voyons, Manon, plus de chimères'. The aria breathes the spirit of innocence, albeit of innocence ready to be awakened. Temptation is at hand in the person of Chevalier des Grieux, who has come to catch the stagecoach home. He, like Guillot before him, is overcome by the sight of Manon, but the pair are the same age and never was *coup de foudre* more devastating.

As their duet develops, we watch young love grow until it sweeps both celebrants along to a realisation that fate could remove Manon to the convent; they belong together, and a solution to their immediate problem is at hand in the shape of Guillot's carriage. 'Enchanteresse! Au charme vainqueur! Manon, vous êtes la maîtresse de mon coeur!' sings des Grieux; and after a little encouragement from Manon, 'Nous vivrons à Paris, tous les deux'. Most performances end the act here, as permitted in the revised score of 1895, but originally Lescaut, having lost at cards, comes out to find Manon gone and to blame Guillot, who in turn understands he has been duped and vows revenge.

Act II. The lodgings of Manon and des Grieux in the Rue Vivienne, in Paris. A constantly reiterated tune heralds a first sight of the lovers happily together, she interrupting his writing, he gently chiding and then getting her to read aloud the letter explaining her to his father: 'On l'appelle Manon'. The music hints delicately at the confidence and privacy of first love requited but as yet barely explored. Manon feels their love is enough but des Grieux says he wants to make her his wife, and is about to go off to send his letter when he notices some flowers – thrown in at the window, explains Manon.

There is a noise outside and the maid says that two guardsmen demand to be admitted. One turns out to be Manon's cousin and the other, the maid whispers, is the nobleman Monsieur de Brétigny, who lodges nearby. When they come in, it is clear that de Brétigny is masquerading as a soldier in Lescaut's regiment,

and that Lescaut smells more profit for himself in a liaison between Manon and a wealthy nobleman than in her relationship with des Grieux. He demands a firm 'yes' or 'no' to his question as to whether des Grieux intends to marry the girl. Des Grieux shows him the letter and everything appears satisfactory, but de Brétigny contrives to let Manon know that the Chevalier's father has arranged to have him carried off that very night. She threatens to warn des Grieux, an action, says de Brétigny, which would lead to misery all round, whereas if she keeps quiet, he himself will surround her with the wealth and luxury which he believes is her destiny. From the music, there can be little doubt of the genuine nature of de Brétigny's feelings for Manon, and though she protests that she loves des Grieux, in the face of threats she is somehow incapable of translating words into action.

After a lively quartet, Lescaut and de Brétigny take their leave. When des Grieux goes out with his letter, Manon sings sadly and touchingly to the table which she takes as a symbol of her domestic life with des Grieux, then hides her tears as he returns, to tell her that he had a daydream, in which he saw a veritable paradise, which was yet a place of sadness since it lacked one thing: Manon! Des Grieux's dream of Manon is an example of the delicate side of Massenet's art at its best – sensitive, expressive, and full of that indefinable thing called 'style'.

There is a disturbance outside and Manon knows that men have come to snatch her lover away. He is overpowered and she is left alone with a heartfelt exclamation of 'Mon pauvre Chevalier!'

Act III, scene i. Introduced by a graceful minuet, a wholly successful pastiche of eighteenth-century style, we are at a popular fête in the Cours la Reine in Paris. The crowd circulates to the figure heard at the start of the prelude, Poussette, Rosette and Javotte for the moment escape Guillot's vigilance and are out to enjoy themselves on their own, and Lescaut finds an opportunity for an eloquent expression of his gambler's happy-go-lucky philosophy: 'A quoi bon l'économie'. Guillot appears, to the discomfiture of 'his' three ladies, and is discovered by de Brétigny, who has to admit (to Guillot's ill-concealed glee) that he recently refused Manon's caprice to have at her house the Ballet of the Opéra.

It is the moment for the appearance of Manon as the climax to a parade of elegance and at the height of her worldly success, admired by all and not disinclined to bask in her popularity and fame: 'Je marche sur tous les chemins' (I rule as queen of the land). The music of her entrance, a bravura *arioso*, demonstrates the panache of her mood and is succeeded by the famous gavotte: 'Obéissons quand leur voix appelle'.[1]

The Comte des Grieux, the Chevalier's father, comes in and, from a conversation between him and de Brétigny, Manon learns that the Chevalier is about to take holy orders at Saint Sulpice. She timidly, if somewhat disingenuously, approaches Comte des Grieux, of whose knowledge of her identity she is ignorant, and asks, as if enquiring about his experience with an acquaintance of hers, whether the Chevalier has recovered from his recent love affair. The old man makes it very plain that the affair is quite finished and his son recovered. It is a passage of delicacy and economy and a perfect example at the same time of Massenet's conversational style and of his ability to advance drama in a set piece.

The time has arrived for Guillot's moment of triumph, and eventually for his discomfiture. The Ballet arrives and goes through its paces in a four-movement pastiche, together with a Préambule, during whose fourth entrée Manon broods over her lost love before making up her mind and asking Lescaut for her chair – to take her to Saint Sulpice. Guillot is left paying the bill and with no more than a nod of indifference from the preoccupied Manon.

Scene ii. Organ chords take us into the church of Saint Sulpice, where devout ladies enthuse over the maiden sermon of the new Abbé des Grieux, who shortly comes in followed by his father. Nothing the older man can say seems to shake his son's resolve to take orders, not even a calculated plea that he marry a suitable girl with a view to settling down to family life: 'Epouse quelque brave fille'. Assuring him his inheritance from his mother's side will be made over without delay, the old Comte leaves the Chevalier, who launches into an impassioned

wrestling with his past and his conscience, 'Ah, fuyez douce image'.

No sooner has he moved off to take part in the service than Manon appears, asking to speak to the Abbé des Grieux and sailing into a dramatic and heart-felt *arioso* prayer to God for a restoration to her of the love of des Grieux. In a moment, he is at her side, denying her pleas albeit with a note of mounting hysteria, until Manon plays her last card: 'N'est-ce plus ma main que cette main presse?' (Don't you feel my hand on your own hand pressing?) As the melody winds its tendrils round his very heart, des Grieux finds his resolve crumbling into an avowal of eternal love.

N'est ce plus ma main que cet-te main pres-se? N'est ce plus ma voix?

Act IV. A fashionable gambling house at the Hôtel Transylvanie. Lescaut, Poussette, Javotte and Rosette are at the tables and there are signs that not all the play is above board, when Guillot enters to sing a risqué song with gestures about the Regent and his mistress. Manon makes her entrance with des Grieux, whom she urges to play until she wrings from him an avowal of love more complete if possible than any that has gone before. Twice comes the phrase of total surrender before Manon, apparently in an ecstasy of pleasure, sings 'A nous les amours et les roses!', the most frivolous of her musical utterances, in whose refrain the three *filles de joie* join. Lescaut has meanwhile been cleaned out but Guillot challenges des Grieux, who wins and attempts a repetition of his love-song only to have Guillot abruptly close the game with an accusation that his opponent has been cheating. He leaves the gaming room but des Grieux will not escape as Manon urges, believing this would be an admission of guilt. Guillot is quickly back, the police at his side, to demand the arrest of des Grieux as a cheat and of Manon as his accomplice. When des Grieux makes towards Guillot, the old Comte des Grieux interposes himself and tries to shame his son into accepting the situation, which develops into the arrest of the two lovers, des Grieux to prison and a quick release, Manon to trial and the near-certainty

---

[1] At the Opéra-Comique, instead of the Gavotte used to be sung the Fabliau 'Oui, dans les bois', written for Bréjean-Silver.

of transportation as a condemned lady of easy virtue.

Act V. The road to Le Havre is announced in music of which a snatch has already been heard in the prelude. Des Grieux has plotted with Lescaut to effect Manon's escape as she is led towards the ship and transportation, but Lescaut reveals that, at first sight of the guards' muskets, his men have fled. The party is heard approaching and one of the guards tells the sergeant that Manon is at the end of her strength. Lescaut bribes the sergeant and Manon shortly appears in a state of complete exhaustion. With much recall of music already heard but with a new theme as basis of the scene, Manon and des Grieux in their present misery remember past happiness, Manon even finding it in her heart to ask her lover for forgiveness for the wrong she has done him, before dying with a half-smile and a quote from the first meeting on her lips: 'Et c'est là l'histoire de Manon Lescaut' (Now you know the story of Manon Lescaut).

History has tended to put forward *Manon* as Massenet's *chef d'oeuvre*, and it is certainly his most-performed work. If for nothing else, his portrayal of his heroine would proclaim him an operatic master. Manon's solos plot her development, and we see her awakening from child to young woman; the gradual development from the disingenuous 'On l'appelle Manon' and the heartrending 'Adieu, notre petite table' through the proud confidence of Act III's entrance and the touchingly vulnerable scene with des Grieux *père* to the impassioned and wholly sincere *arioso* at Saint Sulpice and the calculating and irresistible 'N'est-ce plus ma main' which closes that scene. The brittle frivolities of the Hôtel Transylvanie give way to cruel reality at its end, and the various strands of Manon's musical character – the genuinely simple, the passionate, the sincere, the mundane – are combined in the music at her death. It is a woman seen through the eyes of a man, but an insidiously compelling portrait nonetheless, which celebrates the glitter and accepts the selfishness, at the same time insisting on the qualities of warmth and ultimately gentleness which bring her lover (and chronicler) back to her at each crook of her little finger. Massenet's celebration of an aspect of the eternal feminine inspired him to write what is, with *Carmen*, the greatest example of the genre created for the Opéra-Comique and its audience, incidentally a more typical specimen than *Carmen*. A good perfor-

mance of *Manon* can easily persuade the listener that Beecham was right when he said he would happily give all the Brandenburg Concertos for *Manon* and feel he had vastly profited by the exchange!   H.

LE CID

Opera in four acts, text by d'Ennery, Gallet and Blau, after Corneille's *Le Cid*. Première Opéra, Paris, 30 November 1885, with Fidès-Devries, Jean and Edouard de Reszke, Plançon, Melchissédec (fifty-three performances in two seasons). First performed in U.S.A., New Orleans, 1890; Metropolitan, New York, 1897, with Litvinne, Jean and Edouard de Reszke, Plançon, Lassalle. Revived in Paris for Rose Caron and Saléza in 1893 and later for Bréval and Alvarez. In Paris there were over 150 performances by 1919.

Chimène, *a noble Spanish lady* ....Soprano
The Infanta, *daughter of the King of Spain* ....Soprano
Rodrigue, *a knight* ....Tenor
Don Diègue, *father of Rodrigue* ....Bass
The King ....Baritone
Count de Gormas, *Chimène's father* ....Bass
A Vision of Saint James ....Baritone
The Moorish Envoy ....Baritone
Don Arias ⎫
                  ⎬ *nobles* ....Tenor
Don Alonzo ⎭   ....Bass

Ladies and Gentlemen of the Court, Priests and
    Bishops, Soldiers, People

Place: Spain
Time: Eleventh Century A.D.
Running Time: 2 hours 20 minutes

*L*e Cid is Massenet's sixth opera (if you don't count five early, unperformed or suppressed works), and immediately follows *Manon*, his greatest success to date. His three attempts at the Grand Opera formula fall within eight years. At the time of *Le Cid*, *Le Roi de Lahore* (1877) was the last work of Massenet's to have been heard at the Opéra, but *Hérodiade*, comparable in scale to *Le Cid*, had been a triumph as recently as 1884 at the Théâtre Italien.

Act I follows an overture built on a scale befitting a grand opera. Rodrigue is to be made a knight in recognition of his military exploits and nobles assure the Count de Gormas that he too will be honoured as guardian of the King's son. Chimène receives her father's blessing on her forthcoming marriage to Rodrigue. The Infanta confesses that she too loves

Rodrigue but that, since he is not of royal blood, there can be no rivalry between her and Chimène.

With much ceremony Rodrigue is dubbed a knight, and receives his ceremonial sword, which he apostrophises: 'O noble lame étincelante', an aria of force and fervour. The ceremony continues in church but the King stays outside and announces that Don Diègue, Rodrigue's father, will become his son's guardian. This news infuriates Count de Gormas, who, when the King has gone, insults Don Diègue and provokes him to a duel. Don Diègue is an old man and is first disarmed and then mocked by Gormas. When Rodrigue reappears, he swears to avenge his father's honour before knowing that the perpetrator of the outrage is none other than Chimène's father.

Act II. Rodrigue challenges Gormas and in the ensuing duel mortally wounds him. Chimène is outraged at her father's death and soon knows that it was Rodrigue who killed him. Mourners sing a Requiem.

It is spring, all rejoice, and the crowd watches an extensive ballet, containing some of Massenet's most attractive dance invention, with the seven movements based on the provinces of Spain: Castillane; Andalouse; Aragonaise; Aubade; Catalane; Madrilène; Navarraise. When the Court hears from Chimène that Rodrigue has killed her father, opinion is divided between those who believe he was provoked and others who demand a life for a life. A Moorish envoy brings a declaration of war and Don Diègue pleads for his son to lead the Spaniards. Rodrigue pledges to return and accept whatever verdict the King – and Chimène – have decided upon.

Act III. Chimène loves the man who killed her father and in a fine utterance reflects on a desperate situation ('Pleurez, pleurez, mes yeux'). Rodrigue comes to bid Chimène farewell and in a duet which reminds the listener of Massenet's finest vein, she makes a move to forgive him, then says she will do so if in battle he saves Spain.

Before the battle, some of Rodrigue's officers are so convinced of impending defeat that Rodrigue sends them packing. In his tent, he himself in one of Massenet's great arias ('O souverain, o juge, o père') prays movingly for victory and a vision of Saint James reassures him. Battle is joined, led by Rodrigue with cries of 'O noble lame étincelante'.

Act IV. The officers who deserted Rodrigue tell his father that he is dead, but the entry of the King brings different news: Rodrigue was the victor. The King asks Chimène for the verdict. She seems unable to pronounce the words she longs to say but when Rodrigue threatens to draw his sword to kill himself she rushes to save him and the opera ends in rejoicing.

Massenet's grand operas are well made and far from negligible, but it is the lyrical set-pieces and incidental felicities, like the motif attached to Chimène, rather than the grand gestures and structures which delight devotees of French opera.   H.

ESCLARMONDE

Opera in four acts and an epilogue, text by E. Blau and E. de Gramont. Première Opéra-Comique, Paris, 15 May 1889, with Sybil Sanderson. The hundredth performance at the Opéra-Comique was on 6 February 1890. First performed Brussels, 1889, New Orleans, 1893. Revived Paris with Fanny Heldy, later Ritter-Ciampi; for Joan Sutherland in San Francisco, 1974, at Metropolitan, New York, 1976, Covent Garden, 1982, with Richard Bonynge conducting; 1992 in Saint-Etienne and at Opéra-Comique, Paris, with Denia Mazzola; Turin, 1992, with Alexandrina Pendachanska.

Esclarmonde, *Empress of Byzantium* ....Soprano
Parséis, *her sister* ....Mezzo-Soprano
The Emperor Phorcas ....Bass
Roland, *Count of Blois* ....Tenor
The Bishop of Blois ....Baritone
Enéas, *a Byzantine knight* ....Tenor
Cléomer, *King of France* ....Bass
A Saracen Envoy ....Tenor
A Byzantine Herald ....Tenor

Nobles of the Empire, Knights, Guards, Monks, Priests, Warriors, Maidens, Children, Spirits, Courtiers, Populace

Place: Byzantium, an Enchanted Island, Blois, the Forest of Ardennes
Time: The Middle Ages
Running Time: 2 hours 45 minutes

Sybil Sanderson, the American soprano, was the daughter of a judge, beautiful and endowed with a voice of striking range – three octaves in the air of the Queen of the Night, 'from lower to upper G' said Massenet, allowing, one imagines, for a cadenza. She sang Manon in Holland in preparation for *Esclarmonde* which Massenet wrote for her, and her success was striking in this opera and in *Thaïs*. She was twenty-two when Massenet met her, only thirty-eight when she died.

The opera was planned to coincide with the Universal Exhibition in Paris in 1889.

Prologue. The Basilica in Byzantium. Emperor Phorcas, magician as well as ruler, abdicates in favour of his daughter Esclarmonde, whom he has instructed in the mysteries of which he is master. The sole condition he makes is that she remain veiled and out of reach of men until she is twenty. At a tournament then, the winner will be awarded her hand in marriage. Esclarmonde appears with her sister Parséis who is charged with responsibility for Esclarmonde.

Act I. Esclarmonde broods on memories of the knight Roland, whom she once saw and fell instantly in love with. To her sister she confesses she feels her father has condemned her to a life of solitude, and Parséis recommends that she use her magic powers to bring the man she loves to her. Enéas, the fiancé of Parséis, tells them that Roland is the only knight to overcome him at a tournament, moreover that he knows he is about to marry the daughter of the King of France. Esclarmonde is greatly put out by the news but summons spirits to bring Roland to her, starting the process with two irresistible top Ds. Esclarmonde and Enéas glimpse him first hunting in the forest of the Ardennes, then as he comes by ship to join her on an enchanted island.

Act II. On the enchanted island, Roland is lulled to sleep. Esclarmonde wakens him and promises him glory and honour in return for his love and pledge to make no attempt to lift her veil. Roland accepts the conditions and the couple join in rapturous duet.

Scene ii. The night of bliss is over, Roland repeats his oath and Esclarmonde tells him he must go to fight the Saracens who are besieging Blois. She will by magic join him every night. She gives him a sword whose powers will render him invincible for as long as he keeps his vow to her.

Act III. The King of France mourns the ruined city of Blois and waits for an envoy to bring him the Saracens' terms, which will involve the surrender as tribute of a hundred virgins. As the envoy arrives and the Bishop adjures the crowd to put their trust in God, Roland stands to challenge the Saracen king to single combat. Soldiers accompany him to the battle; the Bishop leads the people in prayer. Roland is victorious, and King Cléomer offers him his daughter's hand in

recompense, which Roland declines. The King forgives him but the Bishop is determined to find out the reason behind his behaviour.

Scene ii. In King Cléomer's palace Roland waits for night and the magical appearance of Esclarmonde. The bishop comes to demand the reason for his refusal of the princess's hand but Roland says he is bound by an oath to secrecy. The prelate threatens him with damnation if he maintain silence; in the end, Roland, in accents almost of ecstasy, admits that every night the woman to whom he is bound appears mysteriously at his side. The bishop is horrified at what he hears and withdraws. Esclarmonde materialises and celebrates with a top F and an *ossia* G as Roland admits to fear that he may have broken his vow. The bishop returns at the head of a group of monks and soldiery, perceives Esclarmonde as a diabolical manifestation and carries out a rite of exorcism, ending by tearing the veil from her face. Roland tries to protect her, only for his sword to shatter in his hand. Esclarmonde's spirits help her disappear as she curses Roland for his betrayal of trust.

Act IV. Phorcas is living as a hermit in the forests of the Ardennes. Spirits dance before him as heralds appear to announce a tournament in Byzantium whose victor will receive the hand of Esclarmonde. Parséis and Enéas make their appearance and to Phorcas Parséis relates the story of the love of Esclarmonde for Roland and its sad outcome. Phorcas in fury commands his spirits to bring his erring daughter to him. She appears at first not to know what has happened, but Phorcas resumes his powers and decrees that she will not only lose her throne but that unless she renounce his love, Roland will die. She reluctantly accepts the decree, but Roland begs her forgiveness and urges her to escape with him. Phorcas insists she keep to the path of duty, she declares she no longer loves Roland and, with her crime expiated, Roland is reprieved. They are briefly but ecstatically united, then Esclarmonde is recalled to duty. Roland longs for death, then joins the heralds and their escort on their way back to Byzantium.

Epilogue. In the Basilica, Phorcas and Esclarmonde wait for the victor in the tournament to claim his prize. He appears, says his name is Despair, and that he came to the tournament seeking death. He will not accept his reward, but Esclarmonde unveils, and she and Roland are reunited, to the acclamation of the crowd.

Esclarmonde lacks for much of the time genuine dramatic and therefore musical conflict – unless it be the scene between Roland and the Bishop of Blois, and later, Esclarmonde's decision to renounce Roland rather than that he lose his life – but its attractions remain. It contains voluptuous music of real grace, fine exploitation of the higher reaches of the soprano voice, and instrumentation to match the hedonistic quality of the vocal writing. For Sybil Sanderson, it must have been the realisation of a dream, as, in different circumstances more than eighty years later, for Joan Sutherland. Without sopranos of this calibre, it cannot be mounted, but when they become available it would be masochistic not to try.   H.

WERTHER

Opera in four acts, text by Edouard Blau, Paul Milliet and Georges Hartmann, after Goethe's novel. Première in a German version at the Vienna Opera, 16 February 1892, with Marie Renard, van Dyck. First performed Opéra-Comique, Paris, 16 January 1893, with Marie Delna, Ibos; Chicago, 1894; New York, 1894, and Covent Garden the same year, with Eames, Arnoldson, Jean de Reszke. Revived Metropolitan, 1910, with Farrar, Alma Gluck, Clément, Dinh Gilly; 1971, with Christa Ludwig and Franco Corelli; His Majesty's Theatre, London (in English), 1910; la Scala, Milan, 1939, with Pederzini, Schipa; 1951, with Simionato, Ferruccio Tagliavini; Sadler's Wells (in English), 1952, with Marion Lowe and Rowland Jones; Glyndebourne, 1966, with Hélia T'Hézan, Jean Brazzi; English National Opera, 1977, with Janet Baker, John Brecknock, conductor Mackerras.

Werther, *a poet, aged 23*......................................Tenor

Albert, *a young man, aged 25* ....Baritone

The Magistrate, *aged 50*......................................Bass

Schmidt ⎱ *the Magistrate's cronies* ....Tenor
Johann ⎰ ....Bass

Charlotte, *the Magistrate's daughter,*
    aged 20..Mezzo-Soprano

Sophie, *her sister, aged 15* ....Soprano

Children, Neighbours

Place: Frankfurt
Time: About 1780
Running Time: 2 hours 30 minutes

The idea of *Werther* as an operatic subject came to Massenet a dozen years before his opera reached the stage, though that process was itself curiously roundabout. A block in composition was resolved by a visit to the part of Germany where Goethe had written his novel, but the opera was turned down by the Opéra-Comique in favour of the less harrowing *Esclarmonde* and eventually, following the enormous success there of *Manon*, staged in Vienna, with (paradoxically we might now think) the singer of *Manon*'s title role now cast as Charlotte. An attractive picture of Marie Renard as Manon has pride of place in Vienna's Volksoper to this day.

Act I. After a prelude consisting of the music associated with the more forceful as well as the idyllic side of Werther's character, the curtain rises to reveal the garden outside the Magistrate's house. The owner is rehearsing his children in a Christmas song; they sing it badly, but his comment – that they would not dare sing like that if their sister Charlotte were there – has the effect simultaneously of introducing Charlotte and improving the singing. Two friends of the Magistrate's, Johann and Schmidt, pause to listen and to remind the Magistrate of his promise to meet them later that night at the 'Raisin d'or'. Sophie has come in to mention the dreamer Werther and the practical Albert; the last-named will make, says Schmidt, a model husband for Charlotte. Schmidt and Johann go off singing 'Vivat Bacchus', and everyone else goes into the house.

Werther appears, asking for the Magistrate's house, and expressing his pleasure in the country atmosphere in a graceful recitative and aria ('O nature pleine de grâce'). Charlotte, dressed for the dance which is to take place that night, comes out of the house with the children and takes advantage of the lateness of her escort to cut them their bread and butter. Various guests arrive and Charlotte says goodnight to the children, who, the Magistrate says, have been in her charge since their mother's death. Most successful is the way Massenet in a few minutes of music suggests the passage of time while Charlotte and Werther are at the ball: a few sentences for the Magistrate alone and then with Sophie, an empty stage before the entry of Albert, his recognition by Sophie followed by his aria – and night has fallen completely, the moon risen, and the scene is set for the return of the principals.

The music of 'Clair de lune' (Moonlight) is heard in the orchestra as Charlotte and Werther come into the garden, arm in arm. Their mutual attraction is obvious and Werther declares his overwhelming love for Charlotte before Massenet interrupts the duet with an effect that is as simple as it is telling: the Magistrate calls out from the house that Albert is back – the idyll is shattered, and we have taken the turn towards tragedy which is to be the eventual outcome. The 'Clair de lune' duet shows many of Massenet's qualities – the elegant simplicity of the vocal line, the economical role of the orchestra, the shapely, rewarding contours of the tunes, the evocative atmosphere of the whole. It is not undramatic – the vocal line becomes gradually animated as the situation develops, and Charlotte's reticence is influenced by Werther's rising passion – but it remains the world of understatement.

A few hasty sentences explain that Albert is the fiancé Charlotte's mother wished for her, and the curtain falls on Werther's desperate cry, 'Un autre! son époux!' (She'll be another's wife![1])

Act II. In front of the church. The two *bons vivants* Johann and Schmidt are drinking at the inn. Inside the church the golden wedding of the village pastor is being celebrated. Charlotte and Albert appear, apparently full of happiness after three months of marriage, and go into the church. Werther catches sight of them as they disappear: 'Un autre est son époux'. He soliloquises in music of more vigorous character than we have previously heard from him as he laments that marriage with Charlotte is an impossibility for him ('J'aurais sur ma poitrine'). He sinks down overcome with misery, and, when he comes out of the church, Albert takes the opportunity of talking to his friend, who, he thinks, is, or has been, in love with Charlotte. After a painful admission, Werther affirms his loyalty to both: 'Mais, comme après l'orage'. Sophie, in a little song which might have done duty for the immature Manon, 'Le gai soleil', sings of the happiness which is in her heart. Werther resolves to leave, but the sight of Charlotte is too much for him and he renews his protestations of love. She begs him to go and at all events to stay away until Christmas time. Werther is overcome by the situation; unable to give up his love, he prays at the same time for strength to stay away and for the happiness which his return could bring him: 'Lorsque l'enfant revient d'un voyage'. Seeing Sophie, he tells her he is going away, never to return. She loses no time in informing her sister and brother-in-law of this decision, and Albert comments darkly that this can mean only that Werther is still in love with Charlotte.

Act III. It is Christmas. Charlotte realises that she returns Werther's love; merely to re-read the letters he has written her is enough to bring her to the verge of hysteria. Her sister's efforts to cheer her up are in vain, and when Sophie refers to Werther, Charlotte's reserve breaks down and she collapses in floods of tears: 'Va! laisse couler mes larmes'. Left alone, she prays for strength: 'Ah! mon courage m'abandonne'. When she is in contact with other people, Charlotte's words and behaviour are conventional and short of compassion (fortunately, this is not by any means always the case with her music), but this can to a large extent be forgiven her for the depth and vehemence of feeling she shows in this scene. In a moment Charlotte becomes a real and believable person, not the prig we have known in the other two acts.

Suddenly, Werther himself appears, confessing that his reason had urged him to stay away but instinct had proved too strong; he is here on the appointed day of Christmas. They look together at the books they used to read, the harpsichord they used to play, and Charlotte reminds Werther that he was translating Ossian before he went away. The sight of the book awakens memories in Werther's mind, and from it he sings a song of tragic love: 'Pourquoi me réveiller?' This aria has become enormously popular, and in it for the first time in Charlotte's presence Werther uses the directness of musical expression which has hitherto been reserved for soliloquies.

When Charlotte's voice betrays her feelings, Werther abandons restraint and embraces her. The music has a genuine tragic ring about it as Werther becomes more and more excited, and in fact, from the beginning of Act III right through to the end of the opera, there is a straightforwardness and a decisiveness that contrasts with the frustration, the continual second thoughts of the first two acts. Werther draws back and Charlotte rushes from the room, locking the door behind her. Albert returns and connects his wife's agitation with Werther's return, of which he has already learned. The servant comes in with a message from Werther: 'I am going on a long journey, will you lend me your pistols?' Albert tells Charlotte to give them to the servant; she does so mechanically, but fully understands the significance of the message.

---

[1] Translation by Norman Tucker.

Act IV. The scene changes to Werther's apartment (Acts III and IV are played without an interval). Charlotte comes in to find him dying. He prevents her going for help, and is contented when she tells him she has loved him from the moment they first met. As he dies, the voices of the children celebrating Christmas can be heard outside his room.   H.

THAÏS

Opera in three acts, text by Louis Gallet after the novel by Anatole France. Première at Opéra, Paris, 16 March 1894, with Sybil Sanderson, Alvarèz, Delmas, conductor Taffanel.

Athanaël, *a Cenobite monk*.............................Baritone

Nicias, *a young Alexandrian*...............................Tenor

Palémon, *an old Cenobite monk*...........................Bass

Thaïs, *actress and courtesan*...........................Soprano

Crobyle *and* Myrtale,
     two slaves ....Soprano, Mezzo-Soprano

Albine, *the abbess*...............................Mezzo-Soprano

La Charmeuse...Dancer

Cenobites, Actors and Actresses, Friends of Nicias, Nuns

Place: In and near Alexandria
Time: End of the Fourth Century
Running Time: 2 hours 5 minutes

Vincent d'Indy, not only a sharp critic but a rival composer, wrote of the 'discreet and semi-religious eroticism' of Massenet's music and it was *Thaïs* he had in mind. But the central relationship between Thaïs, courtesan turned nun, and Athanaël, the monk drawn irresistibly to the world of the flesh he thought he despised, is a stronger one than d'Indy's *bon mot* suggests. Anatole France, in the novel on which *Thaïs* is founded, mocks more than he pities Paphnuce/ Athanaël, but the figure Massenet and his librettists have created is pivotal to the opera, and the pull between his urge to denounce sin and Thaïs's irresistible attraction provides a powerful basis for musical drama.

Massenet wrote *Thaïs* for Sybil Sanderson, who had created *Esclarmonde* and to whose voice and beauty he was strongly attracted.

Act I. A Cenobite establishment on the banks of the Nile. It is evening and the monks are at table when Athanaël returns from Alexandria scandalised by the sensation caused there by the activities of the shameless courtesan and dancer, Thaïs. Before joining the Cenobites he knew her ('Hélas! enfant encore') and once as a young man hesitated in front of her door. Now, a man of God, he must save her soul. Palémon advises against any such action, but once asleep Athanaël has a vision of Thaïs in the theatre and wakes to proclaim his mission.

Scene ii. A terrace with a view of Alexandria. A grandiose orchestral introduction leads to Athanaël's majestic apostrophising of the city of his birth ('Voilà donc la terrible cité'). The voices of Crobyle and Myrtale can be heard from inside before Nicias comes out to greet his friend. He is a young Alexandrian who has purchased the love of Thaïs for a week, of which there is still one day to run. Nicias will clothe and bathe Athanaël so that he may be introduced to the high priestess of Venus whom he plans to save. Graceful music depicts the adorning of Athanaël, supervised by Crobyle and Myrtale, the meeting of Thaïs and Athanaël, and the act's finale as Athanaël goes off to wait outside her house. Athanaël is a handsome young man and does not appear out of place as the devotees greet Thaïs. He strikes her as angry and her 'Qui te fait si sévère?' is one of the score's most attractive moments.

Act II, scene i. Thaïs's house. Thaïs's mood of introspection as she contemplates herself in a mirror turns to something closer to a celebration of her beauty as she demands reassurance ('Dis-moi que je suis belle'). In a splendid bravura piece, she worries about getting old. Reassurance is not what Athanaël plans to provide in his forceful attempt to convert her. He argues that the word 'Amour' has connotations beyond the physical and her hysterical outburst suggests the breaking down of barriers.

Scene ii is preceded by an interlude, the so-called 'Méditation', which consists of a violin solo over harp and eventually full orchestra and chorus, and is the score's most famous number. Thaïs in a rough woollen dress is prepared to forsake the past and follow Athanaël. She must destroy her possessions, he says, but she begs to be allowed to keep a little statue of Eros: 'L'amour est une virtu rare' – an aria graceful and chaste to set beside the scintillation of the Air du Miroir – but Athanaël dashes it to the ground. Here occurs the ballet, a *divertissement* in seven movements danced for Nicias and his friends, at whose end Thaïs's house disappears in flames (the ballet is often cut in modern performance though once *de rigueur* for the Opéra).

Act III, scene i. The Oasis. This scene was added during the opera's first run, and orchestrally it is full of the shimmering heat and destructive sun which beat down on Thaïs and Athanaël as they make their way towards the nunnery Albine has established far from the contamination of civilisation. Thaïs is at the end of her strength and, in an extended duet, she pleads her exhaustion; he goads her forward, until the extent of her plight moves him to fetch water from a well and she sings 'O messager de Dieu'. Their voices join in the scene's culmination, a duet of exquisite tenderness: 'Baigne d'eau mes mains et mes lèvres'. Thaïs is consigned to Albine for the rest of her earthly life, and only then does Athanaël know the unbearable agony of saying goodbye.

Scene ii. With the Cenobites once more, Athanaël confesses that since he returned from his conversion of Thaïs, he has not known a moment's peace. As he sleeps, a vision of the courtesan invades his mind; she is about to die and he must go to her.

Scene iii. Arrived at the huts of Albine's nunnery, Athanaël's vision is confirmed, and Thaïs's pious thoughts as she dies ('Te souvient-il du lumineux voyage?') are contrasted with the powerless rage of Athanaël. The Méditation returns to haunt the monk in his despair.   H.

LA NAVARRAISE

The Girl from Navarre

Episode lyrique in two acts, libretto by Jules Claretie and Henri Cain, after the former's story *La cigarette*. Première Covent Garden, 20 June 1894, with Emma Calvé, Albert Alvarez, Pol Plançon, Charles Gilibert, conductor Philip Flon. New York, Metropolitan, 1895, with Calvé, Lubat, Castelmary, Plançon; Paris, Opéra-Comique, 1895, with Calvé, Jérôme, conductor Danbé. Widely produced in Europe 1894–1900. Revived Paris, Opéra, 1924; New York, Metropolitan, 1921, with Geraldine Farrar, Giulio Crimi, Léon Rothier, Louis D'Angelo, conductor Albert Wolff; Chicago, 1915, with Julia Claussen, Charles Dalmores, Vittorio Arimondi, and 1930, with Mary Garden, René Maison, Jean Vieuille; London Collegiate Theatre, 1972, with Joyce Blackham.

Anita, *the girl from Navarre*............................Soprano
Araquil, *a sergeant* ....Tenor
Garrido, *the General*..Bass
Remigio, *Araquil's father*................................Baritone
Ramon, *a captain* ....Tenor
Bustamente, *a sergeant* ....Baritone

Basque Women, Officers, Wounded Soldiers, an
    Almoner, a Surgeon, Peasants

Place: Spain
Time: The Carlist Wars in 1874
Running Time: 50 minutes

Within just over two years of the première of *Werther*, some three months after that of *Thaïs*, and influenced perhaps by the success in Italy of *Cavalleria Rusticana*, Massenet placed himself in a position to be accused of emulating the Italians of the *Verismo* school.

Act I. The short prelude, during which the action starts to be revealed, begins with a reiterated and forceful theme heard frequently throughout the opera. The scene is a village square near Bilbao, in the Basque country, with at the back an improvised barricade made from wagons, sandbags, mattresses and anything to hand. Soldiers in considerable disorder cross the scene, some wounded and supported by their mates.

General Garrido, whose troops are investing the Carlists after their capture of Bilbao from him, laments the unsuccessful attack his men have just launched. Zuccaraga is still in possession. Were he dead, Bilbao would fall and peace would be won!

A young girl, Anita, hesitatingly approaches Captain Ramon and asks if he has seen Sergeant Araquil. Ramon has no idea where he is and Anita prays to the leaden image of the Virgin she wears round her neck. Another group of soldiers crosses the square and still Anita does not see Araquil, until with a cry she notices that he is bringing up the rear, encouraging the stragglers. He is very obviously as much in love with her as she with him and their duet is youthful and passionate. Remigio, a rich farmer who is Araquil's father, makes his appearance, hardly able to believe his son is still alive and evidently keen to dismiss 'la Navarraise', whose love for his son is to him totally unwelcome. She describes how she met him first, but Remigio is quite unmoved and demands from her, if it is marriage she is after, a dowry equal to what he will settle on his son. She protests their love and begs him to bless their union. The voices join for a moment in a trio until Remigio, not without irony, renews his insistence on a dowry equal to his son's inheritance.

At this point, General Garrido comes out to question Araquil about the recent action, discovering that all his officers have been killed and that Araquil commanded the retreat. He is promoted Lieutenant on the spot, and father and son leave the square. Garrido mourns the loss of his old companions in arms, takes out a map and starts to plot another attack, while Anita, half-hidden, wonders if Remigio were not right. Ramon brings news of another casualty and Garrido starts to inveigh against his old enemy. Whoever can kill Zuccaraga deserves a fortune! Anita steals out of the shadows and asks if he will give two thousand douros – the dowry Remigio mentioned – if she will rid him of his foe. He seems to agree but she refuses him her name and disappears, leaving Garrido to discuss his plans with his entourage. Araquil, now with a lieutenant's insignia on his uniform, sings sadly and beautifully to himself of his beloved Anita: 'O bien aimée, pourquoi n'es-tu pas là?', the score's longest lyrical passage. Ramon questions him about Anita and says that he himself does not trust her. He has just heard that she was seen leaving the camp and asking the way to Zuccaraga's headquarters. Araquil is furious and leaves, the soldiers, led by Bustamente, indulging after he has gone in a brilliant 6/8 camp song, which ends only as bugles sound 'lights out'.

A beautiful nocturne, all woodwind staccatos and turns, suggests the passage of the night and is interrupted by a succession of single shots and the arrival, observed by the alert Garrido, of Anita, dishevelled, wounded in the arm and in a state of very considerable agitation. She demands her money from Garrido who comes to believe that she has killed Zuccaraga. He gives her a heavy purse of leather and its sight seems to hypnotise her. Now at last Araquil will be hers! Her triumph acts almost as a signal for the reappearance of Araquil, badly wounded and sustained by two soldiers. He says he is dying, and because of her, and asks his friends to leave him. He looked for her everywhere and thought her still at Zuccaraga's side; no amount of indignation on her part can persuade him that she is other than unfaithful to him. She protests that she has done everything for their future happiness.

Remigio appears and his son asks why there is a bell tolling in the distance, only to be told that it is for

the chief of the Carlists who has been murdered that night. Araquil looks at Anita's hands, which she instinctively hides. Araquil dies and the distraught Anita searches frantically for the knife she realises she has left in Zuccaraga's tent. To the sound of the tolling bell she goes mad, and the curtain falls on the motif of the opening prelude.   H.

CENDRILLON

Cinderella

Opera in four acts and six tableaux, text by Henri Cain (after Perrault). Première, Opéra-Comique, Paris, 24 May 1899, with Julie Guiraudon, who later married the librettist, as Cendrillon, Emelen (Prince Charming), Deschamp-Jéhin (Mme de la Haltière), Bréjean-Gravière (the Fairy), Lucien Fugère (Pandolphe), conductor Luigini, with fifty performances by the end of the year. Revived in 1909 with Heilbronner and Geneviève Vix.

Cendrillon (Lucette)	Mezzo-Soprano
Prince Charming	Soprano
Madame de la Haltière, *Cendrillon's step-mother*	Mezzo-Soprano
Pandolfe, *her husband, Cendrillon's father*	Bass-Baritone
The Fairy	Soprano
Pandolfe's stepdaughters Noémie	Soprano
Dorothée	Mezzo-Soprano
The King	Baritone
The Master of Ceremonies	Baritone
The Dean of the Faculty	Tenor
The Prime Minister	Baritone
A Herald	Baritone

Running Time: 2 hours 15 minutes

Massenet conspired with Henri Cain as early as 1894 to write an opera based on Perrault's retelling of the Cinderella story. The opera's première was postponed from 1897 (in favour of *Sapho* with Emma Calvé) until 1899 when it met with immediate success. Fairy music was much to the composer's taste, and the opera never quite lost its hold on the repertory. With the Massenet revival of the 1980s, this was one of the first scores to be re-examined.

Act I. Madame de la Haltière's household is preparing the mistress and her two disobliging daughters for the evening's court ball, while Pandolfe, her husband, wryly reflects on the pleasures of the past when he and his daughter Cendrillon lived in peace in the country. Servants, hairdressers and milliners scurry to considerable effect and all four depart leaving Cendrillon to lament, in a typical Massenet entrance aria and with just a hint of self-righteousness, her exclusion from the party. The Fairy materialises in a great celebration of coloratura, galvanises her entourage to improvise a costume, wakes Cendrillon and packs her off to the palace, giving her a glass slipper to make her unrecognisable and enjoining a return by midnight.

Act II. The Palace. Three musicians (flute, viola d'amore and crystal flute) play mysteriously more or less throughout the scene, but at first nothing will rouse Prince Charming from his melancholy. The King commands him to choose a bride from the company shortly to be assembled, guests arrive, a ten-minute suite of five dances ensues (devised with all Massenet's usual facility for ballet music), and Pandolfe and his three ladies make their entrance. So, shortly after, does Cendrillon, to general admiration. The Prince is plainly captivated, Cendrillon returns his interest, and there ensues a love duet of the greatest simplicity and subtlety – one of Massenet's finest, short and as insinuating as so many of his best lyrical inspirations ('Vous êtes mon Prince Charmant'). But midnight sounds ...

Act III. Cendrillon runs home in despair having mislaid the slipper, but disappears before her father and the three termagants return, praising their own prowess at the ball and disapproving everything else. Pandolfe can't stand up to them, but they eventually disappear and he and his daughter look forward to a happier life in the country together. He leaves, but Cendrillon cannot forget her stepsisters' remark to the effect that the Prince's interest in the unknown girl was no more than a passing fancy, and she rushes despairingly into the night.

The Fairy holds court in the forest, and, when an apparently broken-hearted young man appears, contrives to allow Cendrillon to hear him without being seen. Together, she and the Prince implore the Fairy to dissolve the magic barrier which separates them, then once again pour out their love. However real it seems, it is still only a dream ...

Act IV. Months pass and Pandolfe is seen keeping watch over the sleeping Cendrillon, and, when she wakes, offering comfort. He assures her her ravings – of the Prince whom she has never met, of a glass slipper she never owned – are nothing but a dream. She accepts what he says, but father and daughter make their escape before Madame de la Haltière and her daughters put in an appearance and end tranquillity. A herald announces that this very day all the ladies of the court are summoned to try on the glass slipper found in the palace after the ball. Cendrillon realises that her 'dream' was in fact real, and begs her fairy godmother to make it possible for her to go.

At the palace, ladies of rank and fashion enter to the liveliest possible march and try the slipper, all to no avail. The Fairy announces Cendrillon and she and the Prince greet one another rapturously. The court renders homage as Pandolfe and his wife make their entrance, she brushing past him to embrace Cendrillon with the words: 'My own child!' Pandolfe turns to the audience: 'You see, all has ended well!'   H.

GRISÉLIDIS

Opera in three acts and a prologue, text by Armand Silvestre and Eugène Morand from their play *Le Mystère*. Première Opéra-Comique, Paris, 20 November 1901, with Lucienne Bréval, André Maréchal, Hector Dufranne, Lucien Fugère, conductor André Messager (creators respectively of Pénélope, Julien, Golaud, the Father in *Louise*). First performed la Scala, Milan, 1902, with Monti-Baldini, de Luca, Ruffo; Buenos Aires (in Italian), 1903; Manhattan Opera, New York, 1910, with Garden, Dufranne, Huberdeau, Dalmorès; Chicago, 1917, with Garden, Dufranne, Maguénat, conductor Campanini.

Grisélidis	Soprano
Fiamina, *the Devil's wife*	Soprano
Bertrade, *companion to Grisélidis*	Soprano
Loys, *son of Grisélidis and the Marquess*	Treble
The Devil	Bass or Baritone
Alain, *a shepherd*	Tenor
The Marquess	Baritone
The Prior	Baritone
Gondebaud	Bass or Baritone

Soldiers, Servants, Spirits, Celestial Voices

Place: Provence
Time: Middle Ages
Running Time: 1 hour 50 minutes

Massenet composed *Grisélidis* immediately after *La Navarraise* and while *Thaïs* was being prepared for performance, but it bears only slight resemblance to its neighbours.

The setting is medieval, and the Prologue opens with a convincing expression of sheer joy on the part of Alain, a shepherd, at the prospect of seeing Grisélidis and perhaps winning her love ('Ouvrez-vous sur mon front'). It is the Marquess however whose proposal she accepts. Alain despairingly repeats the phrases of his opening celebration.

Act I. In the Castle, Bertrade sings a love song. The Marquess is off to the Crusades but opposes a suggestion from his Prior that Grisélidis should stay indoors during his absence, capping his protest by defying the Devil himself to disrupt his marriage. The Devil pops up and turns out to be at least superficially a good fellow. He bets against the probability of Grisélidis staying faithful and the Marquess gives a ring as a pledge of his conviction in her strength.

Act II. Six months later. The Devil is in holiday mood ('Loin de sa femme'). His wife comes in to break up his good humour, the Devil prevaricates, Fiamina threatens to pay him out in kind. With some panache, they plot against the Marquise, who presently appears praying sadly for her husband and those in danger. The Devil and Fiamina tell her they are messengers from the Marquess who has bought Fiamina in a slave market and proposes she should be installed in the Castle with full powers until his return, when he will marry her! Grisélidis reluctantly accepts the situation and retires with her son. She has passed her first test but the Devil will find another, not unconnected with the person of the shepherd, Alain. He conjures up spirits who dance and Alain is compelled by a stronger force than himself to sing what turns into a moonlight serenade ('Je suis l'oiseau'). His duet with Grisélidis develops into a declaration of love and, from Grisélidis, a partial admission of its return. The sight of her son breaks the spell but the Devil seizes the child and abducts him. Grisélidis has again resisted – but at what a cost!

Act III. Grisélidis laments the loss of her son and means to pray but the statue of St Agnes has been spirited away. The Devil demands she give a kiss to his abductor as the price of her son's return and she accepts the bargain, failing to notice that when she touches holy water, the Devil writhes in agony. The

Marquess returns, the Devil in disguise accuses Grisélidis, thinking her husband dead, of infidelity, and tells the Marquess to watch her going down towards where waits the supposed abductor of their son. The Marquess hesitates between suspicion of the worst and confidence in his wife's strength of mind. When she comes back, his doubts start to vanish as she enquires after the replacement 'wife' he has sent and a reconciliation is on the cards. The Devil laughs at the Marquess's consternation when he realises his child is gone for good but he and Grisélidis resort to prayer and the opera finishes with their child safely returned.

There is little medieval about Massenet's music for his distantly-rooted subject, unless it be an occasional modal reference. His lyrical gift, as for all his best work, underpins the opera, and there is tenderness in the utterances of Grisélidis and her husband the Marquess, apparent even when he is protesting most sternly. Alain is something of a cypher, ardent in his convincing avowal of love at the opera's start, no more than a typical Massenet tenor in Act II's duet (in which only through the Devil's intervention does he participate), and he plays little part in the drama itself. New is the scherzo-like music allotted to the Devil, evocative of Berlioz in his opening ditty's sardonic humour – worthy at least of Gounod's Mercutio. This is a devil with a grim sense of humour, which must have suited the original singer, the great Lucien Fugère, down to the ground. A hundred years after the event it is not easy to see how *Grisélidis* can have been successful as a play but history suggests Comédie-Française audiences liked it, and the not too frequent revivals of the opera suggest the subject presents little impediment to enjoyment.   H.

LE JONGLEUR DE NOTRE DAME
Our Lady's Tumbler

Opera in three acts, text by M. Léna. Première at Monte Carlo, 18 February 1902, with Charles Maréchal, Renaud. First performed at the Opéra-Comique, Paris, 1904, with Maréchal, Allard, Fugère, Huberdeau (later the part of Jean was taken over by Mary Garden); Covent Garden, 1906, with Laffite, Gilibert, Crabbé; New York, 1908, with Garden, Renaud, Dufranne; London Opera House, 1912, with Fer, Chadal, Combe. Revived Chicago, 1929, with Garden, Formichi, Cotreuil; la Scala, Milan, 1938, with Malipiero, Maugeri, Bettoni, conductor Marinuzzi; la Fenice, Venice, 1948, with

Malipiero; Wexford Festival, 1984, with Patrick Power, Sergei Leiferkus, Christian du Plessis, conductor Yan Pascal Tortelier.

Jean, *a tumbler* ....Tenor (or Soprano)

Boniface, *cook at the monastery* ....Baritone

The Prior ....Bass

A Poet-Monk ....Tenor

A Painter-Monk ....Baritone

A Musician-Monk ....Baritone

A Sculptor-Monk ....Bass

Two Angels ....Soprano, Mezzo-Soprano

Place: Cluny, France
Time: Fourteenth Century
Running Time: 1 hour 20 minutes

*L*e *Jongleur* was the first of Massenet's operas to have its première in Monte Carlo, but four of the remaining six operas to be staged in his lifetime were first seen in the principality.

Act I. The square of Cluny. The façade of the abbey can be seen. It is market-day, and dancing is going on in the square. A hurdy-gurdy is heard in the distance, and Jean, the tumbler, comes into view. He starts his patter, but is mocked by the crowd, and has no sort of success until in desperation and with a bad conscience he sings the so-called 'Alleluiah du vin', in which the chorus joins happily. They are interrupted by the Prior, furious at the near-sacrilege which has been committed outside the monastery.

The Prior vents his wrath on Jean, who alone stays behind. When he finds that the blasphemer is disposed to regret his actions, the Prior bids him dedicate himself to the Virgin. Jean is doubtful about renouncing his freedom at so early a stage of his life; he has valued his liberty: 'Liberté! Liberté! c'est elle que mon cœur pour maîtresse a choisie'. Jean's resolve to repent seems to be weakening, but he is particularly anxious not to have to leave behind the cap and bells, which have been the symbols of his trade. The Prior turns on him with some asperity, but decides to make a last attempt to win him over; he shows him the good things being taken by Brother Boniface into the monastery; all are destined for the monks' table. Boniface goes over the splendid array of provisions which he has brought for the greater glory of the Virgin and the greater comfort of her servants: 'Pour la vierge'. The *Benedicite* is heard from inside the monastery, and Jean follows the others in.

Act II. Interior of the abbey. Monks are at work. A painter is finishing a statue of the Virgin, a musician is rehearsing a hymn with the choir, Boniface prepares vegetables. Only Jean has nothing to do. To the Prior, he confesses that he knows no Latin, and that the songs he used to sing were all profane and in French. His fellow brethren mock him for his idleness, and each advises him that his own profession – be it painting, sculpture, poetry – is the only one for him. The Prior is obliged to intervene and ask for some concord in place of the dispute which seems to be growing. Only Boniface, when the others have gone, tries to comfort Jean; there are other things in life than art – and think of the pride which seems to go with it. He tells him a story to console him – the legend of the humble sage, which opened at the request of the Virgin to hide the Saviour from the sight of the soldiers sent to kill him, and in doing so outshone the rose, which was too proud to perform the service asked of it: 'Fleurissait une rose'. The passage has become the best known in the whole work.

Boniface reflects before dropping the subject that the sage is of course extremely valuable in cooking, and he then leaves to look after his kitchen. Jean is struck with what he has heard, and begins to believe that even the humblest can serve the Virgin in a way acceptable to her. Can he not do so himself?

Act III. The abbey chapel. The painted figure of the Virgin, which we saw early in the previous scene, is now set up, and the monks are singing a hymn. As they leave the chapel, the painter who was responsible for the statue takes a last look at his work. He is about to leave when he catches sight of Jean, coming in with his tumbler's gear. He hides before Jean can see him, and watches while Jean prays at the altar. Jean takes off his monkish garb and arrays himself in his old clothes. He plays a few chords on his hurdy-gurdy, just as he had at his first entrance in the square – but the painter-monk waits for no more; Jean is mad, and he must run and tell the Prior.

In the meanwhile, Jean goes through his repertory, not without some lapses of memory, such as when he starts to hand round his begging bowl. He has not got very far before the Prior arrives, led by the monk who had first seen Jean at his strange occupation. Fortunately Boniface has come too, and he restrains the Prior whose immediate reaction is that Jean is committing sacrilege and must be stopped at once. Eventually Jean dances, just as the monks begin to arrive. They are all horrified by what they can see, but they stay out of sight of Jean, who goes on until he falls exhausted.

As they are about to rush forward and seize Jean as a malefactor, Boniface stops them and points to the Virgin, whose arm is miraculously extended to bless the man lying at her feet. Jean awakes from his trance to find the Prior and the others bending over him. He expects punishment, and cannot understand their talk of a miracle. With a last song of praise, he falls back dead.   H.

CHÉRUBIN

Opera in three acts, text by Francis de Croisset and Henri Cain. Première at Monte Carlo, 14 February 1905, with Mary Garden as Chérubin, Lina Cavalieri as l'Ensoleillad, Marguerite Carré as Nina and Maurice Renaud as the Philosopher, conductor Jéhin. First performed at the Opéra-Comique, Paris, 1905, with Garden, Vallandri, Carré, Fugère; Covent Garden, 1994, with Susan Graham, Maria Bayo, Angela Gheorghiu, Robert Lloyd, conductor Mario Bernardi.

Chérubin, *a young man* ....Soprano
Le Philosophe, *his tutor* ....Baritone
L'Ensoleillad, *a Spanish dancer, the*
   King's mistress...Soprano
Nina, *a young girl*...Soprano
The Count ....Baritone
The Countess ....Soprano
The Baron ....Baritone
The Baroness ....Mezzo-Soprano
The Duke ....Tenor
Captain Ricardo...Tenor
The Innkeeper ....Baritone
An Officer...Bass

Officers, Servants, Travellers

Place: Spain, near Seville
Running Time: 1 hour 55 minutes

Massenet at the age of sixty saw a play by Francis de Croisset which so took his fancy that he determined there and then to take it for the subject of his seventeenth opera. Henri Cain, a seasoned librettist, was called in to work on adapting the text, and Prince Albert of Monaco had no difficulty in persuading Raoul Gunsbourg, general manager of the Monte Carlo Opera, to secure the opera for the Principality. It has little to do with Beaumarchais, though purporting to deal with the later adventures of the playwright's page boy, and for Massenet, though he is said to have been captivated by the subject, it is not much more than a musical confection, a soufflé – brilliant, effervescent, only occasionally verging on the sentimental. The marvel is that its tunefulness and high spirits outlasted its star-studded première and that it can be revived to give pleasure to this day.

Act I. It might almost be Offenbach or Chabrier whose prelude introduces us to Chérubin's palace, although Massenet takes over with alacrity when celebrations of the young man's military commission and his seventeenth birthday are in hand. Nina's love for him is more than a passing affair, but he looks forward to the imminent arrival of the celebrated dancer l'Ensoleillad from Madrid – the King's mistress, no less – then tells his tutor he is sad because he falls in love with every woman he meets. The Count has found a letter to his wife from Chérubin, but calls off the duel he intends when Nina convinces them all that the verses were meant for her by reciting them. Chérubin for his part enthusiastically celebrates l'Ensoleillad's arrival.

Act II. An inn. L'Ensoleillad will have the best rooms. Officers are surprised at their new recruit's small stature, but Chérubin makes a pass at Captain Ricardo's mistress before all are engulfed by the beauty of l'Ensoleillad, her dancing and singing. The tutor warns Chérubin against the dangers of his amorous life and is sent packing; his pupil entices l'Ensoleillad to walk in the garden. Baron, Count and Duke, partly from jealousy, partly because l'Ensoleillad is after all the King's mistress, try to intervene but are thwarted and find Chérubin embracing l'Ensoleillad through the bars of her window. Police arrive and arrest the outraged husbands for inciting a riot. Chérubin escapes. The women, on their balconies, faint.

Act III. Chérubin prepares for three duels and in a moment of seriousness (but not, he maintains, of sadness) draws up his will. His tutor attempts to teach him a duelling ploy but he eventually admits it was l'Ensoleillad he was last night serenading and thus avoids the duels, although he is mightily put out when l'Ensoleillad is summoned by the King back to Madrid. She for her part in a beautiful

Chérubin *(Covent Garden, 1994, director Tim Albery, designer Antony McDonald). Angela Gheorghiu as Nina, Susan Graham in the title role.*

Aubade seems to extol one perfect night of love, but Chérubin is left disillusioned, even prepared to take his tutor's advice and wait for the kind, understanding woman who will look after him when he is in trouble – Massenet's own advice, maybe, to a young man? Or to himself?

Nina, about to retire to a convent, confesses she once loved Chérubin. He falls into her arms, taking care as he does so to pluck from his pocket the Countess's ribbon which was sticking out.

Massenet's songs, ensembles and dances, for what are for the most part puppets, are consistently graceful, though it is hard to be more than superficially involved with most of them. Nina, Chérubin and maybe the Philosopher are the exceptions: Chérubin intoxicated with women and in love with all of them; Nina transparently sincere and in love only with him; the tutor trying to bring a note of sobriety, or at least of the real world, into the madcap proceedings.

It is surely not for nothing that in the last bars Massenet quotes Don Giovanni's serenade and the tutor refers to Donna Elvira!   H.

DON QUICHOTTE

Don Quixote

Opera in five acts, text by Henri Cain, after Le Lorrain's play based on Cervantes's novel. Première Monte Carlo, 19 February 1910, with Lucy Arbell, Chaliapin, Gresse. First performed Paris, 1910, with Arbell, Vanni Marcoux, Fugère; London Opera House, 1912, with Kirlord, Lafont, Danse; New Orleans, 1912; New York, 1914, with Garden, Vanni Marcoux, Dufranne; Metropolitan, 1926, with Easton, Chaliapin, de Luca. Revived Opéra-Comique, 1931; Brussels, 1934; Opéra, Paris, 1947, with Renée Gilly, Vanni Marcoux, Musy, conductor Cluytens; Belgrade, 1956, with Čangalovič (subsequently toured all over Europe including 1962 Edinburgh Festival). Nicolai Ghiaurov and Ruggero Raimondi were responsible for a number of revivals in the 1970s and 1980s. English National Opera, 1994, with Richard Van Allan.

La belle Dulcinée (Dulcinea) ....Contralto

Don Quichotte (Don Quixote) ....Bass

Sancho Panza...Baritone

Admirers of Dulcinée
     Pedro...Soprano
     Garcias...Soprano
     Rodriguez..Tenor
     Juan ....Tenor

Two Servants ....Baritone

Ténébrun, and other Bandits; Friends of Dulcinée

Place: Spain
Time: The Middle Ages
Running Time: 2 hours 30 minutes

*D*on Quichotte was first heard two years before Massenet died, though there were four more operas to follow it, the last two posthumously. He was already ill but seems to have very much enjoyed its writing. It was the fourth of his operas to have a first hearing in Monte Carlo, and, with Chaliapin in the cast, its success was very considerable. Having said which, it would be idle to pretend that Massenet is not here a late nineteenth-century composer, making use of a very famous literary source (as had Gounod, Berlioz and Thomas before him) and turning it from a masterpiece in one sphere into a romantic opera – and perhaps a masterpiece – in another. *Don Quichotte* is also a work of Massenet's old age, and in it inspiration runs surely but is spread with a little more economy than in the great romantic operas of twenty years and more earlier. Nonetheless, it is a work of elegant inspiration, beautifully scored, and, in its simplicity, a by no means unworthy frame for the great figure of the title.

Act I. Outside Dulcinée's house, the fiesta is going great guns (as only French composers engaged on Spanish pastiche know how) and her four admirers (two of them travesti roles) are much to the fore. Will she desert her latest lover and devote herself to them? 'Quand la femme a vingt ans' (When a girl is but twenty) she sings provocatively from her balcony. Rodriguez and Juan stay behind to muse on Dulcinée's charms and the need to enjoy them briefly, then notice the imminent arrival of Don Quichotte. Juan mocks his bizarre appearance and behaviour but Rodriguez perceives the sincerity and benevolence behind the bizarre exterior. The crowd rejoice at the appearance of the Knight of the Long Countenance and Sancho Panza on their redoubtable steeds, and Don Quichotte, lance in air, distributes what little money they have to the delighted populace, whose mockery is full of high spirits and more than a trace of affection.

Don Quichotte blows a kiss towards Dulcinée's window, but Sancho murmurs of thirst and his determination to assuage it at the inn. Don Quichotte is not to be put down and, sending Sancho ahead, proceeds to serenade his lady love: 'Quand apparaissent les étoiles', a gently graceful melody heard later as a symbol of Don Quichotte's unquestioning love. He brushes aside the interruptions of Juan, finishes the song to such effect that Dulcinée from her balcony joins her voice to his, and draws his sword to avenge the earlier insult. Only Dulcinée's tactful flattery in admiring the verses he has previously flung up at her window saves the day, and Don Quichotte easily falls to her blandishments, vowing to recover the necklace she says she lost recently to the bandit Ténébrun. As the others go, the Don hums his serenade to himself, only in his turn to hear Dulcinée's voice in the distance.

Act II. Early morning mist in the country. Don Quichotte searches his mind for rhymes for his song in Dulcinée's honour. Sancho remembers warily the disastrous exploit of yesterday, when the Don charged and routed a flock of sheep and some little black pigs. In any event, Sancho resents being out in the country looking for a mythical bandit simply because Dulcinée took it into her head to ask his master to do so. He launches into a tirade against women in general but Don Quichotte has no time to pay heed as at this moment he catches sight of great giants on the plain. That Sancho thinks them windmills weighs with him not at all and he sets his lance and charges. The curtain falls as he spurs on Rosinante, then rises again to reveal him caught up in the windmill by the seat of his breeches.

Act III follows a gently lyrical entr'acte based on the serenade. Don Quichotte is on all fours examining the ground for tracks of the bandits. Sancho finds it a creepy place, but Don Quichotte will go nowhere except forward to glory. It is not long before the bandits appear, heard first in the distance as they half-heartedly pursue the fleeing Sancho. The band easily overpower Don Quichotte, but for all the fun they make of him, the bandit chief senses something different in his impassive gaze. Don Quichotte prays, then in answer to a question, puts forward his creed of knight errantry: 'Je suis le chevalier errant'; to redress wrongs, to love the poor – even to honour bandits when they are proud of bearing. So moved are the bandits by his strange utterance that they return the jewellery they had stolen, then leave extolling the Knight of the Long Countenance.

Act IV. Dulcinée in her garden is surrounded by admirers but remains pensive and impervious to their compliments. She dreams, she says, of a love of another kind, but the frenzied dancing starts again and Dulcinée changes to a livelier mood. Sancho formally announces his master and he and Don Quichotte wait for the appearance of Dulcinée who greets them playfully but is delighted at the reappearance of her necklace. His reward is a kiss which impels Don Quichotte to express his love extravagantly ('Marchez dans mon chemin'), finishing with a request that Dulcinée become his wife. This provokes a burst of laughter, but Dulcinée attempts to let her beau down lightly, dismissing everyone else and, when they are alone, saying it is her affection for the old man which prevents her accepting his offer. Let him abuse her, but let him stay with them, the same as ever. Their voices join together for a moment and Dulcinée kisses Don Quichotte on the forehead, before the others return. Mockery starts again, but Dulcinée will have none of it ('C'est un fou sublime': He is a

madman of genius) and leaves. Their laughter is too much for Sancho, who turns on them and lashes them with his tongue ('Ça, vous commettez tous un acte épouvantable'), before embracing his old master.

Act V. An interlude takes us into the forest, the cello solo developing a tune which will become important before the short act is over. It is a starlit night, and Don Quichotte rests upright against a tree, watched over by Sancho, plainly overcome at the prospect of his master's death. The Don expects Sancho to be dreaming already of his native village, but bids him spare a thought for the master who fought only for good. Then he thinks of the presents with which he meant to reward Sancho's faithful service – castles, islands – but when Sancho tries to remove his armour, he demurs. He stares at a star, before the voice of Dulcinée singing the cello tune comes with a little magic to illuminate his last moments. That Massenet's sense of music theatre was just as sure in his late sixties as it had been at the time of *Manon*, more than twenty-five years before, is well demonstrated in this death scene, economical, understated, and going straight to the emotional heart of the matter.   H.

PETER MAXWELL DAVIES
See under Davies

RICHARD MEALE
(born 24 August 1932)

VOSS

Opera in two acts, text by David Malouf from the novel by Patrick White. Première, Adelaide Festival, 1 March 1986, by Australian Opera, with Marilyn Richardson, Geoffrey Chard, conductor Stuart Challender.

The expedition

Johann Ulrich Voss, *a German explorer* .... Baritone

Frank Le Mesurier, *a gentleman* .... Tenor

Palfreyman, *a naturalist* .... Baritone

Judd, *an ex-convict* .... Bass-Baritone

Harry Robarts, *a young man* .... Tenor

Dugald and Jacky, *Aboriginal guides* .... Mime

In Sydney

Mr Bonner, *a merchant, backer of the expedition* .... Bass

Mrs Bonner, *his wife* .... Mezzo-Soprano

Belle Bonner, *their daughter* .... Soprano

Laura Trevelyan, *their niece* .... Soprano

Rose Portion, *a servant* .... Soprano

Lt. Tom Radclyffe, *officer, engaged to Belle* ....Tenor
Mr Topp, *Voss's landlord, a music teacher* ....Tenor
Mercy, *Rose's child, adopted by Laura* ....Soprano
A Reporter ....Tenor
A Photographer ....Mime

Outside Sydney
Mrs Judd ....Contralto

Guests, Children

Place: Sydney and Central Australia
Time: 1845 and 1865
Running Time: 2 hours

Richard Meale's education in Sydney seems to have been surprisingly general for someone who was to become one of Australia's leading composers, but study in Los Angeles preceded success at the I.S.C.M. Festival of 1960 in Amsterdam with his Flute Sonata. Later he came to be regarded as the leading avant-gardist in Australia, and was appointed to the University of Adelaide in 1969. He was commissioned to write for Australian Opera and the resulting work was seen at the 1986 Adelaide Festival, where it enjoyed considerable success.

The story-line from Patrick White's novel is simple: the German explorer, Voss, is determined to be the first man to cross the Australian continent. Bonner backs him and at a party he is introduced to Bonner's niece, Laura Trevelyan, who is his equal in temperament and determination. The expedition ends in disaster but Laura and Voss enter into a relationship, mostly by correspondence, which takes no account of time or space but stands as effectively the one monument to the great enterprise.

Act I. Crashing chords introduce Voss. Guests dance at Bonner's house. Voss is a dreamer but that seems not to worry Bonner; the other guests cannot take it all quite so seriously.

In the garden, Belle thinks she is in love with Tom Radclyffe, but Laura dreams of Voss, with whose destiny, like Senta's with the Flying Dutchman (as her aria explains), she feels involved. Voss responds, sings a German song, and they part with a bond established, Laura singing his names as if they were talismanic.

Voss gathers his band: Harry Robarts, the young man with few qualifications but enthusiasm; Le Mesurier, the idealist; Palfreyman, the naturalist. Topp, Voss's landlord, plays the flute, and his music

develops into a march as they leave on the great adventure, Voss confident that Laura's prayers, as she finally admits, will follow them.

Act II. Voss sings another German song, takes on Judd as guide and two Aboriginals, expert on the outback. Much of the action requires a split stage from now on; Laura and Rose sew at one side, Palfreyman is with Voss on the other, Laura affirming that she understands Voss even when she does not agree with him, the others reflecting on the beauties of nature. The colloquy between Laura and Voss, half correspondence, half thought-transference, makes one of the opera's central episodes.

Christmas Day finds the explorers preparing a feast, Laura offering to Voss as a pledge, as it were, of their 'union' the child of the dead Rose, whom she has adopted. Voss sits alone, rejects the food Judd brings him and, somehow at the same time, Laura's offering: 'I will not accept the terms.'

Voss sleepwalks, watched anxiously by Harry, more suspiciously by Judd.

Voss lies delirious – 'I do not accept the terms!' Judd plans to go back, Harry refuses to go with him, and Le Mesurier appears to have gone mad. Reality recedes, Voss and Laura appear able to offer each other strength, but the others are lost. Aborigines seem to attack them, Palfreyman is killed, Le Mesurier cuts his own throat. Harry sings a message of hope, Laura still offers comfort. Voss and Harry are at the mercy of Jacky, who kills them.

Epilogue. Twenty years later, in Tom and Belle Radclyffe's house in Sydney. Children play, guests look askance at the gaunt, black figure of Laura, who is approached by a reporter to talk about Voss, whose statue has just been unveiled. Judd is introduced, half insane, and tells a garbled tale before being led away. Mercy, Rose's child, tries to take Laura away, but she seems somehow at peace, the shadow of Voss's statue falling across her as she stands alone.

It will be apparent that the opera's emphasis is on relationships, particularly that of Voss and Laura, which gradually acquires a heroic character, not on narrative or even the geographic force natural to Australia and a story of exploration. In this respect the libretto of the distinguished Australian writer David Malouf follows the novel, at the same time stressing something which opera is well qualified to achieve.   H.

GIAN CARLO MENOTTI

(born 7 July 1911)

Gian Carlo Menotti was for nearly four decades America's most prolific operatic composer,[1] though his meteoric success of the 1940s and early 1950s was not sustained into the 1960s and 70s. His attempts at innovation, or at all events at a stylisation of traditional operatic form, in for instance *The Unicorn, the Dragon, the Manticore* (1958), were not widely successful, *Maria Golovin* (1957) met with a cold reception from critics, audiences and managements, and *The Saint of Bleecker Street*, for all its obvious appeal in Catholic countries, failed to duplicate the sensational success of the earlier *Medium* or *Consul*.

As a child in Italy, Menotti was taken by his nurse to a shrine, and a little later his crippled leg was found to be cured. It can be seen therefore that, just as *The Medium* stemmed from the vivid impressions of a real-life experience of a séance, so even the most successful of his later operas, *Amahl* and *Bleecker Street*, owe a good deal to experiences towards which Menotti's attitude is, to say the least of it, ambivalent.   H.

AMELIA AL BALLO

Amelia Goes to the Ball

Opera in one act, text by the composer. Première (in English translation by G. Meade), Philadelphia, 1 April 1937, conductor Reiner. First performed at Metropolitan Opera, New York (in English), 1938, with Muriel Dickson, Chamlee, Brownlee, Cordon, conductor Panizza; San Remo, 1938 (in Italian), with Rosina Torri, Ugo Cantelmo, Luigi Borgonovo, Roberto Silva, conductor Votto; Berlin, 1947, with Irma Beilke, Kurt Rehm, Paul Schoeffler.

Amelia	Soprano
Her Husband	Baritone
Her Lover	Tenor
Her Friend	Contralto
The Commissioner of Police	Bass
First Maid	Mezzo-Soprano
Second Maid	Mezzo-Soprano

Neighbours, Passers-By, Policeman

Place: The Luxurious Bedroom of Amelia
Time: Early Twentieth Century
Running Time: 50 minutes

A lively prelude is dominated by a lyrical *andante* passage which refers to the trio in the second half of the work. The curtain rises as Amelia, wife of a wealthy, upper-middle-class citizen of a large European city, is being dressed by her two maids for the first ball of the season, while her friend sits, threatening to leave without her if she does not hurry. The two women sing a duet ('La notte, la notte') in which they agree that nothing in the world, neither love nor honour, is of the slightest importance when a woman wants to go to a ball.

Amelia's husband arrives and announces that they cannot go as he must discuss something privately with her. The others go off as Amelia furiously demands an explanation of such behaviour. The unhappy man tells her that he has found among her papers a love letter in passionate language. Amelia denies any knowledge of it, whereupon her husband reads the letter aloud to her. *Now* will she tell him her lover's name? 'What then?' asks Amelia anxiously, 'Shall we go to the ball?' At last she says she will divulge the name, provided her husband promises to take her to the ball. He agrees and Amelia tells him it is the gentleman upstairs on the third floor. 'When do you see him?' demands the husband. 'Only at night', replies Amelia, and when reproached for her disloyalty to her sleeping husband retorts that, since sleeping is all he ever does do in bed, her infidelity is less than surprising.

Her husband puts on his top hat and coat and hurries to the door. Amelia is incredulous, but the husband says he will keep his promise – but first he would like to have a little chat with the gentleman on the third floor, assisted by his pistol; they can go dancing while her lover patches up his punctured skull.

Amelia reflects irritably that once the men begin to

---

[1] Though continuing to think of himself as an Italian.

fight she will never get to the ball. She runs out on to the balcony to call to her lover to climb down the lattice and thus avoid her husband. While she waits for him, she sings a *romanza* – men demand impossible boons, but all she wants is to go to the ball.

The lover arrives (by rope), full of ideas about defending Amelia against her husband until he hears about the pistol, when he suggests an immediate elopement. The husband comes in, furious at being balked of revenge. 'So, we can go now?' asks Amelia. The husband agrees in the interests of peace to take her to the ball. He notices the rope on the balcony and discovers the hidden man; he aims and fires, only to be rewarded by a loud but unlethal click. The lover advances menacingly, but the husband reasons with him and the two sit down to discuss the situation in a calm masculine manner.

After the lover's sentimental *romanza* ('Fu di notte'), discussion is renewed, to the mounting fury of Amelia. There follows the trio referred to in the prelude, in which action is interrupted for the three to sing directly to the audience ('Chi può saper?' – 'Who knows right from wrong?').

When Amelia, exasperated beyond measure, asks her husband, 'For the last time, will you take me to the ball, yes or no?' and he refuses, she snatches up a vase and hits him over the head with it. He collapses and Amelia, horrified, shouts for help.

To the sound of a short orchestral interlude, a crowd of neighbours and passers-by gather, intent on discovering what has happened. Eventually the Chief of Police himself arrives. Amelia at her most bewitching flatters him and tells him that her husband was assaulted by a robber – she points to her lover who, despite his protests, is dragged off to prison. An ambulance takes away the husband, who, the Police Chief assures Amelia, will soon recover. 'I know,' says that single-minded lady. 'But who will take me to the ball now?' As the chorus sings the moral – when a woman sets her heart on going to a ball, that's where she'll go – the Chief of Police is preparing to transform himself into a gallant escort, and so bring to its ordained end one of Menotti's least pretentious but most sparkling and appreciable scores.   H.

THE MEDIUM

Opera in two acts, text by the composer. Première, Brander Matthews Theatre, Columbia University, 8 May 1946, with Evelyn Keller, Claramae Turner, conductor Luening. First performed New York (revised, and sponsored by Ballet Society), 1947, with Keller, Marie Powers, conducted by Barzin; London, Aldwych Theatre, 1948, with Powers, conductor Balaban; Genoa, 1950, with Pederzini, conductor Sanzogno; Venice, Bari, Palermo, Turin, 1951–52, each time with Pederzini; Paris, Opéra-Comique, 1968, with Eliane Lublin, Denise Scharley.

Monica, *daughter of Madame Flora*	Soprano
Toby, *a mute*	Dancer
Madame Flora (Baba), *a medium*	Contralto
Mrs Gobineau	Soprano
Mr Gobineau	Baritone
Mrs Nolan	Mezzo-Soprano

Place: U.S.A.
Time: 'The Present'
Running Time: 50 minutes

Of *The Medium*, the composer himself has written (in notes to a complete gramophone recording): 'Despite its eerie setting and gruesome conclusions, *The Medium* is actually a play of ideas. It describes the tragedy of a woman caught between two worlds, a world of reality which she cannot wholly comprehend, and a supernatural world in which she cannot believe. Baba, the Medium, has no scruples in cheating her clients ... until something happens which she herself has not prepared. This insignificant incident ... shatters her self-assurance, and drives her almost insane with rage.' He goes on to explain that the idea for the opera came to him in 1936 when he was asked to go to a séance by some friends. It was not so much his own scepticism that struck him as the way his friends were pathetically anxious to believe that the spirit of their dead daughter was talking to them through the medium.

Act I. Madame Flora's parlour. A puppet-theatre in one corner of the room. In a corner a tiny statue of the Virgin. Toby is kneeling near a trunk from which he takes out bits of stuff and improvises a costume. Monica combs her hair and sings to herself. She tells him he is the King of Babylon, and they bow to each other. Madame Flora enters: 'How many times I've told you not to touch my things ... Is anything ready? Of course not.' Monica calms her mother, and they prepare for the séance, Monica putting on a white dress and veil, and Toby testing the various devices hidden in the puppet-theatre.

The clients arrive. One of them has not been before, but the others, who have been coming for two years, tell her how wonderful Madame Flora is. Mrs Gobineau talks about her little child who was drowned in a fountain in their garden in France. The séance begins. All the lights, except the candle in front of the Madonna, are put out, and they sit round the table, their hands touching. Baba moans, and Monica slowly appears in a faint blue light, singing 'Mother, mother, are you there?' Mrs Nolan is convinced it is her daughter, and she asks her various simple questions, which are answered to her satisfaction. Monica asks her about a gold locket, but it appears she has never had one, and immediately the apparition starts to disappear.

Monica next imitates the sound of a child laughing, for the benefit of the Gobineaus. Suddenly, Baba shouts hysterically, and turns on the light. 'Who touched me?' They try to reassure her but she sends them away. As they go they sing a trio: 'But why be afraid of our dead?'

Baba is in a paroxysm of fear, and she seizes Toby from the puppet-theatre, and tries to blame the whole phenomenon on him. Monica takes her away and soothes her with an extended melody, which Toby accompanies on a tambourine: 'O black swan, where, oh where, is my lover gone?' Baba suddenly thinks she can hear voices, and sends Toby to see what is there; when he indicates there was nothing, she falls on her knees and prays.

Act II. Evening, a few days later. Monica sits in front of the puppet-theatre watching a performance which Toby is giving. She applauds, and then sings while he dances barefoot round the room. The dance becomes a sort of love duet, in which Monica sings for both and Toby mimes his part. She has guessed his love for her, and tries to divert it into play-acting, which she knows he enjoys.

Baba drags herself up the stairs, and Toby retreats into a corner before she gets into the room. Baba questions Toby about the incident of a few days back; did he touch her throat? Was he the one? She cannot get him to admit it, tries to keep her temper, then loses it hopelessly, seizes a whip and beats the unfortunate boy unmercifully. The doorbell rings, and the Gobineaus and Mrs Nolan enter. Is it not the night of the séance? Yes, she says; but there will be no more –

they were all frauds. She wants to give them their money back, but they will not admit they have been cheated. Nothing will convince them, and they beg for another séance, until Madame Flora loses her temper suddenly and yells to them to get out. She tries to send Toby too, but Monica pleads for him, helpless as he is. Baba however is insistent.

The voices come back to Baba. In desperation she goes to the cupboard and pours herself several drinks. 'Afraid? Am I afraid?' she asks herself. She passes her life in review, and thinks of the horrible things she has known; then tries to comfort herself with the song of the black swan. For a moment she prays for forgiveness; then falls asleep, exhausted.

Toby comes up the stairwell, tiptoes across to Monica's room, finds the door locked, and hides behind the sofa when Baba stirring in her sleep knocks the bottle over. He starts to look in the trunk, but the lid falls with a bang, Baba wakes up with a start, and Toby hides behind the puppet-theatre. She yells 'Who's there?' but gets no answer, and taking out a revolver from a drawer shoots hysterically at the curtain. There is a moment of stillness, then a spot of blood appears on the white curtain. 'I've killed the ghost,' says Baba. Toby's hands clutch the side of the screen, which collapses with his weight, and he falls dead into the room. 'I've killed the ghost,' says Baba, as Monica pounds on the door to be let out: 'I've killed the ghost.'   H.

THE TELEPHONE

Opera buffa in one act, text by the composer. Première, Heckscher Theater, New York, 18 February 1947, with Marilyn Cotlow, Paul Kwartin, conductor Barzin. First performed New York, Ethel Barrymore Theater, 1947, with Cotlow, Rogier, conductor Balaban; London, Aldwych Theatre, 1948, conductor Balaban; Zürich, 1949, with Oravez, Rehfuss; Hamburg, 1952, with Rothenberger, Günther; Sadler's Wells, 1959, with Bronhill, Sharp, conductor Alexander Gibson; Paris, Opéra-Comique, 1968, with Berton, J.C. Benoit.

Lucy..Soprano
Ben ....Baritone

Place: U.S.A.
Time: 'The Present'
Running Time: 20 minutes

Most performances of *The Medium*, at any rate those in English, have been preceded by performances of *The Telephone*, the little comedy Menotti wrote for the Ballet Society's first New York presentation of *The Medium*. But *The Telephone* would appear to have a life of its own, and it makes a capital curtain-raiser, a modern intermezzo as it were, in the style of Wolf-Ferrari's *Il Segreto di Susanna*.

The scene is Lucy's apartment. The opening music clearly indicates the *opera buffa* nature of the ensuing work. Lucy is busy opening a parcel which Ben has just handed her. 'Oh, just what I wanted,' she exclaims, as she unwraps a piece of abstract sculpture. Ben has something to tell her, he says, before his train goes in an hour's time. He seems to be reaching the point, when the telephone rings. Lucy answers it in a little arietta which seems to comprise all the things she always says to all her friends on the telephone.

Ben is about to start again, is again interrupted, but this time it turns out to be a wrong number. An unfortunate mention of the time prompts Lucy to dial TIM, to discover that it is 'four-fifteen and three and a half seconds'. Another attempt is frustrated by another peal of the telephone bell. This time the conversation is fast and furious, and Lucy seems to quarrel with a boyfriend. Ben comforts her, but she goes off to her bedroom to get a handkerchief. Ben thinks wryly of the impossible rival he has to face, with its 'hundreds of lives and miles of umbilical cord'. He is about to cut the line when the telephone rings loudly and desperately ('like a child crying for help,' says the libretto), and Lucy comes in and takes it protectively in her arms.

Lucy must make a call to tell her friend Pamela about the quarrel with George. Again the conversation makes an arietta, but this time Ben's voice joins in underneath Lucy's, complaining that he will never get the chance to say what he wants to say. He goes out, much to Lucy's surprise ('I have a feeling he had something on his mind'). At one side of the stage Ben now becomes visible dialling in a telephone box. Presently Lucy's bell rings, and she is confident it must be him. This time he gets the proposal in early, and is immediately accepted. Lucy demands only one thing: that he shall not forget ... What? asks Ben; her hands, her eyes, her lips? No, her number, exclaims Lucy, and the opera ends in a skittish waltz tune, in which Ben promises never to forget her number. She dictates it to him ...   H.

THE CONSUL

Opera in three acts, text by the composer. Première, Philadelphia, 1 March 1950, with Neway, Powers, Lane, Marlo, MacNeil, Lishner, McKinley, Jongeyans, conductor Lehman Engel. First performed New York, 1951, by same cast; Cambridge Theatre, London, 1951, with Neway, Powers, Lane, Lishner, Kelly, conductor Schippers; Hamburg, 1951, with Mödl, Koegel, Wasserthal, Ilosvay; Zürich, 1951, with Schulz, Malaniuk, conductor Reinshagen; la Scala, Milan, 1951, with Petrella, Powers, conductor Sanzogno; Vienna, 1951, with Zadek, Schürhoff, Rohs, Braun, Jerger, Szemere, Rus, conductor Zallinger; Berlin, 1951, and Munich, 1952, with Borkh; Sadler's Wells, 1954, with Shuard; New York City Opera, 1960, with Neway.

John Sorel..Baritone
Magda Sorel, *his wife* ....Soprano
The Mother..Contralto
Secret Police Agent..Bass
First and Second Plain-Clothes Men ....Silent
The Secretary ....Mezzo-Soprano
Mr Kofner..Bass-Baritone
The Foreign Woman ....Soprano
Anna Gomez...Soprano
Vera Boronel..Contralto
The Magician (Nika Magadoff)........................Tenor
Assan, *friend of John Sorel* ....Baritone
Voice on the Record....................................Soprano

Place: Somewhere in Europe
Time: After World War II
Running Time: 1 hour 55 minutes

Menotti's first full-length opera deals with a subject which was familiar to every member of every one of its early non-English-speaking audiences. Its immediate success was perhaps due as much to the grippingly theatrical nature of its story as to a corresponding power in its music.

The country in which the action takes place is not identified, any more than is the consulate whose secretary is the embodiment of every form-ridden bureaucrat in every big city in the world.

Act I. The home of John Sorel. It is early morning. The sound of a gramophone record is heard coming from a café across the street: 'Tu reviendras ... ' Suddenly the door is flung open and Sorel staggers into the room and throws himself into a chair. Magda runs to him and immediately starts to bandage the wound which she sees in his leg. He tells her and the Mother the story: there was a secret meeting, the police had been tipped off and shot at them as they made their escape across the roofs, wounding him and killing another. Magda looks out of the window and sees the police. John is helped towards the window, and goes to what is obviously an agreed hiding-place, leaving his wife and her mother to tidy up the room in preparation for the questioning which must shortly follow.

As the secret police agents enter, the Mother is rocking the cradle, in which lies the little child of Magda and John. She sings a mournful lament for the peace which has vanished from their lives: 'Shall we ever see the end of all this?' The agent starts to question Magda. His threats are not just those of a bully, but carry potential danger in them: 'Courage is often a lack of imagination. We have strange ways to make people talk. Oh, not at all the way you think ... People like you can defy strength, but not the beat of your own heart.'

The agents leave, and John comes down from his hiding-place; he must get away. He tells them that the signal which shall tell them that there is a message from him will be the breaking of their window by a stone. They are then to send for Assan, the glass-cutter, who will bring them news. Magda and John say goodbye and their duet becomes a trio when the Mother joins her voice with theirs.

Scene ii. The cheerless waiting-room of the Consulate, in one corner of which is the Secretary's desk, and behind it a door leading to the Consul's room. Mr Kofner comes forward to renew his application for a visa; he has everything now ... but the photographs turn out to be the wrong size. A 6/8 *allegretto* movement suggests the monotonous, automatic nature of the dealings between applicant and Secretary. The Foreign Woman comes up to the desk and starts to make an enquiry. She does not know the Secretary's language, but Mr Kofner volunteers to act as interpreter. It appears that her daughter ran away with a soldier, who has now left her with a three-month-old baby. The daughter is ill and needs her mother's help; can she have a visa to visit her? Yes, says the Secretary; if she fills out the forms and her application is accepted, she may be able to leave in a couple of months' time. She is stunned by this information, but Mr Kofner leads her away to fill in the forms.

Magda advances to the desk. The dialogue between her and the Secretary is typical of Menotti's style:

MAGDA: May I speak to the Consul?
SECRETARY: No one is allowed to speak to the Consul, the Consul is busy.
MAGDA: Tell him my name.
SECRETARY: Your name is a number.
MAGDA: But my name is Sorel, Magda Sorel. The wife of Sorel, the lover of freedom.
SECRETARY: Sorel is a name and a name is a number.
MAGDA: May I speak to the Consul?
SECRETARY: No one is allowed to speak to the Consul, the Consul is busy.

The duet gains in intensity: 'Explain to the Consul, explain ... that the web of my life has worn down to one single thread ... ' But it is still a question of filling in forms and making applications in the customary manner. Nika Magadoff comes forward and starts to do some simple conjuring tricks in an effort to impress the Secretary with his *bona fides*, but a slow ensemble begins ('In endless waiting-rooms'), and he joins in it. As the curtain falls, it has become a quintet in which Magda, Anna Gomez, Vera Boronel, the Magician and Mr Kofner express frustration.

Act II, scene i. Sorel's house, a month later. The same record is being played in the café opposite. Magda and her Mother are discussing the possibility of getting a visa. The Mother tries to cheer up the little baby. She sings him a lullaby, and, after Magda has fallen asleep in a chair, goes out. Magda in a nightmare sees John and the Secretary, whom he introduces as his sister. Magda is terrified of her, more particularly since John seems drawn to her. The nightmare comes to an end with a horrible vision of a dead child.

Magda wakes up with a scream, and is comforted by her mother. Suddenly, a stone shatters the glass of the window, and Magda rushes to the telephone to carry out John's instructions. There is a knock at the door, which opens to reveal the Secret Police Agent. He starts to insinuate that there would be no obstacle to her joining her husband if she would only give him the little information about her husband's friends which he wants. She loses control and yells at him to get out, and threatens to kill him if he returns. Assan arrives to mend the window.

Assan tells Magda that John is still hiding in the mountains, and will not leave the country until he knows that his wife has a visa and can follow him. She says that he must be told that arrangements are complete; it is not true, but there is no other way of compelling him to save his own life. Assan agrees to do as he is asked.

During the scene between Magda and Assan, the Mother suddenly realises that the little half-starved child has died quietly in his sleep. She gives no sign to Magda, but remains quite still by the cradle, not rocking it, not singing to the child. As soon as she looks at her, Magda knows what has happened. She stops her mother weeping, but the Mother says she is thinking of John, 'who will never see his baby again'.

Scene ii, in the Consulate, a few days later. The Secretary is standing by the filing-cabinet, Anna Gomez, the Magician, Vera Boronel, Mr Kofner, and the Foreign Woman are waiting. Magda asks to jump the queue, but the Magician explains that he has been seven times to the Consulate, and always when his turn came it was time for the Consulate to close; he *must* take his turn now. He again demonstrates his professional powers of conjuring and of hypnotism, much to the Secretary's dismay. He puts all the occupants of the waiting-room in a trance, and then makes them dance happily together, until the Secretary becomes quite desperate. She begs Magadoff to return everyone to normal, which done, he leaves the room.

The others allow Magda to go ahead of them. She is frantic with worry and demands to see the Consul but is again refused. Finally, she can bear it no more, and throws self-control to the winds, launching out into a denunciation of the bureaucratic system and the injustice it leads to. The rest of the act is given up to a *scena* for Magda, with interruptions from the Secretary and the others: 'To this we've come: that men withhold the world from men.' Her passionate indignation is finally summed up in a brave phrase: 'Oh, the day will come, I know, when our hearts aflame will burn your paper chains. Warn the Consul, Secretary ...'

The Secretary cannot conceal her own feelings, although she does her best: 'You're being very unreasonable, Mrs Sorel.' She goes into the Consul's office, saying that she will ask if he can see her just a minute. The improbable happens when she comes out and informs Magda that she may go in when the important visitor who is with him has left. Anticipation rises as two shadows are seen on the glass panel of the door. The visitor shakes hands, but,

when he turns into the room, he is seen to be the Secret Police Agent. Magda faints.

Act III, scene i. The Consulate. Magda is waiting to see the Consul, in spite of the Secretary's warning that the place will be closed in ten minutes' time. Vera Boronel comes in, states her name, and is greeted with something like pleasure by the Secretary; at last there is somebody to whom she can give good news – her papers are through!

Assan hurries in, looking for Magda. John has heard that his child and the Mother are dead, and intends to come back over the frontier to fetch his wife. Magda and Assan try to think of a way of convincing him that he must not come back. Magda thinks she knows one, and writes a note which she confides to Assan, refusing however to tell him what she has written.

Everyone leaves, and the Secretary is about to leave when John rushes into the room, looking behind him to see that he is not being followed. He asks if Magda has been there, and is told he may still catch up with her if he hurries after her. But that he cannot do, he protests, since he was followed to the Consulate by the police, who will not allow him to leave. At that moment, a confused noise is heard outside, and the Secret Police Agent comes in, followed by two plain-clothes men. When the Secretary protests that no arrest can be made in the Consulate, the Secret Agent says that Sorel will be coming with him of his own free will, not as an arrested man.

As they leave, the Secretary dials furiously, and when the curtain goes up again on scene ii, after an interlude based on a march rhythm, the telephone can be heard ringing in Magda's room, which she presently enters, though only after the bell is silent. She makes preparations to commit suicide, and turns on the gas.

As she bends over towards the stove with a shawl over her head, the walls dissolve and figures from the Consulate appear, looking exactly as Magda has known them there. Behind them are John and the Mother. Gradually the figures disappear, and all that can be heard is the sound of Magda's deep breathing. Suddenly the telephone begins to ring. Magda stretches out her hand as if to answer it, but her reaction is feeble, and she falls inert over the chair, while the telephone bell continues to ring. The curtain falls as the orchestra gives out the tune associated with Magda's protest at the end of Act II.   H.

AMAHL AND THE NIGHT VISITORS

Opera in one act, libretto by the composer. Originally written for television. Première, N.B.C. studios, New York, 24 December 1951, with Rosemary Kuhlmann and Chet Allen, conductor Schippers. First stage performance, Indiana University, Bloomington, 21 February 1952, conductor Ernest Hoffmann. First performed New York, City Center, 1952; Florence Festival, 1953, with Simionato, Alvaro Cordova, Lazzari, Capecchi, Corena, conductor Stokowski. B.B.C. Television, 1967, with Cantelo; Hamburg State Opera, 1968–69, with Kerstin Meyer; Geneva, 1971, with Kerstin Meyer; Vienna State Opera, 1980, with Helga Dernesch. Frequently performed in Italy, the United States and the United Kingdom.

Amahl, *a crippled boy of about twelve*..................Treble
His Mother..Soprano
King Kaspar...Tenor
King Melchior ....Baritone
King Balthazar ....Bass
The Page ....Baritone

Shepherds, Villagers, Dancers

Running Time: 45 minutes

After a few introductory bars the curtain rises to show the outside of a little shepherd's hut, where Amahl sits playing his pipe. Beside him is his home-made crutch. His mother calls him in. He makes one excuse after another to stay outside, and even after his mother loses her patience he tries to persuade her to go out to look at the beautiful sky and the brilliant new star – 'as large as a window and with a glorious tail'. She thinks it is another of his stories and scolds him for lying, but eventually breaks down in tears at the prospect of going out begging next day. They say goodnight and go to bed.

In the distance can be heard the voices of the three Kings. As they draw near, their way is lit by their black Page, bowed under the weight of rich-looking bundles, everything from a jewel box to a parrot in a cage. They stop at Amahl's home and King Melchior knocks. Amahl goes to the door and scurries back to his mother. Three times she thinks hē is lying, but eventually she follows him to the door, the Kings bid her a grave good evening, and she for her part offers her meagre hospitality to the splendid visitors.

To a jaunty march, the Kings make their way into the hut. As the Page spreads out the treasures on a rug, the woman goes off to look for firewood, telling Amahl not to pester their visitors. As soon as she is out of the way, Amahl goes straight to the Nubian King Balthazar and bombards him with questions, meanwhile looking out of the corner of his eye at Kaspar, who is feeding his parrot with bits of food from his pocket. Amahl cannot resist Kaspar's eccentricity. Kaspar however is deaf and things do not warm up until Amahl asks what is in the box, whereupon Kaspar becomes enthusiastic and shows Amahl the precious stone he keeps against all kinds of misfortune. When his mother scolds him for being a nuisance, Amahl protests: 'It's not my fault; they kept asking me questions.'

Amahl goes off to fetch the other shepherds and the Kings tell his mother that they are looking for the Child, and in an *andante* describe their vision. In her mind the mother identifies the Child with her own son.

The shepherds' calls are heard. As they approach, led by Amahl, they sing a bright pastoral unaccompanied chorus. When they reach the door of the hut with their baskets of fruit and vegetables they are struck dumb by the splendour of the Kings, but the mother urges them to come in and shyly they present their humble gifts. The Kings thank them, and the mother asks the young people to dance for her guests. After some persuasion they do so, at first slowly and formally but gradually accelerating into a kind of *tarantella*.

Balthazar thanks the dancers and they file out, bowing to the Kings. As their song grows fainter, Amahl wistfully asks Kaspar if he has perhaps a magic stone to cure a crippled boy. But Kaspar, as usual, does not hear properly and Amahl goes sadly to his straw bed.

They all settle down for the night, the Kings sitting side by side on the bench and the Page lying at their feet, his arms round the precious gifts. Time passes, dawn breaks. Everyone is asleep except the mother, who sings of the unfairness of all this wealth going to an unknown child while her own is starving. She takes hold of one of the bundles and the Page wakes up. The noise of their struggle disturbs Amahl who flings himself at the Page, beating him and pulling his hair in a desperate attempt to rescue his mother. Kaspar orders the Page to release the woman, and King Melchior says she may keep the gold as the Child they seek has no need of it.

The mother is enthralled with Melchior's glowing description and begs him to take back the gold –

were she not so poor she would herself send a gift to the Child. Amahl wants to send his crutch. He lifts it and then, to everyone's amazement, takes a step without it. For a moment no one believes the miracle, then the Kings give thanks to God, as Amahl dances and leaps about the room until at last he falls down. One at a time the Kings ask Amahl to let them touch him. When the Page in his turn asks, Amahl, a little self-importantly, at first refuses but, at a sign from his mother, relents. Amahl begs to be allowed to go with the Kings to give the crutch to the Child and when the Kings join their voices to his, the mother gives her permission. With a wealth of maternal advice to sustain him, Amahl sets off with the Kings and, as the procession moves away, he plays on his pipe the tune which began the opera. H.

THE SAINT OF BLEECKER STREET

Opera in three acts, text by the composer. Première, Broadway Theater, New York, 27 December 1954, with Virginia Copeland, Gloria Lane, David Poleri, conductor Thomas Schippers. First performed la Scala, Milan, 1955, with Eugenia Ratti, Gloria Lane, David Poleri, conductor Schippers; Volksoper, Vienna, 1955, conductor Hollreiser; England, B.B.C. Television, 1957, with Virginia Copeland, Rosalind Elias, Raymond Nilsson; New York City Opera, 1964–65, with Joan Sena, Beverly Wolff, Muriel Greenspon, Enrico Di Giuseppe; Spoleto, 1968, with Maria Mirandara, Gloria Lane, Anna Assandri, Franco Bonisolli, conductor Schippers.

Assunta	Mezzo-Soprano
Carmela	Soprano
Maria Corona, *a newspaper-seller*	Soprano
Her Son, *sixteen years old and dumb*	Silent
Don Marco, *a priest*	Bass
Annina	Soprano
Michele, *her brother*	Tenor
Desideria, *Michele's mistress*	Mezzo-Soprano
Salvatore	Baritone
A Young Man	Tenor

Neighbours, Wedding-Guests, etc.

Place: A Quarter of New York known as Little Italy
Time: 'The Present'
Running Time: 2 hours

An overture establishes the atmosphere of feverish religiosity; a cold-water flat in Bleecker Street on Good Friday afternoon as a crowd of neighbours wait for Annina. She is a frail, religious girl, subject to mysterious visions.

The crowd is impatient to be blessed by the girl, whom they consider a saint; the hubbub is broken by the sudden appearance of the priest Don Marco, who announces that the vision has begun. At first Annina lies motionless, then suddenly cries out in pain, and begins a detailed description of the Crucifixion; on her hands appear the bleeding stigmata. Don Marco and Carmela try to fend off the hysterical neighbours, but the crowd falls back at the sight of Michele, Annina's brother, who drives them away. With Carmela's help, he carries Annina back into her room, then reproaches the priest, saying her visions are mental delusions. Don Marco warns Michele that his adversary is not a priest but God himself.

Scene ii. An empty lot on Mulberry Street, flanked by tenement houses, from one of which can be heard the voice of Assunta singing a lullaby to her child. On the steps, Annina and her best friend Carmela are sewing gold paper stars on to the white gown of little Concettina, who is to be an angel in the forthcoming procession of San Gennaro, to which Annina says her brother will not let her go. When Carmela tells Annina that she is to be married and so they will not be able to take the veil together as they had planned, Annina says she will gladly go to Carmela's wedding if Carmela will come to hers when she becomes a nun. Assunta laughs at Carmela's dreams of happiness. What is heaven like, they ask Annina. Saint Michael once, says Annina, took her in a dream to the gates of Paradise, and the three are singing in wonder at this splendid vision when Maria Corona rushes in, warning Annina that the Sons of Gennaro refuse to have their procession without their 'Little Saint' and are threatening to take her by force. Annina says she is not afraid. Maria Corona confesses that she once doubted Annina's miracles, but since she touched her son, dumb since birth, he has begun to speak – he is grunting pathetically when Michele enters and angrily sends the women away.

There is an extended scene for Annina and Michele. She is afraid for him, because he makes people hate him; he argues that he loves her and wants to protect her. His arguments seem useless and Michele grows desperate; she is the centre of his life, and he swears he will hide her away and that she shall never take the veil.

The procession is heard approaching. A group of

young men overpower Michele, leaving him helpless as they carry the frightened Annina off to head the procession. As the last stragglers vanish, Desideria appears and unbinds Michele who bursts out sobbing. She embraces him passionately.

Act II. The following May, Carmela's marriage to Salvatore is being celebrated. Desideria comes looking for Michele; let him take her in with him to the wedding party and show he is not ashamed of her. When Michele refuses, Desideria flies into a rage. Why can't Michele leave Annina alone? He is obsessed with her, whereas Desideria and he need each other.

Michele reluctantly agrees to go in with her, but at the door they find Don Marco, who begs Michele not to cause a scandal. Michele immediately swings over to Desideria's side, shouting that she is worth more than any woman there. Annina rushes to him but he pushes her away and sings bitterly of his treatment at the hands of those whom he wished to be his friends.

Annina is distressed at the upheaval and asks Michele to take her home. Desideria suddenly appears from a corner and accuses Michele of being in love with his sister. Michele suddenly seizes a knife from the bar and stabs her in the back. He leaves Annina praying with Desideria, who dies as police sirens are heard in the distance.

Act III, scene i. In a deserted passage near a newspaper kiosk in a subway station, Annina and Maria Corona are waiting nervously for Michele. He comes in with Don Marco, and there is a tender reunion between brother and sister. Annina begs Michele to give himself up but he refuses and they comment on their terrible situation in a tragic duet. When she tells him that she is afraid of dying and is going into a nunnery, Michele is shocked and horrified. Nothing he can say affects her resolve, and the scene ends with Michele cursing her and rushing off in a rage.

Scene ii. Annina's room, a week later. She is dying and wants to take the veil immediately. She has no white dress to wear, but Carmela offers to lend her own wedding dress. A letter arrives for Don Marco – it is the Church's permission for Annina to become a nun. Annina sends everyone out except Don Marco and Carmela, and prays that death will spare her long enough to attain her great wish. As Don Marco robes for the ceremony, Assunta brings the news that Michele has been seen nearby. The ceremony proceeds calmly until at the end Michele bursts in and begs his sister to reconsider. She appears not to hear him and the ritual continues as her hair is cut off and the black veil is put on. Michele watches incredulously as Annina collapses and Don Marco places the ring on her finger just before she dies.   H.

OLIVIER MESSIAEN

(born 10 December 1908, died 28 April 1992)

SAINT FRANÇOIS D'ASSISE

Scènes Franciscaines in three acts and eight scenes, libretto by the composer, based mainly on the Saint's writings. Première by the Opéra de Paris at the Palais Garnier, 28 November 1983, with Christiane Eda-Pierre as the Angel, José Van Dam as St Francis, Kenneth Riegel as the Leper, Michel Philippe as Brother Léon, Georges Gautier as Brother Massée, Michel Sénéchal as Brother Elie, Jean-Philippe Courtis as Brother Bernard, conducted by Seiji Ozawa who toured three scenes (3,7,8) in concert to Tokyo, 1986. Berlin (concert), 1986, with Fischer-Dieskau. Kent Nagano conducted a semi-staged performance of four scenes (3,6,7,8) at the Royal Festival Hall in 1988 with David Wilson-Johnson in the title role. Revived 1992 in Salzburg and Paris, conducted by Esa-Pekka Salonen, directed by Peter Sellars, with José Van Dam.

The Angel	Soprano
Saint François (St Francis)	Baritone
The Leper	Tenor
Brother Léon	Baritone
Brother Massée	Tenor
Brother Elie	Tenor
Brother Bernard	Bass

Place: Assisi
Time: Thirteenth Century
Running Time: 3 hours 50 minutes

As the composer himself makes clear, his only stage work is not a conventional opera, rather, a sequence of 'scenes that show different aspects of Grace in the soul of St Francis'. 'I have always admired St Francis,' he wrote, 'first, because he's the saint who most resembles Christ and then for a wholly personal reason: he spoke to the birds, and I'm an ornithologist.'

Messiaen's opera celebrates the life and work of St Francis of Assisi, and quotes from his writings. It also comprises a whole aviary of birdsong that the composer loved, some of which the saint could never have heard in his native Umbria, such as species native to Morocco, Australia and Japan. These are faithfully recreated in the huge orchestra of 120 players. The prelude to scene vi reproduces the 'organised disorder' of a dawn concert. *St François d'Assise* is rather more than a hagiography or an ornithological compendium, however. Paul Griffiths points out that 'one of the attractions of birdsong for Messiaen may have been that it allowed him to abolish or ignore the distinction between reality and representation. He spoke of "trying to trace as exact as possible a musical portrait" of a bird, but the portraits he produced are icons, doing duty for the real, and in the same way *Saint François* is an iconic opera.'[1]

Act I, scene i. The Cross. When Brother Léon admits he is frightened on the road as night falls, St François comforts him with the thought that perfect joy is not found in curing the sick, in prophesying the future, in converting others or in knowledge, but in bearing suffering patiently and cheerfully, for the love of Christ.

Scene ii. Lauds. St François prays alongside his fellow monks. Led by him, they praise God for Brother Wind, Sister Water, Brother Fire and Mother Earth. St François accepts that God created ugliness, the poisonous mushroom alongside the dragonfly; he confronts his own horror of lepers, asking God to let him meet a leper and make him capable of loving him.

Scene iii. The Kissing of the Leper. The Leper refuses to be comforted by St François. An Angel's voice is heard, promising that God is greater than the Leper's heart: he who dwells in love, dwells in Him. The Leper begs for forgiveness. St François calls him his brother, his friend, his son and asks the Leper to forgive him: he hasn't loved him enough. Suddenly, all the Leper's sores disappear: he is healed. The Choir draw the moral, 'To those who have loved greatly, all is forgiven!'

Act II, scene iv. The Journeying Angel. The Brothers fail to recognise an Angel when it knocks at the monastery door and asks them about predestination. The Vicar, Brother Elie, resents being disturbed from his writing and his planning; Brother Bernard asks the name of their visitor. Before the Angel goes to speak to St François, 'better than in words', it tells Bernard that its name is Wonderful. Bernard and Massée wonder, was this an Angel?

Scene v. The Angel-Musician. While St François is meditating on the beauty of creation and on the joy of the blessed a kestrel calls, at a time when he was not expected; the Angel appears to St François, quotes from St Thomas Aquinas and announces that God will speak to him in music 'that suspends life from the ladders of heaven'. The melody is passed between three widely spaced *ondes martenot* at this point, the climax of the opera. The other monks mistake François's rapture for illness. He reassures them, saying, 'If the Angel had played the viol a little longer', his soul might have left his body.

Scene vi. The Sermon to the Birds. St François preaches to the birds, those of Umbria and those he hears in his dreams, from further away. He compares their song to the Angel's music and blesses them. They fly off in four groups, forming a kind of Cross in the sky. For St François, the birds teach man to seek the kingdom of God, for then, 'the rest will be added to us'.

Act III, scene vii. The Stigmata. St François prays to feel in his body the pain Christ suffered on the Cross, as well as the love He felt for man. A Chorus speaks for Christ and promises St François, 'If you carry my Cross with a good heart, it will carry you, and lead you to the desired end.'

Scene viii. Death and the New Life. As he lies dying, St François says farewell to the birds, to Assisi and to the other monks and sings the final verses of his *Cantico del sole*. The Angel assures François that it will be with him when he enters Paradise, along with the Leper, who died holy. He will hear the music of the unseen. The Choir look forward to resurrection through God.

---

[1] Quoted from Philippe Godefroid's conversation with the composer in Paul Griffiths, 'Saint François d'Assise', *The Messiaen Companion*, ed. Peter Hill, London, 1995.

Messiaen anticipated that his opera would be attacked because it calls for such rich means to portray the work of a man dedicated to poverty. In answer, he pointed out that, since his infancy, St Francis had loved the beauty that surrounded him: 'he was rich in the sun, the moon, the stars, the colours of the sky, the clouds, the trees, the grass, the flowers, the sound of the wind, the force of the fire and the limpidity of water. He was rich in everything ... Far from doing him an injury, a music loud in the colours of timbres, of [varying] lengths, of sonorous complexity, seems to me, on the contrary, perfectly in accord with his true inner nature.'

For Messaien, God speaks through music, not words. The opera makes huge demands on its soloists. Messiaen himself said that the central baritone role combines the vigour of Debussy's Golaud with the 'declamatory solemnity' of Boris Godunov.[1] It also makes considerable demands on the chorus of 150 and on its audience, since it moves slowly. It aims to recreate the divine experience, taking us through the exhilaration of nature, the leper's despair, the saint's mystic suffering to a foretaste of heavenly joy. All these are refracted through Messiaen's dazzling patterns of sound to bring us close to what is invisible, ineffable, or simply 'beyond', to quote from the title of his last major orchestral work, *Eclairs sur l'au-delà*.   P.

---

[1] *Idem*

GIACOMO MEYERBEER

(born 5 September 1791, died 2 May 1864)

Born in Berlin, Meyerbeer, with an independent income, set out on a prolonged study of opera. He started in Germany, where he wrote his first works; from 1815 lived in Italy and wrote Italian operas in a post-Rossini style, some (e.g. *Il crociato in Egitto*) outstandingly successful; and from 1825 was active in Paris, where his *Robert le Diable* followed Spontini's Paris operas, Rossini's *Guillaume Tell* and Auber's *La Muette de Portici* in establishing spectacular opera on a grand scale as a French speciality. Though Meyerbeer wrote only four operas in this style, *Les Huguenots* has come to be thought of as the epitome of the genre. He exploited his talent with consummate skill, wrote as effectively for grand voices as he did for the boulevardier audience, and influenced even composers far more gifted, like Verdi and Wagner. Monumental set pieces like the duel septet, the 'Bénédiction des Poignards' and the great fourth-act duet still stir the blood of audiences grown accustomed in succeeding centuries to more direct operatic styles than Meyerbeer's.

ROBERT LE DIABLE

Robert the Devil

Opera in five acts, words by Scribe and Delavigne. Première Grand Opéra, Paris, 22 November 1831, with Dorus-Gras, Cinti-Damoreau, Nourrit, Levasseur. First performed Drury Lane, London, 1832 (in English), as *The Demon, or the Mystic Branch*; Covent Garden, 1832 (in English), as *The Fiend Father, or Robert of Normandy*; Her Majesty's Theatre, 1847 (in Italian), with Jenny Lind (her London début); New York, 1834 (in English), the opera being followed by a *pas seul* by Miss Wheatley, and a farce, *My Uncle John*; Astor Place Opera House, 1851; Academy of Music, 1857, with Formes as Bertram; Metropolitan, 1883, with Fursch-Madi, Valleria, Stagno, Mirabella. Last Covent Garden performance, 1890, with Fanny Moody, Charles Manners, conductor Arditi. Revived Florence Festival, 1968, with Scotto, Merighi, Christoff; Paris, 1985, with June Anderson, Vanzo, Samuel Ramey.

Alice, *foster-sister of Robert*	Soprano
Isabelle, *Princess of Sicily*	Soprano
The Abbess	Dancer
Robert, *Duke of Normandy*	Tenor
Bertram, *the Unknown*	Bass
Raimbaut, *a minstrel*	Tenor

Place: Sicily
Time: Thirteenth Century
Running Time: 4 hours

The production of *Robert le Diable* in Paris was such a sensational success that it made the fortune of the Grand Opéra. Whatever criticism may now be directed against this opera, it was a remarkable creation for its day. Meyerbeer's score not only saved the libretto, in which the grotesque is carried to the point of absurdity, but actually made a brilliant success of the production as a whole.

The story is legendary. Robert is the son of the arch-fiend by a human woman. Robert's father, known as Bertram, but really the devil, ever follows him about, and seeks to lure him to destruction. The strain of purity in the drama is supplied by Robert's foster-sister, Alice, who, if Bertram is the prototype of Méphistophélès in *Faust*, may be regarded as the original of Micaela in *Carmen*.

Act I. Robert, because of his evil deeds (inspired by Bertram), has been banished from Normandy, and has come to Sicily. He has fallen in love with Isabelle, she with him. He is to attend a tournament at which she is to award the prizes. Tempted by Bertram, he gambles and loses all his possessions, including even his armour. Raimbaut, the minstrel, sings of Robert's misdeeds; he is saved from the latter's fury by Alice, who is betrothed to Raimbaut, and who, in an expressive air, pleads vainly with Robert to mend his ways and especially to avoid Bertram, from whom she instinctively shrinks.

Act II. Robert and Isabelle meet in the palace. She bestows upon him a suit of armour to wear in the tournament. But, misled by Bertram, he seeks his rival elsewhere than in the lists, and by his failure to appear there, forfeits his honour as a knight.

Act III. In the cavern of St Irene. There takes place an orgy of evil spirits, to whose number Bertram promises to add Robert. Next comes a scene that verges upon the grotesque, but which is converted by Meyerbeer's genius into something highly fantastic. This is in the ruined convent of St Rosalie. In a big solo ('Nonnes, qui reposez') Bertram summons from their graves the nuns who, in life, were unfaithful to their vows. The fiend has promised Robert that if he will but seize a mystic cypress branch from over the grave of St Rosalie, and bear it away, whatever he wishes for will become his. The ghostly nuns, led by their Abbess (Taglioni at the Paris première), dance about him. They seek to inveigle him with gambling, drink, and love, until, dazed by their enticements, he seizes the branch. Besides the ballet of the nuns, there is a scene for Raimbaut and Bertram – 'Du rendezvous', and 'Le bonheur est dans l'inconstance'.

Act IV. The first use Robert makes of the branch is to effect entrance into Isabelle's chamber. He threatens to seize her and bear her away, but yields to her entreaties, breaks the branch, and destroys the spell. In this act occurs the famous air for Isabelle, 'Robert, toi que j'aime'.

Act V. Once more Bertram seeks to make a compact with Robert, the price for which shall be paid with his soul. But Alice, by repeating to him the last warning words of his mother, delays the signing of the compact until the clock strikes twelve. The spell is broken. Bertram disappears. The cathedral doors swing open disclosing Isabelle, who, in her bridal robes, awaits Robert. The finale contains a trio for Alice, Robert and Bertram, which is considered one of Meyerbeer's finest inspirations.   K.

LES HUGUENOTS

Opera in five acts, text by A.E. Scribe after Deschamps. Première at the Opéra, Paris, 29 February 1836, with Falcon, Dorus-Gras, Nourrit, Levasseur, Serda.

Valentine, *daughter of St Bris,*
    betrothed to de Nevers .... Soprano
Marguerite de Valois, *betrothed to*
    Henri IV of Navarre .... Soprano
Urbain, *Marguerite's page*
    ....Soprano (or Mezzo-Soprano)
Count de St Bris, *Catholic nobleman* ....Baritone
Count de Nevers, *Catholic nobleman* ....Baritone
Raoul de Nangis, *Huguenot nobleman* ....Tenor
Marcel, *Raoul's servant* ....Bass

Catholic and Huguenot Nobles, Ladies and
    Gentlemen of the Court, Soldiers, Pages, Citizens,
    Populace

Place: Touraine and Paris
Time: August 1572
Running Time: 4 hours 15 minutes

The background to *Les Huguenots* is political, just before the Massacre of St Bartholomew, when feeling between Catholics and Huguenots was running murderously high. The feud came to an end only with the accession in 1589 of Henri IV (a Huguenot), who in 1572 had married the Catholic Marguerite de Valois, daughter of Catherine de Medici and sister of François II, Charles IX and Henri III (and therefore sister-in-law of Mary Queen of Scots).

The action revolves round Marguerite's attempt to effect a dynastic and 'politically correct' marriage between the prominent Huguenot, Raoul de Nangis, and Valentine, daughter of a leading Catholic noble. Quite fortuitously, they are already in love, but equally fortuitously de Nangis is led to believe – erroneously – that there exists a liaison between Valentine and de Nevers, a notoriously womanising Catholic leader.

Act I. Touraine. Count de Nevers has invited friends to a party at his château. Among them is the Huguenot Raoul de Nangis, who makes his entrance with considerable musical panache. Invited to toast his love in a song, Raoul obliges: 'Plus blanche que la blanche hermine'. A viola obbligato adds spice to the romance, in which he praises an unknown beauty whom he recently rescued from a group of students. Raoul's retainer, Marcel, defies the Catholics with a stout rendition of 'Ein' feste Burg', which provokes amusement and elicits from Marcel a brisk Huguenot battle song: 'Piff, paff, pouff'. De Nevers is called away, and Raoul sees him outside in the garden with a woman he recognises, to his consternation, as the lady he rescued not so long ago. He immediately assumes a liaison between them.

De Nevers rejoins his guests and Urbain, page to Marguerite de Valois, makes his entrance with a brilliant recitative ('Nobles Seigneurs, salut!') and aria. Urbain has been instructed by his mistress to conduct Raoul, blindfolded and knowing nothing of the circumstances, to a rendezvous with an unknown lady. The Catholics are impressed that Raoul is sought after by so important a Catholic.

Act II. In the garden of the Château de Chenonceaux, Marguerite sings of the beauties of Touraine ('O beau pays de la Touraine'), following with a spectacular cabaletta 'A ce mot tout s'anime'. It was at Marguerite's behest that Valentine has just visited de Nevers to ask him to release her from her engagement to him, a request which, however reluctantly, he granted. A so-called bathers' chorus and a scene for Marguerite and Urbain precede the removal of the

bandage from Raoul's eyes, and his graceful compliments to the beautiful but unknown lady he sees before him (duet: 'Beauté divine, enchanteresse'). Raoul has pledged his word, and when it is proposed that he marry the daughter of St Bris he immediately consents, only, on recognising the woman he thinks is having an affair with de Nevers, to reject her with indignation. The Catholics sense an insult and bloodshed is narrowly averted by the intervention of Marguerite.

Act III. Paris. The Huguenots sing a 'Rataplan' chorus, to the indignation of Catholics assembling for the marriage of de Nevers and Valentine, whose engagement has been renewed. Marcel brings a challenge from Raoul to St Bris; Catholic nobles conspire to lead Raoul into an ambush and thus avenge the insult to St Bris's daughter. But Valentine still loves Raoul and makes haste in an impressive duet to alert Marcel to his master's danger.

Before the duel occurs a stirring septet ('En mon bon droit j'ai confiance'), one of the score's finest numbers, and when the ambush is uncovered and Marcel summons the Huguenots to Raoul's aid, there is an effective climax in a double chorus. Excitement subsides with the arrival of Marguerite, who tells Raoul of his fatal misapprehension, but the finale employs ballet as well as chorus and military band as de Nevers conducts Valentine to their wedding.

Act IV. In her home, where she is now the wife of de Nevers, Raoul seeks out Valentine to hear her confirm what Marguerite has told him. He hides when St Bris, de Nevers and other noblemen enter and discuss a plan to be carried out that very night – the Eve of St Bartholomew – to massacre the Huguenots. They join their voices in an ensemble of dedication, the so-called Bénédiction des Poignards, the blessing of the swords, and only de Nevers opts out of a project which seems to him treacherous and dishonourable.

Valentine's decision to warn Raoul leads to the climax of the opera, the great duet for soprano and tenor in which she entreats him not to go to what she sees as certain death. They proclaim their love in one of Meyerbeer's greatest melodies: 'Tu l'as dit, oui, tu m'aimes'. The voices rise slowly in succession to a high C flat, and Raoul's cadenza involves a D flat taken softly.

Act V. Coligny, the Huguenot leader, has already been killed, Huguenots are being massacred, and Raoul, wounded, rushes into the Hôtel de Nesle where the marriage of Marguerite de Valois and Henri IV is to be celebrated.

In a Huguenot churchyard, Marcel blesses Valentine and Raoul, whose marriage has become a possibility with the death of de Nevers. St Bris and his followers approach, there is a volley of musketry and only too late does he discover that his zealotry has killed his own daughter. (The opera is long and few performances include the whole of Act V.)　　H.

LE PROPHÈTE

The Prophet

Opera in five acts, words by Scribe. Première, Grand Opéra, Paris, 16 April 1849, with Pauline Viardot and Roger. First performed London, Covent Garden, 24 July 1849, with Mario, Viardot-Garcia, Miss Hayes, and Tagliafico; New Orleans, 2 April 1850; New York, Niblo's Garden, 25 November 1853. Revived in German, Metropolitan Opera House, by Dr Leopold Damrosch, 7 December 1884, with Anton Schon as John of Leyden, Marianne Brandt as Fides and Schroeder-Hanfstaengl as Bertha. It was given ten times during the season, in which it was equalled only by *Tannhäuser* and *Lohengrin*. Revived Covent Garden, 1890 (in French), with Richard, Jean de Reszke, Edouard de Reszke; last performed there 1895, with Ravogli, Tamagno. Also, Metropolitan Opera House, 1898-99, with Jean de Reszke, Bréma (Fides), Lehmann (Bertha); 1900, with Alvarèz, Schumann-Heink, Suzanne Adams, Plançon and Edouard de Reszke; 1918, with Caruso, Matzenauer, Muzio, Didur, and Mardones; and 1927, with Corona, Matzenauer, Martinelli. Modern revivals have included those in Zurich, 1962, with McCracken; Turin Radio, 1963, with Rinaldi, Horne, Gedda; Berlin, German Opera, 1966, with Annabelle Bernard, Warfield, McCracken, conductor Hollreiser. Schumann-Heink was a celebrated Fides.

Jean de Leyde (John of Leyden)..........................Tenor

Fides, *his mother* ....Mezzo-Soprano

Berthe, *his bride*..Soprano

Anabaptists
　　Jonas..Tenor
　　Matthisen..Bass
　　Zacharie ....Bass

Count Oberthal ....Baritone

Nobles, Citizens, Anabaptists, Peasants, Soldiers, Prisoners, Children

Place: Dordrecht, Holland, and Münster
Time: 1534–35
Running Time: 4 hours 10 minutes

Act I. At the foot of Count Oberthal's castle, near Dordrecht, peasants and mill hands are assembled. Berthe and Fides draw near. The latter is bringing Berthe a betrothal ring from her son Jean, who is to marry Berthe next day. Permission must first be obtained from Count Oberthal as lord of the domain.

There arrive three sombre-looking men, who attempt to rouse the people to revolt against tyranny. They are the Anabaptists, Jonas, Matthisen, and Zacharie. The Count, however, who comes at that moment out of the castle with his followers, recognises in Jonas a steward who was discharged from his employment. He orders his soldiers to beat the three men with the flat of their swords. Jean's mother and Berthe make their plea to Oberthal. Jean and Berthe have been in love ever since he rescued her from drowning in the Meuse. Oberthal refuses to give permission for her to marry Jean, but, instead, orders her seized and borne to the castle for his own diversion. The people are greatly agitated and, when the three Anabaptists reappear, throw themselves at their feet with threats against the castle.

Act II. In Jean's inn at Leyden are the three Anabaptists and a throng of merrymaking peasants. Jean dreams of Berthe. The Anabaptists discover that he bears a remarkable resemblance to the picture of King David in the Cathedral of Münster. They believe this resemblance can serve their plans. Jean tells them of a strange dream he has had in which he found himself standing under the dome of a temple with people prostrate before him. They interpret it as evidence that he will mount a throne, and urge him to follow them. At that moment, however, Berthe rushes in and begs him to hide her. She has escaped from Oberthal, who is in pursuit. Oberthal and his soldiers enter. The Count threatens that if Jean does not give Berthe up to him, his mother, whom the soldiers have captured on the way to the inn, will die. A soldier with an axe stands over Fides. After a brief struggle of conscience, Jean's love for his mother wins. He hands over Berthe and Fides is released.

The three Anabaptists return. Jean is ready to join them if only for vengeance on Oberthal. They insist that he come at once, without even saying farewell to his mother.

Act III. The winter camp of the Anabaptists in a forest of Westphalia before Münster. On a frozen lake there is skating. The people have risen against their oppressors, Jean has been proclaimed a prophet of God and is besieging Münster.

The act develops in three scenes. The first reveals the psychological medley of fanaticism and sensuality of the Anabaptists and their followers. In the second Jean enters. Oberthal is delivered into his hands. From him Jean learns that Berthe has escaped from the castle and is in Münster. The three Anabaptist leaders wish to put the Count to death but Jean, saying that Berthe shall be his judge, puts off the execution, much to the disgust of the three fanatics, who find Jean assuming more authority than is agreeable to them. The third scene is again in the camp of the Anabaptists. The leaders, nervous of Jean's usurpation of power, have themselves led an attack by their followers on Münster and met with defeat. The rabble is ready to turn against Jean but he by sheer force of personality rallies the crowd to his standard and leads it to victory.

Act IV. A public place in Münster. The city is held by Anabaptists. Jean, swept along on the high tide of success, decides to have himself proclaimed Emperor. Meanwhile Fides has been reduced to beggary. The Anabaptists, in order to make her believe that Jean is dead and so reduce the chance of her suspecting that the new Prophet and her son are one and the same, have left in the inn a bundle of Jean's bloodstained clothes together with a script stating that he had been murdered by the Prophet and his followers.

The poor woman has come to Münster to beg. There she meets Berthe, who, when Fides tells her that Jean has been murdered, vows vengeance upon the Prophet.

Fides follows the crowd into the cathedral. During the coronation scene, Jean announces that he is the elect of God. The poor beggar woman cries out 'My son!' Jean's life is at stake. He has claimed divine origin. If the woman is his mother, the people will denounce and kill him. He meets the emergency and bids his followers draw their swords and thrust them into his breast, if the beggar woman again affirms that he is her son. Seeing the swords held ready, Fides, in order to save him, declares that her eyes, dimmed by age, have deceived her.

Act V. The three Anabaptists, Jonas, Matthisen, and Zacharie, had intended to use Jean only as an instrument to attain power for themselves. The German Emperor, who is moving on Münster with a large force, has promised them pardon if they will betray the usurper into his hands. They have agreed, and are ready on his coronation day to betray Jean.

At Jean's secret command Fides has been brought to the palace. Here she meets her son. He vainly implores her pardon until she, under the illusion that his bloody deeds are occasioned only by his thirst to avenge Berthe's wrongs, forgives him on condition that he returns to Leyden. This he promises to do.

They are joined by Berthe. She blames the Prophet for the supposed murder of her lover and has sworn to kill him, for which purpose she has set a slow fire to the palace. It will blow up the powder magazine, when the Prophet and his henchmen are at a banquet in the great hall.

She recognises her lover. Her joy, however, is short-lived, for at that moment a captain tells Jean that he has been betrayed and that the Emperor's forces are at the palace gates. Berthe understands that her lover and the bloodstained Prophet are one and plunges a dagger into her heart.

Jean determines to die and joins the banqueters at their orgy. Smoke rises from the floor. Fides, in the general uproar and confusion, joins her son and dies with him as the powder magazine blows up.

John of Leyden's name was Jan Beuckelszoon. He was born in 1509. In business he was successively a tailor, a small merchant, and an innkeeper. After he had had himself crowned in Münster, that city became a scene of orgy and cruelty. It was captured by the imperial forces on 24 June 1535. The following January the 'prophet' was put to death by torture. The same fate was meted out to Knipperdölling, his henchman, who had conveniently rid him of one of his wives by cutting off her head.[1]

The music of the first act of *Le Prophète* contains a cheerful chorus for peasants, a *cavatina* for Berthe, 'Mon coeur s'élance', in which she voices her joy over her expected union with Jean; the Latin chant of the three Anabaptists, gloomy yet stirring; the music of the brief revolt of the peasantry against Oberthal, the plea of Fides and Berthe to Oberthal for his sanction of Berthe's marriage to Jean, 'Un jour, dans les flots de la Meuse'; Oberthal's abduction of

---

[1] The story, with its mixture of libertarian idealism (the religious community whose inmates are pledged to work for the common good) and human fallibility (the reformers end up in betrayal, torture and destruction) attracted in the late twentieth century a very different composer from Meyerbeer, the Englishman Alexander Goehr, whose *Behold the Sun* had its première in Düsseldorf in 1985.

Berthe; the reappearance of the three Anabaptists and the renewal of their efforts to impress the people with a sense of the tyranny by which they are oppressed.

Opening the second act, in Jean's tavern, are the chorus and dance of Jean's friends, rejoicing at his prospective wedding. When the three Anabaptists have recognised his resemblance to the picture of David in the cathedral at Münster, Jean, observing their sombre yet impressive bearing, tells them of his dream, and asks them to interpret it: 'Sous les vastes arceaux d'un temple magnifique'. They promise him a throne. But he looks forward to his coming union with Berthe: 'Pour Berthe, moi, je soupire'. Jean's sacrifice of her in order to save his mother from death leads to Fides's solo, 'Ah, mon fils', one of the great airs for mezzo-soprano.

Most attractive in the next act is the ballet of the skaters on the frozen lake near the camp of the Anabaptists.[1]

There is a stirring battle song for Zacharie, in which he sings of the enemy 'as numerous as the stars', yet defeated. Another striking number is the trio for Jonas, Zacharie, and Oberthal, especially the descriptive passage in which, in rhythm with the music, Jonas strikes flint and steel, ignites a lantern and by its light recognises Oberthal. When Jean rallies the Anabaptists and promises to lead them to victory, the act reaches a superb climax in a 'Hymne Triomphal' for Jean and chorus: 'Roi du Ciel et des Anges'.

The great procession in the cathedral with its march and chorus has been, since the first production of *Le Prophète* in 1849, a model of construction for spectacular scenes in opera. The march is famous. Highly dramatic is the scene in which Fides first proclaims and then denies that Jean is her son. The fifth act contains a striking solo for Fides ('O Prêtres de Baal') and a duet for her and Jean. The climax, however, comes with the drinking song, 'Versez, que tout respire l'ivresse et le délire', in the midst of which the building is blown up, and Jean perishes with those who would betray him.   K.

DINORAH ou LE PARDON DE PLOËRMEL

Dinorah or The Pilgrimage of Ploërmel

Opera in three acts, words by Barbier and Carré. Première Opéra-Comique, Paris, 4 April 1859, with Cabel, St Foy, Faure. First performed Covent Garden, 1859 (in Italian), with Miolan-Carvalho; New Orleans, 1861; New York, 1862; Metropolitan, 1892, with van Zandt, Giannini, Lassalle. Revived Paris, 1912; Metropolitan, 1925, with Galli-Curci, Tokatyan, de Luca; Brussels, 1939. Apart from Galli-Curci, famous in the title role were Ilma di Murska, Patti, Tetrazzini.

Dinorah, *a peasant girl*	Soprano
Hoël, *a goat-herd*	Baritone
Corentino, *a bagpiper*	Tenor
Huntsman	Bass
Harvester	Tenor
Goat-Herds	Soprano and Contralto

Place: A Village in Brittany
Time: Nineteenth Century
Running Time: 2 hours 20 minutes

Dinorah is betrothed to Hoël. Her cottage has been destroyed in a storm. Hoël, in order to rebuild it, goes into a region haunted by evil spirits, in search of hidden treasure. Dinorah, believing herself deserted, loses her reason and, with her goat, whose tinkling bell is heard, wanders through the mountains in search of Hoël.

Act I is preceded by an overture during which there is sung by the villagers behind the curtain the hymn to Our Lady of the Pardon. The scene is a rough mountain passage near Corentino's hut. Dinorah finds her goat asleep and sings to it a graceful lullaby, 'Dors, petite, dors tranquille'. Corentino, in his cottage, sings of his fear in this lonely region. He plays on his *cornemuse*. Dinorah makes him dance with her, while she sings.

When she hears someone approaching she jumps out of the window. It is Hoël. Both he and Corentino think she is a sprite. Hoël sings of the gold he expects to find, and offers Corentino a share in the treasure if he will help him. According to the legend, the first one to touch the treasure must die, and Hoël's seeming generosity is a ruse to make Corentino the victim. The tinkle of the goat's bell can be heard. Hoël advises that they follow the sound as it may lead to the trea-

---

[1] A century later heard as the music for *Les Patineurs*, Frederick Ashton's ballet for Sadler's Wells.

sure. The act closes with a trio, 'Ce tintement que l'on entend'. Dinorah stands among the high rocks, while Hoël and Corentino, the latter reluctantly, make ready to follow the sound of the bell.

Act II. A birch wood by moonlight. It is here Dinorah sings of 'Le vieux sorcier de la montagne', following it with the 'Shadow Song', 'Ombre légère qui suit mes pas' – 'Ombra leggiera' is the more familiar Italian version.

The scene changes to a wild landscape. A ravine bridged by an uprooted tree. A storm is rising. Hoël and Corentino enter; later Dinorah. Through the night, she sings the legend of the treasure, 'Sombre destinée, âme condamnée'. Her words make Corentino see through Hoël's ruse. Dinorah sings, in cheerful contrast to the gathering storm. Lightning flashes show her goat crossing the ravine by the fallen tree. She runs after it, the sluice bursts and she is carried away by the flood. Hoël plunges into the wild water to save her.

Act III. Not enough of the actual story remains to make a third act. But as there has to be one, the opening is filled with a song for a Hunter, another for a Reaper, and a duet for Goat-Herds. Hoël enters carrying Dinorah. Hoël here has his principal air, 'Ah! mon remords te venge' (My remorse avenges you). The fainting Dinorah's reason is restored when she finds herself in her lover's arms. The villagers chant the 'Hymn of the Pardon'. A procession forms for the wedding.   K.

L'AFRICAINE
The African Maid

Opera in five acts, words by Scribe. Première, Opéra, Paris, 28 April 1865, with Marie Sasse, Battu, Naudin, Faure.

Sélika, *a slave* ....Soprano

Inès, *daughter of Don Diego* ....Soprano

Vasco da Gama, *officer in the*
    Portuguese Navy ....Tenor

Nélusko, *a slave* ....Baritone

Don Pedro, *President of the Royal Council* ....Bass

Don Diego, *member of the Council* ....Bass

Don Alvar, *member of the Council*.......................Tenor

Grand Inquisitor ....Bass

High Priest of Brahma..................................Baritone

Priests, Councillors, Sailors, Indians, Attendants, Ladies, Soldiers

Place: Lisbon; at Sea; Madagascar
Time: Early Sixteenth Century
Running Time: 4 hours 10 minutes

Meyerbeer worked on *L'Africaine* for more than twenty years but died before the première.

Act I. The Council Chamber, in Lisbon. For two years, nothing has been heard of the ship of Bartholomew Diaz, the explorer, among whose officers was Vasco da Gama, fiancé of Inès, Don Diego's daughter.

The overture foreshadows Inès's attractive aria in the first scene. She is well aware of the rumour of Vasco's death but is determined to ignore it and recalls his song of farewell: 'Adieu, mon doux rivage'. She rejects Don Diego's proposal of a future husband – Don Pedro. The Council meets and interviews a young survivor of Diaz's expedition, none other than Vasco da Gama. He plans to discover the land beyond Africa, and in proof shows them two captives, Sélika and Nélusko, who come from it.

Don Pedro pilfers a crucial chart from Vasco's papers, then persuades the Council that Vasco's plans are futile. Vasco's reaction is to charge the Council with ignorance and bias; he is thrown into prison. The fully choral finale is large in scale and typically Meyerbeerian in spirit.

Act II. In a cell, Sélika watches the sleeping Vasco. At home, she is a queen, a fact known to Nélusko who loves her but not to Vasco with whom she is in love. She sings an aria of considerable originality ('Sur mes genoux, fils du soleil'); her love for Vasco overcomes her jealousy of Inès, whom he still loves, and impels her to protect him from the murderous Nélusko. Nélusko sings impressively: 'Fille des rois, à toi l'hommage'. On a map Sélika shows Vasco the route to the Indies, and their duet ('Combien tu m'es chère') suggests that he returns her love; Inès's arrival in the prison shatters her hopes. In return for Vasco's freedom, Inès will marry Don Pedro, and she bids him farewell. As a gesture and secure in his knowledge of the secret route, he offers her Sélika. Don Pedro announces that he, not Vasco, will lead the new expedition, with Nélusko as his pilot. There is an effective finale, shorter than Act I's but this time without chorus and with solo female voices added.

L'Africaine *(Covent Garden, 1978, director Franco Enriquez, designer Fiorella Mariani). Act III, Don Pedro's ship.*

Act III. Don Pedro's ship, at sea: two levels, Nélusko and the sailors on one, Inès and her ladies on the other, divided from Don Pedro and his entourage. The ladies sing first, then the sailors, who pray for protection. Don Alvaro, who spoke up for Vasco in the Council, warns Don Pedro of treachery from Nélusko, and Nélusko, after an impressive recitative ('Holà! matelots'), savagely invokes sea and storm to destroy his enemies: 'Adamastor, roi des vagues profondes'.

Vasco's boat approaches; Don Pedro treats his warning that they are off course as a mere excuse to see Inès, and he is seized. There is a septet before a violent storm breaks over the ship, which runs upon a reef. Nélusko's tribesmen kill or capture everyone on board.

Act IV. Before a temple, to the sound of a grand march and with elaborate dancing Sélika is welcomed by her subjects. Vasco was saved from the shipwreck,

and in a magnificent aria ('O paradis') he celebrates the beauties of the new country he and his compatriots have braved so much to discover. To save him from death, Sélika asserts he is her husband, and Nélusko is forced to bear witness to her claim. In a beautiful aria, 'L'avoir tant adorée', he sings of his love, then swears to the truth of what Sélika says. The High Priest celebrates the marriage, Vasco tells Sélika he loves her after all, and their duet seems to seal the compact, until that is to say Vasco hears the voice of Inès, who has also been rescued, and old passion revives.

Act V. The garden of Sélika's palace. Sélika threatens Inès with death but contrives to forgive her and Vasco, and even persuades Nélusko to provide them with a ship for escape.

On a promontory overlooking the sea stands a mançanilla tree, whose perfume is lethal (a notion long thought far-fetched, but in the Caribbean, the manchineel tree is famed for its noxious properties;

drips from its leaves cause severe burns and eating its fruit could kill). Sélika lies beneath its shade and watches the ship carrying away the man she loves: 'D'ici je vois la mer immense et sans limite'. It is her farewell at the same time to Vasco and to life, and Nélusko arrives to find her dead.

Meyerbeer is said to have considered *L'Africaine* his masterpiece, and it is true that it has fine set pieces, typical lyrical invention, rare opportunities for stage spectacle. But Scribe's plot is limp in comparison with the historically-based *Les Huguenots*, and if Nélusko as a character possesses a certain rude grandeur and the exotic Sélika an element of sympathy as the faithful, short-changed lover, Vasco himself is an unsatisfactory hero, ambitious and self-seeking and endowed with none of the romantic virtues which place steadfastness and honour above egotism.   H.

DARIUS MILHAUD
(born 4 September 1892, died 22 June 1975)

Milhaud had already collaborated with Paul Claudel on the trilogy *L'Orestie* before accompanying the writer when he was appointed ambassador in Brazil. The five short operas he wrote between 1924 and 1927 were in sharp contrast to the huge *Christophe Colomb* (to a text by Claudel) which followed and was staged in 1930, and the large-scale *Maximilien* of 1932. Operas came regularly from his pen; the last, *Saint Louis, roi de France* (to a text by Claudel), was first performed only two years before his death.

LE PAUVRE MATELOT
The Poor Sailor

Opera in three acts, text by Jean Cocteau. Première Opéra-Comique, Paris, 16 December 1927, with Madeleine Sibille, Legrand, Vieuille, Musy, conductor Lauweryns. First performed Berlin, 1929, with Novotna, conductor Zemlinsky. Revived with new orchestration, Geneva, 1934; Philadelphia, 1937; Vienna, 1937; Opéra-Comique, 1938; Berlin, 1947; London Opera Club, 1950, with Vyvyan, Servant, Loring, Wallace, conductor Renton; la Scala, Milan, 1950, with Favero, Malipiero, Inghilleri, Beuf, conductor Sanzogno.

The Wife ....Soprano
The Sailor ....Tenor
His Father-in-Law...Bass
His Friend..Baritone

Place: A Seaport

Time: 'The Present'
Running Time: 35 minutes

The opera, which is dedicated to Henri Sauguet, is divided into three acts, but is played without intervals and is very short. The action takes place in and near a bar kept by the Wife. Also visible are the street and a wine shop kept by the Friend.

Act I. The Wife and the Friend are dancing. She has waited fifteen years for the return of her husband from abroad, and has steadfastly refused to give up hope of his return. The Friend is disposed to encourage her to hope, and he expresses admiration for the way she has remained faithful. She might have deceived her husband if he had been there, but with his photograph still hanging over the bed, how could she do such a thing?

Her Father takes a very different view; why can't she find herself a man, who could take over the bar and run it properly? The Friend says that he himself has proposed to her, but she makes the obvious retort; supposing one day the bell rang and in walked her husband – his friend? Optimistically she imagines him coming back as rich as Croesus. If he is poor, there is no crime she would not commit to set him up again properly.

The Friend goes back to his shop. The Father repeats his suggestion that they would make a fine pair, but the Wife gives lyrical expression to her resolve to remain true to her husband. Her Father reminds her that she was twenty-five when he left, and is now forty. While they are arguing, the Sailor himself appears unobserved in the street, hesitates in front of their door, and then decides not to open it. What if his own wife does not recognise him? Would it not be best to see first what effect his appearance has on his Friend? He is at first rejected as a drunkard, until he mentions that he has a wife opposite. Then his Friend recognises him. The Sailor congratulates himself that he did not risk going home unannounced. He asks after his wife, and is reassured that she is waiting for him. He has money enough to end all their troubles.

The Sailor suggests he sleep in his Friend's house. He would like to meet his wife as a stranger.

Act II. Next day, the Sailor goes to see what his reception will be like at the bar. He tells his Wife that her husband has returned, but dare not come to her until nightfall, as he is pursued by creditors. His Father-in-Law sneers at the Wife, but she leads a short ensemble of strong rhythmical impulse: 'Cher époux!' She is quite undismayed to learn that had he accepted the love of a cannibal queen her husband might have come home with the treasures which in point of fact devolved upon his shipmate.

The Sailor asks if he may stay the night with them, and is told that no one who brings such good news could be refused so small a request. The Friend is full of curiosity and thinks of the excuse of returning the heavy hammer he borrowed the previous day from the Wife. As she locks up, she is struck with the resemblance which the weary Sailor, stretched out on a bench, bears to her husband.

Act III. The Sailor lies asleep. The Wife comes in with the hammer in her hand, looks at him for a moment, raises the hammer and strikes him on the head with it. When he moves convulsively, she strikes him again, then drops the hammer, and rifles his pockets quickly. The noise arouses her father, whom she instructs to help her carry the body. They will dump it in the rain-water tank, and tell the neighbour that their visitor had to leave early in the morning. There is a knock at the door, but they stay quiet and their neighbour leaves them undisturbed. They prepare to carry the body away, as the Wife sings lyrically of her husband's impending return.   H.

OPÉRAS-MINUTES
Instant Operas

Three one-act operas, lasting about seven or eight minutes each, text by Henri Hoppenot. *L'enlèvement d'Europe* was first given at Baden-Baden, 17 July 1927, in conjunction with Toch's *Die Prinzessin auf der Erbse*, Hindemith's *Hin und Zurück*, and Weill's *Mahagonny*. The same work was performed for the first time with the other two Opéras-Minutes at Wiesbaden, 20 April 1928. First performed Budapest, 1932, in Hungarian; Minneapolis, 1967; Florence, 1970.

These miniature but highly entertaining operas are nothing if not satirical in intent. Mythology in general, and more particularly the classical French interpretation of it, are spoofed to the limit, alike by librettist (who, like Claudel, once represented his country as ambassador) and composer. Milhaud's *Phèdre* bears the same relationship to Racine's as Offenbach's *Orphée* does to Gluck's. The music itself, spiced with South American rhythms, is very attractive, and Milhaud's quick-fire inventiveness seems peculiarly well suited to the original form he has invented.

L'ENLÈVEMENT D'EUROPE
The Rape of Europa

Agénor	Bass
Pergamon, *Europa's suitor*	Baritone
Jupiter, *in the guise of a bull*	Tenor
Europa, *Agénor's daughter*	Soprano
Chorus of 'Maîtresses-Servantes'	One Soprano / One Mezzo / One Contralto
Chorus of Soldier-Labourers	One Tenor / One Baritone / One Bass

The set represents the front of the palace of King Agénor of Thebes. The chorus of women is hanging about near a well, and that of the men near a field. The Chorus reiterates the name of 'Europa', in alternate rising 7ths and 9ths. Pergamon emerges from the palace, and gives vent to his wrath at the discovery that Europa prefers the society of bulls and cows to that of a hero like himself. Agénor agrees that his daughter has never shown much taste for the company of men of warlike accomplishments. She appears with the bull to which she has taken so evident a fancy, and the chorus makes scornful references to her passion for its bellowings.

Jupiter explains his love for Europa, and pleads passionately for satisfaction of 'cette double ardeur du taureau dans mes reins et du Dieu dans mon cœur'. The chorus mocks the beast, and Pergamon, beside himself, draws his bow and looses an arrow at his rival, much to the consternation of the bystanders. The arrow strikes home, but the bull shakes itself free and the missile speeds back to him who dispatched it, and transfixes him. After Pergamon's death, the chorus sings a valediction, in which the 7ths and 9ths of the beginning are prominent. Europa rides away into the distance with the bull.   H.

L'ABANDON D'ARIANE
Ariadne Deserted

Ariane..Soprano
Phèdre, *her sister*..Soprano
Thésée ....Tenor
Dionysos, *the god, in disguise*.........................Baritone

Chorus of Shipwrecked Mariners { One Tenor / One Bass / One Baritone

Chorus of Gypsy Bacchants { One Soprano / One Mezzo / One Contralto

The scene represents part of the island of Naxos; rocks visible in the background. During the piece, darkness falls, and it is almost night at the end. As the curtain rises, the stranded mariners are grouped left, playing dice, the Bacchants are sitting around a cooking pot, looking like gipsies; Dionysos is amongst the Bacchants, dressed as a beggar. Like a 'Greek chorus', the two groups join to convey the information that it is Ariane's custom to come to that part of the island every night in order to escape the attentions of Thésée, whom she cannot abide. Phèdre meanwhile longs unavailingly for his caresses.

Before long, the two sisters, dressed exactly alike, come into view, and each gives vivid utterance to the sentiment ascribed to her by the chorus, which for its part prays to Dionysos to help each in her different affliction. Dionysos, in his capacity as a beggar, laments his blindness and begs for charity. Each sister gives him money. When the sailors announce that Thésée can be seen coming that way, Ariane says she will hurry away, while Phèdre rejoices at the prospect of seeing her beloved.

Thésée cries aloud the name of Ariane, and tenderly asks if anyone can give him information as to her whereabouts. Dionysos offers him a cup of precious wine for which he returns thanks in an exultant musical sentence ending resoundingly on a high B flat. The wine has the effect of making him see double, and when Phèdre comes from her place of concealment he thinks she is the two sisters and goes out with her. The chorus comments in Tango rhythm, and Dionysos informs Ariane that Thésée will in future regard Phèdre as his consort. She thanks him for his kindness towards her, and a moment later Dionysos and the Bacchants shed their beggar's clothes and are revealed in dazzling white. Ariane and her sister gave alms to a god and his reward is to grant their joint wishes. She has one more request; may she finish her days with Diana in the firmament on high? It becomes darker and Dionysos leads her up the rocks; behind her appears the constellation of Ariadne. The chorus rejoices; the opening chorus is repeated in a different rhythm (alternating 6/8 and 5/8 in a bar), and sung over an instrumental accompaniment that has the flavour of a *toccata* from one of Monteverdi's operas.   H.

LA DÉLIVRANCE DE THÉSÉE
Theseus Redeemed

Aricie ....Mezzo-Soprano
Phèdre, *her sister*..Soprano
Hippolyte, *son of Phèdre* ....Baritone
Théramène, *Hippolyte's friend* ....Baritone
Thésée, *husband of Phèdre* ....Tenor
Chorus of Distant Voices ....Mixed Vocal Quartet

A great hall in the palace of Thésée; a throne in the middle. Hippolyte complains to his friend Théramène of the unwelcome attentions of his mother, Phèdre; he is in love with Aricie, to whom he presently pours out his heart, only to be told that Aricie cannot make a decision either way without the consent of Thésée, Hippolyte's father. Enter Phèdre, whose presence causes Aricie and Théramène to withdraw respectfully. She is overjoyed to find Hippolyte alone, but he repulses her, and the trumpets announce the return of Thésée from yet another successful and hazardous exploit. When Thésée appears, Phèdre turns the tables and asks for his protection against her incestuous son. Thésée promptly banishes him and orders him to go out to do battle with the monster which even now threatens the walls of the city.

The chorus takes up the very attractive rhythm of the *Beguine*, which started as Hippolyte left the stage with Théramène; the words are 'Oui, c'est lui! C'est bien lui!' With the chorus as background, Thésée gives an account of his adventure:

> J'arrivai: Ils tremblèrent;
> J'avançai: Ils reculèrent;
> Je dégainai: Ils décampèrent;
> Je les tuai: Ils expirèrent!

Thésée being a tenor, they 'decamp' on a top C, but, by the time his miniature aria has come to an end, the chorus is exclaiming at some new misfortune: 'O douleur! O tristesse!' In spite of the pleas of Phèdre and Aricie, they make no attempt to explain what causes their distress and alarm, but in no time Théramène, who has witnessed all, returns. He takes up his position for 'Le Récit' (a reference to Racine's *Phèdre*) and begins: 'A peine nous sortions', only to be interrupted by the omniscient Thésée: 'Je connais ... finis vite.' There is nothing left for Théramène to do (he makes this quite clear) but to revenge the death of Hippolyte. He takes out his sword and stabs Phèdre to the heart, whereupon Thésée orders the guards to hang him from the nearest tree.

Aricie, aided by the wordless chorus, laments the series of disasters which have befallen them in a single day, but consolation for the two survivors is close at hand. Thésée puts his arm round Aricie, and in phrases of exaggeratedly lyrical character invites her to console herself with him. Poor Aricie, who has earlier been referred to as 'craintive' and 'pudique', seems to be the only one of the characters to benefit from the catastrophes, and by the end we find Thésée addressing her more optimistically as 'la timide Aricie'.   H.

CHRISTOPHE COLOMB
Christopher Columbus

Opera in two parts and twenty-seven scenes, text by Paul Claudel. Première, Berlin, 5 May 1930, with Reinhardt, Scheidl, conductor Erich Kleiber. Given in concert form in Paris, 1936, London, 1937, Antwerp, 1940, New York, 1952, with Dow, David Lloyd, Harrell, Brownlee, Norman Scott, conductor Mitropoulos. In 1968, a one-act opera *The Discovery of America*, drawn by Gunther Schuller from *Christophe Colomb*, was performed in San Francisco.

Isabella, *Queen of Spain*	Soprano
Christopher Columbus I	Baritone
Christopher Columbus II	Baritone
Narrator	Speaker
Counsel for the Prosecution	Speaker
The Representative of the Sailors	Speaker
Major-Domo	Tenor
Master of Ceremonies	Tenor
The Cook	Tenor
The King of Spain	Bass
The Commandant	Bass
Messenger	Baritone
Sultan Miramolin	Tenor

Chorus, Officers, Counsel, Creditors

Place: Genoa; Spain; on the Atlantic Ocean; America
Time: Before and After 1492
Running Time: 2 hours 30 minutes

*C*hristophe Colomb is in the tradition of French operas built on the largest possible scale. Milhaud and Claudel have concentrated on the symbolical aspects of the story of Columbus, and the resulting opera is thus not only highly exacting to stage – it involves a vast apparatus – but anything but easy for the audience to understand. It belongs in fact, as Edward Dent has said in his Pelican *Opera*, to the category of works which one expects to see only once in a lifetime.

Act I. The Narrator and Chorus come on; the Narrator announces: 'The Book of the Life and Voyages of Christopher Columbus, who discovered America.' He prays for light and strength in his endeavour to explain the book. On a cinematic screen at the back of the stage, a globe can be seen spinning; above it is a dove, glowing with light.

A humble inn at Valladolid. Columbus is seen as an old, broken man, his only possession a mule. Narrator and Chorus call on him to join with posterity in looking at his life and the results of his actions.

Prosecution and Defence argue over the behaviour of the King of Spain towards Columbus. He is accused of lying and exaggeration, but defends himself.

The Court of Isabella the Catholic. The Queen is shown as a child. She receives Sultan Miramolin, who gives her a dove in a cage. She accepts the gift, puts a ring on its foot, and releases it. As a boy Columbus read the story of Marco Polo. There is conflict between the views of the Man at the Window, who urges him to seek adventure, and the Chorus, which tries to prevent him leaving his family. His second self bids him follow the call of adventure. As the scene ends, a dove flies in through the window, with a ring on its foot.

Columbus sets out over the seas. He glories in the sea he has conquered, but the cries of his creditors will not be silenced; they agree that a last voyage, however desperate an undertaking, represents their only chance of payment. Columbus goes to the court of the King of Spain, where he is mocked for his pretensions.

Queen Isabella is seen at prayer. On the screen appear representations of events which have led to the unification of Spain. She has played her part by bringing Aragon to Castile; may she not now lay down her life, her duty accomplished? She sees a mystical vision and hears the voice of St James. Had she not another ring besides that she gave her husband? Yes, she put it on a dove's foot and she saw it again on Christopher Columbus's hand.

Cadiz. Recruiting is going on for Columbus's expedition. The Master of Ceremonies calls the roll of the demon gods of America. They refer to the plagues they will inflict on Columbus and his crew. The men wish to return and give up the expedition which they think is condemned by God from above. His senior officers and men all advise Columbus that the expedition is doomed unless he turns back at once. He refuses, and the situation becomes ugly. Columbus is so convinced that he is right in his calculations that he bids the sailors drink the water they have with them and eat the food; sufficient will still remain for their needs. A bird appears, and the scene ends with a cry of 'Land!' from the look-out.

In America, the ships can be seen approaching, and from them is heard the sound of a 'Te Deum'. The first part ends with a large-scale setting of the 'Sanctus'.

Part II. An interlude shows the effect Columbus's discovery has on the whole world. The Narrator tells of the difficulties which follow it; the cruel treatment of the natives leads to revolt and further repression; the New World does not bring profit, and Columbus's enemies are busy in Spain. The King summons three wise men to give him counsel. They warn him against Columbus: 'You must honour him – you must watch him – you must bury him.'

On his fourth voyage, Columbus was put in chains; he is exhorted by his successor to put forth his influence in saving the ship, which has run into dangerous waters. Columbus prays and three times the ship weathers the crises.

Columbus looks back at his past actions and their consequences. He sees the inhabitants of America, on whom his discovery of the new continent has brought ruin and destruction; the slaves he sold to pay his debts; the wife and mother he abandoned; himself as he was at Genoa, and at Lisbon; and his own ghost. The Cook tells him that the New World will not be named after him but after an obscure member of his own crew, Amerigo Vespucci, whom he can scarcely remember.

A Messenger comes from the dying Queen Isabella. She thought of Columbus and his expedition, and now sends words of comfort to him. Her funeral procession can be seen. The servant at the inn comes in to demand payment of Columbus's bill. Will the innkeeper not wait? He once asked his sailors to wait three days before killing him, and in those days he discovered a New World. Will the innkeeper not do the same? That worthy answers that he will take the mule unless he is paid by tomorrow.

The Paradise of the Idea. The scene resembles the court of Isabella in Mallorca. But everything has become the colour of silver. It is paradise. Isabella greets her friends, and is welcomed by the ladies of her court – as children. Sultan Miramolin brings her gifts, and she remembers when he gave her a dove long ago, and she put her ring on its foot. How can she enter into the kingdom of heaven without her friend Christopher Columbus? she asks. No one has been able to find him, she is told; but Isabella can see him in the inn at Valladolid, and she is told that he is dying on a bed of straw. He does not wish to come at her command, but intends to fulfil his destiny, with her ring on his finger.

The image of St James appears on the screen; he it was who guided the Queen safely to heaven. Isabella leads a prayer for Columbus. At the final Alleluiah, a dove flies from the globe. H.

CARL MILLÖCKER
(born 29 April 1842, died 31 December 1899)

DER BETTELSTUDENT
The Beggar Student

Comic opera in three acts, text by Zell and Genée. First performed at the Theater an der Wien, Vienna, 6 December 1882; New York, 1883; London, Alhambra Theatre, 1884 (in English); Royalty Theatre, 1895 (in German). Revived at Vienna, Staatsoper, 1936, with Margit Bokor, Richard Sallaba, Alfred Jerger, conductor Josef Krips; Volksoper, 1949, with Maria Cebotari, Lorna Sidney, Fred Liewehr, Kurt Preger, Walter Höfermayer, conductor Anton Paulik.

Palmatica, *Countess Nowalska*	Mezzo-Soprano
Countess Laura, *her daughter*	Soprano
Countess Bronislawa, *Laura's sister*	Soprano
Simon, *the beggar student*	Tenor
Jan Janitzky, *Simon's friend*	Tenor
Colonel Ollendorf	Bass
Enterich, *prison governor*	Baritone

Saxon officers
  Richthofen
  Wangenheim
  Henrici

Place: Cracow
Time: 1704
Running Time: 1 hour 40 minutes

Like Suppé, under whose baton he played flute at the Theater in der Josefstadt in Vienna, Millöcker was a successful conductor of operetta before he hit the target with *Gräfin Dubarry* (1879) and, even more firmly in 1882, with *Der Bettelstudent*. This operetta's romantic story, together with its richly comic overtones and tunes of melting tenderness, has kept it in the Viennese and German repertories to this day.

Colonel Ollendorf, Cracow's irascible governor, has been badly hurt: he was just starting to make advances to Countess Laura, a proud Polish beauty, when she struck him in the face with her fan – in public, and at an official ball! Honour must be satisfied and he will have his revenge.

Act I. We are in the prison; the prisoners' wives try to persuade Enterich, the prison governor, to let them see their husbands. He is disposed to grant their request, but he confiscates the various delicacies which are intended to cheer the prisoners' lot. To the prison comes Ollendorf, complaining loudly at the treatment meted out to him the night before. His entrance song, with its waltz refrain 'Ach, ich hab' sie ja nur auf die Schulter geküsst', gives an excellent opportunity to a comic bass. The object of Ollendorf's visit is to find two young prisoners and persuade them to aid him in his scheme of revenge: they are to pay court to Countess Laura and her sister, and he will then be able to expose the joke and so avenge the insult to his honour. The two Poles he chooses – political prisoners, both of them – seem light-hearted enough to judge by their duet; they agree to fall in with the scheme, and to say nothing about its origin. Ollendorf will fit them out as Prince Wibicky and his secretary – and they will have their freedom.

The scene changes to a fair in the Rathausplatz in Cracow, which is ushered in with a brisk 6/8 chorus and a march. Palmatica and her daughters are there, too poor to buy anything, but doing their best in their 3/8 trio to disguise this painful fact by sneering at what is exposed for sale. Ollendorf introduces Prince Wibicky and his companion to the Countess and her daughters, and Simon proceeds to tell them of his wanderings over the earth; the flirtations he has indulged in wherever he has been have only proved to him how far superior Polish girls are to those in the rest of the world. His romance, 'Ich knüpfte manche zarte Bände', is an excellent example of the unpretentiousness and graceful charm which is to be found in Millöcker's score. Simon proposes to Laura, and all celebrate the betrothal. Laura sings a Polish song – joy and grief, she says, are closely allied; its solemn *andante* opening soon gives way to a sparkling *allegretto*. The town band puts in an appearance with a march which takes its cue from Schubert rather than Sousa, and the act comes to an end with general rejoicing.

Act II. Laura is at home trying on her wedding dress, assisted by her mother and her sister. She repeats the advice her mother has given her, that husbands can and should be dominated by their wives – not by direct precept but by persuasion, by tears not threats. The Prince's secretary is announced, and Jan makes up to Bronislawa in a charming duet.

Jan reminds Simon that plans are afoot to restore Cracow to the Poles, that the King's nephew, Duke Adam, is preparing a coup, and that only money is wanting. It looks as though their schemes are coming to fruition. Simon is alone with Laura; would she still love him, he asks, if he were poor, untitled, even an impostor? She tells him her love is proof against any such change in his status, and asks him whether he would love her if someone prettier came along, rich and well-born. In a charming duet ('Ich setz' den Fall') Simon reassures her in his turn. Taking courage from what Laura has told him, Simon writes her a note telling her the truth about his deception; he is astonished when he sees later that its reception seems to have made no difference in her attitude towards him, but he does not know that Ollendorf has had it intercepted. The marriage is performed, and Ollendorf waits to savour his triumph, which will not be long delayed. The happy couple are congratulated, their healths drunk in the bride's shoe, the mazurka is danced, when suddenly rowdy singing is heard outside: Simon's fellow-prisoners have come to join in the fun. The truth must come out. Ollendorf explains that the joke was his revenge: after all, he only kissed her on the shoulder, but she slapped his face in public. She may repent now at her leisure.

Act III. The aftermath of Ollendorf's disclosure is still to be reckoned with. People comment on Simon's dastardly behaviour and on the punishment which they cannot help thinking Laura has earned by her behaviour. Bronislawa confesses that she is still secure in her love, and that the day's tragedy has not had the effect of removing her appetite, which she had hoped would be assuaged at the wedding feast.

Simon is disconsolate, but Jan explains to him that all will yet be well. He seems disgraced but he still has a part to play in the freeing of Cracow. Ollendorf has approached Jan and bribed him – with the 200,000 crowns they need to finance Duke Adam's insurrection – if he will give the patriot away. He for his part has promised to do so after the wedding feast, and Simon must pretend, for the sake of Poland, to be the Duke; only by this means can enough time be gained to enable the Duke himself to get inside the gates with his troops. Simon confesses that the game is up for him in his best known aria, 'Ich hab' kein Geld, bin vogelfrei', with its refrain challenging Dame Fortune to another game of chance.

Palmatica takes to abusing poor Simon, in spite of the comment of Ollendorf and Jan, and much to the Beggar Student's rage. Eventually, Ollendorf reveals what he describes as the fact of the matter: he has discovered that Simon is none other than Duke Adam, and he must take him off to prison and there chop off his head. Consternation is general, not least as far as Simon is concerned; Palmatica says she suspected he was noble all along and is delighted to have him as son-in-law, Laura frantically announces she will die with him, and Jan trembles in case Simon should not play his part adequately. All is well, however; a cannon shot is heard, and the news arrives that Duke Adam has won control of the city. Ollendorf admits he must give himself up – whereupon Bronislawa says *she* has already surrendered herself, to the Secretary. Laura says she has done no less, to the Beggar Student, but Jan hastens to correct her: in future he will be known as Count Simon Rymanowitsch. The opera ends in rejoicing.   H.

STANISŁAW MONIUSZKO

(born 5 May 1819, died 4 June 1872)

HALKA

Opera in four acts, libretto by W. Wolski (founded on a story by K.W. Wojcicki). In its original two-act version, produced privately at Wilna on 20 December 1847, but enlarged to the four-act version with première at Warsaw, 1 January 1858. It is the most popular Polish opera ever written; its 500th performance was in Warsaw in 1900 and its 1000th in 1935. First performed in Prague, 1868, Moscow, 1869, Vienna, 1892, and at Volksoper, 1926; New York, 1903 (in Russian) and 1940 (in Polish); Milan, 1905; Hamburg, 1935; Berlin, 1936, with Tiana Lemnitz, Marcel Wittrisch.

Halka, *a peasant girl* ....Soprano

Jontek, *a peasant lad* ....Tenor

Stolnik, *a landowner*...Bass

Zofia, *his daughter* ....Mezzo-Soprano

Janusz, *a young nobleman*..............................Baritone

Dziemba, *Stolnik's major-domo* ....Bass

A Bagpiper ....Baritone

Highlanders, Guests, Noblemen

Place: Podhale, in South Poland
Time: End of the Eighteenth Century
Running Time: 2 hours 30 minutes

Moniuszko studied in Berlin and wrote his first opera, *Halka*, while still in his middle twenties. It is the story of the passionate love of a young girl for the Lord of the Manor, who leaves her in order to marry a girl of his own station. The music speaks with an individual voice, using the arias and ensembles of the period and adding a strong Polish characteristic, most apparent in the dances and choruses. *Halka* was much admired by Hans von Bülow, who wrote about it in Schumann's *Neue Zeitschrift für Musik* in 1858 with enthusiasm. Moniuszko served as Director of the Warsaw Opera before dying at the early age of fifty-three.

Act I. The impressive overture uses material from the opera. At the house of the landowner Stolnik, where a party is taking place to celebrate the engagement of his daughter Zofia to Janusz, a young nobleman, the guests dance a Polonaise of great verve and splendour. Janusz asks Stolnik for a blessing on his bride and himself, which the old man gives in a lyrical trio. Halka's voice, recognised only by Janusz, her lover, can be heard singing outside. Janusz denies any knowledge of the singer, but, when Zofia and Stolnik leave, he is torn between love for his fiancée and guilty passion for Halka and in an aria expresses remorse for his betrayal of the orphan girl, who expects his child.

Halka enters the house and repeats the haunting folk-like melody heard earlier, at first without noticing Janusz, for whom, when she sees him, her greeting is ecstatic. Their duet discloses his continued and genuine remorse, her single-minded devotion, and before it ends, Janusz makes an assignation with her on the outskirts of the town. When Halka has gone, the celebrations start again, Janusz feigns happiness, Stolnik returns thanks to the guests and celebrates his pleasure in a lively song. The act finishes with a brilliant Mazurka.

Act II. After a storm introduction, Halka sings a melancholy song of her betrayed love as she watches outside the house which she knows shelters her beloved Janusz. The aria reaches an impassioned climax before Jontek, her village sweetheart, arrives to take her back to their mountain village. He tries to convince her that Janusz has no more interest in her, but she, he insists in a fine and vigorous aria, still foolishly believes in his love. She is wrong; he has given his heart to another. Halka hears the sound of singing indoors, and Jontek cannot stop her clamouring to be let in. When Janusz appears demanding to know who was making the noise, Halka utterly loses control of her feelings. The confrontation between Janusz and Jontek begins with dignity on both sides, but Jontek does not try to conceal his indignation at the way Halka has been treated. In a short finale Halka and Jontek are thrown out.

Act III. Sunday in a mountain village, the property of Janusz's family. A month later. Villagers are outside the church after Vespers, and their gossip is of the young squire's imminent entry into the state of matrimony, something they say which will not obviate the need for the young girls of the village to be on their guard against him.

There is a brisk mountain dance (Gorale) and Halka and Jontek return to the village. In a scene of some expansiveness, they describe their inhumane treatment at the manor and receive a full measure of sympathy from the villagers. A black raven flies over as the wedding procession of Janusz and Zofia is seen in the distance.

Act IV. Near the village cemetery, Jontek laments the misfortunes of Halka, who would die, he says, if she saw Janusz with his bride. The village bagpiper playing in the distance strikes Jontek as a harbinger of misfortune, and he sings the best-known single number of the score, a beautiful aria ('The trees are rustling in the breeze') once a favourite of recording tenors.

Dziemba is delighted that the villagers are gathered to greet bride and bridegroom, who presently in their turn appear, Janusz to his consternation seeing Halka among the bystanders. Village rejoicing continues but Zofia notices Halka's grief, and she and her father seem to recognise her voice. The scene builds to a beautiful ensemble as all implore God's mercy on the unhappy woman. The wedding party goes into church and Dziemba bids the villagers be merry, an instruction they seem disposed to follow. Halka repeats the words with some bitterness, then sees Janusz in church and again starts to lose control. Even the faithful Jontek cannot comfort her, and the sound of a prayer from inside loosens Halka's hold on reason. In a cavatina, she laments that Janusz has a heart of stone, no pity for her, no pity for his child. She thinks of setting the church on fire, then the sight of the innocents who would lose their lives turns her from her purpose and she throws the firebrand into the river. Janusz she still loves and she can no longer contemplate revenge. Instead she will drown herself and this she does suddenly and dramatically, leaving Jontek calling to her, but Dziemba again rousing the villagers to sing the wedding hymn.   H.

ITALO MONTEMEZZI

(born 4 August 1875, died 15 May 1952)

Although the Metropolitan in New York revived *Giovanni Gallurese* for five performances in 1925 in an attempt to capitalise on the success of *L'Amore dei tre Re*, Montemezzi remains a one-opera composer. His style has been described as unassuming and unadventurous, and he was undoubtedly helped by the excellent subject of Sem Benelli's play, with its heavily symbolical overtones. Nonetheless, the music itself is outstanding for its period in Italy.

L'AMORE DEI TRE RE

The Love of Three Kings

Opera in three acts, text by Sem Benelli, from his play of the same name. Première, la Scala, Milan, 10 April 1913, with Villani, Ferrari-Fontana, Galeffi, de Angelis, conductor Serafin. First performed Metropolitan, New York, 1914, with Bori, Ferrari-Fontana, Amato, Didur, conductor Toscanini; Covent Garden, 1914, with Edvina, Crimi, Cigada, Didur, conductor Moranzoni. Revivals include Metropolitan, 1926, with Ponselle, Gigli, Danise, Didur, conductor Serafin; 1939, with Jepson, Tokatyan, Bonelli, Pinza, conductor Papi; la Scala, 1926, with Cobelli, Lo Giudice, Morelli, de Angelis, conductor Toscanini; 1932, with dalla Rizza, conductor de Sabata; 1953, with Araujo, Prandelli, Valdengo, Rossi-Lemeni, conductor de Sabata; Covent Garden, 1930, with Ponselle, Merli, Inghilleri, Autori (later Pinza), conductor Bellezza; San Francisco, 1941, with Moore, Kullman, Weede, Pinza, conductor Montemezzi.

Archibaldo, *King of Altura*......................................Bass

Manfredo, *son of Archibaldo*...........................Baritone

Avito, *a former prince of Altura*...........................Tenor

Flaminio, *a castle guard*......................................Tenor

Fiora, *wife of Manfredo*...................................Soprano

A Youth, a Handmaiden, a Young Girl, an Old Woman

Place: A Remote Castle of Italy
Time: The Tenth Century
Running Time: 1 hour 50 minutes

This opera is one of the most successful products of twentieth-century Italian music, more popular, it must be admitted, in America, where it has been frequently performed, than in its native Italy. Based upon a powerful tragedy by Sem Benelli, one of the foremost of Italian playwrights, it is a combination of terse, swiftly moving drama with a score which vividly depicts events progressing fatefully toward an inevitable human cataclysm. While there are few set-pieces in Montemezzi's score, nevertheless it is melodious, a glowing medieval tapestry.

Act I. The scene is a spacious hall open to a terrace. A lantern employed as a signal sheds its reddish light dimly through the gloom before dawn.

From the left enters Archibaldo. He is old with flowing white hair and beard, and he is blind. He is led in by his guide Flaminio. As if he saw, the old blind King points to the door of a chamber across the hall and bids Flaminio look and tell if it is quite shut. It is slightly open. Archibaldo in a low voice orders him to shut it, but make no noise, then, hastily changing his mind, to leave it as it is.

In the actions of the old King, who cannot see but whose sense of hearing is weirdly acute, and in the subtle suggestion of suspicion that all is not well, the very opening of this opera casts a spell of the uncanny over the hearer. This is enhanced by the groping character of the theme which accompanies the entrance of Archibaldo with his guide.

There is mention of Fiora, the wife of Archibaldo's son, Manfredo, who is in the north, laying siege to an enemy stronghold. There is mention too of Avito, a prince of Altura, to whom Fiora was betrothed before Archibaldo conquered Italy, but whose marriage to Manfredo, notwithstanding her previous betrothal, was one of the conditions of peace. Presumably – as is to be gathered from the brief colloquy – Archibaldo has come into the hall to watch with Flaminio for the possible return of Manfredo, but the restlessness of the old King, his commands regarding the door opposite, and even certain inferences to be drawn from what he says, lead to the conclusion that he suspects his son's wife and Avito. It is also clear – subtly conveyed, without being stated in so many words – that Flaminio, though in the service of Archibaldo, is faithful to Avito, like himself a native of the country which Archibaldo has humbled.

When Flaminio reminds Archibaldo that Avito was to have wedded Fiora, the blind King bids his guide look out into the valley for any sign of Manfredo's approach. 'Nessuno, mio signore! Tutto è pace!' is Flaminio's reply. (No one, my lord! All is quiet!)

Archibaldo, recalling his younger years, tells eloquently of his conquest of Italy, apostrophising the ravishing beauty of the country when it first met his gaze, before he descended the mountains from which he beheld it. He bids Flaminio put out the lantern, since Manfredo does not come. Flaminio obeys; then, as there is heard in the distance the sound of a rustic flute, he urges upon Archibaldo that they go. It is nearly dawn, the flute appears to have been a signal which Flaminio understands. He is obviously uneasy, as he leads Archibaldo out of the hall.

Avito and Fiora come out of her room. Her hair hangs in disorder around her face, her slender figure is draped in a fine ivory-white garment. The quiet that prevails fills Avito with apprehension. Fiora, confident through love, seeks to reassure him.

There is a brief but passionate love scene. Then Avito perceives that the lantern has been extin-

guished. He is sure someone has been there, that they are spied upon. Once more Fiora tries to give him confidence. Then she herself hears someone approaching. Avito escapes from the terrace into the dim light. The door on the left opens and Archibaldo appears alone. He calls 'Fiora! Fiora! Fiora!'

Concealing every movement from the old man's ears, she tries to glide back to her chamber. But he hears her. 'I hear you breathing! You are breathless and excited! O Fiora, say, with whom have you been speaking?'

Deliberately she deceives him. His keen sense tells him that she lies. For when she sought to escape from him, he heard her 'gliding thro' the shadows like a snowy wing'.

Flaminio comes hurrying in. The gleam of armoured men has been seen in the distance. Manfredo is returning. His trumpet is sounded. Even now he is upon the battlement and embraced by his father. Longing for his wife, Fiora, has led him for a time to forsake the siege. Fiora greets him, but with no more than a semblance of kindness. With cunning, she taunts Archibaldo by telling Manfredo that she had come out upon the terrace at dawn to watch for him, the truth of which assertion Archibaldo can affirm, for he found her there. As they go to their chamber, the old man, suspecting, fearing, thanks God that he is blind.

Act II. The scene is a circular terrace on the high castle walls. A single staircase leads up to the battlements. It is afternoon. The sky is covered with changing, fleeting clouds. Trumpet blasts are heard from the valley. From the left comes Manfredo with his arms around Fiora. He pleads for her love. As a last boon before he departs he asks her to mount the stairway and, as he departs, wave to him with her scarf. Sincerely moved by his plea, a request so simple and yet seemingly meaning so much to him, she promises that she will do it. He kisses her, and runs off to lead his men back to the siege.

Fiora tries to shake off the sensation of her husband's embrace. She ascends to the battlemented wall. A handmaid brings her an inlaid casket, from which she draws a long white scarf. The orchestra graphically depicts the departure of Manfredo at the head of his cavalcade.

Fiora sees the horsemen disappear in the valley. As she waves the veil her hand drops wearily each time. Avito comes. He tells her it is to say farewell. At first, still touched by the pity which she has felt for her husband, Fiora restrains her passionate longing for her lover, once or twice waves the scarf, tries to do so again, lets her arms drop, her head droop, falls into his arms, and they kiss each other as if dying of love. 'Come tremi, diletto' (How you tremble, beloved!) whispers Fiora. 'Guarda in su! Siamo in cielo!' (Look up! We are in heaven!) responds Avito.

But the avenger is near. He is old, he is blind, but he knows. Avito is about to throw himself upon him with his drawn dagger, but is stopped by a gesture from Flaminio, who has followed the King. Avito goes. But Archibaldo has heard his footsteps. The King orders Flaminio to leave him with Fiora. Flaminio bids him listen to the sound of horses' hooves in the valley. Manfredo is returning. Fiora senses that her husband has missed the waving of the scarf. Archibaldo orders Flaminio to go to meet the Prince.

The old King bluntly accuses Fiora of having been with her lover. Cowering on a stone bench that runs around the wall, she denies it. Archibaldo seizes her. Rearing like a serpent, Fiora, losing all fear, in the virtual certainty of death at the hands of the powerful old man, boldly vaunts her lover. Archibaldo demands his name. She refuses to give it. He seizes her by the throat, again demands the name, and when she still refuses, throttles her. Manfredo arrives. Briefly the old man tells him of Fiora's guilt. Yet Manfredo cannot hate her. He is moved to pity by the great love of which her heart was capable, even though it was not for him. He goes out slowly, while Archibaldo lifts the slender body of the dead woman across his chest, and follows him.

Act III. The crypt of the castle. Fiora lies upon her bier. Around her mourn people of her country.

Out of the darkness comes Avito. The others depart in order that he may be alone with his beloved, for he too is of their country, and they understand. 'Fiora! Fiora! – È silenzio!' are his first words, as he gazes upon her. Desperately, he throws himself beside her and presses his lips on hers. A sudden chill, as of approaching death, passes through him. He rises, takes a few tottering steps towards the door.

Like a shadow, Manfredo approaches. He has come to seize his wife's lover, whose name his father could not wring from her, but whom at last they have caught. He recognises Avito.

Upon Fiora's lips Archibaldo has spread a virulent poison, knowing that her lover would come into the crypt to kiss her. With his last breath, Avito says that she loved him as the life that they took from her, aye, even more. Despite the avowal, Manfredo is disposed to wonder at the vast love Fiora was capable of bestowing, yet not upon himself.

Avito is dead. Manfredo, too, throws himself upon Fiora's corpse, and from her lips draws in what remains of the poison, quivers, while death slowly creeps through his veins, then enters eternal darkness, as Archibaldo gropes his way into the crypt. The blind King approaches the bier, feels a body lying by it, believes he has caught Fiora's lover, only to find that the corpse is that of his son.

Such is the love of three Kings; of Archibaldo for his son, of Avito for the woman who loved him, of Manfredo for the woman who loved him not. Or, if deeper meaning is looked for in Sem Benelli's powerful tragedy, the three kings are in love with Italy, represented by Fiora, who hates and scorns the conqueror of her country.   K.

CLAUDIO MONTEVERDI

(born 15 May 1567, died 29 November 1643)

Man's instinct for drama *expressed through* (as opposed to *accompanied by*) music has taken very many forms through the ages – the tragedies and comedies of the Greeks, the Buffalo dances of American Indian Blackfoots, the Ramayana of India, Miracle plays, Mysteries and Masques, the Christian Mass itself – and opera is a culmination of a particular form of Western expression, itself to this day in a constant state of evolution.

Modern opera may conveniently be said to have begun in 1600, the date of Peri's *Euridice*, the first surviving example of the form (his *Dafne*, 1597, has been lost).

At the end of the sixteenth century a small group of aristocratic intelligentsia, known collectively to musical history as the 'Camerata', was meeting in Florence. Under the auspices of Count Giovanni Bardi di Vernio, and later of Jacopo Corsi, it included composers such as Vincenzo Galilei (father of the astronomer), Emilio de' Cavalieri, Jacopo Peri and Giulio Caccini, and the avowed intention was to reproduce as far as possible the combination of words and music which together made up Greek theatre. With this restorative aim in view, the members laid down that the text must at all times be understood, that the words must be sung with a scrupulously correct and natural declamation, and that above all the music must interpret the spirit of the whole, not concentrate on details of incidents and words or even individual syllables. In a word, taking the Greeks as their authorities, the composers and poets concerned were anxious to end the distortion of the words which was inevitable in polyphonic music; in its place they were responsible for putting monody (or solo song), to form something like the opera we know today.

Claudio Monteverdi, already highly successful in polyphonic style, was the composer who was able to build on the foundations which had been laid by the Florentine 'Camerata' and his first opera, *Orfeo*, has been described by Professor Jack Westrup as a landmark 'not because it broke new ground but because in it imagination took control of theory'. It was opera's good fortune that there should appear so soon a composer whose outlook was essentially dramatic, and Monteverdi's *Orfeo* makes the *Euridice* of Peri and Caccini (both set Rinuccini's libretto in the same year, 1600) appear pale and monotonous by comparison.

Monteverdi's career is conveniently divided into two sections: during the first, 1590–1612, he was in the service of the Mantuan court and during the second, 1613–43, he worked in Venice, as Maestro di Cappella of San Marco and as a composer for the theatre. During the first period he wrote three of the twenty-one dramatic (or semi-dramatic) pieces to his credit (*Orfeo* and *Il Ballo delle Ingrate* survive complete, but only a few fragments of *Arianna* exist today); of the remaining eighteen, all but four have disappeared (*Tirsi e Clori*, a ballet-opera; *Il Combattimento di Tancredi e Clorinda*, a dramatic cantata; and the operas *Il Ritorno d'Ulisse in Patria* and *L'Incoronazione di Poppea* survive).

Monteverdi represents not so much revolution as the culmination of a period of change, and he was a composer who was thoroughly at home in both the polyphonic and the monodic styles.   H.

LA FAVOLA D'ORFEO
The Legend of Orpheus

Opera in a prologue and five acts, text by Alessandro Striggio. First produced privately at the Accademia degl'Invaghiti, Mantua, February 1607, with Francesco Rasi as Orfeo, and on 24 February of the same year at the Court Theatre, Mantua. In August 1607 the opera was given in Monteverdi's native town of Cremona, and it is likely that there were stage productions in Turin, Florence and Milan.

Orfeo was revived in 1904 in a concert version in Paris (arranged Vincent d'Indy); in 1909 in Milan and other Italian cities (arranged Giacomo Orefice); in 1910 in Brussels. The first modern staging was at the Théâtre Réjane, Paris, in 1911, in d'Indy's version.

The opera was first heard in America in concert form at the Metropolitan, New York, in 1912 (arranged Orefice), when Hermann Weil was Orfeo. In 1913 Chicago heard a concert version, conducted by Campanini and with Sammarco in the title role. There was a stage performance in Breslau in 1913 arranged by Erdmann-Guckel, and a new realisation by Carl Orff was heard at Mannheim in 1925. Malipiero's arrangement was first performed in Leningrad in 1929. The first American stage performance took place in 1929 at Northampton, Massachusetts, under the auspices of Smith College (in Malipiero's version) with Charles Kullman as Orfeo.

In England, the first performance (in concert form, arranged d'Indy) took place under the auspices of the Institut Français in 1924, and a stage version (arranged J.A. Westrup and W.H. Harris) was seen in Oxford in 1925 and in London in 1929. Italian revivals have been at the Rome Opera, 1934 (arranged Benvenuti), with Franci (Orfeo), conductor Serafin; at la Scala, Milan, 1935 (arranged Respighi), under Marinuzzi and with Carlo Galeffi (Orfeo). *Orfeo* was produced in Budapest in 1936 (in Respighi's version) and remained in the regular repertory for a number of years. Revived New York City Center, 1960, with Souzay, conductor Stokowski; Sadler's Wells Opera (realised by Raymond Leppard), 1965, with John Wakefield; Kent Opera (in Roger Norrington's edition), 1976; Edinburgh Festival, 1978, by Zürich Opera in Harnoncourt's realisation; English National Opera, 1981, produced by David Freeman with Anthony Rolfe Johnson (John Eliot Gardiner conducted his own realisation).

La Musica (Prologue) ....Soprano
Orfeo, *a poet* ....Tenor
Euridice, *his wife* ....Soprano
A Nymph ....Soprano
Four Shepherds............................Three Tenors, Bass
Messenger..Soprano
Speranza (Hope) ....Soprano
Charonte (Charon) ....Bass
Proserpina, *Queen of the Underworld* .... Soprano
Plutone (Pluto), *King of the Underworld* ....Bass
Apollo...Tenor or Baritone

Nymphs, Shepherds, Spirits of the Underworld

Running Time: 2 hours 10 minutes

*O*rfeo was written for performance at court where instrumental resources were lavish. When Monteverdi later wrote for the public theatres of Venice, where profit was a prime motive, the instruments at his disposal were necessarily more limited. It is perhaps worth while to give a list[1] of the instruments called for at the beginning of the score, and of the additional ones mentioned in the inner pages:

Fundamental instruments (i.e. chord-playing)
    2 clavicembalos
    1 double harp (one more needed in performance?)
    2 chitarrones (one more called for in score)
    2 bass cithers (not listed but mentioned in score)
    3 bass gambas
    2 organs with wood (flute) pipes (*Organi di Legno*)
    1 organ with reed pipes (*Regale*)

Stringed instruments
    2 small violins (*alla francese*)
    10 viole de braccio (i.e. a string ensemble, possibly
       4 violins, 4 violas, 2 violoncellos)
    2 contrabass viols

Wind instruments
    4 trombones (one more called for in score)
    2 cornetts
    1 flautino alla Vigesima Seconda (i.e. a high
       recorder; one more (?) called for in score)
    1 high trumpet (*clarino*; possibly referring to use of
       high range of ordinary trumpet)
    3 soft trumpets (*trombe sordine*)

It seems likely that many of the players doubled, and of course not all the instruments were used at once, apart that is to say from the opening *toccata*, some of the *sinfonie*, and the accompaniments of a few of the choruses. Monteverdi indicated what combination of instruments he required, and he used the contrast of orchestral colour for dramatic purposes.

It is a piece of the greatest good fortune that so early in the history of Opera (as opposed to the much longer history of Music Drama), there should in Monteverdi have appeared a master and that his first opera should be a masterpiece. But it is no accident that this first opera should open with a clarion call still unrivalled in its way among operatic introductions. This thrice played *toccata* in C major was perhaps the accompaniment to an entry by Monteverdi's patrons, the Gonzagas, and their guests, but such a circumstance detracts not at all from its effect, which Hans Redlich has rightly called 'shattering'. The Prologue consists of a recitation by La Musica of her powers; there are five verses, composed on a bass, each introduced by a *ritornello* which is played for the sixth time after the last verse. The same *ritornello* recurs for the seventh and eighth times at the end of Act II and at the beginning of Act V. These *ritornelli* are employed throughout the opera to create appropriate atmosphere.

Act I. Shepherds and Nymphs rejoice over the wedding of Orfeo and Euridice. Orfeo himself sings the first of his big solos, 'Rosa del ciel'. This is followed by a stanza for Euridice, and the act ends with a beautiful chorus praying that their happy state may bring no misfortune on the lovers.

Act II is dominated by the great scene for the Messenger, and by Orfeo's lament, but it begins with a long, beautiful pastoral episode. The scene is rounded off by a short chorus in which the Shepherds beg Orfeo to sing. Orfeo sings a strophic song, 'Vi ricordo o boschi ombrosi', each of the four verses being preceded by a *ritornello*. It is a simple, carefree aria, and perfectly establishes the mood of contentment and happiness which is so suddenly broken by the advent of the Messenger with the news of Euridice's death. The unclouded happiness and serenity which have seemed to be Orfeo's have aroused the envy of the gods; the chorus is immediately apprehensive of the nature of

---

[1] The list is quoted in Donald Grout's *A Short History of Opera* (O.U.P.).

Orfeo (Netherlands Opera, 1996, director Pierre Audi, sets Michael Simon, costumes Jorge Jara).
John Mark Ainsley as Orfeo, Russell Smythe as Apollo.

the Messenger's errand; Orfeo alone is unaware of the approach of tragedy. 'Ahi, caso acerbo' sings the Messenger to a phrase which is later repeated by the Shepherds, and the chorus. The solo is one of great emotional and dramatic import, and the few phrases of dialogue with Orfeo at the beginning, ending with his stunned 'Ohimè', produce an extraordinary intensity by the simplest means. The Messenger's narration over, the first reaction of horror comes (to the words 'Ahi, caso acerbo') from the Shepherds. A moment later Orfeo (as if repeating the last words he heard, suggests Leo Schrade[1]) begins his lament, 'Tu se' morta, se' morta mia vita'. It is short, the feeling is restrained, even classical, but the evocative power of the music is unsurpassed, and the simplicity and passion of the ending 'A dio terra, a dio cielo, e Sole, a Dio', is most moving. The chorus and the Shepherds sing an elaborate threnody to the words 'Ahi, caso acerbo', and mourn the tragedies of Euridice bitten by the Serpent, and of Orfeo transfixed by grief.

Act III. In impressively solemn declamation, Orfeo is confronted by Speranza. He resolves to seek Euridice in Hades. The use of trombones is a feature of the orchestration. Charonte's sombre utterance is followed by Orfeo's attempt by means of his powers as a singer to gain admission to Hades. The song with its elaborate ornamentation is a great test of virtuosity, and, as if to emphasise this characteristic, each verse and *ritornello* has a different combination of instruments. It is perhaps surprising that Monteverdi should print an alternative and wholly simple version for the use, one supposes, of singers who were not able to do justice to the more elaborate writing. Charonte admits that he has listened to the song with intense pleasure, but it is only after Orfeo has renewed his pleading in the simplest recitative that he yields; who could resist the rising semitones of the impassioned 'Rendetemi il mio ben, Tartarei Numi' with which he ends his plea? Preceded and followed by a solemn *sinfonia*, the act ends with a most lovely, madrigalesque chorus of Spirits.

Act IV. Proserpina and Plutone discuss Orfeo's plight, and, prompted by his wife and urged by the captive spirits singly and in chorus, the King of the Underworld agrees to release Euridice to her husband. Orfeo is triumphant but his song of rejoicing is interrupted as he looks back to see if Euridice is following. The spirits lament that her short-lived freedom should be snatched from her by her husband's transgression of Plutone's stipulation.

Act V. Orfeo, wandering on the plains of Thrace, laments his broken heart, and summons nature itself, which has so often benefited from his singing, to join him in his mourning. The *ritornello* which begins the act is the same as that used in the Prologue; during the course of the scene, Monteverdi makes use of an echo device. Apollo, Orfeo's father, descends from Heaven and tells his son that he will be translated to divine immortality, and among the stars will be able to see his Euridice again. Father and son ascend to Heaven singing together music full of coloratura ornament. The chorus sings its valediction in a lively 'Moresca'. (It should be noted that Striggio's original libretto brought the legend to an end in accordance with tradition, Orfeo being torn to pieces at a Bacchanalian orgy by the Thracian women, maddened by his unceasing laments for a woman he would not see again.)

'Orfeo', says Professor Westrup,[2] 'is curiously representative of its time. We find in it the new recitative already practised by Peri and Caccini, the rhythmical subtlety of the French *chanson*, the traditional polyphony of motet and madrigal, the conventional practice of embellishing a vocal line with *fioriture*, the chromatic devices of the madrigal transferred to monody ... *Orfeo* is hardly an experimental work; it is rather a successful attempt to combine into a single whole the varied methods of musical expression current at the time.'   H.

ARIANNA

Opera in a prologue and eight scenes, text by Rinuccini. First performed at the Teatro della Corte, Mantua, 28 May 1608, as part of the festivities connected with the wedding of Francesco Gonzaga and Margherita di Savoia. Virginia Andreini was the original Arianna. The score is now lost, apart from the famous lament and a few other fragments, but stage revivals were presented at Karlsruhe in 1926, and in Paris, 1931.

*A*rianna seems to have been enormously successful when first performed, and the great lament of Arianna, 'Lasciatemi morire', became immediately the most popular piece of music of the day. It began a

---

[1] Leo Schrade: *Monteverdi* (Gollancz).

[2] In his essay on the composer in *The Heritage of Music*, vol. III (O.U.P.).

long line of *lamenti*, and Monteverdi himself transformed it into a five-part madrigal (in 1610) and into a sacred 'Pianto della Madonna' (published 1640).

A peculiarity of operatic history is that Alexander Goehr, a leading British composer with several operatic essays to his credit, should have chosen to set Rinuccini's original text to music, which, with its recitative and *ritornelli*, its declamatory solos and frequent vocal 'madrigals', closely follows Monteverdi's patterns if not his style. Goehr's opera, performed in 1995 at Covent Garden, incorporated a version of the Lament.   H.

IL COMBATTIMENTO DI TANCREDI E CLORINDA

The Fight between Tancredi and Clorinda

Dramatic cantata, text by Tasso: verses 52–68 of Canto XII of *Gerusalemme liberata*.

Tancredi ....Soprano
Clorinda...Soprano
Testo (Narrator)... Soprano

Running Time: 30 minutes

Il Combattimento was published in 1638, fourteen years after it was written for performance in the Palazzo of Girolamo Mocenigo. In his introduction to the score, Monteverdi describes the first performance. After some madrigals had been sung as an introduction, Clorinda appeared, armed and on foot, followed by Tancredi, also armed but on a *Cavallo Mariano*.[1] The Narrator began his song, and Clorinda and Tancredi acted, or danced, the story in a way suggested by the words. The Narrator is instructed to sing clearly and firmly and to articulate well; only in the stanza to Night may he employ decoration; for the rest, he must narrate *a similitudine delle passioni dell'oratione*. At the end, says Monteverdi, the audience was moved to tears.

Before the action begins, Tancredi, a Christian knight, has fallen in love with Clorinda, a Saracen maiden. She is a brave and skilful warrior and, dressed in man's armour, has assaulted and burnt, with one companion, a Christian fortification. As she is returning from this victory, she is seen and pursued by Tancredi. He thinks her a man and challenges her to mortal combat.

The Narrator, who remains outside the action but comments throughout, begins by announcing the theme of the story, and straightaway we have, in 6/8 time, a representation of the horseback pursuit. Clorinda and Tancredi defy one another, and Tancredi dismounts for the combat. The Narrator begins his description of the phases of the fight, and before the *sinfonia* which introduces the Invocation of Night, we hear for the first time the string *tremolo*, or *stile concitato*, about which more later. The stanza in praise of Night is a beautiful inspiration; it gives way to a graphic account of the battle, whose musical phases change as often as the various stages of the duel. Not only does Monteverdi use the new device of rapidly repeated notes in the orchestra but he makes the Narrator imitate the device by setting some lines at breakneck speed.

In the middle of the battle, the combatants rest, and their exhaustion is faithfully reflected in the music. Tancredi says that whatever the issue he would like to know the name of his opponent, but Clorinda answers proudly that the warrior who opposes him is one of the two responsible for burning

---

[1] Raymond Leppard has suggested an interesting explanation of the significance of this mysterious term. 'By the time *Combattimento* was published in Book VIII, the circumstances of performance were being *described* and not *prescribed*. The Mocenigo Palace is not large and the courtyard has no place for anyone to sit so it must have been performed on the *piano nobile*, which is also not large. No question then of a real horse. A hobby-horse would seem the most likely and since almost life-size puppets had long been (and still are) a feature of Italian popular theatre, there is the possibility that it was performed by puppets and sung by singers at the side. "Mariano" doesn't exist except in religious or seasonal usage but it is very close to the stem "marionette" (which I believe has a religious origin itself) and I believe that this is the true origin.'

the Christian tower. The music is headed 'Guerra' as they return to fight with renewed zeal. Soon Clorinda is beaten and, transfixed by the sword of her opponent, falls dying at his feet. She forgives him and asks him to mark his forgiveness of her by bestowing Christian baptism on her. He fetches water from a stream which runs nearby, raises her visor and in a moment of horror recognises that his opponent was the Saracen maid he loved so well. He baptises her, and as he does so, she sings a last, rising phrase in which one can feel her soul leaving her earthly body for the heaven which she can see open to receive it: 'S'apre il ciel; io vado in pace.'

In his preface Monteverdi recognises three principal human passions: wrath (*Ira*), temperance (*Temperanza*), and humility or prayer (*Umiltà* or *Supplicazione*). Music, he says, has represented the soft, *molle*, and the temperate, but not the *concitato*, the excited. By means of his invention of the string *tremolo* and by applying it to an appropriate text, he hopes to remedy this defect; with the new device is associated for the first time the string *pizzicato*, like the *tremolo* a commonplace today.

The opera is scored for a quartet of strings (written out in full) supported by contrabass and harpsichord, and it is in Monteverdi's invention of this combination of sound to fit action that the unique quality of this fascinating work lies.   H.

IL RITORNO D'ULISSE IN PATRIA

Ulysses' Return Home

Opera in a prologue and five acts, text by Giacomo Badoaro. First performed in Venice, February 1641, at the Teatro San Cassiano. Doubt was once cast upon the authenticity of the ascription to Monteverdi but it is by now generally agreed that the music is in fact his, and Luigi Dallapiccola, the Italian composer who was responsible for an authoritative arrangement of the opera (1942), did not hesitate to describe the work as a masterpiece. The opera was revived in concert form in Brussels, 1925 (fragments only); in Paris (arranged by d'Indy) in 1925 and 1927; and broadcast from London in 1928 (in d'Indy's version, English translation by D. Millar Craig). The opera was staged in Dallapiccola's arrangement, Florence Festival, 1942, and at la Scala, Milan, 1943; in Paul Daniel's at English National Opera in 1989, and at the Buxton Festival in 1995.

The Prologue

Human Frailty ....Contralto
Time...Bass

Fortune...Mezzo-Soprano
Love ....Soprano

The Gods

Nettuno (Neptune) ....Bass
Giove (Jove) ....Tenor
Minerva ....Soprano
Giunone (Juno)..................................Mezzo-Soprano

The Mortals

Penelope, *Ulysses' wife*........................Mezzo-Soprano
Ericlea, *Penelope's nurse* ....Contralto
Melanto, *Penelope's maid*.....................Mezzo-Soprano
Eurimaco, *Melanto's lover*....................................Tenor
Ulisse (Ulysses) ....Tenor
Eumete, *faithful servant to Ulysses*.......................Tenor
Iro, *a glutton*...Tenor
Telemaco, *Ulisse's son*..Tenor
Antinoo, *one of Penelope's suitors*..........................Bass
Anfinomo, *one of Penelope's suitors*......Counter-Tenor
Pisandro, *one of Penelope's suitors* ....Tenor

Chorus of Phaeacians, Chorus from Heaven, Chorus from the Sea

Place: Ithaca; the Aegean Sea
Time: c. 1270 B.C.
Running Time: 2 hours 50 minutes

In d'Indy's version, Ulisse, Eurimaco and Anfinomo were baritones, and Penelope herself a soprano. Dallapiccola's arrangement adds Mercury to the list of characters and makes Telemaco into a mezzo-soprano. In both versions, Monteverdi's five acts are reduced to three (as they are in the Vienna MS of the score), and this general arrangement is often followed.

When Paris, Prince of Troy, eloped with Helen, wife of Menelaus, King of Sparta, the Greeks, led by Menelaus's brother Agamemnon, sailed to Troy under the protection of Hera/Juno in order to recapture her. Odysseus/Ulysses sailed with the expedition, leaving his wife Penelope behind. After the death of many heroes on both sides, Troy had still not fallen, but Ulysses (as Italian usage has the name) hit on the ruse of leaving a great wooden horse on the seashore while the Greek fleet made believe to sail away. The Trojans, taking the horse for a peace offering, dragged it into the city but that night a party of Greek soldiers hidden inside it broke out and set the city on fire, thus presaging its fall. The Greek fleet sailed for home but Ulysses incurred the special enmity of Poseidon/Neptune, God of the Sea, for injuring his son, Polyphemus, one of the Cyclops, whom he blinded in order to make his escape from the island where he was imprisoned. Neptune has been allowed by Zeus/Jove to wreak vengeance on Ulysses, whose ship he has vowed to destroy. Ulysses meanwhile is under the protection of Minerva, who has stood by him through his adventures.

Prologue. Human Frailty is forced to acknowledge the authority of Time, Fortune and Love.

In a room in the Royal Palace in Ithaca, Penelope is attended by Ericlea as she bemoans her state of loneliness with her husband still not returned from the war. It is a magnificent lament, proof in its own right, say its admirers, that *Ulisse* is by the composer of the *Arianna* lament; 'Torna, torna, deh torna Ulisse' is its poignant refrain. A duet follows between the amorous Melanto and her lover Eurimaco.

Giove and Nettuno discuss the gods' punishment of the sins of men during which Nettuno wins Giove's assent to his continued attempt to destroy Ulisse. The scene changes and we are with Ulisse on board a Phaeacian ship off the coast of Ithaca. The Phaeacians lay the sleeping Ulisse on the shore. He wakes and thinks he has been deposited in an unknown land. Ulisse's lament is not so highly organised as Penelope's in the earlier scene, but it is one of the most effective moments in the opera. There follows a long scene between Ulisse and Minerva, who appears disguised as a shepherd to comfort him and spur him on to return home. Ulisse eventually recognises Minerva, who tells him that she will disguise him and he will return home to rout the suitors who have taken possession of his palace. Ulisse rejoices at the turn in his fortunes.

The flighty Melanto suggests Penelope take another husband but the idea falls on stony ground. Eumete, Ulisse's old herdsman, is discovered alone. He sings of the contrast between his own contented lot and that of princes. The ridiculous Iro breaks in on his reverie, and smacks his lips over the pampered life *he* leads. Eumete sends him about his business: 'Corri, corri a mangiar, a crepar'. Ulisse, disguised as a beggar, comes in and hears Eumete lament his master's absence; he tells him that Ulisse will not fail his country, and the two go off contentedly together.

The scene changes to the ship in which Telemaco, protected by Minerva, is on his way home. He rejoices at the voyage and, joined by Minerva, at the favourable wind. Another change of scene takes us to the grove in which we originally found Eumete. Minerva cautions Telemaco against disregarding her advice. Eumete recognises and greets him, saying that the old man with him (in reality Telemaco's father but not known to either of them) has encouraged him to think Ulisse himself may be on his way to Ithaca. There is a short duet for Ulisse and Eumete on the subject of hope, and Telemaco bids Eumete go to the Queen and warn her that her son has come home and that she should not give up hope of seeing Ulisse himself. Ulisse reveals himself to his son. There is a rapturous duet for father and son and the scene ends with Ulisse telling his son to prepare Penelope for her husband's imminent return.

Penelope is surrounded by her suitors, who beg her, singly and together, to return their love. She will have none of them. Into the palace rushes Eumete, bringing the news that Ulisse may be among them before long. With new danger approaching, the suitors agree that they must dispose of Telemaco and press their claims on the Queen before it is too late.

Minerva intervenes once again, this time to urge Ulisse to go to Penelope, who at Minerva's instigation will offer herself as prize in a contest as to who can string and draw the great bow of Ulisse. Telemaco pours out his heart to his mother Penelope, but it is not long before Antinoo is mocking the poor beggar (in reality Ulisse), who should, he says, be with Eumete and the hogs, not in the palace watching them sup. Iro joins in, stuttering as usual (he is Vašek's forerunner), but is challenged to a wrestling match by Ulisse and soundly beaten. Penelope compliments the old man on his victory. In a moment the other suitors return, and she consents to set them a test: whoever can draw Ulisse's bow shall become her husband. Each in turn fails, but Ulisse asks to be allowed to try his strength. He strings and draws the bow, then, to the accompaniment of war-like music, transfixes each of the suitors in turn. His triumph is complete.

Iro is found alone. His aria, marked *parte ridicola*, is a masterpiece of parody, with the elevated style Monteverdi had done so much to establish as its object. Even the *ciaccona* bass of his own madrigal 'Zefiro torna' is pressed into service to do justice to the spectacle of Iro lamenting the horror which has come upon him: now that all his patrons are dead, he has an empty belly. He can think of no solution to the difficulty of filling it, and resolves on suicide.

Penelope is confronted by Telemaco and Eumete, who try to convince her that the old man who successfully drew the bow was Ulisse himself. Once again the gods have to step in, Minerva asking Giunone to speak on Ulisse's behalf to Giove, in order that he may persuade Nettuno to drop his vengeance. Even the appearance of her husband in his proper form fails to convince Penelope that she is not still the victim of a cruel deception and it is not until Ericlea affirms that she has recognised him by the scar on his leg that Penelope allows caution to be replaced by love. She rejoices in an aria before she and Ulisse join in a final duet to celebrate their reunion.   H.

L'INCORONAZIONE DI POPPEA
The Coronation of Poppaea

Opera in a prologue and three acts, text by G.F. Busenello. Première at Teatro di Giovanni e Paolo in Venice, 1642. Performed in Naples, 1651. Revived in concert form in Vincent d'Indy's arrangement by the Schola Cantorum in Paris in 1905; in 1913 given a stage production there at the Théâtre des Arts with Claire Croiza, conductor d'Indy. Produced in 1926 at Smith College, Northampton, Mass., and the following year at Oxford by the University Opera Club in an English translation by R.L. Stuart. Performed at the Florence Festival of 1937 in the Boboli Gardens in a version by G. Benvenuti, with Gina Cigna, Giuseppina Cobelli, Giovanni Voyer and Tancredi Pasero, conductor Gino Marinuzzi; and in the same year at both the Vienna Volksoper in a German version by Křenek, and at the Opéra-Comique, Paris, in Malipiero's version. Malipiero's realisation was revived at the Teatro Olimpico, Vicenza, and in Venice in 1949, with Hilde Gueden, Elsa Cavelti, Giovanni Voyer and Boris Christoff, conductor Erede. Raymond Leppard's realisation was first performed at Glyndebourne in 1962, and at the Coliseum, London, in 1971, with Janet Baker. Roger Norrington in 1974 prepared and conducted for Kent Opera a version generally believed nearer to the original than perhaps any other since Monteverdi's time, with Sandra Browne as Poppaea and Anne Pashley (soprano) as Nero.

Goddess of Fortune ....Soprano

Goddess of Virtue...Soprano

Goddess of Love ....Soprano

Ottone, Poppea's former lover ....Soprano[1]

Two Soldiers of the Emperor's Bodyguard........Tenor

Poppea (Poppaea)..Soprano

Nerone (Nero), *Emperor of Rome*.................. Soprano[2]

Arnalta, *Poppea's old nurse*.........................Contralto[3]

Ottavia (Octavia), *Empress of Rome* ... Mezzo-Soprano

Ottavia's Nurse .... Mezzo-Soprano

Drusilla, *Ottavia's lady-in-waiting*................. Soprano

Seneca, *philosopher, Nero's former tutor* ....Bass

A Young Attendant on Ottavia (Valletto) .... Tenor[4]

Damigella (Maid) *in Ottavia's service* .... Soprano

Liberto, *Captain of the Guard* ....Baritone

Pallade (Pallas), *Goddess of Wisdom* .... Soprano

Lucano, *Nerone's friend*....................................Tenor

Lictor...Bass

Mercurio (Mercury) ....Bass[5]

Venere (Venus)..Soprano

Soldiers, Disciples of Seneca, Servants, Consuls, Tribunes, Senators, etc.

Place: Rome
Time: About 55 A.D.
Running Time: 3 hours 15 minutes

L'Incoronazione di Poppea is Monteverdi's last opera, written when he was seventy-five and, according to most observers, his finest achievement. Its circumstances are very different from those of *Orfeo*, the composer's first opera reflecting the splendours of the Mantuan court where he was working, while his last, written for the much simpler circumstances of a Venetian public theatre, concentrated directly on character rather than on grandiose surroundings. Monteverdi's pupil, Cavalli (who may have contributed some of *Poppea's* music), had brought about a meeting with the poet Francesco Busenello, a Venetian lawyer and one-time ambassador to the court of Mantua – Busenello, every commentator agrees, was the first great librettist. Throughout, the focus is on dramatic truth and real-life emotions and their expression; illicit (but passionate) love triumphs over 'right', and in the course of the action injustice is more or less manifestly done to Ottavia, Seneca and Ottone.

As far as musical material is concerned, 'all we have is a manuscript written in several hands, a sort of rehearsal or continuo copy ... consisting of a single bass-line, very occasional sketches in parts for *ritornelli*, and a vocal line. Fortunately it has the stamp of

---

[1] Originally male soprano; often a baritone in modern versions.
[2] Originally male soprano; often a tenor in modern realisations.
[3] May have been a tenor originally.

[4] Originally a male soprano.
[1] Originally probably a high tenor.

authenticity about it since remarks, directions and cuts appear throughout in the composer's hand. This manuscript is preserved in Venice, and except for a later copy to be found in Naples, it is the only music we have of the opera, the rest has to be reconstructed.' So writes Raymond Leppard, whose edition of the opera scored a big success at Glyndebourne in 1962. All modern performances have been based on two ingredients: this manuscript, together with the editor's point of view over matters such as orchestration and cuts (the original has some three-and-a-half hours of music).

In Monteverdi's time, music in the theatre was accompanied by strings and continuo, and wind instruments were more or less restricted to church music, being imported into the opera house almost exclusively for representational purposes – horns for hunting scenes; trumpets and drums for a battle, and so on.

After the overture, in a Prologue the goddesses of Fortune and Virtue flaunt their own successes and mock the shortcomings of the other, until the goddess of Love in her turn vaunts her pre-eminence; against her, the others are as nothing, a point of view neither seems able or indeed anxious to refute.

Act I. It is just before dawn and, outside Poppea's house, two of Nerone's guards lie asleep. Ottone, her lover, returning from serving abroad, sings lovingly of the house and of Poppea, until he notices the soldiers and realises that he has been supplanted by no less a person than the Emperor. His world is in ruins around him. The soldiers wake up, gossip about the love of Poppea and Nerone, and grumble tunefully about their lot and the miseries of soldiering in Rome. Suddenly they realise that Nerone is approaching and are heard no more.

We meet Poppea and Nerone in one of the great love scenes of opera, the first of several in the score. After a night in her arms, Nerone must leave, but cannot drag himself away. She, spurred on by ambition as well as her evident love for him, employs every delaying tactic known to woman, and by the time he has gone has obtained a half promise that he will put aside the Empress Ottavia to marry her. Her reiterated 'Tornerai?' has more tenderness than urgency, and it is this ability to portray the contradictory elements of real-life emotions which distinguishes composer and librettist from most others who have tackled similar scenes in the history of opera; here, without hiding underlying motives, they catch the freshness and beauty of passion, which has no regard for conventional ideas of right or wrong.

With Nerone gone but his promise very much in her mind, Poppea seems triumphant and expresses her feelings in an aria, 'Speranza, tu mi vai il core accarezzando'. Her old nurse, Arnalta, tries to warn her against the snare which ambition may set for her – the Empress could seek revenge and Nerone's love cool – but Poppea believes that Love is on her side.

In her palace, Ottavia laments her humiliation and misery, denouncing in a noble utterance the infidelity of Nerone and calling on Jove to punish her erring spouse: 'Disprezzata regina'. Her old nurse tries vainly to comfort her, until Seneca is ushered in by the Empress's page. Gently but firmly he urges that tears and lamentation are unfit for an Empress, who must find refuge in stoicism. Ottavia objects that to promise greater glory from the torments she undergoes is specious and empty comfort, and her page impetuously tries to defend his Empress by attacking the old philosopher for his platitudes.

Alone, Seneca has a vision of Pallade, goddess of Wisdom, who warns him that to interfere in the imperial quarrel will result in his own death. Seneca welcomes the idea of death and claims to have conquered human fear and, as if to reinforce his presentiment, he receives a visit from Nerone, who tells him that he plans to set aside Ottavia and marry Poppea. Seneca warns him that the heart is often a bad counsellor, and begs his erstwhile pupil to avoid arousing the resentment of the people and the Senate, and, if nothing else, to have regard for his own good name. Passions mount, Nerone announces his decision to marry Poppea and leaves Seneca in a fury.

Nerone returns to Poppea and their extended love duet ends with her denunciation of Seneca who, she says, has maintained publicly that Nerone's ability to rule depends on Seneca's counsel. Nerone, to whom providence denied the quality of dispassionate wisdom, in a single sentence orders one of the guards to carry a message immediately to Seneca to the effect that he must that very day die. Then, in lyrical phrases, he reassures Poppea that she will see what true love can do, a power in which recent events must have reinforced her belief.

Ottone makes a last attempt at reconciliation with Poppea but she spurns him and exults in now belonging to Nerone. Ottone is overwhelmed by the disaster which has overtaken him; though his heart contains nothing but love for Poppea, his pride prompts him to plot her murder. In his misery, he turns to Drusilla, who is in love with him. Ottone tries to assure her that he now loves her, but his protestations ring just short of true and when, in answer to her repeated 'You love me? You love me?', he answers 'Ti bramo' (I want you) we are once again confronted by the dispassionate desire for realism which characterises Busenello's writing.

Act II begins with one of the great scenes of the score, the death of Seneca. First, heralded by Mercurio and welcomed by the old philosopher, Nerone's sentence of death is communicated by Liberto, Captain of the Praetorian Guard, and Seneca announces to his pupils that the time has come to prove in deed the stoic virtues he has so long preached in theory. In passionate chorus – a three-part madrigal of high and moving quality – they urge him to live, but he bids them prepare the bath in which his guiltless blood will flow away. The next scene, in which figured Virtue, Seneca and 'Un Choro di Virtù', has been lost, but Busenello and Monteverdi follow it with two in the strongest possible contrast with those leading up to and portraying the death of Seneca. In the first, we have an almost literal precursor of the intermezzos with which composers were in the habit a century later of adorning the intervals of their serious operas. Ottavia's page ('Sento un certo non so che') tells a pretty maid that he has a pain in his heart that he's never known before. Will she help him cure it? As the music flows its spirited way, it is perfectly obvious that she will.

There follows a scene in equally strong contrast, as Nerone, elated at the news of Seneca's death, carouses with his friend Lucano: 'Hor che Seneca è morto, cantiam'. The macabre situation is stressed rather than played down when Nerone, left alone, sings with the utmost conviction of his love for Poppea.

A scene between Nerone and Poppea has been lost and we next see Ottone making up his mind in a soliloquy that his former hatred for Poppea has gone and he must now languish in a state of unrequited love. He cannot kill her, he decides, but it is not long before Ottavia at her most domineering arrives and persuades him, not without threats to slander him to Nerone, that

it is his duty to kill Poppea. His hesitation and evasions are beautifully characterised in the libretto.

Drusilla rejoices in her love for Ottone, and the page asks Ottavia's old nurse what she would give for a day of happy youth such as is Drusilla's. 'Everything' is the answer. The arrival of Ottone brings about a change of mood, but Drusilla rises to the occasion, and, when he confides to her that he has in mind to commit a terrible crime for which he must disguise himself in her clothes, she is happy to offer garments and indeed her life's blood for him.

The scene changes to Poppea's garden, where Poppea opens her dialogue with Arnalta with the same words to which Nerone rejoiced at the news of the death of Seneca: 'Hor che Seneca è morto'. She demands that Love shall guide her ship safe to harbour. Arnalta sings what has perhaps always been the only number known separately from the score, a lullaby of great beauty: 'Oblivion soave'. It has the desired effect and the goddess of Love herself descends while Poppea sleeps and in an aria promises to watch over her as she lies defenceless. Ottone enters in disguise and with murder in his heart, but the goddess intervenes, Poppea wakes up and she and Arnalta think they recognise Drusilla, who runs away. The goddess of Love is triumphant: having defended Poppea, that very day she will see that she becomes Empress!

Act III. Drusilla is at first found singing happily to herself of her love for Ottone, but it is not long before she is identified by Arnalta and arrested for the attempt on Poppea's life. She protests her innocence, and not all the threats of Nerone, who is quickly on the scene, can make her change her story. As she is about to be taken off to torture and death, Ottone himself appears to claim, in spite of Drusilla's protestations, that it was he who was responsible for the attempted crime. A short duet between them leaves Nerone in no doubt of Ottone's guilt and he pronounces sentence of banishment on him. Drusilla says she will share in his exile, and Ottone recognises the good fortune which has suddenly overtaken him in what might have proved his most evil hour. Nerone finishes the scene by announcing his resolve to divorce Ottavia and send her in her turn into exile.

The action has reached a stage where one of the five principal characters is dead and another has been disposed of, together with his appropriate coupling. It only remains for the lonely Ottavia on the one hand and the far from lonely Poppea and Nerone on the other to meet their destinies. Poppea, announcing her re-birth, learns that it was Ottone and not Drusilla who attempted to murder her, and Nerone reveals that he thinks Ottavia was behind the plot. She shall be exiled and Poppea that very day will become Empress! In grave, confident music, which only later develops into coloratura flourishes, the couple privately hymn their love.

Arnalta celebrates her own involvement in Poppea's triumph by recalling in an aria past indignities as a servant and exulting over the prospect of future grandeur.

Ottavia, alone as befits her isolated but still imperial state, bids an unhappy but dignified farewell to Rome, her native land, her friends. She claims, quite falsely, that she is innocent, but her lament is in the great tradition started in *Arianna* by Monteverdi himself.

Poppea is triumphant, and is greeted first by Nerone, who bids her ascend to the apex of sovereignty, then by the consuls and tribunes of Rome itself who hymn her coronation. There is a short intervention by the goddess of Love and Venus (marked in the manuscript as a candidate for a cut, a hint usually taken by subsequent editors), and the opera ends with the idyllic celebration by the two protagonists of their love and their triumph: 'Pur ti miro', whose music, modern scholarship believes, is not by Monteverdi.   H.

WOLFGANG AMADEUS MOZART
(born 27 January 1756, died 5 December 1791)

Mozart's contribution to operatic literature is prodigious, but strictly in accord with the predilections of his time. He was only fourteen when he made his first attempt at *opera seria*, with its grand, archaic themes which accommodated not only musical essays on the characters' emotions and tribulations – their loves, furies, thirst for vengeance, need of consolation, regrets and so on – but the aspirations of leading singers as well. As a boy, he was commissioned to write in this vein for Italian theatres, as a young man in *Idomeneo* he composed the finest example of the form since the days of Handel, and as a leading Viennese composer, already mortally sick, he made a final contribution to the genre the year he died.

With *La finta giardiniera* when only eighteen he took the first steps towards the form he later adorned with incomparable art – called at one time *dramma giocoso*, at another *opera buffa*: a comedy of manners, with its opportunities for probing the human heart as well as embroiling the leading figures in crises which emerge as ensemble. A dozen years later he strode to operatic immortality when he produced *Le nozze di Figaro*, the supreme masterpiece in the form. He followed it up with *Don Giovanni*, a work of altogether different character, and capped the line with *Così fan tutte*, where the ostensibly frivolous comedy half-conceals a vein of deep unease.

Mozart was versatile and his sympathies were not confined to the comedies of high life enjoyed by court and aristocracy. *Die Entführung aus dem Serail* is a deliberate attempt to raise the *Singspiel*, and with it German opera in the vernacular, to a higher level, and his final masterpiece, *Die Zauberflöte*, for all its probing of masonic mysteries, is a celebration of demotic art.

What of tragedy? Mozart at first took Italianate composers (Pergolesi, Traetta, J.C. Bach) as his masters, and followed the inclinations of the time in writing none. All the same, suggestions abound of what might have been, whether in the incidental music to Gebler's play *Thamos, König in Egypten*, in *Idomeneo*, where tragedy seems constantly imminent, in sections of *Die Zauberflöte*, or in *Don Giovanni* and *Così*, whose characters and situations veer between high comedy and near-tragedy.

Mozart died at thirty-five but six operas stand at the core of current repertory. That two of them, *Idomeneo* and *Così fan tutte*, only in mid-twentieth century achieved that status seems now incomprehensible, and makes a much more potent comment on taste than it does on the operas themselves which remain in the list of the supremely great works.

MITRIDATE, RE DI PONTO

Mithridates, King of Pontus

Opera in three acts, libretto by Vittorio Amedeo Cigna-Santi, after Racine's tragedy (libretto originally set by Quirino Gasparini). Première Milan, 26 December 1770, but never again performed in Mozart's lifetime. Revived Salzburg, 1971, with Auger, Lorengar, Edda Moser, Watts, Schreier, conductor Leopold Hager; Wexford, 1989; Covent Garden, London, 1991, with Kenny, Lillian Watson, Ann Murray, Kowalski, Bruce Ford, conductor Hartmut Haenchen (1994, Paul Daniel).

Mitridate (Mithridates), *father of two sons; betrothed to Aspasia* ....Tenor
Aspasia ....Soprano
Sifare (Xiphares), *son to Mitridate* ....Soprano
Farnace (Pharnaces), *son to Mitridate* ....Contralto
Marzio, *a Roman general*.....................................Tenor
Ismene, *a Parthian princess* ....Soprano
Arbate, *Governor of Nymphaeum*....................Soprano

Roman Soldiers, Citizens

Place: Nymphaeum
Time: 63 B.C.
Running Time: 3 hours 40 minutes

Mozart's first commissioned opera, even though it lasted some six hours at the première (including an interpolated ballet), won considerable success. By some, the opera was condemned unheard because of Mozart's extreme youth – he was only fourteen – but its twenty-two performances spoke for its popularity. It is an astonishing feat for so young a composer, though it is not hard, in his first essay in the *opera seria* form, to find Mozart wanting as far as emotional and psychological content is concerned. Nonetheless, the arias he wrote for it – more than twenty, with only a single duet for contrast – are mostly magnificent in scale and achievement.

Mithridates was king of Pontus on the Black Sea for fifty years during which time he fought off the might of Rome until finally defeated in 63 B.C. Only he and his son Pharnaces have a basis in history, but Racine's play, one of his great successes, is fiction.

Act I. Mitridate is rumoured dead in battle against the Romans. His two sons, Farnace and Sifare, the former cruel by nature, the latter noble and honest, become rivals for the affections of Aspasia, who is engaged to their father. Farnace has additionally plotted with the Romans against Mitridate. Arbate assures the two princes that their father is alive and he appears bringing with him Ismene, who was formerly betrothed to Farnace. Mitridate admits to Arbate that he spread the rumour of his own death in order to test his sons.

Act II. Farnace rejects Ismene, and Mitridate doubts the loyalty of Aspasia, whom he nonetheless proposes to marry before leaving for battle. Sifare and Aspasia discover their love is mutual but swear to separate in order to spare Mitridate pain. Mitridate discovers Farnace's treachery on the one hand and Sifare's love for Aspasia on the other and imprisons both sons.

Act III. Aspasia and Ismene plead the cause of Sifare, but Mitridate leaves to command his army in a last attempt to stem the Roman advance. Sifare prevents Aspasia swallowing poison. Farnace is freed from prison by his Roman ally Marzio, but the two sons resolve to support their father and succeed in defeating the Romans, though not before Mitridate himself is mortally wounded. The opera ends with Sifare united with Aspasia, Farnace with Ismene.

As you would expect of *opera seria*, arias of every sort abound, from the ferocity of Mitridate's final aria of Act I (which is itself equalled by his aria condemning Sifare and Aspasia late in Act II) to the expressive lyricism of Sifare's farewell in Act II, 'Lungi da te, mio bene'. This, with its horn obbligato, looks forward you could think to Ilia in *Idomeneo*, and since it is followed immediately by Aspasia's beautiful lament for her own situation and capped by the opera's only duet, one may be tempted to agree with the observation that the quality of the music increases as the opera proceeds. You leave it dazed with the notion that a youth of fourteen could have written it.   H.

LUCIO SILLA

Lucius Sulla

Opera in three acts, text by Giovanni de Gamerra. Première Milan, 26 December 1772, with the castrato Venanzio Rauzzini as Cecilio and Anna de Amicis Buonsolazzi as Giunia, Bassano Morgnoni as Silla. The opera was performed twenty-six times in a month and apparently on the first night with its ballet interludes lasted (like *Mitridate*) some six hours.

Gamerra's libretto was later set among others by J.C. Bach but Mozart's opera disappeared, surfacing in London in 1967 and in Baltimore in 1968.

Lucio Silla, *dictator of Rome* ....Tenor

Giunia, *engaged to Cecilio*................................Soprano

Cecilio, *a senator, once outlawed*.....Soprano (Castrato)

Celia, *Lucio Silla's sister*..................................Soprano

Lucio Cinna, *a patrician, Cecilio's friend*..........Soprano

Place: Rome
Time: c. 100 B.C.
Running Time: 2 hours 40 minutes

After the success of *Mitridate* in Milan in 1770, it was no novice who at fifteen was commissioned for the Ducal Theatre there to compose an opera for Carnival 1772–73, nor was it astonishing that Mozart's opera did not survive its initial showing. Few did – but this was Mozart's last opera written for Italy. The illness of the tenor originally cast in the title role probably affected the final shape of the opera and Mozart certainly had little time in which to work. Commissioned on 4 March 1771, he was to deliver the recitatives by early October 1772, and the arias were to be tailored for the singers during November and December.

Act I. Cecilio, a senator banished from Rome by the dictator Lucio Silla, has secretly returned and is advised by his friend Cinna that his beloved Giunia mourns him believing him to be dead. Silla wants Giunia for himself and Celia, his sister, advises a cautious approach, but even this fails to diminish Giunia's hatred for Silla as her father's murderer. As Cinna predicted, Giunia goes every day to her father's burial place to mourn him, and there Cecilio surprises her to her evident joy.

Act II. Silla has a crisis of conscience but tells Celia she will that day be betrothed to Cinna. Cinna persuades Cecilio to drop his immediate intention of murdering Silla, but then suggests to Giunia that she should appear to agree to marry the dictator in order to kill him on their wedding night. She rejects the plan but Cinna, who in reality hates Silla, decides to undertake the task himself. Silla's renewed protestations do not move Giunia, but his threats make her fear for the life of Cecilio. Even Celia's pleas to Giunia do not move her and she resolves to throw herself on the mercy of the Senate. When Silla asks the Senate to approve his marriage to Giunia, Cecilio draws his sword and is arrested. He and Giunia resolve to die together, their devotion making a deep impression on Silla.

Act III. Cinna enjoins Celia to urge Silla to a more magnanimous course, and comforts Cecilio in prison. Giunia tells her lover that if he is executed she will follow him to death. On the Capitol, Silla executes a *volte-face*, pardoning Cecilio and uniting him and Giunia in marriage. Cinna admits he too, though once his friend, had come to hate the dictator, but Silla gives him Celia as his wife and caps the whole extraordinary episode by resigning his position and vowing in future to live as a Roman among equals. Rejoicing could hardly be more general and an *opera seria* ends, as so often, with a tyrant relinquishing power.

Even more than in *Mitridate*, the arias to which an *opera seria* naturally gives rise are not short of splendour – an achievement for a composer of any age – whether the great utterances of the principal figures, or those of hardly less coloratura magnificence for secondary characters. But the greatest advance on *Mitridate* comes in the composer's writing for the orchestra, not least perhaps in *recitativo stromentato*. The grandeur of set pieces is often suggested so immediately that you feel instinctively that what you are about to hear is from the greatest of Mozart's essays in the genre, *Idomeneo*, than which no praise can be higher.   H.

LA FINTA GIARDINIERA

(Die Gärtnerin aus Liebe)

The Supposed Garden-Girl or *Sandrina's Secret*

Opera in three acts, text by an unknown author (set only a year earlier by Pasquale Anfossi). Première in Munich, 13 January 1775, just before Mozart's nineteenth birthday, with Rosa Manservisi as Sandrina, the tenor Rossi as Belfiore, and a castrato, Tommaso Consoli, as Ramiro. The opera was performed in German in 1779–80 and toured through southwest Germany. After 1797, it disappeared until revived in 1891 in Vienna, but several revivals have taken place in the fourth quarter of the twentieth century, in Munich, Salzburg, and in England.

Don Anchise, *Mayor of Lagonero*........................Tenor

Sandrina, *working for the Mayor;*
in reality Countess Violante Onesti ....Soprano

Count Belfiore, *engaged to Arminda* ....Tenor

Arminda, *the Mayor's niece, once in*
love with Ramiro, now engaged to Belfiore ...Soprano

Ramiro, *in love with Arminda* ....Mezzo-Soprano

Serpetta, *the Mayor's housekeeper;*
in love with him ....Soprano

Nardo, *gardener to the Mayor (in reality,*
Roberto, Countess Onesti's servant) ....Baritone

Running Time: 3 hours 15 minutes

In 1774–75, in his late teens, Mozart 'came of age' as a composer, with the A major Symphony, his Violin Concerto in the same key, and *La finta Giardiniera*, the least-known among his mature, or nearly mature, operas and his first grown-up *opera buffa*, a description he later applied to *Le Nozze di Figaro* and *Così fan tutte*. Soon after its Munich première, it was turned into German and became a *Singspiel*, with spoken dialogue instead of recitative.

The story is much concerned with madness which is treated as comedy, but, before it starts, we should know that Countess Violante, believed dead of a wound sustained in a lovers' quarrel with Count Belfiore, is still in love with him and has pursued him to Lagonero, where she is working as Sandrina in the Mayor's garden. Her servant is working there too, under the name of Nardo.

Act I. Arminda, the mayor's niece, is due to marry Count Belfiore, but the situation has complications. The Mayor himself has fallen for Sandrina, to the fury of Serpetta, who wants him for herself. Nardo for his part is in love with Serpetta. To confuse matters further, Don Ramiro is in love with Arminda. During the first act, Belfiore pays court to Arminda but an encounter with Sandrina leads to mutual recognition. He loves her, she still loves him but is determined to punish him for what she sees as his infidelity. This is the situation at the start of the first finale. Sandrina denies she is Violante, Arminda is furious with Belfiore, the Mayor with Sandrina, Serpetta is jealous and only Ramiro is not wholly displeased by the way things are turning out – a typical mixture for an 'ensemble of perplexity'.

Act II. Misunderstanding and evasion remain the order of the day until the Mayor receives an order to arrest Belfiore on a charge of murdering Countess Violante. Sandrina saves the situation by declaring she is Violante and alive, but, the moment she is alone with Belfiore, denies it roundly; she only said so to rescue him. At this turn of events, Belfiore, not without cause, goes clean out of his mind. Arminda

contrives to have Sandrina transported to a forest full of wild animals, where she laments her predicament. The second finale takes place in semi-darkness. Serpetta lets slip to Nardo some indication of what is going on, and Nardo brings Belfiore to the scene; Arminda and the Mayor follow. Ramiro brings torches to illuminate the scene, but the pressures of the situation are too much for the mental stability of Sandrina, who joins Belfiore in a state of amiable lunacy.

Act III. Nardo does what he can for the two lunatics he feels responsible for, and is lucky that their madness leads them only into pastoral fantasy. They fall asleep and wake, miraculously in their right minds. Sandrina in duet shows initial signs of reluctance, but mass-reconciliation is at hand. Three weddings (but as yet no funeral) are quickly fixed up – Sandrina's to Belfiore, Ramiro's to Arminda, Nardo's to Serpetta; only the Mayor remains a disappointed bachelor.

Mozart's ability to create songs and arias of variety as well as distinction is very much to the fore in this precursor of his finest operatic achievements, and at one moment we seem to be hearing Belmonte, Pedrillo, even Figaro, at another Susanna, the Countess or Donna Elvira; Ramiro's aria in the middle of the second act is, with Belfiore's of a moment later, perhaps the most purely serious of all, forerunner maybe of Idamante. But it is the finales in which the composer shows his burgeoning mastery. Here, as later most notably in the second- and fourth-act finales to *Figaro*, we find the ability to manipulate a kaleidoscopic series of emotions and feelings, full of twists and turns, misunderstandings, disagreements, into a coherent musical movement, an ability unprecedented in a composer no more than eighteen years old. H.

IL RE PASTORE

The Shepherd King

Opera in two acts, text by Pietro Metastasio. Première in Salzburg, 23 April 1775, at the Archbishop's Palace, in the manner of a serenade; with the castrato Tommaso Consoli as Aminta.

Alessandro (Alexander the Great),
King of Macedonia ....Tenor

Aminta, *a shepherd* ....Soprano (Castrato)

Elisa, *a nymph* ....Soprano

Tamiri, *daughter of the deposed*
   King Strato...Soprano

Agenore, *a Sidonian nobleman*...........................Tenor

Place: Sidon
Time: 330 B.C.
Running Time: 2 hours

Il Re Pastore was performed (together with a short opera by Fischietti) in honour of a visit to Salzburg by the Archduke Maximilian; a version of Metastasio's libretto was presumably chosen for Mozart rather than by him and was anyhow a reduction of the original made first in 1774. Metastasio's libretto precludes an opera as ambitious as *Idomeneo*, Mozart's next *opera seria* (1781), and indeed, in spite of a plethora of shapely and purposeful arias and much characteristic music, *Il Re Pastore* breaks less new ground than had *La finta Giardiniera* written a year before.

Act I. Alexander the Great, though not the protagonist, features in the opera as a magnanimous monarch. Aminta is its hero, and after the overture we meet him musing on the future. Elisa tells him Alexander, who has overthrown the tyrant Strato, does not want the throne for himself but aims to find the rightful king. She reassures Aminta of her love. Alexander and his confidant Agenore watch Aminta, and Alexander, impressed by what he observes, decides this must be the rightful claimant to the throne.

Agenore recognises his beloved Tamiri, daughter of the dethroned Strato, in a shepherdess who is sheltering with Elisa from the presumed wrath of the King. All Agenore's blandishments fail to persuade her of Alexander's clemency, but she remains confident of Agenore's love. Elisa tells Aminta she has her parents' agreement to their marriage, but Agenore puts a spanner in the works when he greets Aminta as the King of Sidon. Aminta wants to turn down the throne, but Elisa persuades him otherwise, and the act ends with a pledge of mutual love and dedication.

Act II. Elisa, looking for Aminta who is in conference with Alexander in his tent, is turned away by Agenore who contends that the duty of a king takes precedence over love. Elisa protests and invokes Agenore's love for Tamiri, calling him a heartless barbarian. Aminta adds his voice to Elisa's, for good measure telling Alexander that he does not feel cut out to be a king, but Alexander insists that heaven brings illumination to whomever it ordains to reign.

Not all Alexander's plans take account of people's feelings, and Agenore reacts with less than total enthusiasm when the great monarch proposes that Tamiri should be married to Aminta and so with the new King ascend her father's throne. In the greatest aria of the opera, 'L'amerò, sarò costante', Aminta declares his faithful love for Elisa, a violin obbligato adding elegance to his exquisitely expressed sentiments.

The remainder of the opera is concerned with extricating the lovers from the tangle Alexander's ill-thought-out decisions have got them into. Elisa, when Agenore assures her Aminta and Tamiri will obey Alexander and marry, is ready to die; Tamiri, made perhaps of sterner stuff, berates Agenore for not delivering the news himself, and presses home her advantage by insisting he attend her wedding. Agenore is in an agony of indecision, but finally the ladies, with much invocation of his hard-heartedness, take it into their own hands to throw themselves on the monarch's mercy. He comes to understand the injustice he was in danger of committing and is, with some sycophancy, praised for his decision.   H.

IDOMENEO

Opera in three acts, text by the Abbé Varesco, after a French opera by Campra and Danchet. First performed at Munich, 29 January 1781, with Anton Raaff as Idomeneo, del Prato as Idamante, Dorothea Wendling as Ilia, Elisabeth Wendling as Electra, Panzacchi as Arbace. Revived Vienna, 1786[1]; Karlsruhe, 1917; Dresden, 1925; Vienna, 1931 (revised by Strauss, new text by Lothar Wallerstein), and with Maria Nemeth, Elisabeth Schumann, Joseph Kalenberg, Eva Hadrabova, Richard Mayr; Munich, 1931 (revised by Wolf-Ferrari). First British performance at Glasgow in 1934; first English professional performance at Glyndebourne in 1951, when Fritz Busch conducted a cast including Sena Jurinac (Ilia), Birgit Nilsson (Electra), Richard Lewis (Idomeneo), and Leopold Simoneau (Idamante). First New York performance at Town Hall, 1951. Recent revivals include Salzburg, 1956; Sadler's Wells, 1962, conductor Colin Davis; la Scala, Milan, 1968, conductor Sawallisch; Metropolitan, New York, 1982, with Ileana Cotrubas, Hildegard Behrens, Frederica von Stade, Luciano Pavarotti, conductor Levine; Glyndebourne, 1983, conductor Haitink.

---

[1] When Idamante's role was re-written for tenor.

Idomeneo, *King of Crete* ....Tenor

Idamante, *his son* ....Soprano or Tenor

Ilia, *a Trojan princess* ....Soprano

Elettra (Electra), *a Greek princess*...................Soprano

Arbace, *confidant of Idomeneo*............................Tenor

High Priest of Neptune ....Tenor

Voice of Neptune..Bass

People of Crete, Trojan Prisoners, Sailors, Soldiers,
  Priests of Neptune, Dancers

Place: The Island of Crete
Time: After the Trojan War
Running Time: 3 hours 30 minutes

Mozart's third and greatest essay in the form of *opera seria* (his first two, *Mitridate* and *Lucio Silla*, were written respectively ten and nine years earlier) was first performed in 1781 at Munich, for which Opera it was commissioned. Revived only once in the composer's lifetime (for a private performance in Vienna in 1786), it was fairly frequently heard in Germany and Austria after his death but not performed in Britain until 1934, and never on the English professional stage until its production at Glyndebourne in 1951. It was not heard in America until 1947 when performed at the Berkshire Festival, Tanglewood.

Alfred Einstein describes *Idomeneo* as 'one of those works that even a genius of the highest rank, like Mozart, could write only once in his life'. He was at the height of his powers when it was composed, and the arias are superbly expressive, though on a more rarefied plane than the later comedies have accustomed us to. If drama consists of the interplay of motives and emotions, and tragedy of the ordering of men's destinies by a fate their own actions have provoked, *Idomeneo* is both tragic (in spite of its happy ending) and dramatic. The four main characters, whose conflict reaches its climax with the great quartet in the last act, are sharply defined, and what might well have turned out no more than four stock figures emerge in the course of the musical action as personages no less real, if on an idealised plane, than for instance Susanna or Pamina. In fact we may take Ilia, with the gradual development of her personality through the trials she has to undergo, as a sketch, musically speaking at any rate, for Pamina, Mozart's maturest essay in what one must think of as his conception of the 'perfect' feminine type. It is hardly more fanciful to see in Idamante, her lover, the forerunner of Tamino, even more forceful and generous and dignified for all that he was originally sung by a castrato.

Act I. Idomeneo, King of Crete, has taken part in the Trojan War, and it is many years since he left home. Among the prisoners he has sent home is Ilia, daughter of King Priam, who has fallen in love with Idamante, the son of Idomeneo. The overture immediately establishes the character of an opera whose music, without exception, never relaxes its intense seriousness. Calmly the drama unfolds. In an aria, 'Padre, germani, addio', Ilia reveals that her hatred for the conquerors of her country is as nothing to her love for Idamante. He enters at its conclusion and in veiled terms states his love for Ilia, at the same time announcing that, in honour of his father's imminent return to Crete, the Trojan prisoners are to be set free. A chorus of rejoicing at this news precedes the entrance of Arbace to say that Idomeneo's ship has been sunk; the general consternation is given particular expression by Elettra, who fears that his death will remove all obstacles to the marriage of Ilia and Idamante, with whom she is herself in love. After a chorus of intercession, Idomeneo enters with his followers, whom he dismisses before explaining in an aria the nature of the vow which secured Neptune's intervention in quieting the storm: that he will sacrifice the first living creature he meets in return for deliverance from death. It is, of course, Idamante whom he sees, and their dialogue is made the more poignant because it is some time before Idomeneo recognises his son, whom he has not seen since infancy. In horror, the father orders the son from his presence, and Idamante laments his father's apparent displeasure in an aria 'Il padre adorato ritrovo e lo perdo'. The act ends with a brilliant march and choral *ciaccona* in honour of Neptune.

Act II. The King tells his secret to his counsellor Arbace, who advises that Idamante be sent to a distant country. The scene is usually omitted in modern performance, the act thus beginning with the scene between Idomeneo and Ilia whose aria 'Se il padre perdei' is touchingly beautiful. Idomeneo understands that his vow now involves not only disaster for himself and Idamante but for Ilia as well, but he faces the tragedy with courage and dignity in his great aria 'Fuor del mar ho un mar in seno'. This was written as a showpiece for Raaff, the sixty-six-year-old tenor who created the title role in Munich; whatever may be thought about his musical taste (he wanted an aria for himself substituted for the Act III quartet), his technique must have been very considerable indeed.[1] As Edward Dent said: 'Coloratura for men has gone out of fashion, thanks to Wagner, and, thanks to the late Madame Patti, coloratura for women has been associated with the frail type of heroine rather than the heroic. In the eighteenth century and especially in the early half of it, the grand period of *opera seria*, a coloratura was almost invariably heroic in character ... Donizetti's Lucia is paired off with a flute, Handel's heroes compete with a trumpet.'

A beautiful, lyrical aria for Elettra, whom the prospect of requited love has turned into a happy woman, leads into a march, and thence to the famous barcarolle chorus of embarkation, 'Placido è il mar, andiamo'. Idamante and Elettra take leave of Idomeneo in a superb trio 'Pria di partir', but the music quickens and a storm breaks over the harbour, heralding Neptune's vengeance at this attempt to evade the consequences of the vow made to him. Idomeneo admits his guilt but accuses the god of injustice, and the act ends as the crowd disperses in terror.

Act III. Ilia can think only of her love for Idamante, and her expression of it in her soliloquy 'Zeffiretti lusinghieri' is one of the most perfect moments of the opera. To her comes Idamante; he will fight the monster Neptune has sent to plague the island, and he may not return. Involuntarily, she confesses her love, which leads to a duet. Idomeneo and Elettra interrupt the lovers. Idomeneo still cannot bring himself to explain the exact cause of the disaster which is overtaking them, and Idamante sadly takes his farewell in the noble quartet 'Andrò ramingo e solo'. Einstein calls it 'the first really great ensemble in the history of the *opera seria*' and Edward Dent does not try to disguise his enthusiasm for it when he describes it as 'perhaps the most beautiful ensemble ever composed for the stage'. It shows Mozart at his noblest and most expressive. The scene customarily and appropriately ends with the quartet, Arbace's elaborate aria being cut.

The High Priest exhorts the King to confess his sin to Neptune, and the people are duly horrified to hear that the sacrifice of Idamante is the price they and he will have to pay for deliverance from the god's displeasure. The people are gathered in the temple of Neptune to witness the sacrifice, the priests enter to a march and Idomeneo begins the ceremony with a solemn prayer which is answered by the priests. A shout of triumph is heard outside and Arbace announces that Idamante has killed the monster. However, a moment later Idamante, who by now knows the story of his father's vow, enters and offers himself for sacrifice, and Idomeneo cannot but accept him. The ceremony is about to reach its climax when Ilia interrupts and demands to be sacrificed in Idamante's place. The whole situation is resolved by an oracular pronouncement from Neptune to the effect that the crime can be expiated, the vow fulfilled, if Idomeneo will renounce the throne in favour of his son. In the general rejoicing, only Elettra is left with her worst fears realised; in the most furious of her violent utterances, she gives vent to her despair and rushes from the stage or, as some versions have it, falls dead or commits suicide.

The atmosphere changes to one of peace and fulfilment as Idomeneo in a last recitative and aria, 'Torna la pace al core', presents Idamante to the people as their new ruler, and takes his farewell. At the first performance, this aria had to be cut, much apparently to Mozart's regret. The opera ends with the people celebrating the accession of Idamante in dance and chorus.

When *Idomeneo* was performed privately in Vienna by amateur singers, Mozart added two numbers, transposed the role of Idamante for a tenor, removed most of Arbace's music, and made certain modifications in the rest of the opera. That he gave the role of Idamante to a tenor has been taken by some modern editors to indicate a change of mind as far as the vocal colour of this role was concerned, but this is surely to attach too little importance to the practical conditions of a performance which was after all mostly in the hands of amateur singers; rather few of these would have been likely to be castrati. In any case, however far the colour of the castrato voice must have been from that of a modern soprano, it is hard to believe that it was nearer to a tenor's.   H.

---

[1] A simplified version from Mozart's pen also exists, twenty-two bars shorter and shorn of much embellishment. It has often been assumed that the bowdlerised version dates from Mozart's preparation of the score in 1786 for Vienna, but Daniel Heartz and Stanley Sadie have suggested that it is likelier to represent an acknowledgement of the elderly Raaff's diminished capacity and that it was probably sung at the première. It is sometimes in modern performance, sadly but maybe prudently, preferred by singers of the title role.

Idomeneo *(Glyndebourne, 1951, director Carl Ebert, designer Oliver Messel). Act III, with Sena Jurinac (Ilia), Richard Lewis (Idomeneo), Leopold Simoneau (Idamante), Alexander Young (Priest), Birgit Nilsson (Elettra).*

DIE ENTFÜHRUNG AUS DEM SERAIL
The Escape from the Seraglio

Opera in three acts, text by Gottlieb Stephanie from a play by Bretzner. First performed at the Burgtheater, Vienna, 16 July 1782, with Caterina Cavalieri, Therese Teyber, Valentin Adamberger, Ludwig Fischer. During the first six years of its existence, there were thirty-four performances in Vienna. First performed in London, Covent Garden, 1827, in English, with additional airs by J.B. Cramer, and sung by Madame Vestris, Miss Hughes, Mr Sapio, Mr Benson, Mr Wrenn. The first performance in New York was in 1860. Other performances in London include Drury Lane, 1841 (in German), Her Majesty's, 1866 (in Italian, with recitatives by Arditi). Revived Covent Garden, 1927, with Ivogün, Schumann, Erb, Bender, conducted by Bruno Walter; 1938, with Berger, Beilke, Tauber, Weber, conducted by Beecham. Produced for the first time at Glyndebourne in 1935, with Noel Eadie, Eisinger, Ludwig, Andresen, Heddle Nash (Pedrillo), conducted by Fritz Busch. The first performance in Italy did not take place until 1935, at the Florence Festival, when Bruno Walter conducted a cast including Perras, Schöne, Kullman, and Sterneck. First heard at the Metropolitan, New York, in 1946, in English, with Steber, Alarie, Kullman, Carter, Ernster, conductor Cooper.

Constanze, *a Spanish lady*...............................Soprano
Blonde, *her English maid* ....Soprano
Belmonte, *a Spanish nobleman*...........................Tenor
Pedrillo, *his servant*..Tenor
Pasha Selim ....Speaking Part
Osmin, *overseer of his harem* ....Bass

Turkish Soldiers, Guards, Turkish Women

Running Time: 2 hours 15 minutes

A curious 'springboard' (as Einstein calls it in his *Mozart; his Character, his Work*) exists for *Die Entführung*. In 1779 Mozart began the music for a *Singspiel*, perhaps in desperation at the small prospects for operatic composition and performance which Salzburg offered. It was abandoned, probably owing to the arrival of the commission for *Idomeneo*, was only published in 1838 under the title of *Zaïde*, and did not reach the stage until 1866. The reasons are not far to seek: it was conceived on a modest scale – too modest for Mozart's real requirements – and its subject and style were 'Turkish' and very close to those of the opera he undertook a little later, *Die Entführung*, whose story reads like an amplification of *Zaïde*. *Zaïde* contains some attractive music, and the aria 'Ruhe sanft, mein holdes Leben' is of the greatest simplicity and beauty.

Die Entführung (1782) itself is important among Mozart's works not least because of the ambitious and extended view he takes in it of the hitherto modest German *Singspiel*. The drama is carried on almost exclusively in speech and it is only in moments of high emotion that the characters have recourse to song – but on what a sublimated level is that song when it comes! To expect in a *Singspiel* the extended finales that are a characteristic of *opera buffa* is to wish for something which would have been out of character with the convention and which Mozart was not trying to provide. Nevertheless, the music is highly expressive. Constanze and Belmonte, the latter at any rate, are perhaps loftier in their musical aspirations than they are in the field of human behaviour, where they lay themselves open to charges of ingratitude and deception. Blonde and Pedrillo, though entertaining, are stock comedy figures. Osmin, however, is one of the composer's great dramatic creations, genuinely and consistently comic in music as in action, yet no mere figure of fun, and as potentially dangerous as he is laughable.

Act I. The overture is mainly concerned with establishing the 'Turkish' atmosphere of the piece; Mozart also introduces a reference in the minor to Belmonte's aria, 'Hier soll' ich dich denn sehen, Constanze', which is heard in C major when the curtain goes up. Belmonte is outside the Pasha Selim's house, where he believes his beloved Constanze, who has been carried off by pirates, is a captive. Osmin, in charge of the Pasha's harem and also, it seems, of his garden, appears singing a doleful sort of love song, 'Wer ein Liebchen hat gefunden', one of the delights of the score. He is questioned by Belmonte: is this not the Pasha Selim's house? It is, and he works for the Pasha, but an enquiry for Pedrillo produces an even surlier answer, as this is his *bête noire*, his rival in love for Blonde; Pedrillo should, he says, without delay be hanged, drawn and quartered. He chases Belmonte away, but is immediately confronted with Pedrillo in person, saucier and more impudent than ever. The situation calls for music and he relieves his pent-up feelings with an aria that is a virtuoso expression of rage: 'Solche hergelauf'ne Laffen'.

Belmonte returns to find his former servant; each is delighted at the other's news, Belmonte to hear that Constanze has remained true to him in spite of the Pasha's persuasive powers, Pedrillo that there is a boat waiting to take them all to safety if they can only spirit the women out of the harem. Belmonte sings of love for his absent Constanze: 'O wie ängstlich, o wie feurig'. Its romantic feeling derives in part, we may suppose, from Mozart's love for his own Constanze, whom he married a few weeks after the production of the opera. The orchestral accompaniment, Mozart tells his father in a letter, represents the throbbing of the lover's heart, the heaving of his breast, his sighs and whispers.

Belmonte goes out as Constanze and the Pasha land from a boat. The Pasha once again assures Constanze of his love and of his determination to win hers in return. She sings of the love that she knew before her captivity and protests that she will be true to this memory: 'Ach, ich liebte, war so glücklich'. She leaves, and Pedrillo takes this opportunity to introduce Belmonte to the Pasha as an architect of high standing. The Pasha intimates that he will not withhold his favour from him, but after he has gone Osmin remains unimpressed and tries to bar their way. It is only after a lively trio, 'Marsch, marsch, marsch', that they contrive to outmanoeuvre him and enter the palace.

Act II. Osmin is no match for Blonde in a battle of wits, as she demonstrates in her aria, 'Durch Zärtlichkeit und Schmeicheln', and the duet which follows. He knows she will come off best and can do no more than complain at the folly of the English in allowing their women so much liberty. Constanze unburdens herself to Blonde: 'Traurigkeit ward mir zum Lose'.

It is perhaps the most deeply felt number of the score, and one of Mozart's most sublime expressions of grief (like Pamina's 'Ach, ich fühl's', in the key of G minor). Blonde retires as the Pasha comes once more to urge his suit. Constanze is adamant and launches into one of the most considerable arias Mozart ever wrote for soprano voice: 'Martern aller Arten'. Laid

out on concerto lines with four solo instruments and a lengthy orchestral introduction, it is the one moment in the opera where Mozart definitely sacrifices the stage situation – the Pasha and Constanze can do little more than glare at each other during the introduction – to the possibilities inherent in his singers, of whom Caterina Cavalieri, the Constanze, was perhaps the most eminent. But the aria that results is musically so considerable that few people will grumble at the large scale of the composer's inspiration.

Blonde is wondering if the entreaties of the Pasha have at last been successful when Pedrillo rushes in to tell her that Belmonte is here and a plan afoot for their escape. Osmin is to be drugged to make way for the double elopement. Blonde's joyful song, 'Welche Wonne, welche Lust', contrasts with Pedrillo's definitely nervous reaction to the prospect of dealing with Osmin single-handed ('Frisch zum Kampfe'). However, he tackles as to the manner born the business of persuading Osmin that the Muslim doctrine of teetotalism is better honoured in the breach than the observance, and he soon has him tippling with the best and praising wine in one of Mozart's most exquisite inspirations, the duet 'Vivat Bacchus'. Osmin sinks into a stupor and Pedrillo is able to drag him out of the way and leave the coast clear for a reunion between Belmonte and Constanze. Belmonte in his aria, 'Wenn der Freude Thränen fliessen', is less passionate than Constanze as she begins the quartet which is to end the act. It is a noble piece in spite of the crisis which is contrived to keep drama alive – the men ask to be assured again that their lovers were true during captivity – and the musical integrity is unaffected by the dramatic artifice.

Act III. With much comic pantomime, Pedrillo organises the disposal of the ladders with the help of the captain of the ship which is to take them to freedom. Belmonte enters and is instructed to sing so that no one will notice that he, Pedrillo, is not serenading his Blonde as usual ('Ich baue ganz auf deine Stärke'). A moment later, Pedrillo is back, and ready to give the signal for escape with his enchanting serenade 'Im Mohrenland gefangen war'. Belmonte and Constanze disappear into the darkness, and Pedrillo rushes up the ladder to fetch his Blonde, unaware that his singing has woken up a guard, a mute, who suspects the worst and dashes off to summon Osmin. The latter arrives as the second pair of lovers is on the point of leaving the house, and his suspicions that a double elopement has been planned are confirmed when Constanze and Belmonte are brought back by the guard who has surprised their escape. 'Ha! wie will ich triumphieren' he sings in his joy that at last he is to have the chance of settling a hundred and one old scores with Pedrillo, and several new ones as well with Belmonte. Osmin parades his vengeful notions in an orgy of triumph, touching a top E and sustaining a bottom D in his efforts to give them adequate musical expression.

The Pasha is informed of the intended escape and arrives to question the prisoners. Constanze pleads her love for Belmonte as justification for the attempted escape, and her lover assures the Pasha that his father, a rich Spaniard by the name of Lostados, will pay a high ransom for his freedom. Lostados! exclaims the Pasha: you are the son of my greatest enemy, the man who stole from me my love, my career, and my right to live in my native country. Belmonte and Constanze are face to face with death and perhaps torture, and their extensive duet, 'Welch' ein Geschick', reveals a serious approach to their imminent tragedy. The Pasha comes back, and announces that he scorns to return evil for evil, that they are free to go back to their native Spain whenever they like. The happy couples offer thanks in the form of a *vaudeville*, which Belmonte begins, the others singing a verse each and all joining in the refrain: 'Wer so viel Huld vergessen kann, den seh man mit Verachtung an' (Whoever forgets such kindness should be looked upon with scorn).

Blonde cannot resist a final dig at the discomfited Osmin, whose rage overcomes him so that he disrupts the harmony of the ensemble with another furious outburst before rushing defeated from the scene, leaving the others to finish on a note of suitable gratitude. They take their leave while the chorus sings the praises of the Pasha and his clemency.   H.

DER SCHAUSPIELDIREKTOR

The Impresario

Comedy with music in one act, text by Gottlieb Stephanie the Younger. Première at Schönbrunn Palace, Vienna, 7 February 1786, with Caterina Cavalieri as Mlle Silberklang and Aloysia Lange as Mme Herz, Adamberger (the first Belmonte) as Monsieur Vogelsang, Stephanie as Frank. Cavalieri was the mistress of the composer Salieri, whose *Prima la Musica poi le Parole* was given at the same court festivity; Aloysia Lange was Mozart's sister-in-law and first serious love.

Buff, *a buffo singer* ....Baritone
Monsieur Vogelsang...Tenor
Mme Herz ....Soprano
Mlle Silberklang...Soprano
Frank, *an impresario* ....Spoken Role

There is an *allegro* overture. Frank, with Buff's assistance, is lining up a theatrical company for Salzburg. He has no problem over engaging a couple of actresses but the singers who audition for him are quite another story. The first, Mme Herz, lives up to her name and chooses a pathetic aria, economically going no higher than top D. The second, Silberklang, sings a rousing rondo, contenting herself with a somewhat lower *tessitura* but hardly less brilliance. Each selection needless to say aims to emphasise each singer's strongest points.

There ensues a hilarious trio in which, after protestations of 'Ich bin die erste Sängerin!', one rival soprano advocates '*Adagio!*' followed by a high E and F, the other insists on '*allegro, allegrissimo*' and follows with Cs and then a D, the tenor trying to persuade each of the ladies to accept an accommodation. Eventually, after threats and then promises of large salaries, it all ends with a quartet, and, on the part of the listener, a strong conviction that either Mozart's two prima donnas had a stronger sense of humour in real life than tradition allows, or else he was a remarkable diplomat.   H.

LE NOZZE DI FIGARO

The Marriage of Figaro

Opera buffa in four acts, text by Lorenzo da Ponte after Beaumarchais. First performed at the Burgtheater, Vienna, 1 May 1786, with Laschi (Countess), Storace (Susanna), Bussani (Cherubino), Gottlieb (Barbarina), Mandini (Marcellina), Mandini (Count Almaviva), Benucci (Figaro), Kelly (Basilio and Curzio), Bussani (Bartolo and Antonio), and directed by Mozart. First performed in England (in Italian) at Haymarket Theatre, London, 1812, and (in English) Covent Garden, 1819. First performance in New York, 1824. Revived at Old Vic Theatre, London (Edward Dent's translation), 1920; first performed at Glyndebourne Festival in 1934, conducted by Fritz Busch, produced by Carl Ebert, and with Aulikki Rautawaara, Audrey Mildmay, Luise Helletsgruber, Willi Domgraf-Fassbänder, Roy Henderson, Norman Allin.

Count Almaviva..Baritone
Figaro, *his valet*..Baritone
Doctor Bartolo ....Bass
Don Basilio, *a music-master*............................Tenor
Cherubino, *a page*...Soprano
Antonio, *a gardener* ....Bass
Don Curzio, *counsellor at law* ....Tenor
Countess Almaviva ....Soprano
Susanna, *her maid, engaged to Figaro* ....Soprano
Marcellina, *a duenna* ....Soprano
Barbarina, *Antonio's niece*............................Soprano

Place: The Count's Château of Aguas Frescas, near
   Seville
Time: Eighteenth Century
Running Time: 3 hours 20 minutes

Figaro was Mozart's first venture with his most famous librettist, Lorenzo da Ponte (who incidentally provided the libretti for no fewer than four operas which had their first performance during 1786, the year of *Figaro*'s début). Although he had had no Italian comic opera produced since *La Finta Giardiniera* in 1775, Mozart had in the meanwhile worked on *L'Oca del Cairo* and *Lo Sposo Deluso*, each of which he abandoned. He had also composed the music for *Der Schauspieldirektor*, a slight piece but sufficient evidence of the continuing development of his theatrical and musical craftsmanship. It is surprising in retrospect to note that, in spite of the brilliant libretto and even more brilliant music, *Figaro* made only a moderate success when it was produced in Vienna, where it had to wait until the triumph in Prague before being received into popular affection. It was incidentally the success of *Figaro* in Prague which led to the commission to compose *Don Giovanni* for that city.

Act I. Nothing could make a better prelude to this marriage day of feverish activity than the short *presto* overture. When the curtain rises, Susanna is discovered before the looking-glass. Figaro is measuring out a space on the floor ('Cinque, dieci'). The room, Figaro explains, is to be theirs – 'the most convenient room in the castle, just between milord and milady'.[1] (Not all stage designers have been prepared to admit that, in eighteenth-century castle geography, this is likely to have been a box room or a curtained-off portion of a passage, not a grand room with a veranda and a view of the park.) Susanna astounds him by peremptorily refusing to accept it, but, when he remonstrates ('Se a caso Madama'), explains that while the position may make it easy for her to go to the Countess, it also makes it easy for the Count to get to her. The Countess rings, and Figaro is left alone to contemplate a situation that is by no means to his liking. In the two movements of his duet with Susanna, the mood has been one of light-heartedness, which is hardly interrupted by the hint of intrigue, as Susanna is obviously unperturbed by a situation she feels herself quite capable of dealing with. But 'Se vuol ballare' shows Figaro in a state of mind in which determination to make the Count dance to his tune cannot altogether eliminate apprehension.

No sooner has he left the room than we are shown another aspect of the worry which is to plague him on his wedding-day. Marcellina comes in with Don Bartolo, the pair of them hatching a plot which will compel Figaro to marry Marcellina as he has defaulted on a debt he owes her. He, Doctor Bartolo, with his legal knowledge will ensure that there is no escape for the rascal ('La vendetta') – a splendid example of what such an aria for *basso buffo* can become in the hands of a composer of genius. As he goes out of one door, Susanna enters by another and she and Marcellina meet as they attempt to follow Bartolo; their duet as each offers the other precedence ends in Marcellina's complete discomfiture. Susanna stays behind and is immediately confronted with a disconsolate Cherubino, who wants to enlist her help in getting the Count to reinstate him as the Countess's page. No one takes him seriously except himself. He is at the wrong age: young enough to be allowed liberties, old enough to take advantage of them (as has happened over his latest exploit with Barbarina, for which he has been dismissed) in a way that cannot be tolerated. He is in love with every woman he comes across, and pours out his adolescent aspirations to Susanna in an aria, 'Non sò più cosa son, cosa faccio'.

No sooner has he finished than voices are heard outside and he has only just time to conceal himself before the Count comes into Susanna's room and starts to protest his affections. It is not her lucky day, as the Count is followed a moment or two later by Basilio; in the scramble for concealment, Cherubino

---

[1] Edward Dent's translation.

Le nozze di Figaro *(The Marriage of Figaro/Figaro's Wedding; English National Opera, 1991, director Graham Vick, designer Richard Hudson). Bryn Terfel as Figaro.*

nips into the chair behind which the Count takes refuge. Basilio teases Susanna with gossip about Cherubino and when she will not listen, presses her about the page and the Countess – an intrigue which he says everyone is talking about. The Count can tolerate the situation no longer and emerges from his hiding-place to demand that the gossip-mongers shall be found and punished. In the ensuing trio – since

'Non sò più cosa son' the action has been carried on in recitative – Susanna faints, but revives in time to plead the cause of the unhappy Cherubino, a mere boy she says. Not so young as you think, says the Count, and describes how he caught him the previous day hiding in Barbarina's room. Suiting the action to the word, he draws the cover from the chair – and there is Cherubino again. Only Cherubino's admission that he had heard what passed between the Count and Susanna ('I did all I could *not* to hear, my lord') stays the penalty that he would otherwise incur.

Led by Figaro, a band of locals comes in to sing the Count's praises, and, at its end, the Count yields to the general entreaties, but only to the extent of giving Cherubino a commission in his Regiment, for which he must leave immediately. Figaro speeds him on his way with a spirited description of what his future life has in store for him. Michael Kelly, the Irish tenor who was the Basilio and Curzio in the original production, tells in his memoirs of the splendid sonority with which Benucci, the Figaro, sang the martial air 'Non più andrai' at the first orchestral rehearsal. Mozart, who was on the stage in a crimson pelisse and cocked hat trimmed with gold lace, kept repeating 'Bravo, bravo, Benucci!' It makes a stirring finale to an act.

Act II. We are introduced to the Countess in a soliloquy, 'Porgi amor', in which we are made aware of her intense longing for her husband's love, and also of the reticence which her breeding makes natural to her. Susanna expounds her own view of the situation and opens the door to Figaro. His plan is that the Count shall be given an assignation with Susanna, whose place shall be taken by Cherubino, and that at the same time he shall be told in an anonymous letter that the Countess in her turn has made a rendezvous with an unknown man. Cherubino comes in to see if he can be dressed for the part, but first sings the song he has just composed, 'Voi che sapete'. Not only has Mozart got round the difficulty of introducing a song ('words and music by Cherubino') into a milieu where singing is the natural means of expression, but he has done so in such a way that this piece has become one of the world's most popular tunes. Cherubino tries on the dress to the accompaniment of a song with action, Susanna's 'Venite inginocchiatevi'. No sooner is it ended and Cherubino safely buttoned up than a knock is heard at the door. It is the Count.

Consternation! Cherubino dashes into the Countess's dressing-room and Susanna hides behind a curtain. The Count is suspicious of his wife's all too obvious nervousness, and suspicion that something is being hidden from him becomes certainty when he hears a noise and finds the dressing-room door locked ('Susanna, or via sortite'). He takes his wife with him as he goes off to get tools to break it down with. While he is away Cherubino slips out of hiding and jumps from the window, leaving Susanna to take his place. The little *allegro assai* duet for Susanna and Cherubino is a comedy interlude of the greatest dexterity amidst the ranting and raging of the Count, which redoubles in fury when the Countess tries to explain that Cherubino is in her room without much on because he was being fitted for a charade.

The great finale is begun by the Count to all intents and purposes in a towering passion: 'Esci omai, garzon malnato'. The Countess's pleading seems to be in vain, but both are struck dumb when, at the height of the storm, Susanna emerges coolly from the inner room. The Count rushes in to see if Cherubino is not still there, but, finding he is not, can do nothing but plead for pardon. With Susanna's aid, this is obtained, but with it the Count's suspicions begin to take hold again. The anonymous letter? Written by Figaro, delivered by Basilio. He thinks he has found someone he can safely be angry with, but is told he must forgive everyone if he himself is to be forgiven for his jealousy. There is a moment of peace and relaxation which ends as Figaro bounds in to summon his master and mistress to the wedding dance which is about to begin. But the Count sees a chance of getting his own back and questions Figaro about the anonymous letter. In spite of hints from the Countess and Susanna, Figaro denies all knowledge of it, and has almost turned the Count's suspicions when Antonio, the gardener, bumbles in, protesting that his life is a perpetual trial but that today they have thrown a man out of the window on to his flowerbeds, and that is the last straw. Figaro says that it was he who jumped out, but Antonio thinks it looked more like the page. Figaro sticks to his story until the Count catechises him about a paper Antonio says was dropped near the flowerbed. Figaro searches his pockets and racks his brains, but in the nick of time the Countess recognises it and whispers that it is the page's commission. Why was it left? Again, it is only just in time that the Countess remem-

bers that it had not been sealed. Figaro's triumph is short-lived, as Marcellina comes in, supported by Bartolo and Basilio, to lodge formal complaint before the Count against Figaro for breach of promise. The act comes to an end in pandemonium.

The finale is one of the greatest single movements in all Mozart's operas. For variety of motive, tempo, and texture it is unrivalled; the characterisation is consistent and credible and at no time subordinated to more general musical needs; the level of invention is extremely high; and the whole thing is carried out with resources that make use of the nine principals but involve no chorus or scenic display. It is a marvel of ingenuity, and at the same time a model of simplicity.

Act III. The Count has not yet given up hope of Susanna, and when she comes to borrow smelling salts for her mistress he seems within reach of his prize. She agrees to meet him that night in the garden. Their duet, 'Crudel, perchè finora', reveals the Count as an ardent lover, Susanna as an inattentive beloved, but the result is a masterpiece. As Susanna leaves the room, she meets Figaro and assures him, just a little too loudly, that he is sure now of winning his case against Marcellina. Sure of winning his case? repeats the Count, and launches into a superb recitative and aria, 'Vedrò mentr'io sospiro, felice un servo mio?' (Must I forgo my pleasure, whilst serf of mine rejoices?). Edward Dent has observed that the Count, a man of intense energy, is shown first of all in ensemble, only later in aria, because, one might almost say, he has no time to sing an aria until the moment when he has to take stock of his position. It is an extraordinary piece of self-revelation when it does come, and takes the Count right out of the category of the unsuccessful lover and erring husband into something much more potent. But the balance is redressed when it is discovered, after he has given judgement for Marcellina, that that lady is in fact none other than Figaro's mother. In the great ensemble which follows, the Count is reduced to expressions of impotent fury: what can he do when confronted with this wholly unexpected development? The sextet is one of the most satisfactory instances in all opera of pure comedy purveyed in terms of straight-faced music.

The scene is empty for a moment, and the Countess comes in to sing the most extended and most moving of her utterances in the opera. 'Dove sono' consists of a lengthy recitative followed by a highly expressive aria in two sections, *andantino* and *allegro*. It is her moment of highest self-revelation, just as his aria was the Count's; if his thoughts were of revenge that his desires are not to be satisfied, hers are of the love he once bore her but which she seems to have lost. His aria grew out of the situation created by his duet with Susanna, the Countess's gives audible expression to a situation which can only be resolved with Susanna's aid and therefore leads to a duet between the two. They arrange where Susanna is to meet the Count that evening. The letter duet, 'Che soave zeffiretto', is one of the famous numbers of the score; the mistress dictates a letter to the Count, the maid takes it down, and the voices of both blend as they read it back together.

But the wedding festivities are about to begin and a crowd of village girls presents flowers to the Countess, who is astonished a moment later, when the Count comes in with Antonio, to see one of them unmasked as Cherubino. A tense situation is saved by Barbarina: 'My lord, when you kiss me and tell me you love me, you often say you will give me whatever I want. Give me Cherubino for a husband!' Figaro announces the beginning of the wedding march, the so-called Fandango, the one Spanish element in the score. Like the march in *Idomeneo* and the minuet in *Don Giovanni* it begins as it were in the middle, and returns to what should properly be the opening section later on. There is a chorus in praise of the generosity and right-mindedness of the Count in having abolished the *droit de seigneur*, and the happy couples – Bartolo and Marcellina as well as Figaro and Susanna – receive their wedding wreaths from the Count and Countess, Susanna taking the opportunity to give the Count the letter she and her mistress have concocted for him. He opens it, pricking his finger on the pin – a comedy which is watched all unknowingly by Figaro and commented on with some relish. The Count announces general festivity – song, dance, feasting, and fireworks – and the act ends with a repetition of the chorus in his honour.

Act IV. The last act is devoted to clearing up the various situations which have arisen in the course of Figaro's wedding day, but there is one more complication to be added before the process begins. The atmosphere is more highly charged perhaps than can be put down to the fact that it is night by the time the act begins. The action takes place in a part of the garden which contains arbours and sheltered walks. Barbarina begins it with a little half-finished cavatina; she has been given the pin which sealed the letter to return to Susanna, but has lost it. She tells the story to Figaro, who comes in with Marcellina and is overcome with distress at this apparent indication of his wife's unfaithfulness.

Arias for Marcellina and Basilio occur at this point, but both are often omitted. Before Basilio's, Figaro watches Barbarina hide in one of the arbours (where she is to meet Cherubino), and tells Bartolo and Basilio that they should stay near at hand to witness the seduction of his wife by the Count. Now occurs Figaro's recitative and aria, 'Tutto è disposto' and 'Aprite un po' quegli occhi', at the same time his most serious moment (the recitative is tragic in the extreme) and his most comic (the horns at the end are surely intended to be illustrative as well as musical). Susanna asks the Countess (they have by now changed clothes) to be allowed to walk a little apart from her, and sings an aria of exquisite sensibility, ostensibly to the lover she is waiting for, but in reality knowing full well that Figaro is listening to her, 'Deh vieni non tardar'.

The comedy of mistaken identity begins. Cherubino attempts to flirt with what he thinks is Susanna, in reality of course the Countess. Susanna, the Count, and Figaro observe, and the Count interrupts and starts to make love on his own account to his wife in disguise. Figaro does not know about the change of clothes and it is his turn to interrupt; with the stage empty he invokes the gods to avenge his honour. Susanna (still disguised as the Countess) calls to him and he starts to tell her of the Count's escapade when he recognises that it is in fact Susanna he is talking to. The dramatic tension which may lead to tragedy is shattered, and we are once more safely in comedy. Figaro makes love to her as if she were the Countess, and then laughs at her attempt to disguise herself from him as much as at her indignation. All is forgiven – Susanna does not mind the joke against herself – and the two combine to make the Count think their extravagant love-making is in reality that of mistress and valet. The ruse succeeds, the Count summons anyone within hearing to bear witness to the unfaithfulness of his wife, and in succession hauls Cherubino, Barbarina, Marcellina, and the supposed culprit from the arbour in which they have taken refuge. All pleading is in vain, until the voice of the Countess herself is heard behind them all: 'Almeno io per loro perdono otterrò?' (May I then for pardon at last intercede?). The dramatic suddenness of her entry combines with the Count's noble phrase of contrition to make this a moment that can be set beside that of the emergence of Susanna from the Countess's room in Act II. The Count begs forgiveness in a swelling phrase, receives it, and the opera ends in general rejoicing, voiced though by the principals alone and unsupported by the chorus.

Le Nozze di Figaro is an incomparable masterpiece, one moreover that has been praised throughout its history for a variety of reasons. If it was once the brilliant tunes of the solo songs which attracted audience and performers alike, it would probably nowadays be claimed that the ensembles are the main glories of the work. Nothing, one is inclined to think, could be more perfect than the finale to the second act. Maybe it cannot, but in the last act Mozart has achieved something almost more remarkable in the feeling of anxiety which pervades music and situation alike. It is as though the tapestry of the comedy has been reversed and, instead of dazzling with its brilliance, it is shot through with flashes of light in the darkness; it is not so much that the garden has a thundercloud hanging over it, but that there is lightning in the air. I know I always have something akin to a feeling of relief when Figaro's little B flat tune arrives to prove that once again we have come through the web of intrigue to the safety and resolution beyond it. At no time does the opera break the bounds of comedy, even in this last act, except in so far as Mozart here, as in *Don Giovanni*, appears to acknowledge no bounds where comedy is concerned.   H.

DON GIOVANNI

Opera in two acts, text by Lorenzo da Ponte. First performed at the National Theatre, Prague, 29 October 1787, with Teresa Saporiti, Micelli, Bondini, Luigi Bassi as Don Giovanni, Ponziani, Baglioni, Lolli. In Vienna, 1788, with Aloysia Lange as Donna Anna, Cavalieri, Mombelli, Francesco Albertarelli as Don Giovanni, Morella and Benucci. English première in London, Her Majesty's Theatre, 12 April 1817. Given at Covent Garden (in English) on 30 May 1817, and for the first time in America (as *The Libertine*) in Philadelphia in 1818. Presented at the Park Theatre, New York, in 1826 with da Ponte present, Manuel Garcia senior as Don Giovanni, Manuel

Garcia junior as Leporello, Mme Garcia as Donna Elvira, and Signorina Maria Garcia (afterwards the famous Malibran) as Zerlina. Later revivals: Covent Garden, 1926, conducted by Bruno Walter, and with Frida Leider, Lotte Lehmann, Elisabeth Schumann, Mariano Stabile, Fritz Krauss, and Aquistapace in the cast; 1939 in the same theatre with Elisabeth Rethberg, Hilde Konetzni, Mafalda Favero, Ezio Pinza, Richard Tauber, Virgilio Lazzari and conducted by Sir Thomas Beecham. First performance at Glyndebourne, 1936, when Ina Souez, Luise Helletsgruber, Audrey Mildmay, John Brownlee, Koloman von Pataky, Salvatore Baccaloni were conducted by Fritz Busch.

Faure and Maurel were great Don Giovannis, Jean de Reszke sang the role while he was still a baritone, and Scotti made his debut at the Metropolitan in it. Lablache was accounted the greatest of Leporellos, but earlier in his career he had sung Don Giovanni. The role of Don Ottavio has been sung by Rubini, Mario, John McCormack, Schipa and Simoneau; Lilli Lehmann and Welitsch have been renowned in the role of Donna Anna; and Zerlina has been sung by aspiring *prime donne* from Adelina Patti and Geraldine Farrar to Irmgard Seefried and Mirella Freni.

The Commendatore ....Bass
Donna Anna, *his daughter* ....Soprano
Don Ottavio, *her betrothed*.................................Tenor
Don Giovanni, *a young and
      licentious nobleman* ....Baritone
Leporello, *his servant* ....Bass
Donna Elvira, *a lady of Burgos*.......................Soprano
Zerlina, *a country girl* ....Soprano
Masetto, *betrothed to Zerlina* ....Baritone

Place: Seville
Time: Seventeenth Century
Running Time: 2 hours 55 minutes

It has been asserted that Don Juan Tenorio was a historical personage, but there is little evidence to support this view. His first recorded appearance in literature is in the play *El Burlador de Sevilla* written by Tirso de Molina (1571–1641). Molière's *Le Festin de Pierre* (1665) has little to do with the Spanish play, but introduces an important character, Donna Elvira; Shadwell's *The Libertine* appeared in England in 1676, by which time the story is described as 'famous all over Spain, Italy and France'; Goldoni in 1736 wrote a verse-play, *Don Giovanni Tenorio o sia il Dissoluto*; but it was in 1787 that there appeared the most important of the various sources from which da Ponte's libretto derives. This was Bertati's libretto with music by Giuseppe Gazzaniga. Da Ponte, Edward Dent suggests, may even have proposed the subject to Mozart knowing that he had a convenient source to hand, and certainly he drew copiously on

Bertati's book for his own libretto, which remains one of his best.

It was the huge success of *Figaro* in Prague which brought Mozart a commission to write an opera for the second city of the Austrian Empire.

Don Giovanni no doubt owed some of its initial success to the charismatic and courageous nature of its central figure, part libertine, part blasphemer; some to the speed of its dramatic and musical action, some also to its blend of the comic and the serious. Later twentieth-century opinion, in contrast to the view in the nineteenth century when its popularity was at a peak, has taken a more critical view of the work. Once upon a time, conductors omitted the *envoi* at the opera's end, relying on Mozart's example in Vienna in 1788, and thus reduced emphasis on the comedy on which Mozart and da Ponte had floated their serious commentary on aspects of the human condition – but one could argue that they were forgetting that *dramma giocoso* was after all the description of the work at the head of the score. A true and complete realisation of the opera's possibilities is almost out of reach, has run the modern argument; any performance which satisfies its audience has achieved something against the odds, and to cast it well, conduct it with style, and direct the action with logic is probably not sufficient to guarantee success. The work remains nonetheless a peak of operatic creative achievement and to bring it off satisfactorily an ambition of every conductor and every opera company.

The overture consists of an *andante* introduction which reproduces the scene of the banquet at which the statue appears, followed by an *allegro* which characterises the impetuous, pleasure-seeking Don. Without pause, Mozart links up the overture with the song of Leporello; wrapped in his cloak and seated in the garden of a house in Seville, which Don Giovanni on amorous adventure bent has entered secretly during the night, he is complaining of the fate which makes him a servant to such a restless and dangerous master. 'Notte e giorno faticar' runs his song; the music, like all that Leporello subsequently sings, is in the Italian *buffo* tradition, differing in degree of expressiveness but not in kind of expression from that of other contemporary *buffo* creations. Don Giovanni hurriedly issues from the house, pursued by Donna Anna. There follows a trio in which the wrath of the insulted woman, the

annoyance of the libertine, and the comments of the watching Leporello are expressed simultaneously. The Commendatore hears the noise, finds his daughter struggling with an unknown man, and draws his sword. In spite of the protests of Don Giovanni, who is reluctant to fight so old an opponent, a duel ensues and in it the Commendatore receives a mortal wound. The trio which follows between Don Giovanni, the dying Commendatore, and Leporello is a unique passage in the history of musical art. The genius of Mozart, tender, profound, pathetic, is revealed in its entirety. Written in a solemn rhythm and in the key of F minor, this trio, which fills only eighteen measures, contains in a restricted outline but in master strokes the seeds of the serious side of the drama, just as the recitative which follows – Don Giovanni makes light of the whole affair – re-establishes the opera on a basis of comedy, only to return to seriousness with Anna's grief over the body of her father. In a duet Don Ottavio, her fiancé, tries to comfort her and swears to avenge the dead man.

The scene changes and Don Giovanni and Leporello are on the prowl again; they perceive a woman – or rather, Don Giovanni does – who appears to be inveighing against a lost lover. It is Donna Elvira, whom they do not recognise as yet, but who has been another of the Don's victims. There are in the tears of this woman not only the grief of one who has been loved and now implores heaven for comfort, but also the indignation of one who has been deserted and betrayed. When she cries with emotion 'Ah, chi mi dice mai quel barbaro dov'è?' one feels that in spite of her anger, she is ready to forgive, if only a regretful smile shall recall her to the man who was able to charm her. The character of her music is seen straight away in this aria. It is more pliable than Donna Anna's, but perhaps it is the persistent nature it seems to reveal that makes Don Giovanni run quite so fast from her.

As she finishes her outburst, she turns to find that the stranger who is attempting to console her is none other than Don Giovanni himself. Leaving Leporello to explain the reasons why he deserted her, Don Giovanni makes his escape, and Elvira is obliged to listen while the servant runs through a catalogue – grossly exaggerated we may be sure – of his master's conquests. 'Madamina' is a perfect passage of its kind and one of the most famous arias in the repertory of the *basso buffo*. It is an exquisite mixture of grace and finish, of irony and sentiment, of comic declamation and melody, the whole enhanced by the poetry and skill of the accessories. Every word is illustrated by the composer's imagination without his many brilliant sallies injuring the general effect. According to Leporello's catalogue, his master's adventures in love have numbered 2,065: 640 in Italy, 231 in Germany, 100 in France, 91 in Turkey, and in Spain no less than 1,003. All sorts and conditions of women have contributed to this formidable total, and it is small wonder that Elvira leaves the stage vowing vengeance upon her betrayer.

The scene changes to the countryside near Don Giovanni's palace not far from Seville. A troop of happy peasants is seen approaching. The young and pretty Zerlina with Masetto, her fiancé, and their friends are singing and dancing in honour of their approaching marriage. Don Giovanni and Leporello join this gathering of light-hearted and simple young people. Having cast covetous eyes upon Zerlina and having aroused her vanity and her spirit of coquetry by polished words of gallantry, the Don orders Leporello to get rid of the jealous Masetto by taking the entire gathering – except, of course, Zerlina – to his palace. Leporello complies, but Masetto, while submitting to be removed, makes it clear to Don Giovanni – and to Zerlina as well – that he is not the fool he may look. This aria, 'Ho capito, Signor, si', shows Masetto as an embryo Figaro, duller of wit and in miniature, but a budding revolutionary nonetheless. Don Giovanni, left alone with Zerlina, sings a duet with her which is one of the gems not alone of this opera but of opera in general. 'Là ci darem la mano' (You'll give me your hand) provides ample musical evidence, which is later supported by the Serenade, that though the Don may be unsuccessful in each of the love affairs on which he embarks during the course of the opera, his reputation is still well deserved.

As they are going off arm in arm, Donna Elvira reappears and by her denunciation of Don Giovanni's treachery – 'Ah, fuggi il traditor!' – makes clear to Zerlina that there can be two opinions concerning the character of her fascinating admirer. She takes Zerlina

with her as Donna Anna and Don Ottavio come on to the stage, but no sooner is Don Giovanni in conversation with the two than Elvira is back again on the scene – a true comedy stroke. In a quartet, she again denounces Don Giovanni as a heartless deceiver, while he for his part says that she is mad; Anna and Ottavio are at a loss to know which to believe. Elvira goes out, followed a moment later by Don Giovanni, but in the few sentences he speaks Donna Anna recognises the voice of her father's assassin and her own betrayer. Her narrative of the events of that night is a declamatory recitative 'in style as bold and as tragic as the finest recitatives of Gluck'. The aria which follows, 'Or sai chi l'onore' (Now you know who tried to take my honour), is no less grandiose, and its implacable vengefulness (and implacable *tessitura*) presents a problem for the singer entrusted with the role of Donna Anna. Never elsewhere perhaps did Mozart write music for the soprano voice which is so extremely heavy and taxing.

It is usually after this aria – where it can hardly fail to come as an anti-climax – that Ottavio's interpolated aria 'Dalla sua pace' is sung.[1] This is followed by the Don's exuberant 'Fin ch' han dal vino' which demands a baritone with an immaculate technique and sufficient musical sense to sing it as part of the opera and not just as a sample of his vocal dexterity.

Outside Don Giovanni's palace, Masetto reproaches Zerlina for her flirtation, but she begs his forgiveness in an ingratiating air, 'Batti, batti, o bel Masetto'. This has always been one of the most popular moments in the opera, and it is true that in the quicker 6/8 section you can almost hear Zerlina twiddling her unfortunate admirer round her little finger. But, the aria ended, Masetto's suspicions return when she seems distinctly nervous at the sound of the Don's voice in the distance.

Now begins the finale, one of the great masterpieces of dramatic music. From a hiding place Masetto hears Don Giovanni order his retainers to spare no pains to make the evening a success, and he is able to confront Zerlina and Don Giovanni as the latter attempts to lead her off into an alcove. The situation is well within the Don's compass; he chides Masetto for leaving his bride-to-be alone, and takes

---

[1] Written for the Vienna première of the opera, when the tenor preferred not to sing 'Il mio tesoro', in place of which Mozart introduced the duet for Zerlina and Leporello referred to on page 514 in which she threatens to castrate him with a razor.

them both into the house where the dancing is about to begin. Elvira, Anna, and Ottavio appear, all of them masked. Leporello opens a window to let the fresh evening air into the palace and the violins of a small orchestra within can be heard in the middle of a graceful minuet. He sees the three maskers, and in accordance with tradition, they are bidden to enter. After a moment of hesitation, they decide to accept the invitation, and to carry out their undertaking at all cost and to whatever end. Before entering, they pause on the threshold and, their souls moved by a holy fear, they address heaven in one of the most remarkable prayers written by the hand of man:

Inside the ballroom, the festivities are in full swing. Don Giovanni and Leporello manoeuvre to keep Masetto from Zerlina, but there is a diversion at the entry of the unknown maskers, who are welcomed by Don Giovanni. The dancing begins with the minuet we have already heard. Its graceful rhythm is prolonged indefinitely as a fundamental idea, while in succession two small orchestras on the stage take up, one a rustic quadrille, the other a waltz. Only the ladies and gentlemen engage in the minuet, the peasants in the quadrille; and before Don Giovanni leads off Zerlina into an adjoining room he should have taken part with her in this dance, while Leporello seeks to divert the jealous Masetto's attention by seizing him in an apparent exuberance of spirits and insisting on dancing the waltz with him.

Masetto's suspicions, however, are not without justification. He breaks away from Leporello, who hurries to warn his master. But just as he has passed through the door, Zerlina's piercing shriek for help is heard from within. Don Giovanni rushes out, sword in hand, dragging with him none other than the luckless Leporello, whom he has opportunely seized in the entrance, and whom, under the pretext that he is the guilty party, he threatens to kill. But this ruse fails to

deceive anyone. Anna, Elvira, and Ottavio unmask and accuse Don Giovanni of the murder of the Commendatore: 'Tutto, tutto già si sa'. Taken aback at first, Don Giovanni soon recovers himself. Turning at bay, he defies the threatening crowd. A storm sweeps over the orchestra. Thunder growls in the basses, lightning plays on the fiddles. Don Giovanni, cool and intrepid, dashes through the crowd, which falls back in front of him, and makes his escape.

Act II. A street, with Donna Elvira's house in the background. The beginning of Act II furnishes proof – and proof *is* needed – that *Don Giovanni* is the *dramma giocoso* of its title. The duet with which it opens, 'Eh via, buffone', is in purest *buffo* style, and it is followed by a trio for Elvira, Don Giovanni, and Leporello which points the moral even more sharply. Donna Elvira, leaning sadly on her balcony, gives voice to her melancholy regrets in a tune of exquisite beauty. In spite of the scene which she has recently witnessed, in spite of the wrongs she herself has endured, she cannot hate Don Giovanni or efface his image from her heart. Her reward is that her recreant lover changes clothes with his servant in the darkness below, and, while Leporello disguised as the Don attracts Donna Elvira into the garden, the Don himself mocks her with exaggerated protestations of love, which she takes at their face value. If the scene is to be taken seriously – and the music of 'Ah, taci, ingiusto core' is of a quality to support such an attitude – the way in which sport is made of her pathetic faithfulness would indicate a revolting callousness on the part not only of the man who has loved and left her, but of the composer as well; but if it can be approached by the audience in a spirit of frivolity, of *opera buffa*, this callousness is less in evidence.

Elvira descends, and Don Giovanni sings, to his own mandolin accompaniment (too often played *pizzicato* on a violin), a serenade to Elvira's maid, to whom he has taken a fancy. 'Deh, vieni alla finestra' is one of the most famous numbers of the opera, partly perhaps because of the stress laid on its performance by eminent singers of the title role. Don Giovanni thinks he sees the object of his affections, but, before he can follow up his advantage, round the corner comes Masetto with a band of peasants bent on finding and murdering no less a person than Don Giovanni. They think they are addressing Leporello, and the disguised Don divides them up into parties and sends them off to the four points of the compass in an effective aria, 'Metà di voi qua vadano'. Masetto the ringleader he keeps with him and, having ascertained exactly what weapons he has brought, proceeds to give him a good drubbing and leaves him groaning on the ground. Zerlina, while by no means indifferent to the attentions of the dashing Don, is at heart faithful to Masetto and she comes tripping round the corner when she hears his cries and consoles the poor fellow with the graceful measures of 'Vedrai, carino, se sei buonino'.

The scene changes to the courtyard of a palace in which Elvira and Leporello take refuge. It turns out to be Donna Anna's, and she is on the point of returning home, escorted by the inevitable Don Ottavio and a band of servants bearing torches. Elvira and Leporello make for the doorway, but are intercepted by Masetto and Zerlina, who are lurking in it. Everyone takes Leporello for his master and demands his death, demands they seem rather reluctant to withdraw when they find out that it is the servant they have caught after all.

The sextet is a fine ensemble, with its variety of action and of musical sections. It is plainly intended, says Edward Dent, as the finale of an act, not as a movement in the middle of one.[1] 'It was you then who beat Masetto?' asks Zerlina; 'You who so deceived me?' continues Elvira. 'Spare me, spare my life, I pray',[2] counters Leporello in an aria which dies away while he holds their attention as he creeps to the door and disappears.

Now comes Don Ottavio's famous aria, the solo number which makes the role coveted by tenors the world over, 'Il mio tesoro intanto'. Upon this air praise has been exhausted. It has been called the 'pietra di paragone' of tenors – the touchstone, the supreme test of classical song. In spite of its rather obscure dramatic value, its musical beauty is as undeniable as its difficulty of execution. At this point, it is customary to insert the superb recitative and aria for Elvira, which Mozart composed for Caterina Cavalieri, who sang the role at the Viennese première. She had complained to Mozart that the Viennese public did not appreciate her as did audiences of other cities and begged him for something which would give her voice full scope. The result was 'Mi tradì quell'alma ingrata'. Again its dramatic justification is slight, but in it Elvira rises to her full height.

After the escapade of the serenade and the beating of Masetto, the Don makes off and chances to meet in the churchyard – which he reaches after some other adventure, we may be sure – with none other than Leporello, who for his part is thankful to have got rid of Elvira; Leporello finds it little to his taste that his master's newest conquest has been someone on whom he – Leporello – has made an impression. Don Giovanni is prepared to laugh the whole thing off when he hears a solemn voice, telling him he will cease laughing by morning, which he is not long in tracing to the statue of the Commendatore, whose death is laid at his own door:

Leporello is ordered to invite the statue – 'O vecchio buffonissimo' is Don Giovanni's greeting for him – to supper. This he does in a duet, 'O statua gentilissima', his courage, which fails him at every sentence, being kept at the sticking point by the vigorous encouragement of his master. The statue's utterances in the recitative part of the scene are accompanied by trombones, connected in the opera exclusively with the appearance of the statue and not used, even in the overture, when it is not visible on the stage.

The scene changes once again, this time to a room in Donna Anna's house. Ottavio enters, and she reproaches him when he hints at their forthcoming marriage; at such a time, how could she think of any-

---

[1] This is on the hypothesis that the opera was intended to be in four acts, but was changed to two in the course of rehearsal.

[2] English translations by Edward Dent (O.U.P.).

thing but her murdered father? The scene exists solely to give Anna another aria to sing, and 'Non mi dir', beautiful and famous though it is, contributes little to the dramatic development of the opera. The coloratura section, which is included in the *allegretto* with which the aria ends, was once adversely criticised – amongst other critics, by Berlioz – as having no place in music written for Donna Anna, but we may agree with Edward Dent who says severely that 'Mozart without coloratura is only a very mutilated Mozart'.

The scene changes to Don Giovanni's palace. During the brilliant introduction, he seats himself at table and sings of the pleasures of life. An orchestra (on the stage in many modern performances, but probably not at the première) plays airs from Vicente Martin's *Una Cosa Rara*[1] and Sarti's *I due Litiganti*, and 'Non più andrai' from Mozart's own *Figaro* – the last-named selection greeted by Leporello with the observation that it is a bit old hat. The music is a wonderful picture of the exuberant and devil-may-care nature of Don Giovanni, and is in the brilliant, debonair style which has all along been characteristic of his music, not least the recitative. At this point Elvira enters and begs the man who has betrayed her to mend his ways. Her plea falls on deaf ears. She goes to the door, but her shriek is heard from the corridor and she re-enters to flee the palace by another door. Don Giovanni sends Leporello to find out what has frightened her, but he echoes her scream and babbles that the statue is outside. Seizing a candle and drawing his sword, Don Giovanni boldly goes into the corridor. A moment later, he backs into the room, receding before the statue of the Commendatore. The lights go out. All is dark save for the flame of the candle in Don Giovanni's hand. Slowly, with heavy footsteps that re-echo in the orchestra, the statue enters. It speaks.

'Don Giovanni, you did invite me here to supper, so bid me welcome.' Don Giovanni nonchalantly orders Leporello to serve supper. 'Nay, do not go,' commands the statue. 'They who taste of the food of the angels eat no more the corrupt food of mortals ... Will you come with me to supper?' Don Giovanni accepts and gives his hand to the statue in pledge; it is seized in a grip that is icy cold. 'Think on your sins, repent them' – 'No.' A fiery pit opens. Demons seize him, unrepentant to the end, and drag him down.

The music of the scene is gripping, yet accomplished without other addition than the trombones to the ordinary orchestra of Mozart's day, without straining after effect, without any means save those commonly to his hand.

There is an epilogue in which the characters moralise upon Don Giovanni's end – an important feature of all the plays dealing with the legend. For the Vienna performance of 1788 Mozart cut it out and this was held by the nineteenth century to justify a tragic or at all events a romantic interpretation of the opera; such a view depends on conveniently forgetting the ludicrously comic duet for Leporello and Zerlina which Mozart wrote specially for this same performance and which is still printed at the end of the vocal score though never performed. The comedy device of the moralising finale has been used as recently as Stravinsky's *The Rake's Progress* (page 797), and Alexander Goehr's *Arden Must Die*.

Quite apart from the brilliant speed at which the music of *Don Giovanni* proceeds, quite apart from the juxtaposition of stark tragedy and high comedy in the one work, the opera is distinguished by the fascination attached to its central character. He is a brilliant, irresponsible figure, with a dash of philosophy – sometime, somewhere, in the course of his amours, he will discover the perfect woman, from whose lips he will be able to draw the sweetness of all women. He is a villain with a keen sense of humour; inexcusable in real life, possible only in comedy and represented at the first performance, one should not forget, by a youth no more than twenty-two years old! Leporello is a typical *basso buffo*, except that the quality of the music he has to sing is far higher than customary in this type of role. This is not to say that he is not well characterised, only that there is little new in the conception. At the Viennese première, the singer was Benucci, who had created the role of Figaro there. Ottavio very nearly re-creates the function of the confidant of *opera seria*, so little part does he play in the stage proceedings. The musical side of the role of course is a very different matter; in spite of its difficulty, the part is very much sought after, and not uncommonly a tenor with style and a stage personality astonishes the audience with the positive impression he makes in this basically negative role.

---

[1] Revived at Ledlanet in Scotland in 1967.

More interesting than the lesser figures among the men are the three female members of the cast. Zerlina is often played as if butter would not melt in her mouth, but for the Vienna performance Mozart added the duet for her and Leporello in which she attacks him with a razor but finally, in spite of her threats, contents herself with tying him up. Elvira, though frequently touching in her faithfulness to the memory of the man who has betrayed her (not least in her resolve in the finale that she will finish her days in a convent), is not without a touch of the scold in her make-up. It is perhaps Anna who is the most diversely interpreted of the three female roles. At one extreme, she has been represented as cold and incapable of love, at the other – notably by the German romantic poet E.T.A. Hoffmann – as consumed with passion for Don Giovanni. Einstein finds another solution to the problem: at the rise of the curtain Don Giovanni has in fact succeeded in seducing her, disguised as Don Ottavio. To support this view, he instances the recitative before 'Or sai chi l'onore', Don Giovanni's indifference to Anna (for the same reason as he is indifferent to Elvira), her insistence that Ottavio should revenge her father's murder himself without recourse to the law, and finally her refusal to marry Ottavio until some length of time has elapsed.   K., H.

COSÌ FAN TUTTE
Thus Do All Women

Opera buffa in two acts, text by Lorenzo da Ponte. First performed at the Burgtheater, Vienna, 26 January 1790, with Ferrarese del Bene, Villeneuve (they were also sisters in real life), Dorotea Bussani, Calvesi, Benucci, Signor Bussani. First performed in London, Haymarket Theatre, 1811. Revived by Sir Thomas Beecham at His Majesty's Theatre, London, 1911, with Ruth Vincent, Lena Maitland, Beatrice La Palme, Walter Hyde, Frederic Austin and Lewys James; Metropolitan, New York, 1922, with Florence Easton, Frances Peralta, Lucrezia Bori, George Meader, Giuseppe de Luca, Adamo Didur, conductor Artur Bodanzky; Glyndebourne, 1934, with Ina Souez, Luise Helletsgruber, Irene Eisinger, Heddle Nash, Willi Domgraf-Fassbänder, Vincenzo Bettoni, conductor Fritz Busch. Other revivals include Sadler's Wells, 1944, with Joan Cross, Margaret Ritchie, Rose Hill, Peter Pears, John Hargreaves, and Owen Brannigan, conductor Lawrance Collingwood; Glyndebourne Opera at the Edinburgh Festival, 1948, with Suzanne Danco, Eugenia Zareska, Hilde Güden, Petre Munteanu, Erich Kunz, Mariano Stabile, conductor Vittorio Gui; at Glyndebourne, 1950, with Sena Jurinac, Blanche Thebom, Alda Noni, Richard Lewis, Erich Kunz, Mario Borriello, conductor Fritz Busch; at

Salzburg, 1960, with Schwarzkopf, Ludwig, Sciutti, Kmentt, Prey, Dönch, conductor Böhm. First performance at Covent Garden, 1947, by Vienna State Opera, with Seefried, Höngen, Loose, Dermota, Kunz, Schoeffler, conductor Krips.

Fiordiligi ....Soprano
Dorabella, *her sister* ....Soprano
Ferrando, *Dorabella's fiancé*..............................Tenor
Guglielmo, *engaged to Fiordiligi* ....Bass
Don Alfonso ....Baritone
Despina, *maid to Fiordiligi and Dorabella*.........Soprano

Time: Eighteenth Century
Place: Naples
Running Time: 3 hours 15 minutes

Così fan tutte, ossia La Scuola degli Amanti was written by Mozart to a commission from the Emperor Joseph II; the story is said to have been based on a real-life incident which was the talk of Vienna at the time of its occurrence. Two young officers, confident of the constancy of the sisters to whom they are engaged, enter on a bet with an old bachelor friend of theirs, who maintains that a woman's memory is shorter than they think. At his direction, they put on disguises, and start to pay court to each other's fiancée, having already taken the precaution of securing the aid of Despina, maid to the two sisters. The sisters succumb to their wooing, but at the wedding party the two young men disappear to emerge a moment later in their uniforms and confront the inconstant sisters with their original lovers.

Mozart was at the very summit of his creative powers, and anyone who knows the opera cannot help being surprised at the nineteenth-century suggestion that he in any way disliked the plot he was to use. The truth is inescapable: in *Così fan tutte* Mozart surpassed even himself in the richness and variety of his invention, in the impeccable skill with which the slender drama is adorned with music, in the creation of beauty. The idea is as light as a feather, and yet the music which clothes it suggests not only the comedy which is on the surface and which remains the most important part of the opera, but also the heartbreak which is behind the joke that goes too far and constantly takes a serious turn. All the odder then that various attempts were made in the nineteenth century and later to provide the music with a new libretto, all of them short-lived – and small wonder in view of the quality of the original, which, as Edward

Dent has emphasised, cannot be judged from a summary but must be seen in all its details.

The short overture has eight bars of slow introduction before the theme of the title is enunciated (see page 519). Most of the rest of it is quick, until just before the end when the motto theme recurs.

Act I. The curtain rises on a café where are seated the three men, in the middle apparently of a heated argument, or so one assumes from the vigorous defence of Dorabella, his fiancée, that Ferrando is making as the music begins. There are three trios, the first with the two lovers answering the sceptical Alfonso, the second in the form of an accompanied solo for Alfonso, the third consisting of jubilation on the part of the lovers at the prospect of winning the bet which they enter upon with Alfonso. It is a scene of the purest comedy and the music matches the artificiality of the mood, culminating in a tune of bubbling, infectious gaiety such as even Mozart himself could not surpass:

The scene changes, the clarinets play in thirds over the strings,[1] and we can be sure we are with Fiordiligi and Dorabella, the paragons of faithfulness on whose constancy so much has just been wagered. They are discussing the respective merits of their young men as evinced in their portraits, and their sentimental rapture at what they see is conveyed in music of exquisitely exaggerated cast, which dissolves in the middle into a cadenza in thirds on the word 'Amore'. This day-dreaming is interrupted by the precipitate arrival of Don Alfonso, who makes obvious his distress at the news he is only too

anxious to break to the two young ladies: their lovers are ordered to the wars and are to leave immediately. It is Alfonso's nearest approach to an aria in the whole opera – is in fact described as one in the score; its *allegro agitato* perfectly reflects the breathless agitation he counterfeits so well. The situation is admirably summed up in two quintets, which are separated by a short duet for the two officers and a military chorus. In 'Sento, oh Dio' the ladies are inconsolable, Don Alfonso builds up the situation, while Guglielmo is inclined to leave specific consolation to Ferrando and himself joins with Alfonso in a more general comment. Twice the two men cannot help nudging the sceptic ('There, you see now'),[2] but he remains quite unconvinced. Ferrando and Guglielmo say goodbye, soldiers march across the stage singing of the joys of a military existence, but the farewells are not complete until all four have sung a protracted and beautiful farewell, to pungent comment from Alfonso ('Di scrivermi ogni giorno').

Their lovers departed, Fiordiligi and Dorabella show real feeling so that even Alfonso joins them in a wonderfully evocative trio, 'Soave sia il vento', as they pray for calm sea and gentle breezes for the travellers. The idyllic mood does not for one bar survive their joint exit. Alfonso muses in *secco* recitative on his plans, but as he grows animated at the thought of woman's changeability he launches into an accompanied tirade against the whole sex, the one inescapably bitter moment of the score.

The scene changes, and we meet the chattering Despina, maid to the two sisters, who soon show that their loss has left them in no mood for chocolate or any other such consolation. Dorabella is the first to give vent to her feelings, in an aria of exaggeratedly tragic order, 'Smanie implacabili', a parody one may think of the self-consciously tragic Donna Elvira. Despina advises a more moderate line; she is the female counterpart of Don Alfonso, and in her philosophy a lover's absence affords an opportunity for sport, not for lamentation: 'In uomini, in soldati'. The ladies go out in disgust, and Alfonso seizes the opportunity to enlist Despina as an ally in his attempt to win the wager. Enter the two supposedly departed officers, disguised as Albanians; they are introduced to

---

[1] The richness of the wind writing is unusual, even for Mozart, and there is more than a hint here and elsewhere of the great B flat major Serenade

(K.361) for thirteen instruments.

[2] Translations throughout by the Rev. Marmaduke Browne.

Despina, who laughs at them but does not recognise them, and is quite prepared to help them in their attempt to win the affections of her mistresses. In a moment, the ladies are back on the stage, indignant at finding two strange men in their house and demanding their withdrawal. Alfonso stays in hiding but comments on the situation, and emerges to embrace the Albanians as old friends of his; will the ladies not be kind to them – for his sake? Fiordiligi makes it quite clear that their protestations of love are entirely unavailing: she and her sister are each of them 'firm as a rock' ('Come scoglio'). The aria is parodistic in tone, and, with its wide intervals and absurd jumps from the top to the bottom of the soprano range, seems likely to have been at any rate partly intended to poke fun at the phenomenal range and technique of Ferrarese del Bene, the original singer of Fiordiligi, who was da Ponte's mistress at the time of the première but seems to have been no favourite of Mozart's either artistically or personally. Guglielmo answers for Ferrando as well as himself and is given music of such delicacy and charm – 'Non siate ritrosi'[1] – that one cannot but be surprised that the objects of the two young men's affections turn on their respective heels and leave the room before he has had time to finish the aria, which dissolves in laughter. The rapid laughing trio is charming, but Don Alfonso has his work cut out to persuade his young friends that he has by no means lost his bet at this early juncture. Let them be ready to meet him in the garden in a few minutes' time. Ferrando is left alone to sing of his love in a beautiful aria, in type romantic or even sentimental but hardly comic ('Un'aura amorosa'). Alfonso and Despina reassure themselves that this is only a pair of women, and that there is as yet no danger of losing the bet.

For the finale we are back in the garden, under the blue Neapolitan sky and with the bay of Naples as background. Small wonder that Fiordiligi and Dorabella reflect jointly on the mutability of pleasure in music of exquisite tenderness, whose end is hardly reached before Ferrando and Guglielmo rush on to the stage brandishing bottles of poison which Alfonso is unable to prevent them drinking. The situation is sufficiently complicated to provide Mozart with exactly what he wanted for an extended finale.

As the Albanians sink into a coma, pandemonium breaks loose, and when Alfonso and Despina rush for the doctor, there is even an opportunity for Ferrando and Guglielmo to join in the ensemble. Alfonso returns with a doctor (Despina in disguise) who proceeds to give the corpses the benefit of the most recent scientific discovery, Mesmerism – as much the latest thing in 1790 one may imagine as Virtual Reality in the 1990s and as likely to raise a laugh, particularly when compressed, as here, into the outward form of an oversize, all-healing magnet. The corpses revive, think at first they are in the Elysian Fields, and demand a kiss from the goddesses to set the seal on their cure. In spite of the promptings of Alfonso and Despina this is denied them, and the curtain falls with the sisters defending what they appear to regard as nothing less than honour itself, to a background of derisive exclamations from Despina and Alfonso, and approving comments of 'Great would be my indignation were they not to answer No' from the Albanians themselves.

The music of the finale ranges from the purest beauty – the opening, for instance – to sheer farce – Despina in disguise and her trilling, omnipotent magnet. If there is in this finale less incident than in, for instance, that of Act II of *Le Nozze di Figaro*, there is nonetheless a musical variety and invention which places it in the very highest company.

Act II. Despina loses her patience with her virtuous employers. Make hay while the sun shines, she says, and behave like normal women when men are around; she rounds off her point in an aria, 'Una donna a quindici anni' (A woman has fifteen years). The process of persuasion so well begun is completed by the ladies themselves, who agree that there can be no harm in something so innocent as talk with the strangers. Their minds made up, each selects the appropriate partner – 'Prenderò quel brunettino' – in typically melodious fashion, to find at the end of the duet that they are invited to the garden where an entertainment is planned for their delectation. In truth, Alfonso has not exaggerated: nature has never so well imitated art – not even in the case of Cosima Wagner and the 'Siegfried Idyll' – as to serenade a loved one with music as entrancing as the duet and

---

[1] A magnificent *buffo* aria, 'Rivolgete a lui lo sguardo' (K.584), was originally planned here, but the slighter piece was substituted, one may imagine, as being more in keeping with this situation. Glyndebourne nonetheless substituted it for the more usual 'Non siate ritrosi' in their revival of 1978.

chorus 'Secondate aurette amiche' which Ferrando
and Guglielmo now combine to sing to them. If this is
Mozart's most hedonistically inclined opera, no other
number so perfectly illustrates its prevailing characteristic.

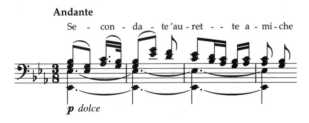

But, the serenade over, neither Albanian seems
able to pursue the advantage gained, and, in disgust,
Alfonso and Despina enact the scene for them. Neither
seems a very apt pupil, but the teachers steal away at
the end of their duet (the few phrases from Ferrando
and Guglielmo make it technically into a quartet),
leaving two rather embarrassed couples behind them
talking animatedly about the weather. Ferrando is led
off by Fiordiligi, and, after some tentative compliments, Guglielmo succeeds in giving Dorabella a
heart-shaped locket, in return for which he removes
the medallion (with its portrait of Ferrando) from her
neck. Their duet, 'Il core vi dono', is charmingly light
in texture and sentiment, and particularly delightful
are the references to the pit-a-pat of their hearts.

The outer defences of Dorabella's constancy have
been rather easily breached; Fiordiligi's are to prove
much harder to carry. She turns a deaf ear to
Ferrando's advances, and he is given a magnificent
aria, 'Ah, lo veggio, quell'anima bella', in which he
alternately expresses doubts and confidence as to the
eventual outcome of his suit. Although it is one of the
highest pieces Mozart wrote for tenor voice, perhaps it
owes its frequent omission from contemporary performances not only to the high *tessitura* and its extended
form, but also to the fact that it is immediately followed by an even longer aria for Fiordiligi which is
much too well known to be omitted under any circumstances. Still, Ferrando's aria is far too good to be
neglected. Fiordiligi's great rondo, 'Per pietà, ben mio,
perdona', is the principal showpiece of the opera; the
extensive range, sudden and precipitous leaps from
high soprano to contralto and back again, the passages of exacting coloratura, the taxing length – all
combine to show off the singer's technique, which is

mocked at the same time as it is used to express the
turmoil of conflicting emotions in Fiordiligi's mind. A
horn obbligato adds to the effect.

Ferrando and Guglielmo meet to compare notes on
their progress to date. Guglielmo is suitably smug
about the apparent constancy of Fiordiligi, but
Ferrando is furiously indignant when he hears of
Dorabella's conduct and sees proof in the shape of the
locket he himself had given her. He will have revenge;
but, he asks Guglielmo, in what form? Don't take it so
much to heart, replies his friend: 'Ladies have such
variations, permutations, combinations' ('Donne mie,
la fate a tanti'). It is a wonderful example of an *opera
buffa* aria, and one of the most delightful moments in
the score, as light of touch and delicate in style as the
best of Mozart's own chamber music. Symmetry being
the thing it is, there follows an aria for Ferrando, less
formidable and shorter than 'Ah, lo veggio', although
by no means easy to sing; it is sometimes omitted, as
the aria for Dorabella, 'È amore un ladroncello', in the
next scene used occasionally to be.

Fiordiligi resolves to make a last effort to extricate
herself and maybe Dorabella as well from the intolerable situation in which they find themselves. She sends
for a couple of old suits of uniform belonging to
Ferrando and Guglielmo which happen to be conveniently in the house, and announces her intention of
going off to the wars taking her equally disguised sister.
She launches into the opening measures of a big aria,
but she has hardly started to express her determination
to reach her lover's side when she is interrupted by
Ferrando, still in his Albanian disguise and protesting
that before she leave him she should run her sword
through his heart and end his agony for ever. Once
more he protests his love, and, in response to a melt-
ingly beautiful tune, resistance crumbles and she falls
into his arms: they sing of their future happiness.

Is it Mozart or the romantic Ferrando who has
overreached himself in this love duet? There is a
school of thought which denies to genius the subtleties which are incidental to the main issue – there
is no indication that he ever actually thought of *that*,
they say, choosing to ignore the part played by the
instinctive and the subconscious in the creative
process. If Ferrando is in love with love as well as with
Dorabella, he will be no less shattered with his new
and involuntary success with her sister than he was
by news of her own infidelity. The joke in fact has

gone too far, and has involved too many emotional ties, old and new, for detachment to be any more a possibility – which is exactly what is conveyed by the uneasiness of the music. Granted that the lovers who began as puppets have suddenly become warm and real; perhaps it is one of music's (and therefore opera's) fascinations that such a transformation is possible, and, when achieved, so moving.

The whole scene is watched by Guglielmo from the side, and Alfonso has his work cut out to keep him quiet until it is over. 'What about your fond Fiordiligi now?' asks Ferrando; 'Fior di Diavolo!' answers the discomfited Guglielmo. They are no worse than all the other women, affirms Alfonso: 'Tutti accusan le donne', and at the end of his short solo, he makes the crestfallen lovers repeat the motto with him: 'Così fan tutte'.

Despina brings the news that her mistresses have made up their minds to make their Albanian suitors happy and marry them on the spot.

The finale carries the plot one stage further and provides the expected dénouement. Servants make ready for the wedding under the direction of Despina, and hail the bridal couples when they appear. The lovers' toast is introduced by one of those unforgettable tunes such as Mozart has a habit of producing at just the moment when abundance has seemed to be sated, and the toast itself is an enchanting canon, led by Fiordiligi, which goes harmoniously on its way until it is the turn of Guglielmo to take up the tune. He contents himself with an angry aside to the effect that nothing would please him more than that the wine should turn to poison on their lips. It has been suggested that the device, which helps to lend variety to the quartet, was dictated to Mozart for the obvious reason that the tune which goes up to A flat was too high for the bass Guglielmo to sing. Alfonso brings in a notary (Despina in yet another costume) who is to take care of the legal side of the weddings, and with much vocal disguise and a spate of pseudo-legal patter (including a punning reference to these 'dame Ferraresi'), the contract is prepared and signed.

This is the signal for a burst of military music from outside, which is immediately recognised by the female signatories as the march to which Ferrando and Guglielmo went off to the wars. Their suspicion turns to consternation when Alfonso confirms that Ferrando and Guglielmo are on their way up to the house at that very moment. The Albanians are bundled out, the sisters try to compose themselves, and their military lovers make an entrance to music which refers back unmistakably to the early part of Act I. Despina is discovered in an ante-room, Alfonso conveniently lets the marriage contracts fall where the young men cannot fail to see them, and they are told that proof of the inconstancy can be found in the next-door room. In a moment they re-appear, bringing with them bits of the Albanian costumes, and moreover singing snatches of the music that helped to bring the wooing to its successful conclusion. Here is a curious anomaly, which I have never yet seen explained. Guglielmo quotes from 'Il core vi dono' and he and Ferrando sing the music associated with Despina's mesmerism in the finale to Act I; but before either of these, Ferrando has quoted something which he in fact never sings at any moment during the opera. Was one of Ferrando's arias changed at rehearsal and did the second thoughts never get as far as this finale, or is there some deeper explanation?

Everything is forgiven, the four lovers are reunited – whether in the original or Albanian combination we are not told – and the six characters sing a valedictory in praise of him who is able to take the rough with the smooth and who can fall back on reason however the world treats him.

Così fan tutte is a comedy but, like every comedy of genius, it comments profoundly and movingly and above all naturally on human life and manners during the course of its action.   H.

LA CLEMENZA DI TITO
The Clemency of Titus

Opera in two acts, text by Mazzolà, adapted from Metastasio. First performed at the National Theatre, Prague, 6 September 1791. First performed in London, King's Theatre, 1806; revived by the City Opera Club, London, 1949; at the Salzburg Festival, 1949, under Josef Krips, with Hilde Zadek, Wilma Lipp, Marta Rohs, Julius Patzak, Richard Holm (in an arrangement by Bernhard Paumgartner, which included much music from other sources, notably *Idomeneo*). First performances in English, Falmouth, 1930, London, 1931. U.S. première, N.B.C. radio, 1940; first stage performance, Tanglewood, 1952. La Scala, Milan, 1966; Covent Garden, 1974, with Janet Baker as Vitellia, Yvonne Minton as Sextus, Eric Tappy as Titus, conductor Colin Davis.

Tito (Titus), *Roman Emperor* ....Tenor

Vitellia, *daughter of the Emperor Vitellius* ....Soprano

Sesto (Sextus), *young Roman patrician* ....Contralto

Annio (Annius), *young Roman patrician* ....Mezzo-Soprano[1]

Servilia, *sister of Sextus* ....Soprano

Publio (Publius), *Captain of the Praetorian Guard* ....Bass

Place: Rome
Time: 79–81 A.D.
Running Time: 2 hours 25 minutes

All his life, Mozart had a hankering for *opera seria*; his attempts began with *Mitridate* (1770), reached their height in *Idomeneo* (1781) and culminated in *La Clemenza di Tito* (1791). Even though *opera seria* was already in 1781 an out-of-date form, it was Mozart, not Gluck, who was in *Idomeneo* to say the final word on the subject. *La Clemenza di Tito* is a rather different matter. Mazzolà's revised version of Metastasio's libretto, though dramatically an update on its model, may not, with its conventional glorification of benevolent despotism, have been particularly congenial material for Mozart. The opera was commissioned to celebrate the coronation in Prague in 1791 of the Emperor Leopold II as King of Bohemia. Mozart had not even finished *The Magic Flute* and was engaged on the *Requiem*, yet *Tito* was written and performed within eighteen days of receipt of the commission, during part of which period the composer was travelling from Vienna to Prague. Small wonder that Mozart entrusted the composition of the *secco* recitatives to his pupil Süssmayer! Three weeks after the première, *The Magic Flute* was brought out in Vienna; nine weeks later still, Mozart was dead. It only remains to add that the work seems to have failed at its first performance, but within a month had turned into a considerable success. It was performed in most German-speaking theatres (in German of course) before the end of the first decade of the nineteenth century, and was actually the first of Mozart's operas to be heard in London, in 1806, when it was given in Italian for Mrs Billington's benefit.

The story is dominated by two considerations: the determination of Vitellia, the daughter of the deposed Emperor, herself in love with Tito, to have revenge on him when he seems disposed to marry another; and the inclination of Tito to show clemency no matter what the provocation.

Act I. Vitellia knows of Tito's plan to marry Berenice, daughter of Agrippa I of Judaea, and she urges Sesto, who is madly in love with her, to fall in with her plans and lead a conspiracy against Tito. No sooner has he agreed than she hears that Berenice has been sent home and that Tito now plans to marry a Roman. Annio asks his friend Sesto to intercede with the Emperor in the matter of his (Annio's) marriage to Servilia, Sesto's sister, but Sesto is forestalled in his plan when Tito tells him that he has chosen none other than Servilia to be Empress. Servilia herself tells the Emperor that she is in love with Annio, and he renounces her, deciding instead to take Vitellia to wife. Vitellia has no knowledge of this change of plans, and sends Sesto off to set fire to the Capitol and murder Tito, only to hear, the moment he is gone, that she is now his destined bride. Sesto succeeds in the first part of his plan, but the conspiracy against Tito's life fails when someone else, wearing his mantle, is killed in his stead. The act ends in general confusion.

Act II. It is known that Tito has escaped death, and moreover that the details of the plot have been revealed to him. Annio advises Sesto to throw himself on the mercy of the Emperor and to show renewed zeal in his cause. Vitellia in contrast is anxious to avoid any risk that her connection with the plot may be discovered, and she urges Sesto to fly the country. Publio, however, settles the matter by arriving to arrest Sesto, who is tried by the Senate and condemned to death. Tito confronts him with proof of his guilt, but when Sesto has left him, tears up the death sentence he has just signed. As Sesto and the other conspirators are about to be thrown to the wild beasts in the arena, Vitellia can bear the load of guilt no longer and confesses her share in the plot, only in her turn to be forgiven by the clement Emperor.

For years, critical opinion was agreed that the music of *La Clemenza di Tito* was written in a hurry at a time when Mozart was exhausted by illness and overwork, and is therefore of little value. Anyone

---

[1] In some modern versions has been sung by a tenor.

hearing it again (or maybe for the first time) will find it hard to agree that it is uninspired, although certainly written against time and in an outmoded form. There is almost no dramatic impetus behind the plot of the opera, and few of the arias have powerful situations behind them. But plot was never the strong point of *opera seria*, which aimed rather at providing a dignified and apt frame for the noble music and virtuoso singing which the aristocracy wanted to hear. Mozart and Mazzolà have between them upset some of the static nature of Metastasio's original libretto but even so they have not succeeded in altering the essentially conventional nature of the entertainment; on the other hand, Mozart has provided a very superior example of the sort of music which went with these eighteenth-century occasions – that he did not write another *Don Giovanni* is logical. He was being asked to write something entirely different.

Of the twenty-six numbers in the score, only eleven are in fact arias – which shows how much alteration was made in Metastasio's original, where there was provision for no ensembles of any sort or kind. They range from a simple arietta such as that for Servilia ('S'altro che lagrime') to the great show-pieces for Sesto ('Parto, parto') and Vitellia ('Non più di fiori'). These latter have elaborate instrumental obbligati, for respectively clarinet and basset horn, and Stadler[1] went specially to Prague to play them. The vocal writing is no less elaborate, and, in this combination of virtuoso styles for voice and instrument, the arias look back to 'Martern aller Arten' (or even 'Possente spirto' from Monteverdi's *Orfeo*), and forward to such different pieces as Schubert's song 'Der Hirt auf dem Felsen' and the Mad Scene in *Lucia*. The duets for Sesto and Annio and for Servilia and Annio are particularly attractive, and there is a fine trio for Vitellia, Sesto, and Publio in the second act just before the arrest of Sesto. But the most notable section of the score is the finale to Act I, after the Capitol has been set on fire by Sesto. An agitated crowd off-stage adds to the terror of the characters on-stage, and Mozart builds up the whole ensemble antiphonally to imposing dimensions. It is genuine dramatic music, and is the only time the composer makes simultaneous use of soloists and chorus together in an extended finale.   H.

DIE ZAUBERFLÖTE
The Magic Flute

Opera in two acts, text by Emanuel Schikaneder. First performed at the Theater auf der Wieden, Vienna, 30 September 1791, with Nanetta Gottlieb (Pamina), Josefa Hofer (Queen of Night), Schack (Tamino), Gerl (Sarastro), Schikaneder (Papageno). First performances in England at the Haymarket Theatre, London, 1811, and at Covent Garden, 1833 (in German). The opera was revived in 1911 by the Cambridge University Music Society in Edward Dent's translation, with Victoria Hopper, Steuart Wilson, Clive Carey; in 1914 at Drury Lane under Sir Thomas Beecham, with Claire Dux, Margarete Siems, Kirchner, Knüpfer, Hans Bechstein; in 1938 at Covent Garden under Beecham, with Lemnitz, Berger, Tauber, Strienz, and Hüsch. It was regularly in the Old Vic and Sadler's Wells repertory from 1921. First performed at Glyndebourne in 1935, with Rautawaara, Walther Ludwig, Andresen, Domgraf-Fassbänder, conducted by Fritz Busch. Revived at Salzburg under Toscanini, 1937, with Novotna, Osvath, Roswaenge, Kipnis, Domgraf-Fassbänder; and under Furtwängler in 1949, with Seefried, Lipp, Ludwig, Greindl, and Schmitt-Walter; Covent Garden, 1962, with Carlyle, Sutherland, Richard Lewis, Kelly, Geraint Evans, conductor Klemperer.

Tamino, *an Egyptian prince*	Tenor
Three Ladies, *in attendance on the Queen of Night*	Sopranos, Mezzo-Soprano
Papageno, *a bird-catcher*	Baritone
The Queen of Night	Soprano
Monostatos, *a Moor in the service of Sarastro*	Tenor
Pamina, *daughter of the Queen of Night*	Soprano
Three Genii	Sopranos, Mezzo-Soprano
The Speaker	Bass
Sarastro, *High Priest of Isis and Osiris*	Bass
Two Priests	Tenor, Bass
Papagena	Soprano
Two Men in Armour	Tenor, Bass

Slaves, Priests, People, etc.

Place: Egypt
Running Time: 2 hours 45 minutes

Emanuel Johann Schikaneder, who wrote the libretto with the aid of a chorister named Gieseke, was a friend of Mozart and a member of the same Masonic Lodge. He was also the manager of a theatrical company and a successful actor,[2] and had persuaded Mozart to compose the music to a puppet show for him. He had selected the story of 'Lulu' by

---

[1] Anton Stadler, virtuoso clarinet player, for whom Mozart's *Quintet* was also written.

[2] According to Einstein, in his youth one of the first German Hamlets.

Liebeskind, which had appeared in a volume of Oriental tales brought out by Wieland under the title of *Dschinnistan*. In the original tale a wicked sorcerer has stolen the daughter of the Queen of Night, who is restored by a Prince by means of magic. While Schikaneder was busy on his libretto, a fairy story by Perinet, music by Wenzel Müller, and treating of the same subject, was given at another Viennese theatre. Its great success interfered with Schikaneder's original plan.

At that time freemasonry was a much discussed subject. It had been interdicted by Maria Theresa and armed forces were employed to break up the lodges. As a practical man Schikaneder saw his chance to exploit the forbidden rites on the stage. Out of the wicked sorcerer he made Sarastro, the sage priest of Isis. The ordeals of Tamino and Pamina became copies of the ceremonials of freemasonry. He also laid the scene of the opera in Egypt, where freemasonry believes its rites to have originated. In addition to all this Mozart's beautiful music ennobled the libretto and lent to the whole the force of the mysterious and sacred.

Because of the opera's relationship to freemasonry, commentators[1] have identified Tamino with the Emperor Joseph II, Pamina with the Austrian people, Sarastro with Ignaz von Born, a freemason and a scientist of great eminence; the vengeful Queen of Night was the Empress Maria Theresa, and Monostatos the clergy,[2] especially the Jesuits and the religious orders.

Mozart was engaged on *The Magic Flute* from March until July 1791, and again in September of that year. On 30 September, two months before his death, the first performance was given.

In the overture, the heavy reiterated chords represent, it has been suggested, the knocking at the door of the lodge room, especially as they are heard again in the temple scene, when the novitiate of Tamino is about to begin. The brilliance of the fugal *allegro* has been commented upon as well as the resemblance of its theme to that of Clementi's sonata in B flat.

Act I. The story opens with Tamino endeavouring to escape from a huge snake. He falls unconscious. Hearing his cries, three black-garbed Ladies-in-Waiting of the Queen of Night appear and kill the

serpent with their spears. The opening *allegro* leads to an extended trio for the Ladies, in which they rejoice that they have been able to foil the serpent, and comment on the good looks of the young man they have rescued. Quite unwillingly they leave the handsome youth, who, on recovering consciousness, sees dancing towards him an odd-looking man entirely covered with feathers. It is Papageno, the Queen's bird-catcher. His song, 'Der Vogelfänger bin ich ja', is punctuated with runs on his pipe and shows us at once that he is a jovial, not to say a popular, type of comedian. He tells the astonished Tamino that this is the realm of the Queen of Night. Nor, seeing that the snake is dead, does he hesitate to boast that it was he who killed it. For this lie he is immediately punished by the three Ladies, who reappear and place a padlock on his mouth. They show Tamino the miniature of a maiden, whose beauty at once fills his heart with an ardent love, which he expresses in one of the most beautiful of Mozart's tenor arias, 'Dies Bildnis ist bezaubernd schön'. The Ladies tell him that she is a prisoner in Sarastro's hands, and he has no sooner sworn to deliver her than the Queen herself materialises from the clouds to reinforce his determination with a description of her desolation now that she has lost her daughter, and a promise that Pamina shall be his once she is free. 'O zittre nicht, mein lieber Sohn', she sings, telling him not to be afraid, and her *scena* develops into a display of coloratura fireworks designed primarily, we may be sure, to display the agile technique of the original Queen, Josefa Hofer, the composer's sister-in-law, but expressive also of her headstrong, passionate nature.

The Ladies return, take the padlock from Papageno's mouth and give him a set of chimes and Tamino a golden flute; by means of these magical instruments they will be able to escape the perils of their journey, on which they will be accompanied by three youths or Genii. The quintet, 'Hm, hm, hm! Der Arme kann von Strafe sagen', apart from being enchanting in itself, serves also to introduce the music associated later with the Genii, which has a curious quality of its own, which one can only ascribe to the lesser supernatural and call 'magical' (in just the sense

---

[1] Beginning with Moritz Zille, 1866.

[2] And he was portrayed accordingly in Michael Geliot's ingenious production for the Welsh National Opera in 1971.

Die Zauberflöte *(The Magic Flute). Wash-coloured engraving by Karl Friedrich Schinkel for the 1816 Berlin production.*

Tippett used the term in *The Midsummer Marriage).*

The scene changes, and a richly furnished apartment in Sarastro's palace is disclosed. A brutal Moor, Monostatos, is pursuing Pamina with unwelcome attentions. Even in this duet, whose basis is surely in comedy, something of the depth which is to be Pamina's can be discerned; compare her feminine warmth with the lack of that quality in the Queen and the three Ladies. The appearance of Papageno puts Monostatos to flight. The Bird-Catcher recognises Pamina as the daughter of the Queen of Night and assures her that she will soon be rescued, and, what is more, by someone who has fallen in love with her without even seeing her – not the sort of thing, he laments, that ever seems to happen to him. Pamina consoles him in an exquisitely simple E flat tune and

assures him that love will yet be his: 'Bei Männern, welche Liebe fühlen, fehlt auch ein gutes Herze nicht'.

The finale takes place in a grove on three sides of which stand three Temples, dedicated to Wisdom, Reason, and Nature. Thither the three Genii lead Tamino, and leave him with the advice that he 'be silent, patient, persevering'. In a recitative which admirably expresses the dawning of understanding in his mind, Tamino decides to enter the Temples, but at the first two he is refused admittance, and from the third emerges a priest who informs him that Sarastro is no tyrant, no wicked sorcerer as the Queen had warned him, but a man of wisdom and of noble character. The solemn atmosphere of their dialogue – an extraordinary example of a musical argument reinforcing words with logic – serves to awaken still further Tamino's desire for knowledge and his recitative 'O ew'ge Nacht' takes the form of question and answer, the answer being supplied by a hidden and encouraging chorus. He takes his flute and sings to its accompaniment: 'Wie stark is nicht dein Zauberton'. Animals come out from their lairs and lie at his feet, but before the end of the aria he hears Papageno's pan-pipe and at its end he rushes off to find him. Papageno comes on from the opposite side of the stage leading Pamina whom he intends to unite with Tamino. Their duet 'Schnelle Füsse, rascher Mut' is punctuated with calls on the pipes and answers from the flute but becomes a trio when they are overtaken by Monostatos, who sends for chains with which to complete their capture.

Disaster seems near, but Papageno remembers that he has a last remedy and sets the Moor and his slaves dancing by playing on his magic chimes. He and Pamina rejoice at their escape, but are interrupted by a flourish of trumpets and the sound of a chorus of praise to Sarastro. Papageno wonders what they are going to say to him. 'Die Wahrheit!' (The truth), proudly answers Pamina, and the phrase serves to end the comedy of the escape and to initiate the solemnity of Sarastro's procession. She kneels at Sarastro's feet and explains that she was trying to escape the unwelcome attentions of the Moor. Sarastro comforts her and assures her that he understands her predicament and that the gods aim to provide a remedy. Monostatos drags Tamino in, and in phrases whose origin is surely in Mozart's 'Turkish' style (see *Entführung*), denounces him to Sarastro, but, instead of the reward he expects, he is sentenced to a sound flogging. Woven into the structure of this section of the finale is the rapturous moment of the first meeting of Pamina and Tamino. By command of Sarastro, the two of them are brought into the Temple of Ordeal, where they must prove that they are worthy of the higher happiness.

Act II. A grove of palms outside the Temple. A solemn *andante* sets the scene. Sarastro informs the Priests of the plans which he has laid. The gods have decided that Pamina shall become the wife of the noble youth Tamino. Tamino, however, must prove that he is worthy of admission to the Temple. Therefore, Sarastro has taken under his protection Pamina, daughter of the Queen of Night. The couple must go through severe ordeals in order to be worthy of entering the Temple of Light. In between his pro-

nouncements the Priests blow their trumpets, repeating the chords which were heard in the overture. Sarastro prays to Isis and Osiris that strength may be granted to the two aspirants after the goal of wisdom: 'O Isis und Osiris'. This solemn prayer is of so noble a nature that it was once described as the only music which could without fear of blasphemy be put into the mouth of God.

The Porch of the Temple. The ordeals of Tamino and Papageno are about to begin. They are warned by the Priests that they may perish in their search for the Truth, and then enjoined to silence as the first step in their probation. Two Priests warn them in a duet of what will happen if they fail to keep their vow of silence in the face of women's wiles ('Bewahret euch vor Weibertücken'), but no sooner are they left alone and in darkness than they are confronted by the three Ladies of the Queen of Night. In the quintet which follows, the Ladies try to persuade them to abandon their quest, but Tamino, and even, with some prompting, Papageno, maintain a rigid silence in the face of the questioning women. The Priests reappear and congratulate them on having passed their first test.

The scene changes to a garden. Pamina is discovered lying asleep. Towards her steals the Moor, and indulges in what Einstein describes as a 'grotesque, phallic dance' and an aria which is not far behind in those qualities: 'Alles fühlt der Liebe Freuden'. The accompaniment to the aria is 'to be sung and played very softly, as if the music was a very long way off' – so runs Mozart's own direction. Monostatos comes up to Pamina but a cry of 'Zurück' (back) causes him to start back: it is the Queen of Night. She flings her daughter a dagger with the command that she take it and kill Sarastro. In 'Der Hölle Rache kocht in meinem Herzen' one can feel the fires of vengeful fury boiling in the music, with its passionate staccato coloratura, its four top Fs, and its headlong impetus. Monostatos returns and, threatening that he will reveal the plot (to which Pamina has never agreed to be a party), demands her love as the price of his silence. Sarastro enters just in time to hurl Monostatos from the defenceless Pamina, but the Moor departs to try his luck with the mother. Pamina pleads for her mother, but Sarastro assures her that vengeance is not in his thoughts: 'In diesen heil'gen Hallen kennt man die Rache nicht'. Again, the nobility of the musical expression equals, perhaps even surpasses, that of 'O Isis und Osiris'.

Enjoined once more to keep silent, Tamino and Papageno are again left by the attendant Priests. Papageno still chatters to himself, and soon enters into a long conversation with an old crone who introduces herself to him as his yet unknown sweetheart, Papagena. A clap of thunder and she departs, to be replaced by the three Genii who appear bringing with them the flute and magic bells, carrying a table spread with food and drink, and singing in strains similar to those we heard at their first entrance. To the two aspirants comes Pamina, unaware of their vow of silence, but overjoyed to have found Tamino at last. But her delight is short-lived and she suspends belief in human constancy when she can get no answer from her beloved. 'Ach, ich fühl's, es ist verschwunden' run the words of her G minor aria; here that mixture of maturity and innocence which she has consistently shown reaches its highest level of expression. Nowhere else in the repertory of the lyric soprano is the grief which passes all bounds given musical expression of such poignant simplicity.

The scene changes to a vault. The Priests sing a solemn *adagio* chorus of praise to Isis and Osiris, after which Sarastro confronts Pamina with Tamino and tells them to take their last farewell of each other: 'Soll ich dich, Teurer, nicht mehr seh'n?' We return to Papageno, who is told he can have one wish but is left vaguely dissatisfied when he has drunk the wine he asks for. What is missing? A girl-friend or a wife: 'Ein Mädchen oder Weibchen wünscht Papageno sich'. At the end of the song, the old woman comes back to him and threatens him with dire penalties if he does not swear to be true to her; when he reluctantly does so, she reveals herself as a young and attractively feathered mate – but poor Papageno is warned off her by a Priest who pronounces him not yet worthy of her.

The three Genii are discovered in a garden singing of the symbolical joys of the rising sun, whose rays drive away the fears of night and herald the reign of light and love: 'Bald prangt, den Morgen zu verkünden'. Nothing more suitable for the beginning of the finale of the opera could be found than these sentiments and the disembodied agents through whom they are expressed. None of the music in the opera stands further away from the conventions of *opera buffa* or *Singspiel* or even *opera seria* – the forms known in Mozart's day – than the conception of this trio of voices, and the hushed beauty of their music seems to convey that sense of being 'different', dedicated even, which characterises the serious side of the music of *The Magic Flute*, and sets it apart from other operas.

Not knowing she is observed, Pamina contemplates suicide ('Du also bist mein Bräutigam? Durch dich vollend' ich meinen Gram'), but is restrained and comforted by the Genii in music of extraordinary tenderness.

Two Men in Armour are seen standing at each side of a doorway, and Tamino is brought in by the Priests for the last stage of his initiation. The test of fire and water is heralded by the Men in Armour, whose scene is constructed in the form of a chorale prelude, the orchestra weaving a *fugato* round the chorale 'Ach Gott vom Himmel sieh' darein'. Tamino proclaims his resolution, but is joined by Pamina for these final ordeals. His joy at being not only reunited with her but even allowed to speak to her freely is expressed in an ardent phrase which prepares us for the moving simplicity of their meeting and the duet which follows and becomes a quartet with the musical entrance of the two guardians of the gates.

Pamina is Tamino's guide as, to the accompaniment of an *adagio* for the solo flute, they undergo successively the ordeals by fire and by water. At the end they are welcomed into the Temple by Sarastro and the Priests.

At this point occurs Papageno's great scene of mock suicide, a parallel trial in comic terms to the serious trials Tamino and Pamina are expected to surmount. 'Papagena! Papagena!' is a song of a more serious cut than the other two Schikaneder had to himself, but, after an appeal to someone in the audience to volunteer to save him and the subsequent intervention of the Genii, the *scena* ends happily with

a jingle of bells, and is followed by an irresistible patter duet for Papageno and Papagena.

Before the Temple, Monostatos leads on the Queen and her Ladies, who are making a last bid for revenge on Sarastro. But their appearance coincides with the stage being flooded with light, and the forces of night disappear before the short chorus extolling the new initiates and the magic flute which was their faithful companion brings the opera to an end.

Nothing is so simple as to be absolutely clear-cut, and in life the serious and the comic are intermingled in a way that is frequently disconcerting but is nonetheless inevitable. Though both *Figaro* and *Così fan tutte* partake of this mixture, they are nevertheless comedies pure though by no means simple: the one a comedy of action, the other of conversation; but the remaining two out of Mozart's four greatest operas present a more complicated problem. In each of them, the close relationship of the comic and the serious is treated as a natural and inevitable thing. *Don Giovanni*, comic in theme and often comic in treatment, yet consistently takes a turn towards the serious considerations which arise out of the comedy; *The Magic Flute*, serious in its presentation of the urge towards an understanding of truth, nonetheless mingles the digressions of Papageno with the aspirations of Tamino and Pamina. A refusal to take the story of *The Magic Flute* seriously is to turn a blind eye to the impeccable skill of the librettist (or librettists) and also to deny to the genius of Mozart the power of discrimination and choice. To what extent the fortuitous circumstances surrounding the commission of *The Magic Flute* – the fact that Schikaneder was an accomplished and popular comedian and that freemasonry was a controversial topic of the day – may have influenced Mozart in an unexpected direction, is likely to be a matter for speculation as long as opera is played, but it is in the end almost irrelevant.   K., H.

MODEST PETROVICH MUSSORGSKY
(born 21 March 1839, died 28 March 1881)

BORIS GODUNOV

Opera in a prologue and four acts; text from Pushkin's play of the same name and Karamzin's *History of the Russian State*. There have been no fewer than four main versions of *Boris*, two by Mussorgsky and two by Rimsky-Korsakov, quite apart from various more recent attempts to prepare performing versions. (**A**), composed and orchestrated between October 1868 and December 1869, consisted of seven scenes: Courtyard of Novodevichy Monastery; Coronation; Pimen's cell; the inn; the Tsar's apartments; before the Cathedral of St Basil in Moscow (including the Simpleton); death of Boris. This version was submitted to the committee of the Imperial theatres and rejected by them. (**B**) Mussorgsky immediately started on a second version, accepting the advice of his friends during composition, and finished by June 1872. In February 1872 the Coronation scene was performed by Napravnik at a concert, and in April Balakirev conducted the Polonaise. This version was also rejected by the committee, but the inn scene and the two scenes of the Polish act were performed publicly in February 1873 at the Mariinsky Theatre with Petrov, the most famous Russian bass of his day, as Varlaam, Komissarzhevsky as Dimitri, Platonova as Marina; the rest of the programme consisted of Act I of *Freischütz* and Act II of *Lohengrin*. As a result of the success of this performance, the entire opera (though with a number of important cuts) was performed on 27 January/8 February 1874, with Melnikov as Boris, and Petrov, Komissarzhevsky, and Platonova in the parts they had played in 1873; Napravnik conducted, and the opera was a great success with the public, although damned by the critics. By 1882 it had dropped from the repertory. (**C**) In 1896 Rimsky-Korsakov revised and re-scored the work, making a large number of cuts and composing some new passages to bridge the gaps caused by the cuts. This was performed in 1896; in 1899 by the Mamontov Company, with Chaliapin in the title role; and in 1904 at the Imperial Theatres, again with Chaliapin in the title role. In 1906–8, Rimsky-Korsakov worked on another edition of the opera (**D**) in which he restored the cuts he had previously made, and retained his own additions to the score. It was in something like version (**D**) that the opera was once most often performed.

(**D**) First produced Paris Opéra, 1908, and la Scala, Milan, 1909, with Chaliapin; Metropolitan, New York, 1913, with Didur, conductor Toscanini; London, Drury Lane, 1913, with Chaliapin; Aldwych, London (in English), 1916. Revived, Metropolitan, 1921, with Chaliapin; 1939, with Pinza; 1943, with Kipnis; la Scala, 1922, with Vanni Marcoux, conductor Toscanini; 1930, with Chaliapin; 1941, with Pasero; 1949, with Christoff, conductor Dobrowen; Covent Garden, 1928, with Chaliapin. In 1935 Mussorgsky's (**A**) was performed at Sadler's Wells, London (in English), with Ronald Stear as Boris; in 1992 by Opera North with John Tomlinson; in 1948, Mussorgsky's (**B**) was produced at Covent Garden (in English), with Silveri in the title role; in 1949 Christoff sang the title role, in 1950 (by which time a retrograde step to Rimsky-Korsakov's (**D**) had been made) Weber was Boris, and in 1952

Rossi-Lemeni sang the title role; in 1958, a reversion to substantially (**B**) was made under Kubelík and with Christoff, but this included the St Basil scene as well as the Forest of Kromy, the Simpleton's utterances being cut from the latter. New production of (**B**) under Abbado in 1983, and substantially uncut, with Robert Lloyd, Randova, Michel Svetlev, Gwynne Howell, Aage Haugland. In Karajan's spectacular production at Salzburg in 1965, Ghiaurov sang the title role with Jurinac, Uzunov, Stolze, Gyuselev, Diakov.

Boris Godunov		Bass
Fyodor, *his son*		Mezzo-Soprano
Xenia, *his daughter*		Soprano
The Old Nurse		Contralto
Prince Shuisky		Tenor
Andrey Chelkalov, *clerk of the Duma*		Baritone
Pimen, *monk and chronicler*		Bass
The Pretender Dimitri, *called Grigory*		Tenor
Marina Mnishek, *a Polish Princess*		Soprano
Rangoni, *a Jesuit*		Bass
Varlaam	} *vagabonds*	Bass
Missail		Tenor
The Hostess of the Inn		Mezzo-Soprano
Nikitich (Michael), *constable*		Bass
The Simpleton		Tenor
Two Jesuits		Bass

Place: Russia and Poland
Time: 1598–1605
Running Time: 3 hours 30 minutes

The subject brings to the stage one of the most curious episodes of the history of Russia in the sixteenth and seventeenth centuries. Boris Godunov, the brother-in-law and chief minister of Tsar Fyodor, son of Ivan, has caused to be assassinated the young Dimitri, half-brother of the Tsar and his heir. On the death of Fyodor, Boris, who has committed his crime with the sole object of seizing power, has himself acclaimed by the people and ascends the throne. But about the same time, a young monk named Grigory escapes from his monastery, discards his habit, and goes to Poland where he passes as the dead Tsarevich Dimitri. The Polish government receives him all the more cordially as it understands the advantage such an event might afford it. Soon the pretended Dimitri, who has married the daughter of the Voyevode of Sandomir, puts himself at the head of the Polish army and marches with it against Russia. Just at this moment they hear of the death of Boris, and the false Dimitri, taking advantage of the circumstances, in turn usurps power.

As a matter of historical fact, Boris's son Fyodor was murdered and his daughter Xenia taken by Dimitri as his mistress (Dvořák's opera *Dimitrij* deals with these events). Dimitri's tenure of power was not long, as he was deposed and killed by Shuisky, who reigned in his stead. History has acquitted Boris of the crime of murdering Dimitri (although for the purposes of the opera it must of course be accepted as true), but Shuisky goes down as an ambitious and cruel Tsar. Marina seems to have been all that is implied in the opera; after the death of Dimitri, she became the wife of yet another pretender to the throne, whom she claimed to recognise as her lost husband.   K. W.

Prologue. After a short prelude the curtain goes up to show the courtyard of the Monastery of Novodevichy, near Moscow. It is crowded with people, who are ordered by a police officer to keep up a prayer for guidance. The moment his back is turned they show clearly by their talk among themselves that they are in entire ignorance of why they are there at all. The prayer rises to a frenzy, but is interrupted by the appearance of Chelkalov, the secretary of the Duma, who informs them that Boris has not yet yielded to the petitions of the government and people, who urge him to accept the crown.

The sound of pilgrims nearing the monastery can be heard, and they distribute alms and relics.

Scene ii. The courtyard of the Kremlin in Moscow. Facing the spectators in the background is the Red Staircase leading to the Tsar's apartments; on the right and near the front, the people on their knees occupy the space between the two Cathedrals of the Assumption and the Archangel.

Bells are pealing and a procession of boyars and guards crosses the stage. Prince Shuisky cries 'Long life to thee, Tsar Boris Fyodorovich', and the people break into song in praise of the new Tsar. Boris himself appears, and, in a mood that is introspective rather than triumphant, prays for the guidance of Tsar Fyodor in his great task; may he justify the people's confidence during the reign that is just beginning. He bids the boyars come with him to pray

before the tombs of Russia's departed rulers; after prayer, the people from beggar to prince shall feast as his guests. The people break out again into acclamation, and the curtain falls.

Act I. It is five years since Boris's coronation. The background is one of famine, and the people have deserted the ways of law and order. For Russia's misfortunes, for the death of his sister, Tsar Fyodor's widow, for the death of his prospective son-in-law, Boris is blamed – and this in spite of his efforts to rule wisely and well.

The scene is a cell in the monastery of Chudov, where the old monk, Pimen, is engaged on his chronicle of the history of Russia. It is late at night, but Pimen is satisfied that he has reached the end of his labours. He will be able to leave his history to be continued in the future by some monk, as anonymous and little anxious for personal glory as himself. The sound of chanting can be heard from another part of the monastery, and suddenly Grigory, Pimen's young companion in his cell, wakes up. For the third time he has dreamed that he stood on the top of a high tower from which he could see all Moscow lying at his feet. The crowd below mocked him with their laughter, and he, overcome with shame and terror, fell from the tower and awoke from his dream (the reference is to a version of Dimitri's murder in which he was thrown from a high tower).

Pimen tries to comfort him, and persuade him to resign himself to a life of contemplation. He himself, before he became a monk and was still young, had fought in the armies of Tsar Ivan the Terrible and lived a sinful life of fighting and feasting. Grigory continues to lament that his whole life has been spent inside the walls of the monastery, that he has never known action and the world. Pimen reminds him that many of Russia's most famous warriors turned to a solitary existence to end their days in peace, not least of them war-like Ivan himself, who died in this very cell. The last Tsar, Fyodor, was a man of peace, but now God has sent to Russia the fierce Tsar Boris, a regicide. At this, Grigory asks Pimen how old would have been Dimitri, brother of Fyodor, had he lived. Pimen tells him that he would have been about his own age, nearly twenty (in version (**A**) Mussorgsky included a passage in which Pimen described the scene after the murder of the young Tsarevich at Uglich, but this was omitted from version (**B**)). The orchestra gives out a theme which is later to be associated both with Grigory's ambition and the murdered Dimitri, whom he pretends to be:

Pimen expresses his hope that Grigory will carry on his work of chronicler when he is dead and gone, and, the bell for matins being heard, he leans on Grigory's arm as he goes to the door of the cell. Grigory remains behind; Boris shall not escape the judgement of heaven for his crime, he says.

Scene ii. An inn on the Lithuanian border of Russia. The hostess sings a little song, half ribald in content, half nonsense. She is interrupted by the sound of singing from outside, and sees that her visitors are monks. When they enter, they are seen to be as disreputable a pair of vagabonds as ever took to the road; their names are Varlaam and Missail, and their time is spent, by their own admission, mainly in begging and converting the proceeds into good liquor. With them is Grigory, who has fled from his monastery, and is even now on his way to Lithuania and freedom, pursued, owing to an unguarded remark before leaving the monastery, by the police.

The hostess provides her reverend guests with wine, and, warmed by it, Varlaam launches into a ferocious song about his achievements as a soldier in Ivan the Terrible's army at the battle of Kazan. It is a moment of splendid vigour. Varlaam curses Grigory for not joining him in either drink or song, and becomes positively maudlin in his reflections. Grigory takes the hostess aside and questions her on the best route to the Lithuanian border. Patrols are out because of some fugitive monk from Moscow, but she confides that there is a safe road by which he may reach his goal unobserved.

Varlaam continues to sing and he is obviously on the verge of falling asleep when the room is suddenly full of the guards of whom the hostess has just been complaining that they never catch their man and serve only to annoy peaceful citizens like herself. They question Grigory, who strikes them as harmless enough, then turn their attention to the vagabond monks, who seem well enough to fit the description of the man they are after. Varlaam and Missail are perfectly accustomed to such cross-questioning, and their answers have the whine of long experience

about them. The captain of the police hands the warrant to Varlaam and orders him to read it, but he pleads lack of practice. Grigory is instructed to read it aloud; he does so, substituting a description of Varlaam for what is written on the paper. When they surround the old monk, he says he will make an effort to decipher the paper, which plainly does not say what Grigory has read out, since he is not the renegade they are after. With much difficulty he spells out the correct sense, and all realise that Grigory is their man. He jumps out of the window and escapes.

Act II. The Tsar's apartments in the Kremlin. The Tsarevich Fyodor is sitting reading, while his sister Xenia sings sadly to herself of the husband who died before they were ever married. The Nurse tries to comfort her, then sings a nursery song about a gnat. Fyodor complains that it is a very depressing song, and leads another, a clapping game, in which the Nurse joins. As it reaches its climax the Tsar himself appears, the Nurse is overcome with terror and vainly tries to explain to Boris that she is an old woman and easily frightened. Boris comforts his daughter in her sadness, and goes over to where his son is looking at a map of the Russian empire. He bids him take his lessons seriously; the time may soon come when he will be called on to rule over the countries he sees outlined on this map.

In his son's presence Boris pours out his agony of mind, the doubts and torments which his rule over Russia has brought him, the enemies who conspire against him, the remorse which fills his soul when he recalls the murdered Dimitri. This great monologue ('I have attained the highest power') rises to a climax of intensity, then falls away as Boris himself sinks under the weight of conscience. Two themes should be quoted; the first is heard again during the scene of Boris's death:

The second is associated with his guilt in relation to the murdered Dimitri:

A noise is heard outside, and the Tsar sends Fyodor to find out its cause. The boyar-in-waiting comes to ask for an audience on behalf of Prince Shuisky. Boris says he will see him. The boyar goes on to warn his master of the rumours that the disaffected nobles have been in touch with the Poles at Cracow, and that Shuisky himself is in league with them. A messenger has even arrived from Cracow ... let him be arrested, says Boris. As the boyar leaves, Fyodor returns, and explains to his father in a charming song that the fuss was about a parrot which escaped and flew at the maids in its panic. Boris is pleased with the way his son tells the story.

Shuisky comes in and is greeted with a storm of abuse from Boris, who accuses him of double-dealing, hypocrisy and treason. Shuisky brushes the accusations aside, but tacitly admits his correspondence with rebels. He has come, he says, to bring Boris grave news; a pretender has arisen in Poland, and has been publicly acknowledged by the King of Poland, and privately by the Pope. After assuring the Tsar that his throne is inviolate and protected by the love his people bear him, he adds that he is in duty bound to warn him that it is possible that the Russian people themselves might be attracted to the pretender's cause if he were to cross the border claiming to be the lost Tsarevich.

At mention of Dimitri's name the Tsar dismisses his son (illogically, Ernest Newman once rightly claimed, since he has already in his presence mentioned the death of his rival for the throne), and is alone with Shuisky. He orders him to confirm or deny that Dimitri's was the body which was buried at Uglich; does he now know the story that the dead can walk again? Shuisky makes as if to soothe his fears. The boy was in truth Dimitri, and he himself watched for five days while the bodies of the prince and the men killed by the crowd as his murderers lay on the cathedral steps. The others began to putrefy, but Dimitri's body alone was as fresh as when it was killed, in spite of the blood-red circle round his neck. On Dimitri's face, an angelic smile was seen.

Boris can bear the story no more, and signs to Shuisky to leave him. Shuisky looks back as he goes out and sees Boris sink exhausted into a chair. He feels that he is suffocating, as much with terror and remorse as from lack of air. A chiming clock (it is known that they were introduced into Russia in

Boris's time) begins to strike. The figures begin to move, and Boris takes them for an apparition of the murdered child. His hysteria verges on madness, and he sinks sobbing to the floor as he prays to God for forgiveness. The sinister power of the music is extraordinary, and Ernest Newman has called it 'one of the most tremendous scenes in all opera'.

Act III. The Polish act. Scene i: the apartments of Marina Mnishek, daughter of the Voyevode of Sandomir. The girls amuse her with their songs, and she in turn sings of her ambition; she is not interested in love songs but in tales of heroic deeds. She dismisses her attendants and sings an air *alla mazurka*, in which she gives further vent to her ambitious plans particularly as they concern the pretender Dimitri, through whom she hopes to ascend the throne of Russia.

Her reveries are interrupted by the sudden appearance of Rangoni, a Jesuit, introduced into the story by Mussorgsky. He exhorts her to remember her duty to her faith when she becomes paramount ruler in Moscow; her aim must be to convert the heretic Russians to the true religion. Marina's angry objections are silenced when he protests that he is heaven's messenger and so the keeper of her soul.

The second scene is laid by a fountain in the garden of Mnishek at Sandomir; it takes place by moonlight. Dimitri has been given a rendezvous by Marina and as he waits for her, he sings ardently of his love. What has been described as an 'oily, snake-like motif' in the shape of a chromatic scale announces that Rangoni has sidled into view. He tells Dimitri (as Grigory is now known by all) that Marina loves him passionately, in spite of the insults she has had to bear on his account. He will lead Dimitri to his beloved, and in return asks for nothing more than that he shall be allowed to follow the Tsarevich and to watch over his spiritual welfare wherever he goes. Rangoni bids him hide as Mnishek's guests are coming out of the house.

A polonaise is danced, during which the nobles pay court to Marina and plan their march on Moscow. Dimitri watches the scene with jealous eyes, and it stings him to a resolution he has not known before (this to a more heroic version of the Dimitri theme). When Marina comes out into the garden, she finds him full of tender phrases and protestations, and it takes all her haughtiness and pride to sting him once again into a determined frame of mind, so that he reacts to her insults with a declaration of his intention immediately to lead an army on Moscow. Marina has got from him what she wanted, and she can afford in the famous love duet to fawn on him. Poor Dimitri was not hard to catch, and he takes Marina in his arms as he protests his love for her. At the moment of their embrace, Rangoni can be seen looking from his hiding-place, while the orchestra runs down his chromatic scale to show the triumph is neither Marina's nor Dimitri's, but his and his Church's. (Apart from the Polonaise and the duet, much of this act is often omitted in performance.)

Act IV. Mussorgsky, advised it is said by his friends, in version (**B**) placed the scene of Boris's death before the so-called revolutionary scene, thus implicitly making the Russian people the real protagonists of his drama. But it is more accurate to refer to (**B**) as Mussorgsky's *latest* work on the score, and to think of it as final and testamentary is perhaps an exaggeration. In (**C**) and (**D**), Rimsky-Korsakov reversed this order of things, and when his versions have been performed, the death of Boris finishes the opera and is preceded by the revolutionary scene.

In Mussorgsky's latest version then, the first scene of Act IV is set in the Granovitaya Palace in the Kremlin, where a session of the Duma has been summoned to discuss the measures necessary to repel the invasion which is threatened. Their deliberations are interrupted by the arrival of Prince Shuisky, just as they were beginning to complain that his absence deprives them of invaluable counsel. Straight away he begins to tell them of the curious sight he saw the previous day, when leaving the Tsar's apartments. Boris was muttering to himself, and seemed to be trying to ward off some spectre, crying, as he did so, 'Away, away'.

No sooner has he uttered the word than Boris's own voice is heard outside, and the same word is on his lips. He staggers into the chamber and seems to see none of the boyars who watch him in frightened silence. Shuisky brings him to his senses, and he takes his seat on the throne, and prepares to listen to the counsel of his boyars. But Shuisky begs to be allowed to speak, and says that a holy man of great age is waiting outside and desires to speak to the Tsar. Boris thinks this may calm his overheated brain and orders that he be admitted.

It is Pimen, and he tells a strange story. A shepherd, blind since birth, was told in a dream to go to the tomb of the Tsarevich Dimitri at Uglich and there to pray beside his tomb. He did so, and immediately his sight was restored. Boris is overcome with horror at this mention of Dimitri, and, calling for light, falls into the arms of the boyars. He understands that he is dying, and sends for his son and for the *skhima* (it was customary for the Tsar to be received into the Church as a monk before he died).

When Fyodor arrives, Boris orders that they be left alone. He bids farewell to his son, and tells him that he is lawful heir to the throne of Russia. Let him beware of the nobles and their plots, and let him care with his life for the Russian people and for his sister Xenia, who will be under his protection. He feels the hand of death upon him, and prays to God that his children may be blessed. The sound of the passing bell can be heard, and then, softly from behind the scenes, the chant of monks praying for the repose of the Tsar's soul. The boyars return to the chamber, and, with a last cry of 'While I have breath I still am Tsar', Boris falls dying in their midst.

Perhaps the opera owed its original popularity in the early years of the twentieth century as much to Chaliapin's performance of the title role as to anything else, and in particular to his singing and acting of this death scene. But its power is such and its effect so moving that it would be wrong to think that only a Chaliapin can do it justice.

Scene ii.[1] A clearing in the forest of Kromy. Dimitri has marched into Russia at the head of his troops, and the country is in a chaotic state of famine and pillage. It is hard to imagine better expression of the disorder and horror, which are the natural consequences of war, than in Mussorgsky's music for this scene. During its course, the mob baits a landlord who has been a supporter of Boris and whom they have cap-

---

[1] The scene in the forest of Kromy replaces one, which would come at the beginning of Act IV, set in Moscow, outside the Cathedral of St Basil. After two years of famine, the people are starving. The crowd does not believe that Dimitri is dead and wonders whether the Tsar's anxiety over Grigory and his claim to be the Tsarevich suggests he is of the same mind. Some ragamuffins steal a kopek from the Simpleton (a half-crazy man, mocked and yet traditionally sustained by Russians), who turns to Boris as he leaves the cathedral and begs the Tsar in retribution to kill them as he killed Dimitri. The Tsar is unnerved by the encounter but stops Shuisky from punishing him and asks the Simpleton instead to pray for him. Even that provides him with no comfort: 'No one can pray for Tsar Herod'. The scene is so effective that many modern productions have included it as well as the scene at Kromy which was intended to replace it, but this not only lengthens the evening but provides an element of solecism by having the Simpleton appear twice, chronologically near but geographically distant.

tured. Children mock a Simpleton, who sings a pathetic song. They steal the few pence he has managed to collect. Varlaam and Missail chant the praises of Dimitri, and, when two Jesuits appear on the scene, denounce them to the crowd, which promptly prepares to string them up on an improvised gallows.

A procession passes across the scene, heralding the approach of Dimitri himself, followed by his troops. He releases the boyar and the Jesuits, and bids the people follow him to Moscow. Then, at the head of his troops and supporters, he leaves the stage. It is empty except for the Simpleton who has taken no part in welcoming the new Tsar. Seated on his stone, he bewails the fate of Russia: 'Woe and sorrow always, lament, Russian folk, poor hungry folk'.

Controversy over whether to use Rimsky-Korsakov's edition (**D**) or to return to Mussorgsky's version (**B**) – the concise, powerful but necessarily limited version (**A**) was heard in England at Sadler's Wells before the war and by Opera North in the 1990s – was for years unresolved. Though most authorities were agreed that the strength of the original's stark scoring is considerably dissipated by Rimsky-Korsakov's bowdlerisation, managements and even conductors were disposed not to drop (**D**), partly because singers already knew it and were disinclined to re-learn their parts, but partly because (**B**) is awkwardly scored and presents difficulties of balance soluble only with almost Festival conditions of rehearsal. Gradually, with repeated performance – as with the Bruckner symphonies – (**B**), even (**A**), have become generally accepted, and there may come a time when the colour and variety of Rimsky-Korsakov's more conventional scoring and lay-out will in its turn suggest revival!

What has been accepted, wherever the work has been performed in virtually whatever version, is the extraordinary power of characterisation which Mussorgsky's music possesses. Boris himself is a towering creation of demonic power, and to sing the role is the summit of ambition of every bass or bass-baritone with Slav tendencies in his make-up. No less remarkable is the way in which the crowd stands out as one of the main influences in the opera. I have never been convinced that it is projected with even greater force than the figure of Boris himself (as some maintain), but the understanding quality of the music Mussorgsky has written for it is extraordinary.   H.

KHOVANSHCHINA
The Khovansky Rising

Opera in five acts, text by the composer and V.V. Stassov. Première 21 February 1886, at St Petersburg. Completed and orchestrated by Rimsky-Korsakov. Official première St Petersburg, 7 November 1911, with Zbrueva, Lobinsky, Sharonoff, Chaliapin, conductor Coates; Paris, 1913, and London, Drury Lane, 1913, with Petrenko, Damaev, Zaporojetz, Chaliapin, conductor Cooper; Drury Lane, 1917 (in English); Covent Garden, 1919, with Thornton, Millar, Richardson, Allin, conductor Pitt; la Scala, Milan, 1926, with Bertana, Dolci, Sdanowsky, Journet; Colón, Buenos Aires, 1933, with Stignani, Ziliani, Morelli, Vaghi; Florence Festival, 1948, with Pini, Parmeggiani, Inghilleri, Christoff, conductor Gui; la Scala, Milan, 1949, with Barbieri, Francesco Albanese, Inghilleri, Christoff, Rossi-Lemeni, conductor Dobrowen; Metropolitan, New York, 1950, with Stevens, Sullivan, Tibbett, Hines, conductor Cooper; Edinburgh Festival, 1962, by Belgrade Company with Bugarinović, Čangalović; Covent Garden, London, 1963, in Shostakovich's version, with Monica Sinclair, Craig, David Ward, Rouleau, conductor Silvestri; and 1972 in Russian in perhaps the first uncut performance anywhere, with Yvonne Minton, Robert Tear, Donald McIntyre, David Ward, Martti Talvela, conductor Edward Downes. English National Opera, 1994, with Anne-Marie Owens, Willard White, Gwynne Howell, conductor Sian Edwards, producer Francesca Zambello.

Prince Ivan Khovansky, *leader of the Streltsy Musketeers*	Bass
Prince Andrei Khovansky, *his son*	Tenor
Prince Vassily Golitsin	Tenor
The Boyar Shaklovity	Baritone
Dosifey, *leader of the Old Believers*	Bass
Marfa, *an Old Believer*	Mezzo-Soprano
A Scrivener	Tenor
Emma, *a girl from the German quarter*	Soprano
Varsonofiev, *attendant upon Golitsin*	Baritone
Susanna, *an Old Believer*	Soprano
A Lutheran Pastor	Baritone
First and Second	Basses
Kuzka *musketeers (Streltsy)*	Tenor
Streshniev	Tenor

Musketeers, Old Believers, Maids-in-Waiting and Persian Slaves in the Suite of Prince Ivan Khovansky, Bodyguards of Peter the Great (Petrovtsy-Poteshny), Populace

Place: In and Near Moscow; Khovansky's Estate
Time: 1682–9
Running Time: 3 hours 10 minutes

Mussorgsky's aim was to picture the struggle between the old and the new in Russian life at the time of the assumption of power by Peter the Great. On the one hand are the reactionary Princes Khovansky, who, with their Streltsy followers, aim to maintain the feudal status quo; on the other, the Westernised Prince Golitsin, established as the favourite and counsellor of the Regent, Tsarevna Sofia, and pledged to reform. On the outer edge of the political spectrum are the Old Believers under Dosifey, who refused to accept reforms imposed as far back as 1654 and who hanker after a return to an old-style Russia founded on religious belief. In Mussorgsky's time, no Romanov was by law allowed to be portrayed on stage but the figure of the young Tsar, known to posterity as Peter the Great, looms over the action and in the course of the opera smashes the opposition. *Khovanshchina*, in contrast to *Boris*, suffers from the lack of a dominating central figure and the legal veto robs the opera of a potential protagonist, or at least a *deus ex machina*.

Mussorgsky, although he began the opera as early as 1872, did not live to finish it himself, the necessary work of scoring and piecing together being done by Rimsky-Korsakov, who also effected a number of changes in his 1883 edition. A more faithful edition by Shostakovich appeared in 1959.

Act I. There is a beautiful prelude beginning *andante tranquillo*. The Red Square in Moscow at sunrise. Kuzka, a musketeer,[1] lies half asleep on guard. A passing patrol sees him and from their conversation it appears that the Streltsy were busy during the night 'making short work' of their opponents in the city. The Scrivener (public letter writer) comes to his place in the square and is soon engaged by the Boyar Shaklovity who dictates a letter to the Tsar and his council warning them of the plots of Prince Khovansky and his son, who, aided by the Old Believers, would become Tsar. The letter must be anonymous and the Scrivener must forget that he wrote it. A mob arrives and forces the Scrivener to read them the proclamation the Streltsy have stuck on the pillar in the middle of the square. The chorus splendidly announces the arrival of Prince Khovansky and causes the Scrivener to quit his place in haste. The Prince arrives and addresses the people, telling them that treason is rife in Russia and that he

is determined to crush the enemies of the Tsars. The people end with an invocation of the 'White Swan'.

As soon as the procession has departed with the crowd, Emma enters pursued by the Prince's son, Andrei Khovansky, who attempts to kiss her in spite of her resistance. Emma's alarm is allayed by the arrival of Marfa, whom Andrei Khovansky has loved and deserted. Marfa upbraids Andrei and bids him repent. The angry youth answers by attacking her with a dagger, but Marfa successfully parries the blow. The arrival of Andrei's father and his Streltsy puts an end to the quarrel. The old Prince likes Emma's looks and orders his guards to take charge of her. His son would rather kill the girl than see her in the hands of the Streltsy, and would do so but for Dosifey, who arrives in time to arrest Andrei's blow. The chief of the Old Believers restores peace. Marfa takes Emma into her care and departs with her. Prince Khovansky and his Streltsy return to the Kremlin, while Dosifey and the Old Believers fall to prayer.

Act II. An apartment in the house of Prince Golitsin, councillor and one-time lover of the Tsarevna. The Prince is discovered reading a love-letter from the Tsarevna. His uneasy conscience tells him, however, not to trust to the favour of the ruler. Varsonofiev announces a Lutheran Pastor who complains of the ill-treatment of Emma by the Khovanskys, a private quarrel in which Golitsin says he cannot intervene. He has invited Marfa to his house to cast his horoscope. A bowl of water is brought, and gazing into it, Marfa in her so-called 'Divination', a celebrated and impressive passage, tells of the disgrace and poverty that will be Prince Golitsin's portion in the time that is coming. He dismisses her angrily and gives orders that she must be seized and secretly drowned. Alone he broods on his past services to Russia. His musing is interrupted by the arrival of Old Prince Khovansky, who has come to complain of Golitsin's interference in his capacity as adviser to the Tsarevna, and of a slight put upon himself. Angry words pass between them until Dosifey appears and advises that differences be reconciled and a return made to government based on the ancient books and customs (Dosifey, he tells Golitsin and Khovansky, was born a noble but in

---

Khovanshchina *(English National Opera, 1994, director Francesca Zambello, designer Alison Chitty).*
The final scene.

youth joined the Old Believers and renounced his title). The song of the Old Believers heard in the distance angers Golitsin, while Khovansky sees in them the saviours of Russia. Marfa rushes in suddenly to ask Golitsin's protection against his servant who attempted to drown her. He was on the point of doing so but the attempt was foiled by the arrival of the Petrovtsy, the bodyguard of Peter the Great. The presence of the Tsar's troops in Moscow, unsuspected hitherto, alarms the Princes. The Boyar Shaklovity comes to tell them that the Khovanskys have been denounced to Tsar Peter as traitors.

Act III. The Streltsy quarter. Marfa sits on a mound near the home of Prince Andrei Khovansky and, to a beautiful tune, sings of her past love. She is overheard by Susanna who accuses her of irredeemable sin. Dosifey appears and comforts Marfa. As they retire, Shaklovity comes in and in an aria, whose mood is one of prophetic dedication, expresses the hope that Russia may be freed from a government which oppresses her. The chorus of the Streltsy approaches and Shaklovity conceals himself. They arrive singing a drinking song and urging one another to repay theft or gossip of neighbours by ravage and destruction. Their womenfolk now enter

and revile them. The uproar is stilled by the arrival of the Scrivener. He has seen foreign mercenaries attack women and children on the outskirts of the Streltsy's own quarters. The Streltsy call in alarm to Prince Khovansky. But the Prince advises submission to the will of Tsar Peter.

Act IV, part i. The residence of Prince Ivan Khovansky, where takes place one of the tautest, most gripping episodes of the entire epic. As the Prince is listening to the singing of his serving girls, Varsonofiev comes from Prince Golitsin to warn him of the dangers which threaten him. Khovansky ignores the warning and orders his Persian slaves to be brought to him to dance. As the dancing ends the Boyar Shaklovity enters to invite Khovansky to the Tsarevna's council. Khovansky at first refuses to go but later appears ready to accompany him. As he leaves the room he is stabbed in the back by Shaklovity.

Part ii. The square in front of the Church of St Basil in Moscow. To the sound of impressively solemn music (in concerts, often known as 'Entr'acte, Act IV'), the people watch the departure of Prince Golitsin in a carriage guarded by troopers. He has been condemned to exile. Dosifey enters lamenting the fall of the two great nobles, Khovansky and Golitsin. After a short dialogue with Marfa he leaves her alone to face Prince Andrei Khovansky, who angrily demands news of Emma. Emma, answers Marfa, is now safe and perhaps wedded to the man she loved, from whom she had been separated by Andrei. He threatens Marfa with the death of a sorceress at the hands of the Streltsy. Marfa defies him and Andrei calls the Streltsy. They come, but not in answer to his call – a mournful procession, carrying blocks on which their heads soon must fall. Andrei is taken to a secret refuge by Marfa. The crowd asks for the death of the Streltsy, but the herald of the Tsar's guards comes to announce that they have been pardoned. (As a matter of historical fact, the Streltsy were not pardoned but tortured and put to death. Peter the Great was ruthless and once in power neutralised Sofia, his half-sister, and confined her to a convent.)

Act V. A pine wood near Moscow. The Old Believers have come to their hermitage for the last time. Their cause is lost, their sect persecuted throughout Russia. The quarrels of princes have brought about their ruin. Rather than yield to the soldiers who surround their retreat they will perish together. Dosifey sings a beautiful prayer in which he says that the world shall see how men can die for its salvation. The Old Believers, amongst whom are Marfa and Andrei, build a funeral pyre which they ascend carrying a lighted taper. As the flames rise and overpower them the troops sent to arrest them arrive and fall back horror-stricken at the sight of the smoking pyre.   F.B., H.

THE FAIR AT SOROCHINTSY
Sorochinskaya yarmarka

Opera in three acts, text by the composer, founded on an episode from Gogol's *Evenings in the Village of Dikanka*. Left unfinished at the time of the composer's death, without the greater part of the last act, and unorchestrated. Given at a concert at St Petersburg, 1911, semi-publicly at the Comedia Theatre, 1911. Another version at the Free Theatre, Moscow, 3 November 1913. In 1917 the opera was produced in a version by César Cui at the Musical Drama Theatre. This version replaced by yet another for which Cherepnin was responsible, Monte Carlo, 1923, with Luart, John McCormack; Buenos Aires, 1929, with Maria Kouznetzova, Davidoff, Sdanovsky, conductor Fitelberg; Metropolitan, New York, 1930, with Müller, Bourskaya, Jagel, Pinza, conductor Serafin; Fortune Theatre, London, 1934; Covent Garden,

1936, with Danieli, de Villiers, Russell, Kassen, conductor Coates; Savoy Theatre, London, 1942, with Daria Bayan, Slobodskaya, Boleslawski, Parry Jones, Arsene Kiriloff, conductor Fistoulari. There is another edition prepared from the original manuscripts by Paul Lamm, with additions by Shebalin, and orchestrated by him; first given in 1931, revised the following year. This is the performing version most widely used now; it has also been recorded.

Cherevik, *an old countryman*................................Bass
Parassia, *his daughter*....................................Soprano
Khivria, *his wife*.................................Mezzo-Soprano
Gritzko, *a young countryman*...........................Tenor
The Priest's Son...Tenor
Cherevik's Crony ....Bass
The Gipsy ....Bass

Young Men and Women, Gipsies, Merchants, Cossacks, Jews, etc.

Place: Sorochintsy, in Little Russia
Running Time: 2 hours

*S*orochintsy *Fair* was written at about the same time as *Khovanshchina*. The story is one of Gogol's, the scene Gogol's own birthplace, in the Ukraine. Mussorgsky wrote the libretto himself, though handicapped in doing so by his scanty knowledge of Ukrainian dialect. Much of the opera was unfinished at his death, but it has had more than a little success outside Russia.

Act I. The introduction is labelled 'A Hot Day in Little Russia', and is an attempt to emulate Gogol's description of the atmosphere in which the story is to take place. The curtain rises to reveal a market scene: 'Mussorgsky constructs' (says Calvocoressi in his 'Master Musicians' volume on the composer) 'a sort of kaleidoscopic musical mosaic which conveys, as realistically as an opera chorus can hope to convey, the confused impression of a country fair'. Cherevik has brought his daughter, Parassia, to a fair for the first time, and she is excited at the bustle, and the variety of things which are for sale. An old gipsy raises his voice above the hubbub to wish everyone well, but also to warn them that the ground on which they stand is cursed by the periodic visitation of a devil, taking the form of a pig and looking, according to legend, for the sleeve (or 'red *svitka*') of a garment he has pawned years ago, but of which he has never been able to recover this one portion.

Parassia has found her young suitor, Gritzko, with whom she sits while the gipsy is telling his story. Cherevik suddenly notices that she is not with him, but Gritzko introduces himself, and asks for Parassia's hand in marriage. The old man can see no harm in such an idea, particularly since Gritzko is the son of an old friend of his, and he gives the couple his blessing. Cherevik disappears, but presently he and his crony reappear from the inn, happily drunk. They are not left long in peace, Khivria, Cherevik's wife, putting in an appearance, and showing little disposition to acquiesce in the notion of acquiring a son-in-law whom she has not yet even seen, much less approved of.

They leave the stage, and Gritzko laments the turn his affairs have taken. Cherepnin's and Lamm's versions have at this point a beautiful aria, but it was intended by the composer for Act III, not Act I at all, the scene in which Gritzko gives way to his sadness having been indicated in the scenario but not (as far as is known) composed. To Gritzko comes the old gipsy, offering, in return for a reduction in the price of the oxen Gritzko wishes to sell him, to convert Cherevik (and, through him, Khivria) to the idea of Gritzko's marriage with Parassia. Gritzko gladly accepts the offer and the bargain which goes with it.

The act should end with the *Hopak* (the best-known bit of the score), but in the Cherepnin and Lamm versions this is transferred to the end of the opera, where it makes an excellent finale. In its place the Cherepnin version has a duet for Parassia and Gritzko, which brings the act to an end.

Act II. Cherevik's house. Khivria is busy in the kitchen. Cherevik is asleep. He wakes up, and there is a short quarrel between husband and wife, during whose course Khivria enquires about the sale of the farm produce. Cherevik leaves the house, and Khivria waits anxiously for her lover, the priest's son, for whom she has prepared the delicacies he cannot resist. He eventually comes into sight, and makes a splendidly comic figure, his pious utterances contrasting nicely with his evidently un-pious intentions. These he is busy making manifest, when suddenly there is a noise outside. Khivria has only just time to hide her lover before Cherevik and his cronies return home, making a deal of noise, and scared at the idea of being where the 'red sleeve' is liable to be found.

They all drink, and, to keep their spirits up, Cherevik sings riotously for their entertainment. The unfortunate priest's son knocks over a tin can but

this is accepted as the work of the 'red sleeve', and no one takes it for what it is. In the end the crony recites the story for the company. When he reaches the climax, the window blows open, and the head of a pig is seen – it is in this form that the devil is said to roam the world looking for his lost garment. General consternation. In the exclamation of horror which follows the revelation, the priest's son loses his balance, and falls into the midst of the assembly, covered by Khivria's nightdress. He is revealed, and Cherevik's friends laugh at the resolute, stiff-necked Khivria, who has given herself away so badly.

Act III. The village square: Cherevik's house visible in the background. Mussorgsky made a special and elaborated version of his *Night on the Bare Mountain* (1867) to act as a ballet-intermezzo between Acts II and III of *Sorochintsy Fair*. The dramatic situation is that Gritzko, the *parobok* (young peasant), is asleep in the open; to him in his dream appears the whole rigmarole of the kingdom of darkness and black magic, and dances round him. In the Lamm version, Gritzko has first extracted Cherevik's consent to marriage with his daughter.

Parassia, alone, sings sadly of her lover, but, looking into a mirror, regains her spirits and sings a charming *Hopak* (marked *allegretto grazioso*). She dances as she sings. Cherevik emerges from the house at the same moment as Gritzko appears. Cherevik loses no time in giving his consent to the marriage – the gipsy's scheme has worked perfectly – and the two young lovers celebrate their future happiness in a lively duet. The rejoicing becomes more general as the other villagers join in, and even the advent of Khivria, emitting story-book step-mother's disapproval from every pore, cannot put a damper on the jollity; Cherevik has acquired new authority from the episode of the priest's son, and will brook no contradiction. The opera ends with the exciting *Hopak* designed by Mussorgsky to come at the end of Act I but transferred by Cherepnin.

The Cherepnin and Lamm versions do not by any means follow Mussorgsky's sketch-plan in every particular. However, as the third act, and even the end of the second, exist in no more than fragmentary form, and as these are the versions most often heard, it seemed more practical to concentrate on them, rather than elaborate on the work in its unfinished state.   H.

OTTO NICOLAI
(born 9 June 1810, died 11 May 1849)

DIE LUSTIGEN WEIBER VON WINDSOR
The Merry Wives of Windsor

Opera in three acts, text by Hermann von Mosenthal, after Shakespeare's play. First produced at the Berlin Hofoper, 9 March 1849 (shortly before the composer's death), with Zschiesche as Falstaff and the composer conducting. First produced Philadelphia, 1863; London, Her Majesty's, 1864 (in Italian), with Tietjens, Vitali, Jura, Santley; Adelphi Theatre, London, 1878 (in English); Metropolitan, New York, 1900 (in German), with Sembrich, Dippel, conducted by Emil Paur; Covent Garden, 1907 (in German), with Jenny Fischer, Minnie Nast, Max Lohfing, Franz Naval. Revived by the Carl Rosa Company, 1943, with Norman Allin.

Sir John Falstaff..Bass
Herr Fluth (Mr Ford) ....Baritone
Herr Reich (Mr Page)...Bass
Fenton ....Tenor
Junker Spärlich (Slender) ....Tenor
Dr Caius ....Bass
Frau Fluth (Mistress Ford) ....Soprano
Frau Reich (Mistress Page).................Mezzo-Soprano
Jungfer Anna Reich (Anne Page)..................Soprano
First Citizen...Tenor

Place: Windsor
Time: Reign of Henry IV
Running Time: 2 hours 30 minutes

Nicolai, who died before he was thirty-nine, had a busy life of professional music-making, and his career embraced such diverse activities as organist at the Prussian Embassy in Rome, Kapellmeister in Vienna, composer in Italy, founder and conductor of the Berlin Philharmonic, and head of the opera in that city. He composed a number of operas, of which *Die lustigen Weiber von Windsor* is by far the most successful, as is hardly surprising in view of the wit, neatness of construction, and light-hearted gaiety for which it is distinguished.

Act I. After an overture which is popular in the concert hall, we find ourselves in the garden between the houses of Messrs Fluth and Reich (Ford and Page, to give them their Shakespearean names), where their respective spouses are comparing notes on the love-letters they have each received that day from no less a person than Sir John Falstaff. They leave the stage to the men. Reich has promised the hand of his daughter in marriage to Spärlich, whom he prefers to her other suitors, Caius and Fenton, in spite of the impassioned pleading of the last-named; Fenton is told Anna is not for a have-not like himself.

Inside Fluth's house, his wife waits for the promised visit from Falstaff. She is furious with all men, and rehearses what she shall say to this particular specimen. She will make as if to give in to him – woman's heart is weak, she observes; he will be taken in and believe her. This is a fine coloratura aria, 'Nun eilt herbei', written on a big scale, with an elaborate recitative and much exacting passage work for the singer.

Falstaff duly arrives, his love scene is interrupted by loud knocking, he hides in the linen basket, and Fluth storms in, announcing he has caught his wife at last and bringing a crowd of witnesses to watch the proceedings. The search begins and the women laugh at the way their well-planned joke is taking shape – Falstaff is to be dumped into the river. The light touch of the duet contrasts well with Frau Fluth's scolding of Fluth for his unworthy suspicion of her. The act ends with a general ensemble.

Act II. We meet Falstaff on home ground for a change, and he leads a drinking song at the 'Gasthaus zum Hosenbande' – The Garter Inn. 'Als Büblein klein' has always been popular and for long a war-horse in the repertory of the German operatic bass. Fluth, calling himself Bach (German for 'Brook'), comes to pump Falstaff on the subject of his relations with Frau Fluth. Their comic duet is admirable, Falstaff's patter being interspersed with horrified interjections from Fluth. 'Wie freu' ich mich' each sings in turn, the one rejoicing at the prospect of his rendezvous, the other at the possibility of catching Falstaff in the act. The audience too should have the chance of rejoicing at the opportunity for the competition the music gives to the two singers, an opportunity not missed in Vienna in the early years of this century when the richly endowed Leopold Demuth and Wilhelm Hesch poured their great voices into the roles of Fluth and Falstaff; a splendid gramophone recording exists to prove the point.

The scene changes to Reich's garden, where no less than three suitors are preparing to serenade Anna. Two of them, Spärlich and Caius, make a decidedly comic effect, the other, Fenton, is distinctly romantic; in fact his 'Horch, die Lerche singt im Hain' is a deliciously pretty tune. There follows a pleasant little love duet for Anna and Fenton and a most ingenious 'quartettino' (as Nicolai calls it) for Anna and the three lovers, the comic pair overhearing what the other two are saying to each other, and handing the tune, which was first sung by Anna, backwards and forwards from one to another until all four are engaged on it. The whole of this garden scene is controlled by the lightest of hands and its delicacy is quite unusual among German comic operas of the period.

We are back in Fluth's house, as in Act I. Fluth tells his wife she will be found out this time; nothing will prevent him catching her lover. He is furious – he even examines the laundry basket which the servants happen to bring through the room at this moment – and his wife laughs at him. Caius, Spärlich, Reich knock at the door saying they are there, as Fluth instructed them. Falstaff is smuggled through dressed as an old woman and guided by Frau Reich. He pretends not to be able to hear Fluth's questions and is got rid of to general acclamation. There is another unsuccessful search, and the act ends with an ensemble.

Act III. The first scene is laid in Frau Reich's house, and there she sings her ballad of Herne the Hunter, an agreeable 6/8 tune. Later Anna delivers herself of the aria which alone makes the role worth a prima donna's while: 'Wohl denn! Gefasst ist der Entschluss'.

The last scene is laid in Windsor Forest, near what the score describes as 'die Eiche des Jägers Herne', or Herne the Hunter's Oak – an English description of *Freischütz* probably sounds just as odd to a German. Here the music we know so well from the overture comes into its own, and is deployed in a succession of choruses and dance movements associated with the preparation and tormenting of Falstaff by the disguised company. Falstaff himself has a trio with the wives of Fluth and Reich – he makes advances to them both; Anna and Fenton, disguised as Titania and Oberon, have a short duet between ballet movements, and finally the big tune of the overture makes its presence felt. All is resolved and the opera ends with a short trio with chorus.   H.

CARL AUGUST NIELSEN
(born 9 June 1865, died 3 October 1931)

SAUL AND DAVID
Saul og David

Opera in four acts, text by E. Christiansen. First produced at the Royal Theatre, Copenhagen, 29 November 1902, with Niels Juel Simonsen (Saul), Peter Cornelius (Jonathan), Helge Nissen (Samuel), Vilhelm Herold (David), Emilie Ulrich (Michal), conductor Nielsen. Revived Copenhagen, 1912, 1929; new production, 1934, with Holger Byrding, Tyge

Tygesen, Einar Nørby, Marius Jacobsen, Else Schøtt, Ingeborg Steffensen, conductor Johan Hye-Knudsen; 1962, with Frans Andersson. Also produced Göteborg, 1928, with Flagstad as Michal; Stockholm, 1930, with Einar Larson, Jussi Björling, Brita Hertzberg, conductor Armas Järnefelt; European Broadcasting Union, 1972 (in English), with Boris Christoff, Willy Hartmann, Michael Langdon, Alexander Young, Elisabeth Söderström, conductor Horenstein.

Saul, *King of Israel* ....Baritone

Jonathan, *his son* ....Tenor

Michal, *his daughter* ....Soprano

David, *a shepherd boy* ....Tenor

Samuel, *a prophet* ....Bass

Abner, *Captain of the King's Guard*.......................Bass

The Witch of Endor ....Mezzo-Soprano

Abisay, *a follower of David's* ....Tenor

Maidens, Priests, Warriors, People

Running Time: 2 hours 15 minutes

From 1889 to the middle of June 1905, Carl Nielsen played second violin in the orchestra of the Royal Theatre in Copenhagen and both his operas, with the exception of the third act of *Maskarade*, were composed during this period. In 1890, on a scholarship to Germany, he went straight to Dresden where he steeped himself in the music of Wagner. He says that the subject of *Saul and David* 'stirred and haunted me, so that for long periods I could not free myself of it no matter where I was – even when I was sitting in the orchestra with my second violin, busy with ballets and vaudevilles.'

The composer and his librettist make Saul into a figure of tragic stature, a man with the intelligence and courage to question the accepted beliefs and superstitions of a primitive society and in contrast to the more naturally representative figure of David, who accepts the existing order and believes in it.

Act I. A short, brilliant martial prelude takes us straight into the action. In front of Saul's dwelling in Gilgal, priests and Israelites together with the King and his son Jonathan wait anxiously for the coming of Samuel, who alone may make sacrifice to the Lord, in order that their stand against the hosts of the Philistines may take place with the blessing of the Almighty. Unable to bear the strain of waiting, Saul turns impatiently on the priests, orders preparations to be completed, and himself performs the priestly office. The scene is one of great urgency, the voices of the soloists, now almost incoherent with fear, now supplicatory to the King, contrast with the choral background of prayer and preparation from priests and people.

The voice of Samuel interrupts the sacrifice to upbraid the King for his presumption, to pronounce him, in spite of his protests of repentance, an outcast in God's sight and unworthy of his kingdom. Saul's

rule is over, an evil spirit will possess him, but the kingdom of Israel will flourish after he is gone. Jonathan alone tries to comfort him, but Saul's spirit is cast down and in solitude he communes with the Lord of Hosts, whom he treats now as his enemy to be defied and overcome. His fine, Iago-like monologue ends in a mood of submissiveness as Jonathan returns, bringing with him his friend, the shepherd boy David. David's singing charms the King and he bids David stay with him as his guest.

Left alone, David tells Saul's daughter Michal that he has loved her since he saw her bathing in the brook with her attendants, and the curtain falls slowly on an idyllic scene of young love.

Act II starts with a martial prelude, more formal in character than that to the first act. While David sings to King Saul, Abner forces his way past the guards to insist that the nearness of the Philistine host requires action, in spite of Jonathan's recent victory over an enemy detachment. The Philistine champion Goliath, a giant of ferocious aspect, has challenged the Israelites to nominate a man to meet him in single combat, the loser's people to become subject to the winner's. David undertakes to defeat him, refusing the King's sword and armour and relying instead on his sling and five smooth stones.

The progress of the fight is followed through the imaginations of Michal and her women, first their apprehension of bloody defeat, then the possibility of victory, until they see the reality of a messenger riding furiously across the valley – Jonathan, with the news of David's triumph over Goliath. A chorus of thanksgiving heralds the return of the Israelite warriors, David and Saul at their head, and the King joyfully gives David the hand of Michal in marriage. Rejoicing is general but when he hears the cry of 'Saul has slain his thousands and David his tens of thousands', Saul's happiness turns to bitterness, so that the act ends with the silencing of the crowd, David's effort to still the King's melancholy with his singing, Saul's hurling of the javelin at his prospective son-in-law and the latter's banishment, and David's defiance of the King.

Act III. A mournful nocturne in 12/8 introduces Saul's sleeping camp at night. Jonathan and Michal, in one of the score's most appealing lyrical passages, mourn the absence of David before they too fall asleep. Suddenly, David and his follower Abisay appear high up among the rocks above the camp. David comes down to stand over the defenceless Saul and then, as a sign that he has been there, takes the spear and the cruse of water which stand by Saul's pillow. David shouts to waken Abner and the King's Guard. Saul cannot remain hostile, faced with David's unrestrained loyalty, and takes him back to his arms. In an impressive and extended polyphonic choral ensemble, the people witness their renewed vows, but the arrival of Samuel fills Saul with new apprehension. Samuel relates his vision of God, telling him to proclaim David King of the Israelites, and solemnly anoints him before falling dead. Saul tries to reassert his sovereignty, bids his soldiers seize David and, when she defies him, Michal his daughter, only to have his authority flouted by his subjects and to be obliged to watch David and Michal walk away unharmed.

Act IV follows a rapid prelude, and two viola solos introduce the scene where Saul and Abner come to consult the Witch of Endor. She insists that if Samuel's spirit is to be conjured from the dead, they must cover their faces and not see him. When he comes it is with accompaniment of trombones and to foretell the death of Saul and his sons at the hands of the Philistines. At the end of an impressive scene, soldiers come looking for Saul to lead them against the advancing enemy.

A vigorous battle interlude leads to the last scene, which takes place on Mount Gilboa. Jonathan enters wounded and dying and supported by Abner. They see on the mountainside the wounded Saul, and Jonathan recognises David behind him and proclaims him 'blest of the Lord' before he himself dies. Saul in a splendid *arioso* demands that Abner kill him so that he may not fall wounded into the hands of the enemy, then cursing God he turns his sword on himself. David arrives with Michal and some Israelite survivors, and together, in music of almost Handelian cast, they mourn Saul and Jonathan and proclaim David their King, chosen of God.   H.

MASKARADE
Masquerade

Opera in three acts, libretto by Vilhelm Andersen, after Ludvig Holberg's play. Première, Copenhagen, 11 November 1906, with Emilie Ulrich/Ingeborg Nørregaard-Hansen as Leonora, Ida Møller/Margrethe Lindrop as Pernille, Karl Mantzius as

Jeronimus, Joanna Neiiendam as Magdelone, Hans Kierulf as Leander, Peter Jerndoff as Leonard, Helge Nissen as Henrik, Lars Knudsen as Arv, conductor Nielsen. Revived fairly frequently in Copenhagen, notably in 1918 when it was restudied, in 1936 when Edith Oldrup sang Leonora, in 1937 when Egisto Tango conducted, in 1943 when Tyge Tygesen sang Leander. Its hundredth performance took place in 1946, and in 1965 there was a new production with Ellen Winther, Else Margrete Gardelli, Willy Hartmann, Ib Hansen, Frans Andersson, conductor John Frandsen. American première, St Paul, 1972. The British première was in Leeds in 1990 by Opera North, conductor Elgar Howarth.

Jeronimus, *a citizen of Copenhagen*	Bass
Magdelone, *his wife*	Mezzo-Soprano
Leander, *their son*	Tenor
Henrik, *Leander's servant*	Bass-Baritone
Arv, *Jeronimus's servant*	Tenor
Mr Leonard, *a citizen of Copenhagen*	Tenor-Baritone
Leonora, *his daughter*	Soprano
Pernille, *Leonora's maid*	Soprano
A Nightwatchman	Bass
A Constable	Baritone
A Mask-Seller	Baritone
A Professor	Bass
A Flower-Seller	Soprano
Master of Ceremonies	Bass-Baritone
A Dancing Master, his Fiancée	Dancers

Students, Officers, Young Girls, Maskers of both Sexes

Place: Copenhagen
Time: Spring 1723
Running Time: 2 hours 15 minutes

In 1905 Nielsen set to work on *Maskarade*, an adaptation of Holberg's comedy of 1724. The influence of *opéra-comique* and a generally French style is apparent, says Jürgen Balzer in an essay published in connection with Nielsen's centenary in 1965, but it is hard when listening to the music not to believe that the composer must have heard – and loved – Verdi's *Falstaff* before setting to work on his own comedy. As it is, he is evidently more interested in the musical possibilities of situation than of character, but the result nonetheless is a work of charm and brilliance. To call it a Danish *Bartered Bride* would be too easy, not only because the subject is less than nationalistic but also because Nielsen is a leading composer in his own right. It is a comedy, thoroughly Danish, and very many works are on the fringe of the international repertory with far lesser claims.

Act I. After a sparkling overture, whose opening arabesque becomes the Masquerade motif, the curtain rises to show us a room in Jeronimus's house. Leander, Jeronimus's son, has been to a Masquerade[1] with his valet, Henrik, and neither finds it easy to wake up next day. Henrik is still dreaming of dancing and even motions to the orchestra to play a cotillion, but Leander in music of fine lyrical flow greets the light and recalls last night's adventure. He is in love, and they must go again to the Masquerade to meet this unknown girl! Unfortunately, there is a snag: his father long ago promised Leander's hand in marriage to Mr Leonard's daughter, whom he has never seen, and in a spirited song Henrik points out that the law deals severely with breach of promise.

Their scene, high-spirited enough to contradict the hangovers they might be expected to be fighting, is interrupted by the entrance of Magdelone, Jeronimus's wife and Leander's mother, who is obviously more than a little envious of Leander's expedition to the Masquerade. She knows of its possibilities only at second hand but plainly would like to sample them, if we are to judge from the dancing in which she now indulges. The gavotte with which she starts is pleasant enough, but there is a change from duple to triple time with a *Folie d'Espagne*, and the combination makes for a charming scene.

The exhibition of Magdelone's prowess is abruptly interrupted by the entrance of Jeronimus himself. He suspects there is a plan to visit the Masquerade, and packs his wife off to her room. Henrik spills the beans about Leander having fallen in love, and Jeronimus, alone, in a monologue which is for the most part reminiscent rather than impassioned, yearns for the old God-fearing days when discipline was discipline and everyone in bed by nine o'clock. Mr Leonard is announced and we find out almost immediately that his daughter is as unwilling to fall in with plans made for her as is Jeronimus's son. Together they plot to prevent a scandal. Jeronimus instructs Arv, a particularly half-witted servant, to keep watch outside the house that night and prevent anyone leaving, then sends for Leander.

When ordered to give an explanation of the previous night's disgraceful behaviour, Henrik distin-

guishes himself by launching, in the jauntiest of songs, not only into a defence of their position but into a piece of special pleading for the few pleasures open to a servant that is so rebellious in its character and content as to be saved only by cheerfulness from being positively revolutionary. Mr Leonard has some sympathy with the young, but Jeronimus demands that Leander make a full apology to Mr Leonard and proceeds to dictate it to him. When it comes to promising to marry Mr Leonard's daughter, Leander jibs, and the finale, a very lively male quintet, is concerned with Leander's reiterated refusal to toe the line.

Act II. The street between the brightly illuminated Playhouse and Mr Jeronimus's home. Though this act is basically concerned with getting everyone to the Masquerade and identifying their costumes, the composer injects considerable lyrical force, beginning in the nocturne prelude with a most poetic evocation of eighteenth-century Copenhagen. There are songs for the nightwatchman and for Arv, the latter of whom is unexpectedly confronted, as it would appear, with a ghost, who bids him confess his sins. Arv clears his conscience, from thefts of flour and wine to that of the cook's virginity, and it is only when the ghost starts to giggle that Arv understands it is Henrik in disguise. If all is not to be revealed, Arv must turn a blind eye when Henrik goes that night with his master to the Masquerade!

In effect, this seems to be the current destination of half the populace, among whom Arv recognises Mr Leonard as he leaves Jeronimus's house. After him come Henrik and Leander, the latter ecstatic at the prospect before him, which indeed promptly materialises in the person of Leonora (of whose true identity he is of course still in ignorance). Nielsen worked many years in the opera house and his admiration for Wagner knew no bounds, but this ecstatic meeting of lovers, even if the composer had his tongue half in cheek, suggests that he was far from despising Puccini. The bustling of Henrik and Pernille round the two lovers and their attempts to parody what is going on by no means invalidate the ecstatic lyricism of the lovers as they sing in sixths.

Interruption comes in the shape of sounds from Mr Jeronimus's house, as it becomes clear he has dis-

---

[1] A carnival ball open to all classes, to which all must go masked.

covered the disappearance of Leander and Henrik. He is sure he knows where to find them, but for the Masquerade he must have a disguise and he goes with Arv to buy it. Enter Mrs Magdelone on pleasure bent, and Mr Leonard equally in search of adventure. Disguised as they are, they meet and agree to go on to the Masquerade together. It remains only for Jeronimus and Arv, got up as Bacchus and Cupid respectively, to make their own way across the street before the nightwatchman, as in Wagner, pre-empts the last word.

Act III. The great hall of the Playhouse. We are plunged into the middle of the festivities with hardly a moment of preluding, and the brilliance and fun of the Masquerade are before us musically as well as visually right from the start. Here is an end of immediate cares and responsibility, here is release. Students seize girls and dance, lovers flirt, there is a charming female trio, and Leander sings happily with his Leonora, even to the extent of exchanging names. The duet[1] of Henrik and Pernille is a deliberate send-up of what their master and mistress have been singing, but warmth is by no means excluded. Soon it is the turn of Mrs Magdelone and Mr Leonard, the former of whom proclaims her unmarried state, though she refuses to unmask. Mr Jeronimus, searching for Leander, interrupts their graceful flirtation, without of course knowing who either is.

There is some danger of a quarrel between students and soldiers, but the master of ceremonies announces the start of the evening's entertainment, and the first item is the very lively *Hanedansen* (Cock's dance), the best-known single number in the score. During its course, Henrik discovers that Jeronimus is here wearing a Bacchus mask, but he somehow persuades a professor who has come with a party of students to side with him and Leander, and together they make Jeronimus drunk.

The next item on the evening's bill has the dancing master and his fiancée act the story of Mars and Venus to graceful waltz music. Jeronimus is inveigled into a round dance and the students sing a song, which does not conceal the intoxicated attempts of the old man to flirt with the dancing girl.

The hour of general unmasking approaches and Nielsen perfectly captures in music the element of sadness implicit in this 'moment of truth'. The master of ceremonies (now dressed as Corporal Mors) calls on everyone present to throw their masks into a big urn placed in the middle of the floor. Mrs Magdelone and Mr Leonard recognise each other and Leonora and Leander, the chance lovers, are revealed as also the objects of the arranged marriage. Only Mr Jeronimus does not at first comprehend that a happy ending seems to be in sight for everyone concerned, but explanations are swallowed up in a final gallop, during which Henrik, Puck-like, solicits the audience's applause.   H.

---

[1] Labelled in the score *Canzone Parodica*.

O

JACQUES OFFENBACH
(born 20 June 1819, died 5 October 1880)

The son of a German cantor who had adopted the name of the town near Frankfurt where he was born, Jacques Offenbach spent most of his working life in Paris. His first comic operas, on a very small scale, were successful at the Bouffes-Parisiens in 1855, and by 1858 larger forces were licensed for the Bouffes, where *Orphée aux Enfers* was an immense and lasting success. Offenbach continued to write one-act operettas for Paris, interrupting his French career to write for Vienna, but in 1864 he inaugurated with *La belle Hélène* a collaboration with the great singer Hortense Schneider which took Paris by storm and lasted until the Franco-Prussian war of 1870 drove Offenbach temporarily from Paris. Other composers – Lecocq, Planquette, Audran – provided competition and his return to France did not bring quite the *réclame* of earlier years. His attempt to invade the precincts of opera with *Les Contes d'Hoffmann* ended with his death and the score still unfinished, but *Hoffmann* became his most performed work.

ORPHÉE AUX ENFERS
Orpheus in the Underworld

Operetta in four acts (originally two), text by Hector Crémieux and Halévy. Première at the Bouffes-Parisiens, 21 October 1858, with Tautin, Léonce, Tayau, Désiré. First performed New York, 1861 (in German); London, Haymarket Theatre, 1865; St James's Theatre, London, 1869, with Hortense Schneider. Revised and enlarged to four-act version, Paris, 1874. Revived Sadler's Wells, 1960, with June Bronhill; Kansas City, 1968, with Sciutti, Monica Sinclair, Driscoll, Cuénod, conductor Rescigno; English National Opera, 1985, produced by David Pountney, designed by Gerald Scarfe, the political cartoonist.

Pluton (Pluto), *god of the underworld* ....Tenor
Jupin (Jupiter), *king of the gods* ....Baritone
Orphée (Orpheus), *a violinist* ....Tenor
John Styx ....Baritone or Tenor
Mercure (Mercury) ....Tenor
Mars ....Bass
Morphée (Morpheus) ....Tenor
Eurydice, *Orphée's wife* ....Soprano
Diane (Diana) ....Soprano
Public Opinion[1] ....Mezzo-Soprano
Vénus (Venus) ....Soprano
Cupidon (Cupid) ....Soprano
Junon (Juno) ....Mezzo-Soprano
Minerve (Minerva) ....Soprano

Running Time: 2 hours 15 minutes

Offenbach's parody of the story of Orpheus originally obtained something of a *succès de scandale*; he was accused of blaspheming antiquity, of poking fun at the music of Gluck, and of satirising the government and prevailing social conditions. Since he was at the time in rather trying financial straits as manager of the Bouffes-Parisiens, success in whatever form it came was by no means unwelcome. History suggests that the role of John Styx was an afterthought and designed especially for the actor Bache, an excellent musician who had just left the Comédie-Française. Within eighteen months of the first night, the Emperor Napoleon III ordered a Command Performance of *Orphée* and congratulated Offenbach afterwards. The original *Opéra-Bouffe* was in two acts and designed by Offenbach's friend, the painter Gustave Doré, but in 1874, when his for-

---

[1] In the 1960 Sadler's Wells production, Calliope, Orphée's mother.

tunes were again at a low ebb, he greatly expanded *Orphée*, adding ballets and transformation scenes and making the whole thing into a four-act operetta on a grand scale. This is what is mostly played today.

The overture as we know it from concert performances is not by a long chalk what Offenbach designed to precede his opera, but was compiled by a certain Carl Binder for the first performance in Vienna; he made use of the overture which Offenbach wrote (an introduction, minuet, and embryonic canon) and added to it the famous violin solo and the Can-Can.

Act I. First tableau. Shepherds and shepherdesses rusticise, Public Opinion introduces the plot, Councillors process with a pomposity worthy of the Mastersingers, and Eurydice sings lightly and prettily of the extramarital love she feels in her heart, while the flutes bill and coo around the vocal line: 'La femme dont le cœur rêve, n'a pas de sommeil'. Orpheus sees her with flowers in her hand; who are they for? It appears that each has lost his or her heart to someone else, and neither intends to renounce the new-found love in favour of connubial bliss. They quarrel and it transpires that Eurydice has a morbid dislike of Orpheus as an artist, hating his fiddle-playing above everything. This is the crowning insult. Orpheus announces he will play for her his latest violin concerto (lasting one and a quarter hours, he says), and the famous violin tune starts. The duet which it initiates is charming, and it is not long before the fiddle tune influences the vocal parts.

Eurydice's lover is Pluto, who appears on earth in the guise of a shepherd and bee-keeper under the name of Aristaeus. He charms Eurydice with a Chanson Pastorale, but admits to her that love for him involves transporting her to the underworld. She says goodbye to life most attractively, and leaves a note behind for Orpheus, telling him that she is dead. This he finds, but his discreet rejoicings are broken in upon by Public Opinion, who threatens him with scandal if he does not follow his wife to Hades; the fact that he does not want to get her back means that his reclamatory action will be even more virtuous than if he did! They start off on their journey, Orpheus complaining, Public Opinion urging him on in a delightful *marziale* duettino.

Act II. The scene changes to Mount Olympus, where the gods are sleeping peacefully. They introduce themselves one by one, until Jupiter is woken by Diana's horn. Diana is unhappy because she could not that morning any longer find Actaeon on earth in his accustomed place. Jupiter reveals that he took it upon himself to change Actaeon into a stag, as he was worried that Diana seemed to be compromising herself rather badly with him. All the gods complain about Jupiter's high-handed, tyrannical ways, but they are stopped in their tracks when Mercury brings news that Eurydice is in hell and that Pluto is on his way to see them. Pluto makes his entrance and is rebuked by Jupiter for having carried off the delightful Eurydice. He defends himself, and soon the gods join in chorus to announce that they are rebelling against the intolerable domination of Jupiter – to say nothing of the monotony of their eternal diet of nectar and ambrosia. In turn, Minerva, Cupid, Venus and Diana remind Jupiter of the disguises he has in the past assumed for his earthly amours, and, in charming and witty 'Couplets', they mock him for his obvious interest in the case of Eurydice. Pluto adds insult to injury by saying that in his view the disguises were necessary because Jupiter was so villainously ugly that he would have got nowhere with the girls without them.

At this juncture, Orpheus and Public Opinion are announced, and Jupiter exhorts the gods to be on their best behaviour when he gives audience to the strangers. Pluto leads off the finale and continues to deny that he has had anything to do with hiding Eurydice. Orpheus starts to ask for Eurydice back, but he has only got as far as the first phrase of 'J'ai perdu mon Eurydice' when the gods and goddesses take up the tune and sing it for him; his demands are obviously granted in advance, since the notoriety of his song has penetrated even to Mount Olympus. Much to Orpheus' dismay, Jupiter orders Pluto to return Eurydice to her husband, and says that he will himself come down to Hades to look for her. Won't he take them too, please, ask the other gods and goddesses, and, when he grants their request, they all join in a hymn of praise which soon becomes a sprightly gallop.

Act III. A sparkling *allegretto* entr'acte introduces the scene in the underworld. Eurydice is being looked after by John Styx, a complete fool on earth and now charged with prison duties in Hades. In a song, with an enchantingly silly melody, he explains that he was once king of Boeotia: 'Quand j'étais roi de

Béotie'. Once he is out of the way, Jupiter comes looking for Eurydice, in whom he is considerably interested. A Tribunal sits to discover the truth, but it is Cupid who comes to Jupiter's aid, preceded by a group of some twenty tiny policemen, singing a very agreeable tune in chorus. This is followed by a wide-ranging slow waltz sung by Cupid himself, who advises Jupiter to disguise himself as a fly. This he does, and imitates its buzzing. Eurydice quickly takes a liking to the fly ('Bel insecte à l'aile dorée'), and they sing and buzz a duet together. At the end, Jupiter in his own voice rejoices at the capture that he seems to have made, and he eventually admits his identity. The scene ends as John Styx repeats his song and is mocked and imitated by Pluto.

Act IV. A splendid *Chœur infernal* opens the scene. Eurydice has by now been turned by Jupiter into a Bacchante, and she is persuaded by Cupid to sing a Bacchic Hymn for their delight. Jupiter proposes a minuet, and all comment on his admirable dancing of it. Then begins the famous Can-Can tune, the best-known piece in the opera. Jupiter is about to go off with Eurydice when Pluto stops him, just at the moment when they can hear the sound of Orpheus' fiddle playing 'J'ai perdu mon Eurydice' for all it is worth. He is warned that he must walk in front of his wife, and that even to glance back at her will lead to the revoking of his permission to take her back with him to earth. Public Opinion urges him to obey the god's injunction, but Jupiter has an unexpected card up his sleeve; he hurls a thunderbolt and the startled Orpheus looks round and forfeits his right to his bride. Everyone is delighted, Eurydice stays on as a Bacchante, and all join in a final version of the Can-Can to express their pleasure at the turn events have taken.

Offenbach wrote startlingly good comic music, full of excellent tunes and humorous invention, and it seems likely to please almost anyone who is at all interested in the best sort of 'light' music (what else can one call it?). *Orphée* itself is a most accomplished and stylish bit of fooling, at its broadest in the spoofing of Gluck's 'J'ai perdu mon Eurydice', its most lyrical in John Styx's song and Eurydice's farewell to life, its most satirical in Diana's entrance song and the couplets on Mount Olympus, its most hilarious and catching in the famous Can-Can.   H.

LA BELLE HÉLÈNE
The Fair Helen

Operetta in three acts, libretto by Meilhac and Halévy. Première at Théâtre des Variétés, Paris, 17 December 1864, with Hortense Schneider as Hélène, Mlle Sully as Oreste, Dupuis as Paris. First performed London, 1866, with Hortense Schneider; New York, 1867 (in German). Revived Paris, 1890, with Jeanne Granier, 1899, with Simon-Girard; 1919, with Marguerite Carré; 1960, with Géori Boué; Berlin, Theater am Kurfürstendam, 1931, with Jarmila Novotna, Gerd Niemar, conductor Korngold, producer Max Reinhardt; London, Adelphi Theatre, 1932, in a new version by A.P. Herbert with Evelyn Laye; Sadler's Wells, 1963, with Joyce Blackham; English National Opera, 1975, with Anne Howells, conductor Mackerras; 1995, with Lesley Garrett.

Paris, *son of King Priam*	Tenor
Ménélas (Menelaus), *King of Sparta*	Tenor
Agamemnon, *King of Argos*	Baritone
Calchas, *High Priest of Jupiter*	Bass
Achille (Achilles), *King of Phthiotis*	Tenor
Oreste (Orestes), *son of Agamemnon*	Soprano
Ajax I, *King of Salamis*	Tenor
Ajax II, *King of Locris*	Baritone
Hélène (Helen), *Queen of Sparta*	Mezzo-Soprano
Bacchis, *Hélène's attendant*	Mezzo-Soprano
Leona, *a courtesan*	Soprano
Parthénis, *a courtesan*	Soprano

Guards, Slaves, People, Princes, Princesses, Hélène's Entourage

Place: Greece
Time: Antiquity
Running Time: 3 hours 10 minutes

La belle Hélène was Offenbach's first collaboration on a grand scale with Hortense Schneider, who at only thirty-one was on the point of retirement but went on to become the toast of the town. The composer and his librettists returned to mockery of classical antiquity and their efforts reveal a new sophistication both dramatically and from the point of view of Offenbach's music.

Act I. The introduction consists of the March of the Kings, and Paris' song played on the oboe. In front of the temple, a chorus pays mock homage to Jupiter during a festivity in honour of Venus. Helen leads the women in their devotions. She sings a mellifluous air in 6/8 ('Amours divins'), then reveals in a conversation with Calchas that she is obsessed with the promise Venus has made to Paris, that he will win the most beautiful woman in the world. This is clearly a delicate situation for her, as who else can lay claim to such a title? To a comic march there enters Orestes, precocious son of Agamemnon, with Leona and Parthénis, the courtesans. He has a skittish song, in whose refrain Calchas joins. Calchas is embarrassed at Orestes' insistence on bringing the two ladies into the temple.

Enter a shepherd asking peremptorily whether a message has yet come from Venus. Even as he speaks the messenger-dove arrives, a little out of breath, and Calchas reads Venus' command – that the shepherd will win the most beautiful woman in the world, clearly Helen. Calchas realises it is Paris, agrees obsequiously to help, and asks rather knowingly for a first-hand impression of Venus. This Paris gives him in his famous song ('Au mont Ida'), perhaps the best known, certainly one of the most attractive of Offenbach's lyrical tunes.

To the accompaniment of a very graceful piece of music, Helen and the women process from the temple, and Helen interrogates Calchas about the handsome young shepherd. Calchas leaves them together, but they have time for only a few words before the Kings of Greece enter in procession. The two Ajaxes, followed by Achilles, announce themselves and their attributes in comic fashion. Next it is the turn of Menelaus, hymning his expectation of imminent cuckoldry, and finally of Agamemnon, King of Kings. The whole episode is Offenbach at his most memorable – and devastatingly comic. It is said that the composer once intended at this point to have a parody of the tournament of song in *Tannhäuser*, but he gave up the idea and we have instead a game of charades,[1] whose winner is to receive his prize from Helen herself. The Kings are bad at the competition, which is won by Paris, still disguised as a shepherd. He announces his identity and, amidst general acclamation ('C'est l'homme à la pomme'), Helen crowns him victor, and invites him to supper. On the side Calchas agrees to try to arrange for Menelaus to be absent. There is a clap of thunder, and Calchas takes the opportunity of announcing a decree from Jupiter: Menelaus must go to Crete ('What the devil to do?' is his aside). The finale gets under way as they all, led by Helen, rapidly admonish Menelaus 'Pars pour la Crète'.

Act II. An entr'acte based on the ripe waltz tune of the act's finale takes us to Helen's apartments, where her women urge her to make a specially fine toilet on this day of all days. Helen for once seems virtuously inclined and chooses a sober dress; let fate not have it *all* its own way. A message comes from Paris, asking Helen to receive him. She tries to refuse, but sighs: 'Pourquoi, ô déesse, as-tu toujours choisi notre famille pour faire tes expériences?' In a song that is a gem of wit and beauty, Helen laments (if that is the right word) her fatal gift:

When one hears it, it is hard to imagine that even Offenbach ever wrote anything more mouth-wateringly appetising. It sums up a whole generation which lived hedonistically but retained the ability to mock itself while doing so.

Paris comes in unannounced, finds her determinedly resistant to love and to threats, and bids her beware of trickery. The music announces the gambling-game of Goose (Snakes and Ladders) – more party games! The Kings bet, Calchas is caught cheating and treated in an ensemble as if he were a welshing bookmaker.[2]

Helen sends for Calchas and asks him if he will through prayer cause her to dream a rendezvous with Paris. She sleeps, Paris enters disguised as a slave, sends Calchas packing, and is alone with Helen. Orestes and the girls can be heard singing outside and soon Helen wakes up. She takes the reality of Paris for the dream she so much wanted, and their extended love duet rivals Gounod in its melodic innocence ('Oui, c'est un rêve'). Their bliss is interrupted by the wholly unexpected arrival of Menelaus, who raises the alarm and summons the Kings who are having supper next door. Orestes with his perpetual song arrives first, but the others are not

---

[1] Napoleon III and Empress Eugénie are known to have been obsessed with party games, which they and their guests played on every possible occasion.

[2] The rather protracted Game of Goose which contains little Offenbach, more Meilhac and Halévy, was omitted in the Paris revival of 1983, to the operetta's distinct advantage.

far behind. Menelaus asks what sort of a show they have made of looking after his honour in his absence. Paris vocalises (like Jupiter as the fly in *Orphée* – did this have an amorous connotation for the composer?), but Menelaus is more taken aback by the suggestion, quickly seized on by Helen, that he is really the most to blame; it is customary for husbands to send warning of their return, is the burden of Helen's delightful song! Agamemnon tries to send Paris away – but, Paris rejoins, in that case he will have to return. To the tune of the waltz of the entr'acte, now with a mocking onomatopoeic verbal accompaniment, they urge him on his way.

Act III. The seaside resort of Nauplia. The entr'acte makes use of Orestes' tune and the curtain goes up to show the Spartans in holiday mood, singing the praises of Venus. Orestes is inclined to think that Menelaus' insistence on the departure of Paris has offended Venus, who seems to have taken revenge on the women of Greece by making them more susceptible than usual to the dictates of the heart. The Kings complain about the crowd now to be found at the seaside – there is no room for decent bathing any more.

Enter Helen and Menelaus quarrelling. Why had Helen said, 'Oh, then it *wasn't* a dream'? Helen explains that Venus had a hand in it, and Paris *is* very attractive. Agamemnon is dissatisfied – Greece is in a sorry moral state due to Venus' displeasure at Paris' departure. It's all Menelaus' fault; if his behaviour could pass as exemplary for a man, it is nothing short of idiotic for a King. In a famous trio, satirising at the same time patriotic moments in *Guillaume Tell* and *La Muette de Portici*, Agamemnon and Calchas try to persuade Menelaus to give up Helen to Paris – in order that Greece may be saved from moral chaos!

Menelaus has had what he thinks is a better idea. He has invited the High Priest of Venus from Cythera to exorcise their troubles, and at that moment he appears in a great ship accompanied by his retinue. The Greeks welcome him and pray for help in their predicament. Of course, it is Paris all the time and he chides them for their melancholy reception – Venus' cult is a bright and breezy affair – and breaks into a *Tyrolienne*, complete with yodelling effects. The High Priest promises them pardon in Venus' name, provided Menelaus allows Helen to embark forthwith for Cythera to make sacrifice to Venus. Helen appears, agrees after some

persuasion to go, and embarks, whereupon Paris reveals himself: Menelaus will not see Helen again – but the implied threat is lost in the final chorus of good wishes for the voyage to Cythera.   H.

BARBE-BLEUE
Bluebeard

Opéra-bouffe in three acts, text by Henri Meilhac and Ludovic Halévy. Première, Théâtre des Variétés, Paris, 5 February 1866, with Hortense Schneider as Boulotte, José Dupuis as Bluebeard and Kopp as Bobèche. Revived in Paris, 1904, with Tariol-Baugé. Schneider played it in London in 1869 and 1870. It was revived at Sadler's Wells in 1966 with Joyce Blackham. The operetta was one of the most successful and long-lived productions of the great Walter Felsenstein at the Komische Oper in East Berlin, with Hans Nocker and Anny Schlemm.

Duke Barbe-Bleue (Bluebeard)	Tenor
King Bobèche	Tenor
Count Oscar, *chief courtier to King Bobèche*	Baritone
Popolani, *court alchemist*	Baritone
Prince Saphir	Tenor
Boulotte, *a peasant girl*	Soprano
Queen Clémentine, *wife of King Bobèche*	Mezzo-Soprano
Princess Hermia, *under the name of Fleurette, Bobèche's daughter*	Soprano
Barbe-Bleue's five former wives	Sopranos, Mezzo-Sopranos
Héloïse	
Rosalinde	
Isaure	
Blanche	
Eléanore	
Alvarez, *a courtier*	Tenor

Running Time: 2 hours

For *Barbe-Bleue*, Offenbach deployed the team which had done such sterling work in *La belle Hélène*, with results which were hardly less satisfactory.

Act I. We meet first the shepherd Saphir (a prince in disguise) paying court to the pretty village florist, Fleurette (a princess in similar case), who is getting fed up with Saphir's excuses every time the subject of marriage comes up. The exuberant Boulotte interrupts proceedings, intent on adding Saphir's to the tally of scalps she carries on her belt. Popolani, Barbe-Bleue's alchemist, is in search of a May Queen

Barbe-Bleue *(Covent Garden, 1989, original production 1963, Komische Oper, Berlin, director Walter Felsenstein, designer Wilfried Werz). Werner Enders as King Bobèche, a role he has sung since 1963.*

for this year's festivity and meets Count Oscar, a dignitary at King Bobèche's court, searching for the King's long-lost daughter, abandoned when Queen Clémentine produced a son. Since the son has turned out an idiot, the King is looking for Princess Hermia; her basket, placed on the river, ought to have come ashore hereabouts, calculates Count Oscar.

Oscar suggests a lottery to find the May Queen. Boulotte wins. Amazement succeeds consternation when the receptacle for the lottery tickets turns out to be the very basket the Princess was placed in eighteen years before, moreover now belonging to Fleurette, who is revealed as the missing Princess. She insists on taking Saphir back with her to court.

Barbe-Bleue is one of King Bobèche's vassals and the demise of successive wives, conveniently before

the celebration of new nuptials, has given him an unsavoury reputation. It is time for his entrance, which he makes in time to catch a glimpse of the Princess as she departs. He is looking for a new wife, five having already been disposed of by the handy alchemist, and his choice falls on Boulotte, dressed up for her May Day coronation and quite unconcerned by her prospective bridegroom's reputation.

Act II. At the palace, courtiers are practising genuflection, but the finger is pointed at Alvarez who is suspected of being the Queen's lover. Count Oscar is to carry out the execution. King Bobèche not only suspects everyone of being the Queen's lover, but he also suspects the behaviour of Barbe-Bleue in the matter of a rapid turnover of wives. There is a snag: Barbe-Bleue's army is much better equipped than

Bobèche's, so he turns to the question of switching Princess Hermia's attention from Saphir to the son of a neighbouring king. A happy ending seems in sight when it is discovered that Saphir is the son of the king in question.

Barbe-Bleue brings his new wife to court, but first sight of Fleurette/Hermia convinces him he has made a bad bargain. Boulotte kisses all the gentlemen, and the outraged Barbe-Bleue resolves to make Hermia wife number seven.

Barbe-Bleue takes Boulotte down to Popolani's cellar, where is the tomb of the first five wives. Boulotte is horrified at the unexpected situation, and makes her plea in an extended duet, but to no avail. Popolani however is a merciful man and offers his prospective victims a choice. One of the phials contains poison, the other nothing more than water – and the hints he drops are broad. Boulotte unerringly chooses wrongly, becomes drowsy and collapses on the sofa.

Barbe-Bleue sees the body of his satisfactorily defunct wife, but no sooner is he gone than an electrical gadget brings her back to life, a situation she finds she shares with each of her predecessors, all of whom have been drugged and then comfortably installed in Popolani's stronghold. Popolani summons the five previous wives for the finale.

Act III. Barbe-Bleue decides to interrupt the wedding of Hermia and Saphir, claiming the Princess as his seventh wife. He threatens the King with his superior artillery, with a blow catches Saphir off guard, and carries the Princess off as his seventh consort. Popolani now puts in an appearance with the earlier wives, all disguised as gipsies. To Oscar he confesses the trick he has played, only to discover that Oscar in his turn has similarly hidden the five men he should have executed as the Queen's lovers. Saphir revives and joins in plotting the future, which discloses Barbe-Bleue furious at his new wife's unwifely attitude towards him, and the Queen, to Bobèche's discomfiture, joining her daughter in what is obviously an early feminist plot. Gipsies are admitted, and Boulotte who is one of them reads the palms of all at court, disclosing the evil-doing of both Barbe-Bleue and Bobèche. The matching sets of putative victims team up together, and Barbe-Bleue patches it up with Boulotte for what may well turn out to be a foretaste of hell. H.

ROBINSON CRUSOË

Operetta in three acts, text by Eugène Cormon and Hector-Jonathan Crémieux. Première Opéra-Comique, Paris, 23 November 1867, with Galli-Marié, the first Carmen eight years later, as Vendredi. The operetta, Offenbach's second for the Opéra-Comique (*Barkouf* in 1860 was the first), was no great success but twentieth-century audiences have taken to it more enthusiastically.

Sir William Crusoë...Bass
Lady Crusoë, *his wife* ....Mezzo-Soprano
Edwige, *their niece*...Soprano
Suzanne, *her maid*...Soprano
Robinson Crusoë, *the Crusoës' son* ....Tenor
Toby, *the Crusoës' general factotum* ....Tenor
Vendredi (Man Friday), *a native*
   of the island....................................Mezzo-Soprano
Jim Cocks, *the cannibal chef, originally*
   from Bristol ....Baritone
Will Atkins, *a pirate chief*....................................Bass

Cannibals and Pirates

Place: Bristol; a Desert Island at the Mouth of the Orinoco
Running Time: 2 hours 45 minutes

The operetta is in many ways a departure from Offenbach's earlier procedure. He writes arias rather than songs, there is less dialogue than in the lighter works, lyricism rather than parody is the order of the day.

Act I follows a jaunty overture. Bristol. Robinson is, as usual, late for Sunday tea with the family. He tells Toby he has booked passage for them both for South America that very night. Suzanne overhears and spills the beans to Edwige, who is in love with Robinson and tries to get him to agree to stay. Toby does.

Act II. A desert island at the mouth of the Orinoco, six years later. Robinson's ship was wrecked and he has saved Man Friday as he was about to be sacrificed. Edwige, who followed him and has arrived on the same island, is there with Suzanne and Toby, now married. Jim Cocks, from Bristol but turned cannibal, tells Suzanne and Toby they are that night to be part of a cannibals' dinner. Edwige is also a prisoner and the cannibals believe that with her blonde hair she will if properly sacrificed become the bride of their god. Man Friday, who fell for Edwige as soon as he set eyes on her, observes the preparations for the funeral pyre, fires Robinson's pistol and rescues the three prospective victims and Jim Cocks.

Act III. Robinson returns to his hut and is reunited with Edwige and the others. He tells them the pirates have sent a boat on shore for supplies and that this is their chance to escape. Robinson sends the pirates off after hidden treasure in the jungle, where they are captured by the cannibals. Robinson now holds the pirates' muskets, with which he rescues them, stipulating that, as they sail for Bristol, Captain Atkins will perform a marriage ceremony for Edwige and him.

Act I is a by no means short, relatively sober-sided affair. With its tale of the Prodigal Son setting the initial tone, its shapely solos and ensembles do not add up to much more than a well-organised *opéra-comique* act, moreover with a protracted farewell. Sparks begin to fly in the second act, where Offenbach writes for mezzo-soprano (Galli-Marié) as opposed to the slipping sopranos he was used to at the Bouffes or the Variétés. Man Friday provides a foretaste of *Hoffmann*! The climax comes with Edwige's waltz song, one of the grandest numbers in any of the composer's operettas.   H.

LA PÉRICHOLE[1]

Operetta in three acts, libretto by Meilhac and Halévy, based on Mérimée's play *Le Carrosse du Saint Sacrement*. Première (in two acts) at the Variétés, Paris, 6 October 1868, with Hortense Schneider. A third act was added for the revival at the same theatre in 1874. First performed New York, 1869; London, 1870. Most recent revivals include those at the Metropolitan, New York, 1957 (in English), with Patrice Munsel, Theodor Uppman, conductor Jean Morel; London, John Lewis Partnership, 1961; Geneva, 1982, with Maria Ewing.

La Périchole, *a street singer* ....Soprano

Piquillo, *another street singer, in love with her* .....Tenor

Don Andres de Ribeira, *Viceroy of Peru* ....Baritone

Don Pedro de Hinoyosa, *Governor of Lima* .....Baritone

Count Miguel de Panatellas, *lord-in-waiting to the Viceroy* ....Tenor

The Marquis de Sartarem.............................Baritone

The Marquis de Tarapote....................................Bass

Two Notaries ....Tenor, Baritone

The Old Prisoner ....Spoken

Joint proprietresses of the 'Three Cousins' tavern
Guadalena ....Soprano
Berginella... Soprano
Mastrilla..Mezzo-Soprano

Ladies of the Court
Manuelita ....Soprano
Ninetta..Soprano
Brambilla ....Mezzo-Soprano
Frasquinella ....Contralto

Courtiers, Citizens, Pages, Guards, etc.

Place: Lima, Capital of Peru
Time: Late Eighteenth Century
Running Time: 2 hours 30 minutes

The story of *La Périchole* is taken supposedly from Prosper Mérimée's play *Le Carrosse du Saint Sacrement*,[2] but the adaptation is a very long way indeed after the original. Offenbach's librettists have abandoned even the bones of the original plot and instead have developed the idea of the situation to make a satire on the Second Empire.

Act I. There is a lively prelude – a march and two airs from the first act – and the curtain goes up on the public square in Lima in front of the café of the 'Three Cousins'. It is the Viceroy's birthday, and he has the habit of roaming round the streets, as he thinks incognito, to find out exactly what is being said and thought about him. Wine is free, and the people of Lima, prompted by the Governor, are perfectly prepared to humour the Viceroy in his masquerade. The proprietresses of the 'Three Cousins' make themselves known in an attractive trio, and then the crowd hears the signal warning them of the Viceroy's approach. His entrance song proclaims his confidence in the impenetrable nature of his disguise, and it is accompanied by the chorus agreeing to respect the incognito of which he is so proud. Across the square come two street singers, la Périchole and Piquillo, her lover. They announce the title of their ballad as 'The Soldier and the Indian Maid' and a very catchy duet it is that they sing. The song finished, they take a collection, not very successfully because Piquillo looks so fierce that he frightens off all the men who want to give la Périchole money, and they are obliged to try another number, a 'séguedille pour soirée'. This time the collection is spoiled by a circus procession, and la Périchole and

[1] Pronounced 'Perikole'.
[2] Mérimée's drama was played in London in 1957 with Edwige Feuillère, and it was from it, too, that derived Jean Renoir's beautiful film *The Golden Coach*, starring Anna Magnani.

Piquillo are left hungry, tired and almost penniless.

Piquillo leaves the stage, and Don Andres can resist the attraction of la Périchole no longer. He asks her if she wouldn't like to be one of the Viceroy's Ladies-in-Waiting – his wife is dead, but he thinks it nice to carry on old customs. She is hungry and she accepts, but first she must write a letter to tell Piquillo what has happened and say goodbye to him. Her attractive song of farewell ('O mon cher amant'), a genuinely touching piece, is in unusually serious vein for Offenbach and his public. She arranges for her letter to be given to Piquillo, but in the meanwhile Don Andres has discovered a snag: nobody but a married woman can become Lady-in-Waiting to the Viceroy, and la Périchole is single. There is a simple solution: he orders Panatellas, his Lord-in-Waiting, to find the lady a husband, and Don Pedro, as Governor of Lima, to collect a notary to perform the marriage ceremony.

In the meanwhile Piquillo receives the letter and in despair is about to hang himself when a diversion occurs. He is selected by Panatellas as the prospective husband of the Viceroy's new lady friend, and in return for money he agrees to go to the Palace.

The finale takes place in an atmosphere of considerable well-being. Both prospective parties to the marriage and the two notaries who are to perform it have had their consciences eased with alcohol. La Périchole in fact sings a charmingly tipsy waltz song ('Ah, quel dîner') as she waits to sign the wedding agreement. She is delighted to recognise Piquillo as the bridegroom, but he is too drunk to have any idea who she is and takes care to explain that he is in love with someone else. The marriage duly takes place and the Chorus works up so much enthusiasm that it seems likely at any moment to break into a can-can. La Périchole and Piquillo, more from force of habit than anything else, sing a snatch of the ballad we heard earlier, and the act comes to an end.

Act II. An elaborate entr'acte takes us to a grand room in the Palace. The situation is complex. The newly created Countess of Tabago must be presented officially by her husband to the Viceroy, but it proves by no means easy to persuade Piquillo to fall in with this scheme, particularly as he now has only one thought in the world and that is to return to la Périchole, wherever she may be. The ladies of the Court are not only jealous of the new arrival but also contemptuous of her lowly birth. When la Périchole appears, Piquillo of course recognises her and loses his temper to such a degree that none of her efforts (even the famous air 'Mon Dieu, que les hommes sont bêtes') serves to calm him. He proceeds to denounce her, for all the world like Alfredo in *La Traviata*, as a heartless and wicked jade, so that the Viceroy has little option but to order him off to prison. There he is to be confined with all other husbands who have proved recalcitrant – to a most seductive waltz tune, great play is made with the individual syllables of the word 'recalcitrant', which comes as the climax to one of Offenbach's most splendid finales.

Act III, scene i. A dungeon in the prison. The court officials conduct Piquillo to his jail, congratulate him on his honourable conduct, and leave him, not however before singing a brilliant trio with him in the form of a bolero. While Piquillo, in a charming song, wonders if his 'wife' is going to do anything about his predicament, la Périchole for her part has procured the Viceroy's permission to visit her husband in prison and, after some mutual recriminations, his heart is melted – as whose wouldn't be? – by her slow waltz song 'Tu n'es pas beau', and its refrain 'je t'adore, brigand'. All is made up between them, and they resolve to bribe the gaoler and procure Piquillo's escape – unfortunately the gaoler turns out to be Don Andres in another of his disguises, this time a successful one. He gets his own back by ordering la Périchole to be chained to the wall opposite Piquillo, but in a delightful trio whispers to her as he leaves the dungeon that she will be released the moment she gives the sign that she loves him.

The lovers are not long together before an old prisoner burrows his way like a mole through the wall. He has been in prison for years, nobody quite knows why, but at last he seems within reach of escape. He helps to free them from their shackles, and they agree that la Périchole shall make the signal to the Viceroy. When he comes in full of ardour, they capture him, tie him up and make their way safely out of the jail.

The second scene is again set in the public square. The soldiers are out and searching the town for the runaways, who for their part have taken refuge in the café of the 'Three Cousins'. There is a very agreeable trio for the cousins and, once the soldiers have left the square, the three escaped prisoners make their appearance. They decide to give themselves up, and la Périchole urges a final appeal to the Viceroy's good nature in the form of a ballad 'La Clémence d'Auguste'. It is completely successful, he grants them their freedom, and the operetta ends with a repetition of the ballad heard in the first act.   H.

LES CONTES D'HOFFMANN
The Tales of Hoffmann

Opera in three acts, text by Barbier and Carré. Première Opéra-Comique, Paris, 10 February 1881, with Adèle Isaac (Stella, Olympia, Antonia),[1] Ugalde, Talazac, Taskin. First performed New York, 1882; London, Adelphi Theatre, 1907; His Majesty's, 1910; Covent Garden, 1910, with Teyte, Nevada, de Lussan, Hyde, conductor Beecham; Metropolitan, New York, 1913, with Hempel, Fremstad, Bori, Macnez, Gilly, conductor Polacco. Revived Metropolitan, 1924, with Morgana, Bori, Fleta, de Luca; Covent Garden, 1936, with Andreva, Delprat, Dino Borgioli, Pinza, conductor Beecham; Metropolitan, 1943, with Munsel, Djanel, Novotna, Jobin, Pinza, Singher, conductor Beecham; Vienna State Opera, 1947, with Lipp, Welitsch, Jurinac, Patzak, Schöffler; Berlin, Komische Oper, 1958, in production and arrangement by Felsenstein; Sadler's Wells, 1970, with Anne Evans, William McAlpine, Geoffrey Chard; Covent Garden, 1980, with Serra, Cotrubas, Baltsa, Domingo, Geraint Evans, Nimsgern, Ghiuselev, Robert Lloyd.

Lindorf, *a councillor of Nuremberg*......................Bass[2]

Andrès, *Stella's servant*....................................Tenor[3]

Hermann, *a student* ....Baritone

Nathanael, *a student*..Tenor

Luther, *innkeeper* ....Bass

Hoffmann, *a poet*...Tenor

Nicklausse, *his companion*..................Mezzo-Soprano

Spalanzani, *an inventor*.....................................Tenor

Cochenille, *his servant* ....Tenor[3]

Coppelius, *a scientist and Spalanzani's rival* ...Baritone[2]

Olympia, *a mechanical doll*.............................Soprano

Antonia, *a singer*..Soprano

Crespel, *her father, a councillor of Munich*.......Baritone

Frantz, *his servant*..Tenor[3]

Dr Miracle, *a doctor* ....Baritone[2]

The Voice of Antonia's Mother ....Mezzo-Soprano

Giulietta, *a courtesan*....................................Soprano

Schlemil, *her lover* ....Bass

Dapertutto, *a sorcerer*..................................Baritone[2]

Pittichinaccio, *an admirer of Giulietta's*.............Tenor[3]

Stella, *an opera singer* ....Soprano

The Muse of Poetry ....Actress

Place: Nuremberg; Munich; Venice
Time: Nineteenth Century
Running Time: 2 hours 45 minutes

Offenbach died during rehearsals of *Hoffmann*, and Ernest Guiraud orchestrated the piece for its Opéra-Comique première, 'tidying' it up and dropping the Giulietta act in the process (in order to retain the barcarolle, he set the Antonia act in Venice!). A dozen years after the first performance Giulietta was brought back, but out of sequence, before Antonia rather than after as Offenbach and his librettists had intended. The episodes of Hoffmann's three loves have little intrinsically in common, and the invention of an evil genius appearing in different disguises to remove the ladies from Hoffmann's grasp (or save his poetic genius from them?) provides continuity rather than a powerful dramatic clash. Editors therefore have seized on the fact that there is no genuinely final version and have cut, added and generally re-worked the opera for almost every revival. Mahler for Vienna scrapped Prologue and Epilogue, but Hans Gregor in Berlin in 1905 restored arias for Coppelius and Dapertutto, taking care however to put Coppelius's tune under Dapertutto's words (the music of the so-called Mirror or Jewel aria was originally written for *Le Voyage dans la Lune* and there is no convincing evidence that Offenbach had finally decided to use it in *Hoffmann*). Felsenstein in Berlin in 1958 and Edmund Tracey and Colin Graham for Sadler's Wells in 1970 are examples of recent attempts to restore Offenbach's intentions as far as they are known or can be deduced. In either case, as in any remotely 'authentic' performance, the order is as given hereafter and the opera is in *opéra-comique* form, with a considerable quantity of spoken dialogue.

The Tales of Hoffmann is recognisably Offenbach in his most lyrical vein and there is little doubt he hoped in it to produce his masterpiece. This he may well have succeeded in doing, and if so it is partly because of the striking level of melodic invention which he sustains throughout, but partly also because he discovered a

---

[1] The Giulietta act was not included in the première.
[2] It is customary for the incarnations of Hoffmann's evil genius (Lindorf, Coppelius, Dapertutto and Dr Miracle) to be undertaken by the same singer,
as are, exceptionally, the three main soprano roles.
[3] Usually taken by the same character tenor.

vein of sardonic musical humour which, particularly in the scenes concerned with Doctor Miracle, gives his music a new sense of the macabre. In whatever version the opera is presented, even the most perverse and furthest removed from what we now believe were Offenbach's latest thoughts, *The Tales of Hoffmann* keeps its central place in the repertory.

Prologue. Luther's Tavern in Nuremberg, situated next door to the opera house, where a performance of *Don Giovanni* is in progress. A drinking chorus can be heard off-stage. Lindorf comes in with Andrès, the servant of the prima donna Stella, who is singing in *Don Giovanni*. Lindorf obtains from him a letter his mistress has written to Hoffmann, making an assignation for that evening and enclosing the key of her room. Lindorf, who assumes during the course of the opera and in various forms the role of Hoffmann's evil genius, in an aria exults over his prospective victim. A crowd of students enter the tavern and immediately start to celebrate the prospect of the beer which Luther brings them.

Enter Hoffmann, with Nicklausse. They sit down with the students, and Nicklausse, with obvious ironical intent, starts to hum 'Notte e giorno faticar' from the first act of *Don Giovanni* which they have just been listening to. Hoffmann seems out of humour, and haunted by the sight of Stella. He is prevailed upon to sing a song to the assembled company, and strikes up the Legend of Kleinzach ('Il était une fois à la cour d'Eisenach'). With the chorus echoing his phrases, he goes briskly through the description of the little dwarf whose knees clicked together as he walked, but when he comes to describe his face, gradually falls into a reverie and instead starts to rhapsodise on the features of his lady-love. He is interrupted, recovers himself, and finishes the song he began.

Hoffmann and the students complain about the quality of Luther's beer, and a punch bowl is brought and duly greeted in song. Hoffmann is by no means pleased to see Lindorf, whom he refers to as haunting his steps and bringing him bad luck. He offers to tell the story of the three great loves of his life, and, in spite of Luther's warning that the curtain is going up on the second act of *Don Giovanni*, all announce their intention of staying behind to listen. The first, says Hoffmann, was called Olympia.

Act I (Olympia) is introduced by a mocking minuet. When the curtain goes up, we are in Spalanzani's room. He is waiting for the arrival of guests who have been invited to witness the astonishing feats of his performing doll, Olympia. Spalanzani mutters that he hopes to make a fortune from his invention, which will recoup him for the loss he suffered when Elias the banker went broke. If only his rival Coppelius does not try to claim a share of the proceeds!

Hoffmann appears, and is immediately impressed by Olympia, whom he takes for Spalanzani's daughter. He sings ardently to her of love. His aria, 'Ah, vivre deux', is one of the loveliest expressions of his romantic spirit to be found in the entire opera. Nicklausse is not at all surprised to find his master in his usual love-lorn condition, but comments tartly on the improbable nature of the new object of his affections – a mechanical doll indeed!

Coppelius comes in to observe Hoffmann gazing fatuously at the doll. He tries to interest him in his own invention; eyes and spectacles to suit every requirement. 'J'ai des yeux' he sings as he shows off his wares. We may guess that the pair he sells to Hoffmann are rose-tinted; at any rate, they seem to increase his delight in beholding Olympia. Spalanzani sees Coppelius, and is forced to acknowledge the latter's share in Olympia; he supplied her eyes, in consideration of which Spalanzani makes him out a bond for five hundred crowns – drawn on Elias's bank.

The guests start to arrive. To the familiar tune of the minuet, they thank Spalanzani for his hospitality. He produces Olympia, whom he describes as his daughter, for their admiration, and accompanies her on the harp while she sings her famous Doll's Song to the assembled company: 'Les oiseaux dans la charmille'. The music perfectly but charmingly imitates the automaton-like delivery that one might expect from a mechanical toy, and in between whiles Spalanzani winds up the spring which brings his 'daughter' to life. She extends her hand to the guests who crowd around to congratulate her, and is left alone with Hoffmann while the others go in to supper. He sings to her, but, when he touches her shoulder, she suddenly rises from the sofa and goes quickly across the room, brushing through the curtains which divide her room from the main part of the house. Hoffmann follows her, in spite of Nicklausse's warning that Olympia is a lifeless doll.

Coppelius returns having found out that he has been cheated by his rival. The dance begins again, and Hoffmann waltzes with Olympia, who, once she is wound up, goes faster and faster so that the other guests wonder if they can save Hoffmann from breaking his neck. When Spalanzani finally manages to catch up with the doll and stop her, she breaks out into coloratura gyrations over the top of the chorus. Olympia is put away in her room, and all bend over to see what damage has been done to the exhausted Hoffmann. Suddenly, the noise of smashing machinery is heard. Coppelius emerges from Olympia's room, laughing with triumph, and Hoffmann is left disillusioned at the discovery that his beloved was only a doll.

Act II (Antonia). Munich; a room in Crespel's house. Antonia, his daughter, sits singing ('Elle a fui, la tourterelle'). Crespel comes into the room, and is distressed to find his daughter in a fainting condition. She has broken her promise not to sing, but she says it was the sight of her mother's portrait that prompted her. Crespel has already seen signs of the consumption which carried away her mother, and he blames her overwrought condition on Hoffmann, to escape whose attentions he has brought her to Munich. Crespel shouts for his deaf old servant Frantz, to whom he gives orders that no one is to be admitted to the house on any pretext whatsoever. When he is alone, Frantz protests that his crotchety master would make his life a misery were it not for the consolation he gets from his singing and dancing, both of which he maintains he does well. After demonstrating the questionable truth of both these assertions, he falls exhausted into a chair, from which Hoffmann, who comes through the door with Nicklausse, at last manages to rouse him.

Hoffmann looks at the song which is lying open on the harpsichord, and has just begun to sing it when Antonia appears. After an impassioned duet, Antonia hears her father coming, and Hoffmann hides as she leaves the room. Crespel comes in, wishes Hoffmann to the devil, but transfers his spleen to Dr Miracle, when Frantz tells him the doctor is at the door. He tries to have him kept outside but is too late, and with a burst of laughter, Miracle enters. Hoffmann from hiding sees Miracle's preparations to treat Antonia, and recognises that he is evil; Crespel is in despair at not being able to get rid of the man who, he is certain, killed his wife and will yet kill his daughter as well. Although she has not yet appeared, Miracle pretends to feel Antonia's pulse and announces his worry at its irregularity. In

response to his command, she sings a brilliant flourish from her room, but still does not appear. Crespel begs Miracle to leave her alone, but he insists that he can cure Antonia, if only he is allowed to. A fine trio for male voices develops in the course of the action.

Hoffmann is alone, but is soon joined by Antonia. He tries to persuade her to renounce her singing for the sake of her health and her love. She agrees, but no sooner is Hoffmann safely out of the way than Dr Miracle is back, pouring temptation into her ear. Can she bear to waste such talent by silencing her voice for ever? Before long, Antonia hears the voice of her mother calling upon her to sing; the portrait glows with life, and Miracle says that he is only there to cause her to give effect to her mother's dearest wish. There is a highly impressive trio, during whose course Miracle seizes a violin from the wall and plays wildly on it. Antonia's voice rises higher and higher until she falls dying to the ground. Miracle disappears, and Crespel rushes in to hear his daughter's last words. When Hoffmann comes in, Crespel blames him for Antonia's death. Hoffmann wants to call a doctor, but, in answer to his summons, it is Miracle who comes.

Act III (Giulietta). Venice. The decorated gallery of a palace overlooking the Grand Canal. The guests of Giulietta are grouped around, and some of them lie on the sofas. Nicklausse and Giulietta in a gondola sing the famous barcarolle, 'Belle nuit, ô nuit d'amour', one of the world's most popular tunes.

Hoffmann objects to its melancholy strains, and responds with a lively song, whose refrain is taken up by the chorus. Giulietta introduces her guests and invites them to a game of cards, Nicklausse seizing the opportunity of telling Hoffmann that he means to take him away the moment he shows the least sign of falling in love with Giulietta. Hoffmann swears that he will not succumb to her charms – may his soul be forfeit to the devil if he does!

Dapertutto is watching him and, when Hoffmann has gone out, produces a huge diamond, with which, he says, he will persuade Giulietta to capture Hoffmann's soul for him as she has done with that of Schlemil. They have only to look into his magic mirror, and their souls stay with their reflections. He is given a powerful aria, 'Scintille diamant',[1] which admirably displays a strong bass voice.

---

[1] From *Le Voyage dans la Lune* and not in the original score.

Giulietta agrees to do Dapertutto's command, and upbraids Hoffmann for wishing to leave just because he has lost his money gambling. Hoffmann is quite unable to resist her, and he sings lovingly of the passion which overwhelms him in her presence ('O Dieu de quelle ivresse'). Like his song to Olympia, this is lyrical expression of a high order.

There is an ecstatic duet for them, 'Si ta présence m'est ravie', during whose course she obtains the reflection which Dapertutto covets. Then Schlemil rushes in and furiously denounces Giulietta's unfaithfulness. Hoffmann discovers he has no reflection when he looks into a mirror, but still he will not leave Giulietta. A septet[1] begins, in which Hoffmann declares his love, Dapertutto and Pittichinaccio their contempt for the poet; Giulietta admits that she found the diamond irresistible, Schlemil furiously anticipates revenge, and Nicklausse and the chorus look with pity at Hoffmann's predicament.

Giulietta saves the situation by suggesting an excursion on the canal, but Hoffmann and Schlemil fight, the former, using Dapertutto's sword, succeeding in killing his rival and removing from a chain round his neck the key of Giulietta's room. The sound of the barcarolle can be heard, but, when Hoffmann rushes away to find his Giulietta, it is to see her float away in the gondola in the arms of Pittichinaccio.

Epilogue. After an intermezzo based on the barcarolle, we are back in Luther's tavern. Hoffmann's story is finished; so too is the performance of *Don Giovanni* in which Stella has been taking part. She is doubtless, as Nicklausse observes, the personification of the three types of womanhood that Hoffmann has idealised in his stories. But Hoffmann is too drunk to care – Lindorf is perfectly confident on that score – and, as the students eddy round him singing the drinking song from the prologue, the Muse of Poetry appears by his side claiming him for her own. Hoffmann seems to be in a stupor. As Lindorf leads Stella from the room, she turns and throws a flower from her bouquet to him. He looks blankly in her direction. There is no doubt that he is dead drunk.   H.

---

[1] Often placed here but by Sadler's Wells restored to its allegedly correct position in the Epilogue.

CARL ORFF

(born 10 July 1895, died 29 March 1982)

Carl Orff was involved in opera from his earliest days and, whatever one may think now of his realisation and version of Monteverdi's *Orfeo* in 1926, it represents an attempt to perform a great masterpiece long before such attempts were in vogue. His operatic ventures have been in a number of apparently unrelated forms, ranging from the 'dramatic cantatas' *Carmina Burana* and *Catulli Carmina*, with their slightly risqué Latin texts and emphasis on the chorus, through the grandiosely tragic *Antigone* (Hölderlin's translation of Sophocles) to *Die Bernauerin*, a work with a specifically Bavarian flavour which is probably impossible to transplant from its native habitat. Common to all are racy rhythms, spicy orchestration, the composer's great sense of theatre and determination to capture his audience's attention. His success, at least in Germany, has been unquestionable.

DIE KLUGE

The Clever Girl

Opera in one act, text by the composer after a story by the Brothers Grimm. Première, Frankfurt, 20 February 1943, with Coba Wackers, Günther Ambrosius, Rudolf Gonszar, conductor Otto Winkler, producer Günther Rennert. First performed Dresden, 1947, with Christel Goltz, Manfred Hübner, Gottlob Frick, conductor Joseph Keilberth; Berlin, Komische Oper, 1948, with Elisabeth Grümmer, Josef Herrmann; Rome, Teatro Valle, 1951, with Ornella Rovero, Sesto Bruscantini; San Francisco, 1958, with Leontyne Price, Lawrence Winters, conductor Leopold Ludwig; London, Sadler's Wells by New Opera Company, 1959, with Heather Harper.

The King	Baritone
The Peasant	Bass
His Daughter	Soprano
The Jailer	Bass

The Man with the Donkey................................Tenor
The Man with the Mule................................Baritone
Three Vagabonds.....................Tenor, Baritone, Bass

Running Time: 1 hour 30 minutes

The Peasant is in prison and bemoans his lot ('O hätt' ich meiner Tochter nur geglaubt!') – if only he had listened to his daughter when she warned him! While ploughing, he found a golden mortar and took it to the King, which immediately put him under suspicion – as his daughter suspected it would – of having stolen the pestle! The King has heard his caterwauling and the Peasant tells him that his daughter gave him wise advice, which causes the King to want to meet her.

The King tells her that he will let her father off all further punishment if she can solve three riddles. She does so without difficulty and the King makes her his wife.

Enter three vagabonds, followed by two men, one with a donkey and the other with a mule, who demand that the King judge their case. Donkey and mule were together in the stable at the inn and the donkey had a foal. The man with the mule insists that as the foal was nearer the mule when they found it, the foal belongs to him, although this goes against every known rule of nature. Curiously enough, the King finds for the man with the mule, and he goes happily off with the vagabonds, leaving the Queen to console the disconsolate donkey man. If he follows her advice for the future, everything will go right. Not only does the donkey man complain in some of the first gentle music heard in the opera but he is put on the right new track in similar vein.

The vagabonds here embark on one of the score's best numbers, a moralistic trio, 'Als die Treue war geboren' (At the time that Truth was born), with a middle section about the eclipse of faith, justice, piety, humility, truth and the rest – William Mann suggested that the only reason these qualities were permitted to be cried out loud and clear in Nazi Germany was because their names were decently veiled in Latin!

The donkey man can now be seen dragging a large fishing-net backwards and forwards over the ground, and the King asks why he does it. If a mule can bear a foal, the man explains, he may perfectly well end up catching fish on dry land! The King is furious and sees the hand of his wife behind such impertinence. The donkey man in his fear confirms that this is true.

In a paroxysm of rage (and in music of similar cast to the peasant's at the start of the opera) the King banishes his wife, telling her she may fill a chest with whichever of his possessions she chooses. She sings lyrically as she gives the King a drink; is it a lullaby, is it a valediction? The donkey man is freed from prison and next morning, the King wakes up in the chest, to discover that his wife gave him a sleeping draught and put him there. She tells him that of all his possessions he himself was the one she most wanted to take with her! The King overflows with admiration and tells her she is the cleverest of women, but she denies this and says it was nothing but pretence because nobody can be really clever and at the same time in love.

The last word is the Peasant's: 'In the end, she found the pestle!'

Die Kluge has been popular from the start, with its easy, catchy music, and skilful dramatic shaping. Orff himself calls the opera 'a little world theatre' and there is no doubt that he saw the King as representing the totalitarian bully, at any stage of history, with the mule-driver a typical 'villain within the law' such as flourishes in a regime of this kind. All the same, to have put such symbolical figures on to the stage under the Nazis is an action not without its own brand of courage.   H.

P

KRZYSZTOF PENDERECKI

(born 23 November 1933)

THE DEVILS OF LOUDUN

Die Teufel von Loudun

Opera in three acts, libretto by the composer, based on John Whiting's dramatisation of Aldous Huxley's *The Devils of Loudun* (German translation by Erich Fried). Première, Hamburg, 20 June 1969, with Tatiana Troyanos, Andre Hiölski, Helmut Melchert, Bernard Ladysz, conductor Henrik Czyz. Stuttgart, 1969, with Colette Lorand, Carlos Alexander, conductor Janos Kulka, producer Günther Rennert; Santa Fe, 1969, with Joy Davidson, John Reardon, conductor Stanislaw Skrowaczewski. British première, Sadler's Wells Opera, 1973, with Josephine Barstow, Geoffrey Chard, Harold Blackburn, producer John Dexter, conductor Nicholas Braithwaite.

Jeanne, *the Prioress of St Ursula's*
    Convent......................................Dramatic Soprano

Ursuline Sisters
    Claire ....Mezzo-Soprano
    Gabrielle ....Soprano
    Louise ....Contralto

Philippe, *a young girl* ....High Lyric Soprano

Ninon, *a young widow* ....Contralto

Father Grandier, *the Vicar of*
    St Peter's Church ....Baritone

Father Barré, *the Vicar of Chinon* ....Bass

De Laubardemont, *the King's Special*
    Commissioner ....Tenor

Father Rangier ....Basso Profondo

Father Mignon, *the Ursulines' father confessor* ...Tenor

Adam, *a chemist*...Tenor

Mannoury, *a surgeon*......................................Baritone

D'Armagnac, *the Mayor of Loudun*........Speaking Part

De Cérisay, *Town Governor*....................Speaking Part

Prince Henri de Condé, *the King's*
    Special Ambassador ....Baritone

Father Ambrose, *an old priest* ....Bass

Bontemps, *a jailer*...................................Bass-Baritone

Clerk of the Court ....Speaking Part

Ursuline Nuns, Carmelites, People, Children, Guards, Soldiers

Place: Loudun
Time: 1634
Running Time: 2 hours 15 minutes

At the première of Penderecki's *The Devils of Loudun* in Hamburg in June 1969, I was vastly impressed by the way the composer had wrung the last drop out of the tensions of the original play, its inexorability and its horrors, and expressed it all through music. Seldom is a texture or a musical movement sustained for long at a stretch, much less developed, and the solo voice – though every word is, exceptionally, audible – is used either in declamation or in isolated expressive phrases. And yet the *effectiveness* of what Penderecki has done is not in doubt. With the precision of an acupuncturist and by musical (i.e. not solely stage) means, he touches nerves unerringly to produce a reaction, thus advancing the drama and manipulating the emotions of his audience at one and the same time.

'Huxley was examining the phenomenon of the Ursuline nuns who claimed to be possessed by devils as one manifestation of mankind's innate urge for self-transcendence, others including drink, drugs, and sexual adventure – though he also compared the witch-hunting of Urbain Grandier with similar persecutions in modern times. For Penderecki, whose earlier works have proclaimed him a devout Christian, Grandier is a Christ-like martyr, proudly set on the road to martyrdom quite early on, and this is the Parson's passion that we are witnessing in his opera.'[1]

---

[1] William Mann, *The Times*, 23 June 1969.

The personal tragedies of Grandier and Mère Jeanne are set against a background of political manoeuvrings in which Grandier, the vicar of St Peter's church in Loudun, comes to champion the independent spirit of the town in opposition to Cardinal Richelieu and his adherents. Grandier is falsely accused of being in league with the devil, the most convincing of his traducers being Mère Jeanne, whose invitation as Prioress to become confessor to her order he had refused. Her dreams and sexual frustrations start to centre on him and the suggestion is that her fixation becomes indistinguishable from love, that she is used by Grandier's enemies, political and social as well as spiritual (he is a womaniser in a provincial society), to secure his downfall.

Act I, scene i. Jeanne is lying on her bed in her cell at night praying. In her vision, she sees Grandier[1] seated on a chair which has been lashed to a litter and is carried by four soldiers. He wears a heretic's shirt impregnated with sulphur, and there is a rope round his neck. His broken legs dangle, he is a ridiculous, hairless, shattered doll. The Clerk of the Court gives Grandier a two-pound taper to hold. During her trance, Jeanne, who is a hunchback, prays to be made straight. The vision fades and Jeanne is brought a letter; it is from Grandier, regretting that he cannot accept her invitation to become director of the Ursuline community. She falls to her knees in convulsions. Bells.

Scene ii. A corpse hangs from the municipal gallows of Loudun as people leave St Peter's church, among them Adam, the chemist, and Mannoury, a surgeon. They comment on the self-importance of the vicar, Grandier, on the contented look of the young widow Ninon, which they say derives from Grandier's visits to her, and then on the new occupant of the gibbet.

Scene iii. Grandier with Ninon in a tub.

Scene iv. Adam and Mannoury have brought the human head from the gallows and they meet and greet Grandier, showing less than total enthusiasm.

Scene v. Grandier kneels at the altar and prays.

Scene vi. Jeanne and the Ursuline nuns enter the church. When Grandier re-enters in full canonicals, Jeanne screams and runs from the church.

Scene vii. Adam and Mannoury plot to indict Grandier.

Scene viii. Grandier in a confessional, with Philippe outside. She confesses to unclean thoughts ... about him, and he draws her into the confessional and pulls the curtain.

Scene ix. D'Armagnac, the town's Governor, confronts de Laubardemont and refuses to obey the latter's order to pull down the town's fortifications. Grandier supports d'Armagnac.

Scene x. Adam and Mannoury prepare their indictment, referring to a small book containing a register of Grandier's movements.

Scene xi. Jeanne is walking with Father Mignon, a foolish old man who has accepted to become the Order's director. She tells him that she has lately suffered from terrible visions straight from the Devil and has recognised Grandier.

Scene xii. Father Mignon, Adam and Mannoury are discussing the Prioress's visions, and Father Mignon says he has sent a message to Father Barré, an expert in exorcism. There is a knock at the door and de Laubardemont enters, asking about Grandier. He seems to have come to the right place.

Scene xiii. The first confrontation of Mère Jeanne with Barré and those who seek to support him in the exorcism. Jeanne is in private prayer and asks God to give her love; immediately she sees Grandier and Philippe walking by the town wall. De Laubardemont, Barré, Mignon, Mannoury, Adam and Father Rangier rush into the room and peals of masculine laughter pour from Jeanne's distorted mouth. Her inarticulate cries form into a single word, 'Grandier!'

Act II, scene i. The church. Jeanne kneels and facing her are Barré, Rangier, Mignon and the Ursuline nuns. The scene of exorcism proceeds but inarticulate whispers and laughter interrupt and Asmodeus speaks in a deep voice through Jeanne. Jeanne demands that they should speak about the sexual activities of priests. Barré diagnoses that the Devil is lodged deep in the lower bowel. Barré and Rangier grab Jeanne and carry her behind a curtain where apothecary and surgeon administer an enema to laughter and screams of protest.

Scene ii. D'Armagnac and de Cérisay, Mayor and Governor of Loudun, warn Grandier that the continual mention of his name by the possessed Jeanne puts him in a dangerous position.

---

[1] Throughout, I have quoted the vocal score's stage directions.

Scene iii. Jeanne lies in her cell, while Barré and his cronies continue to examine her, this time in the presence of de Cérisay. Jeanne screams the name of Grandier, whispering occasionally into Barré's ear, until Barré takes de Cérisay by the arm and draws him aside. While Mignon and the nuns pray (for the first time in the opera, 'normal' choral singing, but soon succeeded by an amazing *glissando* effect), de Cérisay objects that the whole thing is a product of Jeanne's imagination. Three of the sisters have testified that they have engaged in copulation with demons and been deflowered, and Mannoury on examination has found none of them intact. De Cérisay objects that everyone knows about the sentimental attachments between the young women of a convent, and orders the exorcism to cease pending a thorough investigation of the case.

Scene iv. Grandier is grateful to de Cérisay for his intervention, but d'Armagnac says that he has heard from Paris that Grandier, because he has supported d'Armagnac against de Laubardemont, now has a dedicated enemy in Richelieu.

Scene v. Philippe comes to Grandier in the church and tells him she is pregnant. Grandier, not without sympathy, says goodbye; how could he possibly own to being the child's father?

Scene vi. In the pharmacy, Adam, Mannoury and Father Mignon are joined by Fathers Barré and Rangier. The Archbishop has issued an ordinance forbidding further exorcism and their 'mission' seems to be at an end. Their lament for a moment turns into a beautiful quintet, the most 'vocal' number in the score, and at its end Barré says that he must go back to his parish.

Scene vii. The sisters ask Mère Jeanne why the Archbishop has forbidden Father Barré to see them any more. Jeanne laughs at them: 'Why don't you ask the devils to lend a hand?' But the sisters have the last word: 'We have mocked God!'

Scene viii. On the fortifications at night, during a storm Grandier hears from d'Armagnac and de Cérisay that the King has gone back on his word, to Richelieu's evident joy, and the town's fortifications are to be razed to the ground. Grandier paradoxically rejoices: 'Heavenly Father, You have restored strength to my enemies and hope to Your sinful child … You have made the way possible.'

Scenes ix and x. In the church, Mignon incites the sisters to go back on what they had told the Archbishop's doctor – that they were only playing parts and not truly possessed by the Devil – and reveal the truth: that the Devil had them in his power. De Laubardemont is galvanised into action, says he must depart for Paris but will leave Barré to prosecute the cause in Loudun.

The doors are opened and people of every kind and description rush in. The sisters perform their antics to the delight of the townspeople. The noise is only stilled by the arrival of the King's representative, Prince Henri de Condé. Pandemonium breaks loose, with lewd dancing, screaming and shouting. De Condé asks Beherit, concealed in the person of Mère Jeanne, what his opinion is of the King and his adviser the Cardinal. When Jeanne prevaricates, he congratulates Beherit. To have praised would have implied that the King's policy was hellish, to have disparaged could have resulted in a charge of treason! De Condé takes a small box from one of his pages, containing, he says, some true blood of the Saviour; let Barré exorcise the devils with it. Barré does his stuff and is triumphant, but de Condé reveals that the box was empty and, when Barré declares that it was a cruel trick to play, de Condé suggests that he is not the only one to have been playing tricks.

Suddenly, Mignon and Rangier start to run in circles imitating the voices of Leviathan and Beherit, women in the crowd take up the cries, and Barré is once more in his element, plunging into the crowd and wielding his crucifix like a club. De Condé looks at Jeanne and tells her this act will cost her her immortal soul. Now the nuns gossip among themselves, the one delighted that her lovely legs have been so greatly admired, the other that her picture is on sale in the town. Grandier attempts to enter the church but finds his way barred by soldiers and by de Laubardemont, who arrests him.

Act III, scene i. It is night and the stage is divided into three, on one side Grandier in jail, in a second section Jeanne and Father Mignon, and in a third, Mannoury. A crowd has gathered – Bontemps, the jailer, tells Grandier that there are more than 30,000 people come to town to see the execution, and Grandier has to remind him that his trial has not even begun. Grandier prays that he will be able to bear the pain, and Father Ambrose attempts to comfort him. Grandier confesses that he has sinned, with women, in aiming for power, in his worldly attitude.

Scene ii. De Laubardemont joins Mannoury and Adam and announces that Grandier is condemned and will shortly be there. He made something of an impression in court, but Father Barré explained it was the Devil's doing. Grandier enters in full canonicals. Biretta and cape are removed and it is clear he is to be shaved, a process accomplished to a frenzied polyphonic *pizzicato*. De Laubardemont reminds them not to forget the eyebrows, and then instructs Mannoury to tear out his fingernails. The surgeon jibs and de Laubardemont orders Bontemps to complete the process, which he does to a chatter and then a howl of orchestral pain.

Scene iii. A public place. A large number of people watch the Clerk of the Court read out the sentence. With a rope round his neck and a two-pound taper in his hand, Grandier is to ask pardon of God, the King and Justice. Next, he shall be tied to a stake and burnt alive. Before sentence is carried out, he will be subjected to the Question, both Ordinary and Extraordinary. Grandier himself is visible, his hands tied behind his back. De Laubardemont snatches the hat and cap from Grandier's head and the priest is revealed, shaven even to the eyebrows, a bald fool. He calls on God to witness that he has never been a sorcerer and to allow his suffering to atone for his vain and disordered life. Sympathy seems to be turning towards him and de Laubardemont orders the Captain of the Guard to clear the place. He urges Grandier to confess his guilt and sign a confession. Grandier refuses – how can he sign a lie? De Laubardemont threatens him, and says that under torture he will think, first, how can man do this to man; then, how can God allow it; and then, there can be no God. Grandier still refuses to sign.

Scene iv. Jeanne comes in, dressed in a simple white undergarment and with a rope round her neck. Others persuade her that it is too hot for her out of doors and take the rope gently away from her.

Scene v. Barré tries to extract a confession, but Grandier asks him whether he thinks that a man, to save himself pain, should confess to a crime he has not committed. De Laubardemont joins in the attempt to get a confession, Grandier between screams prays to God. At the same time, Mère Jeanne, whose praying voice has been heard throughout, and the nuns sing a litany. Grandier faints. Barré says that the fact that there is no confession means that the Devil has made him quite insensible to pain, but Mannoury asks what the shouts and screams can have been about.

Scene vi. The procession. As in Jeanne's vision at the start, Grandier is seated on a chair which has been lashed to a litter and is carried by four soldiers.

Scene vii. Outside St Peter's church, the procession stops and Ambrose attempts to console Grandier, who kisses his hand. The procession goes on to St Ursula's convent, where a soldier lifts him from the litter so that he collapses. When the Prioress and some other nuns emerge, de Laubardemont demands that Grandier shall ask their pardon but he says he can only ask that God shall forgive them their sins. The Prioress says that she has heard so often of Grandier's beauty which she can now behold with her own eyes, but Grandier answers: 'Look at this thing which I am, and learn what love means.' The procession reaches the site of the execution and Grandier is bound to the stake. De Laubardemont and Barré still try vainly to get him to confess, and when Barré gives him the kiss of peace, there is a shout of 'Judas!' from the crowd. In his fury, Barré snatches up a torch and ignites the pile before the soldiers have had a chance of strangling the victim, a form of relative mercy customary at the time. As the opera ends, Jeanne can be seen in silent prayer.   H.

PEPUSCH, JOHANN (JOHN) CHRISTOPH
see under Gay

GIOVANNI PERGOLESI
(born 4 January 1710, died 16 March 1736)

LA SERVA PADRONA
The Maidservant turned Mistress

Intermezzo in two parts, text by G.A. Federico. First performed at the Teatro di S. Bartolomeo in Naples, 28 August 1733, with Laura Monti and Gioacchino Corrado. The *intermezzo* was played in between the three acts of Pergolesi's serious opera *Il Prigioniero Superbo*. First performed in London, 1750; in Baltimore, 1790. Revivals: Lyric, Hammersmith, 1919; Mercury Theatre, London, 1939; Metropolitan, New York, 1935, with Editha Fleischer and Louis d'Angelo, and 1942, with Bidu Sayao and Salvatore Baccaloni; Paris, 1957, with Elena Rizzieri, Paolo Pedani; Royal Festival Hall, London, 1959, with Rizzieri and Bruscantini; Piccola Scala, Milan, 1961, with Mariella Adani and Montarsolo.

Uberto ....Bass
Serpina, *his servant* ....Soprano
Vespone, *another servant* ....Mute

Running Time: 50 minutes

Pergolesi was born near Ancona and died, very young, near Naples. He was a prolific composer of chamber music, sacred music (including the well-known *Stabat Mater*), and operas both serious and comic. *La Serva Padrona* has been his most frequently performed stage work, and the freshness of the music takes on added interest when it is remembered that the opera was at the very centre of the famous 'Querelle des Bouffons' in Paris. The production of *La Serva Padrona* by an Italian company in 1752 confirmed the division of French musicians and intellectuals into two camps, the one favouring Italian opera, the other French. The Nationalists were known as the 'King's Corner' party, their opponents, who included Rousseau and the Encyclopedists, as the 'Queen's Corner' party. The Nationalists admired Lully (a French composer born Italian!) and the ageing Rameau, the Bouffonists hated what they thought of as the outmoded complexity of French composers. *La Serva Padrona* had one hundred performances at the Opéra before, in 1753, it was transferred to the Comédie-Française, where it had ninety-six more.

La Serva Padrona is on a small scale, the orchestra consisting only of a quartet of strings. The work comprises an overture, and two separate *intermezzi*, each of which includes an aria for both characters and a duet. The overture is a lively piece, and the curtain rises to find Uberto dressing to go out and lamenting that he has had to wait three hours for his chocolate, which has still not arrived. His energetic complaints at the time he is kept waiting are expressed in an aria of a less formal type than the others in the score, each of which is in *da capo* form. His reproaches are directed more specifically at Serpina his maid in the ensuing recitative. However, when it comes to complaints he is no match for her, and after she has finished with her master, she turns on Vespone and sends him briskly about his business. Uberto's aria, 'Sempre in contrasti', is a skittish tune, typical of the score, and demanding more than a little agility from the singer. Serpina tells Uberto that it is much too late for him to go out, and lectures him again in her *allegretto* aria, 'Stizzoso, mio stizzoso'. Uberto can bear the tyranny no longer, and asks Vespone to go and find him a wife. An excellent idea, says Serpina: take me! In a duet, she protests her eligibility and he his intention of, if possible, ridding himself of her altogether (but he confesses to himself that the situation looks like becoming too much for him).

The second *Intermezzo* opens with recitative in which Serpina plans a trick to frighten or cajole Uberto into marrying her. Vespone shall help, and she tells Uberto that she has found a husband for herself, a soldier, by name Captain Tempest. She describes his bad temper and his unreasonable nature, and then in a pathetic aria, 'A Serpina penserete', expresses her hope that she will not be entirely forgotten when she has gone. She seems a different woman, but the moment she sees a change come over her employer's face, the tempo of the music changes too, and we see that it is with the same old Serpina that we have to deal. By the end of the aria, Uberto has taken her by the hand, and she feels her plan is working well. Uberto is in a thorough muddle, and does not know what to think. His E flat aria, 'Son imbrogliato io già', makes clear that he cannot make up his mind whether he is sorry for Serpina or now finds himself in love with her. It is a mixture of *buffo* and mock serious, and its slow refrain,

'Uberto, pensa a te', indicates a very different mood from what we saw at the beginning of the opera.

Serpina returns, bringing with her Vespone dressed up as the gallant captain, and looking as though he would blow up at the least provocation but still, as hitherto, without a word to say to anyone. Uberto is horrified by his disagreeable exterior and by his no less alarming behaviour. Is this a suitable husband for Serpina? She says that the Captain demands a sub-stantial dowry; if it is not forthcoming he will under no circumstances marry her, but he will insist that Uberto himself takes his place. No sooner is the betrothal between master and maid concluded, than Vespone whips off his moustaches and military disguise. Uberto's protests are in vain, and in the concluding duet, he admits that he is in love, and all seems set for the future, with Serpina happily installed as prospective mistress of the house.					H.

HANS PFITZNER
(born 5 May 1869, died 22 May 1949)

Pfitzner was a brilliant if reactionary musician, capable on the one hand as a young répétiteur of going on stage suddenly and without error as Beckmesser to save a performance of *Meistersinger* (without rehearsal – and without need of make-up, his enemies urged), and on the other of an attempt to discredit Berg and his musical intellectualism by an angry and public claim that an inspiration such as 'Träumerei' was a miracle and incapable of analysis (Berg's answer was a cool and scholarly study of Schumann's music). He wrote three operas before *Palestrina*, considered to be his masterpiece, and one of the ironies of operatic history is Pfitzner's far-sighted if embittered prediction in mid-war of the wranglings and miseries of the eventual peace negotiations which must inevitably follow its end.

PALESTRINA

Opera in three acts, text by the composer. Première Munich, 12 June 1917, with Karl Erb, Feinhals, Brodersen, Bender, Gustav Schützendorf, Ivogün, conductor Bruno Walter. First professional British production 1997 at Covent Garden, with Thomas Moser, conductor Christian Thielemann. Famous followers of Erb in the title role have been Julius Patzak, Josef Witt, Fritz Wunderlich and Peter Schreier.

I. Singers

Pope Pius IV ....Bass
Giovanni Morone, *Papal legate* ....Baritone
Bernardo Novagerio, *Papal legate* ....Tenor
Cardinal Christoph Madruscht ....Bass
Carlo Borromeo, *Cardinal from Rome*.............Baritone
Cardinal of Lorraine...Bass
Abdisu, *Patriarch of Assyria* ....Tenor
Anton Brus von Müglitz, *Archbishop of Prague*.....Bass
Count Luna, *envoy from the King of Spain* ......Baritone
Bishop of Budoja, *Italian Bishop*.........................Tenor
Theophilus of Imola, *Italian Bishop*....................Tenor
Avosmediano, *Bishop of Cadiz* ....Bass-Baritone
Giovanni Pierluigi Palestrina ....Tenor
Ighino, *his son, aged fifteen* ....Soprano
Silla, *his pupil, aged seventeen*...............Mezzo-Soprano
Bishop Ercole Severolus, *master-of-ceremonies at Council of Trent*..............................Bass-Baritone

Five Singers from Chapel of Santa Maria Maggiore in Rome........................ Two Tenors, Three Basses

Chorus Singers from Papal Chapel, Archbishops, Bishops, Abbots, Ambassadors, Envoys, Theologians, Servants, Soldiers, People

II. Silent Characters

Two Papal Nuncios, Jesuits, Massarelli, Bishop of Thelesia, Secretary of Council, Giuseppe, Old Servant of Palestrina

III. Singing Apparitions

Apparition of Lucretia, *Palestrina's dead wife* ....Contralto
Apparitions of Nine Dead Composers.....................Tenors, Baritones, Basses
Three Angelic Voices.....................................Soprano
Angels ....Chorus

Place: Rome; Trent at the End of the Council of Trent
Time: November–December 1563
Running Time: 3 hours 30 minutes

Act I. A solemn prelude leads straight into the action which is laid in a room in Palestrina's house. Silla, Palestrina's pupil, is trying over one of his own compositions on the viol (in the last bars of the prelude, this is suggested in the orchestra by two solo violas). Ighino comes in, looking sad. He is worried by the look of unhappiness on his father's face; has Silla not noticed it? Palestrina's pupil admits he can see little wrong with his master, nor can he imagine why he should be unhappy. But Ighino pours out his feelings: fame has brought his father little; he has been desperately lonely ever since the loss of his wife, and has written nothing. His life in fact seemed to come to an end with her death.

Palestrina comes into the room with Cardinal Borromeo, and the two boys leave. The Cardinal is astonished at the music he heard when they came in (Silla was practising his song again), and he asks Palestrina whether he likes that kind of thing. It is perhaps the new music, the music of the future, replies the master. Borromeo admits that Palestrina's attitude of world-weariness, of submission to the new tendencies, makes him impatient. Without him, what is church music to become? He goes into further detail: his object in coming secretly to Palestrina's house is practical. The Council of Trent, which has been sitting these eighteen years, is now coming to an end. Pope Pius was originally not content with reforming the abuses of church music, but wished to return to Gregorian chant and consign to the flames all other sacred music. Only he – Borromeo – resisted this reactionary view, but he had an ally in the Emperor, who opposed so drastic a change. The case is now won, but has yet to be proved: this can only be done if a Mass is written by a contemporary composer of such calibre as to convince the Pope and his Council. Such a work would be a model for future composers, and would secure the future of church music. It is Palestrina's duty to write it!

But Palestrina regretfully says that he is not the right man for the task. Neither the Cardinal's scorn nor his raging nor his pleas are sufficient; Palestrina still insists that even an artist's powers can grow old. Borromeo's anger overflows, and in the end he accuses the composer of blasphemy. He leaves the room in ungovernable fury. Palestrina is moved by what he has seen and heard: there goes my last friend, is his comment. As he muses on the uncertainty of men's conditions and the mysteries of life, looking sadly at the portrait of his dead wife, he is surrounded by a vision of the composers of the past. He recognises them as his predecessors, and they remind him of his youth, when he first came to know them. They encourage him, and tell him that his ultimate duty is not yet accomplished.

As Palestrina's aversion to composition seems to weaken, the ghosts of the composers watch with an interest that is almost knowing; these are the growing pains once familiar to them all! With Palestrina's resistance overcome, they gradually disappear, but immediately he starts to hear the voices of angels, which dictate his Mass to him. At the height of his inspiration, Palestrina sees the ghost of his wife, Lucretia, who appears to him as she had in life, bringing a message of peace, the peace for which he has longed ever since her death. This scene of the dictation of the Mass is the crux of the opera. It is perhaps sufficient praise to say that it succeeds in giving an impression of an artist's exaltation at the moment of creation.

It is dawn, the angel voices die away, the bells of Rome can be heard in the distance, and Palestrina sinks down exhausted. The floor of the room is covered with music-paper, and, when Silla and Ighino come for their morning lesson, they are overjoyed to see that the master has spent the night working. They gather up the sheets of music, and gradually realise that an entire Mass has been written in a single night. As the curtain falls, Silla wonders whether anything written so quickly can possibly add to the master's fame.

Act II. The agitated prelude is in strong contrast to what preceded the first act. The scene is in the great hall in the palace of Cardinal Madruscht at Trent, where preparations are almost complete for renewal of the conference. Cardinal Novagerio makes fun of the farce which always attends the Spanish delegate's efforts to obtain his rightful precedence, and a little later takes the opportunity of warning the servants, who are all of different nationalities, that they will be severely punished if they again start to quarrel in the streets.

Borromeo arrives, and there is a fairly lengthy political discussion between him and Novagerio. Novagerio congratulates Borromeo on the way he has managed the question of church music, but Borromeo reveals that he has been unsuccessful in getting Palestrina to write the Mass he needs. He has had him thrown into prison, but doubts whether the work can be ready in time, even if jail were to break Palestrina's self-imposed silence. Novagerio suggests that there are ways to force men to bend to the will of their masters, but Borromeo starts back in horror at the implication of his remarks.

The other delegates begin to arrive, the Italians suspicious of the Germans, the Spaniards commenting on the Italians who, they say, swarm over the place like ants. Some talk in an indignant way of heretics, others are more concerned over whether or not their expenses to and from the conference will be paid by their diocese. The master-of-ceremonies, Bishop Ercole Severolus, announces that the conference is about to begin and invites the delegates to take their places in proper order of precedence. This done, they are addressed by Morone, the papal legate, who prays that wisdom may attend their deliberations and inform their decisions. He calls down a malediction on all heretics, in which the entire conference joins, apart, that is to say, from the liberal-minded but boorish Bishop of Budoja, who makes the mistake of praying that they may be enlightened rather than destroyed, and gets a number of dirty looks from his fellow-delegates.

Discussion begins on the subject of the musical side of the church service. The Pope's approval is dependent on a work being written which satisfies ritual considerations. Borromeo announces that such a Mass is being written, and that Palestrina is the composer. The business of the conference proceeds, but points of order seem to be preferred for discussion to points of doctrine. The Spanish envoy objects to the speed at which business is being transacted, and his quarrelsome attitude provokes opposition from a number of delegates based on precedence and the exalted position he has claimed as his by right. Some sense of responsibility returns when the Bishop of Budoja shouts at the top of his voice that peace is the last thing likely to be obtained by such a conference divided against itself, but the meeting again degenerates into nationalist quarrelling and, after quelling the shouts, Morone decides to end the session. He calls the delegates for the afternoon, but warns them that the co-operation of them all, and not least of the Spanish envoy, will be needed if this last session of the conference is to accomplish the task set before it.

As soon as the delegates have gone, not without some more sharp remarks, the Spanish servants gather together and mutter that their delegate has been insulted, and it is not long before a free fight develops between the servants. Madruscht appears with soldiers at his back; seeing the disorder, he commands them to open fire and bids them to take any survivors they can catch to the torture chambers. No one shall thus defile the Church's Council with unseemly conduct.

Act III. Palestrina's room as in Act I. The composer is sitting in his chair, barely visible to the audience. Five singers from the chapel stand round him, and Ighino is kneeling by his side. The singers express concern for Palestrina's condition, and when he wakes from his trance, he does not seem to recognise them, though they are from his own choir. He asks Ighino why they are waiting and gazing at him. His son tells him that at that very moment his Mass is being sung at the Pope's Palace. He seems not to grasp the significance of this, but refers to being asked some question about it in prison. The others remind him that they gathered together the pages of the Mass he wrote and that they were subsequently taken away from them.

Suddenly there is a noise from the street, and the people can be heard crying: 'Long life to Palestrina, saviour of music!' People crowd into the room, asking for the master, Palestrina, and saying that the Pope has given it as his opinion that the new Mass is Palestrina's best work. The Pope himself is coming to congratulate him! The Holy Father makes his entrance, followed by his Cardinals, among them Borromeo, and tells Palestrina of the enormous impression his Mass has made on them all. He must remain in his service until the end of his life.

The Pope leaves, blessing Palestrina and his singers. The Cardinals follow the Pope, all, that is, except Borromeo, who makes a sign to the singers to leave him alone with Palestrina. They look at each other for a moment, then with a cry Borromeo falls on his knees in front of the composer, who puts his hands gently on the Cardinal's head. Palestrina raises the Cardinal to his feet and they stay for a moment in an embrace, before the Cardinal goes quickly from the room.

Ighino, who has watched the scene from concealment, rushes out to ask his father if he is not the happiest man in the world. Maybe, says his father, but he is old and shows his happiness less demonstratively than Ighino. Where is Silla, he asks. He guesses he has gone to Florence, and Ighino confirms his impression. There is more acclamation for Palestrina from outside, and he bids his son laugh and dance and sing if he wants to. He himself remains alone in his room.

He goes quietly towards the portrait of his wife, Lucretia, then walks to his organ and plays softly. The crowd is still below, shouting praises to his name, and with these sounds in his ears, the curtain falls.   H.

NICCOLÒ PICCINNI

(born 16 January 1728, died 7 May 1800)

Piccinni was a prolific and successful composer, initially of comic operas, later of more serious works, but his career suffered more than one undeserved setback. In Rome, he lost favour when a lesser composer, Pasquale Anfossi, was precipitated to fame at his expense; in Paris his engagement as a counter-attraction to Gluck produced intense rivalries, more between the 'Gluckistes' and the 'Piccinnistes' than between the composers themselves but heated nonetheless. Both Salieri and Sacchini after Gluck's death threatened Piccinni's standing in Paris, but Piccinni was sufficiently generous apparently to speak at Sacchini's funeral and to propose a concert in Gluck's memory.

'Author of the first real "opera buffa", *Cecchina*', wrote Verdi to his librettist Arrigo Boito in 1887 when recommending Piccinni as a composer to be studied by the students of the newly established school of choral singing. Verdi presumably set aside in his mind not only a whole host of Neapolitan *intermezzi* as not sufficiently structured either musically or in plot to qualify, as well as more developed works like Pergolesi's grander operas such as *Lo Frate 'nnamorato*. Certainly, *La buona Figliuola* is an opera of rare quality, a happy discovery for those who do not know it and hear it for the first time.

LA BUONA FIGLIUOLA

(*Cecchina*)

The Good Maid

Opera in three acts, libretto by Polisseno Fegejo, after Carlo Goldoni, whose text was founded on Richardson's *Pamela or Virtue Rewarded*. Première, Rome, 6 February 1760, and thereafter all over Italy. It reached Vienna in 1764, London in 1766, Berlin in 1768, Paris in 1771. Revived Rome, 1942; la Scala, 1951, with Carteri, Noni, Aimaro, Prandelli, Taddei, Bruscantini; Buxton Festival, 1985; Martina Franca, 1990, with Maria Angeles Peters, Alessandra Ruffini, Giuseppe Morino, Bruno Praticò.

Marchesa Lucinda	Soprano
Cavaliere Armidoro	Soprano
Cecchina, *the gardener*	Soprano
Sandrina, *a peasant*	Soprano
Paoluccia, *a maid*	Mezzo-Soprano
Marchese della Conchiglia	Tenor
Tagliaferro, *a German soldier*	Baritone
Mengotto, *a peasant*	Bass

Place: The Marchese's Palace
Time: Eighteenth Century
Running Time: 2 hours 20 minutes

Act I. Cecchina is happy working in the Marchesa's garden, but can't help wondering about her origins, which are shrouded in mystery. Mengotto is in love with her, but she fancies the Marchese for whom she works but whose mildest advances inspire in her nothing but fear. He tries to get Sandrina to put in a word for him, but Sandrina once thought the Marchese was interested in her, is now after Mengotto herself and so only too keen where Cecchina is concerned to put the boot in. Much to that young gentleman's disgust, she tells Cavaliere Armidoro, engaged to the Marchese's sister Lucinda, that the Marchese's eye has lit on Cecchina, a nobody and a foreigner to boot. Once Lucinda learns of the situation, she loses no time in telling Cecchina, to the girl's distress, that she has found her a good situation elsewhere.

The Marchese has in fact already told his sister

that he loves Cecchina, but the poor girl is stopped as she is about to leave by none other than Mengotto, who offers his love. The Marchese finds them together, suspects the worst and rejects Cecchina. Mengotto, jealous in his turn, does the same.

Act II. The Marchese would call the unfortunate Cecchina back, but, on the instructions of Cavaliere Armidoro, she is being escorted out of the town. Mengotto and his friends free her, but the Marchese intervenes. Mengotto laments but is restrained by Tagliaferro, a German soldier sent, he says, to search for a particular girl. Tagliaferro offers to enroll Mengotto. Lucinda hears Cecchina is still in the city, and Paoluccia and Sandrina assure her she is with the Marchese himself. Cecchina once again rejects the Marchese.

Tagliaferro tells the Marchese that twenty years before, when the Germans were retreating from Italy, his Colonel lost his daughter, by name Mariandel. She has a blue mark on her breast and he is convinced, without much evidence it must be admitted, that Cecchina is in fact Mariandel. They find her asleep, the Marchese withdraws and Tagliaferro stands guard. Cecchina dreams of her father, but Paoluccia and Sandrina put the worst interpretation on the scene and report it immediately to the Marchese, only in their turn to be seen off with contumely.

Act III. Paoluccia is not finished and makes her report to Marchesa Lucinda and Cavaliere Armidoro. The Marchese announces his betrothal to a noble German lady, much to the satisfaction of Tagliaferro. The Marchese teases Cecchina with his planned engagement to the foreigner, then admits that the fiancée he has in mind is none other than her! Mengotto has to make do with Sandrina, and all are offered proof that Cecchina is none other than the long-lost Mariandel.

Piccinni displays fertile invention in shapely arias of all types (more than twenty of them) and witty ensembles. His music, whether romantic or vigorous, is consistently lively and inventive, always elegantly turned, whether to express the ardour of the Marchese, the more high-flown, generalised emotions of the Cavaliere, or the larger-scale coloratura resolve of Marchesa Lucinda. In contrast, we have the gentle, highly expressive lyricism of Cecchina, the hand-wringing of Mengotto, a kind of up-beat Masetto, and the mock heroics of Tagliaferro, a true Sergeant Belcore before his time – all put forward in music of ingratiating quality.   H.

AMILCARE PONCHIELLI
(born 31 August 1834, died 17 January 1886)

LA GIOCONDA
The Ballad Singer

Opera in four acts, text by Arrigo Boito (under the pseudonym of Tobia Gorrio). Première at la Scala, Milan, 8 April 1876, with Mariani, Biancolini-Rodriguez, Barlani-Dini, Gayarre, Aldighieri, Maini.

La Gioconda, *a ballad singer* ....Soprano

La Cieca, *her blind mother*.............................Contralto

Enzo Grimaldo, *a Genoese nobleman* ....Tenor

Alvise Badoero, *one of the heads of the*
      State Inquisition................................ Bass

Laura, *his wife*.....................................Mezzo-Soprano

Barnaba, *a spy for the Inquisition* ....Baritone

Zuane, *a boatman* ....Bass

Isèpo, *a public letter-writer*...................................Tenor

A Pilot ....Bass

Monks, Senators, Sailors, Ladies, Gentlemen,
   Masquers etc.

Place: Venice
Time: Seventeenth Century
Running Time: 2 hours 35 minutes

Ponchielli, some twenty years younger than Verdi, struggled initially to establish a toe-hold in the world of Italian opera. His breakthrough was with a revised version of his first work, *I promessi sposi*, but his one claim to worldwide success came at the age of rather over forty with *La Gioconda*. He became Professor in Milan, where Puccini was his pupil and, briefly, Mascagni.

Act I. The courtyard of the Doge's Palace decorated for a popular festivity. The prelude puts forward la Cieca's aria from Act I, later used to express the indebtedness she and la Gioconda feel towards Laura. The populace sings in festive mood before leaving to watch the regatta, leaving Barnaba to observe Gioconda lead on her blind mother (trio). Barnaba lusts after Gioconda, who has more than once rejected his advances. She for her part loves Enzo, a nobleman proscribed by the Venetian authorities and now clandestinely in the city in the guise of a sea captain. (To complete the amorous tangle, it should be noted that Enzo is still in love with Laura, to whom he was betrothed until she was obliged to marry the much older Alvise.)

Barnaba again makes advances to Gioconda who runs off, leaving her mother a prey to Barnaba's machinations. Opportunity arises when the crowd returns from the regatta with the winner and the loser, Zuane, to whom Barnaba suggests that his defeat was caused by the witchcraft of the old blind woman sitting silently by the steps. His friends help him drag her from the church steps and only the intervention of Enzo ('Assassini!') saves her from the mob. Alvise comes down the great stairs of the palace with Laura, who is masked and who demands justice for the old blind woman. Alvise orders her release and in her gratitude she gives Laura her most cherished possession, a rosary ('A te questo rosario').

Barnaba meanwhile has observed Laura and Enzo exchange meaningful glances. Once the crowd has left, with an eye to the main chance he taxes Enzo with his true identity ('Enzo Grimaldo, Principe di Santafior') and, in a justly renowned tenor-baritone duet, explains that he will bring Laura to Enzo's ship so that they may elope together, thus incidentally advancing his own cause with Gioconda. Enzo departs and Barnaba summons one of his tools, Isèpo, the public scribe, and dictates a letter anonymously informing Alvise of the situation. Gioconda overhears but does not know who the letter is addressed to, and Barnaba drops it into the Lion's Mouth, the infamous method of anonymous denunciation to the state spying system. 'O monumento' is his soliloquy, a dry run one might think for Iago's Credo eleven years later, also with words by Boito. The act ends with the crowd dancing, and a prayer from the church, during which Gioconda laments Enzo's unfaithfulness.

Act II. The deck of Enzo's ship. Sailors sing and Barnaba, with his net laid out for Enzo and Laura, has a fisherman's ballad, 'Ah, pescator affonda l'esca'. Enzo comes on deck to sing one of the two most famous numbers of the opera, 'Cielo e mar', which testifies to his love for Laura, who, ferried by Barnaba, is quickly on the scene. Their love is expressed at first almost formally, as Enzo urges her to put fear behind her ('Deh! non turbare'). She tells him she recognised him instantly in front of the palace, and he again enjoins confidence ('Deh! non tremar'), until their voices combine in a passionate duet, 'Laggiù, nelle nebbie remote'.

Enzo leaves to prepare their elopement, and Gioconda steals on board to confront her rival, who sings what is the most dramatic number of the score: 'L'amo come il fulgor del creato', a high point of the Italian mezzo-soprano's repertory. Gioconda points to Alvise's armed followers approaching in a boat and is about to stab Laura when she sees la Cieca's rosary round her neck. Instantly, she changes plan and bundles Laura into a boat to safety, thwarting Barnaba of his prey and confronting Enzo when he returns. Seeing Alvise's men approaching, he impulsively sets fire to his ship.

Act III. A room in Alvise's palace. Alvise plans vengeance ('Sì! morir ella de'!'), and instructs Laura in a powerful scene to take poison before the serenade heard outside has finished. He has reckoned without Gioconda, who, to save her mother's saviour, has hidden in the palace and now exchanges a powerful sleeping draught for the poison. Laura takes it, Alvise finds the empty phial and believes his orders carried out.

A great hall in the palace. Alvise receives guests for whose benefit is performed the greatly popular Dance of the Hours. Barnaba drags in la Cieca, whom he has found hiding in the house and who says she comes to pray for the recently dead. Barnaba whispers to Enzo that her prayers are for Laura, and when the passing bell is heard, Enzo leads a great ensemble, 'Già ti veggo immota e smorta' at whose end Laura is revealed lying in state and apparently dead.

Act IV. A room in a ruined palace on the Giudecca island. Two men carry the body of Laura into Gioconda's dwelling. She has bargained with

Barnaba to give herself to him in return for Enzo's release from prison, and for a moment in a dramatic soliloquy – a 'terrible song' it has been called – she contemplates suicide: 'Suicidio!' Enzo enters and Gioconda excites his rage by telling him she has had Laura's body removed from the burial vault, where he will no longer find it. He threatens her with a knife when the voice of Laura, waking from her narcotic, is heard. Both Laura and Enzo pour out words of gratitude before they leave and Gioconda is once more alone. The thought of her bargain with Barnaba spurs her to escape, but the spy himself appears in her doorway. He starts to work up a passion ('Ebbrezza! delirio!') as she adorns herself with stage jewellery, but she seizes an opportunity and stabs herself fatally with a dagger. 'You wanted my body, you demon. My body you shall have!' she screams at him, and is dead before he can shout into her deaf ears: 'Last night your mother offended me. I strangled her!'

La Gioconda is Ponchielli's only significant operatic success. Given the relative operatic famine in Italy after Verdi's *Aida* (1871) – his next opera would be *Otello* (1887), with Puccini's *Manon Lescaut* not until 1893 – its initial popularity is perhaps not surprising. One may still find the over-ripe romanticism, not to say obscurity, of the book to a considerable extent compensated by the luscious tunes and skilful pacing of Ponchielli's score.   H.

FRANCIS POULENC
(born 7 January 1899, died 30 January 1963)

LES MAMELLES DE TIRÉSIAS
The Breasts of Tiresias

Opéra-bouffe in a prologue and two acts, text by Guillaume Apollinaire. Première Opéra-Comique, Paris, 3 June 1947, with Denise Duval, Paul Payen, conductor Albert Wolff. First performed in U.S.A. at Brandeis University, Mass., 1953; New York, 1957, with Duval, Singher; in England, at Aldeburgh Festival, 1958, with Jennifer Vyvyan, Peter Pears; Leeds, 1978, with Joy Roberts, Stuart Harling; English National Opera, 1979, with Norma Burrowes, Emile Belcourt.

The Director of the Theatre ....Baritone
Thérèse ....Soprano
Her Husband..Tenor[1]
Monsieur Lacouf..Tenor
Monsieur Presto ....Baritone
The Gendarme...Baritone
The Newspaper Vendor ....Mezzo-Soprano
The Reporter from Paris ....Tenor
The Son ....Baritone

Members of the audience
   An Elegant Lady ....Mezzo-Soprano
   A Woman ....Mezzo-Soprano
   A Bearded Gentleman ....Bass

People of Zanzibar

Place: Zanzibar, an Imaginary Town on the French Riviera, between Nice and Monte Carlo
Time: 1910
Running Time: 55 minutes

'Chabrier', said Francis Poulenc, '... is my true grandfather', and Chabrier, for all his devotion to Wagner, derives some of the flavour of his unique talent from a deliberate cultivation of a robust vulgarity, as evidenced in for instance the overblown music-hall tunes of *España*, a masterpiece and musically a product of some sort of *nostalgie de la boue*. With this musical adherence and his admiration for Guillaume Apollinaire, many of whose poems he had already set, it is not surprising that Poulenc's first opera is a tearaway farce. *Les Mamelles de Tirésias*, says Edward Lockspeiser, 'unites the worlds of surrealism and the music-hall. In his introduction to this fantasy on the change of sexes which, incidentally, he wrote for an intensely serious purpose – Apollinaire believed that the French were neglecting the act of love – he has this to say on the origin of the

---

[1] In the printed score and in the Paris performances of 1947 (and some subsequently abroad), the Husband was sung by a baritone; the composer later revised the role for a tenor.

Surrealist movement: "When man wanted to imitate walking, he invented the wheel, which has no connection whatever with a leg. This was an unconscious surrealist example."'

Other early influences on the composer were the eccentric and talented Erik Satie, and the other composers irrationally joined together with him by contemporary criticism as *Les Six*: Auric, Milhaud, Durey, Tailleferre and Honegger.

Apollinaire's drama was written in 1903 but produced only in 1917. Poulenc finished his first opera in 1945 and it was given at the Opéra-Comique in June 1947, after a preparatory period, the composer used to say, which proved the effectiveness of its motto, 'Français, faites des enfants', since the first two sopranos entrusted with the leading role had to relinquish it on account of pregnancy.

Prologue. There is a quiet orchestral introduction and the curtain rises to reveal the theatre director, who appeals directly to the audience in calm, measured, serious tones: 'Public,[1] attendez sans impatience, je vous apporte une pièce dont le but est de réformer les mœurs. Il s'agit des enfants dans la famille ...' (My friends, your indulgence! We will present you an opera which will try to reform your way of life).[2] His description of what the audience is going to see touches frenzy before returning to the serious tones of the start and the work's motto: 'Et faites des enfants, vous qui n'en faisiez guère' (You must make babies now as you never have before). It is the opera's most extended musical structure and the music is without a hint of irony.

Act I. The curtain rises to reveal the main square of Zanzibar, complete with houses, café, a view of the port – Zanzibar appears to lie somewhere between Nice and Monte Carlo. With the entrance of the charming and energetic Thérèse, the musical mood changes completely to one of bustle and farce. She announces herself feminist, refuses to submit to her husband's desires, wants to be a soldier. His cries from the house – 'Donnez-moi du lard' (Let me have my meat) – only inspire her to a denunciation of love and further proclamations of ambition. At this moment her breasts seem anxious to escape from their owner, she opens her blouse (on a top C) and they escape, two children's balloons attached to her now only by the strings. After celebrating their beauty in a slow waltz,

she reflects that they are a cause of sin and she will get rid of them – 'Débarrassons-nous de nos mamelles'. She feels her beard sprouting, and congratulates herself on the discovery in a brisk *paso doble*.

The husband emerges, a bouquet of flowers in his hands, assumes that what appears to be a stranger in Thérèse's clothing has murdered his wife, but is disillusioned by Thérèse's announcement that she will in future be known as Tirésias. Thérèse-Tirésias disappears into the house and drum rolls accompany the descent from the window of intimate household objects.

A polka starts up and a couple of drunks, Presto the fat one and Lacouf the thin one, come out of the café. In the friendliest possible way they quarrel, arrange a duel and happily shoot each other. It is left to Thérèse, now dressed in the height of masculine fashion, and her husband, disguised as a rather untidy housewife, to mourn the loss of these two worthy citizens, an activity in which the inhabitants of Zanzibar solemnly join.

Quick music and a drum roll precede the appearance of the husband and the gendarme, the latter of whom theoretically pursues crime but seems to prefer to pay court to the husband, whom he takes for a female, to the latter's undisguised mockery.

In an arietta, the husband explains to the gendarme, whom he addresses as 'Fameux représentant de tout autorité', that he feels it essential that Zanzibar should have children and, if women refuse to provide them, he will.

The first half ends with a scene of considerable vivacity, a newspaper-seller denouncing a hoax, the husband assuring the gendarme that if he comes back that night he will show him that he has managed, single-handed as it were, to produce children; even Lacouf and Presto reappear apparently full of life. For the rapid *stretta à la Rossini*, the stage direction has the curtain descend until only the singers' legs are visible.

The Ravel-like entr'acte has a solemn opening before six mixed couples from the chorus dance a kind of farcical gavotte in front of the curtain.

Act II. The scene is filled with cradles. The husband is delighted with his success – forty thousand new children in a single day! – and the voices of the

---

[1] Apollinaire's spelling.

[2] English translations by Robert Goss.

children echo their father's self-satisfaction. In comes a journalist, demanding to know the husband's secret and presuming that he must be very rich to afford so large a family. Not at all, returns the husband, but they should be able to support him once they are grown up. Impressed by the evidence of the husband's income, he tries to touch him for a small loan and is immediately – and literally – kicked out.

The husband seems to read (unaccompanied) a moral from the whole affair: the more children you have, the richer you'll be. He is contemplating further creative activities when he bumps into the gendarme, who remonstrates about the addition of over 40,000 inhabitants to the population of Zanzibar. How are they to be fed? With ration cards, suggests the husband; these can be obtained at the Cartomancienne's (fortune-teller's).

No sooner mentioned than this lady appears, her grandiose cadenzas accompanied on the lyre which she carries. The fortune-teller offers to tell everyone's future and counsels fecundity, revealing herself, when the husband tries to restrain her, as none other than Thérèse. The husband is delighted and even the gendarme revives. The only trouble is that her figure seems, much to her husband's dismay, no more ample than it had in her recent masculine manifestation. She makes light of the problem in a charming arietta and the husband joins her in a lazy, amorous waltz. The inhabitants provide them with vocal accompaniment, and the action ends with a *stretta* and then the moral: 'Ecoutez, O Français, les leçons de la guerre, et faites des enfants, vous qui n'en faisiez guère.'   H.

DIALOGUES DES CARMÉLITES
Dialogues of the Carmelites

Opera in three acts, libretto by Emmet Lavery from the drama by Georges Bernanos, itself inspired by a novel of Gertrude von Le Fort and a scenario of Rev. Fr. Bruckberger and Philippe Agostini. Première la Scala, Milan, 26 January 1957, with Virginia Zeani, Leyla Gencer, Gigliola Frazzoni, Eugenia Ratti, Gianna Pederzini, conductor Nino Sanzogno. First performed at Paris Opéra, 1957, with Denise Duval, Régine Crespin, Rita Gorr, Liliane Berton, Denise Scharley, conductor André Cluytens; Cologne, 1957; San Francisco, 1957, with Dorothy Kirsten, Leontyne Price, Blanche Thebom, Sylvia Stahlman,

Claramae Turner, conductor Leinsdorf; London, Covent Garden, 1958, in English with Elsie Morison, Joan Sutherland, Sylvia Fisher, Jeanette Sinclair, Jean Watson, conductor Kubelík; Vienna, 1959, with Seefried, Zadek, Goltz, Rothenberger, Höngen, conductor Hollreiser; Metropolitan, 1977, in English with Maria Ewing, Shirley Verrett, Mignon Dunn, Betsy Norden, Régine Crespin, producer John Dexter.

Marquis de la Force ....Baritone

Chevalier de la Force, *his son* ....Tenor

Blanche de la Force, *his daughter*
 (Sister Blanche of the Agony of Christ) .....Soprano

Thierry, *a footman* ....Baritone

Madame de Croissy, *the Prioress*
 (Mother Henriette of Jesus) .... Contralto

Sister Constance of St Denis,
 a young novice ....Soprano

Mother Marie of the Incarnation, *assistant
 prioress* .... Mezzo-Soprano

M. Javelinot, *a doctor* ....Baritone

Madame Lidoine, *the new Prioress*
 (Mother Marie of St Augustine) ....Soprano

Mother Jeanne of the Child Jesus ....Contralto

Sister Mathilde.................................Mezzo-Soprano

Father Confessor of the Convent ....Tenor

First Commissary...Tenor

Second Commissary ....Baritone

Officer ....Baritone

Jailer ....Baritone

Eleven Carmelites..............Soprano, Mezzo-Soprano,
 Contralto

Officials of the Municipality, Officers, Policemen,
 Prisoners, Guards, Townspeople

Place: The Carmelite Convent at Compiègne; Paris
Time: Between April 1789 and Summer 1792
Running Time: 2 hours 50 minutes

La Scala asked Poulenc for a new ballet score but were told the composer was thinking of writing an opera, whose première they immediately secured.

Even though the genesis of Bernanos's *Dialogues des Carmélites* is a story by a German writer and an idea for a film scenario by two Frenchmen (it was only the dialogue for this film that Bernanos was asked to supply), 'the psychology of fear which is the main theme of the *Dialogues* is treated in a way entirely characteristic of Bernanos; and the same is true of the interpretation offered in this play of the Communion of the Saints: "One does not die alone;

one dies for others and even in the place of others".'[1]

It is the great merit of Poulenc's setting of Bernanos's *Dialogues* that he preserves all the essential character of the original, that all the words are clearly audible, and that the result is compelling drama.

Act I, scene i. The library in the Paris house of the Marquis de la Force, April 1789. The Marquis is resting, but the Chevalier bursts in; rumour has it there is a mob about and his sister Blanche is out late in the carriage. The Marquis loses his calm as he remembers a ghastly incident of nearly twenty years before when his pregnant wife was jolted in her carriage by a mob and died in giving birth to Blanche. The Chevalier is particularly worried because of Blanche's impressionable, not to say morbid, nature, but when she comes in it is to say that the long and exhausting service that morning has tired her and she will go to bed. A moment later her scream is heard from the passage – she has unexpectedly caught sight of a lamp carried by a servant. It is more than a momentary fear that the shock releases in Blanche, and she formally and with no sign of panic asks her father's permission to join a Carmelite convent; how else is someone as nervous as she to find salvation?

Scene ii. The parlour of the Carmelite convent at Compiègne. The aged Prioress on one side of a screen interviews Blanche who sits on the other. When Blanche professes to be attracted even by the privations of the Order, the Prioress emphasises that prayer is the sole reason for the Carmelites' existence. Under her questioning Blanche breaks down in tears, but the Prioress softens towards her and asks her whether she has already chosen her religious name in case she is admitted to the Order; Blanche answers 'Sœur Blanche de l'Agonie du Christ'.

Scene iii. Blanche and Constance are busy with household work. Constance prattles away about her country upbringing, until Blanche snubs her levity with the reminder that the Prioress is lying near them gravely ill. Constance tries to get Blanche to join her in offering their lives to God in place of that of the old Prioress, but Blanche rejects the idea in an agony of fear. Constance tells her of a dream she has had that she and Blanche will die together.

Scene iv. The cell of the Prioress. The Prioress on her deathbed is obsessed with fear of death, and the Assistant Prioress, Mother Marie of the Incarnation, tries to give her strength. The Prioress entrusts to Mother Marie the care of Blanche, who comes in to say goodbye and is admonished to preserve her innocence of character through trust in God. Mother Marie begs her to concern herself only with God, but the Mother Superior reacts violently: 'Who am I, wretched as I am at this moment, to concern myself with Him? Let Him first concern Himself with me!' Nothing Mother Marie can do will restrain the flood of words that pours from her, and she sends a message that the Sisters cannot be allowed to see the Prioress. Blanche returns, the Prioress tries to speak to her, but falls dead.

Act II, scene i. The chapel of the convent. The body of the old Prioress lies in state. Blanche by herself makes a half-hearted attempt to pray and then rushes towards the door, where she is met by Mother Marie who leads her towards her cell; let her not talk about her failure – tomorrow it will fill her with sorrow, at present it can only cause her shame.

Blanche and Constance are taking flowers to the grave of the old Prioress. Constance wonders at the difficulty the old nun had found in dying; one would have said she had been given the wrong death by mistake, as if it had been someone else's coat in a cloakroom. Perhaps someone when it comes to their turn to die will find a better death than they deserve.

Scene ii. The hall of the chapter house. It is not Mother Marie who is chosen Prioress but a certain Madame Lidoine, from outside.[2] She speaks to the nuns in an aria, praising the old Prioress and bidding them at all times to remember their duty, which is to pray. Anything that may lure them from their duty, even the joy of martyrdom, is to be shunned. She leaves Mother Marie to finish the address, after which in a beautiful ensemble the nuns offer up an 'Ave Maria'.

The bell at the side door rings. It is the Chevalier de la Force asking to see his sister before he goes abroad.

Scene iii. The parlour of the convent. With a screen between them and with Mother Marie in the background, the Chevalier accuses Blanche of staying in the convent because of her fear of fear; Blanche forbids him to leave on a note of anger and

---

[1] *Francis Poulenc* by Henri Hell (1959).
[2] We are told that, as a matter of history, the inhibited and intense Mother Marie was an illegitimate daughter of the King, and that the choice of

Madame Lidoine, daughter of a local tradesman, may have been considered advisable as a sop to the spirit of the time.

misunderstanding. It is an impressively tense scene and reveals in music much of the change that has come over Blanche since she joined the Order.

Scene iv. The sacristy of the convent. The Father Confessor has just finished saying what he tells the nuns is his last Mass. The priesthood has been proscribed and he must go into hiding. When Constance asks rhetorically if there are no men left in France, the Prioress says, 'When there are not priests enough, there will be plenty of martyrs.' Mother Marie seizes on her words: it is the duty of the daughters of Carmel to give their lives so that France may once again have priests. The Mother Superior firmly corrects her: it is not for them to decide if their names shall one day be inscribed among the martyrs.

The bell rings again violently, and a mob pours in. Two commissars announce the expulsion of the nuns from the convent. Mother Marie, now in charge, gets into an argument with the first Commissar, who takes her aside and reveals he was once a sacristan and is at heart a true servant of the Church. He leads the mob out.

Act III, scene i. The ruined chapel of the convent. As the Prioress is away, Mother Marie addresses the assembled nuns. She proposes that together they take a vow of martyrdom to save the order from harm. But, she says firmly, if the vote is not unanimous, the proposal shall be abandoned. Mother Marie announces that there is one voice against. Immediately Constance, to save Blanche from embarrassment, says that that vote was hers: she will retract, and thus they will be unanimous. Blanche and Constance as the youngest go first to take the vow. No sooner has Blanche passed the Father Confessor than she takes advantage of the general confusion to escape.

Outside the convent, an Officer congratulates the nuns, who leave in civilian costume, on their discipline and public spirit, but advises them that they will be watched. The Prioress wants to warn the Father Confessor against coming to celebrate Mass. Mother Marie reacts with smouldering violence: how can they reconcile this caution with their vow? The Prioress says that each is responsible before God as an individual, but she herself must answer for them all and she is old enough to know how to keep her accounts.

Scene ii. The ruined library in the Paris house of the Marquis de la Force. Blanche in peasant costume is cooking when Mother Marie arrives to tell her that

she has come to fetch her. Blanche prevaricates and tells Mother Marie that her father was guillotined and she is now alone. Mother Marie gives her an address, where she will be safe and where she (Mother Marie) will wait for her until the following night. Blanche says that she cannot go, but Mother Marie is quietly confident.

In a street near the Bastille, Blanche hears that they have arrested all the members of the convent.

Scene iii. The prison of the Conciergerie. The Prioress tries to comfort the nuns at the end of their first night in prison; from now on, she will consider herself bound by their vow of martyrdom, though it was made in her absence. Constance is convinced that Blanche will return, because of a dream she has had. The Jailer announces the findings of the tribunal: it is death for each one of them.

Mother Marie hears of the death sentence from the Father Confessor. She must die with them, she says, but the Father Confessor suggests that this may not be the will of God.

Scene iv. The scaffold is prepared and the crowd watches as the Prioress leads in her little band of fourteen Carmelite followers. Singing the 'Salve Regina', one after another they mount the scaffold, and each time the guillotine drops there is one voice the fewer to sustain the singing. When Sister Constance is alone, she sees Blanche in the crowd, stops for an instant, then goes with renewed confidence to her death. Blanche takes up the chant, and with a new serenity follows her sisters to accomplish the vow they swore together.　　　　H.

LA VOIX HUMAINE
The Human Voice

Lyrical tragedy in one act, text by Jean Cocteau. Première, Opéra-Comique, Paris, 6 February 1959, with Denise Duval, conductor Georges Prêtre. First produced at la Scala, 1959; at New York's Carnegie Hall, 1959; by Glyndebourne Opera in Edinburgh, 1960, always with Denise Duval.

The Woman..Soprano

Time: 'The Present'
Running Time: 40 minutes

The score of *La Voix Humaine*, Poulenc's third and last opera, is preceded by two pages of instructions. Jean Cocteau gives general directions about the setting and the action. The composer demands that the only role be taken by a young, elegant woman, since the story is far from being about an ageing woman deserted by her lover. After a rather precise word about the degree of freedom needed in the interpretation of the score, Poulenc emphasises that the whole work needs to be 'bathed in the greatest orchestral sensuality'. And it is, in anything like a good performance, since the transparency of instrumentation is something to marvel at, and it is the orchestra which must establish continuity which is by definition absent from a telephone conversation of which we hear only one side.

The subject is a woman abandoned by her lover. She has tried to commit suicide after he told her that he planned to get married next day, and we may suppose that this is the last time she will talk to him on the telephone. Hysteria is apparent in the orchestra from the start. Throughout, the woman veers between the certainties natural between people who have known each other a long time and the awed tones of familiarity ruined by too many and too explosive past confrontations, to say nothing of the fear that the other and now distant partner may

hang up. She is by turns the betrayed lover and the restorer of trust. She is incoherent; she insists that the past was beautiful, at least in memory; she tells lies; she won't see, still less accept reality; she snatches at optimism when any half sentence half justifies it, she plays outrageously for sympathy. She is wounded, she suffers, she goes off the deep end, she calms herself. Finally it is over, the connection is broken and the receiver drops lifelessly – as she had once planned for herself – to the ground. The essential truths have never been spoken, only the social realities, the conventions, the banalities of such a situation; but with what accuracy they have been pinned to page and score!

The blend of snatches of lyricism with subtly inflected, always expressive, *arioso* is a most effective one. Poulenc's is an exquisitely sensitive setting of French words, as one would expect, and the short opera, in a sensitive performance, redeems an intrinsic sentimentality of situation. Nonetheless, Cocteau's monologue is very far from being a rhapsody and emerges as a strict piece of formal construction.

Perhaps the last word should be Cocteau's. 'Mon cher Francis, tu as fixé, une fois pour toutes, la façon de *dire* mon texte.' H.

SERGEI SERGEYEVICH PROKOFIEV
(born 23 April 1891, died 5 March 1953)

THE GAMBLER
Igrok

Opera in four acts (six scenes), text (after Dostoevsky's novel, *Igrok*, 'The Gambler') by the composer. Première, Brussels, 29 April 1929, in a French translation by Paul Spaak, conducted by Corneil de Thoran. First performed in Italy, Naples, 1953, with Barbato, Gardino, Pirazzini, Annaloro, Sinimberghi, Tajo, conductor Scherchen; in Germany, Darmstadt, 1956; Belgrade, 1961, with Heybalova, Starč, Zarko Cvejč, conductor Danon; Edinburgh Festival, 1962, with Belgrade Company; Amsterdam, 1975 (in Dutch), with Jan Blinkhof; English National Opera, 1983 (in English), with Sally Burgess, Graham Clark, John Tomlinson, conductor Christian Badea (Amsterdam and English National Opera produced by David Pountney).

The General, *a retired army officer* (55) ....Bass
Pauline, *his step-daughter*..............................Soprano

Alexey, *tutor to the General's children* (25) ....Tenor
'Babulenka', the General's
  rich aunt (75)................................Mezzo-Soprano
The Marquis ....Tenor
Mr Astley, *a rich Englishman*.........................Baritone
Blanche, *a demi-mondaine* (25)....................Contralto
Prince Nilsky ....Tenor
Baron Würmerhelm (45) ....Bass
Baroness Würmerhelm ....Mute
Potapich, *Babulenka's steward* ....Baritone

In the gambling scene
The Director..Bass
The First Croupier ....Tenor
The Second Croupier ....Tenor

The Fat Englishman...Bass
The Tall Englishman...Bass
The Florid Lady..Soprano
The Pale Lady ....Mezzo-Soprano
A Respectable Old Lady ....Mezzo-Soprano
A Suspicious Old Lady ....Contralto
A Heated Gambler ....Tenor
A Gambler in Ill-Health...................................Tenor
A Hunch-Backed Gambler ....Tenor
An Unlucky Gambler ....Baritone
An Old Gambler ....Bass

Six Gamblers (Two Tenors, Two Baritones, Two
    Basses)

The Head-Waiter, the Page-Boy; Babulenka's Three
    Servants; Gamblers, People staying in the Hotel,
    Servants, Porters

Place: The Imaginary Town of Roulettenburg
Time: 1865
Running Time: 2 hours 10 minutes

Prokofiev was fascinated by the theatre from the
time his parents took him to Moscow when he was
eight, and he wrote some half a dozen operas before
the end of his student days, one of which (*Maddalena*;
1911, revised 1913) nearly reached the stage.[1] Albert
Coates in the early days of the war was in the process
of replacing Nápravník as head of the Mariinsky
Theatre in St Petersburg, and plans to stage *The
Gambler* in 1917 – the first opera on a subject by
Dostoevsky – were only prevented by the Revolution.
In 1927–28 Prokofiev revised the orchestration and
rewrote certain passages which he had come to regard
as 'mere padding disguised by monstrous chords', for
another projected production (also for Leningrad), but
again it came to nothing and the work received its première in Brussels a year later, and then languished a
further twenty-four before again coming to the notice
of the European opera houses.

    The background of the opera is an imaginary
German spa by the name of Roulettenburg, based on
Wiesbaden. A retired Russian General waits for news
that a rich relation (always referred to as Babulenka –
Grandmama – but in reality his aunt) has died leaving
him her fortune. With him are his young children, his
step-daughter Pauline, and the children's tutor,

Alexey. The General has borrowed large sums of
money from the rich French Marquis and has fallen in
love with Blanche. Alexey for his part loves Pauline,
who has in the past had an affair with the Marquis.

Act I. The garden of the Grand Hotel. In a few
short, halting sentences which seem to epitomise the
ambivalent relationship between them, Pauline
elicits from Alexey that he has staked and lost the
money she gave him to gamble with. Blanche, the
Marquis and Mr Astley appear and watch the
General open a telegram which to their chagrin still
speaks of Babulenka's health, not yet of her death.
They advise Alexey to give up gambling, but he
reacts vigorously: his Tartar nature forbids something so tame as earning merely in order to save. To
Astley, Alexey spits out his dislike of the other's
hypocrisy, then, in a scene with Pauline, explains
that to win he must gamble with his own money –
when that happens he will pay her debts, he will
declare the passion he feels for her.

    Re-enter the General, thanking the Marquis for yet
another loan and signing an IOU. Alone with Alexey
again, Pauline asks if he would live up to his promise
to die for her – would he kill if she named the man?
Alexey refuses to take her seriously, but when she
orders him almost in a frenzy to insult the fat Baroness
Würmerhelm, he reluctantly goes towards his unsuspecting victim, crudely declares himself her slave, and
the curtain falls on a scene of general consternation.

    Act II. In the hall of the hotel casino, the General
tells Alexey off for his conduct, but is unprepared for
Alexey's vigorous reaction: what right had someone
who is neither his father nor his guardian to apologise on his behalf?

    Alexey returns to find only Mr Astley, with whom
he discusses at first his own predicament, then the
General's affair with Blanche, who was originally in
Roulettenburg with an Italian Prince. Now, she has
caught the General and, once he inherits, she will
become his wife – and Pauline will be snapped up by
the money-lending Marquis! At that moment the
Marquis himself puts in an appearance and attempts
rather clumsily to dissuade Alexey from aggravating
the affair with the Germans, supporting his case with
a note from Pauline.

    As Blanche and the General discuss the immi-

---

[1] In 1981 it did, in Graz under Edward Downes, who had completed the orchestration. St Louis followed in 1982.

nence of the General's inheritance, Babulenka herself appears in a wheelchair and attended by her servants – come, she announces, to try her hand at this gambling they all appear to enjoy so much. All salute her in turn, Alexey and Pauline with affection and respect, the General with considerable embarrassment, Blanche and the Marquis somewhat distantly. The old lady tells them that she cured herself by sending the doctors away, that she knows moreover that they have all been waiting for her to die. Blanche departs on the arm of Prince Nilsky.

Act III. Outside the gaming rooms. Inside, the old lady is gambling away her fortune; outside, the General bemoans the turn of events and fails to enlist either the sympathy of Blanche or the help of Alexey, who alone has any influence on Babulenka. Prince Nilsky's announcement of further losses galvanises the General to a last effort, and he rushes into the Casino, leaving Blanche to take the Prince's arm and Alexey to reflect that were it not for Pauline he would be laughing at their imminent downfall. Mention of Pauline's name brings her rapidly to the scene, for him to repeat his declaration that he is always at her service.

The old lady reappears; she has lost all the money she brought with her and is leaving immediately. In music of genuine warmth she asks Pauline to accompany her. Pauline hesitates; at least, warns the old woman, let her beware of the Marquis, from whom can come no good. The General wants to get into the old lady's room, but Potapich bars the way, and the General in his distraught condition falls to lamenting Blanche's unkindness towards him.

Act IV. Alexey's room, where he finds Pauline waiting for him. The Marquis has written to say that, bearing in mind that Alexey has gambled away her share of the family fortunes, he has ordered his agents to preserve for her twenty thousand francs from the sale of the General's property. Alexey is indignant at such insulting behaviour, but his suggestion that she borrow from Astley stings Pauline into asking if she should give herself to the Englishman rather than to him. Alexey's astonishment is complete, but with it comes an idea and he runs off.

A frenzied orchestral introduction takes us to the brilliantly lit gambling rooms. For a moment Alexey watches the play, then it is his turn. He stakes successfully on red, stakes and wins again and eventually in an extraordinary run of luck breaks the bank at the first table. He rushes to the second table, followed by several other gamblers, and repeats his incredible luck; then to a third, always with a winning streak. This is one of Prokofiev's most brilliant scenes, a *Cours à l'abîme* in *scherzo* form, and the voices of the players cross and intermingle without merging into a chorus. The music captures the over-heated atmosphere, the rapt concentration of the players, and the almost ritualistic movements of the croupiers with their incantations of 'Les jeux sont faits ... Rien ne va plus'.

An entr'acte[1] preserves, even enhances, the tension of the previous scene, with the cries of the gamblers coming from behind the lowered curtain, and the last scene returns to Alexey's room. He relives his success, then suddenly remembers Pauline who is watching him, and offers her the money to throw in the Marquis's teeth. She reacts with peals of laughter, and it is in a context of hysteria that they declare they will never part, will together take refuge with Babulenka. Now, Pauline insists, where are the fifty thousand francs? He hands the money over, and with all her strength she hurls it back at him. 'Pauline', he cries after her; then his thoughts go back to the casino and the unrepeatable run of luck, and as the curtain falls, he is staring fixedly at an imaginary roulette wheel. H.

THE LOVE FOR THREE ORANGES
Lyubov k trem Apelsinam

Opera in a prologue and four acts, text by the composer after the comedy of Carlo Gozzi. Première, Chicago, 30 December 1921 (in French), with Koshetz, Pavlovska, Falco, Dusseau, Mojica, Dua, Defrère, Cotreuil, Dufranne, conductor Prokofiev. First performed New York (Manhattan Opera House), 1922, with Chicago cast; Cologne, 1925, conductor Szenkar; Berlin, 1926; Leningrad, 1927; la Scala, Milan, 1947; Edinburgh Festival, 1962, Belgrade Opera, conductor Danon; Sadler's Wells, 1963. Revived with great success, New York City Center, 1949, conductor Halasz; Glyndebourne, 1982 (in French), conductor Bernard Haitink.

The King of Clubs, *ruler of an imaginary kingdom, whose inhabitants are clothed as playing cards*...Bass

The Prince, *his son*..Tenor

---

[1] In the Belgrade production, which was seen in Edinburgh, used as a prologue to the opera (with the curtain up) as well as appearing in its proper place.

Princess Clarissa, *niece of the King*................Contralto

Leandro, *his prime minister, dressed
as the King of Spades*.................................. Baritone

Truffaldino, *jester* ....Tenor

Pantaloon, *friend and adviser of the King* ....Baritone

The Magician Tchelio, *protector of the King*..........Bass

Fata Morgana, *a witch, protectress of
Leandro*..Soprano

Three princesses
Linetta...Contralto
Nicoletta ....Mezzo-Soprano
Ninetta...Soprano

The Cook..Bass

Farfarello, *a devil* ....Bass

Smeraldina, *Fata Morgana's
black servant* ....Mezzo-Soprano

The Master of Ceremonies.............................Tenor

The Herald ....Bass

The Trumpeter ....Bass Trombone

Ten Reasonable Spectators...Five Tenors, Five Basses

Monsters, Drunkards, Gluttons, Guards, Servants,
Soldiers, Jokers, Highbrows, Wits, Romantics,
Lowbrows, Little Devils, Doctors, Courtiers

Running Time: 1 hour 55 minutes

It was in 1918 that the director of the Chicago Opera, the conductor Cleofonte Campanini, commissioned Prokofiev to write an opera, but it had to wait until 1921 for production (largely because of the composer's impossible demands), at a time when the famous singer Mary Garden, still active, had succeeded Campanini. The Russian stage director, Vsevolod Meyerhold, had, immediately prior to the composer's departure from Russia, presented him with a Russian adaptation of the play by Meyerhold himself, and it was this that Prokofiev turned into a libretto. The opera is a farcical but entertaining re-working of the *commedia dell'arte* atmosphere (itself partly parody) of Gozzi's play.

Prologue. A dispute is going on between the protagonists of the various forms of theatrical entertainment, who are put to confusion when ten masked announcers appear to inform them that, whatever they say, they are going to see something quite different from what they are used to, 'The Love for Three Oranges'! The curtain parts to allow a 'trumpeter' (playing a bass trombone) to announce the appear-

ance of a herald, who announces the burden of the story, the apparently incurable hypochondria of the son of the King of Clubs.

Act I, scene i. The King's palace. Doctors inform the King that his son cannot be cured, and the King immediately goes into paroxysms of grief; who will succeed him if his son is removed? His odious niece, Clarissa, presumably. The boy must be made to laugh, as the physicians predicted there was a chance of curing him if that could be achieved. Pantaloon suggests that the most likely way of doing it would be through theatrical performances. He shouts for Truffaldino, who undertakes to arrange everything.

The King orders that plans be put in train. Leandro, who is not at all anxious for the Prince's recovery, tries to raise objections, and the scene ends with Leandro and Pantaloon shouting abuse at each other.

A curtain covered with cabalistic signs descends, and Tchelio and Fata Morgana, surrounded by a chorus of little devils, proceed to play against each other with gigantic cards. Behind their chairs, the representations of the King of Clubs and the King of Spades respectively show that the game is in effect that of the King's protector against Leandro's. Tchelio loses. The music occurs in the orchestral suite[1] as 'Scène infernale'.

The King's palace, where Leandro and the wicked Clarissa have reached an understanding, whereby the Princess undertakes to marry Leandro, who must encompass the Prince's death and so clear the way for her accession. Leandro is confident that his method – to fill the Prince full of tragic prose and boring verse – will yet prove lethal. There is an interruption as the spectators in the boxes get out of hand and invade the stage. When Clarissa demands action, Leandro discovers the black servant Smeraldina is eavesdropping. They threaten to kill her, but she reveals that Tchelio protects the Prince and may yet succeed in his stratagems to make him laugh. Only through the intervention of Fata Morgana, her mistress, can this be avoided. The three voices are raised, calling for Fata Morgana.

Act II. The Prince's room. He is surrounded with medicines – ill and bored, and none of Truffaldino's antics make him laugh. Truffaldino persuades him to dress and watch the diversions which have been planned for his benefit. The well-known march begins

---

[1] The suite consists of Les Ridicules, Scène infernale, Marche, Scherzo, Le Prince et la Princesse, La Fuite.

The Love for Three Oranges *(English National Opera, 1990, director Richard Jones, sets The Brothers Quay, costumes Sue Blane). Donald Maxwell (Leander), Fiona Kimm (Smeraldina), Anne Collins (Princess Clarissa) invoke Fata Morgana.*

in the orchestra, and continues as an interlude to the second scene, which takes place in the great hall of the palace. The King is there with Clarissa, and also in evidence are Leandro and Pantaloon. The Prince is covered in furs to avoid catching cold.

Truffaldino stages a comic battle between 'Monsters', and later turns loose a crowd of drunkards and gluttons to fight for food and drink; all to no avail. In despair, he looks round and catches sight of the witch Fata Morgana. He is horrified that such an old hag should intrude and tries to eject her. In their struggle, she loses her balance, does an involuntary somersault, and achieves the apparently impossible; the Prince starts to laugh. The whole court, and even the spectators, join in, and in their delight, everyone starts to dance – everyone, that is to say, apart from Leandro and Clarissa who are anything but pleased at the turn of events.

Fata Morgana is not long in recovering from her discomfiture. She curses the Prince and, surrounded by her troop of little devils, pronounces his fate; he will fall in love with three oranges, and will pursue them to the ends of the earth. Immediately, the Prince starts to cry out that he will depart forthwith on his journey, accompanied by Truffaldino. Amidst general lamentation, the little devil Farfarello appears and with a pair of bellows wafts the wanderers on their way.

Act III. The desert. Tchelio makes a vain attempt to restrain Farfarello from wafting the Prince and his companion to perdition, but Farfarello tells him that his loss at cards has rendered his magic powers inoperative – and he proves as much by disobeying him. The Prince and Truffaldino appear, and the Magician, having discovered they are seeking the three oranges, advises them, if they ever find them, to cut them open only near water. He also warns them that they are in the keeping of the terrible Creonte, who takes the form of a gigantic cook. In case it may help, he gives Truffaldino a magic ribbon, hoping it may distract the cook's attention while they filch the oranges.

Farfarello appears with his bellows and like light-ning the Prince and Truffaldino are transported towards their destination. This is the *scherzo* of the suite, which, with the March, has become the most popular section of the work.

The two adventurers stand in front of the castle, and are about to go into the kitchen when from it emerges the colossal cook. Both hide, but Truffaldino is quickly discovered and saved from the cook's wrath only because the latter sees and falls hope-lessly for the ribbon round his neck. Meanwhile the Prince creeps silently into the kitchen and emerges a moment later with the three oranges, which are of a calibre that befits their vast guardian. The cook asks for the ribbon, is given it as a present, and capers with delight, while, to the music of the *scherzo*, the Prince and Truffaldino make their escape.

We meet them again in the desert, where the oranges they have been carrying have grown to really huge dimensions, big enough one might think to contain a human being. The Prince falls asleep, but Truffaldino is so thirsty he cannot resist cutting open one of the oranges, which, in spite of Tchelio's warning, he hopes may assuage his thirst. Out steps Princess Linetta. She says that she will die of thirst if she is not immediately given some water, and, when none is forthcoming, demonstrates that she can be as good as her word. The same happens when Princess Nicoletta comes from the second orange. Truffaldino, at his wits' end and unable to wake the Prince, rushes despairingly off into the desert.

The Prince awakes, appears in no way discon-certed by the sight of the two dead girls, but orders four soldiers who conveniently appear to bury them. Then he addresses himself to the third orange, which he is sure contains all that he has ever dreamed of. He cuts it open, and a third girl appears, more beau-tiful than the others; he immediately recognises her as the one being he has waited for since birth. She expresses sentiments that are in no way dissimilar, then sinks into the Prince's arms. It looks as though she will follow the other ladies to the grave, but a bucket of water is produced from one of the boxes, and the Princess's life is saved. The Prince and his prospective bride enthuse over each other but, when the Prince says they must return to his father's palace, she demurs: he must fetch her a suitable dress before she can think of meeting his father.

Princess Ninetta is alone. Towards her glides the figure of Smeraldina, behind whom looms the shadow of Fata Morgana. The occupants of the boxes are in a fever-heat of anxiety, which turns out to be fully justified when Smeraldina sticks a long magical pin into Ninetta's head. She groans long and sadly, and is seen to have been turned into a rat. Fata Morgana tells Smeraldina that she must take Ninetta's place when she meets the King.

The sound of the March is heard, and a procession appears, with the King and the Prince at its head. They come up to Smeraldina, who proclaims herself the Princess. The Prince refuses to marry her, but his father objects, and he is forced to give her his arm and lead her back to the palace.

Act IV, scene i. The cabalistic curtain of Act I, scene ii, is seen once more. Fata Morgana and Tchelio are at it again, abusing one another like pickpockets. Fata Morgana seems to be having the better of the argument, but the spectators leave their boxes, sur-round her, and shove her into a section of the struc-ture from which they have come, shutting the door firmly behind her. For the moment Tchelio is tri-umphant.

Scene ii. The royal throne-room. When the cur-tains round the throne are drawn aside, in the Princess's place is a large rat – Princess Ninetta in her metamorphosed state. All are aghast, the King sends for his guards, but Tchelio does his best to transform the rat into the princess he knows it to be. All of a sudden his efforts work, and Princess Ninetta stands before them. The Prince is beside himself with joy, and Smeraldina's discomfiture is complete. She is recog-nised as an accomplice of Leandro, and is accused with him and Clarissa of treason. For a moment the court watches the King go through the agonising process of making up his mind; then he turns to them full of resolve: all the culprits shall be hanged.

As the guards move towards them, the guilty crew takes flight, and soon the scene is covered with parties chasing each other, all of a dither in case the traitors get away, but none knowing which way they have gone. Suddenly, Fata Morgana appears in the middle of the stage, a trap-door opens, and her followers disappear down it to safety. The courtiers arrive too late, and there is nothing to do but cry 'God save the King' which the King immediately amends to 'God save the Prince and Princess'.   H.

THE FIERY ANGEL
L'Ange de Feu; Ognenniy Angel

Opera in five acts and seven tableaux, libretto by the composer from a novel by Valery Briusoff (published in Russia in 1907). First complete performance (in concert) at the Théâtre des Champs-Elysées, Paris, 25 November 1954, with Lucienne Marée, Xavier Depraz, conducted by Charles Bruck (French translation by André Michel). Stage première, Venice, 14 September 1955, with Dow, Panerai, conductor Sanzogno. First performed la Scala, 1957, with Goltz, Panerai, conductor Sanzogno; Spoleto, 1959, with Gencer, Panerai, conductor Kertesz; Opéra-Comique, Paris, 1964, with Cavalli, Julien Haas, conductor Sebastien; Sadler's Wells, 1965, by New Opera Company with Collier, John Shaw; Frankfurt, 1969 (and Edinburgh Festival, 1970), with Anja Silja, Rudolf Konstantin, conductor Christoph von Dohnanyi (omitting the end of Act II and the whole of Act IV!). Adelaide Festival, 1988, with Josephine Barstow, Rodney Macann, conductor Stuart Challender, producer David Pountney; Covent Garden, 1992 (co-production with Kirov, St Petersburg), with Galina Gorchakova, Sergei Leiferkus, conductor Edward Downes, producer David Freeman.

Ruprecht, *a knight*	Baritone
The Hostess of the Inn	Contralto
Renata	Soprano
The Servant at the Inn	Baritone
The Sorceress	Mezzo-Soprano
Jakob Glock	Tenor
Agrippa von Nettelsheim, *a philosopher*	Tenor
Count Heinrich	Mute
Mathias	Baritone
The Doctor	Tenor
Mephistopheles	Tenor
Faust	Baritone
The Innkeeper at Cologne	Baritone
The Mother Superior	Mezzo-Soprano
The Inquisitor	Bass
Two Young Nuns	Sopranos

Place: Germany, mainly Cologne
Time: Sixteenth Century
Running Time: 2 hours 5 minutes

Prokofiev worked on *The Fiery Angel* between 1920 and 1926, beginning it, that is to say, in America after the failure of *The Love for Three Oranges*.[1] The strongly romantic subject is in great contrast to the ironic rationalism more usually associated with him, but he seems to have been overwhelmed by the possibilities of the story,[2] so that, without immediate prospects of production, he shut himself up from March 1922 for eighteen months at Ettal near Oberammergau, where, as he says, the action might have 'taken place in the back yard'. In the event, the opera seems to have been accepted by Bruno Walter for Berlin in 1926, revised then but never performed. Koussevitzky played an Interlude and the Agrippa scene at a concert in Paris three years later, and the composer planned but did not carry out an extensive revision in the early 1930s, including a re-write of the libretto. The work was then mislaid and its existence even partially forgotten until it turned up in Paris after the composer's death. Prokofiev himself had in the meanwhile used some music from it for his third symphony.[3]

The Fiery Angel belongs to the epoch of *Wozzeck*, but even that masterpiece among products of the post-Freudian era hardly surpasses it in its capacity to evoke and portray neurasthenia. But here a distinction must be made. *Wozzeck* belongs to a different world from the one inhabited by the émigré Prokofiev. His adopted Paris was dominated by Stravinsky's Neoclassicism, the ironies of Cocteau and Satie, the new exploits of Les Six; and the Germany where he retired to write *The Fiery Angel* by the opulence of Richard Strauss, with apparently at the time no more than minority dissension on the part of Schoenberg and his adherents on the one hand and Hindemith on the other.

The work is allegorical on two simultaneous levels. On one plane, Renata symbolises the struggle between good and evil, and the capacity to believe that evil is good and to act on this belief. She is haunted by visions of an Angel, and her passion for him amounts to obsession; to her he is Good, and no one else she meets is of any significance, except as help in her search for the Angel, or his physical embodiment, Heinrich. On another level, this is the account of an all-absorbing (for Briusoff, autobio-

---

[1] After the Chicago première of this opera, Prokofiev may have hoped that Mary Garden, in her double capacity as Director of the Chicago Opera and leading *prima donna*, would mount *The Fiery Angel* and herself sing the title role. But unfortunately, he writes, she resigned the directorship.

[2] It is hardly a coincidence that an earlier opera, *Maddalena* – his first – was also concerned with obsession.

[3] First performed in Paris, spring 1929, under Pierre Monteux.

graphical[1]), but ultimately unsuccessful love affair, seen through the suffering eyes of the male, but more damaging in the final analysis it would appear for the female protagonist than for him.

Musically, the work is dominated by two themes associated with Renata, which with their derivatives occur throughout (Ex. 1 and 2).

(Ex. 1)

(Ex. 2)

Act I. A room in a shabby inn. The hostess conducts Ruprecht to his room for the night. He hears hysterical and terrified imprecations coming from behind an apparently disused door, forces it, and Renata, distraught and dishevelled, throws herself into his arms for protection, continuing to defend herself against her unseen attacker even after Ruprecht has drawn his sword and made the sign of the cross. The music vividly portrays her exhaustion as Ruprecht prays and her terror abates.

She tells her story in an extended narration of considerable musical splendour. It was when she was eight that an Angel first appeared to her, dressed in white with blue eyes and golden hair and surrounded by flames. His name was Madiel and he appeared to her day and night, eventually announcing to her that her destiny was to be a saint. When she was seventeen, her urgent desire for carnal love drove him away, to her utter despair, but eventually he told her in a dream that he would return. As soon as she saw Count Heinrich she knew, in spite of his denial, that he was Madiel in human form. There ensued with Heinrich a year of happiness such as had never been since Eve was expelled from Paradise. In the end he abandoned her, and now Ruprecht has saved her from the fiend who has pursued her with visions and nightmares ever since.

The noise attracts the attention of the hostess and her servant. Renata is a loose woman, the hostess explains to Ruprecht; she bewitched the Count and tormented the villagers, and now she must leave the inn. Ruprecht shrugs his shoulders and decides that, once the hostess goes, this attractive girl, witch or no witch, shall be his. As she looks out of the window yearning for Heinrich, Ruprecht unsuccessfully tries to seduce her. He quickly abandons the attempt, but from that moment Ruprecht becomes as involved in the search for Heinrich as Renata herself.

---

[1] Around 1904 (Richard Taruskin tells us in an article published in connection with the Deutsche Grammophon recording of the opera), Briusoff entered into a liaison with Nina Petrovskaya, a minor writer who had been (and indeed remained) involved with another Russian writer, Andrey Bely. The affair seems to have lasted until 1911, after which Petrovskaya's life disintegrated until her suicide in Paris in 1928; ironically enough, though she was a neighbour of Prokofiev's during the period he was revising *The Fiery Angel*, each lived in ignorance of the existence of the other.

When the hostess brings in a fortune-teller, the contrast with Renata is intentional; the one is up to all the tricks of the trade, the other attracted to sorcery only as a means to an end. The act ends with an impressive musical scene, in which the old fortune-teller makes obscure references to Renata's guilt.

Act II. Cologne. The Introduction features the theme of Ruprecht's disappointment. Renata is alone reading a book of magic when Ruprecht comes in, complaining that the week they have been in the city has been spent only in feverish search for Heinrich; they have looked in every church, in each narrow street, they have tried magic, but all to no avail. Without Heinrich she cannot live, is her answer. Jakob Glock has been commissioned to bring more books of magic, and Renata fastens on them, telling Ruprecht that, despite his uncomplaining love, beside Heinrich he is nothing; were she to be walking with Heinrich and to find Ruprecht's body self-slain in the gutter, she would take no more notice than to ask for its removal.

Renata burns magic herbs, and soon a knock is heard on the wall – it is a spirit, she says, announcing the arrival of Heinrich. With some remarkable *divisi* writing for the strings, Prokofiev expresses Renata's obsession in a scene that is musically of very striking quality with, in its total effect, something of the drama and irresistibility of Berlioz's *Cours à l'abîme*.

The door opens, but the music subsides to impotence and Ruprecht finds nothing. Renata collapses weeping, while Ruprecht swears he will compel the spirits to aid her in her search. Glock reappears; he will take Ruprecht to speak with the philosopher-magician, Agrippa von Nettelsheim.

A fine symphonic interlude takes us to Agrippa's studio, where he sits surrounded by books, bottles of medicine, human skeletons, and three black dogs. In a scene whose impressive music caps even the feverish excitement of its predecessor, Agrippa reveals himself as a master of the diabolical arts, 'cold and steely, immensely powerful and terribly convincing. Here is damnation'.[1] As a philosopher, however, he refuses to help Ruprecht. The first scene of Act II provided most of the music for the third movement of Prokofiev's third symphony (a *scherzo* 'dénué de gaieté' the composer called it), and the interlude and second scene for the last movement.

Act III. Renata is in despair outside the door of a house. It is Heinrich's; she has seen him and been rejected. Ruprecht returns from his encounter with Agrippa and hears the story of Renata's *volte face* – she no longer loves Heinrich, who, she is convinced, was an impostor, not the embodiment of her Madiel. If Ruprecht will kill her seducer, she will be his, and follow him wherever he goes. Ruprecht demands entrance to Heinrich's house, while Renata offers up a prayer to Madiel for forgiveness that she mistook Heinrich for him and for strength for the future. It has the force of a great aria of dedication.

Ruprecht can be seen at a window as he challenges Heinrich, who in appearance is the very incarnation of all that Renata has ever ascribed to Madiel, a true angel of fire. Renata is overwhelmed at the sight of him, and when Ruprecht reappears, in another complete change of heart, she forbids him to shed a drop of Heinrich's blood, rather to let himself be killed.

An interlude depicts the duel (part of it can be heard in the first movement of the third symphony). At its end, Ruprecht is discovered lying seriously wounded on the banks of the Rhine, where Renata tends him, and in a lyrical aria sings of her love, swearing that if he dies she will enter a convent. After Renata's *berceuse*, delirium (Ruprecht's from his wound? Renata's from her obsession? – it is the only moment of the story when Renata and Ruprecht are musically at one) suddenly seizes both in music of uncanny intensity, a chorus of women behind the stage commenting ironically the while on the instability of love. A doctor who has been fetched by Mathias pronounces that Ruprecht will live.

Act IV. In a public garden, Renata tells Ruprecht, who has hardly recovered from his wound, that she must leave him; to accomplish the salvation of her soul, she must take the veil. When Ruprecht protests his love for her, she tries to commit suicide, turning the attack on him as he tries to prevent her. Mephistopheles and Faust have come into the garden and watch the scene. When the pot-boy, in response to their order, only brings wine, Mephistopheles threatens to swallow the child, and later at a gulp makes good his boast, subsequently restoring him to life at the request of the innkeeper.

Act V. The act starts with some beautiful slow

---

[1] Hans Swarsenski, in an excellent article on the opera in *Tempo*, 1956.

music (in Symphony No. 3, the subject of the second movement), chanted by the nuns of the convent of which Renata has become a member. The music is the more welcome by its contrast with the frenzy which has preceded it. The same abstraction from the world is apparent when the Mother Superior asks Renata about her visions: has she seen evil spirits? No, says Renata, she always turned her back on them. The fact remains, the Mother Superior points out, that since she entered the convent, the place has been in an uproar, full of strange noises and the sisters attacked by devils.

The nuns in the meanwhile have filled one side of the crypt, and now the Inquisitor and his followers enter to examine Renata. He asks her to furnish him with proof that her visions have never been inspired by Hell. The spirit who visits her, she tells him, has always spoken of virtue, of the importance of the life to come – are these the words of the devil? Immediately two young sisters cry out in terror, knocks are heard on the wall, and the scene becomes one of pandemonium as one group after another is caught up in the general turmoil, a few supporting Renata but most crying out against her. The exorcism proceeds, but finally, as Mephistopheles and Ruprecht appear, the nuns rush frenziedly at the Inquisitor and his supporters, and the opera ends as he pronounces Renata a heretic and sentences her to death. The final scene, with its intricate part-writing for the women against the *cantus firmus* of the Inquisitor, is masterly in its effect and brings the opera to an overwhelming conclusion.   H.

BETROTHAL IN A MONASTERY

Obrucheniye v monastire

Opera in four acts, text by Mira Mendelson from Sheridan's *The Duenna*. Première planned for 1941 but postponed because of the German invasion of Russia; plans for a 1943 production at the Bolshoi, Moscow, also abandoned. Première, Kirov Theatre, Leningrad, 30 November 1946. First performed New York, Greenwich Mews Playhouse, 1948 (as *The Duenna*), with two-piano accompaniment; Leipzig, 1957; East Berlin, 1958, conductor Lovro von Matacic; Naples, 1959, with Rosetta Noli, Belen Amparan, Agostino Lazzari, Francesco Albanese, Fernando Corena, Guido Mazzini, conductor Fabien Sevitzky; Zagreb Opera, 1960 (and in Paris, 1961); Strasbourg, 1973.

Don Jerome, *a rich man of Seville*	Tenor
Ferdinand, *his son*	Baritone
Louisa, *his daughter*	Soprano
The Duenna (Margaret)	Contralto
Antonio, *in love with Louisa*	Tenor
Clara d'Almanza, *friend of Louisa*	Mezzo-Soprano
Mendoza, *a rich fish merchant*	Bass
Don Carlos, *an impoverished nobleman, friend of Mendoza*	Baritone

Monks

Father Augustine, *Father Superior of the monastery*	Baritone
Brother Elixir	Tenor
Brother Chartreuse	Baritone
Brother Benedictine	Bass
Two Monks	Tenors
Lauretta, *Louisa's maidservant*	Soprano
Rosina, *Clara's maidservant*	Contralto
Lopez, *Ferdinand's servant*	Tenor
Friend of Don Jerome	Non-Singing
Servant of Don Jerome	Non-Singing

Servants, Maidservants, Monks, Guests, Maskers, Tradespeople

Place: Seville
Time: Eighteenth Century
Running Time: 2 hours 25 minutes

Prokofiev's seventh opera is taken from an English literary subject, *The Duenna* by Sheridan.[1]

Act I. An introduction, *moderato ma con brio*, brings us to the house of Don Jerome, a fussy, rich old man of Seville, who has a son and a daughter, Ferdinand and Louisa, for the latter of whom he has engaged a duenna. In front of Don Jerome's house, he and the fish merchant Mendoza are discussing a partnership which they plan to form and they seal the bargain with an agreement for Mendoza to marry Louisa.

Ferdinand comes in with his servant Lopez to lament with considerable romantic ardour the apparent capriciousness of his lady-love Clara. It has grown dark and Antonio enters equipped with a guitar obviously about to serenade Louisa, something which Ferdinand accepts as it would at least keep him from laying siege to the affections of Clara, with whom he was once in love. Antonio sings, and has the gratification of seeing Louisa come out on

---

[1] The subject also of Roberto Gerhard's only opera (see page 241).

her balcony, obviously delighted at his appearance and prepared to join him in song.

Don Jerome has been woken up by it all, but Louisa hides in time, and he is bamboozled by maskers, who dance round him to such purpose that he is driven to reflect that Louisa had better marry soon or she will be the prey of some serenading fool. The act ends with extensive and lively dancing.

Act II. The first scene is set in Louisa's apartment, where she is discussing with her duenna the possibility of marrying the man she has fallen in love with. The duenna has ideas of herself marrying Mendoza and his money, thus leaving Louisa free for Antonio. They plot just as Don Jerome himself appears. He means to impose his will on Louisa in the matter of the marriage with Mendoza, but both his children argue hotly against the plan. Don Jerome loses his patience and swears he will lock Louisa up until she changes her mind.

Ferdinand advises his father to let his sister marry someone she really loves and is disconcerted at Don Jerome's blank refusal, not least as he remembers Antonio's one-time love for Clara. His meditations are interrupted by the sound of the lamentations of the duenna and the insistence of Don Jerome, who has found the incriminating love letter that she and Louisa have planned would fall into his hands. She leaves to go to Louisa's room. Enter Louisa, disguised in the duenna's clothes – cape, hood, veil and all – and pretending to weep. Don Jerome shows her the door, covertly watched by the duenna, and shouts angrily after what is, though he does not know it, his daughter Louisa.

On the waterfront, fishwives are selling their wares, shortly to be observed by Don Mendoza and his impoverished friend Don Carlos. When they leave, Doña Clara and Rosina, her maidservant, come into view, the former delighted at the idea that she has left home at last but furious that it is through the intervention of her lover, who stole at night into her room and has thus by his presumption mortally affronted her.

No sooner have they left than Louisa comes in, lamenting her inability to locate Antonio. Should she look for help from her friend Clara – but then Clara is such a plaster saint! At that moment, Clara catches sight of her but fails to evade her, and they quickly discover that the one is eloping and the other hiding. In a lyrical aria, Clara tells Louisa the story: lying

awake at night, she heard her lover steal into her room but felt she must reject him for his over-ardent behaviour. Louisa attempts to console her but is plainly disconcerted to hear Clara seem to opt for a convent. Suddenly, Louisa catches sight of Mendoza, and immediately decides to ask Clara to allow her to masquerade for a bit as Doña Clara d'Almanza, which Clara agrees to on condition that Louisa, if she sees her brother Ferdinand, will swear not to have seen Clara anywhere, least of all tell him where she has gone – the convent of St Catherine, whose geography Clara proceeds to describe in some detail in the ostensible hope that Louisa will mention not so much as the position of the back door to Ferdinand.

Mendoza and Don Carlos come in and Louisa, pretending to be Clara, makes up to Mendoza and asks him to carry a message to her lover Antonio, thus provoking Mendoza's indignation since, for a moment, he half thought she was attracted to him. All the same, he knows Antonio was Louisa's suitor, and he feels this latest development may suit his purposes. Bidding Don Carlos escort Louisa (whom of course he thinks to be Clara) to Mendoza's house, Mendoza plans himself to visit the house of Don Jerome to see his betrothed.

Back in Don Jerome's house, where he is hearing from Mendoza how Doña Clara has run away from home, Don Jerome cannot refrain from singing his daughter's praises. It soon becomes apparent however that Louisa refuses to put in an appearance if her father is present at her meeting with Mendoza. Eventually he takes his leave, and the duenna enters dressed as Louisa. Mendoza is at first lyrically polite but much taken aback when he contrives to peep at her face. The duenna wins him round with flattery so that he becomes convinced he was mistaken to have found her hideous, and succumbs when she sings him a song. In the end, they are plotting to elope together. Don Jerome and Mendoza finish the act with a drinking song.

Act III. Don Carlos has conducted Louisa to Mendoza's lodgings, whither Mendoza loses no time in bringing Antonio. Antonio smells a rat and cannot believe that it is his old flame Clara who has summoned him, but Mendoza and Don Carlos push him into the room where they say Clara is waiting and then, as the music depicts a tender scene inside, proceed themselves to peer through the keyhole into the room. When Antonio and Louisa re-enter arm-in-arm, Don Carlos is scandalised that Antonio should so lightly steal his friend's beloved, but Mendoza welcomes young love and says that he himself will that very night go to Don Jerome's house in order to abduct Don Jerome's daughter. The scene ends with a quartet, Louisa and Antonio hymning the setting sun while Mendoza and Don Carlos wonder about the compensation available to those of maturer years.

There is jaunty music-making in Don Jerome's house, with the host playing the clarinet, a friend the cornet, and a servant the big drum. Don Jerome cannot understand how it is that his daughter, who yesterday so vehemently refused the bridegroom chosen for her, has now decided to elope with him. Lopez ushers in Don Carlos who has brought Mendoza's letter asking the bride's father for forgiveness. Don Jerome readily grants it. The music-making continues, but now a messenger brings a letter from Louisa herself, again asking Don Jerome to bless the marriage. Again he agrees, interrupting the music to instruct Lopez to organise a wedding banquet, and the scene ends with the music reaching a climax.

Clara, dressed as a nun, is lamenting her fate in the convent garden. To her comes Louisa to plead for Ferdinand, and it is apparent that Clara would give in were he there. Antonio joins them and together he and Louisa read her father's answer to her plea for recognition of her marriage. Antonio cannot understand it, but they leave arm-in-arm and full of delight, only for poor Clara to lament the misery of her predicament. It is not long however before Ferdinand is inside the convent wall, but confusion reigns supreme, and he believes he can see Doña Clara d'Almanza disappearing with his faithless friend Antonio. Clara is overjoyed at his jealousy, and she swears that Louisa will not be the only bride that day.

Act IV. In the monastery, monks are drinking wine. Their mood is one of hilarity, and they toast the sisters of the Order of St Catherine, not forgetting the little dark-eyed novice. The music bubbles on as the wine starts to take control, and it is only gradually that those to whom wine speaks most deeply come to understand that rich clients have been announced and they must rapidly change their tune,

which they proceed – literally – to do. Antonio and Mendoza have come to ask the brethren's help in the project closest to their hearts, which is that they both want to get married. After the mysterious appearance of a purse, the monks agree to do their bit. A complication ensues when Louisa rushes in followed by Ferdinand, who believes that his beloved Clara is to be married to Antonio. Antonio and Ferdinand are about to fight, when Clara enters, minus her veil but still dressed as a nun, and she and Louisa stop the fight. Clara was the black-eyed novice, and the monks are riveted by her appearance. Before long, the lovers' misunderstandings are resolved and the appropriate marriages blessed.

In the ballroom of Don Jerome's house, preparations are in hand for the celebration of Louisa's wedding. But the principal guests seem to be absent. Finally, Mendoza comes in calling for his wife, and the duenna makes her first appearance as a married woman. Don Jerome is taken aback to recognise his old employee, the more so when a moment later he finds Antonio and Louisa kneeling in front of him and asking for his blessing. Guests arrive as efforts are made to clear up the various misconceptions, and soon it is the turn of Ferdinand and Doña Clara to kneel beside Louisa and Antonio. Don Jerome starts to work out that his daughter has married a pauper who has at least the grace to be handsome, and his son has married a lady with a princess's dowry. Things haven't turned out quite so badly as he might have expected and rejoicings proceed more or less unclouded while Don Jerome shows his prowess on the musical glasses.   H.

WAR AND PEACE
Voina y Mir

Opera in thirteen scenes, libretto by the composer and Mira Mendelson, after Tolstoy. The original version (heavily cut) given in concert in Moscow, 7 June 1945,[1] with Nadion (Natasha), Ivanov (Andrei), Pirogov (Kutuzov), conductor Samosud. Première (first eight scenes only) at Maly Theatre, Leningrad, 12 June 1946, with Lavrova, Chishko (Pierre), Shaposhnikov (Andrei), Andrukovich (Anatol), Juravlenko (Old Prince Bolkonsky), conductor Samosud. Part II was heard at a closed première in 1947. Première of so-called 'final' version (eleven scenes only, omitting scenes 7 and 11), Maly

---

[1] The same day as the première of *Peter Grimes* in London.

Theatre, Leningrad, 1 April 1955, with Lavrova, Sokolova, Baskova (Hélène), Gliebov (Pierre), Andrukovich, Shaposhnikov, Modestov (Napoleon), Butiagin (Kutuzov), conductor Grikurov. First non-Russian performance (heavily cut), Florence, 1953, with Rosanna Carteri, Franco Corelli, Ettore Bastianini, Italo Tajo, Fernando Corena, Mirto Picchi, Renato Capecchi, Anselmo Colzani, conductor Artur Rodzinski. First performed Moscow, Nemirovich-Danchenko Theatre, 1957, conductor Shaverdov (thirteen scenes, with internal cuts); N.B.C. TV, New York, 1957, with Helena Scott, Davis Cunningham, Morley Meredith, Kenneth Smith, conductor Peter Herman Alder; Bolshoi Theatre, Moscow, 1959, with Vishnevskaya, Archipova, Grigoriev, Kipkalo, Maslennikov, Vedernikov, Lisitsian, conductor Melik-Pashayev; Leipzig, 1961; Zagreb, 1961. First British performance, Leeds Festival, 1967 (in concert), with Elizabeth Vaughan, Gregory Dempsey, Hans Wilbrink, Ivo Zidek, Donald McIntyre, conductor Edward Downes; Sadler's Wells at the Coliseum, 1972, with Josephine Barstow, Kenneth Woollam, Tom McDonnell, John Brecknock, Norman Bailey, Raymond Myers, conductor David Lloyd-Jones, producer Colin Graham; Australia, for opening of Sydney Opera House, 1973, with Eilene Hannan, Ronald Dowd, McDonnell, Robert Gard, Neil Warren-Smith, Myers, conductor Edward Downes.

Prince Andrei Bolkonsky ....Baritone
Natalya Rostova (Natasha) ....Soprano
Sonya, *Natasha's cousin* ....Mezzo-Soprano
Maria Dmitrievna Akhrosimova ....Contralto
Count Ilya Rostov, *Natasha's father*.....................Bass
Count Pyotr Bezukhov (Pierre) ....Tenor
Hélène Bezukhova, *his wife*.................Mezzo-Soprano
Prince Anatol Kuryagin, *her brother* ....Tenor
Dolokhov, *an officer* ....Baritone
Colonel Vasska Denisov ....Baritone
Field-Marshal Prince Mikhail Kutuzov ....Bass
Napoleon Bonaparte ....Baritone
Platon Karataev, *an old soldier*..........................Tenor
The Host ....Tenor
His Major-Domo ....Tenor
Madame Peronskaya.......................................Soprano
The Tsar...Silent
Prince Nikolai Bolkonsky,
   Andrei's father...............................Bass-Baritone
His Major-Domo ....Baritone
An Old Valet..Baritone
A Housemaid..Soprano
Princess Marya Bolkonskaya,
   Andrei's sister ....Mezzo-Soprano
Balaga, *a troika driver*..Bass
Matriosha, *a gipsy*.............................Mezzo-Soprano
Dunyasha, *Natasha's maid*...........................Soprano

Gavrila, *Akhrosimova's butler* ....Bass
Métivier, *a French doctor*...............................Baritone
A French Abbé ....Tenor
Tikhon Sherbatsky, *a partisan* ....Baritone
Vasilisa ....Mezzo-Soprano
Fyodor, *a partisan*..Tenor
Matveyev, *a Muscovite*...................................Baritone
Two Prussian Generals ....Speaking Roles
Prince Andrei's Orderly...................................Tenor
Two Russian Generals ....Speaking Roles
Kaizarov, *aide-de-Camp to Kutuzov* ....Tenor
Adjutant to General Compans.........................Tenor
Adjutant to Marshal Murat ....Treble
Marshal Berthier ....Baritone
Marquis de Caulaincourt ....Silent Role
General Belliard..Baritone
Adjutant to Prince Eugène ....Tenor
Aide-de-Camp to Napoleon.................................Bass
Off-Stage Orderly ....Tenor
Monsieur de Beausset.......................................Tenor
General Bennigsen...Bass
Prince Mikhail Barclay de Tolly ....Tenor
General Yermolov...Baritone
General Konovnitsin ....Tenor
General Rayevsky ....Baritone
Captain Ramballe ....Bass
Lieutenant Bonnet ....Tenor
Ivanov, *a Muscovite* ....Tenor
Captain Jacqueau..Bass
Marshal Berthier's Adjutant ....Tenor
Mavra Kusminichna, *the Rostovs'*
   housekeeper ....Contralto
Marshal Davout ....Bass
A French Officer ....Baritone
Three Madmen ....Tenor, Baritone, Actor
Two French Actresses ....Sopranos

Place: Russia – Otradnoye, St Petersburg, Moscow,
   Borodino, Fili, near Smolensk
Time: 1806–12
Running Time: 4 hours 20 minutes

According to Mira Mendelson, for whom Prokofiev had left his Spanish-born wife,[1] the composer was thinking of writing an opera on Tolstoy's *Resurrection* when she started to read *War and Peace*

---

[1] Prokofiev and Mira Mendelson met in spring 1940, when the composer was 51 and she was 25.

aloud to him. He was immediately struck by its operatic possibilities, the scene of the meeting between Natasha and the wounded Prince Andrei particularly appealing to him. In April 1941,[1] they started to prepare a scheme for the libretto, by July the German invasion of Russia had provided him with the spur to tackle it and eleven scenes had been decided upon; on 15 August, already evacuated to the Caucasus, he started work on the composition. As a matter of history, he worked at it on and off during the last eleven years of his life and the opera has gone through a number of different versions.

By midsummer 1942,[2] eleven scenes were completed in piano score (two changes from the original eleven), and at this point it was suggested to the composer that there was a lack of heroic quality in the war scenes – not surprising since the original idea had been for something relatively small-scale, with the emphasis on Pierre and the inner struggle of the individual rather than on Kutuzov and the outward struggle of the nation. He had already orchestrated Peace, but he set to work to comply with officialdom's request so that all eleven scenes were finished by April 1943, to form the definitive First Version. Plans for a performance at the Bolshoi Theatre in 1943, Samosud conducting and Eisenstein producing, were shelved,[3] but an idea for an enlarged version in two parts emerged, and in June 1946, the forces of the Maly Theatre, Leningrad, under Samosud gave Part I, consisting of Scenes 1–7 (Scene 2 had been added at Samosud's suggestion to the original scheme) and Scene 8 (the battle of Borodino). Performance of Part II was planned, and during 1946–47 Prokofiev wrote Scene 10 (the Council of War at Fili), only for events to overtake the planners in the shape of the infamous Zhdanov decree of 10 February 1948.

A word of explanation seems necessary. After the première of Muradely's opera *The Great Friendship*, Andrei Zhdanov, acting it is believed after he and Stalin had both intensely disliked the new work, met the Moscow composers in January 1948, to initiate a new 'hard line'. Khrennikov became the new General Secretary of the composers, the over-riding importance of melody in Soviet music was re-emphasised, and war was declared against formalism, naturalism, modernism, and Westernism.

In December 1948, after Part II had been dropped in Leningrad at dress rehearsal stage, Prokofiev, who according to his colleague Kabelevsky 'considered the opera the best thing he had written',[4] started to plan a version suitable for a single evening and suggestions to this end are contained in the preface to the published vocal score. In spite of internal re-arrangements made during the period 1948–52, the thirteen-scene scheme remains, and it is this, together with overture and choral Epigraph, which is now treated as the final version – long (more than four hours of music) and therefore often cut in performance, sometimes only sectionally, occasionally by as much as two complete scenes (usually vii and xi; at the Florence première, ii and ix).

Part I. The granite-hard choral movement called Epigraph in the score, often appropriately substituted at the start of the opera[5] for the much less interesting overture, is a massive piece of block harmony and, with its emphasis on the primordial strength of Russia in the face of her enemies, makes a most effective opening. (The overture itself is concerned with War rather more than Peace, and is usually omitted.) The Epigraph contains a sung reference to Ex. 8 as well as an enunciation of the theme in scene viii symbolising the surge of optimism which is itself the result of fervent patriotism.

Scene i is set in the garden of Count Rostov's estate at Otradnoye. It is a moonlit night in May 1806. The widower Prince Andrei Bolkonsky, who is visiting the estate on business, cannot sleep. His romantic idealism, Ex. 1, gradually becomes associated with Natasha and passes to thoughts of spring, Ex. 2.

It then gives way to a mood of disillusion. From an upstairs room, Natasha, who is preceded by Ex. 2 and sings to a version of Ex. 1, can be heard complaining to her cousin Sonya that she too cannot

[1] I am indebted to Rita McAllister, lecturer in music at Edinburgh University, for much valuable information on chronology.
[2] In November 1941, he moved from Nalchik to Tbilisi in Georgia, and in May 1942, to Alma-Ata in Kazakhstan, where he collaborated with Eisenstein on the film *Ivan the Terrible*.
[3] A private performance of this version with piano accompaniment was

given in Moscow in October 1944, and a public concert in June 1945.
[4] Boris Schwarz: *Music and Musical Life in Soviet Russia 1917–1970* (Barrie & Jenkins).
[5] As in the productions at the Bolshoi Theatre in 1959 and by Sadler's Wells at the London Coliseum in 1972.

(Ex. 1)

(Ex. 2)

could he ever have believed that his life was at an end (Ex. 2)? The mood of the scene is lyrical and expressive – in fact one may doubt if Prokofiev ever elsewhere penned music of such tenderness.

Scene ii takes place on New Year's Eve, 1810, at a ball in a palace in Petersburg. Guests dance a brilliant polonaise, and are invited to listen to a new cantata. Count Rostov enters with Natasha and Sonya, and they are closely followed by Count and Countess Bezukhov – Madame Akhrosimova makes a complimentary remark to Natasha but she and Madame Peronskaya comment with a certain asperity on the beauty of the celebrated Hélène Bezukhova. The Tsar makes his entry, polonaise is succeeded by mazurka, Natasha wonders if no one will ask her to dance (Ex. 1), and then Pierre, rich and unconventional, approaches his friend Prince Andrei and suggests he should ask the young Natasha Rostova to dance. The nostalgic music of the waltz at this point reflects the effect the dance is having on the mind of the impressionable Natasha, whose first ball it is, Ex. 3:

Tempo di Valse

The scene ends on a note of something like rapture, with Andrei murmuring to himself after the dance: 'If she first approaches her cousin and then another lady, she will become my wife'.[1] But he is not the only man to have been impressed by Natasha, the glittering and dissolute Prince Anatol Kuryagin having earlier asked his sister Hélène Bezukhova to arrange an introduction to the new young beauty. The scene ends with an écossaise.

Scene iii. Prince Andrei has proposed to Natasha (February 1812) and Count Rostov brings his daughter (Ex. 1) to see old Prince Bolkonsky, Andrei's father, who has insisted meanwhile that Andrei should spend a year abroad. Count Rostov asks if the Prince and the Princess his daughter are at home. He does not relish the prospect of the interview, but Natasha is a good deal more confident. When she

sleep. Natasha thinks she has never seen anything so beautiful as their garden bathed in moonlight, and Prince Andrei is moved by the romantic situation and the innocence and charm of the young girl. How

[1] Translation by Edward Downes.

sings it, Ex. 1, originally sung by Andrei, seems to stand for the idealism in her character as well as for their mutual love and Ex. 2 for the trust she now feels in Andrei. They are told that the old man cannot see them, but his daughter Princess Marya comes in and Count Rostov quickly makes his excuses to her and departs. No sooner has he gone, than the old Prince puts in an appearance, dressed in night-cap and dressing gown. With boorish insincerity, he apologises for his attire to Natasha, mutters threateningly and leaves. Marya starts to excuse his behaviour – he is perpetually in pain – but Natasha understands all too well that he is the obstacle to her marriage. Count Rostov returns and goes to speak with Princess Marya, leaving Natasha alone. She is outraged at the behaviour of the Bolkonskys but this makes her think, and thought conjures up the image of Andrei, who she realises means everything to her, Ex. 4:

Per-haps he'll come, per-haps he'll come to-
- mor - row

When Princess Marya makes a conscious attempt at conversation, Natasha puts her off with some dignity.

Scene iv takes place in the living room of Pierre Bezukhov's house in May 1812 – the whole scene amounts to a dance on a less grandiose scale than in Scene ii, built up on yet another waltz, with interpolations in 4/4. Hélène compliments Natasha on not staying at home just because she is engaged, then lets slip the information that the previous night her

brother Prince Anatol had admitted to them that he was pining for love of none other than Natasha. Hélène laughs at Natasha's embarrassment and, when a moment later Count Rostov wants to take his family home, insists they stay. In touchingly diffident music, Natasha reflects that neither Hélène nor Pierre seems at all shocked at Prince Anatol having fallen in love with her; she will not be shocked either. The dancing resumes and Anatol proceeds to woo Natasha passionately (this version of the waltz[1] symbolises the fascination Anatol holds for Natasha), Ex. 5.

Pochissimo più mosso

He succeeds in kissing her and gives her a letter of assignation. Natasha is obviously affected by its fervour – but she loves Andrei (Ex. 2). If only he were here now (Ex. 4)! Count Rostov returns to take Natasha and Sonya home.

Scene v. 12 June 1812. Dolokhov's apartments. Anatol's elopement with Natasha is arranged. He sings with the conviction of infatuation, however cynical, and when Dolokhov, who has made all the detailed arrangements, tries to argue his friend out of going through with the mad project, shrugs off his arguments. He likes women young, and anyhow he is in love (echo of the previous scene's waltz: Ex. 5). Here almost incongruously occurs Ex. 1, presumably as ironic counterpoint to Anatol's thoughts. Enter Balaga, with whom Dolokhov has arranged for a carriage and the fastest horses he can procure. He seems to have been implicated in Anatol's escapades before now, and the three of them drink to the adventure as Anatol says a musically nostalgic goodbye to Moscow and to his gipsy mistress Matriosha.

---

[1] From Prokofiev's incidental music to *Yevgeny Onyegin*.

Scene vi. The same night: a room in the house of Maria Dmitrievna Akhrosimova, where Natasha is staying while her father is away. Natasha waits alone for Anatol, until her maid Dunyasha rushes in to say that Sonya has given away the elopement plans. Anatol appears at the door, but the butler, Gavrila, bars the way to him, and Anatol escapes with Dolokhov, Natasha falling in despair on the sofa. Akhrosimova comes in and starts to rate Natasha for her behaviour, but Natasha defies her and begs to be left alone. Suddenly, Akhrosimova softens, the music now in great contrast to her formal denunciation. Can Natasha not think of her father and of Prince Andrei? Natasha runs off sobbing just as Gavrila announces Count Pierre Bezukhov – his theme precedes him, Ex. 6:

Pierre is told of the situation and when Natasha comes back (Ex. 1 swamping Ex. 5), he starts to console her. In answer to Natasha's repeated questions he assures her that Anatol is already married, then succumbs to pity for her – will she not treat him as a friend? Her reaction is to beg him to explain to Andrei and ask him, though all is over between them, to forgive her for the pain she will have caused him (Ex. 4). Pierre promises, and then in an outburst of frankness, tells her that if he were himself free, he would now be on his knees asking for her hand in marriage. He runs out of the room, and Natasha

follows him as Akhrosimova and Sonya come in, Sonya beside herself with worry that Natasha now looks upon her as an enemy.

Scene vii.[1] The same night, Hélène is entertaining guests, among them Anatol. Pierre proceeds to attack his brother-in-law for his infamous conduct, insisting that he leave Moscow immediately. Anatol is taken aback by his vehemence and agrees, leaving Pierre alone to reflect on the pointlessness of his existence, with its unproductive wealth and the worthless friends by whom he is surrounded (the music springs from material already exposed in the previous scene, particularly Ex. 6 and its derivations).

Denisov brings the news that Napoleon is about to cross the Russian frontier. It means war.

Part II. All six scenes of the second part of the opera are concerned with the defence of Russia against the invasion of the French, and the Russian people led by Marshal Kutuzov take the central position. The musical tone fluctuates between a representation on the one hand of patriotic fervour and of devastation on the other, and is very different from that of the preceding scenes – only when Andrei and Pierre appear together on the battlefield of Borodino and in the scene of the death of Andrei do we return to the musical style of Part I – and it is this contrast which has caused some commentators to talk about *War and Peace* as two separate operas on a single evening.

Scene viii. The music starts with Ex. 7, associated with the horrors of war:

25 August 1812. Near Borodino, men are at work digging defences, filling the scene with their fervent working and marching songs. Prince Andrei has raised and trained his own regiment. Lieutenant-Colonel Denisov asks him for the whereabouts of Field-Marshal

---

[1] Prokofiev suggested that this scene might be cut if the opera is found too long in performance, but its excision has the unfortunate effect of greatly reducing the musical portrayal of Pierre.

Kutuzov and, on their way to the Commander-in-Chief, Denisov talks to Andrei of his idea to make use of partisans against the French – a mere five hundred men skilfully deployed could harass Napoleon's lines of communication and ensure his defeat.

Andrei returns. By sheer coincidence he has just met Denisov, who was once engaged to the Natasha in whom he himself thought to realise all his hopes for the future (Exx. 2 and 3). His thoughts are bitter (Ex. 1) when suddenly he recognises the highly unmilitary figure of Pierre Bezukhov. He does not want to be further reminded of Natasha, and his welcome is a little cool. Pierre explains that he has come to Borodino as a mere onlooker. As they talk, two German generals pass by, agreeing that since the object is to rout the enemy one cannot be too concerned with civilian casualties. Andrei is furious: Russia is being devastated, his father has been killed (Ex. 7), and these Prussians, who have unsuccessfully fought Napoleon all over Europe, talk of textbook battles! His orderly tells Andrei that the regiment is drawn up and waiting, and Andrei turns to Pierre, in spite of his presentiments, still patriotically convinced of ultimate victory.

A cry goes up as the Marshal leaves his tent, and Andrei embraces Pierre, both men convinced they have met for the last time. Kutuzov's first appearance is to a wisp of flute tone (Ex. 8a) which brings Ex. 8 softly in the orchestra:

Andante molto

and his first words as he watches the guerrillas at work are sung to this music. He throws each group a well-timed word of commendation, then catches sight of Prince Andrei and sends for him. His intention is to appoint him to his staff, but Andrei declines

the position. The soldiers proclaim their patriotic fervour in a chorus based on Ex. 8, until the sound of a shot heralds the start of the battle (Ex. 7).

Scene ix. In the Shevardino redoubt the same day, Napoleon directs the battle surrounded by his staff. The music is a sinister sort of *scherzo* in Prokofiev's most sardonic vein, with references to Ex. 8 when allusion is made to Russian heroism. The French commander-in-chief broods on the possible outcome of the battle. Moscow is at his mercy; he will earn history's gratitude by showing clemency. He refuses at first to commit his reserves, but eventually gives in. De Beausset tries unsuccessfully to get the Emperor to eat luncheon, and the scene ends with a cannon shot landing almost at their feet. By not succumbing in mid-war to the full temptation of equating Napoleon with Hitler, Prokofiev has achieved the impossible by placing, in the course of a ten-minute scene, one of history's greatest figures convincingly on the musical stage.

Scene x. In a peasant's hut in the village of Fili, Marshal Kutuzov is two days later holding a Council of War, surrounded by his generals (Ex. 7). Two courses are open to them, each potentially disastrous: to defend Moscow puts the army at risk; to retreat would leave the capital at the enemy's mercy. After listening to his generals, it is for Kutuzov to make the momentous decision. He orders a retreat, confident that only through the sacrifice of Moscow is there a hope of final victory. The generals leave and Kutuzov's faith is expressed in soliloquy to a broad tune. Its immediate appeal and memorability have caused some commentators to mutter patronisingly of music aimed at the masses, but others will remember that it is now not so common for an operatic tune to induce a feeling of genuine patriotic fervour, something which must have been just as firmly in Prokofiev's mind in the period 1941–45 as it was in Verdi's at the time of the Risorgimento.

Scene xi. Moscow's inhabitants have set fire to the great city rather than surrender it to the invader (Ex. 7 frequently throughout the scene). Nothing is as the French expect and the soldiers start to loot. Pierre, who feels he could put an end to the horrors by killing Napoleon, learns that the Rostovs have left Moscow taking with them the wounded from their house, Natasha still unaware that Andrei is among them. When soldiers drag in a group of Muscovites accused of having started the fires, Pierre is shoved in with them.

Marshal Davout confirms his order that incendiaries be shot. The veteran Karataev touchingly reassures Pierre of the values to be found in suffering, but most of the incendiaries are reprieved and marched off as prisoners (Ex. 7). French actresses rush into the streets, screaming that the theatre is on fire, and lunatics save themselves as the hospital burns. Introduced by Ex. 7 in the orchestra and surrounded by his staff, Napoleon makes his way through the thick smoke of burning Moscow, defeated by the city's resistance and mightily impressed by the courage of its inhabitants.

Scene xii shows Prokofiev at his most intense and his most dramatic, in this mood one of the great twentieth-century masters of opera. At the back of a peasant's hut at Mitishi, Prince Andrei is lying wounded. He is delirious and the chorus can be heard singing 'Piti-piti-piti' as the blood pounds in his ears. The music returns to the lyricism of the opera's first part. Andrei longs to see Natasha again (Ex. 1) and she has in fact found her way to his death-bed, is recognised (Ex. 4), wonders if he has changed towards her, and then starts to beg for forgiveness. Andrei tells her that he loves her more than he ever has before and their voices join to celebrate what he thinks of as new happiness. He asks her if he will live (Ex. 1) and she tries to reassure him. He falls asleep dreaming of their first dance together (Ex. 3). As his last spasm comes, the sound of 'Piti-piti-piti' becomes ever more insistent until suddenly it stops.

Scene xiii. On the road to Smolensk, November 1812. A storm is raging. French troops are in retreat (a hint of the *scherzo* trumpets of Scene ix), escorting a group of Russian prisoners of war, among them Pierre and Karataev. Karataev can go no further and is shot as a straggler. Guerrillas attack the French and free the prisoners, and Pierre is recognised by Denisov, who assures him of victory and tells him also that Andrei is dead but Natasha safe in Moscow (Ex. 1). In a moment the Russian advance guard appears preceding the Marshal himself (Ex. 8). He is tired, but he knows that the French are beaten and his work done. All join in a great peroration to the eternal Russian spirit.

Prokofiev may on the one hand be thought to have attempted the impossible in turning Tolstoy's novel into a one-evening opera, but there is reason on the other for thinking that his epic will convey some of the novel's essence to the listener who already knows the book, which is to say three out of every four members of *any* Russian audience.

It is not hard to accept the echoes of Tchaikovsky in the first part and, in the second, the thrusting choruses and insistently appealing aria of Kutuzov as equally evocative of the moods Prokofiev wanted to create. The score contains a host of moments which illuminate character and situation and over everything is Prokofiev's rare ability to combine narrative with pathos. In 1972, a quarter of a century distant from the war and in a musical climate when new and (dare I say it?) romantic music had the therapeutic value of water in a desert, to hear as I did rehearsal after rehearsal and half a dozen performances in the space of five weeks was to be convinced all over again – this time from practical experience whereas originally from score, disc and a single Bolshoi performance – that Prokofiev's *War and Peace* is a masterpiece. And that opinion strengthened with each revival over the next dozen years.   H.

GIACOMO PUCCINI

(born 22 December 1858, died 29 November 1924)

Giacomo Puccini came of a line of musicians active in Lucca for five generations. He was the first directly associated with theatre as opposed to church, and his success in the hundred and more years since his breakthrough with *Manon Lescaut* has been little short of phenomenal, certainly unparalleled in Italy since the early years of Verdi's ascendancy. The success contains a paradoxical element in that for much of that century, while audiences basked in the composer's prolific melody and accessible style, fellow composers and even critics had little but contempt for their colleague and his music, muttering about his ability to tailor the length of arias to fit the four-minute format of a gramophone record and holding it against him.

In a career of some forty years cut short by cancer, Puccini wrote only ten mature operas, three of which form part of a triple bill – effectively, seven evenings of opera. There has been much talk of the typical Puccini heroine, put-upon and forlorn, and it is true that Mimì, Butterfly, Suor Angelica and perhaps Manon fulfil the claim; to set against them, Tosca, Minnie, Giorgetta and Turandot come nowhere near the stereotype. On the other hand Liu, a purely secondary figure dramatically, can seem far more interesting than the less sympathetic Turandot.

Rational opinion nearly seventy-five years after his death is likely to take a different tack, admiring his choice of subjects and the care which went into their selection, appreciating the *tinta* (to borrow Verdi's expression) of each new subject and the immediacy with which he establishes local colour, relishing the variety, timing and dramatic skill of his scores. *Manon Lescaut* might be said to look back to tradition, but the skill and pace of *La Bohème* puts it into a new category altogether, and *Butterfly* and *Fanciulla*, for all the latter's relative poverty of invention, represent quite fresh departures. The three components of the *Trittico* contrast effectively, and *Turandot* again breaks new ground. If Puccini wrote tear-jerkers, he did so with a taste so immaculate that few have avoided the need to wipe their eyes when Musetta at the end of the waltz song flies into Marcello's arms, when Butterfly's surmise at sight of the ship turns into certainty, when Rodolfo is the last of the Bohemians to know Mimì dead.

Opera-goers of discernment have appreciated for much of the twentieth century that Puccini is a rare master, capable of delighting the mob with his melody and all but the snob with his masterly workmanship. Neither his publisher nor his bank manager can ever have had doubts on either score.   H.

LE VILLI
The Fairies

Opera in two acts (originally one), text by Ferdinando Fontana after Alphonse Karr's story *Les Willis*. Première Milan, Teatro dal Verme, 31 May 1884; revised version, Turin, 26 December 1884.

Guglielmo, *the head forester* ....Baritone
Anna, *his daughter* ....Soprano
Roberto, *a young man*...Tenor

Place: The Black Forest
Running Time: 1 hour 5 minutes

Puccini, nearing thirty, entered his first opera in a competition organised by the publisher Sonzogno in 1883. It had no success (the score was said to be illegible) but its librettist was a member of a group of avant-garde writers known as the 'Scapigliati' (Bohemians), and the composer Boito, another member, helped to arrange a performance in Milan. There the opera was noticed by Giulio Ricordi, who took the composer on contract, advised a revision into two acts, and asked him to write a new opera for la Scala. Neither *Le Villi* nor *Edgar*, the new opera, a more conventional affair, had much success, but with *Manon Lescaut* a few years later Italy discovered it had another candidate for the mantle of Verdi.

Act I. Mountaineers celebrate the engagement of Roberto and Anna and the news that Roberto is about to leave for Mainz where he has been left a fortune. Anna goes to deposit her bouquet in Roberto's luggage as a keepsake (aria, 'Se come voi piccina'), and a love duet develops before Roberto leaves with the good wishes of all. An Intermezzo of two orchestral movements contains spoken descriptions of Roberto's seduction in Mainz by a witch, of Anna's death and funeral, and of the fate which can befall a faithless lover, danced to death by the Wilis – probably, suggests Julian Budden, intended to be read rather than declaimed from the stage.

Act II. Guglielmo, in one of Puccini's grandest arias for baritone, laments the death of his daughter and hopes for the vengeance of the Wilis on Roberto ('Anima santa'). An extensive solo ('Torna ai felici di'), written for an 1885 revival at la Scala, depicts the remorse of Roberto and the shock he feels when he realises Anna is dead. She reappears as the Wilis take over to wreak vengeance.

The opera is far from negligible, in spite of its curious, untraditional shape, and contains much attractive music, some of it, not unexpectedly, looking towards the past – 'Anima santa', impressive as it is, might be from an opera by Puccini's teacher, Ponchielli. Anna's romance on the other hand is a seductive tune, the tenor solo the longest the composer ever wrote, and the second intermezzo is rare in the composer's output as an orchestral work able to stand alone.   H.

MANON LESCAUT

Opera in four acts, text by Domenico Oliva and Luigi Illica, after the Abbé Prévost's novel. Première in Turin, 1 February 1893, with Cesira Ferrani, Giuseppe Cremonini, conductor Pomé.

Manon Lescaut ....Soprano
Lescaut, *her brother, a sergeant* ....Baritone
Chevalier des Grieux ....Tenor
Geronte di Ravoir, *Treasurer-General* ....Bass
Edmondo, *a student*..Tenor
An Innkeeper ....Bass
Dancing Master ....Tenor
A Singer..Mezzo-Soprano
A Sergeant ....Bass
A Lamp-Lighter ....Tenor
A Naval Captain ....Bass

Citizens, Students, Musicians, Prostitutes, Soldiers, Sailors

Place: Amiens, Paris, le Havre, Louisiana
Time: Eighteenth Century
Running Time: 2 hours

Puccini was thirty-four when his third opera, *Manon Lescaut*, was first heard in Turin, a week before the première of *Falstaff* in Milan. Seven different men, including the composer Leoncavallo, had worked on the libretto, but the result notwithstanding was a resounding success, the first of Puccini's career, and, though Verdi commented that Puccini seemed more a symphonist than an opera composer, the opera maintains a permanent place in the repertory.

Act I. In front of an inn at Amiens. A brilliant orchestral opening introduces Edmondo and fellow students who cavort in front of the townsfolk of Amiens. Des Grieux is persuaded to sing a mocking serenade: 'Tra voi, belle, brune e bionde'. The coach from Arras arrives to disgorge Lescaut, Geronte and Manon, the latter causing all hearts to flutter including that of des Grieux. He addresses her as 'Cortese damigella' to begin a duet which is starting to show the hall-marks of a full-blooded Puccinian love duet when Lescaut calls Manon inside.

Des Grieux muses rapturously in one of Puccini's most immediately attractive arias: 'Donna non vidi mai'. Geronte has his eye on Manon and he and Lescaut seem about to reach an understanding. Geronte arranges for a carriage for two, but Edmondo overhears and warns des Grieux; his duet with Manon ('Vedete? Io son fedele') suggests love returned. He quickly overcomes Manon's reservations, explains Geronte's plot, and together, applauded by the students, they elope in Geronte's carriage, leaving Lescaut and Geronte to plot the future, and Edmondo and the students to mock.

Act II. An elegant room in Geronte's Paris house. Manon at her dressing table is joined by Lescaut. He congratulates her on her present surroundings, splendid in comparison with the humble dwelling she once shared with des Grieux. It is obvious she still carries a torch for des Grieux, as she makes clear in an aria of genuine pathos: 'In quelle trine morbide'. Lescaut, always the instinctive pimp, offers to bring des Grieux to her, and teach him moreover how to win at the tables so that she may continue to enjoy her accustomed comfort. Their voices join in anticipation of the future – Lescaut's finest musical moment. Musicians come to sing a madrigal, but Manon is as bored by them as by the dancing master who follows. A lesson in the minuet starts, watched by Geronte and his friends. Manon sings a brilliant aria, 'L'ora o Tirsi, è vaga e bella', and says she will join Geronte and the others later on the promenade.

She has not long to wait before des Grieux precipitates himself into her room: 'Tu, tu, amore! Tu!' What starts with reproach rapidly becomes an impassioned love duet but it ends when Geronte returns to surprise the lovers. Manon brazens it out: let Geronte look in the mirror if he wants to understand. He promises he will return, and des Grieux urges instant flight, then in an agony of conviction berates her for the dance she leads him and for her incorrigible love of luxury: 'Ah, Manon, mi tradisce'. Lescaut rushes in to tell them Geronte has mobilised guards to arrest them, Manon lingers to collect her jewellery and the delay is fatal. They are arrested as thieves.

An intermezzo represents not only the journey to le Havre but des Grieux's despairing determination to follow Manon to the ends of the earth.

Act III. The harbour at le Havre. The plan des Grieux and Lescaut have hatched to rescue Manon from imprisonment is a failure and the roll is called of the women who are to be transported. When it is Manon's turn, des Grieux stays at her side, defies anyone to take her away from him and in a fine statement sings: 'Guardate! pazzo son!' (Look out! I'm mad!) The ship's captain makes a gesture and offers des Grieux passage to America.

Act IV. A deserted plain. Manon and des Grieux, victims of intrigue and jealousy, have left New Orleans. Manon is exhausted with the journey. The music is a melancholy duet, and when des Grieux goes off to get help, Manon's despair is expressed in a grandiose aria, 'Sola, perduta, abbandonata'. Puccini at one point removed it from the score but later restored it, slightly re-worked. When des Grieux returns, Manon is dying. He collapses by her side.

In spite of some far from negligible music in his first two operas, *Le Villi* and *Edgar*, Puccini found favour only with his third, *Manon Lescaut*, in which critics for the first time discerned an individual voice. That Massenet had written an opera on the same subject caused the composer some concern but it is fair to say that the Italian master-to-be, famous later for his portrayal of frail female heroines, in *Manon Lescaut* placed more emphasis on his hero, des Grieux, than on Manon, and in so doing created one of his most enduring tenor figures. H.

LA BOHÈME
A Bohemian Life

Opera in four acts, text by Giacosa and Illica. Première at the Teatro Regio, Turin, 1 February 1896, with Cesira Ferrani, Pasini, Gorga, Wilmant, Mazzara, Pini-Corsi, conductor Toscanini.

Rodolfo, *a poet*...Tenor
Marcello, *a painter* ....Baritone
Colline, *a philosopher* ....Bass
Schaunard, *a musician*..................................Baritone
Benoit, *their landlord* ....Bass
Alcindoro, *a state councillor and Musetta's admirer*...Bass
Parpignol, *an itinerant toy vendor*......................Tenor
Customs-House Sergeant....................................Bass
Musetta, *a grisette* ....Soprano
Mimì, *a seamstress*...Soprano

Students, Work Girls, Shopkeepers, Soldiers, Waiters, Boys and Girls

Place: The Latin Quarter, Paris
Time: About 1830
Running Time: 2 hours

In *La Bohème*, Puccini's melodic invention and its turn to expressive use is at fullest flood, and he combines it with an epigrammatic, conversational conciseness that is unique in his output, technically adroit though that always is. In the way it puts across conversation economically and with heightened expression, it is without question his highest achievement – something of an Italianate parallel to *Der Rosenkavalier* – but so attractive is the melodic flow, so memorable the lyrical invention that few of its vast army of fans bother to notice that points are made, contrary to the work's reputation for wearing its heart on its sleeve, almost too fast for any but connoisseurs to take in!

Act I. A garret where live four students, Christmas Eve. Rodolfo is writing, Marcello at work on a painting, *The Passage of the Red Sea*. It is freezingly cold and Rodolfo sacrifices his manuscript to keep the stove going. Colline returns from unsuccessfully trying to pawn some books but relief comes with the entry of Schaunard who has been engaged, and well paid, for music lessons by an eccentric Englishman. Nobody listens to his story though they are quite ready to hear his invitation to supper at Café Momus. A knock at the door brings Benoit in search of the rent. They flatter him at first but pretend to be indignant when he boasts of an amorous conquest and chuck him out. The others go off to the café while Rodolfo stays to finish an article.

Again comes a knock at the door; this time a woman's voice. Mimì asks Rodolfo to light her candle, which has gone out as she climbed the stairs. She collapses in a fit of coughing, but quickly revives and makes to leave. This time, she finds she has dropped her key and soon each is searching the by now darkened room for it. Rodolfo's hand meets hers and the flood of melody which has been threatening ever since Mimì's appearance bursts its banks: 'Che gelida manina' (Your tiny hand is frozen). There is perhaps no better known aria for tenor in all Italian opera. Mimì's own description of her work as an embroiderer is no less persuasive: 'Si, mi chiamano Mimì'. The voices of Rodolfo's friends call from below,

Rodolfo is overcome by the sight of Mimì standing in the moonlight, and the act ends with an impassioned avowal of love on both sides: 'O soave fanciulla'.

Act II. A square, with the Café Momus. In a mere eighteen minutes the act introduces Mimì to the other students, and a vital new character, Musetta, Marcello's love, to the narrative. From the bustle of street-vendors and citizens in the last throes of Christmas shopping, tendrils of melody ascend to describe Colline's reaction to a second-hand coat, Schaunard's to a battered horn, Parpignol's to the crying of his wares, and Mimì's to a pink bonnet she wants Rodolfo to buy her. In the end, Rodolfo in a few impassioned phrases introduces Mimì to his friends and all start to order dinner when a commotion precedes the entry of Musetta, attended by the ludicrous Alcindoro, whose efforts to meet her whims provoke her to one excess after another. Marcello tries to hide his interest, but Musetta starts a slow waltz, famous as 'Musetta's waltz song', which she aims provocatively at Marcello. She gets rid of Alcindoro on the pretext that her shoe pinches, and she and Marcello fall into each other's arms to watch a military procession which crosses the square. The sight of the bill causes general alarm, calmed by Musetta's insistence that it be lumped with hers and presented to Alcindoro when he returns.

Puccini's achievement in his second act is no less than in the first, the embroidery of small personal details on the larger Christmas canvas not regularly noticed but nonetheless remarkable for that.

Act III. A toll-gate on the Orléans road into Paris. Open fifths in the orchestra suggest winter's cold, as customs-house men search scavengers and women on their way into town. Mimì comes looking for Rodolfo and Marcello comes out of the inn. He tells her he is painting signboards and Musetta giving music lessons. Won't Mimì join them? In a passage of real feeling, she tells him Rodolfo is so insanely jealous she fears they must part, and her story is fully borne out when Rodolfo emerges to give his side of the picture. 'Mimì è una civetta' (Mimì is a heartless creature), he claims with more than a little passion, but goes on to admit that her coughing worries him to death. A paroxysm gives away her presence, and they agree the time has come to part, less in anger than in sorrow. Tenderness runs through Mimì's farewell: 'Donde lieta uscì', with its closing line: 'Addio, senza rancor'. Marcello inside the pub has caught Musetta flirting and a row flares up to combine in a quartet with the much gentler farewell of Mimì and Rodolfo, whose duetting might be mistaken for an avowal of love.

Act IV. The attic familiar from Act I. Rodolfo longs for Mimì, from whom he hasn't heard, Marcello for Musetta, who is thought to be off with yet another of her rich lovers. Their duet, 'Ah, Mimì, tu più non torni', suggests the withdrawal pangs are anything but over. Schaunard returns and thrusts a bottle of water into Colline's hat as if it were a champagne cooler, the prelude to a riotous student frolic, which culminates in organised dancing and a mock duel between Colline and Schaunard. This is interrupted by the arrival of Musetta, frantic with worry about Mimì, whom she has found half dead of tuberculosis at the foot of the stairs. Rodolfo carries her in and lays her on the bed the others have prepared. Rodolfo's presence restores her strength a little and for a moment she seems happy although it is plain that she is very weak. Her hands are cold, and Musetta gives Marcello her earrings to sell for medicine. Colline is not to be outdone and sings a sad little farewell to his coat ('Vecchia zimarra, senti') before taking it off to the pawnbroker.

When they are alone, Mimì and Rodolfo invoke past happiness and the music of earlier acts reflects their thoughts. Musetta and the others return, but Mimì is beyond help and she dies so quietly that Rodolfo does not at first notice what has happened, then explodes in grief.

Singers from Melba and Caruso, Pavarotti and Freni, to Gheorghiu and Alagna, have always loved *La Bohème*, and for a century its melodic profusion has flattered them as well as audiences. From the opening vocal phrases, there is an individual lilt to the score, its character coming from a combination of rhythmical brilliance, as shown in the extrovert aspects of the action (the Bohemians cavorting at home, the hubbub of Christmas Eve in Act II), with the lyricism of the lovers and the famous arias this generates.   H.

TOSCA

Opera in three acts, text by Giacosa and Illica after the play by Victorien Sardou. Première at the Teatro Costanzi, Rome, 14 January 1900, with Hariclea Darclée, de Marchi, Giraldoni, conductor Mugnone.

Floria Tosca, *a celebrated singer* ....Soprano

Mario Cavaradossi, *a painter* ....Tenor

Baron Scarpia, *Chief of Police* ....Baritone

Cesare Angelotti, *a political prisoner* ....Bass

A Sacristan ....Baritone

Spoletta, *a police agent* ....Tenor

Sciarrone, *a gendarme* ....Bass

A Jailer ....Bass

A Shepherd Boy ....Contralto

Roberti, an Executioner; a Cardinal, Judge, Scribe, Soldiers, Ladies, Nobles, Citizens, Artisans etc.

Place: Rome
Time: 1800
Running Time: 2 hours 10 minutes

The opera is set in the year Napoleon invaded Italy. During the action, the Austrian General Melas is reported to have defeated Napoleon and the consequent celebrations are likely to be attended by Queen Marie Caroline, wife of the Neapolitan King Ferdinand IV, daughter of Empress Maria Theresa of Austria and sister to Queen Marie Antoinette of France. Baron Scarpia, the much-feared Chief of Police, is based on a real-life Sicilian figure, who incidentally affected old-fashioned dress, hence the white wig he wears, more appropriate to an earlier period. Cavaradossi and Angelotti are supporters of the liberal group hoping for Napoleon's victory.

Act I. The Church of Sant'Andrea della Valle. Three chords, played *fff tutta forza* and attached to the sinister Baron Scarpia, introduce the opera before we meet Angelotti, just escaped from prison and in a frenzy to locate the Attavanti chapel in which his sister has hidden a key and clothes. He disappears into the chapel as the Sacristan comes looking for the painter Cavaradossi, not at his easel, the picnic in his basket as yet untouched. The Sacristan kneels for the Angelus, and when Cavaradossi comes in and uncovers the picture he has been painting, recognises in the blonde Mary Magdalene a woman he has seen several times lately at prayer in the church. Yes, he painted her, says Cavaradossi, then abandons his work as he dreams of his love, Floria Tosca: 'Recondita armonia di bellezze diverse'. It is one of the most convincing of all Puccini's tenor arias. The Sacristan grumbles as he cleans the brushes while Cavaradossi sings, then to his delight hears that the painter plans to leave his picnic untouched.

Angelotti comes out of hiding and recognises in Cavaradossi a political sympathiser. Cavaradossi wants to help but, hearing Tosca's voice outside, urges Angelotti to hide in the chapel.

Tosca's jealousy prompts her to think someone is with Cavaradossi but he reassures her and it is not long before she is making an assignation for later that night. Cavaradossi seems less than enthusiastic and it takes all Tosca's blandishments ('Non la sospiri la nostra casetta?') to bring his thoughts round to hers. She recognises the Magdalene as a portrait of Marchesa Attavanti and suspicion flares up again. There is nothing to it, he says; he saw her yesterday, and painted her at prayer, demanding rhetorically what eyes could compare with Tosca's ('Qual'occhio al mondo'). From Tosca's entrance, the entire duet, with its contrasting episodes, constitutes one of Puccini's finest and most detailed scenes, comparable to that in the first act of *Madama Butterfly*.

Tosca leaves, Angelotti comes out of the chapel and he and Cavaradossi refer with hatred to what they describe as the bigoted satyr Scarpia who has consigned Angelotti to prison (the chords of the opera's introduction). In case of necessity, Angelotti should hide in the well in Cavaradossi's garden ('al pozzo del giardino'). A cannon shot is heard and they make a hurried escape as the Sacristan returns. He summons the choristers who dance madly round him only for the chords to announce the arrival of Scarpia in person. His orders are quickly given, and a fan is equally quickly found in the chapel: Marchesa Attavanti's! An agent brings in the basket, now empty of the picnic the Sacristan tells him Cavaradossi wasn't going to eat. Scarpia decides Cavaradossi must have been Angelotti's accomplice. When Tosca returns, Scarpia affects to contrast her seemly behaviour in church with that of others who come perhaps to meet their lovers, and points to the fan which was (he pretends) on the easel. Jealousy comes easily to Tosca, and when she leaves, Scarpia orders one of his men to follow her, then himself joins in the *Te deum*, genuflecting to the Cardinal in procession but singing lustily of the satisfaction he will have in revenging himself on Cavaradossi and bending Tosca to his pleasure.

Act II. Scarpia's apartment in the Palazzo Farnese, where he is at supper. His passions rise as he reflects that he infinitely prefers a forced conquest to a passive surrender ('Ha più forte sapore'), then Spoletta brings the bad news that Angelotti was nowhere to be found when he tracked Tosca to Cavaradossi's villa, followed by the good – he has arrested Cavaradossi. The cantata begins and Tosca's voice can be heard through the open window as Cavaradossi is brought in. Scarpia starts to interrogate his prisoner who denies all knowledge of Angelotti, and continues his questioning as Tosca enters the room. Tosca has no idea that next door is a torture chamber, and she and Scarpia at first converse as if there were no external pressures; but not for long. Her heated denial of any knowledge of Angelotti's whereabouts prompts Scarpia to describe the torments Cavaradossi is undergoing. She is horrified and gasps out that she will tell him the truth. A scream of anguish from the inner room brings an admission: 'Nel pozzo nel giardino'.

Cavaradossi, dragged into Scarpia's room, haltingly asks Tosca if he gave anything away. She reassures him just as Scarpia instructs Spoletta 'In the well in the garden!', but the tables are turned when Sciarrone hurries in with the news that Melas was after all defeated, Napoleon victorious. Cavaradossi finds the strength with a great cry of 'Vittoria!' to hurl defiance at Scarpia.

Scarpia nonetheless holds the cards. Perhaps, he suggests, he and Tosca may together concoct a plan to save Cavaradossi. 'Your price?' demands Tosca. Scarpia laughs at her naïveté. 'Già mi dicon venal' (Venal my enemies call me) he sings in a passage of great power: *she* is the price that must be paid for Cavaradossi's life. Distant drums suggest an escort about to conduct a prisoner to the scaffold. In the opera's most famous aria (one Puccini is said to have grudged its place as interrupting the flow of the action), Tosca prays movingly for strength ('Vissi d'arte, vissi d'amore'). Spoletta announces Angelotti took poison as he was arrested, then waits for instructions about the other prisoner. Tosca reluctantly nods to Scarpia, who tells Spoletta there has been a change of plan. For Cavaradossi there will be a mock execution, simulated only – 'just as we did in the case of Palmieri. You understand: *just* like Palmieri'. Spoletta seems to grasp the emphasis. Tosca demands safe conduct and, as Scarpia writes at his desk, sees a knife on the supper table, picks it up and stabs him to the heart. He falls dying and she searches for the paper, then, placing a candle on either side of the dead man's head, slowly leaves the room.

Act III. A platform high on Castel Sant'Angelo; St Peter's can be seen in the distance. A shepherd sings below, and as dawn approaches Cavaradossi is brought in. He bribes the jailer to deliver a letter to Tosca, before losing himself in memories of her. 'E lucevan le stelle' is in great contrast to 'Recondita armonia', with which he began the opera, a moving farewell to life as opposed to a panegyric to a loved one. Tosca joins Cavaradossi, who listens to the story of Scarpia's killing, then lovingly takes her hands in his: 'O dolci mani mansuete e pure'. They plot their departure and their voices join in a duet ('Amaro sol per te m'era il morire'), which ends on a note less of love than of defiance. When the firing squad, duty done, leaves to a sinister funeral march, Scarpia is found to have kept one last card, a joker, up his sleeve. The mock execution was real after all, and with a last cry, Tosca eludes Spoletta and plunges over the parapet.

In spite of 'Vissi d'arte', Cavaradossi's three splendid arias and Scarpia's two monologues, *Tosca* is not an opera of solos. Puccini has constructed a score which flows, often without recourse to the singers, like the incidental music to a film – introducing and reinforcing dramatic events, regularly raising the temperature, nudging the audience, responding to the ebb and flow of the drama.   H.

MADAMA BUTTERFLY

Opera in three acts, text by Giacosa and Illica. Première at la Scala, Milan, on 17 February 1904, with Rosina Storchio, Giovanni Zenatello, Giuseppe de Luca, conductor Campanini. Revised for Brescia, May 1904, with Salomea Krusceniski and Zenatello.

Cio-Cio-San (Madam Butterfly), *a geisha* ....Soprano

Suzuki, *her servant* ....Mezzo-Soprano

Kate Pinkerton, *Pinkerton's American wife* ....Mezzo-Soprano

Lieutenant B.F. Pinkerton, *U.S. Navy*................Tenor

Sharpless, *American Consul at Nagasaki* ....Baritone

Goro, *a marriage broker* ....Tenor

Prince Yamadori, *a rich Japanese* ....Baritone

The Bonze, *a Priest; Butterfly's uncle* ....Bass

The Imperial Commissioner................................Bass

The Official Registrar ....Baritone

Dolore (Trouble), *Cio-Cio-San's son* ....Silent

Cio-Cio-San's Relations and Friends; Servants

Place: Nagasaki, Japan
Time: Early Twentieth Century
Running Time: 2 hours 5 minutes

Madama Butterfly's first performance in Milan was a fiasco. The public audibly objected to a resemblance it found between the theme of Butterfly's entry (heard again, notably in the love duet) and Mimì's first-act aria in *La Bohème*, and to the fatiguing length of the second act, given without interval. It was heard only once in that form but a revised version (with a much more dramatic soprano than in Milan) triumphed in Brescia. Substantial revision brought a new theme for Butterfly's entrance and the love duet, the second act divided into two, and in the third an aria for Pinkerton.

But that wasn't the end of it. There were further revisions for Covent Garden in 1905, for America in 1906 and, at the behest of the experienced Albert Carré, for the Opéra-Comique at the end of the same year. That 1906 version was the composer's last word. 'Genre' scenes featuring Butterfly's relations were cut from the first act, and revision of the second went far beyond the cosmetic, mainly because the composer had effective second thoughts but also, modern speculation has it, because some of the first thoughts were too 'modern' for an audience in the early 1900s. That Puccini had seventeen years in which to revise the 1906 score but never did has not prevented attempts since the early 1980s to come up with a 'version' for almost any new production.

Puccini was at pains not only to introduce genuine elements of Japanese music into his score but also to imitate Japanese musical style. The result is highly effective, and the exotic, dominating in the scene after Butterfly's entrance and in much of Act II, in no way contradicts Puccini's own brand of lyricism as evidenced in Butterfly's entrance, the love duet, 'Un bel dì', the letter scene with Sharpless, Pinkerton's aria and Butterfly's death.

Act I. A house overlooking Nagasaki harbour. Goro is showing Lieutenant Pinkerton over the house he has leased for the Japanese bride he is to marry ('Tied for 999 years but with the option at every month to cancel the contract'). Goro introduces the servants and is describing the bridal party when the Consul makes his entrance. Pinkerton delights in the elasticity of local law and, in spite of Sharpless's obvious disapproval of the step he is

taking, a rampant sexuality pervades the music of his toast to the future ('Amore o grillo').

The bride's arrival is imminent and her voice soars over those of her relations as she makes her entrance. She discloses her age – fifteen; her mother's poverty; that her father committed *hari kiri*; that her few possessions mean little to her if her new husband does not like them; and that she has abandoned her own religion to take up Pinkerton's. The Commissioner performs the ceremony, the Consul and other officials leave, and Pinkerton is proposing a toast which he hopes will get rid of the relations when there is an interruption. Butterfly's uncle the Bonze has got wind of her conversion and loudly denounces her. The relations follow him out and Pinkerton is left to comfort his bride.

It is the moment for the most extended love duet Puccini ever wrote. It builds slowly while Butterfly rids her mind of the cries of the Bonze, turns to her confused thoughts when it was suggested she should marry an American, passes through an exquisite passage pleading for reassurance ('Vogliatemi bene') until it reaches a climax with a return of the music of Butterfly's entrance.

Act II. Inside Butterfly's house. Three years have passed since Pinkerton left, promising, according to Butterfly, to return 'when the robins nest in spring'. Perhaps they nest less often over there? To comfort herself as much as Suzuki, she sings 'Un bel dì vedremo' (One fine day), a description of his future home-coming which had become possibly the most popular aria of the twentieth century until 'Nessun dorma' swept the board. Sharpless now comes on a mission which is little to his taste – to tell Butterfly he has heard from Pinkerton that he is returning, but does not intend to see her. He is constantly interrupted: by indignation at Goro's suggestion she should take a Japanese husband, by the appearance of her suitor Yamadori, and finally, while reading the letter, by Butterfly's over-enthusiasm. He takes the bull by the horns: what would be her reaction if he were never to come back? She reacts as if struck in the face, then fetches her little boy, born since Pinkerton's departure, and releases her pent-up emotion in an aria ('Che tua madre'). The child's name is 'Dolore', she says, and Sharpless goes resignedly away, his message only partly delivered.

Goro is dragged in and castigated for spreading a false rumour about the baby's parentage, then a cannon shot diverts all attention to the harbour. Through the telescope, Butterfly makes out that it is the *Abraham Lincoln*, Pinkerton's ship, and apprehension turns to jubilation: flowers must be scattered to celebrate Pinkerton's return. She puts on her wedding garment; she, Suzuki and Dolore will together watch until Pinkerton arrives, while a wordless chorus suggests the warm night outside.

Act III. The curtain rises on the same scene, with dawn breaking, Butterfly still on watch. She sings a sad little lullaby as she carries the baby to bed. Suzuki has not long to wait. Pinkerton and Sharpless appear and a moment later Suzuki learns that the woman outside is Pinkerton's wife. The strands of grief and consternation are gathered in a trio, after which Pinkerton, unable to face the situation, sings a tearful farewell to the house he once knew so well (the interpolated, often maligned but effective 'Addio, fiorito asil'), and leaves.

Butterfly is convinced Pinkerton is there and only gradually comes to terms with the reality. She sees Mrs Pinkerton, comforts the weeping Suzuki, then contrives to wish her rival happiness for the future. To Pinkerton she sends a message that, if he will come for his son in half an hour, he may have him. In this last scene, Butterfly acquires tragic dignity, and it is on this level that she reads the words engraved on her father's sword 'To die with honour when one can no longer live with honour', before embracing the child whom Suzuki, in one last effort to avert disaster, has brought in. She sings heartbreakingly to the boy, then blindfolds him, retreats behind a screen and commits *hari-kiri*. Pinkerton returns to find Butterfly dead on the floor and his son waving an American flag.   H.

LA FANCIULLA DEL WEST
The Girl of the Golden West

Opera in three acts, text by G. Civinini and C. Zangarini, from the play by David Belasco. Première at Metropolitan, New York, 10 December 1910, with Destinn, Caruso, Amato, conductor Toscanini. First performed Covent Garden, 1911, with Destinn, Bassi, Dinh Gilly, conductor Campanini; la Scala, Milan, 1912, with Poli-Randaccio, Martinelli, Galeffi. Revived Metropolitan, 1929, with Jeritza, Martinelli, Tibbett; la Scala, 1930, with dalla Rizza, Thill, Viglione-Borghese, conductor de Sabata; 1937, with Cobelli, Merli, Armando Borgioli; San Francisco, 1943, with Kirk, Jagel, Weede; la Scala, 1956, with Corelli; 1957, with del Monaco; Metropolitan, New York,

1961, with Price, Tucker, Colzani; Sadler's Wells, 1963, with Fretwell, Donald Smith, Herincx; Covent Garden, 1977, with Carol Neblett, Domingo, Silvano Carroli, conductor Mehta.

Minnie, *owner of 'The Polka'*	Soprano
Jack Rance, *the Sheriff*	Baritone
Dick Johnson, *a bandit*	Tenor
Nick, *bar-tender at 'The Polka'*	Tenor

Miners

Sonora	Baritone
Trim	Tenor
Sid	Baritone
Handsome	Baritone
Harry	Tenor
Joe	Tenor
Happy	Baritone
Larkens	Bass

Ashby, *agent of the Wells Fargo Transport Co*	Bass
Billy Jackrabbit, *an American Indian*	Bass
Wowkle, *Billy's squaw*	Mezzo-Soprano
Jake Wallace, *a travelling minstrel*	Baritone
José Castro, *a 'greaser' from Ramerrez's band*	Bass
A Courier	Tenor

Place: A Mining Camp
Time: 1849–50
Running Time: 2 hours

Puccini saw David Belasco's play as early as 1907 and the opera seems always to have been intended for the Metropolitan in New York, where with Caruso, Emmy Destinn and Amato in the cast and Toscanini conducting, it was in 1910 a resounding success.

Act I. A large room, forming the inside of 'The Polka', the inn where the miners come to drink and gamble. It is presided over by Minnie, whom they respect, love and protect, and who in return has even ventured to set up a sort of elementary school for the roughest of the inhabitants. She is looked after by two American Indian servants, Billy and Wowkle. There is a bar, a notice offering a reward for the arrest of Ramerrez, and a sheet-iron screen to protect a person from pistol shots.

Miners greet each other, and a game of faro starts up. Larkens is observed to be melancholy – he has gold fever, says Nick. Jake comes through singing a melancholy song, in whose refrain all join. Larkens breaks down, and Sonora takes up a collection for him. Sid is caught cheating and the miners are for meting out justice to him themselves, but Rance, the Sheriff, who has been in and out of the bar since the beginning, dominates the scene, and tells them rather to pin a card on Sid's chest as a token that he must not play; pass the word round the camp, and string him up if he takes off the mark of shame. Ashby comes in, asks after Minnie, and tells Rance that he is close on the heels of the notorious Ramerrez. Minnie sends in hot whisky and lemon, and they all drink to her, Rance taking the opportunity of mentioning that she is likely soon to become Mrs Rance. Sonora mocks him, and they fight, but are separated after a moment by a woman's strong arm. It is Minnie. She tells them all off, and they bring one or two small gifts for her. Rance and Ashby talk apart, as Minnie takes down the Bible and starts to teach from it.

The post arrives, and Ashby has a letter from Nina Micheltorena, a cast-off girlfriend of Ramerrez's, indicating where he is to be found that night. He rejoices at the prospect of catching him at last. Everyone reads letters and newspapers.

A stranger is outside, Nick says, asking for whisky with water. They all laugh at the notion. Rance comes up to Minnie and starts to tell her how much he loves her, but she interrupts and will have none of it. He goes sulkily away, and bursts out into an avowal of his passion: 'Minnie della mia casa son partito'. He left everything without regret when his gambler's heart impelled him to come out West, but now he would give a fortune for a kiss from her. Minnie says that she has happy memories of her parents and her home-life, and would not take a husband unless she loved him as they loved each other: 'Laggiù nel Soledad'.

Nick brings in the stranger, Dick Johnson. Rance is rude to him, but Minnie recognises him and talks about the time they first met. Rance comes over and knocks his glass off the counter, saying that he is Sheriff and demanding to know what is the stranger's business. The miners are about to take Rance's part when Minnie says she will vouch for him. Johnson takes Minnie off to dance. While they are away, Castro is brought in; he is a member of Ramerrez's band and has been captured. He will lead them to the bandit's camp if they will spare him, then, seeing Johnson's saddle lying on the ground, thinks they have already captured him. When his chief comes from the other room, he tells Johnson that he has given nothing away, and that the gang is all round, waiting to fall on the defenceless camp and pillage it.

Johnson remains behind with Minnie when the others ride off. He comments on her defenceless state and on the strange fact that she is guarding the miners' gold. She tells him that she loves the life she lives and would have no other. Nick says that a bandit has been seen skulking round the camp but Johnson comforts her, and agrees to come up later that evening to her cabin to continue the conversation and have a meal. As he goes out, she bursts into tears, but he tells her: 'You've the face of an angel.'

Act II. Minnie's hut – a single room, above which is a loft. Wowkle is singing a lullaby to her papoose. She and Billy talk for a moment – shall they get married? – before Minnie comes in, sends Billy about his business and tells Wowkle that there will be two for supper. She starts to dress up, obviously hoping to make a real impression on Johnson when he comes. He knocks at the door and they sit down to supper, Johnson commenting that the life up here must be lonely. 'Oh, you've no notion how exciting my life is,' says Minnie: 'O, se sapeste.'

They sing of their happiness, and Minnie makes up a bed for herself in front of the fire. She has persuaded Johnson to spend the night there, as he would inevitably get lost in the heavy snow. Voices demand admittance. Minnie hides Johnson behind the curtains of the bed, and lets in Rance, Nick, Ashby, and Sonora. They were worried for her safety – Dick Johnson, they have discovered, is none other than the notorious Ramerrez. They were led by Castro to his hiding-place.

She says goodnight to them, then rounds furiously on Johnson. He admits he came to rob, but at sight of her, changed his purpose. In an aria he explains his upbringing: his father was a bandit, and when he died six months ago ('Or son sei mesi') left nothing for him, his mother and his brothers, but the gang of thieves he led. He was fated to take to the road, but from the moment he met Minnie he longed to lead an honest life. He does not expect forgiveness, only understanding.

Johnson rushes out, and a moment later there is the sound of a shot. A body falls against the door; Minnie opens it, and he staggers in, telling her not to shut the door as he will leave again. She cries that she loves him and will help him, and drags him to concealment in the loft. No sooner is he in hiding than Rance is again at the door. He searches everywhere for his quarry, then, asking Minnie to swear that he is not hidden there, tries to embrace her. She backs away from him; he accuses her of loving the bandit. With a gesture of defiance, Rance swears to Minnie that she shall never be Johnson's. A drop of blood falls on his outstretched hand, then another. Rance calls to Johnson to come out of hiding; he descends the ladder, helped by Minnie, and collapses at the bottom. Minnie tries a last desperate expedient. She will play poker with Rance: if she wins, Johnson's life is hers, if she loses, Rance wins her love. He cannot resist the gamble. They play two hands, each winning one, but before the last Minnie shows signs of distress and asks Rance to get her a drink from the bottle in the corner. She secretes some cards in her stocking, and substitutes them for the hand she has been dealt. Rance returns, and against his three kings, Minnie is able to show three aces and a pair. He leaves the house, and Minnie is left alone with the lover whose life she has saved.

Act III. A clearing in the forest. Nick, Rance, and Ashby are sitting round a fire. They are members of a party hunting for Ramerrez. They reflect bitterly on the change that Johnson's arrival has brought into their lives. Ashby shouts that his men seem to have caught up with their quarry, but it is a false alarm. Rance raises his arms towards Minnie's cabin, and shouts triumphantly that she will not see her lover again, except at the end of a rope. There is another false alarm, and then Sonora gallops in shouting that they have caught him at last. Ashby hands over Johnson to the Sheriff, who suggests that they string him up forthwith. All unite in calling down curses on his head, but he protests that he stopped short of murder, and asks for one thing only, that he be allowed to speak before he dies. He makes an impassioned plea that Minnie shall think he has gone free, and never know the ignominious fate which overtook him: 'Ch'ella mi creda libero e lontano' (Let her believe that I am free and far away). It is one of Puccini's most famous arias, and one that is familiar to every Italian that has ever been to the opera. In the 1914–18 war it was even a favourite song with troops on the march.

Almost before Johnson has finished speaking, Rance rushes up to him and hits him in the face, to sounds of disapproval from the bystanders. They are about to hang their prisoner when Minnie's voice is heard. In a moment she is among them, threatening the first man that takes a step towards Johnson, and defying them to do their worst. For years she shared

their troubles and their dangers – will they deny her the first thing she has ever asked of them? She and Johnson were planning to start a new life together, the bandit having died in her cabin a week before, when the honest man was born. Sonora goes to her side and takes her part; they agree that they owe her too much to deny her this. She and Johnson go off arm-in-arm, to seek a new existence together.　　H.

LA RONDINE

The Swallow

Lyric comedy in three acts, text by G. Adami, from the German libretto by A.M. Willner and H. Reichert. Première at Monte Carlo, 27 March 1917, with dalla Rizza, Ferraris, Schipa, Francesco Dominici, Huberdeau, conductor Marinuzzi. First performed Bologna, 1917; Rome, 1918; Metropolitan, New York, 1928, with Bori, Fleischer, Gigli, Tokatyan, Ludikar, conductor Bellezza. Revived Metropolitan, 1936, with Bori, Martini, conductor Panizza; la Scala, Milan, 1940, with Favero, Malipiero, conductor Marinuzzi; Rome, 1940, with Favero, Gigli, Gobbi, Taddei. First performance in England, 1966, by Opera Viva; English Opera Group, 1974, with June Bronhill.

Magda, *Rambaldo's mistress*	Soprano
Lisette, *her maid*	Soprano
Ruggero, *a young man*	Tenor
Prunier, *a poet*	Tenor[1]
Rambaldo, *a wealthy Parisian*	Baritone
Périchaud	Bass-Baritone

His friends
Gobin	Tenor
Crébillon	Bass-Baritone

Ladies of pleasure and friends of Magda
Yvette	Soprano
Bianca	Soprano
Suzy	Mezzo-Soprano
A Steward	Bass

Ladies and Gentlemen of the World, Citizens, Students, Artists, Demi-Mondaines, Dancers, etc.

Place: Paris
Time: The Second Empire
Running Time: 1 hour 50 minutes

It was while he was in Vienna in 1912 that Puccini was asked by an Austrian publisher to write a light opera in something approaching the Viennese manner. The war prevented fulfilment of the sug-

---

[1] Originally baritone, later tenor.

gested contract, but Puccini decided to set the libretto which had been prepared for him, albeit in a somewhat different form from that originally envisaged. The music is light in character and frequently employs waltz rhythms, but the composer has abandoned any attempt to write an operetta.

Act I. A luxuriously furnished room in Magda's house in Paris. Magda and Rambaldo are entertaining their friends, among whom is Prunier, a poet. He sings his latest song sitting at the piano. It tells the story of one Doretta, who dreams that the king looked upon her one day. When Prunier says that the end evades him, Magda takes up the tale ('Chi il bel sogno di Doretta'). Rambaldo produces a necklace he has been meaning all evening to give Magda. Lisette the maid, about whose cheeky habits Prunier is not slow to complain but whom Magda praises as a ray of sunshine in her life, asks Rambaldo whether he will at last see the young man who has been waiting for nearly two hours to see him. He is the son of an old friend of Rambaldo's.

Magda talks to her friends of the old days when she was still an innocent girl and went to Bullier's café in search of adventure and, maybe, love. The dancing was something that she can never forget, nor the memory of the man she met there, into whose eyes she gazed, but whose name she never knew. 'Ore dolci e divine', she sings, and the music traces every stage of that never-to-be-forgotten experience of her carefree youth.

Ruggero is brought in just as Prunier starts to tell everyone's future from their hands; Magda's is that, like a swallow, she will migrate far away from Paris, perhaps to find love. The conversation turns to where Ruggero shall spend his first evening in Paris; Bullier's is chosen, and Lisette agrees that the choice is an excellent one.

All leave, except Prunier who stays on the verandah. It is Lisette's day off, she reminds Magda, who goes off to her room. Lisette reappears, dressed in an assortment of her mistress's finery. She runs into Prunier, who takes her in his arms with obvious affection – objecting, though, a moment later, that her clothes do not match. She rushes out and reappears more suitably dressed and they go off together. Magda herself comes in, hardly recognisable in that her hair has been redone and she is dressed simply and as a grisette.

Act II. Chez Bullier. The room is crowded with artists, grisettes, demi-mondaines and men about town. Ruggero is sitting alone at one of the tables, apparently oblivious of the confusion and noise around him, and quite unresponsive to the various girls. Magda comes in and has some difficulty in fending off any number of would-be escorts, which she does by saying she is meeting the young man sitting in the corner.

Ruggero is delighted when she sits by him. They dance, and Magda is irresistibly reminded of her adventure long ago; they even write their names in pencil on the marble-topped table at which they are sitting. Prunier and Lisette come in, and Lisette thinks she recognises her mistress, but is persuaded by her escort that she is mistaken. They are introduced to each other, and sing a quartet expressing their different views and requirements of love.

Magda sees Rambaldo come in, and Prunier hastens to get Ruggero and Lisette out of the way. Rambaldo comes over to Magda, brushes Prunier aside, and asks her if she is coming home with him. She tells him she has found love and is not leaving with him, now or at any time. In spite of the blow he preserves his dignity, and leaves her sitting where he has found her. Ruggero returns and together they leave the restaurant.

Act III. A little cottage, near Nice, in which live Magda and Ruggero, secure in their love. The two lovers are blissfully happy, and Ruggero, who says he has written to ask his father's consent to their marriage, tells her of his confidence that his family will receive her as one of themselves. Magda wonders how best to let him know the details of her past.

Lisette and Prunier can be heard in the distance, and they appear just after Ruggero and Magda have left. It appears that Prunier tried to turn Lisette into a successful actress, only to have to listen to the hisses of the audience at her solitary appearance. Lisette now wants her old job back with Magda. Magda agrees, and Lisette immediately seems more natural in her accustomed surroundings – so too would Magda, hints Prunier, if she were to return to Paris and gaiety. Magda understands that Rambaldo has sent her a message through Prunier and that she can return to him whenever she wishes.

Prunier prepares to go, saying he has finished with Lisette for ever – but he does not omit to find out when she is going out that night. Ruggero comes in with a letter he has had from his mother, and makes Magda read it. She tells him she cannot deceive him any longer; he must know that she has been ready to sell her favours for money, that she has lived in guilty splendour. She can love him, but she cannot marry him and come to meet his mother as if she were a virgin bride. They must part, she insists, and, supported by Lisette and with breaking heart, she goes out, back to her own existence, leaving behind her the one love of her life. (In a revised version of the opera's end, Puccini has Ruggero discover Magda's past and, and as a result, throw her out.) H.

IL TABARRO
The Cloak

Opera in one act, text by G. Adami, after the play by Didier Gold, *La Houppelande*. Première at Metropolitan, New York, on 14 December 1918, with Muzio, Crimi, Montesanto, Didur, conductor Moranzoni. First performed in Rome, 1919, with Maria Labia, di Giovanni (Edward Johnson), Galeffi, conductor Marinuzzi; Covent Garden, 1920, with Quaiatti, Tom Burke, Gilly; la Scala, Milan, 1922, with Concato, Piccaluga, Noto, conductor Panizza; Sadler's Wells, 1935 (in English), with Winifred Kennard, Wendon, Matters. Revived Metropolitan, 1946, with Albanese, Jagel, Tibbett; Covent Garden, 1965, with Collier, Craig, Gobbi, conductor Pritchard.

Michele, *owner of a barge, aged fifty* ....Baritone
Luigi, *a stevedore, aged twenty* ....Tenor
'Tinca', *a stevedore, aged thirty-five*.....................Tenor
'Talpa', *a stevedore, aged fifty-five*..........................Bass
Giorgetta, *Michele's wife, aged twenty-five* ......Soprano
Frugola, *Talpa's wife, aged fifty* ....Mezzo-Soprano

Place: The Seine, in Paris
Time: Early Twentieth Century
Running Time: 1 hour

Puccini, against his publisher's inclinations, had long wanted to work on a triptych of contrasting subjects and *Il Tabarro* came first to his notice. Forzano suggested the other two subjects, which he seems to have composed without difficulty, and the *Trittico* was first performed, in the composer's absence, at the Metropolitan in New York.

Attempts to pair *Tabarro* with *Gianni Schicchi*, thus shortening the evening and omitting the least satisfactory element of the *Trittico*, seem doomed to failure. Puccini, the mature theatrical craftsman, may have slightly misjudged the length of his triple bill but unquestionably not its shape, and to alter it

in this way is like leaving out the slow movement of a symphony: self-defeating.

The action of *Il Tabarro* takes place on board a barge, whose master is Michele. It is moored in the Seine and the imposing shape of Notre-Dame can be seen in the distance. The barge takes up most of the stage, but beyond it can be seen the shore, to which it is connected by a gangway.

The curtain rises before the music begins. A swaying orchestral figure denotes the gentle movement of a boat tied up to the shore. It is the end of the day, and workmen are finishing their job of loading the barge. Michele and Giorgetta take little notice of them as they work, but Giorgetta suggests that they should be offered a drink before they go. Michele goes up to embrace her, but she only offers him her cheek, and he goes discontentedly on shore. The workmen crowd round Giorgetta, and drink to her in a well-defined triple time. An organ-grinder goes by on the shore and Luigi calls to him to play for them. Giorgetta says she only understands music which sets her feet dancing. The phrase is later considerably developed in her love scene with Luigi.

Tinca is immediately at her side offering himself as a partner. His clumsiness becomes too much for her, and Luigi pushes him aside and takes his place, holding Giorgetta closer than is perhaps necessary. Talpa sees Michele coming and the dancing stops hurriedly as Giorgetta asks Michele about arrangements for the morrow, when they are due to leave for Rouen; he will take the three – Tinca, Talpa, and Luigi – who have been helping him in Paris.

Frugola, Talpa's wife, appears and talks of her occupation as a rag-picker. Her one love, it appears, is her cat, for whom she buys the best meat available. Talpa, Tinca and Luigi with other stevedores come up from the hold, and Tinca claims that he drinks to forget his sorrows. Luigi takes up the cue: he is right, their fate is a miserable one ('Hai ben ragione'). The solution, says Tinca, is to follow his example: booze!

Talpa and Frugola prepare to go home, dreaming of the cottage in the country they will never be able to afford. Giorgetta admits that her dream is for something quite different; she was born in the suburbs of Paris, and wishes that Michele might one day give up their nomadic existence and settle down: 'E ben altro il mio sogno'. This is one of the opera's purple passages, and Luigi joins his voice to hers as they agree that this former life was the happiest they have known: 'Ma chi lascia il sobborgo'.

Giorgetta and Luigi are alone. They listen to voices singing off-stage; then Luigi moves towards Giorgetta, who stops him with a gesture. They are lovers and Luigi complains of the barrier which prevents them being happy together. There is a short interruption as Michele comes up from down below. Luigi asks him to put him ashore next day at Rouen; he means to try his luck there as a labourer. Michele advises strongly against such a course of action, and Luigi agrees to go on working for him. Michele says goodnight. Luigi's enthusiasm carries Giorgetta away, and the duet rises to a climax as Luigi agrees to come for her in an hour's time; they will use the same signal as last night, a lighted match will mean that all is safe.

Luigi departs and Giorgetta reflects sadly on the difficulties in the way of being happy in this life as Michele comes back and asks her why she has not yet gone to bed. They talk for a moment of their crew, and then Michele comes close to her with an affectionate gesture. Why can they not renew their old love, which seems to have cooled since the death of their child: 'Perchè, perchè non m'ami più?' Why does she no longer come for warmth beneath his cloak? Giorgetta reacts prosaically – they are both getting older.

She goes off to bed, but the moment she has gone, Michele exclaims in fury: 'You whore!' He listens for a moment, then peers in at the window to see Giorgetta still dressed and apparently waiting: for what? Who is her lover? He goes through the men with whom he knows her to be in contact, but dismisses each one in turn. Who can it be? Would he could catch him and crush his life out between his hands. His monologue is a powerful passage, and as his anger rises, so the orchestra boils with emotion.

He raises his pipe and lights it with a match, unwittingly giving as he does so the signal agreed upon by Luigi and Giorgetta. Michele sees a movement, and quickly hides himself before pouncing on the figure which creeps towards the boat. It is Luigi. Michele's hands are round his throat as he demands an admission of guilt. He chokes Luigi, then, as Giorgetta, roused by the noise, appears, hides the body under his cloak and stands as if nothing has happened. Giorgetta comes up to him, and asks him to warm her under his cloak. With a terrible cry, he opens his cloak and reveals what it conceals.   H.

SUOR ANGELICA
Sister Angelica

Opera in one act, text by G. Forzano. Première at Metropolitan, New York, on 14 December 1918, with Farrar, Perini, conductor Moranzoni (in conjunction with premières of *Gianni Schicchi* and *Il Tabarro*). First performed Rome, 1919, with dalla Rizza, conductor Marinuzzi; Covent Garden, 1920, with dalla Rizza; la Scala, Milan, 1922, with Carena, Casazza, conductor Panizza. Revived Covent Garden, 1965, with Carlyle, Fisher, conductor Pritchard.

Suor Angelica	Soprano
The Princess, *her aunt*	Contralto
The Abbess	Mezzo-Soprano
The Alms Collector	Soprano
Mistress of the Novices	Mezzo-Soprano
Suor Genovieffa	Soprano
Suor Osmina	Soprano
Suor Dolcina	Mezzo-Soprano
Aspirant Sisters	Mezzo-Soprano
Nursing Sister	Soprano

Novices, Sisters

Place: The Cloisters of a Nunnery
Time: Seventeenth Century
Running Time: 1 hour

Suor Angelica, the daughter of a noble Florentine family, has taken the veil to expiate the scandal which has overshadowed her life; she is an unmarried mother. Seven years she has spent in the peace and seclusion of a convent, in a state of mind that has alternated between repentance and longing for the child she has never really known. The Abbess tells her that she has a visitor, her aunt, the Princess, towards whom her attitude must be one of reverence and humility.

The Princess has come to obtain from Angelica her signature to a legal document in connection with her sister's forthcoming marriage. She impresses upon her that her life must be given up now and for ever to atoning for the sin she once committed. When Angelica asks for news of the little child which has had to live its life in the great outside world without its mother, she is told coldly that it died two years ago.

In a frenzy of despair, Angelica resolves on suicide. She gathers herbs and flowers and brews a poisonous draught, which she drinks. She prays to the Virgin that she may not die in mortal sin, and, as if in answer to her prayer, sees a vision of the Blessed Virgin leading a little child towards her. An invisible chorus sings of salvation as she dies.

Though hard to separate from its companion pieces in the *Trittico*, the opera has never been popular, and only Angelica's lament, 'Senza mamma', has attained the fame which has attended some of Puccini's other arias. H.

GIANNI SCHICCHI

Opera in one act, text by G. Forzano. Première at Metropolitan, New York, on 14 December 1918, with Easton, Crimi, de Luca, conductor Moranzoni. First performed at Rome, 1919, with dalla Rizza, di Giovanni (Edward Johnson), Galeffi, conductor Marinuzzi; Covent Garden, 1920, with dalla Rizza, Tom Burke, Badini; la Scala, Milan, 1922, with di Voltri, Marion, Badini, conductor Panizza. Revived la Scala, 1928, with Galeffi; 1944, with Menotti, Malipiero, Stabile, conductor Marinuzzi; 1947, with Stabile; Covent Garden, 1962, with Joan Carlyle, André Turp, Geraint Evans, conductor Solti.

Gianni Schicchi, *aged fifty*..............................Baritone

Lauretta, *his daughter, aged twenty-one*..........Soprano

Zita, *called La Vecchia, cousin of Buoso,*
   aged sixty .... Contralto

Rinuccio, *nephew of Zita, aged twenty-four* ....Tenor

Gherardo, *nephew of Buoso, aged forty*...............Tenor

Nella, *his wife, aged thirty-four* ....Soprano

Gherardino, *their son, aged seven* ....Alto

Betto di Signa, *brother-in-law of Buoso,*
   poor and badly dressed, of indefinite age..............Bass

Simone, *Buoso's cousin, aged seventy* ....Bass

Marco, *his son, aged forty-five*.........................Baritone

La Ciesca, *Marco's wife, aged*
   thirty-eight ....Mezzo-Soprano

Maestro Spinelloccio, *doctor*................................Bass

Ser Amantio di Nicolao, *lawyer*.....................Baritone

Pinellino, *cobbler* ....Bass

Guccio, *painter* ....Bass

Place: Florence
Time: 1299
Running Time: 1 hour

Gianni Schicchi, an historical character, has the honour of being mentioned by Dante in the Thirtieth Canto of *The Inferno*, where he appears in company with the incestuous Myrrha of Cyprus as a 'pallid, naked shape' (the connection between the two is that both counterfeited the shape of another for their own ends).

Before the curtain rises, there are a few bars of rapid music, whose impetus is however tempered to become a lament (in the minor) by the time the action begins. A chuckling figure, Ernest Newman once suggested, is used to indicate that the shadow of Gianni Schicchi is already over them.

The opera takes place in a bedroom in the house of Buoso Donati, who has recently died. The dead man is in bed, and his relations are kneeling round him, behaving with proper solemnity, that is all except Gherardino, who is heartily bored by the whole proceedings. A whisper goes round; 'it is rumoured in Signa' that Buoso's wealth has been left to the monks, and the agitation of the mourners resolves itself in a request for the advice of Simone, he having once been mayor of Fucecchio and therefore of them all the wisest as well as the oldest. Simone tells them that if the will is already in the hands of lawyers, there is no hope for them, but if it is still in the room, something may yet be done.

A search for the will begins; first one, then another thinks he or she has discovered it, only to find that it is a false alarm. At last Rinuccio holds it triumphantly aloft, but before giving it up asks for a reward for having found it, in the shape of permission to marry Lauretta, Gianni Schicchi's daughter. Zita is far too much concerned with the will to worry about a little thing like that, and eventually it is opened (in the meanwhile, Rinuccio sends Gherardino off to fetch Gianni Schicchi and his daughter). The will is addressed to Zita and Simone: expectation runs high, and speculation as to what is the portion of each even higher. They read the will in silence and, as they begin to understand its import, mounting horror; the rumour from Signa was by no means an exaggeration. Simone speaks for them all, and gradually they collect their wits sufficiently to be able to utter a rapid curse on the monks who will grow fat on *their* portions. Who would ever have thought, reflects Zita broken-heartedly, that they would shed so many genuine tears when Buoso was taken from them?

A thought seems to strike them all at the same time; if only it were possible ... They appeal to Simone but he can offer them no comfort. Rinuccio suggests that only one man can help them: Gianni Schicchi. Zita furiously says they have heard enough of him and his brood for one day, but Rinuccio is not to be put off, least of all when Gherardino bursts into the room and says the man they are discussing is on his way. He praises Schicchi's resourcefulness and cunning, and urges them to stop their spiteful gossip about his origins and lack of family tree. Has not majestic Florence herself got her roots in the countryside? Rinuccio's aria, 'Firenze è come un albero fiorito', has an antique flavour about it, as if it were a traditional song. It contains in the middle a broad phrase which is later to blossom out into Lauretta's well-known song.

Gianni Schicchi arrives with his daughter, and wonders if the long faces he can see are to be taken as meaning that Donati is better. He is told the sad facts of the will, and comments that this means they are disinherited. Zita repeats the word, and snaps out that he can take himself and his daughter back to where they came from; her nephew shall never marry a nobody. Schicchi bursts out into a vivid denunciation of the snobbish money-grabbing old hag, who would sacrifice young people's happiness to her own greed. An ensemble develops, through which runs the lovers' sad plaint that they had hoped (vainly it seems) to be married before midsummer. Rinuccio prevents Schicchi leaving unceremoniously, and begs him at least to look at the will. Lauretta adds her plea to Rinuccio's and he gives way. 'O mio babbino caro' (O my beloved daddy), built up on the phrase from Rinuccio's aria, has become enormously popular over the years, and is now as well known as 'Un bel dì' or 'Mi chiamano Mimì'. Its lyrical charm must be taken in this context as a masterly piece of tongue-in-cheek writing.

Schicchi walks up and down considering the will; 'it can't be done', he concludes, and immediately there is an outburst of sorrow from the lovers. Finally a ray of hope presents itself to Schicchi's agile mind. Lauretta is sent out on the balcony to feed the bird, and he asks if anyone apart from themselves yet knows of Buoso's death. No one, comes the answer: then there is hope, he concludes, and immediately gives orders that the funeral ornaments, etc., be removed from the room (to the sound of a muffled funeral march rhythm). A knock is heard, and in comes the doctor, not however before Schicchi has had time to jump behind the curtains of the bed. Schicchi answers the doctor's queries in what he hopes is Donati's voice, and tells him he is feeling better; they all bid the doctor goodnight and breathe a sigh of relief at his departure. Schicchi outlines his plan: let them send for a lawyer, giving out that

Buoso has had a relapse and wishes to make his will. Schicchi's monologue is slyness and good humour personified, and at its end the relatives shriek with delight and the ensemble takes on breakneck speed as all congratulate Schicchi (and themselves) on the possibilities of the scheme.

Collectively they tell him to divide the possessions equally among them, but each one then asks for the plums for himself. Schicchi laughs at them all, just as the passing bell is heard – for the mayor's servant, they are told, and heave a sigh of relief. As Schicchi is helped into Buoso's night-clothes, each one in turn offers him some reward if he will leave the particularly coveted things to him. He agrees to each.

When all is ready, he says that before going to bed he must warn them of the danger they are collectively running. The law provides penalties for falsifying a will – exile, and the loss of the right hand for the malefactor and his accomplices – and they are each one of them liable to these penalties. With mock solemnity he bids a sad farewell to the Florence they all love, and the relations, seeing the force of his argument, sadly repeat the phrases after him: 'Farewell, dear Florence ... I wave goodbye with this poor handless arm.'

Then, a knock is heard at the door, and the lawyer and the two witnesses who are to assist him are admitted. Schicchi answers their questions in a thin, assumed voice, and they go through the terms of the new will. Ssomething is left in turn to each, until the moment arrives when there remain only the prizes ... the villa in Florence, the saw-mills at Signa, and the mule. Amid protests from the relations he leaves each in turn to 'his devoted friend, Gianni Schicchi', commenting, when they interrupt, that he knows best what is good for Schicchi. When the interruptions look like becoming too violent, he sings a line or two of the farewell to Florence. They are caught in their own trap, and as if to add insult to injury, he directs Zita to give twenty florins to each of the witnesses and a hundred to the lawyer.

As soon as the lawyer has gone, they all rush at Schicchi and tear the night-shirt off his back. He picks up Donati's stick and deals some shrewd blows with it as he chases them out of the house, which is now his, and which they attempt to pillage before leaving. Lauretta and Rinuccio sing of the happiness they will know together, and Schicchi returns, bringing with him some of the things the relations had filched. He turns to the audience: 'Could you imagine a better use for Buoso's money? ... if you have enjoyed yourselves this evening, I trust you will applaud a verdict of "Extenuating Circumstances".'

Puccini owes an obvious debt to the Verdi of *Falstaff*, but it would be churlish to deny his achievement in writing music of such dexterity and brilliance. *Gianni Schicchi* makes use of a side of the composer's make-up hitherto only revealed in such passages as the interplay of the Bohemians in *Bohème*, the entrance of the Sacristan in *Tosca*: in *Schicchi*, however, the wit is sharper and the tempo of movement faster than anywhere else in his output. H.

TURANDOT

Opera in three acts, libretto by Giuseppe Adami and Renato Simoni. Last duet and final scene completed by Franco Alfano. Première, la Scala, Milan, 2 April 1926, with Raisa, Zamboni, Fleta, Rimini, Nessi, Palai, Carlo Walter, conductor Toscanini. First performed in Rome, 1926, with Scacciati, Torri, Merli, conductor Vitale; Buenos Aires, 1926, with Muzio, Pampanini, Lauri-Volpi, conductor Marinuzzi; Metropolitan, 1926, with Jeritza, Attwood, Lauri-Volpi, conductor Serafin; Covent Garden, 1927, with Scacciati (later Easton), Schoene, Merli, conductor Bellezza. Revived Covent Garden, 1929, with Eva Turner; 1931, with Nemeth, Norena, Cortis, conductor Barbirolli; 1937, with Turner, Favero, Martinelli; 1946, with Turner, Midgley, conductor Lambert; 1963, with Shuard, Kabaivanska, Prevedi, conductor Downes; 1967, with Nilsson, McCracken, conductor Mackerras; Metropolitan, New York, 1961, with Nilsson, Moffo, Corelli, conductor Stokowski. Other famous exponents of the title role have included Mafalda Salvatini, Cigna, Grob-Prandl, Eva Marton, Gwyneth Jones. First (concert) performance of Alfano's complete ending, Barbican, London, 1982, with Sylvia Sass and Franco Bonisolli, conducted by Owain Arwel Hughes; first staged production of this version, Flanders Opera, Antwerp, 1993.

Princess Turandot ....Dramatic Soprano

The Emperor Altoum, *her father* ....Tenor

Timur, *the exiled King of Tartary* ....Bass

The Unknown Prince, Calaf, *his son* ....Tenor

Liù, a *slave girl* ....Lyric Soprano

Ping, *Grand Chancellor of China*......................Baritone

Pang, *supreme lord of provisions* ....Tenor

Pong, *supreme lord of the Imperial Kitchen* ....Tenor

A Mandarin..Baritone

Guards, Executioner's Men, Priests, Dignitaries, Handmaidens, Soldiers, Ghosts of Suitors

Place: Peking
Time: Legendary
Running Time: 2 hours 10 minutes

*T*urandot was Puccini's last opera, and took some four years to compose; it was left unfinished at his death in 1924. The treatment of Gozzi's 'dramatic fable' was first mooted over lunch in Rome with two younger writers, Adami and Simoni. In the event, it was the 1863 Italian translation by Verdi's old friend Andrea Maffei of Schiller's German version (1790) of Gozzi which Simoni handed through the window as Puccini's train was leaving. Puccini immediately responded to the project, although he kept in contact with other authors over versions of *Oliver Twist* and *Sly* (an episode at the start of *The Taming of the Shrew*). Gozzi wrote in 1762: 'I shall stage a fairy tale, one of those stories with which grandfathers and wet-nurses entertain the children on a winter's evening by the fireside, and the Venetians will applaud me more than Goldoni.' His Turandotte sets her riddles in the spirit of Enlightenment feminism, challenging her Venetian audiences with wit and intellect to consider the way they treat women; his comic characters are drawn directly from the *commedia dell'arte*. Gozzi was wrong about his Italian popularity but his fables delighted the young generation of German Romantics. Puccini wrote in March 1920 of his fascination with 'the amorous passion of Turandot that has for so long smouldered beneath the ashes of her great pride... it must be a Turandot by way of the modern mind'. The extraordinary richness of melody as well as the excitingly new orchestral sounds is evidence of a sound world developed with *Elektra*, *L'amore dei tre re* and *Francesca da Rimini* in his ears.

Eager as ever to create an authentic ambience for the opera, he researched Chinese music, and there are five authentic themes in the opera.

By the time of his death in 1924 the libretto had been completed, even if Puccini never ceased to complain about it, and the score itself was fully orchestrated up to the moment in Act III when Liù's funeral procession leaves the stage. Puccini left some twenty-three pages of sketches (some on both sides, amounting to thirty-six in total), and intended to finish the opera when recovering from his operation in the Brussels cancer clinic where he died. Toscanini suggested that his younger contemporary Franco Alfano should complete the score and Ricordi commissioned him to do this, using as much as he could of the sketches. Alfano, himself the composer of an oriental opera, *La leggenda di Sakùntala* (1921), accepted the thankless and controversial task in July 1925, and began work with Giuseppe Adami, one of the librettists. Apparently he did not have access to the full score. When he presented his version, which inevitably contained substantial sections of music which was purely his own, and a different orchestration from Puccini's, it was not well received by Ricordi.

Toscanini, who was to conduct the scheduled production of the opera in April/May 1926, now claimed that Puccini had played him the complete ending on the piano in October 1924, and that Alfano had not been faithful to what Toscanini remembered of the maestro's performance. His objections led to 109 bars being cut from Alfano's score (and consequently the libretto), and much rewriting of other passages. Alfano's second attempts at interpreting Puccini's sketches are sometimes preferable to the first but the cuts in his own music make little musical sense. Toscanini appears to have been adamant in reducing the amount of Alfano in the score. It is this shortened version which has become familiar. Curiously, however, piano-vocal scores had gone into preparation immediately Alfano's version was received, and these – giving the details of the first performers and performance (precisely, where it was *not* performed) – were published. At a London concert performance in 1982 the Alfano ending was restored in full and was heard, as far as was known, for the first time for well over half a century. There is an argument for a new completion to be made now, with all the material available at Ricordi, and a full understanding of Puccini's innovative and unique orchestration.

Act I. 'The walls of the Imperial City. The massive ramparts enclose almost the whole stage in a semicircle.' The crowd listens to a decree that the Princess Turandot will marry only the prince who solves her three riddles. Anyone who stands trial and fails will be executed. The people call for the death of Turandot's latest victim, the Prince of Persia, at moonrise. Timur, the dispossessed and exiled King of Tartary, is among the crowd. His son Calaf, who has also been forced into exile, recognises him after years of separation, and learns that Timur owes his life to a slave-girl, Liù, who accompanies him. They are all unknown in Peking.

The choruses 'Gira la cote' and 'Perchè tarda la luna?' depict the psychotic state of China, of Turandot herself, in music of extraordinary eeriness. As perfect contrast to this, the sound of the boys' chorus (the Chinese melody, Moo-Lee-Whah) accompanies the entrance of the executioner.

The crowd now calls upon Turandot to appear and grant mercy, and she makes her first appearance in silence. She gives the sign for death. Calaf is overwhelmed by what he has seen. Nothing his father or Liù can say will dissuade him from deciding to declare his challenge.

The Imperial functionaries, Ping, Pang and Pong, now break the tension of morbid poetics with a comically grotesque interruption. Their music is one of the authentic Chinese tunes which Puccini carefully researched in J.A. van Aalst's handbook (Shanghai, 1884).

Turandot's handmaidens call for silence (in an ambivalently erotic passage), but the phantoms of her previous suitors urge on the Prince. Nothing, neither the sight of the executioner returning with the head of the Prince of Persia, nor the entreaties of Liù, can dissuade him. Her aria, 'Signore ascolta', is exquisite, and the Prince's response taps a similar vein of tenderness; yet he does not return Liù's love, he simply bids her take his father away ('Non piangere Liù'). With three great beats of the stage gong he signals his challenge, and the start of another ritual trial. The purely musical construction of this act is astonishing, made up as it is of different inspirations and yet welded to one of Puccini's most shattering climaxes.

Act II, scene i. In 'a pavilion, like a vast tent', Ping, Pang and Pong discuss the preparations for what will either be a wedding or a funeral. They compare their recollections of all the princes who have died for Turandot, and grow nostalgic for the country retreats where they could retire if the decree did not hold them to their lugubrious duties. Some of the opera's most beautiful music is contained in their dreams, as the off-stage chorus repeats its bloodthirsty clamour.

Trumpets announce Calaf's trial, and a transformation to scene ii, 'the vast square of the royal palace'. The anthem which now sounds is one of three in a music box belonging to Baron Fassini, formerly in the Italian legation in Peking, where the authors met to discuss the very first draft scenario in 1920. 'Hardly had the manuscript been deposited on a little lacquered table when... the silence was broken by the clear sound

Turandot. *Eva Turner in the title role (Chicago, 1938).*

of a music box playing the ancient Imperial Hymn... In his hands the notes of that Hymn became the massive chorus.' Altoum in vain entreats the Unknown Prince to stand down; his music is almost exactly notated from an Imperial theme played at the opening and closing of ceremonies attended by the Manchu Emperors.

Turandot now sings for the first time, the famous aria 'In questa Reggia'. She recounts how her ances-

tor, the Princess Lo-u-Ling, was raped and murdered by a Tartar prince, and how she is intent upon avenging this memory. As she sings, she seems to weave a spell into which the chorus are hypnotically drawn, and she herself relives the humiliation of her forebear. It is a totally exposed passage demanding a voice of the utmost security. She warns Calaf that, although there are three riddles, death is one. Calaf responds that life is one. Their voices soar to high C, as though the singers dare each other to compete ('Gli enigmi sono tre, una la vita').

Turandot poses the first enigma: what rises at night, invoked by all the world, only to die at dawn reborn in the heart? Calaf rightly answers: hope. The second riddle is: what darts like a flame but is not a flame, that grows cold with death yet blazes with dreams of conquest? Turandot is furious when Calaf solves it with the answer: blood. Thirdly she demands what inflames you, white yet dark, that enslaves if it wants you free, but in taking you captive makes you king? Calaf, after hesitation, answers: Turandot.

The Emperor holds his daughter to her vow to accept the prince who solved her enigmas. Triumphantly Calaf now challenges her: if she can discover his identity before daybreak, he is prepared to die. The Emperor prays for his success, and the court rises to the sound of the Imperial anthem.

Act III. A pavilion in the palace gardens, at night. The Unknown Prince, a captive in the palace, hears the Imperial heralds searching the city for someone who can reveal his name: 'Nessun dorma questa notte in Pekino' (None shall sleep tonight in Peking). This mysterious sound world inspires him to one of Puccini's greatest arias, a reverie on love and death: 'Nessun dorma'. As he dreams of winning his love, the women's voices of the chorus sing 'And we shall have to die...'.

Brusquely interrupting, Ping, Pang and Pong offer him women, wealth or glory if he will leave the Princess alone. Their increasing frenzy comes to a head when he steadfastly refuses; they are threatening him with torture at the moment when guards bring in Timur and Liù. They summon Turandot, who watches as the slave-girl offers herself to protect the old man,

and yet refuses to yield under torture. Asked what gives her such strength, Liù replies that it is love. Turandot is moved for a moment and then orders her ministers to take the secret from her, to tear out her tongue. Liù appeals to the Princess to listen to her in the beautiful aria 'Tu che di gel sei cinta' (You, girded in ice... will love him!). She seizes a dagger and commits suicide. Timur curses the people who have brought about her death, and swears that she will be avenged.

This is the moment where Puccini's full score finishes, and it is here that Toscanini laid down his baton on the first night and said, 'The opera is ending here because at this point the Maestro died'.

Calaf now confronts Turandot, tears off her veil and kisses her. She is mortified, believing that she has lost ('Del primo pianto'); Calaf proclaims that this is only the beginning of their love. Turandot begs him to leave with his secret and Calaf replies that there is no mystery any more – he is Calaf, the son of Timur. Turandot is thrilled that he is now in her power.

The exterior of the imperial palace. Before the whole court Turandot declares that she knows the stranger's name, and that it is Love. Calaf impetuously climbs the stairs, and the two lovers are clasped in an embrace.

Turandot stands at the end of the great Italian lyric tradition and shows Puccini succeeding with a new type of opera, in which the sophisticated orchestration and complex psychology of the libretto were organically conceived. It is, unlike the operas of his contemporaries, full of melody. Yet the callous self-absorption of the protagonists, combined with the enigma of the incomplete score, must leave us wondering how a wholly positive apotheosis could have been achieved, and whether it could ever be satisfactory.   N.J.

HENRY PURCELL
(born 1658, died 21 November 1695)

DIDO AND AENEAS

Opera in a prologue and three acts, text by Nahum Tate. Première at Mr Josias Priest's Boarding School for Girls, Chelsea, London, 1689. Revived by the Royal College of Music under

Stanford at the Lyceum Theatre, London, 1895, for the bicentenary of Purcell's death; in New York, Hotel Plaza, 1923, and Town Hall (in a version by Bodanzky), 1924; Scala Theatre, London, 1929; Sadler's Wells, 1931, with Joan Cross; Florence Festival, 1940, with Gianna Pederzini, conducted by Vittorio

Gui; Rome, 1949, with Simionato. The 1951 Festival of Britain brought three productions to London: by the English Opera Group in Benjamin Britten's new realisation, with Nancy Evans/Joan Cross, Bruce Boyce/Peter Pears; at the Mermaid Theatre with Flagstad; and at Sadler's Wells. It has been widely performed in Europe, including productions with Irmgard Seefried at Schwetzingen, 1966, and with Teresa Berganza at Aix-en-Provence, 1960, and the Piccola Scala, Milan, 1963.

Dido, *or* Elissa, *Queen of Carthage* ....Soprano

Belinda, *a lady-in-waiting*..............................Soprano

Second Woman ....Mezzo-Soprano

Sorceress...Mezzo-Soprano

First Witch..Soprano

Second Witch ....Soprano

Spirit..Soprano (or Tenor)

Aeneas, *a Trojan prince* ....Tenor (or High Baritone)

A Sailor..Soprano (or Tenor)

Chorus of Courtiers, People, Witches, Sailors

Place: Carthage
Time: Following the Trojan War
Running Time: 1 hour

The prologue, which is included in the libretto, appears never to have been set by Purcell, or, at all events, to have been lost.

The overture has the traditional slow and quick sections, and is unmistakably tragic in feeling.

Act I. Dido is discovered surrounded by her court and attended by her lady-in-waiting, Belinda. Belinda's exhortation, 'Shake the cloud from off your brow', is echoed by the chorus, and is in sharp contrast to the grief-laden aria for Dido which follows, 'Ah, Belinda, I am prest with torment'. This magnificent expression of sorrow is worthy of the tragedy it foreshadows and at no point belies the conflict implied in its final words: 'Peace and I are strangers grown'. Belinda does not hesitate to diagnose that it is the presence of the 'Trojan guest' which is at the root of the Queen's unhappiness, and the chorus supports her implied suggestion, that a marriage between the two would solve Carthage's troubles. In the dialogue between Dido and Belinda which ensues, we have a taste of Purcell's extraordinary gift for compressing the most complex emotions into a few bars, and then relieving the tension and crystallising the situation in a set piece for chorus (in this case a *chaconne*), here introduced by a duet for Belinda and an Attendant. Again, her court attempts to encourage her – 'the hero loves as well as you' – and, after Aeneas'

entrance and Dido's cold reply to his opening sentence, all support his suit in music of surpassing freshness. The scene ends with a Triumphing Dance, and Dido's acceptance of Aeneas is celebrated by the whole court to bright, simple music.

This opening scene is short, but Purcell does not rely on understatement and implication so much as on an extraordinary clarity and economy of expression. He says more in a couple of long meaningful phrases than many a lesser composer in a whole aria, and his compression never gives the listener the feeling either that the music is overcharged or that the issues have been only partly stated.

The scene changes to a cave, where lives the Sorceress. She invokes her evil companions to join her in plotting the destruction of Dido and of Carthage. The whole scene, with its laughing choruses, its reference (in the strings) to the horn calls of the hunt now in progress, its echo chorus and its echo dance (phrase and echo are differently harmonised), amounts to an illustration of the insidious beauty which can attend the course of evil just as surely as that of good.

Act II. The Grove. Dido and Aeneas pause in the grove in the middle of the hunt. Belinda and later the Second Woman sing of the peculiar delights of the spot they have reached, of its attractions for the goddess Diana and of how it was the scene of Actaeon's death, torn to pieces by his own hounds. Meanwhile, the scene is one of activity, in the midst of all, Dido and her husband-to-be, Aeneas. The idyll comes to an end as Dido hears distant thunder, and Belinda, always ready to take a hint from her mistress, warns the company to repair as soon as it can to shelter: 'Haste, haste to town', she sings. All leave the stage, but Aeneas is stopped by the appearance of Mercury – in reality, the Sorceress's 'trusty elf' in disguise. He tells Aeneas that he brings Jove's command that the hero shall put off no longer the task which has been allotted him of founding the new Troy on Latin soil. Aeneas replies in a magnificent recitative – one of the highlights of the score. The decision is easily arrived at – it is the gods' command – but to reconcile himself to leaving Dido is something than which, he says, he 'with more ease could die'.

The published versions of the score make Act II end with this recitative, although the oldest version of the libretto has six further lines after the recitative (for the Sorceress and her Attendants) as well as a dance with which to end the act. When his realisation of the opera was produced during the Festival of Britain, 1951, Benjamin Britten wrote as follows: 'Anyone who has taken part in, or indeed heard a concert or stage performance, must have been struck by the very peculiar and most unsatisfactory end of this Act II as it stands; Aeneas sings his very beautiful recitative in A minor and disappears without any curtain music or chorus (such as occurs in all the other acts). The drama cries out for some strong dramatic music, and the whole key system of the opera (very carefully adhered to in each of the other scenes) demands a return to the key of the beginning of the act or its relative major (D minor or F major). What is more, the contemporary printed libretto (a copy of which is preserved in the library of the Royal College of Music) has perfectly clear indications for a scene with the Sorceress and her Enchantresses, consisting of six lines of verse, and a dance to end the act. It is my considered opinion that music was certainly composed to this scene and has been lost ... and so I have supplied other music of Purcell's to fit the six lines of the libretto, and a dance to end in the appropriate key.'

Act III. The scene is set in the harbour of Carthage, with the ships as background. All is in preparation for the Trojan fleet's departure, and the orchestra introduces the sailor's song: 'Come away, fellow sailors, come away'. The tune is briskly compelling, the words cynical, as the singer urges his companions to 'take a boozy short leave of your nymphs on the shore'. Suddenly, the Sorceress is there with her supernatural band, and the first and second Witches sing a lively duet, whose burden is 'Our plot has took, the Queen's forsook' and which ends with peals of highly organised demonic laughter. The Sorceress has a short solo in which she plans the destruction of Aeneas as well. There is a dance for the Witches and Sailors, and the stage clears as Dido and Belinda come down to the harbour to look for Aeneas.

Dido is full of foreboding before Aeneas even appears, and his first words confirm her worst fears. With 'Thus on the fatal banks of Nile weeps the deceitful crocodile' she taunts his attempt at explanation, and, when he announces his determination to defy the gods and stay, she will have none of a lover who once had a thought of leaving her. It is not until his departure that she admits 'Death must come when he is gone'. The chorus sums up the gravity of the situation and prepares the way for Dido's great farewell to life. The recitative is movingly simple, and the aria, 'When I am laid in earth', one of the greatest moments in all opera. Built up on a ground bass,[1] which is first heard as the introduction to the aria after the end of the recitative, this is a piece of controlled vocal writing that is unsurpassed. 'Remember me,' sings the Queen, 'but ah! forget my fate'; and the sense of deep tragedy is increased by the succeeding chorus, 'With drooping wings, ye cupids come, and scatter roses on her tomb'. It is the longest sustained number in the score, and in it Purcell shifts the emphasis of the tragedy from the particular to the universal at the same time as he provides a uniquely beautiful ending to his opera.

Purcell wrote much other music for the stage, but *Dido and Aeneas* must be accounted his only opera proper. *King Arthur* and *The Fairy Queen*, the former with words by Dryden, the latter founded on *A Midsummer Night's Dream*, are included by Dr Alfred Loewenberg in his monumental *Annals of Opera*; but though they contain magnificent music, this is more in the nature of incidental music to a play than of opera, although the masques in these and other works (such as *The Tempest*) offered Purcell a chance of writing in more extended forms. As a writer for the voice, Purcell was supreme, and his output includes a vast quantity of songs, many of them connected with the stage, and all of the greatest beauty. His great mastery is universally admitted, and many of the most gifted of twentieth-century English composers were glad to acknowledge their indebtedness to him not only for his inspiration and example but also for the practical lessons they learned from his music. It is opera's eternal loss that *Dido* should be the only true opera he left behind him; the feeling for dramatic expression, which it shows to have been his, only emphasises what was removed by his death at under forty years of age.   H.

---

[1] In each act there is an aria constructed on this principle: Dido's 'Ah, Belinda' in Act I, the Second Woman's 'Oft she visits' in Act II, and Dido's lament in Act III.

R

SERGEI VASILYEVICH RACHMANINOV

(born 20 March/1 April 1873, died 28 March 1943)

ALEKO

Opera in one act, libretto by Vladimir Ivanovich Nemirovich-Danchenko, based on Pushkin's poem *The Gipsies* (1824). Première, Bolshoi Theatre, Moscow, 27 April/9 May 1893. Chaliapin scored a great success in the title role at the St Petersburg première in 1897. First performed in the U.K. at the London Opera House on 15 July 1915.

Aleko	Baritone or Bass
Zemfira	Soprano
Young Gipsy	Tenor
Old Gipsy Man, *Zemfira's father*	Bass
Old Gipsy Woman	Mezzo-Soprano

Rachmaninov wrote *Aleko*, his first opera, in seventeen days for a competition organised by the Moscow Conservatory, as part of the exam for the diploma. He won a gold medal, the opera was published in a vocal score and his professional career was launched.

A gipsy encampment, evening. Gipsies sing of their free and happy life. The Old Gipsy remembers his youth; his wife Marioula left when another tribe of gipsies camped near them, abandoning their little daughter, Zemfira. Ever since then, he has hated all women, and yet never stopped loving them. Zemfira's husband Aleko, who has joined the gipsies in search of a simpler life, reacts violently to this story, amazed that the old man did not avenge himself. If it happened to him, he himself would not hesitate to kill both the wife and her lover. Zemfira and a Young Gipsy insist that love cannot be bridled. Zemfira tells her father that Aleko frightens her, but her heart longs for freedom. The Young Gipsy knows Aleko is jealous, but that does not frighten him. The Gipsies dance, first the women, then the men, before

everyone falls asleep. Zemfira and the Young Gipsy have fallen in love. They agree to meet when the moon has risen. Zemfira sings a cruel but fearless song about a young wife who dares her old husband to murder her, and makes it clear that her song is addressed to Aleko. When he is alone, Aleko reflects that he left civilisation behind to be free like the gipsies. He remembers how passionately his wife once loved him (cavatina, 'The camp sleeps').

After an intermezzo, the Young Gipsy sings a lovesong. Aleko reminds Zemfira that he gave up his old life to be with her. The young lovers laugh at him. Aleko kills his rival and then Zemfira. The Old Gipsy and the others remind Aleko that, though their people acknowledge no laws or constraints, vengeance and cruelty are alien to them: they do not want to live with a murderer and tell him to leave them. Aleko realises he is condemned to solitude and despair.

Nemirovich-Danchenko's libretto reduces Pushkin's work to a series of nearly incoherent fragments and so obscures its central theme: the sophisticated man of society acts in a more primitive fashion than the supposedly 'savage' gipsies that he has joined. Inevitably in a student work, *Aleko* is full of ghosts: Bizet's influence can be felt in the portrayal of Zemfira; *Cavalleria rusticana* inspired the central Intermezzo, while Rachmaninov's respect for Tchaikovsky colours the duets for the lovers and Aleko's final despair (too reminiscent of the last line of *Eugene Onegin*). The strict fugal form of the gipsies' final chorus demonstrates the composer's technical competence, rather at the expense of the drama. Yet, as Tchaikovsky's approval attests, Rachmaninov's own creativity surges through the opera: it is particularly marked in the distinguished scoring and in the work's melodies, which bring the hackneyed images of gipsy culture to life. Aleko's cavatina has been taken into the bass-baritone concert repertory, thanks partly to Chaliapin's early advocacy.   P.

FRANCESCA DA RIMINI

Opera in two scenes with Prologue and Epilogue, libretto by Modest Tchaikovsky, based on Dante's *Inferno*, canto v (1321). First performance at the Bolshoi Theatre, Moscow, 24 January 1906, conducted by the composer. First U.K. performance at the Chester Festival, 1973.

The Ghost of Virgil ....Baritone
Dante..Tenor
Lanceotto Malatesta....................................Baritone
Francesca ....Soprano
Paolo ....Tenor
Cardinal...Mute

Ghosts, Followers of the Cardinal and of Malatesta

Running Time: 1 hour 15 minutes

In 1893 Rachmaninov had tried unsuccessfully to collaborate with Modest Tchaikovsky on an opera based on the Undine legend. In 1898 he asked him for a libretto based on Shakespeare. Tchaikovsky responded by suggesting canto v of Dante's *Inferno*. Rachmaninov was slow to make anything of the idea, but he was stimulated to return to opera when, in July 1900, he and Chaliapin studied Rimsky-Korsakov's version of *Boris Godunov* together. He composed most of the love duet then, and took up the project again in spring 1904, completing it during the summer. He recognised that there were still structural problems with the libretto: normally he never allowed himself to repeat words (an interesting ambition for a composer), but in the love duet he felt he had no alternative.

Prologue. The First Circle of Hell. The orchestra portrays the groaning of the damned. The ghost of the poet Virgil hesitates, out of pity, he explains to Dante, rather than from fear. Virgil leads Dante to the edge of the abyss in the Second Circle, where those who yielded to lust are tormented by a howling whirlwind. The souls of the damned pass by. Dante questions two of them, as the wind dies down. Paolo and Francesca reply with the first of two quotations from Dante, 'Nothing is sadder than to remember happy times in the midst of grief'.

Scene i. Rimini, the palace of Lanceotto Malatesta. Lanceotto prepares to fight the Ghibellines, on the Pope's orders. Consumed with jealousy, he reflects on his unhappy marriage. He blames Francesca's father, who never told her that Paolo, Lanceotto's brother, was standing proxy for him at the church service. In ignorance of this fact, Francesca fell in love with the man she thought she was marrying. Lanceotto is, as he says, lame, ugly, sullen, while his brother Paolo is graceful, tall and handsome. Lanceotto determines to put his wife and his brother to the test. If she is faithful, he will banish Paolo. When she hears that her husband is going away, Francesca resolves to stay in a convent till he returns. There is no need, Lanceotto tells her, since he has appointed Paolo as her protector. He asks for a single word of affection: as his wife, she knows her duty is to submit, but he longs for her love. She remains silent, refusing to lie to him.

Scene ii. Paolo reads Francesca the story of Lancelot, the knight who fell in love with King Arthur's wife Guinevere. She stops Paolo from mentioning his own love for her, but he throws the book away and falls sobbing at her feet. She reminds him that they must never succumb to passion, that their love will be allowed in paradise. Paolo would forfeit all hope of heaven for a kiss. Eventually, she admits that they belong to one another; they swear fidelity and embrace. Lanceotto appears behind them with his dagger upraised. The lovers' heartrending sobs blend with the cries of the damned.

Epilogue. The Second Circle of Hell. The ghosts of Paolo and Francesca reappear, remembering how, in the text's second quotation from Dante, 'that day we read no more...'. They vanish and their grief is echoed by the chorus of souls of the damned, 'Nothing is sadder than to remember happy times in the midst of grief'.

There are obvious weaknesses in *Francesca da Rimini* but its best features warrant its occasional revival: the role of Malatesta is particularly strong, reflecting the fact that it was written for Chaliapin, the love duet is suffused with passion and Rachmaninov's writing for orchestra generates an aptly lurid power.   P.

JEAN-PHILIPPE RAMEAU

(born before 25 September 1683, died 12 September 1764)

Has any composer ever received such a consistently bad press as Rameau? He was fifty before his first opera *Hippolyte et Aricie* was performed, claiming that modesty inhibited him. He was until then known, if at all, for books on musical theory and collections of harpsichord music, a few cantatas and motets. While his operatic form owed much to precedent, Rameau was an innovator in terms of orchestration, the first in France to use horns and clarinets in opera, as well as to introduce textural devices such as *pizzicato* and *glissando*. His music left a masterful impression – little of such intensity had been heard in French opera. Ironically, he was soon seen as a conservative and suffered later in his career from opposition based on ignorance. Inevitably, some people heard *Hippolyte et Aricie* as a work more indebted to theory than practice. Voltaire called him 'in musical matters ... a pedant ... meticulous and tedious'. Others, however, recognised that a major new talent had appeared fully fledged. The composer Campra remarked that 'There is enough music in this opera to make ten of them; this man will eclipse us all.'[1]

In the twentieth century, some people, such as Debussy, have recognised Rameau's genius, others have repeated earlier canards. New factors exacerbating his neglect surely include the deleterious effects of 'authentic' staging. This approving review for a director (Jean-Louis Martinoty) should be read as condemnation: 'He has always been a dab hand with Baroque opera, creating sumptuous tableaux animated by fancy courtiers.' No wonder the critic concludes, 'But in the end it's all artifice, artifice that cannot surmount the dullness of Rameau's music – page after page of theory-ridden, strait-jacketed stuff.'[2] In such circumstances scenery tends to be sub-Watteau and Tiepolo, while acting is compromised by mannered choreography: Arthur Jacobs once pointed out, 'Those sideways-and-downwards gestures of the hands were assuredly modelled on some historical precedent; but *between* one such gesture and the next, today's singers are still liable to lapse into their customary all-purpose Manrico-meets-Carmen type of acting.'[3] Another fatally inhibiting factor is that French Baroque opera apparently 'lends itself to student performance; there are plenty of solo parts, fine choruses, modest orchestral demands'.[4] No wonder that Stanley Sadie could object (in 1965) that 'Rameau's language is too piecemeal ... [the] deeper emotional responses are never tapped'.[5] Rameau's music cries out for the best choreography, not some lifeless, well researched, historically apt but mortifying twiddling.   P.

HIPPOLYTE ET ARICIE

Tragédie en musique in a prologue and five acts, libretto by Abbé Simon Joseph Pellegrin, based on Euripides' *Hippolytos*, Seneca's *Phaedra* and Racine's *Phèdre* (1677). First performance, Académie Royale de la Musique, 1 October 1733, with Mlle Pellissier as Aricie, Tribou as Hippolyte, Marie Antier as Phèdre, Pierre de Jélyotte as Love and Chassé de Chinée as Thésée. After some forty performances it was dropped, revived in 1742, 1743, 1757 and 1767. Not given again until Geneva, 1903, Paris, 1908, and, in German, Basle, 1931. Birmingham University, in English, 1965, with Robert Tear, Angela Hinckley, Janet Baker and John Shirley-Quirk, conducted by Anthony Lewis. Revived Paris, 1996, conductor William Christie.

Aricie (Aricia), *Athenian princess*	Soprano
Diane (Diana), *goddess of chastity and hunting*	Soprano
Phèdre (Phaedra), *Thésée's wife, Hippolyte's stepmother*	Soprano
Oenone, *Phèdre's confidante*	Soprano
God of Love	Soprano
High Priestess of Diana	Soprano
Hippolyte (Hippolytus), *Thésée's son, in love with Aricie*	High Tenor (Haute-Contre)
Thésée (Theseus), *King of Athens*	Bass
Tisiphone, *a Fury*	Tenor (Taille)
Pluton (Pluto), *ruler of Hades*	Bass
Jupiter, *ruler of the gods*	Bass

---

[1] Quoted in Cuthbert Girdlestone, *Jean-Philippe Rameau, his Life and Work*, rev.ed. New York, 1969.
[2] Charles Pitt, *Opera*, November 1982.

[3] *Opera*, December 1981.
[4] Raymond Monelle, *Opera*, April 1994.
[5] *Opera*, August 1965.

The Fates ....High Tenor (Haute-Contre),
                                         Tenor (Taille), Bass

Nymphs, Forest-Dwellers, Priestesses of Diana,
    Infernal Deities, Shepherds and Shepherdesses,
    etc.

Place: The Forest of Erymanthus, Troezen, Hell,
    Aricie's Forest
Running Time: 2 hours 35 minutes

Prologue. Nymphs pay homage to Diana,
    goddess of chastity, in the first of the opera's
many pageant-like sequences of songs and dances
that celebrate divine or mortal power. Diana
promises those who worship her that they will enjoy
peace. When Love's music is heard she encourages
them to run away. Love insists that he wields power
everywhere, while Diana insists that her kingdom
should remain inviolate and appeals to Jupiter
(*Invocation,* 'Arbitre souverain').

Jupiter descends to give his judgement. He supports Diana's argument, but Destiny has ruled that
Love should exercise supreme power. On one day
each year, his power even reaches into the depths of
Diana's forests, as long as it is blessed by marriage.
Diana leaves to help Hippolyte and Aricie and to
avoid Love's celebrations of his triumph. There
follows a sequence of dances, gavottes, minuets and
a march, while the act ends with a reprise of the
overture's glorious, fanfare-like opening.

Act I. The temple of Diana. Aricie prepares to dedicate herself to serving the goddess. She is the last of
the children of Pallas to survive: Thésée killed her
fifty brothers when he usurped her father's kingdom
of Athens. She has fallen in love with Hippolyte,
Thésée's son, but since Thésée condemned her to
remain a virgin, she has decided to join the priesthood of Diana, the goddess whom Hippolyte serves.
When Aricie meets Hippolyte, he admits he loves
her. Together they appeal to the goddess for help.

The Priestesses of Diana celebrate the fact that
those within the sanctuary remain impervious to
Love. Thésée's wife Phèdre urges Aricie to enter the
sanctuary, but Aricie admits that her heart is
divided; she cannot go through with the ceremony.
Phèdre appeals to Hippolyte to execute his father
Thésée's wishes. When he refuses to force Aricie,
Phèdre threatens to destroy the temple and trumpets
speak for her vindictive power. In response, the
priestesses call on the gods to punish their enemies;

with much emphasis on 'Lancez', they appeal to the
gods to hurl lightning.

Jupiter's thunder is heard. Diana rebukes Phèdre,
promises to look after Aricie and points out that she
can be worshipped in forests, as well as in temples.
Hippolyte leads Aricie into the temple. Phèdre gives
way to fury, partly because Aricie is her rival for the
love of Hippolyte, her stepson.

Arcas, Thésée's confidant, reports that Thésée was
last seen going to the underworld to save his close
friend Pirithous. He is unlikely to return. Oenone
encourages Phèdre: Hippolyte is no longer an enemy
to love, while Phèdre has more to offer him than
Aricie does, namely the crown of Athens. Phèdre
swears that if Hippolyte will not yield, she will die.

Act II. The entrance to the underworld. Thésée
has come to save Pirithous, who was killed by
Cerberus when he attempted to abduct Pluto's wife,
Proserpine. He offers to die in his friend's place but
Tisiphone, one of the fates, implacably insists on
more victims (duet, 'Contente-toi d'une victime').

Pluto's court. Pluto warns Thésée that all he can
expect in Hell as reward for his glory on earth is
eternal torment. Thésée argues that he himself is
innocent: Pirithous may deserve to be punished, but
surely Thésée's loyal friendship is a virtue? Pluto
leaves the decision to his judges and meanwhile
readies all Hell's forces to execute his punishment
('Qu'à servir mon courroux').The three Fates tell
Thésée that Destiny has not yet decreed his death
('Du destin le vouloir suprême'). Thésée turns to the
god Neptune, who promised to come to his aid three
times. The first occasion was when Thésée was
allowed to cross the Styx into Hell. Thésée now begs
to be allowed to go back. Neptune sends Mercury to
plead with Pluto. The ruler of Hell yields, but asks the
Fates to tell Thésée his fate. They warn him that he
leaves the infernal empire only to find Hell at home
('Quelle soudaine horreur').

Act III. Thésée's palace on the sea. Phèdre begs the
goddess Venus, her ancestress, for mercy. When
Hippolyte comes in answer to her summons, she offers
him the throne, her son by Thésée and herself. He
swears fidelity to her as Queen but renounces his
rights of succession, since all that matters to him is his
love for Aricie. Phèdre threatens Aricie and Hippolyte
asks her why she hates her so much (duet, 'Ma fureur
va tout entreprendre'). Phèdre reveals that she consid-

ers Aricie her rival. Hippolyte is horrified. In despair, Phèdre seizes his sword and asks him to kill her. He refuses. At that moment Thésée returns, haunted by the Fates' prediction. Appalled by what he sees, he demands an explanation from Phèdre's confidante, Oenone. She hints that Hippolyte tried to rape Phèdre. The people of Troezen celebrate the return of Thésée who is forced to conceal his anguish. There follow a *Marche*, a chorus, songs for sailors and a series of rigaudons. Alone, for the third and last time, Thésée calls on Neptune to avenge him and punish his son ('Puissant maître des flots'). The sea's sudden disturbance assures him his plea has been heard.

Act IV. A wood sacred to Diana. Hippolyte has been banished; he prepares to go into exile ('Ah! faut-il, en un jour'). Aricie begs him to stay, defend and comfort her ('Dieux! pourquoi séparer deux cœurs'). Although he cannot name her, Hippolyte hints at Phèdre's guilty secret and begs Aricie to accompany him as his wife. The young lovers swear to be true to one another and invoke the aid of Diana (duet, 'Nous allons nous jurer une immortelle foi'). A group of hunters sing in praise of their sport, and a huntswoman invites Hippolyte and Aricie to join them in hunting. Her companions reinforce her argument with appropriate songs and festive minuets. Neptune sends a monster. Only Hippolyte dares to confront it: flames and clouds surround him and he disappears. Aricie faints. When Phèdre comes she is stricken with remorse and confesses her guilt. She promises the gods that she will reveal her crime and Hippolyte's innocence to Thésée.

Act V. Diana's sacred wood. Thésée has heard the truth from Phèdre, who has committed suicide. Now he too wants to die. Neptune stops him: the world needs his courage. Furthermore, Destiny has decided that Hippolyte should live, though in exile. Thésée's punishment will be that he can never see his son again.

Aricie's forest. Aricie recovers from her faint to the sound of soft music. Diana reveals that she has chosen a mortal hero to rule over her kingdom and orders zephyrs to restore Hippolyte to Aricie. The lovers rejoice (duet, 'Que mon sort est digne d'envie'). Diana presents Hippolyte to the shepherds and shepherdesses, and the opera ends with a series of gavottes.

It may only be retrospective knowledge that conditions our hearing, but the overture to *Hippolyte et Aricie* does sound splendidly appropriate: from the beginning, Rameau's first opera sets out to impress. Those increasingly bold intervals and that majestic pace are endowed with dazzling confidence and seem to announce something new, authoritative, masterful. The opera itself provides for much in the way of spectacular transformations and machinery – the *merveilleux* – with descents by Diana, Love, Jupiter, Mercury; a vision of Hell, a monster, as well as a religious ceremony, a civic festivity and an extended pastorale, complete with a flight of zephyrs who bear in a (tenor) hero. These vividly realised pantomimes are far from extraneous, however: from the beginning, this is a story of conflicting authorities, each of whom is entitled to his or her rites of honour, divertissements reinforcing their status.

All the characters' private identities and conflicts are seen in relief against these sharply etched public festivities. The first music we hear is a chorus of homage to Diana; her authority is subsequently disputed by Love – the central conflict of the opera – but he is overruled on appeal by Jupiter, who is then forced to yield to Destiny's supreme power. All this in the prologue, which sets the theme for the work as a whole. Where Lully (1632–87) celebrated the status quo in his operas, all of which were preceded by a prologue in praise of Louis XIV, Rameau has no certain answers but proceeds to establish who rules the world. Act I sees Diana's powers disputed by Phèdre, who is rebuked by Jupiter. Act II in Hades celebrates Pluto's power, but this has to negotiate with Destiny, with Neptune, Mercury and Jupiter. In Act III, Thésée has to curb his own impulses, while Act IV reinforces the debate between Neptune and Diana and Act V brings in Destiny as well as those two deities.   P.

LES INDES GALANTES
The Amorous Indies

Opéra-ballet in a prologue and two entrées, 'Le turc généreux' and 'Les incas du Pérou'; libretto for 'Le turc généreux' by Louis Fezelier, based on a true incident reported in the *Mercure de France*, January 1734. First performance, Académie Royale de la Musique, 23 August 1735. 'Les Fleurs, Fête Persane' added at third performance (revised at eighth). 'Les Sauvages' added 10 March 1736. 'Les Fleurs' revived Opéra Comique, 1925; entire work staged at Paris Opéra, 1952, Edinburgh, 1977.

Prologue

Hébé, *goddess of youth and pleasure*.................Soprano

Bellone, *god of war* ....Baritone

God of Love ....Soprano

First Entrée: 'Le Turc généreux'

Osman Pacha, *in love with Emilie*........................Bass

Emilie, *in love with Valère* ....Soprano

Valère, *in love with Emilie* ....Tenor

Second Entrée: 'Les Incas du Pérou'

Huascar, *high priest*..Bass

Phani, *Inca princess*.......................................Soprano

Don Carlos, *conquistador*....................................Tenor

Third Entrée: 'Les Fleurs, Fête Persane'

Tacmas, *a Persian prince* ....Tenor

Ali, *his favourite courtier*................................Baritone

Zaire, *one of Ali's slaves*.................................Soprano

Fatime, *one of Tacmas's slaves*.........................Soprano

Fourth Entrée: 'Les Sauvages'

Adario, *commander of the savages*...................Baritone

Damon, *French officer* ....Tenor

Don Alvar, *Spanish officer*.....................................Bass

Zima, *the savage chieftain's daughter* ....Soprano

Running Time: 2 hours 30 minutes

Rameau was as concerned with ballet as with opera, though posterity has tended to disregard the former even more than the latter. *Les indes galantes* is nevertheless an extraordinary achievement, whose dimensions now seem astonishingly varied and generous: ballet, opera, flower-fête, lesson in politics, and so on.

Prologue. Hébé's palace. Hébé commands her followers to sing, dance and enjoy love. *Entrée des Quatre Nations*: French, Spanish, Italian and Polish youths enter and dance 'gracefully'. Hébé urges them to enjoy themselves and sing without revealing love's mysteries. She calls for musettes, the bagpipes considered indispensable for pastoral scenes. Suddenly Bellone's drums summon them to war and glory, splendidly accompanied by trumpets ('La Gloire vous appelle'). This occasions more dances and a chorus for the women who stay and the men who leave. Outraged that her votaries abandon her, Hébé summons Love who rallies his troops with a rousing showpiece for soprano and two violins. The prologue ends with a duet for Love and Hébé and a chorus, with the inevitable, apt melismas on 'Volez' to suggest love's flight.

First Entrée: 'Le Turc généreux'. The gardens of Osman Pacha with a view of the sea. Emilie is courted by Osman but tries to discourage him by revealing that she was abducted by a pirate on the eve of her marriage to a devoted lover. She calls her enforced residency with Osman 'a second slavery'. He retires, warning her that she will never see her lover again. The sky darkens and the sea rises. When the sky clears, prisoners lament that they have been saved only to become slaves. Emilie recognises one of them as the lover she lost, Valère. Rameau makes surprisingly little of this encounter. Osman overhears them and warns that he will exact punishment.

Suddenly, he gives them both their freedom, explaining that he himself was once Valère's slave and was freed by him. Valère's ships are filled with presents from the Pacha, loaded by his African slaves. The rest of the entrée celebrates the lovers' departure. They appeal to the breezes to lead their ships home again in a beautiful duet, taken up by the chorus ('Volez, Zéphyrs, tendres amants de Flore'). Dances follow for the African slaves, as well as rigaudons, tambourins, solos and choruses appealing for storm winds to disappear. The finale moves with an increasingly exhilarating pace, as Rameau responds emphatically to the text's series of injunctions, 'Volez, Hatez, Régnez, Fuyez, Partez, Embarquez, Voguez, Bravez'.

Second Entrée: 'Les Incas du Pérou'. A desert with a volcano. The Inca princess Phani has fallen in love with her people's enemy, the Spanish officer Carlos. He begins to doubt the sincerity of her conversion to Christianity. She warns him to beware of the violence of the Incas, who are about to celebrate the Festival of the Sun. Alone, she longs to be united with her conqueror ('Viens, hymen'). The Inca high priest Huascar (one of Rameau's most interesting characters) suspects that he has a rival in his love for Phani. He tells her that the sun has chosen a husband for her. When she shivers, he reminds her that heaven's dictates must be obeyed, in a characterful, forceful air ('Obéissons sans balancer'). He accuses her of loving one of the Incas' enemies.

The festival begins. Huascar's solemn invocation is followed by the Incas' act of adoration and ceremonial dances, evoked in music of considerable gravity: there is nothing frivolous or merely exotic about it. Gavottes follow until an earthquake occurs and the volcano erupts. Huascar exploits the occasion to announce that heaven wants Phani to submit to marriage. She appeals to heaven for help. Carlos intervenes to reveal that the earthquake does not signal the sun's displeasure: his men have arrested Huascar's accomplices, who threw a rock into the volcano to stimulate an eruption. Huascar wanted to terrify Phani so she would yield to him. The lovers are united in the face of Huascar's fury, in a tremendous ensemble, still occasionally shaken by the after-effects of the shock ('Pour jamais, l'amour nous engage'). Huascar sees the volcano erupt again, and incites it to destroy him for his treachery to his religion ('Abîmes embrasés'). Flaming rocks crush him to death.

Third Entrée: 'Les Fleurs, Fête persane'. Gardens of Ali's palace. Prince Tacmas has disguised himself as a woman of the seraglio in order to test Zaire's sincerity – she is a slave in the household of his favourite courtier Ali. Ali is relieved to hear that Tacmas cares nothing for Fatime, since Ali himself has fallen in love with her. Zaire appears, lamenting her sad treatment at the hands of Love ('Amour, Amour, quand du destin'). Tacmas tries to find out the name of his rival. He shows Zaire his own portrait but misinterprets her shocked reaction as distaste. When Fatime appears, disguised as a male, Polish slave, Tacmas assumes this is his rival. Fatime explains that she is also in love and in need of help. Fooled by her disguise, Tacmas assumes this 'man's' problem is that Zaire loves Ali. Tacmas is about to stab his rival, when Fatime reveals her real identity. Zaire explains that Tacmas misunderstood her reaction to his portrait. He proposes marriage to Zaire and unites Ali with Fatime. They all swear that their love will bind them together forever, in a suddenly transcendental quartet whose music imitates the 'chains' that link them ('Tendre amour, que pour nous ta chaîne dure à jamais'). The Festival of Flowers follows, an elaborate, extended divertissement, complete with dances and songs. 'Action' is limited to floral display (dangerous temptation to a designer), such as 'Delightful odalisques of various nations of Asia wear the most lovely flowers in their headdresses and on their clothes.' In terms of its

music, however, it represents the meat in the entrée. There is an appealing, aptly crepuscular chorus inviting night to fall; a splendid air for Tacmas, accompanied only by continuo ('L'eclat des roses'), as well as more for both Zaire and Fatime, whose inventive air asking a butterfly to stay in one place is the last vocal number in the entrée ('Papillon inconstant'). It ends with the *Ballet des Fleurs*, whose richly varied and expressive dances purport to represent the fate of flowers in a garden. A rose is exposed to the fierce North Wind, Borée, but rescued by a loving breeze, Zéphyr.

Fourth Entrée: 'Les Sauvages'. 'A grove in a forest of America, bordering the French and Spanish colonies, where the ceremony of the Great Pipe of Peace is to be celebrated.' Adario is about to sign a peace treaty between his nation, the French and the Spanish, but worries that the leaders of both colonies may have designs on his beloved, Zima. Damon, the French officer, lives up to his nation's reputation and justifies inconstancy in love to Don Alvar, the Spanish officer. Rameau lavishes the most enchanting music of the whole opera on Zima herself. The orchestra weaves elaborate garlands to support her exquisitely simple vocal line ('Nous suivons sur nos bords l'innocente nature'). Each of the men assumes she means to bless his suit and, further, that nature backs him up on the subject of inconstancy. Zima explains that their custom is to allow emotions to wander freely until marriage ('Le cœur change à son gré'). Alvar attacks the habits of the French, who are never less faithful than when married. In exchange, Damon singles out those suspicious husbands who live along the Tagus and keep their wives in chains. Zima tells the Spaniard he loves too much, and the Frenchman, not enough.

Adario comes to receive Zima's tribute. She celebrates their ideal moderation ('Sur nos bords l'amour vole'). This is the air that inspired Cuthbert Girdlestone to unwonted enthusiasm: 'For sheer beauty and power to move, the palm must go to Zima's second air ... Here ... is distilled the essential Rameau: his grace, his limitless poignancy, his nostalgia, his power to bring the infinite within a simple eight-bar phrase ...'[1] The two savages swear fidelity to each other in a touching, intimate duet. A ballet follows, celebrating the new reign of peace and love. The

---

[1] *Jean-Philippe Rameau*, 1969.

most remarkable sequence is the *Danse du Grand Calumet de la Paix*, in which Rameau reworks one of his harpsichord pieces, the deceptively simple 'Les Sauvages', from the *Nouvelles pièces* of 1730, as an orchestral passage, a duet and a chorus in praise of pastoral bliss. This was inspired by seeing some Native Americans dancing in Paris in 1725. It has a rhythmic pattern as hypnotically addictive as Ravel's *Boléro* and just as suited to inventive choreography; the whole sequence lasts only four and a half minutes. There is a splendid, festive, trumpet-graced air for Zima ('Régnez, plaisirs et jeux') and a *chaconne* of unexpectedly grand dimensions to crown this spectacular *opéra-ballet*.   P.

CASTOR ET POLLUX

Tragédie in a prologue and five acts, libretto by Pierre-Joseph Bernard. First performance, Académie Royale de la Musique, Paris, 24 October 1737, with Tribou as Castor, Chassé de Chinais as Pollux, Mlle Pellissier as Télaire. Revised 1750. Revived Montpellier, 1908; Frankfurt, 1980, with Elizabeth Gale and Philip Langridge, conductor Harnoncourt. 1750 revision, English Bach Festival, Covent Garden, 1981, with Peter Jeffes, Ian Caddy and Jennifer Smith, conductor Farncombe.

Vénus (Venus), *goddess of love*.........................Soprano
Mars, *god of war*...Baritone
Minerve (Minerva), *divinity of arts*
    and pleasures..Soprano
God of Love...................................Soprano (or Tenor)
Castor, *son of Tyndarus and Leda,*
    Pollux's twin ....Tenor (Haute-Contre)
Pollux, *son of Jupiter and Leda* ....Bass
Télaire, *daughter of the Sun*.............................Soprano
Phébé, *Princess of Sparta* ....Soprano
Jupiter ....Bass
The High Priest of Jupiter ....Tenor
A Happy Spirit ....Soprano
A Planet...Soprano
A Follower of Hébé ....Soprano
A Pleasure ....Soprano
Two Athletes....................................Tenor, Baritone

Arts and Pleasures, Spartans, Athletes, Priests,
    Shades, Hébé's Followers, etc.

Place: Sparta; Hades; The Elysian Fields
Running Time: 2 hours 45 minutes

Rameau's third opera had to wait eighteen years after its première to be properly appreciated. One of its most successful features, its integration of dance-spectacle and drama, probably impedes its wider acceptance even today, since it calls for resources that are rarely available and, even more, presupposes the will to link the arts together. The divertissements play a very interesting role, since they punctuate the action with extended moments of contemplation, reflection on what matters in life. It might be possible even to integrate the prologue into this sequence, though it was conceived as a *pièce d'occasion* to celebrate the Peace of Vienna in 1736 concluding the War of the Polish Succession.

Prologue. The stage represents the destruction wrought by war on the Arts and Pleasures. In chorus, supported by their tutelary deity Minerva and by Love, they implore Venus to subdue Mars, the god of war. When he appears, bound, at Venus's feet, his surrender is celebrated with gavottes, minuets and tambourins.

Act I. A monument erected for the funeral of Castor, King of the Spartans. Castor was murdered by Lincée, leaving his beloved Télaire, Princess of Sparta, inconsolable. Princess Phébé promises her that Castor's brother, Pollux, who is immortal because he is Jupiter's son, will avenge Castor's murder. Télaire herself renounces the light, and repudiates her father the sun in a magnificent air accompanied by bassoons, that Berlioz called 'one of the sublimest conceptions of dramatic music'[1] ('Tristes apprêts'). A *Symphonie Guerrière* follows, as Pollux brings the corpse of Lincée. When Pollux reveals that he adores Télaire, she asks him to persuade Jupiter to restore Castor to life.

Act II. The temple of Jupiter. Pollux is torn between nature and love, between his fraternal feelings and his love for Télaire ('Nature, Amour, qui partagez mon cœur'). 'Debussy found this air so personal and so modern that he felt one should be able to go up to Rameau after the performance and congratulate him on it.'[2] Pollux decides to help Télaire recover Castor. The High Priest, in a splendid, awesome air, warns that Jupiter will descend and appear in terrifying glory ('Le souverain des Dieux'). Moved by Pollux's pleas, the god decrees that Castor can return to life, but only if Pollux takes his place in Hades. Jupiter then presents

---

[1] *Revue et Gazette musicale*, 1842.

[2] *Gil Blas*, 2 February 1903, quoted in Girdlestone, *op. cit.*

a series of divertissements to remind Pollux of the delights that he will forgo in Hades. Hébé enters with her attendants and they celebrate pleasure and love in an unexpectedly touching chorus and two airs, all of which breathe a seriousness associated with religion. Pollux remains adamant.

Act III. Outside the entrance to Hades. Phébé, who loves Pollux, appeals to the monsters, ghosts and demons that guard the entrance to keep him away, but fails to dissuade him from entering. Télaire responds to her plea by recounting her dream in which new gods appeared, a thunderbolt struck the earth and blood was shed – a remarkably accurate prophecy. Phébé realizes that Pollux loves Télaire. In an intensely vivid, concerted passage the three lovers contemplate their unhappiness or joy. Pollux fights the monsters and demons barring his way (to some impressively busy music) and, with help from Mercury, enters Hades. Phébé, in despair, contemplates joining him there.

Act IV. In the Elysian Fields. Castor is unable to enjoy the peace of eternity, since he cannot forget the love he has lost ('Séjour de l'éternelle paix'). He refuses to be comforted by the Happy Shades, who also stage dances to entertain him. One of the shades celebrates the eternal dawn of the Elysian Fields, where love brings only happiness. Pollux comes to take Castor's place, but when he learns what his brother has sacrificed for him, Castor resolves to return to earth for one day only, in order to bid farewell to Télaire. He will then come back to Hades, so as to allow Pollux to enjoy life and love on earth. Mercury transports Castor, while the Happy Shades appeal to both brothers to live with them.

Act V. Outside Sparta. When Phébé learns that Castor is alive again, she at first determines to avenge what she presumes is an insult to Pollux, but then resolves to commit suicide, so as to join her beloved in Hades. Télaire is devastated that as soon as Castor has come back to her, he must leave again forever. Télaire accuses Castor of having never loved her, and the gods of cruelty and indifference to love. Peals of thunder are heard. Télaire faints; Jupiter descends, releases Castor from his vow and promises him immortality. Pollux joins them, bringing news that Phébé has committed suicide. Jupiter orders that his celestial empire become visible and then stages a final divertissement, 'la fête de l'univers'. The genies, stars and planets watch as Télaire becomes a goddess and the twins join the

Zodiac. A Planet welcomes these new stars, the Dioscurides or Gemini, who will also guide mortals at sea ('Brillez, brillez Astres nouveaux'). The work ends with a *chaconne* and chorus celebrating the fête ordained by the master of the universe.

Apart from a brief over-indulgence in nobility, as the brothers compete to behave well, *Castor et Pollux* keeps up a pace and intensity that never falter. As in *Hippolyte et Aricie*, the scorned woman tends to steal the show, but *Castor et Pollux* keeps Phébé firmly in her place. There is real strength to the relation between the brothers: the prevailing stoicism probably reflects the opera's setting in Sparta. Rameau's score is particularly rich in incidental music for dances and for minor characters: one of the most brilliant numbers occurs right at the end, as a Planet welcomes the new stars into the skies with appropriately festive, glittering figuration. P.

DARDANUS

Tragédie lyrique in a prologue and five acts, libretto by Charles-Antoine Le Clerc de La Bruère. First performed Académie Royale de la Musique, Paris, 19 November 1739, with Jélyotte as Dardanus, Mlle Pellissier as Iphise, Le Page as Teucer and Isménor and Mlle Fel as the Phrygian Woman. Altered ten days later, revised drastically in 1744 with help from Pellegrin. Revived 1908 by Vincent d'Indy in Paris and in Dijon, Rameau's home town. The Paris Opéra combined elements from both versions in 1983.

Vénus (Venus), *goddess of love*........................Soprano
God of Love ....Soprano
Iphise, *Teucer's daughter*.................................Soprano
Dardanus, *Jupiter's son* ....Tenor
Anténor, *Teucer's ally*.....................................Baritone
Teucer, *King of Phrygia*..................................Baritone
Isménor, *magician* ....Bass
A Phrygian Woman ....Soprano
Dreams.............Soprano, Tenor (Haute-Contre), Bass
Followers of Vénus and Love, Sports and
 Pleasures, etc.

Place: Phrygia
Running Time: 2 hours

Objections to the central role played by the super-natural in Rameau's fifth opera convinced the composer to revise it for the revival in 1744. In so doing, however, while he strengthened the plot, he also cut out such major parts as the dream sequences, the scenes involving the monster and Iphise's second monologue.

Prologue. Love's palace on Venus's island of Cythaera. Venus asks the Pleasures to reign, and to keep Jealousy under strict control. But the Pleasures' dance around Love's throne slows down and soon (in 24 bars) they fall asleep. Irritated, Venus commands Jealousy to wake them. Human beings 'of all conditions and ages' pay homage to Love in a merry 'Marche pour les différentes Nations'.

Act I. A place filled with funerary monuments. Iphise, Princess of Phrygia, has fallen in love with her father's enemy, Dardanus, son of Jupiter. She appeals to Love to relinquish his hold on her heart, and to those whom Dardanus has killed to make her hear the voice of reason ('Cesse, cruel amour, de régner sur mon ame'). Her father tells her that he has promised to give her in marriage to Anténor, who will lead his army against Dardanus. Teucer and Anténor swear on the tombs to destroy Phrygia's enemies, while a celebratory chorus, an *Entrée Majestueuse pour les Guerriers*, a further ensemble appealing to the gods of war and several rigaudons enhance the solemnity of the occasion. The act ends, as it began, with Iphise contemplating her secret distress. She resolves to consult the magician Isménor.

Act II. A wilderness. Isménor boasts that his arts make him the equal of the gods. Dardanus comes to consult him and to see Iphise, whom he loves secretly. Isménor's chorus of infernal spirits perform their magical rites and Isménor commands the sun to disappear in an impressive passage ('Suspends ta brillante carrière'). A solemn 'Air Grave' is followed by an exhilarating 'Air Vif'. Isménor confirms that as long as Dardanus holds on to a talisman he can appear as Isménor himself. The spirits warn him to obey. First Anténor comes to consult the magician: Iphise seems indifferent to him; does he have a rival? He does not receive an answer. Then Iphise herself appears, and confesses to 'Isménor' that she loves Dardanus ('Par l'effort de votre art terrible'). Dardanus-as-Isménor assures her that her love is returned and then reveals his own identity. She is appalled and runs away, leaving him heartened but vulnerable: he is taken prisoner.

Act III. A gallery inside Teucer's palace. Iphise is torn between guilt at loving Dardanus and fear that he will die at the Phrygians' hands. She delays her marriage to Anténor, on the grounds that the times are too disturbed. Anténor accuses her of loving the enemy and insists that he will marry her immediately, if only to enjoy her unhappiness. His is a memorably dark, intense air ('Le désespoir et la rage cruelle'). All celebrate their triumph with a divertissement, rigaudons, minuets and tambourins, till King Teucer reveals that Neptune has sent a dragon to lay waste the kingdom because the Phrygians dared put Jupiter's son Dardanus in chains. Anténor resolves to fight the monster. A warlike Sinfonia follows.

Act IV. A prison, where Dardanus despairs in a tremendous, bleak air, whose extended introduction with prominent horns and bassoons foretells *Fidelio* ('Lieux funestes'). Isménor appears and suggests that since the god of love is really to blame, Dardanus should ask him to appease the Furies. Dardanus' appeal ('Amour, Amour, quand tu veux nous surprendre') is answered when Venus descends in her chariot, and commands Dreams to soothe him as he sleeps – in a delectable lullaby, a trio and chorus promising him a future rich in glory and love. The idyll is briefly interrupted – in other words, the divertissement is enriched by contrasting spectacle and incidents – when Dardanus dreams that a monster emerges from the sea, to some moderately disturbed music. Dardanus awakes. Anténor arrives, longing for death to end his sufferings. After a storm, Anténor is attacked by the monster. Dardanus intervenes to save his rival's life, but refuses to say who he is. Anténor hands his saviour his sword as a pledge, promising that he can ask anything of him. Dardanus immediately asks Anténor to allow Iphise 'the freedom to refuse your hand'. Anténor refuses, he would rather lose his life. Dardanus reminds him that his oath has more power than love itself. (In the 1744 version Iphise enters Dardanus's cell and they sing a moving duet, 'Frappez! frappez!' Anténor dies after confessing his treachery. Dardanus escapes and takes Teucer prisoner, after which the King eventually allows Dardanus and Iphise to marry. Venus descends for the wedding.)

Act V. King Teucer's palace. Phrygians welcome Anténor back, assuming that he has saved them from the dragon. Furthermore, Neptune relents, as long as Iphise marries the man who subdued the monster. Dardanus appears, to general astonishment, and asks Anténor to kill him: if he cannot live with Iphise, he will die before her. He hands Anténor back his own sword. This forces Anténor to acknowledge Dardanus as Phrygia's saviour. He also accepts that this is the man the gods have destined for Iphise. Iphise and Dardanus describe Pleasure's impact on the world (duet, 'Un jour plus dur embellit l'univers'), and Venus herself descends, accompanied by Hymen and Love. She calls on the Pleasures to celebrate Love's triumph, and the opera ends as everyone joins in praising Venus.

Dardanus is a great opera, certainly one of Rameau's best; it would hold its own in a conventional opera company's repertory. It is not just the richness of characters, or the variety of the action, the amazing orchestral invention of the centrally placed introduction to Act III, or the great choral and solo numbers (Teucer and Anténor's oath; the magic ceremonies) that deserve to be highlighted. It is the way the varying course of the drama dictates the musical form: repeatedly, free-flowing recitative flares up into 'aria', into a more elaborate musical expression, as the temperature momentarily rises. This occurs when, for example, Iphise faces up to the irrational strength of her feelings and longs to be ruled by reason again, 'Arrachez de mon cœur'; or, in Act IV, when Anténor claims that destiny has no impact on a heart given up to love and flutes briefly lend their support to the still declamatory vocal line. Such variations in the pace and texture of the vocal line look forward to Janáček. They are not so good in excerpt: what is needed is the long stretch, the paragraph or page, rather than the sentence.   P.

PLATÉE

Plataea

Ballet Bouffon in a prologue and three acts, libretto by Andrien-Joseph Le Valois d'Orville, based on Jacques Autreau's ballet *Platée ou Junon Jalouse*. First performed Versailles, 31 March 1745, with Pierre Jelyotte as Platée, Marie Fel as Folie, Le Page as Cithéron, De Chassé as Jupiter, Berard as Mercure. Commissioned to celebrate the Dauphin's wedding, it was given only one performance; revived 1749 and 1759, Paris Opéra. Revived in German, Munich, 1901; Monte Carlo, 1917; in concert (in a new edition by Graham Sadler) by the English Bach Festival, 1983.

Prologue

Thespis, *inventor of comedy*	Tenor
A Satyr	Baritone
Two Grape-Pickers	Sopranos
Thalie (Thalia), *muse of history*	Soprano
Momus, *god of mockery*	Bass
Love	Soprano

Satyrs, Maenads, Grape-Pickers

Platée, *nymph in the marsh below Mount Cithaeron*	Tenor
Cithéron, *King of Greece*	Bass
Jupiter, *King of the gods*	Bass
Junon (Juno), *his wife*	Soprano
Mercure (Mercury), *messenger of the gods*	Tenor (Haute-Contre)
Iris, *goddess of the rainbow*	Soprano
Momus, *god of mockery*	Tenor
God of Folly	Soprano
Clarine, *follower of Platée*	Soprano
A Naiad, *follower of Platée*	Soprano

Naiads, Aquilons, Sad and Serious Followers of Folly, Momus's Followers etc.

Place: A Vineyard in Greece; a Marsh at the Foot of Mount Cithaeron
Running Time: 2 hours 20 minutes

The overture announces the theme of the opera, incongruity, as a grandly consequential opening is followed by an inconsequential, strange figure harping repeatedly on one note, like bitter laughter. The plot hinges on the fact that Platée is so ugly that Jupiter's wife Juno is cured of jealousy when she finds that her husband is supposedly erring with *her*. Before we can work out how offensive that is to single, physically challenged marsh nymphs, we should remember that the role is meant to be sung by a man. This highlights the role's ludicrous side without damaging its sympathetic aspects: how could *he* imagine he would attract the ruler of the gods? Platée emerges as an endearingly, rather than merely repellently, vain creature, but Rameau ends the work on a decidedly acrid note, stressing the humiliation of Platée.

Prologue. 'The Birth of Comedy'. A vineyard in Greece. As Thespis lies in a drunken stupor, a Satyr pays tribute to Bacchus, the god of wine. Thespis wakes to sing in praise of Bacchus, and emphasises how wine licenses mockery: he questions the Maenads' faithfulness, suggests that the Satyrs are cuckolded and that everyone knows the Maenads' secrets ('Charmant Bacchus'). Naturally, everyone invites him to go back to sleep. Thalia has come with Momus to present a spectacle that will correct the faults of mortal men and, as Momus adds, of the gods. After all, Jupiter himself once used a comic trick to cure his wife of jealousy and pride. Thespis invites the spectators to become actors and they agree in a surprisingly serious ensemble which serves to warn us there is nothing trivial in this enterprise. The prologue ends with lively songs and dances in honour of Bacchus, Momus and Love.

Act I. A country scene with a stormy sky, evoked by some splendidly blustery music. Cithéron begs the gods to end the elements' war on earth; Mercury descends and explains that the bad weather has been caused by Juno, who is tormented by jealousy. Mercury has come to find some amusement to distract Jupiter. He likes Cithéron's suggestion that Jupiter pretend to want to marry someone else, particularly since the 'beloved' is so ugly there is no danger. He explains that Platée is a nymph with no idea how hideous she is. Mercury goes to tell Jupiter of the scheme, as Platée herself emerges, determined to 'lose her liberty', i.e. find a husband ('Que ce séjour est agréable!'). She assumes Cithéron must be attracted to her, since he avoids her, as a shy lover would. Seeing him coming, she appeals to the marsh's inhabitants to celebrate the moment: frogs and cuckoos join in with their vocal contribution. She encourages the hesitant Cithéron, but gradually realises that he does not love her. She weeps, asking him why ('Pourquoi?'), echoed by the animal chorus in a frog-like croak ('Quoi? Quoi?').

Mercury descends and presents Jupiter's suit. She can hardly believe her luck. Lightning proclaims Juno's fury with her husband, but, undaunted, Platée again calls on the marsh nymphs to celebrate the occasion. Clarine, Platée's confidante, and a Nymph tell the sun that the 'damp Naiads' reject him, in a duet more memorable for its music than its words ('Soleil, tu luis en vain'). The act ends with a spectacular display of orchestral fury, as a band of Aquilons (north winds) make a 'very lively entrée' and force the nymphs to retire.

Act II. Mercury has pacified Juno, who is now planning to catch Jupiter with his new love. Jupiter appears, rebukes the Aquilons and looks forward to seeing the beautiful nymph he has been promised. He first appears to Platée as a donkey. Assuming this is a test, she advances on it unabashed, indeed amorously. Jupiter brays in response and then turns into an owl. Platée praises its plumage, but the other birds turn on it and it flies away. Jupiter then appears in his own shape and calls on Momus to celebrate his new conquest. She is alternately annoyed and delighted as Momus's followers salute her funny looks and her beauty.

An 'extraordinary symphony' is heard, heralding the arrival of Folly with Apollo's lyre, on which she accompanies dances for her own and Momus's followers. She celebrates the power of love to transform, as it did Daphne for Apollo, in a brilliant, comic air ('Aux langueurs d'Apollon Daphné se refusa'). She asks Hymen to prepare a new marriage for Jupiter and crown his 'new Juno'. Platée is delighted at these words and, as everyone joins in the dancing, they take up her ecstatic, ludicrous cries of 'Hé, bon, bon, bon'.

Act III. Juno gives in to her jealous fury at her husband. Mercury persuades her to hide and see for herself how Jupiter really loves her. A troupe of Dryads, Satyrs, and Nymphs, followers of Platée, arrive to celebrate love's triumph. Platée herself enters in a chariot drawn by frogs, ready to receive either Love or Hymen, the god of marriage. When Jupiter asks where these gods are, Mercury explains that they rarely appear together. Instead, Momus, the god of mockery, appears, bearing a 'ridiculously big' bow and arrow. Momus has come in place of Love (busy elsewhere), but all he can offer is tears, pains, cries and flattering hope (all of which are represented in the music). Three of Momus's followers appear as the Graces and dance comically, accompanied by Folly strumming her lyre. Cithéron appears with some country people to suitably rustic music to celebrate Platée's conquest. At Folly's behest everyone sings in praise of Platée. Jupiter takes her by the hand and pretends to initiate the marriage ceremony. He reassures her that Juno's anger is impotent but, just as he is about to swear the oath, his wife intervenes. When she tears off Platée's veil and sees how ugly she is, the goddess is confused but instantly reassured that Jupiter still loves only her. Together, the gods reaffirm their marital bond. They rise up to heaven while Platée is mocked by the country people, who repeat the chorus sung previously in her honour. Shaking with rage, she threatens to make her waters overflow and blames Cithéron before jumping back into her marsh. Everyone else celebrates Jupiter's reconciliation with Juno.

Platée functions as a satire on contemporary conventions for operatic and ballet performance. The very notion of the divertissement, the celebration of someone's authority in a sequence of songs and dances, is repeatedly turned on its head. Many of these incidental subtleties are lost to us, as the original conventions are not familiar. Rameau also wrongfoots us with games on stresses (huge intervals on the last, neutral syllable of a word such as 'timide'), unsuitable melodic lines and ridiculous melismas, more common in Italian opera (on the vowel 'ou', for example, in Folly's Act II air).   P.

ZOROASTRE

Zarathustra

Tragédie lyrique in five acts, libretto by Louis de Cahusac. First performance Académie Royale de Musique, Paris, 5 December 1749, with Jélyotte as Zoroastre and Mlle Fel as Amélite; revised version (three acts largely rewritten) 20 January 1756, revived by Schola Cantorum, Paris, 1908, and Opéra-Comique, Paris, 1964. First U.K. performance (1756 version), Queen Elizabeth Hall, London, 1979. First U.S performance (1756 version), Sanders Theatre, Harvard University, 1983.

Zoroastre, *founder of the Magi* ....Haute-Contre

Abramane, *high priest of Arimane*........................Bass

Amélite, *heiress to the throne of Bactria* ....Soprano

Erinice, *a Bactrian princess* ....Soprano

Zélize[1], *a Bactrian woman at
    Amélite's court* ....Soprano

Zopire, Narbanor[2], *priests of Arimane*...............Basses

Oromasès[2], *King of the Genies* ....Bass

Céphie, *a Bactrian woman at
    Amélite's court* ....Soprano

Abénis[1], *an Indian savage* ....Haute-Contre

Cénide[1], *an Indian savage*..............................Soprano

Orosmade, *a voice from a cloud of fire*......Haute-Contre

A Salamander[1] ....Baritone

A Sylphide[1] ....Soprano

Vengeance ....Bass

Arimane, *a subterranean voice* ....Bass

Three Furies[1] ....Soprano, Hautes-Contres

Five Furies[2].......................Sopranos, Hautes-Contres

Bactrian People, Indians, Magi, Elemental Beings, Priests of the False God, Demons, etc.

Place: Bactria
Time: Sixth Century B.C.
Running Time: 3 hours 5 minutes

The extraordinarily graphic overture lays out the stark polarity in the opera between evil and good: the cruelty of Abramane and the suffering of the Bactrian people, Zoroastre's beneficence and the happiness of those he has freed from oppression.

Act I. Abramane swears to have revenge on Amélite, who spurned him and loves Zoroastre. A bassoon adds a suitably dark colour to a sung couplet that recurs during his recitative – Rameau's characteristically lively way of breaking down the barriers between sung and declaimed passages. The King who favoured Zoroastre has died; Zoroastre has been outlawed. Abramane now longs for the throne itself and is prepared to ally himself with Erinice to thwart Amélite, the legitimate heiress. Erinice knows he is motivated by ambition, but since Zoroastre rejected her, she is determined to see Amélite suffer. They agree to join forces, in three lines of cold formality, 'Unissons nous'. Abramane breaks his magic ring and gives her half, to signify that he shares his power with her.

A chorus of young Bactrians try to comfort Amélite. Longing for Zoroastre to return, she collapses, overwhelmed by grief. The mood of soft melancholy is enriched by a 'Gavotte Tendre', until a sudden 'Subterranean Noise' causes panic. Amélite sees Erinice and runs to comfort her, only to learn that Erinice is bent on tormenting her. A Chorus of Cruel Spirits drag Amélite away. The first part of the overture returns aptly to remind us that this scene of oppression is part of a larger picture.

Act II. The palace of Oromasès, King of the Genies. Zoroastre remains sunk in grief since he is separated from his beloved Amélite. The high register of his part speaks eloquently for his heroism, though it is vital to remember that this Zoroastre has nothing to do with any other Zarathustra. Oromasès urges Zoroastre to free the universe and summons the Spirits of the Elements to enlighten him. Rameau's music moves to the slow, dignified pace of a ritual ceremony, but the solemnity never entirely

[1] Original version only.   [2] 1756 version only.

masks a gentle playfulness, as it describes Zoroastre's initiation.

Amélite is held captive inside the castle of the Kings of Bactria. Demons torment her in a vicious little chorus and Erinice offers her a bleak choice, 'Renounce the throne, or die!' Amélite remains defiant but before Erinice can stab her rival, an iron door bursts open to reveal Zoroastre, who causes the dagger to drop from her hand and the demons to vanish. The lovers are reunited in bliss. Zoroastre frees the innocent who are imprisoned and makes the prison walls disappear, revealing a public square. He presents Amélite to the people as their next sovereign. They celebrate her return with a lively chorus, a procession whose springy pace always seems about to become a dance, the 'Entrée des Peuples, Air Majestueux', irresistibly lighthearted minuets and rigaudons. Céphie's slow, sensual air ('Ah! Que l'absence est un cruel tourment') is balanced by Amélite's lively, melismatic air reflecting that happiness is sometimes born from disaster ('Non, ce n'est pas toujours pour ravager la terre'). The act ends with rejoicing.

Act III. Outside Bactria, before dawn. Abramane has set a trap for Zoroastre but he worries that Erinice's resolve will falter. He envelops her in a cloud and reflects that 'great crimes' will lead him to glory. He hides as the people led by Zoroastre assemble to salute the rising sun and love itself. An 'Entrée de Peuple Différents' brings on young maidens who will marry at dawn, and Zoroastre sings a 'Hymn to the Sun'. Their grooms join them and after a gigue, Amélite asks Love to discharge his quiver at their hearts. An exhilarating Tambourin en Rondeau is followed by the solemn marriage ceremony. As Zoroastre and Amélite are about to swear an oath, thunder erupts, darkness descends and Abramane calls on his gods and the North Winds (the Aquilons) to destroy them. Zoroastre summons Beneficent Spirits who carry Amélite to safety, while he prepares to do battle. Columns of fire rain down on Bactria.

Act IV. Inside Arimane's secret temple. In a magnificently dark air, Abramane prays not to be afflicted with remorse ('Cruels tyrans'). His confederates Zopire and Narbanor report that Zoroastre turned the troops' weapons back on them, while a clear sky dis-perses Abramane's dark enchantments. Abramane strengthens Erinice's faltering resolve. He conjures the evil deity he worships and sacrifices animals to nourish its wrath. Hatred, the Furies and Despair appear with a crowd of evil spirits and, in their midst, Vengeance, armed with an iron-studded club. In another ballet sequence a statue of Zoroastre on the altar is consumed by flames. Joyful dances are interrupted by 'a frightening symphony': hell itself urges them 'to make virtue tremble and courage pale'. A great ensemble takes up the theme, anticipating victory, death and carnage ('Cours aux armes').

Act V. Zoroastre's ancient domain. The mood changes dramatically, and even before Erinice sings of being torn apart by love and hate (in a superbly vivid, sympathetic air), we know which emotion has won. She now wants to save Zoroastre's life and urges him to flee hell's onslaught. Zoroastre assumes that 'a loud symphony' means the people applaud Amélite. Suddenly, Erinice feels less remorseful.

Bactrians run on in despair: as Amélite was being carried to her coronation, a whirlwind carried her away. In her place, Erinice comes to be crowned, attended by the Priests of Arimane. Abramane stops Zoroastre interfering by revealing that Amélite lies at his feet in chains. But lightning strikes Abramane, Erinice and the Priests and the earth opens to swallow them up. The scene changes to reveal a building filled with the Spirits of the Elements.[1] Amélite is seen in the clouds freed from her chains. Oromasès explains that Heaven wanted to test Zoroastre's virtue once more and invites him to reign over the people he loves. The opera ends in a pastoral vision of bliss: Amélite and Zoroastre are crowned with garlands of flowers while Shepherds and Herdsmen join the festivities in an Andante that might have been written for Mark Morris's idealised form of walking. In Amélite's splendid air, 'Love flies here at the sound of the oboes', oboes imitate musettes. Shepherds assure them that she and Zoroastre will be as happy as they are.

Zoroastre gains from the comparative informality of Rameau's writing: thoughts and feelings prompt the vocal line to soar into lyrical flights of singing, even if only for a line or so. At the same time, music rescues

---

[1] 'It is the first temple dedicated to light, of the composite order, its vaulting is open to the sky, showing various symbols in the air, the goods, the arts and virtues that Zoroastre is going to distribute on earth.'

the polarised characterisation from crude stereotypes: Abramane's ambitious, evil nature emerges with a unique stamp in syncopated rhythms and a vaulting vocal line, while the forces of good are portrayed in serenely balanced music. The fourth act is particularly strong, the equivalent of the Underworld act in *Hippolyte et Aricie* some sixteen years earlier: it builds through a sequence of increasingly fast tempi (*grave, vif, très vif*) to an almost hysterical climax.   P.

LES BORÉADES
The Boreads[1]

Tragédie in five acts, libretto by an unknown author, possibly Louis de Cahusac. Completed in 1764; in rehearsal when Rameau died. Not performed until O.R.T.F. broadcast, 1963. Concert performance, Queen Elizabeth Hall, London, 1975; first staging, Aix-en-Provence Festival, 1982, with Jennifer Smith, Philip Langridge, John Aler, Gilles Cachemaille, Jean-Philippe Lafont, conducted by John Eliot Gardiner.

Alphise, *Queen of Bactria*................................Soprano

Semire, *her confidante*....................................Soprano

Polyhymnie, *muse of song and mime*...............Soprano

A Nymph...Soprano

Abaris, *Alphise's lover* ....Tenor

Calisis, *Alphise's suitor* ....Tenor

Borée (Boreas), *god of the North Wind*...................Bass

Borilée, *Alphise's suitor* ....Baritone

Adamas, *high priest of Apollo* ....Baritone

Apollon (Apollo), *god of light*...............................Bass

God of Love..Soprano

Pleasures and Graces, Priests of Apollo, Seasons, Muses, Zephyrs, Hours, Arts etc.

Place: Bactria
Running Time: 2 hours 50 minutes

Act I. Queen Alphise confides in Sémire: by tradition she is expected to marry a Boread, a descendant of Borée, the North Wind, but she is actually in love with a foreigner, Abaris. Two Boreads, Borilée and Calisis, press their suits on Alphise, who refers the decision to Apollo. Calisis presents an entertainment performed by Pleasures and Graces. The act ends with a contredanse.

Act II. The temple of Apollo. Abaris complains that the god ignores his pleas for help, even though he has been brought up in the temple by the priests. Alone, Adamas the high priest remembers how Apollo entrusted him with the infant and commanded that his divine birth be concealed from him until he proved himself worthy of it. When Abaris confesses his love for Alphise, Adamas commands the priests to obey him as they would the King. The Queen arrives and begs the priests to intercede with Apollo for her. She recounts a dream in which Borée threatened to destroy her palace and country. Abaris declares his love for her; she responds delightedly and, when the priests and courtiers arrive, she pretends that her exclamations of joy are a hymn to Apollo. It is Borilée's turn to present a dance-spectacle: dancers mime the legend of Borée and Orithée: the North Wind abducts a princess. Calisis draws the moral, that we cannot avoid the dictates of Love. A Nymph celebrates love's freedom from passion and its waywardness ('C'est la liberté ... Comme un zéphir'). Dances follow. The people anticipate the arrival of a god, but it turns out to be Love, rather than Apollo. He approves of Alphise's choice of lover and hands her a magic arrow. The act ends with songs in honour of Love and of Apollo. The divertissement is varied in pace and mood, richly scored, graceful and makes a sensuous ending.

Act III. Alphise remembers her terrible dream ('Songe affreux, image cruelle'). Abaris worries that he will lose her to the Boreads, but she reassures him. People sing in praise of Hymen, god of marriage, and a further divertissement is staged. The moral is drawn by Calisis in a charming, bassoon-inflected air and chorus with an elaborate, high-lying vocal line: why fight against love – surrender and save time. Bassoons feature in two delicious gavottes, paired with oboes and strings, then Borilée begs Alphise to choose a husband. When Adamas presses her, however, Alphise abdicates, asks the people to choose their king and hands Abaris Love's arrow. Calisis and Borilée both claim the throne. Abaris is outraged by their behaviour but calmed by Alphise, who declares her love for him. The people beg Alphise to continue as Queen, while they hope she will marry Abaris. This inspires Calisis and Borilée to appeal to their ancestor Borée. A storm erupts and Alphise is carried away in a whirlwind.

---

[1] Descendants of Boreas.

The act ends with a brief and solemn lament sung by Abaris and the people.

Act IV. The storm continues while the people try to calm Borée. Borilée gloats at their distress and swears to destroy Alphise. As the storm ends, Abaris returns in despair at having lost Alphise ('Lieux désolés'). Adamas begs him to save the country and renounce his love. Abaris responds by trying to kill himself. Adamas prevents him: the arrow may help him defeat his rivals. Abaris appeals to Apollo for help. The muse Polyhymnie descends and offers to transport him on the zephyrs' wings. This calls for a series of dances, a gavotte for the Hours and Zephyrs in which 'the string instruments imitate a clock' striking, and two rigaudons. Abaris sets off on his aerial journey, calling on the winds to retire into their caves.

Act V. In Borée's cavern of the Winds. Borée asks the Winds to punish earth ('Obeissez, quittez vos cavernes obscurs'). But Alphise remains constant to her love for Abaris, even when she is forced by the North Wind and the suitors to choose between marriage to one of them and a life in chains. Her undaunted reply ('Qu'on me donne des fers') so irritates Borée that he orders new tortures. Abaris appears and uses the arrow to calm the suitors' fury. Apollo descends in majesty and reveals that Abaris is his son, by a charming young nymph descended from Borée himself. Reunited with Alphise, Abaris frees the rival suitors from their enchantment. Before he leaves, Apollo establishes eternal day in Borée's dark world. Dances for Sports, Love and Pleasure celebrate the occasion. Abaris and Alphise enjoy the triumph of love (duet, 'Que ces moments sont doux') and Abaris compares love to a stream that becomes a torrent when its path is blocked, in a charming air whose violin figuration imitates the stream ('Que l'amour embellit la vie'). The opera ends with several jolly *contredanses*.

In the introduction to the facsimile edition of the score (1982), Antoine Geoffroy-Dechaume remarks that 'It is finally in the amplitude of the truth of the dramatic emotion or of its tenderness that he achieves in *Les Boréades* the perfection of his musical ideal.'   P.

MAURICE RAVEL

(born 7 March 1875, died 28 December 1937)

L'HEURE ESPAGNOLE
The Spanish Hour

Opera in one act, text by Franc-Nohain. Première, Opéra-Comique, Paris, 19 May 1911, with Vix, Périer. First performed at Covent Garden, 1919, with Donalda, André Gilly, Dua, Maguénat, Cotreuil, conductor Percy Pitt; Chicago and New York, 1920, with Gall, Maguénat, Defrère, Warnéry, Cotreuil, conductor Hasselmans; Metropolitan, 1925, with Bori, Errolle, Bada, Tibbett, Didur, conductor Hasselmans; la Scala, Milan, 1929, with Supervia, Menescaldi, Damiani, Baccaloni, conductor Santini.

Concepcion, *wife of Torquemada*	Soprano
Gonzalve, *a poet*	Tenor
Torquemada, *a clock-maker*	Tenor
Ramiro, *a muleteer*	Bariton-Martin
Don Inigo Gomez, *a banker*	Bass

Place: Toledo
Time: Eighteenth Century
Running Time: 50 minutes

Several false operatic starts preceded *L'Heure Espagnole*, a product of one of the composer's most prolific periods, which included the *Rapsodie Espagnole* as well as sketches for *Daphnis et Chloé*, much piano music, songs and chamber music.

The action takes place in the shop of Torquemada, an absent-minded clock-maker of Toledo. It is his day for attending the public clocks in various parts of the town. It is also the one day that his wife Concepcion can enjoy her love affairs with complete freedom. As the clock-maker leaves his house, Ramiro, a muleteer, arrives to have his watch fixed. It is a family heirloom and most important to him. Much to Concepcion's annoyance, Torquemada invites the customer to await his return. In despair Concepcion wonders what to do with the unwelcome visitor. Equally embarrassed, he offers to carry to her room one of the large clocks which her husband has declared too heavy for him to lift.

As he takes the clock to the other room Concepcion's lover Gonzalve appears. While the muleteer is out of the room he is hidden in a grandfather clock. There follows an interchange of clocks, and the unsuspecting muleteer carries Gonzalve inside a clock to Concepcion's room. Inigo, a banker, who is another admirer of Concepcion's, enters. He in his turn is hidden in a clock. Another switching of timepieces effects a change in lovers. But neither turns out to be satisfactory, the one perpetually indulging in flights of poetic fancy, the other proving simply ridiculous, and it is the muleteer who by his prowess and strength wins Concepcion's admiration; she transfers her temporary affections to him and takes him up to her room. While they are away, Torquemada returns. He finds two dejected philanderers hidden in his clocks and takes the opportunity of selling one to each of them. Concepcion and Ramiro re-enter. The husband, however, probably believes that there is safety in numbers and the opera ends with a sparkling quintet, whose moral, say the characters, comes from Boccaccio:

Entre tous les amants, seul amant efficace,
Il arrive un moment, dans les déduits d'amour,
Où le muletier a son tour!

From the delightful clock noises of the opening to the Habanera quintet of the end, *L'heure espagnole* is full of charming music. It is however designed to point up the witty stage action, and there are in the accepted sense hardly any 'numbers' (Concepcion's exasperated 'Ah, la pitoyable aventure' – Oh, what a miserable affair – is the nearest) as one might expect from Ravel's injunction to his singers: '*dire* plutôt que *chanter*' (say it rather than sing it). Gonzalve is the only exception to this rule, and he waxes positively lyrical at times (e.g. his characteristically Spanish opening song). It is all very light, and we may for once legitimately call it very French as well.   K.W., H.

L'ENFANT ET LES SORTILÈGES
The Child and the Magic

Opera in two parts, text by Colette. Première Monte Carlo, 21 March 1925, with Gauley, Warnéry, Lafont, conductor de Sabata. First performed Opéra-Comique, Paris, 1926, with Gauley, Féraldy, Calvet, Sibille, Bourdin, Hérent, Guénot, conductor Wolff; San Francisco, 1930, with Queena Mario, conductor Merola; Florence Festival, 1939, by company from Opéra, Paris (where the work was revived that year), with Micheau, Branèze, Cernay, conductor Previtali; la Scala, Milan, 1948, with Branèze, Danco, Schenneberg, Gianotti, conductor de Sabata. Revived London, Sadler's Wells, 1965, conductor Matheson; in John Dexter's production with designs by David Hockney at Metropolitan, 1981, Covent Garden, 1983.

L'Enfant (The Child) ....Mezzo-Soprano
Sa Mère (His Mother).................................Contralto
La Bergère (The Louis XV Chair) ....Soprano
La Tasse chinoise (The Chinese
  Cup)..Mezzo-Contralto
Le Feu[1] (The Fire)................................Soprano Léger
La Princesse[1] (The Princess) ....Soprano Léger
La Chatte (The Cat) ....Mezzo-Soprano
La Libellule (The Dragonfly)...............Mezzo-Soprano
Le Rossignol[1] (The Nightingale) ....Soprano Léger
La Chauve-Souris (The Bat) ....Soprano
La Chouette (The Little Owl).........................Soprano
L'Ecureuil (The Squirrel) ....Mezzo-Soprano
Une Pastourelle (A Shepherd Girl) ....Soprano
Un Pâtre (A Shepherd)................................Contralto
Le Fauteuil (The Armchair) ....Basse Chantante
L'Horloge Comtoise (The Grandfather
  Clock)..Baritone
La Théière (The Tea Pot) ....Tenor
Arithmetic[2] (The Little Old Man)......................Tenor
Le Chat (The Tom Cat) ....Baritone
Un Arbre (A Tree) ....Bass
La Rainette[2] (The Frog) ....Tenor
Le Banc (Settle), Le Canapé (Sofa), Le Pouf
  (Ottoman), Fauteuil en Vannerie
  (Wicker Chair) ....Children's Chorus
Les Chiffres (Numbers) ....Children's Chorus

Shepherds, Frogs, Animals, Trees

Running Time: 45 minutes

Colette's libretto originally began as a scenario for a ballet, which she sent to the director of the Opéra in Paris, who in turn sent it on to Ravel, who was then serving with the French Army at the front. It was not until the summer of 1920 that the composer started work in earnest, by which time the ballet scenario had become an operatic libretto.

[1, 2] These roles *must* (according to the score) be sung by the same singer.

Ravel interrupted his work more than once, but it was finished towards the end of 1924.

A room in an old Norman country house, giving on to a garden. Big armchairs, a grandfather clock, wallpaper with shepherds and shepherdesses on it. A round cage with a squirrel in it hangs near the window. Remains of a fire in the grate, kettle singing. The cat also singing. It is afternoon. The Child, aged six or seven, is sitting at his lessons, at the height of a fit of laziness. He bites his penholder, scratches his head and mutters under his breath. Work exasperates him and he only wants to do the things he is not allowed to do.

His mother comes in with his tea, and is vexed to see that he has done nothing but make a blot on the tablecloth. When she asks him to promise to work, the Child puts out his tongue at her. She leaves him saying he will be left alone until supper-time as a punishment. The Child suddenly loses control, and dashes about the room indulging in an orgy of destruction. He smashes the cup and teapot, pricks the pet squirrel with his pen, pulls the cat's tail, flourishes the poker, stirs up the fire, and upsets the kettle into it to produce clouds of steam and ashes. Then, brandishing the poker like a sword, he swoops on the wallpaper and pulls great strips of it off the wall. He opens the grandfather clock, swings on the pendulum, and finally makes a dash at his books and tears them up with a scream of delight. All this takes place in a few seconds and to the accompaniment of suitably vivacious music.

From now until the end of the opera, the Child is going to experience the consequences of his destructive actions in a way that is likely to astonish him more than any other – from the objects of his temper themselves. He sinks into a chair, but, to his infinite surprise, it moves slowly away from him, to the creaking sound of a contra-bassoon, and, bowing gravely to a Louis XV chair, leads her in a stately but grotesque dance. Their conversation, to which the Child listens in amazed silence, is to the effect that they will never again have to put up with the weight and the pranks of the naughty child they have had to stand for so long. They are joined in vigorous expression of this sentiment by Settle, Sofa, Ottoman, and Wicker Chair.

Next comes the mutilated clock, striking uncontrollably and complaining bitterly of the treatment which has deprived him, literally, of his balance. From the floor come the voices of the Chinese cup and teapot ('Wedgwood noir' says the score): 'How's your mug? Rotten ... better had ... come on! ... I punch, Sir, I punch your nose ... I boxe you, I marm'lad you.' The words are nonsense, compounded from English and the more nebulous orientalisms such as 'Mah-jong', 'kong-kong', 'Harakiri' and even 'Caskara'; the music is a brilliant parody of the foxtrot of American jazz (1920s style), and the nostalgic tune is sustained now by the voices, now by the first trombone. The foxtrot is justly one of the most famous moments of the score, but it evoked more hostility at the first performances than almost any other passage.

The Child suddenly feels very much alone and goes towards the fire, which however spits in his face and announces to coloratura music that warmth is only for those who are good; bad children will be burnt. The fire pursues the Child round the room until it succumbs quietly to the ashes, which dance with it for a moment and then extinguish it altogether. There is a procession, half comic, half pathetic, of the shepherds and shepherdesses from the torn wallpaper, after which the Fairy Princess rises out of the torn picture book, on which the Child has rested his head. He was half-way through her story, but now that the book is torn he will never know how it will turn out. The Child tries to hold her back as she sinks through the floor, and his lyrical phrases after she has gone are really moving in their mixture of simplicity and intensity.

There is just a chance that the end of the story may be among the pages which lie round his feet, and he looks for it. All he can find are the torn sheets of an arithmetic book, from which emerges an old man covered with arithmetical symbols and crowned with a Pi. Without even pausing to look round him, the little old man starts to reel off problems of the sort which begin 'If two taps fill a bath in ... ' He and the Child catch sight of one another at the same moment, and immediately he and his platoon of figures start to torment the Child with quick-fire arithmetical nonsense. The Child is whirled into the dance, and sinks down exhausted.

He does not notice the black cat come out from under the armchair, yawn, and start to wash itself. It is playing with a ball when the Child notices it and says wearily that he supposes it too has acquired the habit of speech. The cat signs that it has not, and spits at him, before going off to the window, where a white cat has appeared. Now comes the famous Cats'

L'enfant et les sortilèges *(Covent Garden, 1983, director John Dexter, designer David Hockney).*
Ann Murray as the Child.

love duet, which caused such a storm at the first performance. No word is spoken, but the 'Mi-inhou' and
'Mornaou', which Colette has chosen to represent
cat's speech, are set to exact notes and marked
'nasal'. The result is brilliantly real, and the animals
work themselves up to a frenzy of excitement before
bounding out of the window into the garden.

The Child follows them hesitatingly, and at this
point the stage directions require that the room walls
fall away, the ceiling disappear, and the Child with the
two cats be transported into the garden, which is lit by
the last rays of the setting sun. The short and very
beautiful orchestral interlude is for strings; piccolo and
Swanee whistle imitate bird noises and the whole
atmosphere is one of pure magic. A chorus of frogs can
be heard from behind the scenes, and the Child is
delighted to be out in the garden he loves so well.

But even here he is not to escape the accusing
voices which have haunted him indoors. The tree
complains about the cuts made in his flanks; a dragonfly flashes across the scene calling for the mate she
has lost, and who is now pinned to the wall in the

Child's room; a nightingale is heard against the background of the frogs' chorus, and a bat complains that
his mate was killed by the Child. Frogs come out of
the water and sit round the edge until the pool is completely ringed with them. They dance. One lays its
head on the Child's knee, and is immediately admonished by a squirrel for taking such a risk with so dangerous a creature. She herself was able to escape, but
another squirrel was caught and now languishes in a
cage in the Child's room. The Child tries to explain
that it was so as to be able to gaze for ever into the
squirrel's beautiful eyes that he took her captive, but
this answer proves anything but satisfactory to the
squirrel, who makes a moving plea for the freedom
she and her kind love above everything else.

The Child realises that the animals are happy all
round him, and begins to feel lonely with no one
paying any attention to him. Suddenly he cries out
'Maman'. Immediately the atmosphere of peace is
broken. Animals form a menacing chorus, with the
Child as the object of their dislike. Each one has a
grudge to pay off, and together they rush at the

Child, catch hold of him, buffet him, turn him round, shove him, and then forget all about him as, in their anxiety to be the first to down him, they become excited at the battle and turn on each other.

The Child is pushed over into a corner of the stage, when all of a sudden a little squirrel who has been wounded limps over towards him. The Child takes a ribbon and binds up the squirrel's paw, watched by the other animals. Their animosity turns to something quite different as they exclaim in amazement at the Child's kindly action. 'He has stifled the bleeding, he has bound up the wound.' What can they do to help him, now that he looks so helpless and lonely all by himself in the garden? Just now he cried out; what

was the word? They try to call 'Maman', thinking that will help the Child, whom they now believe to be good and kind. The animals help him up and start to lead him towards the house whose windows have just been lit up. The opera ends as the Child calls simply and confidently 'Maman'.

Ravel was at the very height of his powers at the time of *L'enfant,* and working well within them to produce a work whose inventiveness appears to be equal to every facet of the situations he undertook. Above all, the subject is one that exactly suits his peculiar type of genius; the work brilliantly switches from parody to the most moving lyricism, to onomatopoeic representation of the story.   H.

ARIBERT REIMANN

(born 4 March 1936)

LEAR

Opera in two parts, text by Claus H. Henneberg after William Shakespeare. Première, Munich, 9 July 1978, with Fischer-Dieskau, Julia Varady, Colette Lorand, Helga Dernesch, David Knutson (Edgar), Werner Götz (Edmund), Rolf Boysen (Fool), Hans Günter Nöcker (Gloucester), conductor Gerd Albrecht. First performed Düsseldorf, 1978, with Günter Reich. San Francisco (in English), 1981, with Thomas Stewart, conductor Albrecht; Komische Oper, Berlin, 1983; English National Opera, 1989 (in English), with Monte Jaffe, conductor Paul Daniel.

King Lear..Baritone

The King of France...............................Bass-Baritone

Duke of Albany ....Baritone

Duke of Cornwall...Tenor

Kent...Tenor

Gloucester..Bass-Baritone

Edgar, *Gloucester's son*................Tenor/Countertenor

Edmund, *Gloucester's bastard*............................Tenor

King Lear's daughters
    Goneril ....Dramatic Soprano
    Cordelia ....Soprano
    Regan..Soprano

The Fool..Speaking Role

A Servant ....Tenor

A Knight..Speaking Role

Servants, Soldiers, Followers of the King, Followers of Gloucester

Place: England
Time: Medieval
Running Time: 2 hours 15 minutes

Lear, Reimann's third opera (*Melusine* won considerable success in Berlin in 1969), was commissioned in summer 1975 by the newly-appointed Intendant of the Bavarian State Opera, August Everding, with Reimann's partner in many Lieder recitals, Dietrich Fischer-Dieskau, very much in mind for the title role. The première, during the Munich Festival 1978, was a public and critical success rare among modern operas, moreover with a score which, though highly effective by any standards, is firmly in line from Schoenberg and Berg and by no means makes concessions to public taste.

Part I. Lear divides his kingdom among his three daughters. Goneril and Regan respond in florid though hardly graceful manner, but Cordelia cannot articulate her feelings for her father and is banished. Kent speaks up for Cordelia and himself loses place with the King. Cordelia and the King of France make a stammering effort at farewell, then join in an ensemble with her sisters, Lear, Gloucester and his two sons, Edgar and Edmund. It is interrupted only for a rueful comment from the Fool. Goneril and Regan divide Cordelia's portion between them.

The Fool introduces the Gloucester sub-plot, the mirror image of Lear's, as he says, and in a few sentences Edmund has manoeuvred Edgar into flight from his father and, by means of a forged letter, successfully poisoned Gloucester's mind against his son.

A short frenzied interlude takes us to the palace, where Lear's servants carouse and Kent, anonymously and in disguise, after some badinage with the Fool, enters the King's service. Goneril and Regan use the unruly behaviour of their father's servants as pretext to expel them from the court, instructing that the protesting Kent be set in the stocks. Lear's outrage avails him nothing. The sisters combine to banish Lear, and Kent and the Fool lead him away.

The storm, which has already started to blow up, increases in the interlude to become a howling tempest, and 'Blow winds and crack your cheeks' ('Blast, Winde, sprengt die Backen!'), much of it on a baritone's high D, E and F, has epic power, the singer's declamation interspersed with the storm's raging brass and wind (the voice intermittently falling and rising in 7ths). As the fury dies down, the Fool and Kent plan a mission to Cordelia, but Lear is soon back to battle with the elements as his wits start to give way.

The interlude, starting gently and lyrically on solo bass flute, changes the atmosphere if not to one of calm at least to introspection as the scene changes to the hut where Edgar has taken refuge. Bass, alto and normal flute alternate and Edgar's voice, in countertenor range, mysteriously (like Quint's, from a distance) is heard singing off-stage, all possibility of calm vanishing as he assumes more and more the personality of poor Tom, and with it an extreme *tessitura*. Kent and the Fool lead in Lear. The Fool announces that the hut contains a ghost as Lear in his madness edges nearer and nearer in vocal line to Wozzeck. Edgar soars to countertenor's top E, Lear continues to rave about his daughters, Kent joins his voice to theirs, Gloucester and his followers are heard in the distance, then enter to escort the King towards Dover.

Part II. Gloucester's castle. Cornwall, Edmund and Regan discuss Gloucester's 'treachery' in helping the King, accuse him to his face, and then proceed to blind him. A servant in revulsion wounds Cornwall and is himself killed. Gloucester calls for Edmund's help but Regan's mocking laughter confirms that his son is in league with them against him. They turn Gloucester out.

The interlude, with slow muted violins, brings us to a passage in which Reimann takes a leaf out of Bernd Alois Zimmermann's pluralistic book (see page 990) and alternates episodes taking place simultaneously in Albany's palace and in the French camp at Dover. In the one, Goneril plots evil with Edmund, in the other Cordelia plans her father's deliverance. The effect is maintained as we continue to see and hear Goneril, but Cordelia is succeeded by Edgar and Gloucester, the former watching over his unknowing father whose aim is somehow to reach Dover. Edgar's compassion reaches its climax in another vocal flourish connected with his 'poor Tom' assumption. Albany, who both knows of Cornwall's crime against Gloucester and has had news of his death, begs Goneril to be moderate, but she remains unswerving in purpose.

The interlude returns us to Edgar and Gloucester who arrive, as Gloucester thinks, at the cliffs of Dover. In his blindness, he attempts suicide, comes to believe he is to die, but nonetheless proves quicker to recognise Lear, when he appears, simply by his voice, than Lear, with his sight but without his wits, is to make him out. Lear babbles, but with his recognition of the blinded Gloucester starts to regain his senses only, as the French soldiers appear, to seem to lose them again.

Another short interlude takes us to the French camp, where Cordelia, in music of touching simplicity, succours Lear and promises to restore his rights and his powers, to his infinite comfort.

Edmund rejoices in the way fortune has gone his way, with Lear and Cordelia now in his power, Goneril and Regan competing for his favours, and England's throne tottering. He orders Lear and his daughter to prison and enjoins the Captain who has charge of them to fulfil his instructions. Albany inclines towards clemency for Lear and Cordelia, but Edmund challenges his authority. Regan is poisoned by Goneril and dies, leaving Edgar to avenge his father and in single combat kill Edmund, while Goneril stabs herself and dies.

Lear carries in the murdered Cordelia, lays her body on the ground, then sings her dirge – and his – before he in his turn dies and the orchestra sinks murmuringly away.   H.

ERNEST REYER
(born 1 December 1823, died 15 January 1909)

SIGURD

Opera in four acts, text by Camille du Locle and Alfred Blau. Première Brussels, 7 January 1884, with Jourdain, Rose Caron, Bosman, Deschamps-Jéhin, Renaud, Devries, Gresse, conductor Dupont. First performed Opéra, Paris, 1885, with Sellier, Caron, Lassalle, Gresse; London, 1884 (in Italian), with Jourdain, Albani, Fursch-Madi, Edouard de Reszke, Soulacroix. At the Opéra in Paris it was until 1935 played 252 times with singers such as Litvinne, Bréval, Marjorie Lawrence, Escalais, Plançon and Journet, and has since been revived intermittently elsewhere.

Sigurd, *a French hero* ....Tenor

Gunther, *King of Burgundy* ....Baritone

Hagen, *Gunther's companion* ....Bass

The High Priest of Odin ....Baritone

Attila's ambassadors
    Rudiger ....Baritone
    Irnfrid ....Tenor
    Hawart ....Tenor
    Ramunc ....Bass

A Bard...Bass

Brunehild, *a Valkyrie* ....Soprano

Hilda, *Gunther's sister* ....Soprano

Uta, *Hilda's nurse* ....Mezzo-Soprano

Soldiers, People of Burgundy and Islande, Priests etc.

Time: The Dark Ages

A friend of Berlioz's during the senior composer's later life, and of Gautier's, Reyer collaborated with the poet in early symphonic as well as operatic essays, but devoted the middle part of his life to journalism, working as critic on the *Journal des Débats*, where Berlioz had worked before him. After the success of *Sigurd* in 1884 and *Salammbô* in 1890, Reyer was looked on as one of the leaders of French operatic life. He admired Wagner as well as Berlioz, but his music looks more obviously to Weber, Meyerbeer and his French antecedents than to the German, of whose work on the *Ring* he is believed to have been in ignorance at the time of *Sigurd*'s gestation in the 1860s.

Act I. An extended overture introduces women at work in the castle, peacefully preparing for their men to go into battle. Uta supports Hilda, who has rejected Attila the Hun's offer of marriage and now to Uta discloses dreams she has had of Sigurd, who once rescued her when she had been carried off prisoner. Uta assures Hilda that by her magic arts Sigurd will be brought to Gunther's castle and when he drinks a potion his love will be hers. Gunther greets Attila's envoys and a Bard tells the story of Brunehild, punished for her disobedience by the god Odin and held captive in a fire-girt fortress until released by an indomitable warrior. Gunther proclaims that he will win her, then returns Hilda's negative answer to Attila's proposal of marriage. A hero is announced and Sigurd comes to challenge Gunther (Aria: 'Prince du Rhin') with his own determination to win Brunehild. Gunther greets him as the hero who saved his sister and together (as in *Götterdämmerung*) they swear blood brotherhood. They will join in delivering Brunehild, who will become Gunther's bride. Sigurd drinks the magic potion and falls in love with Hilda.

Act II. A forest in Islande. The High Priest celebrates public sacrifice to Freia, consort of Odin (Aria: 'Et toi, Freia'). Sigurd, Gunther and Hagen proclaim their intention to free Brunehild but the High Priest warns them against the attempt. Sigurd puts himself forward (Aria: 'J'ai gardé mon âme ingénue'); he will deliver Brunehild a virgin to Gunther. The High Priest gives him the sacred horn and he prepares for his ordeal (Arioso: 'Le bruit des chants s'éteint'; aria: 'Esprits gardiens'). With lowered visor and through distracting visions, he advances towards the sleeping Brunehild, who in a fine aria worthy of Gounod at his grandest greets the day ('Salut! splendeur du jour!') and announces herself the hero's bride. Sigurd, his unsheathed sword between himself and Brunehild, prepares to conduct her to Gunther.

Act III. The garden of Gunther's palace. Hilda and Uta in some trepidation await the return of the warriors. To Gunther, Sigurd announces his success (Aria: 'Oui, Sigurd est vainqueur'), and Brunehild is greeted by Gunther as the warrior who braved death to free her. They exchange vows. Hilda in spite of Uta's forebodings delights in the prospect of Sigurd's love.

Hagen announces Gunther's wedding. The King

and his future queen are acclaimed, as is Sigurd when he arrives to claim Hilda as his bride. Brunehild falters as she attempts to join her voice with theirs. Notwithstanding Uta's presentiments, the procession continues on its way.

Act IV. Gunther's palace. Brunehild is a prey to sorrow and she laments her predicament (Aria: 'O palais radieux'): she is Gunther's wife but love for Sigurd courses like poison through her veins. Hilda attempts to comfort her but Brunehild recognises in Hilda's gift from Sigurd the girdle he took from her. Hilda is proud that it was her husband who defied the fiery ramparts to claim Brunehild for Gunther. Brunehild reminds her of the electricity which passed between her and Sigurd when she tried to join in their rejoicings, but each remains confident of Sigurd's

love. Brunehild is convinced Hilda exercised magic powers to win Sigurd and Hilda shows signs of remorse. Brunehild accuses Gunther of falsely representing himself as a hero and Hilda admits she has told Brunehild the truth. Gunther is overcome with shame, but Hagen urges him to exact vengeance. Sigurd laments his deception of Brunehild (Aria: 'Un souvenir poignant'). She bids him repeat after her a magic formula which will release him from his situation (Duet: 'Avec ces fleurs'). Gunther rouses himself to hunt down Sigurd, and as Hilda and Brunehild skirmish as to the possibility of saving him, Sigurd is brought in dying. Brunehild will die with him on his funeral pyre; Hilda feels avenged at the prospect of Attila's hordes descending on Gunther, summoned by the talisman brought once by his ambassadors.   H.

NIKOLAI ANDREYEVICH RIMSKY-KORSAKOV
(born 18 March 1844, died 21 June 1908)

In his late teens, Rimsky-Korsakov came under the influence of Mili Balakirev. Balakirev, Rimsky, Mussorgsky, Cui and Borodin together formed a group of five young, nationalistic composers who came to be dubbed the Mighty Handful. Like the last three of the group, Rimsky-Korsakov followed another profession for at least part of his adult life, honouring his family's tradition by joining the Russian Navy as a midshipman at the age of eighteen. His musical interests were never in danger of being stifled and, after a two-and-a-half-year round-the-world voyage during which he wrote his first symphony, he became so inextricably involved in music as in 1873 to resign his commission (he was appointed to the well-paid job of Inspector of Naval Bands). He was already a prolific though by his own admission semi-trained composer when in 1872 he became Professor of Free Composition at the St Petersburg Conservatory, where pride forced him to keep a lesson or two ahead of the pupils he was teaching; in later years they included Igor Stravinsky (a private pupil) and Prokofiev.

Rimsky-Korsakov wrote fifteen operas, unevenly spaced, with no more than three before 1890 (*The Maid of Pskov*, *A May Night* and *The Snow Maiden*), but a further twelve in the last eighteen years of his life during which opera had become a main preoccupation, stimulated in 1889 when for the first time he heard Wagner's *Ring* cycle. His works remain in Russia mainstays of the native repertory, and their wide range comprises essays in the historical (*The Maid of Pskov*), folk comedy (*A May Night*), straight fairy-tale (*The Snow Maiden*, *Christmas Eve*), opera-ballet (*Mlada*), fantastic epic (*Sadko*, *Kashchey the Immortal*), romantic-historical (*The Tsar's Bride*), mystical-psychological (*Kitezh*), and a glittering, satirical fairy-tale form all his own (*Tsar Saltan* and *The Golden Cockerel*), each of them steeped in – indeed, helping to create – Russian tradition. The composer himself viewed opera as an entirely musical affair, and thought of the dramatic side as secondary, a point of view which close acquaintance with his works does nothing to contradict.

It would be wrong in the context to forget his unselfish contribution to operas by his contemporaries: César Cui (one scene of whose *William Ratcliff* he orchestrated), Dargomizhsky (whose *Stone Guest* he orchestrated), Mussorgsky (whose unfinished *Khovanshchina* he completed as well as undertaking the entire orchestration, and of whose *Boris Godunov* his editions acted for many years as a passport to stage performance), and Borodin (whose *Prince Igor* was orchestrated and put into performing shape by Rimsky and Glazunov).　　　　　　　　　H.

A MAY NIGHT

Maiskaya Noch

Opera in three acts, libretto by the composer founded on a story by Gogol. Première Moscow, 21 January 1880, conducted by Napravnik. First performed in London, Drury Lane, 1914, with Petrenko, Smirnoff, Belianin. Revived Oxford, in English, 1931; Cardiff, 1959, by Welsh National Opera Company, with Heather Harper, conductor Warwick Braithwaite (and at Sadler's Wells, 1961).

The Mayor ....Bass
Levko, *his son*..Tenor
The Mayor's Sister-in-Law ....Mezzo-Soprano
Hanna ....Mezzo-Soprano
The Mayor's Clerk...Bass
The Distiller ....Tenor
Kalenik...Baritone
Pannochka, *a water sprite*.............................Soprano
Three Water Sprites...........Sopranos, Mezzo-Soprano

Place: A Small Village in Russia
Time: Nineteenth Century
Running Time: 2 hours 25 minutes

The story is taken from Gogol, and, as well as a very strong nationalist quality, it introduces without any apparent strain a supernatural element which might come straight from *Sadko*. The overture was once well-known from concert performance and was for a long time a favourite of Sir Thomas Beecham's.

Act I. In a small village in the heart of Russia, the peasants are celebrating Whitsuntide with dances and games. A game of 'Millet' is going on, while Kalenik, the best dancer in the village, demonstrates his skill. The crowd moves on, and Levko appears to serenade his sweetheart, Hanna. He sings an attractive and lively romance to the accompaniment of his bandura (piano and harp in the orchestra), and it is not long before she comes out to him. Their extended duet suggests that they are very much in love, but Hanna is still worried that Levko's father, the Mayor, may consider it a bad match and forbid their marriage. Levko does his best to reassure her, and she asks him to tell her again the legend of the deserted castle across the lake.

His story is an odd one. Long ago, an old nobleman lived there with his beautiful daughter, Pannochka. When Pannochka discovered her stepmother was a witch, her father drove her out; she drowned herself, and became a Rusalka, or water spirit. One day she and her companions seized the witch and pulled her into the lake, but through her magic powers she turned herself into a Rusalka, indistinguishable from the others. Not until Pannochka discovers which of her companions is the witch can she free herself of the evil spell.

The lovers say goodnight as they hear the revellers returning. The women of the village sing a little chorus in honour of Pentecost, and Kalenik leads a *Hopak*, singing as vigorously as he dances. Levko stays behind when they go, and is startled to hear someone call up to Hanna's window. He is furious when he finds it is his own father, the Mayor, who pays court to her and abuses Levko as a fledgling while doing so! Levko attracts the attention of his friends, who drive the old man away with their mockery. He suggests to them that they disguise themselves that night, and teach the Mayor a lesson by singing a mocking song outside his house.

Act II. That night the Mayor, with the aid of his spinster sister-in-law, is entertaining a rich crony who hopes to open a distillery on the site of the old castle. But their jollity is due for interruption, first by Kalenik, who is drunk and difficult to get rid of, then by a stone flung through the window, and finally by the sound of Levko and his friends singing their 'Song of the Village Mayor' at the tops of their voices outside the window. The Mayor grabs Levko, but a gust of wind blows out the candles and in the general confusion Levko escapes and the Mayor instead bundles his protesting sister-in-law into a cell. The Mayor's Clerk, who has heard the ribald singing, enters to say that *he* has caught the principal culprit and has locked him up. Puzzled, they investigate, and out of the first cell bursts the infuriated sister-in-law to run screaming from the house.

Mayor, Clerk and Distiller now investigate the Clerk's prisoner. The Mayor peeps through the keyhole, and reacts to what he sees with impotent cries of 'Satanas', which the others take up when they have had a look in their turn. The solution is clearly to burn the devil – obviously it is he – and only the protestations of the sister-in-law (who has now twice been bundled into a cell, the second time by the crowd after they have liberated the Clerk's prisoner, Levko) save her from a witch's fate. Once free, she turns on the Mayor; it is all a plot on his part to prevent her seeing his philanderings, which have become a byword throughout the village. The Mayor tries to rescue what is left of his dignity by ordering the Watch to clear the streets of the band which so grievously insulted him.

The music of the whole act has a most agreeable *buffo* character, and the role of the Mayor, which was created by Stravinsky's father, is rich in comic possibilities. The second scene has something of the variety and even the flavour of a Rossini finale, on which it would appear to be modelled.

Act III. The deserted castle by the lake. Levko sings a hauntingly beautiful love song ('Sleep my beloved'). Suddenly a troop of water nymphs emerges from the lake. There is a delightful 6/8 chorus for them before Pannochka, their Queen, asks Levko if he will help her spot her wicked stepmother, who is concealed in their midst. Each in turn pretends to be a raven, until one does so with such spiteful conviction that Levko points to her and the others fall on her and drag her down into the lake. Pannochka in a little duet thanks Levko and gives him a paper, which she says will settle his father's opposition to his marriage with Hanna.

No sooner have the water nymphs gone than Levko is seized by the Watch as the author of the previous night's disturbances. The Clerk however looks at the paper Pannochka has given Levko, recognises the Governor's seal, and proceeds to read out an indictment of the Mayor's incompetence, and an order for the immediate celebration of the wedding of Levko and Hanna.

The villagers sing their Whitsuntide song, Hanna is reunited with Levko, while the Mayor is overjoyed at the official letter's news that the Governor is to dine with him – even the way his hand has been forced over the matter of Hanna and Levko, even the muttered threats of his sister-in-law, cannot spoil *that*.   H.

THE SNOW MAIDEN
Snegurochka

Opera in a prologue and four acts, text by the composer from a play by N. Ostrovsky. Première St Petersburg, 10 February 1882. First performed Metropolitan, New York, 1922, with Bori, Telva, Harrold, Laurenti, conductor Bodanzky (in French); Buenos Aires, 1929, with Kouznetsova, conductor Fitelberg; Sadler's Wells, 1933, with Olive Dyer, Cross, Tudor Davies, Austin, conductor Collingwood.

Snegurochka	Soprano
Shepherd Lehl	Alto
Coupava	Soprano
Fairy Spring	Mezzo-Soprano
Bobilicka	Mezzo-Soprano
Spirit of the Woods	Tenor
Page	Mezzo-Soprano
Tsar Berendey	Tenor
Misgir	Baritone
King Frost	Bass
Bobil	Tenor
Bermate	Bass

Place: The Fabled Kingdom of Tsar Berendey
Running Time: 3 hours 30 minutes

*S*negurochka was written in 1880, and in his autobiography Rimsky-Korsakov tells us how he became enamoured of the subject and how he came to write it in the 'genuine Russian village' of Stlelyovo in the brief period of three months. The orchestration took longer. The full score was begun on 7 September 1880, and completed on 26 May of the following year. The composer's friends Balakirev, Borodin and Stassov were pleased with it, but each in his own way. 'Stassov and Balakirev were gratified chiefly with the folk-like and fantastic portion of the opera. Borodin, on the other hand, seemed to appreciate it in its entirety.' Balakirev 'could not curb his passion for meddling', and suggested the transposition of the Introduction into B minor. Rimsky-Korsakov declined to do it, because it would have meant, among other things, the transposition of the theme representing Spring, which was indissolubly linked in his imagination with the key of A minor. He also tells us without any false modesty that in writing it he felt 'a matured musician and operatic composer who had finally come to stand on his own feet'. This opinion was confirmed by the public, who found the work more ingenious and distinguished than anything Rimsky-Korsakov had previously written.

Prologue. The Red Mountain near the capital. It is early spring, but although the snows are melting the wind is cold. Flocks of birds arrive from the south carrying with them the Fairy Spring. Many years ago she wooed icy Winter, who now treats her like a slave. Hence the cold which endures and makes the very birds shiver. Their love is dead, but Spring and Winter have a bond in the child of their love, the maid Snegurochka. They fear for her, for she is now sixteen years old and can no longer be kept hidden and protected; if the sun-god, Yarilo, should glimpse her she would die. They entrust her to the keeping of the Spirit of the Wood, who promises to guard her from mischance. Snegurochka, who has a beautiful aria here, is free to go into the world.

A carnival rout invades the stage as Spring and Winter depart. Snegurochka goes among the people and her beauty makes a deep impression on Bobil and Bobilicka, who adopt her.

Act I. The village of Berendey. Snegurochka begs Lehl, a young shepherd and singer, to perform for her. He sings two charming folk-like songs for her, but her artless advances are little to his liking, and he goes off eagerly enough at the invitation of the other girls. The little daughter of Spring and Winter knows now the pangs of unrequited love. The situation is complicated by the arrival of a wealthy youth, Misgir, who comes to wed Coupava, but seeing Snegurochka, falls in love with her and bluntly refuses to proceed with the marriage ceremony. Even though Snegurochka refuses to take any notice of Misgir's impassioned advances, Coupava is desolate, and only saved from suicide by the large-hearted Lehl.

Act II. In the palace of the Tsar, Coupava comes to claim redress for the affront Misgir has put upon her. The Tsar orders a court of justice to be held and commands the presence of Misgir and Snegurochka. The Tsar, impressed by Snegurochka's beauty, asks her who her lover is. When she replies that she has no lover, the Tsar protests that not to love is a sin against the sun-god, Yarilo, and ends the trial by promising a reward to anyone who succeeds in winning the love of Snegurochka.

The music of this act, with its serene aria for the Tsar, has a unity, and the action an economy and suspense that are not always apparent in this rather loosely knit opera.

Act III. There is feasting and jollity in the Sacred Forest. Even the great Tsar sings a cavatina. It is followed by the celebrated Dance of the Tumblers. Lehl is of the company, and, at the command of the Tsar, sings a delicious song. As a reward he is allowed to claim a kiss from any of the girls present. He passes by Snegurochka, who runs away in tears, and chooses Coupava. Snegurochka, broken-hearted, will not listen to Misgir. When the two are left alone and Misgir would urge his love, Snegurochka vanishes and the Spirit of the Wood, faithful to his trust, prevents Misgir from following.

Act IV. Snegurochka in despair appeals to her mother. She wants to love and be loved. Spring grants her wish, and when Misgir returns she hails him lovingly as her hero. The Tsar greets the couples waiting to be married, among them Misgir and Snegurochka. But all is not well. The sun-god has warmed Snegurochka's heart with a ray of sunshine and her destiny must be fulfilled; the little daughter of Spring and Winter must die. As the mist rises she melts away. Misgir throws himself into the lake, but the Tsar interprets his death and Snegurochka's as a removal of the obstacle to Yarilo's granting his blessings. From now on, says the Tsar, Yarilo may be expected to pour his bounty on them. A white-clad youth appears on the mountain top bearing a sheaf of corn in his hand, and the opera ends with an invocation to Yarilo.   F.B., H.

CHRISTMAS EVE

Noch'pered rozhdestvom

'Bil'-kolyadka' (Carol-come-to-life) in four acts and nine scenes, libretto by the composer, based on the tale by Gogol, from his collection *Evenings in the Village of Dikanka* (1831–32). Première, Mariinsky Theatre, St Petersburg, 28 November (10 December) 1895, with Ivan Yersov as Vakula, Yevgenia Mravina as Oxana, M.D. Kayenkaya as Solokha, Koryakin as Panas, conducted by Eduard Nápravník. British première, English National Opera, Coliseum, London, 1988, with Anne-Marie Owens as Solokha and Tsarina, Nigel Douglas as the Devil, Cathryn Pope as Oxana, Edmund Barham as Vakula, conducted by Albert Rosen. U.S. première, Indiana University Opera Theatre, Bloomington, 1977.

Vakula, *the blacksmith* ....Tenor

Oxana, *the beauty he loves* ....Soprano

Chub Korniy, *old Cossack, Oxana's father*..............Bass
Solokha, *Vakula's mother, a witch*.......Mezzo-Soprano
Panas, *Chub's friend* ....Bass
The Mayor..Baritone
The Devil ....Tenor
The Sexton, *Ossip Nikiforovich*..........................Tenor
Patsyuk, *old Cossack, doctor and wizard*.................Bass
The Tsarina, *Catherine the Great*.........Mezzo-Soprano
First Woman, *with a purple nose*....................Contralto
Second Woman, *with a normal nose*...............Soprano

Young Girls and Boys, Witches and Wizards, Good
and Bad Spirits, Ovsen and Koliada, Stars, Lords
and Ladies, etc.

Place: Ukraine; the Palace in St Petersburg; Space
Time: The Reign of Catherine the Great (1762–96)
Running Time: 2 hours 15 minutes

Rimsky-Korsakov felt drawn to Gogol's Ukrainian stories as early as 1868, when he started to compose *Marriage*, based on one of his short stories. In 1877 he wrote *May Night*, based on a story in Gogol's collection, *Evenings in the Village of Dikanka*, but he avoided 'Christmas Eve', because Tchaikovsky had written an opera on the same material for a competition, when Rimsky-Korsakov himself served on the jury. Tchaikovsky's death in 1893 freed Rimsky-Korsakov to return to the story. His major innovation was to expand the supernatural element, which had fascinated him when he worked on *May Night*, *Snegurochka* (*The Snow Maiden*) and *Mlada*. Rimsky-Korsakov focuses on the winter solstice, the year's shortest day, identified here with Christmas Eve, so that Christianity's moment of birth merely re-echoes the older rebirth of the world from winter. Rimsky-Korsakov called the work a *kolyadka* or Ukrainian carol, filled it with *kolyadki* and even brought on a personification. These carols were sung for money or gifts such as 'Sausages, lard and dumplings', between Christmas and Epiphany. The word derives from the Latin *calendae* (the first of a month). As David Pountney (who directed it for English National Opera) once pointed out, *Christmas Eve* itself marked the rebirth of the composer's creativity, frozen in a wintry grip while Tchaikovsky lived.[1]

Act I, scene i. The village of Dikanka in the Ukraine. The witch Solokha flies out of a chimney on her broom-

stick, while the Devil appears on a neighbouring roof. They know that their evil power over human beings ends tonight. The Devil determines to have his revenge on Solokha's son Vakula the blacksmith, who painted a picture showing the Devil being hit with a stick. He decides to make the moon disappear from the sky: it will be so dark that Vakula will not be able to visit his beloved Oxana and will have to stay at home.

Meanwhile, the old Cossack Panas comes to visit Chub, Oxana's father. They mean to go together to dinner at the Sexton's house. But the moon and then the stars disappear as the snow falls. Chub decides to stay at home. When Vakula arrives, the two men quarrel. But when Chub realises that if the blacksmith is here, his mother must be on her own, he decides to end the evening with Solokha.

Scene ii. Oxana admires her reflection in the mirror. Vakula surprises her. She is unfriendly towards him and rejects his advances. Some of Oxana's young friends arrive, singing a *kolyadka* in praise of her. Seeing that one of her friends is wearing smart new slippers, Oxana teases Vakula, promising to marry him if he gives her the same slippers the Tsarina wears.

Act II, scene iii. In Solokha's house. The Devil has stayed with her to keep warm and together they sing a *kolyadka*. They are interrupted by a knocking at the door from the village Mayor. The Devil hides in an emptied coal sack. Like Chub, the Mayor had been invited to dine with the Sexton, but the snow storm persuaded him to take refuge with the hospitable Solokha. Someone else knocks at the door: the Sexton, who has come looking for company, as his guests have not arrived. The Mayor hides in another coal sack. The Sexton enters and begins singing in praise of Solokha to a plainchant. When a third suitor arrives – old Chub – the Sexton bolts into a sack. Chub drinks some vodka and sings a Ukrainian song. Suddenly, Vakula's voice can be heard outside, and Chub hides in the sack containing the Sexton. Vakula sings a song about how a girl's beauty has deprived him of strength. Then, since the sacks look so untidy, he takes them away with him.

Scene iv. A street in Dikanka. Vakula leaves the sacks outside his forge, except for the smallest, containing the Devil, which he carries on his shoulders.

[1] *Opera*, December 1988.

Boys and girls (including Oxana) sing *kolyadki* under the houses' windows. Old Panas arrives, drunk, starts singing and dancing and making a fool of himself. When the boys and girls begin teasing Vakula he leaves, furious and in despair, talking of committing suicide. This worries Oxana, briefly. The boys open the sacks, Solokha's unlucky suitors emerge, embarrassed and repentant. They all curse her: to have made such fools of them, she must be a witch.

Act III, scene v. In Patsyuk's home. He is said to be in league with devils. Vakula has come to him in desperation, wanting to make a pact with the Devil. Patsyuk is eating magic dumplings that leap into his mouth all by themselves, but gives Vakula a useful hint: 'The man who has the Devil at his back has no need to look far'. Vakula takes the sack off his shoulder and the Devil emerges, promising to do anything he likes as long as he will sell him his soul. The blacksmith seems about to accept the offer, but then threatens him with the sign of the cross and forces the terrified Devil to turn himself into a winged horse. Vakula leaps on to its back and orders him to the Tsarina's palace in St Petersburg.

Scene vi. In space. The stars gather in constellations, play games and dance Mazurkas and Czardas. Patsyuk, Solokha and a whole mass of devils try unsuccessfully to stop Vakula. The lights of St Petersburg are seen in the distance.

Scene vii. In the Tsarina's palace. Courtiers praise her in song. A group of Zaporozhye Cossacks beg her to look on them favourably. Vakula kneels and asks tactfully for a pair of her slippers. Touched by such simplicity, the Tsarina offers him one of her most beautiful pairs. Vakula leaves on his winged horse.

Scene viii. In space. As day breaks, Koliada arrives in the form of a young girl in a carriage, accompanied by Ovsen, a handsome youth, mounted on a boar with gold bristles. They end the winter squalls and mark the sun's rebirth. Dikanka's church bells and a Christmas carol can be heard.

Act IV, scene ix. A courtyard by Chub's house. Oxana hears one woman swear Vakula drowned himself; the other, that he hanged himself. She is consumed by remorse, knowing she will never find anyone as handsome and loving as Vakula. Suddenly he appears, with the pair of slippers he promised. He also has some clothes for Chub, and asks for permission to marry his daughter. Chub agrees and they all celebrate. When the villagers pester Vakula for information, he promises to tell the whole truth to Panko the Redhead, who will then write a wonderful story about Christmas Eve. The villagers will find a setting for it, assemble the musicians and sing a *kolyadka* about... Christmas Eve (finale, To the Memory of Gogol, 'Did I go to the Tsarina or not?').

Rimsky-Korsakov's words and music for *Christmas Eve* are lovingly embroidered with references to Ukrainian and Russian traditions, above all the *kolyadki*, but the score also refers to the Ukrainian cittern, the bandura or pandura; much local food and the fasting that should mark the day itself; a Cossack saddle; the Cossacks' worship of their little mother the Empress, while the anthem-like end (and the way the composer dedicates the finale to Gogol) suggests that the whole evening has been an exercise in community feeling. These factors account for its sad fate in Russian and Slavic opera houses, where it tends to be buried under perfunctory local colour and routine sentimentality. The experience of its revival at English National Opera and its evident musical strength suggest that it deserves a better fate: behind the legend of Koliada that Rimsky-Korsakov celebrates is the rather more widely available myth of the annual rebirth of the sun.   P.

SADKO

Opera in seven scenes (three or five acts), text by the composer and V.I. Bielsky. Première, Moscow, 7 January 1898. Metropolitan, New York, 1930, with Fleischer, Johnson, Basiola, Ludikar, conductor Serafin (in French); London, Lyceum Theatre, 1931, conductor Goossens; Rome, 1931, conductor Marinuzzi; la Scala, Milan, 1938, with Carosio, Giani, Parmeggiani, de Franceschi, Sdanowski, conductor Marinuzzi; Staatsoper, Berlin, 1946, with Berger, Klose, Suthaus, Schock, Neumann, Prohaska, conductor Schüler. Currently in repertory of Russian companies.

The King of the Ocean...Bass
Volkhova, *his daughter*...................................Soprano
Sadko, *a singer of Novgorod* ....Tenor
Lubava, *his wife* ....Mezzo-Soprano
Nejata, *a gousli player from Kiev* ....Mezzo-Soprano
A Viking Merchant ....Bass
A Hindu Merchant ....Tenor
A Venetian Merchant...................................Baritone
Four Buffoons ....Mezzo-Sopranos, Tenor and Bass

Two Elders, *merchants of Novgorod* .....Tenor and Bass

Place: Novgorod, and the Bottom of the Sea
Running Time: 3 hours 35 minutes

Tableau I. The merchants of Novgorod sit down to a feast, rejoicing in their prosperity. Nejata, singer and *gousli* player who comes from Kiev, sings a song about the heroic days of old. The merchants would like one of their own countrymen to perform the same service for Novgorod, and Sadko, who enters at that moment, is asked if he will oblige. But his song worries them; he suggests that Novgorod is on a lake, and that, if their ships could only reach the ocean, they could bring back fortunes from all over the world. They mock him and bid him goodbye. Feasting goes on to the accompaniment of song and dance.

Tableau II. On the shores of Lake Ilmen, Sadko sings of his distress and disillusionment: 'Oh, yon dark forest'. Fascinated by Sadko's singing, swans swim towards him, and as they reach him, become young women, Volkhova, the Sea Princess, among them. He sings again for them, they dance, and the Princess tells him that he has won her love. When dawn comes, she parts from Sadko, but tells him that he will catch three golden fish in the lake, that he will make a journey to a foreign land, and that she will wait faithfully for his return. She goes back to the deep, where her father, the King of the Ocean, holds sway. The sun rises.

Tableau III. Lubava at home laments the absence of her husband Sadko. Only yesterday he assured her of his love. She is overjoyed when he comes in, broken-hearted when he leaves her again.

Tableau IV. The quayside at Novgorod, on Lake Ilmen. Ships lie at anchor, and the people of the town crowd round the rich foreign merchants, who come from every land known to man. Soothsayers ply their trade, Nejata sings to the accompaniment of his *gousli*, buffoons sing and dance, the sound of a pilgrim's chant can be heard. Sadko appears and is greeted with laughter, which increases when he tells them he knows a secret: golden fish can be caught in the lake. He bets his head against the wealth of everyone assembled there that he can prove that he speaks the truth. A net is let down, the song of the Sea Princess is heard, and sure enough, when it is drawn up, there are three gold fishes in the net. Sadko invites all the adventurous men of the port to join him in his journey, and they go off to make their preparations.

Nejata sings of the nightingale that became a great merchant. When he returns, Sadko says he will restore the wealth of the merchants, but would take only their ships. He asks three of the merchants, the Viking, the Venetian and the Indian, to sing to him of their native lands, so that he may decide which to visit. The Viking sings first: his country's shores are rugged, the sea rough, and his countrymen fierce fighters. The slow, *pesante* aria is one of the best known in the Russian bass's repertory. Next comes the Indian merchant, with music and story of much more exotic cast. India is a land of gems and mystery, and his song, any hearer would admit, is the stuff of which dreams are made. It is one of the world's famous melodies, known from having been sung by half the sopranos and tenors who have ever appeared on the concert platform, and by its frequent appearance on violin recitalists' programmes. In its original setting it is a tenor melody. Third representative of the merchants of the world is the Venetian, a baritone, who sings a barcarolle. Sadko settles that Venice shall be his destination. He asks the Novgorod people to look after Lubava, and sets sail.

Tableau V. Sadko is on his way home laden with treasure. The ship is becalmed – due to their not having sacrificed to the King of the Ocean all the twelve years they have been away, says Sadko. They pour treasure over the side, but still the ships remain becalmed. Next at Sadko's command they throw wooden logs over the side: Sadko's sinks, and he descends by a ladder to the water's edge, stepping on to a plank which has been thrown overboard. Immediately a breeze gets up, the ship sails away leaving Sadko abandoned. A mist comes up.

Tableau VI. When the mist clears away we are at the bottom of the sea, at the court of the King of the Ocean. The King and Queen sit on thrones, their daughter, Volkhova, sits spinning seaweed. Sadko sings for the King and Queen, and is promised the hand of Volkhova in marriage. The wedding guests arrive – every denizen of the deep seems to have been invited – and the marriage is celebrated fittingly. Dances are performed for their entertainment, Sadko sings again and arouses such enthusiasm among his hearers that they join in the dance. So fast become the movements of the dancers that the waves are lashed into a fury and ships are sunk. Suddenly an apparition warns them that the reign of the King of the Ocean is at an end. Sadko and Volkhova seated in a shell are drawn away by seagulls.

Tableau VII. It is morning. Sadko sleeps by the side of Lake Ilmen, watched over by Princess Volkhova, who sings a lullaby as she watches. She bids a last farewell to the still-sleeping minstrel, then vanishes in mist, becoming the great river Volkhova and flowing thenceforth from Lake Ilmen to the sea.

Lubava is still distractedly looking for her husband, and she is filled with delight to see him lying by the lake asleep. He thinks he has been asleep ever since he last saw her, and that he has dreamed his voyage. But the sight of his fleet coming up the new river convinces him that it has all taken place, and that he really has become the richest man of Novgorod. All the citizens of that town welcome him, not least the three merchants who sang to him before he left home.   H.

MOZART AND SALIERI

Motsart i Sal'yeri

'Dramatic scenes' in one act, text from Alexander Pushkin's *Little Tragedy* (1830). First performed at the Solodovnikov Theatre, Moscow, on 6 [18] November 1898 with Vasily Shkafer as Mozart and Fyodor Chaliapin as Salieri, conducted by Giuseppe Truffi; in London in 1927, Royal Albert Hall; in the U.S.A. in 1933 at the Unity House, Forest Park, Pennsylvania.

Mozart ....Tenor
Salieri...Bass

Place: A Room (Vienna)
Time: 1792
Running Time: 40 minutes

Once he had completed *Sadko*, Rimsky-Korsakov felt he was 'entering upon some new period' in his work. In the summer of 1897 he wrote some forty songs and set Pushkin's play of 1830 almost word for word in what he called 'recitative-arioso style',[1] where the melody was suggested by the text. In this he was inspired by Dargomïzhsky, from whose *Stone Guest* he quoted in the last bars and to whose memory he dedicated *Mozart and Salieri*. It may have held some autobiographical meaning for him: just as Pushkin identified with Mozart, so the hard-working, painstaking and somewhat embittered Rimsky-Korsakov felt an affinity with Salieri.

Scene i. Salieri looks back on his life and career

and concludes that there is no justice, in heaven as on earth. He was born with a love of music, slowly developed his craft and learned to analyse music with forensic skill. As a composer he gradually found fame. He never felt envy for others' success, until he learnt the final injustice: genius is not given to the hard-working, who deserve it, but to the foolish and idle, such as Mozart. Mozart himself appears. He tells Salieri that on his way he passed an inn, where he heard a fiddler playing an aria from *Figaro*, 'Voi che sapete'. It was funny and charming. He has brought the blind violinist, who plays an *andantino grazioso* based on a theme from *Don Giovanni*. Salieri is not amused, however. Mozart plays on the piano some music he composed one night when he couldn't sleep. He suggests it portrays himself, maybe a bit younger; in love, but only slightly, whose happiness is disrupted by a ghost or a sudden gloominess ('*Allegretto Semplice*').

Impressed, in spite of himself, Salieri calls Mozart a god. Mozart agrees to dine with him and goes to tell his wife that he won't be back for supper. Salieri accepts his fate: Mozart must be stopped, since his achievements show up the 'hollow glory' of Salieri's and others' compositions and leave them dissatisfied, frustrated. Salieri has some poison; he'll use it on his enemy, his friend.

Scene ii. In the inn, Mozart explains why he seems sad. A stranger came to see him, commissioned a Requiem and then disappeared. Since then the 'man in black' has haunted Mozart's dreams, like a shadow; he even feels his presence now. Salieri repeats the advice that Beaumarchais once gave him: 'If you're depressed, open a bottle of champagne or reread *Figaro*'. Mozart himself hums a tune Salieri once composed for a text by Beaumarchais (from the opera *Tarare*). Mozart wonders whether the story that Beaumarchais once poisoned someone can be true: surely genius and crime cannot co-exist? Salieri poisons Mozart's wine. Mozart drinks to the friendship that unites them as two sons of harmony, and then plays Salieri an extract from his Requiem (the opening, with optional, off-stage chorus). Salieri is moved. Mozart feels ill and goes to lie down. Salieri wonders, perhaps Mozart was right, perhaps genius and crime are incompatible? He thinks of

---

[1] Nikolai Andreyevich Rimsky-Korsakov, *My Musical Life*, ed. Carl Van Vechten, transl. Judah A. Joffe, London, 1974.

Michelangelo (who was said to have had someone crucified, so that he could paint Christ in agony): but perhaps that was just a story, and he wasn't a murderer ...?

Mozart and Salieri is a product of centennial reverence; like *Andrea Chenier* or *Tosca*, it looks back a hundred years and is imbued with a Tchaikovskian, *fin-de-siècle* nostalgia for the rococo. Rimsky-Korsakov writes an aptly tacky, tavern variation on 'Là ci darem' from *Don Giovanni*, but he also creates something entirely new and 'Mozartian', in the piano solo '*Allegretto Semplice*'. He sets nearly every word of Pushkin's text, yet the opera represents a bold declaration of individuality. This strange and strangely demanding work calls for singers who can move an audience through declamation as much as singing, through implication as much as statement. The emotional impact of the ending depends on what is not said, as Salieri sentences himself to mediocrity. Chaliapin, who created the role of Salieri, called it 'a task more difficult than all previous ones' and endowed the role with great dignity, even with a heroic quality.[1]   P.

THE TSAR'S BRIDE

Tsarskaya Nevesta

Opera in four acts, libretto by the composer and I. Tyumenev after the drama by Lev Mey (1849). First performed on 3 November 1899 by the Association of Russian Private Opera, Moscow, with Mootin as Sobakin, Zabelya as Marfa, Shevelyev as Griaznoy, Tarasov as Malyuta, Syekar-Rozhansky as Lykov, Rostovstseva as Lubasha, Shkaffee as Bomelius, conducted by M.M. Ippolitov-Ivanov. First performance in U.K. 1931, London, Lyceum Theatre. First U.S. performance by the Russian Grand Opera Company on 17 May 1922 at the New Amsterdam Theatre ('in a vile manner'[2]). It was revived by Stanislavsky on 28 November 1926 for the State Opera Studio's first performance at the Dmitrovsky Theatre, Moscow. Galina Vishnevskaya brought the opera back into the mainstream once she started to sing Marfa, in 1970.

Vassily Stepanovich Sobakin, *a merchant from Novgorod*..Bass

Marfa, *his daughter, fiancée to Ivan Lykov*........Soprano

Grigory Grigoryevich Griaznoy,
    an Oprichnik ....Baritone

Grigory Lukanovich Malyuta Skuratov,
    head of the Oprichniki..Bass

Ivan Sergeyevich Lykov, *a Boyar,*
    Marfa's fiancé..Tenor

Lubasha, *Griaznoy's mistress* ....Mezzo-Soprano

Elisey Bomelius, *the Tsar's physician* ....Tenor

Domna Ivanovna, *a merchant's wife* ....Soprano

Duniasha, *her daughter, Marfa's friend*.................Alto

Petrovna, *Sobakin's housekeeper* ....Mezzo-Soprano

The Tsar's Valet ....Bass

A Maidservant..................................Mezzo-Soprano

A Young Boy ....Tenor

Tsar Ivan Vassilyevich the Terrible ....Mute

Two Horsemen, the Oprichniki, Singers, Dancers, Boyars, Maidservants, the People

Place: Alexandrovsky, a Suburb of Moscow
Time: Autumn 1572
Running Time: 2 hours 30 minutes

When Rimsky-Korsakov started to compose *The Tsar's Bride* in February 1898 he determined that the 'style of this opera was to be cantilena par excellence [i.e. predominantly vocal]; the arias and soliloquies were planned for development within the limits of the dramatic situations; I had in mind vocal ensembles, genuine, finished, and not at all in the form of any casual and fleeting linking of voices with others, as dictated by the present-day requirements of quasi-dramatic truth, according to which two or more persons are not supposed to talk simultaneously.'[2] It is surely because the composer set out consciously to emphasise the vocal element in *The Tsar's Bride* that he made use of traditional, Italian numbers in its musical structure (given in brackets in the synopsis below). Some commentators have seen these as evidence of Italian style in the opera, but in fact it sounds, unmistakably, very Russian. The only folk melody Rimsky-Korsakov quotes is the traditional salute to the Tsar, 'Slava', but he invents convincing ones for the various 'folk' numbers. The shape of the melodies and their orchestral colouring remain very much a home product: the bells, most obviously, heard at the end of Act I, summoning Griaznoy to matins, and at the beginning of the next act, as

---

[1] In his biography, *Chaliapin* (London, 1988), Victor Borovsky assembles fascinating eyewitness accounts of his Salieri.

[2] Carl Van Vechten, n.11, Nikolai Andreyevich Rimsky-Korsakov, *My Musical Life*, ed. Carl Van Vechten, transl. Judah A. Joffe, London, 1974.

vespers end, but also in the music for Lubasha, one of those richly characteristic Russian voice-types, the neglected mezzo, and for the chorus of Oprichniki. At one point they have a 'Fughetta a 3 voci', but there is nothing Italian about its boisterousness, which scarcely masks their Tsar-sanctioned brutality.

Marfa Sobakin is engaged to be married to Ivan Lykov, who has just returned from travel abroad.

Act I. The Banquet. Inside Griaznoy's house. The proud nobleman Griaznoy asked for the hand of the merchant's daughter Marfa and was rejected. He looks back regretfully to his carefree youth, when he raped whichever girls he fancied. Marfa's innocence disarmed him, but he still defies Lykov to marry her (aria). He has invited several guests tonight. First to arrive are the Oprichniki, the elite guardsmen who attend the Tsar; led by Malyuta, they drink his health. They are followed by Lykov and Bomelius. Lykov describes what he saw abroad and toasts the Tsar who let him travel (arioso).

Singers entertain the guests with a Song of Glory to the Tsar. Malyuta answers Lykov's remarks, that some say Ivan is 'terrible': the storm wind is welcome, because it breaks off dead branches and allows the forest to grow. Young girls perform the Song of the Hops, in which a girl longs for her lover. Malyuta asks for Lubasha, Griaznoy's longstanding mistress, and invites her to entertain them. They applaud her tragic song about a girl who dies when her mother forces her to marry an old miser. The Oprichniki go to attend the Tsar at matins. Griaznoy asks to be left alone with Bomelius. Lubasha hides and listens. Griaznoy asks, on behalf of an old friend, for a love potion. She realises Griaznoy wants it for himself, which means he no longer loves her. When they are alone, Griaznoy rejects her brutally and leaves for matins (duet). She determines to consult Bomelius.

Act II. The Love Potion. Outside Sobakin's house. Townsfolk are leaving the monastery after vespers. They comment on the mild autumn evening but fall silent in fear when the Oprichniki appear. Cowed, the crowd talk instead of whom the Tsar will choose to marry. Two young men emerge from Bomelius's house. When the crowd tell them they have re-nounced their faith by going to see the heathen sor-cerer, one of them throws away the herbs he had been given. Marfa tells her friend Duniasha that she has loved Lykov since they were children, playing in

his garden (aria). Tsar Ivan the Terrible briefly passes by. She does not recognise him, but his intense stare disquiets her. Her father Sobakin brings Lykov and all four look forward to the marriage (quartet).

Lubasha watches Marfa and the others through the window (intermezzo). She calls on Bomelius, refuses to enter his house and asks him for an imper-ceptible, slow-acting poison. He rejects her jewels in payment and demands she respond to his love. When Lykov leaves, Lubasha overhears him say that he will return tomorrow with Griaznoy. Bomelius brings Lubasha the poison. She agrees to Bomelius's price and goes inside with him. The act ends with the Oprichniki anticipating the effects of their vengeance as they execute the Tsar's supreme power.

Act III. The Betrothal. A banqueting room inside Sobakin's house. Sobakin tells Lykov that his mar-riage to Marfa cannot take place immediately. The Tsar is looking for a wife and has asked to see Sobakin's daughters. The news fills Lykov with dread. Griaznoy determines to use the love potion immedi-ately and asks to be invited to the wedding (trio). He also tells Lykov to follow his example: if the wedding is called off, he should not grieve (arietta). Domna Ivanovna, a fellow merchant's wife, brings news that when the Tsar inspected the girls, he spoke to Duniasha and looked at Marfa for a long time. His decision has not yet been announced (arioso). For Lykov, the outlook looks black, but he remains opti-mistic (aria). Sobakin ushers in his daughters and Griaznoy uses the occasion of the toasts to doctor Marfa's drink (sextet with chorus). They all drink to the couple's happiness (quartet). The women sing an Engagement Song. Malyuta arrives, as envoy from the Tsar: Marfa has been chosen as his future bride, the Tsarevna – here Rimsky-Korsakov introduces the theme of Ivan the Terrible from *The Maid of Pskov*. Sobakin collapses.

Act IV. The Bride. Inside the Tsar's palace. Sobakin stands near the throne reserved for the Tsarevna. His happiness over the honour done to his daughter and to him (he is now a Boyar) is clouded by anxiety over his daughter's long illness (aria). Griaznoy greets Sobakin, who is now his equal, and tells him that the man who poisoned Marfa has confessed. Marfa rushes out of her apartments, haggard, with a golden crown falling off her head. She escapes from her attendants, sits on her throne and tells Griaznoy to speak. Malyuta arrives with several Boyars who watch from a doorway. Griaznoy tells her that Lykov confessed under torture that he poisoned Marfa. The Tsar condemned him to death and Griaznoy himself executed the sentence. Marfa faints and all comment on the news, most of them disbelieving Griaznoy (quintet with chorus). Marfa recovers consciousness, but she mistakes Griaznoy for Lykov. Griaznoy repents, confesses his crime and blames Bomelius for substituting a poison for the potion. In a delirium, Marfa invites Lykov to join her in the garden (aria). Lubasha then confesses that she switched the potions. She blames Griaznoy, because he never took pity on her, and invites him to kill her. He stabs her to death and is dragged away by the Boyars. Everyone asks God to have pity on them.

Marfa is 'The Tsar's Bride', but the issue of his marriage is not even discussed until Act II; it does not affect the characters' lives until Act III. This is because the marriage is itself part of something bigger, the tyranny of the Tsar, whose power is as all-pervasive as he is remote.

Stanislavsky understood that the central point of the opera is when the Tsar himself appears in Act II, even though it lasts only a moment (eight bars of music) and passes in silence. Typically, Stanislavsky prepared for his entry: as the bassoons renewed the theme of glory to the Tsar, two guardsmen emerged from the monastery and stood either side of the portal, then six nuns ran out and knelt in front. When the brass took over the theme the Tsar appeared from the monastery (not as in the score), wearing a rich fur coat over a monk's habit and a huge silver cross on his chest. 'He walks like a sinner laden with chains. Paying no attention to the nuns he moves towards the well and devoutly crosses himself. A sharp chord comes from the orchestra and he stops short, having glimpsed, beyond the ikon on the well, a young girl thoughtfully looking up to the sky. Under the insistent gaze of the monk she turns abruptly towards him and is transfixed. "Suddenly towering over you," said Stanislavsky to Marfa, "you see a horrible face, a mask, a fateful figure. You see your future as you look deep into his eyes. And you," this to the actor playing Ivan the Terrible, "first

study the ikon and then are aware of Marfa ... The moment should be drawn in various shades: first your hand is frozen in mid-air as you cross yourself, then you are full of admiration, which passes on into the smile of a tiger as you let your arm down mechanically ... until, finally, you give a relieved sigh, as much as to say 'She belongs to me!'"[1]   P.

TSAR SALTAN

Opera in a prologue and four acts, libretto by V.I. Bielsky, after Pushkin's poem, and planned as a centenary tribute to Pushkin. Première Moscow, Solodovnikov Theatre, 3 November 1900, with Ippolitov-Ivanov conducting. First performed Buenos Aires, 1927, with Eva Turner, Antonio Melandri, Ezio Pinza, conductor Panizza (revived in seven seasons of the next twenty-five, with such singers as Gina Cigna, Slobodskaya, Umberto di Lelio, Baccaloni); la Scala, 1929, with Bruna Rasa, Melandri, di Lelio, conductor Panizza; London, Sadler's Wells, 1933, with Joan Cross, Henry Wendon, conductor Lawrence Collingwood; Strasland, 1962, and Dresden, 1967, in new German version by Harry Kupfer.

Tsar Saltan	Bass
Three sisters	
Militrissa, the Youngest	Soprano
The Middle *(the Court Weaver)*	Mezzo-Soprano
The Eldest *(the Royal Cook)*	Soprano
Barbarikha, *their mother*	Contralto
Prince Guidon	Tenor
The Swan-Princess	High Soprano
An Old Man	Tenor
A Messenger	Baritone
A Court Jester	Bass
Three Sailors	Tenor, Baritone, Bass

Boyars, Courtiers, Nurses, Secretaries, Guards, Warriors, Sailors, Servants, People; Thirty-Three Heroes and their Leader Cernomor

Place: The City of Tmutarakania; the Island of Buyan
Time: Legendary
Running Time: 3 hours 15 minutes

During winter 1898–99, Rimsky-Korsakov and Byelsky worked on Pushkin's fairy-tale of *Tsar Saltan*, making as much use as possible of Pushkin's

---

[1] Pavel Rumyantsev's fascinating account of Stanislavsky's rehearsals for his 1926 production shed light on the opera as well as on Stanislavsky. Act I, for example, 'is in dark tones. This is a centre of vice, debauchery, evil passions. ... Griaznoy is a wild beast in a cage, he is prowling around like a tiger.' When the curtain goes up, Griaznoy has 'been drinking continuously for two weeks'; he is 'bloated from drunkenness, but [he] can get no rest.' During the party, 'Malyuta is treated like an archpriest. He must fill up as much room as possible, puff himself up, spread himself out!' On her first appearance, the Oprichniki 'look over Lubasha as experts in prize horseflesh.' Constantin Stanislavsky and Pavel Rumyantsev, *Stanislavsky on Opera*, New York, 1975.

words, and Rimsky-Korsakov set it scene by scene, finishing half the orchestration by summer 1899 and the remainder the following year. He seems to have been particularly pleased with the symphonic construction of the score and, when he published it, even started his preface with a warning against the damaging effect of cuts on the musical shape. With twenty-five years of experience behind him, he was by now a most practised operatic composer and easily able to invest music and structure with a fairy-tale quality, now folk-like, now lyrical, now dramatic. The recitatives, he said, had a special character of fairy-tale naïveté, but in contrast he was pleased with the use he made of Leitmotifs.

A brass fanfare begins each scene or movement, and out of the preludes to Acts I, II and IV, the composer made a suite called *Little Pictures for the Fairy Tale of Tsar Saltan*.

Prologue. On a winter's night, three sisters sit spinning, watched by their mother and a black cat. The youngest seems to be treated as a kind of Cinderella, so it is a folk-style duet that the two elder sing; it occasionally becomes a trio when their mother joins in. If I were Queen, says the eldest, I should cook the most sumptuous meals in the world. If *I* were Queen, says the second sister, I would weave the finest cloth ever known. If *I* were Queen, says the youngest sister, I should bear the Tsar a son who was strong and brave. A march announces the Tsar, who sounds like a more serious cousin of King Dodon, and he chooses the youngest because of what he has just heard her say. Jobs as the Royal Cook and the Court Weaver are found for the other sisters, but the idea of being subservient to the youngest is abhorrent to them and with their mother they plot that, after the wedding and with the new Tsarina pregnant, the Tsar must go off to war. Then they will spread a scandal: the Tsarina has given birth to a monster, not a son!

Act I. The entr'acte gets the Tsar safely off to war and the curtain rises on the court and the gentle sound of off-stage singing by the nursery maids. The Tsarina's son has been born, and she has sent a message to the Tsar, but why has no messenger as yet come back from him? The wicked Barbarikha has of course set the plot in motion. The Court Jester tries to entertain them while they wait for the messenger, the cook-sister plies her food, and an old man has a story to tell. He and the Jester bandy words and the resulting laughter wakes

the baby. The nursery maids sing again, with Barbarikha again adding her macabre descant, and the baby falls asleep so that the old man finally gets his chance. The baby wakes up and the nursery maids sing a clapping song. The Tsarevich, by now grown to be big enough to run in on his own, holds the Tsarina's hand while the people sing his praises.

The chorus is interrupted by the arrival of the fatal messenger, who has returned from the Tsar. His pronouncement is portentous, to the effect that the Queen and her offspring are to be thrown into the sea. The Tsarina is in despair, but the Boyars, egged on by Barbarikha, dare not disobey.

Militrissa sings affectingly of her lost happiness, of the unfairness of the Tsar's condemnation without having even seen his son, but she accepts her bitter fate. Together Tsarina and Tsarevich contemplate the sea, then climb into a barrel and pray that they may find land and eventual freedom. The barrel is sealed and thrown into the sea and the people are left weeping behind.

Act II. The orchestral introduction has the stars gleaming in a deep blue sky and the barrel tossing on the ocean. The child grows hour by hour more worthy of his father – so Pushkin's verses appended as motto in the score assure us and so the orchestra seems to emphasise. It is a beautiful passage.

When they land, it is on the island of Buyan, which seems to be a desert on which grows a single small oak tree. The Tsarina and Prince Guidon, now grown to full tenorhood, rejoice at being on dry land after all that time in the barrel, he full of optimism, she still pessimistic and inclined to suspicion. He fashions a bow and arrow out of wood he finds on the shore then, hearing the lamentation of a swan, transfixes with his arrow the kite which has been attacking it so that it falls dead into the sea. The kite, represented by male voices off-stage, is a malevolent magician, the swan a princess, who now comes from the sea and sings sweetly, for all the world like a cousin of the Queen of Shemakha, to the man who has saved its life.

Militrissa sings to her son and he asks what they can have done to his father to deserve such a fate. She can tell him nothing and both fall asleep; a short orchestral interlude depicts the darkness of night.

When they wake up it is to see against the dawn sky that the swan has conjured up a great domed city, sparkling in the new light and fabulously beautiful as well as extravagantly rich. They advance towards the city, bells ring out, cannons are fired and the people flock to greet them. On the Tsarina's advice, Guidon accepts the throne when it is offered him and the act ends with general rejoicing.

Act III. From the now flourishing seashore of the island of Buyan, Prince Guidon watches a ship leave bearing a message from him to his father. His aria is full of longing for home – if only his father will listen to his message! He asks the swan for help and is advised to transform himself into an insect, overtake the ship and visit his father (the Russian translation for Pushkin's choice of his first alias is 'mosquito', but Rimsky-Korsakov jumped the gun and chose Pushkin's third).

The orchestral interlude is the now famous chromatic passage (sometimes played on solo string instrument) known as the Flight of the Bumble Bee and it transports us again to Tmutarakania. The trumpet introduces Tsar Saltan on his throne, with the Royal Cook, the Court Weaver and Barbarikha not far away. Three sailors come in attended by the bumble bee; Pushkin's literary device of three separate journeys revealing three marvels is replaced by the sailors each telling of a particular experience.

The second sailor speaks first and tells of an extraordinary phenomenon. An island which used to be deserted, with a single oak tree on the shore, is now a great city with gilded churches, mansions, gardens and a court. There lives Prince Guidon – and he sends his respects to the Tsar. The Tsar says he must visit him but the Royal Cook and Court Weaver aided by Barbarikha pour cold water on the whole idea. The bumble bee, who has been observing, cannot bear to remain a spectator and flies down and stings the Cook-Sister on the eye. The first sailor proceeds to relate his marvel. Underneath a fir tree, a squirrel sits singing and cracking nuts – each nutshell is made of gold and inside is an emerald. The Weaving-Sister is totally scornful and is also stung on the eye. Now it is the turn of the third sailor, who says that on the same island on which the new city stands, every day a great wave floods the shore leaving behind thirty-three knights in gleaming armour, led by an old man, Cernomor. The Tsar rather crossly makes up his mind to visit the island but Barbarikha puts her oar firmly in and is in her turn stung by the bumble bee, which has no trouble evading the Tsar's guards.

Act IV. Back on the island, Prince Guidon is lonely and becoming conscious that he has no wife. He asks the swan for advice and is told of a beautiful princess, just such a one as he is dreaming of, not living far away as he imagines but close at hand. As they sing together in duet, the swan first reads him a lesson on the responsibilities of taking a wife, then reveals herself as a princess. Guidon is beside himself with delight and their duet ends in total accord (with a top C from each on the way). Female voices rejoice in their happiness and herald the appearance of the Tsarina, from whom Guidon asks a blessing on their marriage. Signalled by the brass, the orchestra launches into a lengthy and episodic description of the three marvels.

Guidon and his mother watch Tsar Saltan's fleet sail towards the island, then with the whole populace welcome the Tsar. Prince Guidon asks him to tell his story, which he does in an aria, with melancholy references to his wife, whom he loved and can't forget, and to his warlike expedition, after which he lost her and his son to his infinite regret. Guidon comforts him but Barbarikha and the two wicked sisters try to distract his attention. In succession, he sees three marvels – the miraculous squirrel, the thirty-three guards led by Cernomor, and then the Swan Princess in her full glory and with her high-flying song as fluent as ever.

Tsar Saltan asks for a boon: may he see his Tsarina again? The Swan Princess gratifies his wish and he expresses his delight, rather belatedly one may think, in duet with Militrissa, then greets his son whom he now recognises.

The wicked sisters and their mother beg for mercy. The Tsar at first threatens them, then, in his happiness and encouraged by Militrissa and Guidon, relents. All rejoice in a scene of festivity, including the old man who promises to tell the story accurately – and to have a drink on it.   H.

THE LEGEND OF THE INVISIBLE CITY OF KITEZH AND THE MAIDEN FEVRONIYA

Opera in four acts, libretto by Vladmir Ivanovich Belsky after a Russian legend. Première St Petersburg, 20 February 1907.

Fevroniya ....Soprano

Prince Vsevolod Yurievich ....Tenor

Prince Yuri Vsevolodovich ....Bass
Grishka Kuterma, *a drunkard*............................Tenor
Fyodr Poyarok ....Bass
Man with a Bear ....Tenor
Gusliar, *a minstrel*..Baritone
Beggar Singer ....Baritone
Young Boy..Mezzo-Soprano
Burundai, *a Tartar warrior* ....Bass-Baritone
Biediai, *a Tartar warrior* ....Baritone
Birds of Paradise*........Two Sopranos, Mezzo-Soprano

Place: In and Near Kitezh
Time: Medieval
Running Time: 3 hours 20 minutes

Act I. A forest. The maiden Fevroniya lives with her young brother, revelling in the animals who abound there and singing of the joys and sorrows of nature. Suddenly, she sees a stranger who might have been part of a hunting party and lost his way. She offers him hospitality and assures him that she needs no church in which to worship as God is all around them. They fall in love and their duet grows in rapture. The stranger gives her a ring but hears hunting horns nearby and goes off to join his companions, who shortly appear and tell Fevroniya that the ring with which she has been betrothed belongs to Prince Vsevolod, son of the ruler of Kitezh.

Act II. The town of Little Kitezh, a short way from the citadel of Great Kitezh. The crowd buzzes with excitement as it waits for the procession of Fevroniya on her way to her wedding in the great city. An old bard prophesies doom, a trained bear dances, and a group of well-off citizens persuades the drunken Grishka to insult Fevroniya, whose lowly birth makes her in their view an unsuitable bride for the Prince. The crowd nonetheless acclaims Fevroniya until panic-stricken people pour into the marketplace and announce a Tartar attack. The invaders prove utterly ruthless but take two prisoners, Grishka, to guide them to the great city, and Fevroniya, because of her beauty. The citizens depart in panic but Fevroniya prays that by a miracle the great city become invisible to the enemy.

Act III. The cathedral square of Great Kitezh. It is night, the citizens have assembled outside the cathedral and Fyodr Poyarok, who has been blinded by the Tartars, tells them of the destruction wrought by the advancing enemy. Prince Yuri prays for the city

and sends his page up a tower to stand guard and warn of the Tartars' approach. The young prince leads the army against the enemy, bells toll and a golden mist descends as by a miracle to hide the city.

An entr'acte portrays the battle of Kerzhenets, where the Russians are defeated and Prince Vsevolod killed.

Grishka has led the Tartars with Fevroniya as their prisoner to the banks of Lake Svetly Yar, from where they should be able to see the city. But it is invisible and all they can hear is the sound of bells. The Tartars accuse Grishka of deceit and threaten to torture him next day if he has misled them, offering to execute him quickly if Kitezh becomes visible, beheading being the least due to traitorous behaviour such as his. Biediai and Burundai quarrel, as if they were Fafner and Fasolt, as to which will have Fevroniya, and Burundai kills Biediai. Burundai goes to rape Fevroniya but she manages with a superhuman effort to subdue him with a look and mesmerise him to sleep. She cuts the ropes which tie her and releases Grishka, who is about to escape when he hears the bells of Kitezh tolling and resounding inside his skull. It is his punishment for cowardice and he rushes towards the Lake, only to stop short when he sees the great city's reflection in the waters. He and Fevroniya escape as the Tartars awake, in their turn see the reflection and decide a mystical power battles against them. They retreat in disarray.

Act IV. A forest, the next night. Fevroniya and Grishka are by now exhausted and he has gone raving mad. Nothing Fevroniya can do will comfort him and he runs off howling into the distance. She falls asleep and the scene around her changes from marsh to garden, where she is magically reunited with Prince Vsevolod. The voices of birds tell her she is to die but the Prince reveals that Kitezh and its inhabitants have survived.

Together they are taken to the great city and the wedding party, interrupted in the second act, resumes. The opera ends as Fevroniya pleads for the salvation of Grishka and she and Vsevolod look forward to everlasting happiness.

Its most ardent admirers have described *Kitezh* as a Russian *Parsifal*, citing the powerful Christianity embodied in the figure of Fevroniya and the Wagnerian overtones throughout the opera. It is one of Rimsky-Korsakov's most ambitious works and its combination of pantheistic folklore and Christian mystery has not interfered with his depiction of the remarkable figure of Grishka, a figure of almost Mussorgskian power and imagination. H.

LE COQ D'OR

Zolotoy Pyetushok/The Golden Cockerel

Opera in three acts, text by V. Bielsky after Pushkin. Première Moscow, 7 October 1909. First performed Paris Opéra, 1914; Drury Lane, London, 1914, with Dobrowolska, Petrenko, Petroff, Altchevsky, conductor Emil Cooper; Metropolitan, New York, 1918, with Barrientos, Didur, conductor Monteux (in French). Revived Covent Garden, 1919 (in English), with Nelis, Richardson, conductor Beecham; Buenos Aires, 1937, with Carosio, Melnik; Metropolitan, 1937, with Pons and Pinza, 1942, with Bok and Pinza, 1945, with Munsel and Cordon; Rome, 1940, with Carosio, Pasero, conductor Serafin; Covent Garden, 1954, with Dobbs, Cuénod, Glynne, conductor Markevitch (in English); New York, City Opera, 1967, with Sills, Treigle; Scottish Opera, 1975, with Catherine Gayer, John Angelo Messana, Don Garrard, conductor Gibson; Edinburgh Festival, 1979.

King Dodon	Bass
Prince Guidon	Tenor
Prince Afron	Baritone
General Polkan	Bass
Amelfa, *the royal housekeeper*	Contralto
The Astrologer	Tenor
The Queen of Shemakha	Soprano
The Golden Cockerel	Soprano

Running Time: 2 hours 25 minutes

*L*e Coq d'Or was Rimsky-Korsakov's last opera. The censor refused to sanction its performance – rather surprisingly, unless he found the references to military incompetence a little too apt – and it was not until after the composer's death that it was performed. When the work was given in Petersburg, it was thought to be over-taxing for the singers who are obliged to dance, or for the dancers who are obliged to sing. Fokine, the choreographer, ingeniously devised the plan of having all the singers seated at each side of the stage, while the dancers interpreted in pantomime what was sung. In spite of the protests made by the composer's family, this was done in Paris, London, and New York, but a return has been made to the directions laid down by Rimsky-Korsakov.

The story of *Le Coq d'Or* is taken from Pushkin. It is

quite possible to fill it with symbolical meaning, although the librettist, Bielsky, preferred to think of it as dealing with human passions and weaknesses in their essence and quite apart from any particular context.

Prologue. A muted trumpet gives out the theme associated with the cockerel, and it is immediately followed by a descending chromatic melody on the clarinet, which is characteristic of the Queen of Shemakha, Ex. 1:

Much of the music of this short prelude is derived from the Queen's aria of Act II. The thin, *staccato* sound of the xylophone heralds the appearance of the Astrologer before the curtain. By his art, he says, he will conjure up for the audience a tale from long ago; though it is only a fairy story, its moral is excellent. The Astrologer's music is instrumental rather than vocal in character and its *tessitura* abnormally high.

Act I. The court of King Dodon. The council-room is magnificently decorated, and the King is seated in the middle of his ministers and advisers, his two sons, Guidon and Afron, on either side of him. He complains that his neighbours treat him unfairly; when he was young and vigorous, he used to go out to attack them at the head of his armies; now that he is old, they are inclined to invade him, in spite of the fact that he finds it more and more troublesome to engage in warfare. What advice can his councillors give him to meet the present invasion threat? Guidon, his elder son, is the first to speak. His recommendation is that the King withdraw his army inside the capital of his kingdom, and there, supplied with a vast stock of provisions and necessaries, think out the whole problem at leisure. All applaud the suggestion, except old General Polkan, the King's chief minister, who finds the whole notion futile and impractical. Afron spurns his brother's plan, and advises that the army be disbanded and sent home; once the enemy is past them, they may re-unite and fall upon him from the rear and destroy him. Dodon

Le Coq d'Or *(Covent Garden, 1945). Mattiwilda Dobbs as the Queen of Shemakha, Howell Glynne as King Dodon.*

is delighted, but Polkan demolishes Afron's proposal as quickly as he had Guidon's. There seems no reasonable and practical solution.

Suddenly, preceded by the same music as we had heard in the prologue, the Astrologer appears at the top of the stairs, dressed in a blue robe covered in golden stars, and with a long white astrakhan hat on his head. In music of characteristic cast, he offers the King a magic golden cockerel, which has only to be placed so that it has a view of the surrounding country, and it will crow to give warning of any danger. When it is quiet, the King may rest peacefully and take his ease with no fear of danger. Dodon rejoices, and offers the Astrologer any reward he likes to name, but the old man says he will not take money or honours, but would like to have the King's promise in writing so as to take advantage of his offer at some future date. This request is refused, the King saying in effect that his word is his bond.

The cock bids the King take his ease heedless of danger. Dodon rejoices at the prospect of never again having to be on his guard; he will indulge his pleasures and his desire for sleep from now on for ever. He begins to feel sleepy, and the royal nurse, Amelfa, has his bed brought in by servants. He lies down, eats sweetmeats out of a bowl, and plays with his parrot, which sings to him (in the orchestra). As he goes to sleep, watched by the faithful Amelfa, the orchestra begins the slumber scene (as it is known in the orchestral suite), in which the woodwind quietly repeat the cockerel's assurance that he can rest undisturbed while the cellos play a gentle lullaby. Even Amelfa falls asleep, and the sound of Ex. 1 shows that the King in his dream is anticipating his amorous encounter of the next act.

But the King has not slept for long before he is roused by the warning cry of the cockerel, which is echoed by the instruments of the orchestra. Polkan manages to wake his master, who gives orders for a general mobilisation of the army. It gets under way to the sound of a march. Soon all is quiet, and Dodon is allowed by his watchful bird to return to his slumbers. He cannot recapture his attractive dream – cannot even remember what it was about. Amelfa tries to help him and makes one or two suggestions, finally hitting upon the right one. All go to sleep once more, only to be awakened by an even more urgent summons from the cockerel than previously. This time Polkan warns the King that he is in danger

himself, and that he must gird himself and lead his army to victory. With much grumbling, Dodon prepares to don his armour. It is found to be rusty, his sword is too heavy, his cuirass is too tight for him and will hardly meet round his middle. But in the end, he is sufficiently arrayed to go off to the wars, which he does to the acclamation of the crowd.

Act II. The war goes badly, and moonlight in a narrow pass reveals the bodies of the soldiers and the King's two sons, lying dead and unattended. The march of the preceding act is now oppressed with gloom, and Dodon bursts into lamentation when he finds the bodies of his slain sons.

The mists which have shrouded the pass lift, and reveal a tent. General consternation. Could it belong to the enemy general? Reluctantly the soldiers are persuaded to drag a piece of comic artillery which is trained on the tent, and eventually with much difficulty fired. But its only effect is that a beautiful young woman emerges from the tent; the soldiers, all but Dodon and Polkan, take to their heels and disappear. The young woman, with nothing but the clarinet phrase of Ex. 1 as prelude, sings the praises of the sun, which gives life and beauty to her native land. This is the famous 'Hymn to the Sun', whose sensuously beautiful melody has made it among Rimsky-Korsakov's vocal compositions second in popularity only to the Song of the Indian Guest from *Sadko*.

When she is questioned, the girl reveals that she is the Queen of Shemakha, come to subdue Dodon, not by force of arms but by her own physical beauty. Dodon is shyer than Polkan, but eventually Polkan's bluntness goes too far and she asks for him to be sent away. Dodon promptly complies, and Polkan watches proceedings from behind the Queen's tent (the bodies of the soldiers have by now been cleared away, and the scene is bathed in sunlight).

Beginning with a little 6/8 tune in which she describes her unclothed beauty, the Queen proceeds to vamp Dodon in seductive snatches of song. Even an orchestral reference to the cockerel's warning makes not the slightest difference to the King, who appears to enjoy the process of becoming ensnared. The Queen tells him he must sing for her, as he no doubt once did in his youth, and at her orders he starts an incredibly primitive-sounding melody, much to her glee. The Queen tries new tactics. At home everyone obeys her slightest whim, and her caprice rules her kingdom;

Oh, for contradiction, even domination! Timidly Dodon offers himself as dominator, and she asks him to dance for her – as he must once have danced when he was young. She rigs him up with a fan and scarf in place of his cumbersome armour, and has her slaves play a slow melody to accompany him. She joins him and mocks his efforts, which land him, as the music gets quicker, on some cushions in a state of collapse.

By now, the King is completely under the Queen's spell. He repeats his offer of his hand, his possessions, his throne, his kingdom. She accepts with the proviso that Polkan shall forthwith be whipped; Dodon offers to go further and behead him. Preparations are immediately put in hand for a return to Dodon's kingdom, and, while the Queen's slaves mock at her newest capture, Dodon's army lines up to escort their monarch and his bride to their capital.

Act III. We are back in Dodon's court. The crowd is wondering if and when he will return. Rumours are noised abroad: he has won a great victory, but lost his two sons, and is escorting home as his bride a young queen whom he rescued from a dragon. All must be well, argue the people, since the cockerel is quiet. Then the cry goes up that the procession is at hand. Eventually the King and his bride appear in their gilded chariot.

Suddenly, proceedings are interrupted by the appearance of the Astrologer, preceded by his characteristic music. He has come to claim his reward from the King; it shall be the Princess who rides by the King's side! The King angrily refuses, but the Astrologer persists, emphasising his determination to risk marriage even at his age with a sustained top E

(Rimsky-Korsakov, in his preface to the score, underlines the fact that the role of the Astrologer requires a tenor with a highly developed falsetto voice). The King orders his guards to remove the old man, and when he seems still anxious to continue the dispute, Dodon strikes him on the head with his sceptre, and kills him. The sky darkens, thunder is heard, and Dodon has the grace to appear embarrassed at the turn events have taken; such a bad omen on one's wedding day! The Queen laughs at the whole episode, but, when Dodon tries to embrace her, repulses him in disgust. The cockerel suddenly comes to life, utters a piercing cry, flies over the crowd and pecks the King on the head. He falls dead, and the crowd loyally break into lamentation for him. The sky becomes completely dark, and when light returns, both Queen and cockerel have disappeared.

In the epilogue, the resuscitated Astrologer announces that the story is only a fairy-tale and that in Dodon's kingdom only the Queen and he himself were mortals.

Le Coq d'Or is more compactly shaped than Rimsky-Korsakov's other stage works, and the gorgeous orchestration has a new economy and is treated with a more directly pointed sense of style than elsewhere. The spectacular staging which the work requires, and the hardly less spectacular vocal writing for the coloratura-soprano Queen, are qualities which have contributed to the opera's popularity; they also constitute a direct link with Rimsky-Korsakov's most famous pupil, Stravinsky, whose first opera, *Le Rossignol*, begun a year after *Le Coq d'Or*, makes use of exactly the same characteristics.   H.

GIOACCHINO ANTONIO ROSSINI
(born 29 February 1792, died 13 November 1868)

Rossini is a bundle of paradox, or at least of superficial contradiction. He was a man of celebrated wit and apparent worldliness, yet consumed by nerves and cursed with the thinnest of skins; he has been famous for the two hundred years since his birth for his comedies, yet in his own time

just as well known as a composer of *opera seria*; he wrote prolifically and fast (thirty-nine operas in nineteen years) yet during the last twenty-nine years of his life produced no operas and, some short vocal and piano pieces apart, only two full-length works, both to sacred texts. Even his birthdate, 29 February

1792 – Leap Year – marks him out as an exception.

The twentieth century's view of Rossini has tended therefore to be lopsided. To think of him as a jovial *bon vivant*, who wrote superb, if slightly farcical comic operas, who was as much interested in culinary as musical pursuits, who gave up composition for a life of luxury in Paris, is as far from the point as to rate Winston Churchill primarily a brilliant if sharply-angled historian. Rossini was almost as much a prodigy as Schubert, his near-contemporary, or Mendelssohn, his early music (such as the six *Sonate a quattro* for strings, written about 1804) suggesting a classical grounding as much as it foreshadows the *buffo* writing of his mature operas. *La Cambiale di Matrimonio* was performed when he was eighteen, he had written twelve successful operas by the time he was twenty-two, and he became proficient in all operatic forms, serious as well as comic, so as in Italy to dominate the first half of the nineteenth century as Verdi did the second.

He was pioneer as well as practitioner; he developed the Italian *buffo* tradition to its ultimate; he wrote in *Guillaume Tell* the finest specimen to date of the French Grand Opera; and at the Théâtre Italien in Paris, he was an influence for good on a number of composers and singers. That his operas, apart from *The Barber*, fell into disuse after his death is a comment more on fashion than on their quality, but interest in the comedies began to revive in the 1920s with the appearance of the great coloratura mezzo, Conchita Supervia, continued with the advocacy of the conductor Vittorio Gui, not least at Glyndebourne, and in the second half of the century, the *opere serie* were once again performed, now in reliable editions. As a result, a festival devoted to his operas has been started in Pesaro, recordings have been made of what would once have been considered his most obscure works, and a new view is rapidly developing of one of opera's greatest figures.   H.

LA SCALA DI SETA
The Silken Ladder

Farsa comica in one act, libretto by Giuseppe Maria Foppa, based on François-Antoine-Eugène de Planard's libretto for the *opéra comique L'Échelle de soie*, set by Pierre Gaveaux (1808). First performance at the Teatro San Moisè, Venice, 9 May 1812, with Maria Cantarelli as Giulia, Carolina Nagher as Lucilla, Rafaele Monelli as Dorvil, Nicola Tacci as Blansac, Nicola de Grecis as Germano and Gaetano Del Monte as Dormont. First U.K. performance by the Piccolo Teatro dell'Opera Comica at Sadler's Wells Theatre, London, 1954. U.S. première at University of Cincinnati, 1989, conducted by H. Teri Murai. Revived at the Rossini Opera Festival, Pesaro, 1988, with Luciana Serra as Giulia, Cecilia Bartoli as Lucilla and William Matteuzzi as Dorvil, and has since entered the general repertory.

Giulia, *secretly married to Dorvil*....................Soprano
Lucilla, *her cousin* ....Mezzo-Soprano
Dorvil, *Giulia's husband*......................................Tenor
Germano, *a servant*..Bass
Blansac ....Bass
Dormont, *Giulia's tutor*......................................Tenor

Place: The Countryside, outside Paris
Running Time: 1 hour

Rossini's first operatic effort was at the age of thirteen, in 1805, when he contributed several arias and ensembles to the *opera seria Demetrio e Polibio*, not staged until 1812. Rossini entered Bologna's Accademia Filarmonica in 1806 but left early, and was already composing an opera for the Teatro San Moisè, Venice, in 1810 (*La cambiale di matrimonio*). *La scala di seta* is the earliest of Rossini's operas to have made it into the general repertory.

Giulia has married Dorvil without permission from her tutor/guardian Dormont, who promised her to Dorvil's friend, Blansac. Husband and wife spent the night together in Giulia's apartment.

Giulia has to get rid of the servant, Germano ('Va, sciocco, non seccarmi') and then of her cousin, Lucilla (trio, 'Un altro malanno'), before Dorvil can leave secretly via the silken ladder that will be waiting for him again at midnight. Dormont warns her to be ready to welcome Blansac as her husband. Having noticed that Blansac appeals to Lucilla, Giulia has determined to marry them off. She appeals to Germano to spy on them (duet, 'Io so ch'ai buon core'). Blansac himself comes to call on Giulia, bringing his friend Dorvil with him. Dorvil warns Blansac that Giulia does not care for him. This merely piques Blansac, who is so confident he will inspire her with love that he invites Dorvil to hide and observe him in action. Dorvil agrees, so as to test his wife's fidelity ('Vedrò qual sommo incanto'). Germano also hides, so he can watch and learn how to woo a woman, but he notices that someone else is watching already. Giulia quizzes Blansac on his fidelity, for the sake of her cousin Lucilla. This misleads Blansac and the two men watching (quartet, 'Si che unito a cara sposa'). Dorvil leaves in fury. Blansac bumps into Lucilla, who strikes him as much more beautiful than Giulia. Lucilla is equally attracted to him ('Sento talor nell'anima').

Giulia longs for midnight, so she can clear up the misunderstanding with Dorvil ('Il mio ben sospiro e chiamo'). Germano overhears and assumes that her rendezvous involves Blansac. He determines to listen in on it, in case he can learn something ('Amore dolce-mente'). Overcome with sleep and, perhaps, the effects of drink, he manages to let Blansac as well as Lucilla know about the rendezvous. Germano and Lucilla hide separately in Giulia's room and watch as Dorvil arrives via the silken ladder, shortly followed by Blansac (finale, 'Dorme ognuno in queste soglie'). The noise wakes Dormont, who arrives in his night-dress and discovers all the others in hiding. His anger is easily mollified, however: he allows them all to do as they wish, since there is no arguing with love.

Rossini cracks the whip four times at the start of his fizzing overture to *La scala di seta*, to summon orchestral players and audience to attention. The opera itself is ruled by an equally strict hand: vocal fireworks are matched by some brilliantly inventive woodwind writing, with piccolo often prominent. Charming arias for all the voices are supplemented by a series of remarkable ensembles, which give the work its intense, slightly sharp flavour. A flirtatious duo for mistress and servant anticipates some of *Il barbiere*'s humour, but is charged with a cruder, more obviously erotic edge; the fugal quartet 'Si che unito a cara sposa', as rigorously worked out as *Idomeneo*'s 'Andrò ramingo e solo', works to ruthlessly comic, rather than tragic effect: the characters are driven not by fate but by the composer. The arbitrarily resolved plot matters less than the musical forms Rossini imposes with such bravura.   P.

LA PIETRA DEL PARAGONE

The Touchstone

Melodramma giocoso in two acts, libretto by Luigi Romanelli. First performance at la Scala, Milan, 26 September 1812, with Carolina Zerbini as Aspasia, Marietta Marcolini as Clarice, Claudio Bonoldi as Giocondo, Filippo Galli as Asdrubale, Pietro Vasoli as Pacuvio. First U.K. performance, St Pancras Town Hall, London, 1963, Glyndebourne, 1964, in Günther Rennert's radically intrusive German version, with Ugo Trama as Asdrubale, Josephine Veasey as Clarice and Anna Reynolds as Ortensia (i.e. Aspasia), conducted by John Pritchard. Wexford Festival, 1975. First U.S. performance, Hartford College of Music, 1955.

Fulvia	Mezzo-Soprano
Baroness Aspasia	Soprano
Marchioness Clarice, *in love with Asdrubale*	Contralto
The Cavalier Giocondo, *Asdrubale's friend*	Tenor
Count Asdrubale	Bass
Pacuvio, *poet*	Bass
Count Macrobio, *journalist*	Bass
Fabrizio	Bass

Guests, Gardeners

Place: A Country Villa
Time: 'The Present' (1812)/Eighteenth Century
Running Time: 2 hours 35 minutes

The libretto by la Scala's resident poet was tailor-made for Rossini, who was making his début in Italy's most important opera house, and for his cast: Luigi Romanelli manoeuvred brilliantly to suit the star contralto Marietta Marcolini, who wanted to appear in soldier's dress, and he provided Rossini with a witty comedy, distinguished by its topical references to journalistic conditions in Milan, and, more unexpectedly, by its reserves of human feeling. It inspired Rossini with a new quality of music, and was performed fifty-three times during the season.

Count Asdrubale has not decided which of three widows he wishes to marry, since he cannot be sure whether any of them is motivated by love or merely by a longing for his money.

Act I. A garden. Asdrubale's guests and his gardeners admire his wisdom, but observe that he seems in no hurry to choose a wife. They ignore the poet Pacuvio when he tries to read them his new poem, as do Fabrizio and the Baroness. Donna Fulvia is less rude: intending to marry the Count for his money, she promises to look after Pacuvio. The journalist Macrobio tries to offer his services to the Cavalier Giocondo but is firmly rejected. When Clarice thinks aloud about the way the Count claims he doesn't love her, her words are echoed by the Count himself (duet, 'Quel dirmi, oh dio! non t'amo'). For a moment, she believes that he does love her; the Count, however, dare not trust his own feelings ('Se di certo io non sapessi').

They fence with one another (duet, 'Conte mio').

Donna Fulvia has brought a rose to present to the Count. First, Pacuvio insists on reading her his poem ('Ombretta sdegnosa del Missipipi' [sic]). She presents her rose and Pacuvio recites some more verses to explain its overblown state. Asdrubale determines to test the women using a 'pietra del paragone'. The Count and Giocondo attack Macrobio, but Clarice intervenes to point out that none of the men acts reasonably (quartet, 'Voi volete, e non volete'). As pre-arranged, Fabrizio hands the Count a piece of paper and he pretends to make light of some bad news. Macrobio refuses to publish Pacuvio's new poem ('Chi è colei chi s'avvicina?'). When everyone learns that Count Asdrubale has lost his fortune, the Baroness and Fulvia congratulate themselves that they got away before marriage. Wearing a disguise, the Count pretends to be his own creditor, bent on sequestering his assets, which will all be sealed ('Sigillarà'). The Baroness, Fulvia, Pacuvio and Macrobio abandon the Count to Clarice, who accepts the responsibility happily. All react with amazement to the news that the Count does not owe any money after all (finale, 'Qual chi dorme e in sogno crede').

Act II. The Baroness and Fulvia determine to exact revenge for what happened; Macrobio and Pacuvio apologise to the Count. The Baroness forces Macrobio to challenge the Count to a duel. The Count invites everyone to come hunting. Pacuvio fails to shoot anything as a storm blows up. Giocondo is wracked by jealousy at the thought of Clarice in another's arms ('Quell'alme pupille'). Clarice explains that she loves the Count, but Giocondo is welcome to keep hoping that her affections will change ('Sperar se vuoi'). The Count overhears and misunderstands. Macrobio teases them by discussing the plot of his poem, which echoes their situation (trio, 'Su queste piante incisi').

Clarice also decides to play the 'touchstone' trick. She pretends her long-lost twin brother Captain Lucindo is coming to see her. Fulvia forces Pacuvio to fight a duel on her behalf. Giocondo also challenges Macrobio to a duel, but first he and the Count pretend they will fight for the right to kill Macrobio. The Count explains that the laws of hospitality oblige him to yield this right to his guest, Giocondo. Having forced Macrobio to admit he is an idiot, they spare him (trio, 'Prima fra voi coll'armi'). Clarice appears, disguised in military uniform as her brother,

Lucindo, and is welcomed by the troops. She announces that she is returning to the Italy she left as a child, for the sake of the soldiers ('Se per voi le care io torno'). Fulvia and the Baroness are both attracted to this military figure. Lucindo announces that he has come to take the unhappy Clarice away. This at last forces the Count to disclose his feelings ('Ah! se destarti in seno'). Clarice reveals her identity, which astonishes everyone ('Voi Clarice?') and delights the Count, who swears to respect women from now on. During the course of the finale, Macrobio and Pacuvio refuse to rush into marriage with the other widows; Clarice and the Count forgive each other and celebrate their happiness.

La pietra del paragone is the best, the funniest and the most serious of Rossini's early comic operas. Its unusually literate text offers opportunities for apt characterisation, of the three different types of widow, of the sinisterly available, unscrupulous journalist Macrobio, of the appalling poet Pacuvio. At the opera's centre stands Asdrubale, the cynic who reforms, as though *Così fan tutte*'s Don Alfonso learnt that some women are indeed phoenixes. This involves a touching journey from experience to innocence. It was probably only an accident that gave Rossini a bass as the hero, while the tenor was relegated to second place as his chum, the worthy but unsuccessful lover (whose presentation is not entirely free of irony). Rossini makes the most of this vocal donnée, just as he does of the fact that the heroine is a contralto. For once, this opera is about grown-ups, its closest parallel with Lehár's *Merry Widow*. The scenes for the central couple cover much emotional and stylistic ground, from sentimentality to barbed fencing via real intimacy. Rossini marks each stage with differentiated orchestration, melodies and rhythms: the pace of the music slows and cellos or horns suddenly suggest the darker implications of their dialogue.

Asdrubale himself begins as a partial echo, invisible, disembodied and genderless, in the delicious horn-accompanied duet with Clarice in Act I; he then battles with his own prejudices before resolving, in a rather savage cabaletta, to be pitiless. When ultimately he repents, in 'Ah! se destarti in seno', Rossini throws in a passage of Mozartian seriousness, reminding us not of *Così* so much as of that other trial opera, *The Magic Flute*, before the music erupts in suitably frivolous roulades.   P.

L'OCCASIONE FA IL LADRO ossia IL CAMBIO DELLA VALIGIA

*The Occasion Makes the Thief or
The Exchange of a Suitcase*

Burletta per musica in one act, libretto by Luigi Prividali, probably based on M.A.E.***'s (i.e. Augustin-Eugène Scribe)'s *comédie Le prétendu par hasard, ou L'Occasion fait le larron* (1810). All the recitatives are by someone else.[1] First performed Venice, 24 November 1812, with Giacinta Canonici as Berenice, Carolina Nagher as Ernestina, Gaetano Del Monte as Don Eusebio, Tommaso Berto as Conte Alberto, Luigi Pacini as Don Parmenione. Staged in Barcelona, 1822, Lisbon, 1826, St Petersburg, 1830, and Vienna, 1834. In Britain, it was first seen performed by Italian marionettes at the Little Theatre, London, on 4 January 1929, and staged live at the Opera House, Buxton, on 8 August 1987. Revived in 1987 as part of the Rossini Opera Festival, in Pesaro, with Luciana Serra as Berenice, Luciana D'Intino as Ernestina, Raul Gimenez as Conte Alberto, Claudio Desderi as Martino and J. Patrick Raftery as Don Parmenione, conducted by Salvatore Accardo.

Don Eusebio..Tenor

Berenice, *his niece, an heiress*...........................Soprano

Count Alberto...Tenor

Don Parmenione...Bass

Ernestina, *Berenice's servant* ....Soprano

Martino, *Don Parmenione's servant*......................Bass

Waiters in the Inn, Don Eusebio's Servants

Place: In and Near Naples
Running Time: 1 hour 15 minutes

The fourth of the farces Rossini was contracted to write for the Teatro San Moisè in Venice, *L'occasione fa il ladro* is the story of an inspired improvisation, an apt theme for an opera composed in only eleven days. Rossini reuses the storm music from *La pietra del paragone* in place of an overture, but such recycling in Rossini rarely signals parsimoniousness.

The hall of an inn, one dark and stormy night. Don Parmenione is pursuing the sister of a friend of his, who has eloped with a seducer. He takes refuge from the storm which leaves him indifferent but frightens his servant Martino (duet, 'Frema in ciel il nembo irato'). They are joined by a stranger, Count Alberto, who seems to arrive from a different operatic world. With his first words he heroically defies fate (i.e. the weather) to obstruct love's progress. Alberto explains that he is on his way to meet the woman he is engaged to marry, whom he has never seen. They toast the god of wine in a spirited Allegro vivace ('Viva Bacco il Dio del vino'). When Alberto and his servant leave, by mistake they take Parmenione's suitcase in place of Alberto's. Martino encourages his master to take Alberto's money and his passport. Parmenione is struck by the portrait inside the bag. Assuming that it shows Alberto's fiancée, he determines to have her for himself ('Che sorte, che accidente').

A hall in Berenice's house. She is about to marry Count Alberto, the man her father chose for her before he died. Her uncle Don Eusebio explains to Ernestina that they will need her help today. Ernestina is a woman of good birth who ran away with a man who abandoned her. She has since been acting as Berenice's confidante, rather than her maid. Berenice is determined to take control of her own destiny: to test her future husband's sincerity she will change places with Ernestina. Parmenione arrives, pretending to be Alberto. Although he begins his scene with Ernestina in an apparent parody of courtly lovemaking, he is genuinely attracted to her – though she looks nothing like the portrait – and she in turn likes his charm and his 'brio' ('Quel gentil, quel vago oggetto').

Meanwhile, over pizzicato strings and tripleting woodwind, Alberto and Berenice no sooner meet than they fall in love ('Se non m'inganna il core'). Eusebio tries to sort out the confusion caused by two Count Albertos in an exquisite quintet, 'Che strana sorpresa'. When Ernestina tells Alberto she can never marry him, he assures her he would never force the issue, as long as her reluctance is not because she doesn't trust him ('D'ogni più sacro impegno'). Berenice's suspicions about Parmenione are reinforced when he flirts with her, presuming on her status as a servant. Eventually, she reveals that she is Count Alberto's future wife and tries to test him on his family knowledge (duet, 'Voi la sposa!').

When Ernestina and Don Eusebio interrogate Martino he adroitly gives nothing away ('Il mio padrone è un uomo'). Alberto and Parmenione find themselves in an impasse which is relieved when Alberto agrees to let Parmenione marry Ernestina, if she is indeed the one intended for him. Berenice reminds them that she has her own doubts and needs to be consulted (aria, 'Voi la sposa pre-

---

[1] See the critical edition by Giovanni Carli Ballola, Patricia Brauner and Philip Gossett, Pesaro, 1994.

tendete'). Parmenione boldly reveals his identity. It turns out that the woman he was pursuing, the fugitive sister of his friend, is Ernestina. He offers her his hand to restore her honour, and she accepts (finale, 'Quello, ch'io fui, ritorno'). Alberto ties up one loose end when he explains that the portrait in his suitcase was of his sister, and what Eusebio calls the *burletta* (farce) finishes with a double marriage.

Once the storm in the overture has yoked together two disparate characters and fates, Rossini delights in the contrasts they evoke: on the one hand, the freewheeling, unscrupulous but endearingly improvisatory (even Rossinian) genius, the bass Don Parmenione, whose own servant says 'he looks like a gentleman and may also be one', and on the other, the quintessentially aristocratic, tenor lover Count Alberto. To enrich the mix, it is the bourgeois who tries to exploit his social superiority over the 'servant', while the aristocrat heroically defends liberty with spectacularly ingenious roulades over a martial rhythm ('D'ogni più sacro impegno'). In post-revolutionary Italy two régimes, two classes are now forced to shelter under the same roof.

The opera explores the collision between humorous, go-getting realism and serious, romantic idealism. The music inspired by each aspect is so disparate that their collocation makes for an uncomfortable, explosive combination. Rossini expands the conventional forms to encompass all this, so that the scene that begins as a duet ('Quel gentil, quel vago oggetto') is actually part of a quintet that goes on for 398 bars. This novelty may explain why *L'occasione fa il ladro* proved unpopular in Venice in 1812. Perhaps it is time to make a case for Berenice's proto-feminism: it takes her feisty coloratura to insist on what is right and so resolve the situation. Her determination to be 'Arbitra de se stessa' (arbiter of her own destiny) in the second, faster section of her first aria ultimately leads to the truth. On the way, Rossini paints a fascinatingly complete portrait, whose facets range from cunning interrogator, via vituperative insulter, to magisterial *grande dame*. Yet her vocal acrobatics are not inconsistent with heartfelt emotions, as exquisite horn and clarinet doubling suggest when she intervenes with 'Voi la sposa pretendete', raises the temperature of the debate and brings them all to their senses.   P.

SIGNOR BRUSCHINO
Il Figlio per Azzardo
His Son by Chance

Farsa giocosa in one act, libretto by Giuseppe Maria Foppa, based on Alissan de Chazet and E.T.M. Ourry's play *Le fils par hasard ou Ruse et Folie* (1809). First performance Teatro S. Moisè, Venice, 27 January 1813, with Nicola De Grecis as Gaudenzio, Teodolinda Pontiggia as Sofia, Luigi Raffanelli as Bruschino the father and Tommaso Berti as Florville. First U.K. performance 1960 by the Kentish Opera Group at Orpington. First U.S. performance 1932 at the Met, in a double-bill with *Elektra*, with Giuseppe de Luca and Ezio Pinza, conducted by Tullio Serafin. Offenbach's adaptation of the score to fit a new libretto by Desforges was first performed in Paris on 29 December 1857; August 1988 at the Rossini Opera Festival, with Mariella Devia as Sofia, Enzo Dara as Gaudenzio, Dalmacio Gonzalez as Florville, Alberto Rinaldi as Bruschino, the father, conducted by Donato Renzetti. Opéra-Comique, Paris, co-production with Cologne Opera and Schwetzingen Festival, July 1992; Pimlico Opera in Oxford, June 1993, conductor Martin Merry; Vienna Chamber Opera, 1993, conductor Vronsky.

Gaudenzio Strappapuppole, *Sofia's tutor* ....Bass[1]
Sofia...Soprano
Bruschino, *the father* ....Bass
Bruschino, *his son*..Tenor
Florville, *in love with Sofia*.................................Tenor
Police Commissioner ....Tenor
Filiberto, *innkeeper*..Bass
Marianna, *Sofia's maid*......................Mezzo-Soprano

Servants

Place: Gaudenzio's Castle
Running Time: 1 hour 20 minutes

Rossini's great opera *Tancredi* had its première in Venice only ten days later, but it shows few affinities. *Signor Bruschino* was written, like *L'inganno felice* and *La scala di seta*, to a text by Foppa, who provided most of the libretti for farces at the Teatro S. Moisè. *Il signor Bruschino*'s mechanical plot encourages Rossini to move in symmetrical patterns, occasionally at the expense of human feelings. Rossini makes two novel, musical jokes. In the overture the second violins are repeatedly instructed to strike the metal parts of their desk-lights with their bows: according to Stendhal, their parody of the overture's serious opening theme was perceived as an 'audacious insult' to the audience. When the real Signor

---

[1] *Basso comico* according to the score.

Bruschino (i.e. the son) enters, he does so to a disconcerting, mock funeral march.

A room on the ground floor, with a view of the garden and the park. Florville appeals to love to help him to marry Sofia ('Deh tu m'assisti amore'). He learns from her maid that Sofia has been promised to another. The lovers are delighted to see each other. Now that Florville's father, whom Gaudenzio hated, has died Florville assumes there will be no barrier to their marriage. Sofia explains that Gaudenzio has arranged for her to marry Signor Bruschino's son, though neither she nor her tutor has ever seen him. He is due to arrive today. Luckily, Gaudenzio has never seen Florville either. Filiberto comes to force Signor Bruschino to settle his son's debts. Pretending to be Gaudenzio's business agent and a cousin of the younger Bruschino, whose surname he also takes, Florville pays off some of the debt ('Io danari vi darò!'), on condition that Filiberto keeps the younger Bruschino locked up. Gaudenzio has observed that everyone is ambitious for what they haven't got; he determines to be satisfied with what he has (cavatina, 'Nel teatro del gran mondo').

Florville makes Gaudenzio believe that he is the younger Bruschino, now repentant. Gaudenzio tries to persuade the elder Bruschino to forgive his son (trio, 'Per un figlio già pentito'). The father refuses to recognise the impostor. For everyone else, this demonstrates his implacability. The father goes for the police. Sofia then begs him to give her his son ('Ah! donate il caro sposo'). After a test involving handwriting, Bruschino is further confounded and everyone else is struck by his obstinacy ('Ho la testa o è andata via?'). Filiberto confirms that Florville is indeed Bruschino (meaning the 'cousin', not the son). Gaudenzio examines his pupil Sofia on the subject of marriage and establishes that she is in love (duet, 'È un bel nodo che due cori'). Bruschino the father discovers that Florville is really the son of Gaudenzio's enemy, and therefore pretends that he now recognises his son (finale, 'Ebben, ragion, dovere'), to spite Gaudenzio. The man who really is Bruschino, the son, arrives, stammering his repentance. Gaudenzio is forced to accept Florville as a husband for his pupil and ward. Everyone salutes the power of love.   P.

TANCREDI

Melodramma eroico in two acts, libretto by Gaetano Rossi, based on Voltaire's play *Tancrède* (1760). First performed at the Teatro La Fenice, Venice, 6 February 1813, with Adelaide Malanotte-Montresor as Tancredi, Elisabetta Manfredini-Guarmani as Amenaide, Pietro Todràn as Argirio, Luciano Bianchi as Orbazzano. The first two performances were broken off because the Tancredi and the Amenaide were indisposed, so it was not given complete until 12 February. Later, the young Giuditta Pasta had an immense impact in the title role. First U.K. performance 1820, Covent Garden. First U.S. performance 1825, New York. It was revived for Giulietta Simionato in 1952 at the Maggio Musicale, Florence; for Marilyn Horne during the 1970s and 1980s. More recently, Vesselina Kasarova has recorded it, 1995.

Argirio, *nobleman*...Tenor
Amenaide, *his daughter, in love
  with Tancredi*...Soprano
Tancredi, *of royal blood, in love
  with Amenaide*...Contralto
Orbazzano, *nobleman, in love with Amenaide*.........Bass
Isaura, *Amenaide's friend*..............................Contralto
Roggiero, *Tancredi's friend*...............Soprano or Tenor

Noble Men and Women, Knights, Warriors and Guards

Place: Syracuse, Sicily
Time: 1005 A.D.
Running Time: 2 hours 50 minutes

Rossini's first operatic effort was *Demetrio e Polibio*, an *opera seria* which he wrote for the tenor Domenico Mombelli's small touring company in 1805 at the age of thirteen, though it was not staged until 1812, at the Teatro Valle, Rome. He entered Bologna's Accademia Filarmonica the next year but left early, and was already composing an opera for the Teatro San Moisè, Venice, in 1810 (*La cambiale di matrimonio*, text by Gaetano Rossi). This *farsa comica* was followed by four more for the same theatre, *L'Equivoco stravagante, L'inganno felice, La Scala di seta, L'Occasione fa il ladro*, while he was commissioned to write his first serious opera (the *dramma con cori, Ciro in Babilonia*), for Ferrara's Teatro Communale in 1812. His second, *Tancredi*, for Venice's rather more important la Fenice, became immensely popular and very influential. The first Tancredi, Malanotte-Montresor, rejected the spectacular but conventional aria (complete with solo violin part and echo effect) that Rossini had provided for her first entrance. Forced to improvise at the last minute, Rossini composed the touching aria whose cabaletta, 'Di tanti palpiti', became an early universally popular song. In 1824 Stendhal claimed it had 'enjoyed a wider and more universal popularity than perhaps any other aria in the world'.[1] Wagner famously parodied it in a chorus in Act III of *Die Meistersinger* – but could Tancredi's selfless, anonymous intervention to defend Amenaide have inspired *Lohengrin*? In its first form, *Tancredi* ended happily. For the revival in Ferrara in March 1813, Rossini made several changes and reworked the finale in collaboration with Luigi Lechi to restore Voltaire's original, tragic ending. This second Ferrara ending is now usually given.

Under attack from Byzantine and Saracen forces, Syracuse has also suffered from a civil war between two noble families, one led by Argirio, the other by Orbazzano. In Byzantium, Amenaide met Tancredi, who was born into the royal family of Syracuse but had been banished unfairly. They fell in love. Meanwhile in Syracuse, all Tancredi's property was confiscated and awarded to Orbazzano. When Amenaide returned to Syracuse, she sent anonymously and unaddressed a letter to Tancredi, imploring him to come.

Act I. A gallery in Argirio's palace. A chorus celebrates the end of the civil war. Argirio and Orbazzano lead them in an oath of loyalty to Syracuse, agreeing that anyone who communicates with the Saracen enemy should be sentenced to death. Amenaide is delighted that peace has returned to Syracuse ('Come dolce all'alma mia'), but she is appalled when Argirio announces that he will marry her to Orbazzano to seal the agreement between them.

The garden outside the palace. Roggiero lands with Tancredi, who resolves to be worthy of Amenaide, or to die ('Di tanti palpiti'). He commands his squires to set up his insignia (inscribed not with his name, but with 'Fede, Onore' (Faith, Honour) in the square and say that an unknown knight offers his services in the defence of Syracuse. He hides when he sees Argirio and Amenaide approaching. Argirio tells her that Solamir, the Saracen commander, has surrounded the city and demanded the hand of Amenaide. He knows that Tancredi has landed, and presumes he is bent on revenge. Argirio insists that Amenaide's duty to her father and to her

country oblige her to marry Orbazzano ('Pensa che sei mia figlia'). When Tancredi reveals himself to Amenaide, she warns him to keep away, but cannot bring herself to reveal that she is due to marry Orbazzano ('L'aura che intorno spiri').

A public space near the city's walls. The nobles appeal to love to unite two hearts ('Amori, scendete'). Soldiers salute their hero Orbazzano. Roggiero begs Tancredi to keep his identity secret. Tancredi offers his services in Syracuse's cause, but, as Amenaide realises, he still thinks she was unfaithful to him. She refuses to marry Orbazzano. Enraged, Orbazzano reveals the letter she wrote to Tancredi, which everyone assumes was intended for the Saracen Solamir. They are horrified (sextet and finale 'Ciel, che lessi'). Amenaide is repudiated by her father and even by Tancredi.

Act II. A gallery in Argirio's castle. Orbazzano swears to persecute Amenaide as fervently as he once courted her. The senate has decreed her death, but the sentence lacks Argirio's signature. Torn between loyalty to the state and love for his daughter, he nevertheless signs the decree. Isaura has remained faithful to Amenaide and prays that she will receive divine comfort ('Tu che i miseri conforti').

Inside the prison. Amenaide is ready to die for love, hoping that one day Tancredi will learn that she is innocent ('No, che il morir non è'). Orbazzano comes to lead her to her death, but Tancredi intervenes: as her champion, he challenges Orbazzano to single combat. Argirio begs Tancredi to reveal his identity; he refuses. Neither can bring himself to hate Amenaide ('Ah, se de' mali miei'). The two men embrace before Tancredi goes off to prove her innocence, which he does not believe in. Amenaide prays for his success ('Giusto Dio che umile adoro').

The great square in Syracuse. The crowd salute Tancredi, who has killed Orbazzano. However, since he still assumes Amenaide's letter was addressed to the Saracen, he rejects and refuses to listen to her ('Lasciami: non t'ascolto'). Isaura assures Roggiero that Amenaide has remained true to Tancredi. Roggiero wishes that were true ('Torni alfin').

Ferrara Finale. In the mountains, with a view of Etna, sunset. The savage landscape reminds Tancredi of his dilemma: he still adores the woman who betrayed him ('Ah! che scordar non so').

---

[1] *Life of Rossini*, ed. and transl. Richard N. Coe, London, 1970. Stendhal's detailed analysis in the fascinating chapter he devoted to *Tancredi* is well worth reading.

Syracusan knights appeal to Tancredi to save them from the Saracens. He again refuses to listen to Amenaide; instead, he determines to die for her in the battle and let love itself avenge him ('Perché turbar la calma'). Amenaide and Isaura learn from Argirio that Tancredi saved the day, though it cost him his own life. When he is brought in, mortally wounded, Argirio reveals that Amenaide was faithful: she wrote the letter to him. Tancredi asks to be married to her and as he dies, he begs her to live, as his widow.

Venice Finale. In the mountains, with a view of Etna, sunset. The savage landscape reminds Tancredi of his dilemma: he still loves the woman who betrayed him. Saracens look forward to victory in the forthcoming battle. Realising that he is among the enemy, Tancredi resolves to sacrifice himself for Amenaide's sake. Argirio reveals that Amenaide was faithful – she wrote the letter to him. The Saracens bring in Solamir's last offer: if he is allowed to marry Amenaide, he will spare Syracuse. Tancredi rebukes Amenaide, but admits he still adores her ('È questa la fede'). He leads the Syracusans into battle. Argirio follows, while Amenaide awaits the outcome. Tancredi returns victorious, having heard from Solamir, before he died, that Amenaide is innocent. He asks to be forgiven and Argirio invites him to rule over Syracuse. Amenaide leads the rejoicing ('Fra questi soavi palpiti').

Tancredi does not convince completely. There is a perfunctory quality to the choruses, for example, while some of the extraordinary vocal feats Rossini calls for remain technical exercises, athletics rather than dancing: syllables routinely divided into quavers and semiquavers can sound like miraculously disciplined hiccupping. Nevertheless, at its best, there is a special quality to *Tancredi*'s music, which Stendhal identified first as its youthfulness. As for the tragic ending Rossini provided for the revival in Ferrara, its power is built on stoic discretion. It is tempting to assume that this is obviously the one to perform now. There is an argument on the other side, however, as Andrew Porter points out: 'The artificially sustained tensions of this florid opera are perhaps more fittingly released by the brilliant, if rather trivial, trio of Rossini's original finale.'[1]   P.

L'ITALIANA IN ALGERI
The Italian Girl in Algiers

Opera in two acts, text by A. Anelli (originally written for L. Mosca and performed at la Scala in 1808). Première at Teatro San Benedetto, Venice, 22 May 1813. First performed in London, Haymarket Theatre, 1819 (in Italian); Princess's Theatre, 1844 (in English); New York, 1832 (in Italian). Revived Metropolitan, New York, 1919, with Besanzoni, Hackett, Didur, de Luca, conductor Papi; Turin, 1925, with Supervia, conductor Gui; Rome, 1927, with Supervia; Paris, 1933; la Scala, Milan, 1933, with Castagna; Covent Garden, 1935, with Supervia, Ederle, Bettoni, Scattola, conductor Bellezza; Florence Festival, 1941, with Pederzini; la Scala, 1953, with Simionato; Glyndebourne, 1957, with Dominguez, Oncina, Montarsolo, Cortis, conductor Gui; Sadler's Wells at London Coliseum, 1968, with Patricia Kern, conductor Mario Bernardi; Metropolitan, New York, 1974, with Marilyn Horne.

Mustafa, *Bey of Algiers*		Bass
Elvira, *his wife*		Soprano
Zulma, *her confidante*		Contralto
Haly, *in the service of the Bey*		Bass
Lindoro, *an Italian in love with Isabella*		Tenor
Isabella		Contralto
Taddeo, *an old Italian*		Baritone

Running Time: 2 hours 20 minutes

Rossini's *L'Italiana in Algeri* is *commedia dell'arte* set to music. The plot and the words are less those of a well-constructed play, rather the situations used by the actors of the *commedia dell'arte* for their free invention. The nearest parallel to it is the Edwardian music hall, where the comedian relied very largely on 'gags' to hold his audience's attention. Improvisation was out of the question the moment music entered into the partnership, but the plot provides plenty of evidence as to its origin.

On its first performance, the opera was immediately successful. 'When Rossini wrote *L'Italiana*', notes Stendhal, 'his youthful genius was bursting into flower.' And the brilliant character of the work shows clearly the spirit, optimism, and geniality of youth (Rossini was only twenty-one at the time). The whole work was written in twenty-seven days.

Act I. The overture, one of the composer's most famous, begins with a strong feeling of latent drama, but this soon gives way to an enchanting *allegro*. The interplay of the woodwind, and in fact the writing for

[1] *New Yorker*, 6 June 1983, repr. *Musical Events*, New York, 1987.

this section of the orchestra throughout the opera, is particularly attractive.

The palace of the Bey of Algiers. A chorus of the eunuchs of the harem laments the sad lot of women, while Elvira, the Bey's wife, assisted by her confidante, Zulma, bemoans her own tragedy – her husband no longer loves her. Enter the Bey in person. With a multitude of roulades he inveighs against the arrogance of women, and, the moment Elvira speaks directly to him, protests that his eardrums are broken. A lively ensemble ensues (it is a quartet, Haly, the captain of the Bey's corsairs, having joined the family quarrel), and at its end Haly is told by the Bey that he must go off and find him an Italian wife – nothing else will satisfy him.

The Bey has in his service an Italian slave, by name Lindoro. In a slow cavatina, 'Languir per una bella', he laments the absence of his beloved. It is a particularly attractive example of Rossini's highly decorated lyric style, and is followed by a vigorous *cabaletta*, no less full of coloratura and with its high Cs, B naturals, and B flats calculated to try the technique of any but the most agile of tenors. The Bey asks Lindoro whether he would like to get married. Not unless he was in love, is Lindoro's reply. A charming duet ensues between the two. The subject is marriage, with particular reference to the qualifications necessary in the prospective partner.

Scene ii. Isabella, who has been roaming the seas in search of her lost lover Lindoro, is involved in a shipwreck, conveniently on the shore of Algeria. Haly's men exclaim on the beauty of the women, and on Mustafa's good fortune in securing so many additions to his harem. 'Cruda sorte!' (Cruel fate) sings Isabella; she is in this danger only because of her faithfulness to Lindoro – but the cabaletta leaves us in no doubt whatsoever as to her ability to look after herself. All are made prisoner, and Haly is overjoyed to find that Isabella and Taddeo, an ageing and comic admirer she has brought with her for company on the voyage, are indeed Italians; they shall go to the Bey. Left alone with Taddeo, Isabella seems less dismayed than he at the indication that she is destined for the Bey's Seraglio. They argue about the situation in their duet, 'Ai capricci della sorte', but all is made up in a charming *allegro vivace*, in which they agree that the status of uncle and niece (which they have decided shall be their official relationship) has its advantages.

At the palace, Elvira and Zulma reason with Lindoro because he seems disinclined to marry the former, even though the Bey has offered him freedom (and money) if he will take her off his hands. Haly brings the news of Isabella's capture, and the Bey rejoices at his good fortune in an aria whose coloratura difficulties rival those of a Handel bass: 'Già d'insolito ardore'. After he has gone, Elvira admits she still loves her inconstant husband, but Lindoro comforts her: if she comes to Italy with him, she will find husbands and lovers as she pleases.

The finale begins with the eunuchs singing the praises of 'Mustafa the scourge of women, who changes them from tigresses to lambs'. Isabella is led in and cannot contain her amusement at the sight of Mustafa; her tune is irresistibly comic, and the duet as she makes up to the bemused Mustafa very funny. Taddeo pushes himself forward: is he not her uncle? A quartet follows between Isabella, Taddeo, Haly, and Mustafa, and at its end, Elvira, Zulma, and Lindoro enter the hall. Isabella and Lindoro recognise each other, and the quartet becomes a septet, dominated by a florid figure for Lindoro and Mustafa. Isabella voices objections when she discovers that Elvira is the Bey's wife whom he is discarding, and the complications mount until the end of the act.

Act II. The eunuchs comment on Mustafa's lovelorn condition. Mustafa sends his wife and her slave to tell the Italian girl he wishes to drink coffee with her later. Isabella, alone with Lindoro, reproaches him because of his forthcoming marriage to Elvira, but eventually accepts his protestations of unchanging affection for herself, and together they plan an escape, the prospect of which spurs Lindoro to an even more exuberant expression of devotion than before. Mustafa tells Taddeo that he will make him, in honour of his niece, Grand Kaimakan of Algeria. The chorus sing his praises, and Taddeo follows with an amusing aria, 'Ho un gran peso sulla testa'.

Isabella is in front of her looking-glass, finishing dressing. Elvira and Zulma come to deliver the Bey's message, and Isabella orders coffee for three from her slave, Lindoro, saying she would not dream of excluding the Bey's wife from the party. She will in fact, as woman to woman, give her a much needed lesson in man-management. Sitting in front of her looking-glass and watched from behind by Lindoro, Haly and Mustafa, she sings 'Per lui, che adoro', which is in effect an aria with comments and later accompaniment from the three men. Mustafa cannot wait to be alone with Isabella. At the beginning of the quintet, he makes formal and florid presentation to Isabella of Taddeo, Grand Kaimakan; this over, he sets about getting rid of the men, but with little success. Coffee comes in, and, after a moment, so does Elvira, and what has begun as a quartet becomes a quintet. Mustafa loses his temper and the ensemble ends in a *crescendo* of pandemonium.

Haly is alone. In a pleasantly straightforward aria, 'Le femmine d'Italia', he praises the wiles of Italian women and the way in which they insinuate themselves into men's affections. No sooner has he left than Taddeo and Lindoro appear, the former telling the latter in confidence that he loves Isabella, who he once thought loved a certain Lindoro, but who he finds loves him (Taddeo) truly after all. Lindoro is suitably impressed by the announcement, but privately finds the time to express pleasure that his rival should be so obviously insignificant. As Mustafa comes in, Lindoro whispers to his compatriot to back him up in the plan he is about to put forward. Mustafa seems disposed to complain of the treatment he has received at Isabella's hands, but he is reassured, and told she waits only until he joins that ancient and noble Italian order of the 'Pappatacci' (literally 'eat and be silent', but implying the convenience of a complaisant husband). Mustafa, who is quite unaware of the *double entendre*, consents to be enrolled, and the trio which ensues, known as the trio of the 'Pappatacci', once sent the public raving with delight. Lindoro has a flowing, high tune and he is supported by the two lower voices to make a very comic effect. Haly meanwhile is suspicious: why, he asks Zulma, does Isabella give too much to drink to the eunuchs and the Moors? For fun, she tells him – and to make it into a true holiday.

In preparation for the ceremony to enrol Mustafa in the glorious ranks, Isabella gathers together all the Italians in the Bey's service and appeals to their patriotism to help her carry out her plans, which include escape for them all during the course of the initiation ceremony. They greet her in a chorus, and she sings her recitative ('Amici, in ogni evento') and rondo ('Pensa alla patria'), taking the chance of having a dig at Taddeo and a kind word for Lindoro. This is bravura writing on a big scale, and contains in its opening section one of Rossini's few overt references to patriotism (that is to say, before the time of *Guillaume Tell*).

Announced by Lindoro, the 'Pappatacci' chorus comes on with horns blowing. Mustafa, prompted by Isabella, swears to obey all the rules of the order, which he then repeats after Taddeo; what it amounts to is that the duty of the model husband is to eat and sleep soundly – nothing else. Isabella and Lindoro indulge in a display of affection as a 'test' for Mustafa – he fails, but is prompted by Taddeo, and swears he will not offend against the rules again. A chorus of European slaves can be heard from outside, where the boat Isabella has chartered to take them all home is waiting in full sight of the Bey's palace. Isabella and Lindoro prepare to go on board, and Mustafa treats it all as part of his initiation, although Taddeo is worried at the turn events are taking. In an *allegro*, Mustafa discovers his mistake through the intervention of Elvira, Zulma, and Haly, who convince him he has been hoodwinked. He turns to Elvira as his true love – Italians were only a passing fancy. Isabella and her party are still within sight of the palace, and the opera ends with mutual congratulations from both parties, escapers and erstwhile captors.   H.

IL TURCO IN ITALIA
The Turk in Italy

Opera in two (now customarily three) acts, libretto by Felice Romani. Première, la Scala, Milan, 14 August 1814. First performed King's Theatre, London, 1821, with Giuseppina and Giuseppe Ronzi de Begnis (their London débuts); New York, 1826; Edinburgh, 1827. In Italy, not given between 1855 and its revival at the Teatro Eliseo, Rome, in 1950, with Callas, Valletti, Stabile, Bruscantini, conductor Gavazzeni; la Scala, 1955, with virtually the same cast; Edinburgh Festival, 1957, by Piccola Scala; Glyndebourne, 1970, with Sciutti, Benelli, Roux, Montarsolo, conductor Pritchard.

Selim, *the Turk*	Bass
Fiorilla, *a young Neapolitan wife*	Soprano
Geronio, *her husband*	Bass
Narciso, *in love with Fiorilla*	Tenor
Zaida, *a Turk*	Mezzo-Soprano
Albazar, *a Turk*	Tenor
Prosdocimo, *a poet*	Baritone

Place: In and Around Naples
Time: Eighteenth Century
Running Time: 2 hours 10 minutes

One of Rossini's most closely worked comedies, this was the victim of adverse circumstances from the time of its relative failure in Milan (because the public thought it was being fobbed off with a number of self-borrowings), through corrupt editions from as early as 1820, until it was triumphantly vindicated in 1950 when revived in Luchino Visconti's highly successful production headed by Maria Callas.

Act I. After a witty and typical overture, of which more than one version exists, the first scene shows a gipsy encampment on the outskirts of Naples. Members of the crowd are having their fortunes told, and among the most active fortune-tellers are two runaway Turks, Zaida and Albazar by name. Zaida is unhappy: a slave in Turkey, she loved her master and despairs of ever seeing him again.

To the camp in search of inspiration comes Prosdocimo, a poet, ordered by his patron to produce a stage comedy. He is unable to believe that yet another piece on the theme of flirtatious wife and ridiculous husband – as are in real life Donna Fiorilla and Don Geronio – would be found acceptable. Just then, none other than Don Geronio appears, looking for a gipsy to read his palm and advise him how to cope with his high-mettled wife. It appears that the stars are not propitious, and he is thoroughly disgruntled at the gipsy's predictions. The scene concludes (although this section is often omitted) with the questioning of Zaida by Prosdocimo. She reveals that she was driven away from her master, Selim Damelec of Erzerum, by the intrigues of her rivals, and Prosdocimo comforts her with the news that a Turkish Pasha is due to sail into Naples at any moment; perhaps he would intercede for her with her master.

The harbourside. Donna Fiorilla is introduced in a bravura aria ('Non si dà follia maggiore') on the agreeable complications of her love life; she turns her attention to a ship flying the Turkish flag which nears the quayside. Announced in the minor, as befits a late eighteenth- or early nineteenth-century musical Turk, Selim's cavatina ('Bella Italia') is in the florid style Rossini favoured for his comic basses. Fiorilla is obviously ripe for a flirtation, and Selim abruptly diverts his praises from the country to its inhabitants, particularly those of the female sex. Fiorilla joins in the concluding phrases of the aria, there is an exchange of compliments, and the scene ends with a quick duet for her and Selim.

As well as an ageing husband, Fiorilla is blessed with a young lover, Narciso, and he gives vent to his feelings in an aria ('Un vago sembiante di gioia'). But the conclusion of the scene in the harbour is dominated by the Pirandellian Prosdocimo, who sees in the way events are shaping a perfect theme for his comedy. As he reflects on the subject – a stupid husband, a flighty wife, a lover supplanted by a handsome and amorous Turk; what more can one ask for? – he is overheard by the husband and the lover he refers to, and the soliloquy becomes a trio. To the ingredients he mentions, they wish to add another, a poet quickened by immediate physical chastisement, but Prosdocimo eludes them.

An apartment in Fiorilla's house. Fiorilla is entertaining Selim to coffee – a pastime, judging from this opera and *L'Italiana*, that librettists seem to have thought particularly suitable when Italian women flirt with Turks. When he protests his devotion, she makes some sly remarks about the hundred women of his harem, and the fine quartet (which in modern versions often ends Act I) begins with their amorous fencing. When Geronio enters, Selim flies at him in a passion, but Fiorilla turns the whole incident in her favour, has Geronio paying compliments to Selim, and only Narciso is put out by her handling of events. The quartet bubbles along, and before it is over Selim has managed to make an assignation with Fiorilla for that night at the harbour.

The penultimate scene of Act I (or, usually, the first of Act II) starts in Geronio's house. He is full of lamentation about his marriage to someone so much younger than himself, someone moreover he cannot control. Firmness and decision are necessary, suggests Prosdocimo, but, alone with Fiorilla, Geronio has no sort of success with the new formula. At the start of their duet ('Per piacere alla Signora, che ho da far') he is already apologetic, by the middle she is feigning love and (in a graphic musical phrase) imitating weeping, and telling him that it is *he* who has caused *her* such sorrow; by the end he is eating out of her hand.

The finale moves to the gipsy quarter, to which comes Selim to find out if the omens are good for his planned elopement with Fiorilla. Zaida recognises him and a reconciliation seems likely, much to the discomfiture of Prosdocimo, since this is the last turn he wants events to take if his story is to come up to scratch. The arrival of Narciso in obvious distress

Il Turco in Italia *(Théâtre de la Monnaie, Brussels, 1995, directors and designers Karl-Ernst and Ursel Herrmann).*
José Van Dam as Selim, Tiziana Fabbricini as Fiorilla.

does little to rectify the situation, but the appearance of an apparently lovelorn Fiorilla is a distinct improvement – better still, she is pursued by her irate husband. As Fiorilla and Zaida confront one another, all is ready for an ensemble of misunderstanding. The fight of the two women finally convinces Prosdocimo that nature has imitated art to perfection: he could not wish for a better finale.

Act II (Act III more often). Prosdocimo, intent on the development of his plot, urges Geronio to catch Fiorilla and Selim together that night and so put an end to the intrigue. No sooner has the poet left than Selim appears, proposing a solution that would resolve the present difficulties: why should Geronio not follow Turkish custom and sell him Fiorilla – after six years of marriage to one woman he must be a bit tired of her! Their duet, with its extended *crescendo* in the final section, is one of Rossini's masterpieces and the equal of that for Dandini and Don Magnifico in *Cenerentola*.

Fiorilla has an aria with chorus of a delicacy that can only be described as Mozartian ('Se il zefiro si posa'), after which she proclaims her intention of worsting anyone who dares set herself up as a rival. When she is joined by Zaida, Selim is bidden to choose between them, but before he can make up his mind, Zaida renounces a claim that she does not want to press in such circumstances. The field is apparently free for a clearing up of misunderstandings between Fiorilla and Selim, and their duet ('Credete alle femmine') with its florid writing is a moment of near-seriousness. It is left to Prosdocimo to re-introduce the note of comedy – at a masked ball planned for that evening Selim is to carry off Fiorilla, he tells Geronio and Narciso. Why should Zaida not dress up as Fiorilla, and Geronio disguise himself as Selim? The plot thickens when Narciso, beside himself with unhappiness, decides to take advantage of the scheme and appear as a third Selim.

At the ball, a festal chorus and a waltz set the scene for the comedy of errors which is worked out in a splendid quintet ('Oh guardate, che accidente, non conosco più mia moglie'). All the conspirators express consternation about their respective futures; the early part of the ensemble, partly unaccompanied, brings to mind nothing so much as *Così fan tutte*, but the *allegro* is full of high spirits that are pure Rossini – he even, at one point, adds a trumpet to the voices for good measure.

The upshot is that Fiorilla's escapade is unmasked, and in an aria she laments her disgrace and the loss at one and the same time of honour, husband and peace of mind. In the end, all is well; Selim bids farewell to Italy in order to return to Turkey with Zaida; Fiorilla remains 'faithful' to Geronio; Narciso decides to profit from the examples before him; and Prosdocimo has the ending for his play. All join in the moral: 'Restate contenti, felici vivete'.   H.

ELISABETTA, REGINA D'INGHILTERRA
Elizabeth, Queen of England

Opera in two acts, libretto by Giovanni Schmidt. Première at San Carlo, Naples, 4 October 1815, with Isabella Colbran, Dardanelli, Nozzari, Garcia the elder. First performed Dresden, 1818; London, 1818; Paris, 1822. Revived by Radio Italiana for Coronation of Queen Elizabeth II, 1953, with Maria Vitale, Lina Pagliughi, Campora, Pirino. No stage performance can be traced from 1841 to 1968, when the opera was produced at the Camden Festival, London. Revived Palermo, 1971 (and Edinburgh Festival, 1972), with Leyla Gencer; 1975 at Aix Festival with Caballé, Masterson, Gösta Winbergh, Benelli.

Elisabetta (Elizabeth) I, *Queen of England* ....Soprano
The Earl of Leicester, *Commander of the army* ....Tenor
Matilda, *his secret wife*....................................Soprano
The Duke of Norfolk ....Tenor
Enrico (Henry), *Matilda's brother*........Mezzo-Soprano
Guglielmo (Fitzwilliam),
    Captain of the Royal Guard............................ Tenor

Courtiers, Soldiers and People

Place: London
Time: Late Sixteenth Century
Running Time: 2 hours 10 minutes

After his successes in the North of Italy, Rossini was in 1815 engaged by the famous impresario Domenico Barbaia to work for the San Carlo in Naples.[1] Barbaia, who had recently rebuilt the theatre after it had burnt down and was in high favour with King Ferdinand, is one of the most extraordinary figures in the history of opera. He started life as a waiter, was the first to think of mixing whipped cream with coffee or chocolate, speculated in army contracts during the Napoleonic Wars, and made a fortune at the gambling rooms in Milan. He is traditionally supposed to have been illiterate, but there is no doubt as to his brilliant success as an impresario – no contradiction involved, maybe, either.

The libretto of Rossini's first opera for Barbaia was adapted from a contemporary play, which had been taken from an English novel called *The Recess* written by a certain Sophia Lee in 1785. Rossini wrote it for Isabella Colbran, Barbaia's mistress and later to become the composer's wife. It has two noteworthy musico-historical features: for the first time Rossini gave his recitatives orchestral accompaniment throughout, and, also for the first time, he wrote out all the vocal ornaments in full – he had heard the castrato Velluti indulge in such prodigality of ornamentation in *Aureliano in Palmira* that he became alarmed at what a less musical singer might do. Rossini was writing for a new audience and he would leave nothing to chance in his efforts to conquer it.

Act I. For the overture Rossini borrowed from his own less successful opera *Aureliano*, a trick he was to repeat less than two years later when he used exactly the same piece of music for *Il Barbiere di Siviglia*, the one overture thus doing duty for three operas.

Leicester's military triumph in Scotland is being celebrated at the Palace of Whitehall in London, where Norfolk makes no attempt to hide his jealousy. The Courtiers salute the Queen, who greets them in dignified (and florid) music and gives vent to her feelings of joy in music hardly distinguishable from 'Io sono docile' (*Barbiere*) – there are a few, but a very few, differences between the two arias, written only eighteen months apart. Leicester is announced, proclaims the defeat of the Scots and is welcomed by the Queen, to the chagrin of Norfolk. Leicester says he has brought the sons of the nobility as hostages from Scotland, but, in an aside, cannot hide his surprise at seeing among

---

[1] Between 1815 and 1822, Rossini wrote nine serious operas and one comic for Barbaia. Andrew Porter, in an article for the Edinburgh Festival in 1972, has suggested that it was only later in Paris that the composer had his chance to realise to the full the ideals he had adumbrated in the Neapolitan operas of 1815–22.

them, disguised as a boy, his secretly married wife, Matilda. The Queen takes them all into her service as pages. Alone, Leicester reproaches Matilda with her foolhardy behaviour – as a relation of Mary, Queen of Scots, she is in great danger – in a duet ('Incauta, che festi?'), an immediate success at the première according to Stendhal. Matilda, who has revealed her knowledge of Elizabeth's love for Leicester, is left with her brother Henry, one of the hostages, to bewail her ill fortune in a mellifluous aria ('Sento un intorna voce').

The false Norfolk, under the pledge of friendship, learns from Leicester the secret of his marriage. Norfolk hastens to tell the news to the Queen, who herself has planned to marry Leicester and whose reaction to the news is expressed with a mixture of fury and dignity in the duet for her and Norfolk ('Perchè mai, destin crudele'). Its vigorous quick section foreshadows *Guillaume Tell* or even early Verdi.

In a few bars before the finale begins, Elizabeth orders Fitzwilliam, who already suspects Norfolk's perfidy, to have the guard stand by and sends for Leicester and the Scottish hostages. Matilda she quickly recognises from her obviously anxious manner, and she proceeds to confront Leicester as her principal adviser and the hero of the moment. When she offers to make him her Consort, he is thrown into complete confusion and tries to refuse. The Queen flies into a passion, denounces the unhappy pair and summons the guard to arrest them. The finale, described by Stendhal as magnificent, is an impressive piece, at one moment full of sound and fury, at the next reminiscent of Mozart.

Act II. Elizabeth sends for Matilda and demands, in what is perhaps the finest scene of the opera, that she sign a paper renouncing all claim to Leicester in return for the safety of her husband and her brother ('Pensa che sol per poco sospendo l'ira mia'). Stendhal describes at some length the great success in this scene of Colbran for whom (or for her Royalist connections) he usually reserves little but scorn. Bellini may well have taken the duet, particularly its slow second section, as a model for his famous 'Mira, o Norma'. Enter Leicester to read the document, to defy the Queen by tearing it up, and to turn the splendid duet into a no less notable trio. They are led off under arrest, but the Queen in a moment of revulsion and

understanding orders the banishment of the false Norfolk, whose duplicity she has now seen through.

Outside the Tower of London, people lament the impending fate of Leicester, and there follows a scene in which Norfolk, now under sentence of exile, tries, in an aria with chorus, to act the part of rabble-raiser.

An evocative prelude leads us to a dungeon in the Tower, where Leicester laments his fate. Flute and cor anglais continue the tale of his uneasy, half-voiced dreams. The false Norfolk brings him promises of help; and their florid duet, 'Deh, scusa i trasporti', is something of a rarity, an extended movement for two tenors. To the prison comes the Queen, anxious to see her favourite before his execution. Norfolk has meanwhile concealed himself, and Matilda and Henry have managed to insinuate themselves into the dungeon. Leicester hears that it was Norfolk who accused him, the Queen comes to understand the extent of Norfolk's treachery, and Norfolk himself draws his dagger and is about to stab the Queen when Matilda throws herself in between them.

In the splendid and (Stendhal tells us) in its day much admired finale, the Queen denounces Norfolk and condemns him to death, then, in a slow and increasingly decorated section in triple time ('Bell'alme generose'),[1] turns to Matilda and Leicester and, in gratitude for their loyalty, grants them their freedom. The voices of the people pleading Leicester's cause can be heard from outside, Elizabeth shows them their liberated hero, and the opera comes to an end with roulades from the Queen, who is acclaimed by the crowd.   H.

IL BARBIERE DI SIVIGLIA

The Barber of Seville

Opera in two acts, text by Sterbini founded on Beaumarchais's play. Première at Teatro Argentina, Rome, 20 February 1816, with Giorgi-Righetti, Manuel Garcia, Zamboni, Vitanelli, Botticelli, conductor Rossini (as *Almaviva, ossia L'Inutile Precauzione*).

Count Almaviva	Tenor
Doctor Bartolo	Baritone
Don Basilio, *a singing teacher*	Bass
Figaro, *a barber*	Baritone

---

[1] Familiar to English ballet audiences as Lisa's flute tune in *La Fille Mal Gardée*.

Fiorello, *servant to the Count*.................................Bass
Ambrogio, *servant to the doctor* ....Bass
Rosina, *Dr Bartolo's ward* ....Mezzo-Soprano
Berta, *Rosina's governess*.............................Soprano

Notary, Constable, Musicians, Soldiers

Place: Seville, Spain
Time: Seventeenth Century
Running Time: 2 hours 35 minutes

The contract for *Il barbiere* was signed a mere two months before the first night, but there can be no doubt that Beaumarchais's play, already the subject of a highly successful opera by the composer Paisiello, had been in Rossini's mind for some time. He took pains to extol the virtues of Paisiello's score, but circumstances, including stage mishaps and disruptions by followers of Paisiello, conspired to make the new opera's première into a nightmare fiasco.

The subsequent history of what was to become one of opera's most enduring successes is full of changes and second thoughts. Rossini allowed the tenor's extended aria, which originally preceded the dénouement, first to be taken over by Rosina and finally to become the finale of *La Cenerentola*; the mezzo-soprano role of Rosina came often to be transposed for soprano, usually with high-flying decoration; baritones cast as Dr Bartolo at one time preferred to sing 'Manca un foglio', a straightforward aria by Pietro Romani, instead of the taxing but much superior 'A un dottor della mia sorte'; and an overture written for the earlier *Aureliano in Palmira* (and therefore thematically irrelevant to *The Barber*) was placed by the composer at the start of the score where it is paradoxically considered wholly apt to the comedy which follows.

Yet few Italian operatic comedies rival *The Barber* in popularity and it has been played in every operatic centre since its première, its tunes adapted for every conceivable musical combination, its wit, timing and invention admired by every composer from Beethoven to Richard Strauss and for that matter by every audience as well.

Act I. A square in which stands Dr Bartolo's house. Count Almaviva has fallen in love with Rosina, Dr Bartolo's ward, and his servant Fiorello leads a band of musicians as with grace but no apparent effect he serenades his beloved: 'Ecco ridente in cielo'. He pays off the musicians and tells

Il barbiere di Siviglia *(Lyric Opera of Chicago, 1963, director Riccardo Moresco). Alfredo Kraus as Count Almaviva, Mario Zanasi as Figaro.*

them to leave quietly, but his generosity provokes a hubbub. From outside the square, the sound of Figaro's insistent self-advertisement starts to intrude and he dances in, singing the famous bravura air, 'Largo al factotum della città', a patter song without equal in the baritone repertory. Figaro turns out to be Dr Bartolo's barber and immediately starts plotting with the Count to bring about an introduction to Rosina.

Bartolo keeps a strict watch on his ward, whom he plans himself to marry, but Rosina has noticed her unidentified suitor, and now contrives to drop from her balcony a letter asking his name. In an aria of the utmost refinement ('Se il mio nome') he somewhat disingenuously tells her it is Lindoro. The Count and Figaro improvise the next move in a bril-

liantly elegant duet ('All'idea di quel metallo'): the
Count will disguise himself as a soldier newly arrived
and demanding to be billeted on Dr Bartolo, who will
not be able to refuse him. The ruse cannot fail!

A room in Dr Bartolo's house. Rosina sings an
aria – once recorded by any high soprano, now by
every mezzo – suggesting that she is all sweetness
and light until crossed, when she becomes the very
devil: 'Una voce poco fa'. Meanwhile, Dr Bartolo
makes known to Don Basilio his suspicions about
Count Almaviva – Rosina's unknown lover, he calls
him. In order to run him out of town Basilio advocates a campaign of rumour and intrigue which may
start as a gentle breeze but will surely swell to roar
like a cannon: 'La calunnia'. When they've gone,
Figaro contrives to tell Rosina his cousin Lindoro is
madly in love with her. She has a note already prepared: 'Dunque io son, tu non m'inganni?' Bartolo
comes in to tax her, crossly but accurately, with
having dropped a letter from the balcony, then,
refusing to accept any excuse, reads her a lecture on
the futility of trying to deceive him. 'A un dottor della
mia sorte' is a *buffo* patter song on the grandest scale.

To gain admittance to Bartolo's house, the Count,
who has followed Figaro's suggestion and disguised
himself as a soldier, now tries to barge his way in,
claiming the right to be billeted there. He reveals
himself to Rosina, then refuses to recognise the
waiver which Bartolo shows him. Berta and Don
Basilio add their voices to the din, which attracts
Figaro. Vigorous knocking at the outside door
heralds the appearance of the police, to whom all at
breakneck speed give what rapidly becomes a hilari-
ously contradictory explanation of events. The officer
in charge is about to arrest the Count when that
worthy shows him a piece of paper. He springs to
attention. Dr Bartolo observes events, thunderstruck
and motionless, and all in an irresistibly comic sextet
comment *staccato* on his plight before the act ends in
rushing scales and general pandemonium.

Act II. A room in Dr Bartolo's house. Dr Bartolo
has begun to suspect that the drunken soldier was an
emissary of Count Almaviva's, but his rêverie is
interrupted by the arrival of a music teacher, ostensibly sent by the sick Don Basilio to give Rosina her
music lesson. Nothing seems to divert the newcomer
from his obsequious and incessantly reiterated greeting of 'Pace e gioia sia con voi' until Dr Bartolo

explodes with irritation and brings him to the point.
'Don Alonso' succeeds in winning his confidence by
producing Rosina's letter to the Count and offering to
persuade the girl that it was given him by a mistress
of the Count's. The lesson – a grand scena in two
parts: 'Contro un cor' and 'Cara immagine' – proceeds smoothly and at its end, Dr Bartolo demonstrates how much better music was in his day, only
to be interrupted by the arrival of Figaro. He won't be
shaved today, protests Bartolo, but Figaro declines to
be put off and creates a diversion during whose
course he obtains the key of the balcony and the disguised Count and Rosina contrive a word together.

At that moment, Basilio puts in an appearance,
and it is all Figaro and the Count can do to persuade
him (with the aid of a purse) to admit that he has a
fever and should be home in bed. 'Buona sera, mio
signore' begins the delightful ensemble as they –
even including Dr Bartolo – join in removing the
intruder, after which Figaro prepares to shave the
doctor while the Count and Rosina plan their elopement. The planning turns out to be insufficiently sur-
reptitious, Dr Bartolo gets wind of the whole affair,
catches the plotters and sends them all packing.

Berta in an aria mocks the old for wanting to
marry the young, the young for wanting to get
married at all, herself for exhibiting the same symptoms as everybody else, after which Bartolo
manages, with the aid of the letter Almaviva felt
obliged as a pledge of good faith to give him, to excite
Rosina's jealousy. In her pique, she discloses the plan
for the elopement and agrees to marry her guardian.

A storm blows up – a Rossinian musical speciality
– and as the last drops of rain fall Figaro and the
Count make their appearance. The lovers are reconciled and Figaro joins as they celebrate in a delightful
trio, 'Ah qual colpo', before Figaro discovers that the
escape-ladder is gone and their plot rumbled. Still, all
is far from lost. When the notary appears with Don
Basilio, he is easily persuaded to perform – and Don
Basilio to witness – the marriage of the young couple
rather than Dr Bartolo's with his ward, and even Dr
Bartolo is reconciled to the loss of Rosina and her
dowry by a gift from the Count of an equal sum. The
most famous of Italian comic operas comes to an end
with an *envoi*, led by Figaro, taken up by Rosina and
the Count, and celebrating the triumph of love over
all obstacles.   H.

OTELLO

Opera in three acts, text by Francesco Maria Berio. Première Naples, 4 December 1816.

Otello, *a Moor in service with the Venetian Army*..Tenor

Desdemona, *daughter of Elmiro*.....................Soprano

Iago, *Otello's ensign*...Tenor

The Doge of Venice..Tenor

Rodrigo, *the Doge's son*.....................................Tenor

Emilia, *Iago's wife, Desdemona's companion* ....Soprano

Elmiro, *a Venetian Senator* ....Bass

Lucio, *a Venetian*...Tenor

A Gondolier ....Tenor

Venetian Senators, Populace

Place: Venice
Time: End of the Fifteenth Century
Running Time: 2 hours 15 minutes

*O*tello is Rossini's nineteenth opera, written when he was twenty-six, between *The Barber of Seville* and *La Cenerentola*, with neither of which comedies can this *opera seria* be seen superficially to have much in common. *Otello* was written for Naples, where Rossini arrived nearly two years before. One of the features of the company, apart from its magnificent orchestra, was the very high quality of the tenors at its disposal, particularly Andrea Nozzari, who was the original Otello, and Giovanni David, the Rodrigo. Each was proficient in florid music, David the higher of the two, and Barbaia, the impresario, had in addition an excellent local tenor for Iago. For all three, Rossini wrote music of the utmost virtuosity.

Act I. The overture is bright and breezy with little hint of tragedy. Doge, Senators and populace of Venice wait for the victorious Otello to return from successful battle with the Turks. He disembarks to the sound of a march, lays his trophies at the Doge's feet and is himself crowned with a laurel wreath. Iago and the Doge's son Rodrigo meanwhile plot in the background against Otello, who confesses in an aside that he will not be happy until love crowns his successes (aria: 'Ah! si, per voi già sento'). Rodrigo can get from Elmiro no clue as to why Desdemona, whom he loves, is so patently unhappy, but, left alone, he and Iago agree concerted action against Otello (duet: 'No, non temer').

Desdemona at home takes no comfort from Emilia's attempts to reassure her as to Otello's love, which she has started to doubt. Her father hates him and she fears he may have been alienated by a piece of bad luck: a love letter she sent him together with a lock of hair was intercepted by her father, who took it to be for Rodrigo, an error she mistakenly encouraged for the sake of domestic peace. If Otello has got wind of it, it would explain his coolness (Duet: 'Vorrei, che il tuo pensiero').

Perceiving the approach of Iago, who once aspired to marry Desdemona and whom, as he knows, she despises, they leave, and Iago and Rodrigo are free to hear Elmiro agree to give Rodrigo the hand of Desdemona. Elmiro plans to bring down Otello and believes a family alliance with the Doge's son would facilitate his scheme. Desdemona, on the other hand, hearing her father has plans for her betrothal, hopes inwardly that Otello's exploits have softened his hostility and waits in some trepidation for the arrival of the man her father has chosen. The finale starts as Elmiro introduces Rodrigo as the prospective bridegroom, followed by Rodrigo's agitation and Desdemona's confusion, which together produce a trio of strong lyrical beauty. Matters come to a head with the arrival of a furious Otello, demanding from Elmiro Desdemona's hand and calling on her to reaffirm her love. All lament the latest turn of events, and Rodrigo and Elmiro challenge Otello for what they see as his insolence. A fine musical edifice ends as Elmiro drags Desdemona away and she looks back fondly at Otello.

Act II. To Desdemona alone in her garden comes Rodrigo to be told he is the cause of her unhappiness. He offers to do anything in his power to allay her sadness and is told 'Placate my father! Otello is my husband!' His despair is expressed in a graceful aria: 'Ah, come mai non senti'. Desdemona is still uncertain of Otello's love and as they leave Emilia fails to reassure her.

Otello enters in despair. His honour and his glory have been sacrificed and Desdemona is still not his. Iago sees his chance, hands him Desdemona's letter which, since Otello has no idea it was meant in the first place for him, produces an outburst of fury. Otello's vengeance duet is highly effective, even in its rhythmic thrust anticipating Verdi's 'Si, vendetta!' of thirty-three years later.

Though Rodrigo now enters in conciliatory mood it is not long before a quarrel between him and the intransigent Otello seems about to end in a duel, when the arrival of Desdemona turns impressive duet to mellifluous trio, and the departure of the duellists leaves her fainting on the ground. Emilia brings her round and she hears from a group of women that Otello has survived the duel. The Finale is mainly concerned with the fury of Elmiro at the course of events, and he rails against Desdemona's disloyalty; his love has turned to hatred and scorn.

Act III. Otello has been banished and Desdemona shares her misery with Emilia. As they sit, they hear a gondolier singing mournfully in the distance, and his song reminds Desdemona of a friend now dead. She sings sadly and beautifully a song of willow: 'Assisa a piè d'un salice'. Harp features prominently in prelude and accompaniment, and a short prayer rounds off the scene as Desdemona prepares for bed. Otello makes his entrance; their duet has no note of tenderness, only force and resignation, and he stabs her as a party arrives to press for reconciliation – the Doge will pardon Otello, Elmiro bless his marriage, and Rodrigo proffer friendship. But it is too late: Otello has been duped, and his only refuge is death and the hope of meeting his beloved in a better life.

Rossini's *Otello* is an *opera seria* of the early nineteenth century, not a work, like Verdi's, consciously bringing the essence of Shakespeare to the lyric stage. Approached in that spirit, it has great riches to offer, not only in the beauties of the last act, which is incidentally the shortest, but in the virtuoso possibilities of the tenor roles. Verdi's opera may have supplanted it to a great extent in public favour, but it does not deserve to be forgotten.   H.

LA CENERENTOLA
Cinderella

Opera in two acts, text by Jacopo Ferretti (founded on Etienne's French libretto for Isouard's *Cendrillon*, 1810). Première at the Teatro Valle, Rome, 25 January 1817, with Giorgi-Righetti in the title role. First performed in London, Haymarket Theatre, 1820 (in Italian); New York, 1826 (in Italian); Covent Garden, 1830 (in English), with Paton. Revived Pesaro, 1920, with Fanny Anitua; Rome, 1920; Paris, 1929, with Supervia, Ederle, Bettoni; Vienna, 1930, with Kern, von Pataky; Berlin, 1931, with Schoene, Hüsch, Kandl; Florence Festival, 1933, with Supervia, conductor Serafin; Covent Garden, 1934, with Supervia, Dino Borgioli, Ghirardini, Pinza, conductor Marinuzzi; la Scala, 1937, with Pederzini, conductor Marinuzzi; la Scala, 1946, with Barbieri, conductor Serafin; Glyndebourne, 1952, with de Gabarain,

Oncina, Bruscantini, Ian Wallace, conductor Gui; Sadler's Wells, London, 1959, with Kern, conductor Balkwill; Covent Garden, 1990, with Anne Sofie von Otter.

Don Ramiro, *Prince of Salerno*...........................Tenor
Dandini, *his valet*...Bass
Don Magnifico, *Baron of Mountflagon* ....Buffo Bass
Clorinda ⎫ ....Soprano
Thisbe ⎬ *his daughters*
 ⎭ ....Mezzo-Soprano
Angelina, *known as Cenerentola,*
 his step-daughter ....Contralto
Alidoro, *a philosopher* ....Bass

Running Time: 2 hours 30 minutes

La Cenerentola, like many other of this and other composers' operas, was written in a hurry, the libretto agreed upon (it is said) just before Christmas, the first night less than five weeks later. Its popularity nonetheless rivals that of *The Barber* itself.

Act I. Cenerentola is, of course, Cinderella, and after the curtain rises she is seen making coffee for her half-sisters, singing a pathetic little song the while. The friend and counsellor of the Prince, Alidoro, enters disguised as a beggar. The two sisters curtly dismiss him; Cenerentola pities him and offers him refreshment, to the intense annoyance of her sisters. The quarrel is interrupted by the entrance of the Prince's followers. Clorinda and Thisbe feel convinced that he must fall an easy victim to their charms. They go to make ready for the Prince, who arrives disguised as his valet, Dandini, to find Cenerentola alone. Cenerentola and the Prince fall in love at first sight and express their feelings in a love duet which has all the wit and melodiousness characteristic of its composer. The sisters clamour for Cenerentola's services. The Prince, left alone, does not know what to think of his charmer. His musings are interrupted by the arrival of Dandini (masquerading as the Prince).

While Dandini misquotes Latin to give himself an air, the voice of Cenerentola is heard begging the Baron to allow her to go to the ball. Neither the Baron nor her sisters will listen to her; the third daughter is dead, they tell the Prince, and Cenerentola is only a servant. They leave, but Alidoro, touched by the sweetness of her nature, promises to help Cenerentola.

The Prince's palace. The ball is in progress. The Baron has been appointed chief butler to the Prince and is busy tasting the wines. The disguised Prince has seen enough of Clorinda and Thisbe by this time to know that neither could make him happy. The girls, for their part, set about capturing the 'Prince', Dandini, and are not best pleased when the arrival of a distinguished but unknown lady is announced. The unknown, however, looks too much like their step-sister to arouse their alarm.

Act II. Clorinda and Thisbe are no longer on friendly terms, as each believes she has made a conquest of the Prince, but Dandini himself has fallen for Cenerentola and asks her to marry him. She refuses, confessing her love for his 'valet'. The Prince, overhearing, himself proposes to her. Cenerentola admits that she loves him, but before she consents to be his bride he must find out who she is. She gives him a bracelet which matches another she is wearing and departs.

The Baron asks Dandini whether it would be possible to speed up the wedding. Dandini asks, if he were to marry one of the Baron's daughters, how should she be treated? The Baron tells him: thirty lackeys always at hand; sixteen horses; a dozen dukes, a coach with six footmen and 'dinners with ices' always ready. Dandini thereupon confesses that he is but a valet, to the Baron's rage.

The Baron's house. Clorinda and Thisbe scowl at Cenerentola, who resembles the hateful stranger of the ball. A storm rages outside – brought about by the incantations of the philosopher, Alidoro. The coach carrying the Prince and Dandini is damaged and they seek refuge; the Baron orders Cenerentola to bring the best chair forward for the Prince. Cenerentola, trying to hide herself, puts her hands up to cover her face, and the Prince notices the bracelet, the companion of which he holds. All the knots are gradually unravelled. The Baron, Clorinda, and Thisbe, unable to understand, rudely order Cenerentola away. The Prince grows angry and threatens them with his displeasure. At the palace, Cenerentola in her famous rondo 'Nacqui all'affano e al pianto' forgives the insults and harsh treatment she has suffered. She intercedes on behalf of the Baron and his daughters, and all ends merrily.   F.B.

La Cenerentola, like other Rossini operas, went through a period of comparative unpopularity, not least because of the florid nature of the vocal writing. The title role, like that of *L'Italiana*, is written for coloratura contralto, and though attempts have been made to arrange the music for a soprano (as has been done with Rosina), the opera really requires a low voice with phenomenal agility. The unmatched ensembles show a modern audience the stuff a comic opera was made of in the days when every singer was a master of the bravura coloratura style, and most of them brilliant actors and actresses as well. Nobody has surpassed Rossini in the surface brilliance of his comic invention. In *Cenerentola*, it is not the motives of the characters which matter – apart from the charming duet early in Act I, the love of Prince Ramiro for the heroine plays little part in the music – nor even primarily their reactions to their own and other people's motives, but the situations these motives get them into. And situations with Rossini lead not so much to arias as to ensembles. Rossini's ability to catch hold of the verbal rhythm of a chance phrase and turn it into music (e.g. the ensemble after Alidoro's announcement of Cenerentola's arrival at the ball), his dexterity with patter, his astonishing manipulation of the simplest material until it becomes a towering invention of quicksilver sound – these qualities are heard at their best in the quintet which begins 'Signore, una parola'; in the finale of Act I, which ends with the *crescendo* first heard in the overture; in the brilliantly comic duet of Dandini and Magnifico in Act II. The climax of the opera comes, not with the rondo at the end, fine though it is, but with the great E flat ensemble of stupefaction after the Prince and Dandini have taken refuge from the storm in the astonished Don Magnifico's house. This sextet is built up on a slow, *staccato* tune (marked *maestoso*: majestically) from which each singer in turn breaks away with a florid phrase, the others meanwhile keeping up the steady rhythm with a constant repetition of the tune and a maximum use of the words and particularly of the opportunities given by the rolled Italian 'r'. This is an ensemble to set beside the *Barber*'s matchless 'fredda ed immobile' as high-water marks of comedy in music.   H.

LA GAZZA LADRA
The Thieving Magpie

Opera in three acts, libretto by Gherardini. Première, la Scala, Milan, 31 May 1817, with Teresa Belloc. First performed London, King's Theatre, 1821, with Violante Camporese and Vestris in the cast; Covent Garden, 1830 (in English, as *Ninetta*;

or The Maid of Palaiseau; music adapted by Bishop), with Mary Anne Paton; Covent Garden, 1847, with Grisi, Alboni, Mario, Tamburini; 1863, with Patti, Didiée, Neri-Baraldi, Faure, Ronconi; and 1883, with Patti, Scalchi, Frappoli, Cotogni; New York, 1830 (in French), 1833 (in Italian). Revived Pesaro, 1941, in new edition arranged by Zandonai with Lina Aimaro, conducted by Zandonai. Subsequently heard in this version in Rome, 1942; Wexford, 1959, with Mariella Adani, Janet Baker, conductor Pritchard; and at Florence, 1965. Première at Sadler's Wells, London, 1966, the score reconstructed from the manuscript in the Bibliothèque Nationale, Paris, and new English version by Tom Hammond, with Catherine Wilson, Patricia Kern, conductor Balkwill.

Fabrizio Vingradito, *a rich farmer*	Bass
Lucia, *his wife*	Mezzo-Soprano
Giannetto, *his son, a soldier*	Tenor
Ninetta, *a servant in their house*	Soprano
Fernando Villabella, *Ninetta's father, a soldier*	Baritone
Gottardo, *the village mayor*	Bass
Pippo, *a young peasant in Fabrizio's service*	Contralto
Isaac, *a wandering pedlar*	Tenor
Antonio, *the jailer*	Tenor
Giorgio, *the mayor's servant*	Bass
Ernesto, *friend of Fernando, a soldier*	Bass
A Magpie	Dancer

An Usher, Armed Men, Villagers, Fabrizio's Employees

Place: A Large Village not far from Paris
Running Time: 3 hours 20 minutes

Immediately after the success of *La Cenerentola* in Rome in January 1817, Rossini went via Bologna to Milan, where he had a contract to write an opera for la Scala. This commission he approached with some circumspection as the Milanese audience had not, according to Stendhal, taken kindly to his earlier operas and their suspicion of the composer would have been anything but assuaged by his recent successes in Rome and Naples. Since he was already in Milan at the beginning of March, ready to start work on whatever libretto the management might provide him with, and the première did not take place until the end of May, it was for Rossini an unusually long period for the writing and preparation of an opera.

In the event, the composer achieved one of the greatest triumphs of his career, and Stendhal describes the first night as the most successful he had ever attended. Perhaps because the score contained something for everyone – pathos, comedy, tragedy,

gaiety – perhaps because, as Toye says, 'things of startling originality were presented in a manner that anybody could follow and understand', nothing in the opera failed to please. The overture, with its opening drum roll (two of the main characters are soldiers returning from the wars), is one of Rossini's most lively and splendid, one moreover whose music has considerably more connection with the rest of the opera than is customary with Rossini.

Act I. The curtain rises on the courtyard of the house of Fabrizio, a rich merchant. A magpie is sitting by an open cage. The people of the village, among them Pippo, who works for Fabrizio, are rejoicing at the prospect of the return of Giannetto, the son of the house, who is expected back from the wars. Everything is going with a swing when suddenly Pippo's name is called. The disembodied voice turns out to be the magpie's and the bird, in answer to Lucia's question as to whom Giannetto shall marry, answers pertly 'Ninetta!' Lucia clearly finds such a match unthinkable, and in fact she seems inclined to pick on Ninetta for anything, even blaming her because one of the silver forks is missing. Ninetta enters and sings of her happiness at the prospect of the return of Giannetto, with whom she is secretly in love ('Di piacer mi balza il cor'), an attractive aria whose layout and even the cast of whose music reminds the listener of 'Una voce poco fa'. Fabrizio, who hints that he would not oppose a match with Giannetto, and Lucia, who charges Ninetta to look after the silver canteen with special care, go off to wait for their son, and the old pedlar Isaac starts to hawk his wares in a cracked voice.

At last Giannetto arrives, and it is apparent that he has eyes only for Ninetta, to whom he sings an aria full of love. In a spirited brindisi led by Pippo all rejoice and then leave the courtyard empty.

As Ninetta says a temporary goodbye to her beloved, a man enters, whom she does not at first recognise as her father but whom she greets rapturously once he makes himself known. He has infringed military law and is in fact even now condemned to death. A long duet ensues between father and daughter but Ninetta's efforts at consolation turn to fear as she sees the mayor coming towards them.

The mayor makes his entry with a *buffo* aria 'Il mio piano è preparato', and he soon makes it plain that Ninetta is the objective his plan is designed to achieve.

The mayor starts to pay court to her when a message is brought to him. Ninetta tells her father to make his escape, but he says he has no money and asks her to sell on his behalf a silver spoon, which is all he has left, and bring him the money to a hiding place he designates. As he is about to go, the mayor stops him and insists that Ninetta read the message aloud as he cannot make it out without his spectacles. As soon as it becomes plain to her that the letter describes her father as a deserter and asks the mayor to help bring him to justice, she changes name and description and there occurs the famous trio 'Oh Nume benefico', Fernando hiding behind the doorway and joining his voice with Ninetta's in thanking heaven for its intervention, the mayor calling down a benediction on his amatory designs.

Once he thinks himself alone with Ninetta, the mayor makes a proposition to her, but she withstands him so firmly that even an old roué could be forgiven for thinking her a spitfire in ingénue's clothing. Fernando can bear the scene no longer and interrupts with a vigorous protest: 'Uom maturo e magistrato'. The scene ends with a lively *stretta*, as each of the three characters realises he or she has gone a good deal further than originally intended. As the mayor retreats and Ninetta's father also makes good his escape, the magpie snatches up one of Lucia's spoons and flies off with it.

The scene changes to a room in Fabrizio's house. Isaac's voice is heard outside and Ninetta sells him the silver spoon which her father has entrusted to her. As she is about to take him the money, Giannetto appears, closely followed by his father, who makes to join the hands of the two lovers. The mayor greets the returned Giannetto, while Lucia goes to count the silver. When she reports a spoon missing, the mayor, with maximum pomposity, sits down to make a legal report. 'Who can the thief be?' asks Giannetto. 'Ninetta,' answers the magpie.

A sextet develops as the mayor takes down the evidence and when he asks Ninetta her father's name and gets the answer 'Fernando Villabella' he suddenly realises that the deserter in the official dispatch was her father and that she was shielding him when she read it out. Things look black when Ninetta pulls out her handkerchief and some money tumbles to the ground. Lucia asks where it comes from, and all Ninetta's protestations are insufficient to divert suspicion, even Pippo's testimony that it came from Isaac only eliciting from the old pedlar himself the information that she sold him a spoon, moreover with the initials F.V. on it – since Isaac has now sold it, it cannot be compared with those in Fabrizio's canteen. Even Giannetto now starts to believe her guilty, and, at the lowest ebb of her fortunes, unable to give her father away, Ninetta movingly leads the ensemble: 'Mi sento opprimere'. The arrival of an armed escort triggers off a frenzied *stretta* to the finale, a typically brilliant, typically solid Rossinian edifice. Nothing will soften the mayor's wrath and apparent zeal for justice, and Ninetta is marched off as a criminal.

Act II. Outside the prison cells of the Town Hall. Antonio, the jailer, tries to comfort Ninetta, then brings in Giannetto, who is intent on persuading her to prove her innocence. She assures him in a beautiful duet that though her lips are now sealed, one day her innocence will be apparent to all. Giannetto leaves as the mayor approaches and that worthy suggests that if she will trust him, she may yet be saved. Unfortunately for the mayor, the judicial Tribunal arrives and his presence is necessary to greet it (the interruption is accompanied by the crescendo from the overture). Pippo is Ninetta's next visitor; she asks him to take the three crowns she got for the silver to her father's hiding place. Pippo himself is to keep her cross as a sign of the affection that was between them. To the *allegro* of the overture, Ninetta gives him her ring to deliver to Giannetto in memory of her.

The scene changes to Fabrizio's house where Lucia is a prey to doubts about Ninetta's guilt, doubts which are resolved in favour of the accused when Fernando enters and proclaims his passionate conviction of his daughter's innocence.

The great hall in the Town Hall. The Tribunal assembles and, in a scene which has been much admired, sings imposingly of its powers and the inexorable manner in which it exercises them. The judge reads out Ninetta's conviction, sentences her to death, and when not even the pleas of Giannetto and Fabrizio persuade her to bring evidence to prove her innocence, the sentence is confirmed. At this point Fernando rushes in and demands in a dramatic *scena* that his innocent daughter be freed. He is overpowered by the guards, but continues to hurl defiance at the Tribunal, which reiterates its decision. A solemn ensemble develops during whose course

Giannetto joins Ninetta in leading a chorus of protest, but all is in vain; Fernando is taken to the cells and Ninetta towards the place of execution.

The village square. Lucia laments the tragic turn events have taken. Pippo is counting his money, and when he puts it down for a moment to talk to the mayor's servant, Giorgio, the magpie flies down and steals a coin. They pursue it out of sight.

Ninetta, surrounded by armed men, is taken towards the scaffold amidst the lamentations of the bystanders. Her last thought is of her father ('Deh tu reggi in tal momento'). Suddenly Pippo and Antonio rush in shouting to Giorgio that they have discovered the real thief: the magpie. Everything has been found in a secret hiding place and Ninetta is innocent after all. To mounting orchestral excitement, Ninetta returns thanks in a tune of delightful innocence, but admits her joy is not complete until she knows what is to happen to her father. At this very moment he appears, released from prison by order of the King himself. It remains only for Lucia to join the hands of Ninetta and Giannetto in token of recognition of the happiness so long delayed, which Rossini loses no time in expressing in music.   H.

ARMIDA

Dramma per musica in three acts, libretto by Giovanni Federico Schmidt, based on Torquato Tasso's poem *Gerusalemme liberata* (1581). First performance at the Teatro San Carlo, Naples, 11 November 1817, with Isabella Colbran as Armida, Andrea Nozzari as Rinaldo, Giuseppe Ciccimarra as Goffredo and Carlo, Claudio Bonoldi as Gernando and Ubaldo, Michele Benedetti as Idraote and Gaetano Chizzola as Eustazio and Astarotte. Revived for Maria Callas at the Maggio Musicale, Florence, in 1952 (along with five other rare Rossini operas); for Christina Deutekom in Venice in 1970 and in Bregenz in 1973; for June Anderson in Aix-en-Provence in 1988; for Renée Fleming as part of the Rossini Opera Festival, Pesaro, 1993. Not yet performed in the U.K. First U.S. performance Tulsa, 29 February 1992.

Armida, *Idraote's daughter* ....Soprano

Rinaldo, *a Frankish knight*................................Tenor

Carlo, *a Frankish paladin* ....Tenor

Goffredo (Geoffroi de Bouillon),
    leader of the crusaders.................................... Tenor

Eustazio, *his brother*..Tenor

Gernando, *a Frankish paladin*...........................Tenor

Ubaldo, *a Frankish paladin*................................Tenor

Idraote, *King of Damascus*....................................Bass

Astarotte, *leader of the demons*............................Bass

Place: Outside Jerusalem
Time: c. 1100 A.D.
Running Time: 2 hours 40 minutes

*A*rmida reflects the determination of Barbaia, the impresario of the Teatro San Carlo in Naples, and of Rossini to offer the public something new and thrilling. Barbaia was reopening the opera house, which had burnt down in February 1816. Rossini faced the challenge of success, in this his third serious opera for Naples (after *Elisabetta Regina d'Inghilterra* and *Otello*). Rossini was also consciously looking for a spectacular role for the great soprano Isabella Colbran, who was shortly to become his wife, which is perhaps why he spent three months working on it – for Rossini, an exceptionally long period of composition. The opera is notable for its structural integrity: the music follows the drama seamlessly, from the beginning, when a military march aptly replaces the usual overture. Apart from Gernando's 'Non soffrirò l'offesa', all the arias are incorporated into larger sequences and ensembles.

Jerusalem is being besieged by the Christians, led by Goffredo.

Act I. The battlefield, as day dawns. Trumpets summon the soldiers, before Goffredo explains that instead of fighting they will hold the funeral of Dudon who died a hero's death. Armida appears, dazzling everyone with her beauty ('Quell'astro mattutino'). She asks the Christians to let her have ten champions to back her in her fight for justice, pretending that her father is conspiring against her. Goffredo explains that she must wait until they have freed Jerusalem. Everyone is moved by her tears (quartet, 'Sventurata! or che mi resta?'). Eustazio's plea on her behalf eventually convinces Goffredo, who asks the soldiers to choose a new leader from their ranks who will then select ten champions. Eustazio proposes Rinaldo, whom Armida has loved ever since she saved his life some time ago. This arouses the jealous fury of Gernando, who swears to be avenged ('Non soffrirò l'offesa'). Idraote encourages his daughter to enslave the Christians, even Rinaldo, though she knows it will not be easy to tame his spirit. Rinaldo is delighted to find Armida in the camp. She rebukes him for deserting her for glory, appeals against his sense of duty and calls on his love for her (duet, 'Amor ... possente nome!'). He yields to her and they leave together. But when Rinaldo overhears Gernando accusing him of cowardice and insulting him, partly because he is Italian, he challenges him to a duel (finale, 'Se pari agli accenti'). Having killed him, to everyone's horror, Rinaldo leaves the camp, in thrall to love.

Act II. A forest. Astarotte and his troop of demons have been summoned by Armida to support her. Armida and Rinaldo approach in a chariot, which she changes into a throne of flowers. As long as he is with Armida, Rinaldo defies fate itself and will think only of their love (duet, 'Dove son io!'). Armida celebrates love's power over all creation (finale, 'No; d'Amor la reggia è questa').

Act III. An enchanted garden. Ubaldo and Carlo, sent to find Rinaldo, recognise that this garden is an infernal deception (duet, 'Come l'aurette placide'). Nymphs try to seduce them ('Qui tutto è calma'), but Ubaldo sends them packing. The Christians hide and watch as Rinaldo and Armida celebrate the 'soft chains' that bind them to each other (duet, 'Soavi catene'). When Armida is forced to leave Rinaldo briefly, Ubaldo uses an adamantine shield to show Rinaldo how cowardly he appears (trio, 'In quale aspetto imbelle'). Shamed into remembering who he is, Rinaldo appeals to heaven to inspire him to leave Armida. On returning, she finds that her infernal powers cannot bring him back and rushes away.

Outside Armida's palace. Rinaldo tries to conceal the pain he feels in leaving Armida, who begs to be allowed to follow him as his squire. He tells her to stay; she accuses him of ruthlessness, asks him to kill her and then faints (finale, 'Se al mio crudel tormento'). Ubaldo and Carlo remove Rinaldo by force. Armida summons the figure of Revenge and resolves to punish Rinaldo. At her command, demons destroy the palace and then carry her away as she rages with vindictive fury.

Armida stands alone, not merely the only woman, but also the major character. Rossini complicates our attitude to this unscrupulous enchantress when he makes the Christian Rinaldo less than her equal antagonist. For a start, because of Naples's casting strength, he is a tenor surrounded by several other tenors – one of the score's high points is the delectable trio for three tenors in the last act. When he is under her spell, Rinaldo rises to Armida's peak of voluptuousness. Stendhal was thinking of their Act I duet when he commented, 'Not infrequently it appears that the fundamental quality of some of Rossini's finest compositions is not true *emotion*, but *physical excitement*, developed to the most extraordinary degree ... One Sunday morning,' Stendhal went on, 'after a truly superlative performance at the *Casino di Bologna*, I observed that many of the ladies present were actually too embarrassed to praise it.'[1] Yet when Rinaldo does abandon Armida, his repentance lacks heroic focus: he has to be dragged away from her by force.

The role of Armida calls for supreme technical ability harnessed to dramatic, seductive ends. This was Maria Callas's particular achievement – as Giorgio Gualerzi put it, her Armida reminded us 'that expressivity is inseparable from technique'.[2] On the other hand, as Andrew Porter put it bluntly in 1952, *Armida*'s 'dramatic action is feeble and the writing for soprano terrific. So that only when a Maria Callas is found to play the enchantress can the revival of *Armida* be an exciting and triumphant success.'[3] P.

ERMIONE

Azione tragica in two acts, text by Andrea Leone Tottola, based on Racine's tragedy *Andromaque* (1667). First performed at the Teatro San Carlo, Naples, 27 March 1819, with Isabella Colbran, Rosmunda Pisaroni, Andrea Nozzari, Giovanni David, Giuseppe Ciccimarra, Gaetano Chizzola, Maria Manzi, De Bernardis *minore*. It was revived only in 1977, in concert, in Siena and restaged in 1987 at the Rossini Festival, Pesaro, for Caballé. First performance in London, in concert at the Queen Elizabeth Hall in 1992, with Anna Caterina Antonacci, conducted by Mark Elder and in the U.S.A. in June the same year, also in concert, San Francisco. First staged in the U.S.A. in 1992 in Omaha, and in Britain at the Glyndebourne Festival in 1995, with Antonacci, conducted by Andrew Davis.

Ermione (Hermione), *Helen's daughter*	Soprano
Andromaca (Andromache), *Hector's widow*	Contralto
Astianatte (Astyanax), *Andromaca's son*	Mute
Pirro (Pyrrhus), *King of Epirus, Achilles' son*	Tenor
Oreste (Orestes), *Agamemnon's son*	Tenor

[1] Stendhal, *Life of Rossini*, revised edition transl. and annotated by Richard N. Coe, London, 1970.

[2] 'Voci Rossiniane', *Opera*, March 1992.

[3] *Opera*, July 1952.

Pilade (Pylades), *Orestes' friend*..........................Tenor
Fenicio (Phoenicius), *Pirro's tutor*........................Bass
Cleone, *Ermione's confidante*...........................Soprano
Cefisa, *Andromaca's confidante*........................Soprano
Attalo, *Pirro's servant* ....Tenor

Place: Epirus
Time: Around 430 B.C.
Running Time: 2 hours

After the fall of Troy, Princess Andromaca and other Trojans are held prisoner by Pirro, King of Epirus. As the widow of Hector, who was slain by Pirro's father Achilles, and as mother of the young Prince Astianatte, Andromaca embodies the future as well as the past of Troy. Even though she therefore represents a threat to political stability, Pirro has fallen in love with her, to the fury of Ermione, Princess of Sparta, who was going to marry him.

Act I. The remarkable, grief-laden overture incorporates the Trojan prisoners' choral lament for the fallen glory of Troy. Andromaca comes to the prison to see her son, whose features remind her of her husband. Attalo points out that to secure her son's freedom, all she has to do is marry Pirro. Fenicio rejects the idea brutally; Andromaca leaves, weeping.

Cleone and a group of young Spartan maidens invite Ermione to go hunting, to distract her from her unhappy love. She is wracked by jealousy, however, and longs for revenge. At first, Pirro tries to reassure her that he still loves her, but she scorns his pretences. When he warns her against pride, she threatens him, but he remains fearless. The news that Oreste has arrived as ambassador from the Greek kings disquiets Pirro and delights Ermione: Oreste loves her; he will defend her interests.

Oreste dreads seeing Ermione, whom he loves, but who rejoices in his suffering. His emotional state worries his friend, Pilade, who begs Oreste to remember his diplomatic mission and be guided by reason and duty. When Pirro sees Andromaca he invites her to sit near him, to the outrage of Ermione. Oreste announces his mission: Astianatte represents a threat to the security of Greece, and must be killed. Pirro reminds Oreste that as the victor of Troy he will do as he wishes with the spoils of war: Astianatte may even share the throne with him ('Balena in man del figlio'). He publicly offers Andromaca his heart and tells Ermione to go back to Sparta ('Deh serena i mesti rai'),

which infuriates her. He departs. Andromaca prepares to leave and tells him she can never marry him.

Ermione tells herself that her love for Pirro has turned to revenge. Oreste is not quite convinced.

Pirro announces that pity has yielded to duty: he is prepared to hand over Astianatte to Oreste, which throws everyone into confusion ('Sperar...temer... poss'io?'). Andromaca begs for time to reconsider her refusal to marry Pirro. Privately, she resolves to die before she loses her son.

Act II. When Pirro learns that Andromaca is ready to marry him he orders Astianatte be set free. In fact, faithful to her dead husband, she intends to ensure that Pirro swear to guarantee her son's safety, then she will commit suicide ('Ombra del caro sposo!').

Andromaca refuses to answer Ermione's threats and insults; she forgives her. Ermione sends Fenicio to remind Pirro of her love and the oaths that he once swore her ('Di, che vedeste piangere'). She still loves and will always love Pirro ('Amata, l'amai'). Pirro is seen to lead Andromaca in a wedding procession across the stage. Ermione accepts that she has lost him, but she can't believe heaven will not punish such treachery. She determines on revenge, hands Oreste a dagger and tells him that if he loves her, he must kill Pirro. She hopes this crime will bring comfort to her ('Se a me nemiche stelle').

Fenicio confirms that Pirro is determined to marry Andromaca. Pilade is appalled: he foresees war, since Agamemnon will avenge this insult to Greece. They both deprecate the power of love ('Quanto sei sempre infausto').

Ermione now regrets her impulsive behaviour. Imagining that Pirro is already remorseful ('Parmi, che ad ogni istante'), she is ready to pardon him. Oreste returns, drenched in Pirro's blood: when the King promised to save Astianatte's life and give him the throne of Epirus, all the Greeks rose and killed him ('Gia di Andromaca sul crine'). Ermione tells Oreste that she loved Pirro and commands the furies to destroy his murderer. Pilade and other Greeks come to save Oreste from the people's fury. Ermione curses him and faints. Oreste is led away, frenzied and nearly unconscious.

Ermione's structure relies on the architecture of mutual loathing and love, complicated by political alliances and underpinned by conflicts rooted in the past, the Trojan war. Tottola and Rossini made two major changes to Racine's play: they shift attention

Ermione (Glyndebourne, 1995, director Graham Vick, designer Richard Hudson).
Anna Caterina Antonacci as Ermione, Jorge Lopez-Yanez as Pirro.

away from Andromache (whose conflict between her duties as a widow and as a mother must end in suicide), to the more dynamic Hermione, the woman scorned, who employs the man who adores her to kill the man she adores. A remarkable sequence of arias and ensembles takes the audience inside her soul. Their other innovation was to flesh out the character of Orestes in an appropriately Romantic way: when he first appears, the orchestral introduction to his cavatina on its own makes it clear that he is already, as the stage direction insists, 'beside himself', in a sense, already pursued by the furies that assail him in the last scene. Rossini called *Ermione* his 'little, Italian *Guillaume Tell*'. It has only recently been recognised, in the words of Philip Gossett, who co-edited the critical edition, as 'one of the finest works in the history of nineteenth-century Italian opera'.   P.

LA DONNA DEL LAGO
The Lady of the Lake

Opera in two acts, text by A.L. Tottola, after Sir Walter Scott's narrative poem *The Lady of the Lake*. Première, San Carlo, Naples, 24 September 1819, with Isabella Colbran. First produced London, King's Theatre, Haymarket, 1823; New York, 1829 (in French). Performed regularly in London in the 1840s and 1850s with Grisi and Mario. Revived Florence Festival, 1958, with Rosanna Carteri, conductor Serafin; London, 1969, Camden Festival, with Kiri Te Kanawa; Italian Radio, 1970, with Caballé; Covent Garden, 1985, with von Stade, Marilyn Horne, Rendall, Chris Merritt.

Elena (Ellen)	Soprano
James V of Scotland (Hubert)	Tenor
Roderigo (Roderick Dhu)	Tenor
Malcolm Groem	Mezzo-Soprano
Archibald Douglas, Earl of Angus	Bass

Serano, *Douglas's retainer*.......................................Bass

Albina, *Ellen's confidante*.....................Mezzo-Soprano

Clansmen, Huntsmen, Pages, Ladies and Gentlemen
  of the Court

Place: Scotland
Time: First Half of the Sixteenth Century
Running Time: 2 hours 15 minutes

Between the beginning of December 1818 and the
end of December the following year, Rossini had
no fewer than four operas on the stage – two at the
San Carlo in Naples, one in Venice and one at la
Scala.[1] Of the four, the only one likely to be known
even by name nowadays is *La Donna del Lago*. The
opera swiftly went the international rounds, was
heard thirty-two times in its first season at la Scala,
remained popular in London until 1851 but seems not
to have been revived between 1860 and 1958, when
the Maggio Musicale Fiorentino mounted it. It is full of
graceful, expressive music and amounts to one of
Rossini's most attractively lyrical scores. That it suffered a century of neglect may perhaps be attributed to
three factors: the role of Ellen was written for Colbran
and is lyrical until the taxingly brilliant final aria[2]
which puts it out of consideration for most sopranos or
mezzos; the two principal tenor roles bristle with high
notes, cascade with runs and roulades, and yet
demand to be sung with a consistent smoothness out
of reach of most singers for the past hundred years or
so; and – most important – the story is concerned with
characters of a much lower voltage than the Normas,
Lucias, or early Verdi heroines who supplanted them
in the imagination of a later generation.

Rossini's opera, like Scott's poem, relates a romantic story of the young King James V of Scotland (born
1512, died 1542). For two years from 1526,
Archibald Douglas, Earl of Angus, kept the King
imprisoned, until he escaped. Douglas fled to England,
and the King took revenge on his relations. At the
start of the opera, Douglas has returned to Scotland
and is living under the protection of Roderick Dhu,
who belongs to a faction opposing the young King. In
gratitude for shelter, Douglas has promised the hand
of his daughter Ellen in marriage to Roderick.

Act I, scene i. The shores of Loch Katrine, with

the Ben Ledi mountains in the background. A
hunting party greets the dawn and Ellen comes into
view in a boat. In a flowing, 6/8 cavatina, 'O mat-
tutini albori', she expresses her hopes that her young
lover Malcolm may be with the hunting party, but
she is surprised by Hubert, who is impressed by her
beauty and tells her that he has lost the other
hunters. She offers him shelter, their voices join in
the melody of Ellen's cavatina, and they leave
together, just as Hubert's companions return.

Scene ii. Douglas's cottage. Ellen reveals to Hubert
that she is the daughter of the famous Douglas who
has been exiled from the court, a decision which
Hubert in an aside says the King much regrets. It is
obvious that Hubert is attracted towards Ellen, and
when her friends refer to the love her father's friend,
Roderick, feels for her and she openly admits in duet
that she loves not Roderick but another, Hubert mistakenly dares to hope that it may be he.

All leave, and Malcolm, the object of Ellen's affections, enters and reveals his hopes and fears in a
soliloquy. Serano, Douglas's servant, announces that
Roderick and some soldiers are already in the valley.
Ellen dares to oppose Douglas's wish that she may be
united with Roderick, to Malcolm's joy and her
father's displeasure. In an aria he commands her
obedience, but when he leaves, Ellen and Malcolm
sing of their love in a slow movement of great charm.

Scene iii. An open field surrounded by high mountains. Roderick is greeted by his clansmen and
responds in a brilliantly florid aria. Tenderly, he
declares his love for Ellen, who herself tries to hide her
apprehension. Malcolm at the head of his followers
has arrived to join Roderick, and Douglas begins to
understand who it is that his daughter loves.
Roderick refers to Ellen as his consort-to-be, and
Malcolm is about to give himself away when Ellen
restrains him, and the four protagonists of the drama,
together with Albina and the chorus, comment on
the situation. With the announcement by Serano
that they are threatened by the enemy, patriotism
replaces private emotions, and the act ends with a
warlike ensemble of defiance and determination.

Act II, scene i. A cave by the lake. Hubert has
returned to seek out the girl with whom he has fallen

---

[1] Though he was under contract to Barbaia as musical director and principal composer, he had frequent leave of absence.

[2] In Florence in 1958 it was apparently omitted.

in love and he sings of his passion ('O fiamma soave'). Ellen appears and he bares his heart, but she says she loves another and offers him only her friendship. He gives her a ring, telling her that he had it from the King of Scotland, whose life he saved; if any member of her family is in danger, she should take it to the King, who will grant any wish she may ask. Their extended duet is overheard by Roderick, whose voice joins with theirs (the music demands high Cs from both tenors and a pair of Ds from Hubert) before he surprises them and challenges Hubert to reveal his identity. He says he does not fear the King's enemies but, at a cry from Roderick, the lakeside is covered with his followers, who have been hiding in the undergrowth. Ellen stops them falling on Hubert without more ado, and a scene of splendid effect ends as Hubert and Roderick prepare to fight, much to Ellen's dismay.

Scene ii. A great room in Stirling Castle. Ellen was born in the castle and she returns to it to ask the King to help her father, who is in prison. Her feelings as she beholds the place of her birth are by no means unmixed, as here she found nothing but misfortune, in contrast to the humble cottage where she has been happy. She enquires for the King and is amazed to find that he and Hubert are one and the same person. When she pleads for her father, he is restored to her and eventually a pardon granted to Malcolm. Roderick is by now dead. (The quartet, 'Cielo il mio labbro inspira', for Ellen, Malcolm, Hubert/James and Douglas, was taken, with Rossini's sanction, from his opera *Bianca e Falliero* and even printed in scores and libretti of the 1830s and 1840s.) The opera ends with a brilliant and very appealing finale, 'Tanti affetti in tal momento', dominated by Ellen, and, it appears, the one passage to find favour at the première.   H.

MAOMETTO II
Mohammed II

Dramma in two acts, libretto by Cesare della Valle, duca di Ventignano, based on his play *Anna Erizio* (1820), which was inspired by Voltaire's play *Mahomet, ou Le fanatisme* (1742). First performance Teatro San Carlo, Naples, 3 December 1820, with Isabella Colbran, Adelaide Comelli, Andrea Nozzari, Filippo Galli. Rossini's own revision was first performed in 1822 at the Teatro la Fenice, Venice, revived in 1985 by the Rossini Opera Festival, Pesaro. First U.S. performance 1988 San Francisco Opera House. Not yet staged in the U.K.

Anna Erisso ....Soprano
Calbo, *Venetian warrior*.......................Mezzo-Soprano
Paolo Erisso, *Anna's father,*
   Governor of Negroponte ....Tenor
Maometto II (Mohammed the Conqueror),
   Turkish Sultan..Bass
Condulmiero, *Venetian warrior*.........................Tenor
Selimo, *Maometto's vizier*..................................Tenor

Place: Negroponte
Time: 1470
Running Time: 3 hours 10 minutes

*M*aometto II represents a further stage in Rossini's development: with its still greater structural complexity and larger-scale musical forms, it shows him building on his Neapolitan experience. Although (or perhaps partly because) *Maometto II* was not a popular success in 1820, Rossini seems to have felt a particular affection for it, choosing to stage it in Venice (in a revised form, with a happy ending) in 1823 and, in a reworked French version, as *Le siège de Corinthe* for his début in Paris in 1826.

When Paolo Erisso was Governor of Corinth, his daughter met and fell in love with a man who told her his name was Uberto – he was, in fact, Maometto. Now Maometto leads the Turks in their siege of Negroponte, whose Governor, Erisso, intends his daughter Anna to marry Calbo, a Venetian soldier.

Act I. Condulmiero proposes that they surrender to the Turks. Calbo convinces everyone that they should still resist and they swear allegiance to Erisso.

Anna's room. Erisso's daughter is torn between concern for the danger her father faces and the love she has concealed ('Ah! che invan su questo ciglio'). He comes to tell her he has decided that she needs a husband to protect her, who will be Calbo. She reveals that she already loves another man whom she met in Corinth, Uberto of Mytiline. Erisso tells her that the real Uberto was with him at that time, on board ship: she realises she has been tricked (terzettone – Rossini's manuscript variant, i.e. *big trio* – 'Ohimè! qual fulmine'). A cannon shot outside summons the men to battle and Anna to pray in church.

Outside the church, Anna hears that a traitor opened the gates to the Turks. She leads the women in prayer ('Giusto cielo'). News comes that Maometto has taken the walls but will not venture further until daybreak. Erisso says goodbye to Anna, who offers to fight (trio, 'Figlia, mi lascia'). Instead, Erisso gives her a dagger with which to kill herself if taken by the Turks.

Turks threaten the inhabitants with fire and death ('Dal ferro, dal foco'). Maometto acknowledges his followers (cavatina, 'Sorgete, sorgete'). When his vizier Selimo is impressed by Maometto's knowledge of the city he reveals that he once travelled throughout Greece as a spy for his father. Turks bring news that the Venetian forces have been defeated and the leaders captured. Calbo and Erisso are brought in, in chains. When Erisso reveals his identity and, in answer to Maometto's questions, that he was once Governor of Corinth and that he is a father, Maometto offers to spare the Venetians' lives if Erisso will persuade the citadel to surrender. Erisso consults Calbo, who is equally adamant in refusing these terms. Enraged, Maometto orders them to be taken away and tortured (finale, 'Guardie, olà'). Anna rushes from the church, confronts her beloved Uberto/Maometto and threatens to kill herself unless he releases her father and Calbo, whom she calls her brother. Maometto frees them and when Erisso rejects his daughter, Maometto offers Anna a life at his side.

Act II. Inside Maometto's tent. Anna is surrounded by luxury, but remains overwhelmed by grief. Moslem girls urge her to enjoy her youth. When Maometto offers his love and his throne, she rejects both and weeps. Yet they both realise that she loves him (duet, 'Anna, tu piangi?'). He orders the tent to be opened at the back and rebukes the Turkish troops who are bent on pillage. Maometto prepares them for another assault on the citadel, which he will lead. When Anna asks for a token of her security in his absence Maometto entrusts her with his imperial seal of authority. He takes the standard to lead his troops into battle ('All'invito generoso'), while Anna feels inspired by a heavenly voice to undertake her 'task of honour'.

The burial vaults of the church. As Erisso kneels before his wife's tomb he accuses his daughter of treachery. Calbo assures him that Anna could never act dishonourably ('Non temer'). When she appears, Erisso continues to reject her until she swears on her mother's tomb that she was true to him. She hands him Maometto's seal and asks to be married to Calbo at the family tomb, as Erisso had once wanted. The two men then leave Anna, knowing she will almost certainly be killed (trio, 'In questi estremi').

Anna hears the women praying in the church. She learns that Erisso and Calbo's appearance at the citadel inspired the Venetians who routed the Turks. They are now looking for Anna, to punish her for her treachery (finale, 'Sventurata! fuggir sol ti resta'). Anna refuses to fly and prepares to meet her fate. When the Turks rush at her, her calmness so surprises them that they stop. Maometto asks for his seal. She reveals that she gave it to her father and to Calbo, whom she names as her husband. She then stabs herself and dies on her mother's tomb.

Maometto II boasts astonishingly elaborate vocalism, but the artifice is never for its own sake. The vocal lines are strongly incised with the characters' different qualities and with their relations with one another. The conflict between Islam and Christianity results in some fairly conventional 'exotic' orchestral colours, and unfrightening jaunty bloodlust from the Turkish soldiers. Maometto's 'military and Asiatic splendour', on the other hand, is a gift to a charismatic bass. More importantly, Anna's dedication to her task inspired Rossini to dramatise a martyrdom. From the prelude to the vault scene, tellingly inflected by the clarinet, she leaves the confusions of profane love for a serenity that finds an echo in the ritual sacrifice, as she herself realises. There is a special, numinous quality to the music that Rossini writes for the last scenes: in the solemn women's chorus with its harp accompaniment, in the dazed reaction of the Turks to Anna's heroism, in Anna's apotheosis, as she foresees the garland heaven will offer her martyrdom, and as she consecrates her last breath to the Virgin Mary. P.

LE SIÈGE DE CORINTHE
The Siege of Corinth

Tragédie lyrique in three acts, libretto by Luigi Balocchi and Alexandre Soumet, based on Rossini's opera *Maometto II*. First performed Opéra, Paris, 9 October 1826, with Laure Cinti-Damoreau, Adolphe Nourrit, Henri Étienne-Dérivis, Louis Nourrit. First performance in U.K. at Her Majesty's Theatre, London, 1834. First U.S. performance, New York, 1834. Revived in Florence (in Italian) in 1949 for Renata Tebaldi; staged in Genoa in 1992, with Luciana Serra, Maurizio Comencini, Marcello Lippi and Dano Raffanti, and given in concert at the Queen Elizabeth Hall, London, in the same year.

Pamyre ....Soprano
Néoclès ....Tenor

Mahomet II ....Bass
Cléomène..Tenor
Hiéros...Bass
Omar..Bass
Ismène...Mezzo-Soprano
Adraste..Tenor

Place: Corinth
Time: 1459
Running Time: 2 hours 30 minutes

Rossini's contract with the Théâtre Italien in Paris obliged him to supply opera in the French style. After the *pièce d'occasion Viaggio à Rheims* and the pastiche of his own works which Pacini compiled, loosely nailed to a framework even more loosely based on Scott, *Ivanhoé*, Rossini reworked two operas that he had written for Naples, *Maometto II* and *Mosè in Egitto*, before he attempted to write new, French operas from scratch. With a beady eye to the main chance, Rossini moved the action of *Maometto II* across the Mediterranean to Corinth, because Paris was aflame with enthusiasm for the cause of Greek independence. You could buy clocks with Lord Byron dying on their top. In April 1826 Rossini conducted a charity concert to raise money for the Greek cause and in October he produced *Le siège de Corinthe* to exploit this wave of Philhellenism.

Some time ago in Athens, Pamyre met and fell in love with a man who told her his name was Almanzor – he was, in fact, Mahomet. Now he leads the Turks in besieging Corinth, whose leader is Pamyre's father, Cléomène.

Act I. The vestibule of the Senate Palace. Cléomène has assembled the troops: should they continue to resist or yield to the Turks? Once the young warrior Néoclès rallies them, they all swear to fight and to die if necessary.

Néoclès reminds Cléomène that he promised to let him marry his daughter. Cléomène is horrified when Pamyre reveals that she has already committed herself to another man, Almanzor. News is brought that the Turks have mounted the city's ramparts. Before he leaves to join the struggle, Cléomène gives Pamyre a knife so she can defend or kill herself.

The square in Corinth. Turks boast of their triumph in the city. Mahomet looks forward to conquering the entire universe. Omar tells him that the Greeks are holding out inside the citadel but that one of their leaders has been captured. Instead of having him executed, Mahomet orders him to be brought for interrogation and explains to Omar that he is merciful now, in memory of a beautiful young woman whom he met once in Athens. The prisoner is Cléomène, who refuses to order the Greeks to surrender, even when Mahomet threatens to punish him for his audacity. When Pamyre runs in, Mahomet's fury yields to love: he offers to save Greece if she will marry him. Cléomène curses his daughter, who is torn between them.

Act II. Inside Mahomet's pavilion. Ismène has observed how Pamyre's remorse poisons her happiness. Pamyre admits that she looks forward only to death and prays that the spirit of her mother will watch over her destiny ('Du séjour de la lumière'). She has a presentiment that Greece will one day be free. Mahomet offers her the spoils of victory, but she grieves at being unfaithful to her God and cursed by her father. Mahomet threatens that if she will not yield to him, her father will suffer. He then stages a fête to celebrate the wedding (ballets). An altar is being erected for the ceremony when Omar leads in Néoclès, who has been captured, but remains defiant: he tells Mahomet that even the Greek women fight to defend Greek liberty from a tyrant. Mahomet's fury is disarmed when Pamyre says, to save Néoclès's life, that he is her brother. Mahomet invites him to witness his 'sister's' wedding and serenades her ('Idole de mon âme'). The tent's flap is lifted and they see that Greek women have joined the men in defending the citadel. At that moment, Pamyre's love dies: like the other Greeks, she now longs for the palm of martyrdom. When Mahomet reminds her that she holds the fate of Greece in her hand, she asks to die with them. Mahomet, enraged, declares that tomorrow the sun will look in vain for Corinth.

Act III. The tombs of Corinth. Néoclès managed to escape and make his way here, which he calls the Greeks' last refuge, the only exile for a people escaping from slavery. He tells Adraste that he is bringing back the remorseful Pamyre, whose voice is then heard in prayer, along with those of the Greek women. Néoclès asks God whether He will allow a people who adore Him to suffer, and thanks Him for saving Pamyre from her fate. Cléomène refuses to forgive his faithless daughter, even when he hears she now wishes to die for Greece. She wishes to marry Néoclès, at her mother's tomb. Cléomène blesses the couple and together they pray God to end the Greeks' suffering ('Céleste providence!'). Hiéros tells them that they have no hope now, the Turks are so near. At Cléomène's request, Hiéros blesses the Greek soldiers' flags and then, inspired, prophesies that after five centuries of slavery, Greece will be free again. Surrounded by the Greek women, Pamyre prays that heaven's mercy will soon end their grief ('Juste ciel. Ah? Ta clemence'). The Turks burst in, bent on slaughter. Pamyre stops Mahomet in his tracks when she threatens to kill herself. With a terrible noise, a wall gives way and Corinth can be seen, consumed by flames.

When Rossini changed *Maometto II* into *Le siège de Corinthe* he wrote one major new number, the patriotic set piece, Hiéros's blessing of the flags, but the revision had many smaller effects as well. The soprano's lover was no longer a mezzo-soprano, because Paris did not share Italy's adherence to the castrato tradition of *bel canto*. Instead, the role of Calbo becomes the tenor Néoclès. Rossini also diminishes the Neapolitan score's florid vocalism and shifts the balance away from individual enterprise to communal effort: the soprano now joins, rather than leads, the chorus's martyrdom. More subtly, Rossini modifies the character of the Turkish Sultan, who now stops the Turkish troops from pillaging Corinth. Suddenly concerned with posterity, he reminds them that 'without the arts, glory's brother, there is no such thing as immortality'. The rhetoric serves no dramaturgical purpose and has little to do with Islam, but in Paris, in 1826, it surely played opportunistically on nostalgia for Napoleon.   P.

MATILDE DE SHABRAN, ossia BELLEZZA E CUOR DI FERRO

Matilde de Shabran, or Beauty and Ironheart

Melodramma giocoso in two acts, libretto by Jacopo Ferretti based on J.M. Boutet de Monvel's play *Mathilde* (1799). First performed at the Teatro Apollo, Rome, 24 February 1821, with Caterina Lipparini as Matilde, Annetta Parlamagni as Edoardo, Giuseppe Fusconi as Corradino, Giuseppe Fioravanti as Aliprando, Antonio Parlamagni as Isidoro, conducted by Paganini (Giovanni Pacini contributed the *Introduzione* to Act II and a late trio). Revived at the Teatro del Fondo, Naples, on 11 November 1821 as a *dramma per musica* and called *Bellezza e cuor di ferro* (Beauty and Ironheart). The Rome version was first performed in the U.K. at Her Majesty's Theatre, London,

1823, New York, 1834. Revived Florence, 1892, Genoa, 1974. The Naples version was presented at the Rossini Opera Festival, Pesaro, 1996, with Elizabeth Futral as Matilde.

Matilde di Shabran	Soprano
Edoardo	Mezzo-Soprano
Raimondo Lopez, *his father*	Bass
Corradino, *known as Ironheart*	Tenor
Ginardo, *his gatekeeper*	Bass
Aliprando, *his physician*	Bass
Isidoro, *a poet*	Bass
Contessa d'Arco, *Corradino's fiancée*	Mezzo-Soprano
Egoldo, *leader of the peasants*	Tenor
Rodrigo, *leader of the Armigeri*	Tenor
Ubaldo, *jailer*	Mute

Place: Spain, in and around Corradino's Castle
Time: The Middle Ages
Running Time: 3 hours 10 minutes

At the last minute, Rossini asked Jacopo Ferretti to provide the libretto for *Matilde*, the opera he had contracted to deliver for the Roman Carnival of 1821. Ferretti handed over his *Corradino*, changing the heroine's name Isabella to Matilde. With no time to set it all, Rossini asked his friend Pacini to compose several parts of the second act. The delayed first night was so rushed that the sets were not all ready. That autumn, in Naples, Rossini rewrote the score, replaced Pacini's contributions and some borrowings from his own operas with new music, wrote the duet between Edoardo and Corradino ('Da cento smanie') to replace Corradino's aria, gave Raimondo's great aria in Act II to Edoardo (which makes greater dramatic sense) and rewrote Isidoro's part in the impenetrable Neapolitan dialect. In so doing he restored the integrity of a work that has only just been recognised as one of his great *semi-seria* operas.

Act I. The Gothic courtyard of an ancient castle. A group of peasants approach cautiously. Aliprando describes the cruelty and misogyny of his master, who is known as Ironheart ('Se all'intorno qui leggete'). Warned by a bell of his arrival, they run away. Isidoro, a Neapolitan poet wracked by hunger and in need of a patron, improvises a song to a guitar ('Intanto Armenia ... Nfra la famma'). Outraged that Isidoro dared cross his threshold, Corradino sends him to prison (quartet 'Alma rea'). Aliprando reminds Corradino that Matilde di Shabran is due to arrive today. Her father was a brave soldier who, before he died in battle, made Corradino promise to look after her. Corradino orders his prisoner Edoardo to be brought to him. Edoardo refused to acknowledge himself beaten in battle by Corradino and now still resolutely defies his captor: his tears are for his father, not for himself ('Piange il mio ciglio').

A gallery in the castle. Matilde expects Corradino to fall in love with her but Aliprando knows he will not yield easily (duet, 'Di capricci, di smorfiette'). The Contessa d'Arco, 'bilious by nature', according to Aliprando, is also staying at the castle and equally determined to marry Corradino, who has been engaged to her for some time. The two rivals for his hand quarrel. When Corradino arrives, Matilde answers his rudeness with equal abruptness, which shocks and even moves him (quintet, 'Questa è la Dea').

Corradino consults his physician Aliprando, who diagnoses love, an illness without remedy. Corradino suspects Isidoro has put a spell on him and sentences him to death. Matilde hints that she loves him and asks if she should leave, while Isidoro and Ginardo watch and laugh. At her command, he disarms, kneels and they declare their love (finale, 'Ah! capisco: non parlate'). Edoardo's father is sighted at the head of an army coming to rescue his son.

The courtyard of the castle. Rodrigo prepares to lead the castle's troops. Isidoro holds Corradino's banner, ready to commemorate the expedition in verse. Edoardo weeps at the thought of the danger threatening his father. Matilde's compassion for him arouses Corradino's jealousy, which convinces the Countess that he loves her rival. Matilde urges Corradino to act humanely. He leaves her in charge of the castle.

Act II. Outside the castle. Isidoro prepares to write his memoirs, in which he will feature heroically. Raimondo's troops have abandoned him; now he despairs of seeing his son Edoardo again. Meanwhile, Edoardo, who has been freed from prison, assumes his father has died. In an aria that includes a virtuoso part for solo horn (decorated, as so often in this opera, by the clarinet) Edoardo also longs to die, until he hears his father's voice ('Sazia tu fossi alfine ... Ah! perchè, perchè la morte'). Corradino is furious to discover Edoardo at liberty, particularly when he hears that Matilde herself freed him.

In the castle's gallery. It turns out that the Countess bribed the jailer to free Edoardo, to turn Corradino against Matilde. When Isidoro appears, the two women question him for news. He claims sole responsibility for the victory. A drum-roll announces Corradino's return. He accuses Matilde of having set Edoardo free and reads out a letter from Edoardo thanking her for letting him go. Convinced of her treachery, Corradino orders Isidoro to throw Matilde off a mountain (sextet, 'È palese il tradimento'), in spite of the pleas of peasant women. Isidoro reports, the Countess exults, but Edoardo reveals that it was the Countess who bribed Edoardo's jailer. Corradino is stricken by remorse, while Edoardo sympathises with Matilde (duet, 'Da cento smanie, e cento').

The rocky mountainside. Isidoro has fled from the castle. Corradino is bent on suicide – until Edoardo leads Matilde forward. Isidoro explains that he only killed her 'metaphorically'. Corradino begs Matilde to forgive him. She insists he open his heart to goodness and embrace his enemy Raimondo. She then commissions a sonnet from Isidoro, celebrates love's triumph and reminds women 'that we are born to conquer and reign'.

Until the 1996 revival at Pesaro, Stendhal's report ('Execrable libretto, but pretty music – such was the general verdict') carried disproportionate weight. In fact, *Matilde di Shabran* is a considerable work, deserving to be more widely seen. Its genre, the *semi-seria*, can cause difficulties. In order to give equal weight to both aspects, its first act lasts over two hours. At its best, *Matilde di Shabran* is a markedly truthful work: Rossini reworks the old forms so that they express an unusual complexity of feeling. Simple names for musical forms such as Act I's quartet and quintet and the sextet in Act II misrepresent them, since they contain any number of smaller groupings chained together to embody the drama's psychological implications.   P.

ZELMIRA

Dramma in two acts, libretto by Andrea Leone Tottola, based on Dormont de Belloy's *tragédie Zelmire* (1762). First performed Naples, 16 February 1822, with Isabella Colbran as Zelmira, Anna Maria Cecconi as Emma, Antonio Ambrosi as Polidoro, Giovanni David as Ilo, Andrea Nozzari as Antenore, Michel Benedetti as Leucippo. For the revival at the Kärntnertortheater, Vienna, on 13 April 1822, Rossini added a chorus and an aria for Emma. London, 1824, Théâtre des Italiens, Paris, 1826. The U.S. première was in New Orleans around 1835. It was revived for Virginia Zeani at the Teatro San Carlo, Naples, in 1965 and, in concert, for Cecilia Gasdia at the Teatro la Fenice, Venice, in 1988.

Zelmira, *Polidoro's daughter* ....Soprano

Emma, *her friend* ....Contralto

Ilo, *Trojan prince, Zelmira's husband* ....Tenor

Antenore, *an adventurer*....................................Tenor

Polidoro, *King of Lesbos* ....Bass

Leucippo ....Bass

Eacide ....Tenor

High Priest ....Bass

Chorus of Ilo's Soldiers

Running Time: 2 hours 40 minutes

When Rossini wrote *Zelmira*, his last opera for Naples, he knew it would be performed in Vienna and then in London: intended to please cosmopolitan ears, it is more richly scored than any of his previous works. The accompanied recitatives, in particular, suggest he was writing with the Viennese tradition of Gluck, Mozart and Beethoven in mind. Stendhal compared *Zelmira* to Mozart's *Clemenza di Tito* and predicted that Rossini 'by the end of his career [may well] have become more *German* than Beethoven himself'.[1]

Polidoro, King of Lesbos, was deposed by Azor, once an unsuccessful suitor for Princess Zelmira's hand while her husband Ilo was absent. Zelmira hid Polidoro among the tombs of the kings of Lesbos and, to protect him further, she let it be known that she hated her father and that he took refuge in the temple of Ceres. Azor had it burnt down, so everyone now assumes that Polidoro is dead. Meanwhile, Azor has been killed by Antenore, with the help of his confederate, Leucippo.

Act I. Outside the city walls, near the tombs of the kings of Lesbos. The army mourns for the dead Azor. Leucippo swears he will be avenged; Antenore promises the assassin will soon die. Leucippo leads the army in proclaiming Antenore as the next king. While Ilo is absent, their only obstacle is likely to be Zelmira. Leucippo tells Antenore that he will accuse her of the murder he himself committed.

Like everyone else, Emma assumes Zelmira has betrayed her father. To prove her innocence, Zelmira leads her friend inside the tombs.

Inside the tombs. Polidoro longs for his beloved daughter to return to him (cavatina, 'Ah! già trascorse il dì'). They meet and comfort one another (trio, 'Soave conforto'). When they hear soldiers approaching they pray for heaven's help in a stupefyingly florid ensemble, before they part once more.

A square, with a temple to Jupiter. The people welcome Ilo back. Ilo longs to see his wife and son ('Qual contento in sen m'ispira'). Zelmira's hesitations trouble him (duet, 'A che quei tronchi accenti?'). Emma tells them that Antenore accused Zelmira of killing Azor. Antenore and Leucippo persuade Ilo that Zelmira betrayed him while he was away and killed Polidoro to keep it secret ('Mentre qual fiera ingorda'). Priests announce that a voice inside the temple said Antenore should be king. Nobody believes Zelmira's assertions of her innocence, not even Emma (duettino, 'Perchè mi guardi').

The throne-room of the royal palace. Antenore enters in triumph to a festive march. He promises to return Lesbos to its days of glory ('Si figli miei').

Ilo cannot find his son and imagines someone has killed him. When he faints, Leucippo moves to assassinate him. Zelmira prevents him, but Leucippo manages to convince Ilo that his wife was about to kill him. Antenore joins in the general amazement at her criminal behaviour (quintet, 'La sorpresa ... lo stupore'). She is taken away to prison.

Act II. The throne-room, as before. Leucippo intercepted a letter from Zelmira to Ilo, which suggests Polidoro is still alive. Antenore resolves to have her followed. Zelmira's son, her friends and Emma emerge cautiously. The women pray that heaven will look after the boy ('Ciel pietoso, ciel clemente').

Outside the city walls. Ilo grieves over his wife's apparent treachery, until Polidoro comes from the tombs and reveals that Zelmira is innocent and has saved his life. Ilo is ecstatic (duet, 'In estasi di gioja'). They separate, Ilo to fetch help, Polidoro to take refuge among the tombs. Zelmira has been freed on Antenore's orders. When he overhears her talk to Emma he realises that Polidoro is still alive. Antenore has Polidoro arrested and boasts of his success (quintet, 'Ne' lacci miei cadesti'). Warriors bring an urn containing Azor's ashes. Believing that Zelmira murdered him, they demand her death and lead her

---

[1] *Life of Rossini*, revised edition, transl. and ed. by Richard N. Coe, London, 1970.

away with Polidoro. Emma meets Ilo at the head of his troops and explains what has happened.

A horrible underground cell. Antenore and Leucippo threaten Polidoro, but he refuses to let Zelmira offer his throne in exchange for his life. At that point, fighting is heard from outside. Zelmira bravely stops Antenore from killing Polidoro. A wall of the cell gives way, revealing part of the square. Ilo enters through the breach. He frees his wife and her father, while Antenore and Leucippo are arrested and led away. Zelmira exults that she saved her father's life and his throne ('Riedi al soglio: irata stella'). Her joy is echoed by everyone.

With no overture, *Zelmira* begins in the most dramatic way possible. It goes on to engineer several exceptional encounters, such as those between husband and wife, between father and daughter, and yet fails entirely to add up as a drama. Rossini seems to delight in scenes, rather than in the individuals involved. He may have been awed by the prospect of presenting the opera in Vienna: the dungeon scenes can be read (and heard) as homage to *Fidelio*. Tottola's libretto has been rightly criticised for incoherence. The characterisation certainly has its problems, alternately unfocused and clichéd: Rossini cannot help giving the tenor villain Antenore some spectacularly heroic music, while the relentlessly wronged wife Zelmira never quite engages our sympathies in the way that Cenerentola does.   P.

SEMIRAMIDE

Semiramis

Opera in two acts, text by Gaetano Rossi, after Voltaire's tragedy *Sémiramis*. Première, Fenice Theatre, Venice, 3 February 1823. London, Haymarket, 1824; Covent Garden, 1842 (in English), with Adelaide Kemble; opened the Royal Italian Opera, Covent Garden, 1847, with Grisi, Alboni, Tamburini, Lavia, Tagliafico, conductor Costa; New York, 1845; Metropolitan, New York, 1893, with Melba, Scalchi, E. de Reszke; Florence Festival, 1940, with Gatti, Stignani, Ferruccio Tagliavini, Pasero, conductor Serafin. Revived at la Scala, Milan, 1962, with Sutherland, Simionato, Raimondi, Gazarolli, conductor Santini.

Semiramide, *Queen of Babylon*	Soprano
Arsace, *Commander of the Assyrian Army*	Contralto
Ghost of Nino	Bass
Oroe, *High Priest of the Magi*	Bass
Assur, *a Prince*	Baritone
Azema, *a Princess*	Soprano
Idreno, *an Indian Prince*	Tenor
Mitrane, *Captain of the Guard*	Tenor

Magi, Guards, Satraps, Slaves

Place: Babylon
Time: Antiquity
Running Time: 3 hours 35 minutes

Rossini married Isabella Colbran nearly a year before the first night of *Semiramide*, in which she created the title role, and it was the last opera he was to write in Italy. Via Milan, Naples and Vienna, it reached London in spring 1824, when Giuditta Pasta took the title role. Maria Malibran sang it in Paris in 1828 and Grisi was heard in it in London in 1847. Aspirant prima donnas sang it for many years and Melba starred in it at the Metropolitan in 1894. In 1962, after a long gap when it seemed to be in eclipse, Joan Sutherland sang it triumphantly at la Scala, Milan. There was a distinguished revival at the Metropolitan as late as 1990, when Marilyn Horne was Arsace, and June Anderson and Lella Cuberli alternated in the title role.

Semiramide is as much a villainess as Lucrezia Borgia and before the opera begins, she and Prince Assur have murdered her husband, King Nino. She even tried to do away with her son, Arsace, but he has survived and, unaware of his true identity, commands a detachment of the army.

Act I. The Temple of Baal. The overture, one of Rossini's most powerful, is unusual in that it is based on themes which occur in the opera itself. A sinister atmosphere pervades the temple as the crowd gathers to hear news of the chosen successor to King Nino. Prince Idreno is there to ask for blessings on his love for Princess Azema. So is Assur and they all acclaim the arrival of Semiramide. An explosion extinguishes the sacred flame on the altar, but, once calm is restored, Arsace can be seen to have returned to the city, an occasion he salutes in his cavatina, 'Ah, quel giorno ognor rammento'. Assur is suspicious of him, and Arsace for his part is resolved never to recognise, if it should come to that, Assur as king.

Semiramide, in a magnificent aria, 'Bel raggio lusinghier', rejoices that Arsace has returned (she does not realise who he is). In duet with him, she not only refers to what she sees as the treachery of Assur but even mistakes Arsace's love for Azema as passion for herself.

The finale takes place in the palace. It is one of Rossini's grandest structures, and during its course Semiramide announces that Arsace will not only be king but become her husband, to the discomfiture of Assur as well as of the young man himself. The ghost of King Nino interrupts what is planned as a celebration of the marriage of Azema to Idreno, and promulgates not only the accession of Arsace to the throne but also a requirement for crimes to be expiated, which will entail Arsace offering a sacrifice to the shade of Nino.

Act II. Semiramide and Assur engage in mutual recrimination over the crime they have committed; their duet is one of the significant passages of the score. Oroe, about to take Arsace to Nino's tomb, tells him that he is in point of fact the son of the late monarch, who was murdered by Semiramide and Assur. Arsace hopes that Nino's ghost will prove clement towards Semiramide. Arsace admits to Semiramide that he is privy to all her secrets and, when Semiramide puts her life in his hands, demonstrates not only his generosity but his genuine love for his mother.

By the tomb of King Nino, Assur reveals his intent to kill Arsace, then hears that Oroe has spoken of his crimes before the people. His frenzy develops into madness but before the end of the scene he has come close to repentance. Within the monument itself, Arsace is followed by Semiramide who is convinced her son is in danger. Her prayer, 'Al mio pregar t'arrendi', is succeeded by a trio, in which she is joined by Arsace and Assur. Attacked by Assur, Arsace succeeds only in striking Semiramide who dies as the people rejoice in their new King.   H.

IL VIAGGIO A REIMS

The Journey to Rheims, or The Hotel Golden Lily

Opera in three parts, text by Luigi Balocchi. Première at the Théâtre-Italien in Paris, 19 June 1825, to celebrate the coronation of Charles X and with a cast of incomparable grandeur including Giuditta Pasta (Corinna), Laure Cinti (Folleville), Domenico Donzelli (Belfiore) and Nicolas-Prosper Levasseur (Alvaro) – the original Norma, Mathilde, Pollione, Moïse, among other creations. Revived Pesaro, 1984, with Gasdia, Valentini Terrani, Cuberli, Ricciarelli, Edoardo Gimenez, Araiza, Ramey, Ruggero Raimondi, Dara, Nucci, conductor Abbado (this cast recorded the opera).

Corinna, *a celebrated Roman improvising poetess* ....Soprano
Marquise Melibea, *the Polish widow of an Italian general* .... Mezzo-Soprano
Countess of Folleville, *a young, fashion-conscious widow* .... Soprano
Madame Cortese, *a lively Tyrolean lady, owner of the Spa hotel* ....Soprano
Chevalier Belfiore, *a young French officer* ....Tenor
Count Libenskof, *a Russian general* ....Tenor
Lord Sidney, *an English colonel* ....Bass
Don Profondo, *an antique-collecting man of letters* ....Bass
Baron Trombonok, *a German, music-loving major* ....Bass
Don Alvaro, *a Grandee of Spain and an admiral* ....Baritone
Don Prudenzio, *a doctor* ....Bass
Don Luigino, *the Countess of Folleville's cousin* ....Tenor
Maddalena, *housekeeper of the hotel* ....Mezzo-Soprano
Delia, *a young Greek orphan* ....Soprano
Modestina, *the Countess of Folleville's chambermaid* .... Soprano
Antonio, *hotel manager* ....Baritone
Zefirino, *a courier* ....Tenor
Gelsomino, *a valet* ....Tenor

Place: A Spa Town
Time: May 1825
Running Time: 2 hours 15 minutes

Ten leading singers were assembled for a festive performance in honour of the coronation of Charles X. Each singer was given a magnificent solo opportunity, well contrasted with its neighbour, replete with embellishments and designed to display his or her special capabilities. The ensembles break up a succession of solos or duets and include what Rossini calls a 'Gran Pezzo Concertato a 14 Voci', a truly splendid set-piece which was cannibalised, albeit with only seven voices, for the first finale of *Le Comte Ory*. Four performances followed before Rossini withdrew the score. Three years later, he used several of the numbers for his successful opera *Le Comte Ory*, after which the opera was forgotten until fragments started to reappear in the 1970s and the score was reconstructed, to be revived with outstanding success at Pesaro in 1984.

Travellers of various nationalities on their way to Rheims for the King's coronation are stuck in a spa town when they find there are no horses to take them further. The hotel wants to make them feel welcome, and the personnel supervised by Madame Cortese (aria) prepare for the party. The Countess of Folleville is impatiently waiting for her wardrobe to arrive, and is mightily cast down to hear from her cousin Don Luigino that the carriage which is bringing it has met with an accident (aria). But her maid Modestina arrives with a hat she has salvaged from the wreck (cabaletta). Baron Trombonok, the German music-lover, who was elected to take charge of the party's travel finances, is interrupted in his reflections on the world's follies (aria) by the Italian man-of-letters Don Profondo. Don Alvaro, the Spanish grandee, and the Polish Marquise Melibea, sadly widowed on the day of her wedding to an Italian general, join the travellers, to be followed by the insanely jealous Russian general, Count Libenskof, who is, like Don Alvaro, in love with her (sextet). Corinna, arrived from Rome, contrives by singing of brotherly love (with harp accompaniment) to prevent a duel (aria). All rejoice (ensemble).

Madame Cortese worries about the continued absence of horses for her guests' onward journey and is baffled by the strange behaviour of the English Lord Sidney, who has fallen in love with Corinna but is too shy to say so and compromises by leaving flowers outside her room (aria with flute obbligato). Don Profondo unavailingly plies Lord Sidney with questions about certain English antiques, and offers to find out for Corinna the latest news about the party's likely time of departure. The young Chevalier Belfiore tries his luck with Corinna, who he is convinced finds him irresistible in spite of her firm rejection of his protestations (duet).

Don Profondo at Baron Trombonok's request makes a list of the valuables held by the travellers, but in his turn starts to show anxiety about the time of departure. The Countess of Folleville asks him where to find Chevalier Belfiore, and is furiously jealous when she hears about his interest in Corinna. Baron Trombonok tells them all that Zefirino has arrived with bad news about their onward journey: there are no horses to be found anywhere. Madame Cortese consoles them by telling them Paris is about to celebrate the King's return to the city, where

Countess Folleville invites them to be her guests (fourteen-voice ensemble). They can travel next day on the public coach, and the funds they had planned for their private travel will pay for a banquet that night in the hotel garden, before which Baron Trombonok contrives to patch up peace between Count Libenskof and Marquise Melibea (duet).

All is prepared for the banquet. The entertainment consists of a toast by each of the travellers in the traditional style of his native country, seven in all (German, Polish, Russian, Spanish, English, French, Swiss), and to crown it all Corinna is prevailed upon to improvise. All join her in praise of the French monarchy.

Such an array of music, owing virtually nothing to dramatic stimulus though much to situation, suggests that there was at least a grain of truth in Tullio Serafin's contention that in Italian opera you went to Verdi for drama but to Rossini for music. Here in his last Italian opera Rossini is at a peak, invention apparently without limit, and the result is one of his most delectable scores, built on a series of attitudes and encounters, and on a sovereign ability to make capital from them.   H.

MOSÈ IN EGITTO/MOÏSE ET PHARAON
Moses in Egypt

Opera in four acts (originally three) by Gioacchino Rossini, Italian libretto by A.L. Tottola. Première at San Carlo, Naples, 5 March 1818, with Benedetti as Mosè, Isabella Colbran and Nozzari. First performed in Vienna, 1821 (in German); London, 1822 (in Italian, as *Pietro l'Eremita*), and in 1833 at Covent Garden (in English under the title *The Israelites in Egypt* and with additions from Handel's oratorio); New York, 1832. Rossini very substantially revised the opera for Paris (as *Moïse et Pharaon*), where it was first given in the new version in 1827, with a new libretto by Jouy, with Levasseur as Moïse, Cinti as Anaï, and Nourrit the younger as Aménophis (its hundredth performance in Paris in this version was in 1838). First performed in second version in Perugia, 1829; Covent Garden, 1850 (as *Zora*), with Zelger as Moses, Castellan as Anaïs, Tamberlik and Tamburini; New York, 1860. Revived la Scala, 1918, with Nazzareno de Angelis, Giannina Russ, Dolci, Merli, conductor Serafin; 1937, with Tancredi Pasero, Cigna, Pagliughi, conductor Marinuzzi; 1950, with Pasero; 1959, with Christoff; 1965, with Ghiaurov; Rome, 1948, with Rossi-Lemeni; Falmouth, 1953 (first performance in England since 1850); Welsh National Opera (also in London), 1965, with Michael Langdon; Paris, 1983, with Samuel Ramey; English National Opera, 1986, with John Tomlinson.

Moses/Mosè/Moïse,[1] *leader of the Israelites* ....Bass
Pharaoh/Faraone/Pharaon,
    King of Egypt ....Baritone
Anaïs/Elcia/Anaï, *Moses' niece* ....Soprano
Amenophis/Osiride/Aménophis,
    Pharaoh's son...Tenor
Sinais/Amaltea/Sinaïde, *Pharaoh's wife* ....Soprano
Aaron/Elisero/Eliézer, *Moses' brother* ....Tenor
Miriam/Amenofi/Marie,
    Moses' sister ....Mezzo-Soprano
Auphis/Mambre/Ophide, *an Egyptian officer* .....Tenor
Osiris/Oziride, *high priest of Isis* ....Bass

Hebrews, Egyptians, Priests, Guards, Soldiers,
    Dancers

Place: Ancient Egypt
Running Time: 1 hour 35 minutes (*Mosè*), 2 hours 30
    minutes (*Moïse*)

Before 1820, Rossini was in the habit of finishing as many as four operas in a single year, and 1818, when the first version of *Mosè* was written for Naples, saw three operas written though only two performed. Like others commissioned for the San Carlo by Barbaia at this time, it was written for Isabella Colbran, once Barbaia's mistress and soon to be Rossini's wife, and the librettist achieved something of a feat in making the female role of Moses' niece the pivot round which the antagonism of Moses and Pharaoh revolved.

The opera's initial success was surpassed at the revival a year later – a rare enough honour in itself at that date – when Rossini added the famous prayer in the last act, purely and simply to divert the audience's attention from the inadequacies of the San Carlo's staging of the Red Sea! Stendhal tells us that it took the composer only a few minutes to write the piece out, but the story is apocryphal and we know from Rossini's own correspondence that he wrote the tune first and had Tottola fit words to it after it was complete. It was this number which had the Italian ladies literally in paroxysms after its first performances – doctors were called in to deal with them – and it is the only one now known separately (not surprisingly since in the second version this is an opera of duets and ensembles and not at all of arias), but it is appropriate that it was this prayer which was sung on the

steps of Santa Croce in Florence when in 1887 the body of Rossini was removed from Paris, where he had died almost twenty years before, and was re-buried in the great Florentine church. Appropriate, too, that on this occasion the vast crowd insisted on a repeat!

It was the work of two months, Francis Toye tells us in his biography of the composer, to turn *Mosè* into *Moïse*, on which later version modern revivals have been based, although often in Italian rather than the French which was heard in Paris in 1827. The second version involved extensive re-writing, with a new first act; for all that it embodies much of the Neapolitan version, there is much new music and much earlier music omitted. Its success was instantaneous, even Balzac praising the opera as 'an immense musical poem', and saying that in this opera he seemed to be watching the liberation of Italy.

Act I. The camp of the Israelites in Egypt is suggested atmospherically in the short *andante* Prelude, an *allegro* leading straight into the first scene. In a fine chorus, the Israelites pray for relief from their bondage and to be allowed to return to their fatherland. Moses appears and demands that his followers cease their lamentations; if they had faith in Him, God would reward them by leading them home. Moses' brother, Aaron, has gone to Pharaoh to plead the Israelite cause and he now returns, together with Moses' sister Miriam, and her daughter Anaïs, who was kept hostage by the Egyptians but whom Pharaoh, influenced by Queen Sinais, has now restored to the Israelites as an earnest of his good faith and decision to set the people free. Pharaoh's son Amenophis has, according to Miriam, fallen in love with Anaïs.

Moses feels that God is about to reward their faith, and a rainbow appears in the sky at the same time as a mysterious voice can be heard reminding Moses and the Israelites that God has kept His promises to them and ordering him to receive God's laws. All swear in an *a cappella* ensemble to observe these laws. Moses leads the people as they give thanks to God and urges them to hasten their preparations to leave Egypt and return home.

All depart except Anaïs, who loves the Egyptian prince Amenophis. He presently appears and begs her to stay with him, abandoning her mother and the

---

[1]English, Italian, French versions of the names.

Israelite people. Amenophis is a passionate lover, but Anaïs seems proof against his pleas, even when he threatens to influence Pharaoh to revoke the order for the liberation of the Israelites, who must now by command of his father bow to Amenophis' edicts. Stendhal esteemed this duet beyond anything in the opera except perhaps the introduction (then to Act I and later to Act II) and the two prayers: 'This is not a piece of music of the moment; it must last as long as powerful feeling itself shall endure.' Amenophis leaves, and Aaron and Miriam lead the company in a thanksgiving hymn. Only Anaïs cannot associate herself with the rejoicing and in a duet of charmingly intimate character she admits her predicament to her mother.

Amenophis is as good as his threat and, as the finale starts, he tells Moses that Pharaoh has reversed his decree and that the Israelites are to return to captivity. Anaïs attempts unsuccessfully to intercede, and Moses threatens God's vengeance on Egypt if His people's departure is put off. For this threat, Amenophis orders his soldiers to slay Moses, but the crime is prevented by the appearance of Pharaoh and Sinais. A great ensemble develops, and Pharaoh announces that Amenophis has spoken the truth and that he has withdrawn his original promise to allow the Israelites to depart. A splendid finale reaches its climax as Moses raises his staff to heaven, the sun is eclipsed and the plague of darkness descends upon Egypt.

Act II. Pharaoh's palace.[1] Darkness lies over Egypt and Sinais, Pharaoh and Amenophis lament the apparently eternal night in a magnificent trio with chorus, whose quality explains Stendhal's comment that, at the première, in spite of his inherent suspicion of such Biblical scenes as a representation of the plagues of Egypt, he found himself surrendering completely and almost instantly to the music. (One must not forget that, in the original version, this was the opera's opening scene.) Pharaoh summons Moses, who arrives with his brother and is faced with Pharaoh's demand that the curse of darkness be lifted from his kingdom; with the return of light, the Israelites may depart. In a splendid prayer ('Eterno! immenso! incomprensibil Dio!'; 'Arbitre suprême du Ciel et de la Terre'),[2] Moses asks God to restore light to the land and, as he waves his staff, light returns.

Reaction to the new situation is in the form of a most expressive canon, enunciated by solo horn, led by Moses and taken up in succession by Aaron, Sinais, Amenophis and Pharaoh. Aaron is optimistic that this light will pierce to the heart of Pharaoh, who is now disposed to allow the Israelites out of captivity, in spite of the efforts of Amenophis to restrain him. Throughout the *stretta*, Amenophis opposes his will to that of the otherwise rejoicing Israelites.

The act sometimes ends with the scene between Pharaoh and Amenophis in which the King tells his son that he is to marry the daughter of the King of Assyria, much to the despair of Amenophis, who still loves Anaïs. There is, however, properly a scene for Amenophis and his mother Sinais in which the Queen, although she had earlier supported the Israelites' efforts to obtain liberation, laments in a fine aria the impending departure of Anaïs, Moses and the Hebrews, while Amenophis works himself into such a passion at the idea of losing Anaïs that he declares, to his mother's consternation, that he himself will kill Moses.

Act III. The Temple of Isis. Egyptians are worshipping the goddess, whose High Priest, Osiris, joins Pharaoh in making offerings to the deity. There follows a three-movement ballet, written of course for the Paris version and attractive in invention. Moses comes to claim the fulfilment of Pharaoh's promise, but the High Priest insists that the Hebrews should first render homage to Isis, to Moses' considerable indignation. Auphis, an Egyptian officer, reports a series of new plagues, the Nile's waters having turned red, earthquakes shaking the land, and the air being filled with insects. The High Priest tries to prevail on Pharaoh to punish Moses for these new disasters, while Sinais' voice urges her husband to keep his original promise. Again Moses lifts his staff, and this time the altar fire is extinguished. The fraught nature of the situation is celebrated in a fine ensemble, after which Moses and Osiris in turn demand justice from Pharaoh. The Egyptian King decrees that the Israelites shall be expelled from Memphis in chains and the finale ends as impressively as it began.

Act IV. The desert, in the distance the Red Sea. Amenophis renews his pleading with Anaïs, telling her

---

[1] Introduced in *Moïse*, as in *Mosè*, by three reiterated Cs, which originally made a unique and effective start to the evening.

[2] 'This entrance of Moses recalls everything that is sublime in Haydn ...' writes Stendhal.

he is prepared to renounce his claim to the throne of Egypt if she will marry him. He urges his devotion, but Anaïs is torn between her loyalty to the Israelites and her love for the prince who is their enemy; the situation is unresolved and they hide when a march announces the arrival of Moses and the Israelites, guarded and chained. This is the day on which they shall return to the Promised Land, Moses announces, but Miriam is sad that her daughter has stayed behind. Suddenly, Anaïs reappears to the joy of all, and announces that her freedom she owes to Amenophis who himself stands before them to demand her hand in marriage. When Moses bids her make her choice, Anaïs, torn as she is, decides in an aria to follow the Israelites in spite of her love for Amenophis. The Prince warns Moses that Pharaoh plans a treacherous assault on them as they march undefended, and admits that he himself must join this Egyptian army.

The scene changes to the shore of the Red Sea. Faced with an impossible crossing in front of him and an implacable army behind him, Moses prays to God in the most famous passage of the score, the prayer, added for the revival in Naples the season following the première, 'Dal tuo stellato soglio' ('Des cieux où tu résides, grand Dieu'), in which he is joined by the voices of Anaïs, Aaron and Miriam.

Anaïs sees the Egyptians about to attack, but Moses leads the Israelites into the sea, which miraculously parts leaving a passage for them to pass through. As the Egyptians follow, with Pharaoh and Amenophis in the vanguard, the waters close upon them, there is an orchestral depiction of the catastrophe which befalls the Egyptian army and the opera ends with a *Cantique* of thanksgiving for the Israelite leaders (cut in the Italian score of the French version).   H.

LE COMTE ORY

Count Ory

Opera in two acts, libretto in French by Scribe and Delestre-Poirson. Première, Paris, 1825, with Cinti-Damoreau. Outstandingly successful in Paris, where 400 performances by 1884. First performed King's Theatre, London, 1829; Covent Garden, 1854, with Bosio, Marai, Lucchesi. Revived Florence Festival, 1952, with Barabas, Monti, conductor Gui; Glyndebourne at Edinburgh Festival, 1954, with Barabas, Oncina, Bruscantini, Wallace, conductor Gui; Berlin, Städtische Oper, 1957, with Barabas, Häfliger; Piccola Scala, Milan, 1958, with Sciutti, Berganza, Oncina; Sadler's Wells, 1963, with Elizabeth Harwood, Patricia Kern, Alexander Young; 1972, with Valerie Masterson and John Brecknock.

Raimbaud, *friend to Comte Ory*	Baritone
Alice, *a peasant girl*	Soprano
Comte Ory, *a young and profligate nobleman*	Tenor
Ragonde, *companion to Comtesse Adèle*	Contralto
The Tutor	Bass
Isolier, *page to Comte Ory*	Mezzo-Soprano
A Young Nobleman, *friend to Comte Ory*	Tenor
Comtesse Adèle	Soprano

Place: Touraine
Time: The Crusades
Running Time: 2 hours 25 minutes

Rossini's first work for Paris was *Il Viaggio a Reims*, performed in June 1825 with an astonishing cast of ten stars. Rossini used four numbers a couple of years later for his first opera in French, *Le Comte Ory*. Here they make a fine effect, but not so great, argue with some justification the admirers of *Il Viaggio*, as in the original.

Following the great success of *Moïse* in Paris, Rossini set to work on a light-hearted comedy in French style – this in spite of the fact that his mother, to whom he was devoted, had recently died. Scribe and Delestre-Poirson reworked a vaudeville they had written a dozen years before, doubling its length by adding another act (the first). The result has been very much admired, not least in France, where composers as different as Berlioz and Milhaud have praised it warmly, and revivals have been many and successful.

The story is of the dissolute young Comte Ory and his efforts (as unsuccessful as Don Giovanni's) to win the favours of a lady. The Comte de Formoutiers is away on the Crusades, leaving his sister, Adèle, and her companions without male protection in the castle. Determined to reach her, Comte Ory and a young scapegrace friend, Raimbaud, have dressed themselves up as hermits and are hanging about the gate of Adèle's castle, waiting for a chance to get in.

Act I. After a mainly martial introduction, Raimbaud summons the peasantry to the hermit's presence; let them put their offerings over on the bank – and no ribaldry. Ragonde comes to rebuke the crowd for its levity at a time when Countess Adèle is mourning her brother's absence; she and her mistress mean to consult the hermit with a view to alleviating their present distress.

Just then the Count appears; the *tessitura* of his cavatina ('Que les destins prospères') is high, like the rest of the role, and in it he offers his help to all and sundry, particularly those of the fair sex who lack husbands. In a typical *crescendo* ensemble, all ask for benefits which he confers. Ragonde, whom he has earlier addressed as 'dame trop respectable', tells him that the Countess and the other ladies of the castle have made vows Lysistrata-like to shun the society of men until the Comte de Formoutiers is back from the Crusades. Now she is lonely and depressed and, to the Count's delight, wants his advice.

In come the Count's tutor and his page, Isolier; the former looking for his elusive charge, the latter suggesting that he may find his lordship in this vicinity, for no better reason than that Isolier himself is in love with his cousin Adèle and sees a chance of being near her. In an aria the tutor complains of his unhappy lot, but he starts to smell a rat when he hears some girls singing the praises of a hermit who arrived eight days before – exactly the time the Count has been gone. Isolier in contrast suspects nothing: he sings a delightful, sprightly duet with his master, whom he does not recognise, and to whom (in search of spiritual advice) he unwittingly reveals his love for Adèle and his plan to gain admission to the castle disguised as a pilgrim. Ory resolves to adopt the plan himself.

Adèle now emerges to consult the hermit, and in an agitated aria ('En proie à la tristesse') admits that her self-denying vow has induced a fit of melancholy. The cure is simple, says the Count; she must fall in love – and forthwith he absolves her from her vow. In her cabaletta she accepts his advice and seems likely to fix her affections on her cousin Isolier until the hermit warns her against the machinations of the page of the notorious Comte Ory. At that moment the tutor arrives, recognises his charge and gives the show away. From different points of view all express horror at such a turn of events in a beautiful unaccompanied septet, at whose end the Countess receives news that her brother and his companions are likely to return home within a day. Reflecting on the short time he now has in which to accomplish his design, the Count leads off a brilliant *allegro spiritoso* ensemble, as delectable in invention as it is affirmative in effect.

Act II. Inside the castle, Adèle, Ragonde and their companions are waiting for the return of the crusaders. Surrounded by the women, they sing a duet, 'Dans ce séjour calme et tranquille', and congratulate themselves on their recent escape from the wiles of Comte Ory. Through the noise of a storm can be heard the sound of pilgrims intoning their chant. The Countess cannot refuse hospitality to the travellers and sends Ragonde, who comes back to say that they are nuns fleeing from the wicked Comte Ory. She brings with her the Mother Superior, who is of course the Count in disguise.

The Mother Superior protests the gratitude of all the nuns in a duet ('Ah, quel respect, madame') and slyly confides to the Countess that rumour has it that the Count loves her – which news causes that lady much indignation. Food is provided for the weary travellers and once they are alone their delight in their situation is expressed in a rollicking chorus. Only one thing is missing – and Raimbaud comes in to tell them in an aria that he has found it: wine! The drinking chorus is merry and infectious, but it changes quickly to the pilgrims' plaint when a footstep is heard approaching. It is the Countess to tell them that their accommodation for the night is prepared.

Isolier brings Adèle news of the imminent arrival of her brother, and when he hears of the nuns lodged within the walls he is filled with suspicion. He warns Adèle that she may be sheltering the Count himself, and, when they hear someone coming, volunteers to save her from the fate which seems to be in store for her. The Count attempts to make up to Adèle, but his advances are intercepted in the dark by Isolier, who loses no time in passing them on, one might say with interest, to his beautiful cousin. The trio ('A la faveur de cette nuit obscure') is the most celebrated number in the score; says Francis Toye: 'for loveliness of melody, originality of harmony, charm of part-writing, it is beyond praise, worthy of Mozart at his best. Berlioz, who cannot be suspected of undue tenderness towards Rossini, writes ... that this particular trio was, in his opinion, the composer's absolute masterpiece.'[1]

Suddenly, trumpets are heard signalling the return of the crusaders. Ory is discovered, Isolier reveals himself, counters his master's fury with the threat to disclose all to his father, but relents to help him escape. The opera ends with the anticipated arrival of the returning warriors.   H.

---

[1] *Rossini: a study in tragi-comedy* by Francis Toye, Heinemann, 1934.

GUILLAUME TELL
William Tell

Opera in four acts, text by V.J. Etienne de Jouy and L.F. Bis, based on Friedrich Schiller's play. Première at the Opéra, Paris, 3 August 1829, with Cinti-Damoreau, Adolphe Nourrit, Henri-Bernard Dabadie, conductor Habeneck. The four acts were reduced to three in June 1831. First performed in London, Drury Lane, 1830 (in English); Her Majesty's, 1839 (in Italian); Covent Garden, 1845 (in French); New York, 1831 (in English), 1845 (in French), 1855 (in Italian). Revived, London Opera House, 1911, with Victoria Fer, Orville Harrold, conductor Ernaldy; at Metropolitan, New York, 1923, with Ponselle, Martinelli, and 1931, with Lauri-Volpi; Colón, Buenos Aires, 1923, with Spani, O'Sullivan, Galeffi; la Scala, Milan, 1930, with Bruna Rasa, Lauri-Volpi, Franci; Paris Opéra, 1932, with Norena, O'Sullivan, Huberty, Journet; Berlin, 1934, with Heidersbach, Roswaenge, Bockelmann, Bohnen, Kipnis, conductor Heger; Florence Festival, 1939, with Gatti, Mazaroff, Sved, Pasero, conductor Marinuzzi.

Guillaume (William) Tell ....Baritone
Hedwige, *his wife* ....Soprano
Jemmy, *their son* ....Soprano
Arnold, *a Swiss patriot* ....Tenor
Walter Fürst, *a Swiss patriot*...............................Bass
Melcthal, *Arnold's father*.....................................Bass
Gessler, *Austrian governor of Switzerland* ....Bass
Mathilde, *an Austrian princess*.......................Soprano
Rudolph, *commander of Gessler's archers*............Tenor
Leuthold, *a herdsman*....................................Baritone
Ruodi, *a fisherman*...Tenor

Peasants, Knights, Ladies, Pages, Soldiers, Hunters, Three Bridal Couples

Place: Switzerland
Time: Thirteenth Century
Running Time: 3 hours 40 minutes

Rossini's last opera was written to fulfil the terms of an agreement with the French government. It is a noble work and must be considered, with Verdi's *Don Carlos*, the finest example of French Grand Opera; in it Rossini demonstrates a new interest in folk music, nature and the picturesque.

Switzerland is governed by a repressive Austrian regime, personified by its Governor, Gessler. Arnold, a young patriot, has saved the life of a Habsburg princess, and as a result they have, from the Swiss point of view unfortunately, and in spite of her nationality, fallen in love.

The overture has four distinct movements: five solo cellos evoke, according to Berlioz, 'the calm of profound solitude'; next, a storm; then a pastoral scene, with a Swiss herdsman's *ranz des vaches*; finally, a patriotic call to arms (*allegro vivace*).

Act I. On the shores of Lake Lucerne. At a village festivity, a triple wedding celebration presided over by Melcthal, a fisherman sings a charming song which turns into a quartet with Tell and his family; Melcthal would like to see his son as one of the bridegrooms. Arnold is reluctant to reveal his love for Mathilde, but in a fine duet ('Ah, Mathilde, idole de mon âme') Tell senses in him a certain ambivalence when open defiance of the occupying force is demanded. In the end, there is no doubt of his love for Mathilde but equally little about his patriotism. Nonetheless, he contrives to leave, and Tell, goaded by the sound of the distant hunt in which Gessler is doubtless active, goes to look for him.

The weddings proceed, a most attractive *Pas de Six* starts the dancing, but interruption comes with the precipitate arrival of Leuthold, who has killed an Austrian who attempted to rape his daughter. Tell volunteers to row him to safety. The Austrians headed by Rudolph arrive breathing fire and slaughter and, baulked of their prey, unavailingly question the villagers before carrying off Melcthal as hostage.

Act II. The mountains overlooking Lake Lucerne and neighbouring cantons. An Austrian hunting chorus is answered by a contrasting chorus of Swiss in devout mood. Mathilde, separated from the hunting party, in a beautiful aria celebrates her love for Arnold ('Sombre forêt'), who himself makes an appearance. Though the obstacles to their love are clear, they pledge faith in a duet and Arnold says that, in order to be worthy of Mathilde, he will win honour fighting in the Austrian army away from Switzerland. Tell and Walter Fürst work on his patriotic instincts (trio: 'Quand l'Helvétie est un champ de supplices') and clinch his support by revealing the murder of his father – one of the score's grandest movements, where moreover the high notes of the tenor cast as Arnold make most effect.

The second part of the act has the gathering of the Cantons, each differently and grandly characterised in music, and, at Tell's urging, the swearing of an oath to join in casting off the Austrian yoke (the music foreshadowing Meyerbeer's 'Bénédiction des Poignards', but celebrating a nobler cause).

Act III. A chapel in the grounds of the Governor's

palace. Arnold tells Mathilde he must adhere strictly to the Swiss cause, partly out of patriotism, partly out of respect for his murdered father, and she reacts with sympathy. They suspect patriotism will keep them apart for ever (this scene is usually omitted in modern performance).

The Square at Altdorf. Celebration of one hundred years of Austrian occupation has been decreed, and orders are out for the Swiss populace to genuflect to Gessler's hat symbolically displayed. A series of vividly contrasted dances follows, some with chorus, and at their end Tell refuses to bow to the Austrian symbol and is recognised as having helped Leuthold escape. Gessler orders him to shoot an apple from his son Jemmy's head. Tell addresses his son in a fine aria: 'Sois immobile' (Hold yourself still). The shot succeeds but Tell has no compunction in admitting to Gessler that the second arrow he held was intended for him. When Gessler condemns both Tell and Jemmy to death, Mathilde makes a spirited intercession and demands in the King's name that Jemmy be handed over to her. Tell is taken off to prison.

Act IV. Melcthal's house. Arnold wants vengeance for his father's murder and at the same time recognises that with Tell in prison he is the natural leader of the revolt. He gazes sadly at his ruined home and pours forth his feelings in an aria ('Asile héréditaire'), famous in its own right and bristling with top Cs. In Rossini's day these were sung in a 'mixed voice' and only later (notably by the French tenor Gilbert Duprez) and to Rossini's distaste by the *tenore di forza* of modern times.

A rocky shore of Lake Lucerne. A storm is rising. To Hedwige Mathilde restores her son Jemmy (trio: Je rends à votre amour un fils digne de vous'). Mathilde pledges herself as surety for Tell, Jemmy lights the beacon as a signal of revolt, all pray for Tell's safety, and Leuthold announces the appearance of Tell's storm-bound boat, which he is piloting but which also contains Gessler. He lands, pushes the boat away from the shore and fires an arrow straight to Gessler's heart. The Swiss are triumphant, Arnold laments that his father did not live to see the day, and a *ranz des vaches* banishes the storm and brings back the sun.

Guillaume Tell is a long opera and by 1831 Rossini had already prepared an abridged edition in three acts. This was subsequently revised but the four-act version did not return to the Paris stage until 1856; in 1868, the Paris Opéra celebrated 500 performances of Rossini's work, which remained in the repertory until 1932. Modern practice tends towards as nearly complete a version as the audience is thought able to stand, and there is little doubt that the opera's nobility and grandeur are most apparent when cuts are at a minimum.   H.

ALBERT ROUSSEL
(born 5 April 1869, died 23 August 1937)

PADMÂVATÎ

Opera-ballet in two acts, libretto by Louis Laloy. Première at the Opéra, Paris, 1 June 1923, with Ketty Lapeyrette, Jane Laval, Paul Franz, Eduard Rouard, conductor Philippe Gaubert. Revived 1946, with Hélène Bouvier, Renée Mahé, Charles Fronval, Marcel Clavère. First produced Buenos Aires, 1949, with Bouvier; 1968, with Lyane Dourian, Jon Vickers, conductor Georges Prêtre; Naples, 1952, with Janine Micheau, Tygessen, Vieuille, conductor Cluytens; London, Coliseum (concert performance), 1969, with Rita Gorr, Jane Berbié, Albert Lance, Gérard Souzay, conductor Jean Martinon; Dortmund, 1997.

Ratan-Sen, *King of Chitoor* ....Tenor

Padmâvatî, *his wife* ....Contralto
Alauddin, *the Mogul Sultan of Delhi* ....Baritone
The Brahmin ....Tenor
Gora, *steward of the Palace at Chitoor* ....Baritone
Badal, *Ratan-Sen's envoy* ....Tenor
Nakamti, *a young girl* ....Mezzo-Soprano
The Sentry ....Tenor
A Priest ....Bass
Two Women of the Palace ....Soprano, Contralto
A Woman of the People ....Soprano
A Warrior ....Tenor

A Merchant ....Tenor

An Artisan ....Baritone

Warriors, Priests, Women of the Palace, Populace

Dancers: A Woman of the Palace, A Female Slave, A Warrior, Kali, Durga, Prithivi, Parvati, Uma, Gauri; Girls of the Palace, Female Slaves, Warriors

Place: Chitoor
Time: 1303
Running Time: 1 hour 40 minutes

Roussel was first in the East during his naval service and returned there in 1909 on a cruise, visiting among other places in India, Bombay, Ellora, Jaipur, Benares, as well as Ceylon, Singapore and Saigon. On his return, he wrote his orchestral triptych *Evocations,* in which his memories of Ellora, Jaipur and Benares live fully up to the title rather than indulging in any form of Oriental reminiscence. In 1914, Jacques Rouché became Director of the Opéra; he had been at the head of the Théâtre des Arts where in 1913 Roussel's ballet *Le Festin de l'Araignée* was given, and one of his first actions after his new appointment was to commission a lyric work from Roussel. The composer chose a subject which had attracted him during his Indian journey, and had finished the vocal score by the outbreak of war, orchestrating it in 1918, after ill health caused his retirement from the Navy, to which he had been recalled.

Roussel never attempted to superimpose Hindu melodic or rhythmic patterns on his music except where the works were of directly Oriental character, and his music remained entirely European. Certain sections of *Padmâvatî,* particularly those lyrical in character, make use of Hindu scale forms not usually found in Western music. The pantomime of the third scene of Act II starts with an imitation of the *arpeggio*-like sweep down the sympathetic strings with which sitar or sarode recitals customarily begin.

Chitoor has for ruler the noble and just Prince Ratan-Sen, married to the beautiful Padmâvatî, whose name denotes the sacred lotus or Padma. In the past, a Brahmin priest had fallen in love with Padmâvatî and was banished from Chitoor. He has now taken service with the Mogul ruler of Delhi, Alauddin, and to avenge himself on Ratan-Sen, he persuades Alauddin to attack Chitoor.

Act I. After a prelude, which starts slowly and atmospherically, the curtain rises to show the people of Chitoor in the public square in front of the palace. They await the arrival of Alauddin and his envoys, who are to discuss peace with Ratan-Sen, and girls garland the sacred images as a watchman announces the approach of the Mogul prince. Gora, steward of the palace, tries to reassure the crowd about their traditional enemies, but his own suspicions are roused when Badal tells him that behind the screen of the peaceful delegation the Mogul army is gathering in the plain.

The music, already full of anticipation of events to come, gathers momentum as Alauddin makes his appearance with the Brahmin priest in his entourage, and is hailed in a wordless chorus. Ratan-Sen proposes a pledge to their future alliance. Gora demands that the Brahmin leave them while they confer, but Alauddin insists on his favourite counsellor remaining. At his guest's suggestion, Ratan-Sen orders a display of dancing, first to vigorous 5/4 and 3/4 rhythms by his soldiers, then by the female slaves to a less energetic but still lively 6/8 with a slow central section. Alauddin asks to see the Hindu palace dancers themselves, a right denied to unbelievers, saying that he has been converted to Hinduism by the Brahmin. After a languorous dance in triple time accompanied by wordless chorus, Alauddin makes his request to see Padmâvatî, the fame of whose beauty has travelled far, and the Brahmin in a beautiful aria passionately sings her praises. Ratan-Sen, in spite of misgivings, feels that he cannot refuse, and Padmâvatî appears veiled on a balcony among her women, among whom Nakamti in a song of considerable allure compares her beauty to the sun, which disperses night and awakens the flowers ('Elle monte au ciel où rêve le printemps'). The opening and often-repeated phrase of Nakamti's aria serves as motif for Padmâvatî and is unusually successful in that not only is it associated with her beauty, which Nakamti is specifically hymning, but it does not exclude the quality of modesty, by tradition all-important among Indian women.

When Ratan-Sen bids Padmâvatî lower her veil, Alauddin seems overcome by what he has seen and makes an excuse to leave. He puts off signing the treaty until the next day when he may bring appropriate gifts.

As the Brahmin is about to follow his master, he is recognised by one of the guards. He waits to hear the watchman report that Alauddin has left the city, then delivers his master's challenge: if Padmâvatî is not handed over to Alauddin (reference to Nakamti's song), the Mogul army already encamped in the plain will sack the city of Chitoor. Ratan-Sen's refusal is brusque and to the point, but the crowd lynches the Brahmin, who dies prophesying death for Ratan-Sen and Padmâvatî and destruction to the people of Chitoor.

In the final scene of this act, against a background of distant calls to arms, Padmâvatî laments that she should be the innocent occasion of disaster – a sacrilegious death has already occurred – and prays that she may meet death rather than be separated from Ratan-Sen.

Act II. A solemn prelude introduces the act, which takes place in the Temple of Siva,[1] containing a gigantic statue of the god, with a door in its base leading to the crypt. It is night. At dawn next day, if Padmâvatî has not been handed over to Alauddin, Chitoor will be sacked. Ratan-Sen is leading his warriors in a last desperate sally against the Moguls, and Padmâvatî has come to the temple to add her supplications to those which we hear rising solemnly from the crypt. The priests tell Padmâvatî that a supreme sacrifice at dawn is required, but when Padmâvatî offers herself to die, she is told that there must be more than one victim.

Ratan-Sen appears in the temple, wounded and with the news that his soldiers are defeated and a truce granted only until dawn. He tries to explain the full horror of the situation to Padmâvatî, but she cannot imagine him allowing more than her dead body to fall into the hands of the Mogul king. He describes the suffering the people of Chitoor will have to undergo if Alauddin is refused, and she at last understands what he means. To forestall the sacrilege which she sees he is planning to commit, she stabs him to the heart in full knowledge that custom demands that she commit suttee[2] on her husband's funeral pyre.

The third scene is a great ritual of death. First,

Padmâvatî is prepared for her immolation. As she sings a lament ('O mes sœurs fidèles') she is attired as a bride by the priestesses. Next comes an extended dance sequence. A fire is lit which provides the illumination for a mime-dance by four vampire-like figures. These are succeeded by the two figures presaging death, Kali and Durga[3], who dance in narrowing circles round Padmâvatî, the chosen victim. The funeral ceremony reaches a climax when the priests garland first the body of Ratan-Sen, then that of the living Padmâvatî, at the same time as are heard the first lamentations of the crowd outside the palace.

At the first rays of sunlight, the procession starts to move. The body of Ratan-Sen is carried slowly to the crypt, Padmâvatî following half walking, half carried. As Ratan-Sen's funeral pyre begins to blaze and Padmâvatî with a supreme gesture of terror is gently carried into the crypt, the music reaches its final climax. There is a great shout as Alauddin bursts through the temple door, but all that he can see is the smoke slowly drifting up from the crypt, as the orchestra recalls Nakamti's celebration of Padmâvatî's beauty.

The opera is Roussel's most ambitious project. It could be argued that he is less than perfectly served by his poet, and certainly there is more urgency in music than libretto. The composer deals in sustained musical shapes, and drama for him lies in the musical expression of the powerful overall theme rather than in portrayal of immediate situation, of clash of motive or will, of violent incident. Characterisation is incidental, but what is notable is the composer's ability to organise, whether the long opening movement with its processions and its messengers, the extended and contrasted dance scenes in both acts, or the quasi-finale of the first act (taking the concluding scene of that act as reflective comment on its main action). The musical splendours of the choral funeral procession bring to a most impressive end an opera whose almost complete neglect ever since it was written seems unbelievable. H.

---

[1] Siva: one of the major gods of the Hindus. 'In the worship of Siva', says Benjamin Walker's *Hindu World*, 'was centred that element of dread and uncertainty that is associated with the unknown and the unfathomable.' Siva is at the same time destroyer, creator and preserver.

[2] Suttee: the ancient Hindu custom where the widow commits suicide (preferably voluntarily) on the funeral pyre of her husband.

[3] Kali and Durga: Kali, an aboriginal goddess, wife of Siva and black of visage, is associated with death, as is Durga, a renowned slayer of demons.

ANTON RUBINSTEIN
(born 28 November 1829, died 20 November 1894)

Anton Rubinstein was not only a magnificent pianist but a prolific composer in all forms, and a highly effective organiser. He was instrumental in founding the Russian Musical Society, which became the Leningrad and later the St Petersburg Philharmonic; also the State Conservatory, where he was the teacher of Tchaikovsky. Balakirev said of him 'He is not a Russian composer, but a Russian who composes.' He was highly successful out of Russia, and half his nineteen operas were written in German. Even his greatest admirers describe his work as uneven: *Nero*, for instance, commissioned by Paris, was rejected and, in spite of some early success – Caruso made a striking recording of one of the arias – has disappeared. Only *The Demon* remains even remotely a candidate for the repertory, although revivals suggest life left in it yet.   H.

THE DEMON

Opera in a prologue, three acts and an epilogue, text by Pavel Viskovatov after the poem by Lermontov. Première Mariinsky Theatre, St Petersburg, 13/25 January 1875, with Ivan Melnikov as the Demon, Wilhelmina Raab as Tamara, conductor Eduard Nápravník (100 performances in St Petersburg by 1884). Performed at Covent Garden, 1881, with Lassalle, Albani (in Italian); Wexford, 1994, with Anatoly Lochak, Marina Mescheriakova, conductor Alexander Anissomov.

The Demon...Baritone
The Angel...Mezzo-Soprano
Tamara, *daughter of Gudal* ....Soprano
Gudal, *a Georgian prince* ....Bass
Prince Sinodal, *Tamara's fiancé* ....Tenor
An Old Servant ....Bass
Tamara's Nanny ....Mezzo-Soprano
A Messenger ....Tenor

Servants, Guards, Monks, Mourners

Running Time: 3 hours

Prologue. Near Prince Gudal's castle in the Caucasus. To the spirits of hell, earth and heaven, the Demon expresses his disillusionment (Monologue: 'Accursed world'). An Angel reminds him that love can restore him to heaven. He rejects the notion.

Act I. By the river Aragva, Tamara and her Nanny, dreaming happily of her forthcoming wedding, first hear and then see the Demon. In a wild place Prince Sinodal is menaced by the Demon, then set on by Tartars and killed.

Act II. Guests gather for the wedding and there is dancing. Suddenly, the mood changes, and the body of the dead Prince is brought in. Tamara weeps but the Demon's voice with great solemnity forbids her to mourn (Romance: 'Do not weep, child'), then equally majestically tells her he will come for her when night falls (Romance: 'On the ocean of the air'). She seems in a daze and her father reluctantly agrees when she begs to be allowed to retire to a convent.

Act III. The Convent. The Demon gazes at Tamara's window and declares Tamara is already his. An Angel bars the way.

Tamara's cell. Tamara's romance begins the second scene, which is cast in the form of an extensive seduction duet. She is troubled by dreams of the stranger. She and the Demon gaze at one another and he sings gravely 'I am he whom you heard'. She orders him to be silent but he pours out his woes and confesses she is all he sought before he was cast out of heaven. She feels compassion, and asks him to forswear evil, then at first light begs him to leave her. She struggles and eventually admits her love for the Demon and seals it with a kiss. She dies.

Epilogue. The Angel appears to save Tamara's soul, and the Demon curses heaven and earth. Apotheosis: voices of angels bearing Tamara to heaven can be heard, and the Demon is denied redemption through love of Tamara.

This is a fine, romantic score, replete with grand choral movements and a number of good solo parts. The Prince, though confined to a single act, is far from negligible, Tamara has attractive music to sing, but the finest role is that of the eponymous baritone. He is powerfully declamatory and grandly lyrical by turns, and the monologues with which he dominates the action, static though they mostly are, make a splendid effect in the right hands. The role is essentially baritone but Fyodor Chaliapin made good use of its opportunities, as his gramophone recordings bear witness.   H.

S

CAMILLE SAINT-SAËNS
(born 9 October 1835, died 16 December 1921)

SAMSON ET DALILA
Samson and Delilah

Opera in three acts, text by Ferdinand Lemaire. Première at Weimar (at Liszt's instigation), 2 December 1877, with Müller, Ferenczy, Milde, conductor Lassen. First performed in France, Rouen, 1890, with Bossy; Paris, Opéra, 1892, with Deschamps-Jéhin, Vergnet, Lassalle, Fournets, conductor Colonne.

Dalila (Delilah), *a Philistine*.................Mezzo-Soprano
Samson, *a Hebrew*...Tenor
High Priest of Dagon ....Baritone
Abimelech, *Philistine satrap of Gaza*.....................Bass
An Old Hebrew ....Bass
A Philistine Messenger ....Tenor

Hebrews, Philistines

Place: Gaza
Time: B.C.
Running Time: 1 hour 55 minutes

Saint-Saëns was composer, scholar and pianist of erudition and sensibility, editor of Rameau, performer of Mozart, with a wealth of chamber and symphonic music to his credit. It is in some ways surprising that his most famous opera should be noted mainly for its sensuous melody, though Dalila's solos and the last-act Bacchanale are in their own way quite unsurpassed. *Samson* as a whole is a powerful work, full of contrast, and remains a sure-fire hit given a mezzo-soprano with a fine voice and physique to match, and a tenor as heroic an actor as he is in voice.

Samson et Dalila got off to a bad start. Saint-Saëns's friends did not like the music when he played it to them, Pauline Viardot's advocacy cut little ice, the biblical subject caused managerial heads to shake, Liszt's interest at one time seemed unlikely to survive the Franco-Prussian War of 1870, and the first French staging did not occur until thirteen years after the Weimar première. The opera's subsequent popularity suggests its early history is a more accurate comment on the period than on the work itself.

Act I. Gaza. The Hebrews are forced by the Philistines to work (fugue: 'Nous avons vu nos cités renversées'). Only Samson has faith in God's promise of liberty and addresses his compatriots in stirring terms: 'Arrêtez, o mes frères' and 'L'as-tu donc oublié?' His third outburst induces in the Hebrews a new spirit of defiance and attracts the attention of Abimelech, who comes in with guards and pours scorn on the God who so signally fails his people in their plight. Samson slays Abimelech and then, as Israel's champion, sets out to complete the work of liberation ('Israel! romps ta chaîne!').

Dagon's High Priest may rage ('Maudite à jamais soit la race') but he cannot rouse the Philistines to effective resistance, and the Hebrews are left masters of the centre of Gaza. They sing God's praises and a group of Philistine girls, Dalila at their head, appears to pay tribute to the victorious Samson: 'Je viens célébrer la victoire'. An old Hebrew solemnly warns Samson against the wiles of Dalila but he is besotted with his old love for her and his prayer for strength to resist is doomed to failure from the start. To a seductive tune, the girls dance, and Dalila, in spite of the reiterated warning of the old Hebrew, completes her ensnarement of Samson in the languorous aria 'Printemps qui commence'.

Act II. The Valley of Sorek. A rich orchestral introduction paints a dark picture as the seductress waits for her victim and in an aria invokes love to further her revenge: 'Amour, viens aider ma faiblesse'. Here we have a new mixture, steely determination added to the voluptuous quality already apparent in 'Printemps qui commence' – a potent combination indeed!

To her comes the High Priest. The Hebrews have overrun the town, he tells her, Philistine soldiers fleeing before Samson, who is rumoured to have renounced the love he once had for her. The Priest offers her money if she will deliver Samson to him, but she is confident he is still her slave and she will trap him for her own reasons of revenge. Their duet ends with a ferocious joint declaration of hate.

To an orchestral background which foreshadows the accompaniment to her forthcoming aria, Dalila wonders if Samson's love will bring him to her. When he arrives, it is plain that the struggle between infatuation and duty has ended in victory for the former; a love scene develops, culminating in Dalila's 'Mon coeur s'ouvre à ta voix' (Softly awakes my heart), than which opera contains few more seductive melodies. Samson joins in the second verse, then, after protesting his love, somehow summons up reserves of resistance and refuses to tell her the secret of his strength. She rushes into her house, and after a moment of indecision Samson goes after her. Dalila's cry followed by Samson's howl of anguish summons the Philistines, who burst into the house.

Act III. A prison in Gaza. If Act II is Dalila's, Act III is unquestionably Samson's. The orchestra suggests the grinding of the mill, which the blinded giant must push on its punishing round, and his voice mingles with the plaints of captive Hebrews who blame him for their plight as he gives magnificent expression to his despair and repentance ('Vois ma misère, hélas').

Philistines drag him to the celebration of their triumph in the Temple of Dagon (to which the scene changes); the singing is reminiscent of the first act's elegant greeting to spring. The Bacchanale which follows initially contains pastiche eastern music of a distinctly elegant cast, then a wonderfully sumptuous passage before it degenerates into orgy. Samson, led in by a child, is mocked for his love of Dalila by all and sundry, including the false temptress herself, who does not scruple to reveal that hatred, not love, prompted her to seduce him. Samson's rage strikes fear into nobody and as libations are poured the High Priest with Dalila leads a spirited chorus of praise for Dagon ('Gloire à Dagon'). Samson prays for strength, then quietly asks the child to lead him between the two pillars which support the Temple. While the intoxification of the feast seizes everybody, he clasps the pillars, then, with a terrible crash, pulls them down and buries the Philistines and himself in one last gesture of defiance.   H.

AULIS SALLINEN

(born 9 April 1935)

Aulis Sallinen studied in Helsinki under Aare Merikanto and Joonas Kokkonen. He has written music in all forms, including three operas and a ballet. To Western ears Sallinen's music is in line from Sibelius and, in his operas, from Mussorgsky, and is plainly influenced by Russian neighbours, Prokofiev and Shostakovich. Echoes of Janáček, Britten and Tippett may suggest themselves but the effect on his style of successful Finnish operatic composers such as Aare Merikanto with his *Juha* and Leevi Madetoja with *Pohjalaisia* may be less immediately apparent. The point is that a Finnish operatic style exists, however little it has travelled, and that Sallinen belongs to it and is not, with his teacher Kokkonen (whose opera *The Last Temptations* appeared about the same time as *Ratsumies*), its begetter.   H.

THE HORSEMAN

Ratsumies

Opera in three acts, libretto by Paavo Haavikko. Première at Olavlinna Castle, 17 July 1975, during Savonlinna Festival, with Matti Salminen as Antti, Taru Valjakka, Anita Välkki, conductor Ulf Söderblom. First performed in Germany, Kiel, 1980.

Antti, *the Horseman* ....Baritone

Anna, *his wife* ....Soprano

A Merchant of Novgorod.................................Tenor

The Merchant's Wife ....Mezzo-Soprano

A Judge ....Bass

The Woman ....Mezzo-Soprano

The Yeoman..Baritone

Matti Puikkanen, *an outlaw* ....Bass

Peasants, Guards, Soldiers

Place: Russia (Novgorod), Finland
Time: The Middle Ages
Running Time: 2 hours 10 minutes

*T*he Horseman is an original libretto by Finland's leading contemporary poet, who places the story in Russia and Finland at the time of the union with Sweden. Its theme is partly patriotic and historical – Finland is a small, lonely country, caught between the hammer of Russia and the anvil of Sweden; partly human, about two people caught inside a situation; partly allegorical, about an involuntary spreader of division and dissent, authority and the individual, choice and its effect. The libretto seems highly poetic, even in translation, but the effect of the opera and its music is direct and powerful.

Prologue (spoken). 'A man's life fits into the area of his skin ... written in a small hand, a man's skin suffices for the story of his life ... Well now, if you want to hear a tale that tells of a man and a woman, of war, horses, women, luck, death, then listen.'

Act I. An off-stage chorus has already started to sing before the prologue finishes, and it continues into the first act (Easter in Novgorod). The house of a Merchant, where Anna and her husband Antti, the horseman, are bonded servants. The Merchant cannot rest and decides he wants to sleep with Anna. Is it true, she asks him, that a bear comes to the house at Easter time? Yes, to find itself a maiden – but you are hardly a maiden, he answers. What will you give me, asks Anna. I am a Merchant, I have already bought you once and never pay twice for anything, he answers. But in a short, ejaculatory aria, he articulates his sad Merchant's creed. To a surge of emotion in the orchestra, the Merchant says he can hear his Wife stirring, and he is sure she has a man there.

The chorus still chants as the Merchant's Wife circles round the Horseman, who is intent only on finding Anna. He must dress up as the bear who visits each household, seeking a maiden for itself and foretelling the future. She cajoles him (*adagio con rito*), and he puts on the bear skin in time to confront Anna and the Merchant, the latter pretending not to know who is inside the bear skin. What is the sweetest thing in the world, the bear asks; for a man, it is a woman's lap. He prophesies: the Merchant will always sleep with his present wife, will never lose in a business deal.

Anna takes her husband to task: in Novgorod, bears that talk out of turn are hanged. The Merchant's Wife demands that her husband kill these knowing slaves, but he instead commands the bear to tie her hands. He wants to know from the way the Horseman looks at her whether he has slept with her or not. The Horseman ties her hands, demands that the Merchant test the bond to see if it is well tied, then traps him too. Only fire will part these bonds, says the Horseman, and the Merchant, resigned to death, foretells that Antti will become a great king, and at his coronation will be lit two hundred candles, and a forest will move and walk before him.

Anna and Antti make their escape from the burning house, the Horseman delirious at his deed, Anna trying to recall him to reality and convince him that the others have died. Do you want the bear, he asks. If I don't want it, I don't want you. And you I want.

Act II. The law court at Olavlinna is introduced in forthright, energetic music. A Woman is accused of having killed her bastard child. She denies the charge but the Judge says her appearance is against her and, when he asks whether he shall have women milk her breasts before the court, she admits that she is guilty but accuses a dark man who rode along the highway of being the father. Her description awakens memories in the Judge's mind – of a man from whom the thief (who will appear) says he bought a horse. Anna, Antti's wife, is in court and says quietly that, now she is a widow, she would wait for that dark unknown man.

It is the turn of the Yeoman, who insists that a horse he is accused of stealing, but on which he sent a man to the wars, is in fact rightly his. The Judge intervenes to say that he himself bought the horse, but the Yeoman says he would know it anywhere by the white blaze on its head. The Judge describes the man who sold him the horse, and names him as Antti.

Anna now steps forward and claims to be officially

recognised as a widow, a demand the Judge refuses for lack of supporting evidence. Let her come back in a year and a night, and, if her husband has not returned – from Finland, from Russia, or wherever – he will make her a widow. A year is too long a time, she says, for one who sleeps alone; it is a cruel sentence. In an aria (*misterioso*) 'He comes in sleep', she graphically describes her loneliness, and the Judge appeals for evidence from the body of the court. The peasants speak up for her, saying among other things that she is in a cruel situation where anyone could claim to be her returning husband, whom she will know only if she sleeps with him. 'A night and a year' is the period which must elapse before he pronounces her a widow, says the Judge, threatening to add a further day every time from now on she protests the judgement.

Now the Horseman appears disguised as an old man and apparently to corroborate her evidence by saying he has on his travels met her husband and he knows he is now dead. But the peasants are saying he has a way with horses and even now tried to get away with one from the courtyard. First the Woman, in a beautiful solo utterance, then the Yeoman, then the Judge recognise the man's voice as respectively the seducer, the man to whom he lent his horse for the wars, and the man from whom he bought the horse he now claims is his. Anna knows him as her husband who disappeared after they had fled together after the crime in Novgorod. The Judge indicates that Anna, the Horseman, the Yeoman and the Woman be taken to the cells.

To the dungeon comes the Judge himself, his desire for the Woman awakened by seeing her in court, and she lures him into setting her free, whereupon the other prisoners tie him up and flee the prison.

Act III (the Attack). Anna, the Horseman, the Woman and the Yeoman are living a savage existence in the hut of an outlaw, Matti Puikkanen, which is to be found somewhere in Sääminki Forest in Finland. The Yeoman is happy that they are in a land where men can call themselves free, but he recognises that here there are three men and two women, a combination potentially dangerous except when one man is on guard and those who sleep even in number. The Woman complains of their life and Anna says she is waiting for her husband, Antti

having become just another man. Matti has lost control of his wits, an example, the Yeoman says, of what happens if a man lives too long alone. Matti in a bold, bantering song says that before they came he and another man lived there with two sisters. He killed all three and they are still sitting there because he has never told them that they are not.

The Horseman comes in to raise the alarm but the Yeoman says it was he who roused the people round about to resist the claim that they fight for others in the war between Russia and Sweden.

There is a fine scene between Anna and the Horseman, as she tries to persuade him to leave with her. But he cannot bear the idea of being on the run again and feels himself part of the movement which is developing.

The Yeoman urges the peasants to accept his plan to capture the royal manor at Liistonsaari. The women will bake a great pie as a present for the sheriff, and they will take it to Liistonsaari with Matti inside. He will open the gates and they will capture the manor. The Horseman doubts the efficacy of the device, but the Yeoman plays on the greed of the peasants, telling them the manor is full of what they need to be rich, and popular feeling rises until Antti rather than the Yeoman is elected leader, and against his better judgement agrees to accept the challenge.

He reveals his plan. The men will be hidden under a net covered with branches, the women will approach the manor complaining of their treatment in the forest, a log will be thrust between the gates and the men will rush in. The new forest state they will found will stand between Russia and Sweden. They start to prepare their ruse, and the guards and the sheriff can be heard saying that it is only women approaching the gates, but are seen preparing in case an ambush is on hand. When the men rush forward, guns appear at the firing slits in the log defences and the attack is repulsed with great loss of life.

Antti is left alone dying, and sings of a great bird flapping towards its death. Anna and the women sing a lament (*tranquillo*) over his body and their dead hopes, and the sheriff is left with the last (spoken) lines: 'I have two hundred rat-chewed candles in the storehouse ... ', whereupon the guards light the candles on the defensive walls and on the ground round Antti's body.   H.

THE RED LINE

Punainen viiva

Opera in two acts, text by the composer, based on a novel of the same name by Ilmari Kianto. Première, Helsinki, 30 November 1978, with Taru Valjakka, Jorma Hynninen, conductor Okko Kamu. Toured extensively by Finnish National Opera with substantially this cast to London, 1979; Stockholm, 1980; Zürich, 1981; Moscow, Leningrad and Tallin, 1982; Metropolitan, New York, 1983. First performed in Germany, Osnabrück, 1985, Dortmund, 1985.

Topi, *a crofter*..Baritone

Riika, *his wife*...Soprano

Puntarpää, *an agitator*....................................Baritone

Simana Arhippaini, *a pedlar*................................Bass

A Young Priest...Baritone

The Vicar...Tenor

Neighbours
    Kisa ....Soprano
    Jussi ....Tenor
    Tina ....Actor

Raappana, *a cobbler*...Actor

Kunilla, *his wife*...Actress

Epra, *an idler*..Actor

Pirhonen, *a policeman*....................................Baritone

Place: Finland
Time: 1907
Running Time: 1 hour 45 minutes

The opera, short but an epic nonetheless, is set in Finland in 1907, the year of the first election there under universal suffrage. The title refers both to a mark on the ballot paper and the line of blood which the bear leaves on Topi's throat at the end – the bear which throughout has symbolised not only the forces of nature against Topi and his like but inevitably Finland's great, sometimes sleeping, sometimes hostile, Eastern neighbour.

Act I, scene i. The house of Topi, a crofter. A bear has taken a sheep (we hear the reaction of the dogs to it on horn and off-stage chorus in a six-note motif) and Topi swears revenge, to the indignation of his wife Riika, who mocks him that he cannot even catch the smaller game they need to supplement what they grow. Their existence is miserable and Riika laments the present and thinks of the past, when she herself worked for farmers who not only had money but manners to go with it. Topi berates her for eternally harping on the same subject and for making her previous life out a paradise. When he

was a kid, he worked in a lumber camp – hard, back-breaking work – and not until he was sixteen did he ever taste bread made from other than pine-bark. So much for the paradise of the past!

Touchingly, Topi tries to comfort her, but she tells him to fetch flour for their porridge and he comes back horrified that there is none left.

Scene ii. Topi collapses but gets little comfort when he dreams he asks the priest for poor-aid, but that worthy is unhelpful and scolds him for coming so seldom to church; through prayer comes help. The Church warms people's souls, says the Vicar, demanding to know what Topi has on his sledge. It is a coffin with the bodies of his three children inside, dead because the poor-aid did not arrive in time. He left it too late, says the Vicar, offering a cut-rate for the burial since there is but a single coffin.

Topi wakes up under the spell of his nightmare, then tells Riika he will go into the village and sell some birds he has caught, and buy grain. Riika watches him go, then in a monologue, gives way to sadness that she was cross with him. She knows he does his best to keep his family going, but worries about his babbling in his sleep, and particularly that he seems obsessed with the Vicar. Is he ill? What would happen to them if he died?

Scene iii. Simana Arhippaini, the pedlar, comes jauntily in with his followers, on his way to Karelia from a trading journey. In a folk-style melody he asks for shelter for the night; in return he will entertain the children. They ask him questions – do they smoke in Heaven, does God have a beard? Arhippaini can't tell them about God but the Emperor has got a beard. To stem the children's flow, Arhippaini starts in his turn to pose riddles, singing a strophic, folk-derived ballad which rattles along. 'What is swifter than a bird? What is blacker than a raven? What are whiter than swans? What cries louder than cranes? A thought is fleeter than a bird; a sin is blacker than a raven; angels are whiter than swans; thunder cries louder than cranes.'

Riika envies someone who can sing so cheerfully. She and her family have little to sing about – it will soon be Christmas, and they have nothing.

Topi returns home, bringing with him some coffee but somehow also changed in himself. He tells Riika he has been to a meeting where he has heard that there will be a new order. It wasn't a prayer meeting but there were speeches, and it all took place, not at the church, but at the nearby house of Kunilla, the cobbler's wife. She read a paper to them – 'the poor of the country have always been downtrodden, but there will soon be an end to this diabolical system' and so on. In March will be the election, and the poor of the country will draw a red line – a red line from the people's own blood, wonders Riika. Could that be sinful? But Topi is fired with the new message, particularly the bit which says every crofter and his wife will come to draw this red line which will set the upper classes by the ears.

Scene iv. We meet Puntarpää, the professional agitator, who has come with skilful insinuations to stir the poor and the downtrodden into action. His routine is well rehearsed. The people *demand* dignity; if it is not given them voluntarily, they will take it by force. The priests lie when they say the poor must be humble. A young priest interrupts to say that it is good someone is taking up the cause of the poor but wrong to let fanaticism destroy reason. If we are all spurred into anger and hatred, we shall be in worse case than before. The bystanders shout in protest but the priest demands to know which is better, hatred or love, revenge or forgiveness?

In a fury, the Agitator turns and denounces the young priest as a class enemy. There are three words to revolutionise the world: equality, liberty and fraternity. Equality means there will be no more rich and poor; liberty means you can speak as he is speaking now without fear of reprisal; fraternity that all will unite against such as priests and warmongers. It is a scene of real dramatic impact as he whips the crowd to a frenzy of agreement, then ends the meeting with a call to vote for the right candidates and so enable the Party to help them all.

Act II, scene v. Discussion is of the forthcoming election, and Riika, Topi and their neighbours read the tracts aloud. It is not nature which makes the poor miserable, reads Riika, but the heartless through their exploitation. Kisa in contrast predicts disaster, as she has seen terrifying omens – sun spots, and black-faced rats sweeping out of the forest like a fire, or like the new political poison, which seeks to destroy God's eternal order.

Argument is general but ill-informed, but their yearning after something they can't define is evident. How should a man draw this red line on the paper?

With your thumb, explains a neighbour – but you can't draw on paper with your thumb, retorts Topi. Press hard, until blood spurts, suggests the neighbour. Nonsense, says Riika; the Emperor will provide them with pencils. But how will we draw, asks Topi, with hands which have held axes and shovels, never pencils. As they speculate, the dogs start to howl (off-stage horn in the six-note theme), but they are too obsessed (in sextet) with the new problems to understand what the dogs can sense, that the big bear is turning in his winter sleep.

Scene vi. It is the time of the election, 15 March 1907, and there is a group of people round the young priest and another round the Agitator, arguing. Even the usually friendly village policeman puts on a show of formality as Riika and Topi come to the polling station to draw their red line on the paper.

Scene vii. The orchestra laments as Riika waits alone for Topi to return from the logging camp. In a monologue which expresses her despair, she prays that he will return soon, that someone, anyone, will come to relieve her misery. When someone appears, it is the low-spirited Kisa, the neighbour's wife, who has heard that the children are ill and wonders if they have been poisoned by the fearful red bird, the political plague, that has flown over the countryside. One has already died, and Riika and Kisa are singing a lament as Topi arrives. He is shattered to find his children are dead, and he goes off muttering to himself that if they are buried in one coffin, the Vicar may charge a reduced fee.

An orchestral threnody introduces the Epilogue. Kunilla is triumphant; the Party has won the election! All will henceforth be different, with land redistributed, the poor exempt from taxes, the rich and the clergy bereft of power. As the orchestra continues to lament, Kisa is unimpressed; can't Kunilla see that God has already punished this household for the wickedness of all? It's all the fault of the oppressors, snaps Kunilla; they have given no help.

Again the dogs, to the distinctive horn-choral theme, howl, and the family cow can be heard lowing in terror. Riika sees the bear, sees too Topi wrestling with it. 'Topi, are you alive? Topi!' But Topi, as the story ends, can no longer reply. He is lying quite still on a patch of snow, with blood seeping from his throat, across which runs a red line.   H.

THE KING GOES FORTH TO FRANCE
Kuningas Lahtee Ranskaan

'A chronicle for music theatre about the coming ice age' in a prologue and three acts, libretto by Paavo Haavikko based on his radio play. First performed at the Savonlinna Festival, 1984; Kiel, 1986. U.S. première, Santa Fe, 1986, conducted by Richard Buckley. U.K. première (in English), Royal Opera, Covent Garden, 1987, with Ian McDiarmid as Froissart, Kim Begley as the Guide, Mikael Melbye as the Prince, Stafford Dean as the Prime Minister, Eileen Hannan and Sarah Walker as the Carolines, Valerie Masterson and Jane Turner as the Annes and Nuala Willis as the Queen, conducted by Okko Kamu.

Guide ....Tenor

The Prince, *later the King*..............................Baritone

The Prime Minister, *later his son,*
    the Young Prime Minister .... Bass

The Nice Caroline ....Soprano

The Caroline with the Thick Mane.....Mezzo-Soprano

The Anne who Steals...................................Soprano

The Anne who Strips.........................Mezzo-Soprano

The Queen ....Contralto

The Blind King of Bohemia ....Silent

English Archer ....Baritone

Froissart ....Spoken

French Prisoner...Spoken

Six Burghers of Calais, Subjects, Courtiers,
  Mercenaries

Running Time: 2 hours 10 minutes

Aulis Sallinen worked with his librettist Paavo Haavikko and the director Kalle Holmberg on a television series based on the Finnish epic, the *Kalevala*, called *The Iron Age*, out of which grew *The King Goes Forth to France*. Sallinen himself described it as 'a kind of fairy-tale for adults'.[1]

Prologue. The English court; a garden in May. The Guide and Chorus describe England's plight as it enters a new Ice Age. The Prime Minister tells the Prince that it is time he married and introduces the four candidates he has chosen, two Carolines and two Annes.

Act I, scene i. The Nice Caroline, the Caroline with the Thick Mane, the Anne Who Steals and the Anne Who Strips encounter one another and work out which one of them will marry the Prince.

Scene ii. The Prince decides to take control. He means to leave England and cross the Channel, accompanied by his people and the army, as well as by all four candidates and Parliament (a large cannon). He decrees that from now on the Prime Minister's office will be hereditary.

Scene iii. The four ladies prepare to leave England. The Caroline with the Thick Mane imagines she is going to marry the Prince. The Nice Caroline persuades the others not to disabuse her.

Scene iv. The English coast. The Guide announces that there is a bridge on the ice across the Channel, so strong it could carry an army. The ladies take a sad leave of Britain as it is submerged in ice. As they cross the Channel, the Prince, now the King, makes friends with the Prime Minister.

Act II, scene v. The French coast. The Caroline of the Thick Mane waits for the King to declare himself, assuming that she will be his wife. The other ladies sing sarcastic songs to her but later, when they hear that the King has married a German princess, they comfort her.

Scene vi. As they march through northern France the Prime Minister becomes aware that the King and his army are recreating the route taken by King Edward when he invaded France and initiated the Hundred Years War. He also criticises the King for funding the campaign by pawning not only his crown but his Queen as well. Allies of the French King arrive, the blind King of Bohemia and a mercenary army of crossbowmen from Genoa on their way to Crécy.

Scene vii. The Battle of Crécy. The King watches its confused progress from a windmill, while his Prime Minister is on the ground, making notes. Suddenly the French King orders the destruction of his own Genoese crossbowmen, because they are in his way. The Prime Minister fires Parliament and so defeats the French.

Scene viii. The King of Bohemia and the crossbowmen have been killed in the battle and now long to return to Paris. An English archer brings in a French prisoner to show to the King, in the hope of getting a ransom. He tells the four ladies to look after him. The Prime Minister thinks the army should march on Paris but the King insists they next attack Calais.

Act III, scene ix. An encampment, autumn.

---

[1] *Full Score*, summer 1995.

During the siege of Calais an English Archer asks to be discharged so he can spend the winter in Paris. The King orders his back to be flayed, so that the discharge can be written on his skin. When the Archer begs to be allowed to retract his demand, the King orders his ears to be cut off and threatens that his tongue will be cut out if he presses his retraction.

Scene x. The Caroline with the Thick Mane looks after the maimed Archer, but is disgusted by his flirtation. She sinks deeper into her own fantasies.

Scene xi. Morning. The King has dreamed of the Nice Caroline. In the night, the Archer has been shackled to the Caroline with the Thick Mane by order of the King. The King is enraged when the Anne Who Steals and the Anne Who Strips quarrel. The ladies try to calm him down. The Nice Caroline reflects on women's role: they give birth and continue life.

Scene xii. The Prime Minister has died: his son takes over his role and introduces his secretary Froissart, who will chronicle history as it happens. The Guide asks the King to have mercy on the starving inhabitants of Calais. The King promises to let them live if the town's most important citizens plead for mercy.

Scene xiii. The Ladies prepare to welcome the Queen back: enough money has been collected to ransom her for one day, the King's birthday.

The Queen arrives and the Guide presents Six Burghers of Calais who beg for mercy. They accuse the peasants of treachery and cruelty, producing the maimed Archer's head as evidence. At first the King sentences the Burghers to death. Then he relents and appoints them to his War Tribunal, explaining that he is engaged in this war to conquer Paris, intending to capture and kill the King of France and finally to march south and meet the new wine. The King tells the Nice Caroline that he loves her and wants to go with her towards spring.

When someone asks why he wants to imprison the King of France, the King explains that he broke the rules of war by attacking in the rain. He orders the War Tribunal to decree that the French King's back be flayed.

The King orders the army to march on Paris. They hear cranes flying north, which signifies the advent of summer. A storm breaks. As they set off, the King orders Froissart to omit his part in history, for the King can take no responsibility for making himself; he is a product of time.

The King Goes Forth to France's combination of satire, history, fantasy and pageant proved a powerful experience in the theatre. Max Loppert described it as 'exciting, disturbing and continuously surprising'. The libretto seems by turns poetic and bizarrely portentous: its obliqueness failed to convince all listeners that it held enough meaning, whereas Sallinen's music had no problem in encompassing extremes of both humour and cruelty and in communicating vividly.   P.

KULLERVO

Opera in two acts, libretto by the composer based on the epic poem *Kalevala* and Aleksis Kivi's play *Kullervo* (1864). Commissioned by Finnish National Opera to celebrate the seventy-fifth anniversary of Finnish independence. Because the new opera house in Helsinki was not ready, it was first performed in Los Angeles, 25 February 1992, with Juha Kotilainen as Unto, Jorma Hynninen as Kullervo, Jorma Silvasti as Kimmo, Vesa-Matti Loiri as the Blind Singer and Martti Wallén as Kalervo, conducted by Ulf Söderblom. Finnish première, Helsinki, 30 November 1993, with the same cast and conductor (but Tapani Valtasaari as Unto). First French performance (of any Finnish opera), Nantes, in Finnish, 1995, conducted by Koen Kessels.

Kullervo, *Kalervo's son*....................................Baritone

Kullervo's Mother..........................Dramatic Soprano

Kalervo, *also Kalervoinen*......................Bass-Baritone

Kimmo, *Kullervo's childhood friend*............Lyric Tenor

Ainikki, *Kullervo's sister*.........................High Soprano

The Smith's Young Wife ....Mezzo-Soprano

Hunter..Tenor

Unto, *also Untamo, Untamoinen,*
    Kalervo's brother...Baritone

Unto's Wife ....Contralto

Tiera..Bass

First Man ....Tenor

Second Man...Baritone

Blind Singer[1] ....Middle-Range Voice[2]

Running Time: 2 hours 25 minutes

---

[1] Sallinen has said that he was inspired to introduce this character as 'scenic relief', by a blind singer in the Provençal village where he spends half the year (*Ars Lyrica*, XII, I, 96).

[2] The composer's description from the score.

In turning to Finnish legend and the epic *Kalevala* for his fourth opera, Sallinen was at once returning to the roots of Finnish culture and making something of universal relevance: the grim brutality of inherited, internecine feuds based on the chain of revenge is familiar from Greek tragedy. That also provides a precedent for the equally grim humour that is so much a trademark of Sallinen's operas. There are suggestions that Kullervo's rearing is to blame for the boy turning out so badly, but such gestures in the direction of societal analysis carry nothing like the weight of the work's emotional impact.

Act I. In the Prologue the Chorus describe the feud between the brothers Kalervo and Unto. Gradually the dark palette of bass voices and timpani is lightened by sopranos and full orchestra. The story darkens, however, as the brothers meet in battle: Unto kills Kalervo's family and burns his house to ashes.

Scene i. Unto tells his wife that he dreamed of killing his brother and burning his house down. She blames him for not killing Kalervo's son Kullervo, who is now their slave. The chorus relates how Kullervo, now an orphan, was left to die on the ice.

Kullervo tells his childhood friend Kimmo that he longs for revenge. Kimmo saw how Unto's men trapped Kullervo's family in his house and set fire to it. In his anger and frustration, Kullervo tries to kill Kimmo and asks, how did he become so evil? Kimmo explains that while he was born a slave, Kullervo was forced into slavery. The Chorus ask God never to let a child suffer as he has.

Unto sells Kullervo to the Smith as a cattleherd. Kullervo refuses to say goodbye. The Chorus list the worthless goods the Smith gave in exchange.

Scene ii. The Smith's Young Wife is attracted to Kullervo. She gave him a loaf that she had baked in which she had put a stone to make him hard for her. Now it is evening and she waits for him to return from guarding the herd.

A Hunter passes by and reveals that Kullervo let wolves slaughter the cattle in revenge, because he broke his father's knife on the stone in the loaf. After a tense interlude punctuated by fortissimo timpani, Kullervo returns and quarrels with the Smith's Young Wife: she laughed at him for his inexperience when they went to bed together. She offers to ask the Smith to show mercy to him, but 'mercy' has poisoned his life. When she repeatedly calls him a slave (*orja*), he

kills her with the knife. The Chorus call on Ukko, the ruler of the gods, to punish Kullervo with death.

A mysterious entr'acte interleaves three stories, each with its own sound world: while Kalervo describes how he survived the fire and his wife mourns for their daughter Ainikki, who disappeared, Kimmo makes a toy horse for Kullervo: now he knows that Kullervo's parents survived he plans to reunite the family.

Scene iii. Kullervo arrives at his parents' house. They guess who he is. Kullervo confesses that he murdered a woman but his mother will not let her husband banish their son. Kimmo blames himself for arriving late.

Act II, scene iv. Kullervo's Dream. According to the composer's own synopsis, 'Kullervo's rage, his humiliatingly unsuccessful affair with the Smith's Young Wife, and the fact that he does not get on with his father – all this erupts in a dream.' In it, the Blind Singer sings 'The Song of the Sister's Ravishing', an oblique account of how Kullervo made his sister Ainikki pregnant, before either realised who the other was. She committed suicide.

Scene v follows an Interlude. Kalervo refuses to acknowledge his son, but Kullervo has his revenge: he admits that he slept with his sister before he knew who she was. Kullervo is expelled from his home. He decides to burn down Unto's house. In what is probably the opera's greatest single number, his Mother tells him she will always weep for him.

Scene vi. Kullervo has joined up with self-interested accomplices, Tiera and two other men. For a fee the Hunter agrees to guide them to Unto's house. Kimmo tells Kullervo that his parents and his sister have all died. While the Chorus sings a lament, Kimmo describes how grief killed Kullervo's mother, Kalervo committed suicide and his sister disappeared into the forest. Kullervo swears revenge. Over a pounding timpani bass, the Chorus narrates Kullervo's slaughter of Unto and his family. Kullervo then goes to find Kimmo, 'in whom he sees a glimmer of hope and light' (composer's synopsis).

Epilogue. Kimmo has gone mad: he raves that he is on his way to the land of the fortunate with a vital message. He does not recognise Kullervo but identifies him as a Christ-like figure, bearing the world's sins on his shoulders. The opera ends as Kullervo says goodbye to his friend and throws himself into the fire, unafraid of death: 'It cannot be worse than life. That is how the world treated me.'

Sallinen has said he was attracted to the nineteenth-century treatment of the epic *Kalevala* by its modernism: the composer explained how exactly he understood this by his comment that *Kullervo*'s own modernism was made concrete a few days after the première in Los Angeles, when the city's streets were filled with 'thousands of Kullervos in revolt'.[1]   P.

THE PALACE
Palatsi

Opera in a prologue and three acts, English libretto by Irene Dische and Hans Magnus Enzensberger based on Ryszard Kapuscinski's *The Emperor*, in the composer's Finnish translation. First performance at the Savonlinna Festival, 26 July 1995, with Jaana Mäntynen as Constance, Ritva-Liisa Korhonen as Kitty, Sauli Tiilikainen as Valmonte, Jorma Silvasti as Petruccio and Tom Krause as Ossip, conducted by Okko Kamu.

The King..Tenor
Constance, *his wife*..Soprano
Valmonte...Baritone
Petruccio ....Tenor
Ossip ....Bass-Baritone
Kitty, *his wife, lady-in-waiting
   to the Queen*......................................High Soprano
Physician..Tenor
Pillow Bearer ....Tenor
Keeper of the Purse ....Baritone
Executioner...Bass
Cuckoo ....Male or Female Voice[2]
First Petitioner ....Bass
Second Petitioner..Contralto
Third Petitioner...Baritone
Fourth and Fifth Petitioners...........................Tenors
A Servant...................................Middle-Range Voice
Defence Counsel ....Spoken

Courtiers

Running Time: 1 hour 55 minutes

The unique flavour of *The Palace* owes much to the libretto. The central characters are borrowed from Mozart's *Entführung*, but the theme also reflects the debate that ensued after the *Wende*, the fall of the Berlin Wall and the reunification of Germany. Before it fell, Enzensberger once wrote a poem for *Fidelio* beginning, 'Nein, die Bastille ist noch nicht gefallen' (No, the Bastille has not yet fallen). *The Palace* is in a sense a sequel to that vision, in the form of a witty parable on power and its abuse. The libretto's poetry ensures, however, that this is not a simple, didactic tale: it has room for different qualities and moods and inspired Sallinen to write a breathtakingly varied opera, covering much musical and emotional ground within a brief span, without a wasted note. The overture's grand scale – it lasts almost seven minutes – alerts us to the more serious implications of the story.

Prologue. For three days Ossip and Petruccio, the King's closest courtiers, have been waiting for him to emerge from his bedroom. They dare not enter, in case he is offended by this break in protocol. Courtiers are aware that no one seems to be in charge; they try to sing the Morning Chorale, but without success. Valmonte stops Ossip from entering the bedchamber and sends in the Physician in Ordinary, whose diagnosis is always positive, since displeasing the King incurs hanging. Valmonte takes charge: he tells the Pillow Bearer and the Keeper of the Purse what to do. He tells everyone to reach into their pockets. They do so and discover giant chocolate coins covered in gold paper. Valmonte is joined by his henchmen dressed like the K.G.B.

Act I. The Palace Hall, three days earlier: the rest of the opera traces the way the 'fascist' coup at the end of the prologue was prepared. Petruccio is rehearsing the chorus when Valmonte introduces himself: recently returned from abroad, he now intends to 'get his foot in at the palace', through Petruccio, who has access to Constance, the King's spokesperson. The Cuckoo announces the time, the 'Hour of the Most Venerable Body', and the Physician gives a favourable report on the King's stool. The King emerges and tosses coins to the crowd, who present petitions. Until the last scene we do not hear the King speak: Constance relays his answers. When the Cuckoo announces the Hour of the Assignments, Valmonte offers his services as a spy. He is appointed Keeper of the Imperial Door and Secretary of Future Affairs. At the Hour of Justice, a

---

[1] *Ars Lyrica*, XII, I, 96.

[2] The composer's own definition in the score.

man is condemned to death for sneezing. His Defence Counsel sneezes and is also condemned. Meanwhile Constance quizzes Valmonte on life outside.

Act II. Later the same afternoon a series of dialogues traces the course of corruption within the palace, though this takes very different forms. Ossip advises the King in his private gardens that Valmonte has got the palace wired, while Petruccio tells him that the Department of the Interior needs watching. In another part of the gardens Ossip's wife Kitty longs to sample such aspects of life outside as fashions and Harrods' catalogue. Sallinen's music alerts us to the more serious gulf between husband and wife. They are watched by the King and by Constance. She repeats the riddles he asks her in an inaudible whisper, and answers them. Ossip leads the King away, leaving the women together. Kitty no longer loves her husband; Constance feels the palace is a prison. They resolve to taste life outside.

Petruccio shows off the goods he has smuggled in from abroad: mobile telephone, fax machine, vodka, pornography etc. In a splendidly catchy, jazzy duet, he tempts Ossip who agrees to embrace 'Graft, corruption, filth and greed'. Valmonte gradually tempts Constance with visions of life outside, where there is no ritual, but she remains afraid of change. In the same scene, Kitty and Petrucchio dream of the more trivial benefits of Western consumerism: 'silicone' rhymes with 'gramophone'. While Sallinen deploys jazz melodies and a sax-

ophone for their duets, a richly eloquent, serious idiom is used for Valmonte's dialogues with Constance. The King overhears their conversation.

Act III. During a banquet in the Palace Hall (attended by beggars, who bash their plates to great aural effect), the King, who has disguised himself as one of the beggars, pleads with Constance to stay. Ossip does not recognise him and orders his arrest as a troublemaker. Constance knows she has failed her husband. Ossip declares a state of emergency. Constance and Kitty find themselves locked out of the Palace and 'on their way to escape'. The last scene shows the empty Palace Hall: the doors of the royal bedchamber open from within to reveal Valmonte, wearing the King's decorations and carrying his baton. The anarchy and despair of the banquet scene have died and yielded to electronic noise and then to a dry timpani march. When Valmonte raises his hand, the music stops 'in the middle of the bar'.

The Palace's sound worlds are so disparate that it almost seems to comprise several different operas: conversational jazz co-exists with comic patter, with the most serious, lyrical intensity (some wonderful writing for soprano voice) and, at the end, with electronic desolation. David Murray in the *Financial Times* commented that 'Nobody who appreciates Sondheim would find the least difficulty with Sallinen here.' P.

ARNOLD SCHOENBERG
(born 13 September 1874, died 13 July 1951)

ERWARTUNG
Expectation

Monodrama in one act (four scenes), libretto by Marie Pappenheim (composed 1909, published 1916). Première, Prague, 6 June 1924 (during I.S.C.M. Festival), with Marie Gutheil-Schoder, conductor Alexander Zemlinsky. First performed Wiesbaden, 1928; Berlin, 1930, with Moje Forbach, conductor Klemperer; Hamburg, 1955, with Helga Pilarczyk; Holland Festival, 1958, with Pilarczyk, conductor Hans Rosbaud; Sadler's Wells, 1960, by New Opera Company, with Heather Harper; Covent Garden, 1961, with Amy Shuard, conductor Georg Solti.

The Woman..Soprano
Running Time: 30 minutes

Schoenberg completed the enormously complex though short score in the unbelievably short space of seventeen days, in the period when to all intents and purposes he had abandoned tonality but had not yet evolved the twelve-note system.

Written for a single voice and full orchestra, the opera – called 'Monodrama' by its composer – is concerned with the half-demented ravings of a woman

Erwartung *(Netherlands Opera, 1995, director Pierre Audi, sets Jannis Kounellis, costumes Jorge Jara).*
Isolde Elchlepp as the Woman.

searching along a moonlit path through a forest for her lover (maybe in a nightmare). She sings in broken phrases of 'their' garden, of the night, the forest, the moon, is terrified by imagined pursuit and wild beasts and shadows, by a log she mistakes for a body. At the end of the third brief scene, she rushes out into the woods leaving the orchestra to give a vivid impression of a thudding, terror-ridden heart such as is found nowhere else in music.

In the fourth and last scene, which amounts to nearly half the work, the woman finds herself near a darkened house and is terrified by the deathly silence. She stumbles over her lover's body, shot dead by her rival, and the rest of the scene consists of hysterical mourning, references to the involvement of another woman, attempts to revive the dead man and cries for help. Eventually, she rises from the corpse and wanders off, muttering 'I was seeking ...' as the orchestral sound evaporates into the air with a cold shiver of ascending semi-quavers as if an icy finger were running down the spine.   H.

DIE GLÜCKLICHE HAND
The Fateful Hand

Drama with music, text by the composer. Première Vienna, 14 October 1924, with Alfred Jerger, conductor Fritz Stiedry (production by Josef Turnau). First performed Royal Festival Hall, London (in concert), 1962.

A Man ....Baritone
A Woman ....Silent
A Gentleman...Silent

Chorus: Three Each of Soprano, Alto, Tenor, Bass

Running Time: 20 minutes

The Expressionist opera was begun a year after *Erwartung*, but Schoenberg allowed other works, notably *Pierrot Lunaire*, to intervene and finished it only in 1912–13. The music – freely atonal – nonetheless remains closer to *Erwartung* than to Schoenberg's later work. The action is short, and involves only one singing character, although two others invade the stage from time to time. Schoenberg specifies highly detailed stage directions and, more particularly, constantly changing lighting effects, and it is not surpris-

ing that the period of composition coincided with one of the composer's intense periods of activity as a painter.

The action, dream-like, is of course symbolical, and differing scenarios have from time to time been imposed. The protagonist is lying on the ground with a monster – a hyena, with bat-like wings, says the libretto – on his back. Through the backcloth can be spied the faces of the chorus – the Man's inner voices – asking why the Man wastes his time looking for earthly rather than spiritual fulfilment (he is doomed somehow to fail, and this is his fate). When the Man stands, he is seen to be ragged and bleeding. He sings of his love for the Woman who enters, but her regard for him wanes as she offers him a goblet and she turns towards a well-dressed Gentleman, into whose arms she rushes. She asks the Man's forgiveness but then turns away once again.

Workmen are active in one of two grottoes, fruitlessly it would appear, until the Man constructs a jewel and throws it to them. A wind gets up amounting to a storm and the Man displays horror until the Woman emerges from the other grotto with a bit torn from her dress, which the Gentleman she had earlier preferred to the Man is seen holding. When the Man tries to keep her with him, she kicks a large rock on to him. The rock turns into the monster of the beginning, the chorus reappears and the work ends much as it had begun.   H.

VON HEUTE AUF MORGEN
From One Day to the Next

Opera in one act, text by 'Max Blonda'.[1] Première, Frankfurt, 1 February 1930, with Else Gentner-Fischer, Benno Ziegler, Elisabeth Friedrich, Anton Maria Töplitz, conductor Wilhelm Steinberg. First performed Naples, 1953, conductor Hermann Scherchen; Holland Festival, 1958, with Erika Schmidt, Magda Laszlo, Derrik Olsen, Herbert Schachtschneider, conductor Hans Rosbaud; Vienna, Theater an der Wien, 1965.

The Wife ....Soprano
The Husband ....Bass-Baritone
The Friend ....Soprano
The Tenor...Tenor
The Child...Spoken

Time: 'The Present'
Running Time: 55 minutes

---

[1] The composer's second wife, Gertrude Kolisch.

Von heute auf morgen *(Netherlands Opera, 1995, director Pierre Audi, sets Jannis Kounellis, costumes Jorge Jara).*
David Wilson-Johnson as the Man, Marilyn Schmiege as the Woman.

Written in 1928, twenty years after the completion of *Erwartung, Von heute auf morgen* is the only genuine comedy in the composer's output and his choice of subject was influenced, it is said, by his admiration for Hindemith's *Neues vom Tage*. The comedy has, however, serious overtones, portrayed along almost Aesopian lines, Schoenberg's moral being that 'the so-called modern, the merely modish, exists only "from one day to the next"'. The tale is set in the framework of a domestic scene which is quickly told.[1] A husband and wife return from a party and discuss their fellow guests. He has been particularly taken with a woman, a childhood friend of his wife's, whose elegance and sophistication are in contrast to his wife's more familiar domesticity, she with a famous tenor who has flattered her. Each ridicules the other's infatuation and they soon quarrel. The wife, nettled by her husband's words, transforms herself into a dazzling figure of fashion. He woos her passionately but she treats him with scorn and even rejects her little boy who has been woken by the argument.

The gasman arrives – much to her husband's astonishment as it is the middle of the night – and demands to be paid. The wife says she has spent all the money on dresses and insists they move to a hotel. She starts to pack. The telephone rings. It is the tenor who, to the husband's disgust, resumes his flattery. He has had a bet with their mutual friend from the party, he maintaining that the light they can see through the window must be from the wife's shining eyes, she that it is an ordinary electric light; if she wins, she must persuade the wife and her husband to accompany them to a nearby bar and if he does, he must get the husband – with his wife of course – to agree to do the same.

The whole thing strikes the wife as eminently reasonable (although her husband does not agree and curses away in the background), and she promises that they will meet in ten minutes. She changes into a cocktail dress, an action which provokes her husband to a jealous fury. Her scorn redoubles and he has no alternative but to admit with some reluctance that he really loved her as she was but never realised it. Will she not come back to him? She at once reverts to her real self and in a tender scene they pledge mutual fidelity. They are interrupted by the singer and the friend who, having been kept waiting in the bar, have come to fetch them. Each of the visitors tries to woo his or her respective prey but the couple, resisting all temptation and attempts to jeer at their old-fashioned ideas, send them packing and the work ends with the family at breakfast discussing their tempters. 'Mummy, what's up-to-date people?' asks the child.

The music, written in clear and easily perceptible forms, is at the same time elaborately textured and extremely expressive, although by the time it was written Schoenberg had evolved the twelve-note system and contained himself firmly within it. It is scored for a wide variety of instruments including, apart from the normal orchestral complement, two saxophones, mandolin, guitar, banjo, celesta, piano and flexatone, and divides itself naturally into short arias and ensembles, very 'vocal' in character, between which are conversational links in recitative. The characters and their moods and actions are sharply defined by the orchestra and, considering its complexity, the piece is amazingly accessible.   H.

MOSES UND ARON
Moses and Aaron

Opera in three acts, text by the composer. Première in concert, 12 March 1954, N.W.D.R. Hamburg, with Helmut Krebs, Hans Herbert Fiedler, conductor Hans Rosbaud. Stage première (first two acts), Zürich, 6 June 1957, supervised by the composer's widow, with Helmut Melchert, Fiedler, conductor Rosbaud. First performed Berlin, 1959, with Melchert, Greindl, conductor Scherchen (the Berlin production was later seen in Vienna in 1960, and in Paris and Milan in 1961); Covent Garden, 1965, with Richard Lewis, Forbes Robinson, conductor Solti, producer Peter Hall; Boston, 1966, with Richard Lewis, Donald Gramm, staged by Sarah Caldwell, conductor Osborne McConathy.

Moses	Bass Speaking Role
Aron (Aaron), *his brother*	Tenor
A Young Girl	Soprano
An Invalid Woman	Contralto
A Young Man	Tenor
A Naked Youth	Tenor
Another Man	Baritone
Ephraimite	Baritone
A Priest	Bass
Four Naked Virgins	Two Sopranos, Two Contraltos

The Voice from the Burning Bush:
    Sopranos, Trebles, Altos, Tenors, Baritones,
    Basses (3–6 to each part)

Six Solo Voices in the orchestra: Soprano, Mezzo-Soprano, Contralto, Tenor, Baritone, Bass

Beggars, Elderly Persons, Elders, Tribal Chieftains, Israelite People

Running Time: 1 hour 40 minutes

---

[1] Based on an episode from the life of the composer Franz Schreker.

Schoenberg started work on the music of his only full-length opera, his last, in 1931 and the second act was finished in Barcelona in 1932, but he seems to have had the work in mind from the mid-1920s. The circumstances of the third act remain something of an enigma. The text exists: in 1949 he wrote that he had already to a great extent conceived the music and could write it in 'only a few months', in 1950 that he had found 'neither time nor mood for the composing of the third act ... that depends upon my nervous eye affliction'; later the same year, 'it is not entirely impossible that I should finish the third act within a year'. But in the year in which he died: 'Agreed that the third act may simply be spoken, in case I cannot complete the composition.' In the event, most people who have heard the two acts of the opera in performance are agreed that it is in no sense a fragment, but a complete and stageworthy work as it stands. Scherchen's experiment in Berlin, where he performed the third act with music taken from Act I, met with little approval.

The text is the composer's own and represents his religious and philosophical thoughts. The drama lies in the conflict between Moses the thinker and Aaron the man of action; Aaron's every attempt to give practical expression to Moses' thoughts results in compromise and a debasing of ideals. To realise his conception, Schoenberg makes very considerable demands on his vocal forces. There are only two long solo parts, Moses and Aaron, but the smaller roles and solo ensembles are complicated and vitally important. The emphasis laid on the chorus is quite out of the ordinary, and there are various semi-chorus groups to be contrasted with the main body. They are asked to speak as well as sing, and often the two methods of expression are combined to remarkable effect. 'The speaking is part of the music and, in the score, written out in musical notation. Within the ensemble of voices its effect is similar to that of the percussion in the orchestra, especially in respect of rhythmic precision; at the same time the notes also indicate the intonation of the spoken phrases, so that spoken melodies are heard; and spoken chords are produced by the different voices of the chorus (though the pitch remains indefinite).'[1]

Act I. The Calling of Moses. There is no prelude, but soft, slow chords (including six solo voices in the orchestra pit) introduce Moses at prayer. The six solo voices in the orchestra and a spoken semi-chorus answer him from the Burning Bush. He is called to lead the Israelites out of Egyptian bondage, and to his protest that he is old and unable to convince the unbelieving people, the answer comes that Aaron his brother will be his mouthpiece. The singing and speaking choruses proclaim God's promise to the Israelites that they are His chosen people.

Moses meets Aaron in the Wasteland. *Grazioso* music of almost chamber music delicacy introduces the second scene (it is associated with the character of Aaron). Though Aaron immediately understands the part he must play in fulfilling the destiny of the Israelites, it is apparent that he and Moses approach their task from opposite points of view. 'To Moses, God is pure thought – unimaginable because any attempt at an image distorts the idea. "Thou shalt not make unto thyself any graven image ... " The disparity between an idea and its realisation, which Schoenberg symbolises in the figures of Moses and Aaron, penetrates into every field of human affairs. Things are never as they were expected. Any work of art is an inadequate image of the artist's original conception. Religious, political, social ideals become idols in reality. Aaron however is simpler-minded and his view of things dictated by emotions. He greets the mission of liberating his people with great enthusiasm, but does not understand what is implied in Moses' conception of God. He asks: "Invisible? unimaginable? ... can you love what you dare not imagine?" Moses sternly replies: "Dare not? Unimaginable? ... Purge your thinking, free it from the trivial, devote it to truth; no other reward will thank your sacrifice".[2] The duet, with its unique combination of singing tenor and speaking bass, is most impressive.

Moses and Aaron bring God's message to the people. Three young Israelites have seen Aaron in a state of religious exaltation, but others, particularly the priests, are less inclined to believe that a new God will deliver them from Pharaoh. A great chorus, partly singing, partly speaking, develops as Moses and Aaron are seen approaching from the distance. Together they proclaim God and his purpose. When the people

---

[1] Erwin Stein, writing in *Opera*, August 1957.

[2] *ibid.*

demand a God they can understand if they are to follow him, Moses feels that he has failed in the task for which he was chosen, but Aaron snatches his rod and rouses the people to a state of religious mania with his miracles – the turning of the rod into a serpent, the leprous hand, and the transforming of the Nile water into blood. The people express their fervour in a march, Aaron celebrates his moral victory in a big aria – the victory which has at the same time won over the people and betrayed Moses' ideals – and, to the tune of the march, the Israelites prepare to set out on their journey through the desert.

Act II. Between the acts, there is an interlude, sung and spoken in a whisper by the chorus in front of the curtain: 'Wo ist Moses?' – an extraordinary, hushed, mystical *scherzo* of a movement, of the greatest beauty.

Aaron and the Seventy Elders before the Mountain of Revelation. The Israelites are encamped below Mount Sinai and now even the Elders grumble at Moses' continued absence: 'Forty days now, yet we're still waiting.' Aaron tries to pacify them, but the sound of a mob can be heard approaching and in a moment the angry people burst on to the scene, shouting for Moses' blood. When they threaten to vent their rage on the priesthood as well as on Moses, Aaron regains command of the situation by promising to give the gods comprehensible form. He sends for gold and the people rejoice in chorus.

The Golden Calf and the Altar. *The Dance before the Golden Calf* is the climax of the opera, as vast a conception musically as it is complicated visually, with its rapid rises and falls in temperature and a gamut running from drunkenness and dancing through the fury of destruction and suicide to the erotic orgy with which it ends. As Aaron announces the casting of the image, processions of camels, asses, horses, porters and wagons come on to the scene and unload their riches, while animals of all sorts are brought in, decorated and finally sacrificed, all this to the accompaniment of the orchestra alone in music of the richest texture. The butchers dance to a vivid rhythm, but the music dies down in a lyrical episode as a sick woman is carried to the image and healed the moment she touches it. Beggars bring their last possessions, old men sacrifice themselves in front of

the calf, and the tension mounts again as, to the sound of trombones, the tribal leaders gallop in to worship it. A youth tries to break up the idolatry and recall the people to their former state of grace, but he is slaughtered almost casually by an Ephraimite. The rejoicing soon turns to ecstasy, ecstasy to a savage frenzy as four naked virgins (in a contrasting and delicately beautiful vocal quartet) offer themselves for sacrifice upon the altar. Destruction and suicide are followed by an orgy of rape until gradually the people pass into exhaustion and sleep. The music dies down, the fires are extinguished and the stage is in almost complete darkness when a man turns on his side, seems to see something in the distance, and cries: 'Moses is descending from the mountain.'

Moses appears, the tablets of the Laws in his hands, and commands: 'Begone, thou image of impotence.' The people are terrified as the Golden Calf disintegrates, and they leave Moses alone with Aaron.

Moses and Aaron. In answer to Moses' angry question, Aaron does not so much defend himself as explain that his actions were the logical outcome of Moses' idea; as Moses' mouthpiece he must interpret his ideas in terms which the people can understand. Moses in his fury smashes the tablets of stone, which he sees in their turn as no more than images. The theological argument is dramatic in character, as Moses unswervingly reiterates his faith, and Aaron in music of florid cast defends the integrity of the people. In the background, led by a pillar of fire, the children of Israel can be heard and seen as they resume their march to the promised land (the march from the end of Act I is heard again). Moses is left alone and in despair. 'O Wort, du Wort, das mir fehlt' (O word, thou word that I lack) is his moving last utterance.

Act III, which remains uncomposed, consists for the most part of a dialogue between Moses and Aaron, the latter now a prisoner and in chains. In the presence of the Seventy Elders, Moses restates his conviction of the ideal nature of the Godhead, and of the misrepresentation of His word as Aaron voiced it. Aaron attempts unsuccessfully to defend his actions, and at the end, when he is given his freedom, he falls down dead.　　　　H.

FRANZ SCHREKER
(born 23 March 1878, died 21 March 1934)

DER FERNE KLANG
The Phantom Sound

Opera in three acts, libretto by the composer. Première Frankfurt, 18 August 1912, with Lisbeth Sellimn, Karl Gentner, conductor Ludwig Rottenberg. Much performed all over Germany, and revived as far apart as Venice (1984) and Leeds (1992).

Greta	Soprano
Fritz, *a playwright*	Tenor
Old Man Graumann, *Greta's father*	Bass
Frau Graumann	Mezzo-Soprano
The Innkeeper	Bass
An Old Woman	Mezzo-Soprano
An Actor	Baritone
Doctor Vigelius	Baritone
Milli	Mezzo-Soprano
Mizzi	Soprano
Mary	Soprano
A Spanish Girl	Mezzo-Soprano
Two Performers	Tenor, Bass
A No-Hoper	Tenor
The Count	Baritone
The Chevalier	Tenor
The Baron	Bass
A Policeman	Bass
Rudolf	Bass

Running Time: 2 hours 20 minutes

Schreker was an Austrian, the son of a successful court photographer and himself born in Monte Carlo. His father died when he was ten, and his musical education was in Vienna. His first opera, a one-acter, was written in 1901 and shortly afterwards he started on a full-scale operatic work, *Der ferne Klang*. He wrote the libretto with its autobiographical overtones himself and had within a short space of time completed the first two acts, which aroused nothing less than consternation. As a result, he put the work aside and finished it only in 1910. The impact of Richard Strauss's opera *Salome* in 1905 and his own success with a ballet in 1908

probably provided him with the impetus to go forward. In the event, the huge success of *Der ferne Klang* in 1912 started Schreker on a quite unusual career which with hardly a setback brought him one operatic success after another. By the later 1920s, his success had run its course and by the time, with the advent of the Nazis, he was forced to resign as Director of the Berlin Hochschule für Musik, his career was in decline.

From the start Schreker's orchestral palette was rich, multi-coloured, seductive, conceding nothing in its shot-silk tapestry to his contemporaries, Richard Strauss, Zemlinsky and Schoenberg. It is curious that he should have conducted the première of Schoenberg's *Gurrelieder* (1911), when the genesis of this work and *Der ferne Klang* had so much in common, each started early in the century, each interrupted for one reason or another, each orchestrated in 1910. The trouble with Schreker's initially successful operas is easier to recognise with hindsight than at the time. In his orchestral tapestry he had the new clothes but was ineffectively looking for an Emperor to hang them on.

Act I. Fritz tells Greta of his aspirations and of his search for the elusive sound of the opera's title. Her father, old Graumann, is gambling, and the game ends when he loses his daughter to the innkeeper, whom she forthrightly rejects. She opts to follow Fritz, but is overwhelmed by a wave of sensual longing and follows a mysterious old woman who promises to show her the way.

Act II. The scene is an establishment near Venice, of which Greta has become the star attraction. Her greatest admirer is the Count but she is thoroughly world-weary and promises herself as the prize in a song contest. The Count and the Chevalier compete, the latter apparently aiming in his description of a flower girl at Sorrento at a Lehár-style hit number. Greta has to choose between them until an unknown makes his appearance. It is Fritz, and his song of love lost and now rediscovered – the phantom sound – is chosen by Greta as the winner. But Fritz has been singing to the Greta he remembers and he denounces and rejects the woman he now sees is a whore.

Act III. In the café in front of a theatre, old acquaintances gossip of the prank played on old Graumann's daughter. Fritz's play is having its première that night, and at the end of two acts seems like a success. Greta is helped out of the theatre by a policeman. Doctor Vigelius recognises her and, when she understands not only that Fritz's last act has been a disaster but that he himself is mortally ill, the doctor takes her to him. Fritz is dying, his friend Rudolf encourages him to rewrite the last act, but the opera ends as he dies in Greta's arms.

Schreker's most successful opera was *Der Schatzgräber* which had 350 reported performances between 1920 and 1925, 385 before being forbidden by the Nazis in 1932. It is saturated in orchestral magic and contains a colossal love duet, but this occurs at the centre of an overwrought medieval tale which it is hard now to take seriously.   H.

FRANZ SCHUBERT
(born 31 January 1797, died 19 November 1828)

Received opinion on the subject of Schubert's operas is simple if, one might be tempted to think, not too well-informed: he wrote a vast number of songs of genius and almost as much instrumental and chamber music on just as high a level, but his dozen or so completed operas (several more unfinished) demonstrate little feeling for the stage. It could be spelled out a little differently. Though only one of the operas was performed in his lifetime, he seems to have developed something of a feeling for the genre during his study with Salieri – he heard works by Cherubini and Spontini for instance, studied the operas of Gluck, Mozart and Salieri himself, in 1814 saw *Fidelio*, and later *Freischütz*. From the time he was sixteen until just before he died he was either writing for the stage or contemplating doing so.

Internal evidence does not always support received opinion. In *Des Teufels Lustschloss*, for example, an ambitious piece written when he was sixteen, after an act of not much more than desultory dramatic interest (though full of musical invention), Schubert wrote two more in which he takes full advantage of the situations offered by the libretto of his *Zauberoper*. His hero and heroine endure trials of a paltry nature (which are later revealed as charades devised by her uncle to test if her husband is worthy of her), but the music they spark off is of sufficiently high voltage to suggest that, if their composer had early on had the luck to encounter a Schikaneder, operatic history might have been different.

As a matter of record, performances of his stage works during Schubert's lifetime consisted of a production of *Die Zwillingsbrüder*, a one-act farce in which his friend the singer Johann Michael Vogl played the twins (1820); eight performances in 1820 of *Die Zauberharfe*, a play with music; and a further two of the unsuccessful play *Rosamunde*, in which his incidental music was considered the redeeming feature. The Italian impresario Domenico Barbaia took over the management of Vienna's operatic theatres in 1821 and, though he was sufficiently intrigued to commission from Schubert what became *Fierrabras*, the failure of Weber's *Euryanthe* put paid to the chances of German romantic opera in Vienna for the time being.   H.

ALFONSO UND ESTRELLA

Opera in three acts, text by Franz von Schober. Composed 1821–22; the première was not until 24 June 1854 in Weimar in an abridged version supervised by Liszt. The conductor Johann Nepomuk Fuchs rearranged the plot and edited the music for Karlsruhe in 1881, and there were further performances in Vienna and Germany. Modern revivals have been at Reading in 1977, Graz in 1991 and Vienna in 1997.

Mauregato, *King of Leon* ....Baritone
Estrella, *his daughter* ....Soprano
Adolfo, *his general* ....Bass
Froila, *deposed King of Leon* ....Baritone

Alfonso, *his son*...Tenor
A Young Girl ....Soprano
A Youth...Tenor
Chief of the Royal Bodyguard...........................Tenor

Place: Leon, Spain
Time: Middle Ages
Running Time: 2 hours 45 minutes

Schubert in autumn 1821 took what must have been a conscious decision to write an opera in a style which suited him, and went with his friend Franz von Schober to Lower Austria to work on it. There was no commission, only the overture seems to have been performed publicly in his lifetime (before *Rosamunde* in 1823), and abortive attempts to mount the opera in Vienna, Dresden, Berlin and Graz came to nothing. Even Liszt's advocacy seems to have been half-hearted.

Act I. Mauregato has ousted Froila from the throne of Leon, but Froila, who now rules the neighbouring area, designates his son Alfonso as his prospective successor, presenting him with a chain as pledge for the future: Eurich's chain. Estrella, Mauregato's daughter, vigorously rejects Adolfo as aspirant to her hand in marriage and Mauregato proclaims that only the man who brings him Eurich's chain shall marry his daughter.

Act II. At Alfonso's request, Froila sings the ballad of a huntsman who falls to his death in pursuit of a beautiful girl. In the woods Alfonso encounters Estrella, is convinced the ballad has come true, declares his love and gives Estrella the chain his father gave him. Adolfo and his adherents plot to overthrow Mauregato. Mauregato laments the disappearance of Estrella until she reappears with a tale of the chain given her by a young man. Mauregato is warned of the plot against him and resolves to resist the rebels.

Act III. Adolfo wins, attempts to force himself on Estrella, then is himself taken prisoner by Alfonso. Froila arrives with his warriors, forgets old hatred when he realises Mauregato is Estrella's father and, with the triumph of 'good', even Adolfo is pardoned.

The opera lacks dramatic energy, still a year or so later shown less than consistently in *Fierrabras*, but comes to life vividly in the finales to Acts I and II; also in the highly effective battle scene of Act III, at first quite graphically described by anonymous observers, then building to a climax. This, unfortunately for the drama, is interrupted by set pieces. Earlier, the conspirators, conventionally conceived, generate an effective head of steam, and the spacious arias given to Froila in the first two acts, as well as the more energetic utterances of Adolfo and Mauregato, are successful enough, though not always dramatically helpful. The most attractive section of the opera is however the sequence of arias and duets in the second scene of Act II, when Alfonso and Estrella fall in love and Schubert deploys his lyrico-dramatic gift for all the world as if starting a song cycle of love requited and eventually triumphant.   H.

DER HÄUSLICHE KRIEG, oder DIE VERSCHWORENEN

Domestic Warfare, or The Conspirators

Opera in one act, text by J.F. Castelli (after Aristophanes' *Lysistrata*). Première (in concert), Vienna, 1861, conductor J. Herbeck; on stage, Frankfurt, 29 August 1861. Given on many German-speaking stages and abroad and by far the most often produced of Schubert's operas.

Count Heribert von Lüdenstein ....Bass
Ludmilla, *his wife*...Soprano
Astolf von Reisenberg, *a knight*..........................Tenor
Helene, *Astolf's wife* ....Soprano
Luitgarte, *wife of Garold von Nummen* ....Contralto
Camilla, *wife of Friedrich von Trausdorf*.........Contralto
Isella, *the Countess's maid*...............................Soprano
Udolin, *Count Heribert's page*..............................Tenor

Place: Vienna
Time: The Crusades
Running Time: 40 minutes

Schubert wrote *Die Verschworenen*, as the opera was called before the censors got their hands on it, in 1823, between his two grand romantic operas, *Alfonso und Estrella* and *Fierrabras*, but put it away as a hopeless case when he heard that Castelli's text had been successfully set in Berlin by a local composer. Alfred Einstein pours scorn on the bowdlerisation of Aristophanes' brilliant political comedy, but the fact is that the libretto is well made and produced from the composer a graceful if unexceptional score.

The Countess persuades the wives of the other knights to deny their beds to their husbands in protest against their long absence at the wars. Udolin, the Count's page, in disguise overhears the plot and betrays it to his master, with the result that the knights repay the coldness of their wives with indifference. Isella tells the Countess that her husband is planning to go off again to the wars, and their confrontation comes close to bringing capitulation on his side. Udolin comes up with a cock-and-bull story to the effect that in a hopeless situation the men swore that if they were rescued, they would re-enlist and would not allow any sign of affection for their wives. The Countess is unpersuaded and dresses herself in armour, but at sight of her husband is about to remove it when the other ladies appear and insist she maintain her position. The men confess they are defeated, and all ends happily. H.

FIERRABRAS

Opera in three acts, libretto by Josef Kupelwieser, after J.G.G. Büsching and F.H. von der Hagen's story in *Buch der Liebe* (1809) and F. de la Motte Fouqué's *Eginhard und Emma* (1811). Première in Karlsruhe, 9 February 1897 (music revised by Felix Mottl). First performed Philadelphia, 1980; Oxford, 1986; Vienna, 1988, with Karita Mattila, Studer, Protschka, Gambill, Hampson, conductor Abbado (recorded at the same time).

King Karl (Charlemagne).....................................Bass

Emma, *his daughter*...Soprano

Eginhard, *a young knight at Karl's court*.............Tenor

Frankish knights
    Roland ....Baritone
    Ogier ....Tenor
    Olivier ....Tenor
    Gui von Burdgund ....Tenor
    Richard von Normandie ....Bass
    Gérard von Mondidur ....Bass

Moors
    Boland, *Prince of the Moors* ....Baritone
    Fierrabras, *his son* ....Tenor
    Florinda, *Boland's daughter* ....Soprano
    Maragond, *her companion* ....Mezzo-Soprano
    Brutamonte, *Moorish army commander* ....Baritone

Frankish and Moorish Knights, Soldiers, Young Women

Place: King Karl's Castle, Frankish–Moorish Border, Boland's Castle
Time: Eighth/Ninth Centuries
Running Time: 2 hours 25 minutes

*F*ierrabras was commissioned for the Kärnthnertortheater in 1821, but the overwhelming success of Rossini's operas, the engagement of Italian singers and the departure of Germans and Austrians (including Schubert's friend, Vogl) combined with the failure of *Euryanthe* to remove *Fierrabras* from the theatre's schedule even though it had been advertised. Schubert was apparently paid no fee and the opera was unperformed until 1897, a sorry comment on operatic history and practice.

Fierrabras is German romantic opera written at a time when problems of censorship beset most serious work during Prince Metternich's reactionary administration. Kupelwieser, though (as the Kärntnertor's so-called secretary) experienced in theatre, was a novice as librettist, and the resulting book with its themes of chivalry and magnanimity, its melodrama and its spoken dialogue, is hardly the work of a stage expert. On the other hand, in spite of moments of naïveté, it is Schubert's grandest opera, packed with beautiful music, and it is nothing short of scandalous that Abbado's famous revival of 1988 is effectively the work's only important staging in 175 years of existence.

Act I. Scene i follows a large-scale overture. Emma, at home among the women (Spinning chorus), hears from Eginhard that her father has returned from war. They sing of their love.

Scene ii. The Franks are victorious and Roland begs the King to release the Moorish prisoners, among whom is Fierrabras. Roland admires his foe, but Fierrabras recognises Emma as the girl he once fell in love with in Italy. The King will offer the Moors peace if they accept Christianity. Fierrabras admits to Roland his love for Emma, and hears that Roland himself in Rome fell for Fierrabras's sister, Florinda. The scene ends in a rousing friendship duet.

Scene iii. Eginhard charmingly serenades Emma, who is confident he will return a hero. Fierrabras cannot repress his passion for Emma (aria). Eginhard is observed leaving Emma's room, Fierrabras covers for him and the King has him arrested as her seducer. Eginhard departs conscience-stricken with the knights, leaving Emma, Fierrabras and the King in their various ways more than a little perturbed (quartet).

Act II, scene i. The Frankish peace mission advances. Roland yearns to meet Florinda, Eginhard longs for death – or at least to repair the injustice to Fierrabras. They agree on a horn signal in case of danger. Eginhard is captured, but, in spite of the horn signal, his comrades cannot help him.

Scene ii. Florinda admits to Maragond that she longs to see Roland. Eginhard, led in by Brutamonte, confesses to Boland the wrong he has done Fierrabras, and in a quintet all mull over the situation.

Scene iii. The Frankish knights bringing messages of peace are amazed when Boland denounces his son as a renegade, and imprisons them. Florinda, seeing Roland, vainly begs for mercy and, in an aria of great vehemence, threatens to spread terror and death.

Scene iv. The imprisoned knights fear death but Florinda intervenes (duet with Roland). Moorish warriors besiege the tower but Florinda knows a cache of arms and in a highly dramatic melodrama followed by a trio the knights prepare to defend themselves. Florinda watches from the tower as their escape is frustrated and they return to captivity.

Act III, scene i. Emma confesses to her father her love for Eginhard as well as the noble sacrifice of Fierrabras, who is immediately released. Eginhard despairs (quartet); Fierrabras revives his and Emma's hopes (trio).

Scene ii. In the Moorish castle, Florinda laments the prospect before them (aria). A funeral march is heard, a scaffold prepared for Roland, but Florinda surrenders with the knights.

Scene iii. In spite of Florinda's pleas, Boland orders the execution of his prisoners, but the Frankish army successfully overcomes Moorish resistance. Fierrabras, who has fought with the Franks, rescues his father but then witnesses the uniting of Eginhard and Emma, Roland and Florinda, even – in Christian brotherhood – Charlemagne and his father. He himself remains alone.

It would be peculiar if the influence of *Fidelio* were not felt in *Fierrabras*, and indeed it is, notably when the solo trumpet heralds the arrival of the King at the start of the finale. Nonetheless, the music throughout is Schubertian, the melodramas highly dramatic, and such numbers as Act II's duet for Florinda and Maragond and the ensuing quintet would be outstanding in any context. If only Schubert had heard his opera, what riches might have ensued!   H.

ROBERT SCHUMANN
(born 8 June 1810, died 29 July 1856)

GENOVEVA

Opera in four acts, libretto by Robert Reinick and the composer, after plays by C.F. Hebbel and L. Tierck. Première, Leipzig, 25 June 1850. First performed Weimar, 1855, conducted by Liszt; Karlsruhe, 1867, Vienna, 1874; London, 1893 (in English). Revived Florence, 1951, with Maud Cunitz, Martha Mödl, Lorenz Fehenberger, Kurt Gester, conductor Cluytens.

Hidulphus, *Bishop of Trier* ....Bass

Siegfried, *a knight*..Baritone

Genoveva, *his wife* ....Soprano

Golo, *his friend* ....Tenor

Margaretha, *a sorceress* ....Mezzo-Soprano

Drago, *Siegfried's steward* ....Bass

Balthasar, *a servant*..Bass

Caspar...Bass

Servants, Soldiers

Place: Trier, Strasburg

Time: Medieval
Running Time: 2 hours 30 minutes

Schumann, with a single opera to his credit and his dislike of Italian opera, to say nothing of his celebrated denunciation of Meyerbeer's *Huguenots*, might be thought of as remote from the stage and its blandishments, but the truth seems otherwise. In 1842 he had written of his interest in the establishment of true German opera, before *Genoveva* had considered a number of subjects (*Faust* led to the formidable concert piece, *Szenen aus Goethes Faust*), and he even wrote to Wagner for his advice on *Genoveva's* libretto which his operatically untutored eye found less than adequate. The opera was no success under his baton in Leipzig and Liszt's advocacy in Weimar, months only before the première of *Lohengrin*, brought no more than a *succès d'estime*. Modern productions have elicited rather kinder reaction, but

Genoveva remains far from even the fringe of the repertory.

Act I. A grandiose overture, gloomy and stormy by turns, leads to an opening scene in church. Siegfried, Count Palatine, is to take command of Charles Martel's army against the Moors and Bishop Hidulphus and the congregation in sonorous accents wish him well. His friend Golo, a bastard, in an aria bemoans that he is to be left in charge of the castle where he will be responsible for Genoveva's safety. Siegfried and Genoveva, relatively newly married, bid each other a heartfelt farewell, little knowing that Golo has conceived a clandestine passion for Genoveva. When she briefly faints as her husband leaves, Golo steals a kiss, an action secretly observed by Golo's foster-mother, Margaretha, who has returned to the castle after years of absence. She hates Siegfried, who banished her on suspicion of witchcraft, and she now sees a chance of revenge in supporting Golo in his attempt on Genoveva's virtue. In spite of old animosities, the two form an alliance to break down Genoveva's resistance.

Act II. The loud roistering of Siegfried's retainers makes Genoveva nervous and when Golo comes late at night to bring her news of the Christian victory, she asks him to restore order. His reaction is to admit to the kiss he stole when she was unconscious and to proclaim his love. She furiously repulses him with a cry of 'erlöser Bastard!' (shameless bastard!), a taunt which brings an instant threat of revenge. He sets up Drago to hide in her room to observe her behaviour, so that, when Margaretha incites the servants to search the castle, Drago is found and, before he can explain his presence, killed. Genoveva is imprisoned on a charge of adultery.

Act III. In Strasburg, Siegfried is recovering from battle wounds, Margaretha in disguise by his side. Golo brings news of Genoveva's proven adultery, a message which throws Siegfried into despair and causes Golo deep misgivings as to the role he has played in bringing Siegfried to such a pitch of misery. Margaretha has offered help; let him look into a magic mirror she possesses and he will see the truth. The scene changes to Margaretha's room, where in the mirror by witchcraft she shows Genoveva with Drago. Siegfried cries out for her to be punished by death, and smashes the mirror. Drago's ghost emerges from it and orders Margaretha on pain of death to tell Siegfried the truth.

Act IV. Not far from Siegfried's castle, Genoveva, in spite of protestations of innocence, is about to be executed. Golo offers mercy if she will yield to his importunities but she remains firm and he cannot bring himself to strike. He disappears to wrestle with his conscience. Balthasar and Caspar, entrusted with Genoveva's execution, try to persuade her to confess her crime. The sword is poised to strike when Siegfried and his troops appear and the opera ends with a renewal of marriage vows and the blessing of the bishop.   H.

DMITRI DMITREVICH SHOSTAKOVICH
(born 25 September 1906, died 9 August 1975)

THE NOSE
Nos

Opera in three acts, libretto by the composer based on a short story by Nikolai Gogol. Première at the Mikhailovsky Theatre, Leningrad, 18 June 1930, conductor Samosud. First performed Florence, 1964, and la Scala, 1972, with Renato Capecchi, conductor Bruno Bartoletti; Santa Fé, 1965, with John Reardon; London, 1973, by New Opera Company at Sadler's Wells with Alan Opie, conductor Leon Lovett, producer Anthony Besch; revived, English National Opera at the Coliseum, 1979, conductor Maxim Shostakovich. Revived with great success 1974 by Moscow Chamber Music Theatre, conductor Rozhdestvensky, and toured in Russia and abroad.

Platon Kuzmich Kovalyov .... Baritone
Ivan Yakovlevich, *a barber* .... Bass-Baritone
A Police Inspector .... Very High Tenor
Ivan, *Kovalyov's valet* .... Tenor
The Nose .... Tenor
Pelagia Grigorievna Podtochina .... Mezzo-Soprano
Her Daughter .... Soprano
The Old Countess .... Contralto
Praskovya Ossipovna, *wife of Ivan Yakovlevich* .... Soprano
A Bread-Seller .... Soprano

A Clerk in a Newspaper Office...............Bass-Baritone

Iarizhkin, *a friend of Kovalyov's*..........................Tenor

Eight Footmen, Ten Policemen, Nine Gentlemen, Four Eunuchs, Passers-By, People at Coach Station, etc.

Place: St Petersburg
Time: The 1830s
Running Time: 1 hour 40 minutes

Gogol's short story was written in 1835 when he was twenty-six. Its mixture of high spirits, social satire and theatricality appealed to the young Shostakovich, who when he wrote it in 1927–28 had, at the age of twenty-one, two symphonies and a quantity of chamber music behind him and who professed to have found it impossible to find either a Soviet subject for an opera or a Soviet writer with whom to collaborate. When the work was first performed, a few saw in it the dawn of a new era in Soviet music, but most (not least the original performers, apparently) found it complex and baffling and one critic headed his denunciation 'an anarchist's hand-grenade'. Sixteen performances were clocked up in Leningrad before the opera fell foul of the new Soviet sin of 'formalism' and was buried until its triumphant revival of 1974, a year before the composer's death.

It is important to recognise that it was conceived and indeed performed in a climate of opinion in which Hindemith, Schoenberg, Stravinsky, Berg, Křenek, Milhaud and Schreker were staged; *Wozzeck* had just been produced in Leningrad; and Lenin's original People's Commissar of Public Education, Anatol Lunacharsky, had been able to pronounce: 'Communism should lead to *multi*formity not *con*formity. Artists should not be cut according to any single pattern.'[1]

The story concerns Platon Kuzmich Kovalyov, who is asleep as it begins. He has little seniority in the civil service as a mere college assessor with the courtesy title of Major, but his anxiety about his status amounts to obsession and he thinks and dreams of little else but his plans for advancement.

In his miniature overture, all brass fanfares and solo snatches of anything from xylophone to piccolo, Shostakovich seems to cock a snook at all academicism. During it, we see Kovalyov being shaved and telling Ivan Yakovlevich that his hands stink.

Act I, scene i. The home of Ivan Yakovlevich, barber. Praskovya Ossipovna, the barber's wife, wakes him up with rolls and coffee for breakfast. Inside his roll he finds a nose, and his wife, with the assiduity of a shrew, drives him from the house with orders to get rid of it.

Scene ii. A quay. Ivan Yakovlevich does his best to obey his wife's instructions and dispose of the nose, but passers-by and acquaintances constantly frustrate his endeavour. In the end with much subterfuge he succeeds in dropping it into the river, but the police inspector catches him in the act, questions him (at the top of his voice – literally – with an E flat in the first phrase!), and detains him for interrogation.

A famous and highly effective interlude for percussion (ten players) leads to scene iii: Kovalyov's house. As a trombone breaks wind for him, the owner wakes up and comes to realise that his nose has disappeared. No amount of looking in the shaving mirror will bring it back and when his servant Ivan has fetched him his clothes he rushes off – the intermezzo is a Galop – to report the disaster to the police.

Scene iv. Kazan Cathedral. On his way, Kovalyov stops at the cathedral where a service is in progress, and to his astonishment perceives his nose there, apparently at its devotions and sporting the outward trappings of a State Councillor. Kovalyov begs his nose, with blandishments appropriate to its status, to come back to him, but his cajoling has no effect and it will have nothing to do with someone so totally inferior in rank. He catches sight of a pretty girl and his momentary move towards her is enough to allow the nose to make its escape.

Act II, scene i. A cab is taking Kovalyov to the office of the Police Inspector but he is told by the assistant Chief of Police that the Inspector is out.

Scene ii. A newspaper office. A newspaper advertisement enquiring about the current whereabouts of his nose seems to Kovalyov the only course, and he attempts to jump the queue at the newspaper office in order to ask the clerk in charge to insert such an advertisement as soon as possible. Queue-jumping is not popular, and Kovalyov's eloquence is of little avail, the clerk claiming that an advertisement of this nature could be deemed to hide a potentially dangerous message in code, moreover one that might be

---

[1] From Edward Downes's introduction to *The Nose* in the programme of its 1979 English revival, an article to which I am indebted for much other information.

held damaging to the newspaper's public repute. Let Kovalyov consult a doctor or get the whole episode written up as a short story. The scene ends with the servants in eight-part *fugato* dictating eight different advertisements to the bewildered clerk.

Scene iii. Kovalyov's house. Ivan, Kovalyov's servant, is singing to himself when his master returns (the song is borrowed from Dostoevsky's *The Brothers Karamazov*), and a flexatone plays the postlude. Despair at the unlikelihood of recovering his nose overwhelms Kovalyov, and the future, whether professional or social, seems indeed bleak.

Act III, scene i. Outside a posting-inn. The Police Inspector is hot on the trail of the nose, which he thinks may be trying to escape from the city. His men, to their considerable chagrin, have orders to scrutinise the passengers due to leave in the stage coach, and they sing a kind of chorale to keep up their spirits. A pulchritudinous female bread-seller interests them far more than the elusive fugitive. Goodbyes are being said amid the general hubbub and the coach is about to leave when the nose rushes in and tries to stop it. The Inspector orders the nose's arrest and the prospect of a victim or scapegoat engages everyone's attention, not least that of an aristocratic old lady who is convinced that the nose has stolen her shawl. All seems won until at the last moment their victim eludes them in the sense that it returns to its initial and appropriate shape and size. The Police Inspector wraps it up and carries it off to Kovalyov's house.

Scene ii. Not without a sense of triumph, the Police Inspector comes to restore the nose to its proper owner. Kovalyov makes no bones about his pleasure and seems to think he must provide the rewards which are plainly demanded by the constantly out-stretched hand of the Inspector. But when he is alone, Kovalyov's rejoicing turns to despair when he finds he can't stick his nose on again and he is driven to send Ivan to fetch the doctor who lives not far away. The doctor arrives full of solicitude but with no effective remedy, so that he is obliged to depart, remembering however to collect his fee and to suggest that the nose might become a pickled curiosity for medical posterity. Iarizhkin, one of Kovalyov's friends, arrives opportunely to offer comfort, but his apprenticeship seems to be to Job, and it dawns on Kovalyov that he is the victim of a quite novel situation. Madame

Podtochina has for some time been keen for him to marry her daughter and is indeed furious that he has never proposed to her; it must be *her* witchcraft which has placed him in his present predicament! He writes a letter to demand that she remove the spell. Ivan takes it and Madame Podtochina and her daughter read it in a spirit of total amazement. They return the only possible answer – that they are in no way responsible for Kovalyov's disastrous predicament and he must forthwith exonerate them. Iarizhkin and Kovalyov come to understand that there is no escape down this avenue. The writing and reading of the letter, its answer and the reaction to the denial of witchcraft take place more or less simultaneously, which constitutes something of an anticipation of Zimmermann's theory of 'Kugelgestalt der Zeit' (see page 990).

In a scenic intermezzo, gossip about the whereabouts of the nose seems to pervade the city, and people collect together looking for it quite unaware that it has already been restored to Kovalyov. Information has got around that the nose is hiding in Junker's department store and a crowd gathers, with a speculator going so far as to sell seats to the public. For a moment they think they have found it, but a senior officer persuades them that what they have is only an old woollen sweater. The latest news is that the nose itself is taking a walk in the Summer Garden and the rush there threatens to become a riot.

Khosriv Mirza, a visiting foreign prince, is carried in attended by his eunuchs and in search of the rumoured nose. He admits that he can see nothing but his status demands that he make some pretence at identification. The crowd is overjoyed and its excitement reaches such a pitch that the police are obliged to break up a potentially subversive gathering.

Epilogue: scene iii. Kovalyov's house. Kovalyov wakes up in a frenzy to understand that his nose is back in its rightful place. Ivan Yakovlevich comes as usual to shave him and he submits to that worthy's ministrations, with his customary complaint that the barber's fingers smell.

Scene iv. The Nevsky Prospect. Kovalyov is now intent on rehabilitation and he must persuade the world and indeed himself that his nose is fully restored, and with it somehow his manhood. He is so delighted to see his acquaintances that he brings himself to be civil to Madame Podtochina and her daughter, even though he mutters to himself that he will have nothing further to do with them. The full extent of his recovery is signalled when he makes an assignation with a passing flower-girl who must come up to his apartment and so reassure him that he is now in full possession of his faculties. H.

KATERINA ISMAILOVA
Lady Macbeth of Mtsensk

Opera in four acts (nine scenes), libretto, after N. Leskov, by A. Preis and D. Shostakovich. Première Leningrad, 22 January 1934, conducted by Samosud. First performed Moscow, 1934, produced by Nemirovich-Danchenko; Cleveland (in Russian), 1935, conductor Rodzinski; London, Queen's Hall (in concert), 1936, with Slobodskaya, Hughes Macklin, Harold Williams, conductor Albert Coates. Revived in original version, Düsseldorf, 1959, with Erika Wien, Rudolf Francl, Randolph Symonette, conductor Erede. Revised by the composer and first performed in new version, Leningrad, January 1963; outside Russia, Covent Garden, 1963, with Marie Collier, Charles Craig, Otakar Kraus, conductor Edward Downes; San Francisco, 1964, with Marie Collier, Jon Vickers, Chester Ludgin, conductor Leopold Ludwig; English National Opera, 1987, with Barstow, conductor Elder, producer Pountney.

Boris Timofeyevich Ismailov, *a merchant* ....High Bass

Zinovy Borisovich Ismailov, *his son, a merchant* ....Tenor

Katerina Lvovna Ismailova, *wife of Zinovy Borisovich* .... Soprano

Sergei, *employed by the Ismailovs*.......................Tenor

A Drunk..Tenor

Aksinya ....Soprano

Mill-Hand ....Baritone

Steward..Bass

Two Workmen...Tenors

Coachman..Tenor

Porter...Bass

A Nihilist ....Tenor

Priest...Bass

Police-Sergeant ....Baritone

Policeman...Bass

Drunken Guest ....Tenor

Sergeant..Bass

Sentry ....Bass

Sonyetka, *a convict*.......................................Contralto

Old Convict ....Bass

Female Convict..Soprano

Workpeople, Foremen, Policemen, Guests, Convicts

Place: Kursk Gubernia, Russia
Time: Mid-Nineteenth Century
Running Time: 2 hours 30 minutes

Leskov's original story, a masterpiece in its way, is dated 1865. Shostakovich and his librettist decided to retain little of its ironical character, choosing instead, with an eye perhaps to political capital, to accentuate the dislikable qualities of the characters of the old regime to the point in some cases of caricature. The exception to this rule is Katerina, to whom the composer has given sympathetic characteristics and the lyrical music to go with them.

Act I, scene i. Katerina's room. She is lying on her bed, bored with the tedium of her life and the loveless marriage she contracted five years ago. Heralded by a bassoon tune, Boris Timofeyevich, her disagreeable old father-in-law, comes upstairs to rail at her and complain that she has not yet given his son an heir – no doubt she would like to take a lover, but his watchfulness will prevent any idea of that sort. As he goes out he tells Katerina to get ready the rat poison, and she mutters that nothing would please her better than to feed it to him. Boris is back in a moment with his son, Zinovy, and some servants. A dam has broken and must be mended and Zinovy himself prepares to set off to superintend the work. The servants set up a mock plea to persuade him not to leave them, but Zinovy pays little attention and introduces to his father Sergei, whom he has just engaged. Boris insists that Zinovy make his wife swear on oath to be faithful to him while he is away and, in spite of Zinovy's protests, crowns the performance by forcing her to kneel. They all go out and Aksinya comments on the saucy looks of Sergei who was dismissed from his last place for having an affair with the mistress.

Scene ii follows an orchestral interlude. The Ismailovs' yard. The servants, among them Sergei, have caught Aksinya and are pinching and prodding her as if she were a pig ready for market, and her complaints are loud and continuous. Katerina appears and rates them for their unkindness and for wasting time. Sergei insists on shaking her by the hand, and in a moment Katerina is wrestling with him. He throws her just as Boris Timofeyevich comes out of the house and sends them all about their business. He threatens to tell Zinovy about his wife's behaviour.

Scene iii. Another interlude takes us to Katerina's

Katerina Ismailova *(Lady Macbeth of Mtsensk; English National Opera, 1987, director David Pountney, designer Stefanos Lazaridis). Josephine Barstow in the title role, Jacque Trussel as Sergei.*

bedroom. As usual she is bored, but she is not alone for long before the voice of her father-in-law is heard outside scolding her for wasting the candle. When he has gone, she looks out of the window and sings a beautiful song contrasting her lonely state with the freedom of the birds she sees outside her window. On the pretext of wanting to borrow a book, Sergei appears at the door, reminds her how agreeable their wrestling was just now and, seizing her, offers to start it again. They embrace, make passionate love and are only momentarily disconcerted when the voice of Boris Timofeyevich can be heard outside the door asking if Katerina is safely in bed.

Act II, scene iv. The yard. To the accompaniment of highly suggestive music, Boris Timofeyevich is prowling up and down like a tom cat underneath Katerina's window, remembering the sexual prowess of his youth and making comparisons between such joys of the past and his son's present avoidance of them. What wouldn't he do if he were ten years younger – he seems about to show us when Sergei can be seen at the window kissing Katerina goodbye. During the rapturous farewell, Boris recognises Sergei and when he climbs down the drainpipe catches him by the collar. Boris shouts for help, has Sergei stripped

and tied to a post, and after summoning Katerina to the window to watch, proceeds to flog him. Katerina screams to be let out of her room, but no one moves, and in the end she slides down the drainpipe and throws herself at her father-in-law. The flogging over, Sergei is carried away and Boris Timofeyevich demands supper from his daughter-in-law.

With Sergei safely locked up in the store-room, Boris sends a message to his son to tell him there is trouble at home. But Katerina's revenge is not long delayed. She has poisoned the mushrooms and Boris begins to feel the pain gnawing at his vitals. He cries for a priest, but Katerina is implacable, takes the keys from his pockets and leaves him to die alone. Some workmen coming back from a drink cannot understand his babbling, but the priest arrives in time to hear him accuse his daughter-in-law of murder. She for her part mourns so eloquently that the priest is left to muse, in music of inanely popular style, on the mysteries of dying. As the curtain falls, an extra battery of brass, not so far heard, lets loose with shattering effect a series of discords which lead into the entr'acte, itself the opera's biggest single movement, a massive *passacaglia* which power-fully sums up the overheated drama.

Scene v. Katerina's bedroom. The lovers are

together. Katerina's passion is reflected in her music, but Sergei is already more disposed for sleep – an erotic predicament fully reflected in the music. Sergei worries, he tells Katerina, at the thought of Zinovy's return, which will inevitably mean the end of their love. If only he were her husband and not her lover! The train of thought is not hard to follow, and Sergei eggs her on until, satisfied, he falls asleep. Her thoughts about the future are interrupted by the appearance of the ghost of Boris Timofeyevich (bass chorus off-stage), at first unable to frighten her, but in the end producing shrieks of terror which wake up Sergei. Sergei cannot see the ghost and they fall asleep again, until Katerina thinks she hears someone stealthily approaching her door. They realise it is Zinovy Borisovich, and Sergei hides.

Zinovy calls to Katerina who eventually lets him in. How has she spent her time? Father's death was very sudden. Why is the bed made up for two – and why is there a man's belt on it? He knows all about her scandalous behaviour, he says, and picking up the belt he starts to beat her with it, until Sergei rushes out from his hiding place. Zinovy scrambles to the window, but Katerina pulls him back and starts to throttle him. Sergei helps her and soon Zinovy is dead. To the tune of a grotesque march, they carry the body down to the cellar, Katerina lighting the way with a candle. What starts as a jaunty, light-hearted tune finishes in something sinister and woebegone as they bury the body.

Act III, scene vi. Katerina and Sergei on their wedding day brood about the crime which lies hidden behind the cellar door. As they leave to go to the party, a drunk enters on the prowl for more liquor. In a brilliantly funny scene, he runs through a whole catalogue of reasons why it is essential for him to get supplies from the cellar, breaks down the door but emerges almost immediately holding his nose and complaining about the appalling stink. Further investigation convinces him that he has found the decomposing corpse of Zinovy Borisovich.

Scene vii, preceded by an entr'acte drawn from the music of the previous scene, takes place in the local police station, where the Sergeant and his men are sitting, frantically doing nothing. In a parody of an operetta chorus, they hymn their unceasing importance but lament their present unemployment. Things look up when a nihilist teacher is brought in and questioned, but even this cannot compensate for what really riles them – that they have not been invited to the Ismailov wedding feast. When the drunk bursts in with news that he has found a corpse in the Ismailovs' cellar, the Sergeant and his men behave as if they have been expecting some such information and hurry off to make their arrests.

A short and brisk entr'acte takes us to scene viii, where, in the Ismailovs' garden, the wedding feast is in progress. Suddenly Katerina notices that the padlock of the cellar is broken. She tells Sergei the game is up and they must leave immediately. He is just coming back from the house with some money, when the Sergeant and his men enter the garden. His tone is bantering, but Katerina quickly realises there is no point in pretence and holds out her wrists for the handcuffs. Sergei tries to escape but they catch him, beat him and secure him too. Completely happy, the police march their prisoners off to jail.

Act IV, scene ix. It is evening and a large band of convicts, all of them shackled, has halted temporarily near a bridge. Men and women are in separate groups. In contrast to the grotesque and even farcical happenings of the previous act, this last scene is entirely tragic and mostly lyrical. An old convict, Dostoevskian in his resignation and in his musical utterance taking after Mussorgsky, sings movingly of the long unforgiving road they must travel to Siberia. A subdued Katerina bribes a guard to let her go through to the men and she makes her way to Sergei. His reception of her caresses is thoroughly disagreeable – has she forgotten that it's entirely her fault he is here at all? She goes sadly back to the other women, lamenting (in a beautiful *arioso* with cor anglais obbligato) that, hard as were the sentence and the flogging, harder still is it to know from Sergei's every gesture that he hates her.

Meanwhile Sergei goes up to Sonyetka and in music of deliberate banality starts to flirt with her. She is a mercenary little baggage and insists that her favours must be paid for. Her stockings are torn; she will be Sergei's if he can get her another pair – from Katerina for instance. On the pretext that his legs hurt him, Sergei wheedles her only spare pair out of Katerina. Immediately he gives them to Sonyetka and carries her off triumphantly, leaving Katerina in an agony of jealousy. The women mock her and their noise brings the sentry running up. Katerina laments slowly and agonisingly before the Sergeant in charge wakes everyone up and gets the column ready to move off. The old convict rouses the stupefied Katerina, and she gets slowly to her feet, goes up to Sonyetka who is standing on the bridge, seizes her and jumps with her into the river. The Sergeant looks after them, decides there is nothing to be done as the current is too strong, and orders everybody to move off. With the old convict trying to brace up their morale, they start on their way.

Katerina Ismailova is undeniably a mixture of styles, parody jostling lyricism, and farce elbowing tragedy. But, if it is the creation of a young opera composer, it is also a work of flair and brilliance and unfailing vitality. Its early success was very considerable, but in January 1936 (a few days after Stalin and Molotov had publicly approved Dzerzhinsky's opera *And Quiet Flows the Don*, based on Sholokhov's novel) an article appeared in *Pravda* entitled 'Muddle instead of Music'. It denounced *Katerina Ismailova* as modernist and confused, its music 'leftist' and discordant. From then on, Shostakovich enjoyed an up-and-down career in Soviet Russia, mostly applauded for his earnest endeavour to live up to the ideals of Socialist Realism, occasionally disapproved for palpably falling short of them. The once popular *Lady*

Macbeth of Mtsensk (abroad, the opera usually carried the name of Leskov's story) became something of a legend, never performed in its native land and very seldom outside owing to the tight control kept on orchestral material.

After the war, there were only two Western productions of the opera in its original form, in Venice in 1947, and in Düsseldorf in 1959 – and no sooner was permission given for the second of these than it was withdrawn, but only after a contract between the publisher and the Düsseldorf theatre had been signed. Those of us who saw this production could have been excused for wondering wryly if it would turn out to be the last performance in our time of a contemporary masterpiece, but the composer's revision, nearly thirty years after the opera was written, removed the work from the realms of conjecture and allowed a new generation to make up its own mind. When it was finally heard, the revision turned out to consist of no more than some smoothing out of the extremities of the vocal line, of some changes in the words and stage directions, and of the composition of new interludes between scenes i and ii and scenes vii and viii. Ten years later still, the original version again became available.   H.

BEDŘICH SMETANA

(born 2 March 1824, died 12 May 1884)

Smetana's life and reputation are replete with contradictions. He is thought of inside as well as outside Czechoslovakia as the most Czech of composers, but had in middle age to work at the Czech language in order to write his operas. He was regarded with suspicion in Prague as an admirer of Wagner's, yet his music has little Wagnerian about it, and his models were French and Italian, the latter by default since he overtly criticised the Italian repertory. He came to be regarded as the epitome of Czech music (in Japan he would have been considered, at least after his time, a national treasure), yet his contemporary compatriots regarded him with suspicion and schemed to remove him from the conductorship of the so-called Provisional Theatre (the first opera house devoted to

Czech use), only for the onset of deafness in 1874 to accomplish their work for them. The rest of his life became an increasing martyrdom to disability, although his last three operas were written after its onset and show little diminution of powers.

Looking for Czech characteristics in Smetana's music has elicited the comment that it was his music which provided the recognised characteristics in the first place. In his operas, folk-song was occasionally imitated, never quoted, and their Czech quality derives particularly from dance rhythms – polka, waltz, furiant – which, like spices in Indian cooking, not only permeate dance scenes but also serve as a basis for highly sympathetic vocal writing. The operas are full of spacious arias taken at the highest level of inspiration; choruses, duets and ensembles contribute to the scheme of things. Look no further than the most popular, *The Bartered Bride*, for examples – Mařenka's last-act aria, her first-act duet with Jeník, the sextet. And so on, throughout.

With hindsight, you can see that Smetana provided exemplars for future Czech opera: historical and heroic works like *Dalibor* and *Libuše*, even *The Brandenburgers in Bohemia*; folk operas like *The Bartered Bride*, *The Two Widows*, *The Kiss*; operas of a peculiarly Smetanian character, somewhere between the two, *The Devil's Wall* and *The Secret*. It is a powerful list and its achievement amounts to something like a mission; taken with his extensive output of orchestral and chamber music, it adds up to a substantial oeuvre. H.

THE BRANDENBURGERS IN BOHEMIA
Braniboři v Čechách

Opera in three acts, text by Karel Sabina. Première Provisional Theatre, Prague, 5 January 1866, with Ferenczy, Polák, and Josef Lev[1] (Tausendmark), Smetana conducting.

Volfram Olbramovič, *Lord Mayor of Prague* ....Bass
Oldřich Rokycansky, *a knight* ....Baritone

Young citizens of Prague
　　Junoš...Tenor
　　Jan Tausendmark ....Baritone

Varneman, *a Brandenburg captain* ....Tenor
Jíra, *a runaway serf*...Tenor

Daughters of Volfram
　　Ludiše...Soprano
　　Vlčenka...Soprano
　　Děčana ....Contralto

Old Villager ....Bass
Town Crier ....Baritone

Knights, Soldiers, Villagers, Brandenburg Soldiers, Beggars, Judges

Place: In and Near Prague
Time: 1279
Running Time: 2 hours 20 minutes

Smetana's first opera was written for a competition, which, after the first night, he was judged to

have won. After the death of the medieval Czech king, Přemysl Otakar II, his young son Václav was held prisoner by his guardian Otto of Brandenburg, in an attempt to gain control over Bohemia. The opera's subject is the Czech reaction to occupation.

Act I. The Mayor of Prague discusses with Bohemian knights the state of Bohemia, occupied – brutally, relates Oldřich – by Brandenburgers. Junoš brings news of fresh atrocities, including the kidnapping of young King Václav. Volfram agrees the knights must resist. Ludiše, the eldest of Volfram's daughters, loves Junoš and, not knowing of developments, resents his precipitate departure, but offers up a prayer for peace. She is interrupted by Tausendmark, whose proffered love she rejects, not least since he is an open supporter of the Brandenburgers. Tausendmark tells the Brandenburgers they may plunder Volfram's possessions as they choose, leaving only the three daughters for him.

Back in Prague, the citizens loot the cellars of the rich, breezily egged on by Jíra, a runaway serf, whom, after dancing, they elect leader. Jíra responds to Ludiše's appeal for help but Brandenburgers take them prisoner and in the confusion which follows, Tausendmark accuses Jíra of abducting the girls. Volfram orders his arrest.

Act II. Villagers, led by an old man, expansively pray for God's mercy but are set on by Brandenburgers, whose captain holds prisoner Volfram's daughters. A Herald proclaims an official end to occupation but Captain Varneman (curiously, the opera's only official Brandenburger) insists his authority still stands, and sends the old man to Prague to demand ransom for his daughters from Mayor Volfram.

In Prague, Jíra, in spite of a vigorous defence, is sentenced to death and Tausendmark entrusted with freeing the Mayor's daughters. Junoš's pleas for Jíra are disregarded, as is his denunciation of Tausendmark. Volfram's daughters lament their fate. Junoš contrives to find them, and in urgent duet confirms to Ludiše his love for her. Meanwhile, Captain Varneman, in default of the ransom, threatens to keep the daughters for himself. Only the courage of the dauntless Ludiše sustains her sisters' morale.

Act III. The third act's muddled and unsatisfactory

---

[1] Josef Lev was an excellent lyric baritone with limited dramatic talent. He became a favourite of Smetana, who wrote an over-sympathetic aria for Tausendmark in Act III out of regard for Lev's talent, and is said to have given up casting villains as baritones because Lev's *legato* was so much better than his acting!

action is said to have militated from the start against the opera's success. Varneman hears from Tausendmark that the Praguers know he holds the sisters, and at first accepts Tausendmark's financial offer for them but, when he insists on safety for himself outside Bohemia, Varneman reneges on the bargain. In pursuit of his intent, Tausendmark persuades the old man (who really means to free them) to help him. He gets two out, but Tausendmark catches Ludiše and forces her into hiding. Junoš and his men question Varneman, then search successfully for Ludiše and Tausendmark. Volfram exonerates Jíra and offers him a place to live, and the opera, which has somehow contrived to combine aspects of a French rescue opera (like Cherubini's *Les Deux Journées*) with those of Czech patriotism, ends with vociferous rejoicing.   H.

THE BARTERED BRIDE

Prodaná Nevěsta

Opera in three acts, text by Karel Sabina. Première, Prague National Theatre, 30 May 1866; some alterations were made to the work in 1869 and the final version produced 1870. First performed Chicago, 1893 (in Czech); Drury Lane, London, 1895 (in German); Covent Garden, 1907 (in German), with Bosetti, Nast, Naval, Marx, conductor Schalk; Metropolitan, New York, 1909 (in German), with Destinn, Jörn, Reiss, Didur, conductor Mahler; Sadler's Wells, 1935 (in English), with Cross, Tudor Davies, Powell Lloyd, Matters, conductor Collingwood. Revivals include Covent Garden, 1939 (in German), with Hilde Konetzni, Tauber, Tessmer, Krenn, conductor Beecham; 1955 (in English), with Morison, Lanigan, Pears, Dalberg, conductor Kubelík; Metropolitan, 1926, with Müller (later Rethberg), Laubenthal, Meader, Bohnen, conductor Bodanzky; 1941, with Novotna, Kullman, Laufkoetter, Pinza, conductor Walter; Sadler's Wells (at the New Theatre), 1943, with Hill (later Sladen), Servent, Pears, Donlevy, conductor Collingwood.

Krušina,[1] *a peasant* ....Baritone
Ludmila, *his wife*................................Mezzo-Soprano
Mařenka,[2] *their daughter*...............................Soprano
Micha, *a landlord* ....Bass
Hata, *his wife* ....Mezzo-Soprano
Vašek, *their son*...Tenor
Jenik, *Micha's son by his first marriage* ....Tenor
Kecal,[3] *a marriage broker* ....Bass
Ringmaster *of a troupe of circus artists*...............Tenor
Esmeralda, *a dancer*...Soprano
An 'Indian'..Bass

Place: Bohemia
Running Time: 2 hours 10 minutes

The Bartered Bride is so much of a national institution in the Czech Republic, and has been so accepted by the outside world as typical of 'folk opera', that it is surprising to remember that Smetana was looked upon during his lifetime as insufficiently nationalist in feeling. *The Bartered Bride* won him immediate recognition as a musical patriot, but the public attitude to some of his other works so angered the composer that he claimed to have written this popular comedy without either conviction or much enthusiasm.

The overture, written before the rest of the opera so great was Smetana's enthusiasm for the subject he was to tackle, is immensely and justifiably popular as a concert piece. Its themes are later used in connection with Kecal and the marriage contract (in the finale to Act II, the Inn Scene), but whatever their associations, their dashing quavers, Mozartian in their gaiety and appropriately marked *vivacissimo*, give the opera an irresistible start.

Act I. Spring in a Bohemian village. The village inn is on one side of the stage. It is holiday time, and the villagers are rejoicing at the prospect of the dancing which will take place to celebrate it. Only Mařenka and Jenik seem left out of the general gaiety, gloomy because Mařenka has just learned that her parents plan a rich marriage for her, in spite of her heart having long since been given to the handsome but impecunious Jenik. Mařenka tells Jenik that her heart would break were he to desert her; her love is his, even though she knows so little of his antecedents and background. Their love duet leaves little doubt of their mutual affection; the lyrical main section is heard fairly frequently during the course of the opera as a love motif.

On come Mařenka's parents, who are being harangued by that typically Czech institution, the marriage broker. He has the gift of the gab, and when his listeners can get a word in, it is clear that they are prepared to accept his suggestion that Mařenka should marry the son of Tobias Micha, a

---

[1] š = approximately 'sh'.   [2] ř = approximately 'rj' (as in Dvořák).   [3] c = approximately 'ts'.

The Bartered Bride *(Welsh National Opera, 1982, director Rudolf Noelte, sets Jan Schlubach, costumes Elisabeth Urbancic). Helen Field as Marenka, Warren Ellsworth as Jenik.*

rich neighbour. Krušina knows Micha, but he cannot remember the names of his two sons. Kecal protests that there is only one; the other, by Micha's first marriage, disappeared from home years ago and is now presumed dead. In spite of Kecal's enthusiastic description of the prospective bridegroom, who was only prevented by natural modesty from meeting them now, Ludmila thinks the final decision should be left in Mařenka's hands.

The trio becomes a quartet when Mařenka herself appears on the scene. She has one small objection to the scheme, she says: she has become engaged to Jenik. Kecal refuses to take such objections seriously, Krušina is furious that his permission has not been asked, and even Ludmila thinks Mařenka might have handled the whole affair more tactfully. Mařenka knocks the contract out of Kecal's hand, and leaves her parents wishing Kecal had brought the bridegroom along with him; a sight of him might have caused her to change her mind.

The act ends with a spirited polka, danced and sung by the assembled villagers.

Act II. Inside the inn, the men are busy drinking; in a chorus, they sing the praises of beer. Kecal is there looking for Jenik, who seems sunk in reflection. Both, however, join in the chorus, Kecal vaunting money as the most desirable of possessions, Jenik preferring love. The villagers dance a brilliant and energetic Furiant, known, like the overture, in the concert hall.

All leave the inn, and the coast is clear for a first sight of Vašek, who comes shyly in, stammering out that he has been sent off by his mother to woo his prospective bride. He is an enchantingly silly figure, with his stutter and his transparent guilelessness. Mařenka realises this is the bridegroom who has been picked out for her. She is horrified, and tells him that she, like all the other village girls, is really sorry that so handsome a lad is contracted to Mařenka, a flighty girl who will lead him an awful dance once they are married. Vašek is frightened at what his mother may say, but Mařenka paints a much brighter prospect for him with another girl, prettier than Mařenka and already very much attracted to him from a distance. He eventually agrees to give up Mařenka, and tries to kiss the pretty girl in front of him; she evades him, but he follows her out.

Kecal has the prospect of a sizeable commission if he brings off the matter of Mařenka's betrothal to the son of Tobias Micha, and he does not intend to lose it. He is prepared to invest a proportion of it in buying off the tiresome suitor whom Mařenka appears to favour. He takes Jenik to the inn for a drink, and talks the matter over. Things do not seem to be getting very far, but Kecal is at pains to point out that there are as good fish in the sea as ever came out of it. He seems to have made some headway as a result of his monologue, and he attempts to clinch the matter by offering Jenik a match in which there would be some money for him. However, even the brilliant and lively tune of their duet, which Jenik repeats after him, is not enough to persuade the young man to give up his sweetheart, and Kecal is eventually reduced to offering him money. Jenik takes some persuading, but finally agrees to do so – but only in favour of the eldest son of Tobias Micha, the money to be paid to him and to be reclaimable under no circumstances whatsoever.

Kecal goes off well satisfied with the bargain he has made, but he leaves behind him a Jenik who knows quite well that the eldest son of Micha, presumed dead, is none other than himself. He has acquired a marriage contract to his beloved and a dowry from his cheese-paring stepmother at the same time! The plan must succeed! We can have no doubts as to the sincerity of Jenik's love for Mařenka after the beautiful love song which he sings the moment Kecal's back is turned. He has not only outwitted the broker, but deserves his reward!

Kecal returns with Krušina and the villagers to celebrate his successful handling of what turned out to be by no means a simple affair. The finale uses the material already heard in the overture. Kecal wants everyone to witness the legality of the document he is about to have signed in their presence. It is to the effect that Jenik has agreed to renounce Mařenka. Krušina and Kecal are delighted, so apparently is Jenik, but the villagers cannot quite understand the position until Kecal adds that the whole thing is in consideration of the sum of three hundred gulden. Then popular fury knows no bounds; even Krušina is shocked that Jenik should abandon Mařenka for money, and Jenik signs amid a general demonstration of hostility.

Act III. Vašek is in stuttering despair that he cannot find the girl who gave him such good advice and whom he found so attractive. His genuinely comic aria is marked *lamentoso*. His thoughts are interrupted by the arrival of a circus troupe, headed by a redoubtable Ringmaster and heralded by the so-called March of the Comedians. The attractions include the great dancer, Esmeralda, and a real, live, American bear. Let all the bystanders stay and watch a sample of what the company can do! To the accompaniment of the delightfully varied and tuneful Dance of the Comedians, the clowns and dancers go through their paces, watched by an admiring throng.

Vašek is left behind admiring the beautiful Esmeralda. One of the clowns comes running in to tell the Ringmaster that the man who plays the bear is too drunk to go through with his role. He himself has looked for a suitable substitute, but he is at his wits' end. Esmeralda solves the problem by suggesting that the dimwit who has been gawping at her for some minutes would be just the right build. The Ringmaster asks Vašek if he would like to dance with the beautiful girl, Esmeralda assures him that she will teach him how, and the agreement is completed. He will make his début that night – all this to an enchanting dance tune sung by the two circus professionals, but made into some kind of trio by the prancing if silent Vašek.

Vašek is just practising some steps to himself, when he sees his parents. Hata wants him to come with them to meet his future bride, but he is unwilling, and downright determined when he hears that it is Krušina's Mařenka who is his destined spouse. He does not know who it is he wants to marry, or rather he does not know her name, but he *is* sure that it is not Mařenka. He escapes, and a moment later in comes Mařenka, furious and mortified at the news her father tells her, that Jenik has sold her love for money. The orchestra reminds her of Jenik's protestations of undying affection, and she is inconsolable.

Vašek reappears and is overjoyed to hear that the girl who stands before him, whom he found so attractive, is Mařenka after all. Poor Mařenka asks for time in which to make up her mind, and the parents of the prospective bride and bridegroom join with Kecal in exhorting her to give the matter serious thought. The sextet (Mařenka joins them just before it finishes) is a lovely, contemplative piece. The mood is continued when Mařenka is left alone to lament in an aria her unhappy position.

To her comes Jenik, apparently in the best of spirits. Mařenka is furious with him, and even more so when he seems to treat the whole affair as an excellent joke. Nothing he can do will reconcile her to hearing him out. The argument is by no means over when Kecal comes to tell Jenik he can have his money as soon as Mařenka has signed the contract. Jenik urges her to do so, which naturally only increases her fury against him, and gives Kecal an even worse opinion of the type of man with whom he is dealing – these sentiments find expression in a trio.

Everyone in the village comes together for the finale which is to see the betrothal of Mařenka and (as Jenik insists the description shall run) 'the son of Tobias Micha'. Everyone congratulates Mařenka on the match, nobody louder than Jenik, who has no sooner opened his mouth than he is recognised by Hata and Micha as the long-lost son of the latter. He asks Mařenka whether she will have him or Vašek, and her triumphant answer leaves Kecal babbling with fury at having been outwitted. He makes himself so conspicuous in fact that everyone laughs at his discomfiture.

All is now set for a happy ending, but there is an interruption as a couple of small boys rush in shouting that the bear is loose! He shambles in, but it is not long before Vašek can be heard inside the skin saying that nobody need be frightened, as the bear is only him. Hata takes him off, and all rejoice at the betrothal of the bartered bride and her faithful lover.   H.

DALIBOR

Opera in three acts, German text by J. Wenzig, Czech translation by Špindler. Première at Prague, 16 May 1868, with Benevicová-Miková (Milada), Lukes (Dalibor). First performed in Vienna, 1892; revived 1938, with Hilde Konetzni, Réthy, Mazaroff, Destal, Kipnis, conductor Walter. First performed Chicago, 1924; Berlin, 1940, with Lemnitz, Scheppan, Völker, Bockelmann, von Manowarda; Edinburgh Festival, 1964 (first performance in Great Britain), by Prague Opera with Miková, Domaninská, Přibyl, Bednař, Haken, conductor Jaroslav Krombholc; English National Opera, 1976, with Anne Evans, John Mitchinson, conductor Charles Mackerras.

Vladislav, *King of Bohemia* ....Baritone
Dalibor, *a knight* ....Tenor
Budivoj, *captain of the guard* ....Baritone
Beneš, *the jailer* ....Bass
Vítek, *Dalibor's squire* ....Tenor
Milada, *sister of the dead Burgrave* ....Soprano
Jitka ....Soprano
Zdeněk's Ghost ....Silent

Nobles, Soldiers, Men and Women

Place: Prague
Time: Fifteenth Century
Running Time: 2 hours 20 minutes

The story of *Dalibor* was a legend[1] which symbolised Czech aspirations long before Smetana took it as a subject for an opera. It is hard to believe that his librettist's treatment of the story owed nothing to *Fidelio* and that dramatic resemblances between the two are pure coincidence. After 1919, when Czech independence ceased to be a dream and became reality, the opera took on new significance for the Czech people, and it has since been looked on, with *The Bartered Bride*, as a national institution, a position which its theme and the splendid music in which it is clothed seem amply to justify.

Act I. There is no extensive overture, and the curtain rises after fifteen bars of music on the judgement hall of the King's palace in Prague. Dalibor has been engaged in strife with the Burgrave of Ploskovice; his friend Zdeněk was captured and put to death, and, in revenge, Dalibor has killed the Burgrave. For this he is coming up for judgement in front of the King. The people, among them Jitka, an orphan whom Dalibor has befriended, are waiting for the assembly of the court; they praise Dalibor as their friend and protector. The King enters with his judges, and rehearses the charges against Dalibor. He calls Milada, the sister of the dead Burgrave, to substantiate her accusations.

Amid expressions of sympathy for her bereavement, she tells the dramatic story of Dalibor's entry into the castle, and of how he killed her brother. The King assures her Dalibor will pay for his crime with his life, and he orders that the accused may be brought in. As he enters, murmurs of admiration are heard on all sides, and even Milada is compelled to comment on his fearless, noble appearance. Dalibor does not deny his action; only, it was not murder but vengeance for murder. In an aria he tells of his love for his friend and of his violin playing (the solo violin is throughout associated with Zdeněk). Zdeněk was captured in battle, and when Dalibor asked what ransom was required to redeem him, he was sent his head on the end of a lance. Milada begins to feel pity for her former foe. Dalibor defies the King; he has committed no crime, only revenged the murder of his friend. If now his life is spared, he will continue to exact vengeance; not the King himself shall stand in his way!

The verdict of the court is imprisonment for life; Dalibor invokes the free spirit of Zdeněk – did he hear the sentence? Milada pleads for him, but the judges say he has openly threatened the King; even when Milada protests that she herself, whom he has most wronged, is prepared to forgive him, they are unimpressed. Milada, thinking she is alone, admits to herself that she is in love with Dalibor. Jitka overhears her and begs her to exert herself to free him. In a vigorous concluding duet, they agree together to free him from prison.

Act II. A street below the castle in which Dalibor is imprisoned. From an inn comes the sound of lively singing. Jitka and Vítek, Dalibor's page, greet each other eagerly in a charming duet. They discuss Dalibor's plight and Jitka reveals that Milada is already inside the prison disguised as a boy. They are optimistic that their cause has not received so severe a setback in the imprisonment of Dalibor as might have been feared. The music has an exuberance that is positively Weberian in character.

The scene changes to the house of Beneš, the jailer, inside the castle. Sentries patrol up and down. Budivoj warns Beneš that there is danger of a rising in favour of Dalibor; he, as head jailer, is answerable with his life for the prisoner's safe-keeping. Budivoj looks at Milada who is standing nearby in disguise, and enquires who it is; Beneš tells him it is his new assistant. The parallel of the whole situation with that of *Fidelio* is too obvious to need pointing out. In music of sombre character, Beneš reflects on the gloomy nature of his calling.

Milada comes to tell Beneš that his meal is ready. The jailer refers most sympathetically to Dalibor, who, he says, has asked for a fiddle to play in his dungeon. He tells Milada to take the instrument down to the prisoner, and says he himself will go to fetch it. Milada rejoices at the prospect of seeing Dalibor for the first time face to face. Beneš returns and gives Milada instructions on how to find the appropriate dungeon.

The scene changes again, this time to Dalibor's cell.

---

[1] The original legend concerns, says Brian Large, 'the rebellious knight, Dalibor, imprisoned in the Daliborka Tower near Hradčany … in 1498 for leading an uprising for the recognition of peasant brewing rights. During captivity, Dalibor learnt to play the violin so beautifully that people came from all over the city to hear him. Though tortured … and later executed for his part in inciting serfs to rebel against their tyrannical masters, Dalibor became a symbol of just revolt against royal power.' (*Smetana*, 1970).

Dalibor has a vision of Zdeněk, who appears to him and plays his violin; when he has gone, Dalibor invokes his reappearance in a beautiful aria. Presently Milada brings him the instrument he has asked for. She admits that she was his accuser at his trial, and that she hated him. She tells of her useless pleas that he should be allowed to go free, and of the preparations which are in hand for his escape. Will he pardon her for what she has done to him; ever since the trial she has loved him from afar. The whole scene is one of extraordinary power, and the lyrical duet itself of haunting beauty.

Act III. The throne room of the King, brightly lit. He is surrounded by his councillors. Budivoj and Beneš appear in front of him, the former saying that he has news of a rising which is plotted in Dalibor's favour. Beneš tells his story; he had an apprentice, who suddenly disappeared, leaving behind him some money and a note of thanks. But at least Beneš was in time to prevent Dalibor's escape – the lad had certainly something to do with the preparations he discovered for freeing the prisoner. Beneš pleads for leniency for himself. The King, in spite of misgivings as to the justice of his action (voiced in a beautiful aria), finally accepts the judgement of his council that Dalibor be condemned to instant death.

Plans are afoot for Dalibor's escape, and he stands in his cell, free of fetters and rejoicing in a brilliant aria as he thinks of the freedom he can bring to his people. But Budivoj rushes in with his guards, secures his prisoner and informs him of the court's decision that he shall die. Dalibor muses on his coming death in music of poignant sadness.

During a march interlude, the scene changes to an open square in front of the castle. Milada, clad for battle, with Jitka, Vítek, and their armed supporters, waits for the signal. They hear the tolling of a bell and the sound of a chorus of monks, and Milada is afraid that Dalibor is being done to death inside the prison while they wait for his signal to attack it. They prepare to assault the castle.

Women comment on what they can see, and presently Dalibor comes out of the castle carrying Milada, who is wounded. She dies in his arms, and, when Budivoj appears with troops, Dalibor stabs himself and dies with his beloved. (There is an alternative ending to the opera, in which Dalibor is executed before Milada and the rescue party can reach him; Milada is killed in the attack.)   H.

LIBUŠE

Opera in three acts, text (originally in German) by Josef Wenzig, translated into Czech by Erwin Spindler. Première, Prague, for the opening of the Czech National Theatre (Národní Divadlo), 11 June 1881, with Marie Sittová, Irma Reichová, Betty Fibichová, Josef Lev, Karel Čech, Antonín Vavra, František Hynek, Leopold Stropnicky. The theatre was burnt down two months later, and a new building inaugurated in 1883, again with *Libuše*. The thousandth performance of operas by Smetana in Prague was celebrated with this work on 27 August 1905. First performed Vienna, 1924, by Olomouc Opera Company; Zagreb, 1933. Frequently revived all over the Czech Republic and Slovakia. No record of either British or U.S. productions.

Libuše, *a Bohemian princess*............................Soprano
Přemysl of Stadice ....Baritone
Chrudoš from Ottava ....Bass
Šťáhlav from Radbuza, *his brother*...................Tenor
Lutobor, *their uncle*..Bass
Radovan, *head of the Council*.........................Baritone
Krasava, *Lutobor's daughter* ....Soprano
Radmila, *sister of Chrudoš and*
  Šťáhlav..Contralto
Four Reapers ....Sopranos, Contralto, Tenor

Elders and Noblemen, Maidens at Libuše's Court,
  Přemysl's Retinue, People

Place: Vyšehrad and Stadice in the Bohemian
  Mountains
Time: Pagan Era
Running Time: 2 hours 55 minutes

Smetana had been appointed conductor at the Provisional Theatre rather over a year before he completed *Dalibor*. He tried to improve every aspect of the theatre but was particularly concerned with a representative repertory, if possible of Czech music. Between 1866 and 1872, eighty-two different operas were performed, thirty-three of which were new productions prepared and conducted by Smetana himself. In 1869, he wrote a concert piece called *Libuše's Judgement*, and this seems to have been the seed from which came what was, chronologically speaking, the fourth of his operas, though the penultimate to reach the stage. From the start, he said of *Libuše*, 'I desire it to be used only for festivals which affect the whole Czech nation. *Libuše* is not an opera of the old type, but a festive *tableau* – a form of musical and dramatic sustenance.'

In the event, he had his way, but at a cost. The composition lasted from 1869 to 1872, but it was another nine years before the opera reached the stage, for the simple reason that Smetana refused it performance at the other Prague theatres and insisted that it should inaugurate the National Theatre when it was eventually opened. The overture was played before, but by the time the work reached the stage, Smetana himself was deaf and could hear nothing at all. Dr Brian Large in his biography[1] of Smetana says: 'Whereas *The Brandenburgers in Bohemia* unfolds like a historical novel, *The Bartered Bride* reads like an idyll, and *Dalibor* develops with epic pathos, it is *Libuše* alone which has the grandeur of an ode. It is not opera in the traditional sense but a magnificent pageant, a hymn to the nation, cast in six tableaux.' He compares it with two other monuments of the nineteenth century, Wagner's *Die Meistersinger* and Berlioz's *Les Troyens*, and the last scene, with its prophetic note, certainly recalls Berlioz's Dido.

The noble overture opens with a splendid fanfare, and is built up on two further ideas, the first associated throughout the opera with Libuše and first heard on the oboe, another associated with Přemysl, first heard on horns.

Act I, scene i. Vyšehrad, overlooking the Vltava valley. Libuše, as her father's only child, is ruler of Bohemia. In measured tones, Radmila introduces the case which she has to try and which concerns Radmila's two brothers, who are in dispute over their dead father's estate. From her anguished comments, Krasava, who stands to one side, is plainly concerned with the way matters will turn out. A solemn orchestral introduction leads to Libuše's majestic prayer for enlightenment, 'Eternal Gods'. Libuše leaves for the council chamber, but Krasava and Radmila remain behind, Krasava admitting her guilty involvement but refusing to elaborate on it.

Scene ii. An open space at Vyšehrad. The two litigants, Chrudoš and Šťáhlav, wait for Libuše's arrival, and the music is urgent as befits the heat of the brothers' quarrel. Chrudoš interrupts the bystanders' conventional regrets at the fraternal strife, and Šťáhlav states his opposition though in more measured terms. Their uncle Lutobor thinks reconciliation most unlikely, and for his part wishes that the Princess might decide to take a husband to sustain her in her heavy task.

The sounds of a march introduce Libuše's procession, and in another big public statement she makes plain the purpose of the meeting and the purport of the brothers' quarrel. Chrudoš angrily proposes that they follow German custom, under which the elder brother inherits all. Šťáhlav adopts a more conciliatory tone and agrees to abide by whatever is decided. Libuše gives judgement that, according to ancient custom, the estate of a father shall be managed jointly by the brothers or, if they prefer, divided between them. Chrudoš dissents, and Libuše turns judgement over to the Council. Radovan affirms the Elders' agreement with Libuše, at which point Chrudoš furiously rejects her as a suitable judge on the grounds that she is a weak woman, and rushes from the spot. Libuše decides to abdicate her power, bidding the people choose her a husband to whom she may hand over rule. In an ensemble, the choice is referred back to her and, amid general rejoicing, she chooses Přemysl of Stadice, whom she has loved since childhood.

Act II, scene i. A burial mound in the country. Lutobor bemoans his fate in having fathered a daughter so different in temperament from him. But Krasava, who follows him, plainly wishes to confess her fault – that she loves Chrudoš, having rejected him at first in order to lead him on, and now knows she is the cause of near disaster – and she does so in music of vibrant passion. Šťáhlav and Radmila overhear her confession and join their voices to her plea to her father, who relents to demand that she achieve reconciliation with Chrudoš and herself persuade him to bow the knee to Libuše. Otherwise, he will see Krasava no more.

Chrudoš comes in, full of resentment – against the idea of accepting Libuše's rule, against his beloved Krasava, who he thinks loves his brother. When Krasava herself appears and admits her fault before pleading her genuine love for him, he at first resists, then, after she has invoked his father's memory, succumbs to the love that has been choking him – to the obvious approval of Radmila, Šťáhlav and Lutobor. The two brothers embrace.

Scene ii. The countryside in the neighbourhood of Stadice. In the background stands Přemysl's beautiful farmhouse, surrounded by lime trees. Voices of harvesters off-stage precede Přemysl's famous aria ('Již plane slunce'; The sun is blazing), a pinnacle of Czech

---

[1] *Smetana* by Brian Large (Duckworth, London, 1970).

operatic literature which runs the gamut of idealised masculine emotions: disciplined if perhaps hopeless love for a good woman, ardour for patriotic duty, the whole tempered by a belief in the solvent qualities of the natural order. The farm workers return home and are greeted by Přemysl, but he himself remains outside and alone, lost in thoughts of Libuše and the deep peace of the countryside – a beautiful lyrical passage.

A crowd of people, led by Radovan and the Elders, come to bring the news that Přemysl has been chosen as Libuše's consort. Přemysl voices his gratitude towards the people and the circumstances of his life as a farmer, then goes with the Elders, the more willingly when he learns from them the possibility of danger from the dissident Chrudoš. There is a vigorous finale for Přemysl, Radovan and the crowd.

Act III, scene i. Libuše's court. Festively clad, she awaits the arrival of her chosen bridegroom, but first, with Radmila and Lutobor watching, she solemnises the reconciliation of Chrudoš and Šťáhlav, then the betrothal of Chrudoš and Krasava. She promises to intercede on Chrudoš's behalf with Přemysl, to whom in future her supreme power will belong.

Libuše is left alone, praying to the spirit of her dead father Krok for blessings on this solemn moment in her life. Her maidens reappear to escort her towards her waiting bridegroom and the scene ends with their bridal chorus.

Scene ii. The great meeting place in Vyšehrad. Chrudoš and Lutobor, together with Šťáhlav, Radmila and Krasava, await the appearance of Libuše and Přemysl. Chrudoš's rebellious spirit is again in the ascendant and it takes all the persuasion that Lutobor, Šťáhlav and Krasava can command before he vows to give soft answers rather than display the stiff-necked pride which is his natural instinct.

A ceremonial procession of noblemen and Elders, headed by Radovan, is followed by Libuše and Přemysl. Přemysl greets the people and promises to serve them to the best of his ability. He and Libuše ask for the blessing of the gods – the nearest Smetana could get, surmises Brian Large, to finding love music for two heroic leaders of the Bohemian people. The scene of general rejoicing turns to the specific as Přemysl applauds the reconciliation of Chrudoš and Šťáhlav, then demands that Chrudoš make amends for his insult to Libuše. As Chrudoš makes to bow the knee, Přemysl embraces him as a man of spirit and the onlookers rejoice in an act of generosity which augurs well for Přemysl's reign.

Libuše meanwhile has been gazing in front of her in a state of prophetic rapture. She starts to foretell the heroic destiny of the Czech people and in six 'pictures' (the word is Smetana's own) we see successively Prince Břetislav, who united Bohemia and Moravia and defeated a German invasion; Jaroslav of Sternberk, who defended the country against the Tartars; King Ottokar II, who increased the Slavonic empire, together with his granddaughter Elisabeth and her son Charles IV, who improved the status of Bohemia in Central Europe; then Žižka, Prokop the Great and the Hussites; the wise King George of Podiebrad, who consolidated the results of the Hussite revolution; and ultimately, as Libuše's vision dims into a general conviction of a great Czech destiny, the royal castle in Prague which dominates the whole scene. In spite of attempts to illustrate each tableau, and Smetana's use of the Hussite chorale 'Ye who are God's warriors' as the basis for the music, this has more solemnity and grandeur than true drama, but the final quarter of an hour nonetheless makes a fitting ending to a festive work, even though one may think that in general the score is notable more for lyrical expansiveness than for economy of means, for Smetana's peculiar – and moving – expressiveness rather than for urgency or concise dramaturgy.　　H.

THE TWO WIDOWS
Dvě Vdovy

Opera in two acts, libretto by Emmanuel Züngel founded on a comedy by P.J.F. Malefille. Première, 27 March 1874, in Prague with Marie Sittová, Ema Saková, Antonín Vávra, Karel Čech, conductor Smetana. New version, with recitatives instead of spoken dialogue, Prague, 1878. First performed in Germany, Hamburg, 1881; in Vienna by company from Olomouc, 1924; London, Guildhall School of Music, 1963; English National Opera, 1993 (in English). Very frequently heard in Czechoslovakia and fairly often in Germany in the years after 1945.

Karolina Záleská, *widow and*
　　heir of a rich Colonel ....Soprano
Anežka Miletinská, *a widow, her cousin* ....Soprano
Mumlal, *gamekeeper in Karolina's service* ....Bass
Ladislav Podhajsky, *a neighbouring landowner* ...Tenor
Toník, *a peasant* ....Tenor
Lidka, *a maid*..Soprano

Villagers, Servants

Place: Karolina's House
Time: Late Eighteenth Century
Running Time: 1 hour 50 minutes

Smetana deliberately set out to write an opera in, as he himself said, 'a distinguished salon style'. In his output *The Two Widows* is, so to speak, the equivalent of *Onegin* or *Traviata* or *Così fan tutte*, and for us it is peculiar to read that it succeeded straight away in spite of accusations of being Wagnerian in style.

Act I. A bustling overture leads to a lively chorus as villagers come to invite Karolina, the lady of the manor, to the harvest festival. She gently mocks her cousin Anežka for continuing to wear nothing but black so long after her husband's death. In a charming aria Karolina explains her philosophy: she is independent and busy, she runs her estate well, and she finds it a highly satisfactory existence. Her advice to her cousin is to remarry – and she'd better begin her new regime by going to the harvest festival dance that very night.

Enter Mumlal, Karolina's gamekeeper and general factotum, and a born grumbler. A trio bubbles away and we might be in the agreeable world of *Die lustigen Weiber von Windsor* as Mumlal explains that the bane of his life at the moment is a poacher who, to add insult to injury, never even hits what he shoots at. A shot is heard, Mumlal is sure it is his tormentor, and Karolina sends him off to arrest the culprit.

The two ladies withdraw as Ladislav comes into view. In an excellent example of the tenor-bass duets which figure regularly in Smetana's operas, Ladislav makes it clear that his one object is to be taken to the manor, there to meet his beloved Anežka, and his only complaint is at Mumlal's slowness in effecting his capture. Karolina insists they put him on trial straight away, Ladislav is brought in, and all comment on his capture in a quartet, to which he and Anežka make contributions which are full of feeling. In a fervent solo and with a plea of unrequited love, Ladislav defends his action to an audience that is by no means unresponsive. A lively trio for the ladies and Ladislav leads to the reading out of the description of the prisoner which Mumlal has been laboriously concocting: 'Height – average; hair – average ... etc.', and then to his sentence to half a day's imprisonment in the house. The scene ends with an exhilarating reprise of the trio, this time with Mumlal adding his voice to make it a quartet.

Mumlal takes Ladislav off, and on his return is surrounded by the young people of the village, among them Toník and Lidka, all eager to know the story of the arrest he has made. Has it something to do with love, they ask? Mumlal abuses the tender passion, only to have Toník and Lidka mock him for his cynicism, and to find the gentry supporting the majority opinion as the curtain falls.

Act II. A large hall with a sun porch. A lively prelude leads to Ladislav's lyrical song in praise of Maytime and love, sung from his room (off-stage). Anežka listens but, in course of conversation with Karolina, agrees to renounce any pretensions to Ladislav's affections in favour of Karolina, who well knows that Anežka is in love with Ladislav and hopes to force her to admit it by making her jealous; the attractive duet is based on Karolina's opening aria.

Anežka alone reads a letter she has received from Ladislav; she goes to burn it, then snuffs the candle and hides the letter as Ladislav appears. In a long scene, Ladislav gently pleads his cause, and recites from memory the letter, which Anežka pretends not to have read. In the end she tells him she can never be more to him than a friend, and they say goodbye. Throughout the scene, Smetana has written music of the utmost tenderness for his lovers, and even when Anežka appears to reject Ladislav's pleading, her real feelings are never in doubt – the music is as touching and genuine as for instance that of Mařenka's aria in *The Bartered Bride*.

The plot thickens as Karolina, dressed for the dance, pretends to appropriate Ladislav herself. Anežka's big *scena* is an extended and shapely aria of considerable appeal – she laments her unhappy and lonely situation. When Mumlal comes in, it is to complain to Anežka at the way his mistress is carrying on, kissing as is the local custom the man with whom she dances. In a comic song, he expounds his philosophy – he thunders with anger on every possible occasion, it seems – but Anežka can stand him no longer and flounces out. Mumlal hides as Lidka, who has been dancing, runs in pursued by Toník demanding the kiss that is his due. She is coy, Mumlal fulminates from behind a pillar for all the world like a Czech Osmin and interposes himself when Lidka finally grants the kiss – 'it tasted like pepper and salt' is the young couple's comment. But they get their own back a minute later and box the old man's ears soundly. The trio is one of the most delightful numbers of the score.

In a scene with Ladislav, Karolina makes him

admit that it is love that has brought him to her estate; they are observed together by Anežka, who jumps to obvious but mistaken conclusions. In a quartet (Mumlal comes in too) each admits his or her true reaction to the situation, and finally in a *stretta* three, with Mumlal vigorously dissenting, proclaim their faith in the power of love. Ladislav runs off, Anežka is constrained to admit to Karolina that she loves him after all, he hears the admission from his hiding place, and as the banquet is announced, only Mumlal is left grousing away. A chorus of rejoicing and a polka bring to an end an opera that is one of the most tuneful and delightful of any that has *not* yet been accepted into the world's repertory.　　H.

THE KISS
Hubička

Opera in two acts, text by E. Krásnohorská. Première, Prague, 7 November 1876. First performed in Chicago, 1921; in England, Carl Rosa, 1948, with Packer, Myrrdin, conducted by Tausky (there had been an amateur performance at Liverpool in 1938). Revived Cambridge University, 1969.

Paloucky, *a peasant* ....Bass-Baritone
Vendulka, *his daughter*....................................Soprano
Lukáš, *a young widower*......................................Tenor
Tomeš, *brother-in-law of Lukáš*......................Baritone
Martinka, *Vendulka's old aunt* ....Contralto
Matouš, *an old smuggler*.......................................Bass
Barče, *a servant girl*.......................................Soprano
A Frontier Guard...Tenor

Place: In the Mountains on the Borders of Bohemia
Running Time: 1 hour 45 minutes

The librettos of Smetana's last three operas (four, if you count the fragmentary *Viola*, an attempt at Shakespeare's *Twelfth Night*) are by Eliška Krásnohorská, a librettist of skill and forceful personality. She determined subject and shape, specifying for instance duets and ensembles (of which in opera she was a determined supporter) and received a minimum of feedback from the composer. The three operas she wrote for Smetana are basically comedies, but comedies with a serious basis, always concerned with the mending of a relationship which, at some time in the past, has been broken or at least bruised. As the same goes to some extent at least for *The Bartered Bride* and

The Two Widows (*not* by Krásnohorská), Smetana's hand in the choice of subjects must not be discounted. But Krásnohorská's influence on the last phase of Smetana's operatic career – the period during which he was deaf – cannot be ignored either.

The Kiss is at least superficially an undemonstrative opera, with only a mild joke for subject – the superstitious reluctance of a bride-to-be to give her lover a kiss before their marriage, and their subsequent quarrel (Act I) and reconciliation (Act II, scene ii). The first scene of Act II is devoted to the frustration of the principal characters, with a band of smugglers (a virtually unexplained interruption) as background. But Vendulka is shown as sufficiently headstrong to risk her future for her 'superstitious reluctance' and the opera's serious undertone must not be totally passed over. Smetana has provided attractive, melodious and singable music, which may not have quite the point of his *Bartered Bride* score but is full of charm.

Act I. A room in Paloucky's cottage. Through the open window can be seen the village square. Lukáš, a young peasant, was always in love with Vendulka, but, at the wish of his parents, he married another woman. Now she is dead and he is free to marry Vendulka. Martinka is delighted at the way things have worked out, but Vendulka's father has some misgivings; both Vendulka and Lukáš are headstrong, determined people – she would do better to refuse him, he tells his daughter. Her unhappiness is so obvious at this piece of advice, that he relents; but he does not appear to alter his view that this marriage is a risky affair.

Barče rushes in to say that the wooing party is about to put in an appearance, and soon Lukáš and Tomeš appear at the window, followed by a crowd of curious villagers. Tomeš explains that Lukáš has come a-wooing; Paloucky gives his consent, but in such a way that Lukáš takes offence that it was not done more gladly. Paloucky explains that he thinks the prospective couple are too hot-tempered to keep peace for long, but he gives them his blessing and all is forgiven and forgotten in a moment. There is a duet for the two lovers, at the end of which Lukáš makes as if to kiss Vendulka; she refuses to allow him to do so. Lukáš insists, she continues to refuse, and the fat is in the fire as Paloucky predicted. But all is well again when Tomeš starts up a drinking song, in which everyone joins, before leaving the happy couple alone together.

They sing of their love, and presently Lukáš's child is brought in a cradle, much to Vendulka's joy. He tries to kiss her again – after all, they are alone now – but she will still not allow him to do so, not until after their wedding. The quarrel breaks out again, and eventually Vendulka threatens to throw Lukáš out of the house, to the surprise of everyone except her father, who had anticipated just such a situation arising. Lukáš makes a last demand for what he has come to think of as his right, and, when it is refused, leaves in high dudgeon.

Martinka advises Vendulka to make up the quarrel, and bids her good night. Vendulka sits herself by the cradle of the child and sings as she rocks it to sleep. She sings two separate songs, which together make a most appealing aria, at the end of which Vendulka herself falls asleep. She is woken up by the sound of a polka outside her window, and she sees Lukáš dancing merrily in front of the house, and kissing the girls with whom he dances. She is furious, but even Tomeš's endeavours are not sufficient to quieten Lukáš, whose blood is up, and who is determined to get his revenge publicly on Vendulka. As the curtain falls, Vendulka exclaims that she must go away from the place where she has been so publicly humiliated.

Act II. A thick wood near the frontier of Bohemia. Matouš appears at the head of a band of smugglers, all carrying heavy bundles. There is a smugglers' chorus, after which the stage is left empty until the arrival of Lukáš, who in an aria expresses his despair at the disappearance of Vendulka, whom he dearly loves in spite of his impetuous behaviour. Tomeš is looking for him, and presently appears along the same path, to be overjoyed at the sight of his brother-in-law, for whose safety he was becoming really worried. Lukáš is anxious to restore himself in Vendulka's favour, and Tomeš in a fine example of Smetana's tenor-baritone duets bids him only have the courage to admit he was in the wrong, and she will have him back at once.

Matouš, who has overheard the conversation between Lukáš and Tomeš, comes out into the open when they have left and has a good laugh at Lukáš's expense. He is waiting for Martinka, who lives nearby and is in league with the smugglers, but when she comes into sight, she has Vendulka with her. Vendulka is frightened by the loneliness of the forest, but Martinka comforts her before giving a signal,

which brings Matouš out of hiding. Vendulka begins to lament her fate, but Matouš knows that the happy ending to her story is being prepared by Lukáš himself, who is only too anxious to make up their quarrel.

When Matouš goes his way, he gives some of his contraband to Martinka, who shares the burden with Vendulka. A frontier guard appears but leaves them unmolested. Martinka continues her efforts to persuade Vendulka to return home, where she is sure Lukáš will be waiting for her.

Next morning, outside Martinka's cottage. Barče is trying to find Martinka or Vendulka to tell them the news she has heard from Matouš. She thinks she can hear them coming – but it is the sound of a lark. She rejoices in the lark's singing in an attractive aria, but one so tricky as to be beyond the capacity of almost any soprano willing to take secondary roles.

Up the path to Martinka's cottage come Matouš, Paloucky, Lukáš and Tomeš, with a whole crowd of villagers. Barče wrings her hands in frustration that Martinka and Vendulka are not there to welcome them and so make the reconciliation possible. Lukáš apologises to Paloucky for his behaviour, and soon afterwards Vendulka appears. She and Lukáš are obviously overjoyed to see each other again, but when Vendulka comes towards him with open arms, Lukáš refuses to kiss her – until he has openly begged her pardon for his behaviour towards her.   H.

THE SECRET
Tajemství

Opera in three acts, libretto by Eliška Krásnohorská. Première at the New Czech Theatre, Prague, 18 September 1878, with Sittová, Fibichová, Mareš, Lev. First performed Vienna (in German), 1895; Oxford (in English), 1957, with a cast including Janet Baker as Rose, conductor Jack Westrup.

Councillor Malina	Bass
Councillor Kalina	Baritone
Miss Rose, *Malina's sister*	Contralto
Blaženka, *Malina's daughter*	Soprano
Vít, *a forester, Kalina's son*	Tenor
Boniface, *an old soldier, Kalina's nephew*	Baritone
Skřivánek, *a ballad singer*	Tenor
The Builder	Baritone
The Innkeeper	Soprano
Jirka, *the bellringer*	Tenor

The Ghost of Friar Barnabáš ....Baritone

Councillors, Neighbours, Boys and Girls, Harvesters,
Bricklayers

Place: In and Near the Bezděz Mountain
Time: End of the Eighteenth Century
Running Time: 1 hour 40 minutes

*T*he Secret was written at a time when the last ves-
tiges of Smetana's hearing were disappearing,
and when he had lost his job as conductor at the
Opera. It was immediately successful, but soon lost
favour with a public which wanted more than anything else a follow-up to *The Bartered Bride*. Its
present popularity in the Czech Republic dates from
its re-studying by Karel Kovařovic in Prague twenty-
five years after the première.

The overture, on an extended scale, is lively in spite
of the almost foreboding nature of the C minor theme
(the secret) with which it opens. From the rise of the
curtain, any lover of *The Bartered Bride* will feel on safe
ground, as chorus and solo, aria and duet alternate in
an open-air setting of village activity. Rose, Malina's
sister, and Kalina were years ago prevented from marrying by her family on the grounds that he was too
poor for her. The families have remained rivals and lose
no opportunity for insult and recrimination. Now, on
one side of the street the harvest is being threshed in
Malina's barn, on the other the bricklayers and their
foreman are rejoicing at the completion of Kalina's new
house. Before long the two factions are quarrelling, but
the arrival of the musician, Skřivánek, provides a distraction, until each side bribes him to sing a derogatory
song about the other. In a charming piece, he gently
mocks each until for a moment it looks as though there
will be a reconciliation. But the quarrel breaks out
anew, and it is only prevented from becoming a brawl
by the intervention of Blaženka and Vít. The rioters disperse, and in a charming *arioso* piece Vít makes an
assignation with Blaženka for that evening.

Rose (who is described as 'a little over thirty') has
earlier mentioned a secret, supposed to have been left
after his death by Friar Barnabáš so that Kalina
might find a treasure. Kalina denies any knowledge
of it, but Boniface has found a piece of old mouldy
paper in a bit of wood he picked up to use as a
weapon. He gives it to Kalina, who recognises it as
Friar Barnabáš's instruction, which must remain his
secret. The jealous Boniface, himself a suitor for

Rose's hand, tells the builder, who immediately communicates the news to whomever he meets, and the
finale to Act I has the news being broadcast to all
and sundry by the bell-ringer, while Blaženka and
Vít murmur tenderly of love.

Act II. A ruin on Mount Bezděz. The 'secret' motif
opens the prelude to an impressive *scena* for Kalina,
who has come to look for the treasure, rails against
his rejection on the score of poverty, and reveals that
his present affluence is all bluff. In music of energetic
cast, he wonders if it is money he craves – but why,
he asks himself. Because of Rose? Kalina falls asleep,
but as he dreams the ghost of Friar Barnabáš spurs
him on to find the treasure, and he wakes to watch a
procession of maidens and pilgrims on their way to
the chapel. He determines to follow them, not sure
whether his dream was inspired by heaven or hell.

Blaženka and Vít have arranged to meet here, and
their scene is a big-scale love duet, dominated by a solo
for Blaženka. When Blaženka makes it clear that she
wishes their idyll to continue in a series of lovers' meetings, Vít protests that he wants her for his wife. They
are about to say goodnight, when they are observed by
Boniface, who fetches the parents. An ensemble of
almost Rossinian brilliance develops as the elders
watch the lovers parting. When they are discovered,
they plead with their relations, until Rose denounces
any Kalina as certain to be untrue. Vít cannot bear to
hear his father slandered and says that he and
Blaženka would refuse money but will elope together.

At the end of an impressive octet, Rose is left alone
to muse longingly on the contrast between this love
which knows no hindrance, and her own for Kalina
which was so early blighted. Boniface enters stealthily, and in a martial air offers himself as her bridegroom, but before Rose can answer, they see Kalina
advancing with his lantern and spade. They watch
him start to dig, but suddenly he cries out Rose's
name and disappears into the hole, leaving Rose and
Boniface aghast behind him.

Act III. In Malina's house there is rejoicing at the
end of the hop harvest, and Rose encourages Blaženka
to ask her father directly if she may get married. She
sings a touching aria in which she compares her love
to a stream; let it not dash against the stones and be
split up and wasted. A patter ensemble develops as they
discuss Kalina's debts, and a loud banging is heard
behind the wall, but no one takes much notice as at

that moment Vít comes to say goodbye before leaving to seek his fortune. His account of his future moves even Malina to pity, but he says he will give Blaženka's hand in marriage only if Kalina himself comes to beg for it on his son's behalf. Just as Boniface puts himself forward as a suitor for Rose's hand, more knocks are heard, and the general reaction is one of fear of the supernatural. Skřivánek improvises a song in praise of Barnabáš's good nature, and the knocking is heard again. To repetitions of the 'secret' motif, Kalina bursts through the wall by the great stove. He has found Friar Barnabáš's treasure: it is Rose! There is a happy ending, with Kalina asking Malina to bestow the hand of his daughter on Vít and that of Rose on Kalina himself.   H.

THE DEVIL'S WALL
Čertova Stěna

Opera in three acts, text by Eliška Krásnohorská. Première 29 October 1882, with Josef Lev as Vok. The performance was apparently ill-prepared and unsuccessful and the work has been revived only spasmodically.

Vok Vítkovic, *a middle-aged,*
    bachelor nobleman......................................Baritone

Záviš Vítkovic, *Vok's nephew*........................Contralto

Jarek, *a knight in Vok's service*...........................Tenor

Hedvika, *Countess of Šauenburk*......................Soprano

Míchálek, *steward of Rožmberk Castle*................Tenor

Katuška, *his daughter*....................................Soprano

Beneš, *a hermit*..Bass

Rarach, *the devil*..Bass

The King's Messengers, Knights, Female Retainers, Peasants, Monsters

Place: Rožmberk; on the River Vltava near Vyšší Brod Monastery
Time: Mid-Thirteenth Century
Running Time: 2 hours 15 minutes

Smetana's illness was sufficiently far advanced to impede the process of composition; the opera's failure hit him terribly hard, critics disliking the portrayal of the devil in a nineteenth-century opera almost as much as they hated the botched staging. Within months he was losing his mental balance, and, though he continued to compose sporadically, he died in a lunatic asylum eighteen months after the première.

The Devil's Wall has never been considered an entirely satisfactory work, partly because of the strain under which it was written, partly because composer and poet never reached accord as to the exact nature of the libretto Smetana required. It was to be a comedy – but Smetana wrote that he had run out of wit and gaiety, and he was most interested in the dark side of Krásnohorská's drama. There is little comedy except for the uninvolving figures of the cheating hermit and the under-achieving Rarach. Even so, the opera, with all its internal contradictions, has excited real admiration among specialists and is perhaps the work of this composer most likely to work its way into the fringes of the repertory.

The name of the opera derives from a group of rocks in the river Vltava at Vyšší Brod, by tradition the remains of a wall the Devil built in order to flood the neighbouring land. The opera concerns the lonely situation and state of mind of the nobleman Vok Vítkovic, who as a young man was disappointed in love and with whom Smetana during composition came more and more to identify.

Act I. Jarek tells Míchálek that his latest attempt to find a bride for Vok has ended once again in failure. The hermit Beneš would much prefer Vok to die single and leave his considerable wealth to a monastery. A comic devil, Rarach by name (characterised by a recurring pantomime-style laugh), tends to act in double harness (though by no means always in strict accord) with Beneš, which is perhaps fortunate since he is physically Beneš's double. Besides Jarek, Vok's entourage includes Katuška, Míchálek's daughter, who is in love with Jarek, and his nephew Záviš. Jarek in excess of loyalty vows not to marry before Vok, who, prompted by the devil, complicates matters by offering himself to marry Katuška, a notion Míchálek takes rather too seriously. When news comes that Vok's beloved from time long ago has in her will left her daughter to his care, he is stirred to remember the past in one of the composer's most successful arias. The act ends as Beneš summons up courage to defy Rarach with, it must be admitted, only partial success, as he is damned by his lies and self-serving behaviour as Rarach is by his out-and-out devilry.

Act II. Jarek's efforts to find Vok a wife continue to be frustrated by Rarach, and Míchálek continues to enjoy lording it as Vok's potential father-in-law. Meantime there arrives Hedvika, daughter of Vok's lost love, a patent threat to Beneš's plans. With the help of Rarach he persuades Vok, in spite of his obvious attraction to Hedvika, to tell the others he plans to finish his days in a monastery. This is generally seen as a disaster, and in a great ensemble they beg him to think again. He changes his mind and says he will marry if there is someone who that night, before his vows are complete, comes to him at the monastery.

Act III is not only packed with action but short of coherence because of cuts made by the composer in the libretto. Beneš confesses to Míchálek that he schemed regardless of consequences to get Vok's wealth for his monastery with himself as abbot, then repels the devil's attempt to cross the river; village girls, to the discomfiture of the village men, queue up at the monastery to offer themselves to Vok; and Rarach's devils feverishly dance a kind of Mephisto waltz before they dam the river. Hedvika sees that Vok and the monastery are in mortal danger but it is out of love that she makes her way across the river. Vok accepts her – and Jarek and Katuška are free to marry. Beneš makes the sign of the cross, for once successfully, over the wall and it breaks, to allow the river to return to its course. Messengers arrive from the King announcing the appointment of Vok to be Marshal of the Kingdom.   H.

ETHEL SMYTH
(born 22 April 1858, died 9 May 1944)

Ethel Smyth bravely insisted on studying abroad, at the Leipzig Conservatoire. Her first opera, *Fantasio*, was performed in Weimar in 1894 and her second, *Der Wald*, in Berlin in 1901. *The Wreckers*, her third and most successful opera, was inspired by a holiday in Cornwall and the Scilly Isles. She wrote three more operas, *The Boatswain's Mate* (1914), the opera-ballet *Fête Galante* (1923) and the ballad-opera *Entente Cordiale* (1925). Though supported by conductors from Nikisch to Beecham, her work was seldom taken as seriously as she hoped. Her eight volumes of memoirs attracted more attention in Britain, where her campaigns for serious opera and for the Suffragettes attracted notoriety but contributed to both causes. Bruno Walter believed that 'her work is destined permanently to succeed although its recognition, like the recognition of all true originality, only comes gradually and in the teeth of opposition.'[1]   P.

THE WRECKERS

Lyrical Drama in three acts, English text translated by the composer and A. Strettel from Henry Brewster's 'Les Naufrageurs'. Première as *Strandrecht* in a German translation by John Bernhoff, Neues Theater, Leipzig, 11 November 1906. Two acts were performed in concert, conducted by Arthur Nikisch in London at the Queen's Hall in 1908, and it was staged on 22 June 1909 at His Majesty's Theatre, with John Coates as Mark and Mme de Vere Sapio as Thirza, conducted by Thomas Beecham. Revived at Covent Garden 1910, conducted by Bruno Walter, at Sadler's Wells in 1939, and in concert at the Proms, 1994, conducted by Odaline de la Martinez, with Justin Lavender and Anne-Marie Owens.

Pascoe, *headman of the village and*
    local preacher, aged 55..............................Baritone

Lawrence, *keeper of the lighthouse*..................Baritone

Harvey, *Lawrence's brother-in-law*........................Bass

Talbot, *landlord of the tavern*..............................Tenor

Jack, *Talbot's son, aged 15* ....Mezzo-Soprano

Mark, *a young fisherman* ....Tenor

Thirza, *Pascoe's wife, aged 22*..............Mezzo-Soprano

Avis, *daughter of Lawrence, aged 17* ....Soprano

A Man ....Bass

Place: Cornwall
Time: Second Half of the Eighteenth Century
Running Time: 2 hours 15 minutes

---

[1] Bruno Walter, *Memoirs*.

The inhabitants of a Cornish village survive by robbing the ships they lure on to their rocky coast. Pascoe, their headman and preacher, supports the wreckers but has alienated his young wife, Thirza. She has fallen in love with Mark, formerly promised to Avis, the daughter of Lawrence, the lighthouse keeper.

Act I. A Cornish village, Sunday evening. The overture leads to the first chorus, 'God's Chosen People shall not pay the price of sin!', sung by the villagers on their way to chapel. They stop to drink and look forward to plunder. Pascoe rebukes them for drinking on the Sabbath: they have forgotten God, so He now guides ships away from their shores, and leaves them near to starvation. Lawrence has another explanation: someone has lit beacons to warn ships away from the coast. The villagers swear to hunt the traitor to death.

Thirza refuses to join the villagers at prayer. Mark sings a folksong and throws a flower in at her window. Avis forces him to admit he no longer loves her and erupts in fury against Thirza. When Thirza emerges, she wears Mark's flower and sings the song that he sang. She longs for love, even though it may cost her shame and death.

Avis hints to Pascoe that his young wife is betraying him. Thirza tells her husband that she longs to leave 'these cruel shores' and has nightmares about the wrecks. The congregation's hymns in the chapel provide an ironic counterpoint to their scene. Pascoe explains that God has provided them with a harvest and flocks on sea, since their land is so barren: 'In God's mighty name we shed blood!' Thirza runs out.

The villagers emerge from chapel, delighted with their hellfire sermon, since they know that they themselves are saved. Storm clouds gather. Avis accuses Pascoe of betraying them, and blames his infatuation with his young wife. The men plan to keep watch for beacons. They will signal their progress by sounding horns. A ship is sighted off shore. The villagers begin a wild dance as they anticipate plundering the wreck.

Act II. A prelude, 'On the cliffs of Cornwall', sets the scene on the seashore. Mark gathers driftwood for a warning beacon and sings the 'Ballad of the Bones'. Thirza warns him not to light the fire, since the villagers will see it: their horns can be heard coming close. Mark persuades her to leave Cornwall with him. They start the fire and then go. Pascoe faints when he recognises Thirza's shawl near the fire. The villagers assume he lit the beacon.

Act III. A cave giving on to the sea: dawn. The villagers have assembled in judgment. They do not want to believe that Pascoe betrayed them, but he refuses to defend himself. To save Pascoe, Mark and Thirza confess they lit the beacon. Avis lies that Mark spent the night with her, but no one believes her. Lawrence disowns his daughter.

The sea can be heard more and more clearly, as the tide rises. The villagers sentence the 'adulterers and traitors' to death. As the villagers leave, singing a psalm, Mark and Thirza greet the waves that flood the cave as their bridal song, 'Our last ecstasy thy embrace, O sea!'

Beecham blamed *The Wreckers'* infrequency of performance on 'the apparent impossibility of finding an Anglo-Saxon soprano who can interpret revealingly that splendid and original figure the tragic heroine Thirza. Neither in this part nor that of Mark, the tenor, have I seen more than a tithe of that intensity and spiritual exaltation without which the characters must fail to make their mark. But the ability to play tragedy with great and moving force has departed for a while from the English stage, and we must wait for a sign of its return there before there can be the slightest hope of *The Wreckers* coming into its own.'[1] Another problem is that the libretto is markedly less effective in the English translation than in the original French. In 1931 Virginia Woolf noted in her diary that the opera was 'vigorous & even beautiful; & active & absurd & extreme; & youthful: as if some song in her had tried to issue & been choked'.[2] Under cover of its historicalism, *The Wreckers* celebrates heterodoxy. The community's corrupt, self-righteous morality ensures that their attack on 'immorality' makes it seem the better option. 'Love in sin' probably has a wider meaning than merely adultery: Ethel Smyth made little secret of her homosexuality. In this respect, as well as in such features as the central role played by the sea and the off-stage service heard behind an on-stage duet, *The Wreckers* anticipates *Peter Grimes*.   P.

[1] Thomas Beecham, *A Mingled Chime*, London, 1944.

[2] Entry for 15 October 1931, *The Diary of Virginia Woolf*, ed. Anne Olivier

Bell and Andrew McNellie, 1977–84, IV.

THE BOATSWAIN'S MATE

Comedy in one act (two parts), libretto by the composer based on W.W. Jacobs's short story of the same name (*Captains All*, 1905). Première, promoted by Thomas Beecham, at the Shaftesbury Theatre, London, 28 January 1916, conducted by the composer and afterwards by Eugene Goossens. Revived in 1919 by the British National Opera company at Covent Garden; in 1922 by Lilian Baylis at the Old Vic (rescored for small orchestra).

Harry Benn, *ex-boatswain*...................................Tenor
Ned Travers, *ex-soldier* ....Baritone
Mrs Waters, *landlady of 'The Beehive'* ....Soprano
Mary Ann, *servant girl* ....Mezzo-Soprano
A Policeman ....Tenor

Chorus of Agricultural Labourers; Cats behind the scenes

Place: England
Time: Twentieth Century
Running Time: 1 hour 30 minutes

At the time she wrote *The Boatswain's Mate* Ethel Smyth was deeply involved with the Suffragette cause. The overture features a reworking of her 'March of the Women', which she wrote while serving a two-month sentence in Holloway Prison, for 'hurling a large-sized brick through the front window of the house of the Home Secretary'.[1] Nevertheless it is a comedy that touches unexpectedly lightly on the theme of women's greater competence. As something of an in-joke, she renamed George Benn, as he was in the original, Harry, in reference to her devoted friend Harry Brewster, the librettist of *The Wreckers*, whose persistent courtship was rewarded with her virginity in 1895, when he was 45 and she was 37.

Part I. Outside 'The Beehive'. Harry Benn, ex-boatswain, has long been in love with the tavern's landlady, Mrs Waters, a widow. Her servant girl Mary Ann tells him that her mistress will be on her own that night. As their first duet ('I know what I want when I see it') makes clear, Mrs Waters obstinately resists Benn's advances. Hope springs, however, as he says, eternal: 'Without a husband to love, obey and cherish, a woman's just like ivy without a tree! She'll run along the ground but she'll soon turn round and look for a tree, or maybe a post. And up it she will climb in a very short time, and cling on tight to the tree's delight'. Travers appears, an ex-soldier down on his luck. Benn explains that he is trying to persuade the landlady to marry him and offers Travers £3 to pretend to burgle 'The Beehive' that night, so that Benn can rescue Mrs Waters. He is sure she will then marry him, 'in her gratitood'. Benn writes out a confession, to prove this is no trick. Mrs Waters reflects on her independent but lonely state in an *allegretto grazioso* ('Suppose you mean to do a given thing'). When a group of labourers arrive and demand beer, she refuses to serve them and they go peacefully. An intermezzo follows.

Part II. The interior of the kitchen of 'The Beehive', 2.30 a.m. Moonlight and the sound of squalling cats. Travers enters through the window and Benn hands him the money. When Travers sees that Mrs Waters is armed with a gun, he hides in the cupboard. She has seen someone go in, however, and locks the door. Travers pushes Benn's confession underneath it and she lets him out. They are each struck by the other. To teach Benn a lesson, Mrs Waters pretends she has shot and killed Travers. In a waltz-time trio ('The first thing to do is get rid of the body') she orders Benn to dig a grave in the garden. He is horrified and leaves. Before she can explain, he returns, conscience-stricken, with a policeman, whose investigations are accompanied by the fate theme from Beethoven's Fifth Symphony. Mrs Waters produces Travers, and says he is working on her plumbing and gas fitting. Benn blames 'the drink or love', the theme of an animated quartet, before Mrs Waters pushes him out, along with the policeman. While she makes breakfast, Travers mends her stiff tap. He confesses that his one ambition is to be landlord of a country tavern. He leaves, promising to return in the evening. Alone, Mrs Waters looks in a mirror and spots a wrinkle. She sings a snatch of the song 'Springtime, the only pretty ring time' but adds, in a touching final aria, marked to be sung 'with passion', 'Summer, summer time for me!'

The text's whimsy has dated; its length has also not helped its cause. Beecham objected that while the first act 'with its mixture of lyrical numbers and dialogue is perfect in style and structure ... in the second this happy scheme is thrown overboard for an uninterrupted stream of music involving the setting of portions of the text that one feels would have been more effective and congruous had they been kept in speech'.[1] Ethel Smyth makes refreshing use of folksongs in her score, which also contains much real feeling. P.

---

[1] Sir Thomas Beecham, *A Mingled Chime*, London, 1944.

STEPHEN SONDHEIM
(born 22 March 1930)

Starting his career in the American musical as a lyricist for other composers (notably Bernstein in *West Side Story* and Jule Styne in *Gypsy*), Sondheim, who studied composition with Milton Babbitt, began his public career as a composer with *A Funny Thing happened on the Way to the Forum*, a farce, and continued with *Company*, *Follies* and *A Little Night Music*, three trail-blazing musicals with serious subjects. Both *Pacific Overtures*, with its strong Kabuki influence, and *Sweeney Todd*, the latter much better suited to a big theatre than the former, have been successfully produced by opera companies and are built to a scale that belongs as much to opera as to operetta or the musical. Sondheim's lyrics range from total simplicity to a dazzling complexity of metre and rhyme that are hard to rival in modern times. His collaboration with the well-known director Hal Prince has been notable and began with the staging of *Company*.   H.

PACIFIC OVERTURES[1]

Musical in two acts, book by John Weidman; additional material by Hugh Wheeler; orchestration by Jonathan Tunick. Première Winter Garden Theater, New York, 11 January 1976. First performed in England, Wythenshawe, 1986; London, English National Opera, 1987, conductor James Holmes.

Reciter	Lord Abe
Manjiro	Three Councillors
Kayama	Tamate, *Kayama's wife*
The Story Teller	A Fisherman
A Thief	Commodore Matthew Galbraith Perry
Shogun's Wife	Shogun's Companion
Four Geisha Girls	The Shogun
The Shogun's Mother	A Madam
An Old Man	A Boy
The American Admiral	The Dutch Admiral
The British Admiral	The Russian Admiral
The French Admiral	Three British Sailors
Samurais, Servants, Observers, Nobles	

Musicians on Stage: Shamisen, Percussion

Place: Japan
Time: July 1853; from then on
Running Time: 1 hour 55 minutes

Pacific Overtures started as a play, was taken over by Hal Prince and rejigged to allow for songs by Sondheim, then re-thought. Sondheim explained: 'What we actually did was to create a mythical Japanese playwright who has come to New York, seen a couple of Broadway shows, and then goes back home and writes a musical about Commodore Perry's visit to Japan. It is this that gives the tone and style for the show.' The original cast was oriental and all-male, roles rarely last more than a scene and doubling is the rule rather than the exception.

The opera, presented in Kabuki style as a series of vignettes, is concerned with the opening up of Japan to Western influence. There are effectively twelve large-scale numbers, each amounting to a separate scene. There is no story, rather a progress from Japan as a world where nothing changes much to Japan taking its place in a modern world. A reciter puts his oar in from time to time, dispensing comments and information, as two friends, Manjiro (who has been to America) and Kayama (a traditionalist), come to terms with the new. Manjiro tries to return to old *samurai* values, Kayama adapts to new ways and becomes Governor.

The episodes build up a picture and the Reciter sets the isolationist scene with 'In the middle of the sea'. A Fisherman (Manjiro) warns of the arrival of the Americans. Lord Abe, the Shogun's chief councillor, appoints an unimportant Samurai, Kayama, as Chief of Police charged with fending the invaders off Japan's sacred soil. Kayama goes to tell his wife, Tamate, of his daunting task. In 'Tamate's Dance' ('There is no other way'), two observers comment. In 'Four Black Dragons', Fisherman, Thief and Reciter graphically describe the arrival of the American fleet, a Samurai pausing to lop off the thief's hand. Kayama fails to deter the Americans who demand an

---

[1] The phrase is a political euphemism coined by Commodore Perry in 1853.

important personage to receive them. The Shogun's councillors dress up Manjiro, who has after all been to America, to look important. He brings back an ultimatum that in six days' time Commodore Perry will land. In 'Chrysanthemum Tea', his family remind the irresolute Shogun that the fleet is still at anchor in the bay, though, having given him poison, they agree he's not in much of a position to react.

Kayama and Manjiro suggest *tatami* mats be laid to avoid foreign feet treading on sacred soil. Kayama is made Governor of Uraga and in 'Poems', he and Manjiro indulge in the Japanese pastime of making up poems while walking home, where they find Tamate has committed suicide. In 'Welcome to Kanagawa', the madam of a brothel reminds the girls the Americans are expected. The Americans land and in 'Someone in a tree', an Old Man, his Younger Self, a Warrior and the Reciter, challenged to remember the scene, describe it in what Rodney Milnes after the Coliseum première called 'the most persistently haunting number in the score'. The Americans return to their ships, the mats are burned, and the act ends with a triumphant Kabuki Lion dance.

The second act addresses the new phenomenon of Japan under the influence of the West, from 1854 to the present. Manjiro is elevated to the rank of Samurai. Five Western Admirals in turn greet Lord Abe in pidgin English and present demands, displaying outrageous and completely non-p.c. national characteristics. Kayama and Manjiro sit before tea tables, Manjiro studying the ancient ceremony, Kayama singing 'A Bowler Hat' as over ten years he becomes progressively more westernised. In the penultimate scene and to a slow waltz, three sailors mistake girls in a garden for geishas, until their father draws his sword and kills one of them. On a journey, Lord Abe and his adherents are ambushed by dissidents from the south determined to restore the old order. Manjiro challenges and kills Kayama. In the thoroughly show-biz finale entitled 'Next', Japan takes its not wholly elegant place in the modern world.

Pacific Overtures is a masterpiece, not of pastiche because that is avoided, but of delicate miniatures, hints and understatement. Its adherents prize it above anything else Sondheim has written and, in spite of initial failure at Broadway's box office, revivals are hailed with an enthusiasm that is rare for something conceived as a Broadway show.   H.

SWEENEY TODD
The Demon Barber of Fleet Street

Opera in two acts (orchestration by Jonathan Tunick), libretto by Hugh Wheeler; lyrics by the composer. Première, Uris Theater, New York, 1 March 1979, with Angela Lansbury, Len Cariou, conductor Paul Gemignani (and recorded the same year). First performed 1980, Drury Lane, London, with Denis Quilley, Sheila Hancock; Houston, 1984, with Timothy Noble, Joyce Castle, conductor John DeMain; New York City Opera, 1984, with Noble, Rosalind Elias, conductor Gemignani; Detroit, 1984; Royal Academy of Music, London, 1986; State Opera of South Australia, Adelaide, 1987, with Lyndon Terracini, Nancy Hayes, conductor Andrew Greene; Wormwood Scrubs, London, 1991, by Pimlico Opera; National Theatre, London, 1993; Tel Aviv, 1993, with Timothy Nolen, Robin Weisel-Capsouto, producer David Alden.

Sweeney Todd, *a barber* ....Baritone
Anthony Hope, *a young sailor* ....Tenor
A Beggar Woman ....Soprano
Mrs Lovett, *a seller of meat pies* ....Mezzo-Soprano
Johanna, *ward of Judge Turpin* ....Soprano
Tobias Ragg, *Pirelli's assistant* ....Tenor
Adolfo Pirelli, *a mountebank barber* ....Tenor
Beadle Bamford ....Tenor
Judge Turpin...Bass-Baritone

Workmen, Londoners, Inmates of an Asylum

Place: London
Time: Late 1840s
Running Time: 2 hours 15 minutes

Sondheim on a visit to England for the London production of *Gypsy* in 1973 saw Christopher Bond's play *Sweeney Todd* at the Theatre Royal, Stratford, in London's East End and decided straight away that its melodrama should be his next project. The result is probably the most ambitious of his many stage ventures, a riveting subject, in form a ballad opera not through-composed, with dialogue and recitative to link the numbers.

The subject itself may have come originally from a tale of a Scottish cannibal family of around 1600; or of a London murder around 1780; or from a French story of murders by a barber in the early nineteenth century. Its modern form dates from 1846 when an English 'penny dreadful' serialised it over eighteen issues; it was dramatised the following year by one George Dibdin Pitt, and this stage version was the first of many. Christopher Bond's play elaborates the social commentary and introduces an element of revenge into the original – Todd as a victim of society driven to crime.

Prologue. 'Attend the tale of Sweeney Todd' sings the company by way of overture; 'He served a dark and vengeful god'.

Act I. From a small boat come Sweeney Todd and Anthony Hope, rejoicing at seeing London again. The latter is accosted by a Beggar Woman, who seems to hope for what she calls 'a little jig jig'. She half-recognises Sweeney, who proceeds to excoriate London but falls to remembering a certain barber and his wife, the latter stolen away by a 'pious vulture of the law'.

Anthony leaves and Mr Todd encounters Mrs Lovett. She serves him a specimen of what she describes as 'probably the worst pies in London', and Todd asks to rent the room over her shop – it's haunted, she says; once lived in by a barber called Benjamin Barker. His wife was raped by a Judge and he was transported for life – 'Poor thing!' comes the refrain of her song. She's dead now, their daughter a ward of the Judge. By the end of the song she has convinced herself Todd was once Barker. Mrs Lovett kept Barker's razors and fetches them from a back room: he can be a barber again, now, she says! He recognises them – 'My friends' – and the company salutes him with a reprise of the opening ballad.

Johanna from Judge Turpin's house wonders how a bird incarcerated in a cage can still sing so sweetly ('Green finch and linnet bird'). Anthony appears, falls in love as soon as he sees her, and, after hearing from the Beggar Woman whose house it is, sings 'I feel you, Johanna'.

Tobias sings to attract a crowd to Pirelli's caravan, but Todd pronounces Pirelli's Miracle Elixir for bald heads as no more than 'piss with ink', and enlists the Beadle to judge whether he or Pirelli can provide the faster, smoother shave, or better pull a tooth. The Beadle confirms his victory, then promises to visit Todd's shop before the week is out.

Mrs Lovett calms the impatient Sweeney – 'Wait'; planning is half the fun. Anthony tells them he has fallen in love with a beautiful girl kept locked up at Judge Turpin's. She has given him the key and will elope with him – but where to? Bring her to Fleet Street, says Sweeney. Pirelli arrives with Tobias. He worked for Barker years ago and has recognised his razors. He tries blackmail on Todd, who bundles him into a trunk, and, when he's got rid of Tobias, extracts Pirelli from the trunk and cuts his throat.

Another verse of the Ballad introduces Judge Turpin, who sings conscience-stricken of Johanna, whom he loved once as a daughter, now pants after as a dirty old man. He strikes himself with a whip – then tells Johanna to forget the young sailor. He has someone else in mind for her; himself! Johanna tells Anthony of her predicament and together they rather frantically plot their escape. The Judge tells the Beadle he plans to marry Johanna; he must smarten up first, says the Beadle – by means of a visit to Sweeney Todd's barber shop. The young lovers continue their by no means placid duetting, while Judge and Beadle move towards the barber's.

Mrs Lovett is at first horrified but later mollified when Sweeney tells her why he killed Pirelli, then announces that the Judge is waiting below. Todd gleefully plots revenge while the Judge complacently contemplates marriage ('Pretty woman'). Todd raises his arm to slash the Judge's throat but Anthony's sudden arrival causes the intended victim to run outside. Mrs Lovett tries to console the frustrated executioner, and they come up with a plan which will dispose of Pirelli, keep Todd's hand in for the Judge's return, and ensure plentiful fresh meat for Mrs Lovett's pies. In a swinging waltz rhythm, one of the score's best and most exhilarating numbers, they rehearse: 'Now let me see ... We've got tinker. No, no, something pinker. Tailor? Paler. Butler? Subtler. Potter? Hotter. Locksmith? Lovely bit of clerk. Maybe for a lark. Then again, there's sweep if you want it cheap and you like it dark'.

Act II. Mrs Lovett is in the money, Tobias is working as a waiter and drumming up trade while Todd waits restlessly upstairs. A barber's chair arrives and Todd and Mrs Lovett elaborately rehearse the procedure; once someone is in the chair he'll pound three times then pull a lever and down the body'll go to feed the customers. Anthony and Todd can be heard singing dreamily of Johanna but customers arrive to be shaved and it is to the accompaniment of 'Johanna' that they are prepared for the oven.

Smoke billows from Mrs Lovett's chimney and the Beggar Woman sings 'City on fire! Mischief!' Todd continues to feed customers down the chute, while Anthony searches for Johanna, who has disappeared; he finds her in Fogg's Asylum.

Mrs Lovett is in amorous mood but as she waxes

lyrical about a wedding by the seaside Todd remains monosyllabic. Anthony's news that he has found Johanna in a madhouse suggests a plan. Wigmakers get hair from madhouses; ergo, Anthony will masquerade as a wigmaker come to buy hair of precisely Johanna's shade. Todd writes to tell Judge Turpin Johanna can be found at his house.

Tobias meanwhile affirms his loyalty to Mrs Lovett in a song ('Not while I'm around'), and during its course convinces her he has smelled more than a rat in Pirelli's disappearance. She runs to look for Todd, only to find the Beadle sitting at the harmonium while he enquires about the stink coming from their chimney. Mrs Lovett diverts him until Todd returns and gives the Beadle the treatment. His body comes down the chute just as Tobias finds evidence of human remains in the pies.

Anthony in the asylum cannot bring himself to shoot the owner but Johanna does it for him, before, to sounds of the lunatics singing 'City on fire!', they make their escape. Todd and Mrs Lovett look for Tobias, while the Beggar Woman nearly surprises Johanna in Todd's parlour had she not providentially hidden in a trunk. Todd senses the Judge's approach and gets rid of the Beggar by slitting her throat and pulling the lever before welcoming the Judge. He makes sure the Judge knows whose chair he's sitting in before cutting his throat too. In his madness, he is about to do the same for Johanna but she escapes. In the bakehouse, Mrs Lovett tries to bundle Judge and Beggar Woman into the oven, but Todd recognises his wife. Mrs Lovett pleads that she has looked after him better. But it's no good, and Todd flings her into the oven. Tobias blunders in, his hair white from shock, picks up the razor and with it slashes Todd's throat. Anthony, Johanna and two policemen watch Tobias start to turn the handle of the meat-grinder, before a repetition of the Ballad of Sweeney Todd brings down the curtain.   H.

GASPARO SPONTINI
(born 14 November 1774, died 24 January 1851)

LA VESTALE
The Vestal Virgin

Opera in three acts, libretto (in French) by Etienne de Jouy, originally written for Boïeldieu, later refused by Méhul. Première, Paris Opéra, 15 December 1807. Given at the Opéra 213 times by 1857. First produced la Scala, 1824, with Ferron; King's Theatre, Haymarket, London, 1826, with Biagnoli; Philadelphia, 1828. Revived Covent Garden, in German, 1842; la Scala, 1908, with Mazzoleni, Emilio de Marchi, Stracciari, de Angelis, conductor Toscanini; Metropolitan, 1925, with Ponselle, Matzenauer, Edward Johnson, de Luca, Mardones, conductor Serafin; Florence Festival, 1933, with Ponselle, Stignani, Melandri, Pasero, conductor Gui; la Scala, 1955, with Callas, Stignani, Corelli, Rossi-Lemeni. As can easily be deduced, La Vestale has, like Norma, through the decades been considered an opera to be revived only when a star of the brightest magnitude has been available.

Licinio, *a Roman general*......................................Tenor
Giulia, *a young Vestal virgin* ....Soprano
Cinna, *a centurion*..............................Tenor/Baritone
The Pontifex Maximus..Bass
The Chief Priestess............................Mezzo-Soprano
A Consul ....Bass

Vestals, Priests, People, Matrons, Young Women, Senators, Consuls, Lictors, Warriors, Gladiators, Dancers, Children, Prisoners

Place: Ancient Rome
Running Time: 2 hours 25 minutes

Act I. After a spacious overture, the scene is the Forum in Rome, in front of the Temple of Vesta. Preparations for the triumph of the Roman leader Licinio are in progress. Licinio admits to his friend Cinna that he still loves one of the Vestal priestesses, Giulia by name, who was once affianced to him. He has returned from the wars to find her vowed to the service of Vesta. Licinio and Cinna join their voices in a duet.

The Chief Priestess and Giulia lead the Vestals in a processional hymn towards the temple, to prepare to crown the hero of the triumph. They withdraw, and Giulia and the Priestess are left alone, for the latter to attempt in a recitative and aria that is Gluck-like in its intensity to strengthen the resolve of the former to keep her vows of chastity. Giulia prays for help and begs that she may not be in the Temple to receive the victor of the wars, but the High Priestess insists that she fulfil her duties. Giulia, left alone, sings of her guilty love.

A vast procession comes towards the temple and the people hymn the victorious general. Licinio plots with Cinna the abduction of Giulia, but in a moment it is time for her to crown him with a golden laurel wreath. An ensemble develops during which Licinio tries to tell Giulia of his plans for them to elope that very night. Licinio is congratulated on his victory, and, in a tune which might have come from *Tannhäuser* or *Rienzi*, all praise his valour which has brought them peace. The act ends with extended triumphal dances.

Act II. Night. In the temple of Vesta, the virgin priestesses worship the goddess and the High Priestess consigns to Giulia the duty of tending the sacred flame, which must never be extinguished. Alone, Giulia, in the best-known scene of the opera, prays for the goddess's intervention to release her from the profane love which torments her. The sweeping phrases, the classical shape, the underlying drama of this *scena* convincingly argue Spontini's claim (made in conversation with Wagner) to be recognised as the natural successor of Gluck, rather than as we today might think of him the contemporary and rival of Cherubini. The intense lyricism of the prayer ('Tu che invoco con orrore') is succeeded by a dramatic section ('Su questo sacro altare') in which Giulia admits to herself that her love for Licinio is all-powerful, and the aria ends with an impassioned avowal of her betrayal of trust as a priestess ('Sospendete qual che istante'). It was Rosa Ponselle's magnificent recording of this music, with its classical inevitability and its climax adorned by the most beautiful soprano voice on record, which Maria Callas used to play as her own touchstone of quality, of what she aimed at in her own singing.

Licinio enters and declares the strength of his love. Soon their voices are joined in passionate duet, and too late they notice that the flame has died out. Cinna warns them to fly while there is still time, but voices can be heard approaching and Licinio rushes off to get help. The Pontifex Maximus denounces Giulia for the neglect of her sacred duties, and she begs for death as the just reward of her impiety. In a beautiful aria ('O nume tutelar'), Giulia prays to the gods, not for herself but that Licinio may not be involved in her fate. She refuses to reveal his name to the Pontifex Maximus, who curses her and orders that she be first divested of the veil and ornaments of her priestly office and then buried alive.

Act III. Giulia's tomb lies open and waiting for her. Licinio inveighs against the cruelty of her impending fate. His friend Cinna begs him not to resort to force but to try to persuade the Pontifex Maximus to clemency. Licinio's efforts to this end meet with a blank refusal, until in despair he declares himself Giulia's fellow transgressor and in a duet denounces the cruelty the Pontifex Maximus dispenses in the name of religion.

In spite of a warning from the Augurer, the Pontifex Maximus will not relent, and Giulia is led in conducted by lictors and surrounded by Vestals, wearing the black veil of her shame. She bids farewell to her companions and to the High Priestess. Her veil is placed on the altar; if the goddess pardons her, then she will cause the veil to burn with sacred fire as a sign of forgiveness. The Vestals pray, the Pontifex Maximus orders Giulia to descend to her tomb and she tenderly bids farewell to her unnamed lover ('Caro oggetto'). Even the precipitate arrival of Licinio cannot change the course of events; Giulia denies that she even knows him, and descends into the tomb. Suddenly the sky darkens, and a shaft of lightning ignites the veil on the altar. Vesta has forgiven, Giulia is released, and the opera ends with choral and balletic rejoicings, dedicated to the glory of Venus.   H.

JOHANN STRAUSS
THE YOUNGER
(born 25 October 1825, died 3 June 1899)

DIE FLEDERMAUS
The Bat

Operetta in three acts, text by Haffner and Genée, from a French vaudeville 'Le Réveillon' by Meilhac and Halévy. First performed at the Theater an der Wien, Vienna, 5 April 1874, with Marie Geistinger, Mme Charles Hirsch, Mme Nittingwe, Szika, Rudinger, Lebrecht, Rott, conducted by the composer. First performed in London, Alhambra Theatre, 1876; New York, 1879; Vienna Opera, 1894; Metropolitan Opera, New York, 1905, with Sembrich, Alten, Edyth Walker, Dippel, Reiss. Revived in London at Covent Garden, 1930, with Lotte Lehmann, Schumann, Olszewska, Willi Wörle, Karl Jöken, Hüsch, Habich, conducted by Bruno Walter; Sadler's Wells, 1934, with Joan Cross, Ruth Naylor, Gladys Parr, Tudor Davies, Arthur Cox, Redvers Llewelyn, Percy Heming, conducted by Warwick Braithwaite. Revived at Metropolitan, New York, 1950, with Welitsch, Munsel, Stevens, Svanholm, Tucker, Brownlee, Hugh Thompson, conducted by Eugene Ormandy. A successful film in English, 'O Rosalinde!' (1955–56), starred Michael Redgrave as Eisenstein and Anneliese Rothenberger as Adele, each singing and acting; Ludmilla Tcherina acted Rosalinde while Sari Barabas sang, and Anton Walbrook was Falke.

Gabriel von Eisenstein ....Tenor

Rosalinde, *his wife*..Soprano

Frank, *the governor of the prison*....................Baritone

Prince Orlofsky, *a rich Russian*............Mezzo-Soprano

Alfred, *a singer* ....Tenor

Dr Falke, *a friend of Eisenstein* ....Baritone

Dr Blind, *Eisenstein's attorney*............................Tenor

Adele, *the Eisensteins' maid*.............................Soprano

Frosch, *the jailer*...................................Speaking Part

Place: A Spa, near a Large City (Vienna)
Time: Late Nineteenth Century
Running Time: 2 hours 30 minutes

Johann Strauss the younger was already famous as a composer of Viennese dance music before he turned his hand to operetta, his first being *Indigo* (1871), his second *Der Karneval in Rom* (1873), his third *Die Fledermaus*. The work as a whole – plot as well as score – is a masterpiece, the finest product of the Viennese operetta school, and a cornucopia of fresh, witty, pointed, memorable melody.

The overture, a potpourri, is one of the most popular ever written. The first three tunes are from the prison scene in the last act, the third being associated with the dénouement. Then comes the famous waltz with its lilting refrain, followed after a short interlude by a mournful tune on the oboe (also in 3/4), with a contrasting section (the tunes associated with Eisenstein's mock-serious farewell before going to prison). The material is repeated, the overture as a whole being dominated by its waltz.

Act I. Eisenstein's house. Outside can be heard the sound of Alfred's voice, as he serenades Rosalinde. He is, it appears, an old flame of hers, and he addresses her fittingly as his dove. Adele, the Eisensteins' maid, makes her entrance on a cadenza and proceeds to read a letter from her sister, Ida. The Ballet, of which Ida is a member, has been invited *en bloc* that night to a party[1] which is being given by Prince Orlofsky, a rich young Russian eccentric who is Vienna's latest host. If Adele can get hold of a dress, Ida can take her along – the orchestra fairly bubbles with Adele's excitement. But Rosalinde, who has heard Alfred's serenade and suspects who it is, is far too preoccupied to pay much attention to Adele's plea that she be allowed to go and look after her sick aunt. With Eisenstein due that night at the prison for the start of a five-day prison sentence, she cannot possibly think of sparing anybody; he must have a good supper before he leaves. Alfred waits until Adele has gone and then tells Rosalinde he has heard that Eisenstein will be away for a few days; he will call again that evening. Rosalinde is beside herself: as long as he doesn't sing she is all right – but he is a tenor and who could resist the sound of his top A?

Eisenstein storms in with his advocate, Dr Blind, who, says Eisenstein, is to blame for the whole affair of the prison sentence, most of all that he is now being

---

[1] The 1870s saw a period of considerable moral permissiveness, in Vienna as elsewhere, even though the rules of conduct were outwardly strict. 'Pleasure', as represented by escape from the 'rule' and the family, was mainly a masculine preserve, and the dancers at Prince Orlofsky's party show the *demi-monde* in contact with society, whose pleasure-ground it was and off whom it lived. Masks covered so wide a multitude of sins that some 'respectable' ladies with their help might hope for a little discreet adventure on their own account. It is sometimes forgotten that *Fledermaus* is Strauss's only opera set virtually in Vienna itself.

sent down for eight days, not five. There is a lively trio for Rosalinde, Eisenstein, and Blind, in which Rosalinde protests her grief – perhaps a shade too much – Eisenstein rages at Blind, and the lawyer runs through a list of legal expedients he will call into play.

The lawyer leaves, Adele, still in tears about her mythical aunt, is sent off to order a delicious supper for the master, and Rosalinde goes to look out some old clothes for him to go to prison in. Enter Dr Falke, a friend of Eisenstein's, who has, we should know, been secretly nursing a grievance against him ever since Carnival. It seems that Falke, dressed as a bat (hence the title), was left asleep by Eisenstein to find his way home in broad daylight and in his unconventional costume. He has a plan, though Eisenstein has not the least suspicion of it, for revenge. Why, he says, should Eisenstein not accept the invitation from Prince Orlofsky which Falke brings him, and go in disguise to the ball, giving himself up to the prison authorities next morning? Rosalinde need never know – nor need Eisenstein guess that Rosalinde is also being asked to the party, at which she will wear a mask. The Bat's revenge is taking shape, and Eisenstein receives the invitation to the strains of the same polka which accompanied Adele's reading of the letter from her sister earlier on. He accepts it with a minimum of shilly-shallying.

Rosalinde is astonished to hear that her husband is going off to prison in style, in evening dress in fact, but she is so preoccupied with the prospect of Alfred's disturbing promise to come back at supper-time that she accepts a flimsy excuse. All is prepared; Rosalinde, Adele (who has, after all, been given the night off, in preparation for Alfred's expected visit), and Eisenstein sing a farewell trio, which is one of the most delicious moments of the score. Rosalinde still grieves in exaggerated fashion in the *moderato espressivo*, but none of the three can keep long faces for ever, and the refrain to each of Rosalinde's utterances glitters and sparkles as gaily as the parties they each of them enjoy in anticipation. Rosalinde ends with a ringing top C, and Eisenstein bustles off.

Alfred keeps his promise, and Eisenstein is hardly out of the house before his wife's admirer is eating the supper that was originally prepared for him. 'Trinke, Liebchen, trinke schnell', sings the tenor, and Rosalinde joins in the refrain, although she cannot help noticing that her companion is beginning to show the effects of the wine he so melodiously urges her to drink. The drinking song is interrupted by the sound of voices below and Frank, the new prison governor, appears, with the information that he has come to escort Herr von Eisenstein, who is to be his guest for the next eight days, to prison. Alfred ropes him in to sing the chorus of his song, but denies hotly that he is Eisenstein when Frank addresses him by name. The situation looks compromising, but Rosalinde carries it off with impressive bravado: does the governor think she would be at supper as late as this with someone who is not her husband? 'Mein Herr, was dächten Sie von mir?' (What inferences would you draw?) she sings, and reconciles Frank to the delay and Alfred to his probable fate in the enchanting slow waltz refrain to her song. Rosalinde fears the worst – Alfred and her husband will almost certainly meet in prison – but what can she do? A farewell kiss, and Frank, who is also going to Orlofsky's party, hurries Alfred off, a brisk trio bringing the act to its end.

Act II. The party at Prince Orlofsky's is in full swing, and the opening chorus leaves us in no doubt as to its successful nature. Although he is too blasé to enjoy them himself, Prince Orlofsky likes his parties to go well – but woe betide anyone who refuses to drink with him; he will get a bottle thrown at his head. His song, 'Ich lade gern mir Gäste ein', a mixture of languid nonchalance and adolescent gaucherie, is perfect characterisation. With its repeated A flats, it is not exactly the easiest music for a mezzo-soprano to sing, requiring as it does a rich lower register if the refrain (ending with a reiterated 'Chacun à son goût') is to make its full effect.

Eisenstein, who is introduced as Marquis Renard, feels sure that he can recognise in one of the guests his wife's maid, Adele, but Orlofsky and the rest laugh at him for his curious mistake and Adele herself sings a delightful soubrette song, 'Mein Herr Marquis', in whose laughing refrain she is able to make fun of her employer to her heart's content. Apart from the famous waltz, this is possibly the best-known number of the score.

Eisenstein has recognised his maid, although he is persuaded to the contrary, but he does not know his wife when she comes in masked and announced as a Hungarian Countess. She excites his curiosity straight away, and it is not long before he is showing her his chiming watch, a bait which has worked the trick on many an unsuspecting Miss. This time, though all seems to be beginning well and Eisenstein is soon timing his Countess's heart-beats, something goes wrong, and the lady ends up with the watch, which is not at all according to plan. It is a delicious moment, this seduction duet, as anyone who has heard Julius Patzak and Hilde Gueden sing it in the recording of the opera will know, just as those who know this recording and that by Richard Tauber and Vera Schwarz will have a shrewd idea of the contrasting styles of Vienna and Berlin in this kind of music. We hear the watch chime before the singers launch into a gallop, and Rosalinde ends with peals of mocking coloratura.

Rosalinde will not unmask and it is suggested by Adele that the reason for this is that she is not a Hungarian at all. 'I will prove it,' says Rosalinde; 'the music of my native country shall speak for me.' It is a flimsy pretext for the Czardas and Frischka which follows, but once it starts the music is exhilarating enough to make us forget why it began in the first place. If there were no other reason – and there are, in fact, plenty of reasons – this Czardas would make it certain that nobody but a really capable soprano could do justice to the role of Rosalinde. It is not only a display piece of a high order, but it demands something unusual in the way of a dramatic technique. Ernest Newman has written that the Czardas 'shows what depths of expression there were in Strauss had he chosen to explore them more consistently. No genuine Hungarian could sing more movingly of the pain of separation from the beloved homeland, or of the fire in the Hungarian breast that drives them to the dance ... '.

The finale begins. It opens with a short section in praise of champagne, *allegro con brio*. First Orlofsky, then Adele and finally Eisenstein lead the company, which joins in the chorus after three verses. Eisenstein and Frank (who has been introduced as the Chevalier Chagrin) toast each other, and Falke, looking round at the assembled couples, proposes in a beautiful slow waltz that they shall pledge each other in eternal brother- and sisterhood. Coherent expression seems out of place, and in their efforts to do justice to the toast, they resort to 'Duidu' and 'la, la, la', relapsing before long into silence for the ballet which, with its dancers, has been mentioned all along as one of the attractions of the party. At the end of the ballet, Orlofsky suggests that the professional dancers should have a rest, and that the guests should show that they are no less adept at the

waltz themselves. It is the famous *Fledermaus* waltz, heard first in the overture but now unmistakably staking a claim as rival to 'The Blue Danube'. It takes the foreground for most of the time, but also serves as background for the continued flirtation of Eisenstein and Rosalinde and for much comic byplay between Eisenstein and Governor Frank. Finally, the clock strikes six, Eisenstein remembers it is high time for him to go to prison, and the curtain comes down as he and Frank help each other from the ballroom.

Act III. An entr'acte, part march, part waltz, introduces us to the prison, where Frosch the jailer (a speaking part) has been doing his best to emulate in his own quiet way the grander drinking exploits of Governor Frank; in a word, he is drunk, a situation of which full advantage is taken by the professional comic engaged to play the role. His inebriated gambollings are interrupted from time to time by snatches of song from cell No. 12, where Alfred is relieving the tedium of prison life with reminiscences of his serenade to Rosalinde, and with snatches of tunes from other operas as well, if the truth be known. Frosch staggers off to make another attempt to curb this nuisance, and no sooner has he gone than Frank comes in, only a little less the worse for wear than his underling. He makes his entrance to musical accompaniment, whistles the tune of the ballroom waltz, sings a bit of the champagne song, and soon falls asleep to reminiscences of the waltz.

But his is not to be the sleep of the just, for Frosch has pulled himself together sufficiently to be able to make his morning report in the usual way. Nothing untoward has happened, he says, except that Herr von Eisenstein has been restive and, having asked for a lawyer, is to see Dr Blind almost immediately. The door-bell rings, and Frosch announces the two young ladies who have so taken Frank's fancy at the ball, to wit Adele and her sister. Adele, it is explained, is not yet an artist in fact, only one by nature. Cannot Frank help her to start a stage career? She sings to him of her versatility ('Spiel' ich die Unschuld vom Lande') and says there is nothing she cannot play on the stage, from country wench to Queen – to say nothing of a flirtatious French Marquise. There is another ring at the door, and the Marquis Renard is admitted. When he hears that the Chevalier Chagrin (whom he at first assumes to have been arrested for insobriety) is none other than the prison governor, he laughs aloud at what he thinks is a particularly good jest. Frank for his part cannot take seriously the announcement that his friend from the ball is Herr von Eisenstein; did he not himself escort that gentleman from his home to the prison, and is he not at this moment incarcerated within twenty feet of where they sit?

Frosch announces that another lady is without (the first two have been shown into cell No. 13), and Frank goes to greet her, leaving Eisenstein to waylay Blind and borrow his wig, glasses and legal paraphernalia in the hope that he may discover who was arrested in his place the previous night.

Rosalinde (she it was at the door just now) has come to see what can be done about getting Alfred out of prison, with the help maybe of the lawyer who is waiting for them. Eisenstein comes in in place of Blind and proceeds to cross-question the two with a vigour more becoming to a prosecuting counsel than to someone engaged for the defence, and they begin to wonder why he is so very strict. He demands the unvarnished truth, which he gets from Alfred in an agreeable tune, punctuated by his own frequent bursts of indignation as the story unfolds. After one of them, Rosalinde defends herself as the victim of a husband who is himself a monster of deceitfulness. Eventually, unable to bear the insults any longer – Alfred asks how they can between them throw dust in the husband's eyes – Eisenstein rises in fury and denounces (to the tune which opens the overture) what he describes as their treachery, whereupon she produces the watch.

The explanation is not long in forthcoming. No sooner is the rather grandiose trio between Rosalinde, Eisenstein and Alfred over, than the rest of the company at last night's ball appears as if summoned by magic, all that is to say apart from Adele and her sister – and news of them is quickly forthcoming when Frosch complains to Frank that the two ladies in No. 13 are proving obstructive and have refused to let him give them their regulation bath! Falke explains that Eisenstein's predicament is of his engineering, is in fact his vengeance for the shabby trick played on him a year ago. Alfred and Rosalinde are quick to take advantage of the situation and add that their supper was also an invention designed as part of the joke. Eisenstein is delighted at the way things have turned out, and Rosalinde sings the only possible moral: let all join with her in praising the sovereign reconciling power of King Champagne!   H.

EINE NACHT IN VENEDIG
A Night in Venice

Operetta in three acts, libretto by F. Zell and Richard Genée. Première, Friedrich-Wilhelmstädtische Theater, Berlin, 3 October 1883. First produced in Vienna at Theater an der Wien a week later; New York, 1884. Revived Berlin, 1925, with Richard Tauber, conductor Korngold; Vienna, 1948, with Esther Réthy, Helge Roswaenge, Kunz, Fritz Krenn, conductor Paulik; Komische Oper, Berlin, 1954, with new libretto by Walter Felsenstein, who produced; London, English National Opera, 1976 (arrangement by Murray Dickie and Anton Paulik), with Valerie Masterson.

The Duke of Urbino	Tenor
Caramello, *a barber*	Tenor (or Baritone)
Delacqua, *a senator*	Baritone
Barbara, *his wife*	Mezzo-Soprano
Barbaruccio, *a senator*	Baritone
Pappacoda, *a cook*	Tenor (or Baritone)
Annina, *a young fish-seller*	Soprano
Ciboletta, *Barbara's maid*	Soprano
Agricola	Mezzo-Soprano
Enrico Piselli	Speaking Part

Senators, Senators' Wives, Fishermen, Gondoliers

Place: Venice
Time: Late Eighteenth Century
Running Time: 2 hours

The first night in Berlin appears to have been a fiasco, mainly because of the libretto. Revision (as with so many operettas) was embarked on almost immediately, to considerable effect, and the operetta has proved – often in a 'new version' – one of the most successful from Strauss's pen.

The overture is a bright compilation of tunes from the opera, in which waltzes play their accustomed part – this is eighteenth-century Venice observed through the eyes and ears of late nineteenth-century Vienna. The famous 'Lagunenwalzer' is a particularly delectable component.

Act I. A crowd of Venetians are rejoicing in the splendour of their city, when Pappacoda congratulates them in a song on having acquired what they have hitherto lacked, a real maker of macaroni – from Naples of course. Young Enrico Piselli, nephew of Senator Delacqua and admirer of the Senator's young wife Barbara, finds in Pappacoda a convenient messenger for the note he means to send to Barbara telling her he will meet her that night.

Along comes Ciboletta, Pappacoda's own sweetheart and Barbara's maid, to engage Pappacoda in a duet that is bright enough in spite of Ciboletta's insistence that the duplicity of men will always defeat their urge towards straight dealing.

Enter Annina, crying her wares to a delicious slow waltz: 'Frutta di mare'. Annina has a suitor, Caramello, who works for the Duke of Urbino as barber and general factotum, and Pappacoda loses no time in teasing her about him. The beautiful Barbara Delacqua now appears, and Pappacoda delivers the message from Enrico.

It is the turn of the older generation, and on to the scene come Delacqua himself and another senator, Barbaruccio, discussing the carnival festivities and the invitation to a masked ball which the Duke has as usual extended to them and their wives. Delacqua is concerned to gain the vacant position of steward to the Duke. Unfortunately, the Duke is a well-known libertine, and Delacqua has thought it prudent to send Barbara by gondola on a visit to the island of Murano.

Now appears Caramello, who hears from Pappacoda of Delacqua's plot to have Barbara safely out of harm's way at carnival time. He immediately decides that he himself will take the gondolier's place and convey her to the palace of the Duke who, he knows, was captivated by her beauty during last year's carnival. Barbara for her part has been told that she is to spend a little time at Murano, but, anxious not to miss her rendezvous with Enrico, she hastily arranges for Annina to take her place in the gondola.

In a brilliant duet with Caramello, Annina keeps him at arm's length and compares him to the migratory swallow, which by its very nature denies constancy – 'Pellegrina rondinella'. Not everyone is so lighthearted; Ciboletta is in tears because Pappacoda has no money to take her dancing. The problem is solved by Caramello handing out invitations to his master's masked ball and all is happiness again – the four lovers rejoice in a quartet at the prospect of the dance, although Ciboletta feels the need to make it clear that dancing is what she is going for and nothing else.

At last it is the turn of the Duke to appear from his gondola and apostrophise his favourite city: 'Sei mir gegrüsst, du holdes Venezia'.[1] When he encounters the senators, they tell him that unfortunately their wives cannot accept his kind invitation to the dance. Caramello whispers to the Duke that it is all a plot to keep the fair Barbara from him but that he, Caramello, is taking care of the whole problem. Delacqua thinks that the coveted stewardship may be brought a little nearer if he can somehow dangle Barbara in front of the Duke's nose, and he therefore sets about procuring someone to take her place in his scheme. He bids a fond farewell to his wife and a typically operetta intrigue is under way. Caramello loses no time in confiding to the Duke that he has arranged to identify himself to Barbara by a particular song. From now on almost nobody will ever again appear as him- or herself.

The Duke's song breathes the very spirit of joyful anticipation, and it is wholly appropriate in the circumstances that, as he sings it, his voice should be joined by those of Annina, Ciboletta, Barbara, and Pappacoda. It is not long before the voice of Caramello (or it could be that of the Duke himself) can be heard singing the pre-arranged gondolier's song ('Komm' in die Gondel'), a richly swaying waltz. Annina waves to Delacqua, who smiles as he sees (as he thinks) his wife off to Murano. Delacqua's attention is attracted to a party of serenaders, who greet him in terms of exaggerated praise: 'O Delacqua, qua, qua, qua, qua'. It is typical of Strauss's prodigal tunefulness that it is not easy to decide whether the mock serenade to the old cuckold or the romantic serenade of the mock gondolier is the more attractive! The ruse is entirely successful and the 'Ho-a-ho' of the gondolier's song is heard from the distance as the act comes to an end.

Act II. The entr'acte is a reprise of the gondolier's song and the curtain rises on the ballroom of the Duke's palace. Agricola leads the ladies in greeting the Duke, who wants to pursue his latest adventure, with the beautiful Barbara. Annina seems delighted at the predicament her substitution has led her into ('Was mir der Zufall gab')[2] and nothing Caramello can say (duet, 'Hör mich, Annina') will divert her from her intention of extracting as much enjoyment as she can from the situation. The Duke pursues his advantage with reminders of what she said to him last year.

---

[1] Imported by Erich Wolfgang Korngold, for his successful 1923 edition of the operetta, from Johann Strauss's *Simplizius* (1887).

[2] With new words ('Treu sein das liegt mir nicht') transferred in Korngold's edition to the Duke and frequently recorded with the new text by German tenors.

The complications are by no means over. Pappacoda cannot find Ciboletta and is beside himself with worry. His friends from all over the town are on the other hand delighted with the party that the invitations passed out by Caramello have brought them to.[1] Now Delacqua introduces his 'wife', and the Duke, for all that Annina points out that it is Ciboletta in disguise, greets her with studied elegance. Here a snag ensues, because Delacqua's drilling of Ciboletta hopelessly misfires, and instead of asking the Duke for the position of steward for her husband, she begs him, with Pappacoda in mind, for that of chief cook! The Duke now takes Annina and Ciboletta to supper and pays compliments quite indiscriminately to each, much to the dismay of Caramello and Pappacoda, who are waiting at table. The announcement that, at midnight, by custom all must repair to the Piazza San Marco, precipitates a lively end to the act.

Act III. The Piazza San Marco. As the opening chorus proclaims, the carnival spirit is still very much in evidence and the pigeons are extolled as symbols of love. But while it is given to some to enjoy the fun, others are inevitably roused to jealousy, though few give vent to their feelings in music of such hypnotically melodious a cast as does Caramello when he sees Annina on the Duke's arm: 'Ach, wie so herrlich zu schau'n' he sings to the music of the *Lagunenwalzer*, and only the refrain (purely verbal!) of 'La donna è mobile' suggests the feeling he says he has.

It is time for the general disentanglement. From Ciboletta, Delacqua finds out that Barbara is by no means on Murano as he had thought. Pappacoda is easily consoled for anything he may have suffered when Ciboletta gives him the news of his appointment as the Duke's chef, and he celebrates in a brisk little song in which, rather generously, he lets Ciboletta join. Ciboletta tells the Duke that what he thought was Barbara was Annina all the time, but he takes the news with aristocratic equanimity. To Delacqua's extreme gratification, Barbara explains that she took the wrong gondola and Enrico was kind enough to look after her. To Caramello's delight, he is made the Duke's steward – and, no doubt to the Duke's, his intended wife Annina will never be far away. All ends with suitable carnival rejoicing.   H.

DER ZIGEUNERBARON
The Gipsy Baron

Operetta in three acts, text by Ignatz Schnitzer, adapted from Jókai Mór's story *Saffi*. First performed at the Theater an der Wien, Vienna, 24 October 1885; at the Staatsoper, Vienna, 1910; New York, 1886; London, Rudolf Steiner Theatre, 1935 (amateur production). Revived, New York City Center, 1944; Volksoper, Vienna, 1948, with Esther Réthy, Laszlo Szemere, Walter Höfermayer, Alfred Jerger, conducted by Anton Paulik; Metropolitan, 1959, with Della Casa, Gedda, conductor Leinsdorf; Sadler's Wells, 1964, with June Bronhill, Nigel Douglas, conductor Vilem Tausky.

Graf Peter Homonay ....Baritone
Conte Carnero ....Baritone
Sandor Barinkay ....Tenor
Kalman Zsupan, *a pig-farmer*.........................Baritone
Arsena, *his daughter*......................................Soprano
Mirabella, *her governess* ....Contralto
Ottokar ....Tenor
Czipra, *a gipsy leader* ....Mezzo-Soprano
Saffi, *her foster-daughter* ....Soprano
Pali, *a gipsy*..Bass

Place: Hungary
Time: Eighteenth Century
Running Time: 2 hours 10 minutes

One of the most successful of Johann Strauss's works, *Der Zigeunerbaron* may be thought of as nearer in style to folk opera than operetta. Its place at the heart of the repertory of the Volksoper in Vienna has nonetheless never been in doubt.

Act I. The overture, as is Strauss's custom, is based on tunes from the opera. The scene is the edge of a village, where stands a deserted and partly ruined castle and a small peasant house. Nearby is a gipsy's hut. Rustic noises in the orchestra introduce a lazy, typically Straussian tune in 6/8 rhythm which is sung by the chorus. Ottokar, a young peasant, comes in vigorously cursing his continued lack of success in finding the treasure which is supposed to be hidden in the castle. Czipra, an old gipsy woman, mocks him for his love of Arsena, daughter of the rich pig-farmer, Zsupan, who lives nearby.

On to the scene comes a little group, headed by Sandor Barinkay, to whom by rightful inheritance belongs the castle; he is about to get it back with the

---

[1] Here for many years has been introduced a *Schwipslied* (or Tipsy Song) for Annina. The conductor Anton Paulik chose the Annen-Polka for a revival for Esther Réthy, and woe betide the Annina who now omits it!

help of Conte Carnero, Commissioner of Morals, who accompanies him. Barinkay gives a vivid account of his experiences in a song ('Als flotter Geist') which has a swinging waltz refrain in which the chorus joins and which is familiar to anyone who has ever seen a Strauss film. Carnero wants witnesses for the official reinstatement, but Czipra, pressed into service, says she cannot write and proceeds to read the hands of Barinkay and Carnero. Barinkay will find both happiness and fortune through a faithful wife, who will tell him through a dream how he can discover hidden treasure. Carnero too will find a treasure, now much increased in size, which he had thought lost years before. This mystifies the Commissioner, who cannot remember any such loss.

Zsupan is to be the other witness, and he appears, explaining in the thickest of country accents and the most comical of tunes ('Ja, das Schreiben und das Lesen') that reading and writing have never come his way; he is content with his pigs and their products. When he hears that Barinkay is to be his neighbour, he warns him to expect some litigation in the matter of property; Barinkay suggests that a match with Zsupan's daughter would prevent any such unpleasantness, and Zsupan calls his daughter from the house. It is not Arsena who answers his summons but Mirabella, her governess, who turns out to be no other than Carnero's long-lost wife (*Schatz* = darling, as well as treasure). She explains in a song that she had thought him lost these twenty-four years. Czipra's first prophecy is fulfilled.

Arsena eventually makes her appearance, veiled and by no means overjoyed at the prospect of another suitor, as she makes quite clear in a charming song. In spite of Barinkay's graceful proposal of marriage, in spite of the charm of her song, Arsena has fully made up her mind not to marry Barinkay, for the very good reason that she already has a lover; she says she requires a noble suitor and warns Barinkay not to singe his wings moth-like at the candle flame.

Barinkay is left alone, disconsolate at his failure. He overhears Saffi, Czipra's daughter, sing a gipsy song in praise of the loyalty the gipsy prides himself on showing to his friend ('So elend und so treu'); it ends with an impassioned *allegretto*. Barinkay is not slow to accept the invitation of the beautiful gipsy girl and her mother and joins them for supper.

It turns out to be Ottokar with whom Arsena is in love, and their after-dark flirtation is observed and overheard by Barinkay, Saffi, and Czipra, the former swearing to be revenged on Arsena for her cavalier treatment of him. The gipsies can be heard in the distance singing the song Saffi has already made known to us, and when they appear Czipra tells them that Barinkay is the true owner of the castle. They make him their chief, and he loses no time in knocking on Zsupan's door and telling him that he now has the title on which Arsena insisted: he is a Gipsy Baron. 'Er ist Baron' sings the ensemble, and Saffi welcomes him to the land of his childhood in a tune already familiar from the overture. Zsupan starts to tell Barinkay he is not the right sort of Baron, but Barinkay makes it quite clear that his ideas have changed; he does not want to marry Arsena, but Saffi! Zsupan is furious, but all join in the big tune of the overture which comes as it were as the coda of the finale.

Act II. The entr'acte, consisting of the tune of the opening chorus of Act I, introduces the dawn. Barinkay has spent the night in the ruins of the castle, with Czipra and Saffi, and the three greet the day in a trio ('Mein Aug' bewacht') which ends in something more like a love duet for the two young people. Czipra tells of a dream she has had in which she found the treasure which legend has always associated with the castle; Barinkay laughs at the idea, but agrees to look where she directs – what's the harm? Czipra and Saffi have a little tune in which they mock his scepticism, and all three join in the rapturous treasure waltz ('Ha, seht es winkt') when they uncover the treasure itself – one of Strauss's most charming inspirations.

The gipsies arrive to start work at their forge. They sing as they come, and the skit on the anvil chorus from *Trovatore* is unmistakable. Zsupan appears with the object of getting help for a wagon which has stuck in the mud, but he insults the gipsies who get their own back by stealing his money and his watch. His cries of fury bring Carnero, Mirabella, Ottakar, and Arsena on to the scene, and they are followed by Barinkay and Saffi. Barinkay is by now dressed as a Gipsy Baron and he greets them with the information that he and Saffi are man and wife. Carnero starts to ask certain questions about the legal side of the affair, and Saffi and Barinkay answer him in a duet which has become the most famous number of the opera: 'Wer uns getraut?' (Who married us?). The birds have performed the ceremony and acted as witness, says Barinkay, and he joins Saffi in the slow refrain.

This is too much for Carnero, who leads Mirabella and Zsupan in a comic ode to morality, the so-called 'Sittencommissions Couplets'.

There is a diversion when Ottokar finds a few pieces of gold and thinks he is on the track of the treasure at last, but Barinkay disillusions him, and the next moment the stage is full of a recruiting party, headed by Barinkay's old friend, Graf Peter Homonay. Led by Homonay, they sing a recruiting song and follow it up with a stirring Czardas. Homonay refuses to be shocked at Barinkay and Saffi and in spite of the protestations of Carnero congratulates them on the match.

During the course of the finale, Czipra makes it known that Saffi is not really her daughter but a princess whom she has brought up, and who is descended from the last Pasha of Hungary – she even has documentary proof. 'Ein Fürstenkind', sings the whole company to the music of a gallop, and Saffi joins in with a couple of top Cs. Barinkay alone cannot play his part in the rejoicing: Saffi is now unapproachably above him, and he will join Ottokar and Zsupan, who have been impressed as soldiers, and go off to the wars. His regret is touchingly shown, but the act ends with the 'Werberlied' repeated by the whole company.

Act III. The entr'acte makes use of the treasure waltz, and the scene is laid in Vienna, where all are assembled to welcome the victorious army, among which are Barinkay, Ottokar, and Zsupan. Arsena sings a little song about the incompatibility of courtship and propriety, but the group is soon joined by the returning heroes. Zsupan sings to them of his exploits, which are hardly of the most military nature but which seem to have been entirely successful. Again, this is an opportunity for the comedian. In the finale, all difficulties are resolved, Arsena flies into Ottokar's arms, and Saffi appears from nowhere to greet Barinkay, who leads the full company in a final statement of the waltz refrain of his opening song.   H.

WIENER BLUT
The Viennese Spirit

Operetta in three acts, libretto by Victor Léon and Leo Stein. Première, Carl Theater, Vienna, 26 October 1899 (a failure); revived with great success at Theater an der Wien, Vienna, 1905.

Prince Ypsheim-Gindelbach,
Prime Minister of Reuss-Schleiz-Greiz .... Baritone
Balduin, Graf Zedlau, *Ambassador of
Reuss-Schleiz-Greiz to Vienna* ....Tenor
Gabriele, Gräfin Zedlau, *his wife* ....Soprano
Graf Bitowski ....Acted
Demoiselle Franziska Cagliari, *a Viennese dancer,
Zedlau's mistress* ....Soprano
Kagler, *her father, a circus manager*......................Buffo

Diplomats
    Marquis de la Fassade ....Acted
    Lord Percy..Acted
    Principe de Lugando ....Acted
Pepi Pleininger, *a mannequin* ....Soprano
Josef, *Graf Zedlau's valet* ....Baritone
Anna, *Demoiselle Cagliari's maid* ....Acted

Place: Vienna
Time: The Congress of Vienna, 1814–15
Running Time: 1 hour 40 minutes

The project for a new operetta, with music from various earlier works of Strauss's, and to a libretto of the time of the Congress of Vienna by Léon and Stein (who six years later wrote *The Merry Widow*), was handed over by Strauss himself before his death to Adolf Müller, a leading Viennese theatrical conductor. The result is a compilation, not a newly minted work, but it has, unlike most of Strauss's operettas, a first-rate book, much enchanting music and it is no accident that it should have obtained a popularity after Strauss's death won by only a few of his own original stage works.

Act I. The scene is the villa of Count Zedlau, Ambassador to Vienna of Reuss-Schleiz-Greiz, a small (and mythical) state whose Prime Minister is also in Vienna for the Congress. At the villa, where Count Zedlau whiles away the time with the dancer Franziska Cagliari, the intrigue is introduced by Josef, the Count's valet, who has secret papers for his master's perusal but who can't find him anywhere. Josef's urgent calls for Anna, the maid, produce instead Franzi, who is also anxious to know where the Count is; after all he has been away for five whole days. Her father, Kagler, a richly comic figure of impeccably Viennese background, now calls at the villa to make sure that his daughter is to perform that night at the ball at Count Bitowski's house. He disappears when Count Zedlau is announced.

At first, Franzi is a little cool; hasn't the Count been with another woman? Only with his wife, for appearance's sake, he replies to a caressing waltz tune that would melt harder hearts than Franzi's. When Franzi has gone, the Count tells the faithful Josef that he and the Countess were seen together by the Prime Minister, who appears to have taken her for his mistress, not his wife. Anyhow, he (the Count) has discovered a most attractive mannequin, with whom he wants to arrange a rendezvous as soon as possible. Why not the fête at Hietzing that very evening, suggests Josef, and the Count insists, in a charming duet, that Josef should write her the letter making an assignation ('O komm, zum Stelldichein').

When the Count has gone, there enters Josef's girl-friend, Pepi, the model – it is she, of course, for whom the Count has fallen and to whom Josef has just unsuspectingly written the letter. She is going to Hietzing that night, but unfortunately Josef cannot take her as he will be on duty – their Polka duet ('Leichter Blut') is suitably fetching. Pepi has come about the dress Franzi is to wear at Count Bitowski's party, and she finishes her business just as the Prime Minister arrives to see his ambassador. Josef tries to gain time by saying that neither the Count nor the Countess is at home, but Kagler, who chooses this moment to reappear and thinks the reference is to his daughter, contradicts him roundly. When therefore Franzi comes in a moment later (finale), it is hardly surprising that the Prime Minister thinks she is Countess Zedlau, and starts to sympathise with her husband's wayward behaviour. Nothing Franzi can say makes him understand the true situation, but when she goes out in a huff, he laments the *faux pas* he seems obviously to have made.

It is the moment for a new complication, and the real Countess makes her entrance; to the charming tune of 'Morgenblätter' she greets the room she knows so well. When the Prime Minister returns, he takes the Countess for the Count's mistress and seizes the opportunity of upbraiding the Count for his lack of taste in bringing his mistress to the villa. Appropriately Franzi comes in, and the Count is faced with his wife and his mistress each asking 'Who is the lady?', and with his Prime Minister mistaking the one for the other and treating each – as he thinks – appropriately. The Count has a brainwave: to save the situation, will the Prime Minister help him by introducing 'the lady' as *his* wife? No sooner said than done; unfortunately the Prime Minister chooses the wrong lady, and it is the Countess whom he presents to Franzi as his wife. The ensemble ends with doubts distinctly unresolved.

Act II. Count Bitowski's ball starts with a Polonaise sung by the guests, but soon Count and Countess Zedlau are discussing their marriage, which went wrong, they agree, because of his lack in its early stages of the Viennese spirit – at the words 'Wiener Blut' there is the obvious musical reference. Now, he agrees in a song, he seems to have substituted the attitude of a Viennese Don Juan for the serious temperament natural to Reuss-Schleiz-Greiz. The Count is in danger of falling in love again with his own wife and is only mildly disconcerted when Franzi tells him she thinks the woman the Prime Minister introduced as his wife was in fact a mistress of the Count's. Suddenly, however, he sees Pepi in the crowd and takes the chance of slipping the note of assignation into her hand; to a reprise of the waltz tune, she reads it, recognises the writing as Josef's and takes it as having come from him. When Josef appears, seeming preoccupied with his duties, he consoles her in a languorous tune and explains that he cannot take her to Hietzing. She is at first vexed with him, but later realises that the note must have been from the Count. The invitation is one she feels she can under the circumstances accept.

The comedy of mistaken identity becomes rapidly more intricate. First, pointing to the Countess, the Prime Minister warns Kagler (the father, as he thinks, of the Countess) that his daughter has a rival. Next, the Countess, seeing her husband confirming the rendezvous with Pepi, assumes that Pepi is his mistress Franzi, of whom she has heard. When the Countess asks her husband to take her that night to Hietzing, he refuses on the grounds that he has business with the Prime Minister, repeating the excuse to Franzi when she makes a similar request. The Prime Minister tells Franzi that he will prevent the Count taking his mistress (in reality the Countess) to Hietzing, but, as the finale begins, is persuaded by the Countess (whom he still thinks is the mistress) to take her there himself.

A further twist: when Franzi and the Countess meet, the Prime Minister introduces them as each other. They burst out laughing and the Countess indicates Pepi, who she thinks is Franzi. Pepi will have none of it, and points to Franzi. When Josef is appealed to, he over-simplifies matters by denying that any of the three is the real Franzi. The Count laughs the whole matter off and leads the company in praise of the Viennese waltz. This finale contains sections from both 'Wine, Women and Song' and 'The Blue Danube', as well as 'Wiener Blut'.

Act III. The fête at Hietzing. Three couples have arranged rendezvous: the Countess and the Prime Minister, Franzi and Josef, the Count and Pepi, and their individual duos, interrupted by the popping of three champagne corks, become a sextet when the Count from his arbour leads a drinking song ('Wine, Women and Song'). One after the other emerges from seclusion – the Prime Minister unfortunately falls asleep – and discovers one or more of the complications around them. In the end everyone knows who everyone else is, the Count vouches for Pepi's innocence, and the motto is supplied when the Prime Minister gives it as his opinion that it is all due to – 'Wiener Blut!' H.

RICHARD STRAUSS
(born 11 June 1864, died 8 September 1949)

Strauss grew up immersed in music and opera, since his father, Franz, was principal horn in the Munich Court Orchestra. Richard Strauss made his name as a composer with a series of spectacular tone-poems, but in his first two operas he wrestled with the ghost of 'Richard I', Richard Wagner, his Munich predecessor in so many ways. *Salome*, his third opera, was his first completely successful work for the stage. Hugo von Hofmannsthal wrote the libretto for *Elektra*, and so began one of the most successful partnerships in operatic history. For all its apparent daring, Strauss's music owes its allegiance to the first Viennese school. With Hofmannsthal he found the ideal collaborator, one who looked back to the past and explored new ground as well. *Der Rosenkavalier* fulfilled his aim of writing 'a Mozart opera', a twentieth-century reinvention of *Le nozze di Figaro*. Later, they tackled *Die Zauberflöte* in *Die Frau ohne Schatten* and, in their last collaboration, they revisited Johann Strauss's territory in *Arabella*. They were also inspired by Molière (*Ariadne auf Naxos*) and continued to find their sources in classical myth (*Aegyptische Helena*). Strauss himself wrote the text for one of his most radical works, *Intermezzo*, based on his marriage to the soprano Pauline de Ahna. After

Hofmannsthal died, Strauss worked with several different writers: he returned to the 'safe' territory of myth in *Daphne* and *Die Liebe der Danae*. Less successful were Stefan Zweig's libretto for *Die schweigsame Frau*, based on Ben Jonson, and Joseph Gregor's realisation of Zweig's synopsis for *Friedenstag*. Richard Strauss's last work, *Capriccio*, aptly celebrates opera itself, as it explores the triangular relationship formed by words, poetry and a soprano. P.

GUNTRAM

Opera in three acts, libretto by the composer, inspired by Alexander Ritter. First performance at the Grossherzogliches Hoftheater, Weimar, 10 May 1894, with Heinrich Zeller as Guntram, Pauline de Ahna (then the composer's fiancée) as Freihild, Karl Bucha as the Old Duke, Franz Schwarz as Duke Robert, conducted by the composer. Presented in Munich, unsuccessfully, 1895. Staged 'with enormous cuts' in Frankfurt, 1900, Prague, 1910.[1] Berlin Radio broadcast 'a concert performance with extensive cuts' for Strauss's seventieth birthday in 1934, conducted by Hans Rosbaud. Strauss himself cut it by forty-five minutes for a revival at the Nationaltheater, Weimar, in 1940, conducted by Paul Sixt. This version of *Guntram* has since prevailed. Staged by the Berlin Staatsoper, 1942, conducted by Robert Heger. U.S. première, Carnegie Hall, New York, 19 January 1983, with

---

[1] Richard Strauss, *Erinnerungen an die ersten Aufführungen meiner Opern*.

Reiner Goldberg as Guntram, conducted by Eve Queler. B.B.C. broadcast, 1981, with William Lewis as Guntram, Carole Farley as Freihild, Patrick Wheatley as the Old Duke, Terence Sharpe as Duke Robert, conducted by John Pritchard; Munich Festival, in concert, 1988.

The Old Duke ....Bass

Freihild, *his daughter*......................................Soprano

Duke Robert, *her husband*..............................Baritone

Singers, members of the league of 'Love's Champions'
    Guntram ....Tenor
    Friedhold ....Bass

The Duke's Jester..Tenor

Poor people
    An Old Woman ....Alto
    An Old Man ....Tenor
    Two Younger Men ....Basses

Three Vassals...Basses

A Messenger...Baritone

Four Minnesingers.............................Tenors, Basses

Vassals, Minnesingers, Monks, Servants, Vagrants

Place: Germany
Time: Mid-Thirteenth Century
Running Time: 3 hours 15 minutes (revised version: 2 hours 30 minutes)

The story came from Alexander Ritter, the composer and violinist, who was married to Wagner's niece Franziska. He introduced Strauss to Wagner's music and philosophy and directed his attention to an article in the Viennese *Neue Freie Presse* which referred to 'secret, artistic-cum-religious orders, which were founded in Austria to combat the wordiness of Minnesang'.[1] This rang a bell for those who subscribed to Bayreuth's self-righteous cult. After working as assistant to Hermann Levi on *Parsifal* at Bayreuth in the summer of 1889 Strauss conducted *Lohengrin* in Weimar. The Lohengrin later created the title role in *Guntram* and the Telramund, Duke Robert. In terms of his name, Guntram = Gunther + Wolfram; in terms of the story, Guntram is at once Tannhäuser (as minstrel); Lohengrin, in that he saves Freihild/Elsa from suicide; and also Parsifal, as a 'compassionate fool' (the Old Duke's description, cut in 1940). Strauss's music also refers to many other operas by Wagner.

But *Guntram* is not merely, passively 'Wagnerian', like, say, Chabrier's *Gwendoline*. The opera comments on the phenomenon, as *Parsifal* rehearses and improves on Christianity and *The Magic Flute* rescinds Freemasonry.

Strauss's first draft of the libretto ended with Guntram repentant, about to seek atonement in a pilgrimage to the Holy Land. While on holiday in Athens, he rewrote it, probably under the joint influence of Nietzsche and Dostoevsky[2]: Guntram now leaves the league and resolves to live by his own judgement. This action represents the new Parsifal's heroic act of self-definition: as a senior member of the league, Friedhold stands for Gurnemanz and, behind him, Wagner and/or Bayreuth. The story ends with Strauss putting Wagnerism behind him, in theory at least. This is clearer in the opera's first version, when Parsifal told Freihild that it was 'Vain folly to preach redemption, if one is oneself unredeemed!' Ritter understood perfectly what this ending meant, told Strauss he had ruined his work, that its tendency was 'now eminently *immoral*', that he should burn it and for his 'inner purgation read a chapter from the Gospels or from Schopenhauer's *Ethics* or Wagner's *Religion and Art*'.[3] Strauss dedicated *Guntram* to 'My beloved parents' but wrote at the end of the score, 'Thanks be to God and to St Wagner'.

[Note: the passages in square brackets cover important details omitted in 1940 from the 1894 edition.] Duke Robert, the tyrannical ruler of a German state, has recently put down a revolution by his starving people.

Act I follows a Prelude.[4] A woodland glade by a lake, one morning in spring. Guntram gives his food to some refugees, who have fled from Duke Robert's tyranny; now, even the Duke's wife, Freihild, has been forbidden to help them. Friedhold reminds Guntram that he must do his duty as a member of the league of Love's Champions and then leaves him. Guntram wonders whether he has now reached his destination. An Old Woman curses the Duke, while the Old Man blesses Guntram, who accepts his divine mission: he resolves to intercede with Duke Robert, to use his art, his singing, to restore peace and love.

---

[1] Richard Strauss's words to Arthur Seidl, quoted in Willi Schuh, *Richard Strauss: a chronicle of the early years 1864–1898*, transl. Mary Whittall, Cambridge, 1982.
[2] Strauss first thought of calling his first opera *Schuld und Sühne* ('Crime and Atonement', *Crime and Punishment* in German).
[3] Letter of 17 January 1893, quoted in Willi Schuh, *op. cit.*
[4] The preludes to both Act I and Act II are on the scale of Strauss's tone-poems and may have been intended to have an independent life.

A woman rushes in, intending to drown herself in the lake. Guntram will not let her. [She assumes he is merely one of the Minnesingers, the minstrels, for whom she has little respect.] When her father the Old Duke is heard calling for her, Guntram learns that she is Freihild.

The Old Duke is delighted to find his daughter and asks Guntram to name his reward for rescuing her. Duke Robert appears, using his riding crop to drive the refugees in front of him. Guntram asks for mercy on their behalf. Unwillingly, Duke Robert grants his request, but his jealousy is aroused by Freihild's interest in this minstrel. Everyone sets off for the court, where a feast will mark Freihild's return.

Act II. In the court. Following the Prelude, 'Victory Celebrations at the Duke's Court', four Minnesingers praise Duke Robert obsequiously, ignoring the Fool's sarcastic comments. Inspired by Freihild, Guntram sings in praise of peace and freedom ('Friedenserzählung'). Everyone except Duke Robert is moved. Guntram then sings of war and destruction. News arrives that the rebels have risen again. Some of the vassals murmur against Duke Robert. When Guntram denounces him explicitly as the enemy of peace, the Duke draws his sword, Guntram defends himself and kills Robert. Everyone is appalled. The Old Duke challenges the vassals to kill him as well. Guntram is so shocked that he can say and do nothing. He is arrested and imprisoned, before the Old Duke goes to lead a new campaign against the rebels. Freihild realises that she is free now and that she loves Guntram. [She persuades the Fool to help him escape. Even though he knows he will not see her again, he agrees to drug the jailers and take Freihild to Guntram's cell.]

Act III. In the dungeon, under the chapel. Monks can be heard chanting above, as they watch over the corpse of Duke Robert. Guntram, haunted by remorse, seems to see the Duke's ghost. When Freihild comes, she confesses the love that Guntram's song aroused in her and urges him to flee with her. He is so confused that he faints, but recovers, to hear her insist that he was motivated entirely by love for her. His ecstasy gives way to anguish and then to certainty: he must leave her. Friedhold appears and tells him he has sinned; Guntram must now answer to the

league of Love's Champions for having broken their law of non-violence. But Guntram no longer feels subject to the league; he heeds only his own judgement. Insisting that his crime was not murdering the Duke, but the fact that he was motivated by love for Freihild, Guntram punishes himself by renouncing her forever. Meanwhile he urges her to undertake a new, benevolent role in leading society and asks her for her blessing. [The Fool enters with the news that the Old Duke has been killed: Freihild is the new ruler. Guntram bids her assume the office for the sake of the poor and suffering.] She kneels in silence and kisses his hand; he bids her farewell and leaves, alone.

'No doubt', Ernest Newman wrote in 1908, 'its Wagnerian tinge is one of the causes of the failure of *Guntram* to keep the stage; the world is growing a little weary of all these good but rather tiresome people who are continually renouncing, or being redeemed, or insisting on redeeming someone else; it finds it a little hard to bear even in Wagner, and will not stand much of it from any other musician.' He went on, however, '*Guntram* is a remarkable piece of work... curiously enough, in spite of the occasional Wagnerism of the music, the style throughout gives one the impression of being personal to Strauss... Some depth of thought and very considerable depth of feeling have gone to the making of the work.'

Strauss certainly felt warmly towards it; he claimed it had been 'dogged by misfortune from the beginning' and erected a tombstone to its memory in the garden of his Garmisch villa. Its epitaph recorded that 'the honourable and virtuous youth Guntram... had been cruelly stricken down by the symphonic orchestra of his own father'. Such terms reinforce the work's association with a son who must leave his father's home (literally, Munich; metaphorically, Wagnerism) in order to establish his own identity. In 1945 Strauss told Joseph Gregor that 'the text is no masterpiece... but it provided the 'prentice Wagnerian, sloughing his skin in the process of gaining independence, with the opportunity to write a great deal of fresh, tuneful, sappy music'.

If Bayreuth were run on rational lines, *Guntram* would be staged there, where the covered pit would suit the work ideally, as Strauss knew, and the ambience would make its own point.   P.

FEUERSNOT
The Need for Fire

Singgedicht ('poem for singing') in one act, libretto by Ernst von Wolzogen, based on J. Ketel's report 'Das erloschene Feuer zu Audenaerde' (Oudenaerde's extinguished fire) in the *Oudenaarde Gazette*, Leipzig, 1843. First performance 21 November 1901 at the Hofoper, Dresden, with Anny Krull as Diemut, Karl Scheidemantel as Kunrad, conducted by Ernst von Schuch. First U.K. performance, His Majesty's Theatre, London, 1910, conducted by Thomas Beecham, with Maude Fay and Mark Oster. First U.S. performance, Philadelphia, 1927. Strauss himself conducted a revival in 1902 in Berlin, starring Emmy Destinn, and another in 1905 in Munich. Revived at la Scala, Milan, 1912, conducted by Tullio Serafin, and by the Munich Festival in 1980 with Sabine Hass and Siegmund Nimsgern, conducted by Gustav Kuhn.

Schweiker von Gundelfingen,
    the bailiff...Low Tenor[1]

Ortolf Sentlinger, *the mayor*..........................Low Bass

Diemut, *his daughter*..............................High Soprano

Her friends
    Elsbeth ....Mezzo-Soprano
    Wigelis ....Low Contralto
    Margret ....High Soprano

Kunrad, *the alchemist*[2] ....High Baritone

Jorg Poschel, *the Leitgeb*................................Low Bass

Hämerlein, *the haberdasher*.............................Baritone

Kofel, *the blacksmith* ....Bass

Kunz Gilgenstock, *the baker and brewer*.................Bass

Ortlieb Tulbeck, *the cooper* ....High Tenor

Ursula, *his wife*...Contralto

Ruger Asbeck, *the potter* ....Tenor

Walpurg, *his wife* ....High Soprano

Citizens, Women, Children, Retainers

Place: Munich
Time: Legendary (Twelfth Century), Midsummer Eve
Running Time: 1 hour 30 minutes

Discouraged by *Guntram's* failure, particularly in Munich, Strauss did not write for the theatre for six years. But the new direction forecast in *Guntram's* last scene is evident in the tone-poems *Till Eulenspiegel* and *Tod und Verklärung*. *Feuersnot* reflects Strauss's determination to 'wreak some vengeance on my dear native town where I ... like the great Richard the First thirty years before, had such unpleasant experiences'.

The Sentlingergasse in Munich, with a view of the Gate, shortly before sunset on Midsummer Eve. Children collect wood for the bonfire that evening. The Burgomaster sets a good example by letting down to them a basket full of wood. His daughter, the beautiful Diemut, offers them some sweets. One of her three girlfriends prophesies that Diemut will be married by evening. The innkeeper warns the children to beware of Kunrad, the strange, solitary man who lives next door. Kunz Gilgenstock defends Kunrad but the old cooper Tulbeck reveals that the original inhabitant of the gruesome house was an ogre. Kofel, another old man, corrects him: the owner was a great wizard, one who did the city a lot of good – a covert reference to Richard Wagner. The children hammer on the door and when Kunrad appears he invites them to strip the wood they need from his house. The girls tease Kunrad and Diemut, suggesting that she already has her eye on him. Kunrad determines that nature and life will lead him to the magic his old master tried to teach him ('Dass ich den Zauber lerne'). He asks Diemut to leap over the fire with him (a traditional custom for engaged couples) and then kisses her on the lips. Humiliated, she swears she will have her revenge, while her friends point out that she rather likes him.

The street clears as the bailiff, Schweiker von Gundelfingen, hears what happened. Diemut's father sides with Kunrad, while the bailiff rebukes him gently. Kunrad is absorbed by his new love for Diemut, as irresistible as fire itself – the bonfire burns in the distance ('Feuersnot! Minnegebot!').

Diemut comes out on to her balcony. The bonfire's glow reminds her of her shame ('Mitsommernacht – wehvolle Wacht!'). Kunrad begs to be allowed to atone for his behaviour. She pretends to be won over and the lovers sing of the flames of feeling that engulf them. When he asks to be allowed up to her room she indicates the basket on the ground, attached to a pulley. Diemut's girlfriends watch and laugh as the basket rises and then stops below the balcony ('Leise, leise! Lasst uns schauen'). Gradually, Kunrad realises this was a trick. Diemut exults as the townsfolk assemble to laugh at him. Only her father rebukes her. Kunrad asks his dead master to extinguish the

---

[1] These descriptions are Strauss's own, from the score.

[2] Strauss specifies 'Ebner' in the cast list, i.e. leveller or joiner, perhaps, but nothing in the opera bears this out.

fires of a people who despise the power of love. All the fires go out. Soon everyone's bewilderment turns to anger, though some young lovers delight in the darkness ('Hollenspuk! Satanstrug!'). In the darkness Kunrad has climbed on to the balcony. He reminds the people of Munich that, out of small-minded fear, they once expelled the great master, Reichhart, who wanted to help them. Kunrad refers to his wizardmaster Reichhart/Richard Wagner as 'a ruler of spirits' (an apt reference to Valhalla in a theme from *Das Rheingold*) and as a daring innovator (another from *Der fliegende Holländer*). Kunrad himself refuses to give in: he is ready for a fight (the war theme from *Guntram's* narration). He explains that he extinguished the city's lights to teach them that he needs woman's love to create. Diemut takes Kunrad by the hand and leads him into her room. Suddenly convinced of Kunrad's nobility, the townsfolk urge Diemut to yield to him, to help them in their 'Feuersnot' (need for fire). The ensemble gathers into a sort of urgent hymn.

A vivid orchestral interlude describes the scene inside her room. When it reaches a climax, all the city's lights and fires start up again. The lovers are heard hoping that the midsummer night will never end. Everyone rejoices.

Richard Strauss in 1942 reflected on *Feuersnot's* lack of success: he admitted that it was 'comparatively difficult, requiring a superior baritone who can easily reach the heights, a good many solo singers capable of good characterisation, and containing difficult children's choruses, which have always been a handicap in repertory performances. And then Kunrad's great address still fails to be appreciated by audiences used to *Il trovatore* and *Martha*. I wonder whether this will ever change.'[1]

Feuersnot's strengths, however, such as the profusion of memorable melodies, many in seductive waltz time, its animated pace and light, transparent orchestration that betrays the influence of *Falstaff*, are offset by an insistent folksiness and bumpy tone. High-minded allegory yoked to low practical jokes makes for an uncomfortable ride and has limited its appeal, even in Bavaria.   P.

SALOME

Opera in one act, words after Oscar Wilde's stage poem, translated into German by Hedwig Lachmann. Première in Dresden, 9 December 1905, with Wittich, von Chavanne, Burian, Perron, conductor von Schuch. First performed Berlin, 1906, with Destinn, Goetze, Krauss, Baptist Hoffmann, conductor Strauss; la Scala, Milan, 1906, with Krusceniski, Bruno, Borgatti; Metropolitan, 1907, with Fremstad, Burian, van Rooy, conductor Hertz; 1909, Manhattan Opera (in French), with Mary Garden; 1910, Covent Garden, with Ackté, Ernst Krauss, Whitehill, conductor Beecham. Revivals at Covent Garden: 1924, with Ljüngberg; 1937, with Ranczak (later Schulz), conductor Knappertsbusch; 1947, by Vienna Opera with Welitsch (later Cebotari), Höngen, Patzak, Rothmüller, conductor Clemens Krauss; 1949 (in English), with Welitsch, conductor Rankl (décor by Salvador Dali, production by Peter Brook); 1970, with Bumbry, conductor Solti. Revived at Metropolitan, 1933, with Ljüngberg, Lorenz, Schorr, conductor Bodanzky; 1937, with Marjorie Lawrence, conductor Panizza; 1942, with Djanel, conductor Szell; 1949, with Welitsch, conductor Reiner; in Berlin, 1942, with Cebotari; Berlin, German Opera, 1963, in Wieland Wagner's production with Silja; English National Opera, 1975, with Josephine Barstow, Emile Belcourt, Howlett, conductor Mark Elder, producer Joachim Herz.

Herod Antipas, *Tetrarch of Judea* ....Tenor
Herodias, *wife of Herod*........................Mezzo-Soprano
Salome, *daughter of Herodias*.........................Soprano
Jokanaan (John the Baptist)........................Baritone
Narraboth, *Captain of the Guard*........................Tenor
Herodias's Page..Alto
Five Jews ....Four Tenors, One Bass
Two Nazarenes ....Tenor, Baritone
Two Soldiers ....Bass
A Cappadocian..Bass
A Slave

Place: The Palace of Herod at Tiberias, Galilee
Time: c. 30 A.D.
Running Time: 1 hour 50 minutes

After the relative failure of *Guntram* and the relative success of *Feuersnot*, Strauss turned for his third opera to an existing subject, Oscar Wilde's stage poem *Salomé*, which he himself shortened for operatic purposes. *Salome* was from the start a sensational success with the public, rather less so with the critics, but it was admired by Mahler, who failed to get it through the censors in Vienna and contemplated resignation. This was the opera by Strauss which most intrigued the *avant garde* of his day.

[1] *Recollections and Reflections*, London, 1953.

Nearly a century after it was written and performed, it remains hypnotic in its vitality and the characterisation of the leading figures. The most detailed character study is contained in the title role, with each and every turn of an emotionally unstable figure mirrored in the music; her final scene with the head of Jokanaan transcends the dramatic implications of the words and is written, through her eyes as it were, as a sort of psychopathic *Liebestod* – the first of Strauss's grandiose operatic statements for female voice. Ernest Newman deduced from internal evidence that this was the first part of the poem which Strauss set so that it became, like the Letter Scene in *Eugene Onegin*, the source of much of the opera's music.

For Jokanaan, Strauss finds music of a very different character, sometimes hectoring when he denounces Herodias or Salome, often granite-like and implacable as he states his mission. Some have found it demonstrates the composer's greater facility for writing music for evil rather than for good operatic characters, but opinion has recently become more sympathetic to Jokanaan's efforts to convert Salome than it used to be. Herod is in very strong contrast, a crazy figure, attempting all the time to hang on to sanity, driven to the edge of dementia by his passion for his stepdaughter, and conveying these states of mind in music no less flexible and demon-ridden than Strauss found for Salome herself. Sir Arnold Bax attended the première in Dresden and wrote about Karel Burian, the Czech Wagnerian tenor who sang Herod, that 'he created a quite horrifying Herod, slobbering with lust and apparently almost decomposing before our disgusted but fascinated eyes'.

The great terrace of Herod's palace, off the banquet hall. The Captain of his bodyguard, Narraboth, a Syrian, cannot keep his eyes off Salome as she sits inside at supper, and he takes no notice of the Page's warning that he is playing a dangerous game. Soldiers' talk is interrupted by the sound of a voice proclaiming that he is the forerunner of a greater Prophet. This is Jokanaan's, imprisoned by Herod because he is constant in his denunciation of Herodias, and speaking from a cistern in which he is held captive.

Salome in considerable excitement runs out. She cannot bear the way Herod, her stepfather, looks at her; he is after all her mother's husband. The Page predicts disaster, but Salome is riveted by the sound of Jokanaan's voice from the cistern and demands to know who it is. She knows that the Prophet has denounced her mother because she has married a man who was her husband's brother, and she knows too that her mother hates him and her stepfather is frightened of him. She refuses to go back to the feast but says she wants to speak with the Prophet. This is of course strictly forbidden but she gradually wheedles Narraboth to do what she wants and he gives the order for Jokanaan to be brought out of his prison.

To a mature statement of the figure associated with him (Ex. 1) he comes slowly into the light, where

he loses no time in denouncing both Herod and Herodias in so forthright a manner that Salome is at first bewildered and then fascinated. Jokanaan is not slow in turning on her ('Wer ist dies Weib, das mich ansieht?') and he rages at her as the daughter of an iniquitous mother. Salome tells him in music of rising intensity of her desire for his body ('Jokanaan, ich bin verliebt in deinen Leib'), his hair ('In dein Haar bin ich verliebt'), and finally his mouth ('Deinen Mund begehre ich').

She does everything she can to tempt him but the sole result is that he bids her do penance, spurning what she offers. When Narraboth in despair kills himself with his own sword, she does not so much as notice it. The Prophet warns her to seek for the only one in whom she can find redemption, the Man of Galilee: 'Es lebt nur Einer, der dich retten kann'. But, realising that his words fall on deaf ears, he curses her and, to an orchestral passage of considerable power, retreats into his cistern.

The first part of the opera is over and the second is dominated by Herod. He comes with his wife and their suite on to the terrace, a strange, neurotic figure, veering between lucidity and a condition not far from madness – soon after leaving his banquet, he has an hallucination that the wind is blowing round his head. Herodias is as cold as a serpent but Herod's lust for Salome stirs him into activity. He asks her in a grand musical paragraph to drink wine from a goblet so that he may place his lips where she placed hers, and follows it by urging her to eat fruit so that he may finish what she has left. In spite of Salome's refusal to

Salome *(Covent Garden/Salzburg Festival, 1995, director Luc Bondy, sets Erich Wonder, costumes Susanne Raschig). Bryn Terfel as Jokanaan and Catherine Malfitano in the title role.*

do what he asks and for all Herodias's objections, he follows this up by asking Salome to sit beside him on his throne in her mother's place. The whole scene stretches all but a Heldentenor and it is an amazing depiction of erotic neurasthenia.

Herod is in considerable awe of the Prophet and he refuses to give him up to the Jews, who have been at the feast and who now clamour to be allowed to judge him. Herod insists that the Prophet is a holy man who has even beheld God. This starts a theological argument among his Jewish guests, who dispute in a fugal quintet. No sooner is it finished than two Nazarenes proclaim their conviction that the Messiah is in their midst; he has even raised the dead from their graves. Herod is immediately filled with misgivings, which are not quieted by the Prophet's continued prediction of doom.

It is almost as much because of his dread of the future as his longing for her that Herod asks as a diversion for Salome to dance. She demurs until he swears to grant any request she may make of him. The Dance of the Seven Veils starts the third phase of the opera, which belongs mainly to Salome. It has a number of contrasting sections. At its end Herod is devastated when she demands the head of the Prophet. He offers her everything else he can name – precious stones, his unique white peacocks, the mantle of the High Priest, even the Veil of the Temple – but Salome refuses to release him from his oath. He senses quite early that he is fighting a losing battle and in the end agrees that she shall have what she demands. Herodias takes the Ring of Death from his finger and gives it to the first soldier, who summons the executioner to go down into the cistern. Salome listens and Jokanaan is beheaded (to the eerie sound of a pinched B flat on a solo double-bass) and his severed head presented to Salome on a silver charger. She is in ecstasy and circles round the head addressing it as though it were still alive. Living, he refused her his lips; now, in a frenzy of lust, she presses hers upon them. The scene is one of Strauss's most magnificent creations, but Herod turns from her in revulsion before she has finished, and orders his guards to kill her.

Strauss uses a large orchestra, 105 in all – but *Elektra* has 112. In the first years of its existence, *Salome* brought objections from almost everyone who thought they had a concern, whether the Church, the German court in Berlin, or the directors of the Metropolitan Opera in New York. But it has stood the test of time to a quite remarkable degree and the virtuosity with which Strauss manoeuvres his orchestra to convey the feelings of his characters and the violence of the drama never fails to fascinate.   H.

ELEKTRA

Opera in one act, text by Hugo von Hofmannsthal, after Sophocles. Première Dresden, 25 January 1909, with Anny Krull, Siems, Schumann-Heink, Sembach, Perron, conductor von Schuch. First performed Berlin, 1909, with Plaichinger, conductor Blech; Vienna, 1909, with Marie Gutheil-Schoder, Mildenburg, Weidemann; la Scala, Milan, 1909 (in Italian), with Krusceniski; New York, Manhattan Opera, 1910 (in French), with Mazarin, Gerville-Réache; Covent Garden, 1910, with Edyth Walker, Mildenburg, d'Oisly, Weidemann, conductor Beecham; Hull, 1912 (in English), with Florence Easton. Revived Covent Garden, 1925, with Kappel, Olszewska, Schorr, conductor Walter; 1938, with Pauly, Hilde Konetzni, Thorborg, Janssen, conductor Beecham; 1953, with Schlüter, conductor Erich Kleiber; 1957 with Lammers, conductor Kempe; 1965, with Shuard, Resnik, conductor Kempe; 1969, with Nilsson, Resnik, conductor Solti. At Metropolitan, 1938, with Pauly, Thorborg, Schorr, conductor Bodanzky; la Scala, 1943, with Rünger; Metropolitan, 1952, with Varnay, Höngen, conductor Reiner. Gutheil-Schoder was one of the most famous of Elektras, Rose Pauly another.

Klytemnestra, *widow of*
  Agamemnon .... Mezzo-Soprano
Elektra ⎫ .... Soprano
Chrysothemis ⎬ *her daughters* .... Soprano
Aegistheus, *Klytemnestra's paramour* .... Tenor
Orestes, *son of Klytemnestra and*
  Agamemnon...Baritone
Tutor of Orestes..Bass
The Confidante of Klytemnestra....................Soprano
The Trainbearer of Klytemnestra ....Soprano
A Young Servant...Tenor
An Old Servant ....Bass
The Overseer..Soprano
First Maidservant..Contralto
Second and Third Maidservants.........Mezzo-Soprano
Fourth and Fifth Maidservants.....................Soprano

Place: Mycenae
Time: Antiquity
Running Time: 1 hour 35 minutes

*E*lektra is now accepted as one of Strauss's most successful operas. But it was not always so. Mme Schumann-Heink, the Klytemnestra of the original production in Dresden, said: 'I will never sing the role again. It was frightful. We were a set of mad women. ... There is nothing beyond *Elektra*. We have lived and reached the furthest boundary in dramatic writing for the voice with Wagner. But Richard Strauss goes beyond him. His singing voices are lost. We have come to a full stop. I believe Strauss himself sees it' – and (comments Kobbé) in his next opera, *Der Rosenkavalier*, the composer shows far more consideration for the voice. Nonetheless, legend has it that at the Dresden dress rehearsal, he called down into the orchestra pit: 'Louder! I can still hear Frau Heink!'

Beyond the fact that Agamemnon was murdered by his wife, Clytemnestra, and her paramour Aegistheus, it is not essential to know the details of the Greek story, but it is nevertheless against this background that Hofmannsthal and Strauss, with all their changes of emphasis, have laid their opera. Agamemnon and Menelaus, the sons of King Atreus, married the sisters Clytemnestra and Helen. The latter was carried off by Paris, son of Priam, King of Troy, and it was to procure her return to her husband and to avenge the insult to Greece that the Trojan War began. On their way to Troy, the Greek fleet touched at Aulis and was caught there by adverse winds, the goddess Artemis being angry with Agamemnon, who had killed one of her sacred hinds. To appease the goddess and to ensure that the fleet reached Troy in safety, Agamemnon sent for his daughter Iphigenia and sacrificed her.[1] The war

---

[1] See page 267.

over, Menelaus and Helen were driven by storms to Egypt, where they stayed for some years (and formed the subjects of Strauss's *Die Aegyptische Helena*[1]), and Agamemnon returned to Mycenae. Here he found that Clytemnestra had installed Aegistheus as her lover. With the excuse of the sacrifice of her daughter to salve her conscience Clytemnestra murdered Agamemnon in his bath. Three children survived their father: Electra, who was reduced to menial status, Chrysothemis, and Orestes, who was sent away to safety, according to some versions by a faithful slave, to others by Electra. Eventually, Orestes returns, gives out that he is dead, gains admittance to the palace, and slays the guilty Clytemnestra and her lover.

The work is in one long act – Strauss was always strongly opposed to having another work given on the same evening – but that act has been divided by analysts into seven sections: (1) Elektra; (2) Chrysothemis; (3) Klytemnestra; (4) Elektra and Chrysothemis; (5) Orestes; (6) the Recognition; (7) the Vengeance.

The curtain rises straight away to show the inner court of the palace of Mycenae. At the back can be seen the palace itself; in the court is a well, from which servants are drawing water as the curtain goes up. They discuss the unpredictable Elektra, who howls like the dogs with whom her mother and stepfather have condemned her to live and eat. Some hate her, others pity her, only the fifth maid reveres and loves her. For her defence of Elektra, she is set upon by the others, and when they have gone inside, the fifth maid can be heard crying out that she is being beaten.

The scene is empty before Elektra comes from the house alone. In a great monologue ('Allein! Weh, ganz allein!') she rehearses the story of her father's murder, calls on his name (Ex. 1), and looks forward

A - ga-mem - - non!

to the time when his death will be avenged by herself and Orestes. When this is accomplished she will dance in triumph round the corpses of her enemies. The motif associated with the children of Agamemnon (Ex. 2) is important.

The second stage begins when Chrysothemis joins Elektra. Hofmannsthal designs her as a weaker, more human contrast to the implacable Elektra, and she is little inclined to join her sister in the schemes for revenge which are constantly being urged upon her. Instead, she issues a warning that further horrors are in store for Elektra. Poor Chrysothemis feels the fires of love frustrated within her ('Ich hab's wie Feuer in der Brust') and longs to escape from her hateful prison, to which she is doomed by the fear which her sister's hatred inspires in Klytemnestra. The ordeal to which both are subjected is leaving its mark on them, she says.

Noises are heard within of running footsteps, torches can be seen, and Chrysothemis says she will not stay to meet Klytemnestra who must surely be coming out. Elektra, however, is determined to speak with her mother.

Stage three begins as Klytemnestra is seen for the first time. She is bloated and decayed, and sleepless nights and debauched days have left her looking as though it were an effort to keep her eyes open. Her first words are to mourn the evil workings of fate which have given her such a daughter, but presently she comes down to the courtyard, and dismissing her attendants, is left alone with the daughter she hates and fears so much.

She is tormented by dreams; does her daughter know no remedy for them? Elektra is wise, and alone can help her. She describes her sleepless nights; is there not some sacrifice she can make to the gods to

Elektra *(Covent Garden, 1966, director Rudolf Hartmann). Martha Mödl as Klytemnestra.*

alleviate the torture she suffers? Elektra answers her insinuatingly, and in terms that admit of two meanings. Yes, there is a victim, who is unconsecrated and roams free; it is a woman, married, who can be killed at any time of day or night, with an axe, by a man, a stranger, but of their kin. Klytemnestra becomes impatient, and Elektra asks whether her mother means to call her brother back from exile. Klytemnestra is uneasy at mention of him, and Elektra accuses her of sending money to bribe those who are looking after him to kill him; the trembling of her body at his name proves as much. But Klytemnestra says she fears nobody. She will find means of dragging from Elektra the secret of whose blood must flow to cause her nightmares to abate. Elektra springs at her; it is *her* blood that is required. *She* is the victim the gods have marked down. Elektra describes the chase which will end with Klytemnestra's death. The librettist indicates:

'They stand eye to eye – Elektra in wild intoxication; Klytemnestra breathing in horrible spasms of fear.'

At this moment the Confidante runs out of the palace and whispers in Klytemnestra's ear. A look of triumph comes into the Queen's face, and she goes into the palace, leaving Elektra alone in the courtyard.

Stage four. Chrysothemis comes out crying that Orestes is dead. Elektra at first will not believe it, but Chrysothemis says that two strangers, one old, the other young, brought the news; Orestes was dragged to death by his own horses. A servant comes out of the palace, demanding a horse as quickly as possible so that he may carry the news to Aegistheus.

Elektra now demands that Chrysothemis shall help her in her task; alone she cannot slay Klytemnestra and Aegistheus but with her sister's help she would be able to accomplish the deed. She flatters Chrysothemis that she is strong, and promises that she will henceforth look after her as if she were her slave. She holds Chrysothemis fast, but when her sister eventually frees herself and rushes from the courtyard, she hurls a curse after her.

The fifth stage begins as Elektra, left alone, begins to dig like an animal at the side of the courtyard. She looks up twice, and then sees someone standing by the gate. Who is interrupting her? He asks her if she works in the palace. She answers bitterly that she does. He tells her that he has business with the Queen; he and another have brought the news of Orestes' death. Elektra's grief at the news is overwhelming; must she look upon him who lives, while someone a thousand times as good as he lies dead? Elektra's utterance takes on the character of a lament for Orestes, whom she will never see again. The stranger asks her if she is of the royal house that she takes Orestes' death as so personal a matter. She says her name, and the stranger exclaims in astonishment. He reveals that Orestes is not dead, and, a moment later, servants come in and kiss his hand. Who is he, demands Elektra? Everyone knows him, he answers, except his own sister.

The Recognition Scene (stage six) is the emotional climax of the opera. Elektra's ferocity drops from her to be replaced by tenderness, and the unremitting tension of the music gives way to lyricism: 'Orest! Orest! Orest!'

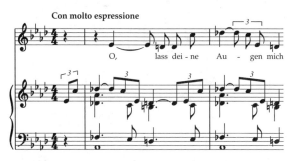

Elektra will not allow her brother to embrace her. She contrasts her former beauty with her present state; she has renounced everything in order to expiate the murder of her father. Together they exult in the prospect of the righteous revenge which they will exact from Agamemnon's murderers. They are recalled to the reality of the situation by Orestes' tutor.

The seventh and last stage of the drama begins when the Confidante appears and leads Orestes and the tutor inside. Elektra is alone, in horrible excitement, waiting for the sounds which will tell her that the first part of the revenge is over. A shriek tells her that

Orestes has found Klytemnestra. By now the palace is aroused, but Elektra bars the entrance with her body.

Aegistheus saunters into the courtyard, and Elektra offers to light him into the palace. Aegistheus wonders at the change that has come over Elektra, who is circling round him in a strange sort of dance. Aegistheus enters the palace, but reappears a moment later at a window, yelling for help.

Women rush out of the palace, among them Chrysothemis, who has discovered that Orestes is back. Their rejoicings are very different in character, and Elektra breaks away from her sister, throwing back her head like a maenad, and dancing about like a demented creature. Her thirst for vengeance is satisfied, and her dance increases to frenzy. Suddenly she collapses dead upon the ground. With a last cry of 'Orest!' Chrysothemis rushes to the door of the palace, and bangs on it. The orchestra continues to give out the motif associated with Agamemnon.   H.

DER ROSENKAVALIER
The Knight of the Rose

Opera in three acts, text by Hugo von Hofmannsthal. Première in Dresden, 26 January 1911, with Margarethe Siems, Minnie Nast, Eva von der Osten (all of whom recorded excerpts) and Karl Perron (who did not); conductor Ernst von Schuch.

Princess von Werdenberg, *the Feldmarschallin (aged 32)*	Soprano
Baron Ochs von Lerchenau	Bass
Octavian, *brother of Count Rofrano (aged 17)*	Soprano or Mezzo-Soprano
Baron von Faninal, *a wealthy parvenu*	Baritone
Sophie, *his daughter*	Soprano
Marianne, *her duenna*	Soprano
Valzacchi, *an Italian intriguer*	Tenor
Annina, *his partner*	Mezzo-Soprano
A Police Commissary	Bass
A Notary	Bass
An Italian Singer	Tenor
An Innkeeper	Tenor

Servants of the Marschallin and of Faninal, Waiters, Mahomet (a little black page), People attending the Levée

Place: Vienna
Time: Reign of Empress Maria Theresa
Running Time: 3 hours 30 minutes

It was Hofmannsthal, the modifier of Sophocles' text for Strauss's fourth opera, *Elektra* – his second success – who suggested the subject of *Der Rosenkavalier*, a comedy to be set in Vienna in Maria Theresa's time. The opera was a success from the start, and has been played more often than any other German opera written in the twentieth century.

It can be claimed as a masterpiece, or alternatively as an edifice of pastiche and paradox – an evocation of an unrealistic, fairy-story Vienna of long ago, where wit and elegance redeemed anything and all could be forgiven provided it were done with style. The result is often magical, but no more realistic than *Die Fledermaus*. The means Strauss and Hofmannsthal employed are undeniably attractive but either anachronistic, like the ubiquitous and seductive waltzes, which perfectly suggest a period atmosphere of which they were never part, or else invented, like the plausible, charming, but unhistorical presentation of a rose to mark an engagement.

The marvel is that one of the fine fruits of the collaboration of Strauss and Hofmannsthal is a fast-moving musical conversation, an outstanding example of speech heightened by music, and that on this basis grow moments of genuine pathos which give the opera memorability, like the Marschallin's reflections on the passing of youth, and set-pieces such as Ochs's waltz, the Presentation of the Rose, or, best of all, the great third-act trio, which provides a splendid and cathartic musical summary of the drama's emotional threads.

Act I. The Marschallin's bedroom. The prelude is explicitly intended to represent the love-making which takes place before the curtain rises. The first seven notes, rampant and assertive, are associated

(Ex. 1)

with Octavian, the Marschallin's music (after a climax) comes a little later and is both passionate

(Ex. 2)

(Ex. 3)

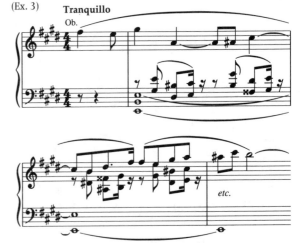

and contemplative. Octavian, a youth of seventeen and certainly not the first of the Marschallin's lovers, is as keen to prolong the moment as she is loath to let him go – it is a scene of great tenderness, with a little jealousy mixed in – but he hides when the breakfast chocolate is brought in and both take alarm when they think the Feldmarschall himself is on his way up. Octavian scampers out, but it is only one of her

Der Rosenkavalier *(English National Opera, 1994, director Jonathan Miller, sets Peter J. Davison, costumes Sue Blane). Sally Burgess as Octavian in Act I.*

relatives, the country-bred Baron Ochs, insisting in spite of the servants' protestations on seeing her.

Octavian returns in a maid's uniform and the Baron is almost diverted from making appropriate obeisance to his cousin by the presence of the pretty 'Mariandel'. He tries to make an assignation for later and comes only reluctantly to the point: will the Princess do him the honour of naming a Knight of the Rose to go on his behalf to his fiancée, Sophie von Faninal? He also needs a notary. A chance remark sets him off on his favourite subject: love-making in all its forms, his monologue consisting partly of reminiscence, partly of pure fancy – if only like Jupiter he could take on disguises for his escapades!

The Princess's morning levée begins, and aspirants to her favour mingle with her notary, chef and hairdresser. An Italian tenor demonstrates his art in a pastiche aria of considerable charm, the Marschallin rejects the attempts of two Italian scandal-mongers, Valzacchi and Annina, to interest her in a gossip sheet, and finally Ochs erupts at the attorney's suggestion that a dowry is due from him to the bride, not the other way round. The Baron and his down-at-

heel retinue depart, leaving the Marschallin prey to autumnal thoughts uttered in some of the score's most expressive music. Was she not herself just such a girl as this poor unsuspecting creature whom Ochs, with all his crudity, plans to marry? Even the return of Octavian, booted and spurred and full of chivalrous talk, only reminds her he will soon find a younger woman. Her reflections on the passage of time are full of melancholy, and Octavian takes an almost formal leave, without even a kiss. The Marschallin sends her little black page after him with the silver rose; Count Octavian, she tells him in an exquisitely poised phrase, will know what to do with it.

Act II. The grand salon in Herr von Faninal's house. Sophie and her duenna are to await her bridegroom, etiquette demanding that Faninal be absent when the bearer of the silver rose arrives. Octavian's entrance triggers what is perhaps Strauss's most magical set-piece, the Presentation of the Rose, with a glittering, ice-cold orchestral texture to support Sophie's soaring vocal rapture, itself a perfect example of the composer's idiomatic writing for soprano voice. The young people engage in polite conversation whose increasingly intimate tone is interrupted by the Baron's entrance. His total lack of manners repels Sophie, Octavian boils with rage and only Ochs's humming of his favourite waltz tune shows a less disagreeable side to his make-up.

Ochs goes into an adjoining room to sign the marriage contract, and the outraged Sophie sinks gratefully into Octavian's arms. Cries from Valzacchi and Annina, anxious to ingratiate themselves with Ochs, bring him in, but he refuses to take seriously Octavian's assertion of Sophie's antipathy. Eventually, Octavian's taunts force him to draw his sword. In the encounter, Octavian lightly pinks the Baron, whose outrage creates commotion, stilled only when recovery sets in after another draught of Faninal's good wine.

Octavian is determined to win Sophie and makes use of the two intriguers. To the Baron alone on the sofa and humming his favourite waltz tune comes Annina to hand him a note purporting to be from the Marschallin's chambermaid and promising him a rendezvous. Delighted with his new conquest, he allows the end of the act to be dominated by his famous waltz.

Act III. An inn near Vienna, where, after a brilliant orchestral *fugato*, Annina and Valzacchi, now in the service of both Octavian and Ochs but inclined to favour the former because he pays better, prepare a room full of surprises for the Baron's assignation. Between him and Octavian, dressed as Mariandel, develops a rude scene of courtship mostly to the accompaniment of a chain of waltzes, to one of which Octavian sings 'Nein, nein, I' trink kein Wein!' (No, no, I don't drink wine!), a tune which will later assume significance. Even the resemblance of Mariandel to Octavian doesn't put the Baron off, but he is soon to discover he is the victim of an elaborate practical joke. First, figures appear at the 'blind' windows, then a disguised Annina insists she is his deserted wife, children claim they are his, a policeman called to defend the Baron against his tormentors turns out to be strict about young women apparently brought to an inn for seduction. When Faninal puts in an appearance, Ochs, who has in desperation described Mariandel as his fiancée, is driven to say he has never seen him before, and the arrival of the Marschallin – summoned by one of Ochs's servants – puts the lid on an evening which for Ochs is fraught with disaster.

She quickly takes in the situation. The Police Commissary was once her husband's orderly and it is easy to persuade him that the whole matter was just a joke. Sophie is heart-broken at the idea that the 'joke' may have included Octavian and herself, but the Marschallin takes things in hand, sends Ochs packing – by a successful appeal to his gentlemanly code; an important sidelight on his character – and pushes Octavian and Sophie together.

The last section of the opera removes something of the impression of musical bustle which has dominated the rest of the act, containing as it does the grandiose trio for the Marschallin, Sophie and Octavian (based paradoxically on the inconsequential little tune of 'Nein, nein, I' trink kein Wein'). Then, with Octavian forgiven, the lovers are left alone to sing an extended duet set to the simplest of tunes and punctuated by an orchestral snatch from the Presentation of the Rose. Sophie and Octavian go hand in hand to the waiting carriage. But it is not quite the end of the opera. Mahomet, the black page, comes to look for Sophie's handkerchief, finds it, and runs out as the curtain falls.   H.

ARIADNE AUF NAXOS
Ariadne on Naxos

In its original form, opera in one act, text by Hugo von Hofmannsthal. The work was designed to follow a condensed version of Molière's *Le Bourgeois Gentilhomme* (translated by Hofmannsthal), for which Strauss provided incidental music. This version was first heard at Stuttgart, 25 October 1912, with Jeritza, Siems, Jadlower, conductor Strauss. First performed Berlin, 1913, with Hafgren-Waag, Bosetti, Jadlower, conductor Blech; His Majesty's Theatre, London, 1913, with von der Osten, Bosetti, Marak, conductor Beecham (Tree was Monsieur Jourdain, and the translation was by Somerset Maugham). Revived Edinburgh Festival, 1950 (by Glyndebourne company), with Zadek, Hollweg, Anders, conductor Beecham (Miles Malleson, who translated the play, also played Jourdain). Subsequently, the opera was revised, the Molière play dropped, the new version, with a prologue and one act, having its première in Vienna, 4 October 1916, with Jeritza, Selma Kurz, Környey, Duhan and Lehmann, substituting as the Composer (according to her autobiography) for the indisposed Gutheil-Schoder, conductor Schalk. First performed Berlin, 1916, with Hafgren-Waag, Hansa, Lola Artôt de Padilla, Kirchner, conductor Blech; Covent Garden, 1924, with Lehmann, Ivogün, Schumann, Fischer-Niemann, conductor Alwin; Turin, 1925, with Arangi-Lombardi, Pasini, Tess, Dolci, conductor Gui; Philadelphia, 1928 (the cast included Helen Jepson as Echo and Nelson Eddy as Harlequin); New York, 1934. Revived Covent Garden, 1936, with Marta

Fuchs, Sack, Wieber, Ralf, conductor Strauss (ensemble of Dresden Opera); Glyndebourne, 1953, with Dow, Dobbs, Jurinac, Lewis, conductor Pritchard.

Characters in the prologue

The Major-Domo ....Speaking Role
Music Master ....Baritone
The Composer..Soprano
The Tenor *(later Bacchus)*................................Tenor
An Officer ....Tenor
The Dancing Master ....Tenor
The Wig-Maker...Bass
A Lackey ....Bass
Zerbinetta ....Soprano
Prima Donna *(later Ariadne)*.........................Soprano
Harlequin ....Baritone
Scaramuccio..Tenor
Truffaldino..Bass
Brighella...Tenor

Characters in the opera

Ariadne...Soprano
Bacchus..Tenor

Three nymphs
    Naiad ....Soprano
    Dryad ....Contralto
    Echo ....Soprano

Characters of intermezzo

Zerbinetta ....Soprano
Harlequin ....Baritone
Scaramuccio..Tenor
Truffaldino..Bass
Brighella...Tenor

(The characters in the opera are the same in both versions; those of the Prologue belong only to the second version, the original conception of the opera calling for the cast of Molière's *Le Bourgeois Gentilhomme* for the first part of the evening.)

Running Time: 2 hours 5 minutes (second version)

One of the first things to strike anyone who reads the correspondence of Strauss and Hofmannsthal is the considerable difference there often is between their first thoughts on the subject of one of their operatic collaborations, and their last. Thus *Rosenkavalier* was thought of as a simple comedy with important roles for a baritone and a soprano in boy's clothes, and in the earlier stages of the correspondence there is no mention of the Marschallin, who was later to become the central figure in the comedy. *Ariadne* went through an even stranger evolution. Originally conceived as a little opera lasting half an hour, and designed as a thank-offering to Max Reinhardt, who produced *Rosenkavalier* in Dresden, it was intended to form the musical divertissement in Molière's *Le Bourgeois Gentilhomme*, taking the place of the Turkish ballet called for by Monsieur Jourdain. In the end the opera became a much more extensive affair than at first envisaged, and lasted about three times as long as projected. Unfortunately, the combination of a theatrical with an operatic company proved beyond the means of most theatres, and the work as it stood was declared impracticable. Strauss therefore revised it and substituted a musical prelude (lasting about thirty-five minutes) for the Molière play, making at the same time some alterations in the body of the opera itself (this, however, remains substantially the same as in the first version, although the role of Zerbinetta[1] has been slightly shortened).

Ariadne has usually been performed in its second version, but such an authority on Strauss's music as Sir Thomas Beecham wrote (in his autobiographical *A Mingled Chime*): 'In this, the earlier version of *Ariadne*, I have always considered that the musical accomplishment of Strauss attained its highest reach, yielding a greater spontaneity and variety of invention, together with a subtler and riper style, than anything that his pen had yet given to the stage ... the Bacchus section of the opera is one of the purple patches in the operatic literature of the twentieth century. ... The later version has not only failed to hold the stage,[2] but has dimmed the public recollection of the far superior and more attractive original.'

The original version of the opera calls for an abbreviated version of *Le Bourgeois Gentilhomme* to form the first part of the evening's entertainment. The theme of this is that Monsieur Jourdain, the bourgeois who is determined to become a gentleman by sheer concentrated hard work and who means to learn to dance, sing, fence, compose, philosophise, is at the same time laying siege to the affections of a certain Marquise Dorimène. She for her part is in love with

---

[1] Margarethe Siems was not only the original Zerbinetta but had earlier created Chrysothemis and the Marschallin.

[2] History suggests this judgement was, to put it mildly, premature.

the shady Count Dorante, who has undertaken to bring her to the lavish dinner party which is given in their honour by Jourdain. The play is garnished with some delightful incidental music by Strauss, and the three principal characters remain at the side of the stage while the opera is performed for their benefit.

In the revised version, the **Prologue** takes place at the house of a Viennese *nouveau riche* (not in Paris, as in the Molière). We see musicians, singers, actors, carpenters, and stage hands preparing for the first performance of a serious opera which has been specially commissioned by the owner of the house to entertain his guests. There is consternation when the Major-Domo announces that after the opera there will be a Harlequinade entertainment; moreover, the two shows must not overrun their allotted span of time, as the fireworks will begin precisely at nine o'clock! Worse is to come, as a little later the Major-Domo comes in to inform the two troupes that his master has changed his mind, and now both entertainments will be played simultaneously, the serious opera being punctuated by intervals of dancing from the comedians.

The dominating figure of the prologue is the composer, a creation of the second version and a touching figure which has found admirable exponents almost every time the opera has been performed. He extemporises an aria which he intends for the tenor (this is derived from a little song heard during the course of the play in the first version), he languishes at the idea of his masterpiece being combined with a common dancing show, he tries to explain to Zerbinetta that Ariadne prefers death to the embraces of any man other than her beloved, and, proving unsuccessful in this, he indulges in a duet with Zerbinetta in which he comes perilously close to declaring that he loves her. There is some trouble with both tenor and prima donna, after which the composer brings the prologue to a suitable end by declaring his conviction in the power of music, the most sacred of the arts.

Opera. After an interval, the curtain rises on the opera itself, which is watched from boxes by the owner of the house and his guests. The setting, which we have hitherto seen only from its reverse side, is now seen from in front. At one side of the set is a cave, in whose entrance Ariadne can be seen asleep, watched by Naiad, Dryad and Echo. In a trio,

these creatures express a certain sympathy with Ariadne's sorrow, to which however they have become accustomed with the passage of time.

A great *scena* begins for Ariadne. She is speaking as if in a dream, and takes no notice when the Harlequinade quartet and Zerbinetta comment on her distress and try to think of means of comforting her. Ariadne welcomes the idea of death, and not even a determined effort by Harlequin to cure her of her madness – for he thinks that's what must surely be wrong with her – can stop her for long. 'Es gibt ein Reich, wo alles rein ist; es hat auch einen Namen: Totenreich' (There is a land where all is purity: it also has a name – Death's domain)[1] she continues, and at mention of death's messenger, Hermes, her monologue becomes more urgent. The last section of the monologue, where Ariadne rejoices in the idea of the deliverance death will bring to her, is ecstatic in import, and (from the singer's point of view) Wagnerian in weight.

The four comedians make another attempt to cheer up the melancholy Ariadne, but their dancing and singing have not the slightest effect, even when they are joined by the sprightly Zerbinetta. Eventually, Zerbinetta bids them leave her to see what she can do on her own. Her *scena* is one of the most taxing ever written for coloratura soprano. After a recitative, 'Grossmächtige Prinzessin', she appeals to Ariadne as woman to woman. Ariadne is not the first to be abandoned by her lover, and will not be the last. Zerbinetta expounds her own fickle philosophy, and is quite unconcerned when Ariadne disappears inside her cave. She goes into details of her amorous career in an *allegretto scherzando* ('So war es mit Pagliazzo') at which point the vocal writing parts company with what is normally considered advisable to write for a singer and becomes a fantastic display of fireworks (even the transposition into D major from the E of the original leaves something which is technically beyond all but the most accomplished of coloratura sopranos).

The section of the opera which begins at her recitative is entirely Zerbinetta's. She is pursued by the four comedians, each of whom seems amorously inclined. Zerbinetta encourages and eludes them all, until Scaramuccio, Brighella, and Truffaldino are left on the stage. Much to their annoyance, Zerbinetta is immediately heard conversing tenderly with Harlequin,

---

[1] English translation by Tom Hammond.

whom they had thought safely out of the way. They rush out to see what they can do about it.

No sooner are they gone than the three attendant nymphs return to the stage, full of the sight they have just seen. A youthful god is coming, Bacchus, fresh from the embraces of Circe, but eager for new adventure. They call to Ariadne, who emerges from the cave in time to hear Bacchus off-stage calling for Circe. The nymphs beg him to continue singing, and Ariadne hails him as the longed-for messenger of death. The opera ends with an extended love duet, Wagnerian in its length and weight if not in its character. In Bacchus' arms, Ariadne finds consolation, and Strauss even allows Zerbinetta to pop in for a moment to comment that all has turned out exactly as she would have expected. Bacchus and Ariadne go together into the cave. (In the first version, soon after Bacchus is first heard off-stage, there is a fairly lengthy interruption by Zerbinetta, during which Ariadne is arrayed in fine clothes; it is only after this that the god is seen on the stage.)

Ariadne is scored for a small orchestra of thirty-six players. H.

DIE FRAU OHNE SCHATTEN
The Woman without a Shadow

Opera in three acts, text by Hugo von Hofmannsthal. Première in Vienna, 10 October 1919, with Lehmann, Jeritza, Weidt, Oestvig, Manowarda, Mayr, conductor Schalk. First performed Dresden, 1919, with von der Osten, Rethberg, Metzger, Vogelstrom, Plaschke, conductor Reiner; Salzburg, 1932, with Lehmann, Ursuleac, Rünger, Völker, Manowarda, conductor Clemens Krauss; la Scala, 1940, with Pacetti, Roman, Voyer, Franci, conductor Marinuzzi. Munich's rebuilt opera reopened 1963, with Borkh, Bjoner, Mödl, Jess Thomas, Fischer-Dieskau, conductor Keilberth; 1966, London, by Hamburg company; 1966, Metropolitan, New York, with Christa Ludwig, Rysanek, Dalis, King, Berry, conductor Böhm; 1967, Covent Garden, with Borkh, Hillebrecht, King, McIntyre, conductor Solti.

The Emperor ....Tenor

The Empress, *his wife* ....Soprano

The Nurse *(Die Amme)* ....Mezzo-Soprano

A Spirit-Messenger ....Baritone

The Keeper of the Gates of the Temple..........................Soprano or Tenor (falsetto)

Apparition of a Youth ....Tenor

The Voice of the Falcon ....Soprano

A Voice from Above.....................................Contralto

Barak, *the dyer* ....Bass-Baritone

His Wife ....Soprano

Brothers of Barak
    The One-Eyed ....Bass
    The One-Armed...Bass
    The Hunchback ....Tenor

Six Children's Voices........................Three Sopranos, Three Contraltos

Voices of the Nightwatchmen ....Three Basses

Servants of the Emperor, Voices of unborn Children, Spirits

Running Time: 3 hours 15 minutes

Written between 1914 and 1917, *Die Frau ohne Schatten* is in Strauss's oeuvre a counterpart to *Die Zauberflöte* in Mozart's, not quite a 'quest' opera, but hovering between a world of human beings and one of spirits. The 'shadow' is of course fertility, which the Empress lacks, but in the course of the opera she grows from a creature of fairy-tale remoteness to a human being prepared to sacrifice hers and her husband's future rather than force Barak and his wife apart. The opera's première took place, just after the end of the Great War, in Vienna, where Strauss had become joint Music Director with Franz Schalk, who conducted. The exacting demands of its staging were not, it would appear, wholly satisfactorily met, and difficulties of staging and casting have always militated against the work's place in the repertory, towards which it has moved slowly but surely in the second half of the twentieth century. Many admirers of the composer estimate it not only the most ambitious but also the greatest of his operas.

The Emperor of the South Eastern Islands is married to a supernatural being, the daughter of Keikobad, King of the Spirits. She emerged from a white gazelle which he shot while out hunting. Their love is mutual and ardent, but their marriage is childless; in token of her barren state, the Empress throws no shadow. To make love complete, the woman must bear children.

Act I. The opera, which is by no means short, each of the three acts lasting over an hour, starts when the Emperor and Empress have been married twelve moons. It is dark, and the Nurse is crouching on a flat roof above the Imperial gardens. To her appears a messenger. He tells her that he is from Keikobad and has come to inform her that unless the Empress within three days casts a shadow (that is to say, becomes pregnant), she must go back to Keikobad. The Emperor will be turned to stone.

The messenger disappears and the Emperor tells how he first saw and won his wife. He will now go hunting for three days, and he refers to his favourite falcon which he has not seen since the day he met his wife. The Emperor leaves, day dawns, and the Empress comes from her chamber. She too talks of her love, but then catches sight of the falcon, whose voice is heard to say: 'The woman throws no shadow, the Emperor must turn to stone.' The Empress understands that the only way to save him is to acquire a shadow, and she begs the Nurse to help her.

The orchestra represents their journey to earth, and the second scene is set in the hut of the dyer, Barak. When the curtain rises, the three deformed brothers of the dyer are quarrelling.

In the scene which ensues, the contrasting characters of Barak and his wife are made apparent. She nags and complains, he is patient and full of natural goodness. But he upbraids her for not having given him a child in the two and a half years of their marriage. He goes off to market.

No sooner has he gone than the Empress and her Nurse enter the hut, dressed simply as peasants. The Nurse is immediately aware that in the dyer's wife she has found a good subject for her black arts. She praises her for her beauty, and tells her she could sell her shadow and get for it all the luxuries and riches she has always wanted.

The dyer's wife agrees to exchange her own prospect of motherhood for the promise of riches. She will refuse her husband's advances. The Empress and the Nurse leave, saying that they will be back next day. When she is alone, the woman has another vision. This time she hears the voices of her unborn children coming from the flames of the fire.

Barak enters to find his bed separated from his wife's. He is optimistic that this is only a temporary state of affairs. As they lie down, the voices of nightwatchmen can be heard coming from outside.

Act II. In his introduction to the published libretto, Hofmannsthal says: 'The trials continue; all four must be cleansed – the dyer and his wife, the Emperor and the daughter of the spirits. The one pair is too much of the earth earthy, the other too full of pride and remote from the earth.'

The scene is again Barak's hut. The struggle to obtain the shadow continues. The Nurse tempts the woman with the apparition of a handsome youth, who appears each time the dyer is out of the hut. The woman believes it would be simple to deceive her husband, and yet does not quite dare to do so. Barak feels the change in her. He invites some beggar children to share in their meal.

The Emperor's falcon house in the forest. The Emperor has found his falcon, and follows it to the falcon house. There he sees his wife. He senses immediately that she has been in contact with the things of the earth.

Barak's hut. It is the third day and the Nurse continues her efforts to gain the shadow of the dyer's wife for the Empress. The Nurse and the dyer's wife go out of the hut together, leaving the Empress and Barak. As the curtain falls, it is obvious that she feels sympathetically towards Barak, and regrets what she is causing to happen to him and his wife.

The Empress's bedroom in the falcon house. The Nurse lies at the foot of the bed. The Empress has a vision of her husband wandering through tomb-like caves and hears the voice of the falcon: 'The woman throws no shadow; the Emperor must turn to stone.' She is much moved by this, but also touched by Barak's distress, which she is fully aware is caused by her actions.

Back in Barak's hut, the Nurse makes her final attempt to win the wife's shadow. Although it is midday, it is growing dark, a storm is brewing, and the three crooked brothers of Barak are howling in terror. The Nurse senses that there are supernatural powers at work over which she has no control, but assures the Empress of their ultimate attainment of their object. The Empress is appalled by the sufferings of men, but grateful that fate has led her to meet Barak, whose integrity has convinced her of the dignity of humanity. The climax of the scene comes when his wife tells Barak that she has been unfaithful to him and sold her shadow and her unborn children with it. To prove the truth of her words, the brothers light a fire and it is seen that she throws no shadow. Barak threatens to kill her, and as if by magic a sword is there to his hand. The Empress refuses to take the shadow at such a price, but the woman, overcome by remorse when she sees the result of her admission, tells Barak that she has not done what she has confessed, but has only wished in her imagination to do it.

As the Nurse tears the Empress from the scene, the earth opens and swallows up Barak and his hut.

Act III. Subterranean vault, divided by a thick wall in the middle. On one side is Barak, on the other his wife, each however unconscious of the presence of the other. In a famous passage, she wrestles with her conscience ('Schweigt doch, ihr Stimmen': Be silent, you voices), he tries to find consolation and peace for the two of them ('Mir anvertraut, dass ich sie hege': Entrusted to me, I'll cherish you).

The vault disappears, and when the clouds have dispersed we see the Empress and her Nurse enter in a boat. Trombone calls summon the Empress to the judgement hall where her father Keikobad presides. The Nurse wants to prevent her from entering, fearing Keikobad's anger more than death; her purpose now is to persuade the Empress to return to earth to continue her search for the shadow. But the Empress is determined to enter where she knows her husband is being judged. She bids the Nurse farewell for ever; the Nurse does not understand men and their struggles and the price they pay for their guilt. She herself has learned to love and understand them. She enters the Temple. The voices of Barak and his wife are heard calling for each other.

The Empress demands to know her place in the scheme of the universe. A voice from above tells her to drink of the Water of Life and the shadow of the woman will be hers and she will be human. But the voices of Barak and his wife are again heard, and the Empress refuses to drink and destroy them. She demands to see her father, her judge. The alcove is illuminated, and the Emperor appears, turned to stone except for his eyes, which can be seen pleading with her for life. In her desperation, she wants to rush to her husband's side, and her anguish is increased when she hears a voice call: 'The woman throws no shadow, the Emperor must turn to stone.' She is again urged to drink of the Water of Life, to gain the shadow and save her husband. It is her moment of supreme trial, and she falls to the ground in the agony of her inner struggle. Finally, a cry breaks from her lips: 'I will not.'

As soon as this cry is heard, the water disappears, and the Temple is brightly lit from above. The Empress rises to her feet and it can be seen that she throws a shadow. The Emperor descends from his alcove, the voices of their unborn children are heard singing from above, and in their happiness the Emperor and Empress embrace and fall on their knees to give thanks for deliverance from their trial.

The scene changes to a beautiful landscape, with a waterfall in the middle. The Emperor and Empress stand beside it. Below it can be seen the figures of Barak and his wife, who have found each other. The voices of unborn children complete the happiness of each couple.   H.

INTERMEZZO

Opera in two acts, text by the composer. Première, Dresden, 4 November 1924, with Lotte Lehmann, Joseph Correck. First performed Berlin, 1925, with Hussa, Scheidl, conductor Szell; Vienna, 1927, with Lehmann, Jerger, conductor Strauss; Cuvilliéstheater, Munich, 1960, with Steffek, Prey; New York, 1963, with Curtin, Donald Bell; Edinburgh Festival, 1965 (Munich company), with Steffek, Prey; Glyndebourne, 1974, with Söderström.

Christine ....Soprano

Little Franz, *her eight-year-old son* ....Silent

Hofkapellmeister Robert Storch,
    her husband ....Baritone

Anna, *the chambermaid*..................................Soprano

Baron Lummer ....Tenor

The Notary ....Baritone

His Wife ....Soprano

Storch's skat partners[1]
    Kapellmeister Stroh[2] ....Tenor
    Commercial Councillor ....Baritone
    Justizrat[3] ....Baritone
    Kammersänger[4] ....Bass

Place: Grundlsee and Vienna
Time: The Nineteen-Twenties
Running Time: 2 hours 5 minutes

When the opera was first produced, emphasis was laid in newspaper reports on the fact that

---

[1] Strauss played regularly; these particular parties were apparently in Berlin at the beginning of the century.
[2] Stroh was the conductor Joseph Stransky, who was later associated with the New York Philharmonic.

[3] An honour bestowed on legal dignitaries by the Emperor and perhaps equivalent to the British Q.C., or Queen's Counsel.
[4] The Kammersänger was the heroic Wagnerian tenor Ernst Kraus, a member of the Berlin State Opera from 1896 to 1924 who sang at Bayreuth and Covent Garden.

the basis of the work was taken from incidents in the composer's private life. The emphasis can hardly be thought to have been misplaced, since Strauss himself took care that the sets were made to correspond with his own home at Garmisch, and Joseph Correck, the creator of the role of Hofkapellmeister Storch, wore a specially constructed mask to make his resemblance to Strauss more marked.

Act I. The dressing-room of the house of Kapellmeister Storch. Seven o'clock in the morning. Open suitcases everywhere indicate that Storch and his wife are busy packing. She is thoroughly bad-tempered, abusing the servants, complaining incessantly at her husband, and, when he seems inclined to answer back, reminding him that she comes of a much better family than he does; who is he, anyway?

After successive exhibitions of her short temper with maid and cook, Christine admits to the former that not the least of her husband's shortcomings in her view is his unvarying kindness and gentleness; if only he would stand up to her like a man and not give way so much, she would have far more respect for him. The telephone rings, and Christine is asked by a neighbour to go skating. She accepts.

An interlude (there are twelve in the course of the opera, and they constitute the chief means of sustained lyrical expression) leads us to a new scene: the toboggan track. Tobogganists cross the stage, but when it is Christine's turn she runs into a young man on skis. She is furious and abuses him, complaining that the fall hurt her very much – there is no word of whether he is injured or not. But when she discovers that he is the well-connected Baron Lummer, she is all over him and only too anxious that he should know she is the wife of the famous composer Storch. She asks him to come and visit her.

An interlude composed of waltzes and other dances takes us to an inn at Grundlsee, where Christine and the Baron are dancing. They converse, and one gathers that he is there for his health. The whole short scene is brilliantly alive; it is the music of the third act of *Rosenkavalier* transferred, shortened, and without any element of farce.

Dining-room in the Storchs' house. Christine reads a letter which she is writing to her husband, and in which she talks about the excellent young escort she has acquired for herself. At that very moment, in comes the Baron. They sit opposite each other reading the newspaper, and she asks him when he is going to begin his studies. His family apparently want him to read law, but he is anxious to take up the study of natural history, for which, without them, he has not the means. She says that he has only to wait until her husband is back, and he will not lack support.

The wistful music from the moment of the Baron's exit is combined with the interlude which follows it to make a concert excerpt, usually known as 'the Interlude from *Intermezzo*'. When the curtain rises, we are in the Baron's room in the house of the notary. He exclaims with impatience at the demands made upon him by Frau Storch. Can she really expect him to sit about with her in the evenings reading the newspapers! And all that talk about his studies ... and his ill-health. He is interrupted by a girlfriend, obviously come to keep an appointment; he will join her in a minute. He sits down to write a letter to his patroness (as he refers to her); he must have money.

Another interlude brings us again to the Storchs' dining-room. Christine has had the letter – a thousand marks, he asks for! He must be mad! At this moment the Baron himself puts in an appearance, and is immediately sent outside to wipe his shoes. She tells him that what he asks for is impossible; let him not spoil their agreeable relationship by insisting.

At this juncture, the maid brings in a note and hands it to her. It is addressed to Kapellmeister Storch, but Christine opens it, and exclaims in horror. She reads aloud: 'My darling. Do send me two tickets for the opera again tomorrow. Afterwards in the bar as usual! Your Mieze Meier.' The Baron is solicitous, but she sends him away, and when he is gone, she writes out a telegram: 'Who is Mieze Meier? Your infidelity discovered. Am leaving you for good.' She hustles the maid to pack all the suitcases: they are leaving the house – for good.

Another interlude. The child's bedroom. Christine sits by the side of his bed, crying. She abuses her husband, but the child will not listen: his father is good and kind, and it is she who is horrid and makes scenes. She kneels melodramatically at the foot of the bed and prays.

Act II. The 'skat' game. The scene is a comfortable sitting-room in the house of the Commercial Councillor. Round the 'skat' table sit the Justizrat, the Commercial Councillor, the Kammersänger, and Kapellmeister Stroh. The conversation which accompanies the game centres round the agreeable character of Storch, which contrasts so markedly with his highly disagreeable wife. When he arrives, Storch apologises for being late and then joins the game. They ask after his wife, and he tells them of the letter he has had in which she talks of her new-found friend the Baron. They cannot keep a hint of criticism from their tone when they refer to Christine, but Storch explains that he finds her extremely stimulating – in any case, her bristling exterior conceals the proverbial heart of gold.

A telegram comes for Storch, whose jocularity falls from him as he reads it. He gives it to Stroh and asks him to read it aloud. Stroh's comment is: 'What, do you know her too?' but Storch hurries out of the room in obvious distress, leaving the others to comment ironically but without malice on the surprising news that such an obviously model husband should turn out to be no better than the rest of them.

The scene changes to the office of the notary. Frau Kapellmeister comes in and demands a divorce. The notary assumes that this is because of the Baron, and is distinctly surprised to hear that Christine is convinced she has evidence against her husband.

A stormy interlude leads to the third scene, in the Prater in Vienna. Storm. Storch is seen wandering about. He has had no answer to his telegrams to Christine, no explanation even of the identity of the mysterious Mieze Meier. He cannot leave Vienna and his work on account of so ridiculous a misunderstanding, but his worry is very real. Stroh finds him and explains that the letter must have been meant for him; the two names are not dissimilar, and probably the volatile Mieze looked up his address in the telephone book, assuming that he – Stroh – was no less a man than the famous Hofkapellmeister. Storch is furious; Stroh must put right the whole ghastly muddle.

Christine's dressing-room. Packing and disorder. Christine vents her wrath on everybody and everything in sight, but she wishes she had not sent the Baron to Vienna to check up on Mieze Meier. Storch's telegrams have caused her to wonder whether there is not some mistake. Another telegram arrives, this time containing the news that Stroh is coming with a full explanation of the whole situation. Stroh is announced and the curtain falls as she goes out to hear what he has to say.

The dining-room, decorated for Storch's return. Christine is wildly excited, she must go and greet him. But she stops herself, and when he rushes in and tries to embrace her, she coldly gives him her hand. She contrives to nag in spite of Storch's obvious delight at seeing her, and seems to think that he must make amends in some way for what has happened. When she tells him she is sick of him and all other men, and he can go and make arrangements for a divorce, he rounds on her and gives her a much needed piece of his mind, then he leaves. She is astonished at his change in attitude, but at this juncture in comes the Baron. It appears that he has bungled the meeting with Mieze.

Storch comes back and pretends to be jealous of the Baron. Christine says he was quite agreeable for a bit, but rather a bore, particularly when he asked her for a thousand marks. Storch is delighted at this, and thinks it a great joke. All is set for their reconciliation, and when the curtain falls, they have made up all their differences, Christine even going so far as to comment what a happy marriage theirs is.   H.

DIE AEGYPTISCHE HELENA
The Egyptian Helen

Opera in two acts, text by Hofmannsthal. Première at Dresden, 6 June 1928, with Rethberg, Rajdl, Taucher, Plaschke, conductor Busch. First performed Vienna, 1928, with Jeritza, Graarud, conductor Strauss; Berlin, 1928, with Müller, Laubenthal, Schorr, conductor Blech; Metropolitan, 1928, with Jeritza, Laubenthal, Whitehill, conductor Bodanzky; Vienna, 1970, with Gwyneth Jones, Jess Thomas, Glossop, conductor Krips. First U.K. performance, Garsington, 1997.

Helena (Helen), *wife of Menelaus*....................Soprano

Menelaus..Tenor

Hermione, *their child*.......................................Soprano

Aithra, *the daughter of an Egyptian King;*
    a sorceress .... Soprano

Altair..Baritone

Da-Ud, *his son* ....Tenor

Servants of Aithra...............Soprano, Mezzo-Soprano

Three Elves..........................Two Sopranos, Contralto

The Omniscient Sea-Shell...........................Contralto

Place: Egypt
Time: 1193–1184 B.C. (after the Trojan War)
Running Time: 2 hours 20 minutes

The Trojan war is over. Menelaus has killed Paris, the seducer of his wife Helena, and is now returning home with her. He has made up his mind that his honour, as well as the blood of the countless Greeks who died fighting for his cause, demands that Helena should pay the supreme price for what has been caused through her beauty, and he is determined to sacrifice her himself, either at sea or when they reach their native soil. But in a storm his ship is wrecked.

Act I. A great room in Aithra's palace. The Sea-Shell assures Aithra of Poseidon's love, but conjures up for her a description of Menelaus' ship, bearing the fairest of women, who is about to be murdered by her husband. Aithra has caused the storm which wrecked the ship, and it is not long before Menelaus enters the room, leading a golden-haired woman behind him. He feels that he must fulfil his vow and slay Helena, but she tries to entice him to her arms once again. Aithra intervenes and causes Menelaus to think he sees Paris and the Trojans once more rising against him. He rushes from the room after them, and Helena is comforted by Aithra, who gives her a potion to drink, which brings forgetfulness.

Menelaus returns convinced that he has killed two of the beings he was pursuing – Paris and Helena. He can see their blood on his dagger – but what he brandishes is spotless and shining. Aithra convinces him that for the past ten years he and the Greeks have been victims of a fantastic delusion; it was not Helena at all who was in Troy – she has been here these ten years, lying in a deep sleep, safe from the touch of man.

Aithra makes a sign, and Helena is visible to Menelaus, waking in all her beauty from her sleep. He is overjoyed, and cannot resist the happiness which the vision affords him. At Helena's insistence, Aithra transports them by her magic arts to a land where the name of Helena means nothing to man or woman. They go together over the threshold of a sleeping chamber, and Aithra watches the triumph of her scheme while she prepares to effect a transformation of their state.

Act II. A tent opening wide on to a palm grove, behind which the Atlas Mountains are visible. Helena and Menelaus awaken after their magic flight. Helena expresses her ecstasy: 'Zweite Brautnacht! Zaubernacht, überlange!' (A second wedding night! Night of magic!). But Menelaus is only half restored to her; for him, she is still a phantom, conjured up by the magic arts of Aithra,

and his conscience is occupied with the murder – he thinks of it as that – of Helena which he accomplished outside the palace of Aithra. It is as the widower of Helena that he thinks of himself.

To visit Helena comes a chieftain of the desert, Altair by name, with his followers. He salutes the Queen reverently, and then, as Menelaus takes his place behind her with drawn sword in his hand, commands his followers led by his son, Da-Ud, to do obeisance before her. Menelaus shows signs of being jealous of Da-Ud – is he not like Paris? – but Helena tries to comfort him. Altair invites Menelaus to join the hunt, and offers him Da-Ud as his guide. As he departs, Altair shows his contempt for Menelaus, but makes no secret of his admiration of Helena.

While Menelaus makes ready for the hunt, Da-Ud throws himself at Helena's feet and declares his devotion and adoration of her, but Helena takes no more notice of his protestations than she has of Altair's. Menelaus departs, but refuses to give up his sword, which Helena wants to take from him but which he insists on having with him for the hunt.

Aithra and attendants come to Helena. Aithra reveals that she has not only given Helena the draught which brings eternal forgetfulness of all that is unpleasant, but has also in error provided her with the antidote. She has come to remove this. But Helena proclaims that this alone can convince Menelaus that she is Helena and not a nymph conjured up by Aithra to take Helena's place in his bed. She bids the slaves mix the potion using the remembrance draught.

Altair appears at the entrance of the tent, and declares his passion for Helena. Slaves describe the progress of the hunt, but their voices change from excitement to horror as they perceive that Menelaus and Da-Ud are engaged in deadly combat. Soon it is evident that Menelaus has triumphed, and Da-Ud's dead body is borne in to the sound of solemn music.

Menelaus appears not to understand that he has slain the son of his host, but, while the slaves gather to bid him and Helena to Altair's feast, Helena and her attendants busy themselves over the mixing of the potion which will restore his memory to him. Helena bids him drink, and herself sets the example. Menelaus takes the cup, and, for a moment after he has drunk, it looks as though he will kill her. Then he drops his sword and gazes at his wife, recognising her and stretching out his arms as though to grasp a shadow.

Altair dashes in as though to take Helena by force and with the help of his slaves separate her from her husband. But at the same moment appears Aithra at the head of cohorts of her supernatural followers, and commands Altair not to presume to raise his hand against her or the woman she would protect. In the middle of Aithra's troops stands Hermione, the daughter of Helena and Menelaus. The opera comes to an end after she has asked her father: 'Where is my beautiful mother?' All is forgiven and forgotten, and Helena and Menelaus enter together upon a new life.   H.

ARABELLA

Opera in three acts, text by Hugo von Hofmannsthal. Première Dresden, 1 July 1933, with Ursuleac, Bokor, Kremer, Jerger, Plaschke, conductor Clemens Krauss. First performed Vienna, 1933, with Lehmann, Jerger, conductor Krauss; Covent Garden, 1934, with artists of première; Genoa, 1936, with dalla Rizza, Jerger, conductor Strauss; Salzburg, 1947, with Reining, della Casa, Hotter, conductor Böhm; Covent Garden, 1953, with della Casa, Uhde, conductor Kempe; New York, Metropolitan, 1955, with Steber, Gueden, London, conductor Kempe; English National Opera, 1980, with Barstow, Burrowes, Glossop, conductor Mark Elder.

Graf Waldner	Bass
Adelaide, *his wife*	Mezzo-Soprano
Arabella, *their daughter*	Soprano
Zdenka, *Arabella's younger sister*	Soprano
Mandryka, *a Croatian landowner*	Baritone
Matteo, *an officer*	Tenor
Graf Elemer	Tenor
Graf Dominik	Baritone
Graf Lamoral	Bass
The 'Fiakermilli'	Soprano
A Fortune-Teller	Soprano

Welko, Djura, Jankel, Servants of Mandryka; Guests at the Ball

Place: Vienna
Time: 1860
Running Time: 2 hours 30 minutes

Strauss asked his librettist Hugo von Hofmannsthal for something in the vein of *Der Rosenkavalier* – a romantic comedy, with a Viennese background and opportunity for waltzes. The libretto was written in 1928 and revised in 1929, the last section reaching the composer only days before Hofmannsthal's sudden death in July 1929. The composer appears to have been inhibited from making changes in his distinguished collaborator's libretto.

Act I. There is no prelude and the curtain rises to show a salon in an hotel in Vienna. We soon learn that the fortunes of the Waldner family are very low indeed. Graf Waldner is a gambler and has been losing heavily, and the only hope for the future seems to lie in matching the beautiful Arabella with a rich suitor. Zdenka, the younger child, has been brought up as a boy, as her parents always wanted one and Adelaide insists that they cannot possibly afford to have two daughters coming out near the same time.

Adelaide is having her fortune told, and Zdenka, dressed in boy's clothes, is making excuses for her parents to the tradesmen who call to talk about their unpaid bills. Zdenka is left alone, and shortly afterwards a young officer, Matteo, who is desperately in love with Arabella, comes in. He asks for news of his beloved from Zdenka whom, like everyone else, he believes to be her brother (and therefore Zdenko). Arabella has not looked at him for days, and if it were not for the wonderful letter she wrote him a day or two ago, he would be in complete despair. He threatens to go away or kill himself if Arabella continues to ignore him. When he has gone, Zdenka reveals her perturbation; she is in love with Matteo herself and it is *she* who wrote him the letter.

There follows a scene between the two sisters. Arabella as usual has presents from her three noble suitors, and from Matteo as well, but she has no real interest in any of them, and Zdenka's pleading for Matteo affects her little. One day the right man will come along, and she will know him straight away ('Aber der Richtige, wenn's einen gibt für mich'):

The two voices join in a charming and typically Straussian duet, whose theme[1] is frequently heard in the course of the opera. Arabella is confident in the future, even though it is the end of Carnival and she should decide which suitor she will accept before the night is over.

Elemer, one of the three suitors, comes to take Arabella for a ride in a sleigh; she says she will be ready in half an hour. When Elemer has gone, Arabella asks Zdenka if she has noticed the stranger whom she has seen during the past day or two from her room, and who, she thinks, looks extremely attractive. No sooner has she spoken than he appears again in the street but he goes away without so much as looking up at the window.

The parents come back into the room and send their daughters out. The Count has been losing again, and is depressed that he finds only bills waiting for him, and no word from any of his regimental cronies, to all of whom he has written for help in his financial embarrassment. There was one in particular, rich and eccentric, Mandryka by name, whom he thought would never fail him. Adelaide tells him she has dreamed all will go well. A servant announces that there is a gentleman to see Graf Waldner. It turns out to be Mandryka, nephew and heir of the Count's old comrade. He has fallen in love with the photograph of Arabella which Waldner sent with his letter, and in a mixture of formality and open-heartedness asks for her hand in marriage. To pay for his journey to Vienna he says he sold some woods, and he offers Waldner a couple of thousand-gülden notes. The latter can hardly believe his senses, and when Mandryka has gone, he imitates his tone of voice: 'Teschek, bedien' dich' (Please, help yourself!).

The listener might be forgiven for believing this the greatest scene for a male singer in any Strauss opera – a totally credible representation in music of the *coup de foudre*, greater than anything he had written for Ochs von Lerchenau, its only musical rival to be found perhaps in the role of Barak in *Die Frau ohne Schatten*. The scene early in Act II when Mandryka finally face to face (as opposed to through the intermediary of her father) confronts Arabella with his declaration of love only acts as corroborative to the earlier scene; it does not supersede it but confirms the impression we have formed. The *coup de foudre* never risked turning into a fly-by-night.

There is a short scene between Zdenka and Matteo, in which the latter shows his desperate anxiety to know whether he can yet have the letter from Arabella which Zdenka promised him she was writing. He is told he may have it that night at the Fiakerball (a ball to which everyone goes in costume: a 'Fiaker' was a two-horse cab). He leaves, and Arabella comes in ready for her drive with Elemer. Zdenka refers to him as 'dein Elemer' (your Elemer), and the sound of the words has a romantic ring in Arabella's ears as she repeats them to start the act's finale. The idea of the romantic stranger is much more attractive to her, and even the horrid thought that he may be already married is not enough to dampen her enthusiasm.

Act II. A ballroom. Arabella, very much the queen of the ball, comes downstairs with her mother and several attendant cavaliers, to be introduced by her parents to Mandryka, who is waiting below, and in whom Arabella recognises the stranger she has seen from her window. She is left alone with him, and sits down, refusing a dance to each of her other suitors in turn. He is a widower, as he gently and touchingly explains. His impassioned language astonishes her, but she is completely fascinated and convinced that she has found the right man in him: 'Und du wirst mein Gebieter sein' (My lord and master you shall be). Their love duet is impassioned enough to suggest to us that she is right. During its course, Mandryka conveys the information that in his country a glass of water is given by a girl to her prospective fiancé in token of engagement.

She asks to be allowed an hour at the ball to say goodbye to the things which have made up her girl-hood. At that moment, the rest of the guests crowd around her, and the Fiakermilli – a pretty girl dolled up to the nines – curtsies and brings her a bouquet. She sings a coloratura polka song for Arabella's entertainment, after which Arabella goes off to dance with Dominik.

Waldner's reaction to the news of Arabella's engagement is naturally one of delight. Matteo, however, is heart-broken, not at the news (which he has not heard), but because Arabella has not looked

---

[1] Slavonic in origin.

in his direction all evening. Zdenka, however, does her best to reassure him, and says that Arabella relies on his love, though she may not find ways of showing it. Mandryka orders champagne for everyone present at the ball; no one shall be left out when he is as happy as he now feels himself. Arabella says goodbye to her three suitors, whom she must relinquish now that she has found the right man.

Zdenka reappears and gives Matteo a letter, which she says is from Arabella. It contains the key of Arabella's room, according to Zdenka, and she insists that if the unbelieving Matteo come to that room in quarter of an hour, he will receive everything that he most longs for. Mandryka overhears the conversation and cannot believe his ears. He decides there must be another Arabella perhaps in the same hotel, but, when he cannot find his fiancée, is forced to the conclusion that his worst suspicions are justified, and that it must be she who made the assignation. In desperation, Mandryka flirts with the Fiakermilli. A note from Arabella is handed to him: she has gone home but will be his tomorrow. Arabella's parents go off to the hotel with Mandryka to find her.

Act III. A lounge in the hotel, with staircase leading upstairs. Night. There is a short prelude,[1] and when the curtain goes up Matteo is seen about to come down the stairs. He hides when he hears a bell. Arabella comes in, smiling happily. Music from the ball plays around her as she sings of the happiness which she and Mandryka will enjoy amidst his fields and forests. Matteo reappears and is astonished to see Arabella in the hall. She can make no sense at all of his ardour and his insinuations, and he for his part cannot understand her coldness and apparent heartlessness.

In the middle of their misunderstanding, Arabella's parents arrive with Mandryka, who immediately recognises Matteo as the man he saw receive the key at the ball and is now convinced of the worst. He remains unpersuaded by Arabella's protestations of innocence, tempers rise, and a duel between Mandryka and Matteo is only prevented by the sudden appearance of Zdenka, in a negligée and with her hair down. She rushes down the stairs, and says that she only wants to say goodbye before throwing herself into the Danube. Arabella says she will stand by her

whatever her trouble, and Zdenka eventually stammers out that it was she who sent the note to Matteo, and the key inside it was to her room, not Arabella's. The room was dark, and Matteo could not have known that it was not Arabella.

Mandryka tries to put his shame and sorrow into words, but Arabella turns to Zdenka without a glance in his direction and thanks her for teaching her to follow the dictates of her heart. Prompted by Arabella and Mandryka – Arabella bears no malice – Waldner agrees to give Zdenka's hand to Matteo, and the crowd, which has been attracted by the noise, begins to disperse. Arabella tells Mandryka that there must be no attempt at explanation between them until morning; she would however be grateful if one of his servants could fetch her a glass of clear, cold water. She would find it refreshing after the tumult of the evening's events. She goes slowly up the stairs without another word.

Mandryka is waiting dejectedly below when at the top of the stairs appears Arabella. Holding the glass of water in her hand she makes her way slowly down and offers it to him. The opera ends with their love duet: 'Das war sehr gut, Mandryka'.   H.

DIE SCHWEIGSAME FRAU
The Silent Woman

Opera in three acts, text by Stefan Zweig, freely adapted from Ben Jonson's comedy *Epicoene, or the Silent Woman*. Première, Dresden, 24 June 1935, with Cebotari, Sack, Kremer, Ahlersmeyer, Plaschke, conductor Böhm. The opera was frowned on by the Nazis,[2] and after very few performances was removed from the Dresden repertory. First performed Zürich, 1936, with Moor, Emmerich, Oeggl, conductor Denzler; la Scala, Milan, 1936, with Carosio, Sinnone, Stabile, Bettoni, conductor Marinuzzi; New York, City Opera, 1955, with Joan Carroll; Komische Oper, Berlin, 1956, in Felsenstein's production, with Arnold, Reinmar; Salzburg, 1959, with Gueden, Wunderlich, Prey, Hotter, conductor Böhm; Covent Garden, 1961 (in English), with Barbara Holt, MacDonald, David Ward, conductor Kempe.

Sir Morosus ....Bass

His Housekeeper ....Contralto

The Barber ....Baritone

---

[1] Used as a bridge passage when Acts II and III are played without interval, a Munich innovation.

[2] Strauss's letter to the Jewish Stefan Zweig (referring to the Nazis as a passing phase in German life) has been much quoted: then, against him, but more recently as expressing his true sentiments *vis-à-vis* Hitler. Zweig committed suicide in 1942.

Henry Morosus...Tenor
Aminta, *his wife*...........................Coloratura Soprano
Isotta ....Coloratura Soprano
Carlotta ....Mezzo-Soprano
Morbio...Baritone
Vanuzzi ....Bass
Farfallo...Bass

Actors and Neighbours

Place: A Room in Sir Morosus's House in a London
    Suburb
Time: About 1780
Running Time: 2 hours 50 minutes

Hofmannsthal died in 1929, leaving behind him the libretto of *Arabella*, but after his death Strauss had to look round for a new collaborator. His choice fell upon Stefan Zweig, and together they turned to Ben Jonson for inspiration, Zweig having already had considerable success with his German version of *Volpone*.

Act I. After an overture, described by the composer as a *Potpourri*, the scene is a room in Sir Morosus's house. It is untidy, and the bric-à-brac about the room indicates that it belongs to a former seaman. We are straight away introduced to the mainspring of the action, Schneidebart, the barber, who is approached by Sir Morosus's housekeeper with the suggestion that he should implant the idea in Sir Morosus's head that he wants to get married and that she is just the person. Life is impossible in the house, what with his exaggerated notions about eliminating any kind of noise, and anyhow he needs a wife. The barber is properly scornful of her suggestion, but at this moment Morosus himself comes in, fulminating about the noise.

While he is being shaved, he launches into a diatribe against the perpetrators of the pollution of noise, by which he is surrounded and from which he can find no means of escape. He sings sadly of his loneliness; could he only find someone to care for him, his life would acquire the purpose which it lacks. At the end of the opera the melody is developed into a grateful hymn of thanksgiving for peace. The barber suggests he should marry a young and silent wife, and, when told there is no such thing, offers to find one. Morosus, although objecting that he is too old, is obviously not averse to considering the suggestion.

The noise of someone trying to gain admittance to his room causes a further tantrum, but when the intruder turns out to be his nephew Henry, whom he had thought dead, his displeasure turns to extravagant rejoicing. He must be received with all honour. Henry starts to tell him he has his troupe with him. Morosus misunderstands him and thinks he has said 'troops', and the initial joy turns to fury when he discovers Henry is a member of a theatrical company. He refuses even to accept Aminta, Henry's wife, as his niece, insults them all, disinherits Henry, and orders the barber to find him a wife forthwith, and moreover to bring a priest with him when he brings her to the house.

Consternation follows Sir Morosus's withdrawal, but it soon gives place to a discussion of ways and means of taking revenge on the old curmudgeon. Henry says he is happy in his love and would not barter it for a house made entirely of gold. The barber reminds him that he is throwing away quite a large fortune, but he and Aminta sing a love duet amid expressions of admiration from the troupe. The barber sees a possible solution in the task which has been set him; it will not be easy to find a silent woman – why should Aminta, Isotta and Carlotta not be dressed up and produced as candidates next morning? Schneidebart says he will take all arrangements into his own hands, and everyone is delighted, except Aminta, who says she would prefer to move the old man to fall in with the situation rather than trick him into it. But she accepts the suggestion, and they make their plans.

Act II. The same room, the afternoon of the next day. Morosus is warned by his housekeeper that some sort of intrigue is brewing, but he will not listen to her, and continues to array himself in his smartest clothes. The barber comes in to say that he has brought three girls with him, and warns the old man that he should not be too ardent with them. Is he likely to eat them? demands Morosus angrily.

When they present themselves for his inspection, the three actresses impersonate three quite different types: Carlotta is a country girl, Isotta a young lady of fashion, and Aminta is dressed simply and unpretentiously. Their conversation matches their clothes: Carlotta is a hopeless bumpkin with a hideous accent, and Morosus soon dismisses her; Isotta's high-flown pretentious talk culminates in an effort to read his hand, and she also is sent packing; but Aminta behaves naturally and Morosus is obviously impressed by her demeanour. After listening to her for a bit, Morosus tells the barber that Aminta is the one for him (she calls herself Timida). When they are left alone it becomes apparent that he is genuinely touched by her youth and beauty, and he attempts to apologise for what must look to her a poor bargain, she is so young, and he so old. Aminta also seems to regret the part she has undertaken to play.

But the scheme is well under way, and Schneidebart returns with two members of the company dressed up as a priest and a notary. The mock marriage is concluded, but no sooner is it over than more members of the company come in, proclaiming that they are old shipmates of Sir Morosus and mean to celebrate with him. This they proceed to do and it is some time before his furious protests are successful in getting rid of them.

Morosus and Aminta are alone, and in an aside she reveals that she has no relish for the part she has to play. It is a question of *Don Pasquale* all over again. Aminta makes scene after scene; she is the mistress of the house, and his wishes have no significance at all. Morosus is dumbfounded, until rescued by Henry, who sends Aminta out and consoles his old uncle. The act ends after a short scene between Henry and Aminta, in which she tells him how she disliked ill-treating the old man; but she consoles herself with the thought that it was only done for her husband's sake.

Act III. The scene is the same. Before the curtain rises, the noise of vigorous hammering is heard, and the scene discloses a troop of workmen redecorating the room under Aminta's orders. Henry, in disguise and with another member of his company as accompanist, gives Aminta a singing lesson. This is the last straw, and Morosus is on the verge of despair when the barber comes in to announce that the Chief Justice of England is on his way to the house, and everything is prepared for a divorce. Aminta rejects the idea out of hand, but the legal party makes its appearance and proceeds to rehearse in dog Latin the grounds on which a divorce can be granted. Isotta and Carlotta witness that Sir Morosus is by no means the first man Timida has known, and Henry, disguised, admits that he has known her intimately. Timida swears she has known but one man – her husband. But the Chief Justice, although agreeing that there is evidence of promiscuity, rules that what took place before marriage is no grounds for divorce. Morosus nears the end of his tether and threatens to

commit suicide if he cannot obtain his freedom.

In his misery he throws himself on his bed, and, at a signal from the barber, Henry and Aminta go up to him and explain the truth; it has all been a hoax. He is at first bewildered, then furious, and then bursts out laughing; he may have been close to suicide, but it cannot be denied they put on a wonderful show! He confesses himself willing to hear all their operas if they can make him laugh as much as he has laughed today, at himself. The rejoicing is general, and when he, Aminta, and Henry are alone, Morosus sings happily of the peace which he has at last found. He sinks back in his chair, and sighs with contentment.   H.

FRIEDENSTAG
Peace Day

Opera in one act, text by Joseph Gregor. Première, Munich, 24 July 1938, with Ursuleac, Patzak, Ostertag, Hotter, Hann, Weber, Wieter, conductor Clemens Krauss (the opera is dedicated to Ursuleac and Krauss). First performed Berlin, 1939, with Ursuleac, Prohaska, Bockelmann, Sinimberghi, conductor Krauss; Zürich, 1939, with Annie Weber, Stig, Emmerich, conductor Denzler; Venice, 1940, with Grandi, Valentino, Rakowski, Cassinelli, conductor Gui. Revived Munich, 1961, with Hillebrecht, Metternich, conductor Keilberth; Los Angeles (University of Southern California), 1967; B.B.C. broadcast (in English), 1971, conductor Edward Downes.

Commandant of the Beleaguered Town........Baritone
Maria, *his wife*...Soprano
Sergeant...Bass
Corporal ....Baritone
A Private Soldier ....Tenor
A Musketeer...Bass
A Bugler...Bass
An Officer ....Baritone
A Front-Line Officer ....Baritone
A Piedmontese ....Tenor
The Holsteiner, *commanding the besieging army*....Bass
Burgomaster...Tenor
Bishop ....Baritone
A Woman of the People................................Soprano

Soldiers of the Garrison and of the Besieging Army, Elders of the Town and Women of the Deputation to the Commandant, Townspeople

Place: The Citadel of a Beleaguered Town during the Thirty Years War

Time: 24 October 1648
Running Time: 1 hour 10 minutes

The scene shows the great circular room in the citadel. A gallery with loopholes runs round at about a man's height. One staircase leads to the upper storey of the fortress, another descends.

The soldiers discuss the garrison's increasingly dire situation, a Piedmontese sings a mournful ditty, but from far off can be heard the sound of the townspeople, already afoot and crying that their hunger can no more be borne.

To the sound of a mournful march and with the cries of 'Hunger! Bread!' still sounding from outside, the town elders enter, led by the Burgomaster and the Bishop. Suddenly, the musket-butts strike the ground, and the Commandant appears on the upper stairway. He is a handsome man of about fifty. He warns the deputation that he will hear them but that his answer to anything they may say which involves a cowardly action on his part will be violent – he seizes a musket from a soldier and throws it down at their feet as he speaks. Burgomaster and Bishop plead with him to allow the surrender of the town, but he will not listen to their arguments.

An officer announces to the Commandant that all the ammunition is spent; will he give the order that more be fetched from the secret cellars, where they all know there is a plentiful supply? The Commandant refuses, but bids them trust him. He reads aloud the Emperor's message which reached him only the previous day; it bids them hold out at all costs. But the cries of the deputation redouble in urgency, the crowd shouts for peace, and eventually the Commandant says he is ready to agree to their demands; let them only wait until midday before the surrender takes effect. He himself will give the signal, a rousing, flashing sign which all will recognise.

The deputation departs well content with what it has achieved, but it is clear a moment later that the Commandant, rather than surrender, plans to set fire to his arsenal and so blow himself and his garrison sky-high.

The stage is empty for a moment, but from below comes Maria, the Commandant's wife. She is younger than he is, and she muses on the situation in which all find themselves. Her monologue ends with a paean of praise to hope, which has returned with the rising sun, which now shines brightly through the loophole.

Maria tries to persuade her husband, who enters at that moment, to confide in her why he looks so different from usual. He urges her to escape since the citadel and all within it are doomed to die. She thanks the sun for the light it has shed on her life; it has melted the heart she had thought frozen, it has removed the look that worried her so much. She will not be parted from the husband she loves so much, be it in life or in death, in peace or in war.

They embrace. The light has grown dimmer during their duet. The soldiers come one by one into the room, last of all the sergeant, with the fuse in his hand. The Commandant motions him towards the arsenal. Suddenly, the sound of a cannon shot is heard. It is the sign the Commandant has hoped for; it means the enemy is attacking. But no enemy can be seen advancing, and instead bells begin to ring out from the town, one after another, bells which have not been heard since the days of peace, almost longer ago than anyone can remember.

A moment later the Burgomaster is up the stairs and into the room, a changed man from the time when he led the deputation to pray for surrender. Peace has now come. The Commandant protests that he will not surrender, but to the sound of a march the Holsteiner's troops enter the citadel, their commander at their head. His voice can be heard from outside demanding to know where his noble, lion-hearted foe is to be found, that he may embrace him. But the Commandant returns harsh words for kind, and refuses to shake the hand which the Holsteiner proffers him. He draws his sword, and the Holsteiner puts his hand on his, but Maria throws herself between the two men. She begs her husband to acknowledge that at long last love and brotherhood have come into the lives of all of them instead of hatred and strife. He looks at her, and then throws away his sword and embraces the Holsteiner. The opera ends with an extended hymn to peace, in which all the soloists join.   H.

DAPHNE

Opera in one act, text by Joseph Gregor. Première, Dresden, 15 October 1938, with Teschemacher, Jung, Ralf, Kremer, conductor Böhm (given in a double bill with *Friedenstag*). First performed Berlin, 1939, with Cebotari, Ralf, Anders, conductor Krauss; la Scala, Milan, 1942, with Cigna, Gallo, conductor Marinuzzi; Buenos Aires, 1948, with Bampton, Kindermann,

Svanholm, Dermota, conductor Erich Kleiber. Revived Munich, 1950, with Kupper, Fischer, Fehenberger, Hopf, conductor Jochum; Vienna, 1950, with Kupper, conductor Moralt; New York, Town Hall, 1960, with Gloria Davy; Munich, 1964, with Bjoner, Madeira, Uhl, conductor Keilberth.

Peneios, *a fisherman* ....Bass
Gaea, *his wife* ....Contralto
Daphne, *their daughter* ....Soprano
Leukippos, *a shepherd*...Tenor
Apollo..Tenor
Four Shepherds ....Baritone, Tenor, Two Basses
Two Maids..Sopranos

Place: Near Peneios' Hut
Time: Antiquity
Running Time: 1 hour 40 minutes

There is a short pastoral introduction, after which the curtain rises to show Peneios' hut and the landscape round it. Heralded by the sound of their flocks, the four shepherds appear in pairs and discuss the forthcoming feast-day in honour of Dionysus, which is traditionally the time for lovers' mating. The last rays of the sun light up the stage as Daphne comes in. In a long monologue she reveals her love of nature and identification of herself with the trees and flowers around her; the prospect of the festivity gives her no pleasure.

Leukippos, her childhood playmate, tells her how much he loves her. She refuses to accompany him to the festival, at the same time, however, telling him that her affection for him is by no means gone although she characterises it as sisterly. Gaea has heard the end of their conversation, and she comes to bid her daughter dress herself for the party. The time will come when she will open her heart to love. Daphne listens to her mother, but will not dress up in the clothes the maids bring for her. The maids hear the sound of Leukippos' lamentations. They determine to help him to win Daphne's love, and offer to dress him up in the clothes she has rejected.

As light dies away, the dignified figure of Peneios appears, accompanied by Gaea and the shepherds. He points to the light which still shines on Mount Olympus; the day will yet come when the gods will return among men. In spite of murmurs of protest from the shepherds, he affirms his belief that Apollo will come to them, and suggests they prepare a great feast to receive him worthily. Peneios laughs and is answered by a mysterious echo. A stranger appears –

Apollo dressed as a herdsman – and greets the company. He tells them his cattle had run wild, and he has only just succeeded in rounding them up. Gaea and the shepherds laugh at Peneios for this mundane realisation of his prophecy that Apollo would visit them. He answers by sending for Daphne and bidding her look after the stranger.

When Daphne appears, Apollo is amazed at her beauty, and calls her 'Sister'. She is taken aback by the compliments he pays her, but starts to do her parents' bidding, and puts a blue cloak round his shoulders. She feels an affinity with him, and asks him his true identity. In enigmatic language, he explains that he saw her from his chariot. She does not understand who he is, but starts to tell him how she hates to be parted from the sun, whereupon he repeats sentences to her from her opening monologue. She sinks on his breast, and rejoices in his promise that she will never again be parted from the sun. For a time she is hidden in the blue of his cloak, but suddenly tears herself free. Apollo declares that he loves her, and tells her to listen to the distant chanting; it is the voice of lovers. But Daphne is full of fear; Apollo told her he was her brother, and now he talks of love.

A procession, led by Peneios and Gaea, approaches, and Daphne joins the women, Apollo the men. They sing the praises of Dionysus, and the feast begins. Leukippos, who is dressed up among the women, invites Daphne to join their dancing. No sooner has she done so than Apollo bursts out in complaint that Peneios and his daughter are the victims of deception. With the sound of a thunderclap, he disrupts the feast, whereupon Leukippos reveals himself as a suitor for Daphne's hand. In a fiery passage he begs her to follow him. Daphne complains that she is being doubly deceived, both by the playmate of her youth, and by the stranger, who is not what he seems to be. Apollo reveals himself as the sun, and in the dispute which follows Daphne's refusal to bind herself to either of her suitors, Apollo wounds Leukippos with an arrow.

In a scene with the dying man, Daphne discovers that her lover was a god, and blames herself for Leukippos' death. Apollo watches her, spellbound by her beauty and full of regret for his action in killing Leukippos. He asks Dionysus to forgive him for having caused the death of one of his disciples, and, begging Zeus to pardon him that he strayed outside his sphere in interfering with mortals, he asks that he be given Daphne, not in mortal guise but transformed into imperishable form as one of the trees she loves so well. From her branches, men will in future cut the wreaths reserved for those who are best and bravest among them. Gradually Daphne changes into a laurel tree, and her voice is heard celebrating her altered state.   H.

DIE LIEBE DER DANAE

The Love of Danae

Opera in three acts, text by Joseph Gregor. The opera was in rehearsal during the late summer of 1944, but a Nazi edict closing the theatres following the plot against Hitler's life prevented a public performance. In the event, *Die Liebe der Danae* was heard at a well-attended dress rehearsal (16 August), conducted by Clemens Krauss and with a cast headed by Ursuleac, Taubmann, and Hotter. The official première was at the Salzburg Festival, 14 August 1952, with Kupper, Gostic, Szemere, Schöffler, conductor Krauss. First performed in Vienna, 1952, with Kupper, Gostic, Patzak, Poell, conductor Krauss; la Scala, Milan, 1952, with Dow, Gostic, Ego, conductor Krauss; Covent Garden, 1953, with Kupper (later Rysanek), Vandenburg, Frantz, conductor Kempe; Los Angeles, 1964 (in English).

Jupiter ....Baritone
Mercury..Tenor
Pollux, *King of Eos* ....Tenor
Danae, *his daughter*......................................Soprano
Xanthe, *her servant* ....Soprano
Midas, *King of Lydia* ....Tenor
Four Kings, *nephews to Pollux* ....Two Tenors, Two Basses

Four Queens
    Semele..Soprano
    Europa ....Soprano
    Alcmene......................................Mezzo-Soprano
    Leda..Contralto

Four Watchmen ....Basses

Chorus of Creditors, Servants and Followers of Pollux and Danae, People

Running Time: 2 hours 20 minutes

As early as the spring of 1920, Hofmannsthal sent Strauss a scenario under the title *Danae, or the prudent marriage*. Strauss had not taken up the suggestion by the time Hofmannsthal died but he remembered it later, and he eventually persuaded Gregor to write a text after Hofmannsthal's theme.

The composition was finished in June 1940, so that though *Die Liebe der Danae* was the last of Strauss's operas to reach public performance, its composition in fact antedates that of *Capriccio* by some two years.

Act I. The throne-room of King Pollux. It is shabby and there is only part of the golden throne left. One can see the former splendour, but now creditors besiege the hall and demand payment. The King appears and tries to pacify them, telling them that his nieces, the four most beautiful women alive, and their husbands, kings of the islands, have set out to find a husband for Danae, and that Midas, the richest man in the world whose touch turns anything to gold, is on his way to marry her. The crowd is sceptical and falls on the throne and plunders what is left.

An interlude depicts the Golden Rain. Bedchamber of Danae. She wakes and tells Xanthe, her maid, of her dream, in which she was surrounded and covered in gold. It fell on her lips and on her breasts, and she can hardly believe it was only a dream, so real and wonderful was the sensation of the gold. A march is heard in the distance, and Xanthe announces a new suitor. But Danae says that she will only accept the man who can bring her the gold.

A pillared hall in the palace; in the distance the sea. A large gathering – the King, his councillors, and his creditors – awaits the return of the emissaries. They announce that Midas is the new suitor, whose touch has turned even the portrait of Danae to gold. He sends a golden garland to Danae. A cry is heard – 'A ship! A ship! A ship of gold!' – and everyone rushes towards the harbour to greet Midas. Only Danae stays behind. It is her dream come true, and she determines that the bringer of gold shall be her bridegroom.

Midas comes in, dressed in simple clothes and saying he is Chrysopher, friend of Midas, come to prepare her to meet the King. She is obviously impressed by him and cannot conceal her disappointment that he is only the forerunner of her suitor. He for his part is reluctant to fulfil his bargain, and hand her over to his master.

The scene changes to the harbour, where the crowd exuberantly welcomes the supposed Midas, in reality none other than Jupiter clothed in golden raiment. Danae recognises him as the master of her golden dreams; but is he the master of her love? She faints, and the curtain falls.

Act II. In a magnificent bed-chamber, the four Queens are decorating the bridal bed. Jupiter enters, clothed from head to foot in gold. The four Queens know him, for in various guises he has been the lover of each of them – as cloud, bull, Amphitryon, and swan. He warns them not to give his disguise away, but they cannot restrain their jealousy that for Danae he is not content to stay in the form of gold, but has taken the form of a real man – and why the double deception over Midas? He explains that his love for Danae is great, and she is made even more desirable in his eyes because of her coldness and disdain of men. He hopes to find true love at last. As for the impersonation of Midas, that is done to deceive Juno, whose jealousy is stronger than ever, and whose punishments for those he has loved grow ever more severe. As he has taken the outward form of Midas, the real Midas can always take his place should Juno approach in anger. The four Queens praise his cunning, and try to entice him back to them.

Midas enters and the women leave the bridal chamber. Jupiter is jealous in case Midas should capture Danae's love, and reminds him that, when he conferred the golden touch upon him, it was with the condition that he should obey his every command. He has been made the richest man on earth, but should he now prove false to his bargain, he will forthwith change back into the donkey-driver Jupiter first knew. Jupiter leaves, a soft march announces the arrival of Danae, and Midas dons the golden clothes which Jupiter has left behind him.

Danae enters accompanied by the four Queens, who tell her that the object of her affections has formerly been the lover of each one of them; when they recognise Midas, they take fright, and disappear. Midas explains as much as he dares; he is the master of the gold, and yet not the suitor on the ship. Danae does not understand the mystery, but it is clear that she wants only him, and, when he turns everything in the room to gold, she knows it must be Midas. They fall into each other's arms. A thunderclap, and Danae is seen turned to a golden statue.

Midas curses himself and his gift. Jupiter appears and claims Danae as his, but Midas objects that she must come to life only for the sake of him whom she truly loves. They both offer her what it is in their power to give: Jupiter – golden dreams, temples, and divine honours; Midas – only his human love and poverty. Her voice is heard as though from afar off, choosing Midas. Danae and Midas disappear, and Jupiter alone laments the loss of what might have been. Danae was offered the fate of the gods, and she has chosen the fate of mortals.

Act III. An open road in the East. Danae and Midas are seen to wake up. Danae slowly begins to understand what has happened. Midas, the favourite of the god, has renounced riches and power and has returned to be the humble donkey-driver on account of his love for her. She is content.

The scene changes to a sunny forest in the mountains. Mercury, half god, half jester, reports to Jupiter that the episode of Danae has caused mirth among the gods, but has thrown everyone on Pollux's island into confusion. Jupiter is confronted by the four Queens, who have found their way to him with Mercury's help. They flatter him, and affect to regard the episode as an amusing trick played on Danae and designed to draw Juno's attention to her while he diverts himself with them. But soon Jupiter tires of them, and bids a final farewell to them, to his last and dearest love, and to earth.

Unfortunately for his plans, Pollux and his nephews and creditors have found him, and demand satisfaction for the deception which has been practised on them. On Mercury's advice, Jupiter lets money fall from the skies, and they all rush after it. Mercury recommends that Jupiter should not abandon his pursuit of Danae; now that she is poor, how much more easily will she succumb to the lure of gold than when she dwelt in a palace!

Midas' hut, simply but tidily kept. Danae sings of her love. Jupiter enters, dressed in the manner Midas has described to Danae as affected by the man who first gave him the gift of the golden touch. He tries to discover if Danae is discontented with her lot; he reminds her of her golden dreams, but she is proof against his temptations, and finally convinces him that she loves Midas. Jupiter is moved by her obvious faithfulness, and tells her the story of Maia, who was loved by the god and brought forth Spring. The duet is one of Strauss's most inspired passages. At its end, Jupiter recognises Danae's greatness, and she too is full of gratitude for his understanding. He thanks her and leaves. Midas' music is heard in the orchestra and she goes out to meet him. H.

CAPRICCIO

Opera in one act, text by Clemens Krauss. Première, Munich, 28 October 1942, with Ursuleac, Ranczak, Taubmann, Hotter, Höfermayer, Hann, conductor Krauss. First performed Zürich, 1944, with Cebotari, Rohs, Dermota, Kunz, Schöffler, conductor Böhm; Salzburg, 1950, with della Casa, Höngen, Dermota, Braun, Schöffler, conductor Böhm; Covent Garden, 1953, with Cunitz, conductor Heger; New York, Juilliard School, 1954, with Gloria Davy, Thomas Stewart; Glyndebourne, 1963, with Söderström, conductor Pritchard.

The Countess ....Soprano
Clairon, *an actress* ....Contralto
Flamand, *a musician* ....Tenor
Olivier, *a poet* ....Baritone
The Count, *the Countess's brother* ....Baritone
La Roche, *director of a theatre* ....Bass
Monsieur Taupe ....Tenor
Italian Singers...................................Soprano, Tenor
A Young Dancer
The Major-Domo..Bass
Eight Servants....................Four Tenors, Four Basses
Three Musicians ....Violin, 'Cello, Cembalo

Place: A Château near Paris
Time: About 1775
Running Time: 2 hours 30 minutes

From the earliest times its practitioners have been concerned with the theory and re-shaping of opera. Every opera ever written constitutes an acceptance of an old form or an attempt to introduce a new, and each example is a particular commentary on operatic form in general. But the commentary is customarily implicit in the work and not explicit as in Strauss's last opera *Capriccio*, in which he and Clemens Krauss took opera itself as subject (*Capriccio* was finished in 1942, and, though performed before *Danae*, was in fact the last opera on which the composer worked).

The scene is laid in France, at the time of Gluck's reform. At the house of the charming Countess, a number of people are discussing the theme 'Prima le parole, dopo la musica' (First the words, then the music), led by Flamand, a musician, and Olivier, a poet, who are rivals for the affections of the Countess as well as in their art. Arguing from a different angle is the Countess's brother, whose interest in music or poetry is mild, but whose regard for the stage, and most of all for Clairon, a leading actress, is quite the

reverse. More professional in his practical attitude than the artists, more knowledgeable in his cynicism than the Count, is La Roche, a theatrical manager, who incidentally emerges as the strongest personality in a cast of types. Each character finds his attitude to opera reflected symbolically in his relationship to the Countess and the other guests.

Originally the opera was intended to be a short, one-act affair, designed to go with *Friedenstag* and *Daphne*, but in its final form it lasts nearly two hours and a half – and there is no interval. The opera has powerful attractions in the skill with which the operatic discussion is argued and the way in which composer and librettist have contrived to diversify the subject – to say nothing of the power of invention Strauss still shows in it.

We are in the salon of a château near Paris where plans are afoot to celebrate the birthday of the young widowed Countess Madeleine. Flamand has written a string sextet for the occasion, and he and Olivier are listening to the music, on whose qualities the theatre director La Roche seems already to have passed judgement by falling asleep in an armchair. He wakes to join in the discussion and they point out that this is the man in whose hands lies the fate of composers. La Roche believes in entertainment – splendid decor, top notes, beautiful women. He is for Italian opera and he cannot resist mentioning that even highbrow creative artists have their foibles: Olivier did not seem to disdain the talent – or the beauty – of the famous Clairon, who by happy chance is not only the subject of the Count's admiration but will arrive soon at the château to play opposite the Count in Olivier's play.

The Count and Countess come in from next door and the others quickly disappear. The Count clearly favours the poetic muse, perhaps because of his interest in Clairon. His sister equally obviously inclines towards music – but by no means to the exclusion of words. The Count is in no doubt about his sister's interest in the two artists and wonders aloud which she will eventually choose.

Re-enter La Roche, Flamand and Olivier, the first-named to announce that all is ready for the rehearsal of the birthday entertainment, which will consist of the new music by Flamand, Olivier's drama and finally an *azione teatrale* by his entire company. All discussion stops with the entrance of Clairon, who dominates proceedings as she greets the Countess and then enquires from Olivier if he has yet finished the play.

He has, and Clairon and the Count read the scene, which culminates in the Count's declamation of a sonnet.[1] He is congratulated and La Roche takes them all off into the theatre, leaving Flamand and Olivier with the Countess.

Olivier criticises the way the Count reads the sonnet and recites it to the Countess as a personal utterance. Flamand goes to the harpsichord and begins to improvise and eventually leaves the room with Olivier's manuscript. It is Olivier's chance to declare his love, which he does delicately and gently. Flamand returns to sing the sonnet he has just set ('Kein Andres, das mir so im Herzen loht') and the Countess and Olivier join their voices to his to make a trio of extraordinary beauty. Flamand and Olivier seem likely to quarrel about the true authorship of the sonnet, but the Countess decides the issue quite neatly: it is now hers!

La Roche takes Olivier away to rehearsal and Flamand in his turn is able to declare his love. He presses Madeleine to decide between him and Olivier, and she promises that he shall hear her answer next morning at eleven o'clock.

The sounds of rehearsal can be heard from next door (where the Prompter, to general amusement, is found to have fallen asleep) and the Countess orders refreshment to be brought in. She and the Count exchange thoughts on the progress of their affairs of the heart. He must not be too easily carried away by his feelings for Clairon, she advises him, only to have to admit that for her own part she is still undecided between poet and composer, but has already started to wonder whether an opera might not be the collaborative outcome of their interest in her.[2]

Rehearsal is over, and refreshments served while La Roche introduces a dancer for their delectation (*Passepied*, *Gigue*, *Gavotte*). During the course of the *Gigue*, Olivier tries unsuccessfully to make up to Clairon, and after the dancing is over the Count comments to Flamand that the dance is an aspect of art where his own contribution is entirely secondary. On the contrary, says Flamand; without music, it would never occur to anyone even to lift a foot.

A fugue ensues, described as 'discussion on the theme "Words on Music"'. Music goes deeper than words; words express thought with greater clarity; music is the art of the sublime; in the theatre, words and music must work together. The Count, Clairon and Olivier are against opera, but the director has a passion for *bel canto*, and at this point introduces two Italian singers who entertain the company with a duet in the Italian style.

The Count offers to take Clairon back to Paris, but the director now takes the opportunity of announcing the form the entertainment will take for the Countess's birthday. The first part of the act of homage will consist of a sublime allegory: 'The Birth of Pallas Athene'. This revelation and the details of the action provoke a torrent of abuse and disbelief and the assembled company expresses its feelings in the first part of a great octet, subtitled 'Laughing Ensemble'.

The Countess tries to mend matters and asks La Roche for an exposition of the second part of the play. This, he says, shall be heroic and highly dramatic: 'The Fall of Carthage'. He has hardly started to describe the magnificent spectacle in prospect when Olivier and Flamand begin to attack him, and the second part of the octet ensues (titled 'Dispute'). But La Roche does not take all this lying down and launches into a most effective defence. Olivier's verse is all right – when Clairon speaks it; Flamand's music will fit the salon, but the theatre needs something of greater moment. For his own part, he serves the eternal art of Theatre itself and he wants drama to show human beings in all their aspects and deal with every problem and possibility of every age. His moving defence ends with his own idea of an epitaph in which he proclaims himself the friend of comedy, a guardian angel of artists, the patron of serious art.

La Roche's declaration has won the day and all congratulate him. The Countess demands a collaboration between Flamand and Olivier, to the dismay of her brother who realises that she has commissioned an opera. In spite of his reservations, they start to discuss a subject – *Ariadne*? *Daphne*? No, says the Count; choose a theme which describes everyday life; write about today's events as all have lived them!

---

[1] A translation of a sonnet by Ronsard.

[2] Strauss wrote the opera without interval but at this point a break has been made, notably (but not exclusively) at Glyndebourne.

The idea is taken up and in the end La Roche sweeps off poet and musician, actress and her admirer, and the Countess retires to her room, leaving the salon to the care of eight servants. No sooner have they left than a voice comes from the darkness. It is Monsieur Taupe, the prompter, who has been asleep and now wonders how on earth he is to get home. The major-domo is almost ready to take him at his own valuation – without him the theatre could not function at all – and offers help in his predicament.

The salon is now lit only by the light of the moon and into it comes the Countess, elegantly dressed. The major-domo follows her in, lights the candles and gives her two messages: that her brother will not be home for supper that evening, and that the poet Olivier will call on her to learn how the opera should

end – tomorrow, at eleven. The stage is set for the great final scene, one of Strauss's most splendid perorations and a hymn in praise of the beauty of the high female voice which leaves one in no doubt as to which side engages the composer's sympathy in the argument between words and music. In the course of the scene, the Countess comes to understand that, since the sonnet, these two men are as inextricably bound up in the art that between them they can produce as they are as rivals for her hand. She sings two verses of the sonnet, looks at herself in the looking-glass and realises that she cannot make the choice which will give the opera an ending. Either alternative seems trivial.

The major-domo solves the problem by announcing that supper is served.   H.

IGOR FYODOROVICH STRAVINSKY
(born 17 June 1882, died 6 April 1971)

Stravinsky is one of the undisputed giants among composers of the twentieth century, over more than sixty years of which he strides as a colossus. Above all perhaps is his contribution to musical theatre. In ballet, he is supreme, prolific, various and consistent; his contribution to opera, if you believe that opera is drama conveyed through music and heightened in the process, is less momentous but also very telling.

Two quotations: 'Perhaps *The Nightingale* only proves that I was right to compose ballets since I was not yet ready for opera ... ';[1] 'If I live to write another opera, I suspect it will be for the electronic glass tube and the Idiot Box, rather than for the early baroque stages of the world's present-day opera houses.'[2] If the first denotes retrospective uncertainty as to his initial approach to opera, surprising perhaps since he had been an operatic enthusiast in youth and was the son of a celebrated singer, the second is consistent with the search for form which is the history of

his operatic endeavour. In over forty years of fairly consistent approach, he produced eight operas[3] in as many forms, only one of full length, another without singing, two more usually associated with the ballet than with opera companies, another for television.

Let us from the outset narrow the field. Stravinsky wrote à propos *The Rake's Progress*: 'I believe music drama and opera to be two very, very different things. My life work is a devotion to the latter.' All the same, though he proclaims himself 'in the line of the classical tradition', right from the start he shows an unwillingness to accept a nineteenth-century concept of opera, inherited, say, from his teacher, Rimsky-Korsakov, for all the latter's influence on *The Nightingale* (1908: 1913–14). His chosen fairy story is quite unheroic in character, and he investigates what one might describe as the more private problems to which it gives rise. In *L'Histoire d'un Soldat*, he has made a virtue out of self-imposed necessity, contriving somehow, while writing a piece whose dimensions by definition are

---

[1] Stravinsky and Craft: *Expositions and Developments*, Faber, 1962.
[2] Stravinsky: 'Working notes for *The Flood*' in *Dialogue and a Diary*, Faber, 1968.

[3] *Rossignol, L'Histoire d'un Soldat, Renard, Mavra, Oedipus Rex, Perséphone* (rated such in Loewenberg's *Annals of Opera*), *The Rake's Progress, The Flood*.

suitable for a village hall, to create something with a far wider relevance, hitting nerve centres unerringly with what the composer himself has described as ' ... characteristic sounds ... the scrape of the violin and the punctuation of the drums. The violin is the soldier's soul, and the drums are the diablerie'. Though his aim was different, one should perhaps note that Stravinsky with this 'economical' piece no more succeeded in creating a cheaper alternative to the standard repertory than did Britten a generation later with his chamber operas. Each produced good art but neither significantly cut costs.

The aftermath of the war coincided with Stravinsky's 'exile' from Russia, and he continued to tap the vein of Russian fairy tale, exotic and fascinating to non-Russian ears, later more fully exploited in *Les Noces*. *Renard* (1917) and *Mavra* (1921), however different from each other, stand in relation to the later masterpiece as a kind of *Parergon*. *Mavra*, with its self-conscious evocation of early, Italian-influenced Russian operas, is almost as dense in texture as *Les Noces* (with of course a quite different vocal idiom). The two works, together with the greater *Les Noces*, represent important aspects of Stravinsky's search for operatic form.

In *Oedipus Rex* (1926–27) stylisation is carried much further than before, a 'dead' language used, action all but eliminated and allowed only at crucial moments, and the story is mostly in the hands of a non-singing narrator. All the same, the music conveys the theme's agonising inevitability every bit as well as any play on the subject, and new aspects of Stravinsky come into play; the violence of the music's hammer blows at critical moments (Jocasta's entry, the mid-way chorus, the Messenger), as well as an ability to convey pathos which contradicts the composer's published tenets (the listener who hears 'Lux facta est' unmoved has a stony heart indeed).

Perséphone (1933–34), with its curiously conceived dialogue between singer and dancer-narrator, could be deemed his least successful stage work, and in fact he did not again attempt musical theatre with words for nearly fifteen years. When he did, the result contained elements of throwback, and was so far from being through-composed as to be nearer Rossini than Wagner or Berg. All the same, *The Rake's Progress* (1948–51) contains its full measure of surprises, whether the extraordinary harpsichord-dominated cemetery scene and its incredibly intense postlude, the ten-bar woodwind-accompanied discovery that Nick's revenge is to leave Tom mad, or the wealth of lyrical melody throughout the score, expressive and moving in a different way from anything in Stravinsky's earlier output. Here Stravinsky comes nearer to comment on human truth on a domestic level than anywhere else, even *L'Histoire du Soldat*: that he did not forge his own new language is less surprising than that here his compassion emerges in such lyrical passages as the trio following Anne's discovery that Tom is married, Baba's Marschallin-like final exit or Anne's cradle song in Bedlam.

All Stravinsky's operas, except for the two greatest, *Oedipus* and *The Rake's Progress*, are direct products of some larger phase of his creative activity, and *The Flood* (1961–62) is representative of a period of serial activity which produced *Movements*; *A Sermon, A Narrative, A Prayer*; *Abraham and Isaac*. It is compact to the point of terseness and invariably powerful. Nothing overall could be less like *The Rake* of eleven years before, and, even though it begins and ends with a hark-back to the choral style of *Noces* and contains more than one echo of *The Rake*'s vocal writing, there is something appropriate in the old innovator finishing, with the first TV opera commissioned from a great composer, an operatic career for whose output we must feel gratitude for what it includes, only strengthened by regret for what we never had – the orchestration and completion of *Khovanshchina*, above all the opera planned with Dylan Thomas but never written. H.

LE ROSSIGNOL
The Nightingale

Opera in three acts, text by the composer and S. Mitousoff after Hans Andersen's fairy tale. Première Paris Opéra, 26 May 1914; first performed Drury Lane, London, 1914, with Dobrovolska, Petrenko, Brian, Andreev, Warfolomeiev, conductor Cooper; Covent Garden, 1919 (in English), with Nelis, conductor E. Goossens (snr.); New York, Metropolitan, 1926, with Talley, conductor Serafin; la Scala, Milan, 1926, with Pasini, conductor Stravinsky; Buenos Aires, 1927, with Dal Monte; Berlin (as ballet), 1929. Revived Holland, 1952, with Mattiwilda Dobbs, conductor Bruck; Sadler's Wells, 1960, by New Opera Company with Marion Studholme (in English); B.B.C. (in concert), 1972, with Elizabeth Harwood, conductor Pierre Boulez (in Russian); Metropolitan, 1981 (with *Sacre* and *Oedipus*), staged by John Dexter, designs by David Hockney and conducted by James Levine (this production was seen at Covent Garden in 1983).

The Fisherman ....Tenor

The Nightingale...Soprano

The Cook ....Mezzo-Soprano

The Chamberlain ....Bass

The Bonze ....Bass

Three Japanese Envoys ....Tenors, Baritone

The Emperor of China ....Baritone

Death..Alto

Chorus of Courtiers and Ghosts

Place: Ancient China
Running Time: 1 hour

Act I. A forest on the seashore at night. At the back of the stage a Fisherman in his boat. He is waiting to hear the Nightingale which delights him every night and causes him to forget his fishing. After a while the Nightingale begins to sing. Other interested spectators arrive – the Emperor's Chamberlain, a Bonze (priest) and the Emperor's Cook, the latter bringing her confederates and other courtiers to give the Nightingale a formal invitation to court to sing before the Emperor. The Nightingale remarks that her voice is far sweeter in the forest than in the palace. Since, however, the Emperor wills it otherwise, the Emperor shall be obeyed. The bird alights on the hand of the Cook, who takes it to the palace while the Fisherman continues to sing the bird's praises.

Act II. The act opens with an entr'acte (with chorus). The chorus inquires of the Cook (who has been appointed 'Grand Cordon Bleu') about the Nightingale. The Cook describes the little bird, whose songs fill the eye with tears. As the curtain rises the Chamberlain announces the Emperor, who arrives in great state with the Nightingale. At a sign from the Emperor the Nightingale begins to sing and the Emperor is so charmed that he offers the Nightingale the order of the Golden Slipper. But the bird requires no other honour than that of having charmed the great monarch. Three envoys from the Emperor of Japan offer the Emperor a mechanical bird which also sings. As soon as the mechanical nightingale's song begins the real one flies away. The Emperor, affronted, condemns it to perpetual banishment. The voice of the Fisherman is heard again.

Act III. The Emperor is ill and Death sits at the foot of his bed wearing the imperial crown and grasping his standard. The Emperor calls for his musicians. The Nightingale answers the call. It has come to banish ghosts and to sing of the dawn. Even Death is persuaded by the loveliness of the song to give back the crown and the standard. The Nightingale's charm has conquered disease, and as the courtiers arrive in solemn procession to salute their ruler whom they expect to find dead, the sun floods the room with light, Death disappears and the Emperor rises from his bed and wishes his courtiers a good morning. The Fisherman bids all acknowledge in the song of the Nightingale the voice of heaven.   F.B.

Le Rossignol was begun in 1908 just before the death of Stravinsky's teacher, Rimsky-Korsakov, but interrupted after the completion of the first act by the commissioning by Diaghilev of *The Firebird*. A request from the newly founded Free Theatre of Moscow to complete the opera led, in 1913, to a resumption of work, but now, of course, by a much maturer composer than the comparative beginner of 1908. The styles of Act I and Acts II and III are, however, not so sharply contrasted that unity is ruled out, particularly taking into account the fact that Act I is little more than a lyrical prologue to the action of the two succeeding Acts; but some critics have found a discrepancy.

The delightful melody of the Fisherman's song, which is used to frame each act, the pageantry of the Chinese March, the delicate, expressive filigree of the Nightingale's exacting coloratura music – these elements are by no means the whole story. The music has charm, the orchestration is masterly without using colour primarily for its own sake, but the truth is that here, as virtually throughout his output, the composer knows as few others how to exercise an iron control over his material; inspiration never leads to excess, a small gesture never produces an over-exuberant musical reaction. It is precisely because the work tells its tale without embellishment, because the nightingale limits her brilliance and does not try to emulate a nineteenth-century heroine – in a word because of Stravinsky's immaculate sense of scale and style – that *Le Rossignol* much more than half a century after it was written can prove so thoroughly rewarding an experience.

Stravinsky made a symphonic poem out of material from the opera (*Le Chant du Rossignol*), using for the first part the prelude and Chinese March from Act II; for the second, the song of the real Nightingale, music associated with the clockwork model from Japan, followed by the Fisherman's song; and for the third, a reworking of music from Act III entitled 'Illness and Recovery of the Emperor of China'. Leonid Massine choreographed it for Diaghilev and its first performance was in Paris in 1920.   H.

L'HISTOIRE D'UN SOLDAT
A Soldier's Tale

A tale to be read, played and danced, libretto by C.F. Ramuz. Première, Lausanne, 28 September 1918. First performed London, in concert at Wigmore Hall, 1920, Arts Theatre Club (staged), 1927; Berlin Volksbühne, 1924; New York, 1926. Revived Edinburgh Festival, 1954, with Moira Shearer, Robert Helpmann, conductor Hans Schmidt-Isserstedt, producer Günter Rennert; Sadler's Wells, 1958, by New Opera Company (in double bill with *Le Rossignol*).

Narrator ....Spoken
The Devil...Actor
The Soldier..Actor
The Princess ....Dancer

Running Time: 50 minutes

An *opera* that has no singing, that was designed to be played in village halls, that has seven instrumentalists accompanying its one dancing and three audible characters? In 1918 Stravinsky was living in Switzerland, short of money and of a theme on which to compose. He and his friend, the Swiss writer Ramuz, decided on a collaboration in which the three elements of music, acting or dancing, and narration, should be almost equal partners. It would involve the smallest forces possible and should be performable in any hall or building or even in the open air. The result is a modern Morality, which makes its not inconsiderable impact as much by means of the pungent, suggestive music as through an ironical text. It is difficult to see exactly what category of musical theatre it fits, but somehow opera seems to be the nearest.

Part I. March of brilliant character (No. 1) sets the scene. A soldier is on his weary way home from the wars. He stops and looks through his pack – there's a picture of his girlfriend and, more impor-

tant, his fiddle, which has been his companion for so long. The fiddle dominates the next section of music (No. 2: Little tunes beside a brook). The Devil, disguised as a little old man with a butterfly net, wants to barter the violin for a book he produces – worth any money, he says, as it foretells the future. The soldier accepts and when the Devil finds he cannot play the instrument, the soldier agrees to teach him.

Off they go together and the soldier lives for two days in great comfort. When he eventually gets home (reprise of the march) he finds that he has been away not three days but three years and that his friends and even his mother and his girlfriend take him for a ghost. Now he understands who was his host for those 'days' of luxury. His dejection and loneliness are shown in a desolate Pastorale (No. 3). He catches sight of his enemy and wants to attack him. But the Devil reminds him of the book he bartered for the fiddle. He starts to read it and its teaching brings him wealth beyond his wildest dreams; only happiness is still out of reach. He is rich, but he begins to suspect that he is dead. The Devil comes now in the guise of an old-clothes woman and begs him to buy something, finally producing an ancient violin, *his* old fiddle – again its sound mocks him (No. 2).

Part II. To the sound of the March (No. 1) the soldier crosses the border to the neighbouring country. In desperation, he has thrown away his possessions and is back as he was at the start, only without his pack. At a frontier inn he hears that the Princess is ill and that the King has promised her hand in marriage to whoever can cure her. Why should he not try his luck? He makes up his mind and to the sound of the royal march (No. 4: a stylised Spanish *Pasodoble*) he arrives at the palace gates and goes inside, only to find the Devil sitting there, disguised as a violin virtuoso. The King promises that he may see the Princess next day.

The narrator eggs the soldier on to play cards against the Devil – if he loses, he'll have no more of the Devil's money and they will be quits. The ruse works and the soldier finds to his joy that he can play the violin again (No. 5: Little concert). Eric White mentions an odd feature of the 'little concert': 'It is curious to find that ... one of the most memorable themes of *The Soldier's Tale* came to Stravinsky in a dream, during which, according to Schaeffner, he saw a gipsy woman seated on the steps at the back of a caravan, playing a violin with the full length of the bow at the same time as she suckled her child. This haunting minor motif is first heard from the cornet followed by the bassoon in the "little concert"[1] and, later, from the violin in the "tango".[2] Although no very extended use is made of it, its character is so strong that in retrospect it seems to flavour the whole work.'[3]

The music rouses the Princess who is cured during the course of three dances (No. 6: tango, waltz and ragtime). Next it is the turn of the Devil, who is obliged to dance till he drops exhausted (No. 7: the Devil's dance). A 'little chorale' (No. 8) celebrates the victory of the lovers, but the Devil in a 'spoken song' (No. 9) swears revenge. There is a 'great chorale' (No. 10) during which the narrator points a moral.

There remains but to finish the 'opera'. The Princess suggests that they might visit the soldier's old home and on the way at the frontier the Devil, who has regained the violin, justifies the title of the last piece of music: 'The triumphal march of the Devil' (No. 11).   H.

RENARD

A burlesque for the stage, to be sung and acted; based on popular Russian folk tales. Words by the composer, French translation by C.F. Ramuz. Première in double bill with *Mavra* at Paris Opéra, 2 June 1922. First produced New York (in concert), 1923; Berlin, 1925; London (B.B.C.), 1935. Revived Edinburgh Festival, 1961, conductor Alexander Gibson.

The Cock..Tenor
The Fox..Tenor
The Goat ....Bass
The Cat..Bass

Running Time: 15 minutes

*R*enard was commissioned by Princesse Edmond de Polignac who expressed the view that, after Wagner and Strauss, the time had come to return to works for small and unusual ensembles and suggested that Stravinsky compose a work of this type to be performed in her Paris house. Stravinsky proposed *Renard*, which had been germinating in his mind for some time – the duet for the cat and the goat was in

fact written some years earlier, while he was working on *Les Noces* in Switzerland. He began work on *Renard* at once and in his enthusiasm he temporarily abandoned the half-finished *Les Noces*.

At this time Stravinsky's friendship with the Swiss writer Ramuz was already well established and, in the course of three years, the two co-operated on the texts of *Les Noces* and *L'Histoire d'un Soldat*, as well as the French translation of *Renard*, whose Russian words Stravinsky himself had already written. This translation took an infinity of time and trouble because of the great importance Stravinsky attached to the relationship of word-sounds and music.

Renard was produced in 1922 for Diaghilev's company by Bronislava Nijinska, the sister of Nijinsky, and the sets were by Larionov, the new work waiting for its première until the completion of *Mavra* (see page 795).

In a note to the score, Stravinsky says, 'The play is acted by clowns, dancers or acrobats, preferably on a trestle stage placed in front of the orchestra.[1] If performed in a theatre it should be played in front of the curtain. The actors remain on the stage all the time. They come on in view of the audience to the strains of the little march, which serves as an introduction, and make their exit in the same way. The actors do not speak. The singers (two tenors and two basses) are placed in the orchestra.' The orchestra is small, containing single woodwind, two horns, trumpet, percussion and single strings, as well as a cembalon, an instrument which had so enchanted Stravinsky when he first heard it in a café in Geneva that he at once bought himself one and learned to play it.

A pompous little *da capo* march introduces the work after which the four singers sing a lively *allegro*, in which they rail against their enemy, the fox. The cock is fidgeting on his perch and we are introduced to him by a broken upward sweep on the cembalon. In a mournful little song he describes his daily life, after which the fox to another cembalon *arpeggio* enters disguised as a nun. He begs the cock to come down and confess his sins, but the cock recognises him and refuses (to a phrase from the first *allegro*). The fox renews his efforts, and reminds the cock of his offensively polygamous domestic arrangements,

---

[1] Sections 13 to 15, 17 and 18.
[2] Sections 4 and 8.
[3] In *Stravinsky: a critical survey*, 1947.
[1] cf. *L'Histoire d'un Soldat.*

to such effect that the silly bird hops down from his perch with a resounding crash on cymbal and drums. Renard, of course, grabs him at once and the cock screeches to the cat and the goat to come to his help. They do so and drive the fox away, after which cock, goat and cat dance triumphantly.

The second part begins with the cock climbing complacently on to his perch, to the same cembalon chord as before, and resuming his sad little song which is again interrupted by the fox, this time not in disguise. The fox once more tries to wheedle the cock down to the ground with flattering words and glittering promises, even at one moment – in an attempt at disguise? – using a bass voice. The idiotic cock resists for a time but in the end jumps down again to a resounding bang from the bass drum. The fox pounces and this time things look very black for the poor cock as his friends the cat and the goat take a good deal longer than before in coming to his aid. The fox begins to pull out all his feathers, and the cock, in desperation, sings a *moderato* aria to the fox, begging for mercy. In the end, realising it is all in vain, the cock prays for the welfare of all his surviving relatives and finally passes out.

The cat and the goat enter and sing a jolly *scherzando*, accompanying themselves on the *guzla*. In their song, they pretend to be well disposed towards the fox who becomes momentarily distracted when they suggest that Mrs Fox is betraying him; this is their chance and they strangle him. The four singers shout triumphantly seven times, after which the actors dance for joy and in conclusion ask for a token of gratitude from the audience if they have been pleased. The opening march is played once more and the performers leave the stage.   H.

MAVRA

Opera buffa in one act, text by Boris Kochno after Pushkin. Première Paris, 2 June 1922, by Diaghilev company with Slobodskaya, Sadoven, Rozovska, Skoupevski, conductor Gregor Fitelberg. First performed Krolloper, Berlin, 1928, London (B.B.C.), 1934, Philadelphia Orchestra, 1934; Rome, 1942, with Iris Adami-Corradetti, Elvira Casazza, Augusto Ferrauto, conductor Previtali; la Scala, 1942; Edinburgh Festival, 1958, by Hamburg Opera with Melitta Muszely, Gisela Litz, Jürgen Förster, conductor Leopold Ludwig.

Parasha	Soprano
The Neighbour	Mezzo-Soprano
The Mother	Contralto
The Hussar	Tenor

Place: Russia
Time: The Reign of Charles X
Running Time: 30 minutes

Stravinsky has said that *Mavra* was conceived because the natural sympathy he had always felt for the melodic language, vocal style and conventions of the old Russo-Italian opera induced him to experiment with this style at a time when it was almost extinct. He wrote *Mavra* 'in the direct tradition of Glinka and Dargomizhsky'.[1]

The work was composed while the composer was living at Biarritz but was interrupted by orchestration he had to do for Diaghilev for the London revival of *The Sleeping Beauty*. It was completed in March 1922, except for the overture which was added later in Paris.

The scene is a Russian village. The opera opens in the living-room of the house occupied by Parasha and her mother. Parasha, in love with the Hussar who lives nearby, sings of her impatience as she sits at her embroidery.[2] Her lover comes to the window and the two sing a duet. The Hussar goes away and the Mother appears, complaining at length of the difficulty of getting a servant now that her old and apparently perfect cook has died. She urges Parasha to find her a new maid. The Mother grumbles on and is joined by the Neighbour; the two women complain happily about the servant problem, the state of the weather and the price of clothes these days.

Parasha comes triumphantly back with a young woman who, she says, will be just right. Her name is Mavra and she used to be in service with old Anna next door. It is, of course, the Hussar in disguise, but the Mother and the Neighbour are both taken in and the four unite in a quartet, the women telling Mavra that the new girl has a lot to live up to, and the Hussar joining in sympathetically. The Neighbour goes home, the Mother upstairs and the scheming lovers sing ecstatically of the success of their plan and the happiness it will bring them.

The Mother reappears, gives Mavra a mass of work to do and takes Parasha off for a walk, saying

---

[1] Stravinsky: *Poetics of music: in the form of six lessons* (O.U.P., 1947).

[2] This aria is sometimes heard in Stravinsky's own arrangement for solo violin.

in an aside that she is going to return early just to make sure the girl is a good worker. Left alone, the Hussar sings of his love for Parasha and the wonderful days which lie ahead, after which he decides to make the most of his solitude and shave himself. In the middle of this operation, complicated as it is by unfamiliar furniture and female attire, the Mother comes back and is so shocked at what she sees that she faints. The Neighbour rushes in, and the curtain falls as the Hussar jumps out of the window leaving Parasha calling plaintively after him.   H.

OEDIPUS REX
Oedipus the King

Opera-oratorio in two acts, text by Jean Cocteau after Sophocles, translated into Latin by J. Daniélou. Première, Théâtre Sarah Bernhardt, Paris, 30 May 1927 (in concert), conducted by Stravinsky. First performed on the stage in Vienna, 1928; Berlin, 1928, conductor Klemperer; New York (concert), 1928; New York (stage), 1931, conductor Stokowski; London, Queen's Hall (concert), 1936, with Slobodskaya, Widdop, Harold Williams, Norman Walker, conductor Ansermet; la Scala, Milan, 1948, with Danco, Demetz, conductor Sanzogno; Cologne, 1951, with Mödl, Pears, Rehfuss, conductor Stravinsky (concert); Holland Festival, 1952, with Bouvier, Vroons, conductor Bruck; Sadler's Wells, 1960, with Monica Sinclair, Dowd, conductor Colin Davis; New York, City Opera, 1959, with Claramae Turner, Cassilly, conductor Stokowski; la Scala, Milan, 1969, with Horne, Lajos Kozma, conductor Abbado; Metropolitan, 1981 (with *Sacre* and *Rossignol*), staged by John Dexter, sets by David Hockney, conducted by James Levine.

Oedipus, *King of Thebes* ....Tenor
Jocasta, *his wife*..................................Mezzo-Soprano
Creon,[1] *Jocasta's brother* ....Bass-Baritone
Tiresias, *a soothsayer*..Bass
The Shepherd ....Tenor
The Messenger[1]..................................Bass-Baritone
Narrator ....Spoken

Chorus (Tenors and Basses)

Place: Ancient Greece
Running Time: 1 hour

The action is continuous, although divided into two acts. It is put forward in the shape of six tableaux, with a minimum of action (the characters are directed to give the impression of living statues), and that explained beforehand in the language of the audience by a narrator. The text is in Latin.

Act I. 1st tableau. The Narrator sets the scene for the audience; of Oedipus he says: 'At the moment of his birth a snare was laid for him – and you will see the snare closing'. In the opening chorus, 'Kaedit nos pestis,'[2] the men of Thebes lament the plague which is destroying the inhabitants of the town. They beg their king, Oedipus, to help them in their affliction. This he promises to do: 'Liberi, vos liberabo.'

2nd tableau. Creon, who has been sent to Delphi to consult the oracle, returns. In an aria, 'Respondit deus', he reports that the god has revealed that Laius' murderer still lives on in Thebes, undetected and unpunished. He must be discovered. Oedipus answers that he himself, with his skill in solving riddles, will track down the murderer: 'Non reperias vetus skelus.'

3rd tableau. The chorus prays to Minerva, Diana and Phoebus (or Athene, Artemis, and Apollo, as they would be in Greek), and welcomes Tiresias, whom Oedipus has decided to consult. Tiresias is blind, and referred to by the Narrator as 'the fountain of truth', but at first he refuses to answer the King's questions. Oedipus taunts him, and he makes it clear that he will hold nothing more back; the King's assassin is a king! ('Dikere non possum'). Oedipus is furious at the implication behind the words, and suggests that Creon and Tiresias are in league to oust him from the throne: 'Stipendarius es' he snarls at Tiresias. The aria ('Invidia fortunam odit') dies away in silence, and is succeeded by a magnificent chorus of greeting and praise to Queen Jocasta: 'Gloria!'

Act II begins with a reprise of the sonorous 'Gloria' chorus.

4th tableau. Jocasta is now seen on the stage. She

---

[1] These roles may be taken by the same singer.

[2] The spelling used is often onomatopoeic, to ensure uniform pronunciation.

has come, says the Narrator, attracted by the dispute of her husband and her brother. How can they raise their voices thus in anger in the stricken city ('Nonn' erubeskite, reges')? Oracles, she says, are accustomed to deceive those who consult them ('Mentita sunt oracula'); did they not predict that her former husband, Laius, would be killed by his own son, and was he not in fact murdered by robbers at the cross-roads ('trivium') between Daulia and Delphi? The chorus takes up the word 'trivium', but its repetition has the effect of filling Oedipus with horror. In a duet with Jocasta ('Pavesco subito, Jocasta') he explains that on his way from Corinth to Thebes he himself killed a stranger at that very crossroads. Jocasta makes an attempt to reassure him ('Oracula mentiuntur'), but it is of little avail.

5th tableau. The messenger steps forward to inform Oedipus that King Polybus is dead, and that Oedipus, so far from being his son, was only adopted by him. Oedipus as a baby was rescued by a shepherd after he had been abandoned on the mountain side and then handed over to King Polybus ('Reppereram in monte puerum Oedipoda'). The shepherd corroborates his evidence, and his words so overwhelm the Queen that she disappears from the scene, convinced and horror-stricken by what she has heard. Oedipus, however, thinks she is merely ashamed of his apparently lowly birth ('Nonne monstrum reskituri'), and it is only after the messenger and the shepherd unite to accuse him of parricide and incest that he is conscious of his crime and its enormity. The chorus repeats the words of the King's accusers, after which shepherd and messenger withdraw. With a quiet dignity that has not been in evidence in his previous utterances, Oedipus resigns himself to acknowledge the truth. On the words 'Lux facta est', he disappears.[1]

6th tableau. The messenger reappears, and the Narrator explains that the audience is about to hear the monologue: 'The divine Jocasta is dead'; he describes how she has hanged herself and how Oedipus has pierced his eyeballs with the golden pin Jocasta wore. He bids farewell to Oedipus – Oedipus whom his people loved.

The great scene in which the messenger and the chorus bewail Jocasta's suicide ('Divum Jocastae caput mortuum!') brings the work to its emotional climax.

As the messenger disappears, and Oedipus is seen with his pierced eyes, the chorus comments gently on his broken condition and bids him a last farewell.

The work is short, and from the opening chorus the expression is direct and, whether Stravinsky liked it or not, emotional. Oedipus himself is a fascinating character study, passing as he does from the heights of power and self-confidence, through arrogance (in his attitude to Creon and Tiresias) and self-pity ('Amiki, amiki' in the aria 'Invidia fortunam odit'), until he reaches a condition of understanding and horror at his position. It is interesting to note that he uses a musical language that is, in its vocal line, curiously like that of Monteverdi's *Orfeo*, particularly in its expressive use of coloratura (e.g. Ex. 1). Oedipus is the central figure, but the climaxes are often associated with his surroundings. Successive heights of intensity are reached with the magnificent 'Gloria' chorus which closes the first act and begins the second, the aria for Jocasta and her duet with Oedipus, and the very powerful section in which the Messenger and the chorus lament the suicide of Jocasta. The form of the work might sound anti-operatic to those who have not heard it; but the music expresses drama and character in every bar, and even if stylisation had been avoided and movement included at every possible moment, nothing would have been added to the total effect, which remains shattering. H.

THE RAKE'S PROGRESS

Opera in three acts and an epilogue, text by W.H. Auden and Chester Kallman. Première, Venice Festival, 11 September 1951, with Schwarzkopf, Tourel, Tangeman, Rounseville, Otakar Kraus, Cuénod, Arié, conductor Stravinsky. First performed Zürich, 1951, with Harvey, Malaniuk, Lichtegg, Wolff, conductor Reinshagen; Stuttgart, 1951, with Wissmann, Marta Fuchs, Holm, Neidlinger, conductor Leitner; la Scala, Milan, 1951, with Schwarzkopf, Elmo, Picchi, Kraus, Cuénod, conductor Leitner; London (B.B.C. broadcast), 1953, with Catley, Pollak, Alexander Young, Kraus, conductor Sacher; Metropolitan, New York, 1953, with Gueden, Thébom, Conley, Harrell, conductor Reiner; Sadler's Wells, 1962, with Morison, Young, Herincx, conductor Colin Davis.

Trulove ....Bass
Anne, *his daughter* ....Soprano

---

[1] By means of a trap-door, according to the original stage directions.

Tom Rakewell, *her sweetheart*............................Tenor
Nick Shadow ....Baritone
Mother Goose, *a brothel-keeper*............Mezzo-Soprano
Baba the Turk, *bearded lady* ....Mezzo-Soprano
Sellem, *the auctioneer*..Tenor
Keeper of the Madhouse......................................Bass

Whores and Roaring Boys, Servants, Citizens,
   Madmen

Place: England
Time: Eighteenth Century
Running Time: 2 hours 25 minutes

It was a post-war viewing of Hogarth's prints *The Rake's Progress* which suggested the subject to Stravinsky, who was quick to contact W.H. Auden who in his turn brought in Chester Kallman as co-librettist. Stravinsky's publishers, Boosey and Hawkes, planned the première for Covent Garden, but the composer himself sold the world première to Venice and the European to Milan, a hard-fought compromise bringing the company of la Scala to perform *The Rake* in Venice at the Festival. The opera, in spite of a less than auspicious start, began a journey which has taken it round the world as one of the operas of the second half of the century likely to last well into the next. It is, incidentally, the climax of the composer's Neoclassical phase.

Act I, scene i. After a very short prelude, the scene shows the garden of Trulove's house in the country. It is spring. In an arbour, Anne and Tom are seated. A trio develops, Anne and Tom rejoicing in the season which seems made for their love ('The woods are green'), and Trulove in the background expressing the hope that his fears about Tom's future may prove unfounded. Anne goes indoors and Trulove tells Tom that he has secured for him the offer of a city position. When Tom declines, he comments that his daughter may choose a poor husband, but he will see to it she does not marry a lazy one.

Tom is scornful of his prospective father-in-law's attitude; why should he waste his time in an office? He has other plans, and proposes to rely primarily on the goddess of fortune. 'Since it is not by merit we rise or we fall' is the burden of his aria, whose vigorous expression suggests that Tom underestimates his own energies. He breaks off: 'I wish I had money.' Immediately a figure appears at the garden gate, and asks for Tom Rakewell. It is Nick Shadow, the bearer,

so he says, of good tidings for Tom and anyone else who wishes him well. Tom calls into the house for Anne and Trulove, and Nick tells all three that Tom has been left a fortune by an unknown uncle.

Tom rejoices in his good luck and thanks Nick for his tidings. Nick in his turn thanks him that he has found a new master, and Anne and Trulove thank God for the turn in Tom's fortunes. The words 'Be thanked' for each character are set to a dropping minor ninth. For a moment, Tom and Anne sing happily to one another ('O clement love'), but Nick interrupts to say that the inheritance of a fortune entails certain business transactions; they must go up to London immediately. Anne starts to say goodbye to Tom, Nick returns to say the carriage awaits, and Tom agrees to reckon up what his services have been worth a year and a day after his engagement. A further farewell, a further warning on the part of Trulove that fortune so easily come by may prove an inducement to idleness, and the stage is clear. Nick turns to the audience: 'The Progress of a Rake begins.'

Scene ii is set in Mother Goose's brothel. It opens with a brilliant introduction and chorus for Whores and Roaring Boys. Nick asks Tom to recite to Mother Goose what he has been taught, and only when Nick mentions the word 'love' does Tom falter in his lesson. According to custom, Tom is asked to sing. 'Love too frequently betrayed' is the theme of his beautiful cavatina, with its rippling clarinet accompaniment.

Mother Goose claims Tom as hers for the night, and the chorus sings away merrily (in a manner not far removed from 'Oranges and Lemons'), their refrain, 'Lanterloo', bringing the scene to an end.

Scene iii has the same setting as scene i. Anne is sad that no word has come from Tom since he left for London. 'Quietly, Night, O find him and caress' she sings in a full-scale aria. There is an interruption as Trulove calls from the house, and Anne makes up her mind that Tom needs her more than her father does. This gives the cue for the cabaletta (Stravinsky actually uses the word in the score – perhaps the only time a composer has ever done this); it is a lively tune punctuated by a brilliant little orchestral *ritornello*: 'I go to him. Love cannot falter.'

Act II, scene i. The morning room of Tom's house in London. Tom is at breakfast. He sings of the city's disillusion, which he contrasts with life as it would have been at the side of the one true person he knows and of whom now he dare not even think. The music is in the form of an extended, loosely knit *scena*: 'Vary the song, O London, change!'

At Tom's words 'I wish I were happy', Nick appears and shows his master an advertisement for a circus, in which is featured Baba the Turk, the bearded lady. Let him advise his master: marry Baba! The music of Nick's aria for the first time suggests the sinister purpose behind the façade of bonhomie. It is agreed that Tom shall marry Baba the Turk.

Scene ii. Outside Tom's house in London. Anne has arrived and is waiting apprehensively for him to return home. A procession of servants carries parcels into the house, and Anne wonders what their significance can be. A sedan chair is borne in. Tom gets out of it and comes quickly up to Anne. She must leave London, where 'Virtue is a day coquette', and forget him; he is not worthy of her. At that moment a head is poked out of the sedan chair; it is Baba, heavily veiled, demanding to know how much longer she is to be kept waiting. Tom admits she is his wife. There is a trio in which Anne and Tom sing of their might-have-beens, and Baba expresses her extreme dislike of being kept waiting. Anne leaves, Tom helps Baba from the chair, and, as a climax to the scene, she unveils and reveals her beard.

Scene iii. The same room as Act II, scene i, except that it is now cluttered with every conceivable kind of object: stuffed animals and birds, cases of minerals, china, glass, etc. Tom and Baba are at breakfast. Tom sulks, but Baba chatters on breathlessly. After a bit she becomes conscious that Tom has not spoken, and turns lovingly to him. He repulses her, and, losing her temper, she paces furiously about the room, smashing the more fragile but less valuable parts of her collection, and proclaiming angrily that Tom must be in love with the girl he met when they first came to the house. She embarks on a florid phrase, but Tom, throwing patience to the winds, seizes his wig and shoves it over her face back to front so that she is cut off in mid-note.

His misery is complete, and there is only one remedy: sleep. Nick comes in, wheeling an object covered with a dust sheet. He removes it and discloses a fantastic baroque machine, into which he puts first a loaf of bread, and then above it a piece of broken china. He turns the handle, out comes the loaf. Tom wakes up with the words 'I wish it were true', and explains to Nick that he has had a dream in which he invented a machine which turned stones to bread, and so relieved the sufferings of mankind. Nick asks him if it was anything like what he sees beside him, and Tom demonstrates it to his own complete satisfaction. Nick suggests he ought to tell his wife. 'My wife?' says Tom with a gesture in her direction, 'I have no wife. I've buried her.'

Act III. The first scene is laid in Tom's room, as for Act II, scene iii, except that now everything is covered in dust and cobwebs. Baba is still sitting motionless at the table, with the wig over her face. An auction is about to take place, and the citizens are examining the objects up for sale. Anne comes in but no one can give her any definite news of Tom.

The door is flung open and in comes Sellem, preceded by servants carrying an auctioneer's apparatus. He gets down to business straight away, and his patter is as resourceful (and as meaningless) as one would expect. It is all carried off with great style, and the waltz tune as Sellem puts up the various items is positively elegant in its inconsequentiality (as witness the incomparable performance of Hugues Cuénod at the première). Finally he comes to Baba, whom he introduces in an awe-struck whisper:

An unknown object draws us, draws us near.
A cake? An organ? Golden Apple Tree?

The bidding rises higher and higher, and Sellem, to calm the crowd, snatches off the wig. Baba finishes her phrase, and turns to strike consternation into the bystanders. Even the sound of the voices of Tom and Nick off-stage (singing a ballad tune which resembles 'Lilliburlero') in no way disconcerts her: 'The pigs of plunder' is her only comment. She comforts Anne: 'You love him, seek to set him right: He's but a shuttle-headed lad'; then, with the greatest dignity, announces her intention of returning to the stage and her interrupted career.

Again, the voices of Tom and Nick are heard below, and Anne leads the *stretto-finale*. Baba tells Sellem to fetch her carriage, and orders the crowd out of her way: 'The next time you see Baba, you shall pay.'

The scene changes to a churchyard. The smell of death is in the music, with the harpsichord somehow providing a colour which is deeply sinister, and

The Rake's Progress (*Glyndebourne, 1975, director John Cox, designer David Hockney*). *The auction scene, Act III: 'Ruin, disaster, shame'.*

Tom's utterances have a new sense of seriousness:

Nick reveals himself in his true colours (to the tune of the ballad):

> A year and a day have passed away
> Since first to you I came ...
> 'Tis not your money but your soul
> Which I this night require.

The vocal writing for Tom, caught in the trap of his own devising, in some respects recalls that for Oedipus in a similar situation; it is Stravinsky at his most expressive and his most powerful, and the crucial scene of the opera. Nick relents to the extent of inviting Tom to play cards in a last effort to save himself from hell. Tom wins the game, but in his rage Nick condemns him to insanity.

Nick sinks into a nearby grave and the stage remains dark for a moment. When the lights come up again, Tom is sitting on a green mound, putting grass in his hair and singing in a child-like voice: 'With roses crowned, I sit on ground, Adonis is my name' (the ballad-tune again). The scene is very short, but the musical suggestion of madness is achieved with economy of means but extremely moving results.

The scene changes to Bedlam. Tom is surrounded by madmen. In his own mind he is still Adonis, and he exhorts the company to prepare for his wedding with Venus. The sound of a key turning in the lock is heard, and the chorus's reaction is swift. But it is the jailer bringing with him Anne, who has come to visit Tom. Anne addresses Tom as Adonis, and in a moment he is happy not only that she has come, but that he has disproved his fellow madmen, who predicted that no Venus would answer his call. There is a love duet, and at its end Anne helps the exhausted Tom on to the straw pallet which lies in the middle of the room. She rocks him to sleep with a Lullaby ('Gently, little boat'). The jailer brings in her father, who leads her gently away.

When she has gone, Tom wakes and raves of his Venus, who was with him and has disappeared. The others will not believe that she was ever there, and he sinks back dead on the mattress. The curtain descends and in front of it step the five principal characters, Anne, Baba, Tom, Nick, and Trulove, to sing an epilogue. The Moral:

> For idle hands
> and hearts and minds
> The Devil finds
> A work to do.   H.

FRANZ von SUPPÉ
(born 18 April 1819, died 21 May 1895)

BOCCACCIO

Opera in three acts, libretto by F. Zell and R. Genée. Première at Carl Theatre, Vienna, 1 February 1879, with Fräulein Link as Boccaccio, and Fräulein Streitmann as Fiametta. First performed New York, Thalia Theater, 1880; London, Royal Comedy Theatre, 1882. Revived New York, Metropolitan (with recitatives by Bodanzky), 1931, with Jeritza as Boccaccio, conductor Bodanzky; Vienna, Volksoper, 1951, with Fred Liewehr as Boccaccio and Réthy, Lorna Sidney, Carl Dönch, Szemere, conductor Paulik.

Fiametta, *foster-daughter of Lambertuccio*	Soprano
Boccaccio, *a writer*	Tenor[1]
Lambertuccio, *a grocer*	Tenor
Beatrice, *wife of Scalza*	Soprano
Peronella, *wife of Lambertuccio*	Contralto
Pietro, *Prince of Palermo*	Tenor
Scalza, *a barber*	Baritone
Leonetto, *a student*	Baritone
Isabella, *Lotteringhi's wife*	Mezzo-Soprano
Lotteringhi, *a cooper of Florence*	Tenor
Checco, *a beggar*	Bass
A Bookseller	Baritone
Major-Domo	Baritone

Place: Florence
Time: 1331

Born in Dalmatia of Austrian parents of Belgian descent who were members of the civil service, Suppé took to the theatre at an early age, wrote theatre music of all kinds in Vienna, sang in smaller theatres, and conducted operas. He was the first composer to write, in imitation of the French, operettas in what became the Viennese style. His greatest successes came with *Fatinitza* and *Boccaccio*, the latter of which is his only operetta, apart from the short *Die schöne Galathee*, regularly performed today. Like Smetana in Czechoslovakia, he had to learn the language in which he wrote for the stage, and his German is said never to have been perfect.

The overture, compounded, apart from the romantic horn tune at the start, of lively tunes from the operetta, is one of the most satisfactory in the genre and well-known as a concert curtain-raiser on Viennese nights.

Act I. The square in front of the church of Santa Maria Novella, where a crowd of beggars, led by Checco, is preparing to use the opportunities offered by a public holiday. Leonetto slips unnoticed into the house of Scalza, whose wife Beatrice has thoughtfully provided him with a key. Students and townspeople celebrate the holiday with a tarantella. A bookseller

---

[1] Sometimes, as at the première, sung by a soprano.

comes by plying his trade, but the offer of some of Boccaccio's stories, which breathe the very scandal of Florence, incenses the worthy citizenry and the bookseller is driven off, in spite of protests from the students.

When Scalza returns home, his wife is by no means alone – Boccaccio as well as his friend Leonetto look out in alarm at the appearance of her husband. Beatrice decides to save herself embarrassment by calling for help, Boccaccio and Leonetto emerge and stage a mock duel, which Scalza tries to stop and which is aggravated when the townspeople take sides and join in the fun. Scalza drags his wife indoors, leaving the others to discuss the ethics of love, a subject Boccaccio takes up in a lively song ('Ich sehe einen jungen Mann dort stehn') – it may become one of his tales, he explains.

Boccaccio hides to listen to Fiametta and Peronella talking of Fiametta's forthcoming marriage to a man of high position. Fiametta sings a romance ('Hab' ich nur deine Liebe'): love without faithfulness has made many a maiden happy, fidelity without love has brought joy to none. Boccaccio joins enthusiastically in the refrain.

Boccaccio devises a scheme to approach Fiametta again, and dresses himself up as a beggar. Meanwhile Pietro is mistaken by Lambertuccio and Lotteringhi for Boccaccio, whose writings they all fear, but he evades them and leaves the coast clear for the disguised Boccaccio to beg for alms from Fiametta. She recognises his voice, and it is clear from their charming duet that what starts as a flirtation is likely to become something more.

Lotteringhi and Lambertuccio lead the older citizens of Florence – particularly the married men – in the hunt for Boccaccio; they enlist the help of Scalza, and he saves Pietro, who has been captured in error but who is quickly recognised by Scalza as the Prince of Palermo. There is nothing left for it but to turn on the offending books themselves; they seize them from the bookseller, build a fire and burn them, while the students, led by Boccaccio, cry to be avenged on stupidity. Truth and honour will survive, they maintain, will rise in fact like a phoenix from the ashes. In spite of its dramatic action, the music of this finale remains merry and charming.

Act II. Boccaccio, Pietro and Leonetto join together in serenading their loved ones, Fiametta, Isabella and Peronella, and hide when Lotteringhi makes his appearance. His wife, Isabella, scolds him for the row he's making with his assistants, and in revenge he sings the Cooper's Song: his wife has got so used to nagging that it has become her favourite pastime and he can get his own back only by banging away at his barrels. Boccaccio meanwhile has taken advantage of the interruption to write love letters to each of the three recipients of the recent serenades, and their delighted reaction to the letters produces one of the most attractive numbers in the score, a trio ('Wie pocht mein Herz so ungestüm') with an enchanting waltz refrain – a tune good enough to make the fortune of any operetta. Peronella and Leonetto, Isabella and Pietro, declare their love for each other, but are interrupted by the return of Lotteringhi.

Boccaccio, again in disguise to be near Fiametta, tells Lambertuccio that there is a magic tree in his garden, whose property is to make anyone who sits in its branches believe that the couple beneath is making love – he proves his point with Fiametta. Meanwhile Isabella entices her husband Lotteringhi into an empty wine cask, while she and Pietro, Leonetto and Peronella add to the demonstration of the tree's unusual qualities, and musically the sextet of lovers is turned into an octet by the addition of one husband up a tree and another in a barrel.

The idyllic scene is interrupted by Scalza bringing news that Boccaccio has been seen entering the house. Positions are reversed, the lovers hide, the husbands emerge to join in the hunt, but the women are able to reveal that the supposed culprit is the man who brings the money to pay for Fiametta's board and lodging! He has now come to take her away, much to her consternation. Boccaccio and his two friends have therefore not only to make their own escape but also to contrive the release of Fiametta as well. Fiametta greets the news of his plan with a reprise of the waltz tune, and as she is borne off in her sedan chair, Boccaccio springs out, dressed as the devil, and scares the crowd away.

Act III. In the garden of the Duke's palace, Pietro admits to Boccaccio that he is the mysterious nobleman to whom Fiametta is due to be married; she is the Duke's natural daughter and has now been granted the title of Princess. Fiametta for her part discovers that her lover is none other than the famous writer Boccaccio and not at all the humble student she had taken him to be. Their misunderstandings are made up in a charming 6/8 duet ('Mia bella fiorentina').

Boccaccio next has to defend himself against the attacks on his writings by Lotteringhi, Lambertuccio and Scalza (who of course do not know him by sight). The women support his contention that it is a writer's job to fight with wit, humour and honesty against the folly of the world. He even counsels the men to do all in their power to prevent their wives becoming bored – therein will lie their undoing.

It remains only for Boccaccio to persuade Prince Pietro to give up Fiametta, and this he succeeds in doing during a theatrical entertainment given in the Duke's house. A reprise of his motto – wit, humour and honesty are sharp-edged weapons; victory is to him who uses them well – brings to an end a Viennese score which must be among the best specimens of the kind not written by Johann Strauss.   H.

KAROL SZYMANOWSKI
(born 6 October 1882, died 29 March 1937)

Karol Szymanowski in his lifetime occupied a curious position as the first Polish composer since Chopin to make an impact on the greater musical world, indeed the first since Moniuszko to write his name in the history books at all. Born of a land-owning family, after the Russian Revolution he led a life of poverty, in spite of a considerable reputation as both composer and pianist, and was repeatedly forced back on the charity of his friends for sheer survival. As well as a substantial list of compositions he was a fairly extensive writer, and his novel *Efebos* has a homosexual theme, an *apologia pro vita sua*. *King Roger* is his second opera; the first, *Hagith* (1912–13; performed 1922), is a one-acter with a lurid plot, modelled according to his biographer B.M. Maciejewski on *Salome*. Before 1914, Szymanowski travelled rather extensively in Russia and Europe and even ventured as far as Algiers, developing a strong taste for the Orient, sufficiently deep for no less a judge than Kaikhosru Sorabji to praise him as 'no European in Eastern fancy-dress'.

KING ROGER
Król Roger

Opera in three acts, libretto by J. Iwaszkiewicz. Première, Warsaw, 19 June 1926, with Stanislava Korwin-Szymanowska (the composer's sister), Eugeniusz Mossakowski as King Roger, Adam Tobosz as the Shepherd, conducted by Emil Młynarski.

First performed in German, Duisburg, 1928; in Czech in Prague, 1932; in Italian, Palermo during I.S.C.M. Festival, 1949, with Clara Petrella, Annaloro, Inghilleri, conductor Mieczyslaw Mierzejewski; in English, 1955 (B.B.C. broadcast), with Joyce Gartside, Rowland Jones, Redvers Llewellyn, conductor Stanford Robinson; London, New Opera Company, 1975, with Janet Gail, David Hillman, Peter Knapp, conductor Charles Mackerras.

Roger II, *King of Sicily*......................................Baritone
Roxana, *his wife*...Soprano
Edrisi, *an Arab scholar* ....Tenor
The Shepherd ....Tenor
The Archbishop ....Bass
An Abbess..Contralto

Priests, Monks, Nuns, the King's Guard, Norman Knights, etc.

Place: Sicily
Time: Twelfth Century
Running Time: 1 hour 45 minutes

The genesis of *King Roger* seems to have come in conversations between the composer and his cousin Iwaszkiewicz, in which Szymanowski made clear his enthusiasm for the beauties of Sicily and particularly for its unique mixture of Greek, Arabic, Byzantine and Latin elements able to coexist there just as had, until the end of the twelfth century, men of differing creeds. Intellectually, the opera represents conflict between Christian and pagan ideals, or between the pulls of the Dionysian and the Apollonian within each of us.[1] The music has some-

---

[1] See Henze's *The Bassarids*, pages 348–52.

thing of the opulence and texture of Szymanowski's contemporaries Strauss and Scriabin, with occasionally the sharp insight of Debussy.

Act I. The interior of a Byzantine cathedral, rich with characteristics of East and West. It is filled with worshippers and the Archbishop stands in front of the altar as the sound is heard of a great psalm of praise to God. The King and his court enter ceremoniously to a musical climax, and Archbishop and Abbess enjoin him to protect the Church from her enemies and in particular from a new voice who corrupts men and women alike. Edrisi explains that they are speaking of a young shepherd boy, and Roxana raises her voice to beg the King at least to hear the boy in his own defence. The King commands that he be brought before him as the throng calls for his destruction.

To the King's questions, the Shepherd answers elliptically in a long, ecstatic utterance of considerable lyrical impact – his god is young, beautiful and full of life. To the King's obvious discomfiture, Roxana's reaction to his words is favourable, and for a moment he is disposed to order the Shepherd's instant death but relents and agrees to let him go free. Finally, to the fury of the worshippers, he orders his appearance that very night at the palace gate. The Shepherd leaves on the same note of ecstasy as had characterised the explanation of his philosophy.

Act II. The inner courtyard of the King's palace, where that night the King awaits his visitor. The gorgeous texture of the music perfectly conveys the hot Mediterranean night, as well as the tension in the King's mind, much of it, as Edrisi finds when he tries unavailingly to comfort him, on account of the sympathy he senses between his beloved Roxana and the Shepherd. In the distance they hear the sound of tambourines and zithers and immediately, on high A flat, Roxana starts to sing, wordlessly at first, but with rapt concentration and in a highly evocative manner. This is the score's best-known moment, more, unfortunately, from Pawel Kochanski's transcription for violin and piano than from performances of the opera.

The King is enraptured by the song but knows it is sung in honour of the Shepherd. Watchmen announce the Shepherd's appearance and, with a group of four followers carrying musical instruments, he advances towards the King's throne. He greets the King in the name of eternal love and tells him he comes from

Benares in India. He proclaims that it is God who has sent him, from God that he derives his powers, and in another extended lyrical passage sings the praises of his faith, until the King stops him, horror-stricken at what he brands as blasphemy. Immediately, Roxana's song starts again, arousing the Shepherd's evident delight and the King's no less evident jealousy.

Eventually, the Shepherd's followers start an Arabic dance, initially in 7/8, and gradually all join in, until Roxana herself becomes visible in the gallery above the courtyard and in her turn starts to sing with the Shepherd and the others. Beside himself with rage, King Roger orders the guards to bind the Shepherd with chains, so that he stands fettered by Roxana's side. Angrily, the Shepherd breaks the bonds and casts them at the King's feet, then calls to Roxana and the people and leads them slowly from the King's presence into what he describes as the Kingdom of Light. The King is left alone in his grief with Edrisi, then suddenly throws aside crown, mantle and sword, announcing that he too will follow the Shepherd, as a pilgrim, no longer as king.

Act III. Among the ruins of a Greek temple appear King Roger and the faithful Edrisi, the former still lamenting his powerless state in the face of his lost love, the latter begging him to call aloud to the echoes. At last he does so, and his cry of 'Roxana!' gets from the distance an immediate answer in the unmistakable voice of Roxana, only for his second attempt to receive a similar answer in the Shepherd's voice. The King's consternation is only partly assuaged by the Shepherd's admonition to leave his fear where he left his sword, and when a moment later Roxana reaches her hand towards him, he still cannot believe that the Shepherd is not playing a cruel joke. Roxana tries to persuade him that the Shepherd is in fact all round him, in every natural thing, and it is not long before Roxana and the King begin to throw great heaps of flowers on the fire which burns on the altar. The Shepherd has by now turned into the Greek god Dionysus and the members of his train into bacchants and maenads, and they whirl into a mad dance, in which Roxana joins, until gradually all disappear, leaving Roger alone with Edrisi. But through his trials the King has grown and it is with confidence, indeed rapture, that he greets the rising of the sun in a splendid paean of thanksgiving as the opera comes to an end.   H.

T

PETER ILYICH TCHAIKOVSKY

(born 7 May 1840, died 6 November 1893)

Tchaikovsky wrote no fewer than ten operas, which together constitute a bulky argument to set against the idea that he was primarily an instrumental composer with a dramatic work or two to his credit. Their success has been decidedly varied, but eventually two of them have established themselves in the world's restricted operatic repertory – *Eugene Onegin* and *The Queen of Spades*. Desmond Shawe-Taylor wrote in 1950:[1] 'It is insular ignorance to regard them as interesting failures, or even as obscure local successes. In Russia their great popularity not only survived the Revolution but positively increased: Tatiana is now the beloved heroine of the factory, as formerly of the drawing-room; though gambling and superstition are officially frowned upon, Herman and the ghost of the Countess have lost nothing of their glamour.'

EUGENE ONEGIN

Yevgeny Onyegin

Opera in three acts, text by the composer and K.S. Shilovsky, after Pushkin. Première 29 March 1879, Imperial College of Music, Little Theatre, Moscow; publicly, Moscow, 1881; 1892, Olympic Theatre, London (in English); la Scala, Milan, 1900; Covent Garden, 1906, with Destinn, Battistini, Journet, conductor Campanini; Metropolitan, New York, 1920, with Muzio, Martinelli, de Luca, Didur, conductor Bodanzky; revived 1957, with Amara, Tucker, London, conductor Mitropoulos. Sadler's Wells, 1934, with Cross, Wendon, Austin, conductor Collingwood; revived 1952, with Shuard. Vienna, 1937, with Lehmann, conductor Walter; Berlin, 1945, with Lemnitz, Domgraf-Fassbaender; Vienna, 1950, with Welitsch, Schock, London, Frick; Glyndebourne, 1968, with Söderström, Ochman, Selimsky, Kim Borg, conductor Pritchard; Covent Garden, 1971, with Ileana Cotrubas, Robert Tear, Victor Braun, conductor Georg Solti, producer Peter Hall.

Madame Larina, *who owns an estate* ...Mezzo-Soprano
Tatiana } *her daughters* ....Soprano
Olga } ....Contralto
Filipievna, *Tatiana's nurse* ....Mezzo-Soprano
Lenski, *Olga's fiancé* ....Tenor
Yevgeny Onyegin, *his friend* ....Baritone
Prince Gremin, *a retired general*............................Bass
A Captain..Bass
Zaretski ....Bass
Monsieur Triquet, *a Frenchman*.........................Tenor

Place: A Country Estate; St Petersburg
Time: Late Eighteenth Century
Running Time: 2 hours 30 minutes

The idea of setting Pushkin's poem, *Yevgeny Onyegin*, as an opera was suggested to Tchaikovsky in 1877, by which date he had already written four operas. After a short hesitation, he accepted the subject, and with it the risk of being accused of misrepresenting a classic – for Pushkin's poem was already looked upon in Russia as being in that class. He set the Letter Scene straight away, and at the time he wrote that he loved Tatiana and was terribly indignant with Onyegin, who seemed to him a cold, heartless coxcomb. It was during the course of work on his opera that he himself received a passionate avowal of love from a girl who had apparently made his acquaintance while he was teaching at the Conservatory in Moscow; his determination not to emulate Onyegin was so strong that he took the fatal decision to embark on a loveless marriage. The results

[1] In *Opera*.

were disastrous, and the composer, a homosexual, seems to have been lucky to escape with nothing worse than a severe nervous breakdown before doctors insisted that the marriage come to an end.

Much of Pushkin's social commentary finds no place in the libretto, but in general the latter follows fairly closely the lines of the poem, apart that is to say from the emphasis thrown on Tatiana as opposed to Onyegin, and the ending which has been amplified and slightly romanticised so that there is a duet between Tatiana and Onyegin before Tatiana leaves him to contemplate a future without her.

Act I. The short prelude is built up on the phrase (Ex. 1):

It is wonderfully apt to the purpose, and produces on the listener a curious effect of anticipation.

The curtain rises to reveal Madame Larina's garden. She is sitting with Filipievna making jam, and through the open window of the house can be heard the voices of Tatiana and Olga as they practise a duet. The two older women listen to the first stanza in silence but start to talk (like all country house audiences, big or small) during the second, and the duet of necessity becomes a quartet. Outside the garden can be heard the sound of a chorus of reapers coming nearer. They present Madame Larina with a decorated sheaf, singing the while an attractive tune of evident folk-song connections. The chorus is followed by a rapid choral dance.

Tatiana timidly says that these country songs transport her in imagination to far-off regions, but Olga takes a matter-of-fact line and says she has no time for such dreams; they do nothing but make her want to dance too. In a little song which is not without tenderness, she gives expression to her light-hearted philosophy. Madame Larina congratulates her daughter, and thanks the reapers for their song. She and Filipievna notice that Tatiana looks pale, but she says (and the clarinet plays a theme associated with her) she is only absorbed in her book, with its

tale of lovers' troubles. A carriage is heard on the drive; Lenski must be here – and is it not Onyegin with him? Tatiana's imagination flies ahead of her and she tries to get away, but is restrained.

Madame Larina greets her guests, but leaves her daughters to entertain them. A quartet begins, the men and the women conversing separately. Finally, Lenski goes towards Olga, Onyegin to Tatiana, and the first pair talk of their mutual pleasure in meeting – they are engaged and have not seen each other since yesterday – and the second of the pleasures, or otherwise, of existence in the country. This conversational music sounds wonderfully natural. Lenski has an *arioso* passage of rapturous import, which is both sincere and immature, conventional and poetic – but then the characters in this opera have a tendency to be life-like persons, rather than romantic giants. Before the scene ends there is a short passage during which Onyegin and Tatiana return from their stroll down the garden, the former finishing a story; it gives Filipievna the chance of speculating aloud as to the possibility of Tatiana being interested in the young neighbour.

The scene changes to Tatiana's bedroom, where Filipievna is saying goodnight to her charge. There is delicate, suggestive orchestral writing in the short prelude. Tatiana and her nurse have been talking, but Tatiana cannot get to sleep and asks Filipievna to tell her a story – about her own early life, and her marriage. Tatiana listens for a bit but her thoughts soon wander and the gradually mounting tension in the orchestra shows the way her feelings are rising. Filipievna asks her if she is ill; no, she is not, but she is in love, Tatiana tells her – and Filipievna must keep it a secret.

The moment she is alone, the violence of her emotion finds full expression in an orchestral passage which precedes the ecstatic phrase with which she releases her pent-up feelings:

She starts to write and the orchestra with a wealth of detail supplies what she does not say aloud.

She makes a fresh start and, as Gerald Abraham[1] has admirably put it, 'the simple oboe line crossed by the dropping fourths and fifths of flute, clarinet and horn and the light splash of the harp magically not only conveys the naive character and romantic mood of the writer but suggests, almost pantomimically, the act of writing in a way comparable with, though not like, the "writing" passages in *Boris Godunov* and *Khovanshchina* (the scene in Pimen's cell and the scene of the public scribe)':

Snatches of recitative are interspersed with the letter writing, and the music is now lyrical and reflective, now impassioned and almost declamatory, the contrasting moods being bound together by the commentary of the orchestra. Could she love another, she asks herself? Never!

Everything she has ever done has been done for him, as if in his presence. The horn answers the voice in an expressive phrase: Gerald Abraham has called

it a motto theme for the whole opera, though an unconscious one, which is particularly apt since the Letter Scene is known to have been composed before the rest of the music, Tchaikovsky having even thought at one time of setting it as a song quite apart from its context.

Each stage of the fateful letter which is to change Tatiana's life is expressed in the music until finally it is finished and nothing is left but to send it. Day is dawning, the sound of a shepherd's pipes can be heard, and Filipievna comes to waken Tatiana. She is sent to deliver the note to Onyegin, and the curtain falls as the orchestra recapitulates Tatiana's longing.

The third tableau of the first act takes place in a different part of the garden which we already saw in the first scene. Girls sing a graceful, folk-like chorus as they gather the crop of berries, and Tatiana comes on the scene in a state of considerable emotion; she has seen Onyegin making his way towards her, and in a minute she will know the answer to her letter – would she had never written it! Onyegin in his aria expresses himself calmly and collectedly. She has written frankly to him, he will answer her no less frankly, as is her due. He is not cruel, but discouraging within the code of manners. Love and marriage are not for him; he loves her like a brother, no more. The chorus is heard again as Onyegin gently leads the humiliated Tatiana from the scene.

Act II. A ball is in progress at Madame Larina's house in honour of Tatiana's birthday. The guests are engaged in an old-fashioned waltz, and they sing of their enjoyment as they dance. Onyegin is dancing with Tatiana, a combination which gives rise to some ill-natured gossip among the more senior element of the neighbours, who look upon Onyegin with anything but favour. He is bored with the whole business and chooses to direct his spite against Lenski, who insisted he should come, by stealing a dance from Olga that she had promised to her fiancé. Lenski's remonstration is in vain, and Olga defends her behaviour when he reproaches her with it, giving the Cotillon as well to the persistent and – says Lenski – flirtatious Onyegin.

There is a diversion as Triquet, the old French tutor, consents to sing a song, which he dedicates to Tatiana. It is a charming piece of pastiche, as good in its way as its equivalent in *The Queen of Spades* – how perfectly Tchaikovsky did this kind of thing! The Cotillon begins with a Mazurka, and Onyegin and Olga dance, watched angrily by Lenski. Onyegin provokes him by asking why he does not join in, and a quarrel slowly works up until Lenski challenges his erstwhile friend to give him satisfaction. Madame Larina is in a great state that this sort of thing should happen in her house. In music of melting tenderness,[2] Lenski recalls the happiness he has known in just this house which he has now made the scene of a quarrel

[1] In the symposium on Tchaikovsky published by Lindsay Drummond.

[2] When I heard this opera in Moscow in 1961, Lenski was the great Sergei Lemeshev, advertised outside in letters as big as the opera's title and cheered to the echo by the younger element of the audience. His singing of the

opening of this great ensemble was unforgettable, full of *ritardando* and the nearest thing I have met in real life to the poetic *bel canto* to be found in the records of, for instance, Fernando de Lucia.

and a scandal. In the ensemble which follows, Onyegin bitterly regrets his provocative and thoughtless behaviour, and everyone else, including by now Tatiana, is filled with consternation at the prospect of the duel. Onyegin makes up his mind that the affair has gone too far for reconciliation, and he and Lenski insult each other, rush together and are separated as the scene comes to an end.

Early next morning the duel is to take place. The melancholy prelude anticipates Lenski's great scene of farewell to life and all he has loved. He and his second, Zaretski, exchange a few words and he is then left alone. He sings of his past, his carefree youth, and contrasts it with his present state, when he cares little whether as a result of the duel he is left alive or dead; the loss of Olga will be his one regret. It is a fine lyrical outpouring, supreme among tenor scenes in Russian opera, and unbearably pathetic in its context.

Onyegin arrives, rather late – Pushkin describes how he overslept – and Zaretski immediately demands to know where his second is; duels cannot be fought except according to the rules, and he owns that he is a stickler for etiquette. Onyegin introduces his servant as his second, and hopes that Zaretski will have no objection; he is a man of the highest character. The two seconds go off to discuss the conditions of the duel, and Lenski and Onyegin stand apart without looking at one another and sing a canon whose form exactly expresses the relationship – the thoughts of the two men are similar but divided by form and come together only as they regret that etiquette precludes a reconciliation at this late hour. The bleak tune has just that dead-pan nervousness which the situation might be expected to produce, and the repetition of the word 'No' at the end has a chilling finality. The opponents measure up, and Lenski is killed. Students of irony will remember that Pushkin himself was killed in a duel only six years after writing *Yevgeny Onyegin*.

Act III. Some years have passed and the end of the story takes place in St Petersburg. A ball is in progress in a fashionable house – the contrast with the country dance at Madame Larina's cannot be overemphasised. As the curtain rises, a Polonaise begins (*the* Polonaise often heard in concert performance, just as the Waltz in the previous act was *the* Waltz). Onyegin is there, just returned at the age of twenty-six to civilisation after the years he has spent in the

wilderness to atone for the death of the friend he killed in a duel. An Ecossaise begins but the tempo changes to a slow waltz in D flat as Prince Gremin and his wife – Tatiana, no less – come into the ballroom. The guests, Onyegin among them, comment on her beauty. The Prince goes to talk to his kinsman, Onyegin, who questions him as to the identity of the lady with whom he has come to the ball, while Tatiana asks those nearest her who it is her husband is talking to. The beauty of the waltz theme and the skill with which Tchaikovsky uses it as a background for conversation are equally notable.

In an aria Gremin tells Onyegin of the love and beauty Tatiana has brought into his life since their marriage two years ago. The aria is a favourite of every Russian bass, and it has the important effect in the opera of maintaining Gremin as no lay figure but a thinking, feeling person, part of Tatiana's background it is true, but real enough to make her loyalty entirely plausible. The solitary aria in fact creates the impression of a truly noble presence.

Gremin introduces his cousin to his wife, and Tatiana asks to be taken home, leaving Onyegin to vent his feelings in an impassioned aria, whose final section is the same (a minor third lower) as the opening section to Tatiana's Letter Scene. The scene ends with a repeat of the Ecossaise.

The last scene plays in a reception room in Prince Gremin's house. Tatiana has had Onyegin's letter and there is no doubt that he is now hopelessly in love with her, to such an extent that words fail him at his entrance and he sinks on his knees at her feet. Tatiana recalls their former meetings – the letter, and his lecture to her on the subject of maidenly reticence – to a tune (derived from Gremin's aria) which is heard played by flute and clarinet in octaves in the orchestral prelude to the scene. She contrives to make some show of indignation at his return; is he only looking for the notoriety of having his name coupled with that of a woman prominent in society? But he is so obviously sincere and in earnest that she cannot restrain her tears for long. For a moment they recall the happiness that could have been theirs long ago, but which, through fate's decree, is now out of their reach. She is Gremin's wife, says Tatiana, and they must part. But Onyegin urges his love once more, and Tatiana sings grandly in D flat, a motif which is to dominate the rest of the scene. Characteristically,

Andante molto mosso

f

though it stands for her admission of her love, it is first heard as she admonishes Onyegin to remember the path of honour and leave her, and only later as an avowal of love. For a moment they sing this theme together, as Tatiana prays for courage, but suddenly she finds the strength to go out of the room, leaving Onyegin distraught behind her as the curtain falls.

The music of *Onegin* can be seen to have grown outwards from the Letter Scene, so much of it is derived from that great central episode. This is not surprising, since for the most part the other characters are seen in relation to Tatiana, and therefore naturally take their cue from her great moment of self-revelation (the duel scene is the only one in which Tatiana does not appear at all; otherwise, only the Waltz and the Polonaise may be said to take place without paying much attention to her or her style of music). A successful performance reveals one of the great romantic masterpieces of the operatic form.   H.

THE MAID OF ORLEANS

Orleanskaya Dyeva

Opera in four acts, text by the composer, founded on Zhukovsky's Russian version of Schiller's tragedy. Première, St Petersburg, 25 February 1881, with M.D. Kamenskaya, M.D. Vasiliev, F.I. Stravinsky (Igor Stravinsky's father) as Dunois. First performed Prague, 1882 – the first of Tchaikovsky's operas to be heard outside Russia. Revived Brno, 1940, conductor Rafael Kubelík; Perugia, 1956, with Marcella Pobbe, David Poleri, Enzo Mascherini, conductor Perlea; Saarbrucken, 1967; Leipzig, 1970; Royal Northern College of Music, Manchester, 1994.

Joan of Arc......................Mezzo-Soprano or Soprano[1]
Charles VII, *King of France*................................Tenor
Agnès Sorel, *his mistress*................................Soprano
Thibaut, *Joan's father* ....Bass
Raymond, *a young man in love with Joan*............Tenor
Dunois, *a French soldier* ....Baritone
Bertrand, *an old peasant*.......................................Bass
Lionel, *a Burgundian soldier* ....Baritone

The Archbishop ....Bass
A Soldier ....Bass
Lore...Bass
An Angel Voice..Soprano

Place: France
Time: 1430–31
Running Time: 3 hours 10 minutes

Act I. An extended prelude introduces immediately a yearning, compassionate theme, *andante* and very Slav in its expression. There follows a fiery *allegro vivo* (associated with the sound of the tocsin and the crowd's fear in face of English military successes) and an *allegro giusto* (associated with Joan's hearing of the angel voices at the end of Act I and her determination to pursue a course of resistance).

In the village of Domrémy, girls sing as they decorate an ancient oak. Thibaut, Joan's father, comes in with a young man, Raymond, whom he envisages as the husband Joan will need to defend her in the troubled times in which they are living. There is a trio started by Raymond during whose course Joan is introduced musically to the opera. The mood changes with the sound of a tocsin and the populace expresses dread of the successful English invasion (the *allegro vivo* of the overture). An old peasant, Bertrand, describes the incipient disaster, and Joan alone refuses to react in terms of despair. In a mood of inspiration, she prophesies the victory of the French troops and the death of the leader of the enemy forces, Salisbury. No one believes her, her father tending to think that she is influenced by the devil; but a soldier comes in to confirm the death of Salisbury and immediately hope is renewed. In ecstasy, Joan leads them in prayer, Raymond and Bertrand joining their voices to the general mood of confidence.

Left alone, Joan expresses her conviction that the time has come to act, to leave home and join the troops. Her aria of decision is a splendid and justly famous utterance, simple of melody, warm and emotional in its appeal.[2] Joan hears a chorus of angels saying that the day of decision has arrived, and the act ends as she prophesies victory to the tune of the overture's *allegro giusto*.

Act II. The royal castle at Chinon. A martial

---

[1] The original Joan was a mezzo-soprano and Tchaikovsky modified some sections of the score for her.

[2] Popularly known as 'Adieu forêts', and once a favourite recording piece for sopranos and mezzos alike.

entr'acte, based on Joan's rallying of the French in the previous scene, leads us to the King's presence. Minstrels and tumblers entertain the King and his mistress Agnès Sorel, first in a beguiling and gently lyrical tune whose melody is assigned by Tchaikovsky to the chorus but has sometimes been sung by tenor solo, and later in a succession of musically attractive dances. The soldierly Dunois in a duet tries to persuade Charles to place himself at the head of his army and lead the French against the English, but the King is irresolute, and cannot bring himself to leave Agnès. Suddenly, a wounded soldier brings news of further losses in battle and expires before he can even finish his message. The King loses what courage he had, and Dunois indignantly leaves him to the consolation of Agnès, which is gently and effectively accomplished, first in an *arioso* then in duet.

Fanfares are heard and Dunois re-enters to announce a near-miracle, victory snatched from the hands of the English, a fact immediately confirmed to the incredulous King by the Archbishop himself. This dignitary further relates that the instrument of the enemy's discomfiture was an unknown warrior maid. The people rejoice, bells are rung, and Joan enters. Dunois has previously on instruction taken the King's place on the throne, but Joan immediately picks out her sovereign from the surrounding courtiers. To his astonishment, she can tell him the purport of his secret prayers but her finest moment – writing no less expressive than Mussorgsky's for Marfa in *Khovanshchina* – comes in an inspired passage when she tells the story of her life. The Archbishop leads a massive general ensemble of approval which mounts to enthusiasm when the King places her at the head of the army.

Act III, scene i. Vigorous introductory music brings the rise of the curtain to show Joan in single combat with Lionel, a Burgundian fighting on the English side. She has him at her mercy but spares his life and, as she sees him face to face, they fall in love. After an extended duet, Lionel prefers to surrender to Dunois as prisoner rather than make his escape.

A march leads to scene ii, the Coronation of the King as Charles VII at Reims (it was this scene which at the time of the first performance brought critical complaints of the influence of Meyerbeer on the composer). After appropriate ceremonial business, Thibaut

and Raymond reappear, the King proclaims Joan the saviour of France, Thibaut denounces her as diabolically inspired, and a splendid ensemble follows. Joan, urged by King and Archbishop to defend herself but believing her sparing of Lionel's life and her love for him to be a sign of inner guilt, remains silent. Dunois throws down a gauntlet, a challenge to someone to pick up as defender of Joan's innocence. Loud claps of thunder are taken as a sign from heaven that she is guilty and all leave except Lionel and Joan herself. When he offers to protect her, she recoils from him in horror as the enemy who has brought destruction upon her. At the end of the act she is left alone to contemplate the King's sentence of banishment upon her.

Act IV, scene i. A wood. Introduced by turbulent music, Joan sits alone, torn by thoughts of her love for Lionel, who presently appears by her side. Their impassioned duet is one of the crucial episodes of the score, its course interrupted by sounds of heavenly voices telling her that she will atone for her sins with suffering and death. Enemy soldiers appear and Lionel is killed, Joan taken prisoner.

Scene ii. A square in Rouen. Joan has been condemned to death at the stake and a funeral march ushers in the final scene. The crowd is moved by her imminent fate, Joan's courage momentarily fails but her angel voices bring consolation, and the music moves on inexorably as she is tied to the stake and the fire lit.   H.

MAZEPPA

Opera in three acts, libretto by the composer and V.P. Burenin (founded on Pushkin's *Poltava*). Première Moscow, 15 February 1884, and in St Petersburg, 19 February 1884. First performed in England, Liverpool, 16 August 1888 (in Russian, by a touring company); in Germany, at Wiesbaden, 1931; in New York, 1933, by a Ukrainian company. Revived Florence, 1954, with Magda Olivero, Marianna Radev, David Poleri, Ettore Bastianini, Boris Christoff, conductor Jonel Perlea; English National Opera, 1984, with Janice Cairns, Felicity Palmer, Rowland Sidwell, Malcolm Donnelly, Richard Van Allan, conductor Mark Elder.

Mazeppa, *the Cossack Hetman*[1] ....Baritone
Kochubey, *a wealthy Cossack*..............................Bass
Maria, *his daughter*...Soprano

---

[1] Hetman is derived through Polish from the German 'Hauptmann', Captain.

Andrei, *a young Cossack* ....Tenor

Orlik, *Mazeppa's henchman* ....Bass

Iskra, *Governor of Poltava, Kochubey's friend* ......Tenor

Liubov, *Kochubey's wife* ....Mezzo-Soprano

A Drunken Cossack ....Tenor

Cossacks and their Women, Kochubey's Servants, Monks

Place: Little Russia
Time: Beginning of the Eighteenth Century
Running Time: 2 hours 35 minutes

Tchaikovsky first told his publisher about the project of an opera on the subject of *Mazeppa* in June 1881, less than four months after the production of *The Maid of Orleans*. He seems to have vacillated in his enthusiasm for the project, writing four numbers, breaking off to sketch out a duet made from the material of the symphonic *Romeo and Juliet*, and then embarking on another love duet, inspired by a play by Antropov. Before long this last had become the great duet of Mazeppa and Maria in Act II, and from then on, apart from some disappointment over the time he took over the orchestration, he seems to have been fairly satisfied with progress.

The story is based on fact. Mazeppa, a noted amorist, was over sixty when he married his goddaughter Maria. He was a learned man, educated partly in Warsaw, and his friendship with the young Tsar, Peter the Great, was based as much on the latter's insatiable curiosity and thirst for knowledge as on political expediency. In 1708 Mazeppa took an army of Cossacks to join Charles XII of Sweden in his campaign against Peter. Defeated at the Battle of Poltava, he fled to Turkey, where he died in 1709. In Russia he was regarded as a traitor of epic proportions, his name solemnly anathematised, it appears, once a year from every altar in Russia until 1918!

Act I. The overture is a brilliant piece, containing a foretaste of the *Hopak*, and a beautiful *andantino con moto* melody. The first scene takes place in the garden of the rich Cossack, Kochubey. Girls sing a flowing 5/4 chorus as they tell their fortunes by throwing garlands into the river, but Maria, Kochubey's daughter, will not join in their game. She loves the powerful Mazeppa, her father's contemporary and guest, and when the girls have gone, she makes it clear that his

grey hair and a wide difference in age seem to her no obstacles to enduring love. Her soliloquy is interrupted by Andrei, a young Cossack madly, but as he knows hopelessly, in love with her. In their lyrical duet, Maria asks for his forgiveness for the pain she causes him.

Mazeppa comes out and renews his thanks to Kochubey for the extent of his hospitality. To all he wishes good fortune for the future, and Kochubey orders his retainers to provide entertainment for their honoured guest. This they do, in chorus and a rousing *Hopak*, the latter a particularly attractive piece.

Alone with Kochubey, Mazeppa loses no time in asking for the hand of Maria in marriage. At first his friend, with many protestations of affection, tries to put him off, urging that Mazeppa is the girl's godfather; how could he marry her? But Mazeppa insists, until Kochubey gives him a round refusal and demands that he leave the house. The quarrel attracts attention, and Liubov, Andrei and Iskra, followed by Kochubey's retainers and guests, come to see what is the matter. A great ensemble develops, with Maria torn between duty to her father and love for Mazeppa, who resolves the situation by summoning his followers to carry off Maria by force. Maria makes her choice to go with Mazeppa willingly and, with a last threat to his hosts, Mazeppa takes his bride away.

The second scene plays in a room in Kochubey's house. Women, led by Liubov, are lamenting the departure of Maria. Liubov, supported by Iskra and Kochubey's retainers, urges revenge on Mazeppa for the injury he has done them, and Kochubey resolves to unmask what he describes as Mazeppa's false patriotism and to reveal to the Tsar[1] that Mazeppa is secretly intriguing with the Swedes. Andrei's offer to carry the information to the Tsar is accepted by Kochubey in music of grave conviction, and the finale ends with general support for the expedition.

Act II, scene i. A dungeon in Mazeppa's castle. The Tsar, who trusts Mazeppa, has delivered his accusers into his hands. Kochubey is chained to a pillar. He bemoans his fate. Orlik comes specifically to discover where he has hidden his treasure. The old man will give nothing away, and Orlik summons the torturer to add force to his interrogation. The scene is one of Tchaikovsky's finest, packed with conflict, from the sombre and beautiful prelude, through

---

[1] The period is some twenty years later than that of *Khovanshchina*.

Kochubey's fine and gloomy monologue to the intensely dramatic interview between him and Orlik.

Scene ii. A room in the castle. Mazeppa is looking out of the window and Tchaikovsky shows him in a very different light from the tyrant postulated in the previous scene, as he poetises in a lovely passage over the beauty of the Ukrainian night. He stills his conscience with reminders of Kochubey's ambition; he must die, and when Orlik comes to tell him that torture has wrung nothing from the old man, he gives orders for his execution in the morning. Left alone, Mazeppa gives passionate expression in a big *arioso* in G flat to his love for Maria, who, he says, has brought spring into an old man's life (this *arioso* was interpolated after the opera's initial production).

With the entrance of Maria we reach the key scene of the opera, the equivalent of the Letter Scene in *Onegin*, whose achievement sets the rest of the opera in motion, giving body to the central dramatic figures, though not quite permeating the music as in the case of *Onegin*. Maria reproaches Mazeppa because he has lately seemed cold to her, and he replies with a warmth that is entirely consistent with that shown in the preceding *arioso*. He goes on to tell her of his plan to set up an independent state in the Ukraine with himself at its head.

Maria does not hide her enthusiasm or her confidence in him, even when he says that the adventure may lead him to a throne or the gallows. Mazeppa tests her: whom she would choose to see saved if it came to a question of death for him or for her father? She would sacrifice anyone rather than Mazeppa.

Left alone, Maria starts to think of her parents, but is suddenly joined by her mother who has stolen into the castle unobserved by the guards. Will her daughter use her influence to save her father from the sentence of death under which he lies? Maria does not understand what she is talking about, and Liubov explains that Kochubey's actions against Mazeppa have brought him to his present miserable situation. Maria is aghast at the news, and both rush out to do what they can to save Kochubey.

Scene iii. A field by the scaffold. People are waiting for the arrival of the executioner's victims. Tchaikovsky describes this as a 'folk scene', and it is punctuated by the song of a drunken Cossack, who sings a ribald song (musical ancestry held in common with the Inn Scene in *Boris*), much to the discomfiture of the crowd – an admirable piece of dramatic irony. The procession comes into sight with Mazeppa on horseback, Kochubey and Iskra heavily guarded. Kochubey prays movingly, and at the moment the axe falls, Maria and her mother rush in to try to save him, but too late.

Act III begins with a symphonic picture 'The Battle of Poltava', sometimes played in the concert hall. As musical symbols of the Russian victory, Tchaikovsky makes use of the famous 'Slava' (used also by Beethoven in his second Rasumovsky quartet, by Mussorgsky in the Coronation Scene in *Boris*, and by Rimsky-Korsakov in *The Tsar's Bride*), as well as of a liturgical chant, which he himself had employed earlier in the *1812 Overture*, and, most extensively, of a military march of the period of Peter the Great.

When the curtain rises it is to show the same scene as the first scene of Act I, but now neglected and half ruined. Andrei in an aria vigorously voices his regret that he has not been able to revenge himself on Mazeppa in the battle. He has returned now to the spot which was once the centre of all his thoughts, the place where he was happy in the company of Maria. He hears the sound of horses' hooves and hides. Mazeppa comes in with Orlik, in flight from the Tsar's troops. Mazeppa turns and abuses Orlik who has addressed him by his title of Hetman – the title he has lost in his vain attempt to win supreme power.

Andrei recognises Mazeppa's voice, and challenges him to answer for his misdeeds in mortal combat. Andrei attacks Mazeppa but is fatally wounded, and lies dying when Maria emerges from the house. Mazeppa calls to her, but she has lost command of her senses, half recognises him only and babbles of her father's death, of which the direct cause has been her own elopement. Orlik drags Mazeppa away, urging him to forget a woman who is mad and who has brought him to his present pitch of disaster.

Maria is left alone in her misery. She takes Andrei's head in her hands and sings softly to him of their happy childhood. He dies in her arms and an opera in which blood, battle and ambition have figured large, ends with the gentlest of cradle songs.[1]   H.

---

[1] The conventional grand finale heard at the first performance was subsequently cut by the composer, who quickly saw that the quiet ending not only kept Maria in the centre of the picture but was also more effective.

THE QUEEN OF SPADES
Pikovaya Dama/Pique Dame

Opera in three acts, text by Modest Tchaikovsky (the composer's brother), based on Pushkin. Première St Petersburg, 19 December 1890, with Nicola Figner and Medea Mei. First produced at la Scala, Milan, 1906, with Corsi, Zenatello, Stracciari, Didur; Metropolitan, New York, 1910, with Destinn, Meitschek, Slezak, Didur, Forsell, conductor Mahler; London Opera House, 1915, with Rosing; Vienna State Opera, 1946, with Hilde Konetzni and Welitsch, Hoengen, Lorenz, Schoeffler, conductor Krips; Covent Garden, 1950 (in English), with Zadek, Coates, Edgar Evans, Rothmüller, Walters, conductor Erich Kleiber. Revived Metropolitan, New York, 1965, with Stratas, Resnik, Vickers, conductor Schippers; Glyndebourne, 1971, with Kubiak, Maievsky, conductor John Pritchard; English National Opera, 1983, with Graham Clark, conductor Mark Elder, producer David Pountney.

Officers
Tchekalinsky	Tenor
Sourin	Bass
Herman	Tenor
Count Tomsky	Baritone
Prince Yeletsky	Baritone
The Countess	Mezzo-Soprano
Lisa, *her grand-daughter*	Soprano
Pauline, *Lisa's companion*	Contralto
Governess	Mezzo-Soprano
Masha, *Lisa's maid*	Soprano
Master of Ceremonies	Tenor
Tchaplitsky	Tenor
Narumoff	Bass

In the interlude
Chloë	Soprano
Daphnis (Pauline)	Contralto
Plutus (Tomsky)	Baritone

Servants, Guests, Gamblers, Children

Place: St Petersburg
Time: End of the Eighteenth Century
Running Time: 2 hours 55 minutes

Quite a number of changes of emphasis as well as of detail were made before Pushkin's poem could become an opera libretto – and these have often come in for hostile criticism. Pushkin's story is cynical in character, with a mixture of the grotesque, and his hero is a cold-blooded, unromantic officer, interested only in the secret of the cards and not in any way concerned with Lisa, except in so far as she brings him into contact with the old Countess.

Tchaikovsky and his brother have turned Herman into a romantic, almost Byronic character nearly as much in love with Lisa as with gambling, and they have elevated Lisa to become the Countess's granddaughter, at the same time providing the story with a tragic ending. That they have made something that differs from Pushkin's original story is undeniable; but whether it is less good is a moot point.

Act I, scene i. A short prelude leads to the first scene, which is laid in an open space in the Summer Garden, St Petersburg. It is spring, and seated on the benches are nurses and governesses chatting together. Children are playing. After a chorus, Sourin and Tchekalinsky enter, discussing the gambling propensities of Herman; it seems that he was last night at his usual habit of watching the players, never risking a throw.

As they speak, Herman comes in with his friend Tomsky, who is questioning him about the sorrow which seems to hang over his life, and has quite changed him from the spirited boy he once knew. Herman explains the change by saying that he has fallen in love, but does not even know the name of the object of his affections. His *arioso* in praise of the unknown lady has a typical Tchaikovskian ardour. Tomsky suggests that the first thing to do is to learn the lady's name, but Herman is afraid she is above him in station and will prove beyond his reach. Tomsky is amazed at Herman's mixture of devotion and despair, and they go off together.

The promenade continues, Tomsky and Herman return, and the former greets Prince Yeletsky, who has that very morning become engaged. Yeletsky points out his Lisa to Tomsky, and Herman recognises her as his own beloved. Lisa and her grandmother, the Countess, exclaim as they catch sight of Herman; they have noticed his ardent looks, but are unaware of his identity. A short quintet ensues, after which Tomsky greets the Countess, who asks Herman's name, and Yeletsky goes towards Lisa.

Presently the Countess takes her grand-daughter away, and the others speculate as to the rumours which surround the Countess's past. She was a great gambler it seems. Is it possible to believe such stories? Tomsky is surprised that her history is not better known, and proceeds to tell it in a ballad. The Countess was a beauty when she was young, and one of her most ardent admirers was the Count

Saint-Germain; but, alas, she preferred gambling to love. One day at the tables she had lost everything; her depression was noticed by the Count, who followed her from the room, and offered to reveal to her the secret of 'three cards', would she but grant him one rendezvous. Her indignation at such a suggestion was quickly overcome, and next morning she was back at the tables, where nothing could stop her winning run. It was whispered that she subsequently passed the secret on to her husband, and years later to a young gallant who had taken her fancy; but in a dream she had been warned that she would die when next anyone tried to win her secret from her.

The recital is not lost on Herman, and Tchekalinsky and Sourin hasten to repeat the refrain mockingly in his ear. A storm is brewing, and all take shelter except Herman, who stays as if in a trance. He broods on the story – what use would the secret be to him with Lisa beyond his reach? – and then gives expression to his determination to win her.

Scene ii. Lisa's room. She sits at the harpsichord, surrounded by girls of her own age. She and Pauline together sing an old-fashioned duet, which, no less than for instance the opening duet of *Eugene Onegin*, shows how much life Tchaikovsky can breathe into what is no more and no less than pastiche. The listeners applaud, and demand more; Lisa asks Pauline to sing alone, and she follows her romance with a lively peasant song, too lively it appears for the peace of the house, for the governess comes in to ask for a little less noise.

Lisa sees her friends to the door, and tries to fob off Pauline's enquiries about her gloomy look. When she is alone, she gives vent to her feelings in a beautiful aria. Is this marriage to which she is contracted the fulfilment of her dreams? Nobody could have better qualifications than the Prince – he is kind, good-looking, clever, well-born, rich – and yet her heart is full of heavy foreboding.

Suddenly Herman appears at the window. Lisa makes as if to rush through the door, but Herman persuades her to stay and listen to him for a moment. In music of passionate tenderness, he declares his love, and it is immediately evident that Lisa is far from indifferent to what he says. Their conversation is interrupted by a loud knocking at the door; it is the Countess, come to see if Lisa is yet asleep. Herman hides, Lisa calms the Countess's fears, while Herman

softly echoes the refrain of Tomsky's ballad; can it be true that she will die when a third man 'impelled by despair' demands to know the secret? When they are left alone, Lisa sinks into Herman's arms.

Act II, scene i. A large reception room. A masked ball is taking place at the house of a rich dignitary. The Master of Ceremonies invites the guests into the garden to see the firework display, and Tchekalinsky and Sourin plan to play a trick on Herman, who, they say, is obsessed by the idea of the Countess's 'three cards'. The Prince is there with Lisa, to whom he addresses an aria whose sentiments are both noble and touchingly chivalrous: 'I love you, dear, beyond all reckoning'. They go off together, and Herman appears reading a note which Lisa has sent him: 'After the performance wait for me in my room. I must speak with you.' Did he but know the secret of the 'three cards', he could be wealthy, and then aspire to Lisa's hand. As if to echo his thoughts, he hears Tchekalinsky and Sourin whisper: 'Are you then that third man? ... three cards?' Herman wonders whether he is hearing the voice of a ghost.

The Master of Ceremonies announces: 'Our host now prays you all to take your seats, to see a pretty pastoral called *The Faithful Shepherdess*.' It is the story of Daphnis, Chloë, and Plutus. A chorus and saraband are followed by a Mozartian duet for Chloë and Daphnis (the latter is played by Pauline). There is an impressive entry for Plutus (Tomsky), riding in a golden chariot, but Chloë spurns his love, and she and Daphnis plight their troth to the tune of their earlier duet. The chorus rejoices in the happiness of the two lovers.

The interlude over, Herman waits for Lisa. She gives him a key and tells him to gain access to their house through her grandmother's room – the old woman will still be playing cards at midnight – and then with the key open the secret door which is situated behind the portrait of the Countess, and which leads to her own apartments. Herman says he cannot wait until the following day, but will come that very night; Lisa is submissive to his desire. The act ends as the Master of Ceremonies announces the imminent arrival of the Empress herself, and the guests join in welcoming her.

Scene ii. The Countess's bedroom, which is empty. Herman enters, hesitates for a moment, and then hearing the sound of voices conceals himself. The Countess herself, preceded by maids and attendants,

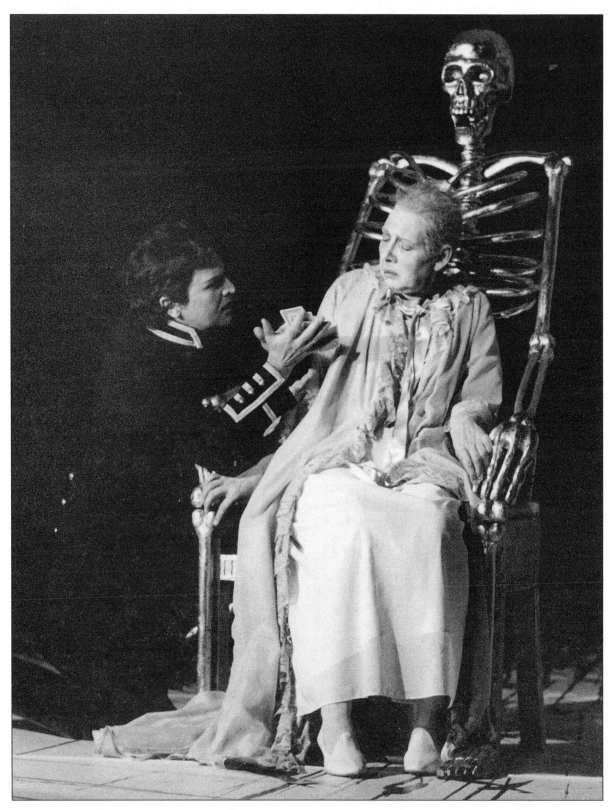

The Queen of Spades *(Glyndebourne, 1992, director Graham Vick, designer Richard Hudson).*
Felicity Palmer as the old Countess, Yuri Marusin as Herman.

comes in. She takes off her evening dress and puts on a nightgown, then stops the sycophantic chorus which has been accompanying her preparations for bed and says she will sit in a chair for a few minutes. Some reflections on the decline of society are followed by reminiscences of 'the old days', when things were done as they should be, when people really could dance, when Madame de Pompadour was queen of Paris, when she herself – the Countess – sang before the King. She sings very softly to herself an air from Grétry's *Richard Cœur de Lion*; then, suddenly aware that the room is still full of servants, their eyes and ears bursting with curiosity, sends them all packing.

She is alone, and again starts to hum the tune which is in her head. But the words die on her lips as she catches sight of Herman in front of her. She does not speak another word, but mouths incoherently as if she had lost the power of speech. Herman begs her not to be frightened; he wants nothing but that she should tell him her secret, the secret of the 'three cards'. In desperation Herman draws his pistol, and the Countess dies of shock at the sight. With a despairing cry that he can now never know the secret, he turns to find Lisa entering the room, alarmed by the noise. She is horrified by the sight which meets her eyes, and no less horrified to learn why it was that Herman was there. So it was for love of gambling, not for her sake, that he came here at midnight! She bids him leave.

Act III, scene i. Herman's quarters in the barracks. The sound of drums and trumpets, suggestive of a funeral march, can be heard; Herman sits reading a letter from Lisa, in which she apparently forgives him for the slight she had read into his action, understands that he did not intend to kill her grandmother, and makes an appointment for midnight by the canal. Herman is obsessed by memories of the Countess's funeral, which he attended. Suddenly, the door opens, and the ghost of his victim can be seen in the doorway. She tells Herman that he must marry Lisa, and that the secret of the three cards shall be his: 'Three! Seven! Ace!' He mutters the formula as the curtain falls.

Scene ii. By the canal. Lisa waits for Herman: 'It is near to midnight'. Can he deceive her, and will she wait in vain? Her nerves are worn with sorrow and waiting. Lisa's aria is particularly fine.

Her fears are quieted when Herman appears, and sings to her of their future together. All seems well,

until Herman tells her they must leave for the gaming-house. Lisa thinks he is mad, but he blurts out his obsession, and, deaf to her pleading, goes his way. Lisa rushes to the parapet of the canal, and throws herself over the edge.

Scene iii. The gambling house. Supper is in progress, and a few are playing cards. Tomsky greets the Prince with some surprise, since he is no longer a habitual gambler. Yeletsky admits that it is to take his revenge he has come: unlucky in love, lucky at cards. Tomsky is persuaded to sing for their entertainment, which he does to a lively tune. Herman enters, and asks who will play with him. Tchekalinsky accepts, and Herman stakes hugely and wins twice, on the three and seven. He rejoices in his fortune: 'What is our life? A game!', then challenges anyone to stake once more. No one accepts, until the Prince steps forward and offers to play with him. Herman reluctantly agrees, and turns up a card, announcing an ace without even looking at it. But the Prince calmly rejoins: 'No, it's your Queen of Spades'. With a wild cry, Herman sees the ghost of the Countess. Everyone moves away from him, as he gibbers with fear and rage. He stabs himself, and with his dying breath asks for the Prince's pardon for what he has done to him. A prayer goes up for his soul, and he dies.   H.

IOLANTA

Opera in one act, libretto by Modest Tchaikovsky, the composer's brother. Première St Petersburg, 6/18 December 1892, with Medea Mei-Figner, Nicola Figner. Revived Leipzig, 1955; Moscow, 1957; London, Camden Festival, 1968, with Josephine Barstow, Adrian de Peyer, Norman Welsby, conductor David Lloyd-Jones; Opera North, 1992, with Joan Rodgers.

René, *King of Provence* ....Bass
Robert, *Duke of Burgundy* ....Bass-Baritone
Count Vaudémont, *a Burgundian knight* ....Tenor
Ebn-Hakia, *a Moorish doctor* ....Baritone
Almeric, *King René's armour-bearer* ....Tenor
Bertrand, *the gate-keeper* ....Baritone
Iolanta, *the King's daughter* ....Soprano
Martha, *Iolanta's nurse and Bertrand's wife*...Contralto
Brigitte, *Iolanta's friend* ....Soprano
Laura, *Iolanta's friend*.........................Mezzo-Soprano

Servants and Friends of Iolanta, Members of the
    King's Retinue, the Duke of Burgundy's Retainers

Place: Provence
Time: Fifteenth Century
Running Time: 1 hour 30 minutes

*I*olanta was commissioned to be produced in double harness with the famous ballet *Nutcracker*. Tchaikovsky began work on it some six months before the première, but soon after he had finished it, he confessed that 'Medieval Dukes and Knights and Ladies captivate my imagination but not my *heart*'. As so often before, the composer approached the libretto through a crucial scene, here the duet between Iolanta and her lover Vaudémont, and this music permeates the whole score. The libretto has its origins in a story by Hans Andersen.

A sombre prelude perhaps suggests Iolanta's blindness. The curtain rises on a beautiful garden, outside the palace of René, King of Provence. To the accompaniment of graceful music, Princess Iolanta is picking fruit with her friends. Iolanta is blind but, at the King's express command, she has never been allowed to know that she is different from everyone around her. She finds the fruit by touch and puts it in the basket, but gradually she becomes listless: how do they know she is crying without having *touched* her eyes? In an *arioso* of some feeling, Iolanta contrasts her present mood of unrest with her former happiness. Martha tries to calm her fears; girls bring in the flowers they have picked, and sing an attractive chorus in 6/8 time, and Martha and Iolanta's friends lull her to sleep in a trio of considerable beauty.

Retainers appear to announce the King's arrival. King René tells the famous Moorish doctor, Ebn-Hakia, that in him rests Iolanta's last hope, and the doctor goes to look at his prospective patient as she lies asleep. When he is alone, the King prays in an aria ('When I, Lord, rouse thy wrath') for God's mercy on his innocent daughter. Ebn-Hakia says he can cure Iolanta's blindness on two conditions: that she be told she is blind, and that she acquire the will to be able to see. The King laments that such a price is more than he is prepared to pay, and even when Ebn-Hakia has (in an *arioso* full of oriental suggestions) emphasised how much the body is dependent on the spirit, he refuses to agree.

The King and the doctor leave and into the garden come Robert, Duke of Burgundy, and Count Vaudémont, who have lost their way. Vaudémont is immediately taken by the beauty of the garden, and

Robert is glad of anything that delays his business with the King – he has never seen Iolanta, to whom he is engaged, but he loves another and wants the King to release him from the betrothal. When Vaudémont suggests that Iolanta may be very beautiful, Robert exclaims in a fine quick-moving outburst: 'Who can compare to Mathilde?' Suddenly they come upon the sleeping girl; Vaudémont is overcome by her beauty, but Robert fears the work of a sorcerer and wants to drag him away. When she wakes, Robert leaves to fetch their companions, and Iolanta brings wine to Vaudémont.

The duet which ensues is the central piece of the opera. Love dawns in a G major theme of great tenderness, and the music quickens as Vaudémont asks Iolanta for a red rose to add to the white one she has already picked for him. She brings him another white one and seems not to understand the difference, and suddenly Vaudémont realises that she is blind. He comforts her and sings of the beauties of the world around them. The climax comes at Vaudémont's impassioned description of light, to which Iolanta's response is no less rapturous.

The King, Ebn-Hakia and Iolanta's attendants enter, expecting to see her asleep, and are astonished instead to find her with a young man, who, she tells them, has given her an idea of the meaning of the word 'light'. The King is overcome with horror, but Ebn-Hakia feels there is now hope of curing Iolanta's blindness. Ebn-Hakia leads a powerful ensemble as everyone reacts to the situation. The King begins to understand and decrees that the stranger's life shall be forfeit if she does not acquire the power of sight. To the big G major theme (now a semitone higher) Iolanta proclaims her determination to save the life of the Knight with whose voice she has fallen in love. She leaves and the King explains to Vaudémont that his threat was intended solely to provide Iolanta with the incentive to see.

Burgundy returns and admits his secret, the King agrees that Vaudémont shall marry Iolanta, and when news is brought of the success of Ebn-Hakia's ministrations, happiness seems to be within the grasp of everyone. The women come out rejoicing, and Iolanta can hardly believe what meets her eyes. She thanks God for his mercy, for the wonders she can now comprehend, and not least for the love she feels in her heart for Vaudémont. H.

AMBROISE THOMAS
(born 5 August 1811, died 12 February 1896)

MIGNON

Opera in three acts, words, based on Goethe's *Wilhelm Meister*, by Barbier and Carré. Produced Opéra-Comique, Paris, 17 November 1866, with Galli-Marié. London, Drury Lane, 5 July 1870, with Christine Nilsson, Volpini, Bettini, Faure. New York, Academy of Music, 22 November 1871; Metropolitan Opera House, 1883, with Nilsson, Capoul, Scalchi (Frédéric). Revived Metropolitan, 1926, with Bori, Gigli; Sadler's Wells, 1932, with Rose Morris, Tudor Davies; la Scala, Milan, 1933, with Besanzoni, Schipa; Metropolitan, 1938, with Risë Stevens; la Scala, 1945, with Pederzini, Schipa; 1947, with Simionato, di Stefano. Frédéric, since Trebelli appeared in the role in London, has become a contralto instead of a buffo tenor part. The 'Rondo Gavotte' in Act II, composed for Trebelli, has since then been a fixture in the score.

Mignon, *stolen in childhood from an Italian castle*	Mezzo-Soprano
Philine, *an actress*	Soprano
Frédéric, *a young man*	Buffo Tenor or Contralto
Wilhelm Meister, *a student on his travels*	Tenor
Laerte, *an actor*	Tenor
Lothario	Bass
Jarno, *a gipsy*	Bass
Antonio, *a servant*	Bass

Townspeople, Gipsies, Actors and Actresses, etc.

Place: Germany; Italy
Time: Late Eighteenth Century
Running Time: 3 hours 10 minutes

Ambroise Thomas was for years a pillar of the French musical establishment. The revered teacher of Massenet, he became Director of the Conservatoire at the age of sixty, but even his best-known operas – *Mignon* and *Hamlet* – dwindled in repute soon after his death.

Notwithstanding the popularity of two airs in *Mignon* – 'Connais-tu le pays?' and the Polonaise – the opera has lost much of its hold on the repertory. It is a work of delicate texture, of charm rather than passion, with a story that is, perhaps, too ingenuous to appeal to the sophisticated audience of the modern opera house.

Act I. Courtyard of a German inn. Chorus of townspeople and travellers. Lothario, a wandering minstrel, sings, accompanying himself on his harp,

'Fugitif et tremblant'. Philine and Laerte, on the way with their troupe to give a theatrical performance in a neighbouring castle, appear on a balcony. Mignon is sleeping on straw in the back of a gipsy cart. Jarno, chief of the gipsy band, rouses her. She refuses to dance. He threatens her with a stick. Lothario and Wilhelm protect her. Mignon divides a bouquet of wild flowers between them.

Laerte, who has come down from the balcony, engages Wilhelm in conversation. Philine joins them. Wilhelm is greatly impressed with her blonde beauty. He does not protest when Laerte takes from him the wild flowers he has received from Mignon and hands them to Philine.

When Philine and Laerte have gone, there is a scene between Wilhelm and Mignon. The girl tells him of dim memories of her childhood – the land from which she was abducted. It is at this point she sings 'Connais-tu le pays?' (Do you know the land?). Wilhelm decides to purchase her freedom, and enters the inn with Jarno to conclude the negotiations. Lothario has been attracted to her, and, before leaving, bids her farewell. They have the charming duet 'Légères hirondelles'. There is a scene for Philine and Frédéric, a young man, who is in love with her. Philine is after bigger game, setting her cap at Wilhelm. Lothario wishes to take Mignon with him, but Wilhelm fears for her safety with the old man, whose mind sometimes appears to wander. Moreover Mignon ardently desires to remain in the service of Wilhelm who has freed her from bondage to the gipsies, and, when Wilhelm declines to let her go with Lothario, is enraptured, until she sees her wild flowers in Philine's hand. Already she is passionately in love with Wilhelm, and jealous when Philine invites him to attend the theatricals at the castle. Wilhelm waves adieu to Philine, as she drives away. Lothario, pensive, remains seated. Mignon's gaze is directed towards Wilhelm.

Act II. The entr'acte is the tune of the famous gavotte. Philine's boudoir at the castle. The actress sings of her pleasure in these elegant surroundings, and of Wilhelm. Laerte is heard off-stage, singing a madrigal to Philine ('Belle, ayez pitié de nous').

He ushers in Wilhelm and Mignon, then withdraws. Mignon, pretending to fall asleep, watches Wilhelm and Philine. While Wilhelm hands to the actress various toilet accessories, they sing a graceful duet, 'Je crois entendre les doux compliments'. Meanwhile Mignon's heart is tormented with jealousy. When Wilhelm and Philine leave the boudoir the girl dons one of Philine's costumes, seats herself at the mirror and puts on rouge and other cosmetics, as she has seen Philine do. In a spirit of abandon she sings a brilliant *Styrienne*, 'Je connais un pauvre enfant'. She then withdraws into an adjoining room. Frédéric enters the boudoir in search of Philine. He sings the gavotte, 'Me voici dans son boudoir'. Wilhelm comes in, in search of Mignon. The men meet. There is an exchange of jealous accusations. They are about to fight, when Mignon rushes between them. Frédéric recognises Philine's costume on her, and goes off laughing. Wilhelm, realising the awkward situation that may arise from the girl's following him about, tells her they must part. 'Adieu, Mignon, courage'. She bids him a sad farewell. Philine re-enters. Her sarcastic references to Mignon's attire wound the girl to the quick. When Wilhelm leads out the actress on his arm, Mignon exclaims: 'That woman! I loathe her!'

The second scene of this act is laid in the castle park. Mignon, driven to distraction, sings a *scena* of real dramatic power: 'Elle est là, près de lui?' She is about to throw herself in the lake, when she hears the strains of a harp. Lothario, who has wandered into the park, is playing. There is an exchange of affection, almost paternal on his part, almost filial on hers, in their duet, 'As-tu souffert? As-tu pleuré?' Mignon hears applause and acclaim from the conservatory for Philine's acting. In jealous rage she cries out that she wishes the building might be struck by lightning and destroyed by fire; then runs off and disappears among the trees. Lothario vaguely repeats her words. '"Fire," she said! "Ah, fire! fire!"' Through the trees he wanders off in the direction of the conservatory, just as its doors are thrown open and the guests and actors issue forth.

They have been playing *A Midsummer Night's Dream*, and Philine, flushed with success, sings the brilliant *Polonaise*, 'Je suis Titania'. Mignon appears. Wilhelm, who has sadly missed her, greets her with so much joy that Philine sends her into the conservatory in search of the wild flowers given to Wilhelm the day before. Soon after Mignon has entered the conservatory it is seen to be in flames. Lothario, obedient to her jealous wish, has set it on fire. At the risk of his life Wilhelm rushes into the burning building and reappears with Mignon's fainting form in his arms. He places her on a grassy bank. Her hands still hold a bunch of withered flowers.

Act III. A gallery in an Italian castle, to which Wilhelm has brought Mignon and Lothario. Mignon has been dangerously ill. A boating chorus is heard from the direction of a lake below. Lothario, standing by the door of Mignon's sick-room, sings a lullaby, 'De son cœur j'ai calmé la fièvre'. Wilhelm tells Lothario that they are in the Cipriani castle, which he intends to buy for Mignon. At the name of the castle Lothario is strangely agitated.

Wilhelm has heard Mignon utter his own name in her delirium during her illness. He sings, 'Elle ne croyait pas'. When she enters the gallery from her sick-room and looks out on the landscape, she is haunted by memories. There is a duet for Mignon and Wilhelm, 'Je suis heureuse, l'air m'enivre'. Philine's voice is heard outside. The girl is violently agitated. But Wilhelm reassures her.

In the scenes that follow, Lothario, his reason restored by being again in familiar surroundings, recognises in the place his own castle and in Mignon his daughter, whose loss had unsettled his mind and sent him, in minstrel's disguise, wandering in search of her. The opera closes with a trio for Mignon, Wilhelm, and Lothario. In it is heard the refrain of 'Connais-tu le pays?'   K.

HAMLET

Opera in five acts, text by Michel Carré and Jules Barbier. First performed Opéra, Paris, 9 March 1868, with Christine Nilsson and Jean-Baptiste Faure.

Hamlet, *Prince of Denmark*............................Baritone
Ophélie (Ophelia), *daughter of Polonius* ....Soprano
Claudius, *King of Denmark*....................................Bass
Gertrude, *Queen of Denmark,*
    Hamlet's mother..............................Mezzo-Soprano
Laerte (Laertes), *son of Polonius* ....Tenor

Marcellus, *an officer* ....Tenor

Horatio, *Hamlet's friend* ....Baritone

The Ghost of Hamlet's Father ....Bass

Polonius, *Lord Chamberlain* ....Bass

Grave-Diggers...Tenor, Bass

Lords and Ladies, Soldiers, Actors, Servants,
   Peasants

Place: Denmark
Time: Sixteenth Century
Running Time: 3 hours

Ambroise Thomas was a pillar of the French musical establishment, the creator of a dozen works for the Opéra-Comique including the highly popular *Mignon*, but, a couple of early works apart, not associated with the Opéra until *Hamlet*. He seems to have taken with noticeable ease to the five-act form which the Opéra demanded, and the work is full of contrast, characterisation and energy, the baritone protagonist one of the plum roles of the romantic repertory, the soprano a favourite of prima donnas. The great French teacher of composition, Nadia Boulanger, asked for an example of well-written opera, is said to have recommended *Hamlet* and indeed it is as this that it will commend itself to anyone who looks less for insight into Shakespeare, more for a notable (and thoroughly enjoyable) example of French nineteenth-century opera.

The King of Denmark has died in mysterious circumstances, rumoured murdered by his brother, Claudius, who has assumed the crown and married Gertrude his brother's widow, herself conceivably implicated in the crime.

Act I. Celebrations of the marriage of Gertrude and Claudius are afoot, to the undisguised dismay of Prince Hamlet. In music of rather formal cut he protests his love for Ophélie ('Doute de la lumière'), listens to Laerte in a short song bid farewell before going abroad, and hears a report of the appearance on the battlements of the ghost of the recently deceased king, his father. On the stroke of midnight, he witnesses the wonders of the previous night and in suitably sepulchral accents calls on the Ghost to speak to him ('Spectre infernal'). Revenge for a murdered father is its simple but devastating demand, and it goes on to adjure Hamlet to spare his mother.

Act II. The moment he catches sight of Ophélie, Hamlet disappears and the Queen arrives to find her in tears and talking of forsaking the court. Gertrude in a grand arioso ('Dans son regard plus sombre') begs her not to leave as in his love for her lies Hamlet's only hope of recovering from what she sees as his madness. The King and Queen speculate as to whether Hamlet has stumbled on evidence of their crime, but Hamlet himself announces that a group of actors will that night entertain the court. The King is reassured.

The actors announce themselves in breezy chorus. Hamlet instructs them on the play they should perform, then calls for wine and sings an irresistibly brilliant drinking song, the best-known number of the score ('O vin dissipe la tristesse'). The court assembles to the sound of a so-called Danish March and the players act out in dumb show 'The murder of Gonzalez'. An old King enters on the arm of his Queen, falls asleep, and is poisoned by what Hamlet describes in his commentary as a demon tempter. The King in a frenzy orders the actors to leave and Hamlet in a fit of feigned madness, and to the court's consternation, denounces him as a murderer.

Act III. A sombre introduction leads to Hamlet's 'J'ai pu frapper le misérable' and 'Etre ou ne pas être' (To be or not to be), a low-key but by no means unworthy setting of Shakespeare's most famous monologue. Kneeling in prayer, the King murmurs of his crime, and when Polonius warns him against betraying both of them Hamlet is convinced that Ophélie's father is Claudius's accomplice.

The Queen fails to persuade Hamlet to marry Ophélie that very evening – his revenge on his father's murderers will inevitably reveal Polonius's involvement – but the trio is fine, even though Ophélie's pleas fail to move Hamlet. In an impressive scene, Hamlet forces his mother to compare the portraits of his father and the man she is presently married to, only the appearance of the Ghost to remind him of his vow not to harm his mother calming him sufficiently to avoid the violence which seems inevitable. Since she can't see the Ghost, Gertrude is confirmed in her view that he is mad.

Act IV. A country site near a lake is the scene of the ballet which was obligatory at the Opéra – attractive music which needlessly interrupts the flow of the drama and is succeeded by Ophélie's mad scene and death. She appears to believe she is married to Hamlet, and at one moment sings a waltz, at another a Swedish folk song the original Ophélie

Hamlet. *Jean-Baptiste Faure in the title role, portrait by Edouard Manet, 1877.*

asked the composer to include for her sake. Its several sections – unusually for a nineteenth-century mad scene, without reference to music previously heard – build up to a highly impressive whole and the scene has remained a favourite of prima donnas equipped to do it justice, from Melba and Tetrazzini early in the twentieth century to Callas and Joan Sutherland towards its end.

Act V. Grave-diggers are at work but can't tell Hamlet for whom the grave is intended. The Prince knows Ophélie has gone mad but not that she is dead and bitterly regrets his cruelty to her ('Comme une pâle fleur'). He misunderstands the hostility of the returning Laerte but accepts his challenge. A funeral procession interrupts their duel and for the first time Hamlet knows whose is the coffin at its head. The appearance of the Ghost galvanises him to denounce the King as a murderer and kill him. Gertrude must go to a convent and Hamlet is proclaimed King, a so-called 'happy ending' which the composer changed for the London première in deference to the supposed wishes of the English public.   H.

VIRGIL THOMSON

(born 25 November 1896, died 30 September 1989)

The 'creative friendship' between Virgil Thomson and Gertrude Stein, says Robert Marx in a perceptive sleeve note for a recording, 'lasted off and on for twenty years and resulted in numerous songs, a motion picture (never filmed, unfortunately), and two operas ... In the best sense the operas are works of poetic theater: the texts are musical in language and harmony, and each opera discards traditional conventions to generate its own panoramic world ... ' He goes on to say 'although sumptuously melodic, they are not easy to sing, and mere vocal beauty in performance is not enough for success'.

'The music of religious faith, from Gregorian Chant to Sunday School ditties, was my background, my nostalgia' the composer has written, and that nostalgia and that background, together with the sense of style imparted by his French training (under Nadia Boulanger), permeates the operas. He met Gertrude Stein in 1925, and, although more than twenty years younger and in spite of tensions and wartime separation, remained on terms of friendship with her until her death in 1946, some ten months before the première of *The Mother of Us All*.

Apart from Stein, Thomson drew for stylistic inspiration on the French composer Erik Satie, of whose music he wrote: 'It has eschewed the impressive, the heroic, the oratorical, everything that is aimed at moving mass audiences ... it has valued quietude, precision, acuteness of auditory observation.' The phrases could have been used to sum up his first opera.   H.

FOUR SAINTS IN THREE ACTS

Opera in four acts, text by Gertrude Stein (*an opera to be sung*). First given in concert form, Ann Arbor, Michigan, 20 May 1933; on the stage, at Hartford, Connecticut, 8 February 1934, by the Society of Friends and Enemies of Modern Music, conducted by Alexander Smallens, staged by Frederick Ashton. The opera was sung by a black cast, including Edward Matthews as Saint Ignatius, Beatrice Robinson Wayne and Bruce Howard as Saint Teresa I and II, Embry Bonner as Saint Chavez, Bertha Fitzhugh Baker as Saint Settlement, and Abner Dorsey and Altonell Hines as Compère and Commère. First performance in New York, 44th Street Theater, 20 February 1934. The work has since been heard in both concert and radio performances, and in May 1952 was presented by a black company in Paris during the Festival of Twentieth Century Art, with Inez Matthews, Edward Matthews, conductor Virgil Thomson; February 1973, Mini-Met Forum, New York; London, Trinity College, 1996; Houston and Edinburgh Festival, 1996, with Ashley Putnam, Gran Wilson, Sanford Sylvan.

Compère...Bass
Commère ....Mezzo-Soprano
Saint Teresa I..Soprano
Saint Teresa II..Contralto

Saint Ignatius Loyola ....Baritone

Saint Chavez...Tenor

Saint Settlement ....Soprano

Double Chorus of Named and Unnamed Saints, Six
Dancers

Place: Spain
Time: Sixteenth Century
Running Time: 1 hour 35 minutes

From the start, *Four Saints* was a success, with a brilliantly stylised production by Frederick Ashton, evocative scenery and remarkably compelling singing and acting by performers many of whom had no stage experience whatsoever. There was a total of sixty performances in its first year.

The surrealist nature of the work is emphasised by the fact that the scenario used for the original production was written (by Maurice Grosser) *after* the words and music had been completed. The original act headings (which are the only indications of 'story' the libretto contains) are given in italics in the following synopsis.

Prelude. *A narrative of Prepare for Saints.* The choral overture in triple time on the following words:

To know to know to love her so.
Four saints prepare for Saints,
Four saints make it well fish.
Four saints prepare for saints it makes it well fish
it makes it well fish prepare for saints

leads to some conversation between the chorus, Compère, Commère, and various saints, and ends with the Commère and Compère reading out a lengthy list of saints, many of whom are not mentioned at any other point in the opera.

Act I. *Saint Teresa half indoors and half out of doors.* The scene is the steps of the Cathedral at Ávila. Saint Teresa enacts for the instruction of saints and visitors seven scenes from her own life. The first has the Compère and Commère and two choruses singing antiphonally, then an aria for Saint Teresa. Saint Ignatius joins the guests just before the end of the first tableau, which gives way to the second, in which Saint Teresa, holding a dove in her hand, is photographed by Saint Settlement. In the third and fourth tableaux Saint Ignatius serenades Saint Teresa, and then offers her flowers. In tableau five Saint Ignatius and Saint Teresa II admire the model of a Heavenly Mansion. In tableaux six and seven, Saint Teresa II is shown in an attitude of ecstasy, and rocking an unseen child.

Act II. *Might it be mountains if it were not Barcelona.* The scene is a garden party near Barcelona. The Compère and Commère sit at the side in an opera box from which they can watch the proceedings and where they are presently joined by both Saint Teresas and Saint Ignatius. A Dance of Angels is performed for their pleasure and there is a party game, after which everyone goes out except the Compère and Commère. There is a love scene between them, and the two Saint Teresas return in time to see it. A telescope is brought in and as the two Saint Teresas look through it a vision of a Heavenly Mansion appears. 'How many doors how many floors and how many windows are there in it?' ask the saints.

Act III. *Saint Ignatius and one of two literally.* The scene is a garden of a monastery on the sea coast. The men saints are mending a fish net. The introductory *allegro moderato* for the orchestra alone leads to a conversation about monastic life between Saint Ignatius, the two Saint Teresas and Saint Settlement, but the men stop their work and listen as Saint Ignatius describes to them his vision of the Holy Ghost. This is his well-known aria, 'Pigeons on the grass alas'; the vocal line is occasionally taken over by the chorus or the Compère, and there is an off-stage heavenly chorus. Saint Chavez lectures to the men, there is a dance in the Spanish style, a storm is quieted by Saint Ignatius, who predicts the Last Judgement. It grows dark, there is a devotional procession, and the Intermezzo recalls the opening of the Prelude.

Act IV. *The sisters and saints reassembled and re-enacting why they went away to stay.* The Compère and Commère discuss whether there shall be a fourth act, and when they have made up their minds, the curtain rises to show all the saints in heaven. They join in a hymn of communion 'When this you see remember me', the Compère announces 'Last Act', and the chorus and principals reply *fortissimo* 'Which is a fact'.   H.

THE MOTHER OF US ALL

Opera in three acts, libretto by Gertrude Stein. Première, Brander Matthews Hall, Columbia University, 7 May 1947, with Dorothy Dow, Ruth Krug, Teresa Stich, William Horne, Bertram Rowe, conductor Otto Luening; London, Trinity College, 1996.

Susan B. Anthony, *a feminist of the 1870s* ....Soprano

Anne, *her confidante; 1870s*.........................Contralto

Gertrude S., *a cheerful woman of middle age* ....Soprano

Virgil T., *a pleasant master of ceremonies*.........Baritone

Political dignitaries of the 1850s (V.I.P.s)
    Daniel Webster...Bass
    Andrew Johnson..Tenor
    Thaddeus Stevens...Tenor

Recently discharged Civil War soldiers
    Jo the Loiterer ....Tenor
    Chris the Citizen ....Baritone

Indiana Elliot, *pretty provincial; 1860s* ....Contralto

Angel More, *sweetheart of Daniel Webster,*
    now dead; about 1845 ....Soprano

Henrietta M., *a feminist of the 1890s* ....Soprano

Henry B., *a poetic gentleman*
    of the 1870s.......................................Bass-Baritone

Anthony Comstock, *a Victorian capitalist*.............Bass

John Adams, *once President of the*
    United States, 1825 ....Tenor

Constance Fletcher, *a beautiful*
    lady, 1905–10 ....Mezzo-Soprano

Intellectuals about 1890–1900
    Gloster Heming...Baritone
    Isabel Wentworth ....Mezzo-Soprano

Anna Hope, *feminist, about 1900*.................Contralto

Lillian Russell, *a theatre star, 1890–1910*.....Soprano

Jenny Reefer, *a comical*
    feminist, 1870s..............................Mezzo-Soprano

Ulysses S. Grant, *an opinionated politician* ......Baritone

Herman Atlan, *a French painter, 1860s* ....Baritone

Donald Gallup, *a college professor, 1920s* ......Baritone

A.A. & T.T., *page boys*..Silent

Negro Man and Woman, *1860–70*...................Silent

Indiana Elliot's Brother, *1870s*....................Baritone

Running Time: 1 hour 50 minutes

In autumn 1945, Gertrude Stein and Virgil Thomson met again in Paris after five years of separation, the writer having already accepted the musician's proposal for a further operatic collaboration. She finished the libretto just before she died in the summer of 1946, and the music was written between October 1946 and January 1947. The première was at Columbia University in May 1947, and by the time the opera was recorded thirty years later, it had received more than 1,000 performances in nearly 200 productions.

Its central figure is the American feminist, Susan B. Anthony, who campaigned all her life for women's rights and particularly for the vote for women, and of whom there stands a statue in Washington. Composer and librettist said it was a musical and dramatic 'landscape' they worked to create, and other characters from American history appear in the opera, anachronistically and with the intention of weaving an American tapestry, into which are introduced figures from Gertrude Stein's own life, both Parisian and American. To identify Susan B. and her companion Anne with Stein and Alice B. Toklas does not require a feat of imagination, but Miss Toklas once specifically rejected the autobiographical analysis.

Just as he had for *Four Saints*, Maurice Grosser wrote a scenario, with the composer's collaboration and with the specific intention of reducing problems of staging.

As for the music, nostalgia remains one of the composer's sources of inspiration, and Robert Marx has suggested he means to 'stimulate memories of experiences we have never had, of small town American life in times long ago'. Virgil Thomson himself described the score as 'a memory-book of Victorian play-games and passions ... with its gospel hymns and cocky marches, its sentimental ballads, waltzes, darned-fool ditties and intoned sermons ... a souvenir of all those sounds and kinds of tunes that were once the music of rural America'.

Act I, scene i. A room in the house of Susan B. Anthony. She is shown in conversation with her constant companion, Anne; Gertrude S. and Virgil T., acting throughout (though intermittently) as narrators, stand down-stage, and the elegantly conversational music passes easily from one participant to another as they discover among other things the failings of men and the tendency of Susan B. to be right.

Scene ii. A political meeting in a tent. The meeting's subject is economic and political injustice.

Politicians parade across the stage, Daniel Webster chanting a dirge with which he once won a legal case, Andrew Johnson, John Adams, Ulysses S. Grant, Anthony Comstock and Thaddeus Stevens following him ('London Bridge is falling down' is the march's theme, the only non-original tune in the score). Susan B. Anthony introduces herself and, after the politicians have marched and counter-marched and various other characters have introduced themselves, including the lyrical (and ghostly) Angel More, Constance Fletcher, and Lillian Russell, a debate develops between Susan B. and Daniel Webster. This consists mostly of quotations from the political utterances of these two historical figures (who historically probably never met), and Maurice Grosser tells us it is out of parliamentary punctilio that Webster constantly refers to Miss Anthony as 'he'. Just before the end of the scene, which has been punctuated by lyrical utterances, short ariettas and duets, Jo and Angel More resume the banter on the subject of mice which they started during the parade.

Scene iii, a public square in front of Susan B. Anthony's house, is preceded by an icily impressionistic orchestral passage. We encounter Andrew Johnson and Thaddeus Stevens as political enemies, Jo and Chris as satirical philosophers, and Constance Fletcher and John Adams as protocol-ridden lovers, the latter more concerned with etiquette ('If I had not been an Adams I would have kneeled at your feet') than anything more passionate. There is an enjoyable waltz, part Parisian in its elegance, part American in its directness, and Jo rounds it all off with a whimper, not a bang, by asking, quietly but with doubtful relevance: 'I just want to know if everybody has forgotten Isabel Wentworth?'

Scene iv. The same place. A short, slow prelude introduces Susan B., day-dreaming about her mission and its problems. Though she has helped to enfranchise the blacks, those she conjures up in her dream will not, she realises, help her in her fight for female suffrage. Nor can Donald Gallup, a college professor, do anything for her, nor yet the V.I.P.s, whose bugle-like interest in their own privileges injects a note of comedy into the proceedings. Jo and Chris ask Susan B. the difference between rich and poor. If people are rich, she tells them, they do not listen; if they are poor they listen but all they perceive is that they are listening.

Scene v. The marriage of Jo the Loiterer and Indiana

Elliot. A beautiful interlude, marked *sereno* and delicately scored, introduces the wedding tune which pervades the scene and haunts the memory, like the melody of a hymn known in childhood and not heard since. Susan B. sings it in aria form as she muses on the subject of women. The wedding party enters, and there is a rather inconclusive discussion between Jo and Indiana about the ring. John Adams and Constance Fletcher continue their theory-ridden duetting of love and non-marriage – one of the most elevated flirtations in all opera, which is not surprising since Adams was the sixth President of the United States and Constance Fletcher a contemporary of Gertrude Stein's!

Daniel Webster and Angel More seem about to follow their lilting example, but Ulysses Grant calls attention to the ceremony, which is almost immediately interrupted by the brother of Indiana who forbids the marriage, whereupon Indiana renounces her brother. The music shifts between the lyrical, epitomised by the wedding hymn tune, and a kind of wry musical humour (including a reprise of the waltz). The various flirtations are pursued, and one has sympathy with the chorus which suddenly demands: 'Why don't you all get married?'

Act II, scene i. Susan B. Anthony's drawing-room. The music starts with the direction 'Smoothly, like a carpet sweeper', but the 'contained' effect it makes sounds much better than that. Still, Susan B. might be doing housework when Anne and Jenny Reefer come to tell her the politicians want her to speak at a meeting – she knows nonetheless that they will never give her what she wants most. Though they are married, Indiana wants to stay Elliot and won't take Jo's name. The politicians come to plead with Susan B., but hers is the response of a spitfire. After renewed pleas, she changes her tune and starts to sound like a statesman before finally agreeing. The carpet sweeper music resumes.

Scene ii is introduced by 'Last Intermezzo', very bright and full of movement. We are still in Susan B.'s drawing-room, whither Susan B. and Anne return from the meeting to discuss the former's philosophy of men. For the first time the word 'male' is written into the constitution and Susan B. decides men 'have kind hearts, but they are afraid'. A short but very impressive scene builds up on this theme, interrupted eventually by a march introducing the suffragettes (the tune is 'London Bridge is falling down').

Lillian Russell has been converted and will give all she earns to the cause. The lady herself thinks it is 'so beautiful to meet you all' (is she quite steady on her feet?), and John Adams and Constance Fletcher seize the opportunity to pay each other compliments. Daniel Webster is in pontifical mood, but there is a new turn of events in that Indiana has decided that Indiana Loiterer is a pretty name, and that her husband must now become Jo Elliot, even though, as he says, nobody will know it's him. The chorus defines Susan B.'s success as having worked for the franchise for women and for blacks, but having succeeded in getting the word 'male' written into the constitution.

Scene iii. Epilogue. A statue of Susan B. Anthony is being unveiled in the Halls of Congress. Anne comes in alone, rejoicing that women finally have the vote, and Angel More, by now unequivocally a ghost, haunts proceedings, as does John Adams, wondering why Constance Fletcher, who shortly enters almost blind, has not been included in the statue, if only because of her wonderful profile. Politicians remain politicians, romantics are still romantic, Indiana insists on some detailed talk about marriage, but Lillian Russell, who is due to make a speech, is plainly tight, in spite of which fact General Grant defends her by insulting those who comment on her state of less than grace. Lillian Russell clings to her conviction that it is 'so beautiful to meet you all here', and when the statue is unveiled, Susan B. herself is revealed, to finish the opera impressively with a monologue about her long life and a reminiscence of the wedding hymn.

One of the curiosities of *The Mother of Us All* is that the listener every now and then hears pre-echoes of Auden's turn of phrase in the as yet unwritten *The Rake's Progress*, and indeed of Stravinsky's turn of phrase in setting Auden's words. It remains a fascinatingly individual opera, not easy perhaps to export but deserving a very high place among operas written by Americans.   H.

LORD BYRON

Opera in three acts, text by Jack Larson. Première at Juilliard Theater, New York, 20 April 1972, with Grayson Hirst, Carolyn Val-Schmidt (Mrs Leigh), Lenus Carlson (Thomas Moore), conductor Gerhard Samuel.

Lord Byron	Tenor
Thomas Moore, *the poet*	Baritone
John Hobhouse, *Byron's friend*	Bass
John Murray, *Byron's publisher*	Tenor
Count Gamba, *his companion in the Greek War*	Baritone
John Ireland, *Dean of Westminster*	Bass
Two English Noblemen	Baritones
Abbey poets	
Gray and Thomson	Tenors
Spenser and Dryden	Baritones
Milton and Johnson	Basses
Mrs Leigh, *lady-in-waiting to the Queen; Byron's sister*	Soprano
Annabella Milbanke, *later Lady Byron*	Mezzo-Soprano
Contessa Guiccioli, *Byron's last mistress*	Soprano
Lady Melbourne, *a former mistress*	Soprano
Lady Charlotte, *a former mistress*	Soprano
Lady Caroline, *a former mistress*	Soprano
Lady Jane	Mezzo-Soprano

People of London, Abbey Choir, Sailors

Place: London
Time: 1812–24
Running Time: 2 hours

*L*ord Byron had a peculiar genesis. After the death of Gertrude Stein, Virgil Thomson in 1962 found a librettist in Jack Larson, who shared with Thomson a fascination with Byron. Work proceeded and in late 1965 an article about the new opera caught the attention of the Metropolitan Opera who organised a commission for the new house, due to open in late 1966. To fit the big new theatre, some re-thinking seemed essential, and early public readings suggested success so that by 1969 the first draft was finished. But a new management at the Met lost interest and in 1972 the work was given at the Juilliard School. It remained a favourite with the composer, who tinkered with the score up to his death, altering and abbreviating it, often – according to informed criticism – to its disadvantage. At the first performance, a ballet was danced to Thomson's Third Symphony.

The libretto, in contrast to the composer's two earlier operas, is, for all its twists and turns of time and place, in fairly straightforward narrative form, the music more romantic than before and inclined to parody and quotation ('Auld Lang Syne', 'Ach, du lieber Augustin', 'Believe me, if all these endearing young charms' among others). There is an impressive choral start; grateful solo writing, with Byron himself a true leading role; ensembles of poets and friends, and, in the last scene of Act II, of women, then men, then, settling into a slow waltz, of both together.

Act I. Westminster Abbey, 1824. London mourns the death of Byron, whose body has recently arrived from Greece. In Poets' Corner, former colleagues join in lament. A committee led by Hobhouse petitions the Dean for burial in the Abbey and we learn that a statue of the poet by Thorwaldsen is on the way. Byron's last love, Contessa Guiccioli, together with her brother, Count Gamba, his companion in Greece, are received by Lady Byron, but there is consternation at the publisher Murray's news that a memoir exists whose revelations may put paid to their efforts to secure Abbey burial.

The statue arrives. Byron's shade sings a sardonic apostrophe to London, and the curtain falls on the admiring throng.

Act II. The Abbey. The friends dispute as to whether or not to destroy the possibly incriminating manuscript. Moore insists they read it.

Four memory scenes follow. In the first (1812), at Lady Melbourne's, Byron is protected by her niece, Miss Milbanke, from young women who want him to expose his club-foot by dancing, and there is a tender scene between them. In the second, at a Victory Ball in 1814, Byron delights in taking his sister, the pregnant Augusta Leigh, on his arm. There is gossip, he is accosted by a former lover, Lady Caroline (who is given an arietta), and to quieten gossip proposes to Miss Milbanke, who accepts. Augusta Leigh seems abandoned. The last scene (New Year's Eve, 1814) is split, with three women nervously contemplating the marriage of one of them to Lord Byron; and four men at a bachelor party in alcoholic enthusiasm mocking marriage and denouncing all women.

Act III. 1815. Lord and Lady Byron, the latter pregnant, visit Augusta Leigh, to whom Byron is still powerfully attracted and with whom he duets skittishly. Lady Byron catches them embracing, Byron protests Augusta is the only woman who ever loved him, but Lady Byron insists she swear not to see him again. Augusta refuses to elope with him to the continent, and at the end of a scene of considerable power, Byron furiously accepts that he must leave the country.

In the Abbey, as in Act I. Hobhouse burns the manuscript, with Mrs Leigh's consent but over Moore's protest and to the Contessa's horror. The Dean, with the facts suppressed and believing completely in Byron's impiety, refuses Abbey burial. The Contessa and her brother denounce British hypocrisy and leave, the statue is re-crated, the crowd laments, but the poets are joined by Byron, whom in a song of unashamed rejoicing they welcome to their company.   H.

MICHAEL TIPPETT

(born 2 January 1905)

Like Stravinsky, Tippett is one of the great 'sports' of opera, scarcely belonging to a 'national' tradition, consistent within himself yet constantly shifting his stance, with his five full-scale works building a considerable oeuvre, acknowledging no obvious ancestor and resolutely declining to enter some hypothetical mainstream. Like Wagner, he wrote his own texts, and there is no doubt they aptly served his purpose, yet from the start public (and even performers) have pronounced themselves perplexed by their precise meaning even when they were convinced by the logic of the music they inspired. Much of his operatic life seems to contain paradox and yet, contrariwise, in many ways he is the least contradictory of composers.

In the course of nearly fifty years of operatic career, Tippett has encompassed a 'quest' opera which amounts to something like a modern *Magic Flute*; a tragedy founded on antiquity and dealing avowedly with the matter of choice; a critique of human behaviour positioned in something like a drawing-room comedy though very distant in subject matter; a penetrating discussion of the violent issues which human beings confront however honourable their intentions; and a postscript he never thought he would write, an opera finished when he was eighty-three and confronting, this time more obliquely, the kind of problem he tackled in *Midsummer Marriage* more than forty years before.

During that lengthy period he progressed from the great enigma of British music to its Grand Old Man, a much-loved sage with an impressive list of major concert works to his credit, whose gnomic pronouncements would be pondered and analysed by British composers of every generation to their eventual benefit. Any one of Tippett's operas, had it stood solitary, might have been seen as the culmination of a lifetime's work – a conscious *magnum opus* – and the delight is that four had a successor. If three of them are not constantly revived in the late twenty-first century, I should be astonished. They are prime candidates.

THE MIDSUMMER MARRIAGE

Opera in three acts, text by the composer. Première Covent Garden, 27 January 1955, with Joan Sutherland, Adèle Leigh, Oralia Dominguez, Richard Lewis, John Lanigan, Otakar Kraus, conductor John Pritchard. Revived Covent Garden, 1957, 1968, with Joan Carlyle, Elizabeth Harwood, Helen Watts, Alberto Remedios, Stuart Burrows, Raimund Herincx, conductor Colin Davis. B.B.C. studio performance, 1963, with Catherine Gayer, Jeannette Sinclair, Janet Baker, Richard Lewis, John Dobson, Howell Glynne, conductor Norman Del Mar; Karlsruhe, 1973; Welsh National Opera, 1976, with Gomez, Mary Davies, John Treleaven, Arthur Davies, Raimund Herincx, conductor Richard Armstrong; Adelaide Festival, 1978, with Marilyn Richardson, Gregory Dempsey, Raimund Herincx, conductor Myer Fredman; Stockholm, 1982; San Francisco, 1983; English National Opera, 1985, with Helen Field, Lesley Garrett, Treleaven, Anthony Raffell, conductor Mark Elder; Opera North, 1985, with Rita Cullis, conductor David Lloyd-Jones.

Mark, *a young man of unknown parentage* ....Tenor

Jenifer, *his betrothed* ....Soprano

King Fisher, *Jenifer's father, a businessman* .....Baritone

Bella, *King Fisher's secretary* ....Soprano

Jack, *Bella's boyfriend, a mechanic* ....Tenor

Sosostris, *a clairvoyante* ....Contralto

The Ancients, *priest and priestess*
of the temple ....Bass, Mezzo-Soprano

Strephon ....Dancer

Chorus of Mark's and Jenifer's Friends; Dancers Attendant on the Ancients

Time: 'The Present'
Running Time: 2 hours 40 minutes

Wilfrid Mellers wrote at the start of an article[1] some years ago, "Of its nature opera is to some degree mythical (in which sense it is "universal"), to some degree social (in which sense it is tied to an historical past and an immediate present).' Tippett's 'quest' opera, written consciously under the influence of T.S. Eliot's verse drama (he once corresponded with Eliot with a view to getting the poet to write the libretto or at least the lyrics) is of course a comedy, and it is concerned, as he says,[2] 'with the unexpected hindrances to an eventual marriage', the hindrances basically 'our ignorance or illusion about ourselves'. In it Tippett emphasises myth, investigating the problems of carnal and spiritual union and the nature of self-knowledge. Mark and Jenifer are the young lovers, and we see their misunderstandings, clashes, adjustments of personality, reaction to opposition – the predicament of most young couples in love, though here made explicit and symbolical where usually implicit and matter-of-fact. Like Pamina and Tamino, Mark and Jenifer have the need for a hard, conscious, uncompromising development of the inner being, and they explore the male and female elements of their own personalities, the understanding of which in self as in the other is a basis for a happy relationship between two people. The opera is essentially the story of their inner development. The 'social' element in *The Midsummer Marriage* is one of place rather than time – as one reviewer[3] put it after the 1968 Covent Garden revival, 'the hilltop clearing in the wood, the burgeoning summer, the sense of the past, the presence of England (and in particular of the West country), with which libretto and music are saturated.'

[1] *New Statesman*, 31 March 1967.
[2] Michael Tippett: *Moving into Aquarius*, Routledge & Kegan Paul.
[3] David Cairns in *The Spectator*, April 1968.

Act I. Morning. 'When fully lighted the stage ... presents a clearing in a wood, perhaps at the top of a hill ... At the back of the stage is an architectural group of buildings, a kind of sanctuary, whose centre appears to be an ancient Greek temple.' Steps to the right lead upwards and end abruptly in mid-air; to the left, steps lead down through gates into the hill-side itself. It is the half-light before sunrise on a mid-summer day, and the music is of the utmost vigour and brilliance. To keep an assignation with Mark and Jenifer, who plan to marry, come their friends. Caution and purpose are immediately apparent. They greet the rising sun on midsummer morning, then perceive the temple building and hear the music coming softly from it (Ex. 1.) Magic is in the air, the

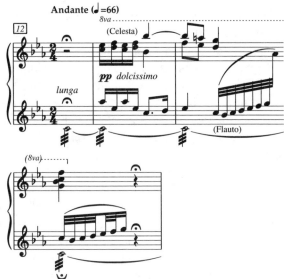

magic of the eternal ritual before which mundanity recedes, the magic which 'seems much nearer than expected'. The chorus hides as the dancers emerge, led by Strephon and followed by the Ancients (Ex. 2). The dance is formal and interrupted by the entrance of Mark calling for a new dance for his wedding day. He is told to watch, with the admonition 'change the unchanging ritual, there'll be no point of rest', but after a few bars of the dance, the He-Ancient to Mark's indignation trips Strephon with his stick, eventually ordering the party back into the temple with the warning: 'We do not seek ... to hold you longer from your dreams; you shall learn a new dance before you leave this place today'. They depart to Ex. 2.

In an extended, florid aria, ranging from B natural at the bottom to A natural nearly two octaves above, Mark exhorts them to celebrate his love with him: 'Ah, the summer morning dances in my heart', he sings, and Tippett's exuberant music catches the words; a splendid affirmation.

Jenifer appears, dressed much to Mark's surprise for a journey and not a wedding; their duet (with six-part chorus beneath it) is rapturous enough, but all Mark's pleading makes little difference: 'It isn't love I want, but truth,' says Jenifer (anticipating in her inherited determination the appearance of her head-strong father, King Fisher). Her feminine instinct for chastity and intellectual independence is affronted by Mark's masculine desire and assertion. They have to learn to accommodate each other's point of view – hence the events of the drama.

Jenifer starts to climb up[1] the broken stairs, disap-pearing suddenly on a *diminuendo* top B flat. Mark is half-laughingly consoled: 'She'll come back', but hearing the voice of Jenifer's businessman father, King Fisher, he decides complementarily to emulate Jenifer and go in search of that element in himself which corresponds with the feminine principles of instinct, fertility and love – the qualities for whose

---

[1] In mythology, the upper regions stand broadly speaking for the masculine principle, Mother Earth for the feminine.

lack he appears temporarily to have lost Jenifer. He goes down through the gates and into the hillside.

Tippett himself in a broadcast has compared King Fisher to Boss Mangan in Shaw's play *Heartbreak House*, and King Fisher stands for all elements, parental and otherwise, which are hostile to Jenifer and Mark and obstructive to their development. Summoning his secretary Bella, he proceeds, with her as intermediary, to enlist the help of the Ancients (derivation of Ex. 2) in tracing his daughter who has, he assumes, eloped with Mark. When they refuse to open the gates, he sends Bella for her boyfriend Jack, a workman who will do the job for them, and himself turns on the men and women who crowd round: 'So you are Mark's fine brood of friends.' In a vigorous monologue, he suborns the men with money and drives them off, but has less luck with the women, who refuse to work for him.

Enter Jack, who with Bella represents the uncomplicated, Papageno-Papagena, pair of lovers, able to live their lives by means of intuition and needing no deeper knowledge of the currents which lie beneath the surface of human love. Jack agrees to do the job, spends a moment of wishful thinking in duet with Bella, but is confronted by a warning voice from behind the gates (derivation of Ex. 1). King Fisher wants action, but the voice of Sosostris is even more vehement in urging caution. The men cry forward, the women are for restraint, but King Fisher gets his way until at the decisive moment Jenifer reappears at the top of the steps partially transformed.[1]

She has hardly started to explain her experience when Mark too becomes visible, also transfigured, in his case towards Dionysus. In their dangerous exaltation – this is still an early stage of the road they have to travel – they postulate different points of view and the Ancients and the dancers come impressively from the temple and demand that each shall put a case.

First Jenifer in a splendid statement, full of musical embroidery and elaboration and with a magical slow section with soft trumpet *obbligato*, then Mark in a

hardly less magnificent aria, 'As stallions stamping', refer in rather oblique terms to their experiences. The dancers and their friends meanwhile force King Fisher further and further away from the protagonists, until Jenifer moves across the stage to confront Mark and show him the animal she feels he has become. She starts to descend as he climbs the steps up which she had formerly sought enlightenment, each now attempting to recover the spiritual balance which is tottering with the symbolical reversal of roles. King Fisher fulminates and rushes out, while the friends of Mark and Jenifer understand, proclaiming themselves 'the laughing children' as the act comes to an end in something close to ecstasy.

Act II. Afternoon. The same physical scene is shown, from a rather different angle. The magical side of the atmosphere of Act I is immediately heard in enhanced (though musically different) form. Strephon starts to dance below the temple steps, then hides when the chorus is heard off-stage, celebrating the longest day. Jack and Bella come on and Bella brings up the subject of marriage. They look forward to future bliss in a scene which is full of tenderness, for all that it is the most nearly conventional of the opera.

They go into the wood, Strephon takes up a dancing position and there begins the central section of the act, an elaborate and closely worked out ballet sequence[2] in which the unconscious conflict between the sexes is shown at its most savage,[3] albeit in music of unusual and persuasive richness even for Tippett. The sequence is as follows:

I   The Earth in Autumn: the Hound chases the Hare.
II The Waters in Winter: the Otter chases the Fish.
III The Air in Spring: the Hawk chases the Bird.

At the start (Ex. 1) some of the trees of the wood represented by dancers begin to move and take up position to form a kind of race-course. The course is set and announced for the first two dances by solemn, grand chords. Round it in succession (and in its differing

---

[1] The score tells us: 'The ancient Greek prototype towards which Jenifer's transfiguration is tending would be Athena ... no exact imitation of Athena is meant, for the natural Jenifer is still visible behind the supernatural transfiguration.'
[2] The Ritual Dances (three in Act II, the Fire Dance in Act III) were first publicly performed in February 1953, in Basle under Paul Sacher, who had

offered Tippett a commission and received these dances in return.
[3] ' ... the man dances all the evasive tricks and the woman pursues him with shrewish relentlessness... the reconciliation of these dancers in Act III shows us the true union of opposites after Mark and Jenifer have achieved their inner resolution'. Robert Donington in *The Music Review*, May 1957.

manifestations for each dance) the hare is pursued by a hound, the fish through the river by an otter, the broken-winged bird in a cornfield by a hawk. The first two with difficulty escape, the fish not before being pinned to the bank by the otter, but it is apparent that the hawk will catch the bird until Bella, who has been watching with Jack, screams and breaks the spell.

A prelude ushers in the splendid musical sequence, and each of the three sections of the ballet consists of transformation, preparation for the dance, and the dance itself. The movements of pursuer and quarry are graphically depicted, sometimes ritually, sometimes almost naturalistically, and there is strong differentiation between the backgrounds – forest for the hare, water for the fish, air and the cornfield below it for the bird.

Jack comforts Bella, who retrieves the situation with mirror and powder-puff, singing a charming arietta as she refurbishes her make-up ('They say a woman's glory is her hair')[1] before confiding to Jack that King Fisher has plans for both of them. The act ends with off-stage cries in praise of midsummer.

Act III. Evening and night. What we have had so far is a look in depth at the problems of one couple – the efforts of each to get inside the mind of the other, parental opposition, misunderstandings and so on; a glance at the way another couple, instinctively and not bothering about the motives behind their thoughts and actions, solve theirs. We have also sensed (and sometimes seen) the usually unseen forces behind our actions: ritual, tradition, the instinct for what we can only inexactly call 'magic' that resides in all of us. Now, Tippett takes us nearer the magical and ritual forces which influence our actions; we hear the one in the voice of Sosostris, see the other in terms of the ritual fire dance, and gain insight into the power of each as we watch the death of the defiant and obstinately mundane King Fisher, and the symbolical transfiguration of Mark and Jenifer. The opera will end with the triumph of young love in its new-found understanding and a sense that the eternal mysteries go on unchanged.

The scene is as at the opera's start; it is plain that some kind of picnic has taken place and on one side of the stage is dancing. The action is languid until the revitalising influence of King Fisher is felt, announcing that he has brought his own brand of magic to counteract that of the Ancients: Madame Sosostris, a clairvoyante. The crowd is to escort her to the spot where he will have a confrontation with the Ancients, whom Bella now calls (Ex. 2). In spite of the Ancients' attempts to dissuade him, King Fisher persists, and a procession comes up the hill bearing a litter, on which is a cloaked figure whom Bella wastes no time in recognising as Jack.

When the fun subsides and the crowd moves, a contraption is seen, of vaguely human form and covered in veils, to which King Fisher explains the situation briefly, calling upon Madame Sosostris to locate his absent daughter. In music of impressive cast, at first slow and measured, Sosostris begins her invocation, 'I am what has been, is and shall be', gradually mounting in tempo and intensity and rising in *tessitura* as she follows it with a divination of the union of Jenifer and Mark, both physical in that they are in love and symbolical in that Jenifer is now ready to accept the masculine in Mark which she has come to understand (and vice versa). It is the most extended vocal movement in a score full of notable vocal writing.

King Fisher interrupts the vision and dashes the bowl to the ground, in the next breath demanding that Jack undertake another role, this time as his agent to unmask Sosostris's imposture. At the end of an ensemble, in which Jack and Bella, the two Ancients, and King Fisher battle for supremacy, Jack throws down belt and holster, his symbols of office, and turns his back on King Fisher who reluctantly picks them up. He moves to unveil Sosostris, and his actions are the subject of comment by the Ancients and the bystanders, who watch the last veil fall of itself to disclose an incandescent bud, which falls open like huge lotus petals. Inside, transfigured, are Mark and Jenifer.[2] King Fisher threatens, but when Mark and Jenifer turn towards him, he falls dead to the ground. Chorus and She-Ancient antiphonally sing his threnody over a Purcellian bass. It is not only the funeral march of an archetypal villain but of a Priest-King, who must die that life can be re-born.

Introduced by the same music as the other ritual dances, Strephon and a female dancer, with wooden

[1] Like the 'Ritual Dances', this section of the score was also heard publicly before the first night when Adèle Leigh, the original Bella, sang it for B.B.C. Television when I interviewed the composer a few days before the première.

[2] 'In Indian mythology, Mark and Jenifer would be transfigured as Siva-Sakti (Siva and Parvati). All the gestures and poses are hieratic', Robert Donington in *Michael Tippett: A Symposium on his 60th Birthday* (1965).

stick and block, begin to make ritual fire. The chorus joins in, and Mark and Jenifer celebrate their vision: 'Sirius rising as the sun's wheel rolls over at the utter zenith', and all including He- and She-Ancient proclaim their belief in carnal love and fertility. As the fire dance proceeds, Mark, Jenifer and Strephon seem to be drawn inside the lotus bud, whose petals close upon them so that finally nothing but the torch lighted at the start of the dance can be seen. Eventually even this is drawn into the veils, which break into flame, glow, die out and leave the stage dark.

'Was it a vision? Was it a dream?' The light starts to return but the temple is shrouded in dawn mist as at the opening. As warmth pervades the music again, Mark and Jenifer can be heard, and soon they are visible too as their mortal selves, proclaiming that they have found truth, and that 'All things fall and are built again, and those that build them again are gay' (Ex. 2). The curtain falls on an empty stage.

From the time of the first performance, the opera has divided opinion, most at first fastening on obscurity in the action, clumsiness in the libretto, which they felt invalidated Tippett's musical vision. Others fell immediately under the composer's spell, myself among them – I was lucky to be working at Covent Garden at the time the opera was, not without controversy, put into rehearsal and first produced. As David Cairns said at the time of the 1968 revival: 'The score has the power to intoxicate the listener, to possess his imagination and to secure his devotion for life, to sweep aside reservations.' It is not hard to believe that it will be one of the works of the mid-twentieth century which will be revived long past its own generation, which has in fact the possibility of becoming a true classic, in the sense that it reveals to its own and succeeding generations a truth which we (and they) need to know – and reveals it in major musical terms.   H.

KING PRIAM

Opera in three acts, words by the composer. Première at Coventry, 29 May 1962 (and later at Covent Garden), with Forbes Robinson, Marie Collier, Josephine Veasey, Margreta Elkins, Richard Lewis, conductor John Pritchard. First performed in Germany, Karlsruhe, 1963, with Howard Vandenburg,[1] con-

ductor Arthur Grüber. Revived Covent Garden, 1967, with Forbes Robinson, Anna Green, Patricia Johnson, Yvonne Minton, Richard Lewis, conductor Pritchard; 1972, conductor Colin Davis; Kent Opera, 1984, with Rodney Macann, Janet Price, Anne Mason, Sarah Walker, Howard Haskin, Omar Ibrahim, Neil Jenkins, conductor Roger Norrington, producer Nicholas Hytner.

Priam, *King of Troy*...............................Bass-Baritone
Hecuba, *his wife* ....Dramatic Soprano
Hector, *their eldest son* ....Baritone
Andromache, *Hector's wife* ...Lyric Dramatic Soprano
Paris, *Priam's second son* (Boy Soprano
    in scene ii) .... Tenor
Helen, *wife to King Menelaus of Sparta,*
    then Paris' lover .... Mezzo-Soprano
Achilles, *a Greek hero*.............................Heroic Tenor
Patroclus, *his friend* ....Light Baritone

Characters and chorus in the scenes and interludes

Nurse ....Mezzo-Soprano
Old Man ....Bass
Young Guard...Lyric Tenor
Hermes, *messenger of the Gods*..........High Light Tenor

Chorus of Hunters, Wedding Guests, Serving Men, Warriors etc.

Place: Troy
Time: Antiquity
Running Time: 2 hours 15 minutes

In his second opera, Tippett breaks to some extent with the luxuriant writing of *The Midsummer Marriage*, something which initially disturbed the nostalgic admiration of many lovers of the earlier work. As *The Midsummer Marriage* refers in its musical proliferation to such works as the song cycle *The Heart's Assurance* (1951) and the Piano Concerto (1953–55), the isolated orchestral textures and starker lines of the music of *King Priam* relate to the Concerto for Orchestra (1962–63).

The composer has prefaced the score with the German words 'Es möge uns das *Schicksal* gönnen, dass wir das innere Ohr von dem Munde der Seele nicht abwenden' (May *Fate* grant that we never turn our inner ear away from our soul's lips), and explained at the time of the first performance that the work was concerned with Choice – Priam's after the

---

[1] Vandenburg started his career in America as a baritone, sang tenor roles in Germany and at Covent Garden (including Radames), and then reverted to baritone to include even this bass role. In 1972, he was enough of a tenor again to audition Siegfried for Sadler's Wells!

prophecy over the fate of Paris, Paris' after the hunting episode to go to Troy, Priam's to accept him, Helen's to leave Sparta with Paris, Paris' between the three Graces, and so on throughout. But, essentially, it is Tippett's reaction to the events and circumstances of one of the world's greatest myths, with its tensions and heroic loves, its themes of courage and suffering, and public and private trial.

Act I. Heralds with trumpets in front of the curtain and a wordless chorus behind it (the latter much used throughout the opera to express stress and particularly battle, the former as 'links' between the episodes of the heroic drama) usher in the action, which starts with discussion of Hecuba's dream – that her newly-born son Paris will cause his father's death. Hecuba's reaction to the Old Man's reading of the dream comes in an aria, 'Then am I no longer mother to this child', which quickly reveals her forthright, passionate nature. Priam's reaction is less positive and exposed in a ruminative soliloquy, whose first words, 'A father and a King', are used later to pinpoint the moment when choice was available to him and he allowed heart (typified in this phrase) to rule head (which insisted on the child's death), and, more culpably, did not hide this reaction from the Young Guard, to whom he gave the job of killing the child and who knew that Priam's feelings contradicted his words.

A vocal Interlude, involving the Nurse, Old Man and Young Guard – the opera's 'Greek Chorus' – discusses choice in its relation to the particular situation.

Priam's son Hector, attempting to demonstrate his physical prowess by subduing and capturing a wild bull single-handed, is dismayed when a young lad jumps on its back and rides it away. Eventually, the boy comes in, reveals that he loves the bull as his best friend but would like to join the young heroes of Troy. Hector offers to teach him the arts of war, a proposition Priam accepts provided the boy's father agrees and he makes a free choice. This the boy does, saying that his name is Paris, a revelation which startles Priam into a soliloquy. He cannot conceal his joy that the gods have reversed his 'choice' of long ago, and his fear that Hecuba's dream may yet prove inspired; in effect, he accepts the new turn of fate.

Nurse, Old Man and Young Guard witness the decision and comment in a second Interlude on its importance.

Guests come rejoicing from the wedding feast of Hector and Andromache, at the same time admitting that the mutual hostility of Hector and Paris has caused Paris to set sail from Troy to the court of Menelaus at Sparta.

We see Helen and Paris, obviously already consumed with passion. Paris insists that Helen must choose between him and Menelaus and at the end of their duet exacts her promise to leave with him if he comes to fetch her. Even Paris in his soliloquy admits to dismay at the prospect their planned elopement opens before him, but turns to wonder whether there is in fact any element of choice in human affairs – do he and Helen 'choose' when, having been apart, their bodies rush together as one? Hermes, as if in answer to his question, comes to tell him he must choose between three Graces: Athene, Hera and Aphrodite (sung by Hecuba, Andromache, Helen). How in choosing one can he escape the wrath of the others? Hermes answers that he will not escape – but he must still choose. Athene offers him courage on the battlefield, Hera satisfaction in marriage, and each curses him when it is obvious he will choose Aphrodite, elope with Helen and plunge Greece and Troy into war.

Act II.[1] Troy is besieged and Hector taunts Paris with having run away in battle from Menelaus. Priam tries to patch up their quarrel, and Paris eventually follows Hector to battle.

The first Interlude has the Old Man asking Hermes to let him see Achilles sulking in his tent.

Except in one short crucial scene, it is the private Achilles whom we meet in the opera, and he is found in his tent with Patroclus, singing sadly to the sound of guitar, 'O rich soiled land', a song of longing for peace and beauty quite at variance with the actions for which Achilles, here as in any other version of the legend, is renowned. Patroclus weeps that Achilles should have so taken to heart the loss of a girl, given as booty after the sack of Thebes and then taken away again, as to refuse to join the battle. Together they cook up the idea that Patroclus shall wear Achilles' armour against the Trojans, and Achilles pours a libation to the gods in order that Patroclus may return safely.

---

[1] Scored for wind, guitar, percussion and piano, unlike the outer acts which include strings.

The act's second Interlude has the Old Man begging Hermes to warn the Trojans of their peril at Patroclus' hands.

Paris comes to tell Priam that Hector has killed Patroclus in single combat, and Hector to parade before his father in Achilles' armour. A fine trio celebrates the victory and the prospect the Trojans now have of destroying the Greek fleet, but it is interrupted at its climax by the sound of Achilles' war cry. This is the finest *coup de théâtre* the composer achieved (the only one, you might argue, he ever truly attempted), and the blood-curdling challenge has haunted whoever heard the opera since Richard Lewis first superbly delivered it at Coventry in May 1962, a reaction Tippett undoubtedly anticipated, to judge by the stage direction he allows himself at this point: 'Hector stands as though transfixed!'

Act III. Cellos alone introduce Andromache, waiting like a fighter pilot's mate for her warrior to return from single combat, knowing that each vigil so far has had a happy ending but aware that the credibility gap is narrowing. In her aria, she remembers her foreboding the day Achilles killed her father and brothers, but she refuses to yield to Hecuba's entreaty to go on to the walls of Troy in order to call Hector back from the field of battle; why does King Priam not end the war by sending Helen back to Sparta? Hecuba retorts that it is not for Helen that the Greeks have gone to war, but to win Troy itself. When Helen appears, Andromache can assuage her nerves with insults about Helen's low priority among war objectives, marriage 'vows' to Menelaus, and so on. Helen's answer takes the form of a great aria, its burden: 'women like you, wives and mothers, cannot know what men may feel with me'. The voices of the three women join in perhaps the most inspired section of the score, a fine trio in which each invokes the name and attributes of her mate and predicts death.

In the Interlude serving women pretend to go about their business in Hector's house, but they have already heard the rumour: ' ... we could tell the story too, the pathetic story of our masters, viewed from the corridor'.

Priam feels alone, isolated by his subjects from some disaster. Only Paris has the courage to tell him that Hector is dead; he cannot accept his father's reproaches and regrets at the result of the choice of twenty and more years ago and proclaims his intention of absenting himself until he has worked out his destiny by killing Achilles.

The last section of the opera begins as Paris leaves and Priam moans to himself: 'A father and a King'. Had the augurs predicted Hector's death and not his own, he would not only have ordered but also willed the killing of the infant Paris. His conscience speaks in the guise of the Young Guard, the Old Man and the Nurse who make him recite the dread chain of events, with vengeance inevitably following military murder, and he gradually accepts the inexorable laws by which men of all ages have lived.

The second Interlude, purely orchestral, ushers in the scene in Achilles' tent, climactic if undemonstrative, in which King Priam begs the body of Hector from the Greek who slew him. Achilles seems to start to urge the law of retribution, but his mention of the name of Patroclus shows the full extent of the wound his friend's death caused him. Priam kisses his hands, 'the hands of him who killed my son', and Achilles grants him the body of Hector. Just as he stood to pour a libation when Patroclus went off to fight, so he stands now to ask his friend's forgiveness for the act of non-hostility which might seem to negate the vengeance he has so bloodily exacted. Achilles and Priam discuss the destiny of each, Achilles' to die at the hands of Paris, Priam's to be killed by Achilles' son Neoptolemus.

The third Interlude has Hermes announcing the deaths of the protagonists and hymning music's all-healing supremacy.

Paris offers to fight to defend Priam, who has refused to leave Troy with him. Priam prays and fails to recognise Hecuba. Stress mounts in the chorus, Andromache spurns Paris and his defence of Priam, and Helen takes her place. 'They stand silent together, the beautiful ill-fated pair', and Priam sends Paris on his way to a hero's death, leaving Helen to make her peace with her lover's father. Priam comforts her – and himself – with the idea, which she enunciates, that neither he nor Hector ever reproached her for her part in events. Finally, Helen goes and as the off-stage sound of the chorus dies away, Priam sinks inaudibly down before the altar where, as Hermes appears before him and departs, Neoptolemus runs his sword through him to kill him instantly. 'Choice' is at an end.   H.

THE KNOT GARDEN

Opera in three acts, words by the composer. First performed at Covent Garden, 2 December 1970, with Jill Gomez, Josephine Barstow, Yvonne Minton, Robert Tear, Thomas Hemsley, Raimund Herincx, Thomas Carey, producer Peter Hall, conductor Colin Davis; U.S.A., Northwestern University, Illinois, 1974; Opera Factory, London, 1984, with Janis Kelly, Marie Angel, Christine Botes, Nigel Robson, Philip Doghan, Tom McDonnell, Omar Ibrahim, London Sinfonietta conducted by Howard Williams.

Faber, *a civil engineer, aged
  about 35* ....Robust Baritone[1]
Thea, *his wife, a gardener*...................Dramatic Mezzo
Flora, *their ward, an
  adolescent girl*...........................Light High Soprano
Denise, *Thea's sister, a freedom-
  fighter* ....Dramatic Soprano
Mel, *a black writer in his late
  twenties*...................................Lyric Bass-Baritone
Dov, *his white friend, a musician* ....Lyric Tenor
Mangus, *an analyst* ....High Tenor-Baritone

Place: A High-Walled House-Garden
Time: 'The Present'
Running Time: 1 hour 35 minutes

In a preface to the published score, the composer has written: 'The scene, whether labyrinth or rose garden, changes with the inner situations. If the garden were ever finally visible, it might be a high-walled house-garden shutting out an industrial city. The labyrinth on the other hand can never be actual. It appears, if at all, as a maze which continually shifts and possibly (in Act II) spins.

'Time is the present. Although the duration is obviously within one day, from getting up to bedtime, the dramatic action is discontinuous, more like the cutting of a film. The term used for these cuts is Dissolve,[2] implying some deliberate break-up and re-formation of the stage picture.'

He has further told us 'Parolles' defiant realism in *All's Well that Ends Well*, "simply the thing I am shall make me live", is the motto of the whole work.'

As an introduction in Act I, which has the sub-title Confrontation, Tippett wrote in the original Covent Garden programme: '*The Knot Garden* is about the loves and hates of seven people in modern England. Mangus, a psychoanalyst, has been invited to stay in the house of Faber and his wife Thea. She hopes that

Mangus can help with the problems of their young ward Flora, who is obsessed by the half-real, half-imagined sexual threat of Faber. Mangus discovers that it is not Flora that is sick but the marriage, and engineers a series of confrontations and "games" to resolve the difficulties. He sees himself as a modern Prospero, manipulating the characters. Dov, a musician, and his lover Mel, a young black writer, are also staying in the house, but as Thea's guests rather than Faber's. The arrival of Thea's sister Denise, a revolutionary, changes all the relationships.'

Act I. Uncompromising, strenuous, wide-striding music (the storm) introduces Mangus, who at his first appearance is described as 'a still point in a whirling storm'. Straight away, he alludes to Prospero and seems full of self-confidence. Here occurs the first Dissolve, ten bars of loud *allegro molto* followed by five of *diminuendo* timpani roll and a soft horn call (sometimes on cellos); it is the same each time it occurs in Acts I and II, but varies in Act III. Thea comes slowly from the inner garden stopping occasionally to tend the flowers. Mangus offers to help, but Thea's authority in the garden is absolute. Flora screams off-stage and rushes still screaming into Thea's arms. Faber follows her, but Thea sends Flora away with Mangus and turns harshly to Faber. Flora is their ward, and Thea continues her gardening analogy before saying that, if she may mother her, he – Faber – should father her, not play the lecher. Thea leaves, and Faber, who has been put in the wrong, wonders how this now happens so regularly. As to his relationship with Flora, he says, half to himself and half to Mangus, 'I do not flirt with Flora; Flora screams before I ... Impossible!', then goes off to work. Mangus is left to muse on the way each withdraws to the refuge of either factory or garden, and again refers to the possibility that, Prospero-like, he may put all to rights. Dissolve (music as before).

Thea recommends flower therapy to Flora – or, more prosaically, tells her to arrange some roses in a bowl – and Flora hums enigmatically to herself before telling Thea that her sister Denise has sent a message that she will be arriving later that day. Flora's desultory and now solitary humming turns more purposefully into 'eeny, meeny, miny, moe', but is interrupted by the rumbustious arrival of Dov

---

[1] The composer's own descriptions of the voices required.　　[2] There are two in Act I, one in Act II, five in Act III.

and Mel in fancy dress, the one tricked out as Ariel, the other as Caliban (jazz drummer's kit in the orchestra). Dov tries to hook Mel, whose Caliban disguise is fish-like, they hold a tableau and Flora stares at them until they suggest that if she thinks they are waxworks, she should pay, and if alive, she should speak. They introduce themselves, Mel as a writer, Dov as a musician, then sing a nonsense rhyme together as Thea and Mangus come from the house.

Mangus is of course delighted at the augmentation of *The Tempest* cast, which now has Ariel, Caliban, Ferdinand and Miranda as well as his Prospero. He takes Flora off to look for costumes and each of the two men who are left takes a glass from Thea's tray until Mel seems hypnotically drawn to Thea, leaving Dov alone to smash his glass to smithereens and start to howl like Ariel's dog. Faber is amazed at what he sees on his return, but Dov's reprise of the ditty he and Mel have already sung leads to an explanation of identities, and Dov moves towards Faber at exactly the moment when Thea and Mel reappear on the opposite side of the stage (the composer explains that the resultant tableau cannot become a vocal ensemble because the tensions are not yet ready for such expression).

Tension builds but is exploded by the sound of Flora's renewed screams as she starts half-hysterically to describe the disconcerting nature of Denise's arrival, explained the moment Denise comes into view and it can be seen that she is disfigured by the torture she has endured in her one-woman efforts to set the world to rights. She knows the effect she will have on them and starts in an extended and passionate aria to explain what she has been through (she is a musical cousin to Queen Hecuba in *King Priam*, although her defiance has occasionally a hint of Achilles' war-cry about it). She wants no pity and her rhetorical question 'How can I turn home again to you, the beautiful and damned?' receives no direct reply until Mel attempts to relieve the tension by starting a blues, itself developed into a considerable ensemble which eventually includes even Mangus and finally Denise herself, soaring to top C and D flat just before the act comes to an end with Mel's softly spoken 'Sure, baby'.

Act II. Labyrinth. The composer's programme note tells us all the action of the opera takes place in Thea's garden, and especially in the Knot Garden of the title. He specifies that 'it appears as if the centre of the stage had the power to "suck in" a character at the back of the stage, say, and "eject" him at the front. During their passage through the maze, characters meet and play out their scenes. But always one of the characters in these scenes is about to be ejected while a fresh character has been sucked in and is whirled to the meeting point.'

The music is violent from the outset and the first to be whirled in are Thea and Denise, aware of each other, not dissimilar in their sentiments but not properly conversing. Thea is whirled off and Faber makes some kind of contact with Denise, who riposts that she is just as tough as Thea before being herself whirled off and replaced by Flora (her ditty again), who backs away from Faber with renewed screams. No amount of reasoning from Faber can change her attitude towards him, she drops the flowers she has been carrying and is whirled off as Thea reappears to strike Faber with a horse-whip. When Thea disappears, Dov, dressed now as himself, takes her place, still howling like a dog, but prepared to sympathise with Faber's predicament – each of them, he feels, humiliated by a woman. Faber is obviously attracted in spite of himself, but his 'Come, I never kissed a man before' only just precedes his disappearance, as Mel is whirled on. Mel's very effective scene with Dov, directed to be played 'like a song and dance number' and with jazz-kit accompaniment, has as its burden the discovery that two souls, who thought they were twin, need to discover their true natures. Dov is whirled off as the music calms and Denise appears to play on Mel's feelings for oppressed men anywhere (the tune of 'We shall overcome'[1] appears in the orchestra and in Mel's vocal line). As Mel turns to Denise, Dov is thrown from the labyrinth, Thea returns and so does Faber until Flora and Dov, after the act's first Dissolve, are left together.

'As the sense of nightmare clears away, Dov comes to life first. He sees the plight of Flora and goes to comfort her,' say the stage directions – and he comforts her with music, in an infinitely touching scene, first getting her to sing the opening phrases of Schubert's *Die liebe Farbe*, orchestrated with magical touch (and ending with a direct quotation of the first chord of Beethoven's G major Piano Concerto, a key

---

[1] The marching song of Martin Luther King's civil rights movement.

work in Tippett's musical evolution). Dov ripostes with his own song, much less simple in outline: 'I was born in a big town, in a home without a garden' (a most appreciable product of the lyrical side of Tippett's genius which gave us *Boyhood's End* and *The Heart's Assurance*). The magic of love is in the air but, the stage directions tell us, 'as the song ends a shadow enters the garden. It is Mel. He taps the lovers on the shoulder: "Come, I taught you that."' For all Dov's denial, the spell is broken and the music fades.

Act III. Charade. In his programme note, Tippett says, 'Mangus, continually dreaming of himself as Prospero, has from the start of the opera been cajoling the other characters to play a series of short charades with him on scenes from *The Tempest*.' There is magic in the air as Mangus attempts to set the scene and Denise is stung into stepping into Mangus's circle to proclaim 'Power is in the will'. But Thea, not to be outdone, steps into the circle herself and cries out, 'Forgiveness. Blood from my breast. Here on this island, I know no god but love.'

In the first Charade, Mangus-Prospero explains the island and its inhabitants to Flora-Miranda, conjuring Mel-Caliban to stand upright, to his daughter's delight, and Dov-Ariel to leave the tree where Sycorax has imprisoned him. But Dov-Ariel flings himself on Mel-Caliban and belabours him, far beyond the calls of the script. Dissolve (with the music this time varied).

There is an exchange between Thea and Denise. The first seems to understand that things go wrong, the second does not accept confusion. Both agree that Mel could be Denise's salvation. Dissolve.

Flora-Miranda is asleep; Dov-Ariel is on guard; Mangus-Prospero watches through a telescope. Mel-Caliban creeps up on the sleeping girl, leaps on her and tries to tear her clothes off. Denise protests and Mel says he is only playing the role he was given and no more. Let Denise lay her head against his pounding heart (where, says Dov, *his* head often lay), and she will understand, but she will not – yet. There is a short duet for Dov and Mel, 'Black earth for white roses?', at the end of which Thea asks Mangus whether he is man of power or voyeur. Mangus's answer is to disclose Faber-Ferdinand and Flora-Miranda playing chess – but not for long, as Flora-Miranda upsets the board. 'That scene went wrong!' says Faber; 'that scene went right!' says Mangus.

The board is set again, and Thea, left alone, expresses new-found confidence in an *arioso* full of melismas: 'I am no more afraid. So we swing full circle back towards the sanctity of marriage.' Dissolve.

A dénouement seems called for, according to Flora-Miranda, and Mangus-Prospero offers to provide it, at least for Dov and Mel. As judge, with Faber-Ferdinand as some sort of jailer, he tries first Dov-Ariel and frees him, then Mel-Caliban. The Charades are at an end, and it is a time for quotation, musical and Shakespearean. Voices off join in with incoherent cries, coalescing at last into the first word of Dov-Ariel's 'Come unto these yellow sands', which words dominate the ensemble. Mel leaves with Denise, Flora goes off alone in spite of Dov's anxiety to follow her, so that in the end he follows Mel and Denise. Mangus can see only Thea and Faber alone in the garden (Dissolve: modified version of original), and they begin to speak, though not to each other. 'I put away the seed packets. I put away the factory papers ... Our enmity's transcended in desire.'

That the problems of each couple, or of each individual, are resolved is evident; but their catalyst seems to have been musical rather than explicitly contained in the events of the drama.　　　H.

THE ICE BREAK

Opera in three acts, words by the composer. Première Covent Garden, 7 July 1977, with Heather Harper, Josephine Barstow, Beverly Vaughn, Clyde Walker, Tom McDonnell, John Shirley-Quirk, conductor Colin Davis. First performed Kiel, 1978; Boston, 1979, with Arlene Saunders, Leigh Munro, Cynthia Clarey, Curtis Rayam, Jake Gardner, Richard Fredricks, conductor Sarah Caldwell.

Lev, *50-year-old teacher; released after
　20 years of prison and exile* .... Bass

Nadia, *his wife, who emigrated*...............Lyric Soprano

Yuri, *their son, a student*.................................Baritone

Gayle, *Yuri's white girlfriend*...........Dramatic Soprano

Hannah, *a black hospital nurse* ....Mezzo-Soprano

Olympion, *a black champion,
　Hannah's boyfriend* ....Tenor

Luke, *a young doctor*...Tenor

Lieutenant of Police ....Baritone

Astron, *a psychedelic
　messenger*................Lyric Mezzo and Countertenor

Time: 'The Present'
Running Time: 1 hour 15 minutes

In his fourth opera, which long before it was completed he claimed was to be his last, Michael Tippett is concerned with whether the humanistic ideal to which he subscribed all his life can survive in a world which seems to be increasingly finding solutions in violence. 'I hold for myself that the composition of oratorio and opera is a collective as well as a personal experience', once wrote Tippett, and in *The Ice Break* he discusses the culture shock involved in the meeting of East and West; the generation gap; racial tensions and hatred. Resolution of the conflicts may not be achieved, but a moral is drawn to the effect that only in the individual and his rebellion against the mass can salvation be found.

The opera is very short, moves rapidly about in its non-realistic dramaturgy, and the words are used at least as often to inspire the composer as to convey information to the audience.

Act I. An airport. Nadia and Yuri, a cross-grained student, wait for the arrival of Lev, the forgotten father of one and much-loved husband of the other. Yuri doesn't go along with Nadia's high-flying romantic notions but it is no surprise when Lev's voice over loudspeakers joins hers in thought before their physical reunion.

Gayle, in a state of near hysteria as usual, and her black friend Hannah are also at the airport, but they have come as two of a crowd acclaiming the returning black champion Olympion. Gayle, exaggeratedly 'with it' and hotly cool, quickly quarrels with Yuri who takes up a racist position not least because of Gayle's enthusiasm for Olympion.

Yuri refuses to make any effort to comfort Nadia, who wonders if the cheering could be for Lev. Cheerleader and fans burst onto the scene, Olympion's grateful vocal flourishes stem from a mixture of Monteverdi's reiterations and the panache of Achilles' war cry and, when the airport is empty, the drab figure of Lev is seen.

There is a dissolve into Nadia's tiny flat, where her vision of a new life and Lev's belief in a poetic ideal are contrasted in a slow, sad duet, full of melismata, devoid of sustained lyricism.

At Olympion's party, there is less joy than in *Midsummer Marriage* though even more jollity.

Olympion continues his bragging and eventually provokes Yuri, who is infuriated when Gayle makes a play for Olympion – to make amends, as she says, for years of injustice. Yuri attacks the black champion, who strikes him to the ground.

Nadia tries to explain to Lev her love for Yuri, who bursts in, dragging Gayle with him and rounding angrily on Lev: 'What have you come here for?'

Act II. In Nadia's flat, four people express each his or her own private world: Nadia's conviction that light emerges from darkness; Lev's sense of the burden he bears; Gayle's instinct that life is there to be lived; Yuri's apprehension of the gap between him and his parents. Lev is convinced that his experiences give him the right to speak, but Yuri insists that in this new country it would be thought shameful to be locked up unresisting. Gayle sings of life's reality, Lev wants an end to brutality, and Nadia laments the ritual dance of death.

Gayle and Yuri are subsumed in a masked white chorus, and Olympion and Hannah are together in recognising the blacks' need of him as their champion. For all its bravado speech, theirs is a love duet.

Hannah's long solo, introduced by oboes, all wide leaps, repeated syllables, and emphasis on solitary words, is perhaps the heart of the opera. Can even she make sense of the violence?

A ritual confrontation and mutual defiance between whites and blacks follows. The composer calls it Tribal Dancing.

Lev and Nadia are in something like despair, and Lev wonders whether Gayle could be right in her insistence on reality.

Black clashes with white in a scene of mindless violence, screaming, shots, at the end of which a white person has been beaten up, a black shot, and a moment later another white shot. Sirens can be heard approaching and the Lieutenant of Police asks the doctor about casualties. Olympion and Gayle are dead, Yuri badly injured.

A solo violin over various instruments dominates the sad slow music with which the act ends as Lev seems inclined to follow the doctor's advice and turn to Hannah.

Act III. Lev reads to Nadia, who lies dying. She hears that Yuri will probably survive but has herself released her hold on life. Lev's monologue is full of bitterness, but it is the sound of the sleigh-bells of her youth which introduces Nadia's aria of death. It might almost be Jenifer in a visionary moment, at least as far as the accompaniment is concerned. She hears the sound of the ice breaking on the river, and dies.

'Seekers of all kinds, tough and tender, past, present and future' are preparing for a psychedelic trip. The stage is full of colours, and the voice of Astron (Mezzo-Soprano and Countertenor, mostly an octave apart) sounds from the distance, but he rejects the idea that he is a saviour.

Doctor Luke reminds Lev that Nadia is dead and that he, who was close to death in the camp, must now choose Yuri. Lev watches as Yuri is wheeled into the operating theatre, and waits outside. 'Seekers' after the psychedelic experience rush into the hospital, third cousins perhaps of the laughing children of twenty-two years before.

The operation has been successful and Yuri will walk again. Hannah quotes from her own aria from the centre of Act II ('Much deeper, O much deeper'), and it is plain that she, Lev and even Yuri have succeeded in separating themselves from the mass to become individuals.   H.

NEW YEAR

Opera in three acts, libretto by the composer, based partly on H.G. Wells's story *Men Like Gods* (1921). First performed (with reduced orchestration) Houston Grand Opera, 27 October 1989, with Helen Field as Jo Ann, Peter Kazaras as Pelegrin, Krister St Hill as Donny, Richetta Manager as Regan, John Schiappa as the Presenter, James Maddalena as Merlin and Jane Shaulis as Nan, conducted by John DeMain. First U.K. performance (première of the full orchestration), 1990, at Glyndebourne, with Helen Field and Philip Langridge, conducted by Andrew Davis.

From Somewhere and Today

Jo Ann, *a trainee children's doctor* ....Lyric Soprano

Donny, *her young brother* ....Light Baritone

Nan, *their foster-mother* ......Dramatic Mezzo-Soprano

From Nowhere and Tomorrow

Merlin, *the computer wizard* ....Dramatic Baritone

Pelegrin, *the space pilot* ....Lyric Tenor

Regan, *their boss* ....Dramatic Soprano

Outside the Action

Voice, *presenter* ....Microphoned Male Singer

Dancers, Singers

Place: Jo Ann's Room; Futuristic Interior; Urban Public Space; Visionary Landscape
Running Time: 1 hour 40 minutes

Completed in 1988, when the composer was eighty-three, *New Year* crowns his career in opera as *The Midsummer Marriage* initiated it thirty-six years earlier. They have affinities, not just in terms of the central rituals (winter solstice/summer solstice), but in the rapturous mood and in the works' coherence. Dance plays an organic role: *New Year*, Tippett has said, 'comes close to being a musical, in that dance is an important and integral element'.[1]

Act I. Prelude. The Presenter's first words, 'Our world is wicked', refer to 'the terror town' outside Jo Ann's flat. The opera traces her journey from traumatised retreat to the moment when she is ready to confront reality outside.

Scene i. Inside her flat, Jo Ann reassures herself that she is 'safe ... from the storm out there', though 'never safe from the wound within'. As yet she can only dream of helping the children of the town (Jo Ann's Dreamsong). Donny bursts in, to 'jazz style solo' for trumpet. In an exaggeratedly upbeat mood, he dances around before retreating to his room. The Voice repeats Jo Ann's Dreamsong. Nan arrives, to the sound of characteristic bells. She loves both her foster-children but worries that Jo Ann's 'cocoon of love' may destroy Donny. He returns, to perform his 'Skarade', expressing his dilemma as a foster-child in comic form. He briefly fantasises a 'real' home, first in the Caribbean, then 'back further' to Africa. Dancers and Singers introduce the idea of 'Nowhere', the alternative dream world to our reality. The chorus question sets the agenda for Nowhere's role in the rest of the opera: 'Is it Science or Love will show the way?'

Scene ii takes us inside Tomorrow's laboratory, where Merlin, who stands for science and is fond of phrases like 'Digit to digit particle instruction', shows off his new computer to Pelegrin. They drink a toast to 'the New Year, the voyage out' in 'florid song' (a

---

[1] Introduction to the score.

wonderful, ecstatically melismatic duet). Merlin tries to show the future on his computer, but instead Jo Ann appears on the screen. Pelegrin is immediately fascinated. Regan appears but she is only interested in the future. In case we are not sure what she stands for, she helpfully begins the ensemble by asking, 'Manifest am I? Of that Eternal Feminine that draws us on?' Her dogmatism and the heroic, jagged intervals in her vocal line suggest a kinship with the Monstrous Feminine that haunted Britain in the eighties, Mrs Thatcher. Pelegrin wants to 'offer comfort and visionary courage' to the 'harrowed face': he determines to be Jo Ann's 'coal-haired stranger' (traditionally invited across the threshold at New Year to ensure good luck). He journeys to her in his spaceship (taped sound effects that recur whenever it moves).

Scene iii. Pelegrin's first brief encounter with Jo Ann is one of ideas hauntingly expressed in music, rather than as people.

Act II. Prelude. The Voice explains the ritual in which the scapegoat (the old year) must be driven out.

Scene i. Outdoors in a city at night: the crowd (which includes Jo Ann, Nan and Donny) prepares to find and expel the scapegoat. A Shaman whirls his body into a trance (the Shaman Dance, coloured by electric guitars and saxophone). In the second part of the ritual, the hunt for the scapegoat, Donny is chosen and 'ritually beaten', to fortissimo chords from trombone, tuba and guitars, vividly marked 'blurt'. The spaceship lands.

Scene ii. Thinking they have reached the future, Merlin introduces himself, Pelegrin and Regan – 'our mistress, our leader, our star'. Donny addresses her, 'speaking dub-style' (i.e. rapping), which she then imitates. When she realises Pelegrin has not brought them to the future she accuses him of betraying her for Jo Ann, 'this pathetic floozy from the past', and asks, 'What power has she that I have not?' To the sound of divided flutes, Pelegrin answers, 'Could it be the power of love?' With authoritative octave leaps up and down, backed by a 'lyric' clarinet, Nan rebukes Regan as 'that illusion men and women have to forge a realm of future good by power alone', as mistaken as Jo Ann's reliance on love alone. A tremendous ensemble builds up. Each character sings in turn, while the others accompany with col-

oratura on open vowels. It is, perhaps, the highpoint of the opera ('No way'). A trio for women's voices becomes a quartet when Pelegrin explains to Jo Ann that their relationship must continue in dreams, rather than reality. Nan points out that dreams can be dangerous in crowds. 'As if to exemplify' her words, the crowd becomes restive, while Donny becomes manically exalted again. He confronts Regan and spits in her face. She leaves with Merlin and Pelegrin in the spaceship.

Scene iii. In a fury the crowd turn on Donny and beat him up. The act ends in a theatrical climax as Jo Ann manages to carry him away, the bell strikes midnight and everyone sings 'Auld lang syne'.

Act III. Prelude. In Jo Ann's room Dancers and Singers reflect that after New Year, 'Our world's still wicked'.

Scene i. Nan has come to take Donny back. Jo Ann acknowledges that she has failed, 'for all [her] love'. In *Sprechgesang* and over agonised guitar, brass and percussion Donny reflects that his problems stem from his broken childhood, in particular his lack of a father: 'No loving, curbing hand on me'. He hands Jo Ann a 'magic video', a cassette of his dreams. Alone, she plays it and enters 'Donny's Dream', whose brilliant string writing recalls *Midsummer Marriage*. His dreams of being carried on a condor, of a tiger, of the wondrous family of whales, mean nothing to her. In her own dream Pelegrin invites her aboard the spaceship. An Interlude covers its journey to 'the countries of the mind'.

Scene ii. A symbolic ritual presents Jo Ann's turning-point: racked with thirst, she follows Pelegrin's encouragement to sip, rather than drink, at the 'fountain of forgetting', but then drinks deep at the lake of remembering. Musically the scene boasts virtuoso use of wind instruments, rippling flute and piccolo, oboes paired with trombone. At its climax, she hears 'a deeper sound, a richer song' (bassoon with double-bass). Her lyrical duet with Pelegrin ('Moments out of time and space') is followed by a dance expressing her new sense of freedom. This sarabande for flutes is cousin to the flute-sarabande portraying Paradise in *The Masque of Time* (1984). Pelegrin picks a rose and an Interlude portrays their return journey.

Scene iii. Pelegrin presents Jo Ann with the rose,

promising that when she is ready to go out, the rose will fly from her hand to him. Pelegrin leaves in the spaceship. As she dances towards the door of her flat, the rose disappears from her hand. A brief scene fills in what happened in the spaceship: Regan and Merlin curse Pelegrin. Suddenly the rose appears in his hand: he manipulates the computer so Nowhere disappears.

In her flat, Jo Ann at last opens the door to go out. Though she is momentarily daunted by a barrage of sound, the Voice reminds her of *her* dream, 'One humanity; One justice'.[1] 'The door is shut sharply behind her, cutting off all sound'. The opera, like *The Mask of Time*, ends without any 'empty bombast',[1] as the light fades.

All his life Tippett has offered an inspiring vision of otherness. Not least among his contributions is that fearlessly un-English, playful love of ideas. He dares to want us to think, as well as feel. 'Moral and metaphysical ideas and symbols are indispensable to Mr Tippett ... even when they are obscure, they convey to the straining, often puzzled, but always moved and at times wholly transported listener a vision of experience about whose authenticity there can be no doubt.'[2] How right that this tribute was paid by the seldom straining or puzzled Isaiah Berlin. Occasionally, Tippett's words grate because they do not reflect the unsentimentality of his vision.[3] But such words are reborn, transfigured in the immaculately controlled sensuousness of his setting. *New Year* charts the course of psychic growth in a way that would be ludicrous if it were merely verbal. Music, in Tippett's hands, celebrates its transcendental power to change the way we think and feel: the opera finds a model for its action in the transforming visitations of the spaceship, guided by that breakaway pilgrim Pelegrin.   P.

---

[1] Spoken by Mark Knoepfler of the group Dire Straits at the 70th birthday concert for Nelson Mandela in 1988. 'For me,' Tippett has commented in his autobiography *Those Twentieth Century Blues* (1991), 'that said everything.'

[2] Isaiah Berlin, *Michael Tippett: A Symposium on his 60th Birthday*, ed. Ian Kemp, 1965.

[3] 'O if we could see them in their saucer ... His rapt face tensed for navigation Her wondering hands strong upon his shoulder'.

MARK-ANTHONY TURNAGE
(born 10 June 1960)

GREEK

Opera in two acts, text by Steven Berkoff from his play of the same title. Première at the Munich Biennale, 17 June 1988, with Quentin Hayes as Eddy, conductor Sian Edwards, producer Jonathan Moore. First produced Edinburgh Festival, 1988; English National Opera, 1990; Montepulciano, 1991 (in Italian), Wuppertal, 1992 (in German). In both Italy and Germany the coarseness of the language was criticised, partly on the grounds that there was no easy Italian or German equivalent!

Eddy ....Baritone
Dad/Café Manager/Chief of Police .... Baritone
Wife/Doreen/Waitress 1/
    Sphinx 2 ....Mezzo-Soprano
Mum/Waitress 2/Sphinx 1 ....Soprano

Running Time: 1 hour 20 minutes

*G*reek was one of twentieth-century opera's instantaneous successes. The first-night audience in Munich (of which I was lucky enough to be part) gave it the kind of reception one associates with *Peter Grimes* and there is no doubt that the demotic immediacy of the libretto, combined with the composer's brilliantly individual mixture of jagged rhythms, demonic energy and often graceful lyricism, was entirely to the taste of a predominantly youthful audience.

Turnage studied with Oliver Knussen and John Lambert and then worked at Tanglewood with Hans Werner Henze, who invited him to write an opera for the first Munich Biennale, where *Greek* won B.M.W. prizes for music and text. 'I realise ... that it took a great deal of daring on Henze's part to commission an unknown, twenty-five-year-old English composer who had never written a piece longer than fifteen minutes', commented the composer, who acknowledges such disparate influences as Stravinsky and Miles Davis, Puccini, Britten, Janáček and rock. The 1988 première, with its seventeen-piece orchestra, sparked off a run of successful works in all forms, and for the last decade of the century Turnage has been composer-in-residence first with the City of Birmingham Symphony Orchestra and then with English National Opera, one striking composition after another resulting from the associations.

Greek is a re-working of the Oedipus myth by Steven Berkoff 'into the contemporary East End of London. Racism, violence and mass unemployment appear as metaphors for the plague that afflicts London ... '

Act I. Eddy is fed up with pub life in the East End and doesn't get on much better with the boredom of family life (Breakfast Quartet). Dad tells him a fortune-teller once said he would murder his Dad and marry his Mum, which strikes Eddy as a good enough reason to leave home (Eddy's Farewell). Mum, Dad and Doreen, Eddy's sister, ruminate on the plague, while Eddy gets involved with the police (Police Riot). After an interlude, he goes to a café, and gets into a fight with the Manager, whom he kicks to death (Fight). He discovers the Waitress is the Manager's widow, finds her attractive (Love Duet), and, even though she discerns a likeness to her long-lost son (The Story of Kid), prepares to marry her. Mum and Dad at home brood on the fortune-teller's prophecy.

After the rhythm-based, highly organised first act, the second is far more lyrical.

Act II. Ten years later, Eddy and his wife have done well (Duet; then Wife's Love Aria, a celebration of physical love and the longest set-piece of the opera). Eddy's parents come to pay them a visit and Eddy decides to take action to end the plague which still rots London. He will visit the Sphinx on the city's outskirts, guarded as it is by a pair of outrageous punk lesbians. It is an extended section and at its end Eddy solves the riddle, then kills the Sphinx.

His parents tell him he is not their son but a foundling they picked up carrying an oil-soaked teddy bear (Dad's Story of Kid). With a piercing scream, Eddy realises the truth (Soliloquy of Regret), is comforted by Mum, Wife and Dad, threatens to do the right thing, then thinks better of it: 'Oh Oedipus, how could you have done it? Never to see your wife's golden body again ... ' There is a mock Funeral March, but Eddy seems not to be blind, and Eddy's final monologue is spoken, not sung: 'Bollocks to all that!' H.

U

VIKTOR ULLMANN
(born 1 January 1898, died 17 October 1944)

DER KAISER VON ATLANTIS
The Emperor of Atlantis

Opera in four scenes, libretto (in German) by Peter Kien. Written in 1944 in the concentration camp of Terezín, in Czechoslovakia, the opera was not publicly performed, though rehearsed with Marion Podolier, Hilde Aronson-Lindt, David Grünfeld (Pierrot and Soldier), Walter Windholz (Emperor), Karel Berman (Death). Première (in German), Amsterdam, 16 December 1975, with Roberta Alexander, Inge Frölich, Adriaan van Limpt (Pierrot), Rudolf Ruivenkamp (Soldier), Meinard Kraak, Tom Haenen, conductor Kerry Woodward.

Emperor Überall ....Baritone
Death ....Bass
Pierrot ....Tenor[1]
The Loudspeaker...Bass
The Drummer.....................................Mezzo-Soprano
A Soldier..Tenor[1]
A Girl ....Soprano

Two Female Dancers

Place: Here
Time: Now
Running Time: 50–60 minutes

*D*er *Kaiser von Atlantis* was written for performance in Teresienstadt (Terezín), the so-called 'show place' concentration camp in the north of Czechoslovakia, but at dress rehearsal stage in October 1944, its explicitly anti-war, anti-Hitler theme caused the camp authorities to prohibit performance. The Czech composer, Viktor Ullmann, was for a while a pupil of Schoenberg's but the score shows more obviously the influence of Stravinsky and Weill, though the descent from Mahler is easy to find in the intermezzos, in Pierrot's aria early in the opera, in the scene for him and the Drummer, and in Death's aria in the last scene. Peter Kien, the librettist, much younger than Ullmann, was primarily a painter and architect; he, like the composer, was moved in 1944 from Teresienstadt to Auschwitz, where both were murdered.

Der Kaiser von Atlantis is laid out in four scenes, with a prelude and two intermezzos. It is scored for string quintet, flute, oboe, clarinet, alto sax, trumpet, percussion, tenor banjo and keyboard (harpsichord, piano, harmonium), and among the original singers was the Czech bass, Karel Berman, for more than thirty years after the war's end well known in Czechoslovakia and East Germany for roles as far apart as Boris Godunov and Leporello.

The appalling circumstances of the opera's gestation and abortive première, to say nothing of the sardonically appropriate choice of subject, make it hard to form a dispassionate estimate of its merits. The original libretto was neatly typed on the back of discarded concentration camp admission forms. But on any reckoning and whatever its origin, *The Emperor of Atlantis*, with its skilful mixture of styles and unerring sense of the dramatic, is a remarkable work and can make an extraordinary effect.

The first notes heard (G, D flat, E flat, A), played on solo trumpet, are from Josef Suk's well-known symphony, *Asrael*. Suk wrote the symphony after the death of his father-in-law, Dvořák, and of his wife, Dvořák's daughter; it was often played in connection with the deaths of famous Czechs. The four notes constitute a Death theme. The loudspeaker announces the opera's title ('Death Abdicates'), its characters, and theme: Death in disgust takes a holiday and

---

[1] Originally intended for one performer.

won't let anyone die. Pierrot is disillusioned, can make no one laugh, and longs to die (aria, duet, aria). Death laments the good old days when war was a matter of spectacle and pageantry, a great contrast to the motorised legions of the present (aria). In the name of the Emperor of Atlantis, the Drummer proclaims total war – to the finish. His aria contains in its introduction a minor-key parody of 'Deutschland über alles'. The curtain falls as Death breaks his sabre.

A Dance Intermezzo, in the tempo of a *Ländler* and with strong overtones of Ullmann's Viennese past, takes us to a room in the Emperor's palace, with a desk, microphone and switchboard. There is a large frame, like a mirror, draped in black. The Emperor shouting his orders into the telephone is answered by the Loudspeaker as he checks on the royal guard, a besieged city, executions, an epidemic, only to get the same report from everywhere: no one seems able to die! Even taking official credit (in a short aria) for the novel situation strikes the Emperor as a hollow form of consolation.

A man and a girl from the two enemy camps meet and in the new situation are driven to make love, not war. The music turns lyrical, the girl seeming to find it all very surprising, the Drummer fruitlessly attempting to reassert the Emperor's authority (trio), until the Girl and the Soldier sing a love duet.

Another Dance Intermezzo, this time slow and funereal ('the living death'), returns us to the Emperor's study, where he is witnessing the collapse of society as he in his deliberate isolation has known it. Pierrot seems to sing a lullaby, but the Emperor is beside himself at the horrible turn of events and first the Drummer and then the Emperor himself join their voices to Pierrot's in a trio. The Emperor pulls the sheet off the mirror and finds Death standing behind it. Death in his *andante* aria sees himself as comforter rather than tormentor but, when the Emperor begs him to return among men, consents only on condition that the Emperor is the first victim of the new order. The Emperor at first demurs, saying that people don't deserve it, but eventually agrees and sings an impressive farewell – to the war, to life itself. Death leads him through the mirror, and in front of the curtain, a magnificent setting of the chorale 'Ein' feste Burg', sung by the Girl, the Drummer, Pierrot and the Loudspeaker (with the music of the Prelude acting as a kind of *ritornello*) brings the opera to a grand, cathartic end.   H.

V

RALPH VAUGHAN WILLIAMS

(born 12 October 1872, died 26 August 1958)

HUGH THE DROVER

Opera in two acts, text by Harold Child. Première, Royal College of Music, London, 4 July 1924. First performed His Majesty's Theatre, 1924, with Mary Lewis, Tudor Davies, Collier, conductor Sargent; Washington, 1928; Toronto, 1932; Royal College of Music, London, 1933; Sadler's Wells, 1937, with Cross, Tudor Davies, Llewellyn, conductor Collingwood; New York, 1952. Revived Sadler's Wells, 1950, with Joyce Gartside, James Johnston, Roderick Jones, conductor Robertson; Royal College of Music, London, 1972, for Vaughan Williams's Centenary.

A Showman...High Baritone

Mary, *the constable's daughter* ....Soprano

Aunt Jane, *the constable's sister*.....................Contralto

The Turnkey...Tenor

The Constable ....Bass

John the Butcher ....Bass-Baritone

Hugh the Drover ....Tenor

A Cheap-Jack...Baritone

A Shellfish-Seller...Bass

A Primrose-Seller...Contralto

A Ballad-Singer ....Tenor

Susan...Soprano

Nancy..Alto

William...Tenor

Robert ....Bass

A Fool...Bass

An Innkeeper ....Bass

A Sergeant ....Baritone

Townspeople, Toy-Sellers, Boys, Soldiers, Stall-Keeper, Juggler, Dancing-Girl, Trumpeter, etc.

Place: A Small Town in the Cotswolds
Time: About 1812
Running Time: 2 hours 10 minutes

The composer of *Hugh the Drover* has made extensive use of English folk songs in his score, giving the music a peculiar flavour and affecting also the treatment of the story, which bears a distinctly original stamp. Although all the melodies seem to bear some resemblance to folk songs, five authentic traditional tunes ('Cockles', 'Toy Lambs', 'Primroses', 'Maria Martin', and 'Tuesday Morning') are used in the first act and one (the psalm-tune 'York') in the second.

Act I. The scene represents a May fair with booths and stalls among which the crowd of sightseers moves slowly, admiring, laughing, jesting with showmen, ballad-singers and Cheap-Jacks. The Showman has a dummy of Napoleon 'Boneyparty', which is to be set on fire to delight the patriots of Cotsall. The voice of Mary is heard singing 'I'm to be married on Tuesday morning'. Mary is to marry John the Butcher, but the thought of the wedding gives her no joy; she does not love John, the strongest and richest man in the town. Her Aunt Jane persuades her to accept her fate, when a stranger, Hugh the Drover, comes by; it is love at first sight for both Hugh and Mary. 'Sweet little linnet' he calls her, and instead of riches he offers her a roaming life of toil. Hugh's rousing song of the open road stirs Mary's fancy; she is not afraid; with him and with him alone can she find peace.

John enters with the crowd and eagerly embraces the proposal to fight Hugh for Mary. The crowd makes a ring for the two champions; they fight, and John does not fight fair, but Hugh, undismayed, in the end beats him. But John accuses Hugh of being a French spy. Mary is sure that Hugh cannot be a traitor; the crowd is not as faithful, and now acclaims the Constable (Mary's father), who will put Hugh in the stocks. Hugh is dragged off while the crowd jeers at the 'French spy'.

Act II, scene i. The market-place of the town.

Afternoon. (The composer directs that this scene[1] may be omitted if the opera is found to be too long.) Hugh, guarded by John and four other men, is brought in and about to be put in the stocks. The Constable asks John whether it might not be more prudent to let Hugh go; how can they prove he is a spy? John shows him money; *that* can prove anything.

Mary comes in, asks her father's pardon, and says she is now willing to marry John. The Constable is for taking her at her word, but John is still suspicious, the more so when she asks for Hugh to be freed since it is on her account that he is in the stocks. The Constable suggests they let him go – they have no evidence against him – but John sees through Mary's stratagem, and urges them to bind Hugh fast lest he should escape. Mary and Aunt Jane lament the failure of their scheme, and they leave Hugh alone in the stocks.

Scene ii. The church bells play the psalm-tune 'York'. Early morning the next day. Hugh is in the stocks.

John and his friends have made a night of it. In passing they come to taunt and hit Hugh who, of course, cannot retaliate. As soon as they go Mary comes to set Hugh free, having taken the key from her father. The lovers are on the point of running away when voices are heard – the alarm has been raised. Hugh goes back to the stocks and hides Mary under his cloak. The Turnkey and the Constable are pacified at the sight of him, but no sooner have they gone when other sounds of May festivities come to the lovers' ears. It is John, who comes to wake up Mary, bringing a spray of mayflowers. Mary cannot be found. The Constable, Aunt Jane, and the Turnkey, coming to inquire into the new mystery, discover Mary sitting in the stocks side by side with Hugh. They want to set Mary free; she refuses to go. The Constable disowns her; John declares that a trollop from the stocks is not a fit wife for him, but the crowd sympathises with the generous girl. There is every likelihood of a fight between the friends of John and those of Mary and Hugh, when the arrival of soldiers called to take away Hugh puts an end to the dispute.

John is anxious that Hugh should be instantly arrested and tried. As soon, however, as the sergeant looks at Hugh he discovers an old comrade; His Majesty has no better friend in England than Hugh the Drover. Annoyed at having come on a wild-goose chase, he refuses to go away empty-handed. He takes John and promises to make a soldier of him. The Constable apologises to Hugh; their friends beg them to stay. In a final homily Hugh tells them that he does not love the smooth, sleek life of the town, and prefers 'the windy wolds of life', where man has to do and dare or die. It is a call that he and Mary must obey. They go, followed by the farewells of their friends.   F.B.

THE POISONED KISS

Opera in three acts, libretto by Evelyn Sharp, derived partly from a tale by Richard Garnett and partly from Nathaniel Hawthorne's story *Rapaccini's Daughter*. First presented at Cambridge on 12 May 1936, and later the same year at Sadler's Wells Theatre, London; Juilliard School, New York, 1937; London Opera Centre, 1975.

Hob		..........................Actor
Gob	*assistants to Dipsacus*	..........................Actor
Lob		..........................Actor
Dipsacus, *a professional magician* ....Bass		
Tormentilla, *his daughter* ....Soprano		
Angelica, *her maid* ....Soprano		
Amaryllus, *son of the Empress of Golden Town*....Tenor		
Gallanthus, *his jester* ....Baritone		
Three Mediums, *assistants to the Empress* ....Soprano, Mezzo-Sopranos		
The Empress Persicaria................................Contralto		

Running Time: 2 hours

Described as a romantic extravaganza, the opera is really a fairytale set to characteristic and very charming music, and with spoken dialogue to help along the action. It was written in 1927–29, revised twice in the 1930s, and then again in 1956–57, when the composer's wife Ursula rewrote the dialogue. Vaughan Williams is said to have thought the work essentially unimportant though nonetheless something he was keen to write. But he was timid about showing it to his friend Gustav Holst!

The overture, compounded of tunes heard later, is directed to be played with the house lights up.

---

[1] Added for the 1933 revival at the Royal College of Music, London, when Beecham conducted, the scene never, it would appear, entirely convinced its composer, who, however, did not specifically discard it.

Act I. Near the house of Dipsacus on the edge of a forest, rival choirs, representing the powers of good and evil, sing of the beauty of day and night. But as soon as they have gone Angelica is left to lament the fate of an attractive young girl whose life passes in complete seclusion. All unknown to her, however, the prince and his jester have been roving in the forest and now the jester, Gallanthus, arrives. Angelica, who has never seen a young man before, falls in love with him and he with her. Their billing and cooing is interrupted by the coming of Dipsacus who means to expel the strangers by magic. The stage is emptied, but now Tormentilla arrives followed by Amaryllus. He met her in the forest nursing a cobra and, fearing for her life, has struck the snake a blow with his cane. Tormentilla does not fear snakes. She has been fed on poisons by Dipsacus, who has his own reasons for the strange diet. Amaryllus cannot understand why Tormentilla instead of thanking him weeps over her pet. An understanding is, however, soon reached when youth calls to youth; in their love duet, Amaryllus sings 'Blue larkspur in a garden, White clouds in summer skies', while Tormentilla, reared on poisons, uses the same tune for 'Black henbane in a thicket, Slime of the serpent's trail'. The two are about to go roving in the forest when Dipsacus intervenes. Tormentilla whispers the word Love, upon which Dipsacus tells her his plans. When he was young he was scorned by the Empress of Golden Town and has vowed to be revenged. He has fed Tormentilla on poisons solely in order that her kiss should be death to any lover. She will have to make the Empress's son kiss her and thus kill him. Tormentilla refuses to be a party to such a murderous plot and the angry magician banishes her. They, for their part, are not unwilling to go, especially as Angelica has abstracted a piece of the philosopher's stone which has the same virtue as Aladdin's lamp. They rub the stone and the stage is filled with a host of milliners and dressmakers with their latest creations.

Act II. Tormentilla's apartments in Golden Town. The room is filled with flowers sent by Tormentilla's admirers. Her beauty has excited such interest that when abroad she must wear a veil to avoid the unwelcome attentions of Golden Town gallants. She loves the prince whom she believes to be a shepherd boy. Part of the act is taken up with the plots of the three assistants of the Empress and counterplots of three assistants of the magician. The assistants of the

Empress have been instructed to poison Tormentilla; the assistants of the magician plot to bring the young lovers together so that the prince should kiss Tormentilla and die. The assistants of the Empress fail. They present Tormentilla with a box of poisoned chocolates, which she eats with relish. The assistants of the magician are more successful. They bring the prince to Tormentilla's apartment, where the lovers kiss and the prince falls, apparently dead.

Act III. The palace of the Empress. The prince is not dead, having been fed on antidotes since childhood, but he is ailing. The doctor bluntly tells the Empress that the only way to cure him is to bring to his side the woman whose name is ever on his lips. The Empress is angry, but if neither her spells nor the art of the physician will serve, Tormentilla will have to come and stay till the prince is restored to health.

Meanwhile Dipsacus comes to gloat over the distracted woman who once jilted him. He boldly tells the Empress that he and his magic alone are responsible for the prince's illness. They quarrel at first, but the old love is not dead; they grow sentimental and fall into each other's arms. They are found in this position by the prince and Tormentilla. Marriages are arranged – not excluding the marriage of Gallanthus and Angelica. The act which began with a waltz and a tango (the composer's touch is ever light) ends in a glorious hornpipe dance. No magic has power against true love, and love has conquered once more.   F.B.

RIDERS TO THE SEA

Opera in one act, text by J.M. Synge. Première, London, Royal College of Music, 1 December 1937. Produced Cambridge Arts Theatre, 1938, with Janet Smith-Miller, Margaret Field-Hyde, Olive Hall, Marcus Dods. Revived Wolverhampton, 1950; Sadler's Wells, 1953, with Marjorie Shires, Elizabeth Robinson, Olwen Price, John Faasen, conductor John Matheson; Naples, 1959, with Pina Malagrini, Elena Todeschi, Miriam Pirazzini, Guido Mazzini, conductor Francesco Molinari-Pradelli.

Maurya, *an old woman* ....Contralto

Bartley, *her son* ....Baritone

Cathleen, *her daughter* ....Soprano

Nora, *her younger daughter* ....Soprano

A Woman ....Mezzo-Soprano

Chorus of Women

Place: An Island off the West Coast of Ireland
Time: Early Twentieth Century
Running Time: 40 minutes

This short music drama, based almost word for word on J.M. Synge's one-act play about a fishing community on the Isle of Aran, is probably the composer's most successful opera. Begun in 1925, it was finished in 1932 and first performed at the Royal College of Music in December 1937. Its relative neglect by opera companies is due to the difficulty of finding a suitable companion piece, which only makes it the more regrettable that the composer abandoned his original idea of setting Synge's *The Tinker's Wedding* which would have made the appropriate contrast.

The opera begins with a short prelude[1] in which we hear the sea swelling from ominous calm to the growing storm heard as the door opens on scene i to admit Nora to the cottage kitchen where her sister Cathleen sits spinning. Nora has brought with her some clothes taken from a drowned man to discover if they belong to Michael, their brother, who, like his father and four other brothers, has been lost at sea. Maurya, their mother, is trying to rest in the next room, and the two younger women, over menacing orchestral sounds of rising wind and sea, quietly talk of their mother's wretchedness and hide the clothes away from her in the loft.

Maurya cannot sleep. She no sooner expresses her anxiety that Bartley, her only remaining son, intends to take the horses in the boat to the Galway Fair than Bartley himself arrives to collect a rope for a halter. In spite of the entreaties of his mother and sisters, he calmly gives them instructions on how to manage during his absence and goes out saying that he will ride the red mare with the grey pony running behind. Cathleen and Nora reproach their mother for not giving Bartley her blessing, and make the excuse that they have forgotten to give him his bread for the journey in order to send her after him. She stands for a moment in the doorway and sings mournfully 'in this place it is the young men do be leaving things behind them for them that do be old', then sets out into the wind, strongly expressed in strings and woodwind.

In Maurya's absence her daughters, at times unaccompanied or over a wandering solo oboe, decide to open the bundle of clothes. They find to their horror that they were certainly Michael's. Their mourning is heartfelt but, on hearing their mother return, they hide the clothes and compose themselves.

Maurya comes in and sits keening to herself. Cathleen tries to discover what has so terribly distressed her and Maurya tells them that she has seen Bartley riding to the sea on the red mare with Michael dressed in fine clothes and new shoes riding behind him on the grey pony. But, Cathleen tells her, they now know Michael is dead. Maurya is adamant and says that this vision means she will lose Bartley as well. Over an off-stage chorus of wailing women she sings of the deaths of all her men one after the other. As she describes the bringing home of the body of Patch, the door opens and behind the old women who come in is carried the dripping corpse of Bartley. He has been knocked into the sea by the grey pony.

Against the keening of the women, Maurya in a majestic aria sings of her resignation, which amounts almost to relief, as the sea has now taken from her everything that it could and is powerless to hurt her further. No longer will she worry about the wind and the tide; at last she can rest. Over a sustained F minor background she blesses all her dead one by one. Then as the music slides into E major she calls on God to bless the soul of everyone left living in the world. The sound of orchestra and wailing women surges up as Maurya sings proudly that Michael has had a clean burial and Bartley will have a fine coffin and a deep grave, but calm returns as she says, 'No man at all can be living for ever and we must be satisfied.' She kneels submissively by the bier. A sudden gust blows open the cottage door through which we hear the ceaseless noise of the sea. A soprano voice grows fainter and fainter in the distance as the stage fades into darkness and we are left only with the sound of the wind.   H.

THE PILGRIM'S PROGRESS

A morality in a prologue, four acts and an epilogue, founded on Bunyan's Allegory of the same name. Première, Covent Garden, 26 April 1951, with Arnold Matters, Inia Te Wiata,

---

[1] Vaughan Williams uses a small orchestra: single woodwind apart from a second flute (the only clarinet is a bass clarinet); brass confined to two horns and one trumpet; and a limited string section.

Norman Walker, Edgar Evans, conductor Leonard Hancock; B.B.C. (in studio), 1960, with John Noble, Herincx, conductor Boult; Royal Northern College, Manchester, 1992.

John Bunyan, *the writer*	Bass-Baritone
The Pilgrim	Baritone
Evangelist	Bass

The four neighbours
Pliable	Tenor
Obstinate	Bass
Mistrust	Baritone
Timorous	Tenor

In the House Beautiful
Three Shining Ones	Soprano, Mezzo, Contralto
The Interpreter	Tenor

Watchful, *the porter*	High Baritone
A Herald	High Baritone

In the Valley of Humiliation
Apollyon	Bass
Two Heavenly Beings	Soprano, Contralto

In Vanity Fair
Lord Lechery	Buffo Tenor
A Jester	Dancer
Demas	Baritone
Judas Iscariot	Baritone
Simon Magus	Bass
Worldly Glory	High Baritone
Madam Wanton	Soprano
Madam Bubble	Mezzo-Soprano
Pontius Pilate	Bass
Usher	Buffo Tenor
Lord Hate-Good	Bass
Malice	Soprano
Pickthank	Contralto
Superstition	Tenor
Envy	Bass

A Woodcutter's Boy	Soprano or Treble
Mister By-Ends	Buffo Tenor
Madam By-Ends	Contralto
Three Shepherds	Tenor, Baritone, Bass
The Voice of a Bird	Soprano
A Celestial Messenger	Tenor

Chorus of the Men and Women of the House Beautiful, of 'Certain Persons clothed in Gold', of Doleful Creatures, of Traders in Vanity Fair, of Angels in the Celestial City

Running Time: 2 hours

Act I, prologue. 'Bunyan is sitting in Bedford Jail and is writing the last words of *The Pilgrim's Progress*, "So I awoke, and behold it was a dream." Then he stands and, turning to his hearers, reads

from the beginning. As he reads there appears a vision of the pilgrim with a burden on his back, with his lamentable cry "What shall I do?" A curtain falls hiding Bunyan, and the Pilgrim is left alone reading his book and lamenting' – thus the synopsis printed as an introduction to the piano score.

The Evangelist appears and directs the Pilgrim to the Wicket Gate, encouraging him to bear his burden until he comes 'to the place of deliverance'. The Pilgrim is about to go when four neighbours, Pliable, Obstinate, Mistrust, and Timorous, attempt to dissuade him from his perilous undertaking. At the behest of the Evangelist, he starts again in quest of 'Life, eternal life!'

The Wicket Gate: behind it, the House Beautiful. The Pilgrim stumbles in and kneels in front of the Cross. He hears the voices of Three Shining Ones, who presently appear, take the burden off his back and lay it on the Sepulchre, then raise him to his feet and lead him to the gate. An Interpreter receives him, and a chorus of men and women welcome him to the house. The Pilgrim kneels while the Interpreter places the mark of the seal on his forehead. A procession appears, carrying a white robe, which the Three Shining Ones place on the Pilgrim's shoulders. The Interpreter slowly leads the Pilgrim into the house.

Act II. A Nocturne interlude leads straight to the act (and should only, says the composer, be included if it is wished to perform Acts I and II without a break). Watchful, the porter of the house, goes his rounds and prays for the blessing of sleep on all that rest within.

An open road stretches out straight from the back of the stage. A Herald steps forward: 'This is the King's highway ... It is straight as a rule can make it. Who will go on that way?' The Pilgrim asks for his name to be set down in the book, and while the scribe enters it and the Pilgrim is provided with armour, the chorus sings Bunyan's hymn, 'Who would true valour see, Let him come hither.'

The Valley of Humiliation, a narrow gorge, shut in at the back by a bare grey hill. A Chorus of Doleful Creatures is howling when the Pilgrim appears. He is hailed by Apollyon, who proclaims that he is King of the region wherein the Pilgrim was born and challenges him to fight for his soul. The Pilgrim is victorious in the combat, but sinks down weak with his wounds until revived by two Heavenly Beings, bearing a branch of the Tree of Life and a cup of the Water of Life. The Evangelist appears and announces new trials for the Pilgrim; he shall pass through Vanity Fair, where he will be ill-treated by the inhabitants: 'Be thou faithful unto death, and the King shall give thee the Crown of Life.' The Pilgrim is invested with the Staff of Salvation, the Roll of the Word and the Key of Promise.

Act III. Vanity Fair. Booths are up against the house walls on each side of the stage. A lane runs upstage between the booths. The Chorus stands round the booth dressed in fantastic dresses of all periods. 'All that the world can provide is for sale. The Pilgrim enters and the crowd surrounds him. "What will ye buy?" But the Pilgrim prays to keep his eyes from vanity. A procession enters of various well-known characters who succumbed to the lure of gold or power, Demas, Judas Iscariot, Simon Magus, Worldly Glory, and Pontius Pilate. Then the mood changes, Madam Bubble, Madam Wanton, and Lord Lechery offer him the lust of the flesh and the pride of life, but the Pilgrim waves them away. "I buy the truth." He defies their Prince Beelzebub, the father of lies. At this moment appears Lord Hate-Good, who, after hearing the witnesses against the Pilgrim, condemns him to prison and death' (from the synopsis to the score).

The Pilgrim in prison laments his condition. Why has God forsaken him? Suddenly he remembers the Key of Promise which has been entrusted to him. He puts it into the lock and the gates fly open. The moon gradually illuminates the landscape and reveals the Pilgrim's Way, up which the Pilgrim strides.

Act IV. The edge of a wood. The Pilgrim's Way is seen stretching out into the distance with the Delectable Mountains far off. When the curtain rises, a Woodcutter's Boy is chopping firewood. He sings brightly as he works. The Pilgrim asks him how far he still has to go before he reaches the Celestial City. He is told that it is not far from the Delectable Mountains. Enter Mister and Madam By-Ends. They are full of talk, but admit that though some 'are for religion in rags and contempt', they themselves 'are for him when he walks in his golden slippers in the sunshine and with applause'. They refuse to accompany the Pilgrim on the terms he proposes, preferring their old principles, 'since they are harmless and profitable'.

The Delectable Mountains, near the Heavenly City. This is the episode known as 'The Shepherds of the Delectable Mountains' and performed separately under that title as early as 1922[1] (though it lasts little more than quarter of an hour, it achieved considerable popularity in the twenty-nine years between its first performance and its incorporation in the longer work). Three shepherds are kneeling in prayer just before sunset. The Pilgrim enters and asks them if he is on the way to the Celestial City. They reassure him and ask him to stay with them for a while, to solace himself with the good of the Delectable Mountains. The voice of a bird is heard singing, and the shepherds join in the hymn. But a Celestial Messenger appears to summon the Pilgrim to the Celestial City, and, as a symbol of his mission, ceremonially pierces the Pilgrim's heart with an arrow. He leads the Pilgrim off, and points the way forward. As the Pilgrim is seen entering the River of Death, the shepherds raise their voices in song, joined by the sound of an invisible chorus.

The stage is quite dark. A distant trumpet sounds, and the voices from the Celestial City are heard a long way off but gradually getting nearer. Men and women on earth join in with them. Darkness gradually gives way to light, and the Pilgrim is seen climbing the stairs to the Gates of the City. They open and he is welcomed by angels. His Pilgrimage is over.

Epilogue. The vision fades. Bunyan addresses his hearers and shows them his book. 'O come hither, and lay my book, thy head and heart together.'

It has been rightly said that the key to the work lies in its title: it is a Morality, not an opera. The composer has been more interested in evoking a half-mystical, half-pastoral atmosphere than in creating dramatic tension through concentration on character and situation. *The Pilgrim's Progress* stands as a monument to the composer's life-long seriousness of purpose (he was seventy-eight when it was first given) and equally long preoccupation with the subject of Bunyan's allegory. In his score, he has not only incorporated the episode of 'The Shepherds of the Delectable Mountains' but has also drawn extensively upon material already familiar from his fifth symphony (when this was first performed, it was explicitly stated that the composer had used themes from his then unfinished opera).   H.

---

[1] Première, Royal College of Music, London, 1922. First performed Sadler's Wells, 1947; Cincinnati, 1949.

GIUSEPPE VERDI

(born 9 or 10 October 1813, died 27 January 1901)

For Italy, in the second half of the nineteenth century Verdi dominated opera even more than Rossini had in the first. His career and his aspirations were totally different from Wagner's and he was never the iconoclastic innovator his great German contemporary was perceived to be. Verdi's influence was great though not so great as Wagner's, and his reputation since his death, nearly a hundred years before I write this, has fluctuated in a way that is with hindsight astonishing though not too hard to elucidate.

Verdi's career divides, like those of most creative artists, into three: first, from *Oberto* to *Luisa Miller* and *Stiffelio*; then, when he had become a respected, much-in-demand composer, from *Rigoletto* to *Don Carlos*; and finally, as a venerated maestro from whom a new work was expected only once in a decade, from *Aida* to *Falstaff*, taking in the Requiem and the *Quattro Pezzi Sacri* on the way. *Macbeth* is an awkwardly placed forerunner of the future in the first phase, where it nonetheless has to remain, and some would include *Don Carlos* in the last phase, arguing its unsurpassed characterisation and the composer's masterly exploitation of colour. The final masterpieces have been highly esteemed from the start, though *Don Carlos* is a relatively late candidate for acceptance on this level. The middle group, apart from the universally accepted trio of *Rigoletto*, *Trovatore* and *Traviata*, has taken time to grow in public estimation since the German revival of the 1920s.

The amazing transformation in public perception has been with the operas of Verdi's first period, what he described as his *anni di galera* (years in the galley), when he was writing up to three operas a year – easy apparently for Rossini and Donizetti, hard for Verdi. Crudities of construction and of detail notwithstanding, the sheer vitality and intensity of the music speak immediately to late-twentieth-century audiences and will I suspect continue to speak to audiences of the next century.

Fifty years ago, the notion of Verdi scholarship, let alone Verdi Conferences and a Verdi Institute, would have seemed peculiar, unnecessary, beside the point.

Nowadays, versions, revisions, Paris options are discussed as ardently as Mozartian or Wagnerian variations, and the results have just as much practical effect on performance. Conceptual directors choose *Nabucco* as soon as *Tannhäuser*, conductors go for *Rigoletto* before *Aida*, audiences delight in *Stiffelio* as readily as in *Turandot*. The grand old man of Busseto needs at the approach of the millennium no special pleading.　　　　H.

OBERTO, CONTE DI SAN BONIFACIO
Oberto, Count of San Bonifacio

Opera in two acts, text officially by Temistocle Solera, although, says Julian Budden, most of it was probably by Antonio Piazza. Première at la Scala, Milan, 17 November 1839, with Rainieri-Marini, Mary Shaw (an English contralto, whose only claim to fame is this creation), Salvi, and the bass Ignazio Marini, the soprano's husband and a famous exponent of Rossini's Mosè. The opera was revived at la Scala for the fiftieth anniversary of Verdi's death, in 1951, with Caniglia, Stignani, Poggi and Pasero, conductor Capuana; and in Leeds by Opera North in 1994, with John Tomlinson in the title role.

Cuniza, *sister of Ezzelino da Romano* ....Contralto
Riccardo, *Count of Salinguerra* ....Tenor
Oberto, *Count of San Bonifacio* ....Bass
Leonora, *his daughter*......................................Soprano
Imelda, *Cuniza's confidante*..................Mezzo-Soprano

Knights, Ladies, Vassals

Place: Bassano, Italy
Time: 1228
Running Time: 2 hours 25 minutes

There is some doubt as to whether Verdi's first opera was a re-hash of an earlier work, but it was certainly written over some four years. Its success was sufficient for la Scala's impresario, Bartolomeo Merelli, to commission further operas and to maintain the connection with Verdi after the failure of *Un Giorno di Regno*. On the other hand, revivals of *Oberto* – even with a cast like la Scala's of 1951 – reveal no more than the burgeoning of talent and nothing approaching a neglected masterpiece.

Ezzelino da Romano has defeated in battle Oberto, who has taken refuge in Mantua. Oberto's daughter, Leonora, has been seduced by Riccardo, who is now due to marry Cuniza, Ezzelino's sister. Oberto and Leonora make their way to Bassano where the marriage will take place, and denounce Riccardo to Cuniza, who in her turn condemns him in front of the full chorus. When Riccardo in the second act asks to speak with her, Cuniza declines to see him, and Oberto shortly after waits to fight him. Riccardo on Cuniza's insistence agrees to marry Leonora, but is unlucky enough in his much delayed duel to kill Oberto. He leaves a letter saying he will go into voluntary exile, leaving his property to Leonora.

Perhaps the most interesting feature of a not very remarkable score is the first of a long sequence of father-daughter duets which occurs in the first act, when Oberto makes it plain to Leonora that he will only forgive her if she will interrupt the wedding feast and herself denounce her seducer.   H.

UN GIORNO DI REGNO

King for a Day

Opera in two acts, text by Felice Romani (subtitle: *Il finto Stanislao* – first set in 1818 by Gyrowetz). Première, la Scala, Milan, 5 September 1840. Not revived after the 1840s until broadcast by Radio Italiana during the Verdi celebrations of 1951, with Pagliughi, Laura Cozzi, Oncina, Capecchi, Bruscantini, Dalamangas, conductor Simonetto. Performed New York, Amato Opera Theatre, 1960; London, St Pancras, 1961; Como, 1973; Bregenz, 1974; Genoa, 1979, with Dessi, Corbelli, Alaimo, Mori; Wexford, 1981, with Aliberti, Feeney, Benelli, Bruscantini, conductor James Judd; San Diego, 1981, with Saunders, J. Patrick Raftery, conductor Calvin Simmons; Vienna Volksoper, 1995.

Cavalier di Belfiore, *a French officer impersonating Stanislao (Stanislas) of Poland*....................Baritone

Baron di Kelbar...Basso Buffo

The Marchesa del Poggio, *a young widow, the Baron's niece, in love with Belfiore*.........Soprano

Giulietta di Kelbar, *the Baron's daughter*..Mezzo-Soprano

Edoardo di Sanval, *a young official, la Rocca's nephew* .... Tenor

La Rocca, *Treasurer to the Estates of Brittany*................................Basso Buffo

Count Ivrea, *Commander of Brest, engaged to the Marchesa* .... Tenor

Delmonte, *esquire to the false Stanislao*..................Bass

Place: Baron di Kelbar's Castle near Brest
Time: August 1733
Running Time: 1 hour 55 minutes

After the favourable reception of Verdi's first opera *Oberto* at la Scala in 1839, the impresario Merelli commissioned the young composer to write him three operas in the next two years, to be produced either at la Scala or the Imperial Theatre in Vienna. The first of these was to be an *opera buffa*, and the circumstances of its composition and première have become famous – the illness of the composer, the death of his wife, an inadequate performance, a disastrous public reception and the withdrawal of the opera to Verdi's intense chagrin. The composer never forgave the Milanese public for what he thought an act of cruelty to a young composer badly in need of encouragement, and years later, when congratulated by a friend on a recent success, refused to show satisfaction at the public's favourable reaction, which he thought as capricious and lacking in seriousness as its former disapproval. Revivals of *Un Giorno di Regno* are rare, but in 1951 a carefully prepared Italian broadcast showed it, in spite of obvious indebtedness to Rossini and Donizetti, to be musically delightful.

The story is taken from an incident which took place during the wars of Polish succession in the eighteenth century, when Stanislas Leszczynski, whose right to the throne had been challenged and who had been hiding in France, made his way secretly back to Poland and reappeared with dramatic suddenness at a service in Warsaw Cathedral, to be recognised as the rightful claimant. There is, however, little historical basis for the incidents which form the subject of Romani's libretto.

Act I. After a brilliant overture referring to the opening and closing scenes of the opera, the first scene takes place in a hall in the castle where servants are excitedly making preparations for the double wedding of the Baron's daughter Giulietta to the rich old Treasurer, La Rocca, and of his niece, the Marchesa, to Count Ivrea. In point of fact, rejoicing is slightly out of place as Giulietta is in love with young Edoardo di Sanval and the Marchesa is marrying the Count in a fit of temper, having been, she thinks, jilted by Cavalier di Belfiore. The Baron and the Treasurer congratulate one another on the great honour which may be accorded them in having the King of Poland as witness to the double ceremony. Delmonte announces the arrival of his master and in comes the 'King', in reality the Cavalier di Belfiore, disguised (Il finto Stanislao – the false Stanislas) in order to distract attention from the real Stanislao's bid for power. In a lyrical aside he sings of his wish that his companions in Paris could see him, the wildest drinker of them all, playing so dignified a role, then in the cabaletta reiterates his desire that the company should treat him not as a king but as a friend.

The Baron invites him to the double wedding and Belfiore is most disturbed to hear that one of the brides is to be the Marchesa, with whom he is in love. He writes urgently to the Polish Court in hope that Stanislao has by now been enthroned and that he may therefore be released from his impersonation. In his turn Edoardo di Sanval, who is in despair at the prospect of Giulietta's marriage, begs, now that life for him is over, to be enlisted in the service of Poland ('Proverò che digno io sono'). Belfiore accepts him, determined, even if his spurious court goes up in smoke, to get the better of the Baron. To a martial air the two sing of glory and heroism, but as they go off together, the Marchesa enters unseen and recognises Belfiore. She wonders if he will reveal himself when he hears of her approaching marriage, and sings of the impossibility of hiding her love.

Scene ii. The garden of the castle. Peasant girls sing and Giulietta reflects that it is a young man she wants to marry, not an old one. Her father the Baron, in company with her elderly fiancé, comes in and reproaches her for hiding at a moment when she is about to meet a king and her future husband is nearby. The Treasurer comforts her. Belfiore enters and presents Edoardo as his new squire. In order to give the thwarted lovers an opportunity to talk, he says he requires the advice respectively of the Baron in military and the Treasurer in political matters. Edoardo is to entertain his future aunt, while the important discussion takes place. That Edoardo makes the most of his chance does not go unnoticed by his jealous uncle, who is so infuriated that he interrupts the strategical discussion and has to be admonished by the 'King'.

Belfiore finally calls a halt, much to the Treasurer's relief, but at this point the Marchesa arrives, whispering to Giulietta that she has come only because of her. When the Baron makes haste to rebuke her for her rudeness to the noble visitor, she apologises to Belfiore,

and each wonders what the other is thinking. After an *allegro* sextet, Belfiore, the Baron and the Treasurer depart, but Edoardo and Giulietta are disappointed to find the Marchesa at first so disinclined to discuss their problems. She apologises and promises to help them. The scene ends with a spirited trio.

Scene iii: the same as scene i. Belfiore tells La Rocca that, if he were not about to be married, he would, because of his brilliant financial brain, give him a ministry in the government, and the hand of a rich Polish princess into the bargain. La Rocca finds this prospect irresistible, agrees to it and, when the Baron comes in to discuss the marriage contract, timidly suggests that he is unworthy of Giulietta. The Baron, incredulous and scandalised by turns, challenges the terrified Treasurer to draw his sword. Everyone runs in and the Baron tells them his daughter has been insulted; Giulietta of course is delighted and the Marchesa cunningly puts forward the idea to the Baron of avenging his honour and humiliating the Treasurer by marrying Giulietta to Edoardo. Belfiore's entrance causes general embarrassment and the Baron apologises for their behaviour. Each participant hopes to enlist the King's aid, and accordingly all together begin to explain the situation, until Belfiore demands they speak one at a time. But it is no use: they are too anxious and upset to obey and the act ends with all begging the King for pardon and agreeing to accept his decision.

Act II, scene i. The menservants of the Baron are undecided whether any wedding will ever take place, as these aristocrats seem to change their minds every five minutes. Their perplexity is not allayed by Edoardo, who in an ecstasy of happiness tells them that love has at last come to him and that he is to marry Giulietta. The servants leave and Belfiore, Giulietta and La Rocca enter, the 'King' questioning his squire and his newly-appointed 'minister' as to why the Baron is adamant in refusing to allow the marriage of Edoardo to Giulietta. When told it is because he is penniless, Belfiore promptly orders the luckless Treasurer to endow Edoardo with one of his several castles and an income for life. The poor Treasurer asks for time, but is interrupted by the still furious Baron, demanding an explanation. The two apoplectic old men rush off, hurling insults at one another.

Scene ii. A conservatory overlooking the garden. The Marchesa and Belfiore enter separately, the latter unseen by his beloved. The Marchesa is angry and puzzled at Belfiore's attitude and vows to force an explanation. Belfiore, still disguised as the King, discloses his presence and says it is easy to see she is thinking of the Cavalier. 'Yes,' says the Marchesa, 'I am trying to think how to punish him for his faithlessness and have decided not to marry him.' Belfiore does not believe her and each thinks the other's cunning quite transparent. The Baron rushes in to say that the Count will be arriving at any moment. Good, says the Marchesa, she is eager to marry him. 'What about the Cavalier?' asks Belfiore. 'Why is he not here?' she asks. In an *andante cantabile* aria, she sings sadly that all she wants is for him to appear to the one who adores him and ask her forgiveness. The servants announce the arrival of the Count, and the Marchesa goes to meet her bridegroom, vowing to forget her faithless lover.

Giulietta comes in, delighted that her father has consented to her marriage with Edoardo and overcome with gratitude to the King. When Edoardo enters and tells her that he must leave with Belfiore, Giulietta insists that as her future husband his place is with her. The two, in an *allegro* duet, are eventually reunited.

The Marchesa's fiancé, Count Ivrea, has now arrived, and the Baron assures the Count that his beloved has no longer any thought of the Cavalier. The Marchesa promises to marry the Count, provided the Cavalier does not appear within an hour. Belfiore enters with Giulietta and Edoardo, and announces that he must leave at once on urgent business. The Marchesa says she hopes he will stay for her wedding but is mortified when he tells her that the Count must accompany him. Belfiore is delighted to observe her dismay, but the rest of the company is taken aback by this sudden, apparently churlish, act.

Delmonte now brings a message from the Polish Court; Belfiore is excited but will only reveal the news after Giulietta has been safely betrothed to Edoardo with himself and La Rocca as witnesses. Once this is accomplished, Belfiore announces that Stanislao has been accepted in Warsaw, that if he himself is no longer a King he has at least been made a Marshal and can now resume his identity as Belfiore. He embraces the delighted Marchesa, and Baron, Count and Treasurer give in to the inevitable, for the opera to end with rejoicing at the restoration of Stanislao and at the happiness of the reunited lovers.   H.

NABUCCO

Opera in four acts, text by Temistocle Solera (refused by Nicolai). Première at la Scala, Milan, 9 March 1842, with Giuseppina Strepponi (who, years later, became Verdi's wife), Bellinzaghi, Miraglia, Ronconi, Derivis. First performed in London, Her Majesty's Theatre, 1846, as *Nino* (in Italian); Covent Garden, 1850, as *Anato*, with Castellan, Costi, Tamberlik, Ronconi, Tagliafico, conductor Costa; New York, 1848. Revived Florence Festival and la Scala, 1933, with Cigna, Stignani, Galeffi, Pasero, conducted by Gui and produced by Ebert; la Scala, 1946, for the reopening of the rebuilt theatre, with Pedrini, Barbieri, Binci, Bechi, Siepi, conductor Serafin; Rome, 1951, with Caniglia, Bechi, Rossi-Lemeni, conductor Gui; Welsh National Opera, 1952, with di Leo, Tom Williams; at Sadler's Wells, London, 1955, with Packer, Ronald Jackson, Hervey Alan, conductor Groves; New York, Metropolitan Opera, 1960, with Rysanek, MacNeil, Siepi, conductor Schippers; la Scala, Milan, 1986, with Bruson, Dimitrova, Burchaladze, conductor Muti; Paris, 1995, with Guleghina, Lafont, Ramey, conductor Pinchas Steinberg.

Abigaille, *a slave, believed to be the elder
    daughter of Nabucco* .... Soprano
Fenena, *daughter of Nabucco* ....Soprano
Ismaele, *nephew of the King of Jerusalem* ....Tenor
Nabucco (Nabucodonosor),
    King of Babylon ....Baritone
Zaccaria, *High Priest of Jerusalem* ....Bass
High Priest of Babylon ....Bass
Abdallo, *an old officer in Nabucco's service* ....Tenor
Anna, *sister of Zaccaria* ....Soprano

Place: Jerusalem; Babylon
Time: 586 B.C.
Running Time: 2 hours 15 minutes

*N*abucco was Verdi's first great success, the opera that established him as one of the leading composers of Italy, the theme which identified him for the first time publicly with his country's political aspirations. Its success was huge, mainly because of its musical quality but also to some extent because of the vivid way in which the composer gave expression to his countrymen's aspirations towards the liberty and self-government which had never yet been theirs. No Italian who heard 'Va, pensiero' could fail to identify himself with the chorus of exiles who were singing it, and it soon became one of the most popular tunes of the day. Franz Werfel has described the scene of Verdi's second funeral in Milan a few months after his death (the first, as directed in his will, was very simple): ' ... then came one of the great and rare moments when people and music become one. Without any preconcerted plan, by some inexplicable inspiration, there suddenly rose out of the monstrous soul of the multitude the chorus from *Nabucco* with which Giuseppe Verdi had become the voice of consolation and hope for his people, sixty years before. "Va, pensiero sull'ali dorate!"'

The rather conventional overture makes effective use of various tunes from the opera, notably the big choral themes.

Act I. In passionate choruses, the priests and people of Jerusalem lament their defeat at the hands of Nabucco, and beg Jehovah to prevent the capture of the Temple. In an impressive solo, 'Sperate, o figli', Zaccaria exhorts them to have faith in God, but the news that Nabucco is advancing on the Temple itself throws them once more into consternation.

Ismaele, who brought the news of the enemy's further advance, is left alone with Fenena, a hostage in the hands of the Jews, whom he loves. Their colloquy is interrupted by the appearance of Abigaille, Fenena's supposed sister. She threatens the two lovers with instant death, but admits to Ismaele that she loves him and says she has it in her power to save him. The trio which follows has the mixture of intensity and suave vocal writing which distinguishes similar moments in *Norma* (though the dramatic situation is by no means similar). Zaccaria rushes in saying he has seen the King riding towards the Temple itself; in a moment Babylonian troops fill the Temple, and Nabucco himself rides to the door. Zaccaria threatens to kill Fenena, Nabucco's daughter, if he desecrate the holy place, but Nabucco taunts the defeated Jews ('Tremin gl'insani'), and Zaccaria's attempt on Fenena's life is frustrated by Ismaele. Nabucco orders the sacking of the Temple.

Act II. The Jews have been carried captive into Babylon, and Nabucco has left Fenena as Regent. Abigaille, jealous of her sister's position and burning to know whether or not she is Nabucco's daughter or, as rumour has it, only a slave, finds a document which proves that the latter estimation of her birth is the true one. Her fury is unbridled, but she remembers her love for Ismaele, and the first part of her great aria is smooth and expressive. The High Priest of Bel informs her that Fenena is setting free the Jewish prisoners; he urges her to seize power, and says he has already spread the report that Nabucco has been killed in battle. Abigaille's reaction to this situation is expressed in a cabaletta suitably vigorous and determined.

In a noble example of Verdian prayer ('Tu sul labbro'), Zaccaria invokes the guidance of God. The people curse Ismaele, but Zaccaria reminds them that Fenena, for whose sake he committed the act of treachery, has become a convert to their faith.

Abdallo comes in to tell them that the popular cry goes up that the King is dead, and Abigaille plans Fenena's death. In a moment she comes to demand the crown from Fenena. It is, however, Nabucco who steps between them, seizes it, and places it on his own head, defying Abigaille to take it from him. Nabucco leads off an ensemble[1] which is extraordinarily effective and notable for its skilful contrasting of soloists and chorus. Nabucco proclaims himself God, there is a clap of thunder, and the crown is torn from his head by a supernatural force. When the crowd has recovered from its consternation, the King is seen to be mad, babbling of persecution and complaining that not even his daughter will help him. Zaccaria proclaims the punishment of heaven on the blasphemer, but Abigaille snatches up the crown crying that the glory of Babylon is not yet departed.

Act III. Abigaille has been installed as Regent. Nabucco is led into her presence and the rest of the first scene consists of an extended duet between the King and his supposed daughter. Abigaille taunts him into sealing the death sentence of the Jews, and, when she tells him he is a prisoner in her hands, his mood changes to one of supplication. Throughout his career, Verdi was to entrust crucial development in his operas to these lengthy, multi-sectioned duets. Here and in *Oberto* are the forerunners, in manner if not in matter, of that great line which was to include the scene for Macbeth and his wife after the murder, the first-act duet for Rigoletto and Gilda, the meeting between Violetta and Germont, the two great duets for Simon Boccanegra and Fiesco, the love duet from *Ballo*, Leonora's scene with Padre Guardiano in *Forza*, Philip's interviews with Posa and the Grand Inquisitor in *Don Carlos*, the two examples in the third act of *Aida*, the love duet in *Otello* and the second-act scene between Otello and Iago, and Falstaff's conversation with Ford.

The second scene of the act takes place on the banks of the Euphrates, where the enslaved Jews sing the psalms of their lost fatherland. 'Va, pensiero' is the first of Verdi's patriotic choruses, and its poignant

---

[1] The section beginning 'le folgori intorno' must have been suggested by the sextet in Donizetti's *Maria Stuarda*.

melody is typical of the composer's writing in this vein. Zaccaria upbraids the Jews for their defeatist attitude and prophesies the imminent fall of Babylon.

Act IV. Nabucco in prison hears the crowd down below crying 'Death to Fenena'. He sees her being led to execution, and prays movingly to Jehovah to pardon him his sin of pride and spare her life: 'Dio di Giuda'. Abdallo frees his master, who rushes out to rescue his daughter.

The scene changes to the place of execution. A funeral march is heard and Fenena has a beautiful prayer as she and the Jews prepare for death. The arrival of Nabucco and his followers arrests the sacrifice, the false idol is thrown down as if by magic, and all join in a prayer of thanksgiving to Jehovah. The general rejoicing is interrupted by the arrival of Abigaille, who in her remorse has taken poison and dies. Zaccaria promises glory to his convert, Nabucco.

Nabucco represents something important in Verdi's output: it was his first success, and in it he can be seen making a serious attempt at the musical portrayal of character.   H.

I LOMBARDI
The Lombards

Opera in four acts, text by T. Solera. Première, la Scala, Milan, 11 February 1843, with Erminia Frezzolini, Guasco, Derivis. First produced London, Her Màjesty's Theatre, 1846, with Grisi, Mario; New York, 1847 (first Verdi opera to be performed there); Paris Opéra, 1847 (as *Jérusalem*, in an extensively revised version) with Frezzolini, Duprez, Alizard. Retranslated into Italian as *Gerusalemme* and produced la Scala, Milan, 1850. Paris heard *Jérusalem* again in 1984 with Cecilia Gasdia, Veriano Luchetti, Silvano Carroli, but *I Lombardi* has generally been preferred and was revived London, Her Majesty's, 1867, with Tietjens, Mongini, Santley; Turin, 1926; la Scala, Milan, 1931, with Scacciati, Merli, Vaghi, conductor Panizza; Florence Festival, 1948; Birmingham, 1935 (by the Midland Music Makers); Berne, 1954, in a new version by Stephen Beinl; London, Sadler's Wells, 1956, by the Welsh National Opera Company; Covent Garden, 1976 (from Budapest), with Sass, Carreras, Ghiuselev, conductor Gardelli; New York, 1993, Metropolitan Opera, with Millo, Pavarotti, Ramey, conductor Levine.

Arvino, *son of Folco*..Tenor
Pagano, *son of Folco* ....Bass
Viclinda, *wife of Arvino*..................................Soprano
Giselda, *her daughter* ....Soprano
Pirro, *Pagano's henchman* ....Bass
Prior of the City of Milan ....Tenor
Acciano, *tyrant of Antioch*....................................Bass
Oronte, *son of Acciano* ....Tenor
Sofia, *wife of Acciano*......................................Soprano

Priests, People of Milan, Retainers of Folco, Muslim Envoys, Crusader Knights and Soldiers, Pilgrims, Muslim Women, Lombard Ladies

Place: Milan, Antioch, the Country near Jerusalem
Time: 1099
Running Time: 2 hours 15 minutes

The commission to write *I Lombardi* for la Scala was the direct result of the success of *Nabucco* a year earlier. As soon as the opera was announced, the Archbishop of Milan drew the attention of the police to religious references in the libretto – a baptism and the like – which could cause offence if represented on the stage. Artistic considerations finally prevailed over the scruples of the Chief of Police, and the opera was given with only one minor alteration, the words 'Ave Maria' changed to 'Salve Maria'. In the event the authorities are likely to have been more worried by the patriotic demonstrations which were, in the Italy of the time, the natural result of a subject like this.

Act I, scene i. A short prelude full of foreboding leads to the curtain rising on the Piazza di Sant'Ambrogio, Milan. Sounds of rejoicing come from within the Cathedral, and the crowd outside comments on the strange turn of events. Many years ago the brothers Arvino and Pagano loved Viclinda, who favoured Arvino. As the young couple went one day to church, Pagano struck and wounded his brother and was in consequence banished to the Holy Land, where it was hoped he might repent of his crime. Now, his offence expiated, he has been forgiven and has returned home; but, comments the crowd, there is still the glint of evil in his eye. As they emerge from the Cathedral, Pagano ostensibly prays for Heaven's forgiveness, and an ensemble develops ('T'assale un tremito!'). Giselda and Viclinda are apprehensive, Arvino is seized with sudden foreboding, Pagano and his henchman Pirro plot revenge, and the crowd worries whether to take outward signs of peace at their face value. The Prior proclaims the appointment of Arvino as Leader of a Crusade, and all call down anathema on anyone who shakes the solidarity of the holy enterprise.

All leave except Pagano and Pirro. Nuns pray within as Pagano broods outside, advancing disappointment in love as the reason for wandering from the paths of virtue ('Sciagurata! hai tu creduto'). Pirro says that Pagano's followers are assembled, and in his cabaletta Pagano rejoices at the prospect of revenge.

Scene ii. A room in the palace of Folco, the father of Pagano and Arvino. Viclinda, Giselda and Arvino believe that Pagano's repentance is feigned, and in a lovely passage, Giselda prays to Heaven ('Salve Maria – di grazie il petto'). The Gallery is empty as Pirro leads Pagano towards Arvino's room. A moment later the interior of the palace is lit up by flames. Pagano tries to carry off Viclinda, but, hearing the voice of Arvino, finds that he has killed his own father and not his brother. The scene fills, all curse Pagano for his crime and in his horror he joins in the general execration. His attempt at suicide is prevented; he must end his days in solitary exile.

Act II, scene i. Acciano's palace in Antioch. Acciano on his throne receives a group of Muslim ambassadors, who call down Allah's vengeance on the invading army of Crusaders. They depart at the entrance of Oronte and Sofia, Acciano's son and wife. Sofia, who is veiled, is secretly a Christian. Oronte reveals his love for Giselda, now a captive in Antioch, in an aria ('La mia letizia infondere') whose lyrical beauty rivals in Verdi's early output the equally inspired 'Quando le sere al placido' (*Luisa Miller*). As he shows in the cabaletta (two versions of which exist), Oronte is so persuaded of the perfection of his beloved that he is convinced that her God must be the true God.

Scene ii. A cave on a mountain overlooking Antioch. A Hermit, Pagano as will be revealed much later, prays in a fine aria ('Ma quando un suon terribile') that he may soon have a chance of aiding the crusading army to capture Antioch from the Saracens. To the Hermit comes Pirro, now a converted Muslim, to ask for spiritual guidance. Their colloquy is interrupted by the sound of the invading Crusaders; they disappear into the cave and the Hermit emerges in military array just as Arvino, the leader of the Crusaders, appears. Arvino approaches the Hermit, little knowing it is his own brother and most deadly enemy from whom he is asking prayers for the safety of his daughter, now a prisoner. The Hermit gives comfort and the scene ends with an *allegro vivace* hymn of hate against the Saracens.

Scene iii. The harem in Acciano's palace. Taunted by the other women, Giselda prays to Heaven ('Oh madre, dal cielo soccorri al mio pianto'). Suddenly women flee through the harem pursued by soldiers, and Queen Sofia reveals that her husband and her son have been killed by the attacking Crusaders – she points to Arvino as their ferocious leader. In music of considerable conviction ('No, Dio non vuole'), Giselda denounces her father for the blood he has shed.

Act III, scene i. The Valley of Jehoshaphat; the Mount of Olives and Jerusalem in the distance. A procession of pilgrims sings a devotional chorus of typically *Risorgimento* cut. They go on their way, and Giselda appears, desolate at the loss of her lover Oronte, whom she presumes dead in the slaughter which followed the capture of the city. But the man who now appears in Lombard clothing is none other than Oronte himself, lamenting that his love for Giselda has caused him to take on a coward's disguise in the hope of seeing her again. Their duet reveals their mutual determination to give up everything for their love, and Oronte even says he means to adopt Giselda's faith. Warlike shouts from the Crusaders' camp make Giselda afraid for Oronte's life and they flee together.

Scene ii. Arvino's tent. He inveighs against the treachery of his daughter's flight, but his thoughts are interrupted as his men tell him of a rumour that Pagano has been recognised in the camp. Arvino's anger turns against his wicked brother.

Scene iii. A cave on the banks of the River Jordan. The prelude is in the form of a violin solo with orchestral accompaniment, so elaborate in the writing that it might be the end of a movement of a concerto. Oronte has been mortally wounded in the attempt to escape, and Giselda, beside herself with grief at this new blow, cries out at the injustice of God's ways, only to be rebuked by the Hermit who appears in the entrance to the cave. The extended trio, 'Qual voluttà trascorrere', always with the violin obbligato in the background and with Oronte's interrupted cantilena as he gasps for breath, is one of the most famous of Verdian death-scenes. The Hermit baptises Oronte as he dies in Giselda's arms.

Act IV, scene i. A cave near Jerusalem. Giselda asleep sees a vision of Oronte among the blessed and even hears his voice. She expresses her perturbation in an agitated quick solo ('Qual prodigio').

Scene ii. The Crusader camp near the Tomb of Rachel. The scene opens with a great chorus of longing ('O Signore del tetto natio'), which, as a hymn of the *Risorgimento*, ranks as companion-piece to, and in its own day achieved comparable popularity with, 'Va pensiero' from *Nabucco* (this line of patriotic music culminates as late as 1865 in the chorus in the last act of *Macbeth*). The Crusaders are preparing an assault on Jerusalem, and Arvino and the Hermit lead them to battle.

Scene iii, set in another part of Arvino's camp, follows an orchestral interlude. Arvino and Giselda attend the Hermit who has been carried in wounded. At mention of Arvino's name, the Hermit comes out of his delirium to mutter of parricide. It is not long before he reveals his name and, in a moving death-scene, Giselda joins her voice to his in begging Arvino to forgive his past wrongs. The opera ends as Pagano begs for a last sight of the Holy City, over whose walls the banner of the Cross can be seen flying.   H.

ERNANI

Opera in four acts, text by Francesco Maria Piave, after the drama by Victor Hugo. Première at the Fenice Theatre, Venice, 9 March 1844, with Löwe, Guasco, Superchi, Selva. First performed at Her Majesty's Theatre, London, 1845; New York, 1847; Metropolitan, 1903, with Sembrich, de Marchi, Scotti, Edouard de Reszke, conductor Mancinelli; 1921, with Ponselle, Martinelli, Danise, Mardones; 1928, with Ponselle, Martinelli, Ruffo, Pinza. Revived la Scala, 1935, with Cigna, Merli, Armando Borgioli, Pasero, conductor Marinuzzi; Berlin, 1935, with Lemnitz, Wittrisch, Janssen, Bohnen, conductor Blech; Rome, 1951, with Mancini, Penno, Silveri, Christoff; Metropolitan, 1956, with Milanov, del Monaco, Warren, Siepi; Florence Festival, 1957, with Cerquetti, del Monaco, Bastianini, Christoff, conductor Mitropoulos; London, Sadler's Wells, 1967, with Tinsley, Donald Smith, Bickerstaff, Clifford Grant; Welsh National Opera, 1979, with Murphy, Ken Collins, Opthof, R. van Allan, conductor Richard Armstrong; la Scala, Milan, 1982, with Freni, Domingo, Bruson, Ghiaurov, conductor Muti; Metropolitan, New York, 1983, with Leona Mitchell, Pavarotti (singing the Act II finale for tenor and chorus which Verdi added after the première), Milnes, Raimondi, conductor Levine. Don Carlos was one of the favourite roles of the great baritone Mattia Battistini.

Don Carlos, *King of Castile* ....Baritone

Don Ruy Gomez de Silva, *Grandee of Spain* ....Bass

Ernani, or John of Aragon, *a bandit chief* ....Tenor

Don Riccardo, *esquire to the King* ....Tenor

Jago, *esquire to Silva* ....Bass

Elvira, *kinswoman to Silva* ....Soprano

Giovanna, *in Elvira's service*..........................Soprano

Mountaineers and Bandits, Followers of Silva, Ladies of Elvira, Followers of Don Carlos, Electors and Pages

Place: Spain
Time: Early Sixteenth Century
Running Time: 2 hours 20 minutes

*E*rnani was Verdi's first opera for Venice, his first on a subject by Victor Hugo and his first with Francesco Maria Piave who became, until he had a stroke in 1867, his preferred (because most compliant) librettist. Its success in the middle of a Venetian season, which had seen *I Lombardi*, even under the composer's supervision, fail and two other operas booed off the stage, was instantaneous.

His father, the Duke of Segovia, having been slain by order of Don Carlos's father, John of Aragon has become an outlaw. Proscribed and pursued by the emissaries of the King, he has taken refuge in the fastnesses of the mountains of Aragon, where, under the name of Ernani, he is leader of a large band of rebel mountaineers. Ernani is in love with Donna Elvira, who, although she is about to be united to her relative, the aged Ruy Gomez de Silva, a grandee of Spain, is deeply enamoured of the handsome, chivalrous bandit chief.

Don Carlos, afterwards the Emperor Charles V, also has fallen in love with Elvira. By watching her windows he has discovered that at dead of night a young cavalier (Ernani) gains admission to her apartments. He imitates her lover's signal, gains admission to her chamber, and declares his passion. Being repulsed, he is about to drag her off by force, when a secret panel opens, and he finds himself confronted by Ernani. In the midst of a violent scene Silva enters. To allay his jealousy and anger at finding two men, apparently rival suitors, in the apartment of his affianced, the King, whom Silva does not recognise, reveals himself, and pretends to have come in disguise to consult him about his approaching election to the empire, and a conspiracy that is on foot against his life. Then the King, pointing to Ernani, says to Silva, 'It doth please us that this, our follower, depart,' thus insuring Ernani's temporary safety – for a Spaniard does not hand an enemy over to the vengeance of another.

Believing a rumour that Ernani has been hunted

down and killed by the King's soldiers, Elvira at last consents to give her hand in marriage to Silva. On the eve of the wedding however Ernani, pursued by the King with a detachment of troops, seeks refuge in Silva's castle disguised as a pilgrim. He is under Spanish tradition his guest, and from that moment entitled to his protection.

Elvira enters in her bridal attire. Ernani is thus made aware that her nuptials with Don Silva are to be celebrated on the morrow. Tearing off his disguise, he reveals himself to Silva, and demands to be delivered up to the King, preferring death to life without Elvira. But true to his honour as a Spanish host, Silva refuses. Even his enemy, Ernani, is safe in his castle. Indeed he goes so far as to order his guards to man the towers and prepare to defend the castle, should the King seek forcible entry. He leaves the apartment to make sure his orders are being carried out. The lovers find themselves alone. When Silva returns they are in each other's arms. But as the King is at the castle gates, he has no time to give vent to his wrath. He gives orders to admit the King and his men, bids Elvira retire, and hides Ernani in a secret cabinet. The King demands that Silva give up the bandit. The grandee proudly refuses. The King's wrath then turns against Silva. He pardons him, but bears away Elvira as hostage for the loyalty of her kinsman.

The King has gone. From the wall Silva takes down two swords, releases his guest from his hiding-place, and bids him cross swords with him to the death. Ernani refuses. His host has just protected his life at the risk of his own. If Silva insists upon vengeance, let grandee and bandit first unite against the King, with whom the honour of Elvira is unsafe. Elvira rescued, Ernani will give himself up to Silva, to whom, handing him his hunting-horn, he avows himself ready to die, whenever a blast upon it shall be sounded from the lips of the implacable grandee.

Silva sets in motion a conspiracy against the King. A meeting of the conspirators is held in the Cathedral of Aix-la-Chapelle. It is resolved to murder the King. A ballot decides who shall do the deed. Ernani's name is drawn.

The King, however, has received information of the time and place of this meeting, and has been an unobserved witness. Booming of cannon outside tells him of his choice as head of the Holy Roman Empire.

Emerging from the tomb, he shows himself to the awed conspirators. At the same moment the doors open. The electors of the Empire enter to pay homage to Charles V.

'The common herd to the dungeon, the nobles to the headsman,' he commands.

Ernani advances, discovers himself as John of Aragon, and claims the right to die with the nobles – 'to fall, covered, before the King'. But upon Elvira's fervent plea, the King, now also Emperor, commences his reign with an act of grace. He pardons the conspirators, restores to Ernani his titles and estates, and unites him with Elvira.

Silva, thwarted in his desire to marry Elvira, waits to sound the fateful horn until Ernani and Elvira, after their nuptials, are upon the terrace of Ernani's castle in Aragon. Ernani, too chivalrous to evade his promise, stabs himself in the presence of the grim avenger and of Elvira.

In the opera, this plot develops as follows.

Act I opens in the camp of the bandits in the mountains of Aragon. In the distance is seen the Moorish castle of Silva. The time is near sunset. Ernani's followers sing, 'Evviva! beviamo'. Ernani sings Elvira's praises in the air 'Come rugiada al cespite'. This expressive number is followed by one in faster time, 'O tu, che l'alma adora'. Enthusiastically volunteering to share any danger Ernani may incur in seeking to carry off Elvira, the bandits go off in the direction of Silva's castle.

The scene changes to Elvira's apartment in the castle. It is night. She is meditating upon Ernani. When she thinks of Silva, 'the frozen, withered spectre', and contrasts with him Ernani, who 'in her heart ever reigneth', she voices her thoughts in that famous air for soprano, one of Verdi's loveliest inspirations, 'Ernani! involami':

Young maidens sing a chorus of congratulation. To this Elvira responds with a graceful cabaletta, the sentiment of which however is expressed as an aside, since it refers to her longing for her young, handsome lover, 'Tutto sprezzo che d'Ernani':

The young women go. Enter Don Carlos, the King. There is a colloquy, in which Elvira protests against his presence; and then a duet, which the King begins, 'Da quel dì che t'ho veduta'.

A secret panel opens. The King is confronted by Ernani, and by Elvira. She interposes between the two men. Silva enters. What he beholds draws from him the melancholy reflection 'Infelice! e tuo credevi', an exceptionally fine bass solo. He follows it with the vindictive 'Infin, che un brando vindice', added after the première. Men and women of the castle and the King's suite come on. The monarch makes himself known to Silva, who does him obeisance and, at the King's command, is obliged to let Ernani depart. An ensemble brings the act to a close.

Act II. Grand hall in Silva's castle. Doors lead to various apartments. The persistent chorus of ladies, though doubtless aware that Elvira is not thrilled at the prospect of marriage with her 'frosty' kinsman and has consented to marry him only because she believed Ernani dead, enters and sings 'Esultiamo!'

To Silva is brought in Ernani, disguised as a monk. He is welcomed as a guest; but, upon the appearance of Elvira in bridal array, throws off his disguise and offers his life, a sacrifice to Silva's vengeance, as the first gift for the wedding. Silva, however, learning that he is pursued by the King, offers him the protection due to a guest under the roof of a Spaniard.

Silva, even when he returns and discovers Elvira in Ernani's arms, will not break the law of Spanish hospitality, preferring to wreak vengeance in his own way. He therefore hides Ernani so securely that the King's followers, after searching the castle, are obliged to report their complete failure to discover a trace of him.

Then come the important episodes described – the King's demand for the surrender of Silva's sword and threat to execute him; Elvira's interposition; and the King's sinister action in carrying her off as a hostage, after he has sung the significant air 'Vieni meco, sol di rose'. Ernani's handing of his hunting horn to

Silva and his arousal of the grandee to an understanding of the danger that threatens Elvira from the King are followed by the finale, a spirited call to arms by Silva and Ernani.

Act III. The scene is a sepulchral vault, enclosing the tomb of Charlemagne in the Cathedral of Aix-la-Chapelle. It is to this sombre but grandiose place that the King has come in order to overhear, from within the tomb of his greatest ancestor, the plotting of the conspirators. His soliloquy, 'Oh, de' verd'anni miei', derives impressiveness both from the solemnity of the situation and the music's flowing measure. The principal episode in the meeting of the conspirators is their chorus, 'Si ridesti il Leon di Castiglia'. Dramatically effective too in the midst of the plotting is the sudden booming of distant cannon. The bronze door of the tomb swings open and the King presents himself at its entrance. Three times he strikes the door of bronze with the hilt of his dagger. The principal entrance to the vault opens. To the sound of trumpets electors enter. Elvira approaches. The banners of the Empire are displayed. The act closes with the pardon granted by the King, and the stirring finale, 'Oh, sommo Carlo!'

Act IV, on the terrace of Ernani's castle, is brief. Ernani asks Silva to spare him till his lips have tasted the chalice filled by love. He recounts his sad life: 'Solingo, errante misero'. Silva's grim reply is to offer him his choice between a cup of poison and a dagger. In the end there is left only the implacable avenger, to gloat over Ernani, dead, and Elvira prostrate upon his form.

Early in its career the opera experienced various vicissitudes. The conspiracy scene had to be toned down for political reasons before the production of the work was permitted. Even then the chorus, 'Let the lion awake in Castilia', caused a political demonstration. In Paris, Victor Hugo, as author of the drama on which the libretto is based, raised objections to its representation, and it was produced in the French capital as *Il Proscritto* (The Proscribed) with the characters changed to Italians. Victor Hugo's *Hernani* was a famous play in Sarah Bernhardt's repertory during her early engagements in America, and her Doña Sol (Elvira in the opera) was one of her finest achievements.   K.

Ernani, old-fashioned as it is, remains a fine opera. Since 1844, the whirligig of fashion has made perhaps four revolutions, and now, more than a hundred and fifty years since the first performance and after a period when it was looked upon as crude and empty, the opera is once again, in adequate performances and with singers who can do justice to the music, accepted by audiences as a thrilling and rewarding experience. Its whipcrack melodies have the energy of youth, and, for all its occasional lack of subtlety, the genius of the composer is very much in evidence.   H.

I DUE FOSCARI
The Two Foscari

Opera in three acts, libretto by Piave after the play by Byron. Première, Rome, 3 November 1844, with Barbieri-Nini, Roppa, de Bassini. First produced London, Her Majesty's, 1847, with Grisi, Mario, Ronconi; New York, 1847. Revived Halle, 1927; Stuttgart, 1956 (as *Der Doge von Venedig*), with Kinas, Traxel; Venice, 1957, with Gencer, Picchi, Giangiacomo Guelfi, conductor Serafin; Wexford Festival, 1958; English National Opera, 1978, with Lois McDonall, Neil Howlett, conductor Charles Groves; Covent Garden, 1995, with June Anderson, Dennis O'Neill, Vladimir Chernov.

Francesco Foscari, *octogenarian*
    Doge of Venice ....Baritone

Jacopo Foscari, *his son* ....Tenor

Lucrezia Contarini, *wife to Jacopo*..................Soprano

Jacopo Loredano, *member of the Council of Ten* .....Bass

Barbarigo, *Senator, member of the Council*..........Tenor

Pisana, *friend and confidante of Lucrezia* ....Soprano

Attendant on the Council of Ten ....Tenor

Servant of the Doge..Bass

Members of the Council of Ten and of the 'Giunta';
    Lucrezia's Maids; Venetian Ladies; Maskers and
    Venetians of both Sexes; Jailers, Gondoliers,
    Pages, Two Sons of Jacopo Foscari

Place: Venice
Time: 1457
Running Time: 1 hour 35 minutes

Byron's verse play, with its less than flattering portraits of Venetian worthies many of whose descendants might have been in boxes at la Fenice, was deemed unsuitable for Venice and became therefore, just under a year after the première of *Ernani* in Venice, the basis of Verdi's first opera for Rome. The original singers were undistinguished and the opera obtained no more than a moderate success. Hindsight suggests its taut if gloomy subject and the composer's increas-

ingly precise characterisation of leading figures deserved better.

There is a short prelude, whose *adagio* theme is associated with the despair of the opera's hero, Jacopo Foscari. The curtain rises on a room in the Doge's Palace in Venice, where the Council of Ten sings in solemn chorus of the implacable nature of its deliberations, and then leaves for the Council Chamber. Jacopo Foscari is brought in and left to wait while the Council decides his fate. He is the son of the aged Doge and has been exiled after an accusation of murder. Now he has illegally returned in order to see his family and his beloved native city, and it is this transgression of the law that the Council is at present considering (Byron's play has him accused by his enemies of conspiring with the Milanese against the Venetians, but this complication is virtually absent from the opera). In a beautiful aria ('Brezza del suol natio') he sings of his love for Venice and, in the brisk cabaletta, of his determination to prove his innocence.

The scene changes to a room in the Palazzo Foscari. Jacopo's wife, Lucrezia, eludes her female attendants and rushes into the room to plead with the Doge for clemency for Jacopo. In a cavatina ('Tu al cui sguardo onnipossente') she prays for heaven's help in her misery. Lucrezia's companion Pisana tells her that the Council has decided again to condemn Jacopo to exile, and Lucrezia rails against the injustice of the sentence.

In his private apartments, the old Doge laments the fate which opposes in him the judge's duty to a father's love for his son. The dilemma is expressed in an aria of great dignity and pathos, 'O vecchio cor che batti', the only moment of the score known out of context (Pasquale Amato's pre-1914 gramophone record was for many years a bestseller). Lucrezia is announced and pleads vehemently that the Doge publicly recognise what the father instinctively knows, that Jacopo is guiltless. In tender music, the old man makes it clear that he is convinced his son is innocent, but equally clear that he feels himself powerless, caught between paternal feeling and the obligations of his position.

Act II. The State Prison. In the darkness of the dungeon, Jacopo laments his misfortunes in a state of mounting delirium. One moment he thinks he sees the ghost of another victim of the Council of Ten and a little later he fails at her entrance to recognise his wife. The scene between husband and wife maintains the intensity of Jacopo's monologue, and, when singing is heard outside, Jacopo bursts into furious condemnation of those who are tearing his loved ones from him. The Doge comes to bid farewell to his son. In a fine trio ('Nel tuo paterno amplesso') Jacopo takes comfort in his father's embrace and affirms his innocence, the Doge describes himself as a dying man, and Lucrezia asks for heaven's vengeance on the authors of their misfortunes. Loredano, a member of the Council of Ten who has sworn vengeance on the Foscari family for their responsibility, as he maintains, for the death of his father and uncle, comes into the prison to conduct Jacopo to hear the judgement of the Council of Ten, and the impressive scene ends with a *presto* quartet.

In the great hall, the Council waits for Jacopo and discusses the crime for which he was once sentenced to exile; its re-affirmation of the sentence now confirms the incorruptible nature of Venetian justice. When the Doge is seated, Loredano announces the 'clemency' of the Council, but Jacopo protests and asks them to believe in his original innocence. The Doge confirms the sentence as Lucrezia brings in her children to reinforce the plea. Jacopo now pleads for pardon, kneeling with his children at the Doge's feet, and the act ends in a grandiose finale, during whose course Lucrezia begs in vain to be allowed to accompany her husband into exile.

Act III. It is carnival, and the Square of St Mark's fills with masked revellers. Gondoliers sing a barcarole. Jacopo is escorted from the Doge's Palace to the state barge, which waits to take him into exile. His mournful song of farewell turns into a cry of despair when he recognises his enemy Loredano.

In his private rooms, the Doge sings movingly of the fate which has deprived him of three sons in infancy and now banishes a fourth, leaving him to die alone. Barbarigo brings news that another has confessed to the murder of which Jacopo was accused, but Lucrezia is not far behind him to assure them that this cannot avert the inevitable tragedy, as Jacopo breathed his last the moment the barge left the confines of the lagoon. The vigour of the Foscari family has passed to Lucrezia, who alone has the strength to proclaim retribution for their enemies.

The Doge receives the Council of Ten, which, through the mouth of Loredano, demands his abdication on grounds of age and the bereavement he has recently suffered. The Doge at first refuses – when he for his part asked to abdicate years ago, was he not constrained to swear to remain in office until death? – but they press their demands with threats. The Doge at first defies them ('Questa dunque è l'iniqua mercede'), and turns on them for removing his last hope of happiness ('Ah, rendete il figlio a me'). Eventually he takes the ring off his finger, the cap off his head, but summons up a last gesture of defiance to order Loredano away from the ducal emblems. Lucrezia arrives in time to hear the great bell toll for the election of a Malipiero as Doge. Old Foscari sinks down exhausted and broken, and sobs out his life, watched by the Council, among them the exultant Loredano.   H.

GIOVANNA D'ARCO
Joan of Arc

Opera in a prologue and three acts, text by Temistocle Solera (after Schiller's *Die Jungfrau von Orleans*). Première at la Scala, Milan, 15 February 1845, with Erminia Frezzolini-Poggi, Antonio Poggi and Filippo Colini. First performed Rome, 1845, Vienna, 1857, Paris, 1868. Revived Naples, 1951, with Tebaldi, Penno, Savarese, who took the opera to Venice (with Bergonzi instead of Penno), Strasbourg and Paris; Teatro Nuovo, Milan, London (in concert), Toulouse, 1963; New York, 1966, with Stratas, conductor Cillario; Royal Academy of Music, London, 1966; Venice and Florence, 1972, with Katia Ricciarelli; Wexford, 1976; Covent Garden, 1996, with June Anderson, Dennis O'Neill, Chernov.

Charles VII, *King of France* ....Tenor
Giacomo, *a shepherd in Dom Rémy* ....Baritone
Giovanna d'Arco (Joan of Arc), *his daughter*..Soprano
Delil, *a French officer* ....Tenor
Talbot, *the English commander*.............................Bass

Officers of the King, Villagers, Townspeople, French and English Soldiers, Nobles

Place: France
Time: 1429
Running Time: 2 hours

That *Giovanna d'Arco*, Verdi's seventh opera, has not found more favour with public and commentators is particularly due to the uninspired nature of Solera's libretto, which makes little of Schiller's play (any connection with which Solera specifically denied). Nonetheless it provides Verdi with the epic he presumably wanted and of which he took advantage to write something grander, as Andrew Porter has described it, than either *Nabucco* or *I Lombardi*, its predecessors in the style. Sadly, the lowering of standards at la Scala under the impresario Bartolomeo Merelli (whose belief in the composer had begun with *Oberto*) led to a break with that theatre, which staged no more Verdian premières for 36 years.

The overture, one of Verdi's most successful, has a lovely *andante pastorale* episode in slow 3/8, mostly intertwined woodwind solos, flanked by two conventional, quick and mostly loud sections (concerned with storm and military marching).

Prologue. At Dom Rémy, villagers and a group of the King's officers wait to hear him reveal his plans for his troops to lay down their arms and surrender to the invading English army. In an aria ('Sotto una quercia') he describes a vision he has had in which he received the Virgin's command to lay his arms at the foot of a great oak tree. Such a tree grows nearby in the forest, say the villagers, and when the King insists that he will find peace there in abdication, they try to dissuade him by describing it as a place of horror and death.

The scene changes to the forest with a shrine in the background and an oak in the foreground. Giacomo, Giovanna's father, prays agitatedly that his daughter may not as he fears be in thrall to the devil. He sees her kneel before the shrine and muse sadly on the fate which seems to be France's, then in a gentle and melodious cavatina, with a couple of moments of contrasting fire, wonder whether it is to her that will fall the task of freeing her country. Giovanna sleeps and the King appears in order to fulfil what he sees as his mission and lay his weapons at the foot of the oak. Demons, in 3/8 time, tempt Giovanna in her sleep with sensual visions, and they are followed by more sedate angel voices inviting her to don sword and helmet and save France. The voices are of course audible only to Giovanna and she cries that she is ready, her cry being heard by the King, who takes courage from her evident preparedness to fight for her country. The scene ends in a *stretta* of some brilliance for King and Maid, joined by the sorrowing Giacomo, convinced that out of love for the King his daughter has given her soul to the devil.

Act I. Near Rheims. The English soldiers sense defeat and Talbot, their commander, tries to encourage them to believe that this is not due to forces of evil ranged on the French side. Both Francis Toye and Julian Budden find in the soldiers' music a half quotation of 'Hearts of Oak', a conscious reference (like Donizetti's of 'God Save the Queen' in the overture to

Roberto Devereux), suggests the latter. Giacomo in an extensive aria offers to join them and deliver up the warrior girl whom they fear – even though she be his daughter! She is in thrall to the powers of evil.

At the Court of Rheims, preparations are in hand for the coronation of the King. Giovanna expresses her longing for the country life she once knew, in a simple and affecting aria of melting tenderness, 'O fatidica foresta', whose recitative has nonetheless been troubled by a reminiscence of the prologue's tempting voices in their insistent 3/8 rhythm. Resolved on a homeward journey she may be, but this is not at all to the liking of the King, who admits that he has loved her from the day he first saw her. She seems at first disposed to listen to his pleas, but the voices continue to speak to her and her alone, warning of the fatal dangers of worldly love and, in spite of his melting pleas and her own responsiveness, she draws away from the King. A similarity with the situation in the love duet in *Un Ballo in Maschera* – an ardent tenor, a soprano tormented by guilt but unable to resist – has been observed.

Delil comes to escort the King to the cathedral where he is to be crowned, and the latter sings beguilingly to Giovanna, who is nevertheless assaulted by her inner voices proclaiming victory for the forces of evil.

Act II. The cathedral square of St Denis in Rheims. The people proclaim the victory of the Maid and soldiers precede the King in procession into the cathedral. Giacomo alone speaks of stripping himself of the character of a father and becoming the voice of the Lord in denouncing Giovanna for her pact with the devil. Giacomo joins the crowd as Giovanna hurries from the cathedral, sustained by the King but soon to be denounced by her father for having sold her soul. The King will not listen but the credulous populace is immediately impressed and, when Giovanna makes little attempt to defend herself, convinced. The King tries to persuade her to speak out on her own behalf but in face of Giacomo's implacable insistence, she is as resigned as Violetta will be in the finale of Act II of *La Traviata*, and the impressive finale sees her condemned by popular acclamation.

Act III. Giovanna has been handed over to the English and awaits death at the stake. She seems to see the battlefield but her father, who observes her, can only believe that she is dreaming of the King. In a passage of gentle beauty, she implores God not to forsake her, and Giacomo wonders whether he could have been mistaken. He is soon convinced of her redemption and, in an impressive duet, loosens her bonds to allow her escape with his blessing.

To the sound of battle music, Giacomo watches from the tower as she turns French defeat into victory. The King rushes in to proclaim Giovanna his saviour and Giacomo begs first for punishment and then for forgiveness. The King pardons him and asks for news of the battle, only to hear that the enemy is routed but Giovanna dead. His lament is touchingly simple, but after a funeral march during which Giovanna's body is carried in procession, she revives sufficiently to be acclaimed by her father and by the King who loves her. The voices of angels proclaim salvation and those of demons admit defeat. Giovanna dies, her standard in her hands.   H.

ALZIRA

Opera in a prologue and two acts, text by Salvatore Cammarano after Voltaire's play *Alzire, ou Les Américains*. Première Naples, 12 August 1845, with Eugenia Tadolini as Alzira (when she was later proposed for Lady Macbeth, Verdi objected that she 'had the voice of an angel'), his favoured tenor Gaetano Fraschini as Zamoro, and Filippo Coletti as Gusmano. Revived Rome, 1967, with Zeani, Cecchele, MacNeil, conductor Bartoletti; London (highly successful, in concert), 1996, with Veronica Villaroel, Keith Ikaia-Purdy, Alexandru Agache, conductor Mark Elder.

Alvaro, *father of Gusmano*......................................Bass
Gusmano, *Governor of Peru* ....Baritone
Ovando, *a Spanish Duke* ....Tenor
Zamoro, *leader of a Peruvian tribe* ....Tenor
Ataliba, *a Peruvian leader*......................................Bass
Alzira, *Ataliba's daughter*...............................Soprano
Zuma, *her maid* ....Mezzo-Soprano
Otumbo, *a Peruvian warrior*...............................Tenor

Spanish Officers and Soldiers, Peruvians

Place: Lima and Elsewhere in Peru
Time: Mid-Sixteenth Century
Running Time: 1 hour 30 minutes

Alzira was written for the San Carlo in Naples, where Cammarano, the senior Italian librettist of the day, was resident poet. It had little success when first performed and until recently revivals have not tended vastly to improve its reputation.

Prologue. Alvaro has been taken prisoner by an Indian tribe, but Zamoro, their chief, returns in time to save him from a cruel death, then tells of his own capture by Gusmano, a Spanish leader. When he hears that his beloved Alzira is in Lima in the hands of the Spaniards, he vows to rescue her.

Act I. In the main square of Lima, Alvaro hands over power to his son Gusmano. Gusmano announces peace between Spaniards and Incas, the latter led by Ataliba, whose daughter Alzira will become Gusmano's bride by the terms of the treaty. Gusmano knows that she is still in love with an Indian and Ataliba urges him to be patient. He declares he cannot wait.

Alzira wakes to tell of a dream in which she successfully fled from Gusmano's power, her boat eluding the storm which breaks out. Zamoro helped rescue her, and she openly declares her love for him. Ataliba comes in to beg her to agree to marry Gusmano but she insists she would prefer death to that fate. Zamoro contrives to find her, but their vibrant declaration of love is surprised by Gusmano, who orders Zamoro's instant execution. Alvaro's pleas followed by a report that an army is demanding Zamoro's release together persuade Gusmano that, as long as his father returns safely, he should release Zamoro. As he does so, he warns Zamoro that they will surely meet on the battlefield.

Act II. Spaniards celebrate with a rollicking brindisi the defeat of the Incas, and Zamoro and his followers go apparently to death. Alzira pleads for mercy, and in the end a bargain is struck: Zamoro's life for Alzira's agreement to marry Gusmano.

Otumbo has bought Zamoro's release from the Spaniards, but Zamoro is broken and cannot face life without Alzira. Otumbo does not improve the situation by revealing that she is at that very moment about to marry Gusmano. Zamoro swears revenge.

The marriage will secure peace and there is general rejoicing in Lima, headed by Gusmano. At the moment when the ceremony begins, Zamoro bursts in and stabs Gusmano, waiting for the retribution which must surely follow. But closer acquaintance with Alzira has brought with it in Gusmano a change of heart, and he gravely blesses the lovers before slowly expiring.

Verdi in later life is said to have dismissed *Alzira* as 'proprio brutta', but it shows him often in exploratory mood and able, in ensemble still more than in the solo arias, to create the kind of music which gives even his minor works an element of after-life. Maybe, at the start, the Incas sing a little too blithely of the impending murder of Alvaro just as the Spaniards in Act II are too light-hearted in victory, but in the prologue and Act I the solos of Zamoro and Gusmano return us effectively to the near-gravitas of an opera of this kind. Energy overflows, the drama proceeds at Verdi's habitual breakneck speed, and the finales impress. Alzira's early cavatina, 'Da Gusman, su fragil barca', is an example of Verdi's sensitivity to the predicaments in which his heroines so often find themselves. Alzira hovers somewhere between the Leonora of *Trovatore* and Amelia Boccanegra, the formula already working and Verdi showing he can vary its application. In his duet with Alzira, Gusmano demonstrates he is a man of substance, and if his final aria of renunciation and benediction does not quite attain the heights of *Simon Boccanegra* of eleven years later, it plainly points the way.   H.

ATTILA

Opera in a prologue and three acts, libretto by Temistocle Solera. Première, Venice, 17 March 1846, with Sophie Loewe, Guasco, Constantini, Marini. First produced London, Her Majesty's, 1848, with Sophie Cruvelli, Italo Gardoni, Velletti, Cuzzoni; New York, 1850. Revived Venice Festival, 1951 (concert performance), with Mancini, Penno, Giangiacomo Guelfi, Italo Tajo, conductor Giulini; Sadler's Wells, London, 1963 (in English); Rome, 1964, with Roberti, Limarilli, Zanasi, Arie, conductor Previtali; Trieste, 1965, with Christoff; Berlin, 1971, with Janowitz, Franco Tagliavini, Wixell, van Dam, conductor Patanè; Edinburgh Festival, 1972, with Ruggero Raimondi; Florence, 1972, with Gencer, Luchetti, Mittelmann, Ghiaurov, conductor Muti; Covent Garden, 1990, with Barstow, O'Neill, Zancanaro, Raimondi, conductor Downes; Opera North, 1991, with John Tomlinson.

Attila, *King of the Huns*..Bass
Uldino, *a Breton slave of Attila's* ....Tenor
Odabella, *daughter of the Lord of Aquileia*........Soprano
Ezio, *a Roman general*.....................................Baritone
Foresto, *a knight of Aquileia*..............................Tenor
Pope Leone (Leo) I..Bass

Place: Italy
Time: Fifth Century A.D.
Running Time: 1 hour 50 minutes

Verdi switched librettists from Piave to Solera for his second Venetian opera and was himself unwell during much of the time spent on composition. With its adumbration of the founding of Venice, the overt patri-

otism of the great duet of the Prologue, to say nothing of the brilliant writing for the leading singers, it must have greatly appealed to early audiences.

Prologue. After a short prelude, the curtain rises to show a piazza in Aquileia. Attila's army has sacked the city and is celebrating victory, with invocations to Wodan and praise of their general, who presently appears amongst his troops and takes his seat on the throne. He is angry to see that, in spite of his strict orders, some of the enemy women have been saved. In an aria, Odabella, who leads them, proclaims the invincible spirit of the Italian women, who fought alongside their men, unlike the women who have accompanied his army. The spitfire coloratura of her music is as full of venom as that of Lady Macbeth, and Attila in admiration offers her any gift she wants – she settles for a sword, and he gives her his own. In a cabaletta, she swears to herself that with it she will exact vengeance for all that she has lost.

Ezio, the emissary of the Roman Emperor, is announced. In an extended duet, he offers Attila the hegemony of the world – the Emperor of the East is old, the ruler of the West a mere boy, he himself requires only that Italy be left to him. At the climax of the duet come the words 'Avrai tu l'universo, resti l'Italia a me', and one can guess at the effect these words and the proud and challenging musical phrase must have had in *Risorgimento* Italy.

Attila reacts against this apparent act of treachery; how can Italy, whose most valiant leader is a traitor, ever hope to defy him? Ezio reminds him of his defeat at Châlons and announces the defiance of Rome.

Scene ii. Foresto, once one of the leaders of Aquileia, has led a band of refugees out to the lagoons, where they have built a sad little group of huts, miserable now, but later to become the proud city of Venice. They salute the dawn, and Foresto comes to greet them, still in his aria mourning his beloved Odabella, but proclaiming to the undisguised satisfaction of his followers their determination to raise from the lonely lagoon a city no less splendid than the one they have left – a compliment to Venice by Verdi's librettist not likely to be missed by the Fenice audience in 1846.

Act I. A wood near Attila's camp. In heartfelt phrases over cor anglais and then full woodwind accompaniment, Odabella laments the death of her father. To her comes Foresto, in spite of her joy at seeing him, full of reproaches that she has betrayed him with the slayer of her family. She justifies herself and reminds him of Judith who saved Israel.

The second scene takes place in Attila's tent, where the conqueror lies asleep, covered by a tiger skin. He wakes, clearly under the influence of a dream, and tells his attendant, Uldino, that he has been visited in his sleep by a vision of an old man, who warned him solemnly against continuing his march on Rome. Shaking off his forebodings, Attila calls together the priests and the army and orders that the march be resumed. From a distance a group can be heard approaching, and, when it turns out to be children and virgins headed by the old man he saw in his dream, Attila's resolution is no longer proof against his superstitions, least of all when the old man (described in the score as Saint Leo) repeats the very words we have just heard Attila recount to Uldino. The act ends with a great ensemble, not unlike the finale to the banqueting scene in *Macbeth*, in which Attila decides to bow to what is evidently the will of heaven.

Act II. In his camp, Ezio reads a letter from the Emperor Valentinian, commanding him to return to Rome. Such a boy to *command* him! In a beautiful aria ('Dagli immortali vertici'), he gives expression to his love of his country, then, urged by Foresto to join the forces resisting Attila, resolves to die if need be in defence of his country.

Attila's camp as in Act I. The troops are feasting in honour of the truce, and Attila, in spite of the warnings of the priests, entertains Ezio. The sudden extinguishing of the torches by a squall of wind appals the guests, but Attila refuses to be diverted even by so ill an omen from his purpose. When Uldino gives Attila a cup in which to pledge the guests, Odabella, who knows it is poisoned, warns Attila against drinking it. Foresto proudly acknowledges that he was responsible for the attempt on Attila's life, but, when Odabella demands his safety as the price of her warning, Attila

consents to spare him, announcing at the same time that Odabella shall be his bride. Foresto bitterly reproaches Odabella and leaves.

Act III. A wood dividing Attila's camp from Ezio's. Foresto and Ezio are still determined to carry out their plan, and Foresto in a fine aria laments the faithlessness of Odabella. Ezio joins him, and they proclaim their common resolve, but even the arrival of Odabella does not quieten Foresto's suspicions of her conduct, exacerbated as they have been by the sound of what he takes – rightly – for her wedding chorus. In a beautiful trio ('Te sol quest'anima') she tries to convince him that her heart has always been his and his alone.

Attila comes to claim his bride and is astonished to find her in the arms of Foresto. He bitterly reproaches all three – the slave he was to marry, the criminal whose life he spared, the Roman with whom he has a truce – but they defy him and his threats in a lively quartet. As the Roman soldiers who have been organised by Ezio and Foresto rush in to kill Attila, Odabella stabs him to the heart: 'E tu pure, Odabella?'   H.

MACBETH

Opera in four acts, text by Francesco Maria Piave. Première in Florence, 14 March 1847, with Barbieri-Nini, Varesi. First performance in New York, 1850; Dublin, 1859, with Pauline Viardot-Garcia as Lady Macbeth and Arditi conducting. Revised for Paris and first performed there in French, 21 April 1865, with Rey, Balla, Ismael. Revived Dresden, 1928, with Eugenie Burckhardt, Robert Burg, Willy Bader; Berlin, 1931, with Bindernagel and Onegin (Lady Macbeth), Reinmar, Andresen; Rome, 1932, with Scacciati, Franci, conductor Guarnieri; Vienna, 1933, with Rose Pauly; Glyndebourne, 1938 (for the first time in England, though productions had been scheduled for seasons of 1861 and 1870 but abandoned), with Vera Schwarz (in 1939, Grandi), Valentino, conductor Busch, producer Ebert; la Scala, Milan, 1938, with Cigna, Sved, conductor Marinuzzi; Edinburgh Festival, 1947, with Grandi, Valentino (Glyndebourne production); la Scala, 1952, with Callas, Mascherini, conductor de Sabata; Metropolitan, 1958, with Rysanek, Warren; Covent Garden, 1960, with Amy Shuard, Gobbi; la Scala, Milan, 1975, with Verrett, Cappuccilli, conductor Abbado, producer Strehler; Chicago, 1982, with Barstow, Cappuccilli; Salzburg Festival, 1984, with Dimitrova, Cappuccilli; English National Opera, 1990, with Kristine Ciesinski, Summers, conductor Mark Elder.

Lady Macbeth ....Soprano
Macbeth, *a general* ....Baritone
Banco (Banquo), *a general* ....Bass
Macduff, *a Scottish nobleman* ....Tenor
Duncano (Duncan), *King of Scotland* ....Mute

Lady-in-Waiting to Lady Macbeth ....Soprano
Malcolm, *son of Duncano* ....Tenor
Fleanzio (Fleance), *son of Banco* ....Mute
Doctor ....Bass

Witches, Hecate

Place: Scotland
Time: 1040 and After
Running Time: 2 hours 40 minutes

If it is legitimate to single out one of the operas of the first period of Verdi's creative life as the vessel of his most concentrated attention and fervour it would have to be *Macbeth*. It has been described as his most idealistic opera to date, and he – in any case, the most meticulous of composers in rehearsal – spent more time working with the singers and on details of staging than on anything hitherto.

After the première in Paris of the revised version (1865), Verdi was accused among other things of not knowing Shakespeare. The accusation moved him to fury, and he, the most modest of composers, wrote: 'I may not have rendered *Macbeth* well, but that I do not know, do not understand and feel Shakespeare, no, by heavens, no! He is one of my very special poets, and I have had him in my hands from my earliest youth, and I read and re-read him continually.'

Macbeth remained a favourite of Verdi's among his own works. He spent a considerable time revising it, and its comparative lack of success in his lifetime was a constant source of irritation to him. Piave the librettist was provided with a detailed scenario by the composer before he was allowed to put pen to paper, so that the dramatic construction is Verdi's. Faced with the difficulty of putting a long play on to the operatic stage, Verdi concentrated on three principals: Lady Macbeth, Macbeth, and the Witches – he was emphatic on this last point. Lady Macbeth is explicitly (as in Shakespeare implicitly) the dominating figure, although her husband remains at the centre of the tragedy; Macduff is reduced to little more than a member of the ensemble (even his solitary aria forms part of the moment of stillness before the turning point in the action); and Banquo, a considerable figure until his murder, disappears well before the halfway mark. Malcolm is almost entirely eliminated, and the Doctor and the Gentlewoman are retained mainly for the sleep-walking scene.

Act I. The prelude concentrates on material later used in the sleep-walking scene. The first scene takes place on the heath, where the Witches sing a fantastic chorus while waiting for Macbeth, and then in awesome tones prophesy his future. A messenger arrives to announce that Macbeth has been granted the title and estates of the rebel Cawdor, and Macbeth and Banquo meditate in a duet on the implications of the prophecy, half of which has already come true (the other half being that Macbeth will be King, and Banquo's heirs will succeed him). The scene concludes with a chorus and dance for the Witches.

Lady Macbeth reads the letter from her husband in which he tells her of the meeting with the weird band, and launches into a determined recitative. 'Vieni, t'affretta' has been described by some as an inadequate setting of the great soliloquy of Act I, but it is strikingly effective in its context, and anyone who heard Margherita Grandi sing it at Glyndebourne or Edinburgh knows that it can, with its cabaletta, 'Or tutti, sorgete, ministri infernali', produce an effect of tigerish ferocity.

Macbeth arrives and in a few pregnant sentences, with hardly a direct word spoken, the murder is decided upon, as the march which announces the King's arrival is heard off-stage. The march itself is commonplace enough, but by no means unsuitable to accompany the pantomime which goes with the King's procession – no word is spoken throughout his passage across the stage.

Macbeth, alone, sees a dagger in front of him, and with his soliloquy, in itself highly expressive, begins the great duet between the two principal characters. The murder done, Macbeth staggers down the stairs with the dagger still in his hands: 'Fatal mia donna! un murmure, com'io, non intendesti?' He describes the scene, the murmuring of the grooms in the antechamber, the way 'Amen' stuck in his throat, and in the end it is Lady Macbeth who has to take the dagger back into the King's chamber.

Characteristically, this duet is marked to be sung 'sotto voce, e cupa', that is to say in a half voice and with dark, stifled tone. Only a few phrases, such as Macbeth's outburst of agonised horror when he catches sight of his blood-stained hands, 'Oh, vista orribile', are to be sung out, and they are specifically marked 'a voce aperta'. The original Lady Macbeth records that there were 151 rehearsals of this duet before the composer was satisfied, and that the sleep-walking scene – Verdi always maintained that these were the opera's two crucial moments – cost her three months of ceaseless worry before her movements and singing were judged to be satisfactory.

Banquo and Macduff arrive to accompany the King on his way, and Banquo broods impressively in C minor on the horrid portents of the night, while his companion goes to rouse the King. The murder is discovered, and all gather together for the magnificently sonorous and excitingly written finale, one of the most splendid in any of Verdi's earlier operas.

Act II. Macbeth is discovered on stage (the orchestral prelude is a reminiscence of 'Fatal mia donna'), where he is quickly joined by Lady Macbeth, who accuses him of avoiding her. They decide that the death of Banquo is necessary to their schemes, and Lady Macbeth is left alone to sing an expressive aria, 'La luce langue', whose ferocious determination (it dates from 1865) puts it into quite another class from the much tamer piece it replaces, and whose layout reminds us that 'O don fatale' (*Don Carlos*) was written less than two years after the revision of *Macbeth*.

The scene changes to a park, where a band of assassins is waiting for Banquo. Their chorus is a particularly fortunate example of the conventional music given to bands of murderers in Italian opera of the period (or indeed to any felonious nocturnal gathering for that matter; cf. the chorus near the end of Act I of *Rigoletto*). Banquo's aria which follows is a beautiful example of Verdi's writing for bass voice; at its end, the murderers fall upon him, but his son Fleance escapes.

The opening music of the banquet scene has a feverish, spurious gaiety, which it may be going too far to ascribe solely to the composer's sense of dramatic character (as if it were the inn scene in *Wozzeck*) but which is uncannily apt in its context. The same quality is evident in the graceless, nerve-ridden Brindisi, which Lady Macbeth sings to the assembled guests; the close relationship of its tune to the flowing 6/8 Brindisi in *Traviata* and the strong contrast of mood between the two has been pointed out by Desmond Shawe-Taylor, writing in the *New Statesman*. In between verses, Macbeth has a conference with a representative of the band charged to murder Banquo and learns that Fleance has escaped. Returning to his guests, he complains that Banquo's absence detracts from the pleasure of the occasion and says he himself will sit for a moment in his place. As he

goes to the chair, he sees the ghost of the murdered man, and bursts into an agonised denial of his guilt, to the astonishment of the company, which naturally sees nothing. Lady Macbeth's remonstrances finally nerve him to face his guests again, which he does with an attempt at making light of the lapse. Lady Macbeth sings another verse of the Brindisi, but Macbeth's frenzy breaks out again as the ghost makes another appearance. His nerve has gone, and the assembly draws away from him, sensing the guilt he makes little attempt any longer to conceal. His sombre tune, 'Sangue a me', begins the finale, which is musically and dramatically no less effective than that to Act I.

Act III. The Witches sit round their cauldron in a dark cave. Their chorus is in the same vein as that of the first act, and is succeeded by a ballet, written of course for Paris (1865) and interrupted in the middle by the appearance of Hecate to instruct her followers as to their conduct when they are visited, as they will shortly be, by Macbeth. The dance continues and at its end Macbeth appears and demands to know his future destiny. The music is extraordinarily suggestive and Verdi has perhaps nowhere else so successfully evoked the supernatural as in the scene of the apparitions, which is punctuated by the distraught comments of Macbeth himself. The King loses consciousness, and the Witches dance round him.

The mood changes, Lady Macbeth appears searching for her husband, and asks what he has learnt from the Witches. He tells her and finishes by revealing that he has seen foretold the line of kings which Banquo will sire. The energy of Lady Macbeth's denial that this shall come to pass communicates itself to her husband and arouses something of his old military spirit, so that their short but vigorous duet makes a very striking end to the act.

Act IV. We are at the turning-point in the drama, the zenith of the ambitious career of the Macbeths and the nadir of the fortunes of the people of Scotland. As we might expect from the Verdi of 1847, the force opposed to Macbeth's tyranny is not only retribution but the less tragic and more immediately topical one of patriotism, which is implied throughout and personified in Macduff, Banquo, the Chorus, and, of course, in the minor figure of Malcolm. 'Patria oppressa', the chorus of the Scottish exiles, is in direct line from 'Va, pensiero' in *Nabucco*, with its wailing minor second in the accompaniment, sometimes ascending, sometimes descending (it appears again in the sleep-walking scene) and its wonderfully evocative contours. The words of the chorus date from the opera's first version, the music from its second.

Macduff's beautiful aria completes the still moment at the centre of the dramatic action, and is succeeded by a quick movement as Malcolm's army crosses the stage; Malcolm and Macduff sing a duet with the chorus.

Nothing in the score of *Macbeth* is more worthy of admiration than the sleep-walking scene, which is cast in the form of the old soprano 'mad scene', but has a freedom of movement and an expressiveness that Verdi was not to excel in a similar set piece, one is tempted to say, until Aida's arias nearly twenty-five years later. Much of the preliminary orchestral music has been heard in the prelude, but the expressive quality of the vocal writing is quite extraordinary, and the scene itself very exacting for the singer,

comprising as it does every shade of expression, and a very wide compass, from C flat at the bottom to top D flat in the last phrase of all (marked 'un fil di voce').

Macbeth is at bay, furious that Malcolm is marching on him with an army reinforced by English troops but confident in his knowledge that the Witches have prophesied for him immunity from death at the hands of anyone 'born of woman', unaware that Macduff was 'from his mother's womb untimely ripp'd'. He curses the low friendless state which his way of life has brought him, but when he hears that his wife is dead, leads his men defiantly to war. The battle is accompanied by a fugue, which persists through the short encounter of Macbeth and Macduff and eventually gives way to a general chorus of rejoicing at the defeat of the tyrant.

Apart from the ballet, which was written specially for Paris, four pieces were inserted in 1865 in place of material which now finds no place in the revised opera: in Act II, Lady Macbeth's aria, 'La luce langue'; in Act III the final duet; in Act IV the chorus of exiles (replacing one similar in feeling and with the same words), and the whole of the battle scene (i.e. after Macbeth's aria). Originally, the opera ended with a short *scena* for Macbeth and this has in fact been used in Glyndebourne's production of the opera, Busch and Ebert inserting it after the fugue and before the entrance of Macduff and Malcolm. Even with the inclusion of this material, which the composer himself had discarded, there is no doubt that the last section of the opera, with its brilliantly descriptive fugue and firm, 'national' final chorus, is a vast improvement on the rather ordinary ending of the original version. There are changes in the rest of the opera, notably in the *presto* section of the big duet of Act I, Macbeth's reaction to the first appearance of the ghost in the banquet scene, the E major section of the first chorus of Act III, and the apparitions scene.

All his life, Verdi strove towards an expression of character, and nowhere previously had he been so successful in its portrayal as in *Macbeth*. Macbeth himself is shown as dominated, even more than in the play, by the other two main characters, his wife and the Witches; that is to say, his own personality plays proportionately a lesser part in determining events, and he is shown often at his worst and most susceptible, hardly ever at his best as poet or soldier. All the same, the working of remorse on his conscience – Verdi, like Shakespeare, obviously thinks of him as a better man than his actions – is excellently shown, and the long duet after the murder subtly and admirably expresses his terror at his deed and its inevitable consequences, and constitutes, with the sleep-walking scene, the most complete musical expression of the element of tragedy and destiny in the composition of the two leading figures.

Macbeth's loss – if loss it can be called – is, of

course, Lady Macbeth's gain, and she dominates music and action alike. Judged purely as a role for a singing actress, it is one of the finest Verdi ever wrote, but its significance goes further than that and it is perhaps the earliest Verdian role in which a complete musical development can be traced along with the dramatic and psychological growth in a character. The progress from the aria in the first act, 'Vieni, t'affretta', which is in form a conventional aria with cabaletta (although a most exciting and successful one), through the increasingly unnerving events of the intermediate scenes, to the final, long, wailing curve of the sleep-walking scene is a remarkable musical study of gradual disintegration under the influence of conscience.

Macbeth may be said to sum up, better perhaps than any other opera, this period of Verdi's career; for the first time he had achieved a combination of the three characteristics which dominate his music: the theatre, patriotism, and character.   H.

I MASNADIERI

The Bandits

Opera in four parts, text by Andrea Maffei after Schiller's *Die Räuber*. Première Her Majesty's Theatre, London, 22 July 1847, with the immensely popular Jenny Lind, Italo Gardoni (Carlo), Filippo Coletti, and the veteran Luigi Lablache as Massimiliano, conductor Verdi (later, the composer Michael Balfe). The opera has been not infrequently revived but seldom with quite the success that could have been anticipated.

Massimiliano, *Count Moor* ....Bass
Carlo, *his elder son*..Tenor
Francesco, *Carlo's brother*.............................Baritone
Amalia, *the Count's niece, an orphan*...............Soprano
Arminio, *the Count's treasurer* ....Tenor
Moser, *a pastor* ....Bass
Rolla, *Carlo Moor's fellow bandit*.........................Tenor

Youths (later Bandits), Women, Children, Servants

Place: Germany
Time: Early Eighteenth Century
Running Time: 2 hours 20 minutes

Verdi's new contract for London was a prestigious affair, with a fine cast and much publicity – Queen Victoria attended the gala première. Success was slightly muted, a circumstance put down variously to the librettist's distinction as poet rather than man of the theatre, and to Verdi's unfamiliarity with the expectations of the London public. The music for Amalia is full of the kind of ornamentation which best suited Jenny Lind, whom Verdi admired but thought a little old-fashioned for 1847, but the opera remains somehow marginalised to this day.

The prelude concerns itself almost entirely with a lengthy 'cello solo, written specially to show the talents of Alfredo Piatti, the leading player at Her Majesty's Theatre and an old friend of Verdi's from Milan days.

Act I. Carlo, estranged from his father as a result of some madcap behaviour, reflects on his homeland and on his love for Amalia, then hears in a letter from his scheming brother that, so far from being forgiven, he is in effect disinherited. He and his disreputable friends in a rollicking cabaletta decide to cut loose, turn their backs on society and live on their wits as bandits.

Francesco, the villain of the piece, having removed the threat of his brother, plans to speed up his father's demise and decides news of Carlo's death in battle (fictitious, but convincing) will do the trick.

Amalia sings as she watches the sleeping Massimiliano, who wakes to lament that he may die without again seeing his favourite son, Carlo. Arminio brings a false report of Carlo's death, together with his dying wish that Francesco may marry Amalia. The act ends with a quartet between the deeply contrite Massimiliano, Amalia and Arminio consolatory, and Francesco crowing in ferocious triumph. At its end, Massimiliano falls, apparently dead.

Act II. Francesco has succeeded his father, at whose tomb Amalia muses, rejecting the sounds of rejoicing within and turning lament to rejoicing when a penitent Arminio tells her that both Massimiliano and Carlo are still alive. Her confrontation with the importunate Francesco comes in the form of a gradually evolving duet of the kind Verdi particularly favoured and during whose course she resists his attempts to bend her to his will.

Bandits celebrate the freeing of Rolla, one of their number, who was condemned to be hanged. Carlo, alone, laments his life of crime, but the alarm is raised and the gang prepare to defend themselves.

Act III. Amalia escapes from Francesco, but she takes fright when she hears the bandits singing until totally by chance she meets Carlo, with whom she joins her voice in rapturous, even confident, duet.

In the forest, Carlo is full of regret that his present

life will separate him forever from Amalia and he contemplates suicide. He and the bandits surprise Arminio taking food to someone imprisoned in a deserted tower. This turns out to be Massimiliano, who does not recognise his son but reveals he was imprisoned by Francesco when he recovered from his earlier collapse. Carlo calls on his gang to help him gain revenge.

Act IV. Francesco suffers a crisis of conscience, relates the terrifying dream he has had, and rushes out after Moser has assured him only God can grant forgiveness for his sins.

Carlo does not reveal his identity to Massimiliano but nevertheless requests from him a father's blessing. The robbers capture Amalia, Carlo's identity is revealed and the opera ends in an unusual manner, with Carlo undergoing a crisis related to the criminal nature of his life, Amalia offering to stay with him in his outlawed state, and Carlo suddenly stabbing her and going off to meet his fate on the gallows. But the trio inspired by the bizarre situation makes a not unworthy finale.

Julian Budden once called it 'a grandiose work in the composer's early manner', and 'not a masterpiece ... moments of genuine greatness – and never a dull one'.   H.

JÉRUSALEM

Opera in four acts, text by Alphonse Royer and Gustave Vaëz, after Verdi's earlier opera *I Lombardi*. Première at the Opéra, Paris, 22 November 1847, with Madame Julian van Gelder, Gilbert Duprez, Adolphe Alizard.

Gaston, *Vicomte de Béarn* ....Tenor
The Count of Toulouse ....Baritone
Roger, *the Count's brother*.....................................Bass
Adémar de Montheil, *Papal Legate* ....Bass
Raymond, *Gaston's squire*.................................Tenor
A Soldier ....Bass
A Herald...Bass
The Emir of Ramla ....Bass
An Officer of the Emir ....Tenor
Hélène, *daughter of the Count* ....Soprano
Isaure, *her companion*....................................Soprano

Knights, Ladies, Soldiers, Pilgrims, Arab Sheiks,
    Women of the Harem, People of Ramla

Place: Toulouse; Palestine
Time: 1095–99
Running Time: 2 hours 20 minutes

Invited to compose for Paris as early as 1845, Verdi finally agreed, partly because of the prestige involved but also for financial considerations. He followed the example of Rossini (whose *Maometto II* became for Paris *Le Siège de Corinthe*) in adapting *I Lombardi* as *Jérusalem*, and the result was a success though subsequent commentators, until the time of Julian Budden, have condemned the 'new' work as inferior to the original. Budden ascribes the hostile view partly to Italian chauvinism, partly to a tendency to insist that music written for one context cannot work in another, partly to a reluctance to examine the new score, whose revisions, insists Budden, are, apart from the ballet, improvements. The plot is more concentrated, the casting of one rather than two principal tenors is an advantage, and all new music an improvement over what it replaced. It was translated into Italian but found little favour there, and is performed far less often than its predecessor, the first English performance for instance waiting until 1990. (See page 856 for a synopsis of *I Lombardi*.)

Act I. A marriage between Gaston and Hélène will reconcile two warring families, Gaston's father having been killed by Hélène's. Roger, Hélène's uncle, has incestuous designs on his niece and, as the men are about to depart on a crusade, hires an assassin to murder Gaston. The attempt is bungled and it is the Count who is apparently killed, although the assassin has the presence of mind to lay the blame on Gaston on whom anathema is pronounced.

Act II. Roger, disguised and penitent, lives in Palestine and offers water to pilgrims dying of thirst. Once he is out of sight, one of them turns out to be Hélène, who believes in Gaston's innocence and has come to Palestine where he is rumoured to be living. She recognises in one of the pilgrims Gaston's squire and hears he is a prisoner nearby in Ramla. She rejoices in the quick solo from *Lombardi*'s Act IV (known on old records – quaintly, as it is in common time – as the 'Polonaise from *I Lombardi*'!). Pilgrims appear to sing a French version of 'O signore del tetto natio', Count Raymond makes an appearance miraculously preserved from the assassin's knife, and his brother Roger asks for his blessing.

Gaston, a prisoner in the Emir's Palace, is given Oronte's solo from Act II scene i of *Lombardi*. Hélène too is a prisoner and she and Gaston sing the duet from the earlier opera's Act III, but fail to make their escape.

Act III. Hélène is mocked by fellow inmates of the harem; there ensues a fifteen-movement ballet. The Count succeeds in capturing Ramla, but denounces his daughter, whom he finds with the man he thinks attempted to kill him. Gaston is to be executed and the Papal Legate proclaims his name henceforth dishonoured – an impressive ensemble new to the score and a forerunner of similar events in later Verdi operas.

Act IV. The act starts with the famous Risorgimento-style chorus of *Lombardi*'s Act IV scene ii, after which it is Roger's task to absolve Gaston before his execution. Hélène stays behind and joins Gaston and Roger for a version of the trio from the end of Act III scene iii in the earlier opera (now with flute rather than violin obbligato), but at its end Roger hears the sounds of battle and restores Gaston's arms to him. In the last scene, Gaston covers himself with glory in battle and is recognised by the Count, who also recognises and forgives his dying brother Roger.   H.

IL CORSARO
The Corsair

Opera in three acts, text by Francesco Maria Piave after Byron's poem. Première in Trieste, 25 October 1848, with Gaetano Fraschini, Verdi's most favoured tenor, as Corrado, Barbieri-Nini (already the first Lady Macbeth) as Gulnara, and Achille de Bassini (who had sung the Doge in *I due Foscari* and would later be Miller in *Luisa Miller*) as Pasha Seid. The opera had little success at first and has been revived only spasmodically.

Corrado, *captain of Corsairs*................................Tenor
Giovanni, *a Corsair*..Bass
Medora, *Corrado's beloved* ....Soprano
Gulnara, *Seid's favourite slave* ....Soprano
Seid, *Pasha of Coron* ....Baritone
Selimo, *a Turkish dignitary*...........................Baritone
A Black Eunuch..Tenor
A Slave ....Tenor

Corsairs, Guards, Turks, Slaves, Odalisques

Place: An Aegean Island, the City of Coron
Time: Early Nineteenth Century
Running Time: 1 hour 35 minutes

Long ago *Il Corsaro* acquired a reputation, not quite fairly, as the least interesting of Verdi's operas, an estimate which grew from the indifference Verdi appears to have shown when he did not even bother to attend the first night, much less look after the opera's initial preparation as he had with all his previous premières. He chose the subject for Piave's attentions as early as 1844–45 and probably worked on it before *Macbeth*, which became something of a watershed in his output, but seems eventually to have set the libretto partly to fulfil an obligation to the publisher Francesco Lucca, Ricordi's competitor, with whom he had fallen out some years before.

Act I. On their island in the Aegean, pirates roister. Their leader, Corrado, laments a life of exile and crime, then sets off in search of plunder. The second scene brings Corrado to his beloved Medora, who sings a melancholy romance before joining him in a duet of partial reassurance before he leaves.

Act II. In Seid's harem, odalisques sing to pass the time and Gulnara bemoans her life as the favourite of Seid, whom she hates. At the harbour, Seid himself joins in a hymn to Allah before a Dervish appears asking for protection from the pirates. A short duet follows before the dervish unmasks to reveal Corrado who, with his followers, leads an unsuccessful attempt to free the women of the harem; his efforts are derided by Seid but admired by the women. Seid threatens his prisoners with death by torture.

Act III. In a magniloquent utterance, Seid regrets the uncompromising hostility of his beloved Gulnara, before in an extended duet refusing her plea for the life of Corrado. In a prison scene Corrado curses his fate, then falls asleep to be wakened by Gulnara, who will help him escape. In spite of her pleading, he rejects her offer to kill Seid but tells her of his constant love for Medora. She returns to tell him Seid is dead and they escape together.

On the corsairs' island, we find that Medora, despairing of ever seeing Corrado again, has taken poison and is not far from death. To her amazement, a ship comes into sight bearing her beloved and Gulnara; Corrado and Medora fall into each other's arms. The situation is explained – that Gulnara, driven by her unrequited love for Corrado, has saved his life – but the finale finds Medora exhausted and she dies. Corrado throws himself over the cliff.

Modern opinion may tend to disagree with history's too hasty verdict. Interestingly, Julian Budden has made a rough equation of Medora with Verdi's memory of his first wife and her early death (in 1840); of Gulnara with Giuseppina Strepponi, with whom he was already associated at the time of *Corsaro*'s première. What had seemed when he embarked on it almost a parable of his situation later became a matter of history rather than a burning issue, hence his distancing of himself from the subject.

The opera, if simplistic and not Verdi's most dramatically intense, is far from negligible. It is concise and full of the exciting kind of music which late twentieth-century experience of Verdi's early operas has convinced audiences they enjoy. Pirates and odalisques chorus away to appropriately different effect; Medora and Gulnara are given an introductory romance and cavatina respectively which are graceful and rewarding; Corrado sings with extraordinary grace for a pirate; Seid is, musically speaking, a baritone of some nobility. Cabalettas and ensembles are impressive even if sometimes a bit short of individuality. However, the final trio (a rarity, with two leading sopranos) was something of which Verdi, with good reason, appears to have been proud.   H.

LA BATTAGLIA DI LEGNANO
The Battle of Legnano

Opera in three acts, libretto by Salvatore Cammarano. Première, Teatro Argentina, Rome, 27 January 1849, with Teresa de Giuli-Borsi, Gaetano Fraschini, Filippo Colini. First performance in Great Britain, 1960, by Welsh National Opera (in a World War II setting, libretto by John and Mary Moody under the title of *The Battle*), with Heather Harper, Ronald Dowd, Ronald Lewis, Hervey Alan, conductor Charles Groves. Revived la Scala, Milan, 1916, with Rosa Raisa, Crimi, Danise, Cirino; Parma, 1951, with Guerrini, Penno, Savarese; Florence Festival, 1959, with Leyla Gencer, Gastone Limarilli, Giuseppe Taddei, conductor Gui; la Scala, Milan, 1961, with Antonietta Stella, Franco Corelli, Ettore Bastianini, conductor Gavazzeni; Carnegie Hall, New York, 1987, with Millo, Malagnini, Manuguerra (in concert).

Federico (Frederick) Barbarossa ....Bass
First Consul of Milan ....Bass
Second Consul of Milan ....Bass
The Mayor of Como ....Bass
Rolando, *Duke of Milan*....................................Baritone
Lida, *his wife* ....Soprano
Arrigo, *a warrior from Verona* ....Tenor
Marcovaldo, *a German prisoner*......................Baritone
Imelda, *Lida's servant*.........................Mezzo-Soprano
A Herald ....Tenor

Time: Twelfth Century
Place: Como and Milan
Running Time: 1 hour 50 minutes

The theme for *La Battaglia di Legnano* was suggested to Verdi by the poet Cammarano, at a time when the composer was uneasy at the way the liberal and nationalist revolution was going and anxious to express his patriotism. He was able to embark on the work at once through the lapse of a previous contract with the San Carlo in Naples and devoted himself to it throughout the summer of 1848, finishing it at the end of the year. The première was received with such delirious excitement – partly because the theme of the victory of the Lombard League over Frederick Barbarossa was so topical – that the entire fourth act was repeated. A little later the opera was suppressed by the Austrian censorship, but it was revived in 1861 in Milan, the title being changed to *L'Assedio di Haarlem*, the Emperor to a Spanish duke and the Italian patriots to Dutchmen; on this occasion however it was a failure.

Act I. An overture of distinctly military flavour introduces the first scene, set in Milan, where a League, composed of contingents from the various cities of Lombardy, is forming to repulse the imminent invasion by Barbarossa. Rolando, leader of the Milanese troops, discovers that the group from Verona is led by his beloved friend, Arrigo, whom he had long believed killed in battle. Arrigo explains that he was taken prisoner and the two comrades rejoice at their happy reunion. In a chorus of great fervour all the patriots vow to die for their cause.

Scene ii opens in a shady place where we find Lida and her ladies. After a gentle chorus, Lida's lyrical and highly ornamented aria is interrupted by Marcovaldo, who is a captive and has fallen in love with Lida. She repulses him angrily.

Arrigo and Rolando arrive, and the embittered Marcovaldo, noticing Lida's agitation at the sight of Arrigo, jumps at once to the conclusion that she is secretly in love with him. Lida and Arrigo are left alone, and in a highly emotional duet we learn that they had indeed been betrothed years before. Arrigo reproaches Lida for her marriage to Rolando; even her eminently valid excuse that she thought he was dead does not seem to satisfy him.

Act II. Arrigo and Rolando are in Como to persuade the local leaders to join forces with them against Barbarossa. The Mayor's refusal on the grounds that he has a treaty with Barbarossa infuriates Rolando and Arrigo, who argue that the whole future of Italy is at stake and beg him to reconsider. 'What answer are we to take back?' they ask. They are soon answered by the sudden and startling appearance of Barbarossa himself, who tells the two envoys to return with the news of imminent and inescapable disaster and shows them a great German camp outside the city. In spite of this show of Barbarossa's power, Arrigo and Rolando retain their confidence in eventual victory, and the act ends with a rousing chorus in which all the Lombards swear to fight to the death.

Act III. In the crypt of Milan Cathedral, Arrigo is initiated into the ranks of the Death Riders (*Cavalieri della Morte*), a band of warriors all of whom have taken a solemn and terrible oath to rid their country of the invaders or die in the attempt.

The second scene takes place in Lida's rooms. Convinced he is going to be killed in battle, she has written a letter to Arrigo which her maid is to deliver, and she sings of her grief in phrases which cast distinct foreshadows of *Traviata*.

Rolando has premonitions of death as he says goodbye to his wife and child, and when Arrigo enters, he draws him aside to tell him that he, Rolando, has been made leader of the Death Riders, an honour which will almost certainly result in his death. Arrigo promises that if Rolando is killed he will look after his family, and the men leave separately. At this point the treacherous Marcovaldo intercepts Rolando and gives him Lida's letter to Arrigo, which he has bought from her servant Imelda – the letter in which Lida implores Arrigo for the sake of what they once meant to each other, to see her before the battle. Rolando swears to be revenged on them both.

The third scene finds Arrigo in his room writing to his mother. Lida comes to him, saying that she still loves him but that they must never meet again. She is on the point of explaining that she has come to see him because he has ignored her letter when Rolando is heard at the door. Arrigo hastily conceals Lida on the balcony, but Rolando, pretending to see if it is time to set off for the battle, discovers her. He is about to kill Arrigo without more ado, but, on hearing the trumpets sounding the call to arms, he realises that a far greater punishment would be to bring dishonour on Arrigo by preventing him from joining the patriot army; he locks him in his room. The thought of the shame which he

will suffer spurs Arrigo to leap from the balcony with a cry of 'Viva Italia!' Franz Werfel, in his edition of Verdi's letters,[1] illustrates the inflammatory effect that Verdi's music had on the patriotic Italians of his day. 'At this very point a sergeant of dragoons in the gallery of the Teatro Costanzi did the same thing that the tenor was doing on the stage. Deprived of his reason by the irresistibly tempestuous rhythm of the music, he tore off his tunic, and leapt from the parapet of the gallery into the orchestra, where, surprisingly enough, he neither broke his back nor seriously injured anyone else.'

Act IV. In the cathedral, the people of Milan, among them Lida, are waiting to hear news of the battle which will have been joined at Legnano. News comes of the complete rout of the German army. Arrigo himself has dragged the Emperor from his horse but has been mortally wounded and is being brought to die in the cathedral. He is carried in by the Death Riders and swears to Rolando that he and Lida are innocent. Rolando believes him, forgives him and embraces Lida. Arrigo kisses the flag and dies while the citizens of Milan rejoice at the victory.　　H.

LUISA MILLER

Opera in three acts, text by S. Cammarano from Schiller's play *Kabale und Liebe*. Première at the Teatro San Carlo, Naples, 8 December 1849, with Gazzaniga, Salandri, Malvezzi, Selva, de Bassini. First performed in Philadelphia, 1852; London, Her Majesty's Theatre, 1858, with Piccolomini, Giuglini, Vialetti, Beneventaro. Revived Berlin, 1927; Metropolitan, 1929, with Ponselle, Lauri-Volpi, de Luca, Pasero, Ludikar, conductor Serafin; Florence Festival, 1937, with Caniglia, Lauri-Volpi, Armando Borgioli, Pasero, conductor Gui; Metropolitan, New York, 1968, with Caballé, Tucker, Sherrill Milnes, Tozzi, conductor Schippers; la Scala, Milan, 1976, with Caballé; Covent Garden, 1978, with Ricciarelli, Pavarotti, Nucci, conductor Maazel; Paris, 1983, with Ricciarelli, Pavarotti, Cappuccilli.

Count Walter	Bass
Rodolfo, *his son*	Tenor
Miller, *an old soldier*	Baritone
Luisa, *his daughter*	Soprano
Federica, Duchess of Ostheim, *Walter's niece*	Mezzo-Soprano
Laura, *a peasant girl*	Contralto
Wurm	Bass

Ladies attending the Duchess, Pages, Servants, and Villagers

---

[1] *Verdi: The Man in His Letters* (edited Franz Werfel and Paul Stefan: translated by Edward Downes. L. B. Fisher, New York, 1942).

Place: The Tyrol
Time: First Half of the Eighteenth Century
Running Time: 2 hours 20 minutes

Schiller's play *Kabale und Liebe*, its fierce social criticism much subdued by Cammarano in deference to Neapolitan censorship, provided the basis for Verdi's second opera for the San Carlo. After a somewhat fraught première in Naples which involved the composer threatening to ask for asylum on a French warship, the opera was well received.

The overture is a notable success and Julian Budden invokes Mozart, Weber and Schubert in his description.

Act I. Luisa's birthday is being celebrated in the village square. In spite of her father's rather nebulous misgivings, she loves a young local whom she knows as Carlo (aria: 'Lo vidi, e'l primo palpito'). Wurm, Count Walter's sinister retainer, himself in love with Luisa, urges her father to support his claims, but Miller in a spacious aria insists his daughter will make her own choice of husband. Wurm reveals that Carlo is in reality Rodolfo, Count Walter's son only recently returned from abroad; a man with such connections would never be allowed to marry a girl from the village. Miller is left to fulminate in cabaletta.

In the castle, Wurm tells his master that Rodolfo is in love with Luisa, news not at all to the liking of Count Walter (aria: 'Il mio sangue') who plans a more suitable alliance with the recently widowed Duchess Federica, with whom Rodolfo was brought up. He tells his son that the Duchess is due to arrive at any minute and instructs him to propose to her. Before Rodolfo can protest, the Duchess is announced and their duet ('Dall'aule raggianti di vano splendor') suggests onetime intimacy which is shattered by Rodolfo's resolve to tell her the truth: he cannot ask for her hand in marriage because he loves another woman. Federica has long been in love with him and is disconcerted by the news.

Miller tells Luisa that her lover is the Count's son, engaged moreover to the Duchess, but in a moment Rodolfo is in the house asking for Miller's blessing on his marriage to Luisa. With all the authority he can muster, the Count intervenes and describes Luisa as a seductress. This is more than Miller can stomach and he draws his sword at the same time as Rodolfo breathes threats against anyone frustrating his intentions. The Count orders Luisa and her father arrested, but releases them when it is clear Rodolfo will reveal the guilty secret of how he came by his title if he proceed with his plan. It is an impressive finale.

Act II. Luisa learns that her father has been arrested and Wurm insists she can only save him from death by writing a letter disclaiming her love for Rodolfo and promising herself to Wurm in marriage. She writes (aria: 'Tu puniscimi, o Signor'), but there is more; she must come to the castle and in front of the Duchess admit her love for Wurm.

Wurm tells Count Walter that his scheme is successful, but then as they discuss their crime learns that Rodolfo knows he and the Count murdered the previous holder of the title. Federica hears Luisa falsely confess her love for Wurm.

Rodolfo has seen Luisa's letter and expresses his misery in the score's most famous aria, 'Quando le sere al placido', one of Verdi's finest melodic inspirations. He challenges Wurm to a duel, then tells his father that Luisa has betrayed him and he now only wishes for death. The Count seizes the chance to urge him to marry the Duchess. He agrees.

Act III. Miller has heard the price his daughter paid for his release and makes an attempt to comfort her. She has written to Rodolfo admitting she was betrayed but has sworn to reveal no details. She suggests a suicide pact but her father's distress convinces her to tear the letter up.

Luisa is at prayer when Rodolfo enters the room, which gives him the chance to empty a phial of poison into a decanter he sees on the table. Confronted with her letter to Wurm, she admits writing it and Rodolfo asks for a drink. She pours, then drinks in her turn, and together in impressive duet ('Piangi, piangi') they lament their situation. With Rodolfo's avowal that the wine was poisoned, Luisa feels freed from her vow and admits the letter was a lie. They make ready for death, and Miller is in time to join a final trio. Count Walter arrives to see Rodolfo kill Wurm.   H.

STIFFELIO

Opera in three acts, libretto by Francesco Maria Piave, after the play *Le Pasteur, ou L'Evangile et le Foyer* by Eugène Bourgeois and Emile Souvestre. Première at Trieste, 20 November 1850, with Marietta Gazzaniga-Malaspina, Gaetano Fraschini and Filippo Colini. Produced in Barcelona, 1856. Revived Parma, 1968, with Gulin, Limarilli, Alberti;

Covent Garden, 1993, with Malfitano, Carreras; Metropolitan, New York, 1994, with Sharon Sweet, Domingo, Vladimir Chernov.

Stiffelio, *a Protestant preacher* ....Tenor

Lina, *his wife* ....Soprano

Count Stankar, *an old Colonel, Lina's father* ...Baritone

Jorg, *another preacher* ....Bass

Raffaele von Leuthold, *a nobleman*.....................Tenor

Dorothea, *Lina's cousin* ....Mezzo-Soprano

Federico von Frengel, *Lina's cousin*....................Tenor

Members of Stankar's Household; Friends and Followers of Stiffelio

Place: Count Stankar's Castle near Salzburg
Time: Beginning of the Nineteenth Century
Running Time: 1 hour 45 minutes

The première of *Le Pasteur* by Bourgeois and Souvestre took place in Paris in February 1849, but it had been published in Italian in 1848 and in this version presumably came to the notice of Piave, Verdi's librettist. Not only was this, together with Dumas's *La Dame aux Camélias*, the most 'modern' play Verdi turned into an opera (both in terms of subject matter and of proximity of stage and operatic premières), but the subject – the adultery of a Protestant clergyman's wife – was highly likely in censor-ridden Italy to cause official consternation. *Stiffelio* attracted the attention of the censor from the start, and the text was in effect butchered before the première in Trieste. Stiffelio and Jorg were turned from ministers into what the libretto was forced to call 'sectarians', and overtones of Church and quotations from the Gospel reduced to negligible proportions. The audience's reaction was unenthusiastic and Verdi set out to make his libretto proof against outside interference, rejecting a possible performance at la Scala and eventually seven years after the première re-writing the opera as *Aroldo* (see page 893), with Protestant clergymen turned into crusaders. 'It is difficult not to feel he took the dramatic heart from the opera,' wrote Julian Budden, 'often replacing the new and the arresting with stage cliché.' In its original form, *Stiffelio* was for years hardly known and often assumed to be inferior to the re-written *Aroldo*.

Stiffelio has been travelling and preaching; during his absence, his wife Lina has had a brief affair with a neighbour, Raffaele von Leuthold, which she is now anxious to end and to forget.

Act I. The overture (a potpourri of melodies from the opera) takes us to a hall in Count Stankar's castle. Jorg invokes heaven's blessing on Stiffelio's work as a preacher and allows himself the hope that Stiffelio's love for his wife may prove no impediment to his zeal – Jorg throughout the opera seems to stand as an embodiment of the spiritual side of Stiffelio's life. Stiffelio tells his assembled friends that he has heard that a man, apparently in the grip of terror, has been observed making his escape from the castle. The fugitive left some papers behind, and these Stiffelio, spurning to uncover what he supposes a guilty intrigue, throws into the fire. In an effective septet, the characters give vent to their feelings, Stiffelio of brotherly mercy towards brother, Jorg, Dorothea and Federico in tune with him, Lina and Raffaele of their joint guilt, and Stankar of his suspicions of his daughter's secret – feelings they continue to vent during the *stretta* which succeeds it.

When Lina is left alone with Stiffelio, she calls him by the name by which she first knew him, Rodolfo Müller, at the time when her father provided him with refuge from a hostile crowd. He tells her how deeply he missed her during his journeys, but speaks with some severity of the infidelities he all too frequently observed. He does not find it easy to forgive them. Stiffelio senses something is wrong, then finds that Lina's ring given her by his mother is missing. In a moment we feel welling up the fury he has so far successfully disguised and which given sufficient cause could at any moment erupt.

Stankar calls him away and Lina is left alone to pray in a beautiful aria to God for pardon ('A te ascenda, o Dio clemente'). She resolves on a letter of confession to Stiffelio, but her father reproaches her for lack of nerve which is in itself unworthy, and, if she confess her sin, will bring about her husband's death. She must dissemble so that not only is Stiffelio's honour saved but that of the Stankar family as well. This powerfully developed scene between father and daughter is worthy of one of the lines which run so productively through Verdi's operas.

Raffaele is bent on arranging an assignation and secretes a letter for Lina in a book, locking it with a key to which only she has a duplicate. Federico picks up the book and walks off with it.

In a reception hall of the castle, a party has gathered to celebrate Stiffelio's return. Jorg hints to Stiffelio that an intrigue is afoot and that the guilty man carry-

Stiffelio *(Covent Garden, 1995, director Elijah Moshinsky, designer Michael Yeargan, costumes Peter J. Hall). Act I: Stiffelio (Placido Domingo) notices the ring is missing from the hand of his wife Lina (Catherine Malfitano).*

ing a book is now with Lina. When Federico, who holds the book, starts to question Stiffelio about the theme of his sermon, the latter replies in peremptory tones: 'The base treachery of the wicked'. As his temper mounts, he snatches the book and demands that Lina open it, then himself breaks the lock so that a letter falls out. Stankar retrieves it and tears it up, whereupon Stiffelio turns his impotent rage on his father-in-law. This is one of those full-blooded finales which belong essentially to Verdi's middle period, with a slow meditative middle section before the eruption of Stiffelio's full fury. Stankar, who is in full knowledge of the intrigue, challenges Raffaele to a duel.

Act II. The prelude is full of atmosphere – Julian Budden finds in it a foreshadowing of the music leading to the gallows scene in *Ballo*. Lina comes to the graveyard to pray for her dead mother's help ('Ah! dagli scanni eterei').

Raffaele, still intent on resuming his affair, urges his love for Lina, who demands he prove it by returning her letters and her ring. In a spirited cabaletta she reiterates her demand that he leave her in peace. He refuses, but Stankar intervenes to dismiss his daughter and press Raffaele to meet his challenge. The latter refuses, but Stankar threatens to reveal him as an adventurer who is no count but a mere foundling. Raffaele seizes a sword but as they start to fight they are interrupted by Stiffelio, who demands they reconcile their differences.

Stankar lets slip that Raffaele was the guilty seducer of Lina and when she reappears but can find no word to deny her guilt, Stiffelio knows the truth and the finale is under way. A hymn can be heard coming from the church and Jorg joins his voice to the off-stage singers who beg Stiffelio for comfort and spiritual sustenance. The act ends with Stiffelio calling down malediction on the head of the faithless woman while the others pray for divine mercy.

Act III. We are again inside Stankar's castle and a fiery orchestral introduction precedes Stankar's denunciation of Raffaele who has fled the district and is trying to persuade Lina to follow him. Stankar contemplates suicide but seems to reject the idea of abandoning Stiffelio and his daughter for whom his love is unabated. The music's gentle cantilena suggests an unsuspectedly tender side to Stankar. Jorg enters and Stankar hides the pistol he was about to turn on himself. Jorg says he has overtaken Raffaele in his

flight, and the prospect of revenge causes a sudden if totally unchristian revulsion in Stankar, whose feelings burst forth in a cabaletta (marked *pianissimo* by Verdi, who found suspect the dramatic stamina of his original baritone and preferred to rely on his soft singing, broken only by a sudden *fortissimo* towards the end).

Stiffelio, in quieter mood than when we last saw him, has sent for Raffaele and asks him what he would do if Lina were free to marry him. He conceals Raffaele nearby and tells Lina he will leave her to the man she loves. Since they were married under a false name, divorce can end their marriage with no complications. Lina protests her love but Stiffelio seems determined and Lina is prevailed upon to sign. She turns to Stiffelio, addressing him as 'Minister', not husband, and begging him to hear her confession ('Ministro, Ministro, confessatemi!'). This was one of the cuts insisted upon by the censor before the first performance. The transparent sincerity of her protestation that her love has been only for Stiffelio moves husband as well as priest, but they are interrupted by the appearance of Stankar, bloodied sword in hand, announcing Raffaele's death. Stiffelio finds the building accursed and urges them to the church.

Inside a Gothic building, organ music plays as the congregation assembles. All pray for God's grace, Lina disguised among them, and Stankar joins his voice with the others, comparing himself, with more than a hint of disingenuity, to the repentant David. Stiffelio does not at first recognise the veiled Lina, but when she lifts her disguise is inspired to read from the gospel the passage describing Jesus's mercy towards the woman taken in adultery: 'Whichever among you is without sin, let him cast the first stone'. His cries of 'perdonata' are taken up by the congregation and Lina raises herself from her knees. Her pleas have been heard.   H.

RIGOLETTO

Opera in three acts, text by Francesco Maria Piave, after Victor Hugo's *Le Roi s'amuse*. Première at Teatro la Fenice, Venice, 11 March 1851, with Teresina Brambilla, Raffaele Mirate and Felice Varesi.

The Duke of Mantua..Tenor

Rigoletto, *his jester, a hunchback* ....Baritone

Count Ceprano, *a nobleman* ....Bass

Count Monterone, *a nobleman* ....Baritone

Sparafucile, *a professional assassin* ....Bass

Matteo Borsa, *a courtier* ....Tenor

Cavaliere Marullo, *a courtier* ....Baritone

Countess Ceprano ....Mezzo-Soprano

Gilda, *Rigoletto's daughter* ....Soprano

Giovanna, *her duenna* ....Mezzo-Soprano

Maddalena, *Sparafucile's sister* ....Contralto

Courtiers, Noblemen, Pages, Servants

Place: Mantua
Time: Sixteenth Century
Running Time: 2 hours 10 minutes

Both Victor Hugo's play and the libretto of Verdi's opera ran into trouble with the censors, not surprisingly since the only character with moral fibre in a licentious court is a court jester, who moreover plots the assassination of an absolute ruler, his master. Hugo's play was proscribed after the first night and the censor caused the venue of Verdi's opera to be removed from real-life France under François I to a fictitious court of Mantua under a Duke. The essence of a closed society, where one man's word was absolute, was of course preserved, as also the elegant and light-hearted figure of the ruler-as-seducer, the Duke's music running the gamut from the throwaway brilliance of the start through the romantic fervour of his wooing of Gilda, the tenderness of his aria of regret at losing his latest love up to the grandeur of the great quartet in the last scene. The dominating role nonetheless is that of Rigoletto, the climax one might say of Verdi's obsession with the baritone voice as protagonist. He wrote for a higher-based baritone than had Rossini, Bellini or Donizetti, and here the overall *tessitura* is perhaps higher than in any other of his scores.

By contrast, the other roles are less extensively developed, though so plentifully endowed with music that singers since early performances have queued to undertake them. Gilda is no more than an *ingénue* but few others have every turn of their feelings so acutely characterised; Maddalena emerges as a personality in a few bars of music; Sparafucile is more than just a 'bravo' and Monterone in a role lasting no more than two or three minutes stands as one of the most rewarding small parts in Italian opera.

The story is concerned with the conflict between Rigoletto's public position as licensed jester and his private life as devoted but clandestine father. To a superstitious man the collision between them seems inescapable when at court he mocks the heartbreak of Monterone only in his turn to feel the lash of a father's curse.

Act I. The music associated with the curse dominates the prelude, leading into a brilliant court scene, which serves as background to the amorous activities of the Duke, who enters with Rigoletto in attendance. A fresh young beauty has recently caught his eye but Countess Ceprano is his immediate quarry, variety being central to his escapades: 'Questa o quella' (This one or that one). He dances a minuet with the Countess and disappears with her, heedless of comment, least of all from her husband, who falls victim to Rigoletto's caustic tongue. Marullo tells anyone who will listen that he has discovered Rigoletto has a young *innamorata*, which suggests to Ceprano a possible line of revenge. Monterone bursts in and with dignity and grandeur denounces the Duke as the seducer of his daughter. Rigoletto volunteers to receive him and makes sport of a father's misery. In his turn Monterone calls down a curse on Rigoletto's head as retribution. Rigoletto's reaction is almost pathological – this is his Achilles heel – and the idea of the father's cursing haunts him throughout the opera.

Scene ii. A street outside Rigoletto's house, Ceprano's palace at one side of it. Memories of Monterone and his curse haunt Rigoletto, but he is confronted by the figure of Sparafucile, who announces himself, to a subtly contrived 'nocturne' accompaniment, as a 'sword' for hire. Rigoletto says he has no need of such services, but we are left in little doubt that he has stored up information about Sparafucile's whereabouts against possible future use. It is a scene of extraordinary subtlety, conducted mostly in a kind of musical whisper. Rigoletto's soliloquy, 'Pari siamo' (How like we are!), impressively contrasts his own and his master's situations, but it is the father's curse which has seized his imagination and it is still on his mind when he unlocks the door to his garden and Gilda runs out to meet him.

Their scene, full of musical invention, is one of great tenderness, as the music successively mirrors Rigoletto's injunction that she must never leave the garden except to go to church, his constant grief over the death of Gilda's mother, and Gilda's protestations of filial love and absolute fidelity to his wishes, the first a more accurate representation of her attitude than the second of her behaviour. As he consigns Gilda to the care of Giovanna ('Ah, veglia, o donna'), there are noises off and the Duke, with Giovanna's help, contrives to conceal himself inside the garden. Rigoletto leaves.

Gilda is a prey to worry that she has concealed from her father the attentions of a young man who followed her from church; when she turns she is confronted with none other than the young man himself, who tells her he is a student and that he loves her. 'E il sol dell'anima', he declares, and their duet celebrates young love until sounds of movement outside precipitate an impassioned farewell. Gilda's graceful aria, 'Caro nome', confirms her romantic involvement. She has no sooner gone up to her room than a group of courtiers appears in the street intent on abducting Rigoletto's mistress and so avenging Ceprano. When Rigoletto returns he is blindfolded, under guise of fitting a mask, and then roped in to help in what he is assured is the capture of Countess Ceprano (Chorus: 'Zitti, zitti, moviamo a vendetta'). The scheme works, the courtiers are triumphant and Rigoletto is left frenziedly lamenting Monterone's fateful curse.

Act II. The ducal palace. The Duke is disconsolate – the cut of the music of 'Parmi veder le lagrime' leaves no doubt that, however free with his affections, he is a man of feelings. He learns from the courtiers that they have abducted Rigoletto's *innamorata*, and once he has gone, they lie in wait to torment the jester. Rigoletto is obviously on edge, searching for any clue as to Gilda's whereabouts and only convinced she is already with the Duke when a page is turned away with obviously fabricated excuses. He rounds on the courtiers, who for the first time learn that it is his daughter and not his mistress they have turned over to the Duke's pleasure, and in a magnificent outburst denounces them for their cruelty: 'Cortigiani, vil razza dannata' (Oh you courtiers, vile rabble, accursed).

In a moment, Gilda is in the room, the courtiers have been thrown out, and she is telling her father of the young man who followed her from church ('Tutte le feste al tempio'). Rigoletto gently consoles her ('Piangi fanciulla'), then, after watching Monterone led towards his death, hurls himself into a violent pledge of vengeance, which may purge at the same time the crime against his daughter and the curse laid on him ('Si! vendetta! tremenda vendetta!').

Act III. Sparafucile's house – an inn – which must be split to show both outside and inside. With him lives his sister, who acts as decoy for his victims. From outside, Rigoletto and Gilda observe Sparafucile greet the Duke, who is in disguise and proceeds to sing what has become perhaps the most famous song in all opera: 'La donna è mobile'. Legend has it Verdi withheld it from rehearsal until the last possible moment for fear it would, even before the first night, become known all over Venice.

Sparafucile finalises his bargain with Rigoletto, who will pay half the agreed money in advance, the rest on delivery of the body of the Duke. Maddalena, Sparafucile's sister, makes her appearance, to the discomfiture of Gilda, who still assures her father that she loves the man she now watches making advances to another woman. A great quartet develops, led by the Duke who in a soaring melody seems to be serenading not so much the relatively inconsequential figure of Maddalena as womankind in general ('Bella figlia dell'amore'). Maddalena responds in a quick *staccato* melody, Gilda laments around the top of the stave while Rigoletto at the bottom mutters vengeance. There is no more famous (and no better) ensemble in nineteenth-century Italian opera.

Rigoletto sends his daughter away with instructions to disguise herself and ride to Verona, meanwhile reviewing his bargain with Sparafucile and reserving for himself the satisfaction of throwing the body in due course into the river. A storm blows up and during its course Maddalena, who finds the young man attractive, proposes her brother kill Rigoletto instead of the Duke and pocket the second half of his fee. But he will have none of what he sees as an immorality, and when Gilda surreptitiously returns, the original bargain is still in place. In the end, Sparafucile relents and agrees to kill whoever next arrives at the inn. Gilda overhears and, at the end of a dramatic trio, knocks on the door. The lights are extinguished, there is a half-stifled cry, more storm music and, when Rigoletto returns with the money and accepts the corpse-filled sack, he is taken aback to hear the Duke's 'La donna è mobile' coming from inside the inn. As the last top B natural dies away, he tears open the sack to find Gilda's body. She dies after a long, sad farewell to her father, who is left to lament the father's curse laid nearly three acts earlier ('Lassù in ciel').

With *Rigoletto* Verdi began what was to become a

trio of operas of unparalleled popularity, completed by *Trovatore* and *Traviata* and all performed within the space of two years. There are substantial differences between them but the mastery is consistent, whether the inimitable concision of the first scene of *Rigoletto* and the tunefulness of the rest of the score, the demotic appeal of Manrico in *Trovatore* contrasting with the aristocratic manners of his opponent di Luna and his lover Leonora, or the novelty in *La Traviata* of the contemporary theme and its impact on the composer. H.

IL TROVATORE

The Troubadour

Opera in four acts, text by Salvatore Cammarano from the Spanish play of the same title by Antonio Garcia Gutiérrez. Première at the Teatro Apollo, Rome, 19 January 1853, with Penco, Goggi, Baucardé, Guicciardi, Balderi.

Count di Luna, *a young nobleman* ....Baritone

Ferrando, *captain of his guard* ....Bass

Manrico, *supposed son to Azucena and a rebel under Prince Urgel* ....Tenor

Ruiz, *a soldier in Manrico's service* ....Tenor

An Old Gipsy ....Baritone

Doña Leonora, *lady-in-waiting to the Princess of Aragon* .... Soprano

Inez, *confidante of Leonora* ....Soprano

Azucena, *a gipsy woman from Biscay*...................................Mezzo-Soprano

Followers of Count di Luna and of Manrico; Messenger, Gipsies, Soldiers, Nuns

Place: Aragon and Biscay
Time: Fifteenth Century
Running Time: 2 hours 15 minutes

In Verdi's output *Il Trovatore* is unsurpassed for prodigality of melody, energy and sheer popular appeal. It is also notorious for incomprehensibility of plot, a reputation which is not entirely fair. It is however a fact that crucial elements of the story occur before the stage action starts, so that the prospective listener must bone up on it beforehand; moreover the complications of the original story are retained and compressed, with results which are telegraphic in the terse way they re-tell a story which was never without convolutions.

Verdi encountered the subject in early 1850, but composition was not started until autumn 1851.

The legend that virtually the entire opera was composed between 1 and 29 November 1852 is probably false, but Verdi was a quick worker and nowhere in his output is there more evidence of the white heat of inspiration.

Spain is torn by civil war. Leonora is lady-in-waiting to the wife of the Prince of Aragon, in whose cause Count di Luna is fighting; Manrico, the so-called gipsy with whom she is in love, fights for the insurgents led by Prince Urgel. The mystery of Manrico's birth raises its head from time to time but is not finally resolved until the opera's last moments, when it transpires that Azucena, in her overwrought attempt to avenge the murder of her mother (on the orders of di Luna's father), had thrown her own son rather than the Count's into the flames. She knows the truth and it haunts her throughout the action.

Act I. The guardroom of the Palace of Aliaferia. Ferrando, captain of the guard, with a shout wakes his companions, warning them not to be sleeping when the Count returns from his nightly vigil beneath the windows of Leonora's apartments, a vigil necessitated by his fear that a rival is preferred by Leonora. Ferrando recounts, not for the first time we may imagine, the story of how a gipsy woman put a spell on one of the sons of the Count di Luna, was apprehended and burnt at the stake ('Abbietta zingara'). Her daughter contrived to make away with the boy and a little later the charred bones of a child were found not far away. The old Count looked in vain for his son and made the surviving brother, now their master, swear to continue the search.

The gardens of the palace. Leonora and Inez wait for Leonora's unknown but favoured suitor. 'Tacea la notte placida' is one of the grandest and most effective of the arias in which Verdi in his early operas liked to introduce a leading female character. Leonora's graceful cabaletta, 'Di tale amor', is no less appealing. The ladies re-enter the palace and Count di Luna comes into the garden, to be met almost immediately, and thoroughly disconcerted by, the sound of the troubadour preparing to serenade Leonora. 'Deserto sulla terra' he sings until Leonora, hearing his voice, comes out of the palace and, mistaking the Count for the serenader, hastens towards him. Manrico comes out of the shadows, and Leonora cannot prevent the two men drawing their swords and fighting (trio: 'Di geloso amor sprezzato').

Act II. The gipsy camp in Biscay. The gipsies sing the so-called Anvil Chorus, one of nineteenth-century opera's most famous numbers. Azucena, who is sitting with them, seems mesmerised by the fire (aria: 'Stride la vampa'), and recalls her mother's death at the stake and cry for revenge. Her son Manrico asks her to tell him the story once again and she goes through the narrative ('Condotta ell'era in ceppi'), amazing him by her incoherent references to the death of her own son in the flames rather than the Count's. She reassures him, but in her turn questions him as to why he spared the life of di Luna in battle when he had him at his mercy. In the splendidly martial 'Mal raggendo all'aspro assalto', Manrico explains that a hidden force caused him to stay his hand: he felt he could not kill his adversary. A messenger from the Prince brings an order for Manrico to go immediately to defend Castellor, adding that Leonora, believing him dead, plans to enter a nunnery. Manrico springs into action and Azucena's pleas ('Perigliarti ancor') fail to move him from his decision.

The cloister of a convent. Stealthily at night the Count and his followers group themselves in order when she appears to abduct Leonora. He sings of his love for her in one of the most beautiful solos of the baritone repertory: 'Il balen del suo sorriso'. It is followed by a determined *cabaletta alla marcia*, 'Per me ora fatale', which suggests di Luna is very much a man to be reckoned with. A chorus of nuns is heard from the convent and they are about to process to the cloister when the Count makes his move only for Manrico and his followers to forestall him, to Leonora's infinite relief. 'E deggio! e posso crederlo' she sings, leading an impassioned finale at whose end Manrico frees Leonora and departs.

Act III. Di Luna's camp. He is laying siege to Castellor, where Manrico has taken Leonora, and his army sings stirringly of the pleasures of gambling. The Count emerges from his tent to be confronted with a gipsy woman captured as she was prowling round the camp. She protests she is a poor traveller ('Giorni poveri vivea'), but Ferrando claims to recognise her as the gipsy who, to avenge her mother, kidnapped the old Count's son. When she calls on Manrico for help, di Luna in a paroxysm of rage condemns her to be burnt.

A hall in Castellor. Leonora is about to become Manrico's bride, and he sings of his love in expansive phrases culminating in a marvellous lyrical inspira-

tion: 'Ah sì, ben mio coll'essere'. Happiness is to be short-lived as Ruiz rushes in with word that Azucena has been captured and will shortly be burnt alive. Manrico seizes his sword and launches into the vigorous cabaletta 'Di quella pira', a rousing solo crowned in many performances with the most famous unscripted top C in opera (or, transposed, with a B natural) – Verdi did not write the note but he must have heard it many times and it is far from contradicting the spirit of the music.

Act IV. Outside a tower in the palace of Aliaferia. Manrico's sortie to rescue his mother has failed and he is a prisoner in the tower. Leonora is led in by Ruiz, and in a magnificent aria she prays for him in his captivity, 'D'amor sull'ali rosee', with its long lines a test of any Verdian soprano's capacity. There follows the Miserere, when, to the sound of chanting within, Leonora sings brokenly of her foreboding and Manrico despairingly of his love for her. Few nineteenth-century Italian operatic tunes are more famous, few more effective in context. Leonora caps the scene with an impassioned *stretta*, 'Tu vedrai che amore in terra'.

The Count confronts Leonora. She promises to become his if he will free Manrico. Di Luna's passion urges him to agree. There is a solo for Leonora, 'Mira d'acerbe lagrime', followed by a duet between her and the Count, who little suspects that, Manrico once at liberty, she will take the poison hidden in her ring and escape his clutches.

The interior of the tower. Manrico and Azucena lie in prison. Azucena raves of the pyre on which her mother perished, and Manrico tries in long, expressive phrases to calm her spirit. In a mood between sleeping and waking, she intones a haunting melody 'Ai nostri monti', while Manrico continues his attempt to soothe her forebodings. Leonora comes to urge him to escape, but he immediately suspects the price she has paid, suspicions confirmed as the poison starts to take effect. Leonora dies in Manrico's arms; di Luna returns to find her dead and promptly orders Manrico's execution. He drags Azucena to the window to witness her son's death, and it is a Pyrrhic victory she wins as she calls out 'He was your brother!'

Il Trovatore was never easy to cast and has always required, as Caruso is supposed to have pointed out, no less than 'the four best singers in the world'. Di Luna and Leonora are representatives of an energetic aristocratic world whose aspirations are perfectly mirrored in their consistently grand utterances, but the powerfully characterised Azucena is another story, one of Verdi's most original creations and a challenge to any leading mezzo. Manrico has, wrongly and over the years, become associated with a muscular top C, whereas for most of the role the music requires a singer combining delicacy and refinement with the energy which is an equally essential part of Manrico's armoury.   H.

LA TRAVIATA
The Fallen Woman

Opera in three acts, text by Francesco Maria Piave after Alexandre Dumas's play *La Dame aux Camélias*. Première at Teatro la Fenice, Venice, 6 March 1853, with Salvini-Donatelli, Graziani, Varesi.

Alfredo Germont...Tenor
Giorgio Germont, *his father* ....Baritone
Gastone de Letorières ....Tenor
Baron Douphol...Baritone
Marchese d'Obigny ....Bass
Doctor Grenvil ....Bass
Giuseppe, *Violetta's servant*..............................Tenor
Violetta Valéry, *a courtesan*............................Soprano
Flora Bervoix, *her friend*.....................Mezzo-Soprano
Annina, *Violetta's maid*..................................Soprano

Ladies and Gentlemen, Servants and Masks, Dancers and Guests

Place: Paris and Vicinity
Time: 1850
Running Time: 2 hours 10 minutes

Alexandre Dumas *fils* at the age of twenty fell in love with the brilliant courtesan, Marie Duplessis, a girl from the country whose praises were sung even after her death by all who had met her. She died from tuberculosis in 1847, and Dumas published his novel, *La Dame aux Camélias*, in 1848, deriving a play from it the following year. That was not performed until 1852 but Verdi and Piave, searching for an operatic subject for the Carnival in Venice in 1853, decided on it in November 1852. Legend once had it that initial failure was because the audience could not accept a risqué story played in a contemporary setting, but the fact is that in Venice it was played in the costumes of 1700 (even though Verdi's contract stipulated modern dress) and that scores continued to specify that period until well after the composer's death.

The prelude's opening section is concerned with the music before Violetta's death, its second with her impassioned cry of 'Amami Alfredo' in Act II. Violetta is giving a party and Gastone informs her that Alfredo, who is there, has fallen seriously in love with her. Alfredo leads a spirited brindisi ('Libiamo ne' lieti calici'), and there is dancing in the next room which Violetta is about to join when she feels faint. Alfredo remains behind and gracefully admits his love: 'Un dì felice, eterea', Violetta echoing his mood while appearing to mock. The phrase 'Di quell'amor ch'è palpito' (All that has life has its breath from you) in the course of the opera takes on something of the character of a love motif, and before the end of the act Violetta repeats it in her aria.

Alfredo and the other guests retire and Violetta is lost in contemplation, her heart perhaps touched for the first time: 'Ah, fors'è lui'. At the end of the aria, her mood changes from introspection and she bursts into what is musically a celebration of dawning love at the same time as the words she sings deny any such possibility. A scene of marvellous power, as the music develops to echo Violetta's burgeoning love.

Act II. Violetta and Alfredo are living together in the country. He sings of his joy in his life with her ('De' miei bollenti spiriti'), but is disturbed when he learns from the maid Annina that Violetta has been selling her jewellery in order to pay the bills. He will go to Paris to raise money! Violetta opens a note from Flora inviting her to a party in Paris and smiles at the mere idea she might return there. When a visitor is announced she assumes it will be her lawyer but it turns out to be Alfredo's father, come to persuade her to give up his son in order that no breath of scandal may attach to the forthcoming wedding of his daughter. His harsh tone soon softens when it is apparent she is not the gold-digger he had assumed he would find. Their scene together, cast in the loosely-knit duet form Verdi mined so productively throughout his operas, is the centrepiece of the opera, and we pass through Germont's plea for his daughter's happiness ('Pura siccome un'angelo'), and Violetta's attempt to put the opposite case, to reach the moment when in a tune of infinite pathos ('Ah, dite alla giovine') she ceases to resist what she now accepts is inevitable. Germont does not find it hard to love her for what she has promised to do and he assures her – not too convincingly – that she will not regret it. He for his part will at some time in the future tell Alfredo that in spite of appearances to the contrary her love for him never faltered.

In its way, nineteenth-century opera contains no more involving, indeed moving, scene, and yet no twentieth-century listener fails to condemn the elder Germont for his heartless destruction of a vulnerable woman's life – a tribute to the internal dramatic logic of the situation, given acceptance of the principle on which it is based, or to the power and beauty of Verdi's music?

Violetta writes Alfredo a note telling him she is going back to her old life, to be kept by Baron Douphol, but when he appears, she hides what she has been writing. He says he has heard from his father that he is on his way in an attempt to separate them, and Violetta, as she says goodbye, pours out her heart in an almost wordless protest against the unfairness of her position ('Amami Alfredo'), for the soprano, one of the opera's emotional touchstones.

Alfredo is handed Violetta's letter, but he has hardly digested its contents before his father enters and, in one of the most famous of baritone arias, offers comfort ('Di Provenza, il mar, il suol'). Alfredo nonetheless dashes off to Paris.

The second scene is at Flora's party, where festivities are in full swing. Alfredo comes in on his own, closely followed by Violetta on the arm of the Baron. 'Unlucky in love, lucky at cards' is Alfredo's comment, and he and the Baron play before supper is announced. Violetta has asked Alfredo to meet her alone, but her words only fan the flames of his jealousy and he summons the other guests to insult her in front of them all. His father intervenes, the Baron issues a challenge, and Violetta recovers from a fainting fit to sing lyrically of the love for Alfredo she still holds within her heart ('Alfredo, Alfredo, di questo core').

Act III. Violetta lies mortally ill in bed. The slow, sad prelude echoes that of the first act, but with nothing this time to contrast with the tragedy. Violetta wakes to read, for the hundredth time, the letter she has had from Germont telling her that the Baron was wounded in the duel and that Alfredo now knows of her sacrifice and is on his way to see her. She senses the approach of death and her aria, 'Addio del passato', suggests a sigh from the depths of a purified soul. Revellers can be heard below and in a moment Alfredo is in the room and holding her in his arms. 'Parigi, o cara, noi lasceremo' (We shall fly from Paris, beloved) he sings, and Violetta seems at first to believe him. But she knows she is dying ('Gran Dio! Morir si giovane': O God, to die so young), and, watched by Annina, Germont and the doctor, at peace with the world, she breathes her last.

La Traviata is Verdi's second setting of a contemporary subject, *Stiffelio* his first, and this is only the second time he wholly abandoned the grand public events and gestures which had so far provided him with subjects and accepted something more intimate (*Luisa Miller* preceded *Traviata*). It represents a logical build on the intimate scenes of *Rigoletto*, and for its unheroic, bourgeois world the composer had to find what amounted to a new style, an achievement the more remarkable since for much of the time he was writing *Traviata* he was preoccupied with *Trovatore*, whose première took place less than two months before that of *Traviata*. Form is more flexible, vocal writing on the whole more delicate than in earlier operas, and one may wonder what nineteenth-century Italian opera rivals in subtlety this extraordinary work, which may owe much of its naturalness and the credibility of its dialogue to the original play but is transformed by Verdi's score from a comment on the life and times of its heroine into one on life itself. He wrote it at a time when he had for some time been living more or less openly with Giuseppina Strepponi, a retired opera singer and a remarkable woman, with several liaisons and more than one illegitimate child in her past. He was not to marry her until six years after the première of *La Traviata*. Verdi brooked no interference with his private life and criticism of his liaison with Giuseppina caused him to come close to severing connections with the small town of Busseto where he was born. Asked once which of his operas he considered his best the composer is said to have replied: 'Speaking as a professional, *Rigoletto*, as an amateur, *Traviata*'.   H.

LES VÊPRES SICILIENNES
I Vespri Siciliani – The Sicilian Vespers

Opera in five acts, text in French by Scribe and Charles Duveyrier. Première at the Opéra, Paris, with Cruvelli as Hélène, 13 June 1855. First performed in Italy, Parma, 1855; at la Scala, Milan, 1856 (as *Giovanna de Guzman*); at San Carlo,

Naples, 1857 (as *Batilde di Turenna*); Drury Lane, London, 1859; New York, 1859. Revived Stuttgart, 1929; Berlin, 1932, with Anni Konetzni, Roswaenge, Schlusnus, List, conductor Erich Kleiber; Palermo, 1937, with Arangi-Lombardi, Franco lo Giudice, Guicciardi, Vaghi, conductor Capuana; Genoa, 1939, with Scacciati, Olivato, Armando Borgioli, Pasero, conductor Gui; Florence Festival, 1951, with Callas, Kokolios, Mascherini, Christoff, conductor Erich Kleiber; la Scala, Milan, 1951, with substantially the same cast, conductor de Sabata; Cardiff, 1954, by Welsh National Opera. Successful modern revivals in productions by John Dexter with sets by Josef Svoboda have been in Hamburg, 1969; Metropolitan, 1974, with Caballé, Gedda, Milnes, Diaz, conductor James Levine; Paris, 1974 (in Italian), with Arroyo, Domingo; Florence, 1978, with Scotto, Luchetti, Bruson, Raimondi, conductor Muti; English National Opera, 1984, with Plowright, Ken Collins, Howlett, R. van Allan, conductor Mark Elder. La Scala, Milan, 1989, with Studer, Merritt, Zancanaro, Furlanetto, conductor Muti.

Hélène (Elena), *sister of*
    Frederick of Austria ....Soprano

Henri (Arrigo), *a young Sicilian*...........................Tenor

Guy de Montfort (Monforte),
    Governor of Sicily.......................................Baritone

Giovanni da Procida, *Sicilian doctor* ....Bass

De Béthune, *a French officer* ....Bass

Count Vaudemont, *a French officer* ....Bass

Ninetta, *in attendance on Hélène* ....Soprano

Danieli, *a young Sicilian* ....Tenor

Thibault (Tebaldo), *a French soldier*...................Tenor

Robert (Roberto), *a French soldier* ....Bass

Manfredo, *a Sicilian*..Tenor

Place: Palermo
Time: 1282
Running Time: 3 hours 10 minutes

*L*es Vêpres Siciliennes was commissioned for the Great Exhibition of 1855. Much as Verdi disliked the conditions of work in Paris, he could not but find it an honour to be asked to write music for so great an occasion in the artistic capital of the world. In the event, he hated the libretto, as offending the French because of the massacre at the end, and the Italians because of the treacherous behaviour of the Sicilian patriots, and his relations with Scribe were even the subject of comment in the newspapers. As if Verdi had not enough to bear, Cruvelli, the admirable soprano entrusted with the role of Hélène, elected to disappear without a word to anyone during rehearsals. 'She seems to have gone', says Francis Toye, 'on a kind of anticipatory honeymoon with one Baron Vigier, whom she married shortly afterwards.'

The opera is concerned with the occupation of Sicily by French troops during the thirteenth century, and the efforts of the Sicilians to dislodge them. The overture is one of Verdi's best, and is dominated by a long cello tune, taken from the duet in Act III between Henri and de Montfort.

Act I. A detachment of French troops is in the great square at Palermo, some of them drinking, others watching the crowd of Sicilians which eyes them sullenly from the other side of the square. The French sing of their enforced absence from their native land, the Sicilians of their hatred of their oppressors. An exchange between de Béthune, Robert, and Thibault indicates that there is nothing new about the proprietary attitude of occupying troops towards the women of the country.

At this moment the French notice Hélène crossing the square. She has been praying for her brother, who was executed by order of de Montfort for his patriotic activities. A drunken soldier is struck by her beauty and orders her to sing to entertain the French conquerors. Somewhat to his surprise she consents, but her song is not at all what it was expected to be. The loosely knit opening phrases and the long *cantabile* line lead to a sudden and inflammatory *allegro giusto*, which whips up the courage of the downcast Sicilians. It is a scene of considerable theatrical power and makes a great effect when sung by a soprano of the calibre of Maria Callas, who was in the revival at the Florence Festival in 1951. No one who heard her will forget her repeated 'Votre salut est dans vos mains' (Il vostro fato è in vostra man), nor the brilliant effect of her coloratura and top notes in the cabaletta itself.

The Sicilians rush at the French, but the abortive rising is quelled by the appearance of de Montfort, alone and unarmed, at the door of his palace. The square clears as if by magic, and Hélène, supported by her attendants Ninetta and Danieli, is left alone with de Montfort. Their quartet is mostly unaccompanied, and at its end Henri, who has been imprisoned, rushes up to Hélène with the news of his release. He does not notice de Montfort but, in spite of his openly expressed patriotic sentiments, is ordered by him to remain behind. The act ends with a duet between the two, in which de Montfort offers Henri fame in the service of the French. His offer is indignantly spurned, as is his command that Henri associate no more with the rebel Hélène, into whose palace without more ado Henri betakes himself.

Act II. Outside the city, in a valley. Procida, until his banishment leader of the Sicilian patriots, now returns secretly to stir up resistance. He salutes his beloved native land in a recitative and aria which has become perhaps the most famous number of the opera, 'O toi, Palermo'. In a cabaletta, he exhorts the small band of chosen patriots to prepare with him the deliverance of Sicily.

Hélène and Henri have been bidden to meet the exiled patriot, and he leaves them together while he goes off to set plans afoot, but not before he has enrolled Henri as one of the leaders of the projected revolt. Henri declares his love to Hélène and swears to avenge the death of her beloved brother. A messenger arrives from de Montfort bringing an invitation to Henri to attend a ball. He indignantly refuses it, and is surrounded by soldiers and led away.

Procida returns to learn of this new mishap, but he sees an opportunity of stirring up feeling against the French in the betrothal festivity which is about to take place, and for which a crowd can be seen approaching. He will suggest to the French that they carry off the young women, an outrage which may perhaps rouse the Sicilians from their apathy. Couples in festive attire dance a tarantella, but Procida's plan works all too well, and in a moment the French soldiers have fallen on the women, carried off some and put the rest to flight.

Only a few patriots are left behind with Procida and Hélène and together in half-strangled sentences they give vent to their feelings, which are further exacerbated by the sound of a complacent barcarolle being sung at sea by a boat-load of French pleasure-seekers. The two choruses combine effectively as the act comes to an end.

Act III. De Montfort is found alone in his palace. He reflects on the injustice he did years ago to the woman who became the mother of his son but escaped from him and brought up that son to hate his father as the oppressor of the Sicilians. Now, on her death-bed, she has written to him that the son he has not seen for eighteen years is no other than Henri, his sworn enemy. De Montfort's soliloquy 'Au sein de la puissance' (In braccio alle dovizie) gives effective expression to his indecision and agony of mind, and is in many ways more satisfactory than

the big duet between de Montfort and his newly found son which immediately follows it. Here occurs the tune first heard on the cellos in the overture, which, memorable though it is, has more than a little complacency about it when heard in its proper context – and complacency is the last thing felt by either father or son in their peculiar predicament.

The scene ends with Henri calling on his mother's memory, but at the beginning of the ballroom scene he is apparently sufficiently reconciled, at any rate temporarily, to accompany his father to the great hall, where together they watch the lengthy ballet of the seasons, which de Montfort has planned for the entertainment of his guests. This is a French ballet on a grand scale and, whatever its importance to the devotees of Grand Opera in its heyday, it tends nowadays to impress listeners mostly with its length – it lasts for half an hour – and the way it holds up the dramatic action at a crucial point.

Amongst the invited guests are to be seen a number of masked figures with silk ribbons fastened to their cloaks. These are the Sicilian conspirators, led by Procida and Hélène. The tension of Henri's predicament – whether to allow his father to be murdered, or to betray his friends – is skilfully suggested by the snatched conversations he has with Hélène and Procida in the midst of the general festivity. Finally, he makes an attempt to warn de Montfort that his life is in danger, but the governor refuses to leave the ball. When Procida advances upon him, Henri steps in between, the conspirators are arrested, and the act ends with an impressive concerted piece, in which the Sicilians unite in cursing the treachery of Henri.

Act IV. The great courtyard of the fortress. Henri has come, armed with a pass from de Montfort, to see the prisoners. In a sombre E minor aria, 'O jour de peine' (Giorno di pianto), he reflects on the situation he is in, when his dearest friends are likely to look upon him as their worst enemy. The thought of Hélène's hate is too much for him, he thinks he hears her coming up from her cell, and in an ecstasy he prays for her forgiveness. When Hélène appears, she does in fact greet him as a traitor, and repeats his words, 'Malheureux et non coupable' (Non son reo) after him ironically, until he admits to her that their enemy is his own father. Her tone changes to one of pity, and later she admits in a ravishing Bellini-like cantilena that her greatest sorrow in prison was the

Les vêpres siciliennes *(English National Opera, 1984, director John Dexter, designer Josef Svoboda).*
Rosalind Plowright as Hélène in the final scene.

necessity to think of the man she loves as a traitor. Their music takes on the character of a love duet, before Procida is led out of the prison by the guards. He sees Henri, but ascribes his apparent repentance to yet another treacherous trick.

De Montfort enters and orders that the preparations for the double execution shall go forward straight away, in spite of the pleading of Henri, who demands to die with them – such an honour, says Procida, is too great for so notorious a traitor. De Montfort bids Henri pay no attention to the insults of his erstwhile comrades; let him but remember that he is his son. Procida is stupefied at this totally unexpected revelation, and in a few moving phrases bids farewell to the country for whose ideals he has fought. His phrases lead to a quartet (with Hélène, Henri, de Montfort) of considerable beauty, which in its turn gives way to the execution music, heard already in the overture but now assuming considerable poignancy, with de Montfort urging that pardon will only be given if Henri will address him as Father. Henri is hesitant, Hélène and Procida emphatic that death is preferable to dishonour, and all the time the sound of the funeral hymn accompanies the victims as they draw nearer to the block and the headsman's axe.

At last Henri gives in to de Montfort's dearest wish, pardon is forthwith granted and with it a general amnesty. The troth of Hélène and Henri is announced, and the curtain falls on a general ensemble.

Act V. The gardens of de Montfort's palace. The wedding of Hélène and Henri is about to be celebrated. After a chorus, Hélène sings her well-known *Bolero*, 'Merci, jeunes amies' (Merce, dilette amiche), a lively and appropriate display piece. Henri joins her and sings a charming air, 'La brise souffle au loin plus légère et plus pure' (La brezza aleggia intorno a carrezzarmi il viso), an entirely lyrical interlude in what is by no means otherwise a predominantly lyrical score.

Henri disappears and Hélène is joined by Procida, now more than ever the plotter with a dagger ever conveniently to hand, for whose over-simplified drawing Verdi so much reproached Scribe. He congratulates Hélène on having provided with her wedding the opportunity for the Sicilian patriots to fall on the unarmed French, and tells her that the ringing of the bells will be the signal for the massacre.

Nothing she can say will deflect the fanatic from his purpose and he defies her to denounce him to the French and so prevent the carrying out of his plan. Hélène's only reply is to refuse to go through with the wedding, much to Henri's consternation. There is an impressive and extended trio for Hélène, Henri, and Procida, which dominates the finale. De Montfort enters, sweeps aside Hélène's objections, the cause of which has not been revealed to him, and himself pronounces the betrothal, at the same time ordering the bells to ring out. The Sicilians rush from their hiding-places, and Procida's revenge is complete.

Les Vêpres Siciliennes has been much criticised and it is true that it does not reach the heights of *Don Carlos* or *Simon Boccanegra*. On the other hand, recent revivals have been attended by a good deal of success, and the unfamiliar music is in the habit of striking its listeners as vastly better than commentators have made out. In the first act, Hélène's aria and the unaccompanied quartet are brilliantly successful numbers, and in the second, 'O toi Palermo' is one of Verdi's most famous bass arias. De Montfort's monologue at the beginning of Act III is of an expressive quality worthy of Philip himself, and the choral finale after the attempted murder is most effective. The whole of the fourth act is on Verdi's highest level, the solo for Henri and that for Hélène in the middle of their scene together being outstandingly successful, and the moment of suspense before the execution most movingly done. The fifth act can seem rather long in performance, but Henri's lyrical tune and the large-scale trio are first-rate.   H.

SIMON BOCCANEGRA

Opera in three acts and a prologue, text by Francesco Maria Piave, from a play by Gutiérrez. Première at the Teatro la Fenice, Venice, 12 March 1857, with Bendazzi, Negrini, Giraldoni, Echeverria, Vercellini. First performed in revised version (textual alterations by Boito), la Scala, Milan, 1881, with d'Angeri, Tamagno, Maurel, Edouard de Reszke, conductor Faccio. Revived Vienna (in Werfel's version), 1930, with Nemeth, von Pataky, Rode, Manowarda, conductor Krauss; Berlin, 1930, with Reinmar; Metropolitan, New York, 1932, with Müller, Martinelli, Tibbett, Pinza, conductor Serafin; la Scala, 1933, with Caniglia, Bagnariol, Galeffi, de Angelis, conductor Gui; Sadler's Wells, 1948, with Gartside, Johnston, Matters, Glynne, conductor Mudie; Metropolitan, New York, 1949, with Varnay, Tucker, Warren, Szekely, conductor

Stiedry; Covent Garden, 1965, with Gobbi. Revived la Scala, Milan, 1972, with Freni, Raimondi, Schiavi, Ghiaurov, conductor Abbado, producer Strehler.

Amelia Boccanegra *(sometimes called Maria, and under the name of Amelia Grimaldi during Act I)*..Soprano
Gabriele Adorno, *a patrician* ....Tenor
Simon Boccanegra, *a plebeian, later Doge*.......Baritone
Jacopo Fiesco, *a patrician*....................................Bass
Paolo Albiani, *a plebeian*..............................Baritone
Pietro, *a plebeian*...Bass
A Captain ....Tenor

Place: In and Near Genoa
Time: Fourteenth Century
Running Time: 2 hours 35 minutes

*S*imon Boccanegra was unsuccessful when first performed in Venice, and indeed Verdi himself referred to this first version as 'monotonous and cold', so that it is not surprising that he chose to revise the opera over twenty years after the first performance. At this time he had written *Aida* and the *Requiem* and plans for *Otello* already existed in his mind, and it was to Boito, as his prospective collaborator in the greater enterprise of *Otello*, that he entrusted the revision. In this version the opera has gradually and deservedly won its way into the international repertory.

Genoa in the fourteenth century was ruled by an elected Doge, who had hitherto always been chosen from the ranks of the patricians. Fiesco, who is in office when the story begins, has a daughter, Maria, who has fallen in love with a plebeian, Simon Boccanegra, and borne him a daughter. Simon's seafaring exploits, in the course of which he cleared the seas of the African pirates who so impeded the smooth course of Genoa's trade, have won him considerable fame but not the right to treat the Doge's daughter as his equal. Their child was looked after at Pisa by an old woman while he was at sea, until one day on his return home he found the old lady dead, and his daughter vanished. Since then, he has sought her in vain, and he does not know that she was found wandering on the sea shore by Count Grimaldi and brought up by him as his own child.

Prologue. Paolo, political leader of the plebeians, and Pietro, an influential member of the movement, are in conversation, the latter proposing that

Lorenzino shall be the plebeian choice for Doge, the former suggesting that Boccanegra would be a better candidate. Pietro agrees to organise the people's vote for Boccanegra in return for honour and riches for himself. Boccanegra has been specially called to Genoa by Paolo, and agrees to accept the position, which should win him permission to marry his beloved Maria. The people are called together, and Paolo announces to them that Boccanegra is to be their candidate; they unite in cursing Fiesco, in whose palace they see mysterious lights.

The whole of this section is set to music that is extraordinarily suggestive of underground movement and conspiracy under the cover of darkness, from the mysterious prelude to Paolo's cursing of the haughty patricians and his *sotto voce* working up of the crowd in fear of the nameless doings in Fiesco's palace.

The square empties, and Fiesco leaves his home, lamenting the loss of his daughter, from whose death-bed he has just come. His noble, restrained cry of grief, 'Il lacerato spirito', with its moving orchestral postlude, establishes him straight away as a flesh-and-blood personality whose emotions may be subdued to his sense of position, but who is nonetheless anything but an insensitive, cardboard figure. He sees

Boccanegra enter the square and confronts him again with an accusation of the wrong he has done Maria. It is the first of the two great duets between the adversaries, Fiesco's fury contrasting well with Boccanegra's pleading as he tells the story of the loss of the little daughter, which has robbed one of them of his only child, the other of the grand-daughter he has never seen (Ex. 2). Fiesco leaves Boccanegra, telling him that only the sight of his grand-daughter can bring peace between them. He watches from a distance as the distracted man knocks on the palace door, then, seeing it open, goes up, only to find that his Maria is dead. Boccanegra reappears to hear the plaudits of the mob, as they crowd into the square (to a most democratic-sounding march) and salute their new Doge.

Act I. Twenty-five years have passed. Amelia, Boccanegra's daughter, is standing in the garden of the Grimaldi palace, near the sea. It is dawn, and she salutes the beauty of the scene and memories of her childhood in a gentle aria, 'Come in quest'ora bruna', whose shimmering accompaniment might have been sketched by a French Impressionist painter. She hears the voice of Gabriele, her lover, serenading her from a distance, and when he appears, tells him of her fears for his safety and that of Andrea (in reality, Fiesco in disguise), who she knows is plotting against the Doge. Her warning, and Gabriele's answer, turn to thoughts of their mutual love, which take on a greater urgency when Pietro comes to announce that the Doge asks to be received by Amelia on his way back from hunting, for no other purpose, as she well knows, than that of asking her hand in marriage for his henchman, Paolo. Gabriele resolves immediately to ask the blessing of Andrea, Amelia's guardian now that Count Grimaldi has been banished from Genoa for political intrigue, on their marriage. When he does so, Fiesco tells him the story of Amelia's adoption (he has, of course, no idea of her actual identity), Gabriele swears eternal love to her, and Fiesco blesses Gabriele in his affection for Amelia and his patriotic love of Genoa.

The Doge greets Amelia, shows her the pardon he is granting to Count Grimaldi, and asks her if she is content with her life of seclusion. She answers that she has a lover, and is pursued by one she hates – Paolo.

Simon Boccanegra *(La Scala, Milan/Paris Opéra, 1976, director Giorgio Strehler, designer Ezio Frigerio).*
Mirella Freni as Amelia, Piero Cappuccilli as Boccanegra.

In any case she confides to the Doge that she is not Grimaldi's daughter, but an orphan, whose only clue to her identity is a locket containing the portrait of her mother. With great emotion, Boccanegra comes to recognise it as that of Maria, and knows he has found his daughter at last. Their duet mounts in intensity, through Simon's lyrical reaction to the possibility of having found his daughter, until uncertainty gives way to proof, and he gratefully acknowledges her. The direct expression of the latter part of the duet gives way to unique tenderness as it comes to an end, and the orchestral postlude, with Boccanegra's final, ecstatic 'Figlia!' (Daughter) on a high F, makes a fitting end to a remarkable scene, one of the most rewarding in the long line of father–daughter duets in Verdi's operas – incidentally, one of the few pre-supposing a happy outcome. It remains only for Boccanegra to deny any hope of Amelia to the waiting Paolo and for Paolo to plot her abduction with his crony Pietro, before we return to the political struggle.

The finale of Act I, which plays in the Council Chamber of the Doge, dates entirely from Boito's revision, and amounts to fifty pages of vocal score, or almost one half of the entire act. It is one of the finest scenes in all Verdi, and an extraordinary and entirely worthy anticipation of the work of the composer and librettist in *Otello*; it has been not inaccurately said that if Otello had ever been depicted in council, this is how it might have sounded.

We find the Doge surrounded by the plebeian and patrician members of his Council (the former in the majority) and receiving emissaries from the King of Tartary, who pledges himself to keep his waters open to the ships of Genoa. He goes on to read and support a message from Petrarch, which urges that peace should immediately be made with Venice, which, like Genoa, acknowledges a common fatherland, Italy. Rioting is heard in the distance, and Paolo sees through the window that the crowd is dragging Adorno to the palace; the words 'Morte ai patrizi' (Death to the nobles) can now be distinguished. In a moment, the Council has divided itself into patricians and plebeians, each group with swords drawn. Simon hears the cry 'Morte al Doge', and sends his herald to open the doors of the palace and say to the crowd that he awaits them in his Council Chamber, if they wish to find him. The sound of the trumpet can be heard calling them to silence, but the herald's words cannot be distinguished,

only the sound of 'Evviva il Doge' as he ends. It is a scene of breathless drama achieved by the simplest means, and the domination of Boccanegra is nowhere better shown than in his efforts to keep peace, not only in the city but within his own Council as well.

The mob rushes in, crying for vengeance on Gabriele Adorno and Andrea (or Fiesco), whom they drag into the Doge's presence. It seems from Adorno's own account that he has slain Lorenzino, who had abducted Amelia, and that before he died, the villain admitted he was the agent of a mightier man than he, 'a man of high position'. He is about to stab Boccanegra for the crime which he supposes to be his when Amelia, who has entered through the crowd, throws herself between the two men. Her story corroborates Gabriele's, but before she can name the offender, patrician and plebeian accuse and counter-accuse each other of the crime. Only Boccanegra's intervention prevents bloodshed. His great plea for peace and unity, 'Piango su voi, sul placido raggio del vostro clivo', leads to an extended ensemble, led by Amelia, who echoes the prayer that peace may return to all their hearts.

Adorno surrenders his sword to Boccanegra, who accepts it, before turning 'con forza terribile' to Paolo. He speaks with ever-increasing intensity of his determination to find the traitor who raised his hand against Amelia, and in a terrible voice calls on Paolo to join with him in cursing the villain. This Paolo cannot avoid doing, and his curse is taken up by the bystanders, in whom the scene seems to induce something approaching hysteria, to judge from their first *forte* cry of 'Sia maledetto!' (Let him be accursed), and the subsequent and ever softer repetitions. Boccanegra and his daughter are left alone at the end of a scene whose atmosphere has been at any rate partly induced by the uncanny nature of the principal motif, played by cello and double-bassoon.

Act II. Paolo is alone, a prey to acute fear of the consequences of his action and of the curse he was obliged by the implacable Boccanegra to deliver against himself. He sees himself as rejected by all, patricians and plebeians alike, but rears himself like a snake to threaten the absent Doge with the most terrible and the most secret vengeance at his command – poison. Fiesco and Adorno are brought in, and he offers the former his liberty if he will perform one vital action: kill the Doge. If he refuse, the details of the patrician plot will go forthwith to the Doge himself. Fiesco indignantly rejects the offer, but Paolo has one weapon left; as Adorno prepares to leave with Fiesco, he asks him if he knows that Amelia is here in the palace, as Boccanegra's mistress?

Adorno accepts Paolo's slander all too easily, and launches into a magnificent tirade in A minor against the Doge, who once ordered his father's execution and has now ravished the girl he loves. He prays, in the dominant major, that his fears may be groundless and that Amelia's love may still be his. Amelia comes in and he confronts her with the accusation, which she indignantly denies. She attempts to persuade him to leave, but the Doge can be heard approaching, and Adorno hides, still breathing threats of revenge.

Boccanegra notices that his daughter has tears in her eyes, and tells her that he knows the reason, which she has already revealed to him: she is in love. When he hears the name of Adorno, his worst fears are realised; Adorno is a traitor and a plotter against the state. She entreats him to pardon Gabriele, the Doge tells her to leave him, and wonders whether it is strength or weakness which prompts him to pardon an enemy. He pours water from the jug which Paolo has poisoned, drinks from it, and, in a sad phrase, reflects on the melancholy destiny of those who wear a crown. He feels himself falling asleep, and murmurs Amelia's name while the orchestra softly adumbrates the theme of their duet in Act I.

Adorno steps from concealment; the man who murdered his father and who is now his rival is at his mercy! But Amelia steps between the two men. Boccanegra wakes, takes in the situation and defies Adorno to kill a defenceless man. Gabriele says Boccanegra's life is forfeit in return for his father's. Boccanegra replies that his revenge is already complete since he has taken from him the thing in life that he values most, his daughter. Adorno is overcome at the news, and begs for forgiveness from Amelia, whom he says he has pursued with too jealous a love. He begs for death at the Doge's hands,

in music whose virility and youthful, heroic quality is as good as anything of the kind Verdi ever wrote. Boccanegra's humanity does not desert him and he pardons his would-be murderer in a phrase whose nobility dominates the latter part of the splendid trio:

Warlike sounds are heard outside, and Boccanegra, remembering the conspiracy, orders Adorno to join his friends, whose rebellion has evidently started. But Adorno swears loyalty to the Doge and the act ends as he promises to do what he can to put an end to the fighting.

Act III. The scene changes from Simon's private apartments to a great hall, whose window reveals a view of Genoa harbour. The city is lit up with torches in honour of the crushing of the revolt. Fiesco's sword is returned to him and he is released. As he turns to go, he sees Paolo with an escort of guards, and learns that he took part in the rebellion and, when captured, was immediately condemned to death by Boccanegra – but Paolo can exult in the knowledge that the Doge will follow him quickly to the grave, slain by the slow poison he has prepared for him. The strains of the wedding hymn of Gabriele and Amelia can be heard, and Paolo is conducted to the scaffold with its sound ringing in his ears, leaving Fiesco full of regret that Boccanegra's end should be brought about in so treacherous and dishonourable a manner, but still determined to see him again.

A proclamation is read from the balcony, ordering that the lights be extinguished in honour of the valiant dead. The Doge himself enters the hall, already affected by the poison he has taken. The sight of the sea and the feel of the salt wind on his brow restore his confidence, and bring back to him memories of the life he once led as a free man on the sea he loved and understood so well. It is a moving, expansive moment, one of those pieces of unforced self-revelation in which this opera abounds, and whose beauty is so intense that one finds oneself waiting for them at every performance. Why, asks Boccanegra, did he not find death at this early, happy stage of his career? As if in answer to his question comes an echo from the concealed Fiesco. The Doge makes an effort to summon his guards, but Fiesco reveals himself as the ancient enemy long thought dead. It is the moment, not of Fiesco's revenge, but of Boccanegra's atonement, and he proudly announces that there can be peace between them now that in Amelia he has found the daughter he had lost. Fiesco's hate turns to pity for the man he knows has only a short time to live. As is appropriate the second of the two great duets is on an even more generous scale than that of the prologue, when Fiesco first imposed his conditions for reconciliation on the unfortunate Boccanegra. The passionate declamation of the bass is matched here by the mature, conciliatory tone of Boccanegra's music.

Boccanegra summons up strength to tell Amelia of her descent, and to appoint Adorno as his successor before he dies in the arms of his children and surrounded by his friends and counsellors. Fiesco goes to the balcony and announces to the assembled crowd that Gabriele Adorno is their new Doge; when they shout for Boccanegra, he reveals to them that he is dead.

Much has been made of the complication of the original libretto, and of the difficulty Boito apparently had in rationalising it, but the truth is that very little is needed to make the story entirely comprehensible, even easy to follow. Apart from a general tidying up of the dialogue, Boito was responsible for the finale of Act I, generally conceded to be the finest section of the opera. Verdi's revision was even more thorough. Details of the orchestration, of the vocal line, and of the harmony are altered all over the place, in much the same way as they had been in *Macbeth* but on a more extensive scale. Entirely new is the opening scene of the prologue up to Fiesco's aria (apart from Paolo's 'L'altra magion'); the introduction to Act I, the duet for Gabriele and Fiesco, the climax of the recognition duet, and of course the Council Chamber scene; Boccanegra's short solo in Act II and Paolo's *Credo*-like soliloquy which precedes it; the opening of Act III up to the entrance of Boccanegra and to a large extent the final quartet with chorus.

That Verdi entertained such high regard for the opera is perhaps to some extent due to his love for Genoa itself. Certainly his music communicates this love as well as the city's dependence on the sea. But the most remarkable thing about the opera is its central figure, a puissant character and among Verdi's greatest creations; all the way through, one cannot help but be impressed by the amazing consistency of the characterisation. Never before perhaps had a composer been wholly successful in putting the unspectacular quality of statesmanship on to the stage. Boccanegra is a mature creation, whose insight and integrity are expressed in music as well as in the drama. It is not only that Verdi has been provided with striking situations for his main character – the sudden recognition of a long-lost daughter, the cursing of the abductor, the falling asleep and waking to find his daughter's prospective bridegroom standing over him with a dagger, the confronting by his ancient enemy apparently risen from the dead – but that the music shows exactly the same consistent understanding that we are asked to believe was Boccanegra's. Not a bar of recitative, not a note in the great solos and ensembles in which he takes part but contributes to this picture of the central figure, which is in addition perhaps the most exacting baritone part Verdi ever wrote, certainly one of the most rewarding.   H.

AROLDO

Opera in four acts, text by Francesco Maria Piave, based on his libretto for *Stiffelio* (1850), which was in three acts. Première Rimini, 16 August 1857, with Marcellina Lotti (later known as Lotti della Santa), Giovanni Pancani, Carlo Poggiali, Cornago, Gaetano Ferri. First produced New York, Academy of Music, 1863; London, St Pancras Town Hall, 1964. Revived Florence Festival, 1953, with Antonietta Stella, Gino Penno, Aldo Protti, conductor Tullio Serafin; Hamburg, 1954, with Anne Bollinger, Peter Anders, Josef Metternich; Wexford Festival, 1959, conductor Charles Mackerras; New York, 1961, Amato Opera Company, with George Shirley in the title role; Venice, 1985.

Aroldo, *a Saxon knight* (Stiffelio[1])......................Tenor
Mina, *his wife* (Lina) ....Soprano
Egberto, *Mina's father* (Stankar)....................Baritone
Godvino, *a knight* (Raffaele)..............................Tenor
Briano, *a holy man* (Jorg)......................................Bass
Enrico, *Mina's cousin* (Federico) ....Tenor
Elena, *Mina's cousin* (Dorothea) ....Mezzo-Soprano

Place: England and Scotland
Time: About 1200
Running Time: 2 hours 10 minutes

Verdi was already interested in the French and Spanish plays which were to become *Rigoletto* and *Il Trovatore* when he accepted Piave's suggestion of a French play less than two years old whose subject was the curious one, for a Catholic country, of a Protestant clergyman whose wife has committed adultery and whom he finds it in his heart, after her father has killed her lover, to forgive. This became *Stiffelio*, which Verdi in a letter of 1854 mentions as one of two operas which had not taken the public's fancy but which he would not like to see forgotten. The other is *La Battaglia di Legnano*. In 1856, he worked with Piave to revise the libretto, and in 1857 the revised work was produced as the inaugural production of a new opera house in Rimini. The outline of the story has stayed the same, except that time and place have been moved from early nineteenth-century Germany to England and Scotland around 1200, with the principal figures Crusaders rather than Protestant clergymen and their colleagues. Much of the music remains the same, although alterations are frequent, and one or two numbers have been re-written. The main difference comes in the final scenes of the two operas, *Stiffelio*'s Act III scene ii being set in a church where the congregation first prays and Stiffelio later preaches on the gospel story of the woman taken in adultery before publicly forgiving his wife. *Aroldo*'s Act IV, as will be seen later, provides quite a different ending for the opera.

Act I. After an effective overture whose slow opening section is dominated by a horn solo, the curtain rises to show a great hall in Egberto's castle. It is empty, but sounds of rejoicing come from within, the half-heard music making in the empty space a curious effect of foreboding, an impression not belied at the entrance of Mina, who in her soliloquy reveals

the torment of a conscience labouring under a guilty secret: during her husband's absence, she has been unfaithful to him with Godvino, a guest in her father's castle. Her anguished recitative and heartfelt prayer could hardly be in stronger contrast with the bravura writing frequently heard in an introductory aria for a nineteenth-century opera's heroine.

Aroldo enters with Briano, who has campaigned with him on the crusade and is now acting as a kind of spiritual adviser. Aroldo immediately notices his wife's perturbed condition, but Briano leaves them alone together and there is tenderness in Aroldo's cavatina, in which he describes his longing for Mina while he was abroad. Mina punctuates his cavatina with exclamations of remorse, and Aroldo finally demands a smile of welcome instead of the tears with which she has greeted him. He notices that the ring his mother had given her has gone, and in a cabaletta denounces its loss.

Briano returns and takes Aroldo off to join in the celebrations for his return, while Mina, observed by her father who begins to suspect Godvino's role, resolves to confess all to Aroldo in a letter. Egberto interrupts, reads what she has written, and succeeds in persuading her not to confess her adultery to Aroldo in case the shock of learning of the family's shame should kill him.

The second scene takes place in the great hall of the castle. When it is left momentarily deserted by the knights and their ladies, Godvino, observed by Briano, comes with a letter he has written to Mina and leaves it in a huge locked book which lies on the table and of which he carries the key. Briano does not recognise Godvino except as a friend of Aroldo's, and, when Egberto and his daughter and then his son-in-law and the other guests re-appear, Briano describes what he has seen to Aroldo, but by mistake points out the man who hid the letter as Enrico, Mina's cousin. Aroldo is asked to describe the crusade to the guests, but instead he starts to talk about the book and the letter and then, in music which to some extent presages *Otello*, demands that Mina unlock the book that he may see what is inside. He breaks the lock and the letter falls out, but Egberto retrieves it and, denying it to Aroldo, himself destroys it. Aroldo's rage knows no bounds, but it is Egberto who orders Godvino to meet him later in the graveyard for a duel.

---

[1] The names of the corresponding characters in *Stiffelio* (page 875) are in brackets.

Act II. The ancient graveyard of the castle, with a church visible on one side and the castle on the other. The music is darkly suggestive, as Mina in a splendid aria prays at her mother's tomb, comparing the purity of her mother with her own guilt ('Ah! dagli scanni eterei'). Godvino comes to plead his love, but she orders him not to profane the place where her mother is buried, then demands that he give her back her ring. He refuses and insists that he will defend her in her predicament, but she makes it quite clear that she will have no more to do with him.

Egberto arrives to confront them and challenges Godvino to fight to the death. Godvino at first refuses to fight a man so much older than himself, but Egberto goads him, and they are separated only by the arrival of Aroldo. Aroldo greets Godvino warmly, but this is too much for Egberto who denounces Godvino as the man who has betrayed Aroldo's honour. Mina appears, cannot deny Aroldo's charge, and Aroldo's impassioned outburst of jealous fury is not unworthy of the Verdi of thirty years later. A most impressive quartet follows, at the end of which Aroldo challenges Godvino to fight him. Sounds of prayer come from the church, and Briano attempts to persuade Aroldo to temper his rage, as a Christian who has fought for his faith. Aroldo is still beside himself with fury, and the act ends as, in his emotion, he collapses unconscious.

Act III. An ante-chamber of the castle. Egberto, planning vengeance, finds that Godvino has escaped and in a fine aria bemoans the dishonour which has fallen on him and his family. He contemplates suicide, but Briano intervenes with the news that Godvino is back in the castle. One of them must die, says Egberto, and celebrates the prospect in a cabaletta of splendid impact, marked, most unusually, *pianissimo*, a direction Verdi underlines in a footnote in the vocal score enjoining the singer to sing it 'extremely quietly apart from the last phrase'.

Aroldo enters with Godvino and, demanding that he choose whether he values his own freedom more or the future of the woman he had betrayed, sends him to wait in a neighbouring room. Then he confronts Mina with the news that he himself will leave that very night and, so that she may be free to join the man she truly loves, he offers her a divorce. The duet is in Verdi's extended manner, and at its end

Mina signs the paper he offers her. Egberto rushes in with a blood-stained sword in his hand, having killed Godvino, and Mina stays behind to pray forgiveness while Aroldo goes into the church.

Act IV. The banks of Loch Lomond (*sic*), some time later. In the introduction, imitation bagpipes are followed by a huntsmen's chorus, and, as the sun sets, there is even a hint of 'The Campbells are Coming' – could Verdi have known it? In a rustic hut, Aroldo and Briano have retired from the world, and Aroldo admits to himself that he still loves Mina; as the sound of the angelus is heard, he and Briano join in the evening prayer.

A storm breaks out, stunningly portrayed in the music with pre-echoes of *Otello*, and from the boat which is driven up on the shore emerge Egberto and Mina. They go to the hut for shelter, and Aroldo immediately recognises Mina. He tries to repulse her, but Egberto urges that her trials in exile have brought her to a state of repentance, and Briano quotes the scriptures so that finally, after a short but impressive quartet, love triumphs – unexpectedly, in this quasi-tragedy.

Modern revivals suggest that *Stiffelio* is just as viable as *Aroldo* and that each has claims to figure among Verdi's unjustly neglected works.   H.

UN BALLO IN MASCHERA
A Masked Ball

Opera in three acts, text by Somma based on Scribe's libretto for Auber's opera *Gustave III, ou le Bal Masqué*. Première at Apollo Theatre, Rome, 17 February 1859, with Julienne-Déjean, Scotti, Sbriscia, Fraschini, Giraldoni.

Gustavus III (Riccardo, *Count of Warwick*)[1] ..... Tenor

Amelia, *Anckarstroem's wife* ....Soprano

Anckarstroem, *the King's secretary*
   (Renato)..Baritone

Conspirators against the King
   Count Ribbing (Samuele) ....Bass
   Count Horn (Tommaso) ....Bass

Cristian (Silvano), *a sailor*.............................Baritone

Oscar, *the King's page* ....Soprano

Mlle Arvidson (Ulrica), *a fortune-teller* ....Contralto

A Judge, Amelia's Servant, Populace, Courtiers

Running Time: 2 hours 15 minutes

---

[1] Names for Swedish setting first, for Boston second.

The opera was written for Naples in 1858, and
rehearsals were in progress when an Italian revolutionary, Felice Orsini, made an unsuccessful
attempt on the life of Napoleon III, with the result
that the performance of a work dealing with the
assassination of a king was forbidden. In spite of
protests and the popular slogan 'Viva Verdi!' (= *Viva
Vittorio Emmanuele Re D'Italia*), the opera was
withdrawn, but mounted a year later in Rome, when
Verdi accepted the unlikely setting of Boston for the
assassination of an English Governor in place of the
historical Swedish monarch.

Ballo has been claimed as the best-shaped opera of
Verdi's middle period, with a precise balance
between the music's romantic and tragic elements
on the one hand and its strongly ironic characteristics on the other, the latter evinced not only in what
the conspirators (particularly at the end of Act II)
and Oscar have to sing, but most of all in the well
characterised musical picture of the tenor hero. The
actual King Gustavus III of Sweden was a liberal in
politics and a lover of the arts, married but homosexual, but Verdi's portrait is more conventional.
Nothing could be more romantic than his opening
aria, the love duet, or the aria in the last act, but this
monarch rejects the portentous and in the opera
constantly brings the music to the boil with his exuberance, never running the risk of taking himself too
seriously, as seen particularly in his mocking reaction to Arvidson's prophecy of doom. For Oscar, his
page, Verdi seems to have taken something from the
lighter world of French opera and Oscar is evidently
licensed to mock pretension of any kind. Amelia and
Anckarstroem, given a wealth of splendid music, are
figures less strikingly characterised, but the music
associated with King and page brings a colour to this
musical suggestion of a historical court which is
unlike anything else in Verdi.

The short prelude is concerned with Court, conspirators, and the love of the King for Amelia.

Act I. A hall in the palace. Conspirators (Ribbing
and Horn) mutter through the opening chorus but
the King is overjoyed to notice on a list of invitations
to a masked ball the name of his beloved Amelia, wife
of his faithful secretary, Anckarstroem ('La rivedrà
nell'estasi'). Anckarstroem warns the King that the
court contains plotters as well as loyal subjects and a
judge denounces a certain Mlle Arvidson for sorcery.

Un ballo in maschera. *Jussi Björling as Riccardo/King
Gustav III, New York, 1941.*

Oscar takes her side ('Volta la terrea') and the King
decides to go in disguise to investigate whether she is
genuine or not.

Arvidson's abode. The sorceress conjures a spell
for the crowd ('Re dall'abisso, affrettati!'), the King
arrives, and Arvidson finishes her solo in a mood of
exaltation. She predicts good fortune for a young
sailor, and the King fulfils the prophecy by slipping a
note into his pocket. Next, none other than Amelia is
advised to cure a guilty love by gathering a herb at
the foot of the public gallows (trio). The courtiers, in
disguise like the King, arrive and he in a barcarolle
('Di tu se fedele') asks Arvidson to foretell his future.
He will die by the hand of a friend, she predicts. The
King pokes fun at the whole issue (Quintet: 'È
scherzo, od è follia') and when it is further foretold
that his murderer will be the first to shake his hand
and this turns out to be Anckarstroem, he mocks the
sorceress for failing to recognise him. The finale
starts with a 'National Anthem' theme but ends in
high spirits as the King and his page take over.

Act II. Midnight, beside the gallows. Amelia,

heavily veiled, comes to pick the magic herb and in a magnificent aria betrays her nervousness and desperate need for reassurance ('Ma dall'arido stela divulsa'). The duet with the King which follows sees her initial reticence blossom into an admission of love, and is one of the most expansive Verdi ever wrote. At its end, Anckarstroem, who has heard that murderers are on the King's tracks, comes to rescue him and the apparently unknown woman. In a short, agitated trio they discuss escape, and the finale is concerned with the unsuccessful efforts of Anckarstroem to get his (still unrecognised) wife past the plotters, her unmasking and the consequent rage of the one and remorse of the other. With the mocking laughter of the conspirators, this is one of Verdi's most fascinating scenes. During its course Anckarstroem makes an assignation with the leaders of the conspiracy to meet at his house next day.

Act III. A room in Anckarstroem's house. Anckarstroem intends to kill Amelia but yields to her plea ('Morrò, ma prima in grazie') that she may first say goodbye to their son. The King is the more guilty of the two, he decides, and in a dramatic recitative and grandiose aria, 'Eri tu', inveighs against him. Anckarstroem receives the leaders of the conspiracy and agrees to make common cause with them, Amelia draws lots to decide who shall kill the King at tonight's masked ball – Anckarstroem's name emerges – and finally there is a brilliant solo for Oscar which becomes a quintet of reaction to the news of that night's party.

The last scene, at the masked ball, is preceded by an aria for Gustavus, introspective in the recitative and full of romantic stress in the aria ('Ma se m'e forza perderti'), in which he declares his intention to send Amelia and her husband on a foreign mission.

The masked ball works up the tension slowly but unerringly: a dramatic recitative from the King, chorus and dancing, then Oscar's brilliant solo in reply to Anckarstroem's question about Gustavus's disguise: 'Saper vorreste'. Much of the scene is carried on over dance music and the farewell duet between the King and Amelia is particularly moving, as is the King's death. A shot rings out, Gustavus falls into the arms of Oscar, Amelia rushes to him, the dance music stops, he forgives his enemies and dies.   H.

LA FORZA DEL DESTINO
The Force of Destiny

Opera in four acts, text by Francesco Maria Piave, founded on a Spanish drama by the Duke of Rivas, *Don Alvaro o La Fuerza de Sino*. Première, St Petersburg, 10 November 1862, with Barbot, Didiée, Tamberlik, Graziani, Angelini. First performed New York, 1865; London, Her Majesty's Theatre, 1867, with Tietjens, Trebelli, Mongini, Santley, Gassie, conductor Arditi. Revived Metropolitan, 1918, with Ponselle, Caruso, de Luca, Mardones, conductor Papi; 1942, with Milanov, Baum, Tibbett, Pinza, conductor Bruno Walter; Dresden, 1926, with Seinemeyer, Pattiera, Burg, Plaschke, conductor Fritz Busch; Vienna, 1926, with Angerer, Piccaver, Schipper, Mayr; la Scala, 1928, with Scacciati, Merli, Franci, Pasero, conductor Toscanini; Covent Garden, 1931, with Ponselle, Pertile, Franci, Pasero, conductor Serafin; la Scala, 1949, with Barbato, Filippeschi, Silveri, Christoff, conductor de Sabata; Metropolitan, New York, 1952, with Milanov, Tucker, Warren, Siepi; Covent Garden, 1962, with Cavalli, Bergonzi, John Shaw, Ghiaurov, conductor Solti.

Donna Leonora di Vargas	Soprano
Preziosilla, *a gipsy*	Mezzo-Soprano
Don Alvaro	Tenor
Don Carlo di Vargas, *Leonora's brother*	Baritone
Padre Guardiano, *a Franciscan monk*	Bass
Marchese di Calatrava, *Leonora's father*	Bass
Fra Melitone, *a Franciscan monk*	Baritone
Curra, *Leonora's maid*	Mezzo-Soprano
The Mayor of Hornachuelos	Bass
Trabuco, *a muleteer*	Tenor
A Surgeon	Tenor

Place: Spain and Italy
Time: Middle of the Eighteenth Century
Running Time: 3 hours 20 minutes

After *Ballo*, Verdi, newly married, preoccupied with his estate and his support for Garibaldi's increasingly successful campaign for Italian independence, seemed determined to retire from the operatic arena. When the great tenor Enrico Tamberlik, a regular singer in St Petersburg, wrote to ask him if he would write an opera for Russia, the omens seemed unpropitious, but Verdi was inclined to seek new pastures and even the censor's uncompromising refusal to allow Victor Hugo's *Ruy Blas* as subject was not enough to deter him. He settled on a Spanish drama by the Duke of Rivas, a writer from the same liberal and romantic school as Victor Hugo though with less than Hugo's talent. Julian Budden neatly describes one half of the antagonists: the Calatravas 'swing from one vehement extreme to another without any transition of mood. They are twice as large as life and half as life-like'.

Forza is customarily criticised for its rambling libretto, and because the destiny which is proclaimed in the title tends to be replaced in the story by the less compelling factor of coincidence. Francis Toye is at some pains to point out that Rivas's play, *Don Alvaro*, is dominated by the principle of the blood-feud, in which facts were more important than intentions, and that to understand the original significance of the play entails an imaginative reconstruction of this out-moded attitude. He also suggests that Rivas, a liberal, may have intended to show that life should be influenced by other considerations than that of the honour of noble Spanish families – in any case, his scenes of popular life were, like Verdi's, particularly successful.

In spite of a good if not outstanding success in St Petersburg, Verdi was not entirely happy with his new opera and contemplated modifications and a new ending. By 1868 when he was minded to effect these changes, his librettist Piave had suffered a stroke; Antonio Ghislanzoni undertook the alterations which were first heard at la Scala in February 1869 (an event which marked a *rapprochement* with that theatre), with Teresa Stolz and Mario Tiberini as Leonora and Don Alvaro, described by the composer in a letter as no less than superb.

The overture is a vividly exciting affair, probably Verdi's best, dominated by Leonora's aria from Act II, and the music concerned with 'fate' (Ex.1). Reference is

Allegro agitato e presto

also made to Alvaro's *cantabile con espressione* (in A minor) from the fourth-act duet, and to themes from the duet between Leonora and Padre Guardiano.

Act I. Leonora's room. She says goodnight to her father but is overcome with remorse at the idea of leaving him so precipitately – for she has arranged

that very night to elope with her lover, Don Alvaro. In an aria, 'Me pellegrina ed orfana', she pictures her friendless lot in a foreign country, for which even the prospect of marriage with her lover cannot console her. It is late; he surely won't come now – but no sooner are the words out than the sound of his horses can be heard and he bounds in through the window, proclaiming his eternal love. His passionate description of the preparations for their elopement provokes, after a little hesitation, an equally demonstrative response from Leonora, but the delay is disastrous, and, before they can escape, the Marchese is in the room, denouncing his daughter's seducer. Alvaro protests his and her innocence, and throws down his pistol in token of surrender. It goes off and fatally wounds the old man, who curses Leonora as he dies.

Act II. Leonora has been separated from Alvaro in their flight. Each believes the other dead, but Don Carlo, Leonora's brother, is convinced that they are alive and scours the land to revenge himself on the sister who has brought dishonour to his family and on what he sees as the murderer of his father.

The first scene is laid in the inn at the village of Hornachuelos, where are gathered various village worthies, muleteers, servants and a mysterious student, who is no other than Don Carlo in disguise. The company revels until the meal is announced; Leonora appears for a moment at the door looking for shelter, just as the student says grace, but she recognises her brother and leaves. Preziosilla, a gipsy, comes in, telling the guests that war has broken out and that all should go off to Italy to fight the Germans. She sings flamboyantly in praise of war and its incidental delights, and proceeds to tell the fortunes of the assembled company, incidentally informing the student that his being in disguise does not fool her.

Pilgrims are heard outside, and all join in their prayer, not least Leonora, who observes from the door and prays to be saved from her brother's vengeance. It is a splendid piece of choral writing. Don Carlo plies the muleteer with questions about the traveller he brought to the inn, and is asked in his turn, since he is so curious about others, to tell the company his own story. This he does in a ballad: he is Pereda, a young student, who has followed his friend Vargas in his quest for the murderer of his father. The murderer, he says, has escaped to South America, and the sister of Vargas, whom the murderer seduced, is dead. The mayor says it is late, all bid each other good night, and the scene ends with a dance.

Leonora goes on her way and at the opening of the next scene we find her outside the monastery of the 'Madonna degli Angeli', near Hornachuelos, looking for sanctuary. In the most extended aria of the opera, she prays for forgiveness for her sin, and takes courage from the sound of the hymn which can be heard coming from the church. At the start can be heard the 'fate' motif familiar from the overture, then, after a dramatic recitative, the aria 'Madre, pietosa Vergine', whose climax comes with the great phrase (in the major) of which such use has already been made in the overture: 'Deh, non m'abbandonar' (Ex. 2). Leonora rings the bell, and Fra Melitone pokes

con passione

his head through a window in the door. He is impressed to hear that Father Cleto sent her and will inform the Father Superior of her presence. He receives her kindly, and knows immediately who she is when she tells him who sent her. He warns her of the extreme loneliness of the solitary life she proposes to lead in the cave where once before a female penitent lived out her life, but she is determined to go through with her plan, and he agrees to allow her request. He himself will bring her food daily and she can ring a bell to summon help; otherwise, she will never again set eyes on a human being. He gathers the monks together and tells them that once again the cave will be occupied; no one is to approach it or make any attempt to discover the identity of the penitent.

Leonora's scene with Padre Guardiano is one of the finest in all Verdi, and belongs to the line of great duets. The expressive vocal line is enhanced by the contrasting nature of the various sections, whether it be the loose-limbed tune in which Leonora first tells of the gradual awakening of peace in her soul, or the closely knit E major duet in which Padre Guardiano immediately afterwards warns her of the danger she runs in living alone, the long sentences in which he urges her to draw closer to God, or the passionate phrases she employs to voice her thanks for the sanctuary she feels she has found. The finale (the short service in which the Father Superior blesses Leonora and warns the monks to keep away from her solitary

cave) is the perfect pendant to a great scene. Padre Guardiano leads them in pronouncing a curse on anyone who violates the sanctity of the cell, and then the sound of Leonora's voice floats out over the male voices of the monks in the prayer to the Virgin, 'La Vergine degli angeli'.

Act III. The scene changes to Italy, near Velletri, where the fighting referred to at the beginning of the previous act is taking place. In the War of the Austrian Succession, Spain allied to the King of Naples drove the Austrians out of southern Italy. Don Alvaro and Don Carlo di Vargas, each under assumed names and unknown to the other, have enlisted in the Spanish contingent which is taking part in the battles. The sound of gambling is heard as Alvaro comes forward to sing his long recitative and aria, 'O tu che in seno agli angeli', one of Verdi's major inspirations. Alvaro's is a tortured and lonely soul, and the thinly accompanied opening phrases hovering between F minor and A flat major, together with the leaps of major and minor sixths and octaves, most acutely convey his neurosis – he has deserted the woman he loves after having inadvertently killed her father, and he alternately proclaims the shame of his mixed blood and prison birth, and the glory of his noble ancestry.

There is a cry for help, he rushes off-stage, and reappears with none other than his old enemy Don Carlo, whom he has saved from death at the hands of a gang of ruffians. Having exchanged false names, they swear friendship and go off together in answer to an urgent call to arms.

The scene changes, and we see a military surgeon surrounded by soldiers watching the battle from a distance. Victory is to the Italians and the Spaniards, but Don Carlo brings in Alvaro grievously wounded. When Carlo seeks to give his friend the military decoration of the order of Calatrava, he shudders at the name, but a moment later he entrusts Carlo with his last instructions. He has a small casket which contains a letter and which must be burnt unopened after his death; will his friend do this for him? Carlo swears to carry out the commission faithfully. The duet, 'Solenne in quest'ora', has become world-famous, partly perhaps initially because of the celebrity of the recording made of it by Caruso and Scotti, but also because of its graceful tune and remarkably apt relationship to the situation.

Alvaro is carried away by the surgeon, and Carlo

reflects on the secret which lies hidden in the fateful box. His friend trembled at the name of Calatrava; could it be his enemy in disguise? He soliloquises on the temptation the casket presents even to a man of honour, 'Urna fatale del mio destino', but finds a portrait inside which no oath prevents him from inspecting. It is Leonora's! The secret is out, and his newly found friend is recognised as his old enemy! At this moment a messenger tells him that Alvaro's life is saved; he rejoices at the prospect of revenge.

The scene changes to a military camp near Velletri. A patrol passes, and as dawn approaches Don Alvaro can be seen crossing the camp. Carlo calls him, and asks him if he is strong enough to fight a duel. With whom? Has he had no message lately from Don Alvaro, the Indian? Alvaro's protests and offers of friendship are in vain; Carlo insults him until he has provoked the duel he is seeking, only to be interrupted by the patrol on its way home. Alvaro, left alone, resolves to seek sanctuary in a monastery. The scene is in the splendid tradition of Verdian duets for tenor and baritone and it is to be regretted that Italian custom was for so long to omit it altogether. In any case, the duet is in a false position, as Toye points out, and was originally designed to end the act.

It is dawn. Soldiers polish their equipment, pedlars offer their wares, food and drink is for sale, and Preziosilla offers to tell fortunes until the appearance of a band of recruits gives her an opportunity of leading a tarantella in an effort to dispel their gloom. Mixed up in the dance is Fra Melitone, who extricates himself and treats the company to a discourse on its several vices, the whole thing dressed up in a series of outrageous puns. The soldiers make an attempt to give him a drubbing, but Preziosilla interrupts to sing a spirited 'Rataplan', which ends the act.

Act IV. The scene shows the cloister of the Convent of the 'Madonna degli Angeli', where a crowd of beggars is assembling to collect the free soup which the monks regularly dole out. Fra Melitone is in charge, and his marked lack of patience and intense annoyance at being compared unfavourably by the crowd with Padre Raffaello (in reality Alvaro in disguise) make him more than usually short-tempered. Finally, he can't bear any more of their torments and importunities, and kicks over the cauldron with what remains of the soup inside. The Father Superior, who has been watching, reproaches him

gently for lack of patience, and bids him not complain if Raffaello be preferred to him. Melitone says he likes Raffaello but cannot understand his odd, haunted look – caused, says the Father Superior, by his frequent fasts and his concentration on his duty.

The music of Melitone is always cited as among the most interesting in *Forza*, as giving a foretaste of the methods Verdi employed years later when writing *Falstaff*. The rhythms and orchestral accompaniment as well as the shape of the vocal line certainly suggest an entirely new type of character for Verdi.

The monastery door-bell rings violently, and Melitone admits Don Carlo himself, asking for Padre Raffaello. Melitone says there are two of that name in the monastery, but from the description he easily knows which is meant. He goes off to fetch him, while Don Carlo reflects on how his hatred for Alvaro was sufficient to penetrate the most unlikely of hiding-places. Alvaro comes in, Carlo discloses himself and immediately challenges him to a duel, producing two swords from under his cloak. Alvaro pleads with him to renounce thoughts of vengeance and believe what he now hears from the mouth of a priest, that his sister Leonora was never dishonoured, that he has nought to avenge but the misfortune which has dogged them both. Alvaro will even do what he says he has never before done, kneel at Don Carlo's feet. Carlo says this act proclaims the baseness of his birth and for a moment Alvaro's feelings threaten to get the better of him, but he chokes back his anger until Carlo strikes him across the face, branding him a coward. Alvaro's vows are forgotten; he is ready to fight! They rush off to expiate the blood-feud which has dogged their steps so long.

The duet is a splendid passage, perhaps the finest for tenor and baritone Verdi achieved before the days of *Otello*. It is immediately followed by a quick change of scene; the 'fate' motif sounds, and Leonora is seen outside her grotto. In great long phrases of supplication she prays for the peace which she has never known since the day she first secluded herself from the world: 'Pace, pace, mio Dio'. She sees the bread which has been left for her and which serves only to prolong, as she says, a wretched life. Suddenly, the sounds of fighting can be heard, and, calling down a curse on whoever dares to profane her solitude, she rushes back to her cell.

In a moment, the voice of Carlo can be heard

begging for absolution; he is wounded, and Alvaro, distraught that he has once again Vargas blood on his hands, bangs on the door of Leonora's cell for help. Leonora rings the bell in her alarm but a moment later appears and is recognised by Alvaro, who tells her what has happened. She goes to the spot where her brother lies and a few seconds later her cry is heard as Carlo stabs her, revenge even at his last moment uppermost in his mind. Alvaro can restrain himself no longer when he sees Leonora supported by Padre Guardiano, and he curses the fate which has brought so much misery on them all. The old Father Superior in music of great nobility bids him not to curse but to prostrate himself before the might of Heaven, whither the angel, who now lies dying, is going. In the presence of her lover and of the old priest who brought her such salvation as earth can offer, Leonora dies, and so expiates the curse which fell on them all with the death of her father.   H.

DON CARLOS

Opera in five acts, text by G. Méry and C. du Locle (in French), after Schiller. Première at Opéra, Paris, 11 March 1867, with Marie Sass, Gueymard, Morère, Jean-Baptiste Faure, Obin, David, conductor Emil Perrin. First performed at Covent Garden, 1867,[1] with Pauline Lucca, Fricci, Naudin, Grazziani; New York, 1877. Produced in Italian in four acts (but re-worked with du Locle and only turned into Italian after revision was finished), at la Scala, Milan, 1884, with Bruschi-Chiatti, Pasqua, Tamagno, Lhérie, Silvestri, Navarrini. Revived Metropolitan, 1920, with Ponselle, Matzenauer, Martinelli, de Luca, Didur (later Chaliapin), conductor Papi; la Scala, 1926, with Scacciati, Cobelli, Trantoul, Pasero, conductor Toscanini; Vienna, 1932 (in revised version by Werfel), with Ursuleac, Rünger, Völker, Schipper, Manowarda, conductor Krauss; Covent Garden, 1933, with Cigna, Giani, Lappas, Rimini, Autori, Tomei, conductor Beecham; Florence Festival, 1950, with Caniglia, Stignani, Picchi, Silveri, Christoff, Neri, conductor Serafin (five acts);[2] Metropolitan, 1950,[3] with Delia Rigal, Barbieri, Björling, Merrill, Siepi, Hines, conductor Stiedry (four acts); Covent Garden, 1958, with Brouwenstijn, Barbieri, Vickers, Gobbi, Christoff, Langdon, conductor Giulini, producer Visconti (five acts); Salzburg Festival, 1958, with Jurinac, Christa Ludwig, Fernandi, Bastianini, Siepi, under Karajan (four acts); la Scala, Milan, 1978 (five acts, with additions), with Freni, Obraztsova,

Carreras, Cappuccilli, Ghiaurov, Nesterenko, conductor Abbado; Covent Garden, 1996 (in French), with Karita Mattila, Roberto Alagna, José van Dam, Thomas Hampson.

Elisabeth (Elisabetta) de Valois, *later Queen of Spain*	Soprano
Princess Eboli, *her lady-in-waiting*	Mezzo-Soprano
Don Carlos (Carlo), *heir to the Spanish throne*	Tenor
Rodrigue (Rodrigo), *Marquess of Posa*	Baritone
Philippe (Filippo; Philip) II, *King of Spain*	Bass
The Grand Inquisitor	Bass
A Monk	Bass
Thibault (Tebaldo), *Elisabeth's page*	Soprano
Count Lerma	Tenor
The Royal Herald	Tenor
A Heavenly Voice	Soprano

Place: France and Spain
Time: Mid-Sixteenth Century
Running Time: 3 hours 30 minutes

*D*on Carlos for many years suffered from an inherent disadvantage; it was written for Paris, in the five-act, display-conscious tradition which Meyerbeer did so much to establish at that house, and it was therefore too long for non-Gallic taste. In 1882–3 Verdi undertook, with Ghislanzoni, his librettist for *Aida*, to produce a shorter version, but this entailed, as well as the omission of the ballet music, the jettisoning of most of the important first act, which is hard to justify artistically. Since then, most satisfactory revivals of the opera have made an attempt at including the first act, whatever they may have cut later on,[4] and the opera, with its magnetic subject, fecund musical invention, and splendid opportunities for leading singers, in the second half of the twentieth century has established itself close to the heart of the international repertory.

Spain is nearing the end of a war with France, and one of the conditions of peace is that the heir to the throne of Spain, Don Carlos (in reality, a near-psychopath, but represented in Verdi as well as in Schiller as a brilliant young man), would marry Elisabeth, the daughter of the King of France.

Act I. Don Carlos has come secretly to France to see

---

[1] Escudier for this production removed Act I and the ballet, reinstating Carlos's aria in the Garden scene of what then became Act II.

[2] First performance in this version at Modena in 1886. Andrew Porter describes it as 'a scissor-and-paste job, in which Act I as published in 1867 was joined to the four revised acts of 1883'. This was Florence's version of 1950, Covent Garden's of 1958, but there is no evidence that Verdi had

anything to do with it, though he must have allowed it.

[3] Opening performance of Rudolf Bing's first season as General Manager of the Metropolitan.

[4] In 1866, writing to Tito Ricordi, Verdi had insisted that *Don Carlos* be given complete; in 1874 he was angry at cuts made for Reggio; in 1875 he said that cuts for the Vienna production would be difficult.

Don Carlos *(Covent Garden, 1958, director Luchino Visconti, designers Visconti and Maurizio Chiari).*
Act II: Boris Christoff as Philip II, Tito Gobbi as Posa.

the bride who has been chosen for him. A hunt is in progress near Fontainebleau (there is no prelude to the opera) and Elisabeth and her page Thibault are separated from the main body of riders. They disappear in search of their companions and Carlos, alone, sings of the love which the sight of his bride has awakened in his heart. His romance was salvaged in somewhat reduced version when Verdi discarded Act I in his attempt at revision. Elisabeth reappears and Don Carlos offers to escort her home, saying he is a member of the staff of the Spanish envoy. He lights a fire and is questioned by the Princess about the young Spanish Prince to whom she is betrothed but whom she has never met. She fears for her marriage if love does not enter into it. Carlos tells her she need have no fear; the Prince will love her – and he shows her a portrait, which she naturally recognises as his. He declares his love, which she

tells him she returns. Their duet, which was omitted in the 1884 version, is a particularly lovely inspiration, and the delicate beauty of Elisabeth's phrase, 'De quels transports poignants et doux' (Di qual amor, di quant'ardor), as she recognises the love in her heart, is something that can ill be spared, not only for its own sake but because it is used later in the opera in something approaching the manner of a motif (Ex. 1).

Thibault returns and warns Elisabeth that the Spanish envoy is approaching to make a formal request for her hand in marriage for his master, the King of Spain himself, not for Don Carlos as had originally been arranged. The two lovers are filled with consternation, but Elisabeth accedes to the prayers of the crowd who beg her to acquiesce and so put an end to the war. The acclamations of the crowd mingle with the agonised regrets of Elisabeth and Carlos as the curtain falls.

Act II. In an effort to forget the misery of the world, Carlos has taken refuge in the Convent of San Yuste, where his grandfather, Charles V, before him had gone to end his days. Monks are praying before the tomb of the great Emperor, and one of them proclaims the uselessness of expecting peace in this life. Don Carlos remembers the curious stories to the effect that Charles V is not really dead at all but still living peacefully as a monk, and fancies he sees and hears a resemblance to his grandfather. The bass solo with the chorus is gravely impressive, the more particularly since this is the first contact we have with the influence of the Church, which is to be one of the dominating features of the opera. In the four-act version, at this point occurs Don Carlos's romance.

Carlos is overjoyed to see Rodrigue, Marquess of Posa, his greatest friend, lately returned from Flanders. Carlos confides to him that he loves none other than his own stepmother – will his friend turn from him at the news? Rodrigue expresses his determination to help him, and begs him to devote himself to the cause of the oppressed people of Flanders, and forget his own troubles in his efforts to right their wrongs. They swear eternal friendship, 'Dieu, tu semas dans nos âmes un rayon' (Dio, che nell'alma infondere amor), to a theme which is heard frequently throughout the opera (Ex. 2). A procession passes in front of the tomb, and the King himself is seen leading his Queen by the hand. The sight is almost too much for Carlos, but he is sustained by Rodrigue and by the voice of the mysterious monk, who leads the chanting. The scene ends with a reiteration of the friendship theme.

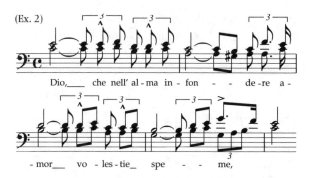

(Ex. 2)

Dio,___ che nell' al-ma in-fon - - de-re a-
- mor__ vo-les-tie_ spe - - me,

The scene changes to a garden outside the monastery. The Queen's entourage wait for their mistress, and Princess Eboli, supported by the irrepressible Thibault, whiles away the time by singing the song of the veil, a Moorish love-romance. With its ambitious cadenzas and rapid coloratura, it is a fine display piece for the mezzo-soprano.[1]

The Queen leaves the church and makes her way to where her ladies are waiting for her. Posa is announced, and gives her a letter he has brought from her mother in Paris, at the same time slipping a note from Carlos into her hand. She reads the message, while Rodrigue takes Eboli aside to tell her the latest news from Paris. The conversation between the two and the asides from Elisabeth are carried on to the accompaniment of a graceful dance rhythm, which most successfully suggests the elegant court atmosphere. Elisabeth thanks Rodrigue and bids him ask some favour. He will, but not for himself. In a short aria 'L'Infant Carlos, notre espérance' (Carlo ch'è sol il nostro amore) he asks for her help and influence with the King in acquiring for Carlos what he most desires, an interview with his father. Eboli, who is in love with Carlos, is struck with the thought that the agitation she has noticed in him when she has been in attendance on the Queen may be due to undeclared love for herself. Elisabeth signifies to Rodrigue that she will see her stepson, and he contrives to manoeuvre the ladies out of hearing so that the interview takes place in private.

Carlos enters and greets his stepmother formally, asking for her influence in persuading the King to send him to Flanders. But his outward calm is not proof against contact with the woman he loves, and he bitterly reproaches her for her seeming indiffer-

---

[1] According to Andrew Porter (Proceedings of Royal Musical Association, 15.iv.72) originally written in G when Eboli was cast before the Paris première with a young French mezzo-soprano; the aria was transposed up a tone by the composer when Pauline Gueymard, a soprano hardly less celebrated than Marie Sass herself, was given the role. This accounts, says Andrew Porter, for the role of Eboli – begun for an Azucena and completed for a Leonora – still proving so difficult for a single mezzo (or a soprano) to compass.

ence, which, she tells him, is no more than the duty she owes his father. In music of melting tenderness, Carlos shows that he understands her meaning, but it is clear that love for her still dominates his thoughts.

Suddenly, he passes into a mood of exaltation and falls senseless at Elisabeth's feet (the only reference in the opera to the fits which appear to have been so common with the real Don Carlos). Elisabeth for a moment fears he is dying, but in his delirium he once again proclaims his love for her. Coming to himself, he takes her in his arms, but she tears herself away, demanding whether he means to murder his father and then lead his mother to the altar. With a cry of grief, Carlos rushes from her presence, and she is left asking for Heaven's assistance in her predicament.

The King leaves the church to find that the Queen, contrary to his strict orders, has been left unattended. He dismisses the offending lady-in-waiting. Elisabeth ignores the affront to herself, and does her best to console the unhappy woman in a tender aria 'O ma chère compagne' (Non pianger, mia compagna).

Philippe watches until the Queen withdraws, followed by her ladies, but bids the Marquess of Posa remain behind. Why, he asks, has so tried and trusted a servant of Spain never asked him for a favour – preferment, or even an audience? Rodrigue answers

that service is his reward; but there is a favour he would like to ask, not for himself, but for others. He pleads for a relaxation of the measures being taken against the people of Flanders, who are even now dying by the sword and starvation. Only severity, answers the King, can cure such infidels and rebels of their heresies; and he cites the contentment and peace of the people of Spain as an example of what he hopes to bring to the Flemish. It is the peace of desolation that he brings, replies Rodrigue. Let the King beware lest history say of him: 'This man was Nero!' Let him instead build an empire founded on freedom. The King tells him his dreams are those of youth; but let him have no fear of the throne, rather beware of the Grand Inquisitor, not only for his own sake but because the King wants him as counsellor. He confides his fear over Elisabeth and Carlos to Rodrigue, who takes this confidence in him as a sign that happier times may be at hand for all whom he loves. With a last warning to beware the Inquisition, the King dismisses Rodrigue.

The second act is dominated by the two duets. That for Elisabeth and Don Carlos is a most moving affair, with its characterisation of Carlos's hopeless love for Elisabeth and the suggestive description of his delirium. The interview between Philippe and Rodrigue shows Verdi's mastery in setting to music not only the clash involved between differing personalities but also the logical type of argument which takes place when the personalities involved are what we think of as reasoning, intelligent beings.

Act III. A masked ball is in progress at the palace in Madrid (it was here that the ballet music originally occurred), and Carlos waits in the Queen's gardens in response to an anonymous note which he has received making the assignation. He sees what he thinks is Elisabeth, and pours out his love to her, until she unmasks and reveals that it is Eboli. He cannot conceal his dismay, and just as the watchful Posa comes upon them she accuses him of loving the Queen. Carlos, he says, is not well and can be held responsible for neither his words nor his actions; but Eboli is not deceived, and in spite of Posa's threat against her life, she promises to exert her power in bringing about their downfall. Posa persuades Carlos to give him any incriminating papers he may possess in case Eboli carries out her threats, and the curtain falls on a *fortissimo* statement in the orchestra of the theme of the oath of friendship.

The second scene is placed in the square in Madrid,

where preparations are afoot for an *auto-da-fé*, the ceremonial burning of heretics at the stake. The people rejoice in the might of Spain as a procession of monks precedes the mournful band of victims of the Inquisition. The members of the court, headed by the Queen, enter in procession, and to the acclamation of the crowd and announced by a herald, Philippe himself comes ceremonially through the doors of the cathedral, the crown of Spain on his head. He repeats the oath which he swore before his coronation, to wage war against the enemies of the Faith. There is an unexpected interruption as six deputies from Flanders, led by Carlos, fling themselves at his feet protesting their own loyalty and that of his Flemish subjects but begging for relief from their suffering. The King is adamant in his attitude towards them, and an ensemble develops in which some of the court and part of the crowd join in begging for mercy, others, led by the priests, demand death for the traitors and heretics.

Don Carlos stands before his father and asks that he may begin his training for the Crown which will one day adorn his brow by being appointed the King's deputy at the head of his Flemish subjects. The King refuses a request that would create a weapon which might one day be used against Spain itself. Carlos in desperation draws his sword and announces that he will save Flanders; consternation fills the bystanders that he should have dared to draw his sword in the presence of the King. Philippe orders that he be disarmed, but no one dare obey, until Rodrigue, who sees that he is otherwise lost, quietly asks for his sword and gives it to the King. The procession advances, the sound of the monks singing the death-knell of the heretics can be heard, and over all a voice from heaven promises peace in the next world to those who are suffering in this.

Act IV. The first scene takes place in Philippe's own room, high above the altar of the Escorial. Here, for the first time in the opera, we see him alone, as man rather than as monarch. In his monologue he betrays his anxiety, more, his acute misery over the failure of his marriage, his loneliness not only as a king, because his state demands it, but as a man, because his wife has no love for him in her heart.

The Grand Inquisitor is announced, an old man, ninety years of age, blind but walking erect with the aid of a stick. He has been sent for; may he know why? The King explains that his son has offended grievously and has publicly taken the part of the heretic Flemish; he intends either to exact no penalty from him at all, or else to punish him with nothing less than death. If he decides on the latter alternative, has he the support of Holy Church in so extreme a measure? The Inquisitor says that God was not afraid to give His only Son that the world might be saved. Has the King nothing more to ask of him? No. Then it is his duty, as Inquisitor, to speak to him as the King. The fault of the impetuous Carlos is as nothing to that committed by the man he wishes to denounce: the Marquess of Posa. The King will not agree to sacrifice his new confidant, and is castigated by the Inquisitor as a man whose heart is not wholly given to God. Refusing to make any concession whatsoever, the Inquisitor goes his way, leaving behind him a sadder man.

No sooner has the Inquisitor left than Elisabeth rushes into the King's presence, demanding his help in regaining her casket of jewels, which has disappeared from her room. He asks her coldly if what she seeks is the casket on his table; on his instruction she opens it to reveal a portrait of Carlos. Philippe denounces what he describes as her adultery in phrases of ever mounting tension, and Elisabeth faints. Eboli and Rodrigue answer the King's call for help, and Philippe himself expresses his bitter regret at his rash and cruel suspicion. Eboli is stricken with conscience at what her jealousy of Carlos and Elisabeth has brought about – it was she who suggested the King look in the jewel case – and Rodrigue sees in the crisis a situation from which he can only rescue Carlos by taking his place as an offering on the altar of liberty. The Queen revives and voices her loneliness and desolation. The two men leave the room and Eboli throws herself at the feet of the Queen to confess a double fault: that she has excited the King's suspicions because of her own jealousy, and that she herself has been guilty of the adultery of which she suspected Elisabeth – she has in fact been the King's mistress. Elisabeth's dignity remains unshaken, but she orders Eboli to leave her presence for ever and to expiate her crime by choosing between exile and life in a nunnery. Left alone, Eboli pours forth her grief and misery at what her fatal beauty has brought about; one thing only remains for her before she leaves the court for the last time – she must do whatever is in her power to save Carlos from the threat of death which hangs over him.

The first scene of Act IV is one of the finest in all

Verdi's operas. A mere catalogue of what it contains is perhaps enough to give some idea of its varied, many-sided nature, and yet to suggest the strong dramatic line which runs through it all. It begins with the greatest of Verdi's bass arias, the *scena* 'Elle ne m'aime pas' (Ella giammai m'amo), a remarkable portrayal of the King's anguish and loneliness.

There follows the duet between the two basses, a uniquely varied piece of writing, whose strength is unsurpassed, one makes bold to say, in any operatic music. The clash of personalities is extraordinary, the King, bigot though he is, still relying on logic and reason for his argument, the Inquisitor, impregnable in his privileged stronghold, defying logic and argument in his religious conviction. At the end, after the King has twice made unsuccessful attempts at reconciliation or at least at a kind of working peace, his reserve breaks down, and in a mighty two-octave phrase spanning the bass's top and bottom Fs he demands rhetorically whether the throne must always bow the knee to the altar. The short scene between Philippe and Elisabeth, particularly the King's measured cursing of his wife's infidelity, is excellent, as is the equally brief but no less expressive scene between Eboli and Elisabeth, and the quartet which divides the two is equally remarkable. It is dominated by Philippe's rising phrase, but the Queen's revival from her swoon is exquisitely done, and the whole quartet is a fine example of Verdi's ensemble writing. To crown an act of almost unmatched richness, we have 'O don fatal' (O don fatale), a superb, economical piece of construction, which brings the act to an appropriate close and crowns Eboli's appearances in a blaze of musical glory.

Scene ii is set in Carlos's prison. To him comes Rodrigue, knowing that the letters from Flanders which were originally addressed to Carlos have been found in his possession and that his days are therefore numbered. He bids farewell to his friend in an expressive aria, 'C'est mon jour, mon jour suprême' (Per me giunto è il dì supremo). A shot rings out and he falls mortally wounded by an assassin who has crept into the prison after him and discharged his arquebus into his back. He tells Carlos ('Carlos, écoute'; O Carlo ascolta) that the Queen will wait for him on the following day outside the Convent of San Yuste and will see him for the last time. He dies happy at the thought that in Carlos a champion of liberty survives him. The act sometimes ends here.

Philippe makes an attempt to give back his sword to his son, but Carlos spurns him as the murderer of his friend. A noise can be heard; it is a mob which has gained entrance to the prison building, crying for liberty and the release of Don Carlos. Eboli herself is with them, making a last effort to save Carlos from the results of his folly. The people demand that Carlos be given up to them, but at this moment the Inquisitor appears as if from nowhere and castigates the crowd which has dared to raise its hand against the Lord's anointed; let them go down on their knees before him. Once more, the Church has come to the rescue of the throne.

Act V. The scene is the cloister of San Yuste. Elisabeth kneels at the tomb of Charles V. She sings sadly of the joys she once knew, of her native France and her love for the youthful Don Carlos, and of the sorrow she now has in parting from him for ever: 'Toi qui sus le néant des grandeurs de ce monde' (Tu che le vanità conoscesti del mondo). The wide-ranging melody shows Elisabeth in full stature as a mature person, and does something to give the lie to those who look upon this as not one of Verdi's most interesting heroines. The exquisite phrase, originally

S'an - cor si pian - ge in cie - - lo,

heard in the duet in Act I and since then associated with her youth in France, recurs as she remembers her past happiness. The aria finishes with a renewal of her prayer for peace, ending exquisitely *ppp*.

Elisabeth and Carlos meet for a last farewell, and recall the happiness that might have been theirs, turning their attention however from the past and present towards the future, which holds for Carlos a career devoted to the liberal causes that Rodrigue loved so well. It is the last of their three extensive duets, and worthy of the richness of the two that went before. As they take their leave of one another, Philippe comes from his hiding-place, seizes Elisabeth, and demands that the Grand Inquisitor, who is with him, shall do his duty towards Carlos. The old priest orders his guards to seize the prince, but Carlos defends himself and backs towards the tomb of Charles V at the rear of the cloister. Suddenly, a voice can be heard coming from it, and the Emperor himself (or a monk in his guise) appears and takes his grandson into the safety of the cloister. The ending has been much criticised as a weakened version of Schiller, where Philippe hands his son over to the mercy of the Inquisition, and in some productions an attempt has been made to return to Schiller's original.

Don Carlos is a magnificent opera, weakened only by its unusual length. It contains Verdi's greatest bass role and one of the greatest of his mezzo-soprano roles; two superb singing roles in Elisabeth and Carlos; and an opportunity for a notable baritone to re-create out of the slightly reduced figure of Posa the great liberal of Schiller's play. It also contains one of the most perfect climactic scenes in all Verdi, the first of the fourth act, in which the diverse threads of the drama, which have been developed in the five preceding scenes, are drawn together. The two scenes which follow resolve the conflicts which it has brought to a head – in Act IV, scene ii, Catholic Spain *v.* Protestant Flanders, liberal Rodrigue *v.* established authority (Crown and Church), Church *v.* State; in Act V, Elisabeth *v.* Eboli (over Carlos), and Philippe *v.* Carlos (over Elisabeth and Flanders). With these five major issues at stake, it is hardly surprising that the opera is a long one, any more than it is surprising that the subject elicited some of Verdi's most memorable music.   H.

AIDA

Opera in four acts, text by Antonio Ghislanzoni from the French prose of Camille du Locle, on an original scenario by Mariette Bey. Première at Cairo, 24 December 1871; at la Scala, Milan, 8 February 1872, with Stolz, Waldmann, Fancelli, Pandolfini, Maini, conductor Verdi.

The King of Egypt..Bass
Amneris, *daughter of the*
    King of Egypt..................................Mezzo-Soprano
Aida, *her Ethiopian slave*...............................Soprano
Radames, *captain of the Egyptian Guard* ....Tenor
Ramfis, *High Priest of Isis* ....Bass
Amonasro, *King of Ethiopia and*
    Aida's father..Baritone
A Messenger ....Tenor

Priests, Egyptian Soldiers, Ethiopians, Egyptians

Place: Memphis and Thebes
Time: Epoch of the Pharaohs
Running Time: 2 hours 15 minutes

*A*ida was commissioned by the Khedive of Egypt for the Italian Theatre in Cairo (not for the opening of the Suez Canal as is sometimes supposed), and written in Italian from a French prose text on an original scenario by a French Egyptologist. Taking a cue from the Triumph Scene of Act II, *Aida* has often been the subject of spectacular productions, and the scale of the voices needed to do justice to the score supports this view. But a case can also be made for a sparer view of *Aida*. The prelude and the first scene (all but the finale) are concerned with soliloquies and private meetings, as is, a dance of priestesses apart, the dedication of Radames to his role as army commander in the scene which follows, and indeed the long encounter between Amneris and Aida in Act II. Act III is entirely an affair of solo, duet and trio, and the last act has Amneris in confrontation with Radames, Radames silent in face of his judges, and finally Radames entombed with Aida. Only the return of the triumphant Egyptian army in Act II scene ii is on a truly big scale, and perhaps the end of the opening scene when the citizenry wishes its forces well. Otherwise it is individual emotions, conflicts and resolutions with which Verdi is concerned. A slimline *Aida* may be rare, but is not self-contradictory and can be a revelation.

Act I. The prelude puts forward Aida, gentle and feminine, contrasted with the implacable Egyptian priesthood of Isis. Ethiopia has recovered quickly from war with Egypt and news has been received to the effect that an Ethiopian army menaces Thebes. In his aria, 'Celeste Aida', Radames hopes he will be chosen to lead the Egyptian army, not least because this might facilitate his plan to marry Aida. But the King's daughter, Amneris, as is plain from her entrance, is herself in love with Radames, and, in spite of feigned friendship, already jealous of Aida whom she has taken as her slave (trio). On to the scene come King and court; first a messenger brings news that Amonasro, the Ethiopian king, is himself leading the enemy forces, then Radames is proclaimed Egyptian commander-in-chief. General rejoicing culminates in a cry of 'Ritorna vincitor!' (Return as victor), which, the crowd departed, is paradoxically taken up in a magnificent aria by Aida, more immediately anxious for Radames's success than concerned for Ethiopian aspirations. Her aria ends with a *cantabile* prayer ('Numi, pietà').

The second scene is in the Temple of Vulcan,

where priests chant, dancers celebrate, and Radames with some solemnity is invested with consecrated weaponry.

Act II. In Amneris's apartments, the princess, plainly languishing with love for Radames, is being prepared for the festivity which will welcome the now victorious army. Amneris commiserates with Aida over the Ethiopian defeat, advancing the (fictitious) news of Radames's death as comfort. Aida's despairing reaction provides Amneris with ammunition to taunt her slave that the King's daughter is her rival. There is no greater scene for soprano and mezzo in Italian opera.

Scene ii. Before one of the gates of Thebes, King and court assemble to greet the triumphant Egyptian army. Trumpets start the processional March – one of the most famous in or out of opera – and soldiers with trophies file past. Finally it is Radames's turn; he asks for the prisoners to be brought before the King, and Aida recognises her father, whose identity as leader remains hidden. Radames requests they be set at liberty, priests and populace demand death, while Aida, Amneris, Radames and Amonasro express conflicting emotions in a magnificent scene. The King announces a compromise: the prisoners will be freed with Aida's father remaining as surety; Amneris rejoices, and the King announces that her hand in marriage shall be Radames's reward for victory.

Act III. From the Temple of Isis on the banks of the Nile, priests chant as Amneris goes to pray before her nuptials with Radames. In an aria of subtle beauty ('O patria mia, mai più ti rivedrò'), Aida wonders why Radames has asked her to meet him here and yearns for Ethiopia. Before she can find out, her father confronts her with a demand that, if she would outflank her rival, she must discover from Radames the Egyptian army's route for the forthcoming battle. She recoils at the suggestion, he savagely denounces her prevarication, and his insistence wears her down. The meeting with Radames is partly one of the great love scenes of opera, partly pure seduction, as Aida entices him to agree they must flee together and then asks how they will avoid the Egyptian army. No love music could be more fragrant than Aida's, no triumph more complete than Amonasro's when he learns the chosen route. Radames is horror-stricken; Amneris and Ramfis denounce him as a traitor and, as Amonasro and Aida flee, he surrenders.

Act IV. A hall in the King's palace. Amneris, now bitterly regretting the doom her jealous denunciation will bring upon Radames, sends for him and interrogates him. In a passage as taut as advocates making points in a courtroom, she alternately implores Radames to exculpate himself and rages at his refusal to do so. When he is three times silent in face of a priestly accusation of treason, Amneris's fury is turned on his accusers in a passage which for sheer mezzo-soprano power rivals Ortrud's in the third act of *Lohengrin*.

Scene ii. Above, the Temple of Vulcan; below, a dungeon. Radames is, as he thinks, doomed to perish alone, but a voice utters his name: Aida has hidden herself to die with him. Their farewell to life ('O terra addio') has a stillness and finality that finds echo in the almost monotone Amneris, a desolate mourner in the temple above.

Aida stands as one of the romantic nineteenth century's operas which have best stood the test of time. It can be saturated with spectacle but the musical characterisation is unsurpassed; the tunes are immediate but the writing as subtle as if it were a string quartet; Aida is part seductress, part faithful lover; Radames as robust as a games captain but as un-selfseeking as a biblical hero; Amneris outwardly a power-conscious virago but inside a love-lorn maiden. The music is consistently of the highest quality and there can have been few performances in the last hundred-odd years without the 'house full' signs outside.   H.

OTELLO

Opera in four acts, text by Arrigo Boito, after Shakespeare's play. Première at la Scala, Milan, 5 February 1887, with Pantaleoni, Tamagno, Maurel, conductor Faccio. First performed in New York, 1888, with Eva Tetrazzini, Marconi (later Campanini), Galassi; Lyceum Theatre, London, 1889, with Cataneo, Tamagno, Maurel, conductor Faccio; Covent Garden, 1891, with Albani, Jean de Reszke, Maurel; Metropolitan, New York, 1894, with Albani, Tamagno, Maurel. Revived Covent Garden, 1926, with Lehmann, Zenatello, Stabile; 1928, with Zanelli; 1937, with Ciani (later Norena), Martinelli, Formichi (later Tibbett), conductor Beecham; 1950, by Company of la Scala, Milan, with Tebaldi, Vinay, Bechi, conductor de Sabata; 1955, with Brouwenstijn, Vinay, Otakar Kraus, under Kubelík. Revived at Metropolitan, 1902, with Eames, Alvarez, Scotti; 1937, with Rethberg, Martinelli, Tibbett, conductor Panizza. Revived at la Scala, 1927, with Scacciati, Trantoul, Stabile, conductor Toscanini; 1938, with Caniglia, Merli, Biasini, conductor de Sabata; 1942, with Caniglia, Lauri-Volpi, Stabile, conductor Marinuzzi; 1947, with Caniglia, Vinay, Bechi, conductor de Sabata. After Tamagno's death, Zenatello and Slezak became the leading international exponents of the title role, to be followed by Zanelli and later Martinelli, and (after 1945) by Vinay, del Monaco and Placido Domingo. Other famous singers of the title role have included Pertile, Vickers, McCracken and (in England) Frank Mullings and Charles Craig.

Otello, *a Moor, general in the Venetian army*...Tenor

Iago, *his ensign*..Baritone

Cassio, *his lieutenant* ....Tenor

Roderigo, *a Venetian gentleman*..........................Tenor

Lodovico, *ambassador of the Venetian republic* ....Bass

Montano, *Otello's predecessor as Commander in Cyprus*......................................Bass

A Herald ....Baritone

Desdemona, *wife to Otello* ....Soprano

Emilia, *Iago's wife and Desdemona's lady*..Mezzo-Soprano

Soldiers and Sailors of the Republic, Venetian Ladies and Gentlemen, Cypriot Men and Women

Place: A Seaport in Cyprus
Time: End of the Fifteenth Century
Running Time: 2 hours 10 minutes

In the 1860s Arrigo Boito, a young man in his early twenties and a champion of the new (not least Wagner), caused Verdi deep offence, yet it was he nearly twenty years later who was to write for Verdi the libretti of his two last operas, *Otello* and *Falstaff*. It took years of coaxing on the part of his astute publisher, Giulio Ricordi, years of patient and skilful bridge-building on the part of Boito, before Verdi in 1879 was induced to contemplate *Otello* as an idea and just as skilful discussion of the musico-theatrical possibilities before the composer would admit to a genuine interest. He was nervous of committing himself, of being unable to finish what he had started, and the secrecy surrounding the project was as deep as if it were a military operation.

Nearly sixteen years elapsed between the appearance of *Aida* and that of *Otello*, and between the two only the composition of the *Manzoni Requiem* (1884) told the public that the veteran composer had not actually abandoned composition. The enthusiasm engendered by the opera's first performances gave way as the years went by to something closer to respect, but in the second half of the twentieth century a performance of *Otello* which did not sell

out was a rarity and the opera has become as much a part of the repertory – in spite of the difficulty of casting the title role – as *Don Giovanni* or *Tristan*.

In *Otello* as in *Macbeth*, his previous Shakespearean opera, Verdi had a hand in the construction of the libretto, although Boito must have the credit for the remarkable feat of compression which has gone towards it. In Shakespeare's play there are nearly 3,500 lines; in the opera under 800. The Venetian scenes have been removed and each of the four acts plays without a break with (in the modern, not the Shakespearean sense) no more than a single change of scene (in Act III).

Act I. In the background, a quay and the sea. After the *fortissimo* crash of the opening chord, Otello's ship can be seen making for port through a heavy storm. Among the crowd of watchers who exclaim upon the danger to the vessel are Iago and Roderigo. The storm prepares vividly for our first encounter with Otello, who is, as it is obvious he must be, the dominating figure of the opera. His opening shout of triumph, 'Esultate! l'orgoglio musulmano sepolto è in mar', makes a splendid entrance, and shows the warrior in all his glory, unhurried and unrivalled, in a way that without the help of music is perhaps out of reach of Shakespeare.

Otello is acclaimed by the crowd, and proceeds to the castle followed by Cassio, Montano, and soldiers. The people start a wood fire and gather about it dancing and singing: 'Fuoco di gioia'. It transpires in talk between Iago and Roderigo that Iago hates Otello, to whom he is outwardly so devoted, because he has advanced Cassio over him, and that Roderigo is in love with Desdemona.

The fire dies out, the storm has ceased. Now comes the scene in which Iago purposely makes Cassio drunk, in order to cause his undoing. He sings a drinking song, 'Inaffia l'ugola', which Cassio tries unsuccessfully to repeat after him; under the influence of the liquor Cassio resents the taunts of Roderigo, which Iago has instigated. Montano tries to quiet them, Cassio draws, and in the fight that follows Montano is wounded. The tumult brings Otello to the scene, and, with an imperious call, he brings the brawl to an end (Boito's use of 'Keep up your bright swords' – 'Abbasso le spade' – at this point is evidence of his care for detail). Cassio is dismissed from the Moor's service and Iago has scored his first triumph.

Otello. *The great tenor Francesco Tamagno (1850–1905) in the title role, which he created in 1887 in Milan; portrait by F. Keller, 1889.*

The people disperse, quiet settles upon the scene, and Otello and Desdemona are alone. So far, we have seen only the man of authority, but in the love duet Otello the poet is put forward with a persuasiveness that is to keep this side of him fresh in the minds of the audience, however low he may later fall. For the duet Boito has used lines from the Senate scene of Shakespeare's Act I, and also from Othello's welcome to Desdemona in Cyprus. This is Verdi's only full-scale love duet in which there is no sense of urgency or restriction; all the previous examples, however beautiful, have been either illicit or liable to interruption at every moment. In his music, the composer encompasses the sensitivity of both lovers, the mature yet impetuous Otello, the serene but passionate Desdemona, frequently giving them the same phrases to sing, yet always differentiating the one from the other with the surest and most delicate touch imaginable. Just before the close of the act, Otello embraces Desdemona; the musical phrase is used again before the end of the opera:

Act II. A hall in the castle. Iago, plotting to make Otello jealous of Desdemona, advises Cassio to induce the Moor's wife to plead for his reinstatement. When he is alone, Iago sings his famous Credo: 'Credo in un Dio crudel che m'ha creato simile a sè' (I believe in a cruel God, who has fashioned me in his own image). The lines and the sentiments are original to Boito, and the soliloquy could be thought of as simplifying the essential complications of Shakespeare's Iago – a mighty declaration of belief, nonetheless. Declamatory trumpets are conspicuous in the accompaniment.

Iago, seeing Otello approach, looks fixedly in the direction of Desdemona and Cassio, exclaiming, 'Ha! I like not that.' As in the corresponding scene in the play, this leads up to the questioning of him by Otello and to Iago's crafty answers, which not only apply the match to, but later fan the flame of Otello's jealousy. The temptation of Otello by Iago is set to music that is suggestive and fluid to a marked degree and the rising temperature of the music throughout the act is exactly calculated to fit the growing and unremitting intensity of the play at this point.

Now comes the interruption of the madrigal; by its end, Otello is once more under the spell of Desdemona's beauty and transparent innocence, and is prepared to put suspicion behind him. But in a moment she has

asked him to pardon Cassio, has asked again when he gently refuses to consider the subject at such a juncture, and then accused him of ill-temper in his answer. During the ensuing quartet for Desdemona, Emilia, Otello and Iago, the poison works, and at its end Otello dismisses Desdemona, but not before Iago has had the opportunity to steal the handkerchief on which so much of the rest of the plot is to hang.

Otello and Iago are alone again, and Otello voices his grief at his loss of peace of mind: 'Ora e per sempre addio' (Now and for ever, farewell). It is the equivalent of the play's farewell to arms, and the type of musical expression used here is far more straightforward than in the earlier part of the act, as befits Otello decided as compared with Otello perplexed.

Iago makes pretence of calming him, but to such a fury is the Moor roused that he seizes Iago, hurls him to the ground, and threatens to kill him should his accusations against Desdemona prove false. Iago ventures on a bolder step, and describes a dream he says Cassio has had while sharing a room with him. He talked openly in his sleep of his love for Desdemona, and Iago describes what ensued in wonderfully suggestive music. He caps it all by telling Otello that he has even seen the handkerchief, which Otello gave his wife when they were married, in the hands of Cassio.

Otello's rage knows no limits, and in music of relentless fury, he pledges himself to prove Desdemona's guilt, and to avenge it; Iago joins him in his oath: 'Si, pel ciel marmoreo giuro'.

Act III. The great hall of the castle. After a brief scene in which the approach of the ambassadors is announced, Desdemona enters. Wholly unaware of the cause of Otello's strange actions towards her, she again begins to plead for Cassio's restoration to favour. Boito has used Otello's insistence on the handkerchief while Desdemona urges Cassio's reinstatement, and combined it with part of the so-called 'brothel' scene. Upon her knees, Desdemona vows her constancy: 'Esterrefatta fisso', but Otello's mixture of fury, irony and hysteria proves too much for her, and she rushes from his presence.

Left alone, Otello soliloquises in the introspective mood of the temptation scenes ('Dio mi potevi scagliar'), and there is nothing of the character of the outburst at the end of Act II about his monologue until its close, when Iago re-enters and tells him that

Cassio is at hand, and the music rises suddenly to a strident climax.

Otello hides and Iago brings in Cassio, who is led into banter about Bianca, which Otello half hears and takes to refer to Desdemona. During the course of the trio, Iago contrives that Cassio shall reveal the handkerchief so that Otello may see it (Iago has conveyed it to Cassio's chambers, after stealing it from Emilia). Cassio disappears when the trumpets are heard announcing the arrival of the Venetian ambassadors, and, in a few bars of music and with the acclamation of the crowd as background, Otello plots with Iago that Desdemona shall die that very night in the bed she has fouled.

The Venetian ambassadors arrive. There follows the scene in which the recall of Otello to Venice and the appointment of Cassio as Governor of Cyprus in his stead are announced. In the presence of the ambassadors, the Moor strikes down Desdemona, and all join her in a plea for mercy, at the end of which ensemble Otello orders them to leave the hall. Overcome by his rage and emotion, Otello falls in a swoon, while the people, believing that their deliverer is to return to Venice to receive new honours at the hands of the Republic, shout his praises from outside. Iago reaches the heights of his power with his triumphant 'Ecco il Leon!' over the prostrate body of the general who trusts him and has just granted him promotion, but whom he hates so much.

Act IV. Desdemona's bedchamber. There is an orchestral introduction of great beauty; then, as in the play, comes the brief dialogue between Desdemona and Emilia. Desdemona sings the pathetic Willow Song: 'Piangea cantando'. Her singing is interrupted as she talks to Emilia, and at its end she says goodnight, the song dying away into silence as Emilia goes out, only to be called back by Desdemona's heartrending cry of 'Ah! Emilia, Emilia, addio!' It is the most moving moment of a moving scene.

Emilia leaves, and Desdemona kneels and intones an exquisite 'Ave Maria', beginning and ending in pathetic monotone. The violins end Desdemona's prayer on a high A flat, and double basses herald Otello's entrance with a *pianissimo* bottom E, five octaves and a half below. He moves towards Desdemona's bed, hesitates, and then kisses her three times. He vainly tries to force her to admit the crime he thinks she has committed, and then smothers her in

spite of her pleas for mercy. The sound of knocking is heard and Emilia runs into the room crying that Cassio has killed Roderigo. She hears a dying gasp from Desdemona, and rushes from the room screaming that her mistress has been murdered. Cassio, Iago, and Lodovico answer her summons, and Emilia reveals Iago's villainy, which is confirmed by Montano, who has heard the confession of the dying Roderigo.

Iago escapes, and Otello seizes his sword from the table, defying anyone present to require it of him. 'Niun mi tema' he sings before addressing himself to the dead Desdemona in music whose pathos is doubled by its contrast with what has gone before. He stabs himself, and the music associated in the Love Duet with his kiss is heard: 'Un bacio, un bacio ancora, un altro bacio', before he lies dead beside his wife. In his last utterance he has resumed the nobility of the earlier part of the opera, and his death scene musically has much of the quality of the great closing speech of the last act of Shakespeare's play.   K., H.

FALSTAFF

Opera in three acts, text by Arrigo Boito. Première at la Scala, Milan, 9 February 1893, with Stehle, Zilli, Pasqua, Garbin, Maurel, Pini-Corsi, Paroli, Arimondi, conductor Mascheroni. First performed Opéra-Comique, Paris, 1894; Covent Garden, 1894, with Ravogli, de Lussan, Olgina, Pessina, Arimondi; Metropolitan, New York, 1895, with Eames, de Lussan, Schalchi, Russitano, Maurel, Campanari, conductor Mancinelli. Revived at la Scala, 1921, with Canetti, Marmora, Casazza, de Paolis, Stabile, Badini, conductor Toscanini; 1936, with Caniglia, Favero, Casazza, Landi, Stabile, Badini, Bettoni, conductor de Sabata; 1950, with Tebaldi, Noni, Barbieri, Francesco Albanese, Stabile, Silveri, Siepi, conductor de Sabata; Covent Garden, 1926, with Stabile; Sadler's Wells, 1938; Cambridge Theatre, 1948, with Stabile, conductor Erede; Covent Garden, 1950, by la Scala company; Metropolitan, 1925, with Bori, Alda, Telva, Gigli, Scotti, Tibbett, conductor Serafin; 1938, with Tibbett, conductor Panizza; Salzburg, 1935, with Caniglia, Mason, Cravcenco, Dino Borgioli, Stabile, Biasini, conductor Toscanini; Covent Garden, 1961, with Geraint Evans, conductor Giulini.

Sir John Falstaff..Baritone

Fenton, *a young gentleman*.................................Tenor

Ford, *a wealthy citizen*....................................Baritone

Dr Caius..Tenor

Bardolfo (Bardolph), *a follower of Falstaff*...........Tenor

Pistola (Pistol), *a follower of Falstaff*....................Bass

Alice Ford, *Ford's wife* ....Soprano
Nannetta, *her daughter* ....Soprano
Mistress Page, *Alice's friend*................Mezzo-Soprano
Dame Quickly ....Contralto

Burghers and Street-Folk, Ford's Servants, etc.

Place: Windsor
Time: Reign of Henry IV
Running Time: 2 hours 10 minutes

If Verdi surrounded the writing of *Otello* with mystery, this was as nothing compared with the secrecy which shrouded its successor, which Verdi insisted, almost until it was finished, was being written purely for his own pleasure and with no thought or intention of public performance. The aged composer seems to have laid down the score with a feeling of real regret and a conviction that his life's work was ended with its completion. As far as opera was concerned, this turned out to be true, but the anything but negligible *Quattro Pezzi Sacri* testify to his continued energy as a musical creator.

In both *Otello* and *Macbeth*, Verdi and his librettists had kept as close to Shakespeare as operatic form would allow them; but in *Falstaff*, they contrived to inject a considerable measure of the great Falstaff of *Henry IV* into the veins of the Falstaff of *The Merry Wives of Windsor*, and so the operatic adaptation is in certain ways an improvement on the original.

Act I. A room at the Garter Inn – the 'Giarrettiera', as the Italian has it. Dr Caius comes to complain that Falstaff has beaten his servants, and that Bardolfo and Pistola made him drunk and then robbed him. Falstaff laughs and talks him out of countenance, and he swears that he will never get drunk again, save in the society of honest, sober people, noted for their piety. As he leaves after this grandiloquent statement, Pistola and Bardolfo, beating time as they do so, sing an antiphonal 'Amen', until Falstaff stops them with his complaint that they sing out of time.

He looks at his bill, compares the total with what is left in his purse, and starts to complain that the prodigal living of his two cronies is reducing him to a state of beggary, and, what is worse, is bringing him perilously close to reducing his weight – and Falstaff, as he rightly says, without his corporation would be a shadow of his real self. The others applaud such

self-revelation – 'Falstaff immenso! enorme Falstaff!' – and Falstaff proceeds to tell them that he is currently enamoured of no less than two ladies, the wives of Ford and Page. He has written two love letters, and Bardolfo and Pistola are to bear them to their destinations. But this the two worthies refuse to do; their honour will not allow them to take part in such a transaction. Cursing them, Falstaff sends the notes off by a page, and rounds on the pair of them. What right have they to talk of honour, ruffians that they are? Boito has transplanted the Honour monologue, and here Verdi sets it with incomparable aptness and relish: 'L'onore! Ladri!' At its end, Falstaff picks up a broom and chases Bardolfo and Pistola out of the room.

The scene changes to the garden of Ford's house, and the orchestra tells us clearly we are in the presence of the merry wives, Alice Ford, Meg Page, and Mistress Quickly. With them is Anne Ford[1] (Nannetta). In company with Quickly, Meg has come to pay a visit to Alice Ford to show her a letter which she has just received from Falstaff. Alice matches Meg's with one of her own, and the four read the two letters which, save for a different address, are exactly alike. The women are half amused, half annoyed at the presumption of the fat knight, and plan to avenge themselves upon him.

Meanwhile Ford goes walking before his house together with Caius, young Fenton (who is in love with Nannetta, but frowned on as a suitor by Ford), Bardolfo and Pistola. The last two have deserted their master, and from them Ford has learned that Falstaff is after his wife. He too meditates revenge, and the female quartet and the male quintet sometimes mingle, sometimes are heard separately. Fenton and Nannetta remain behind for a fleeting kiss, and sing a miniature love duet together, ending with a phrase of melting beauty:

---

[1] Anne Page in Shakespeare, with a new patronym.

The women return, but quickly disappear when they think they are being overheard, and once again the two young lovers are alone and can indulge in their battle of kisses. The men reappear, so do the women, and separately they put the finishing touches to their schemes of revenge. This is the famous ensemble in which Verdi combines what was previously sung separately by the men and women, the men singing *alla breve*, the women in 6/8 (Ex. 2).

Act II. The Garter Inn, where Falstaff is still at table. Beating their breasts in mock penitence, Bardolfo and Pistola beg to be forgiven for their previous infidelity, and tell Falstaff that an old woman is outside asking to be admitted to his presence. Dame Quickly comes in, and, with the orchestra, makes deep obeisance to the knight: 'Reverenza' is set characteristically to a musical representation of a curtsey. Falstaff is all condescension and affability – 'Buon giorno, buona donna': and Quickly delivers

her messages, one from each of the ladies, to the effect that Alice will receive the knight, but that Meg's husband guards her too jealously ever to leave her alone. Alice can see him from two till three ('Dalle due alle tre') when her husband is always out. Falstaff repeats the words with evident delight, and assures Quickly that he will not default on the assignation.

Quickly starts to leave, and is tipped by Falstaff as he dismisses her, again with a magnificent sense of the appropriate gesture. He is left alone with thoughts of his impending success: 'Alice è mia' (Alice is mine) he sings (orchestrally this is the epitome of Falstaff's delight and anticipation), and has time for

a little strutting march of anticipatory triumph ('Va, vecchio John') before his next visitor is announced.

It is Ford. He introduces himself to Falstaff under the name of Master Brook (Signor Fontana), presents the knight with a purse of silver as a bait, then tells him that he is in love with Mistress Ford, whose chastity he cannot breach, and begs Falstaff to lay siege to her and so make the way easier for him. Falstaff catches up the suggestion of music from him, and breaks mockingly into a little song of delicious triumph ('L'amor, l'amor che non ci dà mai tregue Finchè la vita strugge').

Falstaff gleefully tells him that he has a rendezvous with her that very afternoon, and that he (Signor Fontana) may be quite sure that he will be able eventually to attain what he so much desires. When Ford asks if Falstaff knows the husband of Alice, he hears himself described with contumelious abuse. The comedy is rich and never underlined and this duet stands as the last of the long line of similarly conceived scenes.

Falstaff goes out for a moment to change his clothes, and Ford is left alone, a prey to jealousy in its most tormenting form. His soliloquy in celebration of that emotion might be expected to put Verdi in a dangerous position after his completely successful portrayal of tragic jealousy in *Otello*, but peril is circumvented, and this is one of the great moments of the opera, moreover a complete re-creation of the Elizabethan delight in the comedy of the outraged cuckold. Falstaff returns, and, after some argument as to who shall go through the door first, they leave arm in arm.

The scene changes to Ford's house, where the four women get ready to give Falstaff the reception he deserves. We learn, quite casually from talk between Mistress Ford and Nannetta, that Ford wants to marry off the girl to the aged pedant, Dr Caius, while she of course will marry none but Fenton, with whom she is in love. Her mother promises to aid her plans. Alice leads an ensemble with a *staccato* melody, and Quickly gives warning of Falstaff's approach.

Alice sits herself down and starts to play on the lute, to whose accompaniment Falstaff begins to sing her praises in extravagant terms. He sings a little song of irresistible melody: 'Quand'ero paggio del Duca di Norfolk', in which he describes his own slender and comely build when he was a boy. They are interrupted by Quickly, who announces that Ford can be seen approaching. The fat lover must be concealed. This is accomplished by getting him behind a screen, just before Ford enters with his followers, hoping to surprise the man who has invaded his home. They begin a search of the rooms.

While they are off exploring another part of the house, the women hurry Falstaff into a big washbasket, pile the soiled linen on top of him, and fasten it down. Scarcely has this been done when Ford comes back and hears the sound of kissing behind the screen. No longer any doubt! Falstaff is hidden there with his wife. He gathers everyone together, marches them towards the screen and knocks it down – to find behind it Nannetta and Fenton, who have used to their own purpose the diversion of attention from them. Ford, more furious than ever, rushes out, while his wife and her friends call in the servants, who lift the basket and empty it out of the window into the Thames

below. When Ford comes back, his wife leads him to the window and shows him Falstaff striking out for the shore.

Act III. Falstaff is sitting recovering at the Garter. His thoughts are gloomy and he calls for more wine, but even that prospect does not seem to cheer him up. The world is in a sorry state, he reflects, when such a pearl of knighthood as himself can be bundled unceremoniously into a basket full of dirty linen and dropped into the water. Everything is going to the dogs – even a subdued memory of the little march only reminds him that he is the last of the old brigade. The host appears with wine, and Falstaff's mood alters perceptibly at the prospect of swamping some of the Thames water inside him with some good wine. The scene has begun as invective against an ungrateful world but finishes as a panegyric in praise of wine, with the full orchestra trilling in sympathy as the wine mounts to colour his view of humanity.

Once more Quickly curtseys to him (considerably, it must be admitted, to his dismay), and offers him a rendezvous with Alice. Falstaff wants to hear no more of such things, and it takes all Quickly's powers of persuasion to get him even to listen, much less to agree to a meeting-place. However, in the end, he cannot resist the temptation which is being dangled in front of him, and settles for midnight at Herne the Hunter's Oak in Windsor forest, where he is to appear (as we learn a moment later from the concealed Alice and her friends) disguised as the black hunter himself, who, according to legend, hanged himself from the oak, with the result that the spot is haunted by witches and sprites.

The scene ends with an ensemble as the women and Fenton arrange the details of the evening's fun, and Ford and Caius plot that Caius's betrothal to Nannetta shall be announced that very night. The women call to each other off-stage and the strings offer fifteen bars of idyllic commentary as night falls.

The last scene takes place by moonlight under Herne's Oak. Horn-calls and references to the love music form the basis for the prelude to Fenton's aria 'Dal labbro il canto estasiato vola', which begins the act. It is filled with the same sweetness as can be found in the love music. Disguises are hastily donned, and in a moment Falstaff is heard arriving. He is wearing a pair of antlers on his head and is wrapped in a heavy cloak. Midnight strikes, echoed at each stroke by Falstaff, who consoles himself for the incongruity of his disguise by remembering that Jove disguised himself as a bull for love of Europa. For a moment he is alone with Alice, but they are immediately interrupted by noises, and Alice disappears into the darkness leaving Falstaff to fend for himself.

Nannetta, who is disguised as Queen of the Fairies, calls her followers around her, and they pirouette until she begins to sing. Verdi has given them music of exquisite delicacy and the choral writing is as delicious as that for the soloist: 'Sul fil d'un soffio etesio'.

Bardolfo in disguise stumbles on the recumbent figure of Falstaff (who has hidden his face so as not to see the fairies), and calls everyone to him. The merry women, Ford's entourage, and about a hundred others, all disguised and masked, unite in mystifying, taunting and belabouring Falstaff, until the knight at last recognises Bardolfo among his tormentors. Everyone unmasks in turn, and Falstaff's enormity and folly are displayed for his discomfiture. He makes a valiant attempt to recapture the initiative by complaining that without his participation a joke seems to have no wit in it, and all – even Ford – agree that his wit alone is sufficient to redeem him, in spite of his egregious faults.

Ford takes Nannetta by the hand and announces her betrothal to Caius, and does the same to another disguised young couple whom Alice leads up to him. He bids them all unmask – to find that Bardolfo has been dressed up in Nannetta's clothes and is now therefore betrothed to Caius, and that the other couple were Nannetta and Fenton in disguise. Falstaff cannot resist the temptation to turn Ford's question back on him: who is the dupe now? But Alice will not let him get away with it; he is to be placed beside Ford and Caius; if they are dupes, so is he. Ford is induced to bless his daughter and her sweetheart, and Falstaff leads the company in a final fugue: 'Tutto nel mondo è burla. L'uom è nato burlone' (Jesting is man's vocation. Wise is he who is jolly). For the second time in his career,[1] Verdi, who despised academicism, finished a Shakespearean opera with what is traditionally the most academic of forms, a fugue.

It would take most of a book to describe *Falstaff* in sufficient detail to do anything like justice to the kaleidoscopic variety of the score. There is a sparkle, a rapidity of utterance, a speed of movement, an economy of means in the ensemble writing that has no equal in music written since Mozart, and every bar is endowed with a refinement of expression and a restraint that it would be difficult to imagine in the composer of the operas before *Macbeth*. The music is even more fluid than in *Otello* and rhythmic ideas are caught up, dropped, and used again with a dexterity which Shakespeare himself never excelled in his own medium. It is all as light as air, and yet out of it has been fashioned Shakespeare's Falstaff drawn appropriately in the round, speaking Italian but more English at heart than in any English musical recreation of him.

H.

---

[1] *Macbeth* was the first.

PARAM VIR

(born 6 February 1952)

SNATCHED BY THE GODS

Chamber opera in one act, libretto by William Radice, based on the poem *Dvatar Gras* by Rabinranath Tagore. Commissioned by the Munich Biennale; first performed Amsterdam, 11 May 1992, with *Broken Strings*, conducted by David Porcelijn, then in Munich. Revived Almeida Theatre, London, 1996, conducted by Markus Stenz.

Maitra, *a well-to-do Brahmin*		Baritone
Moksada, *a young widow*		Soprano
Rahkal, *her son*		Treble

Ananda, *her elder sister*.......................Mezzo-Soprano

Boatman ....Bass

A Young Wife ....Soprano

Her Aunt...Contralto

Pilgrims
    A Young Man ....Tenor
    A Middle-Aged Man........................High Baritone
    An Old Blind Man...Bass

At sunrise Maitra is to lead a group of pilgrims to a festival where everyone will wash away their sins by bathing in the Ganges. He agrees to allow the young widow Moksada to come too. She means to leave her young son Rakhal with her sister Ananda. While she is fetching her things, Rakhal is discovered hiding in the boat. He also wants to go to the festival. Moksada returns and orders him to get out. Maitra is impressed by his eagerness and lets him stay, even though the Boatman warns that the boat is over-loaded. Without thinking, Moksada curses the boy: 'The sea can have you!' At once she regrets saying it. Ananda arrives, worried that she cannot find Rakhal, and is full of dread at his going. The journey begins.

The orchestral Interlude paints an extremely engaging picture of the voyage and the festival, complete with all manner of bell and gong sounds.

Afterwards, the passengers wait for the tide to turn so they can return home. Rakhal is homesick, Moksada is still beset with guilt at her curse. A strong wind drives the boat and soon builds into a storm. The Boatman loses control. He explains that the gods have been enraged: 'Someone among you has cheated the gods, has not given what is owing: hence these waves.' The passengers hurl their possessions into the water, but to no avail. Maitra points out that Moksada kept back the son she promised to the sea. All the passengers demand that Rakhal be thrown overboard. Moksada tries in vain to protect him. As he drowns he screams for his 'Aunt Ananda'. Maitra cries out, 'I shall bring you back', jumps in after the boy and drowns. The sun sets slowly in the river.

In a note on his double bill, the composer wrote of the meaning of the end: 'For the dying light of the setting sun, as it embraces the crumpled form of Moksada, contains the gentle promise of sunrise and rebirth.'   P.

BROKEN STRINGS

Opera in one act, libretto by David Rudkin, based on a traditional Buddhist story, *Guttil Jatak*. Commissioned by the Munich Biennale; first performed Amsterdam, 11 May 1992, with *Snatched by the Gods*, conducted by David Porcelijn, then in Munich. Revived Almeida Theatre, London, 1996, conducted by Markus Stenz.

The King ....Bass

Musil, *a brilliant young musician*........................Tenor

Guttil, *a forgotten old musician* ....Bass

Magical creatures
    The Elephant...Contralto
    The Fish ....Soprano
    The Peacock...Tenor

The Presiding Judge ....Baritone

The Second Judge ....Tenor

The Third Judge...................................High Baritone

The King asks for a play to be performed. An actor offers a work called 'To Play before the King', set during the last stages of a competition for the post of royal musician. Musil assumes he has won, since no one's mastery comes near to his. The music he plays is 'a high scherzando, dancing, rapid, glittering, impressive; but empty, cold'. Worried that the judges remain impassive, he tunes his instrument down and plays 'something more melodic... phrases in high middle register, arching, plaintive', but the judges are unimpressed; they thought he was tuning his instrument. Rodney Milnes in *Opera* magazine wickedly noted 'a hint of Stravinsky' in the music of Musil, that 'insufferably arrogant and priggish young virtuoso'. The composer himself has denied the allusion but volunteered that he embedded in Musil's music a flaw 'which can be taken both literally and symbolically. His music *lacks a bass line*.' Musil himself remains certain of success and waits to hear the final candidate.

Guttil emerges in rags, 'a man reduced to his own minimum'. He strikes his (four-stringed) instrument and creates 'sour "rusty" tones'. He tries again, 'searching, as though tuning in to what he hears'. A lower string breaks but that does not perturb him: 'We can make music yet. On higher strings...' He plays 'a defiant high glittering scherzando, angry somewhat, shallow, shrill...' Somehow, a new, deep note emerges, which rouses a magical elephant to life, a dancing and trumpeting personification of rhythm, a role beautifully written for a real contralto. A second string breaks but Guttil is undaunted: 'With even less,' he resolves, 'play on.' With the two remaining strings he creates 'halting, fragmentary, spare' music, which summons, touches and teases the Fish (harmony), sung by a coloratura soprano. Her delicious, silvery music (including a laughing song) makes all the more impact, partly because no high voice has been heard until now. A third string breaks but Guttil continues to play. A fierce pizzicato passage yields to an exquisite cor anglais solo as Guttil plays on the last string, 'an unearthly arching birdlike calling', and the Peacock (melody), a lyrical tenor, responds, enraptured. The three creatures dance as their musics fuse and 'glow with incandescent intensity... Through it all sounds more and more the penetrating note of the final string about to break...'.

The King has been watching appalled. He intervenes to stop the play but the last string breaks. A magical light appears about Guttil as he becomes a radiance and 'the song itself burns all the instrument away'. Musil, unmoved, laughs satanically, calls it a 'great trick' and Guttil a charlatan. He nevertheless determines to pay Guttil to teach his 'freak effect' to him. First, however, he breaks his own instrument hoping to repeat the effect. No sound emerges, Musil flees, 'uttering a long howl of one damned'.

The King bursts on to the stage and dismisses the actors. The opera ends with his exposed, heroic baritone solo, in which he applies to himself the lesson that Guttil has taught. Tom Sutcliffe in *The Guardian* rightly praised Param Vir's 'melodic writing for this final passage, the object of the whole opera, [as] both touching and memorable'. Holding Guttil's broken instrument the King asks, 'Is this... myself? Some song I thought I was?... Must less sustain me too?' David Rudkin's insubstantial, oblique version of Buddhist teachings ensures that the opera ends on a note of poetry, rather than didactic philosophy, as the King wonders whether he must continue the process, 'Till I must make whatever song is mine... from nothing...? The song I am... from nothing? Nothing? Only then... I begin...?'

When *Broken Strings* was revived in 1996, the critics of *The Times* and *The Guardian* (in rare agreement) united in saluting 'a born opera composer'. P.

AMADEO VIVES

(born 18 November 1871, died 1 December 1932)

Vives studied in Barcelona, where he later founded with Luis Millet the famous choir, Orfeó Català. A success in his native city with an opera, *Artus*, brought a move to Madrid, where for the rest of his life he composed operas and *zarzuelas* – more than a hundred works for the stage in the space of thirty-five years. He was stricken with infantile paralysis as a boy and this, together with a badly set shoulder after a fracture, so severely limited his movement that he was unable for instance to attend the triumphant première of *Doña Francisquita*. In spite of his success with lighter works, he longed for recognition as a wholly serious composer, particularly of Catalan operas, but only *Maruxa* in this genre rivalled the popularity of *zarzuelas* like *Bohemios* and *Doña Francisquita*. Vives died in Madrid but is said on his deathbed to have asked the priest to be allowed to pray in Catalan. H.

DOÑA FRANCISQUITA

Lyric comedy in three acts, text by Frederico Romero and Guillermo Fernández Shaw, after Lope de Vega's *La discreta enamorada*. Première in Madrid, 17 October 1923, with Mary Isaura, Cora Raga, Juan de Casenave (an inexperienced singer, hence the diffident nature of the role), Antonio Palacio, conductor Juan Antonio Martínez. The composer, who was in love with Mary Isaura, is rumoured to have restricted the number of encores allowed to the brilliant Cora Raga in the secondary role of Beltrana. *Doña Francisquita* has from the start captivated the Spanish public.

Doña Francisquita, *in love with Fernando*.......Soprano
Fernando Soler, *a student*...................................Tenor
Aurora 'la Beltrana', *an actress*...........Mezzo-Soprano
Cardona, *Fernando's friend*................................Tenor
Doñã Francisca, *Francisquita's mother*.........Contralto
Don Matías, *Fernando's father* ....Bass
Lorenzo Perez, *refreshment stall owner*...........Baritone

Lañador, *a tinker*..Baritone
A Pedlar..Mezzo-Soprano
A Nightwatchman ....Tenor

Street Vendors, Bullfighters, Townspeople

Place: Madrid
Time: Mid-Century, at Carnival Time
Running Time: 1 hour 40 minutes

It is as hard to avoid making some element of comparison between Spanish *zarzuela* and Viennese operetta as it is between Offenbach and Johann Strauss; neither's virtues are reduced by the appraisal. A composer like Franz Lehár is not diminished by the suggestion that his grandiloquent, full-frontal assaults on popular taste are at least matched by the Spaniard's subtler, rhythmically more varied, and scarcely less muscular effusions. The best of the *zarzuelas*, like the best of the operettas, are surely robust enough to travel.

Doña Francisquita provides a perfect exemplar of the 'high' *zarzuela* style – large of scale, with strong, lyrical writing for the soloists; lively rhythmical underpinning from the orchestra; 'big', potentially popular numbers to launch the work's fame into the popular media; and an atmosphere quintessentially Spanish. The invention seems inexhaustible, one delectable scene succeeds another, bolero attempts to outdo mazurka, lighter numbers somehow sound distinguished and larger statements contrive to sound popular. Vives is not afraid of writing an elaborate quintet just before the end of Act II, and solos like Francisquita's haunting waltz-time Song of the Nightingale and Fernando's heart-felt romance in Act II are candidates, one might think, for any aspiring artist's recital disc.

The action proceeds in a series of short scenes, several of them without music.

Act I. A square in Madrid, where tinker and pedlar are crying their wares and where Fernando meets his friend Cardona. Fernando is in love with the actress Beltrana, who makes fun of so inexperienced a suitor. From the church emerge Doña Francisca and her daughter Francisquita, the latter of whom has fallen for Fernando and resents the way he has eyes for no one but the actress. Francisquita's ploy of dropping her handkerchief works well and they strike up a conversation. Cardona praises Francisquita's beauty, but Fernando, not responding, can think only of the more sophisticated Beltrana.

Fernando's father, Don Matías, with none of his son's well-known shyness, has his eye on Francisquita, his manoeuvres unfortunately suggesting to that young lady's mother that she is his potential quarry rather than her daughter, a misunderstanding cleared up in a trice. Francisquita decides to take full advantage of what she sees as a chance to make Fernando jealous.

When la Beltrana puts in an appearance, she continues her not so subtle taunting of Fernando, and is promptly told off by Cardona. She retreats to a neighbouring refreshment booth, whose owner, Lorenzo, is another of her admirers. Cardona prevents an incident by stopping Fernando following her.

An encounter between Don Matías and the two young students produces another misunderstanding, this time suggesting to Fernando that he might make la Beltrana jealous by pretending to be interested in Francisquita. Students dance attendance on a wedding party, which Cardona and Fernando toast. When la Beltrana reappears, with Cardona's help Fernando makes up to Francisquita, noticing at the same time how genuinely attractive she is but not to the extent of extinguishing the torch he continues to carry for la Beltrana, who with a band of street musicians sings a *pasacalle* before disappearing with them. Francisquita is quietly confident she will still turn Fernando's head in her direction. The act ends with acclaim for the wedding party.

Act II. Near a tavern on the canal. La Beltrana sings; members of a noisy group reply. Cardona enters in drag, followed by 'admirers'. Fernando too comes in, with Doña Francisca and Don Matías not far behind, the latter intent on introducing his son to Francisquita, who he hopes will soon become Fernando's step-mother. This has the effect of making Fernando for the first time truly notice Francisquita's attractions and, in an appropriately wistful duet, regret that she contemplates matrimony with so old a man. He sounds more than half in love himself. When he hears la Beltrana's song, he is torn two ways and sings the romance which has become the best-known number of the opera.

Misunderstandings proliferate, with Cardona pretending to be Fernando's sweetheart, thus successfully provoking la Beltrana's fury; Fernando quite genuinely starting a break with la Beltrana and then declaring his love for Francisquita, so that she pretends to faint; and Don Matías reacting with extreme displeasure. The act finishes with Fernando dancing with Francisquita; la Beltrana flirting with Lorenzo, who takes it all seriously; Don Matías for a moment successfully wrestling with Lorenzo; then dancing with la Beltrana – all to the strains of a mazurka.

Act III. In the street. A nightwatchman sings. Carnival in a slow waltz relaxes between bouts of energy, and Doña Francisca and her daughter tell Don Matías that Fernando is pestering Francisquita and on that account they will not go dancing. He for his part decides to stay at home too. Francisquita schemes to get her mother to believe Fernando fancies her, then gets ready to go out. Things take a serious turn when Cardona quarrels with la Beltrana, who takes out her bad temper on Lorenzo, who decides that she really loves Fernando, leaving him no option but to challenge the young student to a duel.

In the patio of a house Carnival continues, and la Beltrana is joined by Cardona, watched by Fernando, who wonders how, with Francisquita at hand, he can ever have been so infatuated by her. La Beltrana with Cardona sings the 'Marabú', a gipsy bolero. After a fandango, Lorenzo, ready for the duel, is convinced Fernando's interest in la Beltrana is at an end. The situation clears rapidly, with Francisca disabused of the notion that Fernando loves her, Don Matías convinced by Cardona that he is too old for Francisquita, and finally celebrations in train for the wedding of Fernando and Francisquita.   H.

W

RICHARD WAGNER

(born 22 May 1813, died 13 February 1883)

If Monteverdi was the progenitor of opera as we know it today and Gluck its first great reformer, Wagner with his reappraisal of the entire art form two hundred years after Monteverdi and nearly a hundred after Gluck caused an explosion so powerful that opera never regained the equilibrium it possessed in, say, the time of Handel, Mozart or Rossini. The sheer innovation of his music – *Tristan* once heard could never be forgotten – and the scale of his works, even the early ones, produced nothing less than revolution.

Wagner's earliest operas, *Die Feen*, *Das Liebesverbot* and *Rienzi*, are written without much regard for public taste – two of them are too long, for one thing – but the composer was pouring his music into moulds which are relatively conventional and obviously derived from the operas he knew in the theatre, some of which he himself was at the time conducting. It is only with *The Flying Dutchman* that his imagination soars (at the age of twenty-nine), that he starts to write to a theme – in this case what became an obsession, redemption through love – and that the path his career was to follow can with hindsight be seen mapped out in front of him. The difficulties were nonetheless enormous. Not only did musicians have inordinate problems with his music, but impediments to his career were the norm. His revolutionary activities led to exile and a cutting off from performance centres – he did not see *Lohengrin* on stage until a dozen years after it was finished – but no setback seems to have had the slightest effect on his convictions. He broke off work on the mightiest of his enterprises, *The Ring*, for a period of no less than a dozen years (during which he wrote in strict contrast *Tristan* and *Meistersinger*), and yet returned apparently unperturbed to finish the colossal endeavour. In his final years, he was enabled, partly through the favour of King Ludwig II of Bavaria, to build a Festival theatre at Bayreuth specifically for the performance of his mature works, a privilege accorded by fate to no other composer.

A random opinion poll would probably equate Wagner with huge enterprises – vastly long operas (music dramas he called them), huge themes, super-human protagonists – and yet he wrote music of delicacy and subtlety beyond the reach of almost any of his contemporaries. The love of Lohengrin for Elsa is suggested in music of unparalleled lyrical beauty – unparalleled until you call in evidence the burgeoning love of Eva for Walther von Stolzing in the second act of *Die Meistersinger* and find confirmation there. At the start of the last act of *Götterdämmerung*, Siegfried is within an ace of returning the ring to the Rhinemaidens, and his lyrical reaction to them and to nature is of an enchantment which comes close to matching their own incomparably melodious pleas. Siegfried draws back, and part of Wagner's mastery lies in moving within twenty minutes from an expressiveness worthy of Schubert to the implacable tragedy of the Funeral March, the music of what might be thought of as contrasting episodes perfectly balanced within a music drama whose inexorable flow is never at any point in doubt. Not only an architect of huge vision but a musical magician!   H.

DAS LIEBESVERBOT

The Ban on Love

Opera in two acts, words by the composer (libretto adapted from Shakespeare's *Measure for Measure*). Première, Magdeburg, 29 March 1836 (for a single night). Revived Munich, 1923; Berlin, 1933; Munich, 1983, with Sabine Hass, Pamela Coburn, Marianne Seibel, Robert Schunk, Hermann Prey, conductor Sawallisch, producer Ponnelle.

Friedrich, *the King's German*
  Viceroy in Sicily ....Baritone

Luzio ⎫
Claudio ⎭ *young noblemen* ....Tenor
          ....Tenor

Antonio ⎫
Angelo ⎭ *their friends* ....Tenor
          ....Bass

Isabella, *Claudio's sister*.................................Soprano

Mariana...Soprano

Brighella, *captain of the watch*..............................Bass

Danieli, *an innkeeper* ....Baritone

Dorella ....Soprano

Pontio Pilato, *a bawd* ....Tenor

Nuns, Judges, Guard, Townspeople, Musicians

Place: Sicily
Time: Sixteenth Century
Running Time: 2 hours 35 minutes

Wagner's second opera (his first, *Die Feen*, was performed only posthumously in 1888) was written when he was twenty-two, first performed in Magdeburg, where he worked as a conductor, and coldly received – not surprising, since it was long and complicated and had been allowed (according to accounts) only ten days of rehearsal. It had no success whatsoever during the composer's lifetime (Wagner, giving the manuscript to his patron, King Ludwig of Bavaria, referred to it as a youthful sin[1]); it did not until 1923 get to Munich, where all the rest of the composer's *oeuvre* had been performed by 1888, and was only finally accepted there as late as 1983, when the work was mounted in exemplary fashion to celebrate the centenary of Wagner's death.

Wagner moved the action from Vienna to Palermo but kept the bones of Shakespeare's plot, Friedrich taking on Angelo's role as the stand-in Viceroy of Sicily and with it overtones of comedy absent from the original; Mariana (presumably to placate contemporary susceptibilities about seduction) becoming his wife, cast off as a burden once he has gained the favour of the King. The result is less an indictment of hypocrisy as in Shakespeare, more a comedy of licentiousness and intrigue.

The overture, *molto vivace* with castanets to the fore, puts forward leading motifs and anticipates the liveliness of the action.

Act I. Much to the displeasure of the crowds, Brighella and his watch attempt to close down the bars and places of amusement proscribed by the new edict promulgated in the King's absence by Friedrich. This vetoes Carnival and all its accoutrements and allows him to place anyone who contravenes it under arrest; even one 'taken in drunkenness or lechery' faces a death sentence. Danieli, the publican, is arrested, as is Claudio, a young grandee, and also Dorella who now works for Danieli but who used to be lady's maid to Isabella, Claudio's sister. Claudio – arrested for love, he says – in a solo of Weber-like cut prevails on his friend Luzio to find Isabella (who has been in a convent since the death of her parents) and beg her to intervene on his behalf with the Viceroy.

A convent. Isabella and Mariana, friends from girlhood, commune like sisters from *Così* re-set by Weber. Mariana reminds her friend that she has returned to the convent following Friedrich's repudiation of their secret marriage. Luzio comes to beg Isabella's assistance for Claudio, whose crime is to have seduced one Julia but who now intends to marry her. For the first time Isabella hears of Friedrich's law-giving and determines to help her brother. Luzio meanwhile is smitten with Isabella's charms and asks her to marry him, something she, in view of his reputation as a philanderer, resolutely refuses to contemplate.

A courtroom. Brighella in the absence of Friedrich sets up as judge (*buffo* song) and for running a brothel sentences Pontio Pilato to exile. One look and Brighella has fallen head over heels for Dorella; only the intervention of the crowd frustrates his advances, which appear by no means unwelcome. Friedrich's arrival puts paid to Brighella's brief period on the bench. A petition asking him to grant permission for the forthcoming Carnival is handed in but he tears it up unread.

Both Claudio and Julia are condemned to death for transgressing the new law, but Isabella comes to demand a private interview with the Viceroy. This he grants, and, after hearing her plea for mercy, loses little time in offering Claudio's life in return for a night with her. She yells for bystanders to witness his hypocrisy but he warns her the accusation will be laughed out of court and she appears to give in (ensemble). But all is not the plain sailing Friedrich imagines. Isabella has had the notion of sending

[1] In 1939 it passed into Hitler's hands and disappeared.

Mariana to keep the assignation and thus expose Friedrich. Her apparent acceptance of his proposition brings Friedrich's agreement to free Claudio, but he declares publicly that he has no mind to go against the law. An ensemble of cross-purposes ends the act.

Act II. The prison. In music of some spirit, Isabella tells Claudio Friedrich's price. When Claudio's initial horror turns to pleas for her to make the sacrifice, Isabella is minded to punish what she sees as his selfishness and gives him no inkling of the Mariana plot. Dorella is given letters to Mariana and the Viceroy telling them the whereabouts – in Carnival costume – of the assignation. Luzio, reassured about Claudio's fate, turns his attentions to Isabella and is mocked by Dorella, to his considerable discomfiture (trio). However, when he hears of Friedrich's dastardly plan, his fury is so real that Isabella is convinced of his sincerity. She will play a trick on him nonetheless.

Pontio has been promoted, if only temporarily, to the rank of jailer. Luzio rails at him for such a breach of faith, but Isabella knows that to get hold of Claudio's reprieve will cost her only a purse full of money.

Friedrich's palace. The Viceroy recognises that falling for Isabella has turned his well-ordered world upside down (aria). Dorella brings him Isabella's note and he succumbs to temptation, but determines to send Claudio to execution. The infatuated Brighella asks Dorella for a rendezvous, to which she agrees on condition he comes masked.

Palermo disregards the new laws and is celebrating Carnival. Luzio sings a carnival song and prevents a brawl by getting the roistering citizens to unmask. Brighella dons pierrot costume for his rendezvous with Dorella. Isabella and Mariana are identically masked and Mariana waits for her assignation with the unsuspecting Friedrich (aria). Before clarification confusion must become worse confounded. Luzio recognises the Viceroy and conducts him towards other maskers, railing the while at the injustice of the new laws. He spies on Friedrich's meeting with Mariana and naturally takes her, to his jealous fury, for Isabella. Dorella throws her arms round his neck and will release him only at the price of a kiss, an action which infuriates both Brighella and Isabella who are watching. Luzio chases Friedrich and the putative Isabella, Dorella flees from Brighella, while Pontio Pilato gives the real Isabella Claudio's reprieve. She realises the 'safe conduct' is a fraud and as a last resort denounces Friedrich to the roistering populace as an arrant hypocrite. The Viceroy is unmasked and accepts to be judged by his new law, then, in a turn-up for the book, is let off; Isabella and Luzio are reconciled, Brighella even finds Dorella, and a masked procession led by Friedrich and Mariana goes off to find the King, who has just returned to Sicily.

The score of *Das Liebesverbot* has many signs of an early work, among others that it is far too long (nearly 600 pages of Breitkopf's vocal score). It is not hard to see it initially as a victim of operatic fashion, later as unrelated to other works of Germany's greatest operatic composer. There is plainly some looking back to Beethoven and more particularly Weber, also forward to *Tannhäuser* and to *The Flying Dutchman*, some reflection of Marschner and other German contemporaries, but an unprejudiced ear can notwithstanding find in it a lively opera, easy to accept in a well-integrated performance.					H.

RIENZI

Opera in five acts, text by the composer after Bulwer Lytton's novel of the same name. First performed at the Hofoper, Dresden, 20 October 1842, with Schröder-Devrient, Wüst, Thiele, Tichatschek, Dettmer, Wächter, Vestri, Reinhold, Risse, conductor Reissiger. New York, 1878; London, Her Majesty's (in English), 1879, conductor Carl Rosa; Metropolitan, New York, 1886, with Lilli Lehmann, Marianne Brandt, Emil Fischer, conductor Anton Seidl; revived Berlin, 1933, with de Strozzi, Klose, Lorenz, conductor Blech; Stuttgart, 1957, with Windgassen, producer Wieland Wagner; English National Opera, 1982, with Kenneth Woollam.

Cola Rienzi, *Roman Tribune*	Tenor
Irene, *his sister*	Soprano
Stefano Colonna, *a nobleman*	Bass
Adriano, *his son*	Mezzo-Soprano
Paolo Orsini, *another patrician*	Bass
Raimondo, *Papal Legate*	Bass
Baroncelli, *Roman citizen*	Tenor
Cecco del Vecchio, *Roman citizen*	Bass
A Messenger of Peace	Soprano

Ambassadors, Nobles, Priests, Monks, Soldiers, Messengers, Populace

Place: Rome
Time: Middle of the Fourteenth Century
Running Time: 4 hours 25 minutes (with cuts)

With two operas to his credit, Wagner in his mid-twenties pined for success, perhaps on Grand Opera lines – he had seen Spontini's *Fernand Cortez* in Berlin – and perceived in Bulwer Lytton's novel just what he needed. Politically, he was for the middle class and against the nobility and he hoped to have his new opera produced in Paris, where in 1840 he wrote Acts III, IV and V. Rebuffed in Paris, he offered the score to Dresden, where it was accepted and, in 1842, performed. The great Schröder-Devrient, whom Wagner had so much admired as Fidelio, undertook the male role of Adriano, and so early in his career Wagner found a nearly ideal Heldentenor in Joseph Tichatschek. In spite of cuts, the performance seems to have lasted from six until midnight, and Wagner set out to shorten the opera, but met strong objections from the chorus master and the singer of the title role. An attempt to divide it into two was not a success and eventually more cuts were adopted.

The overture is a brilliant affair, full of music which is heard to major effect in the opera, and five themes are particularly to be noted: the slow introduction, which has three long sustained notes on the trumpet, later used as a signal for the people to rise against the nobles; a broad melody well known as Rienzi's prayer in Act V; a theme heard first in the finale to Act I and associated with the people; the battle hymn; the march heard first in the finale to Act II.

The story is concerned with Rienzi, the people's Tribune, who succeeds in outwitting and then defeating the nobles and their followers and in raising the power of the people. Magnanimous at first, he is forced by events to crush the nobles' rebellion against the people's power, but popular opinion changes and even the Church, which has earlier urged him to assert himself, turns against him. In the end the populace burns the Capitol, in which Rienzi and a few adherents have made a last stand.

Act I. A Roman street. The Pope has fled Rome, violence has erupted between the noble houses of Orsini and Colonna, and now Orsini attempts to abduct Irene, Rienzi's sister, and she is saved only by the arrival of Adriano Colonna. Cardinal Raimondo tries unsuccessfully to quell the riot until the Tribune, Rienzi, appears with his henchmen, Baroncelli and Cecco del Vecchio, to restore order. The nobles and their followers leave Rome to con-tinue their quarrel outside the city walls, and Rienzi orders his adherents to shut the city gates against them. Raimondo promises that the Church will support any attempt to break the tyranny of the nobles, and Rienzi bids the people be prepared to gather as soon as the trumpet signals the alarm.

Adriano, a noble, saved her honour, Irene tells her brother. Nevertheless, much as he hates the lawlessness of the nobles, Adriano finds it difficult to support the force against his family which Rienzi must use if Rome is to be his. Reminded that it was a Colonna who murdered Rienzi's brother, Adriano eventually agrees to join his cause. Irene is given over to the care of Adriano, who finds strength in their mutual love.

The trumpet sounds, and the finale has Rienzi and the Cardinal invoke Rome's ancient tradition of freedom and in its name proclaim peace in the city and death to Rome's enemies. Rienzi's 'Erstehe, hohe Roma, neu!' (Arise, great Rome, anew!) rouses the people to great enthusiasm and Cecco takes advantage of the situation to urge that the people make Rienzi king, a proposition he vigorously rejects.

Act II. In the Capitol, peace is the topic of the day, with youth groups from the leading Roman families forming a chorus of Messengers of Peace and processing in front of Rienzi to affirm their conviction that the surrounding countryside is free from trouble. Colonna and Orsini follow them and overtly accept Rienzi's leadership while covertly continuing to plot against him. Their colloquy becomes a trio when their plot is overheard by Adriano, who protests vehemently against their plans to murder Rienzi.

Rienzi returns to greet visiting ambassadors and order the public entertainment to begin, refusing to listen seriously to Adriano's warning of the plot to assassinate him. The ballet music was written in Riga in some haste and, apart from that written for *Tannhäuser*, is Wagner's only essay in this form.

Rienzi has already proclaimed Rome's refusal to recognise the Holy Roman Emperor, usually chosen from among the German Princes, and has demanded that the Emperor's powers be vested in him and the people of Rome, which provides added reason for the assassination attempt by the nobles. In the event, it is unsuccessful (Rienzi has chain-mail beneath his robe) and the people demand that the nobles be punished with the utmost severity. They are condemned to death by the Senators, but Irene joins Adriano in pleading for the life of Adriano's father. Rienzi, moved by their pleas and hearing the distant chant as the nobles are led to execution, agrees to spare their lives on condition that they swear a new oath of allegiance. This they agree to do and, in spite of the opposition of Baroncelli and Cecco, they are forgiven and the act ends with the energetic march from the overture.

Act III. In front of the Forum, the people, outraged by the treachery of the nobles who have broken their oath, call for Rienzi to crush the new insurrection and this time to show no mercy. He again rouses them to enthusiasm and they disperse to raise forces to fight the nobles.

It is the moment of decision for Adriano, who in a great aria, 'Gerechter Gott!', wonders how to choose between his beloved's brother, Rienzi, whose actions have caused his predicament, and his father, to whom he must be loyal but who threatens the safety of Rome. He prays that the two may be reconciled.

Rienzi makes a patriotic appeal and the people answer with the battle hymn (whose music has already been heard in the overture). Adriano cannot deflect Rienzi from his intention to do battle with the nobles and he is left behind with Irene and the Roman women. Fighting can be heard in the distance, and with the sounds of the battle hymn the people return victorious, leaving the nobles vanquished and Colonna and Orsini dead. Adriano mourns his father but Baroncelli is more concerned with the numerous ordinary Romans who have been killed in the fighting. All prepare to march in triumph to the Capitol.

Act IV. The heavy casualties have shaken the people's allegiance to Rienzi, and, in the square in front of the Lateran Church and led by Baroncelli and Cecco, they start to plot against him. With rumours afoot of the Pope and Emperor united against the regime, Adriano resolves to kill Rienzi. A procession reaches the church, Irene at Rienzi's side, and the Tribune addresses the crowd. When he mounts the steps, monks can be heard chanting a malediction and the Cardinal appears to announce his excommunication. The people leave in confusion, and Adriano tries unsuccessfully to persuade Irene to desert Rienzi; at curtain fall, brother and sister stand alone to the sound of the malediction from inside the church.

Act V. Rienzi prays movingly to God: 'Allmächt'ger Vater', to music heard in the overture. It is a moment of truth, with Rienzi for once seen not in public but in private, face to face with crisis and potential disaster.

In spite of his suggestion that if she stay with him she may also be cursed, Irene declares that she will not leave Rienzi. He is determined through his oratory to bring the people of Rome back to his side. In a short duet, Adriano warns Irene that the people seem likely to burn the Capitol and that she must leave Rienzi. But she refuses and he departs. Baroncelli and Cecco have done their work well, and the people are determined on Rienzi's death and will not even allow him to address them. They set the Capitol on fire, Rienzi and Irene can be seen inside it, and, as the nobles return to attack the people, the Capitol collapses in flames.

Rienzi, in spite of some foreshadowing of the future, is mostly written in a style which seems conventional in comparison with what Wagner later wrote and which reappears only at the most 'public' moments in the next three operas. Nonetheless, I find it difficult to agree with commentators who find in the score little of value; on the contrary, Wagner was a towering genius and even his earlier works are not without interest, *Rienzi* standing as a major essay in the field of Grand Opera, and, one drawback apart, more effective than most of its peers. The rock on which all revivals risk shipwreck is of course the opera's sheer length. Nevertheless, with drastic pruning of some of the weaker numbers and a bold approach to the great ensembles and finales, an exciting evening can be ensured and it is an unheeding ear which cannot find in the score's very considerable musical edifices something much more effective than in, for instance, the operas of Meyerbeer.   H.

DER FLIEGENDE HOLLÄNDER
The Flying Dutchman

Opera in three acts, text by the composer, founded on an episode in Heine's *Memoirs of Herr von Schnabelewopski*. Performed at the Hofoper, Dresden, 2 January 1843, with Schröder-Devrient, Thérèse Wächter, J.M. Wächter, Reinhold, Risse, Bielezizky, conductor Wagner; Drury Lane, 1870 (in Italian; first Wagner opera to be performed in London), with Ilma di Murska, Santley, conductor Arditi; Lyceum, 1876 (in English), by Carl Rosa Company; Philadelphia, 1876 (in Italian); Metropolitan, 1889, with Sophie Weisner, Reichmann, Kalisch, Fischer, Mittelhauser, conductor Seidl.

Daland, *a Norwegian sea captain* ....Bass

Senta, *his daughter* ....Soprano

Eric, *a hunter* ....Tenor

Mary, *Senta's nurse* ....Contralto

Daland's Steersman..Tenor

The Dutchman ....Baritone

Sailors, Maidens, Hunters, etc.

Place: A Norwegian Fishing Village
Time: Eighteenth Century
Running Time: 2 hours 30 minutes

From *Rienzi* Wagner took a great stride forward to *The Flying Dutchman*. This is the first milestone on his road from opera to music drama. Of his *Rienzi* the composer was in after years ashamed, writing to Liszt: 'I, as an artist and man, have not the heart for the reconstruction of that, to my taste, superannuated work, which, in consequence of its immoderate dimensions, I have had to remodel more than once. I have no longer the heart for it, and desire from all my soul to do something new instead.' He spoke of it as a youthful error, but in *The Flying Dutchman* there is little, if anything, which could have troubled his artistic conscience.

Wagner's libretto is based upon the picturesque legend of the Flying Dutchman – the Wandering Jew of the ocean. A Dutch sea-captain, who, we are told, tried to double the Cape of Good Hope in the teeth of a furious gale, swore that he would accomplish his purpose even if he kept on sailing forever. The devil, hearing the oath, condemned the captain to sail the sea until Judgement Day, without hope of release, unless he should find a woman who would love him faithfully until death. Once in every seven years he is allowed to go ashore in search of a woman who will redeem him through love.

In *The Flying Dutchman* Wagner employs several leading motifs, not indeed with the resource which he displays in his music-dramas, but with considerably greater freedom of treatment than in *Rienzi*. The overture, which may be said to be an eloquent and beautiful musical narrative of the whole opera, contains all these leading motifs. It opens with a stormy passage out of which there bursts the strong but sombre Motif of the Flying Dutchman himself, the dark hero of the legend. The orchestra fairly seethes and rages like the sea roaring under the lash of a terrific storm. And through all this furious orchestra-

tion there is heard again and again the motif of the Dutchman, as if his figure could be seen amid all the gloom and fury of the elements. There he stands, hoping for death, yet indestructible. As the excited music gradually dies away there is heard a calm, somewhat undulating phrase which occurs in the opera when the Dutchman's vessel puts into the quiet Norwegian harbour. Then, also, there occurs again the motif of the Dutchman, but this time played softly as if the storm-driven wretch had at last found a moment's peace.

We at once recognise to whom it is due that he has found this moment of repose, for we hear like prophetic measures the strains of the beautiful ballad which is sung by Senta in the second act of the opera, in which she relates the legend of The Flying Dutchman. It would not be too much to call this opening phrase the Senta Motif. It is followed by the phrase which indicates the coming to anchor of the Dutchman's vessel; then we hear the Motif of the Dutchman himself, dying away with the faintest possible effect. With sudden energy the orchestra dashes into the surging ocean music, introducing this time the wild, pathetic plaint sung by the Dutchman in the first act of the opera. Again we hear his motif, and again the music seems to represent the surging, swirling ocean when aroused by a furious tempest. Even when we hear the measures of the sailors' chorus the orchestra continues its furious pace, making it appear as if the sailors were shouting above the storm.

Characteristic in this overture, and also throughout the opera, especially in Senta's ballad, is what may be called the Ocean Motif, which most graphically depicts the aspect of the ocean during a storm. The overture ends with an impassioned burst of melody based upon a portion of the concluding phrases of Senta's ballad; phrases which we hear once more at the end of the opera when she sacrifices herself in order to save her lover.

Act I. The opera opens just as a term of seven years has elapsed. A wild and stormy scene is disclosed. Daland's ship has sought shelter in a little cove formed by the cliffs of the coast of Norway. The orchestra depicts the raging of the storm, and above it are heard the shouts of the sailors at work.

As the storm abates the sailors descend into the hold and Daland goes into the cabin to rest, leaving his Steersman in charge of the deck. The Steersman, as if to force himself to remain awake, intones a sailor song, but sleep overcomes him and the phrases become more and more detached, until at last he falls asleep.

Suddenly the ship of the Flying Dutchman, with blood-red sails and black mast, enters the harbour over against the ship of the Norwegian; then silently and without the least noise the spectral crew furl the sails. The Dutchman goes on shore.

Here now occur the weird, dramatic recitative and aria 'Die Frist is um' (The term is passed, and once again are ended seven long years). Daland perceives the Dutchman and going ashore questions him; in the course of their dialogue he discloses that he has a daughter. The Dutchman asks Daland to take him to his home nearby and allow him to woo his daughter, offering him his treasures. The storm having subsided and the wind being fair, the crews of the vessels hoist sail to leave port.

Act II. After an introduction in which we hear a portion of the Steersman's song, the curtain rises upon a room in Daland's house. On the farther wall the portrait of a pale man with a dark beard. Senta is absorbed in dreamy contemplation of the portrait. Her old nurse, Mary, and her young friends are spinning. Here we have that charming musical number famous all the musical world over, the 'Spinning Chorus'. It may be cited as a striking instance of Wagner's gift of melody. The girls tease Senta for gazing so dreamily at the portrait of the Flying Dutchman, and finally ask her if she will not sing his ballad. This begins with the storm music familiar from the overture, and with the strange measures of the Flying Dutchman's motif which sound like a voice calling in distress across the sea.

Senta repeats the measures of this motif, and then we have the simple phrases beginning 'A ship the restless ocean sweeps'. Throughout this portion of the ballad the orchestra depicts the surging and heaving of the ocean, Senta's voice ringing out dramatically above the accompaniment. She tells how he can be delivered from his curse, finally proclaiming that she is the woman who will save him. The girls about her spring up in terror and Eric, who has just entered the door and heard her outcry, hastens to her side. He brings news of the arrival of Daland's vessel, and Mary and the girls hasten forth to meet the sailors. Senta wishes to follow, but Eric restrains

her and pleads his love for her in melodious measures. Senta, however, will not give him an answer. He tells her of a dream in which he saw a weird vessel from which two men, one her father, the other a ghastly-looking stranger, made their way.

Senta, worked up to the highest pitch of excitement by Eric's words, exclaims, 'He seeks for me and I for him,' and Eric rushes away. The door opens and the Dutchman and Daland appear. Senta turns from the picture to him, and remains standing as if transfixed without removing her eyes from the Dutchman. Daland in an aria tells her of the stranger's request, and leaves them alone. There follows a duet for Senta and the Dutchman, in which Senta gives herself up unreservedly to the hero of her romantic attachment, Daland finally entering and adding his congratulations on their betrothal.

Act III. The scene shows a bay with a rocky shore, with Daland's house in the foreground on one side, and the background occupied by his and the Dutchman's ships. The sailors and the girls in their merrymaking call loudly to the Dutch ship to join them, but no reply is heard. The sailors call louder and louder and taunt the crew of the other ship. Suddenly the sea, which has been calm, begins to rise. The wind whistles, and as blue flames flare up in the rigging, the weird crew show themselves and sing a wild chorus, which strikes terror into all the merrymakers. The girls have fled, and the Norwegian sailors quit their deck, making the sign of the cross. The crew of the Flying Dutchman, observing this, disappear with shrill laughter.

Senta now comes with trembling steps out of the house. She is followed by Eric. He pleads with her and entreats her to remember his love for her, and speaks also of the encouragement which she once gave him. The Dutchman has entered unperceived and has been listening. Eric, seeing him, at once recognises the man whom he saw in his vision. When the Flying Dutchman bids her farewell, deeming himself abandoned, and Senta endeavours to follow him, Eric holds her and summons others to his aid. Senta seeks to tear herself loose. The Flying Dutchman announces who he is, thinking to terrify her, and puts to sea. Senta, freeing herself, rushes to a cliff overhanging the sea, proclaims herself faithful unto death, and casts herself into the water, with her arms outstretched towards him. The phantom ship sinks, the sea rises high and falls back into a seething whirlpool. In the sunset glow the forms of Senta and the Dutchman are seen rising in each other's embrace from the sea and floating upwards. The work ends with the portion of the ballad which brought the overture and spinning scene to a close.

Wagner intended *The Flying Dutchman* to be played in a single act – another example of his efforts to break with tradition – and at Bayreuth in 1901 his original design was adhered to. For this purpose, Ernest Newman tells us in his invaluable *Wagner Nights*, cuts were made from bar 26 before the end of the orchestral postlude to Act I to bar 19 of the prelude to Act II, and a dozen bars were omitted at the end of Act II.   K.

TANNHÄUSER

und der Sängerkrieg auf Wartburg

Tannhäuser and the Song Contest on the Wartburg

Opera in three acts, text by the composer. Première Dresden, 19 October 1845, with Johanna Wagner, Schröder-Devrient, Tichatschek, Mitterwurzer, Dettner, conductor Wagner. Revised and performed (in what is now known as the 'Paris version') Opéra, Paris, 1861, with Marie Saxe, Fortunata Tedesco, Niemann, Morelli, Cazaux, conductor Dietsch. First performed New York, 1859; Covent Garden, 1876 (in Italian) with Albani, d'Angeri, Carpi, Maurel, Capponi, conductor Vianesi; Metropolitan, New York, 1884, with Seidl-Kraus, Slach, Schott, Adolf Robinson; Covent Garden (in French, in 'Paris version'), 1896, with Eames, Adini, Alvarez, Ancona, Plançon, conductor Mancinelli. Famous Tannhäusers include Max Alvary, Winkelmann, Urlus, Slezak, Schmedes, Melchior.

Hermann, *Landgrave of Thuringia* ....Bass

Minnesingers
    Tannhäuser ....Tenor
    Wolfram von Eschenbach ....Baritone
    Walther von der Vogelweide ....Tenor
    Biterolf..Baritone
    Heinrich der Schreiber................................Tenor
    Reinmar von Zweter ....Bass

Elisabeth, *the Landgrave's niece*........................Soprano

Venus..............................Soprano or Mezzo-Soprano

Nobles, Knights, Ladies, Pilgrims, Sirens, Naiads, Nymphs, Bacchants

Place: Near Eisenach
Time: Early Thirteenth Century
Running Time: 3 hours 20 minutes

Wagner drafted his libretto in 1842, conflating two medieval legends, one concerning the crusading knight Tannhäuser, the other involving the song contest on the Wartburg. He finished the score in 1845 and it was first performed in Dresden, where it had limited success. Within ten years however it had been played in more than forty German houses.

In 1861, the composer remodelled *Tannhäuser* for an ill-starred production in Paris. Dissatisfied with the music for the Venusberg ballet which followed the rise of the curtain, he re-wrote it, maintaining however the original form of the overture. It was not apparently until 1872 that a re-worked overture was joined to the new Venusberg music to give the opera's opening its final form. Not surprisingly and particularly in Vienna, there was something approaching a public outcry over the sensuous nature of the new music.

Evidence exists to suggest that even before 1861, Wagner contemplated a revised bacchanale, but it was unquestionably for Paris that he recast the scene of the Hall of Song, removing a solo for Wolfram von Eschenbach but retaining much solo music in the earlier style. For Paris, too, the orchestral introduction to Act III was shortened, and the end of the opera rewritten with Venus brought on to the stage in order to clarify her role in Tannhäuser's internal drama. One problem facing Wagner with his new version of the opera was that his Paris revision had been with French words, and not all of the new music went easily with the regular metric scheme of the German he had already written.

The opera takes place in and near the Wartburg, where the Landgraves of the Thuringian Valley presided over contests between the famous Minnesingers. Near the castle stands the Venusberg, inhabited by Holda, the Goddess of Spring, who had in time become identified with the Goddess of Love. She seduced the Knights of the Wartburg and held them captive. One such knight was Tannhäuser, who, in spite of Venus's beauty, has by the time the opera starts grown weary of her charms and longs for a glimpse of the real world.

The overture, as with that of *The Flying Dutchman*, amounts to little less than the story of the opera told in orchestral form. It is based on four episodes: the pilgrims' chorus, the seductive Venusberg music,

Tannhäuser's impassioned song in praise of Venus, and the threatening music of the Landgrave.

Act I. The Venusberg. Tannhäuser lies in the arms of Venus (originally a soprano, in the Paris version a mezzo-soprano), as nymphs, satyrs and sirens dance about them. Music familiar from the overture is heard during this scene but to it is added the distant voices of the sirens and the dances of the denizens of Venus's court. Tannhäuser sings his hymn to Venus, but loses no time in proclaiming his longing to return to the world. Venus tries to tempt him to remain with her but he insists on leaving. She warns him that misfortune awaits him and predicts he will some day ask to be taken back.

The scene is highly effective in the original version but unquestionably gains in power through the additions Wagner made for Paris. As later re-thought, the overture does not come to a formal close but leads directly into the Venusberg scene. The dances are elaborated and planned on an allegorical basis, and Venus's music is substantially strengthened.

The scene changes to the valley of the Wartburg. Tannhäuser kneels before a crucifix as a young shepherd pipes a pastoral tune. The voices of pilgrims are heard in the distance and, as they cross the scene, swell into an eloquent hymn of devotion. Tannhäuser is deeply affected. Hunting horns are heard and gradually the Landgrave and his party gather. Tannhäuser is recognised by Wolfram von Eschenbach and is greeted in a septet. They are intent on persuading Tannhäuser to return with them to the Wartburg instead of following the pilgrims to Rome. Wolfram in a fine solo ('Als du in kühnem Sange uns betrittest') tells him that Elisabeth, the Landgrave's niece, has mourned him ever since he left, and Tannhäuser, who was in love with her, is profoundly moved and agrees to return.

Act II. The Hall of Song. The introduction depicts Elisabeth's overwhelming joy at the prospect of Tannhäuser's return and when the curtain rises she radiantly greets the scene of his former triumphs ('Dich teure Halle'). Wolfram brings Tannhäuser to her and she asks where he has been. He is evasive but finally tells her that she attracted him back to the castle. They sing a rapidly flowing and dramatic duet ('Gepriesen sei die Stunde'). The Landgrave tells Elisabeth that he will offer her hand as prize to the man who wins the song contest. To an effective grand march, the singers make their entrance. After an address by the Landgrave, they draw lots to determine the order of singing. The Minnesingers in turn sing tamely of the beauty of virtuous love, to the increasing contempt of Tannhäuser, who finally, no longer able to restrain himself, repeats his hymn in praise of the unholy charms of Venus ('Dir, Göttin der Liebe, soll mein Lied ertönen'). Horrified, the Knights draw their swords as Elisabeth, in spite of Tannhäuser's betrayal of her love, throws herself protectingly in front of him ('Zurück von ihm!'). In short and excited phrases the men inveigh against Tannhäuser's crime. He is overcome by guilt, and the ensemble reaches a splendid climax ('Erbarm' dich mein!').

Voices of pilgrims are heard from the valley. The Landgrave, moved by Elisabeth's willingness to sacrifice herself for Tannhäuser, announces he will be allowed to join the pilgrimage to Rome and plead with the Pope for forgiveness.

Act III. The Valley of the Wartburg. Elisabeth, waiting for Tannhäuser's return, prays before the crucifix, watched by Wolfram. A chorus of returning pilgrims sings the melody heard in the overture and in the first act. Vainly Elisabeth looks for Tannhäuser, then sings her prayer ('Almächt'ge Jungfrau'). She rises and slowly returns to the castle.

It is night. The evening star glows in the sky, inspiring Wolfram to sing the beautiful 'Song to the Evening Star' ('O du mein holder Abendstern'), privately confessing his love for Elisabeth. Tannhäuser appears, weary and dejected. He asks Wolfram to show him the way back to the Venusberg. Wolfram persuades him to tell the story of his pilgrimage. In a passage of great splendour, Tannhäuser tells how he suffered on his way to Rome, where the Pope passed judgment: he can expect forgiveness only when the Pope's staff sprouts leaves. Tannhäuser thinks he has lost all chance of salvation and intends to yield to the delights of the Venusberg. Venus stretches out her arms to him in welcome, and when he seems unable to resist, Wolfram invokes the memory of Elisabeth. Venus disappears. A tolling of bells and mournful voices precede a funeral procession and Tannhäuser, recognising the body of Elisabeth, falls upon her bier in anguish. The pilgrims arrive with the Pope's staff, which has burst into leaf, and the opera ends amid their hallelujahs.

Wagner's allegory of a man's struggle between sacred and profane love is in itself a highly dramatic theme but it evolves into the notion of redemption through love, the theme which runs through almost all his mature work.   K., H.

LOHENGRIN

Opera in three acts, text by the composer. Première, Weimar, 28 August 1850, with Agthe, Fasztlinger, Beck, von Milde, Hoder, conductor Liszt. First performed Covent Garden, 1875 (in Italian), with Albani, d'Angeri, Nicolini, Maurel, Seiderman, conductor Vianesi; Drury Lane, 1882 (in German), with Sucher, Dily, Winkelmann, Kraus, Koegel, conductor Richter. First performed in New York, 1871; Academy of Music, New York, 1874 (in Italian), with Nilsson, Cary, Campanini, del Puente; Metropolitan (in German), 1885, with Seidl-Kraus, Brandt, Stritt, Robinson, Fischer, conducted by Seidl.

Heinrich der Vogler (Henry the Fowler),
   King of Germany .... Bass
Lohengrin ....Tenor
Elsa of Brabant...Soprano
Duke Gottfried, *her brother* ....Silent
Friedrich of Telramund, *Count of Brabant* .....Baritone
Ortrud, *his wife* ....Mezzo-Soprano
The King's Herald ....Baritone

Saxon, Thuringian, and Brabantian Counts and
   Nobles, Ladies of Honour, Pages, Attendants

Place: Antwerp
Time: First Half of the Tenth Century
Running Time: 3 hours 40 minutes

Wagner intended *Lohengrin* for the opera in Dresden but his sympathy with the unsuccessful Dresden revolution of May 1849 led to his banishment and abandonment of the project. In the end, it was taken by Liszt for Weimar, but Wagner himself remained in exile in Switzerland and he is supposed not to have heard the entire opera until May 1861 in Vienna.

Owing to the lyric character of its story, the opera, while by no means lacking in dramatic situations, is characterised by a subtler and more subdued melodiousness than *Tannhäuser*, and is in fact more lyrical than any other Wagner opera except *Parsifal*. The score contains typical themes but they are not treated in the manner of leading motifs. On the other hand,

Wagner uses the orchestra with rare imagination: the brass chiefly to accompany the King and the martial choruses; the plaintive, yet spiritual high woodwind for Elsa; the English horn and bass clarinet for Ortrud; the violins, especially in high harmonic positions, to indicate the Grail and its representative, Lohengrin. Even the keys employed are distinctive. The Herald's trumpets are in C; F sharp minor, dark and threatening, is used for Ortrud; and A, the purest for strings and most ethereal in effect, announces the approach of Lohengrin and the influence of the Grail.

The Prelude is based on a single theme: the beautiful and expressive one of the sanctity of the Grail. It opens with long, drawn-out high chords on violins and flutes, then on violins alone, and works up through a *crescendo* to a magnificent climax, after which it dies away again to the ethereal harmonies.

Act I. A plain near the River Scheldt. King Heinrich has summoned the Brabantians to join his army to defeat the threatened Hungarian invasion of Germany. The King has found Brabant in factional strife over Friedrich of Telramund's claim to the ducal succession. Telramund tells the King how the late Duke placed his children, Elsa and Gottfried, in his care. Gottfried, the heir, has disappeared, and Telramund accuses Elsa of murdering him in order to claim the title. Telramund says he was so horrified by this that he rejected his right to marry Elsa and has instead married Ortrud, daughter of the Prince of Friesland. He leads her forward and she bows to the King. The King has no choice but to appeal to the immediate judgment of trial by combat between Telramund and whoever may appear as champion for Elsa. The King summons Elsa.

So far, the music has been vigorous, even harsh, reflecting Telramund's excitement; but with Elsa's appearance the music becomes gentle and plaintive, without however renouncing hope.

As violins whisper the Grail Motif, Elsa, enraptured, describes her dream of a Knight in white, sent by Heaven to defend her cause: 'Einsam in trüben Tagen' – the passage usually known as Elsa's Dream. After a triple summons by the Herald, a Swan can be seen in the distance on the river, drawing a boat in which stands a Knight in silver armour. Elsa, hardly daring to trust her senses, gazes heavenward, and Ortrud and Telramund look at each other in amazement and alarm.

The Knight bids farewell to the Swan ('Nun sei bedankt, mein lieber Schwann'). He bows to the King and approaches Elsa, offering his hand in marriage and declaring his willingness to fight for her. But he warns her never to ask where he is from or what his name is ('Nie sollst du mich befragen'). The Warning Motif is one of the significant themes of the opera. Elsa agrees to the conditions.

Before the combat begins, the King intones a prayer ('Mein Herr und Gott'), in which the principals and later the chorus join to noble effect. Three Saxons for the Knight and three Brabantians for Telramund pace off the circle within which the two men are to fight. The King strikes his sword on his shield, and the fight begins. The Knight fells Telramund but spares his life and bids him rise. The King leads Elsa to the Knight while all praise him in a great ensemble as her champion and betrothed.

Act II, scene i. The fortress of Antwerp; outside the Knights' palace. It is night, and skulking in the darkness are Telramund and Ortrud, who have been banished by the King. He is dejected ('Erhebe dich, Genossin meiner Schmach!'; Arouse yourself, companion of my shame!). She still trusts in the power of the heathen gods she worships. Telramund is unaware of Ortrud's scheming to ruin Elsa and restore him to power and denounces her in an outburst of rage and despair, his bitterness fuelled by sounds of revelry from inside the palace. Ortrud unfolds her plot: as tomorrow's bridal procession reaches the steps of the Minster, Telramund will accuse the Knight of treachery and demand he disclose his name and origin. Thus will Elsa begin to doubt.

At this very moment, Elsa comes onto the balcony, enraptured by her approaching marriage ('Euch Lüften die mein Klagen'). Ortrud, sending Telramund away, calls to Elsa, who, moved by her apparent misery, descends to lead her into the palace. Ortrud has already begun her persuasive work but she has time to call on her gods to help in her plan of revenge ('Entweihte Götter!'). The scene ends with a beautiful duet as Ortrud is conducted by Elsa into the fortress.

Scene ii. In front of the Minster. After a spirited chorus the bride herself appears, followed by her ladies. Ortrud throws herself in her path, saying that Elsa still does not know who her Knight is, and casting doubt on his reasons for secrecy. The King,

the bridegroom and the nobles enter from the palace and Elsa shrinks from Ortrud to her champion's side. At this moment, Telramund, taking his cue from Ortrud, appears and repeats his wife's accusations. The poison has already begun to take effect. Bride and groom go into the church, but the trembling Elsa catches sight of Ortrud and goes to the altar with feelings of love mingled with doubt and fear.

Act III, scene i. The bridal chamber. The wedding festivities are described in a brilliant introduction, followed by the famous bridal chorus (whose popularity in isolation Wagner deplored). The King ceremonially embraces the couple and the procession makes its way out, leaving Elsa and her champion alone for the first time.

It should be a moment of supreme happiness for both, and indeed, Elsa exclaims as her bridegroom takes her into his arms that words cannot express all love's hidden sweetness. When he tenderly says her name, Elsa is reminded that she cannot respond by uttering his. The Knight realises that the seeds of mistrust have been sown. Elsa begins to question him and, in a passionate musical phrase, he begs her to trust him. Elsa imagines she sees the Swan approaching to take her Knight away from her, and she asks him the forbidden questions. Immediately, Telramund and four of his followers burst in, intending to kill the Knight, but he fells Telramund with a single blow. The followers kneel in front of the Knight, who tells them to bear the corpse to the King.

This section is an extended love duet of quite extraordinary beauty, as Lohengrin throws open the window, points to the flowery garden below illuminated by the moon, and sings 'Atmest du nicht mit mir die süssen Düfte?'. Gradually the magic yields to suspicion, and, as Elsa collapses, the Warning Motif can be heard. The duet is in linked sections, but the flow is marvellously sustained as it proceeds from pure lyricism to the dramatic end. It is a high point of its kind in Wagner's output.

Scene ii. The banks of the Scheldt, as in Act I. The assembled nobles and Brabantians hail the King in a brilliant march and chorus. The Knight enters, saying he has come to bid them all farewell. Elsa has been induced to break her vow and he will now answer the forbidden questions. His narration, 'In fernen Land', is beautifully set to the music already heard in the Prelude. He reveals he is from

Montsalvat, the Temple of the Holy Grail. The Grail gives its Knights the power to right wrong and protect the innocent, but only so long as the secret of their power remains intact. His father, Parsifal, rules as King, and he, a Knight of the Grail, is called Lohengrin. As he proclaims his name, we hear the same measures which Elsa sang in the second part of her dream in Act I. The Swan returns and Lohengrin bids Elsa a sorrowing farewell ('Mein lieber Schwann'). He hands Elsa his horn, his sword and his ring to give to her brother should he return; then enters the boat.

A triumphant Ortrud pushes her way through the spectators. She exclaims that the Swan is Elsa's brother, Gottfried, whom Ortrud changed into his present form. Had Elsa kept her vow, Gottfried would have been freed from the spell. Lohengrin prays and a white dove descends over the boat, as the Swan vanishes. In its place Gottfried stands on the bank. Ortrud falls with a shriek, while the crowd kneels and Gottfried bows to the King. Elsa gazes at her brother in rapture, as Lohengrin is drawn away in his boat by the dove. 'My husband! my husband!' she calls, and sinks back dead. The opera ends with a repetition of the music of the second portion of Elsa's dream, followed by a splendid climax of the Motif of the Grail.

The music of *Lohengrin* is so beguiling that no lesser advocate of Wagner's achievement than Ernest Newman once said that a true lover of Wagner's music might have wished that he had never turned from this aspect of his development to write his later masterpieces.   K., H.

TRISTAN UND ISOLDE
Tristan and Isolde

Opera in three acts, text by the composer. Première Munich, 10 June 1865, with Malvina and Ludwig Schnorr von Carolsfeld (the Tristan and Isolde were husband and wife), Anne Deinet, Zottmeyer, Mitterwurzer, Heinrich, conductor Hans von Bülow. Bülow was still married to Cosima, Liszt's daughter, at the time of the première of *Tristan* and did not divorce her until a year later, after which she became Wagner's wife. The first production after Munich was not until 1874, at Weimar. First performed Drury Lane, London, 1882, with Rose Sucher, Brandt, Winkelmann, Gura, Landau, conductor Hans Richter; Bayreuth, 1886, with Malten, Gisela, Staudigl, Gudehus, Gura, Plank, conductor Mottl; Metro-

politan, New York, 1886, with Lilli Lehmann, Brandt, Niemann, Robinson, Fischer, conductor Seidl; Covent Garden, 1892, with Sucher, Schumann-Heink, Alvary, Knapp, conductor Mahler. Jean de Reszke was a great Tristan and others were Schmedes, Vogel, Urlus, Melchior, Vinay and Windgassen. Famous Isoldes have included Nordica, Ternina, Fremstad, Mildenburg, Wittich (the first Salome), Litvinne, Gadski, Kappel, Leider, Larsen-Todsen, Marta Fuchs, Lubin, Flagstad, Traubel, Varnay, Mödl, Birgit Nilsson. Giuseppe Borgatti and Giuseppina Cobelli were well-known exponents of the title roles in Italy.

Tristan, *a Cornish knight,*
    nephew to King Marke ....Tenor
Marke, *King of Cornwall* ....Bass
Isolde, *an Irish princess* ....Soprano
Kurwenal, *one of Tristan's retainers* ....Baritone
Melot, *a courtier, Tristan's friend* ....Tenor
Brangäne, *Isolde's companion* ....Soprano
A Young Sailor ....Tenor
A Shepherd...Tenor
A Helmsman ....Baritone

Place: A Ship at Sea; outside King Marke's Palace in
    Cornwall; Tristan's Castle in Kareol
Time: Legendary
Running Time: 4 hours 15 minutes

Wagner subjected the *Tristan* legend to a thorough re-modelling before turning it into a music drama. Everything was pared down to essentials and the main episodes have been worked into a concise, vigorous, swift-moving drama, showing particularly keen insight in the matter of the love-potion. In the legends, the love of Tristan and Isolde is the result of the love-philtre, but Wagner presents them as in love from the outset, so that the potion does no more than quicken a passion already active. In the past, the story had been a favourite of the troubadours, whose fantasy decorated the tale as they told it. Dante mentions Tristan in the *Inferno*, Tennyson retold the story in *Idylls of the King*, and Frank Martin derived a chamber opera, *Le Vin Herbé*, from the same source.

Wagner mentions the subject as a definite project in a letter to Liszt in 1854 at a time when he was writing *Die Walküre*. He started to compose the music in mid-1857, when he was engaged on *Siegfried*, and during the twelve-year gap (1857–69) between finishing Act II of *Siegfried* and resuming with Act III, he wrote not only *Tristan* but *Die Meistersinger* as well – the need to write music in absolute contrast to

Tristan und Isolde (Metropolitan Opera House, New York, c. 1936). Lauritz Melchior and Kirsten Flagstad in the title roles.

what had seemed appropriate for the Nibelung legend must truly have been overpowering! *Tristan* was published in 1860 but for years considered unperformable.

The opera is less a dramatic action brought to the stage, rather a musico-poetic idea remote from anything physical. Nonetheless, it is based on a story and, before the opera begins, we should know that Tristan, having lost his parents in infancy, had been brought up by his uncle Marke, King of Cornwall. He slew in fair combat Morold, an Irish knight, who came to Cornwall to collect the tribute that country had been paying to Ireland. Morold was betrothed to his cousin Isolde, daughter of the Irish King, and Tristan, who was dangerously wounded in the fight, placed himself, under the pseudonym of Tantris, in care of Isolde, whose healing skills were legendary. Isolde cured Tristan but became aware that she was harbouring the slayer of her intended husband; in spite of her thirst for vengeance, she fell in love with him. Tristan too fell in love, but each believed their love unrequited. After his return to Cornwall, Tristan was sent to Ireland by King Marke to win Isolde as his Queen.

The Prelude to *Tristan* tells in music the story of the two lovers. Its first bars contain the two Motifs of Tristan and Isolde and the Motif of the Love Glance – which expresses the couple's sensuous yearning; these motifs recur throughout the Prelude.

Act I. On the ship in which Tristan is taking Isolde to Cornwall, Isolde occupies the forward deck. A young sailor is heard singing a farewell song to his 'Irish Maid'. Brangäne replies to Isolde's question as to the ship's course and the orchestra seems to surge wildly around Isolde's outburst of impotent anger when she learns that Cornwall is near, breaking into fury as she invokes the elements to destroy the ship and all on it.

Isolde's mood is dominated by her passion for Tristan and her anger that he is taking her as bride to another man. For Tristan, she wishes for nothing less than death, but Brangäne sings his praises as Isolde demands she send Tristan to her. Tristan declines to leave the ship's helm and his retainer Kurwenal answers for him with a song. Isolde's anger at Kurwenal's taunts – his song amounts to

nothing less – finds vent in a narrative in which she tells Brangäne how she came to love Tristan, bringing the story to a splendid climax with a furious outburst against his treachery. Brangäne whispers of the love potion and takes a phial from a casket. As Kurwenal brusquely calls to her and Brangäne to prepare to go ashore, Isolde orders Kurwenal to send Tristan to her and tells Brangäne to prepare the death potion. The motif which announces Tristan's approach is full of tragic defiance, as if he were prepared to meet death. Isolde claims she wants to drink to their reconciliation, but in a sombrely impressive passage, he asks Isolde to slay him with the sword she once held over him as he lay sick.

The sailors hail the land as Isolde hands Tristan the goblet containing, as she thinks, the death-draught, for which Brangäne has substituted the love potion. He seizes it and drinks and Isolde grabs it from him. The Love Glance motif is heard as they sink into each other's arms. Brangäne separates the lovers as people crowd the deck and the act ends as Isolde's motif is heard above the general jubilation.

Act II. A garden outside King Marke's castle. The King and his entourage are hunting. With them is Melot, who is outwardly devoted to Tristan but whom Brangäne suspects of double-dealing, with the hunt no more than a trap. As the sound of the hunt grows distant, Isolde urges Brangäne to extinguish the torch as a signal for Tristan to join her, laughs as Brangäne warns of Melot's treachery, says the love potion merely intensified her passion, and proclaims she will signal to Tristan even at the risk of putting out the light of her life.

Impatience leads to ecstasy as Isolde and Tristan rush into each other's arms, the music awash with passion. In a rapid exchange of phrases, they declare their mutual love. As day sinks into night, the music turns from urgency to rapture and the lovers commence their great duet, 'O sink hernieder, Nacht der Liebe'. Brangäne's voice interrupts, warning that night will soon be over ('Einsam wachend') and the arpeggios which accompany her warning are like the first grey streaks of dawn. The lovers refuse to listen to her, preferring to express their yearning for death through love: the *Liebestod*.[1]

---

[1] The word, now customarily applied to the music of Isolde's death, was intended by Wagner to characterise the Prelude, which contains the seeds of death through love. He used it for the first time for concert performances he was giving in Paris in 1860. When the opera's closing section was given in concert in conjunction with the Prelude it was described as 'Verklärung' (Transfiguration).

As early as their declaration of love after drinking the potion, Tristan had pledged himself and Isolde to the mystical other-world of Night, and insisted that is where he and Isolde belong: Night protects their love while Day destroys it. Act II propounds the opposites of Night, where Tristan knows he thrives, and Day, from which all evil flows and which when it arrives at the end of the Act – the only period effectively they spend together – will separate them for ever.

Brangäne calls again, but Isolde exclaims that night will protect them. With the dawn, the dream ends. There is a cry from Brangäne and Kurwenal rushes in, calling to Tristan to save himself. Surrounded by the King's followers, including the treacherous Melot, the lovers awaken to the terror of the situation. The King, who is no commonplace cuckold but a saddened, noble, mature figure, in a philosophical soliloquy tries to understand the unfathomable nature of events.

Tristan turns to Isolde. Will she follow him to the bleak land of his birth? This is too much for Melot, who draws his sword. Tristan rushes upon him but, as Melot thrusts, allows his guard to drop and is wounded.

Act III. Tristan's castle at Kareol in Brittany. The melancholy introduction is prophetic of the desolation which broods over the scene. A long, ascending phrase seems to represent the broad waste of ocean overlooked by Tristan's castle. Tristan himself is lying under a great tree, Kurwenal by his side. A shepherd pipes a melancholy tune (solo cor anglais), then tells Kurwenal that the ship he has sent to Cornwall to bring Isolde to Kareol is not yet in sight. Eventually Tristan, to Kurwenal's great joy, wakes from his coma and loses himself in sad memories of Isolde. Kurwenal tells him Isolde is coming to try to heal his wound. The ship is still not in sight and jubilation gives way to yearning. Tristan's mind wanders until, in a paroxysm of anguish not far from insanity, he curses love. Three times the music reaches climax as Tristan pushes his physical resistance to the limits and after each climax he sinks into total exhaustion, so that Kurwenal wonders if his master can survive another bout of such hysteria. Tristan inveighs against sun and light, symbols of Day; against the loss of father and mother before he could do anything for himself; against the absence of Isolde. Gradually, his vision of Isolde becomes calmer

and the music takes on an incomparably expressive quality with the passage beginning 'Wie sie selig'.

Suddenly the shepherd's piping takes a joyful turn. The ship is in sight! Kurwenal runs off to meet Isolde and Tristan struggles to rise, to music of frenzied urgency tearing the bandage from his wound. Isolde rushes in and Tristan, murmuring her name, dies in her arms. A second ship arrives with King Marke and his entourage. Kurwenal thinks they have come in pursuit of Isolde, attacks the newcomers, killing Melot, but in turn receives a mortal wound. Brangäne hurries in to tell Isolde she has confessed to the King that she switched the potions, but Isolde is beyond the understanding of mere events. In what we now call her *Liebestod* ('Mild und leise'), which reaches its climax with a stupendous crash of instrumental forces, she gazes in rapture on her dead lover, then sinks upon his corpse and dies.

Tristan is the most influential opera in all musical history. Hans Redlich, the German musicologist, wrote: 'The orchestral Prelude alone, in which the implicit tonality of A minor is never so much as touched upon, is to all intents and purposes the first piece of practical atonalism, conceived half a century before Schoenberg and Busoni had drafted their first tentative experiments in the direction of a music of undefined tonality.' Musicians since they came to know *Tristan* have known that this is true. Wagner knew it too, claims Ernest Newman, but his conviction was deep enough to convince him to leave the opera's music to speak for itself. Commentators and analysts would make claims on its behalf and he himself could remain silent. H.

DIE MEISTERSINGER VON NÜRNBERG
The Mastersingers of Nuremberg

Opera in three acts, libretto by the composer. First performed Munich, 21 June 1868, with Mathilde Mallinger as Eva, Sophie Dietz as Magdalene, Franz Betz as Sachs, Gustav Holzel as Beckmesser, Franz Nachbaur as Walther and Max Schlosser as David, conducted by Hans von Bülow. First U.K. performance at Drury Lane, 1882, conducted by Hans Richter; Covent Garden, 1889, in Italian, with Emma Albani, Jean de Reszke and Jean Lassalle. Friedrich Schorr sang Sachs there in 1925, succeeded by Hans Hotter, Josef Greindl, Norman Bailey, Hans Sotin, Bernd Weikl and John Tomlinson;

as Eva, Lotte Lehmann, Elisabeth Schumann, Elisabeth Grümmer, Elisabeth Schwarzkopf, Irmgard Seefried, Joan Sutherland, Lucia Popp, Felicity Lott and Nancy Gustafson. Conductors have included Bruno Walther, Thomas Beecham, John Barbirolli, Karl Rankl, Reginald Goodall, Rudolf Kempe, Georg Solti, Christoph von Dohnanyi and Bernard Haitink. First U.S. performance, New York, 1886, with Seidl-Kraus, Marianne Brandt, Emil Fischer, Josef Staudigl, Kemlitz, Stritt, Kraemer, conducted by Anton Seidl; in Italian, 1892.

Walther von Stolzing, *a young knight from Franconia*..Tenor

Eva, *Pogner's daughter*.....................................Soprano

Magdalene, *Eva's companion*...............Mezzo-Soprano

David, *apprenticed to Hans Sachs* ....Tenor

Veit Pogner, *a goldsmith*.......................................Bass

Sixtus Beckmesser, *town clerk* ....Baritone

Kunz Vogelsang, *a furrier* ....Tenor

Konrad Nachtigall, *a tinsmith*.............................Bass

Hans Sachs, *a cobbler*....................................Baritone

Fritz Kothner, *a baker* ....Bass

Hermann Ortel, *a soap-boiler*...............................Bass

Balthasar Zorn, *a pewterer* ....Tenor

Augustin Moser, *a tailor* ....Tenor

Hans Foltz, *a coppersmith*.....................................Bass

Hans Schwarz, *a stocking-weaver* ....Bass

Nightwatchman ....Bass

People of Nuremberg, Members of the Guilds, Journeymen, Apprentices, Girls

Place: Nuremberg
Time: Mid-Sixteenth Century
Running Time: 4 hours 55 minutes

Wagner first thought about *Die Meistersinger von Nürnberg* in 1845. The story of a young man whose radical ideas about art triumph over the hostile judgement of the establishment and win him the beautiful daughter of a goldsmith (and all her father's property) had considerable charm for the late-developing thirty-two-year-old composer. At one point, he thought of it as the 'satire play' to follow another opera about a singing competition, *Tannhäuser*: his satire against the mastersingers and their rules was originally much harsher than in the completed opera. Wagner himself reported that the Viennese critic Eduard Hanslick took offence when he attended a reading of the text in 1862. He may well have known that Wagner's original name for Beckmesser was Veit Hanslich. Wagner returned to the story after he had written *Tristan und Isolde* as a

sort of light relief. He promised the publisher Franz Schott that it would be 'easily staged': every theatre, 'even the smallest', would be able to produce it.

It is the day before the Feast of St John the Baptist, when the Guild of Mastersingers stage their annual competition for the best composition and performance of a song by one of their members. The young knight Walther von Stolzing has come to Nuremberg to sell his land. The goldsmith Veit Pogner has been helping him and Walther has fallen in love with Eva, Pogner's daughter. Pogner is a mastersinger, devoted to the guild. He has decided that Eva will marry the winner of this year's competition. She can refuse the winner, but she must marry a mastersinger.

The opera's prelude gives, as Kobbé said, 'a complete musical epitome of the story'. The stately Motif of the Mastersingers is opposed by the Lyric Motif, which in turn is checked by the Mastersingers' March. The Motif of the Art Brotherhood leads to a climax in the Motif of the Ideal. The Motif of Longing leads to 'Walther's Prize Song' and then to the Motif of Spring and the Motif of Ridicule. At the end, the Prize Song 'soars above the various themes typical of the masters, [as] the new ideal seems to be borne to its triumph upon the shoulders of the conservative forces which, won over at last, have espoused the cause with all their sturdy energy.'

Act I. In St Catherine's church, the service is ending with a chorale. Walther succeeds in attracting Eva's attention. She sends her companion and chaperone Magdalene on various errands, and the young couple establish their mutual attraction. She swears she will marry only Walther. Magdalene tells David, who is apprenticed to the great Hans Sachs, the leading mastersinger, that he must instruct Walther, so that he becomes a mastersinger. As the apprentices convert the church into a song-school, David points out that it takes years of study. He warns Walther about Beckmesser, the mastersinger who acts as 'Marker' at auditions, chalking up faults on a blackboard. More than seven marks means failure.

Pogner assumes that Beckmesser himself will win the competition. Beckmesser shares this assumption, though he knows that he has not yet won Eva's heart. He resolves to serenade her that evening. The other mastersingers arrive and take their places. Pogner explains why he offers his daughter (as well as all he owns) as a prize in the competition. It is in order to counter the prevailing view that the middle classes are only interested in material values. Hans Sachs suggests they let the people at the festival choose the winner, but cannot secure the other mastersingers' agreement. Pogner introduces Walther as the new candidate to join the guild. The mastersingers' unease at a nobleman trying to join is confirmed when Walther sings an apparently improvised song in praise of spring. He also reveals that his only teachers have been old books and nature (he puns on Walther von der Vogelweide, whose name means 'bird-pasture'). Long before its end Beckmesser has filled his slate with faults (including 'no coloratura'). Only Sachs hears in its unconventionality that the noble-man's 'heart is in the right place'.

Act II. A square with Pogner's house opposite Sachs's. Magdalene is sad to hear from David that Walther was rejected by the mastersingers. Eva sits with her father under the lime tree (whose rustling is deliciously evoked by Wagner). He confirms that she must marry a mastersinger.

Hans Sachs sits up late. He doesn't work, but reflects on the song Walther sang: 'It sounded so old and yet it was so new, like birdsong in May.' Eva comes to find out more about the knight. She flirts playfully with Sachs, who tells her he is finishing a pair of shoes for Beckmesser, her eager suitor. But when he realises that she cares for the knight, Sachs determines to help him succeed in the competition.

Eva and Walther meet in the street and he per-suades her to elope with him. He bitterly resents the way he was treated and draws his sword in protest. His tirade climaxes on a discord, which is resolved by the sound of the Nightwatchman's horn as he passes on his round. It is a magical moment. The Night-watchman, incidentally, is one of the few roles in which a young, talented bass can make a consider-able impact.

Sachs has overheard the lovers' plans. He positions a lamp so they cannot get away in the darkness. Beckmesser comes to serenade Eva, but Magdalene takes her place at the window. Eva stops Walther from killing his rival and draws him into the bushes. While Sachs works at his cobbling, he sings a song warning Eva that he knows what's going on. Beckmesser asks Sachs to comment on the song that he will perform tomorrow. Sachs offers to act as 'marker' and, as Beckmesser sings, hammers the sole

on to the shoe every time he finds a fault. It drives Beckmesser into a frenzy, and the noise eventually wakes the town. David recognises Magdalene at the window and presumes he has a rival. He starts to fight Beckmesser. Their fight attracts the neighbours who soon turn it into a general mêlée. Walther is about to cut his way through with his sword when Sachs drags him inside his shop. The riot's climax repeats the sequence of Walther's protest. Music, in the form of the Nightwatchman's call, restores order once again.

Act III. Sachs's workshop, where David asks to be forgiven. His master is in abstracted mood. He reflects on everyone's madness in a monologue that is one of the highpoints of the score ('Wahn, Wahn, überall Wahn'). He encourages Walther to use the dream he had overnight as inspiration for his 'prize song'. Sachs writes the notes down, as Walther recounts his dream of a beautiful garden ('Morgenlich leuchtend in rosigem Schein').

Beckmesser limps in, aching from his beating, and discovers the pages with Sachs's handwriting. He assumes this is Sachs's own 'prize song' and steals it. When Sachs comes, Beckmesser accuses him of being his rival for Eva's hand. Sachs assures him he is not. Noticing that his papers have disappeared from his desk, he says Beckmesser may have them and promises he will never reveal his authorship.

Eva comes. While Sachs tackles one of her new shoes (which manages to be both too broad and too tight), she gazes at Walther and inspires him to improvise the last verse of his prize song. The emo-tions that have been hidden until now burst out: Eva weeps on Hans Sachs's breast, Walther presses his hand. She thanks Sachs for teaching her what love is; he replies that he did not want to share King Mark's fate, referring to the husband Isolde betrayed for Tristan. When David and Magdalene conve-niently appear, Sachs arranges a mock christening for the new song. Since apprentices can't act as wit-nesses, Sachs releases David from his indentures. There follows a marvellous quintet.

The last scene is set in an open meadow outside the city, prepared for St John's Day. Guilds process, apprentices and journeymen dance, till the master-singers march in with considerable pomp. When Hans Sachs arrives, the people sing the chorale 'Wach' auf', to the original Hans Sachs's words, in his honour. He addresses the crowd and reminds them that Pogner's promise demonstrates the respect in which art is held in Nuremberg. Beckmesser mangles the words of Walther's song, which reinforces the idea that he could not compose music that was worthy of the poetry. Everyone laughs at him. Sachs introduces Walther. His performance of his prize song wins the approval of both the people and the mastersingers. Pogner offers Walther the chain with a picture of King David that represents membership of the guild, but Walther refuses it. Hans Sachs intervenes and, in the last of his great monologues, he credits the mastersingers with preserving what is good and true in German art ('Verachtet mir die Meister nicht'). The opera ends as the mastersingers and the people unite in acclaiming Hans Sachs.

Die Meistersinger von Nürnberg's special strength is that, like the best comedies, it is a serious work. This is what justifies its inordinate length: when it was new it was the longest opera ever written (or, perhaps more properly, ever performed). At its heart is not the plight of the young lovers, but the role of art in the community. It is an opera about opera, but this is never a narcissistic exercise. Hans Sachs is one of the greatest bass-baritone roles in the repertory. His character combines aspects of both Wotan and the Marschallin, but more importantly, he encapsulates a humaneness that must represent Wagner's best aspects, those that were sometimes submerged by other instincts. This is why his final admonition to respect 'holy German art' carries such weight and has to be heard in context. Beckmesser can seem a more problematic portrayal. It is partly that the humour of his beating has lost its savour. The problem becomes more acute when we know that Wagner wrote into the role vocal characteristics that he associated with Jews.[1] On the other hand, recent productions have emphasised Beckmesser's normality: with singers of the calibre of Hermann Prey and Thomas Allen prepared to lend their weight to the role, Beckmesser has emerged as less of a caricature, more of a complex character, the Malvolio of opera.   P.

---

[1] His serenade is 'a parody of Jewish cantorial style, with long melodic wailing syllables sung in a near-falsetto *tessitura*', Paul Lawrence Rose, *Wagner Race and Revolution*, 1992.

DER RING DES NIBELUNGEN
The Nibelung's Ring

Wagner's vast *Ring* cycle may or may not be the greatest event inside the form loosely known as opera but it is certainly the grandest. What is curious is that Wagner, the great musical architect, did not initially conceive it as the four-part structure we know, though he clearly always envisaged a huge canvas: modern commentators have compared it in scale with *The Oresteia*. He started work as early as 1848 and by 1850 had completed the book of what he called *Siegfrieds Tod* (Siegfried's Death), which subsequently became *Götterdämmerung* (The Twilight of the Gods) and ended originally with Brünnhilde leading Siegfried to Valhalla. He had considered immediately starting to compose *Siegfried's Death*, but came to feel the need to explain events which led up to it and in turn wrote *The Young Siegfried*, *The Valkyrie* and *The Rhine Gold*, thus creating the cycle as it were in reverse. The whole cycle was first performed at Bayreuth, 13–17 August 1876; *Rhine Gold* première, Munich, 22 September 1869; *Valkyrie*, 26 June 1870. The Bayreuth cast included Franz Betz (Wotan), Amalie Materna (Brünnhilde), Georg Unger (Siegfried).

Composition of *The Rhine Gold* was started in 1853 and the full score of *Twilight* finished in 1874, but amazingly there occurred an interregnum of nearly twelve years (1857 to 1869) during which he not only composed *Tristan und Isolde* (1857–59) and *Die Meistersinger* (1862–67), but attempted to cope with so severe a dip in his fortunes as to lead him at one stage to contemplate abandoning composition altogether. He must have felt an overpowering need to write music of a quite different nature from what he was composing for *The Ring*, music which in *Tristan* was to come close to parting company with tonality and to pointing a way for the future not fully taken up (though highly influential) until the time of Schoenberg's earliest experiments some fifty years later. *The Ring*, for all its inventiveness and innovative construction, was fashioned from music of slightly less iconoclastic cast.

Wagner's studies of Teutonic and Norse myth undertaken over many years provided him with the subject matter of *The Ring*, which involves gods, demigods, giants, earth-dwellers and inhabitants of the underworld. The fierce competition between them for wealth and ultimate dominance constitutes the stuff of the drama, but there is room for examination in depth of the more human motives of the characters involved. The music is held together by a large number of motifs, sometimes with meanings and attachments as straightforward as 'the Rhine Gold', 'the Ring', 'Valhalla', 'The Giants', 'the Sword', even concepts like 'Renunciation of Love'; often with strong initial attachments but shifting connotations, as, to take an example, that of 'the Rhine', specifically descriptive of the river during the prelude to *The Rhine Gold* but later taking on wider references as when two hours later and to its accompaniment Erda sings of her own all-pervading wisdom. To think of them as labels or visiting cards is not only confusing and inadequate but does an injustice to Wagner's incredibly dexterous and fertile use of his materials, which he employs hardly ever as musical shorthand but rather as means towards the creation of musical edifices great enough to carry the burden of a colossal epic drama whose overtones and ramifications later generations have not succeeded in exhausting.

In *The Ring*, the antagonists play for great stakes but their not infrequent moral transgressions are subject to high moral laws. Both Wotan, the King of the Gods, and Alberich, ruler of the underworld Nibelungen, aspire to ultimate heights of wealth and power. In order to rob the Rhinemaidens of the Rhine Gold, Alberich renounces Love (but later in the drama fathers Hagen by an act of near rape). From the gold he forges a Ring which will make its owner all-powerful. Wotan by an act indistinguishable from theft obtains gold and Ring from Alberich, who curses the Ring. Instead of returning it to the Rhinemaidens, Wotan ransoms Freia, goddess of youth, from Fafner and Fasolt, to whom he had promised her as fee for building Valhalla. No sooner have the giants obtained the Ring, than Alberich's curse claims its first victim,

Fafner killing his brother and retiring to guard Ring and treasure in the obscurity of a cave.

Wotan takes twofold precautions against the future: first, the fathering with Erda of a race of warlike Valkyries. They carry to Valhalla dead heroes who will with the Valkyries defend it in case of war with the Nibelungs. The second is more complex. The Ring can be redeemed from Fafner, restored to the Rhinemaidens, and the curse lifted from the race of the gods only through the intervention of a hero impelled by pure and unselfish motive. The gods are ruled out because they have too much to gain. Wotan therefore casts off his divinity and fathers twins, Siegmund and Sieglinde. Siegmund, to steel him for his role of hero, is subjected to trials (like Tamino in *The Magic Flute*, like him magically supported, in his case by a sword), but the scheme founders when he and Sieglinde fall in love.

Their offspring Siegfried, fortuitously raised by the dwarf Mime, Alberich's brother, knows no fear, kills Fafner and becomes master of the gold, and at the same time the object of high-level plotting on the part of Alberich and Mime, who mean to regain what they lost, and of his grandfather Wotan, who must persuade or coerce him to part with the gold if he is to restore it to the Rhinemaidens. The foremost representative of the Valkyries, offspring of Wotan and Erda, is Brünnhilde, whose valour and sympathetic understanding of his own efforts make her her father's favourite. When she defies Wotan in an effort to save Siegmund's life (and incidentally saves the unborn Siegfried), Wotan puts her to sleep surrounded by magic fire which only a hero may penetrate. Armed with Siegmund's sword which he has succeeded in reforging, Siegfried smashes Wotan's hitherto invincible spear and with it Wotan's power, rescues Brünnhilde and claims her as his bride, only to be bamboozled through a drug by Hagen (Alberich's son) into surrendering her to Gunther, king of the Gibichungs. Siegfried comes within an ace of voluntarily giving up the gold to the Rhinemaidens, regains his memory of Brünnhilde, and is slain by Hagen. It remains for Brünnhilde to perform the final act of renunciation, ignite the funeral pyre she has caused to be built, ride into the flames and at the same time return the gold to its owners, reunite with the slain Siegfried and expiate the crimes and follies of the gods, thus fulfilling Wotan's will to end the rule of the gods. H.

RHEINGOLD	WALKÜRE	SIEGFRIED	GÖTTERDÄMMERUNG	
Gods				
Wotan	Wotan	Wanderer		...........Bass-Baritone
Donner				...................Baritone
Froh				.......................Tenor
Loge				.......................Tenor
Fricka	Fricka			........Mezzo-Soprano
Freia				...................Soprano
Erda		Erda		.................Contralto
	Valkyries			
	Brünnhilde	Brünnhilde	Brünnhilde	...................Soprano
	Gerhilde			...................Soprano
	Helmwige			...................Soprano
	Ortlinde			...................Soprano
	Waltraute		Waltraute	........Mezzo-Soprano
	Rossweisse			........Mezzo-Soprano
	Siegrune			........Mezzo-Soprano
	Grimgerde			........Mezzo-Soprano
	Schwertleite			.................Contralto
			Three Norns	.....Contralto, Mezzo, Soprano
Rhinemaidens				
Woglinde			Woglinde	...................Soprano
Wellgunde			Wellgunde	...................Soprano
Flosshilde			Flosshilde	.................Contralto
Giants				
Fasolt				........................Bass
Fafner		Fafner		..................Baritone
Nibelungs				
Alberich		Alberich	Alberich	...................Baritone
Mime		Mime		.......................Tenor
	Mortals			
	Siegmund			.......................Tenor
	Sieglinde			..................Soprano
	Hunding			........................Bass
		Siegfried	Siegfried	.......................Tenor
			Gibichungs	
			Hagen	........................Bass
			Gutrune	..................Soprano
			Gunther	..................Baritone
			Gibichung Vassals and Women	
		Woodbird		..................Soprano
Running Time: 2 hours 35 mins	4 hours	4 hours 5 mins	4 hours 35 mins	

DAS RHEINGOLD
The Rhine Gold

The prelude sets *The Ring* on its way with a soft low E flat from the depths of the Rhine; a horn intones the Rhine motif. In lyrical music, the Rhinemaidens sing, Alberich splashing lecherously around them until his eye is caught by the glint of the gold, a ring made of which he learns from the Rhinemaidens will invest its owner with great power – but only if he renounces love. Alberich, rejected by the Rhinemaidens, makes such a vow and seizes the gold, thus committing the first crime in its name.

Across the Rhine can be made out Valhalla, the castle of the Gods, and Fricka wakes Wotan who sings of its glories. Fricka reminds him he must pay for it by yielding Freia to the Giants who have built it, and Freia appears in flight from them. Froh and Donner, her brothers, try ineffectively to defend her against the Giants' insistence, but Wotan takes courage with the appearance of Loge. Loge tells Wotan of Alberich's theft of the gold, cunningly inciting the curiosity of the Giants as he describes his own wanderings and Alberich's renunciation of love. The Giants decide to accept the gold rather than Freia but retain her as hostage until Wotan can

Das Rheingold *(Covent Garden, 1996, director Richard Jones, designer Nigel Lowery). Matthias Hölle (Fafner), Peter Rose (Fasolt), Rita Cullis (Freia).*

deliver. As she is led off, the Gods wilt in the absence of their sister, Goddess of Youth. Wotan's problem, urged by their predicament and his own by now overmastering desire for gold and Ring, is how to obtain both. 'Durch Raub!' (By theft!) says Loge in one of *The Ring*'s more startling moments.

An orchestral passage takes us to the underworld of the Nibelungs, where Alberich is brutally insisting Mime give him the magic Tarn helmet he has just manufactured. Its wearer can assume any shape he chooses. To test his invisibility, Alberich pinches and punches Mime, who is alone when Wotan and Loge descend the shaft and enter the cave. Alberich forces a crowd of Nibelungs to pile up the treasure, then with a gesture of the Ring drives them off. He boasts that the Ring's power will soon allow him to threaten Valhalla, but Loge flatters him and he turns successively into a serpent, then a toad. Wotan is not slow to put his foot on the toad, Loge wrenches off the Tarn helmet and Alberich materialises writhing under Wotan's boot.

He is bound and dragged off towards the light, where it is clear his lease on power was brief. The gold shall be the price of his release, and Alberich with the Ring summons the Nibelungs with their hoard. When Wotan tears the Ring from the Nibelung's finger, he turns in his rage and not without dignity curses the Ring and all who henceforth possess it, until it be returned to him. Then he is allowed to slink off into Nibelheim.

It is the moment for Freia to be ceded to the Giants or for the ransom to be paid. They measure out a space the height and width of Freia, the gold is piled up, the Tarn helmet added and finally, to Wotan's fury, they demand the Ring. He seems about to refuse, but Erda slowly manifests herself and majestically warns Wotan against so rash an action. He chucks the Ring on the pile and Freia is free. But not so the Giants from the curse, as Fafner quarrels with Fasolt over his share and beats his brother to death, dragging Ring and gold out after him. Another crime has been committed but Loge congratulates Wotan on having given up the curse-laden Ring.

The curse rests on anyone who has touched the Ring and Wotan cannot forget that it has been through his hands. Finally, in a burst of not wholly justified optimism, Donner ascends to the top of a rock, swings his hammer and a flash of lightning dispels the clouds so that a rainbow bridge spans the valley to Valhalla. In a magnificent peroration ('Abendlich strahlt der Sonne Augen'), Wotan greets Valhalla and leads a procession of the Gods across to the castle. Wagner adds six harps to the orchestra to accompany the rainbow, but Wotan is to be denied full triumph as the Rhinemaidens beg him to restore the Ring to them, and Loge decides to defect before the Gods are overcome by the disaster he predicts. H.

DIE WALKÜRE
The Valkyrie

If *The Valkyrie* is the slow movement in the symphonic construction of *The Ring*, then *Rhine Gold* has been just as plainly its expository first movement, *Siegfried* the scherzo and *Twilight* the grandiose last movement in which all threads are to be pulled together and the grand design completed. Lyricism has flowered in *Rhine Gold* in such episodes as the long scene for the Rhinemaidens and the beautiful music associated however briefly with Freia and the idea of Eternal Youth, but it is sinewy narrative and argument, harsh dramatic collision between Gods, Nibelungs and Giants, or grand statements like Wotan's and Erda's with which we have been mainly concerned. This is music drama in its most epic form, but much of *The Valkyrie*, the first act in particular, is in marked contrast, full of lyrical outpouring, as in the entire encounter of Siegmund and Sieglinde, or in the tenderness of the second half of the third act, when Wotan proves unable to resist the pleas of his favourite daughter Brünnhilde.

Sieglinde, Wotan's daughter by a human woman, has been forced into a loveless marriage with Hunding and has no idea of the identity of her father whom she knows only as Wälse.

Act I. The orchestra suggests not only a storm sweeping through the forest but the headlong flight from his enemies of the fugitive Siegmund. He staggers exhausted into Hunding's hut and is found a moment later by Sieglinde. As his strength returns and she looks into his eyes, it becomes obvious from the music that the bond between them is so strong as to amount to love at first sight, but he protests he brings misfortune to anyone who helps him and is about to leave when the approaching Hunding is heard outside. Ordering her to prepare food, Hunding questions the stranger and discovers that Siegmund, whose name is as yet undisclosed, is a sworn enemy to him and his family. Hunding will respect the laws of hospitality, but in the morning his guest, who is his foe, must be prepared to defend himself in the working out of their blood feud.

Siegmund is alone. The Sword motif comes softly from the orchestra and light from the fire falls on a sword buried to the hilt in the tree round which Hunding's hut is built. From this point to the end of the act occurs what can only be described as one of Wagner's most inspired passages. Siegmund muses on his weaponless state ('Ein Schwert verhiess mir der Vater'), on his father's promise to provide him with a sword when his need is greatest and on the sympathy between him and the woman he has just met. He calls on his father – 'Wälse! Wälse!' – to help him. The image of the woman and the gleam from the tree link inextricably in his subconscious and when Sieglinde appears all becomes clear, as she tells the story of her wedding to Hunding and of the stranger who buried a sword deep in the ash trunk. Now she has found the hero who will draw the sword and so achieve what Hunding's relations failed to do! Her words seem to release a new spirit in Siegmund, who declares he will claim both weapon and bride for himself.

One side of the hut flies open and lets in the full moon which rouses Siegmund to new lyrical outpouring: 'Winterstürme wichen dem Wonnemond'. A love duet develops by the end of which Sieglinde has recognised Siegmund as her twin brother. He glories in his name and draws the promised sword from the tree before they rush off together into the night.

Act II. We leave the humans for a different world, dominated by the Gods and their power struggle. The orchestra, with forward references to the Ride of the Valkyries, introduces Wotan and Brünnhilde, the latter eager, as she shows in her war-cry 'Ho-jo-to-ho!', to accept his command to aid Siegmund in his forthcoming fight with Hunding.

It is not to be as sentiment might direct, and Fricka's intervention reminds Wotan that Hunding is calling for vengeance on a breaker of marriage vows, vows moreover that she herself is sworn to uphold. Wotan urges the sanctity of true love against the false values of loveless marriage but Fricka will have none of it, denouncing the incestuous twins and prophesying the end of the Gods' glory now that Wotan casts aside honour by whoring in cavern and on mountainside. Worse, he is prepared to stoop to abandon his wife and her honourable precepts in order to protect the fruits of his union with an earth-woman. Wotan reminds her of the need the Gods have for a pure hero to win back the Ring, but Fricka will not let him off the hook of the laws of morality, nor allow him to trick her by pretending that Siegmund is free to fight unaided when Brünnhilde will be by his side. To uphold Siegmund means exposing his own consort to the scorn of mankind, and in the end he has to agree that Siegmund shall die.

The motif of Alberich's Curse punctuates the return of Brünnhilde, who listens to her father's paroxysms of anger and despair before he embarks on his multifaceted narrative of the theft of the Gold, his own tricking of Alberich, the birth of the Valkyries, and his hopes, now thwarted, that an unsullied hero might regain the ground he – and the Gods – have lost. As it is, his plans are in ruins, and rumour has it Alberich has lovelessly impregnated a woman who will bear him a son and seal the fate of the Gods. His orders are plain: at Fricka's behest, Brünnhilde is to abandon Siegmund and sustain Hunding! Though it is clear from the early part of his narration that Wotan, while initially planning a world subject to good laws, had become embroiled in what Ernest Newman once called a network of evil, the music in which he expresses his rage, his hopes, his disappointments and now, as he sees it, looming disaster, is consistently grand in scale. The baring of his soul reveals on the one hand an unnerving tendency to believe the end justifies the means but, in apparent contradiction, a genuine nobility. Though vast narratives of past events have come to be accepted as part of Wagner's musico-dramatic scheme, they were once deplored as dealing mainly with events with which we are already to a greater or lesser extent familiar.

Terror of being overtaken by Hunding and his kinsmen has stretched Sieglinde's nerves to breaking point, and Siegmund tells her they will rest from their flight and wait for Hunding where she has collapsed. Brünnhilde appears to him in a foreshadowing of his death: 'Todesverkündigung'. She describes the joys of Valhalla in music of the utmost solemnity but Siegmund rejects any possibility which rules Sieglinde out of his life. When he makes as if to kill his sister with his drawn sword, Brünnhilde is moved to defy Wotan: she will throw her resources behind him in his fight with Hunding!

Hunding's horn calls sound nearer and nearer and Sieglinde wakes to hear his voice. As Siegmund raises his magic sword to fight, Wotan interposes his spear – the symbol of his power – and shatters it; Siegmund falls a defenceless victim to Hunding. Wotan orders the victor to kneel in thanks before Fricka, but a contemptuous gesture of his spear leaves Hunding dead on the ground. Brünnhilde gathers up the splintered sword and flees with Sieglinde, while Wotan breathes threats against the disobedient Valkyrie.

Act III. As the eight Valkyries gather on their rock, the act opens on a musical scene of wild energy founded on Brünnhilde's battle cry heard at the start of Act II, now become the motivating force of a great descriptive scene, the Ride of the Valkyries. Brünnhilde arrives pleading with her sisters to help her hide Sieglinde, who at first seems deaf to any notion of a future without Siegmund. She is eventually roused to pulsating life by reference to the child she is yet to bear him and with a stirring cry greets the future before making her escape (Wagner called this motif 'the Glorification of Brünnhilde' and it is heard again in full glory at the end of *Twilight*).

As Wotan approaches calling for her, Brünnhilde leaves her sheltering sisters and is face to face with the father whose orders she has defied. It is not he who is sentencing her, he tells her, but she herself. His will woke her to life, but now that she has rebelled against him she has chosen another fate for herself. No more will she ride as a Valkyrie, no more – and here his heart seems on the point of breaking – may she be considered his favourite child. Instead she will lie defenceless, asleep and shorn of divinity on the Valkyrie rock until claimed by the first man who wakes her.

The Valkyries are driven off by Wotan's wrath and the savagery of Brünnhilde's sentence, and it is to the sound of the bass clarinet, continuing on lower strings and taken up by cor anglais, that Wagner introduces the motif of Brünnhilde's pleading: 'War es so schmählich?' (Was it so shameful?). Did not Wotan himself originally favour Siegmund's cause? Was what she did so disgraceful that she must

herself be disgraced? His tone towards her softens and she pleads passionately for a mitigation of sentence: let the rock on which she sleeps be guarded by fierce flames so that only a dauntless hero may penetrate the barrier and claim her as bride.

Wotan, hedonist as well as master-strategist, has no defence against either her pleas or the inclinations of his heart, and there has been nothing in *The Ring* so far grander of scale or more touching in its examination of the human motives involved than his farewell to Brünnhilde. His last kiss is preceded by a lyrical hymn to the beauty of her eyes from which he has so often derived courage, before the orchestra meditates on the sleep which will envelop her, and Wotan with his spear invokes Loge to girdle the rock with fire. H.

SIEGFRIED

Sieglinde has died giving birth to Siegfried, who has been reared by Alberich's brother Mime. Mime believes the young hero he recognises Siegfried to be will help him forge the broken but potentially all-powerful sword of his father (whose identity Mime knows but of which Siegfried is ignorant). With it Mime hopes Siegfried will kill Fafner, who has turned himself into a dragon, and regain Ring and treasure. Mime will then himself dispose of Siegfried and possess the Ring. Wotan, still with hopes that Siegfried may prove the hero of pure motive that he willed Siegmund to become, watches the development of events, as does Alberich, the two thus playing jackal to Fafner's (and in the end Siegfried's) lion.

The prelude suggests Mime brooding on Ring, hoard of gold and how to re-possess them. When the curtain rises, he is making a further attempt to forge the sword, with which he will attain his objective but which, every time repaired, is smashed at a single blow by the precocious Siegfried. Siegfried's music is initially hyper-active, Mime's plangent but full of venom and spite. Siegfried, whose horn call precedes him, torments Mime by bringing a captive bear into the cave they share, then shatters the latest product of Mime's work at the smithy before impatiently listening as Mime reminds him that it is to him, Mime, that he owes life and upbringing. How then, asks

Siegfried, does he finds his foster-father so repellent? Who indeed is his mother? Because Mime alone knows the answer to that question must be why he constantly returns to share the cave, says Siegfried. Mime admits Siegfried's mother died giving birth to him, and that his father, who was killed in battle, left nothing behind him but the fragments of the sword Mime spends his time attempting to mend. Siegfried rejoices at the prospect of his father's sword reforged then runs from the cave, leaving Mime even more depressed than at the start of the act.

The second scene reintroduces Wotan, no longer recognisably a God but disguised as the Wanderer. He wagers his head that he can correctly answer any three questions which Mime may put to him, and, in music very recognisably belonging to Wotan, comes up with the Nibelungs as the race born in the earth's deep bowels, the Giants as those dwelling on the earth's back, and the Gods as inhabiting the cloudy heights, each answer accompanied by appropriate and by now largely familiar motifs. The Wanderer in his turn, postulating but not expecting the same forfeit and castigating Mime for failing in his questioning to search for knowledge, puts three questions to Mime. 'What noble race did Wotan treat harshly and yet hold most dear?' 'The Wälsungs' (Siegmund and Sieglinde). 'Name the sword with which Siegfried must strike to regain the Ring.' 'Notung' correctly answers Mime. 'Whose hand can forge the sword?' Mime cannot answer but the Wanderer assures him only a hero who does not know fear can weld the pieces together; moreover, though he may keep his forfeit head for a while, it is through that hero that Mime will lose his life.

Mime collapses behind the anvil, where he is found by Siegfried, returning full of the confidence of youth and impatient that Mime has again failed to forge the sword. Mime, remembering the Wanderer's warning, asks Siegfried if he has ever known fear, which the young hero denies, while affirming he is ready to learn if that will help him face the future. Mime describes Fafner in his guise as dragon, but that only inspires Siegfried to demand the sword with which to face Fafner. Impetuously he starts to file down the pieces, then, hearing from Mime that it is called Notung and addressing it by name, he blows up the fire with the bellows and in a scene crackling with energy and excitement heats the metal to melting point before pouring it off into a mould, thence into water to cool, finally heating it in the fire and beating it out with a hammer on the anvil. It is the most physical scene of the entire *Ring* cycle, and Siegfried with a shout of triumph splits the anvil in two with his newly-forged weapon, Mime, part menace, part comic, collapsing in terror behind the anvil.

Act II. Night, in the depths of the forest, near Fafner's cave. Alberich lying in wait recognises the Wanderer as Wotan, his enemy, the thief of the Ring. That his curse will bring about Fafner's downfall causes him satisfaction, but the Wanderer predicts that a young hero, guided by none other than Mime, will win the Ring, and even risks waking Fafner to warn him of what is in store. Mime leads Siegfried into the space in front of the cave and warns of the perils to be faced when Fafner emerges, but Siegfried drives him off and is left by himself.

There follows one of the supreme lyrical episodes of the cycle, a pastoral poem to nature which marks a crucial stage in the awakening of Siegfried's sensibilities. As he lies under a lime-tree and listens to the rustling of the leaves (the 'Waldweben' or Forest Murmurs it is called in the concert hall), he reflects on his parentage, then listens to the song of the Woodbird and plays on a reed in an effort to communicate with the bird. That effort ends in fiasco and he decides to blow his horn instead (the grandest manifestation of his horn call we shall hear). This rouses Fafner from his sleep, but in fight he is no match for Siegfried and his sword and it is not long before he is demanding who it is has mortally wounded him. The motif of the Curse sounds as he dies, and as he pulls the sword from Fafner's body Siegfried licks the scalding blood from his hand. Instantly, he acquires the power to understand the bird's song, hearing first of the gold, the Tarn helmet and the Ring, which he goes into the cave to fetch.

Alberich and Mime scuttle scavenger-like into the clearing in front of the cave, snarling and snapping like a couple of cur dogs and desisting only when Siegfried comes out of the cave with the booty Mime craves. The bird warns him first against Mime's wiles and eventually he understands that the dwarf is plotting to poison him. He gets in first and kills Mime with his sword, the motif of the Curse ringing out from the orchestra to remind us not only that it has claimed a second victim in this segment of the cycle but that the

Siegfried *(Metropolitan Opera House, New York, c. 1933). Lauritz Melchior in the title role.*

Ring is now in Siegfried's possession. But that hero's thoughts are on the present, in the form of the beauty of the forest, and on a future in which the bird seems to be promising him Brünnhilde as bride.

Act III. The opening scene sees Wotan/Wanderer musically at the height of his powers, apparently dominant and carrying all before him. But in reality he is full of fear that through Siegfried and Brünnhilde, whose partnership he sees as inevitable, the rulership of the world may pass from the Gods to the human race. In his perplexity he calls in music of power and passion on Erda for counsel, but she can give no advice and he appears to abdicate not only hope but responsibility. Let human love supplant Gods and Nibelungs; perhaps the twilight of the Gods will be the dawn of a more glorious epoch.

The bird has guided Siegfried to the spot where Brünnhilde lies asleep and Wotan's final attempt to hold back the inevitable by barring the way with his spear ends as Siegfried smashes it with a single blow. The flames which surround the sleeping maiden are now visible and Siegfried advances towards his destiny.

The last scene is an extended duet, starting with Siegfried's first view of the sleeping Brünnhilde, his attempt to loosen the breastplate which covers her, and his discovery that this is no man but a woman, the first he has seen. The music swells to magnificence as she wakes, greets the sun, refers to her rescue of his mother, then turns to thoughts of their mutual love. For a moment of exceptional musical richness, Brünnhilde dwells on her once supernatural status ('Ewig war ich'), then Siegfried plights his troth with the curse-laden Ring, and the scene finishes with a magnificent hymn to love.   H.

GÖTTERDÄMMERUNG
The Twilight of the Gods

Prologue. The first scene has the three Norns, daughters of Erda and guardians of fate, discussing the progress of events and passing a golden rope from one to the other until, as they foresee the end of the Gods and wonder whether Alberich is destined to supplant them, the rope breaks and they see catastrophe impending.

An orchestral interlude returns us to Siegfried and Brünnhilde striding heroically and in an aura of requited love through the dawn, Brünnhilde preparing him for the heroic deeds he must accomplish ('Zu neuen Thaten'), he leaving her with the fatal Ring as pledge. The orchestra describes Siegfried's journey down the Rhine, which takes us into the first act.

Act I. Siegfried arrives at the castle of the Gibichungs, where live Gunther, his sister Gutrune, and their half-brother Hagen, son of Alberich. Through Hagen, the product of Alberich's loveless union with Queen Grimhilde, the curse hurled by Alberich at all who possess the Ring will be worked out – with Siegfried betrayed and the rule of the Gods brought to an end. Hagen excites Gunther's concupiscence with ideas of Brünnhilde as his bride, even though he stipulates that she must be won by a stronger man than Gunther. Such a man is Siegfried, a worthy mate for the unwed Gutrune. Hagen plots to trick Siegfried with a magic potion into forgetting Brünnhilde and falling in love with Gutrune, after which it will not be hard to persuade him to stand in for Gunther and win him a bride. Siegfried is greeted, drinks from the cup Gutrune offers him, and Hagen's trick starts to work. Siegfried and Gunther swear an oath of Blood Brotherhood (introduced by the Curse motif), and Siegfried goes off to win Brünnhilde for Gunther, leaving Hagen to brood alone (Hagen's Watch: 'Hier sitz ich zur Wacht': I sit here and wait).

Back at the rock to which she was once bound asleep, Brünnhilde hears from her sister Waltraute that Wotan has passed into a near-catatonic state, brooding over his splintered spear and the imminent end of the power of the Gods. Only the return of the Ring to the Rhinemaidens can lift the curse. Will Brünnhilde take it on herself to cast the Ring back into the Rhine where it belongs? Brünnhilde refuses. The Ring symbolises her and Siegfried's love and she will yield it to no one.

The notes of Siegfried's horn are heard, but it is apparently a stranger who braves the flames, transformed by the Tarn helmet to look like Gunther. Brünnhilde tries to defend herself but she is powerless against the intruder, who tears the Ring from her finger and subdues her – laying his sword between them as pledge to his blood-brother's honour.

Act II. In front of the hall of the Gibichungs,

Alberich appears to Hagen, who sleeps, spear in hand, against a pillar. He exacts an oath from his son that he will murder Siegfried and seize the Ring from his finger, then dematerialises. Siegfried returns with Brünnhilde from his mission, wearing the Ring and boasting of his exploit. Hagen summons the Gibichung vassals to the double wedding, and in a moment Gunther is there dragging Brünnhilde by the hand. It is when she sees Siegfried standing, Ring on finger, with Gutrune and apparently oblivious to what has passed between them that Brünnhilde is consumed with the idea of vengeance. She accuses Siegfried of having passed himself off as Gunther, stolen the Ring from her, and delivered his own bride to another. His defence is to swear on spear-point that he found the Ring among the dragon's treasure and has never been parted from it and that the sword stayed between them when he found her. Hagen offers his weapon for the oath, in the knowledge that, should he swear falsely, Siegfried's death is certain at the point of that very spear. Siegfried takes his oath, and is followed by Brünnhilde in full knowledge that he has sworn falsely. She dedicates the weapon to his destruction.

Tension mounts, if that is possible, in the last scene of the act, when Hagen manipulates Brünnhilde and Gunther, the one in a state of fury and the other humiliated beyond endurance, so that they plot the murder of Siegfried in the course of a forthcoming boar hunt, intending to strike him from behind (his 'Achilles heel') with Hagen's spear on which the oath has just been sworn.

Act III. The final act is an extraordinary succession of melodic grace, Wagnerian narrative and high drama, followed by a peroration of unique and tragic grandeur. The hunt has taken its followers to the banks of the Rhine, where the Rhinemaidens in a scene of great melodic beauty endeavour to coax the Ring from Siegfried. He seems on the point of handing it over but one threat too many from the Rhinemaidens causes him to change his mind: he will never give in to pressure.

The hunting party assembles, and Hagen presses on Siegfried a drinking-horn containing an antidote to the potion before getting him to relate the story of his life. Memories of Mime precede those of Brünnhilde now coming back to his mind, and he relates in some detail the story of how he penetrated

the wall of flame to claim her for his bride. Gunther now knows Brünnhilde's accusation was true, and Hagen loses no time in plunging the spear into Siegfried's defenceless back. Siegfried rears himself up on his shield and relives the moment when he awakened Brünnhilde from sleep, before he falls back dead. His Funeral Music is of overwhelming grandeur. In the hall of the Gibichungs, Gutrune awaits the return of the hunt. Hagen announces Siegfried's death and when Gunther refuses to allow him to take the Ring from Siegfried's finger, kills his half-brother and adds a further death to the day's tally. Siegfried's hand with the Ring upon it raises itself threateningly from the bier, and even Hagen falls back in some consternation as Brünnhilde advances solemnly.

The rest of the drama is Brünnhilde's. Gutrune falls in a faint on Siegfried's body as Brünnhilde bids the men erect a funeral pyre and place the body on it. She apostrophises the dead hero, who at the same time betrayed her and was the most faithful of men, then, the Ring upon her finger, mounts her Valkyrie charger and rides into the flames. She will expiate the crimes of lust and greed which started with the wresting of the Rhine gold from the Rhinemaidens, and Wotan's crisis will be at an end. The Rhine overflows, from Brünnhilde's finger the Rhinedaughters pluck the ring and, when Hagen tries to seize it, draw him down with them into the eternal waters. In the heavens, Valhalla is consumed in flames. It is *Götterdämmerung*, the Twilight of the Gods, and Brünnhilde through love – the emotion Alberich renounced to gain power – has caused a new human era to dawn in place of the old mythological one of the Gods.

It is the grandest example in all Wagner of redemption through woman's heroic love, from the time of *The Flying Dutchman* a constant motif in his writing. In that at least his thesis holds good today. Otherwise, the satirists are due a field day with Wagner's moral – the bastard daughter of the King of the Gods, through love of Wotan's doubly illegitimate grandson, her own nephew, purges her father's crime and rids the world of the curse which it precipitated. Or, as George Bernard Shaw would have it, we have the ultimate exposé of the Capitalist system, and only in the transcendent love of a decent woman can it have any hope of redemption.   H.

PARSIFAL

Bühnenweihfestspiel (festival work for the initiation of a stage) in three acts, libretto by the composer, based on Chrétien de Troyes' *Percival le Galois* (1190), Wolfram von Eschenbach's *Parsifal* and the fourteenth-century *Mabinogion.* Composed specifically for Bayreuth's covered pit, first performed there 26 July 1882, with Winkelmann as Parsifal (later, Gudehus and Jäger), Materna as Kundry (later, Marianne Brandt and Malten), Scaria as Gurnemanz (later, Siehr); Reichmann as Amfortas, Hill as Klingsor (later, Fuchs), conducted by Hermann Levi. U.S. première, Metropolitan, New York, 24 December 1903, with Burgstaller, Ternina, Blass, Van Rooy and Goritz, conducted by Hertz. U.K. première, 2 February 1914, with von der Osten, Heinrich Hensel, Vender, Knüpfer, August Kiess, Murray Davey, conducted by Bodanzky.

Amfortas, *son of Titurel, ruler of the*
    Grail kingdom ....Baritone
Titurel, *former ruler* ....Bass
Gurnemanz, *a veteran Knight of the Grail*..............Bass
Parsifal ....Tenor
Klingsor, *a magician* ....Bass
Kundry ....Soprano
Two Grail Knights ....Tenor, Bass
Four Esquires ....Sopranos and Tenors
Klingsor's Magic Girls ...Three Sopranos, Three Altos

The Brotherhood of the Grail, Boys, Esquires

Place: Domain and Castle of the Guardians of the
    Grail; Monsalvat; Klingsor's Magic Castle
Running Time: 4 hours 40 minutes

Gustav Kobbé attended the first performance of *Parsifal* in 1882. His confident description of what happened (or, rather, what happens) when the Grail is uncovered was reprinted unchanged until this edition: 'a ray of brilliant light darts down upon the sacred vessel, which shines with a soft purple radiance that diffuses itself through the hall'. There was no need to change that description because, once upon a time, wherever *Parsifal* was performed, the same events always took place on stage. This was a consequence of Wagner's own attempt to reserve performances of his last opera for Bayreuth itself. It no longer holds true.

Some time ago, Titurel led a group of Christian knights. When they were most threatened by heathen attack, angels appeared and brought two holy relics to sustain them. The Chalice is the cup from which Jesus drank at the Last Supper and which later received his blood when he bled on the Cross. It is known as the Grail. The Spear is the weapon that wounded him. Titurel built a sanctuary for these relics. His Knights were fortified by superhuman nourishment provided by the Grail. Only the pure were allowed to join the order. Klingsor applied but was refused. When he then castrated himself to stop himself sinning, he was rejected scornfully. He turned in fury to magic and is now bent on destroying the Christian Knights. He uses women to seduce them, led by Kundry, a woman cursed to live forever unless she can find someone who resists her charms. She was punished for laughing at Jesus when he was on his way to be crucified. Now she is in thrall to Klingsor, since he can resist her. But in an attempt to expiate her crime she also serves the Knights as their messenger. They do not know of her other life.

In old age Titurel abdicated and his son Amfortas became King of the Grail. Impatient to free the Knights from Klingsor, Amfortas went to fight him, armed with the holy Spear. He was seduced by Kundry; Klingsor seized the Spear and wounded Amfortas with it. Returning to the sanctuary, Amfortas found his wound was incurable. He prayed for salvation and was told by angels to wait for 'the pure fool, the man made wise by compassion'.

Act I. Gurnemanz, Titurel's former esquire, hears the morning call and rebukes the esquires who guard the wood for being asleep. Amfortas will soon pass by on his way to bathe in the lake. Gurnemanz hears that the herb Gawan (Gawain) brought has not relieved Amfortas's pain. Kundry herself brings a balsam from Arabia for Amfortas, who is temporarily restored by the sight of the lake. He knows, however, that there is only one remedy: he must wait for the pure fool. He is still grateful for Kundry's trouble. The esquires mistrust her, but Gurnemanz reminds them that Kundry helped them in the past, though she cannot help them regain the Spear. He recalls how Amfortas was seduced by 'a fearsomely beautiful woman', which enabled Klingsor to seize the weapon and wound him. No one realises that this woman was and is Kundry.

The esquires return and Gurnemanz tells them of the Knights' history: how Titurel was entrusted with the Grail and the Spear, how Klingsor attempted to join the brotherhood and then resorted to magic. Cries are heard: someone has killed a wild swan flying over the lake. Amfortas had greeted it as a good omen. A young man boasts that he killed the swan, not knowing that the Grail's domain is a sanctuary for all creatures. Gurnemanz asks him how he could kill it, where he has come from, what his father is called, who sent him and what his own name is. The only answer the young man makes is that he does not know. All he knows is that his mother is called Herzeleide (heart's sorrows) and that they lived in the woods. Kundry interrupts and explains that his mother brought him up in ignorance of knightly arms, so that he would not die young, as his father Gamuret did. She also reveals that his mother is dead. Seeing he is about to faint, she fetches water from a spring. Gurnemanz thanks her for her good deed. Kundry denies that she ever does good. Against her will, she falls into a deep sleep.

Bells toll and Gurnemanz invites the young man to join him at the hallowed feast of the Grail Knights in their temple. If he is pure, the Grail will provide him with sustenance. The young man asks, 'Who is the Grail?' Gurnemanz explains that, if he is chosen to join the fellowship, he will understand. As they talk, the wood turns into the temple of the Grail because here, as Gurnemanz says, 'time becomes space'.

The Knights take their places for the ceremony and the young man watches as Titurel calls on his son Amfortas to officiate and uncover the Grail. Amfortas begs to be relieved of his office: each time he performs it, his wound bleeds and causes him terrible agonies. The Knights remind him that he must wait for 'the pure fool'. In the meantime he performs the office and his wound bleeds again. The young man watches but understands nothing. Disappointed, Gurnemanz sends him away. Unseen voices remind us of that 'pure fool, made wise by compassion'.

Act II. Klingsor waits in his magic castle for the young man. He summons Kundry from her sleep and calls up the renegade knights, those who fell victim to his spells. They fight the young man, and are defeated. Klingsor then turns the castle into a magic garden. Beautiful women invite the young man to join in their games. He is about to run away when he hears Kundry's voice calling him 'Parsifal', a name he remembers from his dreams. She describes how she saw him when he was still a baby, how he broke his mother's heart when he left home one day and did not return. Parsifal blames himself for her death. Kundry offers him, 'as a last token of his mother's blessing, the first kiss of love'. But this only reminds

Parsifal of Amfortas's wound: suddenly, Parsifal himself suffers as Amfortas suffered during the Grail ceremony. As Kundry attempts to seduce him, Parsifal realises this is how Amfortas was seduced. He rejects her, knowing that if he yielded it would only increase her torment. He asks her to show him the way back to Amfortas. She refuses, curses him violently and calls on Klingsor to destroy him. But when the magician hurls the Spear at Parsifal, it remains suspended above his head. Parsifal seizes it and with it makes the sign of the Cross: the castle collapses and the magic garden withers. As he goes, Parsifal reminds Kundry, 'You know where you can find me again.'

Act III. It is Good Friday, some years later. Gurnemanz has become a hermit. He hears groaning from inside a thicket and discovers Kundry lying there in a cold trance. He restores her numb circulation and she wakes with a cry. All she wants to do now, she says, in the only two words she utters in this act, is to serve ('Dienen, dienen'). Gurnemanz comments that she won't have much to do, now that the Knights have given up fighting and travelling.

He sees someone approaching in dark armour. It is Parsifal, who has spent years trying to find his way back to the Grail sanctuary. He remains silent. Gurnemanz reminds him that this is Good Friday, when the weapons of war are most out of place, but then he recognises the Spear in Parsifal's hand. Parsifal has come to bring Amfortas salvation. Gurnemanz tells him that the whole brotherhood are in need of his healing power: since Amfortas refused to perform the office, the Grail has remained covered. Deprived of sustenance, the Knights wander about pale and unhappy. Gurnemanz himself has retreated to this corner of the wood: now that his old warrior-lord Titurel has died, he himself longs for death.

Parsifal's intense remorse that it took him so long to return brings him near to fainting. Kundry fetches him some water but, knowing that Parsifal will perform the holy office today, Gurnemanz leads him to the spring. Parsifal learns that Amfortas has agreed to uncover the Grail for the last time at the funeral of Titurel. Kundry and Gurnemanz prepare Parsifal for the rite. The 'pure, wise, compassionate healer', as Gurnemanz calls him, baptises Kundry. He notices that the meadow has never looked as beautiful as it does today. Gurnemanz explains that this is the magic of Good Friday – not a day of mourning, but of rejoicing at the salvation brought by suffering.

As the bells toll, the scene changes once more to the Temple of the Grail. The Knights assemble for Titurel's funeral. When they insist that Amfortas uncover the Grail, he asks them to kill him, rather than make him suffer renewed agony from his wound. Parsifal steps forward and touches it with the Spear: it is healed. As everyone gazes at the uplifted Spear they see its point bleeding, as it yearns to be united with the blood in the Grail. Parsifal promises that the Grail will never be enclosed again. As the Grail glows at its brightest, a white dove descends and hovers over Parsifal's head. Unseen voices from on high celebrate the miracle: the redeemer has been redeemed ('Erlösung dem Erlöser').

Doubts about *Parsifal* begin with Wagner's own definition of the work and end with the work's last words. For many people, ignorance is bliss and *Parsifal* can still be enjoyed as a Christian mystery. Others ignore the Christian symbolism or try to go behind it. Mike Ashman's essay, 'A Very Human Epic', works hard at this tack.[1] *Parsifal* makes rather more sense as a sequel to *The Magic Flute*, as an initiatory journey, a riddle that we can only partially solve at each performance. We then experience the enigmas of the deliberately obscure narrations, of Kundry, of Amfortas's wound, of the Grail ceremony, as Parsifal does: we know nothing. Music solves the enigmas because it evades logic. The opera becomes a symphony. Those who do not want to know what Wagner himself intended should stop here.

On the other hand, Wagner's now unread essays 'Religion and Art' and its supplements, published in the *Bayreuther Blätter* 1880–81, his letters and comments that Cosima recorded in her diary, provide overwhelming evidence of the anti-semitic programme he wrote into *Parsifal*. He defined it as a *Bühnenweihfestspiel*, meaning that it was conceived as the cornerstone of his Bayreuth crusade to free Christianity of its Judaic stain. This was why he could not bear the idea of Hermann Levi conducting the première. In a letter of 25 August 1879 Wagner told King Ludwig II that he wanted to preserve 'this most Christian of all artworks from a world which fades in cowardice in the face of the Jews'. He told the King on 28 September 1880 that because *Parsifal* represented the 'most sublime mysteries of the Christian faith', it could not be staged outside Bayreuth. Wagner tried very hard but unsuccessfully to convince Levi to convert to Christianity; at the last performance, he seized the baton from him at the beginning of the last act.

According to Wagner's 'thinking', Jesus wasn't Jewish; Judaism had corrupted Christianity (as Klingsor corrupted the Knights). Wagner assured Liszt in a letter of 7 June 1855 that 'modern research has succeeded in showing that pure and unalloyed Christianity was nothing but a branch of that venerable Buddhism which Alexander's Indian expedition spread to the shores of the Mediterranean'. Compassion ('Mitleid') mattered, because it was the virtue that Schopenhauer denied the Jews. The philosopher also blamed man's cruelty towards animals on Judaism and 'Jewish Christianity'.[2] Christianity can only be saved by the Aryan hero, Parsifal, once he has learned not to kill swans. Which is why the opera ends with unseen voices celebrating Parsifal's kingship of the Grail as 'Redemption to the redeemer'. Never has D.H. Lawrence's injunction, to trust the tale, not the teller, made more sense.   P.

---

[1] 'The "baptism" of Parsifal and Kundry, and the anointing of Parsifal in Act III, use the elements of oil and water present in initiation ceremonies since recorded time'; 'A dove is not a specifically Christian symbol', etc.,

Parsifal, Opera Guide Series 34, ed. Nicholas John, 1986.
[2] Paul Lawrence Rose, *Wagner Race and Revolution*, 1992.

VINCENT WALLACE
(born 11 March 1814, died 12 October 1865)

MARITANA

Opera in three acts, text by Edward Fitzball, based on the play *Don César de Bazan* by d'Ennery and Dumanoir. Première, Drury Lane, London, 15 November 1845. First performed Philadelphia, 1846; New York, 1848; Her Majesty's Theatre, London (in Italian), 1880. Revived Lyceum, London, 1925; Old Vic and Sadler's Wells, 1931, with Kennard (later Cross), Morris, Cox, Austin, Brindle. Continuously in the repertories of British touring companies until about 1930.

Maritana, *a handsome gitana* ....Soprano
Don Caesar de Bazan ....Tenor
Don José de Santarem, *an unscrupulous*
    courtier ....Baritone
Lazarillo, *a poor boy* ....Mezzo-Soprano
The Marchioness of Montefiore ....Mezzo-Soprano
Captain of the Guard ....Baritone
Marquis of Montefiore..Bass
The King ....Bass
The Alcalde ....Bass

Soldiers, Gipsies, Populace

Place: Madrid
Running Time: 3 hours 10 minutes

*M*aritana deals, like Balfe's *Bohemian Girl*, with the very poor on the one hand, and the very rich and powerful on the other. The essential difference is that while there is no humour of any kind in *The Bohemian Girl*, the librettist of *Maritana*, Edward Fitzball, has contrived to invest the character of Don Caesar de Bazan with a lighthearted, whimsical humour. As regards the music, the soprano aria 'Scenes that are brightest' and the tenor's 'Yes, let me like a soldier fall' are the equals of Balfe's 'I dream that I dwelt in marble halls'.

Act I. Don José, a young and wealthy courtier of Madrid, is enamoured of the Queen of Spain. Don José believes that the Queen would be his if he could only persuade her that the King does not care for her. The King himself is of a roving disposition and he has been much attracted lately by the simple charms of Maritana, a street singer, whom we meet engaged in her occupation and surrounded by an admiring crowd. Don José naturally determines to do his utmost to further the King's interests in this quarter, although he well knows that Maritana is above the temptations of wealth and position. Since she does not care for the King, José has to wait until chance comes to aid his desires. The opportunity comes with the return to Madrid of Don Caesar de Bazan, a nobleman as poor as a church mouse and as proud as Satan. Don Caesar, the hero of countless duels, when told by Don José that duelling has been forbidden on pain of death, declares his intention never to fight again. He learns that anyone who forfeits his life to the law on this particular day of the year is not going to be shot in a clean, soldierly fashion, but hanged. But when Lazarillo, a poor apprentice, is pursued by the guards, he does not hesitate to challenge their captain so as to give Lazarillo a chance of escaping. Don Caesar wounds the captain, but is himself apprehended and marched to jail.

Act II. Interior of a fortress. The prospect of dying a felon's death horrifies him, and he accepts eagerly a strange proposal from Don José. The Don, believing that if Maritana could be married to a nobleman she could be got more easily to comply with the King's wishes, proposes a bargain. Don Caesar will be shot and not hanged if he consents to marry a veiled lady. Don Caesar is ready to do anything if he can escape the rope, and sings one of the best arias of the opera, extolling the advantages of a soldier's death: 'Yes, let me like a soldier fall'. Don José recalls his first sight of the Queen: 'In happy moments day by day', and resolves to go through with his scheme. The marriage takes place there and then and so does the execution – apparently, since Lazarillo, to show his devotion to the man who risked death to save him, has abstracted the bullets from the executioners' rifles. The soldier of the song fell only to rise again. As soon as the firing squad has gone, Don Caesar goes in search of the unknown lady he has wedded.

Meanwhile, the King, remembering Don Caesar's former services to the State, has pardoned him. But the pardon has fallen into the hands of Don José, who hides it and so frees himself of Don Caesar's presence.

Scene ii. Maritana has now been taken to the

castle of the Marquis of Montefiore. There she is introduced to the King: 'Hear me, gentle Maritana'. Her heart has been given to the gallant Don Caesar and she refuses to listen to the advances of her royal master. Don Caesar comes to the Marquis's house, in search of his wife, whom he is sure he will recognise, although he has only seen her once heavily veiled: 'There is a flower that bloometh'. At Don José's instigation, the Marchioness poses as the wife of Don Caesar, who is completely disillusioned when he sees her age. He is about to sign away all claim on her, when he hears and recognises Maritana's voice and suspects that some intrigue is in progress. Don José has Don Caesar rearrested.

Act III. A magnificent apartment. Maritana laments the loss of her liberty: 'Scenes that are brightest'. The King comes to her pretending to be her husband. Lazarillo, ordered by Don José to guard their privacy and to shoot anyone who attempts to enter,

fires on an approaching stranger. His aim is not accurate enough to hit Don Caesar, who climbs in through the window to meet the King, whom Maritana has left to nurse his disappointment alone. 'What are you doing here?' he asks, without recognising the King. 'I am the master here, the Count of Bazan,' replies His Majesty. 'Oh, well', retorts the nobleman, 'I, then, must be the King.' In the course of the wrangle, Don Caesar finds out from the King that he has been pardoned and that the execution which nearly cost him his life need never have taken place. The King leaves, and Don Caesar is face to face with Maritana. They recognise each other as husband and wife. The Queen arrives, escorted by Don José, who meant to show her her spouse's infidelity. Explanations ensue; Don Caesar runs his sword through Don José's body to save the Queen from his importunity, and all ends happily for Don Caesar and his true love, the street singer Maritana.   F.B.

WILLIAM WALTON
(born 29 March 1902, died 8 March 1983)

TROILUS AND CRESSIDA

Opera in three acts, text by Christopher Hassall. Première, Covent Garden, London, 3 December 1954, with Magda Laszlo, Monica Sinclair, Richard Lewis, Peter Pears, Otakar Kraus, Frederick Dalberg, conductor Sir Malcolm Sargent. First performed San Francisco, 1955, with Dorothy Kirsten, Richard Lewis, conductor Erich Leinsdorf; New York, City Center, 1955, with Phyllis Curtin, Jon Crain; la Scala, Milan, 1956, with Dorothy Dow, David Poleri. Revived Covent Garden, 1963, with Marie Collier, Josephine Veasey, André Turp, John Lanigan, conductor Sargent; Covent Garden, 1976, with Janet Baker, Richard Cassilly, Gerald English, Benjamin Luxon, Richard Van Allan, conductor Lawrence Foster; Opera North, Leeds, 1994, with Judith Howarth, Arthur Davies, conductor Richard Hickox.

Calkas, *High Priest of Pallas* .... Bass

Antenor, *Captain of Trojan spears* .... Baritone

Troilus, *Prince of Troy* .... Tenor

Pandarus, *brother of Calkas* .... Tenor Buffo

Cressida, *daughter of Calkas* .... Soprano

Evadne, *her servant* .... Mezzo-Soprano

Horaste, *a friend of Pandarus* .... Baritone

Diomede, *Prince of Argos* .... Baritone

A Woman's Voice within the Temple; Priests, Soldiers, Trojans, Greeks, etc.

Place: Troy
Time: About the Twelfth Century B.C.
Running Time: 2 hours

Sir William Walton's only full-length opera was commissioned in 1947 by the B.B.C. Its first performance was at Covent Garden towards the end of 1954 and it was an immediate success, its straightforward manner and late romantic style appealing to the London public and press. It was no more successful in its foreign productions than were other British operas of the period – *Gloriana*, *The Midsummer Marriage*, *Billy Budd* – but revival has suggested that the music's strong lyrical impulse, from the same source as that of the composer's Violin Concerto, puts it into a longer-lasting category than that of the 'well-made' opera.

Act I. Before the temple of Pallas in the citadel of Troy. Quiet timpani and a murmuring chorus of worshippers from within the temple set the scene, but soon the muttering becomes desperate, and it is apparent that the starving population of Troy is liable to riot in protest against conditions. Calkas tries to quieten them and reminds them that the oracle at Delphi has already spoken. His unequivocal if defeatist interpretation is to advise them to parley with the Greeks while there is still time. Antenor, intent on a foray with his warrior companions, over-hears him and challenges his right to utter such counsel of despair. He rouses the crowd, and Calkas is obviously in some danger until Troilus appears and restores order. He wishes Antenor luck on his mission and is hardly ruffled when his friend guesses that it is the presence of the beautiful Cressida which draws him to the temple.

In a gently lyrical aria Troilus admits to himself that he loves Cressida, and as the music reaches a climax the temple doors open and Cressida, preceded by two priests, appears in the doorway. Troilus has never spoken to her before and her first musical utterance is subdued: 'Morning and evening I have felt your glance follow me out of sight.' She is a widow and is soon to take her vows as a priestess; in Pallas, she feels, lies her only hope for the future.

Troilus unavailingly protests his love, and as Cressida disappears her place is taken by her uncle Pandarus, whose arrival produces a complete change of musical mood, from the lyrical to something much more volatile. He takes in the situation at a glance and proceeds to win Troilus' confidence. Pandarus is about to enter the temple in search of Cressida when the doors open and Calkas emerges, followed by Cressida and Evadne. Pandarus listens to Calkas admit to his daughter and her companions that he plans to quit the city and desert to the enemy. Cressida's pleas fail and he departs, leaving her to sing of an incident in childhood which she now recognises as representing presentiments of desertion, always connected with her father ('Slowly it all comes back'). Warmth enters the music as she interprets the warrior in her dream of long ago as the Troilus of today – the Troilus they (and the gods who preside over our destinies at birth) will not allow her to love!

Pandarus and Evadne confirm that Calkas has deserted, and Pandarus prays to Aphrodite to ensure that his tongue has not lost its golden touch; only with its aid can he rescue the family from crisis. In lively, flexible music, he starts to plead Troilus' cause with Cressida but is interrupted by the arrival of the prince himself. Troilus is met by Antenor's soldiers with the news that their captain has been taken pris-oner. Troilus swears that he will be rescued, either by means of an exchange of prisoners, or else by force of arms. As Troilus goes to look for Calkas, Pandarus persuades Cressida to come next day to a supper party at his house, then, before she leaves, prevails upon her to leave her crimson scarf as a token of esteem for Troilus. Troilus for his part has discovered that Calkas, the father of his beloved, is a traitor, but the music returns, as he catches sight of Cressida's scarf, to the ecstatic lyricism of his earlier aria.

Act II. A room in Pandarus' house the following evening. The music, with its syncopated rhythms, immediately recalls us to the mood induced by Pandarus' arrival in the previous act. Supper is over and the guests are playing chess, Cressida with Horaste. A storm is blowing up and Pandarus, think-ing this will suit his book, dispatches a messenger to fetch Troilus. At the first sign of rain, Pandarus urges Cressida and the other guests to stay the night and promptly shows her an alcove furnished with a bed. In gently decorative music, her ladies prepare Cressida for the night. She cannot sleep and in an aria admits to herself that she is in love – her basi-cally cool music (the languor of beauty long accus-tomed to admiration?) soon turns to passion as she proclaims 'friend and foe, Troilus my conqueror'.

Pandarus comes in to say that Troilus is in the house, racked with jealousy and begging to see her. 'On jealousy's hot grid he roasts alive', begins the ensemble, which becomes a trio when Troilus over-hears Pandarus' barefaced fabrication – one of the liveliest moments of the score, cut by the composer for Covent Garden's 1963 revival. Troilus interrupts, denounces the trickster who admits he has made it all up, and starts to woo Cressida from her tears. A love duet develops, under the star, as it were, of Aphrodite, whose protection the lovers invoke. Pandarus looks in, is delighted at what he sees, snuffs the candles and tiptoes away.

The storm breaks in an orchestral interlude, which depicts the love-making within as well as the wind and rain outside and which might not have been as it is without *Peter Grimes* but is nonetheless essentially Walton. It ends with peaceful dawn.

Scene ii opens as Troilus and Cressida together watch the sun rise over the roofs of Troy. Like Pandarus, they are disturbed to hear the sound of approaching drums, and Pandarus is particularly concerned for the good name of his family. A military deputation is at the door and Troilus must not be discovered; Pandarus will cope with the visitors.

It is Diomede, a young Greek commander, who explains that Calkas wishes to have his daughter restored to him and that the commanders of the army have agreed that Cressida shall go to the Greek camp in exchange for the Trojan warrior Antenor. When Pandarus claims that Cressida is not in his house, Diomede searches, discovers her and marvels at her beauty. Troilus emerges at Diomede's departure and says he will not rest until the agreement is revoked and Cressida back in Troy. In the meanwhile, he will send daily messages and will corrupt the sentries so that he may visit her in the Greek camp. There is a moving vocal postlude, as it were, to their grand duet, and, as Cressida leaves, Troilus gives her back the crimson scarf which she had given him and which she must keep as a token of their love.

Act III. The Greek encampment. Early evening ten weeks later. Calkas' tent can be seen at the side, and at the back the battlements. A sad cor anglais solo (marked *lugubre*) introduces the scene and the sound of nightwatchmen's voices can be heard. Cressida, whose distraught loneliness is all too apparent in every bar she sings, implores Evadne to see if there is a message from Troilus at the palisade. She has not heard from him since they parted and is beginning to despair. Evadne knows Cressida's coldness to Diomede jeopardises their safety, and her solo ('Night after night the same') offers her mistress no comfort. Cressida for her part is a prey to every kind of fear, most of all that Troilus is already dead, and she prays movingly to the goddess either to allay or confirm her fears. Calkas interrupts her reverie and protests that it is madness to continue to flout Diomede, whom Cressida admits to finding attractive. No sooner has she mentioned his name than Diomede is standing in front of her, demanding her final decision as to whether she will become his wife. Abandoning all hope of seeing Troilus again (return of cor anglais solo), Cressida yields to Diomede's

demands, even ceding him the scarf he begs from her as a favour. Evadne overhears and secretly destroys the last of the many messages Troilus has sent Cressida, all of which at Calkas' behest she has concealed from her mistress.

Troilus and Pandarus have gained admittance to the Greek lines in an hour of truce, and they urge Evadne to fetch Cressida, whose ransom has at last been arranged. Cressida comes from her tent, richly dressed to meet Diomede, but her music speaks of heartbreak rather than rejoicing, and only the sound of Troilus' voice brings a quickening of the musical pulse. His pleading is full of tenderness, but, in spite of the many messages he protests he has sent, the news of her ransom obviously perplexes Cressida. Before she can convince Troilus that he has come too late, Greeks can be heard acclaiming her as Diomede's bride.

Diomede himself comes into view wearing the crimson favour on his helmet and in time to hear Troilus claim Cressida as his, body and spirit. Diomede orders Cressida to denounce him, and when she hesitates, he is overcome by the public humiliation and begins an embittered lament which develops into a full-scale and impressive sextet eventually swelled by the chorus. It is broken off by the infuriated Diomede, who stamps on Cressida's scarf. Troilus falls on him with his sword and is getting the better of their fight when Calkas stabs him mortally in the back. Diomede gives orders that the body of the gallant Trojan prince be carried away with due honours, that Calkas be sent in fetters back to Troy, and that Cressida shall stay in the camp of the Greeks for the enjoyment of whoever chooses her. Left alone for a moment, she utters a final lament to the gods, then, seeing Greek soldiers approach, snatches up Troilus' sword and, binding it with her scarf, kills herself.   H.

THE BEAR

Opera in one act, libretto by Paul Dehn. Première Aldeburgh Festival, 3 June 1967, with Monica Sinclair, John Shaw, Norman Lumsden, conductor James Lockhart (later the same year at Sadler's Wells, London, and in Montreal). Première B.B.C. TV, 1970, with Regina Resnik, Thomas Hemsley, Derek Hammond-Stroud, conductor Walton.

Yeliena Ivanovna Popova,
a young widow ....Mezzo-Soprano

Grigory Stepanovich Smirnov,
a middle-aged landowner .... Baritone

Luka, *Madame Popova's servant* ....Bass

Place: The Drawing Room of Madame Popova's
House in the Country in Russia
Time: 1888
Running Time: 55 minutes

This light-hearted one-acter was commissioned by the Serge Koussevitzky Music Foundation in 1965; its completion was interrupted when the composer had to undergo a serious operation, and the opera waited for first performance until the 1967 Aldeburgh Festival.

Written on a framework of Chekhov's short story of the same name, the plot concerns Madame Popova, the pretty young widow of a landowner, who clings, against the strongly proffered advice of her old manservant, Luka, to the idea of a virtuous, life-long widowhood, although, as she well knows, her late husband was no paragon of virtue. It seems that, while he was impervious to her reproaches during his lifetime, she intends, perhaps for this reason, to pursue him with them into the hereafter.

Luka announces that a man has arrived, saying he is determined to see her on what he describes as urgent business. The visitor forces his way in and introduces himself as Grigory Stepanovich Smirnov, landowner and retired lieutenant of artillery. The late Popov owed him 1,300 roubles for oats. His bank is demanding interest on a loan tomorrow, and, if his estate is not to be forfeit and he himself declared a bankrupt, he must be paid at once. Refusing to listen to Madame Popova's promise that her bailiff will pay, he insists that she alone can help. When his language becomes too strong, Madame Popova sweeps out slamming the door and leaving the frustrated Smirnov bemoaning the fact that all his debtors vanish when he pursues them while his creditors are all too readily available.

As Smirnov works himself up into a fine state of rage and indignation at his evil fortune and emphasises his total aversion to dealing with women, Luka enters to say that Madame Popova is indisposed and can see no one. Smirnov announces that he will get his own back even if he has to stay for a year and he orders the servant to unharness his horses and bring him a bottle of vodka. Catching sight of his unkempt reflection in the looking-glass, he is temporarily disconcerted at his own boorishness but soon flies again into a passion when reproached by Luka for his behaviour.

Madame Popova returns, eyes modestly cast down. Will Smirnov not wait until the end of the week? He is adamant; unless he is paid at once, he will hang himself! With Smirnov's insistence that he will remain there until he is paid deadlock seems to have been reached. Their quarrel is lively but capped by a sprightly aria from Madame Popova who, stung by Smirnov's assertion that men are more faithful than women, tells him the dreadful tale of her husband's infidelities and emphasises her own hyper-virtuous conduct and her intention of remaining pure for evermore.

Unconvinced, Smirnov makes the point that her clinging to widow's weeds has not made her forget to powder her face. This is too much for Madame Popova and she orders him out. At the argument's height, Smirnov proposes they settle the quarrel with a duel. Let there be real equality between the sexes! Madame Popova accepts the proposition with alacrity and goes off to fetch her late husband's pistols. Smirnov is full of admiration for her spirit and regrets the need to kill such a splendid creature. Madame Popova returns with the pistols (to the horror of Luka) and asks Smirnov to instruct her in their use as she has never handled them before. By the end of the lesson, Smirnov is head-over-heels in love and says he will fire into the air. She mistakes his infatuation for fear and orders him out. They gaze at each other and Smirnov declares his love for her. She threatens to shoot. He announces that to be shot by her would be a pleasure. She clings rather shakily to her dignity and rings for Luka to show Smirnov out but, by the time the old man arrives, the couple are in a tender embrace.

The charm of the piece is enhanced by its liberal spicing with parodies of other composers, including Stravinsky and Britten, and the connoisseur will enjoy picking them out like sixpences from a Christmas pudding.   H.

CARL MARIA VON WEBER

(born 18 November 1786, died 5 June 1826)

Weber's place in operatic history is secure as the high priest of German romanticism and an important precursor of Wagner. His death before he was forty limited his output to six operas, one of which was short, another unfinished. Only three remain as candidates for the repertory, for which the quality of their music undoubtedly fits them.

Der Freischütz was by far Weber's biggest success but its story now seems old-fashioned. Fifty years ago there would have been half a dozen new productions each season in Germany, now its appearance is a rarity. Yet the music is masterly, consistent, even popular, and, in the Wolf's Glen, it contains a scene which continues to stir the blood in anything like a decent production. *Oberon* is a different case altogether. It has always been claimed that sublime music is left to waste away in the desert of an impossible libretto. Yet the fairy-tale theme is by no means unattractive and, given a bold approach to story and casting, success should be assured.

The most consistent and ambitious of all Weber's operas remains *Euryanthe*, handicapped again according to tradition by an awkward libretto. The first hurdle to overcome is the theme, which belongs less to the romantic era than to the age of chivalry and courtly love, to evoke which must be the producer's first task; his next, to present the serpent, from which Euryanthe saves Adolar, in such a way as to avoid the obvious risk of risibility.

Weber is one of the great composers of opera, and it is little short of scandalous that most opera-goers outside Germany have not witnessed a stage performance of his work.   H.

DER FREISCHÜTZ

The Free-Shooter

Opera in three acts, text by Johann Friedrich Kind. First produced at the Schauspielhaus, Berlin, 18 June 1821, with Mmes Seidler, Eunicke, Messrs Stümer and Blume. First performed in London at the English Opera House, 1824, with Miss Noel, Miss Povey, Mr Braham, Mr Baker, Mr Bartley, and Mr Bennett; in German at Her Majesty's Theatre, 1832. First performance in New York (in English), 1825; (in German) 1845; at Metropolitan Opera, 1884. For the performance in Italian at Covent Garden in 1825, Costa wrote recitatives to replace the spoken dialogue, as did Berlioz for the production at the Opéra, Paris, 1841.

Prince Ottokar	Baritone
Cuno, *the head ranger*	Bass
Max, *a forester*	Tenor
Caspar, *a forester*	Bass
Kilian, *a rich peasant*	Tenor
A Hermit	Bass
Samiel, *the wild huntsman*	Speaking Part
Agathe, *Cuno's daughter*	Soprano
Aennchen, *her cousin*	Soprano

Place: Bohemia
Time: Middle of the Seventeenth Century
Running Time: 2 hours 40 minutes

The overture to *Der Freischütz* is the first in which an operatic composer has unreservedly made use of melodies from the opera itself. Beethoven, in the *Leonora* overtures, utilises the theme of Florestan's air and the trumpet call. Weber has used not merely thematic material but complete melodies. Following the beautiful passage for horns at the beginning of the overture is the music of Max's outcry when, in the opera, he senses the passage of Samiel across the stage, after which comes the sombre music of Max's 'Hat denn Himmel mich verlassen?' This leads up to the music of Agathe's outburst of joy when she sees her lover approaching.

Act I. At the shooting range. Kilian, a peasant, has defeated Max, the forester, at a prize shooting, a *Schützenfest*. Max, of course, as a forester accustomed to the use of firearms, should have won, and it is disgraceful for him to have been defeated by a peasant. Kilian rubs it in and the men and girls of the village join in the mocking of Max.

The hereditary forester, Cuno, is worried over the poor showing Max has made not only that day but for some time past. There is to be a shoot on the morrow before Prince Ottokar. In order to win the hand in marriage of Agathe, Cuno's daughter, and the eventual succession as hereditary forester, Max must carry off the honours in the competition now so near at hand. There is an expressive trio for Max, Caspar, and Cuno with chorus ('O diese Sonne!'), which is followed by a short waltz as the peasants bring the competition to a suitable end.

Max is in despair; life will be worthless to him without Agathe, yet he seems to have lost all his cunning as a shot, and without it he cannot win her hand. The first part of this *scena*, 'Durch die Wälder, durch die Auen', is a melody of great beauty, but the music takes on a more sinister character as Samiel, unseen of course by Max, hovers, a threatening shadow, in the background. It is now, when the others have gone, that his comrade Caspar, another forester of dark visage and of morose and forbidding character, approaches him. He hands him his gun, points to an eagle circling far above, and tells him to fire at it. Max shoots, and from its dizzy height the bird falls dead at his feet. It is a wonderful shot, but Caspar explains to him that he has shot with a magic bullet and that such bullets always hit what the marksman wills them to. If Max will meet him in the Wolf's Glen at midnight, they will mould bullets with one of which, on the morrow, he will be able to win Agathe's hand and the hereditary office of forester. Max, to whom victory means all that is dear to him, consents. Caspar's effective drinking song, which precedes his tempting of Max, is forced in its hilarity and ends in grotesque laughter, Caspar being the familiar of Samiel, the wild huntsman. The act ends with an aria for Caspar, whose wide range and rapid passages are in keeping with his sinister character.

Act II. Agathe's room in the head ranger's house. The music opens with a delightful duet for Agathe and Aennchen and a charmingly coquettish air for the latter ('Kommt ein schlanker Bursch gegangen'). But Agathe has gloomy forebodings, and even her sprightly relative is unable to cheer her up. Left alone, she opens the window and, as the moonlight floods the room, intones a prayer so simple, so exquisite, so expressive: 'Leise, leise, fromme Weise'.

This is followed after a recitative by a rapturous passage leading into an ecstatic melody as she sees her lover approaching. It is one of the best-known tunes in all opera, but gains immeasurably from being heard in its context as part of one of the greatest scenes for solo soprano:

Max comes in and is quickly followed by Aennchen. Very soon, however, he says he must leave, because he has shot a deer in the Wolf's Glen and must go after it. The scene ends with a trio in which the girls try vainly to warn him against the locality, which is said to be haunted.

The scene changes to the Wolf's Glen, the haunt of Samiel the wild huntsman (otherwise a devil), to whom Caspar has sold himself, and to whom he now plans to turn over Max as a victim, in order to gain for himself a brief respite on earth, his time to Samiel being up. The younger forester joins him in the Wolf's Glen and together they mould seven magic bullets, six of which go true to the mark, the seventh wherever Samiel wills it. The music has long been considered the most expressive rendering of the gruesome that is to be found in a musical score – its power is undiminished today whatever may be thought of the naïveté of the stage apparatus which goes with it. The ghost of Max's mother appears to him and strives to warn him away. Cadaverous, spooky-looking animals crawl out from caves in the rocks and spit flames and sparks. But the music is a fascinating essay in the grotesque – nothing comparable had been tried before – and the way in which it avoids the excessive but yet cunningly mixes the speaking voice and singing, the purely musical effect of Max's entrance with the atmospheric climax of the moulding of the bullets, is entirely admirable. The music remarkably anticipates Wagner, who got more than one hint from this scene – but its merits are particular and far beyond any prophetic qualities it may incidentally possess.

Act III. After a brief introduction, with suggestions of the hunting chorus later in the action, the act opens with Agathe's lovely cavatina 'Und ob die Wolke', a melody of such pure and expressive beauty that even Weber was never able to surpass it. Agathe is attired for the shooting test, which will make her Max's bride if he is successful. Aennchen sings a solo (composed after the rest of the opera), and then comes the enchanting chorus of bridesmaids who wind the bridal garland.

The concluding scene – the shooting test – begins with a spirited hunting chorus. Only the seventh bullet, the one which Samiel controls, remains to Max, the others having been used up during the hunt. Caspar, who expects Max to be Samiel's victim, climbs a tree to watch the proceedings from a safe place of concealment. Before the whole village and Prince Ottokar himself the test shot is to be fired. The Prince points to a flying dove and Max raises his gun. At that moment Agathe appears, accompanied by a Hermit, and calls out to Max not to shoot, that she is the dove. But Max has already pulled the trigger; Agathe falls – but only in a swoon – and it is Caspar who tumbles from the tree and rolls, fatally wounded, on the turf. Samiel has had no power over Max, for the young forester had not come to the Wolf's Glen of his own free will, but only after being tempted by Caspar; therefore Caspar had himself to be the victim of the seventh bullet. There is general uproar, Agathe is seen to be alive and Caspar dying, but Max's confession results in a sentence of banishment from the Prince. Only through the intercession (in a chorale-like aria) of the Hermit, a holy man revered by the whole district, is disaster for Max averted and the Prince's forgiveness obtained. The opera ends with the jubilant melody from Agathe's second-act scene.

No less notable as portent than as music, *Der Freischütz* holds an important position in the logical development of music and particularly of opera. If anyone can be said to qualify for such a title, Weber was the founder of the German romantic school – a school which reached its climax with Wagner, its culmination perhaps with Richard Strauss.

But Weber is much more than just Wagner's fore-runner – just as Bellini and Donizetti have importance of their own beyond being predecessors of Verdi. He is one of the great melodists of musical history, and perhaps no other composer of the romantic movement so completely preserved musical freshness at the same time as he introduced the literary element into music. K., H.

EURYANTHE

Opera in three acts, book by Helmine von Chezy, adapted from *L'Histoire de Gérard de Nevers et de la belle et vertueuse Euryanthe, sa mie*. This is Weber's only 'Grand Opera', i.e. without spoken dialogue. Produced Vienna, Kärnthnertor-theater, 25 October 1823, with Henriette Sontag; London, Covent Garden (in German), 1833; Drury Lane (in German), 1882, with Mmes Sucher, Peschka-Leutner, Messrs Nachbaur, Gura, conductor Hans Richter. Probable American première, Metropolitan, New York, 1887, with Lilli Lehmann, Marianne Brandt, Max Alvary, Emil Fischer, conductor Anton Seidl. *Euryanthe* was re-staged in Vienna under Mahler in 1904, with Förster-Lauterer and Weidt, Mildenburg, Winkelmann and Slezak, Weidemann and Mayr.

Euryanthe of Savoy ....Soprano
Eglantine of Puiset.............................Mezzo-Soprano
Count Lysiart of Forêt.................................Baritone
Count Adolar of Nevers ....Tenor
Louis VI..Bass
Rudolph, *a knight*......................................Tenor
Bertha...Soprano

Ladies, Knights, Peasants

Place: France
Time: Beginning of the Twelfth Century
Running Time: 2 hours 40 minutes

Much of Weber's theatrical life, in Prague as a young man and then for most of the rest of its short duration in Dresden, was spent consciously promoting the cause of German opera. These persistent endeavours combined with a preoccupation with the supernatural and a love of the Gothick to produce *Euryanthe*, itself a cornerstone of the edifice of German romantic opera. Wagner, who pronounced the funeral oration when Weber's body was returned from London to Germany eleven years after his death, was not only an admirer but a prime beneficiary of his pioneering efforts, the debt *Lohengrin* owes to *Euryanthe* being too obvious to need emphasis.

The weaknesses of *Euryanthe*'s libretto have been so notorious from the outset as to cause cuts within months of the première and a series of new versions and perversions throughout its history. Even so fervent an admirer of Weber's as Mahler – the most constant of revisers but also the most sensitive – tried his hand and at the revival in Vienna in 1904 omitted the ghostly element and the serpent. Particular objections have been to the impossible naïveté of Euryanthe's non-reaction to the public accusations of Lysiart, to the obdurate refusal of Adolar in the desert to consult reason, and to the slightly absurd manifestation of the serpent in the same scene. Defence has urged a comparable innocence in Desdemona and comparable obduracy in Othello, and the last quarter of the twentieth century at least has been more inclined than past generations to accept the supernatural as, in certain circumstances, a plausible explanation of events. Perhaps the truth is that *Euryanthe* needs, indeed can stand, no special pleading, and requires only a straightforward performance – which is not easy to achieve, not least since the opera's conventions are those of the medieval Courts of Love, the attitudes those of the Troubadours; their restrained though ardent actions sometimes fit a little strangely to our eyes and ears with the romantic music they inspire in *Euryanthe*.

The overture, like that of *Freischütz*, is full of thematic references to the material of the opera, notably at the start Adolar's defiance of Lysiart and affirmation of his faith in Euryanthe; Adolar's romance from the second scene of the second act introduced on violins; and the ghostly apparitions (eight muted violins over tremolo violas). Because of the complicated nature of the story, Weber once went so far as to suggest that a *tableau vivant*, depicting Euryanthe at prayer by the tomb of Emma, Adolar's deceased sister, should be acted during the overture.

Act I, scene i. The Royal Court at Prémery. King Louis VI has successfully waged war against his rebellious barons and his kingdom is now at peace. The graceful conventions of the court are straight away apparent from the gently swaying chorus of Ladies, soon echoed by the returning Knights and succeeded by a stately dance. The King perceives Adolar's melancholy, says he will invite Euryanthe to court and, in response to the King's request, Adolar sings a graceful *Minnelied*, 'Unter blüh'nden Mandelbäumen'. Adolar and Lysiart are rivals and the latter provokes a quarrel by casting doubt on the virtue of Euryanthe, which Adolar vehemently defends: 'Ich bau' auf Gott und meine Euryanth', to the music of the opening of the overture. The rival noblemen pledge their lands on a trial of her fidelity and Lysiart swears to prove that she is untrue.

Scene ii. At their castle in Nevers, Euryanthe longs for Adolar's return from the wars and her sweetness of character is fully apparent from her cavatina, 'Glöcklein im Thale'. Eglantine, her family outlawed as a result of the rebellion and herself once in love with Adolar but now ostensibly Euryanthe's friend and guest, reproaches her that her trust is less

than absolute. Her own, she says, is a passionate nature ('O mein Leid ist unermessen'), and, stung by the reproach, Euryanthe reveals the secret which she and Adolar share but which she has sworn not to give away (ghost music). His sister Emma once appeared to them in spirit and revealed how she had taken poison from her ring, mad with grief at the death in battle of her betrothed Udo. Her guilty soul cannot be at peace until the tears of an innocent girl have been shed on the ring. Euryanthe is aghast at what she has done but she and Eglantine pledge faith in a duet, falsely on Eglantine's side as is immediately apparent from her aria of jealous hatred: 'Bethörte! die an meine Liebe glaubt', a grand piece of bravura in which she shows herself the true ancestress of Ortrud, and plans to ransack Emma's tomb in search of a proof of Euryanthe's betrayal of trust which she may proffer to Adolar.

Trumpets proclaim the arrival of Lysiart who announces that he has come to escort Euryanthe back to court. The peasants' chorus of welcome is answered by the Knights, and Euryanthe greets Lysiart and his party in music of such carefree elegance that the tension audible earlier in both music and text eases under the gentle influence of her personality.

Act II, scene i. Nevers. Lysiart has come to understand that his task is hopeless and has even started to fall in love with the guileless Euryanthe himself. The music ('Wo berg ich mich?') is a grand expression of frustrated longing for Euryanthe, jealousy of Adolar and thirst for vengeance, and the spirit of Caspar hangs over it as it harks back to Beethoven's Pizarro and forward to Wagner's Telramund. Lysiart hides to hear Eglantine admit to having stolen Emma's ring from her tomb and to her plan to use it as a weapon with which to destroy the innocent Euryanthe. But how? In return for the ring she has stolen, he himself will be her instrument, promises Lysiart, and they will be married with Adolar's lands hers for ever! The unholy alliance is sealed in a duet vibrant with exultancy and purpose.

Scene ii. Prémery. Adolar, alone, voices his love for Euryanthe in music of such inspiration, poise and ardour as to convince the most sceptical of listeners of its purity and enduring nature ('Wehen mir Lüfte Ruh'). Here is Weber at his most lyrically evocative, here the pure spirit of courtly love which this opera is almost unique in celebrating. The tune provides the lyrical core of the overture, and the mood it sets is continued in a rapturous short duet for Euryanthe and Adolar as they are reunited, but disrupted when, the King and court having made their entrance, Lysiart announces that he has won his wager. Adolar is again defiant (music from the finale of I.i) and Euryanthe cannot understand what Lysiart is trying to establish until he produces Emma's ring, saying he knows its secret. Euryanthe knows she is guilty of a betrayal of trust, Adolar is convinced that she has been unfaithful, and all are prepared to believe Lysiart's assertion of his triumph. Dressed now in black armour, Adolar leads Euryanthe from the court with general opinion apparently united against her.

Act III, scene i. The music is in stark contrast to what has gone before as we move from court and castle to a deserted place at night. The Wolf's Glen seems not far away and Euryanthe, urging that she has unquestioningly followed Adolar through the wilderness, pleads for some sign of tenderness, even forgiveness. Adolar continues to reproach her but Euryanthe can only protest her innocent love, contrasting states of mind which carry through a short duet. It is plain that Adolar means to kill her but Euryanthe warns him of the approach of a serpent and even throws herself between it and Adolar, who fights and kills it. As recompense for her attempted self-sacrifice, Adolar determines not to kill her but rather to abandon her to heaven's will. Bassoon and flute introduce Euryanthe forsaken and her prayer is that Adolar may visit her grave and hear the trees and flowers hymning her innocence. The sound of a royal party approaching can be heard (hunting chorus, accompanied by horns and trombones), and the King is quickly – too quickly – convinced of Eglantine's treachery and Euryanthe's guiltlessness, assuring her that she will soon see Adolar again, so that the scene finishes with an ecstatic cabaletta for Euryanthe and chorus, at the end of which she collapses.

Scene ii. Nevers. Lysiart is now lord of Adolar's castle and domain, and his wedding to Eglantine in preparation, first in a dance (added by Weber for the Berlin première) and then in a charming chorus sung by Bertha and the villagers. When Adolar appears, he is at first not recognised but it is not long before the villagers pledge their renewed loyalty. As the sound of the wedding procession draws near, it is plain that Eglantine is in the grip of hallucinations and haunted by visions of Emma (ghost music). When he recognises him, Lysiart defies Adolar, but the knights hail him with joy and only the King's appearance prevents a duel. The King says that Euryanthe is dead and at the news, Eglantine becomes possessed with fury and confesses not only that she herself once loved Adolar but also that she has been the author of the plot which has precipitated the tragedy. Lysiart kills her, but when the King orders his arrest, Adolar urges his own guilt as being the more heinous, until Euryanthe, borne in on a litter by the hunters, revives and is restored to her husband. As her tears fall on Emma's ring, which she sees on Adolar's finger, the ghostly music, now reassuringly diatonic, makes it clear that that troubled spirit can rest for ever.

Euryanthe is one of those operas which gets more honourable mentions in operatic commentaries than it receives serious stage productions. Yet the generous Schumann[1] was able to write in 1847, 'this music is as yet far too little known and recognised. It is heart's blood, the noblest he had; the opera cost him part of his life – truly. But it has also made him immortal'; and Liszt, 'We find in Weber a marvellous divination of the future shaping of the drama; and the endeavour to unite with opera the whole wealth of instrumental development'. John Warrack in his admirable book[2] on the composer pinpoints the reasons for the musicologist's interest: 'in no other work does Weber take chromatic harmony to such extreme limits; indeed it was not until Liszt and Wagner that certain passages of *Euryanthe* were overtaken – principally, the ghost music of the overture, some of Eglantine's scenes and the extraordinary opening to Act III as the unhappy Adolar and Euryanthe pick their way through the desert, while bleakly shifting harmonies reflect, with true romantic imagery, their misery against the desolation of the scene. The loosening of the closed forms also allowed him a much greater range of harmonic relationships.' H.

[1] Robert Schumann: *Theaterbüchlein.*

[2] John Warrack: *Carl Maria von Weber* (Hamish Hamilton 1968).

OBERON

Opera in three acts, text, in English, by James Robinson
Planché. The original story appeared in *La Bibliothèque Bleue*
under the title of *Huon de Bordeaux*. Wieland adapted this story
to form his poem *Oberon*, and Planché took his libretto from
Sotheby's translation of Wieland. First performed at Covent
Garden, 12 April 1826, with Miss Paton as Reiza (Rezia only
in German versions), Mme Vestris as Fatima, Braham as Huon
and Bland as Oberon, the composer conducting. First performance in New York, 1828. Revived, Metropolitan Opera,
1918, with Ponselle, Martinelli, conducted by Bodanzky (with
recitatives composed by Bodanzky, instead of spoken dialogue); Salzburg, in German under Walter, with, in 1932,
Maria Müller, Lotte Schoene, Helge Roswaenge; Holland
Festival, 1950, with Gré Brouwenstijn, Frans Vroons, conducted by Monteux (in German); Florence Festival, 1952, in
the Boboli Gardens in a production by Herbert Graf, with Doris
Doree, Gianna Pederzini, Tyge Tygesen, Gino Penno, conducted by Fritz Stiedry (in Italian); Opéra, Paris, 1953, with
Araujo, Gedda, conducted by Cluytens.

Sir Huon of Bordeaux ....Tenor

Sherasmin, *his squire*......................................Baritone

Oberon, *King of the Fairies* ....Tenor

Puck ....Soprano

Reiza,[1] *daughter of Haroun el Rashid*...............Soprano

Fatima, *her attendant* ....Mezzo-Soprano

A Sea Nymph...Soprano

Speaking parts
    Charlemagne, *Emperor of the Franks*
    Haroun el Rashid, *Caliph*
    Babekan, *a Saracen Prince*
    Almanzor, *Emir of Tunis*
    Abdullah, *a Corsair*
    Titania, *Oberon's wife*
    Roshana, *wife of Almanzor*
    Namouna, *Fatima's grandmother*
    Nadina, *a female of Almanzor's harem*

*O*beron has always resisted the efforts which have
from time to time been made to fit it neatly into
the category of German romantic opera. Its pattern is
undeniably unconventional, and the signs are that
Weber himself was disturbed by several aspects of
the dramatic plan. Various attempts have been made
to adapt the opera for performance. Bodanzky composed recitatives in place of the spoken dialogue for
the production at the Metropolitan in 1918, but otherwise left the score intact. More important is the
version prepared by Mahler in conjunction with the
scenic designer Alfred Roller, with a new German

translation by Gustav Brecher. Mahler arranged a
number of musical sections, usually (but not always)
in conjunction with spoken dialogue as opposed to
singing, which he designated 'Melodram'; these are
not given separate numbers in his edition but are
clearly indicated as 13a and 13b in the score. There
are eight of these additions, and they have the effect
of connecting certain sections of the music very
closely with the dramatic action, most particularly of
course the horn call, which is heard at the beginning
of the overture, and which in Mahler's arrangement
assumes a musical status comparable to that of
Papageno's pipes. A section of music is introduced to
lead up to the vision of Reiza in Act I, and another to
reinforce the giving of the magic horn by Oberon to
Sherasmin before the ensemble during which takes
place the transformation from France to Baghdad. In
Act II, the bewitching of Haroun's court is made
more plausible by means of musical accompaniment,
and the flight of the two pairs of lovers has orchestral
accompaniment from the moment the horn invokes
Oberon's aid, Oberon and Reiza later between them
singing the short aria of Oberon which occurs in the
finale of the third act (in Mahler's version it is thus
heard twice). After Reiza has been carried away by
the pirates (which occurs immediately after she has
sung 'Ocean, thou mighty monster'), Oberon
laments the hard nature of their trials in a shortened
version of his first aria, and Puck anticipates the fairy
music of the finale by singing a reminiscence (shortened, and in C instead of F) of the fairy chorus at the
opening of Act I. In Act III, Huon's return just before
the trio with Fatima and Sherasmin is heralded by a
melodrama for Puck, and Mahler omits entirely the
rondo for Huon which should follow Reiza's F minor
aria. The preparations for the public burning of
Huon are made to the sound of the march which,
later in the finale, reintroduces Huon to the court of
Charlemagne.

The overture, which is one of the best known and
most popular of concert pieces, is made up entirely of
music employed elsewhere in the opera. The horn
call (Ex. 1) with which it opens plays a prominent
part throughout and is used in rather the same way
as the magic instruments in *The Magic Flute*. It is fol-

---

[1] Reiza is the original form, as found in the libretto and in the first English edition of the score. It appears as Rezia in the earliest German score,
where Huon is spelled Hüon.

lowed by a figure of soft, quickly descending wood-wind chords (Ex. 2), which at once suggests the

atmosphere of fairyland; its light, airy quality sets the scene for the opening fairy chorus. Two themes follow, still played softly and mysteriously; they are heard again at the end of the opera, as a triumphant march. Atmosphere and tempo change and we hear a stormy figure in the strings; this returns as an accompanying figure to the quartet in Act II, when the four lovers escape to the ship. The fairy chords have the effect of calming down the violent *allegro* section, and a theme of great beauty (Ex. 3),

which Huon later sings in the big *scena*, is heard on the clarinet and is then taken over by the strings. This leads straight into an exultant tune (Ex. 4),

which is typically and unmistakably Weber – most people will recognise it as from the closing section of Reiza's great aria 'Ocean, thou mighty monster'. As is so often his way with his triumphant themes, Weber first introduces it quietly and unpretentiously, and it is not till after a recapitulation of the existing material and the introduction of a new, strong theme (later associated with Puck), that he allows us to feel the full force of this exhilarating tune. It brings the overture to an exciting close.

Act I. The curtain rises to reveal Oberon's bower, where a group of fairies sing over their sleeping King a chorus which breathes the very atmosphere of enchantment. Ex. 2 punctuates the various sentences, and the composer's marking is *Andante quasi allegretto* (sempre tutto pianissimo possibile). Puck appears and explains that Oberon, having quarrelled with his fairy partner Titania, has vowed never to be reconciled to her until he shall have found two lovers constant through every peril and temptation. To seek such a pair, Puck, his 'tricksy spirit', has ranged through the world in vain. Oberon wakes and, in an aria which fulfils the implications of its *agitato* introduction, laments the 'fatal oath' he has sworn. He learns that Puck has heard sentence passed on Sir Huon of Bordeaux, a young knight, who, having been insulted by the son of Charlemagne, has killed him in single combat and for this has been condemned by the Emperor to proceed to Baghdad, slay him who sits on the Caliph's right hand, and claim the Caliph's daughter as his bride.

Oberon instantly resolves to make this pair the instrument of his reunion with his Queen, and for this purpose he conjures up Huon and Sherasmin asleep before him, and enamours the knight by showing him Reiza, daughter of the Caliph, in a vision. Introduced by the horn call of the overture (Ex. 1), she begs for help.

Oberon wakes Huon to the sound of fairy music, Huon promises to be faithful to his mission, and Oberon with a wave of his wand transports him and his squire to Baghdad. The contrast between the utterances of the mortal Huon and the immortal Oberon is most marked, and the transformation (an enharmonic change from F minor to D major) makes as lovely an effect musically as it should when staged. Huon rejoices at the prospect before him in music of florid cast accompanied by the chorus, and prepares, with the help of the magic horn Oberon has given him, to fulfil his mission.

Two non-musical episodes follow. In the first, Huon and Sherasmin rescue Prince Babekan from a lion. He turns out to be the betrothed of Reiza, but his evil disposition is soon apparent when he and his followers set on their rescuers; they are, however, put to flight. The knight next learns from an old woman, Namouna, that Reiza is to be married next day, but the Princess has been influenced, like her lover, by a vision and is resolved to be his alone. She believes that fate will protect her from her nuptials with Babekan.

Huon exults in his chivalrous role in a great *scena*,

whose music exactly fits his youthful heroic character. The magnificent flourish of the opening section is succeeded by a lovely *andante* for the cello (Ex. 3) which later expresses Huon's sentiments as opposed to his heroic resolves. The *scena* returns to the *Allegro energico* of the beginning and the close is strenuous and forthright.

The scene changes to the palace of Haroun el Rashid, where Reiza tells Fatima that nothing will induce her to marry anyone other than her destined knight; better death than union with the hated Babekan. The finale begins with a big solo for Reiza, in which she swears to be true to the knight she has as yet seen only in a vision. Fatima tells Reiza that her deliverer is at hand, and mistress and maid contemplate their coming bliss in a simple duettino. The sound of a march is heard and Reiza sings jubilantly above a soft chorus of palace guards and eunuchs.

Act II. We are at the court of Haroun el Rashid. A chorus of attendants and slaves sings the praises of the mighty Caliph, who sits serenely in their midst with Prince Babekan at his right. The Prince asks that there shall be no more delay before he is married to his promised Reiza, and Haroun orders that she be led into his presence. Preceded by dancing girls (to a short orchestral *allegretto grazioso*) she comes in. No sooner is the music ended than the clash of swords is heard outside and in a moment Reiza is in the arms of her rescuer. Huon fights Babekan and vanquishes him, and having spellbound the rest by a blast of the magic horn, he and Sherasmin carry off Reiza and Fatima.

A scene without music serves to establish the flight of the four fugitives (they are set on by palace guards, but frighten them off with the help of the horn); it also gives them an opportunity to lose the horn in the course of the fight. Later, we find Fatima and Sherasmin together, and, in the course of a love scene, Fatima finds occasion to sing a song of nostalgic import, 'A lonely Arab maid', marked by the composer *Andante amoroso*. The four lovers take ship to the sound of a quartet, the two women answering the two men, all four later joining in a rapturous ensemble to the accompaniment of the string figure of the overture.

The scene changes to a rocky seashore. Puck calls together his spirits and instructs them to bring about the wreck of the ship in which Reiza and Huon are crossing the sea; the music ends with the rousing of the storm. No sooner are they gone about their work

than Huon appears supporting the fainting figure of Reiza. His short *adagio* prayer for her recovery is one of the most beautiful passages in the score and reveals a tender, poetic side to Huon's character. His prayer is answered, Reiza revives, and Huon goes off to see if there are other survivors of the wreck.

Reiza is alone. She apostrophises the sea, whose very repose carries menace but whose fury is terrible indeed. 'Ocean, thou mighty monster' is a justly famous aria for dramatic soprano, and, with the overture, it is the one number of *Oberon* which will be familiar to everybody. It is an extended *scena*, modelled on the lines of Agathe's great solo in *Freischütz* but more dramatic in content. It opens with a grand recitativic introduction, continues with a swelling *allegro con moto* section describing the storm still in progress, sinks to the comparative calm of the *maestoso assai*, but rises again steeply as Reiza catches sight of something moving, reaching a climax of excitement as she realises it is a ship; the concluding *Presto con fuoco* is one of the most thrilling passages in opera and is familiar as the final section of the overture (Ex. 4).

But the ship Reiza has seen turns out to be manned by pirates, who pause only to make her prisoner, and leave Huon, who attempts to rescue her, senseless on the shore.

For the finale, we are back in an atmosphere which is Weber at his most idyllic. The sensuously graceful song of the Sea Nymphs in 6/8 has a magic of its own, but the whole scene, with its short duet for Oberon and Puck and its extended and mostly *pianissimo* chorus of fairies, is wonderfully beautiful. This is pure fairy music, which even such a specialist as Mendelssohn never excelled (the *Midsummer Night's Dream* overture, like *Oberon*, was written in 1826), and its delicacy and soft charm can never fail to astonish an unsuspecting listener and ravish his musical susceptibilities.

Act III. Fatima, saved with Sherasmin from the wreck but now like him a slave in Tunis, laments her changed fortune in a song with a pronounced Oriental flavour, 'O Araby, dear Araby, my own native land'. But she cannot prevent her natural cheerfulness breaking into the refrain with its repeated 'Al, al, al, al, al, al'. Sherasmin, who works in the same establishment for one Ibrahim, joins her and together they reflect sadly on the distance each of them has come since childhood; again, they finish by looking on the bright side – at least they are together in their slavery, and have a kind master. But a surprise is round the corner and Puck brings in Huon. There is a great recognition, and Fatima says she has even heard that Reiza is in Tunis, but where she does not know. They plan to dress Huon up and get him employment with Ibrahim.

The scene changes to the palace of the Emir of Tunis, where Reiza lies a captive, and has become, like Mozart's Constanze before her, the principal object of a noble master's affections. She grieves for her lost love in an F minor aria of pure and mournful beauty, the counterpart of Huon's prayer in the previous act, 'Mourn thou poor heart'. Like the Pasha Selim, Almanzor respects the grief of his prisoner and tells her he will not force her to yield to his love.

Huon receives a message, conveyed in the symbolic language of the East by means of flowers. Fatima interprets it for him and tells him it is from Reiza; he is to go at once to her. Huon's rondo, 'I revel in hope and joy again', is likely to test the agility of the tenor but is of comparatively conventional musical value. He is led to the Emir's palace where, in fact, Reiza is incarcerated, but is confronted instead with the Emir's wife, Roshana, thirsting for revenge on the husband who has discarded her in favour of the beautiful captive. She assures Huon that he will have earned her love and the throne of Tunis if he will help her dispose of her erring husband. Neither the prospect of power nor of her love can turn the hero from his purpose, which is to free Reiza, and he has little difficulty in resisting the efforts which Roshana employs to seduce him; his musical answers to the blandishments of Roshana's attendants are nothing if not firm.

As Huon is rushing from her presence he is surprised and seized by Almanzor and his guard; Roshana tries to stab her husband and is arrested in her turn and led off by attendants. Almanzor commands that a pyre be erected and Huon burnt within the hour, and the efforts of Reiza to obtain his pardon only succeed in gaining for her a similar sentence. At this juncture, Sherasmin, who has contrived entrance to the palace, has the magic horn miraculously restored to him, and with its help he is able to change the situation completely.

The sound of music has an exactly similar effect on Almanzor's court as it had on Monostatos' slaves; they no longer have a desire to do anything but dance, and the four lovers, now reunited, resolve to summon the aid of Oberon in an effort not only to suspend but to dissolve completely the nightmare situation in which they find themselves. The Fairy King appears in answer to the horn's blast, and in a short but beautiful aria hails the faithful, loving pair and tells them that their prayers are answered and he will restore them to safety and happiness. They are transported to the court of Charlemagne, who takes his place with his entourage to the sound of a march. Huon tells him his commands have been fulfilled, and he is here with Reiza to claim the promised pardon. This is granted and the opera ends with a chorus of praise and thanksgiving.　　　　H.

KURT WEILL

(born 2 March 1900, died 3 April 1950)

AUFSTIEG UND FALL DER STADT MAHAGONNY

Rise and Fall of the City of Mahagonny

Opera in three acts, libretto by Bertolt Brecht. Première, Leipzig, 9 March 1930, with Mali Trummer, Marga Dannenberg, Paul Beinert, conductor Gustav Brecher, producer Walter Brügmann, designer Caspar Neher. First produced Berlin, 1931, with Lotte Lenya, Trude Hesterberg, Harold Paulsen, conductor Alexander von Zemlinsky, producer Ernst Anfricht, after which it was banned in Germany under the Nazis. A Paris production of the *Songspiel* was agreed to by Weill in 1932, and this version was heard in Venice, 1949, with Hilde Gueden; Cologne, 1952; and on the Turin Radio, 1953. First post-war stage performances (in a garbled version) Darmstadt, 1957, and Kiel, 1961. Operatic (Leipzig) version, Heidelberg, 1962; Hamburg, 1962, with Helga Pilarczyk, Gisela Litz, Helmut Melchert, conductor Janos Kulka; London, Sadler's Wells, 1963, with April Cantelo, Patricia Bartlett, Ronald Dowd, conductor Colin Davis; English National Opera, 1995, with Lesley Garrett, Sally Burgess.

Leokadja Begbick ....Contralto
Fatty, *the book-keeper* ....Tenor
Trinity Moses ....Baritone
Jenny ....Soprano
Jim Mahoney ....Tenor
Jake Schmidt ....Tenor
Alaska Wolf Joe...Bass
Pennybank Bill...Baritone
Toby Higgins[1] ....Tenor

Six Women of Mahagonny; the Men of Mahagonny

Running Time: 2 hours 10 minutes

Brecht's first collaboration with Kurt Weill, a pupil of Busoni's,[2] was in 1927, when at Baden-Baden a *Songspiel* [*sic*], *Kleine Mahagonny*, was given on 17 July in the same programme as short operas by Milhaud, Toch and Hindemith. This work consisted of five songs of Brecht's set to music by Weill (it is interesting to note that Brecht himself had earlier set them to music) and it was not until after their collaboration on *Die Dreigroschenoper* (a play with music, 1928), *Der Lindberghflug* (a cantata, 1928) and *Happy End* (a play with music, 1929), that they were able to finish the full-length opera which they had straight away started to develop from the material of the *Songspiel*. Later collaboration was on *Der Jasager* (a children's opera, 1930), *Mann ist Mann* (a play with songs, 1931) and *Die sieben Todsünden* (*The Seven Deadly Sins*: a ballet-opera, 1933).

Whatever else it may be, *The Rise and Fall of the City of Mahagonny* is an opera, written for opera singers (it was not until the Berlin production that Lotte Lenya took over the role of Jenny), and designed in what can only be described as the operatic convention, that is to say with the characters singing not just songs but frequently when in real life they would speak. Brecht on the one hand had the strongest antipathy to what he described as 'culinary' opera – opera with 'a hedonistic approach' – and on the other believed that the theatrical art of the future would make frequent use of music, not least as a means of halting the action and driving home a message; music to his way of thinking even in an opera would be at the service of the dramatist. Most

theoreticians believe that in opera, on the contrary, whatever the *content* of the piece, the *form* is dictated by the music. Here comes a fundamental clash. After his stage collaboration with Weill came to an end, Brecht went on to write a series of committed plays (his study of Marx began only in 1927) and to found in East Berlin after the war one of the great theatrical companies of our time.

In the years after his early death, Weill came to be identified in the minds of many listeners in the first place with the Berlin of the Weimar Republic and its overtones, and in the second with the singing of his wife, Lotte Lenya. Lenya was an extraordinary interpretative singer, endowed with a voice essentially more suited to cabaret than to opera, a fragile instrument moreover for which Weill and even later musicians had over the years progressively to transcribe what she sang in order that she could sing it. She was a great artist but the results of transposition, and of her success in the recording studio late in her career, often produced results rather different from what Weill wrote, or originally intended.

The première in Leipzig[3] provoked demonstrations by the Nazis, who were later to banish composer and author and ban their works, and every subsequent revival has been attended by controversy, the Hamburg production scheduled for autumn 1961 being postponed until the following year because it was felt unwise to risk such a work in the weeks following the building of the Berlin wall. It remained for Lotte Lenya, the composer's widow, in her notes on the complete recording in which she sang Jenny, to remind readers that the opera, which is now solemnly worked over by the critics, had once – for her and Brecht and Weill – been such fun to create.

Act I. As the music[4] dashes energetically into action, a much battered truck comes to a stop in a desolate part of America, and from it emerge Leokadja Begbick, Trinity Moses and Fatty the book-keeper, all on the run from the police. If they can't go any further, why not stay here and found a new city, where no one has to work and where there are prize fights every third day – so explains Leokadja in an extended *arioso* ('Sie soll sein wie ein Netz').

---

[1] This part is sometimes taken by the singer of Jake.
[2] Busoni at one time accused Weill (before the collaboration with Brecht, by which time Busoni was dead) of attempting to become a 'poor man's Verdi'.
[3] Klemperer refused to do it at the Kroll Oper in Berlin, and years later (in

Conversations with Klemperer, edited by Peter Heyworth) referred to it as a 'complete failure'.
[4] For a small orchestra with emphasis on saxophone, banjo, bass guitar, piano, zither, accordion.

And so the city was founded and called Mahagonny, and the first sharks moved in. Enter Jenny, the mulatto from Cuba, and six other girls, who sit on their suitcases and introduce themselves in the famous 'Alabama-song', written originally in Brecht's peculiar pidgin-English[1] and set to one of Weill's most haunting tunes, Ex. 1:

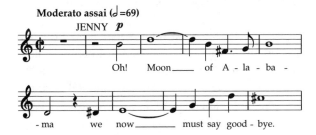

The news of the founding of a city of pleasure reaches the big cities, where the inhabitants hymn their misery while Fatty and Moses cry the praises of Mahagonny. In the next few days, all the malcontents of the continent move to Mahagonny, notably the lumberjacks Jim, Jake, Bill and Joe, who sing a quick fox-trot in anticipation of the pleasures to come (including a parodistic phrase from the Bridesmaids' Chorus in *Freischütz*).

The hero of the story is Jim Mahoney, and he and the others are greeted by Mrs Begbick, Trinity Moses losing no time in proffering pictures of the available girls from whom they may care to choose. Jenny and the six girls are produced, and Jake offers $30 for Jenny, who protests in a song: 'Ach, bedenken Sie, Herr Jakob Schmidt' – just think how little you get for $30. Jim says perhaps he'll take her, and when the others have gone, he and Jenny exchange to a wistful tune such vital information as whether Jenny shall comb her hair forward or back, shall or shan't wear underwear under her skirt.

Disillusion has set in and, says Mrs Begbick, people are starting to leave town. Fatty counters with the news that the police are catching up with Begbick. Jim comes in, planning to leave because he has just seen a notice 'Forbidden'! Jake, Bill and Joe sing the praises of the city with its everlasting freedom, but Jim's blues come straight from the purposelessness of it all.

In front of the inn, which is known as 'Nothing

barred', the men are sitting drinking and listening to the strains of 'The Maiden's Prayer' – eternal art, thinks Jake. Jim's mock ballad of the sufferings he underwent in Alaska in order eventually to reach a haven of rest complains of the inadequacy of what he has found, and it takes a concerted effort to prevent him carving up everything in sight with his famous knife.

The loudspeaker announces a 'typhoon', and a *fugato* introduces an impressive set piece of lamentation. The next scene is called 'The Night of the Hurricane'. The men sing determinedly in chorus (echoes of the chorale from *Die Zauberflöte*), Jake laments and Jenny sadly repeats the Alabama-song. Jim mockingly expounds his philosophy: what sort of horror is a hurricane when compared to man? The long *scena*, in whose course we learn that the hurricane is heading straight for Mahagonny and that the police who were pursuing Mrs Begbick have been killed, reaches its climax with Jim leading what is perhaps the best (as well as the best-known) of the songs: 'Denn wie man sich bettet, so liegt man' (As you make your bed, you must lie there), Ex. 2.

As the curtain falls, there can be seen a map with an arrow moving slowly across it towards Mahagonny.

Act II. Again the map, with the arrow still moving towards Mahagonny and successive radio announcements indicating the imminence of danger, until 'the hurricane has been diverted past Mahagonny and continues on its way'! The citizens rejoice; if they have learnt anything, it is to enjoy what luck has unexpectedly sent them. From now on the motto is 'nothing barred'. First, gluttony. To a slow parodistic waltz (zither and accordion), Jake sits down to dine and eats three entire calves, expiring as he asks for more.

Next, love. In the room at the back can be seen a girl and a man with Mrs Begbick between them. She

---

[1] Brecht thought at one time that a form of pidgin-English would be the world's first universal language!

admonishes the man to spit out his gum, wash his hands and behave decently. The lights go out, the chorus sings the Mandalay-song and urges him to get on with it, but when the lights go up, Jenny and Jim are seen sitting a little way apart, he smoking, she making up. They sing tenderly about two cranes flying in the sky, a duet in which Brecht's lyrical invention is matched by Weill's to form one of the most purely 'operatic' numbers in the whole score. It was placed here in the published score apparently at the behest of Weill's publishers, though intended by author and composer for the third act.

Next, prize fights. Trinity Moses and Alaska Wolf Joe are matched to the astonishment of Fatty and the other men, who predict a walk-over for Trinity Moses. Jim and Joe rather sentimentally remember the seven winters they spent together in Alaska, and Jim puts his money on Joe, who duly fulfils expectations and is knocked out. 'Dead!' says the referee. The crowd laughs, and the men come forward with a reminder that here nothing's barred, that we may now expect the boozing as well.

Jim, Bill and Jenny are playing billiards, and Jim invites everyone to drink with him. Jim finds he has run out of money and asks Jenny to help him. They make a boat out of the billiard table, and Jim, Bill and Jenny climb on it, until Jim announces that they have arrived back in Alaska. Trinity Moses and the widow Begbick demand payment, but Jim has nothing left and everyone except Bill and Jenny move away from him, and even they refuse to come to his financial rescue. As Jim, who has committed the ultimate capitalist crime of running out of money, is bound and led away, Jenny repeats, 'Denn wie man sich bettet, so liegt man'. The act ends with Jim alone in the forest, tied by one foot to a tree and longing in an impressive *scena* (which rises to a 'culinary' top C) for the night to continue and for the day never to arrive.

Act III. Jim is to be tried in what passes for a Court of Justice in Mahagonny – the widow Begbick sits as judge, Fatty is defence counsel and Trinity Moses prosecutes. One Toby Higgins is being tried for murder, and as Trinity Moses waxes eloquent on the depravity of the crime, the accused can be seen bargaining in mime with the judge. Apparently he offers a big enough bribe because defending counsel is allowed to ask for the injured party to be produced, and nobody coming forward the case goes by default.

It is Jim's turn and he asks his friend Bill to let him have $100 so that his case can be conducted decently. Again they remember their seven winters together in Alaska, but sentiment cannot interfere with financial considerations as far as Bill is concerned and he refuses the loan. As the prosecution starts its case, Begbick again bargains, but Jim is unable to respond and the prosecution gets down to details. Jim is accused of the seduction of Jenny, of singing cheerfully during the approach of the 'typhoon', of corrupting the entire city, of sending his friend to certain death in a prize fight merely to win his bet, of not being able to pay for the whisky which he drank and the curtain rod he broke. Each time the question is, 'Who is the injured party?'

The men demand Jim's acquittal on the grounds that his behaviour during the typhoon injured nobody, that it certainly wasn't he who killed Alaska Wolf Joe, but as he is undoubtedly guilty of the last charge, he is sentenced on all five, and the penalty becomes increasingly stiff, ending with death for the failure to pay for the whisky.

People are sitting around in a bar reading a newspaper and displaying the disillusion which has once again overtaken Mahagonny. Jointly they long for a change. The loudspeaker announces the impending execution of Jim Mahoney and suggests that, though many will dislike seeing the spectacle, most of the spectators in the audience would be no more willing than have been the inhabitants of Mahagonny to stump up money for him. A tender farewell between Jenny and Jim, who consigns her to his best friend Bill, precedes his walk to the place of execution. Jim in rather lugubrious music proclaims that he has no regrets, that his philosophy is unchanged and that life is meant to be drained in gigantic draughts. Jim is seated on the electric chair but asks whether they do not know that there is a God. During his execution the others act out the coming of God to Mahagonny, Trinity Moses taking the chief role.

The loudspeaker announces that giant processions took place in protest against the tremendously high cost of living, and that these heralded the end of the 'City of Nets'. During the march-finale which is dominated by 'Denn wie man sich bettet, so liegt man' and the Alabama-song, the processions appear, each of them carrying an appropriate banner, and the opera ends with 'Können uns und euch und niemand helfen!' (We can't help ourselves or you or anyone).   H.

DIE SIEBEN TODSÜNDEN
The Seven Deadly Sins

Ballet chanté in one act, text by Bertolt Brecht, scenario by Edward James and Boris Kochno. Première Paris, 7 June 1933, with Lotte Lenya and Tilly Losch as the singing and dancing Anna. Choreography was by Balanchine; Maurice Abravanel conducted. First performed 1933, Savoy Theatre, London; 1958, City Center, New York; 1961 in Italy, in Brussels (by Béjart), and at the Edinburgh Festival with Cleo Laine, Anya Linden, choreographed by Kenneth Macmillan; 1978, English National Opera, with Julie Covington, Siobhan Davies.

Anna I ....Soprano
Anna II ....Dancer
The Family ....Two Tenors, Baritone, Bass

Running Time: 35 minutes

Weill arrived in Paris in March 1933, and only days later Edward James had commissioned him to write a work for Les Ballets 1933, the company founded by Balanchine and Kochno which he backed. The original cast was packed with ambivalence: Tilly Losch was James's estranged wife, Lenya and Weill were in the throes of a divorce (and the music had to be transposed to fit her vocal resources), and Lenya's current lover, Otto Pasetti, sang one of the tenor members of the family. Casper Neher, with whose wife Weill was having an affair, designed the sets. The season lost money, but the work was an artistic success and it seems to have been during this season that Lincoln Kirstein recognised the genius of Balanchine and made up his mind to take him to America, where between them they later founded the New York City Ballet. Brecht appears to have been less than enthusiastic about the project and the scenario but, for what turned out to be his last stage collaboration with Weill, contrived to inject enough social criticism to suit his own agenda.

Prologue. Anna I and Anna II set out from Louisiana to make enough money in seven years in the big cities of the U.S.A. to build a house for their Family. Anna I is practical, Anna II pretty and romantic, though they are in reality two halves of one personality, with a single savings-bank account. The Family (the bass is the Mother) don't do much to help beyond biblical exhortations to avoid sin, which reduces earning power and is therefore to be avoided for practical reasons.

Sloth. The Family hopes Anna II will become industrious, but she falls asleep, accosts strange men

in the park, and only quick thinking extracts a fee for removing her.

Pride. In Memphis Anna II wants her dancing to be treated as Art, but this is show-business and the cabaret audience prefers striptease. Pride is something for the rich.

Anger. Working in film in Los Angeles, Anna II is fired for complaining of the ill-treatment of a horse. The Family complains of the poor financial results so far.

Gluttony. In Philadelphia Anna has problems over her weight and the specifications of the contract. The Family is confident – and eating well.

Lust. In Boston, they find Edward, who has money and pays for love, and Fernando, whom Anna loves but who has none.

Avarice. Anna II ruins Edward who kills himself. In Baltimore she is famous, but if she's not careful, avarice will turn fame to notoriety.

Envy. In San Francisco, Anna envies the people who get away with anything. Her sister rebukes her. The world is not for idealists. Don't try to do good when you're doing well.

Epilogue. The sisters go back to live in Louisiana.

Weill's achievement is to have created a synthesis of popular music, often jazzy or barber-shop in style, within a classical framework, the music constantly prompting the mood, underlining the irony, insisting the practical trips up the romantic. By the end, Anna II can only respond, crushed, to Anna I's 'Nicht wahr, Anna?' with 'Ja, Anna'. Too downbeat an ending to be bittersweet?   H.

STREET SCENE

Opera in two acts, libretto by Elmer Rice and Langston Hughes (based on Elmer Rice's play). Première Philadelphia, 16 December 1946, and New York, 9 January 1947, with Polyna Stoska, Anne Jeffreys, Brian Sullivan, Sydney Rayner, Norman Cordon, conductor Maurice Abravanel; 1989, Scottish Opera; English National Opera.

Abraham Kaplan...Tenor
Greta Fiorentino ....Soprano
Carl Olsen...Bass
Emma Jones.......................................Mezzo-Soprano
Olga Olsen...Contralto
Shirley Kaplan.....................................Speaking Role

Henry Davis ....Baritone
Willie Maurrant...Treble
Anna Maurrant...Soprano
Sam Kaplan..Tenor
Daniel Buchanan ....Tenor
Frank Maurrant.....................................Bass-Baritone
George Jones...Baritone
Steve Sankey ....Speaking Role
Lippo Fiorentino ....Tenor
Jenny Hildebrand ....Mezzo-Soprano
Mrs Hildebrand.................................Mezzo-Soprano
Rose Maurrant ....Soprano
Harry Easter ....Baritone
Mae Jones ....Dancer/Singer
Dick McGann.......................................Dancer/Singer
Two Nursemaids.................Soprano, Mezzo-Soprano

Inhabitants of the Street, Policemen, Milkman, Old
   Clothes Man, Interne, Ambulance Driver,
   Neighbours, Passers-By, Children, etc.

Place: New York City
Time: The Present (1946)
Running Time: 2 hours 35 minutes

Kurt Weill left Germany for America in 1935 and, once naturalised, lost few opportunities to emphasise his identification not only as an anti-Nazi but as an American. His European successes (which included American references in *Happy End*, *Seven Deadly Sins* and particularly *Mahagonny*) were followed by a number of shows written for wartime New York and eventually an American folk-ballad opera, *Down in the Valley* (written in 1945).

It is easy with hindsight to see that, from the moment he arrived in the U.S.A., Weill had been inching his way towards writing an American opera; his association with theatrical success in Berlin made it more or less inevitable that this should be a Broadway opera. By late 1945 he was in discussion with Elmer Rice, and the new work was ready for performance a year later. It was critically panned in Philadelphia but had considerable success in New York, though its total of 148 performances on Broadway was considered a disappointment. It was not revived in his lifetime but when he visited London in 1947 he seems to have had hopes that it might have an English production, perhaps at Covent Garden. This never eventuated and when after his death it was heard in Germany, it was

greeted with total misunderstanding, though increasingly successful in revival elsewhere.

Act I. An evening in June. The Prelude opens with a phrase from Sam Kaplan's aria 'Lonely house', which Weill emphasised to Langston Hughes is one of the show's centrepieces. An off-stage radio introduces us to the action. It is indescribably hot and neighbourhood talk is of little else: 'Ain't it awful, the heat.' The slow-moving but highly effective ensemble gives way to a blues sung by Henry, the Janitor. Willie Maurrant yells up to his mother which doesn't please Mrs Jones, who is not slow to lead a trio of neighbours gossiping about the man they have more than once seen Mrs Maurrant with recently. Mrs Maurrant's return pushes the gossip in other directions and we discover in quick succession that she thinks she and her daughter don't always have the same tastes as her husband; that the neighbourhood harbours considerable xenophobic sentiment; that Sam Kaplan is more than a little interested in Rose Maurrant. But the most urgent topic is Mrs Buchanan's pregnancy and in slow 6/8 her husband emphasises how difficult having a baby can be, particularly for the husband; he is interrupted by a scream from his wife at the top of the building.

We meet for the first time the cross-grained Mr Maurrant. Rose staying out late is a particular bone of contention, and he is quite happy to blame it on his wife. 'Somehow I never could believe that life was meant to be all dull and grey' she sings, and her substantial aria tells us about her early hopes. Steve Sankey the Milk Company Collector strolls by on his way to the drugstore. Mrs Maurrant says she must look for her son Willie, and the field is clear for the gossips: 'Get a load of that!' But life on the Street is not all gossip and threat and Lippo Fiorentino, the Ice Cream Salesman, leads a substantial Ice Cream Septet. His high-flying tenor soars over everyone (originally sung by an ex-Metropolitan tenor, Sydney Rayner), though Mrs Fiorentino is not to be outdone and finishes the extended ensemble on a top D flat.

Kaplan and Maurrant, liberal and traditionalist, disagree vigorously on the handling of children and Maurrant rams home his point of view in an aria 'Let things be like they always was'. Children march in (to a tune belonging to a New York High School) which gives place, as girls come from graduation, to one of the score's most obviously popular numbers: 'Wrapped in a ribbon and tied in a bow'.

Mrs Maurrant dances for a moment with Lippo Fiorentino, Sankey passes by on his way home (Maurrant wonders why he's hanging around), and Willie Maurrant has apparently been fighting with another boy who has been rude about his mother. When the Maurrants leave, he for a drink with a neighbour, she and Willie to go up to their room, gossip breaks out again, but Sam explodes with indignation and, when the others have left, embarks on his big arioso, 'Lonely house, lonely me!' He disappears as Rose comes in with Harry Easter, manager of her office, who sneaks a kiss and attempts to entice her away from the neighbourhood: 'Wouldn't you like to be on Broadway?' Rose is obviously tempted, but at the moment more worried by the notion that the neighbours might see her with a stranger and tell her father. Still, Rose doesn't figure on being a mistress: 'What good would the Moon be, Unless the right one shared its beams?' Maurrant nearly catches them saying goodnight and bawls Rose out, which provokes an element of rebellion in her before she reverts to a reprise of 'What good would the Moon be'.

When Mr Buchanan rushes from the house Rose says she will telephone the doctor. The arrival of Dick and Mae brings a complete change of mood in the most obviously Broadway-style number in the score, 'Moonfaced, starry-eyed', designated Song, Scene and Dance, and ending with a Blues on the trumpet. Vincent Jones, a slob if ever there was one, makes a pass at Rose and then knocks down the unfortunate Sam who answers her cry for help. He is obviously not seriously hurt and Rose asks him, rather shyly, if he thinks it's true what they are saying about her mother. His awkwardness confirms her fears but their duet not only makes a fine ending to the act but, when Sam quotes Walt Whitman, 'In the door yard ... Stands the lilac bush', an emblem for their love.

Act II. Daybreak, the next morning. Neighbourhood comings and goings precede a game for the children, 'One, Two, Three, for Superman, come and catch me if you can', during whose course a scrap breaks out. Mrs Buchanan has had a baby girl and Mary Hildebrand makes a passing reference to the fact that she and her family are to be evicted that day because they are behind with the rent. Rose attempts to get her father to be gentler with her mother but when Mrs Maurrant comes in, he is just as brusque as ever. An impassioned trio follows, full of expostu-

lation from all three participants, and when his wife asks when he'll be back he rounds on her, 'In case somebody came calling, huh?' Rose tries without much success to comfort her mother, then makes an effort to tidy Willie before he goes off to school, but he'll have none of it until his mother intervenes: 'A boy like you'.

Shirley Kaplan quite gently tries to warn Rose off Sam, who will have another three years before he is a fully-fledged lawyer. When Sam comes out, the two young people fantasise of a happier future away from their dreary neighbourhood and, above everything, together: 'We'll go away together'. They are interrupted by the reappearance of Easter, who offers Rose a lift to the office funeral. Rose and Sam show considerable embarrassment but in the end she walks off with Easter and leaves the coast clear for Sankey to reappear and, on hearing from Mrs Maurrant that her husband is away for the day, to go into the house with her. Sam has noticed all this but is distracted by the appearance of the Marshal whose job is to supervise the eviction of the Hildebrands. When Maurrant reappears, Sam can't block his way and he goes menacingly upstairs, leaving Sam to yell a warning to Mrs Maurrant. There is a scream of terror, then shots and a moment later Maurrant reappears covered in blood, and disappears down the cellar steps. The crowd erupts in general hubbub before the Marshal regains control of them and Rose reappears. There is a threnody for the tragedy, then Rose makes an attempt to talk to her mother as she is carried out on a stretcher. It is in many ways the most impressive number in the score.

An interlude takes us to mid-afternoon the same day. The eviction of the Hildebrands is over but some of their furniture is still on the sidewalk. Two Nursemaids go by with a pram and stop under the Maurrant windows to sing a satirical lullaby in 6/8, partly quieting their charges, mostly reading from the sensational tabloids.

Maurrant is captured but the police let him have a word with his daughter. It is his moment of truth. In 'I loved her too', he seems to ask for understanding, not mercy. Sam is left attempting to console Rose. She says she will go away, alone, and no argument Sam can advance will dissuade her, not even a reference to the lilac bush. They say goodbye, Mrs Jones not missing the opportunity for an acid comment;

the neighbours go back to moaning about the heat.

Street Scene works at every level: it strikes a blow for Weill's instinctive feeling for popular contact; it is in no sense a betrayal of his former work; though rather long and certainly downbeat in content, it is unmistakably a Broadway show; and it is no less obviously an opera. At the time it was being produced Weill quoted his teacher Busoni as having insisted to him 'the fear of triviality is the greatest handicap for the modern artist ... the main reason why "modern" got more and more removed from reality'. Weill's greatest admirer would never deny that he harboured no such fear.   H.

JAROMÍR WEINBERGER
(born 8 January 1896, died 8 August 1967)

SCHWANDA THE BAGPIPER
Švanda Dudák

Opera in two acts, text by M. Kareš. Première, Prague, 27 April 1927, conductor Ostrčil. First performed Berlin, 1929, with Müller, Branzell, Soot, Scheidl, Schützendorf, Helgers, conductor Erich Kleiber; Vienna, 1930, with Angerer, Rünger, Piccaver, Hammes, Mayr, conductor Krauss; Metropolitan, New York, 1931, with Müller, Branzell, Laubenthal, Schorr, Andresen, Schützendorf, conductor Bodanzky; Covent Garden, 1934, with Ursuleac, Rünger, Kullmann, Schoeffler, Kipnis, Sterneck, conductor Krauss. Revived Sadler's Wells, 1948; Düsseldorf, 1949.

Schwanda the Bagpiper ....Baritone
Dorotka, *his wife* ....Soprano
Babinsky, *a romantic robber* ....Tenor
The Queen ....Mezzo-Soprano
The Magician ....Bass
The Judge ....Tenor
The Executioner ....Tenor
The Devil...Bass
The Devil's Familiar Spirit ....Tenor
The Captain of Hell's Guard ....Tenor
Two Forest Rangers.................................Tenor, Bass

Running Time: 2 hours 10 minutes

Though Weinberger wrote other operas, only *Schwanda* caught the public imagination, to such a tune in this case that its publisher claimed it had been performed some 2,000 times in its first five seasons. Its lively story and jaunty rhythms – the Polka and Fugue survives as an occasional concert piece – carried it round the world, but success evaporated after 1939 and the composer, described as a recluse in his life in exile in Florida, committed suicide in 1967.

Act I. Close to a forest is the cottage where Schwanda dwells with his young wife, Dorotka. As the curtain rises, two armed foresters hasten to the cottage to enquire whether a suspicious stranger has been seen in the neighbourhood. They are after the robber, Babinsky. Dorotka, however, cannot help them; she has seen no one.

No sooner have they gone than Babinsky, who has been hiding in the high branches of a tree, drops to the ground before the astonished Dorotka. She learns that Babinsky has never heard of her famous husband, Schwanda, the bagpiper of Strakonitz. Why, the devil himself envies Schwanda his gift. 'Are you the Devil?' asks the gentle Dorotka. Babinsky is rather hurt. Schwanda arrives from the fields where he has been working, and courteously asks his unknown guest to share their meal. In the course of the conversation Babinsky tells the story of the great robber Babinsky, the friend of the poor, the hero of a thousand adventures. The story makes an impression on Schwanda.

'A man gifted as you are,' says Babinsky, 'could easily make his way.' He tells of people who are wealthy and bored and of the Queen whose heart is ice. Schwanda's ambition is on fire. Dorotka would hold him back but, while she is out of sight, Schwanda departs with Babinsky.

The second scene shows the chamber of Queen Iceheart, who vainly hopes to find a cure. To the tune of the now famous polka, Schwanda enters. His music is simply irresistible; the Queen's maids-of-honour and pages dance. 'Who art thou, bringer of jollity?' asks the Queen. 'I am Schwanda,' replies the piper in a jovial aria, in which the chorus joins; 'I go where there is bitterness and sorrow; I blow on my pipe and at once the clouds melt and the whole world rejoices.' The Queen is so much enamoured of the music that she decides to wed the musician forthwith. Schwanda, fascinated by the prospect of sharing a throne, agrees and kisses the Queen.

But if Schwanda can forget the faithful Dorotka, Dorotka, far from forgetting Schwanda, has followed him, and now overtakes him to tax him with infidelity. Schwanda's forgetfulness, however, was but a moment's aberration. The Queen, learning this, orders both to appear before the judge, who will condemn them to death.

Sentence is passed on Schwanda and Dorotka. Just as the execution is about to take place, the executioner discovers that his axe has been stolen. It is Babinsky who has come to the rescue of his friend, and now hands him the pipes. Schwanda plays and the public are helpless; they *must* dance while Schwanda and his friends move slowly towards the gate (Furiant).

Once they are well away Dorotka turns on him and taunts her errant husband. Schwanda denies everything: 'If I have given the queen a single kiss may the Devil take me'. Schwanda disappears.

Act II. Hell. The Devil is playing cards by himself; no one trusts him, and he is reduced to Patience. Schwanda is there too. Since he has not been sent there but came of his own free will, the rules of Hell do not apply to him. The Devil is very bored, and begs Schwanda to play for him. His requests meet with a blank refusal. The Father of Lies is at a loss for arguments, but he overhears Schwanda's lament for Dorotka, who made life pleasing to him. Here is his opportunity. He shows Schwanda the spectre of Dorotka and tells him he has but to sign a paper to get her. Schwanda signs the paper giving away his soul. The Devil tells him that now he is bound to obey and, to begin with, he must play on his pipes.

The timely arrival of Babinsky saves Schwanda for the moment. The robber is, of course, well known to the Devil. Moreover, he is only too pleased to welcome a man who is not afraid of having a game of cards with him. They gamble and in the end the Devil loses everything.

Babinsky, however, is generous. He will leave the Devil his kingdom and his insignia; only Schwanda must be free to go with him. The servants of Hell cheer Babinsky, while the Devil thanks him and promises that should he ever return he will be welcomed as 'a son of the house'. To crown it all the piper will play them a tune so that they may learn what the playing of the great master Schwanda of Strakonitz is like. This is the ingenious fugue.

Schwanda's cottage. Babinsky makes a last attempt to divide the lovers. He tells Schwanda that, although he may not have known it, he has lived twenty years in Hell; that Dorotka is now an old peasant woman who, most likely, will not know him again, and invites him to go back to the great world.

Schwanda has learnt his lesson. Never again will he depart from his beloved. 'Dorotka! Dorotka!' he calls, and Dorotka comes to him as beautiful as ever. Babinsky retires discomfited. Peasants rush to congratulate Schwanda on his return.   F.B.

JUDITH WEIR

(born 11 May 1954)

Judith Weir's first two major music-theatre works, the ten-minute 'Grand Opera in Three Acts' *King Harald's Saga* of 1979 and the twenty-five-minute song-cycle *The Consolations of Scholarship* of 1985, were not intended to be staged. As she said later (in a 'Note on the Opera' to *A Night at the Chinese Opera*)

'the constant quick character changes in the soloist's part ensure that unstageability is perhaps their most striking dramatic feature'. In this context it is notable that 'the most formative experience of [her] early opera-going life was a performance of the Stravinsky-Cocteau *Oedipus Rex*'.

A NIGHT AT THE CHINESE OPERA

Opera in three acts, libretto by the composer based on Chi Chun-hsiang's drama *The Chao Family Orphan* (thirteenth century). Commissioned by the B.B.C., first performed by Kent Opera, Everyman Theatre, Cheltenham, 8 July 1987, with Tomos Ellis as Nightwatchman/Marco Polo, Michael Chance as Military Governor, Gwion Thomas as Chao Lin, Meryl Drower as Little Moon/Actor, Enid Hartle as Mrs Chin/Old Crone, conducted by Andrew Parrott. First U.S. performance, Santa Fe Festival, 1989, conducted by George Manahan.

A Nightwatchman/Marco Polo.........................Tenor

A Military Governor............................Counter-Tenor

A Mongolian Soldier ....Bass

Chao Sun, *an explorer and mapmaker/*
   A Fireman...Baritone

Little Moon, *wife of Chao Sun/*An Actor ....Soprano

Chao Lin, *their son, as a boy*.................................Silent

Chao Lin, *as a young man*.......................High Baritone

Mrs Chin, *housekeeper/*Old Crone........Mezzo-Soprano

Old P'eng, *a scholar/*Old Mountain-Dweller ......Tenor

An Actor...Mezzo-Soprano

An Actor...Tenor

In Act II the roles are shared as follows

Chao-the-Loyal-Civil-Servant's-Wife ⎱ .... Soprano
Kung-Sun Ch'u Chiu, *the pig farmer* ⎰ .... Actor

General Tu-an-Ku ⎱
General Han Chueh ⎰ ....Mezzo-Soprano Actor

Chao-the-Loyal-Civil-Servant ⎱
Wang Piao, *Personal Assistant to*
   General Tu-an-Ku ⎰ ....Tenor Actor
Ch'en Ying, *the loyal retainer*
The Immortal, T'ai-Po

Judith Weir's interest in Chinese music-theatre fuses with her liking for plays-within-plays. Here, she sets a real Chinese play, Chi Chun-hsiang's *The Chao Family Orphan*, reduced from five acts to one operatic act. For this Act II, Weir avoids chinoiserie but aims at 'imaginative reconstructions of Chinese originals', using a reduced Western orchestra of flutes, violas, basses and percussion with occasional reeds. This is a numbers opera: each scene of the outer acts is a self-contained musical unit with its own musical form (a trace of the influence of Berg's *Wozzeck*).

Act I takes place in Loyan, a small, provincial city on the north-west borders of late thirteenth-century China.

Scene i. Nightwatchman's Song with three sky pictures. These are evoked poetically by the Nightwatchman, who fails to notice Kublai Khan's army invading the city.

Scene ii. Sextet. Chao Sun goes into exile, leaving behind his wife, Little Moon, and baby son. She dies soon afterwards.

Scene iii. Kite, in Moto Perpetuo. His son, Chao Lin, is brought up by neighbours in ignorance of his parents and becomes influenced by the invaders' martial culture.

Scene iv. Aria, with rising floodwaters. Fifteen years later, China has been flooded. The Military Governor relates how the invaders lacked Chinese expertise in irrigation and agriculture. They turn to Chao Lin for help.

Scene v. Chansonette. One of the actors who once served the Chinese Emperor strums a lute: they have no work now. In a seven-part motet Chao Lin conscripts three of these ex-actors to work on his project to dig a canal from the city to the mountain. Chao Lin's neighbours surprise him when they talk approvingly of his father's escape into exile. They hand him the map his father started but never completed. It covers the mountains that Chao Lin's canal must run through.

Scene vi. Finale. Before he leaves, he hears from the Nightwatchman that the actors will stage an old Chinese play this evening, in defiance of the Mongolian curfew, *The Poor Orphan of the Chao Family*, in which an orphan is befriended by his father's enemy. Chao Lin decides to go and see it.

Act II. 'The Orphan of the Chao Family'. The Wedge (or Prelude). The wicked General Tu-an-Ku plots against Chao-the-Loyal-Civil-Servant, his rival for the Emperor's trust. The General hands Chao an order to commit suicide, pretending that it came from the Emperor. Chao obeys and asks his pregnant wife to ensure that if she has a son, he will avenge him.

First Act of *The Orphan*. Chao's Wife gives her son, the Orphan of Chao, to her loyal physician Ch'eng Ying and then kills herself. Ch'eng Ying hides the baby in a medicine chest. He is allowed through the city gates by General Han Chueh, who then commits suicide, to avoid revealing this to General Tu-an-Ku.

Second Act of *The Orphan*. Ch'eng Ying leaves the baby with Kung-Sun Ch'u-Chiu, a former colleague

A Night at the Chinese Opera *(Kent Opera, 1987, director Richard Jones, designer Richard Hudson).*
Three Citizens (Tomos Ellis, Alan Oke, Frances Lynch) peer at pictures of the Emperor Kubilai Khan.

of Chao-the-Loyal-Civil-Servant and now a pig farmer. General Tu-an-Ku is heard approaching in pursuit of the Orphan of Chao. A pig is substituted for the baby and Ch'eng Ying then escapes into the mountains. Kung-Sun Ch'u-Chiu tells the General that the baby is in the medicine chest, and the General stabs it with his sword. To reward Kung-Sun for collaborating, the General offers to adopt the baby he assumes is Kung-Sun's child, but who is in fact the Orphan of Chao.

Third Act of *The Orphan.* Twenty years have passed. The General plots to dethrone the Emperor. An immortal is shocked by this plan to upset the natural, divinely ordained order and sends a mina-

tory earthquake which the General ignores. He invites his adopted son to join him and gives him a coin that he has had minted to commemorate his putsch.

Ch'eng Ying has returned from exile. He leaves a scroll commemorating the events of twenty years ago where the Orphan finds it. Ch'eng Ying helps him understand it and the Orphan realises who he is. In a radiant aria he swears revenge on General Tu-an-Ku.

Fourth Act of *The Orphan.* The Orphan has arranged to meet the General secretly but when the Orphan is about to kill him, the Fireman and the Soldier interrupt the performance in a coda with news of a small earthquake in the north. The audience is asked to leave and rebuked for breaking the curfew by gathering after dark. Chao Lin reflects on what he knows.

Act III. Marco Polo, in Italian, sketches in the historical background: China's elaborate feats of canal-building in the fourteenth century.

Scene i. Prisoners' Chorus. Chao Lin is about to set off the morning after the play with his team, the three Actors. The Military Governor congratulates him on his work which will 'overcome the laws of nature', and presents him with a seal of office, which increases his authority and his anxiety.

Scene ii. Misterioso. Chao Lin marks out the route his canal will take. An Old Crone suggests he use a nearby mountain as a vantage point. It is where those who ran away from the city took refuge.

Scene iii. The Ascent. Chao Lin longs to know what happened to his father. He uses his map to go up the mountain.

Scene iv. Scena. On the summit he sees an Old Mountain-Dweller who tells him that Chao Sun, his father, was among those who died in the mountains. Chao Lin decides to exact revenge.

Scene v. Nocturne. The Military Governor has come to the mountain, along with a Soldier, in response to a message from Chao Lin. Chao Lin hesitates before striking and is arrested.

Scene vi. Finale. The Actors have been released and now prepare to rehearse. Chao Lin is sentenced to death for treason. After he is led away the Actors present the final events of their play, which were not performed at the end of (the opera's) Act I. The Orphan of Chao prevents General Tu-an-Ku's treason, the Emperor sentences the General to death and rewards the Orphan and all those who assisted him.

A Night at the Chinese Opera is that rarity, a genuinely popular new opera. It revels in the exotic and yet finds poetry in the perfunctory. The original thirteenth-century Chinese play was greatly admired by Voltaire, who knew it in a French translation by the Jesuit Father Joseph Prémare (1735). Weir has said that Voltaire's remark about the play, 'everything is of the most brilliant clarity', 'was always in [her] mind as a compositional ideal for [her] own opera'. Genuinely curious, the opera is more than picturesque, however, and exerts a strong emotional and theatrical hold on its audiences.   P.

THE VANISHING BRIDEGROOM

Opera in three parts, libretto by the composer, based on J.F. Campbell of Islay's edition of *Popular Tales of the West Highlands*, vol. 2 (1860) and Alexander Carmichael's edition of *Carmina Gadelica*, vol. 2 (1900). First performed by Scottish Opera, Theatre Royal, Glasgow, 17 October 1990, with Peter Snipp, Virginia Kerr, Robert Poulton and Harry Nicoll, conducted by Alan Hacker. First U.S. performance, St Louis, Missouri, 1992, conducted by Scott Bergeson.

The Inheritance

Narrator	Tenor/High Baritone
Youngest Son	Tenor
Middle Son	Tenor/Baritone
The Doctor	Low Baritone
The Dying Man	Tenor
The Bride	Soprano
The Bride's Lover	Tenor
The Bridegroom	High Baritone
Two Bad Robbers	Baritones
A Good Robber	Tenor/High Baritone

The Disappearance

Three Women	Soprano, Soprano or Mezzo, Mezzo-Soprano
The Wife	Soprano
The Husband's Friend	Tenor
The Husband	High Baritone
The Policeman	Low Baritone

The Stranger

The Daughter	Mezzo-Soprano
The Stranger	Low Baritone
The Mother	Soprano
The Father	High Baritone
The Preacher	Tenor

Two Little Girls, Fairies, etc.

Running Time: 1 hour 30 minutes

For her libretto, Judith Weir assembled three entirely separate stories from an 1860 anthology of Scottish tales, attracted by the language's 'severity and barrenness, which seems utterly truthful and documentary'. In so doing, she constructed a narrative about one particular marriage. She created very different sound pictures for each part of her opera. Male voices dominate the first part, which suits the story of a Bride victimised by men. 'Translated out of Gaelic into English, the language and themes have a formality and severity that recall the dourest and least religious parts of the Old Testament.' Apart from brief interventions from the female chorus, representing the Thick Wood, there is only one female voice, surrounded by the stern, judgemental choir who open and close the act, and by the Three Sons who 'voyeuristically follow her, in close harmony, through the events of the story'.

In the second part, 'the balance in the opera between male and female voices is redressed ... by a group of three women who, together with the deserted wife, sing a progressively developing refrain which motivates the musical development of the act'.

The composer herself described the action of the third part as follows: 'The romantic lead proposes marriage to the heroine, she decides this would not be in her best interests and destroys him; she leaves the stage perfectly content and in control. It is an unusually optimistic ending.'[1]

The Inheritance. A man dies but his legacy is missing: one of his three sons must have stolen it. The Doctor decides to find out which one did it, by telling this parable:

A woman who is not allowed to marry her lover is married off to another man, who is rich. When the Bridegroom hears that his Bride loved someone else, he sends her back to him. But her Lover rejects her because she is married and sends her back to her husband. As she is goes through a thick wood she is robbed. However, one of the robbers takes her back to her husband.

The Doctor asks the three sons whose behaviour they admire most, out of all the people in the story. The Eldest Son answers, 'The rich husband'; the Middle Son says, 'The forbidden lover'; the Youngest Son says, 'The robbers who got away with all the money'. And it was he who stole the legacy.

The Disappearance. When the Bride of the previous story gives birth to a daughter, the Bridegroom goes to fetch the Priest, but he is lured into a hillside and is not seen again. His Friend (his wife's former lover) is accused of his murder but allowed to stay and watch for his return. Many years later, the Husband returns, having spent the intervening time with the fairies, in the Land of the Young. He is unwilling to believe any time has passed, until he sees that the Daughter, whose christening he had gone to arrange, is now an adult.

The Stranger. A handsome Stranger courts the Daughter, encouraged by her parents. A Preacher identifies him as the Devil and advises her to stand on a piece of earth that is holy when the Stranger returns. Frustrated that he cannot get any closer to her, the Devil reveals himself and, in the words of the composer's own synopsis, 'assails her with the worst perils of the Highlands – inclement weather and voracious insects – but eventually he has to retire defeated, while the sanctified ground blooms beautifully'.

In *The Vanishing Bridegroom* Judith Weir demonstrates a masterly control of her material, in terms of both the language and the music. She conjures up whole worlds of feeling with the most elegant economy of means: vast issues (feminism, satanism et al.) are summoned, made to dance to her tunes, which deftly transform the given in terms of melodies based on folksongs, and then playfully dismissed.   P.

BLOND ECKBERT

Opera in two acts, libretto by the composer, based on Ludwig Tieck's tale, 'Der blonde Eckbert'. First performed by English National Opera, Coliseum, London, 20 April 1994, with Nerys Jones as the Bird, Anne-Marie Owens as Berthe, Christopher Ventris as Walther/Hugo/An Old Woman and Nicholas Folwell as Blond Eckbert, conducted by Sian Edwards.

A Bird	Soprano
Berthe, *Blond Eckbert's wife*	Mezzo-Soprano
Walther, *his friend*	
Hugo, *his friend*	Tenor
An Old Woman	
Blond Eckbert	Baritone

Running Time: 1 hour 5 minutes

Act I. Flying Prelude. A Bird tells a story to a dog. 'Far away and long ago', Blond Eckbert and his wife Berthe lived quietly in the Harz mountains. 'They appeared to love each other deeply.'

Scene i. Eckbert and Berthe at home. One night Eckbert sees his only friend, Walther, approaching. Eckbert reflects how sometimes 'it is a grief to have any secrets at all', but revealing them to a friend can be dangerous: 'it can happen that one can recoil with fear from the face of the other'.

Scene ii. Walther has arrived. Walther tells Berthe

---

[1] Quotations are from the composer's own programme note, 1990.

and Eckbert how he was deep in the mountains listening to the rushing water and the birdsong. He sang a huntsman's song, 'Through the woods the horns resounding'. Then he thought of his friends, 'at home and safe', and came to see them. Eckbert invites him to stay and hear Berthe tell the story of her life. She does so, but first asks Walther not to take her story as a fairy tale.

Scene iii. Berthe's ballad. When she was a child, her parents worried that they could not afford to feed or clothe her. Her father beat her, so she ran away. She was brought up elsewhere by a strange old woman who had a dog (whose name Berthe has forgotten) and a magic bird which laid jewels instead of eggs.

Berthe learnt to spin and looked after the dog and the bird. Eventually she became curious about the world and escaped, taking the jewels and the bird with her. She heard the bird warning her 'You did wrong and you'll pay'. When Berthe reached her original home, she found that both her parents had died. She married Blond Eckbert and they settled down, selling the jewels to live. Blond Eckbert comments, 'She brought me prosperity – our marriage has caused us no regrets.' As they go to bed, Walther tells her that she told her story so vividly that he can just imagine 'the bird and that friendly little dog, Strohmian'.

Scene iv. Strohmian! Berthe is amazed that Walther knew the name of the dog that she had forgotten. She leaves for bed. In a monologue Eckbert reviews his suspicions ('And when he said goodnight'): will Walther abuse their trust and want to steal their jewels?

Act II. Prelude. Walther's death. Eckbert has gone hunting in the forest. He sees an object moving in the distance. It is Walther. 'Scarcely knowing what he did' (the words from the original story are quoted in the score) he shoots and kills Walther.

After a moving orchestral passage, the bird is heard singing (in German) of repentance.

Scene i. Berthe's last breath. On her deathbed, Berthe writes to Eckbert, still worrying how Walther knew her dog's name ('My dearest husband'). On another part of the stage, Eckbert is seen reading her letter, repeating her terrified phrases.

Scene ii. Accusation. Eckbert goes to the city to distract himself. The Chorus's repeated exclamation 'Ah!' punctuates the scene to suggest what the score calls 'the brutal business of an urban scene'. Eckbert meets a man called Hugo (doubled by the tenor who sang Walther) who hears his tale and reassures him. Eckbert becomes suspicious of him, however: he even thinks that Hugo looks like Walther. He rushes away.

Scene iii. Eckbert, fugitive. He finds himself in a landscape that looks familiar, because it is the countryside that Berthe had described. He hears the same bird singing of 'truth's clear, blinding light'.

Scene iv. At the end. He arrives at the hut of the Old Woman who reared Berthe. She asks him if he is bringing back her bird and her jewels and tells him that she was Walther as well as Hugo. She also reveals that Berthe was his sister. Eckbert realises that he had suspected this. The Old Woman tells him that he had heard his father mention it when he was a child. In agony, Eckbert sings only 'Ah!' The Bird tells us that Eckbert lies on the ground, 'insane and dying'. The Bird flies away, chased by the dog.

From the overture on, as themes are fragmented, repeated and passed urgently from one section of the orchestra to another, *Blond Eckbert* grips the listener remorselessly. Eventually the Bird takes up one of the themes, singing wordlessly 'Ah!', the sound that returns at the end of the opera as Eckbert's raving. The composer said she was drawn to Ludwig Tieck's original tale partly by 'the way it was told ... there's a seeming simplicity, yet the more you read it, the more the complexities of the story come out'.   P.

HUGO WOLF
(born 13 March 1860, died 22 February 1903)

DER CORREGIDOR
The Magistrate

Opera in four acts, text by Rosa Mayreder-Obermayer, founded on P. de Alarcón's story *El sombrero de tres picos*. Première in Mannheim, June 1896. First performed in Vienna, under Mahler, 1904, with Förster-Lauterer, Breuer, Demuth and Hesch; London, Royal Academy of Music, 1934; Salzburg Festival, 1936, with Novotna, Thorborg, Bella Paalen, Gunnar Graarud, Jerger, Zec, Ludwig Hoffmann, conductor Bruno Walter; London, 1955, by City Opera Club; New York, 1959, in concert form; Wiesbaden, 1960; Zürich, 1972.

Don Eugenio de Zuniga,
    the Corregidor (magistrate) ....Buffo Tenor

Doña Mercedes, *his wife*...............................Soprano

Repela, *his valet*...Buffo Bass

Tio Lucas, *a miller*...Baritone

Frasquita, *his wife* ....Mezzo-Soprano

Juan Lopez, *the alcalde (mayor)* ....Bass

Pedro, *his secretary* ....Tenor

Manuela, *a maid* ....Mezzo-Soprano

Tonuelo, *a court messenger* ....Bass

A Neighbour..Tenor

A Duenna, *employed by the*
    Corregidora ....Mezzo-Soprano

Running Time: 2 hours

Wolf was established as the late nineteenth century's most renowned writer of *Lieder* when, after completing the *Spanisches Liederbuch* in 1890, he contemplated more than one possible operatic subject with a Spanish theme. He settled in 1894 on the story popularly known as *The Three-Cornered Hat* (from Massine's later ballet on music by Manuel de Falla), wrote it fast as was his invariable habit, but had it turned down by more than one theatre before it was accepted for Mannheim. *Der Corregidor* contains many incidental felicities but it shows overall a limited sense of either drama or the stage. Mahler conducted a slightly revised version of the opera in Vienna in 1904, and his disciple Bruno Walter revived it in Salzburg in 1936, but success constantly eluded it. Nonetheless, Wolf embarked on another Spanish subject, *Manuel Venegas*, which remained unfinished at his death.

Act I. The miller, Tio Lucas, is living a happy life with his beautiful wife, Frasquita. Her love is so true that jealousy, to which he is inclined, cannot thrive. Yes, he has a bump of jealousy. True, the Corregidor, who is keenly interested in the Miller's pretty wife, has one too. But no matter, he is a high, very influential functionary. Meanwhile Frasquita loves her Tio Lucas so truly that she can even allow herself a dance with the Corregidor. Perhaps she will cure him, perhaps she will obtain in addition the wished-for official place for her nephew. Frasquita flirts with the Corregidor and makes him so much in love with her that he becomes impetuous. As she eludes his attempt to kiss her he loses his balance and falls in the dust, out of which the miller, unsuspecting, raises him up. But the Corregidor swears revenge.

Act II. The opportunity for this comes very quickly. As the miller one evening is sitting with his wife in their cosy room, there comes a knock at the door. It is a drunken court messenger, Tonuelo, who produces a warrant of arrest. Tio Lucas must follow him without delay to the alcalde who has fallen in with the Corregidor's scheme. Frasquita is trying to calm her anxiety with a song when outside there is a cry for help. She opens the door and before it stands the Corregidor dripping with water. He has fallen in the brook. Now he begs admission from Frasquita, who is raging with anger. He has even brought with him the appointment of the nephew. But the angry woman will pay no attention and sends the Corregidor away. He falls in a swoon. His own servant now comes along. Frasquita admits both of them to the house and herself goes into town to look for her Tio Lucas. When the Corregidor hears this, full of anxiety, he sends his valet after her; he himself, however, hangs his wet clothes before the fire and goes to bed in the miller's bedroom.

Scene ii. In the meantime Tio Lucas drinks the alcalde and his fine comrades under the table and seizes the occasion to flee.

Act III. In the darkness of the night, Tio Lucas and Frasquita pass by without seeing each other.

Scene iii. The miller's house. Everything is open.

In the dust lies the deed of appointment for the nephew; before the fire hang the Corregidor's clothes. A frightful suspicion arises in Tio Lucas's mind which becomes a certainty when through the keyhole he sees the Corregidor in his own bed. He is already groping for his rifle to shoot the seducer and the faithless woman, when another thought strikes him. The Corregidor also has a wife, a beautiful wife. He quickly slips into the Corregidor's clothes and goes back to town. In the meantime the Corregidor has awakened. But he does not find his clothes and so he crawls into those of the miller, and in them is almost arrested by the alcalde who now enters with his companions and Frasquita. When the misunderstanding is cleared up, they go to the town after the miller.

Act IV. Now comes the explanation and the punishment of the Corregidor, at least in so far as he receives a sound thrashing. The miller too is recognised and likewise beaten black and blue – *that* he must suffer in reparation for his churlish doubt of the faithful Frasquita.

The comedy of *Der Corregidor* is through-composed. The overture opens with the Corregidor theme (later played on the trombones), and makes play also with the E major love music, which is later heard in the first scene of the second act. Two of Wolf's songs are worked into the libretto of the work, the first, 'In dem Schatten meiner Locken', sung by Frasquita to the Corregidor, the second to words by Heine, 'Herz, verzage nicht geschwind', sung by the Corregidor at the end of the first scene of Act II.   K.W.

ERMANNO WOLF-FERRARI
(born 12 January 1876, died 21 January 1948)

A Bavarian father and Venetian mother gave Wolf-Ferrari musical dual nationality, compounded by musical education in Germany, some Italian librettos and frequently Italianate musical style, and the fact that he spent much of his life in German-speaking countries. His best operas are comedies which build on the legacy of the Verdi of *Falstaff*, but the Great War, with Germany and Italy on opposite sides, found him traumatised in Zürich, and, in spite of *Sly* (1920), it was years before he regained his touch with three further comic operas. He was an industrious composer and the years between the operas are filled with instrumental music of one kind or another, none of which had quite the impact of his operas.

I QUATTRO RUSTEGHI
The School for Fathers

Opera in four acts, text by G. Pizzolato from Goldoni; German text by H. Teibler. Première Munich, 19 March 1906, in German. First performed Teatro Lirico, Milan, 1914; la Scala, Milan, 1922, with Labia, Soster, Fabbri, Azzolini, Scattola, conductor Panizza; Buenos Aires, 1927, with Cobelli, Cravcenco, Marengo, Azzolini, Vanelli, conductor Panizza; Berlin, 1937, with Berger, Heidersbach, Marherr, Spletter, Prohaska, Neumann, Helgers, Fleischer; Sadler's Wells, London, 1946; City Center, New York, 1951.

Lunardo, *merchant* ....Bass
Margarita, *his second wife* ....Mezzo-Soprano
Lucieta, *his daughter by his first wife*..............Soprano
Maurizio, *merchant* ....Bass or Bass-Baritone
Filipeto, *his son* ....Tenor
Marina, *aunt to Filipeto* ....Soprano
Simon, *her husband* ....Bass-Baritone
Canciano, *a wealthy merchant* ....Bass
Felice, *his wife* ....Soprano
Count Riccardo Arcolai, *a visitor to Venice* ....Tenor

A Young Maid

Place: Venice
Time: End of the Eighteenth Century
Running Time: 2 hours 25 minutes

Wolf-Ferrari set to music more than one of Goldoni's Venetian comedies, which, written mostly in dialect, have a somewhat limited appeal. *I*

Quattro Rusteghi is one of the finest of them. The character-drawing is finished and the action moves quickly to its climax. The provincial colours of the picture have militated against rapid and wide acceptance of the opera, as of the comedy. But Germany has given it a welcome – indeed its première was in German translation – and the London production, whose translator, Edward Dent, transferred the action from Venice to London, met with success.

The 'rusteghi' (in no sense 'rustics') are the honest, plain-speaking, conservative, domestic tyrants who, believing that woman's place is the home, forbid anything that might enliven the tedium of domestic work. The opera has been called a comedy of bad manners.

Act I. Lunardo's wife, Margarita, and her stepdaughter, Lucieta, are sitting knitting and embroidering. It is carnival and their thoughts turn to the amusements and gaiety of more fortunate people. Margarita remembers that before she married Lunardo there were parties at home and occasional visits to the theatre. Lucieta is of marrying age and hopes for a husband and better times. Lunardo enters silently, desiring to speak with his wife yet unwilling to interrupt her occupation. When the two are finally alone he tells her as an important secret that he and his friend Maurizio have arranged to wed Lucieta to Maurizio's son, Filipeto. The fact that the young people have never seen each other is, to them, immaterial. Margarita's very reasonable objections are rudely ignored. Lunardo's will is law. He answers Margarita's arguments with: 'I am the master.' Maurizio is announced and Margarita retires. The two 'rusteghi' now discuss the details of the contract – Lucieta's dowry, her clothes (no silk but good, honest home-spun), jewels which must not be re-set as the fashionable people do who thus pay twice for the gems. The dour, rigid character of the domestic bears is well described in this scene.

The second part of the act takes us to the house of Marina and her husband – even more of a 'rustego' than Lunardo. Marina is singing the tune familiar from its use as an interlude before Act II. Filipeto enters and begins by asking whether his uncle is in. He is in great dread of his uncle and means to avoid him. The purpose of his visit is to enquire whether his aunt has heard anything about his own wedding. His father has informed him abruptly that he intends to give him a wife and the homely youth is flustered, yet determined not to marry a girl he does not like; he begs his aunt to help him. If having seen the girl he does not like her, he will run away rather than marry her: 'Lucieta! Xe un bel nome' (Lucieta! her name at least is pretty). Simon arrives and unceremoniously dismisses Filipeto. Marina has another caller, the talkative Felice, accompanied by her husband and her 'cavalier servente', Count Riccardo. The husband, Canciano, stands mute and disapproving. The two women put their heads together determined that the men shall not be allowed to have it all their own way.

Act II. The act is preceded by the famous intermezzo, which serves admirably as an example of the composer's light, graceful style. When the curtain rises, we are back in Lunardo's house. Lucieta has persuaded Margarita to lend her a few trinkets but Lunardo arrives on the scene and orders the girl to take off her borrowed finery. They are joined by Marina and Simon. When the women retire the men rail at them and lament the passing of the good old days when women were women and did as they were told ('What has become of the old sort of women?'). The appearance of Felice is the signal for their departure. The other women join her, and Lucieta is congratulated on her betrothal. 'Shall I see my future husband?' she asks and hears that Felice and her friends have found a way to bring the young people together. It is carnival and Filipeto, escorted by Riccardo, plans to arrive disguised as a girl. If they should be discovered they will pass him off as a distant female relative. He soon arrives, and in a charming little scene Marina persuades him to take off the mask. Meanwhile the men have settled their business and Filipeto's father, Maurizio, has gone off to bring the youth to the betrothal. Now Lunardo surprises the women who have just time to hide Filipeto in a closet and Riccardo in another. The situation is tense. Maurizio returns very angry with the news that Filipeto is not to be found anywhere. All that is known is that he left the house with Riccardo. Canciano then begins to show himself in his true colours. He dislikes Riccardo; he will have no dealings with him; he must be an impostor. But Riccardo is a man of spirit and, hearing all that Canciano is saying, comes out of hiding and challenges him. Filipeto is found, the whole conspiracy discovered, and a very angry Lunardo orders the callers to leave his house. There will be no wedding for Lucieta.

Act III. The act begins with Lunardo, Simon, and Canciano considering in gloom the wickedness of the women's conduct. What is the next step to be? Lucieta can be sent away to the country but how can the other women be punished? The plain truth is that the women are necessary to their own comfort and, if they were sent away, the men themselves would suffer. This homely commination is interrupted by the arrival of Felice. She is received with hostility at first, for she is the arch-plotter. But her arguments are unanswerable, and, delivered with the speed and accuracy of aim which she commands, irresistible. What harm has been done? Would it not have been much worse if the young people had *not* liked each other's looks? Slowly, slowly the men begin to relent and finally and not very graciously are won over. The opera ends like a fairy story with wedding bells.

At the time of the first performance of the opera at Sadler's Wells (1946), *The Times* wrote as follows of the music: 'It flows spontaneously; it has a touch of distinction which saves it from the obvious; it is technically modern yet picks up the *opera buffa* tradition of the eighteenth century with the utmost grace and learning; it has a vein of lyrical melody and excels in ensemble.'   F.B.

IL SEGRETO DI SUSANNA

Susanna's Secret

Opera in one act, text by Enrico Golisciani (German version by Kalbeck). Première Munich, 4 December 1909 (in German), conductor Mottl. First performed New York (by Chicago company), 1911, with Carolina White and Sammarco; Rome, 1911; Covent Garden, 1911, with Lipkowska, Sammarco; Metropolitan, 1912, with Farrar, Scotti, conductor Polacco. Revived la Scala, Milan, 1917, with Vallin, Parvis, conductor Panizza; Covent Garden, 1919, with Borghi-Zerni, Sammarco, conductor Coates; Metropolitan, 1921, with Bori, Scotti; la Scala, 1934, with Oltrabella, Biasini; Glyndebourne, 1958, with Costa, Roux, conductor Pritchard. The little opera is a direct descendant of the eighteenth-century *Intermezzo*.

Count Gil, *aged thirty* ....Baritone

Countess Susanna, *his wife, aged twenty* ....Soprano

Sante, *their servant, aged fifty* ....Silent

Scene: Piedmont
Time: 'The Present'
Running Time: 45 minutes

Given in Munich in German translation only three and a half years after the successful production there of *I Quattro Rusteghi*.

After a short overture suitably labelled *vivacissimo*, the curtain rises to show a handsome apartment in the Count's house. Gil in walking clothes enters hurriedly: 'The light grey cloak, pink hat and feather ... could I be mistaken?' He goes out quickly, and a moment later Susanna comes in wearing a grey cloak and a pink hat. She gives her coat and hat and a parcel to the servant, and goes out again, having first made sure that her husband is in his room. No sooner has she gone than Gil reappears, and listens at the door of *her* room, seeming relieved to find that she is there. He must be mistaken – and yet: he has distinctly caught a smell of tobacco in his house – and he is a non-smoker. He catches himself out being unmistakably jealous. He questions Sante whether he is a smoker ... or his mistress? The old servant shakes his head at each question. Who can it be then?

Gil is in even more of a state by the time Susanna comes into the room. He comments on having seen someone just like her while he was out walking; it could not be her because he has forbidden her to go out alone. But why does she blush? Only because he is unkind for the first time. Rapturously, Gil assures her of his undying, unswerving devotion: 'Il dolce idillio'; a love duet follows, and at its end Gil is about to embrace his wife, when he smells the hated tobacco smell. She is horrified that he should notice – she knows how much he hates the smell – and he thinks he has turned suspicion that she is visited by an admirer into certainty. In a moment they are at cross purposes: Susanna suspects he knows her secret – 'If I'm left at home and you're late at the club, the time goes quicker ... Do like other husbands, and shut one eye discreetly to my little secret'; but Gil suspects something quite different, and smashes the vases in his fury. Susanna escapes to her room ('to have a good cry'), and Gil throws himself into a chair in a paroxysm of grief. Sante surveys the room in comic dismay, and proceeds to tidy up the mess.

After an intermezzo, during which Sante gets the room straight again, Susanna comes out and brings Gil his gloves, hat, and umbrella; she is sure he must want to go out. Just before he goes, she sings sweetly to him; will he not give her a word of love, one tender look, before he goes ('Via, così non mi lasciate')? He relents to the extent of kissing her on the forehead, and departs.

Susanna, alone, relaxes and Sante brings her the cigarettes she has been out to buy. No sooner has she lit one than Gil is back. He hunts everywhere but finds no one, only the smell of tobacco. Beside himself with rage, he goes out again. This time, Susanna has time to sing an aria to the cigarette for whose refreshing perfume she so yearns: 'O gioia, la nube leggera.' But she is not undisturbed for long. Gil suddenly appears through the window, and confronts his wife. She puts her hand behind her back, he snatches to see what she is hiding, and burns himself. The secret is out: she smokes. All is forgiven, and they each light a cigarette, dancing round each other with joy.   H.

I GIOIELLI DELLA MADONNA

The Jewels of the Madonna

Opera in three acts, text by Golisciani and Zangarini; German version by H. Liebstöckl. Première Berlin, 2 December 1911; Chicago and New York, 1912, with Carolina White, Bassi, Sammarco; Covent Garden, 1912, with Edvina, Martinelli, Sammarco; Metropolitan, New York, 1926, with Jeritza, Martinelli, Danise, conductor Papi. Revived Covent Garden, 1925, with Jeritza, Merli, Noto, conductor Bellezza. Italian stage première not until 1953, in Rome, with Clara Petrella, Prandelli, Gobbi.

Gennaro, *a blacksmith*...Tenor
Maliella, *adopted daughter of Carmela*..............Soprano
Rafaele, *leader of the Camorrists*.....................Baritone
Carmela, *Gennaro's mother* ....Mezzo-Soprano
Biaso, *a scribe*..Tenor
Ciccillo, *a Camorrist* ....Tenor

Friends of the Camorrists
    Stella ....Soprano
    Concetta...Soprano
    Serena ....Contralto

Rocco, *a Camorrist* ....Bass
Totonno, *a young peasant*...................................Tenor

Grazia, a Dancer; Vendors, Monks, Populace

Place: Naples
Time: 'The Present'
Running Time: 2 hours 20 minutes

After his comedies Wolf-Ferrari, surprisingly, turned to *verismo* at its crudest, a violent story set in Naples and more popular in the U.S.A. and England than in either Germany or Italy, in which latter country it found no favour in Fascist times as showing Italy in a poor light.

Act I. A small square in Naples, near the sea. Carmela's house, Gennaro's smithy, an inn, and the little hut of Biaso, the scribe, among many other details. 'It is the gorgeous afternoon of the festival of the Madonna, and the square swarms with a noisy crowd, rejoicing and celebrating the events with that strange mixture of carnival and superstition so characteristic of Southern Italy.' This describes most aptly the jolly, crowded scene, and the character of the music with which the opera opens. It is quite kaleidoscopic in its constant shifting of interest.

Gennaro in his blacksmith's shop is seen giving the finishing touches to a candelabrum. He places it on the anvil, as on an altar, kneels before it, and sings a prayer to the Madonna – 'Madonna, con sospiri'.

Maliella rushes out of the house pursued by Carmela. She is a restless, wilful girl – a potential Carmen, from whom opportunity has as yet been withheld. Striking an attitude of bravado, and in spite of Gennaro's protests, she voices her rebellious thoughts in the 'Canzone di Cannetella'.

A crowd gathers to hear her. From the direction of the sea comes the chorus of the approaching Camorrists. Maliella and the crowd dance wildly. When Carmela reappears with a pitcher of water on her head, Maliella is dashing along the quay screaming and laughing.

Carmela tells her son the brief story of Maliella. Once when he was ill as a baby, she vowed to the Madonna that she would adopt a baby girl and treat her as her own daughter if only her beloved son were allowed to recover. There is a touching duet for mother and son ('T'eri un giorno ammalato bambino'), in which Carmela bids him pray to the Madonna, and Gennaro asks for her blessing before he leaves to do so.

Maliella runs in. The Camorrists are in pursuit of her. Rafaele, the leader of the band, is a handsome, flashy blackguard. When he advances to seize and kiss her, she draws a dagger-like hat-pin. Laughing, he throws off his coat, like a duellist, grasps and holds her tightly. She stabs his hand, making it bleed, then throws away the skewer. Angry at first, he laughs disdainfully, then passionately kisses the wound ('Bacio di Lama'). The Camorrists buy flowers from a passing flower-girl and make a carpet of them, Rafaele picks up the hat-pin, kneels before Maliella, and hands it to her. Maliella slowly replaces it in her hair, and then Rafaele sticks a flower on her breast, where she permits it to remain. She throws it away but Rafaele picks it up, and carefully replaces it in his button-hole. A little later he goes to the inn, and raises his filled glass to her, just as a subtle influence compels her to turn and look at him.

Tolling of bells, discharge of mortars, cheers of populace, announce the approach of the procession of the Madonna. While hymns to the Virgin are chanted, Rafaele pours words of passion into Maliella's ears. The image of the Madonna, bedecked with jewels, is borne past. Rafaele brags that for love of Maliella he would even rob the sacred image of the jewels and bedeck her with them.

Gennaro warns her against Rafaele as 'the most notorious blackguard in this quarter', and orders her into the house. Rafaele's mocking laugh infuriates him. The men seem about to fight, but the procession returns, and they are obliged to kneel. Rafaele's looks, however, follow Maliella. He tosses her the flower she has previously rejected. She picks it up, puts it between her lips, and flies indoors.

Act II. The garden of Carmela's house. It is late evening. Intermezzo. Carmela, having cleared the table, goes into the house. Gennaro starts in to warn Maliella. She insists she must have freedom, rushes up the staircase to her room, where she is seen putting her things together, while she hums, 'E ndringhete' (I long for mirth and folly).

She is ready to leave but Gennaro pleads with her. With eyes half-closed, she recalls how Rafaele offered to steal the jewels of the Madonna for her. Gennaro, at first shocked at the sacrilege, appears to yield. He bars the way to Maliella, locks the gate, and stands facing her.

Her laugh still ringing in his ears, he goes to a cupboard under the stairs, takes out a box, selects from its contents several skeleton keys and files, wraps them in a piece of leather which he hides under his coat, crosses himself, and sneaks out.

From the direction of the sea a chorus of men's voices is heard. Rafaele appears at the gate with his Camorrist friends. To the accompaniment of their mandolins and guitars he sings to Maliella a lively waltz-like serenade: 'Aprila, o bella, la fenestrella.' The girl, in a white wrap, a light scarlet shawl over her shoulders, descends to the garden. There is a love duet: she promises she will join him.

Left to herself, she sees in the moonlight Gennaro's open tool box. As if in answer to her presentiment of what it signifies, he appears with a bundle wrapped in red damask. He is too distracted by his purpose to question her presence in the garden. He spreads out on the table for Maliella the jewels of the Madonna.

Maliella – in an ecstasy, half mystic, half sensual, and apparently seeing in Gennaro the image of the man who promised her the jewels, Rafaele – no longer repulses Gennaro, but yields herself to his embrace.

Act III. A haunt of the Camorrists on the outskirts of Naples. Intermezzo, to the tune of Rafaele's serenade.

The Camorrists gather. There is singing with dancing – the 'Apache', the 'Tarantelle'. They do not anticipate Maliella's expected arrival with much pleasure. When Rafaele comes in, they ask him what he admires in her. In his answer, 'Non sapete ... di Maliella la preziosa qualità' he tells them her chief charm is that he will be the first man to whom she has yielded herself.

In the midst of an uproar of shouting and dancing, while Rafaele, standing on a table, cracks a whip, Maliella rushes in. In an agony she cries out that, in a trance, she gave herself to Gennaro. The women laugh derisively at Rafaele, who has just sung of her as being inviolable to all but himself. For Rafaele she is a plucked rose to be left to wither. Furiously he rejects her. The jewels of the Madonna fall from her cloak.

Gennaro, who has followed her to the haunt of the Camorrists, enters, half mad. Maliella, laughing hysterically, flings the jewels at his feet. The crowd recoils from both intruders. Rafaele curses the girl. At his command, the band disperses. Maliella goes out to drown herself in the sea. 'Madonna del dolor! Miserere!' prays Gennaro. His thoughts revert to his mother: among the débris he finds a knife and plunges it into his heart.   K.

Z

RICCARDO ZANDONAI

(born 30 May 1883, died 5 June 1944)

FRANCESCA DA RIMINI

Opera in four acts, text by Tito Ricordi after D'Annunzio's play of the same name. Première, Teatro Regio, Turin, 19 February 1914, with Canetti, Crimi, Cigada, Paltrinieri, conductor Panizza. First performed Covent Garden, 1914, with Edvina, Martinelli, Cigada, conductor Panizza; la Scala, Milan, 1916, with Raisa, Pertile, Danise; Metropolitan, 1916, with Alda, Martinelli, Amato, conductor Polacco. Revived la Scala, 1929, with dalla Rizza, Pertile, Maugeri, conductor Panizza; 1937, with Cigna, Parmeggiani, Maugeri, conductor Zandonai; 1942, with Somigli, Ziliani, Maugeri, conductor Guarnieri; 1946, with Carbone, Ziliani, Stabile, conductor Guarnieri; 1950, with Caniglia, Prandelli, Biasini, conductor Capuana; 1959, with Olivero, del Monaco, Giangiacomo Guelfi; San Francisco, 1956, with Gencer; Metropolitan, 1984, with Scotto, Domingo, Cornell MacNeil, conductor Levine.

The son and daughters of Guido Minore of Polenta
  Francesca...Soprano
  Samaritana ....Soprano
  Ostasio ....Baritone

Sons of Malatesta of Verrucchio
  Giovanni (Gianciotto) lo Sciancato
  (the Lame) ....Baritone
  Paolo il Bello (the Handsome)......................Tenor
  Malatestino dall'Occhio (the One-Eyed) ....Tenor

Francesca's women
  Biancofiore..Soprano
  Garsenda..Soprano
  Altichiara....................................Mezzo-Soprano
  Donella.......................................Mezzo-Soprano
  The Slave...Contralto

Ser Toldo Berardengo, *a lawyer* ....Tenor

A Jester..Bass

An Archer ....Tenor

A Torchbearer...Baritone

Archers, Torchbearers, Musicians

Place: Ravenna; Rimini
Time: End of the Thirteenth Century
Running Time: 2 hours 15 minutes

Zandonai, a pupil of Mascagni's, had a round dozen operas to his credit before he died at the age of sixty-one. Several are of more than passing interest, but only one, *Francesca da Rimini*, has been the subject of regular revival, D'Annunzio's play inspiring him to effects of real delicacy and to music of greater passion than elsewhere.

Act I. The scene is a court in the house of the Polentani, in Ravenna. A colloquy between Francesca's brother Ostasio and the notary Ser Toldo Berardengo informs us that for reasons of state Francesca is to be married to one of the three sons of Malatesta da Verrucchio, who, although named Giovanni, is known as Gianciotto, the Lamester, because of his deformity and ugliness. A plot has been formed by which she is introduced to his handsome younger brother Paolo, with whom, under the impression that he is her destined bridegroom, she falls in love at first sight, a passion that is fully reciprocated.

Act II. The interior of a round tower in the fortified castle of the Malatestas. The summit of the tower is crowned with engines of war and arms. The castle is a stronghold of the Guelfs. In the distance, beyond the city of Rimini, are seen the battlements of the highest Ghibelline tower.

Soon after the act opens, an attack takes place. Amid the tumult occurs the first meeting between Francesca and Paolo since the marriage into which she was tricked. Their love is obvious enough. Paolo despairingly seeks death, to which Francesca also exposes herself by remaining on the platform of the tower during the combat.

The Malatestas are victorious. The attacking foes are driven off. Gianciotto comes up on the platform and brings news to Paolo of his election as Captain of the people and Commune of Florence, for which city Paolo presently departs. Malatestino is carried in wounded (he has lost the sight of an eye), but he exhibits great courage and wishes to continue the fight.

Act III. The scene is the apartment of Francesca, where she is reading to her women the story of Lancelot and Guinevere. The women dance and sing until Francesca dismisses them. Paolo has returned. The greeting from her to him is simple enough: 'Benvenuto, signore mio cognato' (Welcome, my lord and kinsman), but the music is charged with deeper significance. Even more pronounced is the meaning in the musical phrase at Francesca's words, 'Paolo, datemi pace' (Paolo, give me peace).

Together they read the story which Francesca had begun reading to her women. Their heads come close together over the book, and when, in the ancient love tale, the queen and her lover kiss, Francesca's and Paolo's lips meet and linger in an ecstasy of passion.

Act IV. The scene is an octagonal hall of grey stone. A grated door leads to a subterranean prison.

Malatestino is desperately in love with Francesca, and even hints that he would go to the length of poisoning Gianciotto. Francesca repulses him. Cries of a prisoner from the dungeon have disturbed Francesca. When she complains of this to Malatestino, he says he will go down into the prison and kill the captive.

Gianciotto enters the room and Francesca complains to him of Malatestino's cruelty and of his attitude towards her – what it is she does not specify. Francesca has prepared food for her husband before his journey, and he removes his sword and helmet before eating. Suddenly there is a terrible cry from the dungeon; it is evident that Malatestino has carried out his intention of beheading the prisoner. A moment later, knocking is heard at the door through which Malatestino went down to the dungeon; Francesca quickly goes out so as not to have to see him again.

Out of revenge for his slighted passion, Malatestino excites the jealousy of Gianciotto by arousing his suspicions of Paolo and Francesca. Gianciotto works himself into a passion and demands to be shown proof of the accusation. Malatestino bids him wait until nightfall.

The scene changes to Francesca's chamber. It is night. Francesca is lying on the bed. From her sleep she is roused by a wild dream that harm has come to Paolo. Her women try to comfort her. After an exchange of gentle and affectionate phrases, she dismisses them.

A light knocking at the door, and Paolo's voice calls, 'Francesca!' She flings open the door and throws herself into the arms of her lover. There is an interchange of impassioned phrases. Then a violent shock is heard at the door, followed by the voice of Gianciotto, demanding admission. Paolo spies a trap-door in the floor of the apartment, pulls the bolt, and bids Francesca open the door of the room for her husband, while he escapes.

Gianciotto rushes into the room. Paolo's cloak catches in the bolt of the trap-door. He is still standing head and shoulders above the level of the floor. Seizing him by the hair, the Lamester forces him to come up. Paolo unsheathes his dagger. Gianciotto draws his sword, thrusts at Paolo. Francesca throws herself between the two men, receives her husband's sword full in the breast, and falls into Paolo's arms. Mad with rage, her deformed husband with another deadly thrust pierces his brother's side. Paolo and Francesca fall to the floor. With a painful effort, Gianciotto breaks his blood-stained sword over his knee.   K.

ALEXANDER VON ZEMLINSKY
(born 14 October 1871, died 15 March 1942)

Zemlinsky, who was born in Vienna, was a man of the theatre. As a student of the Vienna Conservatory, he was enthusiastic about Brahms but equally enthralled by Wagner. His first opera, *Sarema*, had its première in Munich in 1897 with Milka Ternina, the great Wagnerian and Covent Garden's first Tosca, in the title role, and his second, *Es war einmal* (1900), was conducted in

Vienna by Mahler with a cast which included Selma Kurz and Erich Schmedes, two of the stars of the Vienna Opera. From 1900 he conducted in various theatres in Vienna, resigning from the Court Opera when Mahler left and later joining the Volksoper where he conducted *Salome* when it was first heard in the Austrian capital. In 1911 he moved to the Deutsches Theater in Prague, conducting in 1924 the première of Schoenberg's *Erwartung*, and from 1927 he was with Klemperer at the Krolloper in Berlin. With the advent of the Nazis, he moved back to Vienna, and after the Anschluss to America. He was the teacher and later brother-in-law of Arnold Schoenberg, but his outlook was essentially romantic and Expressionist and his music, which was always eclectic, remained by and large tonal.   H.

EINE FLORENTINISCHE TRAGÖDIE

A Florentine Tragedy

Opera in one act, text translated by Max Meyerfeld from Oscar Wilde. Première Stuttgart, 30 January 1917, with Helene Wildbrunn, Rudolf Ritter, Felix Fleischer, conductor Max von Schillings, and the same year in Vienna. The opera was revived in 1980 for the Florence Festival, with Sigune von Osten, Werner Götz, Heinz Jürgen Demitz, conductor Friedrich Player; and with even greater success in 1981 in Hamburg, with Elisabeth Steiner, Kenneth Riegel and Guillermo Sarabia, conductor Gerd Albrecht; this production was taken to the Edinburgh Festival in 1983.

Guido Bardi, *Prince of Florence*............................Tenor
Simone, *a merchant*...Baritone
Bianca, *his wife* ....Mezzo-Soprano

Place: Florence
Time: Sixteenth Century
Running Time: 50 minutes

Zemlinsky's operas span most of his life, from *Sarema* in 1897 to *Der Kreidekreis* in 1933, with two (*Der König Kandaules* and *Circe*) unfinished at his death. The Oscar Wilde double bill, of which *Eine florentinische Tragödie* is the first, re-established his reputation in the last quarter of the twentieth century, but, partly because of his outstanding conducting, he was never truly sidelined during his lifetime, except when the Nazis ruled the German-speaking theatre.

The overture graphically compensates for the opera's lack of an explicit love scene, Simone surprising his wife Bianca and the Prince as the curtain rises in what is evidently an assignation. Simone is the opera's central figure, and he at first seems to pretend that Guido is a customer. He sells him a robe of state, then proceeds to offer him anything in his house. He is disconcerted when Guido opts for Bianca and says she is fit only for housework. Simone digresses into a discussion of English merchants and Italian politics before going into the garden. When he returns, he recognises the strength of his wife's spleen but this seems to galvanise him into a state of hyper-activity, and, to a frenzied waltz rhythm, he invites the Prince to play the lute, then to drink wine. Left alone again, Bianca and Guido indulge in a love scene, after which Simone cannot hide his thoughts of revenge and hands Guido his sword, reminding him that those who steal from him do so at their own risk. Guido is caught in a trap as lethal as the one Pirandello devised in his play *Rules of the Game*. The duel mounts in tension and ends with Simone disarming and then strangling his victim. He turns to kill his wife but instead embraces her, aware at last of her beauty as she is in her turn of his strength.

The music is saturated in orchestral magic, the virtuosity of *Salome* and the *Gurrelieder*, and the work is as representative of the Viennese Secession as Mahler's later music, the early works of Schoenberg, Berg or Webern, Korngold's opera *Violanta*, or Schreker's *Die Gezeichneten* (it is an odd reflection that for some time Puccini contemplated Wilde's play for his own purposes). Zemlinsky's opera was begun just before the start of the Great War and finished in 1916, and is a product of his most fecund period, when he was in Prague and, like Mahler before him, composed every summer. Schoenberg, no easy critic even of his adherents of which Zemlinsky was certainly one, described *Eine florentinische Tragödie* as 'ein prachtvolles Werk' – a magnificent work.   H.

DER ZWERG

The Dwarf or The Birthday of the Infanta

Opera in one act, text by Georg C. Klaren after Oscar Wilde's story *The Birthday of the Infanta*. Première Cologne, 28 May 1922, with Erna Schröder, Karl Schröder, conductor Otto Klemperer. Revived Hamburg, 1981, with Janet Perry, Kenneth Riegel, conductor Gerd Albrecht (and at the Edinburgh Festival, 1983).

Donna Clara, *Infanta of Spain*..........................Soprano

Ghita, *her favourite maid and confidante* ....Soprano

Don Estéban, *the Major-Domo* ....Baritone

The Dwarf..Tenor

Three Maids ....Sopranos

Playmates of the Infanta

Running Time: 1 hour 15 minutes

In 1911, Zemlinsky commissioned his colleague Franz Schreker to write him a libretto, the result being *Die Gezeichneten*, which Schreker eventually set himself. Its principal figure is an ill-favoured dwarf, not unlike the central character of Wilde's story and, it would appear, not unlike Zemlinsky himself, who is said never to have recovered from a rebuff at the hands of Alma Schindler-Mahler, who was his pupil and with whom he was in love (in her memoirs she described him as 'a horrible dwarf'). Klaren's libretto differs some-what from Wilde's original in that the Infanta is no longer an innocent girl but a young woman whose cruelty is more intentional than inadvertent.

The opera was successful from the start, has been a significant feature in the new focus on the composer, and is generally thought of as Zemlinsky's masterpiece. For the highly successful production in Hamburg, Adolf Dresen rewrote a text closer to Wilde's original, with the dwarf no longer a courtier accustomed to royal circles, instead a rough peasant lad unused to sophisticated behaviour.

Don Estéban, the court major-domo, is supervising preparations for the Infanta's birthday. Ghita, the Infanta's confidante, swiftly emerges as the most sympathetic member of her entourage, indeed of the entire cast. The Infanta herself joins in a dance, then insists on seeing her presents until Don Estéban persuades her to the contrary. She is dressed for the

Der Zwerg *(Hamburg State Opera at Edinburgh Festival, 1983). Kenneth Riegel in the title role, Janet Perry as the Infanta.*

birthday festivities and the great mirror is afterwards covered over. One of the presents, it transpires, is from the Sultan and consists of a dwarf, who has no idea that others find him hideous. The major-domo addresses him as Prince and, when they meet, it is obvious he finds the Infanta attractive. He sings a romance and when she starts to play with her new 'toy' and asks him to name a 'wife' from among her companions, it is she whom he predictably chooses. They are left alone, the Infanta sings wistfully and the dwarf's narrative makes plain that he thinks of himself as some kind of latter-day knight, handsome and romantic. With no regard to consequences, she lets him think she loves him, details what he must do to be worthy of her, and only narrowly avoids his kiss when Ghita surprises them.

The Princess tells Ghita that the dwarf has no idea of his ugliness and instructs her to show him his face in a mirror. This Ghita has not the heart to do, though she urges him to understand the futility of his chase after the Infanta. She leaves him near the Infanta's throne with the Infanta's white rose in his hand and, as he goes towards the ballroom, he sees himself for the first time in the mirror and screams in horror. He is near hysteria and, when the Infanta reappears, begs her to tell him he is not ugly: 'I am a dwarf and I love you.' But she has made it clear that she finds him repulsive and he falls down. Ghita tries to comfort him but sees that he is dead. The Infanta's reaction is that her new toy is broken; let them get on with the dance – and music is heard from the ballroom.

The brilliance of the music at the outset has the effect of conjuring up an exotic Spanish ambience, just as the lazy rhythms early on suggest the hedonistic atmosphere of the court. The score waxes romantic for the long scene between Princess and dwarf, but follows the action minutely through the dawning of the dwarf's disillusion and his long monologue up to the agony of his full understanding of how others see him, then the disaster of rejection by the Infanta. An extraordinary, bittersweet score and a total success as an opera.   H.

BERND ALOIS ZIMMERMANN
(born 20 March 1918, died 10 August 1970)

DIE SOLDATEN

The Soldiers

Opera in four acts, fifteen scenes, libretto from the play (1775) by Jakob Michael Lenz. Première in Cologne, 15 February 1965, with Edith Gabry, Liane Synek, Helga Jenckel, Anton de Ridder, Claudio Nicolai and Zoltan Kelemen, conductor Michael Gielen, producer Hans Neugebauer. First performed Cassel, 1968, conductor Gerd Albrecht; Munich, 1969 (after a reported thirty-three rehearsals for orchestra and no less than 377 for soloists), with Catherine Gayer, Charlotte Berthold, Gudrun Wewezow, de Ridder, Hans Wilbrink, Keith Engen, conductor Gielen, producer Václav Kašlík, designer Josef Svoboda; Düsseldorf, 1971, conductor Günther Wich, and in 1972 at Edinburgh Festival; first British production, 1996, at English National Opera, conductor Elgar Howarth.

Wesener, *a fancy goods merchant in Lille* .... Bass

Marie } *his daughters* .... High Soprano
Charlotte } .... Mezzo-Soprano

Wesener's Old Mother .... Contralto

Stolzius, *a draper in Armentières* .... High Baritone

Stolzius's mother .... Contralto

Obrist, *Graf von Spannheim* .... Bass

Desportes, *a young nobleman in the French Army* .... High Tenor

A Young Gamekeeper, *in the service of Desportes* .... Actor

Captain Pirzel .... High Tenor

Eisenhardt, *an Army chaplain* .... Baritone

Major Haudy .... Baritone

Major Mary .... Baritone

Three Young Officers
.... High Tenor (or High Soprano)

Comtesse de la Roche .... Mezzo-Soprano

The Young Count, *her son* .... High Lyric Tenor

An Andalusian Waitress .... Dancer

Three Cadets .... Dancers

Madame Roux, *hostess of the coffee house* ....Silent
Servant of Comtesse de la Roche........................Actor
Young Cadet ....Actor
A Drunken Officer ....Actor
Three Officers ....Actors

Eighteen Officers and Cadets; Ballet, doubles of the actors and dancers

Place: French-Speaking Flanders
Time: Yesterday, Today, and Tomorrow
Running Time: 1 hour 50 minutes

'What are the requirements for a modern opera?' asked Zimmermann. 'The answer can be given in one sentence: opera as total theatre! This is the way to think about opera, or rather about theatre, by which I mean the concentration of all theatrical media for the purpose of communication in a place created specially for this purpose. In other words: architecture, sculpture, painting, musical theatre, spoken theatre, ballet, film, microphone, television, tape and sound techniques, electronic music, concrete music, circus, the musical, and all forms of motion theatre combine to form the phenomenon of pluralistic opera ... I have employed speech, singing, screaming, whispering, jazz, Gregorian chant, dance, film, and the entire modern "technical" theatre to serve the idea of the pluralistic form of musical theatre.' But this pluralism of Zimmermann's goes far beyond the combining of the many factors in the one art-form of opera and refers just as much to 'the simultaneous occurrence of past, present and future as *one* complicated cross-relationship of inseparable factors in our lives, ever-present to each other, as if they were taking place on the inside surface of a vast globe with the audience suspended somewhere in the middle taking in the sweep of cause and effect simultaneously.'[1]

It was presumably because it deliberately ignored the classical unities of time, place and action in favour of a rapid cross-cutting of the often very short scenes – which approached his own notion of a pluralistic scene – that Zimmermann chose a play by Jakob Michael Lenz, the German dramatist of the second half of the eighteenth century, whose work exhibited a certain iconoclastic turn of mind (a lesser, though earlier, worker in Büchner's field) and whose play was distinctly anti-establishment. Zimmermann's attraction was not of course to the relatively prosaic events of Lenz's play – the seduction of the middle-class Marie by the upper-class Desportes and her decline from respectability to the miserable existence of a soldiers' whore; rather it sprang from his conviction that Lenz's characters 'inevitably collide with an inescapable situation – innocently rather than guiltily – which directly leads towards rape, murder and suicide and finally towards the destruction of everything existing'.

In the event, neither Zimmermann's theories nor his practice led as smoothly and inevitably to performance as the quality of his work would suggest. He started work on the opera in 1957 and in 1958 it was officially commissioned by the Opera in Cologne, his native city. It was not long however before the Opera House's direction, the producer Oscar Fritz Schuh and the conductor Wolfgang Sawallisch, decided that it was impossible to perform in its original form. In 1963–64 the composer prepared a simplified score, which had its première in early 1965. What was lost was mainly due to Zimmermann's acceptance, reluctant we may suppose, of standard theatrical architecture instead of a 'theatre of the future' capable of giving more vivid expression to his attempt to show the inevitability of events and the unimportance of the time-order in which they take place – 'Kugelgestalt der Zeit' is the expression he used; 'the spherical shape of time', you might translate it. He wanted to surround the audience with action either live or on film, so that in, for instance, scene vii or xiii, the use of twelve surrounding stages, each with its attendant musicians together making up the vast orchestral resources required, would force listeners to focus on either the past, the present or the future, each a candidate for their attention.

Act I. An extended and violent prelude, dominated by an obsessive drum beat, leads us straight into Scene i (*Strofe*), which plays in Wesener's house in Lille. Marie asks the advice of her sister Charlotte as she writes a bread-and-butter letter to Madame Stolzius in Armentières, where she has recently been staying. What she does not want her sister to know is that she has fallen in love with young Stolzius and hopes to see him again.

---

[1] James Helme Sutcliffe in *Opera*, June 1969.

Die Soldaten *(English National Opera, 1996, director David Freeman, designer Sally Jacobs).*
Foreground: Nicholas Folwell (Major Mary), Roberto Salvatore (Stolzius), David Burrell (Major Haudy).

Scene ii (*Ciacona I*). Stolzius's house in Armentières. Stolzius is obviously labouring under stress, and it is some time before his mother shows him a letter from Marie, with whom he in his turn has fallen in love. Immediately the clouds lift, for him at least though not for his mother, since she plainly has been less taken with the girl's charms than has her son.

A short interlude (*Tratto I*) takes us to Scene iii (called *Ricercari I*), again in Lille. Baron Desportes, a young officer in the French army, calls on Marie in her father's house. He opens his courtship of her with a florid, wide-ranging phrase, 'Mein göttliche Mademoiselle' (a kind of modern 'Reverenza!'[1]), which effectively characterises an ardent, not too

sincere young man used to expressing himself in formal fashion and which remains typical of his music throughout the opera. He affects to be shocked when Marie tells him that her father has warned her that men are false, and his 'göttliche Mademoiselle' becomes even more fulsome and exaggerated than before. When Wesener comes in, Desportes tries to take advantage of the situation by inviting Marie to the theatre, but Wesener is adamant that she cannot go. Her disappointment is quite apparent, and Wesener tries to read her a lecture on the situation, excusing his severity by assuring her, not without tenderness, that she is his only joy in life.

Scene iv (*Toccata I*). Armentières, where we meet for the first time the military in force. Haudy, Pirzel,

---

[1] Mistress Quickly's greeting to Falstaff in Verdi's opera.

and the chaplain Eisenhardt lead a discussion about the comparative merits of the theatre and the sermon as opportunities for moralising, and the others, particularly three young officers, join in spasmodically. 'A whore will always be a whore,' announces Haudy at the top of his voice, only to have the chaplain rebuff his contention with, 'a whore never became a whore without being made one'.

Scene v (*Nocturne I*). Lille. Marie is alone in her room and her father comes to ask whether Desportes' intentions towards her are honourable. She shows him the letter in the form of a love poem which he has written her, and Wesener reads it over with some satisfaction. Though he advises her not to accept presents from him, it is quite apparent that the prospect of a Baron for a son-in-law is not unattractive to him, but he wants her to hedge her bets by not breaking off with young Stolzius before Desportes has proposed to her formally. Marie left alone reveals in an important *arioso* not only that she still has misgivings but her love for Stolzius is far from dead. Thunder and lightning outside the window and a comparable turmoil in the orchestra seem to bode no good.

Act II, scene vi (*Toccata II*). Armentières – the café where Madame Roux holds sway, with the Andalusian waitress as one of the principal attractions of her establishment. Zimmermann specifies the layout of tables, partly to secure ensemble balance, and partly because he makes provision for the occupants of each one to tap with tea or coffee spoon, fist, open or closed hand, on table or vessel in the course of the action (an exactly notated effect). A drunken young officer announces to all and sundry, 'If I had a wife, I should give you permission to sleep with her, if you could persuade her to it.' The chaplain and Pirzel take their places well to the front, as also the young Count de la Roche. An elaborate dance begins, full of jazz complications and led by the Andalusian (it is during this dance that the percussion effects on glass, cup and table-top are most in evidence). Stolzius comes in and is unmercifully teased with insinuations about the behaviour of Marie in Lille. He pretends not to know what they're talking about and certainly not to have heard of their brother officer Desportes. It is not long before he precipitately leaves. An *Intermezzo* with organ, stage

music, a variety of percussion leads to the next scene.

Scene vii. Lille (*Capriccio, Corale and Ciacona II*). Marie sits in tears after reading a reproachful letter from Stolzius, and hands it to Desportes, who is indignant at what he describes as the impertinence of the writer, then says he will dictate an answer. But the letter is soon lost sight of in the hysteria of coloratura laughter as the physical seduction of Marie begins. At this point the scene, like the means the composer employs throughout, becomes for the first time pluralistic as Zimmermann simultaneously shows the seduction, Stolzius's far-off instinctive reaction to it, and a third party ruminating on the situation. As well as Marie and Desportes, we see Wesener's old mother, perhaps in the centre, foretelling misfortune for her beloved granddaughter and, on the side of the stage opposite to Marie's room in Lille, Stolzius in Armentières miserable at the tone of Marie's letter which has in effect broken off the engagement. He tries to defend Marie to his mother but vows vengeance on Desportes. Meanwhile, the wordless love scene has continued and we have effectively reached the halfway point in the action with Marie's seduction complete and her downfall therefore more or less assured – a musical scene of remarkable complexity and brilliant invention.

Act III. After a short prelude, scene viii (*Rondino*) takes place in Armentières, where, in the principal square, the chaplain and Captain Pirzel are engaged on one of their interminable discussions. The chaplain wants to discuss the implications of Mary's intended move to Lille, but Pirzel insists on philosophising. The chaplain observes that you cannot go out of the door without finding a soldier embracing a girl, but this provokes further theoretical stuff from Pirzel, whose lengthy military service seems to have driven him into some kind of private mental corner, as a refuge presumably from the irrationality of what has been going on around him.

Scene ix (*Rappresentazione*). Mary's room. A knock at the door heralds the arrival of a stiff and nervous Stolzius, dressed in uniform and applying to become Major Mary's batman. Mary accepts him.

The tenth scene (*Ricercari II*) follows after a single silent bar and takes place in Wesener's house in Lille. Charlotte is scolding her sister for taking up with Major Mary the moment Desportes has left the town. Marie tries to excuse herself, but Charlotte is not to be put off and, as Marie makes up in the looking glass, hisses 'Soldier's hussy!' at her back. Major Mary comes in to be greeted by Marie with a sort of parody of Desportes' greeting in the third scene, a gallantry he echoes in his turn. All three prepare to leave, but the girls notice before doing so a resemblance between Mary's batman, standing discreetly in the background, and 'a certain person'. The interlude is called *Romanza*, and is one of the score's most considerable pieces.

Scene xi (*Nocturne II*). The house of Comtesse de la Roche. It is evening, and the Countess is waiting up for the return of her son, musing that it seems inevitable that children regularly cause their parents pain from the womb to the grave. Her thoughts are conveyed in a wide-ranging solo *arioso*, which becomes, with the entrance of her son (the young Count whom we have already rather unobtrusively met in the two regimental scenes), an extended and vocally grateful duet, vociferously and aptly applauded by the audience when I first heard the opera. The burden of their conversation is basically the unsuitability of Miss Wesener as a potential consort for the young Count. Countess de la Roche herself will take responsibility for the girl's future.

Scene xii (*Tropi*). Lille, Wesener's house. From the conversation of Charlotte and Marie, it seems that Major Mary, like the Count, has in his turn deserted Marie, but their discussion is interrupted by the arrival of a servant asking on behalf of the Countess de la Roche if the young ladies are at home. With a perfectly contrived mixture of condescension and warmth, the Countess insists that she is Marie's best friend, commiserates with her on the gossip which is rife in the town, bids her in a firm but kindly way to forget all about the young Count, and offers to take her as a companion into her own house. The scene develops into a splendid trio for female voices and the Countess leaves.

Act IV, scene xiii (*Toccata III*). The café in Armentières. Zimmermann's pluralistic theories are here put more extensively and effectively into practice. The subject is the various stages of Marie's downfall, represented simultaneously as if in a kind of dream on different levels on the stage, one with dancers, another with all the performers, a third

with their doubles, and yet again in film on three screens.[1] The whole thing is conceived as if Marie were on trial. Mixed on the three screens and cross-cut from one to another, the salient events of the action are shown. Major Mary has quickly found out where Marie is to be found, and the Countess has surprised them in a garden rendezvous. Marie has run away from the Countess's house and is not to be found at her father's. At the same time, Desportes, who, the original play tells us, has been trying, even though Wesener has guaranteed debts he left behind him in Lille, to rid himself of his discarded mistress by getting her well and truly involved with Mary, has written to his gamekeeper at home to say he has found a woman for him. Marie, homeless and terrified, is raped by the gamekeeper, and becomes a common prostitute. Stolzius, apprised of events, buys poison with which to effect his revenge. The threads of the very complex scene are drawn together in a great common utterance on the part of all the participants: 'And must those who suffer injustice tremble, and only those who do wrong be happy.'

An interlude (*Tratto II*) leads to scene xiv (*Ciacona III*). Armentières, Major Mary's room. Desportes is dining with his friend, and Stolzius keeps on fetching them fresh napkins so as to overhear the conversation. Desportes speaks in the most callous manner imaginable of Marie, who wrote to tell him she planned to visit him at home, and goes on to explain that he quickly arranged for his keeper, a strong masculine sort of chap, to give her the kind of reception she deserved. Mary protests at so revolting a stratagem, but Desportes thinks that Marie would have nothing to complain about if his keeper were to marry her. Major Mary insists that he himself would have married her if the young Count de la Roche had not got in the way. At this point, Stolzius serves soup, into which he has put the poison he bought, and its effect on Desportes is almost immediate. Stolzius seizes Desportes by the ears and yells 'Marie!' in his face, then, as he watches Desportes' agony, drinks poison himself and dies.

The last scene (*Nocturne III*) takes place on the road. To the accompaniment of stylised and amplified vocal noises, a miserable beggar woman – Marie of course – accosts old Wesener and begs for money.

---

[1] And this is the composer's simplified, compromise version!

At first he refuses but then he thinks of the possible plight of his daughter and relents. He does not recognise her. While the end of the tragedy is being played out, various scenes are enacted in contrapuntal contrast, from a view of groups of officers having recourse to Madame Roux's café to films of soldiers of all ages and all nationalities marching relentlessly over the cobblestones, until the latter idea takes over the scene entirely to the accompaniment of an amplified march on the drums. Marie lies motionless on the stage throughout and it is emphasised that the soldiers are only symbolical of those who are responsible for the misery of others, by no means intended as exclusive perpetrators of those crimes against humanity which Zimmermann so cogently protests.

Zimmermann has written a complicated serial score, involving vast stage and musical resources, but what impresses the listener at the end of a performance is the clarity of organisation, the audibility of text, the subtlety of the sounds he has heard. His vocal line is often angular and complex but also lyrical and expressive, his orchestra is filled with colour as well as weight of sonority. Above all, he has written an opera that is full of compassion and humanity, that speaks to the hearts of audiences which see and hear it.   H.

INDEX